D1383982

THE
MILITARY AND NAVAL
HISTORY OF THE REBELLION
IN THE UNITED STATES.

Miller & Mathews Photo^rs — H W Smith, N.Y.

A Lincoln.

PRESIDENT OF THE UNITED STATES

New York, D. Appleton & Co.

THE

MILITARY AND NAVAL

HISTORY OF THE REBELLION

IN THE UNITED STATES.

WITH

BIOGRAPHICAL SKETCHES OF DECEASED OFFICERS.

Illustrated with Steel Plate Portraits.

BY

W. J. TENNEY,

EDITOR OF THE "AMERICAN ANNUAL CYCLOPÆDIA."

1866 EDITION

STACKPOLE
BOOKS

Published by
STACKPOLE BOOKS
5067 Ritter Road
Mechanicsburg, PA 17055-6921
www.stackpolebooks.com

Printed in the United States of America

10 9 8 7 6 5 4 3 2 1

Originally published by D. Appleton & Company, New York, 1866
From the old War Department Library

Cover Design by Wendy Reynolds

Library of Congress Cataloging-in-Publication Data

Tenney, William Jewett, 1814–1883.
The military and naval history of the rebellion in the United States : with biographical sketches of deceased officers / by William Jewett Tenney.
p. cm.
Originally published: New York: D. Appleton & Co., 1866.
Includes bibliographical references and index.
ISBN 0-8117-0028-3 (alk. paper)
1. United States—History—Civil War, 1861–1865—Campaigns. 2. United States—History—Civil War, 1861–1865—Naval operations. 3. United States. Army—History—Civil War, 1861–1865. 4. United States—History—Civil War, 1861–1865—Biography. I. Title.

E470 .T46 2003
973.7'3—dc 2002075949

THE

MILITARY AND NAVAL

HISTORY OF THE REBELLION

IN THE UNITED STATES.

WITH

BIOGRAPHICAL SKETCHES OF DECEASED OFFICERS.

Illustrated with Steel Plate Portraits.

BY

W. J. TENNEY,

EDITOR OF THE "AMERICAN ANNUAL CYCLOPÆDIA."

NEW YORK:

D. APPLETON & COMPANY, 443 & 445 BROADWAY.

1866.

PREFACE.

THE design of this work is to present in one volume the military and naval scenes of the great contest recently closed. It contains not only all the principal battles by land and sea, but every important skirmish. The plans and objects of the various campaigns are clearly stated, and the progress of the armies, step by step, in their execution, is described and illustrated with distinct topographical maps, chiefly obtained from official sources. The important naval conflicts are described and illustrated in a similar manner. Portions of the work have been submitted to the inspection of distinguished military officers, relating to operations by armies under their command, and received their approval for its completeness and accuracy. By a reference to the Index at the end of the volume, the military or naval careers of General or Commanding officers can be traced.

But it is not merely a work of skirmishes and battles. The manner of raising, organizing, and equipping the armies and fleets is stated in detail; also the sanitary measures for their preservation, including hospitals and charitable organizations; the improvements in the weapons and forts and floating batteries of military and naval warfare; the treatment of prisoners, and the action relative to those military questions arising between combatants.

It also embraces a statement of the civil and political proceedings incidental to the war, which took place previous to its commencement or during its progress; such as the succession of the Southern States, and the organization of their Confederacy; the political issues of the war and the triumph of emancipation, with the treatment of colored men, whether soldiers or freedmen, and all other subjects properly a portion of its direct history. It concludes with biographical tributes to the principal military and naval officers who have fallen in the contest.

CONTENTS.

CHAPTER XVIII.

PAGE

CHAPTER XIX.

CHAPTER XX.

CHAPTER XXI.

CHAPTER XXII.

CHAPTER XXIII.

CHAPTER XXIV.

CHAPTER XXV.

CHAPTER XXVI.

CHAPTER XXVII.

CHAPTER XXVIII.

CHAPTER XXIX.

CHAPTER XXX.

CHAPTER XXXI.

CHAPTER XXXII.

CHAPTER XXXIII.

CHAPTER XXXIV.

CHAPTER XXXV.

CHAPTER XXXVI.

CHAPTER XXXVII.

CHAPTER XXXVIII.

CHAPTER XXXIX.

CHAPTER XL.

CHAPTER XLI.

CHAPTER XLII.

CHAPTER XLIII.

CHAPTER XLIV.

CHAPTER XLV.

CHAPTER XLVI.

CHAPTER XLVII.

CHAPTER XLVIII.

CHAPTER XLIX.

CHAPTER L.

CHAPTER LI.

MILITARY AND NAVAL HISTORY OF THE REBELLION.

INTRODUCTION.

THE recent war in the United States broke out under circumstances so unusual, and displayed such a grandeur of military scenes, such perfection in implements of destruction, and such vastness of operations, as to deserve some preliminary notice. Within less than the limits of a century is comprised the existence of the nation. During that period, its previous great war had been known among the people as that of the Revolution. On its scenes their minds have ever loved to dwell; its conflicts have been unceasingly rehearsed as illustrations of American bravery and fortitude; and the few lingering survivors have been cheered by a veneration due only to a superior class of men. The population of the country at the time of that war is unknown, no census having been taken until 1790. But the number of soldiers furnished by each State, and the population at the first census, were about as follows:

STATES.	Soldiers.	Population in 1790.
New Hampshire	12,497	141,899
*Massachusetts (including Maine)	67,907	475,257
Rhode Island	5,908	69,110
Connecticut	31,959	238,141
New York	17,781	340,120
New Jersey	10,726	184,139
Pennsylvania	25,678	434,373
Delaware	2,386	59,096
Maryland	13,912	319,728
Virginia	26,678	748,308
North Carolina	7,263	393,751
South Carolina	6,417	249,073
Georgia	2,589	82,548
Territories.		
Vermont	....	85,416
Tennessee	....	35,791
Kentucky	....	73,077
	231,701	3,929,827

The territories were then without any distinct civil organization, and as such furnished no soldiers. Their recruits were doubtless included among those of the adjoining States.

The battles of this war, together with the place and commander of each, and the losses, were as follows:

Where fought.	American commanders and loss.		British commanders and loss.	
Lexington	....	84	....	245
Bunker Hill	Warren	453	Howe	1,054
Flatbush	Putnam	2,000	Howe	400
White Plains	Washington	300	Howe	300
Trenton	Washington	9	Rahl	1,000
Princeton	Washington	100	Mawhood	400
Bennington	Stark	100	Baum	600
Brandywine	Washington	1,200	Howe	500
*Saratoga	Gates	350	Burgoyne	600
Monmouth	Washington	230	Clinton	400
Rhode Island	Sullivan	211	Pigott	260
Briar Creek	Ash	300	Prevost	16
Stony Point	Wayne	100	Johnson	600
Camden	Gates	720	Cornwallis	375
Cowpens	Morgan	72	Carleton	800
Guilford	Greene	400	Cornwallis	523
Eutaw Springs	Greene	555	Stewart	1,000

The surrender of Cornwallis at Yorktown, October 19, 1781, closed the war. The number surrendered was 7,073.

* The figures do not truly represent the aid given by the respective States. Thus the number of soldiers furnished by Pennsylvania is set down at 22,678; but to Massachusetts there is set down 67,507, although the population of the two States was then about the same in numbers. In one sense this is correct. Pennsylvania did furnish but 25,000 recruits, while Massachusetts sent 67,000. But there was this difference between the recruits: those from Pennsylvania were mostly enlisted for three years, or for the war; while those of Massachusetts generally entered the army for nine months. Thus, the Pennsylvania line was renewed only once every three years, while, during this interval, the Massachusetts line was renewed four times, or once every nine months. In this manner the latter nominally furnished four men, while the former furnished one, and this while having only the same number in the field.

* 5,752 British prisoners taken.

On the sea there was no organized navy. A few ships, as national vessels, had a brief, though bold and destructive career.

Perhaps it may be interesting to add, that the amount of currency, known as "Continental money," issued, was as follows:

Amount issued in 1775	$2,000,000
" " in 1777	20,000,000
Total amount issued to July, 1779	358,000,000

The whole expenses of the war, estimated in specie, amounted to $135,193,703.

In the next war, known as that of 1812, between the same combatants, General Brown crossed the Niagara River for the invasion of Canada with about 3,500 men. Three weeks afterwards, on July 25th, 1814, the battle of Lundy's Lane was fought between 3,000 Americans and 4,500 British troops. The loss of the former was 753 in killed and wounded, and that of the latter 878. The most celebrated battle of this war was that fought at New Orleans. The entire force of the British army landed above the mouths of the Mississippi for the capture of that city, was 12,000 men. On January 1st, 1815, an artillery duel took place, in which the British had thirty heavy guns behind a breastwork of hogsheads of sugar, which, it was supposed, would be as protective as sand-bags; and the Americans ten guns behind cotton bales. The sugar hogsheads were demolished, and the cotton bales set on fire. After a loss of seventy men, the British force drew off. The American loss was thirty-four. On January 8th the decisive battle was fought. The British advanced with 10,000 men against 6,000 under Gen. Jackson, of whom 3,500 were defended by breastworks. The British were repulsed with a loss of more than 2,000 men, while that of the Americans was but 27 in killed and wounded. In this war the United States had an organized navy of comparatively small wooden ships, the exploits of which were very brilliant and successful.

Peace now existed for thirty years, when the war with Mexico took place. On May 8th, 1846, Gen. Taylor, marching with 2,288 men from Point Isabel to Fort Brown, opposite Matamoras, on the Rio Grande, was attacked at Palo Alto by a Mexican force estimated at 6,000 men. The most celebrated battle in northern Mexico, that of Buena Vista, was fought by Gen. Taylor with about 6,000 men against 14,000, partially exhausted by crossing a desert previous to the action. The march from Puebla to the city of Mexico was made by Gen. Scott, with a force consisting of 10,738 men, rank and file. He fought the battles of Contreras, Churubusco, &c., August 20th, 1847, with 8,497 men. At Molina del Rey there were only three brigades, with some cavalry and artillery, making in all 3,251. The operating force in the battles of Sept. 12 and 13, was 7,180 men, and the city of Mexico was entered with less than 6,000. The opposing force in these battles is stated by Gen. Scott, "upon accumulated and unquestionable evidence," to have been not less than three and a half times greater in numbers than his own. The total losses of Gen. Scott in all these battles, including killed, wounded, and missing, amounted to 2,703, of whom 383 were officers.

The amount of the public debt on June 21st, 1848, after peace had been concluded, was $48,196,321; of which $31,868,762 had been incurred subsequent to July 1st, 1846. The first battle of the war was on May 8th, 1846. The Union consisted, in 1847, of thirty States, and by an estimate of the Government made at that time, the number of the militia of all the States was 1,821,093.

A period of profound peace now ensued. The standing military force of the Government was reduced to the smallest number practicable, being, in 1860, about 16,000 men, most of whom were required on the Western frontier to preserve the peace with the Indians. Officers of the army, after the close of the Mexican war, resigned their commissions, and devoted their talents to the pursuits of private life. Inventors of implements of war found their ingenuity to be unappreciated, and their manufactures profitless. The national Military School at West Point was regarded by the mass of the people as an expensive and useless establishment, and motions to suspend or refuse appropriations for its support were often made in Congress. Militia service in the several States had become almost disreputable. If laws existed to promote an efficient organization, they were not enforced. Private establishments for the manufacture of arms had, with one or two exceptions, ceased to exist, and the Federal armories at Springfield and Harper's Ferry were inactive. Meanwhile the warnings of another and more terrible conflict, given by gathering clouds, were unheeded, except in Massachusetts, where Governor Banks secured the adoption of legislative measures for a reorganization of the militia of the State, and in South Carolina, where the authorities, in 1860, secretly procured a considerable importation of muskets, which were at an early period of invaluable service to the cause she had espoused. Thus unprepared, and amid the most overflowing prosperity which the pursuits of peace ever yielded to an industrious people, the nation was alarmed by the sounds of an internal war that called every man to the field, and brought to pass the scenes described in the following pages.

CHAPTER I.

Secession Movements in South Carolina, Florida, Mississippi, Alabama, Georgia, and Louisiana.

THE Legislature of South Carolina assembled on the 4th of November, 1860, and having chosen the Presidential electors, adjourned.

The election for President was held on the 6th of November, 1860. On that day the vote of the State was given by the electors to John C. Breckinridge for President. On the next day the Legislature again assembled, and the subject of withdrawal from the United States was taken up, and an act passed calling a State Convention to meet at Columbia on the 17th of December. Other measures were then introduced and adopted, the object of which was to place the State in a suitable position to meet the crisis about to be inaugurated.

On the 10th of December Francis W. Pickens was chosen Governor by the Legislature. He was inaugurated immediately after his election, and improved the occasion to declare the cause of the movement on the part of South Carolina to separate from the Union. In his view it was as follows:

For seventy-three years this State has been connected by a Federal compact with co-States, under a bond of union for great national objects common to all. In recent years there has been a powerful party, organized upon principles of ambition and fanaticism, whose undisguised purpose is to divert the Federal Government from external and turn its power upon the internal interests and domestic institutions of these States. They have thus combined a party exclusively in the Northern States, whose avowed objects not only endanger the peace, but the very existence of nearly one-half of the States of this Confederacy. And in the recent election for President and Vice-President of these States, they have carried the election upon principles that make it no longer safe for us to rely upon the powers of the Federal Government, or the guarantees of the Federal compact. This is the great overt act of the people in the Northern States at the ballot-box, in the exercise of their sovereign power at the polls, from which there is no higher appeal recognized under our system of Government in its ordinary and habitual operations. They thus propose to inaugurate a Chief Magistrate, at the head of the army and navy, with vast powers, not to preside over the common interests and destinies of all the States alike, but upon issues of malignant hostility and uncompromising war, to be waged upon the rights, the interests, and the peace of half the States of this Union.

In the Southern States there are two entirely distinct and separate races, and one has been held in subjection to the other by peaceful inheritance from worthy and patriotic ancestors, and all who know the races well know that it is the only form of government that can preserve both, and administer the blessings of civililization with order and in harmony. Any thing tending to change and weaken the Government and the subordination between the races, not only endangers the peace, but the very existence of our society itself. We have for years warned the Northern people of the dangers they were producing by their wanton and lawless course. We have often appealed to our sister States of the South to act with us in concert upon some firm and moderate system by which we might be able to save the Federal Constitution, and yet feel safe under the general compact of Union; but we could obtain no fair warning from the North, nor could we see any concerted plan proposed by any of our co-States of the South calculated to make us feel safe and secure.

Under all these circumstances we now have no alternative left but to interpose our sovereign power as an independent State to protect the rights and ancient privileges of the people of South Carolina. This State was one of the original parties to the Federal compact of union. We agreed to it, as a State, under peculiar circumstances, when we were surrounded with great external pressure, for purposes of national protection, and to advance the interests and general welfare of all the States equally and alike. And when it ceases to do this, it is no longer a perpetual Union. It would be an absurdity to suppose it was a perpetual Union for our ruin.

After a few days the Legislature took a recess until the 17th of December, the day on which the State Convention was to assemble. Preparations for the Convention were commenced immediately after the bill was passed by the Legislature. Candidates for membership were nominated. All were in favor of secession, and the only important distinction to be seen among them consisted in the personal character of individuals. Those who were known to be men of moderate and conservative views were generally successful over individuals of a radical and ultra stamp.

The Convention assembled in the Baptist church at Columbia, the capital of the State, at noon, on the 17th of December. Unlike the conventions of the other States, its sessions were at first held with open doors, and its proceed ings published to the country. When the Con vention was called to order, David F. Jamison was requested to act as president *pro tem.*

The names were called, but an oath was not administered to the delegates. For president of the Convention, on the fourth ballot, David F. Jamison received 118 votes, J. L. Orr 30, and James Chesnut, jr., 3. Mr. Jamison was elected.

A motion was next made that the Convention adjourn, to meet in Charleston on the afternoon of the next day, owing to the prevalence of small-pox in Columbia. This motion was opposed by W. Porcher Miles, who said:

"We would be sneered at. It would be asked on all sides, Is this the chivalry of South Carolina? They are prepared to face the world, but they run away from the small-pox. Sir, if every day my prospects of life were diminished by my being here, and if I felt the certain conviction that I must take this disease, I would do so, and die, if necessary. I am just from Washington, where I have been in constant, close, continual conference with our friends. Their unanimous, urgent request to us is, not to delay at all. The last thing urged on me, by our friends from Georgia, Mississippi, Florida, North Carolina, Alabama, Texas, and Louisiana, and every State that is with us in this great movement, was, take out South Carolina the instant you can. Now, sir, when the news reaches Washington that we met here, that a panic arose about a few cases of small-pox in the city, and that we forthwith scampered off to Charleston, the effect would be a little ludicrous, if I might be excused for that expression."

The motion was adopted, and the Convention assembled on the next day at Charleston.

The following committee was then appointed to draft an ordinance of secession: Messrs. Inglis, Rhett, sen., Chesnut, Orr, Maxcy Gregg, B. F. Dunkin, and Hutson, and another committee, as follows, to prepare an address to the people of the Southern States, viz.: Messrs. Rhett, sen., Calhoun, Finley, J. D. Wilson, W. F. De Saussure, Cheves, and Carn.

The following committees were also appointed, each to consist of thirteen members:

A Committee on Relations with the Slaveholding States of North America; a Committee on Foreign Relations; a Committee on Commercial Relations and Postal Arrangements; and a Committee on the Constitution of the State.

On the same day Mr. Magrath, of Charleston, offered the following resolution:

Resolved, That so much of the Message of the President of the United States as relates to what he designates "the property of the United States in South Carolina," be referred to a committee of thirteen, to report of what such property consists, how acquired, and whether the purpose for which it was so acquired can be enjoyed by the United States after the State of South Carolina shall have seceded, consistently with the dignity and safety of the State. And that said committee further report the value of the property of the United States not in South Carolina; and the value of the share thereof to which South Carolina would be entitled upon an equitable division thereof among the United States.

Upon offering the resolution, he said:

"As I understand the Message of the President of the United States, he affirms it as his right and constituted duty and high obligation to protect the property of the United States within the limits of South Carolina, and to enforce the laws of the Union within the limits of South Carolina. He says he has no constitutional power to coerce South Carolina, while, at the same time, he denies to her the right of secession. It may be, and I apprehend it will be, Mr. President, that the attempt to coerce South Carolina will be made under the pretence of protecting the property of the United States within the limits of South Carolina. I am disposed, therefore, at the very threshold, to test the accuracy of this logic, and test the conclusions of the President of the United States. There never has been a day—no, not one hour—in which the right of property within the limits of South Carolina, whether it belongs to individuals, corporations, political community, or nation, has not been as safe under the Constitution and laws of South Carolina as when that right is claimed by one of our own citizens; and if there be property of the United States within the limits of South Carolina, that property, consistently with the dignity and honor of the State, can, after the secession of South Carolina, receive only that protection which it received before."

Mr. Miles, who had just returned from Washington, stated the position of affairs to be as follows:

"I will confine myself simply to the matter of the forts in the harbor of Charleston, and I will state what I conceive to be the real condition of things. I have not the remotest idea that the President of the United States will send any reënforcement whatsoever into these forts. I desire no concealment—there should be no concealment—but perfect frankness. I will state here that I, with some of my colleagues, in a conversation with the President of the United States, and subsequently in a written communication, to which our names were signed, after speaking of the great excitement about the forts, said thus to him:

Mr. President, it is our solemn conviction that, if you attempt to send a solitary soldier to these forts, the instant the intelligence reaches our people, (and we shall take care that it does reach them, for we have sources of information in Washington, so that no orders for troops can be issued without our getting information,) these forts will be forcibly and immediately stormed.

"We all assured him that, if an attempt was made to transport reënforcements, our people would take these forts, and that we would go home and help them to do it; for it would be suicidal folly for us to allow the forts to be manned. And we further said to him that a bloody result would follow the sending of troops to those forts, and that we did not believe that the authorities of South Carolina would do any thing prior to the meeting of this convention, and that we hoped and believed that nothing would be done after this body met until we had demanded of the General Government the recession of these forts. This was the substance of what we said. Now, sir, it is my most solemn conviction that there is no attempt going to be made to reënforce these forts."

Resolutions were offered and referred, which proposed a provisional government for the Southern States on the basis of the Constitution of the United States; also to send commissioners to Washington to negotiate for the cession of Federal property within the State, &c.; also, the election of five persons to meet delegates from other States, for the purpose of forming a Confederacy, &c.

On the 20th the committee appointed to draft an ordinance of secession made the following report:

The committee appointed to prepare the draught of an Ordinance proper to be adopted by the Convention in order to effect the secession of South Carolina from the Federal Union, respectfully report:

That they have had the matter referred to under consideration, and believing that they would best meet the exigencies of the great occasion, and the just expectations of the Convention by presenting in the fewest and simplest words possible to be used, consistent with perspicuity and all that is necessary to effect the end proposed and no more, and so excluding every thing which, however proper in itself for the action of the Convention, is not a necessary part of the great solemn act of secession, and may at least be effected by a distinct ordinance or resolution, they submit for the consideration of the Convention the following proposed draught:

AN ORDINANCE *to dissolve the Union between the State of South Carolina and other States united with her under the compact entitled "The Constitution of the United States of America."*

We, the people of the State of South Carolina, in Convention assembled, do declare and ordain, and it is hereby declared and ordained, that the ordinance adopted by us in Convention on the twenty-third day of May, in the year of our Lord one thousand seven hundred and eighty-eight, whereby the Constitution of the United States was ratified, and also all acts and parts of acts of the General Assembly of the State ratifying amendments of the said Constitution, are hereby repealed, and the Union now subsisting between South Carolina and other States, under the name of "The United States of America," is hereby dissolved.

The ordinance was then taken up and immediately passed by the unanimous vote of the Convention. After its passage, the following ordinance was passed to preserve the order of affairs under the altered political relations of the State:

Be it ordained by the People of South Carolina, by their Delegates in Convention assembled, That, until otherwise provided by the Legislature, the Governor shall be authorized to appoint collectors and other officers connected with the customs, for the ports within the State of South Carolina, and also all the postmasters within the said State; and that until such appointments shall have been made, the persons now charged with the duties of the said several offices shall continue to discharge the same, keeping an account of what moneys are received and disbursed by them respectively.

The Convention adjourned to meet at Institute Hall, and in the presence of the Governor, and both branches of the State Legislature, to sign the ordinance of secession.

At the close of the ceremonies the president of the Convention announced the secession of the State in these words: "The ordinance of secession has been signed and ratified, and I proclaim the State of South Carolina an independent Commonwealth." The ratified ordinance was then given to the Secretary of State to be preserved among its archives, and the assembly dissolved.

On the 21st the committee to prepare an address to the Southern States made a report, reviewing the injuries to South Carolina imputed to her connection with the Federal Union. An ordinance was then adopted which prescribed the following oath, to be taken by all persons elected and appointed to any office:

I do solemnly swear, (or affirm,) that I will be faithful and true allegiance bear to the Constitution of the State of South Carolina, so long as I may continue a citizen of the same; and that I am duly qualified under the laws of South Carolina, and will discharge the duties thereof to the best of my ability, and will preserve, protect, and defend the Constitution of this State. So help me God.

In secret session, Messrs. Robert W. Barnwell, J. H. Adams, and James L. Orr, were appointed commissioners to proceed to Washington, to treat for the delivery of the forts, magazines, light-houses, &c., within the limits of the State, also the apportionment of the public debts and a division of all other property held by the Government of the United States, as agent of the confederation of States, of which South Carolina was recently a member, and to negotiate all other arrangements proper to be adopted in the existing relations of the parties.

Active movements immediately commenced for resisting any attempt on the part of the United States to exercise Federal powers within the limits of the State. Rumors that vessels of war had started for Charleston harbor, and that the commissioners to Washington were on their way home, created great excitement in the State, and all thought of peaceable secession was abandoned. A collector for the port of Charleston was nominated to the Senate by President Buchanan, but that body failed to confirm the nomination.

Meantime, Governor Pickens organized his Cabinet, as follows: Secretary of State, A. G. Magrath; Secretary of War, D. F. Jamison; Secretary of the Treasury, C. G. Memminger; Postmaster-General, W. H. Harlee; Secretary of the Interior, A. C. Gurlington.

On the 31st of December, the State troops, which had been for some time acting as a guard to the arsenal, under orders from the Governor, took full possession, and relieved the United States officer who had been in charge. At half-past one o'clock on Sunday, the Federal flag was lowered after a salute of thirty-two guns. The State troops were drawn up in order and presented arms. The Palmetto flag was then run up, with a salute of one gun for South Carolina.

The arsenal contained at the time a large amount of arms and other stores. Meanwhile military preparations were actively pushed forward, and several volunteer companies from other Southern States tendered their services. Notice was given by the collector at Charleston that the masters of all vessels from ports outside of South Carolina must enter and clear at Charleston. Bank bills were also made receivable for duties.

The flag of the State, adopted by the Legislature, to whom the subject had been referred by the State Convention, consisted of a plain white ground with a green Palmetto tree in the centre, and a white crescent in the left upper corner on a square blue field.

On the 14th of January the Legislature unanimously passed a resolution declaring that any attempt by the Federal Government to reënforce Fort Sumter would be considered as an act of open hostility, and as a declaration of war. At the same time they adopted another resolution, approving the act of the troops who fired on the Star of the West, and also resolved to sustain the Governor in all measures necessary for defence.

The forts in Charleston harbor, occupied by a small garrison of regular troops of the United States, afforded a standing denial of the sovereignty and independence of South Carolina. The first object to be accomplished by the State authorities to secure that respect due to an independent nation, was to obtain possession of these forts. For this object the following correspondence took place:

STATE OF SOUTH CAROLINA,
EXECUTIVE OFFICE, CHARLESTON, *Jan.* 11, 1861.

To Major Robert Anderson, commanding Fort Sumter.

SIR: I have thought proper, under all the circumstances of the peculiar state of public affairs in the country at present, to appoint the Hon. A. G. Magrath and Gen. D F. Jamison, both members of the Executive Council, and of the highest position in the State, to present to you considerations of the gravest public character, and of the deepest interest to all who deprecate the improper waste of life, to induce the delivery of Fort Sumter to the constituted authorities of the State of South Carolina, with a pledge, on its part, to account for such public property as is under your charge. Your obedient servant,

F. W. PICKENS.

MAJOR ANDERSON TO GOV. PICKENS.

HEADQUARTERS FORT SUMTER, S. C., January 11, 1861.

His Exc'y F. W. Pickens, Governor of S. Carolina.

SIR: I have the honor to acknowledge the receipt of your demand for the surrender of this fort to the authorities of South Carolina, and to say, in reply, that the demand is one with which I cannot comply.

Your Excellency knows that I have recently sent a messenger to Washington, and that it will be impossible for me to receive an answer to my despatches, forwarded by him, at an earlier date than next Monday. What the character of my instructions may be I cannot foresee. Should your Excellency deem fit, prior to a resort to arms, to refer this matter to Washington, it would afford me the sincerest pleasure to depute one of my officers to accompany any messenger you may deem proper to be the bearer of your demand.

Hoping to God that in this, and all other matters, in which the honor, welfare, and lives of our fellow-countrymen are concerned, we shall so act as to meet His approval, and deeply regretting that you have made a demand of me with which I cannot comply, I have the honor to be, with the highest regard, your obedient servant, ROBERT ANDERSON,

Major U. S. Army, commanding.

Other States soon followed the example of South Carolina. Of these Florida was foremost. Her Senators in Congress assembled, in secret caucus, with those from other States to devise the plan of action. Prompt measures were also taken by the State authorities to secure success. At an early day a State Convention was called to meet on the 5th of January, to which delegates were at once elected. The Convention assembled at Tallahassee on the day appointed. It consisted of sixty-seven members, one-third of whom were regarded as in favor of coöperation. On the 7th, a resolution declaring the right and duty of Florida to secede was passed —ayes, 62; noes, 5.

On the same day the ordinance of secession was passed by a vote of 62 ayes to 7 noes. The following is the ordinance:

Whereas, All hope of preserving the Union upon terms consistent with the safety and honor of the slaveholding States, has been fully dissipated by the recent indications of the strength of the anti-slavery sentiment of the free States; therefore,

Be it enacted by the people of Florida, in convention assembled, That it is undoubtedly the right of the several States of the Union, at such time and for such cause as in the opinion of the people of such States, acting in their sovereign capacity, may be just and proper, to withdraw from the Union, and, in the opinion of this Convention, the existing causes are such as to compel Florida to proceed to exercise this right.

We, the people of the State of Florida, in Convention assembled, do solemnly ordain, publish, and declare that the State of Florida hereby withdraws herself from the Confederacy of States existing under the name of the United States of America, and from the existing Government of the said States; and that all political connection between her and the Government of said States ought to be, and the same is hereby totally annulled, and said Union of States dissolved; and the State of Florida is hereby declared a sovereign and independent nation; and that all ordinances heretofore adopted, in so far as they create or recognize said Union, are rescinded; and all laws, or parts of laws, in force in this State, in so far as they recognize or assent to said Union, be and they are hereby repealed.

The Convention, at a subsequent date, was addressed by the Commissioner from South Carolina, L. W. Spratt. In his address he admits that, if the Southern people had been left to consult their own interests in the matter, apart from the complications superinduced by the action of South Carolina, they would never have felt it their duty to initiate the movement in which, for reasons partly long conceived and partly fortuitous, she had now, as she thinks, succeeded in involving them.

The other acts of the Convention completed the work commenced by the ordinance of secession. Delegates were appointed to a Confederate Congress, with instructions to coöperate with those from other States in the formation of a Government independent of the United States. A session of the Legislature was held at the same time, in order to pass such measures as would give strength to the executive officers in their new position.

The forts and arsenals of the United States and the U. S. schooner Dana were seized, under instructions from the Governor, at the same time those in Alabama were occupied by the troops of that State. At the most important forts, as Pickens, Jefferson, and Taylor, there were such garrisons as were able to defend them. The investment of the former was immediately made by the troops from Florida, with reënforcements from Georgia, Alabama, and Mississippi. The navy yard and forts on the mainland at Pensacola were thus occupied, but Pickens defied all the efforts of the besiegers.

Mississippi moved next. A session of her Legislature was held at Jackson early in November, 1860, for making the preliminary arrangements for a State Convention. It passed an act calling such Convention on the 7th of January, and fixed the 20th of December as the day upon which an election should be held for members. The measures were passed unanimously. The following resolutions were also adopted unanimously:

Resolved, That the Governor be requested to appoint as many Commissioners as in his judgment may be necessary to visit each of the slaveholding States, and designate the State or States to which each Commissioner shall be commissioned, whose duty it shall be to inform them that this Legislature has passed an act calling a Convention of the people of this State to consider the present threatening relations of the Northern and Southern sections of the Confederacy, aggravated by the recent election of a President upon principles of hostility to the States of the South, and to express the earnest hope of Mississippi that those States will coöperate with her in the adoption of efficient measures for their common defence and safety.

Resolved, That, should any Southern State not have convened its Legislature, the Commissioner to such State shall appeal to the Governor thereof to call the Legislature together, in order that its coöperation be immediately secured.

One of the members, Mr. Lamar, advocated separate secession of the State, and recommended that the Senators and Representatives in the Federal Congress from the Southern States should withdraw and form a Congress of a new republic, and appoint electors for President of a Southern Confederacy. The Legislature adjourned on the 30th of November, 1860.

The people of the State were divided on the question of secession. The election of members of the State Convention took place on the 20th of December. The number of members to be elected was ninety-nine. Of these more than one-third were coöperationists. This distinction into coöperationists and secessionists only referred to the manner of proceeding which the State should adopt. The latter advocated immediate and separate secession, the former preferred consultation and coöperation with the other slaveholding States. The ultimate object of each was the same, as expressed in the following language by one of the citizens: "These are household quarrels. As against Northern combination and aggression we are united. We are all for resistance. We differ as to the mode; but the fell spirit of abolitionism has no deadlier and we believe no more practical foes than the coöperationists of the South. We are willing to give the North a chance to say whether it will accept or reject the terms that a united South will agree upon. If accepted, well and good; if rejected, a united South can win all its rights in or out of the Union."

The State Convention organized on the 7th of January, and immediately appointed a committee to prepare and report an ordinance of secession with a view of establishing a new confederacy to be comprised of the seceded States. The Committee duly reported the following ordinance, and it was adopted on the 9th—ayes, 84; noes, 15:

The people of Mississippi, in Convention assembled, do ordain and declare, and it is hereby ordained and declared, as follows, to wit:

SEC. 1. That all the laws and ordinances by which the said State of Mississippi became a member of the Federal Union of the United States of America be, and the same are hereby repealed, and that all obligations on the part of the said State, or the people thereof, be withdrawn, and that the said State does hereby resume all the rights, functions, and powers which by any of the said laws and ordinances were conveyed to the Government of the said United States, and is absolved from all the obligations, restraints, and duties incurred to the said Federal Union, and shall henceforth be a free, sovereign, and independent State.

SEC. 2. That so much of the first section of the seventh article of the Constitution of this State, as requires members of the Legislature and all officers, both legislative and judicial, to take an oath to support the Constitution of the United States, be, and the same is hereby abrogated and annulled.

SEC. 3. That all rights acquired and vested under the Constitution of the United States, or under any act of Congress passed in pursuance thereof, or any law of this State, and not incompatible with this ordinance, shall remain in force, and have the same effect as if the ordinance had not been passed.

SEC. 4. That the people of the State of Mississippi hereby consent to form a Federal Union with such of the States as have seceded or may secede from the Union of the United States of America, upon the basis of the present Constitution of the United States, except such parts thereof as embrace other portions than such seceding States.

Delegations from South Carolina and Alabama were invited to seats in the Convention, and were greeted with much applause. Efforts were made to postpone action, but these were voted down, and only fifteen voted nay on the final passage of the measure. The vote was subsequently made unanimous. The first aggressive movement was made by Governor Pettus on the 12th of January, when he ordered a piece of artillery to Vicksburg to be used in stopping for examination boats passing on the Mississippi. Movements were at the same time commenced to complete the organization of the militia of the State. Judge Gholson, of the United States Court, resigned. South Carolina was recognized by the Convention as sovereign and independent, and steps were taken to cut asunder every tie to the United States, excepting the postal arrangements. The subsequent movements were reported to the Legislature by the Governor in a Message on the 15th of January. He says:

"As soon as I was informed that the Governor of Louisiana had taken the arsenal at Baton Rouge, I sent Col. C. G. Armstead with a letter to Gov. Moore, requesting him to furnish Mississippi with ten thousand stand of arms on such terms as he might deem just. Col. Armstead informs me that his Excellency has responded to my request by ordering eight thousand muskets, one thousand rifles, and six twenty-four pound guns, with carriages, and a considerable amount of ammunition, to be delivered to him, which will be shipped to Mississippi as soon as possible."

Alabama soon followed. The southern portion of the State was strongly in favor of secession. Early in December, 1860, commissioners were sent to the authorities and people of the other slaveholding States, to urge forward a movement in favor of secession, and a union of these States in a separate Confederacy. All represented that the purpose of Alabama was fixed to secede, even if no other State did. The announcement of the secession of South Carolina was hailed with great joy in Mobile. One hundred guns were fired. Bells were rung. The streets were crowded by hundreds expressing their joy, and many impromptu speeches were made. A military parade ensued.

The first official movement in Alabama toward secession was the announcement by Governor Moore of his intention to order an election of Delegates to a State Convention. He advised the people to prepare for secession. This election was held on the 24th of December, 1860, and the Convention subsequently assembled on January 7th. At the election, the counties in North Alabama selected "coöperation" members. The members throughout the State were classed as immediate secessionists, and coöperationists. The coöperationists were divided into those who were for secession in coöperation with other cotton States, those who required the coöperation of a majority, and those who required the coöperation of all the slave States. Montgomery County, which polled 2,719 votes on the Presidential election, now gave less than 1,200 votes. The inference drawn from this at the time was, that the county was largely in favor of conservative action. The vote reported from all but ten counties of the State was: for secession, 24,445; for coöperation, 33,685. Of the ten counties, some were for secession, others for coöperation.

The Convention met at Montgomery on the 7th of January. All the counties of the State were represented. Wm. M. Brooks was chosen President. A strong Union sentiment was soon found to exist in the Convention. On the day on which it assembled, the Representatives from the State in Washington met, and resolved to telegraph to the Convention, advising immediate secession, stating that in their opinion there was no prospect of a satisfactory adjustment.

On the 9th the following resolutions were offered and referred to a committee of thirteen:

Resolved, That separate State action would be unwise and impolitic.

Resolved, That Alabama should invite the Southern States to hold a Convention as early as practicable, to consider and agree upon a statement of grievances and the manner of obtaining redress, whether in the Union or in independence out of it.

Mr. Baker, of Russell, offered a resolution requesting the Governor to furnish information of the number of arms, their character and description, and the number of military companies, etc., in the State, which was adopted. Also the following was offered and discussed:

Resolved, by the people of Alabama, That all the powers of this State are hereby pledged to resist any attempt on the part of the Federal Government to coerce any seceding State.

After a lively discussion of some days, a brief preamble and resolution refusing to submit to the Republican Administration, were proposed in such a form as to command the unanimous vote of the Convention. It was in these words:

Whereas the only bond of union between the several States is the Constitution of the United States; and whereas that Constitution has been violated by a majority of the Northern States in their separate legislative action, denying to the people of the Southern States their constitutional rights; and whereas a sectional party, known as the Republican party, has, in a recent election, elected Abraham Lincoln for President and Hannibal Hamlin for Vice-President of these United States, upon the avowed principle that the Constitution of the United States does not recognize property in slaves, and that the Government should prevent its extension into the common territories of the United States, and that the power of the Government should be so exercised that slavery should in time be extinguished: Therefore be it

Resolved by the people of Alabama in Convention assembled, That the State of Alabama will not submit to the Administration of Lincoln and Hamlin, as President and Vice-President of the United States, upon the principles referred to in the foregoing preamble.

On the 10th, the ordinance of secession was reported, and on the 11th it was adopted in secret session by a vote of ayes, 61; noes, 39. It was as follows:

AN ORDINANCE *to dissolve the Union between the State of Alabama and other States united under the compact styled "The Constitution of the United States of America."*

Whereas the election of Abraham Lincoln and Hannibal Hamlin to the offices of President and Vice-President of the United States of America, by a sectional party, avowedly hostile to the domestic institutions and to the peace and security of the people of the State of Alabama, preceded by many and dangerous infractions of the Constitution of the United States by many of the States and people of the Northern section, is a political wrong of so insulting and menacing a character as to justify the people of the State of Alabama in the adoption of prompt and decided measures for their future peace and security: Therefore,

Be it declared and ordained by the people of the State of Alabama in convention assembled, That the State of Alabama now withdraws, and is hereby withdrawn, from the Union known as "the United States of America," and henceforth ceases to be one of said United States, and is, and of right ought to be, a sovereign and independent State.

SEC. 2. *Be it further declared and ordained by the people of the State of Alabama in convention assembled,* That all the powers over the territory of said State, and over the people thereof, heretofore delegated to the Government of the United States of America, be and they are hereby withdrawn from said Government, and are hereby resumed and vested in the people of the State of Alabama.

And as it is the desire and purpose of the State of Alabama to meet the slaveholding States of the South who may approve such purpose, in order to frame a provisional as well as permanent government, upon the principles of the Constitution of the United States,

Be it resolved by the people of Alabama in convention assembled, That the people of the States of Delaware, Maryland, Virginia, North Carolina, South Carolina, Florida, Georgia, Mississippi, Louisiana, Texas, Arkansas, Tennessee, Kentucky, and Missouri, be, and are hereby, invited to meet the people of the State of Alabama, by their delegates, in convention, on the 4th day of February, A. D. 1861, at the city of Montgomery, in the State of Alabama, for the purpose of consulting with each other as to the most effectual mode of securing concerted and harmonious action in whatever measures may be deemed most desirable for our common peace and security.

And be it further resolved, That the president of this Convention be, and is hereby, instructed to transmit forthwith a copy of the foregoing preamble, ordinance, and resolutions, to the Governors of the several States named in said resolutions.

Done by the people of the State of Alabama in Convention assembled, at Montgomery, on this, the 11th day of January, A. D. 1861.

WM. M. BROOKS, President of the Convention.

A majority and minority report were presented on the ordinance of secession. Trouble arose in the Convention, because a portion of the members desired that the ordinance should not take effect until the 4th of March. A number refused to sign it for this reason; and as late as the 17th of January, a despatch was sent to the Senators and Representatives of the State in Congress at Washington, to retain their seats until further advised.

A proposition was also made in the Convention to submit their action to the people, for ratification or rejection. This was refused, and an exciting scene ensued.

Nicholas Davis, of Huntsville, declared his belief that the people of North Alabama would never abide the action of that Convention, if denied the right of voting upon it. Mr. Yancey thereupon denounced the people of North Alabama as tories, traitors, and rebels, and said they ought to be coerced into a submission to the decree of the Convention. Mr. Davis replied that they might attempt coercion, but North Alabama would meet them upon the line and decide the issue at the point of the bayonet.

The ordinance was adopted about two o'clock in the afternoon. Subsequently in the afternoon an immense mass meeting was held in front of the Capitol, and many coöperation delegates pledged their constituents to sustain secession. A flag which had been presented by the ladies of the city to the Convention, was then raised over the building, amid the ringing of bells and firing of cannon.

In Mobile the news was received at once, and the day became one of the wildest excitement. The people were at the highest point of enthusiasm until a late hour at night. To add to the excitement, news was received that the State of Florida had passed a secession ordinance.

Immediately on the receipt of the news, an immense crowd assembled at the "secession pole" at the foot of Government Street, to witness the spreading of the Southern flag, and it was run up amid the shouts of the multitude and thunders of cannon. One hundred and one guns for Alabama and fifteen for Florida were fired, and after remarks from gentlemen, the crowd repaired to the Custom-House, walking in procession with a band of music at the head, playing the warlike notes of the "Southern Marseillaise."

Arrived at the Custom-House, a lone star flag was waved from its walls amid enthusiastic shouts. The balcony of the Battle House, opposite, was thronged with ladies and gentlemen, and the street was crowded with excited citizens. Standing upon the steps of the Custom-House, brief and stirring addresses were delivered by several speakers.

The military paraded the streets. The Cadets were out in force, bearing a splendid flag which had been presented to them a day previous, and, with the Independent Rifles, marched to the public square, and fired salvos of artillery. The demonstration at night was designed to correspond to the importance attached by the people to the event celebrated. An eye-witness declares the display to have been of the most brilliant description. When night fell, the city emerged from darkness into a blaze of such glory as could only be achieved by the most recklessly extravagant consumption of tar and tallow. The broad boulevard of Government street was an avenue of light, bonfires of tar barrels being kindled at intervals of a square in distance along its length, and many houses were illuminated. Royal Street shone with light, the great front of the buildings presenting a perfect illumination. Rockets blazed, crackers popped, and the people hurrahed and shouted as they never did before. The "Southern Cross was the most favored emblematic design in the illumination, and competed with the oft-repeated 'Lone Star' for admiration and applause from the multitude."

By previous concert with the Governors of Georgia and Louisiana, "all the positions in these three States which might be made to follow the fashion set by Fort Sumter" were seized. The arsenal at Mt. Vernon, forty-five miles above Mobile, was seized at daylight on the morning of January 14th; Fort Morgan was taken on the same day, without opposition. Previously, however, and on the 9th of January, five companies of volunteers, at the request of the Governor of Florida, left Montgomery for Pensacola. They were sent to assist in capturing the forts and other property there belonging to the United States. In order to place the city of Mobile in a better state of defence, the Mayor issued a call to the people for a thousand laborers. These were at once supplied, and also money sufficient to meet all demands. The Common Council of the city passed an ordinance changing the names of various streets. The name of Maine Street was changed to Palmetto Street; Massachusetts was changed to Charleston Street; New Hampshire was changed to Augusta Street; Rhode Island was changed to Savannah Street; Connecticut was changed to Louisiana Street; New York was changed to Elmira Street; Vermont was changed to Texas Street; Pennsylvania was changed to Montgomery Street.

The Union feeling in the northern part of the State continued very strong. Many delegates from that region refused at first to sign the ordinance of secession which passed the State Convention, unless the time for it to take effect was postponed to the 4th of March. Some of them withheld their signatures entirely. The sessions of the Convention were conducted wholly in secret, and only such measures were made known to the public as were of such a character as to prevent secrecy.

Upon the adjournment of the Convention the President made an address, expressing the most decided views upon the permanency of the secession of the State. He said:

"We are free, and shall any of us cherish any idea of a reconstruction of the old Government, whereby Alabama will again link her rights, her fortunes, and her destiny, in a Union with the Northern States? If any one of you hold to such a fatal opinion, let me entreat you, as you value the blessings of equality and freedom, dismiss it at once. There is not, there cannot be, any security or peace for us in a reconstructed Government of the old material. I must believe that there is not a friend or advocate of reconstruction in this large body. The people of Alabama are now independent; sink or swim, live or die, they will continue free, sovereign, and independent. Dismiss the idea of a reconstruction of the old Union now and forever."

After the adjournment of the Convention, a Commissioner, Thomas J. Judge, was sent by the State authorities to negotiate with the Federal Government for the surrender of the forts, arsenals, and custom-houses within the limits of the State. It appears that the President declined to receive him in any other character than as a distinguished citizen of Alabama. In this capacity he declined to be received, and returned home.

At this time, previous to the surrender of Fort Sumter, a considerable Confederate force was, in a manner, besieging Fort Pickens at Pensacola, under the command of Gen. Bragg. Meanwhile, the Federal fleet lay off at anchor. Supplies having been taken to the fleet by the sloop Isabella, Capt. Jones, of Mobile, the vessel was seized and turned over to the military authorities, and the captain arrested. The charge was that he had attempted to convey supplies on his own private account, or that of his owners, to the United States vessels. On a writ of habeus corpus Jones was irregularly discharged. The reputed owners of the sloop refused to receive her, intending to hold the captors responsible for all loss.

Georgia was one of the latest of the first group of States to secede. The session of the Legislature commenced in November, and its attention was early attracted to the movement. Various propositions were offered and discussed, and on the 7th of December the following preamble and resolutions were adopted in the Assembly—yeas 101, nays 27:

The grievances now affecting the Southern States must be effectively resisted.

The interests and destiny of the slaveholding States of this Union are and must remain common.

The secession of one from the Union must, more or less, involve or affect all; therefore

Resolved by the General Assembly of Georgia, That in the judgment of this General Assembly, any State in this Union has the sovereign right to secede from the Union, whenever she deems it necessary and proper for her safety, honor, or happiness; and that when a State exercises this right of secession, the Federal Government has no right to coerce or make war upon her because of the exercise of such right to secede; and should any Southern State secede from the Amercan Union, and the Federal Government make war upon her therefor, Georgia will give to the seceding Southern State the aid, encouragement, and assistance of her entire people. And should the State of Georgia secede from the Union by the action of the Convention of her people on the 16th of January next, she asks the like sympathy and assistance from her Southern sisters which she hereby offers to them.

This resolution was subsequently, under the indications of the strength of the popular feeling against separate State secession, rescinded by a vote of yeas 50, nays 47.

The Senate had previously indefinitely postponed all the resolutions on this subject which had been pending in that body, for the reason that a large majority of its members were indisposed to interfere with a matter upon which they had called a Convention of the People to act.

Numerous public meetings were at this time held in many counties of the State, at which resolutions were adopted expressing apprehensions of the consequences of the "election of Lincoln and Hamlin," but manifesting a disinclination to proceed to acts of immediate secession, until other measures had been tried. They were dignified and conservative in language, and clearly indicated that hostility to the Union was neither deep-seated nor bitter.

The election for delegates to the State Convention took place on the 4th of January. The vote on that occasion was thus spoken of soon after:

"We know as well as any one living that the whole movement for secession, and the formation of a new Government, so far at least as Georgia is concerned, proceeded on only a *quasi* consent of the people, and was pushed through, under circumstances of great excitement and frenzy, by a fictitious majority. With all the appliances brought to bear, with all the fierce rushing, maddening events of the hour, the election of the 4th of January showed a falling off in the popular vote of 25,000 or 30,000, and on the night of that election the coöperationists had a majority, notwithstanding the falling off, of nearly 3,000, and an absolute majority of elected delegates of 29. But, upon assembling, by coaxing, bullying, and all other arts, the majority was changed."

This Convention assembled at Milledgeville on the 16th of January. General W. Crawford was elected President. Commissioners Orr, from South Carolina, and Shorter, from Alabama, were invited to seats in that body. On the 18th, a resolution declaring it to be the right and duty of Georgia to secede, and appointing a committee to draft an ordinance of secession, was offered and put to vote. On a division, the vote was—ayes, 165; noes, 130. The ordinance was as follows:

AN ORDINANCE *to dissolve the union between the State of Georgia and other States united with her under the compact of Government entitled "The Constitution of the United States."*

We, the people of the State of Georgia, in Convention assembled, do declare and ordain, and it is hereby declared and ordained, that the ordinance adopted by the people of Georgia in Convention in the year 1788, whereby the Constitution of the United States was assented to, ratified, and adopted, and also all acts and parts of acts of the General Assembly ratifying and adopting the amendments to the said Constitution, are hereby repealed, rescinded, and abrogated; and we do further declare and ordain, that the Union now subsisting between the State of Georgia and other States, under the name of the United States of Americo, is hereby dissolved; and that the State of Georgia is in full possession and exercise of all those rights of sovereignty which belong and appertain to a free and independent State.

The vote on its adoption was—ayes, 208; noes, 89.

On the night after its passage, great demonstrations of joy were made at the Capital, including the firing of cannon, torch-light processions, sky-rockets, music, speeches, &c. In Augusta there was an illumination with fireworks, ringing of bells, and firing of cannon.

A substitute was introduced for the ordinance of secession, but was lost. It was also moved to postpone the operation of the ordinance to March 3d. This motion failed. Subsequently a preamble and resolution were adopted, the object of which was to remove the unfavorable impression created by the large vote given in opposition to the ordinance of secession. The preamble was in these words:

Whereas, as a lack of unanimity in this Convention on the passage of the ordinance of secession indicates a difference of opinion amongst the members of the Convention, not so much as to the right which Georgia claims or the wrongs of which she complains, as to a remedy and its application before a resort to other means for redress; and *whereas*, it is desirable to give expression to that intention which really exists among all the members of the Convention to sustain the State in the course of action which she has pronounced to be proper for the occasion; therefore, &c.

The resolution required every member to sign the ordinance. This was adopted unanimously.

Before the Convention proceeded to sign the ordinance, a resolution was offered, proposing to submit it to a vote of the people, through the proclamation of the Governor, and that the question should be "secession" or "no secession" at the ballot-box. If a majority of votes were for secession, then the ordinance was to take effect, and not otherwise. The resolution was rejected by a large majority.

Representatives to the Montgomery Congress were appointed on the 24th. Before voting, an assurance was given to the Convention, that none of the candidates were in favor of forming a Government having in view an immediate or ultimate union with the Northern States. No such idea could be entertained. All were for the establishment of a Southern Confederacy on the basis of the old Constitution, and never, under any circumstances, to connect themselves with the Northern States. Notwithstanding this unanimity in the Convention, there was a great reaction in some parts of the State, and the flag of the United States was kept flying without regard to the ordinance of the Convention. This was done also in North Alabama, and in portions of Mississippi and Louisiana. Fears were expressed by former members of Congress from Georgia, that the reaction might be greatly increased in the popular mind in the Gulf States, if a compromise was effected satisfactory to the Border States.

Two regiments were ordered by the Convention to be organized as the army for the Republic of Georgia, over which a number of officers were appointed by the Governor, chiefly those who had resigned from the army of the United States.

In Louisiana the authorities were undoubtedly early enlisted in the plans for the secession of the Southern States from the Union, and ready to use all their efforts to secure success. In November, 1860, Governor Moore issued a proclamation for an extra session of the Legislature on the 10th of December. The reason requiring this session was thus stated:

Whereas the election of Abraham Lincoln to the office of President of the United States by a sectional and aggressive anti-slavery party, whose hostility to the people and the institutions of the South has been evinced by repeated and long-continued violations of constitutional obligations and fraternal amity, now consummated by this last insult and outrage perpetrated at and through the ballot-box, does, in my opinion, as well as that of a large number of citizens of all parties and pursuits, furnish an occasion such as is contemplated by the Constitution; and *whereas* some of our sister States, aggrieved like ours, are preparing measures for their future security, and for the safety of their institutions and their people, and both patriotism and the necessity of self-preservation require us to deliberate upon our own course of action; now, therefore, I, Thomas O. Moore, Governor of the State of Louisiana, do hereby convene the Legislature of this State in extra session, and do appoint Monday, the 10th day of December next.

On the day appointed this body met at Baton Rouge, and caused to be prepared an act providing for a State Convention, to be held on the 23d of January, and for the election of delegates. On the next day the act was passed by the Senate and House. In the Senate it was eloquently opposed by Randall Hunt. In the House a strong effort was made to cause the question "Convention or no Convention" to be submitted to a vote of the people. It, however, failed of success. At the same time an act passed both Houses, which appropriated $500,000 for military purposes, and provided for the appointment of a military commission, the organization and arming of volunteer companies, and for the establishment of military depots. On the 12th, Wirt Adams, commissioner from Mississippi, was introduced to the Legislature in joint session, and made an address, announcing the action of Mississippi, and asking the coöperation of Louisiana. The speech was eagerly listened to by a crowded audience. On the next day the Legislature adjourned to January 21st.

Friends of secession became active in New Orleans, the great city of the State, as soon as the movement commenced in South Carolina, and the sentiment had gathered so much volume that as early as December 21st a general demonstration of joy was made over the secession of that State. One hundred guns were fired, and the Pelican flag was unfurled. Speeches in favor of secession were made by distinguished citizens, and the Marseillaise hymn and polkas were the only airs played.

The movement had now commenced in earnest. The influence and efforts of New Orleans were expected to carry the rest of the State. Only four days later a mass meeting was held to ratify the nomination of the "Southern Rights" candidates, as they were called, for the Convention. It was the largest assemblage of all parties ever held in the city. Speeches were made by prominent citizens advocating immediate secession amid unbounded enthusiasm. The Southern Marseillaise was again sung as the banner of the State was raised, with reiterated and prolonged cheers for South Carolina and Louisiana. A citizen of eminence in the southern part of the State, writing upon the condition of affairs at this time, thus says: "In our section the excitement is confined to the politicians, the people generally being borne along with the current, and feeling the natural disposition of sustaining their section. I think that ninety-nine out of every hundred of the people sincerely hope that some plan will yet be devised to heal up the dissensions, and to settle our difficulties to the satisfaction of both the North and the South; and a combined effort will be made to bring about such a result, even after the States withdraw from the Union."

A State Convention was early called, and the vote in New Orleans for members was close enough to defeat a portion of the secession candidates. The city was entitled to twenty "representative delegates" and five "senatorial delegates." The "immediate secessionists" succeeded in electing all of the latter class and fifteen of the former, whilst the "coöperationists" obtained five of the "representative delegates." The majority of the secessionists for the senatorial delegates was about 350. The number of votes polled was little upwards of 8,000, being less than one-half the voters registered in the city. Their success, however, was regarded as sufficient to be made the occasion of great rejoicing. This election took place on the 8th of January. On the next day three separate military organizations departed to take possession of Forts Jackson and St. Phillip at the mouth of the Mississippi, and also the arsenal at Baton Rouge.

On the 13th the United States revenue cutter, Lewis Cass, was seized by a military company at Algiers, opposite New Orleans. The vessel was laid up and undergoing repairs. Her armament, consisting of one long 24-pounder and six 8-pounder carronades, with a large quantity of cannon-balls, powder, and other military stores, had been placed in the Belleville Iron Works, an extensive and unoccupied brick building. About the same time the barracks below the city, which had been for several months occupied as a marine hospital, were taken possession of in the name of the State of Louisiana. They contained at the time 216 invalids and convalescent patients. The collector at New Orleans was required to remove the convalescents immediately, and the sick as soon as practicable. The reason assigned for this act by the State authorities was that they wanted the buildings for quarters for their own troops.

On the 24th the State Convention met at the same place and organized. A committee of 15 was ordered to report an ordinance of secession. Over the capital waved a flag with 15 stars.

On the 26th the ordinance of secession was adopted by a vote of ayes 113, noes 17. The following is the ordinance:

AN ORDINANCE *to dissolve the union between the State of Louisiana and other States united with her under the compact entitled "The Constitution of the United States of America."*

We, the people of the State of Louisiana, in Convention assembled, do declare and ordain, and it is hereby declared and ordained, that the ordinance passed by us in Convention on the 22d day of November, in the year 1811, whereby the Constitution of the United States of America, and the amendments of said Constitution, were adopted, and all laws and ordinances by which the State of Louisiana became a member of the Federal Union, be, and the same are hereby, repealed and abrogated; and that the union now subsisting between Louisiana and other States, under the name of the "United States of America," is hereby dissolved.

We do further declare and ordain, that the State of Louisiana hereby resumes all rights and powers heretofore delegated to the Government of the United States of America; that her citizens are absolved from all allegiance to said Government; and that she is in full possession and exercise of all those rights of sovereignty which appertain to a free and independent State.

We do further declare and ordain, that all rights acquired and vested under the Constitution of the United States, or any act of Congress or treaty, or under any law of this State and not incompatible with this ordinance, shall remain in force, and have the same effect as if this ordinance had not been passed.

The undersigned hereby certifies that the above ordinance is a true copy of the original ordinance adopted this day by the Convention of the State of Louisiana.

Given under my hand and the great seal of Louisiana, at Baton Rouge, this 26th day of the month of January, in the year of our Lord, 1861.

[L. S.] A. MOUTON, Pres. of the Convention.
J. THOMAS WHEAT, Secretary of the Convention.

The aspect of New Orleans at the time of the passage of this ordinance is thus reported:

Every thing in this city appears to be in rapid progress toward a war establishment. Trade is at a stand still; the importation of merchandise has almost entirely ceased; the warehouses of the Federal Government are everywhere literally glutted with bonded goods; the banks are remorselessly curtailing their discounts; ordinary creditors are endeavoring by all means short of legal pressure to lessen the liabilities of their debtors; stores and manufactories, traders and mechanics, are diminishing their expenses by the discharge of hands, and, save the office-holders, an influential, wealthy, and important body, electorially considered, everybody looks dubious and bewildered, not knowing what to expect or what may happen. The proceedings at Baton Rouge will take no one by surprise. The Legislature is engaged in spending money profusely, and the Convention is engaged in laying down a broad foundation for the erection of a monstrous superstructure of debt.

In the Convention on the 31st, a resolution was offered to instruct the delegates to the Montgomery Convention, who had been previously appointed, to resist any attempt to reopen the African slave trade. This was laid on the table by a vote of 83 to 28.

On the same day the United States Mint and Custom-House at New Orleans were quietly taken possession of by the State authorities, and the oath was subsequently administered to the officials under the ordinance. In the mint was $118,311, and in the sub-Treasury $483,984. A draft of the United States for $300,000 was presented soon after, which the sub-Treasurer refused to pay, saying that "the money in his custody was no longer the property of the United States, but of the Republic of Louisiana."

CHAPTER II.

Preparations for a Southern Confederacy—Meeting of Congress at Montgomery—Members and Organization—Inauguration of a President—His Addresses—Cabinet—Proceedings of the Congress—New Constitution.—Its Features.

No sooner was secession an organized fact in South Carolina, with a certainty that other States would soon reach the same result, than suggestions were made for a Southern Confederacy. A committee in the Legislature of Mississippi, on Jan. 19, reported resolutions to provide for a Confederacy and establish a Provisional Government. Florida, Alabama, and Georgia at once approved of this general object, and delegates were appointed to a Congress to be held at Montgomery. The design of this Congress, as then understood, was to organize a new Confederacy of the seceding slaveholding States, and such other slaveholding States as should secede and join them; and to establish first, a Provisional Government, intended to prepare for the general defence of those States which were linked together by a common interest in the peculiar institution, and which were opposed to the Federal Union; second, make treaties with the United States and "other foreign" countries; third, obtain decisive legislation in regard to the negro; and fourthly, determine what States should constitute the Confederacy.

On the 4th of February this Congress met at Montgomery, in a hall, on the walls of which, portraits of Marion, Clay, Andrew Jackson, and several of Washington, were hanging. It was composed of the following members, except those from Texas, who were not appointed until Feb. 14:

South Carolina.—R. B. Rhett, James Chesnut, jr., W. P. Miles, T. J. Withers, R. W. Barnwell, C. G. Memminger, L. M. Keitt, and W. W. Boyce.

Georgia.—Robert Toombs, Howell Cobb, Benjamin H. Hill, Alexander H. Stephens, Francis Bartow, Martin J. Crawford, E. A. Nisbett, Aug's B. Wright, Thomas R. R. Cobb, and Augustus Keenan.

Alabama.—Richard W. Walker, Robert H. Smith, Colin J. McRae, John Gill Shorter, S. F. Hale, David P. Lewis, Thomas Fearn, J. L. M. Curry, and W. P. Chilton.

Mississippi.—Willie P. Harris, Walker Brooke, A. M. Clayton, W. S. Barry, J. T. Harrison, J. A. P. Campbell, and W. S. Wilson,

Louisiana.—John Perkins, jr., Duncan F. Kenner, C. M. Conrad, E. Spencer, and Henry Marshall.

Florida.—Jackson Morton, James Powers, and J. P. Anderson.

Texas.—L. T. Wigfall, J. H. Reagan, J. Hemphill, T. N. Waul, Judge Gregg, Judge Oldham, and Judge W. B. Ochiltree.

All the members were present except Mr. Morton, of Florida, and the members from Texas. A permanent organization was made by the election of Howell Cobb, of Georgia, as Chairman, and J. J. Hooper, of Montgomery, Alabama, Secretary.

Mr. Cobb, on taking the chair, made an address, saying:

"Accept, gentlemen of the Convention, my sincere thanks for the honor you have conferred upon me. I shall endeavor, by a faithful and impartial discharge of the duties of the Chair, to merit, in some degree at least, the confidence you have reposed in me.

"The occasion which assembles us together is one of no ordinary character. We meet as representatives of sovereign and independent States, who, by their solemn judgment, have dissolved the political association which connected them with the Government of the United States. Of the causes which have led to this decision it is unnecessary now to speak. It is sufficient to announce that by the judgment of our constituents they have been pronounced ample and sufficient. It is now a fixed and irrevocable fact. The separation is perfect, complete, and perpetual.

"The great duty is now imposed upon us of providing for these States a Government for their future security and protection. We can and should extend to our sister States—our late sister States—who are identified with us in interest, feeling, and institutions, a cordial welcome to unite with us in a common destiny—desirous at the same time of maintaining with our former confederates, as with the world, the most peaceful and friendly relations, both political and commercial.

"Our responsibilities, gentlemen, are great, and I doubt not we shall prove equal to the occasion. Let us assume all the responsibility which may be necessary for the successful completion of the great work committed to our care, placing before our countrymen and the world our acts and their results, as the justification for the course we may pursue, and the policy we may adopt. With a consciousness of the justice of our cause, and with confidence in the guidance and blessings of a kind Providence, we will this day inaugurate for the South a new era of peace, security, and prosperity."

The rules of the Convention were drawn on the principle that it was a Congress of sovereign and independent States, and the members should therefore vote by States.

On the 7th of February, the Committee on a Provisional Government reported a plan which was discussed in secret session. On the 8th, the Constitution of the United States was adopted with some amendments, as follows:

Alterations.—1st. The Provisional Constitution differs from the Constitution of the United States in this: That the legislative powers of the Provisional Government are vested in the Congress now assembled, and this body exercises all the functions that are exercised by either or both branches of the United States Government.

2d. The Provisional President holds his office for one year, unless sooner superseded by the establishment of a permanent government.

3d. Each State is erected into a distinct judicial district, the judge having all the powers heretofore vested in the district and circuit courts; and the several district judges together compose the supreme bench—a majority of them constituting a quorum.

4th. Wherever the word "Union" occurs in the United States Constitution the word "Confederacy" is substituted.

Additions.—1st. The President may veto any separate appropriation without vetoing the whole bill in which it is contained.

2d. The African slave trade is prohibited.

3d. Congress is empowered to prohibit the introduction of slaves from any State not a member of this Confederacy.

4th. All appropriations must be upon the demand of the President or heads of departments.

Omissions.—1st. There is no prohibition against members of Congress holding other offices of honor and emolument under the Provisional Government.

2d. There is no provision for a neutral spot for the location of a seat of government, or for sites for forts, arsenals, and dock-yards; consequently there is no reference made to the territorial powers of the Provisional Government.

3d. The section in the old Constitution in reference to capitation and other direct tax is omitted; also the section providing that no tax or duty shall be laid on any exports.

4th. The prohibition against States keeping troops or ships of war in time of peace is omitted.

5th. The Constitution being provisional merely, no provision is made for its ratification.

Amendments.—1st. The fugitive slave clause of the old Constitution is so amended as to contain the word "slave," and to provide for full compensation in cases of abduction or forcible rescue on the part of the State in which such abduction or rescue may take place.

2d. Congress, by a vote of two-thirds, may at any time alter or amend the Constitution.

Temporary Provisions.—1st. The Provisional Government is required to take immediate steps for the settlement of all matters between the States forming it and their late confederates of the United States in relation to the public property and the public debt.

2d. Montgomery is made the temporary seat of government.

3d. This Constitution is to continue one year, unless altered by a two-thirds vote or superseded by a permanent government.

The tariff clause provided that "Congress shall have power to lay and collect taxes, duties, imposts, and excises for revenue necessary to pay the debts and carry on the Government of the Confederacy, and all duties, imposts, and excises shall be uniform throughout the Confederacy."

The first section of Article I. is as follows:

"All legislative powers herein delegated shall be vested *in this Congress, now assembled,* until otherwise ordained."

The fifth article is as follows:

"The Congress, by a vote of two-thirds, may, at any time, alter or amend this Constitution."

The other portions of the Constitution are nearly identical with the Constitution of the United States.

On the next day after the adoption of the Provisional Constitution, at the opening of Congress, the President of the body was sworn by R. W. Walker to support the new Constitution, and the oath was then administered in turn by the President to all the members, in the order in which they were called by States.

At a quarter past twelve o'clock in the afternoon the Congress threw open its doors, after having previously gone into secret session, and proceeded to elect a President. The ballots were taken by States, each State being allowed one vote. On counting, it was found that Jefferson Davis, of Mississippi, had received six votes, the whole number cast. The same formality was gone through in the election of Vice-President, resulting likewise in the unanimous election of Alexander H. Stephens, of Georgia.

An immense crowd had gathered on the floor and in the galleries to witness the election of the first President of "the Confederate States of America." The election of Davis and

Stephens was greeted with loud cheers and applause from the spectators.

The President of the Convention was directed to appoint Committees on Foreign Affairs, Finance, Military and Naval Affairs, the Judiciary, Postal Affairs, Commerce, Patents, and Printing.

A bill was passed continuing in force, until repealed or altered by Congress, all the laws of the United States which were in force on the 1st of November, 1860, not inconsistent with the Constitution of the Provisional Government.

A resolution was adopted instructing the Finance Committee to report promptly a tariff bill for raising a revenue for the support of the Provisional Government.

A resolution was also adopted authorizing the appointment of a Committee to report a Constitution for a permanent Government of the Confederacy.

The name "Confederate States of North America" was also adopted for the Union represented at Montgomery.

At the session on the next day, Mr. Stephens appeared and announced his acceptance of the office of Vice-President, and said:

"I have been notified by the committee of my election as Vice-President of the Provisional Government of the Confederate States of America. The committee requested that I should make known to this body, in a verbal response, my acceptance of the high position I have been called upon to assume, and this I now do in this august presence—before you, Mr. President, before this Congress, and this large concourse of people, under the bright sun and brilliant skies which now smile so felicitously upon us.

"I take occasion to return my most profound acknowledgments for this expression of confidence on the part of this Congress. There are especial reasons why I place an unusually high estimate on it. The considerations which induced me to accept it, I need not state. It is sufficient for me to say that it may be deemed questionable if any good citizens can refuse to discharge any duty which may be assigned them by their country in her hour of need.

"It might be expected that I should indulge in remarks on the state of our public affairs—the dangers which threaten us, and the most advisable measures to be adopted to meet our pressing exigencies; but allow me to say, in the absence of the distinguished gentleman called to the Chief Executive Chair, I think it best that I should refrain from saying any thing on such matters. We may expect him here in a few days—possibly by Wednesday—if he is not providentially detained. When he comes you will hear from him on these difficult questions; and I doubt not we shall cordially and harmoniously concur in any line of policy his superior wisdom and statesmanship may indicate.

"In the mean time, we may be profitably employed in directing attention to such matters as providing the necessary postal arrangements, making provision for the transfer of the custom-houses from the separate States to the Confederacy, and the imposition of such duties as are necessary to meet the present expected exigencies in the exercise of power, and raise a revenue. We are limited in the latter object to a small duty, not exceeding ten per centum upon importations. We can also be devoting attention to the Constitution of a permanent Government, stable and durable, which is one of the leading objects of our assembling.

"I am now ready to take the oath."

The oath was accordingly administered.

A committee of two from each State was appointed to form a permanent Constitution for the Confederacy.

On the 12th resolutions were offered to continue in office the revenue officers of the respective States.

It was also resolved "That this Government takes under its charge all questions and difficulties now existing between the sovereign States of this Confederacy and the Government of the United States relating to the occupation of forts, arsenals, navy-yards, custom-houses, and all other public establishments, and the President of this Congress is directed to communicate this resolution to the Governors of the respective States of the Confederacy."

On the 13th of February, the Committee on Naval Affairs, and also the Committee on Military Affairs, were instructed to include in any plans they might propose for the army and navy, provisions for such officers as might tender their resignations.

A resolution was also adopted instructing the Committee on Commercial Affairs to inquire and report upon the expediency of repealing the navigation laws.

A debate took place on the subject of a National flag, proposing to make only such changes as might be necessary to distinguish it easily from that of the United States.

Mr. Brooks, in the course of his remarks, said the flag of stars and stripes is the idol of the heart, around which cluster memories of the past which time cannot efface, or cause to grow dim.

Mr. Miles, in reply, said he had regarded from his youth the stars and stripes as the emblem of oppression and tyranny.

The Committee to whom the subject was referred made a report, which was unanimously adopted. It recommended that the flag of the Confederate States should consist of three bars of red and white—the upper red, middle white, lower red. The lower bar should extend the whole width of the flag, and just above it, next to the staff in the upper left hand corner of the flag, should be a blue Union with seven stars in a circle.

The form of Government adopted by the Congress was chiefly objected to, so far as it held out any encouragement for reconstruction, or any inducement to the Border Slave States to remain in the Union with the North.

On the 15th, Congress made arrangements for the reception and inauguration of Jefferson Davis. An official copy of the Texas secession ordinance was presented, and the deputy present invited to a seat, although the ordinance had not been ratified.

There was then a secret session, during which a resolution was passed removing the injunction of secrecy from an act continuing in office the officers connected with the collection of customs at the time of the adoption of the Constitution of the insurrectionary States, with the salaries and powers as heretofore provided; the compensation not to exceed five thousand dollars. The collectors were required, within two weeks, to execute the same bonds as heretofore, and the subordinates to give bond. One week after the collectors were required to take the oath to discharge their duties and support the Constitution of the Provisional Government. The Secretary of the Treasury had been instructed to report a plan, to go into effect on the first of April, diminishing the expenses of collecting the revenue at each custom-house at least fifty per cent.

On the 16th of February Mr. Davis arrived at Montgomery, to be inaugurated and to enter upon the duties of his office. He was greeted with an ovation, to which he responded in an address reviewing the position of the South. He said: "The time for compromise has now passed, and the South is determined to maintain her position, and make all who oppose her smell Southern powder and feel Southern steel if coercion is persisted in. He had no doubts as to the result. He said we will maintain our rights and government at all hazards. We ask nothing, we want nothing; we will have no complications. If the other States join our Confederation they can freely come in on our terms. Our separation from the old Union is now complete. No compromise, no reconstruction is now to be entertained."

After reaching the Exchange Hotel he again addressed the crowd from the balcony as follows: "Fellow-citizens and brethren of the Confederated States of America—for now we are brethren, not in name merely, but in fact—men of one flesh, one bone, one interest, one purpose of identity of domestic institutions—we have henceforth, I trust, a prospect of living together in peace, with our institutions subject to protection and not to defamation. It may be that our career will be ushered in in the midst of a storm; it may be that, as this morning opened with clouds, rain, and mist, we shall have to encounter inconveniences at the beginning; but as the sun rose and lifted the mist, it dispersed the clouds and left us the pure sunlight of heaven. So will progress the Southern Confederacy, and carry us safe into the harbor of constitutional liberty and political equality. We shall fear nothing, because of homogeneity at home and nothing abroad to awe us; because, if war should come, if we must again baptize in blood the principles for which our fathers bled in the Revolution, we shall show that we are not degenerate sons, but will redeem the pledges they gave, preserve the rights they transmitted to us, and prove that Southern valor still shines as bright as in 1776, in 1812, and in every other conflict."

In concluding his speech, Mr. Davis said: "I thank you, my friends, for the kind manifestations of favor and approbation you exhibit on this occasion. Throughout my entire progress to this city I have received the same flattering demonstrations of support. I did not regard them as personal to myself, but tendered to me as the humble representative of the principles and policy of the Confederate States. I will devote to the duties of the high office to which I have been called all I have of heart, of head, and of hand. If, in the progress of events, it shall become necessary that my services be needed in another position—if, to be plain, necessity require that I shall again enter the ranks of soldiers—I hope you will welcome me there. And now, my friends, again thanking you for this manifestation of your approbation, allow me to bid you good night."

The inauguration took place at Montgomery, on the 18th of February. The hill on which the Capitol is situated, was crowded with the wealth and beauty, the soldiers and citizens from the different States. In the evening the city was gorgeously illuminated. The President held a levee at Estelle Hall—bands of music played, fireworks were displayed, and a grand and general demonstration was made.

The cabinet officers of this new Government were as follows: Secretary of State, Robert Toombs; Secretary of the Treasury, Chas. G. Memminger; Secretary of War, L. Pope Walker.

On the 19th, measures were adopted to admit, duty free, all breadstuffs, provisions, munitions of war, or materials therefor, living animals, and agricultural products in their natural state; also goods, wares, and merchandise from the United States purchased before the 1st of March, and imported before the 14th of March. Texas was excepted from the operation of the tariff laws.

On the next day the Departments of War, Navy, Justice, Postal Affairs, State and Treasury, were organized.

On the 22d an act was unanimously passed declaring the free navigation of the Mississippi River to be established.

Subsequently the nomination of Gustave T. Beauregard, of Louisiana, as Brigadier-General of the Provisional Army, was confirmed.

An act to raise provisional forces for the Confederate States and for other purposes was passed. It directed, among other provisions, that the President should take charge of all the military operations between the Confederacy and other Powers.

An act was also passed to raise money to support the Government. It authorized the

President to borrow $15,000,000, payable in ten years, at an interest of eight per cent. The last section directed an export duty of one-eighth per cent. on each pound of cotton exported after the 1st of August following, to create a fund to liquidate principal and interest of the loan.

The postal system of the Confederate States was adopted on the report of the Committee of Congress, made on the 25th of February.

On Monday, 7th March, an act was passed anthorizing a military force of 100,000 men to be raised. The first section was in these words:

SEC. 1. *The Congress of the Confederate States of America do enact,* That in order to provide speedily forces to repel invasion, maintain the rightful possession of the Confederate States of America in every portion of territory belonging to each State, and to secure the public tranquillity and independence against threatened assault, the President be, and he is hereby, authorized to employ the militia, military, and naval forces of the Confederate States of America, and ask for and accept the services of any number of volunteers, not exceeding one hundred thousand, who may offer their services, either as cavalry, mounted rifle, artillery, or infantry, in such proportion of these several arms as he may deem expedient, to serve for twelve months after they shall be mustered into service, unless sooner discharged.

On the 11th of March the permanent Constitution was adopted by Congress. In nearly all its parts it adopts the precise language, and follows in its articles and sections the order of arrangement of the Constitution of the United States. The parts in which it differs from the latter, either by variations from, or additions thereto, are herewith presented. It begins with the following preamble:

We, the people of the Confederate States, each State acting in its sovereign and independent character, in order to form a permanent Federal Government, establish justice, insure domestic tranquillity, and secure the blessings of liberty to ourselves and to our posterity—invoking the favor and guidance of Almighty God—do ordain and establish this Constitution for the Confederate States of America.

The second section of the first article imposed the following restriction on the rights of suffrage in order to correct an abuse which had sprung from the action of certain States in the Union which have granted the right of voting to unnaturalized aliens:

The House of Representatives shall be composed of members chosen every second year by the people of the several States; and the electors in each State shall be citizens of the Confederate States, and have the qualifications requisite for electors of the most numerous branch of the State Legislature; but no person of foreign birth not a citizen of the Confederate States, shall be allowed to vote for any officer, civil or political, State or Federal.

In adjusting the basis of representation and direct taxation, "three-fifths of all slaves" were enumerated, as in the Constitution of the United States, which substitutes for the word "slaves" the term "other persons." The number of Representatives given prior to an actual enumeration of the population, appointed to take place within three years after the first meeting of the Congress of the Confederate States, and within every subsequent term of ten years, was as follows:

The State of South Carolina shall be entitled to choose six, the State of Georgia ten, the State of Alabama nine, the State of Florida two, the State of Mississippi seven, the State of Louisiana six, and the State of Texas six.

On the subject of impeachments, the following provision was made:

The House of Representatives shall choose their Speaker and other officers, and shall have the sole power of impeachment, except that any judicial or other Confederate officer, resident and acting solely within the limits of any State, may be impeached by a vote of two-thirds of both branches of the Legislature thereof.

It was provided that the Senators of the Confederate States should be chosen by the State Legislatures "at the regular session next immediately preceding the commencement of the term of service."

It was provided that the concurrence of "two-thirds of the whole number" of each House should be necessary to the expulsion of a member.

Congress was authorized to make the following provision in reference to heads of the Executive Departments:

Congress may by law grant to the principal officer in each of the Executive Departments a seat upon the floor of either House, with the privilege of discussing any measures appertaining to his Department.

The President was authorized to make the following discrimination in giving his assent to appropriation bills:

The President may approve any appropriation and disapprove any other appropriation in the same bill. In such case he shall, in signing the bill, designate the appropriations disapproved, and shall return a copy of such appropriations with his objections to the House in which the bill shall have originated, and the same proceeding shall then be had as in case of other bills disapproved by the President.

The following prohibition of the "protective policy" was engrafted in the Constitution in enumerating the powers of Congress:

No bounties shall be granted from the Treasury, nor shall any duties or taxes on importations from foreign nations be laid to promote or foster any branch of industry.

Internal improvements by the Confederate Government were also prohibited:

Congress shall have power to regulate commerce with foreign nations and among the several States, and with the Indian tribes; but neither this nor any other clause contained in the Constitution shall ever be construed to delegate the power to Congress to appropriate money for any internal improvement intended to facilitate commerce; except for the purpose of furnishing lights, beacons, and buoys, and other aids to navigation upon the coasts, and the improvement of harbors and the removing of obstructions in river navigation, in all of which cases such duties shall be laid on the navigation facilitated thereby as may be necessary to pay the costs and expenses thereof.

The Post-Office Department must pay its expenses from its own resources "after the first day of March, 1863."

In relation to the slave trade, the following provision was made:

The importation of negroes of the African race from any foreign country other than the slaveholding States or Territories of the United States of America, is hereby forbidden; and Congress is required to pass such laws as shall effectually prevent the same. Congress shall also have power to prohibit the introduction of slaves from any State not a member of or Territory not belonging to this Confederacy.

The imposition of export duties was restricted by the following provision:

No tax or duty shall be laid on articles exported from any State, except by a vote of two-thirds of both Houses.

The appropriation of money for other objects than those indicated and estimated for by the several Executive Departments is thus restrained:

Congress shall appropriate no money from the Treasury except by a vote of two-thirds of both Houses, taken by yeas and nays, unless it be asked and estimated for by some one of the Heads of Department, and submitted to Congress by the President, or for the purpose of paying its own expenses and contingencies, or for the payment of claims against the Confederate States, the justice of which shall have been judicially declared by a tribunal for the investigation of claims against the Government, which it is hereby made the duty of Congress to establish.

All bills appropriating money shall specify in Federal currency the exact amount of each appropriation, and the purposes for which it is made; and Congress shall grant no extra compensation to any public contractor, officer, agent, or servant, after such contract shall have been made or such service rendered.

Akin to these regulations was the following provision:

Every law or reselution having the force of law shall relate to but one subject, and that shall be expressed in the title.

Tonnage duties when levied by the several States were thus regulated:

No State shall, without the consent of Congress, lay any duty of tonnage, except on sea-going vessels, for the improvement of its rivers and harbors navigated by the said vessels; but such duties shall not conflict with any treaties of the Confederate States with foreign nations; and any surplus of revenue thus derived, shall, after making such improvement, be paid into the common treasury; nor shall any State keep troops or ships of war in time of peace, enter into any agreement or compact with another State, or with a foreign Power, or engage in war, unless actually invaded, or in such imminent danger as will not admit of delay. But when any river divides or flows through two or more States, they may enter into compacts with each other to improve the navigation thereof.

The President and Vice-President of the insurrectionary States hold office for the term of six years, the President not being reëligible. The qualifications of eligibility were as follows:

No person except a natural born citizen of the Confederate States, or a citizen thereof at the time of the adoption of this Constitution, or a citizen thereof born in the United States prior to the 20th of December, 1860, shall be eligible to the office of President; neither shall any person be eligible to that office who shall not have attained the age of thirty-five years, and been fourteen years a resident within the limits of the Confederate States, as they may exist at the time of his election.

Appointments and removals were regulated as follows:

The principal officer in each of the Executive Departments, and all persons connected with the diplomatic service, may be removed from office at the pleasure of the President. All other civil officers of the Executive Department may be removed at any time by the President, or other appointing power, when their services are unnecessary, or for dishonesty, incapacity, inefficiency, misconduct, or neglect of duty; and when so removed, the removal shall be reported to the Senate, together with the reasons therefor.

The President shall have power to fill all vacancies that may happen during the recess of the Senate, by granting commissions which shall expire at the end of their next session; but no person rejected by the Senate shall be reappointed to the same office during their ensuing recess.

The following provisions were made in reference to the rights of transit and sojourn with slave property, recovery of fugitive slaves, &c.

The citizens of each State shall be entitled to all the privileges and immunities of citizens in the several States, and shall have the right of transit and sojourn in any State of this Confederacy, with their slaves and other property; and the right of property in said slaves shall not be thereby impaired.

A person charged in any State with treason, felony, or other crime against the laws of such State, who shall flee from justice, and be found in another State, shall, on demand of the Executive authority of the State from which he fled, be delivered up to be removed to the State having jurisdiction of the crime.

No slave or other person held to service or labor in any State or Territory of the Confederate States, under the laws thereof, escaping or lawfully carried into another, shall, in consequence of any law or regulation therein, be discharged from such service or labor, but shall be delivered up on claim of the party to whom such slave belongs, or to whom such service or labor may be due.

The following was the provision in reference to the admission of States into the new Confederacy:

Other States may be admitted into this Confederacy by a vote of two-thirds of the whole House of Representatives and two-thirds of the Senate, the Senate voting by States; but no new State shall be formed or erected within the jurisdiction of any other State, nor any State be formed by the junction of two or more States, or parts of States, without the consent of the Legislatures of the States concerned as well as of the Congress.

The "Territorial question" was thus disposed of:

The Congress shall have power to dispose of and make all needful rules and regulations concerning the property of the Confederate States, including the lands thereof.

The Confederate States may acquire new territory; and Congress shall have power to legislate and provide governments for the inhabitants of all territory belonging to the Confederate States lying without the limits of the several States; and may permit them, at such times and in such manner as it may by law provide, to form States to be admitted into the Confederacy. In all such territory the institution of negro slavery, as it now exists in the Confederate States, shall be recognized and protected by Congress and by the Territorial government; and the inhabitants of the several Confederate States and Territories shall have the right to take to such Territory any slaves lawfully held by them in any of the States or Territories of the Confederate States.

Amendments to the Constitution were to be thus initiated and consummated;

Upon the demand of any three States, legally assembled in their several Conventions, the Congress shall summon a Convention of all the States to take into consideration such amendments to the Constitution as the said States shall concur in suggesting at the time when the said demand is made; and should any of the proposed amendments to the Constitution be agreed on by the said Convention—voting by States—and the same be ratified by the Legislatures of two-thirds of the several States, or by Conventions in two-thirds thereof—as the one or the other mode of ratification may be proposed by the General Convention—they shall thenceforward form a part of this Constitution.

The following temporary provisions were enumerated:

The Government established by this Constitution is the successor of the Provisional Government of the Confederate States of America, and all the laws passed by the latter shall continue in force until the same shall be repealed or modified; and all the officers appointed by the same shall remain in office until their successors are appointed and qualified, or the offices abolished.

All debts contracted and engagements entered into before the adoption of this Constitution shall be as valid against the Confederate States under this Constitution as under the Provisional Government.

The mode of ratification and the number of States necessary to put the Constitution in force were thus designated:

The ratification of the Conventions of five States shall be sufficient for the establishment of this Constitution between the States so ratifying the same.

When five States shall have ratified this Constitution, in the manner before specified, the Congress under the Provisional Constitution shall prescribe the time for holding the election of President and Vice-President, and for the meeting of the Electoral College, and for counting the votes, and inaugurating the President. They shall also prescribe the time for holding the first election of members of Congress under this Constitution, and the time for assembling the same. Until the assembling of such Congress, the Congress under the Provisional Constitution shall continue to exercise the legislative powers granted them; not extending beyond the time limited by the Constitution of the Provisional Government.

An act was also passed authorizing the issue of one million dollars in Treasury notes, and an appropriation bill to meet current expenses.

CHAPTER III.

Inauguration of President Lincoln—Commissioners sent to Europe and Washington—Time for War had come—Despatches from Montgomery to Gen. Beauregard at Charleston—Condition of Fort Sumter—Occupied by Major Anderson—Excitement—Surrender demanded by Gov. Pickens—Negotiations at Washington—Preparations for attack on the Fort—Women and Children removed—Evacuation demanded by Gen. Beauregard—Correspondence—Attack on the Fort—Its Surrender—Action of the Federal Government to relieve it.

The ceremonies at the inauguration of Mr. Lincoln were in some respects the most brilliant and imposing ever witnessed at Washington. Nearly twenty well-drilled military companies of the district, comprising a force of more than two thousand men, were on parade. Georgetown sent companies of cavalry, infantry, and artillery of fine appearance. The troops stationed at the City Hall and Willard's Hotel became objects of attraction to vast numbers of both sexes. At noon the Senate Committee called upon President Buchanan, who proceeded with them to Willard's Hotel to receive the President-elect. The party thus composed, joined by other distinguished citizens, then proceeded, in open carriages, along the avenue at a moderate pace, with military in front and rear, and thousands of private citizens, in carriages, on horseback, and on foot, crowding the broad street. The capitol was reached by passing up on the north side of the grounds, and the party entered the building by the northern door over a temporary planked walk. During the hour and a half previous to the arrival of President Buchanan and the President-elect in the Senate chamber, that hall presented a gayer spectacle than ever before. The usual desks of the senators had been removed, and concentric lines of ornamental chairs set for the dignitaries of this and other lands with which this country was in bonds of amity and friendship. The inner half-circle on the right was occupied by the judges of the Supreme Court, and by senators. The corresponding half-circle on the extreme left was occupied by the members of the cabinets of Mr. Buchanan and Mr. Lincoln, mingled together, and further on by senators. The concentric circle further back was filled by senators. The next half-circle on the right by the members of the diplomatic corps, all in the full court dress of their respective countries. In the half-circle immediately in the rear of that occupied by the ministers were the secretaries and attachés. The half-circles on the left, corresponding to those occupied by the corps diplomatique, furnished places for senators and governors of States and Territories. Outside of all, on both sides, stood—for there was no further room for seats—the members of the House of Representatives and chief officers of the executive bureaus. The galleries all round the Senate were occupied by ladies.

At a quarter-past one o'clock the President of the United States and the President-elect entered the Senate chamber, preceded by Senator Foot of Vermont, and the marshal of the

District of Columbia, and followed by Senators Baker and Pearce. They took seats immediately in front of the clerk's desk, facing outward; President Buchanan having the President-elect on his right, and the senators equally distributed right and left.

In a few minutes Vice-President Hamlin, who had been previously installed, ordered the reading of the order of procession to the platform on the east of the capitol, and the line was formed, the marshal of the District of Columbia leading. Then followed Chief Justice Taney and the judges of the Supreme Court, the sergeant-at-arms of the Senate, the Committee of Arrangements of the Senate, the President of the United States and President-elect, Vice-President of the United States and Senate, the members of the diplomatic corps, governors of States and Territories, and members of the House of Representatives. In this order the procession marched to the platform erected in the usual position over the main steps on the east front of the capitol, where a temporary covering had been placed to protect the President-elect from possible rain during the reading of his inaugural address. The greater part of an hour was occupied in seating the procession on the platform, and in the delivery of the address of Mr. Lincoln, which he read with a clear, loud, and distinct voice, quite intelligible to at least ten thousand persons below him. At close of the address Mr. Lincoln took the oath of office from the venerable chief justice of the Supreme Court. After the ceremony of inauguration had been completed the President and ex-President retired by the same avenue, and the procession, or the military part of it, marched to the executive mansion. On arriving at the President's house Mr. Lincoln met Gen. Scott, by whom he was warmly greeted, and then the doors of the house were opened, and thousands of persons rapidly passed through, shaking hands with the President, who stood in the reception-room for that purpose. In this simple and quiet manner was the change of rulers made.

At Montgomery, on the other hand, commissioners were now appointed to the courts of Europe and to the Federal Government. The latter arrived at Washington on the 5th of March. They were John Forsyth, Martin J. Crawford, and A. B. Roman, appointed under a resolution of Congress requesting it, and for the purpose of making a settlement of all questions of disagreement between the Government of the United States and that of the Confederate States "upon principles of right, justice, equity, and good faith." Upon the arrival of the commissioners at Washington, an informal notice was given to the Secretary of State, and the explanation of the object of their mission was postponed to the 12th of March. On that day they addressed Secretary Seward, informing him of the purpose of their arrival, and stating their wish to make to the Government of the United States overtures for the opening of negotiations, and assuring that Government that the President, Congress, and people of the Confederate States desired a peaceful solution of the questions of disagreement between them; and that it was neither their interest nor their wish to make any demand which was not founded on the strictest principles of justice, nor to do any act of injury to their late sister States.

A memorandum, bearing date March 15th, was delivered, as the reply to this communication, on the 8th of April, and then upon the request of the secretary of the commissioners, for an answer to their note. This length of time was permitted to elapse by the commissioners, who waived all questions of form with the design of avoiding war if possible. All negotiation, upon the basis on which the commissioners desired to place it, failed. Official intercourse with them was declined by Secretary Seward.

Meanwhile the United States Government had prepared to send supplies to the handful of troops besieged in Fort Sumter. Notice of this intention was given to the Governor of South Carolina, and if the Confederate Government was in earnest in what had been done, the hour had come when the sword must be drawn.

On the 8th of April, the following telegraphic correspondence commenced between the Secretary of War for the insurrectionary States and the commander of their forces at Charleston harbor:

CHARLESTON, April 8th.

L. P. Walker, Secretary of War:

An authorized messenger from President Lincoln just informed Governor Pickens and myself that provisions will be sent to Fort Sumter peaceably, or otherwise by force. G. T. BEAUREGARD.

MONTGOMERY, 10th.

Gen. G. T. Beauregard, Charleston:

If you have no doubt of the authorized character of the agent who communicated to you the intention of the Washington Government to supply Fort Sumter by force, you will at once demand its evacuation; and if this is refused, proceed in such a manner as you may determine, to reduce it. Answer.

L. P. WALKER, Secretary of War.

CHARLESTON, April 10.

L. P. Walker, Secretary of War:

The demand will be made to-morrow at twelve o'clock. G. T. BEAUREGARD.

MONTGOMERY, April 10.

General Beauregard, Charleston:

Unless there are especial reasons connected with your own condition, it is considered proper that you should make the demand at an early hour.

L. P. WALKER, Secretary of War.

CHARLESTON, April 10.

L. P. Walker, Secretary of War:

The reasons are special for twelve o'clock.

G. T. BEAUREGARD.

CHARLESTON, April 11, 1861.

To Hon. L. P. Walker:

The demand was sent at 2 P. M., and until 6 was allowed for the answer. G. T. BEAUREGARD.

MONTGOMERY, April 11, 1861.

General Beauregard, Charleston:

Telegraph the reply of Major Anderson.

L. P. WALKER.

CHARLESTON, April 11, 1861.

To Hon. L. P. Walker:

Major Anderson replies: "I have the honor to acknowledge the receipt of your communication demanding the evacuation of this fort, and to say in reply thereto that it is a demand with which I regret that my sense of honor and of my obligations to my Government prevent my compliance." He adds verbally, "I will await the first shot, and, if you do not batter us to pieces, we will be starved out in a few days." G. T. BEAUREGARD.

MONTGOMERY, April 11, 1861.

To General Beauregard:

Do not desire needlessly to bombard Fort Sumter. If Major Anderson will state the time at which, as indicated by himself, he will evacuate, and agree that in the mean time he will not use his guns against us unless ours should be employed against Fort Sumter, you are authorized thus to avoid the effusion of blood. If this or its equivalent be refused, reduce the fort, as your judgment decides to be the most practicable.

L. P. WALKER.

CHARLESTON, April 12, 1861.

To Hon. L. P. Walker;

He would not consent. I write to-day.

G. T. BEAUREGARD.

CHARLESTON, April 12, 1861.

To Hon. L. P. Walker:

We opened fire at 4:30. G. T. BEAUREGARD.

Vigorous operations had been commenced on Fort Sumter, which is one of the defences of Charleston, in the month of August, 1860, with a view of placing it in a good defensive position as soon as possible. The casemate arches supporting the second tier of guns were all turned; the granite flagging for the second tier was laid, on the right face of the work; the floors laid, and the iron stairways put up in the east barrack; the traverse circle of the first tier of guns reset; the blue-stone flagging laid in all the gun-rooms of the right and left faces of the first tier; and the construction of the embrasure of the second tier commenced, at the time that the fort was occupied by Major Anderson. Then the fears of an immediate attack and disloyal feelings induced the greater portion of the engineer corps to leave. But those that remained of this corps, fifty-five in number, reduced toward the end of the investment to thirty-five, were made very effective in preparing for a vigorous defence.

This fort was occupied by Major Anderson on the night of the 26th of December. It is the largest of the forts in Charleston harbor. It is a work of solid masonry, octagonal in form, and pierced on the north, east, and west sides with a double row of port-holes for the heaviest guns, and on the south, or land side, in addition to openings for guns, loop-holes for musketry. It stands in the middle of the harbor, like a monster on the bosom of the waters, and near the edge of the ship channel. The armament consists of one hundred and forty guns, many of them being the formidable ten-inch columbiads. The wharf, or landing, is on the south side, and exposed to a cross-fire from all the openings on that side. At twelve o'clock on the 27th, the stars and stripes were hoisted over the fort, and Charleston knew for the first time that Major Anderson was in full possession. The garrison now consisted of eighty men, as follows:

NAMES.	Rank.	Regiment or Corps.	Original Entry into Service.	Where Born.
R. Anderson....	Major	1st Artil'y	July 1, '25	Ky.
S. W. Crawford.	As'tSurgeon	Med. Staff	M'h 10, '51	Penn.
A. Doubleday...	Captain.....	1st Artil'y	July 1, '42	N. Y.
T. Seymour.....	Captain.....	1st Artil'y	July 1, '46	Vt.
Theo. Talbot....	1st Lieut...	1st Artil'y	M'y 22, '47	D. C.
Jeff. C. Davis...	1st Lieut...	1st Artil'y	J'e 17, '48	Ind.
J. N. Hall.......	2d Lieut....	1st Artil'y	July 1, '59	N. Y.
J. G. Foster.....	Captain	Engineers	July 1, '46	N. H.
G. W. Snyder...	1st Lieut...	Engineers	July 1, '56	N. Y.
R. K. Meade....	2d Lieut....	Engineers	July 1, '57	Va.

Officers, 10; Band, 15; Artillerists, 55. Total, 80.

There were in addition fifty-five of the engineer corps, which was subsequently reduced, as before mentioned, to thirty-five. This movement on the part of Major Anderson created great excitement in Charleston. The State authorities immediately commenced the preparation of batteries to reduce the fort, and also opened negotiations for its surrender. An effort had been made by the Government to send provisions to the garrison in the fort. The Star of the West arrived off Charleston on Jan. 9th, and attempted to enter the harbor, but being fired on she withdrew.

Governor Pickens first demanded a surrender of the fort from Major Anderson. He replied, on the 11th of January, that he had "no power to comply with such a demand." On the same day a demand on the President for the fort was despatched to Washington by J. W. Hayne, envoy of South Carolina. On his arrival, he was addressed by several Senators from the other seceded States, under date of January 15th. They desired him to postpone for a time the delivery of the letter with which he was charged to the President of the United States, and urged their community of interest, of destiny, and of position, as a reason why he should postpone action, and allow time for consultation. He agreed to do this, upon the condition that, "until he can hear from his Government, no reënforcements shall be sent to Fort Sumter, pledging himself that, in the mean time, no attack shall be made upon that fort."

The Senators, through Messrs. Fitzpatrick, Mallory, and Slidell, transmitted the correspondence between them and Mr. Hayne to the President, asking him to take into consideration the substance of the said correspondence. The reply came through Mr. Holt, who gave no pledge that he would not attempt to reënforce Fort Sumter. The only remark was, that it was not at present deemed necessary to reënforce Fort Sumter, but, if deemed necessary, every effort would be made to reënforce it.

The Senators to whom this was addressed did not regard it as satisfactory, but told Mr. Hayne that they felt certain that at present no attempt would be made to reënforce Sumter, and upon their judgment he postponed the deli ery of his letter to the President. On the 24th, he stated to the Senators, that he had, the day before, forwarded the correspondence to Charleston. The reply of the State Government was lengthy, and bore down heavily upon the tone of Mr. Holt's answer to the letter of the Senators.

Col. Hayne was instructed to deliver his letter conveying the demand for the surrender of Fort Sumter; also, to ask if the President was to be understood as asserting the right to send reënforcements to Fort Sumter, stating that the assertion of such right, with the attempt to exercise it, would be regarded by South Carolina as an act of war. If the President refused to deliver the fort, then Col. Hayne was to communicate that fact immediately. The President's answer could be transmitted within a reasonable time to the Government at Charleston, and Col. Hayne was not instructed to wait for it.

The final reply of the President, through Mr. Holt, the Secretary of War, was made on the 6th of February. That reply closes with these words: "If, with all the multiplied proofs which exist of the President's anxiety for peace, and of the earnestness with which he has pursued it, the authorities of that State shall assault Fort Sumter, and peril the lives of the handful of brave and loyal men shut up within its walls, and thus plunge our common country into the horrors of civil war, then upon them and those they represent must rest the responsibility."

The question of attacking the fort was finally referred to the Confederate Congress at Montgomery. By that body all military matters were placed under the charge of the President of the Confederate States.

As it had been resolved to remove the women and children from the fort, they were, by the permission of the South Carolina authorities, taken to Charleston and placed on board the steamer Marion, bound to New York. She left on Sunday, February 3d; and as she proceeded down the harbor, having among the passengers the wives—twenty in number—and the children of the soldiers stationed in the fort, quite an exciting scene occurred, which an eye-witness thus described: "On nearing the fort, the whole garrison was seen mounted on the top of the ramparts, and when the ship was passing, fired a gun and gave three heart-thrilling cheers as a parting farewell to the dear loved ones on board, whom they may possibly never meet again this side the grave. The response was weeping and 'waving adieus' to husbands and fathers—a small band pent up in an isolated fort, and completely surrounded by instruments of death, as five forts could be seen from the steamer's deck with their guns pointing towards Sumter."

Major Anderson, writing to the War Department, about March 1st, expressed his conviction that Fort Sumter would soon be attacked. He could then clearly discern with the naked eye the arrangements for the assault, which he believed would be of the most determined character. The fortification was only then entirely completed. The utmost ingenuity of himself and brother officers had been employed to strengthen every part, and to provide means for resisting the attack, which was certain to come.

Preparations were made under the direction of the Confederate Government to capture the fort, until the 11th of April, when the following correspondence took place between the commander of the Confederate forces, Gen. Beauregard, and the commander of the fort, Major Anderson:

HEAD-QUARTERS PROVISIONAL ARMY C. S. A.,
CHARLESTON, S. C., *April* 11, 1861—2 P. M.

SIR: The Government of the Confederate States has hitherto forborne from any hostile demonstration against Fort Sumter, in the hope that the Government of the United States, with a view to the amicable adjustment of all questions between the two Governments, and to avert the calamities of war, would voluntarily evacuate it. There was reason at one time to believe that such would be the course pursued by the Government of the United States; and under that impression my Government has refrained from making any demand for the surrender of the fort.

But the Confederate States can no longer delay assuming actual possession of a fortification commanding the entrance of one of their harbors, and necessary to its defence and security.

I am ordered by the Government of the Confederate States to demand the evacuation of Fort Sumter. My aides, Colonel Chesnut and Captain Lee, are authorized to make such demand of you. All proper facilities will be afforded for the removal of yourself and command, together with company arms and property, and all private property, to any post in the United States which you may elect. The flag which you have upheld so long and with so much fortitude under the most trying circumstances, may be saluted by you on taking it down.

Colonel Chesnut and Captain Lee will, for a reasonable time, await your answer.

I am, sir, very respectfully,
Your obedient servant,
G. T. BEAUREGARD,
Brigadier-General Commanding.

Major ROBERT ANDERSON, Commanding at Fort Sumter, Charleston Harbor, S. C.

HEAD-QUARTERS, FORT SUMTER, S. C.,
April 11th, 1861.

GENERAL: I have the honor to acknowledge the receipt of your communication demanding the evacuation of this fort, and to say in reply thereto that it is a demand with which I regret that my sense of honor and of my obligations to my Government prevent my compliance.

Thanking you for the fair, manly, and courteous terms proposed, and for the high compliment paid me, I am, General, very respectfully,

Your obedient servant,
ROBERT ANDERSON,
Major U. S. Army, Commanding.

To Brig.-Gen. G. T. BEAUREGARD, Commanding Provisional Army C. S. A.

HEAD-QUARTERS PROVISIONAL ARMY C. S. A.,
CHARLESTON, *April* 11, 1861—11 P. M.

MAJOR: In consequence of the verbal observations made by you to my aides, Messrs. Chesnut and Lee, in relation to the condition of your supplies, and that you would in a few days be starved out if our guns did not batter you to pieces—or words to that effect;—and desiring no useless effusion of blood, I communicated both the verbal observation and your written answer to my communication to my Government.

If you will state the time at which you will evacuate Fort Sumter, and agree that in the mean time you will not use your guns against us, unless ours shall be employed against Fort Sumter, we will abstain from opening fire upon you. Colonel Chesnut and Captain Lee are authorized by me to enter into such an agreement with you. You are therefore requested to communicate to them an open answer.

I remain, Major, very respectfully,
Your obedient servant,
G. T. BEAUREGARD,
Brigadier-General Commanding.

Major ROBERT ANDERSON, Commanding at Fort Sumter, Charleston Harbor, S. C.

HEAD-QUARTERS, FORT SUMTER, S. C.,
2.30 A. M., *April* 12, 1861.

GENERAL: I have the honor to acknowledge the receipt of your second communication of the 11th inst., by Col. Chesnut, and to state, in reply, that cordially uniting with you in the desire to avoid the useless effusion of blood, I will, if provided with the proper and necessary means of transportation, evacuate Fort Sumter by noon on the 15th instant, should I not receive, prior to that time, controlling instructions from my Government, or additional supplies; and that I will not, in the mean time, open my fire upon your forces, unless compelled to do so by some hostile act against this fort, or the flag of my Government, by the forces under your command, or by some portion of them, or by the perpetration of some act showing a hostile intention on your part against this fort, or the flag it bears.

I have the honor to be, General,
Your obedient servant,
ROBERT ANDERSON,
Major U. S. Army Commanding.

To Brig.-Gen. G. T. BEAUREGARD, Commanding Provisional Army C. S. A.

FORT SUMTER, S. C.,
April 12, 1861—3.20 A. M.

SIR: By authority of Brigadier-General Beauregard, commanding the provisional forces of the Confederate States, we have the honor to notify you that he will open the fire of his batteries on Fort Sumter in one hour from this time.

We have the honor to be, very respectfully,
Your obedient servants,
JAMES CHESNUT, JR., Aide-de-Camp.
STEPH. D. LEE, Capt. S. C. A., and Aide-de-Camp.

Major ROBERT ANDERSON, U. S. Army, Commanding Fort Sumter.

At thirty minutes past 4 o'clock on the morning of Friday, April 12, the first gun of civil war was fired, discharging a shell from the howitzer battery on James' Island. The sending of this deadly messenger to Major Anderson was followed by a deafening explosion, caused by the blowing up of a building that stood in front of the battery.

While the white smoke was melting away into the air another shell pursued its swift way towards the silent fortification. The missive described its beautiful curve through the balmy air, and falling within the hostile fortress, scattered its deadly contents in all directions.

Fort Moultrie then took up the assault, and in a moment the guns from the Gun Battery on Cummings' Point, from Captain McCready's Battery, from Captain James Hamilton's Floating Battery, the Enfilade Battery, and other fortifications, sent forth their wrath at the grim fortress rising so defiantly out of the sea.

Major Anderson received the shot and shell in silence. But the deepening twilight revealed the stars and stripes floating proudly in the breeze. The batteries continued at regular intervals to belch forth iron shells, and still no answer was returned by the besieged. About an hour after the firing began, two balls rushed hissing through the air and glanced harmless from the stuccoed bricks of Fort Moultrie. The embrasures of the besieged fortress gave forth no sound again till between six and seven o'clock, when, as if wrathful from enforced delay, from casemate and parapet there poured a storm of iron hail upon Fort Moultrie, Stevens' Iron Battery, and the Floating Battery. The broadside was returned with spirit by the gunners at those posts.

The firing now began in good earnest. The curling white smoke hung above the angry pieces of hostile brothers, and the jarring boom rolled at regular intervals on the anxious ear. The atmosphere was charged with the smell of foul saltpetre, and, as if in sympathy with the melancholy scene, the sky was covered with heavy clouds, and every thing wore a sombre aspect.

A brisk fire was kept up by all the batteries until about 7 o'clock in the evening, after which hour the guns fired at regular intervals.

The effect during the night was grand and terrific. The firing reached its climax at about ten o'clock. The heavens were obscured by rain-clouds, and the horizon was as dark as Erebus. The guns were worked with vigor, and their booming was heard with astonishing distinctness, because the wind was blowing in-shore. At each discharge a lurid sheet of flame was belched forth, and then another and another was seen before the report reached the ears. Sometimes a shell would burst in mid-air, directly over the doomed fortress, and at all times the missiles of this character could be distinguished in their course by the trail of fire left momentarily behind them.

The fire from all the forts, Sumter included, and from the batteries of the Confederate States, was kept up with vigor till early dawn. Then the rapidity of the discharges gradually diminished.

Such was the appearance of the contest during the first day and night.

The batteries firing upon Sumter were, as nearly as could be ascertained, armed as follows:

On Morris' Island.—Breaching battery No. 1, 2 42-pounders; 1 12-pounder, Blakely rifled gun.

Mortar battery, (next to No. 1,) 4 10-inch mortars.

Breaching battery No. 2, (iron-clad battery,) 3 8-inch columbiads.

Mortar battery, (next to No. 2,) 3 10-inch mortars.

On James' Island.—Battery at Fort Johnson, 3 24-pounders, (only one of them bearing on Fort Sumter.)

Mortar battery, south of Fort Johnson, 4 10-inch mortars.

Sullivan's Island.—Iron-clad (floating) battery, 4 42-pounders.

Columbiad battery No. 1, 1 9-inch Dahlgren gun.

Columbiad battery No. 2, 4 8-inch columbiads.

Mortar battery, west of Fort Moultrie, 3 10-inch mortars.
Mortar battery, on parade, in rear of Fort Moultrie, 2 10-inch mortars.
Fort Moultrie.—3 8-inch columbiads; 2 8-inch S. C. howitzers; 5 32-pounders; 4 24-pounders.
At Mount Pleasant.—1 10-inch mortar.
Total, firing on Fort Sumter, 30 guns, 17 mortars.

Of the 43 workmen constituting the engineer force in Fort Sumter, nearly all volunteered to serve as cannoniers, or to carry shot and cartridges to the guns.

The armament of the fort was as follows:

Barbette Tier.—Right flank—1 10-inch columbiad; 4 8-inch columbiads; 4 42-pounders.
Right face.—None.
Left face.—3 8-inch sea-coast howitzers; 1 32-pounder.
Left flank.—1 10-inch columbiad; 2 8-inch columbiads; 2 42-pounders.
Gorge.—1 8-inch sea-coast howitzer; 2 32-pounders; 6 24-pounders.
Total in barbette, 27 guns.
Casemate Tier.—Right flank.—1 42-pounder; 4 32-pounders.
Right face.—3 42-pounders.
Left face.—10 32-pounders.
Left flank.—5 32-pounders.
Gorge.—2 32-pounders.
Total in casemate, 21 guns. Total available in both tiers, 48 guns.

Besides the above, there were arranged on the parade, to serve as mortars, 1 10-inch columbiad to throw shells into Charleston, and 4 8-inch columbiads to throw shells into the batteries on Cummings' Point. The casemate guns were the only ones used. Of these, those that bore on Cummings' Point were the 42-pounder in the pan-coupé of the right gorge angle; the 32-pounder next to it on the gorge, which, by cutting into the brick wall, had been made to traverse sufficiently; and the 32-pounder next the angle on the right flank, which, by cutting away the side of the embrasure, had been made to bear on a portion of the point, although not on the breaching batteries.

The guns of the first tier, that bore on Fort Johnson, were 4 32-pounders, on the left flank; of these one embrasure had been, by order, bricked up.

The guns that bore on the three batteries on the west end of "Sullivan's Island" were 10 32-pounders, situated on the left face, and one at the pan-coupé of the salient angle, (four embrasures being bricked up.)

The guns bearing on Fort Moultrie were 2 42-pounders, situated on the right face, and one at the pan-coupé of the right shoulder angle.

The supply of cartridges, seven hundred in number, with which the engagement commenced, became so much reduced by the middle of the day, although the six needles in the fort were kept steadily employed, that the firing was forced to slacken, and to be confined to six guns, two firing towards Morris' Island, two towards Fort Moultrie, and two towards the batteries on the west end of Sullivan's Island.

At 1 o'clock on the 12th, two United States men-of-war were seen off the bar, and soon after, a third appeared.

The effect of the fire was not very good, owing to the insufficient calibre of the guns for the long range, and not much damage appeared to be done to any of the batteries except those of Fort Moultrie, where the two 42-pounders appeared to have silenced the gun for a time, to have injured the embrasures considerably, riddled the barracks and quarters, and torn three holes through the flag. The so-called "floating battery" was struck very frequently by shot, one of them penetrating at the angle between the front and roof, entirely through the iron covering and wood work beneath, and wounding one man. The rest of the 32-pounder balls failed to penetrate the front or the roof, but were deflected from their surfaces, which were arranged at a suitable angle for this purpose.

The columbiad battery and Dahlgren battery, near the floating battery, did not appear to be much injured by the few shots that were fired at them. Only one or two shots were fired at Fort Johnson, and none at Castle Pinckney or the city.

The fire towards Morris' Island was mainly directed at the iron-clad battery, but the small calibre of the shot failed to penetrate the covering when struck fairly. The aim was therefore taken at the embrasures, which were struck at least twice, disabling the guns for a time. One or two shots were thrown at the reverse of batteries "3" and "4," scattering some groups of officers and men on the lookout, and cutting down a small flagstaff on one of the batteries.

The barracks caught fire three times during the day, from shells apparently, but each time the flames, being in the first or second stories, were extinguished by a pump and application of the means at hand.

The effect of the Confederate fire upon Fort Sumter during the day was very marked in respect to the vertical fire. This was so well directed and so well sustained, that from the seventeen mortars engaged in firing 10-inch shells, one-half the shells came within or exploded above the parapet of the fort, and only about ten buried themselves in the soft earth of the parade, without exploding. In consequence of this precision of vertical fire, Major Anderson decided not to man the upper tier of guns.

Saturday dawned a bright and lovely day, but the flags of each of the combatants were still flying in stately defiance, and the cannon continued to send forth their fiery thunder. Within Fort Sumter, the last of the rice was cooked that morning, and served with the pork, the only other article of food left in the mess-room. After this the fire was reopened, and continued very briskly as long as the increased supply of cartridges lasted. The surrounding batteries had reopened fire at daylight, and continued it with rapidity. The aim of their guns was better than on the previous day.

It soon became evident that they were firing

hot shot from a large number of their guns, especially from those in Fort Moultrie; and at nine o'clock volumes of smoke issued from the roof of the officers' quarters, where a shot had just penetrated. From the exposed position, it was utterly impossible to extinguish the flames, and permission was given to remove as much powder from the magazine as was possible, before the flames, which were only one set of quarters distant, should encircle the magazine and make it necessary to close it. All the men and officers not engaged at the guns worked rapidly and zealously at this; but so rapid was the spread of the flames that only fifty barrels of powder could be taken out and distributed around in the casemates before the fire and heat made it necessary to close the magazine doors and pack earth against them. The men then withdrew to the casemates on the faces of the fort. As soon as the flames and smoke burst from the roof of the quarters, the surrounding batteries redoubled the rapidity of their fire, firing red-hot shot from most of their guns. The whole range of officers' quarters was soon in flames. The wind, being from the southward, communicated fire to the roof of the barracks, and this, being aided by the hot shot constantly lodging there, spread to the entire roofs of both barracks, so that by twelve o'clock all the wood work of quarters and of upper story of barracks was in flames. Although the floors of the barracks were fire-proof, the utmost exertions of the officers and men were often required to prevent the fire communicating down the stairways, and from the exterior to the doors, window-frames, and other wood work of the east barrack, in which the officers and men had taken their quarters.

The clouds of smoke and cinders which were sent into the casemates by the wind, set on fire many boxes, beds, and other articles belonging to the men, and made it dangerous to retain the powder which had been saved from the magazine. Orders were accordingly given that all but five barrels should be thrown out of the embrasures into the water, which was done.

The small stock of cartridges now only allowed a gun to be fired at intervals of ten minutes.

As the fire reached the magazines of grenades that were arranged in the stair towers and implement rooms on the gorge, they exploded, completely destroying the stair towers at the west gorge angle.

About this time information was brought to the commanding officer that Mr. Wigfall, bearing a white flag, was on the outside and wished to see him. He accordingly went out to meet Mr. Wigfall, passing through the blazing gateway, accompanied by Lieutenant Snyder. In the mean time, however, Mr. Wigfall had passed to an embrasure on the left flank, where, upon showing the white flag upon his sword, he was permitted to enter; and Lieutenant Snyder, entering immediately after, accompanied him down the batteries to where some other officers were posted, to whom Mr. Wigfall commenced to address himself to the effect that he came from General Beauregard to desire that, inasmuch as the flag of the fort was shot down, a fire raging in the quarters, and the garrison in a great strait, hostilities be suspended, and the white flag raised for this object. He was replied to that the flag was again hoisted on the parapet; that the white flag would not be hoisted, except by order of the commanding officer; and that his own batteries should set the example of suspending fire. He then referred to the fact of the batteries on Cummings' Point, from which he came, having stopped firing, and asked that his own white flag might be waved to indicate to the batteries on Sullivan's Island to cease also. This was refused; but he was permitted to wave the white flag himself, getting into an embrasure for this purpose. Having done this for a few moments, Lieutenant Davis, First Artillery, permitted a corporal to relieve him. Very soon, however, a shot striking very near to the embrasure, the corporal jumped inside and declared to Mr. Wigfall that "he would not hold his flag, for it was not respected."

At this moment, the commanding officer, having reëntered through an embrasure, came up. To him Mr. Wigfall addressed nearly the same remarks that he had used on entering, adding some complimentary things about the manner in which the defence had been made, and ending by renewing the request to suspend hostilities in order to arrange terms of evacuation. The commanding officer desiring to know what terms he came to offer, Mr. Wigfall replied: "Any terms that you may desire; your own terms—the precise nature of which General Beauregard will arrange with you."

The commanding officer then accepted the conditions, saying that the terms he accepted were those proposed by General Beauregard on the 11th; namely, to evacuate the fort with his command, taking arms and all private and company property, saluting the United States flag as it was lowered, and being conveyed, if he desired it, to any Northern port.

With this understanding Mr. Wigfall left, and the white flag was raised and the United States flag lowered by order of the commanding officer.

Very soon after, a boat arrived from the city, containing three aides of General Beauregard, with a message to the effect that, observing the white flag hoisted, General Beauregard sent to inquire what aid he could lend in extinguishing the flames, &c. Being made acquainted with the condition of affairs and Mr. Wigfall's visit, they stated that the latter, although an aide of General Beauregard, had not seen him for two days.

The commanding officer then stated that the United States flag would be raised again; but yielded to the request of the aides for time to report to their chief and obtain his instructions.

They soon returned with the approval of all the conditions desired, except the saluting the flag as it was lowered; and this exception was subsequently removed after correspondence.

The evacuation was completed after saluting the flag; in doing which, one man was instantly killed, one mortally and four severely wounded, by the premature discharge of a gun and explosion of a pile of cartridges.

After the cessation of fire, about 600 shot marks on the face of the scarp wall were counted, but they were so scattered that no breached effect could have been expected from such fire, and probably none was attempted except at the right gorge angle. The only effect of the direct fire during the two days was to disable three barbette guns, knock off large portions of the chimneys and brick walls projecting above the parapet, and to set the quarters on fire with hot shot. The vertical fire produced more effect, as it prevented the working of the upper tier of guns, which were the only really effective guns in the fort, being columbiads, 8-inch sea-coast howitzers, and 42-pounders principally, and also prevented the use of the columbiads arranged in the parade to be used as mortars against Cummings' Point.

The weakness of the defence principally lay in the lack of cartridge bags, and of the materials to make them, by which the fire of the fort was all the time rendered slow, and toward the last was nearly suspended.

The contest continued thirty-two hours, and the weapons used were of the most destructive character, and in skilful hands, but no life appears to have been lost on either side.

The garrison was taken by the steamer Isabel to the Baltic, which lay off the harbor, and thence transported to New York. The naval force and supplies which had been sent to the relief of the fort by the Government, arrived off Charleston harbor previous to the commencement of the assault, but were prevented from entering the harbor by a gale of wind, until after the attack began. The vessels, however, continued outside, and there was no communication between them and the fort.

The force and supplies thus sent by the Government were composed as follows:

Vessels.	Guns.	Men.
Sloop-of-war Pawnee,	10	200
Sloop-of-war Powhatan,	11	275
Cutter Harriet Lane,	5	96
Steam transport Atlantic,	—	353
Steam transport Baltic,	—	160
Steam transport Illinois,	—	300
Steamtug Yankee,	Ordinary crew.	
Steamtug Uncle Ben,	Ordinary crew.	
Total number of vessels,		8
Total number of guns (for marine service),		26
Total number of men and troops,		1,380

Nearly thirty launches, whose services are useful in effecting a landing of troops over shoal water, and for attacking a discharging battery when covered with sand and gunny bags, were taken out by the Powhatan, and by the steam transports Atlantic, Baltic, and Illinois. The official notification of the surrender of the fort, sent by Major Anderson to the War Department, was as follows:

STEAMSHIP BALTIC, off Sandy Hook,
April 18, 1861—10:30 A. M., via New York.

Having defended Fort Sumter for thirty-four hours, until the quarters were entirely burnt, the main gates destroyed by fire, the gorge walls seriously injured, the magazine surrounded by flames, and its door closed from the effects of heat; four barrels and three cartridges of powder only being available, and no provisions remaining but pork, I accepted terms of evacuation offered by General Beauregard—being the same offered by him on the 11th instant, prior to the commencement of hostilities—and marched out of the fort on Sunday afternoon, the 14th instant, with colors flying and drums beating, bringing away company and private property, and saluting my flag with fifty guns. ROBERT ANDERSON,

Major First Artillery Commanding.

Hon. SIMON CAMERON, Sec'y of War, Washington.

CHAPTER IV.

State of Affairs—Action of the Union States—Proclamation of the President calling for men on the surrender of Fort Sumter—Response of the Northern and Central States—Attack on Massachusetts troops in Baltimore.

WHAT was the posture of affairs at the time of President Lincoln's inauguration, especially as compared with their situation on the day of election in November? Seven Southern States had voted themselves out of the Union, the officers of the Federal Government had resigned, and there were no persons to represent its powers or execute its duties within their limits, excepting in the Post-Office Department. Within these States, also, all the forts, arsenals, dockyards, custom-houses, revenue cutters, etc., embracing all the movable and stationary articles connected therewith, had been taken possession of by the authority of these States individually, and were held by persons and officers denying any allegiance to the Federal Government, and avowing it to be due by them only to a Government created by the united action of these seven States. Only Forts Pickens, Taylor, and Jefferson, near the Florida coast, and Sumter, in Charleston harbor, continued under the flag of the Union.

The other forts thus seized were put in an improved condition, new ones built, and armed forces had been organized, and were organizing, avowedly to protect this property from recapture, and to capture those not yet seized. Around Fort Sumter batteries had been erected, with guns equal or heavier in calibre than hers, and in far greater number. Officers of the army and navy of the Union from these States, had chiefly resigned, and had been reappointed in the service of the latter. A complete Government for a nation was in operation in these States, and the property thus seized was held, as the new Government avowed, to be accounted for in a peaceful settlement with the Federal Union, or to be used for the defence of those States, if assaulted by the same Union. They asked for peace, and to be "let alone," but were determined to hazard a war sooner than return to their former allegiance.

Among the other States, Kentucky made an application to Congress to call a National Convention to amend the Constitution of the United States, and requested the Legislatures of all the other States to make similar applications, and appointed commissioners to a conference of the Border States to consider and, if practicable, agree upon some suitable adjustment of the present unhappy controversies. Some of the States of the North appointed commissioners to this conference, which agreed upon terms for an adjustment, but no State action followed. Not a single slaveholding State complied with the request of Kentucky to apply to Congress to call a National Convention, whilst three non-slaveholding States so complied, and several others prepared to follow.

A Peace Conference was called by Virginia, in which twenty States were represented. Such measures would have been recommended as were desired by the seceding States if they had been present by their votes to secure their adoption. Three territorial bills were passed by Congress, in no one of which was inserted the prohibition of slavery as insisted upon hitherto by the Republicans. The North condemned the personal liberty bills of the States, declared in favor of a faithful execution of the fugitive slave law, and concurred in proposing, by the requisite constitutional majority, an amendment of the Constitution guaranteeing positively and forever the exemption of slavery in the States from the interference of Congress. This was one of the guarantees embraced in the scheme of Mr. Crittenden, and also in the scheme of the Peace Conference.

Rhode Island repealed its personal liberty law outright, whilst Vermont, Maine, Massachusetts, Pennsylvania, and Wisconsin had under consideration the repeal or essential modification of their respective laws of this description. Not less than a quarter of a million of the people of the North, besides societies and representative bodies without number, petitioned Congress for the adoption of any adjustment satisfactory to the States of the Southern border.

The attack on Fort Sumter began on the 12th. The fort surrendered on the afternoon of the 13th, and was evacuated on Sunday, the 14th. As the news flashed over the country by the telegraph it was instantly followed by the summons of the President, "to arms; to arms." His proclamation, ordering seventy-five thousand men into the field, was issued on the night of the 14th, as follows:

By the President of the United States.

A PROCLAMATION.

Whereas the laws of the United States have been for some time past and now are opposed, and the execution thereof obstructed, in the States of South Carolina, Georgia, Alabama, Florida, Mississippi, Louisiana, and Texas, by combinations too powerful to be suppressed by the ordinary course of judicial proceedings, or by the powers vested in the marshals by law:

Now, therefore, I, Abraham Lincoln, President of the United States, in virtue of the power in me vested by the Constitution and the laws, have thought fit to call forth, and hereby do call forth, the militia of the several States of the Union, to the aggregate number of seventy-five thousand, in order to suppress said combinations, and to cause the laws to be duly executed.

The details for this object will be immediately communicated to the State authorities through the War Department.

I appeal to all loyal citizens to favor, facilitate, and aid this effort to maintain the honor, the integrity, and the existence of our National Union, and the perpetuity of popular Government, and to redress wrongs already long enough endured.

I deem it proper to say that the first service assigned to the forces called forth will probably be to repossess the forts, places, and property which have been seized from the Union; and in every event the utmost care will be observed, consistently with the objects aforesaid, to avoid any devastation, any destruction of or interference with property, or any disturbance of peaceful citizens in any part of the country.

And I hereby command the persons composing the combinations aforesaid to disperse and retire peaceably to their respective abodes within twenty days from this date.

Deeming that the present condition of public affairs presents an extraordinary occasion, I do hereby, in virtue of the power in me vested by the Constitution, convene both Houses of Congress.

Senators and Representatives are therefore summoned to assemble at their respective Chambers, at 12 o'clock, noon, on Thursday, the fourth day of July next, then and there to consider and determine such measures as, in their wisdom, the public safety and interest may seem to demand.

In witness whereof, I have hereunto set my hand and caused the seal of the United States to be affixed.

Done at the city of Washington, this fifteenth day of April, in the year of our Lord one thousand [L. S.] eight hundred and sixty-one, and of the independence of the United States the eighty-fifth.

ABRAHAM LINCOLN.

By the President:

WILLIAM H. SEWARD, Secretary of State.

A call for troops was issued by the Secretary of War, Mr. Cameron, in accordance with this proclamation, and sent to the Governors of the respective States, giving the quotas allotted to each, as follows:

DEPARTMENT OR WAR, WASHINGTON, April 15, 1861.

To His Excellency the Governor of ——— :

SIR: Under the act of Congress for calling for the "Militia to execute the laws of the Union, suppress insurrections, repel invasions," etc., approved February 28, 1795, I have the honor to request your Excellency to cause to be immediately detached from the militia of your State the quota designated in the table below, to serve as infantry or riflemen, for the period of three months, unless sooner discharged.

Your Excellency will please communicate to me the time at or about which your quota will be expected at its rendezvous, as it will be met as soon as practicable by an officer or officers to muster it into the service and pay of the United States.

These documents were spread through the country on Monday, and on Wednesday the 6th regiment of Massachusetts, completely equipped, passed through New York for Washington, so prepared was that State as to be the first in the field.

A most uncontrollable excitement now existed in the country. Both North and South rushed to arms—the former to maintain the Government and to preserve the Union, the latter to secure the independence of the Confederate States and the dissolution of the Union.

The national city of Washington became the most conspicuous object before the country. Northern troops hastened thither to secure its possession in the hands of the Government, and Southern troops gathered on its outskirts to seize it as their first prize.

The manner in which the requisition of the Secretary of War for troops was received by the authorities of the respective States, indicates the controlling sentiment of the people in those States at this time. The Governor of Kentucky replied on the same day: "Kentucky will furnish no troops for the wicked purpose of subduing her sister Southern States." The Governor of North Carolina answered: "You can get no troops from North Carolina." The Governor of Virginia wrote on the next day to the Secretary of War, saying: "The militia of Virginia will not be furnished to the powers at Washington for any such use or purpose as they have in view." The Governor of Tennessee replied: "Tennessee will not furnish a single man for coercion, but fifty thousand, if necessary, for defence of our rights, or those of our Southern brothers." The Governor of Missouri answered that "the requisition is illegal, unconstitutional, revolutionary, inhuman, diabolical, and cannot be complied with."

The Governor of Rhode Island replied by tendering the services of a thousand infantry and a battalion of artillery.

The Governor of Massachusetts immediately ordered out troops, and in fifty hours three regiments had been gathered, equipped, and had left for Washington.

The Governor of Connecticut also issued his proclamation at once, calling for troops.

The Legislature of New York adjourned on the 16th; but previously to adjournment appropriated three millions of dollars to defend the Federal Government.

Orders for four regiments were issued by the Governor of New Jersey on the 17th.

A detachment of five hundred men left Philadelphia on the night of the 17th for Washington.

The first regiment from Indiana left for Washington on the 18th. The Legislature also resolved, "That the faith, credit, and resources of the State in both men and money are hereby pledged in any amount and to every extent which the Federal Government may demand to subdue rebellion;" etc. At the same time, the State Bank tendered to the Governor a loan for the State of all the money necessary to fit out the required quota.

In New York, the great city of the Union, all shades of opinion seemed to vanish before the one great fact, that the country was in danger and must be saved. Citizens of all classes breathed but one spirit of patriotism, and the Mayor of the city issued the following:

MAYOR'S OFFICE, NEW YORK, April 15, 1861.

To the People of the City of New York.

As Chief Magistrate, representing the whole people, I feel compelled at this crisis to call upon them to avoid excitement and turbulence. Whatever may be or may have been individual positions or opinions on questions of public policy, let us remember that our country now trembles upon the brink of a precipice, and that it requires a patriotic and honest effort to prevent its final destruction. Let us ignore the past, rising superior to partisan considerations, and rally to the restoration of the Constitution and the Union, as they existed in the days and in the spirit of our fathers. Whether this is to be accomplished by fratricidal warfare, or by concession, conciliation, and sacrifice, men may differ; but all will admit that here at least harmony and peace should prevail. Thus may we, under the guidance of Divine Providence, set an example of peace and good will throughout our extended country. In this spirit and with this view, I call upon the people of New York, irrespective of all other considerations or prejudices, to unite in obedience to the laws, in support of the public peace, in the preservation of order, and in the protection of property.

FERNANDO WOOD, Mayor.

All citizens were now decorated with the national emblem in every variety of form, while from store, dwelling, church, and public buildings, signs, and lamp-posts, fluttered the Stars and Stripes in every variety of form and in the greatest profusion.

Instantly the military were in motion; every drill-room and armory was alive with active officers calling for and enrolling men. On the 16th several regiments were already partly equipped. The 1st National Guard, Col. Allen, the 7th Regiment, 79th Highlanders, the 71st, the Fire Zouaves of Ellsworth, the 70th, the 55th, the 12th, and others, were rapidly organizing to march. On the 17th the 6th Massachusetts, Colonel E. J. Jones, arrived in New York on its way to Washington, and met the most enthusiastic reception. It made a triumphal march through the city on the 17th of April.

The intelligence that the favorite New York regiment, the 7th, would leave for Washington on the 19th, created an immense excitement. Although it was announced that the departure would not be before 3 P. M., the streets were thronged at an early hour of that day. Lafayette Place, where the regiment was to form previous to marching, was very attractively dressed—a huge flag being displayed from the

Astor Library, with many others from private buildings. The aspect of Broadway was very gay. The Stars and Stripes were floating everywhere, from the costliest silk, 20, 30, 40 feet in length, down to the homelier bunting, and the few inches of painted calico. But the gayest and, in this respect, the most remarkable thoroughfare, was Cortlandt Street, which showed a gathering of flags, a perfect army of them. They were not, in that comparatively brief space, from Broadway to the Jersey City Ferry, to be numbered by dozens or by scores; every building seemed like "Captains of Fifties," flag over flag waving. From every window, from the first floor to the roof, from every doorway, they waved responsive to the fluttering banners that were held in every hand.

Through this gay and expectant throng marched the 8th Massachusetts, Col. Timothy Monroe, accompanied by Gen. B. F. Butler, who had been the Breckinridge candidate for Governor at the election in November, and was now leading the Massachusetts troops. The regiment was presented with colors on the way. This, which would have been an absorbing ceremony at another time, merely filled a portion of the time till the 7th came.

They formed in Lafayette Place about 4 P. M., in the presence of an immense crowd, each window of each building being filled with applauders. Before moving, the excitement of the crowd was made wild by the news of the attack upon the 6th Massachusetts in Baltimore, and there were served out to the 7th forty-eight rounds of ball cartridge. Once in line, they proceeded through Fourth street to Broadway, down that great throroughfare to Cortlandt Street, and across the ferry, in boats provided for the purpose, to Jersey City. The line of march was a perfect ovation. Thousands upon thousands stood on the sidewalks. The regiment was escorted by a band of Zouaves, who volunteered for the occasion. Their gay uniform and peculiar step revived the excitement that had begun somewhat to droop among the crowd that had waited for hours, as the regiment did not reach the Park till half-past five. After the Zouaves came a strong body of police, and after the police the regiment. The officers were Col. M. Lefferts, Lieut.-Col. W. A. Pond, Major A. Shaler.

The public bodies at once began to adopt measures to supply and move the troops. An immense mass meeting, without distinction of party, was called for, April 20, in Union Square. It proved one of the largest and most enthusiastic ever held. It was addressed by J. A. Dix, Secretary of the Treasury under Mr. Buchanan, D. S. Dickinson, Senator Baker of Oregon, Robert J. Walker, formerly Secretary of the Treasury, Mayor Wood, Ex-Gov. Hunt, James T. Brady, John Cochrane, Hiram Ketchum, D. S. Coddington, Esq., and a number of Irish and German citizens, all breathing the one unanimous sentiment of ignoring the political opinions of the past, and standing by the Government with their whole heart, regardless of who might administer it for the time. The fortunes and lives of the citizens were pledged to that end.

A meeting of the merchants of New York City was held at the Chamber of Commerce, April 19th. The proceedings were characterized by the utmost harmony and unanimity. Resolutions upholding the Federal Government, and urging a strict blockade of all ports in the secession States, were unanimously adopted. It being announced that several of the regiments needed assistance to enable them to leave—on motion, a committee was appointed to receive donations, and in ten minutes the subscription had reached over $21,000. What was still more important was the appointment of a large committee of the most influential capitalists, to use their exertions to secure an immediate taking of the $9,000,000 remaining of the Government loan.

On Monday, April 22, the Mayor of the city of New York recommended, and the Board of Aldermen voted, $1,000,000 to aid in the defence of the Government.

At a meeting of the whole New York Bar on the same afternoon, the announcement was received with enthusiastic cheers, and the Bar raised $25,000 on the spot.

The city appropriated the Park to the erection of extensive barracks for the entertainment of the troops, which from North and East made New York their halting-place *en route* for the capital. The Worcester Rifles, the 1st Regiment of Rhode Island, per steamer Osceola, passed through on Sunday the 21st, and on the same day departed the 6th, 12th, and 71st New York State Militia.

The people were early astir on that day, and by ten o'clock every available spot where a human being could stand, was occupied, through the entire length of Broadway; and from near Canal street to Grace Church, not only the sidewalks, but the whole of the street, was densely thronged. Every window, door, stoop, balcony, and housetop was alive with human beings, of every age, sex, and condition, in expectation of this most novel and exciting scene. From almost every housetop and store, from the windows of almost every private dwelling, from the masthead of every ship, from the flagstaff of every manufactory, from all the public buildings, from the Roman Catholic cathedral, from the lofty spire of Trinity Church, from St. Paul's Church, the national ensign was flying The other streets were thronged as on a gala day. On all coats were pinned the red, white, and blue cockade, and in every lady's bonnet ribbons of the same colors were tastefully tied. In the Park, cannons were booming at different times during the day. At the arsenal, regiments, just raised, were formally organized and equipped.

At the armories of the 6th, 12th, and 71st, from early dawn all was bustle and animation, preparing for the afternoon departure. At the rendezvous of the several regiments, the character of the day was ignored, and the maxim realized that in war times there are no Sundays.

At the wharves great steamers were alive with the bustle of preparation for conveying large numbers of troops. In the stream at anchor was the steamer Osceola, with troops from Rhode Island. At the railroad depot in Jersey City the greatest activity prevailed, and means of transportation were being got in readiness for moving as many regiments as might present themselves.

Young men in uniforms, with knapsacks strapped, were seen leaving luxurious homes in aristocratic parts of the town, prepared to rough it with the roughs in defence of the country. Firemen were gathered at their engine-houses, and busy in doing what they could to help off companions who had enrolled themselves in Ellsworth's regiment of Firemen Zouaves.

At noon, the 6th, 12th, and 71st regiments, comprising three thousand men, marched down Broadway, fully armed and equipped. The occasion was without hardly a parallel, and the march a complete ovation. The 6th embarked in the steamer Columbia, the 12th in the steamer Baltic, and the 71st in the steamer R. R. Schuyler. A Massachusetts battalion and some regulars went on board the Ariel. As the fleet left, the harbor was a scene of great excitement. The piers, landings, and housetops of the city, Jersey City, Hoboken, and Brooklyn, were crowded. The Battery was covered with people, and thousands of boats saluted the steamers crowded with the troops. Flags were dipped, cannons roared, bells rang, steam-whistles shrilly saluted, and thousands upon thousands of people sent up cheers of parting.

On the same Sunday many congregations mingled practical patriotism with piety, and took occasion to make contributions for the outfit of volunteers, or for the support of their families. In a church in Brooklyn a letter was read from the 13th Regiment N. Y. S. M., asking for uniforms for recruits, and the response was a collection of about $1,100 for that patriotic purpose. In the Broadway Tabernacle, the pastor preached a sermon in the evening on "God's Time of Threshing." The choir performed "The Marseillaise" to a hymn composed for the occasion by the pastor. A collection was taken for the Volunteers' Home Fund, amounting to $450, to which a member of the congregation afterwards added $100. Dr. Bethune's sermon was from the text: "In the name of our God we will set up our banners." In Dr. Bellows' church the choir sang "The Star-Spangled Banner," which was vigorously applauded by the whole house. At Grace Church (Episcopal), Dr. Taylor began by saying, "The Star-Spangled Banner has been insulted." At Dr. McLane's Presbyterian church, Williamsburgh, "The Star-Spangled Banner" was sung. Dr. T. D. Wells (Old School Presbyterian) preached from the words: "He that hath no sword, let him buy one." Dr. Osgood's text was: "Lift up a standard to the people."

On Monday, the march of troops continued through the city, and on the 23d again New York was alive with excitement to witness the departure of the 8th, 13th, and 69th regiments. The 8th, one thousand strong. Col. Geo. Lyon, formed in Sixteenth Street, and at four o'clock proceeded, amidst the cheering citizens, to pier No. 36, North River, where they embarked on board the steamer Alabama. The 69th Irish, Col. Corcoran, assembled at their armory, No. 42 Prince Street, at three o'clock. They received the order to march, and they proceeded down Broadway amidst such greetings as the excited Irish citizens alone could demonstrate. At half-past six they left in the James Adger. The 13th, Col. Abel Smith, left on board the Marion. Thus through more than two months the living stream of troops went out of New York to support the Government.

During that period of time New York continued to pour out an average, in round numbers, of 1,000 men per day at the call of the Government, not only supplying and equipping the men, but furnishing the money, and lending large sums to the Government in addition.

All the Northern or free States responded alike and instantly to the summons from Washington. The defence of the Government was proclaimed to be a most sacred cause, more especially such a Government as this of the United States had been. Arms, money, men, railroads, and all other "sinews of war," were freely offered. Men of wealth, influence, and position, without regard to party, stepped forth patriotically at this call.

Some apprehensions existed relative to the manner in which Northern troops would be received in Maryland on their way to Washington. On the 19th a body of them were expected to arrive at Baltimore by the Philadelphia and Baltimore Railroad. At the depot a crowd of two or three thousand persons gathered. Soon after 11 o'clock in the forenoon, the train from Philadelphia, comprising twenty-nine cars, arrived. Without disembarking the soldiers from the train, horses were attached to the several cars, which were drawn along Pratt Street to the Camden station. Six cars were permitted to pass without any particular disturbance except hooting and yelling. The horses attached to the seventh car becoming restive, were detached, and the car moved without their aid nearly to Gay Street, where a body of laborers were engaged in repairing the bed of the street, and for this purpose removing the cobble stones.

Some thirty or forty men assembled at this point, having followed the car from the depot, and with cheers for President Davis and the Southern Confederacy, hurled bitter taunts at the Northern Black Republicans, as they termed them. The troops remained in perfect silence.

This continued for several minutes, when, as the horses were again attached and the car moved off, it was proposed to stone it. Before the car had gone twenty yards, almost every window therein was broken to pieces, and a portion of the crowd followed a considerable distance hurling paving-stones. The eighth car was treated in the same manner, but the ninth car, apparently being empty, or at least no person being visible except the driver of the team, escaped with only one stone thrown.

The tenth car was observed approaching from Pratt street bridge, when a number of persons, seizing the picks in the hands of the laborers, made an ineffectual effort to tear up the track. Finding that they could not succeed, as a last resort they took up the paving-stones, and threw them on the track, almost covering it from observation. They also dumped a cart-load of sand on the bed of the track, placing also four or five large anchors thereon, having bodily removed them from the sidewalk. This being accomplished, they, with loud hurrahs, dared the troops to come on; but the latter, observing the posture of affairs, deemed it more prudent to turn back to the President street depot.

Mayor Brown hastened to the President street depot, and endeavored to prevent any disturbance. At this point there still remained upwards of twenty cars filled with the troops, and five or six cars which had been used for the reception of ammunition, baggage, &c.

After the lapse of a quarter of an hour, the command was given for the troops to disembark and form on the outside. While forming, they were surrounded by a dense mass of people, who impeded their march, up President street by every possible means. Stones were thrown in great numbers. At Fawn street two of the soldiers were knocked down by stones and greatly injured.

After the cars had been checked and returned to the depot, as above stated, the military formed and prepared to march through the city.

From the President street depot to Pratt street bridge they were pursued by the excited crowd, who continued to hurl stones, and, it is stated, fired at them with muskets, &c. Mayor Brown had put himself at the head of the column, with a strong body of police. The soldiers continued on up Pratt street over the bridge, where several more were badly injured by the stones thrown at the rear ranks. They came along at a brisk pace, and when they reached Market Space, an immense concourse of people closed in behind them and commenced stoning them.

When they reached Gay street, where the track had been torn up, a large crowd of men armed with paving-stones showered them on their heads with such force that several of them were knocked down in the ranks. These, after lying a few moments crawled on their hands and knees into some of the stores on Pratt street. After they fell there was no further attack made on them, and those thus wounded were taken to apothecary stores for medical attendance.

At the corner of South and Pratt streets a man fired a pistol into the ranks of the military, when those in the rear ranks immediately wheeled and fired upon their assailants, and several were wounded. The guns of the soldiers that had fallen wounded were seized, and fired upon the ranks with fatal effect in two instances.

After they reached Calvert street they succeeded in checking their pursuers by a rapid fire, which brought down two or three, and they were not much molested until they reached Howard street, where another large crowd was assembled. Some stones were thrown at them, but their guns were not loaded, and they passed on through the dense crowd down Howard street towards the depot.

The scene on Pratt street, as stated, was of a startling character. The wounded soldiers, three in number, were taken up carefully and carried to places of safety by the citizens along the street.

The rear portion of the troops received the brunt of the attack of the assailants. The paving-stones were dashed with great force against their backs and heads, and marching thus in close ranks, they were unable to effectually defend themselves. When they did turn and fire, it was without halt, and being thus massed together, their shots took effect mostly on innocent spectators who were standing on the pavement. They stood the assault with stones without resistance, the entire distance from the President street depot until they reached the vicinity of South street, and then fired obliquely on to the pavements, rather than turning on their assailants. The police did their utmost to protect the troops from assault, and partially succeeded until they reached Gay street, where the crowd, armed with paving-stones, were collected. They rushed in between the police and the rear ranks, driving them back, and separating them from the military. After the firing commenced, the assaulting party dispersed, and for the balance of the route there was no attack upon them. The four soldiers who fell wounded in the street, were struck down between Gay and Calvert streets, where the fiercest of the attack was made on them. The troops composed the Sixth regiment of Massachusetts Infantry, commanded by Colonel E. F. Jones, in all eleven companies, with an aggregate of eight hundred and sixty men, rank and file.

It was about half-past twelve o'clock when the train left the Camden station. A few minutes afterwards, a discharge of firearms attracted the attention of the crowd to the corner of Pratt and Howard streets, where a body of infantry from one of the Northern States, about one hundred and fifty strong, were seen rapidly approaching the depot, and no doubt anxious to reach the cars.

The excitement now was beyond description, and a man displaying the flag of the Confederate States seemed to be the rallying point of the disaffected people. Some of these assaulted the command with stones, when a number of the latter discharged their muskets. At least twenty shots were fired, but it happily proved that no person was injured. There seemed to be but little discipline among the troops, especially as they rushed along pell-mell. Whilst they were entering the cars a crowd of young men gave them several volleys of bricks and stones, some of which demolished the windows of the cars, whereupon three or four of the privates pointed their muskets through the car windows and fired, but no one was injured.

The baggage and munitions, in two cars, were seized by the crowd, but rescued by the police. Other troops were sent back to the borders of the State by orders of Gov. Hicks. The military of the city were called out, and quiet was restored at evening. Among the killed was Robert W. Davis, a member of a mercantile firm, and a person held in high esteem by a large circle of friends and acquaintances. Nine citizens of Baltimore were killed, and many wounded. Twenty-five of the wounded Massachusetts troops were sent to the Washington hospital.

During the night following a report prevailed that more Northern troops were approaching by the Northern Central Railway. It was immediately resolved to destroy the bridges nearest the city, on both the Northern roads ending in Baltimore. The bridge at Canton was thus destroyed, and two bridges between Cockeysville and Ashland; also the bridges over Little Gunpowder and Bush rivers. This was ordered to be done by the authorities of Baltimore. Upon a representation of the events to President Lincoln, he ordered that "no more troops should be brought through Baltimore, if, in a military point of view, and without interruption or opposition, they can be marched around Baltimore."

The public mind continued in a feverish state from the excitement of Friday, when unfounded reports that Northern troops were approaching the city, aroused a most indescribable tumult, like ten thousand people bereft of reason. The error of the rumors becoming finally known, peace and order were restored.

The transmission of the mails, and the removal of provisions from the city, however, were suspended by the orders of the Mayor and Board of Police. Four car loads of military stores, clothing, tents, and other army equipments, sufficient for the accommodation of a thousand men, and the property of the Government, were thus detained. On the 24th, the city presented much the appearance of a military camp. The number of volunteers there enlisted, was put as high as 25,000. Large quantities of provisions were seized, and its departure from the city stopped. About four hundred picked men left the city for the Relay House, on the Baltimore and Ohio Railroad, for the purpose of seizing and holding that important strategic point. They were followed by a force of about two hundred men, having with them four field-pieces and an abundance of ammunition. It was the intention of the military authorities to concentrate there about 1,200 men. The object of the seizure was to cut off the communication of the Pennsylvanians with Washington by that route.

The troops at Cockeysville were removed to York, Pennsylvania.

Immediately upon the departure of the train, the authorities of Baltimore County despatched a body of armed men to follow in the rear, and destroy the bridges, which they did; burning all the bridges, large and small, from Ashland to the Maryland line, with one exception, the "Big Gunpowder Bridge."

The turnpike from Ashland to York was literally black with vehicles of every description, containing whole families from Baltimore, who were hurrying to the country. A great many strangers were also proceeding to Pennsylvania, for the purpose of getting into the more Northern States.

Unparalleled as was the excitement in Baltimore, after one week quiet was not only restored, but a counter-revolution took place, which by its mere moral force reëstablished the control of reason and judgment.

On the 5th of May, the volunteer militia were dismissed by the authorities.

On the 10th of May, thirteen hundred troops landed near Fort McHenry from transports, and were thence transferred by trains to Washington.

The Board of Police Commissioners had at noon detailed a large police force, who were present at Locust Point, and acted with great efficiency, under the direction of Marshal Kane. The Board of Commissioners were present in person, as also the Mayor. Few spectators were present at Locust Point, but the wharves on the city side were filled with persons, who quietly looked on the scene of the disembarkation, which was very tedious, and was not concluded until between six and seven o'clock in the evening.

The troops were Sherman's Battery, five companies of the Third Infantry from Texas, and a Pennsylvania Regiment.

On the 5th of May, the United States Volunteers under the command of General Butler, had taken possession of the Relay House on the Baltimore and Ohio Railroad, and proceeded to fortify their position. Subsequently, on the 13th, he moved a portion of his troops to Baltimore. It soon became known in the city, and a number of people went to the Camden station to witness the arrival.

About half-past seven o'clock a long train came, containing a portion of the troops. They disembarked in good order, and marched from the depot down Lee street and other streets to Federal Hill, and, moving to the high ground surrounding the Observatory, stacked arms, and made preparations for a long rest.

The force under command of General Butler was composed of a portion of the Boston Light Artillery, Major Cook; a strong detachment of the 6th Massachusetts regiment, Col. Jones, and about five hundred of the 8th New York regiment, Lieut.-Col. Waltenburg.

On the route to the Hill the streets were thronged with people, who greeted the military with cheers at every step, the ladies at the windows and the doors joining in the applause by waving their handkerchiefs.

Thus quietly was military possession taken of the city of Baltimore. On the next day considerable reënforcements arrived.

On the 16th of May, the regular passenger trains between Baltimore and Washington resumed their usual trips. Baltimore subsided into one of the most quiet cities of the Union. The military encampment was, however, maintained. Meantime the action of States to secede from the Union was renewed.

CHAPTER V.

Proceedings in Texas to effect Secession, and Military Movements—Action in Virginia and Military Movements—Action in Arkansas and Military Movements—Action in North Carolina and Military Movements—Action in Tennessee and Military Movements.

The secession of more Southern States now commenced. Of these Texas was foremost. The call for her Convention was revolutionary. It was signed by sixty-one individuals. Upon this call delegates were elected.

About the same time one of the members of the Legislature took the responsibility of issuing a call for the meeting of that body in extra session. To avoid a conflict between the State authorities and the revolutionists, Governor Houston convened the Legislature in extra session at Austin on January 22d.

The following is the proclamation issued by the Governor:

Whereas, there has been and yet is great excitement existing in the public mind, arising from various causes, touching our relations with the Federal Government and many of the States, and a portion of the people have expressed a desire that the Legislature should be convened in extra session; and *whereas* the Executive desires that such measures should be adopted as will secure a free expression of the popular will through the ballot-box upon the question at issue, involving their peace, security, and happiness, and the action of the whole people made known in relation to the course which it may be proper and necessary for Texas, as one of the States of the Union, to pursue, in order to maintain, if possible, her rights in the Union, as guaranteed by the Federal Constitution; and *whereas* our frontier is now invaded by Indians, and the lives of our citizens taken and their property destroyed; and *whereas* the treasury is without means either to defend the frontier or meet ordinary expenses of Government;

Now, therefore, I, Sam Houston, Governor of the State of Texas, for the reasons herein set forth, do hereby issue this my proclamation, ordering the Legislature of the State of Texas to convene in extra session at the Capitol, in the City of Austin, on Monday, the 21st day of January, A. D. 1861.

When the Legislature assembled, he addressed a message to them, in which he favored delay as long as possible in holding a State Convention. He was himself opposed to calling one, and believed that the Union could be preserved.

The Legislature sanctioned the election of delegates to the State Convention, which assembled one week later, by the adoption of the following

JOINT RESOLUTION *concerning the Convention of the people of Texas, called in pursuance of the Bill of Rights.*

Whereas the people of Texas, being much concerned for the preservation of the rights, liberties, and powers of the State and its inhabitants, endangered by the political action of a majority of the States, and the people of the same have, in the exercise of powers reserved to themselves in the Bill of Rights, called a Convention, composed of two members for each representative in the Legislature, from the various districts established by the apportionment law of 1860, to assemble on the 28th day of January, 1861, at the city of Austin; which Convention, by the terms of the call, made by numerous assemblages of citizens in various parts of the State, was, when elected and assembled, to have power to consider the condition of public affairs; to determine what shall be the future relations of this State to the Union, and such other matters as are necessarily and properly incident thereto; and in case it should be determined by said Convention that it is necessary for the preservation of the rights and liberties aforesaid that the sovereignty of Texas should resume the powers delegated to the Federal Government in the Constitution of the United States, and by the articles of annexation, then the ordinance of said Convention resuming said delegated powers, and repealing the ratification by the people of Texas of said articles of annexation, should be submitted to a vote of the qualified electors of this State for their ratification or rejection. Therefore

Be it resolved by the Legislature of the State of Texas, That the Government of the State of Texas hereby gives its assent to and approves of the Convention aforesaid.

SEC. 2. That this resolution take effect and be in force from and after its passage.

With a protest against the assumption of any powers on the part of said Convention beyond the reference of the question of a longer connection of Texas with the Union to the people, approved 4th February, 1861. SAM HOUSTON.

Resolutions had been offered for delaying the secession movement, but these were twice laid on the table. A resolution was also passed repudiating the idea of using forcible means for coercing any seceding State, and declaring that any such attempt would be resisted to the last extremity. A bill was passed requiring the ordinance of secession, if adopted by the State Convention, to be submitted to the people.

On the 28th of January, the State Convention assembled. The call having been irregular, the vote for members was very light. There are 122 counties in the State, of which nearly half held no election, and were not represented in the Convention. Some of these were: Old Nacogdoches, with 1,023 legal voters; Lamar, with 1,123 voters; Blanco, with 1,139 voters; Cherokee, with 1,644 voters; Fannin, with 1,183 voters.

The vote in some of the counties was as follows: Anderson, with 1,093 voters, only 387 voted; Bastrop, 769 voters, 153 voted; Collin, 1,119 voters, 211 voted; Grayson, 1,217 voters, 280 voted; Hays, 296 voters, 67 voted; Jackson, 296 voters, 40 voted; Lampasas, 285 voters, 50 voted; Red River, 879 voters, 60 voted; Travis, 1,011 voters, 342 voted. This county has Austin within its limits.

On the 5th of February an ordinance of secession was passed in the Convention by a vote of ayes 166, nays 7. The following is the ordinance:

AN ORDINANCE *to dissolve the Union between the State of Texas and the other States under the compact styled "The Constitution of the United States of America."*

SEC. 1. Whereas the Federal Government has failed to accomplish the purposes of the compact of union between these States, in giving protection either to the persons of our people upon an exposed frontier, or to the property of our citizens; and whereas the action of the Northern States is violative of the compact between the States and the guarantees of the Constitution; and whereas the recent developments in Federal affairs make it evident that the power of the Federal Government is sought to be made a weapon with which to strike down the interests and property of the people of Texas and her sister slaveholding States, instead of permitting it to be, as was intended—our shield against outrage and aggression; therefore, "We, the people of the State of Texas, by delegates in the Convention assembled, do declare and ordain that the ordinance adopted by our Convention of delegates on the fourth (4th) day of July, A. D. 1845, and afterwards ratified by us, under which the Republic of Texas was admitted into the Union with other States, and became a party to the compact styled 'The Constitution of the United States of America,' be, and is hereby repealed and annulled."

That all the powers which, by the said compact, were delegated by Texas to the Federal Government are resumed. That Texas is of right absolved from all restraints and obligations incurred by said compact, and is a separate sovereign State, and that her citizens and people are absolved from all allegiance to the United States or the Government thereof.

SEC. 2. The ordinance shall be submitted to the people of Texas for their ratification or rejection, by the qualified voters, on the 23d day of February, 1861; and unless rejected by a majority of the votes cast, shall take effect and be in force on and after the 2d day of March, A. D. 1861. Provided that in the representative district of El Paso said election may be held on the 18th day of February, 1861.

Done by the people of the State of Texas, in convention assembled, at Austin, the 1st day of February, A. D. 1861.

Public sentiment was in favor of joining a Southern Confederacy, and on the 11th an ordinance was passed favoring the formation of such a Confederacy, and electing seven delegates to a Southern Congress.

On the 14th the Convention adjourned to the 20th of February.

The vote to refer the ordinance of secession to the people was quite as unanimous in the Convention as was that on the adoption of the ordinance. The election of delegates being to some extent informal, and scarcely half of the vote of the State having been cast, it was thought best that the ordinance of secession should receive the sanction of the people before it should be declared final. It was submitted to the voters of the State on the 23d of February, which election was legalized by the Legislature, and approved by the Governor under a protest against the shortness of time intervening between the passage of the ordinance and the day of election. The vote in eighty counties of the State was: For secession, 34,794; against secession, 11,235. Majority for secession, 23,559. The vote at the Presidential election in November previous was: Lincoln, ———; Douglas, ———; Breckinridge, 47,548; Bell, 15,438.

On the 2d of March the Convention reassembled without a quorum, and on the 4th the vote was counted. When the result was announced in the Convention, and the President declared that Texas was a free and independent State, there immediately ensued a tremendous burst of cheers and enthusiastic applause.

On the 5th the Convention passed an ordinance instructing the delegates, whom it had previously appointed to the Southern Congress, to apply for the admission of Texas into the Southern Confederacy, and to that end to give the adhesion of Texas to the Provisional Constitution of the said Confederacy.

The numerical strength of the United States army in Texas was about 2,500 men, divided into thirty-seven companies—twenty-two infantry, five artillery, and ten cavalry. Twenty companies were on the Rio Grande—fifteen infantry, and five artillery. The other seventeen companies were stationed in the interior, from Camp Cooper, Phantom Hill, in the northern part of the State, south as far as San Antonio and Fort Inge, near Fort Duncan, on the Rio Grande.

On the withdrawal of these troops, their places on the Rio Grande were supplied by State militia from Galveston and the neighboring counties.

Previous to this time, the surrender of Major-General Twiggs, the United States commander in that Department, to the authorities in Texas, took place. This caused great astonishment at Washington, where it was hardly anticipated. The secession of the State was not then, in fact, concluded. There had been no vote of the people upon the ordinance. The United States army was allowed to march to the coast by the articles of agreement, and to take with them their side-arms, facilities for transportation and subsistence, as well as two batteries of flying artillery of four guns each. The means of transportation were to be surrendered, and left upon arrival at the coast. By this treaty, without one drop of bloodshed, and "without sullying in the least the honor of the United States army," Texas came into possession of over thirteen hundred thousand dollars' worth of property, principally consisting of munitions of war.

The seizure of all the property of the United States was complete. The revenue cutter was surrendered, and the lighthouse supply-vessel for the coast was captured. This vessel, the Guthrie, sailed from New Bedford, Massachusetts, November 8, 1860, with a full cargo of supplies for one year for all the lighthouses and light vessels between Amelia Island, Georgia, and the Rio Grande, Texas. The master in charge reached the bay at Galveston on the 5th of March, for the purpose of delivering the year's supply of oil, &c., to the Bolivar Point and other lighthouses in that vicinity. While he was absent from the vessel, attending to the delivery of the supplies, the Guthrie was boarded by several men, accompanied by an individual calling himself General Sherman, claiming to act by authority, and under the orders of the "Committee of Safety at Galveston." These men got the vessel under weigh, and proceeded with her nearer the cutter, where she was detained.

Some detachments of United States troops still remained in the State, and these were made prisoners, and released upon parole. On the 24th of April, Colonel Van Dorn, with a Texan force on steamers, came down from Indianola to Saluria, and anchored near the schooners having on board the United States troops under Major Sibley, numbering 450. An interview took place during the next day between the commanding officers, which ended in the surrender of the entire Federal force as prisoners of war. The officers were to be released on parole, and the men on their oaths that they would not take up arms against the Southern Confederacy, after surrendering their arms and all the property of the companies; such of the men and officers as desired were to be received into the Confederate army. Private property was not to be molested, and the soldiers were not permitted to leave the State except by way of Galveston and the Mississippi River.

On the 9th of May, six companies of the 8th United States infantry, under command of Lieut.-Colonel Reeve, surrendered to a Confederate force under Colonel Van Dorn, near San Lucas Springs, about twenty-two miles west of San Antonio, and on the Castroville road. Colonel Reeve's command consisted of 366 rank and file, with their appropriate officers, together with Colonel Bumford and several other officers who were on leave, or under orders to report at other points, and who, taking advantage of the troops coming to San Antonio, sought and obtained the escort of the same.

Colonel Van Dorn left his camp on the Leon at four o'clock on Thursday morning, the 8th, and took a position previously selected, about two miles to the westward on the road leading to Castroville, where he formed his command into line of battle. Shortly after daylight the pickets and spies reported Colonel Reeve as having left his camp at two o'clock A. M., as had been his custom on this march, and having reached the high ridge of land near San Lucas Springs, and at the ranche of Mr. Adams, where he had halted his command, taken possession of the large stone house, barricaded the road with his wagons, and placed his troops in position behind the strong corral fences and in the stone house, apparently to await the assault.

Upon this being announced to the colonel commanding the Confederate troops, he ordered a forward movement of the whole command, and gave directions for the forming of the line of battle. The infantry, under the command of Lieut.-Col. Duff, were placed on the right; the battery of flying artillery—six pieces, 12-pounders—under Capt. Edgar, in the centre, with the cavalry and mounted troops under Col. H. E. McCulloch on the left; the whole command, numbering some 1,500 troops of all arms, presenting a very fine appearance, with banners flying, drums beating, sabres and bayonets glittering in the meridian sun, horses pawing and neighing, the field officers flying from one end of the field to another, carrying the commands of their chief.

Under a flag of truce, borne by Capts. Wilcox and Majors, a demand was made of an unconditional surrender of the United States troops as prisoners of war, and five minutes given to answer it. Col. Reeve would not agree to the terms unless Col. Van Dorn would convince him that he had sufficient strength to enforce them, by permitting an officer of his command, whom he would designate, to see the troops and report to him; the prompt answer returned was, that he should have that opportunity to see the troops, and the more he saw of them the less he would like it. The officer designated by Col. Reeve was Lieut. Bliss, a young officer of distinguished bravery, well known in the United States army, who mounted a horse, rode down the line of Confederate troops, and was repeatedly cheered. Suffice it to say, on his report Col. Reeve surrendered with his command, together with all the public property in his possession, unconditionally, as prisoners of war, giving his word of honor that he would report himself and command at Col. Van Dorn's camp on the Leon that evening at 6 o'clock.

The Confederates then retired to camp, where they arrived about 3 o'clock P. M. At 5 o'clock P. M. Col. Reeve's command arrived in camp, and their ground being designated by the proper officer, they pitched their tents as orderly, and stacked their arms with as much precision, as if on inspection parade. Next morning at 5 o'clock the infantry and cavalry struck their tents and marched into San Antonio, where they arrived in good condition at 6 o'clock. Col. Reeve's command marched to the San Pedro Springs, two miles above San Antonio, to a camp designated by a proper officer, where all the arms and Government property were given up. Other States now rapidly followed in the secession movement.

The State Convention of Virginia met at Richmond on the 13th of February. John Janney, of Loudon, was elected President of the Convention, and upon taking the chair he made an address friendly to the Union, but said that Virginia would insist on her own construction of her rights as a condition of her remaining in the present Union. The next day was devoted to perfecting the organization.

The object of the people of Virginia, as expressed by their Legislature, and by their vote at the election for delegates to the Convention, was, if it could be done, honorably "to restore the Union of the States, and preserve that Union for all time to come."

On the 16th numerous resolutions were offered, which, while expressing a hope that the difficulties then existing might be reconciled and the Union perpetuated, yet denounced the idea of coercing in any way the seceding States.

Mr. Wise, of Princess Anne, reiterated his policy of fighting in the Union, and counselled speedy action.

Mr. Moore, of Rockingham, opposed haste. He would not be driven by the North, nor dragged by the cotton States, who had acted without consulting Virginia.

Addresses were also made to the Convention by the Commissioners from other States who were present. Mr. Preston, from South Carolina, in his remarks, said that the Union could never be reconstructed "unless power should unfix the economy of good. No sanctity of human touch could reunite the people of the North and South."

On the 20th of February, numerous resolutions were offered and referred. They generally expressed an attachment to the Union and the desire for an equitable settlement, but denounced coercion, and declared a purpose to resist it. Others maintained that the union of the South was the safety of the South, and that each State should speedily resume the powers delegated to the General Government. A resolution was offered to raise a committee to inquire whether any movement of arms or men had been made by the General Government toward strengthening any fort or arsenal in or bordering on Virginia, indicating preparations for an attack or coercion. It was laid on the table without further action, but taken up the next day and adopted. The report of the committee on the election of members stated that all the counties except sixteen had sent in returns thus far, and the majority for referring the action of the Convention to the people was 52,857.

The Convention was occupied with debates on general subjects until April 13th. On that day the debate turned exclusively upon the surrender of Fort Sumter. Messrs. Carlile and Early deprecated the action of South Carolina in firing upon the fort, and expressed devotion to the flag of their country. Others applauded the gallantry of South Carolina, and maintained that whatever the Convention might do, the people would take Virginia out of the Union.

A communication was received from the Governor, submitting a despatch from Gov. Pickens, giving an account of Friday's bombardment. He said: "There was not a man at our batteries hurt. The fort fired furiously upon us. Our iron battery did great damage to the south wall of the fort; the shells fell freely into the fort, and the effect is supposed to be serious, as they are not firing this morning. Our 'Enfield' battery dismounted three of Anderson's largest columbiads. We will take the fort, and can sink the ships if they attempt to pass the channel. If they land elsewhere we can whip them. We have now 7,000 of the best troops in the world, and a reserve of 10,000 on the routes to the harbor. The war has commenced, and we will triumph or perish. Please let me know what your State intends to do."

Governor Letcher replied: "The Convention will determine."

On the 15th the reply of the President was presented by the Commissioners. A resolution was offered to go into secret session to consider this report. A debate followed. The proclamation of President Lincoln, calling for seventy-five thousand men, constituted the principal theme. Messrs. Scott and Preston (Unionists) declared, that if the President meant subjugation of the South, Virginia had but one course to pursue. A difference of opinion existed as to whether it would be best to secede immediately, or await the coöperation of the Border States, and it was believed the alternative propositions would be submitted to the people. Some delegates doubted the authenticity of the proclamation, and, in deference to their wishes, the Convention adjourned.

The reply of the Governor to the requisition of the Secretary of War was made on the 16th, as follows:

EXECUTIVE DEPARTMENT, RICHMOND, VA., April 16, 1861.
Hon. Simon Cameron, Secretary of War.

SIR: I received your telegram of the 15th, the genuineness of which I doubted. Since that time I have received your communication, mailed the same day, in which I am requested to detach from the militia of the State of Virginia "the quota designated in a table," which you append, "to serve as infantry or riflemen for the period of three months, unless sooner discharged."

In reply to this communication, I have only to say that the militia of Virginia will not be furnished to the powers at Washington for any such use or purpose as they have in view. Your object is to subjugate the Southern States, and a requisition made upon me for such an object—an object, in my judgment, not within the purview of the Constitution or the act of 1795—will not be complied with. You have chosen to inaugurate civil war, and, having done so, we will meet it in a spirit as determined as the administration has exhibited toward the South.

Respectfully, JOHN LETCHER.

On the 16th the Convention assembled in secret session. This was immediately after the surrender of Fort Sumter.

On the 17th an ordinance of secession was passed by the Convention. The vote was 88 in its favor and 55 against it. Only 91 delegates had signed it at the expiration of the first month after its passage. It is stated by a member that when the Convention assembled, a clear majority was for the Union, at which a mob excitement existed in Richmond. It was then calculated that if ten Union men could be kept away, there would be a majority for secession. Accordingly, ten members were waited upon and informed that they were given the choice of doing one of three things: either to vote for the secession ordinance, to absent themselves, or to be hanged. Resistance was found to be useless, and the ten yielded and were absent. The report of the vote, however, shows that at the final moment the majority in favor of the ordinance was large.

The following is the Ordinance of Secession:

An Ordinance to repeal the ratification of the Constitution of the United States of America, by the State of Virginia, and to resume all the rights and powers granted under said Constitution.

The people of Virginia, in the ratification of the Constitution of the United States of America, adopted by them in Convention, on the 25th day of June, in the year of our Lord one thousand seven hundred and eighty-eight, having declared that the powers granted under the said Constitution were derived from the people of the United States, and might be resumed whensoever the same should be perverted to their injury and oppression, and the Federal Government having perverted said powers, not only to the injury of the people of Virginia, but to the oppression of the Southern slaveholding States;

Now, therefore, we, the people of Virginia, do declare and ordain, that the Ordinance adopted by the people of this State in Convention on the twenty-fifth day of June, in the year of our Lord one thousand seven hundred and eighty-eight, whereby the Constitution of the United States of America was ratified, and all acts of the General Assembly of this State ratifying or adopting amendments to said Constitution, are hereby repealed and abrogated; that the union between the State of Virginia and the other States under the Constitution aforesaid is hereby dissolved, and that the State of Virginia is in the full possession and exercise of all the rights of sovereignty which belong and appertain to a free and independent State. And they do further declare that said Constitution of the United States of America is no longer binding on any of the citizens of this State.

This Ordinance shall take effect and be an act of this day, when ratified by a majority of the votes of the people of this State, cast at a poll to be taken thereon, on the fourth Thursday in May next, in pursuance of a schedule hereafter to be enacted.

Done in Convention in the city of Richmond, on the seventeenth day of April, in the year of our Lord one thousand eight hundred and sixty-one, and in the eighty-fifth year of the commonwealth of Virginia.

A true copy, JNO. L. EUBANK,
Secretary of Convention.

At the same time the Convention passed an ordinance requiring the Governor to call out as many volunteers as might be necessary to repel invasion, and to protect the citizens of the State. The following is the Governor's Proclamation:

Whereas seven of the States formerly composing a part of the United States have, by authority of their people, solemnly resumed the powers granted by them to the United States, and have framed a Constitution and organized a Government for themselves, to which the people of those States are yielding willing obedience, and have so notified the President of the United States by all the formalities incident to such action, and thereby become to the United States a separate, independent, and foreign Power; and whereas the Constitution of the United States has invested Congress with the sole power "to declare war," and until such declaration is made the President has no authority to call for an extraordinary force to wage offensive war against any foreign Power; and whereas on the 15th instant the President of the United States, in plain violation of the Constitution, issued a proclamation calling for a force of seventy-five thousand men, to cause the laws of the United States to be duly executed over a people who are no longer a part of the Union, and in said proclamation threatens to exert this unusual force to compel obedience to his mandates; and whereas the General Assembly of Virginia, by a majority approaching to entire unanimity, declared at its last session that the State of Virginia would consider such an exertion of force as a virtual declaration of war, to be resisted by all the power at the command of Virginia; and subsequently, the Convention now in session, representing the sovereignty of this State, has re-affirmed in substance the same policy, with almost equal unanimity; and whereas the State of Virginia deeply sympathizes with the Southern States in the wrongs they have suffered and in the position they have assumed, and having made earnest efforts peaceably to compose the differences which have severed the Union, and having failed in that attempt through this unwarranted act on the part of the President; and it is believed that the influences which operate to produce this proclamation against the Seceded States will be brought to bear upon this Commonwealth if she should exercise her undoubted rights to resume the powers granted by her people, and it is due to the honor of Virginia that an improper exercise of force against her people should be repelled:

Therefore I, John Letcher, Governor of the Commonwealth of Virginia, have thought proper to order all armed volunteer regiments or companies within this State forthwith to hold themselves in readiness for immediate orders, and upon the reception of this proclamation to report to the Adjutant-General of the State their organization and numbers, and prepare themselves for efficient service. Such companies as are not armed and equipped will report that fact that they may be properly supplied.

[L. S.] In witness whereof, I have hereunto set my hand, and caused the seal of the Commonwealth to be affixed, this 17th day of April, 1861, and in the eighty-fifth year of the Commonwealth. JOHN LETCHER.

During the next day, it was announced from the hall of the Convention, that an ordinance of secession had been passed, to take effect as an act of that day, should the same be ratified by the people on a vote to be taken thereon on the fourth Thursday of May. The intelligence spread throughout Richmond and produced immense excitement. Loud and prolonged cheering proceeded from the assembled crowds. In a very short time a rush was made by a party of citizens to the custom-house, for the purpose of signalizing the act of secession in a more demonstrative manner. The gilt letter sign, "United States Court," over the portico was speedily displaced and taken down, and the occupants of the building notified that the United States jurisdiction over the property had ceased. The next act was to raise a Southern Confederacy flag, with eight stars, over the capitol, in which the Convention held its sessions.

The Confederate flag was displayed on the same day from the custom-house, hotels, and private residences, eight stars being generally the number on the flag—one having been added for Virginia. The custom-house was also taken out of the hands of the United States officials, and placed under a guard of State troops. The steamships Yorktown and Jamestown (belonging to the Virginia and New York Steamship Company) were both seized and put in charge of Virginia State troops. Many other seizures were also made.

The Traders' Bank at Richmond tendered the State a loan of $50,000.

A proclamation was issued by the Governor, prohibiting the exportation of flour, grain, and provisions from Virginia, and another was issued ordering all private vessels and property recently seized or detained, with the exception of the steamers Jamestown and Yorktown, to be released and delivered up to their masters or owners. For this purpose proper officers of the State were assigned to each of the rivers Rappahannock, York, Potomac, and James, with orders to release such vessels and property, and give certificates for damages incurred by their seizure or detention.

The supply of troops, under the call of the Governor authorized by the State Convention, was so great that further orders were issued directing no more troops to proceed to Richmond until called for. About 6,000 had assembled there, and 4,000 at Harper's Ferry.

An intelligent citizen of Richmond thus describes the military spirit existing there on the 25th of April: "Our beautiful city presents the appearance of an armed camp. Where all these soldiers come from, in such a state of preparation, I cannot imagine. Every train pours in its multitude of volunteers, but I am not as much surprised at the number as at the apparent discipline of the country companies. Some of them really march like regulars, and with their stalwart forms, dark, fierce countenances, and the red-coated negro fifers and drummers in front, present quite a picturesque as well as most warlike aspect.

"General R. E. Lee, late of the United States Army, has been appointed by the Governor to the chief command of the Virginia forces. Colonel Walter Gwynn, formerly of the United States Army, received a commission of Major-General.

"Yesterday evening, in addition to the large force pouring in from all parts of the country, five hunded troops arrived from South Carolina, under command of Brigadier-General M. D. Bonham. About the same number from the same State will arrive to-day.

"The Cadets of the Virginia Military Institute, under the Superintendent and officers, are here drilling and disciplining the various companies of military who require such aid. But I can give you no idea of the military spirit of the State. Augusta County, a strong Whig Union county in Western Virginia, and Rockingham, an equally strong Democratic Union county, lying side by side with Augusta, each contribute 1,500 men to the war. These are like all our volunteer companies, farmers, mechanics, professional men, the bone and sinew of the country. It was of Augusta that Washington said in the darkest hour of the Revolution that, if defeated everywhere else, he would unfurl a banner on the mountains of Augusta, and raise the prostrate form of Liberty from the dust. Amherst County, with a voting population of only 1,500, contributes 1,000 volunteers.

"But the war spirit is not confined to the men nor to the white population. The ladies are not only preparing comforts for the soldiers, but arming and practising themselves. Companies of boys, also, from ten to fourteen years of age, fully armed and well drilled, are preparing for the fray. In Petersburg 300 free negroes offered their services, either to fight under white officers, or to ditch and dig, or any kind of labor. An equal number in this city and across the river in Chesterfield have volunteered in like manner."

The lights on the Virginia shore of Chesapeake Bay were removed or extinguished, by order of the authorities of the State.

The accession of Virginia to the Southern Confederacy was announced by the Governor in the following proclamation:

Whereas the Convention of this Commonwealth has, on this, the 25th day of April, 1861, adopted an ordinance "for the adoption of the Constitution of the Provisional Government of the Confederate States of America;" and has agreed to a "Convention between the Commonwealth of Virginia and the Confederated States of America, which it is proper should be made known to the people of this Commonwealth and to the world:

Therefore, I, John Letcher, Governor of the Commonwealth of Virginia, do hereby publish and proclaim that the following are authentic copies of the Ordinance and Convention aforesaid.

[L. S.] Given under my hand as Governor, and under the seal of the Commonwealth at Richmond, this twenty-fifth of April, one thousand eight hundred and sixty-one, and in the eighty-fifth year of the Commonwealth.

JOHN LETCHER.

By the Governor.

GEO. W. MUNFORD, Secretary of the Commonwealth.

An Ordinance for the adoption of the Constitution of the Provisional Government of the Confederate States of America.

We, the delegates of the people of Virginia, in Convention assembled, solemnly impressed by the perils which surround the Commonwealth, and appealing to the Searcher of hearts for the rectitude of our intentions in assuming the grave responsibility of this act, do by this Ordinance adopt and ratify the Constitution of the Provisional Government of the Confederate States of America, ordained and established at Montgomery, Alabama, on the eighth day of February, eighteen hundred and sixty-one; provided that this Ordinance shall cease to have any legal operation or effect if the people of this Commonwealth, upon the vote directed to be taken on the Ordinance of Secession passed by this Convention, on the seventeenth day of April, eighteen hundred and sixty-one, shall reject the same. A true copy.

JNO. L. EUBANK, Secretary.

Convention between the Commonwealth of Virginia and the Confederate States of America.

The Commonwealth of Virginia, looking to a speedy union of said Commonwealth and the other slave States with the Confederate States of America, according to the provisions of the Constitution for the Provisional Government of said States, enters into the following temporary Convention and agreement with said States, for the purpose of meeting pressing exigencies affecting the common rights, interests, and safety of said Commonwealth and said Confederacy:

1st. Until the union of said Commonwealth with said Confederacy shall be perfected, and said Commonwealth shall become a member of said Confederacy, according to the Constitutions of both powers, the whole military force and military operations, offensive and defensive, of said Commonwealth, in the impending conflict with the United States, shall be under the chief control and direction of the President of said Confederate States, upon the same principles, basis, and footing as if said Commonwealth were now, and during the interval, a member of said Confederacy.

2d. The Commonwealth of Virginia will, after the consummation of the union contemplated in this Convention, and her adoption of the Constitution for a permanent Government of said Confederate States, and she shall become a member of said Confederacy under said permanent Constitution, if the same occur, turn over to said Confederate States all the public property, naval stores, and munitions of war, etc., she may then be in possession of, acquired from the United States, on the same terms and in like manner as the other States of said Confederacy have done in like cases.

3d. Whatever expenditures of money, if any, said Commonwealth of Virginia shall make before the union under the Provisional Government, as above contemplated, shall be consummated, shall be met and provided for by said Confederate States.

This Convention entered into and agreed to in the city of Richmond, Virginia, on the twenty-fourth day of April, 1861, by Alexander H. Stephens, the duly authorized commissioner to act in the matter for the said Confederate States, and John Tyler, William Ballard Preston, Samuel McD. Moore, James P. Holcombe, James C. Bruce, and Lewis E. Harvie, parties duly authorized to act in like manner for said Commonwealth of Virginia; the whole subject to the approval and ratification of the proper authorities of both Governments respectively.

In testimony whereof the parties aforesaid have hereto set their hands and seals, the day and year aforesaid and at the place aforesaid, in duplicate originals.

[L. S.] ALEXANDER H. STEPHENS,
Commissioner for Confederate States.

[L. S.] JOHN TYLER, WM. BALLARD PRESTON, S. McD. MOORE, JAMES P. HOLCOMBE, JAMES C. BRUCE, LEWIS E. HARVIE, Commissioners for Virginia.

Approved and ratified by the Convention of Virginia, on the 25th day of April, 1861.

JOHN JANNEY, President.

JNO. L. EUBANK, Secretary.

In Western Virginia, on the 23d of April, at a public meeting held in Clarksburg, Harrison County, eleven delegates were appointed to meet delegates from other northwestern counties at Wheeling on May 13th, to determine what course should be pursued in the present emergency. This movement resulted in the separation of Western from Eastern Virginia.

The State Convention adjourned from the first of May to the eleventh of June. The injunction of secrecy was still retained as to their proceedings relative to the secession ordinance. The acts of violence which had been committed thus far, such as the march upon Harper's Ferry, and the sinking of vessels at the mouth of the Elizabeth River, were done in opposition to the authority of the State. The Governor refused to consent that troops should be ordered to the Ferry. It was his purpose to preserve the State in an uncommitted position until after the vote on the Ordinance of Secession. The seizure at Harper's Ferry was, however, afterwards approved by him, and his thanks given to the party who made it. He also issued his proclamation calling out troops, in accordance with the requisition of the Confederate Government. Whatever might have been his previous purposes, he seems now to have had only one object in view, which was, to secure Virginia to the Southern Confederacy. The vote on the Ordinance of Secession in the Convention was not published by that body. It was rumored to have been—ayes 88, nays 55. Many of the negatives were subsequently induced to acquiesce with the majority.

The popular vote on the Ordinance was almost unanimously against it in Western Virginia, while with equal unanimity Eastern Virginia voted in favor of it. It was carried by a large majority of the votes cast. The vote in the city of Richmond was 2,400 in favor to 24 against it, being less than half the vote (5,400) polled at the Presidential election in November previous.

Great activity took place in Eastern and Southwestern Virginia in the organization and equipment of troops. It was claimed as early as the 20th of May, that the whole number volunteered was 85,000, and that 48,000 of these were under arms, and distributed at Richmond, Norfolk, Petersburg, Lynchburg, Fredericksburg, Alexandria, Staunton, and Harper's Ferry. These points were nearly all connected by railroad. There were said to be, in addition, about 8,000 from other States.

As the troops arrived from the South, Richmond became the general rendezvous whence, as soon as inspected and properly outfitted for active duty, they were distributed wherever most needed. By another estimate there were, by the 5th of June, in active service in Virginia, about fifty thousand Confederate troops, namely: about eight thousand at or near Manassas Junction; about five thousand at Fredericksburg and Aquia Creek; about twelve thousand at Norfolk and its neighborhood; about five thousand at Yorktown and Williamsburg; and about fourteen thousand at Harper's Ferry. Of this aggregate, nearly all, exclusive of the force at Harper's Ferry, were so posted that they could be concentrated by railroad at any point between Norfolk and Alexandria within twenty-four hours. About forty thousand, it was calculated at Richmond, could be thrown almost at once upon the Union troops whenever they might present themselves along the line. Such a movement, however, had a certain degree of hazard connected with it, as any concentration by which they withdrew their troops from the seaboard, exposed them to invasion by forces from the fleet.

Arkansas also had become ripe for the movement. On the 16th of January her Legislature unanimously passed a bill submitting the Convention question to the people on the 18th of February. If a majority were in favor of a Convention, the Governor should appoint the time for the election of its members.

On the day appointed an election was held throughout the State, and the vote in favor of holding a Convention was 27,412; against it, 15,826; majority for a Convention, 11,586. The vote of the State at the Presidential election in November was, for Douglas, 5,227; Breckinridge, 28,732; Bell, 20,094.

At the election of delegates to the Convention, the Union vote was 23,626; Secession, 17,927; Union majority, 5,699.

The Convention assembled on the 4th of March, and organized by the election of Union officers, by a majority of six. On the 6th, the inaugural of President Lincoln was received, and produced an unfavorable impression on the minds of the people. Secession was strongly urged upon the Convention, which had been regarded as containing forty members opposed to it, and thirty-five in favor of it.

Various resolutions were offered and referred to appropriate committees, looking to an endorsement, on the one hand, of the doctrine of secession, and the right and duty of Arkansas to secede, and on the other to a clear definition of the position Arkansas should take, stopping short of secession, with a view to the security of her rights in the Union.

A conditional ordinance of secession was debated, with a clause referring it back to the people for ratification or rejection. This was defeated by a vote of ayes, 35; noes, 39. The Convention was disposed to pass resolutions approving the propositions of Missouri and Virginia for a conference of the border slave States, and providing for sending five delegates to said Conference or Convention, and agreeing with Virginia to hold said Conference at Frankfort, Kentucky, on the 27th of May.

At Van Buren a salute of thirty-nine guns was fired in honor of the thirty-nine members of the Convention who voted against the secession ordinance. The same number of guns were fired at Fort Smith.

On the 17th, an ordinance was reported by a self-constituted committee composed of seven secessionists and seven coöperationists, as a compromise measure between the two parties. It was adopted as reported, unanimously, in the Convention. It provided for an election to be held on the first Monday of August, at which the legal voters of the State were to cast their ballots for "secession," or for "coöperation." If on that day a majority of the votes were cast for secession, that fact was to be considered in the light of instructions to the Convention to pass an ordinance severing the connection of Arkansas with the Union. If, on the other hand, a majority of the votes of the State were cast for coöperation, that fact would be an instruction to the Convention immediately to take all necessary steps for coöperation with the border or unseceded slave States, to secure a satisfactory adjustment of all sectional controversies disturbing the country.

The next session of the Convention was to be held on the 17th of August; and to secure the return of all the votes of each county, each delegate was made a special returning officer of the Convention to bring the vote of his county to the Capitol.

Besides this ordinance submitting the proposition of "secession" or "coöperation" to the vote of the people, resolutions were passed providing for the election of five delegates to the border slave State Convention, proposed by the States of Virginia and Missouri, to be held some time during the month of May. Thus the proceedings of that Convention would be before the people, amply canvassed and understood, when the vote of the State was cast on the first Monday of August.

The result of the labors of the Convention, although not exactly what either party desired, was regarded as probably more nearly satisfactory to the public than any other action which could have been taken by that body. Time was given for investigation and deliberation as to consequences.

Affairs remained quiet; the friends of the Union were hopeful; those who sympathized with the seceded States were sanguine that Arkansas would be one of them. The capture of Fort Sumter, and the subsequent events, roused Arkansas to take a stand either with the North or with the South. Together with the news of the fall of the fort, there came also the President's Proclamation, and the requisition of the Secretary of War for a quota of troops from Arkansas. The reply of the Governor to this requisition was dated the 22d of April. It proved him to be decided in his friendship to the secession movement. He wrote to the Secretary of War thus: "In answer to your requisition for troops from Arkansas, to subjugate the Southern States, I have to say that none will be furnished. The demand is only adding insult to injury. The people of this Commonwealth are freemen, not slaves, and will defend to the last extremity their honor, lives, and property, against Northern mendacity and usurpation."

The President of the State Convention, entertaining similar views, immediately issued a call requiring it to reassemble on the 6th of May. The call was dated on the 20th of April.

On the 6th of May the State Convention met, and immediately took the necessary steps to prepare an ordinance to sever the relations existing between the State and the other States united with her under the Constitution of the United States. The ordinance was prepared and reported to the Convention at three o'clock in the afternoon, and was passed immediately, with only one dissenting vote. There were sixty-nine votes in the affirmative, and one in the negative. An eye-witness describes the passage of the ordinance as "a solemn scene." Every member seemed impressed with the importance of the vote he was giving. The hall of the House of Representatives was crowded almost to suffocation. The lobby, the gallery, and the floor of the chamber were full, and the vast crowd seemed excited to the highest pitch. A profound stillness prevailed all the time as vote after vote was taken and recorded, except occasionally, when some well-known Union member would rise and preface his vote with expressions of stirring patriotic Southern sentiments, the crowd would give token of its approbation; but the announcement of the adoption of the ordinance was the signal for one general acclamation that shook the building.

A weight seemed suddenly to have been lifted off the hearts of all present, and manifestations of the most intense satisfaction prevailed on all sides. Immediate steps were taken by the Convention to unite with the Confederation of States. The ordinance was as follows:

Whereas, in addition to the well-founded causes of complaint set forth by this Convention, in resolutions adopted on the 11th March, A. D. 1861, against the sectional party now in power at Washington City, headed by Abraham Lincoln, he has, in the face of resolutions passed by this Convention, pledging the State of Arkansas to resist to the last extremity any attempt on the part of such power to coerce any State that seceded from the old Union, proclaimed to the world that war should be waged against such States until they should be compelled to submit to their rule, and large forces to accomplish this have by this same power been called out, and are now being marshalled to carry out this inhuman design, and to longer submit to such rule or remain in the old Union of the United States would be disgraceful and ruinous to the State of Arkansas;

Therefore, we, the people of the State of Arkansas, in Convention assembled, do hereby declare and ordain, and it is hereby declared and ordained, that the "ordinance and acceptance of compact," passed and approved by the General Assembly of the State of Arkansas, on the 18th day of October, A. D. 1836, whereby it was by said General Assembly ordained that, by virtue of the authority vested in said General Assembly, by the provisions of the ordinance adopted by the convention of delegates assembled at Little Rock, for the purpose of forming a constitution and system of government for said State, the propositions set forth in "an act supplementary to an act entitled an act for the admission of the State of Arkansas into the Union, and to provide for the due execution of the laws of the United States within the same, and for other purposes, were freely accepted, ratified, and irrevocably confirmed articles of compact and union between the State of Arkansas and the United States," and all other laws and every other law and ordinance, whereby the State of Arkansas became a member of the Federal Union, be, and the same are hereby in all respects and for every purpose herewith consistent repealed, abrogated, and fully set aside; and the Union now subsisting between the State of Arkansas and the other States, under the name of the United States of America, is hereby forever dissolved.

And we do further hereby declare and ordain, that the State of Arkansas hereby resumes to herself all rights and powers heretofore delegated to the Government of the United States of America—that her citizens are absolved from all allegiance to said Government of the United States, and that she is in full possession and exercise of all the rights and sovereignty which appertain to a free and independent State.

We do further ordain and declare, that all rights acquired and vested under the Constitution of the United States of America, or of any act or acts of Congress, or treaty, or under any law of this State, and not incompatible with this ordinance, shall remain in full force and effect, in nowise altered or impaired, and have the same effect as if this ordinance had not been passed.

The Convention also passed a resolution authorizing the Governor to call out 60,000 men, if necessary. The State was divided into two grand divisions, eastern and western, and one brigadier-general from each appointed. Gen. Bradley was elected to the command of the eastern, and Gen. Pearce, late of the U. S. Army, to the western.

The Governor was authorized to call out the military force, and two millions of dollars in bonds were ordered to be issued in sums of five dollars and upwards.

The first movement after the secession of the State, was to get possession of the property of the United States. The United States arsenal, located at Little Rock, became the first object for seizure. On the morning of February 5th that city was thrown into high excitement by the unexpected arrival of a steamboat with a body of troops from Helena, with the avowed purpose of taking the arsenal. In a few hours another boat arrived with more troops, and on the next day others arrived, until a force of four hundred men was collected. The City Council was assembled, and on application to the Governor, it was informed that the troops were not there by his orders. The troops themselves were of a different opinion, and came there, as they thought, at his command; but whether so or not, they were there to take the arsenal, and they determined to accomplish that object before leaving. The Governor was then requested to assume the responsibility of the movement, and in the name of the State to demand the arsenal of the officer in command of it. It was believed that Captain Totten would surrender to the authorities of the State rather than have a collision, but would not to a body of men disavowed by the Governor and acting in violation of law; and that as the troops were determined on taking the arsenal at all hazards, there would of course be a collision, and probably much sacrifice of life. Consequently, the Governor consented to act, and immediately made a formal demand upon Captain Totten.

To the Governor's demand for the surrender of the arsenal, Captain Totten asked until three o'clock the next day to consider the matter, which was agreed to. At the time appointed Captain Totten made known his readiness to evacuate the arsenal, and, after the details were finally agreed upon, it was arranged that, at twelve o'clock the next day, the arsenal should be delivered to the authorities of the State, which was done.

About the same time the public property at Fort Smith was seized in behalf of the State.

On the 18th of May Arkansas was admitted as one of the Confederate States, and her delegates took their seats in Congress. They were R. W. Johnson, A. Rust, A. W. Garland, W. H. Watkins, and W. F. Thomason.

Equally prompt was North Carolina in her movement. The Legislature being in session in December, 1860, previous to the meeting of the State Convention in South Carolina, a series of resolutions were offered proposing to appoint Commissioners to the South Carolina Convention for the purpose of urging that body to await a general consultation of the slaveholding States, and to provide also that the Commissioners should attend the Conventions in other States. They were made a special order, but did not pass.

A strong Union sentiment was shown in the State during the session of the Legislature, but it was in favor of requiring additional guarantees. The public sentiment at this time, being the first of January, has been described in these words:

"The general feeling of North Carolina is conservative. She would respond to any fair proposition for an equitable adjustment of present national difficulties, but will insist on her rights at all hazards."

On the 8th of January Forts Caswell and Johnson were occupied by unauthorized persons, who presented themselves with some show of force and demanded their surrender. Governor Ellis ordered them to be immediately restored to the proper authority. In a letter to President Buchanan, on the 12th of January, he thus describes his action:

SIR: Reliable information has reached this Department, that, on the 8th instant, Forts Johnson and Caswell were taken possession of by State troops and persons resident in that vicinity, in an irregular manner.

Upon receipt of this information, I immediately issued a military order requesting the forts to be restored to the authorities of the United States, which order will be executed this day.

My information satisfies me that this popular outbreak was caused by a report, very generally credited, but which, for the sake of humanity, I hope is not true, that it was the purpose of the Administration to *coerce* the Southern States, and that troops were on their way to garrison the Southern ports and to begin the work of subjugation. This impression is not yet erased from the public mind, which is deeply agitated at the bare contemplation of so great an indignity and wrong; and I would most earnestly appeal to your Excellency to strengthen my hands in my efforts to preserve the public order here, by placing it in my power to give public assurance that no measures of force are contemplated toward us.

Your Excellency will pardon me, therefore, for asking whether the United States forts will be garrisoned with United States troops during your Administration.

This question I ask in perfect respect, and with an earnest desire to prevent consequences which I know would be regretted by your Excellency as much as myself.

Should I receive assurance that no troops will be sent to this State prior to the 4th of March next, then all will be peace and quiet here, and the property of the United States will be fully protected as heretofore. If, however, I am unable to get such assurances, I will not undertake to answer for the consequences.

The forts in this State have long been unoccupied, and their being garrisoned at this time will unquestionably be looked upon as a hostile demonstration, and will in my opinion certainly be resisted.

To this communication the Secretary of War replied on the 15th, as follows:

Your letter of the 12th instant, addressed to the President of the United States, has by him been referred to this Department, and he instructs me to express his gratification at the promptitude with which you have ordered the expulsion of the lawless men who recently occupied Forts Johnson and Caswell. He regards this action on the part of your Excellency as in complete harmony with the honor and patriotic character of the people of North Carolina, whom you so worthily represent.

In reply to your inquiry, whether it is the purpose of the President to garrison the forts of North Carolina during his administration, I am directed to say that they, in common with the other forts, arsenals, and other property of the United States, are in charge of the President, and that if assailed, no matter from what quarter or under what pretext, it is his duty to protect them by all the means which the law has placed at his disposal. It is not his purpose to garrison the forts to which you refer at present, because he considers them entirely safe, as heretofore, under the shelter of that law-abiding sentiment for which the people of North Carolina have ever been distinguished. Should they, however, be attacked or menaced with danger of being seized or taken from the possession of the United States, he could not escape from his constitutional obligation to defend and preserve them. The very satisfactory and patriotic assurance given by your Excellency justifies him, however, in entertaining the confident expectation that no such contingency will arise.

The bill for calling a State Convention was under debate a number of days; so, also, was the resolution proposing the appointment, on the part of North Carolina, of Commissioners to a Peace Conference at Washington, as proposed by Virginia. The Convention bill finally passed on the 24th of January.

Ultimately, the Legislature seconded the movement of Virginia, by appointing several eminent men, of both parties, to represent the State in the National Conference at Washington. Commissioners were also appointed to represent the State in the Southern meeting at Montgomery, Alabama, the avowed purpose of which was to establish a Provisional Government over a Southern Confederacy, but with instructions, adopted by a vote of 69 to 38 in the Commons, that they were "to act only as mediators to endeavor to bring about a reconciliation." This vote was hailed as an unmistakable sign that North Carolina was not prepared for disunion and a Southern Confederacy.

The Convention bill, as it finally passed the Legislature, provided for putting the question to the people at the time of electing delegates; Convention or no Convention.

It further provided that the election should be held on the 28th of January, and that ten days should be allowed the sheriffs to make their returns. If a majority of the people voted for the Convention, the Governor should issue his proclamation fixing the day for the meeting. If the Convention was called, its action should be submitted to the people for ratification or rejection. If a majority of the people voted against the Convention, the Governor should make known the fact by proclamation. The action of the Convention was required to be confined to Federal matters, and the members would be sworn to that effect.

A more guarded and restricted form could hardly have been adopted and permit any liberty of action to the Convention.

On the 4th of February a resolution was passed unanimously in the House, declaring that, in case reconciliation fails, North Carolina goes with the slave States. The military bill passed in the House, authorized the arming of ten thousand volunteers, and provided for the entire reorganization of the militia.

The election for members of the State Convention resulted in the choice of a considerable majority who were in favor of the Union, and opposed to secession. As expressed at the time, "They, as Unionists, would not submit to the administration of the Government on sectional principles, but they were anxious to preserve the Union on a constitutional basis, and to obtain such guarantees as would lead to a permanent reconstruction of it."

The official vote of the State on the question of Convention or no Convention, including the vote of Davie and Heywood counties, which were reported, was: for Convention, 46,672; against a Convention, 47,323. Majority against a Convention, 651. The vote of the State was smaller by about twenty thousand than at the election in August previous.

Of the whole number of delegates, eighty-two were constitutional Union men, and thirty-eight secessionists. The Union majority, therefore, was rather more than two to one.

After this election, the Governor determined not to call the Legislature of the State together in extra session unless something more urgent than was known should occur.

No events of unusual interest occurred until the attack upon Fort Sumter and the call by the President for troops. To the requisition of the Secretary of War, the Governor immediately replied by telegraph as follows:

RALEIGH, *April* 15, 1861.

Your despatch is received, and, if genuine—which its extraordinary character leads me to doubt—I have to say, in reply, that I regard the levy of troops made by the Administration, for the purpose of subjugating the States of the South, as in violation of the Constitution and a usurpation of power. I can be no party to this wicked violation of the laws of the country, and to this war upon the liberties of a free people. You can get no troops from North Carolina. I will reply more in detail when your call is received by mail. JOHN W. ELLIS,
Governor of North Carolina.

HON. SIMON CAMERON, Secretary of War.

The forts in the State which had been once seized on a popular outbreak and restored by the Governor, were once more seized, and at this time by his orders. Guns and ammunition were obtained in Charleston for use at Fort Macon and Fort Caswell. An extra session of the Legislature was immediately summoned to assemble on the 1st of May. The proclamation of Gov. Ellis convening that body was as follows:

Whereas, by proclamation of Abraham Lincoln, President of the United States, followed by a requisition of Simon Cameron, Secretary of War, I am informed that the said Abraham Lincoln has made a call for seventy-five thousand men, to be employed for the invasion of the peaceful homes of the South, and the violent subversion of the liberties of a free people, constituting a large part of the whole population of the late United States; and whereas this high-handed act of tyrannical outrage is not only a violation of all constitutional law, utter disregard of every sentiment of humanity and Christian civilization, and conceived in a spirit of aggression unparalleled by any act of recorded history, but is a direct step toward the subjugation of the entire South, and the conversion of a free Republic inherited from our fathers, into a military despotism to be established by worse than foreign enemies, on the ruins of the once glorious Constitution of equal rights;

Now, therefore, I, John W. Ellis, Governor of the State of North Carolina, for these extraordinary causes, do hereby issue this my proclamation, notifying and requesting the Senators and Members of the House of Commons of the General Assembly of North Carolina, to meet in special session at the capital in the city of Raleigh, on Wednesday, the 1st day of May. And I furthermore exhort all good citizens throughout the State to be mindful that their first allegiance is due to the sovereignty which protects their homes and dearest interests, as their first service is due for the sacred defence of their hearths, and of the soil which holds the graves of our glorious dead.

United action in defence of the sovereignty of North Carolina, and of the rights of the South, becomes now the duty of all.

Given under my hand and attested by the great seal of the State. Done at the city of Raleigh, the 17th day of April, A. D. 1861, and in the eighty-fifth year of independence. JOHN W. ELLIS.

A call was also issued by the Governor, for the enrolment of thirty thousand men, to be held in readiness to march at a day's notice.

On the 1st of May the Legislature convened in special session. In his Message, the Governor recommended that, in view of the secession of North Carolina from the Northern Government, and her union with the Confederate States at as early a period as practicable, a Convention of the people be called with full and final powers. The powers of the Convention should be full because the sovereignty of the people must be frequently resorted to during the war, and it therefore became necessary that it should be temporarily reposed in the Convention. The action of the Convention should be final, because of the importance of a speedy separation from the Northern Government, and the well-known fact that upon this point the people were as a unit.

He also recommended "the raising and organization of ten regiments, to serve during the war, and that appropriate bounties be offered to all persons thus enlisting."

The Governor further said that the Northern Government was concentrating a large force in the District of Columbia, ostensibly to protect the seat of Government. But such a force cannot be allowed to remain within the limits of Maryland and on the borders of Virginia without seriously endangering the liberties of the people of those States. If they be conquered and overrun, North Carolina would become the next prey for the invaders. Policy, then, as well as sympathy, and a feeling of brotherhood, engendered by a common interest, required them to exert their energies in the defence of Maryland and Virginia. Every battle fought there would be a battle in behalf of North Carolina. The Legislature met at 12 o'clock M., and at 1 P. M. both Houses had unanimously passed a bill calling an unrestricted Convention, whose action was to be final. The election of delegates took place on the 13th of May, and the Convention met on the 20th.

The Legislature unanimously repealed the section of the Revised Code, which required all officers in the State to take an oath to support the Constitution of the United States before entering upon their duties. The act further provided that it should not be lawful to administer any such oath or affirmation to any officer, civil or military.

After a session of eleven days, the Legislature adjourned, to meet again on the 25th of June. Among other measures, it passed a stay law, to take effect immediately, and authorized the Governor to raise ten thousand men, to serve during the war, and also appropriated $5,000,000 for the use of the State, giving the Treasurer power to issue Treasury notes to the amount of $500,000, in bills ranging from five cents to two dollars, and with a conditional clause, authorizing the issue of a larger amount if necessary.

The forces of the State, under orders of the Governor, seized the Federal forts on the coast, and took possession of the mint at Charlotte and the arsenal at Fayetteville, gaining, by the seizure of the latter, 37,000 stand of arms, 3,000 kegs of powder, and an immense supply of shells and shot. Of course, these acts placed the State in the same category with the seceded States, and the ports of North Carolina were, therefore, included in the blockade ordered by the Government.

The State Convention assembled on the 20th of May, the eighty-sixth anniversary of the Mecklenberg Declaration of Independence.

On the 21st the ordinance of secession was passed by the State Convention, as follows:

We, the people of the State of North Carolina, in Convention assembled, do declare and ordain, and it is hereby declared and ordained, that the ordinance adopted by the State of North Carolina, in the Convention of 1789, whereby the Constitution of the United States was ratified and adopted, and also all acts and parts of acts of the General Assembly, ratifying and adopting amendments to the said Constitution, are hereby repealed, rescinded, and abrogated.

We do further declare and ordain that the Union now subsisting between the State of North Carolina and the other States, under the title of the United States of America, is hereby dissolved, and that the State of North Carolina is in the full possession and exercise of all those rights of sovereignty which belong and appertain to a free and independent State.

Done at Raleigh, 20th day of May, in the year of our Lord 1861.

The following ordinance was also passed:

We, the people of North Carolina, in Convention assembled, do declare and ordain, and it is hereby declared and ordained, that the State of North Carolina does hereby assent to and ratify the Constitution for the Provisional Government of the Confederate States of America, adopted at Montgomery, in the State of Alabama, on the 8th of February, 1861, by the Convention of Delegates from the States of South Carolina, Georgia, Florida, Alabama, Mississippi, and Louisiana, and that North Carolina will enter into the federal association of States upon the terms therein proposed, when admitted by the Congress or any competent authority of the Confederate States.

Done at Raleigh, 20th day of May, in the year of our Lord 1861.

Military preparations were immediately commenced, and as early as the 15th of June the State had raised a force of twenty thousand volunteers.

The following delegates to the Confederate Congress were elected by the Convention: For the State at large, W. W. Avery and George Davis; 1st district, W. N. H. Smith; 2d, Thomas Ruffin; 3d, T. D. McDowell; 4th, A. W. Venable; 5th, John M. Morehead; 6th, R. C. Puryear; 7th, Burton Craige; 8th, A. D. Davidson.

The flag agreed upon for the State was said to be handsome. The ground was a red field, with a single star in the centre. On the upper extreme was the inscription, "May 20, 1775," and at the lower, "May 20, 1861." There were two bars, one of blue and the other of white.

The Governor now set to work to place the coast defence in a satisfactory condition. At the same time troops were sent forward to the Confederate army as fast as they could be equipped. No notice was taken by the Secretary of War of the request for a few well-drilled regiments for the coast defence, although the Governor offered fresh levies in their place. The State, like South Carolina and others, was expected to defend herself. The subsequent capture of the forts at Hatteras Inlet occasioned intense excitement; and although the work of the expedition extended no further than to "take and hold" those positions, it revealed such a degree of weakness to resist any naval attack, that it awakened the first serious apprehensions among the people for the cause of the Confederacy.

In Tennessee, in particular, of all the States attempting to secede, a controlling conservative sentiment manifested itself in the Legislature, which, while it endorsed the position that the grant of additional guarantees to the South should be made a condition of Tennessee's remaining in the Union, determined that the State should not be precipitated into secession. The bill calling for a convention of the people of the State, provided that any ordinance or resolution which might be adopted by said Convention having for its object a change of the position or relation of the State to the National Union, or her sister Southern States, should be of no binding force or effect until it was submitted to or ratified by the people, and required a vote equal to a majority of the votes cast in the last election for Governor to ratify it. Thus the people had an opportunity, in voting for delegates, to declare for or against secession; and should the action of the Convention contemplate any change in the Federal relations of the State, they had still the opportunity of endorsing or overruling alike their former decision and the action of the Convention. The election for members of the Convention was to be held on the 9th of February, the Convention to assemble on the 25th.

The result of the election was highly successful to the friends of the Union. Even West Tennessee gave a Union majority. The following returns, except a few counties, show the relative strength of union and disunion in the State:

	Union.	Disunion.
East Tennessee..................	30,903	5,577
Middle Tennessee..............	36,809	9,828
West Tennessee................	24,091	9,344
Total..........................	91,803	24,749
Union majority............		67,054

The returns from all the counties made the actual majority 64,114. The question of holding a convention was determined in the negative by a large majority, thus declaring that there was no need for a convention at all to determine where Tennessee should stand. The Union delegates at Memphis were elected by a majority of 400. The vote of the State on the Convention question was as follows:

East Tennessee voted no convention by 25,611 majority, or four and a quarter to one. Middle Tennessee 1,382 majority; but West Tennessee gave for a Convention 15,118 majority. The vote for no Convention was 69,673. The total vote for and against Convention was 127,471, with a majority against the meeting of a Convention of 11,875.

The people decided that no Convention should be held, chiefly because they had seen that all the conventions which had been held in the Southern States had withdrawn their States from the Union, and then had proceeded to sit on their own adjournments, as if they conceived they possessed the right to continue their own existence indefinitely. The loyal people of Tennessee now flattered themselves that they had thus put an effectual stop to the secession movement in the State, and so the secessionists thought as well; and even the Governor seemed, for a time, to have abandoned the scheme.

The proclamation of the President on the 15th of April, however, produced an intense feeling throughout the State. The Governor immediately called an extra session of the Legislature, to be convened on the 25th of April. He refused the requisition of the President for troops, saying:

Hon. Simon Cameron:

SIR: Your despatch of the 15th inst., informing me that Tennessee is called upon for two regiments of militia for immediate service, is received.

Tennessee will not furnish a man for purposes of coercion, but 50,000, if necessary, for the defence of our rights, and those of our Southern brothers.

ISHAM G. HARRIS, Governor of Tennessee.

On the 25th of April the Legislature assembled for the third time, although the members had been elected without any reference to the momentous questions now about to be considered. In the Assembly, on the same day, the following resolution was offered.

Resolved, That upon the grave and solemn matters for our consideration, submitted by the Governor's Message, with a view to the public safety, the two Houses of this Legislature hold their sessions with closed doors whenever a secret session in either House may be called for by five members of said House, and that the oath of secrecy be administered to the officers and members of said House.

The resolution was adopted—ayes 42; noes 8. The Message of the Governor was very strong and decided in urging immediate secession.

On the 30th of April, Henry W. Hilliard, commissioner from the Confederate States, appeared before the Legislature and made an address. He said his object was to establish a temporary alliance between Tennessee and the Confederate States, to continue until Tennessee should decide for or against adopting the Constitution of that Government, and becoming one of the Confederate States. He regarded the issue now pending between the North and the South something more than a mere right to hold slaves. It was a question of constitutional liberty, involving the right of the people of the South to govern themselves. "We have said that we will not be governed by the abolition North, the abolition North says we shall," and he would not hesitate to say there was not a true-hearted man in the South but would rather die than submit. He repudiated the idea of settling the pending questions between the North and South by reconstruction "by going back to our enemies." He regarded the Southern system of government established at Montgomery, and based upon slavery, as the only permanent form which could be established in this country.

On the 29th of April Governor Harris had ordered to be seized sixty-six thousand dollars' worth of Tennessee bonds and five thousand dollars in cash, belonging to the United States, which were in possession of the collector at Nashville. He said:

"This seizure was conditional; the property was to be held in trust until the Government restored the property of the State and its citizens involved in the seizure of the steamer Hillman by troops of the Federal Government."

The steamer Hillman was seized at Cairo by the Illinois troops, because she was laden with munitions and other articles contraband of war. The boat, and property not contraband, was subsequently surrendered to the owners.

The Legislature in secret session, immediately, on the 1st of May, passed a joint resolution directing the Governor to enter into a military league with the Confederate States, subjecting "the whole military force of the State" to the control of the Confederate States. Acting upon this authority, the Governor immediately appointed Gustavus A. Henry, Archibald O. W. Totten, and Washington Barrow, as commissioners for that purpose. On the 7th of May he sent a Message to the Legislature, stating that he had appointed the said commissioners on the part of Tennessee, etc., as follows:

To enter into a military league with the authorities of the Confederate States, and with the authorities of such other slaveholding States as may wish to enter into it; having in view the protection and defence of the entire South against the war that is now being carried on against it.

The said commissioners met the Hon. Henry W. Hilliard, the accredited representative of the Confederate States, at Nashville on this day, and have agreed upon and executed a military league between the State of Tennessee and the Confederate States of America, subject, however, to the ratification of the two Governments, one of the duplicate originals of which I herewith transmit for your ratification or rejection. For many cogent and obvious reasons, unnecessary to be rehearsed to you, I respectfully recommend the ratification of this league at the earliest practical moment.

The Convention was as follows:

Convention between the State of Tennessee and the Confederate States of America.

The State of Tennessee, looking to a speedy admission into the Confederacy established by the Confederate States of America, in accordance with the constitution for the provisional government of said States, enters into the following temporary convention, agreement, and military league with the Confederate States, for the purpose of meeting pressing exigencies affecting the common rights, interests, and safety of said States, and said Confederacy:

1st. Until the said State shall become a member of said Confederacy, according to the constitutions of both powers, the whole military force and military operations, offensive and defensive, of said State, in the impending conflict with the United States, shall be under the chief control and direction of the President of the Confederate States, upon the same basis, principles, and footing, as if said State were now and during the interval a member of the said Confederacy—said forces, together with those of the Confederate States, to be employed for the common defence.

2d. The State of Tennessee will, upon becoming a member of said Confederacy, under the permanent Constitution of said Confederate States, if the same shall occur, turn over to said Confederate States all the public property, naval stores, and munitions of war, of which she may then be in possession, acquired from the United States, on the same terms and in the same manner as the other States of said Confederacy have done in like cases.

3d. Whatever expenditures of money, if any, the said State of Tennessee shall make before she becomes a member of said Confederacy, shall be met and provided for by the Confederate States.

The vote in the Senate, on the adoption of this treaty, was 14 to 6—absent or not voting, 4; in the House, 42 to 15—absent or not voting, 18.

Meanwhile, the Legislature had not been idle. On the 6th of May it passed an ordinance entitled, "An Act to submit to a vote of the people a Declaration of Independence, and for other purposes." The first section provided that the Governor should, by proclamation, require the respective officers in each county to hold the polls open in their several precincts on the 8th day of June ensuing. The second section provided that the following declaration should be submitted to a vote of the qualified voters for their ratification or rejection:

Declaration of Independence and Ordinance dissolving the Federal relations between the State of Tennessee and the United States of America.

1st. We, the people of the State of Tennessee, waiving an expression of opinion as to the abstract doctrine of secession, but asserting the right as a free and independent people to alter, reform, or abolish our form of Government in such manner as we think proper, do ordain and declare that all the laws and ordinances by which the State of Tennessee became a member of the Federal Union of the United States of America, are hereby abrogated and annulled, and that all obligations on our part be withdrawn therefrom; and we do hereby resume all the rights, functions, and powers which by any of said laws and ordinances were conveyed to the Government of the United States, and absolve ourselves from all the obligations, restraints, and duties incurred thereto; and do hereby henceforth become a free, sovereign, and independent State.

2d. We furthermore declare and ordain, that Article 10, Sections 1 and 2 of the Constitution of the State of Tennessee, which requires members of the General Assembly, and all officers, civil and military, to take an oath to support the Constitution of the United States, be and the same are hereby abrogated and annulled, and all parts of the Constitution of the State of Tennessee, making citizenship of the United States a qualification for office, and recognizing the Constitution of the United States as the supreme law of this State, are in like manner abrogated and annulled.

3d. We furthermore ordain and declare that all rights acquired and vested under the Constitution of the United States, or under any act of Congress passed in pursuance thereof, or under any laws of this State, and not incompatible with this ordinance, shall remain in force and have the same effect as if this ordinance had not been passed.

The third section provided that the election should be by ballot, and that those voting for the declaration and ordinance should have on their ballots the word "Separation," and those voting against it should have on their ballots the words "No separation;" the returns should be made to the Secretary of State by the 24th of June, and if a majority of votes were given for separation, the Governor was required immediately to issue his proclamation declaring "all connection by the State of Tennessee with the Federal Union dissolved, and that Tennessee is a free, independent Government, free from all obligations to, or connection with the Federal Government."

The fourth section authorized all volunteers to vote, wherever they may be in active service. By the fifth section it was provided that, under the rules and regulations prescribed for the election above ordered, the following ordinance should be submitted to the popular vote:

AN ORDINANCE *for the adoption of the Constitution of the Provisional Government of the Confederate States of America.*

We, the people of Tennessee, solemnly impressed by the perils which surround us, do hereby adopt and ratify the Constitution of the Provisional Government of the Confederate States of America, ordained and established at Montgomery, Alabama, on the 8th of February, 1861, to be in force during the existence thereof, or until such time as we may supersede it by the adoption of a permanent Constitution.

The sixth section provided that all voters in favor of adopting the Provisional Constitution, and thereby securing to Tennessee equal representation in the deliberations and councils of the Confederate States, should have written or printed on their ballots the word "Representation;" opposed, the words "No Representation."

The seventh section provides for an election of delegates to the Confederate Congress in case the Provisional Constitution was adopted. The vote on the Declaration of Independence in the Senate was—yeas 20, nays 4; in the House, yeas 46, nays 21.

By this act, provision was made to submit to the vote of the people of the State, the adoption or rejection of a "Declaration of Independence," whereby they were to separate themselves from the Union, and adopt the insurrectionary States' Constitution, and abrogate that part of their own Constitution which required every person chosen or appointed to any office of trust or profit under it, or any law made in pursuance of it, before entering on the duties thereof, to take an oath to support the Constitution of the State and of the United States; and requiring each member of the Senate and House of Representatives, before proceeding to business, to take an oath to support the Constitution of the State and of the United States. (Constitution of Tennessee, art. x., sections 1, 2.)

By another act the Governor was required to raise, organize, and equip, a provisional force of volunteers for the defence of the State, to consist of 55,000 men; 25,000 of whom, or any less number demanded by the wants of the service, were to be fitted for the field, at the earliest practicable moment, and the remainder to be held in reserve, ready to march at short notice. It authorized the Governor, should it become necessary for the safety of the State, to "call out the whole available military strength of the State," and to determine when this force should serve, and direct it accordingly. To defray the expenses of this military organization, the Governor was authorized "to issue and dispose of $5,000,000 of the bonds of the State," in denominations of not less than $100, or greater than $1,000, to run ten years, and bear interest at the rate of 8 per cent.

Thus provided with a semblance of authority, the Governor hastened the organization of the provisional force of 25,000 men, and before the day of the election, June 8, 1861, he had most of it on foot, and distributed in camps around Nashville and elsewhere, armed and equipped, so far as it could be, with the munitions of the United States in possession of the State, and with such as could be obtained from the arsenal at Augusta, Georgia, from which they were brought by Gen. Zollicoffer. Thus, on the morning of the election, the people of Tennessee, for the first time in their lives, went to the polls conscious that they were no longer a free people; knowing that the Executive and Legislative Departments of the State, with its Treasury in their hands, and with all the arms of the State in their possession, and with a formidable army in their pay, had joined a conspiracy to overthrow their Government, and that nothing remained for them but to reverse their vote of the 9th of February, and to ratify what their self-constituted masters had already accomplished. Even by voting against the Declaration of Independence, and by refusing to absolve their officers from the oath to support the Constitution of the United States, and declining to accept the Constitution of the insurrectionary States, they could not free themselves from the military incubus which had been imposed upon them. In these circumstances it is not to be wondered at that the election showed an apparent majority of 57,667 for secession. It must not be concluded, however, that this majority was real; for the men who could so wantonly contemn the obligations of the law as to resort to the measures above detailed, could not escape from the suspicion of having filled the ballot-box with spurious votes.

By such means was Tennessee carried over to the insurrectionary States, and in the employment of these means there does not appear to have been any semblance of regard, among the actors, for oaths or for the observance of the most solemn obligations of legal and constitutional duty.

The aggregate votes in the several divisions of the State were announced to be as follows on the ordinance of separation:

	For Separation.	No Separation.
East Tennessee	14,780	32,923
Middle Tennessee	58,265	8,198
West Tennessee	29,127	6,117
Military Camps	2,741	.....
	104,913	47,238
	47,238	
Majority	57,675	

The Governor made an agreement with the Governor of Kentucky at this time, that no troops should cross the Tennessee line for any purpose, unless upon the invitation or permission of the latter. This proved worthless when the Confederate Government deemed it necessary to move a force into Kentucky. The rights of the State of Tennessee as a sovereign were not taken into account.

Confederate troops were sent at the earliest moment to take possession of the three gaps in the mountains of East Tennessee, known as the

Fentress, Wheeler, and Cumberland. Cleveland was also declared a military station. The mails of the United States were, by order of the proper department, continued in twenty-six of the counties of East Tennessee at this time, in consequence of the Union feeling which was manifested. They were as follows: Anderson, Bledsoe, Blount, Bradley, Campbell, Carter, Claiborne, Cocke, Grainger, Green, Hamilton, Hancock, Hawkins, Johnson, Knox, Marion, McMuir, Meigs, Monroe, Morgan, Polk, Rhea, Sevier, Sullivan, and Washington.

On the other side every effort was made to procure arms. The Governor sent instructions to the clerks of all the county courts, requesting them to issue to each constable in their respective counties an order requiring him to make diligent inquiry at each house in his civil district for all muskets, bayonets, rifles, swords, and pistols belonging to the State of Tennessee, to take them into possession, and deliver them to the clerks. A reward of one dollar was to be paid to the constable for each musket and bayonet or rifle, and of fifty cents for each sword or pistol thus reclaimed. The arms thus obtained were to be forwarded, at public expense, to the military authorities at Nashville, Knoxville, and Memphis, as might be most convenient, and information sent to the military and financial board at Nashville, of the result.

Stringent measures were adopted with the Union people of East Tennessee. Many, upon bare suspicion, were arrested and taken prisoners, insulted, abused, and carried into camps, there to be disposed of as the insurrectionary mob thought proper. Squads of cavalry and infantry were scouring over the country, offering the people, male and female, every indignity that ruffian bands are capable of; destroying crops and substance without regard to the condition or circumstances of the persons; pasturing their horses in corn-fields; wasting hay-stacks, taking provisions of every description without regard to quantity, not even asking the price or tendering an equivalent therefor in any shape whatever. Nashville was put under martial law, passports were required, and all baggage was examined under directions of the Committee of Safety.

CHAPTER VI.

Effects of the President's Proclamation—Assembling of Troops at Washington—Destruction at Harper's Ferry—Destruction and abandonment of the Norfolk Navy Yard—Capture of the Star of the West—Other Events—Capture of Camp Jackson, St. Louis—Other Events—Attack on Sewell's Point—Seizure of Ship Island—Occupation of Harper's Ferry by Southern Troops—Movement of Troops from Washington into Virginia—Occupation of Alexandria—Blockade of the Mississippi—Attack on the Batteries at Aquia Creek—Dash into Fairfax Court House.

THE appearance of the proclamation of the President, calling for seventy-five thousand men, caused the most active efforts both at the North and South to raise and equip troops. This was immediately followed by hostile movements of Southern forces upon the most important positions. At the North it was feared that Washington would be captured at once, unless it was quickly garrisoned. Thither, therefore, the troops from Pennsylvania, New York, and Massachusetts immediately moved. The advance of the 6th Massachusetts regiment through Baltimore on April 19th, has already been described.

At Washington, in the meanwhile, preparation for defence was commenced with the small military and naval force on hand. But on the 18th, three days after the appearance of the proclamation, several car loads of troops, numbering about 600 men, arrived from Harrisburg *via* Baltimore, and were quartered in rooms in the Capitol. Other troops were also expected soon to arrive, and the Massachusetts regiment was the next which reached there.

During the whole day and night of the 18th, the avenues of the city were guarded and closely watched. Cannon were planted in commanding positions so as to sweep the river along that front, and these were supported by infantry. A proclamation was also issued by Mayor Berret, exhorting "all good citizens and sojourners to be careful so to conduct themselves as neither by word or deed to give occasion for any breach of the peace." After the outbreak at Baltimore on the 19th, no mail was received at Washington, either from the North or South, except from Alexandria on the one side and Baltimore on the other, until the 25th. On the 27th the New York 7th regiment arrived, having left New York on the 18th. A delay took place between Annapolis and Washington, in consequence of the damage done to the railroad track. The news brought to Washington by the 7th was that four New York regiments were at Annapolis, with a part of a Massachusetts regiment, the remainder of which was at the Junction. The 7th, therefore, as they marched up Pennsylvania Avenue, preceded by their band, and making a fine appearance, were received with the wildest demonstrations of pleasure on the part of the citizens. On the next day another body of troops arrived. They consisted of one-half of the Rhode Island regiment, 1,200 strong, commanded and headed by Gov. Sprague; and the Butler brigade, under Brig.-Gen. Butler, of Massachusetts, numbering nearly 1,400 men. They were met at the depot by the 6th Massachusetts regiment, stationed in the Capitol, who greeted their friends with the heartiest cheers. These men, though severely worked by the toilsome labor requisite to repair the bridges and road track from Annapolis to the Junction, presented a fine appearance as their long and serpent-like lines wound through the streets. Troops now began to arrive daily, and Washington soon became the most military city on the continent.

Meantime hostile movements were commenced at Harper's Ferry, where a United States Armory and a National Arsenal were located. The situation of this town is at the confluence of the Shenandoah River with the Potomac, in Jefferson County, Virginia, on the line of the Baltimore and Ohio Railroad. At the armory 10,000 muskets were made annually, and the arsenal often contained 80,000 to 90,000 stand of arms. On the 2d of January, orders were received from Washington for the Armory Guard, Flag Guard, and Rifles to go on duty, as a precautionary measure. A few days afterwards a detachment of unmounted United States Dragoons, numbering sixty-four, under command of Lieut. Jones, arrived there. Affairs remained in a quiet condition until the excitement created through the country by the capture of Fort Sumter, and the issue of the first proclamation by the President calling out troops. A movement was immediately made by friends of the rebellion in Northern Virginia, to take possession of Harper's Ferry Arsenal. As early as the 18th of April, Lieut. Jones was informed that between 2,500 and 3,000 State troops would reach the ferry in two hours. Deeming the information positive and reliable, he gave orders to apply the torch to the buildings. In ten minutes or less both the arsenal buildings, containing nearly 15,000 stand of arms, together with the carpenter's shop, which was at the upper end of a long and connected series of workshops of the armory proper, were in a complete blaze. Lieut. Jones then withdrew his small force, and marching all night, arrived at Carlisle barracks at half-past 2 o'clock the next afternoon. This was done by orders of the Government. The place was then taken possession of by the Virginian troops. Most of the machinery which was not destroyed was removed to Richmond. About six hundred arms were recovered.

But the severest blow at this time was given near Norfolk, a city in Norfolk County, Va., situated on the right or north bank of Elizabeth River, eight miles from Hampton Roads. A navy-yard was located at Gosport, a suburb of Portsmouth, on the side of the river opposite, accessible to the largest ships. A naval hospital and a large dry-dock were also prepared there.

At the time of the secession of Virginia, April 18th, the marines and Government forces at the yard numbered nearly eight hundred men. The vessels of war there at that time were as follows;

Ships of the Line.—Pennsylvania, 120 guns; Columbus, 80; Delaware, 84; New York (on stocks), 84. *Frigates.*—United States, 50 guns; Columbus, 50; Raritan, 50. *Sloops-of-War.*—Plymouth, 22 guns; Germantown, 22. *Brig.*—Dolphin, 4 guns. *Steam frigate*—Merrimac, 40 guns.

As to their condition, there was the liner Columbus, useless; liner Delaware, useless; liner New York, never launched; frigate Columbus, out of order; frigate Raritan, out of order; steam-frigate Merrimac, needing full repairs; corvette Germantown, almost ready for sea. The force of the Government was distributed as follows: The flag-ship Cumberland, 300 men; receiving-ship Pennsylvania, 350; marines at the barracks, 70; steamer Pocahontas, 60; total, 780.

Upon the first excitement, a party of men, without any authority, had seized the light-boats, and floating them to the shallowest point at the mouth of the harbor, had sunk them, to prevent the removal of the vessels of war from the navy-yard.

On the 19th Gen. Taliaferro and staff arrived at Norfolk. He had command of all the Virginia troops in that section, and was waited on shortly after his arrival by the captains of the several military companies of the city and vicinity for the purpose of reporting their strength, condition, &c., and receiving orders.

On Saturday, the 20th, the greatest excitement prevailed in the city. It was reported that the Cumberland was about to sail from the navy-yard, and preparations were made to prevent her. At twelve o'clock an officer came from the yard bearing a flag of truce, and was conducted to Gen. Taliaferro's headquarters, where a consultation was held, which resulted in a promise from Com. Macauley, the commandant of the yard, that none of the vessels should be removed, nor a shot fired except in self-defence.

This quieted the excitement; but it was renewed at a later hour, when it was ascertained that the Germantown and Merrimac had been scuttled, and that the heavy shears on the wharf at which the Germantown was lying had been cut away and allowed to fall midships across her decks, carrying away the main topmast and yards. It was also perceived that the men were busily engaged in destroying and throwing overboard side and small arms, and other property, and boats were constantly passing between the Pennsylvania, Cumberland, and other vessels.

About midnight a fire was started in the yard. This continued to increase, and before daylight the work of destruction extended to the immense ship-houses known as A and B (the former containing the entire frame of the New York, 74, which had been on the stocks, unfinished, for some thirty-eight years), and also to the long ranges of two-story offices and stores on each side of the main gate of the yard. The flames and heat from this tremendous mass of burning material were set by a southwest wind directly toward the line of vessels moored on the edge of the channel opposite the yard, and nearly all of these, too, were speedily enveloped in flames.

The scene, at this time, was grand and terrific beyond description. The roar of the conflagration was loud enough to be heard at a distance of miles; and to this were added occasional discharges from the heavy guns of the old Pennsylvania, ship-of-the-line, as they became successively heated.

When the destruction of the ship-houses was certain, the Pawnee, which arrived on Saturday, and had been kept under steam, was put in motion, and, taking the Cumberland in tow, retired down the harbor, out of the reach of danger, freighted with a great portion of valuable munitions from the yard, and the commodore and other officers. The ships proceeded as far down as the barricades at the narrows, where the Cumberland was left at anchor, and the Pawnee continued on to Fortress Monroe. The Cumberland subsequently passed out.

It afterwards appeared that the ship Pennsylvania was burnt, and the Merrimac, Columbus, Delaware, and Raritan, Plymouth, and Germantown were scuttled and sunk, and a vast amount of the machinery, valuable engines, small arms, chronometers, &c., had been broken up and rendered entirely useless. Besides the ship-houses and their contents, the range of buildings on the north line of the yard (except the Commodore's and Commander's houses), the old marine barracks, and some workshops were burnt. Much of value, however, was not destroyed. The great dry-dock was uninjured. The large number of two thousand five hundred cannon, of all kinds and sizes, fell into the hands of the State of Virginia; also shot, shell, and other warlike missiles to a very large amount. Besides these, the machinery of the yard was generally uninjured. A collection of ship-building and outfitting material, large and valuable, including a number of steel plates and iron castings, was found ready for use, and capable of being turned to account.

Old Fort Norfolk, used as a magazine, was taken by the Virginia authorities without resistance. Within were three thousand barrels of powder, containing three hundred thousand pounds; also, a large number of shells and other missiles, loaded, and for that reason necessary to be kept in magazines.

The value of the property destroyed was estimated at several millions. The cost of the immense and magnificent ship-houses and their contents formed a considerable item in the account, and so did that of the Pennsylvania. "It brings tears into our eyes," said a citizen of Norfolk, "when we realize the destruction of this noble ship, so long the ornament of our harbor, and the admiration of thousands from all parts of the country who visited our waters." That splendid specimen of naval architecture, the new and beautiful frigate Merrimac, and four or five other vessels, were given to the flames, or with their valuable armament sunk in the deep water.

On the same day an order was issued by Gen. Taliaferro, prohibiting the collector of the port from accepting any draft from the United States Government, or allowing the removal of deposits, or any thing else, from the custom-house. The collector, being informed that on his refusal to obey the order a file of men would be sent down to occupy the premises, acquiesced.

On the 20th the Richmond Grays, a fine company numbering one hundred rifle muskets, arrived. They brought with them fourteen pieces of rifle cannon of large size, one of the pieces weighing ten thousand pounds, and three box cars filled with ammunition of various kinds, to be distributed to the patriotic companies by the wayside.

On the night previous, four companies of Petersburg riflemen and infantry, numbering in all four hundred men, reached Norfolk. They were followed by two additional companies of one hundred each.

On the 22d, three companies of troops from Georgia arrived in the express train from Weldon; the Light Guards, from Columbus, numbering eighty men; the Macon Volunteers, eighty men; and the Floyd Rifles, from Macon, eighty men. The first and last commands marched immediately to the naval hospital.

About the same time the hull of the old ship United States, in which Com. Decatur captured the Macedonian, was taken possession of at the navy-yard by an efficient crew, and towed down to the narrow part of the channel, a mile below Fort Norfolk, where she was moored across the channel and sunk. Only a few feet brought her in contact with the bottom. Any naval force that might attempt to pass up the harbor must remove the hulk, while, in the mean time, the shot and shells from the two forts above—one on the right and the other on the left—would be poured into them. Norfolk thus was occupied by Confederate troops, who remained in undisturbed possession through the year.

Excitement both at the North and the South now ran high. Events daily occurred which added fuel to the flame. Besides those already narrated in connection with the secession of the several States, space will permit here merely a summary of other isolated incidents in the order of time in which they took place. On April 19th, the steamer Star of the West was boarded off Indianola, by a party of volunteers from Galveston, and captured without resistance. She had been sent out to convey to New York the force of regular troops to be withdrawn from that State. On the same day the President issued another proclamation declaring a blockade of the Southern ports.

On the 21st, Senator Andrew Johnson, of Tennessee, was mobbed at Lynchburg, Va., and narrowly escaped.

On the 22d, the arsenal at Fayetteville,

North Carolina, was surrendered to a force of about eight hundred men, with thirty-five thousand stand of arms and some cannon, and considerable quantities of ball and powder.

On the 25th, the Legislature of Vermont, being in session, appropriated $1,000,000 to equip her volunteers.

At this time a large number of the officers of the army and navy who were natives of Southern States, sent in their resignation.

On the 26th, twenty-one thousand stand of arms were removed, by order of the Federal Government, from the arsenal at St. Louis, and taken to Springfield, Illinois, for safety.

On the 29th, the Legislature of Indiana being in session, appropriated five hundred thousand dollars to equip her volunteers. On the same day a number of Northern steamers at New Orleans were seized and appropriated.

On the 30th, the Legislature of New Jersey assembled in extra session, and authorized a loan of two millions of dollars to fit out her troops. The command of her force was given to Gen. Theodore Runyon. It immediately started from Trenton for Annapolis, in fourteen propellers, by canal to Bordentown, thence down the Delaware River. The whole brigade was armed with Minié rifles, and took also four pieces of artillery. It was stated that "the fleet of transports with a strong convoy made a novel and splendid appearance steaming in two lines up the Chesapeake Bay."

On May 3d, the Connecticut Legislature appropriated two millions of dollars for the public defence. These appropriations continued to be made in the first months of the war, by States, cities, and towns, until the amount exceeded thirty-seven millions of dollars.

On the same day, May 3d, Gov. Letcher, of Virginia, called out the State militia to defend Virginia from invasion by Northern troops.

On the 9th, a resolution was adopted by the Congress at Montgomery, authorizing their Government to accept all the volunteers who might offer.

On the 13th, a Convention assembled at Wheeling, in Western Virginia, for the purpose of separating the counties represented from being a part of Virginia, and forming a Union State Government. On this same day the proclamation of Victoria, Queen of England, was issued, recognizing the insurrectionary States as belligerents.

On the 14th, a schooner at Baltimore found to be loaded with arms was seized by the Federal authorities.

On the 16th, the first injury was done to the Baltimore and Ohio Railroad, by the destruction of several bridges and portions of the track.

On the same day, the brigade of State militia under Gen. Frost at St. Louis, Missouri, surrendered to Gen. Lyon, an officer in the United States service. A camp of instruction had been formed under Gen. Frost in the western suburbs of the city, in pursuance of orders from the Governor of the State. He had directed the other militia districts also to go into encampments with a view of acquiring a greater proficiency in military drill. It had been reported to Gen. Frost that Gen. Lyon intended to attack him, and, on the other hand, it had been reported to Gen. Lyon that it was the intention of Gen. Frost to attack the arsenal and United States troops. On the 16th, Gen. Frost addressed a note to Gen. Lyon alluding to these reports.

About the same time Gen. Lyon's troops were put in motion, to the number, as was represented, of four or five thousand, and proceeded through the city to the camp of Gen. Frost, and surrounded it, planting batteries on all the heights overlooking the camp. Long files of men were stationed in platoons at various points on every side, and a picket guard established, covering an area of two hundred yards. The guards, with fixed bayonets and muskets at half cock, were instructed to allow none to pass or repass within the limits thus taken up.

By this time an immense crowd of people had assembled in the vicinity, having gone thither in carriages, buggies, rail cars, baggage wagons, on horseback, and on foot. Numbers of men seized rifles, shot-guns, or whatever other weapons they could lay hands on, and rushed to the assistance of the State troops, but were, of course, obstructed in their design. The hills, of which there are a number in the neighborhood, were literally black with people—hundreds of ladies and children stationing themselves with the throng, but as they thought out of harm's way. Having arrived in this position, Gen. Lyon addressed a letter to Gen. Frost demanding an immediate surrender.

Immediately on the receipt of the foregoing, Gen. Frost called a hasty consultation of the officers of his staff. The conclusion arrived at was that the brigade was in no condition to make resistance to a force so numerically superior, and that only one course could be pursued —a surrender.

The State troops were therefore made prisoners, but an offer was made to release them on condition they would take an oath to support the Constitution of the United States, and not to take up arms against the Government. These terms they declined on the ground that they had already taken the oath of allegiance, and to repeat it would be to admit that they had been in rebellion.

About half-past five the prisoners left the grove and entered the road, the United States soldiers enclosing them by a single file stretched along each side of the line. A halt was ordered, and the troops remained standing in the position they had deployed into the road. The head of the column at the time rested opposite a small hill on the left as one approaches the city, and the rear was on a line with the entrance to the grove. Vast crowds of people covered the surrounding grounds and every fence and house top in the vicinity. Suddenly the sharp reports of several fire-arms were heard from the front of the column, and the spectators that lined the adjacent hill were seen fleeing in the greatest dismay and terror. It appeared that several members of one of the German companies, on being pressed by the crowd and receiving some blows from them, turned and discharged their pieces. Fortunately no one was injured, and the soldiers who had done the act were at once placed under arrest. Hardly, however, had tranquillity been restored when volley after volley of rifle reports was suddenly heard from the extreme rear ranks, and men, women, and children were beheld running wildly and frantically away from the scene. Many, while running, were suddenly struck to the sod, and the wounded and dying made the late beautiful field look like a battle-ground. The total number killed and wounded was twenty-five. It was said that the arsenal troops were attacked with stones, and two shots discharged at them by the crowd before they fired. Most of the people exposed to the fire were citizens with their wives and children, who were merely spectators. It was now night, and the excitement in the city was indescribable. On the next afternoon a large body of the German Home Guard entered the city from the arsenal, where they had been enlisted during the day, and furnished with arms. They passed unmolested until they turned up Walnut Street, and proceeded westward. Large crowds were collected on the corners, who hooted and hissed as the companies passed, and one man standing on the steps of a church fired a revolver into the ranks. A soldier fell dead, when two more shots were fired from the windows of a house near by. At this time the head of the column, which had reached as far as Seventh Street, suddenly turned, and levelling their rifles, fired down the street, and promiscuously among the spectators, who lined the pavements. Shooting, as they did, directly toward their rear ranks, they killed some of their men as well as those composing the crowd. The shower of bullets was for a moment terrible, and the only wonder was that more lives were not lost. The missiles of lead entered the windows and perforated the doors of private residences, tearing the ceilings, and throwing splinters in every direction. On the street the scene presented, as the soldiers moved off, was sad indeed. Six men lay dead at different points, and several were wounded and shrieking with pain upon the pavements. Four of the men killed were members of the regiment, and two were citizens. Immense crowds of people filled the streets after the occurrence, and the whole city presented a scene of excitement seldom witnessed. Among the arms taken at Camp Jackson were three thirty-two pounders, a large quantity of balls and bombs, several pieces of artillery, twelve hundred rifles, of the late model, six brass field-pieces, six brass six-inch mortars, one ten-inch iron mortar, three six-inch iron cannon, several chests of new muskets, five boxes canister shot, ninety-six ten-inch and three hundred six-inch shells, twenty-five kegs of powder, and a large number of musket stocks and barrels, between thirty and forty horses, and a considerable quantity of camp tools.

The number of prisoners taken to the arsenal was six hundred and thirty-nine privates and fifty officers. On the same day a body of secessionists were dispersed at Liberty, Missouri.

On the 17th a number of persons were arrested at Washington, on the charge of being spies from the insurrectionary States. The transportation of any articles by express, to any point further south than Washington, was also forbidden. Some fortifications were commenced by Southern troops at Harper's Ferry. The yacht Wanderer, formerly noted as having brought a cargo of slaves from Africa into the State of Georgia, was at the same time seized off Key West by the Federal steamer Crusader.

On the 19th the light ship in the Potomac River was seized by a body of Virginians, but they were pursued and the vessel recaptured.

On the 19th a collision took place at Sewell's Point, which is the projection of land on the right shore, where the Elizabeth River turns from a north to an easterly course, becoming then what is called Hampton Roads. It is on this river that Norfolk in Virginia is situated. The point was fortified immediately after the secession of Virginia. The battery placed there by her troops was the exterior of the line of batteries intended to guard the Elizabeth River, through which Norfolk is approached. This line of batteries consisted of seven, the heaviest of which was at Craney Island, mounting about thirty guns. Two batteries further inland mounted about twelve and fifteen guns respectively. The other batteries mounted from seven to ten guns. The battery at Sewell's Point commanded the vessels blockading James River, and if the guns were sufficiently heavy and effective, it could cause them to remove. A party being observed perfecting the earthworks, the gunboat Star opened fire upon them with two ten-inch guns and shell. Subsequently the Freeborn, Capt. Ward, arrived, and taking a position near the shore, drove the defenders out of the works, and disabled the battery.

The Star was struck by five shots of small calibre, all of which took effect. One ball, a six-pounder, penetrated the hull on the larboard bow, a few inches above the water line. Two of her crew were injured, and one of them, a boy, seriously. This was the first skirmish between the floating batteries of the North and land batteries of the South. On the other side, Vice-President Stephens, in an address at Atlanta, Ga., on the 23d of May, spoke of the affair as resulting in "the vessel being repulsed and disabled."

Southern troops now marched for Harper's Ferry, and on the 20th of May there were on the spot 8,000, made up from Kentucky,

Alabama, South Carolina, and Virginia. They occupied all the neighboring heights on both sides of the Potomac and Shenandoah Rivers, and claimed to hold a position impregnable to 40,000 men, so eligible were the points of defence. They expected accessions to their number, under the belief that the United States Government intended to make an effort to replant the national flag wherever it had been displaced.

A small force was thrown over the river to the heights on the Maryland shore, thus occupying a position important to the security of Harper's Ferry. The invasion of Maryland by Virginia caused a remonstrance from Governor Hicks, addressed to Governor Letcher, of Virginia. The latter replied that the movement was unauthorized and should be countermanded. On the 14th of June the ferry was evacuated by the troops. Their total force on that day in and around the place was about 10,000.

On the day when the evacuation commenced the bridge over the Potomac was destroyed, having been partly blown up and then set on fire by the retiring force. It was a long and costly structure. This retreat of the Southern troops was made in consequence of the movement of Union troops up the Potomac, from Washington, and from Chambersburg, in Pennsylvania, toward Harper's Ferry. At a later day, a small force of Confederate troops returned and burned the bridge over the Shenandoah and other property. After the passage of the Union troops across the Potomac at Williamsport, under General Patterson, the Confederate forces retired, and the ferry remained in possession of the former permanently.

On the 22d a body of men from the mainland reoccupied Ship Island, near the mouth of the Mississippi, on which the construction of an extensive fort had been commenced by the Federal Government, and destroyed the wooden work and the lighthouse structure.

On the night of the 23d of May troops from Washington proceeded to occupy the heights on the opposite side of the Potomac in Virginia. The large camps of southern troops formed in such places in Virginia, that a rapid concentration by railroad could be made, rendered it prudent for the Government to occupy these positions, which, in consequence of the railroad connections between Alexandria and Richmond, were of great importance to the security of Washington. The night of the 23d was beautiful on the Potomac. A full moon looked peacefully down, and perfect quietness prevailed over all the shores in the neighborhood of Washington. Companies of infantry, cavalry, and artillery, were stationed near and on the Long Bridge. About midnight two companies of rifles were advanced across the bridge to the neighborhood of Roach's Spring. Scouts were sent out in all directions, who managed to get past the line of Virginia pickets. Somewhat later the latter, getting the alarm, set spurs to their horses, and made off in haste down the road toward Alexandria. Volunteers of the District of Columbia were also advanced toward Alexandria. At Georgetown, above, a movement was made about half-past eleven over the aqueduct by the Georgetown battalion. They drove off the two or three pickets on the Virginia side of the river, and soon established themselves in position. Next followed the 5th Massachusetts regiment, 28th Brooklyn regiment, Company B of the U. S. cavalry, and the 69th regiment. The last-named regiment scoured Alexandria County, and went back as far as the Loudon and Hampshire Railroad. The sight of the troops crossing the aqueduct, with their burnished weapons gleaming in the bright moonlight, was strikingly beautiful. About 2 o'clock in the morning another large body of troops passed over from Washington and the neighborhood. The 7th New York regiment halted under orders at the Virginia end of the Long Bridge; the 2d New Jersey regiment went to Roach's Spring, half a mile from the end of the bridge; the New York 25th and one cavalry company, and the New York 12th and the 3d and 4th New Jersey regiments, proceeded to the right, after crossing the bridge, for the occupation of the heights of Arlington. They were joined by the other troops, which crossed at the Georgetown aqueduct.

Ellsworth's Zouaves, in two steamers, with the steamer James Guy as tender, left their camp on the East Branch, directly for Alexandria by water. The Michigan regiment, under Col. Wilcox, accompanied by a detachment of United States cavalry and two pieces of Sherman's battery, also proceeded by way of the Long Bridge to Alexandria. At 4 o'clock A. M. the Zouaves landed at Alexandria from the steamers, and the troops, who proceeded by the bridge, also reached that town. As the steamers drew up near the wharf, armed boats left the Pawnee, whose crews leaped ashore just before the Ellsworth Zouaves reached it. The crews of the Pawnee's boats were fired upon by a few Virginia sentries as the boats left the steamship, by way of giving the alarm, but these sentries instantly fled into the town. Their fire was answered by scattering shots from some of the Zouaves on the decks of the steamers. Immediately on landing, the Zouaves marched up into the centre of the town, no resistance whatever to their progress being offered. Thus quiet possession was taken of that part of Alexandria, in the name of the United States, by that portion of the troops immediately commanded by Col. Ellsworth. The Michigan regiment, at the same time, marched into the town by the extension of the Washington turnpike, and the cavalry and artillery came in two or three streets below. The destination of both these detachments was the depot of the Orange and Alexandria Railroad, which they instantly seized. They also found there a disunion company of cavalry, of thirty-five men, and as many horses, who were made prisoners, not having heard the alarm made by the firing of the sentries below. A portion of the Virginia force escaped in cars. Thus was possession taken of the Virginia shore. Intrenching tools were conveyed over from Washington; the next day intrenchments were thrown up, and about noon a large national flag was raised within them, and thrown out to the winds. Great numbers of spectators, of both sexes, lined the heights on the east bank of the Potomac, watching the movements of the troops with eager interest. The only disastrous event occurring was the death of Col. Ellsworth, commander of the Fire Zouave regiment of New York. The intrenchments thus commenced subsequently became of immense extent, and, with those on the other sides of Washington, consisted of forty-eight works, mounting 300 guns. The whole defence perimeter occupied was about thirty-five miles.

During the next day after the occupation of Alexandria, the bridges on the railroad from that city to Leesburg were destroyed. Martial law was at once declared in Alexandria, and the command of the troops in the vicinity of Washington was given to Brig.-Gen. Irvin McDowell. From Fortress Monroe Gen. Butler advanced his forces and formed an intrenched camp at Newport News on the 27th. His object was to command Sand Island, which is about midway in, and completely guards the entrance of the James River.

A blockade of the Mississippi was commenced at this time by the Southern troops, and also a regular blockade of the ports of Savannah and Mobile by the Federal fleet.

On the 30th, Grafton, in Western Virginia, was occupied by Col. Kelly. A small force of the enemy retired on his approach. In Missouri Gen. Lyon superseded Gen. Harney, and at Washington commissions were issued to Gens. Fremont and Banks.

On the 31st an attack was made on the batteries erected by the Virginia troops at Aquia Creek, below Washington, by Commander H. J. Ward in the gunboat Freeborn, supported by the Anacostia and Resolute. He thus reported the affair:

"After an incessant discharge, kept up for two hours by both our 32-pounders, and the expenditure of all the ammunition suitable for distant firing, and silencing completely the three batteries at the railroad terminus, the firing from shore having been rapidly kept up by them until so silenced, and having been recommenced from the new batteries on the heights back, which reached us in volleys, dropping the shot on board and about us like hail for nearly an hour, but fortunately wounding but one man, I hauled the vessel off, as the heights proved wholly above the reach of our elevation. Judging from the explosion of our ten-second shells in the sand-batteries, two of which were thrown by the Anacostia, it is hardly possible the enemy can have escaped considerable loss. Several others of the Anacostia's shells dropped in the vicinity of the battery."

Another attack was made on the batteries on the 1st of June, by the Freeborn and Pawnee gunboats. Just as the firing opened the men at the batteries burned the depot houses at the end of the wharf, probably to prevent them from being in the way of their shot. They continued burning throughout the whole engagement, as it was not safe for any one to leave the batteries to extinguish the fire. The entire wharf to the water's edge was also burned.

A slight affair had taken place on the 29th of May, previous to these two attacks, which was the first hostile collision on the waters of the Potomac.

On June 1st the first collision took place between the hostile forces in the neighborhood of Washington. Lieut. Tompkins, with a company of regular cavalry, consisting of forty-seven men, made a dash upon the village of Fairfax Court-House. A body of Southern troops were in possession of the village, who made a vigorous and determined resistance. The cavalry charged through the principal street, and upon their return were met by two detachments of the enemy. Again wheeling, they encountered another detachment, through which they forced their way and escaped, bringing with them five prisoners. They lost nine horses in the skirmish.

CHAPTER VII.

Southern Congress adjourns to meet at Richmond—Speeches of Howell Cobb and Vice-President Stephens—The Federal Army—Skirmish at Philippi—Attack on Pig's Point—Great Bethel—Movements in West Tennessee—Romney—Advance of Gen. Lyon to Jefferson City—Vienna—Locomotives Destroyed—Mathias Point—Other Events—Southern Privateers.

BLOODY conflicts soon began to occur in various quarters, which renders it necessary to notice more fully the preparations each side had been making. On April 29th the insurrectionary Congress had assembled at Montgomery, in compliance with a proclamation from their President. At the opening of the session he delivered a message recommending such measures as were necessary to conduct a vigorous defensive war. They were promptly passed, and on the 21st of May Congress adjourned to meet at Richmond, in Virginia, on July 20th. The reasons for this change of capital are given by the President of the Congress, Howell

Cobb, in a speech at Atlanta, Ga., on the 22d of May:

"I presume that a curiosity to know what we have been doing in the Congress recently assembled at Montgomery, has induced you to make this call upon me. We have made all the necessary arrangements to meet the present crisis. Last night we adjourned to meet in Richmond on the 20th of July. I will tell you why we did this. The 'Old Dominion,' as you know, has at last shaken off the bonds of Lincoln, and joined her noble Southern sisters. Her soil is to be the battle-ground, and her streams are to be dyed with Southern blood. We felt that her cause was our cause, and that if she fell we wanted to die by her. We have sent our soldiers on to the posts of danger, and we wanted to be there to aid and counsel our brave 'boys.' In the progress of the war further legislation may be necessary, and we will be there, that when the hour of danger comes, we may lay aside the robes of legislation, buckle on the armor of the soldier, and do battle beside the brave ones who have volunteered for the defence of our beloved South.

"The people are coming up gallantly to the work. When the call was made for twelve-months' volunteers, thousands were offered; but when it was changed to the full term of the war, the numbers increased! The anxiety among our citizens is not as to who shall go to the wars, but who shall stay at home. No man in the whole Confederate States—the gray-haired sire down to the beardless youth—in whose veins was one drop of Southern blood, feared to plant his foot upon Virginia's soil, and die fighting for our rights."

On the next evening the Vice-President, Mr. Stephens, being at Atlanta, also made an address, in which the plan of the Government was more fully unfolded: "The time for speech-making has passed. The people have heard all that can be said. The time for prompt, vigorous, and decisive action is upon us, and we must do our duty. Upon the surface affairs appear to be quiet, and I can give you no satisfaction as to their real condition. It is true that threats of an attack on Pensacola have been made, but it is uncertain whether any attack will be made. As you know, an attack was made at Sewall's Point, near Norfolk, but the vessel making it was repulsed and disabled. But the general opinion and indications are that the first demonstration will be at Harper's Ferry, and that there, where John Brown inaugurated his work of slaughter, will be fought a fierce and bloody battle. As for myself, I believe that there the war will begin, and that the first boom of cannon that breaks upon our ears will come from that point. But let it begin where it will, and be as bloody and prolonged as it may, we are prepared for the issue! Some think there will be no war; as to that I know not. But whatever others wanted, the object of the Confederate Government is *peace*. Come peace or war, however, it is determined to maintain our position at every hazard and at every cost, and to drive back the myrmidons of Abolitionism. We prefer and desire peace if we can have it; but if we cannot, we must meet the issue forced upon us."

Richmond was promptly occupied by the Southern authorities, and was made the capital of the new Confederacy.

Meanwhile President Lincoln had issued another call for troops. On the 4th of May a second proclamation appeared calling for volunteers to serve during the war. So patriotic and enthusiastic were the people in favor of preserving the Union, that, under this call, two hundred and eight regiments had been accepted by July 1st. A number of other regiments were also accepted, on condition of being ready to be mustered into service within a specified time. All of those regiments accepted under this call were infantry and riflemen, with the exception of two battalions of artillery and four regiments of cavalry. Many regiments, mustered as infantry, had attached to them one or more artillery companies; and there were also some regiments partly made up of companies of cavalry. Of the two hundred and eight regiments above mentioned, one hundred and fifty-three were in active service on the 1st of July, and the remaining fifty-five within twenty days afterwards. The total force in the field on July 1st, was computed as follows:

Regulars and volunteers for three months and for the war		232,875
Add to this 55 regiments of volunteers for the war, accepted and not then in service.	50,000	
Add new regiments of regular army	25,000	
		75,000
Total force at command of Government		307,875
Deduct the three-months' volunteers		77,875
Force for service after the withdrawal of the three-months' men		230,000

Of this force, 188,000 men were volunteers, and 42,000 men computed for the regular army.

The proclamation of the President of May 4th also called for an increase of the regular army. This increase consisted of one regiment of cavalry of twelve companies, numbering, in the maximum aggregate, 1,189, officers and men; one regiment of artillery, of twelve batteries, of six pieces each, numbering, in the maximum aggregate, 1,909, officers and men; nine regiments of infantry, each regiment containing three battalions of eight companies each, numbering, in the maximum aggregate, 2,452, officers and men, making a maximum increase of infantry of 22,068, officers and men.

The system adopted for the organization of the volunteers was different from the one which had existed in the regular army. The French regimental system of three battalions to a regiment was adopted.

Such gatherings of forces along an irregular and disputed line from east to west, soon led to collisions before the earnest work of war could commence. A camp of insurrectionary troops in the neighborhood of Philippi, Barbour County, Western Virginia, were completely surprised by Union troops, consisting of Western Virginia and Indiana volunteers, under Cols. Kelly and Dumont, both under the command of Brig.-Gen. Morris. On the morning of the 2d of June, five regiments, formed in two divisions, left Grafton, Virginia, for an attack on the forces of the insurrectionists. The first division consisted of the 1st Virginia, part of the 16th Ohio, and the Indiana 7th, under Col. Kelly; the other consisted of the Indiana 9th and the Ohio 14th, accompanied by Col. Lander, formerly engaged against the Western Indians. The division under Col. Kelly moved eastward by railroad, to Thornton, five miles from Grafton, and thence marched to Philippi, a distance of twenty-two miles. The Indiana 9th, uniting at Webster with the 14th Ohio, forming the second division, pushed on to Philippi, twelve miles distant, on foot. The march of both divisions was performed on the night of the 2d, through rain and mud. The division under Col. Dumont arrived on the hill across the river from and below Philippi early on the morning of the 3d. They at once planted two pieces of artillery on the brow of the hill, and prepared to open on the enemy as soon as four o'clock should arrive. This division was to attack the enemy in front, while the other, under Col. Kelly, made an attack in the rear; but the darkness of the night and the violence of the rain so impeded the march as to render it impossible for the division to arrive before Philippi at the appointed hour. The artillery of the division under Col. Lander, opened fire soon after four o'clock, when the enemy began to retire at once, leaving their camp behind. At this moment Col. Kelly, with the division, came up across the river and below the camp. At the same time Col. Dumont's force rushing down the hill and over the bridge to unite in the attack, the retreat of the enemy became a complete rout, and he fled, leaving seven hundred stand of arms, a number of horses, and all his camp equipage and provision. The loss on both sides was small. Among the badly wounded was Col. Kelly; he, however, subsequently recovered from the wound. The town was occupied by the Federal force.

On the 5th of June an attack was made by the steam-cutter Harriet Lane, upon a battery located at Pig's Point nearly opposite Newport News, to guard the entrance of James River. The cutter was proceeding up the river to reconnoitre and look out for batteries. She soon observed a large and heavy one planted upon the point, and about five miles distant from Newport News, and opened fire, which was briskly returned by the batteries, for nearly a half hour. It was found that but one gun of the cutter could reach the battery, the guns of which being heavier, easily reached the former, and several shot struck her. These were supposed to come from a rifled 32-pounder. Several shells were thrown into the battery by the gun from the cutter. There were five injured on the Harriet Lane.

On the 9th of June a movement of troops up the Potomac took place from Washington. The Rhode Island battery, under Col. Burnside, was sent to join the force under Gen. Patterson at Chambersburg, and on the next day three bodies of District of Columbia volunteers, numbering 1,000 men, moved up the Rockville road along the Potomac toward Edwards' Ferry. This point is about thirty miles from Georgetown, and equidistant from Washington and Harper's Ferry. It is the only crossing for teams between the Point of Rocks and the District. The road passed from Frederick, Md., across a bridge over the Chesapeake and Ohio Canal, to the established ferry across the Potomac, and terminated in Leesburg, Va., which is only four miles distant from the crossing. At the same time Gen. Patterson advanced from Chambersburg toward Harper's Ferry.

Meanwhile the most important movement which had yet taken place was ordered by Gen. Butler against Great Bethel. This place is about twelve miles from Fortress Monroe, on the road from Hampton to Yorktown, and between two and four miles beyond Little Bethel on the same road. This latter spot, consisting chiefly of a small church, is about ten miles from Hampton and the same distance from Newport News, in Elizabeth City County, Virginia. At Little Bethel a Confederate outpost of some strength was established, the main army being in the vicinity of Yorktown. From Little Bethel the Virginia troops were accustomed to advance, both on Newport News and the picket guards of Hampton, to annoy them. They had also come down in small squads of cavalry and taken a number of Union men, and forced them to serve in their ranks, besides gathering up the slaves of citizens who had moved away and left their farms in charge of their negroes, and sent them to work on the intrenchments at Williamsburg and Yorktown. Gen. Butler, being in command at Fortress Monroe, determined to drive out the enemy and destroy his camp. At Great Bethel, which is a large church near the head of Back River, there was another outpost, and a considerable rendezvous with works of some strength in process of erection. Brig.-Gen. E. W. Pierce was appointed to the command of the expedition, and issued the following orders:

HEADQUARTERS CAMP HAMILTON, June 9, 1861.

General Order No. 12.—A plan of attack to-night is herewith enclosed and forwarded to Col. Duryea, commanding 5th Regiment New York State troops, who will act accordingly. Col. Townsend, commanding 3d Regiment New York State troops, will march his command in support of Col. Duryea; Col. Carr, commanding 2d Regiment New York volunteers, will detach the artillery company of his regiment, with their field-pieces, caissons, and a suitable supply of ammunition, and take their position at the burnt bridge, near Hampton. Cols. Allen, Carr, and McChesney will hold their entire commands in readiness, fully prepared to march at a moment's notice. All the troops will be supplied with one day's rations, and each man with twenty rounds of ball cartridges. That no mistake may be made, all the troops as they charge the

enemy, will shout "Boston." Cols. Allen, Carr, Townsend, Duryea, and McChesney will take notice, and act accordingly. By command of
Brigadier-General E. W. PIERCE.

Some notes were added to this order, the principal points of which were as follows:

A regiment or battalion to march from Newport News. A regiment or battalion to march from Camp Hamilton, Duryea's; each to be supported by sufficient reserves under arms in camp, and with advance-guard out on the line of march. Duryea to push out two pickets at 10 P. M.; one also two and a half miles beyond Hampton, on the county road, but not so far as to alarm the enemy. This is important. Second picket half so far as the first. Both pickets to keep as much out of sight as possible. No one whosoever to be allowed to pass through their lines. Persons to be allowed to pass inward towards Hampton, unless it appear they intend to go around about and dodge through the front. At 12 M., (midnight,) Col. Duryea will march his regiment, with twenty rounds of cartridges, on the county road towards Little Bethel. Scows will be provided to ferry them across Hampton Creek. March to be rapid but not hurried. A howitzer with canister and shrapnell to go, and a wagon with planks and materials to repair the New Market bridge. Duryea to have the two hundred rifles. He will pick the men to whom they are to be intrusted. Newport News movement to be made somewhat later, as the distance is less. If we find the enemy and surprise them, we will fire a volley if desirable, not reload, and go ahead with the bayonet. As the attack is to be made by night, or gray of morning, and in two detachments, our people should have some token, say a white rag, or nearest approach to white attainable, on left arm.

Accordingly, on that night, the regiment of New York Zouaves, under Col. Duryea, and the Albany (N. Y.) regiment, under Col. Townsend, were despatched from Fortress Monroe, while the New York Steuben (German) regiment, under Col. Bendix, with detachments from the First Vermont and the Third Massachusetts, were ordered from Newport News. With the division from Fortress Monroe, or Camp Hamilton, as it was called, there was a small detachment of United States Artillery, Lieut. Greble commanding, with three pieces of light artillery.

The Zouaves were ordered to proceed over Hampton Creek at 1 o'clock in the morning, and to march by the road up to New Market Bridge; thence, after crossing, to go by a by-road, which would put them in the rear of the enemy, and between Little Bethel and Great Bethel. This was to be done for the purpose of cutting off the enemy and then to make an attack on Little Bethel. This movement was to be supported by Col. Townsend's regiment with two howitzers, which was to march from Hampton one hour later. The companies of Massachusetts and Vermont were to make a demonstration upon Little Bethel in front, supported by Col. Bendix's regiment with two fieldpieces. The regiments of Cols. Bendix and Townsend were to effect a junction at a fork of the road leading from Hampton to Newport News, about a mile and a half from Little Bethel. Col. Townsend, in his report, thus describes the manner in which this junction was made:

"In obedience to these orders, with the concerted sign of a white badge upon our left arm, (at midnight,) I marched my regiment to Hampton, where the general met the command and accompanied it.

"On approaching a defile through a thick wood, about five or six miles from Hampton, a heavy and well-sustained fire of canister and small-arms was opened upon the regiment while it was marching in a narrow road, upon the flank, in easy step and wholly unsuspicious of any enemy, inasmuch as we were ordered to reënforce Col. Duryea, who had preceded us by some two hours, and who had been ordered to throw out, as he marched, an advance guard two miles from his regiment, and a sustaining force half-way between the advance and the regiment; therefore, had Col. Duryea been obliged to retreat upon us before we reached his locality, we should have heard distant firing, or some of his regiment would have been seen retreating.

"The force which fired upon us was subsequently ascertained to be only the regiment of Col. Bendix, though a portion of the Vermont and Fourth Massachusetts regiments was with it, having come down with two 6-pounder fieldpieces from Newport News to join the column. These regiments took up a masked position in the woods at the commencement of the defile. The result of the fire upon us was two mortally wounded, (one since dead,) three dangerously, and four officers and twenty privates slightly, making a total of twenty-nine. At the commencement of the fire, the general, captain chamberlain, his aide-de-camp, and two mounted howitzers were about 250 paces in advance of the regiment; the fire was opened upon them first by a discharge of small-arms, and immediately followed by a rapidly returned volley upon my regiment and the field-pieces; my men then generally discharged their pieces and jumped from the right to the left of the road, and recommenced loading and firing. In a few minutes, the regiment was reformed in the midst of this heavy fire, and by the general's directions, retired in a thoroughly military manner, and in order to withdraw his supposed enemy from his position. On ascertaining that the enemy were our friends, and on providing for the wounded, we joined Cols. Duryea and Bendix."

Col. Duryea, who was on the advance, thus describes his movement:

"At half-past 11 o'clock, at night, we commenced the march, and for the first two miles to Hampton Bridge, proceeded leisurely, waiting for the howitzer which should be placed at the head of the column. Arriving at Hampton Creek, much delay was occasioned by the non-arrival of the surf-boats which were to convey the regiment across the river, and it was 1 o'clock before the column was formed, ready to push forward on the other side. We now advanced rapidly, and soon came up with our two companies of skirmishers, who had been despatched ahead an hour and a half previous. Proceeding steadily on without resting a moment, we came about 4 o'clock in the morning to Little Bethel, a distance of about ten miles. At this point we discovered and surprised the picket-guard of the enemy, and a mounted officer with four or five foot were taken prisoners. While pushing forward towards Big Bethel, we suddenly heard a heavy fire of musketry and cannon in our rear, bespeaking a severe engagement. Supposing it to be an attempt of the enemy to cut off our reserve, we immediately countermarched in quick and double-quick time, when, having proceeded about five miles, we came upon two of our regiments, and learned that in the darkness of the night they had mistaken each other for enemies, and an unfortunate engagement, accompanied with some loss, had taken place."

Up to the time of this fatal mistake, the plan had been vigorously, accurately, and successfully carried out. As a precaution, the commanding general had ordered that no attack should be made until the watchword had been shouted by the attacking regiment. Ten of Col. Townsend's regiment were wounded, and one mortally. All hope of surprising the enemy above the camp at Little Bethel was now lost, and it was found, upon marching upon it, to have been vacated, and the cavalry had pressed on towards Great Bethel. Gen. Pierce now consulted with his colonels, and it was concluded to attempt to carry the works of the enemy at Great Bethel, and measures were taken for that purpose. The force proceeded on, and Great Bethel was reached about 10 o'clock. Over a small stream twelve miles from Hampton, a bridge, called County Bridge, crosses on the road to Yorktown. On the opposite side, and to the right, the enemy were posted behind sand batteries. In front of their batteries was a broad open field, and nearer to the bridge than that, and on the right of the advancing force, was a wood, and in front and to the left, a corn-field. Between the wood and the corn-field, ran a road connected with that by which the advance was made. Col. Duryea's regiment now advanced over the fence and into the corn-field, and deployed into an apple orchard on the enemy's right flank. The Albany regiment took a supporting position on the right and rear of Col. Duryea, while it in turn was supported in like manner by Col. Allen's regiment. In the road in front of the enemy's batteries, Lieut. Greble's howitzers were placed, having in their rear Col. Bendix's regiment, which deployed on the right, in the wood, and on the enemy's left flank with three companies of the Massachusetts and Vermont regiments. The fire of the enemy became at once incessant and galling on the Federal right. The howitzers of Lieut. Greble, supported only by the ordinary force of gunners, opened fire with great rapidity and effect, and were steadily advanced to within 200 yards of the enemy's position. Several attempts were now made to charge the batteries, but were unsuccessful, owing to a morass in their front and a deep ditch or stream requiring ladders to cross it. The troops were, however, gradually gaining ground, although the action had continued nearly two hours and a half, when the order was given by Gen. Pierce to retreat. The howitzers maintained their position until their ammunition began to give out, when Lieut. Greble was struck on the back part of the head by a cannon ball, killing him instantly. The gunner having been disabled, the pieces were withdrawn by a small force under Col. Washburn.

On the right, the Vermont companies had outflanked the enemy, gaining a position in their rear and pouring such a hot fire as to silence the battery there. A statement by one of the Confederate force, says: "One company under Capt. Winthrop attempted to take the redoubt on the left. The marsh over which they crossed was strewn with their bodies. Their captain, a fine-looking man, reached the fence and leaping on a log, waved his sword, crying, 'Come on, boys; one charge and the day is ours.' The words were his last, for a Carolina rifle ended his life the next moment, and his men fled." The force retired from the field in order, about half-past 12 o'clock, and the enemy on the same day fell back to Yorktown. The number of Federal troops was between three and four thousand, while that of the enemy was nearly fifteen hundred. The loss on the Federal side was sixteen killed, thirty-four wounded, and five missing. The loss on the Confederate side was small.

A statement was made by an officer of Col. Bendix's regiment, that the latter had not received any intimation that the troops would wear white badges round the arm for the purpose of mutual recognition, and if he had, he would not have been able to distinguish such badge at the distance and in the dusk of the morning. Col. Bendix's command did not wear such badges. The uniform of Col. Townsend's regiment was very similar to that of the enemy. It was also further stated, that when Col. Townsend's troops approached the junction over a slight ridge, they appeared to be a troop of cavalry, because Gen. Pierce and staff and Col. Townsend and staff, in a body, rode in advance of their troops, and without any advance guard thrown out.

The expedition was originally undertaken with the object of cutting off a body of the enemy supposed to be near Newport News, and it was undertaken at night in order to surprise their batteries. This surprise was frustrated by the mistaken engagement between the two regiments. Some of the officers were opposed to an advance after this occurrence.

The bravery of the Federal troops was admitted even by the enemy, and if proper knowledge had been obtained beforehand of the position, and no order for retreat had been given, the attack would have been successful. No investigation has ever been made of the affair, nor has the generalship displayed ever been approved.

The progress of military affairs in the western part of Tennessee had been such that at this time there were established on the Mississippi River five or six batteries of heavy guns, including mortars, columbiads, and 32 and 24-pounders, commanding the river from Memphis to the Kentucky line. About fifteen thousand troops were concentrated in West Tennessee under Maj.-Gen. G. J. Pillow, as commander-in-chief, with Brig.-Gens. Cheatham and Sneed. Eight thousand troops of all arms from Mississippi had passed up the Mobile and Ohio Railroad, at Corinth, and at Grand Junction, on the Mississippi Central Railroad, on their way to a rendezvous near the Kentucky line, to act under Maj.-Gen. Clark, of Mississippi, in concert with Maj.-Gen. Pillow, of Tennessee. With these troops were some cavalry and two light batteries. At least seventy-five or one hundred heavy guns had been placed in battery, and other large guns were in the State ready for use. A *corps d'armée*, under command of Brig.-Gen. Foster, had assembled in Camp Cheatham. Gen. William R. Caswell had assembled, and armed and equipped, a force of considerable strength in East Tennessee, ready to repel any attack in that division of the State.

On June 11th a body of Virginia troops at Mill Creek, a few miles from Romney, Northern Virginia, were surprised by an Indiana regiment under Col. Wallace. The Virginians fled through Romney, on the road to Winchester, abandoning their tents and arms. Some prisoners were taken with a small loss on both sides.

Meanwhile active operations commenced in Missouri by the movement of troops from St. Louis to Jefferson City.

On the 13th the steamer Iatan left St. Louis with the second battalion of the First Regiment Missouri volunteers, one section of Totten's Light Artillery, and two companies of regulars, and the steamer J. C. Swan, with the first battalion of the First Regiment, under Col. Blair, and another section of Totten's battery, and a detachment of pioneers, and Gen. Lyon and staff, numbering fifteen hundred men. Horses, wagons, and all necessary camp equipage, ammunition, and provisions for a long march, accompanied the expedition.

On the 15th they arrived at Jefferson City. Five companies of Missouri volunteers, under Lieut.-Col. Andrews, and a company of regular artillery under Capt. Totten, all under Gen. Lyon, disembarked and occupied the city. Gov. Jackson and the officers of the State Government, and many citizens, had left on the 13th. A company of regulars, under Maj. Conant, thoroughly searched the country for contraband articles, and found some wheels and other parts of artillery carriages. No violence was offered, but, on the contrary, the boats containing the Federal troops were received with cheers by a large concourse of the citizens. On the next day Gen. Lyon left for Booneville. Previously, however, he placed Col. Henry Boernstein, of the Second Missouri volunteers, in command.

Meantime Gov. Jackson, on leaving Jefferson City, summoned the State troops to his support at Booneville, which is situated on the south bank of the Missouri River, and forty-eight miles northwest of Jefferson City. Several companies from the adjacent counties joined him, under Col. Marmaduke.

Leaving Jefferson City on the 16th, Gen. Lyon proceeded on the steamers A. McDowell, Iatan, and City of Louisiana, up the river, and stopped for the night about one mile below Providence. Early in the morning he started with his force, and reached Rochefort before six o'clock, when he learned that a small force of the State troops was a few miles below Booneville, and preparing to make a vigorous defence. Proceeding on, they discovered, about six miles from Booneville, on the bluffs, a battery, and also scouts moving. A landing was made about 7 o'clock two miles lower down, on the south bank of the river, and the troops began to move on the river road to Booneville. Following it about a mile and a half to the spot where it begins to ascend the bluffs, several shots announced the driving in of the enemy's pickets. On the summit of the bluffs the enemy were posted. The Federal force advanced and opened the engagement by throwing a few nine-pounder shells, while the infantry filed to the right and left, and commenced a fire of musketry. The enemy stood their ground manfully for a time, then began to retire, and withdrew in order. The Federal force was two thousand; only a small portion of which was engaged, and its loss was two killed and nine wounded. The number of the State troops was small. They admitted ten as killed, and several as having been taken prisoners. Some shoes, guns, blankets, etc., were taken by the Federal troops. This was the first hostile collision in the State like a skirmish or battle between those representing the authority of the United States and any of the officers of the State Government or forces under them. Gen. Lyon, therefore, deemed it necessary to issue the following proclamation:

BOONEVILLE, June 18, 1861.

To the People of Missouri:

Upon leaving St. Louis, in consequence of war made by the Governor of this State against the Government of the United States, because I would not assume on its behalf to relinquish its duties, and abdicate its rights of protecting loyal citizens from the oppression and cruelty of the secessionists in this State, I published an address to the people, in which I declared my intention to use the force under my command for no other purpose than the maintenance of the authority of the General Government, and the protection of the rights and property of all law-abiding citizens.

The State authorities, in violation of an agreement with Gen. Harney on the 2d of May last, had drawn together and organized upon a large scale the means of warfare, and, having made a declaration of war, they abandoned the capital, issued orders for the destruction of the railroad and telegraph lines, and proceeded to this point to put into execution their hostile purposes toward the General Government. This devolved upon me the necessity of meeting this issue to the best of my ability, and accordingly I moved to this point with a portion of the force under my command, attacked and dispersed the hostile forces gathered here by the Governor, and took possession of the camp-equipage left, and a considerable number of prisoners, most of them young and of immature age, and who represent that they have been misled by frauds, ingeniously devised and industriously inculcated by designing leaders, who seek to devolve upon unreflecting and deluded followers the task of securing the object of their own false ambition.

Out of compassion for these misguided youths, and to correct the impressions created by unscrupulous calumniators, I liberated them upon the condition that they will not serve in the impending hostilities against the United States Government.

I have done this in spite of the well-known facts that the leaders in the present rebellion, having long experienced the mildness of the General Government, still feel confident that this mildness cannot be overtaxed even by factious hostilities, having in view its overthrow; but lest, as in the case of the late Camp Jackson affair, this clemency shall still be misconstrued, it is proper to give warning that the Government cannot always be expected to indulge in it to the compromise of its evident welfare.

Hearing that those plotting against the Government have falsely represented that the Government troops intended a forcible and violent invasion of Missouri for the purposes of military despotism and tyranny, I hereby give notice to the people of this State that I shall scrupulously avoid all interference with the business, right, and property of every description recognized by the laws of the State, and belonging to law-abiding citizens. But it is equally my duty to maintain the paramount authority of the United States with such force as I have at my command, which will be retained only so long as opposition makes it necessary, and that it is my wish, and shall be my purpose, to visit any unavoidable rigor arising in this issue upon those only who provoke it.

All persons, who, under the misapprehensions above mentioned, have taken up arms, or who are preparing to do so, are invited to return to their homes and relinquish their hostilities toward the Federal Government, and are assured that they may do so without being molested for past occurrences.

N. LYON, Brigadier U. S. Army, Commanding.

On the 18th Gov. Jackson was at Syracuse, about twenty-five miles south of Booneville, with about five hundred men. Property was taken from Union citizens, also the rolling stock of the railroad by the force, when they further retired to Warsaw, destroying the Lamoine bridge, a costly structure, six miles west of Syracuse. On the same day a skirmish took place near the town of Cole, between a force of Union Home Guards and State troops from Warsaw and that region, in which the former were put to flight.

Military affairs now progressed so rapidly that the force concentrated in the State reached 10,000 men, 2,500 of whom were stationed at Herman and Jefferson City, 3,200 at Rolla, the terminus of the southwest branch of the Pacific Railroad, 1,000 on the North Missouri Railroad, and 1,000 at Bird's Point, opposite Cairo. In addition to this there was a force of 2,500 remaining at St. Louis, which could be increased to 10,000 in a few hours by accessions from the neighboring camps in Illinois. These troops held the entire portion of the State north of the river, the southeast quarter lying between the Mississippi and a line drawn southward from Jefferson City to the Arkansas border, thus giving to the Federal Government the important points of St. Louis, Hannibal, St. Joseph, and Bird's Point as a base of operations, with the rivers and railroads as a means of transportation.

On the 24th the State Treasurer, the Auditor, and Land Register, who had retired with the Governor, returned to Jefferson City and took the oath of allegiance, and entered upon their duties. The Home Guard of the capital were furnished with arms, and drilled under the direction of Col. Boernstein, and intrenchments for the defence of the place against attacks were erected. Several expeditions were sent by Gen. Lyon to various parts of the State where collections of secessionists were reported, but the latter succeeded in getting away before the arrival of the Federal troops.

In the latter part of June Gen. Fremont was ordered to take command of the Department of the West. Since Gen. Harney had been ordered to another post, Capt. Lyon, who had been promoted to a brigadier-generalship, had been in command.

The movement to separate the Union portion of Western Virginia from the State was now carried through. The Convention declared its separation, elected Frank H. Pierpont Governor, and established a seat of Government at Wheeling, which was acknowledged by President Lincoln, and Senators and Representatives admitted to seats in Congress.

On June 17th, Vienna, a small village on the railroad from Alexandria to Leesburg, was the scene of surprise and disaster to the 1st Ohio regiment, Col. McCook. On the day previous a train of cars passing over this portion of the road had been fired upon, and one man killed. In consequence, the Government resolved to place pickets along the road, and this regiment, accompanied by Brig.-General Schenck, set out in a train of cars, and the men were distributed in detachments along the line. As the cars approached Vienna, Col. Gregg, with six hundred South Carolinians, and a company of artillery and two companies of cavalry, on a reconnoitring expedition, heard the whistle of the locomotive. He immediately wheeled his column and marched back to Vienna, which he had just left. This force had scarcely time to place two cannon in position, when the train, consisting of six flats and a baggage car, pushed by the locomotive, came slowly around the curve. As the train was about to stop, the artillery opened a well-directed fire, which raked the cars from front to rear. At the same time the coupling of the locomotive became detached or destroyed, and the engineer retired, leaving the cars in their exposed position. The Ohio volunteers immediately took to the woods on each side, and were pursued a short distance by the Confederate infantry and cavalry. The Federal loss was five killed, six wounded, and seven missing. The cars were burned, and a considerable quantity of carpenters' tools, blankets, and other baggage was taken by the enemy, who suffered no loss.

At the same time the Potomac was crossed at Williamsport by the Union forces under the command of Gen. Patterson, and Piedmont, a village on the Manassas Gap Railroad, sixty-one miles west of Alexandria, was occupied by the enemy. As an offset a small squad of Missouri troops, numbering thirty-five men, was captured at Liberty in that State.

On the 23d, by an order of Gen. J. E. Johnston, in command of the Southern troops, forty-six locomotives and three hundred and five cars of the Baltimore and Ohio Railroad were gathered at Martinsburg, and with wood from the company's supply, piled around them, set on fire and destroyed. The destruction of property was estimated at $400,000.

On the 26th an attack was made on a small force sent on shore to clear the wood from Mathias Point, on the Potomac, fifty miles below Washington. The party were about to go on board the gunboat Freeborn, when they were attacked. They escaped without loss under the cover of the gun of the Freeborn, but Capt. Ward, her commander, while sighting the gun was wounded, and died a few hours' afterwards.

On July 1st, Gen. Morris, commanding the 3d and 4th Ohio regiments, near Buckhannon, on the east fork of the Monongahela River, attacked a body of Virginia troops under Gen. Henry A. Wise, and routed them with a loss of twenty-three killed and a number taken prisoners. On the same day a skirmish took place at Falling Water, Virginia, and on the next day another at Martinsburg, with a very small loss on either side. On the next day an entire company of Confederates were captured at Nesho in Missouri. This was followed by the seizure of the Louisville and Nashville Railroad by Tennesseans on the 4th, and a battle at Carthage, Missouri, on the 5th, between some of Gen. Lyon's troops under Col. Sigel, assisted by Col. Solomon, and a body of State troops under Gen. Rains and Col. Parsons. The Union loss was thirteen killed and thirty-one wounded. The movement of Gen. Lyon up the Missouri River and through the central part of the State, it now appeared, had the effect to restrain the secessionists and prevent them from organizing a formidable force. Two days later another skirmish occurred at Brier Forks near Carthage, in which neither party gained any special advantage. Meantime a skirmish occurred at Middle York bridge, near Buckhannon, in which a part of a company of the 3d Ohio regiment encountered a body of Virginians unexpectedly, and escaped without serious loss.

On July 8th a communication was brought to President Lincoln from Jefferson Davis by Col. Taylor, relative to prisoners who had been taken with vessels which sailed from Southern ports as privateers. Col. Taylor, in displaying a flag of truce before the Federal lines in Virginia, opposite Washington, was brought blindfolded into camp, and his letter sent to Lieut.-Gen. Scott, who delivered it to the President. Gen. Scott sent back as an answer, that the President would reply. No reply was ever made. The President of the new Confederacy had issued a proclamation as early as April 17th, proposing to grant letters of marque and reprisal on certain conditions. The announcement of this privateering policy caused at the North, where there was so much at risk, a great sensation, after it was seen that the insurrectionists would be successful in obtaining vessels, and were determined to do all the injury possible to Northern commerce. President Lincoln, in anticipation of these efforts at privateering, closes his proclamation of April 19, announcing a blockade of Southern ports, with this threat:

> And I hereby proclaim and declare that if any person, under the pretended authority of the said States, or under any other pretence, shall molest a vessel of the United States, or the persons or cargo on board of her, such person will be held amenable to the laws of the United States for the prevention and punishment of piracy.

Among the first vessels to take out letters of marque at the South, under the proclamation of Jefferson Davis, was the Petrel, formerly the revenue-cutter Aiken, which had been surrendered to the Confederates in Charleston harbor, and the crew of which had volunteered under the new government. This vessel had run the blockade, but was no sooner at sea, July 28, than she fell in with the United States frigate St. Lawrence, and was captured. The captain of the St. Lawrence observed the Southern vessel in the distance, and immediately hauled down his heavy spars and closed his ports. Then, with the men below, the old frigate looked very much like a large merchant vessel, and the privateer bore down, hoping to take a good prize. The commander of the Petrel, William Perry, of South Carolina, gave the St. Lawrence a round ball over her bows and some canister over the stern, but the frigate sailed on as if trying to get away, when the Petrel gave chase, and when in fair range of the frigate the latter opened her ports and gave the Petrel a compliment of three guns, two of grape and one of round shot. The latter was a 32-pounder, and struck the Petrel amidships, below the water line, and she sunk in a few minutes. Four of the crew were drowned, and the rest, thirty-six in number, were rescued. Some of the men, when fished out of the water, were at a loss to know what had happened to them. The suddenness of the St. Lawrence's reply, the deafening roar of the guns, and the splinters and submerged vessel, were all incidents that happened apparently in a moment.

The Calhoun, a side-wheel steamer of 1,058 tons, was built in New York in 1851. She was 175 feet long, 27 feet wide, 11 feet hold. She was commanded by George N. Hollins, formerly of the United States navy, and carried one 24-pounder, and two 18-pounder Dahlgren guns. By the 27th of May she had captured and sent into New Orleans two schooners, the John Adams and the Mermaid, of Provincetown, and the brig Panama. Their united crews numbered 63 men, and they had on board 215 bbls. whale and sperm oil. She captured also the ship Milan, from Liverpool, with 1,500 sacks of salt, worth $20,000; the bark Ocean Eagle, from Rockland, Maine, with lime, worth $20,000; and the schooner Ida, from Tampico, with fruit, worth $5,000. The Calhoun was commander Hollins's flag-ship when the attack on the Union fleet was made on the Mississippi, October 11.

The schooner William C. Atwater, Capt. Allen, belonged to New Haven, and was in the service of the Government. The crew numbered eight men. Off Cedar Keys, Florida, on the 10th of May, she was captured by the steamer Spray, which had on board thirty-one men, armed with bowie-knives, revolvers, muskets with bayonets, etc. The captors took her to Appalachicola, where she arrived on the 13th of May.

The Ivey, a small steamer of 200 tons, was armed with two 8-inch rifled 32-pounder guns. She captured the ship Marathon, from Marseilles, in ballast, worth $35,000; and the ship Albino, from Boston, with a cargo of ice, worth $20,000. The armed steamer Murie captured the Marshall Sprague, of Providence, from Havre, in ballast, worth $50,000; and the ship John H. Jarvis, from Liverpool, worth $10,000.

The steamer Wm. H. Webb was formerly a towboat in New York, where she was built in 1856; she was 650 tons, draught 7 feet, 197 feet long, 31 feet beam, 12 feet hold, and was one of the strongest and largest boats of that class. A few years previous she had been purchased by some of the New Orleans merchants for the purpose of towing the heavily-laden ships to and from that city. She was converted into a gunboat and seized three vessels laden with oil, on the 24th of May.

The Dixie, a schooner of about 150 tons burden, was fitted out as a privateer in Charleston, from which place she ran the blockade on the 19th of July, and on the 23d encountered the bark Glen, of Portland, Maine, of which she at once made a prize. On the 25th she captured the schooner Mary Alice, of New York, with a cargo of sugar, from the West Indies, bound to New York, and placed a prize crew on board; she was, however, retaken by the blockading fleet almost immediately after. On the evening of the 31st the Dixie came up with the Rowena, a bark laden with coffee, bound to Philadelphia; she was taken possession of, and the captain of the Dixie himself took the place of prize-master, and successfully reached Charleston on the 27th of August, after several narrow escapes from the vessels of the blockading fleet. The following were the officers of the Dixie: captain, Thomas J. Moore; first lieutenant, George D. Walker; second lieutenant, John W. Marshall; third lieutenant, L. D. Benton; gunner, Charles Ware; boatswain, Geo. O. Gladden; steward, C. Butcher. She had also twenty-two seamen and a cook, and her armament consisted of four guns.

The Jeff. Davis, early in June, appeared on the eastern coast, running in as near as the Nantucket Shoals, and making on her way prizes that were roughly estimated at $225,000. She was formerly the slaver Echo, that was captured about two years previous, and was condemned in Charleston harbor. She was a full-rigged brig, painted black on the outside, and had a rusty, dull appearance, that would not be likely to alarm any vessel of ordinary sailing qualities; crew 260 men. Her armament consisted of a 32-pounder gun, placed amidships, mounted on a pivot, so that it might be used in all directions, and on each side a 32-pounder and a 12-pounder, so as to equalize the strength of the broadside. Captain Coxetter was her commander. His first lieutenant, named Postel, was at one time a midshipman in the United States navy, and also held a position in the Savannah custom-house.

The Davis had previously taken three prizes; one of these, and the most valuable, was the J. G. Waring, captured within 200 miles of New York. The captain, mates, and two seamen, were taken out, and five of the Davis crew put on board. The colored steward, W. Tillman, was allowed to remain. The vessel then made for Charleston. On the 16th of July Tillman, aided by McLeod, a seaman, killed the prize-captain and mates, and sailed for New York, where he arrived with two prisoners of the prize-crew. Tillman was awarded salvage. The Jeff. Davis also took the ship John Crawford, from Philadelphia, for Key West, with arms and coal for the United States. She drew 22 feet water, and was burned.

In attempting, August 17, to cross the bar at St. Augustine, Fla., the brig grounded on the North Breakers. This was about half-past six o'clock, Sunday morning. A small boat was sent ashore with Dr. Babcock and Lieut. Baya, and the prisoners landed. The officers and crew of the privateer then went ashore, and were greeted with the most enthusiastic demonstrations by the inhabitants. About half-past nine two lighter-boats went off to the brig with Capt. Coxetter and other officers. The starboard guns were thrown overboard to lighten the vessel, in order to clear her decks of water, and save as much as possible of the supplies on board the brig. Every effort was finally made to change her position, but it was supposed that the guns when thrown overboard stove her in and caused her to bilge. The lighter boats, however, were filled with a large amount of provisions and baggage, and finally succeeded in saving all the small-arms on board. About two o'clock all hands left, and were conveyed to St. Augustine. The crew afterwards arrived at Charleston. The brig became a total loss.

The Bonita, a brig built in New York, 1853, was 276 tons burden and 110 feet long, 25 feet wide, and 11 feet deep. She was previously engaged in the slave trade, but was captured on the coast of Africa and was taken to Charleston, and afterwards to Savannah, where she was seized by order of Gov. Brown, and converted into a vessel of war. She had always borne the character of a fast sailer, and was in perfect order.

The Sallie was a fore-and-aft schooner of one hundred and forty tons burden, mounted one long gun amidships, and had a crew consisting of forty men. She was previously the schooner Virginia, of Brookhaven, and was built at Port Jefferson in 1856. Her dimensions were: length, 97 feet 6 inches; breadth, 29 feet 4 inches; depth, 10 feet. She was commanded by Capt. Libby. She ran out from Charleston and made several prizes, among them the Betsey Ames and the brig Granada; both these vessels were sold in Charleston, under decree of Judge Magrath, of the Admiralty Court.

In New Orleans, by the end of May, there were the following prizes:

Name.	Master.	Where from.
SHIPS.		
Abælino	Smith	Boston.
Ariel	Delano	Bath, Maine.
American Union	Lincoln	Bath, Maine.
C. A. Farwell	Farwell	Rockland.
Express	Frost	Portsmouth, N. H.
J. H. Jarvis	Rich	Boston.
Marathon	Tyler	New York.
Marshall	Sprague	Providence.
Milan	Eustis	Bath, Maine.
Robert Harding	Ingraham	Boston.
State of Maine	Humphrey	Portland.
Toulon	Upshur	New York.
BARKS.		
Chester	Bearse	Boston.
Ocean Eagle	Luce	Thomaston.
BRIG.		
Panama		Provincetown.
SCHOONERS.		
E. S. Janes	Townsend	
Henry Travers	Wyatt	Baltimore.
Ella	Howes	Philadelphia.
John Adams		Provincetown.
Mermaid		Provincetown.

The seizure of vessels made by the Confederate States, up to the close of 1861, is thus enumerated:

Off the different ports	13
In port	30
Steamers captured on the Mississippi	15
Total	58

These prizes were sold under a decree of the Confederate Admiralty Court. In respect to some of them there were points raised as to the legal boundary of the "high seas;" but this was decided to be low-water mark.

The following vessels were formerly United States revenue-cutters, but were taken possession of by the Confederate Government, and armed for its service:

Schooners: Lewis Cass, Savannah, 40 men, one 68-pounder pivot; Washington, New Orleans, 42-pounder pivot; Pickens, Pensacola, 8-in. columbiad, four 24-inch carronades; Dodge, 100 tons, one long pivot; McClellan, Breshwood, one pivot, four side-guns.

Steamer: Bradford, formerly Ewing.

In addition to the above, the Navy Department of the insurrectionary Government purchased or fitted out the following vessels, which acted as privateers:

The Gordon was a small sea steamer of about 500 tons burden, drawing from seven to nine feet of water, and making an average of twelve miles an hour. She was about ten years old, and the most of that time she had been running in and out of Charleston harbor. In 1859 she was purchased by the Florida Steamship Company, and ran on the line between Charleston and Fernandina as consort to the Carolina, a steamer of her own size and build. The Gordon was fitted out as a vessel of war. She was employed along the coast islands at Hatteras, in and out of Pamlico Sound *via* Hatteras Inlet, when it was occupied by Union troops. She succeeded in running the blockade at Charleston, with some vessels which she had made prizes. She was armed with two guns, and was commanded by Capt. Lockwood, who was formerly engaged on the New York and Charleston line of steamers. His last employment, previous to this position, was as commander of the Carolina, on the Charleston and Fernandina line of steamers. He had succeeded in running the blockade with his vessel seventeen times. The last feat of the Theodora, to which the name of the Gordon had been changed, was to carry to Cuba the ministers, Slidell and Mason.

The Coffee, a side-wheel steamer carrying 2 guns, the steamer Marion, and the schooner York, were consorts of the Gordon in Hatteras Inlet. The Coffee was wrecked—a total loss.

The McRea, formerly the steamer Habana, plying between the ports of New Orleans and Havana, was a propeller of 500 tons burden; she was built in Philadelphia in 1859, and was owned in New Orleans previous to her being used as a privateer. She carried a 64-pounder, mounted on a pivot, four 8-inch columbiads, and a rifled 24-pounder. She succeeded in running the blockade at the mouth of the Mississippi River.

The steamer Lady Davis was one of the first vessels prepared in Charleston, and was intended for the harbor defence. She was purchased by Gov. Pickens, at Richmond. She received her name in honor of the wife of Jefferson Davis. She was armed with two 24-pounders, regularly equipped, and commanded by Capt. T. B. Huger.

The Nina was a small steam gunboat, mounting one light gun.

The Jackson was a steamer, 200 tons, armed with two 8-inch columbiads. She was commanded by Capt. Gwathemy.

The Incarora, steamer, carried one 8-inch columbiad, and a 32-pounder rifled cannon.

The little steamer George Page, operating

on Occoquan River and Quantico Creek, was famous for her boldness in running down to within gunshot of the Federal batteries, and occasionally throwing a shell into them, thereby keeping up continuous alarm.

The Judith, schooner, of 250 tons, armed with a heavy pivot-gun, and four broadside guns, was destroyed in Pensacola harbor, September 13. The Union loss was 3 killed, 12 wounded.

The Yorktown was formerly used in the New York and Virginia line of steamers. She was a side-wheel steamer of 1,400 tons burden, built in New York in 1859; length, 251 feet; breadth, 34 feet; depth, 18 feet. She had been completely fitted out at Norfolk, her sides having been plated with iron, and other means taken to strengthen her, and to render her formidable. She was commanded by Capt. Parish, her old commander, and carried two pivots, and six broadside guns.

The Everglade was a small side-wheel steamer, purchased by the State of Georgia for the sum of $34,000. She was made a gunboat, for the purpose of cruising as a coast-guard at the mouth of the Savannah River. Her officers, as at first appointed, were as follows: commander, J. McIntosh Kell; midshipmen, R. F. Armstrong, S. N. Hooper, J. A. Merriweather; chief engineer, Joshua Smith; assistant engineer, Norval Meeker; clerk, William J. Bennett.

The North Carolina steamer Winslow, Lieut. Crossman commanding, captured off Cape Hatteras the schooner Transit, Knowles master, last from Key West. The prize was in ballast, having sailed from New York for Key West with provisions, shot, etc., about the 27th of May. Having landed her cargo safely at Key West, the Transit was upon her return north when captured. She was a fine schooner, of 195 tons burden, and was built at a cost of $13,000. She was copper-fastened up to 9 feet, and had galvanized iron fastenings above that. She belonged to New London, Conn. The prize was carried to Newbern, by Lieut. Seawell. Lieut. Crossman also captured off Cape Hatteras, the Hannah Balch, a hermaphrodite brig, which was captured previously off Savannah by the United States ship Flag, Lieut. Sarton. She was just from Cardenas, and laden with 150 barrels of molasses.

The little schooner Savannah was formerly pilot boat No. 7, doing duty in Charleston harbor, 54 tons burden. She carried one 18-pounder amidships, and was commanded by T. Harrison Baker, of Charleston, and had a crew of 20 men. On the 1st of June she captured the brig Joseph, of Maine, from Cuba, loaded with sugar, and sent her into Georgetown, S. C., in charge of eight men. On the 3d of June, off Charleston, she fell in with the U. S. brig Perry, which she mistook for a merchantman, and immediately engaged, but was soon taken. Her crew were placed in irons on board the United States steamer Minnesota, and she was sent to New York, in charge of prize-master McCook. Her appearance created great interest among the people, on account of her being the first privateer captured, and crowds of people flocked to the Battery, off which she lay, to see the little craft. She was afterward taken to the navy yard.

CHAPTER VIII.

March of Gen. McClellan into Western Virginia—His Address to the Inhabitants—Surprise at Philippi—Battle at Laurel Hill—Defeat and Surrender of the Enemy—Manassas—Position of the Northern and Southern Armies—Forces of Gen. McDowell—Advance to Centreville—Battle of Bull Run—Retreat.

Military operations now began to be conducted with more concentrated forces. From the first moment great activity in raising troops had prevailed in the State of Ohio.

Gen. George B. MClellan was invited from his duties in connection with the Ohio and Mississippi Railroad by the Governor of Ohio, and appointed to the chief command in the State. Under his directions the volunteers were organized, and preparations for a campaign made. Early in May the forces were ready to cooperate with the two or three regiments organized in Western Virginia, to oppose the advance of Virginia troops. The occupation of Western Virginia, which had voted against the ordinance of secession, and its control, was early an object with the Confederate Government. To oppose them, Gen. McClellan pushed forward, under the orders of the United States Government.

On the 26th of May he issued the following proclamation to the people of Western Virginia, from his headquarters at Cincinnati, Ohio:

To the Union Men of Western Virginia.

Virginians: The General Government has long enough endured the machinations of a few factious rebels in your midst. Armed traitors have in vain endeavored to deter you from expressing your loyalty at the polls. Having failed in this infamous attempt to deprive you of the exercise of your dearest rights, they now seek to inaugurate a reign of terror, and thus force you to yield to their schemes and submit to the yoke of traitorous conspiracy dignified by the name of the Southern Confederacy. They are destroying the property of citizens of your State and ruining your magnificent railways.

The General Government has heretofore carefully

abstained from sending troops across the Ohio, or even from posting them along its banks, although frequently urged by many of your prominent citizens to do so. It determined to wait the result of the State election, desirous that no one might be able to say that the slightest effort had been made from this side to influence the free expression of your opinions, although the many agencies brought to bear upon you by the rebels were well known. You have now shown, under the most adverse circumstances, that the great mass of the people of Western Virginia are true and loyal to that beneficent Government under which we and our fathers lived so long.

As soon as the result of the election was known, the traitors commenced their work of destruction. The General Government cannot close its ears to the demand you have made for assistance. I have ordered troops to cross the river. They come as your friends and brothers—as enemies only to armed rebels, who are preying upon you; your homes, your families, and your property are safe under our protection. All your rights shall be religiously respected, notwithstanding all that has been said by the traitors to induce you to believe our advent among you will be signalized by an interference with your slaves. Understand one thing clearly: not only will we abstain from all such interference, but we will, on the contrary, with an iron hand crush any attempt at insurrection on their part. Now that we are in your midst, I call upon you to fly to arms and support the General Government; sever the connection that binds you to traitors; proclaim to the world that the faith and loyalty so long boasted by the Old Dominion are still preserved in Western Virginia, and that you remain true to the Stars and Stripes.

G. B. McCLELLAN,
Major-General Commanding.

On the same day he issued the following proclamation to his troops:

SOLDIERS: You are ordered to cross the frontier and enter on the soil of Virginia. Your mission is to restore peace and confidence, to protect the majesty of the law, and secure our brethren from the grasp of armed traitors. I place under the safeguard of your honor the persons and property of the Virginians. I know you will respect their feelings and all their rights, and preserve the strictest discipline. Remember, each one of you holds in his keeping the honor of Ohio and of the Union. If you are called upon to overcome armed opposition, I know your courage is equal to the task. Remember, that your only foes are armed traitors, and show mercy even to them when in your power, for many of them are misguided. When, under your protection, the loyal men of Western Virginia shall have been enabled to organize and form until they can protect themselves, you can return to your homes with the proud satisfaction of having preserved a gallant people from destruction.

G. B. McCLELLAN,
Major-General Commanding.

The instructions to General McClellan were to cross the Ohio, and, in conjunction with the forces of Western Virginia under Colonel Kelly, to drive out the Confederate force, and advance on Harper's Ferry. On the night of the 26th of May, orders were given to Colonel Kelly at Wheeling, to march on Grafton, which he proceeded to execute early the next morning with the First Virginia Volunteers. He was followed on the same day by the Sixteenth Ohio, Colonel Irvine, which had been stationed at Bellair, Ohio. These forces advanced by the Baltimore and Ohio Railroad. At the same time, the Fourteenth Ohio, Colonel Steadman, crossed the Ohio at Marietta, and occupied Parkersburg. These, advancing on the railroad, were welcomed by crowds at every station. On the same night, a Confederate force of 1,500 men evacuated Grafton, and that place was occupied, on the 29th, by the Virginia and Ohio Volunteers. Here they were joined by the Seventh and Ninth Indiana. The Confederate force, in the mean time, had retired to Philippi, where they prepared to make a stand with considerable strength. Philippi is twenty-four miles from Grafton, and General McClellan determined to surprise the Confederate force. On the night of June 2, two divisions moved forward to accomplish this purpose. The surprise was complete, and the Confederate force, under Colonel G. A. Porterfield, was forced to retire, abandoning a large amount of stores and arms, with a loss of fifteen killed. Owing to the storm and the darkness of the night, the first division, under Colonel Kelly, was unable to arrive in the rear of the Confederate force soon enough to cut off its retreat. This force retired to Laurel Hill, in the vicinity of Beverly, where the enemy was concentrated in a strongly fortified position, which not only commanded the road to the southern part of the State, whence the Confederate supplies were obtained, but from which an attack upon the Federal forces was constantly threatened. Laurel Hill is on the western slope of a range of the Alleghany Mountains, which runs from northeast to southwest, and which is impassable for an army except at certain points. The Confederate encampment was on a slope which declined gradually to the valley, and was strongly fortified in front, below which passed the only road to southern Virginia. The plan of General McClellan was to occupy the attention of the enemy, by the appearance of a direct attack, while a strong force marched round to his rear to take possession of the road by which his supplies came. The enemy must then either come out of his intrenchments and fight, or starve. Taking the main body of his army, composing a force of ten thousand men, General McClellan moved to Clarksburg, and thence to Buckhannon, on the west of Laurel Hill. Previously however, and on the 7th of July, he ordered General Morris to march upon Laurel Hill, to occupy the enemy. Taking with him the Ninth Indiana, Colonel Milroy, the Fourteenth Ohio, the First Virginia, the Cleveland Artillery, the Sixth and Seventh Indiana, and the Sixth Ohio, in the order named and making a force of about 4,000 men, he left early in the morning, and reached Bealington in front of the enemy at eight o'clock, with his right, having flanking parties on each side, and two companies of skirmishers ahead. The Confederate pickets fired and retreated. A slight skirmish ensued with a party of the enemy in a wood beyond the town, about two miles from the Confederate camp, which the Federal force had occupied. On the 8th, a brisk skirmishing was kept up all the afternoon with the Confederates, and some were killed on both sides. On the 9th, the skirmishing was renewed, and every outlet of the Confederate camp was watched except that back to Beverly, where General McClellan was soon expected to be. Thus the enemy was held in check on the north and occupied, while General McClellan was attempting to get in his rear. Meantime, as General McClellan reached Buckhannon, he found that the rear of the enemy was strongly fortified at a position called Rich Mountain, which was defended by one to two thousand men, under Colonel Pegram. He now formed the plan of capturing this entire force. For this purpose, General Rosecrans with about three thousand men was sent to attack his rear, while General McClellan himself made a direct attack in front. General Rosecrans with the Eighth, Tenth, Thirteenth Indiana, and Nineteenth Ohio, therefore proceeded, on the 11th, along the line of hills southeast of the enemy's intrenched camp on the Beverly road, to make an attack on the east side, while General McClellan made it on the west side, as soon as he heard from General Rosecrans. A courier, who mistook the road through the enemy's camp for the route of the troops, gave the enemy intelligence of the movement. Their position was about two miles west from Beverly, which is on the east side of what is called Rich Mountain, a gap in the Laurel Hill range, through which the southern road passes. General Rosecrans arrived in the rear of the enemy at four o'clock, and meeting a small force, immediately began the attack, to which they made a vigorous resistance, but were unable to withstand it. The effect was to alarm Colonel Pegram, and upon finding out his exposed position he silently moved off with his main body, with the hope of being able to join the camp at Laurel Hill. Meanwhile General McClellan was in position with his whole force during the afternoon ready to make an assault, but heard nothing from the other column except distant firing. Early in the morning he was about proceeding to plant cannon upon an eminence commanding a portion of the Confederate camp, and preparing to attack the whole next in front, when it was ascertained that the enemy had evacuated his position during the night, moving towards Laurel Hill, leaving only a few men in charge of the sick, cannon, and camp equipage and transportation.

The following despatch from General McClellan thus announced these movements:

RICH MOUNTAIN, VA., 9 A. M., *July* 12.

Col. E. D. Townsend, Assistant-Adjutant General:

We are in possession of all the enemy's works up to a point in sight of Beverly. We have taken all his guns; a very large amount of wagons, tents, &c.; every thing he had; and also a large number of prisoners, many of whom are wounded, and amongst whom are several officers. They lost many killed. We have lost in all, perhaps twenty killed and forty wounded, of whom all but two or three were in the column under Col. Rosecrans, which turned the position. The mass of the enemy escaped through the woods entirely disorganized. Among the prisoners is Dr. Taylor, formerly of the army. Col. Pegram was in command.

Col. Rosecrans' column left camp yesterday morning and marched some eight miles through the mountains, reaching the turnpike some two or three miles in the rear of the enemy. He defeated an advanced force, and took a couple of guns. I had a position ready for twelve guns near the main camp, and as the guns were moving up I ascertained that the enemy had retreated. I am now pushing on to Beverly—a part of Colonel Rosecrans' troops being now within three miles of that place. Our success is complete and almost bloodless. I doubt whether Wise and Johnston will unite and overpower me. The behavior of our troops in action and towards prisoners was admirable. G. B. McCLELLAN,
Major-General Commanding.

By the retreat of Colonel Pegram, the rear of the Confederate force at Laurel Hill was entirely exposed. On the 11th, General Garnett first learned that General McClellan was in his rear. He immediately evacuated his camp, and retired before General Morris, hoping to reach Beverly in advance of General McClellan, and thus be able to withdraw his forces by the road to southern Virginia. Upon arriving within three miles of Beverly, the fugitives of Colonel Pegram's force were met, and finding escape impossible by that route, General Garnett returned towards Laurel Hill, and took the road branching off to the northeast towards St. George, in Tucker County. His aim was now to press along the base of the mountains down the Cheat River, with the hope of finding some practicable path across the mountains into the valley of Virginia. The following despatch of General McClellan describes the precise state of affairs at this time:

BEVERLY, VA., *July* 13, 1861.

To Col. E. D. Townsend:

The success of to-day is all that I could desire. We captured six brass cannon, of which one was rifled; all their camp equipage and transportation, even to their cups. The number of tents will probably reach two hundred, and more than sixty wagons. Their killed and wounded will fully amount to one hundred and fifty. We have at least one hundred prisoners, and more coming in constantly. I know already of ten officers killed and prisoners. Their retreat is complete. We occupied Beverly by a rapid march. Garnett abandoned his camp early this morning, leaving his camp equipage. He came within a few miles of Beverly, but our rapid march turned him back in great confusion, and he is now retreating on the road to St. George. I have ordered Gen. Morris to follow him up closely. I have telegraphed for the Second Pennsylvania Regiment at Cumberland to join Gen. Hill at Rowlesburg. The General is concentrating all his troops at Rowlesburg, to cut off Garnett's retreat, if possible, to St. George. I may say we have driven out some ten thousand troops, strongly intrenched, with the loss of eleven killed and thirty-five wounded. Provision returns were found showing Garnett's force to have been ten thousand men. They were Eastern Virginians, Georgians, Tennesseans, and, I think, Carolinians. To-morrow I can give full particulars, &c. Will move on Huttonsville to-morrow and endeavor to seize the Cheat Mountain pass, where there are now but few troops. I hope that Gen. Cox has by this time driven Wise out of the Kanawha valley. In that case I shall have accomplished the object of liberating Western Virginia. I hope the General will approve my operations. G. B. McCLELLAN,
Major-General Commanding.

Up the mountains, through defiles, and

over rugged ridges, guided by the tents, camp-furniture, provisions, and knapsacks thrown away, the hot pursuit of the flying enemy was pressed. Capt. Bonham led the advance, and Gen. Morris the rear, and after fording Cheat River four times, they came up with the enemy's rear guard at Carrick's Ford, where the enemy attempted to make a stand, but were attacked on the right flank and forced to retire. At another turn in the river, about a quarter of a mile below, the enemy again attempted to stand. Gen. Garnett tried in vain to rally his men and gather them around him. While he was thus standing with his back to the Federal forces, he received a Minié ball on the left of the spine. It made a terrible wound, piercing the heart and coming out at the right nipple. He threw up his arm and fell dead. The Confederate rout was now complete. Only about two thousand of the troops with which Gen. Garnett left his intrenchments, escaped. Gen. McClellan's despatch was as follows:

HUTTONSVILLE, July 14, 1861.

To Edw. Townsend.

Garnett and forces routed. His baggage and one gun taken. His army demoralized. Garnett killed.

We have annihilated the enemy in Western Virginia, and have lost thirteen killed and not more than forty wounded. We have in all killed at least two hundred of the enemy, and their prisoners will amount to at least one thousand. Have taken seven guns in all.

I still look for the capture of the remnant of Garnett's army by Gen. Hill.

The troops defeated are the crack regiments of Eastern Virginia, aided by Georgians, Tennesseans, and Carolinians.

Our success is complete, and secession is killed in this country. G. B. McCLELLAN,
Maj.-Gen. Commanding.

Meantime Col. Pegram, hearing of the retreat of Gen. Garnett, surrendered the remnant of his force to Gen. McClellan, who now issued the following address to his soldiers:

WESTERN VIRGINIA, BEVERLY, VA., July 19, 1861.

Soldiers of the Army of the West:

I am more than satisfied with you. You have annihilated two armies, commanded by educated and experienced soldiers, intrenched in mountain fastnesses and fortified at their leisure. You have taken five guns, twelve colors, fifteen hundred stand of arms, one thousand prisoners, including more than forty officers. One of the second commanders of the rebels is a prisoner, the other lost his life on the field of battle. You have killed more than two hundred and fifty of the enemy, who has lost all his baggage and camp equipage. All this has been accomplished with the loss of twenty brave men killed and sixty wounded on your part.

You have proved that Union men, fighting for the preservation of our Government, are more than a match for our misguided and erring brothers. More than this, you have shown mercy to the vanquished. You have made long and arduous marches, with insufficient food, frequently exposed to the inclemency of the weather. I have not hesitated to demand this of you, feeling that I could rely on your endurance, patriotism, and courage. In the future I may have still greater demands to make upon you, still greater sacrifices for you to offer. It shall be my care to provide for you to the extent of my ability; but I know now that, by your valor and endurance, you will accomplish all that is asked.

Soldiers! I have confidence in you, and I trust you have learned to confide in me. Remember that discipline and subordination are qualities of equal value with courage. I am proud to say that you have gained the highest reward that American troops can receive—the thanks of Congress and the applause of your fellow-citizens. GEORGE B. McCLELLAN,
Major-General.

Gen. McClellan was subsequently called to the active command of the Army of the Potomac.

Frequent collisions or skirmishes continued to take place between detached parties or at small advanced posts, as at Bunker Hill in Virginia, on July 15th; Millville, Missouri, on the 16th, Barboursville, Virginia, and Fulton, Missouri, on the 17th. Some loss was thus inflicted on each side.

But movements of a more important character were now progressing in Virginia near Washington.

The Southern Government having inclined to the defensive policy as that upon which they should act, their first object was to prevent an advance of any Federal force into Virginia. Early in the month of May troops were assembled in Richmond, and pushed forward toward the northeastern boundary of the State, to a position known as Manassas Junction. The name is given to this hilly region, as it is here that a railroad from Alexandria, another from Staunton up the valley and through Manassas Gap, and another from Gordonsville unite. At Gordonsville the railroad from Richmond and the line from East Tennessee unite. As a point for concentration none more eligible exists in northeastern Virginia. The advantages for fortification are naturally such that the place can be rendered impregnable. Here the centre of the northern force of the Southern army was posted, with the left wing pushed forward to Winchester, and the right extended to the Potomac, and sustained by heavy batteries which served to blockade the river.

The Federal force, the advance of which was assembled at Washington for the defence of that city against any attack by the Southern troops, was posted on the Virginia side of the Potomac, on Arlington Heights, which were strongly fortified. Their right was pushed some distance up the Potomac, and chiefly on the Maryland side, while their left occupied Alexandria. The armies of both sides consisted of raw militia hastily brought together, and of volunteers who for the first time had put on the uniform, and taken up the weapons of the soldier. On both sides the forces were constantly accumulating. On the morning of June 27th, the consolidated report of Gen. Mansfield, commanding the Department of Washington, gives the number of troops in that city and vicinity. The privates, including regulars and volunteers present for duty, numbered 22,846 men. The grand aggregate of the force, including officers, etc., present and absent, was 34,160 men. The force of Gen. Patterson, commanding in Maryland above Washington, and also on the Virginia side of the Potomac, on the 28th of June, was returned, embracing officers and men enlisted and present for duty, 15,923. Of these about 550 were reported as sick.

The Confederate force was largely increased by troops from South Carolina, Georgia, Mississippi, Alabama, and Texas. On the night after the battle Mr. Davis sent a despatch to Richmond by telegraph, saying: "The battle was mainly fought on our left. Our force was 15,000; that of the enemy estimated at 35,000.

Gen. McDowell in his official report says: "We crossed Bull Run with about 18,000 men, of all arms." "The numbers opposed to us have been variously estimated. I may safely say, and avoid even the appearance of exaggeration, that the enemy brought up all he could, which were not kept engaged elsewhere."

The force under Gen. McDowell, on the 8th of July, was organized into five divisions. The first division, under Brig.-Gen. Tyler, consisted of four brigades. The regiments in each brigade were as follows: First brigade, under Col. Keyes, First, Second, Third, Connecticut; Fourth Maine; Varian's battery, and Company B, Second Cavalry. In the second brigade, under Col. Schenck, the regiments were as follows: First, Second, Ohio; Second New York, and Company E, Second Artillery. In the third brigade, under Col. W. T. Sherman, were the Thirteenth, Sixty-ninth, Seventy-ninth, New York; Second Wisconsin; and Company E, Third Artillery. In the fourth brigade, under Col. Richardson, Second, Third, Michigan; First Massachusetts; Twelfth New York.

In the second division, under Col. David Hunter, were two brigades. These contained the following regiments: In the first brigade, under Col. Porter, were the Eighth, Fourteenth, New York; battalion of regular infantry; Companies G and L, Second Cavalry; Company —, Fifth Artillery. In the second brigade, under Col. Burnside, were the First, Second, Rhode Island; Seventy-first New York; Second New Hampshire; battery of Light Artillery, R. I.

In the third division, under Col. Heintzelman, were three brigades with the following regiments: In the first brigade, under Col. Franklin, were the Fourth Pennsylvania; Fifth Massachusetts; First Minnesota; Company E, Second Cavalry; Company I, First Artillery. In the second brigade, under Col. Wilcox, were the First Michigan; Eleventh New York; Company D, Second Artillery. In the third brigade, under Col. Howard, were the Second, Fourth, Fifth, Maine; Second Vermont.

In the fourth division, under Brig.-Gen. Runyon, as a reserve, were the following regiments: First, Second, Third, Fourth, New Jersey three-months' volunteers, and First, Second, Third, New Jersey three years' volunteers.

In the fifth division, under Col. Miles, were two brigades. In the first brigade were the following volunteers, Col. Blenker commanding: Eighth, Twenty-ninth, New York; Garibaldi Guard, and Twenty-fourth Pennsylvania. In the second brigade under Col. Davies, were the Sixteenth, Eighteenth, Thirty-first, Thirty-second, New York; Company G, Second Artillery.

The movement of troops to attack the Southern army commenced on the 16th of July. It was first made known to the inhabitants of Washington by their sudden disappearance from the opposite or Virginia side of the Potomac. The force comprised in this movement consisted of five divisions, as above mentioned, but a few of the details were altered. A body of five hundred mariners was also added. On the 17th, the advance of Gen. McDowell's entire command was begun. It was made by four different routes. The right wing, composed of the first division of four brigades under Gen. Tyler, moved by the Georgetown road. The centre, composed of the second division of two brigades under Col. Hunter, advanced by the Leesburg and Centreville road. The left wing, consisting of the third division of three brigades, under Col. Heintzelman, moved by the Little River turnpike, and the other part of the wing, consisting of the fifth division of two brigades, under Col. Miles, proceeded by the old Braddock road. The reserve consisted of the fourth division of New Jersey troops, under Gen. Runyon.

The following order, issued by Gen. McDowell from his headquarters at Arlington on July 5th, shows the condition of the men when ready to march:

When troops are paraded in light marching order, they will be equipped as follows: Their arms, accoutrements, and ammunition—the cartridge-boxes filled. Their haversacks, with three days' cooked rations; their blankets in a roll, with the ends tied to each other, across the shoulder; and where it is possible, a pair of stockings inside of the blanket. Their canteens and cups; knapsacks will be packed and left in the tent under a guard of the regiment, consisting of those men least able to march, and to the number to be specially designated for each corps. Knapsacks should be numbered or marked in such way as will enable them to be readily claimed by their owners. Commanding officers of brigades will take measures to diminish as quickly as possible the baggage of the regiments under their commands, by sending away every thing not absolutely necessary. This will apply to the personal effects of the officers and men, as well as to military property.

Near Fairfax Court House obstructions had been placed by the Southern troops upon all the roads upon which the divisions advanced. The division of the centre marched with the left brigade in front. This placed the Rhode Island troops, under Col. Burnside, in advance. The Second regiment was employed as skirmishers in front of the division. Their lines extended from half a mile to two miles on each side of the road. The Confederate troops retired as fast as the head of the advancing column made its appearance. Within three miles of the Court House the division encountered the first barricade, consisting of trees felled and thrown across the road. The second was of a similar character. They occasioned only a few moments' delay. The third barricade was more formidable. It was at the entrance of a deep cut, about half way up a steep hill, crowned on one side by a thick wood, and on the other by an open field. A road was made through the field, and the army passed around. When the central division reached the village of Fairfax Court House, an order was sent to the left wing to halt, and Gen. McDowell with his staff, escorted by a squadron of dragoons, proceeded to Germantown, where the right wing was halted. It was his desire to push forward without delay to Centreville.

Germantown is a small village on the road from Fairfax Court House to Centreville, and about one-fourth of the distance beyond the former.

The order to move forward was first given to all divisions of the army on the 15th. Gen. Tyler, of the right wing, communicated it to his troops that evening, with orders to be ready to move at 2 P. M. on the 16th, provided with cooked rations for three days. Precisely at that hour the right wing began to move forward, and reached Vienna, and encamped for the night.

At 5 o'clock the next morning, the onward march was renewed. It was necessarily slow, owing to the obstructions placed in the road. The enemy during the day rapidly retreated upon the approach of the Federal army. Germantown was reached soon after noon. Col. Miles' division of the left wing was at the crossing of the old Braddock road with the road from Fairfax Court House to Fairfax Station, on the railroad, when ordered to halt. On the 18th it was ordered forward to Centreville by the old Braddock road. The other brigades of this wing halted at Fairfax Station and below. Eleven of the enemy's force were made prisoners at this station.

The right wing, Gen. Tyler, resumed its march from Germantown to Centreville at 7 o'clock on the morning of the next day, the 18th. Upon coming in sight of Centreville, the town proved to have been evacuated. Part of the division proceeded through the village, and turning into a by-road to the right, advanced a short distance toward Bull Run, a valley traversed by a creek about three miles from Centreville. A halt was then commanded, and the whole division encamped on both sides of the road.

About 11 o'clock, Gen. Tyler proceeded to make a reconnoissance in force. He took the fourth brigade of his division, composed of the Second and Third Michigan, First Massachusetts, and Twelfth New York, under Col. Richardson, together with Ayres' battery, and four companies of cavalry. Advancing south on the road from Centreville to Manassas, which crosses Bull Run at Blackburn's Ford through a long stretch of timber, for about two miles, they came to an opening, when sight was caught of a strong body of the enemy. Ayres' battery was ordered to advance and open on them from a commanding elevation. Hardly had the firing well commenced, when it was replied to by a battery which had not been seen, at a distance down the road. Some of the grape shot from this battery killed two horses of the cavalry drawn up in a body on a hill, and wounded two of the men. A vigorous response being kept up by Ayres' battery, the enemy soon retired into the woods, when the firing ceased. The Second Michigan was then ordered to deploy as skirmishers on the left of the road, and advance into the wood. They briskly moved forward and entered the timber, and quickly after their disappearance a lively exchange of rifle shots took place for a few minutes. This was soon followed by a succession of volleys, evidently discharged by large bodies of men. The Third Michigan, the First Massachusetts, and the Twelfth New York, composing the remainder of the brigade, were then ordered to advance toward the wood. This was promptly done. They then drew up in battle array in front and on the right of the timber. All this time the firing in the woods went on in the liveliest style. Companies G and H and others of the First Massachusetts, and some companies of the New York Twelfth, were then ordered into the woods as skirmishers, at the same time the cavalry and two howitzers advanced to their edge. Meanwhile the firing within was kept up. The howitzers then threw some grape shot into the timber, when a terrific series of volleys of musketry was discharged from the woods upon the troops outside. At the same time a battery opened from an elevation in the rear, and poured a storm of grape and canister at the Federal troops. Fortunately the fire was aimed too high, and few outside the woods were hit. A retreat was now ordered, and the whole brigade retired, and formed behind their battery on the hill. In doing this, the Twelfth New York and a portion of the First Massachusetts broke ranks and scattered in different directions for some distance on their retreat.

At this time the third brigade, under Col. Sherman, came up, headed by the Sixty-ninth New York. The fire was now reopened from the battery, and continued about an hour, to which the enemy's battery vigorously replied. Their shot and shells struck the houses in front of the battery, and raked the woods in the rear for a considerable distance. A retreat was then ordered by Gen. McDowell, who had come up, and the entire force fell back, having suffered a loss of one hundred killed and wounded.

This reconnoissance developed a degree of strength and preparation on the part of the enemy greater than had been anticipated. During the day the centre and left wings came up, and the whole force was concentrated at Centreville.

The next two days were passed by the Federal force in strengthening its position. Meantime the Commander-in-Chief was occupied in obtaining more accurate knowedge of the position and strength of the enemy, and arranging his plans for an attack. The result of these reconnoitrings is shown in the order of battle subsequently issued.

Meanwhile it would appear that an attack upon the Federal forces was contemplated by the Commander of the Confederate army. Probably he was anticipated by the attack of Gen. McDowell. This appears from documents found in the camp at Manassas, after its evacuation by the Confederate force early in 1862. One of these papers contains the plan of battle, and shows by the details that the Confederate force was not inferior to that of the Federal army. It is as follows:

[CONFIDENTIAL.]

Special Order No.—.

HEADQUARTERS ARMY OF POTOMAC, July 20, 1861.

The following order is published for the information of division and brigade commanders:

1. Brig.-Gen. Ewell's brigade, supported by Gen. Holmes' brigade, will march *via* Union Mills Ford and place itself in position of attack upon the enemy. It will be held in readiness either to support the attack upon Centreville, or to move in the direction of Santer's Cross Roads, according to circumstances. The order to advance will be given by the Commander-in-Chief.

2. Brig.-Gen. Jones' brigade, supported by Col. Earl's brigade, will march *via* McLane's Ford to place itself in position of attack upon the enemy on or about the Union Mills and Centreville road. It will be held in readiness either to support the attack on Centreville, or to move in the direction of Fairfax Station, according to circumstances, with its right flank toward the left of Ewell's command, more or less distant, according to the nature of the country and attack. The order to advance will be given by the Commander-in-Chief.

3. Brig.-Gen. Longstreet's brigade, supported by Brig.-Gen. Jackson's brigade, will march *via* McLane's Ford to place itself in position of attack upon the enemy on or about the Union Mills and Centreville roads. It will be held in readiness either to support the attack on Centreville or to move in the direction of Fairfax Court House, according to circumstances, with its right flank toward the left of Jones' command, more or less distant, according to the nature of the country. The order to advance will be given by the Commander-in-Chief.

4. Brig.-Gen. Bonham's brigade, supported by Col. Bartow's brigade, will march *via* Mitchell's Ford to the attack of Centreville. The right wing to the left of the third division, more or less distant, according to the nature of the country and of the attack. The order to advance will be given by the Commander-in-Chief.

5. Col. Cooke's brigade, supported by Col. Elzy's brigade, will march, *via* Stone Bridge and the fords on the right thereof, to the attack of Centreville. The right wing to the left of the fourth division, more or less distant, according to the nature of the country and of the attack. The order to advance will be given by the Commander-in-Chief.

6. Brig.-Gen. Bee's brigade, supported by Col. Wilcox's brigade, Col. Stuart's regiment of cavalry, and the whole of Walton's battery, will form the reserve, and will march *via* Mitchell's Ford, to be used according to circumstances.

The light batteries will be distributed as follows:

1. To Brig.-Gen. Ewell's command—Capt. Walker, six pieces.

2. To Brig.-Gen. Jones'—Captains Albertis' and Stonewood's batteries, eight pieces.

3. To Brig.-Gen. Longstreet's—Col. Pendleton's and Capt. Imboden's batteries, eight pieces.

4. To Brig.-Gen. Bonham's—Captains Kemper's and Shields' batteries, eight pieces.

5. To Col. Cooke's—Col. Hemton's and Captains Latham's and Beckwith's batteries, twelve pieces.

Col. Radford, commanding cavalry, will detail to report immediately, as follows:

To Brig.-Gen. Ewell, two companies cavalry.

To Brig.-Gen. Jones, two companies cavalry.

To Brig.-Gen. Longstreet, two companies cavalry.

To Brig.-Gen. Bonham, three companies cavalry.

To Col. Cooke, the remaining companies of cavalry, except those in special service.

7. The fourth and fifth divisions, after the fall of Centreville, will advance to the attack of Fairfax Court House *via* the Braddock and Turnpike roads, to the north of the latter. The first, second, and third divisions will, if necessary, support the fourth and fifth divisions.

8. In this movement the first, second, and third divisions will form the command of Brig.-Gen. Holmes. The fourth and fifth divisions, that of the second in command.

The reserve will move upon the plains between Mitchell's Ford and Stone Bridge, and, together with the fourth and fifth divisions, will be under the immediate direction of Gen. Beauregard.

By command of Gen. BEAUREGARD.

THOMAS JORDAN, A. A. Adjt.-Gen.

Special Order No. —.

HEADQUARTERS ARMY OF THE POTOMAC, July 20, 1861.

The plan of attack given by Brig.-Gen. Beauregard, in the above order, is approved, and will be executed accordingly.

J. E. JOHNSTON, Gen. C. S. A.

Mitchell's Ford, spoken of in the above orders, is a short distance above Blackburn's Ford. McLane's Ford is about the same distance below Blackburn's Ford. Union Mills is still further below, near the crossing of the Alexandria and Orange Railroad.

The result of observations on the part of Gen. McDowell convinced him that the mass of the Southern force had not been advanced from Manassas to the back of the creek called Bull Run. This tortuous stream runs from northwest to southeast, through the entire field of battle. At the extreme part on the northwest, is Sudley's Spring, where it is fordable; three miles lower down is a crossing known as the Stone Bridge, and still lower is Blackburn's Ford; further down is Union Mills, mentioned in Gen. Beauregard's order. Centreville is a village of a few houses, mostly on the west side of a ridge running nearly north and south. The road from Centreville to Manassas Junction was along this ridge, and crossed Bull Run about three miles from the former place. Through Centreville, running nearly east and west, passes the Warrenton turnpike, and crosses Bull Run about four miles distant.

The conviction of Gen. McDowell was that the mass of the enemy's force was at Manassas. He says in his report: "On the evening of the 20th my command was mostly at or near Centreville. The enemy was at or near Manassas, distant from Centreville about seven miles to the southwest." Thus conceiving the mass of the Confederate army to be at Manassas, the order of battle was prepared accordingly, and issued on the night of the 20th, to be executed the next day. It was manifest that the crossing of Bull Run would be disputed; but the greatest contest, anticipated the next day, was expected to come when the attempt should be made to destroy the railroad leading from Manassas to the valley of Virginia. The orders for the 21st were as follows:

HEADQUARTERS DEPARTMENT ARMY EASTERN VA., CENTREVILLE, July 20, 1861.

The enemy has planted a battery on the Warrenton turnpike to defend the passage of Bull Run; has seized the Stone Bridge and made a heavy abatis on the right bank, to oppose our advance in that direction. The ford above the bridge is also guarded, whether with artillery or not is not positively known, but every indication favors the belief that he proposes to defend the passage of the stream.

It is intended to turn the position, force the enemy from the road, that it may be reopened, and, if possible, destroy the railroad leading from Manassas to the valley of Virginia, where the enemy has a large force. As this may be resisted by all the force of the enemy, the troops will be disposed as follows:

The first division (Gen. Tyler's), with the exception of Richardson's brigade, will, at half-past two o'clock in the morning precisely, be on the Warrenton turnpike to threaten the passage of the bridge, but will not open fire until full daybreak.

The second division (Hunter's) will move from its camp at two o'clock in the morning precisely, and, led by Capt. Woodbury, of the Engineers, will, after passing Cub Run, turn to the right and pass the Bull Run stream above the ford at Sudley's Spring, and then turning down to the left, descend the stream and clear away the enemy who may be guarding the lower ford and bridge. It will then bear off to the right and make room for the succeeding division.

The third division (Heintzelman's) will march at half-past two o'clock in the morning, and follow the road taken by the second division, but will cross at the lower ford after it has been turned as above, and then, going to the left, take place between the stream and second division.

The fifth division (Miles') will take position on the Centreville Heights (Richardson's brigade will, for the time, form part of the fifth division, and will continue in its present position). One brigade will be in the village, and one near the present station of Richardson's brigade. This division will threaten the Blackburn Ford, and remain in reserve at Centreville. The commander will open fire with artillery only, and will bear in mind that it is a demonstration only he is to make. He will cause such defensive works, abatis, earthworks, etc., to be thrown up as will strengthen his position. Lieut. Prime, of the Engineers, will be charged with this duty.

These movements may lead to the gravest results, and commanders of divisions and brigades should bear in mind the immense consequences involved. There must be no failure, and every effort must be made to prevent straggling.

No one must be allowed to leave the ranks without special authority. After completing the movements ordered, the troops must be held in order of battle, as they may be attacked at any moment.

By command of Brig.-Gen. McDOWELL.

JAMES B. FRY, Adjt.-Gen.

The position of the Federal forces on the night previous to the battle can be briefly told. The first division, which had been the right wing thus far, was stationed on the north side of the Warrenton turnpike and on the eastern slope of the Centreville ridge, two brigades on the same road and a mile and a half in advance, to the west of the ridge, and one brigade on the road from Centreville to Manassas, where it crosses Bull Run at Blackburn's Ford, where the engagement on the 18th was. The second division was on the Warrenton turnpike, one mile east of Centreville. The third division was about a mile and a half out on the old Braddock road, which comes into Centreville from the southeast. The fifth division was on the same road as the third division, and between it and Centreville.

The fourth division (Runyon's) had not been brought to the front further than to guard our communications by way of Vienna and the Orange and Alexandria Railroad. His advanced regiment was about seven miles in the rear of Centreville.

At half-past two, on the morning of the 21st, the division under Gen. Tyler, which had heretofore been the right wing, moved, with the exception of Richardson's brigade, to threaten the passage of the Warrenton turnpike bridge, or Stone Bridge, on Bull Run. After moving a short distance Col. Keyes' brigade was halted by order of Gen. McDowell, to watch the road coming up from Manassas. This was about two miles from the run. The two remaining brigades of this division, being those of Cols. Schenck and Sherman, with Ayres' and Carlisle's batteries, proceeded on and arrived in front of the bridge about 6 A. M. An examination of the position was made, and the brigades and artillery got into position. The first gun, as a signal that they were in position, was fired at half-past six o'clock. As the design was to threaten the brigade, Col. Schenck's brigade was formed into a line, with its left resting in the direction of the bridge and the Confederate battery, which had been established to sweep the bridge and its approach, so as to threaten both. Col. Sherman's brigade was posted to the right of the turnpike, so as to be in position to sustain Col. Schenck or to move across Bull Run, in the direction to be taken by Col. Hunter's division.

A 30-pounder gun attached to Carlisle's battery was posted on the turnpike, with Ayres' battery considerably in its rear, while Carlisle's battery was posted on the left of Col. Sherman's brigade. In this position they were ordered to remain, awaiting the appearance of the divisions of Cols. Hunter and Heintzelman on the other side, until such time that the approach to the bridge could be carried and the bridge rebuilt by the engineers, who had on the spot materials for that purpose.

While this had been going on with the first division, the first brigade of the second division, under Col. Porter, had been silently paraded in light marching order at two o'clock in the morning. Owing to frequent delays in the march of troops in front, it did not reach Centreville until half-past four. It proceeded out on the Warrenton turnpike, and it was an hour after sunrise when its head was turned to the right to commence the flank movement by crossing at Sudley's Spring. The second brigade of the division, which was now in advance, made such slow and intermittent progress through the woods, that it was four hours be-

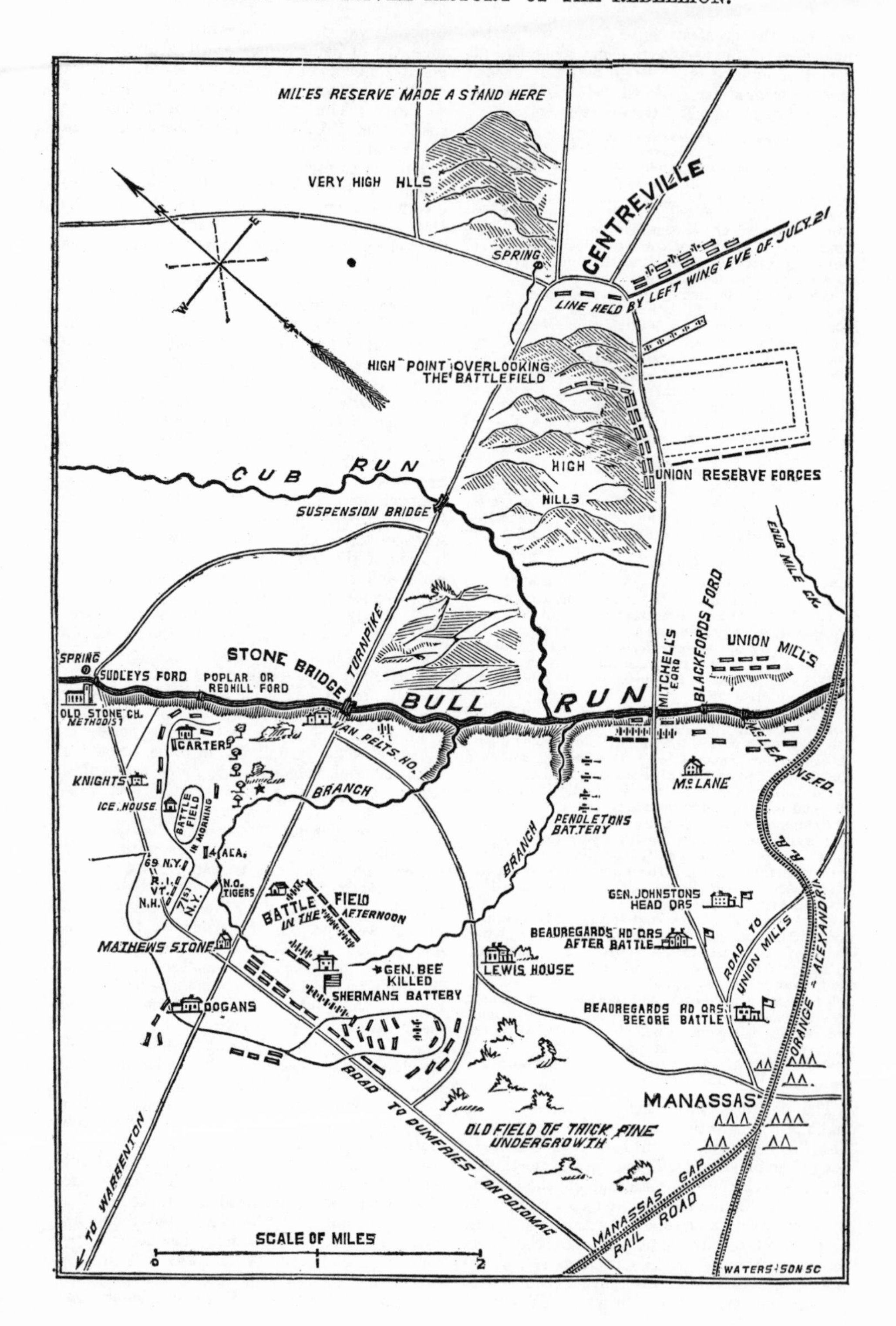
MILES RESERVE MADE A STAND HERE
VERY HIGH HILLS
CENTREVILLE
SPRING
LINE HELD BY LEFT WING EVE OF JULY 21
HIGH POINT OVERLOOKING THE BATTLEFIELD
CUB RUN
HIGH HILLS
UNION RESERVE FORCES
SUSPENSION BRIDGE
FOUR MILE CK.
TURNPIKE
BLACKFORDS FORD
MITCHELL'S FORD
UNION MILLS
SPRING
SUDLEYS FORD
POPLAR OR REDHILL FORD
STONE BRIDGE
BULL RUN
OLD STONE CH. METHODIST
CARTERS
VAN PELTS HO.
McLEANS FD.
KNIGHTS
McLANE
BRANCH
ICE HOUSE
BATTLE FIELD IN MORNING
PENDLETONS BATTERY
4 ALA.
69 N.Y.
R.I.
VT.
N.H.
7 (S) N.Y.
N.O. TIGERS
BRANCH
BATTLE FIELD IN THE AFTERNOON
GEN. JOHNSTONS HEAD QRS
BEAUREGARDS HD QRS AFTER BATTLE
MATHEWS STONE
GEN. BEE KILLED
LEWIS HOUSE
SHERMANS BATTERY
DOGANS
BEAUREGARDS HD QRS BEFORE BATTLE
ROAD TO UNION MILLS
ORANGE & ALEXANDRIA R.R.
MANASSAS
ROAD TO DUMFRIES ON POTOMAC
OLD FIELD OF THICK PINE UNDERGROWTH
TO WARRENTON
MANASSAS GAP RAIL ROAD
SCALE OF MILES
0
1
2
WATERS & SON SC

fore the head of the division reached Bull Run. This was about half-past nine o'clock, and intelligence was here received that the Confederate troops were in front with considerable force. A halt of half an hour was now ordered, to obtain a supply of water, and to rest and refresh the men. The shade of the green and waving foliage of the trees, and the water of the creek, on this hot summer morning, were delightful to the perspiring men. Only the gleam of bayonets and the equipments of war in sight on every side, indicated the terrific conflict so close at hand.

Not only was the intelligence received that the enemy was in front with a considerable force, but from the heights where the troops rested, a vast column could be plainly descried, at the distance of a mile or more on the left, moving rapidly towards the line of march in front, which the halting troops were about to resume. Skirmishers were now thrown out upon either flank and in front, by Col. Slocum, of the Second Rhode Island. The column moved forward, however, before this was completed, and in about thirty minutes emerged from the timber, whence the rattle of the musketry and occasional crash of round shot through the branches of the trees indicated the opening of the battle. The Second Rhode Island, of the second brigade, under Col. Burnside, was immediately sent forward with its battery of artillery, and the balance of the brigade was formed in a field to the right of the road. At the same time the head of the first brigade was turned slightly to the right, in order to gain time and room for deployment on the right of the second brigade. Griffin's battery found its way through the timber to the fields beyond, followed promptly by the marines, while the Twenty-seventh took a direction more to the left, and the Fourteenth followed upon the trail of the battery—all moving up at double-quick step.

Since this division left the Warrenton turnpike by turning to the right, it had moved in a semicircle, crossing Bull Run at Sudley's Spring, and it was now approaching the turnpike again. Along this turnpike the enemy now appeared drawn up in a long line, extending from a house and haystack upon the extreme right of the advancing division to a house beyond its left. Behind that house there was a heavy battery which, with three others along the Confederate line, but on the heights behind it, covered with all sorts of projectiles the ground upon which the Union force was advancing. A grove in front of the enemy's right wing afforded it shelter and protection, while the shrubbery in the fences along the road screened somewhat his left wing. The battery of Griffin advanced within a thousand yards, and opened an unerring and deadly fire upon the enemy's batteries, (on the right,) which were soon silenced or driven away. The right of the Union force was now rapidly developed by this first brigade of the second division—the marines, the Twenty-seventh, Fourteenth, and Eighth, with the cavalry in the rear of the right. The enemy retreated in more precipitation than order, as this part of the line advanced. Meanwhile, it appearing that the Second Rhode Island, of the second brigade, was closely pressed by the right of the enemy, Col. Burnside ordered the Seventy-first New York and Second New Hampshire to advance, intending to hold the First Rhode Island in reserve; but, owing to delay in the formation of the Seventy-first and Second, the First Rhode Island was at once ordered on the field. It performed most efficient service in assisting its comrades to repel the attack of the enemy's forces, which the Second Rhode Island had steadily borne, and had bravely stood its ground, even compelling him to give way. Soon the Seventy-first came into action, planting the two howitzers belonging to the regiment upon the right of its line, and working them most effectively. Next came the Second New Hampshire into the field; and the whole of the second brigade was engaged in action on the right of the enemy.

The enemy now clung with so much tenacity to the protecting wood, and the Rhode Island battery became so much endangered, as to impel the commander to call for the battalion of regulars. This battalion was composed of two companies of the Second, five companies of the Third, and one company of the Eighth U. S. Infantry. It was a part of the first brigade, and was at once ordered to support the second brigade, under Col. Burnside, which was now suffering from a severe fire in its front. The line of the battalion was rapidly formed, opening fire, and a column under Col. Heintzelman appearing at the same moment on the left of the battalion, the enemy fell back to the rising ground in his rear.

The third division, consisting of three brigades, under Col. Heintzelman, was under arms, in light marching order, with two days' cooked rations in their haversacks, and commenced the march at half-past two in the morning. It followed immediately in the rear of the second division, Col. Hunter, and with that division, turning to the right from the turnpike by a country road, and crossing Bull Run at Sudley's Spring. It was the intention that this division should turn to the left and cross a ford about midway between the Warrenton turnpike and Sudley's Springs. But the road was either missed or did not exist. Probably missed, as there is a ford called "Poplar or Red Hill Ford," midway between the Stone Bridge and Sudley's. Before the third division reached Sudley's the battle had commenced. Smoke could be seen rising on their left from two points a mile or more apart. Two clouds of dust were also visible, showing the advance of troops from the direction of Manassas. Two regiments were at this time ordered forward, to prevent the enemy from outflanking the second division, under Col. Hunter. Accordingly, the Minnesota advanced on the left of the road which crossed the run, the Eleventh Massachusetts moved up it, followed by the remainder of the division, except Arnold's battery, which, supported by the First Michigan, was posted a little below the crossing of the run as a reserve.

The advance of the battalion of regular infantry and the regiment detached from Col. Heintzelman, to support the second brigade, under Col. Burnside, above mentioned, caused the enemy to come flying from the woods towards the right, and the Twenty-seventh completed their retreat by charging directly upon their centre in the face of a scorching fire, while the Fourteenth and Eighth moved down the turnpike to cut off the retiring foe, and to support the Twenty-seventh, which was standing the brunt of the action, with its ranks thinning in the dreadful fire. Now the resistance of the enemy's left became so obstinate that the beaten right retired in safety. This retreat of the enemy's right afforded an opportunity for the brigades of Cols. Sherman and Keyes, belonging to Gen. Tyler's division, to cross over, as will be presently noticed.

The appearance of the head of Col. Heintzelman's column upon the field at the moment of the obstinate resistance of the enemy's left, enabled the Fifth Massachusetts and Eleventh New York (Fire Zouaves) to move forward to support the centre of the first brigade of Col. Hunter's division, which had been on the right and constantly engaged. At this time the Eighth New York, under Col. Lyons, of this brigade, had broken. They were only partially rallied again. This was the first regiment to break ranks and retire on the field that day. The Fourteenth also broke, but was soon rallied in rear of Griffin's battery, which soon took a position further to the front and right, from which its fire was delivered with such precision and rapidity as to compel the batteries of the enemy to retire far behind the brow of the hill in front.

At this time the first brigade of Col. Hunter's division occupied a line considerably in advance of that first occupied by the left wing of the enemy. The battery was pouring its withering fire into the batteries and columns of the enemy wherever exposed. The cavalry were likewise engaged in feeling the left flank of the enemy's position, during which some captures were made. Early in the action Gen. Hunter had been wounded and conveyed from the field, and the command of the division had devolved on Col. A. Porter.

The orders to Gen. Tyler were to threaten the passage of the Stone Bridge. Soon after getting into position, it was discovered that the enemy had a heavy battery with infantry in support, commanding both the road and bridge approaches, on which both Ayres and Carlisle at different times tried the effect of their guns without success. The banks of the run proving impracticable for the passage of artillery, the batteries remained comparatively useless until the approach to the bridge was cleared. During this period of waiting, the 30-pounder was occasionally used with considerable effect against bodies of infantry and cavalry, which could be seen from time to time moving in the direction of Col. Hunter's column, and out of the range of the ordinary guns. When it appeared that the divisions of Cols. Hunter and Heintzelman were arrested in their progress, and the enemy seemed to be moving heavy reinforcements to support their troops, the brigade of Col. Sherman was ordered by Gen. Tyler to cross over and support the columns engaged. The brigade of Col. Keyes was also ordered to follow. This brigade, on reaching the high ground across the run, was ordered to form on the left of Col. Sherman's brigade, which was done with great steadiness and regularity. After waiting a few minutes, the line was ordered to advance and come into conflict on its right with the enemy's cavalry and infantry, which, after some severe struggles, it drove back, until the further march of Keyes' brigade was arrested by a severe fire of artillery and infantry, sheltered by some buildings standing on the heights above the road leading to Bull Run. A charge was here ordered, and the Second Maine and Third Connecticut, which were opposed to this part of the enemy's line, pressed forward to the top of the hill until they reached the buildings which were held by the enemy, and drove them out and for a moment held possession. The gallantry of this charge upon infantry and artillery, says Col. Keyes, "was never, in my opinion, surpassed." At this point, finding the brigade under the fire of a strong force behind breastworks, it was ordered to march by the left flank across an open field until the whole line was sheltered by the right bank of Bull Run, along which the march was conducted, with a view to turn the battery, which the enemy had placed on the hill below the point at which the Warrenton turnpike crosses Bull Run. The enemy were forced to retire for a considerable distance below the Stone Bridge, and an opportunity was afforded to Capt. Alexander to pass over the bridge, cut out the abatis which had been placed there, and prepare the way for Col. Schenck's brigade and two batteries to pass over.

Meanwhile Col. Sherman's brigade, which had been ordered by Gen. Tyler to cross over in advance of Col. Keyes, found no difficulty in the movement and met no opposition in ascending the steep bluff with the infantry. Advancing slowly and continuously with the head of the column to give time for the regiments in succession to close up their ranks, the brigade proceeded with caution towards the field, and soon formed in rear of Col. Porter's brigade. Here orders were given to Col. Sherman to join in pursuit of the enemy, who were falling back to the left of the road by which the army had approached from Sudley's Spring. The brigade moved in the following order: Thirteenth New York in advance, followed by the Second Wisconsin, Seventy-ninth and Sixty-ninth New York. The Thirteenth advanced steadily down the hill and up the ridge, from which it opened fire upon the enemy who had made another stand on ground very favorable to him, and the regiment continued advancing as the enemy gave way.

The position which the battle had now attained was as follows: Early in the morning the force of the enemy had been stationed along Bull Run, from the Stone Bridge down to the Union Mills, below Blackburn's Ford. But owing to the crossing of the Federal troops at Sudley's Spring, further up than the extreme left of the enemy at the Stone Bridge, the line of the latter was entirely changed. It formed, as has been stated, along the Warrenton turnpike, which crosses at the Stone Bridge, and continues on in a due western course. In this position the enemy was found by the first troops that crossed over. On the Federal side, Col. Richardson's brigade, of the first division, was posted at Blackburn Ford, to prevent the enemy from crossing, and also to make a feint to cross when the firing of Gen. Tyler at the Stone Bridge above should be heard, which was so done. Gen. Hunter's division opened the attack upon the enemy's line formed on the Warrenton turnpike. The brigade of Col. Porter on the right had been strengthened by Col. Heintzelman's division, consisting of Cols. Wilcox's and Howard's brigades and a part of Col. Franklin's. To these was now added Col. Sherman's brigade, from Gen. Tyler's first division. Further on the left the attack was commenced by Col. Burnside, with the second brigade of Col. Hunter's division, and sustained with great gallantry and resolution, especially by the First and Second Rhode Island and the Rhode Island battery, until strengthened by Major Sykes' battalion of regulars, and still further by a portion of Col. Heintzelman's force and Keyes' brigade, of Gen. Tyler's division. All the Federal force was now on the field of battle, excepting the division of Col. Miles, consisting of Cols. Blenker and Davies' brigades, and also the brigade of Col. Richardson at Blackburn's Ford, and the brigade of Col. Schenck at the Stone Bridge, with the accompanying batteries. The effect of this strong and firm attack on the enemy's line had caused it to yield at all points. The Federal force was in possession of the Warrenton turnpike from the Stone Bridge westward. On their right the enemy had retreated nearly a mile and a half. On the left they had also given way so that Col. Schenck's brigade was about to cross over the Stone Bridge.

The road taken by the troops from Sudley's Spring down to the Warrenton turnpike, deflects to the left somewhat, near the turnpike, and crosses it at about right angles. On the left of this road, after it crosses the turnpike, is a hill with a farm-house on it, where the enemy had, early in the day, planted some of his most annoying batteries. Across the road from this hill was another hill, or rather elevated ridge, or table land. The hottest part of the contest was for the possession of this hill, with the house on it. General McDowell thus describes it: "The force engaged here was Heintzelman's division of Wilcox's and Howard's brigades on the right, supported by part of Porter's brigade, of Hunter's division, and the cavalry under Palmer, and Franklin's brigade, of Heintzelman's division, Sherman's brigade, of Tyler's division, in the centre, and up the road, whilst Keyes' brigade, of Tyler's division, was on the left attacking the batteries near the Stone Bridge. The Rhode Island battery, of the Burnside brigade, also participated in this attack, by its fire from the north of the turnpike. Ricketts' battery, together with Griffins' battery, was on the side of the hill and became the object of the special attention of the enemy, who succeeded, through a mistake by which one of his regiments was thought to be a Federal force, in disabling the battery, and then attempting to take it. Three times was he repulsed by different corps in succession, and driven back, and the guns taken by hand, the horses having been killed, and pulled away. The third time, it was supposed by us all that the repulse was final, for he was driven entirely from the hill, and so far beyond it as not to be in sight, and all were certain the day was ours.

"The enemy was evidently disheartened and broken. But we had been fighting since half-past 10 o'clock in the morning, and it was after 3 o'clock in the afternoon; the men had been up since 2 o'clock in the morning, and had made what to those unused to such things, seemed a long march before coming into action, though the longest distance gone over was not more than nine and a half miles; and though they had three days' provisions served out to them the day before, many no doubt did not eat them, or threw them away on the march, or during the battle, and were therefore without food. They had done much severe fighting. Some of the regiments which had been driven from the hill in the first two attempts of the enemy to keep possession of it, had become shaken, were unsteady, and had many men out of the ranks."

Colonel Porter, in command of Hunter's division after Colonel Hunter was wounded, thus reports the same scenes: "The flags of eight regiments, though borne somewhat wearily, now pointed towards the hill, from which disordered masses of the enemy had been seen hastily retiring. Griffin's and Ricketts' batteries were ordered by the Commanding General to the top of the hill on the right, as supporting with the Fire Zouaves and marines, while the Fourteenth entered the skirt of wood on their right, to protect that flank as a column composed of the Twenty-seventh New York, and Eleventh and Fifth Massachusetts, Second Minnesota, and Sixty-ninth New York moved up towards the left flank of the batteries; but so soon as they were in position, and before the flanking supports had reached theirs, a murderous fire of musketry and rifles opened at pistol range, cut down every cannonier and a large number of horses. The fire came from some infantry of the enemy, which had been mistaken for our own forces; an officer in the field having stated that it was a regiment sent by Colonel Heintzelman to support the batteries.

"The evanescent courage of the Zouaves prompted them to fire perhaps a hundred shots, when they broke and fled, leaving the batteries open to a charge of the enemy's cavalry, which took place immediately. The Marines, in spite of their gallant officers, gave way in disorder. The Fourteenth, on the right, and the column on the left, hesitatingly retired, with the exception of the Sixty-ninth and Thirty-eighth New York, who nobly stood and returned the fire of the enemy for fifteen minutes. Soon the slopes behind us were swarming with our retreating and disorganized forces, while riderless horses and artillery teams ran furiously through the flying crowd."

Colonel Sherman, in his report of this part of the conflict, says: "At the point where the road from Sudley's Spring crossed the bridge to our left, the ground was swept by a most severe fire, by artillery, rifle, and musketry, and we saw in succession several regiments driven from it, among them the Zouaves and battalion of marines. Before reaching the crest of the hill, the roadway was worn deep enough to afford shelter, and I kept the several regiments in it as long as possible. But when the Second Wisconsin was abreast of the enemy, it was ordered to leave the roadway by the left flank, and attack the enemy. This regiment ascended to the brow of the hill steadily, received the severe fire of the enemy, returned it with spirit, and advanced, delivering its fire. It was repulsed, rallied, and repulsed again. By this time, the Seventy-ninth New York had closed up, and in like manner it was ordered to cross the brow of the hill, and drive the enemy from cover. It was impossible to get a good view of the ground. In it there was one battery of artillery, which poured an incessant fire upon our advancing column, and the ground was irregular, with small clusters of pines, affording shelter, of which the enemy took good advantage. The fire of rifles and musketry was very severe. The Seventy-ninth, headed by its Colonel, charged across the hill, and for a short time the contest was severe. They rallied several times under fire, but finally broke, and gained the cover of the hills. This left the field open to the Sixty-ninth New York, Colonel Corcoran, who, in his turn, led his regiment over the crest, and had in full open view the ground so severely contested. The firing was very severe, and the roar of cannon, rifles, and musketry incessant. It was manifest the enemy was here in great force, far superior to us at that point. The Sixty-ninth held the ground for some time, but finally fell back in disorder. At this time, the Thirteenth New York occupied another ridge to our left, overlooking the same field of action, and similarly engaged. Here, at 3½ P. M., began the scene of disorder."

Colonel Burnside reports from another part of the field:

"The battery of the Second Rhode Island changed its position into a field upon the right, and was brought to bear upon the force which Colonel Porter was engaging. The enemy's infantry having fallen back, two sections of Captain W. H. Reynolds' battery advanced, and succeeded in breaking the charge of the enemy's cavalry, which had now been brought into the engagement. It was nearly 4 o'clock P. M., and the battle had continued for almost six hours since the time when the second brigade had been engaged, with every thing in favor of our troops, and promising decisive victory, when some of the regiments engaging the enemy upon the extreme right of our line broke, and large numbers passed disorderly by my brigade, then drawn up in the position which they last held."

The position of the battle described in these extracts was its turning point. The view taken of the contest at this time, by the Commander-in-Chief of the Confederate forces, is of great interest. In his official report, General Beauregard thus speaks:

"The topographical features of the plateau, now become the stage of the contending armies, must be described in outline. A glance at the map will show that it is enclosed on three sides by small water courses, which empty into Bull Run within a few yards of each other, half a mile to the south of the Stone Bridge. Rising to an elevation of quite one hundred feet above the level of Bull Run at the bridge, it falls off on three sides, to the level of the enclosing streams in gentle slopes, but which are furrowed by ravines of irregular direction and length, and studded with clumps and patches of young pines and oaks. The general direction of the crest of the plateau is oblique to the course of Bull Run in that quarter, and on the Brentsville and turnpike roads, which intersect each other at right angles. Completely surrounding the two houses before mentioned, are small open fields, of irregular outline, and exceeding 150 acres in extent. The houses, occupied at the time, the one by widow Henry, and the other by the free negro, Robinson, are small wooden buildings, densely embowered in trees and environed by a double row of fences on two sides. Around the eastern and southern brow of the plateau, an almost unbroken fringe of second-growth pines gave excellent shelter for our marksmen, who availed themselves of it, with the most satisfactory skill. To the west, adjoining the fields, a broad belt of oaks extends directly across the crest, on both sides of the Sudley road, in which, during the battle, regiments of both armies met and contended for the mastery. From the open ground of this plateau the view embraces a wide expanse of woods and gently undulating open country of broad grass and grain fields in all directions, including the scene of Evans' and Bee's recent encounter with the enemy—some twelve hundred yards to the northward. In reply to the play of the enemy's batteries, our own artillery had not been idle or unskilful.

The ground occupied by our guns, on a level with that held by the batteries of the enemy, was an open space of limited extent, behind a low undulation, just at the eastern verge of the plateau, some 500 or 600 yards from the Henry house. Here, as before said, some thirteen pieces, mostly six-pounders, were maintained in action. The several batteries of Imboden, Stanard, Pendleton, (Rockbridge Artillery,) and Alburtis', of the Army of the Shenandoah, and five guns of Walton's, and Heaton's section of Rogers' battery, of the Army of the Potomac, alternating to some extent with each other, and taking part as needed; all from the outset displaying that marvellous capacity of our people as artillerists which has made them, it would appear, at once the terror and the admiration of the enemy. As was soon apparent, the Federalists had suffered severely from our artillery, and from the fire of our musketry on the right, and especially from the left flank, placed under cover, within whose galling range they had been advanced. And, we are told in their official reports, how regiment after regiment, thrown forward to dislodge us, was broken, never to recover its entire organization on that field. In the mean time, also, two companies of Stuart's cavalry (Carter's and Hoge's) made a dashing charge down the Brentsville and Sudley road upon the Fire Zouaves—then the enemy's right on the plateau—which added to the disorder wrought by our musketry on that flank. But still the press of the enemy was heavy in that quarter of the field, as fresh troops were thrown forward there to outflank us; and some three guns of a battery, in an attempt to obtain a position apparently to enfilade our batteries, were thrown so close to the Thirty-third Regiment, Jackson's brigade, that that regiment, springing forward, seized them, but with severe loss, and was subsequently driven back by an overpowering force of Federal musketry.

"Now, full 2 o'clock P. M., I gave the order for the right of my line, except my reserves, to advance to recover the plateau. It was done with uncommon resolution and vigor, and at the same time, Jackson's brigade pierced the enemy's centre with the determination of veterans, and the spirit of men who fight for a sacred cause; but it suffered seriously. With equal spirit the other parts of the line made the onset, and the Federal lines were broken and swept back, at all points, from the open ground of the plateau. Rallying soon, however, as they were strongly reinforced by fresh regiments, the Federalists returned, and by weight of numbers pressed our lines back, recovered their ground and guns, and renewed the offensive. By this time, between half-past 2 and 3 o'clock P. M., our reinforcements pushed forward, and directed by General Johnston to the required quarter, were at hand just as I had ordered forward to a second effort for the recovery of the disputed plateau, the whole line, including my reserves, which, at this crisis of the battle, I felt called upon to lead in person. This attack was general, and was shared in by every regiment then in the field, including the Sixth (Fisher's) North Carolina Regiment, which had just come up and taken position on the immediate left of the Forty-ninth Virginia Regiment. The whole open ground was again swept clear of the enemy, and the plateau around the Henry and Robinson houses remained finally in our possession, with the greater part of the Ricketts and Griffin batteries, and a flag of the First Michigan Regiment, captured by the Twenty-seventh Virginia Regiment, (Lieutenant-Colonel Echolls,) of Jackson's brigade. This part of the day was rich with deeds of individual coolness and dauntless conduct, as well as well-directed embodied resolution and bravery, but fraught with the loss to the service of the country, of lives of inestimable preciousness at this juncture. The brave Bee was mortally wounded, at the head of the Fourth Alabama and some Mississippians, in an open field near the Henry house; and a few yards distant, the promising life of Bartow, while leading the Seventh Georgia Regiment, was quenched in blood. Colonel F. J. Thomas, Acting Chief-of-Ordnance, of General Johnston's staff, after gallant conduct, and most efficient service, was also slain. Colonel Fisher, Sixth North Carolina, likewise fell, after soldierly behavior, at the head of his regiment, with ranks greatly thinned. Withers' Eighteenth Regiment, of Cocke's brigade, had come up in time to follow this charge, and, in conjunction with Hampton's Legion, captured several rifle pieces, which may have fallen previously in possession of some of our troops; but if so, had been recovered by the enemy. These pieces were immediately turned, and effectively served on distant masses of the enemy, by the hands of some of our officers.

"While the enemy had thus been driven back on our right entirely across the turnpike, and beyond Young's branch on our left, the woods yet swarmed with them, when our reinforcements opportunely arrived in quick succession, and took position in that portion of the field. Kershaw's Second, and Cash's Eighth South Carolina regiments, which had arrived soon after Withers', were led through the oaks just east of the Sudley-Brentsville road, brushing some of the enemy before them, and, taking an advantageous position along and west of that road, opened with much skill and effect on bodies of the enemy that had been rallied under cover of a strong Federal brigade posted on a plateau in the southwest angle, formed by intersection of the turnpike with the Sudley-Brentsville road. Among the troops thus engaged, were the Federal regular infantry. At the same time, Kemper's battery, passing northward by the S.-B. road, took position on the open space—under orders of Colonel Kershaw—near where an enemy's battery had been captured, and opened with effective results upon the Federal right, then the mark also of Kershaw's and Cash's regiments. Preston's Twenty-eighth Regiment, of Cocke's brigade, had by that time entered the same body of oaks, and encountered some Michigan troops, capturing their brigade commander, Colonel Wilcox.

"Another important accession to our forces had also occurred about the same time, at 3 o'clock P. M. Brigadier-General E. K. Smith, with some 1,700 infantry of Elzey's brigade, of the Army of the Shenandoah, and Beckham's battery, came upon the field, from Camp Pickens, Manassas, where they had arrived by railroad at noon. Directed in person by General Johnston to the left, then so much endangered, on reaching a position in rear of the oak woods, south of the Henry house, and immediately east of the Sudley road, General Smith was disabled by a severe wound, and his valuable services were lost at that critical juncture. But the command devolved upon a meritorious officer of experience, Colonel Elzey, who led his infantry at once somewhat further to the left, in the direction of the Chinn house, across the road, through the oaks skirting the west side of the road, and around which he sent the battery under Lieutenant Beckham. This officer took up a most favorable position near that house, whence, with a clear view of the Federal right and centre, filling the open fields to the west of the Brentsville-Sudley road, and gently sloping southward, he opened fire with his battery upon them with deadly and damaging effect.

"Colonel Early, who, by some mischance, did not receive orders until two o'clock, which had been sent him at noon, came on the ground immediately after Elzey, with Kemper's Seventh Virginia, Hay's Seventh Louisiana, and Barksdale's Thirteenth Mississippi regiments. This brigade, by the personal direction of General Johnston, was marched by the Holkham house, across the fields to the left, entirely around the woods through which Elzey had passed, and under a severe fire, into a position in line of battle near Chinn's house, outflanking the enemy's right. At this time, about half-past 3 P. M., the enemy, driven back on their left and centre, and brushed from the woods bordering the Sudley road, south and west of the Henry house, had formed a line of battle of truly formidable proportions, of crescent outline, reaching on their left from the vicinity of Pittsylvania, (the old Carter mansion,) by Matthew's, and in rear of Dogan's, across the turnpike near to Chinn's house. The woods and fields were filled with their masses of infantry, and their carefully preserved cavalry. It was a truly magnificent, though redoubtable spectacle, as they threw forward in fine style, on the broad, gentle slopes of the ridge occupied by their main lines, a cloud of skirmishers, preparatory for another attack. But as Early formed his line, and Beckham's pieces played upon the right of the enemy, Elzey's brigade, Gibbon's Tenth Virginia, Lieutenant-Colonel Stuart's First Maryland, and Vaughn's Third Tennessee regiments, and Cash's Eighth, and Kershaw's Second South Carolina, Withers' Eighteenth, and Preston's Twenty-eighth Virginia, advanced in an irregular line almost simultaneously, with great spirit, from their several positions upon the front and flanks of the enemy, in their quarter of the field. At the same time, too, Early resolutely assailed their right flank and rear. Under the combined attack, the enemy was soon forced, first over the narrow plateau in the southern angle made by the two roads, so often mentioned, into a patch of woods on its western slope, thence back over Young's branch and the turnpike, into the fields of the Dugan farm, and rearward, in extreme disorder, in all available directions, towards Bull Run. The rout had now become general and complete."

In his report, General McDowell thus remarks on the position of the battle:

"It was at this time that the enemy's reinforcements came to his aid, from the railroad train, understood to have arrived from the valley with the residue of Johnston's army. They threw themselves in the woods on our right, and opened a fire of musketry upon our men, which caused them to break, and retire down the hillside. This soon degenerated into disorder, for which there was no remedy. Every effort was made to rally them, even beyond the reach of the enemy's fire, but in vain."

A line drawn through the battle-field to Manassas Junction, would run about due south. The railroad from Winchester to Manassas Junction comes in on a southeast course. Consequently, the line above mentioned, and the railroad, converge, and meet at the Junction. The Dumfries road, bounding the west side of the battle-field, and running straight south, crosses the Winchester railroad about two miles from the Junction. Up this road came the last reinforcements of the enemy, from General Johnston's command at Winchester. This was nearer than to proceed to the Junction, and caused the clouds of dust seen.

Colonel Porter, commanding the division of Colonel Hunter, thus continues his report:

"All further efforts were futile. The words, gestures, and threats of our officers were thrown away upon men who had lost all presence of mind, and only longed for absence of body. Some of our noblest and best officers lost their lives in trying to rally them. Upon our first position, the Twenty-seventh New York was the first to rally, under the command of Major Bartlett, and around it the other regiments engaged soon gathered their scattered fragments. The battalion of regulars, in the mean time, moved steadily across the field from the left to the right, and took up a position where it held the entire forces of the enemy in check until our forces were somewhat rallied.

"The Commanding General then ordered a retreat upon Centreville, at the same time directing me to cover it with the battalion of regulars, the cavalry, and a section of artillery.

The rear-guard thus organized followed our panic-stricken troops to Centreville, resisting the attacks of the Confederate cavalry and artillery, and saving them from the inevitable destruction which awaited them, had not this body been interposed."

A prompt retreat of the fragments of his army was resolved upon by Gen. McDowell; and while the stragglers had pushed on from the battle-field to Washington without halting, the organized masses commenced leaving about nine o'clock that night. By midnight all but the wounded and the dead of that well-equipped army which commenced its march from Washington five days previous, proud, exultant, and confident of victory, was panic-stricken, groping its way, under cover of the darkness of night, to the intrenchments opposite Washington. Never had the flag of the Union trailed so low in the dust before; never was so brilliant a career opened before it as that which commenced on the day after that dreadful night.

Fortunately for the remnants of the Federal army, the Southern forces did not pursue their flying foe. The reasons for this omission are thus stated by Gen. Johnston in his official report:

"The apparent firmness of the United States troops at Centreville who had not been engaged, which checked our pursuit; the strong forces occupying the works near Georgetown, Arlington, and Alexandria; the certainty, too, that Gen. Patterson, if needed, would reach Washington, with his army of thirty thousand men, sooner than we could; and the condition and inadequate means of the army in ammunition, provisions, and transportation, prevented any serious thoughts of advancing against the capital. It is certain that the fresh troops within the works were, in number, quite sufficient for their defence; if not, Gen. Patterson's army would certainly reënforce them soon enough."

The loss on the Federal side, according to the official returns, was 481 killed, 1,011 wounded, and 1,216 missing. Among the killed were Col. Cameron, of the New York 79th; Lieut.-Col. Haggerty, of the New York 69th; Col. Slocum, 2d Rhode Island; also Maj. Ballou and Capt. Tower.

The artillery lost was as follows:

Company D, 2d artillery, 6 rifle guns.

Company I, 1st artillery, 6 rifled Parrott 10-pounders.

Company E, 2d artillery, 2 rifled guns and 2 howitzers.

Company —, 5th artillery, 1 rifled gun.

Company G, 1st artillery, 1 30-pounder Parrott gun.

Rhode Island battery, 5 rifled guns.

To this should be added 180 boxes of small arm cartridges, 87 boxes of rifled cannon ammunition, 30 boxes of old fire-arms, 12 wagons loaded with provisions, and 3,000 bushels oats, a large number of muskets thrown away, and an immense number of blankets and knapsacks.

Gen. Beauregard, in his report, states the number of his force on the 18th of July at 17,000 effective men; and on the 21st 27,000, which includes 6,200 sent from Gen. Johnston, and 1,700 brought up by Gen. Holmes from Fredericksburg. The report states the number killed to have been 269, wounded 1 483, aggregate 1,852. The same report states the number of prisoners taken at 1,460.

On the left the Southern force was commanded by Brig.-Gens. Evans, Jackson, and Cocke, and Col. Bartow. The centre was under Gens. Jones, Longstreet, and Benham. On the extreme right was Gen. Ewell. Early in the day an order was sent to him by Gen. Beauregard to attack and attempt to turn the left flank of the Federal force. The messenger was killed, and the orders were not received.

It is manifest that this battle was well fought. In the fore part of the afternoon the Southern troops were nearly outflanked. At three o'clock the Federal force believed they had the victory; and that, indeed, they had, and would soon have reached and obtained possession of the railroad leading to Winchester. But the arrival of four fresh regiments, who entered the field with great spirit and energy, changed the result.

CHAPTER IX.

Extra Session of Congress—Its Action—Strength of the Army—Southern troops organized—Skirmishes in Missouri—At Monroe Station, Millville, and Fulton—Movements of Gen. Lyon—Battle of Wilson's Creek—Surrender of Major Lynch in New Mexico—Skirmishes—Attack on Galveston—Expedition against the forts at Hatteras Inlet.

THE Congress of the United States assembled in extra session at Washington on July 4th. The President in his message asked for authority to enlist 400,000 volunteers for three years or the war, and for an appropriation of $400,000,000. The wants of the War Department were estimated by Secretary Cameron above $185,000,000. These were distributed to the several branches of the service as follows:

Quartermaster's Department	$70,289,200 21
Subsistence Department	27,278,781 50
Ordnance Department	7,468,172 00
Pay Department	67,845,402 48
Adjutant-General's Department	408,000 00
Engineer Department	685,000 00
Topographical Engineer Department	50,000 00
Surgeon-General's Department	1,271,841 00
Due States which have made advances for troops	10,000,000 00
Total	185,299,397 19

The Navy Department asked for $32,000,000 for immediate use.

Immediately after the disaster at Bull Run, Congress authorized the enlistment of 500,000 men, and appropriated $500,000,000. An appropriation for the navy was also passed. The enlistment and organization of troops were entered upon with great activity and warm popular approbation during the ensuing three months, when it was restricted. Many circumstances aided the enlistment. The cause of the Union was approved by every one; a general stagnation or inactivity pervaded all industrial pursuits, and multitudes were partially or wholly unemployed, and the wages offered to the soldier were then extremely liberal. The pay offered to privates by the United States was $13 per month, and a bounty of 100 acres of land at the close of the war. In addition, many of the States gave to each married citizen volunteer about one dollar per week for his wife, and in proportion for each child of his family between certain ages. Where such a sum was not given to the family of the private by the State, it was in numerous instances bestowed by the city or town in which he lived.

The pay of officers was on an equally liberal scale; and civilians in profitable social positions, as well as those in no position, aspired, in the rawest state, to obtain the rank of officers. Too many unworthy persons were successful. It cost the Government millions, and required the efforts of all the military skill in the country, to bring the accumulated mass up to the discipline and order of an approved army.

On the 1st of December, 1861, the entire strength of the army, both volunteers and regulars, was estimated as follows:

Volunteers for the War.

California	4,608
Connecticut	12,400
Delaware	2,000
Illinois	80,000
Indiana	57,332
Iowa	19,800
Kentucky	15,000
Maine	14,239
Maryland	7,000
Massachusetts	26,760
Michigan	28,550
Minnesota	4,160
Missouri	22,130
New Hampshire	9,600
New Jersey	9,342
New York	100,200
Ohio	81,205
Pennsylvania	94,760
Rhode Island	5,898
Vermont	8,000
Virginia	12,000
Wisconsin	14,153
Kansas	5,000
Colorado	1,000
Nebraska	2,500
Nevada	1,000
New Mexico	1,000
District of Columbia	1,000
	640,637
Estimated strength of the regular army, including the new enlistments under act of Congress of July 29, 1861	20,334
Total	660,971

This estimate, which was prepared at the War Department, as representing the force of the army, varied unquestionably from the amount of troops in the field. It was not to be expected that the precise force could be stated with strict accuracy while the enlistment was not closed. The quota of New York in the field was about the amount stated; the same was the case with the force assigned to other States. The several arms of the service were estimated as follows:

	Volunteers.	Regulars.	Aggregate.
Infantry	557,208	11,175	568,383
Cavalry	54,654	4,744	59,398
Artillery	20,380	4,308	24,688
Rifles and Sharpshooters	8,395	....	8,395
Engineers	....	107	107
	640,637	20,334	660,971

The appropriation asked for to sustain the army, by the Secretary of War, on the 1st of December, was $360,159,986.

The appropriation was computed for a force of 500,000 men. Some portion was to cover deficiencies arising from an excess of force in the field over the estimate for the previous six months.

In the beginning of July, also, a session of the Southern Congress commenced at Richmond. The report of the Secretary of War stated the number of regiments of troops then accepted was 194, and 32 battalions, besides various detachments of artillery, and companies of cavalry. He urged the continued acceptance of troops until the number reached 300 regiments. The success at Bull Run awakened such a degree of enthusiasm and confidence in the ultimate triumph of the Confederacy, that the army, in a short time, increased to a greater number than had been anticipated. Forward movements were made from Manassas and Centreville, and the flag of the "Stars and Bars" was flaunted from the summit of Munson's Hill, where the inhabitants of the city of Washington could see its folds proudly waving. For some time a division of opinion existed, even in the Cabinet of Mr. Davis, on the policy of a forward movement of the army. It was apprehended by those who were opposed, that an attack upon and destruction of Washington would thoroughly arouse the North. Some asserted that the true policy at that time, was to await the action of the French and English Governments, and thus the difficulties might be arranged without further effusion of blood. At the same time the army was desirous of a forward movement, the capture of Washington, the recovery of Maryland, and the possession of Baltimore for their winter-quarters. The final decision was adverse to a forward movement. The rapid increase in the Federal force, its improving discipline and reorganization, rendered doubtful the result. A change was also made in the war policy of the Federal Government, the design of which now was to attack the Confederate States elsewhere than in Virginia. All these circumstances exerted a controlling influence when united with others which existed within the Confederacy itself. These consisted in a lack of transportation, and those more indispensable means to the success of an attempt at invasion, an abundance of money. Nevertheless, the military efforts of the Government were on a most extensive scale. Troops were organized and sent to intrenched camps in Kentucky. Forces were maintained in Western Virginia, and an active campaign carried on. In Missouri, although left in a manner by the Southern Government to take care of herself, the most active military operations took place. The talents and skill of their Commanding General, Price, enabled him to sustain himself, and carry on an active campaign with less assistance and encouragement from the Government than any officer in the army.

At this time, the solvent or specie-paying banks refused to receive the Confederate Treasury notes, and were calling in all their own circulation. They also refused to receive the bills of suspended banks, and both Treasury notes and suspended bills sunk from eight to fifteen per cent., and in the cities of the Gulf States were refused by mechanics and tradesmen. Embarrassment, discouragement, and uncertainty settled upon whole communities. The valuable paper was rapidly decreasing and disappearing, while the other was as rapidly increasing. All who could, drew specie from the banks, and millions of dollars were hid away or buried.

From the month of September, the favorable aspect of affairs in the Confederate States began to decline, and before the close of the year the subject of drafting soldiers to serve in the army was actively discussed.

On July 22d Gen. George B. McClellan, having left Western Virginia, took the command of the troops in and around Washington. Their reorganization was immediately commenced. It was realized now by every one that the country was engaged in a great war, and all the appliances required for mighty and victorious armies were to be prepared.

Meanwhile bloody conflicts on a limited scale were constantly occurring in other parts of the country.

In the northern counties of Missouri the division of sentiment rapidly aroused a hostile spirit. Squads of troops from Illinois were soon stationed at important places, while State troops gathered to oppose them. The destruction of property and bloody skirmishes soon followed. At Monroe station, thirty miles west of Hannibal, an attack was made by secession troops, on July 11th, on the railroad station-house, which was burned with six passenger and eighteen freight cars. A portion of the railroad track was torn up on each side of the town. On the same night the bridge of the Hannibal and St. Joseph's Railroad was burned. On the 15th Brig.-Gen. Hurlburt, in command of the volunteer force, issued a lengthy proclamation to the people of the northeastern counties, warning them that the men or body of men who ventured to stand in defiance of the supreme authority of the Union, endangered their lives.

On the 16th a skirmish took place at Millville, about thirty miles above St. Charles, on the North Missouri Railroad. About eight hundred Union troops had reached this point, when the track was torn up, and they were fired upon by a secession force, and an engagement followed, in which a small number were killed and wounded on each side.

A little further south, near Fulton, in Calloway County, about twenty-three miles northeast of Jefferson City, a skirmish took place on the 17th, between Col. McNeil, with about six hundred men, and Gen. Harris, with a considerable force, in which the latter were routed with a loss of several as prisoners. On the 19th Gen. Pope, who had been assigned to the command in Northern Missouri, issued a proclamation addressed to the inhabitants.

He had previously proceeded from St. Louis to St. Charles, where his headquarters were established, in order to take charge of that department. His command in North Missouri was seven thousand strong, and so posted that Jefferson City, Booneville, Lexington, and all the principal points in the northern parts of the State, were within easy striking distance.

About the same time that Gen. Lyon left St. Louis for Jefferson City, June 15, other troops, consisting of ten companies, left for Rolla, which is the termination of the southwest branch of the Pacific Railroad, and one hundred and thirteen miles from St. Louis. This force was increased subsequently, and active operations took place in that section of the State.

On the 1st of August Gen. Lyon ordered his entire command, with the exception of a small guard, to rendezvous at Crane's Creek, ten miles south of Springfield. The command was composed as follows: Five companies 1st and 2d regiments regulars, Maj. Sturgis. Five companies 1st regiment Missouri volunteers, Lieut.-Col. Andrews. Two companies 2d regiment Missouri volunteers, Maj. Osterhaus. Three companies 3d regiment Missouri volunteers, Col. ——. 5th regiment Missouri volunteers, Col. Salomon. 1st regiment Iowa volunteers, Col. J. F. Bates. 1st regiment Kansas volunteers, Col. Deitzler. 2d regiment Kansas volunteers, Col. Mitchell. Two companies 1st regular cavalry, Capts. Stanley and Carr. Three companies 1st regular cavalry (recruits), Lieut. Lathrop. Capt. I. Totten's battery regular artillery, six guns, six and twelve-pounders. Lieut. Dubois' battery regular artillery, four guns, six and twelve-pounders. Capt. Shaeffer's battery Missouri volunteer artillery, six guns, six and twelve-pounders. Brig.-Gens. Sweeny and Sigel, and Maj. Sturgis, were intrusted with the most important secondary commands.

The march commenced that afternoon, and the camp was reached at ten o'clock at night.

The next morning the march was resumed, and about five o'clock that afternoon a body of the enemy were overtaken, when a brisk interchange of shots between the skirmishers took place. Upon this, a body of the enemy's infantry, about five hundred in number, approached, apparently with the design of cutting off an advanced body of the Federal infantry. Several volleys were interchanged, when a charge was made by a body of regulars. The enemy's ranks were thus broken, and they retreated. The place of this skirmish was Dug Springs. The march was continued as far as Curran, twenty-six miles from Springfield, but the heat of the weather, shortness of provisions, and the fact that a strong Confederate force was posted in front, and a large division had also moved in the direction of Sarcoxie, while it was necessary that communication should be kept open to Springfield, led Gen. Lyon to determine to return to that town.

On the 5th Gen. Lyon, learning that Gen. Price, of the Confederate army (Missouri State Guards), had effected a junction with Gen. Ben. McCulloch, and that the consolidated force was within ten or twelve miles of Springfield, resolved, though aware of the hazard of the movement, as a last resource, to attack the Confederates at their camp on Wilson's Creek, nine miles from Springfield. His entire force amounted to 5,200 men, of whom one regiment, the 5th Missouri, were three-months' men, whose time had expired nine days before the battle, but who had been retained by the urgency of Col. Sigel. There were in all less than 500 cavalry, while the Confederates had over 6,000, according to Gen. Ben. McCulloch's report. He had also three batteries, comprising in all sixteen guns, all of light calibre. This force marched from Springfield at 8 P. M. on the 9th of August, intending to commence the attack at daybreak the next morning. They were in two columns, the larger consisting of three small brigades and not quite 4,000 men, under the command of Gen. Lyon himself, the brigades being severally commanded by Major Sturgis, Lieut.-Col. Andrews, and Col. Deitzler; the smaller column, of about 1,300 men and one battery of six pieces, was commanded by Col. (afterwards Maj.-Gen.) Sigel. The enemy's camp was situated along Wilson's Creek for a distance of five or six miles, and in the ravines, and on the heights west of the creek; and Gen. Lyon's plan of attack was to march his main column, which he divided into two, giving the command of one to Maj. Sturgis, in front and to the left flank of the enemy, so as to enfilade their position on the creek; while Col. Sigel with his column, taking another road from Springfield, and crossing the creek, which here assumes the form of an inverted U, lower down, should endeavor to turn their right flank. Sigel's column fell into an ambuscade, and suffered severely, losing five of his six cannon, and was thus unable to render as efficient service as had been intended. The fight was continued in front, and on the enemy's left, with terrible effect for over six hours; the Confederates twice, in the course of the battle, came up to the Federal lines with the Union flag flying, and thus deceived the Federal troops till they could get so close as to pour a most destructive fire upon them, but they themselves fell back, when the artillery, which was served by officers and men of the regular army, was brought to bear upon them. Gen. Lyon, who was thrice wounded early in the engagement, and had had his horse killed under him, mounting another horse, led the 2d Kansas regiment, which had lost its colonel, for a charge upon the enemy; but was killed instantly by a rifle ball, which struck him in the breast. His death did not, however, throw the Federal troops into confusion, and the battle, in which Maj. Sturgis now commanded, was continued for nearly three hours longer, when the enemy were forced from their camp and the field. Finding his force too much reduced to hold the position, Maj. Sturgis gave the order to fall back on Springfield, and there resigned the command to Col. Sigel, who made a masterly retreat with the remnant of his army, his baggage trains, and $250,000 in specie, to Rolla. The loss of the Federal force in this battle was 223 killed, 721 wounded, 292 missing, mostly prisoners. The enemy's loss, according to their own account, was 517 killed, about 800 wounded, and 30 missing. Three of their generals were wounded, two of them mortally.

This battle at Wilson's Creek, in its effects, proved quite disastrous to Gens. McCulloch and Price. It not only served to check their progress, but discouraged many lukewarm sympathizers. Meanwhile the accumulation and organization of Union troops at St. Louis and other points added to the strength of Gen. Fremont, who had been ordered to the command of the Department.

In New Mexico a loss was suffered by the Union cause in the surrender of Maj. Lynde, with 750 men, on August 2d, without resistance. Again, on the 7th, the village of Hampton, two and a half miles from Fortress Monroe, having been previously evacuated by the Federal troops, was burned by a body of Virginians under the orders of Gen. Magruder. This was done to prevent its reoccupation by the Union troops. A few minutes after midnight the torch was applied. Most of the five hundred houses composing the village having been built of wood, and being very dry, were soon in flames, and a strong south wind fanned them into a terrible conflagration. The fire raged during the remainder of the night, and on the next day, at noon, only seven or eight buildings remained. Four churches were among the buildings burned. On the 28th the 7th Ohio regiment, under Col. Tyler, was surrounded at Summersville, Va., while at breakfast, and attacked on both flanks and in front simultaneously. The troops, about nine hundred strong, although surprised, fought bravely, and forced their way through the enemy with considerable loss. No permanent advantage was gained by the Virginians, as Gen. Cox, with a larger Federal force, was stationed at Gauley's bridge.

On the other hand, an advantage was gained over the enemy at Athens, Missouri, on August 5th, by which their loss was between thirty and forty. At Potosi, in the same State, on the 9th, an affair occurred in which the enemy suffered some loss. An advantage was also gained in a small skirmish at Lovettsville, in Virginia, on the 8th; and another at Grafton on the 13th, at which the Virginians met with some loss.

At Fortress Monroe, Gen. Wool, of the regular army, had taken command, and Gen. Butler had been relieved for duty elsewhere. A passport system had been adopted by the authorities at Washington under a non-intercourse proclamation issued by the President on Aug. 16th, by which no person was permitted to go to the seceding States without an official permit.

On the water some movements had taken place. At Pokomoke Sound in Virginia, a number of small vessels belonging to the enemy had been destroyed, with some stores, on Aug. 2d.

At Galveston in Texas, on the 3d, a few shots were fired from the blockading Schooner Dart at the batteries on the island. This was intended as a sort of reconnoissance. Again, on the 5th, the steamer North Carolina opened fire upon the same batteries, and threw some sheels into the city. A large number of persons having collected on the sand hills a little east of the batteries, a shell fell among them, killing one, and wounding three others.

A protest was made by the foreign consuls, and Capt. Alden, on the next day, sent a reply, stating the facts to have been as follows:

Early on the morning of the 3d, our gunboat found herself near the shore, and shortly after, as the result proved, within range of some of the batteries. The first warning she got was a shot—not a blank cartridge, but a shot—not fired ahead or astern of her to warn her off, but straight at her. She of course fired back, and some shots were exchanged; then she came back and reported the facts to me. This was in the morning. I waited till nearly five in the afternoon hoping explanation, some disavowal, of the act would be sent off. None came. I then got under way and stood in for the batteries, which, you are aware, are in the rear and close to the town, merely to see if they could, when they knew the town must be injured by our return fire, repeat such an act of aggression by commencing upon us. We were no sooner within range of their guns, however, than they opened their fire, when we, after exchanging a few shots, retired, preferring that it should appear that we were beaten off rather than continue a contest where, as the result shows, so many unoffending citizens must necessarily suffer.

Again, you protest against my firing a shell into a crowd of unarmed citizens—amongst whom were many women and children. Good God! gentlemen, do you think such an act was premeditated? Besides, was it not the duty of the military commandant, who by his act in the morning had invited me to the contest, to see that all such were out of the way? Did he not have all day to prepare? It was evident to my mind they knew we were coming, or why was that demonstration of the steamer Gen. Rusk?

In conclusion, let me add that no one can regret the injury done to unoffending citizens more than I do. Still, I find no complaints of my acts of the 3d instant coming from military or civil authorities of Galveston, and with due deference to your consideration and humanity, I must respectfully remark that it is the first time I have ever heard that the women and children and unarmed citizens of an American town were under the protection of foreign consuls.

Yours, etc., etc., JAMES ALDEN.

On the 13th of August, when General Wool took command at Fortress Monroe, he found that preparations had already been made for an expedition to the North Carolina coast. Hatteras Inlet, the point of destination, was a gap in the sandy barrier which lines the coast of North Carolina, about 18 miles southwest of Cape Hatteras, and 160 miles below Fortress Monroe. Its channel was intricate, but accessible without difficulty to those who were accustomed to it, provided the weather was good. This and Ocracoke Inlet were the principal entrances to Pamlico Sound, a large body of water lying between this sandy beach and the mainland of North Carolina. Hatteras Inlet would admit vessels drawing 7 feet water, but its tortuous channel, from which all the buoys had been removed, made it difficult to enter in rough weather, without danger of grounding. On the sandy beach, commanding the inlet, the Confederate forces had erected, during the summer, two forts—the larger, named Fort Hatteras, being intended for 15 guns, though only 10 had been mounted; the smaller for 7 guns, of which 5 had been mounted. These forts were built of sand, and were 20 feet wide at top, and turfed. They had each a bombproof, the one at the larger fort capable of protecting about 400 men; that at the smaller 300. The guns were mounted *en barbette* (that is, on the top of the earthworks). The guns on both forts were thirty-two pounders, except one eight-inch shell gun on Fort Hatteras. Most of these particulars had been communicated to the Federal authorities about the 1st of August by Mr. Daniel Campbell, master of the schooner Lydia Frances, which had been wrecked about the 1st of May on the coast near Hatteras Inlet, who had been detained as a prisoner at the inlet for three months. The expedition intended for the capture of these forts consisted of the United States steamers Minnesota, Capt. Van Brune; Wabash, Capt. Mercer; Monticello, Commander Gillis; Pawnee, Commander Rowan, and Harriet Lane, Capt. Faunce; the U. S. chartered steamers Adelaide, Commander Stellwagen, and George Peabody, Lieut. Leroy, and the steamtug Fanny as transports, together with schooners towed by the steamers having surf-boats on them. The steam-frigate Susquehanna and the sailing frigate Cumberland were ordered also to join the expedition. The naval portion of the expedition was under the command of Commodore S. H. Stringham, whose broad pennant was hoisted on the Minnesota. To this naval force was added a body of about 880 troops, consisting of 500 of the

20th Regiment N. Y. Volunteers, under command of Col. Max Weber; 220 of the 9th N. Y. Volunteers, (Hawkins' Zouaves,) under command of Col. R. C. Hawkins; 100 of the Union Coast Guard, Capt. Nixon commanding, and 60 of the 2d U. S. Artillery, Lieut. Larned commanding, who were embarked on the transports George Peabody and Adelaide, and were under the command of Maj.-General Benj. F. Butler. The expedition left Fortress Monroe on the afternoon of Monday, Aug. 26th, and arrived off Hatteras Inlet about 4 o'clock P. M., Tuesday. At daylight the next morning arrangements were made for landing the troops, and for an attack upon the forts by the fleet. The swell upon the beach was so heavy that after landing 315 men, including the regular troops and 55 marines, with two guns, one a 12-pound rifled boat gun, the other a howitzer of the same calibre, the boats were stove and swamped, and no more could be landed that day. Meantime the fleet had opened fire on the smaller fort, which was nearest the inlet, and continued it till about half-past 1 P. M., when both forts hauled down their flags, and the garrison of the smaller escaped to the larger. A small detachment of the troops already landed immediately proceeded to take possession of Fort Clark, and raised the Union flag. The fleet ceased firing, and the Monticello was sent in to the inlet to discover what the hauling down of the flags meant. She entered and proceeded within about 600 yards of Fort Hatteras, when the occupants of that fort commenced firing upon her, and inflicted serious injury to her hull; whereupon the Wabash, Susquehanna, and Minnesota came to her assistance, and the Confederates took themselves to their bomb-proof, and ceased firing. The little force which had landed now withdrew from Fort Clark to a safer position, where they threw up a slight intrenchment, and mounted their two cannon on it, together with one they had taken from the enemy. The General and the force on board the fleet felt much anxiety in regard to this little company, as it was supposed that the Confederates, who were known to have a considerable body of troops on board steamers in the Sound, would be largely reënforced in the night, and would take them prisoners. At 7 o'clock next morning, however, the Union troops were seen advancing in good order upon Fort Clark, and it appeared that Capt. Nixon of the coastguard with his company had occupied that fort during the night, and had hoisted the Stars and Stripes there. As a reënforcement from the fleet approached the shore, they heard firing, which they afterwards found proceeded from the temporary battery erected by the Union troops, and was directed at the Confederate steamer Winslow, which had come down the sound loaded with reënforcements, but which, on meeting with this reception, made the best of its way out of range. The fleet renewed its fire upon Fort Hatteras at a little past 8 o'clock, and, substituting 15-second for 10-second fuzes, dropped almost every shell from their heavy guns inside the fort. At ten minutes past 11, a white flag was displayed from the fort. Gen. Butler went at once on board the steamtug Fanny, and, entering the inlet, sent Lieut. Crosby on shore to demand the meaning of the white flag. He soon returned with the following memorandum from the commander of the fort, who proved to be a former commodore of the U. S. Navy.

FORT HATTERAS, *Aug. 29th*, 1861.

Flag-officer Samuel Barron, C. S. Navy, offers to surrender Fort Hatteras with all the arms and munitions of war. The officers allowed to go out with side-arms, and the men without arms to retire.

S. BARRON,
Commanding Naval Division, Va. and N. Car.

Accompanying this was a verbal communication stating that he had in the fort six hundred and fifteen men, and a thousand more within an hour's call, but that he was anxious to spare the effusion of blood. Gen. Butler sent in reply the following memorandum:

Aug. 29th, 1861.

Benjamin F. Butler, Major-General United States Army, commanding, in reply to the communication of Samuel Barron, commanding forces at Fort Hatteras, cannot admit the terms proposed. The terms offered are these: Full capitulation, the officers and men to be treated as prisoners of war. No other terms admissible. Commanding officers to meet on board flagship Minnesota to arrange details.

After waiting three-fourths of an hour, Lieut. Crosby returned, bringing with him Capt. Barron, Major Andrews, and Col. Martin, the commanding officers of the Confederate force, who informed Gen. Butler that they had accepted the terms of capitulation he had proposed, and had come to surrender themselves and their command prisoners of war. General Butler informed them that, as the expedition was a combined one from the army and navy, the surrender must be made on board the flagship and to Com. Stringham, as well as himself. The party then proceeded to the flagship Minnesota, and the following articles of capitulation were there signed:

OFF HATTERAS INLET, U. S. FLAGSHIP MINNESOTA,
Aug. 29th, A. D. 1861.

Articles of Capitulation between Flag-officer Stringham, commanding the Atlantic Blockading Squadron, and Benjamin F. Butler, U. S. Army, commanding on behalf of the Government, and Samuel Barron, commanding the naval force for the defence of North Carolina and Virginia, and Col. Martin, commanding the forces, and Major Andrews, commanding the same forces at Hatteras.

It is stipulated and agreed between the contracting parties, that the forces under command of the said Barron, Martin, and Andrews, and all munitions of war, arms, men, and property under the command of said Barron, Martin, and Andrews, be unconditionally surrendered to the Government of the United States in terms of full capitulation.

And it is stipulated and agreed by the contracting parties, on the part of the United States Government, that the officers and men shall receive the treatment due to prisoners of war.

In witness whereof, we, the said Stringham and Butler, on behalf of the United States, and the said Barron, Martin, and Andrews, representing the forces at Hatteras Inlet, hereunto interchangeably set our hands, this twenty-ninth day of August, A. D. 1861, and of the independence of the United States the eighty-fifth year.

S. H. STRINGHAM,
Flag-Officer Atlantic Blockading Squadron.
BENJAMIN F. BUTLER,
Major-General U. S. A., Commanding.
S. BARRON,
Flag-Officer C. S. N., Com'g Naval Forces Va. & N. C.
WILLIAM F. MARTIN,
Col. Seventh Light Infantry N. C. Volunteers.
W. L. G. ANDREWS,
Major Com'g Forts Hatteras and Clark.

The results of this capitulation were the capture of 715 men, including the commander, Com. Barron, who was at the time Acting Secretary of the Navy of the Confederate States, and Major Bradford, Chief of the Ordnance Department of the Confederate States army, 2 forts, 1,000 stand of arms, 75 kegs of powder, 5 stand of colors, 31 pieces of cannon, including one 10-inch columbiad, a brig loaded with cotton, a sloop loaded with provisions and stores, 2 light boats, 150 bags of coffee, &c. The forts were held and garrisoned by U. S. troops, and the Fanny and Monticello retained at the inlet to keep off the Confederate gunboats, and capture vessels attempting to run the blockade. On the 30th Sept. a fortification called Fort Oregon at Ocracoke Inlet, about 15 miles below Hatteras Inlet, was abandoned by the Confederate forces, and on the 16th of September an expedition from Hatteras Inlet visited and destroyed it. On the 7th of September, four Confederate vessels, and on the 8th a fifth, attempted to enter Hatteras Inlet, and were all captured by the steam-tug Fanny. On the 2d of October the Fanny was captured by a party of Confederates in armed steam-tugs; her two brass cannon and 35 men belonging to the 9th N. Y. volunteers (Hawkins' Zouaves) were taken, and a considerable quantity of stores.

CHAPTER X.

Campaign of Gens. Wise, Floyd, and Lee, in Western Virginia—The Campaign of Gen. Fremont in Missouri—Affairs in Kentucky—Neutrality abandoned—Occupation of the State by troops—Military Operations.

A CAMPAIGN was now commenced by the enemy in Western Virginia. Gen. Henry A. Wise was at Lewisburg, the capital of Greenbrier County, organizing his brigade for an advance down the Kanawha valley, when Gen. Floyd (ex-Secretary of War) arrived with three regiments of infantry and a battalion of cavalry. After a consultation with Gen. Wise, whom he outranked, he resumed his march westward. At Tyree's, on the west side of Sewall Mountain, he was first met by the Union pickets, who were driven back upon their command with a loss of four killed and seven wounded. At Locust Lane he was overtaken by Gen. Wise, and the two commands advanced to Dogwood Gap at the intersection of the Summerville road with the turnpike from Lewisburg to Charleston. The main body of the Union force was stationed at Hawk's Nest, on New River, seven miles east of Gauley bridge, under Gen. Cox, with outposts at Cross Lanes and Carnifax ferry. Leaving at Dogwood Gap posted two pieces of artillery to keep open his line if a flank movement should be attempted from Carnifax ferry, Gen. Floyd advanced to Pickett's Mills. Here learning that his rear was threatened by the Union troops at Carnifax ferry and Cross Lanes, he left Gen. Wise to hold the turnpike, and moved at once upon Carnifax ferry to attack the Federal troops supposed to be there. He arrived at noon, but the Federal troops were at Hawk's Nest. On attempting to cross the river with his force, the boat was capsized and drawn over the rapids. His infantry and a small portion of his cavalry had crossed, but the mass of the cavalry and four pieces of artillery were still on the eastern side of the river. With great efforts another boat was prepared in a day and the transportation completed. Meanwhile Col. Tyler advanced from Hawk's Nest, but arrived too late to gain an advantage over Floyd, whose forces were now concentrated. On the contrary, the regiment was surprised by Gen. Floyd while at breakfast on the 26th of August, and with difficulty escaped capture.

Gen. Floyd then proceeded to strengthen his position and to bring up supplies for his men. Meanwhile Gen. Rosecrans, on Sept. 10th, advanced to attack the enemy; and about three o'clock in the afternoon he sent forward Gen. Benham, with his brigade, to make a reconnoissance in force. They were soon engaged with the enemy, and after a severe action were about being reënforced, when, from the great difficulties of the position rendering night fighting almost impossible, Gen. Rosecrans ordered his men to form in order of battle and rest upon their arms, intending to renew the attack in the morning. During the night Gen. Floyd and his force withdrew across the Gauley, leaving their camp, baggage, small arms, and munitions of war, and burning the bridge which he had constructed, and the ferry boats. Being unable to effect a crossing of the river, Gen. Rosecrans could not pursue them, but took a few prisoners. The Federal loss was, according to official report, 15 killed and 80 wounded; that of the Confederates was less, as they were protected by the forest and their fortifications.

Meanwhile Gen. Wise had marched down to Big Creek in Fayette County, where a slight skirmish took place with some Union troops.

Gen. Floyd, on retreating from Carnifax ferry, went to the summit of Big Sewell Mountain, having been joined on his way by Gen. Wise. Here a consultation was held, and it was decided to retreat to Meadow Bluff as a position which guarded all the approaches to Lewisburg and the railroad. Gen. Wise, however, refused to retreat, and proceeded to fortify his position, which he called Camp Defiance. Meanwhile Gen. Rosecrans advanced to Tyree's, a public house on the turnpike road in Fayette County. Such was the position of the enemy's forces in the Kanawha valley when Gen. Robert E. Lee arrived and took command.

After the defeat of Garnett and his forces on July 14th, by Gen. McClellan, Gen. Lee was ordered to succeed him, and with as little delay as possible to repair to the scene of operations. He took with him such reënforcements that on joining the remnant of Gen. Garnett's command, his force was about sixteen thousand men. His plan was to dislodge the forces of Gen. Rosecrans from Cheat Mountain, and thus relieve northwestern Virginia. In August he arrived in the neighborhood of the mountain on the Staunton and Parkersburg turnpike, and found Gen. Reynolds in command of the forces under Gen. Rosecrans, who, since the removal of Gen. McClellan to Washington, was in chief command in northwestern Virginia.

The aim of Gen. Lee on perceiving the strength of Gen. Reynolds, was to dislodge him by strategic movements, and capture his forces. With this object he cautiously moved along the road leading from Huntersville to Huttonsville in Randolph County, and, reaching Valley Mountain, halted to arrange his plans for attacking a body of Union troops stationed about eight miles below on Tygert's Valley River, and about five thousand strong. Thence he moved over the spurs of the mountains, and with great difficulty succeeded in getting below this body of Union troops, and at the same time placed a force east and west of them. Meantime fifteen hundred men of the forces of Gen. H. R. Jackson, under Col. Rust, of Arkansas, advanced from Greenbrier River around another position of the Union troops at Cheat Mountain pass, ten miles distant from the former Union force, for the purpose of an attack. This attack was to be the signal for Gen. Lee to attack the force on Tygert's Valley River. But Col. Rust finding the position so well prepared for defence, concluded that the attack could not be made with any hope of success, and ordered a retreat. No signal was thus given to Lee, and no attack therefore made by his forces, which retreated back to Valley Mountain without firing a gun. The attack of Col. Rust was designed merely to hold the force at Cheat Mountain Pass while the contest took place on the Valley river. Probably the attack of Lee would have been successful if it had been made without regard to the retreat of Rust, and would have resulted in giving him control for a time of that portion of West Virginia.

Lee now determined to move to the Kanawha Valley to relieve Gens. Floyd and Wise. Gen. Rosecrans was already on his march thither to oppose Floyd. All their forces were thus concentrated under Lee at Wise's position on Big Sewell Mountain, amounting nearly to twenty thousand men. The position was strengthened by a breastwork extending four miles. Meanwhile Gen. Rosecrans, who had approached within view of the enemy's position, where he remained some days prepared to receive an attack, concluding that it was not likely to be made, and that the enemy's position was too strong for him to assail successfully, quietly withdrew to his former position on the Gauley River, thirty-two miles distant. The reasons given by the enemy for not following, were the muddy roads, swollen streams, and the weakness of his artillery horses.

Meanwhile, on Oct. 2d, Gen. Reynolds, with about 5,000 men, left his camp at Cheat Mountain to make an armed reconnoissance of the forces of the enemy encamped on Greenbrier River and in the neighborhood. He reached the enemy's camp shortly after daylight, drove in the pickets, and his advanced regiments approached to within 700 yards of the intrenchments, and opened fire. A battle followed, of about four hours' duration. The Confederate force at the camp were driven from their guns, three of which were disabled; their reserve came up after the action had continued about two hours, and, thus reënforced, they maintained their position behind their breastworks, but did not sally out to attack the Federal troops. Gen. Reynolds, finding his ammunition exhausted, and having accomplished his purpose, withdrew in order, without being pursued, and returned the same night to his camp. The Federal loss was 8 killed and 32 wounded. The Confederate loss was much larger, and was estimated by Gen. Reynolds as at least 300. Gen. Reynolds brought away 13 prisoners. The enemy state that their loss did not exceed fifty, and estimated that of Gen. Reynolds between two hundred and fifty and three hundred.

On the approach of winter Gen. Lee was ordered to take charge of the coast defences of South Carolina and Georgia; Gen. Wise was ordered to Richmond, and the forces were all withdrawn by the authorities at Richmond, except those under Gen. Floyd, and a force of 1,200 men on the Alleghany Mountain. On December 13th this force, at Camp Alleghany, was attacked by Gen. Milroy.

The Union troops consisted of portions of the 9th and 13th Indiana, the 25th and 32d Ohio, and the 2d Virginia, numbering in all 1,750 men. The Confederate force was under the command of Gen. Johnson, of Georgia, and was estimated at 2,000. The action commenced about daylight and lasted till 3 o'clock in the afternoon, when the Confederates set fire to their camps and retreated to Staunton, in the valley of Virginia, thus vacating Western Virginia, at least that portion west of the Kittatinny range. The loss, as officially reported, was about equal on both sides: the Federal troops having 20 killed and 107 wounded; and the enemy 25 killed, 97 wounded, and about 30 of their men being taken prisoners.

Meantime Gen. Floyd, after the departure of the other Southern troops, moved by the way of Richard's ferry, Raleigh, and Fayette Court House, to Cotton Hill on the west side of the Kanawha River. Cotton Hill is in Fayette county, opposite the mouth of the Gauley River. Gen. Rosecrans was posted on both sides of the Gauley River above the mouth, and the hostile forces were in full view of each other. To cut off the retreat of Gen. Floyd, a movement was planned by Gen. Rosecrans across Miller's, Montgomery's, and Loop Creek ferries, concentrating at Fayetteville. Floyd detecting the movement immediately fell back, barely in time to escape capture. His rear was attacked and pursued some twenty miles, causing considerable loss. He now retired, and was subsequently transferred to Tennessee.

Some skirmishes took place during this period in West Virginia, attended with small loss to either side, but without special importance.

Meanwhile military movements of considerable interest had been made in Missouri. After the battle at Wilson's Creek, the forces of Gens. McCulloch and Price retired to the frontier of Arkansas. Here they remained until the latter part of August, when Price with a considerable force of Missourians began another movement into the State. As he advanced reënforcements joined him. Among others was Gen. Thos. A. Harris with about three thousand men, who been engaged in active guerrilla operations in northern Missouri. On September 7th a skirmish took place between a body of Kansas troops under Gen. Lane, which encountered the advance of Price at a stream called Drywood, near Fort Scott. The Kansas troops, although presenting a bold front, were soon compelled to retire. Fort Scott was also evacuated. Price then continued his march toward Lexington, where Col. Mulligan was in command. Lexington, the capital of Fayette County, is in a high and healthy situation, on the right bank of the Missouri River, 120 miles, by the road, west of Jefferson City. The population was about 5,000.

On the 29th of August a body of Home Guards, with some United States regulars posted at Lexington, were attacked by a large Confederate force. The Federal force numbered 430, and was intrenched. The assailing party had no artillery, and were repulsed with a considerable loss, and subsequently withdrew. This attack showed the importance of sending forward reënforcements. Accordingly, on the 9th of September, the town was occupied by an Irish Brigade under Col. Mulligan, which, in addition to a small force there, consisting of Home Guards, a few Kansas troops, a portion of the Missouri 8th regiment, and seven hundred of the Illinois cavalry, swelled the number to 2,500 men. Soon after a Confederate force under Gen. Price threatened an attack upon them. No time was lost in the work of intrenching their position, chosen about midway between the new and old towns of Lexington, which are about a mile apart, connected by a scattering settlement. Midway stood a solid brick edifice, built for a college, and about this a small breastwork had been already begun. By Col. Mulligan's order this was extended, and the troops commenced the construction of an earthwork, ten feet in height, with a ditch eight feet in width, enclosing a large area, capable of containing a force of 10,000 men. The army train, consisting of numerous mule teams, was brought within this area. The work was pushed with great vigor for three days, or until Thursday, the 12th, at which time that portion assigned to the Irish Brigade was well advanced, that of the Home Guard being still weak on the west or New Lexington side.

The college building, within the fortification, became Col. Mulligan's headquarters. The magazine and treasure were stored in the cellar and suitably protected. The hospital of the troops was located just outside of the intrenchments, in a northwesterly direction. The river, at that point, is about half a mile wide, and about half a mile distant from the fortifications. The bluff there is high and abrupt, the steamboat landing being at New Lexington.

The artillery of Col. Mulligan consisted of five brass pieces and two mortars, but, having no shells, the latter were useless. The cavalry had only side-arms and pistols.

On the 12th, scouts and advanced pickets driven in reported the near approach of the enemy's force. The attack was led by Gen. Rains with a battery of nine pieces of artillery against the point least prepared to resist assault. The Confederates were repulsed, and the result warned them that they had no easy task on hand. The hospital, containing about twenty-four patients, was not spared by the assailants. Some of the sick were pierced with bayonets or sabres in their cots. The chaplain and surgeon of the brigade were taken prisoners.

Skirmishing continued for several days, during which the enemy brought more of their artillery into action. Messengers had been sent to Jefferson City by Col. Mulligan to urge the necessity of reënforcements, but they had been captured. At the same time, sufficient troops were sent out by the enemy to intercept any Federal reënforcements. Thus a party of 1,500 Iowa troops were met and forced to retire when they had arrived within sixteen miles of the river.

The situation of the Federal force was daily growing more desperate. Within their lines were picketed about the wagons and trains a large number of horses and mules, nearly three thousand in all, now a serious cause of care and anxiety; for, as shot and shell plunged among them, many of the animals were killed or wounded, and from the struggles of the latter the danger of a general stampede was imminent. The havoc in the centre of the intrenchment was immense. Wagons were knocked to pieces, stores scattered and destroyed, and the ground strewn with dead horses and mules.

On the 17th the water gave out, and being cut off from the river, the Union troops were reduced to great straits. Rations, also, began to grow short. Meanwhile, the contest continued with little cessation, as a brilliant moon shone all night. Gen. Price had sent to Col. Mulligan a summons to surrender, to which the latter sent a refusal, saying, "If you want us, you must take us." The Home Guard, however, had become discouraged and disheartened, and on the 21st, while Col. Mulligan was engaged in another part of the camp, a white flag was raised by Major Becker, of the Guards, in the portion of the intrenchments assigned to him. As soon as this was made known to Col. Mulligan, he ordered the flag to be taken down, which was done. The severest of the fighting during that day followed in a charge made upon the enemy's nearest battery. Subsequently the Home Guards left the outer work and retreated within the line of the inner intrenchments, about the college building, refusing to fight longer, and here again raised the white flag, this time from the centre of the fortifications, when the fire of the enemy slackened and ceased. Under this state of affairs, Col. Mulligan, calling his officers into council, decided to capitulate, and Capt. McDermott went out to the enemy's lines, with a handkerchief tied to a ramrod, and a parley took place. Major Moore, of the brigade, was sent to Gen. Price's headquarters, at New Lexington, to know the terms of capitulation. These were: that the officers were to be retained as prisoners of war, the men to be allowed to depart with their personal property, surrendering their arms and accoutrements. Reluctantly this was acceded to.

At 4 P. M. on Sept. 21st, the Federal forces were marched out of the intrenchments. They left behind them their arms and accoutrements, reserving only their clothing. The privates, numbering some 1,500 strong, were first made to take the oath not to serve against the Confederate States, when they were put across the river, and, in charge of Gen. Rains, marched on Saturday night to Richmond, sixteen miles; whence, on Sunday, they marched to Hamilton, a station on the Hannibal and St. Joseph's Railroad, where they were declared free to go wherever they pleased. While on this march they experienced generous and humane treatment, both from Gen. Rains and from the residents.

The Federal force at Lexington was composed of the 23d regiment (Irish Brigade), Col. Mulligan, 800; 13th Missouri, Col. Peabody, 840; 1st Illinois, Col. Marshall, 500; Home Guards, Col. White, 500; total, 2,640, with one 4, three 6, and one 12-pounders, and two 4-inch mortars. The Confederate force had been increased from 3,000 by the arrival of reënforcements to a large number, estimated at 10,000. It appears by the official report of Gen. Price, who took command at the outset, that, in addition to the large force he brought with him from the southwest, he was joined, before the battle, by the forces under Martin Green, Harris, Boyd, and Patten, all of whom participated in the siege. Green's force, when he crossed the river at Glasgow, was 2,500 men; Harris had 2,700 when he crossed; and Patten and Boyd had a considerable number. The force of the garrison was only 2,640 men. The loss of water, and the inferiority of numbers caused the surrender. Gen. Price says that the firing was continued for fifty-two hours. The enemy adopted for defence a breastwork of hempen bales, which they rolled before them as they advanced. Their loss they state at 25 killed and 72 wounded. The Federal loss in killed and wounded was estimated from 300 to 500. Gen. Fremont, upon hearing of this surrender, sent the following despatch to Washington:

HEADQUARTERS WESTERN DEPARTMENT,
ST. LOUIS, *Sept.* 23, 1861.

Col. E. D. Townsend, Adjutant-General:

I have a telegram from Brookfield that Lexington has fallen into Price's hands, he having cut off Mulligan's supply of water. Reënforcements 4,000 strong, under Sturgis, by the capture of the ferry boats, had no means of crossing the river in time. Lane's forces from the southwest, and Davis from the southeast, upwards of 11,000 in all, could also not get there in time. I am taking the field myself and hope to destroy the enemy either before or after the junction of the forces under McCulloch. Please notify the President immediately. J. C. FREMONT, Major-Gen. Commanding.

Some remarks appeared in the St. Louis "Evening News" a few days after, commenting upon the neglect of the authorities at St. Louis to send out reënforcements, when the paper was immediately suppressed by Gen. Fremont, and its publisher and editor sent to prison, from which they were subsequently unconditionally released.

As a strategetical point, the loss of the town was a serious affair to the Federal cause, and a gain of no small value to the Confederates. Its possession would tend to retain that part of Missouri on the Union side, while its loss would expose Kansas, as well as the northern and western parts of Missouri.

The capture of Lexington, the most important affair to the Confederates which occurred in the State, doubtless caused Gen. Fremont, on September 27th, to hasten from St. Louis to Jefferson City. On the 3d of October Gen. Price abandoned Lexington, and as the Union force concentrated at Jefferson City, he retired to Springfield and still further south. His force was extravagantly estimated at this time at twenty thousand men and upward. The original purpose of Gen. Price had been to move from Lexington northward and destroy the railroad, and then attack the Federal forces in Northwestern Missouri, but the approach of Fremont prevented its accomplishment. No one of the Confederate generals sustained his position so well as Gen. Price, with the slender resources at his command. It was necessarily, therefore, a part of his system of operations to avoid a doubtful conflict. Retiring produced no discouragement upon his men. At the same time, by retiring, he came nearer to Arkansas, from whence he could expect supplies and reënforcements, whilst the Federal force, on advancing, would be removed further and further from its chief source of supplies. The advance of Gen. Fremont, in the southwest, was made in five divisions, under Gens. Hunter, Pope, Sigel, Asboth, and McKinstry. Each division was subdivided, and was composed of cavalry, artillery, and infantry, ambulances, &c., and whatever was necessary to enable it to act independently. Gen. Fremont accompanied the advance with Gens. Sigel and Asboth.

On the 14th of October he arrived at Warsaw on the Osage River, sixty-five miles southwest of Jefferson City, where he prepared to cross by means of bridges. On the opposite bank was a considerable rebel cavalry force at the time of his arrival, which was dispersed by canister-shot. The bridge was finished about the 21st, and on the 26th the troops reached Bolivar. Gen. Fremont left on Sunday with Gen. Sigel by forced marches, for Springfield. Gen. McKinstry still continued at Warsaw with the reserve, and Gen. Pope was on the other side of the Osage. Gen. Hunter was with the right wing advancing, and Gen. Sturgis with the left. On the 27th Gen. Fremont arrived at Springfield, where the national flag was displayed by the people with every demonstration of joy. On the 25th a dashing charge was made by Maj. Zagonyi with a hundred and fifty of Gen. Fremont's Body Guard, armed with Colt's rifles, upon a force of the enemy about half a mile west of the town, by which the latter were dispersed.

The retreat of Gen. Price had been steadily in advance of the Union troops. On the 13th he was at Clintonville, Cedar County, twenty-five miles south of Papinsville, on the Carthage Road. His entire army had passed the Osage. On the 17th he was expected by the Union general to make a stand, and again on the 19th. On the 24th he was at Nesho, in Newton County, and had united with Gen. McCulloch. The Legislature of the State had convened here at this time. Only a small number of members were present.

In Northwestern Missouri, Col. Morgan, on the 19th, with two hundred and twenty of the 18th Missouri, had a skirmish with a larger rebel force at Big Harrison Creek in Carrol County. Fourteen of the enemy were reported to have been killed, and eight were taken prisoners. The Federal loss was two killed and fourteen wounded. On the 21st the rebel garrison at Fredericktown was surprised by a portion of the 1st Missouri regiment, and the town recaptured.

In Southwestern Missouri, a skirmish took place near Lebanon on the 13th of October between two companies of mounted men under Major Wright and a small body of secession cavalry, in which the latter were surprised and routed with a small loss. On the 17th a skirmish took place near Pilot Knob, and on the 22d another at Fredericktown. Several other skirmishes of small importance, otherwise than as showing the activity of both Federal and secession troops, occurred during the month of October.

So much complaint had been made relative to the management of the Western Department by Gen. Fremont, that the Secretary of War proceeded to St. Louis for the purpose of investigation. An interview with Gen. Fremont took place at Tipton, and when about to return from St. Louis to Washington, the Secretary issued the following order:

St. Louis, October 14, 1861.

General: The Secretary of War directs me to communicate the following as his instructions for your government:

In view of the heavy sums due, especially in the Quartermaster's Department in this city, amounting to some $4,500,000, it is important that the money which may now be in the hands of the disbursing officers, or be received by them, be applied to the current expenses of your army in Missouri, and these debts to remain unpaid until they can be properly examined and sent to Washington for settlement; the disbursing officers of the army to disburse the funds, and not transfer them to irresponsible agents; in other words, those who do not hold commissions from the President, and are not under bonds. All contracts necessary to be made by the disbursing officers. The senior Quartermaster here has been verbally instructed by the Secretary as above.

It is deemed unnecessary to erect field-works around this city, and you will direct their discontinuance; also those, if any, in course of construction at Jefferson City. In this connection, it is seen that a number of commissions have been given by you. No payments will be made to such officers, except to those whose appointments have been approved by the President. This, of course, does not apply to the officers with volunteer troops. Col. Andrews has been verbally so instructed by the Secretary; also, not to make transfers of funds, except for the purpose of paying the troops.

The erection of barracks near your quarters in this city to be at once discontinued.

The Secretary has been informed that the troops of Gen. Lane's command are committing depredations on our friends in Western Missouri. Your attention is directed to this, in the expectation that you will apply the corrective.

Maj. Allen desires the services of Capt. Turnley for a short time, and the Secretary hopes you may find it proper to accede thereto.

I have the honor to be, very respectfully, your obedient servant, L. THOMAS, Adjutant-General.

Major-General J. C. Fremont,
Commanding Department of the West, Tipton.

On the 1st of November an agreement was entered into between Gens. Fremont and Price that a joint proclamation should be signed by both, and issued, which should provide for certain objects therein specified, as follows:

To all peaceably-disposed Citizens of the State of Missouri, greeting: Whereas, a solemn agreement has been entered into by and between Maj.-Gens. Fremont and Price, respectively commanding antagonistic forces in the State of Missouri, to the effect that in future, arrests or forcible interference by armed or unarmed parties of citizens within the limits of said State, for the mere entertainment or expression of political opinions, shall hereafter cease; that families, now broken up for such causes, may be reunited, and that the war now progressing shall be exclusively confined to armies in the field. Therefore be it known to all whom it may concern:

1. No arrests whatever on account of political opinions, or for the merely private expression of the same, shall hereafter be made within the limits of the State of Missouri; and all persons who may have been arrested and are held to answer on such charges only, shall be forthwith released. But it is expressly declared, that nothing in this proclamation shall be construed to bar, or interfere with any of the usual and regular proceedings of the established courts under statutes and orders made and provided for such offences.

2. All peaceably-disposed citizens who may have been driven from their homes because of their political opinions, or who may have left them for fear of force or violence, are hereby advised and permitted to return, upon the faith of our positive assurances that, while so returning, they shall receive protection from both armies in the field whenever it can be given.

3. All bodies of armed men acting without the authority or recognition of the Major-Generals before named, and not legitimately connected with the armies in the field, are hereby ordered at once to disband.

4. Any violation of either of the foregoing articles shall subject the offender to the penalty of military law, according to the nature of the offence. In testimony whereof, the aforesaid Maj.-Gen. John C. Fremont, at Springfield, Mo., on the 1st day of November, A. D. 1861, and Maj.-Gen. Sterling Price, at Cassville, on this 5th day of November, A. D. 1861, have hereunto set their hands, and hereby mutually pledge their earnest efforts to the enforcement of the above articles of agreement, according to their full tenor and effect, to the best of their ability.

JOHN C. FREMONT,
Major-General Commanding U. S. A.
STERLING PRICE,
Maj.-General Commanding Missouri State Guards.

On the 2d day of November, Gen. Fremont, at Springfield, received the order for his removal from the command of the Department of the West. He had arrived there only a few days previous at the head of an army, and was then in the act of marching on after a retiring enemy. Although not altogether unexpected, it occasioned much excitement in the army, and many officers were disposed to resign, declaring that they would serve under no other commander. Gen. Fremont, however, issued a patriotic farewell address, urging the army to cordially support his successor, and expressing regret to leave on the eye of a battle they were sure to win. The following is his address:

HEADQUARTERS WESTERN DEPARTMENT,
SPRINGFIELD, November 2, 1861.

Soldiers of the Mississippi Army: Agreeably to orders received this day, I take leave of you. Although our army has been of sudden growth we have grown up together, and I have become familiar with the brave and generous spirits which you bring to the defence of your country, and which makes me anticipate for you a brilliant career. Continue as you have begun, and give to my successor the same cordial and enthusiastic support with which you have encouraged me. Emulate the splendid example which you have already before you, and let me remain as I am, proud of the noble army which I have thus far labored to bring together.

Soldiers, I regret to leave you. Most sincerely I thank you for the regard and confidence you have invariably shown me. I deeply regret that I shall not have the honor to lead you to the victory which you are just about to win; but I shall claim the right to share with you in the joy of every triumph, and trust always to be personally remembered by my companions in arms. JOHN C. FREMONT,
Major-General.

Gen. Fremont immediately surrendered his command to Gen. Hunter, and returned to St. Louis, where he arrived on the 8th of November.

After his departure, Major-Gen. Hunter, on the 7th of November, addressed a letter to Gen. Price, in which he recapitulated the agreement, and said: "As General commanding the forces of the United States in this Department, I can in no manner recognize the agreement aforesaid, or any of its provisions, whether implied or direct, and I can neither issue, nor allow to be issued, the 'joint proclamation' purporting to have been signed by yourself and Maj.-Gen. Fremont, on the 1st day of November, A. D. 1861."

Some of the objections of Gen. Hunter to this agreement, were that it would render the enforcement of martial law impossible, that it would practically annul the confiscation act of Congress, &c.

The Federal force in Missouri at this time was estimated at 27,000 men, of whom 5,000 had been under the command of Gen. Hunter, 4,000 under Gen. Sigel, 4,500 under Gen. Asboth, 5,500 under Gen. McKinstry, 4,000 under Gen. Pope, under Gen. Lane 2,500, and under Gen. Sturgis 1,000.

When Gen. Fremont left the army was in good spirits, and no battle was soon expected. The chief command was held by Gen. Hunter as the oldest officer in the field, who expected soon to be superseded by Gen. Halleck. Gen. Price fell back near the State line, and remained until the Federal army began to recede, about the 15th. They were accompanied by long trains of emigrant wagons containing Union refugees. As they retired, Gen Price followed up after them. The advance of Gen. Price was made in three divisions, and with the intention of moving upon Kansas, and making that the field of future operations. The opinion in the Southern States was that Gen. Price never had any difficulty to procure men. His only obstacle had been the want of arms.

On the 30th of November his right wing, 6,000 strong, was at Stockton. The left wing held position near Nevada under Gen. Rains, 4,000 strong. The centre, under Gen. Price, 5,000 strong, was near Monticello.

In Boone County, on the 3d, Gen. Prentiss broke up a secession camp, with some loss on both sides.

On the 18th of November Gen. H. W. Halleck arrived at St. Louis, and took command of the Western Department. Gens. Sturgis and Wyman arrived on the same day. The divisions of Gens. Hunter and Pope had reached different points on the Pacific Railroad, there to await the orders of Gen. Halleck. About the 20th the divisions of Gens. Sigel and Asboth arrived at St. Louis.

The plan of Gen. Price now, was to approach the boarders of Kansas, and supply his forces with arms, destroy the track of the Northern Railroad, and thus cut off the communication with St. Louis. This, however, was defeated by the strategical combinations of Gen. Halleck, and on the 25th of December almost a clean sweep had been made of the country between the Missouri and Osage Rivers, and Gen. Price was cut off from all supplies and recruits from Northern Missouri, and in full retreat for Arkansas.

In the last two weeks of December, the Federal army captured 2,500 prisoners, including 70 commissioned officers, 1,200 horses and mules, 1,100 stand of arms, two tons of powder, 100 wagons, and an immense amount of commissary stores and camp equipage. Several skirmishes took place during these operations. On the 22d of November the town of Warsaw was burned by incendiaries, to prevent its further occupation by Union troops. At Salem a skirmish took place on the 3d of December, between a small Federal force and a body of State Guards. Several were killed and wounded on both sides. At Shawnee Mound, on the 18th of December, Gen. Pope captured 150 Confederate prisoners, with wagons, tents, and baggage. At Milford, on the 18th, a body of the enemy were surrounded, and surrendered. Thirteen hundred prisoners were taken, including three colonels and seventeen captains, and one thousand stand of arms, one thousand horses, sixty-five wagons, and a large quantity of tents, baggage, and supplies.

The close of military operations in Missouri at the approach of winter left Gen. Halleck free to use a large part of his army in Western Kentucky. The struggle in the State during the year had been vigorous and active, especially on the part of Gen. Price, under the contracted resources at his command.

It was stated at Richmond, Va., that after the capture of Mulligan, Gen. Price intended to attack Gen. Fremont before he could concentrate his army, but was prevented by a lack of ammunition from executing his design. When Lexington surrendered he had but 2,000 percussion caps in his whole command. He sent to Gen. Hardee and to Gen. McCulloch for a supply, but for some reason it was not sent. It was thought at that time in Richmond that if Gen. Price had been zealously and efficiently seconded, he would soon have driven the Federal force from Missouri, and thus have secured to the Confederacy one of the most important Western States. A consequence of such an acquisition would involve the destinies of Kansas, the Indian nation, Arizona, and New Mexico. The possession of the vast countries which lie to the west and southwest was the occasion of the contest made by the Southern States in Missouri.

On the 21st of November, after Gen. Halleck had taken command, he issued, at St. Louis, an order, setting forth that, as important information respecting the numbers and condition of his forces had been conveyed to the enemy by fugitive slaves, no such persons should thereafter be permitted to enter the lines of any camp, nor of any forces on the march. On the 9th of December he issued an order directing the Mayor of St. Louis to require all municipal officers immediately to take the oath of allegiance prescribed by the State Convention, and also directing the provost-marshal to arrest all State officers who had failed to subscribe the oath within the time fixed, and subsequently attempted to exercise authority.

On the night of December 20, some men who had returned from Gen. Price's army destroyed about one hundred miles of the Missouri Railroad, or rendered it useless. Commencing eight miles south of Hudson, they burned the bridge, wood piles, water tanks, ties, and tore up the rails for miles, bent them, and destroyed the telegraph. It was a preconcerted and simultaneous movement of citizens along the road.

On the 23d Gen. Halleck issued an order fixing the penalty of death on all persons engaged in destroying railroads and telegraphs, and requiring the towns and counties where it is done to repair the damages and pay expenses.

On the 25th he issued the following order, declaring qualified martial law:

In virtue of authority conferred on me by the President of the United States, martial law is hereby declared, and will be enforced in and about all the railroads in this State.

It is not intended by this declaration to interfere with the jurisdiction in any court which is loyal to the Government of the United States, and which will aid the military authorities in enforcing order and punishing crimes.

The attack upon Fort Sumter and the call of President Lincoln for seventy-five thousand men, were turned to the utmost advantage by the friends of the seceded States, to promote their cause. Kentucky, however, refused to take part either with the North or the South.

The State Union Committee issued an address to the people on the condition of the country, declaring it to be the duty of the State to maintain neutrality, and to take no part either with the Government or the Confederates.

The present duty of Kentucky, they said, was to maintain her present independent position, taking sides not with the Government, and not with the seceding States, but with the Union against them both; declaring her soil to be sacred from the hostile tread of either, and if necessary, making the declaration good with her strong right arm. And, to the end that she might be fully prepared for this last contingency, and all other possible contingencies, they would have her arm herself thoroughly at the earliest practicable moment.

Subsequently, Governor Magoffin issued a proclamation with the following warning:

I hereby notify and warn all other States, separate or united, especially the United and Confederate States, that I solemnly forbid any movement upon Kentucky soil, or occupation of any post or place therein, for any purposes whatever, until authorized by invitation or permission of the Legislative and Executive authorities. I especially forbid all citizens of Kentucky, whether incorporated in the State Guard, or otherwise, from making any hostile demonstrations against any of the aforesaid sovereignties, to be obedient to the orders of lawful authorities, to remain quietly and peaceably at home when off military duty, and refrain from all words and acts likely to provoke a collision, and so otherwise to conduct themselves that the deplorable calamity of invasion may be averted; but in the meanwhile to make prompt and efficient preparation to assume the paramount and supreme law of self-defence, and strictly of self-defence alone.

Volunteers from Kentucky entered both the Northern and the Southern armies. Those attached to the former were ordered to Western Virginia, and there entered into active service.

So stringent had the restrictions upon all intercourse between the North and the South now become that commerce was to a great degree cut off, except by the route of the Louisville and Nashville Railroad. It had long become manifest that the blockade of the South would not be complete unless the transit of supplies through Kentucky was stopped. But how this should be effected while Kentucky was herself in so doubtful a position, was a question not easily determined. The authorities of Tennessee solved it, however, by placing a complete embargo on the Tennessee end of the road.

They forbade the exportation of cotton, tobacco, rice, and turpentine to Kentucky. From their own point of view the act was one of folly, for the freight sent North was never one-fifth part of that sent South, and at that moment especially must have been vastly inferior in importance to the constant supply of provisions flowing into Tennessee from Louisville. They thought, however, that they could afford the step, and therefore forbade all exports from Tennessee.

This cut the knot as to the enforcement of the blockade at Louisville. It put an end to all scruples on the part of Kentucky, except among the open sympathizers with secession; it placed the secessionists in the wrong in "neutral" eyes, and gave the Government firm ground on which to stand. The blockade being undertaken with vigor, those who were forwarding supplies to the secessionists attempted to break it by legal proceedings. They crowded the Louisville freight stations with merchandise consigned to Nashville, and sued the company as common carriers for refusing to receive and forward it. The decision of the Court justified the company in its course of obedience to the Federal Government, and gave to the Government the authority of legal approval, as well as the sympathy of right-minded citizens. It still remained, however, for the Tennessee secessionists, in their wisdom, to conceive one more plan for perfecting the work undertaken by the Government. This scheme they carried out on the fourth of July, by stopping the running of cars on the railroad altogether, and by doing this in such a manner as to seriously injure a great interest in Kentucky.

Of this proceeding we have the following account:

The Louisville and Nashville Railway is 286 miles in length, forty-five miles of it lying in Tennessee. These forty-five miles cost $2,025,000, of which Tennessee contributed in all bonds to the amount of $1,160,500, the remaining $864,500 being raised by the Kentucky owners. On the first of July a Tennessee General, named Anderson, ordered the company to keep a larger amount of its rolling stock at Nashville. James Guthrie, president of the company, stated, however, that "there being no provision in the charter to the effect that the company should be subject to the military orders of Tennessee, the order was not complied with." On the 4th of July, General Anderson seized two trains that were about to leave Nashville, and one that came in, together with such machinery as could be found in Tennessee, and then called for a fair division of the rolling stock of the road, and agreed that while arrangements were in progress for this end the trains should be uninterrupted; but to this Mr. Guthrie astutely made answer that he could thus have no guarantee against the interference of others besides General Anderson, who was supposed to be acting under orders. This brought out the Governor of Tennessee as the real actor in the matter, for he at once replied to Mr. Guthrie with a proposition to continue the use of the road while a division of property was made. Mr. Guthrie at once rejoined, disproving the charge made by the Tennessee authorities, that their end of the road had not hitherto had its share of the rolling stock, and showing the impossibility of managing the road under Governor Harris's proposition.

The result was that the road was closed. The Kentucky stockholders declared that their chartered rights in Tennessee had been no protection to their property, and refused to risk any more within the limits of that State. All questions as to the blockade upon this route were therefore disposed of by the breaking up of the route itself. The secessionists felt the extent of their error, for they urged Governor Magoffin to seize the Kentucky end of the road, and to run it in connection with Governor Harris; but it was evident that such a step would only serve to remove the last scruple on the part of Union men as to forcible resistance to the bold plans of the secessionists in Kentucky.

The question as to the transit of provisions to the South by this railroad was thus settled; and, although it did not close other routes through Kentucky, which were equally important, the controversy which had sprung up took such a turn as to have an important effect throughout the State, stimulating the Union men everywhere to a more active support of the Government. A small encampment of Federal troops was formed in Garrard County, which occasioned some excitement, as it was an infringement of the neutrality assumed by Kentucky. Letters were addressed to the commanding officer, Gen. Nelson, asking the special object which the Government had in view in the establishment of the camp called "Camp Dick Robinson." In reply, the commanding officer said: "The troops assembled here have been called together at the request of Union men of Kentucky. They are intended for no hostile or aggressive movement against any party or community whatever, but simply to defend Kentucky in case they are needed for that purpose, preserve its tranquillity, and protect the rights of all the citizens of the State under the Constitution and the laws; and the object of myself and all the officers in command will be, by all honorable means, to maintain that peace and tranquillity." Commissioners were then sent by the Governor to President Lincoln to insist on the neutrality of the State.

Governor Magoffin, in his letter to the President, said: "In a word, an army is now being organized and quartered in this State, supplied with all the appliances of war, without the consent or advice of the authorities of the State, and without consultation with those most prominently known and recognized as loyal citizens. This movement now imperils that peace and tranquillity which from the beginning of our pending difficulties have been the paramount desire of this people, and which, up to this time, they have so secured to the State.

"Within Kentucky there has been, and is likely to be, no occasion for the presence of military force. The people are quiet and tranquil, feeling no apprehension of any occasion arising to invoke protection from the Federal arm. They have asked that their territory be left free from military occupation, and the present tranquillity of their communication left uninvaded by soldiers. They do not desire that Kentucky shall be required to supply the battle-field for the contending armies, or become the theatre of the war.

"Now, therefore, as Governor of the State of Kentucky, and in the name of the people I have the honor to represent, and with the single and earnest desire to avert from their peaceful homes the horrors of war, I urge the removal from the limits of Kentucky of the military force now organized and encamped within the State. If such action as is hereby urged be promptly taken, I firmly believe the peace of the people of Kentucky will be preserved, and the horrors of a bloody war will be averted from a people now peaceful and tranquil."

To this the President replied: "In all I have done in the premises I have acted upon the urgent solicitation of many Kentuckians, and in accordance with what I believed, and still believe, to be the wish of a majority of all the Union-loving people of Kentucky.

"While I have conversed on this subject with many eminent men of Kentucky, including a large majority of her members of Congress, I do not remember that any one of them, or any other person, except your Excellency and the bearers of your Excellency's letter, has urged me to remove the military force from Kentucky, or to disband it. One other very worthy citizen of Kentucky did solicit me to have the augmenting of the force suspended for a time.

"Taking all the means within my reach to form a judgment, I do not believe it is the popular wish of Kentucky that this force shall be removed beyond her limits; and, with this impression, I must respectfully decline to so remove it.

"I most cordially sympathize with your Excellency in the wish to preserve the peace of my own native State, Kentucky. It is with regret I search, and cannot find, in your not very short letter, any declaration or intimation that you entertain any desire for the preservation of the Federal Union."

A similar letter was addressed by the Governor to the President of the insurrectionary States. In the reply, Mr. Davis said: "The Government of the Confederate States of America neither intends nor desires to disturb the neutrality of Kentucky. The assemblage of troops in Tennessee to which you refer had no other object than to repel the lawless invasion of that State by the forces of the United States, should their Government approach it through Kentucky, without respect for its position of neutrality. That such apprehensions were not groundless has been proved by the course of that Government in Maryland and Missouri, and more recently in Kentucky itself, in which, as you inform me, 'a military force has been enlisted and quartered by the United States authorities.'

"The Government of the Confederate States has not only respected most scrupulously the neutrality of Kentucky, but has continued to maintain the friendly relations of trade and intercourse which it has suspended with the people of the United States generally.

"In view of the history of the past, it can scarcely be necessary to assure your Excellency that the Government of the Confederate States will continue to respect the neutrality of Kentucky so long as her people will maintain it themselves.

"But neutrality, to be entitled to respect, must be strictly maintained between both parties; or if the door be opened on the one side for the aggressions of one of the belligerent parties upon the other, it ought not to be shut to the assailed when they seek to enter it for the purpose of self-defence.

"I do not, however, for a moment believe that your gallant State will suffer its soil to be used for the purpose of giving an advantage to those who violate its neutrality and disregard its rights, over those who respect them both."

It should be stated that previous to this correspondence, Kentucky had been invaded by Tennessee forces, and six cannons and a thousand stands of arms taken. The Richmond Congress, on August 7th, passed an act authorizing enlistments in Kentucky. The Legislature assembled on the 2d of September, and on the 5th a large barbecue was to be held in Owens County, about twelve miles from the seat of Government. The apprehensions of the Unionists were greatly excited on this occasion. The State Guard were invited to attend; they consisted of an organized body of troops about fifteen thousand strong, under the control of the friends of secession in the State. Intimidation of the Legislature was feared. Happily the affair passed over without any special interest. A Peace Convention was also to be held on the tenth of the same month, which awakened apprehensions of an attempt to organize the secession force. But these likewise proved groundless. The Legislature stood 27 Union and 11 Southern Rights Senators, and 76 Union and 24 Southern Rights Representatives. The message of the Governor to that body on the 5th of September, asserted that Kentucky had a right to assume a neutral position in the war; that she had no agency in fostering a sectional party in the Free States, and did not approve of separate action and the secession of the Southern States. Lawless raids had been suffered on both sides, private property seized, commerce interrupted, and trade destroyed. These wrongs had been borne with patience, but a military Federal force had been organized, equipped, and encamped in a central portion of Kentucky, without consultation with the State authorities. If the people of Kentucky desired more troops, let them be obtained under the Constitution of Kentucky. He recommended the passage of a law to enable the Military Board to borrow a sufficient sum to purchase arms and munitions for the defence of the State. He also recommended the passage of resolutions requesting the disbanding or removal of all military bodies not under State authority, from the State.

On the same day the Legislature were notified that Confederate troops had invaded the State, and occupied and fortified strong positions at Hickman and Chalk Bluffs. Governor Harris, of Tennessee, replied to a demand of the Kentucky authorities, that the troops "that landed at Hickman last night did so without my knowledge or consent, and I am confident without the consent of the 'President.' I have telegraphed President Davis requesting their immediate withdrawal."

Gen. Polk, in command of the secession forces, in reply to the Governor of Kentucky, stated that he had occupied Columbus and Hickman, in Kentucky, on account of reliable information that the Federal forces were about to occupy the said points. He proposed substantially that the Federal and Confederate forces should be simultaneously withdrawn from Kentucky, and enter into stipulation to respect the neutrality of the State.

In the proclamation issued on the 4th of September, Gen. Polk gives this reason for invading Kentucky: "The Federal Government having, in defiance of the wishes of the people of Kentucky, disregarded their neutrality by establishing camp depots for their armies, and by organizing military companies within the territory, and by constructing military works on the Missouri shore immediately opposite and commanding Columbus, evidently intended to cover the landing of troops for the seizure of that town, it has become a military necessity for the defence of the territory of the Confederate States that a Confederate force should occupy Columbus in advance."

On the 9th, the Governor communicated the following to the Legislature: "The undersigned yesterday received a verbal message, through a messenger, from Gov. Harris. The message was that he (Gov. H.) had, by telegraphic despatch, requested Gen. Polk to withdraw the Confederate troops from Kentucky, and that Gen. Polk had declined to do so; that Gov. Harris then telegraphed to Secretary Walker, at Richmond, requesting that Gen. Polk be ordered to withdraw his troops from Kentucky, and that such order was issued from the War Department of the Confederacy; that Gen. Polk replied to the War Department that the retention of the post was a military necessity, and that the retiring from it would be attended by the loss of many lives. This embraces the message received."

On the same day the Governor also received the following by telegraph from Gen. Polk:

GOV. B. MAGOFFIN: A military necessity having required me to occupy this town, Columbus, I have taken possession of it by the forces under my command. The circumstances leading to this act were reported promptly to the President of the Confederate States. His reply was, the necessity justified the action.

As a matter of course, the invasion of the State by the Tennessee troops brought in a Federal force under Gen. Grant from Cairo. Thus ended the neutrality of Kentucky.

It was on the 6th of September that Gen. Grant, with two regiments of infantry and a company of light artillery, in two gunboats, took possession of Paducah, Kentucky. He found secession flags flying in different parts of the town, in expectation of greeting the arrival of the Southern army, which was reported to be 3,800 strong, and only sixteen miles distant. The loyal citizens tore down the secession flags on the arrival of the Federal troops. Gen. Grant took possession of the telegraph office, railroad depot, and the marine hospital. He found large quantities of complete rations, leather, etc., for the Southern army.

He issued a proclamation saying that he came solely for the purpose of defending the State from aggression, and to enable the State laws to be executed.

On the 11th of September, the Assembly of the Legislature adopted a resolution directing the Governor to issue a proclamation ordering the Confederate troops to evacuate Kentucky soil. The vote was seventy-one against twenty-six. The House refused to suspend the rules to allow another resolution to be offered ordering the proclamation to be issued to both Federals and Confederates.

This resolution was subsequently passed by the Senate, and vetoed by the Governor. It was then passed, notwithstanding the Governor's objections, by a vote in the House of 68 to 26, and in the Senate of 25 to 9. The Governor then issued his proclamation as follows:

In obedience to the subjoined resolution, adopted by the General Assembly of the Commonwealth of Kentucky, the Government of the Confederate States, the State of Tennessee, and all others concerned, are hereby informed that "Kentucky expects the Confederate or Tennessee troops to be withdrawn from her soil unconditionally."

In testimony whereof I have hereunto set my name, and caused the seal of the Commonwealth to be affixed. Done at Frankfort this the 13th day of September, A. D. 1861, and in the seventieth year of the Commonwealth. B. MAGOFFIN.

By the Governor:

THOS. B. MONROE, JR., Secretary of State.

Resolved, by the General Assembly of the Commonwealth of Kentucky, That his excellency Governor Magoffin be, and he is hereby instructed to inform those concerned that Kentucky expects the Confederate or Tennessee troops to be withdrawn from her soil unconditionally.

Preparations were now commenced for different military movements.

While Gen. Polk was thus invading the State on the west, Gen. Zollicoffer was operating on the east. With about four thousand men he came to Cumberland Ford, which is situated near the point where the corner of Virginia runs into Kentucky, and captured a company of Home Guards. On the 17th, the Legislature received a message from Governor Magoffin communicating a telegraphic despatch from Gen. Zollicoffer, announcing that the safety of Tennessee demanded the occupation of Cumberland, and the three long mountains in Kentucky, and that he had done so, and should retain his position until the Union forces were withdrawn, and the Union camp broken up.

Col. Crittenden, of Indiana, who was the first to bring a regiment from another State into Western Virginia in aid of the Federal Government, was also the first to go to the aid of Kentucky. His regiment, well armed, passed through Louisville on the 20th of Sept., toward the Nashville depot, and were enthusiastically received. At the same time Gen. Buckner, once the Inspector-General of Kentucky, but afterwards a Brigadier in the Southern service, advanced on Elizabethtown, the capital of Hardin County, and on the railroad from Louisville to Nashville. Troops were now rapidly concentrated in the State, and despatched to points invaded by the Confederates.

Gov. Magoffin issued a proclamation, directing Gen. Thomas L. Crittenden to call out the State troops to resist the invasion of the State, and Gen. C. accordingly called out the militia. Hamilton Pope, Brigadier-General of the Home Guards, also called upon the people in each ward in Louisville to organize themselves into companies for the protection of the city.

Thus was Kentucky launched with her whole soul into the bloody contest for the maintenance of the Government and the preservation of the Union.

On the 23d the House passed a bill authorizing the Military Board to borrow one million dollars, in addition to a million authorized May 24th, on the State bonds, payable in ten years, and established a tax to pay the bonds and interest. The above sum was to be appropriated to the defence of the State.

On the next day a bill was passed calling out 40,000 volunteers for service from one to three years. The votes were, in the House, 67 to 13, and in the Senate 21 to 5. The Senate also passed a bill providing that Kentuckians who voluntarily joined the Confederate force invading the State, should be incapable of taking estate in Kentucky by devise, bequest, division, or distribution, unless they returned to their allegiance within sixty days, or escaped from the invaders as soon as possible.

A bill was also passed tendering the thanks of the Legislature to Ohio, Illinois, and Indiana, for having so promptly forwarded troops to aid in repelling the invasion of the State; and the Governor was instructed to communicate the same.

The Bank of Kentucky promised her quota of the $2,000,000 for the defence of the State. The Bank of Louisville, whose quota was nearly $100,000, promised $200,000. The Northern Bank promised $25,000 more than her quota; and the Farmers' Bank promptly responded to her quota.

The military operations in the State, though marked by no great achievement during 1861, were nevertheless the forerunner of very important results. Civil, commercial, and agricultural pursuits had engrossed the entire attention of the people. In a military point of view the State, like nearly all her sister States, was entirely defenceless. Men, arms, ammunition, were abundant, but an organized, drilled, and completely-equipped force, ready to take the field and go into active service on a day's notice, could not be expected to exist. Notwithstanding the position of neutrality, after President

Lincoln's proclamation, imperfect organizations were formed, under the name of Home Guards. Their object was to drill novices, and impart the preliminary information needed for the future soldiers. These embraced considerable numbers, and finally formed the chief portion of the force obtained by the secessionists in the State. Large numbers also left the State, and volunteered in the Federal and Confederate armies.

The first appearance of a military force within Kentucky was made under Gen. Polk, commander of Confederate troops from Tennessee, as has been previously stated. They commenced fortifying Hickman and Columbus. The former is situated in the western part of the State, near the Tennessee line, and the latter about twenty-five miles north. Its position is on the southern slope of a high bluff of the Mississippi bank, which commands the stream for about five miles. Wolf's Island is in the centre of the river in its immediate vicinity. The place was occupied on the 4th of September by Gen. Polk's troops. This closed the navigation of the Mississippi to the steamboats belonging to the States above. The fortifications were pushed to such an extent as to render it one of the strongest points held by the Confederate troops. Three one hundred and twenty-eight pounders were placed in such a position as to command the river from the highest part of the bluff, being seventy-five feet above the water. Above on the river was another battery of fourteen guns, most of which were rifled.

On the northern slope of the bluff were two light batteries and a rifle-pit, one mile in length, which were designed specially to protect the place against a land attack from the north, while on the summit of the hills was a strongly-intrenched work, commanding all directions, and manned by eight cannon.

On the south side, and to protect the town from a rear attack, was a small battery of eight guns. The whole number of guns has been estimated at between eighty and a hundred. In addition, there was a floating battery of twenty guns capable of being moved to the most exposed points.

About the same time Gen. Grant, as before stated, commander of the Federal force at Cairo, took possession of Paducah, on the Ohio River. The distance between the two positions is forty-seven miles. It is below the mouth of the Tennessee River, and 340 miles below Louisville. The town was occupied about eight o'clock on the morning of September 6. The 9th Illinois regiment, Major Phelps, the 12th Illinois, Col. McArthur, with four pieces of artillery, left Cairo for Paducah on the previous evening. Upon their arrival the disembarkation was quickly performed. Every place of business was closed.

At the railroad depot it appeared that all the rolling stock had been sent off. A large quantity of contraband supplies, marked for towns in the insurrectionary States, was found in the depot, and immediately seized. They were marked for Fort Gibson, Memphis, Union City, and New Orleans. The whole value of the seizure was over twenty thousand dollars. On the next day, part of the 8th regiment, the 41st Illinois, and the American Zouaves from Cape Girardeau, poured in, increasing the force to about 5,000 effective men. Gen. Polk, it was supposed, intended to seize Paducah, but was barely anticipated by Gen. Grant. It was necessary for the former as a defence for the rear of his positions on the Mississippi. He advanced as far as Mayfield two or three times with a large force, but his prudence caused him to retreat.

In the southeastern part of the State, Gen. Zollicoffer advanced from Tennessee with a considerable force, and on the 18th of September a slight skirmish took place at Barboursville between some of his men and a portion of Home Guards, but without any serious results on either side. The Confederate cavalry scoured the country in the vicinity of their camp, arrested prominent Union men, and destroyed their property. They also occupied the small towns in the vicinity. Subsequently, a portion of the same force entered Manchester, in Clay County, in the vicinity of the Cumberland Mountains. On the 1st of October a retreat was commenced toward Barboursville, which was continued to the Cumberland Ford. This is fifteen miles within the limits of Kentucky, and was fortified by Gen. Zollicoffer; meanwhile, his advance was pushed to London, and the country ravaged. The salt-works in this region were an important possession to the Confederate force. In their rear was also the Cumberland Gap—a most important point—from which the East Tennessee and Virginia Railroad, forty miles below, would be accessible to a Federal force. This railroad was one of the main lines for the transportation of supplies to the troops in Virginia. During this period, a Federal force of Ohio and Indiana troops, with some Kentucky volunteers, were advancing to hold the enemy in check, and, if able, to route them. This force was under the command of Gen. Schœpf. The first affair of any importance took place at a place called Camp Wildcat, on the 21st of Oct. About eleven o'clock in the forenoon, a body of rebel troops, consisting of two regiments of Tennessee volunteers, under Cols. Newman and Bowler, advanced upon four companies of the 33d Indiana regiment, Col. Coburn, and a portion of Col. Woodford's regiment of Kentucky cavalry. The Confederate force opened upon the 33d Indiana on the left wing with cannon, and almost simultaneously their column appeared on the side of the hill, within sixty or seventy yards of the Indiana troops. A charge was ordered upon the latter, which was met with such a galling fire as brought the Tennesseeans to a stand, when a charge by the Kentucky cavalry was made upon them, and they retired with severe loss. At one P. M. another attack was made at another point, and at a late hour a third attack made by Gen. Zollicoffer. It was supposed that the camp was defended only by a small force under Col. Garrard. The attacking force consisted of Mississippians, Georgians, and Tenesseeans. The opposing force was under Gen. Schœpf, consisting of Ohio, Indiana, and Kentucky troops. The Confederates were generally armed with flint-lock muskets and altered locks, buckshot guns, and navy-revolvers. The Federal force carried the Minié rifle. Reënforcements were added to each force during the day, and the different attacks were probably made after they were received by the Confederate commander. The enemy were repulsed with severe loss, and retired to Barboursville.

The small Federal force in Eastern Kentucky was under the command of Gen. Nelson, a Lieutenant in the Navy, who had been detached from his naval duties and sent to Kentucky, of which State he was a native, and well known to her citizens. Being furnished with arms by the Federal Government, he collected and organized a force in the eastern part of the State, near Virginia. With these he advanced, and on the 2d of November occupied Prestonburg without any resistance. The enemy fell back about six miles.

His next movement was on Pikeville, near which a Confederate force under Gen. Williams had taken position. Pikeville is the capital of Pike County, on the west fork of the Big Sandy River. On the forenoon of the 7th he despatched a force, under Col. Sill, of one regiment of infantry with a light battalion of three companies, and two companies of Kentucky volunteers mounted from the teams, and a section of artillery, to march by the way of John's Creek, and pass to the left of Pikeville, where was the enemy's position—a distance of about forty miles—and turn or cut them off. On the 8th, at 5 A. M., Gen. Nelson moved forward with three Ohio regiments, a battalion of Kentucky volunteers, and two sections of artillery, and took the State road direct to Pikeville, distant twenty-eight miles. Eight miles from Prestonburg they met a picket of about forty cavalry, which escaped. At 1 P. M., the cavalry had advanced along the narrow defile of the mountain that ends at Ivy Creek. This mountain is the highest along the river, very precipitous, and thickly covered with brush and undergrowth, and the road, which is but seven feet wide, is cut along the side of it, about twenty-five feet above the river, which is close under the road. The ridge descends in a rapid curve and very sharp to the creek, or rather gorge, where it makes a complete elbow. Behind this ridge, and along the mountain side, the enemy, seven hundred strong, lay in ambush, and did not fire until the head of the Kentucky battalion, Col. C. A. Marshall, was up to the elbow. Four were instantly killed and thirteen wounded, and the Kentuckians were ordered to charge. Col. Harris led his 2d Ohio regiment up the mountain side with much gallantry, and deployed them along its face. Col. Norton, who had just reached the defile, led his 21st Ohio regiment up the northern ridge of the mountain, deployed them along the creek, and made an attack. Two pieces of artillery were got in position on the road, and opened on the enemy. In an hour and twenty minutes the rebel force dispersed and fled, leaving a number killed and wounded, of whom thirty were found dead on the field. The Federal loss was six killed and twenty-four wounded. In their retreat they obstructed the road by felling trees and burning or cutting all the bridges.

On the morning of the 10th Gen. Nelson reached Pikeville, where Col. Sill had arrived, according to orders, on the previous day, having twice encountered mounted men. The result of these movements was so effectual, that, on the 10th, Gen. Nelson issued the following proclamation:

SOLDIERS:—I thank you for what you have done. In a campaign of twenty days you have driven the rebels from Eastern Kentucky, and given repose to that portion of the State. You have made continual forced marches over wretched roads, deep in mud. Badly clad, you have bivouacked on the wet ground, in the November rain, without a murmur. With scarcely half rations, you have pressed forward with unfailing perseverance. The only place that the enemy made a stand, though ambushed and very strong, you drove him from, in the most brilliant style. For your constancy and courage I thank you, and with the qualities which you have shown that you possess, I expect great things from you in future.

Thus closed the campaign in Eastern Kentucky. In the central part of the State the military movements were more extensive. Louisville, the headquarters of the Union Department, is situated on the Ohio River, on the northern boundary of the State, and connected by river and railroad with all the Northern States, and by railroad with the localities of active operations near the borders of Central Tennessee. The level land on which the city is located, extends uninterruptedly south to Rolling Fork River, a stream two hundred feet in width and three feet deep. Crossing by bridge or a ford, a good road leads through a level country for two miles to a series of rugged hills, known as Muldraugh's Hills. The railroad follows a stream called Clear Creek, crossing it about half way up the ascent by a tresselwork ninety feet high, and two miles further south enters at its base Tunnel Hill. It emerges on a smooth level plain, which extends many miles south to Green River. Elizabethtown is four miles from Tunnel Hill and forty-two miles from Louisville. Nolin Creek is the first stream of any importance south of Elizabethtown, and fifty-three miles from Louisville. Munfordsville is on the right bank of Green River, and seventy-two miles from Louisville. Green River empties into the Ohio, and is navigable by steamboats most of the year. The railroad crosses it by an extensive bridge. Bowling Green is on the railroad, one hundred and fourteen miles from Louisville and seventy-one miles from Nashville. It is also at the head of navigation on Barren River, which flows into Green River thirty miles below. A branch railroad to Memphis commences here; the distance by which to Clarksville, on the Cumberland River, is sixty-two miles, and from thence to Memphis one hundred and fifty-seven miles. The importance of Bowling Green is manifest from its position at the junction of two roads leading into Tennessee, furnishing great facilities for transportation. The entrance of hostile forces into the western part of the State, in September, produced great excitement at Louisville. Union Home Guards began to assemble, and other Union troops began to arrive from Ohio, Indiana, and Illinois. On the 18th of September a body of the latter advanced to Rolling Fork, where they found the bridge had been destroyed by a hostile force under Gen. Buckner, formerly commander of the State Guard. This force was then five miles below, on Muldraugh's Hills, but subsequently withdrew to Elizabethtown. At this time Gen. Anderson, formerly in command at Fort Sumter, was ordered to the Department of Kentucky, but was soon compelled to resign his command, in consequence of ill health, and was succeeded by Gen. W. T. Sherman, who for the same reason retired, and was succeeded by Gen. Buell.

As early as the 10th of October, a very considerable Federal force was in Camp Dick Robinson, in Garrard County, which was daily becoming more formidable. At the same time the Confederate General Buckner, who had boasted of an intention to spend the winter in Louisville with his troops, began to retire to Bowling Green, and on the 13th a portion of the iron bridge over the Green River was blown up. Friends in Louisville and throughout the State had given him strong assurances that if he would come to Louisville, or even to Bowling Green, at the head of a force capable of maintaining its position for a short time, reënforcements would immediately pour in by thousands, rendering his army too powerful to be resisted. Unquestionably he came with the full conviction that these assurances would be verified, but he found them all falsified. There was reason to believe that not more than a thousand men joined him.

Accumulations of Federal troops from the States north of the Ohio River, with stores for a vast army, were made during the month of November. On the part of the South the same course was pursued. On the 1st of December, the Federal troops in the State were estimated at 70,000, of which there were 9 regiments from Illinois, 16 from Indiana, 17 from Ohio, 8 from Pennsylvania, 1 from Michigan, 3 from Wisconsin, and two from Minnesota, and at least 25,000 of her own soldiers.

This vast force was looking to Nashville and the State of Tennessee; to withstand it, there was the force of Gen Buckner, estimated at 30,000 men. No affair of importance occurred between these hostile troops during the year, except at Munfordsville. The precise position was on the south bank of the Green River, near the iron bridge of the Louisville and Nashville Railroad. This bridge had been partially destroyed by the rebel troops, to prevent the passage of the Federal force, but a temporary structure had been thrown over the river. Four companies of the 32d Indiana regiment, under command of the lieut.-colonel, had crossed, and were advanced as pickets in squads of eight or ten upon an open meadow at the distance of about one hundred yards from the river bank. At the Munfordsville depot there was a battery of three guns, and another of an equal number about a mile distant, in a southerly direction. A belt of timber skirted the position of the Indiana companies.

Some Confederate soldiers being espied in the wood, two companies were ordered to advance and effect their dislodgement. They retreated half a mile to their main body without firing a shot, and the two companies advanced stealthily as skirmishers. A body of cavalry, consisting of Texan rangers, then made a dash upon the companies, who returned the fire from their shot-guns with a galling effect. When the batteries opened, the Indianians, who reached the wood under cover of the trees, did fearful execution in the ranks of the cavalry.

The rangers fled, leaving their dead upon the field, including the body of Col. Terry, who was killed by a musket-ball. His body was sent back afterwards under a flag of truce.

The enemy's loss was considerable. There were found upon the field sixty-three dead bodies, and the bodies of twelve or fourteen horses. In addition, a large number are known to have been wounded. The Federal loss was thirteen killed and an equal number wounded.

Two regiments of Federal troops, the 36th Indiana and the 16th Ohio, came promptly up to the relief of the four companies from the 32d Indiana, but the fight was not renewed.

The hopes of the Richmond Government that Kentucky would join the Confederacy, were extremely sanguine. Indeed so confident were the friends of the Government of her ultimate secession that a Convention was called by them to organize the forms of that movement. It met at Russellville about the 27th of November, and was in session during three days.

It passed a Declaration of Independence and an Ordinance of Secession. A Provisional Government, consisting of a Governor, Legislative Council of ten, a Treasurer, and an Auditor, was agreed upon. George W. Johnson, of Scott, was made Governor.

The Commissioners to Richmond were H. C. Burnett, W. E. Simms, and Wm. Preston. All executive and legislative powers were vested in the Governor and Council. Acts to be done by the Provisional Government required the concurrence of a majority of its members; the Council were authorized to fill vacancies, but no councilman should be made Governor to fill a vacancy. The old Constitution and laws of Kentucky were declared in force, except where inconsistent with the acts of the Confederate

Government. Bowling Green was fixed as the new capital. Fifty-one counties were said to be represented in the Convention by over two hundred members not elected by the people. Ex-Vice-President Breckinridge and others about this time joined the Southern forces.

CHAPTER XI.

Attack on Wilson's Regiment—Bombardment of Fort Pickens—Burning of Warrenton—Attack on the Federal fleet at the mouths of the Mississippi—Repulse at Ball's Bluff—Expedition against Port Royal: its success—Resignation of Lieut.-Gen. Scott—Battle at Belmont—Capture of Messrs. Mason and Slidell—Occupation of Accomac and Northampton Counties, Va.—The Stone Blockade of Charleston—Affair at Drainesville—Treatment of Slaves—Exchange of Prisoners—Plans of the Government.

SOME operations, too important to be overlooked, but forming no part of a military plan of campaign, arose out of the general situation of the combatants with respect to each other. They indicated an active state of hostilities, and resulted in advantage or loss to each side.

At Pensacola Bay, hostile movements were early commenced as has already been stated. This fine bay is located in the northwest corner of Florida, and at the mouth of the Escambia River. On the east side of the entrance, and on the extremity of Santa Rosa Island, is Fort Pickens. Nearly opposite, being a little further outward or seaward, is Fort McRea. Facing the entrance, on the farther side of the bay, is Fort Barrancas, and nearly one mile to the eastward, along the shore, is the navy yard. On the secession of Florida the Barrancas was abandoned, its guns spiked, and its munitions removed by Commandant Armstrong, of the navy; and on the 12th of January this fort and navy yard were occupied by Florida and Alabama troops. The commandant had a force of about sixty men, and the opposing force consisted of nearly five hundred and fifty. Ultimately all the military positions came into the possession of the Southern troops, except Fort Pickens. They immediately mounted at the navy yard four Dahlgren long 32s, and at Fort Barrancas twenty-five 32s; at Fort McRea were four columbiads and a large number of heavy guns. This work was carried on until the guns were all mounted, additional batteries erected along the shore, and every thing made ready to attack Fort Pickens, or to resist any attack which might be made.

Lieut. A. J. Slemmer, who had been in command of the little Federal force in charge of the forts, took possession of Fort Pickens on the first indication of any thing like an attempt to seize it. It was the strongest and most important of all the fortifications of the bay. In this position he remained securely until relieved of his command. When the Federal Government determined to relieve Fort Sumter, it also resolved to reënforce Fort Pickens, and immediate arrangements were made for that purpose.

On the 7th of April, the steamer Atlantic sailed from New York with 450 troops on board, including two companies of light artillery, and a company of sappers and miners, under command of Col. Harvey Brown, together with 69 horses and a large quantity of munitions of war and supplies. On the 13th she reached Key West, and took on board more troops and ordnance, etc., and arrived at Pensacola on the 16th, in the afternoon. With the assistance of the boats of the squadron then there, the larger portion of the officers and men were landed, and entered Fort Pickens before midnight. Between that time and the 23d the remaining troops, stores, etc., were all safely landed. Before the arrival of the Atlantic, and on the night of the 12th of April, reënforcements, consisting of one company of artillery, being 86 men and 115 marines, were sent to the fort. The old garrison consisted of 82 men and with this addition amounted to 283 men. The arrival of the Atlantic increased the number, and the steamer Illinois followed, until the garrison amounted to about 880 men.

Meantime, farther reënforcements were sent out, and a large amount of stores, while quite a fleet of vessels were stationed outside in the Gulf. The first volunteer troops sent, consisted of a New York regiment, under Col. William Wilson. This regiment encamped on the island near the fort. No serious conflict, however, took place, although the hostile forces were within a short distance of each other. Some daring exploits were performed by Federal troops, one of which, under Lieut. Russel's command, is thus described by a Confederate officer: "The enemy executed, last night, the most brilliant and daring act which has yet marked the history of the war. For some time past they have exhibited unmistakable indications of eagerness for a fight, and have grown more and more audacious. First they fired on one of our schooners. Next they burned the dry dock, and last night, September 13th, they made a most daring and reckless raid upon the navy yard. About three o'clock in the morning, five launches, containing about thirty men each, pulled across from Santa Rosa Island to the navy yard, a distance of about two miles.

Each launch had in it a small brass howitzer on a pivot. Their main object seems to have been to burn the largest schooner of our harbor police, which was anchored near the wharf. They were led by an officer with the courage of forty Numidian lions, and their success was perfect. Under cover of the darkness, silently, with muffled oars, they approached the wharf, and were not discovered until very near it. They then pulled rapidly to the schooner, and grappled to her, when their daring leader shouted, 'Board her,' leading the way himself with a cutlass in one hand, and a blazing fire-ball in the other. He threw the flambeau into the hold of the schooner, and feeling sure that she was on fire, he ordered his men to take to their launches and pull for life, as he said that a shower of grape would soon be rattling after them. They pulled off a short distance; but before going, they sent back a shower of grape from their howitzers, directed upon our men as they were forming. The darkness rendered the fire uncertain, and only two of our men were wounded. The schooner burned rapidly, and we had to cut her loose from the wharf to save it from destruction. She floated off on the tide, emitting a brilliant flood of light over the surrounding darkness of the scene." Such is the brief account of this very daring adventure.

Affairs continued quiet until the night of the 8th of October, when the enemy attempted a daring attack upon the forces on the island. They hoped to break up the encampment of the volunteer regiment. Early in the evening Col. Jackson visited the camp of the 5th Georgia regiment at Pensacola, and informed the troops that he required one hundred and fifty men for an important service, also twenty-seven from the Clinch Rifles, and nineteen from the Irish Volunteers. Every man who was willing to volunteer, was requested to shoulder arms, and every one did so. The captains were then ordered to select the men, who were put under the command of Lieut. Hallenquist. The expedition was accompanied by Col. Jackson. It consisted of 1,200 men, under the command of Gen. Anderson. About two o'clock in the morning they landed on the island, and marched upon the Zouave camp. They were first met by Major Vodges, with 85 men, some distance above the camp. The major was taken prisoner. The Zouaves were taken chiefly by surprise, but as soon as they recovered, fought desperately. The Confederates penetrated the camp, which was almost entirely destroyed. A number of prisoners were taken on both sides. The invader's loss was severe. Of the Zouaves and regulars, fourteen were killed and thirty-six wounded. The officers and men lost almost every thing.

In November, the force at the fort and on the island was thirteen hundred men, and it was supposed that upon the opposite side were near eight thousand, when Col. Brown, the commandant of Fort Pickens, determined to open fire upon the batteries occupied by the Southern troops.

Having invited Flag-officer McKean to coöperate in the attack, on the morning of the 22d of November, Col. Brown opened his batteries on the enemy, to which, in the course of half an hour, he responded from his numerous forts and batteries, extending from the navy yard to Fort McRea, a distance of about four miles, the whole nearly equidistant from Fort Pickens, and on which line he had two forts—McRea and Barrancas—and fourteen separate batteries, containing from one to four guns, many of them being ten-inch columbiads, and some twelve and thirteen-inch seacoast mortars, the distance varying from two thousand one hundred to two thousand nine hundred yards from Fort Pickens. At the same time Flag-officer McKean, in the Niagara, and Capt. Ellison, in the Richmond, took position as near to Fort McRea as the depth of the water would permit, but which unfortunately was not sufficiently deep to give full effect to their powerful batteries. They, however, kept up a spirited fire on the fort and adjacent batteries during the whole day. The fire from Fort Pickens was incessant from the time of opening until it was too dark to see, at the rate of a shot for each gun every fifteen or twenty minutes, the fire of the enemy being somewhat slower. At noon the guns of Fort McRea were all silenced but one, and three hours before sunset this fort and the adjoining batteries ceased firing. The guns of batteries Lincoln, Cameron, and Totten were directed principally on the batteries adjacent to the navy yard, those of Battery Scott to Fort McRea and the lighthouse batteries, and those of Fort Pickens to all. They reduced very perceptibly the fire of Barrancas, entirely silenced that in the navy yard, and in one or two of the other batteries.

The next morning Col. Brown again opened about the same hour, the navy unfortunately, owing to a reduction in the depth of water, caused by a change of wind, not being able to get so near as on the day before; consequently the distance was too great to be effectual. The fire of Fort Pickens, this day, was less rapid, and more efficient. Fort McRea did not fire. One or two guns of the enemy were entirely silenced, and one in Fort Pickens was disabled by a shot coming through the embrasure.

About three o'clock fire was communicated to one of the houses in Warrington, and shortly afterwards to the church steeple, the church and the whole village being immediately in rear of some of the Confederate batteries. Of the largest and most valuable buildings along the street, probably two-thirds were consumed. About the same time fire was discovered issuing from the back part of the navy yard, probably in Wolcott, a village to the north and immediately adjoining the yard, as Warrington does on the west. Finally it penetrated to the yard, and continued to burn brightly all night. Very heavy damage was also done to the buildings of the yard by the shot, shell, and splinters.

The steamer Time, which was at the wharf at the navy yard at the time, was abandoned on the first day. The fire was continued till dark, and with mortars occasionally till two o'clock the next morning, when the combat ceased.

Fort Pickens, at its conclusion, though it had received a great many shot and shell, was reported in every respect, save the disabling of one gun carriage and the loss of service of six men, as efficient as at the commencement of the combat. No serious damage was done to the frigates Niagara or Richmond.

The only hostile movements within the limits of Louisiana in 1861, were made at the mouths of the Mississippi. On the 12th of October, near four o'clock in the morning, as the Federal steamship Richmond, under the command of John Pope, was lying at the Southwest Pass receiving coal from the schooner J. H. Toone, a floating ram, as it was called, was discovered close upon the ship.

By the time the alarm could be given, she had struck the ship abreast of the fore channels, tearing the schooner from her fasts, and forcing a hole through the ship's side.

Passing aft, the ram endeavored to effect a breach in the stern, but failed. Three planks on the ship's side were stove in about two feet below the water line, making a hole about five inches in circumference. At the first alarm the crew promptly and coolly repaired to their quarters, and as the ram passed abreast of the ship the entire port battery was discharged at her, with what effect it was impossible to discover, owing to the darkness.

The sloops of war Preble and Vincennes, and the smaller steamer Water Witch, were lying at anchor a short distance below. A red light was shown from the Richmond as a signal of danger, and the vessels, having slipped their cables, were under way in a few minutes. Soon, three large fire rafts stretching across the river were seen rapidly approaching, while several large steamers and a bark-rigged propeller were astern of them. The squadron, however, moved down the river, and, under the advice of the pilot, an attempt was made to pass over the bar, but in the passage the Vincennes and Richmond grounded, while the Preble went clear. This occurred about eight o'clock in the morning, and fire was opened on both sides. The shot of the fleet fell short, while shells of the enemy burst around them, or went beyond them. About half-past nine o'clock the commander of the Richmond made a signal to the ships outside of the bar to get under way. This was mistaken by Captain Hardy of the Vincennes as a signal for him to abandon his ship. Accordingly, with his officers and crew he left her, after having lighted a slow match at the magazine. But as no explosion occurred for some time, he was ordered to return and attempt to get her off shore. At ten o'clock the enemy ceased firing. No one was killed or wounded on the Federal fleet. No damage was done to any vessel except to the Richmond. The schooner J. H. Toone was captured, having about fifteen tons of coal on board.

The ram, as it was called, was the hull of a steamer, iron-plated with railroad iron, and having a projection on her bow beneath the water line, sufficient to punch a hole in the hull of a wooden vessel when struck with force. It was under the command of Capt. Hollins, formerly of the United States navy, the officer who was in command at the bombardment of Greytown, Nicaragua.

Some events occurred in Mississippi Sound, east of the mouths of the river, which it may not be out of place here to mention. The Sound is bounded on the south by Ship Island. On June 28th the United States steamer Massachusetts visited the island and found it unoccupied, and captured five Confederate schooners in its vicinity. On the 8th of July she again visited the island, and found a considerable force there, who were throwing up intrenchments and had mounted some heavy guns. An attempt was made to dislodge them, but unsuccessfully, and they were allowed to remain in possession till the 16th of September, when, under the apprehension that a large naval expedition was coming to attack them, they abandoned the island and escaped to the shore, taking most of their ordnance with them. During the two months of their occupation they had rebuilt the fort, constructing eleven fine bomb-proof casemates and a magazine, and had mounted twenty guns. They named it Fort Twiggs. On the 17th September the Massachusetts landed a force on the island, who took possession, and having been reënforced, have continued to hold it. They mounted cannon on the fort, and strengthened it still further by the addition of two more bomb-proof casemates, and a formidable armament of Dahlgren 9-inch shell guns and rifled cannon. They also erected barracks for troops, with brick, left on the island by the Confederates, and lumber captured from them. On the 19th October, Com. Hollins, in command of the Confederate gunboat Florida, appeared in Mississippi Sound, and challenged the United States gunboat Massachusetts to a naval battle. The challenge was accepted, and after a sharp engagement of forty-five minutes the Florida retired, seriously disabled, and put into Pass Christian, apparently in a sinking condition. Four of her crew were killed. The Massachusetts was injured, but not seriously, by a 100-lb. shell, which struck her five feet above her water line, but was repaired in a few days. None of her crew were killed, and only one slightly wounded. On the 21st November the gunboat New London arrived in the Sound, and in the course of a fortnight captured five Confederate vessels.

In Virginia, a serious repulse was suffered by the Union troops at Ball's Bluff, or Leesburg

Heights. This is the name given to a part of the bank of the Potomac River, on the Virginia side, east of Leesburg and opposite Harrison's Island. The height of the bluff is variable, in some parts being one hundred and fifty feet. It is steep, with brush, trees, rocks, and logs on its front, and at the point of ascent was, on the day of the battle, rendered soft and muddy by the passage of the troops. Opposite the bluff and about one hundred yards distant is Harrison's Island, a long narrow tract of four hundred acres, between which and the Virginia shore the river runs with a rapid current. On the other side of the island, which is one hundred and fifty yards broad, the distance to the Maryland shore is two hundred yards, and the stream not quite so rapid. At the head of the island passes Conrad's Ferry from the Maryland to the Virginia shore. Six miles below is Edwards' Ferry, which is on the direct road from Poolesville to Leesburg.

On the opposite banks of the Potomac the hostile forces of the North and South had confronted each other for many months. The distance thus occupied extended from Great Falls up the river beyond Harper's Ferry. It was here that the Richmond Government contemplated an advance into the State of Maryland, and an opportunity to flank the force on the Virginia shore opposite Washington, placed for the defence of that city. The Federal Government, anticipating such intentions, had stationed a strong force to prevent them. This was in several divisions: the first, under General Banks, was stationed from Great Falls nearly to Edwards' Ferry. From that point to Conrad's Ferry was the division under General Stone; next was Colonel Lander's force and that of Colonel Geary. The principal points occupied by the Richmond troops on the Virginia borders of the Potomac were Dranesville, Leesburg, and Charlestown. It became an object to learn with what strength the former of these positions was then held. For this purpose a reconnoissance was ordered by the Commander-in-Chief, General McClellan, to be made toward Dranesville, and the duty was assigned to General McCall, who was in command of a division on the extreme right of the force beyond the Potomac opposite Washington. These orders were successfully executed on the 19th of October, and on the forenoon of the 20th he returned to his former position, in compliance with orders received the afternoon previous. At the same time notice was given to General Stone of this movement on the part of General McCall in the following despatch:

To Brigadier-General Stone, Poolesville:
General McClellan desires me to inform you that General McCall occupied Dranesville yesterday, and is still there. Will send out heavy reconnoissances to-day in all directions from that point. The General desires that you keep a good look-out upon Leesburg to see if this movement has the effect to drive them away. Perhaps a slight demonstration on your part would have the effect to move them.
Assistant Adjutant-General, A. V. COLBURN.

Later in the day General Stone replied to this despatch as follows:

OCTOBER 20, 1861.

To Major-General McClellan:
Made a feint of crossing at this place this afternoon, and at the same time started a reconnoitring party toward Leesburg from Harrison's Island. The enemy's pickets retired to intrenchments. Report of reconnoitring party not yet received. I have means of crossing one hundred and twenty-five men once in ten minutes at each of two points. River falling slowly.
C. P. STONE, Brigadier-General.

On communicating General Stone's report of the battle to the Secretary of War, General McClellan, in a note, said: "My despatch did not contemplate the making an attack upon the enemy or the crossing of the river in force by any portion of General Stone's command."

Immediately upon the receipt of these instructions, General Stone went to Edwards' Ferry with General Gorman's brigade, the Seventh Michigan, two troops of the Van Alen cavalry, and the Putnam Rangers. This was at one o'clock P.M. At the same time he ordered four companies of the Fifteenth Massachusetts to proceed to Harrison's Island, under Colonel Devens, who already had one company on the island. To Conrad's Ferry, above, which was in his department, he also ordered Colonel Lee with a battalion of the Massachusetts Twentieth, a section of the Rhode Island battery, and the Tammany Regiment. These three movements of troops were ordered—one to Edwards' Ferry, one to Harrison's Island, and one to Conrad's Ferry above. General Stone says that at this time General McCall's movement on Dranesville had evidently attracted the attention of the enemy, as a regiment appeared from the direction of Leesburg, and took shelter behind a hill about one mile and a half from his position at Edwards' Ferry. This day is Sunday, and at half-past four P. M. Van Alen's battery of two twelve-pound Parrott guns opens with shell upon the Confederate force upon the Virginia side. Their explosion can be distinctly heard. Seven are thrown within ten minutes, and no response comes across the water. The direction given to the shells is varied so as to find out the location of the force, which is supposed to be concealed in a thick wood to the southwest, on the hill. At five o'clock P. M. the battery in charge of Lieut. Frink, a quarter of a mile from the ferry, also opens with shell, and the two batteries keep up the fire with rapidity. Just as the sun is going down the First Minnesota and Second New York come down over the hill and take the road to the ferry. The sun sets gloriously, his rays reflecting from the thousands of bayonets which line the road.

Gen. Gorman is ordered to deploy his forces in view of the enemy, making a feint to cross the river with a view of trying what effect the movement may have upon the enemy. The troops evince by their cheering that they are all ready, and determined to fight gallantly when the opportunity is presented. Three flat-boats are ordered, and at the same time shell and spherical-case shot are thrown into the place of the enemy's concealment. Elsewhere all around the air is perfectly still, and the close of the pleasant Sabbath is impressively beautiful, while the view of the Virginia hills is almost enchanting. Soon something resembling the sound of a drum corps is distinctly heard, and the shelling and the launching of the boats induces the quick retirement of the Confederate force. Three boat-loads of thirty-five men each from the First Minnesota crossed and recrossed the river, each trip occupying about six or seven minutes. At dusk Gen. Gorman's brigade and the Seventh Michigan returned to camp. The other forces at Harrison's Island and Conrad's Ferry remained in position.

Here the movement should have stopped. The orders of Gen. McClellan had been obeyed, and their object had been accomplished. The subsequent orders were not authorized by any superior authority to Gen. Stone, and the responsibility for their consequences must rest upon him. Had a brilliant achievement ensued, the honor of it would likewise have belonged to him.

Previous to one o'clock P. M. four companies of the Massachusetts Fifteenth, as above stated, had been ordered to Harrison's Island, which had for some time been guarded by one company of the same regiment. At night Col. Devens ordered Capt. Philbrick of Company H, and Quartermaster Howe of his staff, with a detachment of twenty men, to cross from Harrison's Island to the Virginia shore, and follow a bridle path which had been discovered, to the vicinity of Leesburg, and report what was seen. The party executed the order by approaching within three-fourths of a mile of Leesburg, and returned to the starting-point by 10 o'clock at night, after having discovered, as they supposed, a small Confederate camp one mile from Leesburg. There appeared to be about thirty tents. No pickets were out any distance, and the party approached within twenty-five rods without being challenged.

Upon receiving this report, Gen. Stone instantly ordered Col. Devens to cross over with four companies to the Virginia shore, and march silently under cover of night to the position of the camp, and to attack and destroy it at daybreak, pursue the enemy lodged there as far as would be prudent, and return immediately to the island—his return to be covered by a company of the Massachusetts Twentieth, to be posted over the landing-place. Col. Devens was ordered to make close observation of the position, strength, and movements of the enemy, and, in the event of there being no enemy there visible, to hold on in a secure position until he could be strengthened sufficiently to make a valuable reconnoissance. At this time orders were sent to Col. Baker to send the First California Regiment to Conrad's Ferry, to arrive there at sunrise, and to have the remainder of his brigade ready to move early. Lieut.-Col. Wood, of the Fifteenth Massachusetts, was also ordered to move with a battalion to the river bank opposite Harrison's Island by daybreak. Two mounted howitzers, in charge of Lieut. French, of Ricketts' battery, were ordered to the tow-path of the canal opposite Harrison's Island.

Col. Devens, in pursuance of his orders, crossed the river and advanced to the point indicated, while one company of the Massachusetts Twentieth, of one hundred men, took position at the landing-place on the bluff, to cover the return of Col. Devens, as ordered. Upon arrival at the point indicated as the position of the enemy's camp, Col. Devens found that the scouts had been deceived by the uncertain light, and had mistaken openings in the trees for a row of tents. He found, however, a wood in which he concealed his force, and proceeded to examine the space between that and Leesburg, sending back at the same time a report that thus far he could see no enemy.

In order to distract the attention of the enemy, during this movement of Col. Devens, and also to make a reconnoissance in the direction of Leesburg from Edwards' Ferry, Gen. Stone now directed Gen. Gorman to throw across the river at Edwards' Ferry two companies of the First Minnesota, under cover of a fire from Ricketts' battery, and send out a party of thirty-one Van Alen cavalry under Major Mix, with orders to advance along the Leesburg road westwardly until they should come to the vicinity of a battery which was known to be on that road, and then turn to the left and examine the heights between that and Goose Creek, and see if any of the enemy were posted in the vicinity, find out their numbers as nearly as possible, their disposition, examine the country with reference to the passage of troops to the Leesburg and Georgetown turnpike, and return rapidly to cover behind the skirmishers of the Minnesota First. This reconnoissance was most gallantly conducted, and the party proceeded along the Leesburg road nearly two miles from the ferry; and when near the position of the hidden battery came suddenly upon a Mississippi regiment, about thirty-five yards distant, received its fire and returned it with their pistols. The fire of the enemy killed one horse, but Lieut. Gouraud seized the dismounted man, and, drawing him on his horse behind him, carried him unhurt from the field. One private of the Fourth Virginia cavalry was brought off by the party a prisoner, who, being well mounted and armed, his mount replaced the one lost by the fire of the enemy.

While this was going on, Gen. Stone received the report of Col. Devens that no enemy could be seen. On the reception of this information, he immediately ordered a non-commissioned officer and ten cavalry to join Col. Devens, for the purpose of scouring the country near him while he was engaged in his reconnoissance, and to give due notice of the approach of any force. At the same time Col. Ward was ordered, with his battalion of the

Massachusetts Fifteenth, to cross over and move half a mile to the right of the landing-place of Col. Devens, and in a strong position to watch and protect the flank of the latter on his return, and secure a good crossing more favorable than the first and connected by a good road with Leesburg. Neither of these orders were carried out to their full extent, for which no reason has been given. The squad of cavalry crossed over to the Virginia side, but were sent back without having left the shore to go inland; thus Col. Devens was deprived of the means of obtaining warning of the approach of any hostile force. The battalion under Col. Ward was detained on the bluff instead of being directed to the right.

At an early hour, Col. Baker, in pursuance of the orders sent at ten o'clock at night, arrived at Conrad's Ferry with the First California Regiment. Leaving his regiment he went to Edwards' Ferry below, and reported to Gen. Stone that his regiment was at Conrad's Ferry, and the three other regiments of his brigade were ready to march.

The orders now given to Col. Baker are thus related in the words of Gen. Stone: "I directed him to Harrison's Island to assume the command, and in a full conversation explained to him the position as it then stood. I told him that Gen. McCall had advanced his troops to Dranesville, and that I was extremely desirous of ascertaining the exact position and force of the enemy in our front, and of exploring as far as it was safe on the right toward Leesburg, and on the left toward the Leesburg and Gum Spring road. I also informed Col. Baker that Gen. Gorman, opposite Edwards' Ferry, should be reinforced, and that I would make every effort to push Gorman's troops carefully forward to discover the best line from that ferry to the Leesburg and Gum Spring road already mentioned; and the position of the breastworks and hidden battery, which prevented the movement of troops directly from the left to right, were also pointed out to him. The means of transportation across, of the sufficiency of which he (Baker) was to be judge, was detailed, and authority given him to make use of the guns of a section each of Vaughan's and Bunting's batteries, together with French's mountain howitzers, all the troops of his Brigade and the Tammany Regiment, beside the Nineteenth and part of the Twentieth Regiments of Massachusetts Volunteers; and I left it to his discretion, after viewing the ground, to retire from the Virginia shore under the cover of his guns and the fire of the large infantry force, or to pass over reinforcements in case he found it practicable and the position on the other side favorable. I stated that I wished no advance made unless the enemy were of inferior force, and under no circumstance to pass beyond Leesburg, or a strong position between it and Goose Creek, on the Gum Spring, *i. e.*, the Manassas road. Col. Baker was cautioned in reference to passing artillery across the river, and I begged if he did do so to see it well supported by good infantry. I pointed out to him the position of some bluffs on this side of the river, from which artillery could act with effect on the other; and leaving the matter of crossing more troops or retiring what where already over to his discretion, gave him entire control of operations on the right. This gallant and energetic officer left me about nine A. M., or half-past nine, and galloped off quickly to his command."

The following orders have been received as true copies of the orders given to Col. Baker, the originals of which were found in his hat after his death. The first is of such date as to have been delivered to him on Sunday night, and the second was delivered to him on the battle-field by Col. Coggswell, who, perceiving that it had no bearing upon the then condition of affairs, said so to Col. Baker, who put it in his hat without reading. Some other order, it may be presumed, preceded these two.

H. Q. CORPS OF [Here the bullet struck and a word is missing.] EDWARDS' FERRY, *October* 21, 1861.

Colonel E. D. Baker, Com. of Brigade:

COLONEL: In case of heavy firing in front of Harrison's Island, you will advance the California Regiment of your brigade, or retire the regiments under Colonels Lee and Devens, now on the [almost rendered illegible by blood] Virginia side of the river, at your discretion —assuming command on arrival.

Very respectfully, Colonel, your most obt. servt.,
CHAS. P. STONE, Brig.-Gen. Commanding.

The second order which follows, was delivered on the battle-field by Col. Coggswell, who said to Col. Baker, in reply to a question what it meant, "All right, go ahead." Thereupon Col. Baker put it in his hat without reading. An hour afterward he fell:

HEAD-QUARTERS CORPS OF OBSERVATION, EDWARDS' FERRY, *October* 22—11.50.

E. D. Baker, Commanding Brigade:

COLONEL: I am informed that the force of the enemy is about four thousand, all told. If you can push them, you may do so as far as to have a strong position near Leesburg, if you can keep them before you, avoiding their batteries. If they pass Leesburg and take the Gum Springs road, you will not follow far, but seize the first good position to cover that road.

Their design is to draw us on, if they are obliged to retreat, as far as Goose Creek, where they can be reinforced from Manassas, and have a strong position.

Report frequently, so that when they are pushed, Gorman can come up on their flank.

Yours respectfully and truly,
CHARLES P. STONE,
Brigadier-General Commanding.

The following are the copies said to have been made by General Beauregard's order and sent to General Stone, of the orders given to Devens and Baker at Ball's Bluff and found on the field by the Confederates.

HEAD-QUARTERS CORPS OF OBSERVATION, POOLESVILLE, *October* 20, 1861—about 11 A. M.

COLONEL: You will please send orders to the canal to have the two new flat-boats now there, opposite the island, transferred at once to the river, and will at 2 o'clock P. M. have the island reinforced by all of your regiments now on duty at the canal and at the New

York battery. The pickets will be replaced by the companies of the Nineteenth Massachusetts there.

Very respectfully, your obedient servant,
CHARLES P. STONE, Brigadier-General.

Col. CHARLES DEVENS, Commanding Fifteenth Regiment Mass. Vols.

A true copy.
WM. R. HYSLOP, Lieut. and A. D. C.

HEAD-QUARTERS CORPS OF OBSERVATION,
POOLESVILLE, *Oct.* 20, 1861—10½ P. M.

SPECIAL ORDERS, No. —. Colonel Devens will land opposite Harrison's Island with four companies of his regiment, and proceed to surprise the camp of the enemy discovered by Captain Philbrick in the direction of Leesburg. The landing and march will be effected with silence and rapidity.

Colonel Lee, Twentieth Massachusetts Volunteers, will immediately after Colonel Devens' departure occupy Harrison's Island with four companies of his regiment, and will cause the four-oared boat to be taken across the island to the point of departure of Colonel Devens.

One company will be thrown across to occupy the heights on the Virginia shore, after Colonel Devens' departure to cover his return.

Two mountain howitzers will be taken silently up the tow-path, and carried to the opposite side of the island, under the orders of Colonel Lee.

Colonel Devens will attack the camp of the enemy at daybreak, and having routed, will pursue as far as he deems prudent, and will destroy the camp, if practicable, before returning.

He will make all the observations possible on the country, will under all circumstances keep his command well in hand, and not sacrifice this to any supposed advantage of rapid pursuit.

Having accomplished this duty, Colonel Devens will return to his present position, unless he shall see one on the Virginia side, near the river, which he can undoubtedly hold until reinforced, and one which can be successfully held against largely superior numbers. In such case he will hold on and report.

CHARLES P. STONE, Brigadier-General.

Great care will be used by Colonel Devens to prevent any unnecessary injury of private property, and any officer or soldier straggling from the command for curiosity or plunder will be instantly shot.

CHARLES P. STONE, Brigadier-General.

A true copy.
WM. R. HYSLOP, Lieut. and A. D. C.

The following is given as the last order to Col. Baker. It could never have reached him. It shows what report he sent to Gen Stone, and indicates under what orders he was acting:

HEAD-QUARTERS CORPS OF OBSERVATION,
EDWARDS' FERRY, *Oct.* 21—3.45 P. M.

Colonel E. D. Baker, Commanding Right Wing:

COLONEL: Yours of 2.30 is received. I am glad you find your position tenable. If satisfied with it, hold on, and don't let the troops get fatigued or starved while waiting.

Please detail plenty of officers to attend to the *food* of the men. Do you need more artillery than the eight pieces now at your disposition?

Respectfully, your obedient servant,
CHAS. P. STONE, Brig.-Gen. Com'g.

A true copy.
WILLIAM R. HYSLOP, Lieut. and A. D. C.

In the morning a skirmish took place between the command of Col. Lee, of the Massachusetts Twentieth, who had been ordered to cover Col. Devens' retreat, and about one hundred Mississippi riflemen. Col. Devens then fell back in good order on Col. Lee's position. Presently he again advanced, his men behaving admirably, fighting, retiring, and advancing in perfect order, and exhibiting every proof of high courage and good discipline. Had the cavalry scouting party sent to him in the morning been with him, then he could have had timely warning of the approach of the superior force which afterward overwhelmed his regiment.

Between twelve and one P. M. the enemy appeared in force in front of Col. Devens, and a sharp skirmish ensued, and was maintained for some time by the Fifteenth Massachusetts, unsupported; and finding he would be outflanked, Col. Devens retired a short distance, and took up a position near the wood, half a mile in front of Col. Lee, where he remained until two o'clock, when he again fell back, with the approval of Col. Baker, and took his place with the portions of the Twentieth Massachusetts and First California which had arrived.

The movement of troops now to the Virginia side was constant—until 700 of the Fifteenth and three companies of the Twentieth Massachusetts, the First California battalion, and some companies of the Tammany Regiment had crossed, and four pieces of artillery.

At one o'clock the order had been given to the right battery detached from the New York Ninth to report to Gen. Baker at the Maryland side of the Potomac, opposite Harrison's Island. In half an hour the four pieces arrived at the spot, in command of Lieut. Bramhall. At this time but little firing was heard upon the opposite shore, and that only desultory.

At about half-past two P. M., however, the firing of musketry suddenly became very brisk, accompanied by occasional discharges of artillery. At this time Col. Baker, who had been actively engaged in superintending the despatch of reinforcements, crossed himself, accompanied by but one officer, Major Young, of his command, leaving word to forward the artillery with all despatch. The means provided for this purpose consisted of two scows, manned by poles, and which, owing to the swiftness of the current, consumed a great deal of time in the trip from the mainland to the island.

Lieut. Bramhall thus describes the crossing in his report: "I took command, and ordered the immediate embarkation of the pieces. I crossed with the first piece, (which happened to be a Rhode Island piece,) accompanied by Col. Coggswell, of the Tammany Regiment, arriving upon the island after a half hour's hard labor to keep the boat from floating down the stream. We ascended the steep bank, made soft and sloppy by the passage of the troops, and at a rapid gait crossed the island to the second crossing. At this point we found only a scow, on which we did not dare to cross the piece and the horses together, and thus lost further time by being obliged to make two crossings. Upon arriving on the Virginia shore we were compelled to dismount the piece and carriage, and haul the former up by the prolonge, the infantry assisting in carrying the parts of the latter to a point about thirty feet up a precipitous ascent, rendered almost impassable with soft mud, where we remounted the piece, and, hitching up the horses, dragged it through a perfect thicket up to the open ground above, where the fighting was going on.

"During all this time the firing had continued with great briskness, and that the enemy's fire was very effectual was evident from the large number of wounded and dead who were being borne to the boats. But a few moments previous to coming into position the firing had ceased, and when I arrived I found that our men were resting, many with arms stacked in front of them. The ground upon which was such of the fight as I engaged in was an open space, forming a parallelogram, enclosed entirely in woods. Our men were disposed in a semicircle, the right and left termini of which rested upon the woods, with, as near as I could discern, skirmishers thrown out upon each flank, while the convexity of our lines skirted the cliff overhanging the river. The ground sloped from a point about forty yards from the cliff sufficiently to afford a very tolerable cover for our men."

The field was about seventy-five yards in breadth by two hundred in length. At the distant front and down the right and left, a thick dark forest skirted its sides. Behind, the bluff fell steeply off to the river. A winding spur of the field extended a few rods into the woods on the left, half way between the opposing lines. Directly on the left, and near where a crooked path led the Federal force to the fight, a ravine fell slightly off, its opposite bank ascending to the thicket of woods which thus totally surrounded the field. About four o'clock P. M., Col. Baker formed his line for action. At this time no enemy was anywhere visible in rank, but from the woods in the extreme front a galling irregular fire poured out upon his men. They were then ranged, in no very exact order, from right to left, the wings partially covered by the thicket—portions of the centre lying close to the edge of the hill—while others boldly stepped forward, delivered their fire at the woods, returned to load, and advance again and again. The men of the Fifteenth and Twentieth Massachusetts were placed on the right, the Californians on the left, while the artillery, with the Tammany companies, were posted in the centre. A quick consultation was held. Intimations of a large hostile force near were received. No retreat could be effected in safety. The fire was growing hot. A retrograde movement would only bring seventeen hundred men to the river's brink, with two boats, capable of carrying sixty persons each, to transport them over a swift channel, while it would cause a rush of the enemy upon them. Their only hope was in maintaining their ground until troops by the Edwards' Ferry could force a way to their aid. The enemy had evidently concentrated here under the apprehension that the principal attack would come from this quarter. The battle now commenced in earnest on the left and was brought on by pushing two companies forward to feel the enemy in the wood. They advanced half the distance, and were met by a murderous fire from the enemy, which was followed by a terrific volley along their whole front. They still kept their cover, but the bullets rattled against the whole Federal line, which gave a quick reply. Instantly both ends of the field were clouded in smoke, and the contest raged hotly for an hour. Feeling their strength, the enemy pressed down the sides of the field, and the fight grew close until Col. Baker fell while cheering his men, and by his own example sustaining them in the obstinate resistance they were making. The command soon devolved on Col. Coggswell, who saw that the day was lost, and that the time for retreat had come.

The enemy pursued to the edge of the bluff, over the landing-place, and poured in a heavy fire as the Federal force were endeavoring to cross to the island. The retreat was rapid, but according to orders. The men formed near the river, maintaining for nearly half an hour the hopeless contest rather than surrender.

The smaller boat had disappeared, no one knew where. The larger boat, rapidly and too heavily loaded, swamped at fifteen feet from the shore, and nothing was left to the soldiers but to swim, surrender, or die. With a devotion worthy of the cause they were serving, officers and men, while quarter was being offered to such as would lay down their arms, stripped themselves of their swords and muskets and hurled them out into the river to prevent them falling into the hands of the foe, and saved themselves as they could, by swimming, floating on logs, and concealing themselves in the bushes of the forest, and to make their way up and down the river bank to a place of crossing.

The fate of the piece of artillery which had been so effective, is thus described by Lieut. Bramhall, who commanded it:

"Finding that the battle was lost to us, and with but one man left to aid me, (Booth, of the California regiment,) and growing weak and stiff from my wounds, of which I received three, none dangerous, I caused the piece to be drawn down to the edge of the cliff, whence it was afterward thrown down, lodging in the rocks and logs, with which the descent was cumbered, and, assisted by two privates of the Fifteenth Massachusetts Regiment, made my way to the boat and over to the island. Here I found my own section and the other piece belonging to the Rhode Island section, one of which I had had; and leaving directions to command the ford at the upper end of the island with two pieces, and to hold the other in reserve to act where circumstances might require aid to cover the retreat of our own infantry, I crossed to the mainland. I had first despatched a messenger for Lieut. Clark, of our battery, who soon after arrived and took command. The only projectile with which the ammunition chest was provided was the James shell, I have been told by those from the right and left who could correctly observe their effect, that they burst, and with great effect. The short range at which they were fired would of course hardly admit of any very appreciable deviation from a direct course, such as has been remarked of the projectile. The piece, I have since learned, was taken by the enemy; with it there were but eight or ten rounds of shell, and about twenty blanks. I do not think it was possible to have saved the piece from capture, for it would have required a full half hour to have gotten it down to the river, when if it were shipped upon the boat it would have been necessarily to the exclusion of the wounded, who were being conveyed to the opposite shore. Indeed, I very much doubt if it could have crossed at all, for the scow sunk with its weight of men the next trip after I returned in it. The horses belonging to the piece were all shot; and I learn from Capt. Vaughan, who has since been over to bury the dead, that five of them lay dead in one heap. I regretted that the canister which was to be sent over to us did not reach us, as with it I might have at least kept the enemy sufficiently in check to have given time to many of the wounded who were left on the Virginia side to have escaped."

The report of the Confederate General Evans states his killed and wounded at three hundred. He speaks of his force as twenty-five hundred men, without artillery, engaged against ten thousand with five batteries. The force to which he was opposed was about twenty-one hundred, with one piece of artillery that was served effectively, the other three being fired only at intervals. The Confederate forces engaged were the Eighth Virginia, and Seventeenth and Eighteenth Mississippi Regiments. The First Mississippi was held in reserve.

The Massachusetts Fifteenth lost, in killed, wounded, and missing, three hundred and twenty-two, including a Lieut-Colonel and fourteen out of twenty-eight line officers who crossed. The Massachusetts Twentieth lost, in all, one hundred and fifty-nine. The Tammany companies lost one hundred and sixty-three. The First California Regiment lost three hundred, killed, wounded, and missing.

Meantime at Edwards' Ferry, where the facilities for transportation consisted of two scows and a yawl boat, Gen. Stone was preparing to push forward to the road by which the enemy's retreat would be cut off, if driven. He says:—"The additional artillery had already been sent, and when the messenger, who did not leave the field until after three o'clock, was questioned as to Colonel Baker's position, he informed me that the Colonel, when he left, seemed to feel perfectly secure, and could doubtless hold his position in case he should not advance. The same statement was made by another messenger half an hour later, and I watched anxiously for a sign of advance on the right, in order to push forward Gen. Gorman. It was, as had been explained to Colonel Baker, impracticable to throw Gen. Gorman's brigade directly to the right by reason of the battery in the woods, between which we had never been able to reconnoitre.

"At four P. M., or thereabouts, I telegraphed to General Banks for a brigade of his division, intending it to occupy the ground on this side of the river near Harrison's Island, which would be abandoned in case of a rapid advance; and shortly after, as the fire slackened, a messenger was waited for, on whose tidings should be given orders either for the advance of General Gorman to cut off the retreat of the enemy, or for the disposition for the night in the position then held.

"At five P. M. Captain Candy arrived from the field and announced the melancholy tidings of Colonel Baker's death, but with no intelligence of any further disaster. I immediately apprised General Banks of Col. Baker's death, and I rode quickly to the right to assume command. Before arriving opposite the island, men who had crossed the river plainly gave evidence of the disaster, and on reaching the same I was satisfied of it by the conduct of the men then landing in boats.

"Orders were then given to hold the island and establish a patrol on the tow-path from opposite the island to the line of pickets near the Monocacy, and I returned to the left to secure the troops there from disaster, and make preparations for moving them as rapidly as possible.

"Orders arrived from Gen. McClellan to hold the island and Virginia shore at Edwards' Ferry at all risks, indicating at the same time that reinforcements would be sent, and immediately additional means of intrenchments were forwarded, and Gen. Gorman was furnished with particular directions to hold out against any and every force of the enemy."

The crossing was ultimately continued, and by Tuesday morning four thousand infantry, a section of Ricketts' battery, and Van Alen's cavalry detachment were safely on the Virginia shore. Five hundred feet of intrenchment was thrown up. At 3 A. M. on Tuesday, Gen. Banks arrived and took command.

All Tuesday night the whistles of the locomotives bringing Confederate reinforcements to Leesburg were distinctly heard. On Tuesday morning Gen. McClellan was disposed to hold the position on the Virginia side, but further information caused a change of purpose. A bridge of boats taken from the canal, together with others passing up and down which were stopped, was formed, and on Wednesday the entire force returned to the Maryland shore.

The first cause of failure consisted in the lack of suitable means of transportation. The Federal force at Ball's Bluff was evidently outnumbered and overpowered. The crossing was at an exceedingly unfavorable spot; it was the same as crossing two ferries at a point where the current being narrow, becomes swifter. The movement should have ceased with what had been done on Sunday night. No suitable preparations were made for that afterward undertaken.

The Hatteras expedition having proved successful, the Government was encouraged to prosecute with all diligence a much greater and more formidable undertaking, which it had already projected. The finest harbor on the Southern Atlantic coast was that of Port Royal in South Carolina—a broad estuary, formed by the junction of Broad and Port Royal Rivers, and Archer's Creek and their debouchure into the Atlantic. The interlacing of these and other rivers in the vicinity has formed a large group of islands, of which Hilton Head, Hunting, St. Helena, Paris, and Port Royal are the principal. This harbor is situated about halfway between Charleston and Savannah, with both which cities it has an interior water communication. The parish, of which these islands form the greater part, was the richest agricultural district in South Carolina. It was the most important seat of the production of the fine long-stapled Sea Island cotton, and was also largely engaged in the rice culture. It was the largest slaveholding parish in that State, having 32,000 slaves to less than 7,000 whites. The village of Beaufort and the adjacent country on Port Royal and the other interior islands was the summer residence of the wealthy planters of South Carolina.

The Government at first seems to have purposed sending the expedition to some other point (perhaps Savannah) on the coast, but wisely referred the final decision of the point to be first attacked, to the thorough professional knowledge and skill of the flag-officer of the expedition, Com. S. F. Dupont, who, after much deliberation and consultation with the Assistant Secretary of the Navy, Mr. Fox, fixed upon Port Royal, as being the best spot from which to move either northward or southward. The preparations for the expedition were on an extensive scale, and required a longer period for the completion of all its equipments than was at first expected. It finally set sail from Hampton Roads on the 29th of October, consisting of fifty vessels, including transports. A fleet of twenty-five coal vessels, to supply the necessary fuel, had been despatched the previous day.

The naval vessels connected with the expedition were the Wabash (the flag-ship), the Susquehanna, and the gunboats Mohican, Seminole, Pawnee, Unadilla, Ottowa, Pembina, Isaac Smith, Bienville, Seneca, Curlew, Penguin, Augusta, R. B. Forbes, and Pocahontas, the steam-tug Mercury, the frigate Vandalia, and the little steam-cutter Vixen. There were also thirty-three transports, many of them of the first class, such as the Baltic, Ocean Queen, Vanderbilt, Illinois, Cahawba, Empire City, Ariel, Daniel Webster, Coatzacoalcos, Ericsson, Oriental, Philadelphia, S. R. Spaulding, Winfield Scott, Atlantic, &c., &c.; and such sailing vessels as the Great Republic, Ocean Express, Golden Eagle, &c. The naval command was, as has already been said, assigned to Com. S. F. Dupont, but the transports carried out an army of about 15,600 troops, under the command of Acting Major-General Thomas W. Sherman. This force was divided into three brigades, commanded respectively by Brigadier-Generals Egbert S. Viele, Isaac J. Stevens, and Horatio G. Wright. The first brigade consisted of the 3d New Hampshire, 8th Maine, 46th, 47th, and 48th New York regiments; the 2d brigade of the 8th Michigan, 50th Pennsylvania, Roundhead Pennsylvania, and 79th New York (Highlanders); the 3d brigade of the 6th and 7th Connecticut, the 9th Maine, the 4th New Hampshire, and the 3d Rhode Island, with Hamilton's (late Sherman's) battery of six rifled cannon, and a battalion of Serrell's volunteer engineers.

The weather, which was unsettled when the fleet left Hampton Roads, soon changed into a storm of wind of great violence, which, increasing on the 31st October, became on Friday, Nov. 2, a hurricane from the southeast, and scattered the ships so widely that, on Saturday morning, but one of the whole fleet was in sight from the deck of the Wabash. On Sunday the wind had moderated, and the steamers and ships began to reappear. The Isaac Smith had been compelled to throw her battery overboard to keep from foundering; the Governor and the Peerless, two of the transports, sank; but the soldiers and crews were saved except seven of the marines on the Governor, who were drowned by their own imprudence. On the morning of the 4th, Com. Dupont anchored off the bar of Port Royal harbor, with twenty-five of his vessels in company. The channel of the harbor was that day found, sounded out, and buoyed under the direction of Commander Davis, the fleet captain. The gunboats and lighter transports were, before dark of the same day, anchored inside of the bar, in the secure roadstead, and Com. Tatnall's (Confederate) fleet chased under their own batteries. The next day a reconnoissance in force was made by the Ottawa, Seneca, Curlew, and Isaac Smith, which drew the fire of the Confederate forts, and showed which was the strongest. On the 5th, the Wabash and Susquehanna, and the large transports crossed the bar, and the buoys which marked the shoal lines were planted. A storm postponed the attack until the 7th, when it was commenced at about half-past nine o'clock, A. M., and continued for four hours, closing with the complete rout and flight of the enemy's force from both forts. The fortifications were Fort Walker, on Hilton's Head Island, at the right of the channel—a strong earthwork mounting twenty-three guns, all of the heaviest calibre and most approved pattern for sea-coast defence, some of them rifled, and several imported from England since the war commenced. A small outwork, mounting a single rifled gun, had been erected near the fort and beyond it on the sea front. Fort Beauregard, at Bay Point, on Phillips or Hunting Island, on the left bank of the channel, 2¼ miles from Fort Walker, was also a strong work, though not as formidable as Fort

Walker. It mounted 20 guns of the same general character as those in the other fort, and was supported by an outwork nearly a half mile distant, mounting 5 guns. About 2 miles above the forts, where the Port Royal or Beaufort River joins the Broad, Com. Tatnall's (Confederate) fleet of six or seven gunboats was stationed.

The circumstances thus detailed influenced Com. Dupont in deciding upon his plan of attack. He first stationed his transports at anchor, beyond the range of the guns of the forts; then leading the way with the Wabash, followed immediately by the Susquehanna, Mohican, Seminole, Pawnee, Unadilla, Ottawa, Pembina, and Vandalia, towed by the Isaac Smith, he passed up the centre of the channel, delivering his fire at the forts on each side, and, sailing in an ellipse, passed down within 600 yards of Fort Walker, firing slowly and deliberately, but never losing the range. Meanwhile the Bienville, Seneca, Curlew, Penguin, and Augusta had passed up on the left side of the channel, pouring their broadsides into Fort Beauregard, and then taking a station where they could cut off Tatnall's fleet from any participation in the fight, and at the same time maintain a destructive flanking fire upon the weak left flank of Fort Walker. Three times the line of vessels traversed their elliptical circuit, the last time aided by the fire of the Pocahontas, the R. B. Forbes, and the Mercury tug, which came up about twelve o'clock, M. At the completion of the third circuit, the guns of the forts were mostly disabled, and the garrisons, consisting in Fort Walker of two South Carolina regiments, and in Fort Beauregard of one, had fled in a terrible panic, leaving their weapons, overcoats, and even their watches and papers behind them. The Federal loss was: killed, 8; wounded seriously, 6; wounded slightly, 17. Total killed and wounded, 31. Confederate loss not known, but considerably larger than this. With these forts were captured 48 cannon, 43 of them of excellent quality, and mostly of large calibre, and large quantities of ammunition and stores. On the 9th of November the Seneca, Lieut. Ammen commanding, proceeded to Beaufort, and found the town in possession of the negroes, the whites having fled. The other islands were successively occupied, and on the 25th Nov. Com. Dupont reported to the Navy Department that he had taken possession of Tybee Island, commanding the entrance of the Savannah River. Meantime the troops under Gen. Sherman, though debarred by the circumstances from any active participation in the capture of the two forts, had not been idle. Having landed on Hilton Head, they occupied and strengthened the fortifications, and made that point the base of further operations on Savannah, Charleston, and other places.

On the 31st of October Gen. Winfield Scott, the Lieutenant-General of the army of the United States, or the executive officer under the President, who is the commander-in-chief, determined to resign his position. Age and its infirmities had imposed this step upon him. This office was created and tendered to General Scott after the close of the Mexican war, in which he conducted the American arms with so much glory into the very halls of the Montezumas.

Born near Petersburg, in Virginia, June 13, 1785, he entered the army as captain of light artillery, May 3, 1808, and served his country with unvarying success for more than half a century. In that time he proved his right to rank with the first commanders of the age. He was twice honored with a gold medal from Congress for distinguished services, and now retired from active duty with the reputation, after fifty years of command, of never having lost a battle when he was present in person.

To accomplish his purpose, he addressed the following letter to the Secretary of War:

HEADQUARTERS OF THE ARMY,
WASHINGTON, *October* 31, 1861.

The Hon. S. CAMERON, Secretary of War:

SIR: For more than three years I have been unable, from a hurt, to mount a horse, or to walk more than a few paces at a time, and that with much pain. Other and new infirmities—dropsy and vertigo—admonish me that repose of mind and body, with the appliances of surgery and medicine, are necessary to add a little more to a life already protracted much beyond the usual span of man.

It is under such circumstances—made doubly painful by the unnatural and unjust rebellion now raging in the Southern States of our (so late) prosperous and happy Union—that I am compelled to request that my name be placed on the list of army officers retired from active service.

As this request is founded on an absolute right, granted by a recent act of Congress, I am entirely at liberty to say it is with deep regret that I withdraw myself, in these momentous times, from the orders of a President who has treated me with distinguished kindness and courtesy; whom I know, upon much personal intercourse, to be patriotic, without sectional partialities or prejudices; to be highly conscientious in the performance of every duty, and of unrivalled activity and perseverance.

And to you, Mr. Secretary, whom I now officially address for the last time, I beg to acknowledge my many obligations for the uniform high consideration I have received at your hands; and have the honor to remain, sir, with high respect, your obedient servant,

WINFIELD SCOTT.

This letter was laid before a Cabinet meeting called for the purpose of considering it, and it was concluded, under the authority of a recent act of Congress, to place Gen. Scott on the retired list of the army, with the full pay and allowances of his rank. At 4 o'clock on the afternoon of the same day the President, accompanied by the Cabinet, proceeded to the residence of General Scott, and read to him the official order carrying out this decision.

The venerable general, oppressed by infirmity and emotion, rose with difficulty to make to the President his acknowledgments, which he did in touching terms, concluding with the declaration that the kindness manifested toward him on this occasion he felt to be the crowning reward of a long life spent in the service of his country, and his deep conviction of the ultimate triumph of the national arms and the happy termination of the unnatural war.

The President responded, expressing the profound sentiment of regret with which the country, as well as himself, would part with a public servant so venerable in years, and so illustrious for the services he had rendered.

The following was the official order:

On the first day of November, A. D. 1861, upon his own application to the President of the United States, Brevet Lieutenant-General Winfield Scott is ordered to be placed, and hereby is placed, upon the list of retired officers of the army of the United States, without reduction of his current pay, subsistence, or allowances.

The American people will hear with sadness and deep emotion that Gen. Scott has withdrawn from the active control of the army, while the President and unanimous Cabinet express their own and the nation's sympathy in his personal affliction, and their profound sense of the important public services rendered by him to his country during his long and brilliant career, among which will ever be gratefully distinguished his faithful devotion to the Constitution, the Union, and the flag, when assailed by parricidal rebellion. ABRAHAM LINCOLN.

On the same day an order was issued by the President, directing Maj.-Gen. George B. McClellan to assume the command of the army of the United States.

It was stated in a previous chapter that Columbus, on the Mississippi River, in Kentucky, was occupied by Gen. Polk with Southern troops, and Paducah, on the Ohio, likewise in Kentucky by Gen. Grant, with troops from Illinois. Meantime a small body of the enemy occupied a position near Belmont, on the Missouri side of the Mississippi River, under Col. Tappan. This force Gen. Grant determined to dislodge or capture. Early on the morning of Sept. 7th, he therefore landed with a force a few miles above Belmont. This movement was detected by the enemy, and Gen. Pillow was ordered to cross from the Kentucky side to aid Col. Tappan. Gen. Grant immediately advanced upon the enemy's position, now reënforced by Gen. Pillow. A sharp contest ensued for some hours, when Gen. Pillow finding it impossible to maintain himself without reënforcements and a further supply of ammunition, fell back in some confusion to the river bank. At this time reënforcements arrived, and a flank movement up the river upon Grant was made by the enemy. Meantime the camp of Col. Tappan's forces had fallen into the possession of Gen. Grant, and he had also planted batteries to attack the steamers bringing reënforcements across the river. The flank movement disconcerted the Federal troops, and, apprehending an attack in the rear, they fell back to the transports and rapidly embarked, leaving many dead and wounded behind. The loss of the enemy was 632 in killed, wounded, and missing. That of Gen. Grant was 84 killed, 288 wounded, and 235 missing.

An event occurred at this time in the capture of Messrs. Mason and Slidell, which produced a profound sensation, from the serious questions which it raised.

The British mail steamer Trent, belonging to the line of English merchant steamers which run from Vera Cruz and Havana to St. Thomas, carrying the mail by contract, and thence connecting with a line to England, left Havana on the morning of the 7th of November, under the command of Captain Moir, having on board Messrs. J. M. Mason and John Slidell—the former sent by the Government of the insurrectionary States, as ambassador to England, and the latter to France. Nothing of interest occurred till about noon on the 8th, when in the narrow passage of the old Bahama channel, opposite the Panador Grande light, a steamer was observed ahead, apparently waiting, and showing no colors.

An officer of the U. S. steamer San Jacinto thus reports the affair: "About 11.40 A. M., the lookout at the masthead reported a smoke as from a steamer from the westward, and about 11 A. M. she was visible from the deck. We were all ready for her, beat to quarters, and as soon as she was within reach of our guns, every gun of our starboard battery was trained upon her. A shot from our pivot gun was fired across her bow. She hoisted English colors, and showed no disposition to slacken her speed or heave to. We hoisted the 'Star Spangled Banner,' and as soon as she was close upon us, fired a shell across her bow, which brought her to. Our captain hailed her, and said he would send a boat on board, and ordered Lieutenant Fairfax to board her; he went in the second cutter; at the same time Lieutenant Greer was all ready in the third cutter to shove from the port side should his assistance be required. On coming alongside the packet, Lieutenant Fairfax ordered the other officers to remain in the boat with the crew until force should become necessary, and he went on board alone. The captain of the mail steamer refused to show his papers and passenger list, knowing very well the object of our visit and the character and mission of the commissioners. But Mr. Mason being recognized, a part of the armed crew was ordered from the boat, and came on board. Messrs. Mason and Slidell were then requested to come on board the San Jacinto, but declined, and said that they would only yield by force; Mr. Slidell making the remark that 'it would require considerable force to take him on board the San Jacinto.' Lieutenant Fairfax then ordered Mr. Houston to return to our ship and report that the Confederate commissioners were on board the mail steamer, and refused to come on board the San Jacinto by other means than force. Lieutenant Greer then shoved off and went alongside the Trent, sent his armed crew and marines on board, and stationed them at both gangways, and then, after a 'gentle application' of force, the four gentlemen were taken in the second cutter and conveyed on board of our ship, where they were received by Captain Wilkes at the gangway, and shown into his cabin, which they afterwards occupied. Two other boats were then sent on board to remove the luggage, and the ladies having declined the hospitalities offered them, at 3.30 we parted company from the Trent."

The commissioners made a protest to Captain Wilkes on the next day, in which they say that when the Trent got withing hailing distance, her captain inquired what was wanted? The reply was understood to be: "They would send a boat." Both vessels were then stationary, with steam shut off. A boat very soon put off from the ship, followed immediately by two other boats, with full crews, and armed with muskets and side-arms. A lieutenant in the uniform of the United States navy, and with side-arms, boarded the Trent, and, in the presence of most of the passengers then assembled on the upper deck, said to Captain Moir that he came with orders to demand his passenger list. The captain refused to produce it, and formally protested against any right to visit his ship for the purpose indicated. After some conversation, implying renewed protests on the part of the captain against the alleged object of the visit, and on the part of the officer of the San Jacinto that he had only to execute his orders, the latter said that two gentlemen, naming Messrs. Slidell and Mason, were known to be on board, as also two other gentlemen, naming Messrs. Eustis and McFarland, and that his orders were to take and carry them on board the San Jacinto. On first addressing the captain, he announced himself as a lieutenant of the United States steamer San Jacinto. The four gentleman named being present, the lieutenant addressed Mr. Slidell and afterwards Mr. Mason, repeating that his orders were to take them, together with Messrs. Eustis and McFarland, and carry them on board his ship. Messrs. Slidell and Mason, in reply, protested in the presence of the captain of the Trent, his officers and passengers, against such threatened violation of their persons and their rights, and informed the lieutenant that they would not leave the ship they were in unless compelled by the employment of actual force greater than they could resist, and Messrs. Eustis and McFarland united with them in expressing a like purpose. That officer stated that he hoped he would not be compelled to resort to the use of force, but if it should become necessary to employ it, in order to execute his orders, he was prepared to do so. He was answered by the commissioners that they would submit only to such a force. The lieutenant then went to the gangway where his boats were, the commissioners going at the same time to their state rooms on the next deck below, followed by Capt. Moir and by the other passengers. The lieutenant returned with a party of his men, a portion of whom were armed with side-arms, and others, appearing to be a squad of marines, having muskets and bayonets. Mr. Slidell was in his state room immediately by and in full view. The lieutenant then said to Mr. Mason that, having his force now present, he hoped to be relieved from the necessity of calling it into actual use. The gentleman again answered that he would only submit to actual force greater than he could overcome, when the lieutenant, and several of his men, by his order, took hold of him, and in a manner and in numbers sufficient to make resistance fruitless; and Mr. Slidell joining the group at the same time, one or more of the armed party took like hold of him, and those gentlemen at once went into the boat.

One account says, an exciting scene took place between Mr. Slidell, his eldest daughter, a noble girl devoted to her father, and Lieut. Fairfax. With flashing eyes and quivering lips she threw herself in the doorway of the cabin where her father was, resolved to defend him with her life, till, on the order being given to the marines to advance, which they did with bayonets pointed at this defenceless girl, her father ended the painful scene by escaping from the cabin by a window, when he was immediately seized by the marines and hurried into the boat. The commissioners were taken by the San Jacinto to Fortress Monroe and transferred to Fort Warren, in Boston harbor, where they remained as prisoners.

A most intense excitement was aroused in England upon the arrival of the news of the transaction. Preparations for war with the United States were commenced, troops were sent to Canada, and a formal demand was made for the surrender of the commissioners, and an apology for the act by the Government.

On the 30th of November, Mr. Seward writes to Mr. Adams that Capt. Wilkes, in the steamer San Jacinto, had boarded a British colonial steamer, and taken from her deck two insurgents who were proceeding to England on an errand of treason against their own country. He then proceeds:

> We have done nothing on the subject to anticipate the discussion, and we have not furnished you with any explanations. We adhere to that course now, because we think it more prudent that the ground taken by the British Government should be first made known to us here, and that the discussion, if there must be one, shall be had here. It is proper, however, that you should know one fact in the case, without indicating that we attach much importance to it, namely, that, in the capture of Messrs. Mason and Slidell on board a British vessel, Capt. Wilkes having acted without any instructions from the Government, the subject is therefore free from the embarrassment which might have resulted if the act had been specially directed by us.

Earl Russell on the same day writes to Lord Lyons, the British Minister at Washington, relating the facts of the case as he had received them from the commander of the colonial steamer Trent, and thus states the demands of his Government in relation to the matter:

> Her Majesty's Government, bearing in mind the friendly relations which have long subsisted between Great Britain and the United States, are willing to believe that the United States naval officer who committed the aggression was not acting in compliance with any authority from his Government, or that if he conceived himself to be so authorized he greatly misunderstood the instructions which he had received. For the Government of the United States must be

fully aware that the British Government could not allow such an affront to the national honor to pass without full reparation, and her Majesty's Government are unwilling to believe that it could be the deliberate intention of the Government of the United States unnecessarily to force into discussion between the two Governments a question of so grave a character, and with regard to which the whole British nation would be sure to entertain such unanimity of feeling.

Her Majesty's Government, therefore, trust that when this matter shall have been brought under the consideration of the Government of the United States, that Government will, of its own accord, offer to the British Government such redress as alone could satisfy the British nation, namely, the liberation of the four gentlemen and their delivery to your lordship, in order that they may again be placed under British protection, and a suitable apology for the aggression which has been committed.

Should these terms not be offered by Mr. Seward you will propose them to him.

Later, on the same day, Lord John Russell addressed another note to Lord Lyons, of a private nature, as follows:

In my previous despatch of this date I have instructed you, by command of her Majesty, to make certain demands of the Government of the United States.

Should Mr. Seward ask for delay in order that this grave and painful matter should be deliberately considered, you will consent to a delay not exceeding seven days. If, at the end of that time, no answer is given, or if any other answer is given except that of a compliance with the demands of her Majesty's Government, your lordship is instructed to leave Washington with all the members of your legation, bringing with you the archives of the legation, and to repair immediately to London.

If, however, you should be of opinion that the requirements of her Majesty's Government are substantially complied with, you may report the facts to her Majesty's Government for their consideration, and remain at your post till you receive further orders.

A copy of the first despatch was sent to Mr. Seward by Lord Lyons, who gave him a reply on the 26th of December. After stating the facts in the case, Mr. Seward proceeds thus:

Your lordship will now perceive that the case before us, instead of presenting a merely flagrant act of violence on the part of Capt. Wilkes, as might well be inferred from the incomplete statement of it that went up to the British Government, was undertaken as a simple legal and customary belligerent proceeding by Capt. Wilkes to arrest and capture a neutral vessel engaged in carrying contraband of war for the use and benefit of the insurgents.

The question before us is, whether this proceeding was authorized by, and conducted according to the law of nations. It involves the following inquiries:

1st. Were the persons named and their supposed despatches contraband of war?

2d. Might Capt. Wilkes lawfully stop and search the Trent for these contraband persons and despatches?

3d. Did he exercise that right in a lawful and proper manner?

4th. Having found the contraband persons on board and in presumed possession of the contraband despatches, had he a right to capture the persons?

5th. Did he exercise that right of capture in the manner allowed and recognized by the law of nations?

If all these inquiries shall be resolved in the affirmative, the British Government will have no claim for reparation.

The first four questions are briefly answered by himself in the affirmative, and only the fifth remained for consideration.

Other nations besides Great Britain took a lively interest in this seizure of Messrs. Mason and Slidell. On the 10th of December, the Minister of France for Foreign Affairs writes to the representative of that court at Washington that "the arrest had produced in France, if not the same emotion as in England, at least extreme astonishment and sensation. Public sentiment was at once engrossed with the unlawfulness and the consequences of such an act." Again he says:

The desire to contribute to prevent a conflict, perhaps imminent, between two powers for which the French Government is animated by sentiments equally friendly, and the duty to uphold, for the purpose of placing the right of its own flag under shelter from any attack, certain principles, essential to the security of neutrals, have, after mature reflection, convinced it that it could not, under the circumstances, remain entirely silent.

After examining the reasons which might be urged to justify the arrest of Mason and Slidell, if the United States approved of the act, he proceeds to show the disastrous effects which their detention would have on the principles governing neutral rights.

There remains, therefore, to invoke, in explanation of their capture, only the pretext that they were the bearers of official despatches from the enemy; but this is the moment to recall a circumstance which governs all this affair, and which renders the conduct of the American cruiser unjustifiable.

The Trent was not destined to a point belonging to one of the belligerents. She was carrying to a neutral country her cargo and her passengers; and, moreover, it was in a neutral port that they were taken.

The Cabinet of Washington could not, without striking a blow at the principles which all neutral nations are alike interested in holding in respect, nor without taking the attitude of contradiction of its own course up to this time, give its approbation to the proceedings of the commander of the San Jacinto. In this state of things it evidently should not, according to our views, hesitate about the determination to be taken.

A vote of thanks to Captain Wilkes passed the House of Representatives of Congress, but the authorities at Washington sent instructions to the commandant at Fort Warren to deliver the Confederate commissioners to the representatives of the British Government. They were, therefore, quietly placed on board of a small steamer and taken to an English steam vessel at anchor near Provincetown, some distance from Boston. In her they were conveyed to the island of St. Thomas, and thence by the line of steam packets took passage to England, where they safely arrived, and were landed without any special official attention.

Next in the order of events was the occupation of Virginia, east of the Chesapeake Bay. It is a peninsula, having the Atlantic Ocean on the east, and the bay above mentioned on the west. It was understood, near the close of the year, that a body of secessionists, who were chiefly residents, were in arms and exercising a hostile control over the inhabitants of these two counties. Gen. Dix, then in command of that Department, with his head-quarters at Baltimore, despatched a body of troops to restore the Federal authority. At the same time he issued a proclamation, stating the objects of the expedition, which produced the happiest results. The troops as they advanced met with no opposition. The people declared their intention to submit to the authority of the United States before the arrival of the military force. On the night of November 15 a force of Confederate troops, in Accomac County, mostly drafted militia, disbanded. They gave as reasons that they were satisfied with the proclamation, and they believed they could not withstand the military force. In Northampton County the secessionists, to the number of 1,800, laid down their arms, and the Union troops held peaceful possession of the entire county. The following was the proclamation of Gen. Dix:

HEADQUARTERS, BALTIMORE, *Nov.* 13, 1861.

To the People of Accomac and Northampton Counties, Va.:

The military forces of the United States are about to enter your counties as a part of the Union. They will go among you as friends, and with the earnest hope that they may not by your own acts be compelled to become your enemies. They will invade no right of person or property. On the contrary, your laws, your institutions, your usages, will be scrupulously respected. There need be no fear that the quietude of any firesides will be disturbed, unless the disturbance is caused by yourselves. Special directions have been given not to interfere with the condition of any person held to domestic servitude; and, in order that there may be no ground for mistake or pretext for misrepresentation, commanders of regiments or corps have been instructed not to permit such persons to come within their lines.

The command of the expedition is intrusted to Brig.-Gen. Henry H. Lockwood, of Delaware—a State identical in some of the distinctive features of its social organization with your own. Portions of his force come from counties in Maryland bordering on one of yours. From him and from them you may be assured of the sympathy of near neighbors, as well as friends, if you do not repel it by hostile resistance or attack.

This mission is to assert the authority of the United States, to reopen your intercourse with the loyal States, and especially with Maryland, which has just proclaimed her devotion to the Union by the most triumphant vote in her political annals to restore to commerce its accustomed guides, by reëstablishing the lights on your coast; to afford you a free export for the produce of your labor, a free ingress for the necessaries and comforts of life which you require in exchange, and in a word, to put an end to the embarrassments and restrictions brought upon you by a causeless and unjustifiable rebellion.

If the calamities of intestine war which are desolating other districts of Virginia, and have already crimsoned her lands with fraternal blood, fall also upon you, it will not be the fault of the Government. It asks only that its authority may be recognized. It sends among you a force too strong to be successfully opposed—a force which cannot be resisted in any other spirit than that of wantonness and malignity. If there are any among you, who, rejecting all overtures of friendship, thus provoke retaliation and draw down upon themselves consequences which the Government is most anxious to avert, to their account must be laid the blood which may be shed, and the desolation which may be brought upon peaceful homes. On all who are thus reckless of the obligations of humanity and duty, and all who are found in arms, the severest punishment warranted by the laws of war will be visited.

To those who remain in the quiet pursuit of their domestic occupations, the public authorities assure that they can give peace, freedom from annoyance, protection from foreign and internal enemies, a guarantee of all constitutional and legal rights, and the blessings of a just and parental Government.

JOHN A. DIX,
Major-General Commanding.

The importance of a stringent blockade of the harbor of Charleston was early apparent. This had been maintained during the temperate months of the year; but on the approach of winter the Government resorted to another method to stop the trade. The attempt was made to seal up the channels with sunken ships. The Secretary of the Navy thus states the plan:

"One method of blockading the ports of the insurgent States, and interdicting communication, as well as to prevent the egress of privateers which sought to depredate on our commerce, has been that of sinking in the channels vessels laden with stone. The first movement in this direction was on the North Carolina coast, where there are numerous inlets to Albemarle and Pamlico Sounds, and other interior waters, which afforded facilities for eluding the blockade, and also to the privateers. For this purpose a class of small vessels were purchased in Baltimore, some of which have been placed in Ocracoke Inlet.

"Another and larger description of vessels were bought in the eastern market, most of them such as were formerly employed in the whale fisheries. These were sent to obstruct the channels of Charleston harbor and the Savannh River; and this, if effectually done, will prove the most economical and satisfactory method of interdicting commerce at those points."

Two fleets of vessels were obtained for the blockade of Charleston and Savannah. The first consisted of twenty-five vessels; the second of twenty. The largest number of these vessels had been used in the whale fisheries and in the trade to India. They were ships and barks of a burden between two and five hundred tons, which had become too old to encounter any longer the hazards of a long voyage at sea. They were purchased by the Government at about ten dollars per ton, principally in the seaports of New Bedford and New London. The vessels, although old, were substantial and generally double-deckers. They were stripped of their copper and other fittings not necessary for so short a voyage, and loaded with picked stone as deeply as was safe. At light-water mark in each vessel one or more holes were bored through the sides, into which a lead pipe was carefully inserted, the ends of which were nailed down on each side of the vessel, a plug was driven in from the outside and another from within, and both secured by a rod passing through them, and fastened within by a nut and screw. Each fleet carried about six thousand tons of stone. The vessels were each manned by about fourteen men. The orders given to the commander were as follows:

"To Captain ——, Sir: The —— now under your command, having been purchased by the Navy Department for service on the Southern coast of the United States, the following are your orders for your proposed voyage:

"You will proceed from this port on ——, the —— instant, or with the first fair wind, and when clear of the land make a direct passage to the port of ——, and there deliver your ship to the commanding officer of the blockading fleet off said port, taking his receipt for her return to me. After the delivery of your vessel, yourself and crew will be provided with passages to the port of New York, by the Navy Department, and on your arrival there you will call on ——, who will furnish you with funds to return to this port.

"On the voyage down it would be well, as far as practicable, to keep in company of your consorts, to exhibit lights by night and sound horns or bells in case of fog near the coast.

"You will also examine daily the pipe in the quarter of your ship under water, to see that it remains safe.

"The only service required of you is the safe delivery of your vessel; and as she is old and heavily laden, you will use special care that she sustains no damage from unskilful seamanship or want of prudence and care.

"On a close approach to your port of destination, begin to put between-decks cargo into lower hold, and, before anchoring permanently, have your second anchor and chain (if you have one) secured on deck. On leaving your vessel, unless otherwise ordered, you will bring away papers, chronometer, charts, compasses, spy-glass, and any other valuable portable articles not required by the commander of the blockading fleet there, and return them safely to me.

"In case of disaster, to preclude going on, you can call at Fortress Monroe, Hampton Roads, to repair damages, reporting to the flag-officer there.

"Wishing you a safe and speedy passage,

"I am yours, respectfully, —— ——."

The effect of sunken vessels upon the channels of a harbor, if uninfluenced by winds and currents, is to stop the navigation. These old hulks become points for the accumulation of alluvials which the rivers bear down, and of the sands which the tides carry back. Becoming thoroughly imbedded in the sand, they cause the accumulations to increase with time, forming unconquerable obstacles to reopening the channels. The strong westerly winds which prevail at Charleston tend to sweep out the channels of its harbor by the increased force of the ebb tide. Two or three hulks which were sunk by the State authorities before the bombardment of Fort Sumter were soon afterwards swept out in this manner. In some instances obstructions of this kind have caused the water to cut out new channels. On the 21st of December seventeen of these vessels were sunk across the principal entrance to Charleston by orders from the Navy Department at Washington. They were placed in three or four rows across the channel, not in uniform, but in a chequered order.

The occupation of Beaufort by the Federal troops with an immense fleet of transports excited great apprehensions at Charleston. An increased military force was gathered; the defences increased and put in a complete state of readiness to resist an attack.

On Dec. 20th an affair occurred at Dranesville, in Virginia, near Washington, which was so favorable to the Federal side that it was regarded with much gratification. A brigade of Gen. McCall's division, under the command of Gen. E. O. C. Ord, having been ordered to advance in the direction of Dranesville, for the purpose of obtaining a quantity of forage known to be in the possession of secessionists, they marched from camp about six o'clock in the morning. Apprehending that they might be attacked, Gen. McCall ordered another brigade, under Gen. Reynolds, to follow at eight o'clock. Meantime Gen. Ord's brigade, having advanced nearly to Dranesville, were assailed by a Confederate force in ambush. A spirited engagement ensued, which lasted nearly an hour, when the enemy's force fled in the direction of Fairfax Court House, abandoning on the field a number of their killed and wounded, besides arms, clothing, and other articles. The force under Gen. Reynolds did not come up until the action was over. The Union force, after remaining at Dranesville till near sundown, returned to their camp, which they reached between nine and ten o'clock at night, bringing with them fifty wagon loads of forage, and the prisoners and abandoned articles.

The enemy's force was composed of the 1st and 11th Kentucky regiments, and the 10th Alabama, with a regiment of cavalry and a battery of cannon, all under the command of Col. John H. Forney, acting Brigadier-General. They left on the field ninety dead bodies and ten of their wounded. Eight of their number, unhurt, were taken prisoners.

On the Union side, about seven were killed and sixty-three wounded.

The position which had thus far been taken by the Federal Government relative to the Confederate States, was to regard them still as a part of the United States, whose inhabitants were in a condition of insurrection against the Government. Those carrying on active hostilities were to be subdued by military force. When all vestiges of military power on the part of the insurgents were destroyed, it was expected that the good sense of the people of those States would convince them of the great blessings of the Union, and induce their hearty return to its support. From the outset the Government was confident of its ultimate success. This was founded upon the peculiar character of the insurgent people, being that of masters rather than laborers, and upon their commercial inability to sustain a long war. The policy of the Government, therefore, was to blockade all the ports, and thereby shut out all foreign manufactures and all foreign aid from a people exclusively devoted to agriculture, and almost entirely dependent upon other States or nations for their market, and for all the comforts and luxuries of life. The military conquest was expected to be very easy and rapid, until the disaster at Bull Run taught the Government that success would result only from the most extensive, careful, and thoroughly organized military preparations.

On the other hand the people of the insurrectionary States had, at first, looked upon secession as hopeless, if it should be powerfully opposed by the Federal Government and Northern people; but within a short period they had become convinced that the North would not fight, and therefore flattered themselves that certain success was within their grasp. Their amazement at the valor, bravery, and vigor of the Northern troops has been inexpressible, and with the loss of all hope of foreign assistance, they have seen their prospects of success fading away.

The course of the Government relative to the slave property in the Confederate States was designed to be in strict conformity with its views of the Constitution and laws. But as the Southern States were in insurrection, there was no obligation to return fugitive slaves to them; consequently all slaves who came within the army lines were treated as freemen.

As to prisoners captured by either side there was no recourse but to exchange, according to the laws of war. This the Federal Government hesitated to do, for the reason that it might be construed into acknowledging belligerent rights on the part of the Confederates. The necessity of exchange became urgent, and the friends of prisoners were clamorous that something should be done for their relief. The Administration practically ignored the question, being impressed with the idea that it would derogate from the dignity of its position to accept any interchange of courtesy. By exchanging prisoners, nothing is conceded or admitted except what is patent to the world—that actual war exists. Previous to the battle of Bull Run the number of prisoners on either side was not large. By that disaster the Southerners captured about 1,400 northern troops. They released numbers at different points on parole, and the matter was compromised in various ways. In September an exchange took place between Gen. Pillow and Col. Wallace, of the Federal army.

On the 1st of November Gen. Fremont made a treaty with Gen. Price, of Missouri, among the provisions of which was one for the exchange of prisoners. Certain parties named are authorized, whenever applied to for the purpose, to negotiate for the exchange of any and all persons who may hereafter be taken prisoners of war and released on parole; such exchanges to be made upon the plan heretofore approved and acted upon, to wit: "grade for grade, or two officers of lower grade, as an equivalent in rank for one of a higher grade, as shall be thought just and equitable." This was signed by both parties. Gen. Hunter, having succeeded Gen. Fremont on the 7th of Nov., repudiated this treaty.

At the close of the year three commissioners were appointed by the Federal Government to proceed to the Confederate States and examine the condition of the Union prisoners there. They were refused admission within the Confederate territory, and thus the fate of prisoners was left to the discretion of each commander, who exchanged them at his will. But, while such were the terms on which exchanges were effected for those taken as prisoners on either side upon land, only an informal regulation had been established respecting the persons detained on a charge of piracy, because found waging war against Federal commerce on the high seas, and in retaliation for whose treatment the Confederate authorities imprisoned in the common jail a corresponding number of United States officers.

In his message to Congress on the 20th of July, Mr. Davis refers to a despatch sent to Washington, as before stated, and after stating the reasons upon which it was sent, thus proceeds: "To this end I despatched an officer under a flag of truce to President Lincoln, and informed him of my resolute purpose to check all barbarities on prisoners of war by such severity of retaliation on prisoners held by us as should secure the abandonment of the practice. This communication was received and read by an officer in command of the United States forces, and a message was brought from him by the bearer of my communication that a reply would be returned by President Lincoln as soon as possible. I earnestly hope this promised reply (which has not yet been received) will convey the assurance that prisoners of war will be treated in this unhappy contest with that regard for humanity which has made such conspicuous progress in modern warfare. As measures of precaution, however, and until this promised reply is received, I shall retain in close custody some officers captured from the enemy, whom it had been my pleasure previously to set at large on parole, and whose fate must necessarily depend on that of prisoners held by the enemy."

The foreign policy of the Government was conducted on the principle that the troubles of the country formed a domestic affair of its own, and the interference of foreign nations was neither desired nor would be allowed. The prompt manner in which the Confederate States were acknowledged as belligerents by France and England is a proof that not a doubt was entertained by the Governments of those nations of the ultimate independence of the new Confederacy.

After the adjournment of the extra session of Congress in July, the plan of the Government was to make the most ample and perfect preparations to recover and repossess the strongholds in the Confederate States. In its progress due regard was had to the will of Congress, and the requirements of the emergency. With a surprising unanimity among the people, its measures were steadily sustained.

The army around Washington was reorganized, greatly increased in numbers, and brought up to the highest state of discipline. In its front the camps of the flower of the Southern States were spread, and the year closed with the two armies watching each other. The one was growing more formidable and better prepared for the approaching strife, while the other was growing weaker by the overstrained effort to maintain a position which it finally yielded without a single blow.

CHAPTER XII.

Views of the Combatants—Condition of the Federal Navy—Its Increase—Iron-Clads—Western Fleet—Numbers and position of the hostile Armies—Campaign in Eastern Kentucky—Battle of Mill Springs—Death of Zollicoffer—Campaign in Western Kentucky and Tennessee—Federal Troops engaged—Capture of Fort Henry—Surrender of Fort Donelson—Advance of Gen. Buell—Surrender of Nashville.

When the new year began, the anticipations of the two antagonists were materially changed. The South, rendered exultant and hopeful by the successes at Bull Run and Leesburg or Ball's Bluff, believed that foreign interference was certain, and that the war would be short. Under these influences a serious state of apathy was beginning to prevail. The enlistment of troops was for the short period of twelve months, and the naval preparations for defence were on a limited scale.

Meanwhile the North had begun to realize the gigantic nature of the contest in which it was engaged, and to put forth corresponding efforts of preparation. Besides the organization of vast armies, naval preparations were commenced on an immense scale, and embracing every variety of improvement. The Federal Government also, in order to strengthen itself, had resorted to the imprisonment of all persons who by words or actions manifested a strong sympathy for the Southern cause. At the same time many newspapers whose general spirit was hostile to the Government, were suppressed, and their circulation forbidden.

The Secretary of the Navy, in his report of July 4th, 1861, presented the following statement of the vessels at that time in service:

"Of the 69 vessels, carrying 1,346 guns, mentioned as available for service on the 4th of March last, the sloop Levant has been given up as lost in the Pacific; the steamer Fulton was seized at Pensacola; and one frigate, two sloops, and one brig were burnt at Norfolk. These vessels carried 172 guns. The other vessels destroyed at Norfolk were considered worthless, and are not included in the list of available vessels.

"These losses left at the disposal of the department 62 vessels, carrying 1,174 guns, all of which are now, or soon will be, in commission, with the exception of the

	Guns.
Vermont, ship-of-line	84
Brandywine, frigate	50
Decatur, sloop, at San Francisco	16
John Hancock, steam tender at San Francisco	3

"There have been recently added to the navy, by purchase, 12 steamers, carrying from 2 to 9 guns each, and 3 sailing vessels. There have been chartered 9 steamers, carrying from 2 to 9 guns each. By these additions, the naval force in commission has been increased to 82 vessels, carrying upwards of 1,100 guns, and with a complement of about 13,000 men, exclusive of officers and marines. There are also several steamboats and other small craft which are temporarily in the service of the department.

"Purchases of sailing ships have been made for transporting coals to the steamers that are performing duty as sentinels before the principal harbors. * * *

"The squadron on the Atlantic coast, under the command of Flag-officer S. H. Stringham, consists of 22 vessels, 296 guns, and 3,300 men.

"The squadron in the Gulf, under the command of Flag-officer William Mervine, consists of 21 vessels, 282 guns, and 3,500 men.

"Additions have been made to each of the squadrons, of two or three small vessels that have been captured and taken into the service. The steamers Pawnee and Pocahontas, and the flotilla under the late Commander Ward, with several steamboats in charge of naval officers, have been employed on the Potomac River, to prevent communication with that portion of Virginia which is in insurrection. Great service has been rendered by this armed force, which has been vigilant in intercepting supplies, and in protecting transports and supply vessels in their passage up and down the Potomac.

"The squadron in the Pacific, under the command of Flag-officer John B. Montgomery, consists of six vessels, 82 guns, and 1,000 men.

"The West India squadron is under the command of Flag-officer G. J. Pendergrast, who has been temporarily on duty, with his flag-ship, the Cumberland, at Norfolk and Hampton Roads, since the 23d of March. He will, at an early day, transfer his flag to the steam-frigate Roanoke, and proceed southward, having in charge our interests on the Mexican and central American coasts, and in the West India Islands.

"The East India, Mediterranean, Brazil, and African squadrons, excepting one vessel of each of the two latter, have been recalled.

"The return of these vessels will add to the force for service in the Gulf and on the Atlantic coast, about 200 guns and 2,500 men."

He also stated in his report that 259 officers of the navy had resigned their commissions, or been dismissed from the service, since the 4th of March; for which reason many of the vessels were necessarily sent to sea without a full complement of officers. Many, however, who had retired to civil pursuits, had promptly come forward in this time of their country's need, and voluntarily tendered their services, while many masters and masters' mates were also appointed from the commercial marine. So promptly did seamen present themselves at the naval rendezvous of all the principal seaports, under the authorized increase and abbreviated term of enlistment, that only one or two ships experienced any detention for want of a crew, and none beyond two or three days. Never, as the Secretary states, has the naval force had so great and rapid an increase, and never have our seamen come forward with more alacrity and zeal to serve the country.

In the need of a substantial class of vessels suitable for performing continuous duty off the coast in all weathers, the department contracted for the building of 23 steam gunboats, each of about 500 tons burden, and made preliminary arrangements for several larger and fleeter vessels, in addition to taking measures for carrying out the order of Congress of the preceding session for the construction of seven sloops of war, with the addition of one more. At each of the Northern navy yards, Portsmouth, Boston, New York, and Philadelphia, two of this last class were directed to be built. The following table comprises a summary of the vessels purchased for naval service during the year 1861:

CLASS OF VESSELS.	No.	Number of guns to each.	Total number of guns.	Tonnage of each.	Total tonnage.	Cost of each.	Total cost.
Side-wheel steamers	36	1 to 10	160	123 to 1,800	26,680	$12,000 to $200,000	$2,418,108
Screw steamers	42	1 to 9	170	65 to 2,100	19,985	5,000 to 172,500	2,187,537
Auxiliary steam bark	1	....	5	....	418	....	27,500
Ships	13	1 to 8	52	334 to 1,375	9,998	7,000 to 40,000	313,503
Barks	17	2 to 6	78	265 to 888	8,136	11,500 to 32,000	343,400
Barkantine	1	....	...	....	296	....	16,000
Schooners	25	1 to 4	50	53 to 349	5,458	6,000 to 18,000	241,790
Brigs	2	2	4	196 to 264	460	9,000 to 10,000	19,000

Of side-wheel steamers nine were first-class steamships, all of them costing from $85,000 to $200,000 each, except one, the Alabama, which was bought for $23,000. Among the steamers were eighteen ferry-boats and tug-boats, the former purchased from the Brooklyn and New Jersey companies.

The armed vessels were almost exclusively ordered, on entering into the service, to proceed to the Southern ports, for the purpose of enforcing their blockade, and the result of their operations is shown in the following summary of vessels, captured and destroyed from April 23 to November 15. These are 7 ships, 12 barks, 9 brigs, 115 schooners, 8 sloops, and 7 miscellaneous, the last including the steamer Salvor, loaded with arms, from Havana, and bound to Tampa Bay. Most of these vessels contained valuable cargoes, and three of them were privateers. A few were recaptured prizes, and were restored to their owners.

The year 1861 will always be famous in naval history for the material change then first fairly established in the construction of vessels of war, by rendering them as nearly impenetrable as possible to the heaviest shot, by means of a coating of iron plates. The superiority of a few guns of the heaviest calibre to the large batteries of the older ships was then first generally appreciated, and the whole system of ship-building in the navies of France and England, as also of some of the minor naval powers of Europe, underwent a more complete change than had followed the introduction of steam. The building of wooden vessels was entirely abandoned, except in some special cases where they were to be covered with plates of iron, and the day of old wooden frigates and line-of-battle ships was looked upon as having passed.

The subject came before Congress in 1861, and on the 3d of August an act was approved, directing the Secretary of the Navy "to appoint a board of three skilful naval officers to investigate the plans and specifications that may be submitted for the construction and completing iron-clad steam-ships or steam-batteries, and on their report, should it be favorable, the Secretary of the Navy will cause one or more armored, or iron or steel-clad steam-ships or floating steam-batteries to be built; and there is hereby appropriated, out of any money in the treasury not otherwise appropriated, the sum of $1,500,000." Commodores Joseph Smith and H. Paulding, with Capt. C. H. Davis, were appointed this board, and their report was presented of the date of Sept. 15. While considering iron-clad ships as without doubt formidable adjuncts to coast and harbor fortifications, the board questioned their advantages and ultimate adoption as cruising vessels, chiefly on account of the enormous weight added to the vessel by the armor, which involved greater power to propel her, and at the same time largely increased the cost of construction. To meet the immediate demand for vessels as far as practicable invulnerable to shot, and adapted by their light draught of water to penetrate our shoal harbors, rivers, and bayous, the board recommended "that contracts be made with responsible parties for the construction of one or more iron-clad vessels or batteries, of as light a draught of water as practicable consistent with their weight of armor." They also advised the construction in our own dock-yards, of one or more of these vessels upon a large and more perfect scale

ERICSSON'S BATTERY—THE MONITOR.

when Congress shall see fit to authorize it. The report concludes with a synopsis of the propositions and specifications submitted, amounting to 17 in number, the terms of construction for the different vessels ranging from $32,000 to $1,500,000. Three only of these were selected as worthy of recommendation, the others being put aside, either owing to too great cost or for other reasons. The three proposals recommended were those of J. Ericsson, New York; Merrick & Sons, Philadelphia; and C. S. Bushnell & Co., New Haven, Conn. Of these the remarks of the board are as follows:

"J. Ericsson, New York.—This plan of a floating battery is novel, but seems to be based upon a plan which will render the battery shot and shell-proof. It is to be apprehended that her properties for sea are not such as a seagoing vessel should possess. But she may be moved from one place to another on the coast in smooth water. We recommend that an experiment be made with one battery of this description on the terms proposed, with a guarantee and forfeiture in case of failure in any of the properties and points of the vessel as proposed. Price, $275,000; length of vessel, 174 feet; breadth of beam, 41 feet; depth of hold, 11½ feet; time, 100 days; draught of water, 10 feet; displacement, 1,245 tons; speed per hour, 9 statute miles.

"Merrick & Sons, Philadelphia.—Vessel of wood and iron combined. This proposition we consider the most practicable one for heavy armor. We recommend that a contract be made with that party, under a guarantee, with forfeiture in case of failure to comply with the specifications; and that the contract require the plates to be 15 feet long and 36 inches wide, with a reservation of some modifications, which may occur as the work progresses, not to affect the cost. Price, $780,000; length of vessel, 220 feet; breadth of beam, 60 feet; depth of hold, 23 feet; time, 9 months; draught of water, 13 feet; displacement, 3,296 tons; speed per hour, 9½ knots.

"S. C. Bushnell & Co., New Haven, Conn., propose a vessel to be iron-clad, on the rail and plate principle, and to obtain high speed. The objection to this vessel is the fear that she will not float her armor and load sufficiently high, and have stability enough for a sea vessel. With a guarantee that she shall do these, we recommend on that basis a contract. Price, $225,250; length of vessel, 180 feet; breadth of beam — feet; depth of hold, 12⅝ feet; time, 4 months; draught of water, 10 feet; displacement, — tons; speed per hour, 12 knots."

The recommendation was adopted by Congress, and the 3 vessels ordered to be built.

The contract made with Capt. Ericsson stipulated for the completion of his battery within 100 days from the signing of the contract, which was October 5, 1861; and the extraordinary provision was introduced, that the test of the battery, upon which its acceptance by the U. S. Government depended, should be its withstanding the fire of the enemy's batteries at the shortest ranges, the United States agreeing to fit out the vessel with men, guns, &c. The vessel was not completed, and delivered to the U. S. Government for trial until March 5, 1862.

Soon after taking command of the Western Department, Maj.-Gen. Fremont became convinced of the necessity of preparing a fleet of gunboats and mortar-boats, for the purpose of commanding the Mississippi and other navigable waters of the West, and decided upon the plans and ordered the construction of the number of each he deemed necessary. Their completion, and the furnishing of them with their armament and crew, and the collection of the requisite land force to accompany them, was not completed till February, 1862.

The fleet consisted of twelve gunboats, carrying an armament in all of 126 guns, viz.:

Benton	16 guns.
Essex	9 "
Mound City	13 "
Cincinnati	13 "
Louisville	13 "
Carondelet	13 "
St. Louis	13 "
Cairo	13 "
Pittsburgh	13 "
Lexington	9 "
Conestoga	9 "
Tyler	9 "

None of these guns were less than 32-pounders, some were 42-pounders, some 64-pounders, and one (on the Essex) threw a shell weighing 128 lbs. In addition to these, each boat carried a Dahlgren rifled 12-pounder boat howitzer on the upper deck. Several of the larger guns on each boat were rifled. Naval officers regarded the 10-inch Dahlgren shell guns as their most efficient weapons. The Benton carried two of these guns in her forward battery; the others carried one each.

Seven of the gunboats were iron-clad, and able to resist all except the heaviest solid shot. These boats cost on an average $89,000 each. The other five were of wood, but strongly and substantially built; all were fast sailers.

Besides these, thirty-eight mortar-boats were ordered, each about sixty feet long and twenty-five feet wide, surrounded on all sides by iron-plate bulwarks, six or seven feet high. The mortar itself weighed 17,200 lbs., had a bore easily admitting a 13-inch shell, and from the edge of the bore to the outer rim was seventeen inches. The mortar bed weighed 4,500 lbs.

The mortar-boats were thoroughly tested before being used in actual service, and were found to produce but slight recoil, and the concussion caused by the iron bulwarks was remedied. With a charge of 11 lbs. of powder the mortars threw a shell, weighing 215 lbs. a distance of 2½ miles; and with a charge of 15 to 23 lbs. the same shell was thrown from 3 to 3½ miles.

There was also a sufficient number of steamboats and tugs provided for towing and transport service. The fleet was placed under the command of Flag-officer Andrew H. Foote, an experienced and able commander in the navy; and each boat was in charge of a lieutenant commanding, who had already seen service.

At the commencement of the year 1862, the position of the Federal and of the Confederate forces were as follows: At Fortress Monroe and Newport News, under the command of Gen. Wool, there were estimated to be 15,000 men in a good state of organization and discipline. Thence proceeding up the Potomac, Gen. Hooker's division, including Gen. Sickles's brigade, was south of Washington, and partly on the Maryland side of the Potomac. They numbered about 10,000 men. Southwest of Washington, and in the neighborhood of that city, was the mass of Gen. McClellan's army, consisting of a large portion of the men who had volunteered from the middle and eastern States, for the war. They were organized into eight divisions, and becoming disciplined for future operations. The divisions of Gens. Keyes and Casey were in and around Washington, that of Gen. Stone was at and near Poolesville, and that of Gen. Banks near Darnestown, with detachments on the Potomac to Williamsport. The entire force thus organized, was not far from 160,000 men, which, in connection with other troops on the line of railroad to Baltimore, at that city, and in the vicinity, was something less than 200,000 men. This force before Washington was subsequently designated as the Army of the Potomac. It was organized into divisions, each commanded by a major-general, or by a brigadier-general acting as a major-general; and each division consisted of three brigades, each brigade of four, a few of five, regiments of infantry, making twelve infantry regiments in a division, one regiment of cavalry, and three and sometimes four batteries of artillery, or about twenty pieces. To each division generally one regiment of cavalry was assigned, and one or two of them had four instead of three batteries.

Further up the Potomac, was Gen. Kelly's force, of which Gen. Lander soon took command, looking up the valley of the Shenandoah, toward Winchester. Gen. Rosecrans was in western Virginia, with a force somewhat less than 20,000 men.

At Louisville, in Kentucky, Gen. Buell had collected and combined the scattered Federal forces, and was now organizing and preparing for future operations, an army of more than 100,000 men. At St. Louis and Cairo, Gen. Halleck was performing a similar service, and at the same time holding in check the Confederate forces in Missouri, and preparing to drive them entirely over its southern border. The force he was thus organizing, was nearly equal to that under Gen. Buell in Kentucky.

On the western frontier preparations were also making for an expedition, which was designed to be more than 20,000 strong, for the purpose of penetrating from Kansas to the Gulf of Mexico. A naval force was also collected at Cairo and St. Louis, to coöperate, by gunboats, with the military force, at important points on the western rivers. The entire Federal force, including the troops under Gen. Sherman in South Carolina, and those under Gen. Burnside on their way to North Carolina, and the regiments designed for the expedition under Gen. Butler, made not more than 450,000 to 475,000 in the field.

The position and force of the Confederate army at the commencement of the year, were nearly as follows: At Norfolk and Yorktown there was a considerable force, probably over 30,000 men. The larger portion of this force was at Yorktown. A small force also manned batteries on the James and York rivers. The army before Washington was fortified on a very extended line. Its right wing rested upon the Potomac, beyond Fredericksburg, and at Stafford Court House, Dumfries, &c., and thus formed a support to the batteries which blockaded the Potomac river, and endangered the navigation between Washington and the lower Potomac into Chesapeake Bay. The main body was at Centreville and Manassas. The former place was strongly fortified, and held not less than 75,000 troops. The left wing occupied Aldie and Leesburg, and considerable forces were stationed at Winchester and Martinsburg. This entire force has been estimated to have reached 175,000 men, under Gen. Joseph Johnston. A small force was in western Virginia.

In Kentucky, the Confederate forces were stationed at Prestonburg, Hazel Green, Bowling Green, Columbus, Hickman, Donelson and Fort Henry, and amounted to 30,000 men.

The points occupied by the Confederate forces in Tennessee, were Cumberland Gap, Nashville, Waverly, Humboldt, Chattanooga, Jonesboro, Memphis, and forts Osceola, Wright, Randolph, Rector and Harris. These troops amounted to 20,000 men.

There were also Confederate troops stationed at Vicksburg, Natchez, New Orleans, Mobile, Savannah, Charleston, and at various points in Missouri. The total force under arms, was not far from 350,000 men.

The Confederate forces at this time occupied half of Missouri, nearly half of Kentucky, including the strong positions of Columbus and Bowling Green, western Virginia, nearly as far north as the Kanawha river, the whole of eastern Virginia, except a few miles around Washington and Fortress Monroe and Newport News, the whole of North Carolina, except Hatteras Inlet, the whole of Florida except Key West, and Santa Rosa Island, and all the rest of the Southern States.

The results of the previous year when compared with the purposes entertained by the citizens of the North, appear most insignificant. But this is not a true view of the case. It was too soon to expect results, and nothing was done which had any influence upon the termination of the war. These gigantic combatants were yet unprepared for the conflict. Armies had been collected and hastily equipped, and the work of organization and discipline to change raw militia into men of war was progressing on both sides. So unused, however, were the people to such events, that a speedy close of the contest had been anticipated by them. War, in their minds, was to be begun, carried on, and closed up with the despatch of ordinary enterprises.

It was not only necessary to organize and discipline armies, but to provide food, munitions, and transportation, and to organize artillery reserves, the engineer corps, the pontoon trains, the telegraphs, and the hospitals; but also to manufacture or import from other countries cannon, carriage harness, cavalry equipments, small arms, artillery, camp equipage, bridge trains, &c. The time required to secure these objects, under the most favorable circumstances, was even longer than had been assigned for the duration of hostilities by the people of both the Northern and Southern States.

The Federal Government proposed to blockade the coast to cut off the Confederate States from all communication with other nations. The recovery of the Mississippi valley, by which the western States of the Confederacy would be separated, and the outlet of the Northwest to the ocean recovered, was also a part of the purpose of the Government. The recovery of the Border Slave States by actual military force, and their protection against invasion by the Confederate Government, which claimed them as a part of its Union, was the occasion of the most active and extensive military operations. It was anticipated that the signal success which would attend the execution of these purposes, would so emphatically convince the Southern people of the irresistible power of the North as to satisfy them that the attainment of their independence was hopeless. At the same time it was believed their efforts of resistance would so exhaust their limited resources as to make a return to the Union on their part a necessity. Such appear to have been the purposes of the Federal Government, and such were the views of the people. On the opposite side, the purposes of the Confederate Government were no less determined, and the views of the people no less sanguine and exalted. A defence was to be made to the last extremity, and if this was successful, an invasion of the enemy was to follow, when the smoking ruins of Philadelphia, New York, and Cincinnati would wring humiliating conditions from the North. The years which passed have thus witnessed most stupendous military operations conducted on a theatre which was almost the size of a continent, with a profusion of expenditure and a waste of resources sufficient to engulf most nations. The actors in these terrific scenes now stand forth to receive the judgment of mankind not only upon their skill, ability, and sincerity, but upon those higher and nobler qualities which are the jewels of humanity.

The military operations in the interior of the country have been conducted chiefly with a reference to the lines of the railroads and the water courses. The facilities for the transportation of supplies and for the concentration of men furnished by these railroads and the rivers, in a country so covered with woods, and so poorly supplied with common roads, has resulted in making some of them the base of all important movements.

At the beginning of the year preparations were vigorously pushed forward both at the West and with the Army of the Potomac. The forces of each side on the line between the Federal and Confederate States maintained their respective positions during the month of January, excepting in eastern Kentucky. There Col. Humphrey Marshall had a few months previous intrenched the Confederate forces under his command, consisting of a few regiments of infantry, one battery of artillery, and five or six companies of cavalry at a town called Paintville. It was expected in the Confederate States that he would be able to sweep the whole of eastern Kentucky, take possession of Frankfort, the seat of the State Government, and set up the authority of the Provisional Governor Johnson. Meanwhile Col. John A. Garfield, commanding a brigade of Union forces, having the 42d Ohio and 14th Kentucky infantry and a squadron of Ohio cavalry, advanced to encounter the Confederate force. Embarrassed by the difficulty of moving supplies at that low stage of the Big Sandy river, it was the 7th of January when his advance, consisting of five companies of the 42d Ohio, under Lieut.-Col. Sheldon, reached Paintville. The Confederate force had then evacuated its intrenchments two and a half miles south of the town, but a part of it was placed in ambush at Jennie Creek, two miles west. This body was driven out immediately by Col. Bolles, of the 1st Virginia cavalry, who had come up. At the same time Col. Garfield, with eight companies of the 42d Ohio and two companies of the 14th Kentucky, moved upon the main position of the enemy, who were found to have hastily retreated. On the next day the 40th Ohio, Col. Cranox, and six companies of the 1st Kentucky cavalry joined Col. Garfield; a part of the 22d Kentucky, under Lieut.-Col. Munroe, had also reached him. With a portion of this force, the pursuit of the enemy was immediately commenced up the road along the Big Sandy river.

The following despatches from Col. Garfield describe his movements:

PAINTSVILLE, *January* 8.

To Capt. J. B. Fry, Assistant Adjutant-General:

I entered this place yesterday with the 42d Ohio, the 4th Kentucky, and 300 of the 2d Virginia cavalry. On hearing of my approach, the main rebel force left their strongly intrenched camp and fled. I sent my cavalry to the mouth of Jennie Creek, where they attacked and drove the rebel cavalry, which had been left as a vanguard, a distance of five miles, killing three and wounding a considerable number.

Marshall's whole army is now flying in utter confusion. He had abandoned and burned a large amount of his stores. We have taken fifteen prisoners. Our loss is two killed and one wounded. I start in pursuit to-morrow morning.

(Signed) J. A. GARFIELD,
Col. commanding Brigade.

SECOND DESPATCH.

To Capt. J. B. Fry, Assistant Adjutant-General:

I left Paintsville on Thursday noon with 1,100 men, and drove in the enemy's pickets two miles below Prestonburg. The men slept on their arms. At 4 o'clock yesterday morning we moved toward the main body of the enemy at the forks of Middle Creek, under command of Marshall. Skirmishing with his outposts began at 8 o'clock, and at 1 P. M. we engaged his force of 2,500 men and 3 cannon, posted on the hill—fought them until dark, having been reënforced by 700 men from Paintsville, and drove the enemy from all their positions. He carried off the majority of his dead and all of his wounded.

This morning we found twenty-seven of his dead on the field. His killed cannot be less than sixty. We have twenty-five prisoners, ten horses, and a quantity of stores. The enemy burned most of his stores, and fled precipitately. To-day I have crossed the river, and am now occupying Prestonburg. Our loss is—two killed and twenty-five wounded.

(Signed) J. A. GARFIELD,
Col. commanding Brigade.

This was a rapid and spirited movement on the part of Col. Garfield, and it resulted in forcing Col. Humphrey Marshall with his troops to retire from eastern Kentucky.

On the 16th of January Col. Garfield issued the following address to the inhabitants:

HEADQUARTERS EIGHTEENTH BRIGADE,
PAINTSVILLE (KY.), *January* 16, 1862.

Citizens of the Sandy Valley:

I have come among you to restore the honor of the Union and to bring back the Old Banner, which you all once loved, but which, by the machinations of evil men and by mutual misunderstanding, has been dishonored among you. To those who are in arms against the Federal Government I offer only the alternative of battle or unconditional surrender. But to those who have taken no part in this war, who are in no way aiding or abetting the enemies of the Union—even to those who hold sentiments averse to the Union, but yet give no aid and comfort to its enemies—I offer the full protection of the Government, both in their persons and property.

Let those who have been seduced away from the love of their country to follow after and aid the destroyers of our peace lay down their arms, return to their homes, bear true allegiance to the Federal Government, and they shall also enjoy like protection. The army of the Union wages no war of plunder, but comes to bring back the prosperity of peace. Let all peace-loving citizens who have fled from their homes return and resume again the pursuits of peace and industry. If citizens have suffered from any outrages by the soldiers under my command, I invite them to make known their complaints to me, and their wrongs shall be redressed and the offenders punished. I expect the friends of the Union in this valley to banish from among them all private feuds, and let a liberal-minded love of country direct their conduct toward those who have been so sadly estranged and misguided, hoping that these days of turbulence may soon be ended and the days of the Republic soon return.

J. A. GARFIELD,
Col. commanding Brigade.

But the most important action of the month was fought at a place called Webb's Cross Roads on the 19th. It is known as the battle of Mill Springs, although this place is about five miles distant from the spot where the battle was fought. For three months previous the Federal General Schoepff had been stationed at Somerset, a small town in south-eastern Kentucky, with a force of about 8,000 men. The object was to prevent the advance of the Confederate force any further north. At the same time the Confederate General Zollicoffer, with nearly the same force, was intrenched directly south on both banks of the Cumberland river, for the purpose of defending the approach to the Cumberland Gap and the road into east Tennessee against any Federal force. About two weeks previous to the action, Gen. Zollicoffer was reënforced by the division under Gen. Crittenden, which had been previously stationed at Knoxville, Tennessee. Gen. Crittenden took command, and issued the following proclamation:

DIVISION HEADQUARTERS, MILL SPRINGS, KY.,
January 6, 1862.

To the People of Kentucky:

When the present war between the Confederate States and the United States commenced, the State of Kentucky determined to remain neutral. She regarded this as her highest interest, and, balancing between hope for the restoration of the Union and love for her Southern sisters, she declared and attempted to maintain a firm neutrality.

The conduct of the United States Government toward her has been marked with duplicity, falsehood, and wrong. From the very beginning, the President of the United States, in his Messages, spoke of the chosen attitude of Kentucky with open denunciation, and on the one hand treated it with contempt and derision, while on the other hand he privately promised the people of Kentucky that it should be respected. In violation of this pledge, but in keeping with his first and true intention, he introduced into the State arms which were placed exclusively in the hands of persons known or believed to be in favor of coercion, thus designing to control the people of Kentucky, and to threaten the Confederate States. Then the Government of the Confederate States, in self defence, advanced its arms into your midst, and offer you their assistance to protect you from the calamity of Northern military occupation.

By the administration of your State Government, Kentucky was being held to the United States, and bound at the feet of Northern tyranny. That Government did not rest upon the consent of your people. And now, having thrown it off, a new Government has been established and Kentucky admitted into the Southern Confederacy. Can Kentuckians doubt which Government to sustain? To the South you are allied by interest, by trade, by geography, by similarity of institutions, by the ties of blood, and by kindred courage. The markets of the North do not invite your products—your State is, to the centre of its trade, society, and laws, but a distant province, despised for its customs and institutions—your heroic lineage forbids association in arms with their warriors of Manassas, of Leesburg, and of Belmont; and your former devotion to the Union must intensify your hatred toward that section which has, in its Abolition crusade, broken to pieces the Constitution, and which is now vainly endeavoring to destroy the liberty of the Southern States!

At first you may have been deceived as to the purposes of the North. They talked of restoring the Union. Do you not see that it is hopelessly lost in the storm of war, and that, while the rotten Government of the North is shaking over its ruins, the South has erected out of them a new, powerful, and free constitutional republic! And now, indeed, the mask is thrown off, and you find the North, through its President, and Secretary of War, and public journals, and party leaders, giving up the claim of Union, and proclaiming the extinction of slavery and the subjugation of the South. Can you join in this enterprise? The South would never in any event consent to a reconstruction. She is contending with unconquerable spirit, with great military power, with unbroken success, for constitutional freedom, and for her own national government. Where is your spirit of other days, that you do not rush to her victorious standard? Shall the sons of Tennessee, Virginia, Mississippi, and other Southern States, with whom you have gathered the laurels on other battle fields, win them all in this war of independence, while you are inactive and lost in slothful indolence? May the proud genius of my native Kentucky forbid it.

In these mountains, where freedom and patriotism stir the human heart, can you sleep with the clarion of a glorious war ringing in your ears? True, you have refused to bear the arms and wear the livery of Northern despotism. Their base hirelings have been among you, but have not seduced you into their ranks. Will you stay at home and let noble bands of soldiers, armed in your cause as in their own, pass on to battle fields, on your own soil, consecrated by no deed of your valor?

Having assumed command of the forces of the Confederate States on Cumberland river, in south-eastern Kentucky, I make this appeal to you. You are already assured that we come among you as friends and brothers, to protect you in your personal liberties and property, and only to make war against the invaders of your home and our common enemies. I invoke you to receive us as brothers, and to come to our camp and share with us the dangers and the honor of this struggle. Come to these headquarters, as individuals or in companies, and you will be at once accepted and mustered in with pay and arms from the Government of the Confederate States. At first many Kentuckians entered the army of the South for the great cause it supports; now this has become the cause of Kentucky, and it is your duty to espouse it. Duty and honor unite in this call upon you. Will you join in the moving columns of the South, or is the spirit of Kentucky dead? GEO. B. CRITTENDEN, Major-General.

Previous to the junction of the force of Gen. Crittenden with that of Gen. Zollicoffer, Gen. Buell, in command of the Federal department, with his headquarters at Louisville, had detached from his main body a division under Gen. Geo. H. Thomas to attack the rear of Gen. Zollicoffer, whose position was a strong one. It was about fifteen miles south-west of Somerset, forty miles south-east of Columbia, and six miles below the head of steamboat navigation. It was considered to be one of the three Confederate strongholds in Kentucky—the first being Columbus, in the extreme West; the second, Bowling Green in central Kentucky; and the third, this one in the south-east, commanding the coal mines and many of the salts wells south of the Cumberland, and suitable to check any Federal advance into east Tennessee. The hills on the immediate bank of the river are between three and four hundred feet in height and their summits were fortified. The actual situation of the Confederate force has been variously represented. It was nearly destitute of supplies, and upon hearing of the approach of the Federal force, the choice was presented to Gen. Crittenden, either to retreat without striking a blow, or to remain in his position and be stormed out, or to surrender upon the approach of starvation, or to make an advance. The latter measure was chosen, and for this reason the Confederate general was found without his intrenchments and making an attack upon the approaching force. It is probable, however, that the Federal force was supposed to be much smaller than it in truth was, and hence the Confederate general was tempted to advance and make an attack. That day (Sunday) he was defeated and retired to his intrenchments. During the night he abandoned his camp, and by the aid of a small steamboat crossed the Cumberland with his entire force. The Federal forces most actively engaged were: the 9th Ohio, Col. McCook; 2d Minnesota, Col. Van Cleve; 4th Kentucky, Col. Fry; 10th Indiana, Col. Munson; with the batteries of Capts. Stanhart and Wetmore. These were supported by the 14th Ohio, Col. Steadman; and the 10th Kentucky, Col. Haskin. The force of Gen. Schœpff came up and joined in the pursuit. The Confederate force consisted of the 15th Mississippi, Col. Walthal; 19th Tennessee, Col. Cummings; 20th Tennessee, Capt. Battle; 25th Tennessee, Capt. Stouton; 17th Tennessee, Col. Newman; 28th Tennessee, Col. Murray; 29th Tennessee, Col. Powell; 16th Alabama, Col. Wood, with two batteries. The Federal loss was 38 killed and 194 wounded; the Confederate loss was 190 killed (among whom was Gen. Zollicoffer), 60 wounded, and 89 prisoners. The forces of Gen. Thomas and Gen. Crittenden were about equal. The force of Gen. Schœpff, however, was equal to a reserve for Gen. Thomas. The artillery of Gen. Thomas was of longer range than the Confederate guns.

The following order of thanks was issued by President Lincoln in consequence of this victory:

WAR DEPARTMENT, *January* 22, 1862.

The President, commander-in-chief of the army and navy, has received information of a brilliant victory achieved by the United States forces over a large body of armed traitors and rebels at Mill Springs, in the State of Kentucky.

He returns thanks to the gallant officers and soldiers who won that victory; and when the official reports shall be received, the military skill and personal valor displayed in battle will be acknowledged and rewarded in a fitting manner.

The courage that encountered and vanquished the greatly superior numbers of the rebel force, pursued and attacked them in their intrenchments, and paused not until the enemy was completely routed, merits and receives commendation.

The purpose of this war is to attack, pursue, and destroy a rebellious enemy, and to deliver the country from danger menaced by traitors. Alacrity, daring, courageous spirit, and patriotic zeal, on all occasions and under every circumstance, are expected from the army of the United States.

In the prompt and spirited movements and daring battle of Mill Springs, the nation will realize its hopes, and the people of the United States will rejoice to honor every soldier and officer who proves his courage by charging with the bayonet and storming intrenchments, or in the blaze of the enemy's fire.

By order of the President.

EDWIN M. STANTON, Secretary of War.

This victory opened the path into east Tennessee, but no advantage was taken of it by the Federal Government. It also produced an exhilaration in the North far above its importance.

Some important reconnoissances were made in western Kentucky at this time, extending even to the Tennessee line. The country around Fort Columbus was fully explored, the length and condition of the roads ascertained, the number of bridges and their strength, the depth of the streams without bridges, and the sentiments of the inhabitants. Fort Henry was twice approached by the gunboat Lexington, and its strength estimated. These reconnoissances were made by forces from the Department of Missouri, then under the command of Maj.-Gen. Halleck. Early in January troops began to concentrate at Cairo, Paducah, and Fort Jefferson from different quarters. To such an extent had this progressed that, in the public mind, it was supposed that a great movement was on foot.

The plan of the campaign in the West now began to be manifest. At the time when Gen. Buell was ordered to the command of the department of the Ohio, the views of the Government were favorable to an expedition to the Cumberland Gap and into east Tennessee, for the purpose of seizing the Virginia and east Tennessee line of railroad and affording aid to the loyal citizens. The Confederate line of defence had now become so fully developed, with its strong positions of Bowling Green and Columbus, that the propriety of an expedition by the forces in Kentucky into east Tennessee became a question for military investigation. The mountainous character of the country through which the Gap had to be reached, the roughness of the roads, rendering the conveyance of artillery extremely difficult and slow, and subjecting an army at every interval to formidable resistance, were discouraging obstacles to an advance in that direction.

On the other hand, the movement of troops from Cairo up the Cumberland river by transports and gunboats against Nashville, so as to reach the rear of the Confederate army under Gen. Buckner, presented an easy manner of breaking the enemy's line and compelling the evacuation of Kentucky. Its successful achievement might be attended with the capture of the Confederate force at Bowling Green. These views finally prevailed and measures were taken to carry them into execution. The original plan of the western campaign had been for a military and naval expedition to proceed from St. Louis and Cairo down the Mississippi river. For this purpose the gunboats were originally constructed. They were found to be of sufficiently light draft to navigate the Cumberland and Tennessee rivers, and the coöperation of the western department under Gen. Halleck was also secured. Indeed the Mississippi river expedition was thus diverted at the outset, and Gen. Halleck, by order of the President, assumed the entire commahd After a union of these two armies, they were expected to control the whole country to New Orleans.

The reconnoissance of Fort Henry had convinced Com. Foote, in command of the western fleet of gunboats, that it could be easily reduced by his gunboats. At an early day he applied to Gen. Halleck for permission to attack the fort. These views undoubtedly had an important influence on the plan of the western campaign.

The States which contributed chiefly to the force organized by Gen. Buell in Kentucky were: Ohio, Kentucky, Indiana, Illinois, Michigan, Wisconsin, Minnesota, Pennsylvania, and Tennessee, as follows: Ohio, thirty regiments of infantry, two and half regiments of cavalry, and eight batteries of artillery; Indiana, twenty-seven regiments of infantry, one and half regiments of cavalry, and five batteries of artillery; Illinois, three regiments of infantry; Kentucky, twenty-four regiments of infantry, four regiment, of cavalry, and two batteries of artillery; Pennsylvania, three regiments of infantry, two regiments of cavalry, one battery of artillery; Michigan, three regiments of infantry, one battery of artillery; Wisconsin, three regiments of infantry; Minnesota, two regiments of infantry, and one battery of artillery; Tennessee, two regiments of infantry. Besides these there were of regulars, three regiments of infantry, and three batteries of artillery. Thus making one hundred and two regiments of infantry, ten regiments of cavalry, and twenty-one batteries of artillery; which might be summed up as follows: infantry 100,000, cavalry 11,000, artillerists 3,000; total 114,000 men, and 126 pieces of artillery. This army was divided into four grand divisions under the command of Gens. Alexander McDowell McCook, Geo. H. Thomas, Ormsby M. Mitchell, Thos. L. Crittenden. Among the brigade commanders, of whom there were twenty, were the following officers: Ebenezer Dumont, Albin Schœpff, Thos. J. Wood, Wm. Nelson, Richard W. Johnson, Jerre T. Boyle, Jas. S. Negley, Wm. T. Ward.

The force organized by Gen. Halleck, with his headquarters at St. Louis, was concentrated at that place and Cairo and Paducah, excepting that portion which was in the field in the State of Missouri. It was somewhat less in numbers than the army of Gen. Buell. For operations in Kentucky and Tennessee it was placed under the command of Gen. Grant. It was drawn chiefly from the States adjacent to Missouri.

The naval force prepared to coöperate with the military consisted of twelve gunboats carrying an armament in all of one hundred and twenty-six guns. None of these guns were less than 32-pounders, some were 42-pounders, and also 9 and 10-inch naval columbiads. In addition, each boat carried a rifled Dahlgren 12-pounder boat howitzer on the upper deck. Several of the larger guns on each boat were rifled.

The boats were built very wide, in proportion to their length, giving them almost the same steadiness in action that a stationary land battery would possess. They were constructed with the sides sloping upward and downward from the water line, at an angle of forty-five degrees. The bow battery on each boat consisted of solid oak timber twenty-six inches in thickness, plated on the exterior surface with iron two and a half inches thick.

The side and stern batteries were somewhat thinner, but had the same thickness of iron over that portion covering the machinery.

The boats were built so that in action they could be kept "bow on;" hence the superior strength of the bow battery. Broadsides were so arranged as to be delivered with terrible effect while shifting position. To facilitate movements in action, the engines and machinery were of the most powerful kind. The boilers were five in number, constructed to work in connection with or independent of each other.

Seven of these boats only were iron clad. The number of mortar boats ordered was thirty-eight. Each one which was built, carried a mortar of 13-inch calibre. The charge of powder for the mortar was about twenty-three pounds. Each boat was manned by a captain, lieutenant, and twelve men. Formidable as this naval force appears, its preparation was very tardily undertaken by the Government, and at the moment when first needed, but few of the boats were ready.

On the 27th of January, the President of the United States appeared as commander-in-chief of the army and navy, and issued the following order:

EXECUTIVE MANSION, WASHINGTON, *Jan.* 27, 1862.

PRESIDENT'S GENERAL WAR ORDER, No. 1.

Ordered, That the 22d day of February, 1862, be the day for a general movement of the land and naval forces of the United States against the insurgent forces.

That especially

The Army at and about Fortress Monroe,
The Army of the Potomac,
The Army of Western Virginia,
The Army near Munfordsville, Kentucky,
The Army and Flotilla at Cairo,
And a Naval Force in the Gulf of Mexico,

be ready for a movement on that day.

That all other forces, both land and naval, with their respective commanders, obey existing orders for the time, and be ready to obey additional orders when duly given.

That the Heads of Departments, and especially the Secretaries of War and of the Navy, with all their subordinates, and the General-in-Chief, with all other commanders and subordinates of land and naval forces, will severally be held to their strict and full responsibilities for the prompt execution of this order.

ABRAHAM LINCOLN.

This order was unproductive of direct military effect, but was viewed as an indication of the President's desire that active measures should be taken speedily toward the initiation of hostilities. Gen. McClellan still continued to be general-in-chief, and all the movements of Gen. Buell up to the occupation of Nashville, and those of Gens. Halleck and Grant, were made under his instructions up to the 11th of March, when the order of the President was issued, relieving him "from the command of the other military departments."

By the "Army near Munfordsville, Kentucky," were designated the forces of Gen. Buell. After the battle of Mill Springs, movements were made by order of Gen. Buell, as if with the purpose of advancing into eastern Tennessee in force. The Cumberland river was crossed at Waitsboro', and a column was pushed toward Cumberland Gap, while two brigades were moved from Gen. Buell's centre toward his left. The Confederates understood that east Tennessee was the destination of these troops, and hastily sent a large force by railroad from Bowling Green through Nashville to Knoxville. But the army of Gen. Thomas, instead of going to east Tennessee, turned back to Danville and subsequently marched to join Gen. Nelson, at Glasgow, and flank Bowling Green on the left. Thus, instead of dividing his forces, Gen. Buell concentrated them by a movement from the left to the centre. Meanwhile the centre of Gen. Buell's force, under Gen. Mitchell, had been advanced toward Munfordsville, on the road to Bowling Green.

By the term "The Army and Flotilla at Cairo," was designated the military force of Gen. Halleck's department, collected at Cairo, Paducah, and Fort Jefferson, under Gen. Grant, together with the gunboats, and intended for the Tennessee river expedition.

A movement against Fort Henry on the Tennessee river was at once undertaken. This fort is situated near the line of Kentucky and Tennessee, on the east bank of the stream. It stands on the low lands adjacent to the river, about the high water mark, and being just below a bend in the river, and at the head of a straight stretch of about two miles, it commands the river for that distance, and very little else. On Saturday night, Feb. 1, the gunboats St. Louis, Cincinnati, Carondolet, Essex, Tyler, and Lexington, in an incomplete state of preparation, being the only ones manned, left Cairo, and proceeded to the mouth of the Tennessee at Paducah. Here they were joined by the gunboat Conestoga and a fleet of transports, with a land force under Gen. Grant, and on Monday afternoon proceeded up the river. By Tuesday all were anchored about eight miles below the fort, which being an unfavorable place for the debarkation of troops, a reconnoissance was made by the Essex, St. Louis, and Cincinnati. A suitable place for the landing, encampment, and general rendezvous of the troops was found just below the range of the guns of the fort. The troops were landed during the afternoon, and the transports returned to Paducah for more regiments. By Thursday morning, Feb. 6, a large force was gathered, and a body of troops under Gen. Smith were also landed on the west side of the river, where it was supposed that a considerable Confederate force was encamped. The troops after being landed were formed into two divisions; the first, consisting of the 8th, 18th, 27th, 29th, 30th, and 31st, making one brigade; and the 11th, 20th, 45th, and 48th Illinois regiments making

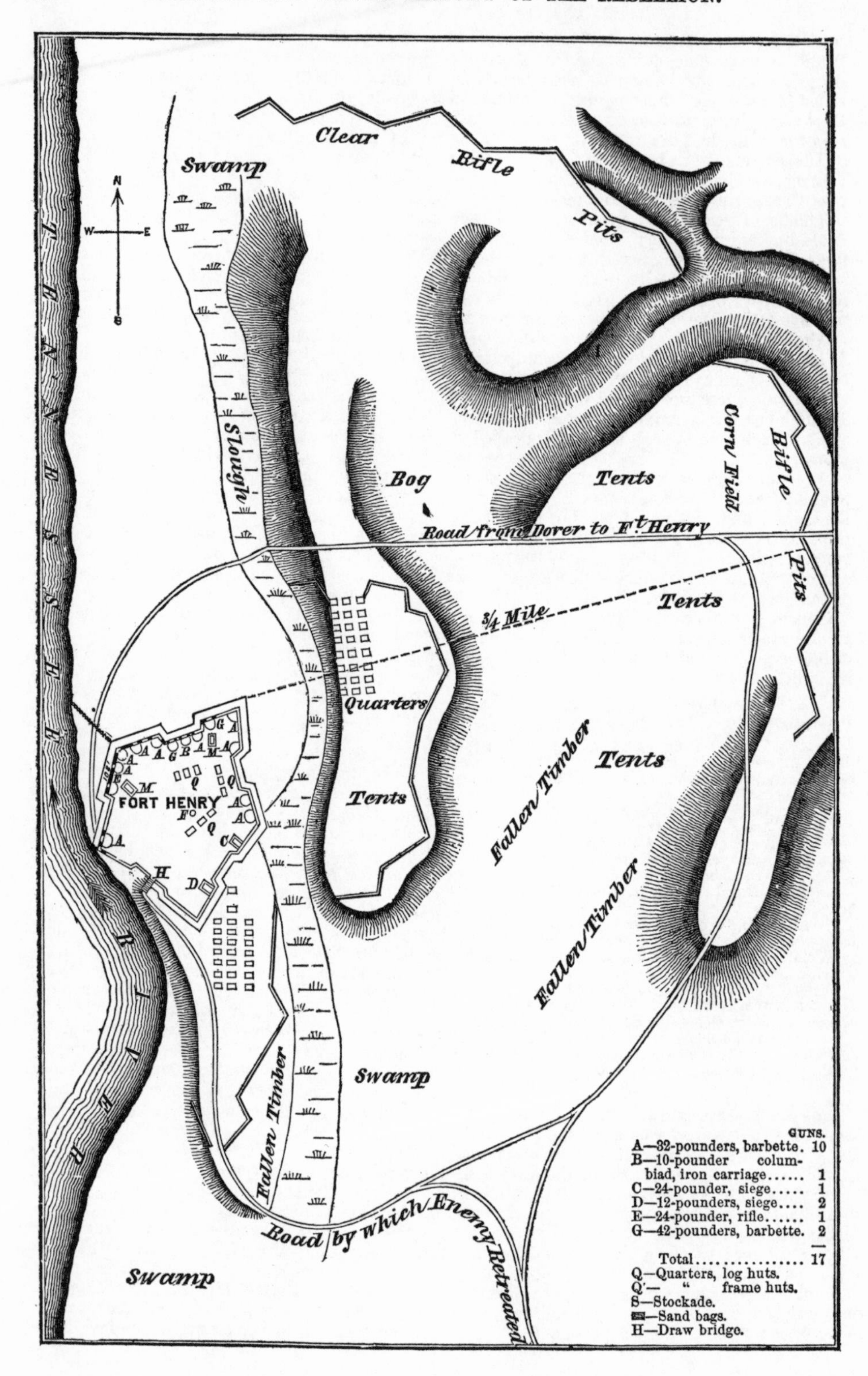
Clear
Rifle
Pits
Swamp
N
W
E
S
TENNESSEE
RIVER
Slough
Bog
Tents
Corn Field
Rifle
Road from Dorer to Ft. Henry
Pits
Tents
3/4 Mile
Quarters
Tents
Fallen Timber
Tents
FORT HENRY
Fallen Timber
Fallen Timber
Swamp
Road by which Enemy Retreated
Swamp
GUNS.
A—32-pounders, barbette. 10
B—10-pounder columbiad, iron carriage...... 1
C—24-pounder, siege..... 1
D—12-pounders, siege.... 2
E—24-pounder, rifle...... 1
G—42-pounders, barbette. 2
Total................ 17
Q—Quarters, log huts.
Q'— " frame huts.
S—Stockade.
—Sand bags.
H—Draw bridge.

another brigade, with one regiment (the 4th Illinois), and four independent companies of cavalry, and four batteries of artillery, under Gen. McClernand. This division was ordered to move across the country to a point on the road leading from the fort to the town of Dover, on the Cumberland river, for the purpose of preventing reënforcements to the enemy and cutting of his retreat. The second division consisted of the 7th, 9th, 12th, 28th, and 41st Illinois regiments, the 11th Indiana, 7th and 12th Iowa, 8th and 13th Missouri, with artillery and cavalry, under Gen. Smith. About ten o'clock the land force commenced the march over the hilltops, and the gunboats began to move under steam toward the fort. Passing up the narrow passage to the westward of the island below the fort, they were protected from its guns until within a mile, and emerged in line of battle, the St. Louis, Lieut. Paulding, on the left, next the Carondolet, Commander Walke, next the flag ship Cincinnati, Commander Stembel, and next upon the right the Essex, Commander Porter. The other boats acted as a reserve. Firing upon both sides soon commenced, but the gunboats continued to approach until within six hundred yards of the Confederate batteries. The action lasted for one hour and a quarter, when the flag on the fort was hauled down. Meantime the high water and muddy roads prevented the arrival of the land forces under Gen. Grant, and the Confederate troops in the fort retired, and escaped. Commodore Foote, commanding the naval portion of the expedition, says: "The garrison, I think, must have commenced their retreat last night, or at an early hour this morning. Had I not felt it an imperative necessity to attack Fort Henry to-day, I should have made the investment complete and delayed until to-morrow, so as to secure the garrison. I do not now believe, however, the result would have been any more satisfactory."

This Confederate force was supposed to number between four and five thousand. The fort was armed with twenty guns, 32 and 34-pounders, including one 10-inch Columbiad. Before the close of the action a shot entered the boiler of the Essex, which resulted in wounding and scalding twenty-nine officers and men. Eighty-three prisoners were taken, among whom was Brig. Gen. Tilghman, and a large amount of stores, and everything belonging to the retiring force. On the gunboats two were killed and nine wounded in the action, and on the part of the Confederates five killed and ten wounded.

The result of this action occasioned great joy in the Northern States. The Secretary of the Navy, Gideon Welles, sent the following despatch to Com. Foote:

NAVY DEPARTMENT, *February* 9, 1862.

Your despatch announcing the capture of Fort Henry, by the squadron which you command, has given the highest gratification to the President, to Congress, and the country. It was received and read in both Houses of Congress in open session. The country appreciates your gallant deeds, and this department desires to convey to you and your brave associates its profound thanks for the service you have rendered.

GIDEON WELLES.
Secretary of the Navy.

Flag Officer A. H. FOOTE, U. S. N., commanding the United States naval forces, Cairo, Ill.

By the possession of Fort Henry the Federal forces were in the rear of Columbus on the Mississippi, and within ten miles of the bridge by which the railroad connection was made between Columbus and Bowling Green. There was now no obstacle to the passage of the gunboats to the sources of the Tennessee river in northern Alabama.

Immediately after the surrender, Commander Phelps was ordered to proceed with the gunboats Conestoga, Tyler, and Lexington, up the river to the railroad bridge, and to destroy so much as would prevent its use by the enemy, and thence proceed as far up the river as the stage of water would permit, and capture the gunboats and other vessels which might be useful to the enemy.

After dark, on the same day, the expedition arrived at the bridge for the railroad crossing about twenty-five miles above Fort Henry, where considerable camp equipage was destroyed. Thence the expedition proceeded as far up the river as Florence in Alabama, at the foot of the Muscle shoals. Here the enemy burnt six of their steamers and two were captured, beside a half complete gunboat and considerable lumber. Two hundred stands of arms, a quantity of stores and clothing were also seized, and the encampment of a regiment destroyed. This sudden appearance of the Federal gunboats was like an unexpected apparition to the inhabitants, and loyal and friendly feelings were manifested on every side.

The next step of Com. Foote was to return to Cairo to prepare the mortar boats for operations against Fort Donelson. He desired a delay of a few days to complete them, believing that thereby the garrison, however extensive, could be shelled out without much loss of life to the Federal force. But Gen. Halleck regarded an immediate attack as a military necessity, and it was made although the fleet was reduced to a crippled state, and the loss of life was considerable. There is no question of the correctness of Gen. Halleck's views relative to the attack; the deficiency resulted from a degree of precipitation in the entire movement after the issue of the President's proclamation.

At this time Gen. Crittenden, in command of the right wing of Gen. Buell's army, having advanced to the left bank of Green river near South Carrollton and manœuvred in front of the Confederate (Gen. Buckner's) force, suddenly retreated to Calhoun on Green river. Steamers were there awaiting him, on which his force was embarked and taken down the Green river to the Ohio, down the Ohio, and up the Cumberland, where a junction was effected with Gen. Grant's army.

Troops were also sent from St. Louis, Cairo, and Cincinnati, until the following regiments and batteries were under the command of Gen. Grant, not including the force brought by Gen. Crittenden:

Illinois Infantry.—7th, Col. John Cook, acting brigadier-general; Lieut.-Col. Andrew J. Babcock; 8th, Col. Richard J. Oglesby, acting brigadier-general; Lieut.-Col., Frank L. Rhodes; 9th, Col. Augustus Marsey; 10th, Col. James D. Morgan; 11th, Col. Thomas E. R. Ransom; 12th, Col. John McArthur; 16th, Col. Robert F. Smith; 18th, Col. Michael K. Lawler; 20th, Col. C. Carroll Marsh; 22d, Col. Henry Dougherty (invalid); Lieut.-Col. H. E. Hart; 27th, Col. Napoleon B. Buford; 28th, Col. Amory K. Johnson; 29th, Col. James S. Riordan; 30th, Col. Philip B. Fouke, absent; Lieut.-Col. E. B. Dennis; 31st, Col. John A. Logan; 32d, Col. John Logan; 41st, Col. Isaac C. Pugh; 45th, Col. John E. Smith; 46th, Col. John A. Davis; 48th, Col. Isham N. Haynie; 49th, Col. Wm. R. Morrison, wounded; Lieut.-Col., Thomas G. Allen; 50th, Col. Moses M. Bane; 52d, Lieut.-Col. John S. Wilcox; 55th, Col. David Stuart; 57th, Col. S. D. Baldwin.

Illinois Artillery.—2d regiment, Col. Silas Noble; 3d regiment, Col. Eugene A. Carr; 4th regiment, Col. T. Lyle Dickey; 7th regiment, Col. William Pitt Kellogg.

Illinois Artillery Batteries.—Schwartz's, Dresser's, Taylor's, McAllister's, Richardson's, Willard's, and Buell's; in all, thirty-four guns.

Troops from other States.—3d Iowa, Col. N. G. Williams; 7th Iowa, Col. John G. Lauman; 11th Iowa, Col. Abraham F. Hare; 12th Iowa, Col. Jackson J. Wood; 13th Iowa, Col. Marcellus M. Crocker; 14th Iowa, Col. William T. Shaw; 8th Missouri, Col. Morgan M. Smith; 13th Missouri, Col. Crafts J. Wright; 1st Missouri Artillery, Major Cavender; 11th Indiana, Col. George F. McGinniss; 23d Indiana, Col. Wm. L. Sanderson; 48th Indiana, Col. Norman Eddy; 52d Indiana, Col. James M. Smith.

Gen. Lewis Wallace commanded a third division, in which were the following regiments who were engaged in the battle at Donelson: 28th Kentucky, Col. James L. Shackelford; 31st Indiana, Maj. Fred. Arn; 44th Indiana, Col. Hugh B. Reed; 17th Kentucky, Col. John McHenry.

The force of Gen. Grant had grown within a few days into almost gigantic proportions. Its numbers have been variously stated. After the surrender of Donelson, Gen. Halleck sent the following despatch to Gen. Hunter:

HEADQUARTERS, DEPARTMENT OF ST. LOUIS, *Feb'y* 19.

To Maj.-Gen. D. Hunter, Commanding Department of Kansas at Fort Leavenworth:

To you more than any other man out of this department, are we indebted for our success at Fort Donelson.

In my strait for troops to reënforce Gen. Grant, I applied to you. You responded nobly, by placing your forces at my disposal.

This enabled us to win the victory. Receive my most heartfelt thanks.

(Signed) H. W. HALLECK, Major-General.

A respectable authority wrote as follows, on the morning of Feb. 14:

At eleven o'clock last night we arrived within two miles of the fort. Here we found the Carondolet at anchor. She had been engaging the enemy during the afternoon, at a distance of a mile, had fired about two hundred shots, and retired without receiving any damage. By six o'clock this morning, sixteen transports had arrived from St. Louis, Cairo and Cincinnati, carrying in all about 10,000 troops, cavalry, artillery and infantry. The debarkation occupied about four hours. The sight of such strong reënforcements encouraged all our men greatly. Knowing already that the fort was surrounded by Gen. Grant's command—estimated at 30,000—we felt that such a large addition to his numbers would make assurance doubly sure.

Senator Trumbull thus stated, in the Senate of the United States, his view of the force engaged: "I think there is a disposition to overestimate the number of men upon both sides in the field. We have seen a statement within a few days going the rounds of the papers, that Fort Donelson was invested by an army of fifty thousand men; I have seen it in a number of papers; but when we come to see what regiments were there, instead of being fifty thousand, there were not thirty thousand men. A gentleman direct from Cairo, well acquainted with all the troops engaged in that gallant affair, informs me that the number of our troops was less than twenty-eight thousand."

The Confederate regiments in the fort were reported as follows:

Regiments.—Tennessee, 11; Mississippi, 8; Texas, 1; Kentucky, 2; Arkansas, 1; Virginia, 4; Alabama, 1.

Cavalry Battalions.—Alabama, 1; Tennessee, 1; Mississippi, 1.

The location of the fort was on a fine slope, one hundred and fifty feet high, on a slight bend on the west side of the Cumberland river. At this point the Cumberland and Tennessee rivers, both running north, approach within about twelve miles of each other. Opposite on the Tennessee is situated Fort Henry. There were two batteries at Fort Donelson—the first about twenty-five feet above the water, consisting of nine guns, eight 32's and one 10-inch; the second having one rifled 32-pounder and two 32-pound carronades, located sixty feet higher up. The main fort was in the rear of these batteries, occupying a high range cloven by a deep gorge opening toward the south. The outworks consisted in the main of rifle pits. Along the front of the extension line, the trees had been felled and the brush cut and bent over breast high, making a wide abatis very difficult to pass through. The Confederate camp was behind the hill and beyond the reach of shot and shell from the gunboats.

At three o'clock on the afternoon of Feb. 14, Com. Foote began the conflict with four iron-clad gunboats and two wooden ones. It continued for an hour and a quarter, and the latter part of the time within four hundred yards of the fort, when the wheel of one vessel and the tiller of another were shot away, and both rendered unmanageable, and drifted down the river. At this time the Confederates appeared to be deserting their batteries along the water. The other boats were injured between wind and water, and fifty-four had been killed and wounded, when all retired. Com. Foote deeming his services to be less required on the spot than at Cairo, "until damages could be repaired, and a competent force brought up from that place to attack the fort," retired to Cairo. At the same time he sent a gunboat up the Tennessee to render the railroad bridge above Fort Henry impassable. This had not been done by Lieut. Phelps who had gone up that river with three gunboats.

The land forces under Gen. Grant left Fort Henry on the 12th of February, in two divisions, stated by Gen. Grant as "about fifteen thousand strong,"—six regiments having been sent round on transports. The head of the marching column arrived within two miles of Fort Donelson at twelve o'clock. The Confederate fortifications were from this point gradually approached and surrounded, with occasional skirmishing on the line. The next day the investment was extended on the Confederate flanks, and drawn closer to their works, with skirmishing all day. That night the gunboats and reënforcements arrived. On the next day the attack of the gunboats was made, and after its failure Gen. Grant resolved to make the investment as perfect as possible, and to partially fortify and await the repairs to the gunboats. This plan was frustrated by a vigorous attack upon his right under Gen. McClernand, by the enemy. The battle was closely contested for several hours, and with considerable advantage to the enemy, when they were finally repulsed, having inflicted upon the Union troops a loss of one thousand two hundred in killed, wounded, and missing. At this time Gen. Grant ordered a charge to be made on the left by Gen. Charles F. Smith with his division. This was brilliantly done, and the contest here, which continued until dark, resulted in giving to him possession of part of the intrenchments. Soon after this charge was commenced, an attack was ordered by Gen. Grant to be made by Gen. Wallace of the third division, and two regiments of the second division, on the other Confederate flank, by which it was still further repulsed. At the points thus gained, all the troops remained for the night, feeling that, notwithstanding the brave resistance, a complete victory awaited them in the morning.

The result of this conflict convinced the Confederate officers that without fresh troops they would be unable to hold their position on the next day. Gens. Pillow and Floyd determined therefore to withdraw as no reënforcements would reach them, leaving Gen. Simon B. Buckner in command. By means of two or three small steamboats these officers retired during the night taking about five thousand troops with them.

Early the next morning a flag of truce was sent to Gen. Grant with the following letter:

HEADQUARTERS, FORT DONELSON, *Feb.* 16, 1862.

SIR: In consideration of all the circumstances governing the present situation of affairs at this station, I propose to the commanding officer of the Federal forces the appointment of commissioners to agree upon terms of capitulation of the forces at this post under my command. In that view I suggest an armistice until twelve o'clock to day.

I am, very respectfully, your obedient servant,
S. B. BUCKNER.
Brigadier-General C. S. Army.

To Brig.-Gen. U. S. Grant, Commanding
United States forces near Fort Donelson.

The reply of Gen. Grant to this letter was as follows:

HEADQUARTERS, ON THE FIELD,
FORT DONELSON, *Feb.* 16, 1862.

To Gen. S. B. BUCKNER:

SIR: Yours of this date, proposing an armistice and the appointment of commissioners to settle on the terms of capitulation, is just received.

No terms, except unconditional and immediate surrender, can be accepted.

I propose to move immediately on your works.

I am, very respectfully, your obedient servant,
U. S. GRANT,
Brigadier-General Commanding.

The answer of Gen. Buckner was as follows:

HEADQUARTERS, DOVER (TENN.), *Feb.* 16, 1862.

Brig.-Gen. U. S. Grant, U. S. Army:

SIR: The distribution of the forces under my command, incident to an unexpected change of commanders, and the overwhelming force under your command, compel me, notwithstanding the brilliant success of the Confederate arms, to accept the ungenerous and unchivalrous terms which you propose.

I am, sir, your servant,
S. B. BUCKNER.
Brigadier-General C. S. Army.

The fort was subsequently given up and occupied by the Union troops.

In the action 231 were killed and 1,007 wounded on the Confederate side. The number was larger on the Union side. About 10,000 prisoners were made, and 40 pieces of cannon and extensive magazines of all kinds of ordnance, quartermasters' and commissary stores were captured.

The following is a list of the regiments which were captured at Fort Donelson: 49th Tennessee regiment, Col. Bailey; 43d Tennessee regiment, Col. Abernethy; 27th Alabama regiment, Col. Jackson; 42d Tennessee regiment, Col. Quarrells; Captain Guy's battery; 26th Tennessee regiment, Col. Silliard; 14th Mississippi regiment, Col. Baldwin; 18th Tennessee regiment, Col. Palmer; 2d Kentucky regiment, Col. Hanson; 20th Mississippi regiment, Major Brown; Captain Milton's company; 15th Virginia regiment, Lieut. Haslep; Texas regiment, Col. Gregg; 15th Arkansas regiment, Col. Lee; Capt. Oreston's cavalry; 15th Tennessee regi-

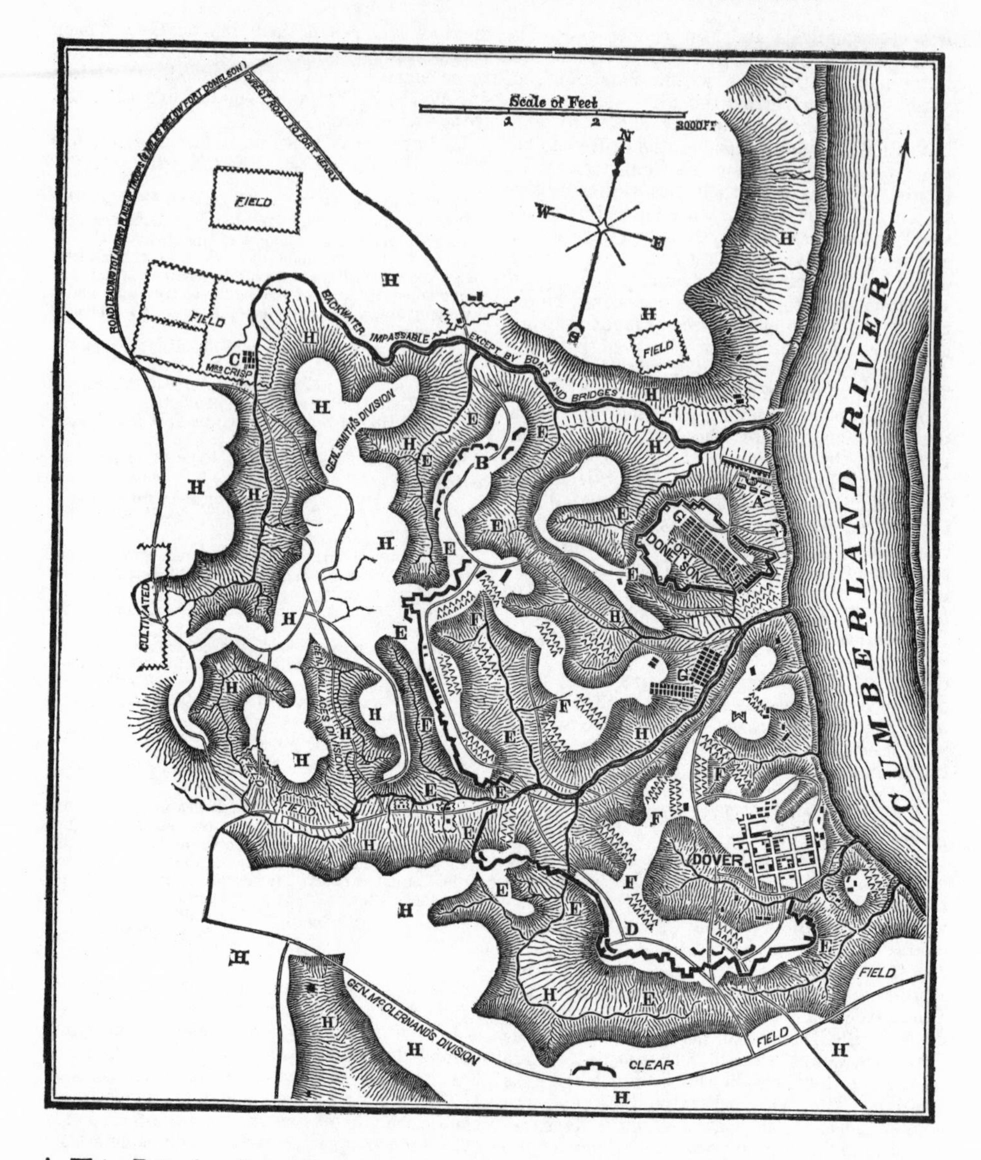

A Water Batteries—Lower Battery, 8 32-pounder guns; 1 10-inch Columbiad.
Upper Battery, 1 32-pounder heavy rifled gun; 2 32-pounder carronades.

B Rifle Pits, carried by General Smith's division.

C General Grant's Headquarters during the siege.

D Part of Confederate Intrenchments, carried by a portion of General McClernand's division.

E Fallen Timber.

F Confederate Tents.

G Confederate Log Huts.

H Woods.

ment, Maj. Clark; one Company, Col. Lugg; Porter's artillery; 3d Tennessee regiment, Col. Brown; 8th Kentucky regiment, Capt. Lyon; 30th Tennessee regiment, Maj. Humphrey; 32d Tennessee regiment, Col. Cook; 41st Tennessee regiment, Col. Forquehanor; Mississippi regiment, Col. Davidson. A portion of the Federal troops in Gen. McClernand's division were under arms two days and nights, amid driving storms of snow and rain.

The fall of the fort occasioned great rejoicing in the Northern cities.

The commanding general (Grant) thus addressed his troops:

HEADQUARTERS, DISTRICT OF WEST TENN., FORT DONELSON, Feb. 17, 1862.

The General commanding takes great pleasure in congratulating the troops of this command for the triumph over rebellion gained by their valor on the 13th, 14th, and 15th instant.

For four successive nights, without shelter during the most inclement weather known in this latitude, they faced an enemy in large force in a position chosen by himself. Though strongly fortified by nature, all the additional safeguards suggested by science were added. Without a murmur this was borne, prepared at all times to receive an attack, and with continuous skirmishing by day, resulting ultimately in forcing the enemy to surrender without conditions.

The victory achieved is not only great in the effect it will have in breaking down rebellion, but has secured the greatest number of prisoners of war ever taken in any battle on this continent.

Fort Donelson will hereafter be marked in capitals on the map of our united country, and the men who fought the battle will live in the memory of a grateful people. By order U. S. GRANT,
Brigadier-General Commanding.

The following is the order of Gen. Halleck:

HEADQUARTERS, DEPARTMENT OF MISSOURI. ST. LOUIS, *Feb.* 19, 1862.

The Major-General commanding the department congratulates Flag-Officer Foote, Brig.-Gen. Grant, and the brave officers and men under their command on the recent brilliant victories on the Tennessee and Cumberland.

The war is not ended. Prepare for new conflicts and new victories. Troops are concentrating from every direction. We shall soon have an army which will be irresistible. The Union Flag must be restored everywhere, and the enthralled Union men in the South must be set free. The soldiers and sailors of the Great West are ready and willing to do this. The time and place have been determined on. Victory and glory await the brave!

By command of Maj. Gen. HALLECK.
N. H. McLEAN, Assistant Adjutant-General.

The Confederate Congress being at that time in session, the following Message was addressed to that body by President Davis:

EXECUTIVE DEPARTMENT, *March* 11, 1862.

To the Speaker of the House of Representatives:

I transmit herewith copies of such official reports as have been received at the War Department of the defence and fall of Fort Donelson.

They will be found incomplete and unsatisfactory. Instructions have been given to furnish further information upon the several points not made intelligible by the reports. It is not stated that reënforcements were at any time asked for; nor is it demonstrated to have been impossible to have saved the army by evacuating the position; nor is it known by what means it was found practicable to withdraw a part of the garrison, leaving the remainder to surrender; nor upon what authority or principles of action the senior Generals abandoned responsibility by transferring the command to a junior officer.

In a former communication to Congress, I presented the propriety of a suspension of judgment in relation to the disaster at Fort Donelson, until official reports could be received. I regret that the information now furnished is so defective. In the mean time, hopeful that satisfactory explanation may be made, I have directed, upon the exhibition of the case as presented by the two senior Generals, that they should be relieved from command, to await further orders whenever a reliable judgment can be rendered on the merits of the case. JEFFERSON DAVIS.

The successful operations against Fort Donelson were followed by the immediate evacuation of Bowling Green by the Confederate troops under Gen. Johnston. The centre of Gen. Buell's army under Gen. Mitchell was advancing from Munfordsville upon Bowling Green on the 14th of February, and by a forced march reached the river at that place on the next day. He immediately began to reconstruct the bridge, which had been burned some hours previous to his arrival, and took possession of the fortifications on the next day.

Since the battle of Mill Springs the intention of holding Bowling Green had been given up by the Confederate commander, and the troops were gradually withdrawn. About the 25th of January Gen. Floyd, with a command composed of his brigade and those of Gens. Wood and Breckinridge, left Bowling Green and went to Nashville and east Tennessee. The brigade of Gen. Buckner about the same time moved in the direction of Hopkinsville, near which place he manœuvred in front of Gen. Crittenden until the latter left to join Gen. Grant, when Gen. Buckner fell back and combined his forces with those at Fort Donelson. The force then remaining at Bowling Green consisted of the brigades commanded by Gens. Hardee and Hindman, which were chiefly Arkansas regiments, and twelve in number. This force, being about 8,000 men, was totally inadequate to defend the position against the forces of Gen. Mitchell and the reserve of Gen. Buell commanded by Gen. McCook.

On the 19th of February Com. Foote left Fort Donelson with the gunboats Conestoga and Cairo on an armed reconnoissance. At Clarksville he learned that nearly two thirds of the citizens had fled in alarm, and therefore issued a proclamation, assuring "all peaceably disposed persons that they could with safety resume their business avocations, and requiring only the military stores and equipments to be given up and holding the authorities responsible that it should be done without reservation." Clarksville is on the line of railroad communication between Memphis and Nashville and Memphis and Bowling Green and Louisville. Below the town were two small forts which were taken by the Federal force without any resistance. They mounted three guns each. One span of the railroad bridge had also been destroyed.

The fate of Nashville was now settled. With a high state of the water of the Cumberland river, there were no obstacles to the immediate approach of the gunboats with a force on transports. The centre of Gen. Buell's army had already arrived at Bowling Green, within two days' march of Nashville. Its progress had been attended with many difficulties, and Brig.-Gen. Mitchell in command issued the following address to his soldiers:

BOWLING GREEN, *February* 19, 1862.

Soldiers of the Third Division! You have executed a march of forty miles in twenty-eight hours and a half. The fallen timber and other obstructions opposed by the enemy to your movements, have been swept from your path. The fire of your artillery and the bursting of your shells announced your arrival. Surprised and ignorant of the force that had thus precipitated itself upon them, they fled in consternation.

In the night time, over a frozen, rocky, precipitous pathway, down rude steps for fifty feet, you have passed the advance guard, cavalry, and infantry, and before the dawn of day, you have entered in triumph a position of extraordinary natural strength, and by your enemy proudly denominated the Gibraltar of Kentucky.

With your own hands, through deep mud, in drenching rains, and up rocky pathways next to impassable, and across a footpath of your own construction, built upon the ruins of the railway bridge, destroyed for their protection, by a retreating and panic-stricken foe, you have transported upon your own shoulders your baggage and camp equipage.

The General commanding the department, on receiving my report announcing these facts, requests me to make to the officers and soldiers under my command the following communication:

"Soldiers who by resolution and energy overcome great natural difficulties, have nothing to fear in battle, where their energy and prowess are taxed to a far less extent. Your command have exhibited the high qualities of resolution and energy, in a degree which leaves no limit to my confidence in them in their future movements.

"By order of "Brig. Gen. BUELL,
"Commanding Department of the Ohio."

Soldiers! I feel a perfect confidence that the high estimate placed upon your power, endurance, energy, and heroism, is just. Your aim and mine has been to deserve the approbation of our commanding officer, and of our Government and our country.

I trust you feel precisely as does your commanding General, that nothing is done while anything remains to be done.

By order of Brig.-Gen. O. M. MITCHELL,
Commanding.

The certainty of the capture of Nashville showed to the Confederate generals the danger in which Columbus, their strong position on the Mississippi, was placed. Even the occupation of Clarksville by the Union forces put into their possession that part of the railroad running to Columbus, and opened the way to approach that position from the rear. At the same time the river in front was under the control of the Federal gunboats. Gen. Beauregard, having previously retired from his command at Manassas, was now the commanding officer in this Confederate department with Gen. Johnston. Orders were accordingly issued on the 18th of February to destroy a portion of the track and bridges of the Memphis and Ohio railroad preparatory to a removal of the forces at Columbus to Island No. Ten, about forty-five miles below on the Mississippi river.

At the same time preparations were made to remove the Confederate stores and other public property from Nashville. The near approach of the Federal forces filled the authorities of the State with great alarm. The Legislature, which had just been convened in extra session, retired with Gov. Harris to Memphis, taking the archives and treasury of the State. Extreme measures and the destruction of property were proposed by the Governor to the citizens, but without gaining their approval. The railroad and the suspension bridges over the river were, however, destroyed.

After taking possession of Clarksville, Com. Foote returned to Cairo for the purpose of obtaining an additional gunboat and six or eight mortar boats. Meantime the troops of Gen. Grant, under Brig.-Gen. Smith, were pushed forward to Clarksville, and at the request of Gen. Smith, Lieut. Bryant, of the gunboat Cairo, preceded seven transports with the brigade of Gen. Nelson up the river to Nashville. They arrived on the 24th. The troops were landed without any opposition, as there was not any hostile force on the banks of the river. On the same day the advance of Gen. Buell's centre from Bowling Green arrived on the opposite side of the river, to see the Stars and Stripes already floating in triumph from the staff on the State capitol. The Confederate force under Gen. Albert S. Johnston retired to Murfreesborough, a small town thirty-two miles distant on the Nashville and Chattanooga railroad. Here they were soon after joined by the force under the Confederate General Crittenden.

An invasion having now been commenced within the limits of the States attached to the Confederacy, the Major-General commanding the department of Missouri issued the following order for the regulation of the troops:

HEADQUARTERS, DEPARTMENT OF MISSOURI,
ST. LOUIS, *February* 22.

The Major-General commanding the department desires to impress upon all officers the importance of preserving good order and discipline among their troops as the armies of the West advance into Tennessee and the Southern States. Let us show to our fellow citizens in these States that we come merely to crush out rebellion, and to restore to them peace and the benefits of the Constitution and the Union, of which they have been deprived by their selfish and unprincipled leaders.

They have been told that we come to oppress and plunder. By our acts we will undeceive them; we will prove to them that we come to restore, not to violate, the Constitution and laws in restoring to them the flag of the Union. We will assure them that they shall enjoy under its folds the same protection of life and property as in former days.

Soldiers, let no excess on your part tarnish the glory of our arms. The orders heretofore issued in this department in regard to pillaging, marauding, the destruction of private property and stealing, and the concealment of slaves, must be strictly enforced.

It does not belong to the military to decide upon the relation of master and slave. Such questions must be settled by civil courts. No fugitive slave will, therefore, be admitted within our lines or camps except when especially ordered by the General commanding. Women, children, merchants, farmers, mechanics, and all persons not in arms, are regarded as noncombatants, and are not to be molested in their persons or property. If, however, they aid and assist the enemy, they become belligerents, and will be treated as such. If they violate the laws of war, they will be made to suffer the penalties of such violation.

Military stores and public property must be surrendered, and any attempt to conceal such property by fraudulent transfer or otherwise, will be punished; but no private property will be touched unless by orders of the General commanding.

Whenever it becomes necessary to levy forced contributions for the supply and subsistence of our troops, such levies will be made as light as possible, and be so distributed as to produce no distress among the people. All property so taken must be receipted and fully accounted for, as heretofore directed.

These orders will be read at the head of every regiment, and all officers are commanded to strictly enforce them.

By command of Maj.-Gen. HALLECK.
N. H. MCLEAN, Assistant Adjutant-General.

The effect of these military operations was a great excitement in the neighboring Confederate States. To witness their strongest positions for defence flanked and evacuated without a blow, to see other fortified points compelled to a quick surrender by an irresistible force of men and gunboats, revealed to them the gigantic contest in which they were engaged. They said: "No people were ever engaged in a more serious struggle. It is emphatically a combat for life or death." The Governor of Mississippi issued a proclamation calling upon every citizen able to bear arms to have his arms in readiness. Boards of police in all the counties of the State were required to appoint "enrollers" preparatory to drafting, and to establish gun shops to repair arms. The Governor of Arkansas issued a proclamation drafting into immediate service every man in the State subject to military duty, and requiring them to respond within twenty days. Gov. Harris of Tennessee issued a proclamation, saying: "As Governor of your State and Commander in Chief of its army, I call upon every able-bodied man of the State, without regard to age, to enlist in its service. I command him who can obtain a weapon to march with our armies. I ask him who can repair or forge an arm to make it ready at once for the soldier. I call upon every citizen to open his purse and his storehouses of provision to the brave defenders of our soil. I bid the old and the young, wherever they may be, to stand as pickets to our struggling armies." Thus was set on foot a system of measures which led to the passage of a conscription act by the Confederate Congress and the raising of an immense Confederate army during the ensuing summer months.

Meanwhile, on the morning of the 4th of March, an expedition consisting of the gunboats Louisville, Carondelet, St. Louis, Pittsburg, Lexington and four mortar boats, left Cairo for Columbus on the Mississippi. Transports with the following troops formed a part of the expedition: 42d and 27th Illinois, 6 companies of the 55th Illinois, four companies of the 71st Ohio and one company of the 54th Ohio. On arrival the fort was found to be unoccupied, except by two hundred and fifty of the 2d Illinois regiment, who had reached it by a land march a short time previous. The enemy had commenced the evacuation on the 26th ult. Almost everything difficult to move had been more or less destroyed. Still a large amount of army material was obtained. The enemy had retired down the river.

At Nashville order was speedily restored. Col. Matthews of the 51st Ohio was appointed provost marshal and the troops were all quartered without the city. An immense amount of military stores of the Confederate Government was found in the city. They consisted of pork, beef, rice, corn, and molasses. Gen. Buell removed his headquarters to the city, and the reserve of his army under Gen. McCook had arrived and were in quarters before the 2d of March.

This division in its progress had protected the railroad and repaired the bridges and roads on the route to Louisville. All of Gen. Buell's force was concentrated at Nashville and encamped along the different turnpikes leading from the city in a southerly direction at distances from two to five miles from the city, with pickets extending to the distance of ten miles.

Thus the Confederate line of defence from the Mississippi east to the mountains was swept away. The strongholds were evacuated and the less impregnable positions captured. There was nothing to withstand the triumphant march of the Federal forces southward over the country but the military force which might be gathered from the Confederate States.

Meanwhile the events which occurred in Nashville after the news of the first Southern defeat reached there, are too interesting to be overlooked Intelligence of the capture of Fort Donelson reached the city on Sunday, February 16th, and produced the utmost consternation. The Confederate governor, Harris, immediately convened the Legislature, but they speedily adjourned to Memphis, whither the public archives and money were also removed. On the same day Gen. A. S. Johnston passed through the city on his retreat from Bowling Green, and, before nightfall, hundreds of families were abandoning their homes and making their way southward. The general confusion was increased by the destruction of unfinished steamers at the wharves, and the free distribution of the stores by the military authorities to all who would take them. On Monday the public stores were closed, and an effort was made by Gen. Floyd, who had been placed in command of the city, to recover what had already been given out; but on Tuesday the distribution began again, and continued until Saturday morning. On Tuesday night the troops destroyed the wire bridge and railroad bridge across the Cumberland River, in spite of the earnest remonstrances of the leading citizens. The former cost $150,000, and the latter $250,000. Governor Harris made a speech recommending the citizens to burn their private property, and calling on Tennesseeans to rally and meet him at Memphis; but little or no response was made to his appeal. The machinery was removed from many of the most important workshops and carried to Chattanooga. On the 23d, the rear guard of the Confederates evacuated the city, and the same day the advance of Gen. Buell's column occupied Edgefield, a small town on the opposite side of the river. The next day Mayor Cheatham and a committee from Nashville waited upon the general, and agreed to surrender the city at a certain hour on the following morning (the 25th), receiving assurances that the liberty and property of all citizens should be sacredly respected. Before the surrender was effected, however, Gen. Nelson arrived with his column on transports, accompanied by the gunboat St. Louis, and landed at Nashville. The following proclamation was afterward issued by the mayor:

The committee representing the city authorities and people have discharged their duty by calling on Gen. Buell, at his headquarters, in Edgefield, on yesterday. The interview was satisfactory to the committee, and there is every assurance of safety and protection to the people, both in their persons and property. I therefore respectfully request that business be resumed, and that all our citizens of every trade and profession pursue their regular vocations. The county elections will take place on the regular day, and all civil business will be conducted as heretofore. Commanding Gen. Buell assures me that I can rely upon his aid in enforcing our police regulations. One branch of business is entirely prohibited, viz., the sale or giving away of intoxicating liquors. I shall not hesitate to invoke the aid of Gen. Buell in case the recent laws upon the subject are violated. I most earnestly call upon the people of the surrounding country, who are inside the Federal lines, to resume their commerce with the city, and bring in their market supplies, especially wood, butter, and eggs, assuring them that they will be fully protected and amply remunerated.

R. B. CHEATHAM, Mayor.

The city remained perfectly quiet, and the Federal troops, to use the words of the Southern press, "conducted themselves with marked propriety." The Union feeling in the city, however, was for many weeks extremely faint. A correspondent, writing ten days after Gen. Buell's arrival, says: "The disagreeable, but irresistible conviction forces itself upon the mind of even a superficial observer, that whatever the number and warmness of Unionists may have been at the time when, and for some time after Tennessee was juggled out of the Union, eight out of every ten have been made submissionists by the protracted secession pressure that was brought to bear upon them." The same writer adds: "Most of the stores continued closed. But few male and fewer female inhabitants are visible upon the streets. Victorious soldiery alone enliven them. Half of the private residences are deserted, and add further gloom to the aspect by their closed doors and window shutters and grave-like stillness. Hardly less than a third of the population must yet be absent."

Senator Andrew Johnson, military governor of Tennessee, by appointment of President Lincoln, arrived at Nashville March 12th.

The newspapers of Nashville had all suspended publication on the evacuation of the city, but they soon reappeared, and one of Governor Johnson's first official acts was to place them under military supervision.

On the 25th of March, Governor Johnson requested the municipal officers to take the oath of allegiance. The city council refused, by a vote of sixteen to one.

On the 29th the mayor and several other citizens were arrested for treason, and a few days later Governor Johnson issued a proclamation ejecting from office the mayor and most of the city councilmen, and appointing other persons to fill their places. Numerous arrests were made for disunion practices about the same time. The condition of the city on the 1st of May is thus described by the "Union":

"Our courts are proceeding pretty much as formerly. The United States court is in session, and the regular business pursuing its accustomed channels. Process is being issued daily from the circuit and chancery courts, returnable to their next terms. The magistrates' courts are also in continuous session. Business is beginning to recover and to wear its accustomed appearance, and as facilities are being opened with the country, it is extending in all directions. Our city market is daily improving. Prices are rapidly moderating to a reasonable standard, and custom proportionately increasing. The passenger and freight trains on the Louisville and Nashville railroad are making daily trips.

CHAPTER XIII.

Gen. Burnside's Expedition sails—The Fleet and Transports in a Storm—Advance up Pamlico Sound—Capture of Roanoke Island—Other Operations—Provisional Government set up in North Carolina—Operations in South Carolina—Bombardment and surrender of Fort Pulaski—Operations in Florida—Capture of Fernandina, Jacksonville, and St. Augustine—Other Naval Operations—Treatment of Slaves by the Federal Government—Organized as Troops at Hilton Head.

MEANTIME important events had taken place elsewhere. The military and naval expedition under Gen. Burnside was making important captures in the most populous and fertile part of the State of North Carolina. His force, being engaged at the time in active operations, was not included in the order of the President for a general advance. This army corps comprised three brigades. The first, under the command of Brig.-Gen. John G. Foster, consisted of the 23d, 24th, 25th and 27th Massachusetts, and the 10th Connecticut regiments; the second, under the command of Brig.-Gen. Jesse L. Reno, consisted of the 51st New York, 51st Pennsylvania, 21st Massachusetts, 6th New Hampshire, and 9th New Jersey regiments; the third, under the command of Brig.-Gen. John G. Parke, consisted of the 8th and 11th Connecticut, 53d and 89th New York, and a battalion of the 5th Rhode Island, together with battery F of the Rhode Island artillery. These three brigades numbered about 16,000 men, and required more than 30 transports to take them to their destination—5 vessels to transport the horses, 8 or 10 to carry the supplies, a siege train and 2 pontoon bridge schooners, a division hospital, and one for the signal corps. The naval portion of the expedition was under the command of L. M. Goldsborough, subsequently raised to the rank of rear admiral.

The chief of staff was Commander A. L. Case, staff medical officer S. C. Jones, signal officer H. G. B. Fisher. The names of the steam gunboats and of their commanders were as follows:

Name.	Guns.	Commander.	Rank.
Stars and Stripes	7	A. Herden	Lieut. Commanding.
Valley City	4	J. C. Chaplin	"
Underwriter	2	N. V. Jefford	"
Hetzel	2	H. K. Davenport	"
Delaware	6	S. P. Quackenbush	"
Shawshene	2	T. G. Woodward	Act. Master.
Lockwood	3	G. L. Graves	" "
Ceres	2	J. McDiarmid	" "
Morse	2	Peter Hays	" "
Whitehead	1	Charles A. French	" "
J. N. Seymour	2	F. S. Welles	" "
Philadelppia	2	S. Reynolds	" "
Henry Brincker	1	J. E. Giddings	" "
Granite	1	E. Boomer	" "
General Putnam	2	—— McCook	Lieut. Commanding.
Hunchback	4	E. R. Calhoun	Act. Lieut. Com.
Southfield	4	C. F. W. Behm	Act. Vol. Lieut. Com.
Com. Barney	2	R. D. Renshaw	Act. Lieut. Com.
Com. Perry	2	Chas. W. Flusser	Lieut. Com.
Total	51		

To these may also be added the Virginia, Louisiana, Young America, Jenny Lind. These steamers were of three classes: screw and side wheel tugs, navy screw gunboats, and armed ferry boats. Their armaments consisted chiefly of 30-pounder Parrotts rifled, and long smooth 32's, 64's, and some of much heavier calibre. A coast division of gunboats, with the transports, consisted of the Picket, 4 guns, Pioneer, 4 guns, Hussar, 4 guns, Vidette, 3 guns, Ranger, 4 guns, Chasseur, 4 guns. The transport portion of the expedition was under the command of Samuel F. Hazard of the U. S. Navy.

Nothing had been withheld that was necessary to secure success, and the accomplished officers, the disciplined and gallant men, and the abundant material, awakened the most sanguine expectations on the part of the Government and the people.

The expedition sailed from Hampton Roads on the 12th of January, consisting of over 100 vessels of all classes.

The order to sail was issued on Saturday night the 11th, and by daylight on Sunday morning the largest portion of the fleet had passed outside the capes. Some vessels, and especially the water boats, refused to leave the capes. The first part of the day was pleasant, with a light wind from the southwest. During the afternoon it was thick weather, and the sailing vessels were generally obliged to cast off from the steamers and take care of themselves, and two or three of the canal boats, with hay and horses on board, broke away and were blown ashore. The expedition was bound to Hatteras Inlet, which is an entrance from the ocean to Pamlico Sound. It is a narrow passage with seven feet of water on the bar, and difficult to enter in rough weather without danger of grounding. The entrance to the inlet was commanded by two forts, which were captured by an expedition under Gen. B. F. Butler and Commodore Stringham during the preceding year. (*See* preceding pages, chap 9.)

The wind changed to the southeast and continued blowing in that quarter for several days after the vessels began to arrive. This brought in a considerable sea or swell, which made it dangerous for all the vessels drawing much water to cross the bar and attempt to enter except at the top of the tide. Those drawing the least water got in first, the others anchored outside watching an opportunity. In this perilous situation, with a high sea, a strong wind blowing on shore, and shoal water, with a crooked channel, several days passed during which the fleet was endeavoring one by one to get within the inlet. The steamer City of New York grounded on the bar, and the sea swept clean over her and quickly reduced her to a wreck. The gunboat Zouave sunk in the inlet, and two or three other small vessels were equally unfortunate. Within the inlet the anchorage was narrow and the change of the tide brought the vessels in contact, and the roughness of the water caused a constant chafing of rigging and spars, and crashing of bulwarks.

For two days the wind and sea were so high as to prevent all communication with the outer vessels, or with each other. The New Jersey regiment was then called to enter upon its work, with mourning in its ranks. Its Colonel, J. W. Allen, and its surgeon, F. S. Weller, were drowned by the overturning of a small boat in the breakers at the inlet.

The gale increased; dark clouds swept down from the east and seemed almost to touch the vessels' masts as they swayed to and fro. A single person here and there appeared on some vessel's deck, holding on by the rail or the rigging, and a few scattered groups of the soldiers who had been landed, were seen hurrying on the beach as if in search of shelter from the fury of the blast. The tents of the Massachusetts 24th, which had been pitched on the beach, were swept away, and the poor soldiers spent a fearful night, exposed to the peltings of a pitiless storm, with yet a more fearful night to follow. Even the brave commander of the expedition was heard to exclaim in suppressed tones, "This is terrible! When will the storm abate?"

This violent storm was followed by a high tide, and on the 24th, nearly all the vessels which had arrived were within the entrance, and by the 26th repairs had been made and the force was ready to move. Fortunately the few Confederate gunboats on the sound kept aloof and made no attack.

Preparations were now made for a speedy movement. The object was to proceed up Pamlico Sound, and open the passage into Albemarle Sound. This passage was called Croatan Sound, and was bounded on the one side by the mainland and on the other by Roanoke Island, which is low and marshy. As this was the principal communication between Pamlico and Albemarle, the enemy had erected fortifications in the upper part of the passage, on Roanoke Island, and had also obstructed it by piles and sunken vessels. They had a fleet of seven small gunboats, prepared to contest the passage, and stationed near the batteries.

On the 3d of February, Gen. Burnside issued the following general orders:

HEADQUARTERS, DEPARTMENT OF NORTH CAROLINA,
PAMLICO SOUND, *February* 3, 1862.

GENERAL ORDERS, No. 5.

This expedition being about to land on the soil of North Carolina, the General Commanding desires his soldiers to remember that they are here to support the Constitution and the laws, to put down rebellion, and to protect the persons and property of the loyal and peaceable citizens of the State. In the march of the army, all unnecessary injuries to houses, barns, fences, and other property will be carefully avoided, and in all cases the laws of civilized warfare will be carefully observed.

Wounded soldiers will be treated with every care and attention, and neither they nor prisoners must be insulted or annoyed by word or act.

With the fullest confidence in the valor and the character of his troops, the General Commanding looks forward to a speedy and successful termination of the campaign.

By command of Brig.-Gen. A. E. BURNSIDE.
LEWIS RICHMOND, Asst. Adj.-Gen.

Further orders relative to signals, and to the disembarkation of the troops, were issued on the next day.

Everything being ready, the forward movement commenced at half past seven on the morning of the 5th of February. The naval squadron following the flag officer's vessel, headed the fleet. Their course was at first southward, following the zigzag channel, until it finally became north by west. At regular and short intervals the gunboats filled their places in the line, and with scarcely perceptible motion, steadily stretched away to the horizon. Next came the transports and gunboats carrying the troops, consisting of sixty-five vessels, of all classes and characters. Each brigade formed three columns, headed by the flag ship of the brigade. Each large steamer had one, two, and in some instances, three schooners in tow. The aisles between the three columns of vessels were kept unbroken, through the whole length, which extended almost two miles over the surface of the sound, except by the two or three small propellers whose duty consisted in conveying orders.

At sundown the fleet came to anchor about ten miles from the southern point of Roanoke Island. The next morning, at eight o'clock, it was in motion. The preceding beautiful day was followed by a stormy one, and anchors were again dropped at the entrance of the inlet or strait. This was the day on which Fort Henry was taken. The next morning was clear, and the sun rose in a sky marked only with clouds enough to give it peculiar beauty. By ten o'clock all preparations had been made, and the gunboats moved forward, entering the inlet. The flag ship of Gen. Burnside next followed, but the remainder of the transports were detained nearly two hours. A gun fired from one of the Confederate gunboats announced the approach of the Federal squadron. At half past eleven the conflict commenced between the gunboats at long range, but it was noon before they were engaged in close action. The Confederate boats gradually retired, drawing their opponents within range of the forts, when fire was opened by the latter.

The contest between the boats and the battery continued with varied energy during the next three hours, in which time the barracks within the forts were consumed. At three o'clock the troops began to land, under the protection of the fire of three of the gunboats. At this time the Confederate gunboats drew near and recommenced the action, which was continued until their ammunition was exhausted. They then retired up the inlet or sound. The battery continued to fire until the Union gunboats retired for the night. The bravery of the Confederate defence was admitted on every side. On the Federal side, five had been killed and ten wounded. In the fort, the Confederates reported one killed and three wounded, and in the gunboats five wounded, and the largest gunboat sunk, and another disabled.

By four o'clock the transports had all arrived, and the first body of troops were landed unobstructed at five o'clock. In a short time six thousand were on shore, and the remainder of the force landed soon after.

The next morning the troops started in three columns, the centre under Gen. Foster, composed of the 23d, 25th, and 27th Massachusetts, and 10th Connecticut; the next, or left flanking column, under Gen. Reno, consisted of the 21st Massachusetts, 51st New York, 9th New Jersey, and 51st Pennsylvania; the third, or right flanking column, under Gen. Parke, consisted of the 4th Rhode Island, first battalion of the 5th Rhode Island, and the 9th New York. The approach to the enemy was by a road through a swamp, on each side of which was a thick underbrush. An earthwork about thirty-five yards wide had been erected across the road for defence. The attack was bravely made, as it had been planned, upon the enemy's position, and after a most spirited and splendid defence, as reported by the assailants, they were obliged to give way before this overwhelming force, and retiring further up the island were overtaken, and Col. Shaw, their commander, surrendered. Thus six forts, forty guns, over two thousand prisoners, and three thousand stand of arms were captured. The Union loss was thirty-five killed and two hundred wounded. The Confederate loss in killed was reported to be sixteen, and wounded thirty-nine. The artillery of each side consisted of some heavy pieces, such as 100-pound Parrotts, and a 100-pound Sawyer gun captured by the Confederates some time previous. The contest between the battery and the gunboats, in the morning, was unimportant, and the latter proceeded to remove the obstructions in the channel.

On the reception of the report of Gen. Burnside at Washington the following order was issued by President Lincoln:

WASHINGTON, *Feb.* 15.

The President, Commander-in-Chief of the Army and Navy, returns thanks to Brigadier-General Burnside and Flag Officer Goldsborough, and to General Grant and Flag Officer Foote, and the land and naval forces under their respective commands, for their gallant achievements in the capture of Fort Henry and at Roanoke Island. While it will be no ordinary pleasure for him to acknowledge and reward in a becoming manner the valor of the living, he also recognizes his duty to pay fitting honor to the memory of the gallant dead. The charge at Roanoke Island, like the bayonet charge at Mill Springs, proves that the close grapple and sharp steel of loyal and patriotic citizens must always put the rebels and traitors to flight. The late achievements of the navy show that the flag of the Union, once borne in proud glory around the world by naval heroes, will soon again float over every rebel city and stronghold, and that it shall forever be honored and respected as the emblem of Liberty and Union in every land and upon every sea.

By order of the President.

(Signed) EDWIN M. STANTON,
Secretary of War.
GIDEON WELLES, Secretary of the Navy.

On the afternoon of the next day after the surrender, Commodore Rowan, by order of Com. Goldsborough, with fourteen steamers, proceeded toward Elizabeth city. It is the capital of Pasquotank county, North Carolina, situated on the Pasquotank river, about twenty miles from its mouth and thirty miles from Roanoke Island. That night the fleet anchored about eighteen miles from the city. Next morning, the 10th, on approaching the town, seven Confederate gunboats and one schooner were discovered, and after a brief contest they retired under the guns of a small fort, were set on fire, and abandoned. This fort on Cobb's Point, mounting four guns, was also abandoned. At the same time the town was deserted by the Confederate forces, after having set on fire some of the houses, which were burned. All the Confederate gunboats were destroyed excepting one. Two were killed and about twelve wounded on the Union gunboats. The loss on the other side is not known. Commander Rowan immediately sent the gunboats Louisiana, Underwriter, Commodore Perry, and Lockwood, under Lieut. A. Maury, to Edenton, on the west end of Albemarle Sound. It is the capital of Chowan county and is at the head of Edenton bay, which opens into Albemarle Sound a little below the mouth of Chowan river. On the 12th the town was taken possession of by Lieut. Maury. Part of a light artillery regiment, from one to three hundred in number, withdrew without firing a gun. No fortifications existed, nor was any opposition made. Eight cannon and one schooner on the stocks were destroyed. Two schooners with four thousand bushels of corn were captured on the sound, and six bales of cotton taken from the custom house wharf.

On the next day, the 14th, Lieut. Jeffers was sent by Lieut. Maury with the gunboats Underwriter, Lockwood, Shawshene, and Whitehead, towing a couple of schooners to the mouth of the Chesapeake and Albemarle canal. The enemy were found engaged in placing obstructions in the mouth of the canal. These works were completed by sinking the two schooners and burning all that remained above water. This small expedition then returned to the mouth of North River. This was two days before the surrender of Fort Donelson. On the 18th of February the joint commanders of the Union forces in North Carolina issued the following proclamation, declaring to the people of that State the object of their mission:

ROANOKE ISLAND, NORTH CAROLINA, *February* 18, 1862.

To the People of North Carolina:

The mission of our joint expedition is not to invade any of your rights, but to assert the authority of the United States, and to close with you the desolating war brought upon your State by comparatively a few bad men in your midst.

Influenced infinitely more by the worst passions of human nature than by any show of elevated reason, they are still urging you astray to gratify their unholy purposes.

They impose upon your credulity by telling you of wicked and even diabolical intentions on our part; of our desire to destroy your freedom, demolish your property, liberate your slaves, injure your women, and such like enormities—all of which, we assure you, is not only ridiculous, but utterly and wilfully false.

We are Christians as well as yourselves, and we profess to know full well, and to feel profoundly, the sacred obligations of the character.

No apprehensions need be entertained that the demands of humanity or justice will be disregarded. We shall inflict no injury, unless forced to do so by your own acts, and upon this you may confidently rely.

Those men are your worst enemies. They, in truth, have drawn you into your present condition, and are the real disturbers of your peace and the happiness of your firesides.

We invite you, in the name of the Constitution, and in that of virtuous loyalty and civilization, to separate yourselves at once from these malign influences, to return to your allegiance, and not compel us to resort further to the force under our control.

The Government asks only that its authority may be recognized; and we repeat, in no manner or way does it desire to interfere with your laws constitutionally established, your institutions of any kind whatever, your property of any sort, or your usages in any respect. L. M. GOLDSBOROUGH, Flag Officer,
Commanding North Carolina Blockading Squadron.
A. E. BURNSIDE, Brigadier-General,
Commanding Department of North Carolina.

It may be thought that this part of North Carolina was in a very defenceless condition. In many respects this was not so. It cost the United States two military and naval expeditions before it was reached. The first expedition, under the command of Gen. Benjamin F. Butler and Commodore S. H. Stringham, consisted of the steam frigates Minnesota and Wabash, and armed steamers Monticello, Pawnee, and Harriet Lane, and the steam transports Adelaide and George Peabody, and the tug Fanny. The steam frigate Susquehanna also joined the expedition. The military force consisted of 880 men. These forces captured the forts at the entrance of Hatteras Inlet, and made no further advance. The result of the expedition was the acquisition of the forts captured, the control of the island in which they were located, and the closing of the inlet against the passage of vessels running the blockade. The expedition under Gen. Burnside entered the inlet and captured the fortifications on Roanoke Island and destroyed the Confederate navy, when the country lay at its mercy. Small fortifications and some military force was found, however, at every town of any importance. No civil, commercial, or political changes were made such as to indicate that the inhabitants regarded themselves as restored to the Union. Those in whose hands was held the local civil and political power, retired to safe quarters upon the approach of the Federal force. They acknowledged another allegiance due to a power which they believed or hoped would yet be able to expel the Union troops. So long as that power retained its strength they either feared or declined to acknowledge allegiance elsewhere. That invariable follower of the invasion of hostile armies, the provost marshal, or military governor, attended the footsteps of the Burnside expedition as he has almost every other which has entered within the limits of the Confederate States during this year.

On the 19th of February a reconnoitring expedition left Edenton for Winton, the capital of Hereford county, situated near the head of navigation on the Chowan river, about fifty miles above its mouth. It consisted of the flotilla under the command of Commander Rowan and a company of Col. Hawkins' N. Y. regiment. This force had been informed at Elizabeth City, that five hundred Union men at Winton had raised "the Stars and Stripes" and desired protection. Upon arriving opposite the landing of the town, which was a short distance in the rear, a perfect shower of balls and buckshot were fired upon the advancing vessel. The river here is about a hundred yards wide and the banks high. The boats ascended and brought their guns to bear and fired several shells, and retired about eight miles down the river for the night. The next morning they returned and shelled the village. The military were landed and found it deserted, when the buildings were set on fire and burned.

The movements of the Federal forces caused efforts to be made by the State authorities to resist them. On the 22d Governor Clark issued the following proclamation:

NORTH-CAROLINIANS! Our country needs your aid for its protection and defence against an invading foe. The President of the Confederate States has made a requisition upon our State to complete her quota of troops in the field. Our own borders are invaded by the enemy in force, now threatening an advance to deprive us of liberty, property, and all that we hold dear, as a self-governing and free people. We must resist him at all hazards and by every means in our power. He wages a war for our subjugation—a war forced upon us in wrong and prosecuted without right, and in a spirit of vengeful wickedness without a parallel in the history of warfare among civilized nations.

As you value your rights of self-government and all the blessings of freedom—the hallowed endearments of home and fireside, of family and kindred—I call upon you to rally to their defence, and to sustain the noble and sacred cause in which we are engaged. North Carolina has always proved true, constant and brave, in the hour of trial and of danger. Never let it be said, that in the future she has failed to maintain her high renown. If we are threatened now more than heretofore, and upon our own soil, let our exertions be equal to every demand on our patriotism, honor, and glory. No temporary reverses dampened the ardor of your ancestors, even though the enemy marched in columns through the State. The fires of liberty still burned brightly in their breasts.

They were moved to new energy and resisted by gallant deeds, with abiding hope and unflinching courage and perseverance, bravely contending with enemies at home as well as the foreign foe, until, after a struggle of seven long years, our independence was achieved and acknowledged. Let us imitate their glorious example. The enemy is redoubling his efforts and straining every nerve to overrun our country and subjugate us to his domination—his avarice and ambition. Already it is proposed in their Congress to establish a territorial government in a portion of our State. Now is the time to prove our zeal and animate by example. I call upon the brave and patriotic men of our State to volunteer, from the mountains to the sea.

You are wanted both to fill up our quota in the confederate army and for the special defence of the State. I rely, with entire confidence, on a prompt and cheerful response to this call upon your patriotism and valor. Tender yourselves in companies and squads, under officers of your own selection. You will be at once accepted and organized into regiments under the laws that are or may be made, and which it is my duty to execute. The Adjutant-General will issue the necessary orders for this purpose.

Fellow citizens! Your first allegiance is due to North Carolina. Rally to her banners. Let every man do his duty and our country will be safe.

Given under my hand and the seal of the State, at Raleigh, this twenty-second day of February, 1862.

[SEAL] HENRY T. CLARK.

Preparations were now made by Gen. Burnside for an attack upon Newbern. This city is situated at the confluence of the Neuse and Trent rivers, about fifty miles from Pamlico Sound near its southern extremity. It is second in commercial importance in the State, and is connected by railroad with Raleigh the capital. On the 11th of March the troops intended for the expedition were embarked and ordered with the naval force to rendezvous at Hatteras Inlet. The latter force was under Commander Rowan, Com. Goldsborough having been ordered to Hampton Roads. These forces having combined left Hatteras the next morning and arrived about sunset at Slocum's Creek, eighteen miles below Newbern, and the place selected for disembarking the troops. The landing was effected the next morning with great enthusiasm under cover of the gunboats, and after a toilsome march of twelve miles through the mud, the head of the column reached, that evening, within a mile and a half of the Confederate stronghold. The remainder came up during the night with eight pieces of artillery, chiefly boat howitzers. The gunboats shelled the road in advance of the march of the troops, and covered their encampment at night. Early the next morning Gen. Foster's brigade was ordered by Gen. Burnside to proceed up the main country road to attack the enemy's left, Gen. Reno up the railroad to attack the enemy's right, and Gen. Parke to follow Gen. Foster and attack the enemy in front, with instructions to support either or both brigades. The engagement which ensued continued for four hours, and resulted in carrying a continuous line of Confederate field work, over a mile in length, protected on the river flank by a battery of thirteen heavy guns and on the opposite flank by a line of redoubts over half a mile in length for riflemen and field pieces in the midst of swamps and dense forests. This line was defended by eight Confederate regiments of infantry, five hundred cavalry, and three batteries of field-artillery, each of six guns.

The position was finally carried by a brave charge, which enabled the Federal force to gain the rear of all the batteries between that point and Newbern. This was done by a rapid advance of the entire force up the main road and railroad, while the gunboats proceeded up the river throwing their shot into the forts and in front of the advancing forces. The enemy in retreating destroyed the country road bridge and the draw of the railroad bridge over the river Trent, thus preventing pursuit, and escaped by the railroad. Meantime the gunboats arrived at the wharves and commanded the city, but it was not occupied by the troops until Gen. Foster's brigade was brought up by the vessels. Thus eight batteries containing forty-six heavy guns, three batteries of light artillery containing six guns each, two steamboats, a number of sailing vessels, wagons, horses, a large quantity of ammunition, commissary and quartermasters' stores, forage, and two hundred prisoners were captured. The Union loss was ninety-one killed and four hundred and sixty-six wounded. The Confederate loss was severe, but not so great, as they were effectually covered by their works. They retired to Tuscarora about ten miles from Newbern. Gen. Gatlin being indisposed, they were commanded by Gen. O. B. Branch.

On the next day Gen. Burnside issued the following address to his force:

HEADQUARTERS, DEPT. OF NORTH CAROLINA,
NEWBERN, *March* 15.

General Order, No. 17.

The General Commanding congratulates his troops on their brilliant and hard won victory of the 14th. Their courage, their patience, their endurance of fatigue, exposure and toil, cannot be too highly praised.

After a tedious march, drawing their howitzers by hand through swamps and thickets, after a sleepless night, in a drenching rain, they met the enemy in his chosen position, found him protected by strong earthworks, mounting many and heavy guns, and in an open field themselves—they conquered. With such soldiers, advance is victory.

The General Commanding directs with peculiar pride, that, as a well-deserved tribute to valor in this second victory of the expedition, each regiment engaged shall inscribe on its banner the memorable name "Newbern."

By command of Brigadier-General
A. E. BURNSIDE.

LEWIS RICHMOND, Adjutant-General.

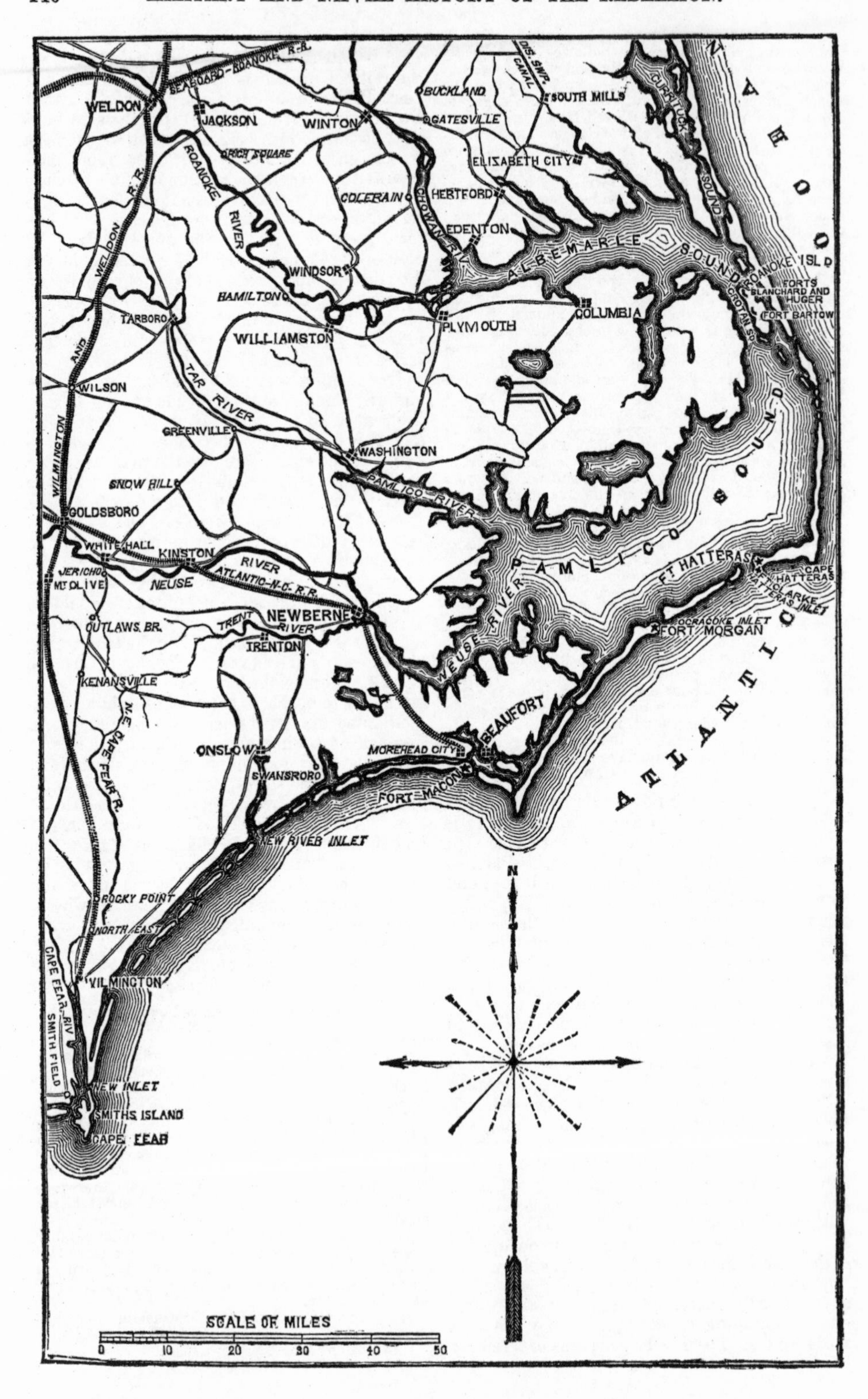
WELDON
SEABOARD-ROANOKE R.R.
JACKSON
WINTON
BUCKLAND
GATESVILLE
SOUTH MILLS
DIS. SWP. CANAL
CURRITUCK SOUND
ELIZABETH CITY
HERTFORD
COLERAIN
CHOWAN R.
EDENTON
ROANOKE RIVER
WELDON AND WILMINGTON R.R.
WINDSOR
HAMILTON
ALBEMARLE SOUND
ROANOKE ISL.D
FORTS BLANCHARD AND HUGER
FORT BARTOW
CROTAN SO.
COLUMBIA
PLYMOUTH
WILLIAMSTON
TARBORO
TAR RIVER
WILSON
GREENVILLE
WASHINGTON
SNOW HILL
PAMLICO RIVER
GOLDSBORO
WHITE HALL
KINSTON
NEUSE RIVER
ATLANTIC-N-C. R.R.
JERICHO
MT. OLIVE
PAMLICO SOUND
FT HATTERAS
CAPE HATTERAS
FT. CLARKE
HATTERAS INLET
OCRACOKE INLET
FORT MORGAN
NEWBERNE
TRENT RIVER
TRENTON
OUTLAWS BR.
NEUSE RIVER
KENANSVILLE
N.E. CAPE FEAR R.
BEAUFORT
MOREHEAD CITY
ONSLOW
SWANSBORO
FORT MACON
ATLANTIC OCEAN
NEW RIVER INLET
N
ROCKY POINT
NORTH EAST
WILMINGTON
CAPE FEAR RIV.
SMITH FIELD
NEW INLET
SMITHS ISLAND
CAPE FEAR
SCALE OF MILES
0 10 20 30 40 50

On the 20th Gen. Parke's brigade commenced to march from Newbern for Beaufort, and on the 23d entered Moorhead city, thirty-six miles from Newbern, and found it evacuated. It is a short distance from Beaufort and connected by a steam ferry. A flag of truce was then sent over to Fort Macon, and a surrender demanded. This was refused, and vigorous measures were at once commenced to reduce it by a siege. Beaufort is the capital of Carteret county, situated at the mouth of Newport river, and a few miles from the sea. The harbor is the best in the State, and its entrance is defended by Fort Macon.

Meanwhile, on the 20th, a naval column consisting of the gunboats Louisiana, Delaware, and Com. Perry, with the transport Admiral, having on board eight companies of the 24th Massachusetts regiment, proceeded to Washington, a small town on the left bank of the Tar river about forty miles from Pamlico Sound. On the 25th, the force arrived before the town, and were received by the authorities without opposition. Below the town obstructions had been placed in the river, and abandoned fortifications were found on each shore adjacent. The commander, A. Maury, thus reported to his superior officer: "I found on further consultation with the authorities, on whom I made my demand for the restoration of the Hatteras Light property, that underlying an apparent acquiescence of the people of the town and neighborhood, in permitting the building of gunboats, and the construction of batteries to repel the approach of the Federal forces, was a deep-rooted affection for the old Union, and not a little animosity for its enemies; the latter element not being diminished by the importation of troops from a distant State. The result of this state of affairs was, as could be anticipated, the abandonment of its defences by the troops, followed by the destruction of what remained of Confederate property by the people. The launched gunboat had been towed several miles up the river, loaded with turpentine, and fired on the night of our arrival. A few hundred bushels of meal and corn left in the commissary store, were distributed to the poor by my orders. All the Hatteras Light property in the town was secured. The woods and swamps were represented as being alive with refugees from the draft. Many of them, encouraged by our presence, came in. They were bitter and deep in their denunciations of the secession heresy, and promised a regiment if called to aid in the restoration of the flag." This force returned to Newbern.

The force in the neighborhood of Fort Macon, however, was not idle. A detachment from Gen. Parke's brigade, consisting of the 4th Rhode Island and 8th Connecticut, on the night of the 25th, crossed over and took possession of Beaufort without opposition. In the day time this passage would have been resisted by the fort. No military force was found in the town. Preparations were now made seriously to invest the fort. All communication by land or water was cut off, and guns were put into position to reduce it. The garrison consisted of nearly five hundred men under command of Col. White. The regular siege operations commenced on the 11th of April, when a reconnoissance in force was made by Gen. Parke. The pickets of the enemy stationed on Bogue Beach, two miles from the fort, were driven in and a good situation for the siege guns was found. Everything being in readiness, on the morning of the 25th of April, fire was opened upon the fort from a breaching battery eleven hundred feet distant, and flanking mortars planted at a distance of about fourteen hundred yards, and behind sand banks which prevented the garrison from seeing them before the fire was opened. At the same time the blockading gunboats Daylight, Commander Lockwood; State of Georgia, Commander Armstrong; Chippewa, Lieut. Payson and bark Gemsbok, Lieut. Caverdy; approached the fort and began to fire. The three steamers assisted the bark, and kept under way, steaming round in a circle and delivering their fire as they came within range, a mile and a quarter distant from the fort. After an hour and a quarter, the sea became so rough and their fire consequently so inaccurate, that the fleet retired. The action however continued between the batteries and the fort until toward evening, when the latter was surrendered with the honors of war. All the guns on the side of the fort opposite that attacked, were dismounted, and also all but three of those bearing upon the Federal force, when it became untenable. The firing of the fleet did no injury to the fort. The Daylight was struck by an 8-inch solid shot which entered her quarter. Seven of the garrison were killed and eighteen wounded. One was reported killed on the Federal side.

While this siege was pressed forward, Gen. Burnside, in order to create the impression at Norfolk, Va., that he was approaching with his whole force, sent Gen. Reno with the 21st Massachusetts, 51st Pennsylvania, a part of the 9th and 89th New York, and 6th New Hampshire in that direction. Proceeding nearly to Elizabeth City, he disembarked at a point about three miles below, on the night of the 19th of April. Col. Hawkins was ordered forward with the 9th and 89th New York and the 6th New Hampshire toward South Mills, to be followed by Gen. Reno four hours after, upon getting the remaining troops ashore. Col. Hawkins lost his way and came in behind Gen. Reno on the march, and was ordered to follow. Having marched about sixteen miles, and within a mile and a half of South Mills, a Confederate force opened with artillery upon the advanced guard before it was discovered. They were found posted across the road, with their infantry in ditches, and their artillery commanding all the direct approaches. Their rear was protected by a dense forest. Gen. Reno ordered the 6th New Hampshire to form in a line on the left of the road and support the four pieces of artillery, while the 51st Pennsylvania and 21st Massachusetts filed to the right and passed over to the edge of the wood to turn the enemy's flank, and the New York regiments supported them. The effect of these movements, and the sharp firing that ensued, caused the enemy soon to retire in a rapid manner. The force rested until evening, and then withdrew to their boats. The Federal loss was fourteen killed and ninety-six wounded, and two taken prisoners. The Federal force remained on the field for seven hours, buried their dead, and transported all the wounded except fourteen, so severely wounded that they could not be moved, but who were comfortably provided for and left in charge of a surgeon and chaplain. "In obedience to orders," says Gen. Burnside, "Gen. Reno then returned to his fleet and embarked his men." Ten or fifteen prisoners were taken, most of whom belonged to the 3d Georgia regiment. The loss of the Confederate force was unknown; thirty killed and wounded were left on the field. They reported one regiment and three pieces of artillery as the entire force engaged.

On the 23d of April a naval expedition, consisting of the gunboats Lockwood, Whitehead, and Putnam, under Lieut. Flosser, was sent to obstruct the entrance of the Dismal Swamp canal. This was done by means of sinking a schooner, and filling the canal with brush, stumps, rails, and earth, and trunks of trees.

On the 6th of June a sharp engagement occurred eight miles from Washington near Pactolus, between a Confederate force under Col. Singleterry and the 24th Massachusetts under Capt. Potter. This latter officer had been stationed at Washington with a small force, and hearing of the gathering of the enemy, obtained reënforcements, and successfully attacked them. Seven were killed and eleven wounded on the Federal side.

Some other military movements, to be hereafter stated, took place during the succeeding months. This portion of North Carolina was held by the Union forces throughout the year. Its ports were closed to imports for the Confederate States, and its commerce ceased entirely. The principal part of the forces under Gen. Burnside were subsequently brought to Newport News, where they remained in transports until the Army of the Potomac returned to Alexandria. They then united with it under Gen. Pope.

This expedition in its outfit, vigor of action, and complete achievements, showed that it was commanded by an experienced, judicious, and able officer. It was necessarily confined in its operations to the shores of the country, where it could act in concert with the gunboats. It had not been in the field four months, when the Government found itself entirely without soldiers who could be sent to reënforce him.

At the approach of Gen. Burnside's command upon the coast of North Carolina much confidence was felt on the part of the authorities that they would be able to make a successful resistance. A few days served to dispel these delusions, and change the aspect of their situation. The entire coast was exposed to the invasion of the Federal troops. This change quenched a spirit of dissatisfaction with the Confederate Government, which was beginning to prevail under grievances that the State had suffered. Efforts, however, were now made to prevent the advance of the Federal troops into the interior, and to make as successful opposition to their movements as might be possible.

The election for State officers in North Carolina takes place on the second Thursday in August. Some months before this election the person who should be the next governor of the State became a subject of active discussion. One party desired a man who was not a proscriptive secessionist, and the other desired one who was radical and thorough on secession, and who would sustain the Confederate Government, even at the expense of State rights. Both parties sustained the war. The candidates nominated for the office were William Johnson, of Mecklenberg County, and Zebulon B. Vance, of Buncombe County.

The result of the election was the choice of Col. Vance as governor by a large majority.

On the 17th of November the Legislature assembled at Raleigh, and the governor delivered his message. He urged a vigorous prosecution of the war, but complained of the bad faith of the Confederate Government in sending agents into the State to obtain clothing and supplies, after agreeing not to do so if the State undertook to clothe her own troops. He condemned the conscription law, and stated that the soldiers were suffering greatly for want of shoes and clothing. The debt of the State at the beginning of the year was $2,098,361. Flour and corn commanded such prices as to be used only by wealthy persons.

The Legislature adopted the following resolutions on the 27th of November:

Resolved, That the Confederate States have the means and the will to sustain and perpetuate the Government they have established, and that to that end North Carolina is determined to contribute all her power and resources.

Resolved, That the separation between the Confederate States and the United States is final, and that the people of North Carolina will never consent to a reunion at any time or upon any terms.

Resolved, That we have full confidence in the ability and patriotism of his Excellency President Davis, and that his administration is entitled to the cordial support of all patriotic citizens.

Resolved, That we heartily approve of the policy for the conduct of the war set forth by his Excellency Gov. Vance to the General Assembly, and that he ought to be unanimously supported in the manly and patriotic stand he has taken for our independence.

The number of men obtained in the State by the Confederate conscription law was stated to exceed forty thousand, three-fourths of whom were reported by the examining physicians as unfit for military duty.

On the 15th of May, Edward Stanley, formerly a distinguished citizen of North Carolina, arrived at New York from California, for the purpose of entering upon the office of temporary governor of North Carolina, which had been tendered to him by President Lincoln. The part of Carolina placed under his jurisdiction was that in which the Federal arms held control. The instructions of the Federal Government to Gov. Stanley were similar to those given to Gov. Andrew Johnson in Tennessee, and were as follows:

WAR DEPARTMENT, WASHINGTON, D. C., *May* 2, 1862.

Hon. Edward Stanley, Military Governor of North Carolina:

SIR: The commission you have received expresses on its face the nature and extent of the duties and power devolved on you by the appointment of military governor of North Carolina. Instructions have been given to Maj.-Gen. Burnside to aid you in the performance of your duties and the exercise of your authority. He has been instructed to detail an adequate military force for the special purpose of a governor's guard, and to act under your direction. It is obvious to you that the great purpose of your appointment is to reëstablish the authority of the Federal Government in the State of North Carolina, and to provide the means of maintaining peace and security to the loyal inhabitants of that State until they shall be able to establish a civil government. Upon your wisdom and energetic action much will depend in accomplishing that result. It is not deemed necessary to give any specific instructions, but rather to confide in your sound discretion to adopt such measures as circumstances may demand. You may rely upon the perfect confidence and full support of this department in the performance of your duties.

With great respect, I am your obedient servant,

EDWIN M. STANTON,
Secretary of War.

On the 26th of May he arrived at Newbern, and entered upon his duties. On the 17th of June he made an address to the people at Washington, N. C. Permission had been given to the citizens to enter the Federal lines for the purpose of hearing this address, and they were present from seventeen counties. The speech was a review of the past, an examination of present affairs, and an urgent appeal to the citizens to resume their allegiance to the Federal Government. The result showed that so long as the Confederate Government retained its organization and power, the citizens could not be expected to turn against it; especially as the fortune of war might soon place them under its control again.

At all the military posts of the Federal Government in the State, the slaves from the interior who had run away collected. This was especially the case at Newbern, where five thousand had come in. When Gov. Stanley arrived there he found schools established for their instruction, but expressed the opinion that it was injudicious, as contrary to the laws of the State, and if upheld by him it must destroy his influence with the people. The schools were temporarily suspended. The course pursued by the governor was designed to restore the confidence and good will of the people, which had been lost by the belief that it was the purpose of the Federal Administration to destroy their institutions and subjugate the people. A conference was proposed by Gov. Stanley to Gov. Vance, for the purpose of restoring peace in the State. The latter refused to meet, but referred the former to the Confederate Government at Richmond. Apparently little had been gained for the Federal cause thus far by the military organization on the borders of the State.

The achievements of the military and naval expedition to the coast of South Carolina and Georgia, should be described in this connection. For an account of its outfit, departure, and occupation of Hilton Head see Chapter XI. Undoubtedly there was a double object in thi expedition. On the one hand it was designed to seize and hold as large a district of the coast as might be practicable, and on the other prepare a base for future operations against Charleston and Savannah, South Carolina, and the great State of Georgia. The point designed for its headquarters, and for the base of future operations, was occupied at once. The first labor was to prepare Port Royal for the purposes in view. Immense cargoes of commissary stores, ordnance, and means of transportation were landed from the large ocean steamers which accompanied the expedition. Extensive warehouses were erected for the preservation of the stores; while for the security of the depot whence supplies were to be drawn for all portions of the command, and to enable as many troops as possible to be spared for distant operations, long lines of defence had to be constructed. While the works were pushed forward reconnoissances were made in every direction to ascertain the position and strength of the enemy, to learn the depth of water in the numerous creeks and inlets, and remove all obstructions that might have been placed in important channels of communication.

At the beginning of the year it was observed to be the design of the enemy to shut up the Federal troops in Port Royal Island, by placing obstructions in Coosaw River and Whale Branch, by constructing batteries at Port Royal Ferry, at Seabrook, and at or near Boyd Creek, and by accumulating men in the vicinity so as to be able to throw a force of twenty-five hundred or three thousand upon any of these points, at a short notice. It was determined to arrest their designs peremptorily, and in such a manner as would serve a subsequent purpose. Commander E. R. P. Rodgers had charge of the naval force of the expedition, consisting of the gunboats Ottawa, Lieut. Stevens, Pembina, Lieut. Bankhead, and four armed boats of the Wabash, carrying howitzers, and under the command of Lieuts. Upsher, Lane, Irwin, and Master Kempff, which were to enter the Coosaw by Beaufort River; and the gunboat Seneca, Lieut. Ammen, and tugboat Ellen, Master Budd, which were to move up Beaufort River, and approach the batteries at Seabrook and

Port Royal Ferry by Whale Branch. The tug boat E. B. Hale, Master Foster, was added to the expedition after it started. The part assigned to the naval force was to protect the landing of the troops at Haywood's plantation, the first point of debarkation, to cover the route of the advancing column, and the second point of debarkation, and to assail the batteries on their front. The military force consisted of the 47th and 48th New York regiments, Cols. Frazer and Perry, the 79th New York, 50th and 100th Pennsylvania, and 8th Michigan, with a naval howitzer force of forty men, under Lieut. Irwin. After the forces, landed at the two points, had marched, driving all of the enemy who were seen before them, and formed a junction, they were divided into centre, right, and left wings, and ordered forward to attack the batteries of the enemy. A sharp skirmish of half an hour ensued upon their approach to the battery, when the enemy retired, and the works were completely destroyed. An incomplete work at Seabrook, two miles from Port Royal Ferry, was destroyed at the same time. The result of the expedition was the destruction of the two batteries, driving the enemy five miles into the rear, and rendering the Broad and Coosaw rivers secure for the gunboats. The land force was commanded by Gen. Stevens. Eleven privates were wounded and two of them missing. Four of the enemy were found dead.

While all the improvements were urged forward at Hilton Head, reconnoissances were constantly made. The next movement of interest took place on the 26th of January, in consequence of explorations which had been previously made, and which were of such an adventurous nature as to entitle to honor the parties engaged. The city of Savannah is about fifteen miles from the mouth of the river of that name, and situated on its right or southern bank. The approach to it by water is defended by Fort Pulaski (captured by the Georgians in 1861), a casemated work on Cockspur Island, at the mouth of the river, and Fort Jackson, a barbette work on the mainland, only four miles below the city. The left bank of the river is formed by a succession of islands, and the channel is also interrupted by large and numerous ones. The network of creeks and bays which surround Hilton Head terminates to the southward in Calibogue Sound, which is separated from Savannah river at its mouth by Turtle and Jones Islands. The waters that bound two sides of Jones Island, which is triangular in shape, are called Mud and Wright rivers; the latter is the more southern, and separates Jones from Turtle Island, which lies next to Dawfuskie Island, the western shore of Calibogue Sound. The water on the third side of Jones Island is the Savannah river. This island is about five miles long, and between two and three broad. About half way between its upper and lower angles, and fronting on the Savannah, is Venus Point, where a Federal battery was subsequently placed to cut off communication between Savannah and Fort Pulaski.

Lieut. J. H. Wilson, of the topographical

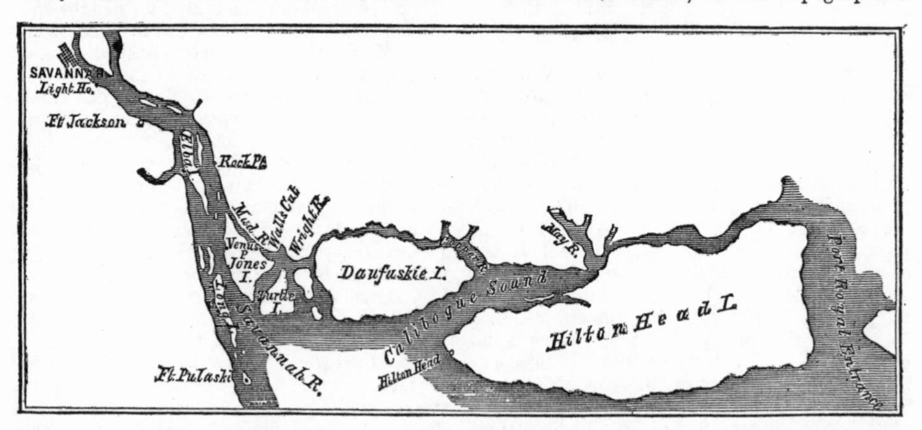

engineers, becoming convinced, from information obtained of negro pilots and others, that an interior passage existed, connecting Calibogue Sound with the Savannah river, and which, if passable by gunboats, might lead to cutting off Fort Pulaski from communication with Savannah, was despatched by Gen. Sherman on a reconnoissance. Taking with him two row boats, and about seventy men of the Rhode Island regiment, he left Calibogue Sound with his negro crew and pilots, and ventured by night through the intricate passages. At this time the Union troops had not advanced beyond Dawfuskie Island, and on some of these rivers Confederate pickets were still stationed. The oars of the reconnoitring party, however, were muffled, and they passed by the pickets without discovery. Under cover of the darkness they penetrated several miles up one of these streams, leaving the pickets in their rear. If discovered, retreat or escape would have been impossible for them, as there was no opportunity of returning except on the same route by which they came. The river which they thus explored led into no other channel, but wasted away in a marsh. They got back into another stream. Finally the creeks became so shallow as to be unnavigable for any but the smallest craft. At one point an artificial channel had been constructed about two hundred yards long, called Wall's Cut. This led to the rear of Jones Island, and into both the Mud and Wright rivers, both of which, as stated above, empty into the Savannah, the former about six miles, and the latter about two miles above Fort Pulaski. This cut had, however, been obstructed by three rows of piles driven across its entire width, and by a large brig sunk in the same direction, across the channel. At high tide the reconnoitring party were able to get over the piles and pass the brig. The reeds on both banks were very high, and the cut altogether invisible from Savannah, while the marshy nature of the region prevented any approach by land. There was danger of meeting pickets or stray parties of sportsmen, shooting wild ducks abounding in those waters. The party remained concealed by the reeds during the day, and at night pursued their explorations. They found the channel of Mud river impassable for large vessels by reason of its shallow water, but got easily through the Wright river, and rounding the point of Jones Island, entered the Savannah. There they remained nearly all night, moving at times under the guns of Fort Pulaski, near enough to hear the challenge of the lonely sentinels, or the conversation of the gunners on the parapets before tattoo. They found the depth and bearings of the channel in all directions; went up the river beyond Venus Point, and even passed the entrance of Mud river, and then returned into the Wright, establishing to their own satisfaction that gunboats of ten feet draught could pass by that route into the Savannah, without incurring any material risk from the guns of Pulaski, which were at the nearest point a mile and three-fourths distant.

Upon this report Gen. Sherman caused another and fuller reconnoissance to be made. Major Beard of the 48th New York was sent to remove the obstructions in Wall's Cut. A party of volunteer engineers and a company of the 7th Connecticut accompanied him; and while some kept a careful watch, others were engaged at the obstructions. They were removed in three weeks of unremitting night labor. All the piles were sawn off a foot below the bottom of the cut, and the brig turned lengthwise, leaving a passage wide enough for the gunboats. All this was accomplished without awakening the suspicions of the enemy, whose pickets had been withdrawn. All stragglers, white or black, who approached were seized; of these, four or five whites seemed to have been hunting, for they were in boats loaded with game; others were slaves who had escaped from Savannah. All were astonished to see their captors there. No scouts were ever detected, and no boats passed on the Savannah river except the steamers plying to Fort Pulaski from Savannah. On some nights the rain fell furiously, but the work proceeded. After the obstructions had been removed, a violent storm that lasted for several days rendered any further operations impracticable; still the pickets kept up their watch on the dismal and muddy marsh, and every straggler or spy was seized.

A naval reconnoissance was now made by Capt. John Rodgers and Lieut. Barnes, in company with Lieut. Wilson. Like all the others it was made in the night. The party were able to pass through the cut, take soundings in the Wright river, enter the Savannah, and ascertain all that was necessary to determine the practicability of the passage of gunboats. Capt. Rodgers reported favorably, and was willing to command the movement. It was determined therefore that a reconnoissance in force should be made, and preparations were commenced for that purpose.

It had always been known that a passage existed on the right side of the Savannah, leading from Warsaw Sound through the Wilmington river until it narrows into St. Augustine Creek, and finally empties into the Savannah just below Fort Jackson. This passage was defended by a battery. Information was however obtained from negroes of another passage leading up also from Warsaw, but much nearer to the Savannah and entering it lower down than St. Augustine Creek. This second passage is called Wilmington Narrows. Several reconnoissances were made along its course and the result was a determination by Gen. Sherman and Com. Dupont to send a force up Wilmington Narrows, at the same time that operations should begin in the vicinity of Wall's Cut. Accordingly on the 26th of January, Gen. Wright with the 4th New Hampshire, Col. Whipple, 6th Connecticut, Col. Chatfield, and 97th Pennsylvania, Col. Guess, on the transports Cosmopolitan, Boston, and Delaware were convoyed by the gunboats Ottawa, Seneca, and others under Capt. C. H. Davis to Warsaw Sound. The force then proceeded up the Wilmington Narrows for some miles and in the rear of Fort Pulaski until it arrived at a place where piles had been placed to obstruct its further progress. The gunboats remained at this spot a short distance from the Savannah during the night, while reconnoissances were made on land and water. In the morning Capt. John Rodgers with three gunboats appeared on the opposite side of the Savannah in Wall's Cut. Two of these vessels passed into Wright river. About eleven o'clock in the forenoon Com. Tatnall and the five Confederate steam gunboats attempted to pass down the river with scows in tow, when fire was opened upon them by the gunboats on each side. The country on each side is so flat that but little obstruction to the sight intervened. In less than half an hour Com. Tatnall and one of his vessels were driven back; the other three escaped injury apparently and mado good their passage down to Fort Pulaski. They returned at low water and escaped uninjured. The objects of the reconnoissance being now attained the forces returned to Hilton Head. The gunboats in Wright river did not go down as far as the entrance to the Savannah, as they would be in reach of the guns of Fort Pulaski, and Capt. Rodgers feared that they might get aground. This withdrawal of the boats from Wall's Cut was regarded by the Confederate commander as an abandonment of the purpose to enter the Savannah by that route. Confidence was thus restored in the minds of the citizens of Savannah, and the wisest hoped that the fort, which was the key of the city, might be enabled to detain their enemy for an indefinite length of time. The greatest consternation therefore prevailed in Savannah when the fort was ultimately captured.

Gen. Sherman now commenced a series of measures by which to cut off all communication between the city and the fort. This consisted in the planting of batteries on the river. The most important one was at Venus Point on the river side of Jones Island. A road was made with almost herculean labor across its marshy surface from Wall's Cut, by the 48th New York regiment. Over this road the cannon were brought and placed in the battery. An attack was made on this battery by the Confederate gunboats on the 14th of March. After an engagement of an hour they were driven off. Another battery was placed on the extremity of Long Island, which was on the other side of the channel of the river, and still another was placed on floats at the mouth of Mud river. Some weeks were passed before this work was done and the communication entirely cut off. Preparations were next commenced for the reduction of the fort. This was to be done by batteries established on Tybee Island adjacent to Cockspur Island, on which the fort is located. These were not completed until the 9th of April, when the following order for the bombardment of the fort was issued:

General Orders—No. 17.

HEADQUARTERS UNITED STATES FORCES,
TYBEE ISLAND, GA., *April* 9, 1862.

The batteries established against Fort Pulaski will be manned and ready for service at break of day to-morrow.

The signal to begin the action will be one gun from the right mortar of Battery Halleck (2,400 yards from the work), fired under the direction of Lieutenant Horace Porter, chief of ordnance; charge of mortar 11 lbs., charge of shell 11 lbs., elevation 55°, and length of fuse 24″.

This battery (two 13-inch Mortars) will continue firing at the rate of fifteen minutes to each mortar alternately, varying the charge of mortars and length of fuse, so that the shells will drop over the arches of the north and northeast faces of the work, and explode immediately after striking, but not before.

The other batteries will open as follows, viz:

Battery Stanton (three 13-inch mortars, 3,400 yards distant), immediately after the signal, at the rate of fifteen minutes for each piece, alternately from the right; charge of mortar 14 lbs., charge of shell 7 lbs., elevation 45°, and length of fuse 23″, varying the charge of mortar and length of fuse as may be required. The shells should drop over the arches of the south face of the work, and explode immediately after striking, but not before.

Battery Grant (three 13-inch mortars, 3,200 yards distant), immediately after the ranges for Battery Stanton have been determined, at the rate of fifteen minutes for each piece, alternately from the right; charge of shell 7 lbs., elevation 45°, charge of mortar and length of fuse to be varied to suit the range, as determined from Battery Stanton. The shells should drop over the arches of the south face of the work, and explode immediately after striking, but not before.

Battery Lyon (three 10-inch columbiads, 3,100 yards from the work), with a curved fire, immediately after the signal, allowing ten minutes between the discharges for each piece, alternating from the right; charge of guns 17 lbs., charge of shell 3 lbs., elevation 20°, and length of fuse 20″; the charge and length of fuse to vary as required. The shell should pass over the parapet and into the work, taking the gorge and north face in reverse, and exploding at the moment of striking, or immediately after.

Battery Lincoln (three 8-inch columbiads, 3,045 yards from the work), with a curved fire, immediately after the signal, allowing six minutes between discharges for each piece, alternating from the right; charge for gun 10 lbs., charge of shell 1½ lbs., elevation 20°, and length of fuse 20″, directed the same as Battery Lyon, upon the north face and gorge in reverse, varying the charge and length of fuse accordingly.

Battery Burnside (one 13-inch mortar, 2,750 yards from the work), firing every ten minutes, from the range as obtained for Battery Sherman; charge of shell 7 lbs.; elevation 45°; charge of mortar and length of fuse varying as required from those obtained for Battery Sherman. The shells should drop on the arches of the north and northeast faces, and explode immediately after striking, but not before.

Battery Sherman (three 10 inch-mortars, 2,650 yards from the work), commencing immediately after the ranges for Battery Grant have been determined, and firing at the rate of fifteen minutes for each piece, alternating from the right; charge of shell 7 lbs.; elevation 45°; charge of mortar and length of fuse to be fixed to suit the range as determined from Battery Grant. The shells should drop over the arches of the north and northeast faces.

Battery Scott (three 10-inch and one 8-inch columbiads, 1,677 yards from the work), firing solid shot and commencing immediately after the barbette fire of the works has ceased. Charge of 10-inch columbiads 20 lbs., elevation 4½°; charge of 8-inch columbiad 10 lbs., elevation 5°. This battery should breach the pancoupé between the south and southeast faces, and the embrasure next to it in the southeast face: the elevation to be varied accordingly, the charge to remain the same. Until the elevation is accurately determined each gun should fire once in ten minutes; after that, every six or eight minutes.

Battery Sigel (five 30-pounder Parrotts and one 24-pounder James', 1,620 yards from the work), to open with 4¾″ fuse on the barbette guns of the fort at the second discharge from Battery Sherman. Charge for 30-pounders, 3¼ lbs.; charge for 24-pounder, 5 lbs.; elevation, 40° for both calibers.

As soon as the barbette fire of the work has been silenced, this battery will be directed, with percussion shells, upon the walls, to breach the pancoupé between the south and southeast face, and the embrasure next to it in the southeast face, the elevation to be varied accordingly, the charge to remain the same. Until the elevation is accurately determined, each gun should fire once in six or eight minutes; after that, every four or five minutes.

Battery McClellan (two 42 and two 32-pounder James', 1,620 yards from the work) opens fire immediately after Battery Scott. Charges for 42-pounder, 8 lbs.; charge for 32-pounder, 6 lbs.; elevation of 42-

pounder, 4½°, and 32-pounder, 4°. Each piece should fire once every five or six minutes after the elevation has been established, charge to remain the same. This battery should breach the works in the pancoupé between the south and southeast faces, and the embrasure next to it in the southeast face. The steel scraper for the grooves should be used after every fifth or sixth discharge.

Battery Totten (four 10-inch siege mortars, 1,685 yards from the work) opens fire immediately after Battery Sigel, firing each piece about once in five minutes; charge of mortar, 3¼ lbs.; charge of shell, 3 lbs.: elevation, 45°.; and length of fuse, 18¼". The charge of mortar and length of fuse vary, so as to explode the shell over the northeast and southeast faces of the work.

If any battery should be unmasked outside the work Battery Totten should direct its fire upon it, varying the charge of mortars and length of fuse accordingly.

The fire from each battery will cease at dark, except especial directions be given to the contrary.

A signal officer at Battery Scott, to observe the effects of the 13-inch shells, will be in communication with other signal officers stationed near Batteries Stanton, Grant, and Sherman, in order to determine the range for these batteries in succession.

By order of Brig.-Gen. Q. A. GILLMORE.

Before the bombardment was commenced on the 10th, the fort was summoned to surrender. The following is the correspondence:

HEADQUARTERS DEPARTMENT OF THE SOUTH,
TYBEE ISLAND, GA., *April* 10, 1862.

To the Commanding Officer, Fort Pulaski:

SIR: I hereby demand of you the immediate surrender and restoration of Fort Pulaski to the authority and possession of the United States.

This demand is made with a view to avoiding, if possible, the effusion of blood which must result from the bombardment and attack now in readiness to be opened.

The number, caliber, and completeness of the batteries surrounding you, leave no doubt as to what must result in case of refusal: and as the defence, however obstinate, must eventually succumb to the assailing force at my disposal, it is hoped you will see fit to avert the useless waste of life.

This communication will be carried to you under a flag of truce by Lieut. J. H. Wilson, United States Army, who is authorized to wait any period not exceeding thirty minutes from delivery for your answer.

I have the honor to be, sir, your most obedient servant,
DAVID HUNTER,
Major-General Commanding.

Gen. Hunter had been placed in command of the Federal forces, and Gen. Sherman, before completing the enterprises he had commenced, was recalled. The Confederate commander of the fort replied to this demand as follows:

HEADQUARTERS, FORT PULASKI, *April* 10, 1862.

Maj.-Gen. David Hunter, commanding on Tybee Island:

SIR: I have to acknowledge receipt of your communication of this date, demanding the unconditional surrender of Fort Pulaski.

In reply I can only say that I am here to defend the fort, not to surrender it.

I have the honor to be, very respectfully, your obedient servant,
CHAS. H. OLMSTEAD,
Colonel First Volunteer regiment of Georgia, commanding post.

On this refusal, and at twenty-three minutes of eight o'clock in the morning the fire was opened. Three minutes after the fort replied from a 10-inch barbette gun, and soon after the firing became general on both sides. After eighteen hours the fort was breached in the southeast angle, and at the moment of surrender, 2 o'clock P. M. of the 11th, preparations had been commenced for storming. Forty-seven guns, a great supply of fixed ammunition, forty thousand pounds of powder, and large quantities of commissary stores, and three hundred and sixty prisoners were taken.

It was expected at Savannah that an attack would be immediately made upon Fort Jackson, to be followed by its surrender, and that of the city also. Nothing of the kind, however, was contemplated. The Union commander was in no condition to underteke such an enterprise, and actually was obliged to content himself with holding what had been acquired. The possession of Fort Pulaski prevented any further attempts to run the blockade into Savannah by the mouth of the river.

While these operations had been going on against Fort Pulaski, the other portion of the military and naval forces at Hilton Head had not been idle. On the 28th of February Com. Dupont sailed from Port Royal in the steam frigate Wabash, accompanied by the following vessels: Ottawa, Mohican, Ellen, Seminole, Pawnee, Pocahontas, Flag, Florida, James Adger, Bienville, Alabama, Key Stone State, Seneca, Huron, Pembina, Isaac Smith, Penguin, Potomska, armed cutter Henrietta, armed transport McClellan, the latter having on board the battalion of marines under the command of Maj. Reynolds, and the transports Empire City, Marion, Star of the South, Belvidere, Boston, and George's Creek, conveying a brigade under the command of Brig.-Gen. Wright.

On the 2d of March the expedition came to anchor in St. Andrew's Sound, and on the next morning a portion of the gunboats and transports, under Commander Drayton, proceeded down Cumberland Sound toward Fernandina on the north extremity of Amelia Island. Cumberland Sound is the passage between Cumberland Island and the mainland. Amelia Island is next in order below Cumberland Island; the north point of the former and the south point of the latter being nearly opposite. The remainder of the fleet proceeded down outside to the entrance between Cumberland and Amelia Islands. The object of sending a portion of the fleet through Cumberland Sound was to turn the works on the south end of Cumberland and the north end of Amelia Islands. The enemy having received information of the expedition, abandoned their works on its approach and retired. Fort Clinch on Amelia Island was taken possession of and garrisoned. The town of Fernandina, which was almost deserted, was occupied by the Union force, and a small steam boat loaded with stores was overtaken and captured. The Confederate force stationed at Fernandina consisted of the 4th Florida, Col. Hopkins, with a number of companies of cavalry and light artillery. Reconnoitring expeditions were sent out in different directions with successful results. New Fernandina on Amelia Island, about a mile and a half from Old Fer-

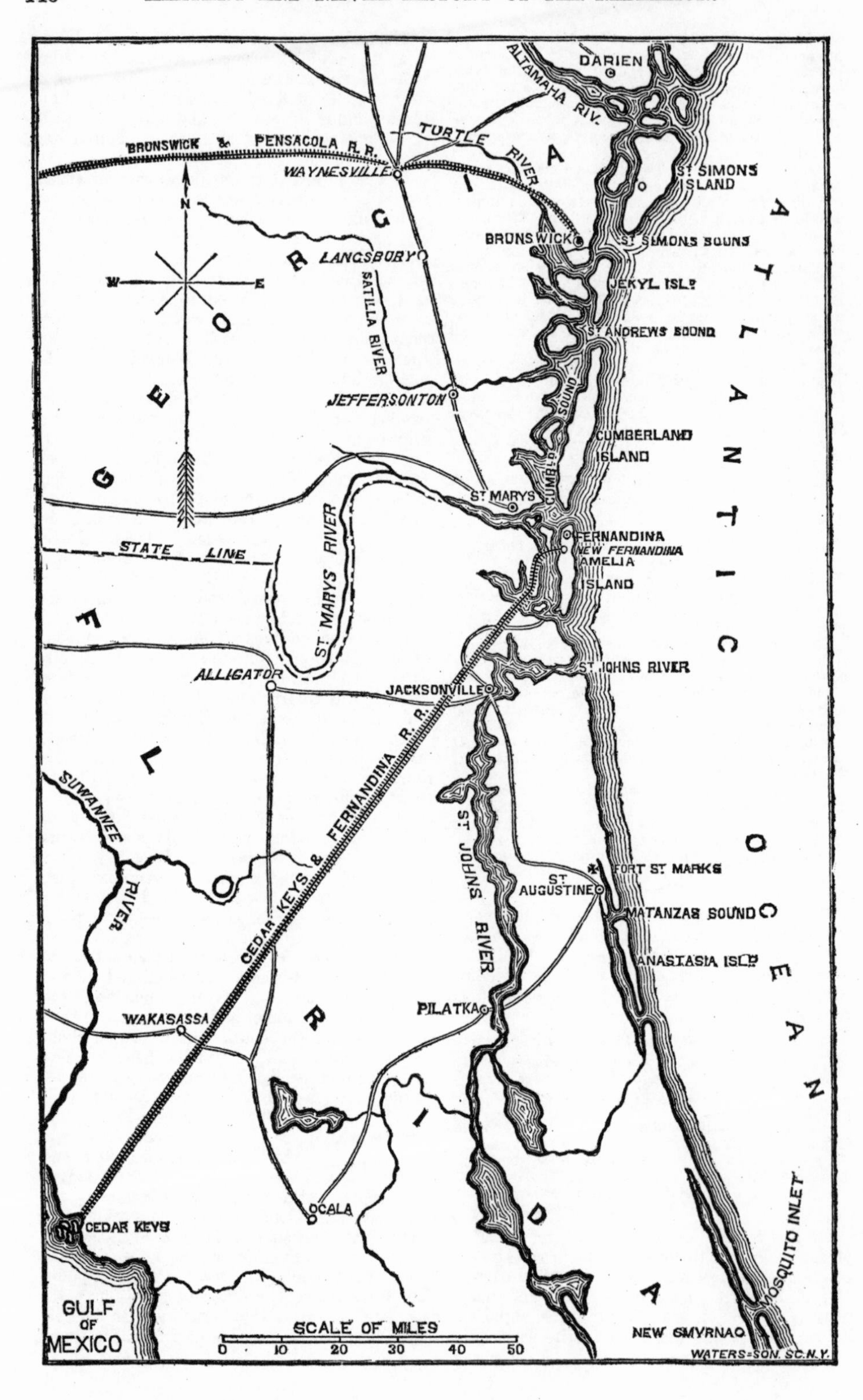
DARIEN
ALTAMAHA RIV.
TURTLE RIVER
BRUNSWICK & PENSACOLA R.R.
WAYNESVILLE
ST SIMONS ISLAND
BRUNSWICK
ST SIMONS SOUNS
LANGSBURY
SATILLA RIVER
JEKYL ISLD
ST ANDREWS SOUND
JEFFERSONTON
CUMBLD SOUND
CUMBERLAND ISLAND
ST MARYS
FERNANDINA
NEW FERNANDINA
AMELIA ISLAND
STATE LINE
ST. MARYS RIVER
ST JOHNS RIVER
ALLIGATOR
JACKSONVILLE
CEDAR KEYS & FERNANDINA R.R.
SUWANNEE RIVER
ST JOHNS RIVER
FORT ST MARKS
ST AUGUSTINE
MATANZAS SOUND
ANASTASIA ISLD
PILATKA
WAKASASSA
OCALA
CEDAR KEYS
MOSQUITO INLET
NEW SMYRNA
GULF OF MEXICO
SCALE OF MILES
0 10 20 30 40 50
GEORGIA
FLORIDA
ATLANTIC OCEAN
N
W
E
WATERS=SON. SC.N.Y.

nandina, is the eastern termination of the railroad across the peninsula. The western termination is Cedar Keys, a small town located on one of a group of small islands close to the west coast of Florida. It was captured by a Union force on the 16th of January. On the same night that Fernandina was taken Commander E. R. P. Rodgers in the Ottawa ascended the St. Mary's river, and took possession of the town of that name, driving out a picket of the enemy's cavalry. This town and Fernandina were uninjured. Preparations for a most vigorous defence were found to have been made at both places, but the State troops were probably required for the Confederate army. The difficulties arising from the indirectness of the channel and from the shoalness of the bar would have added to the defences by keeping approaching vessels a long time exposed to fire under great disadvantages. Having turned the property over to the military power the expedition was ready for further movements.

A principal and ultimate object of this entire expedition was, in its first conception, to take and keep under control the whole line of seacoast, especially of the State of Georgia. Having heard at Fernandina that the works at Brunswick in Georgia had been abandoned, Com. Dupont on the 7th of March despatched a force, consisting of the Mohican, Pocahontas, and Potomska, under Commander Gordon, to hold the place. It is a port of entry in the extreme southeastern part of the State of Georgia, pleasantly situated on Turtle river, and has a spacious harbor. It is the eastern terminus of the Brunswick and Florida railroad. Commander Gordon with his vessels crossed the bar on the 8th, and anchored at sundown within two miles of the forts commanding the channel. The next day he took possession of the batteries on St. Simon's Island and on Jekyl Island. When abandoned, all their guns and ammunition had been removed. The town also was entirely deserted, and nearly all the property which could be removed had been taken away. Proclamations were posted by Commander Gordon on several public buildings, urging the inhabitants to return to their homes and promising protection to the property of all good citizens. The force then retired to the vessels.

On the 13th with the Potomska and Pocahontas Commander Gordon proceeded from St. Simon's Sound through the inland passage to Darien on the Altamaha river. Piles had been driven in two places across the passage, which were removed. Darien like Brunswick was entirely deserted, and also all the plantations on St. Simon's Island. But one white man was found on the island, and one old negro, although about fifteen hundred troops had been quartered there a few months previous. The former appeared to be in great dread of the coming of the Union force, and had been told that they would destroy even women and children.

At the same time when this force was ordered to Brunswick on the 7th of March, Com. Dupont sent the gunboats Ottawa, Seneca, Pembina, and Huron, with the Isaac Smith and Ellen under Lieut. Stevens to St. John's river with instructions to cross its difficult and shallow bar, feel the forts if still held, and push on to Jacksonville and even Pilatka and capture river steamers. St. John's river empties into the Atlantic some twenty-five miles south of Fernandina. On the 11th Lieut. Stevens succeeded in crossing the bar and anchored for the night. During the evening large fires were seen in the direction of Jacksonville, which proved to have been made under the order of the Confederate commander, Gen. Trapier, by the burning of mills, houses, and property belonging to Northern men suspected of entertaining Union sympathies. On arriving at Jacksonville during the next day, the corporate authorities came off to Lieut. Stevens and gave up the town. The 4th New Hampshire, Col. Whipple, was landed and took possession. The location of the town is on the northern bank of the St. John's, about twenty-five miles from its mouth. It contains about three thousand inhabitants. From almost all the houses a white flag was displayed on the approach of the force, and men, women, and children of all colors turned out to see the display. A Union feeling was aroused and encouraged. A public meeting was called and resolutions adopted in favor of organizing a Union State Government and calling a convention to meet at Jacksonville for that purpose on the 10th of April, then approaching. On the 8th of April the Union commander, Gen. Wright, evacuated the town, and then sent information of his movement to the Confederate commander, Gen. Trapier, inviting him to come and re-occupy the town, and requesting him to take care of the women and children remaining. On the 9th the Confederate officers stood on the dock and watched the vessels sailing away. On the 10th, the Union convention, which had been warmly encouraged by these retiring officers with their force, was called to assemble. Of course it was not held. The more active Unionists had through fear left with the fleet.

Com. Dupont, immediately after having despatched Commander Gordon to Brunswick and Lieut. Stevens to Jacksonville, as above stated, proceeded himself toward St. Augustine. Arriving off the harbor he ordered Commander Rodgers to approach the city with a flag of truce, presuming that if there were any people along the coast likely to remain in their houses, they would be found at St. Augustine. As Commander Rodgers approached the city, a white flag was hoisted upon one of the bastions of Fort Marion. As he landed upon the wharf and inquired for the chief authority, he was soon joined by the mayor and conducted to the city hall, where the municipal authorities were assembled. His report to Com. Dupont proceeds as follows:

I informed them that, having come to restore the

authority of the United States, you had deemed it more proper to send in an unarmed boat to inform the citizens of your determination, than to occupy the town at once by force of arms; that you were desirous to calm all apprehensions of harsh treatment, and that you should carefully respect the persons and property of all citizens who submitted to the authority of the United States; that you had a single purpose to restore the state of affairs which existed before the rebellion.

I informed the municipal authorities that so long as they respected the authority of the Government we serve, and acted in good faith, municipal affairs would be left in their own hands, so far as might be consistent with the exigencies of the times. The mayor and council informed me that the place had been evacuated the preceding night by two companies of Florida troops, and that they gladly received the assurances I gave them, and placed the city in my hands.

I recommended them to hoist the flag of the Union at once, and in prompt accordance with the advice, by order of the mayor, the national ensign was displayed from the flag staff of the fort. The mayor proposed to turn over to me the five cannon mounted at the fort, which are in good condition and not spiked, and also the few munitions of war left by the retreating enemy. I desired him to take charge of them for the present, to make careful inventories and establish a patrol and guard, informing him that he would be held responsible for the place until our force should enter the harbor.

I called on the clergymen of the city, requesting them to re-assure the people, and to confide in our kind intentions toward them. About 1,500 people remain in St. Augustine, about one-fifth of the inhabitants having fled. I believe there are many citizens who are earnestly attached to the Union, a large number who are silently opposed to it, and a still larger number who care very little about the matter. There is much violent and pestilent feeling among the women; they have a theatrical desire to figure as heroines! Their minds have doubtless been filled with the falsehoods so industriously circulated in regard to the lust and hatred of our troops.

On the night before our arrival a party of women assembled in front of the barracks and cut down the flag staff, in order that it might not be used to support the old flag. The men seemed anxious to conciliate in every way. There is a great scarcity of provisions in the place. There seems to be no money, except the wretched paper currency of the rebellion, and much poverty exists.

In the water battery at the fort are three fine army 32-pounders and two 8-inch sea coast howitzers, with shot and some powder. Several good guns were taken away some months ago. The garrison of the place left from St. Augustine at midnight on the 18th, for Smyrna, where are said to be about 800 troops, a battery, the steamer Carolina, and a considerable quantity of arms and ammunition.

The fort at this place is the second one of the old forts in Florida of which possession had then been recovered. The other is Fort Clinch at Fernandina. St. Augustine is farther south than Jacksonville and situated on the north shore of Matanzas Sound about two miles from the sea, from which it is separated by the island of Anastasia. The population exceeds two thousand.

The next object of Com. Dupont was to visit Musquito Inlet, fifty miles farther south. It had been reported to him that the inlet was resorted to by vessels of light draft for the introduction of arms transhipped from English vessels and steamers at the English colony of Nassau. Accordingly the Penguin, Lieut. T. A. Budd, and the Henry, Andrew S. W. Mather, master, were sent in advance and ordered to cross the bar and establish an inside blockade and guard from incendiarism the live oak timber on the Government lands. On their arrival they started with four or five light boats and forty-three men and moved southward into Mosquito lagoon, but when returning, they were unexpectedly fired on, upon landing, and the commanding officers and three men were killed, and several wounded, and two taken prisoners.

By these operations along the Florida coast some small steamers and other vessels were captured, and the blockade was rendered more effective by the actual occupation of the principal ports. The country appeared to be undefended and entirely unprepared to make any resistance against the overwhelming Union force. Many fortified positions were found, but the soldiers were not seen. The white population in Florida in 1860 was 77,778, and during the previous year the State sent about ten thousand men to the Confederate army. Her military strength was thus reduced to a feeble condition. Whatever progress was made in restoring the Union was defeated by the sudden evacuation of Jacksonville and the abandonment of many Union citizens there. It taught the people of the State that so long as the Confederate Government existed in security, it might at any time return and demand their allegiance.

Commodore Dupont now returned to Port Royal, leaving a small force at all the points taken. On his arrival on the 27th of March, he learned that the formidable Confederate batteries on Skidaway and Green islands had been abandoned, by which complete control was obtained of Warsaw and Ossibaw sounds and the mouths of Vernon and Wilmington rivers, which form a part of the approaches from the south to Savannah.

Toward Charleston the only movement of importance which had been made by Gen. Sherman was the occupation of Edisto Island by the 47th New York. This took place on the 11th of February. This island is about twelve miles long and nine broad, and is about ten miles from the mainland, twenty miles from the Charleston and Savannah railroad, and forty miles from Charleston. The island was found to be entirely deserted except by the negroes. Considerable cotton was gathered, although the greater portion of that produced had been burned.

On the 31st of March Maj.-Gen. David Hunter assumed the command of the department of the South, consisting of the States of South Carolina, Georgia, and Florida. Thus Gen. Sherman was relieved of the command and assigned to another post. In a proclamation issued on the same day, Gen. Hunter announced the division of his department into three districts as follows:

1. The first, to be called the Northern District, will comprise the States of South Carolina, Georgia, and

all that part of Florida north and east of a line extending from Cape Canaveral northwest to the Gulf coast, just north of Cedar Keys and its dependencies, and thence north to the Georgia line. The headquarters of this district will be at Port Royal, South Carolina, and Brig.-Gen. H. W. Benham (who will relieve Brig.-Gen. Sherman) is appointed to command this district and the troops therein, which troops will constitute a division, to be called the First Division of the Department of the South.

2. The second, to be called the Southern District, will comprise all of Florida and the islands adjacent, south of the said line from Cape Canaveral, extending northwest to the Gulf coast, just north of Cedar Keys. The headquarters of this district and the troops will remain, as at present, under command of Brig.-Gen. J. M. Brannan.

3. The third, to be called the Western District, will comprise that part of Florida west of the line before described as running north from Cedar Keys to the Georgia line. The headquarters of this district will remain at Fort Pickens, as at present, with Brig.-Gen. L. G. Arnold commanding.

The preparations, commenced by Gen. Sherman for the capture of Fort Pulaski, were pushed forward by Gen. Hunter, until the fort surrendered in April, as has been above described. The subsequent movements under Gen. Hunter consisted in reconnoissances in force toward Charleston. The southern boundary of the harbor of Charleston is formed by James Island. This island is bounded on the north by the harbor of Charleston and the Ashley River, on the northwest by Wappoo Creek, on the south and southwest by Stono River, and on the east are a few small islands and the ocean. Wappoo Creek connects with the Ashley River in the immediate rear of Charleston, and by entering Stono River and into Wappoo Creek, gunboats can reach Charleston. The next island south of importance is John's Island, and the next Edisto Island. Between these and Hilton Head are a number of islands of much less size. Early in May Com. Dupont ordered the channel of Stono River to be sounded out and buoys to be placed. This was completed on the 20th of May, and the gunboats Unadilla, Pembina, and Ottawa crossed the bar and entered the river. Along the river, owing to its great importance as a means of access to the city, a vast number of earthwork fortifications had been erected. All of these were abandoned as the gunboats proceeded. The distance from the mouth of the Stono to Wappoo Creek is about eight miles. Little was done in the river by the fleet for many days, except silencing some of the Confederate batteries, and preventing the erection of others in commanding points likely to be needed on the march toward Charleston, of which this was designed as a preliminary movement. No signs of the approaching army appeared for two weeks, during which several reconnoissances were made by the fleet. The fire of the forts at the entrance to Wappoo Creek was drawn from two large rifled cannon at the lower battery of seven guns. The Huron and Pembina were anchored within range of these guns and within three miles of Charleston. From their mastheads could be seen a dozen spires, cupolas and observatories, the top-masts of two or three large ships, and nearly all the north-western part of the city. On the 2d of June the military advance with Gens. Hunter and Benham arrived and were landed on James Island, to await the coming of Gen. Wright with cavalry, artillery, and additional infantry from the Edisto. An important fortification which had been vacated was occupied on James Island. On the 5th the additional forces arrived, and a series of skirmishes ensued for the next ten days both on James and John's Islands. On the 13th a sharp contest occurred between several new York and Pennsylvania regiments and the 47th Georgia.

Meanwhile a diversion was made by a small Southern force against Hilton Head, which caused much consternation there, but effected nothing further.

It was soon manifest that the Confederate force had been increased, and nothing of importance could be further effected by Gen. Hunter without reënforcements. As the Government had none at this time to send, not being able to reënforce the more important army in Virginia, military operations were comparatively suspended.

Some operations of the South Atlantic and West Gulf squadrons during the year are worthy of notice in this place. On the first of January a combined attack was made by land and water upon a Confederate post at Port Royal Ferry, S. C., the naval forces, consisting of three gunboats, two tugs, and four armed boats from the Wabash, being under the direction of Commander C. R. P. Rogers.

On January 27th a fleet of two gunboats, four armed steamers, and two armed launches under Fleet Captain C. H. Davis, accompanied by 2,400 men on transports commanded by Brig.-Gen. Wright, made a reconnoissance of Little Tybee River and the adjacent waters, with a view of preparing for the cutting off communication between Fort Pulaski and Savannah and the ultimate capture of the fort. While on this duty they were attacked by five Confederate vessels under Commodore Tatnall, which they repulsed after a half hour's fight, two of the enemy being driven back to Savannah, and the others running under the guns of the fort.

On April 29th Lieut. Rhind, with the steamer E. B. Hale, captured and destroyed a battery near the junction of the Dawho, Pow Pow, and South Edisto Rivers.

On May 13th the steam-tug planter, an armed despatch and transportation steamer attached to the engineer department at Charleston, under Brig.-Gen. Ripley, was brought out by her pilot, Robert Small, a very intelligent slave, and surrendered to the blockading squadron. She had on board eight men, five women, and three children, all negroes, and was armed with a 32-pounder pivot gun and a 24-pounder howitzer, besides which she had four large guns, one of them belonging to Fort Sumter, which she was to have transported that morning to the new fort on the middle ground. At 4 o'clock in the morning, while the captain was on shore, she left her wharf with Palmetto and Confederate flags flying, passed the forts, saluting as usual by blowing her steam whistle, and after getting out of reach of the last gun, hauled down the Confederate flags and hoisted a white one. The steamer, from her excellent machinery and light draught, proved a valuable acquisition to the blockaders.

On the 19th, Flag-Officer Dupont, having been led to believe, chiefly by the information given by Robert Small, that the Confederates were erecting batteries on Stono Inlet, caused a reconnoissance to be made which established the truth of the report. The inlet was immediately occupied by the gunboats and an important base thus secured for future operations against Charleston.

The military forces sent to occupy Jacksonville, Fla., after its capture in March, were afterwards withdrawn, and a battery was planted by the Confederates on St. John's River, some distance below the town, which caused considerable annoyance to the gunboats employed on the inside blockade of the river. Commander Steedman and Gen. Brannan accordingly moved on the 30th of September with a joint naval and land force, silenced and occupied the battery, capturing nine guns, and afterwards ascended the river as far as Lake Beresford, a distance of two hundred and thirty miles, and captured a transport steamer.

The East Gulf squadron was under the command of Flag-Officer McKeon. Early in January he sent the steamer Hatteras, Commander Emmons, to Cedar Keys, where about the 10th she captured or destroyed a quantity of artillery and military stores, and several schooners, the place being an important depot of the enemy.

In the latter part of March Commander Stellwagen of the Mercedita arrived off Appalachicola with that vessel and the Sagamore, and organized a boat expedition, the immediate object of which was the capture of a number of vessels understood to be at or above that city. The place, however, had already been evacuated by the enemy's troops, and the expedition met with no resistance. The inhabitants received the sailors favorably and raised the United States flag. Several vessels were brought out and others were destroyed.

On the night of April 6th a boat expedition from the bark Pursuit, under Acting Master Elnathan Lewis, surprised and captured at St. Andrew's the rebel steamer Florida, of five hundred tons, with two hundred bales of cotton on board, and brought her safely out.

On the 4th of October a boat expedition from the steamer Somerset proceeded to the main land near Cedar Keys for the purpose of destroying some salt works, but was fired upon from a house on which a white flag was flying, and compelled to return without thoroughly accomplishing their purpose. On the 5th a stronger force, consisting of four boats from the Somerset and four from the gunboat Tahoma, landed at the same place, completing the destruction and dispersing a small guerrilla force.

The movements already described brought the Federal forces into more immediate contact with the slaves, hence the questions relative to the political, civil, and social position of "colored persons of African descent," became more prominent during 1862 than in any previous period. An elaborate opinion was prepared by the U. S. Attorney-General, Mr. Bates, on the question, "Are colored men citizens of the United States?" The chief points of the opinion were—that the Constitution does not define the word citizen, the Attorney-General therefore examines history and the civil law from the existence of the Roman Empire to the present day to discover its meaning. His conclusion is—that all free persons, without distinction of race or color, if native born, are citizens. A distinction is made between the inherent rights of citizens and the political privileges of certain classes. All citizens have a right to protection, but only certain classes enjoy the privileges of voting and holding office. Hitherto not only the public but jurists have often confounded the two. A child or a woman is a citizen, though not always privileged to vote or hold office. The Dred Scott opinion is pronounced void and of no authority, since the province of the Supreme Court was only to settle the questions of the jurisdiction of the Circuit Court. They are simply entitled to the respect due to the views of eminent gentlemen, and no more.

In Massachusetts, Governor Andrew ordered negroes to be enrolled as well as white persons for the purpose of drafting soldiers. The Attorney-General of the State justified the order on the ground that—"Congress and the war department both leave out the word *white* from the description of the class to be enrolled." He further adds: "The only possible question now open is whether colored men are citizens of Massachusetts, which no one, I presume, will have the hardihood to deny, inasmuch as they are tax-payers, voters, jurors, and eligible to office, and there is no inequality founded on distinction of races known to our laws."

On the other hand the Circuit Court of Illinois sitting in Montgomery County decided that negroes were not citizens.

The operations of the Federal forces within slaveholding States necessarily released many slaves from the restraints of their masters. The mass of them took advantage of this circumstance to escape from servitude. Their presence within the Federal lines led to the adoption of various measures by the commanding officers and by the Federal Government relative to them, all looking toward their ultimate freedom.

In January the Marshal of the District of Columbia was instructed by order of the President "not to receive into custody any persons claimed to be held to service or labor within the District, or elsewhere, and not charged with any crime or misdemeanor, unless upon arrest or commitment, pursuant to law, as fugitives from such service or labor, and not to retain any such fugitives in custody beyond a period of thirty days from their arrest and commitment, unless by special order from the civil authority." The effect of this order was to relieve from any fears of apprehension all the fugitives that had escaped to the District from Virginia. Thousands of slaves flocked to the District and were sustained throughout the year by rations furnished by the Government.

In Missouri, Gen. Halleck had, previous to this time, issued an order that fugitive slaves should not be permitted to enter the lines of any camp, or any forces on the march. This order occasioned much discussion, especially in Congress, as it cut off an opportunity for escape to thousands of slaves. It was explained by Gen. Halleck in these words: "unauthorized persons, black or white, free or slave, must be kept out of our camps, unless we are willing to publish to the enemy every thing we do, or intend to do."

In Arkansas, Gen. Curtis issued orders of immediate emancipation under confiscation of a number of slaves who had been at work for the Confederate Government by the consent of their masters.

Similar orders were issued by Gen. Hunter, under like circumstances, in the Department of South Carolina. These were extended until he at length issued an order confiscating and emancipating all the slaves in his military district, embracing South Carolina, Georgia, and Florida. This was countermanded by the President.

At Baton Rouge, in Louisiana, Brig.-Gen. Williams issued an order that, in consequence of the demoralizing and disorganizing tendencies to the troops of harboring runaway negroes, the commanders should turn all such fugitives beyond the limits of their respective guards and sentinels. Col. Paine of this brigade refused obedience, and justified himself by the following act of Congress:

Be it enacted by the Senate and House of Representatives of the United States of America in Congress assembled, That hereafter the following shall be promulgated as an additional article of war for the government of the Army of the United States, and shall be obeyed and observed as such:

ART. —. All officers or persons in the military or naval service of the United States are prohibited from employing any of the forces under their respective commands for the purpose of returning fugitives from service or labor who may have escaped from any person to whom such service or labor is claimed to be due, and any officer who shall be found guilty, by a court-martial, of violating this article, shall be dismissed from the service.

SEC. 2. *And be it further enacted*, That this act shall take effect from and after its passage.

The effect of all the regulations adopted, except in Missouri and Baton Rouge, was to secure freedom to every slave that would make the effort to obtain it. Wherever permanent headquarters for Federal troops were established within slaveholding States, they soon became crowded with hundreds and thousands of fugitive slaves. The Government was immediately obliged to feed them or starvation would ensue. At Washington, at Fortress Monroe, Newbern, and Port Royal were large numbers furnished with quarters and fed at the national expense. Various schemes were devised for the occupation of these negroes, particularly in the department of South Carolina.

Subsequently the Secretary of War issued orders, which developed the following plan for a social experiment with the negroes:

General Order No. 17.

HEADQ'RS E. C., HILTON HEAD, S. C., March 3, 1862.

1. Mr. Edward L. Pierce having been appointed by the Hon. Secretary of the Treasury General Superintendent and Director of all persons engaged in the cultivation of the land and the employment of the blacks, he is hereby announced as such.

2. The following instructions to the general commanding are hereby published for the information of all concerned; and commanding officers of all posts and stations within the limits of this command, will be governed in strict conformity thereto:

WAR DEPARTMENT, February 13, 1862.

To Gen. T. W. Sherman, Commanding at Port Royal, S. C.;

GENERAL: You are hereby directed to afford protection, subsistence, and facilities, so far as may be consistent with the interests of the service and the duties and objects of your command, to all persons who may present to you written permits, issued to them under the authority of the Secretary of the Treasury, setting forth that said persons have proceeded to Port Royal under the sanction of the Government, for the collection, safe keeping, and disposition of cotton, rice, and other property abandoned by the possessors within your military department, and for the regulation and employment of persons of color lately held to service or labor by enemies of the United States, and now within the occupying lines and under the military protection of the army.

Such permits, signed by the Collector of Customs at New York City, will be considered by you as emanating from the Treasury Department.

Under the head of subsistence will be included rations to such persons as may be employed under the direction of the Treasury Department, in the temporary charge of the abandoned plantations; or, with its sanction, to labor for the instruction and improvement of the laboring population.

EDWIN M. STANTON, Secretary of War.

Several societies undertook to take charge of the matter, and seventy-two persons, farmers, mechanics, physicians, and teachers, were sent out by the Government, receiving each one ration a day from the commissariat, and paid salaries by the affiliated societies. They were "to teach Christianity and civilization to the freed men of the colored race, to imbue them with notions of order, industry, and economy, and self-reliance, and to elevate them in the scale of humanity, by inspiring them with self-respect." The cost of rations to the Government, a part of which were consumed in this experiment, was estimated at $100,000 per day. Educational associations were formed in Boston and other places, by whom the teachers were procured. On the 2d of June the agent, E. L. Pierce, made a report to the Secretary of the Treasury, Mr. Chase, in which he stated that seventy men and sixteen women were engaged in missionary work among the negroes, under the auspices of the Treasury Department. The number of plantations under the care of these persons was 189, having on them 9,050 Africans, classified as follows: 309 mechanics and house servants, 693 old, sickly, and unable to work, 3,619 children, not useful for field labor, 4,429 field hands, of whom 3,202 were full hands, 295 three-quarter hands, 597 half hands, and 335 quarter hands. The amount of labor performed was as follows:

The aggregate result makes (adding the negro patches to the cornfields of the plantations) 8,314.12 acres of provisions (corn, potatoes, &c.) planted, 4,489.11 acres of cotton planted—in all, 13,795.23 acres of provisions and cotton planted. Adding to these the 2,394 acres of late corn, to a great extent for fodder, cowpens, &c., to be planted, and the crop of this year presents a total of 16,189.2 acres. The crops are growing, and are in good condition.

The sum of $5,479 has been distributed among 4,030 negroes in payment for labor on the plantations. The rate is $1 per acre for cotton.

After the novelty had passed away very little was accomplished by the slaves. A report in September makes the effective hands 3,817, non-effective 3,110; acres of corn, 6,444; potatoes, 1,407; cotton, 3,384; which was considered more than enough for their own support, but not sufficient to reimburse the Government. The whole experiment finally failed, and was abandoned by order of Gen. Hunter, and the negroes fell upon the Government for support.

The negroes near Fortress Monroe made a better use of their advantages. The military commission to examine into their condition, stated that by the report of the provost marshal at Camp Hamilton, it appears that for the five months ending 1st January, 1862, he had drawn rations amounting to about three hundred and eighty-three per day, which was issued to about six hundred and fifty women and children and old infirm men, all of whom returned little or no equivalent to the Government. But since the 1st of January the rations issued there have not exceeded seventy, and for part of the time were less than forty per day. As a consequence the negroes have been thrown very much upon their own exertions to provide for themselves; and the commission of inquiry do not find that any amount of suffering has ensued; but in many instances the effort at self-support has been successful and improving.

Schools have been in successful operation at Camp Hamilton under the charge of clergymen, assisted by other teachers, black and white, where children and adults were daily instructed in reading, writing, and the elements of arithmetic; also religious instruction, and meetings were regularly held on Sunday and stated evenings during the week.

Another measure undertaken, in order to put the negroes to a useful purpose, was to organize the able-bodied ones into regiments of soldiers. The most conspicuous friends of the negroes, who have long urged the measure, have doubtless hoped that so much military spirit might thereby be infused into a considerable number as to qualify them to strike for the emancipation of their race.

On the 9th of June resolutions of inquiry relative to the organization of a negro regiment in South Carolina were offered in the House of Representatives in Congress, and adopted soon after. The resolution was referred to Gen. Hunter by the secretary, who replied as follows:

HEADQUARTERS DEPARTMENT OF THE SOUTH,
PORT ROYAL, S. C., June 23, 1862.

Hon. Edwin M. Stanton, Sec'y of War, Washington:

SIR: I have the honor to acknowledge the receipt of a communication from the adjutant-general of the army, dated June 13, 1862, requesting me to furnish you with the information necessary to answer certain resolutions introduced in the House of Representatives, June 9, 1862, on motion of the Hon. Mr. Wickliffe, of Kentucky, their substance being to inquire—

1st. Whether I had organized or was organizing a regiment of "fugitive slaves" in this department?

2d. Whether any authority had been given to me from the War Department for such organization? and

3d. Whether I had been furnished by order of the War Department with clothing, uniforms, arms, equipments, &c., for such a force?

To the first question, therefore, I reply that no regiment of "fugitive slaves" has been or is being organized in this department. There is, however, a fine regiment of persons whose late masters are "fugitive rebels"—men who everywhere fly before the appearance of the national flag, leaving their servants behind them to shift as best they can for themselves. So far, indeed, are the loyal persons composing this regiment from seeking to avoid the presence of their late owners, that they are now, one and all, working with remarkable industry to place themselves in a position to go in full and effective pursuit of their fugacious and traitorous proprietors.

To the second question I have the honor to answer that the instructions given to Brig.-Gen. T. W. Sherman, by the Hon. Simon Cameron, late Secretary of War, and turned over to me by succession for my guidance, do distinctly authorize me to employ all loyal persons offering their services in defence of the Union and for the suppression of this rebellion, in any manner I might see fit, or that the circumstances might call for. There is no restriction as to the character or color of the persons to be employed, or the nature of the employment, whether civil or military, in which their services should be used. I conclude, therefore, that I have been authorized to enlist "fugitive slaves" as soldiers, could any such be found in this department. No such characters, however, have yet appeared within view of our most advanced pickets; the loyal slaves everywhere remaining on their plantations to welcome us, aid us, and supply us with food, labor, and information. It is the masters who have in every instance been the "fugitives," running away from loyal slaves as well as loyal soldiers, and whom we have only partially been able to see—chiefly their heads over ramparts, or, rifle in hand, dodging behind trees—in the extreme distance. In the absence of any "fugitive master law," the deserted slaves would be wholly without remedy had not the crime of treason given them the right to pursue, capture, and bring back those persons of whose protection they have been suddenly bereft.

To the third interrogatory it is my painful duty to reply that I never have received any specific authority for issues of clothing, uniforms, arms, equipments, and so forth, to the troops in question—my general instructions from Mr. Cameron to employ them in any manner I might find necessary, and the military exigencies of the department and the country, being my only, but, in my judgment, sufficient justification. Neither have I had any specific authority for supplying these persons with shovels, spades, and pickaxes when employing them as laborers, nor with boats and oars when using them as lightermen; but these are not points included in Mr. Wickliffe's resolutions. To me it seemed that liberty to employ men in any particular capacity implied with it liberty also to supply them with the necessary tools; and acting upon this faith I have clothed, equipped, and armed the only loyal regiment yet raised in South Carolina.

I must say, in vindication of my own conduct, that had it not been for the many other diversified and imperative claims on my time a much more satisfactory result might have been hoped for; and that in place of only one, as at present, at least five or six well-drilled, brave, and thoroughly acclimated regiments should by this time have been added to the loyal forces of the Union.

The experiment of arming the blacks, so far as I have made it, has been a complete and even marvellous success. They are sober, docile, attentive, and enthusiastic, displaying great natural capacities for acquiring the duties of the soldier. They are eager beyond all things to take the field and be led into action; and it is the unanimous opinion of the officers who have had charge of them, that in the peculiarities of this climate and country they will prove invaluable auxiliaries, fully equal to the similar regiments so long and successfully used by the British authorities in the West India Islands.

In conclusion, I would say it is my hope—there appearing no possibility of other reënforcements owing to the exigencies of the campaign in the Peninsula—to have organized by the end of next fall, and to be able to present to the Government, from forty-eight to fifty thousand of these hardy and devoted soldiers.

Trusting that this letter may form part of your answer to Mr. Wickliffe's resolutions, I have the honor to be, most respectfully, your very obedient servant,

D. HUNTER, Major-General Commanding.

On the 18th of October Gen. Saxton, in command of the Department, issued an order to organize the 1st regiment of South Carolina volunteers as soon as possible. The enlisting of the negroes had proceeded very slowly. Thirteen dollars a month, with army rations and clothing, was to be the pay of the soldier. By the close of the year the regiment was completed.

The attempt was made in Kansas by Gen. Lane to enlist negroes, but it failed of success.

An attempt was made by Gen. Sprague, of Rhode Island, to raise a regiment of free negroes, but it met with no success. An attempt was also made at New Orleans to organize negro troops, but at the close of the year it was still an experiment.

Another measure proposed relative to the slaves was their colonization in Chiriqui, in Central America. For this purpose Senator Pomroy, of Kansas, who had been very successful in organizing "Emigrant Aid Expeditions" from Massachusetts at the time of the Kansas disturbances, received a kind of general permission from the President to settle at any suitable point within the tropics, being charged "to maintain the honor of the republic abroad." Some progress was made in organizing this enterprise, but it was abandoned. Another measure proposed was the removal of a portion of those at Fortress Monroe to Massachusetts and other Northern States, both for "humane and military reasons."

Notwithstanding all the measures proposed, the Southern slaves remained a great burden on the hands of the Government, excepting those who had pressed forward to the free States, already well supplied with white labor. The action of the President relative to emancipation will be stated in a subsequent page.

CHAPTER XIV.

Military Operations in Missouri and Arkansas—Advance of Gen. Curtis—His Address to the People of the Southwest—Battle of Pea Ridge—Retreat of Gen. Price—Further Operations—Advance of the Fleet against Columbus, Ky.—Evacuated—Further progress down the Mississippi—Island No. 10: its Bombardment—Gunboats pass the Batteries in the night—Evacuation of the Island—Advance of the Fleet toward Memphis—Naval Battle before the City—Its Surrender—Occupied by Federal Troops—Proceedings during the Year.

Up to this time movements of some importance had taken place in Missouri and Arkansas. Two sharp skirmishes took place—the one at Mount Zion, eighteen miles southwest of Sturgeon, on December 28, 1861, and the other near Fayette, on January 8, 1862. In the former Brig.-Gen. Prentiss commanded, and in the latter Major Torneru. They produced no special influence on the campaign in that department. On the 29th of January, Gen. Earl Van Dorn took command of the Confederate forces in the trans-Mississippi district, which comprised a considerable portion of the State of Missouri, with his headquarters at Little Rock. On the preceding day, the division of the Union army under the command of Col. Jeff. C. Davis left Marseilles for Springfield. It consisted of four regiments—the 8th and 22d Indiana, 37th Illinois, and 9th Missouri, with two batteries, and three companies of cavalry. The other forces immediately moved forward, and combined under Gen. Curtis. On the 11th of February this army moved forward from Lebanon, formed in three divisions—the right under Col. Davis, the centre under Gen. Sigel, and the left under Col. Carr. Six miles from Springfield on the 12th, a skirmish took place between the advance of this force and a body of Confederate troops, with serious loss to both sides. During the night a continuous fire was kept up between the pickets. On the next morning the Confederate force had retreated, and Gen. Curtis occupied Springfield without opposition. About six hundred sick and a large amount of stores were left behind by the Confederate General Price. Gen. Halleck, in command of this department, sent the following despatch to the commander-in-chief, Gen. McClellan, at Washington:

ST. LOUIS, *February* 14, 1862.

The flag of the Union floats over the court house in Springfield. The enemy retreated after a short engagement, leaving a large amount of stores and equipments, which were captured by Gen. Curtis. Our cavalry are in close pursuit.

H. W. HALLECK, Major-General.

Such had been Gen. Halleck's skilful management of this department, that a few days previous he had received the following despatch from the Secretary of War:

WASHINGTON, *February* 8, 1862.

Maj.-Gen. Halleck, St. Louis: Your energy and ability received the strongest commendation of this Department. You have my perfect confidence, and you may rely upon my utmost support in your undertakings. The pressure of my engagements has prevented me from writing you, but I will do so fully in a day or two.

EDWIN M. STANTON, Secretary of War.

As Gen. Price retreated Gen. Curtis followed rapidly in pursuit. On the 16th his army had advanced sixty-nine miles south of Springfield, and on the 18th had crossed the Arkansas line. Several skirmishes took place in the mountain defiles. The following despatch was sent to Washington by Gen. Halleck:

ST. LOUIS, *February* 18, 1862.

To Maj.-Gen. McClellan, Washington:

The flag of the Union is floating in Arkansas. Gen. Curtis has driven Price from Missouri, and is several miles across the Arkansas line, cutting up Price's rear, and hourly capturing prisoners and stores. The army of the Southwest is doing its duty nobly.

H. W. HALLECK, Major-General.

On the 19th Gen. Price had been reënforced by Gen. McCulloch, and made a stand at Sugar Creek crossing, but was defeated after a short engagement, and retreated. Squads of recruits from Missouri, on their way to join the Confederate force, were captured at this time, among whom was Brig.-Gen. Edward Price, son of Gen. Price. On the 26th Gen. Price had been driven from his stronghold at Cross Hollows, leaving his sick and wounded, and such stores as he could not destroy. He burned his extensive barracks at that place. The Federal forces had now, for some days, been subsisting chiefly on provisions which they had captured.

On the 27th, Gen. Halleck sent the following despatch to Washington:

HEADQUARTERS, ST. LOUIS, *February* 27.

Maj.-Gen. McClellan:

Gen. Curtis has taken possession of Fayetteville, Arkansas, capturing a large number of prisoners, stores, baggage, &c.

The enemy burnt a part of the town before they left. They have crossed the Boston Mountains in great confusion. We are now in possession of all their strongholds.

Forty-two officers and men of the Fifth Missouri cavalry were poisoned at Mud Town by eating poisoned food which the rebels left behind them. The gallant Capt. Dolfort died, and Lieut. Col. Von Dutch and Capt. Lehman have suffered much, but are recovering. The anger of our soldiers is very great, but they have been restrained from retaliating upon the prisoners of war. H. W. HALLECK, Major-General.

Gen. Price thus reported his retreat from Missouri, under date of Feb. 25:

"About the latter part of January my scouts reported that the enemy were concentrating in force at Rolla, and shortly thereafter they occupied Lebanon. Believing that this movement could be for no other purpose than to attack me, and knowing that my command was inadequate for such successful resistance as the interests of my army and the cause demanded, I appealed to the commanders of the Confederate troops in Arkansas to come to my assistance. This, from correspondence, I was led confidently to expect, and relying upon it, I held my position to the last moment, and, as the sequel proved, almost too long; for on Wednesday, February 12, my pickets were driven in, and reported the enemy advancing upon me in force. No resource was now left me except retreat, without hazarding all with greatly unequal numbers upon the result of one engagement. This I deemed it unwise to do. I commenced retreating at once. I reached Cassville with loss unworthy of mention in any respect. Here the enemy in my rear commenced a series of attacks running through four days. Retreating and fighting all the way to the Cross Hollows in this State, I am rejoiced to say my command, under the most exhausting fatigue, all the time with but little rest for either man or horse, and no sleep, sustained themselves, and came through, repulsing the enemy upon every occasion with great determination and gallantry. My loss does not exceed four to six killed and some fifteen to eighteen wounded."

On the 1st of March, Gen. Curtis issued the following address to the people of the Southwest:

HEADQUARTERS ARMY OF THE SOUTHWEST,
CAMP HALLECK, ARK., *March* 1, 1862.

I have received a private communication from an intelligent writer, a citizen of Arkansas, who says: "We, as citizens, have left our homes and firesides for the purpose, as we supposed, of having to defend ourselves against a brutal soldiery that would lay waste our humble homes, and outrage the chastity of our wives and daughters, and place our own lives in jeopardy. We have organized what is called Home Guard Companies, partly of Union men and partly of Southern men, all of whom are anxious to return to their homes. We are happy to find that you and your men are not composed of that class of persons commonly called jayhawkers, who do not regard the rights of citizens and property, but confine the war to its legitimate object."

The falsehoods circulated concerning us have driven thousands from their homes, and I take the liberty of responding publicly to the sentiments expressed by the writer, because these falsehoods have involved the whole community in the troubles which he seeks to mitigate.

The only legitimate object of the war is peace, and the writer only does me justice when he says I adhere to this legitimate object. Peaceable citizens shall be protected as far as possible. I act under strict orders of Maj.-Gen. Halleck. The flight of our foes from their camps, and the imitation of their conduct by the citizens, in fleeing from their homes, leaving their effects abandoned as it were for the victors, have much embarrassed me in my efforts to preserve discipline in my command, as these circumstances offered extraordinary temptations.

The burning of farms and fields of grain in Missouri, and extensive barracks and valuable mills in Arkansas by the enemy, has induced some resentments on the part of my troops, which I have severely punished. Necessary supplies for my command could not keep up with my rapid movements, and peaceable citizens not being at home to sell them to my quartermasters, I am compelled to take them without purchase, making settlement difficult and doubtful; occasioning irregularities which I have always labored to counteract. If peaceably disposed citizens will stay at home, or return home, and check the clandestine, stealthy warfare that is carried on under the cover and cloak of peaceable citizens, much of the havoc of war will be avoided, and many poor families can be protected from distress and misery. I have followed the war-path through the entire State of Missouri, have seen the havoc and devastation surrounding it, and I deplore the prospect of these disasters in the virgin soil of Arkansas.

Armed men, in the garb of citizens, are concealed by citizens, and the unfortunate condition of Missouri will be transferred to Arkansas, if you allow this complicity of yourselves in the struggle. If you do not discriminate by requiring soldiers to wear some distinctive badge, you must not complain if we cannot discriminate.

There is no honor, no glory, no good that can be gained by taking up arms in this way, to defend your homes, for we do not wish to molest them if you are peaceably disposed. We only wish to put down rebellion by making war against those in arms, their aiders and abettors. We come to vindicate the Constitution, to preserve and perpetuate civil and religious liberty, under a flag that was embalmed in the blood of our Revolutionary fathers. Under that flag we have lived in peace and prosperity until the flag of rebellion involved us in the horrors of civil war.

We have restored the Stars and Stripes to northwestern Arkansas, where I am glad to find many who rejoice to see the emblem of their former glory, and hope for a restoration of the peace and happiness they have enjoyed under its folds. A surrender to such a flag is only a return to your natural allegiance, and is more honorable than to persist in a rebellion that surrendered to the national power at Forts Henry and Donelson, at Nashville and at Roanoke, and throughout the most powerful Southern States. Why then shall the West be devastated to prolong a struggle which the States of Maryland, Virginia, Kentucky, North Carolina, and Tennessee cannot successfully maintain?

Disband your companies; surrender your arms; for in all instances where men in arms have voluntarily surrendered and taken the oath of allegiance to our common country, they have been discharged. No prisoners have, to my knowledge, been shot or hung, or cruelly treated by us.

I know of no instance where my troops have treated females with violence, and I have not heard of a complaint of any kind. I enjoin on the troops kindness, protection, and support for women and children. I shall, to the best of my ability, maintain our country's flag in Arkansas, and continue to make relentless war on its foes, but shall rejoice to see the restoration of peace in all the States and Territories of our country —that peace which we formerly enjoyed and earnestly desire; and I implore for each and all of us that ultimate, eternal peace "which the world cannot give or take away." I have the honor to be,

Very respectfully, your obedient servant,

SAMUEL R. CURTIS,

Brig.-Gen. Commanding Army of the Southwest.

On reaching Arkansas the forces of Gen. Price were rapidly reënforced by regiments which had been stationed in Arkansas and the Indian Territory. Knowing this fact, Gen. Curtis expected an attack would soon be made upon him. He therefore selected Sugar Creek, as the strongest of several strong places taken from the enemy, to make a stand against any and all odds. The position of Gen. Curtis's force on the 6th of March was as follows: The first and second divisions, under Gens. Sigel and Asboth, were four miles southwest of Bentonville under general orders to move round to Sugar Creek about fourteen miles east. The third division, under Col. Jeff. C. Davis, had moved to take position at Sugar Creek, under orders to make some preparatory arrangements and examinations for a stand against the enemy. The fourth division was at Cross Hollows under command of Col. E. A. Carr, about twelve miles from Sugar Creek on the main telegraph road from Springfield to Fayetteville. The number of his force is stated by Gen. Curtis to have been not more than 10,500 cavalry and infantry with forty-nine pieces of artillery. The following were the forces engaged in the battle of Pea Ridge: 1st division, under command of Col. Osterhaus,—36th Illinois, 12th Missouri, 17th Missouri, battalion of 3d, two battalions of Benton Hussars cavalry, one battalion 39th Illinois cavalry, batteries A and B, twelve guns. A brigade, consisting of the 25th and 44th Illinois, was commanded by Col. Coler. Another brigade was commanded by Col. Greusel.

The second division, commanded by Brig.-Gen. Asboth, consisted of the 2d Missouri, Col. Schæfer; 2d Ohio battery, six guns, Lieut. Chapman; 15th Missouri, Col. Joliet; 6th Missouri cavalry, Col. Wright; light battery of six guns, Capt. Elbert; battalion 4th Missouri cavalry, Maj. Messaur. These two divisions were commanded by Gen. Sigel.

The third division, commanded by Brig.-Gen. Jeff. C. Davis, consisted of 2 brigades: the 1st, commanded by Col. Barton, was composed of the 8th, 18th and 22d Indiana, and an Indiana battery of six guns. The 2d brigade, commanded by Col. White, was composed of the 37th Illinois, 9th Missouri, 1st Missouri cavalry, and a battery of four guns.

The fourth division, commanded by Col. Carr, consisted of 2 brigades; the 1st, commanded by Col. Dodge, was composed of the 4th Iowa, 35th

Illinois, and an Iowa battery. The 2d brigade, commanded by Col. Vandever, consisted of the 9th Iowa, 25th Missouri, 3d Illinois cavalry, and a battery. There were also two battalions of the Iowa 3d cavalry and a mountain howitzer battery of four guns. A considerable number of sick soldiers belonging to many of these regiments had been left at Rolla and Lebanon.

On the 5th of March, a cold, blustering day, snow having fallen so as to cover the ground, as Gen. Curtis was engaged in writing, not apprehending an immediate attack, he was informed by scouts and fugitive citizens that the enemy were rapidly approaching to give battle. His cavalry would be at Elm Springs, twelve miles distant, that night, and his infantry had then passed Fayetteville. Couriers were immediately sent to Gen. Sigel and Col. Carr to move with their divisions to Sugar Creek.

The Confederate forces were under the command of Gen. Van Dorn, who had arrived at their camp on the 2d of March. They were stated to be composed of between twenty-five and thirty thousand men, as follows: Missouri troops under Brig.-Gen. Price; Arkansas, Louisiana, and Texan troops under Brig.-Gen. McCulloch; Choctaw, Cherokee, and Chickasaw Indians under Brig.-Gen. Pike.

Gen. Sigel, upon receiving the orders of Gen. Curtis to march to Sugar Creek, and becoming aware of the dangerous position of his command, immediately ordered Col. Schæfer to break up his camp, and send the cavalry company to Osage Springs to cover his right flank and to march with his regiment to Bentonville. All the other troops he ordered to be prepared to march at two o'clock on the next morning. Commencing his march in the morning, he reached Bentonville, and, retaining a small force to set as a rear guard, he sent his train forward. At ten o'clock it was reported that large masses of troops, consisting of infantry and cavalry, were moving from all sides toward the front and both flanks of the rear guard at Bentonville. By a mistake a part of this force designed to act as rear guard had gone forward, leaving about six hundred men with five pieces of the light battery. These troops were ordered by Gen. Sigel to march in the following order: two companies of the 12th Missouri regiment at the head of the column deployed on the right and left as skirmishers, followed by the light battery; one company of the same regiment on the right and one on the left of the pieces, marching by the flank, and prepared to fire by ranks to the right and left, the remainder of the regiment being behind the pieces; two companies of cavalry to support the infantry on the right and left, and the rest of the cavalry with one piece of artillery following in the rear. Thus the troops advanced slowly in this formation, modified from time to time according to circumstances, fighting and repelling the enemy in front, on the flanks, and rear, whenever he stood or attacked, for five hours and a half, when reenforcements from Gen. Curtis arrived. What made this march a more difficult achievement, was the condition of the roads, which were in many places very narrow and badly cut up. This movement brought Gen. Sigel's division to the west end of Pea Ridge, where he formed a junction with Gen. Davis and Col. Carr.

On this day Gen. Curtis had been engaged in diligently preparing earthwork defences and cutting timber to check the progress of the enemy along the Fayetteville road, where they were confidently expected by him. But during the day and the ensuing night Gen. Van Dorn moved his entire army around the west side of Gen. Curtis's army, so that Gen. Price occupied the Fayetteville road north of Gen. Curtis's camp, while Gens. McCulloch and McIntosh lay north of Gen. Sigel. Thus the Confederate forces fronted south, and the division under Gen. Price formed their left wing. The distance apart of the main bodies of the two wings of each army was nearly three miles, thus forming in fact four distinct armies. Gens. Van Dorn and Price were opposed to Gen. Curtis, who had with him Gen. Davis and Cols. Carr and Asboth, leaving one division to Gen. Sigel opposed to Gens. McCulloch and McIntosh. Gen. Curtis was thus compelled to make a change of front, and formed it almost two miles further north and resting on the brow of a range of hills fronting north, called Pea Ridge. In this position the enemy occupied the line of retreat for Gen. Curtis, if defeated. The battle commenced on the 7th on the right of Gen. Curtis's column, and raged furiously during the entire day. The brunt of it was borne by Col. Carr's division. The Confederate forces, owing to their superior numbers, the numerous and deep ravines and the thick brush which covered the hills, succeeded in driving the Union right from the ground occupied in the morning, with a severe loss on both sides. They encamped on the battle ground during the night, and the right wing of Gen. Curtis fell back nearly a mile. The field occupied by this portion of both armies during the day did not exceed three fourths of a mile in diameter.

On the left wing Gen. McCulloch commenced in the morning by moving his force to the south and east, evidently intending to form a junction with Gens. Van Dorn and Price. Gen. Sigel, perceiving this movement and the effect it would have toward surrounding the Federal force, sent forward three pieces of light artillery, with a supporting force of cavalry, to take a commanding position and delay the movement of the enemy until the infantry could be brought into proper position for an attack. Hardly had the artillery obtained their position and opened fire, when an overwhelming force of the enemy's cavalry came down upon them, scattering the cavalry and capturing the artillery. This terrible onslaught of the enemy allowed their infantry to reach unmolested the cover of a dense wood. On the west of this wood was a large open field. Here and in the surrounding wood a protracted struggle ensued between Gen. McCulloch and the forces of Col. Osterhaus. But the arrival of Gen. Davis's force, as a reënforcement, so strengthened Gen. Sigel that the enemy were finally routed and driven in all directions. At the same time Gens. McCulloch and McIntosh and a number of the Confederate officers were killed.

Thus the right wing of Gen. Curtis was defeated, and his left was victorious. The discipline of the right wing, however, was such as to keep the troops completely together, while the right wing of the enemy, which was defeated, was greatly disorganized in consequence of their loss of officers and lack of discipline. During the night all the Confederate forces formed a junction on the ground held by their left wing, which was a strong position, and they felt confident of a complete victory on the next day. On the Federal side the prospect was gloomy. The night was too cold to sleep without fires, and their position and nearness to the enemy would not allow fires along the advance lines. The men were exhausted by two days' fighting and the loss of sleep. The enemy's forces, in far superior numbers, held the only road for their retreat, and nearly a thousand of their companions were dead or wounded. No alternative was presented to them but to conquer or be destroyed.

With the rising sun the battle commenced. Col. Carr's division had been reënforced by a large part of that of Gen. Davis, thus enabling the right barely to hold its position. Gen. Sigel began to form his line of battle by changing his front so as to face the right flank of the enemy's position. For this purpose he first ordered the 25th Illinois, Col. Coler, to take a position along a fence in open view of the enemy's batteries, which at once opened fire upon the regiment. He next ordered a battery of six guns, partly rifled twelve-pounders, into a line one hundred paces in the rear of the 25th infantry, on a rise of ground. The 15th Missouri then formed into a line with the 25th Illinois on their left, and another battery of guns was similarly disposed a short distance behind them. Thus more infantry with batteries in their rear was placed until about thirty pieces of artillery, each about fifteen or twenty paces from the other, were in continuous line, the infantry in front lying down. Each piece opened fire as it came in position, and the fire was so directed as to silence battery after battery of the enemy.

For two hours the Confederate forces stood unshaken before that fire, with their crowded ranks decimated and their horses shot at their guns. One by one their pieces ceased to reply. Then onward crept the infantry and onward came the guns of Gen. Sigel. The range became shorter and shorter. No charge of the enemy could face those batteries or venture on that compact line of bayonets. They turned and fled. Again the Union line was advanced with a partial change of front, when an order to charge the enemy in the woods was given. Then the infantry rising up pressed forward into the dense brush, where they were met by a terrible volley, which was fiercely returned; volley followed volley, still the line pushed forward until more open ground was obtained, when the Confederate force broke in confusion. As Gen. Sigel advanced, Gen. Curtis also ordered the centre and right wing forward. The right wing turned the left of the enemy and cross-fired into his centre. This placed him in the arc of a circle. The charge was then ordered throughout the whole line, which utterly routed their forces as above stated, and compelled them to retire in complete confusion, but rather safely through the deep and almost impassable defiles of Cross Timbers. Gen. Sigel followed toward Keetsville, and the cavalry continued the pursuit still further. The Union loss in this battle was 212 killed, 926 wounded, and 124 missing. The Confederate killed and wounded was larger in numbers, with a loss of nearly 1000 prisoners. Among their killed were Gens. McCulloch and McIntosh.

On the 9th Gen. Van Dorn, under a flag of truce, requested permission to bury his dead, which was readily granted. In the reply to this request Gen. Curtis said: "The General regrets that we find on the battle-field, contrary to civilized warfare, many of the Federal dead, who were tomahawked, scalped, and their bodies shamefully mangled, and expresses the hope that this important struggle may not degenerate to a savage warfare."

To this statement, Gen. Van Dorn replied: "He hopes you have been misinformed with regard to this matter, the Indians who formed part of his forces having for many years been regarded as civilized people. He will, however, most cordially unite with you in repressing the horrors of this unnatural war; and that you may coöperate with him to this end more effectually, he desires me to inform you that many of our men who surrendered themselves prisoners of war, were reported to him as having been murdered in cold blood by their captors, who were alleged to be Germans. The general commanding feels sure that you will do your part, as he will, in preventing such atrocities in future, and that the perpetrators of them will be brought to justice, whether German or Choctaw."

Gen. Curtis in answer further said: "I may say, the Germans charge the same against your soldiers. I enclose a copy of a letter from Gen. Sigel, addressed to me before the receipt of yours, in which the subject is referred to. As 'dead men tell no tales,' it is not easy to see how these charges may be proven, and the General hopes they are mere 'camp stories,' having little or no foundation. The Germans in the army have taken and turned over many prisoners, and the General has not before heard murder charged against them; on the contrary, they have seemed peculiarly anxious to exhibit the number of their captured as evidence of their valor. Any act of cruelty to prisoners, or those offering to deliver themselves as such, on the part of the soldiers of this army, coming to the knowledge of the General commanding, will be punished with the extreme penalty of the law."

The following is Gen. Halleck's despatch to Washington, announcing this battle:

ST. LOUIS, March 10, 1862.

To Maj.-Gen. McClellan:

The army of the Southwest, under Gen. Curtis, after three days' hard fighting near Sugar Creek, Arkansas, has gained a most glorious victory over the combined forces of Van Dorn, McCulloch, Price, and McIntosh. Our killed and wounded are estimated at one thousand. That of the enemy still larger. Guns, flags, provisions, &c., captured in large quantities. Our cavalry is in pursuit of the flying enemy.

H. W. HALLECK, Major-General.

The Confederate force retired south of the Boston Mountains unpursued by Gen. Curtis, to obtain reënforcements and to recover from their loss. Meantime reënforcements were sent to Gen. Curtis from Kansas and Missouri. He fell back to Keetsville, and remained through the month. On the 5th of April, it being supposed that Gen. Price was moving on Springfield, Missouri, Gen. Curtis began a march in that direction. On that day he advanced eighteen miles and on the next twenty, to the junction of Flat Rock with James river. Failing in an attempt to cross the James, the force moved to Galena, where a crossing was effected in a rain storm. On the next day, the 9th, Bear Creek, thirteen miles, was reached, and on the 10th Forsyth, eighteen miles, where the army was concentrated. The high water of the river delayed active operations. Gen. Price, with a body of mounted men, was encamped about five miles south and on the other side of the river. On the 16th of April an expedition was sent out under Col. McCrellis to destroy some saltpetre works located eight miles below the Little North Fork, south side of White river. It was entirely successful. About ten thousand pounds nearly prepared for transportation were destroyed. The army next moved to West Plains, eighty-seven miles, thence to Salem, Arkansas, which is southeast of Forsyth, Mo., and distant one hundred and seventeen miles. Thence it advanced to Batesville, crossed the White river, and took the route to Little Rock, the capital of the State. It advanced to Searcy, fifty miles from Little Rock, where an order was received from Gen. Halleck to send ten regiments by a forced march to Cape Girardeau and thence to Corinth. The army then fell back to Batesville, which is the capital of Independence county and the most important town in the northeastern part of the State. It is situated on the White river about four hundred miles from its mouth. The river is navigable to this point for small steamers. Such was the scarcity of supplies that the army suffered severely. An expedition was fitted out in June from Memphis to descend the Mississippi to the mouth of Arkansas and thence up the White river to Batesville. (See page 168.) It was unsuccessful. Supplies were subsequently sent by land from Missouri, which reached Gen. Curtis about the 1st of July. His position during this period was critical, and excited much apprehension, as he was known to be nearly destitute of provisions, far distant from the sources of supply, and surrounded in the midst of a wilderness by foes. From Batesville he now advanced to Jacksonport at the confluence of the White and Black rivers, thence passing through Augusta and Clarendon he reached Helena on the Mississippi river, one hundred and seventy-five miles from Batesville.

It was reported soon after that Confederate troops under Gen. Price were crossing the Mississippi at a point between Napoleon and Vicksburg, and Gen. Curtis started with a body of troops on transports to make an exploration. The steam ferry boat at Napoleon, upon the approach of Gen. Curtis, was withdrawn up the Arkansas river, whither he followed and captured it with fifteen other ferry and flat boats. A large number of boats were destroyed on the Arkansas by this expedition, which soon after returned to Helena. Gen. Curtis was then absent until the close of September, when he was appointed to command the department of Missouri, containing the States of Missouri and Arkansas and the adjacent Indian Territory, with his headquarters at St. Louis. Helena continued to be occupied by the Federal troops, but active military operations were suspended. This closed the campaign of Gen. Curtis.

After the departure of Gen. Curtis from Helena on the 15th of November, an expedition under Gen. Alvin P. Hovey, consisting of eight thousand infantry and cavalry, started for the White river; but in consequence of new bars which had formed, and the low stage of the water, it entirely failed of the object intended, and returned. The command of the post was then taken by Gen. Steele, who had arrived with a division of troops. Subsequently Gen. Hovey was sent upon an expedition from Helena into Mississippi to coöperate with Gen. Grant on his advance into that State. The particulars of this expedition are stated in connection with the campaign of Gen. Grant.

The subsequent military operations in Arkansas exerted no special influence on the conduct of the war. They may be briefly stated in this place. The Confederate forces in the State, in October, were estimated to consist of five thousand men under Gen. Hindman, posted five miles north of Little Rock; five thousand men under Gen. Roan, posted fifty miles southeast of Little Rock at White Sulphur Springs, near Pine Bluff on the Arkansas river; at Cross Hollows in the northwestern part of the State, between four and five thousand men, chiefly conscripts under Gen. Rains; Gen. Holmes, in chief command, was at Little Rock with two thousand men; Gen. McBride was at Bates-

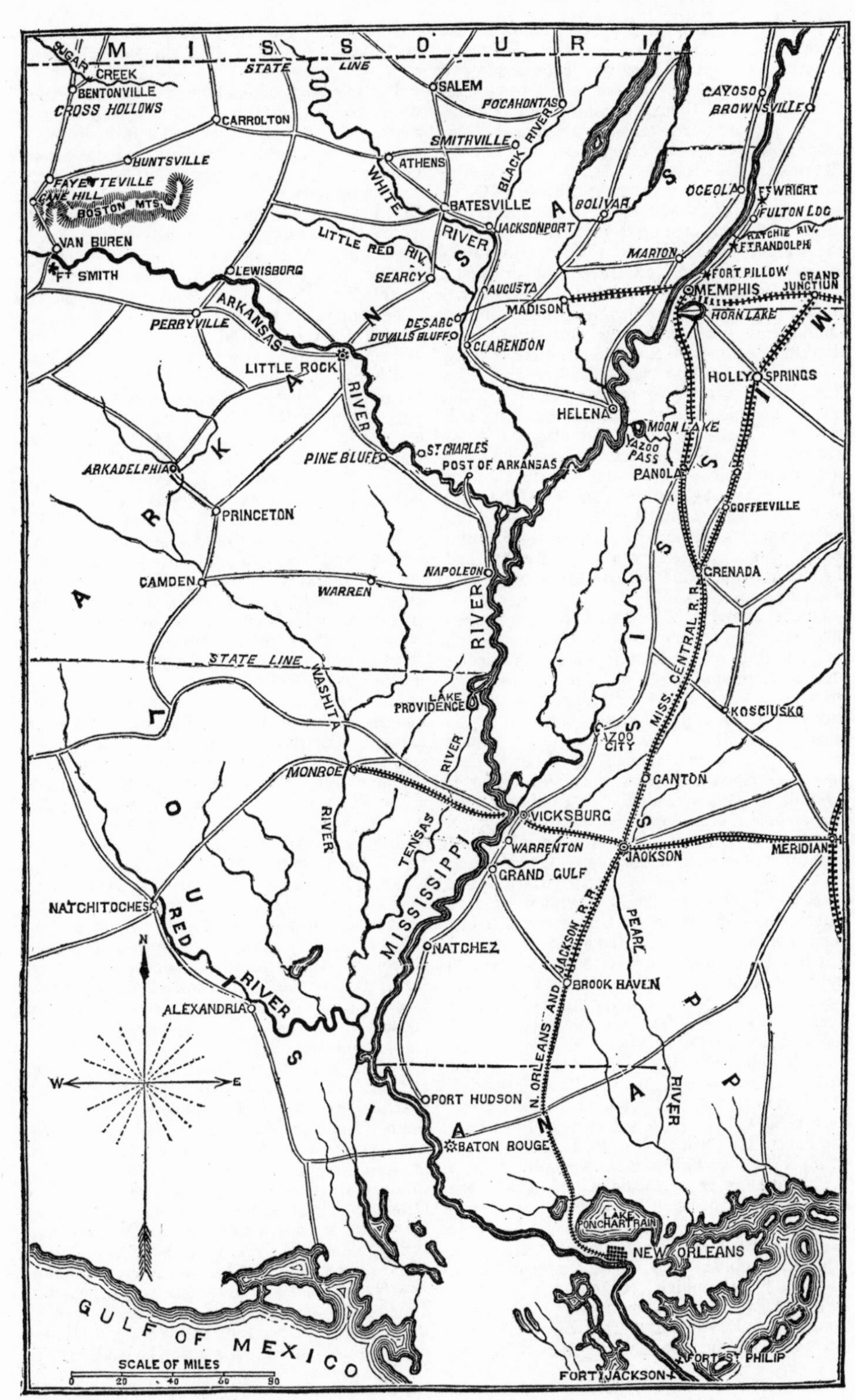
M I S S O U R I
STATE LINE
SUGAR CREEK
BENTONVILLE
CROSS HOLLOWS
CARROLTON
SALEM
POCAHONTAS
CAYOSO
BROWNSVILLE
SMITHVILLE
BLACK RIVER
HUNTSVILLE
ATHENS
WHITE RIVER
FAYETTEVILLE
CANE HILL
BOSTON MTS.
BATESVILLE
BOLIVAR
OCEOLA
FT. WRIGHT
FULTON LDG
JACKSONPORT
RAYCHIE RIV.
FT. RANDOLPH
LITTLE RED RIV.
VAN BUREN
FT SMITH
LEWISBURG
SEARCY
MARION
FORT PILLOW
MEMPHIS
GRAND JUNCTION
AUGUSTA
MADISON
HORN LAKE
ARKANSAS
PERRYVILLE
DESARC
DUVALLS BLUFF
CLARENDON
LITTLE ROCK
RIVER
HOLLY SPRINGS
HELENA
MOON LAKE
YAZOO PASS
ST. CHARLES
PINE BLUFF
POST OF ARKANSAS
PANOLA
ARKADELPHIA
PRINCETON
COFFEEVILLE
A R K A N S A S
NAPOLEON
CAMDEN
WARREN
GRENADA
STATE LINE
WASHITA
MISS. CENTRAL R.R.
LAKE PROVIDENCE
KOSCIUSKO
YAZOO CITY
MONROE
RIVER
CANTON
VICKSBURG
TENSAS
WARRENTON
JACKSON
MERIDIAN
GRAND GULF
MISSISSIPPI
NATCHITOCHES
RED RIVER
PEARL
NATCHEZ
N. ORLEANS AND JACKSON R.R.
BROOK HAVEN
ALEXANDRIA
N
W
E
PORT HUDSON
BATON ROUGE
LOUISIANA
MISSISSIPPI
LAKE PONCHARTRAIN
NEW ORLEANS
GULF OF MEXICO
SCALE OF MILES
0 20 40 60 80
FORT JACKSON
FORT ST. PHILIP

ville with two thousand more. Small forces were also at Arkansas, Crystal Hill, and Arkadelphia. The latter post had been made the seat of government. These forces were estimated at twenty thousand men with a deficient outfit. In the northwestern part of Arkansas, near Cross Hollows, twelve miles south of Fayetteville, Gen. Herron had a severe conflict with a Confederate force near the end of October. Again on the 28th of November Gen. Blunt made an attack on Gen. Marmaduke with about eight thousand men, at Cane Hill, forty-five miles north of Van Buren, which caused the Confederate force to retreat to Van Buren. Again, on the 7th of December, the combined Confederate forces under the command of Gen. Hindman, estimated at fifteen thousand men, made an attempt to cut off reënforcements for Gen. Blunt, ten miles south of Fayetteville. The Confederate forces advanced on the flank of Gen. Blunt's position, and attacked Gen. Herron with the reënforcements, who held them in check until they were attacked in the rear by Gen. Blunt at Crawford's Prairie. The fight continued obstinate until dark, when the Confederate forces retreated across Boston Mountains. The loss was severe on both sides, and the advance of the Confederate troops into Missouri was checked.

The campaign in the West was now pushed through. The evacuation of Columbus, and the flanking of other Confederate positions on the Mississippi river by the force on the advance up the Tennessee river, led to the fitting out of an expedition to move down the Mississippi. On the 4th of March an armed reconnoissance, commanded by Flag Officer Foote and General Cullum, was made as far as Columbus. This consisted of six gunboats, four mortar boats, and three transports having on board two regiments and two battalions of infantry under Gen. Sherman. On arriving at Columbus, it was found to have been evacuated and subsequently occupied by two hundred and fifty of the 2d Illinois on a scouting expedition. The Confederate troops had chiefly retired down the river to Island No. 10 and New Madrid. The evacuation was a consequence of the position being flanked on both sides of the river. The distances to various points down the river are as follows: Cairo to Columbus, 20 miles; Hickman, 37; Island No. 10, 45; New Madrid, 55; Point Pleasant, 87; Plumb Point, 154; Island No. 33, 164; Fort Wright, 167; Fulton Landing, 168; Hatche River, 170; Island No. 34, 170; Fort Randolph, 175; Fort Pillow, 238; Memphis, 242;

This force returned to Cairo, and on the 14th a formidable expedition left to move down the river. The following vessels formed the fleet: flag ship Benton, Lieut. Phelps acting flag captain; gunboats Cincinnati, Commander R. N. Stembel; Carondelet, Commander Walke; Mound City, Commander Kelly; Louisville, Commander Dove; Pittsburgh, Lieut. Thompson commanding; St. Louis, Lieut. Paulding commanding; Conestoga, Lieut. Blodgett commanding—the only boat in the fleet not iron-clad.

The mortar boats assigned to the expedition were designated numerically. Each had a mortar of 13-inch calibre and discharging a round shell weighing two hundred and fifteen pounds without its contents. The "sailing" or "running" crews of these mortar boats consisted of one captain and two men. The force to fire the mortars in action was one captain to each brace of mortars, and one lieutenant and twelve men to each boat. The Nos. of the vessels were, 5, 7, 11, 19, 22, 23, 27, 29, 30, 38, under command in chief of Capt. H. E. Maynadier, U. S. Army. The steamers Hammit and Wilson, lashed together, towed four; the Pike and Wisconsin four others; Lake Erie, No. 2, towed two others. Then followed a steamer with a barge laden with coal in tow, after which came the two ordnance steamers, and two transports with the 27th Illinois, Col. Buford, and 15th Wisconsin, Col. Hey, infantry—the latter regiment being composed exclusively of Norwegians—and also a battery of the 2d Illinois artillery. With the gunboats on the right, followed by the mortar fleet, ordnance boats, and transports with troops, the gunboat Conestoga brought up the rear, protecting the transports, while eight or ten little screw propellers, used for conveying orders and despatches from the flag ship to the fleet, were busily darting in all directions.

The expedition reached Columbus at 1 P. M., and at 3 o'clock left for Hickman, where it arrived between five and six o'clock. A small force of Confederate cavalry left upon its approach. The town was partly deserted; a few Union flags, however, were waved. The next morning it proceeded down the river to within half a mile of the Missouri point above Island No. 10, which by an air line was two and a half miles distant, while by the river, owing to the bend, it was four miles distant. In this position the flagship opened fire upon a Confederate battery discovered on the Kentucky shore, but, owing to the distance, without effect. Two of the mortar boats then, having got into position, opened upon and soon silenced it. A large Confederate force appeared to be encamped on that side.

Island No. 10 is situated in the corner of that bend of the Mississippi river which touches the border of Tennessee, a few miles further up the river than New Madrid, although nearly southwest of that point. It is situated about two hundred and forty miles from St. Louis, and nine hundred and fifty from New Orleans. The average depth of the water at this point is from ninety to one hundred and twenty feet, and the breadth of the stream from mainland to mainland about nine hundred yards. The current runs by the island at a moderately fast rate, and with the power of three rivers—Mississippi, Missouri, and Ohio—combined. The island is near the southern, or what might be termed the eastern bank of the river, but at this point the stream varies from its southern course and turns abruptly to the northwest, leaving this island in the southern angle of the bend. It is about forty-five miles, by the course of the river, south of Columbus, and about twenty-six miles from Hickman. It is near Obionville, which is in Obion county, in the northwest extremity of Tennessee, where it borders on Kentucky and Missouri. The Mississippi river passes to the north and to the south of Obionville, leaving a land distance between the two waters very inconsiderable, and easily walked across in less than an hour, although the voyage by water between the same points, owing to the bends in the river, is about twenty miles. The surface of the surrounding country is nearly level. Obionville is connected by a turnpike road with Columbus, in Kentucky, via Hickman, and with Troy, the capital of the county.

The fortifications on the island and mainland adjacent consisted of eleven earthworks, with seventy heavy cannon, varying in caliber from thirty-two to one hundred pounders, rifled. The bombardment commenced on the 16th of March, and continued with more or less vigor until the 7th of April. A different plan, however, was arranged for the capture of the island. This consisted in cutting a canal across a portion of the narrow and low peninsula, by which the transports could pass below the island, and a part of the troops with Gen. Pope at New Madrid be taken across the river, and thus completely invest the island.

On the 21st of February, by orders of Gen. Halleck, Gen. Pope proceeded to Commerce in Missouri above Cairo, and was followed by a force numbering in the aggregate about forty thousand men. With this army Gen. Pope proceeded southwardly in the early part of the last week in February, destined for New Madrid. In a direct line the distance from Commerce to New Madrid is about fifty miles, but by the road it is between sixty and seventy-five miles. On the 3d of March he arrived with his forces before New Madrid, and found the place occupied by five regiments of infantry and several companies of artillery. The defensive works consisted of one bastioned earthwork, mounting fourteen heavy guns, about half a mile below the town, and another irregular work at the upper end of the town, mounting seven pieces of heavy artillery, together with lines of intrenchment between them; six gunboats, carrying from four to eight heavy guns each, were anchored along the shore between the upper and lower redoubts. The country being perfectly level and the river so high that the guns of the boats looked directly over the banks, Gen. Pope found the approaches to the town commanded for miles by guns of heavy caliber.

His first step was to occupy Point Pleasant, twelve miles below, in such a manner that his force could not be driven out by the Confederate gunboats, and thus blockade the river from below. He next procured siege guns from Cairo, which arrived on the 12th of March, and were placed in battery during the night within eight hundred yards of the enemy's main work, so as to command that and the river above it. The battery consisted of two small redoubts connected by a curtain, and mounting four heavy guns, with rifle pits in front and on the flanks for two regiments of infantry. As soon as day dawned on the 13th, these batteries opened fire, and were replied to by the whole of the enemy's heavy artillery on land and water. In a few hours several of the gunboats were disabled, and three of the heavy guns dismounted in the enemy's main work. The cannonading continued all day without producing any impression on the position of Gen. Pope, other than the disabling of one gun by a round shot. The effect of the contest during the day convinced the Confederate commander that he could not hold the town, although he had previously reënforcements of men and guns from Island No. 10. Accordingly in the night, during a violent storm of rain, he evacuated the town by crossing over to the Kentucky shore. This evacuation was made with considerable precipitation. Almost everything was left behind. Even the pickets were abandoned. "Thirty-three pieces of artillery, magazines full of fixed ammunition, several thousand stand of small arms, hundreds of boxes of musket cartridges, tents for an army of ten thousand men, horses, mules, wagons, &c., were among the spoils."

The Confederate fleet was commanded by Com. Hollins, and their land force by Gens. McCown, Stewart, and Gantt. The Union loss was fifty-one killed and wounded; the Confederate loss was estimated by Gen. Pope to be larger. A number of their dead were left unburied. By the possession of these works Gen. Pope commanded the river, so as to cut off all communication with Island No. 10 from below. It was on the day after this evacuation that the fleet left Cairo.

In order to cut off entirely the retreat of the Confederate force from Island No. 10, it was necessary that a portion of Gen. Pope's army should be taken across the Mississippi to the Tennessee shore. To bring down transports a channel was made, twelve miles long, six of which were through heavy timber. The trees standing in water, had to be cut off four feet below its surface. While this work was pushed forward the bombardment of the island was continued. On the night of the 1st of April, under the cover of darkness and storm, a boat expedition from the fleet, with a small force under the command of Col. Roberts of the 42d Illinois, landed at the upper or No. 1 Fort on the Kentucky shore and spiked the six guns mounted, and retired without injury. The pickets of the enemy fired and fled, and the troops in the vicinity also retreated. As the work on the canal approached

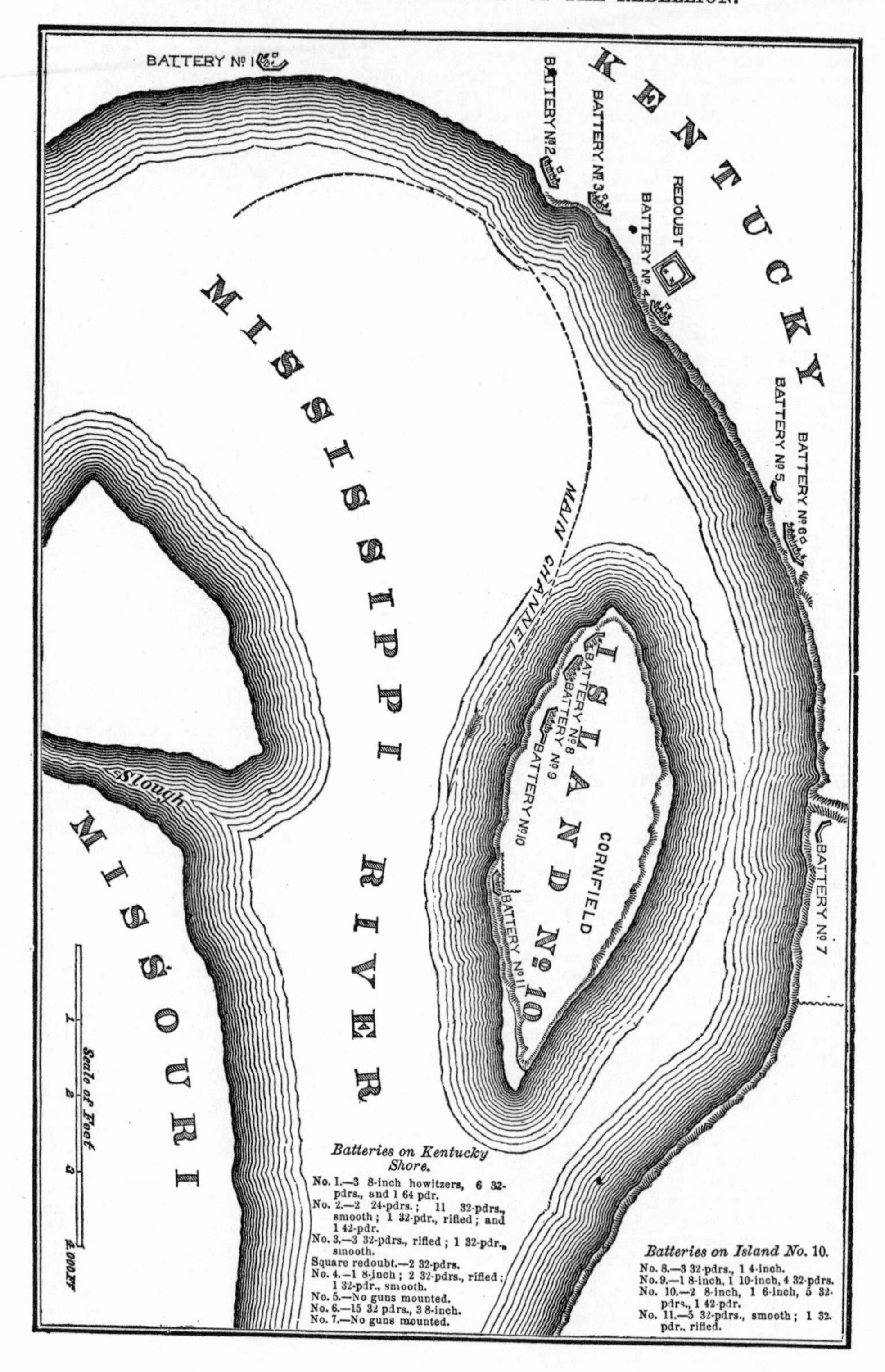
KENTUCKY
BATTERY No 1
BATTERY No 2
BATTERY No 3
REDOUBT
BATTERY No 4
BATTERY No 5
BATTERY No 6
BATTERY No 7
MISSISSIPPI RIVER
MAIN CHANNEL
ISLAND No 10
BATTERY No 8
BATTERY No 9
BATTERY No 10
BATTERY No 11
CORNFIELD
Slough
MISSOURI
Scale of Feet
1
2
3
4.000FT
Batteries on Kentucky Shore.
No. 1.—3 8-inch howitzers, 6 32-pdrs., and 1 64 pdr.
No. 2.—2 24-pdrs.; 11 32-pdrs., smooth; 1 32-pdr., rifled; and 1 42-pdr.
No. 3.—3 32-pdrs., rifled; 1 32-pdr., smooth.
Square redoubt.—2 32-pdrs.
No. 4.—1 8-inch; 2 32-pdrs., rifled; 1 32-pdr., smooth.
No. 5.—No guns mounted.
No. 6.—15 32 pdrs., 3 8-inch.
No. 7.—No guns mounted.
Batteries on Island No. 10.
No. 8.—3 32-pdrs., 1 4-inch.
No. 9.—1 8-inch, 1 10-inch, 4 32-pdrs.
No. 10.—2 8-inch, 1 6-inch, 5 32-pdrs., 1 42-pdr.
No. 11.—5 32-pdrs., smooth; 1 32-pdr., rifled.

completion, it was evident that the assistance of the gunboats would also be required to make a successful landing of the troops across the river. The enemy, to oppose any attempt that might be made to cross the river, had planted field pieces along the left bank for the distance of several miles above and below New Madrid. Gunboats were also needed to protect the transports from any gunboat of the enemy that might appear during the passage across the river. For these reasons the gunboat Carondelet, Capt. Walke, undertook to run down past the batteries of the island on the night of the 4th of April. For this purpose her hull was protected in all weak places by additional covering, and a barge laden above with hay was taken in tow on her left side. Starting at ten o'clock on the night of the 4th, amid the darkness of an impending storm, she proceeded on in silence. Twice as she approached the batteries of the enemy the soot in the chimneys caught fire, and a flame five feet high leaped out from their tops, lighting brightly the upper deck of the vessel, and everything around. It was seen by the enemy, and the anxious listeners for the signal of her safety in the fleet above now heard the long roll beat in the camps on the island. At the same time five rockets were sent up from the mainland and the island, and were followed by a cannon shot from Fort No. 2. A full head of steam was now let on, to make the greatest possible speed; and while vivid flashes of lightning lit up the hurried preparations of the enemy, while peal after peal of thunder reverberated along the river, and the rain fell in torrents, the moment for coolness and heroism came. For thirty minutes the discharge of cannon and musket ball at the dark and silent object, revealed on the waters only by the lightning flash, was furious, but no injury was done. Then stopping her machinery, her officers fired the signal guns to inform their companions in the fleet that she was safe. On the night of the 6th, the gunboat Pittsburg, Lieut. Thompson, also passed the batteries. On the morning of the 7th the transports were brought into the river from the bayou where they had been kept concealed, and while the division of Col. Paine was embarking, the gunboats ran down the river and silenced the enemy's batteries at the place of landing. Then the passage of the wide and swift river commenced, and was completed at the hour of midnight.

As soon as the troops began to cross the river the enemy began to evacuate the island and his batteries along the Kentucky shore. The divisions were pushed forward as fast as they landed, that of Col. Paine leading. The Confederate force was driven before him, says Gen. Pope; and although it made several attempts to form in line of battle and make a stand, Col. Paine did not once deploy his columns. It was pushed all night vigorously until, at four o'clock A. M., it was driven back on the swamps and forced to surrender. "Three generals, seven colonels, seven regiments, several battalions of infantry, five companies of artillery, over one hundred heavy siege guns, twenty-four pieces of field artillery, an immense quantity of ammunition and supplies, several thousand stand of small arms, a great number of tents, horses, and wagons were taken." The force that surrendered was under the command of Gen. Mackall. Before abandoning Island No. 10, the Confederate officers sunk the gunboat Grampus and six transports. The force surrendered consisted of Tennessee, Arkansas, Mississippi, Alabama, and Louisiana regiments, and numbered about five thousand. At the island a large amount of commissary stores was found with the tents and baggage of the enemy. Besides there were eleven earthworks, with seventy heavy cannon varying in caliber from 32 to 100-pounders, rifled. The works, erected with the highest engineering skill, possessed great strength. There appeared to be no concert of action between the force on the island and that on the shore. Gen. Pope did not lose a man or meet with an accident in crossing the river or afterward. The canal was made on the suggestion of Gen. Schuyler Hamilton. A part of the distance the route was through a bayou. The cut made was about four miles, sufficient for steamboats of moderate size, and about one thousand trees, ranging from six inches to three feet in diameter, were sawed off about four feet under water by means of long saws worked by hand. When the canal was finished, the water came through with such a current that the boats had to be dropped by lines nearly the whole distance. The work was done by an engineer regiment, under the superintendence of Col. Bissell.

The position thus taken was regarded by the Confederate officers as one of the highest importance to the new line of defence proposed by them. Upon their ability to hold it depended the safety of Memphis, and of the entire Mississippi valley thereabout. This line was adopted by the Confederate commander, with his left resting on the Mississippi, his centre between Jackson, Tenn., and Corinth, Miss., and his right between Florence and Decatur.

On the 12th of April the gunboats under Com. Foote, with the mortar boats, followed by the transports, left New Madrid, and stood down the river. The order of a line of battle was observed. A part of Gen. Stanley's division, and those of Gens. Hamilton and Palmer, were on the transports. Their destination was Fort Pillow or Wright, which is situated on the first Chickasaw Bluffs, near Islands Nos. 33 and 34, and about seventy miles above Memphis. At Plum Point the Mississippi makes a sharp bend, running for some distance eastwardly, and at the first Chickasaw Bluffs turns off abruptly south-southwest, which course it continues below Island No. 34, where it again bends; the convex side of the curve being to the Tennessee shore. Here are the second Chickasaw Bluffs, surmounted by Fort Randolph, some twelve miles below Fort Pillow. The location of these fortifications was admirably adapted for defence, and in case of a determined stand it would have been very difficult to reduce them. Opposite Plum Point is the village of Osceola in Arkansas.

On the next day, at evening, the fleet arrived at Plum Point and anchored. A force of three Confederate gunboats were in sight most of the time during that day, but kept at a safe distance. The anchorage was about three and a half miles from the fort. Operations against the fort were commenced by moving the mortars to the Arkansas shore at Craighead Point, and opening upon the enemy's gunboats and batteries with shells. The distance of the contending forces across the point was three fourths of a mile, although by the river around the point it was three miles. In the afternoon of the 17th of April fire was opened from the mortars, and rapidly and accurately answered by the fort. This continued until midnight and then ceased; daily afterward it was repeated without any expectation of an immediate reduction of the fort. The high water of the river prevented coöperation of the land forces. On the 4th of May a battle occurred between the gunboats and a Confederate ram and gunboats, which has been thus related:

"The enemy appeared with four boats—three gunboats and a ram—the latter a powerful contrivance, combining immense weight and strength with high speed and admirable steering facilities. Her hull and boilers, as well as all the Confederate rams, were those of old New Orleans towboats. The upper works of these were cut away; their sides protected, in some instances with a layer of railroad iron, and in others only with bales of tightly compressed cotton, hooped and bound together, one to the other, with iron bands. Their bows were pointed and sharp, and apparently of solid iron.

"At their first appearance the gunboats manifested no disposition to come up the river, but sent the ram ahead to attack and destroy the Cincinnati, thinking then, doubtless, to run up and make an easy prey of the defenceless mortar boats. The commander of the Cincinnati perceived the movement and apprehended its intent. The ram was already halfway up to her before she was cut loose, and then the accumulated driftwood on her bows prevented her getting her head out into the stream. To back out would be to run directly upon the enemy while they were seeking to run into her, thus adding to the force of the blow with which they would strike her. In this dilemma she let fly her stern guns full into the face of the enemy, and at the same time attempted to crowd along up the shore, hoping, before moving far, to succeed in getting her head out. Her guns made not the slighest apparent impression upon the ram, which still held its course and was rapidly coming upon the entangled gunboat.

"Again the stern guns were let go full into the face of the enemy, but still her progress was not retarded in the slightest. A moment more and her tremendous weight came with terrible force upon the starboard stern quarter of the gunboat, but without inflicting any serious damage The force of the blow, however, threw the stern of the vessel in and enabled her to get headway from the shore. Then, in turning out, her broadside was discharged directly into the Confederate craft, which was backing off preparatory to renewing the assault.

"Again the gunboat prepares to open fire on her assailant, and the ram seeks an apportunity to renew the assault. The Cincinnati has worked herself away from the shore and is now more easily handled. Turning to and fro, she gives her antagonist broadside for broadside, with no apparent result. Still he comes on. As he nears his object, his steam apparatus is got ready, and his crew, armed with small arms, prepare to board the Federal craft. Commander Stembel, seeing these demonstrations, orders out carbines, boarding pikes, and cutlasses, and also puts his steam battery in readiness to give the enemy a warm reception. On they come, closer and closer, and strike! The boats collide with fearful violence, followed by the crashing of timbers, and the bending of iron, and the shouts of men, and the discharge of musketry, and, above all, another broadside directly into the enemy now immediately alongside. Amid this general uproar Commander Stembel rushes upon deck, and, seizing a pistol, with admirable aim discharged its contents into the head of the Confederate pilot, killing him instantly. The pilot's mate seized a gun in retaliation, and shot the gallant commander, just as he was turning to give his attention to some other duty, the ball entering high up on his shoulder behind, and, passing in at an upward direction through his neck, went out under his chin. He fell instantly, and was carried below.

"While this fierce engagement was in progress, the shots from the other vessels had exploded the boiler on one of the Confederate gunboats, and set fire to another which was burned to the water's edge.

"The Cincinnati, thus released from her antagonist, sought others of the foe. It was soon after this withdrawal that the Mallory, which is also fitted as a ram, though carrying a heavy armament, moved up and singled out the crippled Cincinnati as her special victim. This craft was more lumbering and slower than the rams proper, and could not be so easily moved about. She worked very hard to get her nose into the Cincinnati's side, but every time was foiled by the movements of the latter. At last she had apparently secured the desired opportunity, and was crowding all steam to make good headway, when an unlooked-for adversary appeared. The St. Louis bore down upon her, unseen, until close on her, and then came the unavoidable collision—the ram was cut half into and sunk immediately. Her crew perished with her, but half a dozen or so escaping by clinging to the St. Louis. This was a brilliant manœuvre on the part of the St. Louis, relieving and probably saving the Cincinnati, which was already half sunk and almost unmanageable from the weight of water in her hold. Seeing her condition, the acting flag officer signalled her to withdraw, and she was run upon the shoal at the foot of the island, and sunk to the bottom.

"The action had now lasted about forty-five minutes. One of the enemy's boats had been sunk and two blown up. The rest of their fleet was crippled. To prolong the fight was to insure its destruction. They therefore gradually fell back, under cover of the smoke, around the point to the protection of their land batteries. The Cincinnati was the only boat injured in the Union fleet. Four were wounded on board of her."

On the night of the 4th of June Fort Pillow was evacuated. Everything of value was either destroyed or removed by the Confederate officers. On the same night Fort Randolph, some miles below, was evacuated. The few guns were dismantled. Com. Ellet, in his report to the Secretary of War, said: "Randolph, like Pillow, is weak, and could not have held out long against a vigorous attack." The remark is worthy of notice, as it raises an inquiry why such an attack was not made. The forts were not attacked because this expedition, was not sustained at the critical time for its success. There were no land forces to coöperate with the fleet.

On the 13th of April the gunboats and transports arrived before Fort Pillow, and on the 4th of June this fort and the one below were evacuated, and the way clear for the fleet to attack Memphis. On the 7th of April the battle of Pittsburg Landing took place between the Federal forces, under Gen. Grant, and the Confederate forces, under Gen. Beauregard, which resulted in the withdrawal, by Gen. Beauregard, of all his forces from the battle field to the strong position at Corinth. Reënforcements were required by the Federal army, and Gen. Pope was ordered to join it. On the 21st of April he arrived in transports up the Tennessee river at Pittsburg Landing. His force numbered between twenty and twenty-five thousand men, and were taken on some thirty transports. This withdrawal of the force of Gen. Pope put a stop to the progress of the Mississippi river expedition. The gunboats, however, were obliged to remain in such force as to prevent any movement of the Confederate gunboats up the river. Soon after the withdrawal of Gen. Pope, Com. Foote obtained leave of absence, and the command of the fleet was taken by Charles Ellet, jr., until the arrival of Charles H. Davis, the successor of Com. Foote.

As has been stated, Forts Pillow and Randolph were evacuated on the night of the 4th of June. This evacuation was in consequence of the withdrawal of a large portion of the Confederate army from Tennessee, and their abandonment of Corinth. The positions of Fort Pillow, Randolph, and Memphis could not be held under these circumstances, and were therefore wisely evacuated.

Nothing now remained to oppose the Federal fleet but the Confederate gunboats. On the 5th of June the fleet arrived within two miles of Memphis, and came to anchor for the night. On the 6th, at 4½ o'clock in the morning, the gunboats Benton, Cairo, Carondelet, Louisville, and St. Louis, and the four rams Monarch, Lancaster, No. 3, and Queen of the West, weighed anchor, and dropped slowly down toward the city. The Confederate gunboats were seen approaching in order of battle. This was in two lines, the first consisting of the Beauregard, Little Rebel, Gen. Price, and Gen. Bragg, the second of the Gen. Lovell, Gen. Van Dorn, Jeff. Thompson, and the Sumter. When within three fourths of a mile, a shot from the Little Rebel, the flag ship, fell within a short distance of the Cairo, which replied with a broadside, and soon the engagement became general. The Confederates had fewer guns than their opponents, but exceeded them in the number of gunboats. The scene of the battle was in front of the city of Memphis, and the shores were crowded with spectators. After half an hour two of the rams, Monarch and Queen of the West, which had been lying on the Arkansas side, in rear of the line of battle, steamed out toward the scene of action. The Queen of the West started directly for the Beauregard, and that gunboat fired at, but missed her. A second shot struck the ram but did her no injury, and she steamed steadily and swiftly toward her adversary. When she was within ten feet the latter swung round, and the ram missed her prey. Not discouraged, however, the Queen ran toward the Gen. Price, which fired several shots but did no damage, and thrust her iron prow into the wheelhouse of the Price, crushing it to pieces, and causing the vessel to leak so badly that she was run to the Arkansas shore, to prevent her from sinking. The Beauregard now determined to avenge the Price, and hurried toward the Queen, while the ram in full motion was dashing toward her foe. They bore down upon each other bravely, but the skilful pilot of the enemy contrived to evade the shock of the Queen, and struck her aft so heavily that the ram was disabled and began to leak. The Monarch, seeing the state of affairs, dashed boldly at the Beauregard. The latter fired four times at the ram, and struck her bulwarks once, the ball glancing harmlessly. She could not, however, avoid the unerring aim of the Monarch, which crashed through her bow, and caused her to fill in a few minutes and go down as far as her cabin, the shallowness of the water preventing her sinking lower, and the white flag she had run up stopping further damage from the fleet. The Monarch then looked after her disabled consort, the Queen of the West, and towed her ashore, placing her in a position of security. The gunboats now increased their fire against the enemy, when the flag ship, having obtained an excellent range, threw a 50-pound ball from a rifled Parrott, striking the Gen. Lovell aft above the water line, tearing a great hole in her, through which the water rushed like a torrent. She began to sink at once, giving few of the officers and crew time to save themselves. In less than four minutes the vessel had sunk in seventy-five feet of water, and passed entirely out of sight. Some of the crew went down with the Lovell, but about fifty of them leaped into the river, and were struggling in the water, when the Benton's crew arrived in advance of several other cutters from the flotilla, and just in time to see the chimneys of the hostile gunboat disappear beneath the water. Many of the crew had already begun to swim for the shore. Some six or seven, however, were rescued by the cutter, but the current was so strong that a large number were carried off and drowned. The engagement still continued warm and desperate. The smoke of the battle so obscured the boats that it was difficult to see them at any distance, yet the levee of Memphis was black with the crowd of human beings. From the time the rams made their appearance, the Confederate gunboats had been steadily falling back, though continuing to fire heavily, before the advance of the Federal gunboats.

The Jeff. Thompson, Gen. Bragg, Sumter, and Van Dorn were the only vessels remaining, and these were so frequently struck and saw so little opportunity of escaping, that they turned their bows ashore. As soon as the Thompson reached the shore her officers and crew leaped off, and ran through the woods; but a shell exploding on the vessel, she took fire and was burned to the water's edge. The Gen. Bragg reached the shore about half a mile below the Thompson, and her officers and crew escaped. The Sumter followed next, and the Gen. Van Dorn, which was a swift vessel, alone escaped down the river. The Federal fleet now came to anchor before the city. The engagement had lasted over an hour. No one was killed on the fleet. The loss of the other side could not be stated. About one hundred were made prisoners. The other mortar boats, owing to a misconception of orders, were not engaged.

The following correspondence then ensued between Com. Davis and the city authorities:

UNITED STATES FLAG STEAMER BENTON,
OFF MEMPHIS, *June* 5, 1862.

SIR: I have respectfully to request that you will surrender the city of Memphis to the authority of the United States, which I have the honor to represent.

I am, Mr. Mayor, with high respect,
C. H. DAVIS, Flag Officer commanding, etc.
To His Honor the Mayor of the City of Memphis.

The answer of the mayor was as follows:

MAYOR'S OFFICE, MEMPHIS, *June* 6, 1862.

SIR: Your note of this date is received, and contents noted. In reply I have only to say that, as the civil authorities have no means of defence, by the force of circumstances the city is in your hands.

Respectfully, JOHN PARK, Mayor.
To C. H. DAVIS, Flag Officer commanding, etc.

Commander Davis wrote in reply as follows:

UNITED STATES FLAG STEAMER BENTON,
OFF MEMPHIS, *June* 6, 1862.

SIR: The undersigned, commanding the naval military forces of the United States in front of Memphis, has the honor to say to the Mayor and the city that Col. Fitch, commanding the Indiana brigade, will take military possession immediately.

Col. Fitch will be happy to receive the coöperation of His Honor the Mayor and the city authorities in maintaining peace and order. To this end he will be pleased to confer with His Honor the Mayor at the military headquarters at 3 o'clock this afternoon.

Yours, etc., C. H. DAVIS,
Flag Officer commanding, etc.
To the Mayor of the City of Memphis.

The military occupation of the city followed, and the appointment of a provost marshal. Memphis is the most populous and important town, on the Mississippi river, between St. Louis and New Orleans. Its population in 1860 was 22,625.

About the 10th of June the gunboats St. Louis, Mound City, Lexington, and Conestoga, with the transport New National, having on board the 46th Indiana regiment, Col. Fitch, left Memphis, on an expedition up the White river, to open communication with the army of Gen. Curtis, and to remove the obstructions in that river. The White river is formed by the junction of three small branches, which unite a few miles east of Fayetteville, Arkansas. It flows first northwesterly into Missouri, and after making a circuit of about one hundred miles, returns into Arkansas, and pursues a southeasterly course to the mouth of Black river. Thence its direction is nearly south, until it enters the Arkansas fifteen miles above its mouth. It is navigable by steamboats to the mouth of Black river, three hundred and fifty miles, in all stages of water.

As the expedition approached St. Charles, the Mound City, being in advance, was fired on from two concealed batteries. This was returned. Meantime the troops were landed below for the purpose of marching in the rear and capturing the batteries. At this juncture a ball from a siege gun on the bluff struck the forward and left side of the Mound City and penetrated the casemate and passed through the steam drum. The vessel was immediately filled with the escaping vapor and nearly every one on board was scalded; only twenty-three of the officers and crew, numbering one hundred and seventy-five, escaped uninjured. A horrible scene ensued. Many of the crew, frantic with pain, jumped overboard, and some were drowned. The boats from the Conestoga, which was coming up at the time, were sent to their relief, but the enemy fired on the men in the water with grape and canister from their field pieces, killing most of those who were attempting to escape. Meantime Col. Fitch, learning the facts, pushed forward with his regiment and carried the works at the point of the bayonet. They consisted of two batteries, the lower of which mounted six field-pieces, and the upper one three heavy siege guns. About thirty prisoners were taken, among whom was Col. Frye, commanding the post. This expedition failed to open communication with Gen. Curtis, as has been heretofore stated.

As Memphis was the second important city in the West captured by the Federal troops, a more full statement of affairs there after its occupation will serve as a general illustration of the proceedings in the captured cities.

A satisfactory arrangement was made as aforesaid with the civil authorities, all the more readily as the mayor and a great many of the citizens—according to some accounts the majority—were Union men. Although previously Col. Ellet, commanding the ram fleet, had made an independent movement toward placing the city under the Federal authority, of which the following is his official report to the Secretary of War:

U. S. RAM SWITZERLAND,
OPPOSITE MEMPHIS, *June* 7, P. M.

Hon. E. M. Stanton, Secretary of War:

SIR: Yesterday, after the engagement with the rebel fleet had nearly terminated, and the gunboats and one of my rams had passed below, I was informed that a white flag had been raised in the city. I immediately sent my son, a medical cadet, Chas. R. Ellet, ashore with a flag of truce and the following note to the authorities:

"OPPOSITE MEMPHIS, *June* 6. I understand that the city of Memphis has surrendered. I therefore send my son, with two United States flags, with instructions to raise one upon the custom house and the other upon the court house, as evidence of the return of your city to the care and protection of the Constitution.

"CHAS. ELLET, JR., Commanding."

The bearer of the flags and the above note was accompanied by Lieut.-Col. Conkell, of the Fifty-ninth Illinois regiment, and sixty-two men of the boat guard.

The following is the reply of the mayor of the city:

MEMPHIS, *June* 6.

"*Col. Chas. Ellet, Jr., Commanding, &c.:*

"SIR: Your note of this date is received and the contents noted. The civil authorities of this city are not advised of its surrender to the forces of the United States Government, and our reply to you is simply to state respectfully that we have no power to oppose the raising of the flags you have directed to be raised over the custom house and post office.

"JOHN PARK, Mayor

On receiving this reply the small party proceeded to the post office to raise the national flag, and were there joined by the mayor. It is proper to say that the conduct of the mayor and some of the citizens was unexceptionable. The party was surrounded by an excited crowd, using angry and threatening language, but they ascended to the top of the post office and planted the flag, though fired upon several times and stoned by the mob below. Still I believe this conduct was reprobated by the people of standing in the place; indeed, many evidences of an extensive Union feeling there reach me.

Respectfully,
CHAS. ELLET, JR., Commanding Ram Fleet.

The same evening the citizens, to the number of some two thousand, reported themselves, armed and equipped, to the provost marshal to prevent the destruction of property by the mob, who it was feared would fire the city, in fulfilment of a threat which had been made some time previously; but, beyond the breaking open of the Mississippi and Tennessee Railroad depot, little or no disorder occurred. The same day Col. Fitch issued a proclamation to the citizens, announcing that he had taken military possession of the city. "Residents who may have fled from their homes," he continues, "are exhorted to return; merchants and others who have abandoned their business are requested to reopen their stores and shops, excepting those dealing in intoxicating liquors, who are forbidden to resume that traffic under penalty of having the stock immediately destroyed. The mayor and common council will continue in the exercise of their municipal functions, the military authorities simply coöperating with them in enforcing all proper ordinances, unless some exigency arises rendering it imperative to place the city under martial law. It is hoped and believed, however, nothing will occur to render this step necessary." In fact, the most perfect tranquillity continued to prevail; the municipal authorities coöperated cordially with the military in preserving order; and great numbers of citizens, who had fled on the destruction of the Confederate fleet, began to return to their homes. Before the surrender, 1,494 bales of cotton, and large quantities of sugar and molassses, had been destroyed by order of the Confederate Government; but the citizens had succeeded in concealing probably $150,000 worth of these staples, which now began to find their way to the levees. Any person was allowed to go North, or ship goods thither, on taking the oath of allegiance. Trade was extremely dull for a week or two; many of the shops remained closed, and owing to the lack of every species of currency except Confederate scrip, Northern merchants, who had sent goods to Memphis, were in several instances compelled to reship them.

The Memphis post office was reopened on June 13th.

On the same day Col. James R. Slack, of the 47th Indiana volunteers, assumed command of the city, and immediately issued the following order:

General Orders No. 3.

HEADQUARTERS UNITED STATES FORCES,
MEMPHIS, TENN., *June* 13, 1862.

Hereafter the dealing in and passage of currency known as "Confederate Scrip" or "Confederate Notes" is positively prohibited, and the use thereof as a circulating medium is regarded as an insult to the Government of the United States, and an imposition upon the ignorant and deluded.

All persons offending against the provisions of this order will be promptly arrested and severely punished by the military authorities.

By order of JAS. R. SLACK,
Colonel Commanding Post.

The Mayor and Board of Aldermen addressed

a letter to Col. Slack, representing that in the absence of almost all other money the order above cited was certain to cause great distress and suffering among the laboring class, and requesting him to leave the matter for sixty days "to the judgment and discretion of the people." Their request was not granted, Col. Slack reminding them, in his answer, "that the so-called Confederate States issued all their notes in bills of the denomination of $50's and $20's," and that consequently the laboring class probably had very few of them in their possession. "The ruinous effect to which you allude," he continued, "will strike a different class altogether. The calamity of having to contend with a depreciated currency, and to which you refer, will come upon the people sooner or later, and I see no reason why it may not as well come now as sixty days hence.

"Those who have been the most active in getting up this wicked rebellion, are the individuals whose pockets are lined with Confederate notes; and if sixty days' time should be given them, it is only giving that much time for those who are responsible for its issue to get rid of it without loss, and the worthless trash will be found in the hands of the unsuspecting and credulous, who have always been the dupes of designing Shylocks, by inducing them to accept of a circulating medium which was issued to aid in the destruction of the first and best Government ever known to civilization."

On the 17th Gen. Lewis Wallace arrived at Memphis, and assumed the chief command by virtue of his rank. His principal official act, during the few days that he remained in Memphis, was to take possession of the "Argus" newspaper office, where he installed the correspondents of the "New York Herald" and "New York Tribune" as editors. The provost marshal also issued orders to the guard to shoot any one tearing down United States flags, and imprison citizens carrying concealed weapons.

On the 20th Col. Slack issued the following "General Orders No. 8:"

Members of the Board of Aldermen, the Mayor, City Recorder, and all other persons discharging any official duty within the city of Memphis, and under the charter thereof, are required to come before the Provost Marshal and take the oath of allegiance to the Government of the United States within three days, or, in default thereof, will be regarded as sympathizing, aiding, and abetting rebellion, and will be arrested and treated as only traitors deserve.

On the 25th a Union meeting was held in Court House Square, at which some 350 or 400 persons were present, about 200 of them being citizens. After several speeches had been made, a series of resolutions were passed pledging the support of the meeting to the Union ticket at the municipal election to be held the next day; and the meeting then adjourned, to reassemble in the evening for the purpose of nominating candidates. The election on the 26th passed off quietly, not more than 700 votes being cast. John Park, the Union candidate, was reëlected mayor without opposition. All persons offering to vote were required to take the oath of allegiance.

The city was now for some weeks the headquarters of Gen. Grant, and Col. J. D. Webster was appointed commandant of the post. The editors of the "Argus" were permitted to resume the direction of their paper, with the understanding that their immediate arrest and the suppression of the paper would follow the appearance of any disunion article in it.

The Northern shipments from Memphis up to the 27th of June were, according to the report of the Trade Committee, 9,206 hhds. of sugar, 8,117 hhds. of molasses, and 7,061 bales of cotton. The number of persons who had taken the oath of allegiance in the city at the same date was estimated at 3,000.

On the 1st of July the "Memphis Avalanche" was suppressed, but its reissue being allowed on condition of the retirement of the chief editor, it appeared the next day as a "Bulletin."

On the 10th of July Gen. Grant published the following order:

The families now residing in the city of Memphis, of the following persons, are required to move South beyond our lines within five days from the date hereof:

1. All persons holding commissions in the so-called Confederate army, or who are voluntarily enlisted in said army, or who accompany and are connected with the same.

2. All persons holding office under or in the employ of the so-called Confederate Government.

3. All persons holding State, county, or municipal offices, who claim allegiance to the said so-called Confederate Government, and who have abandoned their families and gone South.

Gen. Grant went to Corinth on the 11th, and was succeeded at Memphis by Gen. A. P. Hovey, who published an order on the 16th requiring all male residents of the city, between 18 and 45 years of age, to take the oath of allegiance within six days or go South. About 1,300 took the oath and 500 were sent South. On the 17th it was discovered that a Confederate telegraph operator had interrupted the line between Memphis and Corinth, over which passed Gen. Halleck's messages to Flag-Officer Davis, Gen. Curtis, and the commandant at Memphis, and with the aid of a pocket instrument had read all the official despatches sent over the wires for four days.

Maj.-Gen. W. T. Sherman reached Memphis with reënforcements on the 20th, and took command of the post. On the 24th he published an order reopening trade and communication with the surrounding country under certain restrictions. Travel into and out of the city, over five specified roads, without passes or any hindrance except the right of search by the guard at the discretion of the officer in command, was freely permitted to farmers, planters, and business men with their families and servants. This travel must in all cases be by daylight, except in the case of market and supply carts. Another order prohibited the payment of gold, silver, or treasury notes for cotton, and ordered quartermasters to seize all cotton purchased after that date and send it North to be sold, the proceeds to be held subject to the claim of the owners. Tennessee or Southern paper might be used for the purchase of cotton, or buyers might give obligations to pay at the end of the war, or at the pleasure of the Government, or might deposit the value of it with the quartermaster, to be held in trust for the planters. This order was soon afterward modified by direction of the Government at Washington.

A few days later Gen. Grant directed Gen. Sherman to "take possession of all vacant stores and houses in the city, and have them rented at reasonable rates, and to be paid monthly in advance." These buildings, with their tenants, were to be turned over to the proprietors on proof of loyalty. Houses which had been leased by disloyal owners were also to be seized, and the rents appropriated by the United States. Early in August he also ordered the families of all persons absent in the Confederate States to be sent out of Memphis.

On the 9th of the same month it was announced that one artillery and three infantry companies, comprising in the aggregate 400 men, had been enlisted in Memphis for the Federal army and had taken the field, and two others were recruiting.

Toward the close of the month Gen. Sherman issued an order prohibiting the importation and sale, except by permit, of arms, ammunition, salt, and salt meat; and commanding dealers to keep an account of goods received and the disposition made of them, said account to be subject to inspection at all times by the provost marshal. Dealers in arms and medicines, detected in endeavoring to get the same outside the Union lines, were to suffer the extreme penalty of military law.

A meeting of citizens was called by the General on the 7th of September, at which he made an address in answer to various complaints which had been made of his administration. The attendance was very large, and an unmistakable feeling of loyalty was indicated by the assembly.

About the 10th a joint order was issued by Gen. Sherman and W. D. Gallagher, agent of the Treasury Department, for the regulation of commercial intercourse between Memphis, Helena, and other points. No boats were to receive goods without permits, and persons who had never encouraged secession were to receive facilities for shipping supplies on their taking oath that no part of the same were to be sold to disloyal parties.

On the 25th of October Gen. Sherman published stringent regulations for the government of the city. A military commission of three army officers was to sit daily to try offenders under the laws of war. Vagrants, thieves, and other disreputable characters, were to be organized into gangs and set to work in the trenches or on the streets. Citizens lurking about the camps were to be treated as spies. The inhabitants were to keep within doors between tattoo and reveille, unless attending church, places of amusement, a party of friends, or necessary business. After midnight all persons must be in their houses, except the guard. Assemblages of negroes were forbidden, except by permission previously obtained from the provost marshal.

On the 7th of November another Union meeting was held at Memphis.

About the same time the general commanding prohibited the importation of liquors, except by gentlemen-citizens and officers, for the exclusive use of themselves and their families; by regular apothecaries for medicinal purposes, to be retailed on a physician's prescription; or by keepers of hotels and licensed saloons, in limited quantities, not exceeding one month's supply at a time.

Gen. Sherman took the field about the middle of December, and the command of Memphis devolved upon Gen. Hurlbut, who immediately caused all drinking saloons to be closed.

On the 21st of December the guerrillas, who had been for some time growing daily bolder in their operations about Memphis, burning cotton, intercepting supplies, and forcing conscripts into the Confederate army, attacked the suburbs of the city, committed great depredations, and carried off 100 head of cattle and 180 mules. The next day a meeting of the citizens was held to provide means of defence. On the 24th the guerrillas appeared again, drove the Federal pickets within the fortifications, and plundered the neighboring shops and houses. Two companies of citizens were immediately enrolled for home defence, and the provost marshal interdicted for the time all trade with the surrounding country. The arrival of two regiments of Federal troops, however, soon quieted the public alarm. In consequence of these occurrences, the election for member of Congress in the district of which Memphis forms a part, which was to have been held, under Gov. Johnson's proclamation, on the 29th of December, was postponed twenty days. A quiet state of affairs ensued. The population of Memphis in 1860 was 22,623.

CHAPTER XV.

Advance of Gen. Grant up the Tennessee River—Position of the Southern Forces—Movements of Gen. Buell—Advance of Gen. Johnston to attack Gen. Grant—Commencement of the Battle at Shiloh—Arrival of Gen. Buell—Second day of Battle—Retreat of Southern Troops—Message of Mr. Davis to Congress at Richmond—Arrival of Gen. Halleck—March on Corinth—Its Evacuation—Movements of Gen. Mitchel—Provisional Government in Tennessee—Its Proceedings.

The military operations in Tennessee, which finally controlled the movements of the Mississippi River expedition, had paused after the capture of Nashville, as above described, but were soon resumed again. The first step consisted in fitting out a great expedition to proceed under Gen. Grant up the Tennessee River. More than fifty-seven steamers and two gunboats were required to transport and convoy the force. It was organized in five divisions, each consisting of infantry, cavalry, and artillery. The advance was under the command of Gen. Sherman, 2d division under Gen. Hurlbut, 3d division under Gen. McClernard, 4th division under Gen. L. Wallace, and 5th division under Col. Lauman of the 7th Iowa regiment. On the 11th of March the transports began to arrive at Savannah in Tennessee. On the night of the 12th the Tyler and Lexington were sent up the river to reconnoitre as far as Eastport, forty miles above Savannah. The enemy was found constructing fortifications and with a considerable force. It was known that the Confederate forces were also concentrated along the lines of railroad south and southwest of the river.

The line of defence now adopted by the Confederate commander after his first line was broken up, had for its base the Charleston and Memphis Railroad, the preservation of which was absolutely necessary to any pretence of resistance through northern Mississippi, Alabama, and Georgia. Along this railroad are Tuscumbia and Florence, at the foot of the Muscle shoals in the Tennessee River and the junction with the Florence and Nashville Railroad; Decatur, near the head of the lower Muscle Shoal; Huntsville and Bellefontaine; Stevenson, important as the junction with the railroad from Nashville through Murfreesboro' and Chattanooga, a strong position. All these points are east of Corinth. On the west of Corinth the railroad runs in a nearly straight line to Memphis, ninety-three miles distant; and northwest runs the road to Jackson, almost in the centre of West Tennessee.

The Union line was the Tennessee River, extending from Paducah, Kentucky, to Eastport in Mississippi. The gunboats Lexington and Tyler, by moving up and down the river, prevented the erection of batteries. Above Eastport, at Chickasaw Bluffs and at some other points, Confederate batteries were placed to command the navigation of the river.

On the 5th of March Gen. Beauregard assumed the command of the Southern forces in this department, when he issued the following address to his soldiers:

> SOLDIERS: I assume this day the command of the army of the Mississippi, for the defence of our homesteads and liberties, and to resist the subjugation, spoliation, and dishonor of our people. Our mothers and wives, our sisters and children, expect us to do our duty, even to the sacrifice of our lives.
>
> Our losses since the commencement of this war, in killed, wounded, and prisoners, are now about the same as those of the enemy.
>
> He must be made to atone for the reverses we have lately experienced. Those reverses, far from disheartening, must nerve us to new deeds of valor and patriotism, and should inspire us with an unconquerable determination to drive back our invaders.
>
> Should any one in this army be unequal to the task before us, let him transfer his arms and equipments at once to braver, firmer hands, and return to his home.
>
> Our cause is as just and sacred as ever animated men to take up arms; and if we are true to it and to ourselves, with the continued protection of the Almighty we must and shall triumph.

Associated with Gen. Beauregard in command were Gens. Albert Sidney Johnston, Bragg, Polk, Pillow, Cheatham, and others. The Confederate force consisted not only of the troops from the adjacent States which had been in service for months, but also of new levies now called out by the governors on the requisition of Mr. Davis. They were encamped principally at Corinth, with detachments at various points on the railroad, so situated that they could be easily concentrated on any point.

Corinth is at the intersection of the Mobile and Ohio and Memphis and Charleston Railroads, in Tishemingo Co., Mississippi, forty miles from Grand Junction, fifty-eight miles from Jackson, Tennessee, and about eighteen miles from Pittsburg on the Tennessee River. It is situated in a hilly, semi-mountainous country.

The Federal forces at first concentrated at Savannah, a small town of two hundred inhabitants, on the Tennessee River, about one hundred and seventy miles above Fort Henry. The number of transports which arrived by the 13th of March, was eighty-two. This force comprised all of Gen. Grant's original command, with an additional force of infantry, almost entirely from the State of Ohio. All the steamers that formed the regular line of packets between Louisville and New Orleans and between Louisville and St. Louis were in the fleet, carrying from 1,200 to 1,500 men each, and heavily laden. The demonstrations of the inhabitants along the shore of the river were of the most extravagant character. One declared it to be "the second coming of Christ." The command of the army was taken by Gen. Grant soon after its arrival at Savannah, and it was advanced seven miles to Pittsburg Landing. Savannah was made a depot for stores, with only a few troops. Here troops and supplies were sent to Gen. Grant by Maj.-Gen. Halleck, both from St. Louis and Cairo. There had also been such a change in the position of the enemy before Gen. Buell at Nashville, that the original plan was altered, and he was directed by Maj.-Gen. Halleck to make a junction of his forces with those under Gen. Grant. By General War Order No. 3 of the President, dated March 11th, the Departments of Kansas and Kentucky, respectively under the command of Gen. Hunter and of Gen. Buell, were united with that of the Missouri, under the designation of the Department of the Mississippi, and of this consolidated Department Gen. Halleck was assigned the command.

It was the original plan of Gen. Buell to advance with his army in several columns upon northern Alabama over the principal roads leading to that region from Nashville. With this object in view, the divisions of Gens. Mitchell, Nelson and McCook left Nashville on the same day, and by different roads. But the Confederates, having retired from Murfreesboro and formed along the new line they proposed to defend, rendered necessary a corresponding change in the plan of Gen. Buell. A direct advance upon Alabama by Gen. Buell's forces would not only have involved an unnecessary amount of labor and slowness of movement, owing to the destruction of bridges over the watercourses, and other impediments, but the passage of the Tennessee into northern Alabama being practicable for a large army at a few places only, the Confederates could by means of the railroad have easily collected a large force to dispute it at any point. This concentration of the main body of the Confederate forces in localities within the contemplated field of the operations of Gen. Grant's army, not only gave to the latter an opportunity to employ the whole of his force to the best possible advantage, but enabled Gen. Halleck to order Gen. Buell to turn his army toward western Tennessee, to coöperate with Gen. Grant and cross the river. Thus combined, they were regarded as certain to be superior to the Confederate army in the number, armament, and fighting trim of their commands.

On the 28th of March, Gen. Buell left Nashville and passed the advance of his divisions at Columbia. On the 28th, 29th, and 30th the divisions of his army had crossed Duck river on a new bridge, and advanced through Columbia, distant eighty-two miles from Savannah.

Meantime most active preparations had been made to assemble a large Confederate force at Corinth, and to fortify that position, which is about eighteen miles south of Pittsburg Landing. The force of Gen. Grant was posted at Pittsburg and along both sides of the river toward Crump's Landing and Savannah, but kept in active service scouring the country. The importance of the approaching contest to the Confederate States could not be concealed. If Corinth fell, Memphis would also fall, and the whole territory of the Gulf States would be open to an army larger than that of the Potomac. The plan adopted by Gens. Johnston and Beauregard was to strike an unexpected blow before the arrival of Gen. Buell's forces. On the 3d of April, Gen. Johnston issued the following address to his soldiers:

HEADQUARTERS ARMY OF MISSISSIPPI,
CORINTH, MISS., *April 3.*

Soldiers of the Army of the Mississippi:

I have put you in motion to offer battle to the invaders of your country, with the resolution and discipline and valor becoming men, fighting, as you are, for all worth living or dying for. You can but march to a decisive victory over agrarian mercenaries sent to subjugate and despoil you of your liberties, property, and honor.

Remember the precious stake involved; remember the dependence of your mothers, your wives, your sisters, and your children on the result. Remember the fair, broad, abounding lands, the happy homes that will be desolated by your defeat. The eyes and hopes of eight million people rest upon you. You are expected to show yourselves worthy of your valor and courage, worthy of the women of the South, whose noble devotion in this war has never been exceeded in any time. With such incentives to brave deeds, and with the trust that God is with us, your general will lead you confidently to the combat, assured of success.

(Signed) A. S. JOHNSTON,
General Commanding.

The orders accompanying the address divided "the Army of the Mississippi" into three corps. Gen. Beauregard was proclaimed to be in command of the whole force. The first corps was assigned to Gen. Polk, and embraced all the troops of his former command, excepting detached cavalry and artillery, and reserves detached for the defence of Fort Pillow and Madrid Bend. The second corps was assigned to Gen. Bragg, and was to consist of the second division of the army of the Mississippi, less artillery and cavalry "hereafter detached." The third corps was assigned to Gen. Hardee, and consisted of "the Army of Kentucky." To Gen. Crittenden was assigned a command of reserves, consisting of not less than two brigades.

From two to three miles out on the road to Corinth from Pittsburg Landing lay the five divisions of Gen. Grant's army. The advance line was formed by three divisions: Brig.-Gen. Sherman's, Brig.-Gen. Prentiss's, and Maj.-Gen. McClernand's. Between these and the landing lay the two others, Brig.-Gen. Hurlbut's and Maj.-Gen. Smith's, commanded in his absence by Brig.-Gen. W. H. L. Wallace. On the extreme left of the line was one brigade of Gen. Sherman's division, while the other brigades were some two miles distant, forming the extreme right of the advance line. To the left, though rather behind a portion of the line

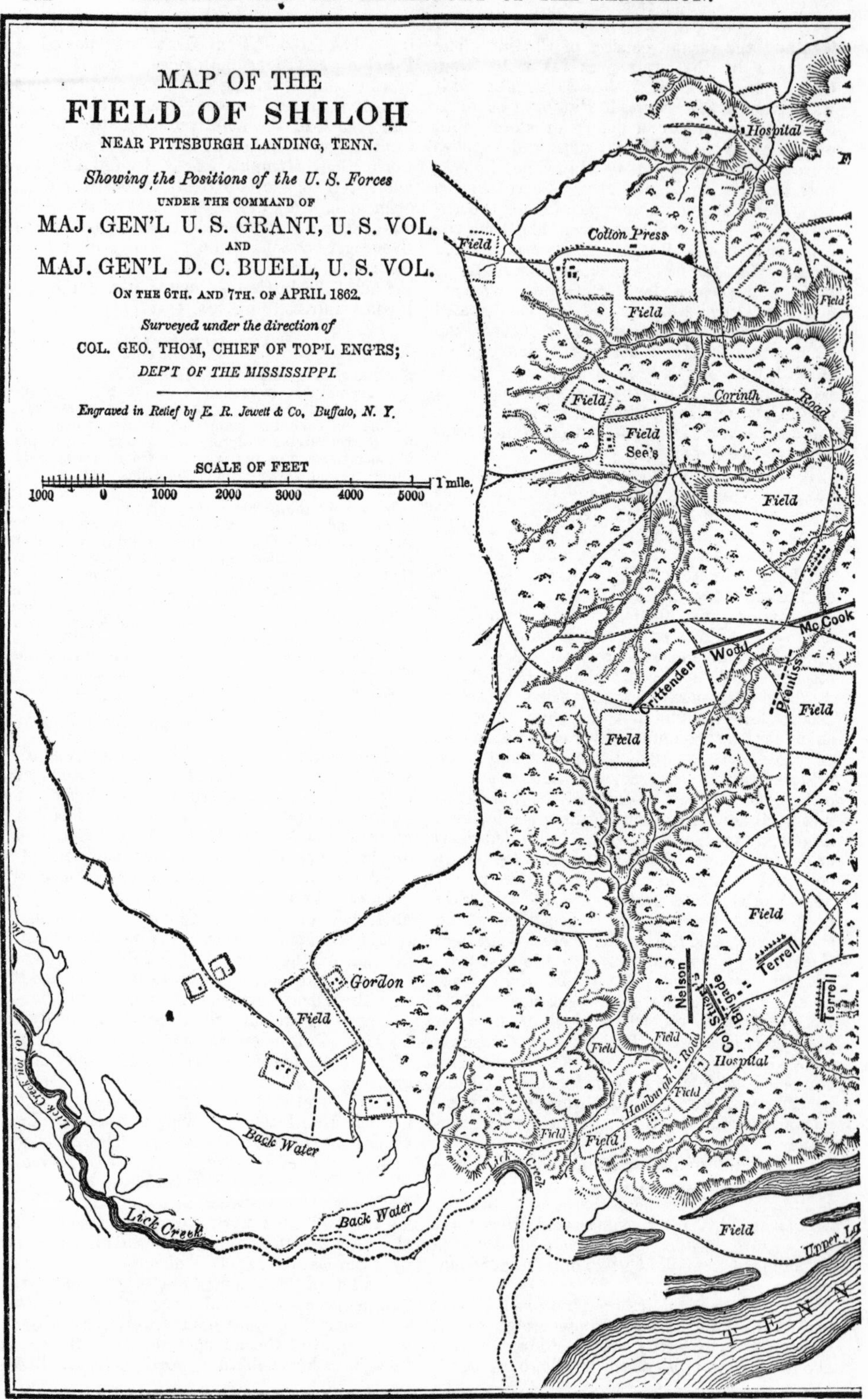
MAP OF THE
FIELD OF SHILOH
NEAR PITTSBURGH LANDING, TENN.
Showing the Positions of the U. S. Forces
UNDER THE COMMAND OF
MAJ. GEN'L U. S. GRANT, U. S. VOL.
AND
MAJ. GEN'L D. C. BUELL, U. S. VOL.
ON THE 6TH. AND 7TH. OF APRIL 1862.
Surveyed under the direction of
COL. GEO. THOM, CHIEF OF TOP'L ENG'RS;
DEP'T OF THE MISSISSIPPI.
Engraved in Relief by E. R. Jewett & Co, Buffalo, N. Y.
SCALE OF FEET
1000 0 1000 2000 3000 4000 5000 1 mile.
Hospital
Cotton Press
Field
Field
Field
Corinth Road
Field
Field
See's
Field
McCook
Wood
Crittenden
Prentiss
Field
Field
Field
Gordon
Field
Nelson
Col. Stuart's Brigade
Terrell
Terrell
Field
Field
Hospital
Hamburgh Road
Field
Field
Field
Back Water
Lick Creek
Lick Creek
Back Water
Field
Upper L
TENN

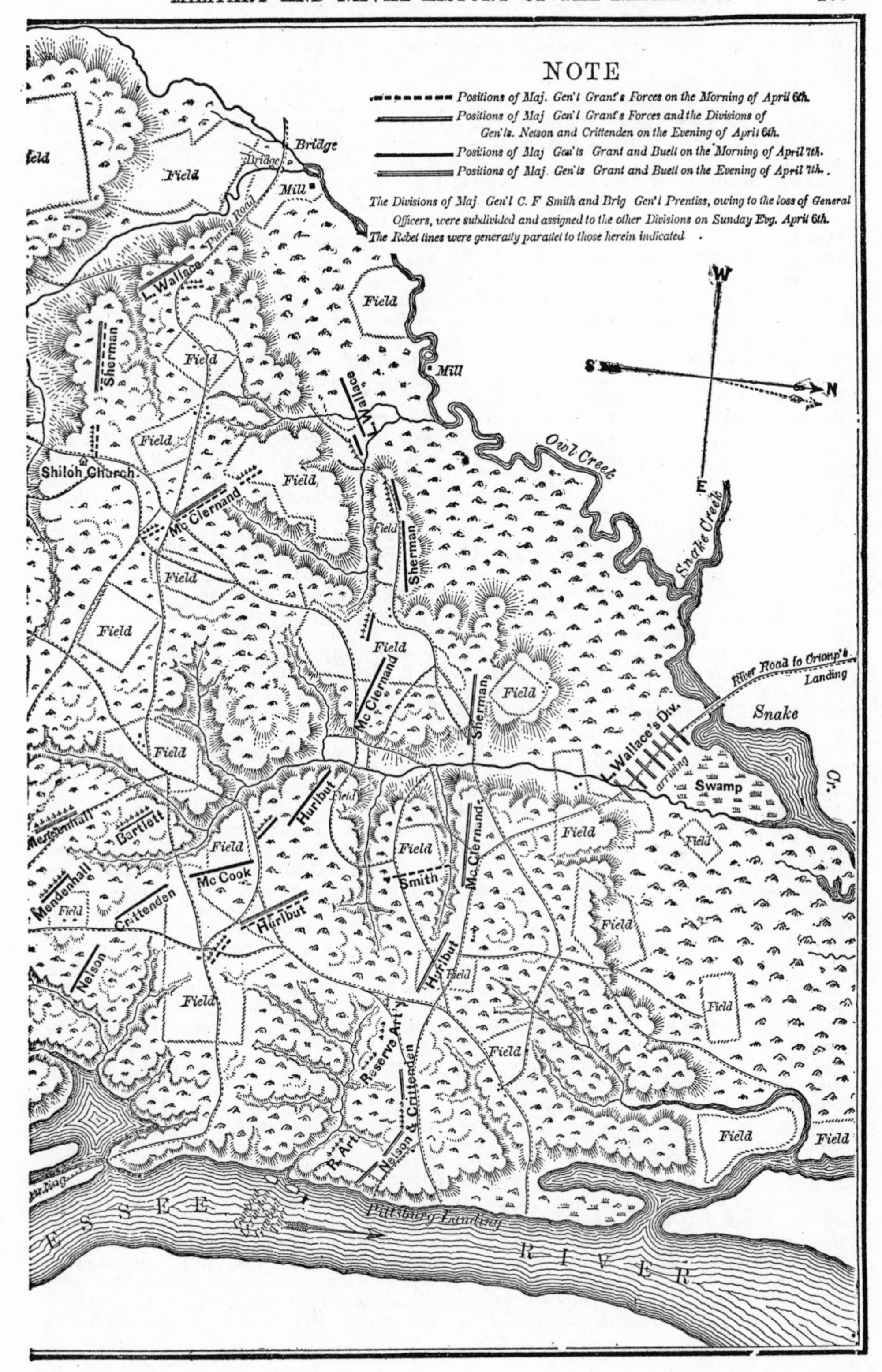
NOTE
Positions of Maj. Gen'l Grant's Forces on the Morning of April 6th.
Positions of Maj Gen'l Grant's Forces and the Divisions of Gen'ls. Nelson and Crittenden on the Evening of April 6th.
Positions of Maj Gen'ls Grant and Buell on the Morning of April 7th.
Positions of Maj. Gen'ls Grant and Buell on the Evening of April 7th.
The Divisions of Maj Gen'l C. F Smith and Brig Gen'l Prentiss, owing to the loss of General Officers, were subdivided and assigned to the other Divisions on Sunday Evg. April 6th.
The Rebel lines were generally parallel to those herein indicated.
W
S
N
E
Bridge
Bridge
Mill
Purdy Road
Field
L. Wallace
Sherman
Mill
Owl Creek
Snake Creek
Shiloh Church
Mc Clernand
Sherman
Mc Clernand
Sherman
River Road to Crump's Landing
Snake
Cr.
L. Wallace's Div.
arriving
Swamp
Hurlbut
Bartlett
Mendenhall
Mc Cook
Crittenden
Smith
Mc Clernand
Hurlbut
Nelson
Hurlbut
Reserve Art'y
Nelson & Crittenden
R. Art.
Pittsburg Landing
RIVER

formed by Sherman's main brigades, lay Gen. McClernand's division, and between it and Gen. Sherman's brigade, on the extreme left, lay Gen. Prentiss's division. No preparations had been made for any means of defence in case of attack, although the position was an exposed one.

The information that Gen. Buell was near at hand, determined Gen. Beauregard to make the attack at once. The movement of his troops from Corinth commenced on the 3d of April. Owing to the difficulties of the roads, they did not reach the vicinity of the Federal forces until Saturday afternoon, the 5th. It was then determined that the attack should be made on the next morning, at the earliest hour practicable, and in three lines of battle: the first and second extending from Owl Creek, on the Confederate left, to Lick Creek on their right—a distance of about three miles—supported by the third and the reserve. The first line consisted of Gen. Hardee's corps, augmented on his right by Gladden's brigade of Bragg's corps, deployed in line of battle, with their respective artillery following immediately, and the cavalry in rear of the wings. The second line followed the first at a distance of five hundred yards, in the same order as the first. The corps under Gen. Polk followed the second line, at the distance of about eight hundred yards, in lines of brigades, deployed with their batteries in rear of each brigade, the left wing supported by cavalry. The reserve followed closely the third line in the same order, its right wing supported by cavalry. These two corps constituted the reserve, and were to support the front lines of battle by being deployed, when required, on the right and left, or otherwise act according to the exigencies of the battle.

At half past five on the morning of April 6, the Confederate lines and columns were in motion. Like an Alpine avalanche they came, attacking first the left of Gen. Grant, under Gen. Prentiss, who, with two thousand of his men, were soon made prisoners. This attack was in part a surprise. Scarcely had the men time to seize their weapons and form, after knowing of the approach of the Confederates. Gen. Grant himself was at Savannah at the commencement, but early reached the raging field. Gradually, as the Confederate line came up, the engagement had become general, and as Gen. Prentiss's division fell back, abandoning their camp, they were supported by Gen. Hurlbut, and thus for a time checked the progress of the Confederates. At the same time the left of Gen. Sherman's division on the right was forced back, and the brunt of the battle, in the centre, fell upon Gen. McClernand's division. Desperate as was their determination, yet at eleven o'clock this division had been pressed back in a line with Gen. Hurlbut. It still did some gallant fighting; once its right swept round and drove the Confederates for a considerable distance, but again fell back, and at the last it brought up near the position of the camps of Gen. Smith's division, commanded by W. H. L. Wallace. Thus the divisions of Prentiss, Sherman, and McClernand were driven back, their camps were all in the hands of the Confederates, and the whole front line, for which Hurlburt and Wallace were but the reserves, was gone, excepting Stuart's brigade of Sherman's division, on the extreme left. The position of this brigade was along the circuitous road from the Landing to Hamburg, some two miles distant from the former, and near the crossing of Lick Creek. They had remained isolated until after the division of Gen. Prentiss fell back, when the Confederates advanced upon them in such force as to be irresistible in their position, and they fell back a fourth of a mile and made a stand for three fourths of an hour. At this juncture a brigade of Gen. Wallace's reserve, under McArthur, was sent over to their support. They were, however, soon forced to fall back to one ridge, and then to another, and finally at twelve o'clock, badly shattered and disordered, they retreated to the right and rear of McArthur's brigade to reorganize.

Six hours had passed since the approach of the Confederates, and at this time only the divisions of Gens. Hurlbut and Wallace stood between the army and destruction or surrender. Still all was not lost. The divisions of Gens. Hurlbut and Wallace began to make a most gallant stand. The brigade of the latter had been sent to reënforce McArthur's, and thus reunited, filled the space in the line on the left made vacant by the falling back of Gen. Prentiss's division and Stuart's brigade of Gen. Sherman's division, and thus were on the left of Hurlbut's division. By the early breaking of Gen. Prentiss's line, the onset of the Confederates had been made to veer chiefly to the Union left. Here the contest continued stubborn. Four times the Confederates attempted to charge on Gen. Wallace's men. Each time the infantry poured in rapid volleys, and the artillery redoubled their efforts, thus compelling them to retreat with heavy slaughter. Farther to the right, Gen. Hurlbut's division, which had taken an advanced position, was compelled to fall back through its camp to a thick wood behind. Here, with open fields before them, they could rake the approach of the Confederates. Three times their heavy masses bravely charged upon the division, and each time they were repulsed with severe loss. The troops from the driven divisions were reorganized so far as available, and re-sent to the field. Thus the right of Gen. Hurlbut, which was almost wholly unprotected, and the weakness of which does not appear to have been discovered by the Confederates, was in a measure patched out. It had been previously determined that in case of an attack at Pittsburg Landing, the division under Gen. L. Wallace at Crump's Landing, five miles below, should come up on the right and flank the enemy. But no message was sent to this division until nearly noon, and it missed the way on coming up, and did not arrive until night. The division of Gen. Hurlbut at length became exhausted, and fell back out of sight of their camps to a point within half a mile of the Landing. Iu consequence of losing this support, the division of Gen. Wallace, thus in isolated advance, was compelled to fall back, the last to leave the field. Just at this moment its commander was mortally wounded.

It was now half past four o'clock. The front line of the divisions had been lost since eleven o'clock, and the reserve line was gone too. The Confederates occupied the camps of every division except Smith's, commanded during his sickness by Gen. Wallace, who had just been wounded. The whole army was crowded in the region of Wallace's camp, and to a circuit of one half to two thirds of a mile around the Landing. The next repulse would put it into the river, and there were not transports enough to cross a single division before the enemy would be upon them. Nearly half the field artillery was lost, nearly all the camps and camp equipage. Prisoners had been taken in great numbers.

At this time a lull took place in the firing, the first which had occurred since sunrise. It was thought that the enemy were either preparing for the grand final rush that was to crown the day's success, or that they were puzzled by the last retreat, and were moving cautiously. These few minutes were golden ones for that driven and defeated army, and they were impróved. Col. Webster, chief of staff, arranged the guns which he could collect of those that remained, in a sort of semicircle to protect the Union centre and left, upon which it was thought the enemy were now sure to advance. Corps of artillerists to man them were gathered from all the batteries. Twenty-two guns were thus placed in position, two of which were long 32's. In front was a victorious enemy; behind were the remnants of the repulsed divisions of the army driven within half a mile of the Landing, beyond which was a deep and rapid river. Gen. Wallace's division at Crump's Landing had not been heard from. Across the river now was seen the first glitter of the advance of Gen. Buell, but it could not be brought over in time to do much good. Suddenly a broad flash of light leaped out from the darkening woods, and the whistling leaden hail swiftly followed. The enemy were about to make their crowning effort for the day. Instantly the artillery replied, and as they approached nearer, the infantry fired volley after volley. At this time the gunboats, Lexington and Tyler, approached the mouth of Lick Creek, and were able with their guns to reach the field occupied by the Confederates near the river. This was a fire in their flank, which disconcerted their plans. Amid this terrible conflict darkness came on. The enemy had been held at bay.

Meantime Gen. Wallace had arrived with his division, and Gen. Buell with his forces, part of which took part in the battle of the afternoon, and it was decided after the sounds of battle had ceased, to attack the Confederates as soon as possible after daybreak. Gen. Wallace's division was to take the right and sweep back toward the position from which Gen. Sherman had been driven during the morning, and Gen. Nelson was to take the extreme left. Gen. Crittenden was to take a position during the night next to Gen. Nelson, and Gen. McCook with his division next to Crittenden. The space between Gens. McCook and Wallace was to be filled with the reorganized divisions of Gen. Grant's army. Stealthily the troops crept to their new positions, and lay down in line of battle on their arms. All through the night, Gen. Buell's men were marching up from Savannah to the point opposite Pittsburg Landing, and were ferried across, or were coming up on transports. At nine o'clock, the gunboats commenced a cannonade of the Confederate position, which was kept up all night. It produced little or no effect.

Gen. Beauregard thus reported his position on Sunday night: "At six o'clock P. M., we were in possession of all encampments between Owl and Lick creeks but one. Nearly all of his field artillery, about thirty flags, colors, and standards, over three thousand prisoners, including a division commander (Gen. Prentiss) and several brigade commanders, thousands of small arms, an immense supply of subsistence, forage, and munitions of war, and a large amount of means of transportation—all the substantial fruits of a complete victory—such indeed as rarely have followed the most successful battles; for never was an army so well provided as that of our enemy.

"The remnant of his army had been driven in utter disorder to the immediate vicinity of Pittsburg, under the shelter of the heavy guns of his iron-clad gunboats, and we remained undisputed masters of his well-selected, admirably provided cantonments, after over twelve hours of obstinate conflict with his forces, who had been beaten from them and the contiguous covert, but only by a sustained onset of all the men we could bring into action."

The Federal forces arranged for the battle of the next day were: the divisions of Gens. Nelson, Crittenden, McCook, Hurlbut, McClernand, and Sherman, including in the three latter the shattered and disorganized commands of Prentiss and W. H. L. Wallace, which were without commanders, and the fresh division of Gen. L. Wallace. These divisions were arranged in the order above named, beginning on the left. The change produced in the position of the Confederate forces, by the shells of the gunboats during the night, prevented them from opening the battle at daylight.

At seven o'clock in the morning, Gen. Nelson on the extreme left formed his line of battle, and advanced, with skirmishers thrown out, for nearly a mile before meeting the enemy in force. They immediately became engaged. There was no straggling, as upon the previous day. Gen. Nelson slowly but steadily advanced, pushing the exhausted enemy before him until half past ten, when under cover of the timber and a furious cannonading they made a general rally. Suddenly the masses of the enemy were hurled with tremendous force against the Federal lines, which now halted, wavered, and fell back. At this moment Terrill's battery of 24-pounder howitzers rushed up, and in a few minutes was unlimbered and firing into the compact and advancing ranks of the enemy. Here was the turning point of the battle on the left. The enemy were only checked, not halted; then followed for two hours a contest of artillery and musketry at short range. The enemy began to waver, when Gen. Buell coming up, saw at a glance the chance and ordered a charge by brigades, at "double quick." The Confederates fell back for a quarter of a mile, became more confused, and at half past two that point of the field was cleared. The next divisions, of Gens. Crittenden and McCook, after an obstinate struggle, were equally successful. The divisions of Gens. McClernand and Hurlbut, nothing daunted by the reverses of the preceding day, fought with much bravery. On the right the contest was more severe, and longer continued. A design was manifested by the enemy to turn the flank of Gen. Wallace's division. This was thwarted, and the enemy steadily driven back until four P. M., when a general retreat took place on the right. Thus the original plan of the enemy was frustrated. It was his design to drive Gen. Grant into his transports and the river, or to capture his force in time to profit by the victory, and remove to the rear all the stores and munitions that would be taken. This was to be done before the arrival of Gen. Buell.

On the retreat of the Confederate army, the original ground, and even the tents of Gen. Grant's army, were recovered. No regular pursuit was attempted until the next day. The number of the Federal army engaged on Sunday, was estimated by Gen. Beauregard at five divisions of nine thousand men each, or forty-five thousand men. The reënforcements of Sunday night were estimated by him at twenty-five thousand from Gen. Buell's army, and eight thousand under Gen. Wallace, and the entire force on Monday fifty-three thousand. This estimate slightly exceeds the Federal force engaged, especially in the number of reënforcements furnished by Gen. Buell. On the other hand, the Confederate force was estimated at sixty thousand by the Union officers, which was undoubtedly an overestimate. Gen. Grant had a force somewhat less than the enemy on Sunday, but on Monday he outnumbered them. No official statement of numbers has been afforded on either side. The Federal loss was 1,735 killed, 7,882 wounded, and 3,956 taken prisoners. Total, 13,573. The Confederate loss was killed 1,728, wounded 8,012, missing 959. Total, 10,699.

At the close of the battle on the first day Gen. Beauregard sent the following despatch to Richmond:

BATTLE FIELD OF SHILOH, *April* 6,
via Corinth and Chattanooga.

General S. Cooper, Adjutant-General:

We have this morning attacked the enemy in a strong position in front of Pittsburg, and after a severe battle of ten hours, thanks to Almighty God, gained a complete victory, driving the enemy from every position.

The loss on both sides is heavy, including our Commander-in-Chief, Albert Sidney Johnston, who fell gallantly leading his troops into the thickest of the fight.

(Signed) G. T. BEAUREGARD, Gen'l Com'd'g.

In consequence of the reception of this message, President Davis sent the following Message to the Confederate Congress, then in session at Richmond, on the 8th of April:

To the Senate and House of Representatives of the Confederate States of America:

The great importance of the news just received from Tennessee induces me to depart from the established usages, and to make to you this communication in advance of official reports. From official telegraphic despatches, received from official sources, I am able to announce to you, with entire confidence, that it has pleased Almighty God to crown the Confederate arms with a glorious and decisive victory over our invaders.

On the morning of the 6th, the converging columns of our army were combined by its Commander-in-Chief, Gen. A. Sidney Johnston, in an assault on the Federal army, then encamped near Pittsburg, on the Tennessee river.

After a hard-fought battle of ten hours, the enemy was driven in disorder from his position, and pursued to the Tennessee river, where, under cover of the gunboats, he was at the last accounts endeavoring to effect his retreat by aid of his transports. The details of this great battle are yet too few and incomplete to enable me to distinguish with merited praise all of those who may have conspicuously earned the right to such distinction, and I prefer to delay our own gratification in recommending them to your special notice, rather than incur the risk of wounding the feelings of any by failing to include them in the list.

When such a victory has been won over troops as numerous, well-disciplined, armed, and appointed, as those which have just been so signally routed, we may well conclude that one common spirit of unflinching bravery and devotion to our country's cause must have animated every breast, from that of the Commanding General to that of the humblest patriot who served in the ranks. There is enough in the continued presence of invaders on our soil to chasten our exultation over this brilliant success, and to remind us of the grave duty of continued exertion, until we shall extort from a proud and vain-glorious enemy the reluctant acknowledgment of our right to self-government.

But an All-wise Creator has been pleased, while vouchsafing to us his countenance in battle, to afflict us with a severe dispensation, to which we must bow in humble submission. The last long, lingering hope has disappeared, and it is but too true that Gen. Albert Sidney Johnston is no more. The tale of his death is simply narrated in a despatch from Col. William Preston, in the following words:

"Gen. Johnston fell yesterday at half past two o'clock, while leading a successful charge, turning the enemy's right, and gaining a brilliant victory. A Minie ball cut the artery of his leg, but he rode on until, from loss of blood, he fell exhausted, and died without pain in a few moments. His body has been intrusted to me by Gen. Beauregard, to be taken to New Orleans, and remain until directions are received from his family."

My long and close friendship with this departed

chieftain and patriot forbids me to trust myself in giving vent to the feelings which this sad intelligence has evoked. Without doing injustice to the living, it may safely be asserted that our loss is irreparable. Among the shining hosts of the great and good who now cluster around the banner of our country, there exists no purer spirit, no more heroic soul, than that of the illustrious man whose death I join you in lamenting.

In his death he has illustrated the character for which through life he was conspicuous—that of singleness of purpose and devotion to duty—with his whole energies. Bent on obtaining the victory which he deemed essential to his country's cause, he rode on to the accomplishment of his object, forgetful of self, while his very life-blood was fast ebbing away. His last breath cheered his comrades on to victory. The last sound he heard was their shout of victory. His last thought was of his country, and long and deeply will his country mourn his loss. JEFFERSON DAVIS.

On the 10th of April, President Lincoln, having received reports of the battles at Pittsburg Landing, or Shiloh, issued the following proclamation:

WASHINGTON, *April* 10, 1862.

It has pleased Almighty God to vouchsafe signal victories to the land and naval forces engaged in suppressing an internal rebellion, and at the same time to avert from our country the dangers of foreign intervention and invasion.

It is therefore recommended to the people of the United States that, at their next weekly assemblages in their accustomed places of public worship, which shall occur after the notice of this Proclamation shall have been received, they especially acknowledge and render thanks to our Heavenly Father for these inestimable blessings; that they then and there implore spiritual consolation in behalf of all those who have been brought into affliction by the casualties and calamities of sedition and civil war, and that they reverently invoke the Divine guidance for our national counsels, to the end that they may speedily result in the restoration of peace, harmony, and unity throughout our borders, and hasten the establishment of fraternal relations among all the countries of the earth.

In witness whereof I have hereunto set my hand and caused the seal of the United States to be affixed.

Done at the city of Washington, this tenth day of April, in the year of our Lord one thousand eight hundred and sixty-two, and of the independence of the United States the eighty-sixth.

ABRAHAM LINCOLN.

By the President—WM. H. SEWARD, Secretary of State.

On the 8th Gen. Sherman, with a body of cavalry and infantry, advanced on the Corinth road. His progress was at first checked by a force of the enemy's cavalry, which afterward was driven back. The roads were found in a bad state, in consequence of the heavy rain on Sunday night, and strewn with abandoned wagons, ambulances, and limber boxes. A general hospital, containing about two hundred and ninety wounded Confederate soldiers, was also found. The force of Gen. Sherman returned to camp at night.

It was charged against Gen. Grant that the commencement of the battle was a surprise to the Federal forces, and that he was absent from the field until some hours after. In reply he said: "As to the talk of our being surprised, nothing could be more false. If the enemy had sent us word where and when they would attack, we could not have been better prepared. Skirmishing had been going on for two days between our reconnoitring parties and the enemy's advance. I did not believe, however, that they intended to make a determined attack, but simply to make a reconnoissance in force. My headquarters were at Savannah, though I usually spent the day at Pittsburg. Troops were constantly arriving to be assigned to the different brigades and divisions. All were ordered to report at Savannah, making it necessary to keep an office and some one there. I was also looking for Buell to arrive, and it was important that I should have every arrangement complete for his crossing and transit to this side of the river."

Gen. Beauregard issued the preliminary orders for his troops to move from Corinth at one o clock on the morning of the 3d of April. The movement did not commence until during the forenoon. It was expected to reach the Federal lines in time to commence the attack on the 5th. They arrived too late in the afternoon of that day to attack. It could not have been with the advance of this force that "skirmishing had been going on for two days."

On the 9th of April, Maj.-Gen. Halleck, with a portion of his staff, left St. Louis for Pittsburg Landing, to assume command in the field. His first efforts were devoted to reorganizing the army. Two days after his arrival, an expedition was sent under convoy of the gunboats to destroy the railroad bridge over Bear Creek, seven miles inland from Chickasaw. This was successfully done by Gen. Sherman, and cut the communication between Richmond, Va., and Corinth. The state of the roads delayed for some days any movement of importance. Frequent skirmishes, however, took place with the Confederate infantry and cavalry hovering near. On the 22d of April, Gen. Pope, with his division, numbering about 25,000, arrived at Pittsburg Landing from New Madrid. On the 27th, orders were issued by Gen. Halleck for the army to hold itself in readiness for an immediate movement. Gen. Grant's divisions formed the right wing of the army, those of Gen. Buell the centre, and those of Gen. Pope the left wing. Gens. Grant and Buell retained the immediate command of their respective armies. The advance of the army was now gradually commenced. Day after day a division or a brigade was moved a few miles, and the outposts extended. On the 1st of May, Monterey was occupied. It is a small village in McNairy Co., Tenn., four miles from the Mississippi line, and about midway between Pittsburg Landing and Corinth. A few days previously, an expedition under Gen. Wallace had gone as far as Purdy, about twenty miles west of Pittsburg Landing, and destroyed the bridge of the railroad connecting Corinth with Jackson.

On the 2d of May, Gen. Beauregard issued the following address to his soldiers:

HEADQUARTERS OF THE FORCES AT CORINTH, MISSISSIPPI, *May* 2, 1862.

Soldiers of Shiloh and Elkhorn: We are about to meet once more, in the shock of battle, the invaders of our soil, the despoilers of our homes, the disturbers of our family ties, face to face, hand to hand. We are to decide whether we are to be freemen or vile slaves of those who are free only in name, and who but yesterday were vanquished, although in largely superior numbers, in their own encampments, on the ever-memorable field of Shiloh. Let the impending battle decide our fate, and add a more illustrious page to the history of our revolution—one to which our children will point with noble pride, saying, "Our fathers were at the battle of Corinth." I congratulate you on your timely junction. With your mingled banners, for the first time during this war, we shall meet our foe in strength that should give us victory. Soldiers, can the result be doubtful? Shall we not drive back into Tennessee the presumptuous mercenaries collected for our subjugation? One more manly effort, and, trusting in God and the justness of our cause, we shall recover more than we have lately lost. Let the sound of our victorious guns be reëchoed by those of the army of Virginia on the historic battle field of Yorktown.

G. T. BEAUREGARD,
General Commanding.

J. M. Otey, Acting Assistant Adjutant-General.

On the 3d of May, the army, commanded by Gen. Halleck, numbering 108,000 men, was within eight miles of Corinth. The bridges burned had been rebuilt, and the roads had become dry enough to render transportation easy. Few can conceive the difficulty of moving such a mass of men with their tents, baggage, artillery, and supplies, over an uneven, marshy country, covered with woods, and without roads.

Corinth is a small village in the northeast corner of Mississippi, ninety miles east from Memphis, and about twenty miles west from the Tennessee river. The Memphis and Charleston railroad runs through it from east to west, and the Mobile and Ohio from north to south. The country between it and the Tennessee river is very uneven, broken into ridges of hills and abrupt valleys, and covered with a heavy forest. The bridges over the creeks had been destroyed; the roads over the marshes had been torn up, and timber had been felled in great quantities over them.

On the same day Gen. Paine, with his division, made a reconnoissance to Farmington, five miles northwest of Corinth, and found about 4,500 Confederate troops, who, on being attacked, retreated with a loss of 30 killed and 200 taken prisoners. At the same time an artillery reconnoissance to Glendale on the Charleston and Memphis railroad, destroyed two trestle bridges and some of the track.

At this time the organization of Gen. Halleck's force had been somewhat changed. Gen. Thomas was assigned to the command of the right wing, composed of five divisions, viz.: his own, Hurlbut's, Sherman's, that of Gen. Smith, deceased, and Gen. Davies'; the centre consisted of four divisions under Gens. McCook, Wood, Nelson, and Crittenden; the left under Gen. Pope, to which was added one division of Gen. Curtis's army from Arkansas. Gen. Grant was appointed second in command. The reserve under Gen. McClernand consisted of his own and Gen. Wallace's divisions. The advance upon Corinth was made with the extremity of each wing thrown back in echelons to prevent a flank attack.

Meantime the Confederate forces at Corinth were active in strengthening their position and accumulating reënforcements. Pensacola and New Orleans had at this time been captured by the Federal forces, and Gen. Lovell had with his force arrived at Corinth from the neighborhood of the latter city. On the 9th, a strong Confederate force drove in the Federal pickets beyond Farmington, and advanced upon the brigade occupying the farther side of the creek in front of the Federal camp. The brigade maintained its position for some time, but Gen. Pope, finding it would be necessary to move his whole force across the creek, contrary to orders, in order to sustain it, directed it to retire.

Great as was the army of Gen. Halleck, the Confederates were believed to be stronger, and the people of the Southern States now looked forward to a signal and brilliant victory.

The advance of the Federal lines was slow, and on the 21st their batteries were within three miles of Corinth. The skirmishing of the pickets now increased every day, and soon became constant along the entire line. Almost daily the artillery was engaged, and the hour for battle was close at hand.

The railroad communication to the northward and eastward of Corinth had been destroyed at Purdy and Glendale. With a view to prevent still further, so far as it was in his power, either the reënforcement or the retreat of the Confederate armies at Corinth, Gen. Halleck directed that the railroad to the southward of Corinth and in the direction of Mobile should be also cut. To effect this, Col. Elliott, with two regiments of cavalry, started on the night of the 27th, and early on the 30th reached Booneville, 24 miles south of Corinth. A large amount of stores was found and destroyed, consisting of five railroad cars loaded with small arms, five loaded with loose ammunition, six with officers' baggage, and five with subsistence stores, harness, saddles, &c. Some hundreds of sick Confederate soldiers were paroled. The trains, engines, and depot were burned.

On the 28th, Gen. Halleck sent the following despatch to Washington:

Headquarters Department Mississippi,
Camp on Corinth Road, *May* 28.

Hon. E. M. Stanton, Secretary of War:

Three strong reconnoitring columns advanced this morning on the right, centre, and left, to feel the enemy and unmask his batteries. The enemy hotly contested his ground at each point, but was driven back with considerable loss. The column on the left encountered the strongest opposition. Our loss was twenty-five killed and wounded. The enemy left thirty dead on the field. The losses at other points are not yet ascertained. Some five or six officers and a number of privates were captured. The fighting will probably be renewed to-morrow morning at daybreak. The whole country is so thickly wooded that we are compelled to feel our way.

H. W. HALLECK, Major-General.

The following despatches were sent on the 30th:

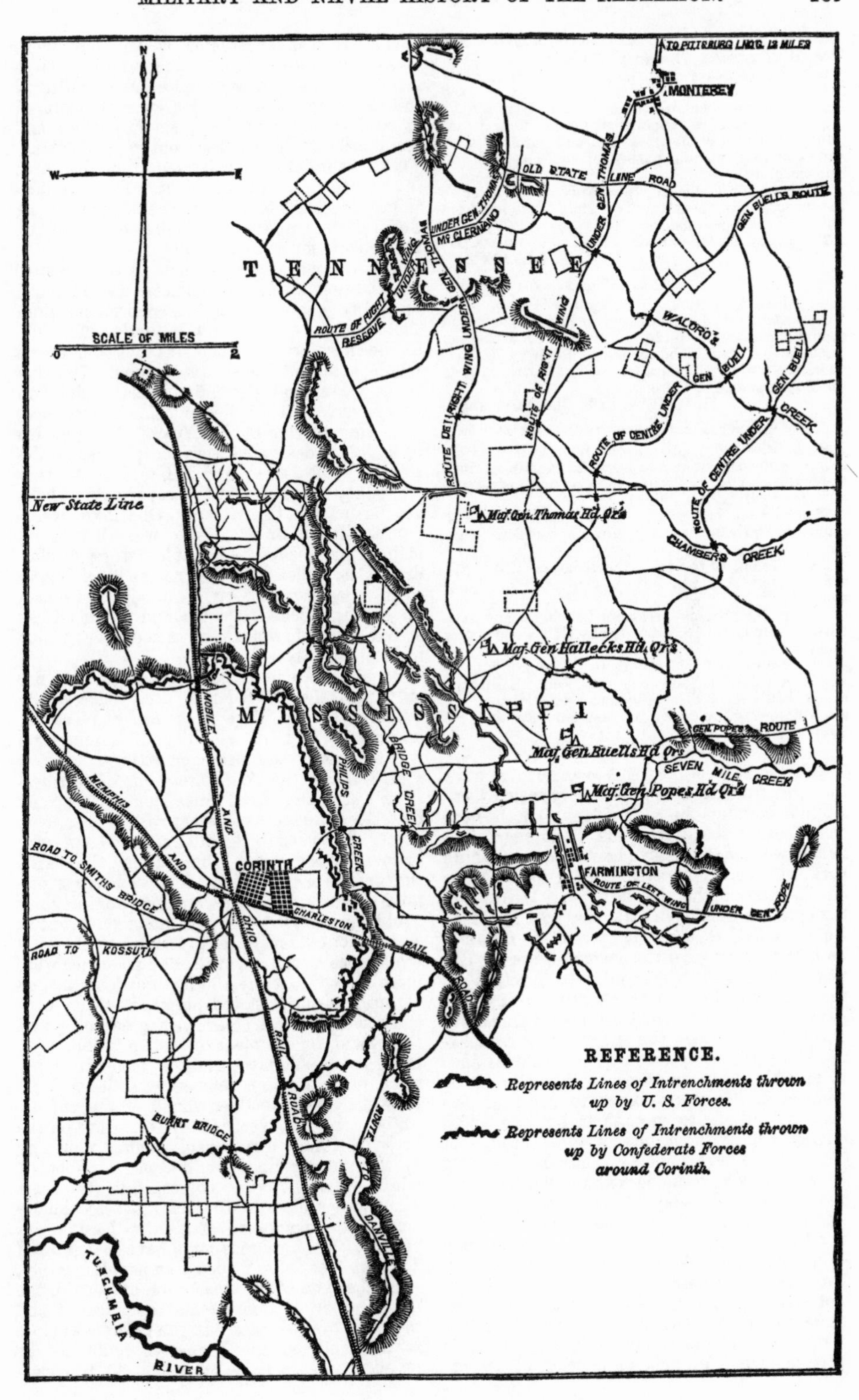
N
W
E
SCALE OF MILES
0 1 2
TO PITTSBURG LNDG. 12 MILES
MONTEREY
OLD STATE LINE ROAD
TENNESSEE
UNDER GEN. THOMAS
MC CLERNAND
ROUTE OF RIGHT RESERVE
ROUTE OF RIGHT WING UNDER GEN. THOMAS
ROUTE OF RIGHT WING
GEN. BUELL'S ROUTE
WALCRO'S
ROUTE OF CENTRE UNDER GEN. BUELL
CREEK
CHAMBERS CREEK
New State Line
Maj. Gen. Thomas Hd. Qrs
Maj. Gen. Hallecks Hd. Qrs
MISSISSIPPI
Maj. Gen. Buells Hd. Qrs
GEN. POPES ROUTE
SEVEN MILE CREEK
Maj. Gen. Popes Hd. Qrs
MOBILE AND OHIO RAIL ROAD
MEMPHIS AND CHARLESTON RAIL ROAD
PHILIPS CREEK
BRIDGE CREEK
CORINTH
FARMINGTON
ROUTE OF LEFT WING UNDER GEN. POPE
ROAD TO SMITHS BRIDGE
ROAD TO KOSSUTH
BURNT BRIDGE
ROUTE TO DANVILLE
TUSCUMBIA RIVER
REFERENCE.
Represents Lines of Intrenchments thrown up by U. S. Forces.
Represents Lines of Intrenchments thrown up by Confederate Forces around Corinth.

NEAR CORINTH, *May* 30, 1862.

Hon. E. M. Stanton, Secretary of War:

Gen. Pope's heavy batteries opened upon the enemy's intrenchments yesterday, about 10 A. M., and soon drove the rebels from their advanced battery.

Maj.-Gen. Sherman established another battery yesterday afternoon within one thousand yards of their works, and skirmishing parties advanced at daybreak this morning.

Three of our divisions are already in the enemy's advanced works, about three quarters of a mile from Corinth, which is in flames.

The enemy has fallen back of the Mobile railroad.

H. W. HALLECK.

NEAR CORINTH, *May* 30, 1862.

Hon. Edwin M. Stanton, Secretary of War:

Our advanced guard are in Corinth. There are conflicting accounts as to the enemy's movements. They are believed to be in strong force on our left flank, some four or five miles south of Corinth, near the Mobile and Ohio railroad.

H. W. HALLECK, Major-General.

HEADQUARTERS CAMP NEAR CORINTH, *May* 30.

Hon. E. M. Stanton, Secretary of War:

The enemy's position and works in front of Corinth were unexpectedly strong. He cannot occupy a stronger position in his flight.

This morning he destroyed an immense amount of public and private property, stores, provisions, wagons, tents, &c.

For miles out of the town the roads are filled with arms, haversacks, &c., thrown away by his flying troops.

A large number of prisoners and deserters have been captured, and are estimated by Gen. Pope at two thousand.

Gen. Beauregard evidently distrusts his army, or he would have defended so strong a position. His troops are generally much discouraged and demoralized. In all their engagements for the last few days their resistance has been weak.

H. W. HALLECK, Major-General.

The Confederate officers began to remove their sick from Corinth preparatory to an evacuation on Monday, the 26th of May. On the next day, Tuesday the 27th, Gens. Beauregard and Bragg were making arrangements for falling back, which process was completed in great haste on Thursday night, the 29th. On Wednesday the entire line of Gen. Halleck was advanced from one half to three quarters of a mile and up into easy range of the enemy's works. The heavy siege guns were put into position on that day on the works thrown up by the advanced column. This movement throughout was hotly contested, the enemy doubtless seeking to keep their opponents at a safe distance if possible, until their evacuation should be completed. They continued to show an unbroken front and to work their batteries with energy and without interruption throughout that and the next day. On Thursday morning operations were resumed with the same earnestness as on Wednesday. The enemy appeared still in position, and contested every inch of the Union advance with the utmost determination. At nine o'clock on that morning, however, their musketry firing ceased, and was not again resumed. After that hour there were no further close engagements. The batteries on both sides, however, were kept in play, though a gradual diminution of the enemy's fire was observable as the day wore away, and before night it had wholly ceased. During the night heavy explosions were heard in the enemy's works, which were conjectured to be the destruction of their magazines and ammunition, which subsequently proved true. Flames were also seen issuing from the town in the latter part of the night. These indications were plain to those in the advance of the Federal lines, and were understood to be the movements for an evacuation.

As no opposition was made to the advance on Friday morning, some officers dashed ahead to satisfy themselves of the enemy's position. The first party rode into the town at 6h. 30m. in the morning, and then was discovered the whole extent of the success gained. Destruction, waste, and desolation were visible on every hand. Huge piles of commissary stores were smouldering in the flames. The remains of buildings destroyed were conspicuous on the streets. The enemy had fled, taking care that what they could not carry away should at least not be left for the victors. One large warehouse, filled with provisions, was all that remained undamaged of boundless stores of similar goods, sufficient to withstand a much longer siege. Sacks were torn open, barrels broken, hogsheads knocked to pieces, and their contents mixed in common piles, upon and about which huge bonfires had been lit.

So complete was the evacuation that not only was the Confederate army successfully withdrawn, but they took every piece of ordnance. A large quantity of ammunition was left behind in a damaged state.

At Corinth the Confederate line of fortifications was about fifteen miles long, with strong batteries or redoubts at every road or assailable point. Between the fortifications and a marshy stream covering the whole front, the dense timber had been cut down to form a very strong abattis, through which no cavalry or artillery could have passed, nor even infantry except as skirmishers. The lines thrown up by the Federal troops at the end of the day's advance were mere rifle pits, while the fortifications around Corinth were, as stated above, a strong continuous line, constructed with great care and labor, and, independent of their position, were in themselves immeasurably stronger than the mere precautionary defences on the Federal part against any sudden sortie of the enemy. The Confederate works, moreover, were on the brow of a ridge considerably higher than any in the surrounding country, at the foot of which was a ravine correspondingly deep. The zigzag course of the line gave to the defenders the command of all the feasible approaches, and hundreds could have been mowed down at every step made by an assailing army.

At the time of the evacuation of Corinth the hot weather of summer had commenced and the period of low water in the rivers was close at hand. Even the Tennessee could not be relied upon as a route by which to transport all the supplies required for the Federal army. Gen. Halleck consequently took immediate steps to open a new line direct to Columbus, Ky., to which place the railroad was speedily repaired. These circumstances would impose a limit upon the military operations of Gen. Halleck's army for some months. Even if Corinth was evacuated and a part of the Confederate force withdrawn entirely, no serious blow could be struck by Gen. Halleck. These considerations must have presented themselves to the Confederate Government at the time when Richmond was closely pressed by Gen. McClellan, and really in danger of capture. Without doubt they exerted an influence in producing the determination to evacuate Corinth. And when it became evident that the position could not be held against the force that was advancing upon it, they pointed out the manner in which this evacuation could be turned to advantage.

At this time Gen. McClellan had crossed the Chickahominy, Gen. Banks was retreating before Gen. Jackson up the Virginia valley, Forts Pillow and Randolph and the city of Memphis had surrendered, and a Federal force was making an attack on Vicksburg.

The pursuit of the retreating forces of Gen. Beauregard was made as follows: On the morning after the evacuation, Gen. Pope's forces entered the town about twenty minutes before seven o'clock, just as the last of the Confederate cavalry were leaving. One company of cavalry, being Gen. Pope's escort, pushed after them, and had a brisk skirmish, in which several were killed and captured. The pursuit, however, was arrested by the burning of a bridge over a swampy creek, and the cavalry returned. A brigade of cavalry and a battery under Gen. Granger were then sent out by Gen. Pope on the Booneville road. It left Farmington at noon on the 30th, and the same day came up with the rear guard of the enemy posted on Tuscumbia Creek eight miles south of Corinth. The next day they were driven out, and on Sunday, June 1, the pursuit was recommenced. Gen. Granger passed Rienzi only two hours behind the retreating army, and found the bridges between that place and Booneville so recently fired that the timbers were nearly all saved. That afternoon the advance overtook the retreating Confederate rear four miles from Booneville, and pursued it within one mile of the town, and halted for the night. At five o'clock on the next morning the town was entered, and skirmishing was kept up all day with the Confederates on every road leading westward or southward as far as Twenty Mile Creek. On the next day a reconnoissance with force was made toward Baldwin, and the Confederate force driven across Twenty Mile Creek; and on the 4th another reconnoissance was made by Col. Elliot via Blocklands, with similar results. On the 10th Baldwin and Guntown were occupied by Federal troops, which was the termination of the pursuit. Booneville, above mentioned, is twenty-four miles by the railroad from Corinth. The Confederate force fell back to Tupello. The position of the forces at Corinth remained unchanged until the 10th of June, when Maj.-Gen. Buell, under instructions from Gen. Halleck, moved his army along the line of railroad toward Chattanooga. He was then between Huntsville and Stevenson, when it became necessary to move upon Louisville to counteract the designs of Gen. Bragg. Meantime the army under Gen. Grant occupied the line of west Tennessee and Mississippi extending from Memphis to Iuka, and protecting the railroads from Columbus south, which were then their only channels of supply. On the 23d of July Gen. Halleck left the department to take the position of general-in-chief at Washington. Gen. Grant continued in the position above stated until a portion of his troops were withdrawn from Mississippi and sent to Kentucky and Cincinnati to give confidence to the new levies brought into the field upon the invasion of Kentucky by Gen. Bragg.

It will have been observed that the division of Gen. Buell's army, under the command of Gen. Mitchell, has not been spoken of as coöperating with the other divisions at Pittsburg Landing and Corinth. This division left Nashville on the same day with the others, but took the road to Murfreesboro. There it remained in occupation of the place and repairing the bridges until the 4th of April. Long before this time the Confederate troops, which occupied Nashville and retreated to Murfreesboro, had withdrawn and united with those under Gen. Beauregard on the new southern line of defence.

On the 4th of April, Gen. Mitchell marched to Shelbyville, the county seat of Bedford county, Tenn., twenty-six miles distant. On the 7th he advanced to Fayetteville, twenty-seven miles farther, and the next forenoon, the 8th, fifteen miles beyond, he crossed the State line of Alabama. Continuing his march six miles farther, and being within ten miles of Huntsville, Ala., he halted for the artillery and infantry to come up. No tents were pitched. The men lay round camp fires. Just as the moon was going down, the shrill bugle call was sounded. All were up, and in a few minutes ready to move. A battery was put in advance, supported by two brigades. Four miles from Huntsville, the shrill whistle of a locomotive was heard, and in a few minutes the train came in sight, and was stopped by the call of the brass guns of the battery. The train was captured together with 159 prisoners. On to the town was now the order. The citizens were quietly sleeping as the army entered. Says a spectator of the scene: "The clattering noise of the cavalry aroused them from their slumber ere the dawn of the morning, and they flocked to door and window, exclaiming with blanched cheek and faltering tongue, 'They come, they

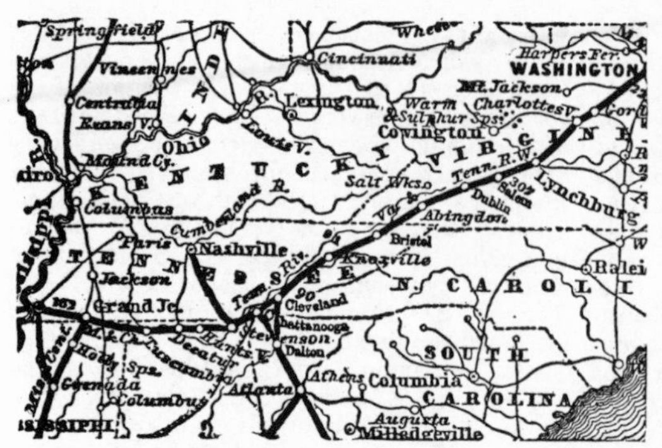

come, the Yankees come!' Never in the history of any military movement was surprise so complete. Men rushed into the streets almost naked, the women fainted, the children screamed, the darkies laughed, and for a short time a scene of perfect terror reigned. This state of affairs soon subsided."

Col. Gazley, of the 37th Indiana regiment, was appointed provost marshal, and his regiment occupied the city as guard. Then commenced an examination of the results of this bloodless capture. At the railroad depot were found seventeen first-class locomotives and a great quantity of passenger and freight cars, and at the foundery two or three cannon, together with several small arms. Gen. Mitchell soon made good use of the engines. Before the close of day, one hundred miles of the Memphis and Charleston railroad were in his possession, stretching in one direction as far as Stevenson, and in the other as far as Decatur. At the latter place, the entire camp equipage of a regiment was captured. From Decatur he pushed on at once to Tuscumbia.

Thus, without the loss of a single life, Gen. Mitchell placed his army midway between Corinth and Chattanooga, prevented the destruction of a fine bridge at Decatur, opened communication with Gen. Buell, and also the navigation of the Tennessee. The occupation of Huntsville also cut off all communication between the east and west by the Memphis and Charleston railroad. The expedition east on the railroad, under Col. Sill, penetrated as far as Stevenson at the junction of the Chattanooga road, at which place five locomotives and an amount of rolling stock were captured. An expedition went as far south from Tuscumbia as Russelville. Lagrange and Florence were also visited, and Confederate property of the military kind was found.

This extension of Gen. Mitchell's lines to hold the railroad rendered his situation precarious. Soon the enemy began to gather in force and threaten him. His course however received the commendation of the War Department. He was raised to the rank of a major-general, and ordered to report directly to the department, and his force was constituted an independent corps. But he got no reënforcements. He was left in such a condition that he at first hardly had anything to report but that he had been gradually driven from those positions, the gaining of which had made him a major-general. On his right, the enemy were now in force, and picket skirmishing was constant. On his left, at Chattanooga, a strong force threatened his rear and the safety of Nashville. In his front, cavalry came up and attacked his line at times. Gen. Halleck sent to him 100,000 rations under convoy of a gunboat. Of these 40,000 were burned to prevent their capture. On the 24th of April, the retreat from Tuscumbia commenced. On the 26th the bridge at Decatur was crossed, when it was fired and burned. It was the only crossing of the Tennessee east of Florence, above the head of navigation, and west of Bridgeport near Chattanooga. The bridge was destroyed in an hour and a half, but before its destruction was complete, the enemy's cavalry appeared on the opposite side. Having returned to Huntsville, the right wing of the force commenced operations toward Chattanooga.

On the 30th of April, an expedition was sent to Bridgeport near Stevenson, the result of which placed under the control of Gen. Mitchell the bridge across the river. As there was no bridge below his position since the destruction of the one at Decatur, and as he had control of the one above near Chattanooga, and as his communication between the extremes of his line was by railroad, which was in his possession, and the Tennessee river lay in front of him, on the farther side of which was all the enemy he anticipated, he thus closed his report to the Secretary of War under date of May 1: "The campaign is ended, and I now occupy Huntsville in perfect security, while all of Alabama north of the Tennessee river floats no flag but that of the Union." It was stated that if Gen. Mitchell had been sustained with a sufficient force, he would have crossed the Tennessee river at its extreme southern point in Alabama, and reached Gunter's Landing—a march of forty miles thence would have placed in his possession Gadsden on the Coosa river, where he could have destroyed the steamboats on the river, or seized them and proceeded to Rome and destroyed large armories and founderies. From Gunter's Landing there is also a fine road to Rome, eighty miles distant. In two days his cavalry could have passed that distance, destroyed the founderies at Rome, and captured engines and cars enough at that place and Kingston to have enabled him to proceed up the road with an armed force to protect them in burning the bridges. This movement would have cut off Gen. E. Kirby Smith, then advancing upon Huntsville, from reënforcements or retreat. The Confederate forces in Knoxville, Greenville, and Cumberland Gap, in east Tennessee, and even in western Virginia, would all have been dangerously exposed by little more extended operations along the railroads by Gen. Mitchell.

Subsequently he advanced upon Chattanooga, which compelled the Confederate forces in Eastern Tennessee to make a backward movement. Only a single stem of railroad connects Chattanooga with Atlanta, and thence connects with other parts of Georgia, Alabama, and South Carolina, and its loss would compel evacuation above, as in the case of Bowling Green. Several expeditions were sent out by Gen. Mitchell during the month of May against small bands of cavalry upon the same side of the river. One or two skirmishes of considerable spirit, and with respectable numbers, also took place. On the 6th of June Gen. Negley, from the opposite side of the river, made an attack with his artillery upon Chattanooga. This was replied to from some earthworks. On the next day a considerable force under Gen. E. K. Smith opened fire upon Gen. Negley, but were compelled to retire. Chattanooga was finally abandoned by the Federal force in consequence of the difficulty of procuring supplies.

On the advance of Gen. Buell, this division of his army under Gen. Mitchell was placed under the command of Gen. Rousseau, and Gen. Mitchell was ordered to the command at Port Royal, South Carolina.

The result of the military operations that have been thus far described, was at this time of the year such as to leave in the hands of the Southern Government a large military force, which it could use without additional hazard wherever it pleased, while the Federal Government, struck with panic from other causes, was actually calling upon the governors of the loyal States to hurry forward to its protection even three months' volunteers. The acquisition of territory, however, was all on the side of the Federal Government, which had got its hands so full in proportion to its military preparations, that it must either relinquish some portion of it or submit to defeat somewhere, if its antagonist was active, skilful, and dexterous. This state of affairs culminated in the midst of the Virginia campaign, and it was decisive not only of that campaign, but it presented to the world magnificent displays of the skill and power of the respective antagonists.

It has been said that the Southern Government had a large military force with which it was free to act, without additional hazard. This force consisted of part of the levies of the previous year, some of the levies raised by the governors of the States, under a call from President Davis in February of this year, and some of the troops beginning to come up under the conscription act passed by the Richmond Congress early in April. In Missouri the success of Gen. Curtis had been such as to drive out all the regular Confederate troops, and he had established himself just within the borders of Arkansas. But the requisition upon him to send ten regiments to the assistance of Gen. Halleck, so limited his ability for offensive operations, that the troops of Arkansas were to a considerable extent free to act wherever the Southern Government needed. Kentucky and Middle and Western Tennessee had been evacuated by the Confederate forces, which held them at the beginning of the year. These forces congregated at Corinth, and, upon its evacuation, the vast army was not in a condition, at that hot season of the year, to follow the fugitives any considerable distance, or to push forward its offensive operations, as has been before observed. A limited Confederate force was therefore kept in the field, to observe the operations of Gen. Halleck. The cessation of military operations against Charleston and Savannah, and also in North Carolina, by the Federal Government, caused the Confederate Government to keep no more than a force of observation in the field, and left it at liberty to concentrate its other troops wherever their presence might be most needed. These troops were therefore sent to Virginia, to engage in the campaign going on in that State.

On the 23d of February the Confederate troops evacuated Nashville; and on the 25th the city was occupied by the advance of the Federal army under Gen. Nelson. A large portion of the State having now been reconquered to the Union, President Lincoln nominated Andrew Johnson Military Governor of Tennessee, with the rank of brigadier-general of volunteers, and the nomination was confirmed by the Senate on the 5th of March. Governor Johnson, a native of North Carolina, had been five times a Representative in Congress, and twice Governor of Tennessee, and at the time of his appointment was United States Senator from that State. He reached Nashville March 12th, in company with Emerson Etheridge, Clerk of the House of Representatives, and Horace Maynard, Member of Congress from Tennessee, and the next evening, in response to a serenade, he made an address, which he afterwards published as an "Appeal to the People of Tennessee." After briefly recounting the history of the secession movement, and the measures adopted by the Federal Government, he proceeded as follows:

The President has conducted this mighty contest, until, as commander-in-chief of the army, he has caused the national flag again to float undisputed over the Capitol of our State. Meanwhile the State Government has disappeared. The executive has abdicated; the Legislature has dissolved; the judiciary is in abeyance. The great ship of State, freighted with its precious cargo of human interests and human hopes, its sails all set, and its glorious old flag unfurled, has been suddenly abandoned by its officers and mutinous crew, and left to float at the mercy of the winds, and to be plundered by every rover upon the deep. Indeed, the work of plunder has already commenced. The archives have been desecrated, the public property stolen and destroyed; the vaults of the State bank violated, and its treasures robbed, including the funds carefully gathered and consecrated for all time to the instruction of our children. In such a lamentable crisis the Government of the United States could not be unmindful of its high constitutional obligation to guarantee to every State in this Union a republican form of government, an obligation which every State has a direct and immediate interest in having observed toward every other State; and from which, by no action on the part of the people in any State, can the Federal Government be absolved. A republican form of government in consonance with the Constitution of the United States, is one of the fundamental conditions of our political existence, by which every part of the country is alike bound, and from which no part can escape. This obligation the national Government is now attempting to discharge. I have been appointed, in the absence of the regular and established State authorities, as Military Governor for the time being, to preserve the public property of the State, to give the protection of law actively enforced to her citizens, and, as speedily as may be, to restore her Government to the same condition as before the existing rebellion.

In this grateful but arduous undertaking, I shall avail myself of all the aid that may be afforded by my fellow citizens. And for this purpose I respectfully but earnestly invite all the people of Tennessee, desirous or willing to see a restoration of her ancient Government, without distinction of party affiliations or past political opinions or action, to unite with me, by counsel and coöperative agency, to accomplish this great end. I find most, if not all of the offices, both State and Federal, vacated either by actual abandonment, or by the action of the incumbents in attempting to subordinate their functions to a power in hostility to the fundamental law of the State, and subversive of her national allegiance. These offices must be filled temporarily, until the State shall be restored so far to its accustomed quiet, that the people can peaceably assemble at the ballot box and select agents of their own choice. Otherwise anarchy would prevail, and no man's life or property would be safe from the desperate and unprincipled.

I shall, therefore, as early as practicable, designate for various positions under the State and county Governments, from among my fellow-citizens, persons of probity and intelligence, and bearing true allegiance to the Constitution and Government of the United States, who will execute the functions of their respective offices until their places can be filled by the action of the people. Their authority, when their appointments shall have been made, will be accordingly respected and observed.

To the people themselves, the protection of the Govarnment is extended. All their rights will be duly respected, and their wrongs redressed when made known. Those who through the dark and weary night of the rebellion have maintained their allegiance to the Federal Government will be honored. The erring and misguided will be welcomed on their return. And while it may become necessary, in vindicating the violated majesty of the law, and in reasserting its imperial sway, to punish intelligent and conscious treason in high places, no merely retaliatory or vindictive policy will be adopted. To those, especially, who in a private, unofficial capacity have assumed an attitude of hostility to the Government, a full and complete amnesty for all past acts and declarations is offered, upon the one condition of their again yielding themselves peaceful citizens to the just supremacy of the laws. This I advise them to do for their own good, and for the peace and welfare of our beloved State, endeared to me by the associations of long and active years, and by the enjoyment of her highest honors.

The address was listened to with respect and some favor; but the Union feeling developed in Nashville and other parts of Middle Tennessee, after their occupation by the Federal forces, was far from answering the expectations of the North, or even of the Tennessee Unionists themselves. On the 9th of March the citizens of Shelbyville, in Bedford County, burned a quantity of stores, to prevent them from falling into the hands of the Confederates; and soon afterwards the people of Gallatin, a place in which the Southern party had before been strongly in the ascendant, held a town meeting, and expressed a readiness to return to their allegiance; but these were exceptional instances, and the Federal occupation did not become popular until there seemed reason to think it would be permanent.

On the 20th the following letter was addressed to the governor by seven Tennessee officers, confined at Camp Chase, near Columbus, on behalf of themselves and "a great many others whose names were not subscribed":

To Andrew Johnson, Governor, &c., of the State of Tennessee.

We the undersigned, citizens of Columbia, Tenn., having gone into service, under the last call of Gov. Harris, the circumstances of which call, and our enlistment, you have by this time become fully aware of; are very desirous of returning to loyalty by taking the oath of allegiance to the Federal Government, and will ever feel grateful to you for our deliverance from our present confinement.

Several other letters of like import, from Tennesseans who had served in the Southern army, were published about the same time.

Trade, for some time after the occupation of Nashville, gave no sign of reviving. Northern merchants had followed the national armies into Tennessee, in the expectation of buying cotton, and obtaining markets for their own commodities, but there was little or no cotton at Nashville and other river ports, and the planters of the interior showed no disposition to send it forward. Northern products of nearly all sorts were in great demand, and quoted at high prices; but the people had no money except the currency of the Southern Confederacy, which the Northern speculators, of course, refused to take. In a few weeks' time, however, United States money became comparatively plentiful throughout Middle Tennessee, confidence in the depreciated bills of Tennessee banks was restored, and cotton gradually found its way to the ports of outlet.

Buyers began to scour the country in all directions, within, and sometimes even beyond the Federal lines. The reluctance of the cotton planters to sell was soon entirely overcome. Good middling brought, in April, 16 and 17 cents in specie, or United States Treasury notes, and 22 and 25 cents in current Tennessee paper.

Rice was also shipped to some extent, and the quantity of both these staples sent into the loyal States would have been much greater but for guerrilla bands, who made it their object to prevent the crops from being sold. A proclamation was issued by the governor, threatening to imprison five or more secessionists of the neighborhood where such things occurred.

On May 12, in pursuance of a call signed by a number of prominent citizens, requesting "their fellow-citizens of the State of Tennessee, who are in favor of the restoration of the former relations of this State to the Federal

Union, to be present at a public meeting to be held at the Capitol, in the city of Nashville," a large gathering of persons from different parts of the State took place in the Hall of Representatives. Ex-Gov. Wm. B. Campbell (now brigadier-general) was chosen president of the convention, and on taking the chair made a few remarks, in the course of which he said:

We invite all to help us in restoring the supremacy of law over Tennessee, and reinstating her in all the privileges and immunities of the Union. We wish to welcome back all our deluded fellow-citizens cordially. The Government intends no sweeping confiscation, nor wild turning loose of slaves against the revolted States. It designs no infringement on the rights of property. All will be protected who will be loyal to the Government. We bear no malice toward any one, but deep sympathy for the deluded. He had dear friends and dear relations who had gone astray, and his heart yearned for their return. The Federal Government will pursue a kind, liberal, and benevolent policy toward the people of the South, to bring them to the Union.

Addresses were made by W. H. Wiseman, Hon. W. B. Stokes, Edmund Cooper, Col. W. H. Polk, Gov. Johnson, Col. L. D. Campbell, Gen. Dumont, and others.

At the request of many persons present at this convention, the chairman appointed Allen A. Hall, John Lellyett, Russell Houston, Horace H. Harrison, and M. M. Brien, a "State Central Union Committee," for the purpose of communicating with the friends of Union in various parts of the State.

The United States Circuit Court opened at Nashville on the 13th, and in his charge to the Grand Jury Judge Catron instructed them to ferret out and indict all persons guilty of aiding and abetting the marauding parties who infested the State.

On the 14th Ex-Gov. Neil S. Brown, one of the leaders of the secession party in Tennessee, was arrested, by order of Gov. Johnson, on charge of treason, but was afterward released on parole. He took the oath of allegiance, and became a prominent advocate of the Union.

The following notice was issued at Nashville on May 18:

After this date no shipment of merchandise from this city or State will be allowed, except upon permits therefor issued by the proper constituted officers of the Government of the United States.

On the 21st, D. F. Carter, president, and John Herriford, cashier of the Bank of the Union at Nashville, were arrested on charge of treason, and placed in confinement.

An election for judge of the circuit court of Nashville, held on the 22d, resulted in the choice of Turner S. Foster, secessionist, by a majority of about 190. The Union vote was about 1,000; the vote against separation in Nashville, in June, 1861, was only 300.

Judge Foster received his commission from the provisional governor on the 26th of July, and the same day was arrested and sent to the penitentiary.

On the 24th of May a Union meeting was held at Murfreesboro', at which speeches were made by Gov. Johnson and others, and the resolutions of the Nashville Union Convention of the 12th were unanimously adopted. Thirty-four soldiers of a Tennessee regiment in the Southern army came before the provost marshal on that occasion, and took the oath of allegiance.

On the same day, under the provisions of the general confiscation act of August 6, 1861, the United States Marshal for the Middle District of Tennessee seized at Nashville the offices of the "Republican Banner," "Union and American," and "Gazette" newspapers, and the Southern Methodist Publishing House, and on the 26th the Baptist Publishing House, and "Patriot" newspaper office, all having been active supporters of the secession movement. He also seized two gun factories in South Nashville, belonging to stock companies.

Governor Johnson, about the same time, issued an order providing that all persons who should be arrested for using treasonable and seditious language, and who should refuse thereafter to take the oath of allegiance and give bonds in the sum of $1,000 for future good behavior, should be sent South beyond the Federal lines, with the distinct understanding that if they returned they would be treated as spies.

On the 7th a Union meeting was held at Shelbyville, Gov. Johnson, Col. May of Kentucky, and James L. Scudder, formerly a prominant secessionist and assistant inspector general of State troops under Gov. Harris, being among the orators.

On June 17th Gov. Johnson summoned six prominent secession clergymen of Nashville to meet him at the Capitol, and requested them to take the oath of allegiance to the Federal Government. At their urgent desire, a few days were granted them for deliberation. On the 28th, as they refused to take the oath, five were sent to the penitentiary, to be kept in close confinement until arrangements could be made for escorting them beyond the lines: the sixth, being in feeble health, was paroled. On the same day Dr. J. P. Ford, and on the next day the Rev. C. D. Elliott, principal of a girls' boarding-school, and Dr. Cheatham, superintendent of the State Lunatic Asylum, were arrested at Nashville, and similarly disposed of. At a Union meeting held in Pulaski June 17, Mr. George Baber, formerly identified with the Southern party as editor of the Nashville "Banner," delivered an address in which he disavowed his past course. Another meeting of the people of Giles County was held at the same place on the 21st, when resolutions were passed, whereby the citizens pledged themselves to use their influence for the speedy restoration of the State to her Federal relations. Giles County is one of the most flourishing in Middle Tennessee. It was largely engaged in cotton growing, and works over 5,000 negroes. On the 23d five of the most prominent secessionists of Pulaski, including the Rev. Mr. Mooney, a Methodist clergyman, were arrested and sent beyond the Federal lines under an escort of cavalry.

A Union meeting was held at Valley Springs Meeting House, Dickson county, on the 21st.

The anniversary of American independence was celebrated with great enthusiasm, and Union speeches were delivered at the capital and in other parts of the State.

Arrests continued frequent, and in the early part of July twenty-eight persons were arrested at Goodlettsville, but were all released on taking the oath of allegiance.

In the mean time, the Union citizens of the State had been almost incessantly harassed by roving bands of guerillas and marauders, of whom the cavalry forces of Cols. Forrest and Morgan acquired the greatest notoriety. Scarcely a day passed which did not bring a report of their seizing horses, cattle, and stores, burning bridges, tearing up railroad tracks, destroying telegraphic communications, and not unfrequently killing prominent Union men or falling unexpectedly upon small detachments of Federal troops. On the 1st of May a party of Col. Morgan's horsemen entered Pulaski and destroyed the goods of a shop keeper of that place. A military commission examined the case on the 20th, and ordered the provost marshal to collect from the secession authorities of the town, or failing in that, from certain well-known Confederate citizens, a sum sufficient to cover all the damages. As soon as Memphis had fallen the Confederate cavalry began to infest the line of the Memphis and Charleston railroad, burning cotton, carrying off Union citizens, and threatening to seize the person and destroy the property of any one who attempted to enter Memphis upon whatever pretext. On the 7th of July the pickets of a Minnesota brigade were attacked near Murfreesboro' by a party of civilians, and two of the soldiers were killed. The next day 90 guerillas were captured between Gallatin and Hartsville. On the 9th a wagon master and a sutler were fired upon from an ambush near Franklin, the the latter being killed and the former severely wounded. Similar murders were perpetrated near Memphis. On the 13th Colonels Forrest and Warner, with a regiment of Texan Rangers and a strong force of other Confederate troops, captured Murfreesboro'; and on the 21st a party of Forrest's guerillas captured the Federal pickets on the Lebanon road.

The greatest excitement now existed at Nashville, and the loyal citizens proceeded to enroll themselves in anticipation of an attack upon the city, but in a few days reënforcements arrived and the guerillas fell back toward McMinnville. On the 17th an attack was made by about 60 guerillas upon a small scouting party belonging to Gen. Negley's command, between Mount Pleasant and Columbia. The Federal soldiers, only 8 in number, took refuge in a house and defended themselves for 6 hours, the guerillas finally retiring. On the 19th a party of 11 guerillas entered Brownsville and destroyed a large quantity of cotton. On the 2d of August Gen. Nelson occupied McMinnville, the Confederates falling back before his arrival. Gen. Negley about the same time led an expedition against the guerillas in the direction of Columbia, dispersing a large assemblage of the marauders at Williamsport, and engaging them again with success at Kinderhook. On the 12th a detachment of Col. Morgan's guerillas surprised Gallatin, on the Louisville and Nashville railroad, making 130 prisoners and capturing a quantity of government stores, with a train of grain and 65 horses on the way from Louisville to Nashville. A force was immediately sent from Nashville to intercept them, but arrived only in time to capture a wagon load of arms, and exchange shots with stragglers on the outskirts of the town. On the 16th a party of workmen sent to repair the railroad which had been injured by Morgan near Gallatin were captured by guerillas, and the same day two Federal couriers were made prisoners a few miles south of Nashville. Railroad communication with the latter place was now entirely cut off on every side, bridges being burned and the track torn up for considerable distances, but the interruption lasted only a short time. On the 18th a railroad train was fired into near Columbia, a woman and child and two Federal soldiers being killed. The day afterward Clarksville was captured by a guerilla force, assisted by the disunion inhabitants of the town, Col. Mason of the 71st Ohio and about 300 men surrendering without resistance.

On the 20th a guard of 20 men under Captain Atkinson of the 50th Indiana volunteers, being attacked at Edgefield junction by an overwhelming force of guerillas under Col. Morgan, defended themselves for 3 hours behind a stockade, repulsing their assailants three times, and saving the train to Bowling Green which it seems to have been Morgan's intention to capture.

A second engagement with Morgan at Gallatin on the 22d proved a much more disastrous affair than the raid on the 12th. Gen. R. W. Johnson was taken prisoner, and more than half his command of 800 men were killed or captured. The guerillas emboldened by success now became more than ever troublesome. Travel ceased to be safe even within a few miles of the capital; the mails were robbed; Union citizens were seized and sent to the South, and small detachments of Federal troops were frequently surprised by these daring horsemen, whose rapid movements generally set pursuit at defiance. At McMinnville they attacked the stockade, but the little guard repulsed them with heavy loss; and on the 28th Col. Forrest's band had a severe engagement with a Federal Kentucky regiment near Woodbury, losing 8 killed, 30 wounded, and 15 prisoners. On the 10th of September some Federal officers were captured by guerillas while dining at a house two or three miles from Nashville. At Covington, Tipton county, in the western part of the State, where such raids had been common, the citizens gave bonds in the sum of $50,000 to protect Union residents, and declared their purpose of hanging all guerillas who fell into their hands. The interior of the State was not only harassed by organized bands, such as those of Forrest and Morgan, who held regular commissions in the Confederate army, but were also ravaged by marauders of the worst description, who had no object but plunder, and robbed both parties alike. The guerillas also gathered in considerable force in the counties bordering on the Mississippi, and attacked transports and other vessels on the river, generally with musketry alone, but sometimes with light field artillery. On the 23d of September a party of twenty-five or thirty men at Randolph, armed with rifles, muskets, and shot-guns, signalled the steamer Eugene to land. As the boat had two passengers and some freight for that point, she rounded to, none of the officers perceiving the guerilla band, who in fact had kept in the background up to that time. It was now apparent, as the guerillas sprang from their hiding place, that the intention was to seize the boat; and the captain, regardless of the demand to surrender, boldly pushed back into the stream amid several volleys of musketry. There were a great many passengers on board, including women and children, but no one was killed or hurt.

The outrage having been reported the next day to Gen. Sherman, at Memphis, he sent the forty-sixth regiment of Ohio volunteers and a section of Willard's Chicago battery to destroy the town. These troops took passage on the steamers Ohio Belle and Eugene, which arrived at Randolph on the 25th. The inhabitants seemed to have been impressed with the conviction that the town would be destroyed, and consequently most of them had left the place. The quartermaster of the regiment went through the town and took an inventory of the buildings and their probable worth, with their owners' names, as far as they could be learned. This having been done, and everything in each house having been removed, every house in the town was burnt to the ground, except the Methodist church, which was left standing for the accommodation of the few persons turned out of doors by the fire. All the cotton and other property of value as merchandise was brought away.

The town of Randolph, thus destroyed, contained about ninety houses, said to be mostly in a dilapidated condition. It is situated about sixty miles above Memphis, and was the site of extensive Confederate fortifications before the Mississippi river was opened.

To prevent similar occurrences in future, General W. T. Sherman, commanding at Memphis, ordered that for every boat fired upon ten disloyal families should be expelled the city.

On Oct. 21st the President recommended an election for members of Congress to be held in several districts of Tennessee, and instructed the military commanders to take measures to facilitate the execution of the order.

The progress of the campaign had now brought the Confederate forces almost within sight of Nashville, and the guerillas, hovering over the route of the regular forces, carried off stragglers from the Federal columns and rendered important service to their cause by burning bridges, skirmishing with pickets, and threatening the Union supply trains. On the 19th of October, Col. Forrest was defeated on the Gallatin turnpike about 7 miles from Nashville by a Union brigade under Col. Miller. On Nov. 5th Morgan made a dash at a Federal camp north of the Cumberland, but was repulsed with some loss. The same active chieftain on the 9th was driven out of Gallatin by a detachment of Gen. Crittenden's corps, and the next day was beaten at Lebanon, where the Federalists captured a quantity of stores and some prisoners. On the following morning Morgan returned and carried off thirty men from the Union camp, soon after which exploit he joined the rebel army near Murfreesboro'.

Col. Forrest's cavalry was also active in the same part of the State, but the vigorous measures of the Federal generals soon succeeded in checking this species of irregular warfare.

Some of the Federal soldiers, however, had been guilty of excesses hardly less outrageous than those of the guerillas, and rigid orders were issued by Gen. Grant to prevent it.

On the 7th of November, a portion of one of the Illinois regiments broke open a shop at Jackson, Tenn., and plundered and destroyed property to the value of some $1,242. Gen. Grant ordered that sum to be assessed against the regiment, and such of its officers as were absent without leave at the time when the depredations were committed, the money when collected to be paid to the persons who had suffered by the outrage; and two officers who had failed to prevent it were mustered out of the service.

Toward the close of the same month, a plan was matured by the governor and Gen. Rosecrans for requiring bonds and sureties for good behavior from persons suspected as disunionists, or known to have been formerly secessionists.

On the 7th, a brigade of Gen. Dumont's division was captured by Col. Morgan, at Hartsville, near Nashville, having been surprised in their camp, and forced to surrender after a short and desultory resistance. The Confederate military authorities proclaimed a general conscription in Tennessee, and proceeded to draft into the Confederate army all able-bodied men under 40, in the portions of the State under their control. The Union men made a determined resistance. but in general, as might be supposed, with little effect. Even in Middle and West Tennessee, where the national arms were nominally paramount, the guerrillas were employed to drive conscripts into the ranks. East Tennessee suffered still more severely, and it is stated that particular care was had to draft into the Confederate ranks those persons who were most conspicuous for their devotion to the Union.

In accordance with the President's order of October 21st, Governor Johnson, in the early part of December, issued a proclamation, calling for an election of Representatives to the 37th Congress, to be held on the 29th, in the Ninth and Tenth Districts of Tennessee. The Ninth District embraces the counties of Henry, Weakly, Dyer, Oberon, Lauderdale, Tipton, Gibson, Carroll, and Henderson, and the Tenth includes the counties of Haywood, Madison, Hardeman, Fayette, and Shelby. The governor ended his proclamation with the notice that "no person will be considered an elector qualified to vote who, in addition to the other qualifications required by law, does not give satisfactory evidence to the judges holding the election, of his loyalty to the Government of the United States."

About the same time Gov. Johnson reissued a former order assessing the wealthy secessionists of Nashville and the vicinity to the amount of $60,000, for the support of the poor during the winter. The first order was as follows:

NASHVILLE, August 18, 1862.

SIR: There are many wives and helpless children in the city of Nashville and county of Davidson, who have been reduced to poverty and wretchedness in consequence of their husbands and fathers having been forced into the armies of this unholy and nefarious rebellion. Their necessities have become so manifest, and their demands for the necessaries of life so urgent, that the laws of justice and humanity would be violated unless something was done to relieve their suffering and destitute condition.

You are therefore requested to contribute the sum of dollars, which you will pay over within the next five days to James Whitworth, Esq., Judge of the County Court, to be by him distributed among these destitute families in such manner as may be prescribed. Respectfully, &c.,

ANDREW JOHNSON, Military Governor.

Attest: EDWARD H. EAST, Secretary of State.

On the 20th a body of Confederate horsemen made a raid on the railroad near Jackson, in the western part of the State, burned a long trestle work, and tore up the track for a considerable distance. The day following a small guerrilla force entered the suburbs of Memphis, pillaged several shops, and carried off 100 cattle and 180 mules. As the armies of Gens. Bragg and Rosecrans began to prepare for battle, the guerrilla raids became more numerous and more destructive; Nashville was again almost isolated, and the situation of the Union troops, in continual danger of having their supplies cut off, became extremely precarious. Soon after the close of the year, the Chattanooga "Rebel" published the following from an official source:

Gen. Morgan's report of his expedition shows that 2,000 prisoners were paroled, and several hundred of the enemy killed and wounded, and an immense quantity of arms and property destroyed.

Forrest's report shows 1,500 prisoners taken, 1,000 of the enemy killed and wounded, an immense quantity of arms, ammunition, and stores destroyed, and his whole command splendidly equipped from their captures.

Our operations at Murfreesboro', including the capture of 5,000 prisoners and the capture of 2,000 at Hartsville and around Nashville, sum up 10,000 prisoners in less than a month.

We have also captured and sent to the rear 30 cannon, 60,000 small arms, with 2,000 more in the hands of our troops; 1,500 wagons destroyed, and the mules and harnesses secured. The enemy's loss in killed and wounded is estimated at 20,000, including 7 generals.

The exploits of Cols. Forrest and Morgan referred to in this summary were performed principally in the latter half of December and early part of January, 1863.

CHAPTER XVI.

Preparations for the capture of New Orleans—Occupation of Ship Island—The Mortar Fleet—Arrival of Captain Farragut—Bombardment of the Forts on the Mississippi—Preparation to run past the Forts—The Scenes which ensued—Arrival of the Fleet before New Orleans—Surrender of the City—Advance up the River—Surrender of the Forts to Commodore Porter—Gen. Butler occupies New Orleans—His Administration—Superseded by Gen. Banks.

PREPARATIONS for the capture of New Orleans had early in the war been commenced. As a preliminary movement an expedition to Ship Island was projected in September, 1861, almost immediately after Gen. Butler's return from the expedition to Hatteras Inlet, and he was authorized to enlist troops for it in New England. Coming into collision with Gov. Andrew of Massachusetts, in relation to the appointment of persons as field-officers for the regiments he raised in Massachusetts, whom the Governor regarded as unfit for their posts, and refused to commission, the expedition was delayed for a time. The first instalment of troops for it were embarked at Boston, on the 19th of November, on the U. S. transport Constitution, and sailed at first for Portland, Me., and thence for Fortress Monroe, which they reached on the 26th November, and sailed the next day for Ship Island, where they arrived on the 3d December. They consisted of the Twenty-sixth Massachusetts regiment, Col. Jones, the Ninth Connecticut, Col. Cahill, and the Fourth battery of Massachusetts artillery, Capt. Manning, and were under the command of Brig.-Gen. John W. Phelps, a native of Ver-

Bogardus Photr H. W. Smith

U.S. NAVY

mont, and graduate of West Point in 1836. He served for 23 years in the army, but resigned in 1859, and was living at Brattleboro', Vt., at the commencement of the war.

Having completed the debarkation of his command, Gen. Phelps issued a proclamation to the loyal citizens of the Southwest, for which there seemed no occasion, as his superior in command, Maj.-Gen. Butler, had not arrived, and there were on the island none but U. S. troops, and no invasion had been made upon the territory claimed by the Confederate Government. The proclamation was not circulated upon the mainland to any considerable extent; but it created much dissatisfaction among Gen. Phelps's own command.

The Constitution left Ship Island on the 7th of December on her return to the North, and arrived at Fortress Monroe on the 15th; in January, 1862, she returned with another considerable body of troops. Thus the military part of the expedition for the capture of New Orleans under Gen. B. F. Butler, was transferred to a position in the neighborhood of that city.

On the 3d of February Capt. D. G. Farragut sailed from Hampton Roads in the U. S. steamer Hartford to assume the duties of flag-officer of the Western Gulf blockading squadron. In addition to the ordinary duties of the blockade, he was specially charged with the reduction of the defences guarding the approaches to New Orleans. "There will be attached to your squadron," said the Secretary of the Navy in his letter of instructions, "a fleet of bomb vessels, and armed steamers enough to manage them, all under command of Commander D. D. Porter, who will be directed to report to you. * * * When these formidable mortars arrive, and you are completely ready, you will collect such vessels as can be spared from the blockade and proceed up the Mississippi River, and reduce the defences which guard the approaches to New Orleans, when you will appear off that city and take possession of it under the guns of your squadron, and hoist the American flag therein, keeping possession until troops can be sent to you. If the Mississippi expedition from Cairo shall not have descended the river, you will take advantage of the panic to push a strong force up the river to take all their defences in the rear."

This fleet of mortars spoken of by the Secretary was fitted out at the Brooklyn Navy Yard, and was for some months in preparation. It consisted of one gunboat, the Octorara, mounting 18 guns, and serving as Com. Porter's flag-ship, but subsequently diverted from the expedition to Fortress Monroe, and 20 schooners, of from 200 to 300 tons each, of great strength and solidity, and carrying each a mortar, weighing 8½ tons, of thirty-nine inches length of bore, forty-three inches external and fifteen inches internal diameter, and intended to throw a 15-inch shell, weighing, when unfilled, 212 lbs. They are elevated or depressed by means of projections on the breech. Each vessel also carried two 32-pounders, rifled.

This class of vessels had been selected because they were stronger in proportion to their size than larger ones, at the same time that their light draft enabled them to go into shallow water; and from their small tonnage they could be handled by a small number of men.

To fit them to receive the mortars, a bed had been prepared, which was supported by an almost solid mass of wood, built from the keel to the deck. This consisted of timbers over one foot square and twelve feet in length, interlaced and firmly fastened. The bed rose two or three inches above the deck, and consisted of a solid horizontal surface, circular in form, with a truck near its edge, upon which run rollers bearing a revolving platform. The bed itself was carefully braced and supported by the entire strength of the vessel, so as to sustain the recoil of the mortar.

The circular platform surmounting the bed and bearing the mortar carriage, was constructed of heavy timbers, and was one foot in depth and nearly twelve feet in diameter. When in position for a discharge, it laid flat and firmly on the bed, but by ingenious mechanism it might be made to revolve, in order to aim the mortar in any direction, or to resight it if the vessel shifted its position. The change of direction was easily and quickly accomplished. By means of four eccentric axles in the platform, to which levers were fitted, the mortar and machinery (weighing altogether over ten tons) might be raised, and the weight transferred by the same movement to a great number of metallic rollers attached to a framework of immense strength under the platform. Then, by means of tackle, already arranged, the whole mass might be moved to its desired position, and instantly, by a reverse movement, replaced on the bed. In the centre of the platform, and extending into the solid mass beneath, was an iron cylinder or spindle which prevented any side movement.

The mortar carriage was constructed almost exclusively of wrought-iron. Its length was about nine feet, and its height and width each four feet. In form it had the slightest possible resemblance to a land carriage—gradually sloping at the point where the mortar rested, in the direction of the breech; and having wheels, yet not resting on them when the mortar was discharged. The carriage was composed principally of plate iron, riveted together, braced and bolted. It was a framework of excellent design, and though weighing probably not more than two tons, was capable of resisting a pressure of one to two hundred tons.

Two wheels were set close to the framework, directly under the mortars; and connected with them were eccentric axles, so arranged as to permit so large a part of the weight to be thrown on the wheels, that the carriage might be moved on them.

It was not intended, however, that the recoil of the mortar should in any degree be taken up or lessened in its effect by the moving of the wheels. The carriage laid firmly on the platform when the mortar was discharged, and the only possible motion was that of the vessel in the water.

The bombs were the most formidable ordnance missile known, except those used in the Rodman columbiad of 15-inch bore. In addition to the two 32-pounder guns, the vessels were provided with pikes, cutlasses, and other necessary weapons.

The mortars could not be fired directly over the sides of the vessels, and therefore the latter were partially headed toward the point of attack. The vessels were therefore anchored, and a part of the rigging removed. The extraordinary weight and strength of the mortars, the unprecedentedly large charge of powder, the long range and high velocity of the projectiles, with their destructive character, combined to render this novel expedition one of the most important undertaken during the war. The vessels made their first rendezvous at Key West, and subsequently proceeded to Ship Island, Mississippi.

Captain Farragut arrived at Ship Island on the 20th, having been detained for some time at Key West, and immediately began to organize his squadron for the important duty which had been assigned to him. There are two routes by which New Orleans may be approached by water, one through Lake Borgne and Lake Pontchartrain, and the other directly up the Mississippi River; but the former, on account of the shallowness of the water, is impracticable for any but vessels of very light draft. The Confederates had consequently devoted their labors chiefly to the fortification of the Mississippi. Some seventy-five miles below the city, and about twenty-five miles from the "Passes" or mouths of the river, they had possession of two strong works constructed many years before by the United States Government, Fort St. Philip on the left, or north bank, and Fort Jackson on the right. Their united armament was one hundred and twenty-six guns, many of them of the very largest calibre. Starting opposite Fort Jackson and extending to a point a quarter of a mile below Fort St. Philip, a stout chain cable was stretched across the stream (here seven hundred yards wide) supported by a raft of logs and eight hulks securely moored. Adjoining Fort Jackson was a water battery. Under cover of the forts was a fleet of thirteen gunboats, the powerful iron-clad battery Louisiana, and the iron-clad ram Manassas, the naval forces being commanded by Commodore G. N. Hollins. Between New Orleans and the forts several earthworks, well armed, commanded the channel. "Our only fear," said the press of New Orleans of April 5, "is that the Northern invaders may not appear. We have made such extensive preparations to receive them that it were vexatious if their invincible armada escapes the fate we have in store for it."

To reduce these formidable defences, Capt. Farragut was able to collect the following vessels: steam sloops Hartford, 24 guns (flag-ship), Richmond, 26, Pensacola, 24, Brooklyn, 24, Mississippi, 12, Iroquois, 9, Oneida, 9, sailing sloop of war Portsmouth, 17, gunboats Varuna, 12, Cayuga, 6, and Winona, Katahdin, Itasca, Kineo, Wissahickon, Pinola, Kennebeck, and Sciota, 4 each. The frigate Colorado, 48, could not pass over the bar, and the entrance of some of the other large ships was only effected with the expenditure of much time and labor. The mortar fleet comprised twenty schooners, each mounting one large mortar and two small guns. They were accompanied by the steamers Harriet Lane, 4, the flag-ship of Commodore Porter, Miami, 7, Westfield, 6, Clifton, 6, and Owasco, 5. Some of these were merely armed tugs, intended principally to serve the purpose of towing the bomb vessels into position. Including the coast-survey steamer Sachem, the number of vessels under Capt. Farragut's command was therefore forty-six, and their aggregate armament, counting boat howitzers placed in the maintops, was about three hundred guns and mortars. There were no iron-clads in the fleet.

Nearly three weeks were consumed in getting all the ships of the squadron over the bars at the mouths of the Mississippi. Capt. Farragut found the depth considerably less than it had been laid down on the official maps; no doubt for the reason that the daily passing of large ships, before the port was blockaded, had kept the channel open. On the 28th of March, Fleet Captain H. H. Bell made a reconnoissance with two gunboats from the head of the Passes up toward the forts. He found the left bank quite clear of trees and bushes, but on the west side a thick wood extended about four miles below Fort Jackson. By the 8th of April the Mississippi and Pensacola were over the bar, and the mortar boats were moving up toward their appointed stations. On the 13th a detachment from the coast survey party set out under protection of the Owasco, and spent three days in making a minute boat survey of the river and banks, much of the time under fire, and marking the positions which the mortar vessels were to occupy. On the 18th two divisions of Commander Porter's flotilla were moored under the lee of the wood on the right bank of the river, screened from observation by the thick growth of trees interwoven with vines; the masts and rigging were dressed off with bushes, which were renewed as often as they were blown away. The head vessel was 2,850 yards from Fort Jackson and 3,680 from Fort St. Philip. The remaining division, composed of six vessels, was stationed under the opposite bank, the nearest being 3,680 yards from Fort Jackson. There was nothing on this side to screen them from observation, but their hulls were covered with reeds and willows.

The bombardment opened on the 18th, the mortar vessels taking the lead, and the gunboats

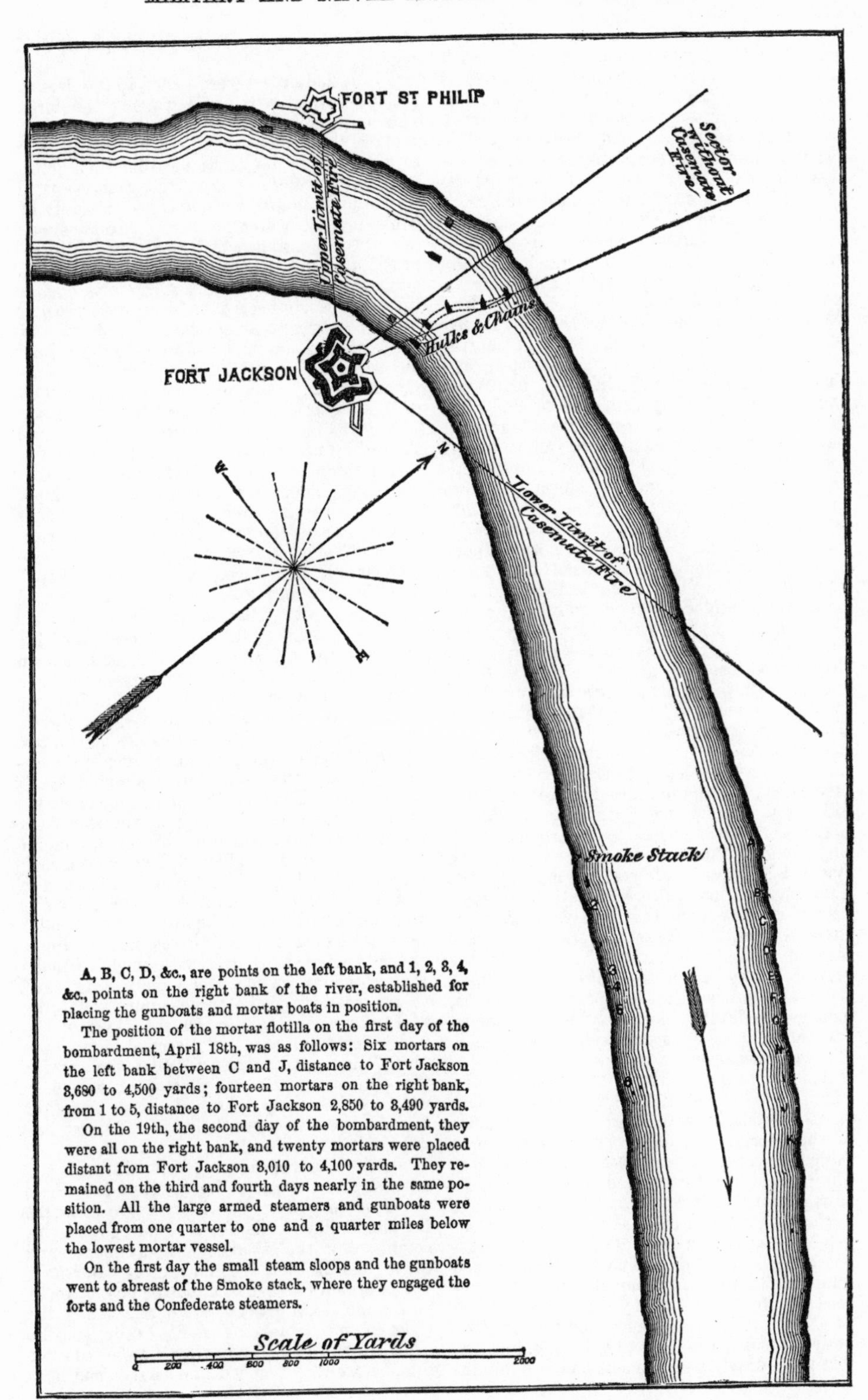

A, B, C, D, &c., are points on the left bank, and 1, 2, 3, 4, &c., points on the right bank of the river, established for placing the gunboats and mortar boats in position.

The position of the mortar flotilla on the first day of the bombardment, April 18th, was as follows: Six mortars on the left bank between C and J, distance to Fort Jackson 3,680 to 4,500 yards; fourteen mortars on the right bank, from 1 to 5, distance to Fort Jackson 2,850 to 3,490 yards.

On the 19th, the second day of the bombardment, they were all on the right bank, and twenty mortars were placed distant from Fort Jackson 3,010 to 4,100 yards. They remained on the third and fourth days nearly in the same position. All the large armed steamers and gunboats were placed from one quarter to one and a quarter miles below the lowest mortar vessel.

On the first day the small steam sloops and the gunboats went to abreast of the Smoke stack, where they engaged the forts and the Confederate steamers.

running up occasionally to draw the enemy's fire when the mortars required relief. Each boat having its precise distance from the forts marked out by the surveyors, the firing was remarkably accurate. At the given signal they opened in order, each one throwing a shell every ten minutes. Fort Jackson was the principal object of attack. On the first day the citadel was set on fire and burned until two o'clock the next morning, all the clothing and commissary stores in the fort being destroyed, and great suffering caused by the intense heat. During the night the firing ceased on both sides. Two of the mortar vessels had been injured by the enemy's fire and were accordingly moved to another position. On the 19th the mortar schooner Maria J. Carleton was sunk by a rifle shell passing down through her deck, magazine, and bottom, but nearly all her stores and arms were saved. One or two men were wounded, but very little other damage was done except to the masts and rigging of some of the schooners. On the other hand the officers' quarters in Fort Jackson were set on fire and entirely consumed, the artillerists were driven from the parapet guns, and the batteries were silenced every time the shells were concentrated on any one point. The fuzes being bad, however, a great many exploded prematurely in the air. Commander Porter accordingly gave up timing them and put in full-length fuzes, to burst after they had entered the ground. The soil being wet and soft, the shells penetrated 18 or 20 feet into the ground, and then exploded with an effect like an earthquake. The levee was broken in more than 100 places, and the water rushing into the fort flooded the parade ground and casemates. On the night of the 20th an expedition was sent up under Commander Bell to break the obstructions across the river. With the gunboats Pinola, Lieut.-Com. Crosby, and Itasca, Lieut.-Com. Caldwell, he made for the hulks, under a heavy fire, while all the mortars opened at once upon the forts to distract the enemy's attention. Petards were arranged to blow up the boom by means of a galvanic current, but they failed to ignite. Lieutenant Caldwell however, boarding one of the hulks, managed to slip the chain, and thereby made an opening sufficiently large for the fleet to pass. His vessel was swept ashore by the current, which was running with great violence, but the Pinola got her off after about half an hour's labor in full sight of the forts, the terrible fire of the mortar fleet being probably the only thing that saved the two boats from destruction. The bombardment continued with undiminished vigor for 3 days longer, with little damage to the squadron. Almost every night the Confederates sent down fire rafts, but Capt. Farragut easily avoided them, and had them towed ashore. On the 23d Commander Porter succeeded in breaking a heavy rifled gun on Fort St. Philip, which had been annoying him seriously for some time. Wth this single exception the 6 days' bombardment had not diminished the fire of the forts in any perceptible degree.

On the 23d orders were issued to the fleet to prepare for attacking and passing the forts. The mortars were to continue the bombardment while this movement was in progress, and to try to drive the garrisons from their guns. The five steamers of Porter's flotilla, assisted by the Portsmouth, were assigned the duty of enfilading the water battery of six guns, and the barbette of guns which commanded the approach to the forts. The rest of the ships and gunboats were to push on past the forts, engage the Confederate fleet, and if victorious proceed to New Orleans, leaving the final reduction of the forts to Commander Porter and the land forces under General Butler. Flag-Officer Farragut now separated his gunboats into two divisions, of six boats each, the first under Capt. Theodorus Bailey, his second in command, and the second under Fleet Capt. H. H. Bell. The first division of ships comprised the flag ship Hartford, Commander Wainwright; Brooklyn, Captain Craven; and Richmond, Commander Alden. The second was composed of the Pensacola, Captain Morris, and Mississippi, Commander Melancton Smith. "Every vessel," says Captain Farragut, "was as well prepared as the ingenuity of her commander and officers could suggest, both for the preservation of life and of the vessel, and perhaps there is not on record such a display of ingenuity as has been evinced in this little squadron. The first was by the engineer of the Richmond, Mr. Moore, by suggesting that the sheet cables be stopped up and down on the sides in the line of the engines, which was immediately adopted by all the vessels. Then each commander made his own arrangements for stopping the shot from penetrating the boilers or machinery that might come in forward or abaft, by hammocks, coal, bags of ashes, bags of sand, clothes-bags, and in fact every device imaginable. The bulwarks were lined with hammocks by some, with splinter nettings made with ropes by others. Some rubbed their vessels over with mud, to make their ships less visible, and some whitewashed their decks, to make things more visible by night during the fight." On the night of the 23d Lieut. Caldwell made a second visit to the obstructions, and ascertained that the passage was still clear. He was discovered and fired upon by the enemy, who had chosen that time to send down some of their fire rafts, and had lighted fires on the shore near the chain. At two o'clock on the morning of the 24th the signal was given to get under way, and the whole squadron moved up the river in two columns, Captain Bailey in the Cayuga leading the right, composed of the 1st division of gunboats and the second division of ships, and the Hartford, with Captain Farragut, taking the post of honor on the left. On passing the barrier chain the right column attacked Fort St. Philip, and the left Fort Jackson. They were discovered some time before they reached the barrier, and both forts opened upon them a hot fire, to which the squadron at first could only reply with their bow guns. As soon as their broadsides were brought within range the engagement became general. "The flames," said Commander Porter, "seemed to be literally eating the vessels up." In attempting to avoid a fire raft the Hartford grounded on a shoal, and in this position was set on fire, the flames bursting through the ports and running up the rigging; but, with great exertion, they were extinguished, and the ship's guns, which had meanwhile been worked without interruption, were now brought to bear upon Fort St. Philip, and that work was almost completely silenced. In the mean time, the Brooklyn and some other vessels, owing to the darkness and smoke, became entangled in the barrier, and were exposed to a raking fire from the forts for a few minutes, but managed to extricate themselves, and the Brooklyn, finding herself unexpectedly close abreast of Fort St. Philip, poured in such a storm of grape and canister that the garrison were seen, by the flash of the bursting shrapnells, running from their guns. Before the squadron had fairly passed the forts, the Confederate fleet of gunboats and rams appeared, and took part in the fight. They were first encountered by Captain Bailey in the Cayuga, who was considerably in advance of the rest, at a moment when no supporting ship was in sight. By skilful steering he frustrated their attempts to board and butt, and had forced three to surrender, when the Oneida, Commander Lee, and Varuna, Captain Boggs, hove in sight. The Oneida, discovering a Confederate gunboat crossing her bows, ran into her with a full head of steam, and cut her down, leaving her to drift down the stream with the current. The Varuna, after passing the forts, and destroying or driving ashore a gunboat and three transports, found herself, about daylight, completely surrounded by the enemy. The Governor Moore, iron-clad about the bow, first attacked her, butting her twice, and sending a raking fire along her port gangway, killing four and wounding nine of the crew; but Captain Boggs, by a few well-directed shells, drove her off, partially disabled. While still engaged with her, another Confederate steamer, iron-clad, with a prow under water, struck the Varuna in the port gangway, doing considerable damage. She backed off for another blow, and struck again in the same place, crushing in the side; "but by going ahead fast," says Captain Boggs, "the concussion drew her bow around, and I was able, with the port guns, to give her, while close alongside, five eight-inch shells abaft her armor. This settled her and drove her ashore in flames. Finding the Varuna sinking, I ran her into the bank, let go the anchor, and tied up to the trees. During all this time, the guns were actively at work crippling the Morgan (Governor Moore), which was making feeble efforts to get up steam. The fire was kept up until the water was over the guntrucks, when I turned my attention to getting the wounded and crew out of the vessel." Just at this moment the Oneida came up, took off some of the men from the Varuna, and completed the destruction of the Gov. Moore, which was run ashore and set on fire by the crew, part of whom afterward surrendered to Commander Lee. Three of the gunboats were obliged to put back, one having been disabled early in the action, and the others caught in the barrier chain and delayed until the day had broken and the rest of the fleet had gone past the forts. Within two hours from the commencement of the fight, nearly the whole Confederate fleet was captured or destroyed, and the victory was secured; but, "just as the scene appeared to be closing," writes Captain Farragut, "the ram Manassas was seen coming under full speed to attack us. I directed Capt. Smith, in the Mississippi, to turn and run her down. The order was instantly obeyed by the Mississippi turning and going at her at full speed. Just as we expected to see the ram annihilated, when within fifty yards of each other, she put her helm hard a-port, dodged the Mississippi, and ran ashore. The Mississippi poured two broadsides into her, and sent her drifting down the river a total wreck." As she came into the midst of Porter's flotilla, several of the mortar boats and steamers opened fire upon her; "but I soon discovered," writes Porter, "that the Manassas could harm no one again, and I ordered the vessels to save their shot. She was beginning to emit smoke from her ports, or holes, and was discovered to be on fire and sinking. Her pipes were all twisted and riddled with shot, and her hull was also well cut up. She had evidently been used up by the squadron as they passed along. I tried to save her as a curiosity, by getting a hawser around her and securing her to the bank, but just after doing so she faintly exploded. Her only gun went off, and emitting flames through her bow port, like some huge animal, she gave a plunge and disappeared under the water." About 5 o'clock the Cayuga came upon the camp of the Chalmette regiment, Col. Szymanski, on the right bank of the river. Casting anchor, Captain Bailey opened upon it with canister, and obliged the whole force to surrender, with their arms, camp equipage, &c. Soon afterward, the signal was given to cease action, and 12 vessels dropped anchor above and out of range of the forts, and began to prepare for further operations. Two of the gunboats were immediately sent ahead to cut the telegraph wires in various places, and one was sent, by way of the Quarantine bayou, to communicate with Commander Porter and General Butler. With his nine remaining vessels, Captain Farragut then proceeded up to New Orleans, meeting on the way abundant evidence of the panic which prevailed in that city. "Cotton-loaded ships, on fire, came floating down, and working implements of every kind, such as are used in shipyards." "I never witnessed such vandalism in my life," he writes to the Secretary of the Navy, "as the destruction of property; all the shipping, steamboats, &c., were set on fire and consumed." The squadron reached the English Turn about 10.30 A. M. on the 25th, and soon descried the new earthwork forts on the old lines on both shores, some 6 or 7 miles below the city; these were known as the Chalmette batteries. The fleet formed, as before, in two lines, each taking its own work, but Captain Bailey, with the Cayuga, was far in advance, not having noticed the signal for close order, and sustained alone a cross fire for about 20 minutes, at the end of which time the Hartford ranged up ahead, and gave the batteries a broadside of shells, shrapnell, and grape, the first discharge driving the men on the right bank from their guns. The Pensacola, the Brooklyn, and then the rest of the fleet, came up in quick succession, and in about 15 or 20 minutes "the forts were silenced, and those who could run were running in every direction." From this point no obstacles were encountered, except burning steamers, cotton ships, fire rafts, and the like, and at one o'clock P. M. the squadron anchored in front of New Orleans.

A terrible and melancholy spectacle was presented to the victors. The whole levee, for miles, was wrapped in smoke from the burning gun carriages and cotton which the authorities had ordered to be consumed. In the river were many hulls of burning ships, and the utmost ingenuity was required to avoid them. As the squadron neared the levee the sailors gave a cheer which was answered by some persons in the crowd on shore. Pistol shots were immediately fired at these latter by the excited multitude, and several persons were wounded. After a delay of half an hour or so, Capt. Bailey was sent ashore to demand the surrender of the city. He was received by the mob with the most violent demonstrations, but under escort of a number of citizens proceeded unmolested to the mayor's office, the mob at his heels contenting itself with furiously assaulting citizens suspected of sympathy with the Federal Union. On reaching the City Hall, Capt. Bailey demanded the surrender of the city, and the display of the United States flag over the custom house, post office, mint, and city hall. The mayor replied that he had no authority, the city being under military control, and a messenger was accordingly sent for Gen. Mansfield Lovell, the commander of the department. Gen. Lovell informed Capt. Bailey that he had already evacuated the city, and would now turn over the control to the municipal authorities, leaving them free to act as they saw fit. It was then arranged that Capt. Bailey should return to his fleet, and await the action of the common council. To the demand to haul down the flag of Louisiana from the City Hall the mayor gave an unqualified refusal. The common council was already in session, and the mayor at once sent in a message, recommending that an answer be returned to Capt. Farragut, representing that the city being incapable of offering any resistance yielded to physical force alone, without giving up its allegiance to the Confederate Government; that the custom house, post office, and mint were the property of the Confederate Government, and the municipal authorities had no control over them; and that all acts involving a transfer of authority must be performed by the invading forces themselves. The sentiments expressed in this message were unanimously adopted by the council, and on the next day the following correspondence was opened between Capt. Farragut and the mayor:

U. S. FLAG SHIP HARTFORD, off New Orleans, *April* 26, 1862.

To His Excellency the Mayor of New Orleans:

SIR: Upon my arrival before your city I had the honor to send to your honor Capt. Bailey, U. S. N., second in command of the expedition, to demand of you the surrender of New Orleans to me as the representative of the Government of the United States. Capt. Bailey reported the result of an interview with yourself and the military authorities. It must occur to your honor that it is not within the province of a naval officer to assume the duties of a military commandant. I came here to reduce New Orleans to obedience to the laws of and to vindicate the offended majesty of the Government of the United States.

The rights of persons and property shall be secured. I therefore demand of you, as its representative, the unqualified surrender of the city, and that the emblem of the sovereignty of the United States be hoisted over the City Hall, Mints, and Custom House by meridian this day; and that all flags and other emblems of sovereignty other than those of the United States be removed from all the public buildings at that hour.

I further particularly request that you shall exercise your authority to quell disturbances, restore order, and call upon all the good people of New Orleans to return at once to their vocations, and I particularly demand that no person shall be molested in person or property for sentiments of loyalty to their Government.

I shall speedily and severely punish any person or persons who shall commit such outrages as were witnessed yesterday, by armed men firing upon helpless women and children for giving expression to their pleasure at witnessing the old flag.

I am, very respectfully,
D. G. FARRAGUT,
Flag-Officer Western Gulf Squadron.

U. S. FLAG SHIP HARTFORD, at anchor off the City of New Orleans, *April* 26, 1862.

To his Honor the Mayor of New Orleans:

Your honor will please give directions that no flag but that of the United States will be permitted to fly in the presence of this fleet, so long as it has the power to prevent it; and as all displays of that kind may be the cause of bloodshed, I have to request that you will give this communication as general a circulation as possible.

I have the honor to be, very respectfully, your obedient servant,
D. G. FARRAGUT,
Flag-Officer Western Gulf Blockading Squadron.

MAYOR'S OFFICE, CITY OF NEW ORLEANS, CITY HALL, *April* 26, 1862.

To Flag-Officer D. G. Farragut, U. S. Flag Ship Hartford:

SIR: In pursuance of a resolution which we thought proper to take, out of regard for the lives of the women and children who still crowd the metropolis, Gen.

Lovell has evacuated it with his troops, and restored back to me the administration of its government and the custody of its honor.

I have, in council with the City Fathers, considered the demand you made of me yesterday of an unconditional surrender of the city, coupled with a requisition to hoist the flag of the United States on the public edifices and haul down the flag that still floats upon the breeze from the dome of this hall.

It becomes my duty to transmit to you an answer which is the universal sentiment of my constituents, no less than the promptings of my own heart on this sad and solemn occasion.

The city is without the means of defence, and is utterly destitute of the force and material that might enable it to resist the overpowering armament displayed in sight of it.

I am no military man, and possess no authority beyond that of executing the municipal laws of the city of New Orleans. It would be presumptuous in me to attempt to lead an army to the field, if I had one at command, and I know still less how to surrender an undefended place, held as this is at the mercies of your gunners and your mortars.

To surrender such a place were an idle and unmeaning ceremony. The city is yours by the power of brutal force, not by my choice or the consent of the inhabitants. It is for you to determine the fate that awaits her. As to hoisting any flag not of our own adoption or allegiance, let me say to you that the man lives not in our midst whose hand and heart would not be paralyzed at the mere thought of such an act; nor could I find in my entire constituency so desperate and wretched a renegade as would dare to profane with his hand the sacred emblem of our aspirations.

Sir, you have manifested sentiments which would become one engaged in a better cause than that to which you have devoted your sword. I doubt not that they spring from a noble though deluded nature, and I know how to appreciate the emotions which inspired them. You have a gallant people to administrate during your occupancy of this city—a people sensitive to all that can in the least affect their dignity and self-respect.

Pray, sir, do not fail to regard their susceptibilities. The obligations which I shall assume in their name will be religiously complied with. You may trust their honor, though you might not count on their submission to unmerited wrongs.

In conclusion, I beg you to understand that the people of New Orleans, while unable to resist your force, do not allow themselves to be insulted by the interference of such as have rendered themselves odious and contemptible by their dastardly desertion of our cause in the mighty struggle in which we are engaged, or such as might remind them too forcibly that they are the conquered and you the conquerors.

Peace and order may be preserved without resort to measures which I could not at this moment prevent.

Your occupying the city does not transfer allegiance from the government of their choice to one which they have deliberately repudiated, and that they yield the obedience which the conqueror has a right to extort from the conquered. Yours, respectfully,

JOHN F. MONROE, Mayor.

U. S. FLAG SHIP HARTFORD, at anchor of the City of New Orleans, *April* 28, 1862.

To His Honor the Mayor and City Council of the City of New Orleans:

Your communication of the 26th instant has been received, together with that of the City Council.

I deeply regret to see both by their contents, and the continued display of the flag of Louisiana on the court house, a determination on the part of the city authorities not to haul it down. Moreover, when my officers and men were sent on shore to communicate with the authorities, and to hoist the United States flag on the Custom House, with the strictest order not to use their arms unless assailed, they were insulted in the grossest manner, and the flag which had been hoisted by my orders on the Mint was pulled down and dragged through the streets.

All of which goes to show that the fire of this fleet may be drawn upon the city at any moment, and in such an event the levee would, in all probability, be cut by the shells, and an amount of distress ensue to the innocent population, which I have heretofore endeavored to assure you that I desire by all means to avoid.

The election, therefore, is with you. But it becomes my duty to notify you to remove the women and children from the city within forty-eight hours, if I rightly understood your determination.

Very respectfully, your obedient servant,

(Signed) D. G. FARRAGUT,
Flag-Officer, Western Gulf Blockading Squadron.

CITY HALL, *April* 28, 1862.

To Flag-Officer D. G. Farragut, United States Flag Ship Hartford:

Your communication of this morning is the first intimation I ever had that it was by your strict orders that the United States flag was attempted to be hoisted upon certain of our public edifices, by officers sent on shore to communicate with the authorities. The officers who approached me in your name disclosed no such orders and intimated no such design on your part, nor would I have for a moment entertained the remotest suspicion that they could have been invested with power to enter on such an errand while the negotiations for a surrender between you and the city authorities were still pending. The interference of any force under your command, as long as those negotiations were not brought to a close, could not be viewed by us otherwise than as a flagrant violation of those courtesies, if not of the absolute rights, which prevail between belligerents under such circumstances. My views and sentiments with reference to such conduct remain unchanged. You now renew the demand made in your former communication, and you insist on their being complied with unconditionally, under a threat of bombardment within forty-eight hours; and you notify me to remove the women and children from the city, that they may be protected from your shells.

Sir, you cannot but know that there is no possible exit from this city for a population which still exceeds in number one hundred and forty thousand, and you must therefore be aware of the utter inanity of such a notification. Our women and children cannot escape from your shells, if it be your pleasure to murder them on a question of mere etiquette. But if they could, there are but few among them who would consent to desert their families and their homes, and the graves of their relatives, in so awful a moment. They would bravely stand the sight of your shells tearing up the graves of those who are so dear to them, and would deem that they died not ingloriously by the side of the tombs erected by their piety to the memory of departed relatives.

You are not satisfied with the possession of an undefended city, opposing no resistance to your guns, because of its bearing its hard fate with something of manliness and dignity, and you wish to humble and disgrace us by the performance of an act against which our natures rebel. This satisfaction you cannot expect to obtain at our hands.

We will stand your bombardment, unarmed and undefended as we are. The civilized world will consign to indelible infamy the heart that will conceive the deed and the hand that will dare to consummate it.

Respectfully, JOHN T. MONROE,
Mayor of the City of New Orleans.

UNITED STATES FLAG-SHIP HARTFORD, At Anchor off the City of New Orleans. *April* 29, 1862.

To His Honor the Mayor of the City of New Orleans:

SIR: The Forts St. Philip and Jackson having surrendered, and all the military defences of the city being either captured or abandoned, you are required, as the sole representative of any supposed authority in the city, to haul down and suppress every ensign and symbol of Government, whether State or Confederate, except that of the United States. I am now about to raise the flag of the United States upon the Custom House, and you will see that it is respected with all the civil power of the city.

I have the honor to be, very respectfully, your obedient servant, D. G. FARRAGUT,
Flag-Officer, Western Gulf Blockading Squadron.

UNITED STATES FLAG SHIP HARTFORD, At Anchor off the City of New Orleans, *April* 30, 1862.

GENTLEMEN: I informed you in my communication of the 28th of April, that your determination, as I understood it, was not to haul down the flag of Louisiana on the City Hall, and that my officers and men were treated with rudeness when they landed, even with a flag of truce, to communicate with the authorities, &c., and, if such was to be the determined course of the people, the fire of the vessels might at any moment be drawn upon the city. This you have thought proper to construe into a determination on my part to murder your women and children, and made your letter so offensive that it will terminate our intercourse; and so soon as General Butler arrives with his forces I shall turn over the charge of the city to him and assume my naval duties. Very respectfully, &c.,

D. G. FARRAGUT,
Flag-Officer Western Gulf Blockading Squadron.

His Honor the Mayor and City Council of New Orleans.

Captain Farragut then seized all the steamboats which had not been destroyed,—among them the famous Tennessee, for which the blockaders had long been watching—and sent them down to Quarantine for General Butler's forces. There were several iron-clad rams building, at the time of the capture of the city, the principal one of which, the Mississippi, soon came floating by in flames. Another was sunk in front of the custom house, and there were others at Algiers, opposite New Orleans, just begun.

"I next went above the city eight miles, to Carrolton," writes Captain Farragut, "where I learned there were two other forts; but the panic had gone before me. I found the guns spiked, and the gun carriages in flames. The first work, on the right, reaches from the Mississippi nearly over to Pontchartrain, and has 29 guns; the one on the left had 6 guns, from which Commander Lee took some 50 barrels of powder, and completed the destruction of the gun carriages, &c. A mile higher up there were two other earthworks, but not yet armed.

"We discovered here, fastened to the right bank of the river, one of the most Herculean labors I have ever seen—a raft and chain to extend across the river to prevent Foote's gunboats from descending. It is formed by placing three immense logs of not less than three or four feet in diameter, and some thirty feet long: to the centre one a 2-inch chain is attached, running lengthwise the raft; and the three logs and chain are then frapped together by chains from one half to one inch, three or four layers, and there are 96 of these lengths composing the raft. It is at least three quarters of a mile long. * * *

"I sent on shore and hoisted the American flag on the custom house, and hauled down the Louisiana State flag from the city hall, as the mayor had avowed that there was no man in New Orleans who dared haul it down; and my own convictions are that if such an individual could have been found he would have been assassinated."

The operations of Commander Porter below the forts were as follows: As soon as Captain Farragut was ready to proceed, the five steamers attached to the mortar flotilla moved up and took position under the batteries, the leading vessel 500 yards off, and the others closing up as the fire commenced. As soon as the Hartford, Brooklyn, and Richmond passed they opened with shrapnell on the water battery and forts, having received the fire ten or fifteen minutes before replying to it. As the fire was high and they were close in shore, nearer the forts than the enemy supposed, they occupied, as it turned out, a safer position than the vessels farther out, there being only one killed and one wounded on board the Harriet Lane, while the other steamers remained untouched. The mortars meanwhile poured a heavy fire upon Fort Jackson. In one hour and ten minutes from weighing anchor, the fleet had passed the forts, and Commander Porter, having accomplished his part, hung out the signal to retire, and sent Lieutenant Commanding Guest with a flag of truce to demand the surrender of the forts. The flag was fired upon and put back, but a boat soon came down with an apology and received the summons, to which Lieut.-Col. Higgins, commanding the forts, replied that until he received official information of the fall of New Orleans no proposition for a surrender could be for a moment entertained. Giving the men one day to rest, Commander Porter resumed the bombardment on the 26th, but there was no response. Learning that the formidable iron-clad battery Louisiana, mounting 16 heavy guns, had escaped Captain Farragut, and with three Confederate steamers which the flotilla had also left behind them, was about to make an attack upon the mortar boats, he sent the schooners, which would have been almost defenceless against such an adversary, down the river to refit and prepare for sea, six of them having orders to pass around to the rear of Fort Jackson to prevent supplies from getting in, and two being sent to the rear of Fort St. Philip to assist in landing troops. Three of them drifted over to the mouth of Barataria Bay, and received the surrender of Fort Livingston. On the 27th, the possession of the forts being an urgent necessity, Commander Porter renewed the demand, offering honorable terms, the officers to retain their side arms, and both officers and men to be paroled, private property to be respected, the arms and munitions of war and public property to be surrendered, and no damage to be done by the garrison to the defences. These terms were accepted the next day, partly, no doubt, in consequence of the landing of General Butler at Quarantine in the rear of Fort St. Philip, which entirely cut off reënforcements; and partly, according to Command-

FARRAGUT'S FLEET PASSING THE FORTS
BELOW NEW ORLEANS

er Porter, on account of disaffection in the garrison. Two hundred and fifty in fact of the garrison of Fort Jackson, after spiking the guns bearing up the river, surrendered themselves to Gen. Butler's pickets on the night of the 28th, averring that they had been impressed and would fight no longer. While the capitulation was being drawn up, the Confederate naval officers towed the ram Louisiana to a point above the forts, and having set her on fire, turned her adrift, with guns shotted, in the expectation that she would explode in the midst of the fleet. The final catastrophe, however, took place sooner than they had hoped. Just as the battery got abreast of Fort St. Philip it blew up with a tremendous noise, and sunk immediately. The only injury was to a Confederate soldier in the fort, who was killed by one of the fragments. As soon as the capitulation was completed, the Harriet Lane turned her attention to the three Confederate steamers which were lying about half a mile above. One of them had already been scuttled; the others surrendered without resistance, and 14 officers, 7 engineers, the crews of the steamers, and 300 men and two companies of marine artillery belonging to the Louisiana became prisoners of war. The men were released on parole; the officers, in consequence of their conduct in setting fire to the battery, and attempting to destroy the fleet while a capitulation was in progress, were sent to the North as close prisoners. Gen. Phelps now arrived, and Porter turned over to him the forts, guns, and captured property. The loss of the Confederates during the bombardment was 14 killed and 39 wounded. The casualties in the fleet were, during the six days' bombardment, 2 killed and 24 wounded; during the passing of the forts and the engagement with the Chalmette batteries, 37 killed, and 147 wounded; on board the mortar boats, 1 killed and 6 wounded; total, 40 killed, and 177 wounded. Fort St. Philip was very little injured, only one of the mortars having fired upon it, because its fate evidently depended upon that of Fort Jackson. The latter was described by Commander Porter after the surrender as "a perfect wreck." Over 1,800 shells fell inside the work proper, 170 in the water battery, and by the estimate of the soldiers, about 3,000 in the ditches around the works. All the buildings in and near the fort were burnt; the ramparts were severely damaged on every side, and particularly on the north, but had been repaired with sand bags which were constantly sent down from New Orleans during the bombardment; the walls of the citadel were cracked in many places very badly; the casemates were cracked from end to end, several of them showing wide fissures in the roofs and sides, and their floors were three inches under water. Still there is little question that, but for the interruption of their communications with New Orleans, these works could have held out much longer, the extent of the damage being far from proportionate to the time and powder expended in the bombardment. If the formidable 13-inch mortars did not fully answer the expectations which had been formed of them, this fact must be attributed first to the softness of the soil which allowed the shells to sink 20 feet, by measurement, before they exploded, and secondly to the difficulty of getting accurate range: the forts rose but little above the surrounding bushes, and the vessels which were moored behind the wood often had to fire almost at random; the mortars could only be pointed from sights fixed to the mast heads, and the most curious expedients were resorted to for obtaining correct firing.

After the conquered forts and city had been occupied by the military forces, Commander Porter was ordered to repair to Ship Island. The Portsmouth, the Pensacola, and one gunboat were stationed at New Orleans; seven vessels were sent up the river under command of Captain Craven, "to keep up the panic;" and the smaller steamers, under command of Captain Lee, were ordered to ascend as far as Vicksburg.

Commander James S. Palmer arrived off Baton Rouge with the Iroquois, May 7, and demanded the surrender of the town and all property belonging to the Confederate Government, promising to respect the rights and property of private citizens, but requiring that the United States flag should be hoisted on the arsenal. The mayor, while admitting that the city was without the means of resistance, refused to surrender or to hoist the flag. Com. Palmer accordingly landed a force and took possession of the arsenal, and Flag-Officer Farragut arriving soon afterward took measures to secure proper respect for the national ensign, and to cause all other flags to be suppressed.

On the 12th the Iroquois anchored off Natchez in company with several other vessels, and Commander Palmer sent on shore a demand for surrender which the people at the wharf refused to receive. He then made dispositions for landing an armed force, but was met at the shore by a deputation from the common council with an apology for the previous refusal. The mayor sent a reply to the summons similar to that given by the mayor of Baton Rouge, but he issued a proclamation urging the citizens to commit no act to provoke the displeasure of the United States forces. As Natchez however had never been occupied as a military position, Commander Palmer deferred taking formal possession of it.

Commander S. P. Lee with the advance of the squadron arrived near Vicksburg, May 18, and in reply to his demand for surrender received a defiant refusal. He then gave 24 hours for the removal of women and children, after which time he declared he should consult his own judgment as to the propriety of immediately opening fire. Flag-Officer Farragut arrived a few days afterward, accompanied by a column of troops under General Williams. Subsequently an additional naval and military force was brought up, including Porter's mortar fleet, and the latter opened the bombardment on the night of June 26–27, directing their fire partly against the town and partly against some formidable batteries on the heights. On the morning of the 27th the Owasco, Lieut. Guest, ran up abreast of the town and threw in some incendiary shells, which failed to explode. At 3 o'clock on the morning of the 28th the squadron made a move to pass the batteries, the mortar fleet supporting them as at the battle of Forts Jackson and St. Philip. The Hartford and several other vessels succeeded in passing the range of batteries, which extended full three miles, and did this too in the face of a strong current, but as there was not a sufficient land force to coöperate in the attack, no substantial benefit resulted from the movement. The enemy were several times driven from their batteries, but returned to their guns as soon as the ships had passed. Forming a junction with the western gunboat flotilla of Flag-Officer C. H. Davis, Farragut concerted with that officer and Gen. Williams an expedition up the Yazoo River, consisting of the gunboats Carondelet and Tyler and the ram Queen of the West, strengthened by sharpshooters from the army. They started on the morning of July 15, and near the mouth of the river encountered the Confederate ram Arkansas. A severe fight ensued, in which both the Carondelet and the Tyler were partially disabled, and the Arkansas then entered the Mississippi and passing boldly through the surprised fleets of Farragut and Davis, took refuge under the guns of Vicksburg. Farragut now determined to repass the batteries, for the double purpose of supporting the rest of his squadron and destroying the Arkansas in passing; to assist in which Flag-Officer Davis added to his force the ram Sumter, Lieutenant-Commanding Erben. Toward evening Davis opened a bombardment, for the purpose of covering the movement, and Capt. Farragut succeeded in getting below Vicksburg again with little loss of life, but his designs against the Arkansas were defeated by the darkness of the night. On the 22d Commander W. D. Porter with the iron-clad gunboat Essex, and Lieut.-Col. Ellet, with the ram Queen of the West, made another attempt to destroy the Confederate vessel, but the attack, though executed with great gallantry under the fire of the batteries, did not succeed. The Essex ran down to Farragut's fleet, and Farragut having been instructed by the navy department to drop down the river before the water got too low, it was arranged that Commander W. D. Porter should remain below Vicksburg with the Essex and Sumter.

On the 28th of July Farragut arrived at New Orleans, leaving the Katahdin and Kineo at Baton Rouge. On the 5th of August the Confederates made a vigorous land attack upon the latter place, which was repulsed after a severe contest. The gunboats were not able to assist until toward the close of the action, when they threw their shells directly into the midst of the enemy with great effect. The Arkansas had dropped down the river to take part in the attack, but was not brought into action, one of her engines having broken down. The next morning Porter, who was then at Baton Rouge, with the Essex, moved up to attack her, but before the fight had fairly begun her other engine gave way, and she was run ashore, abandoned, and set on fire by the crew. About an hour afterward she blew up. On the 11th Farragut sailed for Ship Island and Pensacola, which latter place, having been evacuated by the Confederates, was now made the depot of the Western Gulf squadron.

Commander W. D. Porter remained at Baton Rouge until August 23, when the town having been evacuated by the Federal troops, he proceeded up the river to reconnoitre batteries reported to be erecting at Port Hudson, and thence ascended to Bayou Sara to obtain coal, where his boat's crew was fired upon by guerrillas. Some of the buildings were thereupon burned, and a few days afterward, as the firing was repeated, the rest of the place was destroyed. Afterward, a boat's crew from the Essex, sent ashore at Natchez to procure ice for the sick, was attacked by some two hundred armed citizens, one of the sailors being killed, and an officer and five men wounded. Commander Porter immediately opened fire on the town, set a number of houses in flames, and continued the bombardment for an hour, after which the mayor surrendered. On her way down to New Orleans the Essex had a brisk engagement, on the 7th of September, with the Port Hudson batteries.

In the mean time, several vessels of Capt. Farragut's squadron had been employed on the coast of Texas, where acting volunteer Lieut. J. W. Kittredge, with the bark Arthur, the little steamer Sachem, and a launch, captured Corpus Christi, after several spirited engagements with the enemy's batteries, but was unable to hold the town, and was himself made prisoner, September 14, while on shore exploring.

On May 1, several days after the surrender of the city to Flag-Officer Farragut, formal possession was taken of New Orleans by the land forces of the United States under the command of Major-Gen. B. F. Butler, who, after a conference with the municipal authorities and some of the principal inhabitants, issued a proclamation adapted to the circumstances of the captured city and its inhabitants. After assuring protection to all well-disposed persons, natives as well as foreigners, and requiring keepers of public property and manufacturers of arms and munitions of war to make a return of the kind and quantity of material in their possession, the proclamation proceeded as follows:

All the rights of property of whatever kind will be held inviolate, subject only to the laws of the United States. All the inhabitants are enjoined to pursue their usual avocations. All shops and places of amusement are to be kept open in the accustomed manner, and services are to be held in the churches and religious houses, as in times of profound peace. Keepers of all public houses and drinking saloons are to report their names and numbers to the office of the Provost Marshal, and they will then receive a license and be held responsible for all disorders and disturbances arising in their respective places. Sufficient force will be kept in the city to preserve order and maintain the laws. The killing of American soldiers by any disorderly person or mob is simply assassination and murder, and not war, and will be so regarded and punished. The owner of any house in which such murder shall be committed will be held responsible therefor, and the house be liable to be destroyed by the military authority. All disorders, disturbances of the peace, and crimes of an aggravated nature, interfering with the forces or laws of the United States, will be referred to a military court for trial and punishment. Other misdemeanors will be subject to the municipal authority, if it desires to act. Civil causes between party and party will be referred to the ordinary tribunals. The levy and collection of taxes, save those imposed by the laws of the United States, are suppressed, except those for keeping in repair and lighting the streets and for sanitary purposes. These are to be collected in the usual manner. The circulation of Confederate bonds, evidences of debt (except notes in the similitude of bank notes), issued by the Confederate States, or scrip, or any trade in the same, is forbidden. It has been represented to the commanding general by the civil authorities that these Confederate notes, in the form of bank notes, in a great measure, are the only substitutes for money which the people have been allowed to have, and that great distress would ensue among the poorer classes if the circulation of such notes should be suppressed. Such circulation, therefore, will be permitted so long as any one will be inconsiderate enough to receive them until further orders. No publication of newspapers, pamphlets, or handbills giving accounts of the movements of the soldiers of the United States within this department, reflecting in any way upon the United States, intending in any way to influence the public mind against the United States, will be permitted, and all articles on war news, editorial comments, or correspondence making comments upon the movements of the armies of the United States, must be submitted to the examination of an officer who will be detailed for that purpose from these headquarters. The transmission of all communications by telegraph will be under the charge of an officer from these headquarters.

Gen. Butler further requested that outrages committed by the soldiery upon the persons or property of citizens should be reported to the provost guard, prohibited the assemblage of persons in the streets, suspended the municipal authority so far as the police of the city and crimes were concerned (except that, for the effective promotion of order, an armed body of foreigners known as the European Legion, which was employed subsequent to the evacuation of the city by Gen. Lovell to protect the lives and property of the citizens, was invited to coöperate with the military authorities), and in general imposed upon the city the ordinary conditions of martial law. Copies of the proclamation were sent to all the newspaper offices; and upon the editors unanimously refusing to print it, forcible possession was taken of the "True Delta" office, and by the aid of Northern printers, selected from the different regiments of national troops, the document was speedily set up, and was worked off in the edition of the paper for May 2.

The landing of troops at New Orleans and at Algiers, on the opposite side of the Mississippi, meanwhile went vigorously on, and, by the direction of Gen. Shepley, the military governor, the principal points of approach to the city were occcupied in force, with pickets thrown out as far as the crossing of the Jackson and Jefferson Railroad. Gen. Butler established his headquarters at the St. Charles Hotel, and another large hotel, the Evans House, on Poydras street, was converted into a hospital. A sufficient force of gunboats remained in front of the city to oppose any sudden rising of the inhabitants or attack by a Confederate army, while the remainder with a portion of the mortar fleet proceeded up the river to Carrollton, Baton Rouge, and other places. Whether on account of the hopelessness of opposition, or of the indifference with which the large foreign element in the population (about 40 per cent.) regarded the fate of the city, or because perhaps the inhabitants were satisfied with the immense destruction of cotton and sugar which had already been accomplished, the city remained comparatively tranquil. "Our streets," says the "Delta" of May 1, "are remarkably quiet. Most of the stores have been closed since Friday last (April 25), and remain closed, with a few exceptions. The principal hotels are closed, and there is some difficulty among those who have been in the habit of making these establishments their homes in effecting other arrangements. The bar rooms have all been closed since Friday last. For some days there was great difficulty in passing the miserable currency we are cursed with, but, thanks to the judicious measures taken by the authorities, confidence in it has been partially restored. The markets are still very meagrely furnished, and, to provide regular supplies of food for this large population, will require all the wisdom of those who have our welfare in their keeping, for the ordinary intercourse between the city and country must, to a considerable extent, continue broken up." * * * * *

The first consideration brought to the notice of the military and municipal authorities was the destitute condition of a large portion of the population, who were literally at the point of starvation; and in accordance with a recommendation from the mayor and common council Gen. Butler gave orders, on May 2 and 3, for the safe conduct of cargoes of flour, live stock, and other necessaries from Mobile and various places in the interior. These proving ineffectual to relieve the prevailing distress, he issued on the 9th of the month a proclamation, known as General Order No. 25, the purport of which can be best understood by quoting the document in full:

HEADQUARTERS DEPARTMENT OF THE GULF,
NEW ORLEANS, May 9, 1862.

The deplorable state of destitution and hunger of the mechanics and working classes in this city has been brought to the knowledge of the commanding general.

He has yielded to every suggestion made by the city government, and ordered every method of furnishing food to the people of New Orleans that that government desired. No relief by those officials has yet been afforded. This hunger does not pinch the wealthy and influential, the leaders of the rebellion, who have gotten up this war, and are now endeavoring to prosecute it, without regard to the starving poor, the working-man, his wife and child. Unmindful of their suffering fellow-citizens at home, they have caused or suffered provisions to be carried out of the city for the Confederate service since the occupation by the United States forces.

Lafayette Square, their home of affluence, was made the depot of stores and munitions of war for the rebel armies, and not of provisions for their poor neighbors. Striking hands with the vile, the gambler, the idler, and the ruffian, they have destroyed the sugar and cotton which might have been exchanged for food for the industrious and good, and regrated the price of that which is left, by discrediting the very currency they had furnished while they sloped with the specie, as well as that stolen from the United States, as the banks, the property of the good people of New Orleans, thus leaving them to ruin and starvation—fugitives from justice many of them, and others, their associates, staying because too puerile and insignificant to be objects of punishment by the clement Government of the United States.

They have betrayed their country.

They have been false to every trust.

They have shown themselves incapable of defending the State they have seized upon, although they have forced every poor man's child into their service as soldiers for that purpose, while they made their sons and nephews officers.

They cannot protect those whom they have ruined, but have left them to the mercies and assassinations of a chronic mob.

They will not feed those whom they are starving.

Mostly without property themselves, they have plundered, stolen, and destroyed the means of those who had property, leaving children penniless and old age hopeless.

Men of Louisiana, working-men, property-holders, merchants and citizens of the United States, of whatever nation you may have had birth, how long will you uphold these flagrant wrongs, and by inaction suffer yourselves to be made the serfs of these leaders?

The United States have sent land and naval forces here to fight and subdue rebellious armies in array against her authority. We find, substantially, only fugitive masses, runaway property-owners, a whiskey-drinking mob, and starving citizens with their wives and children. It is our duty to call back the first, to punish the second, root out the third, feed and protect the last.

Ready only for what we had not prepared ourselves, to feed the hungry and relieve the distressed with provisions. But to the extent possible within the power of the commanding general it shall be done.

He has captured a quantity of beef and sugar intended for the rebels in the field. A thousand barrels of those stores will be distributed among the deserving poor of this city, from whom the rebels had plundered it; even although some of the food will go to supply the craving wants of the wives and children of those now herding at Camp Moore and elsewhere, in arms against the United States.

Capt. John Clark, acting Chief Commissary of Subsistence, will be charged with the execution of this order, and will give public notice of the place and manner of distribution, which will be arranged as far as possible so, that the unworthy and dissolute will not share its benefits.

By command of Major-General BUTLER,
GEO. C. STRONG, Assistant Adjt.-Gen., Chief of Staff.

In accordance with this proclamation, a public distribution of the captured stores was commenced on the 13th, by which means, together with the subsequent revival of traffic, all apprehensions of immediate distress were dispelled. In reply to the severe strictures of Gen. Butler, several of the city newspapers stated, that since the preceding August the poor had been gratuitously supplied twice a week with provisions, that millions of dollars had been subscribed by private individuals for similar purposes, and that the existing suffering was due to two causes: first, the blockade, or non-intercourse with the country from which provisions had previously been drawn, and, secondly, the derangement of the currency, the United States commander having, in his proclamation, warned the people of the danger of receiving the only currency in circulation, or rather the basis of the only currency in circulation.

With a view to procure a remedy for the latter evil, a committee of the Associated Banks of New Orleans requested permission to restore to their vaults the specie which had been conveyed from the city previous to its occupation by the national forces; to which Gen. Butler replied that the specie should have safe conduct through his lines and be protected, so long as it should be used in good faith to make good the obligations of the banks to their creditors by bills and deposits. "In order," he added, "that there may be no misunderstanding, it must be further observed that I by no means pledge myself that the banks, like other persons, shall not return to the United States authorities all the property of the United States which they may have received. I came to "retake, repossess, and occupy all and singular the property of the United States of whatever name and nature. Further than that I shall not go, save upon the most urgent military necessity."

Acting in the spirit of these words, Gen. Butler had on the 10th of the month taken forcible possession of a large amount of specie deposited in the office of M. Conturié, consul of the Netherlands, and which, it was supposed, belonged to the Confederate Government, or was to be expended in their behalf. The proceeding drew forth a formal protest from the entire consular body of New Orleans, as being in contravention of treaties between their governments and the United States. In reply Gen. Butler expressed his regret that the consuls should have acted without investigating the facts of the case, and stated that it would be demonstrated at the proper time that the flag of the Netherlands had been used to cover and conceal property of an incorporated company of Louisiana, secreted under it from the operation of the laws of the United States. "No person," he concluded, "can exceed me in the respect I shall pay to the flags of all nations and to the consular authority, even while I do not recognize many claims made under them; but I wish it to be most distinctly understood, that, in order to be respected, the consul, his office, and the use of his flag, must each and all be respected."

The rigor and decision which marked Gen. Butler's conduct in this instance characterized his administration from the moment of his arrival in New Orleans, and by a prompt and sometimes severe exercise of the rules of martial law, particularly in the matter of arrests and imprisonments, he kept the city in an orderly condition, although the inhabitants, distrusting his ability to maintain his authority for any considerable period, at first manifested no enthusiasm at the restoration of the national supremacy, and carefully abstained from committing themselves in favor of the Union. A notable exception was found in the conduct of a portion of the female population, who availed themselves of the license usually permitted to their sex, to offer gross insults and indignities to the national soldiers while in the orderly discharge of their duties. Apprehending that, if this conduct should be unrebuked, the soldiers might be induced to retaliate, or brought into such contempt as to provoke open assaults from the disaffected portions of the populace, Gen. Butler issued on May 15 the following order, known as General Order No. 28:

HEADQUARTERS, DEPARTMENT OF GULF, NEW ORLEANS.

As officers and soldiers of the United States have been subject to repeated insults from women, calling themselves ladies, of New Orleans, in return for the most scrupulous non-interference and courtesy on our part, it is ordered hereafter, when any female shall by mere gesture or movement insult, or show contempt for any officers or soldiers of the United States, she shall be regarded and held liable to be treated as a woman about town plying her avocation.

By command of Major-General BUTLER.

Its publication excited violent opposition from disloyal citizens, and the mayor of the city, John T. Monroe, made it the subject of an angry communication to the municipal government, and of a letter to Gen. Butler, placing an exceedingly offensive construction upon the order. The latter immediately directed him to be deprived of his official functions, and committed to Fort Jackson until further orders. At a subsequent interview with the commander-in-chief at headquarters, the mayor was informed that a withdrawal of his letter, and an apology for the language which it contained, would alone relieve him from incarceration; whereupon he made the annexed apology and retraction, and was allowed to resume the functions of his office:

GEN. BUTLER: This communication, having been sent under a mistake of fact, and being improper in language, I desire to apologize for the same, and to withdraw it. JOHN T. MONROE, Mayor.

May 16, 1862.

In explanation of the meaning and intent of the order, Gen. Butler, at the same time, addressed the following letter to the mayor, which was published, together with the apology of the latter, in the daily papers of New Orleans:

HEADQUARTERS, DEPARTMENT OF THE GULF.
NEW ORLEANS, *May* 16, 1862.

SIR: There can be, there has been, no room for misunderstanding of General Order No. 28.

No lady will take any notice of a strange gentleman, and *à fortiori* of a stranger, simply in such form as to attract attention. Common women do.

Therefore, whatever woman, lady, or mistress, gentle or simple, who, by gesture, look, or word, insults, shows contempt for, thus attracting to herself the notice of my officers and soldiers, will be deemed to act as becomes her vocation as a common woman, and will be liable to be treated accordingly. This was most fully explained to you at my office.

I shall not, as I have not, abated a single word of that order; it was well considered; if obeyed, it will protect the true and modest women from all possible insult. The others will take care of themselves.

You can publish your letter, if you publish this note and your apology. Respectfully,

BENJ. F. BUTLER,
Major-General Commanding.

JOHN T. MONROE, Mayor of New Orleans.

The agitation consequent upon the publication of Order No. 28 was not confined to New Orleans or its neighborhood, but throughout all the States, loyal and disloyal, the language of Gen. Butler was made the subject of comments varying with the feelings or circumstances of the writer. Gen. Beauregard read it at the head of his army, as an incitement to renewed efforts against the "Northern hordes;" the Confederate journals denounced it with all the resources of the language at their command; and even in the North many editors and public speakers expressed themselves strongly against the order, and called upon the President to disavow it publicly and rebuke its author. In the European journals unfriendly to the national cause, and in some also of opposite views, it was criticised with characteristic asperity. The order was nevertheless tolerated by the President, and, in spite of the obloquy sought to be associated with it, was, in the opinion of persons competent to judge, in no respect oppressive in its operation, but rather productive of substantial good by preventing an indulgence in wanton insults by any class of the population.

On May 29, the further circulation of Confederate money, which had been permitted for a limited period, ceased, in accordance with an order from the commander-in-chief, and on June 1, the port of New Orleans was declared, by a proclamation of the President, again open to commerce. Charles L. Lathrop, a former resident of the city, was appointed collector, and steam communication was almost immediately resumed with the Northern States.

This change was not effected without a resort to measures which were denounced as arbitrary and tyrannical. Arrests of suspected persons had constantly to be made, at the discretion of the commander-in-chief, including, among others, Pierre Soulé, who was sent North; the "thugs," gamblers, and other desperate characters who had long dominated in the city, were dispersed or intimidated into silence; the newspapers were on one occasion temporarily suppressed for advocating the burning of cotton and produce; and the bakers and other venders of food who had taken advantage of the scarcity of provisions to charge exorbitant prices, were compelled to conform to the tariff fixed by the city ordinances. For the further protection of the citizens, stringent orders were issued on May 27 and June 5, prohibiting officers and soldiers from taking private property or forcibly entering and searching private dwellings without written authority from the proper officers.

On June 7 took place the first military execution since the occupation of the city, the sufferer being one William B. Mumford, who was arrested for hauling down, on the morning of April 26, an American flag hoisted on the Mint by a boat's crew from Flag-Officer Farragut's fleet, and subsequently assisting in tearing it into shreds, and otherwise insulting it in the presence of a large and riotous crowd of citizens. The act, if unnoticed, was deemed to offer so pernicious a precedent for future offences, that Mumford was directed to be tried before a military commission, by whom he was convicted and sentenced to be hung. The sentence was approved by Gen. Butler, and carried into effect in the presence of an immense throng of citizens, who made no demonstrations and dispersed quietly to their homes. A universal cry of indignation at what was denounced as an act of murder went up from the seceded States, the hoisting of the flag, pending the formal surrender of the city, being deemed an unauthorized and unjustifiable proceeding on the part of the United States authorities, and one against which the mayor had protested in a written communication to Flag-Officer Farragut. On the other hand, it was claimed that the flag had been hoisted on a public building of the United States, and that the tearing of it down was an overt act of treason, done for the purpose of exciting other evil-minded persons to further resistance to the laws and arms of the United States.

To the deep feeling of revenge which this execution aroused was due the vindictive retaliatory order subsequently issued by Jefferson Davis, and the rewards for the assassination of Gen. Butler, which have from time to time appeared in the Southern papers. The clemency of Gen. Butler had, however, a few days previous, been successfully invoked in favor of six Confederate soldiers paroled at Fort Jackson, and subsequently sentenced by a court-martial to be shot for being engaged in a conspiracy to raise a company to serve in Gen. Beauregard's army; and on another occasion he manifested his desire to administer justice impartially, by causing sentence of death against two soldiers of the garrison, convicted of robbery by a court-martial, to be carried into effect. These were the only military executions which have taken place in New Orleans during its occupation by the national forces.

The difficulties with which Gen. Butler had become involved at the very outset of his administration, with the foreign consuls in New Orleans, foreshadowed a long series of complications embodying several grave questions of international comity. The news of the proceeding in the case of the consul of the Netherlands made some stir in the Northern States, and the subject having been brought to the notice of Mr. Seward by the British minister in the latter part of May, orders were issued from the War Department directing General Butler to refrain from practising any severities or strictness of doubtful right toward consuls or the subjects of any foreign power.

Business meanwhile began to assume some activity; a degree of order previously unknown in the city was maintained, and, owing to the stringent quarantine regulations enforced by the commander-in-chief, the sanitary condition of all classes of the inhabitants was unusually good. On June 14, the first of a series of Union meetings was held, at which several of the old residents were present and made speeches, and the papers of the 17th announced a gratifying increase of Union sentiment among the population at large.

During the summer no material change in the condition of things was experienced, the attention of Gen. Butler being directed toward the gradual weakening of the latent disunion power which still existed to a considerable extent among the wealthy classes. By an order issued July 25th, all negroes leaving New Orleans by direction of their masters, and who joined the national forces, were declared free; and early in the succeeding month a tax of $312,716 for the relief of the poor was levied on disloyal corporations and firms, being 25 per cent. of their contributions in aid of the Southern Confederacy. Confiscations of the property of prominent secessionists, as Gen. Twiggs and John Slidell, were also ordered. Subsequent to August 11, all the inhabitants of New Orleans were disarmed by order of the military commandant of the city, a proceeding which elicited a remonstrance from the French consul in behalf of French subjects. In reply, Gen. Butler stated that he "could see no just cause for complaint against the order," and promised the protection of the United States troops against any attempts at violence upon disarmed persons, no matter by whom attempted. To the Spanish consul, who protested against the stringency of the quarantine laws, he replied that his object in enforcing these laws in their strictness was "to save the inhabitants of New Orleans, as well Spanish as others, from the epidemic of yellow fever." In the latter part of August the initiatory step in the formation of a negro soldiery was taken by reorganizing the "Native Guards," a colored corps of the Louisiana State militia, raised under the certificate issued by the former governor of the State, and placing them in the service of the United States. Other organizations of a similar kind followed, and by the close of the year this branch of the service was established on a permanent footing.

On September 24, Gen. Lewis G. Arnold

assumed command of all the national troops at New Orleans and Algiers, and on the same day Gen. Butler created a panic among the secession sympathisers, by ordering all Americans, male and female, in his department, to renew their allegiance to the United States Government, under pain of fine and imprisonment at hard labor, and at the same time to submit a return of the amount of their real and personal property. The native population consequently flocked *en masse* to register their allegiance, and within a comparatively short time upward of 60,000 persons had complied with the order. Soon afterwards an order was issued prohibiting all persons in New Orleans holding moneys or other property in trust for persons in or sympathizing with the Confederate service; or from paying over the same without an order from the military headquarters, under penalty of having to refund a similar amount to the United States; and on October 22 the relief commission, whose labors had been regularly prosecuted since the previous May, was directed to supply no family where there was an able-bodied male member over 18 and under 45 years of age, who was either not employed, or had not enlisted in the United States army.

The month of November was distinguished by a further series of orders. The most important of these was one, framed in accordance with the provisions of the confiscation act of July, 1862, declaring sequestered all the property in the district called La Fourche, on the west side of the Mississippi, and all in that part of the State lying east of the Mississippi, except the parishes of Orleans, St. Bernard, and Plaquemines. Within these portions of the State sales or transfers of property were prohibited, and a commission was appointed to take possession of the districts in question, under whose direction the sugar plantations were worked in the absence of their owners, and the property of disloyal persons inventoried and sold for the benefit of the Government. From these sales, which continued until the middle of December, considerable sums were realized. Another order suppressed distilleries and other manufactories of intoxicating liquors; another announced that any officer found drinking intoxicating liquors in any public drinking place, would be recommended to the President for dismissal from the service; and a third prohibited the arrest of any slave unless known to be owned by a Union citizen, or the imprisonment of a slave unless his expenses should be prepaid, the slave to be released when the money was exhausted. Gen. Butler also ordered a list of slaves confined in the police jail in the month of November to be published, and all whose jail fees were not paid within ten days to be discharged, adding: "This is the course taken in all countries with debtors confined by creditors, and slaves have not such commercial value in New Orleans as to justify their being held and fed by the city, relying upon any supposed lien upon the slave."

A prominent feature in the history of this month was a Union meeting, held on the 15th, which was terminated by a grand torchlight procession through the principal streets.

On December 3, in compliance with an order from Gen. Shepley, the military governor of Louisiana, an election for members of Congress was held, at which Benjamin F. Flanders and Michael Hahn were chosen to represent the first and second districts of the State, the elective franchise being accorded to all citizens who had taken the oath of allegiance.

The next event of importance was the arrival, on the evening of December 14, of Gen. Banks, who had been appointed to supersede Gen. Butler in command of the Department of the Gulf. The news excited surprise among all classes, and not a few of those opposed to the restoration of the national supremacy were sorry to part with an officer who, if obnoxious from his zeal in the discharge of his duties, had brought unexampled order and security to the city. A meeting of the two generals took place on the 15th, at which Gen. Butler tendered a cordial welcome to his successor, assuring him that the troops would render a cheerful obedience to his orders; and, on the 16th, Gen. Banks issued a general order assuming command of the Department of the Gulf and of the State of Texas. Another order required all military and civil officers in the department to report to him, and a third suspended all public sales of property on account of the United States until further orders.

On assuming command, Gen. Banks issued the following proclamation:

HEADQUARTERS DEPARTMENT OF THE GULF,
NEW ORLEANS, Dec 16, 1862.

In obedience to orders from the President of the United States, I assume command of the Department of the Gulf, to which is added, by his special order, the State of Texas.

The duty with which I am charged requires me to assist in the restoration of the Government of the United States. It is my desire to secure to the people of every class all the privileges of possession and enjoyment consistent with public safety, or which it is possible for a beneficent and just government to confer. In execution of the high trust with which I am charged, I rely upon the coöperation and counsel of all loyal and well-disposed people, and upon the manifest interest of those dependent upon the pursuits of peace, as well as upon the support of the naval and land forces.

My instructions require me to treat as enemies those who are enemies, but I shall gladly treat as friends those who are friends. No restrictions will be placed upon the freedom of individuals which is not imperatively demanded by considerations of public safety; but, while their claims will be liberally considered, it is due also to them to state that all the rights of the Government will be unflinchingly maintained. Respectful consideration and prompt reparation will be accorded to all persons who are wronged in body or estate by those under my command.

The Government does not profit by the prolongation of the civil contest, or private or public sufferings which attend it. Its fruits are not equally distributed. In disloyal States desolation has its empire, both on sea and on land. In the North the war is an abiding sorrow, but not yet a calamity. Its cities and towns are increasing in population, wealth, and power,

Refugees from the South alone compensate in great part for the terrible decimations of battle.

The people of this department who are disposed to stake their fortunes and lives upon resistance to the Government may wisely reflect upon the immutable conditions which surround them. The valley of the Mississippi is the chosen seat of population, product, and power on this continent. In a few years twenty-five millions of people, unsurpassed in material resources and capacity for war, will swarm upon its fertile rivers. Those who assume to set conditions upon their exodus to the Gulf count upon power not given to man. The country washed by the waters of the Ohio, Missouri, and Mississippi, can never be permanently severed. If one generation basely barters away its rights, immortal honors will rest upon another that reclaims them.

Let it never be said either, that the East and the West may be separated. Thirty days' distance from the markets of Europe may satisfy the wants of Louisiana and Arkansas, but it will not answer the demands of Illinois and Ohio. The valley of the Mississippi will have its deltas upon the Atlantic. The physical force of the West will debouch upon its shores with power as resistless as the torrents of its giant river.

This country cannot be permanently divided. Ceaseless wars may drain its blood and treasure; domestic tyrants or foreign foes may grasp the sceptre of its power; but its destiny will remain unchanged. It will still be united. God has ordained it. What avails, then, the destruction of the best Government ever devised by man, and the self-adjusting, self-correcting Constitution of the United States?

People of the Southwest, why not accept the conditions imposed by the imperious necessities of geographical configuration and commercial supremacy, and reëstablish your ancient prosperity and renown? Why not become founders of States, which, as entrepots and depots of your own central and upper valleys, may stand in affluence of their resources without a superior, and in the privileges of the people without a peer among the nations of the earth?

N. P. BANKS, Maj.-Gen. Com'g.

The commencement of Gen. Banks's administration was marked by much leniency; but a portion of the people abused his clemency by various demonstrations, which brought out the following significant warning:

HEADQUARTERS DEPARTMENT OF THE GULF.
NEW ORLEANS, *Dec.* 21, 1862.

Information has been received at these headquarters that publications, injurious to the character of soldiers of the United States, are circulated in the streets, and that anonymous and threatening letters are sent to officers connected with the public service. Such practices are indecent, offensive, and criminal, and must be suppressed. The troops of this department are instructed to observe a respectful deportment to all persons, and the same deference will be exacted from all persons in their favor. Any attempt on the part of any person whatever by offensive personal conduct to excite passion, or which tends to personal altercation or controversy and the disturbance of the public peace, will be punished with the sharpest severity known to the military laws. The Commanding General requests that any violation of this order may be reported to these headquarters or to the Provost Marshal General.

By command of Maj.-Gen. BANKS.

That this did not immediately produce the effect intended was shown by the riotous conduct of several citizens, who, on Christmas Day, cheered in the public streets for President Davis, and used threatening language toward the military authorities. Prompt measures were taken to prevent the repetition of such acts.

CHAPTER XVII.

Position of the forces near Washington—Movements of Gen. Lander—Fortifications at Manassas—Plans of Gen. McClellan —Evacuation of Manassas—Commanders appointed by the President—Advance of the Army of the Potomac by water—Delay of Gen. McDowell—Safety of Washington—New Departments created—Advance of the Army of the Potomac on Yorktown—Its Siege—Evacuation—Pursuit by the Army of the Potomac—Evacuation of Williamsburg—Naval Battle and destruction of the Iron-clad Merrimac—Capture of Norfolk—Attack on Drury's Bluff—Advance of the Army of the Potomac up the Peninsula—Position on the Chickahominy—Withdrawal of Gen. McDowell.

THE position and number of the Federal troops in Virginia at the beginning of the year have already been stated. The distinct bodies of men were those under Gen. Wool at Fortress Monroe and Newport News; those under Gen. Hooker south of Washington; those under Gen. McClellan southwest of Washington; those under Gens. Keyes and Casey in and around Washington; those under Gen. Stone at and near Poolesville, and those under Gen. Banks near Darnestown with detachments on the Potomac to Williamsport. Cumberland was the headquarters of Gen. Kelly, and Grafton in western Virginia, on the line of the Baltimore and Ohio Railroad, the headquarters of Gen. Rosecrans, while Gen. Cox was up the Kanawha valley.

On the 5th of January Gen. Lander arrived at Hancock, on his way to Cumberland to relieve Gen. Kelly, who was sick. He found the enemy, under Gen. Jackson, on the other side of the Potomac, in considerable strength. It had been designed for two months that General Jackson should move northwest toward Romney; but he was delayed by the impression of the Confederate Government that the Federal army would make a general advance, and risk a battle during the winter. On the 3d or 4th of January he left Winchester and moved northward toward Hancock, a distance of forty miles, and attacked four companies of Federal troops stationed at Bath, driving them to Hancock, where, having been reënforced by Gen. Lander, they made a stand. Here Gen. Jackson made a feint attack by throwing some shells across the Potomac, which did only slight damage. He then moved westward with the intention of coming into Romney, on the Union left, by way of Springfield, and thus cut off the supplies from Cumberland and the railroad. The relative positions of Winchester, Hancock, and Romney are at the points of an equilateral triangle: Hancock north of Winchester, and Romney northwest.

The day before Gen. Jackson retired from before Hancock, Gen. Kelly, who was in Cumberland, sent an order to Col. Dunning, the commandant at Romney, to make an attack on the enemy's force stationed at Blue's Gap, a strong position, sixteen miles from Romney, on the road to Winchester. On the night of the 6th an expedition, consisting of the 4th, 5th, 7th, and 8th Ohio, 14th Indiana, and 1st Virginia, with two companies of cavalry and a battery, was sent to Blue's Gap, and made an attack upon the enemy, who, being in small force, were completely driven out. At this time Gen. Loring, with a considerable Confederate force, was within six miles of the gap, expecting the Federal column to push on and attack him. Meantime, as soon as Gen. Jackson left Hancock, Gen. Lander, anticipating his intentions, proceeded to Cumberland to Gen. Kelly, and assumed the chief command, and thence to Romney, where he arrived on the night of the Tuesday on which the expedition returned from Blue's Gap. Everything was put in readiness for a struggle. On Friday following it was reported that Gen. Jackson, in command of his right wing of ten thousand men, was within twelve miles east of Springfield, resting his men, and waiting for his other forces to get into position. His centre under Gen. Loring, about eight thousand strong, was at Blue's Gap, and his left wing of three thousand had moved up from toward Moorefield, and taken position on the New Creek road, some six miles in the rear of Romney. Thus, excepting at one point, Romney was completely surrounded by Gen. Jackson. If Gen. Lander could march north eight miles, to the Springfield crossing of the South Branch of the Potomac, before Gen. Jackson could march west twelve to Springfield, then Gen. Lander could get beyond him, or fight him with ten thousand men, at a less disadvantage than in Romney, where Gen. Jackson would concentrate twenty thousand. The entire force of Gen. Lander was about four thousand five hundred men. On Friday night everything was ready for the march. The sick, the hospital, and commissary stores were sent forward under a strong guard, and at midnight the rear guard of Gen. Lander withdrew from the town. It had rained during the day, and the rate of advance over the bad roads was a mile and a quarter to the hour. At five o'clock the next morning Gen. Lander reached Springfield. The men were so tired and exhausted that, after making fires of the fences, they lay down in files on the cold, wet ground and slept. In two hours they were again on the march. But Gen. Jackson, instead of following, went to Romney, and thence retired to Winchester, leaving the former place occupied by Gen. Loring. He also evacuated it after a few days, partly in consequence of Gen. Lander having gathered his forces, and prepared for a march upon it. Subsequently Moorefield was captured, and Bloomery Gap, by Gen. Lander. On the 11th of February Gen. Lander telegraphed to Gen. McClellan, the commander-in-chief, as follows: "The railroad was opened to-day to Hancock; also the telegraph. Papers taken, and my own reconnoissance to the south, prove the country clear, and Jackson and Loring in Winchester. The enemy have been driven out of this department."

The failure of Gen. Lander's health compelled him soon after to resign his command.

The time was now approaching when some movement should begin among the vast forces encamped in northeastern Virginia. With the Confederate Government, which still adhered to the defensive policy, the question was, whether it should maintain its advanced position before Washington, or fall back on Richmond? Its position was so well fortified that it could resist any attack in front, but would be in danger if either of its flanks were turned. Winchester, in the Shenandoah Valley, was the extreme point on the northwest occupied by the Confederate army, and Aquia Creek and Matthias Point on the southeast. This extent of line was too great to be maintained before the vast Federal forces organized in front. The flanks might thus be turned by the way of Leesburg on the north, or the Potomac on the south, and serious disaster would ensue. At the same time, the farther Gen. McClellan was drawn from his position before being encountered, so much the easier would his army be overcome, and at a greater cost to the North. These and similar considerations determined the Confederate Government to evacuate the position held by its army at Manassas. This measure was, however, not executed until March.

On the 30th of January, Gen. Beauregard, having been ordered to command in Kentucky and Tennessee, issued the following address to the soldiers at Manassas:

HEADQUARTERS FIRST CORPS ARMY OF THE POTOMAC,
Near CENTREVILLE, *January* 30, 1862.

Soldiers of the First Corps Army of the Potomac:

My duty calls me away, and to a temporary separation from you. I hope, however, to be with you again, to share your labors and your perils, and in defence of our homes and our rights, to lead you to new battles, to be crowned with signal victories.

You are now undergoing the severest trial of a soldier's life; the one by which his discipline and capacity for endurance are thoroughly tested. My faith in your patriotism, your devotion and determination, and in your high soldierly qualities, is so great that I shall rest assured you will pass through the ordeal resolutely, triumphantly. Still, I cannot quit you without deep emotion, without even deep anxiety, in the moment of our country's trials and dangers. Above all, I am anxious that my brave countrymen, here in arms, fronting the haughty array and muster of Northern mercenaries, should thoroughly appreciate the exigency, and hence comprehend that this is no time for the army of the Potomac—the men of Manassas—to stack their arms and quit, even for a brief period, the standards they have made glorious by their manhood. All must understand this, and feel the magnitude of the conflict impending, the universal personal sacrifices this war has entailed, and our duty to meet them as promptly and unblenchingly as you have met the enemy in line of battle.

To the army of the Shenandoah I desire to return my thanks for their endurance in the memorable march to my assistance last July, their timely, decisive arrival, and for their conspicuous steadiness and gallantry on the field of battle.

Those of their comrades of both corps, and of all arms of the army of the Potomac, not so fortunate as yet to have been with us in conflict with our enemy, I leave with all confidence that on occasion they will show themselves fit comrades for the men of Manassas, Bull Run, and Ball's Bluff. G. T. BEAUREGARD,
General Commanding.

Twelve months had now nearly passed since the first soldiers of the Confederate army took the field, and their term of enlistment was about to expire. This fact is not only referred to in the address of Gen. Beauregard, but it was made the occasion of the following address by Gen. Johnston, now in command of the same forces:

HEADQUARTERS, DEPARTMENT OF NORTHERN VIRGINIA, *February* 4, 1862.

SOLDIERS: Your country again calls you to the defence of the noblest of human causes. To the indomitable courage already exhibited on the battle field, you have added the rarer virtues of high endurance, cheerful obedience, and self-sacrifice. Accustomed to the comforts and luxuries of home, you have met and borne the privations of camp life, the exactions of military discipline, and the rigors of a winter campaign. The rich results of your courage, patriotism, and unfaltering virtue are before you. Intrusted with the defence of this important frontier, you have driven back the immense army which the enemy had sent to invade our country, and to establish his dominion over our people by the wide-spread havoc of a war inaugurated without a shadow of constitutional right, and prosecuted in a spirit of ruthless vengeance. By your valor and firmness, you have kept him in check, until the nations of the earth have been forced to see us in our true character—not dismembered and rebellious communities, but an empire of confederate States, with a constitution safe in the affections of the people, institutions and laws in full and unobstructed operation, a population enjoying all the comforts of life, and a citizen soldiery who laugh to scorn the threat of subjugation.

Your country now summons you to a noble and a greater deed. The enemy has gathered up all his energies for a final conflict. His enormous masses threaten us on the west; his naval expeditions are assailing us upon our whole southern coast; and upon the Potomac, within a few hours' march, he has a gigantic army, inflamed by lust and maddened by fanaticism. But the plains of Manassas are not forgotten, and he shrinks from meeting the disciplined heroes who hurled across the Potomac his grand army, routed and disgraced. He does not propose to attack this army so long as it holds its present position with undiminished numbers and unimpaired discipline; but, protected by his fortifications, he awaits the expiration of your term of service. He recollects that his own ignoble soldiery, when their term of service expired, "marched away from the scene of conflict to the sound of the enemy's cannon," and he hopes that at that critical moment Southern men will consent to share with them this infamy. Expecting a large portion of our army to be soon disbanded, he hopes that his immense numbers will easily overpower your gallant comrades who will be left here, and thus remove the chief obstacle to his cherished scheme of Southern subjugation.

The Commanding General calls upon the twelve months' men to stand by their brave comrades who have volunteered for the war, to re-volunteer at once, and thus show to the world that the patriots engaged in this struggle for independence will not swerve from the bloodiest path they may be called to tread. The enemies of your country, as well as her friends, are watching your action with deep, intense, tremulous interest. Such is your position that you can act no obscure part. Your decision, be it for honor or dishonor, will be written down in history. You cannot, you will not, draw back at this solemn crisis of our struggle, when all that is heroic in the land is engaged, and all that is precious hangs trembling in the balance.
JOS. E. JOHNSTON, Major-General C. S. A.

It was not the purpose of Gen. McClellan while commander-in-chief to move on Centreville, but by the lower Chesapeake upon Richmond. His object was to capture and hold Chattanooga, Tenn., before the army of the Potomac advanced. In this, however, he was overruled by the President, who, on the 27th of January, issued an order, as above stated, for a general advance of all the armies on the 22d of February. This order was thus undoubtedly premature; and while it served to present the President before the country as anxious for a movement, it was really of no benefit to the cause, but, on the contrary, an actual injury. Previous to its issue a change had been made in the head of the War Department. Secretary Cameron had resigned and was succeeded by Edwin M. Stanton, who had been a member of the cabinet at the close of the previous administration.

The effects upon the Confederate States of the movements made in consequence of this order were thus described at Richmond: "Had not the impatience of the Northern people and the pressure of the European Cabinets forced the hand of McClellan, and had he been able to assemble and arrange his troops and stores in the position he desired, without a conflict to arouse the attention of the Southern people to what was going on, our condition in April and May would have been tenfold more dangerous than it now is. The disasters we have suffered are mortifying to us and exhilarate our enemies; but they have startled without crippling the Confederacy. Had it lain still two months more, with the army dwindling daily under the furlough system, disgusted with the inaction of stationary camps, while the Government was squabbling with the Generals and the people sinking into indifference, we would have been overrun between the 15th of April and the 1st of May."

Gen. Lander having cleared his department of the forces of the enemy, a movement was now commenced lower down the Potomac by a portion of Gen. Banks's command. On the 24th of February the 28th Pennsylvania regiment, Col. Geary, crossed the Potomac from Sandy Hook and took possession of Harper's Ferry. The object of this movement upon Harper's Ferry was to cover the reconstruction of the Baltimore and Ohio railroad, and at the same time to draw the attention of the Confederates to their left flank, which was threatened by the movement. The operations of crossing the Potomac and the occupation of Harper's Ferry and Charlestown were superintended by Gen. McClellan in person. The bridges were thrown over the Potomac by Capt. J. C. Duane, U. S. engineers, on the 26th of February, and on the same day Gen. Banks occupied Harper's Ferry permanently, and the advance took possession of Bolivar Heights. On the 27th reconnoissances were pushed forward to Charlestown, and some prisoners taken; Loudon Heights were also occupied. On the 28th of February Charlestown was occupied by a strong force with the intention of holding it against any attack. On the 3d of March Martinsburg was occupied by the 13th Massachusetts, who left camp at Williamsport on the previous afternoon. This is an important town on the Baltimore and Ohio railroad between Harper's Ferry and Hancock. It is distant from the former fifteen miles, and is twenty miles north of Winchester, with which it is connected by a turnpike road. All the iron of the double track of the railroad had been removed excepting half a mile of track made of compound rails. On the 2d, Leesburg was occupied by Col. Geary. The retreat of the Confederate army had now commenced along its entire line from Aquia Creek to the Shenandoah. This movement threatening its left flank was undoubtedly the cause of this abandonment of Manassas. All their important positions were occupied by the Federal troops during the next ten days, including the strong one at Centreville. Winchester was evacuated by Gen. Jackson on the night of the 11th of March. Gen. Shields, in command of Gen. Lander's division, soon followed up this retreat, and on the 19th he discovered Gen. Jackson rëenforced in a strong position near New Market, and within supporting distance of the main body of the Confederate army under Gen. Johnston. In order to draw him from this position Gen. Shields fell back rapidly to Winchester on the 20th, as if in retreat, having marched his whole command thirty miles in one day. On the next day the Confederate cavalry under Gen. Ashby showed themselves in sight of Winchester. On the 22d the entire command of Gen. Banks, with the exception of Gen. Shields's division, evacuated Winchester and marched for Centreville. This movement, and the masked position in which Gen. Shields placed his division, led the enemy to believe that the town was evacuated with the exception of a few regiments to garrison it. That afternoon at 5 o'clock Gen. Ashby attacked the pickets of Gen. Shields and drove them in, but was repulsed by a small force pushed forward by Gen. Shields for that purpose, who now made preparations for a contest in the morning. Only a small Confederate force appearing in the morning, Gen. Shields ordered a portion of his artillery forward to open fire and unmask it. This had the desired effect, when a battle ensued, during which Gen. Shields by an attack upon the Confederate left flank forced that wing back upon its centre and placed the enemy in a position to be routed by a general attack, which was made at five o'clock in the afternoon with great success. The Confederates were driven from the field. Two guns, four caissons, three hundred prisoners, and a thousand stand of small arms were captured. The force of Gen. Shields was between seven and eight thousand men. His loss in killed and wounded was between three and four hundred. On the previous evening the arm of Gen. Shields was broken above the elbow by the fragment of a shell. The Confederate loss in killed and wounded was large. Considerable numbers were subsequently found in the houses of the inhabitants as the force of Gen. Banks advanced. The Confederate force was estimated at near ten thousand men. The brigades of Gens. Jackson, Smith, Garnett, and Longstreet were engaged, and prisoners were taken from the 2d, 4th, 5th, 21st, 23d, 27th, 28th, 33d, 37th, and 42d Virginia; 1st regiment of the Provisional Army, and an Irish battalion. For these movements Gen. Shields was complimented by the War Department in the following despatch:

WAR DEPARTMENT, *March* 26, 1862.

To Brig.-Gen. Shields:

Your two despatches relative to the brilliant achievement of the forces under your command have been received. While rejoicing at the success of your gallant troops, deep commiseration and sympathy are felt for those who have been victims in the gallant and victorious contest with treason and rebellion.

Your efforts as well as your success proves that Lander's brave division is still bravely led, and that wherever its standard is displayed rebels will be routed and pursued. To you and to the officers and soldiers under your command the Department returns thanks. EDWIN M. STANTON, Secretary of War.

The following was also received by Gen. Shields:

HEADQUARTERS ARMY OF THE POTOMAC,
SEMINARY, *March* 27, 1862.

To Brig.-Gen. Shields:

The Commanding General congratulates you and the troops under your command upon the victory gained by your energy and activity and their bravery on the 23d. He is pained to learn that the wound you have received in the skirmish on the day before is more serious than at first supposed.

By command of

Maj.-Gen. GEO. B. McCLELLAN.

S. WILLIAMS, Assist. Adj.-Gen.

The following congratulations and instructions were sent to Gen. Banks:

FAIRFAX SEMINARY, *March* 27, 1862.

To Maj.-Gen. Banks:

The General Commanding congratulates you and the brave troops under your command on the splendid achievement commenced in your department, news of which he has just received. He desires you to follow up rapidly the enemy's troops as far as Strasburg if possible. S. WILLIAMS, Assistant Adjutant-General.

This little affair at Winchester is said to have caused orders to be issued which were attended with momentous consequences. They will be stated hereafter. It occurred on the date of March 23d.

The evacuation by the Confederate army of their positions before Washington was conducted in a most successful manner. When the Union troops entered their intrenchments, all were gone. Their evacuation had been effected by means of the railroad from Manassas to Gordonsville, while the state of the roads was such as to prevent an immediate active campaign by the Union army. Their retreat was arrested at the Rappahannock river, and a new line formed for the purpose of defence. It stretched from the Rappahannock by a circle to Cumberland Gap near the extreme southwestern part of the State, embracing the Central and the Virginia and Tennessee railroads, the chief cities of Virginia, and the valley of the James river with its canal and railroads. It was simply a line of defence, and assumed as a necessity in view of the immense Federal force that had been marshalled and put quietly in position.

The design of Gen. McClellan, as above stated, was, so far as he was master of his own movements, to attack Richmond by the water line, on the ground that such a movement would certainly force the Confederate army out of Manassas. By the James river, Richmond could be approached by transports and gunboats of light draft, and without a long line for the transportation of supplies. At this time the President as commander-in-chief issued the following order:

EXECUTIVE MANSION,
WASHINGTON, *March* 8, 1862.

General War Order, No. 2.

Ordered, I. That the Major-General commanding the Army of the Potomac proceed forthwith to organize that part of said army destined to enter upon active operations (including the reserve, but excluding the troops to be left in the fortifications about Washington), into four army corps, to be commanded according to seniority of rank, as follows:

First Corps, to consist of three divisions, and to be commanded by Maj.-Gen. I. McDowell.

Second Corps, to consist of three divisions, and to be commanded by Brig.-Gen. E. V. Sumner.

Third Corps, to consist of three divisions, and to be commanded by Brig.-Gen. S. P. Heintzelman.

Fourth Corps, to consist of three divisions, and to be commanded by Brig.-Gen. E. L. Keyes.

II. That the divisions now commanded by the officers above assigned to the commands of corps, shall be embraced in and form part of their respective corps.

III. The forces left for the defence of Washington will be placed in command of Brig.-Gen. James Wadsworth, who shall also be Military Governor of the District of Columbia.

IV. That this order be executed with such promptness and despatch, as not to delay the commencement of the operations already directed to be undertaken by the Army of the Potomac.

V. A fifth army corps, to be commanded by Maj.-Gen. N. P. Banks, will be formed from his own and Gen. Shields's (late Gen. Lander's) division.

ABRAHAM LINCOLN.

In compliance with this order of the President, Gen. McClellan, on the 13th, issued an order dividing "the active portion of the army of the Potomac" into army corps as follows:

The corps of Gen. McDowell was composed of the divisions of Gens. Franklin, McCall, and King.

The corps of Gen. Sumner was composed of the divisions of Gens. Richardson, Blenker, and Sedgwick.

The corps of Gen. Heintzelman was composed of the divisions of Gens. Kearney, Hooker, and Fitz John Porter.

The corps of Gen. Keyes was composed of the divisions of Gens. Couch, Smith, and Casey.

The corps of Gen. Banks was composed of the divisions of Gens. Williams and Shields.

On the 11th of March, the President issued another order relieving Gen. McClellan from the command of all the military departments except that of the Potomac, and re-arranging the departments as follows:

EXECUTIVE MANSION,
WASHINGTON, *March* 11, 1862.

General War Order, No. 3.

Maj.-Gen. McClellan having personally taken the field at the head of the Army of the Potomac until otherwise ordered, he is relieved from the command of the other military departments, he retaining command of the Department of the Potomac.

Ordered, further, That the two departments now under the respective commands of Gens. Halleck and Hunter, together with so much of that under Gen. Buell as lies west of a north and south line indefinitely drawn through Knoxville, Tenn., be consolidated and designated the Department of the Mississippi, and that until otherwise ordered, Maj.-Gen. Halleck have command of said department.

Ordered, also, That the country west of the Department of the Potomac and east of the Department of the Mississippi be a military department, to be called the Mountain Department, and that the same be commanded by Maj.-Gen. Fremont.

That all the Commanders of Departments, after the receipt of this order by them respectively, report severally and directly to the Secretary of War, and that prompt, full, and frequent reports will be expected of all and each of them. ABRAHAM LINCOLN.

The effect of this order was to put under the charge of the Secretary of War a class of duties which had heretofore been under the direction of the highest military command. It relieved Gen. McClellan from the supervision of military operations in any other department than his own. He retained still under his immediate command the five corps of the army of the Potomac, as is manifest by his despatches, dated March 27, to Gens. Banks and Shields, after the battle at Winchester. It also shows that the corps of Gen. Banks was at that date expected to operate under his command, although he had then embarked a portion of his army to Fortress Monroe.

Assuming the distinct command of the Army of the Potomac, as his forces were now designated, for the purpose of conducting a campaign, Gen. McClellan issued the following address to his soldiers:

HEADQUARTERS ARMY OF THE POTOMAC,
FAIRFAX COURT HOUSE, VA., *March* 14, 1862.

Soldiers of the Army of the Potomac:

For a long time I have kept you inactive, but not without a purpose. You were to be disciplined, armed, and instructed; the formidable artillery you now have, had to be created; other armies were to move and to accomplish certain results. I have held you back that you might give the death blow to the rebellion that has distracted our once happy country. The patience you have shown, and your confidence in your General, are worth a dozen victories. These preliminary results are now accomplished. I feel that the patient labors of many months have produced their fruit; the Army of the Potomac is now a real army—magnificent in material, admirable in discipline and instruction, excellently equipped and armed—your commanders are all that I could wish. The moment for action has arrived, and I know that I can trust in you to save our country. As I ride through your ranks, I see in your faces the sure presage of victory; I feel that you will do whatever I ask of you. The period of inaction has passed.

I will bring you now face to face with the rebels, and only pray that God may defend the right. In whatever direction you may move, however strange my actions may appear to you, ever bear in mind that my fate is linked with yours, and that all I do is to bring you, where I know you wish to be—on the decisive battle field. It is my business to place you there. I am to watch over you as a parent over his children; and you know that your General loves you from the depths of his heart. It shall be my care, as it has ever been, to gain success with the least possible loss; but I know that, if it is necessary, you will willingly follow me to our graves, for our righteous cause. God smiles upon us, victory attends us; yet I would not have you think that our aim is to be attained without a manly struggle. I will not disguise it from you: you have brave foes to encounter, foemen well worthy of the steel that you will use so well. I shall demand of you great, heroic exertions, rapid and long marches, desperate combats, privations, perhaps. We will share all these together; and when this sad war is over we will return to our homes, and feel that we can ask no higher honor than the proud consciousness that we belonged to the Army of the Potomac. GEO. B. McCLELLAN,
Major-General Commanding.

The Prince de Joinville, in a narrative of the campaign on the peninsula, has described with much detail the reasons for the evacuation of Manassas by the Confederate forces, and the change of the plan for the campaign under Gen McClellan. He states as follows:

"While we were riding forward, grave events were occurring in the highest regions of the army. There exists in the American army, as in the English, a commander-in-chief, who exercises over the head of all the generals a supreme authority, regulates the distribution of the troops, and directs military operations. These functions, which have been greatly curtailed in the British army since the Crimean war, were still exercised in all their vigor in America. From the aged General Scott, who had long honorably discharged them, they had passed to General McClellan. We learned, on reaching Fairfax, that they had been taken away from him. It is easy to understand the diminution of force and the restrictions upon his usefulness thus inflicted upon the general-in-chief by a blow in the rear at the very outset of his campaign.

"Yet this was but a part of the mischief done him. McClellan had long known, better than anybody else, the real strength of the rebels at Manassas and Centreville. He was perfectly familiar with the existence of the 'wooden cannon' by which it has been pretended that he was kept in awe for six months. But he also knew that till the month of April the roads of Virginia are in such a state that wagons and artillery can only be moved over them by constructing plank roads—a tedious operation, during which the enemy, holding the railways, could either retreat, as he was then actually doing, or move for a blow upon some other point. In any event, had McClellan attacked and carried Centreville, pursuit was impossible, and victory would have been barren of results. A single bridge burned would have saved Johnston's whole army. Such are the vast advantages of a railway for a retreating army—advantages which do not exist for the army which pursues it.

"We have the right, we think, to say that McClellan never intended to advance upon Centreville. His long-determined purpose was to make Washington safe by means of a strong garrison, and then to use the great navigable waters and immense naval resources of the North to transport the army by sea to a point near Richmond. For weeks, perhaps for months, this plan had been secretly maturing. Secrecy as well as promptness, it will be understood, was indispensable here to success. To keep the secret it had been necessary to confide it to few persons, and hence had arisen the long ill feeling toward the uncommunicative general.

"Be this as it may, as the day of action drew near, those who suspected the general's project, and were angry at not being informed of it; those whom his promotion had excited to envy; his political enemies (who is without them in America?); in short, all those beneath or beside him who wished him ill, broke out into a chorus of accusations of slowness, inaction, incapacity. McClellan, with a patriotic courage which I have always admired, disdained these accusations, and made no reply. He satisfied himself with pursuing his preparations in laborious silence. But the moment came in which, notwithstanding the loyal support given him by the President, that functionary could no longer resist the tempest. A council of war of all the divisional generals was held; a plan of campaign, not that of McClellan, was proposed and discussed. McClellan was then forced to explain his projects, and the next day they were known to the enemy. Informed no doubt by one of those female spies who keep up his communications into the domestic circles of the Federal enemy, Johnston evacuated Manassas at once. This was a skilful manœuvre. Incapable of assuming the offensive, threatened with attack either at Centreville, where defence would be useless if successful, or at Richmond, the loss of which would be a great check, and unable to cover both positions at once, Johnston threw his whole force before the latter of the two.

"For the Army of the Potomac this was a misfortune. Its movement was unmasked before it had been made. Part of its transports were still frozen up in the Hudson. Such being the state of affairs, was it proper to execute as rapidly as possible the movement upon Richmond by water, or to march upon Richmond by land? Such was the grave question to be settled by the young general in a miserable room of an abandoned house at Fairfax within twenty-four hours. And it was at this moment that the news of his removal as general-in-chief reached him; the news, that is, that he could no longer count upon the coöperation of the other armies of the Union, and that the troops under his own orders were to be divided into four grand *corps* under four separate chiefs named in order of rank—a change which would throw into subaltern positions some young generals of division who had his personal confidence. It is easy to see that here was matter enough to cast a cloud upon the firmest mind. But the general's resolution was promptly taken.

"To follow the Confederates by land to Richmond at this season of the year was a material impossibility. An incident had just proved this to be so. Gen. Stoneman, with a flying column, had been sent in pursuit of the enemy. This column came up with the enemy on the Rappahannock, along the railway to Gordonsville, and had two engagements with him of no great importance. Then came the rain. The fords were swollen, the bridges carried away, the watercourses could no longer be passed by swimming; they were torrents. Stoneman's column began to suffer for want of provisions, and its situation was perilous. In order to communicate with the army, Stoneman had to send two of McClellan's aides-de-camp, who had accompanied him, across a river on a raft of logs tied together with ropes.

"Such was the country before the army. Furthermore, the enemy was burning and breaking up all the bridges. Now with the wants of the American soldier and the usual extravagance of his rations, and with the necessity of transporting everything through a country where nothing is to be found, and where the least storm makes the roads impassable, no army can live unless it supports its march upon a navigable watercourse or a railway. In Europe our military administration assumes that the transportation service of an army of one hundred thousand men can only provision that army for a three days' march from its base of operations. In America this limit must be reduced to a single day. I need only add that upon the roads to Richmond there were viaducts which it would have required six weeks to reconstruct.

"The land march was therefore abandoned, and we came back to the movement by water. But this operation also was no longer what it had been when McClellan had conceived it. The revelation of his plans to the enemy had allowed the latter to take his precautions. The evacuation of Manassas had preceded instead of following the opening of the Federal campaign. The movement by water could no longer be a surprise. Unfortunately it was also to lose the advantages of a rapid execution."

The movement of troops had been as follows: The last detachment of the Confederate army left Manassas on the 9th of March. On the morning of the 10th Gen. McClellan moved the Army of the Potomac toward the deserted position. The object of moving to Manassas was to verify its evacuation, to take the chance of cutting off the enemy's rear guard, to deceive the enemy, if possible, as to the real intentions of Gen. McClellan, and to gain the opportunity of cutting loose from all useless baggage, and to give the troops a few days' experience in bivouac and on the march. After reaching Manassas, Gen. McClellan returned to Washington on the 13th, and the army at once countermarched, and on Sunday the 16th it was massed in new positions near Alexandria, ready to embark with the least possible delay. During the ensuing week it began to embark on transports at Alexandria for Fortress Monroe. The number of transports promised was to be sufficient to convey fifty thousand men, but the number collected was found to be hardly enough for the conveyance of half that number. Instead of moving the whole army with its equipage at once, as it had been intended, a number of trips were required. The embarkation commenced on the 17th of March.

By reference to the order of the President issued on the 8th of March (*see* p. 210), it will be seen that the army was divided into five corps. Of these, the corps of Gens. Banks and McDowell did not embark. Of the second corps, under Gen. Sumner, one division, that of Gen. Blenker, was withdrawn and sent to Gen. Fremont in the Mountain Department. There remained therefore to be embarked, two divisions under Gen. Sumner, three under Gen. Heintzelman, and three under Gen. Keyes—being in all eight divisions. The Prince de Joinville, in his statement of the numbers of the entire army, says it consisted of "11 divisions of infantry, 8,000 to 10,000 strong; 1 division of regulars (infantry and cavalry), 6,000 strong; 350 pieces of artillery. The total effective force may have been 120,000 men." From this number are to be deducted the corps of Gen. McDowell and the division of Gen. Blenker. This will make the effective force of Gen. McClellan embarked for Fortress Monroe about eighty-five thousand men. Two weeks were occupied in transporting this force to Fortress Monroe.

It has been stated that Gen. Blenker's division was withdrawn from Gen. Sumner's corps, and sent to Gen. Fremont in the Mountain Department. This was done one or two days before Gen. McClellan sailed. The reason given was "political pressure" exercised to get a command for Gen. Fremont. No military reason was stated for this withdrawal. The following letter from President Lincoln to Gen. McClellan, produced at a court martial in Washington, thus explains it:

WASHINGTON, *April* 9, 1862.

Maj.-Gen. McClellan:

MY DEAR SIR: Your despatches complaining that you are not properly sustained, while they do not offend me, do pain me very much.

Blenker's division was withdrawn from you before you left here, and you know the pressure under which I did it; and, as I thought, acquiesced in it—certainly not without reluctance.

After you left I ascertained that less than twenty thousand unorganized men, without a single field battery, were all you designed to be left for the defence of Washington and Manassas Junction; and part of of this even was to go to Gen. Hooker's old position.

Gen. Banks's corps, once designed for Manassas Junction, was diverted and tied up on the line of Winchester and Strasburg, and could not leave it without again exposing the Upper Potomac and the Baltimore and Ohio railroad. This presented (or would present, when McDowell and Sumner should be gone) a great temptation to the enemy to turn back from the Rappahannock and sack Washington.

My explicit order that Washington should, by the judgment of all the commanders of corps, be left entirely secure, had been neglected. It was precisely this that drove me to detain McDowell. I do not forget that I was satisfied with your arrangement to leave Banks at Manassas Junction; but when that arrangement was broken up, and nothing was substituted for it, of course I was not satisfied; I was constrained to substitute something for it myself.

And now allow me to ask, "Do you really think I should permit the line from Richmond, *via* Manassas Junction, to this city, to be entirely open, except what resistance could be presented by less than twenty thousand unorganized troops?" This is a question which the country will not allow me to evade.

There is a curious mystery about the number of troops now with you. When I telegraphed you on the 6th, saying that you had over one hundred thousand with you, I had just obtained from the Secretary of War a statement taken, as he said, from your own returns, making one hundred and eight thousand then with you, and *en route* to you.

You now say you will have but eighty-five thousand when all *en route* to you shall have reached you. How can the discrepancy of twenty-three thousand be accounted for?

As to Gen. Wool's command, I understand it is doing for you precisely what a like number of your own would have to do, if that command was away.

I suppose the whole force which has gone forward for you is with you by this time; and, if so, I think it is the precise time for you to strike a blow. By delay the enemy will relatively gain upon you; that is, he will gain faster by fortifications and reënforcements than you can by reënforcements alone.

And, once more, let me tell you it is indispensable to you that you strike a blow. I am powerless to help this. You will do me the justice to remember I always insisted that going down the bay in search of a field, instead of fighting at or near Manassas, was only shifting and not surmounting a difficulty; that we would find the same enemy and the same or equal intrenchments at either place. The country will not fail to note—is now noting—that the present hesitation to move upon an intrenched enemy is but the story of Manassas repeated.

I beg to assure you that I have never written you or spoken to you in greater kindness of feeling than now, nor with a fuller purpose to sustain you so far as in my most anxious judgment I consistently can. But you must act.

Yours, very truly, A. LINCOLN.

When Gen. McClellan sailed he supposed that Gen. McDowell's corps would follow him, and it was not until he was before Yorktown that he received the first intimation to the contrary. The reason of this change should also be stated.

By reference to a preceding page, it will be seen that the battle of Winchester took place on the 23d of March, about the time the army of the Potomac was embarking. It startled the Government by revealing a much stronger force of the enemy in their immediate front than they had supposed. At the same time the number of troops at Washington being limited, it was decided that one of the two corps which had not embarked (either McDowell's or Sumner's) should be withheld, and the decision fell upon Gen. McDowell. The same question came up in Congress on the 26th of May, after Gen. Jackson had made his brilliant dash up the Shenandoah, and driven Gen. Banks across the Potomac. Although it may be anticipating some events, it is proper that the explanation of the withdrawal of McDowell's corps should be here noticed. In the Senate, Mr. Wilson of Massachusetts, chairman of the Committee on Military Affairs, said: "I will state that the Secretary of War is not responsible for the movements charged upon him by the Senator from Kentucky. The President alone is responsible for whatever has occurred, both for arresting the advance of General McDowell to Yorktown, and withdrawing a portion of Gen. Banks's forces. The order arresting the advance of Gen. McDowell was made by the President, with the approval of the Secretary of War, General Hitchcock, and several other military men. It was given for the best of purposes, and I am sure there was no intrigue about it, nor personal objects gained. It may have been an error; but, if so, it was an error committed by the President for an honest and patriotic purpose, under the advice of the military men whom he consulted. I understand the fact to be that the President gave written orders—in fact I have seen the orders—that the number of men necessary for the defence of Washington should be left here, and that that number should be agreed upon by the commanders of the various corps of the army. The commanders of corps held a consultation, and decided that forty-five thousand men were necessary to be held for the defence of this city. All the forces were ordered to be withdrawn from this city, with the exception of nineteen thousand, and four thousand of that number were sent for. Nearly all of the regiments left here were recently brought into the service, and four or five of them were cavalry regiments, not mounted, and not in a condition for service. Under these circumstances, apprehending precisely what has taken place, the President withheld thirty thousand men under Gen. McDowell. Ten thousand of this force, under Gen. Franklin, at the urgent request of Gen. McClellan, were sent forward to Yorktown, but McDowell was held back with twenty thousand men on the Rappahannock to protect the capital and menace Richmond. The President then, in order to concentrate a force here and threaten Richmond, and aid Gen. McClellan's movements, ordered Gen. Shields to unite with Gen. McDowell, thus making an army of about forty thousand men, the intention of which was to move on Richmond by land, so as to cover Washington in their movement. This left Gen. Banks a small force, and a movement has been made upon him, and he has been compelled to evacuate the Shenandoah Valley and recross the Potomac. These movements were directed by the President; and he is alone responsible for them. In doing what he did, I have no doubt he was actuated by honest purposes, and he had the sanction and support of his military advisers, including the Secretary of War."

Mr. Trumbull of Illinois said: "While the Senator from Massachusetts is making his statement, I should like to inquire of him if it was not at the urgent and repeated request of Gen. McClellan that troops should be sent to him to aid in his attack upon Richmond that this has been done?"

Mr. Wilson of Massachusetts: "In response to the Senator's question, I will say that I understand that Gen. McClellan desired to have the forces reserved under Gen. McDowell sent forward to him by the steamers. Upon his request, Gen. Franklin with his division was sent forward to Yorktown. The President, to protect Washington, and at the same time to aid Gen. McClellan by menacing Richmond, withdrew Gen. Shields's division from Gen. Banks, thus concentrating on the Rappahannock forty thousand men. This force could move on Richmond, or act directly for the protection of Washington, according to circumstances. Yesterday the President, in view of what has occurred, stated that this force of twenty thousand men, which he had reserved, and for which he takes the entire responsibility, had been reserved by him in apprehension of precisely such a movement of the enemy threatening this city as has already taken place.

"The President may have made a mistake in withdrawing so much of the force of Gen. Banks, but I am sure he acted according to the best lights he possessed. Gen. Banks has been forced to retrace his steps, to abandon the Shenandoah Valley, and to recross the Potomac."

On Dec. 10, before a court martial at Washington, Gen. McClellan, in answer to the question, What communication he received from the President through Gen. Franklin, &c.? said: "The substance of the communication of Gen. Franklin from the President was that the President assumed the responsibility of the change of destination of Gen. McDowell's corps, regarding that corps necessary for the defence of Washington, although the troops actually left in Washington and in front of it, disposable for its defence, were rather more than double the garrison fixed by the engineer and artillery officers, and considerably more than the largest number recommended by any of the corps commanders to be left in the vicinity of Washington."

The following orders of Gen. McClellan will show his plans for the protection of Washington:

HEADQUARTERS, ARMY OF THE POTOMAC, *March* 16, 1862.

Brig.-Gen. James S. Wadsworth, Military Governor of the District of Columbia:

SIR: The command to which you have been assigned, by instruction of the President, as Military Governor of the District of Columbia, embraces the geographical limits of the district, and will also include the city of Alexandria, the defensive works south of the Potomac, from the Occoquan to Difficult Creek, and the post of Fort Washington. I enclose a list of the works and defences embraced in these limits. Gen. Banks will command at Manassas Junction, with the divisions of Williams and Shields, composing the Fifth Army Corps, but you should, nevertheless, exercise vigilance in your front, carefully guard the approaches in that quarter, and maintain the duties of advanced guards. You will use the same precautions on either flank. All troops not actually needed for the police of Washington and Georgetown, for the garrisons north of the Potomac, and for other indicated special duties, should be removed to the south side of the river. In the centre of your front you should post the main body of your troops, in proper proportions, at suitable distances toward your right and left flanks. Careful patrols will be made to thoroughly scour the country in front from right to left.

It is specially enjoined upon you to maintain the forts and their armaments in the best possible order, to look carefully after the instruction and discipline of their garrisons, as well as all other troops under your command, and by frequent and rigid inspection to insure the attainment of these ends.

The care of the railways, canals, depots, bridges, and ferries within the above-named limits will devolve upon you, and you are to insure their security and provide for their protection by every means in your power. You will also protect the depots of the public stores and the transit of the stores to the troops in actual service.

By means of patrols you will thoroughly scour the neighboring country south of the eastern branch, and also on your right, and you will use every possible precaution to intercept mails, goods, and persons passing unauthorized to the enemy's lines.

The necessity of maintaining good order within your limits, and especially in the capital of the nation, cannot be too strongly enforced. You will forward and facilitate the movement of all troops destined for the active part of the Army of the Potomac, and especially the transits of detachments to their proper regiments and corps.

The charge of all new troops arriving in Washington, and of all troops temporarily there, will devolve upon you. You will form them into provisional brigades, promote their instruction and discipline, and facilitate their equipments. Report all arrivals of troops, their strength, composition, and equipment, by every opportunity. Besides the regular reports and returns which you will be required to render to the Adjutant-General of the army, you will make to these headquarters a consolidated morning report of your command every Sunday morning, and a monthly return on the first day of each month.

The foregoing instructions are communicated by command of Maj.-Gen. McClellan.

Very respectfully, your obedient servant,

——— ———,
Assistant Adjutant-General.

HEADQUARTERS, ARMY OF THE POTOMAC, *March* 16, 1862.

To Maj.-Gen. N. P. Banks, Commanding Fifth Corps, Army of the Potomac:

SIR: You will post your command in the vicinity of Manassas, intrench yourself strongly, and throw cavalry pickets well out to the front. Your first care will be the rebuilding of the railway from Washington to Manassas and to Strasburg, in order to open your communications with the valley of the Shenandoah. As soon as the Manassas Gap railway is in running order, intrench a brigade of infantry—say four regiments, with two batteries—at or near the point where that railway crosses the Shenandoah. Something like two regiments of cavalry should be left in that vicinity to occupy Winchester, and thoroughly scour the country south of the railway and up the Shenandoah Valley, as well as through Chester Gap, which might perhaps be occupied advantageously by a detachment of infantry well intrenched. Block houses should be built at all the railway bridges occupied by grand guard, Warrenton Junction or Warrenton itself, and also some still more advanced points on the Orange and Alexandria railroad, as soon as the railroad bridges are repaired.

Great activity should be observed by the cavalry. Besides the two regiments at Manassas, another regiment of cavalry will be at your disposal to scout toward the Occoquan, and probably a fourth toward

Leesburg. To recapitulate, the most important points that should engage your attention are as follows:

First—A strong force, well intrenched, in the vicinity of Manassas, perhaps even Centreville, and another force, a brigade, also well intrenched near Strasburg.

Second—Block houses at the railroad bridges.

Third—Constant employment of cavalry well to the front.

Fourth—Grand guards at Warrenton, and in advance as far as the Rappahannock, if possible.

Fifth—Great care to be exercised to obtain full and early information as to the enemy.

Sixth—The general object is to cover the line of the Potomac and Washington.

The foregoing is communicated by order of Maj.-Gen. McClellan. ——— ———,

Assistant Adjutant-General.

On the 1st of April Gen. McClellan addressed the following additional note to Gen. Banks:

HEADQUARTERS, ARMY OF THE POTOMAC,
ON BOARD COMMODORE, *April* 1, 1862.

Maj.-Gen. N. P. Banks, Commanding Fifth Army Corps:

GENERAL: The change in affairs in the valley of the Shenandoah has rendered necessary a corresponding departure, temporarily at least, from the plan we some days since agreed upon.

In my arrangements I assume that you have a force amply sufficient to drive Jackson before you, provided he is not reënforced largely. I also assume that you may find it impossible to find anything toward Manassas for some days, probably not until the operations of the main army have drawn all the rebel force toward Richmond.

You are aware that Gen. Sumner has for some days been at Warrenton Junction, with two divisions of infantry, six batteries, and two regiments of cavalry, and that a reconnoissance to the Rappahannock forced the enemy to destroy the railroad bridge at Rappahannock Station, on the Orange and Alexandria railroad. Since that time our cavalry have found nothing on this side of the Rappahannock in that direction, and it seems clear that we have no reason to fear any return of the rebels in that quarter. Their movements near Fredericksburg also indicate a final abandonment of that neighborhood.

I doubt whether Johnston will now reënforce Jackson with a view to offensive operations. The time has probably passed when he could have gained anything by so doing.

I have ordered one of Sumner's divisions (that of Richardson) to Alexandria for embarkation. Blenker's has been detached from the Army of the Potomac, and ordered to report to Gen. Fremont. Abercrombie is probably at Warrenton Junction to-day; Geary at White Plains.

Two regiments of cavalry have been ordered out, and are now on the way to relieve the two regiments of Sumner. Four thousand infantry and one battery leave Washington at once for Manassas. Some three thousand more will move in one or two days, and soon after three thousand additional.

I will order Blenker to move on Strasburg and report to you for temporary duty; so that, should you find a large force in your front, you can avail yourself of his aid. As soon as possible, please direct him on Winchester, thence to report to the Adjutant-General of the Army for orders; but keep him until you are sure what you have in front.

In regard to your own movements, the most important thing is to throw Jackson well back, and then to assume such a position as to enable you to prevent his return. As soon as the railway communications are reëstablished, it will be probably important and advisable to move on Staunton; but this would require communications and a force of 25,000 to 30,000 for active operations. It should also be nearly coincident with my own move on Richmond. At all events, not so long before it as to enable the rebels to concentrate on you and then return to me.

I fear that you cannot be ready in time; although it may come in very well with a force less than I have mentioned, after the main battle near Richmond. When Gen. Sumner leaves Warrenton Junction, Gen. Abercrombie will be placed in immediate command of Manassas and Warrenton Junction, under your general orders. Please inform me frequently by telegraph and otherwise as to the state of things in your front. I am, very truly yours,

GEO. B. McCLELLAN,
Maj.-Gen. Commanding.

P. S. From what I have just learned, it would seem that the two regiments of cavalry intended for Warrenton Junction have gone to Harper's Ferry. Of the four additional regiments placed under your orders, two should as promptly as possible move by the shortest route on Warrenton Junction.

I am, sir, very respectfully, your obedient servant,

GEO. B. McCLELLAN,
Maj.-Gen. Commanding.

HEADQUARTERS, ARMY OF THE POTOMAC,
STEAMER COMMODORE, *April* 1, 1862.

To Brig.-Gen. L. Thomas, Adj.-Gen. U. S. A.:

GENERAL: I have to request that you will lay the following communication before the Hon. Secretary of War. The approximate numbers and positions of the troops left near and in rear of the Potomac are about as follows:

Gen. Dix has, after guarding the railroads under his charge, sufficient troops to give him five thousand men for the defence of Baltimore, and one thousand nine hundred and eighty-eight available for the eastern shore, Annapolis, &c. Fort Delaware is very well garrisoned by about four hundred men. The garrisons of the forts around Washington amount to ten thousand men, other disposable troops now with Gen. Wadsworth being about eleven thousand four hundred men. The troops employed in guarding the various railroads in Maryland amount to some three thousand three hundred and fifty-nine men. These it is designed to relieve, being old regiments, by dismounted cavalry, and to send them forward to Manassas. Gen. Abercrombie occupies Warrenton with a force which, including Col. Geary's at White Plains, and the cavalry to be at their disposal, will amount to some seven thousand seven hundred and eighty men, with twelve pieces of artillery.

I have the honor to request that all the troops organized for service in Pennsylvania and New York and in any of the Eastern States, may be ordered to Washington. This force I should be glad to have sent at once to Manassas—four thousand men from Gen. Wadsworth to be ordered to Manassas. These troops, with the railroad guards above alluded to, will make up a force under the command of Gen. Abercrombie to something like eighteen thousand six hundred and thirty-nine men. It is my design to push Gen. Blenker from Warrenton upon Strasburg. He should remain at Strasburg long enough to allow matters to assume a definite form in that region before proceeding to his ultimate destination. The troops in the valley of the Shenandoah will thus—including Blenker's division, ten thousand and twenty-eight strong, with twenty-four pieces of artillery, Banks's Fifth Corps, which embraces the command of Gen. Shields, nineteen thousand six hundred and eighty-seven strong, with forty-one guns, some three thousand six hundred and fifty-three disposable cavalry, and the railroad guard, about twenty-one hundred men—amount to about thirty-five thousand four hundred and sixty-seven men.

It is designed to relieve Gen. Hooker by one regiment—say eight hundred and fifty men—being, with five hundred cavalry, thirteen hundred and fifty men on the Lower Potomac. To recapitulate: At Warrenton there are to be seven thousand seven hundred and eighty; at Manassas, say ten thousand eight hundred and fifty-nine; in the Shenandoah Valley, thirty-five thousand four hundred and sixty-seven; on the Lower

Potomac, thirteen hundred and fifty—in all, fifty-five thousand four hundred and fifty-six. There would then be left for the garrisons in front of Washington and under Gen. Wadsworth some eighteen thousand men, exclusive of the batteries, under instructions. The troops organizing or ready for service in New York, I learn, will probably number more than four thousand. These should be assembled at Washington, subject to disposition where their services may be most needed.

I am, very respectfully, your obedient servant,
GEO. B. McCLELLAN,
Maj.-Gen. Commanding.

Some explanation of these orders is to be found in answers of Gen. McClellan to interrogatories before the court martial above mentioned. In one answer he said: "The force left disposable for the defence of Washington was about 70,000 men, independent of the corps of Gen. McDowell." Again, he said: "My recollection of the suggestions as to the forces to be left varied from forty to fifty thousand. I think Gen. McDowell proposed the latter number. Of one thing I am confident: that, with the facts fresh in my mind, I thought that I left more than was suggested by any corps commander."

As to the necessity that Gen. McDowell should remain for the defence of Washington, he said: "I think that Gen. McDowell was correct in his opinion that it was safe and proper for him to unite with the Army of the Potomac. I think that immediately after the occupation of Hanover Court House by a portion of the Army of the Potomac, there was no rebel force of any consequence between Hanover Court House and Gen. McDowell. I think that the main object of Jackson's movement against Gen. Banks was to prevent reënforcements from being sent to the Army of the Potomac, and expressed that opinion in a telegram to the President within a day of the time I received information of Jackson's movements. I think that if Gen. McDowell had moved direct upon Hanover Court House, instead of in the direction of Front Royal, Jackson would have rapidly retraced his steps to join the main rebel army at Richmond. With a strong army of our own in the vicinity of Richmond, and threatening it, I do not think that the rebels would have detached a sufficient force to seriously endanger the safety of Washington."

Before Gen. McClellan left Washington, an order was issued placing Gen. Wool and all his troops under his command, and he was expressly authorized to detail a division of about 10,000 men from the troops under Gen. Wool and to attach them to the active army. After operations had commenced on the peninsula, on the 3d of April Gen. McClellan received an order from the Secretary of War countermanding all this. No explanation of this has ever been made.

The design of Gen. McClellan was to make a sure and rapid movement upon Richmond, but other causes still occurred to defeat this purpose. The contest between the Monitor and Merrimac took place on the 9th of March (see below pp. 223 &c.), and the insecurity of the transports, while the navy really had not entire control of the James river, caused the troops to be landed at Fortress Monroe, and the march to be commenced overland from that point.

About the 1st of April the force above stated had reached Fortress Monroe, Gen. McClellan arrived on the 2d, and commenced active operations. On the 4th of April the following order was issued from the War Department:

War Department, Washington, *April* 4, 1862.

Ordered, 1.—That the portion of Virginia and Maryland lying between the Mountain Department and the Blue Ridge shall constitute a military department, to be called the Department of the Shenandoah, and be under the command of Maj.-Gen. Banks.

2.—That the portion of Virginia east of the Blue Ridge and west of the Potomac and the Fredericksburg and Richmond railroad, including the District of Columbia and the country between the Potomac and the Patuxent, shall be a military district, to be called the Department of the Rappahannock, and be under the command of Maj.-Gen. McDowell.

By order of the PRESIDENT.
Edwin M. Stanton, Secretary of War.

The effect of this order was to take from under the control of Gen. McClellan the forces of Gens. Banks and McDowell, and the direction of all military operations in his department west of the Richmond and Fredericksburg railroad, and in lower Maryland, and to confine him strictly to the remainder of eastern Virginia. On the 11th of April, the following order was sent to Gen. McDowell:

War Department, *April* 11, 1862.

Maj.-Gen. McDowell Commanding:

Sir: For the present, and until further orders, you will consider the national capital as especially under your protection, and make no movement throwing your force out of position for the discharge of this primary duty.

EDWIN M. STANTON, Secretary of War.

On the 5th of April, firing was opened by the enemy at Yorktown on the extreme Federal right, to repel a bold reconnoissance. While this was going on, Gen. McClellan heard for the first time that Gen. McDowell was withdrawn from his command. Yorktown is a post village, port of entry, and shire town of York county, Virginia. It is situated on rising ground on the right bank or south side of York river, eleven miles from its mouth. It is seventy miles east-southeast of Richmond, and had before the war about sixty houses, four hundred and fifty inhabitants, and several thousand tons of shipping.

The army of the Potomac had commenced its march upon this place wholly in the dark as to the nature of the country, or the position and strength of the enemy. The maps which were furnished by the commanders at Fortress Monroe were found to be entirely erroneous. The peninsula is bounded on the north by York river, which is commanded by Yorktown and Gloucester, on either side. Both places were strongly fortified to obstruct the entrance of the river by gunboats. The Confederate batteries mounted fifty-six guns, many of which were

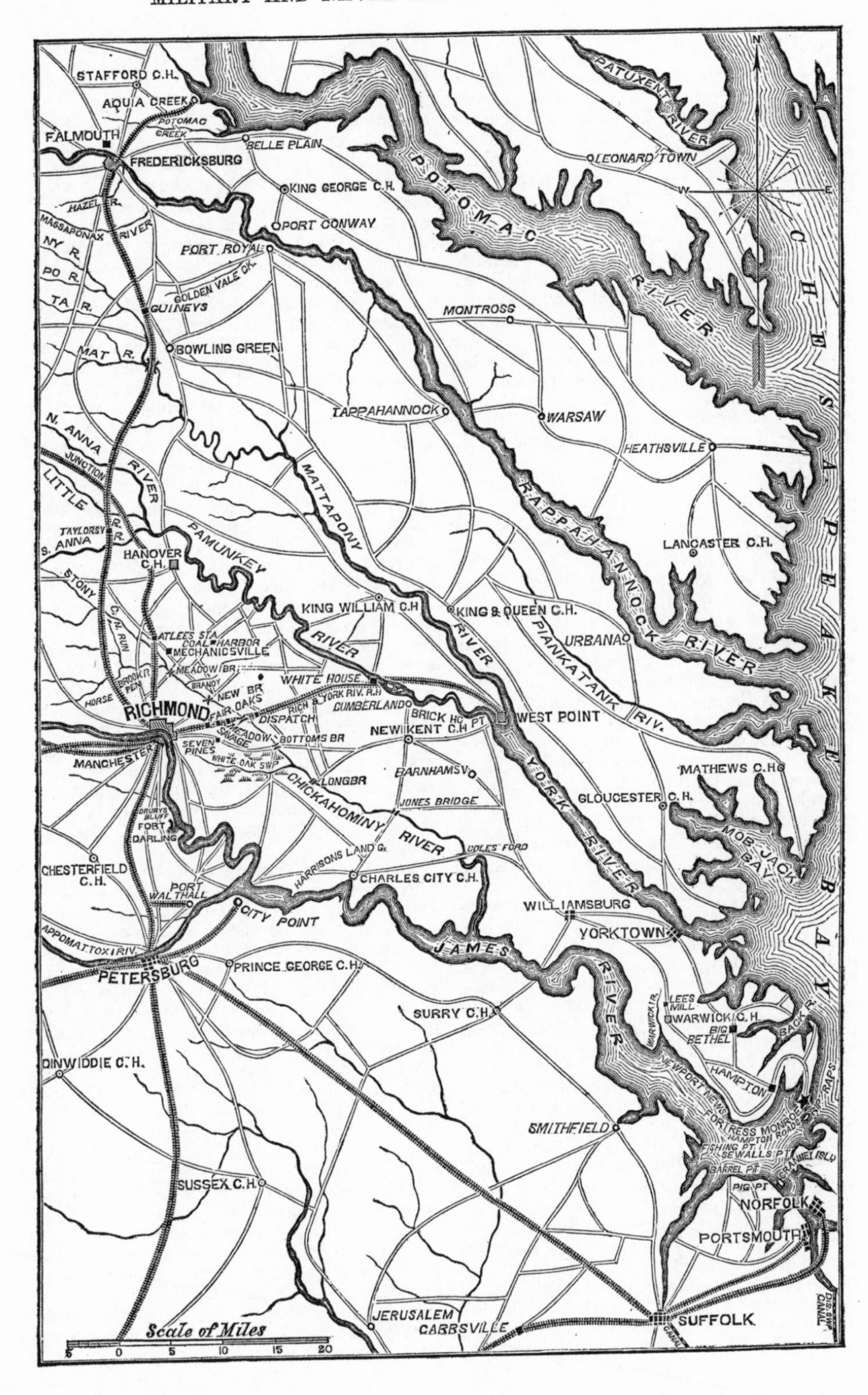
STAFFORD C.H.
AQUIA CREEK
POTOMAC CREEK
FALMOUTH
FREDERICKSBURG
BELLE PLAIN
KING GEORGE C.H.
PORT CONWAY
PORT ROYAL
HAZEL R.
MASSAPONAX RIVER
NY R.
PO R.
TA R.
MAT R.
GOLDEN VALE CK.
GUINEYS
BOWLING GREEN
POTOMAC
RIVER
PATUXENT RIVER
LEONARD TOWN
MONTROSS
TAPPAHANNOCK
WARSAW
HEATHSVILLE
N. ANNA RIVER
JUNCTION
LITTLE
TAYLORSV
R.R.
S. ANNA
HANOVER C.H.
PAMUNKEY
MATTAPONY
RAPPAHANNOCK RIVER
LANCASTER C.H.
STONY
C. N. RUN
ATLEES STA.
COAL HARBOR
MECHANICSVILLE
MEADOW BR.
BRANDY
BROOK R. PEN
HORSE
NEW BR
KING WILLIAM C.H
RIVER
KING & QUEEN C.H.
RIVER
PIANKATANK RIV.
URBANA
WHITE HOUSE
RICH & YORK RIV. R.R.
RICHMOND
FAIR OAKS
DISPATCH
CUMBERLAND
BRICK HO. PT
WEST POINT
MEADOW
SAVAGE
SEVEN PINES
BOTTOMS BR
NEW KENT C.H.
WHITE OAK SWP
MANCHESTER
LONG BR
BARNHAMSV
JONES BRIDGE
CHICKAHOMINY
RIVER
DRURYS BLUFF
FORT DARLING
YORK RIVER
MATHEWS C.H
GLOUCESTER C.H.
MOB JACK BAY
HARRISONS LAND G.
COLES FORD
CHARLES CITY C.H.
CHESTERFIELD C.H.
PORT WALTHALL
CITY POINT
WILLIAMSBURG
YORKTOWN
APPOMATTOX RIV.
JAMES
RIVER
PETERSBURG
PRINCE GEORGE C.H.
SURRY C.H.
WARWICK R.
LEES MILL
WARWICK C.H.
BIG BETHEL
BACK R.
DINWIDDIE C.H.
NEWPORT NEWS
HAMPTON
RIP RAPS
FORTRESS MONROE
HAMPTON ROADS
SMITHFIELD
FISHING PT.
SEWALLS PT.
CRANEY ISL'D
BARREL PT
PIG PT
SUSSEX C.H.
NORFOLK
PORTSMOUTH
DIS. SWP. CANAL
CANAL
JERUSALEM
CARRSVILLE
SUFFOLK
CHESAPEAKE BAY
N
W
E
Scale of Miles
5 0 5 10 15 20

rifled one-hundred pounders, and could have sunk the entire fleet of these gunboats. The James river, which bounded the peninsula on the south, was in full possession of the enemy. The line of defence at Yorktown was selected with great judgment. Taking advantage of the highest ground on the peninsula at that place, and projecting a line of intrenchments and forts bearing a little southwest to a point connecting with the head of Warwick river, the enemy had continued his works down that stream to James river, making the entire distance from point to point eight and a half miles. While the flat and marshy surface of the peninsula, together with streams constantly fed with copious supplies of water from the swamps, afforded peculiar means of defence, it was equally unfavorable to offensive operations, especially when distant from the harbor for supplies and with bad roads. The country was also covered with dense forests of pine, which formed a valuable shield to the positions of the enemy.

From the 5th to the 8th, when the unfavorable weather suspended active hostilities on both sides, there were frequent skirmishes, and firing by artillery, to prevent the enemy from constructing further defences and mounting additional guns, with few casualties on either side. On the 8th, 9th, and 10th there was a succession of extraordinary storms of rain and hail with some sleet and snow. The enemy took advantage of this weather to complete their defences. Much work was done in the interval by the Federal army in making and corduroying roads to the depots, &c.

When the army left Fortress Monroe, Gen. Keyes with three divisions proceeded along the James river until he reached the Warwick. In seeking for a ford he discovered the Confederate line of defence. Dykes had been erected in different parts of this stream, converting it into a kind of pond. These dams were defended by redoubts, artillery, and rifle pits.

The supplies of the army consisted in provisions for two days, which each soldier had taken. After these two days the army was entirely dependent on the wagons for subsistence. It was therefore necessary to construct roads. These were made by cutting down trees of equal size, and from one foot to eighteen inches in diameter, and placing the pieces from twelve or eighteen feet in length, side by side, on the ground. All the infantry that were not on picket duty on the outposts, were employed up to their knees in mud and water in this labor. By this means the cannon and wagons arrived at places where otherwise it would have been impossible to have brought them.

In order to avoid the delays of a siege, Gen. McClellan had formed a plan to turn the position at Yorktown. This was to be done by effecting a landing on the Severn river, north and in the rear of Gloucester, by which this latter position might be carried, and thus render the York river less difficult of entrance by the gunboats. The Federal force could then have advanced up the left bank of the York river, in the direction of West Point, and rendered the position of the Confederate army most perilous, if they had persisted in holding it. The execution of this movement had been confided to the corps of Gen. McDowell, which was to have embarked the last of all, at Alexandria, and arrive at Yorktown at the moment when the rest of the army, coming from Fortress Monroe, appeared before that place. This corps of Gen. McDowell was detained, as has already been stated. The effect of its detention is thus stated by Prince De Joinville:

"We received the inexplicable and unexplained intelligence that this corps had been sent to another destination. The news was received by the army with dissatisfaction, although the majority could not then foresee the deplorable consequences of an act performed, it must be supposed, with no evil intention, but with inconceivable recklessness. Fifteen days earlier this measure, although it would always have been injurious, would not have had so bad an effect; for new arrangements might have been made. Now, it was the mainspring removed from a great work already begun. It deranged everything. Among the divisions of the corps of Gen. McDowell there was one—that of Franklin—which was regretted more than all the rest, both on account of the troops themselves and of the officers commanding them. The commander-in-chief had carefully superintended its organization during the winter. He held it in great esteem and earnestly demanded its restoration. It was sent back to him, without any explanation, in the same manner as it had been withdrawn. This splendid division—eleven thousand strong—arrived, and for a moment the commander thought of intrusting to it alone the storming of Gloucester; but the idea was abandoned."

The next step was to search the Confederate line of defence for weak points. It was believed that if any were found and forced, the result would be, that the enemy would, as is usual in such cases, believe that his position was turned at both extremities, and his forces would become demoralized. Then if he was vigorously pushed with overwhelming force, a serious, if not fatal disaster might be inflicted on his army. This point was supposed to exist about the centre of the line, on Warwick river or creek, below Winn's Mills and near Lee's Mills. Here the Federal forces had thrown up a considerable work, with wings for riflemen, in which guns were mounted. Directly opposite the enemy, were protected by a demi-lune with two embrasures, with long infantry epaulements extending from each wing. An open field some six or seven hundred yards in width intervened. The enemy's works rested on the skirts of a pine forest, while the Federal were in the centre of the field. The forest extended like a curtain clear across the north edge of the field, in which sharpshooters on either side were posted.

On the 16th four Federal batteries of light artillery, under Capts. Ayres, Mott, Kennedy, and Wheeler, opened furiously upon the opposite work, and soon drove the enemy's cannoneers to shelter. Detachments consisting of companies E, F, D, and K, of a Vermont regiment, were ordered forward through the woods to capture the Confederate work. These brave men pushed forward firmly under a scattering fire of musketry, and were struggling through the creek, when the enemy, in superior force, opened upon them a galling fire of rifles and musketry. They still went forward unfalteringly, and their ranks were rapidly thinning, when they were recalled. Not more than half their number had crossed the stream. They reluctantly obeyed, but soon it became more difficult to return than it had been to advance. The enemy suddenly opened a sluice above, and almost overwhelmed them with a flow of water which reached their armpits. They maintained their order firmly, however, under cover of the batteries, which with the sharpshooters kept the enemy within their intrenchments, and in a short time extricated themselves, bringing away all their dead and wounded except six. The casualties exceeded one hundred and fifty. The attempt to force through the enemy's line was afterward abandoned, having presented unforeseen difficulties.

Sharpshooting was a feature of the early part of the campaign on the peninsula. An officer thus describes one or two scenes:

"The operations of our fellows were extremely interesting. One man was securely posted behind an embankment with a glass, and upon discovering an enemy, he signalized the active riflemen. The latter, covered by rifle pits or trees, were constantly blazing away, and at each successful shot would make some satisfactory sign. One of them afforded considerable amusement by his daring antics. Depositing his rifle every now and then behind a tree, he would dash across the field from his cover to our bastion and back again quickly, courting a shot, while his comrades watched for a victim. He must have made twenty trips while we observed him. Once or twice the enemy's balls knocked up the dust a few feet from him, and quicker than thought a leaden messenger would be sent after the unlucky enemy. We left the saucy fellow continuing his hazardous pranks."

The siege of Yorktown was now commenced in earnest. The Federal army was encamped before it in line of battle order. The arrangement of the columns, however, was influenced by the nature and topography of the position invested. It is thus summarily described by Prince de Joinville:

"The last operation, like that on Gloucester, not being accomplished, nothing remained but to begin a regular siege against Yorktown. All this wandering in the dark had, unfortunately, consumed much time, and the siege itself would consume much more, although it should be pushed with the greatest energy. Ten thousand laborers were unceasingly employed cutting through the woods and forming roads, trenches, and batteries. It was a curious spectacle. A straight arm of the sea, fringed by a thick and strong vegetation, mixed with trees of all kinds, living and dead, entangled with withes and moss, approached in a serpentine form to the front of the attack. The first parallel was made. The wood which surrounded us was an admirable protection. This arm of the sea was covered with bridges. Roads were cut along its margin in the midst of tulips, flowers of Judea, and azaleas in full bloom. From this natural parallel others were formed by the hands of man, and we rapidly approached the place. The defenders opened a terrific fire on those works that they could see, as well as upon those which they supposed were in progress. Shells whistled on every side through the large trees, cutting down branches, frightening horses, but otherwise doing very little harm. Nobody cared about it. In the evening, when all the laborers returned in good order, with their rifles on their backs, and their shovels on their shoulders, the fire became more furious, as if the enemy had marked the hour of their return. We went to this cannonade as to a show; and when, on a beautiful night in spring time, the troops gayly marched along to this martial music through the flowering woods; when the balloon, with which we made our reconnoissances, was floating in the air, we seemed to be spectators at a fête, and for a moment were made to forget the miseries of war.

"The siege, however, still went on. Powerful artillery, with great difficulty, had been brought up; 100 and even 200-pounder rifled cannon, and 13-inch mortars were ready to batter the place. Fourteen batteries were constructed, armed, and appointed. If our fire had not been yet opened, it was because it was designed to open all our batteries together along the whole line; and for this reason we waited until nothing was wanting to complete all our preparations. We could not, however, resist the desire to try the 200-pounders. These enormous pieces were handled with incredible ease. Four men sufficed to load and aim them, without any more difficulty than in the working of our old 24-pounders. At a distance of three miles their fire was admirably precise. One day one of these immense pieces had a kind of duel with a rifled piece of somewhat smaller caliber, in position on the bastions at Yorktown. The curious among us mounted on the parapet to see where the missiles might fall, and, while they communicated their observations to one another, the sentry on the lookout would announce when the enemy was about to fire in turn; but the distance was so great that, between the discharge and the arrival of the projectile, everybody had time to descend without any hurry, and to place himself under the shelter of the parapet. Such, however, was the precision of the fire that we were sure to see the enormous projectile passing over the very spot where the group of observers had been standing but a moment before; then it would bound along and tear up the earth some fifty or sixty yards off, and its inflammable composition would burst with a loud explosion, throwing into the air a cloud of dust as high as the water jets of St. Cloud.

"It was evident that with the powerful means at our disposal the capture of Yorktown was but a work of time. Shattered beneath the tremendous fire which was about to be opened upon it, without casemates to cover their soldiers, without any other defence than outworks and palisades, the place had not even the chance of opposing a lengthened resistance. Everything was ready for the final blow. Not only was a terrific bombardment about to be opened upon the town, not only were the most select troops set apart to follow up this bombardment by a grand assault, but the steam transports only awaited a sign to push immediately up the York river, and to land Franklin's troops at the upper part of the stream, on the line of retreat of the Confederate army. A part of these troops were also to remain on board the transports. They would have taken but a few hours to traverse by water the distance it would have taken the enemy's army two days at least to march by land. Driven from the lines of Yorktown by a powerful attack, pursued sword in hand, intercepted on the route by fresh troops, that army would have been in a most critical position, and the Federals would have obtained what they so much desired—an astonishing military success.

"A great success of the Federal army before Yorktown was therefore of vital importance to the Government at Washington. Unfortunately, the Confederate leaders and generals were of the same opinion, and, as able and resolute men, they took the best means to render it impossible."

On the nights of the 3d and 4th of May, Yorktown and the Confederate lines of the Warwick river were evacuated. This work, doubtless commenced several days before, and was conducted with great skill and energy. On the 3d the fire of the enemies batteries was redoubled in severity. This was done to mask their retreat, and it was highly successful. The absence of all signs of them on the morning of the 4th, caused their lines to be closely examined, when it was soon ascertained that they were abandoned. The capture of this strong position of Yorktown and its armament with scarcely any loss of life, was a brilliant military success.

The impossibility for the navy to coöperate with the army, the want of forces to turn the flank of the enemy, as had been originally planned, and their obstinate courage and efforts to prevent the capture of Yorktown, had caused the delay of a month before that place. During this time the defences of Richmond had been pushed forward, and the spring time of the year had so far passed away, that the hot season was at hand, which would produce diseases in the low lands of the peninsula, and thus greatly aid the enemy. The loss thus far on the Federal side was about three hundred. That of the Confederates has not been ascertained. They left in their works at Yorktown two 3-inch rifled cannon, two 4½-inch rifled cannon, sixteen 32-pounders, six 42-pounders, nineteen 8-inch columbiads, four 9-inch Dahlgrens, one 10-inch columbiad, one 10-inch mortar, and one 8-inch siege howitzer, with carriages and implements complete. Each piece was supplied with 76 rounds of ammunition. At Gloucester there was captured nine 9-inch Dahlgrens, two 32-pounders rifled, five 32-pound navy guns, five 42-pound carronades; making at both places a total of seventy-three guns and much ammunition.

Their force has been estimated at 100,000 men. Some of the Federal soldiers were killed and horses injured by the explosion of instruments of destruction left by the enemy. It was at this time that New Orleans was captured.

The next important point before the Federal army was the city of Williamsburg. There were two roads to that city: one direct from Yorktown; and the other, from the left of the Federal army, crossed Warwick river at Lee's Mills, and uniting with the first formed a fork near Williamsburg.

This city is the capital of James City county, and is situated near the narrowest part of the peninsula between the James and York rivers, and is three miles from James river and about five and a quarter from York river. It is one of the oldest towns in the State, and contained a population of about fifteen hundred.

As soon as the evacuation of Yorktown was known, the entire cavalry and horse artillery with five divisions of infantry were advanced in pursuit. Gen. Franklin's division was ordered to move at once by water to the vicinity of West Point to endeavor to check the retreat of the enemy, and to be supported by other divisions as rapidly as water transportation could be obtained. The remaining divisions were massed near Yorktown, ready to move by land or water, as might be necessary. Gen. McClellan meanwhile remained at Yorktown until Monday noon, the 5th, pushing the movement of the troops to West Point by water and awaiting the development of events. It was not until that time that he was made aware of the serious resistance encountered at Williamsburg. All the information up to that time indicated nothing more than an affair of a rear guard. As soon as the true state of affairs was known he moved rapidly to the front and assumed the immediate command.

Gen. Stoneman had led the advance, with his cavalry and four batteries of artillery, on the direct road from Yorktown. After the bridge had been constructed over Warwick river, Gen. Smith advanced on the narrow road from the Federal left to Yorktown. He encountered a Confederate force, which fell back before him.

A report of this was sent to the commander-in-chief, who ordered Gen. Stoneman on the other road to press forward, and endeavor to intercept this retiring force before its junction with the main body, which was supposed to be at Williamsburg. Gen. Stoneman pushed forward with all the rapidity possible in the miry condition of the roads, and as he came out at the point where the road from Warwick Creek united, he was saluted by an artillery fire from numerous fieldworks known as Fort Magruder. A vain attempt was made to take this work with cavalry, during which Major Williams displayed great bravery, but the column was forced to retreat and await the arrival of the infantry. Gen. Smith's division subsequently arrived, but the lateness of the hour and the heavy rain caused the attack to be put off.

The pursuit by Gen. McClellan's forces had been so rapid that the Confederate officers found it to be necessary to give it a check, in order to continue their retreat with success. This led to the battle of Williamsburg on the next day, and the retreat of the Confederate army. Their plan for the campaign was thus developed. It was to delay the Federal army as long as practicable at Yorktown, and thus secure time to place Richmond in a defensive condition, and also to meet them in final battle near the marshes of the Chickahominy river.

The Confederate position at Williamsburg consisted of thirteen works, extending nearly across the peninsula. Excepting two or three narrow roads, it was approachable only through dense forests. These roads were made worse by a heavy rain which commenced on Sunday afternoon, the 4th, and continued during the next day.

When Sunday night came, the division of Gen. Smith, of Keyes's corps, had reached Gen. Stoneman's position after he fell back from Fort Magruder. Gen. Hancock's brigade formed the advance of this division. Gen. Hooker, of Heintzelman's corps, was approaching on the left by the road from Warwick river. His force consisted of the 11th Massachusetts, 5th, 6th, and 7th Wisconsin, 26th Pennsylvania, Sickles's New York brigade, and four batteries. Thus the advance of the Federal line had arrived within about two and a half miles of the works at Williamsburg. The Union troops slept on their arms without tents, without food, and in a hard rain. The Confederates determined to make the attack in the morning upon the Federal left and rear. About eight o'clock they threw out a body of infantry on their right, which soon exchanged fire with the advance of Gen. Hooker's division. This continued intermittently for some time. Some light batteries became engaged, and drove the enemy back until they came within range of his heavy guns, when the former suffered severely. Bramhall's battery lost all its horses, the guns became mired, and the forces of the enemy pressing upon it in greatly increased numbers, it was lost. Encouraged by this success, the enemy pushed forward, and Gen. Hooker was finally forced to give way and fall back, leaving his wounded, about two thousand in number, behind. The Confederates followed him as he fell back, until the division of Gen. Kearney came up and restored the battle. At the same time the enemy was strongly reënforced, and the fight was sharp and fierce. The state of the roads had prevented an earlier arrival of Gen. Kearney's division. His intrepidity was brilliantly shown on this occasion, although Gen. Heintzelman commanded the joint divisions. Meantime the part of the army on the road to the right remained passive. A single division only had come up. Of this the brigade of Brig.-Gen. Peck, of Couch's division of Gen. Casey's corps, was ordered by Gen. Sumner, who was in chief command, into the woods on the left toward the point where the battle was raging against Gen. Hooker's division. This brigade was composed of the 93d, 98th, and 102d Pennsylvania, the 55th and 62d New York, and West's battery. Placed on the right of that division, with other regiments amounting to six thousand men, it stopped the Confederate advance by repulsing with great obstinacy every attempt made. Supported later in the day by Gen. Palmer's brigade, they formed a strong centre.

Gen. Smith's division had formed on the right of the Federal line, and at an early hour a reconnoissance was made with a view of finding a route to the enemy's left flank. One was finally found, which had been overflowed with water by the enemy, and another was cut through the woods. The only obstacles to reaching the flank were two forts, strong from position and construction. To explore this route in force, and if possible occupy these works, Gen. Hancock was sent forward in the afternoon with his brigade. This consisted of the 6th and 7th Vermont, 5th Wisconsin, 33d and 49th New York, and Kennedy's battery. The two works were found to be unoccupied, and garrisoned by his men. A third at a distance he attacked with artillery and silenced. The enemy, seeing the fatal consequences to themselves from this attack, if successful, sent out two brigades to drive back the Federal force. The latter allowed them to come up, and received them with a most destructive fire of artillery. The enemy unshaken pushed forward within thirty yards of the cannon's mouth, when they wavered. Gen. Hancock, seizing the moment, ordered his brigade to charge upon them with the bayonet, which they could not withstand, and broke and fled, leaving their dead and wounded on the field. Gen. McClellan now arrived, and gave orders to support Gen. Hancock, and to press the advantage already gained in that direction. In a few minutes seven thousand men were on the march for that point. Night fell before they reached it, and no more was done that day. The ploughed land and the day's rain made a soft bed on which the weary soldiers sank down during that night.

The success of Gen. Hancock on the Confederate left flank caused them to retreat that night, and at daylight all the forts on the Federal front and Williamsburg itself were found completely abandoned by the entire Confederate army. On the roads and in the woods were found the Confederate dead left unburied, and the wounded in their agonies. Their loss in killed and wounded was estimated at nearly a thousand.

Gen. McClellan evidently had not anticipated so serious a resistance at Williamsburg. In a despatch to the Secretary of War on Sunday evening the 4th, he says: "Our cavalry and horse artillery came up with the enemy's rear guard in their intrenchments about two miles on this side of Williamsburg. A brisk fight ensued just as my aid left. Smith's division of infantry arrived on the ground and, I presume, carried his works, though I have not yet heard. The enemy's rear is strong, but I have force enough up there to answer all purposes."

The force that was actually before Williamsburg would have been routed on the next day, if they had not been sustained by the arrival of fresh troops. These troops were delayed greatly by the bad roads. They were a portion of those whom Gen. McClellan, unaware of the great difficulty of the roads, and uninformed of the true state of the case by correct reports of the front, supposed were before Williamsburg. As it was, Gen. Hooker's division alone for hours withstood the enemy, even within hearing of other troops who were unable to come earlier to his relief.

In the evening after his arrival Gen. McClellan sent a despatch to the Secretary of War, in which he says: "After arranging for movements up York river, I was earnestly sent for here. I find Gen. Joe Johnston in front of me in strong force—probably greater a good deal than my own.

"I shall run the risk of at least holding them in check here while I resume the original plan.

"My entire force is considerably inferior to that of the rebels, who will fight well; but I will do all I can with the force at my disposal."

On a subsequent day Gen. McClellan took occasion to address three of the regiments of Gen. Hancock's brigade, which was engaged on the enemy's left. His remarks indicate the importance which he afterward ascribed to the action of the brigade on that day.

To the men of the Fifth Wisconsin regiment he said:

My Lads: I have come to thank you for the bravery and discipline you displayed the other day. On that day you won laurels of which you may ever be proud —not only you, but the army, the State, and the country to which you belong. Through you we won the day, and Williamsburg shall be inscribed upon your banner. I cannot thank you too much, and I am sure the reputation your gallantry has already achieved will always be maintained.

To the Seventh Maine regiment he said:

Soldiers of the Seventh Maine: I have come to thank you for your bravery and good conduct in the action of yesterday. On this battle plain you and your comrades arrested the progress of the advancing enemy, and turned the tide of victory in our favor. You have deserved well of your country and your State, and in their gratitude they will not forget to bestow upon you the thanks and praise so justly your due. Continue to show the conduct of yesterday, and the triumph of our cause will be speedy and sure. In recognition of your merit you shall hereafter bear the inscription "Williamsburg" on your colors. Soldiers, my words are feeble; but from the bottom of my heart I thank you.

To the Thirty-third New York regiment he addressed the following:

Officers and Soldiers of the Thirty-third: I have come to thank you in person for your conduct and bravery on the 5th of May. I will say to you as I have said to the other regiments engaged with you at that part of the field, that all did well—did all that I could have expected. The other troops engaged elsewhere fought well and did their whole duty, too; but you won the day, and to you and your comrades belongs the credit of the victory of Williamsburg.

You acted like veterans! Veterans of many battles could not have done better. You shall have "Williamsburg" inscribed upon your flag. I have accorded the same privilege to the other regiments engaged with you.

You have won for yourselves a name that will last you through life.

Soldiers, again I thank you.

It has been stated that the division of Gen. Franklin, belonging to the corps of Gen. McDowell, was subsequently sent to the army of Gen. McClellan. This division arrived previous to the surrender of Yorktown, and remained on board of the transports in order to proceed up the York river as soon as the enemy's batteries might be taken. The division was delayed on the 5th by the weather. On the 6th it left Yorktown, and landed at Brick House Point on the same day. This is the point where the Pamunkey river enters the York river and on the right bank of the latter. The Pamunkey is navigable for gunboats of light draft some twenty miles above White House. It unites with the Mattapony and forms the York river. On the tongue of land between the two rivers at their junction is West Point opposite to Brick House Point. From West Point a railroad runs to Richmond, and crosses the Pamunkey at White House. Although at this time an insignificant village, West Point was anciently a place of considerable pretensions. It is about twenty-five miles by water from Yorktown and about thirty-five by railroad from Richmond. The troops were landed on the same night, and encamped on a plain surrounded on three sides by woods, and on the fourth bounded by the river. That evening a part of the division of Gen. Sedgwick, under Gen. Dana, arrived. During the next day the enemy were discovered in the woods, and made an attack in which they had the advantage for a short time, but were repulsed and driven a considerable distance. Two batteries were brought to bear, which caused them to press upon the Federal left. The gunboats then opened upon them and did effective service, contributing materially to the success of the day. The division of Gen. Porter subsequently arrived on transports, but no further skirmishing took place at that position.

The success at Williamsburg proved to be more complete than had been at first expected. The strong works of the enemy, the town, and his sick and wounded being taken, indicated that his loss had been great, and that his retreat was rapid and disorderly. The retreat was followed up by the Federal cavalry for one or two days, and constant skirmishing kept up with the Confederate rear guard. The terrible condition of the roads rendered a more active pursuit out of the question. Three days were spent by the army at Williamsburg looking after their wounded, who were scattered through the woods, and waiting for provisions from Yorktown, the arrival of which was delayed by the state of the roads.

After the movement of General McClellan commenced, a serious blow was given to the strength of the enemy by the destruction of the Merrimac and the breaking up of the blockade of the James River, which had been caused by the Merrimac taking a position off Craney Island, and subsequently by their loss of Norfolk.

The Merrimac was the steam frigate of that name which had been sunk at the Norfolk navy yard at the time it was abandoned. The vessel was subsequently raised by the enemy, razeed or cut down and covered with a roof like a house, but composed of railroad iron. Her sides were also protected with plates of iron. She took a position as above stated, and to watch her the wooden frigates Cumberland and Congress were stationed at Newport News, and the Minnesota, Roanoke, St. Lawrence, and other ships at Fortress Monroe. At the same time iron clads were in process of rapid construction at New York and elsewhere, with the hope of being ready to encounter the Merrimac, or Virginia, as she was called by the enemy, whenever she should come forth.

About half-past eleven A. M., on Saturday, March 8th, the Merrimac, armed with ten guns, appeared to be coming down, accompanied by the Patrick Henry, Com. Tucker, six guns; the Jamestown, Lieut. Barney, two guns; Raleigh, Lieut. Alexander; Beaufort, Lieut. Parker; Teazer, Lieut. Webb, each one gun, and moved directly toward the Cumberland. Immediately all hands were ordered to their places, and the Cumberland was sprung across the channel, so that her broadside would bear on the Merrimac. The armament she could bring to bear was about eleven nine and ten-inch Dahlgren guns, and two pivot-guns of the same pattern. The former came up at the rate of four or five knots per hour, and when she arrived within about a mile, the Cumberland opened on her with her pivot-guns, and soon the whole broadside commenced. The balls bounded from her mailed sides like India-rubber, apparently making not the least impression. Six or eight broadsides had been fired when a shot was received from one of her guns which killed five marines. It was impossible for the Cumberland to get out of her way, and the Merrimac soon crushed her iron horn or ram into the frigate, just forward the main chains, knocking a hole in the side near the water-line, as large as the head of a hogshead, and driving the vessel back upon her anchors with great force. The water came rushing into the hold. The Merrimac then backed out and discharged her guns again, the shot passing through the main bay and killing five sick men. The water was all the while rushing in the hole made by the ram, so that in five minutes it was up to the sick-bay on the berth-deck. In the mean time her broadsides swept the men away, maimed and killed, and also set the frigate on fire in the forward part. The fire was extinguished. The sick-bay, berth-deck, and gun-deck, were almost literally covered with men killed and wounded, but the surviving ones still fought well, and every one displayed the utmost heroism. The fight lasted about three-fourths of an hour. The Cumberland fired rapidly, and all the time the water poured in the hole, and by and by into the ports, as her bow kept sinking deeper and deeper. Near the middle of the fight, when the berth-deck of the Cumberland had sunk below water, one of the crew of the Merrimac came out of a port to the outside of her iron-plated roof, and a ball from one of the guns instantly cut him in two. The Merrimac fired occasionally, but every shot told upon the wooden vessel, as her guns being without the least elevation, pointed straight at the Cumberland, and her nearness, being much of the time within three hundred yards, made it an easy matter to send each ball to its exact mark. Finally, after about three-fourths of an hour, the frigate sank, the stars and stripes still waving. That flag was finally submerged, but after the hull grounded on the sands, fifty-four feet below the surface of the water, the pennant was still flying from the topmast above the waves. None of the men were captured, but many were drowned as the vessel went down. There were about four hundred on board, and from one hundred and fifty to two hundred were killed during the engagement and drowned at the sinking. Lieut. George M. Morris was in command of the vessel, Capt. Radford being absent on the Roanoke at a court of inquiry. Very few of the men swam ashore, most of those who were rescued from the water being saved by small boats. The Merrimac seemed to be uninjured, although her small boats and flagstaff were shot away in the commencement of the action.

The Merrimac next surged up, and gave the Congress a broadside, receiving one in return, and getting astern, raked the ship fore and aft. This fire was terribly destructive, a shell killing every man at one of the guns except one. Coming again broadside to the Congress, the Merrimac ranged slowly backward and forward at less than one hundred yards distant, and fired broadside after broadside into the Congress. The latter vessel replied manfully and obstinately, every gun that could be brought to bear being discharged rapidly, but with little effect upon the iron monster. Finally the ship was on fire in so many places, and the flames gathering such force, that the National flag was hauled down and a white flag hoisted at the peak.

The loss of life on the Congress was about one hundred. The remaining officers and a part of the crew escaped ashore, and the others were taken off by a gunboat of the enemy. During the night the Congress was burned to the water's edge and sunk.

On the first appearance of the Merrimac, the steamship Minnesota left Fortress Monroe for the scene of action. On approaching within a few miles, the ship got aground. She was followed by the frigate St. Lawrence, which also grounded. The Roanoke also made an attempt to get up to the scene, but owing to the shallow water was obliged to return.

After sinking the Cumberland and firing the Congress, the Merrimac, with the Yorktown and Jamestown, stood off in the direction of the steam-frigate Minnesota, aground about three miles below Newport News. This was about five o'clock on Saturday evening. The commander of the Merrimac, wishing to capture this splendid ship without doing serious damage to her, did not attempt to run the Minnesota down. He stood off about a mile distant, and with the Yorktown and Jamestown threw shell and shot at the frigate. The Minnesota, though from being aground unable to manœuvre or bring all her guns to bear, was fought splendidly. She threw a shell at the Yorktown which set her on fire, and she was towed off by her consort the Jamestown. She received two serious shots: one, an eleven-inch shell, entered near the waist; another shot through the chain-plate, and another through the main-mast. Six of the crew were killed outright on board the Minnesota, and nineteen wounded.

About nightfall the Merrimac, satisfied with her afternoon's work of destruction, steamed in behind Sewall's Point. The day thus closed with the most gloomy apprehensions of what would occur on the next. The Minnesota was at the mercy of the Merrimac, and there appeared no reason why the iron monster might not clear the Roads of the fleet, destroy all the stores and warehouses on the beach, drive the troops into the Fortress, and command Hampton Roads against any number of wooden vessels the Government might send there. Meantime the iron-clad, called Monitor, had been completed in New York, and was taken in tow from New York harbor by a steam-tug, on the 6th of March, 1862, and propelled by her own steam-power also, was hurried towards Hampton Roads, to be in readiness, if possible, for the threatened descent of the Merrimac. In case of encountering storms, the original plan was to make a harbor, and thus avoid the dangers to which a vessel of this character would be subjected. The voyage, however, was performed through a heavy gale of wind and rough seas, which the vessel happily weathered, although the waves rolled over the top of the turret, and the water was driven with violence through the apertures necessarily left for ventilation, for the escape of smoke, &c. This threatened several times to extinguish the fires, and caused the engines to work so feebly that they were incompetent to expel the noxious gases, or pump out the water. Several of the men and officers were rendered senseless by the suffocating fumes from the fires, and were only restored by being brought up into the turret, and exposed to the fresh air. In the height of the gale the tiller rope was thrown off the wheel, and but for the strong hawser connecting the battery with the tug-boat ahead, the former must have foundered before her movements could have been brought under any control. During the night, when these dangers were most imminent, no means whatever were available for signalling to the tugboat the need of seeking protection nearer the shore, from which direction the wind came, and all on board were thus kept in constant alarm.

To those upon whom rested the responsibility of the great trial upon which they were about to enter, no sleep was afforded after Friday morning the 7th of March. On Saturday evening the Monitor entered Hampton Roads as the engagement of the day was terminating. During the night the Merrimac lay at anchor near Sewall's Point, and the Monitor remained near the Minnesota, which was fast aground between Fortress Monroe and Newport News. Early on Sunday morning the Merrimac was seen advancing toward the Minnesota, to renew the work of destruction she had so succesfully prosecuted the day before. When within range, her shot were discharged at the frigate aground without any heed being paid to the apparently insignificant stranger within a mile of which she was passing. At this distance, those on board the Merrimac must have been astonished as one of the 11-inch Dahlgrens from the curious little tower upon the raft-like structure opened upon the ship with its hundred and sixty-eight pound shot. From that time the attack upon the Minnesota was abandoned, and attention was directed only to this new antagonist. The vessels soon came into close action, and no effect resulting from the shot of the Merrimac striking the Monitor, an attempt was made by the former to run down and crush or sink the smaller vessel. Five times the two vessels struck each other, and each time one of the guns of the Monitor was discharged directly against the plated sides of the Merrimac. The Minnesota directed her fire against the Merrimac, and two of her balls struck the Monitor, without, however, inflicting any damage. After the contest had raged for some hours, the Monitor, entirely unharmed, withdrew to some distance for the purpose of hoisting more shot into her turret; which being done, the fight was immediately recommenced. The Merrimac soon appeared to be in a disabled condition, and gradually worked away towards the batteries at Sewall's Point. As afterward ascertained, the heavy iron prow, projecting six feet from the stem of the Merrimac, was so wrenched by the concussion against the side of the Monitor, that the timbers of the frame were started, causing the vessel to leak badly. It is not known that the shot of the Monitor penetrated the sides of her opponent; but it has been reported and denied that the timbers behind the iron plating were shattered by the tremendous force of the blows. The Merrimac received some injury, and loss of life was incurred from the shot of the Minnesota. During the fight, the first officer of the Monitor, Capt. A. H. Worden, took his station in the pilot-house, and directed the firing by signals to the First Lieutenant, S. Dana Greene, by whom the guns were trained and fired. One of the last shots of the Merrimac struck the pilot-house near the aperture through which Capt. Worden was looking at the instant. The blow, which was so heavy as to break one of the great wrought-iron beams of the pilot-house, stunned this officer, seriously injuring his eyes and face. On the retiring of the Merrimac, the second officer took charge of the vessel, knowing that another shot striking the pilot-house would be likely to complete its destruction, and render the vessel unmanageable by disabling the steering apparatus; and acting under orders which restricted the Monitor to a defensive course, except so far as might be necessary to protect the Minnesota, declined to pursue the Merrimac, and remained by the Minnesota.

On the 7th President Lincoln arrived at Fortress Monroe, and after examining the fortress and the camp at Newport News, urged a movement on Norfolk, which had already been reported as abandoned in consequence of the advance of the army of the Potomac up the peninsula. An expedition was accordingly organized, under the direction of Maj.-Gen. Wool, which embarked at Fortress Monroe during the night of the 9th of May, and landed at Willoughby's Point, a short distance from the Rip Raps and eight miles from Norfolk, at daylight on the 10th. The force consisted of the 10th New York, Col. Bendix; 20th do., Col. Weber; 99th do.; 1st Delaware, Col. Andrews; 16th Massachusetts, Col. Wyman; 58th Pennsylvania, Col. Bailey; a battalion of mounted rifles, and a company of 4th regular artillery. Gens. Mansfield and Weber proceeded over a good road on the direct route to Norfolk, but finding the bridge over Tanner's Creek on fire, and a small force of the enemy on the opposite side with three small howitzers, a march of eight miles was then made by the Princess Anne road, around the head of the creek to Norfolk. The defences of the city were found to have been abandoned. At the limits of the city Gen. Wool was met at half-past four in the afternoon by the mayor and a committee of the council, who surrendered it. He immediately took possession, and appointed Brig.-Gen. Vielé military governor, with directions to see that the citizens were protected in "all their civil rights." The troops bivouacked on the field outside of the limits of the city for the night. About four o'clock the next morning a bright light was observed from Fortress Monroe, in the direction of Craney Island, which was supposed at first to be a signal of some description from the Confederate iron-clad steamer Merrimac or Virginia. It was closely watched by the officers of the picket boats, as well as by the various naval vessels of the fleet, and precisely at half-past four o'clock an explosion took place, which made the earth tremble for miles around. In the midst of the bright flames that shot up through the distant blaze, the timber and iron of the monster steamer could be seen flying through the air, while immense volumes of smoke rose up, and for a time obscured every thing. No doubt was entertained that the Merrimac had ceased to exist, and had doubtless been abandoned by the crew.

A naval reconnoissance was immediately sent out toward Norfolk. The fortifications on Craney Island were found to have been abandoned. On the main front of the island, commanding the approaches by the river channel, the works were casemated. Nine of these casemates were finished, in each of which were nine or ten-inch guns, principally Dahlgrens, and the work of erecting five more casemates was in progress at the time of the evacuation, in one of which a gun was mounted. The whole number of guns mounted was thirty-nine, of which two were Parrotts and a number rifled Dahlgrens. There were also about six guns in the works which had not been mounted. None of them had been removed.

On the line of the river leading from Craney Island to Norfolk there were not less than six heavy earthworks, mounting in all about sixty-nine cannon, all of which were in position, except those that were in the works near the Naval Hospital. These had been taken to Richmond.

Not far above Craney Island was the river barricade. Although the river is here nearly a mile wide, a line of piles had been driven from shore to shore, with the exception of an opening in the centre of the channel for vessels to pass in and out. Here were two steam pile-drivers which had been used for this work, and near the opening was moored the hulk of the old frigate United States, which it was proposed to sink in case Federal vessels should have succeeded in passing the fortifications.

Immediately commanding this river barricade was a casemated battery, forming a half circle, and mounting eleven heavy guns. On the opposite bank of the river was another battery, with two or three other small works, before old Fort Norfolk on one side of the river, and the Naval Asylum batteries on the other, were reached.

In addition to the amount of ammunition left in the sheds of the batteries, the magazines, of which there was a great number, were well filled. The amount of powder in the magazines was estimated at five thousand pounds, and the fixed ammunition could be enumerated by the cargo. All the workshops, storehouses, and other buildings at the Gosport navy yard were burned, and the dry dock had also been partially blown up with powder on the night after Norfolk was surrendered. While this was taking place, another party was engaged in burning the shipping and steamboats in the harbor. There is no doubt this vast sacrifice was permitted by the Confederate Government, only to enable it to summon to Richmond the troops in and about Norfolk under Gen. Huger. They were about eighteen thousand in number.

At the same time when this movement was made on Norfolk, steps were taken to open the blockade of James river. On the 8th of May the gunboats Galena (iron clad), Aroostook, and Port Royal started up the river, and were successful in silencing the batteries at its mouth and on its banks. They were subsequently joined by the Monitor and Naugatuck, and on the 18th were repulsed by a heavy battery at Drury's Bluff, about eight miles below Richmond. The blockade of the river below that point was raised.

Meantime the army of Gen. McClellan was advancing toward Richmond. On the 8th of May the advance was beyond Williamsburg, on the 11th it was at Barnhamsville, on the 13th at New Kent Court House, and on the 15th at the White House. This was the point where the railroad from West Point to Richmond crossed the Pamunkey river. It took its name from a fine building, once the property of Gen. Washington, but now of his heirs. The railroad was in good order, and locomotives and cars, brought on the transports, were immediately placed on the track. It was intended that the supplies of the army, as it advanced, should be taken over this road. The Pamunkey river, at the White House, was of sufficient depth to float large vessels, and an immense amount of stores was there collected. A reconnoissance was made on the 16th by one of the smaller gunboats, with two companies of infantry under Major Willard, and one section of Ayres' battery, up the Pamunkey river, a distance of twenty-five miles, to a point known as Russell's Landing. A steamboat, a propeller, and fifteen small schooners were found in flames upon their arrival. Most of these vessels were loaded with corn. On the same day the Confederate troops, consisting chiefly of a corps of observation, were driven over the Chickahominy on the main road to Richmond, at Bottom's Bridge, which was burned. When the Federal troops arrived within a half mile of the bridge, a brisk fire of artillery from the opposite side opened upon them. The Confederate army had now retreated across the Chickahominy, determined beyond that river to dispute the possession of Richmond. The Chickahominy river is formed by the junction of Horsepen Branch, Rocky Branch, North Run, and Brook Run, near Meadow Bridge, five miles directly north of Richmond. All these streams, and several others too small to have names, rise within ten miles northwest of Richmond, in a rough, unfertile country, exceedingly broken and unfit for cultivation.

Meadow Bridge is nearly north of Richmond, five miles in a direct line by railroad, and is the outlet of a considerable swamp, and the place of crossing for Meadow Bridge road and the Virginia Central and Louisa railroad. The stream at this bridge is an insignificant brook, receiving another creek from the Richmond side, a short distance below. Less than two miles from Meadow Bridge is the bridge of the Mechanicsville turnpike, four and one half miles from the Confederate capital and fifteen from Hanover Court House.

Two miles further on, it receives a small creek with the name of Brandy Run, and from this point it grows considerably wider, more sluggish, with swampy shores at intervals, and low banks often overflowed. Near this place is a small bridge, and a road crosses, but little used.

Four miles from Mechanicsville turnpike bridge is New Bridge, in a direct line northeast from the city six miles, and seven and a half miles by the road. Four miles farther, and directly east from the city, is a military bridge. From this bridge three miles farther to Bottom's Bridge the banks of the stream are quite swampy, but it is still of no considerable size, although several creeks have emptied their waters into it. A mile before reaching Bottom's Bridge it is crossed by the Richmond and York River railroad, running to White House and West Point. The course of the river from its source is east-southeast, so that it is constantly leaving Richmond, and at Bottom's Bridge is fifteen miles away from the city. Its nearest point is at Mechanicsville bridge. The bank of the stream on the north side is for the most part rolling bluffs, covered with forests, with an occasional opening, where can be seen finely situated plantations. Upon the south side of the stream, and from one to two miles from the bank, a considerable bluff extends the entire distance to the vicinity of the lower military bridge. This bluff is highest opposite New Bridge, where a point of it is known as Lewis Hill. A road runs along on the brow of this hill, and there are some very fine residences situated upon it, which, as it is only some three or four miles, at most, from the city, are very desirable locations. Other bridges were constructed by orders of Gen. McClellan.

The soil along the York River railroad is of too pliable a nature to admit of the transportation of heavy guns, or, in fact, any others, at the time of severe rains. The same may be said of all the localities between the Chickahominy and Richmond. After the passage of a hundred teams it becomes necessary to construct new roads. Some days passed in bringing up the rear of the army, in making preparations to cross the Chickahominy, and in securing the conveyance of the supplies for the army. The railroad from the White House became the base for this purpose, and was kept open until the 25th of June. Meantime the Federal army was diminishing in numbers, while the Confederates were gathering troops by every method they could devise. Prisoners were taken, who belonged to regiments which had opposed Gen. Burnside in North Carolina. And Norfolk had been sacrificed to send her troops to Richmond. The conscription act, passed by the Confederate Congress in April, made every man between the ages of eighteen and thirty-five years a soldier. The new levies were now collecting before Richmond.

On the evening of the 21st Gen. McClellan sent the following despatch to the War Department: "I have just returned from Bottom's Bridge; have examined the country on the other side, and made a reconnoissance on the heels of the enemy, who probably did not like the skirmish of yesterday. The bridge will be repaired by to-morrow morning, and others constructed. All the camps have advanced to-day."

On the next day the troops began to cross both at Bottom's Bridge and at the railroad bridge, and took up a position one and a half miles beyond. Reconnoissances made during the day gave no assurance that the Confederates were in any considerable force near at hand, but led to the impression that it was their purpose to make a stand in a selected position near Richmond. On the next day, the 23d, the advance was within seven miles of Richmond. The Confederates were at the same time attacked with shells on the opposite side of the river near New Bridge. This was followed up on the next day with more skirmishing. During these days, since the army had reached the river, the unusual quantity of rain that fell had rendered the roads almost impassable for artillery, at the same time it had greatly retarded the construction of the numerous bridges which Gen. McClellan wished to build over the Chickahominy. There were two principal objects now before the commander-in-chief: one was to capture Richmond, and the other to secure supplies for his army. For this latter purpose, it was necessary for him to be prepared to defend the railroad against every attack upon it. The Confederate general, Johnston, by having possession of the bridges over the river on the north of Richmond, could at any moment throw a force over and attack Gen. McClellan's line of supplies. The river therefore was necessarily made passable to the Federal army at all times, to enable the commander to mass his troops on either side as might be necessary.

While arrangements were making to render the position of the Army of the Potomac safe and secure its successful advance upon Richmond, Gen. McClellan began to look anxiously for the expected coöperation of Gen. McDowell. It was evident that the retreat of the enemy could be made but very little farther. The campaign had ripened for the battle, and the conflict must be near at hand. The enemy had always declared that Richmond would never be captured so long as any men were left to defend it. They had shown their willingness to wait, and no one believed they would retire within the defences of Richmond until they were forced to do it by the disastrous issue of a battle.

On the 17th of May, the War Department sent the following instructions to Gen. McClellan. Unfortunately the reënforcements spoken of therein, were destined never to arrive:

WAR DEPARTMENT,
WASHINGTON CITY, D. C., *May* 17, 1862.

Maj.-Gen. George B. McClellan, Commanding Army of the Potomac before Richmond:

Your despatch to the President, asking for reënforcements, has been received and carefully considered. The President is not willing to uncover the capital entirely, and it is believed that even if this were prudent, it would require more time to effect a junction between your army and that of the Rappahannock, by the way of the Potomac and York rivers, than by a land march.

In order, therefore, to increase the strength of the attack upon Richmond at the earliest possible moment, Gen. McDowell has been ordered to march upon that city by the shortest route. He is ordered—keeping himself always in position to cover the capital from all possible attack—so to operate as to put his left wing in communication with your right, and you are instructed to coöperate so as to establish this communication as soon as possible. By extending your right wing to the north of Richmond, it is believed that this communication can be safely established, either north or south of the Pamunkey river. In any event, you will be able to prevent the main body of the enemy's forces from leaving Richmond and falling in overwhelming force upon Gen. McDowell. He will move with between thirty-five and forty thousand men.

A copy of the instructions to Maj.-Gen. McDowell is with this. The specific task assigned to his command has been to provide against any danger to the capital of the nation. At your earnest call for reënforcements, he is sent forward to coöperate in the reduction of Richmond, but charged, in attempting this, not to uncover the city of Washington, and you will give no orders either before or after your junction, which can keep him out of position to cover this city. You and he will communicate with each other by telegraph or otherwise as frequently as may be necessary for efficient coöperation.

When Gen. McDowell is in position on your right, his supplies must be drawn from West Point, and you will instruct your staff officers to be prepared to supply him by that route.

The President directs that Gen. McDowell retain the command of the Department of the Rappahannock, and of the forces with which he moves forward.

By order of the President.

EDWIN M. STANTON, Secretary of War.

On the 26th, an order was given for a movement, the design of which was to open a communication with Gen. McDowell, as well as to scatter a force known to be collecting near Hanover Court House to threaten the right of Gen. McClellan and his communications.

About four o'clock on the morning of the 27th, the division of Gen. Morrell, of Gen. Porter's corps, commenced its march in a heavy rain which had continued all night. It turned off from the road to New Bridge, and took that to Hanover Court House. The whole column marched fifteen miles steadily, with great rapidity, and with very little straggling. Soon after noon the enemy's pickets were met and driven in. This was near the railroad and about four miles from the Court House. The advance, consisting of Gen. Martindale's brigade, composed in part of the 18th and 22d Massachusetts, 2d Maine, and 25th New York, had met the enemy in considerable force. The latter regiment suffered severely by the enemy on either flank, until the artillery opened its fire. This continued for half an hour, when the arrival of Gen. Butterfield's brigade soon settled the affair. After an advance of a mile farther the Federal force halted. During this halt the enemy marched so as to flank it and made an attack upon its left, when a severe battle ensued, which finally resulted near sundown in driving the enemy from the field. The Federals, in both contests, had fifty-four killed and one hundred and ninety-four wounded and missing. The loss was chiefly in the 25th New York. The Confederate force was estimated at eight thousand, and wounded prisoners were taken to the hospitals belonging to fourteen different regiments. Their loss was between two and three hundred killed and wounded, and about five hundred taken prisoners. The expedition was under the command of Gen. Porter. The battle was near Peak's Station, on the Virginia Central Railroad. Fredericksburg, the headquarters of Gen. McDowell, was distant about forty-five miles, and his advance was at Bowling Green, distant only fifteen miles. This was the moment for the junction of the two armies. Prince de Joinville thus speaks of the actions of this hour:

"It needed only an effort of the will; the two armies were united, and the possession of Richmond certain! Alas! this effort was not made; I cannot recall those fatal moments without a real sinking of the heart. Seated in an orchard in the bivouac of Porter, amid the joyous excitement which follows a successful conflict, I saw the Fifth cavalry bring in whole companies of Confederate prisoners, with arms and baggage, their officers at their head. But neither the glad confidence of the Federals nor the discouragement of their enemies deceived me, and I asked myself how many of these gallant young men who surrounded me, relating their exploits of the day before, would pay with their lives for the fatal error which was on the point of being committed. Not only did not the two armies unite, but the order came from Washington to burn the bridges which had been seized. This was the clearest way of saying to the Army of the Potomac and to its chief that in no case could they count on the support of the armies of upper Virginia."

Gen. McClellan, in his testimony before the court-martial at Washington in the case of Gen. McDowell on December 10, said: "I have no doubt, for it has ever been my opinion, that the Army of the Potomac would have taken Richmond, had not the corps of Gen. McDowell been separated from it. It is also my opinion that had the command of Gen. McDowell joined the Army of the Potomac in the month of May, by way of Hanover Court House from Fredericksburg, we would have had Richmond in a week after the junction. I do not hold Gen. McDowell responsible for a failure to join with me on any occasion. I believe that anwers the question."

The principal bridge burned was the one over the South Anna River. The report of the destruction of this bridge, made from the army at the time says: "It cuts off the communication by railroad between Richmond and the forces under Gen. Jackson." On the 29th the expedition returned to its original camp.

CHAPTER XVIII.

Junction of Gen. Shields with Gen. McDowell—Both ordered to the Shenandoah Valley—March of Gen. Fremont to the same point—Previous advance of Gen. Banks up the Shenandoah—Position of the Forces—Advance of Gen. Jackson down the Valley—Attack at Front Royal—Retreat of Gen. Banks—Excitement in the Northern States—Gen Jackson falls back—Pursuit by Gens. Fremont and Shields—Battle at Cross Keys—Battle at Port Republic—Advance of Gen. Heath.

THE explanation of this failure on the part of Gen. McDowell to coöperate with the army of Gen. McClellan at this critical moment, involves a statement of the military operations which had been taking place in the Department of the Potomac, the Mountain Department, and the Department of the Shenandoah, and which culminated at this time. On the Confederate side, the design of these military operations was not only to prevent this junction of Gen. McDowell with Gen. McClellan, but also to prevent any reënforcement whatever to the latter. In this last object they were also partly successful.

The corps of Gen. McDowell was not allowed to embark for Fortress Monroe with the other forces of Gen. McClellan by order of the President, as has been stated. The Department of the Rappahannock created soon after, and placed under the command of Gen. McDowell, became the field of his operations. The division of Gen. Franklin having been sent to Gen. McClellan, the forces of Gen. McDowell consisted of the divisions of Gens. McCall and King. These forces were in Virginia, southwest of Washington. On the 15th of April the order for their advance was issued. On the night of that day the advance reached Catlett's Station. On the 17th the march again commenced, and, six miles out, the pickets of the enemy were found and driven in, and several skirmishes took place during the day. On the morning of the 18th the small force of the enemy were driven across the bridges into Fredericksburg, which place they were not prepared to defend, and soon after abandoned it, having destroyed everything of value to themselves which could not be carried away. On the next day the city was surrendered by the authorities. It was so completely under the guns of the Federal force planted opposite the town, that any resistance in its unprotected state would have been useless. The Confederate force which retired before the advance, consisted of one regiment of infantry and one of cavalry. On the 23d of April Gen. McDowell was ordered by the President not to occupy Fredericksburg for the present, but to prepare the bridges and his transportation. On the 30th he was authorized to occupy it. On the 4th of May the bridges across the Rappahannock had been restored, and the city was occupied by the Federal troops. At the same time when the order was given to Gen. McDowell to advance upon Fredericksburg, an order was given to Gen. Shields to withdraw with his division from the corps of Gen. Banks in the Department of the Shenandoah, and to join the corps of Gen. McDowell. Upon the issue of this order detaching Gen. Shields from the command of Gen. Banks, the War Department was warned by experienced military officers that disaster would certainly follow from it. Gen. Shields immediately moved to comply with the order, and on the 19th his division encamped half a mile south of Catlett's Station. He was ordered then to Fredericksburg, and reached Falmouth on the 22d of May.

On the 17th of May the following instructions were given to Gen. McDowell:

WAR DEPARTMENT,
WASHINGTON CITY, D. C., *May* 17, 1862.

To Maj.-Gen. McDowell, Commanding Department of the Rappahannock:

GENERAL: Upon being joined by Shields's division, you will move upon Richmond by the general route of the Richmond and Fredericksburg railroad, coöperating with the forces under Gen. McClellan now threatening Richmond from the line of the Pamunkey and York rivers. While seeking to establish as soon as possible a communication between your left wing and the right wing of Gen. McClellan, you will hold yourself always in such position as to cover the capital of the nation against a sudden dash by any large body of the rebel forces.

Gen. McClellan will be furnished with a copy of these instructions, and will be directed to hold himself in readiness to establish communication with your left and to prevent the main body of the enemy's army from leaving Richmond and throwing itself upon your column before a junction between the two armies is effected. A copy of his instructions in regard to the employment of your forces is annexed.

EDWIN M. STANTON, Secretary of War.

A few days previously a small force had crossed over to Fredericsburg by order of Gen. McDowell, but the main body of his corps remained at Falmouth, where it could sustain the advance if necessary. The enemy had retired only a short distance from the town. So far as related to numbers, the division of Gen. Shields was not needed by Gen. McDowell; but the soldiers of the former had been on many a hard field, while those of the latter had hardly stood the shock of battle. The division of Gen. Shields, just from a march of one hundred and ten miles, was appointed to take the advance upon the enemy. This division consisted of the following brigades: first brigade, Gen. Kimball, 4th and 8th Ohio, 14th Indiana, and 7th Virginia; second brigade, Gen. Terry, 7th, 29th, and 66th Ohio, and 7th Indiana; third brigade, Gen. Tyler, 5th Ohio, 1st Virginia, 84th and 110th Pennsylvania; fourth brigade, Col. Carroll acting brig.-gen., 7th and 62d Ohio, 13th Indiana, and 39th Illinois.

On Saturday evening, May 24, the order was received for the division of Gen. Shields and other forces, to fall back.

The following was the order:

WASHINGTON, *May* 24, 1862.

Maj.-Gen. McDowell:

Gen. Fremont has been ordered, by telegraph, to move to Franklin and Harrisonburg, to relieve Gen. Banks, and capture or destroy Jackson and Ewell's forces. You are instructed, laying aside for the present the movement on Richmond, to put twenty thousand men in motion at once for the Shenandoah, moving on the line, or in advance of the line, of the Manassas Gap railroad. Your object will be to capture the force of Jackson and Ewell, either in coöperation with Gen. Fremont, or, in case want of supplies or transportation interfered with his movement, it is believed that the force which you move will be sufficient to accomplish the object alone. The information thus far received here makes it probable that, if the enemy operates actively against Gen. Banks, you will not be able to count upon much assistance from him, but may have even to release him. Reports received this moment are that Banks is fighting with Ewell, eight miles from Harper's Ferry. ABRAHAM LINCOLN.

The reply of Gen. McDowell to this order was as follows:

HEADQUARTERS, DEPARTMENT OF THE RAPPAHANNOCK,
May 24, 1862.

Hon. E. M. Stanton, Secretary of War:

The President's order has been received, and is in process of execution. This is a crushing blow to us.

IRVIN McDOWELL, Major-General.

To this the President responded as follows:

WASHINGTON, *May* 24, 1862.

Maj.-Gen. McDowell:

I am highly gratified by your alacrity in obeying my orders. The change was as painful to me as it can possibly be to you or to any one.

Everything now depends upon the celerity and vigor of your movements. A. LINCOLN.

The reply of Gen. McDowell to this message is important, as showing the probabilities that his movement would be unsuccessful. It was as follows:

HEADQUARTERS, DEPARTMENT OF THE RAPPAHANNOCK, OPPOSITE FREDERICKSBURG, *May* 24, 1862.

His Excellency the President:

I obeyed your order immediately; for it was positive and urgent, and, perhaps, as a subordinate, there I ought to stop; but I trust I may be allowed to say something in relation to the subject, especially in view of your remark that everything depends upon the celerity and vigor of my movements; I beg to say that coöperation between Gen. Fremont and myself to cut off Jackson and Ewell is not to be counted upon, even if it is not a practicable impossibility; next, that I am entirely beyond helping distance of Gen. Banks, and no celerity or vigor will be available as far as he is concerned; next, that by a glance at the map it will be seen that the line of retreat of the enemy's forces up the valley is shorter than mine to go against him. It will take a week or ten days for the force to get to the valley by the route which will give it food and forage, and by that time the enemy will have retreated. I shall gain nothing for you there, and lose much for you here. It is, therefore, not only on personal grounds that I have a heavy heart in the matter, but I feel that it throws us all back, and from Richmond north we shall have all our large mass paralyzed, and shall have to repeat what we have just accomplished.

I have ordered Gen. Shields to commence the movement to-morrow morning. A second division will follow in the afternoon. Did I understand you aright that you wish that I personally should accompany this expedition? Very respectfully,

IRVIN McDOWELL.

The division of Gen. Shields, accompanied by other portions of McDowell's forces, was on the march at noon of the next day, and moved fifteen miles, and the next day, the 26th, encamped six miles beyond Catlett's Station. Early the next morning, moving again, it passed Manassas Junction during the day, where it met a portion of the force driven from Front Royal, and learned that Gen. Banks was flying before Gen. Jackson, and halted at Haymarket. Twelve days previous this division had left Gen. Banks's army to join Gen. McDowell, on his way, as it was believed, to coöperate with Gen. McClellan before Richmond. It had been the division of Gen. Lander, and had become familiar with the Shenandoah Valley, up which they had pursued the enemy from the Potomac to the northern base of the Massanutten Mountains. Now the work of a whole winter and spring was before them to do over again. In coöperation with Gen. Fremont's forces they prepared to aid in cutting off the retreat of Gen. Jackson after having driven Gen. Banks across the Potomac. On the 27th a column under Gen. Kimball, embracing, as a part of it, the entire division of Gen. Shields, commenced its march for Front Royal, which, without serious opposition, it was expected to reach in three days, and Strasburg in four.

The advance of Gen. McDowell at the time it was countermanded had reached Bowling Green, fifteen miles from Hanover Court House, which was two days later occupied by a force from Gen. McClellan's army under Gen. Porter.

The order creating the Mountain Department was issued by the President on the 11th of March. It was supposed at this time that the plan of the campaign for Gen. Fremont was to move up the left bank of the Big Sandy river in Kentucky, to Prestonville and Pikeville, through Cumberland Gap to Knoxville, and thus command the southern railroad, and cut off any retreat from or any reënforcements to Richmond. On the 29th Gen. Fremont, at Wheeling, assumed the command, and Gen. Rosecrans retired and took command of Gen. Pope's corps under Gen. Grant. The new department was bounded on the east by that of the Potomac under Gen. McClellan, and on the west by that of the Mississippi under Gen. Halleck. Active preparations had been made by Gen. Rosecrans for the spring campaign. On the same day Gen. Fremont issued an order assigning Brig.-Gen. B. F. Kelly to the command of the railroad district, consisting of all of western Virginia, north and east of the counties of Jackson, Roane, Calhoun, Braxton, Lewis, Barbour, and Tucker inclusive, and west of the Alleghanies, Maryland, and Pennsylvania.

Military operations in this department, under Gen. Fremont, commenced about the 1st of April. Gen. Milroy, who had been some time holding the pass of Cheat Mountain in Randolph county in the northern part of the State, advanced twelve miles to Camp Greenbrier, thence nine miles in a northeasterly direction to Camp Alleghany, a position occupied by the enemy, who retreated before him. On the 10th he had occupied Monterey, being an advance of sixteen miles. This position was evacuated by the Confederates, and also Huntersville. The next day he moved toward McDowell, distant ten miles, and occupied it and advanced subsequently to Fort Shenandoah eight miles. Thus far Gen. Milroy had followed the retreating foe from Monterey in the direction of Staunton in the Shenandoah Valley.

On the 3d of May Gen. Fremont left Wheeling and arrived at New Creek on the Baltimore and Ohio railroad, and on the 5th, accompanied by his staff and body guard, and one or two regiments of infantry and a battery, he advanced about six miles; on the 7th he reached Petersburg, a small town twelve miles beyond Moorefield, and forty-four from New Creek. Gen. Schenck's brigade had left Petersburg on the 3d. Their aim was to effect a junction with Gen. Milroy, whose situation was becoming exposed in consequence of forces of the enemy advancing from the east. Gen. Milroy in his advance had driven the Confederates beyond the Shenandoah Mountains, the boundary of Gen. Fremont's department, and had made his headquarters at McDowell. On the 5th of May the 32d Ohio regiment was advanced beyond the Shenandoah Mountains, about sixteen miles from McDowell, for the double purpose of scouting and foraging. The 75th Ohio and 3d Virginia, with Hyman's battery, were encamped at the foot of the mountain on the west side, and the remainder of Gen. Milroy's force was at

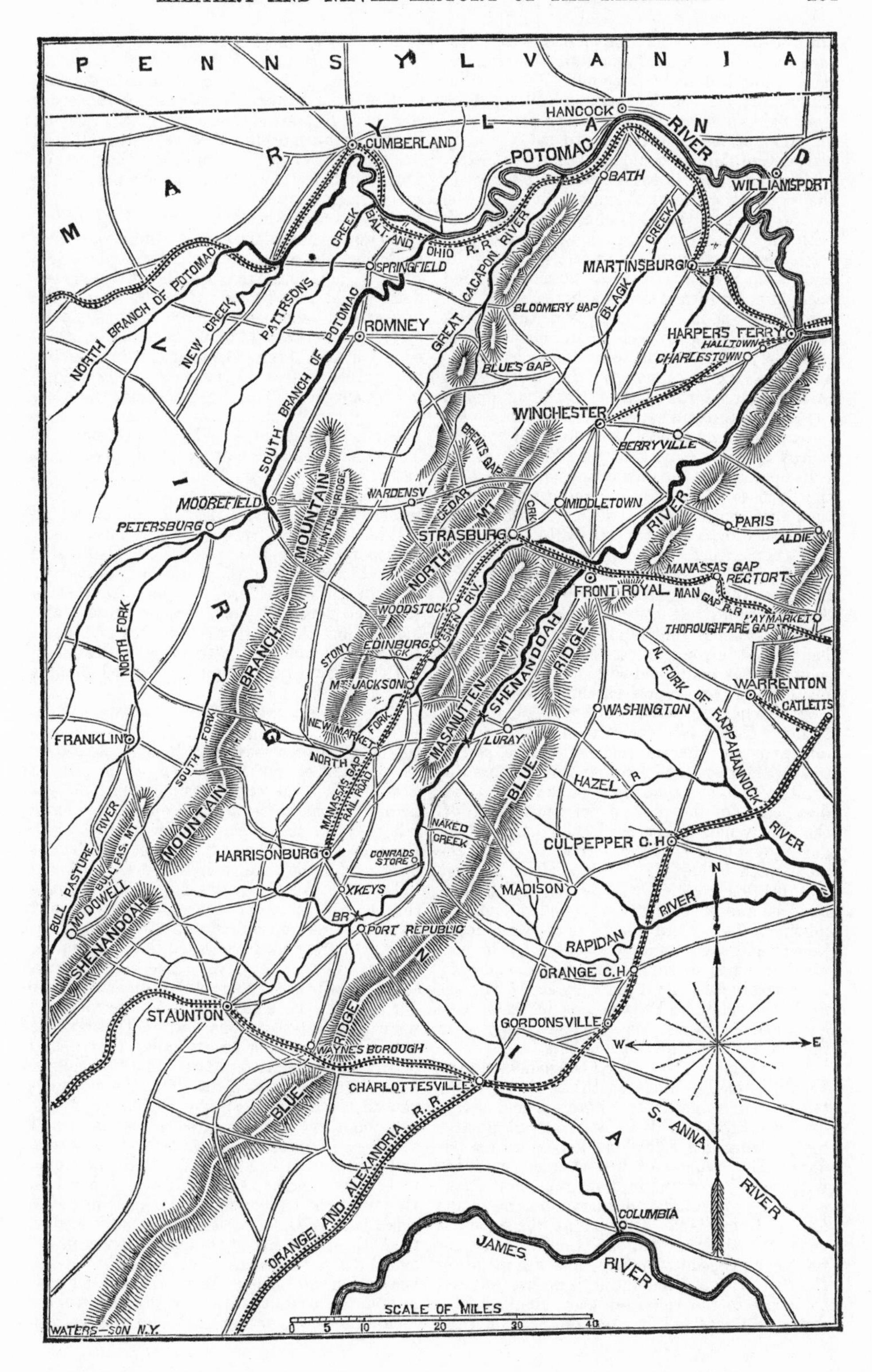
PENNSYLVANIA
MARYLAND
VIRGINIA
HANCOCK
CUMBERLAND
POTOMAC RIVER
BATH
WILLIAMSPORT
BALT. AND OHIO R.R.
SPRINGFIELD
MARTINSBURG
NORTH BRANCH OF POTOMAC
NEW CREEK
PATTERSONS CREEK
SOUTH BRANCH OF POTOMAC
ROMNEY
GREAT CACAPON RIVER
BLOOMERY GAP
BLACK CREEK
HARPERS FERRY
HALLTOWN
CHARLESTOWN
BLUES GAP
WINCHESTER
BERRYVILLE
BRENTS GAP
MOOREFIELD
PETERSBURG
WARDENSV
CEDAR CRK
MIDDLETOWN
STRASBURG
HUNTING RIDGE
NORTH MT
PARIS
ALDIE
MANASSAS GAP
RECTORT
FRONT ROYAL
MAN GAP R.R
HAYMARKET
THOROUGHFARE GAP
WOODSTOCK
EDINBURG
STONY CK
MT JACKSON
NEW MARKET
NORTH FORK
SOUTH FORK
MASANUTTEN MT
SHENANDOAH
BLUE RIDGE
N. FORK OF RAPPAHANNOCK
WARRENTON
CATLETTS
WASHINGTON
LURAY
FRANKLIN
MANASSAS GAP RAIL ROAD
HAZEL R
BULL PASTURE RIVER
BULL PAS. MT
MOUNTAIN
HARRISONBURG
CONRADS STORE
NAKED CREEK
CULPEPPER C.H.
RAPPAHANNOCK RIVER
MADISON
KEYS
M^c DOWELL
BR
PORT REPUBLIC
RAPIDAN RIVER
ORANGE C.H.
STAUNTON
GORDONSVILLE
WAYNESBOROUGH
CHARLOTTESVILLE
ORANGE AND ALEXANDRIA R.R.
S. ANNA RIVER
COLUMBIA
JAMES RIVER
N
W
E
SCALE OF MILES
0 5 10 20 30 40
WATERS—SON N.Y.

McDowell. This is a small town on the Bull Pasture river at the foot of mountains bearing the same name, and about forty miles distant from Harrisonburg in the Shenandoah Valley, where Gen. Banks's forces then were. To prevent the junction of these forces, or to cut them up before Gen. Milroy could be reënforced, Gen. Jackson collected all the Confederate forces in the region, and marched against him. On the 7th he attacked the 32d Ohio, which fell back with the loss of their camp equipage and baggage, through lack of transportation. At the same time the force west of the mountain fell back in order to McDowell, where a stand was determined upon. Gen Milroy at the earliest moment sent despatches to Gen. Schenck, who was thirty miles distant, to hasten to his assistance. In the afternoon the enemy appeared in large force on the tops of the mountains in the rear of the town, arranging for an attack. A force was immediately sent forward by Gen. Milroy to occupy the hilltops adjacent to the ones upon which the enemy appeared, more for the purpose of skirmishing and reconnoitring than for bringing on a battle. A fierce contest ensued, which was increased by the arrival of Gen. Schenck with his brigade, and continued until night. The forces of the enemy being manifestly greatly superior, Gen. Milroy determined to retreat. The march was commenced at midnight, and at daybreak they had retired thirteen miles. After a halt of two hours it was continued with the enemy pressing upon them. Upon reaching the camp of Gen. Schenck, arrangements were made for protection. Every hill was surmounted with cannon, and ten different regiments were placed to support them, and for over thirty hours the artillery by a constant fire kept the enemy at a distance. On the morning of the 14th all of the enemy had disappeared, which was subsequently explained by the arrival of Gen. Fremont with Blenker's division. The Federal loss in this conflict was twenty killed, one hundred and seventy-seven wounded, and two missing. The Confederate loss was forty killed, and two hundred wounded. It was nearly a flight of the Federal forces, and only the arrival of Fremont probably saved it from final capture. The Federal loss in tents, baggage, and stores was great. The enemy were present in much superior numbers.

Gen. Fremont now made his headquarters at Franklin, eighty miles south of New Creek, twenty-four miles from Monterey, and sixty-five from Staunton. Here he remained quietly, reorganizing and refreshing his forces for ten days. This repulse of his advance, with his withdrawal to Franklin, now gave Gen. Jackson the opportunity to carry out the plans against Gen. Banks as soon as the moment came for their execution. Consequently no further movement of importance was made on the part of Gen. Fremont until he was ordered to hurry to the relief of Gen. Banks. This order was received by him on Saturday, the 24th of May, under the form of a despatch from the Secretary of War, directing him to fall back with his entire command to the support of Gen. Banks. That evening the order was given to be ready for a movement early on the following morning. As early as half past three o'clock on Sunday morning the noise of preparation was heard, and at six o'clock the army was in motion.

It seems that when Gen. Fremont was ordered to go to the relief of Gen. Banks, the order prescribed the route by which he should go. (*See* p. 237.) This route, thus specified by the President, would have brought Gen. Fremont in the rear of Gen. Jackson; whereas that taken by Gen. Fremont brought him in front of Gen. Jackson. But Gen. Fremont, judging it to be an impracticable route, took the responsibility of going by another. The President telegraphed to him, saying: "You are ordered to go so and so. I hear of you elsewhere. What does this mean?" To which Gen. Fremont replied, giving the reasons, viz.: that he knew of a shorter and easier route by which he could more effectually perform the service desired, and on which his half-famished troops would meet their transportation and supplies. He also stated that when one is "in the field," it is essentially difficult to obey literally orders transmitted from one necessarily unaware of present exigencies, but that if it was expected of him so to do, he would do it. To this the President, with characteristic simplicity, replied that he was satisfied.

The first six miles of the road were indescribably bad, owing to the recent rains and the heavy wagons that had been passing over it. Wounded and sick had been left at Franklin, but the entire train of wagons was taken. At night the army bivouacked about a mile beyond the upper crossing of the South Branch of the Potomac on the road to Petersburg. The distance marched was fourteen miles. On Monday, the 26th, the advance reached Petersburg after noon, having marched sixteen miles, and halted until the next morning. Orders were here issued that knapsacks, tents, and baggage of every description, which could possibly be dispensed with, should be left behind. Five days' rations of hard bread were given to the troops, and on Tuesday, the 27th, after marching twelve miles, they halted on the highlands east of the village of Moorefield. On Wednesday, the 28th, the army advanced ten miles, passing over Hunting Ridge, and about two o'clock halted to rest and await supplies. The roads continually grew worse, and the rain fell steadily. Thursday, no movement was made. A small force under Col. Downey, on a reconnoissance, encountered a small body of Confederate cavalry. On Friday, the 30th, an advance of twenty miles was made, and the army bivouacked at Wardensville. A heavy rain fell during the afternoon. On Saturday, the 31st, the last of the intervening mountain ranges was crossed, and the western barrier of the Shenandoah Valley alone remained to be traversed. The troops pushed on twelve miles through the rain, and halted at night where the Winchester and Strasburg roads divide. On the narrow ridges, along which the path wound in constant ascent, there was no plane or table land for camp. That rainy night the tired troops dropped and slept by the roadside or in the swimming fields. The next morning, Sunday, June 1, the advance moved at six o'clock, and at eight the whole column was in motion on the road to Strasburg. In about an hour and a half later a skirmish ensued near Strasburg, and Gen. Fremont had reached the position to coöperate with the force of Gen. McDowell against the advance of the enemy upon Gen. Banks.

After the battle of Winchester, on the 23d of March, the retiring Confederate forces in the Shenandoah Valley were followed up by Gen. Banks. On the 1st of April he moved from Strasburg to Woodstock, where his entrance was disputed by a force of cavalry, infantry, and artillery under Col. Ashby. They however retreated to Edinburg, destroying one railroad and two turnpike bridges. The advance was subsequently continued with occasional skirmishes, and on the 26th Harrisonburg was occupied. A considerable body of Confederate troops was in the neighborhood, but in a position from which a retreat could easily be made.

The order of the President, which divided the army in Virginia into five corps, placed the fifth under the command of Gen. Banks. It was to be composed of his division and that of Gen. Shields, which had previously been commanded by Gen. Lander. This was the force now encamped near Harrisonburg. About the 15th of May an order was issued from the War Department withdrawing the division of Gen. Shields from the corps of Gen. Banks, and directing him to report immediately at Catlett's Station on the Orange and Alexandria railroad, as above stated. At the same time orders were given to Gen. Banks to fall back to Strasburg and fortify. Gen. Shields left at once, and on his arrival at Catlett's Station he was ordered to join Gen. McDowell at Fredericksburg immediately.

At Strasburg the Massanutten range of mountains rise in the middle of the valley, and divide it. Strasburg is favorably located for defence against an attack from the south by the western valley. But the eastern valley, by opening out at Front Royal, affords another road to the Potomac, and also a good plank road, which runs direct to Winchester, going round Strasburg.

Gen. Banks had not actually fallen back to Strasburg when Gen. Shields marched over the mountain and down the eastern branch of the valley to Front Royal. At that very time an attack was expected on the front, and a portion of his forces had been daily skirmishing with a Confederate force in the gap of the Massanutten Mountains. It was also known that Gen. Jackson, having attempted to dislodge Gen. Milroy in the Mountain Department, was returning to the Shenandoah Valley, and that Gen. Ewell was with a strong force on the road running from Harrisonburg to Gordonsville, and also that Gen. Taylor was still higher up the valley with another Confederate force. In addition, Gen. Jackson could be easily reënforced from Gordonsville. With this force menacing the valley, Gen. Banks was left with less than six thousand men, including cavalry and artillery, to defend the whole valley, and that, too, before he had time to prepare himself for resistance by fortifications.

Eastward of Front Royal there was another force under Gen. Geary, charged with the protection of the Manassas Gap railroad. The headquarters of Gen. Geary were at Rectortown, and there were only between seven and eight hundred troops at Front Royal. Still farther east, at Catlett's Station, on the Orange and Alexandria railroad, about ten miles south of Manassas Junction, was the brigade of Gen. Duryea, consisting of three New York and one Pennsylvania regiment. These forces formed the connection between Gen. Banks and the main body of the army of the Rappahannock, under Gen. McDowell, at Fredericksburg.

The enemy, knowing the position and strength of these forces, formed a plan to capture the entire force of Gen. Banks. This plan was to be executed on the proper signal being given from Richmond. At this time Gen. McClellan was within fifteen miles of Richmond. Gen. McDowell had been reënforced by Gen. Shields, and orders were expected every hour for him to advance toward Richmond. It was all-important for the defence of that capital that reënforcements should be prevented from reaching Gen. McClellan. After the junction of Gens. Shields and McDowell, dense columns of smoke could be seen at evening ascending for miles south of Fredericksburg, which were caused by the burning of bridges to retard the Federal advance. Something greater than the mere burning of bridges was needed; for it was not only necessary to prevent the Federal reënforcements to Gen. McClellan, but also to gain time to accumulate the Confederate forces before Richmond from such parts of the South as they could be taken, and by the levies of the conscript law. The moment had come for the dash on Gen. Banks, and the signal from Richmond was given. Meanwhile Gen. Banks, according to the orders of the War Department, had fallen back, and now occupied Strasburg. The first movement of the enemy, who had retired from their advance on Fremont, and were already concentrated under Gens. Jackson and Ewell for the purpose, was to advance a heavy column rapidly up the valley between the Blue Ridge and Massanutten mountain range to Front Royal, with the design of capturing the force there, and then press on by a good plank road to Winchester, and thus get in the rear of Gen. Banks. The guard at Front Royal consisted of the 1st Maryland regiment, Col. Kenly, with three companies of the 29th Pennsylvania, two rifled guns of Knapp's battery, and two companies of the 5th New York cavalry. To their bravery is due the partial defeat of the Confederate plan. On Friday noon, May 23, the enemy were reported to be approaching, and Col. Kenly formed in a position about one mile east of the Shenandoah river. The fight commenced by a strong dash of cavalry under Col. Ashby upon this position. After a contest of two hours the enemy were repulsed with considerable loss. Finding that a large force of infantry was approaching to the aid of the cavalry, Col. Kenly ordered his men to fall back to the west side of the Shenandoah and to destroy the bridges after them. This was done in good order and the smaller bridge destroyed; but a flanking force of the enemy fording above came upon them before the larger one was destroyed. Col. Kenly immediately got his guns in position and formed his men, and another struggle ensued, which checked the enemy a couple of hours longer. Finding the force of the enemy increasing, he placed his artillery in the rear and commenced falling back. This was continued for three miles, when the force was overwhelmed by a charge of the enemy, their lines broken, and no further resistance could be made. Col. Kenly was severely wounded, but afterward recovered. This check retarded the Confederate advance.

The news of this affair reached Gen. Banks that evening, with such details as convinced him that the enemy were at hand with a force from fifteen to twenty thousand strong. It was evident to him from the large Confederate force, composed as it must be of all their troops in the valley concentrated, that they were close upon him for some purpose not yet developed. That purpose must be nothing less than the defeat of his own command, or its possible capture by occupying Winchester, and thus intercepting supplies or reënforcements and cutting off all opportunity for retreat. Under this interpretation of the enemy's plans, one of three courses was open for him to pursue: first, a retreat across the little North Mountain to the Potomac river on the west; second, an attack on the enemy's flank on the Front Royal road; third, a rapid movement direct upon Winchester with a view to anticipate the occupation of the town by the enemy, and thus place his own command in communication with its original base of operations in the line of reënforcements by Harper's Ferry, and secure a safe retreat in case of disaster.

To remain at Strasburg was to be surrounded; to move over the mountains was to abandon his train at the outset, and to subject his command to flank attacks, without possibility of succor; and to attack the enemy in such overwhelming force could only result in certain destruction. It was, therefore, determined by Gen. Banks that to enter the lists with the enemy in a race or a battle, as he should choose, for the possession of Winchester, the key of the valley, was, for him and his force, the path to safety.

Accordingly, the advance guard was called in, and at three o'clock on the next morning several hundred disabled men, left in charge by Gen. Shields's division, were put upon the march to Winchester, followed by the wagon train under escort of cavalry and infantry. The rear was protected by nearly the whole force of cavalry and six pieces of artillery. The attack of the enemy was expected in the rear. When all the column except the rear guard had passed Cedar Creek, three miles from Strasburg, information was received from the front that the enemy had attacked the train and was in full possession of the road at Middletown. The danger being now in front, the troops were ordered to the head of the column and the train to the rear. After this change the head of the column encountered the enemy in force, fifteen miles from Winchester, who were attacked with artillery and infantry and driven back some two miles. The neglect of the enemy to attack the train and throw it into confusion when at the head of the column secured a successful continuation of the march. On the remainder of the route to Winchester, the enemy pressed the main column with the utmost vigor, and defeated at every point all efforts of detachments to effect a junction with it. At five o'clock in the afternoon the advance guard arrived at Winchester, and Gen. Banks became satisfied that the force of the enemy was not less than twenty-five thousand men. His command consisted of two brigades of less than four thousand men, with nine hundred cavalry, ten Parrott guns, and one battery of smooth six pounders. To this should be added the 10th Maine regiment of infantry and five companies of Maryland cavalry, stationed at Winchester. During the night Gen. Banks determined to test the strength of the enemy by actual collision, and measures were promptly taken to prepare the troops. The rolling of musketry was heard during the latter part of the night, and before the break of day a sharp engagement occurred at the outposts. Soon after four o'clock the artillery opened its fire, which continued without cessation until the close of the engagement.

The main body of the Confederates was hidden during the early part of the action by the crest of a hill and the woods in the rear.

Their force was massed apparently upon the Federal right, and their manœuvres indicated a purpose to turn them upon the Berryville road, where, it appeared subsequently, they had placed a considerable force with a view of preventing reënforcements from Harper's Ferry. But the steady fire of the Federal lines held them in check until a small portion of the troops, on the right of the Federal line, made a movement to the rear. This was done under the erroneous impression that an order to withdraw had been given. No sooner was this observed by the enemy than its regiments swarmed upon the crest of the hill, advancing from the woods upon the Federal right, which, still continuing its fire, steadily withdrew toward the town.

The overwhelming Confederate force thus suddenly showing itself, made further resistance unwise, and orders were sent to the left to withdraw, which was done in an orderly manner. By this engagement the enemy were held in check five hours.

The retreat was now continued in three parallel columns, each protected by an efficient rear guard, in the direction of Martinsburg, with the hope of meeting reënforcements. The pursuit of the enemy was prompt and vigorous, and the retreat rapid and without loss. At Martinsburg the columns halted two hours and a half, and the rear guard remained in the rear of the town until seven in the evening, and arrived at the river at sundown, forty-eight hours after the first news of the attack on Front Royal. It was a march of fifty-three miles, thirty-five of which were performed in one day. The scene at the river when the rear guard arrived was of the most animated and excited description. A thousand camp fires were burning on the hillside; a thousand carriages of every description were crowded upon the banks of the broad stream between the exhausted troops and their coveted rest. The ford was too deep for the teams to cross in regular succession; only the strongest horses, after a few experiments, were allowed to essay the passage over before morning. The single ferry was occupied by the ammunition trains, the ford by the wagons. The cavalry was secure in its form of crossing. The troops only had no transportation. No enemy appeared in sight. Fortunately there were several boats belonging to the pontoon train brought from Strasburg, which were launched and devoted exclusively to the soldiers. Gen. Banks says in his report: "There never were more grateful hearts in the same number of men than when at midday, on the 26th, we stood on the opposite shore." The loss was as follows: killed, 38; wounded, 155; missing, 711; total, 904. The wagon train consisted of nearly five hundred wagons, of which fifty-five were lost. All the guns were saved. The loss of the enemy has not been stated.

On the morning of the 28th, Gen. Jackson issued the following address to his soldiers:

HEADQUARTERS, V. D.,
WINCHESTER, *May* 28, 1862.

General Order, No. 53.

Within four weeks this army has made long and rapid marches, fought six combats and two battles, signally defeating the enemy in each one, capturing several stands of colors and pieces of artillery, with numerous prisoners and vast medical and army stores, and finally driven the boastful host, which was ravishing our beautiful country, into utter rout. The General commanding would warmly express to the officers and men under his command his joy in their achievements, and his thanks for their brilliant gallantry in action, and their obedience under the hardships of forced marches, often more painful to the brave soldier than the dangers of battle.

The explanation of the severe exertions to which the commanding General called the army, which were endured by them with such cheerful confidence in him, is now given in the victory of yesterday. He receives this proof of their confidence in the past with pride and gratitude, and asks only a similar confidence in the future. But his chief duty to-day, and that of the army, is to recognize devoutly the hand of a protecting Providence in the brilliant successes of the last three days, which have given us the result of a great victory without great losses, and to make the oblation of our thanks to God for his mercies to us and our country in heartfelt acts of religious worship. For this purpose the troops will remain in camp to-day, suspending as far as practicable all military exercises, and the chaplains of the regiments will hold divine service in their several charges at 4 o'clock P. M., to-day.

By order of Maj.-Gen. JACKSON.
R. D. DANBY, Asst. Adj.-Gen.

When the news of the attack on the Maryland regiment at Front Royal on the 23d, reached Gen. Geary, who, with his force, was charged with the protection of the Manassas Gap railroad, he immediately began to move to Manassas Junction. His troops hearing the most extravagant stories of the fate of the Maryland regiment, and supposing they were about to be swallowed up, burnt their tents and destroyed a quantity of arms. Gen. Duryea, at Catlett's Station, became alarmed on learning of the withdrawal of Gen. Geary, took his three New York regiments, leaving the Pennsylvania one behind, and hastened back to Centreville, and telegraphed to Washington for help. He left a large quantity of army stores behind, and also for two days his camp equipage. A panic prevailed at Catlett's Station and Manassas Junction for two days. At night the camps were kept in constant alarm by the sentinels firing at stumps or bowing bushes, which they mistook for Confederate guerillas. The alarm spread to Washington, and Secretary Stanton issued orders calling for the militia of the loyal States to defend that city.

The following is the despatch sent to the Governor of Massachusetts:

WASHINGTON, *May* 25, 1862.

To the Governor of Massachusetts:

Intelligence from various quarters leaves no doubt that the enemy in great force are marching on Washington. You will please organize and forward immediately all the militia and volunteer force in your State. EDWIN M. STANTON, Secretary of War.

This alarm at Washington, and the call for its defence, produced a most indescribable panic in the cities of the Northern States, on Sunday, the 25th, and two or three days afterward.

The Governor of New York, on Sunday night, the 25th, telegraphed to Buffalo, Rochester, Syracuse, and other cities as follows:

Orders from Washington render it necessary to forward to that city all the available militia force. What can Buffalo do? E. D. MORGAN.

Governor Curtin, of Pennsylvania, issued the following order:

HEADQUARTERS PENNSYLVANIA MILITIA,
HARRISBURG, *May* 26.

General Order, No. 23.

On pressing requisition of the President of the United States in the present emergency, it is ordered that the several major-generals, brigadier-generals, and colonels of regiments, throughout the Commonwealth, muster, without delay, all military organizations within their respective divisions or under their control, together with all persons willing to join their commands, and proceed forthwith to the city of Washington or such other points as may be indicated by future orders.

By order A. G. CURTIN, Governor and Commander-in-Chief.

(Signed) A. L. RUSSELL, Adjt.-Gen.

The Governor of Massachusetts issued the following proclamation:

Men of Massachusetts!—The wily and barbarous horde of traitors to the people, to the Government, to our country, and to liberty, menace again the national capital. They have attacked and routed Maj.-Gen. Banks, are advancing on Harper's Ferry, and are marching on Washington. The President calls on Massachusetts to rise once more for its rescue and defence.

The whole active militia will be summoned by a general order, issued from the office of the Adjutant-General, to report on Boston Common to-morrow; they will march to relieve and avenge their brethren and friends, and to oppose with fierce zeal and courageous patriotism the progress of the foe.

May God encourage their hearts and strengthen their arms, and may He inspire the Government and all the people!

Given at Headquarters, Boston, 11 o'clock, this (Sunday) evening, May 25, 1862.

JOHN A. ANDREW.

Over three thousand men responded on Monday.

The Governor of Rhode Island issued the following order:

PROVIDENCE, *May* 25, 1862.

Citizens of the State capable of bearing arms will at once report themselves to the nearest military organizations.

The commandants of the chartered and volunteer military companies will at once organize their companies, and the men so reporting into companies of eighty-three men rank and file, and report to these headquarters, when they will be armed, equipped, and moved under the direction of the Commander-in-Chief to Washington, to protect the national capital from the advance of the rebels who are now rapidly approaching.

Gen. Robbins is directed to organize and command the first regiment, and will order his brigade under arms and form it into a regiment.

The second regiment will be under command of Capt. Bliss, of the United States Army.

The Providence Marine Corps of artillery will be placed under the command of Lieut.-Col. E. C. Gallup as captain, and he is directed to organize the same.

Col. Shaw is ordered to assemble the National Guard for organization.

Rhode Island troops will move through Baltimore, and if their progress is impeded by the rebel mob of that city, they will mete out to it the punishment which it has long merited. Our regiments will move to Washington to defend the capital in common with thousands of our patriotic countrymen, who will rush to arms to ward off the danger which is imminent.

WM. SPRAGUE.

AUG. HOPPIN, Assistant Adjutant-General.

The Governor of Ohio issued the following proclamation:

COLUMBUS, O., *May* 26.

To the Gallant Men of Ohio: I have the astounding intelligence that the seat of our beloved Government is threatened with invasion, and am called upon by the Secretary of War for troops to repel and overwhelm the ruthless invaders.

Rally, then, men of Ohio, and respond to this call, as becomes those who appreciate our glorious Government. Three classes of troops will be accepted:

First. For three years, or during the war.

Second. For a term of three months.

Third. For guard duty within the limits of the State.

All are requested to report for duty at Camp Chase, where the organization will take place.

The number wanted from each county has been indicated by special despatches to the several Military Committees.

Everything is valueless to us if our Government is overthrown.

Lay aside, then, your ordinary duties, and help to bear afloat the glorious flag unfurled by our fathers.

DAVID TOD, Governor.

At the same time the Secretary of War at Washington, caused the following order to be issued:

WASHINGTON, *May* 25, 1862.

Ordered. By virtue of the authority vested by an act of Congress, the President takes military possession of all the railroads in the United States, from and after this date, until further orders, and directs that the respective railroad companies, their officers and servants, shall hold themselves in readiness for the transportation of troops and munitions of war, as may be ordered by the military authorities, to the exclusion of all other business.

By order of the Secretary of War.

M. C. MEIGS, Quartermaster-General.

When the alarm thus indicated in the headquarters of Government had disseminated itself throughout the military and social ramifications of society, the excitement was almost tumultuous. In Baltimore, crowds pursued persons suspected of sympathy with the cause of the South, until all such disappeared from the streets. The display of flags was demanded from public buildings. Almost half a million of men offered themselves for the defence of Washington within twenty-four hours after the issue of the proclamations.

Meanwhile Gen. Jackson, having seen Gen. Banks safely escaping to the ford of the Potomac, turned away from further pursuit to carry out the other details of his plan, little conceiving of the panic his movements had occasioned in the departments at Washington and the offices of the Governors of States. In fact a captured despatch from Gen. Johnston to Gen. Jackson shows that the chief object of Gen. Jackson's movement was to prevent reënforcements to Gen. McClellan. The effect of this causeless panic on the part of the authorities at Washington was extremely disastrous to the Federal cause; fully as much so as the groundless fears for the safety of the capital, which determined the detention of Gen. McDowell's corps from the army of the Potomac in the beginning of the month of April. The War Department manifestly did not realize the self-evident fact, that Washington being strongly fortified, its surest defence consisted in the presence of a large army threatening Richmond from the peninsula.

On the 28th Gen. Jackson advanced upon Harper's Ferry from Charlestown, driving in before him a Federal reconnoitring force consisting of the 111th Pennsylvania infantry, Col. Schlandecker; the 1st Maryland cavalry, Major Deems, and a section of Reynolds's battery. Small bodies of the enemy appeared in the neighborhood during that and the ensuing day, as if with the object of alluring the Federal forces from their strong defensive position to one where they could be more easily attacked and overpowered. This was the opinion of the Federal commander. The whole force of Gen. Jackson was not before Harper's Ferry. Finding the strength of front presented against him, he determined to collect all the plunder he could convey with prisoners, and retire. To effect this object more securely and to deceive his enemy respecting his movements, he left a force with Gen. Ewell, which became his rear guard, and which made the demonstration upon Harper's Ferry. Gen. R. Saxton, who was in command at Harper's Ferry, fearing a flank movement on the part of the enemy, crossing the Potomac above and occupying Maryland Heights on the Maryland side at the same time that an attack should be made in front, determined to defeat it. He therefore withdrew his forces from Bolivar Heights on the Virginia side to an inner line of defence, on the heights known as Camp Hill, immediately above the town of Harper's Ferry. The occupation of this inner line presented a twofold advantage: First, that being much less extended, it could be held by a smaller force—the enemy, from the nature of the ground, being unable to bring into action a larger force than the Federal; secondly, that it would enable Gen. Saxton to bring his naval battery on the Maryland Heights to bear upon the enemy, as they advanced down the declivity of Bolivar Heights into the valley which separates it from Camp Hill. They would thus be exposed for a considerable time to a heavy fire from this formidable battery, where great elevation would enable it to throw shells directly over the heads of the Federal forces on Camp Hill into the face of the advancing foe. With the force rendered by this contraction of his front available for other purposes, he deemed it prudent to occupy the crest of the hill above the naval battery, on the Maryland shore, to frustrate any attempt of the enemy to take this hill in the rear and turn his batteries against him.

On Friday night, the 30th, about dark, the enemy advanced beyond Bolivar Heights to storm the works on Camp Hill. The batteries on Camp Hill, and the one on Maryland Heights, opened upon them. The scene at this time was very impressive. The night was intensely dark; the hills around were alive with the signal lights of the enemy; the rain descended in torrents; vivid flashes of lightning illumined at intervals the green and magnificent scenery, while the crash of the thunder, echoing among the mountains, drowned into comparative insignificance the roar of Federal artillery.

After an action of about one hour's duration the enemy retired. He made another unsuccessful attack at midnight, with regiments of Mississippi and Louisiana infantry, and after a short engagement disappeared. Signal lights continued to be seen in every direction.

A reconnoissance the next day developed that the rear of the Confederate force passed through Charlestown about one hour before the arrival of the Federal reconnoitring force from Harper's Ferry.

Gen. Jackson was now on his retreat. If he had not accomplished all that he aimed at, the result will show that he was completely successful in cutting off nearly all reënforcements to Gen. McClellan. The fear of having his own retreat cut off now caused his rapid movements. Gen. Fremont from the west, and Col. Kimball with the division of Gen. Shields from the east, were on the march to intercept him. The Confederate movements, which had been made to prevent the retreat of Gen. Jackson from being cut off, consisted in the march of Gen. Smith up the Shenandoah from Strasburg to prevent Gen. Fremont from crossing over, as he was ordered, to Harrisonburg. If Gen. Fremont could have successfully crossed to this point, he might have taken up a position so far in the rear of Gen. Jackson as to have effectually cut him off. It has been said that it was impossible for Gen. Fremont to cross to Harrisonburg. When he received the order to come to the aid of Gen. Banks he was at Franklin, sixty-five miles from Staunton, and a less distance from Harrisonburg. Instead of taking this route, he marched a hundred miles to Strasburg. The Confederate forces which attacked Gen. Milroy and drove him back from McDowell, crossed the mountains, whence they retired to Staunton or Harrisonburg. This was some three weeks previous. The enemy also expected Gen. Fremont to cross to New Market or Harrisonburg, thus showing that no local obstacles prevented. The means of transportation were limited; the supplies could hardly have been found by that route.

On Thursday, the 29th, Gen. Jackson ordered a retrograde movement, and sent off his train and prisoners. Early Friday morning, he left camp between Halltown and Charlestown, and his advance rested the first night at or near Middletown, and the next day (Saturday) entered Strasburg. On Saturday morning, Gen. Ewell, disappearing from Harper's Ferry with the rear guard, followed Gen. Jackson, and encamped on Saturday night at Middletown, thus performing a march of thirty-four miles in one day.

Where now were the pursuers of Gen. Jackson, who were to cut off his retreat? On Saturday night the advance of Gen. Fremont arrived at Brent's Gap, about six miles northwest of Strasburg. It was at noon of the previous day that Gen. Fremont was expected to be in Strasburg by Gen. Shields, who was advancing from the east, having been ordered to be in Front Royal at that hour, which he was. The advance of Gen. Fremont's force on Sunday, June 1, encountered the enemy three or four miles from Strasburg, on the road to Winchester. Gen. Jackson had arrived in Strasburg on the previous day, and tarried to secure the safe arrival and departure of all his force. This encounter of the advance of Gen. Fremont was with the rear of Gen. Jackson. Col. Cluseret, with the 60th Ohio and 8th Virginia and a battery, formed this advance. The contest was with artillery, and was continued by Col. Cluseret until about noon, when he was ordered to retire under the hope of drawing Gen. Jackson on to attack the position which Gen. Fremont had in the meanwhile taken. He had formed a line of battle in a strong position, with Gen. Milroy on the left, Gen. Schenck on the right, and Gen. Stahl in the centre, with Blenker's division in reserve. In this affair five of the 8th Virginia and two of the 60th Ohio were wounded. While Gen. Jackson's rear was thus engaged with the advance of Gen. Fremont, the main body of his troops was pushing on through Strasburg, which was accomplished on Sunday. Thus Gen. Jackson reached Strasburg just in time to pass between Gen. McDowell on the one side, and Gen. Fremont on the other. The advance of Gen. McDowell reached Strasburg soon after the advance of Gen. Fremont. The afternoon wore away without any appearance of Gen. Jackson. The truth was that the attack on the advance of Gen. Fremont was made to divert his attention from the retreating movement Gen. Jackson was then making. A reconnoissance was made during the night beyond Strasburg. On Monday morning, June 2, Gen. Fremont pushed on to Strasburg only to find that Gen. Jackson was on his way to Woodstock unchecked and uninjured. The advance of Gen. Fremont's main force as it entered Strasburg met the 1st New Jersey and the 1st Pennsylvania cavalry under Gen. Bayard, then just coming in, as a part of Gen. McDowell's force.

Meanwhile the force of Gen. Shields which had been ordered to coöperate, had left Manassas Junction, and halted at Haymarket on Tuesday, the 27th of May, as has been stated. On the 28th this division, followed by other troops from Gen. McDowell's corps, advanced as far as Rectortown, thirteen miles, having passed over steep and rocky roads through Thoroughfare Gap. On Thursday, the 29th, it started at five o'clock P. M., with orders to be in Front Royal, twenty-eight miles distant, on the next day at noon, at which time Gen. Fremont was to reach Strasburg. Their entire train was left behind and at the appointed time their advance brigade, under Gen. Kimball, struck the enemy at Front Royal, completely routing them and taking a number of prisoners and a large amount of commissary and quartermaster's stores. On the next day a party of eighteen cavalry entered the outskirts of Strasburg. Finding that the enemy had retired before Gen. Fremont, and that he was following them, Gen. Shields moved up the east side of the Massanutten range of mountains to Luray, while Gen. Fremont advanced on the west side. Gen. Shields was in hopes of striking the enemy at New Market, but finding the Whitehouse and Columbia bridges burned, he resolved to push on further up the east side of the Shenandoah, to intercept the enemy at Conrad's Store (Miller's Bridge), Port Republic, or Waynesborough on the railroad eleven miles east of Staunton. Col. Carroll, in command of the 4th brigade, moved rapidly forward with one regiment, followed by the remainder of the brigade. A violent rain on the night of the 3d caused a delay, and various portions of the command were separated by rapid streams overflowing their banks. He, however, reached Port Republic in advance of the enemy.

At this time forces were gathering in other quarters. The 5th New York cavalry, Col. De Forrest, left Williamsport on Friday night, the 30th, at the time the attack at Harper's Ferry was made, and advanced to Martinsburg on Saturday morning, the 31st, and occupied the town. On the 2d of June Gen. Banks, having recrossed the Potomac, reached Bunker Hill, twelve miles from Winchester. Also by special train from Baltimore, Gen. Sigel arrived at Harper's Ferry on Sunday evening, June 1. During the next forenoon, he inspected the positions of the forces, and ordered a march at four o'clock in the afternoon. The next morning the advance of his division, consisting of Gen. Cooper's brigade, was beyond Charlestown, pushing forward to Winchester, where a junction was formed with Gen. Banks.

Meantime Gen. Fremont was in full chase of the swift-footed foe. Finding that the enemy had escaped him at Strasburg, and being joined by an advance of Gen. McDowell's, consisting of Gen. Bayard's cavalry, he ordered the cavalry and artillery to the front, and pursuit to be given.

A stand was made several times by the retreating enemy, during Monday, the 2d. A mile and a half beyond Strasburg, at a narrow and defensible pass called Fisher's Hill, the road, after crossing a bridge, turns abruptly to the right, and curving to the left passes the base of a thickly wooded hill with a deep ravine on the right, and continues up the hill through a deep and densely wooded defile. Here the first stand was made by the rear guard under Gen. Ewell. His artillery occupied elevated positions overlooking the road on his front for a mile, and commanding a range of hills adjacent to the road on the right of Gen. Milroy. Finding it to be impossible to drive the enemy's centre, Gen. Milroy chose other elevated positions for his guns on the right, and a fierce contest ensued for several hours. The enemy at night encamped three miles beyond Woodstock, while the forces of Gen. Fremont occupied the town.

The pursuit was commenced at seven o'clock

on the next morning, Tuesday, June 3. The advance to Edinburg was made without incident. A military bridge constructed by Gen. Banks across Stony Creek, a swift, wide stream, was half burned by the flying enemy. The delay in repairing the bridge and crossing gave the enemy time to move to Mt. Jackson, eight miles beyond Edinburg, where he halted until noon of the next day, the 4th, when he was again in motion, owing to the approach of Gen. Fremont's advance. One mile beyond Mt. Jackson, is a long bridge over the Shenandoah, a river too swift and deep to be forded. Gen. Jackson left his artillery in position long enough to delay the advance of Gen. Bayard's cavalry, then crossed the bridge before the guns of his pursuers could be brought up, and burned the bridge in face of their cavalry. The bridge was rebuilt by noon of the next day, the 5th, and the army of Gen. Fremont was again in motion. At three o'clock the advance entered New Market, a distance of seven miles, and encamped two miles beyond. On the 6th, Friday, the advance reached Harrisonburg about two o'clock P. M. None of the enemy were seen on the way. Almost every bridge, however small, was found to have been burned. Information was immediately received that a body of Confederate cavalry was near the town. Cannon were planted on the highlands north, and a force of cavalry, under Col. Wyndham, was sent out to reconnoitre, with instructions to engage the enemy if the force was only two or three companies, but not if it was in force and supported by infantry. Some three miles beyond the town, Col. Wyndham discovered the Confederate cavalry and made an effort to oppose them, but unfortunately came upon a large force of infantry, which opened such a volley upon him that his troops were thrown into confusion, and suffered severely, and he himself was taken prisoner. Later in the day Gen. Bayard and Col. Cluseret with a force of cavalry and infantry encountered the enemy. One regiment, the Bucktail rifles of Pennsylvania, numbering one hundred and twenty-five, under Col. Kane, suffered a severe loss of fifty-five men. This small force was rashly led against an overwhelming Confederate mass. The Union forces were finally withdrawn, and the enemy subsequently disappeared. Among the killed of the Confederate force was Col. Ashby, a brave and dashing cavalry officer. The forces of Gen. Fremont remained at Harrisonburg on Saturday, the 7th of June. A reconnoissance was made by Gen. Milroy, about seven miles on the road to Port Republic, where the enemy was found in a position well protected by woods. It seems that Gen. Jackson, before reaching the final bridge across the Shenandoah, determined to fight Gen. Fremont, and thereby check his pursuit. For this purpose he had chosen his position as above stated, at a spot called Cross Keys, near Union Church.

At six o'clock on Sunday morning, June 8, the army of Gen. Fremont began to move, and at half past eight his advance opened upon the enemy. Gen. Fremont says:

"The battle began with heavy firing at eleven o'clock, and lasted, with great obstinacy and violence, until four in the afternoon, some skirmishing and artillery firing continuing from that time until dark."

The right wing was under Gen. Schenck, the left under Gen. Stahl, and the centre under Gen. Milroy. The right wing was not assailed, except by skirmish fighting. The contest was hot on the centre, and Gen. Milroy forced the enemy back from point to point. He had penetrated the centre, and almost reached the enemy's guns, when the order to retire was given. This filled him with indignation, but he obeyed.

Gen. Stahl's brigade was all engaged. Of this, the 45th New York and the 27th Pennsylvania first met the enemy, and being threatened by superior numbers, the 8th New York was sent to support them on the left, and the 41st New York on the right. These regiments were soon all engaged, and the enemy appeared to be bearing heavily upon this wing of the army. It finally gave way, and the whole line was ordered back to a more favorable position. The enemy did not advance, but commenced a retreat. The army encamped that night on the ground where their line was first formed in the morning. They drove the enemy's pickets and skirmishers over it at first, for no attempt was made on the other side to support them. The place where the fighting occurred, and the dead and wounded were strewn over the field, was in the enemy's possession all night.

The loss was very severe on both sides. In Gen. Stahl's command the loss was 69 killed, wounded 254, missing 79. The total loss was estimated by Gen. Fremont, immediately after the battle, at 125 killed and 500 wounded. The enemy's loss was less than this, owing to the shelter of their forces.

The despatch of Gen. Fremont to the War Department, dated on the next morning, says:

"There was no collision with the enemy after dark last night. This morning we renewed the march against him, entering the woods in battle order; his cavalry appearing on our flanks. Gen. Blenker had the left, Gen. Milroy the right, and Gen. Schenck the centre, with a reserve of Gen. Stahl's and Gen. Bayard's brigades."

Port Republic is a small town on the south fork of the Shenandoah river, near which is the bridge by which the river is crossed. It is a few miles distant from Cross Keys, where the conflict between Gens. Fremont and Jackson's forces took place. It has already been stated that Col. Carroll, in command of the advance of Gen. Shields's division up the east side of the Shenandoah, arrived at Port Republic in advance of Gen. Jackson. This means, in advance of the main force of the enemy. On Saturday, the 7th, Col. Carroll received orders to move forward to Waynesborough, distant some thirty-five or thirty-seven miles, by the way of Port Republic, for the purpose of destroying the railroad depot, track, and bridge, at that place, and to seize Gen. Jackson's train and throw his force upon Gen. Jackson's flank. Col. Carroll marched in obedience to these orders, on Saturday afternoon. His infantry, cavalry, and artillery had in the mean time come up, and he started for Conrad's Store with less than a thousand of the former, with one hundred and fifty cavalry, and with a single battery of six guns.

Halting, in the night, six miles before reaching Port Republic, Col. Carroll sent forward a party of scouts, who returned with the information that Gen. Jackson's train was parked near Port Republic, with a drove of beef cattle herded near by, and the whole guarded by about two or three hundred cavalry. On learning this he pushed forward, with the design of capturing the train and cattle, as his orders directed. He halted some two miles from the town, made a reconnoissance, and received further information confirming the report of his scouts, and then dashed into the town with his cavalry and two pieces of artillery, driving the enemy's cavalry out and taking possession of the bridge. He halted there for his infantry to come up, and disposed his pieces and little force to prevent a repulse from the train guard, when, before he had occupied the village any length of time, he was attacked by a force of the enemy superior to his own, and forced to retire and abandon his further march to Waynesborough. Thus the enemy recovered possession of the bridge and held it.

Col. Carroll brought his forces to a stand at the first defensible position, about two miles north of the town. At this time the conflict was going on between Gens. Fremont and Jackson at Cross Keys, several miles distant, and it was over this bridge that Gen. Jackson must retreat or be placed between the forces of Gens. Fremont and Shields. At two o'clock in the afternoon Gen. Tyler arrived to the aid of Col. Carrol.. As commanding one of the brigades of Gen. Shields's division, he had also been ordered to proceed to Waynesborough. He left Columbia Bridge on the 7th, and reached Naked Creek on the same day, and went into camp under orders to march at four A.M. When within six miles of Port Republic he learned of the engagement of Col. (acting brig.-gen.) Carroll, and pressed forward immediately with infantry and artillery to his support, and reached him at two P. M.

Gen. Tyler in his report thus explains his proceedings: "From Col. Daum I learned the enemy had eighteen pieces of artillery, planted so as to completely command all the approaches to the town, and from the engagement with Gen. Carroll that morning, had obtained the range of the different points. Immediately on the arrival of my command, Col. Daum urged an attack with the combined force of infantry and artillery, to which I so far consented as to order the infantry into position under cover of a thick wood which skirted the road, and commenced observing the enemy's position myself, which appeared to me one to defy an army of 50,000 men. I at once sent for Col. Carroll, Lieut.-Col. Schriber, Capts. Clark and Robinson, who had been over the ground; they all agreed in the opinion that an attack would result in the destruction of our little force."

The infantry was ordered back to bivouac for the night, and early in the morning Gen. Tyler was informed that the enemy were advancing evidently with the intention of outflanking him on his left. Forces were ordered up to counteract this movement, which was sucessfully done. The enemy retired into the woods, and a part crossed over and joined the forces attacking the right wing. The engagement now became very heavy on the right, additional troops having been brought up on both sides. Under cover of this conflict, the enemy threw another force into the woods, pressed down upon the battery on the left, and with a sudden dash captured it. The contest continued until Gen. Tyler, perceiving additional reënforcements for the enemy approaching, about ten o'clock ordered his troops to fall back, with a view of retreating until he should meet reënforcements. The retreat, he says, "save the stampede of those who ran before the fight, was as orderly as the advance." The number of his force is stated at three thousand, and that of the enemy much larger. This was evidently the rear guard of Gen. Jackson's army, which had been engaged, and some reenforcements were sent back to it. Gen Jackson retired from before Gen. Fremont on Sunday night, and on Monday morning crossed the bridge at Port Republic, and while the main body continued to retreat, Gen. Tyler was thus held in check.

Meanwhile Gen. Fremont, as has been stated, commenced his march for Port Republic that morning, with his army in battle array. During the afternoon his whole army reached the river opposite the town, and he learned that a portion of Gen. Shields's division had engaged the enemy on both Sunday and Monday on the other side of the river. During the march of Gen. Fremont's forces from the battle field of the preceding day to the river, they could hear brisk cannonading, and see the heavy volumes of smoke arising from the valley where the contest was going on. When they arrived the Confederate force was gone. Thus closed the pursuit of Gen. Jackson with a portion of the forces of four major-generals of the U. S. army on his line of retreat, beside those of Brig.-Gen. Shields. The loss of men on both sides occasioned by this expedition was not very great either in killed, wounded, or prisoners. No accurate details are at present accessible; but the destruction of Federal stores was vast.

On the night of the arrival of Gen. Fremont's forces at the river, an alarm was raised in camp. Horses were harnessed, and men placed in a condition for an immediate movement, but affairs finally became quiet, and a part of a night's rest was obtained. On the next morning, the 10th, orders to march were issued, and the army was soon in motion back to Harrisonburg, a distance of twelve miles, which it reached in a pitiless storm during the afternoon. On Wednesday it moved eighteen miles to New Market, and on Thursday reached Mt. Jackson, seven miles, and encamped for rest. Some forces of Gen. Jackson's army returned to Harrisonburg almost as soon as the Federal troops had left it. The division of Gen. Shields also fell back to New Market.

The force of Gen. Jackson was estimated by his opponents at twenty-five thousand men. The force of Gen. Fremont, on leaving Franklin, was stated to be about twenty thousand men.

It should be stated in this connection, that on the very day on which Gen. Jackson attacked the 1st Maryland, under Col. Kenly, at Front Royal, the 23d of May, the Confederate General, Heath, in the western part of the Mountain Department, advanced rapidly and boldly with nearly three thousand men and attacked Col. Crook, acting brigadier-general, at Greenbrier Bridge, thirty-five miles from McDowell, and nine miles from Camp Alleghany. The command of Col. Crook consisted of the 36th and 44th Ohio and some batteries. The advance of Gen. Heath was met with so much vigor and promptness, that his forces were soon defeated, with the loss of his four pieces of artillery, and one hundred and fifty killed and wounded, and three hundred stand of arms, and a number taken prisoners. On his retreat, the Greenbrier bridge was burned to check or prevent pursuit. This affair occurred on the day previous to the reception of the order by Gen. Fremont to march to the aid of Gen. Banks. The ill success of this enterprise was such that it failed to cause any diversion from Gen. Fremont's command.

This exploit of Gen. Jackson, undoubtedly one of the most brilliant and successful thus far of the war, if its objects are considered, introduced into the whole campaign in Virginia a disturbing element of considerable magnitude. It diverted large masses of men from movements designed to accelerate events on the peninsula, delayed the advance of Gen. McClellan, and deprived him of the reënforcements he expected. The time required for the transfer of troops in the South and Southwest, where the Confederate campaign had been a failure, to Richmond, was thus gained, and when Gen. McClellan was next prepared to move, he found the enemy in accumulating force in front of him.

CHAPTER XIX.

General McClellan crosses the Chickahominy—Battle of Fair Oaks—Retreat of the Enemy—March in the rear of Gen. McClellan—Bridges over the Chickahominy completed—Battle at Mechanicsville—Gen. McClellan moves toward the James—Battles at Savage Station, White Oak Swamp, and Charles City Cross Roads—Confusion of the Enemy—Attack at Malvern Hill—Army at Harrison's Landing—Arrival of Gen. Halleck—His Views—Army of the Potomac withdrawn from the Peninsula.

On the 25th of May Gen. McClellan issued a general order, which was read throughout the camps, directing the troops, as they advanced beyond the Chickahominy, to be prepared for battle at a moment's notice, and to be entirely unencumbered, with the exception of ambulances; to carry three days' rations in their haversacks, leaving their knapsacks with their wagons, which were on the eastern side of the river, carefully parked. Besides practical directions as to conduct, this order says to officers and soldiers: "Let them bear in mind that the Army of the Potomac has never yet been checked, and let them preserve in battle perfect coolness and confidence, the sure forerunners of success."

The divisions from the corps of Gens. Heintzelman and Keyes were among the first to cross the Chickahominy. They took a position on the right bank somewhat advanced therefrom. The right wing rested near New Bridge, the centre at Seven Pines, and the left flank on the White Oak Swamp. Gen. Sumner's corps remained on the east side of the river. On the 30th the Confederate Gen. Johnston made arrangements for an attack upon the Federal army, for the purpose of cutting off, if possible, the corps of Gens. Heintzelman and Keyes before they could be joined by Gen. Sumner. He selected the divisions of Gens. Longstreet, Huger, G. W. Smith, D. H. Hill, and Whiting, His plan was that Gens. Hill and Longstreet should advance by the road to Williamsburg and make the attack in front, and that Gen. Huger should move on the road to Charles City and attack in flank the troops assailed by Gens. Hill and Longstreet. Gen. Smith was ordered to the junction of the New Bridge Road and the Nine Mile Road, and to be in readiness to fall on the right flank of Gen. Keyes and to cover the left of Gen. Longstreet. The forces of Gens. Hill, Longstreet, and Smith were in position early on the morning of Saturday, May 31, and waited until afternoon for Gen. Huger to get into position. Prince de Joinville, who was a competent spectator, thus describes the scenes which followed this attack:

"At the moment it was thus attacked the

Federal army occupied a position having the form of a V. The base of the V is at Bottom Bidge, where the railroad crosses the Chickahominy. The left arm stretches toward Richmond, with this railroad and the road from that city to Williamsburg. There stood the left wing, composed of four divisions echeloned, one behind the other, between Fair Oaks and Savage stations, and encamped in the woods on both sides of the road. The other arm of the V, the right, follows the left bank of the river; that is the right wing. There are these five divisions and the reserve. Should one desire to communicate from one extremity to the other of those two wings, going by Bottom's Bridge, the way is very long, not less than 12 or 15 miles. In an air line the distance, on the contrary, is very trifling, but between the two arms of the V flows the Chickahominy. It was to connect both arms, in the space between them, that the construction of 3 or 4 bridges had been undertaken, only one of which was serviceable on the 31st of May. It had been built by Gen. Sumner, nearly halfway between Bottom's Bridge and the most advanced point of the Federal lines. It saved the army that day from a disaster." The other bridges were not ready. They were structures of logs, and time was required to build them. The approaches were always bad, and the tedious labor of corduroying long distances was necessary.

"It was against the left wing of the army that every effort of the enemy was directed. That wing had its outposts at Fair Oaks station, on the York river railroad, and at a place called Seven Pines, on the Williamsburg road. There the Federals had thrown up a redoubt in a clearing, where a few houses were to be seen, and constructed abatis, to increase the field for sharpshooting of the troops posted there. The rest of the country was completely covered with woods. The previous day there had been a frightful storm, with torrents of rain, and the roads were frightful.

"All at once, about one o'clock in the afternoon, the weather being dark and gloomy, a very spirited fusilade is heard. The pickets and sentries are violently driven in; the woods which surround Fair Oaks and Seven Pines are filled with clouds of the enemy's sharpshooters. The troops rush to arms and fight in desperation; but their adversaries' forces constantly increase, and their losses do not stop them. The redoubt of the Seven Pines is surrounded, and its defenders die bravely. Col. Bailey, of the artillery, among others, there upon his pieces finds a glorious death. In vain Gens. Keyes and Naglee exhaust themselves in a thousand efforts to keep their soldiers together: they are not listened to. In this moment of confusion they perceive a little French battalion, known as the Garde Lafayette, which has remained in good order. They rush to it, place themselves at its head, charge the enemy and retake a battery. The battalion loses a fourth of its men in this charge; but, like true Frenchmen, always and everywhere the same, they cry, "They can call us the Garde Lafourchette now?" alluding to an offensive nickname that had been given them.

"Meanwhile Heintzelman rushes to the rescue with his two divisions. As at Williamsburg, Kearney arrives in good time to reëstablish the fight. Berry's brigade, of this division, composed of Michigan regiments and an Irish battalion, advances firm as a wall into the midst of the disordered mass which wanders over the battle field, and does more by its example than the most powerful reënforcements. About a mile of ground has been lost, fifteen pieces of cannon, the camp of the division of the advanced guard, that of Gen. Casey; but now we hold our own. A sort of line of battle is formed across the woods, perpendicularly to the road and the railroad, and there the repeated assaults of the enemy's masses are resisted. The left cannot be turned, where is the White Oak Swamp, an impassable morass; but the right may be surrounded. At this very moment, in fact, a strong column of Confederates has been directed against that side. If it succeeds in interposing between Bottom's Bridge and the Federal troops, which hold beyond Savage's Station, the entire left wing is lost. It will have no retreat, and is doomed to yield to numbers; but precisely at this moment—that is to say, at 6 o'clock in the evening—new actors appear on the scene. Gen. Sumner, who has succeeded in passing the Chickahominy, with Sedgwick's division, over the bridge constructed by his troops, and who, like a brave soldier, has marched straight through the woods to the sound of the cannon, arrived suddenly on the left flank of the column with which the enemy is endeavoring to cut off Heintzelman and Keyes.

"He plants in the clearing a battery which he has succeeded in bringing with him. They are not those rifled cannon, the objects of extravagant admiration of late, good for cool firing and long range in an open country: these are the true guns for a fight—twelve-pound howitzers,* the old pattern, throwing either a round projectile, which ricochets and rolls, or a heavy package of grape. The simple and rapid discharging of these pieces makes terrible havoc in the opposing ranks. In vain Johnston sends against this battery his best troops, those of South Carolina—the Hampton Legion among others. In vain he rushes on it himself; nothing can shake the Federals, who, at nightfall, valiantly led by Gen. Sumner in person, throw themselves upon the enemy at the point of the bayonet, and drive him furiously, with frightful slaughter and fear, back as far as Fair Oaks Station.

"Night put an end to the combat. On both sides nothing was known of the result of the battle but what each one had seen with his

* They were "Napoleon" guns.—[Ed.

own eyes. Friends and enemies, lost in woods they were unacquainted with, lay down amid heaps of dead and wounded, wherever darkness overtook them. The fatigue of this obstinate struggle as well as the obscurity of the night had imposed on the combatants one of those tacit truces so frequent in war.

"Evidently Johnston had flattered himself, in throwing all his forces on the four divisions of the left wing, that he could annihilate them before any aid could come to them from the main body of the army on the left bank of the Chickahominy. For the moment he had recoiled before the energetic resistance of those four divisions, and also before the furious and unforeseen attack of Sumner's troops. No doubt he had counted on the terrible storm of the previous day to have swelled the Chickahominy so as to render the establishment of a bridge impossible, or to sweep away in its overflowing waters those already established; but the capricious river baffled his plans, as it did some hours later those of his adversaries. The effect of the deluge was not immediate; the rise in the water delayed its appearance 24 hours. Was this unhoped-for delay turned to account with all desirable activity on the part of the Federals? That is a question which will remain always in dispute, as are so many others of the same kind, which form one of the necessary chapters of the history of most great battles.

"It was only at one o'clock in the afternoon that the action had commenced. We had waited some time to ascertain if the attack on that side was not a feint, intended to draw the Federal troops to that point while the bulk of the enemy's forces was hastening to debouch on the left bank. We had been promptly relieved of our uncertainty by the violence of the attack and by the reports of the aeronauts, who saw the entire Confederate army marching to the point of attack.

"Then Sumner had received orders to cross the water with his two divisions. He had executed the movement with rapidity, marching at the head of his column, without any other guide than the sound of the cannon, and he arrived at the right moment and at the critical place. But some persons thought then, and still think, that if, at the moment Sumner received the order to cross the river, the same order had been given to all the divisions of the right wing, it would have been practicable. We fancy what might have happened if, in place of throwing 15,000 men on Johnston's flank, 50,000 had been thrown. Sumner's bridge, doubtless, would not have answered for the crossing of so many. At midnight the tail end of his column was still crossing, struggling against all the difficulties which bridges formed of trunks of trees that turn under the feet, muddy sloughs and a dark night—the darkness rendered still deeper by the thickness of the woods—present to horses and artillery. Several bridges were, however, ready to be thrown across at other points. It was necessary to work without a moment's loss to construct them, and not be disturbed by the obstacles the enemy would not have failed to present to the undertaking. A brigade was displayed for full effect and scarecrow fashion, opposite the points naturally marked out for crossing; but the stake was so large, the result so important, and the occasion itself so unforeseen and so favorable for playing a decisive part, that nothing, in our opinion, should have prevented that operation from being attempted.

"Here, again, was evident that American slowness which belongs much more to the character of the army than that of its chief. It was not until 7 o'clock in the evening that the idea of securing all the bridges without delay, and causing the whole army to cross at daybreak to the right bank of the Chickahominy, was entertained.

"It was now too late. Four hours had been lost, and the opportunity—that moment so fleeting, in war as in other circumstances—had gone. The rise, on which Johnston had vainly counted, and which had not hindered Sumner from crossing, came on during the night. The river rose suddenly from two feet, and continued to swell with rapidity, carrying away the new bridges. tearing up and sweeping off the trees which formed the planking of Sumner's bridges, and covering the entire valley with its overflowing waters. Nothing could cross.

"At the earliest dawn of day the combat was resumed with great fury on the left bank. The enemy came on in a body, but without order or method, and rushed upon the Federals, who, knowing that they were inferior in numbers and without hope of being supported, did not attempt to do more than resist and hold their ground. They fought with fierce determination on both sides, without any noise, without any cries, and whenever they were too hardly pressed they made a charge with the bayonet. The artillery, placed on the eminences in the rear, fired shell over the combatants. Ah! I could have wished that all those who, forgetful of the past, and impelled by I do not know what kind of egotistical calculation, have lavished their encouragement on the fatal rebellion of slaveowners, could have been present at this fratricidal struggle. I could have wished them, as a punishment, a sight of this terrible battle field, where the dead and dying were piled up by thousands. I wished that they could have seen those temporary ambulances formed around the few habitations found here and there. Oh! what misery—oh! what suffering! The ambulances had something about them particularly horrible. The houses were altogether too few to contain the smallest proportion of the wounded, and they were therefore compelled to lay them outside; but although they did not make any complaints, and bore their fate with the most stoical courage, their exposure in one position beneath the rays of the sun of the middle of June soon became intolerable. They were then to be seen putting forth all their remaining strength, and crawling to seek a little shade. I will always remember a bed of roses, whose sweet-scented flowers I was admiring while conversing with one of my friends, when he drew my attention to one of these unfortunate men, who had just died beneath its bushes. We looked at each other without saying a word, the heart being oppressed with the most painful emotion. Mournful scenes, from which the pen of the writer, like the eye of the spectator, hastened to turn away.

"Toward midday the fire gradually diminished, then ceased. The enemy retreated; but the Federals were not in a position to pursue them. No one then knew what a loss the Southerners had just suffered in the person of their commander, Gen. Johnston, who was severely wounded. It was to his absence that was owing, in a great measure, the unskilful attacks against the Federal army in the morning. When the firing ceased at midday, the Confederates, tired of the prolonged strife which they had been sustaining, and being no longer commanded, were, it is said (for in the midst of these immense woods one sees nothing, and is compelled to guess everything), in a state of inextricable confusion. Who can say what would have been the result if at this moment the 35,000 fresh troops left on the other side of the Chickahominy had appeared on the flank of this disordered mass after having successfully crossed the bridges?

"Such is the history of this singular battle, which, although complicated by incidents superior to human will, must not be taken otherwise than as a type of American battles. The conflict was a bloody one, for the North had lost 5,000 men, the South at least 8,000; but the results were barren on one side as on the other. Although the losses of the enemy were much greater than those of the Federals, the result was especially distressing to the latter. They had lost a rare opportunity of striking a decisive blow. These occasions did not return, and therefore, in the circumstances in which they were placed, the result was against them."

The crossing of Gen. Sumner's corps commenced about four o'clock in the afternoon. At that time the head of the advance, Gen. Gorman's brigade, turned from the swamps on the left bank of the river to cross by the bridge built by Gen. Sumner,—a battery moved next, then Gen. Burns's brigade, then artillery, and finally Gen. Dana's brigade, all of Gen. Sedgwick's division. In consequence of the morasses, all the batteries except Kirby's were left behind; but all the troops except the 19th Massachusetts, which was detached to assist the artillery, were moved swiftly onward to the scene of action. Gen. Richardson's division was detained until quite late in the evening by the obstructed causeway. At seven o'clock, it was in the position to which it had been assigned. It took no part in the battle on Saturday.

Now was the time to capture the city. The retreat of the army caused great consternation at Richmond. The Confederate force had retired in confusion, and if they had been sharply followed up, the gates of the city would have been reached, if friend and foe had not gone in together. It is useless to speculate on possibilities. The force with which Gen. McClellan commenced his march had been diminished before Yorktown and Williamsburg, and by constant skirmishing. It garrisoned Yorktown and Williamsburg, and occupied the White House, and the line of the railroad. It had received no reënforcements up to this time except the division of Franklin. It was also impossible for him to move the corps of Gens. Porter and Franklin over the Chickahominy at the decisive moment, as even the bridge on which Gen. Sumner had crossed had been so far destroyed by the river, which was swollen by the rains of Friday and Saturday, that it was impassable for a single horseman. The three corps which had been engaged in the battles of Saturday and Sunday were too much cut up and wearied, by their conflict with superior numbers, to be able to pursue the retreating Confederates, particularly as they might probably have been met at the outworks of the city by fresh troops, in numbers fully equal to themselves, and a strong artillery in position. He was in no condition to risk anything. He had fought the enemy in equal or superior numbers, and they had retired in confusion. The corps of Gen. McDowell, if on hand now, might have taken Richmond, but without it the commanding general was not strong enough to risk its immediate attack. There were other considerations to govern his conduct. He was leading an invading army without reserves to fall back upon. A repulse would have ended in serious, if not complete disaster. Such a result to the peninsular campaign would have been fatal to the cause to which the Army of the Potomac was devoted. It would have convinced foreign powers that there was such a degree of military strength in the Confederacy as to render the immediate recognition of its independence both safe and politic. But there was probably one consideration which outweighed all others, and exerted a decisive influence upon the movements. This was the certain and safe reception of sufficient supplies. The single line of railroad was not capable of transporting them. The horses were kept on half forage, and if the distance had been increased, the army itself would have suffered. What hope was there of holding Richmond, even if it had been taken, with a line of transportation not capable of bringing forward sufficient to sustain the army, and one which, from the inadequate force to guard it, was liable at any moment to be broken up? Finally, for many days after the battle, the fields and roads were in such condition as to render it impossible to move any amount of artillery over them. To have advanced without it would have placed infantry in front of works armed with heavy guns.

The danger of his position was soon demonstrated to the commanding general. It was determined in Richmond at this time, to penetrate the lines of the Federal army, and make a full and thorough reconnoissance of its position and strength. For this purpose, early on the 8th of June, Gen. J. E. B. Stuart, with the 1st, Col. Fitz Hugh Lee; 9th, Col. F. H. Fitz Hugh Lee; and 4th Virginia cavalry, Lieut. Gardner; the Jeff. Davis troop, with two pieces of flying artillery, a 12-pound howitzer, and a 6-pound rifled English piece, numbering about fifteen hundred men, left Richmond and proceeded down the Charlottesville turnpike. That night they encamped at Ashland, not deeming it safe to proceed after dusk, and communicated by signal rockets with Richmond. As soon as day dawned, they proceeded carefully and cautiously, and penetrated the Federal lines. Near Hanover Court House, two or three small bodies of Federal cavalry were met, and skirmishing ensued, but the latter, being unable to withstand the heavy Confederate force, were quickly routed. The camps of these Federal outposts were visited and destroyed; wagons on the road were overtaken and burnt, and the entire route from Ashland by Hanover Court House to Tunstall's Station, on the York River railroad, was to this force a continuous scene of triumph and destruction. Commissary and quartermasters' stores were seized and burned; prisoners and horses were taken and sent to the rear. The amount of property destroyed, however, was very small.

Upon approaching the railroad, cars were heard advancing, and the whistle sounded. By orders, every man was instantly dismounted and ranged beside the track. Thinking the force to be a friendly one, the train was stopped, when one company of the troop opening fire, disclosed its character. The train was immediately started under full steam for the Chickahominy, and despite logs placed on the track, made its escape. It consisted chiefly of uncovered platform cars, on which were some soldiers who were fired upon and killed or wounded. A detachment was immediately sent toward the White House on the Pamunkey river, where a number of wagons loaded with stores, and four transport vessels were found. Two of the vessels with their stores were destroyed, and a few wagons at Garlick's Landing. New Kent Court House was made the rendezvous whither the main body had gone, and where they were soon joined by this detachment. Here a halt was made until midnight. Some prisoners were taken, and sutlers' stores consumed or destroyed. At midnight they quietly moved by a lonely road toward the Chickahominy, and passing near a considerable body of the Federal forces, they reached its banks a little before dawn on Sunday, the 11th, and were ready to cross. They had arrived far below the bridges, and where deep water flows, and knew not how to cross. Their perplexity is thus described by a Confederate writer: "Here was an awful situation for a gallant band! Directed to Blind Ford, it was fifteen feet deep! The enemy had blocked up all the main roads, and had thousands scouring the country, eager to entrap or slaughter it. And without means to cross! Quietly taking precautions against all surprise, strict silence being enjoined upon the prisoners, first one horseman plunged into the flood, and then another at different points—all too deep; no ford discoverable, no bridge! The horses, it was thought, would follow each other, and swim the stream—it was tried, and the horses carried away by the current! Breaking into small parties, the cavalrymen swam and reswam the river with their horses, and when some fifty or more had been landed, a strange but friendly voice whispered in the dark, 'The old bridge is a few yards higher up—it can be mended!' 'Twas found, and mended it could be! Quietly working, tree after tree was felled, earth and twigs and branches were carried and piled up on the main props; old logs were rolled and patched across the stream; yet after long and weary labor the bridge was built, and the long and silent procession of cavalry, artillery, prisoners and spoils, safely and quietly passed this frail impromptu bridge, scarcely any sounds being heard but the rush of waters beneath. Once across and in the swamps, all was industry and expedition. Artillery axles sank low in the mire—ten Yankee horses were hitched to each piece, and as the first rays of morning crimsoned the tree tops, the long line rapidly sought the shade of woods away from the Federal lines. Yet the troops had not proceeded far when the advance was halted. 'Who comes there?' cried the Federal horsemen in the swamp. 'Who goes there?' calls another, and quicker than thought the advance guard dashes away into the open ground; the Federals fire half a dozen shots, and rush in pursuit. Into the thicket some half dozen Federal horsemen dart and are surrounded and made prisoners."

The crossing was made thirteen miles from Gen. McClellan's headquarters, and five miles from his pickets. They were now soon within the lines of the Confederate army. The delay caused by the vigorous skirmishing with the enemy encountered, caused them afterward to make so much haste to escape, that the amount of property destroyed was small, and estimated at fifty thousand dollars. Three hundred mules and some prisoners were taken away. This small force of the enemy's cavalry had passed entirely round and in the rear of the Federal army. The hope for the coöperation of Gen. McDowell amid these perilous scenes was again, for the third time, now rekindled in the mind of Gen. McClellan, and not entirely in vain. On the 10th of June, Gen. McDowell wrote as follows:

June 10, 1862.

Maj.-Gen. G. B. McClellan, Commanding Department of Virginia, before Richmond:

For the third time I am ordered to join you, and hope this time to get through. In view of the remarks made with reference to my leaving you and not joining you before, by your friends, and of something I have heard as coming from you on that subject, I wish to say I go with the greatest satisfaction, and hope to arrive with my main body in time to be of service. McCall goes in advance by water. I will be with you in ten days with the remainder by Fredericksburg.

IRVIN McDOWELL,
Major-General Commanding.

On the 12th, he again wrote, as follows:

HEADQUARTERS DEPARTMENT OF THE RAPPAHANNOCK, MANASSAS, *June* 12, 1862.

Maj.-Gen. G. B. McClellan, Commanding Department of Virginia, before Richmond:

The delay of Maj.-Gen. Banks to relieve the division of my command in the valley beyond the time I had calculated on, will prevent my joining you with the remainder of the troops I am to take below at as early a day as I named. My third division (McCall's) is now on the way. Please do me the favor to so place it that it may be in a position to join the others as they come down from Fredericksburg. IRVIN McDOWELL,
Major-General Commanding.

Contrary to the expectation of both, the division of Gen. McCall was the only one of Gen. McDowell's corps which subsequently reached the army of the Potomac.

On the next day after the battle of Fair Oaks, above described, Gen. McClellan recovered without resistance the stations of Fair Oaks and Seven Pines, and the two armies were once more in the same position as before.

On the 2d of June President Davis issued the following address to the Confederate army:

EXECUTIVE OFFICE, *June* 2, 1862.

To the Army of Richmond:

I render to you my grateful acknowledgments for the gallantry and good conduct you displayed in the battles of the 31st of May, and the 1st instant, and with pride and pleasure recognize the steadiness and intrepidity with which you attacked the enemy in position, captured his advanced intrenchments, several batteries of artillery, and many standards, and everywhere drove them from the open field.

At a part of your operations it was my fortune to be present. On no other occasion have I witnessed more of calmness and good order than you exhibited while advancing into the very jaws of death, and nothing could exceed the prowess with which you closed upon the enemy when a sheet of fire was blazing in your faces.

In the renewed struggle in which you are on the eve of engaging, I ask and can desire but a continuance of the same conduct which now attracts the admiration and pride of the loved ones you have left at home.

You are fighting for all that is dearest to men; and, though opposed to a foe who disregards many of the usages of civilized war, your humanity to the wounded and the prisoners was the fit and crowning glory to your valor.

Defenders of a just cause, may God have you in His holy keeping! JEFFERSON DAVIS.

Gen. McClellan now set to work to complete in a substantial manner the bridges across the Chickahominy and put the two wings of his army in communication with each other in spite of any inundations. Entrenchments were then thrown up along the whole line. The right wing, consisting of the divisions of Gens. McCall, Morrell, and Sykes, was posted on the left bank of the Chickahominy from Beaver Dam Creek to a point below New Bridge. The centre, consisting of Gens. Smith's, Sedgwick's, and Richardson's divisions, was stretched in a line from Golding on the right bank of the river to a point south of the York river railroad. The left wing, consisting of Gens. Hooker's, Kearney's, and Couch's divisions, extended from the left of Gen. Richardson's posision to a point considerably south of the Williamsburg stage road, on the borders of White Oak swamp. The Confederate line pressed so close to the Federal line on the right bank of the river that neither could advance a regiment outside their respective breastworks without provoking a contest. In this position the two armies remained until near the close of the month.

The demonstration in the rear of the Federal army had convinced the commanding general that a change of position might become necessary, and some vessels loaded with ammunition, provisions, and other supplies were wisely sent to James river near City Point, but no further steps for this purpose were taken.

On Wednesday, the 25th of June, the first movement on the part of Gen. McClellan was made. This consisted in directing Gen. Hooker to take up an advanced position of a mile on Fair Oaks farm, near the Williamsburg road leading directly to Richmond. It was calculated that this movement might be followed by a general resistance on the part of the Confederates, which would renew the battle of Fair Oaks, and by the advantage of the bridges the whole army could be concentrated. If the battle was not renewed then it would be one step in advance toward Richmond. The ground Gen. Hooker was ordered to occupy was taken, lost and retaken with a loss of from four to five hundred men. He was ably supported by Brig.-Gens. Grover and Sickles. During the ensuing night information was received that Gen. Jackson, returned from the Shenandoah Valley, was in force near Hanover Court House. This indicated that the Confederate army had now been concentrated, and the object of Gen. Jackson in that position was to attack the Federal communications, and cut them off by seizing the York river railway in their rear. The advance upon Richmond could not therefore be further prosecuted by the diminished forces of the Federal army. Gen. Hooker was consequently recalled from his advanced position on the next day.

It appears that on the 25th a council of all the Confederate generals was held at Richmond. Gens. Lee, Baldwin, Jackson, A. P. Hill, D. H. Hill, Huger, Longstreet, Branch, Wise, Anderson, Whiting, Ripley, and Magruder were present. It was determined that Gen. Jackson should move upon the right flank of the Federal army, and if Gen. McDowell remained inactive in his position near Fredericksburg, then a general and simultaneous attack was to be made upon the whole line of Gen. McClellan.

A demonstration along the Richmond road made at that time by Gen. McDowell would have rendered the flank march of Gen. Jackson entirely impracticable. This demonstration was feared by Gen. Lee; but he was unaware that it had then been determined at Washington to concentrate the corps of Gen. McDowell with the other forces before Washington and form the army of Virginia under Gen. Pope. The order for that purpose was issued on the 27th, at Washington, the 2nd day after the council of officers at Richmond; and thus prevented entirely the movement feared by Gen. Lee.

On the 26th Gen. Jackson reached Ashland, there to commence his flanking operations. His advanced guard drove in the little Federal force posted there and pushed on without loss of time to Hanover Court House, where he threw forward Gen. Branch's brigade between the Chickahominy and the Pamunkey rivers to establish a junction with Gen. Hill, who was to cross the former stream at Meadow Bridge. It was the movement of Gen. Hill's troops, seen pouring out of Richmond by the Federal army, in the direction where Gen. Jackson was known to be, which convinced them of the serious work at hand on their right. Gen. D. H. Hill began his offensive operations about 1 P. M. by an attack upon Mechanicsville and met with a brave resistance. Gen. McCall's Pennsylvania reserves were stationed there supported by Gen. Morrell and Gen. Sykes, and strongly intrenched for defence. Storming attacks were made again and again with fury, and were as often repelled with a cool determination. In vain Gen. D. H. Hill sent his aids in quest of Gen. Branch. The latter did not arrive until night, when the conflict had ended.

At this time eight divisions of the Federal army were on the right bank of the Chickahominy occupying entrenchments fronting Richmond. Before these troops lay the mass of the Confederate army also in entrenched positions. Upon the left bank of the river connected by numerous bridges was Gen. Fitz-John Porter with two divisions and Gen. Sykes' regulars. It was against this latter force that the Confederate attack was made. Two separate armies of great force were thus about to attack Gen. McClellan, and his position was extremely critical. If he concentrated on the left bank of the Chickahominy, he abandoned the attempt to capture Richmond, and risked a disastrous retreat upon the White House and Yorktown with the entire Confederate army in pursuit, and where he could hope for no support. If he moved to the right bank of the river, he risked the cutting off of his communications with the White House by the enemy, who might seize the railroad over which his supplies came. He would then be forced to open new communications with James river, and move at once in that direction. There he would receive the support of the navy, and if reënforced could operate against Richmond or Petersburg, the fall of the latter place involving the fall of the former. This latter movement had been thought of some time previous, and transports, with a prudent foresight, had been sent to the James river. It was now determined upon. The distance from Fair Oaks to the James river was about seventeen miles. A single road only existed by which the baggage and stores could be moved. This was exposed in front to the enemy, who, by several roads radiating from Richmond, could throw a considerable force at once upon different points. The activity with which this movement was performed was such that it was nearly completed before it was anticipated by the enemy.

During the night in which Gen. D. H. Hill was held in check at Mechanicsville, the whole of Gen. Porter's baggage was sent over to the right bank of the river and united with the long train which was to set out on the evening of the 27th for James river. At the same time orders were given to reship or destroy all the stores along the railroad to White House and to evacuate that depot. This duty was assigned to Gen. Stoneman with a flying column. He was also ordered to delay the advance of the enemy and to fall back after the execution of these orders on Yorktown. All this was successfully done.

For the next day, Friday, the 27th, the orders to Gen. McCall on the extreme right were to fall back on the bridges thrown across the Chickahominy at Gaines's Mill. Joining the other troops of Gen. Porter's corps, consisting of the division of Gen. Morrell and the regulars of Gen. Sykes, their duty was to make a stand in front of the bridges in order to give the army time to execute its general movement. Gen. Porter, with this force, was not to cross the bridges until evening, and then to destroy them. The manner in which these orders were executed will now appear.

Scarcely had the morning of the 27th dawned, when the Confederate forces, under Gen. D. H. Hill, that had been held in check the previous evening, opened a tremendous fire of artillery upon the front of Gen. McCall, who, upon seeing the brigade of Gen. Branch, ordered on the previous day to support Gen. Hill, advancing to attack his right, began to fall back, fighting, further down the stream. This secured the crossing of the Chickahominy at Mechanicsville to the Confederates, and the first reënforcements ordered from their main body during the night, consisting of the veteran corps of Gen. Longstreet, and the division of Gen. A. P. Hill, now arrived. An order to advance was now given all along the Confederate line, except the right wing under Gen. Magruder, which now confronted Gen. McClellan on the right bank of the Chickahominy. The divisions of Gens. A. P. Hill, Anderson, and Whiting formed the centre, and moved toward Coal Harbor, while Gens. Jackson, D. H. Hill, and Longstreet formed the left nearer the Pamunkey river. Apprehensions were still entertained by Gen.

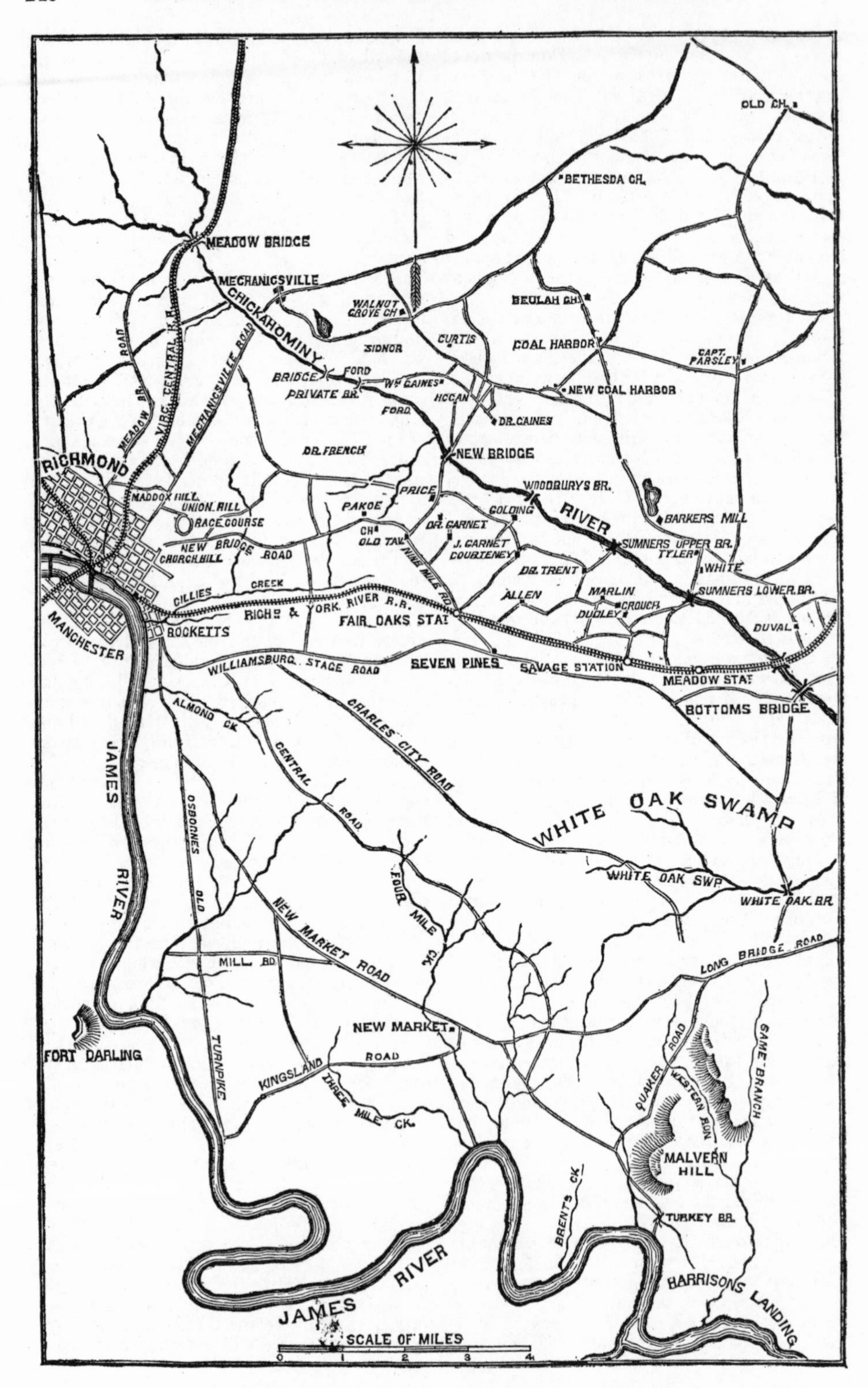
OLD CH.
BETHESDA CH.
MEADOW BRIDGE
MECHANICSVILLE
CHICKAHOMINY
WALNUT GROVE CH.
BEULAH CH.
SIDNOR
CURTIS
COAL HARBOR
CAPT. PARSLEY
BRIDGE
FORD
PRIVATE BR.
Wm. GAINES
HOGAN
NEW COAL HARBOR
FORD
DR. GAINES
DR. FRENCH
NEW BRIDGE
RICHMOND
MEADOW BR. ROAD
VIRG. CENTRAL R.R.
MECHANICSVILLE ROAD
MADDOX HILL
UNION HILL
RACE COURSE
PRICE
WOODBURYS BR.
PAKOE
GOLDING
RIVER
BARKERS MILL
CH.
OLD TAV.
DR. GARNET
J. GARNET
COURTENEY
NEW BRIDGE ROAD
CHURCH HILL
NINE MILE RD.
DR. TRENT
SUMNERS UPPER BR.
TYLER
WHITE
SUMNERS LOWER BR.
MARLIN
CROUCH
DUDLEY
ALLEN
GILLIES CREEK
RICHd. & YORK RIVER R.R.
FAIR OAKS STAT.
DUVAL
MANCHESTER
ROCKETTS
WILLIAMSBURG STAGE ROAD
SEVEN PINES
SAVAGE STATION
MEADOW STAT.
BOTTOMS BRIDGE
ALMOND CK.
CHARLES CITY ROAD
CENTRAL ROAD
JAMES
WHITE OAK SWAMP
OSBORNES OLD TURNPIKE
RIVER
FOUR MILE CK.
WHITE OAK SWP.
WHITE OAK BR.
NEW MARKET ROAD
LONG BRIDGE ROAD
MILL RD
NEW MARKET
FORT DARLING
KINGSLAND ROAD
THREE MILE CK.
QUAKER ROAD
WESTERN RUN
GAME BRANCH
MALVERN HILL
BRENTS CK.
TURKEY BR.
JAMES RIVER
HARRISONS LANDING
SCALE OF MILES
0 1 2 3 4

Lee of the approach of Gen. McDowell, and it was not until he received reliable intelligence of the latter's inactivity that he resolved upon a general attack. As soon, therefore, as he was informed that Gen. Jackson had reached Coal Harbor, steps were taken for an immediate attack on the retiring corps of Gen. Porter, which was supposed to be the mass of Gen. McClellan's army, and which had taken up the position it was ordered to hold on the left bank before the bridges. The Confederate attack was opened by the columns of Gen. D. H. Hill, Anderson, and Pickett. These brave masses rushed with "thundering hurrahs" upon the musketry of Gen. Porter's corps, and whole ranks went down under the terrible fire that met them. After a fierce struggle the Confederate troops began to give way, and at length all orders and encouragements were vain. They were falling back in the greatest disorder. Immediately Gen. Cobb appeared on the field with his legion, and the 19th North Carolina, and 14th Virginia, and renewed the attack, but all their efforts were in vain. Broken to pieces and disorganized, the fragments of that legion came rolling back from the charge. The 19th North Carolina lost eight standard bearers, and most of their officers were either killed or wounded. The shattered regiments of Gens. Hill and Anderson were again led up, but their foes quietly and coolly held out against every attack that was made. During this moment of success for the Federal army, Gen. McClellan hastened to throw upon the left bank all the troops not absolutely necessary to guard the lines in front of Richmond. It was nearly night when some of the divisions reached the river, and at this time the Confederate left and reserves had been brought up. The weight of their attack was made on the Federal left, where the troops had sustained an unequal fight all day, and were worn out, having fired almost their last cartridge. The left gave way and disbanded. This disorder extended until it reached the centre of the Federal lines, which fell back in increasing confusion, until the fresh brigades of Gens. Meagher and French were met. The vigorous shouts of these troops, and the placing a few guns anew in battery and opening fire served to check the enemy, who paused at this final determination, and darkness closed the contest at Gaines's Mill.

The left wing, under Gen. Porter, subsequently supported from the main body, had accomplished the purpose of holding the Confederates in check, and that night the train of five thousand wagons, the seige train, a herd of twenty-five hundred oxen, and other material was in motion for James river. During the night the troops of Gen. McClellan repassed the bridges of the Chickahominy in perfect order, destroying them after they had passed. The field of battle, with the dead, and those most seriously wounded, a few guns and some prisoners. was abandoned. The corps of Gen. Keyes in the advance toward James river took possession of the road across the White Oak Swamp, and the principal lines of communication by which the Federal army could be annoyed by their enemies.

Meantime the Confederate officers and men supposed, from the manner in which the day closed, leaving them in possession of the field of battle and its spoils, that Gen. McClellan was completely cut off from his base of retreat. The capture or destruction of the entire Federal army was regarded as certain. The rejoicing bordered on frenzy. Their demonstration on the 28th was made to the White House, where the immense stores which were expected to fall into their hands were found to have been destroyed, and nothing but ruins remained. The burial of the dead, and the care for the wounded, and repose for the troops, and uncertainty as to the position of the Federal army, caused the day to pass without any movement of the Confederate troops. The mass of them were now on the left bank of the Chickahominy, over which the bridges had been destroyed, while Gen. McClellan's army united was on the right bank. Time now was worth everything to them. Before they could be attacked, however, it was necessary for the Confederate force to rebuild the bridges, or to fall back some distance to the Mechanicsville bridge. It was not until the reports of the state of affairs at the White House were made in the afternoon of the 28th, and the statements of prisoners, that Gen. Lee comprehended the real movements of Gen. McClellan, and that he was on his way to James river to form a junction with the fleet. The twelve brigades of Gens. D. H. Hill and Longstreet were instantly put in motion to give the death blow to the enemy, whom they supposed now to be flying.

The position of Gen. McClellan on Saturday night was such that the Confederate officers, who were unaware of his design, were confident of his capture. Having abandoned, and, as they supposed, been driven from all his strongholds on the north side of the Chickahominy, cut off from all communication with his supplies at the White House, and with the Chickahominy in his rear, and the divisions of Gens. Longstreet, Magruder, and Huger in his front, all hopes of his escape were thought to be impossible.

The morning of the 29th was spent by Gen. McClellan's troops in destroying all that could not be carried away from the camps. A complete railroad train, locomotive, tender and cars, which had been left on the track, was sent headlong over the broken bridge into the river. Nothing was left but three siege guns which could not be moved.

The corps of Gens. Sumner and Franklin had been left in the works at Fair Oaks with instructions to evacuate and protect the baggage and supply trains on their way to the river. Hardly had they commenced to fall back on the railroad and Williamsburg turnpike, when the enemy, perceiving the movement, pressed forward, giving the former barely time to place their men in position. The attack was commenced by the Confederates about two o'clock P. M., about one mile and a half above Savage's Station, and the conflict continued until near night. The enemy, advancing in solid masses to within a short distance of the artillery, suffered severely and were repulsed. During the night Gens. Sumner and Franklin fell back to White Oak Swamp bridge.

On the morning of Monday, the 30th of June, all the troops and all the trains were in safety beyond White Oak bridge, which presented a new obstacle to the Confederates. Gens. Sumner and Franklin were left to act as a rear guard, and hold the passage of the White Oak Swamp, whilst Gens. Heintzelman, with the divisions of Gens. Hooker, Kearny, Sedgwick, and McCall, were placed at the point of intersection of the roads leading from Richmond, called Charles City cross roads. These movements protected the trains until they arrived at the James river, precisely at the time when the transports with provisions and ammunition and hospital stores arrived from Fortress Monroe.

The advance of the Confederate force was actively resumed early in the morning. Gens. D. H. Hill, Whiting, and Ewell, under the command of Gen. Jackson, crossed the Chickahominy by the Grapevine bridge, and followed the Federal retreat by the Williamsburg road and Savage's Station. Gens. Longstreet, A. P. Hill, Huger, and Magruder took the Charles City road with the intention of cutting off the Federal retreat. At the White Oak Swamp the left wing under Gen. Jackson came up with the Federal force under Gens. Franklin and Sumner, about 11 A. M. They had crossed the stream and burned the bridge behind them. An artillery fire was opened upon both sides, which continued with great severity and destruction until night. The result of this battle was to prevent the further advance of the enemy in this direction, which was the single line of road over which the trains had passed.

Late on the same day, a battle was fought between the forces under Gen. Heintzelman and the main force of the enemy, which attempted to advance by the Charles City road to cut off the retreat. This force was led by Gens. Longstreet, A. P. Hill, and Huger. The former, however, being called away, the command devolved upon Gen. Hill. As the masses advanced upon the Federal batteries of heavy guns they were received with such a destructive fire of artillery and musketry as threw them into disorder. Gen. Lee sent all his disposable troops to the rescue, but the Federal fire was so terrible as to disconcert the coolest veterans. Whole ranks of the Confederate troops were hurled to the ground. Says an actor in the conflict, "The thunder of the cannon, the cracking of the musketry from thousands of combatants, mingled with the screams of the wounded and the dying, were terrific to the ear and to the imagination." The conflict thus continued within a narrow space for hours, and not a foot of ground was won by the Confederates. Night was close at hand. The Federal lines were strengthened and the confidence of the Confederate general began to falter. The losses of his exhausted and worn out troops in attempting to storm the batteries were terrible. Orders were given to Gen. Jackson to cover the retreat in case the army should have to fall back, and directions were sent to Richmond to get all the public property ready for removal. The Federal forces, perceiving the confusion, began step by step to press forward. The posture of affairs at this time is thus related by a Confederate officer: "The enemy, noticing our confusion, now advanced, with the cry, 'Onward to Richmond!' Yes, along the whole hostile front rang the shout, 'Onward to Richmond!' Many old soldiers who had served in distant Missouri and on the plains of Arkansas wept in the bitterness of their souls like children. Of what avail had it been to us that our best blood had flowed for six long days?—of what avail all our unceasing and exhaustless endurance? Everything, everything seemed lost, and a general depression came over all our hearts. Batteries dashed past in headlong flight; ammunition, hospital and supply wagons rushed along, and swept the troops away with them from the battle field. In vain the most frantic exertion, entreaty and self-sacrifice of the staff officers! The troops had lost their foot-hold, and all was over with the Southern Confederacy.

"In this moment of desperation Gen. A. P. Hill came up with a few regiments he had managed to rally, but the enemy was continually pressing nearer and nearer; louder and louder their shouts, and the watchword, 'On to Richmond!' could be heard. Cavalry officers sprang from their saddles and rushed into the ranks of the infantry regiments, now deprived of their proper officers. Gen. Hill seized the standard of the Fourth North Carolina regiment, which he had formerly commanded, and shouted to the soldiers, 'If you will not follow me, I will perish alone.' Upon this a number of officers dashed forward to cover their beloved general with their bodies; the soldiers hastily rallied, and the cry 'Lead on, Hill; head your old North Carolina boys!' rose over the field. And now Hill charged forward with this mass he had thus worked up to the wildest enthusiasm. The enemy halted when they saw these columns, in flight a moment before, now advancing to the attack, and Hill burst upon his late pursuers like a famished lion. A fearful hand to hand conflict now ensued, for there was no time to load and fire. The ferocity with which this combat was waged was incredible. It was useless to beg the exasperated men for quarter; there was no moderation, no pity, no compassion in that bloody work of bayonet and knife. The son sank dying at his father's feet; the father forgot that he had a child—a dying child; the brother did not see that a brother was expiring a few paces from him; the friend heard not the last groans of a friend; all natural ties were dissolved; only one feeling, one thirst, panted in every bosom —revenge. Here it was that the son of Major Peyton, but fifteen years of age, called to his father for help. A ball had shattered both his legs. 'When we have beaten the enemy then I will help you,' answered Peyton; 'I have here other sons to lead to glory. Forward!' But the column had advanced only a few paces farther when the major himself fell to the earth a corpse. Prodigies of valor were here performed on both sides. History will ask in vain for braver soldiers than those who have fought and fell. But of the demoniac fury of both parties one at a distance can form no idea. Even the wounded, despairing of succor, collecting their last energies of life, plunged their knives into the bosoms of foemen who lay near them still breathing.

"The success of General Hill enabled other generals to once more lead their disorganized troops back to the fight, and the contest was renewed along the whole line, and kept up until deep into the night; for everything depended upon our keeping the enemy at bay, counting, too, upon their exhaustion at last, until fresh troops could arrive to reënforce us. At length, about half past ten in the evening, the divisions of Magruder, Wise, and Holmes, came up and deployed to the front of our army.

"So soon as these reënforcements could be thrown to the front our regiments were drawn back, and as far as possible reorganized during the night, the needful officers appointed, and after the distribution of provisions, which had also fortunately arrived, measures were adopted for the gathering up of the wounded and the burial of the dead."

In this conflict Gen. McCall was taken prisoner by the Confederates.

During the same day an attack was made upon the corps of Gen. Porter by the divisions of Gens. Wise and Holmes near Malvern Hill, but without success.

On the night of the 30th all the divisions of the Federal army were united at Malvern Hill, a strong position where the whole train, including the siege guns, were sheltered. The army was thus in communication with its transports and supplies. Five days of incessant marching and fighting had passed, during which many had been sun struck by the heat, and others from exhaustion had quitted the ranks and fell into the procession of sick and wounded. Attacked by a force far superior to itself, it had succeeded in reaching a position where it was out of danger and from which, if reënforced, it could have advanced.

Gen. McClellan immediately put his army in a position for defence by arranging his batteries along the high grounds so as not to interfere with the defence by the infantry of the sort of glacis upon which the enemy would be obliged to advance to the attack. About four P. M. on the 1st of July, the Confederate forces advanced to storm the position. But a destructive fire of grape mowed them down until the fragments of their divisions were compelled to seek shelter in the woods. The position being within range of the gunboats they also opened a destructive fire with their hundred pounders upon the enemy. The attack was a failure, the loss of the Confederates being immense while that of the Federal troops was insignificant. On the evening after the battle the exhausted enemy retired to Richmond to appear no more, and the army of the Potomac took up a position at Harrison's Bar, a spot chosen by the engineers and naval officers as the most favorable for defence and for receiving supplies.

These battles were fought at a time when the military strength of the Confederate States had been brought into the field and concentrated at Richmond. Thus the Confederate army greatly outnumbered the Federal force, reduced by losses during the campaign and by sickness, on the banks of the Chickahominy. No official reports have appeared of the losses on either side. They were not far from fifteen thousand men. On the 3d of July the War Department published a despatch from Gen. McClellan dated at Berkeley, Harrison's Bar, stating that he had lost but one gun, which broke down and was abandoned, and that the rear of his train was then within a mile of camp and only one wagon abandoned.

On the 4th of July Gen. McClellan issued the following address to his army:

HEADQUARTERS, ARMY OF THE POTOMAC,
CAMP NEAR HARRISON'S LANDING, *July* 4, 1862.

SOLDIERS OF THE ARMY OF THE POTOMAC: Your achievements of the past ten days have illustrated the valor and endurance of the American soldier. Attacked by superior forces, and without hopes of reënforcements, you have succeeded in changing your base of operations by a flank movement, always regarded as the most hazardous of military operations. You have saved all your guns except a few lost in battle, taking in return guns and colors from the enemy.

Upon your march you have been assailed, day after day, with desperate fury, by men of the same race and nation, skilfully massed and led. Under every disadvantage of number, and necessarily of position also, you have in every conflict beaten back your foes with enormous slaughter.

Your conduct ranks you among the celebrated armies of history. None will now question what each of you may always, with pride, say: "I belonged to the Army of the Potomac." You have reached this new base complete in organization and unimpaired in spirit. The enemy may at any time attack you—we are prepared to meet them. I have personally established your lines. Let them come, and we will convert their repulse into a final defeat.

Your government is strengthening you with the resources of a great people. On this, our nation's birthday, we declare to our foes, who are rebels against the best interests of mankind, that this army shall enter the capital of the so-called Confederacy; that our national Constitution shall prevail, and that the Union, which can alone insure internal peace and external security to each State, must and shall be preserved, cost what it may in time, treasure, and blood.

GEO. E. McCLELLAN,
Major-General Commanding.

On the 5th President Davis issued the following address to the Confederate army:

RICHMOND, *July* 5, 1862.

To the Army in Eastern Virginia:

SOLDIERS; I congratulate you on the series of brilliant victories which, under the favor of Divine Providence, you have lately won, and as the President of the Confederate States, do heartily tender to you the thanks of the country, whose just cause you have so skilfully and heroically served. Ten days ago, an invading army, vastly superior to you in numbers and the material of war, closely beleaguered your capital and vauntingly proclaimed its speedy conquest; you marched to attack the enemy in his intrenchments; with well directed movements and death-defying valor, you charged upon him in his strong positions, drove him from field to field over a distance of more than thirty-five miles, and despite his reënforcements compelled him to seek safety under the cover of his gunboats, where he now lies cowering before the army so lately derided and threatened with entire subjugation. The fortitude with which you have borne toil and privation, the gallantry with which you have entered into each successive battle, must have been witnessed to be fully appreciated; but a grateful people will not fail to recognize you and to bear you in loved remembrance. Well may it be said of you that you have "done enough for glory;" but duty to a suffering country and to the cause of constitutional liberty, claims from you yet further effort. Let it be your pride to relax in nothing which can promote your future efficiency; your one great object being to drive the invader from your soil, and, carrying your standards beyond the outer boundaries of the Confederacy, to wring from an unscrupulous foe the recognition of your birthright, community, and independence.

[Signed] JEFFERSON DAVIS.

Early in July Gen. Halleck resigned his command of the army of the West, and in obedience to an order of the President assumed, on the 23d of July, the duties of general-in-chief of the entire army of the United States. This was the position held by Gen. McClellan, previous to his departure from Washington to conduct the peninsular campaign. Its duties had been subsequently performed by the Secretary of War, under the supervision of President Lincoln, assisted by the counsel of Maj.-Gen. Hitchcock, an elderly officer of the army. Gen. Halleck, upon assuming these duties, had his attention immediately called to the army of the Potomac. He thus relates his action in relation to it:

"The first thing to which my attention was called on my arrival here (at Washington), was the condition of the army at Harrison's Landing, on the James river. I immediately visited Gen. McClellan's headquarters for consultation. I left Washington on the 24th and returned on the 27th. The main object of this consultation was to ascertain if there was a possibility of an advance upon Richmond from Harrison's Landing, and if not to favor some plan of uniting the armies of Gen. McClellan and Gen. Pope on some other line. Not being familiar with the position and numbers of the troops in Virginia and on the coast, I took the President's estimate of the largest number of reënforcements that could be sent to the army of the Potomac.

"On the day of my arrival at Harrison's Landing Gen. McClellan was of opinion that he would require at least 50,000 additional troops. I informed him that this number could not possibly be sent; that I was not authorized to promise him over 20,000, and that I could not well see how even that number could be safely withdrawn from other places. He took the night for considering the matter, and informed me the next morning that he would make the attempt upon Richmond with the additional 20,000, but immediately on my return to Washington he telegraphed that he would require 35,000, a force which it was impossible to send him without leaving Washington and Baltimore almost defenceless. The only alternative now left was to withdraw the army of the Potomac to some position where it could unite with that of Gen. Pope, and cover Washington at the same time that it operated against the enemy. After full consultation with my officers, I determined to attempt this junction on the Rappahannock, by bringing McClellan's forces to Aquia Creek.

"Accordingly, on the 30th of July, I telegraphed to him to send away his sick as quickly as possible, preparatory to a movement of his troops. This was preliminary to the withdrawal of his entire army, which was ordered by telegraph on the 3d of August. In order that the transfer to Aquia Creek might be made as rapidly as possible, I authorized Gen. McClellan to assume control of all the vessels in the James river and Chesapeake Bay, of which there was then a vast fleet. The quartermaster-general was also requested to send to that point all the transports that could be procured. On the 5th I received a protest from Gen. McClellan, dated the 4th, against the removal of the army from Harrison's Landing. On the 1st of August I ordered Gen. Burnside to immediately embark his troops at Newport News, transfer them to Aquia Creek, and take position opposite Fredericksburg. This officer moved with great promptness, and reached Aquia Creek on the night of the 3d. His troops were immediately landed, and the transports sent back to Gen. McClellan.

"About this time I received information that the enemy were preparing a large force to drive back Gen. Pope, and attack either Washington or Baltimore. The information was so direct and trustworthy that I could not doubt its correctness. This gave me serious uneasiness for the safety of the capital and Maryland, and I repeatedly urged upon Gen. McClellan the necessity of promptly moving his army so as to form a junction with that of Gen. Pope. The evacuation of Harrison's Landing, however, was not commenced till the 14th, eleven days after it was ordered."

The following correspondence, respecting this removal of the army of the Potomac, took place between Gen. McClellan and Gen. Halleck:

BERKELEY, VA., *August* 4, 12 M.

Maj.-Gen. Halleck, Commander-in-Chief:

Your telegraph of last evening is received. I must confess that it has caused me the greatest pain I ever experienced, for I am convinced that the order to withdraw this army to Aquia Creek will prove disastrous in the extreme to our cause. I fear it will be a fatal blow. Several days are necessary to complete the preparations for so important a movement as this, and while they are in progress, I beg that careful consideration may be given to my statement. This army is now in excellent discipline and condition. We hold a debouche on both banks of the James river, so that we are free to act in any direction, and, with the assistance of the gunboats, I consider our communications as secure.

We are twenty-five miles from Richmond, and are not likely to meet the enemy in force sufficient to fight a battle until we have reached fifteen to eighteen miles, which brings us practically within ten miles of Richmond. Our longest line of land transportation would be from this point twenty-five miles, but with the aid of the gunboats we can supply the army by water, during its advance, certainly to within twelve miles of Richmond. At Aquia Creek we would be seventy-five miles from Richmond, with land transportation all the way. From here to Fortress Monroe is a march of about seventy miles, for I regard it as impracticable to withdraw this army and its material, except by land. The result of the movement would thus be to march one hundred and forty-five miles to reach a point now only twenty-five miles distant, and to deprive ourselves entirely of the powerful aids of the gunboats and water transportation. Add to this the certain demoralization of this army, which would ensue; the terrible depressing effect upon the people of the North, and the strong probability that it would influence foreign Powers to recognize our adversaries; and these appear to me sufficient reasons to make it my imperative duty to urge in the strongest terms afforded by our language, that this order may be rescinded, and that, far from recalling this army, it may be promptly reënforced to enable it to resume the offensive.

It may be said that there are no reënforcements available. I point to Gen. Burnside's force, to that of Gen. Pope, not necessary to maintain a strict defence in front of Washington and Harper's Ferry; to those portions of the Army of the West not required for a strict defence there. Here, directly in front of this army, is the heart of the rebellion. It is here that all our resources should be collected to strike the blow which will determine the fate of this nation. All points of secondary importance elsewhere should be abandoned, and every available man brought here. A decided victory here, and the military strength of the rebellion is crushed. It matters not what partial reverses we may meet with elsewhere, here is the true defence of Washington; it is here, on the bank of the James river, that the fate of the Union should be decided.

Clear in my conviction of right, strong in the consciousness that I have ever been, and still am, actuated solely by love of my country, knowing that no ambitious or selfish motives have influenced me from the commencement of this war; I do now what I never did in my life before, I entreat that this order may be rescinded. If my counsel does not prevail, I will, with a sad heart, obey your order to the utmost of my power, devoting to the movement, which I clearly foresee will be one of the utmost delicacy and difficulty, whatever skill I may possess, whatever the result may be, and may God grant that I am mistaken in my forebodings. I shall at least have the internal satisfaction that I have written and spoken frankly, and have sought to do the best in my power to arrest disaster from my country.

GEO. B. McCLELLAN, Major General.

GEN. HALLECK TO GEN. McCLELLAN.

WASHINGTON, *Aug* 6, 1862.

Maj.-Gen. Geo. B. McClellan, Commanding, &c., Berkeley, Va.:

GENERAL—Your telegram of yesterday was received this morning, and I immediately telegraphed a brief reply, promising to write you more fully by mail. You, General, certainly could not have been more pained at receiving my order than I was at the necessity of issuing it. I was advised by high officers, in whose judgment I had great confidence, to make the order immediately on my arrival here, but I determined not to do so until I could learn your wishes from a personal interview; and even after that interview I tried every means in my power to avoid withdrawing your army, and delayed my decision as long as I dared, to delay it. I assure you, General, it was not a hasty and inconsiderate act, but one that caused me more anxious thought than any other of my life. But after full and mature consideration of all the pros and cons, I was reluctantly forced to the conclusion that the order must be issued. There was to my mind no other alternative.

Allow me to allude to a few of the facts of the case. You and your officers, at our interview, estimated the enemy's forces in and around Richmond at 200,000 men. Since then you and others report that they have received and are receiving large reënforcements from the south. General Pope's army, now covering Washington, is only 40,000. Your effective force is only about 90,000. You are thirty miles from Richmond, and Gen. Pope eighty or ninety. With the enemy directly between you, ready to fall with his superior numbers upon one or the other, as he may elect, neither can reënforce the other in case of such an attack.

If Gen. Pope's army be diminished to reënforce you, Washington, Maryland, and Pennsylvania would be left uncovered and exposed. If your force be reduced to strengthen Pope, you would be too weak to even hold the position you occupy should the enemy turn round and attack you in full force. In other words, the old Army of the Potomac is split into two parts, with the entire force of the enemy directly between them. They cannot be united by land without exposing both to destruction, and yet they must be united. To send Pope's forces by water to the peninsula is, under present circumstances, a military impossibility. The only alternative is to send the forces on the peninsula to some point by water—say Fredericksburg—where the two armies can be united. Let me now allude to some of the objections which you have urged.

You say that to withdraw from the present position will cause the certain demoralization of the army, which is now in excellent condition and discipline. I cannot understand why a simple change of position to a new and by no means distant base will demoralize an army in excellent discipline, unless the officers themselves assist in the demoralization, which I am satisfied they will not. Your change of front from your extreme right at Hanover Court House to your present position was over thirty miles, but I have not heard that it demoralized your troops, notwithstanding the severe losses they sustained in effecting it.

A new base on the Rappahannock, at Fredericksburg, brings you within about sixty miles of Richmond, and secures a reënforcement of forty or fifty thousand fresh and disciplined troops. The change, with such advantages, will, I think, if properly represented to your army, encourage rather than demoralize your troops. Moreover, you yourself suggested that a junction might be effected at Yorktown, but that a flank march across the peninsula would be more hazardous than to retire to Fort Monroe. You will remember that Yorktown is two or three miles further from Richmond than Fredericksburg is. Besides the latter is between Richmond and Washington, and covers Washington from any attack by the enemy.

The political effect of the withdrawal may at first look unfavorable, but I think the public are beginning to understand its necessity; and that they will have much more confidence in a united army than in its separate fragments. But you will reply, Why not reënforce me here, so that I can strike Richmond from my present position? To do this, you said at our interview that you required 50,000 additional troops. I told you that it was impossible to give you so many. You finally thought you would have "some chance" of success with 20,000; but you afterward telegraphed to me that you would require 35,000, as the enemy was being largely reënforced.

If your estimate of the enemy's strength was correct, your requisition was perfectly reasonable; but it was utterly impossible to fill it until new troops could be enlisted and organized, which would require several weeks. To keep your army in its present position until it could be so reënforced would almost destroy it in that climate. The months of August and September are almost fatal to whites who live on that part of James River; and even after you got the reënforcements asked for, you admitted that you must reduce Fort Darling and the river batteries before you could advance on Richmond. It is by no means certain that the reduction of these fortifications would not require considerable time, perhaps as much as those at Yorktown. This delay might not only be fatal to the health of your army, but in the mean time Gen. Pope's forces would be exposed to the heavy blows of the enemy, without the slightest hope of assistance from you.

In regard to the demoralizing effect of a withdrawal from the peninsula to the Rappahannock, I must remark that a large number of your highest officers—indeed a majority of those whose opinions have been reported to me—are decidedly in favor of the movement. Even several of those who originally advocated the line of the peninsula now advise its abandonment. I have not inquired, and do not desire to know, by whose advice or for what reason the Army of the Potomac was separated into two parts, with the enemy before them. I must take things as I find them. I find our forces divided, and I wish to unite them. Only one feasible plan has been presented for doing this. If you or any one else had presented a better one, I certainly should have adopted it; but all of your plans require reënforcements which it is impossible to give you. It is very easy to ask for reënforcements, but it is not so easy to give them when you have no disposable troops at your command. I have written very plainly as I understand the case, and I hope you will give me credit for having carefully considered the matter, although I may have arrived at different conclusions from your own. Very respectfully, your obedient servant,

H. W. HALLECK, General-in-Chief.

(Official Copy.) J. C. Kelton, Assistant Adj.-Gen.

Thus the campaign was closed. The once proud Army of the Potomac was withdrawn from the peninsula to Aquia Creek and Alexandria, and its corps were immediately ordered into the field to reënforce the army of Gen. Pope southeast of Washington, and to act under his command.

CHAPTER XX.

General Pope takes command of the Army of Virginia—Call of the President for more Men—Advance of Gen. Lee—Battle of Cedar Mountain—Capture of Louisa Court House—Gen. Pope falls back—Dash on Catlett's Station—Further advance of the Enemy—Attack at Manassas—Attack at Bristow's Station—Battle near Manassas—Battle at Gainesville—Battle near Bull Run—Excitement in the Northern States—Retreat of Gen. Banks—Battle at Chantilly—Retreat of Gen. Pope to the fortifications at Washington.

By an order of the President on the 27th of June, Maj.-Gen. Pope, who had been in command of a force in the West, entered upon the chief command of the army of Virginia.

The following is the order of the President creating the Army of Virginia, and putting Gen. Pope in command, dated June 27, 1862:

I. The forces under Maj-Gens. Fremont, Banks, and McDowell, including the troops now under Brig.-Gen. Sturgis, at Washington, shall be consolidated and form one army, to be called the Army of Virginia.

II. The command of the Army of Virginia is specially assigned to Maj.-Gen. John Pope as commanding general.

The troops of the Mountain Department, heretofore under command of Gen. Fremont, shall constitute the First Army Corps, under the command of Gen. Fremont.

The troops of the Shenandoah Department, now under Gen. Banks, shall constitute the Second Army Corps, and be commanded by him.

The troops under the command of Gen. McDowell, except those within the fortifications and the city of Washington, shall form the Third Army Corps, and be under his command.

The creation of the several separate and independent commands which constituted the forces west and southwest of Washington had always been looked upon with distrust. Hence the consolidation of these forces under one commander was regarded with much satisfaction by the public, as a wise and prudent measure.

The appointment of Gen. Pope to the chief command was not favorably received by Maj.-Gen. Fremont. Consequently an order was issued from the War Department, relieving him from command.

On the next day Gen. Fremont issued an order declaring his resignation of the command of his forces and assigning it to Brig.-Gen. Schenck. The ground upon which the resignation of Gen. Fremont was made, was understood to be that Gen. Pope, who had been appointed to the command of the Army of Virginia, was his inferior in rank, and he could not consistently command a corps under him. Gen. Schenck, on assuming command, issued his orders.

At night of the same day he learned that Gen. Rufus King had been ordered to the command of that corps, and sent in his request to be relieved of command in that portion of the army. But on the subsequent day, still further learning that Gen. King had been detached and Gen. Sigel ordered to the same command, he withdrew his resignation.

Meantime Maj.-Gen. Pope was making his arrangements to take the field. On the 14th of July he issued the following address to his army:

To the Officers and Soldiers of the Army of Virginia:

By special assignment of the President I have assumed command of this army. I have spent two weeks in learning your whereabouts, your condition, and your wants, in preparing you for active operations, and in placing you in a position from which you can act promptly and to the purpose. These labors are nearly completed, and I am about to join you in the field. Let us understand each other. I have come to you from the West where we have always seen the backs of our enemies—from an army whose business it has been to seek an adversary and beat him when found; whose policy has been attack and not defence. In but one instance has the enemy been able to place our Western armies in a defensive attitude. I presume I have been called here to pursue the same system, and to lead you against the enemy. It is my purpose to do so and that speedily. I am sure you long for an opportunity to win the distinction you are capable of achieving; that opportunity I shall endeavor to give you. In the mean time I desire you to dismiss certain phrases I am sorry to find much in vogue amongst you. I hear constantly of taking strong positions and holding them—of lines of retreat and bases of supplies. Let us discard such ideas. The strongest position a soldier should desire to occupy is one from which he can most easily advance against the enemy. Let us study the probable line of retreat of our opponents, and leave our own to take care of itself. Let us look before us, and not behind. Success and glory are in the advance—disaster and shame lurk in the rear. Let us act on this understanding, and it is safe to predict that your banners shall be inscribed with many a glorious deed, and that your names will be dear to your countrymen forever.

(Signed) JOHN POPE, Maj.-Gen. Commanding.

Subsequent orders issued by Gen. Pope at this time indicate the manner in which he proposed to conduct the campaign, as follows:

HEADQUARTERS OF THE ARMY OF VIRGINIA,
WASHINGTON, *July* 18, 1862.

General Orders, No. 5:

Hereafter, as far as practicable, the troops of this command will subsist upon the country in which their operations are carried on. In all cases supplies for this purpose will be taken by the officers to whose department they properly belong, under the orders of the commanding officer of the troops for whose use they are intended. Vouchers will be given to the owners, stating on their face that they will be payable at the conclusion of the war upon sufficient testimony being furnished that such owners have been loyal citizens of the United States since the date of the vouchers.

Whenever it is known that supplies can be furnished in any district of the country where the troops are to operate, the use of trains for carrying subsistence will be dispensed with as far as possible.

By command of Maj.-Gen. POPE.

GEO. D. RUGGLES, Col. A. A.-G. and Chief of Staff.

HEADQUARTERS OF THE ARMY OF VIRGINIA, *July* 18, 1862.

General Orders, No. 6:

Hereafter in any operations of the cavalry forces in this command no supply or baggage trains of any description will be used unless so stated especially in the order for the movement. Two days' cooked rations will be carried on the persons of the men, and all villages and neighborhoods, through which they pass, will be laid under contribution in the manner specified by General Orders, No. 5, current series, from these headquarters, for the subsistence of men and horses.

Movements of cavalry must always be made with celerity, and no delay in such movements will be excused hereafter on any pretext.

Whenever the order for the movement of any portion of the army emanates from these headquarters, the time of marching and that to be consumed in the execution of the duty will be specifically designated, and no departure therefrom will be permitted to pass unnoticed without the gravest and most conclusive reasons.

Commanding officers will be held responsible for strict and prompt compliance with every provision of this order. By command of Maj.-Gen. POPE.

GEO. D. RUGGLES, Col. A. A.-G. and Chief of Staff.

Another order was issued on the same day, declaring that the inhabitants along the lines of railroads and telegraphs and the routes of travel, would be held responsible for any injury done to track, line, or road, or for any attacks on trains or stragglers by bands of guerillas in their neighborhood. In cases of damage to roads the citizens, within five miles, would be turned out in mass to repair the damage. If a soldier or legitimate follower of the army was fired upon from any house, the same should be razed to the ground. By another order all disloyal citizens within the lines of the army, or within the reach of its respective officers, were to be arrested at once. Those taking the oath of allegiance, and giving sufficient security for its observance, were to be allowed to remain; all others were to be conducted to the South, beyond the extreme pickets, and if again found anywhere within the lines, were to be treated as spies and subjected to the extreme rigor of military law. These orders of Gen. Pope were followed by the pillaging of private property and by insults to females to a degree unknown heretofore during the war. The Confederate Government, by way of retaliation, issued an order declaring that Gen. Pope and the commissioned officers serving under him, were "not entitled to be considered as soldiers, and therefore not entitled to the benefit of cartel for the parole of future prisoners of war. Ordered, further, that in the event of the capture of Maj.-Gen. Pope, or any commissioned officer serving under him, the captive so taken shall be held in close confinement so long as the orders aforesaid shall continue in force, and unrepealed by the competent military authority of the United States, and that in the event of the murder of an unarmed citizen or inhabitant of this Confederacy by virtue or under pretence of the order hereinbefore recited, it shall be the duty of the commanding general of the forces of this Confederacy to cause immediately to be hung, out of the commissioned officers prisoners as aforesaid, a number equal to that of our own citizens thus murdered by the enemy."

The main divisions of Gen. Pope's army were now stationed at Culpepper Court House and Fredericksburg. Culpepper Court House is about seventy miles from Washington and equally distant from Richmond. The route crosses the Long Bridge at Washington, thence through Alexandria, Fairfax, Manassas, Warrenton, &c. Fredericksburg is connected with Washington by steamboat navigation on the Potomac to Aquia Creek, thence by railroad, fifteen miles, to Fredericksburg, which is sixty miles by railroad from Richmond. Gen. Pope, although not personally in the field until the 27th of July, had been engaged in concentrating his forces. His delay in taking the field was occasioned by the absence of Maj.-Gen. Halleck, who arrived at Washington on the 23d of July, and entered upon the duties of general-in-chief.

A show of force had been kept up in the Shenandoah Valley, and east of the Blue Ridge, by the Confederate Government throughout the month of July, chiefly for the purpose of preventing reënforcements to Gen. McClellan. The knowledge which it had of the position and strength of the Federal forces made it manifest that no reënforcement to the Army of the Potomac would come from any other quarter. The departure of the division of Gen. Burnside from Newport News, where it had been for some weeks ready to coöperate with Gen. McClellan in any forward movements to Aquia Creek on the 1st of August, was immediately known in Richmond. It showed not only that no reënforcements were coming to the Army of the Potomac, but also that this army would soon evacuate the peninsula. The star of their fortune now appeared to be in the ascendant. The day, so long and anxiously looked for, had come, in which they should be able to take their great and powerful adversary at a disadvantage, and demonstrate to civilized nations their own military strength and ability to win that independence which they had proclaimed. Consultations were immediately held at Richmond, and their purposes were soon formed. It was resolved to abandon the defensive policy and to repeat the exploit which Gen. Jackson had performed by driving Gen. Banks out of the Shenandoah Valley, on a scale of national magnitude. Rumors were set afloat that Tennessee, Kentucky, and the whole of Virginia were to be recovered at once; Maryland liberated from her oppression, and not only Washington and Baltimore captured, but also Harrisburg and Philadelphia in the east, and Cincinnati in the west. It was a magnificent enterprise for a people situated like those in the Confederate States at that time. Measures were immediately adopted for the execution of these plans. Gen. McClellan was to be left to retire from the peninsula without any further attacks than were necessary to cover their real designs, and their forces were to be prepared for an immediate movement northward. The Confederate forces at this time were greater than ever before. Not less than one hundred and fifty thousand men were at Richmond and in communication with it. All this force, excepting a strong corps of observation, was to be precipitated at once upon Maryland.

The preparations to advance into Maryland which were making at Richmond, were immediately known at Washington and awakened great anxiety. An order was issued to Gen. Cox in western Virginia to send his main forces, with all possible despatch, by railroad to join Gen. Pope. To facilitate the withdrawal of the army from Harrison's Landing, as stated by Gen. Halleck, and to gain time also by a demonstration against the enemy, Gen. Pope was ordered to push his forces across the Rappahannock, and occupy Culpepper and threaten Gordonsville. At the same time President Lincoln issued the following order, calling out an additional three hundred thousand men to serve for nine months:

WAR DEPARTMENT, WASHINGTON, *August* 4, 1862.

Ordered First—That a draft of three hundred thousand militia be immediately called into the service of the United States, to service for nine months, unless sooner discharged. The Secretary of War will assign the quotas to the States, and establish regulations for the draft.

Second—That if any State shall not by the 15th of August furnish its quota of the additional three hundred thousand volunteers authorized by law, the deficiency of volunteers in that State will also be made up by a special draft from the militia. The Secretary of War will establish regulations for this purpose.

Third—Regulations will be prepared by the War Department, and presented to the President, with the object of securing the promotion of officers of the army and volunteers for meritorious and distinguished services, and of preventing the nomination and appointment in the military service of incompetent or unworthy officers. The regulations will also provide for ridding the service of such incompetent persons as now hold commissions.

By order of the PRESIDENT.

EDWIN M. STANTON, Secretary of War.

The Confederate army began to move immediately after the 1st of August; and the divisions of Gens. Jackson, Ewell, and Hill were hurried to the Rapidan river, which is the south fork of the Rappahannock. On Friday, the 8th of August, Gen. Pope reached Culpepper Court House, from his last encampment near Washington, the county seat of Rappahannock. At the same time the corps of Gen. Banks was in motion in the direction of Culpepper. The corps of Gen. Sigel was encamped at Sperryville, twenty miles from Culpepper, and on the road from Washington, Rappahannock county. At Culpepper Court House was Brig.-Gen. Crawford, with his brigade belonging to Gen. Banks's corps, and Gen. Ricketts's division, belonging to Gen. McDowell's corps. They had arrived two days previous from Warrenton with Gen. McDowell, who took command of all the forces then at Culpepper. Gen. Bayard with his cavalry had been guarding the fords of the Rapidan from Racoon Ford to a point fourteen miles below, and south of the railroad at Burnett's Ford, where he connected with the cavalry of Gen. Buford. At noon on Friday he sent information to Culpepper Court House that the enemy had early that morning crossed the river and driven in his pickets with such force that he was obliged to retire before them. He was retiring to the north and east side of Robertson's river, about eight miles from Culpepper, there to await a supporting force. The numbers of the enemy he estimated at two regiments of infantry, two pieces of light artillery, and three small regiments of cavalry. Gen. Buford at the same time reported the enemy to be advancing in heavy force upon Madison Court House, thus leaving it in doubt whether the movement was directed toward Culpepper or Madison. Wishing to maintain the communication with Fredericksburg at all hazards, Gen. Pope resolved to concentrate at Culpepper, in order to keep his forces interposed between

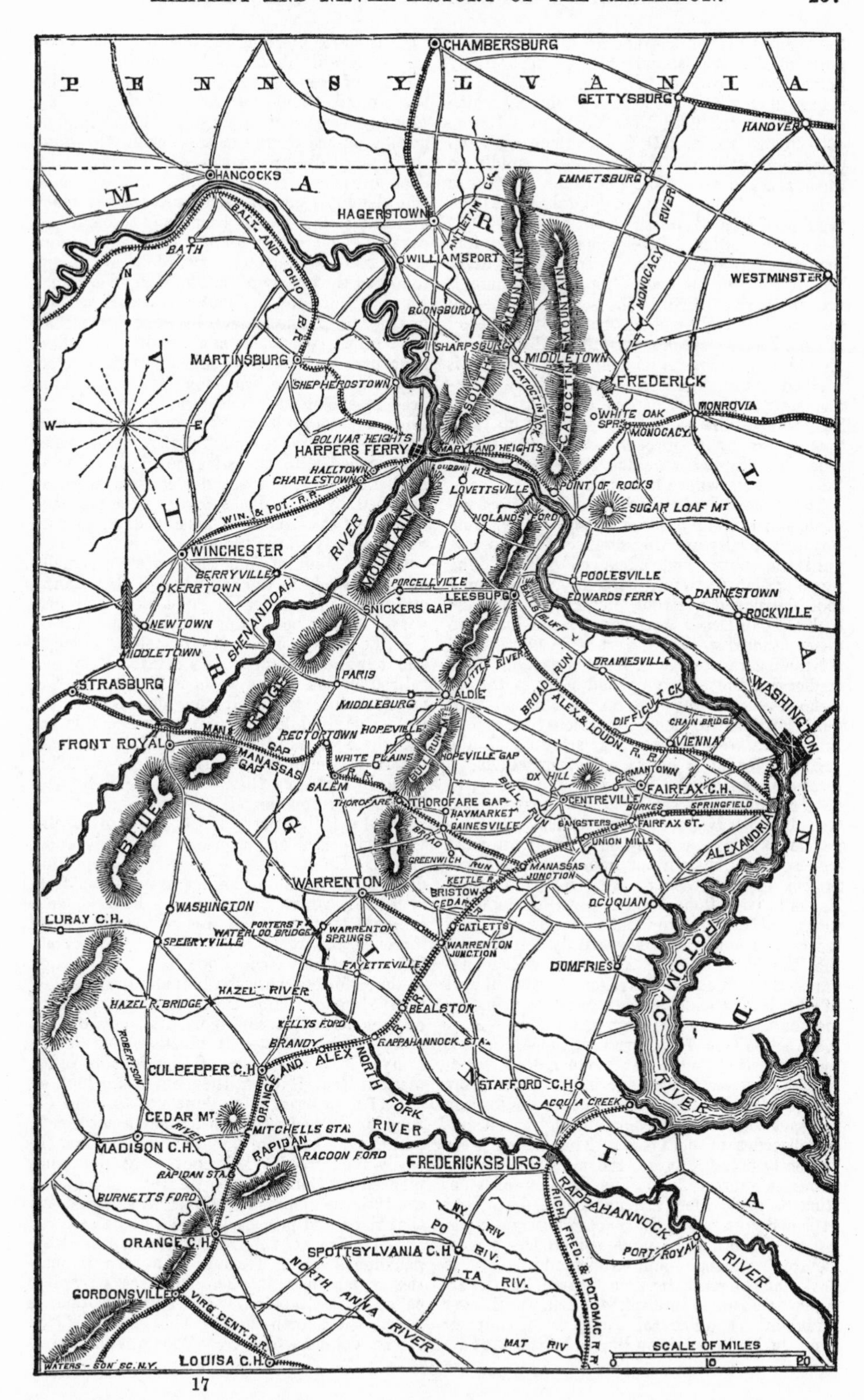
PENNSYLVANIA
MARYLAND
VIRGINIA
CHAMBERSBURG
GETTYSBURG
HANOVER
HANCOCKS
EMMETSBURG
HAGERSTOWN
WILLIAMSPORT
WESTMINSTER
BATH
BOONSBURO
SHARPSBURG
MIDDLETOWN
MARTINSBURG
SHEPHERDSTOWN
FREDERICK
MONROVIA
WHITE OAK SPRS
MONOCACY
BOLIVAR HEIGHTS
HARPERS FERRY
MARYLAND HEIGHTS
HALLTOWN
CHARLESTOWN
LOVETTSVILLE
POINT OF ROCKS
SUGAR LOAF MT
NOLANDS FORD
WINCHESTER
BERRYVILLE
KERRTOWN
NEWTOWN
MIDDLETOWN
STRASBURG
FRONT ROYAL
POOLESVILLE
EDWARDS FERRY
DARNESTOWN
ROCKVILLE
PORCELLVILLE
LEESBURG
SNICKERS GAP
DRAINESVILLE
WASHINGTON
PARIS
ALDIE
MIDDLEBURG
CHAIN BRIDGE
VIENNA
RECTORTOWN
HOPEVILLE
MANASSAS GAP
WHITE PLAINS
HOPEVILLE GAP
OX HILL
GERMANTOWN
FAIRFAX C.H.
SALEM
CENTREVILLE
THOROFARE GAP
HAYMARKET
GAINESVILLE
BURKES
SPRINGFIELD
FAIRFAX ST.
UNION MILLS
ALEXANDRIA
GREENWICH
MANASSAS JUNCTION
WARRENTON
BRISTOW
OCCUQUAN
WASHINGTON
LURAY C.H.
PORTERS F.
WATERLOO BRIDGE
WARRENTON SPRINGS
CATLETTS
WARRENTON JUNCTION
SPERRYVILLE
FAYETTEVILLE
DUMFRIES
HAZEL R. BRIDGE
HAZEL RIVER
BEALSTON
KELLYS FORD
BRANDY
RAPPAHANNOCK STA.
POTOMAC RIVER
CULPEPPER C.H.
ORANGE AND ALEX
NORTH FORK RIVER
STAFFORD C.H.
ACQUIA CREEK
CEDAR MT
MITCHELLS STA.
MADISON C.H.
RAPIDAN
RACOON FORD
FREDERICKSBURG
RAPIDAN STA.
BURNETTS FORD
RAPPAHANNOCK
ORANGE C.H.
SPOTTSYLVANIA C.H.
NORTH ANNA RIVER
PORT ROYAL
RIVER
GORDONSVILLE
VIRG. CENT. R.R.
RICH. FRED. & POTOMAC R.R.
SCALE OF MILES
10
20
LOUISA C.H.
WATERS - SON SC. N.Y.

the main body of the enemy and the lower fords of the Rappahannock. He accordingly immediately ordered Brig.-Gen. Crawford to march to Gen. Bayard with his brigade, which consisted of the 28th New York, 10th Maine, 46th Pennsylvania, 25th Connecticut, with ten pieces of artillery. He proceeded rapidly to the front, and occupied a position about seven miles from Culpepper, immediately in rear of the line of Gen. Bayard's cavalry. Soon after, Gen. Pope ordered the remainder of Gen. Banks's corps to move rapidly from Hazel River bridge, nine miles from Culpepper, where it was the night before, to the scene of expected conflict. By eight o'clock that night, the head of Gen. Banks's column was descried marching around the village to its destination, which it reached before midnight. That point was immediately in the rear of Gen. Crawford. Gen. Sigel was at the same time ordered up from Sperryville by a forced march of twenty miles, his advance reaching Culpepper late in the afternoon, where it was halted.

Throughout Friday night and Saturday forenoon, skirmishing was continued between Gen. Bayard's cavalry and the advance of the enemy, until the latter had advanced within long range of Gen. Crawford's artillery. The enemy soon developed a strong force, and occupied both sides of Cedar Mountain, a sugar-loaf eminence situated two miles west of the Orange and Alexandria railroad at Mitchell's Station. The artillery of the enemy opened early in the afternoon of Saturday, but he made no advance until near five o'clock, at which time a few skirmishers were thrown forward on each side under cover of a heavy wood, in which his force was concealed. A strong force was pushed forward in the rear of the skirmishers, and Gen. Banks advanced to the attack. The engagement did not fairly open until after six o'clock P. M., but for an hour and a half was furious and unceasing. The report of Gen. Banks to Gen. Pope had expressed the opinion that no action was imminent that afternoon, and it was not until after it was fully commenced that the latter ordered Gen. McDowell to advance Gen. Ricketts's division to the support of Gen. Banks, and also Gen. Sigel to bring his men on the ground as soon as possible. At 7 P. M., when Gen. Pope arrived, the action was raging fiercely, but Gen. Banks held the position he took early in the morning. During the action he had fallen back about one mile from the spot where it first commenced, but without any disorder or confusion. The enemy were evidently pressing close, and the artillery was firing at short range. The division of Gen. Ricketts pushed forward and occupied the right of Gen. Banks, taking the place of his right wing, which was ordered to mass upon the centre. Before this change could be effected it was quite dark, and the musketry firing ceased, but the artillery kept up an intermittent firing until near midnight. The Federal troops rested on their arms during the night in line of battle. At daylight the next morning the enemy fell back two miles, and still higher up the mountain, and the pickets of Gen. Pope advanced and occupied the ground. The army rested during the day. Monday was spent in burying the dead and in getting off the wounded, and during the night the enemy disappeared, leaving many of his dead unburied and his wounded on the ground. The slaughter on both sides was severe; much of the fighting having been hand to hand. A cavalry and artillery force under Gens. Buford and Bayard was thrown forward in pursuit, and followed the enemy to the Rapidan, over which his rear guard passed about ten o'clock on Tuesday morning. The Federal loss was fifteen hundred killed, wounded, and missing, of whom near three hundred were taken prisoners. Gen. Pope also lost two Napoleon guns, fifteen hundred muskets, and considerable ammunition. The Confederate loss was severe, among whom were Gens. Winder and Trimble. The battle commenced with the advance of Gen. Ewell, consisting of ten thousand men, who were reënforced by Gen. Jackson with five thousand more, and the balance of his command got into position early in the night.

On the Federal side the contest was maintained entirely by the command of Gen. Banks, and was conducted with great skill and bravery. The object of this attack on the part of Gen. Lee was undoubtedly to feel the strength and temper of Gen. Pope's army. His forces retired across the river, a few miles toward Gordonsville, to await the approach of the main army, while Gen. Pope pushed forward his whole force in the direction of the Rapidan, where he occupied a strong position, extending from Robertson's Rise on the right to near Racoon Ford on the left.

On the 16th a party of Confederate cavalry were surprised and captured at Louisa Court House. Upon them were found important despatches, including an autograph letter from Gen. Lee, which informed the Federal Government that Gen. Lee was moving by forced marches the main body of the Confederate army to attack Gen. Pope before a junction could be formed between him and the Army of the Potomac. Thus their plan was to throw overwhelming forces upon him, cut off his rear, and annihilate, if possible, his entire army. In consequence of this reliable information, Gen. Halleck, the general-in-chief, on the 17th ordered Gen. Pope not to cross the Rapidan, but advised him to take a position in rear of the North Fork, where he could be more easily reënforced. This movement was commenced by Gen. Pope on the 18th, and during the 19th the main body of his forces was behind that river, and prepared to hold its passes.

Ten miles above Fredericksburg the Rappahannock river receives the two tributaries which form it. The southern stream is called the Rapidan, the northern one is called the North Fork. This latter is the stream behind which Gen. Pope was advised to retire, and which he effected on the 18th and the subsequent day. Below the junction of the tributaries the stream is called the Rappahannock. This junction is twenty miles below the spot where the Culpepper or Orange and Alexandria railroad crosses the North Fork.

Gen. Lee commenced reconnoitring on the day that Gen. Pope retired, and at night a considerable body of his troops had crossed the Rapidan. On the 19th he crossed with a large force, comprising cavalry, infantry, and artillery.

Gen. Pope had thus far received some re-enforcements from Gen. Burnside, who landed at Fredericksburg from the mouth of the James river on the 4th of August. On the 6th, at six P. M., Gen. Reno, with his division of Gen. Burnside's corps, left camp to march to Gen. Pope. On the 10th Gen. King, of McDowell's corps, hurried forward to Culpepper Court House for the same purpose, and on the 13th Gen. Stevens, with six regiments of his division, and four of Gen. Wright's, which had been detached from Port Royal, S. C., followed. Thus nearly forty regiments of infantry, fully armed and provided with trains and a large force of artillery and cavalry, were sent forward from Fredericksburg. He was also authorized to call the main portion of Gen. Cox's forces from western Virginia.

The Orange and Alexandria railroad, which runs from Alexandria, and connects with the Virginia Central railroad at Gordonsville, was, at the end near Alexandria, the route by which Gen. Pope received his supplies. The stations on that part of the road were as follows: Alexandria, to Springfield, 9 miles; to Burke's, 14 miles; to Fairfax, 18 miles; to Union Mills, 23 miles; to Manassas Junction, 27 miles; to Bristol, 31 miles; to Catlett's, 38 miles; to Warrenton Junction, 41 miles; to Bealeton, 47 miles; to Rappahannock, 51 miles; to Brandy, 56 miles; to Culpepper, 62 miles; to Mitchell's, 69 miles. The road crosses the North Fork at the Rappahannock station, ten miles beyond Warrenton Junction. At Manassas Junction the Manassas Gap railroad comes in from the northwest. The first station west of Manassas Junction is Gainesville, distant 8 miles; the next is Thoroughfare, distant from Manassas Junction 14 miles. At the Warrenton Junction comes in from the northwest the Warrenton railroad. It connects Warrenton with Warrenton Junction. All these positions were in the rear of Gen. Pope's army on the North Fork, and were involved in the subsequent movements.

When the retreat of Gen. Pope commenced, Gen. Sigel's command was in the advance, Gen. Reno's held the left in the vicinity of Mitchell's Station, on the line of the Orange and Alexandria railroad, and Gen. McDowell's forces, supported by Gen. Banks, occupied the right centre. At half-past ten on the night of the 18th of August, Gen. Sigel commenced moving back toward Culpepper. Previous to this hour, however, the troops in the rear were in motion. The night was dark and cold, and the march slow in consequence of the immense train of transportation wagons placed in advance of the troops. The usual camp fires were extinguished, excepting those necessary for the safe passage of the trains, and all unnecessary noise was avoided. At midnight the advance of Gen. Sigel reached Cedar Mountain, the scene of the late battle, and at a late hour on Tuesday morning, the 19th, it reached Culpepper. The forces of Gen. McDowell, including Gen. King's division, had then passed through the town. Gen. Banks's division was at an encampment on the right of the road, and Gen. Sigel brought up the rear. Far as the eye could reach, there was to be seen nought but moving masses of infantry, cavalry, and artillery; beyond that it could catch an occasional glimmer of the white-covered tops of the wagon trains slowly winding up the distant hills. All the sick and wounded, excepting eighty-five men whose injuries were of such a kind as to prevent their removal, and all the stores of the medical department, had been sent off by railroad before five o'clock that afternoon. The rear guard of the army consisted of the cavalry under Gen. Bayard. The movement of the troops during the day, although made in different directions, all tended toward one point, the Rappahannock station on the railroad, at which was the bridge crossing the North Fork. During the forenoon of the 19th, the advance crossed, and the rear, which was that day under Gen. Sigel, encamped at night some four miles from the bridge. All night, long army trains, infantry, and artillery were moving across the bridge, and by noon on the 20th the cavalry composing the rear guard made its appearance just on the west side of the bridge, and was then drawn up in line of battle to meet the enemy's cavalry, with whom Gen. Bayard had been skirmishing from Cedar Mountain. About one o'clock the Confederate cavalry made a charge, but accomplished nothing except wounding a few men. The Federal cavalry then came across the bridge, and the retreat behind the North Fork of the Rappahannock was complete.

During the afternoon and night, the Confederate artillery came up. On the next day, the 21st, being Thursday, an attempt was made by them to cross a few miles above the bridge. The New York battery of Crowell and the Third Maryland regiment, stationed at the ford, would have been driven off except for the additional batteries sent to their support. At the same time an attack was made at Kelly's Ford; this was also repulsed. An attack of the enemy was expected during the night, and the Federal force slept on their arms. Early the next morning a Confederate battery opened at the spot where the first attempt to cross was made, which kept up a fire for some time. A little farther up the stream a bridge was discovered which the enemy had erected during the night. A Federal battery opened, which slackened fire soon after and appeared to be silenced by the batteries of the enemy. It was apparently withdrawn, when the enemy began to cross. The batteries of Gen. Sigel's command again opened upon their approach, and they were here also driven back. It was on this occasion that Gen. Henry Bohlen lost his life. Attempts to cross were also made at other fords. On Friday afternoon and night of the 22d, rain fell so heavily as to swell the river and make it unfordable between the mountains and a few miles back of Warrenton Springs, which checked the efforts of the enemy. The firing of artillery at nearly all the fords was kept up on the 23d and 24th with more or less spirit, but with no special results. On the 23d the bridge at the Rappahannock station was burned by Gen. Ricketts. While this was going on during the 24th, Gen. Lee made a flank movement, advanced higher up, and attempted to throw a portion of his force over at Waterloo bridge, about twelve miles above the Rappahannock bridge, which was burned. This attempt was defeated. The strategy of the movements of Gen. Pope consisted in the hope that by his falling back across and holding the fords of the North Fork, sufficient time would be gained for the Army of the Potomac to come to his aid.

On Friday evening, the 22d, while the Federal force was thus in possession of the fords of the Rappahannock, a body of Confederate cavalry under Gen. Stuart, consisting of detachments of the 1st, 4th, and 9th Virginia cavalry, made a dash upon Catlett's Station on the Orange and Alexandria railroad, thirty-five miles from Washington, and thirteen miles in the rear of the Rappahannock station. They met with only slight resistance. There were a great number of trains in a circle round the station at the time, which first occupied their attention; but a terrible storm of rain setting in a few moments after their arrival, the wagons could not be destroyed by fire, and only few were injured. They remained some hours, and left at four o'clock in the morning, their pickets having been driven in. They took away over two hundred horses of Gen. Pope's train, and twenty from Gen. McDowell's. They took all Gen. Pope's baggage and everything belonging to his staff officers. All the sick were taken from the hospitals, and most of them put on the captured horses to ride. A few were killed on both sides, and the number of prisoners taken was about two hundred. This force had crossed the North Fork at Porter's Ford, two miles above White Sulphur Springs. The Federal force at Catlett's consisted of a small guard from the Pennsylvania regiment under Col. Kane, and the Purnell Legion of Maryland. In the neighborhood were other trains likewise having small guards, upon some of which an attack was made.

After a body of the Confederate force had crossed at Waterloo bridge on the 24th, as above stated, an attack was made upon them by order of Gen. Pope, with the hope of cutting them off. This was unsuccessful, but the enemy was compelled to retire, move farther up the river, and enter the valley which lies between the Blue Ridge and the Bull Run mountains. The object of this movement was to get in the rear of Gen. Pope and cut off his supplies from Washington.

It put the Confederate army in such a position that it could move either upon Washington or upon Leesburg, for the purpose of crossing into Maryland. Nevertheless, Gen. Pope was successful in preventing the enemy from crossing at any of the fords of the North Fork, and compelling him to move still higher up on the west side of the Bull Run mountains. Thus, during eight days, Gen. Lee had advanced no nearer to Washington. It now remained for Gen. Pope to guard the passes of these mountains in order to prevent the approach of the enemy any nearer to Washington, or to meet him after crossing the mountains and defeat him. On the other hand it was the object of Gen. Lee to pass the mountains and take Gen. Pope in the rear if possible. At all events it was necessary for him to get rid of the army of Gen. Pope if he intended to cross over the Potomac into Maryland.

When it appeared doubtful if the North Fork river could be held long enough to effect a junction of the forces of Gen. McClellan with those of Gen. Pope, a part of the former were ordered to land at Alexandria and move out by railroad as rapidly as possible. After this movement of Gen. Lee, the remainder of Gen. McClellan's forces were ordered to land at Alexandria, and Gen. Burnside was ordered to evacuate Fredericksburg and Aquia Creek.

As soon as Gen. Pope discovered that a large force of the enemy was turning his right toward Manassas, and that the divisions which he expected to be there from Alexandria had not arrived, he broke up his camps at Warrenton and Warrenton Junction and marched rapidly back in three columns. At this time the corps of Gen. Heintzelman from Gen. McClellan's army had reached Warrenton Junction, although without artillery, wagons, or horses for the field and general officers. One division of the corps of Gen. Porter from Gen. McClellan's army coming by the way of Fredericksburg, arrived at Bealston's Station, eleven miles south of Warrenton Junction in advance of Gen. Heintzelman, about four thousand five hundred strong. The other division was at Kelly's Ford. This corps had marched night and day to join the army under Gen. Pope, and was broken down with excessive labor. Both these divisions were immediately concentrated at Warrenton Junction. When Gen. Pope determined to fall back he had no other course to pursue, except to detach a sufficient force to defeat the Confederate troops attempting to turn his flank, and still preserve his front before the main body of the Confederate army. The reason assigned by Gen. Pope for not pursuing the latter course was the lack of a sufficient force to maintain his front after a suitable body had been detached to defeat Gen. Jackson on his flank. He estimates the number of his troops at forty thousand, before the arrival of Gen. Heintzelman with ten thousand. The Confederate army before him was not less than eighty thousand in number. On evacuating Warrenton and Warrenton Junction, Gen. McDowell was ordered to march rapidly with his own corps and that of Gen. Sigel, and the division of Gen. Reynolds, by the turnpike upon Gainesville, the first station west of Manassas Junction, on the Gap railroad, for the purpose of intercepting any reënforcements coming through Thoroughfare Gap to Gen. Jackson, who he learned was on the railroad. At the same time Gen. Reno, from Gen. Burnside's corps, and Gen. Kearny, from Gen. Heintzelman's corps, were ordered to march upon Greenwich, so as to support Gen. McDowell if necessary. Greenwich is a little south of Gainesville, and a little southwest of Manassas Junction. The division of Gen. Hooker, under Gen. Pope, moved back upon Manassas, on the line of the railroad. Gen. Porter was ordered to remain with his corps at Warrenton Junction until relieved by Gen. Banks marching from Fayetteville, and then to push forward in the direction of Gainesville, where the main collision with the enemy was expected.

On Tuesday night, the 26th, the pickets at Manassas Junction were driven in, and two companies of Pennsylvania infantry, one company of Pennsylvania cavalry, and a battery of artillery stationed there were surprised and attacked by a large force under Gen. Ewell. The Union force, after a brief skirmish, retreated across Bull Run. There, at Union Mills, were the 11th and 12th Ohio regiments under Col. Scammon, being a portion of Gen. Cox's division brought on from western Virginia. They immediately advanced to meet the Confederate force, and early on Wednesday morning, the 27th, a conflict took place between Manassas Junction and Bull Run. This continued for a couple of hours, when Col. Scammon was forced to retire across Bull Run bridge, which he attempted to hold. About noon, after considerable loss, he was obliged to retire along the railroad in the direction of Alexandria, halting at a point midway between Centreville and Fairfax Court House. About two o'clock on the same morning, the New Jersey brigade under Brig.-Gen. Taylor, being a portion of Gen. Franklin's division of Gen. McClellan's army, left their encampment near Alexandria, and proceeding out the Fairfax road some distance, made a detour to the left, and during the forenoon arrived on the old battle ground near Manassas. The enemy, being aware of their approach, were drawn up to meet them. As they emerged from the woods the enemy opened upon them with a severe fire of artillery. Gen. Franklin, having no artillery, was compelled either to make a charge or retire. He resolved to charge upon the enemy's battery, but as these were supported by infantry, it proved ineffectual, and he then fell back in order to Sangster's Station, toward Fairfax, holding the enemy in check. At this station two Ohio regiments, sent to reënforce him, came up, who were at first mistaken for a body of the enemy. The troops of Gen. Taylor were now thrown into confusion, but finding out the mistake, rallied and joined in an attack upon the enemy, who now retired toward Manassas. Gen. Taylor then fell back to Fairfax Court House, having left one regiment at Sangster's Station as a guard. The losses during these actions were about three hundred.

On the same night of the 26th, when Manassas Junction was taken, a body of Confederate cavalry, being a detachment of the force of the enemy at Manassas, made an attack upon a railroad train at Bristow's Station, four miles from Manassas Junction. This train was the one which had conveyed, a few hours previous, the division of Gen. Hooker to Warrenton Junction, and was now returning empty. The cars were destroyed and the track torn up for a considerable distance. This force was increased by the arrival of more troops from Gen. Ewell's division, who had taken Manassas Junction, where was an immense depot of Federal stores valued at nearly one million of dollars. This was the body of the enemy which Gen. Pope had designed to intercept by ordering Gen. McDowell to fall back on Gainesville. Unfortunately, his order was too late, for the first reënforcements to Gen. Jackson, then in the rear of Gen. Pope, had passed through Thoroughfare Gap and Gainesville, and were in possession of Manassas at the time when the order was given to Gen. McDowell. The stores captured at Manassas served to sustain the Confederate army in extending its march into Maryland. Vast quantities, however, were burned, because, as Gen. Lee reported, "they had captured more than they could use or carry away." On the 23d, the next day after the attack upon Catlett's Station, Gen. Halleck had sent a despatch to Gen. Pope in these words: "By no means expose your railroad communication with Alexandria. It is of the utmost importance in sending your supplies and reënforcements." Gen. Pope, in his report, says: "The movement of Gen. Jackson toward White Plains and in the direction of Thoroughfare Gap, while the main body of the enemy confronted me at Sulphur Springs and Waterloo bridge, was well known to me, but I relied confidently upon the forces which I had been assured would be sent from Alexandria, and one strong division of which I had ordered to take post on the works at Manassas Junction. I was entirely under the belief that these would be there, and it was not until I found my communication intercepted that I was undeceived. I knew that this movement was no raid, and that it was made by not less than twenty-five thousand men."

The army of Gen. Pope was now on the 27th on the retreat in three columns. The one moving back along the railroad toward Manassas Junction, under Gen. Hooker, was the first to encounter the Confederate forces in the rear. It was the advance of the same force, a portion of which had repulsed Col. Scammon and Gen. Taylor in separate actions during the forenoon. That portion of the force had ceased to follow them beyond Sangster's Station, as they would thereby have been drawn away from the main body, and also from the support of Gen. Lee's army marching upon White Plains and Thoroughfare Gap, and because Gen. Pope was falling back upon them. Upon the approach of Gen. Hooker's force to Bristow's Station the Confederate forces fell back about one and a half miles across Kettle Run, and formed upon its left bank. Their main body was at Manassas, a little farther in the rear, to which their line of battle extended. A severe action ensued, which terminated at dark. Gen. Ewell's force was driven from the field, with the loss of his camp equipage and about three hundred killed and wounded. Gen. Hooker's division had brought with them only forty rounds of ammunition, and at night there were only five rounds to the man left. Upon learning this fact, Gen. Pope immediately sent back orders to Gen. Porter to march with his corps at one o'clock that night, so as to be with Gen. Hooker at daylight in the morning, the 28th, with Morell's division, and also directed him to communicate with Gen. Banks the order to move forward to Warrenton Junction. All trains were ordered this side of Cedar Run, and to be protected by a regiment of infantry and a section of artillery. Owing to insurmountable obstacles and the limited time given him to make the march, Gen. Porter did not arrive as early as expected.

The position of Gen. Jackson after the defeat of Ewell on the night of the 27th was dangerous. Without reënforcements he must retreat before the powerful foe in front. Only two routes were open for him. The one by which he had come, which was through Gainesville and Thoroughfare Gap; and the other toward Centreville. If he attempted the first one, he would meet the forces of Gens. McDowell and Sigel, and the Pennsylvania reserve under Gen. Reynolds, who were already at Gainesville, whither they had been ordered two days previous by Gen. Pope. His only course of safety was to fall back toward Centreville, which he did that night, and took position on the farther line of Bull Run. At noon on the 28th Manassas was occupied by the troops of Gen. Pope, and on the same day Gen. Heintzelman's corps, consisting of the divisions of Gens. Hooker and Kearny, pushed on to Centreville, and entered the place soon after the rear of Gen. Jackson had retired. At this time Gen. Reno, who had coöperated with Gen. McDowell, had reached Manassas Junction, and Gen. Porter was at Broad Run, where he had been ordered to halt. It was now of the utmost importance to Gen. Lee that Gen. Jackson should be reënforced, or he might be cut off. Foreseeing the danger, Gen. Lee had ordered Gen. Longstreet to proceed on the 24th from Warrenton by way of Thoroughfare Gap, a pass in the Bull Run mountains, fifteen miles west of Centreville, and unite with Gen. Jackson. The advance of Gen. Longstreet appears to have reached Thoroughfare Gap on the evening of the 28th, and encountered Gen. Ricket's division, which retired that night to Bristow's Station. The enemy was thus free to join Gen. Jackson both by Thoroughfare and Hopeville Gaps. The advance of Gen. Jackson retiring to join Gen. Longstreet encountered, near Gainesville on the Warrenton turnpike, Gen. Gibbon's brigade of King's division—or all of King's division—which was a part of Gen. McDowell's force. The division behaved handsomely, and suffered severe loss. The contest closed with the darkness, and the division retired to Manassas Junction before day of the 29th. The road was open for the union of Gen. Longstreet with Gen. Jackson, and the junction was effected on the morning of the 29th, at 10 A. M., in person and with large force.

Hopeville is about three miles northeast of White Plains, on the road from White Plains to Aldie. The road across the mountains is some three miles north of Thoroughfare Gap. Gen. Halleck in his report says: "McDowell had succeeded in checking Lee at Thoroughfare Gap; but the latter took the road from Hopeville to Haymarket, and hastened to the relief of Jackson, who was already in rapid retreat."

The next morning found Gen. King's division fallen back from Warrenton turnpike toward Manassas Junction. It had been driven back by the forces of Gen. Jackson. The passage of the Gap was no longer disputed, and reënforcements to Gen. Jackson were passing through during the whole day. Gen. Lee, in his despatch to Richmond, says that Gen. Longstreet reached Gen. Jackson on the 29th. The posture of affairs was now changed. The overwhelming forces of Gen. Lee were at hand, and it became a question with Gen. Pope what the consequences to him might be. He seems to have apprehended the facts. He cautioned Gen. Porter, in his order, not to go farther in his march to effect a junction with Gen. Heintzelman than might be necessary, adding, "as he might be obliged to retire behind Bull Run that night for subsistence, if nothing else." It is worthy of notice that the movements of Gen. Jackson for the last two days had been in the direction of Thoroughfare Gap, in order to be nearer the approaching rëenforcements, which he was confident would surely come. Soon after daylight on the next morning, the 29th, the contest began on the part of Gens. Sigel and Reynolds's divisions of Gen. McDowell's corps and the Confederate forces. The divisions were on the west toward Gainesville. The plan of Gen. Pope was for Gen. Heintzelman, with Gens. Hooker, Kearny, and Reno, to proceed from Centreville toward Gainesville and attack the enemy on that side, and Gen. Porter, with Gen. King's division, to make another attack from the south, and Gens. McDowell and Sigel from the west, thus attacking them on three sides. The contest, as has been stated, commenced early in the morning on the part of Gens. Sigel and Reynolds, and was continued rather feebly until the afternoon, when Gen. Heintzelman's corps joined Gen. Sigel, and soon after Gen. Longstreet had joined Gen. Jackson. Here Gen. Grover's brigade of Gen. Hooker's division made a brilliant bayonet charge through two lines of the enemy and into a third one, losing thirty per cent. of its force in twenty minutes. Gen. McDowell also brought his whole corps into the field in the afternoon, and, as Gen. Pope says, "taking a conspicuous part in that day's operations." Gen. Porter, reduced by the withdrawal of Gen. King's division, was on the direct road to Gainesville, along the railroad from Manassas Junction, holding in check a large force of the enemy's right wing, strongly posted to guard the flank of that portion confronting Gen. Pope's right. About 7 P. M. Gen. Heintzelman's right division under Gen. Kearny turned the enemy's left toward Sudley Springs and went into action, driving them back fully a mile. Thus the day ended successfully for the Federal arms. The entire force of Gen. Pope, except Gen. Banks's corps, was thus engaged with the two wings of Gen. Lee's army. The loss on this day by Gen. Pope was reported at eight thousand, which was an overstatement. Both parties slept upon their arms that night on the same spot, near the old battle ground of Bull Run. The contest was renewed the next day, the 30th. The object now with Gen. Pope was, if possible, to maintain his position. The design of the enemy appeared to be to accumulate such a force on his right as to crush the Federal left and occupy the road to Centreville in its rear. Gen. Lee, of the Confederate army, thus reports the action of this day: "The enemy, being reënforced, renewed the attack on the afternoon of the 30th, when a general advance of both wings of the army was ordered, and after a fierce combat, which raged until after nine o'clock, he was completely defeated and driven beyond Bull Run. The darkness of the night, his destruction of the stone bridge after crossing, and the uncertainty of the fords, stopped the pursuit." The only additional force brought into this part of the field on this day by Gen. Pope was the corps of Gen. Porter, which was moved from the extreme left to the centre, travelling a distance of six miles. Gen. Pope, in his report, thus describes the conflict of the 30th: "The enemy's heavy reënforcements having reached him on Friday afternoon and night, he began to mass on his right for the purpose of crushing our left, and occupying the road to Centreville in our rear. His heaviest assault was made about five o'clock in the afternoon, when, after overwhelming Fitz John Porter, and driving his forces back on the centre and left, mass after mass of his forces was pushed against our left. A terrible contest, with great slaughter, was carried on for several hours, our men behaving with firmness and gallantry under the immediate command of Gen. McDowell. When night closed our left had been forced back about half a mile, but still remained firm and unshaken, while our right held its ground. Gen. Franklin, with his corps, arrived after dark at Centreville, six miles in our rear, whilst Sumner was four miles behind Franklin. I could have brought up these corps in the morning in time to have renewed the action, but starvation stared both men and horses in the face, and, broken and exhausted as they were, they were in no condition to bear hunger also. I accordingly retired to Centreville that night in perfect order."

It appears that the contest with artillery commenced early in the day, and but little damage was done on either side. Early in the afternoon an attempt was made to break the line of Gen. Porter stationed on Gen. Pope's centre. This was unsuccessful, but caused a severe loss to Gen. Porter. In the latter part of the afternoon the enemy's forces were concentrated upon the corps of Gen. McDowell on the left of the centre. The batteries there, Lapine's 5th Maine, Thompson's New York, and Howell's, not being sufficiently supported by infantry, were soon captured, and McDowell's troops were driven irresistibly back. The right and centre still maintained their positions, but the disaster on the left, and the apprehended design of the enemy to occupy the road to Centreville in their rear, made it necessary for them to fall back. In doing so the bridge across Bull Run was destroyed. The field of battle with its dead and wounded was left in the hands of the enemy. The right wing of the army was this day commanded by Gen. Heintzelman, and did not give one inch of ground to the enemy until ordered so to do after the repulse received by the left wing. The losses on both sides were severe, but have never been officially made public. The report of Gen. Pope was made before the reports of his subordinate officers were received. These, in consequence of his absence in the West, had not been made near the close of the year. The entire loss of Gen. Pope was estimated at between 15,000 and 20,000.

At Richmond the following despatch was received from Gen. Lee:

HEADQUARTERS ARMY NORTHERN VIRGINIA, GROVETOWN, *Aug.* 30, P. M., *via* Rapidan.

To President Davis:

This army achieved to-day, on the plains of Manassas, a signal victory over the combined forces of Gens. McClellan and Pope. On the 28th and 29th each wing, under Gens. Longstreet and Jackson, repulsed with valor attacks made on them separately. We mourn the loss of our gallant dead in every conflict, yet our gratitude to Almighty God for His mercies rises higher each day. To Him and to the valor of our troops a nation's gratitude is due. R. E. LEE.

This was followed on the 2d of September by the following Message of President Davis to the Confederate Congress:

To the Senate and House of Representatives of the Confederate States:

I have the gratification of presenting to Congress

two despatches from Gen. Robert E. Lee, commanding the army of Northern Virginia, communicating the result of the operations north of the Rappahannock.

From these despatches it will be seen that God has again extended His shield over our patriotic army, and has blessed the cause of the Confederacy with a second signal victory on the field already memorable by the gallant achievement of our troops.

JEFFERSON DAVIS.

At Washington, on Saturday, the 30th, the War Department invited the citizens to go out to the battle-field and assist in taking care of the wounded soldiers. A large number responded to the invitation. From three to seven o'clock, P. M., the streets swarmed with people and conveyances loaded with blankets and baskets and rolls of lint. Every public carriage and vehicle was impressed into the service. A thousand persons at least went out. More would have gone on Saturday morning, but the invitation was recalled, and passes refused. The entire movement turned out as ill advised. Very few persons were allowed to go far enough to find the wounded they sought, and some were made prisoners by the Confederates. The movement thus begun at Washington instantly extended through all the principal cities of the Northern States. In Boston, Massachusetts, which will serve as an illustration of the others, the greatest excitement prevailed on Sunday, the 31st. A despatch had been received on the previous evening from Washington, by Gov. Andrew, asking that the surgeon-general of the State should send on twenty surgeons with hospital supplies as soon as possible. This demand was made public at an early hour in the morning, with the notice that contributions would be received at Tremont Temple. Those notices were also read from pulpits, which is the usual manner of advertising on Sunday in New England, and many congregations were immediately dismissed to procure contributions. At an early hour these contributions began to be received at the Temple, and continued to pour in during the whole day—old sheets for bandages, shirts, dressing gowns, pillows, liquors, jellies, and sweetmeats of all kinds—in a word, every variety of article which could suggest itself to a kind heart as necessary to the comfort of the wounded soldier. Bundles and packages of every conceivable size and shape were momentarily arriving. Ladies brought bundles, who were never seen to carry bundles before; and stout gentlemen in gold spectacles were seen driving heavy-laden carts through the streets, or lending a hand at the boxes. All these articles were received at the side doors of the Temple and taken within, where corps of packers inclosed them in boxes, which were then taken out of the main entrance to the express wagons, which crowded the streets. Thus twenty-one hundred cases were packed, and all sent forward by the evening train, except about one hundred and fifty. At the same time subscriptions were taken at stands on the sidewalks, and over five thousand dollars collected.

To an application from Gen. Pope for a truce to gather the wounded, Gen. Lee on the same day, August 31st, replied as follows:

SIR: Consideration for your wounded induces me to consent to your sending ambulances to convey them within your lines. I cannot consent to a truce nor a suspension of the military operations of this army. If you desire to send for your wounded, should your ambulances report to Dr. Guilet, Medical Director of this army, he will give directions for their transportation. The wounded will be paroled, and it is understood that no delay will take place in their removal. Very respectfully, your obedient serv't,

R. E. LEE, General.

On Sunday, the 31st, the Confederate army was put in motion toward the Little River turnpike for the purpose of turning the right of Gen. Pope. During Sunday night and Monday morning, Gen. Pope, anticipating this design of the enemy, changed his front by causing his right wing to fall back to the heights of Germantown. Thus when the enemy reached Ox Hill on Monday, he discovered Gen. Pope's army in his front on these heights. The ultimate design of the enemy was to cut the rear of Gen. Pope in the direction of Fairfax Court House. The Little River turnpike runs from Middleburg to Alexandria, and intersects the Centreville turnpike about a mile east of Fairfax Court House. Germantown is a small village between Fairfax Court House and Centreville, and about one-fourth of the whole distance beyond the former.

Meanwhile, during the conflict on Friday and Saturday, Gen. Banks, with his command, was covering the extreme left of Gen. Pope's line, to keep off reënforcements for the enemy, and to be used as a reserve. He crossed to Bristow's Station, on the railroad four miles beyond Manassas Junction, and on Sunday was approached by a large force of the enemy, before which he fell back and joined Gen. Pope. The bridge at Bristow's station having been destroyed by the enemy at the time of their attack upon it, and that over Bull Run not having been repaired, he destroyed the property of the United States before retiring. This consisted of some 200 railroad cars, five locomotives, and a large quantity of fixed ammunition, ordnance stores, &c. The enemy, however, obtained great spoil. On the same day, Sunday, Sept. 1, Fredericksburg was evacuated by Gen. Burnside. Falmouth station was burned, and a quantity of commissary stores. The bridge erected in place of the old railroad bridge, the wire bridge, and the boat bridge were destroyed. The evacuation of Aquia Creek followed.

Gen. Pope states that by the reports of the commanders of corps of his army it consisted on the 1st of September, of less than 60,000 men. The position taken by his orders on this day was as follows: The division of Gen. Couch and one brigade of Gen. Sumner's corps were at Fairfax Court House. Gen. Hooker was posted at or in front of Germantown, and had command of his own troops and those at Fairfax. Gen. McDowell's corps was stationed on the Warrenton turnpike about two miles west of Fairfax. Gen. Reno was pushed north of the turnpike at a point about two and a half miles east of Centreville, and supported by Gen. Kearny's division of Gen. Heintzelman's corps.

Late in the afternoon the force of Gen. Lee, composed of infantry and cavalry, approached Germantown by the Little River turnpike, and were met by Gen. Hooker at that place and by Gen. Reno farther west. The conflict raged for an hour, when they concentrated their force on the left of Gen. Reno's line, which was commanded by Gen. Stevens. Their intention was to turn his left flank. Gen. Stevens was soon killed by a bullet through his head, and his troops were driven back. The Confederate force now began to advance on the main body of Gen. Reno, which was short of ammunition, when the division of Gen. Kearny came up and took the position occupied by the troops of Gen. Stevens. Night had now set in, rendered thickly dark by a thunder storm. The rain fell in torrents, and the position of the contending armies was revealed only by the flashes of lightning. At this time Gen. Kearny, anxious to know the nature of the ground upon which he expected so soon to fight, rode out to examine it. Inadvertently he passed the line of his own pickets and approached those of the Confederate force, when he was shot by one of them. He was soon missed from his camp, and not being found, Gen. Birney took command of the division. During the next day his body was brought in under a Confederate flag of truce. Thus two most valuable officers and brave soldiers were slain in this conflict. After Gen. Birney had taken command, he ordered a bayonet charge to be made by Col. Egan, commanding the 1st and 40th, and Col. Ward, of the 38th New York regiments, before which the enemy retired.

By morning, on the 2d of September, the whole of Gen. Pope's army was massed behind Difficult creek, between Germantown, Flint Hill, and Fairfax. On that day orders were issued by the general-in-chief for the Army of Virginia to fall back within the defences of Washington. The object of the general-in-chief in giving this order was "to reorganize the different corps, to get the stragglers back into the ranks, and to supply deficiencies of ammunition, clothing," &c. This movement was executed on the 2d and 3d of September. During these days might be seen on the roads leading to Alexandria and the fortifications around Washington, the worn and bleeding fragments of the once proud armies of the North, as they straggled in from their fifteen bloody days of fighting and retreating. There were the remnants of the decimated regiments of Maine, New York, New Jersey, Pennsylvania, Ohio, and Michigan—stragglers belonging to every army corps, wounded, weak, and dispirited, retiring before a victorious enemy to obtain safety in the fortifications. Many of them had fought their way up the peninsula, contesting almost every inch from Williamsburg against bullets and bayonets until they stood in sight of the spires of Richmond, and then were required to abandon their position and withdraw.

CHAPTER XXI.

Advance of Gen. Lee into Maryland—His Address to the People—Gen. McClellan ordered to take command at Washington—His Orders—Advances into Maryland to meet Gen. Lee—Confidential Order of Gen. Lee—Battle of South Mountain—Attack of the Enemy on Harper's Ferry—Its Surrender—Battle of Antietam—Retreat of Gen. Lee.

The rebel force which was repulsed near Centreville on Monday night, September 2d, moved toward Vienna, about twelve miles west from Washington, for the purpose of making a demonstration near the Chain Bridge, and the fords of the Potomac above Washington. The chief object in this movement was to divert the attention of the Federal officers from what Gen. Lee was doing elsewhere. The withdrawal of the army of Gen. Pope left the field clear for the army of Gen. Lee to follow it, and assault the strong fortifications of Washington, or to pass over the Potomac into Maryland. The assault upon the fortifications of Washington was not to be thought of. But the invasion of Maryland might be followed by such a welcome from the mass of the citizens, and such coöperation, as to enable Gen. Lee not only to hold a portion of the State, but to attack Washington in the rear, and perhaps invade Pennsylvania. In any event it would be a demonstration to the Federal Government, and to nations in Europe, of the vigorous energy and strength of the Richmond Government. Accordingly, on the 31st of August, while Gen. Pope was resting his exhausted forces at Centreville, Gen. Lee drew off the main body of his army and moved to Leesburg. Thence he moved to the Potomac, near Point of Rocks, and crossed at Noland's Ford, five miles below, and at a ford three miles above on the 5th. His force consisted of the divisions of Gens. Longstreet, Jackson, Ewell, A. P. Hill, and D. H. Hill. It proceeded along the eastern slope of the Catoctin Mountains, in the direction of Frederick, Maryland. On the night of the 5th the advance reached White Oak Springs, about three miles from that city, which is fifty miles from Centreville. On the same night information was received at Frederick of the approach of the Confederate force, and it produced much excitement. A large number of the inhabitants fled toward Pennsylvania and Baltimore. Frederick, the capital of the State of Maryland, is forty-four miles northwest of Washington, and sixty miles west of Baltimore. It is the second city of the State in wealth and commercial importance, and the third in population, containing 8,143 inhabitants. The military force in the city consisted of only one company, which could make no opposition. The Federal provost marshal removed all the military stores possible, and, leaving enough for the hospitals, in which there were about six hundred patients, burned the remainder. About ten o'clock the next morning, the 6th, the Confederate troops quietly entered the city. These soldiers were in a destitute condition, in respect to clothes and shoes, yet the most scrupulous regard was had to private property. They had no tents, nor were burdened with any baggage. Their only trains were ammunition trains. If enduring great hardships without a murmur, and most bravely and heroically fighting, are evidences of good soldiers, seldom has the world witnessed better than those who composed the army of Gen. Lee. A Confederate provost marshal was appointed (Bradley Johnson), and a proclamation issued to the citizens, stating that the army came as friends, and not as enemies, to relieve the people of Maryland from the tyranny by which they were oppressed; that they did not purpose to interfere with any non-combatants, or to disturb private property, or to inquire into the opinions of citizens; and that whatever stores they required would be paid for, either in Confederate notes or United States Treasury notes, as the seller might prefer. At night the soldiers were all ordered to their camps outside of the city. Meantime foraging parties were sent out in various directions, which returned at evening with droves of sheep, cattle, hogs, and horses. These droves were all taken toward the Potomac. Pickets were thrown out from Frederick both east and west for considerable distances. On Sunday they were reported to have advanced within seven miles of Westminster, causing a great excitement in the town, but disappeared during the night. No Confederate force, however, came farther east at that time than Uniontown, twenty miles from Westminster. The main body encamped for some days on a line between Frederick and the Potomac river. Recruiting offices were opened in the city, and citizens invited to enlist. Very few volunteers, however, were obtained.

On the 8th, Gen. Lee issued the following address to the people of Maryland:

HEADQUARTERS, ARMY OF NORTHERN VIRGINIA,
NEAR FREDERICKTOWN, *Sept.* 8, 1862.

To the People of Maryland:

It is right that you should know the purpose that has brought the army under my command within the limits of your State, so far as that purpose concerns yourselves.

The people of the Confederate States have long watched with the deepest sympathy the wrongs and outrages that have been inflicted upon the citizens of a Commonwealth allied to the States of the South by the strongest social, political, and commercial ties, and reduced to the condition of a conquered province.

Under the pretence of supporting the Constitution, but in violation of its most valuable provisions, your citizens have been arrested and imprisoned, upon no charge, and contrary to all the forms of law.

A faithful and manly protest against this outrage, made by a venerable and illustrious Marylander, to whom in his better days no citizen appealed for right in vain, was treated with scorn and contempt.

The government of your chief city has been usurped by armed strangers; your Legislature has been dissolved by the unlawful arrest of its members; freedom of the press and of speech has been suppressed; words have been declared offences by an arbitrary decree of the Federal executive; and citizens ordered to be tried by military commissions for what they may dare to speak.

Believing that the people of Maryland possess a spirit too lofty to submit to such a government, the people of the South have long wished to aid you in throwing off this foreign yoke, to enable you again to enjoy the inalienable rights of freemen, and restore the independence and sovereignty of your State.

In obedience to this wish, our army has come among you, and is prepared to assist you with the power of its arms in regaining the rights of which you have been so unjustly despoiled.

This, citizens of Maryland, is our mission so far as you are concerned. No restraint upon your free will is intended—no intimidation will be allowed within the limits of this army at least. Marylanders shall once more enjoy their ancient freedom of thought and speech. We know no enemies among you, and will protect all of you in every opinion.

It is for you to decide your destiny freely and without constraint. This army will respect your choice, whatever it may be; and, while the Southern people will rejoice to welcome you to your natural position among them, they will only welcome you when you come of your own free will.

R. E. LEE, General Commanding.

On the 10th Gen. Lee began to evacuate Frederick, and by the 12th his entire force had left. His forces moved in the direction of Hagerstown. That same night the city was occupied by the advance of Gen. McClellan's army, under Gen. Hooker.

On the afternoon of the 10th, Hagerstown was entered by a Confederate force. On the 6th and 7th the banks of the town, anticipating this approach, removed their specie to Harrisburg and other places east for safety. The Government stores there were also removed.

Meantime, on the first approach of the Confederate army across the Potomac, the greatest excitement prevailed in Pennsylvania, especially in York and Adams counties, and through the Susquehanna and Cumberland valleys. The farmers sent away their wives, children, and cattle, and hastened to take up arms. In many of the towns of the State stores were closed, bells rung, guns fired, public meetings held, and citizens in their excitement assembled in mass to drill. On the 10th Gov. Curtin issued an order calling upon all the able bodied men of Pennsylvania to organize immediately for the defence of the State, and to be ready for marching orders upon an hour's notice. On the 11th he issued a call for fifty thousand of the freemen of the State to enter immediate service to repel the imminent danger of invasion. On the same day he addressed the following despatch to the mayor of Philadelphia:

We have reliable information this evening that the rebel generals have moved their entire army from Frederick to Cumberland Valley, and their destination is now Harrisburg and Philadelphia. We need every available man immediately. Stir up your population to-night. Form them into companies, and send us twenty thousand to-morrow. No time can be lost in massing a force on the Susquehanna to defend the State and your city. Arouse every man possible and send him here.

Gov. Bradford, of Maryland, also issued a proclamation calling upon the citizens to organize without delay such a force as might effectually assist in defending their homes and firesides. The effect of these appeals, especially in Pennsylvania, was to bring to the governor a response from more than seventy-five thousand men. Harrisburg, the capital, overflowed with troops. The excitement, however, was not confined to Pennsylvania. In the adjacent States, troops under the first call for three hundred thousand men were hurried to Washington and to Harrisburg. It created another military excitement, and volunteers promptly came forward in all the States to fill up the call of the President.

On the 2d of September, the following order was issued by the general-in-chief:

War Department, Adjutant-General's Office, Washington, *September* 2, 1862.
General Orders, No. 122.

Maj.-Gen. McClellan will have command of the fortifications of Washington, and of all the troops for the defence of the capital.

By command of Maj.-Gen. HALLECK.
E. D. Townsend, Assist. Adj.-Gen.

When Gen. McClellan arrived at Washington from Harrison's Landing, he was in the department of Gen. Pope, which included the District of Columbia. This was about the middle of August. Subsequent to that time he was without a command, excepting a body of ninety-six men, until this order was issued. Each corps of his army had been sent forward to Gen. Pope. In fact the active forces under the command of Gen. Pope consisted of the Army of Virginia, embracing the corps of Gens. McDowell, Banks, Sigel, a portion of Gen. Cox's force from western Virginia, a part of Gen. Burnside's force from North Carolina, about ten regiments from Port Royal in South Carolina, under Gen. Stevens, and the Army of the Potomac, consisting of the corps of Gens. Heintzelman, Sumner, Porter, and Franklin, and the divisions of Gens. McCall and Couch, without including the troops stationed in the fortifications around Washington. With this force he was not able to withstand the overwhelming march of the Confederate army. Yet this same Confederate army was the force which the Army of the Potomac, under Gen. McClellan, single handed and unaided, was required to meet and conquer, and thus obtain the capital of the Confederacy, which was in their possession. In this unequal struggle no dishonor ever tarnished the Army of the Potomac.

On the 4th of September, Gen. McClellan, having received the order above stated, issued another assuming command of the forces above mentioned, together with some new levies which had arrived at Washington under the call of the President for three hundred thousand men. His order assuming the command acted like an electric shock upon these dispirited, defeated masses. It was as follows:

Headquarters, Washington, *Sept.* 4, 1862.
General Orders, No. 1.

1. Pursuant to General Orders No. 122, from the War Department, Adjutant-General's Office, of the 2d instant, the undersigned hereby assumes command of the fortifications of Washington and of all troops for the defence of the capital.

2. The heads of the staff departments of the Army of the Potomac will be in charge of their respective departments at these headquarters.

3. In addition to the consolidated morning reports required by circular of this date from these headquarters, reports will be made by corps commanders as to their compliance with the assignment to positions heretofore given them, stating definitely the ground occupied and covered by their command, and as to what progress has been made in obedience to orders already issued to place their commands in condition for immediate service. GEO. B. McCLELLAN, Maj.-Gen.

Official: S. Williams, Assist. Adj.-General.

It was now known that Gen. Lee had marched into Maryland, and the orders given to Gen. McClellan were to pursue him with all the troops which were not required for the defence of Washington. On the next day most of his army was in motion, and rapidly advanced into Maryland. Gen. Couch's division, consisting of three brigades, commanded by Gens. Howe, Devens, and Cochrane, on the morning of the 6th had reached the road from Rockville to Great Falls, eight miles beyond Tenallytown. Other corps were rapidly pressing on. Three days after assuming command, on the 7th, at six P. M., he left Washington to take the field. That night he passed through Rockville, fifteen miles from Washington, stopping only long enough to refresh his horses. On the morning of the 10th, the army had advanced to Damascus, thirty-four miles from Washington and sixteen miles from Frederick. The first movements of the army were such as to occupy positions which commanded all the lower fords of the Potomac, thus presenting to the Confederate army the alternative of meeting him in battle, or retiring before him, and crossing the Potomac higher up, which would take them further from Washington, and oblige them to retreat through the Shenandoah Valley.

Meantime Gen. Lee, after his successes against Gen. Pope, had no reason to apprehend that the same army would soon be in pursuit of him; yet, like a prudent commander, he, upon learning of the approach of Gen. McClellan, immediately took precautions to secure his own safety. His army had met with no such welcome from the citizens of Maryland as to give any hope that the State would, under any circumstances, rise in opposition to the Federal Government. On the contrary the people had shown that it was the Government of their choice. Very few recruits had joined the Confederate army, and no contributions of importance had been made to it. The following is a copy of Gen. Lee's order of march, found at Frederick, on the 13th of September. It discloses his plans:

[CONFIDENTIAL.]

HEADQUARTERS, ARMY OF NORTHERN VIRGINIA, *Sept.* 9, 1862.

Special Order, No. 191.

III. The army will resume its march to-morrow, taking the Hagerstown road. Gen. Jackson's command will form the advance, and after passing Middleton with such portion as he may select, take the route toward Sharpsburg, cross the Potomac at the most convenient point, and by Friday morning take possession of the Baltimore and Ohio railroad, capture such of the enemy as may be at Martinsburg, and intercept such as may attempt to escape from Harper's Ferry.

IV. Gen. Longstreet's command will pursue the main road as far as Boonsboro', where it will halt with reserve, supply, and baggage trains of the army.

V. Gen. McLaws, with his own division and that of Gen. R. H. Anderson, will follow Gen. Longstreet, on reaching Middleton will take the route to Harper's Ferry, and by Friday morning possess himself of the Maryland Heights, and endeavor to capture the enemy at Harper's Ferry and vicinity.

VI. Gen. Walker, with his division, after accomplishing the object in which he is now engaged, will cross the Potomac at Check's Ford, ascend its right bank to Lovettsville, take possession of Loudon Heights, if praticable, by Friday morning, keep the ford on his left, and the road between the end of mountain and the Potomac on his right. He will, as far as practicable, coöperate with Gen. McLaws and Gen. Jackson in intercepting the retreat of the enemy.

VII. Gen. D. H. Hill's division will form the rear guard of the army, pursuing the road taken by the main body. The reserve artillery, ordnance, and supply trains will precede Gen. Hill.

VIII. Gen. Stuart will detach a squadron of cavalry to accompany the commands of Gens. Longstreet, Jackson, and McLaws, and with the main body of the cavalry will cover the route of the army, and bring up all stragglers that may have been left behind.

IX. The commands of Gens. Jackson, McLaws, and Walker, after accomplishing the objects for which they have attached [been detached?], will join the main body of the army at Boonsboro' or Hagerstown.

X. Each regiment on the march, will habitually carry its axes in the regimental ordnance wagons for use of the men at their encampments to procure wood, &c.

By command of Gen. R. E. LEE.

(Signed) R. H. CHILTON, A. A.-General.

For Maj.-Gen. D. H. HILL, Comd'g Division.

It is clear from this order that Gen. Lee intended first to capture the garrison at Harper's Ferry, and then to enter Pennsylvania by the Cumberland Valley; at all events, that he had no idea of abandoning Maryland until forced to do so by the battles of South Mountain and Antietam. He evacuated Frederick, and taking the road to Hagerstown crossed the Catoctin Mountains, passed through the valley in which Middletown is situated, and drew up his forces along the crest of South Mountain there to await the advance of Gen. McClellan. At the same time he detached a portion of his force, amounting to twenty-five thousand men, and sent them to Harper's Ferry by the route of Williamsport, where they crossed the Potomac. The chief command of this force was given to Gen. Jackson. It embraced his division with those of Gens. A. P. Hill and Walker, and one or two others. By this route, although longer, they were more certain to reach Harper's Ferry without the knowledge of the Federal Government than if their movement had been more direct. The distance from Frederick to Williamsport was thirty miles, and from Williamsport to Harper's Ferry thirty miles.

The advance of Gen. McClellan entered Frederick on the 12th, and he immediately sent forward cavalry and artillery to follow and harass the Confederate rear. Gen. Pleasanton was in command of the cavalry, and several skirmishes took place during the succeeding days. The line of the Federal army extended from the Potomac river in the region of Point of Rocks in a north-easterly direction to the region near Frederick, and thence in an easterly and southerly direction along the Baltimore and Ohio railroad to Baltimore. On Saturday the 13th, the main column of Gen. McClellan's army reached Frederick, and was received with the highest demonstrations and encamped two miles beyond. The same afternoon the Confederate rear was driven by his advance out of Middletown, which was held by the latter during the night. West of Frederick and running nearly due south is the Catoctin range of mountains, a continuation of the Blue Ridge. On the south it terminates in Maryland at Point of Rocks, but still continues in Virginia. On the north it unites at the Pennsylvania State line with the South Mountain range, which, tending to the southwest, slopes down to the Potomac at Knoxville four miles east of Harper's Ferry. Between these two ranges, nestles the loveliest valley in Maryland—the valley of Catoctin. The village of Middletown, ten miles from Frederick, is in the centre of this valley. On Sunday morning, the 14th, the Confederate army were found posted on the east side of the South Blue Ridge Mountain and stretching on a line from north to south from points immediately opposite Middletown and Jefferson, both of which villages are about eight miles from Frederick. Middletown is on the road to Hagerstown and Jefferson on the direct road to Harper's Ferry. The right of the Federal army, at that time under Gen. Burnside, rested on Middletown, and the left under Gen. Franklin on Jefferson. Early in the morning, the advance beyond Middletown overtook the Confederate rear, who retreated slowly, contesting the road toward Boonsboro' step by step. The conflict that ensued during the morning was chiefly with artillery, and came to closer quarters in the afternoon. At this time the Confederate line of battle was formed with the left resting upon Turner's Gap and the turnpike road toward Hagerstown which passes through the gap, and the right covering Crampton's Gap.

Preparations for moving the main body of the Federal army had commenced at daylight, and shortly after the whole army was advancing rapidly toward the mountains followed by the ambulances, artillery, and baggage wagons. Middletown was reached with ease, beyond which was now the scene of conflict. As they approached the field the long black lines of infantry were halted and opened to make way for the artillery and ammunition trains which advanced to their positions..

The battle of South Mountain really commenced at a bridge over Catoctin Creek half a mile west of Middletown, where Confederate artillery had been posted to dispute the passage. Dislodged from this position it retreated to a stronger one up the mountain side. The main body was massed on wooded bluffs to the right and left for a distance of more than two miles. On the right of Turner's Gap they were stormed out of their stronghold by Gen. Burnside's corps. Gen. Cox's Kanawha division in Gen. Reno's corps, attacked and carried the crest on the left of the gap. Of this division, the 23d Ohio, known as the "psalm singers of the Western Reserve," here came in contact with the 23d South Carolina, and the encounter was most stormy. So desperate were the Carolinians in the fight that before a single man surrendered he would beat his gun against a rock or tree to render it useless to his enemy. The Kanawha division was supported by the divisions of Gens. Wilcox, Rodman, and Sturgess. After very severe fighting they repulsed several attacks of the enemy, and retained entire possession of the crest. About 3 P. M., Gen. Hooker attacked the heights on the right of the pass, the Pennsylvania reserves leading, and after a desperate resistance carried the crest about dark, and held it. Shortly before dark Gen. Gibbon's brigade of Gen. Hooker's corps, attacked by the main road, and after an obstinate conflict gained the entrance to the pass some time after dark. Only by a display of equal valor in all the other regiments, and often at close quarters, was the enemy driven over the crest of the mountain into the valley on the west side of the South Mountain. In the centre and on the left, equally desperate was the battle. A severe fire of artillery had been opened all along the front. Under cover of this, the infantry advanced, and poured in a fire of musketry; this continued until 3 o'clock P. M. when the battle raged at its height. Success being soon gained on the right, desperate charges were made with the bayonet before which the Confederate troops wavered, broke, and fell back in confusion. The loss sustained by the Union forces was 2,325 killed and wounded. Among the killed was Gen. Reno, who was shot through the body. Turner's Gap, where the last desperate stand of the Confederate force on the right was made, is two miles from the base of the mountain. Six miles south is Crampton's Gap, through which passes the road from Jefferson to Roherville. This strong position on the left was carried by Gen. Franklin's corps, after a succession of brilliant bayonet charges. Gen. Franklin had followed the line of the Potomac closely. On Saturday he reached Sugar Loaf Mountain, and drove out the Confederate cavalry occupying it for a signal station. On Sunday, he passed through the small village of Burkitsville, and advanced about a mile, when he met the Confederate pickets at the South Mountain range, and near Crampton's Gap. The gap was strongly held by a Confederate force under Gen. Howell Cobb, and his artillery immediately opened fire upon the Federal advance, which was under the command of Gen. Slocum. The division of Gen. Slocum consisted of three brigades under Gens. Bartlett, Torbert, and Newton. These were formed in line of battle and ordered to advance up the side of the mountain. They had proceeded only a short distance before they came under the fire of a strong Confederate force concealed behind a stone wall running along the base of the gap. At this point a desperate hand to hand fight ensued which lasted nearly an hour, when the Confederate troops were routed. They did not attempt to make a stand again until they reached the crest of the mountain, where they turned and prepared to hold the Federal advance at bay. It came rushing up, composed of New Jersey, New York, and Pennsylvania regiments, until the top of the mountain was gained, when another bloody struggle ensued. The Confederate force finally gave way and fell back in disorder down into the valley, leaving four hundred prisoners, three regimental colors, two pieces of artillery, and three thousand stand of arms. The Federal loss in this affair was one hundred and five killed, and four hundred and forty-eight wounded. The Confederate loss was still larger. The seizure of this gap exposed the flank of Gen. Lee's army, and brought the Federal left into Pleasant Valley, and within five miles of Harper's Ferry. That night the Federal army occupied the battle ground, and the Confederate army fell behind Antietam Creek and took a position admirably adapted for defence.

Meantime the Federal garrison at Winchester and Martinsburg had been ordered to Harper's Ferry, and the commanding officer at that post had been advised to confine his defence, in case he was attacked by a superior force, mainly to the position of Maryland Heights, which could be held a long time against overwhelming numbers. A large amount of artillery and stores had been collected at Harper's Ferry by the Federal Government, which it would have been necessary to destroy or leave to the enemy if the troops there had been withdrawn. It was therefore determined by the general-in-chief (Halleck) to hold the position until Gen. McClellan could relieve it, or open communication so that it could be evacuated in safety.

On Friday, the 12th of September, two days before the battle of South Mountain, the Confederate force of Gen. Jackson, which had been ordered to Williamsport and thence to Harper's Ferry, commenced an attack on Maryland Heights. As early as the 15th of August Col. Miles, then in command, received orders from Gen. Wool, commanding the department, to fortify Maryland Heights, which is considered to be the key of the position. He, however, disobeyed the orders, and did nothing to improve its defences. On the 5th of September Col. Thomas H. Ford took command of the force stationed on the heights, and, apprehending an attack from the Confederate army, sent a requisition to Col. Miles for reënforcements and for tools necessary to erect defensive works. He received reënforcements, but not the tools; and with a few borrowed axes constructed a slight breastwork of trees near the crest of the hill on the same day upon which the advance of Gen. Jackson appeared. The forces at Harper's Ferry had been increased that day to about thirteen thousand men, of whom twenty-five hundred were cavalry, by the arrival of Gen. Julius White with the garrison from Martinsburg. Gen. White, although entitled to the command, waived his right in favor of Col. Miles. The only position fortified by Col. Miles was Bolivar Heights behind the town of Harper's Ferry. This is commanded by Maryland Heights and by Loudon Heights situated on the Virginia side of the Potomac and on the right bank of the Shenandoah.

The attack of the Confederate force was renewed, on the morning of the 13th, on the forces stationed on Maryland Heights, and they were driven behind the breastwork. This was soon after attacked, and the enemy were repulsed. Subsequently, through the precipitate flight of a portion of the troops and the premature retreat of the remainder, in consequence of a mistake of orders, the heights were about midday entirely abandoned. Col. Miles, who had visited the position early in the morning, left Col. Ford with permission to exercise his discretion in determining whether to hold or abandon the heights. Subsequently Col. Miles sent to him the following order.

HARPER'S FERRY, *Sept.* 13, 1862.

Col. Ford, Commanding Maryland Heights:

Since I returned to this side, on close inspection I find your position more defensible than it appears when at your station, covered as it is at all points by the cannon of Camp Hill. You will hold on, and can hold on until the cows' tails drop off.

Yours, D. S. MILES, Col. 21st Infantry.

The answer of Col. Ford to this order, as stated by Col. Miles, did not indicate that he had the slightest intention of giving up the heights.

Col. Ford, after the events above mentioned, disobeyed this order of Col. Miles, abandoned the position, and withdrew his forces across the river. It was only necessary, after this disgraceful retreat, for the enemy to plant their batteries and the position of Harper's Ferry must surely fall. The heights were not, however, immediately occupied by the enemy, and on the next morning a detachment of the 39th volunteers, sent there by Col. D'Utassy, returned with four field pieces and a wagon load of ammunition. On the 13th the Confederate force began to establish batteries on Loudon Heights, and on the next day opened fire from those heights and also from Maryland Heights. On the night of the 13th, Col. Miles sent a despatch to Gen. McClellan that the position could not be held forty-eight hours longer without reënforcements. This was the night before the battle of South Mountain. On the night of the 14th, the cavalry force under Col. Davis cut their way through the enemy's lines and reached Greencastle, Penn., in safety on the next morning, having captured by the way an ammunition train belonging to the corps of the Confederate general Longstreet. Early in the morning of the 15th Col. Miles surrendered. At that time Gen. McClellan's left wing was in Pleasant Valley, within five miles of him. It has been stated that the ammunition for the batteries was nearly exhausted, and for this reason the place became no longer tenable. The enemy, not perceiving the white flag that had been raised, continued their fire some time afterward, by which Col. Miles was mortally wounded by the fragment of a shell. The principal fighting took place on Saturday; there was very little on Sunday, and none worthy of mention on Monday, when the surrender took place. The military mistake was in abandoning Maryland Heights. No enemy could have occupied the village, or disturbed the railroad or pontoon bridges so long as they were held. Provisions and forage for a siege of four or five days could have been readily transferred to the heights by a road made some months previous. There are abundant springs of good and cool water gushing out from its rocky and wooded sides. When these and the other heights came into the possession of the enemy, surrender or destruction were the only alternatives to Col. Miles. If his entire force had been transferred to Maryland Heights, the Confederate force present could not for many days have taken Harper's Ferry. By the terms arranged for the surrender, the officers were allowed to go on parole with side arms and private property, and the privates with everything except equipments and guns. The forces which surrendered were as follows:

Unit	Number	Unit	Number
Col. Downye, 3d Maryland Home Brigade	600	65th Illinois	850
Col. Maulsby, 1st Maryland Home Brigade	900	Graham's battery	110
115th New York	1,000	McGrath's battery	115
120th New York	1,000	15th Indiana batt'y	142
39th New York	530	Phillips's N. Y. battery	120
111th New York	1,000	Potts's battery	100
125th New York	1,000	Rigby's battery	100
32d Ohio	654	Scatt'd companies	50
12th New York S.M.	504	Officers connected with Headquarters and Commissary Department	50
87th Ohio	900		
9th Vermont	800	Total	11,583

The following guns were surrendered: 12

2-inch rifled, 6 James's rifled, 6 24-pound howitzers, 4 20-pound Parrott guns, 4 12-pounders, 4 12-pound howitzers, 2 10-inch Dahlgrens, 1 50-pound Parrott, and 6 6-pound guns.

The Federal loss in killed and wounded was reported at about two hundred; the Confederate loss has not been stated. In the latter part of the year the circumstances attending this surrender were examined by a court of inquiry at Washington, in accordance with whose suggestions Col. Ford and other officers were dismissed from the United States army. The conduct of Col. Miles was stated in their report to have exhibited "an incapacity amounting almost to imbecility."

The surrender of this position with so little resistance was followed by serious consequences. It took place on the 15th. On the next day, the 16th, most of the Confederate force left it in great haste, crossed the pontoon bridge into Maryland, and joined Gen. Lee at Antietam in time to engage in the great battle on the next day, the 17th. Without the assistance of this force Gen. Lee's army would undoubtedly have been badly defeated and his retreat into Virginia probably cut off. That the importance of their aid was known to their commander, is manifest from the haste of the evacuation and the subsequent celerity of their movements. By their arrival the Confederate army outnumbered the Federal army in the battle of Antietam.

The battle on which was staked "the invasion of Maryland" in the view of the Federal, and "the deliverance of Maryland" in the view of the Confederate Government, but in reality the sovereignty of the Union, was now near at hand.

On the morning of the 15th the whole right wing and centre of Gen. McClellan's forces were pushed forward in pursuit of the enemy, who were found in the strong position made memorable by the battle of the Antietam. The troops were not up in sufficient force to make the attack on that day; but soon after night fell the greater part were in bivouac behind the heights on the left bank of the Antietam, sheltered from, but within range of the enemy's batteries.

On the left the three divisions of Gen. Franklin were ordered to occupy Roherville, and to push in the direction of Brownsville in order to relieve Harper's Ferry if possible. During the morning Gen. Franklin received intelligence of the surrender of Harper's Ferry, and found the enemy in force in a strong position near Brownsville. As he had but two divisions with him, the third not having yet arrived, he was not in sufficient force to dislodge the enemy, and was obliged to content himself with watching them and endeavoring to hold them in check.

The morning of the 16th was occupied in reconnoissances of the enemy's position, in rectifying the position of the Federal troops, and perfecting the arrangements for the attack. Very sharp artillery firing took place without any material loss on the Federal side. The position of Gen. McClellan's forces on that morning was as follows: Gen. Hooker's corps was on the right, next that of Gen. Sumner, with Gen. Mansfield's corps in the rear; in the centre was Gen. Porter's corps, only two divisions being present; on the left was Gen. Burnside's ninth corps. Gen. Franklin was still in Pleasant Valley.

At about 3 P. M., Gen. Hooker crossed the Antietam by the bridge in the village on the Hagerstown road and an adjacent ford, and soon gained the crest of the height on the right bank of the stream. He then turned to his left and followed down the ridge under a strong opposition, until brought to a stand still by the darkness. During the evening Gen. Mansfield was ordered to follow Gen. Hooker so as to be in a position to support him at daybreak.

At daylight on the 17th, Gen. Hooker attacked the forces in his front, and for a time drove them before him. The enemy however rallying, and strengthened from their supporting columns, repulsed him. Gen. Mansfield's corps was then drawn to Gen. Hooker's support, and the two masses repelled the enemy. Gen. Mansfield was killed and Gen. Hooker wounded at this crisis, and obliged to withdraw from the field. Shortly afterward Gen. Sumner's corps reached this portion of the field and soon became hotly engaged. This corps suffered greatly at this period of the contest, Gens. Sedgwick and Crawford being wounded, and portions of the line were compelled to fall back. The enemy were here, however, checked by the Federal artillery. Gen. Franklin shortly arrived to the relief of Gen. Sumner's line with two divisions of his corps, one of which, that of Gen. W. F. Smith, drove back the enemy and recovered the lost ground. The enemy did not retake it. Gens. Richardson's and French's divisions held the extreme left of the Federal right with tenacity during the day. Gen. Richardson was wounded.

In the centre Gen. Porter's corps was held as a reserve with cavalry and horse artillery.

The contest on the right had been most obstinate, and the several corps which participated in it had lost heavily.

Gen. Burnside's corps on the left was ordered early in the day to carry the bridge across the Antietam at Rohrback's farm, and to attack the enemy's right. The approaches to the bridge being in the nature of a defile, and being swept by batteries of the enemy, the opposite bank of the Antietam was only reached after a severe struggle. It was afternoon before the heights were in his possession. The enemy were driven back, and a portion of their line in disorder. By the most desperate efforts, however, the enemy rallied their retreating regiments, strengthened their line with all their available fresh troops, and opened batteries on the hills, from positions which the amphitheatrical character of the ground, it seems, abundantly furnished. Gen. Burnside could not maintain his advantage, and was obliged to withdraw from the extreme position which he had gained near Sharpsburg to one slightly in rear of it. He, however, held his bank of the river completely, and maintained much ground beyond it which he had taken from the enemy. During the advance on the left Gen. Rodman was wounded.

The Federal artillery is represented to have played an important part during this battle.

Notwithstanding substantial and decided successes of the day, the Federal forces had suffered so severely during the conflict, having lost 11,426 in killed and wounded, and among them many general and superior officers, that it was deemed prudent by Gen. McClellan to reorganize and give rest and refreshment to the troops before renewing the attack. The 18th was accordingly devoted to those objects. On the night of the 18th, however, Gen. Lee withdrew his forces hastily across the Potomac, abandoning further contest with the Union forces, and yielding all hope of further remaining on the Maryland soil.

The Confederate army is supposed to have lost nearly 30,000 men during its brief campaign in Maryland. The Federal forces captured 39 colors, 13 guns, more than 15,000 small arms, and more than 6,000 prisoners.

On the 20th Harper's Ferry was evacuated by the Confederate troops, which fell back in the direction of Charlestown and Winchester. Gen. McClellan took a position along the left bank of the Potomac, and active movements were suspended for a short time in order to prepare for a vigorous advance.

CHAPTER XXII.

Message of the President recommending Emancipation with Compensation—His Conference with Members of Congress—Proclamation threatening Emancipation—Finances of the Federal Government—Increase of the Armies—Efforts of the South to raise Armies—Conscription—Officers of the Southern Government—Its Finances—Its Navy Department—Cruisers—The Oreto—The Alabama: vessels destroyed by her—Other Operations—Diplomatic Correspondence with the British Government.

MEASURES to secure the emancipation of the slaves were early adopted by the Government. On March 6th President Lincoln sent a message to Congress, then in session, recommending that a joint resolution should be passed, substantially declaring that the United States, in order to coöperate with any State which might adopt gradual abolition of slavery, would give pecuniary aid to be used by such State, in its discretion, to compensate it for the inconveniences, public and private, produced by such a change of system. Again, on May 19th, after Gen. Hunter had issued an order at Hilton Head, declaring slavery and martial law incompatible, the President issued another proclamation, declaring the emancipation of the slaves to be a question reserved to himself for decision, and he further added, relative to the resolution above mentioned: "The resolution in the language above quoted was adopted by large majorities in both branches of Congress, and now stands an authentic, definite, and solemn proposal of the Nation to the States and people most interested in the subject matter. To the people of these States now I mostly appeal. I do not argue—I beseech you to make the arguments for yourselves. You cannot, if you would, be blind to the signs of the times.

"I beg of you a calm and enlarged consideration of them, ranging, if it may be, far above partisan and personal politics.

"This proposal makes common cause for a common object, casting no reproaches upon any. It acts not the Pharisee. The change it contemplates would come gently as the dews of Heaven, not rending nor wrecking any thing. Will you embrace it? So much good has not been done by one effort in all past time, as in the Providence of God it is now your high privilege to do. May the vast future not have to lament that you have neglected it."

Subsequently, on July 12th, he held a conference with the members of Congress from Maryland, Delaware, Kentucky, and Missouri, in which he urged them to use their efforts to secure with their respective States the adoption of a system of emancipation, with compensation to the owners of slaves. This measure was discussed in those States, but not adopted by any one.

Subsequently, on September 22d, the President issued a proclamation, as follows:

PROCLAMATION.

I, ABRAHAM LINCOLN, President of the United States of America, and Commander-in-Chief of the army and navy thereof, do hereby proclaim and declare that hereafter, as heretofore, the war will be prosecuted for the object of practically restoring the constitutional relation between the United States and each of the States, and the people thereof, in which States that relation is or may be suspended or disturbed.

That it is my purpose, upon the next meeting of Congress, to again recommend the adoption of a practical measure tendering pecuniary aid to the free acceptance or rejection of all Slave States, so called, the people whereof may not then be in rebellion against the United States, and which States may then have voluntarily adopted, or thereafter may voluntarily adopt, immediate or gradual abolishment of slavery within their respective limits; and that the effort to colonize persons of African descent, with their consent, upon this continent or elsewhere, with the previously obtained consent of the governments existing there, will be continued.

That on the first day of January, in the year of our Lord one thousand eight hundred and sixty-three, all persons held as slaves within any State, or designated part of a State, the people whereof shall then be in rebellion against the United States, shall be then, thenceforward, and forever free; and the Executive Government of the United States, including the military and naval authority thereof, will recognize and maintain the freedom of such persons, and will do no act or acts to repress such persons, or any of them, in any efforts they may make for their actual freedom.

That the Executive will, on the first day of January aforesaid, by proclamation, designate the States and parts of States, if any, in which the people thereof respectively shall then be in rebellion against the United States; and the fact that any State, or the people thereof, shall on that day be in good faith represented in the Congress of the United States, by members chosen thereto at elections wherein a majority of the qualified voters of such State shall have participated, shall, in the absence of strong countervailing testimony, be deemed conclusive evidence that such State, and the people thereof, are not then in rebellion against the United States.

That attention is hereby called to an Act of Congress entitled "An Act to make an additional Article of War," approved March 13, 1862, and which act is in the words and figures following:

Be it enacted by the Senate and House of Representatives of the United States of America in Congress assembled, That hereafter the following shall be promulgated as an additional article of war for the government of the army of the United States, and shall be obeyed and observed as such:

ARTICLE.—All officers or persons in the military or naval service of the United States are prohibited from employing any of the forces under their respective commands for the purpose of returning fugitives from service or labor who may have escaped from any persons to whom such service or labor is claimed to be due; and any officer who shall be found guilty by a court-martial of violating this article shall be dismissed from the service.

SEC. 2. *And be it further enacted*, That this act shall take effect from and after its passage.

Also, to the ninth and tenth sections of an act entitled "An Act to Suppress Insurrection, to Punish Treason and Rebellion, to Seize and Confiscate Property of Rebels, and for other Purposes," approved July 17, 1862, and which sections are in the words and figures following:

SEC. 9. *And be it further enacted*, That all slaves of persons who shall hereafter be engaged in rebellion against the Government of the United States, or who shall in any way give aid or comfort thereto, escaping from such persons and taking refuge within the lines of the army; and all slaves captured from such persons, or deserted by them and coming under the control of the Government of the United States; and all slaves of such persons found or being within any place occupied by rebel forces and afterwards occupied by the forces of the United States, shall be deemed captives of war, and shall be forever free of their servitude, and not again held as slaves.

SEC. 10. *And be it further enacted*, That no slave escaping into any State, Territory, or the District of Columbia, from any other State, shall be delivered up, or in any way impeded or hindered of his liberty, except for crime, or some offence against the laws, unless the person claiming said fugitive shall first make oath that the person to whom the labor or service of such fugitive is alleged to be due is his lawful owner, and has not borne arms against the United States in the present rebellion, nor in any way given aid and comfort thereto; and no person engaged in the military or naval service of the United States shall, under any pretence whatever, assume to decide on the validity of the claim of any person to the service or labor of any other person, or surrender up any such person to the claimant, on pain of being dismissed from the service.

And I do hereby enjoin upon and order all persons engaged in the military and naval service of the United States to observe, obey, and enforce, within their respective spheres of service, the act and sections above recited.

And the Executive will in due time recommend that all citizens of the United States who shall have remained loyal thereto throughout the rebellion shal (upon the restoration of the constitutional relation between the United States and their respective States and people, if that relation shall have been suspended or disturbed) be compensated for all losses by acts of the United States, including the loss of slaves.

In witness whereof I have hereunto set my hand and caused the seal of the United States to be affixed.

[L. S.] Done at the city of Washington, this twenty-second day of September, in the year of our Lord one thousand eight hundred and sixty-two, and of the Independence of the United States the eighty-seventh.

ABRAHAM LINCOLN.

By the President:

WILLIAM H. SEWARD, Secretary of State.

The finances of the Federal Government steadily improved after the commencement of the difficulties. There seemed to be a settled purpose on the part of the people to furnish the Government with all the men and money it might need to restore the Union. The vast expenditures incident to the military and naval operations were met with a promptitude and certainty unusual under similar circumstances. On January 1st, 1862, the state banks of the country suspended specie payments, which made large issues of United States notes unavoidable. These were subsequently, by act of Congress, made a legal tender, and constituted the chief circulating medium of the country to the close of the war.

The receipts into the Treasury from all sources during the fiscal year ending June 30th, 1862, were $583,885,247; of this amount the sum of $529,692,460 was raised by loans of various forms. The disbursements for the same period were $570,841,700; of this amount there was expended by the War Department the sum of $394,368,407, and by the Navy Department $42,674,569.

The commerce of the country was shorn of its proportions by the war, and became hazardous on the ocean. No trade of importance took place from ports captured from the enemy.

The forces in the field were largely increased by calls from the President for more men. About June 1st a call for militia to serve three months was made on the States of Massachusetts, Rhode Island, New York, Pennsylvania, and Ohio. Nearly 40,000 men were sent forward. On July 1st the President called for 300,000 more volunteers for the war, and on August 9th for 300,000 for nine months, who were to be drafted unless they volunteered promptly. There was subsequently considerable vacillation on the part of the Government in regard to the force to be raised under these two calls. In Pennsylvania a part of those enlisted under the first call were enlisted for twelve months only; in other States an excess raised under the first was allowed to be credited to the second; and in some instances an excess under the previous calls was allowed to count on these. There was very little drafting; probably up to February 1st, 1863, there were not 10,000 drafted men in the army. This was mainly due to the great exertions made in the loyal States to promote volunteering, and the very liberal bounties offered by States, counties, cities, towns, and individuals, to those who would enlist.

In the new Confederacy formed by the insurrectionary States, the demand for men early became urgent. This arose in part from the short term of enlistment and a disposition on the part of large numbers to desert. On February 1st Mr. Davis called upon the States for an additional quota of men, and on April 16th the Congress at Richmond passed an act declaring every man between the ages of eighteen and thirty-five years, with a few exceptions, to be a soldier owing service to the Confederacy.

On the 16th of April the conscript act, having passed both Houses of Congress, was approved by the President. This act annulled all previous contracts made with volunteers, and by explicit terms made all men under the age of thirty-five years and over eighteen years, soldiers for the war, or until they attained the age of thirty-five years. It drew every male citizen within the prescribed ages immediately and entirely from the control of State action, and placed them at the disposal of the President during the war. It also provided, "That all persons under the age of eighteen years, or over the age of thirty-five years, who are now enrolled in the military service of the Confederate States, in the regiments, squadrons, battalions, and companies hereafter to be organized, shall be required to remain in their respective companies, squadrons, battalions, and regiments for ninety days, unless their places shall be sooner supplied by other recruits, not now in the service, who are between the ages of eighteen and thirty-five years; and all laws and part of laws provided for the reorganization of volunteers, and the organization thereof into companies, squadrons, battalions, and regiments, shall be, and the same are hereby repealed."

The existing organization of companies, regiments, etc., was preserved, but the companies were required to be filled up to the number of one hundred and thirty-five men. When thus filled up, the privates had the privilege of electing their officers in the same manner as under former laws, but the commissions were issued by the President. The provision of the law annulling the contract with volunteers, and requiring those under eighteen years or over thirty-five to continue in service ninety days after its passage, without regard to their term of enlistment, was construed by these volunteers as entitling them to a discharge on the 16th of July. Previous to that date, however, an order was issued by the War Department placing them on the same footing as conscripts, and requiring them to continue in the service. So extreme was this order that it retained in service all enlisted men without regard to the time of their enlistment or their ages. Thus youths of seventeen and men of fifty were not allowed to withdraw, nor any who were in the army at the time of the passage of the law. In a word, the law set aside all contracts, and the Government retained all soldiers in the field, and sought to add to them every man between the required ages. Not even physicians were exempted. Mr. Davis, in a letter to the Governor of Georgia, thus states the reason for this injustice to the volunteers:

> I would have very little difficulty in establishing to your entire satisfaction that the passage of the law was not only necessary, but that it was absolutely indispensable; that numerous regiments of twelve months' men were on the eve of being disbanded, whose places would not be supplied by new levies in the face of superior numbers of the foe, without entailing the most disastrous results; that the position of our armies was so critical as to fill the bosom of every patriot with the liveliest apprehension, and that the provisions of the law were effective in warding off a pressing danger.

The regulations for executing the law detailed an officer in each State to take charge of the enrolment, mustering in, subsistence, transportation, and disposition of the recruits. The coöperation of State officers in making the enrolment was requested of the governors of the States, and in any case in which such assistance might be refused, the duty was performed by officers of the army. Not more than two camps of instruction were established in each State, where the recruits were made ready for the field with the utmost despatch. The recruits were not organized in force as separate bodies, but were sent to supply deficiencies in regiments, battalions, squadrons, or unattached companies, and, so far as practicable, in corps from their own region of country. Recruits were allowed to choose any corps to which they desired to be attached, in which vacancies existed. They could also join any corps, the formation of which had been authorized by the Government. All twelve months' volunteers in service were required to reorganize by the election of new officers within forty days after the act passed. Those who preferred a guerrilla service were authorized to form as partisan rangers by an act specially passed for that purpose. The operation of the act was suspended in Missouri and Kentucky, under a provision authorizing it to be done by the President. Troops from those States were received under the acts passed previous to the conscription law. Maryland was regarded as exempt from the law, as appears by the following from the Secretary of War, dated April 26:

> *Major J. A. Weston:*
>
> In reply to your letter of the 17th inst., you are respectfully informed that Marylanders are not subject to the conscription act.
>
> G. W. RANDOLPH, Sec. of War.

This extreme measure met with much opposition on the part of the people in the Southern States. It was an evidence, in itself, that the ardor of the people had ceased to be a safe medium of reliance in the conduct of the war. It was a measure which had never before been adopted in the States of the Union during any previous war. It necessarily established a consolidated government founded on military principles, and was thus spoken of by some of the Southern leaders:

If it be absolutely necessary to save us from a conquest by the North, we are willing to submit to it; but we fear the public mind must prepare itself for a great change in our government.

Mr. Davis, in the letter to Governor Brown, of Georgia, above mentioned, argued at much length that the act may be pronounced "constitutional" in spite of its seeming invasion of State rights, and said:

There seems to me to be a conclusive test on that whole subject. By our constitution, Congress may declare war offensive as well as defensive. It may acquire territory. Now, suppose that, for good cause and to right unprovoked injuries, Congress should declare war against Mexico and invade Sonora. The militia could not be called forth in such case, the right to call it being limited "to repel invasion." Is it not plain that the law now under discussion, if passed under such circumstances, could by no possibility be aught else than a law to "raise an army"? Can one and the same law be construed into a "calling forth the militia," if the war be defensive, and a "raising of armies" if the war be offensive?

At some future day, after our independence shall have been established, it is no improbable supposition that our enemy may be tempted to abuse his moral power by depredations on our commerce, and that we may be compelled to assert our rights by offensive war. How is this to be carried on? Of what is the army to be composed? If this Government cannot call on its arms-bearing population more than as militia, and if the militia can only be called forth to repel invasion, we should be utterly helpless to vindicate our honor or protect our rights. War has been well styled "the terrible litigation of nations." Have we so formed our government that in litigation we may never be plaintiff? Surely this cannot have been the intention of the framers of our compact?

A permanent form of Government was organized in these States in February, 1862, of which the officers were as follows:

President.—Jefferson Davis, of Mississippi.

Vice-President.—Alex. H. Stephens, of Ga.

The term of office for which they were elected was six years. The cabinet of Mr. Davis was composed as follows:

Secretary of State.—J. P. Benjamin, of La.

Secretary of War.—George W. Randolph, of Virginia.

Secretary of the Navy.—S. R. Mallory, of Florida.

Secretary of the Treasury.—C. G. Memminger, of South Carolina.

Attorney-General.—Thomas H. Watts.

Postmaster-General.—James H. Reagan, of Texas.

In November, 1862, the Secretary of War resigned, and James A. Seddon, of Virginia, was appointed in his place.

The finances of the Government soon began to indicate weakness. The main reliance was paper money, and depreciation began almost with the first issues. Cut off by the blockade from all commerce with foreign countries, their great staples, which would readily command gold in the markets of the world, perished on their hands. The receipts of the Government, including loans and paper issues, amounted in August, 1862, to $302,482,096, and the expenditures $347,272,958. At this date the issues of currency amounted to $183,244,135. Bonds $41,577,240. Whenever there was a danger of the capture of cotton by the Federal troops it was ordered by the Confederate Government to be burned.

The navy department organized by the Government at Richmond, not only devoted its energies to fit out iron-clad vessels in the ports of the States for harbor defence, but to procure armed vessels on the ocean.

The early operations of the privateer Sumter have been stated on a previous page. Her career was closed in the year 1861 by the refuge of the vessel in Gibraltar, where, being unable to procure coal, she remained watched by the Federal ship Tuscarora. The Sumter was finally sold, and the Federal steamer left Gibraltar, January 13th, for the Spanish waters of Algesiras. The efforts of the Confederates were then turned to the formation of an extensive navy by purchasing vessels in England. It very soon became apparent that a number were in process of construction at the shipyards near Liverpool, and the attention of the British Government was called to the fact, which became the basis of diplomatic correspondence. Early in April the American minister, Mr. Adams, addressed Earl Russell relative to the Oreto, then in a forward state, and by general report destined for the rebel service. On her arrival at Nassau she was immediately seized by the captain of her Majesty's steamer Greyhound, but almost as quickly released. Shortly after she was seized again, but, after some difficulty, released again. The authorities appeared to have great doubts as to whether she was or was not intended for the Confederate service. On one occasion, when the British gunboat Bulldog went to seize her, she was discharging shell. The Oreto, on the 4th of September, suddenly appeared off Mobile harbor, which was blockaded by a steamer under Commander George Henry Preble, whose instructions were emphatic against giving offence to foreign nations while enforcing the blockade. The Oreto approached flying the English flag and pennants. Commander Preble hesitated to fire lest the stranger should really prove an English man-of-war. The few moments' time lost in the hesitation sufficed for the Oreto to pass out of range and gain her object, getting safely into Mobile bay with her freight. For this want of success Commander Preble was summarily dismissed from the service without a hearing.

On the 27th of December, the Oreto again left Mobile bay, fully armed for a cruise, under the command of John Newland Maffit, who was born in Ireland, and when quite young was brought to this country by his father, a celebrated preacher of the same name; was appointed to the United States navy from the State of New York. He originally entered the naval service in the year 1832, and became a citizen of Georgia.

After the sale of the Sumter her captain, Semmes, was active in England in building a new vessel, and it was soon ascertained that one was in a forward state for the Confederate service. Complaint was made to the British Government of infringement of the neutrality laws, and means were taken to prevent the departure of the vessel as she approached completion. The orders came, however, too late. Meantime a barque had loaded in London with arms, and sailed from the Thames. The United States ship Tuscarora was at the same time watching for the Alabama to make her appearance, but she avoided her by taking the North Channel out. After a short run she arrived at the Western Islands, giving an excuse to the authorities for making harbor there. Soon after the barque arrived, alleging stress of weather. The Alabama at once hauled alongside of the barque, and cranes were rigged by the order of the Alabama's captain. When in readiness he began to transfer the cargo, and this infringement of quarantine rules excited the ire of the Portuguese authorities, but it was alleged that the bark was sinking and it was necessary to save the cargo. On the following day, when the transfer was nearly completed, the British screw steamer Bahama arrived, bringing Capt. Semmes and other late officers of the Sumter, the remainder of the armament, and 20 more of the crew. This arrival exhausted the patience of the authorities, and all three vessels were ordered to leave at once. The Bahama handed over to the Alabama what was destined for her and left immediately, followed by the "290" towing the bark. They went a few leagues to Angra bay and remained 24 hours, when they were again ordered to leave, which they did, all being now in readiness. The bark left for Cardiff to load coal for the Alabama. Capt. Semmes then took command, mustered the crew, read his commission as post captain in the Confederate navy. It was a document duly attested at Richmond, and bore the signature of "Jefferson Davis, President, Confederate States of America." He then opened and read his sealed orders from the President, directing him to assume command of the Confederate sloop-of-war Alabama, hitherto known as the 290, in which (having been duly commissioned) he was to hoist the Confederate ensign and pennant, and "sink, burn, and destroy everything which flew the ensign of the so-called United States of America." Captain Semmes then ordered the first lieutenant to fire a gun, and run up the Confederate flag and pennant. The gun was fired by the second lieutenant (Armstrong, a relation of the famous inventor), and ere its smoke had cleared away, the stars and bars of the Confederacy were floating on the breeze, and the ceremony was complete; Captain Semmes declared the vessel, henceforth to be known as the Alabama, to have been duly commissioned. The next step was formally to engage the crew to serve and fight under the Southern flag, which having been done, the men were addressed by their captain, who informed them that if any of the crew were dissatisfied they could leave in the Bahama about to take her departure for England. The offer was declined, the two vessels parted company, the Bahama for England and the Alabama in chase of a whaler. The operations of the vessel were very active. The following is a list of vessels captured and destroyed by her:

Sept.	6,	Ship Ocmulgee	Edgartown,	Burned.
"	7,	Schooner Starlight......	Boston,	"
"	9,	Bark Alert..............		
"	9,	Schooner Weather Gauge	Provincetown,	"
"	9,	Bark Ocean Rover.......	Mattapoisett,	"
"	13,	Ship Benjamin Tucker..	New Bedford,	"
		Bark Osceola............		"
		Bark Virginia, Tilton....	" "	"
		Ship Elisha Dunbar, Gifford	" "	"
		Brig Allamaha...........	Sippican,	"
		Schooner Courser.......	Provincetown,	"
Oct.	3,	Ship Brilliant, Hagar....	New York,	"
"	3,	Ship Emily Farnham, Simms..............	" "	Released.
"	10,	Ship Tonawanda........	Philadelphia,	Bonded.
"	15,	Ship Lamplighter.......	New York,	Burned.
"	15,	Ship Manchester........	" "	"
"	15,	Brig Dunkirk...........	" "	"
"	23,	Ship Lafayette, Small...	" "	"
"	23,	Schooner Ocean Cruiser.	" "	"
"	26,	Schooner Crenshaw.....	" "	"
"	28,	Bark Laurietta, Wells...	Boston,	"
"	29,	Brig Baron de Castine, Saunders		Bonded.
Nov.	2,	Schooner Alice..........		
"	8,	Ship I. B. Wales.........	Boston,	Burned.
"	18,	Steamer Ariel...........	New York,	Bonded.
		Ship Levi Starbuck......		
"	30,	Bark Parker Cook, Fulton..................	Boston,	Burned.
Dec.	5,	Schooner Union.........	Baltimore,	Bonded.

Ship Lafayette had a cargo consisting of 13,369 bushels of wheat, 47,663 bushels of corn, and 16,850 lbs. of lard.

Bark Lamplighter had a cargo of 300 hhds. of tobacco.

Bark Laurietta had a cargo of 1,424 bbls. of flour, 225 kegs of nails, 998 bbls. of flour, 205 boxes of herring, and 7,200 staves.

Schooner Crenshaw had a cargo of 1,298 bbls. of flour and 9,272 bushels of wheat.

Ship Manchester had on board 45,141 bushels of wheat and 14,666 bushels of corn.

Brig Dunkirk had a cargo of 2,967 bbls. of flour and 6,000 staves.

Ship Tonawanda, her cargo being insured in England, was released on giving a bond for $80,000. She had a cargo of 48,700 bushels of wheat, 40 bbls. of flour, 36 hhds. of bark, 172 cases of wine, 128 bales of hemp, and 50 bales of hops and rags.

The course of the Alabama was to destroy, since under the regulations of foreign powers she had no means of landing and condemning her prizes. Her case is certainly a very peculiar one. She has neither register nor record, no regular ship's papers nor evidence of transfer, and no vessel captured by her has ever been sent into any port for adjudication and condemnation. All forms of law which civilization has introduced to protect and guard private rights, and all those regulations of public justice which distinguish and discriminate the legalized naval vessel from the pirate, are disregarded and violated by this famous rover, which, though built in and sailing from England, has no acknowledged flag or recognized nationality, nor any accessible port to which to send any ship she may seize, nor any legal tribunal to adjudge her captures. She was built and fitted out in British ports in alleged violation of British law and of the royal proclamation of neutrality, and her crew is composed almost exclusively of British subjects, or persons who, pursuing a lawful voyage, would be entitled to ship and receive protection as British seamen. Most of the crew sailed from Liverpool to join her, and others volunteered from captured vessels, as in the case of the crew of the ship Brilliant. The prize money or half the value of the vessels and cargoes destroyed was, it was stated, regularly paid in money to the crew, who were thus large gainers, and their prosperity tempted the men of captured vessels, from which also supplies were procured. Among the first of the captured were the Virginia and the Elisha Dunbar. The statements of the captains of those vessels indicate the course pursued by the Confederate commander.

Captain Tilton, of the Virginia, says that he was overhauled by the Alabama on the morning of the 17th of September, in lat. 39° 10′, and long. 34° 20′. The enemy showed British colors, but when a quarter of a mile from the Virginia set Confederate colors, and sent an armed boat's crew on board. Captain Tilton was informed that he was a prize to the Alabama, and was ordered to take his papers and go on board that steamer. The Confederates then stripped the ship of all the valuable articles on board, and at 4 P. M. set fire to the vessel. Captain Tilton adds:

I went on the quarter deck with my son, when they ordered me into the lee waist, with my crew, and all of us put in irons, with the exception of two boys, cook and steward. I asked if I was to be put in irons? The reply was that his purser was put in irons and his head shaved by us, and that he was going to retaliate. We were put in the lee waist, with an old sail over us and a few planks to lie upon.

The steamer was cruising to the west, and the next day they took the Elisha Dunbar, her crew receiving the same treatment as ourselves. The steamer's guns being kept run out the side ports could not be shut, and when the sea was a little rough or the vessel rolled, the water was continually coming in on both sides and washing across the deck where we were, so that our feet and clothing were wet all the time, either from the water below or the rain above.

We were obliged to sleep in the place where we were, and often waked up in the night nearly under water. Our fare consisted of beef and pork, rice, beans, tea and coffee, and bread. Only one of our irons was allowed to be taken off at a time, and we had to wash in salt water. We were kept on deck all the time, night and day, and a guard placed over us.

The steamer continued to cruise to the northwest, and on the 3d of October fell in with the ships Brilliant and Emily Farnham—the former of which they burnt, and her crew, with ourselves, were transferred to the latter ship, after signing a parole. On the 6th instant was taken on board the brig Golden Lead, of Thomaston, Captain Smith, from Jersey for New York; was treated with great kindness.

Captain Gifford, of the Elisha Dunbar, stated as follows:

On the morning of the 18th Sept., in lat. 39° 50′, long. 35° 20′, with the wind from the southwest and the bark heading southeast, saw a steamer on our port quarter standing to the northwest. Soon after found she had altered her course and was steering for the bark. We soon made all sail to get out of her reach, and were going ten knots at the time; but the steamer gaining on us under canvas alone, soon came up with us and fired a gun under our stern, with the St. George's cross flying at the time. Our colors were set, when she displayed the Confederate flag; being near us, we hove to, and a boat with armed officers and crew came alongside, and upon coming on board, stated to me that my vessel was a prize to the Confederate steamer Alabama, Captain Semmes. I was then ordered on board the steamer with my papers, and the crew to follow me, with a bag of clothing each. On getting aboard, the captain claimed me as a prize, and said my vessel would be burnt. Not having any clothes with me, he allowed me to return for a small trunk of clothes—the officer on board asked me what I was coming back for, and tried to prevent me from coming on board. I told him I came after a few clothes, which I took and returned to the steamer. It blowing very hard at the time and very squally, nothing but the chronometer, sextant, charts, &c., were taken, when the vessel was set fire to and burnt; there were 65 barrels sperm oil on deck, taken on the passage, which were consumed. We were all put in irons, and received the same treatment that Captain Tilton's officers and crew did, who had been taken the day before. While on board we understood that the steamer would cruise off the Grand Banks for a few weeks to destroy the large American ships to and from the Channel ports. They had knowledge of two ships being loaded with arms for the United States, and were in hopes to capture them. They were particularly anxious to fall in with the clipper ship Dreadnought, and destroy her, as she was celebrated for speed; and they were confident of their ability to capture or run away from any vessel in the United States. The steamer being in the track of outward and homeward bound vessels, and more or less being in sight every day, she will make great havoc among them.

DAVID R. GIFFORD,
Late Master of Bark Elisha Dunbar.

The Brilliant was built in Boston in 1861, was 839 tons, and was valued at $80,000. The Confederate commander, in reply to the captain of the Virginia, on protesting against his detention, stated: "You Northerners are destroying our property, and New Bedford people are having their war meetings, offering $200 bounty for volunteers, and send out their stone fleets to block up our harbors, and I am going to retaliate!" The officers were in some cases ironed in accordance with this view of retaliation. The number of prisoners had now increased to 68, and these were placed on board the Emily Farnham, which was captured on the same day as the Brilliant, and released because the ship's papers showed the cargo to be on English account. The large number of prisoners exceeded the accommodations of the vessel, and eight of the number were put on board the brig Golden Lead. The Alabama landed 170 prisoners at the Island of Flores. Her action in relation to British ownership seemed to be a little eccentric. When the ship

Lafayette was captured, Capt. Small produced his British consular certificate and remarked he supposed that would be sufficient protection. Captain Semmes replied, "The New York people are getting very smart, but it won't save you; it's all a hatched up mess." He then gave orders to burn the ship. It was the case that the property of a large circle of merchants known to Capt. Semmes was respected much more scrupulously than that of strangers. It is obvious that, as 290 merchants were subscribers to build the Alabama, any of their names upon a manifest would be a safe passport.

When the news of these depredations reached New York great excitement was created. The insurance companies advanced the war risks. British consular certificates were in demand, and freights were placed in British bottoms rather than American. The New York Chamber of Commerce held a meeting in relation to the matter, on the 21st day of October, and a series of resolutions were adopted.

Captain C. H. Marshall submitted the following letter from the Secretary of the Navy:

NAVY DEPARTMENT, WASHINGTON, —— 1862.

SIR: I received your letter of the 14th instant, also your letter of yesterday, referring to it, inquiring, as the chairman of a special committee of the Chamber of Commerce, what measures have been taken to capture the rebel pirate Alabama, and also whether the Government will grant commissions to private vessels, if fitted out under promise of reward by citizens, for that purpose. An earlier reply to the inquiry of the committee has been unavoidably delayed. The department has several vessels in search of the Alabama, in addition to the flying squadron of Acting Rear Admiral Wilkes in the West Indies, and other ships of war on the European coast. Additional force will be despatched in this service as early as practicable. There is no authority for granting commissions to private vessels to search for the Alabama or other piratical vessels or privateers. I am, respectfully, your obedient servant,

GIDEON WELLES, Secretary of the Navy.

C. H. MARSHALL, Esq., Chairman.

The events also produced some excitement in England. The vessels destroyed and threatened were those sailing under the Federal flag. But vessels so sailing have hitherto carried more property of British owners than of any others. And as Capt. Semmes burns vessels and cargoes without distinction, and the cargo is commonly much more valuable than the vessel, the English, as a neutral nation, have hitherto been, probably, the chief sufferers. Time, of course, soon changed this aspect of the case. Vessels under the Federal flag became by so much less eligible for safe conveyance; and, though a corresponding premium of insurance will always cover the war risk, it in this case so enhanced the ordinary charges as to put Federal vessels to a very serious disadvantage in the market of freight; thus affording some compensation to English interests.

An attempt was made to obtain redress from the Confederate Government for British losses in the manner indicated in the following correspondence:

To his Excellency the British Minister, Washington:

PHILADELPHIA, *Nov.* 7 1862.

EXCELLENCY: As a British subject and a shipper of merchandise upon the ship Tonawanda, lately overhauled by the Confederate war steamer Alabama, I beg most respectfully to call your attention to this matter.

The Tonawanda, as you are no doubt aware, was released from capture, and allowed to proceed on her voyage under a bond of $60,000, as a ransom, and this sum will be rated upon ship and cargo by the average staters, on her arrival in Liverpool.

I respectfully suggest that your Excellency make application to the Government of the Confederate States that consent be given that all sums so rated upon property belonging *bona fide* to British subjects be remitted, and that the same shall be deducted from amount of said bond of $60,000, with similar proceedings in all such cases as may arise.

I have also merchandise on board the ship Lancaster, American, now in this port, and advertised to sail on Tuesday next. To my bills of lading, which the captain takes with him, I have attached the British consul's certificate that the property belongs to British subjects; but, as it is feared that this may not be sufficient to save from destruction, in the event of capture, I beg that your Excellency will be so good as to furnish me with a letter protesting, as the highest British authority in this country, against the destruction of British merchandise, to be used by the captain of the Lancaster, if necessary. Any cost attending such letter I will gratefully pay, and trust your Excellency will think that I only do right in seeking to protect my friends in England from loss, for whom I have shipped these goods, by appealing thus to our own Government.

It will mitigate the horrors of this war if your Excellency shall succeed in preventing the destruction of ships holding certificates of British property, and it will be but just that British merchants should be exempt from contributing to the ransom of ships and merchandise belonging to belligerents. I cannot but think that your Excellency's protest, which I ask for, will be respected on the seas, and also that the Confederate Government will readily grant the exemption desired.

Your immediate action in these matters will, I feel certain, be satisfactory to yourself, and will be hailed with much gratitude by British merchants everywhere, and meet with the approval of the home Government.

I have the honor to be your Excellency's most obedient servant, W. H. TRENWITH.

WASHINGTON, *Nov.* 3, 1863.

W. H. TRENWITH, Esq., Philadelphia:

SIR: I have received your letter of the 7th instant, in which you suggest that I should make an application to the Government of the so-styled Confederate States with reference to the ransom of British property on board American vessels, in consequence of the recent proceedings of the war steamer Alabama; and that I should furnish you with a letter of protest, for the purpose of protecting some merchandise which you have shipped on board the American ship Lancaster.

While greatly regretting the risk to which British property is exposed by being shipped in belligerent vessels, it is not in my power to accede to either of your suggestions.

You are aware that the so-styled Confederate States have not been recognized by her Majesty the Queen, and for that reason I shall not be justified in entering into communication with the Government of those States, except under special instructions from her Majesty's Government. Neither do I feel at liberty to supply you antecedently with the protest which you desire, having no authority to issue such a document, and seeing no reason to believe that it would insure a more effective protection to your goods upon the high seas than the consular certificate, with which you seem to have supplied yourself.

I am, Sir, your obedient servant, W. STUART.

On the 18th of November the Alabama fell in with the steamship Ariel, on her way from New York to Aspinwall. The steamer was bonded and allowed to proceed with her passengers; but the alarm occasioned by her seizure prevented her from bringing back her usual freight of gold. A United States gunboat was sent to bring it. In the mean time, however, it arrived by the next boat of the company. A number of armed vessels were sent out to cruise in the track of the Alabama, without much success. The Vanderbilt sailed from New York for Fayal, December 11. Two other steamers left New York, one from Boston, one from Philadelphia, and one from Portsmouth, N. H. None of these were, however, of sufficient speed. The U. S. frigate Sabine, Com. Cadwalader Ringgold, left New London, November 3, in search of the Alabama. Arrived at the Azores November 28. Sailed thence December 2, and arrived at Cape de Verde December 23, and left there January 2. Absent 100 days, cruising 93 days, and sailed 10,000 miles in vain.

The Alabama meantime, having captured the Ariel on the 18th, arrived on the 26th, two days before the Sabine reached the Azores, at Martinique, where she took in coal from a British bark. The United States steamer San Jacinto, at the same date, was off St. Thomas watching for the Alabama, which on the 30th captured the Parker, Cook, off the Moro Passage. December 5 she captured the Union off Cape Mais, and was off Havana December 31. Thus she does not appear to have left the American coast, while the Vanderbilt and other vessels sent in search were seeking her elsewhere. In some cases the Alabama released her prizes on a ransom bill being signed by the captain, and agreeing to pay a sum of money after the close of the war. By the general law of nations these bills or contracts are recognized as between belligerents, and a captain may by his contract bind his owners, the whole cargo as well as the ship. Those ransoms were forbidden by the English Government under George III, but have never been prohibited by the United States.

The theory of ransom is that it is a repurchase of the actual right of the captors at the time the bill or bond is given, be that what it may; or, more properly, it is a relinquishment of all the interest or benefit which the captors might acquire or consummate in the property by regular adjudication of a prize tribunal, whether it may be in the interest of the ship and cargo, or a lien on the same, or a mere title to expenses. These ransom bills are, by rules of international law, an exception to the general doctrine that no contract with an enemy is valid.

In the case of the ransom bill given by the Ariel, it seems not to be payable till six months after the recognition of the Southern Confederacy. If then, that contingency should happen, what court would have jurisdiction to enforce the agreement? Primarily, all questions of prize belong to the tribunals of the capturing power; and foreign tribunals will not interfere, unless where their territorial rights have been violated. Ransoms belong to the same jurisdiction, and may there be enforced or set aside, as the facts disclose a good or bad prize. It is, however, competent for the captors to change the *forum* in cases of ransom, and apply for redress in any country where the person of the owner of the Ariel may be found, or the ship itself.

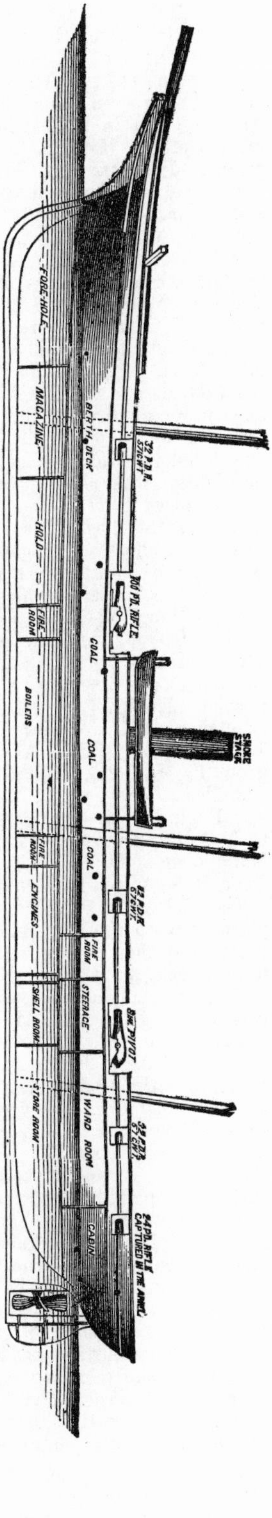

A CORRECT SKETCH OF THE CONFEDERATE STATES STEAMER "ALABAMA'S" HULL, WITH THE POSITION OF THE SHOT HOLES AFTER THE FIGHT WITH THE "HATERAS;" ALSO THE POSITION AND WEIGHT OF HER ARMAMENT.

On the 11th of January, 1863, about 3 P. M., as the Federal squadron, consisting of the steamers Brooklyn, Hatteras, and five others, was cruising off Galveston, a vessel hove in sight at the southeast, which the Hatteras was ordered to proceed to and learn her character. As she came in sight she appeared to the officers of the Hatteras to be endeavoring to escape. Just after dark the officers of the Hatteras could perceive that she was bark rigged, and set a topgallant sail; and, as they approached, found her lying to, under steam. The crew of the Hatteras were at quarters, and Capt. Blake hailed and asked what ship it was. The answer was, "Her Britannic Majesty's ship Spitfire." Capt. Blake replied that he would send a boat aboard. The Alabama ranged a little ahead, her officer declaring that she was the Confederate steamer Alabama, and immediately opened fire on the Hatteras It was returned by the Hatteras, and both started ahead under a full head of steam, exchanging broadsides as fast as they could load and fire,

The heavy guns of the Alabama soon disabled the Hatteras, so that it was impossible to keep her afloat. Two guns were fired to the leeward, the contest ceased, and the officers and crew of the Hatteras, which soon sunk, were taken to Kingston, Jamaica, and paroled.

The following were the principal officers of the Alabama: Captain, Raphael Semmes; First Lieutenant and Executive Officer, J. M. Kell; Second Lieutenant, R. T. Armstrong; Third Lieutenant, J. D. Wilson; Fourth Lieutenant, J. Low; Sailing Master, Arthur St. Clair; Surgeon, F. M. Galt; Assistant Surgeon, R. H. Lewelien; Lieutenant of Marines, B. K. Howell; Engineer, Michael Freeman; Paymaster, C. T. Young (since discharged); Midshipmen, Maffit (son of Capt. Maffit, of the Oreto), St. Clair, Bullock, and Anderson.

The diplomatic correspondence which took place between the Government of the United States and that of Great Britain, relative to these vessels, it may not be out of place here to notice, especially as the subject may at some period be again discussed between the two nations.

On the 18th of February, 1862, Mr. Adams writes to Earl Russell that he had been informed of the preparation at Liverpool of an armed steamer, evidently intended for hostile operations on the ocean. In reply, Earl Russell stated that the commissioners of the customs at Liverpool reported that she was built for certain parties in Liverpool, and intended for the use of Thomas, Brothers, of Palermo, one of whom had frequently visited the vessel during the process of building; that she had taken nothing on board but coal and ballast; that she was not fitted for the reception of guns, nor were the builders aware that she was to be supplied with guns while she remained in England, and the collector at Liverpool stated that he had every reason to believe that the vessel was for the Italian Government—also that special directions had been given to the officers at Liverpool to watch the movements of the vessel. Mr. Adams subsequently writes to Mr. Seward: "The nominal destination of the Oreto to Sicily is the only advantage which appears to have been derived from my attempt to procure the interference of the Government to stop her departure."

On the 25th of March Mr. Adams writes again to Earl Russell, enclosing a letter from the American Consul at Liverpool, stating certain facts relative to the Oreto. Mr. Adams says: "It is with great reluctance that I am driven to the conviction that the representations made to your lordship of the purposes and destination of that vessel were delusive, and that though at first it may have been intended for service in Sicily, yet that such an intention has been long since abandoned in fact, and the pretence has been held up only the better to conceal the true object of the parties engaged. That object is to make war on the United States. All the persons thus far known to be most connected with the undertaking are either directly employed by the insurgents in the United States of America, or residents of Great Britain, notoriously in sympathy with, and giving aid and comfort to them on this side of the water."

On the 8th of April Earl Russell replied to Mr. Adams, enclosing a report from the Lords Commissioners of her Majesty's Treasury, which states that the Oreto was registered on the 3d of March in the name of John Henry Thomas, of Liverpool, as sole owner; that she cleared on the following day for Palermo and Jamaica in ballast, but did not sail until the 22d, having a crew of fifty-two men, all British with the exception of three or four, one of whom was an American. She had no gunpowder, nor even a signal gun, and no colors save Marryatt's code of signals and a British ensign, nor any goods on board excepting the stores enumerated in an accompanying copy of her victualling bill.

On the 15th of April a conference took place between Mr. Adams and Earl Russell. Its close is thus stated by the former:

In the case of the Oreto, upon which I had addressed a note to him, he had directed an investigation to be made and the authorities at Liverpool had reported that there was no ground for doubting the legality of her voyage.

I replied that this was exactly what gave such unpleasant impressions to us in America. The Oreto, by the very paper furnished from the custom-house, was shown to be laden with a hundred and seventy tons of arms, and to have persons called troops on board, destined for Palermo and Jámaica. The very statement of the case was enough to show what was really intended. The fact of her true destination was notorious all over Liverpool. No commercial people were blind to it. And the course taken by her Majesty's officers in declaring ignorance only led to an inference most unfavorable to all idea of their neutrality in the struggle. It was just such action as this that was making the difficulties of our Government in the way of giving the facilities to the supply of cotton, which they hoped to furnish in a short time if the whole control of means to put an end to the contest was left to them.

His lordship concluded by a polite expression of regret at these circumstances, at the same time that he could not see how the Government could change its position.

The assertion of Mr. Adams relative to troops, &c., is not sustained by the copy of the paper from the custom house contained in the diplomatic correspondence. The only part referring to troops and guns is as follows: "Men, 52; passengers or troops, ——; guns, ——; 178 tons."

Again, on the 26th of June, Mr. Seward writes to Mr. Adams that a gunboat called the Oreto, built in England for the service of the insurgents, with ports and bolts for twenty guns, and other equipments, arrived at Nassau; and that the United States Consul, on the basis of the facts relative to her, made a protest upon the subject and she was seized by the authorities. She was, however, released soon after, on the arrival at Nassau of Capt. Semmes, late of the Sumter, and was about to start on a privateering cruise. This release by the authorities of Nassau, Mr. Seward was instructed by the President to protest against, as it seemed to be particularly at variance with her Majesty's proclamation of neutrality—and to ask the consideration of her Majesty's Government upon the proceeding as one calculated to alarm the Government and people of the United States. The subject was duly brought to the notice of Earl Russell, who, on the 29th of August, replied that the Oreto had been seized at Nassau, and was to be tried before the admiralty court for a breach of the foreign enlistment act. This was accompanied by the statements of the collector, surveyor and inspector of the port of Liverpool, and the affidavit of the pilot, that the vessel, when she went to sea, had no munitions of war in her, that is, guns, carriages, shot, shell, or powder.

No further reference is made to the Oreto in this correspondence, but the 290, or Alabama, is introduced as a more formidable object. On the 23d of June, Mr. Adams writes to Earl Russell, saying:—"I am now under the painful necessity of apprising your lordship that a new and still more powerful war steamer is nearly ready for departure from the port of Liverpool on the same errand as the Oreto. This vessel has been built and launched from the dockyard of persons, one of whom is now sitting as a member of the House of Commons, and is fitting out for the especial and manifest object of carrying on hostilities by sea." Accompanying this was a letter from the United States Consul at Liverpool in confirmation of these and other statements.

The subject was immediately referred to the Lords Commissioners of her Majesty's treasury, who, on the 1st of July, report that the fitting out of the vessel had not escaped the notice of the revenue officers, but that as yet nothing had transpired concerning her which had appeared to demand a special report. The vessel was intended for a ship of war, reported to be built for a foreign government, but as yet had neither guns nor carriages on board, and the builders did not appear disposed to reply to any questions respecting the destination of the vessel after she left Liverpool. Their solicitor, however, reported his opinion that there was not at that time sufficient ground to warrant the detention of the vessel, or any interference by the department. The Consul at Liverpool was then instructed by Mr. Adams to lay his evidence before the Commissioners. At the same time, he called Capt. Craven, in command of the U. S. gunboat Tuscarora, to Southampton. To Capt. Craven was given all the information respecting the objects and destination of the 290 in possession of Mr. Adams, who advised him to take such measures as might in his opinion be effective to intercept her on her way out.

Meanwhile evidence was procured of the character and objects of the vessel by the U. S. Consul at Liverpool, which, in the opinion of a Queen's solicitor, was sufficient to justify the collector of the port in seizing the vessel, and laid before the commissioners. While the subject was under their consideration the 290 sailed from Liverpool, without register or clearance. The captain of the Tuscarora was immediately notified by Mr. Adams and he started in pursuit. Earl Russell, in a conference with Mr. Adams, stated that a delay in determining upon the case had most unexpectedly been caused by the sudden development of a malady of the Queen's advocate, Sir John D. Harding, totally incapacitating him for the transaction of business. This had made it necessary to call in other parties, whose opinion had been at last given for the detention of the gunboat, but before the order got to Liverpool the vessel was gone. He should however send directions to have her seized if she went, as was probable, to Nassau.

On the 30th of Sept. Mr. Adams wrote to Earl Russell, relating the injuries done by the 290 or Alabama, saying, "I have strong reasons to believe that still other enterprises of the same kind are in progress in the ports of Great Britain at this time. Indeed they have attained so much notoriety, as to be openly announced in the newspapers of Liverpool and London." Earl Russell, acknowledging the letter, in reply said: "I have to state to you that, much as her Majesty's Government desire to prevent such occurrences, they are unable to go beyond the law, municipal and international.

On the 16th of October Mr. Adams writes home to Mr. Seward that, "It is very manifest that no disposition exists here to apply the powers of the Government to the investigation of the acts complained of, flagrant as they are, or to the prosecution of the offenders. The main object must now be to make a record which may be of use at some future day."

Among the papers laid before Earl Russell by Mr. Adams was an affidavit of a person who sailed from Liverpool in the 290, stating that arms were furnished to her in or near Augra Bay, part of the Azores. To which Earl Russell replies that the transaction does not appear to have taken place in any part of the United Kingdom, or of her Majesty's dominions, but in part of the Portuguese dominions. No offence, therefore, cognizable by the laws of the country, appears to have been committed by the parties engaged in the transaction. Respecting a statement in a letter of the American consul at Liverpool, that a bark was to take out a cargo of coals, either from Cardiff or Troon, near Greenock, for the 290, Earl Russell replies that "there would be great difficulty in ascertaining the intention of any parties making such a shipment, and we do not apprehend that our officers would have any power of interfering with it, were the coals cleared outward for some foreign port in compliance with the law." No further correspondence relative to the 290 and the Oreto took place during 1862.

CHAPTER XXIII.

Guerrillas in Kentucky—Invasion of the State by Gen. E. Kirby Smith—Gen. Buell falls back from Tennessee as Gen Bragg advances toward Kentucky—Movements in Kentucky—Battle at Perryville—Retreat of Gen. Bragg—Cumberland Gap —Invasion of West Virginia—Operations in Mississippi—Battle of Iuka—Battle at Corinth—Retreat of the Enemy—Expedition of Gen. Hovey—Gen. Rosecrans takes command in Tennessee—Position of Gen. Bragg's Forces—Battle of Stone River.

EARLY in June the guerrilla operations became troublesome in some of the lower counties of Kentucky. At Madisonville, in Hopkins county, a descent was made by a small body of them at night. The county clerk's office was broken open and the records of the court carried off or destroyed. In other cases horses and other property were taken. Their own friends, equally with Union citizens, were robbed. In Jessamine, Mercer, Boyle, and Garrard counties bridges over the streams were burned. On the 5th of July Lebanon was taken. It is at the termination of the Lebanon branch of the Louisville and Nashville road. About the same time Murfreesborough in Tennessee was captured by a strong guerrilla force under Col. Forrest. Vigorous opposition was however made by the small body of Federal troops stationed there. The 9th Michigan regiment was captured entirely by surprise, with Brig.-Generals Duffield and Crittenden, of Indiana. On the 18th of July an attack was made by Col. John Morgan on a small Federal force stationed at Cynthiana, Ky. Subsequently he was overtaken near Paris by Gen. Green C. Smith and defeated. About the same time Henderson was occupied by citizens of Kentucky and other States, acting the part of guerrillas, and the hospital and other stores carried off. At the same time Newburg, in Indiana, on the Ohio River, was occupied by a band from Kentucky. They soon, however, left. The activity of the bands under Col. Morgan produced a great excitement in the interior of the State. Many towns were visited and much plunder obtained. It had been his conviction that large numbers of the citizens would flock to his standard. In this he was greatly mistaken, and the indifference and hostility of the people, together with the preparations to resist him, checked his movements. Active operations continued in Tennessee, whither Col. Morgan retired. Clarksville was captured with its military stores.

The increase of guerrilla operations in Kentucky about the 1st of September, with the manifestations of the existence of a Confederate force, indicated some hostile movements. It was soon known that the Confederate general E. Kirby Smith was approaching from Knoxville in Tennessee. On the 22d of August he left Jacksborough with a train of one hundred and fifty wagons, and passed through Big Creek Gap. So difficult were some parts of the route in Tennessee that for two or three days the rear of the trains was only able to reach at night the point from which the advance started in the morning. Rations failed, and the men were obliged for several days to subsist on green corn. Hungry, thirsty, footsore, and choking with dust, his men marched steadily on to a land of plenty. The ordnance stores were brought safely through without the loss of a wagon. On Saturday, August 30, a battle took place between his forces and a Federal force near Richmond, Ky., in which the latter were defeated. Richmond is the capital of Madison County, situated about fifty miles south-southeast of Frankfort, the capital of the State. The Federal force there consisted of one Ohio regiment and five Indiana regiments and part of a sixth, two Kentucky regiments, all raw troops, and a squadron of Kentucky cavalry, under the command of Brig.-Gens. Mahlon D. Manson and Crufts, with nine field pieces. It made an attack upon this Confederate column under Gen. Smith at Rogersville about four miles from Richmond, and after a severe battle, continuing from six o'clock in the morning until night, it was entirely defeated, with a large number killed and wounded and with the loss of eight field pieces. Gen. Nelson, who had come from Lexington, arrived at the commencement of the retreat, and endeavored to rally the troops, was wounded and obliged to retire. At that time the Legislature of the State was in session, and it met on Sunday evening, and passed resolutions adjourning to Louisville, &c. The archives of the State and about one million of treasure from the banks of Richmond, Lexington, and Frankfort were transferred during the night to Louisville.

At the same time the governor of the State issued the following proclamation:

FRANKFORT, KY., *August* 31, 1862.

To the People of Kentucky:

A crisis has arisen in the history of the commonwealth which demands of every loyal citizen of Kentucky prompt and efficient action. The State has been invaded by an insolent foe, her honor insulted, her peace disturbed, and her integrity imperilled. The small but gallant army, raised upon the emergency of the occasion for her defence, under the brave and chivalric Nelson, has met with a temporary reverse, and the enemy is advancing for the accomplishment of his purpose—the subjugation of the State. He must be met and driven from our border, and it is in your power to do so. I, therefore, as Governor of the Commonwealth, deem it my duty to call upon every loyal citizen of Kentucky to rally to the defence of the State; not a moment is to be lost. I appeal to you as Kentuckians, as worthy sons of those who rescued the dark and bloody ground from savage barbarity, by the memories of the past of your history, and by the future of your fame, if you are but true to yourselves, to rise in the majesty of your strength and drive the insolent invader of your soil from your midst. Now is the time for Kentuckians to defend themselves. Each man must constitute himself a soldier, arm himself as best he can, and meet the foe at every step of his advance. The day and the hour, the safety of your homes and firesides, patriotism and duty, alike demand that you rush to the rescue. I call upon the people, then, to rise up as one man, and strike a blow for the defence of their native land, their property, and their homes. Rally to the standard, wherever it may be nearest, place yourselves under the commanders, obey orders, trust to your own right arm and the God of battle, and the foe will be driven back, discomfited and annihilated. To arms! to arms!! and never lay them down till the Stars and Stripes float in triumph throughout Kentucky. I but perform my duty in thus summoning you to the defence of your State, and I am assured that it will be promptly responded to. I promise that I will share with you the glory of the triumph which surely awaits you.

Done in the city of Frankfort, this 31st day of August, 1862.

(Signed) JAMES F. ROBINSON.

By the Governor,
D. C. WICKLIFFE, Secretary of State.

On the 2d the Confederate advance guard entered Lexington. All the Government stores had been previously safely removed. The stock of horses and mules had also been sent off, and all the cars withdrawn from the railroad.

In explanation of the object of the invasion, Gen. Smith issued the following proclamation:

KENTUCKIANS: The army of the Confederate States has again entered your territory under my command.

Let no one make you believe we come as invaders, to coerce your will, or to exercise control over your soil. Far from it. The principle we maintain is, that government derives its just powers from the consent of the governed.

I shall enforce the strictest discipline, in order that the property of citizens and non-combatants may be protected. I shall be compelled to procure subsistence for my troops among you, and this shall be paid for.

Kentuckians: We come not as invaders, but liberators. We invoke the spirit of your resolutions of 1798. We come to arouse you from the lethargy which enshrouds your free thought, and forebodes the political death of your State.

We come to test the truth of what we believe to be a foul aspersion, that Kentuckians willingly join the attempt to subjugate us, and to deprive us of our property, our liberty, and our dearest rights.

We come to strike off the chains which are riveted upon you. We call upon you to unite your arms, and join with us in hurling back from our fair and sunny plains the Northern hordes who would deprive us of our liberty, that they may enjoy our substance.

Are we deceived? Can you treat us as enemies? Our hearts answer NO! E. KIRBY SMITH,
Major-General C. S. A.

On the 6th Frankfort, the capital of the State, was quietly occupied by about fifteen hundred Confederate cavalry. The government of the city was reorganized, and recruiting stations opened. The guerilla force, under Col. Morgan, also joined Gen. Smith.

Meanwhile, on the first approach of the Confederate force toward Lexington, excitement commenced in Cincinnati, and preparations for defence began to be made. Gen. Lewis Wallace took command of Cincinnati, Covington, and Newport on the 1st of September. Martial law was declared, and on the next day all places of business in Cincinnati were ordered to be closed at nine o'clock in the morning, and the citizens were required to assemble at ten o'clock and organize for defence. The street railroad cars were stopped, and no male citizen was allowed to leave. Preparations to throw up intrenchments and to fortify the city were immediately commenced. This excitement extended into the interior of the State and into the adjoining State of Indiana. The governor of Ohio issued the following proclamation:

CINCINNATI, *September* 2, 1862.

To the Loyal People of the River Counties:

Our southern border is threatened with invasion. I have, therefore, to recommend that all the loyal men of your counties at once form themselves into military companies and regiments to beat back the enemy at any and all points he may attempt to invade our State. Gather up all the arms in the country, and furnish yourselves with ammunition for the same. The service will be of but few days' duration. The soil of Ohio must not be invaded by the enemies of our glorious Government. DAVID TOD, Governor.

About the 10th of June Gen. Buell left Corinth with the main body of his army for Chattanooga. On reaching Huntsville he appointed Gen. Rousseau to command the division of his army previously under Gen. Mitchell, and completely reorganized the state of affairs in that part of his department. Depredations by soldiers were stopped, discipline restored, and order established. His army then took positions at Battle Creek, Huntsville, and McMinnville. At the same time the Confederate general Bragg massed his army at Chattanooga and Knoxville. This was done by suddenly moving his force from Tupello, in Mississippi, through the States of Alabama and Georgia, and thus reaching Chattanooga in advance of Gen. Buell. It was divided into three corps under Maj.-Gens. Wm. J. Hardee, Leonidas Polk, and E. Kirby Smith, each of which numbered about fifteen thousand men. The two former of these officers had been at Corinth, and their forces consisted of some of the troops which evacuated that place, increased by new levies under the conscription law. The division of Gen. Smith was stationed at Knoxville, where it safely remained while Chattanooga was occupied by the corps of

Gens. Hardee and Polk. Gen. Smith moving from Knoxville succeeded in flanking the Federal general G. W. Morgan, and with no battle of any consequence, except at Tazewell, effected the design of getting into his rear, and thence advanced into Kentucky as above stated. The next movement was made by the other two corps, for the purpose of forming a junction with Gen. Smith after he had reached Lexington. Accordingly, on the 21st of August, Gen. Bragg crossed the Tennessee river at Harrison, a few miles above Chattanooga, and turning the left of Gen. Buell he marched westward by the mountain road to Dunlap, which he reached on the 27th. His force then consisted of five regiments of cavalry, thirty-six of infantry, with forty pieces of field artillery. Thence he moved up the Sequatchie Valley, and reached Pikeville on the 30th. On the same day he threw a large force forward toward McMinnville, the capital of Warren county, Tennessee, and seventy-five miles southeast of Nashville. The Confederate cavalry advanced far toward McMinnville, and one or two smart skirmishes took place with the Federal cavalry thrown forward from that point. In the mean time the rest of the Confederate army moved northeast toward Crossville, and on the 1st of September reached the mountains at that place, having ascended the Grassy Cave road, while the force thrown toward McMinnville was suddenly withdrawn, and followed the main army. On the 5th of September this Confederate force entered Kentucky, and moved on toward Bowling Green. On the 13th of September an advance of this force appeared before Munfordsville, at the crossing of the Louisville and Nashville railroad, over Green river, and demanded its surrender. Col. Wilder then in command refused, and early on the next morning an attack was made by the Confederate force, under Gen. Duncan, who after a struggle of seven hours was repulsed. The force at Munfordsville, which had been stationed there for the protection of the bridge, consisted of three thousand one hundred infantry with four pieces of artillery. The Federal loss was eight killed and twenty wounded. The Confederate loss was larger. The attack was renewed again on the 16th with great spirit, and on the next day the place was surrendered by Col. C. L. Dunham, who had arrived with his regiment, and then had command. The troops surrendered consisted of the 17th, 60th, 67th, 68th, 69th Indiana, a company of Louisville cavalry, a part of the 4th Ohio, and a section of the 13th Indiana battery; amounting in all to about four thousand five hundred men, and ten guns. The bridge over the Green river was burned at this time.

During this period Gen. Buell had not been idle. While on the Tennessee river, near Chattanooga, his army was dependent on Louisville as its base for the supply of provisions and munitions. To render this available it was necessary to protect over three hundred miles of railroad, over which every pound of these supplies had to be transported. Every care which prudence could suggest was exercised to retain the command of this road. Stockades were built, and guards were stationed at the places most liable to attack, but they were not able

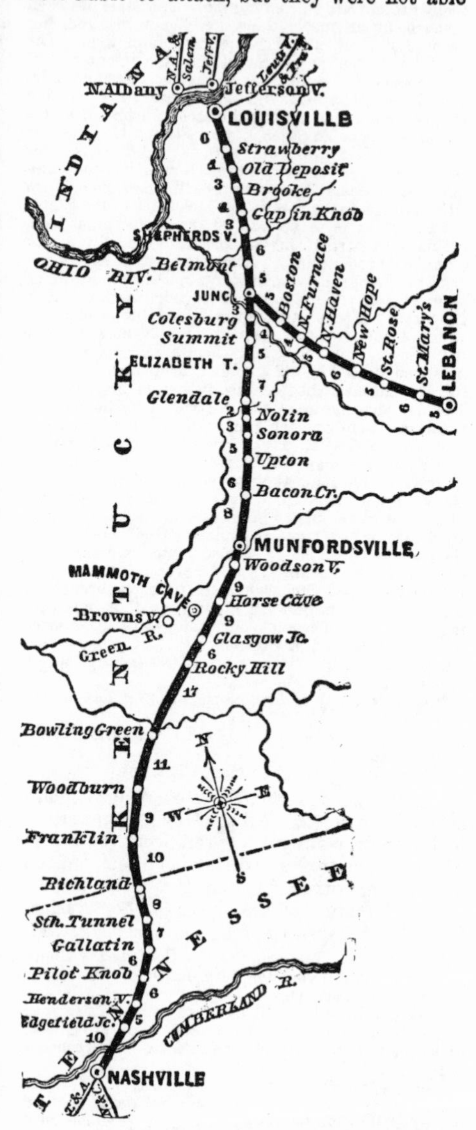

to resist the dashes of the Confederate cavalry, who in many cases were aided by the sympathies of the local residents. In the meanwhile the Confederate conscription act had been rigidly enforced, and a large army under Gen. Bragg was massed near Chattanooga, as above stated, the definite object of which was long unknown. For several weeks the utmost vigilance was exercised over the enemy at Dechard, McMinnville, and the valley of the Sequatchie before it was assuredly ascertained where he intended to strike his blow. It was expected that Nashville was the point he desired to reach, but subsequent movements soon made it evident that was not the projected point of attack. Finally despatches to Gen. Bragg were intercepted, which proved conclusively that Louisville in Kentucky was the point toward which the Confederate strategy was directed. This was to be effected by forced marches of the Confederate force without supplies, subsisting on the country, and reaching the city when in a condition unprepared for defence. It was then intended to destroy the canal around the falls of the Ohio, to seize all the public stores, and to hold the city, under the impression that the Federal army would make no effort to recover it, for fear of injuring it by a bombardment.

While Gen. Bragg made his way slowly toward the Cumberland river, which he struck at Carthage, Gen. Buell was on his left flank, at Lebanon, guarding against his approach to the city of Nashville. The march of Gen. Bragg was commenced on the 21st of August, as above stated, and all the way he was felt by Gen. Buell, whose object was to guard the railroad as much as possible, and allow his enemy to get no distant start of him. All this time Gen. Buell was drawing his supplies from the depots, collecting at Nashville and Bowling Green; but Gen. Bragg was warmly received in many places, and bountifully supplied by friends. Gen. Buell harassed his rear as long as possible, shelled him out of Woodsonville, and forded the Green river and drove him out of Munfordsville, and followed him along the turnpike road from Nashville to Louisville, until the road through Hodgenville to the east was reached, into which Gen. Bragg's forces defiled. It was evident from the movement of Gen. Bragg that he was hurrying in a direction in which he expected to find Gen. E. K. Smith, Gen. Humphrey Marshall, and Col. Morgan with their forces, with whom he could unite and make a combined attack on Louisville. Gen. Buell, however, was forced by the need of supplies to move directly to the city, around which his army encamped.

The chief object of this Confederate movement upon the State of Kentucky was to obtain supplies of meat. There were more hogs and cattle in the State available for general consumption, two or three to one, than were left in all the South besides. The grain growing and provision raising country which stretched from the Potomac at Harper's Ferry to Memphis, on the Mississippi, was now exhausted of its provisions. Much of the productive portions of North Carolina, and of the Gulf States, were also exhausted, and a general scarcity existed. Wheat was two dollars and a half per bushel in the heart of a fine wheat country, and cattle sold for seven cents gross per pound in the chief cattle-raising region of the whole South. Pork could not be had at an advance of four hundred per cent. At the same time it was thought that a powerful force might secure the State to the Southern Confederacy.

On the 18th of September Gen. Bragg issued the following address to the people of the State:

GLASGOW, KY., *September* 18, 1862.

Kentuckians! I have entered your State with the Confederate army of the West, and offer you an opportunity to free yourselves from the tyranny of a despotic ruler. We come, not as conquerors or despoilers, but to restore to you the liberties of which you have been deprived by a cruel and relentless foe. We come to guarantee to all the sanctity of their homes and altars; to punish with a rod of iron the despoilers of your peace, and to avenge the cowardly insults to your women. With all non-combatants the past shall be forgotten. Needful supplies must be had for my army, but they shall be paid for at fair and remunerating prices.

Believing that the heart of Kentucky is with us in our great struggle for Constitutional Freedom, we have transferred from our own soil to yours, not a band of marauders, but a powerful and well-disciplined army. Your gallant Buckner leads the van. Marshall is on the right, while Breckinridge, dear to us as to you, is advancing with Kentucky's valiant sons, to receive the honor and applause due to their heroism. The strong hands which in part have sent Shiloh down to history, and the nerved arms which have kept at bay from our own homes the boastful army of the enemy, are here to assist, to sustain, to liberate you. Will you remain indifferent to our call, or will you not rather vindicate the fair fame of your once free and envied State? We believe that you will, and that the memory of your gallant dead who fell at Shiloh, their faces turned homeward, will rouse you to a manly effort for yourselves and posterity.

Kentuckians! We have come with joyous hopes. Let us not depart in sorrow, as we shall if we find you wedded in your choice to your present lot. If you prefer Federal rule, show it by your frowns, and we shall return whence we came. If you choose rather to come within the folds of our brotherhood, then cheer us with the smiles of your women, and lend your willing hands to secure you in your heritage of liberty.

Women of Kentucky! Your persecutions and heroic bearing have reached our ear. Banish henceforth, forever, from your minds the fear of loathsome prisons or insulting visitations. Let your enthusiasm have free rein. Buckle on the armor of your kindred, your husbands, sons, and brothers, and scoff with shame him who would prove recreant in his duty to you, his country, and his God. BRAXTON BRAGG,
General Commanding.

From Munfordsville the Confederate force moved toward Bardstown, Glasgow, and the central part of the State. Thence guerillas in large and small bands scoured almost every other portion, penetrating in various places to the Ohio river, and even making dashes to within four or five miles of Louisville. Every day, during which they continued these operations, was estimated to afford them a gain of a hundred thousand dollars, and to bring a loss to the loyal people of at least two hundred thousand. Everything which could be of use to the army or to the Southern people was seized. Hundreds of drovers almost daily took away horses, cattle, and hogs, and almost interminable trains were hauling away bacon, pork, and all kinds of breadstuffs. Regarding Kentucky as belonging to the Confederacy,

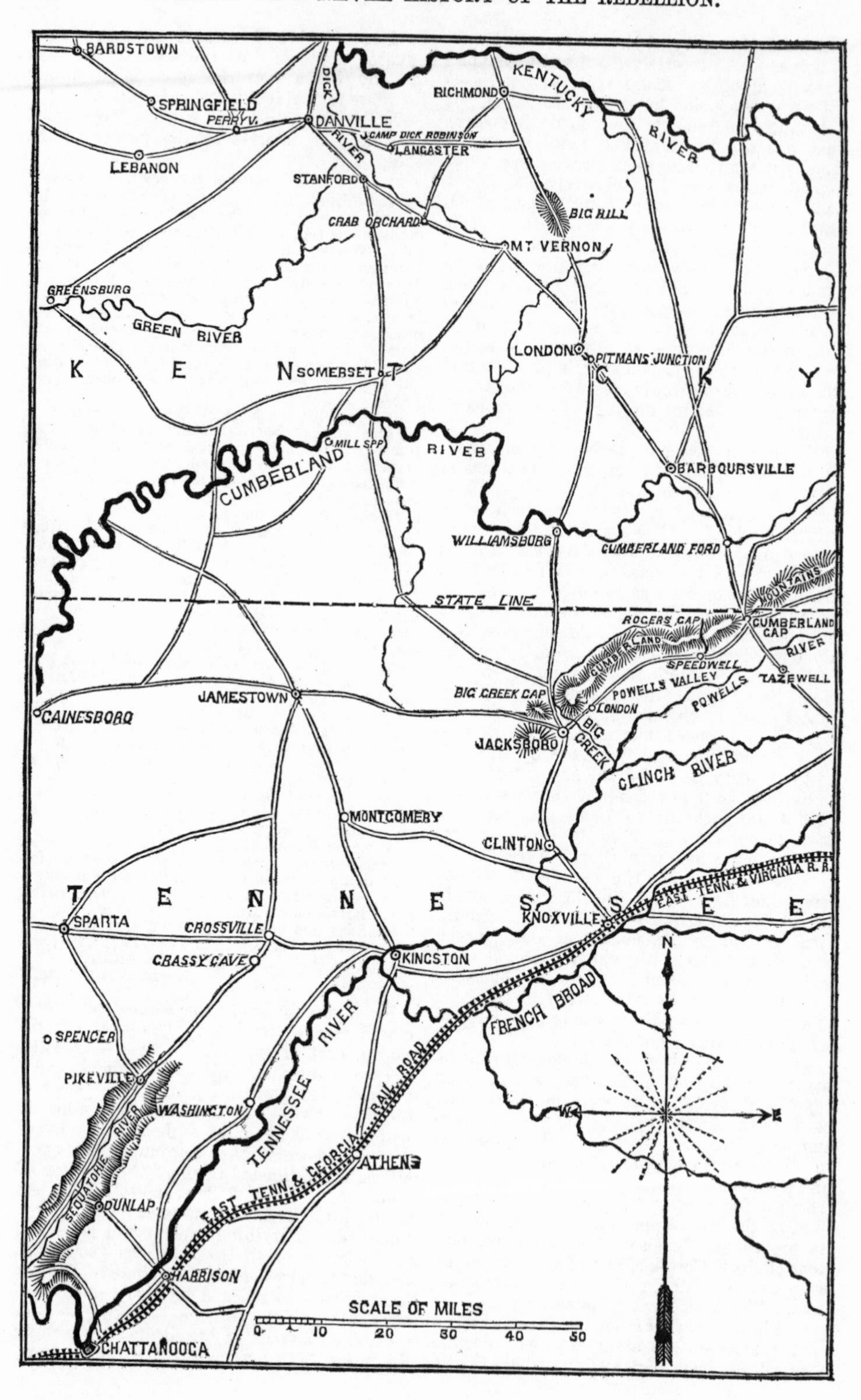
BARDSTOWN
SPRINGFIELD
PERRYV.
DANVILLE
DICK RIVER
CAMP DICK ROBINSON
LANCASTER
RICHMOND
KENTUCKY RIVER
LEBANON
STANFORD
BIG HILL
CRAB ORCHARD
MT VERNON
GREENSBURG
GREEN RIVER
LONDON
PITMANS JUNCTION
K E N T U C K Y
SOMERSET
MILL SPP
CUMBERLAND RIVER
BARBOURSVILLE
WILLIAMSBURG
CUMBERLAND FORD
STATE LINE
MOUNTAINS
ROGERS GAP
CUMBERLAND GAP
CUMBERLAND
SPEEDWELL
POWELLS VALLEY
RIVER
POWELLS
TAZEWELL
BIG CREEK GAP
LONDON
JAMESTOWN
CAINESBORO
JACKSBORO
BIG CREEK
CLINCH RIVER
MONTGOMERY
CLINTON
T E N N E S S E E
EAST TENN. & VIRGINIA R. R.
KNOXVILLE
SPARTA
CROSSVILLE
CRASSY CAVE
KINGSTON
N
FRENCH BROAD
SPENCER
TENNESSEE RIVER
RAIL ROAD
PIKEVILLE
WASHINGTON
W
E
SEQUATCHIE RIVER
EAST TENN. & GEORGIA
ATHENS
DUNLAP
HARRISON
SCALE OF MILES
0
10
20
30
40
50
CHATTANOOGA

the conscription act was enforced, and men were forced into the ranks of the Confederate army by the point of the bayonet. The stores of the towns were ordered to be opened, and the goods taken and paid for in Confederate scrip.

On the 1st of October Gen. Buell, who had been previously removed from command and reinstated again, moved from Louisville, where he had lost thousands by desertion, to meet the Confederate force, and on the 4th his army arrived at Bardstown. On the previous day a force of Gen. Bragg had evacuated that place. This force consisted of about sixty-five regiments, averaging about three hundred men each, and amounting in total to twenty thousand. It moved from Bardstown in the direction of Springfield. The force of Gen. Buell was stated by the general-in-chief to number about one hundred thousand men. From the first approach of the Confederate forces, every effort had been made to collect new troops at Cincinnati and Louisville, and to fortify these places against a *coup de main*. To give confidence to the new levies, a portion of Gen. Grant's army was withdrawn from Mississippi and sent to Kentucky and Cincinnati.

The army of the Ohio, as Gen. Buell's force was designated, was now divided into three corps, commanded by Gens. Gilbert, Crittenden, and McCook. The new regiments sent to Louisville were placed in brigades with the old ones, which had seen nearly a year's service. On the march from Louisville the corps of Gen. McCook, forming the left wing, took the road to Taylorsville, Gen. Gilbert the road to Shepherdsville, and Gen. Crittenden, forming the right wing, the road to Bardstown. With the latter corps Gen. Buell moved.

On the 4th, Richard Hawes was inaugurated at Frankfort as Confederate Provisional Governor, and on the same day the city was evacuated, and he retired with the troops.

On the 6th the army of Gen. Buell arrived at Springfield, sixty-two miles from Louisville. Its slow progress had been owing to its numbers, the difficulty of the route and the conflicts with the Confederate rear guard. The main body of the Confederate army was twenty-four hours in advance when Gen. Buell left Louisville, and thus far had been constantly gaining. The order of Gen. Bragg to his rear guard was to prevent the arrival of Gen. Buell at Bardstown before the 4th, if possible, in order to give time to the Confederate wagon train to gain an advance of some twenty miles. Gen. Crittenden's corps only entered the place, and those of Gens. McCook and Gilbert kept on toward Springfield, retaining their position on the left and centre. Gen. Crittenden followed on the 5th. On the 7th it was reported to Gen. Buell that a considerable Confederate force was at Perryville, forty-two miles south of Frankfort. The three army corps were then marching on that place by different roads. Gen. Buell determined to surround the enemy, if possible, and ordered all the divisions to march without delay, leaving behind their transportation. Gens. McCook and Gilbert continued their march, but Gen. Crittenden lost half a day on a circuitous route to obtain water. Gen. Bragg, learning of the united approach of the Union forces, immediately began to retreat. It was the design of Gen. Buell that the three corps should participate in the battle, but Gen. Bragg hearing of the delay of Gen. Crittenden, immediately determined to fight the corps of Gens. McCook and Gilbert, and defeat them if possible, and then to fall upon Gen. Crittenden or to retreat before his arrival. The Confederate general Hardee's corps, which had retreated six miles, was accordingly ordered back in haste to Perryville. Suddenly, on the 8th, Gen. McCook found himself in front of the Confederate line of battle, with his men marching in columns, and without skirmishers in advance, nothing in front but a small advance guard which attempted to attack the enemy's outpost. The Confederate infantry rushed forward and a division of raw troops had to be formed in line of battle under a heavy fire. The raw troops fled in confusion, but the old troops stood their ground. Gen. McCook had approached Perryville by the Knoxville road. Gen. Gilbert had marched direct from Springfield, and had arrived within two miles of Perryville on the preceding evening, the 7th. To Gen. McCook's request for reënforcements, they were ordered from Gen. Gilbert's corps. At the same time Gen. Crittenden was ordered to push forward on the Lebanon road to attack the Confederate left. The advance of Gen. Gilbert's reënforcements arrived at half-past three o'clock in the afternoon to support Gen. McCook on the left. His forces were found badly cut up and hotly pressed by the Confederate force, having retreated nearly a mile. The contest continued violent until dark, the Federal force retiring from the field. During the evening Gen. Crittenden's corps came up, but no movement was made till noon of the next day, when it was ascertained that the Confederate force had retired. The Federal loss was about four hundred and sixty-six killed, among whom were Brig.-Gens. Jackson and Tyrrell, fourteen hundred and sixty-three wounded, and one hundred and sixty missing. The Confederate loss was nearly the same. The forces of Gen. Bragg, which he had been able to draw from all quarters, were now about sixty thousand. The arrival of Gen. Crittenden's corps undoubtedly induced Gen. Bragg to continue his retreat. On that evening the Federal troops returned to Perryville.

It was now expected that Gen. Bragg would make a stand at Camp Dick Robinson. The position of this place is such that it can easily be defended against an approach in front by a few batteries on the cliffs which line Dick river. It, however, can be easily flanked. It was the plan of Gen. Buell, therefore, to make a feint in front and a strong attack on the flank of the Confederate position. Accordingly, Gen. Crittenden was ordered to march to Dick river, giving the semblance of a contemplated attack in front. Gens. McCook and Gilbert were to approach by different roads, so as to cut off the escape of Gen. Bragg and leave to him no alternative but to fight or surrender. By the night of the 12th the entire army of the Ohio was within a mile of Danville, which is forty-two miles south of Frankfort, in one of the most fertile and highly improved parts of the State. But Gen. Bragg penetrated the designs of his antagonist in consequence of a retrograde movement by the advance of Gen. Crittenden's corps, under Gen. Wood, and determined to frustrate them. His spoils loaded heavily nearly four thousand wagons, a majority of which were branded with the letters U. S., having been captured during the year; in addition there were several thousand head of cattle, a thousand mules, and as many sheep.

The following statement from a highly creditable source at Lexington, Ky., has been made of property taken by Gen. Bragg's forces:

We were here in Lexington and saw something of the removal of Government stores, and witnessed the plunderings of the Confederate armies of our dry-goods stores, groceries, &c. Upon the resumption of the publication of our paper ("Observer") we stated that an immense amount of Government stores, amounting perhaps to $1,000,000, besides arms sufficient to arm eighteen or twenty thousand men, were taken off, and we stated precisely the truth, and there are hundreds here who will bear us out in the statement. We are not inclined to think the "Richmond Examiner" far wrong when it published that the "wagon train of supplies brought out of Kentucky by Gen. Kirby Smith was forty miles long, and brought a million yards of jeans, with a large amount of clothing, boots, and shoes, and 200 wagon loads of bacon, 6,000 barrels pork, 1,500 mules and horses, 8,000 beeves, and a large lot of swine."

From the city of Frankfort it is stated that 74,900 yards of jeans were taken from the establishment of Mr. Watson. From one concern in this city (Lexington) they took $106,000 worth of jeans and linseys, from another $10,000 worth, another $9,000, another $10,000, another $5,000. These different amounts in woollen goods we know to have been removed from this city, as we have the names before us from whom they were taken. Aside from this, in boots, shoes, &c., we know of $30,000 worth that they carried off, and also have the names to show from whom the goods were taken. From one house seven boxes of new Springfield rifles and nine boxes of muskets, with all the tents belonging to Metcalf's cavalry, forty kegs of horse shoes, and one hundred and twenty boxes belonging to four regiments, containing clothing and subsistence. The articles taken from this house were valued by the Confederates themselves at more than $10,000, and they so declared at the time. The Adams Express office was robbed of everything it contained. All the goods that had been sent and deposited in the establishment from all parts of the country were seized and appropriated. For four weeks, during the stay of the enemy here, a train of cars were running daily to Nicholasville, bearing away mess pork and other articles necessary to the subsistence of armies, while trains of wagons—huge in number—were moving out on the Richmond, Versailles, and Nicholasville roads, day and night, loaded with valuable commodities. We were here and saw and know what occurred, and can prove what we assert. Lexington afforded the Confederates, when they entered it, the richest harvest they have reaped during the war, and nothing is to be made by disguising the fact.

On the night of the 11th the evacuation of Camp Dick Robinson commenced. The destination of Gen. Bragg was Cumberland Gap. Two routes for retreat were open to him, both leading to that point; one by the way of Richmond and Big Hill, through Madison county, and the other, called the Crab Orchard road, by the way of Mt. Vernon and Barboursville. These two roads converge at Pitman's Junction, twenty-two miles from Mt. Vernon, and fifty-eight miles from Cumberland Gap.

At midnight, on the night of the 12th, orders were received from the headquarters of Gen. Buell at Perryville, by the army encamped near Danville, for an immediate advance. Transportation of all kinds was ordered to remain behind. Only ambulances were to accompany the troops. Gen. Buell had been informed of the retreat of the Confederate army. At one o'clock the army was in motion toward Stanford, nine miles from Danville, a town through which it was supposed the Confederate force was then retreating. The march was rapid, and the advance arrived in time to see the rear of the Confederate rear guard pass unmolested. Two or three regiments of cavalry, one of which was the Texan Rangers, and two howitzers, was the force of this rear guard. Familiar with the topography of the country, and taking advantage of it whenever favorable to themselves, these troops were able to conceal their small numbers and to check the Union advance until late in the afternoon. Having thus accomplished their object, which was to gain time for the main body, they then retired toward Crab Orchard. From a few prisoners, taken by the Union troops, they learned that the main body of Gen. Bragg's army and half his wagon train had passed through Stanford on the previous day, and the other half of the wagon train had gone safely through Lancaster, and were retreating on the Richmond and Big Hill road. That night the Union army encamped at Stanford. Early the next morning, the 14th, it was on the march, and soon reached Crab Orchard, a distance of ten miles. As it approached the town, the Confederate rear guard made its appearance drawn up in battle array. It had taken possession of two hills, and was in a good position to make a formidable resistance for a short time. This caused the Federal column to halt. The artillery was then brought up into position, a line of battle was formed, a reconnoissance made, an advance of skirmishers thrown out, and other details performed which caused a delay of several hours. During all this time the army of Gen. Bragg was unmolested and in full retreat. When all the Federal preparations were complete, the Confederate rear guard hastily retired. The Union advance, on the next day, reached Mt. Vernon. On the next day, the 16th, the division of Gens. Van Cleave and Smith were ordered forward; the rest of the advance halted. At this time Gen. McCook's corps and a part of Gen. Gilbert's were at Crab Orchard, and all the cavalry had been ordered to the rear in consequence of the difficulty of obtaining forage in the mountainous region. On the hills and in the defiles between Mt. Vernon and the State line, ten thousand men would be as effective as forty thousand in resisting an army. The pursuit of the Confederate forces now lost all of its importance.

The result of the invasion of Kentucky was undoubtedly regarded by the Confederate leaders as successful in obtaining supplies, but they were greatly chagrined at the tardiness of the Kentuckians to rally around the Confederate standard. The desertions from their force exceeded the number of recruits obtained. The Confederate forces now retired into east Tennessee, and Gen. Buell fell back to the line between Louisville and Nashville, where he was superseded in the command by Major-Gen. Rosecrans, under the orders of President Lincoln. Col. Morgan, with a small guerilla force, still remained in the State. The invasion of eastern Kentucky, by the Confederate forces, cut off the line of communication between the Federal forces at Cumberland Gap in east Tennessee and the north. It was followed by the evacuation of that strong position by the Union General, G. W. Morgan.

Cumberland Gap is south and a little east of Lexington, Ky., and about one hundred and fifty miles distant. It is a natural gap in a mountain, nearly eighty miles in length. There are other places in this long mountain which are called gaps, but this name is given more from the fact that the summit at those places is of more easy access than because of any natural depression of the mountain. At the place called Roger's Gap, next to Cumberland, and eighteen miles west, there is actually no gap; but the road, taking advantage of a succession of ridges on the northern side and running diagonally on the southern side, is rendered passable by man and beast, and may, by great exertions, be passed over by wagons and cannon. The distance from the beginning of the ascent on the one side to the ending of the descent on the other is a little more than five miles. Sixteen miles further west is Big Creek Gap, the crossing at which is a little more difficult.

The mountain on each side of Cumberland Gap is about twelve hundred feet high. In the gap it is only four hundred feet. The road through the notch is a good one. On the southern side the mountain is abrupt in some places and almost perpendicular, and the summit is inaccessible without the greatest danger, except by entering the gap and ascending on either the right or left. The northern side is more irregular, breaking off in a succession of smaller mountains and hills, to the valley lying between the gap and Cumberland Ford. But the main mountain towers far above its neighbors. Two roads from Lexington, Ky., lead to the gap. One passes through Nicholasville, Crab Orchard, and Mt. Vernon, by the way of Wild Cat. The other passes through Richmond, by way of Big Hill. From London, Ky., there is but one road. It is flanked on each side by a succession of hills and mountains, and passes through Barboursville, and crosses the Cumberland Ford. Wagons or cannon could scarcely pass by any other route.

This position was important to the Confederate Government, as by its occupation in force they could hold possession of east Tennessee, and prevent any approach from the north to cut their northern railroad line of connection between Richmond and northern Alabama, Mississippi, Nashville, Memphis, and other towns on the Mississippi. Its occupation was also necessary to sustain their advance into eastern Kentucky. A small Confederate force, therefore, took possession of the gap soon after the commencement of hostilities. On the other hand, its possession was important to the Federal Government, as thereby it prevented the invasion of Kentucky from the southeast. It was also the stronghold of east Tennessee, a section in which there existed among the people a stronger and more invincible attachment to the Union than in any other portion of the seceded States. After the defeat of the Confederate forces in southeastern Kentucky, under Gen. Zollicoffer, a body of Federal troops advanced in the direction of Cumberland Gap. On the 15th of February, they were encamped near Cumberland Ford, about ten miles from the gap, which was then occupied by about two thousand Confederate soldiers. Scouting parties were sent out from the camp near the ford, one of which penetrated the gap and captured a few prisoners. On the 13th of March, another expedition consisting of about 12 companies of infantry and 86 cavalry, started from camp near Barboursville, Ky., and crossing the mountain near Big Creek Gap, after four days reached Powell's Valley, five miles from Jacksborough, where a body of about four hundred Confederate cavalry was surprised and routed, and their camp taken possession of. Another body at Jacksborough, about two hundred in number, was next driven out. After remaining four days, the Federal force retired. On the 21st, a strong expedition moved upon the gap and made an attack, and cannonading ensued without any important result except developing the Confederate strength. The Confederate occupation of the gap continued without any serious interference until Chattanooga was occupied by the forces of Gen. Mitchell, as has been stated. This led to its evacuation about the 10th of June. Previous to that date, Gen. Geo. W. Morgan, with a division of Union troops, advanced from Cumberland Ford, and crossing at Roger's Gap, prepared to cut off the supplies for the small force then at Cumberland Gap. Their stock at the time was small; the Confederate forces under Gen. E. K. Smith had moved south from east Tennessee, and the Union forces at hand being large, and threatening in front and rear, no alternative remained to the garrison but to surrender or evacuate the position. On the 14th of July, an expedition was sent against a body of Confederate cavalry at Wallace Cross Roads, and after a brief skirmish the latter retired. Again, on the 9th of August, Col. De Courcy was on a foraging expedition with the 16th and 42d Ohio, 14th and 22d Kentucky, when the 14th Kentucky, being advanced a short distance beyond Tazewell, was attacked by the 11th and 42d Tennessee, 30th Alabama, and 21st Georgia, under Col. Rains. A severe conflict ensued, in which the Confederate forces were compelled to retire before the artillery that was brought to the aid of the Federal forces.

On the 17th of August, a small Confederate force approached in front of the position, and attacked a body of Union cavalry some two miles out in the valley, who were compelled to retire with a loss of two or three killed and wounded. Their camp, however, was protected from the approach of the Confederate force by the guns on the mountain. On the same day information was received by Gen. Morgan that a large Confederate force had appeared at Barboursville and London, Ky., and captured his supply trains nearly as far back as Crab Orchard. Its object was to hold the Blue Grass region of Kentucky, and ultimately to force the entire division of Gen. Morgan to surrender or hastily evacuate the position. The comparative success of Gen. Bragg in his movements in Kentucky, cut off all the communications of Gen. Morgan, and by Sept. 11, his corn was all gone and nothing remained for his troops but a scanty supply of beans and rice. The force, however, had not remained inactive during this period; about three hundred prisoners and two hundred horses had been captured. The destitute condition of the force for clothes and food, caused the evacuation of the gap by Gen. Morgan on the 17th of September. On that day the 23d Indiana and the 9th Ohio battery left with all the ammunition. During the succeeding night all the troops left except a squad that remained to finish the work of destruction. The magazine was blown up, and the commissary building burned. Nothing but ammunition and a few of the most useful cooking utensils were brought away. Tents, wagons, gun carriages, arms, and accoutrements were changed to a mass of fragments and ashes. The line of retreat was two hundred and fifty miles with a large Confederate force intervening. But the position was one of the strongest in the country, and Gen. Morgan had represented that his supplies were abundant. By the 4th of October the division reached the Ohio river. It had foraged on the country, but suffered at times for water. During the entire march, a Confederate cavalry force harassed the retreat. During nineteen nights the troops bivouacked without a tent. New roads were made, trees cut out, provisions gathered, a hovering enemy kept at check, and a large force brought safely through to the borders of Ohio.

This body of troops under Gen. Morgan numbered more than ten thousand men. It brought twenty-eight pieces of artillery, six of which were 20-pounder siege guns, and four hundred wagons. Four heavy siege guns were destroyed before evacuating the gap, and a large number of sick men were left behind.

The march was through a mountainous and unproductive country. A court of inquiry was subsequently ordered to investigate the causes of this evacuation. The position was soon afterwards occupied by a small Confederate force.

It has been stated, that on the advance of the Confederate army from Richmond to attack the forces of Gen. Pope, troops were summoned by the general-in-chief from points adjacent to come to his support. Among others a portion of the troops of Gen. Cox in western Virginia were brought on to unite with the army of Virginia. The effect of thus reducing the force in western Virginia was an invasion by a Confederate force under Gen. Loring. He advanced up the Kanawha Valley as far as Charleston, which he occupied for some time. His troops were finally required to reënforce Gen. Lee's army, when he retired. The chief advantage derived from this invasion by the Confederate people was the seizure of the salt works in the Kanawha Valley. Perhaps there was no article of which they were so destitute in comparison to its importance as salt. It was exchanged by the Confederate colonel Echols, who had charge, for forage for his troops. Affairs remained in this situation until the return of Gen. Cox's forces early in November, when the Confederate forces retired.

It has also been stated that, on the invasion of Kentucky by Gen. Bragg, a portion of Gen. Grant's troops were withdrawn from Mississippi and sent to Kentucky and Cincinnati to give confidence to the new levies, and to reenforce Gen. Buell. The consequence of the withdrawal of these troops was to induce the Confederate officers to renew their operations in north Mississippi and western Tennessee. On the departure of Gen. Halleck to take the position of general-in-chief, Gen. Grant was put in command of the department of west Tennessee, including the districts of Cairo and Mississippi, that part of the State of Mississippi occupied by Federal troops, and that part of Alabama which might be occupied by the troops of his particular command, including the forces heretofore known as the army of the Mississippi.

In the department of Gen. Grant it became apparent in August that the Confederate forces south of his position had assumed a threatening attitude upon his line between Corinth in Mississippi, and Tuscumbia in Alabama. On the 10th of September the 2d brigade of Gen. Stanley's division, commanded by Col. Murphy, evacuated Tuscumbia, and fell back thirty miles upon Iuka. On the next day the Ohio brigade, which had been occupying Iuka, fell back to Corinth, leaving the force with Col. Murphy in its place. Scarcely, however, had it reached Corinth before information was received that a body of Confederate cavalry had dashed into Iuka, and after a slight skirmish put the force of Col. Murphy to flight. A considerable amount of medical and commissary stores was captured, among which were six hundred and eighty barrels of flour that Col. Murphy had neglected to destroy. Col. Murphy was immediately placed under arrest by Gen. Rosecrans, who now commanded the forces previously under Gen. Pope, and the brigade was ordered back to Iuka under Col. Mower, It, however, finally reached the neighborhood of Jacinto, and was there instructed to await further orders. The preparations of the army for an active campaign were now commenced. Transportation and baggage were reduced, and the supply of tents cut down. At this time information was received that the Confederate general Price had not only occupied Iuka in force, but was endeavoring to cross the Tennessee river for the purpose of getting in the rear of Gen. Buell, then falling back toward Nashville. It was also a part of the plan of Gen. Price, by his movement upon Iuka, to draw the Federal forces away from Corinth, and thus render its capture easy by Gen. Van Dorn, who was to attack it during the absence of Gen. Grant's forces. The design was then formed by Gens. Grant and Rosecrans to cut off the retreat of Gen. Price, and force him to surrender. For this purpose eighteen thousand men under Gens. Grant and Ord were to move by way of Burnsville, and attack Gen. Price, while Gen. Rosecrans should move with part of his force by the way of Jacinto, and attack him on the flank; at the same time the remainder of Gen. Rosecrans' force was to move on the Fulton road and cut off Gen. Price's retreat if he should attempt it. With this understanding the army was put in motion on the morning of the 18th of September. The divisions of Gens. Stanley and Hamilton under Gen. Rosecrans, after a fatiguing march in a drenching rain, bivouacked at Jacinto. Early the next morning they were again on the march, and at ten o'clock the advance encountered the Confederate pickets at Barnett's Corners. A sharp skirmish ensued, which resulted in driving them six miles toward Iuka, with a small loss. At this time the entire column had arrived at Barnett's Corners, and awaited, according to the previous understanding, for Gen. Grant to commence the attack, which would be known by the sound of his artillery. After two hours had elapsed a despatch arrived from Gen. Grant, seven miles distant, to the effect that he was waiting for Gen. Rosecrans to open the battle. The column was immediately moved forward within two miles of Iuka, when the Confederate force was discovered posted on a broad ridge commanding the country for some distance. The Confederates opened fire upon the skirmishers as they advanced in sight, under which Gen. Hamilton's division formed in line. They were also received by a hot fire of artillery and musketry, which was replied to by the 11th Ohio battery, that had now got into position. The engagement soon became general, and continued for two hours, when darkness prevented any further advantage to either side. The contest was exceedingly fierce, and the troops behaved with great bravery. The 11th Missouri and the 5th Iowa stood the severest portion of the contest, and the former lost seventy-six, and the latter one hundred and sixteen in killed and wounded. The 11th Ohio battery was exposed to a severe fire of musketry, and in less than half an hour seventy-two of its men were killed or wounded. The Confederate officers, perceiving that it was poorly supported, ordered a charge to be made on it, by which the six guns were captured, and two of them spiked. It was afterward retaken twice by the 5th Iowa at the point of the bayonet, but finally fell into the possession of the Confederates. The night was spent in taking care of the wounded and burying the dead, while the troops lay on their arms awaiting the dawn of the next day to renew the battle.

Early in the morning, as no movement was perceived on the part of the Confederate force like renewing the contest, Gen. Rosecrans ordered his line of pickets to advance. Not meeting with any opposition the whole force was thrown forward, and within a half mile of the town a flag of truce was seen approaching. It reported that Gen. Price had evacuated the town during the night. Pursuit was immediately made and kept up by three companies of cavalry during the day, skirmishing with the Confederate rear guard, and capturing many prisoners. The loss of Gen. Rosecrans's force was 148 killed, 570 wounded, and 94 missing. The Confederate loss was supposed to be larger in killed and wounded, and about one thousand prisoners were taken by Gen. Rosecrans. At Iuka the six pieces of the 11th Ohio battery were found, having been abandoned, and also a large number of wounded, and commissary stores and camp equipage. Among the killed were the Confederate generals Lytle and Berry. Gen. Whitfield also was mortally wounded. The road by which Gen. Price retreated being unobstructed, he marched that day twenty-seven miles to Bay Spring.

The force of Gen. Grant left Corinth at the same time when Gen. Rosecrans marched, and reached Burnsville, Miss., in the afternoon. There it remained one night and the next day, and then pushed forward until it met the Confederate pickets. Then it retired and awaited the next morning, when a flag of truce was sent to the Confederate camp, which did not return until late in the afternoon. Thus while Gen. Rosecrans engaged the Confederates on the south, Gen. Grant was prevented from engaging them on the west and north.

The effect of this battle was to relieve Gen. Buell from all danger of an attack by Gen. Price on his rear, while moving against Gen. Bragg. On the 22d Gen. Grant's forces returned to Corinth, and Gen. Rosecrans to Jacinto. Gen. Van Dorn through delays had not reached Corinth as soon as had been planned, and Gen. Grant by now abandoning Iuka reached the former place in advance of Gen. Van Dorn. On the 26th Gen. Rosecrans proceeded to Corinth, and took command of that position, Gen. Grant having been ordered to Jackson, and Gen. Ord to Bolivar. Jackson is forty-seven miles, and Bolivar nineteen miles by railroad north of Grand Junction, which is forty-one miles by railroad west of Corinth. By the ordinary routes Jackson is fifty-one miles north, and Bolivar forty miles northwest of Corinth. Meantime, Gen. Price retreating southwesterly from Iuka by Bay Spring, reached Baldwin, Miss., thirty miles. Thence he moved northwest to Dumas, fifteen miles, where he joined Gen. Van Dorn; thence to Pocahontas, thirty miles, where he was joined by Gen. Lovell; thence down the Chewalla, and from thence to Corinth by the old State Line road. Gen Van Dorn took the chief command at Dumas.

Meanwhile Gen. Rosecrans, anticipating that an attack would be made on his position at Corinth, prepared to meet it. The fortifications constructed by Gen. Beauregard in the beginning of the year were on the north and east, and two miles from the centre of Corinth, and required an immense force to occupy them. After Gen. Halleck took possession of the town he constructed a line of intrenchments inside those of Gen. Beauregard. Afterward, upon consultation between Gens. Grant and Rosecrans, it was determined to construct a line inside that of Gen. Halleck. This was done under the direction of Capt. Prim of the U. S. engineers. It consisted of a chain of redoubts, arranged for the concentric fire of heavy batteries. Learning the approach of the Confederate forces, Gen. Rosecrans ordered Gen. Oglebey with his brigade to proceed up the Chewalla road and meet them, with instructions to resist strongly enough to draw them under the defences of Corinth. McArthur next went forward and sent back for assistance. Gen. Davis was then ordered to send a small force, but moved with his whole division. This occupied the 30th of September, and the 1st and 2d of October. On the 3d the Confederate force was greatly increased, and the fighting became severe; Gen. Oglesby was wounded, and Gen. Hackelman killed, and the loss in killed, wounded, and prisoners was considerable, and the Union troops were driven back to their defences.

On the north and east of Corinth, hill and swampy ground alternate, which is on the whole heavily timbered. On the left hand side of the railroad there is occasionally an open field. The Union army faced to the north. On the front of its right centre there was a heavily thicketed swamp almost impassable for masses of infantry. On the left centre the ground was quite hilly. Where the right wing was posted it was rolling, but fell off in front into heavily timbered ground, such as to be swampy in rainy weather. The Chewalla road enters the town on the left, and the Bolivar road on the right centre. Excepting at this last named point Corinth was approachable in an unbroken line of battle. The new line of fortifications consisted of four revetted redoubts, covering the whole front of the town, and protecting the flanks. The front of the extreme right was strengthened by the old works of Gen. Beauregard. On the left of the extreme right, which was held by Gen. Hamilton's division, a new five-gun battery was constructed on the night of Friday the 3d. This was in direct range of the point where the Bolivar road entered the town. The previously mentioned fort on the extreme right flanked that road. The hills over which the Chewalla road entered the town were commanded by Fort Williams, which mounted twenty-pounder Parrotts. On a high, narrow ridge was located Fort Robinson, which with Fort Williams enfiladed both the Chewalla and Bolivar roads. Another fort on the extreme left protected the left and strengthened the centre. Several forts in the rear were so located as to be of much service during the action. Their guns were reversed, and turned toward the centre.

On the extreme right was stationed the division of Gen. Hamilton. Its right rested near the fort first mentioned and the old works of Gen. Beauregard, and stretched from the south side of the road to Purdy. Its left rested behind Fort Richardson. On the left Gen. Davies' division joined it, and in consecutive order six companies of Illinois sharpshooters and Burke's Missouri sharpshooters; Gen. Stanley's division, consisting of two brigades, and Gen. McKean's division, with Gen. Arthur's brigade, were on the extreme left. The cavalry, under the command of Col. Misener, was stationed on the wings and in the rear. Suitable forces were held as reserves and to protect the rear. The front line was covered by crests of undulations on the surface. On the night of the 3d, the Confederate line was formed within a thousand yards of the Union position. Before daybreak the Confederates were heard at work planting a battery on a hill in front of and about 200 yards from Fort Robinett, and soon after they opened a furious fire on Corinth. At daylight, the Parrott guns in Fort Williams opened upon this Confederate battery and in a few minutes silenced it. Two of the guns were removed, but the third was taken and drawn within the Federal line. Skirmishing also opened at various points in front, which was constantly increasing to the magnitude of a battle. The Confederate lines, however, were still invisible. About half past nine o'clock dark and threatening masses of Confederate troops were suddenly discerned on the east of the railroad moving up the Bolivar road. They assumed a wedge-like form and advanced impetuously. It was now manifest that the Confederate force had been enticed to attack at the very point where the Federal artillery could sweep it with direct, cross, and enfilading fire. These batteries rent hideous gaps in those massive lines, but they were closed at once and inflexibly pressed forward. Suddenly the Confederate force extended to the right and left, and approached covering the whole field. In front of them, however, was a broad turfed glacis sloping upward to a crest, fringed with determined soldiers and covered with frowning batteries. The few obstructions from fallen timber produced no disorder in the approaching lines but what was quickly restored. The entire Federal line next opened fire, but the Confederate forces, as if insensible to fear, steadily pressed forward undismayed. As they approached the crest of the hill in front and to the right of Fort Richardson, the division of Gen. Davis, although not in immediate danger, began to fall back in disorder. Gen. Rosecrans, seeing the disgraceful scene, dashed forward inflamed with indignation and began thrashing the fugitives with the blade of his sabre. His staff, and even his orderlies, followed his example, and the panic was checked and the line restored. Much space was thus lost, and the enemy reached the headquarters of Gen. Rosecrans and took possession. The loss of fort Richardson now appeared certain. The Confederates gained the crest of the hill, swarmed around the little redoubt, and were swept away. Again they came like infuriated tigers, and with a yell made a desperate dash before which the battery, unsupported, gave way. The guns were seized, but before they could be manned, the 56th Illinois, rising from cover in the ravine, fired a deadly volley and with a shout made a sweeping charge, before which the Confederates fled. When the division of Gen. Davis broke, it was necessary for all to fall back, but this charge of the 56th Illinois recovered the ground. The whole line advanced, and the Confederates were broken and fled to the woods, whither they were pursued. The attack on the Federal right was made by Gen. Price. On the left Gen. Van Dorn was expected to make a simultaneous approach and thus carry Corinth by assault. In the extension of the Confederate right, artificial obstructions interfered. Gen. Van Dorn was obliged to move with his left over a rugged ravine through dense thickets and over a heavy abatis up hill. His centre moved down hill under the fire of Fort Williams, the siege guns in the rear of the town, and under heavy musketry. His right was obliged to move round a ridge and advance over almost insurmountable abatis under the direct fire of both Fort Williams and Fort Robinett well supported by experienced troops. Gen. Van Dorn's advance had necessarily been slower than that of Gen. Price, and the latter was overwhelmed and defeated when the former was ready to commence the attack. His forces advanced steadily, with troops from Mississippi and Texas in front. Huge gaps were made through their ranks by the great guns of the batteries, but they closed and at once moved unflinchingly onward. The slaughter was great, but none wavered. As they reached the ditch a pause, as if for breath, was made. That pause was fatal to them. The two redoubts, Fort Robinett and Fort Williams, were on the same ridge, and the former, which was in front, was commanded by the latter. They were about 150 yards apart. The Ohio brigade, Col. Fuller commanding, was formed behind the ridge on the right of the redoubts. The left of the 63d Ohio rested on Fort Robinett, and its right joined the left of the 27th Ohio; the 39th Ohio was behind the 27th supporting it; the right of the 43d Ohio joined the left of the 63d, forming a right angle with it, and extending to Fort Williams behind the crest of the ridge. The 11th Missouri was formed behind the 63d Ohio, with its left in the angle and the regiment facing obliquely to the right of the 63d. The brigade were required to lie flat on their faces, and reserve their fire until the Confederates were close upon them. At the moment when the Confederate advance paused, as above stated, the 63d Ohio was ordered to fire. An officer has thus described the scene which ensued: "There were only 250 of the 63d in the conflict, but their volley was fearful. It is said 50 Confederates fell at once. Six volleys were fired and the enemy was gone. The 63d again lay down. Directly the supporting Confederate brigade advanced. The 63d was ordered to make a half left wheel to sweep the front of the redoubt, and the manœuvre was handsomely executed. The 11th Missouri moved on the left into line into the vacant space; the 43d moved by the right of companies to the left, and the 27th half-faced to the left. Suddenly the enemy appeared, and a furious storm of lead and grape was launched at them. The 63d fired five or six volleys and the enemy rushed upon them. A terrific hand to hand combat ensued. The rage of the combatants was furious and the uproar hideous. It lasted hardly a minute, but the carnage was dreadful. Bayonets were used, muskets clubbed, and men were felled with brawny fists. Our noble fellows were victors, but at a sickening cost. Of the 250 of the splendid 63d, 125 lay there on the field, wounded, dead, or dying. The last final struggle terminated with a howl of rage and dismay. The foe flung away their arms and fled like frightened stags to the abatis and forests. The batteries were still vomiting destruction. With the enemy plunging in upon him, brave Robinett, with his faithful gunners of the 1st U. S. artillery, double shotted his guns and belched death upon the infuriate host, and now he sent the iron hail after the fugitives with relentless fury. The abatis was full of them, but they were subdued. Directly they began to wave their handkerchiefs upon sticks in token of submission, shouting to spare them "for God's sake." Over 200 of them were taken within an area of a hundred yards, and more than 200 of them fell in that frightful assault upon Fort Robinett. Fifty-six dead were heaped up together in front of that redoubt, most of whom were of the 2d Texas and 4th Mississippi."

The battle was now over. It had begun in earnest about 9 o'clock, and at half past 11 the Confederate force was falling back. The front was so thoroughly masked that it was late in the afternoon before it could be determined whether a second assault was intended. Pursuit in force could not be attempted before rations and ammunition were provided. It was 3 o'clock on the morning of the next day, Sunday the 5th, before the column moved in light order and swiftly. The vigor and determination with which Gen. Rosecrans would pursue a flying foe may be understood from his views expressed to his officers: "Follow close; force them to pass to the rear; compel them to form often in line of battle and so harass and discourage them; prevent them from communicating from front to rear; give them no time to distribute subsistence; don't let them sleep." Meantime, after the Confederate force had retired, Gen. McPherson arrived with 3 regiments from Jackson, and led the van of the pursuit.

The Confederate force retreated by the route on which they had advanced, which was the Chewalla road. It was necessary for them to cross the Tuscumbia river in the neighborhood of Pocahontas. They sent a body of troops to protect the Hatchie river bridge, which is two miles from the bridge across the Tuscumbia. On the 4th Gens. Ord and Hurlbut, from Gen. Grant's force, moved down and encountered this detachment and defeated it, capturing a large number of prisoners and two batteries of 6 guns. The Federal loss here was 50 killed, 493 wounded, and 17 prisoners. This action compelled the Confederate force to retrace their steps and by making a wide circuit they finally crossed the Hatchie at Crum's Mill, about 6 miles farther up. Gen. Rosecrans, however, continued the pursuit to Ripley, whence he was ordered by Gen. Grant to return. He captured nearly 1,000 prisoners, part of the Confederate ammunition and baggage trains, and 11 guns. The Federal loss at Corinth was stated at 315 killed, 1,312 wounded, and 232 prisoners, taken chiefly on Friday, and two Parrott guns. The additional effects of the battle are thus stated by Gen. Rosecrans in an address to his troops, dated October 25:

I have now received the reports of the various commanders. I have now to tell you that the magnitude of the stake, the battle and the results, become more than ever apparent. Upon the issue of this fight depended the possession of west Tennessee, and perhaps even the fate of operations in Kentucky. The entire available force of the rebels in Mississippi, save a few garrisons and a small reserve, attacked you. They were commanded by Van Dorn, Price, Villipigue, Rust, Armstrong, Maury, and others in person. They numbered, according to their own authorities, nearly 40,000 men—almost double your own numbers. You fought them into the position we desired on the 3d, punishing them terribly; and on the 4th, in 3 hours after the infantry went into action, they were completely beaten. You killed and buried 1,423 officers and men; some of their most distinguished officers falling—among whom was the gallant Colonel Rogers, of the 2d Texas, who bore their colors at the head of his storming column to the edge of the ditch of "Battery Robinett," where he fell. Their wounded, at the usual rate, must exceed 5,000. You took 2,268 prisoners, among whom are 137 field officers, captains, and subalterns, representing 53 regiments of infantry; 16 regiments cavalry; 13 batteries of artillery; 7 battalions; making 69 regiments, 13 batteries, 7 battalions, besides several companies. You captured 3,300 stands of small arms, 14 stands of colors, 2 pieces of artillery, and a large quantity of equipments. You pursued his retreating columns 40 miles in force with infantry, and 69 miles with cavalry, and were ready to follow him to Mobile, if necessary, had you received orders. I congratulate you on these decisive results; in the name of the Government and the people, I thank you. I beg you to unite with me in giving humble thanks to the Great Master of all for our victories.

After the battle at Corinth and the pursuit of the Confederate force, the troops of Gen. Grant returned to their respective positions. Gen. Rosecrans, on the 25th of October, was ordered from Corinth to Cincinnati to take command of the forces preparing for a new campaign. On the 4th of November the forces of Gen. Grant advanced from Jackson and Bolivar to Lagrange, 3 miles east of Grand Junction on the Cairo and New Orleans railroad. The scattered forces of Gens. Van Dorn and Price had rallied and were within 20 miles of the same place, at Cold Water and Holly Springs, Mississippi. Their numbers had not been increased by reënforcements, but they had been rendered more effective by concentration. The forces of Gen. Grant had been slightly increased by the new levies. His army was required to garrison Columbus, Humboldt, Trenton, Jackson, Bolivar, Corinth, and Grand Junction, and was now designated as the army of west Tennessee. The position of the army was unchanged until near the end of November. It required reënforcements and supplies. Active efforts were made to repair the Memphis railroad in order that supplies might be brought from that point instead of Columbus in Kentucky. The distance to the latter place is 138 miles, and to the former, from Lagrange, 49 miles. On the south a small body of troops was thrown forward a few miles to Davis's Mills, and on the west a heavy force had been stationed at Moscow. On the 28th, however, the advance of Gen. Hamilton's corps began to move in the direction of Holly Springs, which place was reached on the 29th. By the 1st of December, Gen. Grant's forces had arrived and were chiefly encamped at Lumpkin's Mills, south of Holly Springs, and 7 miles north of the Tallahatchie river. The Confederate force had retired to the river. At the same time that the movement was commenced from Davis's Mills, a division of Gen. Curtis's army left Helena,

Ark., for the purpose of making a flank movement on the Confederate force on the Tallahatchie and getting in their rear, and thus cutting off their retreat while the main army advanced upon them. On the river extensive fortifications had been thrown up as if for the purpose of making a determined stand against the progress of the Federal army. These, however, were abandoned on Dec. 1 by Gen. Van Dorn, and his forces retired farther south. It was supposed that information of the flank movement from Helena led to the evacuation of his strong position on the Tallahatchie. On the 2d his rear guard passed through Abbeville, and on the 3d through Oxford, with some sharp skirmishes with the Federal advance. On the 4th Gen. Grant's headquarters were at Oxford. The main body of the army was at Abbeville. As it advanced, the bridges and culverts of the railroad were repaired, the track restored, and the cars run. At the same time the Confederate force continued to fall back toward Grenada, presenting only a strong rear guard.

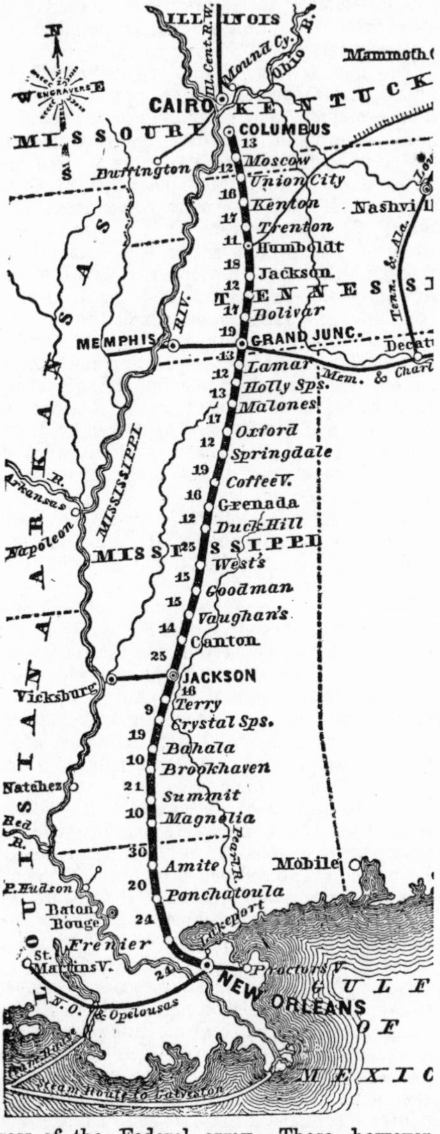

Meantime the expedition from Helena abovementioned, moved on the 27th of November with seven thousand men under Gen. Alvin P. Hovey. On the next day he crossed the Tallahatchie. The passage was disputed by Confederate pickets without loss. On the 30th a second skirmish occurred at the Yacknapatapha, after the crossing of which the Confederate forces retired toward Coffeeville. The next movement of Gen. Hovey was to cut the Mississippi Central railroad and the telegraph line. The railroad line was destroyed for a considerable distance. The Confederate communication on the Mississippi and Tennessee railroad for a short distance was next cut near Panola, by a cavalry force sent out by Gen. Hovey under Col. Washburn. In executing this order, on Dec. 1, Col. Washburn unexpectedly encountered a cavalry force near Oakland, on the Mississippi and Tennessee railroad, and a sharp skirmish ensued. The superiority of the Federal artillery soon put an end to it, and the Confederate forces retired in the direction of Coffeeville, with a loss of five killed, several wounded, and about fifty taken prisoners. The loss of Col. Washburn was fifteen men wounded and fifteen horses killed. The steamboats and small craft on the Tallahatchie river were destroyed, and two locomotives and some cars on the railroad, and the expedition then returned to Helena. The effect of this movement was to cause the Confederate force under Gen. Pemberton to fall back from the Tallahatchie, evacuate Grenada, and retire toward Canton, under the impression that the entire command of Gen. Grant was very strong. The effect of the return of this force to Helena was to restore the confidence of the Confederate general Van Dorn, and an attack upon Gen. Grant's rear, in order to cut off his supplies, was immediately organized, and on the 20th, while Gen. Grant's headquarters were at Oxford, an attack by surprise was made on the garrison at Holly Springs, thirty miles north, by a considerable force of cavalry, to whom the place was surrendered. The prisoners were paroled, the immense stores collected there for Gen. Grant's army were destroyed, also a large quantity of cotton which had been purchased of the people in the vicinity. On the same day a similar attack was made at Davis's Mills, a little farther north, which was bravely repulsed. Near Jackson, in Tennessee, previously the headquarters of Gen. Grant, an attack was made on the 19th by a body of cavalry with artillery, under Col. Forrest. It was first made upon a train loaded with wood. The telegraph wire was also cut, and the road destroyed. On the next day Humboldt was captured, and an attack was made on Trenton, which was soon surrendered by Col. Fry in command. The railroad depot was burned with all the stores and cotton in it. Other stations on the road, as Dyer, Rutherford, and Keaton, were taken on the same day. The purpose was to destroy every bridge on the railroad from Columbus to Corinth and Grand Junction, and thus cut off the route for supplies to Gen. Grant's army. The consequence of destroying his depot of supplies, and disturbing his line of communication, was to make Gen. Grant fall back upon Holly Springs. Subsequently Col. Forrest's force was entirely routed by Col. Sweeney.

Meanwhile troops had been collected at Cairo and Memphis, for an expedition against Vicksburg. This had been done within the department of Gen. Grant, and the commander of the expedition, Gen. Sherman, was stationed at Memphis in the same department, and under the command of Gen. Grant. It was an object of Gen. Grant's movements into Mississippi, just related, to reach Jackson in the rear of Vicksburg, and thus coöperate with Gen. Sherman. In this design he was unsuccessful, and obliged to fall back in consequence of the attacks on his line of communication. After falling back upon Holly Springs, a division of his troops was sent to join Gen. Sherman. The future proceedings of Gen. Grant and of this Expedition properly belong to the record of 1863.

The second campaign in Kentucky and Tennessee during the year was virtually ended. The forces of Gen. Grant were reduced by a detachment of ten thousand men to aid Gen. Sherman in the capture of Vicksburg, which was a part of the new campaign.

Meanwhile the calls of the President for six hundred thousand additional troops were producing their effect. Vast forces were gathering, and new campaigns were about to commence. The great march of the Northwest sweeping everything before it to the Gulf of Mexico, was now to be made. The Government had found that the Western people would bear no longer with its futile efforts to open the Mississippi and to seize the Southern valley. "What we need," said President Lincoln, "is a military success;" money and men had been promptly furnished to the full extent of the request.

This new campaign contemplated the advance of a powerful army under Gen. Rosecrans through Tennessee into Alabama; the movement of a military and naval expedition from Cairo upon Vicksburg; the coöperation of an expedition under Gen. Banks from New Orleans, and thence into Texas; and an advance from Missouri upon Arkansas; and also from Kansas upon the Indian country and northern Texas. Thus the Federal Government would not only open the Mississippi river, but occupy all the Southwestern States, and reduce the Confederate forces to the limits of the Atlantic States.

On the 25th of October, Gen. Rosecrans was ordered to Cincinnati to take command of the army of the Ohio, as already stated. This command consisted of what remained of the splendid army of Gen. Buell, reënforced by new but raw levies, until it became the second army in size of the United States. The preparation for his campaign was no ordinary effort.

The new troops were to be drilled, disciplined, and made reliable; equipments, arms, horses, and stores of every kind were needed.

The country in which he proposed to march had just been swept of its forage by two armies—that of Gen. Buell, and that of Gen. Bragg. His supplies must come from the States of the Northwest. Only two routes existed for their conveyance: the Cumberland river, which was at too low a stage of water for successful navigation, and the Louisville and Nashville railroad, on which the bridges had been burned, and the tunnel at Gallatin destroyed. The work of preparation and organization was vigorously begun, and his army soon began to move southward. On the 1st of November Gen. Rosecrans moved to Bowling Green, and on the 5th three divisions of Gen. McCook's corps moved farther on their way to Tennessee.

The commanders of the corps of the whole army were Gens. Thomas, McCook, Rousseau, and Crittenden. On the 7th the corps of Gen. McCook passed through Nashville.

The Louisville and Nashville railroad was completed on the 8th to Mitchellsville on the northern line of Tennessee. On the 10th, Gen. Rosecrans arrived at Nashville, and from that time to the close of the year he was constantly engaged in concentrating, reorganizing, reëquipping, and disciplining his army, accumulating supplies by the railroad, of which there was only a single track, and preparing for a forward movement. As early as the 25th of November, the Confederate army manifested a purpose to contest the occupation of middle Tennessee. The railroad bridge at Bridgeport was repaired and troops hurried to Murfreesborough. Gen. Joseph Johnston had been placed in command of this Confederate department, although unable to engage in active field operations. The Confederate forces were stationed at Lavergne, Murfreesborough, McMinnville, &c. Their numbers, under Gen. Bragg, were estimated at forty-five thousand effective men. He had been led to believe by the spies of Gen. Rosecrans that the latter intended to go into winter quarters at Nashville, and had despatched one body of cavalry under Gen. Forrest to cut off Gen. Grant's communication, and another body under Col. Morgan to cut the communication of Gen. Rosecrans in Kentucky, and also a body of infantry to the Confederate army of Mississippi. This appeared to be the opportunity for Gen. Rosecrans to strike an effective blow. At this time, the Federal army occupied a line of about ten miles on the southeasterly front of Nashville facing south, the right resting on the right of the Franklin turnpike, the centre extending out to Breakville on the Nolinsville turnpike, and the left covered by Mill Creek, some six or eight miles from Nashville, with outposts describing an irregular semicircle, covering a distance of nine miles from the city. To this front the Confederate army presented its force with outposts about two miles distant. Gen. E. Kirby Smith's corps, with part of Col. Morgan's cavalry, occupied the Confederate right; the corps of Gen. Polk, with Col. Wheeler's cavalry brigade, occupied the centre at Lavergne; Gen. Hardee's corps at Triune and Nolinsville, with Col. Wharton's cavalry in front, occupied the left. On the night of the 25th, Christmas, the determination for an advance the next day was made. The respective columns were so disposed as to move down Wilson's, the Nolinsville, Murfreesborough, and Jefferson turnpikes. The general plan was to move a brigade down Wilson's turnpike to protect the right, while Gen. Negley should endeavor to turn the Confederate left and get into its rear; Gen. McCook's corps was to press directly upon Gen. Hardee at Nolinsville and Triune, while Gen. Crittenden pushed down the Murfreesborough and Jefferson turnpikes. At dawn on the 26th, the troops broke up camp with wild shouts and poured along the highways. Gen. McCook's corps marched steadily down the road with skirmishers widely spread out. The Confederates resisted sharply, but were steadily driven, the Federal loss being small. Gen. Crittenden advanced to Lavergne without opposition. The Confederates retired rapidly before his skirmishers. On the next day, the 27th, the Confederate force continued to retire as the Federals advanced with sharp skirmishing. At four o'clock P. M., the Confederate right had been driven over the bridge across Stewart's Creek, on the Jefferson turnpike, which they were prevented from destroying. They were also driven over the bridge across the same creek on the Murfreesborough turnpike so rapidly as to be unable to destroy it. Both structures came into the possession of the Federal forces, all the columns of which had now closed up. It was now apparent from the course of the Confederate retreat that their purpose was to concentrate near Stone Creek or river. On Sunday the 28th, Gen. Thomas advanced his camp across Stewart's Creek, and joined the left. Next day, Gen. McCook moved within seven miles of Murfreesborough, and Gen. Crittenden moved within three miles, Gen. Negley advanced to the centre, and Gen. Rousseau's division was placed in reserve, on the right of Gen. Crittenden. On the 30th, Gen. McCook advanced through thickets, stubbornly resisted by the Confederates, and pressed Gen. Hardee's corps in his front in line of battle. The front of this Confederate corps crossed the Federal right obliquely, in a position which, if extended, would flank it. The centre, under Gen. Negley, was slightly advanced into a cedar wood, and was engaged in reconnoitring under sharp resistance, and in cutting roads through the dense forest to open communication with the right. The left was in a line corresponding with the course of Stone river. The right division of Gen. McCook now faced to the southeast, and two brigades were thrown out on the extreme right, somewhat in reserve. The Confederate force was concentrated within two miles of Murfreesborough, with its right resting on the Lebanon turnpike, thence extending west across Lytle's Creek and the Nashville turnpike, and under the command of Gen. Leonidas Polk. It consisted of three divisions under Gens. Cheatham, Breckinridge, and Buckner. The Confederate centre was composed of three divisions of Gen. E. Kirby Smith; the left was under the command of Gen. Hardee, and rested on the Franklin and Murfreesborough road. This position of the Confederate army gave to it the advantage of strong natural fortifications, with their centre effectually masked by almost impenetrable cedar forests. Constant skirmishing was going on between both forces, and it was manifest that another day would witness the impending battle. At this time assaults were made by cavalry on the Federal rear, and several trains were captured. During the night it was evident that the Confederate forces were massing on the right of Gen. Rosecrans, and his plan was formed to give ground a little, if necessary, on that wing, and to advance the left at the same time into Murfreesborough. The execution of this purpose was prevented by the great force of the Confederate attack on the right.

Early on the morning of the 31st, the attack was made along the entire line of the Federal right under Gen. McCook. The weather was foggy, and the appearance of the Confederate force was sudden. No preparations up to this time for an advance or an assault had been made. An attack very early in the morning had been anticipated; but as it did not come, a degree of carelessness and indifference had taken possession of both officers and men, and all precautions were in a degree abandoned. The opposing lines of the two hostile wings had formed on the opposite sides of a valley which narrowed toward the Federal left. Gen. McCook's corps consisted of three divisions which formed this line. On the left was the division of Gen. Sheridan, in the centre that of Gen. Davis, and on the right that of Gen. Johnson. The attack was made along the entire front at once by the Confederate force, rapidly advancing in double columns. Before the divisions of Gens. Johnson and Davis could form, the Confederate batteries opened upon them, and their infantry soon after became engaged at short range, rapidly advancing and preparing to charge bayonets. Two batteries of Gen. Johnson's division were taken before a gun was fired; and the irregular fire of the others, many of which had no horses near at hand, and the desultory fire of the incomplete line did not cause the Confederate line to waver, much less repulse it. One brigade of Gen. Johnson's was broken and fled to the rear, leaving the artillery they should have supported, and the men were shot down at the guns. The rest of the division fell back, and with them a few of the guns. The line of Gen. Davis's division, which was attacked at the same time, was also imperfectly formed. In vain it attempted to hold its position. Like that of Gen. Johnson, it was crushed and broken, and three entire batteries lost. The division of Gen. Sheridan, when first assailed, withstood the shock, and forced back the Confederate line; but when the division of Gen. Davis was driven back it stoutly resisted, and endeavored to hold the position until the others could be rallied in the rear, and advanced to its support. The effort, however, was unsuccessful, and like the others, his division retreated. The divisions of Gens. Johnson and Davis had in the mean time formed in the rear, and endeavored to stay the Confederate progress. They were unsuccessful, but maintained their line and fell back in good order, and again formed at the first good position. In like manner Gen. Sheridan proceeded. No guns were captured after the first assault, and the mass of prisoners was taken during this retreat. The object of Gen. Bragg was to turn the right flank, but this failed. Gen. Rosecrans, on the other hand, prepared to stop the progress of the Confederates on his right, without exposing his centre and left to immediate danger. His left wing could not be advanced to Murfreesborough, because his right was gone. He, therefore, massed his artillery upon his centre, at the probable point of assault. These movements were concealed by forests, and were unperceived by the enemy. Gen. Negley now ordered forward the advance of the centre, consisting of two small brigades to protect the retreating forces of Gen. McCook. These were supported by the division of Gen. Rousseau, and served to check the Confederate force in its pursuit of the right wing. As the enemy approached these brigades, they retired slowly. The former, unsuspecting it to be a decoy, rushed forward, and were received with such a cross-fire of double shotted canister from two batteries and a volley from a brigade, as caused their line to waver for a moment. It dashed forward again. In the mean time Gen. Rousseau had come up on the right of Gen. Negley, and his regular troops on his left advanced at the moment when the right of the Confederate left wing dashed forward. The combined fire of Gen. Negley's force and of the regular troops drove the Confederate main force back with terrible loss, and a large number of Confederate prisoners were taken. The struggle was maintained a few moments, when the Federal force under orders fell back, and the Confederate line, flushed with success, and consisting of their centre and right of left wing, rushed in overwhelming mass upon the batteries which had been so placed as to rake them in almost every direction. A horrible slaughter ensued. The Confederate line wavered, fell back, and attempted to rally. On another discharge, they fled from the fire which they could not face. Meanwhile Gen. McCook had got into line on the right of Gen. Rousseau, and received reënforcements of artillery, and was ready for another attack. The Confederate force had now fallen back, and a suspension of fire took place along the entire line. It was midday. The Federal line had been driven back between two and three miles, thirty pieces of artillery had been lost, and the dead and wounded with many prisoners were in Confederate hands. The spirit of the troops was still resolute.

These movements had somewhat changed the position of the Federal line. The left and centre recovered their position at right angles to the Murfreesborough road and across it. They extended from the river to the distance of a mile west of it. The right wing had fallen back until it was nearly parallel to this road, and extending from Stewart's Creek to the right of Gen. Rousseau. The Confederate left was opposite the Federal right and a few hundred yards from it. In this position both of Gen. Rosecrans's flanks were protected by streams with good bridges and fords in his rear.

About three o'clock, the battle opened again by a Confederate attack upon the Federal centre and left. Although this was made by large masses, yet such was the favorable position occupied by the Federal line on a crest or ridge of ground, and such was the strength of its batteries that no advantage was gained by the Confederates. The slaughter on both sides was great and the contest very determined. It continued until five o'clock when the exhausted armies suspended operations for the night. This was so clear and beautiful that some batteries continued their fire. The result of the day was that the Federal right had been driven in almost upon the left, and a change of front had been made under fire, leaving in possession of the Confederate troops that part of the field. They also held the ground occupied in the morning by the Federal pickets on the left, which wing had receded to draw the Confederate troops on. During this time the communication to Nashville had often been cut off, and a strong force of Confederate cavalry had made a dash in the Federal rear within a mile of the front, and captured a considerable amount of hospital stores. The ammunition train of the right wing was twice captured and twice retaken. The Federal loss on that day was estimated at three thousand killed and wounded, twenty-five pieces of artillery, and a large number of prisoners. The Confederate loss in killed and wounded was not less.

On Thursday the 1st of January, 1863, the line of Gen. Rosecrans was restored to its original position by the success of Gen. McCook's efforts to recover and hold it, on the third attempt. The division on the extreme left was also moved across Stone River. The position on the right wing was intrenched and the communications in the rear completed. On the morning of the 2d, sharp demonstrations were made along the whole Federal line by the Confederate army, but nothing serious was attempted until three o'clock in the afternoon. At that time the Confederate force burst in mass upon the division across Stone River, as if having discovered the intention of Gen. Rosecrans to advance it in their rear. This attacking force consisted of their entire right wing. The three brigades of the Federal division under Col. Beatty were prepared for the attack and stood their ground manfully, but the overwhelming force finally drove them back across the creek. Gen. Negley's division, which had been formed in reserve as if for this occasion, now advanced, supported by the division of Gen. Davis and the pioneer battalion of Morton. The most bitter conflict of the battle now ensued. Both sides massed their batteries and used them with desperate vindictiveness. The Confederate line wavered and fell back. Gen. Davis was ordered to cross the stream, and Col. Sirwell of the 78th Pennsylvania, placing his hat on the point of his sword, led the way with a shout. Col. Beatty's division followed. An overwhelming and irresistible charge was made on the Confederate line, and it broke and fled. A battery was captured, and a stand of colors. The entire division of Gen. Negley followed up rapidly, and Gen. Rosecrans's whole line immediately advanced. The enemy's right wing was now broken, and the Federal force was gaining the Confederate flank, when resistance on its part became vain and the entire force receded with the loss of many prisoners. The next morning found the Federal line intrenched in its advanced position, but a storm was raging. Quiet prevailed through the day, excepting one or two sharp conflicts resulting in the capture of a small breastwork. On the next morning the Confederate army had retired from Murfreesborough, which was subsequently occupied by Gen. Rosecrans. Two divisions were soon sent forward in pursuit of the forces of Gen. Bragg, who fell back to Tullahoma. The Federal loss was 8,485 killed and wounded, and 3,600 missing. The enemy's loss is not known.

The original plan of Gen. Rosecrans to turn the right of the Confederate army and cut off its retreat, was entirely defeated by the failure of the right wing to maintain itself.

CHAPTER XXIV.

Conclusion of the Campaign in Virginia—Gen. McClellan crosses the Potomac—Causes of his Delay—Presses Gen. Lee—Gen. Burnside ordered to take Command—His Orders—Gen. Lee falls back—Advance of Gen. Burnside toward Fredericksburg—Its Surrender Demanded—Occupied by Gen. Lee—Battle of Fredericksburg—Withdrawal of Gen. Burnside's Forces—Losses.

THE conclusion of the campaign in Virginia remains to be described. Immediately after the battle of Antietam, the Confederate army retired across the Potomac and occupied strong positions on its right bank. All hopes that the State of Maryland would unite her destinies with the Southern Confederacy were now banished. The invasion had been made by crossing the Potomac within a limit of twelve miles, which is about a mile above the Point of Rocks and five miles below the Monocacy aqueduct on the Chesapeake and Ohio Canal. The army then marched through fields, woods, and roads for Frederick. The line of the Chesapeake and Ohio Canal for twelve miles presented a scene of desolation. It was tapped at five places. Several floodgates were cut to pieces, and from heights above large boulders of rock were dislodged and thrown into the canal. An unsuccessful attempt was made to blow up the aqueduct at Monocacy. The telegraph lines and the track of the Baltimore and Ohio Railroad were much injured. The bridge at Monocacy and portions of the abutments were destroyed. Private property did not escape. Fences were torn down and fields laid desolate.

The army of Gen. McClellan remained on the north bank of the Potomac in the vicinity of Sharpsburg and Harper's Ferry. On the 1st of October it was visited by President Lincoln, who was cordially received and tarried until the 4th. On the 7th Gen. McClellan issued the following order relative to the proclamation threatening emancipation of the Southern slaves:

HEADQUARTERS ARMY OF THE POTOMAC, *October* 7, 1862.

General Order, 163.—The attention of the officers and soldiers of the Army of the Potomac is called to General Orders, No. 139, War Department, September 24, 1862, publishing to the army the President's proclamation of September 22.

A proclamation of such grave moment to the nation, officially communicated to the army, affords to the General commanding an opportunity of defining specifically to the officers and soldiers under his command the relation borne by all persons in the military service of the United States toward the civil authorities of the Government.

The Constitution confides to the civil authorities—legislative, judicial, and executive—the power and duty of making, expounding, and executing the Federal laws. Armed forces are raised and supported simply to sustain the civil authorities, and are to be held in strict subordination thereto in all respects. The fundamental law of our political system is essential to the security of our republican institutions, and should be thoroughly understood and observed by every soldier.

The principle upon which and the objects for which armies shall be employed in suppressing rebellion must be determined and declared by the authorities, and the Chief Executive, who is charged with the administration of the national affairs, is the proper and only source through which the views and orders of the Government can be made known to the armies of the nation.

Discussion by officers and soldiers concerning public measures determined upon and declared by the Government, when carried beyond the ordinary, temperate, and respectful expression of opinion, tend greatly to impair and destroy the discipline and efficiency of the troops, by substituting the spirit of political faction for the firm, steady, and earnest support of the authority of the Government, which is the highest duty of the American soldier. The remedy for political errors, if any are committed, is to be found only in the action of the people at the polls.

In thus calling the attention of this army to the true relation between the soldiers and the Government, the General commanding merely adverts to an evil against which it has been thought advisable during our whole history to guard the armies of the Republic, and in so doing he will not be considered, by any right-minded person, as casting any reflection upon that loyalty and good conduct which have been so fully illustrated upon so many battle-fields.

In carrying out all measures of public policy this army will, of course, be guided by the same rules of mercy and Christianity that have ever controlled its conduct toward the defenceless.

By command of Maj.-Gen. McCLELLAN.

JAS. A. HARDIE, Lieut.-Col.,
Aide-de-Camp and Act'g Ass't Adj.-General.

On Monday night, Oct. 10, a body of Confederate cavalry of about twenty-five hundred, under Gen. Stuart, suddenly appeared at Chambersburg, Penn., and occupied the place. The Government storehouses and machine shops were burned by them; also the Cumberland Valley railroad depot. On the next day Gen. Stuart marched to Emmettsburg, thence to Woodsborough, New Market, and Monrovia, which place he reached early on Sunday morning. Thus far his force had gathered about one thousand horses. He next pushed for the Potomac, at Noland's Ford, at the mouth of the Monocacy; but finding a Federal force there, he divided his troops and crossed at different places, chiefly at Conrad's Ferry, and six miles below the Monocacy. The entire distance of his march north of the Potomac, was a little over one hundred miles. A large number of Federal troops were put in motion to effect his capture, but without success. Reconnoissances made on the 16th and 17th discovered the Confederate army occupying a position extending from Bunker Hill to the Shenandoah river.

It had been expected that Gen. McClellan would take the forces of Gen. Pope's shattered army and march into Maryland and conquer the victorious Confederate force and pursue them even to Richmond. The inactivity of his army after the battle of Antietam became a subject of complaint. It was overlooked that the low water in the Potomac required time to line its north shore with troops to prevent another invasion of Maryland. It was overlooked that most of his troops had been in active service in the field during the previous six months, and might require most important supplies. On the 6th of October the following despatch was sent by the general-in-chief, Gen. Halleck, to Gen. McClellan:

WASHINGTON, D. C., *Oct.* 6, 1862.

Maj.-Gen. McClellan:

I am instructed to telegraph to you as follows: The President directs that you cross the Potomac and give battle to the enemy or drive him south. Your army must move now while the roads are good. If you cross the river between the enemy and Washington, and cover the latter by your line of operation, you can be reënforced with 30,000 men. If you move up the valley of the Shenandoah, not more than 12,000 or 15,000 can be sent to you. The President advises the interior line between Washington and the enemy, but does not order it. He is very desirous that your army move as soon as possible. You will immediately report what line you adopt and when you intend to cross the river. Also, to what point the reënforcements are to be sent. It is necessary that the plan of your operations be positively determined on before orders are given for building bridges and repairing railroads. I am directed to add that the Secretary of War and the General-in-Chief fully concur with the President in these instructions.

H. W. HALLECK, Gen.-in-Chief.

According to the report of Gen. Halleck, Gen. McClellan disapproved of the plan of crossing the Potomac south of the Blue Ridge, and said that he would cross at Harper's Ferry and advance on Winchester. The advance, however, did not take place until the 26th of October. It became the subject of speculation on the part of the public as to the real nature of the causes of delay. Subsequently, upon the removal of Gen. McClellan from the command of the army, on the 7th of November, the following letter was published:

HEADQUARTERS OF THE ARMY,
WASHINGTON, *Oct.* 28, 1862.

Hon. E. M. Stanton, Secretary of War:

SIR: In reply to the general interrogatories contained in your letter of yesterday, I have to report:

1st. That requisitions for supplies to the army under Gen. McClellan are made by his staff officers on the chiefs of bureaus here; that is, for quartermasters' supplies, by his chief quartermaster on the Quartermaster-General; for commissary supplies, by his chief commissary on the Commissary-General, &c. No such requisitions have been, to my knowledge, made upon the Secretary of War, and none upon the General-in-Chief.

2d. On several occasions Gen. McClellan has telegraphed to me that his army was deficient in certain supplies. All these telegrams were immediately referred to the heads of bureaus, with orders to report. It was ascertained that, in every instance, the requisitions had been immediately filled, except one, where the Quartermaster-General had been obliged to send from Philadelphia certain articles of clothing, tents, &c., not having a full supply here. There has not been, so far as I could ascertain, any neglect or delay, in any department or bureau, in issuing all supplies asked for by Gen. McClellan, or by the officers of his staff. Delays have occasionally occurred in forwarding supplies by rail, on account of the crowded condition of the depots, or of a want of cars; but whenever notified of this, agents have been sent out to remove the difficulty. Under the excellent superintendence of Gen. Haup, I think these delays have been less frequent and of shorter duration than is usual with freight trains. An army of the size of that under Gen. McClellan will frequently be for some days without the supplies asked for, on account of neglect in making timely requisitions and unavoidable delays in forwarding them and in distributing them to the different brigades and regiments. From all the information I can obtain, I am of opinion that the requisitions from that army have been filled more promptly, and that the men, as a general rule, have been better supplied than our armies operating in the West. The latter have operated at much greater distances from the sources of supply, and have had far less facilities for transportation. In fine, I believe that no armies in the world, while in campaign, have been more promptly or better supplied than ours.

3d. Soon after the battle of Antietam Gen. McClellan was urged to give me information of his intended movements, in order that, if he moved between the enemy and Washington, reënforcements could be sent from this place. On the first of October, finding that he proposed to operate from Harper's Ferry, I urged him to cross the river at once and give battle to the enemy, pointing out to him the disadvantages of delaying till the autumn rains had swollen the Potomac and impaired the roads. On the 6th of October he was peremptorily ordered to "cross the Potomac and give battle to the enemy or drive him south. Your army must move now, while the roads are good." It will be observed that three weeks have elapsed since this order was given.

4th. In my opinion there has been no such want of supplies in the army under Gen. McClellan as to prevent his compliance with the orders to advance against the enemy. Had he moved to the south side of the Potomac he could have received his supplies almost as readily as by remaining inactive on the north side.

5th. On the 7th of October, in a telegram in regard to his intended movements, Gen. McClellan stated that it would require at least three days to supply the first, fifth, and sixth corps; that they needed shoes and other indispensable articles of clothing, as well as shelter tents. No complaint was made that any requisitions had not been filled, and it was inferred from his language that he was only waiting for the distribution of his supplies.

On the 11th he telegraphed that a portion of his supplies sent by rail had been delayed. As already stated, agents were immediately sent from here to investigate this complaint, and they reported that everything had gone forward. On the same date (the 11th) he spoke of many of his horses being broken down by fatigue. On the 12th he complained that the rate of supply was only "one hundred and fifty horses per week for the entire army there and in front of Washington."

I immediately directed the Quartermaster-General to inquire into this matter and report why a larger supply was not furnished. Gen. Meigs reported on the 14th that the average issue of horses to Gen. McClellan's army in the field and in front of Washington for the previous six weeks had been 1,459 per week, or 8,754 in all. In addition, that large numbers of mules had been supplied, and that the number of animals with Gen. McClellan's army on the upper Potomac was over thirty-one thousand. He also reported that he was then sending to that army all the horses he could procure.

On the 18th Gen. McClellan stated, in regard to Gen. Meigs's report that he had filled every requisition for shoes and clothing: "Gen. Meigs may have ordered these articles to be forwarded, but they have not reached our depot, and, unless greater effort to insure prompt transmission is made by the department of which Gen. Meigs is the head, they might as well remain in New York or Philadelphia, so far as this army is concerned." I immediately called Gen. Meigs's attention to this apparent neglect of his department. On the 25th he reported, as the result of his investigation, that 48,000 pairs of boots and shoes had been received by the quartermaster of Gen. McClellan's army at Harper's Ferry, Frederick, and Hagerstown; that 20,000 pairs were at Harper's Ferry depot on the 21st; that 10,000 more were on their way, and 15,000 more ordered. Col. Ingals, aide-de-camp and chief quartermaster to Gen. McClellan, telegraphed, on the 25th: "The suffering for want of clothing is exaggerated, I think, and certainly might have been avoided by timely requisitions of regimental and brigade commanders." On the 24th he telegraphed to the Quartermaster-General that the clothing was not detained in cars at the depots: "Such complaints are groundless. The fact is, the clothing arrives and is issued, but more is still wanted. I have ordered more than would seem necessary from any data furnished me, and I beg to remind you that you have always very promptly met all my requisitions, so far as clothing is concerned. Our department is not at fault. It provides as soon as due notice is given. I foresee no time when an army of over 100,000 men will not call for clothing and other articles."

In regard to Gen. McClellan's means of promptly communicating the wants of his army to me or to the proper bureaus of the War Department, I report that, in addition to the ordinary mails, he has been in hourly communication with Washington by telegraph.

It is due to Gen. Meigs that I should submit herewith a copy of a telegram received by him from Gen. McClellan.

Very respectfully, your obedient servant,

H. W. HALLECK, Gen.-in-Chief.

UNITED STATES MILITARY TELEGRAPH.

Received, *Oct.* 22, 1862—9 40 P. M.

From McClellan's Headquarters.

TO BRIG.-GEN. MEIGS: Your despatch of this date is received. I have never intended, in any letter or despatch, to make any accusation against yourself or your department for not furnishing or forwarding clothing as rapidly as it was possible for you to do. I believe that everything has been done that could be done in this respect. The idea that I have tried to convey was, that certain portions of the command were without clothing, and the army could not move until it was supplied.

G. B. McCLELLAN, Maj.-Gen.

Nothing has been made public on the part of Gen. McClellan alluding to or explaining the causes of the delay of the movements of the army. Strict justice requires that, in estimating the importance of the preceding letters, the testimony of Gen. Burnside on a subsequent page should be considered. It was generally understood that Gen. McClellan's movement was delayed by the want of clothing and other supplies, and especially on account of his deficiency in cavalry and artillery horses. The purchase and forwarding of these was going on even up to the day of his crossing the Potomac. One army corps did not receive its clothing until it had commenced its march in Virginia. It was stated by several commanders that they made every effort to get the clothing for their troops, repeatedly sent teams to the railroad depots for it, and until a short time previous to the marching of the army they were invariably told that the clothing had not arrived.

Early on the 26th of October a cavalry force, under Col. Pleasanton, crossed the Potomac on the new pontoon bridge at Berlin, and moved on in the direction of Purcellville. Soon after the corps of Gen. Burnside began to cross in light marching order, followed by an immense train of wagons, and took a position near Lovettsville. On the next day a heavy reënforcement joined him. About the same time the Confederate force prepared to abandon the line of the Potomac and to fall back. The crossing of the Federal troops was now constant, until the entire army was south of the river. On the 30th of October Gen. Sedgwick advanced from Boliver Heights, and crossed the Shenandoah in the direction of Shannondale, and Gen. Hancock pushed forward, pressing on the Confederate lines in front of Charlestown. Gen. Burnside moved along the eastern base of the Blue Ridge, followed by the corps of Gen. Porter.

The situation of the respective forces at this time was as follows: The Federal army reënforced by the divisions of Gens. Sigel and Sickles, who had advanced from Washington, occupied all the region east of the Blue Ridge, with the right resting on Harper's Ferry, and the left extending nearly to Paris, on the road from Aldie to Winchester. The centre was at Snickersville; with Snicker's Gap in its possession. The Confederate line was on the south side of the Blue Ridge, with the Shenandoah river immediately in its front, extending from Front Royal down to Charlestown, with the great body of their troops massed between Berryville and Winchester. On the 4th Ashby's Gap was occupied without opposition by the Federal troops. The cavalry corps, under Col. Pleasanton, pushed on from Piedmont, and occupied Marguette, holding the approaches to Manassas and Chester Gap, on the left side of the Blue Ridge. The condition and spirit of the army at this time were unequalled by that of any force before organized. On the 6th Gen. McClellan's headquarters were at Rectortown near Front Royal. The army was steadily advancing and the Confederate force falling back, with some skirmishing. Warrenton was occupied by the Federal troops on the same day. On the 7th a severe snow storm commenced, and continued throughout the day. On the 8th the bridge at Rappahannock Station was taken and held by Gen. Bayard. On the night of the 7th, near midnight, Gen. Buckingham arrived, from Washington, at Gen. McClellan's tent, and delivered to him an order from President Lincoln, to surrender the command of the army to Gen. Burnside, and to report himself immediately at Trenton, the capital of the State of New Jersey. This order was entirely unexpected by Gen. McClellan, and probably by every officer of the army. The only reasons for it which have officially appeared, will be found in the above letter of Gen. Halleck, dated October 28, which was given to the public a few days after this removal.

Gen. McClellan immediately wrote the following address to his troops preparatory to his departure:

HEADQUARTERS OF THE ARMY OF THE POTOMAC,
CAMP NEAR RECTORTOWN, VA., *November* 7.

Officers and Soldiers of the Army of the Potomac:

An order of the President devolves upon Maj.-Gen. Burnside the command of this army. In parting from you I cannot express the love and gratitude I bear to you. As an army you have grown up in my care. In you I have never found doubt or coldness. The battles you have fought under my command will probably live in our Nation's history. The glory you have achieved over mutual perils and fatigues; the graves of our comrades fallen in battle and by disease; the broken forms of those whom wounds and sickness have disabled; the strongest associations which can exist among men unite us by an indissoluble tie. We shall ever be comrades in supporting the Constitution of our country and the Nationality of its people.

(Signed) GEO. B. McCLELLAN.
Major-General U. S. A.

The next day was devoted by Gen. McClellan to the transfer of his command to Gen. Burnside. The most cordial feelings existed between the two officers, the latter of whom accepted a promotion which he had before twice declined, only upon the peremptory order of the War Department. On Sunday evening his officers assembled at his tent, for a final parting of commander and officers. It was such a scene of deep feeling as could occur only where officers reposed the highest confidence in their commander, who had led them successfully through some of the most fearful battles of modern wars. Monday was occupied in passing among the various camps, reviewing the troops, and taking a final leave of both officers and men. A spectator of these scenes has summed them up in these words:

"As Gen. McClellan, mounted upon a fine horse, attended by a retinue of fine-looking military men, riding rapidly through the ranks, gracefully recognized and bid a farewell to the army, the cries and demonstrations of the men were beyond bounds—wild, impassioned, and unrestrained. Disregarding all military forms they rushed from their ranks and thronged around him with the bitterest complaints against those who had removed from command their beloved leader."

On the next day, the 10th, he withdrew, taking the railroad cars at Warrenton. On reaching Warrenton Junction a salute was fired. The troops, which had been drawn up in line, afterward broke ranks, when the soldiers crowded around him and many eagerly called for a few parting words. He said in response, while on the platform of the railroad depot, "I wish you to stand by Gen. Burnside as you have stood by me, and all will be well. Good-bye." To this there was a spontaneous and enthusiastic response.

The troops were also drawn up in line at Bristow's Station and Manassas Junction, where salutes were fired and he was complimented with enthusiastic cheers. On reaching Washington he proceeded immediately to the depot, and passed on to Philadelphia and Trenton, where he arrived early on the 12th.

What was now the military aspect? The movement of Gen. McClellan's army, after crossing the Potomac, was toward Gordonsville. This made a movement on the part of the Confederate general Lee necessary in order to prevent the Federal army from getting between him and Richmond. For this purpose he attempted to move from Winchester through the gaps of the Blue Ridge to Culpepper. The larger part of his force had passed through, when the gaps were taken and held by Gen. McClellan. At the same time Gen. Sigel had advanced from Washington, and lay near the Blue Ridge, covering at once Washington, observing the gaps to the Rappahannock, and protecting the railroad communication to that river. The bridge at Rappahannock Station had already been seized by the cavalry, under Gen. Bayard. The available force of Gen. McClellan was about one hundred and twenty thousand men; that of Gen. Lee consisted of about sixty thousand able men at Culpepper and Gordonsville, and thirty thousand in the Shenandoah Valley, near Strasburg. The distance from Warrenton to Gordonsville is about fifty miles, and from Warrenton to the Rapidan, thirty-five miles; from Strasburg to Gordonsville, by Staunton and Charlottesville, one hundred and thirty-five miles; and by the only other practicable route, one northwest of Gordonsville, and perpendicular to Gen. McClellan's line of advance, about one hundred miles. In his position it was necessary for Gen. Lee to defend the line of the Rapidan, or endeavor to effect a junction with the force in the Shenandoah Valley, under Gen. Jackson, or fall back upon Richmond, in a country without a line of defence, with Gen. McClellan close upon him, leaving Gen. Jackson to shift for himself. The defence of the Rapidan was impracticable from the course of the river from the Alexandria railroad to the Blue Ridge. The efforts to join Gen. Jackson would have uncovered Richmond, and the attempt to fall back on Richmond would have at least hazarded the demoralization of his army, and enabled Gen. McClellan to turn the defensible parts of the Rappahannock, and the line of the North Anna. The appointment of Gen. Burnside was followed by the organization of a portion of the army into divisions, and a movement to concentrate it at Fredericksburg. On the 12th Gen. Burnside issued the following address to the army:

HEADQUARTERS ARMY OF THE POTOMAC, *Nov.* 10, 1862.

In accordance with General Orders, No. 182, issued by the President of the United States, I hereby assume command of the Army of the Potomac. Patriotism, and the exercise of my every energy in the direction of this army, aided by the full and hearty coöperation of its officers and men, will, I hope, under the blessing of God, insure its success.

Having been a sharer of the privations, and a witness of the bravery of the old Army of the Potomac in the Maryland campaign, and fully identified with them in their feelings of respect and esteem for Gen. McClellan, entertained through a long and most friendly association with him, I feel that it is not as a stranger I assume command.

To the 9th army corps, so long and intimately associated with me, I need say nothing. Our histories are identical. With diffidence for myself, but with a proud confidence in the unswerving loyalty and determination of the gallant army now intrusted to my care, I accept its control, with the steadfast assurance that the just cause must prevail.

[Signed] A. E. BURNSIDE,
Major-General Commanding.

On the 12th the general-in-chief (Halleck) and Gen. Meigs proceeded from Washington to the headquarters to confer with Gen. Burnside. On the same day the advance of the army was across the Rappahannock and fifteen miles south of Warrenton. On the 14th Gen. Burnside issued the following order reorganizing a portion of his army:

HEADQUARTERS, ARMY OF THE POTOMAC,
WARRENTON (VA.), *Nov.* 14, 1862.

General Order, No. 184.

First. The organization of a portion of this army in three grand divisions is hereby announced. These grand divisions will be formed and commanded as follows:

The Second and Ninth Corps will form the right grand division, and will be commanded by Maj.-Gen. E. V. Sumner.

The First and Sixth Corps will form the left grand division, and will be commanded by Maj.-Gen. W. B. Franklin.

The Third and Fifth Corps will form the centre grand division, and will be commanded by Maj.-Gen. Joseph Hooker.

The Eleventh Corps, with such others as may hereafter be assigned to it, will constitute a reserve force, under the command of Maj.-Gen. F. Sigel.

Assignments of cavalry and further details will be announced in future orders.

By command of Maj.-Gen. BURNSIDE.

S. WILLIAMS, A. A.-G.

A movement was made at this time by Gen. Jackson for the purpose of detaching a portion of the army of the Potomac. He occupied all the roads west and north of Winchester as far as Big Cacapon Bridge on the northwestern turnpike, and from Pughtown to Bath and Hancock. He was thus looking westward, at the same time he was in a position to cross the Potomac. His movement failed to effect his design.

Meanwhile the mass of Gen. Lee's forces retired to Gordonsville. On the 16th the forces of Gen. Burnside began to move for Fredericksburg, as had been previously determined in consultation on the 12th between Gens. Halleck and Burnside. On the 15th the evacuation of Warrenton and the adjacent places was commenced, and by the morning of the 18th it was entirely completed. The advance was led by Gen. Sumner. At the same time supplies were sent to Aquia Creek, and the repairs of the railroad track to Fredericksburg commenced, and the army concentrated at Falmouth opposite Fredericksburg.

The march to Richmond, it appeared, was to be made by the route from Fredericksburg. This city is on the south bank of the Rappahannock, and sixty-five miles distant from Richmond. It is connected with the latter place by a railroad, of which there is a double line nearly to Hanover Junction, twenty-three miles from Richmond. The railroad crosses the Mattapony river at Milford, thirty-seven miles from Fredericksburg, and the Pamunkey, twenty-five miles from Richmond, besides a number of smaller streams. Between Falmouth, where the Federal army concentrated, and Richmond there are two main and two minor lines of defence. The first that of the Rappahannock river. Above Falmouth its abrupt banks, which are lined with high hills, difficult of access, and its narrow fords and rocky bottom render a rapid crossing for a large force almost impossible. Below, the valley of the river expands, spreading often into spacious plains, while the winding course of the stream forms numerous necks of land, easily commanded from the north side, and giving secure crossing places, and ample ground for the formation of troops. At Fredericksburg the north commands the south bank and much of the distance, which is a mile and a half, to the frowning hills or table land beyond. But these heights equally command this intermediate plain, and are unassailable in front except by infantry. Next in the rear and twelve miles distant, is the line of the Po river and Stannard's Marsh, which is hardly available except to hold a pursuing foe in check. The North Anna is about forty miles from the Rappahannock, and affords another principal line of defence. It is a deep and rapid stream, with a narrow valley. The table land on its north bank is about one hundred feet above the bed of the river, and about one hundred and fifty on the south bank. The extension of its line after it turns to join the South Anna, and becomes the Pamunkey, presents scarcely less obstacles than the river itself, so well is the ground guarded by swamps and flanked by streams. The last and a minor line of defence is the South Anna river, with the southern commanded by the northern bank, and too near the North Anna for a second formation by a force that has been badly defeated. Numerous small streams parallel to the line of advance present suitable points for resistance, and protect foes attacking the line of communication, while the bridges over them are weak points necessary to be securely guarded.

By the 20th a considerable force had reached Falmouth. Gen. Sumner on the next day sent to Fredericksburg the following summons to surrender:

HEADQUARTERS ARMY OF THE POTOMAC, *Nov.* 21, 1862.

To the Mayor and Common Council of Fredericksburg:

GENTLEMEN: Under cover of the houses of your city shots have been fired upon the troops of my command.

Your mills and manufactories are furnishing provisions and materials for clothing for armed bodies in rebellion against the Government of the United States; your railroads and other means of transportation are removing supplies to the depots of such troops.

This condition of things must terminate, and by direction of Gen. Burnside, I accordingly demand the surrender of the city into my hands, as the representative of the Government of the United States, at or before five o'clock this afternoon.

Failing an affirmative reply to this demand by the hour indicated, sixteen hours will be permitted to elapse for the removal from the city of women and children, the sick and wounded, and aged, &c.; which period having expired, I shall proceed to shell the town.

Upon obtaining possession of the city, every necessary means will be taken to preserve order and secure the protective operation of the laws and policy of the United States Government.

I am, very respectively, your obedient servant,
E. V. SUMNER,
Brevet Maj.-Gen. U. S. army,
Commanding Eighth Grand Division.

In reply the mayor of the city, M. Slaughter, stated that the firing complained of occurred in the suburbs, and was the act of the Confederate officer in command, for which neither the citizens nor authorities were responsible. The other matters complained of, he said, should no longer exist, and proceeded thus: "The civil authorities of Fredericksburg have no control; but I am assured by the military authorities of the Confederate army near here that nothing will be done to infringe the conditions herein named, as to matters within the town; but the latter authorities inform us that, while their troops will not occupy the town, they will not permit yours to do so."

The late hour at which the summons was received rendered it impossible to remove the women and children in the time allowed.

The reply of Gen. Sumner to the mayor was as follows:

HEADQUARTERS RIGHT GRAND DIVISION, CAMP NEAR FALMOUTH, *Nov.* 21, 1862.

To the Mayor and Common Council of Fredericksburg:

Your letter of this afternoon is at hand, and in consideration of your pledge that the acts complained of shall cease, and that your town shall not be occupied by any of the enemy's forces, and your assertion that a lack of transportation renders it impossible to move the women, children, sick, wounded, and aged, I am authorized to say to you that our batteries will not open upon the town at the hour designated. Gen. Patrick will meet a committee of representatives from your town to-morrow morning at nine o'clock at the Lacy House.

Very respectfully your obedient servant,
E. V. SUMNER,
Brevet Maj.-Gen. Commanding Division.

An interview was subsequently held as above mentioned, which resulted in the following note from Gen. Sumner:

HEADQUARTERS RIGHT GRAND DIVISION, *Nov.* 22, 1862.

To the Mayor and Common Council, Fredericksburg:

I am authorized to say that so long as no hostile demonstration is made from the town it will not be shelled. I have also to say that there will be no firing upon the cars before 11 o'clock P. M. to-morrow.

I am, gentlemen, your obedient servant,
E. V. SUMNER,
Brevet Maj.-Gen. U. S. A., Commanding.

The firing upon the cars of the railroad above mentioned was in consequence of the belief that they were used to remove military stores from Fredericksburg.

As Gen. Burnside's army concentrated on the north bank, Gen. Lee's forces concentrated on the heights in the rear of Fredericksburg. Had the pontoon bridges required been at hand when the advance reached Falmouth, the line of the Rappahannock would have been taken without opposition. Then, with proper supplies and bridges, thirty of the sixty miles to Richmond would have been placed within the reach of Gen. Burnside, and perhaps a lodgment have been effected on the banks of the North Anna. Nearly thirty days elapsed before the pontoons arrived and the bridges were completed. The ensuing military operations were investigated by a committee of Congress, before whom Gen. Burnside testified as follows:

Gen. Halleck came down to see me on the 11th of November. On the 9th I made out a plan of operations, in accordance with the order of Gen. Halleck, which directed me not only to take the command, but also to state what I proposed to do with it. That plan I wrote on the morning of the 9th of November, and sent it by special messenger to Washington. I can furnish the committee a copy of that plan if they desire it. I do not have it here now.

Question.—State the substance of it, if you please. That may do as well.

Answer.—I stated, in substance, that I thought it advisable to concentrate the army in the neighborhood of Warrenton, to make a small movement across the Rappahannock as a feint, with a view to divert the attention of the enemy, and lead them to believe we were going to march in the direction of Gordonsville, and then to make a rapid movement of the whole army to Fredericksburg, on this side of the Rappahannock.

As my reasons for that, I stated that the farther we got into the interior of Virginia, the longer would be our lines of communication and the greater would be the difficulty we would have in keeping them open, as the enemy had upon our right flank a corps that almost at any time could, by a rapid movement, seriously embarrass us. If we were caught by the elements so far from our base of supplies, and at the same time in the enemy's country, where they had means of getting information that we had not, it might, I thought, prove disastrous to the army, as we had but one line of railway by which to supply it.

In moving upon Fredericksburg we would all the time be as near Washington as would the enemy, and after arriving at Fredericksburg, we would be at a point nearer to Richmond than we would be even if we should take Gordonsville. On the Gordonsville line, the enemy, in our opinion, would not give us a decisive battle at any place this side of Richmond. They would defend Gordonsville until such time as they felt they had given us a check, and then with so many lines of railroad open to them, they would move upon Richmond or upon Lynchburg, and in either case the difficulty of following them would be very great.

In connection with this movement I requested that barges filled with provisions and forage should be floated to Aquia Creek, where they could easily be landed; that materials be collected for the reconstruction of the wharves there, and that all the wagons in Washington that could possibly be spared should be filled with hard bread and small commissary stores, and, with a large number of beef cattle, started down to Fredericksburg on the road by way of Dumfries; and that this wagon train and load of cattle should be preceded by a pontoon train large enough to span the Rappahannock twice. I stated that this wagon train could move in perfect safety, because it would be all the time between our army and the Potomac; or in other words our army would be all the time between the enemy and that train. But at the same time I said that if a cavalry escort could not be furnished from Washington, I would send some of my cavalry to guard the train.

On the morning of the 14th of November, feeling uneasy with reference to the pontoons, as I had not heard of their starting, I directed my chief engineer to telegraph again in reference to them.

He telegraphed to Gen. Woodbury or to Major Spaulding. It subsequently appeared that that was the first they ever had heard of any wish to have the pontoon train started down to Fredericksburg, although the authorities in Washington had had my plans sent to them on the 9th of November; and it had also been discovered by Gen. Halleck and Gen. Meigs, at my headquarters, on the night of the 11th and 12th of November; and after discovering it fully there, they sat down and sent telegrams to Washington, which, as I supposed, fully covered the case, and would secure the starting of the pontoon trains at once. I supposed, of course, that those portions of the plan which required to be attended to in Washington would be carried out there at once. I could have sent officers of my own there to attend to those matters, and perhaps I made a mistake in not doing so, as Gen. Halleck afterward told me that I ought not to have trusted to them in Washington for the details.

In reply to the telegram I had ordered to be sent, Gen. Woodbury telegraphed back that the pontoon train would start on Sunday morning probably, and certainly on Monday morning, which would have been on the 16th and 17th of November, and would have been in time. They did not, however, start until the 20th, and on that day it commenced raining, which delayed them so much and the roads became so bad that when they got to Dumfries they floated the pontoons off the wagons. We then sent to Washington for a steamer, and carried them down to Aquia Creek by water, sending the wagons around by land. The pontoons did not get here until the 22d or 23d of November.

On the 15th of November I started the column down the road to Fredericksburg, not knowing anything about the delay in the starting of the pontoons, because the telegram announcing the delay did not reach Warrenton Junction until I had left to come down here with the troops, and that telegram did not reach me until I arrived here on the morning of the 19th, when it was handed to me by an orderly who had brought it down to Warrenton Junction.

After reaching here I saw at once that there was no chance for crossing the Rappahannock with the army at that time. It commenced raining and the river began to rise—not to any great extent, but I did not know how much it might rise. There were no means of crossing except by going up to the fords, and it would be impossible to do that because of the inability to supply the troops after they should cross.

Gen. Sumner, with his command, arrived here in advance. He sent to me, asking if he should cross the river. He was very much tempted to take his own men across to Fredericksburg by a ford near Falmouth, as there was no enemy there except a very small force. I did not think it advisable that he should cross at that time.

The plan I had in contemplation was, if the stores and these bridges had come here as I expected, to throw Sumner's whole corps across the Rappahannock, fill the wagons with as many small stores as we could, and having beef cattle along for meat, then to make a rapid movement down in the direction of Richmond and try to meet the enemy and fight a battle before Jackson could make a junction there. We knew that Jackson was in the valley, and felt confident that there was force enough on the upper Rappahannock to take care of him. We felt certain that as soon as the enemy knew of our crossing down here, the force of Jackson would be recalled, and we wanted to meet this force and beat it before Jackson could come down on our flank and perhaps cripple us.

I had recommended that some supplies should be sent to the mouth of the Rappahannock with a view of establishing a department at Port Royal. After we had advanced to Fredericksburg, and after the first delay in starting the pontoons, I think they were sent as quickly as they could have been, and the supplies and quartermasters' stores have been always in as great abundance as we could have expected, for after the 19th of November the roads were particularly bad. Horses and mules were sent down to us, so that our cavalry and teams were in very good condition.

After it was ascertained that there must be a delay, and that the enemy had concentrated such a force as to make it very difficult to cross, except by a number of bridges, we commenced bringing up from Aquia Creek all the pontoons we could. After enough of them had been brought up to build the bridges, I called several councils of war to decide about crossing the Rappahannock. It was at first decided to cross at Shinker's Neck, about twelve miles below here, but our demonstration was simply for the purpose of drawing down there as large a force of the enemy as possible.

I then decided to cross here because, in the first place, I felt satisfied that they did not expect us to cross here but down below. In the next place I felt satisfied that this was the place to fight the most decisive battle, because if we could divide their forces by penetrating their lines at one or two points, separating their left from their right, then a vigorous attack with the whole army would succeed in breaking their army in pieces.

The enemy had cut a road along on the rear of the line of the heights where we made our attack, by means of which they connected the two wings of their army, and avoided a long detour round through a bad country. I obtained from a colored man from the other side of the town information in regard to this new road, which proved to be correct. I wanted to obtain possession of the new road, and that was my reason for making an attack on the extreme left. I did not intend to make the attack on the right until that position had been taken, which I supposed would stagger the enemy, cutting their lines in two. And then I proposed to make a direct attack on their front, and drive them out of the works.

By Mr. Gooch: Do I understand you to say that it was your understanding that Gen. Halleck and Gen. Meigs, while at your headquarters in Warrenton, and before you commenced the movement of your army, sent orders to Washington for the pontoons to be immediately forwarded to Falmouth?

Answer: That was my understanding, certainly.

Question: In your judgment, could the pontoons have been forwarded to you in time for you to have crossed the Rappahannock when you expected, if all possible efforts had been made by those charged with that duty?

Answer: Yes, sir, if they had received their orders in time.

Question: Did the non-arrival of these pontoons at the time you expected prevent your crossing when you expected to cross and interfere with the success of your plans?

Answer: Yes, sir.

Thus it was the design of Gen.Burnside that the pontoons should leave Alexandria on Nov. 11, and arrive at Falmouth at the same time with the advance of his army. The right grand division reached Falmouth on Nov. 17. The pontoons left Alexandria on Nov. 19, and arrived at Fredericksburg after the movements of Gen. Burnside had not only become known, but after Gen. Lee had advanced his forces from Gordonsville to the heights in the rear of Fredericksburg, and had fortified them. They were not used until the night of Dec. 10.

A plan for the movements of Gen. Burnside had now been arranged between President Lincoln, Gen. Halleck, and himself, by which it was determined that the army should move across the Rappahannock at a certain place and at a certain time. This was departed from by Gen. Burnside, who was induced to move the army across at a different place and at an earlier day. His reasons for this change he thus states in his report:

During my preparations for crossing at the place I had first selected, I discovered that the enemy had thrown a large portion of his force down the river and elsewhere, thus weakening his force in front, and also thought I discovered that he did not anticipate the crossing of our whole force at Fredericksburg, and I hoped by rapidly throwing the whole command over at that place to separate by a vigorous attack the forces of the enemy on the river below from the force behind and on the crest in the rear of the town, in which case we could fight him with the greatest advantage in our favor. To do this we had to gain a height on the extreme right of the crest, which height commanded a new road lately made by the enemy for the purpose of more rapid communication along his lines; which point gained, his position along the crest would have been scarcely tenable, and he could have been driven from them easily by an attack on his front in connection with a movement in rear of the crest.

During the night of the 10th of December, therefore, the pontoons were conveyed to the river, and the artillery to the number of one hundred and forty-three pieces was placed in position opposite the city. Between four and five o'clock on the morning of the 11th, the work of building four bridges was commenced. One was to be made at the point where the railroad bridge formerly crossed, and two others opposite the city but nearer Falmouth, and the fourth nearly two miles below for the crossing of the left wing under Gen. Franklin. A dull haze so obscured the movement, that it was not discovered for some time by the Confederate pickets. The bridges were thus partly constructed, when a brisk and deadly fire of musketry from along the banks of the river and windows of the houses was opened, which compelled the workmen to stop. They fled to the cover of the surrounding hills where they formed again, and about six o'clock the work was recommenced. The Confederates had now become aroused to a sense of what was going forward, and with reënforcements of sharpshooters swarmed the opposite bank and houses. The pontonniers, nothing daunted by the hot fire poured upon them, went bravely to work. A storm of bullets covered them. The planks and boats were riddled by every volley. Once more they were compelled to withdraw, and again fell back to the cover of the ridge of hills running parallel with the river. Orders were now given to the artillery to open fire on the city. The Federal batteries commenced an almost simultaneous bombardment, directing their fire chiefly at the houses in which the sharpshooters had concealed themselves. At the first fire they became untenable, and the riflemen retreated to the rear of the town, and took shelter behind the buildings unharmed. The fire of the artillery, which commenced at seven o'clock, was continued incessantly until one o'clock. The fog somewhat obscured its results, but bodies of the Confederates with great stubbornness still kept within the city. The Confederate batteries on the heights in the rear continued silent. Not a gun was fired, About ten o'clock, the workmen were again formed for a third attempt to build the bridges. Volunteers joined them from the 8th Connecticut. Some planks were seized and carried out to the end of a string of boats and placed in position, when a galling fire from sharpshooters in rifle pits near the edge of the water again interrupted them, and they were recalled. Meantime the bombardment was continued, and several houses in the city had taken fire. In the afternoon, several pontoon boats, loaded with volunteers from the 7th Michigan and 19th Massachusetts, were sent over. They chased the Confederate sharpshooters from their hiding places, and the bridges were finished without further interruption. On the other side a scene of destruction presented itself. The walls of houses were breached, roofs had fallen in, and the interiors were destroyed.

No sooner were the bridges completed than the troops began to cross, and before dusk Gen. Sumner's grand division had gone over, and a section of Gen. Hooker's. All had rations for three days, and blankets for a bivouac. The grand division of Gen. Franklin, consisting of the corps of Gens. Reynolds and Smith, crossed over at the lower bridge, which was built earlier in the day without interruption, as there was a plain before it which the artillery could easily have swept. The troops commenced crossing again early on the morning of the 12th without molestation. Some sharp resistance had been made by the Confederate soldiers to those who crossed on the previous day, but these were driven out of the city or killed. During the afternoon fire was opened upon the city by the Confederate batteries on the nearest heights, which was replied to by the Federal batteries, and soon ceased. The occupation of Fredericksburg had now been successfully made. No greater opposition had been presented by the forces of Gen. Lee than was sufficient to tempt the Federal troops to press forward with greater ardor.

The next movement was to drive the Confederate forces from their positions on the heights. These positions consisted of two lines of batteries, one a mile in rear of the other, and both overlooking the city. They extended, in the form of a semicircle, from Port Royal to a point about six miles above Fredericksburg. Their right wing, under Gen. Jackson, extended from Port Royal to Guinney's Station on the Richmond and Fredericksburg railroad; the centre, under Gen. Longstreet, extended to the telegraph road; the left, under Gen. Stuart, was west of Massaponax Creek. A reserve corps was commanded by Gen. A. P. Hill. This was the force which had fought at Richmond and in Maryland.

Friday night and Saturday morning, the 13th, were spent by Gen. Burnside in making a proper disposition of his forces. The left was occupied by Gen. Franklin with his grand division, the centre by Gen. Hooker, and the right by Gen. Sumner.

The right of Gen. Franklin rested on the outskirts of the city, his centre was advanced about a mile from the river, and his left was on the Rappahannock, about three miles below. The action commenced on the extreme left by an annoying fire from a Confederate battery, which the 9th New York was ordered to charge and capture. In this attempt they were repulsed. A brigade was brought to their aid by Gen. Tyler, and another attempt made, but the fire was so deadly that it failed of success. The battle now became more general, and another attempt was made to capture the battery. No advantage was gained at this time, but a severe loss was suffered. The conflict now extended along the whole line of the left, and a desperate effort was made to drive the Confederates across the Massaponax Creek by turning their position. The ground was contested most obstinately, but the Confederates gradually fell back, occasionally making a most desperate stand, until night, when Gen. Franklin had succeeded in gaining nearly a mile, and his troops occupied the field. The right of Gen. Franklin's division, under Gen. Reynolds, encountered the fire of the Confederate artillery on the heights, and although the conflict was most deadly, no advantage was gained.

On the right, under command of Gen. Sumner, the action commenced about ten o'clock and was furious during the rest of the day. The Confederate forces occupied the woods and hills in the rear of the city, from which it soon became evident they could not be driven except at the point of the bayonet. The charge was ordered to be made by the division of Gen. French supported by that of Gen. Howard. Steadily the troops moved across the plain, until they were within a dozen yards of the ridge, when they were suddenly met by a galling fire from the Confederate infantry posted behind a stone wall. For a few minutes the head of the column exhibited some confusion; but quickly forming into line it retired back to a ravine within musket shot of the Confederates. Here they were reënforced by fresh troops who fearlessly advanced to their aid under a most destructive fire of artillery. The line of assault was now formed again, and with bayonets fixed and a double-quick step, they rushed forward to seize the Confederate artillery. From the first step they encountered a terrific fire of infantry and artillery. No veterans could face that shock. They were thrown into confusion and brought to a sudden halt. At this juncture the centre quivered, faltered, and fled in disorder, but was afterward rallied and brought back. Three times was the attack thus made to dislodge those batteries. But each time it was in vain. The ranks of the storming party, shrunk to small limits, retired. The entire force of his artillery was now brought by Gen. Sumner to bear upon the enemy, and thus the contest was kept up until dark. At night the Confederate force occupied their original position, and the wounded and the dead remained where they had fallen. Every attempt to remove them by the Federal troops was defeated by the Confederate infantry.

In the centre, under the command of Gen. Hooker, skirmishing commenced early in the morning; and during the forenoon, while the fog prevailed, a terrific contest, chiefly with artillery, was kept up on both sides. The Confederate position appeared to be invulnerable to artillery, and about noon preparations were made for storming it. The troops marched steadily up within musket shot of the batteries, and were there met by such a destructive fire of artillery and rifles as drove them back with a heavy loss. Reënforcements were obtained, and the attempt to take the batteries was repeated in the afternoon, but without success. The contest continued with great fierceness until night. About half past five the firing of musketry ceased, but that of the artillery continued until long after dark.

On the next day, Sunday the 14th, both armies remained comparatively quiet. Some skirmishing and artillery fire took place for a short time. Gen. Burnside sent the following despatch to President Lincoln early in the morning:

HEADQUARTERS ARMY POTOMAC,
FOUR O'CLOCK, A. M., *December* 14.

THE PRESIDENT: I have just returned from the field. Our troops are all over the river and hold the first ridge outside the town and 3 miles below. We hope to carry the crest to-day. Our loss is heavy—say 5,000.

A. E. BURNSIDE,
Major-General Commanding.

On Monday, both armies continued in the same position. The Confederates had strengthened some of their works. During the ensuing night, the army evacuated Fredericksburg and retired across the river to its former position. The artillery crossed first, followed by the infantry, the last of whom left about daylight. The pontoon bridges were then removed and all communication cut off. The movement was not perceived by the Confederates until it was too late to do any injury to the retreating force. The following is the despatch of Gen. Burnside announcing this movement:

HEADQUARTERS ARMY POTOMAC,
SIX O'CLOCK P. M., *December* 16, 1862.

Maj.-Gen. HALLECK: The army was withdrawn to this side of the river because I felt the position in front could not be carried, and it was a military necessity either to attack or retire. A repulse would have been disastrous to us. The army was withdrawn at night, without the knowledge of the enemy, and without loss either of property or men.

A. E. BURNSIDE,
Major-General Commanding.

The Federal loss was as follows: Gen. Sumner's division on the right, killed, 473; wounded, 4,090; missing, 748, Total, 5,311,

Gen. Hooker's division on the centre, killed, 326; wounded, 2,468; missing, 754. Total, 3,548.

Gen. Franklin's division on the left, killed, 339; wounded, 2,547; missing, 576. Total, 3,462. Grand total, killed, 1,138; wounded, 9,105; missing, 2,078. Total, 12,321.

The Confederate loss was comparatively small, having been sheltered by their works.

Gen. Burnside, in his report to the general-in-chief, thus explains his defeat:

How near we came to the accomplishment of our object future reports will show. But for the fog, and the unexpected and unavoidable delay in building the bridges, which gave the enemy 24 hours to concentrate his forces in his strong position, we would almost certainly have succeeded, in which case the battle would have been, in my opinion, far more decisive than if we had crossed at the places first selected. As it was, we came very near success. Failing in accomplishing the main object, we remained in order of battle two days, long enough to decide that the enemy would not come out of his strongholds to fight me with his infantry, after which we recrossed to this side of the river unmolested, without the loss of men or property.

As the day broke our long lines of troops were seen marching to their different positions as if going on parade—not the least demoralization or disorganization existed.

To the brave officers and soldiers who accomplished the feat of thus recrossing in the face of the enemy, I owe everything. For the failure in the attack, I am responsible, as the extreme gallantry, courage, and endurance shown by them were never exceeded, and would have carried the points had it been possible.

To the families and friends of the dead I can only offer my heartfelt sympathies, but for the wounded I can offer my earnest prayer for their comfort and final recovery.

The fact that I decided to move from Warrenton on to this line rather against the opinion of the President, Secretary of War, and yourself, and that you have left the whole movement in my hands, without giving me orders, makes me the more responsible.

Thus closed the third campaign against Richmond. No further hostile demonstrations were made by either army during the year. On the 31st of December, the Confederate general Lee issued the following address to his troops:

HEADQUARTERS ARMY OF NORTHERN VIRGINIA,
Dec. 21, 1832.

General Order, No. 38.

1. The General commanding takes this occasion to express to the officers and soldiers of the army his high appreciation of the fortitude, valor, and devotion displayed by them, which, under the blessing of Almighty God, have added the victory of Fredericksburg to the long lists of their triumphs.

An arduous march, performed with celerity under many disadvantages, exhibited the discipline and spirit of the troops and their eagerness to confront the foe.

The immense army of the enemy completed its preparations for the attack without interruption, and gave battle in its own time, and on ground of its own selection.

It was encountered by less than twenty thousand of this brave army, and its columns, crushed and broken, hurled back at every point with such fearful slaughter that escape from entire destruction became the boast of those who had advanced in full confidence of victory.

The war is not yet ended. The enemy is still numerous and strong, and the country demands of the army a renewal of its heroic efforts in her behalf. Nobly has it responded to her call in the past, and she will never appeal in vain to its courage and patriotism.

The signal manifestations of Divine mercy that have distinguished the eventful and glorious campaign of the year just closing, give assurance of hope that, under the guidance of the same Almighty hand, the coming year will be no less fruitful of events that will insure the safety, peace, and happiness of our beloved country, and add new lustre to the already imperishable name of the Army of Northern Virginia.

R. E. LEE, General.

As a part of the campaign against Richmond undertaken when Gen. Burnside took command of the army in Virginia, the efforts which were made to cut the Confederate line of communication between Richmond and the southwestern States, should be stated. There are three lines of railroad running south and southwest. The one running southwest passes through southwestern Virginia, eastern Tennessee, northern Alabama, and connects with roads to western Tennessee and to New Orleans. One line running south connects Richmond with Wilmington, Charleston, Savannah, and parts of Alabama. A southern line from Richmond, recently completed, passes through central North Carolina and South Carolina. By cutting the former of these roads at Cumberland Gap, reënforcements and supplies could not be brought from the southwest to the Confederate army under Gen. Lee. Neither could reënforcements be taken from Gen. Lee's army to Gen. Bragg at Murfreesborough. By cutting the second line the most direct communication between Richmond and the principal cities of the Confederate States was destroyed.

At the time when Gen. Rosecrans was prepared to move from Nashville to attack the Confederate army near Murfreesborough, an expedition was sent into east Tennessee to destroy the railroad, in order to prevent any reënforcements to Gen. Bragg from Richmond. Gen. Carter, with a force of cavalry numbering one thousand men, left London, in Kentucky, on Dec. 21. They entered Virginia between Cumberland Gap and Pound Gap, and advanced within six miles of Bristol, burned the bridges across the Halston and Watauga rivers, and tore up portions of the track, destroying the rails for a distance of nearly one hundred miles, almost to Jonesborough. They captured nearly five hundred prisoners, seven hundred stand of arms, and a large amount of stores. They reached Manchester, Ky., on the 6th of January, having lost only ten men. The enterprise was a most hazardous one.

The expedition against the second line of railroads was undertaken in North Carolina. It forms the only subsequent military movement of importance, in addition to those heretofore described, which was made in that department during the year. It was a march upon Goldsborough, and the destruction of the railroad at that place. This is the line connecting Charleston and Savannah with Richmond. Gen. J. G. Foster, who commanded the department after the departure of Gen. Burnside, took charge of the expedition. The force consisted of four brigades under Cols. Wessels, Amory, Stevenson, and Lee; the 3d New York and 1st Rhode Island batteries; also sections of the 23d and 24th New York Independent batteries, and the 3d New York cavalry. It left Newbern on the morning of Dec. 11, and moved on the Kinston road fourteen miles. Some parts of the road were obstructed by felled trees. On the next morning it advanced to the Vine Swamp road, having some sharp skirmishing with a small Confederate force. At this point three companies of cavalry were sent up the Kinston road as a demonstration, and the main force took the Vine Swamp road, thereby avoiding the obstructions and the Confederate forces. It was delayed to build the bridge over Beaver Creek, where the 51st Massachusetts and a section of artillery were left to hold it, and support the cavalry on the main road, and halted at a distance of four miles. The next morning the main column advanced, turning to the left and leaving the road it was upon to the right. At the intersection the 46th Massachusetts and a section of a battery were left as a feint and to hold the position. On reaching Southwest Creek a Confederate force was found posted on the opposite bank, about four hundred strong, and with three pieces of artillery. The creek was not fordable, and ran at the foot of a deep ravine. Under the protection of a battery the 9th New Jersey effected a passage and formed on the opposite bank, where it was afterward supported by the 85th Pennsylvania. This caused the Confederate force to retire with some skirmishing. On the next day an advance upon Kinston was made, and the Confederate force found posted in a strong position about one mile from the place. An attack was at once made with the 9th New Jersey in advance, and the position taken. The Confederate force retired across the Neuse river, with a loss of four hundred prisoners. On crossing, the bridge was set on fire, but soon extinguished by the advance of Gen. Foster. The bridge was immediately repaired, and the column crossed, and occupied the town of Kinston. With constant skirmishing the force of Gen. Foster continued to advance until the 17th, when it reached Goldsborough. Here it burned two trestle-work culverts, destroyed a train of four railroad cars, water station, depot, &c., and some small arms, which it was unable to carry off. After destroying other bridges, and capturing some small positions that had been occupied by a Confederate force, the expedition successfully returned to Newbern. This enterprise was very skilfully executed. In connection with movements upon Richmond it would have possessed considerable importance, but in the absence of such movements it only served to interfere for a few days with one line of the Confederate internal communication.

These expeditions, although successful in themselves, secured no important advantages as the great movement upon Richmond had, in the mean time, been suspended. They were useful reconnoissances, and the former may have delayed the arrival of reënforcements from Gen. Lee to Gen. Bragg before the battle of Murfreesborough. They developed the importance of these roads to the Richmond Government, and proved that their permanent loss would have caused serious embarrassment to it.

CHAPTER XXV.

Attempt to capture Washington, North Carolina—Expedition from Port Royal—Attack on Baton Rouge—Contest near Donaldsonville—Attack on Vicksburg—Surrender of Natchez—Capture of Galveston—Attack on the Federal Fleet and capture of several Vessels—Military Operations in New Mexico—Expedition to the Indian Territory—Operations in Arkansas and Missouri—Campaign against the Northwestern Indians—Results of the Year.

SOME military movements took place during the year, which have not been stated in the preceding pages, as they were rather isolated operations than a part of the campaign at the time progressing.

On the 6th of September a body of Confederate troops surprised the garrison at Washington, in the Department of North Carolina. A vigorous resistance was made, and the attacking party was repulsed with a loss of thirty-three killed and nearly one hundred wounded. The Federal loss was eight killed and thirty-three wounded.

On the 22d of October an expedition was sent out from Port Royal in the Department of the South, which was then under the command of Gen. Mitchell, to destroy the trestle-work bridges of the Charleston and Savannah Railroad across the Pocotaligo, Tullifinny, and Coosawhatchie, tributaries of the Broad River, and to make a reconnoissance of these streams. The expedition was under the command of Gens. Brannan and Terry. The main body of the troops was landed at Mackey's Point, about fifteen miles from the railroad, and marched seven miles inland, where the Confederates were met in force. After a sharp fight of an hour they retired to a point two miles distant and made a second stand. From this point they again fell back to the village of Pocotaligo, and having burned the long bridge across the stream, they were inaccessible. Meanwhile Col. Barton, with three hundred and fifty men, penetrated to the railroad at Coosawhatchie, and destroyed some of the rails, cut the telegraph wire, and fired upon a train containing troops. The engagement by the main force was severe, and the Federal loss was thirty-two killed, and one hundred and eighty wounded. The Federal force retired on the next day, having failed in the object of the expedition, except the reconnoissance. The rebel loss has not been stated.

On the 5th of August an attack was made on Baton Rouge, in the Department of the Gulf, which was under the command of Gen. Butler. The Federal force of this city was under command of Brig.-Gen. Williams. The Confederate force making the attack was under the command of Gen. John C. Breckinridge. The contest was sharp and bloody, and the attack was successfully repulsed. The Federal loss was ninety killed, and two hundred and fifty wounded. Among the killed was Gen. Williams. Three hundred of the enemy were reported to have been killed and buried by the force of Gen. Williams. The city was subsequently evacuated by the Federal force on May 16.

On the 24th of October Brig.-Gen. Weitzel commanded an expedition from New Orleans to the west bank of the Mississippi in the La Fourche district. An engagement took place with a considerable Confederate force on the next day, about nine miles from Donaldsonville, in which they were defeated with the loss of their commander, and a large number killed and wounded, and two hundred and sixty-eight prisoners. The Federal loss was eighteen killed, and sixty-eight wounded.

No further resistance was made to his march to Thibodeaux, the capital of La Fourche Interior Parish. On the 9th of November all the property of this parish was confiscated by an order of Maj.-Gen. Butler. Citizens who had been loyal to the Government of the United States were to be secured in their rights of property. The plantations not confiscated were to be worked by hired negroes for the benefit of the United States.

In Mississippi, June 17th, Holy Springs was first occupied by Federal troops from the army of Gen. Halleck. This movement of troops in the northern part of the State and the defenceless condition of the counties on the river against the approach of the Federal gunboats caused the removal of the archives of the State from Jackson, the capital, to Columbus, near the border of Alabama. On June 26th the first attack on Vicksburg was made, which continued for eleven days. On September 10th Natchez surrendered to the commander of the gunboat Essex, after a bombardment of two hours. The result of these operations was the firm occupation of the northern extremity of the State by the Federal forces, while the coast at the southern extremity was completely under the control of the Federal naval forces in the neighborhood. Two points on the Mississippi River within the State, Port Hudson and Vicksburg, were strongly fortified by the Richmond Government in order to preserve its communication with Texas, and to prevent the complete control of the river from falling into possession of the

Federal Government. These were measures of the utmost importance to the insurrectionary States.

Some military movements of interest took place on the coast of Texas. On the 17th of May the commander of the Federal naval forces before Galveston, Henry Eagle, summoned the place to surrender "to prevent the effusion of blood and the destruction of property, which would result from the bombardment of the town," also stating that the land and naval forces would appear in a few days. The reply was that "when the land and naval forces made their appearance the demand would be answered." The city, however, was finally taken on the 8th of October. The military and the municipal authorities retired, and the inhabitants appointed a temporary mayor. On the morning of that day Commander Renshaw, with four steamers, approached so as to command the city with the guns of his vessels, and upon a signal the mayor came off to the flagship. The mayor requested Commander Renshaw to communicate to him his intentions in regard to the city, informing him at the same time of its abandonment by the military, of the absence of the mayor and city council, and of his appointment as mayor *pro tem.* by a meeting of citizens.

Commander Renshaw replied that he had come for the purpose of taking possession of the city; that it was at his mercy under his guns; that he should not interfere in the municipal affairs of the city; that the citizens might go on and conduct their business as heretofore; that he did not intend to occupy the city for the present, nor until the arrival of a military commander; but that he intended to hoist the United States flag upon the public buildings, and that his flag should be respected. Whereupon the mayor *pro tem.* answered that he could not guarantee to him the protection of the flag; that he would do every thing in his power, but that persons over whom he had no control might take down the flag and create a difficulty.

Commander Renshaw replied that, although in his previous communications with the military commander he had insisted that the flag should be protected by the city, still he thought it would be onerous upon the good citizens; and, to avoid any difficulty like that which occurred in New Orleans, he would waive that point, and when he sent the flag ashore, he would send a sufficient force to protect it, and that he would not keep the flag flying for more than a quarter or half an hour—sufficient to show the absolute possession.

Commander Renshaw further said that he would insist upon the right for any of his men in charge of an officer to come on shore and walk the streets of the city, but that he would not permit his men to come on shore indiscriminately or in the night; that, should his men insult citizens, he gave the mayor the right to arrest and report them to him, when he would punish them more rigidly than the mayor possibly could; but, on the other hand, should any of his men be insulted or shot at in the streets of Galveston, or any of his ships or boats be shot at from the land or wharves, he would hold the city responsible and open his broadsides on the same instantly; that his guns were kept shotted and double shotted for that purpose; that it was the determination of his Government to hold Galveston at all hazards until the end of the war.

Commander Renshaw thus held the city, in which a small military force was placed, until the 1st of January, 1863, when it was captured by the Texans. The Federal naval force in possession at this time consisted of the gunboats Westfield, Harriet Lane, Clifton, Owasco, Corypheus, and Sachem, the latter being broken down. The troops on shore were two hundred and fifty men under Col. Burrill, of the Massachusetts 42d regiment. On the night previous information was received by the commanding officers of both the land and naval forces that such an attack would be made. At 1.30 A. M. on the night of the 1st two or three Confederate steamers were discovered in the bay by the Clifton and Westfield. Soon after the force on shore was informed by their pickets that the Confederate artillery was in possession of the market place, about one quarter of a mile distant from the wharf on which they were quartered.

The attack commenced on shore about 3 A. M., by the enemy, upon the Federal troops, which were defended by the Sachem and Corypheus, with great energy, the troops only replying with musketry, having no artillery. About dawn the Harriet Lane was attacked, or, rather attacked two Confederate steamers, one of which, the Bayou City, was armed with 68-pounder rifle guns, had 200 troops, and was barricaded with cotton bales, some twenty feet from the water line. The other, the Neptune, was similarly barricaded, and was armed with two small brass pieces and 160 men—(both were common river steamers). The Harriet Lane was under way in time, and went up to the attack, firing her bow gun, which was answered by the Confederates, but their 68-pounder burst at the third fire.

The Harriet Lane then ran into the Bayou City, carrying away her whole guard, passed her and gave her a broadside that did her little or no damage. The other Confederate steamer then ran into the Harriet Lane, but was so disabled by the collision that she was soon afterwards obliged to back in on the flats, where she sunk in about eight feet of water, near to the scene of action. The Bayou City turned into the Harriet Lane, and she remained secured to her by catching under her guard, pouring in incessant volleys of musketry, as did the other steamer, which was returned by the Harriet Lane, with musketry. This drove the Harriet Lane's men from her guns, and probably wounded Commander Wainwright and Lieutenant-

Commander Lee—the latter mortally. She was then carried by boarding, by the Bayou City; her commander was summoned to surrender, which he refused to do, gallantly defending himself with his revolver until killed. But five of the Harriet Lane's men were killed, and five wounded. One hundred and ten, inclusive of officers and wounded men, were landed on shore, prisoners.

The Owasco, which had been anchored below the town, moved up at the commencement of the attack, and engaged the Confederate artillery on shore. When it was light enough for her to observe the two Confederate steamers alongside of the Harriet Lane, she moved up to her assistance, grounding several times, owing to the narrowness of the channel. Occasionally she brought her 11-inch gun to bear, but was soon driven off by the fire of the Confederate musketry. Soon the howitzers of the Harriet Lane opened on her, and she backed down below, continuing her engagement on shore. All her rifle gun crew were wounded.

The Clifton, before the action commenced, went around into Bolivar Channel to render assistance to the steamer Westfield, which had got under way when the Confederate steamers were first discovered. Soon after, she got hard and fast ashore, at high water, and made a signal for assistance. When the Clifton was in the act of rendering this assistance, the flashes of the Confederate guns were first seen in the town. Commander Renshaw then directed Lieutenant Commander Law to leave him and to return to the town.

The moon had now gone down, and it became quite dark, yet the Clifton, with some difficulty, got around in the other channel, opening her batteries upon Fort Point, which the Confederates now had possession of, shelling them out and driving them out up the beach as she neared the town. Here she anchored, and continued the engagement, but did not proceed up to the rescue of the Harriet Lane, owing to the failure of the Owasco, the intricacy of the channel, and the apprehension of killing the crew of the Harriet Lane, who were then exposed upon her upper deck. It was now about half-past seven A. M. A white flag was hoisted on the Harriet Lane. A boat bearing a flag of truce, with a Confederate officer and an acting master of the Harriet Lane, came down to the Clifton, informing her commander of the capture of the Harriet Lane, the death of her commander and first lieutenant, and the killing and wounding of two-thirds of her crew.

The proposition was made by the Confederate officer that all the Federal vessels should surrender, and one be allowed, with the crews of all, to leave the harbor, or they would proceed to capture them with the Harriet Lane and all their steamers, three more of which were in sight. These were neither armed nor barricaded. Upon being informed of this proposition, Commander Renshaw refused to consent, and directed Lieutenant Law to return and get all the vessels out of port as soon as possible, and, as he could not get the Westfield afloat, he should blow her up, and go on board the army transports Saxon and M. A. Bardman, then near him. Lieut. Law returned to execute these directions. Meanwhile, the Confederates had hauled the Harriet Lane alongside the wharf, and had made prisoners of the troops on shore, although it had been understood that all should remain *in statu quo* until the answer was returned. When the Clifton was half way toward the bar, her commander was informed by a boat from the Westfield, that, in the explosion of that vessel (which they observed some half an hour before), Commander Renshaw, Lieutenant Zimmerman, Engineer Green, and some ten or fifteen of the crew, had perished, the explosion being premature. Lieutenant Commander Law, now being commanding officer, proceeded to cross his vessel over the bar, and finally concluded to abandon the blockade altogether, considering the Owasco as his only efficient vessel, and regarding her as not equal to resist an attack from the Harriet Lane, should she come out for that purpose.

The vessels which were left in possession of the enemy were the Harriet Lane, and two coal barks, the Caralto and Elias Pike. The only injury sustained by the Harriet Lane appears to have been from a twelve-inch shell under her counter, fired by the Owasco, and the damage to her guard from the collision.

New Mexico, during the year 1862, was the theatre of some of the most desperate and hard-fought battles of the war. On the 4th of January, 1862, it was ascertained that a Texan force 1,500 strong, under the command of the Confederate General Sibley, were approaching Fort Craig, 200 miles south of Santa Fé, which Col. E. R. Canby held with about 1,000 regular troops and 1,500 volunteers. Finding the Federal force too strong to be attacked, Sibley and his Texans fell back, and did not again approach Fort Craig till they had been largely reënforced. In the last days of January, having received reënforcements, which brought his force up to fully 3,500, the rebel general again advanced slowly and cautiously, in two columns, toward the fort. Col. Canby, hearing, on the 13th of February, from scouts and deserters that the enemy were within 30 miles from Fort Craig, sallied out with a large force to meet and attack them, but could find no trace of them, and returned to the fort. On the 18th the Confederates appeared in front of the fort, about 2,000 strong, but retired the same day, and it was supposed commenced a retreat. Col. Canby despatched Major Duncan, with a squadron of dragoons and mounted men, to follow and harass them. The Texans retreated down the valley of the Rio Grande to a ravine about eight miles below the fort, where they had a battery of eight guns strongly planted. From this, after a strong skirmish, Major Duncan was recalled. On the 19th and 20th the Texans attempted to cross the Rio Grande, in order to take possession of the heights opposite Fort Craig, but were driven back by the Federal forces without material loss on either side. On the 21st a desperate battle was fought, lasting most of the day, at a place called Valverde, about ten miles below Fort Craig. Early in the morning the Federal forces captured 200 mules belonging to the Texans, and burned many of their wagons, and soon crossed the Rio Grande to attack them, with a battery of six pieces and two mountain howitzers. Both parties fought with the greatest desperation, the Texans, to capture the battery, the deadly execution of which cut them off from access to water, for want of which they and their animals were near perishing, and the Federal troops to hold the ground they had gained. The two howitzers were under command of Lieutenant Hall, who successfully, and with great carnage, repulsed their attempts to capture them; the six-gun battery was commanded by Captain McRea, and to the capture of this the main efforts of the Texans were directed. They would not have succeeded, however, had not the new Mexican volunteers (Col. Pino's regiment) been panic-stricken and fled in great disorder, and the regulars refused to obey their commander. The Texans, repeatedly repulsed by the terrible fire of the battery, which was admirably served by Capt. McRea, finally came up to the charge, armed with only their long bowie knives and Colt's revolvers, and though more than half their number fell before they reached it, they finally succeeded in killing all the gunners, and capturing the battery. The brave McRea and his two lieutenants, Michler and Bell, stood at their guns when all the rest had fled, and defended themselves with their revolvers till they were killed. The loss of this battery compelled Col. Canby to fall back to Fort Craig. His loss was 62 killed and 140 wounded; that of Confederates was very much greater, and effectually crippled their subsequent operations. They did not attempt to capture Fort Craig, but proceeded up the Rio Grande to Albuquerque and Santa Fé, both of which towns were evacuated by our forces, which fell back to Fort Union, 100 miles east of Santa Fé, a strong position, where the Government stores for the department were concentrated. Col. Canby intercepted and captured a force of 400 Texans on their way north to reënforce General Sibley. Colonel Slough, in command of a force of 1,300 Colorado mounted volunteers, reached Apache Pass, on the 26th of March, on his way to reënforce Colonel Donelson at Fort Union, and there met a considerable force of Texans, whom, after a severe action, he routed, capturing 100 men and officers, killing and wounding between 300 and 400, and burning 50 loaded wagons. The Federal loss was less than 150 killed and wounded. On the 28th he had another battle at Pigeon's Ranche, twenty-five miles north of Santa Fé, and captured more prisoners and supplies. He then fell back to Fort Union, and there received orders from Col. (now General) Canby to form a junction with his forces at Galesto, which he accomplished on the 9th of April, and there learned that the Texans were retreating from the Territory. Major Duncan, commanding the advance guard of Gen. Canby's forces, had a battle with a body of Texans in the early part of April, and defeated them. Finding themselves hard pressed in their retreat, the Texans took a strong position at Parillo, on the Rio Grande, and fortifying it hastily, awaited an attack there about the middle of April; General Canby attacked them in front, and sent Major Paul, in command of the Colorado troops, to assail them in the rear. After a sharp action, in which the Federal forces lost 25 killed and wounded, the Texans were defeated with great slaughter, and compelled to fly to the mountains. From this point their retreat was a succession of disasters; the destruction of the greater part of their train reduced them to the verge of starvation, and more than one half of the original number were left in New Mexico, as killed, wounded, or prisoners. They reached Nusilla with five pieces of artillery and seven wagons, and even this scanty supply, the small remainder of the magnificent train with which they had invaded the Territory, was destined to be still further diminished before they reached El Paso. With bitter curses on their leaders, who had gone on in advance, and left them to take care of themselves, the half-starved and wretched remnant of the Texan troops, once the flower of the Texas chivalry, made their way, sadly and slowly, homeward, and every point which they left—as for instance, Nusilla, Fort Fillmore, Fort Bliss, and El Paso, was immediately occupied by loyal troops, under the efficient movements of Gen. Carleton.

In the spring of 1862 an expedition was fitted out in the State of Kansas to go south, through the Indian Territory, to reduce the Indian tribes which had joined the Confederacy to subjection, and repossess the U. S. forts, Gibson, Arbuckle, Washita, and Cobb, of which the Confederates had taken possession. The expedition consisted of about 5,000 troops, of which 2,000 were whites and 3,000 loyal Indians. The expedition was unfortunate in its commanders at first: Gen. Blunt having assigned the command to Col. Charles Doubleday, of the Second Ohio cavalry; but, from some political influences, he was removed, and Col. Wm. Weir, of Kansas, substituted. Col. Weir's management was so inefficient and ruinous that Col. Solomon, of the 9th Wisconsin regiment, who commanded one of the brigades, deemed it necessary to arrest him on the charge of insanity. Under Col. Solomon's management the expedition took possession of the Indian Territory, arrested John Ross, the principal Cherokee chief, as being of doubtful sentiment toward the United States, and received professions of loyalty from about two thirds of the Cherokees and Creeks. The Choctaws they found mostly on the side of the South. Large numbers of the slaves of the Indians enlisted in the army of the expedition as "Woolly-headed Indians." The expedition had subdued and held the country north of the Arkansas River before the 25th of July, and Gen. Blunt, on the 8th of August, taking command in person, routed the Confederate force at Maysville, in the northwest corner of Arkansas, on the 22d of Oct.; on the 28th and 29th of Nov. he again met and defeated, with heavy loss, the Confederate forces under Gen. Marmaduke, at Cane Hill, Ark.; on the 7th of December he defeated and scattered a greatly superior force (28,000) of the enemy under Gen. Hindman, at Prairie Grove, Ark., his loss being about 1,000, and that of the Confederates 1,500, the Confederates retreating in the night, abandoning their dead and wounded; and on the 27th and 28th of Dec. Gens. Herron and Blunt defeated two regiments of rebel cavalry at Dupping Spring, and captured Van Buren, a strong fortress on the Arkansas River, taking one hundred and twenty prisoners, and four steamboats laden with stores.

After the military movements in the northwestern part of Arkansas, including the battle of Pea Ridge, related on a previous page, Gen. Curtis moved to the White River, and occupied Batesville about the 1st of May. Here he was met by many demonstrations of attachment to the Union. Many citizens came forward and took the oath of allegiance to the United States; these were judges of courts, clergymen, and citizens holding positions of influence. His advance being pushed forward on the road to Little Rock, a great excitement was produced there. The governor issued a proclamation calling upon the State militia to repair immediately to its defence. Finding himself not sufficiently supported, Gov. Rector fled, and the State was left without any executive government. Martial law was then declared by Brig.-Gen. Roane, commanding the department, and George C. Watkins was appointed provost marshal. The weakness of Arkansas at this moment was caused by the concentration of all the rebel military strength at Corinth, and her fate was as much involved in the security of that position as the fate of Tennessee or Mississippi. But while the forces of Arkansas were taken to defend Corinth, ten regiments were taken from Gen. Curtis to reënforce the Federal troops attacking it. This left him in no condition to march upon Little Rock, and the capital of the State thus escaped being captured.

On the 19th of May a skirmish took place near Searcy, between one hundred and fifty men of Col. (acting Brig.-Gen.) Osterhaus's division and a State force under Cols. Coleman and Hicks. The loss was small on both sides. Other skirmishes occurred during the march of Gen. Curtis from Batesville to Helena, of small importance. Bridges were burned by the Arkansas troops across Bayou des Arc and Cypress River, and about ten thousand bales of cotton on the Arkansas River, and all the cotton and sugar at Jacksonport. By the first of June, twelve thousand men were collected at Little Rock in answer to the call of the governor, but were very destitute of arms. The State records, however, had been removed to Arkadelphia.

After Gen. Curtis had occupied Helena, the Federal Government appointed John S. Phelps of Missouri, military governor, and Col. Wm. F. Switzler secretary for Arkansas. He left St. Louis on Aug. 19, for Helena. It was contemplated at this time that a movement on Little Rock would be made. This however was not done, and the office of governor became of little importance. Two regiments were organized at Helena, composed of citizens of Arkansas; they were chiefly men who had suffered in consequence of their attachment to the Union, and were refugees.

In Missouri disturbances continued. During the summer the guerrillas became exceedingly troublesome.

On June 22, Gen. Schofield issued an order holding "rebels and rebel sympathizers responsible in their property, and, if need be, in their persons, for damages thereafter committed by guerrillas or marauding parties." This had so so little effect that by the middle of July the whole northern and western parts of the State were disturbed by rumors of guerrilla raids and outrages. In the northeast quarter Col. Porter and Col. Quantrell began, as early as the last week in June, to gather followers about them, and early in July the former was defeated and his band dispersed, at Cherry Grove, in Schuyler County, on the Iowa line.

The increasing alarm in the State, heightened by the apprehension that the sudden rising of the guerrillas was to be followed by another invasion from the South, caused vigorous measures of defence, and on July 22d an order from Gen. Schofield for the immediate organization of all the militia of Missouri. The organization was effected with energy and rapidity, and in a brief space of time the forces of the State were prepared to make vigorous opposition to the guerrillas in all quarters.

On July 28, Cols. Porter and Cobb were defeated in Calloway County, on the Missouri River; but within three days the former captured Newark, in Knox County, with two companies of national troops. About the same time a new partisan leader, Col. Poindexter, began to be active in the central counties on the Missouri, and during the first week in August his movements, together with those of Col. Quantrell in the west, compelled the national commanders to take additional measures of precaution. On August 6th, Col. Porter was disastrously defeated by Col. McNeil, at Kirksville, in Adair County, and for several weeks was compelled to keep aloof from active operations. As a consequence, the war shifted to central and western Missouri, where Cols. Coffee and McBride were reported to have come to the assistance of Col. Quantrell.

After a series of desultory skirmishes, an attack was made on the 13th by the combined bands of these leaders, who had been joined a short time previously by Col. Hughes, and other officers of the Confederate army, upon Independence, resulting in a severe defeat of the State troops; and two days later a body of 800 of the latter were drawn into an ambuscade at Lone Jack, Jackson County, by Cols. Quantrell and Coffee, losing two pieces of cannon, and a number of prisoners. Heavy reënforcements under Gen. Blunt, of Kansas, coming up, however, the guerrillas beat a hasty retreat southward, and never paused until they were over the Arkansas line.

Scarcely was the southwest cleared of guerrillas than their operations commenced in the north with renewed activity. Col. Poindexter, after several defeats, was captured early in September, but so daring were the raids of Col. Porter and his followers in Lewis, Maria, and other northeastern counties, that a Palmyra newspaper declared the whole of that part of the State "to be in the possession of the rebels, with the exception of the posts immediately garrisoned by State or United States troops." It estimated the number of the Confederates at 5,000, divided into numerous small bands, and commanded by reckless and enterprising leaders. On the 12th, Palmyra, occupied by a small Union garrison, was plundered by Col. Porter's force; but, subsequent to the 15th, the efforts of Cols. McNeil, Guitar, and other Union commanders began to discourage the guerrillas, whose strength was gradually frittered away in petty combats.

By an order from the War Department of September 19, the States of Missouri, Kansas, and Arkansas were formed into a military district, under the command of Gen. Curtis, and soon after Gen. Schofield assumed command of the so-called "Army of the Frontier" in southern Missouri. Moving with rapidity and in considerable force, he broke up a formidable camp in Newtonia, and by the 10th of October had driven the enemy completely over the Arkansas border. In the latter part of the same month Cols. Lazear and Dewry defeated the Confederate bands in southeastern Missouri in several engagements, capturing many prisoners, and driving them finally into Arkansas. Col. Quantrell had reappeared in the west in the middle of September, but was almost uniformly beaten in his encounters with the State troops, and by the end of October the war, both there and in the north, was practically ended.

Before this event was consummated in the north an incident occurred in Palmyra, which created no little comment throughout the State. On the occasion of Col. Porter's raid upon Palmyra, in September, he had captured, among other persons, an old and respected resident of the place, by name Andrew Allsman, who had formerly belonged to a cavalry regiment, and had been, from his knowledge of the surrounding country, of great service to scouting parties sent out to arrest disloyal persons. Allsman was not paroled like ordinary prisoners, but was conveyed by the band to one of their hiding places, and from the known hatred of his captors and their repeated threats, it was believed that he would be summarily executed by them. When several weeks had elapsed without intelligence of him, this belief ripened in the minds of his friends into absolute conviction, particularly as several Union men had been barbarously murdered by the guerrillas in the course of the campaign.

When Gen. McNeil returned to Palmyra, and ascertained the circumstances under which Allsman had been abducted, he caused to be issued, after due deliberation, the following notice:

PALMYRA (MO.), *October* 8, 1862.

JOSEPH C. PORTER,—SIR: Andrew Allsman, an aged citizen of Palmyra, and a non-combatant, having been carried from his home by a band of persons unlawfully arrayed against the peace and good order of the State of Missouri, and which band was under your control, this is to notify you that unless said Andrew Allsman is returned unharmed to his family within ten days from date, ten men who have belonged to your band, and unlawfully sworn by you to carry arms against the Government of the United States, and who are now in custody, will be shot, as a meet reward for their crimes, amongst which is the illegal restraining of said Allsman of his liberty, and, if not returned, presumptively aiding in his murder. Your prompt attention to this will save much suffering.

Yours, &c. W. R. STRACHAN.
Provost Marshal General,
District N. E. Missouri. Per order of Brigadier-Gen. Commanding McNeil's column.

A written duplicate of this notice he caused to be placed in the hands of the wife of Joseph C. Porter, at her residence in Lewis County, it being well known that she was in frequent communication with her husband. The notice was published widely, and as Porter was in northeast Missouri during the whole of the ten days subsequent to the date of this notice, it is supposed to be impossible that he should have been unaware of Gen. McNeil's determination in the premises.

The ten days having elapsed without tidings of Allsman, ten prisoners, already in custody, were selected to pay with their lives the penalty demanded.

They received the announcement for the most part with composure or indifference, and were executed at Palmyra, on October 18, in the presence of a multitude of spectators, in literal accordance with the notice of Gen. McNeil.

In order to complete the history of the military operations of 1862, the proceedings against the Indians in Minnesota remain to be described. During the spring and early summer of 1862, reports from various sources reached the United States Government, indicating that the Indian tribes of Utah, Colorado, Dakota, and Western Nebraska, would ravage the Territories and frontier States. It was said that emissaries from the Southern Confederacy had been among them, stimulating them to rise and plunder and destroy the frontier settlements; and to encourage them in this movement, they were told that the United States Government was broken up by the South, and could make no resistance. Adventurers from Canada, too, had visited them in the early part of the year, urging them to bring their furs across the boundary, and assuring them that they should be aided with money and arms to drive the Americans from their lands. The Indians, while thus prompted to insurrection by evil and designing men from both north and south of their hunting fields, had also many imaginary and some real grounds of complaint against the Indian agents sent among them by the United States Government. Some of these had proved unworthy of their trust; had swindled and defrauded the Indians, and had treated them with harshness; and though these were the exceptions, and perhaps rare exceptions, yet the delay in paying the Indian annuities, owing to the negligence of the Indian bureau, and the attempt on the part of some of the agents to pay them in legal tender notes instead of gold, which the Government had furnished, aroused distrust in the minds of the Red men, and led them to plot revenge.

The reports which reached the Department of the Interior had given rise to so much apprehension that the Commissioner of Indian Affairs published in the summer an advertisement warning the public of the dangers in taking the overland route to the Pacific.

Meantime the settlers in Western Minnesota were entirely unsuspicious of danger. A large proportion of these settlers were Germans, especially in Brown and the adjacent counties; a considerable number were Norwegians, and the remainder generally of American birth. Most of them had purchased considerable farms, and they had built up small but thriving villages throughout the tier of western counties. They were on terms of friendship with the Indians, had no apprehension of any treachery from them.

Though an insurrection had been deliberately planned, there is reason to believe that the massacre was precipitated somewhat sooner than was at first intended. On the 17th of August, four drunken Indians belonging to Little Crow's band of Sioux, roaming through the country and becoming intoxicated on whiskey obtained from a white man, had a violent altercation with each other as to which of them was the bravest, and finally determined that the test of their bravery should be the killing of a white man. After committing several murders, and becoming somewhat sober, they fled to their village (Red Wood), and told their chief, Little Crow, who was one of the conspirators, what they had done. He, expecting retaliation for this outrage, at once determined upon commencing the intended attack, and on the morning of the 18th, with a force of two hundred and fifty or three hundred Indians, proceeded to the agency at Yellow Medicine and engaged in an indiscriminate slaughter of all the whites he could find there. Mr. Galbraith, the agent, was absent, having left home three days before, but his family were among the victims of this murderous assault. A force of forty-five soldiers, sent up from Fort Ridgley at the first rumour of disturbance, were attacked by the Indians in ambush, and half their number slain. The marauders, flushed with success, pressed on with their work of death, murdering, with the most atrocious brutalities, the settlers in their isolated farmhouses, violating and then killing women, beating out the brains of infants or nailing them to the doors of houses, and practising every species of atrocity which their fiendish natures prompted. On the 21st of August they had attacked New Ulm, a flourishing German settlement, the capital of Brown County, with a large force, had beleaguered Fort Ridgley, and were advancing upon other settlements. The only Indians engaged in these outrages were Sioux, and that portion of them under the special command of Little Crow. The Chippewas, the inveterate enemies of the Sioux, who had also a reservation in Minnesota, were uneasy, and assumed a threatening attitude. They alleged gross frauds on the part of their agent, who escaped from the reservation and committed suicide; but they took no part in the Sioux massacres, and, indeed, a few weeks later, offered to raise a force of their warriors to fight the Sioux, an offer which the Government did not think it wise to accept. On the first intelligence of this insurrection Governor Ramsey sent four companies of the 6th regiment of volunteers from Fort Snelling, and, two days later, on fuller information, he sent forward seven companies more. Col. (now Gen.) H. H. Sibley, who had thirty years' experience among the Indians on the frontier, was placed in command. Mounted volunteers were also called for by proclamation to join these forces, and large numbers obeyed the call. The 3d Minnesota regiment, then on parole at St. Louis, was also ordered to report at St. Paul, and arrived there on the 4th of September.

On the 23d of August New Ulm was attacked by the Indians, who were repulsed after a severe battle by a body of the citizens, under Judge Flandrau; but remained in the vicinity, intending to renew the assault. The next day a detachment of Col. Sibley's troops relieved them from siege, and scattered the marauders; but as two thousand women and children, who had fled in terror from the surrounding region, had taken refuge there, it was deemed best to evacuate the place, in order to convey them to a place of permanent safety. Fort Ridgley had been besieged for nine days, and its little garrison had sustained and repelled three desperate attacks; they were relieved on the 26th by a force under the command of Lieut.-Col. McPhail, sent forward by Col. Sibley. Finding a large force concentrating on their trail in this direction, the greater part of the Indians proceeded northward, burning and killing every thing in their way, toward Breckinridge, a town at the junction of the Bois des Sioux and Red River of the North, which at that point formed the west boundary of the State, massacred the settlers there, and crossing the river, laid siege to Fort Abercrombie in Dakota Territory. Intelligence of these movements having reached St. Paul on the 27th, two companies were forwarded at once to reënforce Fort Abercrombie. On the 3d of September a force of one hundred and fifty Indians unexpectedly appeared at Cedar City, in McLeod County, in the centre of the State, attacked a company of volunteers there, and drove them to Hutchinson, while another band about as numerous attacked Forest City not far distant, and were repulsed by the citizens. A few days later the Indians attacked Hutchinson, but were repulsed. Troops were sent at once to these points. Driven back here, the savages next extended their raid to Jackson, Noble, and Pipeston Counties, in the S. W. part of the State on the border of Iowa, and Col. Flandrau, who had so valiantly defended New Ulm, was sent with five hundred troops to protect that region. Gov. Ramsey had meantime apprised the United States Government of the condition of affairs, and had called the Legislature of Minnesota together to meet in extra session on the 9th of September. At their assembling he laid before them, in his message, the circumstances of the Indian insurrection, and suggested the measures requiring their action, all of which were promptly passed. Meantime the Government had despatched Maj.-Gen. Pope to command in that department, and aid in suppressing the insurrection. The Indians, finding a force greatly superior to their own ready to take vengeance on them for the terrible and dastardly outrages they had committed, began to withdraw from the region they had desolated. A force of three or four hundred of them made two assaults in September on Fort Abercrombie, but were repulsed in both, the second time with heavy loss; the larger part of those who had invaded the central and southwestern portions of the State, fled toward the western border, but were overtaken and brought to bay at Wood Lake on the 22d of September, where, after a sharp battle they were utterly defeated, and Little Crow, with his women and children, fled to the Yankton Sioux of Dakota Territory. About five hundred Indians were taken prisoners, and four hundred and ninety-eight were tried by court-martial, of whom three hundred were sentenced to be hung. The President ordered, however, that only thirty-eight of these should be executed, while the remainder were kept in confinement until further investigation could be had. One of the thirty-eight executed on the 26th of December was a negro named Godfrey, who had been a leader in the massacres, and it was said had killed more than any one of the Indians.

The whole number of Indian warriors among the Minnesota Sioux did not exceed 1,000 or 1,200, and many of these had taken no part in the insurrection, so that probably the killed and captured constituted the greater part of the insurgents. This defeat and prompt arrest of the assailants carried terror into the hearts of the other Indian tribes in the vicinity; and though there have been occasional symptoms of uneasiness since that time among some of the Indians of that region, and the inhabitants of Minnesota cannot feel safe with such treacherous and bloodthirsty foes so near them, it is hardly probable that there will be another uprising for some years. The citizens are desirous the Government should remove the Indians.

The loss of life in this insurrection has never been accurately ascertained. Gov. Ramsey, in his message, stated it in round numbers at eight hundred, a number undoubtedly larger than subsequent facts would sustain. Some of the writers from the region in which it occurred speak of it as not exceeding one hundred, which is probably as great an error in the other direction. Eighty-five were buried at Yellow Medicine, nearly all of whom were horribly mutilated, and a considerable number at New Ulm, Breckinridge, Birch Coolie, Fort Abercrombie, Red Lake, Red Wood, and Wood Lake, and many more in the isolated farm houses in the extensive tract overrun by the savages. Probably not far from five hundred in all lost their lives, either through the ferocity of the Indians or from the sickness, suffering, and starvation which resulted from their hasty flight from their homes. Between 20,000 and 30,000 persons thus fled for their lives, leaving every thing behind them. A part afterwards returned, others found their way to their friends at the East, but for some months between 6,000 and 7,000, mostly women and children, were necessarily dependent upon charity. The people of the State contributed most liberally to their relief, and considerable sums were forwarded from other States.

The following list of the most important military events, with the date when they occurred, presents a more summary view of the great magnitude of the simultaneous operations in 1862:

Burnside sails	Jan.	12
Mill Springs (Ky.), battle	Jan.	19
Cedar Keys (Fla.) captured	Jan.	16
Fort Henry (Ky.), captured	Feb.	6
Roanoke Island (N. C.), captured	Feb.	7
Elizabeth (N. C.), captured	Feb.	8
Edenton (N. C.), captured	Feb.	12
Springfield (Mo.), captured	Feb.	14
Donelson (Ky.), captured	Feb.	16
Bowling Green (Ky.), evacuated	Feb.	17
Fayetteville (Ark.), occupied	Feb.	18
Clarkville (Tenn.), occupied	Feb.	19
Winton (N. C.), occupied	Feb.	20
Nashville (Tenn.), occupied	Feb.	24
Columbus (Ky.), evacuated	March	1
Fernandina (Fla.), captured	March	3
St. Mary (Fla.), captured	March	3
Pea Ridge (Ark.), battle	March	6, 7
Brunswick (Ga.), captured	March	8
Jacksonville (Fla.), captured	March	12
St. Augustine (Fla.), captured	March	14
Newbern (N. C.), captured	March	14
New Madrid (Mo.), captured	March	14

Washington (N. C.), captured	March	25
Shiloh (Tenn.), battle	April	6, 7
Island No. 10, evacuated	April	7
Huntsville (Ala.), captured	April	8
Decatur and Stevenson (Ala.), captured	April	9
Fort Pulaski (Ga.), captured	April	11
Fort Macon (N. C.), captured	April	25
New Orleans, captured	April	26
Yorktown (Va.), evacuated	May	3
Williamsburg (Va.), evacuated	May	6
Pensacola (Fla.), evacuated	May	9
Norfolk, captured	May	10
Baton Rouge, occupied	May	27
Corinth (Miss.), evacuated	May	29
Fair Oaks (Va.), battle	May	31
Fort Pillow, evacuated	June	5
Memphis (Tenn.), surrenders	June	6
Cross Keys, battle	June	8
Cumberland Gap, occupied	June	18
Seven days before Richmond	June	25, &c.
Malvern Hill, battle	July	1
Baton Rouge, attack	Aug.	5
Cedar Mountain, battle	Aug.	9
Rappahannock Bridge	Aug.	23
Centreville (Va.), battle	Aug.	28
Manassas (Va.), battle	Aug.	30
Chantilly (Va.), battle	Sept.	1
Munfordsville (Ky.), battle	Sept.	14
South Mountain, battle	Sept.	14
Antietam, battle	Sept.	17
Iuka (Miss.), battle	Sept.	19
Corinth (Miss.), battle	Oct.	4
Perryville (Ky.), battle	Oct.	8
Holly Springs (Miss.)	Nov.	13
Cane Hill (Ark.), battle	Nov.	28
Crawford's Prairie (Ark.), battle	Dec.	7
Fredericksburg (Va.), battle	Dec.	13
Murfreesboro (Tenn.), battle	Dec.	31

What had been accomplished by the military operations of the year:—The State of Missouri had been relieved from invasion by the Confederate force. Half of Arkansas had been permanently occupied. The Confederate force has been driven from the Mississippi River except at Vicksburg and Port Hudson. Western and Middle Tennessee were occupied, and the former and part of the latter held. Western Virginia had been retained by the Federal Government. Maryland exhibited her preference for the Union. Norfolk and Yorktown were taken and held. The cities and towns on the coast of North Carolina, with few exceptions, were occupied by a Federal force. Fort Pulaski, commanding the entrance to Savannah, was captured, and the important points on the coast of Florida occupied. Pensacola and New Orleans were also taken, and nearly all of Louisiana brought under Federal control. The forces of the North slowly but firmly advanced upon every side of the Confederacy, and permanently held every important position which they had gained. The battle of Antietam secured the border States, and decided the physical supremacy of the Union in favor of the North.

CHAPTER XXVI.

The Emancipation Proclamation—Action of Congress—Oath of Office required—Organization of West Virginia as a State Proceedings relative to the exchange of Prisoners—The Cartel agreed upon—Difficulties—Officers in the Insurrectionary Service—Condition of Gen. Lee's Army in the Autumn of 1862—Appeal to the Southern People—Condition of the Federal Army—Organization of a Provost Marshal's Department.

On January 1, 1863, the President issued his emancipation proclamation, and its principles were adopted as controlling the policy of the Government in the future. The proclamation was as follows:

Whereas on the 22d day of September, in the year or our Lord one thousand eight hundred and sixty-two, a proclamation was issued by the President of the United States, containing, among other things, the following, to wit:

"That on the first day of January, in the year of our Lord one thousand eight hundred and sixty-three, all persons held as slaves within any States or designated part of a State, the people whereof shall then be in rebellion against the United States, shall be then, thenceforward, and forever free; and the Executive Government of the United States, including the military and naval authority thereof, will recognize and maintain the freedom of such persons, and will do no act or acts to repress such persons, or any of them, in any efforts they may make for their actual freedom.

"That the Executive will, on the first day of January aforesaid, by proclamation, designate the States and parts of States, if any, in which the people thereof, respectively, shall then be in rebellion against the United States; and the fact that any State, or the people thereof, shall on that day be in good faith represented in the Congress of the United States, by members chosen thereto at elections wherein a majority of the qualified voters of such State shall have participated, shall, in the absence of strong countervailing testimony, be deemed conclusive evidence that such State and the people thereof, are not then in rebellion against the United States."

Now, therefore, I, Abraham Lincoln, President of the United States, by virtue of the power in me vested as Commander-in-Chief of the Army and Navy of the United States in time of actual armed rebellion against the authority and Government of the United States, and as a fit and necessary war measure for suppressing said rebellion, do, on this first day of January, in the year of our Lord one thousand eight hundred and sixty-three, and in accordance with my purpose so to do, publicly proclaimed for the full period of one hundred days, from the day first above mentioned, order and designate as the States and parts of States wherein the people thereof respectively are this day in rebellion against the United States, the following, to wit,

Arkansas, Texas, Louisiana (except the parishes of St. Bernard, Plaquemines, Jefferson, St. John, St. Charles, St. James, Ascension, Assumption, Terre Bonne, Lafourche, Ste. Marie, St. Martin, and Orleans, including the city of New Orleans,) Mississippi, Alabama, Florida, Georgia, South Carolina, North Carolina, and Virginia (except the forty-eight counties designated as West Virginia, and also the counties of Berkeley, Accomac, Northampton, Elizabeth City, York, Princess Ann, and Norfolk, including the cities of Norfolk and Portsmouth), and which excepted parts are for the present left precisely as if this proclamation were not issued.

And by virtue of the power and for the purpose aforesaid, I do order and declare that all persons held as slaves within said designated States and parts of States are and henceforward shall be free; and that the Executive Government of the United States, including the military and naval authorities thereof, will recognize and maintain the freedom of said persons.

And I hereby enjoin upon the people so declared to be free to abstain from all violence, unless in necessary self-defence; and I recommend to them that, in all cases when allowed, they labor faithfully for reasonable wages.

And I further declare and make known that such persons, of suitable condition, will be received into the armed service of the United States to garrison forts, positions, stations, and other places, and to man vessels of all sorts in said service.

And upon this act, sincerely believed to be an act of justice, warranted by the Constitution upon military necessity, I invoke the considerate judgment of mankind, and the gracious favor of Almighty God.

In testimony whereof I have hereunto set my name, and caused the seal of the United States to be affixed.

[L. S.] Done at the city of Washington this first day of January, in the year of our Lord one thousand eight hundred and sixty-three, and of the independence of the United States the eighty-seventh.

ABRAHAM LINCOLN.

By the President:

WILLIAM H. SEWARD, Secretary of State.

Congress in the session of 1861–'62 had taken action looking to this object. An act was passed for the abolition of slavery in the District of Columbia. It emancipated all persons of African descent held to service in the District immediately upon its passage; loyal owners of slaves only were allowed ninety days to prepare and present to commissioners appointed for that purpose the names, ages, and personal description of their slaves, who were to be valued by the commissioners. No single slave could be estimated to be worth more than three hundred dollars. The amount of these claims was to be paid to each owner after the final report of the commissioners at the end of nine months. One million of dollars was appropriated to carry the act into effect. The sum of one hundred thousand dollars was appropriated to colonize any of the liberated slaves who might desire to go to Hayti, Liberia, or any country beyond the limits of the United States, as the President might select.

Slavery was forbidden in all the Territories of the United States. Liberia and Hayti were recognized as independent republics, and as belonging to the family of nations. A new treaty, relative to the slave trade, was ratified with Great Britain, which allowed to her the liberty of searching American vessels under certain circumstances. All persons in the army or navy were prohibited from returning slaves, or sitting in judgment on the claim of their masters.

An act was also passed requiring every person afterwards elected or appointed to any office of honor or profit under the Government of the United States, either in the civil, military, or naval departments, except the President, to take the following oath before entering upon the duties of such office:

I, A B, do solemnly swear (or affirm) that I have never voluntarily borne arms against the United States since I have been a citizen thereof; that I have voluntarily given no aid, countenance, counsel, or encouragement to persons engaged in armed hostility thereto; that I have neither sought, nor accepted, nor attempted to exercise the functions of any office whatever, under any authority or pretended authority in hostility to the United States; that I have not yielded a voluntary support to any pretended government, authority, power, or constitution within the United States, hostile or inimical thereto. And I do further swear (or affirm) that to the best of my knowledge and ability, I will support and defend the Constitution of the United States against all enemies, foreign and domestic; that I will bear true faith and allegiance to the same; that I take this obligation freely, without any mental reservation or purpose of evasion, and that I will well and faithfully discharge the duties of the office on which I am about to enter, so help me God.

Meantime steps had been taken to organize an independent State of that portion of Virginia west of the mountains. On a previous page it has been related that on the secession of Virginia a convention of loyal citizens assembled at Clarksburg. This convention declared the ordinance of secession to be null and void; that its provision suspending the election of members of the Federal Government was a usurpation, and that if the ordinance of secession was ratified by a vote they recommended the election on June 4th of delegates to a general convention to be held on the 11th to devise such measures as the welfare of the people might demand. This convention met at Wheeling. Meantime nearly all the judicial and executive officers in that part of the State had fled to Richmond before the Federal forces. Legal protection to life, liberty, or property was given up. This convention declared the office of governor, &c., vacant, "by reason of those who occupied them having joined the rebellion," and proceeded to fill those offices. The action of this convention was not confined to Western Virginia, but intended to embrace the whole State. The governor elected thus stated the object of the convention:

It was not the object of the Wheeling convention to set up any new government in the State, or separate or other government than the one under which they had always lived. They made a single alteration in the Constitution of the State, which prescribes the number of delegates in the General Assembly which shall be necessary to constitute a quorum.

A declaration was made by the convention, and an ordinance adopted for the reorganization of the State Government. According to this ordinance the Government to be reorganized, either in its executive or legislative departments, was not for a part of the State, but for all of Virginia. In conformity with this ordinance a State Government was reorganized in all its branches in every county of the State not occupied by an armed foe.

On the 20th of August, 1861, the convention

passed an ordinance "to provide for the formation of a new State out of a portion of the territory of this State." In compliance with its provisions delegates were elected to a constitutional convention which assembled at Wheeling, November 26, 1861, and proceeded to draft a Constitution, which was submitted to the people on the first Thursday of April, 1862. The vote in favor was 18,862, that against it was 514.

The governor appointed by the convention of June, 1861, which declared the State offices vacant, now issued his proclamation convening an extra session of the Legislature, elected and organized under the same authority, and which claimed to be the Legislature of Virginia. This Legislature met on the 6th of May, 1862, and passed an act, giving its consent to the formation of a new State, and forwarded its consent to the Congress of the United States, together with an official copy of the Constitution adopted by the voters, and with the request that the said new State be admitted into the Union.

On the 31st of December, 1862, the following act of Congress was approved by the President:

An act for the admission of the State of "West Virginia" into the Union, and for other purposes.

Whereas the people inhabiting that portion of Virginia known as West Virginia did, by a convention assembled in the city of Wheeling on the twenty-sixth of November, eighteen hundred and sixty-one, frame for themselves a Constitution, with a view of becoming a separate and independent State; and *whereas* at a general election held in the counties composing the territory aforesaid on the third day of May last, the said Constitution was approved and adopted by the qualified voters of the proposed State, and *whereas* the Legislature of Virginia, by an act passed on the thirteenth day of May, eighteen hundred and sixty-two, did give its consent to the formation of a new State within the jurisdiction of the said State of Virginia, to be known by the name of West Virginia, and to embrace the following named counties, to wit: Hancock, Brooke, Ohio, Marshall, Wetzel, Marion, Monongalia, Preston, Taylor, Tyler, Pleasants, Ritchie, Doddridge, Harrison, Wood, Jackson, Wirt, Roane, Calhoun, Gilmer, Barbour, Tucker, Lewis, Braxton, Upshur, Randolph, Mason, Putnam, Kanawha, Clay, Nicholas, Cabell, Wayne, Boone, Logan, Wyoming, Mercer, McDowell, Webster, Pocahontas, Fayette, Raleigh, Greenbrier, Monroe, Pendleton, Hardy, Hampshire, and Morgan; and *whereas* both the convention and the Legislature aforesaid have requested that the new State should be admitted into the Union, and the Constitution aforesaid being republican in form, Congress doth hereby consent that the said forty-eight counties may be formed into a separate and independent State. Therefore—

Be it enacted by the Senate and House of Representatives of the United States of America in Congress assembled, That the State of West Virginia be and is hereby declared to be one of the United States of America, and admitted into the Union on an equal footing with the original States in all respects whatever, and until the next general census shall be entitled to three members in the House of Representatives of the United States: *Provided, always,* That this act shall not take effect until after the proclamation of the President of the United States hereinafter provided for.

It being represented to Congress that since the convention of the twenty-sixth of November, eighteen hundred and sixty-one, that framed and proposed the Constitution for the said State of West Virginia, the people thereof have expressed a wish to change the seventh section of the eleventh article of said Constitution by striking out the same and inserting the following in its place, viz.: "The children of slaves born within the limits of this State after the fourth day of July, eighteen hundred and sixty-three, shall be free; and that all slaves within the said State who shall, at the time aforesaid, be under the age of ten years, shall be free when they arrive at the age of twenty-one years; and all slaves over ten and under twenty-one years, shall be free when they arrive at the age of twenty-five years; and no slave shall be permitted to come into the State for permanent residence therein:" Therefore,

SEC. 2. *Be it further enacted,* That whenever the people of West Virginia shall, through their said convention, and by a vote to be taken at an election to be held within the limits of the said State, at such time as the convention may provide, make and ratify the change aforesaid, and properly certify the same under the hand of the President of the Convention, it shall be lawful for the President of the United States to issue his proclamation stating the fact, and thereupon this act shall take effect and be in force from and after sixty days from the date of said proclamation.

Approved December 31, 1862.

These conditions were subsequently complied with by the citizens, and the President of the United States issued his proclamation accordingly.

The following is a provision of the Constitution of the United States: "New States may be admitted by the Congress into this Union; but no new States shall be formed or erected within the jurisdiction of any other State, nor any State be formed by the junction of two or more States, or parts of States, without the consent of the Legislatures of the States concerned, as well as of the Congress."

The following is the population of the counties embraced in this new State according to the census of 1860:

COUNTIES.	White population.	Slaves.	COUNTIES.	White population.	Slaves.
Hancock.....	4,442	2	Lewis........	7,736	230
Brooke	5,425	18	Gilmer.......	3,685	52
Ohio.........	22,196	100	Calhoun......	2,492	9
Marshall.....	12,936	29	Braxton......	4,885	104
Wetzel......	6,691	10	Clay.........	1,761	21
Pleasants....	2,926	15	Nicholas......	4,470	154
Wood	10,791	176	Fayette.......	5,716	271
Jackson.....	8,240	55	Raleigh.......	3,291	57
Mason	8,752	886	Wyoming	2,797	64
Cabell.......	7,691	305	McDowell....	1,535	..
Wayne......	6,604	143	Mercer.......	6,428	862
Logan.......	4,789	148	Monroe.......	9,526	1,114
Boone.......	4,681	158	Greenbrier...	10,499	1,525
Kanawha....	13,787	2,184	Pocahontas...	3,686	252
Roane.......	5,309	72	Webster......	1,552	3
Wirt	3,728	23	Upshur.......	7,064	212
Ritchie......	6,809	38	Randolph.....	4,793	183
Doddridge..	5,168	34	Tucker.......	1,396	20
Tyler........	6,488	18	Putnam......	5,708	580
Harrison.....	13,185	582	Pendleton....	5,873	244
Marion......	12,656	63	Hardy........	8,521	1,073
Monongalia..	12,907	101	Hampshire	12,481	1,213
Preston......	13,183	67	Morgan.......	3,613	94
Taylor.......	7,300	112			
Barbour.....	8,729	95	Total, 48 cos..	334,921	12,771

The officers of West Virginia, at the close of 1862, were Francis H. Pierpont, governor; Daniel Palsley, lieutenant-governor; Lucian A. Hugans, secretary; Campbell Tarr, treasurer.

The exchange of prisoners was attended with difficulties through the whole year 1862. After the refusal to receive within the Southern lines the commissioners appointed by the Federal Government at the close of 1861, negotiations were opened by them at Norfolk, which resulted in an agreement for an equal exchange; and the Confederates, having about 300 prisoners in excess of those taken by the national troops, proposed to release them also, on parole, provided the United States Government would agree to release three hundred Confederates who might thereafter fall into their hands. On February 14th the commissioners returned to Washington, and the arrangement entered into by them having been approved by the War Department, Gen. Wool was directed to inform the rebel general Huger, commanding at Norfolk, that he had full authority to settle the terms of the proposed exchange. Gen. Howell Cobb was designated by the Richmond Government to confer with Gen. Wool, and a permanent plan was settled between them on the basis previously established. By the terms of this plan it was agreed that the prisoners of war in the hands of each Government should be exchanged, man for man, the officers being assimilated as to rank, &c.; that the privateersmen captured by the United States forces during the previous year, and who had been held as having lost the rights of war, should be exchanged on the footing of ordinary prisoners of war; that any surplus remaining on either side after these exchanges should be released; and that hereafter, during the continuance of the war, prisoners taken on either side should be paroled. The clause relating to the privateersmen was considered an important concession on the part of the National Government, public opinion in the North having demanded that exemplary punishment should be inflicted on this class of prisoners, for which reason they had been for a number of months held in strict confinement in the city prison at Washington. As a retaliatory measure, the Confederates selected a number of Union prisoners, including Cols. Corcoran and Wilcox, and other high officers, whom they declared hostages for the safety of the privateersmen.

The exchanges commenced in the latter part of February, but had proceeded but a short time when they were interrupted, on March 18, by a message from Mr. Davis to the Confederate Congress, recommending that all the Confederate prisoners who had been paroled by the United States Government be released from the obligations of their parole, so as to bear arms in the defence of the Richmond Government. The reason assigned for this action was an "infamous and reckless breach of good faith on the part of the Northern Government," in neglecting to exchange the privateersmen, and in sending the prisoners captured at Fort Donelson into the interior, instead of releasing them on parole. But, according to their own confession, the Confederates took the first step toward the interruption of the exchange, by questioning, without sufficient cause alleged, the integrity of the United States Government. "At the time of sending North the hostages we had retained for our privateersmen," said a Richmond journal, commenting upon President Davis's message, "Gen. Cobb had reason to suspect the good faith of the Northern Government, and telegraphed in time to intercept the release of a portion of these hostages (among them Col. Corcoran), who were *en route* from points further South than Richmond, to go North under a flag of truce to Norfolk."

The progress of events immediately previous to and succeeding the agreement between Gens. Wool and Cobb had materially changed the relative positions of the belligerents, and the captures of Roanoke Island and Fort Donelson left the North not merely an excess of prisoners, but an excess numbering many thousands. The 3,000 prisoners captured at Roanoke Island, Feb. 8, were, nevertheless, released on parole, in accordance with the agreement, and the privateersmen were placed on the footing of other prisoners, by being removed from Washington to Fort Lafayette, in New York harbor. The latter, indeed, were temporarily withheld from exchange until information should be received from the rebel authorities that Col. Corcoran, and the other officers retained as hostages, were on their way to Norfolk; but in all other respects the terms of the cartel were faithfully observed by the United States Government, until after the capture of the Fort Donelson prisoners, and measures were taken to release these, when the message of President Davis was delivered.

As a consequence of the receipt of this communication by the Richmond Congress, the exchange of prisoners ceased at Craney Island, the point at which the flags of truce from Fortress Monroe and Norfolk were accustomed to meet; and the Confederates having failed, on several succeeding days, to meet the United States officers at this rendezvous, Secretary Stanton issued an order, March 27, prohibiting the release on parole of the Fort Donelson prisoners. Here the matter rested for several weeks, the prisoners in the hands of the Federal authorities meanwhile reaching a formidable number, very largely in excess of those taken by the rebels.

In order, however, not to shut the door entirely to negotiation on a subject of deep interest to the inhabitants of both the Union and the seceded States, Gen. Wool informed Gen. Huger, on May 2, that the privateersmen were held as prisoners of war, and that he was empowered to effect their exchange. On the succeeding day Gen. Huger replied as follows:

HEADQ'RS DEPARTMENT OF NORFOLK, *May* 3, 1862.

GENERAL: I have your letter of the 2d instant. On faith of your statement that our privateersmen are prisoners of war, and will be exchanged, the officers heretofore held as hostages will be exchanged on the same terms as any others.

As it is but fair those longest in captivity should be released first, I request you will let the privateersmen be released, and I will reciprocate, and release those longest confined.

I have requested Gen. Winder to send prisoners from Richmond to Newport News on Monday, the 5th inst.

Very respectfully, your obedient servant,
BENJ. HUGER, Maj.-Gen. Commanding.

Maj.-Gen. J. E. WOOL,
Commanding Department of Virginia.

On the 19th, Gen. Wool wrote that he was prepared to make exchange on the terms proposed by Gen. Huger in the above communication, adding, "I will have the privateersmen sent to this post (Fortress Monroe), to be forwarded to you at any place you designate on James river, provided you will send forward, at the same time, the hostages, Cols. Corcoran, Wilcox," &c.; and, on the succeeding day, Gen. Huger replied from Petersburg:

If you will release upon parole the privateersmen, and send them to me at City Point, I will return you such number of your officers, heretofore retained as hostages for them, as would be their equivalent, according to the rates of exchange prescribed by the cartel between the United States and Great Britain in 1813—the captains of privateersmen to rank as lieutenants of the navy, and the mates of the privateers as master's mates. If you will have the rank and number of the privateersmen made out, and their equivalent of officers now retained as hostages for them, such officers will be released unconditionally and returned to you. Any of the other hostages that may not be required for exchange for the privateersmen will be released upon parole, to be exchanged for officers of equal rank, or their equivalent, according to the cartel above alluded to.

On the 21st, Gen. Wool despatched another letter to Gen. Huger, requesting him to appoint a time for the exchanges to take place, and received the following reply:

HEADQUARTERS, DEPARTMENT OF APPOMATTOX,
PETERSBURG, VA., *May* 23, 1862.

GENERAL: I have detained your boat until to-day, expecting an answer from Richmond as to the time when the prisoners to be exchanged for the privateersmen could reach here. I have not yet received an answer, and I am not aware of the location of these officers, or when they could reach here; but I can assure you I consider the War Department have fully agreed to the terms stated in my letter of the 3d instant to you, and which have been accepted by yourself. I must be responsible that on the delivery of all the privateersmen all the officers retained as hostages will be released upon parole, the details of the exchanges to be arranged between us according to the cartel referred to, and such of the officers as are not exchanged in this way to remain on parole until exchanged for others. If not interrupted by movements in the field, I will promise to have the officers forwarded as soon as possible, and will send notice to any of your vessels, and request you may be notified to send for them.

Very respectfully, your obedient servant,
BENJ. HUGER, Maj.-Gen. Commanding.

Supposing the matter to be definitely settled, Gen. Wool, on June 1, sent the privateersmen, 85 in number, to City Point, on the James river, with instructions to deliver them up on receiving the hostages on parole. The latter not being on the spot, the privateersmen were withheld, and a communication was sent to the Confederate authorities demanding an explanation. An answer came back that Gen. Huger had exceeded his authority, and that further conference would be necessary before the exchange could be effected. With a view to the holding of such a conference, the flag of truce boat remained at the Point until the 6th, when, learning that nothing further was expected from Richmond, she returned to Fortress Monroe.

The following letter from the Confederate Secretary of War, of which a copy was transmitted by Gen. Huger to Gen. Wool, gives his reasons for refusing to abide by Gen. Huger's communication of May 23:

C. S. A. WAR DEPARTMENT, RICHMOND, *June* 3, 1862.

GENERAL: I have received your letter of the 28th ultimo, in which you give a construction in your agreement with Gen. Wool for the exchange of the privateersmen and the persons formerly held as hostages, which requires us to return *all* of the latter for all of the former, and to parole such of the so-called hostages as are not exchanged, and to support this construction you refer me to your letter of May 23 to Gen. Wool.

Upon examining that letter I find that you use the following language: "I must be responsible that on the delivery of *all* the privateersmen all the officers detained as hostages will be released upon parole." If this were the agreement, there could be no doubt of your promise to return all the "officers retained as hostages;" but in the same letter you state that the agreement was contained in your letter of May 3, and you say, "I consider the War Department has fully agreed to the terms stated in my letter of the 3d inst."

The letter of May 3, so far from promising "to return all the officers, as hostages," as you apparently suppose, confines the proposed exchange to such as Gen. Wool might name, and as would be equivalent to the privateersmen according to the tariff agreed upon by the cartel between Great Britain and the United States in 1813, and consents that when that exchange had been made the other officers held as hostages might be exchanged "as usual." There can be no doubt about the agreement; your language is perfectly explicit. You say to Gen. Wool, "I will return such officers as you may name in exchange according to the tariff agreed upon by the cartel between Great Britain and the United States in 1813. As soon as these men are exchanged, any other officers that have been held as hostages will be exchanged as usual."

I am willing to perform the agreement which you stated to Gen. Wool that the department had fully agreed to perform, but I cannot consent to carry out a palpable misconstruction of it, much more disadvantageous to the Government of the Confederate States than the agreement itself, and evidently the result of mere inadvertence on your part. Even this erroneous interpretation of your promise is founded on the supposition that "officers were still retained as hostages," when, in fact, they had all been restored to the condition of prisoners of war, and a colonel and three captains were actually then on parole. It is therefore not only erroneous in its construction of the agreement actually made, but is founded upon such a misconception of facts that it would not bind you as an independent agreement.

You will, therefore, inform Gen. Wool that the War Department will execute faithfully your agreement with him of May 3, without considering whether you were authorized to make it or not; that we will exchange such officers recently held as hostages as he may name for the privateersmen, according to the cartel agreed on, but that we shall hold others to be exchanged hereafter.

I might justly complain that Gen. Wool, after being informed by Gen. Cobb that the "officers hitherto held as hostages for the privateersmen had been placed on the same footing as other prisoners of war," and knowing that a number of them, more than equivalent to the privateersmen, had actually been paroled, should yet negotiate with you as if they were all still held as hostages, apparently taking advantage of the circumstance that you were not so well informed as himself.

Very respectfully, your obedient servant,
G. W. RANDOLPH, Secretary of War.

Major-General B. HUGER,
Commanding Department of the Appomattox.

Accompanying this letter was the following personal explanation of Gen. Huger:

HEADQUARTERS HUGER'S DIVISION, *June* 5, 1862.

SIR: I enclose you a copy of a letter I received from the War Department. I have heard from private persons that the privateersmen whom you promised to send for exchange had arrived at City Point, but no letter to me has as yet been forwarded. As I had charge of the correspondence with yourself on the subject, I hasten to send you this communication, which I must confess I do not clearly understand. The language of one of my letters may not have been the same as another; but I did intend not to give you all the officers once retained as hostages in exchange for all the privateersmen, but to give you such numbers of them in exchange as would be required by the cartel exchanging the equivalent of rank, and the other officers to be exchanged as usual. As you agreed to these terms, and had a sufficient number of our officers, there was no reason why the exchange should not be made at once; and I shall insist, if the privateers have been sent, as I hear, that all the officers referred to above be given in exchange. I think it but fair we should name the officers to be exchanged on our side; and as the most equitable way, I propose to exchange those who have been longest prisoners, including navy officers.

I am, General,
Very respectfully, your obedient servant,
BENJ. HUGER,
Major-General Commanding.

Major-Gen. JOHN E. WOOL,
or Officer Commanding Department of Virginia.

Here the matter rested, and for upward of a month nothing seems to have been done toward a general exchange, notwithstanding in the mean time prisoners had accumulated in large numbers on either side. The Confederates had indeed made certain overtures, by sending to Washington Col. Miller and Major Stone, who had been captured in the battle near Pittsburg Landing, to induce the National Government to adopt some general plan. This the latter declined to do, claiming that certain Confederate officers of rank, as Gen. Buckner, captured at Fort Donelson, had, in consequence of acts done previous to the war, forfeited their right to be considered prisoners of war, and ought to be excepted from any cartel entered into by the belligerents, and to be held amenable for treason. The Confederates, on the other hand, insisted that the rule should be general, although from the reluctance which they had manifested in releasing Col. Corcoran and other prisoners demanded by the people of the Northern States, it was evident that they had been themselves inclined to make exceptions.

In obedience to a very general popular demand the National Government finally decided to yield its point, and on July 17, Gen. Dix, who had meanwhile succeeded Gen. Wool in command at Fortress Monroe, met the Confederate general D. H. Hill, in conference, at Turkey Island Creek on the James river, where on the 22d was signed the following agreement for the exchange of prisoners, based upon the cartel of 1812 between the United States and Great Britain, and which was claimed by the Richmond papers to mark an important era in the war, by acknowledging the quasi nationality of the Confederate Government:

HAXALL'S LANDING, ON JAMES RIVER, VA.
July 22, 1862.

The undersigned, having been commissioned by the authorities they respectively represent to make arrangements for a general exchange of prisoners of war, have agreed to the following articles:

ARTICLE 1.—It is hereby agreed and stipulated that all prisoners of war held by either party, including those taken on private armed vessels, known as privateers, shall be discharged upon the conditions and terms following:

Prisoners to be exchanged man for man and officer for officer; privates to be placed on the footing of officers and men of the navy.

Men and officers of lower grades may be exchanged for officers of a higher grade, and men and officers of different services may be exchanged according to the following scale of equivalents:

A general commander-in-chief or an admiral shall be exchanged for officers of equal rank, or forty-six privates or common seamen.

A flag officer or major-general shall be exchanged for officers of equal rank, or for forty privates or common seamen.

A commodore carrying a broad pennant, or a brigadier-general, shall be exchanged for officers of equal rank, or twenty privates or common seamen.

A captain in the navy, or a colonel, shall be exchanged for officers of equal rank, or for fifteen privates or common seamen.

A lieutenant-colonel, or a commander in the navy, shall be exchanged for officers of equal rank, or for ten privates or common seamen.

A lieutenant commander or a major shall be exchanged for officers of equal rank, or eight privates or common seamen.

A lieutenant or a master in the navy, or a captain in the army or marines, shall be exchanged for officers of equal rank, or six privates or common seamen.

Masters' mates in the navy, or lieutenants and ensigns in the army, shall be exchanged for officers of equal rank, or four privates or common seamen.

Midshipmen, warrant officers in the navy, masters of merchant vessels, and commanders of privateers, shall be exchanged for officers of equal rank, or three privates or common seamen: second captains, lieutenants, or mates of merchant vessels or privateers, and all petty officers in the navy and all non-commissioned officers in the army or marines, shall be severally exchanged for persons of equal rank, or for two privates or common seamen; and private soldiers and common seamen shall be exchanged for each other, man for man.

ART. 2.—Local, State, civil, and militia rank held by persons not in actual military service will not be recognized, the basis of exchange being of a grade actually held in the naval and military service of the respective parties.

ART. 3.—If citizens held by either party on charge of disloyalty or any alleged civil offence are exchanged, it shall only be for citizens, captured sutlers, teamsters, and all civilians in the actual service of either party, to be exchanged for persons in similar position.

ART. 4.—All prisoners of war to be discharged on parole in ten days after their capture, and the prisoners now held and those hereafter taken to be transported to the points mutually agreed upon at the expense of the capturing party. The surplus prisoners not exchanged shall not be permitted to take up arms again, nor to serve as military police or constabulary force in any fort, garrison, or field work held by either of the respective parties, nor as guards of prisoners, depots, or stores, nor to discharge any duty usually performed by soldiers, until exchanged under the provisions of this cartel. The exchange is not to be considered complete until the officer or soldier exchanged for has been actually restored to the lines to which he belongs.

ART. 5.—Each party, upon the discharge of prisoners of the other party, is authorized to discharge an equal number of their own officers or men from parole, furnishing at the same time to the other party a list of their prisoners discharged and of their own officers and men relieved from parole, enabling each party to relieve from parole such of their own officers and men as the party may choose. The lists thus mutually furnished will keep both parties advised of the true condition of the exchanges of prisoners.

ART. 6.—The stipulations and provisions above mentioned to be of binding obligation during the continuance of the war, it matters not which party may have the surplus of prisoners, the great principle involved being:

1. An equitable exchange of prisoners, man for man, officer for officer, or officers of higher grade exchanged for officers of lower grade or for privates, according to the scale of equivalents.

2. That privates and officers and men of different services may be exchanged according to the same rule of equivalents.

3. That all prisoners, of whatsoever arm of service, are to be exchanged or paroled in ten days from the time of their capture, if it be practicable to transfer them to their own lines in that time; if not, as soon thereafter as practicable.

4. That no officer, soldier, or employé in the service of either party is to be considered as exchanged and absolved from his paròle until his equivalent has actually reached the line of his friends.

5. That the parole forbids the performance of field, garrison, police, or guard or constabulary duty.

JOHN A. DIX, Major-General.

D. H. HILL, Major-General, C. S. Army.

Supplementary Articles.

ART. 7.—All prisoners of war now held on either side, and all prisoners hereafter taken, shall be sent with all reasonable despatch to A. H. Aikens, below Dutch Gap, on the James river, in Virginia, or to Vicksburg, on the Mississippi river, in the State of Mississippi, and there exchanged, or paroled until such exchange can be effected, notice being previously given by each party of the number of prisoners it will send, and the time when they will be delivered at those points respectively; and in case the vicissitudes of war shall change the military relations of the places designated in this article to the contending parties, so as to render the same inconvenient for the delivery and exchange of prisoners, other places, bearing as nearly as may be the present local relations of said places to the lines of said parties, shall be, by mutual agreement, substituted. But nothing in this article contained shall prevent the commanders of two opposing armies from exchanging prisoners or releasing them on parole at other points mutually agreed on by said commanders.

ART. 8.—For the purpose of carrying into effect the foregoing articles of agreement, each party will appoint two agents, to be called Agents for the Exchange of Prisoners of War, whose duty it shall be to communicate with each other by correspondence and otherwise, to prepare the list of prisoners, to attend to the delivery of the prisoners at the places agreed on, and to carry out promptly, effectually, and in good faith, all the details and provisions of the said articles of agreement.

ART. 9.—And in case any misunderstanding shall arise in regard to any clause or stipulation in the foregoing articles, it is mutually agreed that such misunderstanding shall not interrupt the release of prisoners on parole, as herein provided, but shall be made the subject of friendly explanations, in order that the object of this agreement may neither be defeated nor postponed. JOHN A. DIX, Major-General.

D. H. HILL, Major-General C. S. A.

Acting in the humane spirit which characterized this agreement, the adjutant-general of the United States a few days afterward issued an order that chaplains should not be held as prisoners of war, and directing the immediate and unconditional release of all chaplains so held.

In accordance with the terms of the cartel, an exchange of prisoners commenced forthwith, and by the middle of August most of the officers of rank on either side, who had been for any lengthened period in captivity, were released. So far as the case of prisoners of this class was concerned, matters worked harmoniously enough; but new complications, the result of circumstances happening subsequent to the cartel, soon occurred, which gave rise to an acrimonious correspondence between the belligerent parties, and a series of retaliatory orders from the Confederate authorities.

Previous to the adoption of the cartel of July 22, however, the Confederate general, R. E. Lee, had written to the authorities at Washington, under date of July 6, requesting information respecting the alleged execution by the national authorities of John Owens and William B. Mumford, citizens of the seceded States, and on certain other points, indicated in the following reply of Gen. Halleck, the general-in-chief of the United States army:

HEADQUARTERS OF THE ARMY, WASHINGTON, *Aug.* 7, 1862.

Gen. R. E. Lee, Commanding, &c.:

GENERAL: Your letter of July 6 was received at the Adjutant-General's office on the 14th, but supposing from the endorsement that it required no further reply, it was filed without being shown to the President or Secretary of War. I learned to day, for the first time, that such letter had been received, and hasten to reply.

No authentic information has been received in relation to the execution of either John Owens or ——— Mumford, but measures will be immediately taken to ascertain the facts of these alleged executions, of which you will be duly informed.

I need hardly assure you, general, that, so far as the United States authorities are concerned, this contest will be carried on in strict accordance with the laws and usages of modern warfare, and that all excesses will be duly punished.

In regard to the burning of bridges, &c., within our lines by persons in disguise as peaceful citizens, I refer you to my letter of the 22d of January last to Gen. Price.* I think you will find the views there expressed as most materially differing from those stated in your letter.

In regard to retaliation, by taking the lives of innocent persons, I know of no modern authority which justifies it except in the extreme case of a war with any uncivilized foe, which has himself first established such a barbarous rule. The United States will never countenance such a proceeding unless forced to do so by the barbarous conduct of an enemy who first applies such a rule to our own citizens.

Very respectfully, your obedient servant,

H. W. HALLECK,
General-in-Chief of U. S. Army.

---

* In this letter Gen. Halleck, then commanding the department of Missouri, reiterated his intention to subject persons, other than soldiers, accused of burning or destroying railroads, bridges, and similar property, to trial by court-martial, notwithstanding such persons had been authorized and instructed by Gen. Price to commit such acts. Armed men, in the garb of soldiers, destroying bridges as a military act, would, if captured, be treated as ordinary prisoners of war.

On July 21, Gen. Lee addressed a communication to Gen. McClellan, then in command at Harrison's Landing, stating that he was informed that many Confederate citizens, engaged in peaceful vocations, had been arrested and imprisoned because they refused to take the oath of allegiance to the United States; while others, by harsh treatment, had been compelled to take an oath not to bear arms against the National Government; adding:

This Government refuses to admit the right of the authorities of the United States to arrest our citizens, and extort from them their parole not to render military service to their country under the penalty of incurring punishment in case they fall into the hands of your forces.

I am directed by the Secretary of War to inform you that such oaths will not be regarded as obligatory, and persons who take them will be required to render military service. Should your Government treat the rendition of such service by these persons as a breach of parole, and punish it accordingly, this Government will resort to retaliatory measures as the only means of compelling the observance of the rules of civilized warfare.

The matter was referred by Gen. McClellan to Gen. Halleck, who in reply to that officer, dated August 13, made the following statement of the policy which the Government would pursue:

The Government of the United States has never authorized any extortion of oaths of allegiance or military paroles, and has forbidden any measures to be resorted to tending to that end. Instead of extorting oaths of allegiance and paroles, it has refused the applications of several thousand prisoners to be permitted to take them and return to their homes in the rebel States.

At the same time this Government claims and will exercise the right to arrest, imprison, or place beyond its military lines any persons suspected of giving aid and information to its enemies, or of any other treasonable act. And if persons so arrested voluntarily take the oath of allegiance, or give their military parole, and afterward violate their plighted faith, they will be punished according to the laws and usages of war.

You will assure Gen. Lee that no unseemly threats of retaliation on his part will deter this Government from exercising its lawful rights over both persons and property, of whatsoever name or character.

On July 22 an important order was issued by Secretary Stanton, acting under instructions from the President, by which military commanders in Virginia and other parts of the seceded States were empowered "in an orderly manner to seize and use any property, real or personal, which may be necessary or convenient for their several commands, for supplies or for other military purpose;" to employ at reasonable wages persons of African descent when needed; and requiring that "as to both property and persons of African descent, accounts shall be kept sufficiently accurate and in detail, to show quantities and amounts, and from whom both property and such persons shall have come, as a basis upon which compensation can be made in proper cases." In accordance with the terms of this document Gen. Pope, then recently appointed to the command of the army of Virginia, directed his division generals to seize all horses and mules in their vicinity, and all stores not absolutely needed by the inhabitants for their maintenance or subsistence; and his General Order No. 11, dated July 23d, required all officers of his army holding independent commands to arrest all disloyal male citizens within their lines or within their reach. "Such as are willing to take the oath of allegiance to the United States," &c., the order continued, were to be discharged.

These several orders did not fail to create excitement among the Confederate authorities at Richmond, and ultimately led to the retaliatory action suggested by the two following documents, of which the first was addressed by President Davis to Gen. Lee:

RICHMOND (VA.), *July* 31, 1862.

SIR: On the 22d of this month a cartel for the general exchange of prisoners of war was signed between Maj.-Gen. D. H. Hill, in behalf of the Confederate States, and Maj.-Gen. John E. Dix, in behalf of the United States. By the terms of this cartel it is stipulated that all prisoners of war hereafter taken shall be discharged on parole till exchanged.

Scarcely had that cartel been signed when the military authorities of the United States commenced a practice changing the whole character of the war from such as becomes civilized nations into a campaign of indiscriminate robbery and murder.

The general order issued by the Secretary of War of the United States, in the city of Washington, on the very day the cartel was signed in Virginia, directs the military commanders of the United States to take the private property of our people for the convenience and use of their armies, without compensation.

The general order issued by Maj-Gen. Pope on the 23d day of July, the day after the signing of the cartel, directs the murder of our peaceful inhabitants as spies, if found quietly tilling the farms in his rear, even outside of his lines; and one of his brigadier-generals, Steinwehr, has seized upon innocent and peaceful inhabitants to be held as hostages, to the end that they may be murdered in cold blood, if any of his soldiers are killed by some unknown persons whom he designates as "bushwhackers."

Under this state of facts, this Government has issued the enclosed general order, recognizing Gen. Pope and his commissioned officers to be in the position which they have chosen for themselves—that of robbers and murderers, and not that of public enemies, entitled, if captured, to be considered as prisoners of war.

We find ourselves driven by our enemies by steady progress toward a practice which we abhor and which we are vainly struggling to avoid.

Some of the military authorities of the United States seem to suppose that better success will attend a savage war in which no quarter is to be given, and no age or sex to be spared, than has hitherto been secured by such hostilities as are alone recognized to be lawful by civilized men in modern times.

For the present we renounce our right of retaliation on the innocent, and shall continue to treat the private enlisted soldiers of Gen. Pope's army as prisoners of war; but if, after the notice to the Government at Washington of our confining repressive measures to the punishment only of the commissioned officers who are willing participants in these crimes, these savage practices are continued, we shall be reluctantly forced to the last resort of accepting the war on the terms observed by our foes, until the outraged voice of common humanity forces a respect for the recognized rules of war.

While these facts would justify our refusal to execute the generous cartel by which we have consented to liberate an excess of thousands of prisoners held by us beyond the number held by the enemy, a sacred regard to plighted faith, shrinking from the mere semblance of breaking a promise, prevents our resort to this extremity.

Nor de we desire to extend to any other forces of the enemy the punishment merited alone by Gen. Pope and the commissioned officers who choose to participate in the execution of his infamous orders.

You are hereby instructed to communicate to the commander-in-chief of the United States the contents of this letter, and a copy of the enclosed general order, to the end that he may be notified of our intention not to consider the officers hereafter captured from Gen. Pope's army as prisoners of war.

Very respectfully yours, &c.,
JEFFERSON DAVIS.

To Gen. R. E. LEE, Commanding.

The substance of this letter was communicated by Gen. Lee, according to President Davis's request, to Gen. Halleck on Aug. 2, with the accompanying General Order No. 54:

Confederate General Order No. 54.

ADJUTANT AND INSPECTOR-GENERAL'S OFFICE, RICHMOND, *August* 1, 1862.

First. The following orders are published for the information and observance of all concerned.

Second. Whereas, by a general order dated the 22d of July, 1862, issued by the Secretary of War of the United States, under the order of the President of the United States, the military commanders of that Government within the States of Virginia, South Carolina, Georgia, Florida, Alabama, Mississippi, Louisiana, Texas and Arkansas, are directed to seize and use any property, real or personal, belonging to the inhabitants of this Confederacy, which may be necessary or convenient for their several commands, and no provision is made for any compensation to the owners of private property thus seized and appropriated by the military commands of the enemy.

Third. And whereas, by General Order No. 11, issued by Major-General Pope, commanding the forces of the enemy in Northern Virginia, it is ordered that all commanders of any army corps, divisions, brigades, and detached commands, will proceed immediately to arrest all disloyal male citizens within their lines or within their reach in the rear of their respective commands. Such as are willing to take the oath of allegiance to the United States, and shall furnish sufficient security for its observance, will be permitted to remain in their houses, and pursue in good faith their accustomed avocations; those who refuse shall be conducted south beyond the extreme pickets of the army, and be notified if found again anywhere within our lines, or at any place in the rear, they will be considered spies and subjected to the extreme rigor of military law. If any person, having taken the oath of allegiance as above specified, be found to have violated it, he shall be shot, and his property seized and applied to the public use.

Fourth. And whereas, by an order issued on the 13th of July, 1862, by Brigadier-General A. Steinwehr, Major William Steadman, a cavalry officer of his brigade, has been ordered to arrest five of the most prominent citizens of Page county, Virginia, to be held as hostages, and to suffer death in the event of any of the soldiers of said Steinwehr being shot by bushwhackers, by which term are meant the citizens of this Confederacy who have taken up arms to defend their lives and families.

Fifth. And whereas it results from the above orders that some of tho military authorities of the United States, not content with the unjust and aggressive warfare hitherto waged with savage cruelty against an unoffending people, and exasperated by the failure of their efforts to subjugate them, have now determined to violate all the rules and usages of war, and to convert the hostilities, hitherto waged against armed forces, into a campaign of robbery and murder against innocent citizens and peaceful tillers of the soil.

Sixth. And whereas this Government, bound by the highest obligations of duty to its citizens, is thus driven to the necessity of adopting such just measures of retribution and retaliation as shall seem adequate to repress and punish these barbarities. And whereas the orders above recited have only been published and made known to this Government since the signature of a cartel for the exchange of prisoners of war, which cartel, in so far as it provides for an exchange of prisoners hereafter captured, would never have been signed or agreed to by this Government, if the intention to change the war into a system of indiscriminate murder and robbery had been made known to it. And whereas a just regard to humanity forbids that the repression of crime, which this Government is thus compelled to enforce, should be unnecessarily extended to retaliation on the enlisted men of the army of the United States who may be unwilling instruments of the savage cruelty of their commanders, so long as there is hope that the excesses of the enemy may be checked or prevented by retribution on the commissioned officers, who have the power to avoid guilty action by refusing service under a Government which seeks their aid in the perpetration of such infamous barbarities.

Seventh. Therefore it is ordered that Major-General Pope, Brigadier-General Steinwehr, and all commissioned officers serving under their respective commands, be and they are hereby expressly and especially declared to be not entitled to be considered as soldiers, and therefore not entitled to the benefit of the cartel for the parole of future prisoners of war.

Ordered, further, That in the event of the capture of Major-General Pope or Brigadier-General Steinwehr, or of any commissioned officers serving under them, the captive so taken shall be held in close confinement, so long as the orders herein expressed shall continue in force, and until repealed by the competent military authorities of the United States, and that in the event of the murder of any unarmed citizen or inhabitant of this Confederacy, by virtue or under the pretext of any of the orders hereinbefore recited, whether with or without trial, whether under the pretence of such citizen being a spy or hostage, or any other pretence, it shall be the duty of the commanding General of the forces of this Confederacy to cause immediately to be hung, out of the commissioned officers prisoners as aforesaid, a number equal to the number of our own citizens thus murdered by the enemy.

By order. S. COOPER,
Adjutant and Inspector-General.

On the same day, August 2, Gen. Lee addressed the following communication on a different subject, but one involving similar principles, to Gen. Halleck:

HEADQUARTERS OF THE CONFEDERATE STATES, NEAR RICHMOND, VA., *Aug.* 2, 1862.

To the General Commanding Army of the United States, Washington:

GENERAL: On the 29th of June last I was instructed by the Secretary of War to inquire of Maj.-Gen. McClellan as to the truth of alleged murders committed on our citizens by officers of the United States army.

The case of Wm. B. Mumford, reported to have been murdered at New Orleans by order of Maj.-Gen. B. F. Butler, and of Col. John Owens, reported to have been murdered in Missouri by order of Maj.-Gen. Pope, were those referred to. I had the honor to be informed by Maj.-Gen. McClellan that he had referred these inquiries to his Government for a reply. No answer has as yet been received.

The President of the Confederate States has since been credibly informed that numerous other officers of the army of the United States within the Confederacy have been guilty of felonies and capital offences which are punishable by all laws, human and divine. I am directed by him to bring to your notice a few of those best authenticated.

Newspapers received from the United States announce as a fact that Maj.-Gen. Hunter has armed slaves for the murder of their masters, and has thus done all in his power to inaugurate a servile war, which is worse than that of the savage, inasmuch as it superadds other horrors to the indiscriminate slaughter of all ages, sexes, and conditions.

Brig.-Gen. Phelps is reported to have initiated at New Orleans the example set by Maj.-Gen. Hunter on the coast of South Carolina.

Brig.-Gen. G. N. Fitch is stated in the same journals to have murdered in cold blood two peaceful citizens, because one of his men, while invading our country, was killed by some unknown person while defending his home.

I am instructed by the President of the Confederate States to repeat the inquiry relative to the cases of Mumford and Owens, and to ask whether the statements in relation to the action of Gens. Hunter, Phelps, and Fitch are admitted to be true, and whether the conduct of these generals is sanctioned by their Government.

I am further directed by his Excellency the President to give notice that, in the event of not receiving a reply to these inquiries within fifteen days from the delivery of this letter, it will be assumed that the alleged facts are true, and are sanctioned by the Government of the United States. In such an event, on that Government will rest the responsibility of the retribution or retaliatory measures which shall be adopted to put an end to the merciless atrocities which now characterize the war against the Confederate States. I am, most respectfully, your ob't serv't,

R. E. LEE, General Commanding.

To both communications but one answer was returned, and that was given in the following note:

HEADQUARTERS OF THE ARMY, WASHINGTON, *Aug.* 9, 1862.
Gen. R. E. Lee, Commanding, &c.:

GENERAL: Your two communications of the 2d instant, with enclosure, are received. As these papers are couched in language insulting to the Government of the United States, I most respectfully decline to receive them. They are returned herewith.

Very respectfully, your obedient servant,
H. W. HALLECK, General-in-Chief, U. S. Army.

The rebels, however, not receiving what they considered a satisfactory answer to the allegations contained in the last-quoted letter of Gen. Lee, of August 2, proceeded to issue two vindictive orders in the nature of retaliatory measures against officers of the United States army. The first, dated August 20, threatened retaliation for the lives of peaceable citizens said to have been taken by Gen. (Colonel) Fitch in Arkansas, and the second, dated on the succeeding day, and known as General Order No. 60, is as follows:

Whereas Maj.-Gen. Hunter, recently in command of the enemy's forces on the coast of South Carolina, and Brig.-Gen. Phelps, a military commander of the enemy in the State Louisiana, have organized and armed negro slaves for military service against theil masters, citizens of this Confederacy:

And whereas the Government of the United States has refused to answer an inquiry whether said conduct of its officers meets its sanction, and has thus left to this Government no other means of repressing said crimes and outrages than by the adoption of such measures of retaliation as shall serve to prevent their repetition:

Ordered, That Maj.-Gen. Hunter and Brig.-Gen. Phelps be no longer held and treated as public enemies of the Confederate States, but as outlaws; and that in the event of the capture of either of them, or that of any other commissioned officer employed in drilling, organizing, or instructing slaves, with a view to their armed service in this war, he shall not be regarded as a prisoner of war, but held in close confinement for execution as a felon, at such time and place as the President may order.

The retaliatory orders against Gen. Pope's command were for several weeks enforced with a considerable degree of strictness; but when he retired from command, they were rescinded.

An event occurring in Missouri in October gave occasion for further retaliatory action on the part of the Confederate authorities. Andrew Allsman, a loyal citizen of Palmyra, in the northeastern part of the State, and a non-combatant, having been forcibly abducted by a band of guerrillas under the command of one Porter, the latter was notified by Gen. McNeil, commanding a portion of the Missouri State Militia, that unless Allsman was returned unharmed to his family by the 18th of October, ten of the captured guerrillas would be summarily shot. Allsman not appearing on the day specified, the death penalty was inflicted on ten men selected from Porter's band, in the presence of a large concourse of citizens.

The following in an official list of general officers in the insurrectionary service in August, 1862. The major and brigadier-generals are said to belong to the Provisional Army, their commissions having been granted under the Provisional Government, or prior to 1862:

General-in-Chief.
*Robert E. Lee....................Virginia.

Adjutant and Inspector-General.
*Samuel Cooper....................Virginia.

Quartermaster-General.
*A. C. Myers....................Louisiana.
*Larkin Smith (Assistant).

Chief of Ordnance.
*Benjamin Huger.......South Carolina.

Generals—Regular Army.
*Samuel Cooper....................Virginia.
*Joseph E. Johnston...............Virginia.
*Robert E. Lee....................Virginia.
*P. G. T. Beauregard........Louisiana.
*Braxton Bragg....................Louisiana.

Major-Generals—Provisional Army.
*Leonidas Polk....................Louisiana.
*Earl Van Dorn....................Mississippi.
*Gustavus W. Smith........Kentucky.
*Theo. N. Holmes......North Carolina.
*William J. Hardee....................Georgia.
*Benj. Huger (rel'd)....South Carolina.
*James Longstreet....................Alabama.
*J. B. Magruder....................Virginia.
*Thomas J. Jackson....................Virginia.
*Mansfield Lovell...District Columbia.
*E. Kirby Smith (rel'd)........Florida.
William W. Loring.....North Carolina.
Sterling Price....................Missouri.
*John P. McCown....................Tennessee.
*Daniel H. Hill........North Carolina.
*Richard S. Ewell....................Virginia.
*John C. Pemberton....................Virginia.
*Ambrose P. Hill....................Virginia.
John C. Breckinridge..........Kentucky.
William S. Cheatham........Tennessee.
Thomas C. Hindman..........Arkansas,
*Richard H. Anderson..South Carolina.
*James E. B. Stewart....................Virginia.
*Simon B. Buckner..........Kentucky.
*James M. Withers....................Alabama.

Brigadier-Generals.
John B. Floyd (rel'd).........Virginia.
Henry A. Wise....................Virginia.
*August R. Lawton....................Georgia.
G. J. Pillow (rel'd)..........Tennessee.
*Daniel S. Donelson.........Tennessee.
*David R. Jones.......South Carolina.
*John H. Winder....................Maryland.
*Jubal A. Early....................Virginia.
*Arnold Elzey....................Maryland.
*Samuel Jones....................Virginia.
*C. C. Sibley (dead)..........Louisiana.
*William H. C. Whiting......Georgia.
*Daniel Ruggles....................Virginia.
Charles Clark....................Mississippi.
*Roswell S. Ripley.....South Carolina.
*Isaac R. Trimble....................Maryland.
*Paul O. Hebert....................Louisiana.
*Richard E. Gatlin.....North Carolina.
L. Pope Walker....................Alabama.
*Albert B. Blanchard.......Louisiana.
*Gab. J. Rains (killed).......Kentucky.
*Lafayette McLaws..........Georgia.
*Thomas F. Dayton....South Carolina.
*Lloyd Tilghman..........Kentucky.
*Nat. G. Evans.........South Carolina.

*Cadmus C. Wilcox.........Tennessee.
Richard E. Rodes..............Alabama.
Richard Taylor...............Louisiana.
*James H. Trapier.....South Carolina.
*Samuel G. French.........Mississippi.
William H. Carroll..........Tennessee.
*Hugh W. Mercer............Georgia.
Humphrey Marshall.........Kentucky.
*Alexander P. Steuart.......Tennessee.
*W. Montgomery Gardner.....Georgia.
*Richard B. Garnett..........Virginia.
William Mahone..............Virginia.
L. O'B. Branch (killed).North Carolina.
Maxey Gregg..........South Carolina.
Robert Toombs.................Georgia.
*George H. Stewart...........Virginia.
*Wm. W. Mackall...District Columbia.
*Henry Heth.....................Virginia.
*Johnson K. Duncan.........Louisiana.
John R. Jackson...............Georgia.
*Edward Johnson.............Virginia.
Howell Cobb....................Georgia.
Joseph L. Hogg...................Texas.
William S. Featherston.....Mississippi.
Roger A. Pryor..................Virginia.
*John H. Forney...............Alabama.
*John B. Villepigue (dead)....Georgia.
*Bushnel R. Johnson.........Tennessee.
*Thomas K. Jackson.........———.
*Thomas Jordan.................Virginia.
*John S. Bowen...............Missouri.
*John B. Hood......................Texas.
*G. B. Anderson (k'd)..North Carolina.
*Thomas M. Jones.............Virginia.
J. J. Pettigrew.........South Carolina.
Albert Rust.....................Arkansas.
James J. Ramsey...............Georgia.
Hamilton P. Bee....................Texas.
Henry McCulloch..................Texas.
William Preston.............Kentucky.
*Henry Little (killed).........Missouri.
*R. Ransom............North Carolina.
Martin E. Greene..............Missouri.
Thomas R. R. Cobb (killed)...Georgia.
——— Wood.........................Alabama.
——— Kemper.........South Carolina.
——— Kershaw........South Carolina.
——— Leadbeater...........Tennessee.
——— Armstrong...........———.
John S. Williams...............Kentucky.
N. B. Forrest....................Tennessee.
Robert E. Garland (killed)....Virginia.
*A. W. Reynolds..................Virginia.
——— Jenkins.........South Carolina.
*——— Pender.........North Carolina.
Edward W. Gantt...............Arkansas.
Solon Borland....................Arkansas.
*M. L. Smith....................Mississippi.
*William B. Taliaferro........Virginia.
*George E. Pickett.............Virginia.
——— Wright......................Georgia.
——— Helm.....................Kentucky.
George Maurey.................Tennessee.
Blanton Duncan...............Kentucky.
*L. A. Armistead..............Virginia.
——— Semmes....................Georgia.
——— Maxey..................———.
S. R. Gist................South Carolina.
*D. M. Frost.....................Missouri.
Beverly R. Robertson.........Virginia.
J. B. S. Roane..................Arkansas.
C. L. Stevenson................———.
Wade Hampton...........South Carolina.
A. G. Jenkins...................Virginia.
——— Fields...................———.
——— Martin..........North Carolina.
*Fitz Hugh Lee..................Virginia.
John R. Jones...................Virginia.
James E. Slaughter.............———.
Henry Hayes....................Louisiana.
Henry W. Hilliard...............Alabama.
*Abraham Buford..............Kentucky.

This list, numbering 137 generals, is divided among the several States as follows: Virginia, 31; South Carolina, 14; Georgia, 14; Kentucky, 11; Tennessee, 11; Louisiana, 9; North Carolina, 9; Alabama, 7; Mississippi, 5; Missouri, 5; Arkansas, 5; Texas, 4; Maryland, 3; District of Columbia, 2; Florida, 1; Unknown, 6.

The following were born in the North: Gen. S. Cooper, New York; Maj.-Gen. John C. Pemberton, Pennsylvania; Brig.-Gens. H. C. Whiting, A. B. Blanchard, Massachusetts; Johnson K. Duncan, Pennsylvania; R. S. Ripley, Ohio; ——— Leadbeater, Connecticut; S. G. French, New Jersey; D. M. Frost.

CASUALTIES, &c.—*Killed.*—Maj.-Gen. A. S. Johnston,* Texas, at Shiloh, April 6, 1862.

Brig.-Gen. R. S. Garnett,* Va., at Carrick's Ford, July 11, 1861.

Brig.-Gen. Bernard E. Bee,* S. C., at Manassas, July 21, 1861.

Brig.-Gen. F. K. Zollicoffer, Tenn., at Somerset, January 19, 1862.

Brig.-Gen. Ben McCulloch, Texas, at Pea Ridge, March 7, 1862.

Brig.-Gen. A. H. Gladden, La., at Shiloh, April 6, 1862.

Brig.-Gen. T. W. Ashby, at ——— ———, May —, 1862.

Brig.-Gen. Robert Hatton, Tenn., at Seven Pines, May 31, 1862.

Brig.-Gen. Richard Griffith, Miss., before Richmond, June 27, 1862.

Brig.-Gen. C. S. Winder,* Md., at Cedar Mountain, August 9, 1862.

Brig.-Gen. J. T. Hughes, Mo., at Independence, August —, 1862.

Brig.-Gen. Robert E. Garland, Va., at South Mountain, September 14, 1862.

Brig.-Gen. Starke, N. C., at Antietam, September 17, 1862.

Brig.-Gen. Law. O'B. Branch, N. C., at Antietam, September 17, 1862.

Brig.-Gen. Henry Little, Missouri, at Iuka, September 19, 1862. Total—15.

Acting Brig.-Gen. F. S. Bartow, Ga., at Manassas, July 21, 1861.

Acting Brig.-Gen. James McIntosh, at Pea Ridge, March 7, 1862. Total—13.

Died.—Brig.-Gen. J. B. Grayson, Ky.; T. A. Flourney, Ark.; Philip St. George Cooke,* Va. (suicide)—3.

Resigned.—Maj.-Gens. David E. Twiggs, Ga. (since dead); M. L. Bonham, S. C.; George B. Crittenden, Ky.; Brig.-Gens. H. R. Jackson, Ga.; T. T. Fauntleroy, Va.; G. W. Randolph, Va.; L. T. Wigfall, Texas; S. C. Anderson, Tenn.; J. R. Anderson,* Va.; Albert Pike, Ark.; W. H. T. Walker,* Ga.—11.

* Graduates of West Point.

The Confederate army in Virginia, near the close of the year, was in a most destitute condition. The following statement, dated at Winchester, Virginia, on September 26, was circulated through the Confederate States, as entirely reliable, and made the basis of appeals to the people to contribute to the relief of the soldiers:

I can recall no parallel instance in history, except Napoleon's disastrous retreat from Moscow, where an army has ever done more marching and fighting, under such great disadvantages, than Gen. Lee's has done since it left the banks of the James river.

This army proceeded directly to the line of the Rappahannock, and, moving out from that river, it fought its way to the Potomac, crossed the stream, and moved on to Frederick and Hagerstown, had a heavy engagement at Boonsboro' Gap, and another at Crampton Gap below, fought the greatest pitched battle of the war at Sharpsburg, and then recrossed the Potomac back into Virginia. During all this time, covering the full space of a month, the troops rested but four days! And let it always be remembered, to their honor, that of the men who performed this wonderful feat one fifth of them were barefooted, one half of them in rags, and the whole of them half famished. The country from the Rappahannock to the Potomac had been visited by the enemy with fire and sword, and our transportation was insufficient to keep the army supplied from so distant a base as Gordonsville; and, when provision trains would overtake the army, so pressing were the exigencies of their position, the men seldom had time to cook. Their difficulties were increased by the fact that cooking utensils in many cases had been left behind, as well as everything else that would impede their movements. It was not unusual to see a company of starving men have a barrel of flour distributed to them, which it was utterly impossible for them to convert into bread with the means and the time allowed to them. They could not procure even a piece of plank or a corn or flour sack upon which to work up their dough.

Do you wonder, then, that there should have been stragglers from the army?—that brave and true men should have fallen out from sheer exhaustion, or in their efforts to obtain a mouthful to eat along the roadsides? Or that many seasoned veterans, the conquerors in the valley, at Richmond and Manassas, should have succumbed to disease, and been forced back to the hospital? I look to hear a great outcry against the stragglers. Already lazy cavalrymen and dainty staff officers and quartermasters, who are mounted and can forage the country for something to eat, are condemning the weary private, who, notwithstanding his body may be covered with dust and perspiration, and his feet with stone bruises, is expected to trudge along under his knapsack and cartridge box, on an empty stomach, and never turn aside for a morsel of food to sustain his sinking limbs. Out upon such monstrous injustice! That there has been unnecessary straggling is readily admitted; but, in a large majority of cases, the men have only to point to their bleeding feet, tattered garments, and gaunt frames for an answer to the unjust charge. No army on this continent has every accomplished as much or suffered as much as the army of Northern Virginia within the last three months. At no period during the first Revolutionary War, not even at Valley Forge, did our forefathers in arms encounter greater hardships, or endure them more uncomplainingly.

But great as have been the trials to which the army has been subjected, they are hardly worthy to be named in comparison with the sufferings in store for it this winter, unless the people of the Confederate States, everywhere and in whatever circumstances, come to its immediate relief. The men must have clothing and shoes this winter. They must have something to cover themselves when sleeping, and to protect themselves from the driving sleet and snow storms when on duty. This must be done, though our friends at home should have to wear cotton, and sit by the fire. The army of Virginia stands guard this day as it will stand guard this winter, over every hearthstone throughout the South. The ragged sentinel who may pace his weary rounds this winter on the bleak spurs of the Blue Ridge, or along the frozen valleys of the Shenandoah and Rappahannock, will also be your sentinel, my friends, at home. It will be for you and your household that he encounters the wrath of the tempest and the dangers of the night, He suffers, and toils, and fights for you, too, brave, true-hearted women of the South. Will you not clothe his nakedness, then? Will you not put shoes and stockings on his feet? Is it not enough that he has written down his patriotism in crimson characters along the battle road from the Rappahannock to the Potomac? And must his bleeding feet also impress their mark of fidelity upon the snows of the coming winter?

It is not necessary to counsel violent measures; but it is not expected that any person will be permitted to accumulate leather and cloth for purposes of speculation. The necessities of the armies rise up like a mountain, and cannot, and will not be overlooked. It was hoped at one time that we might obtain winter supplies in Maryland. This hope was born after the army left Richmond, and has now miserably perished, The Government is unable to furnish the supplies, for they are not to be had in the country. If it had exercised a little foresight last spring and summer, when vessels were running the blockade with cargoes of calico, linen, and other articles of like importance, a partial supply at least of hats, blankets, shoes, and woollen goods might have been obtained from England. But foresight is a quality of the mind that is seldom put in practice in these days.

But whatever may be done by the people should be done immediately. Not one moment can be lost that will not be marked, as by the second-hand of a watch, with the pangs of a sufferer. Already the hills and valleys in this high latitude have been visited by frost, and the nights are uncomfortably cool to the man who sleeps upon the ground. Come up, then, men and women of the South, to this sacred duty! Let nothing stand between you and the performance of it. Neither pride nor pleasure, nor personal ease and comfort, should withhold your hands from the holy work. The supply of leather and wool, we all know, is limited; but do what you can, and all you can, and as soon as you can. If you cannot send woollen socks, send half-woollen or cotton socks; and so with under clothing, coats, and pants; and if blankets are not to be had, then substitute comforters made of dyed osnaburgs, stuffed with cotton. Any thing that will keep off the cold will be acceptable. Even the speculator and extortioner might forego their gains for a season, and unite in this religious duty.

If the army of Virginia could march through the South just as it is—ragged, and almost barefooted and hatless; many of the men limping along, and not quite well of their wounds and sickness, yet cheerful, and not willing to abandon their places in the ranks; their clothes riddled with balls, and their banners covered with the smoke and dust of battle, and shot into tatters, many of them inscribed with "Williamsburg," "Seven Pines," Gaines's Mill," "Garnett's Farm," "Front Royal," "McDowell," "Cedar Run," and other victorious fields—if this army of veterans, thus clad and shod, with tattered uniforms and banners, could march from Richmond to the Mississippi, it would produce a sensation that has no parallel in history since Peter the Hermit led his swelling hosts across Europe to the rescue of the Holy Sepulchre.

The straggling from the army, as the winter approached, was without a parallel. The press, Mr. Davis, and officers of the Confederate and State Governments, appealed to the people, and particularly to the women, to frown upon all stragglers, and use every means to secure their apprehension. It was declared that more than half the men who went into service from the northeastern counties of the State of Georgia were at home without leave, and most of them were skulking in the mountains to avoid being arrested. Others had banded together under a few desperate leaders to resist any attempts that might be made to arrest them, or to release from the jails those who had been arrested. Some of those bands had arms and ammunition, and subsisted by plunder. They were volunteers and not conscripts, as the conscript laws had never been enforced in that section.

So far as regards desertions the condition of the Federal armies at this time was bad. The number of "missing" and of "deserters" in the Eastern volunteer army was more than double the number of those classes in the Western volunteer forces.

Taking the returns of the period from the 1st of June, 1861, to the 1st of March, 1862, as the basis of calculation, it was estimated that to secure in the field a constant force of 500,000 effective men, the nation must not only maintain 58,000 sick men, but must also recruit the ranks of the enlisted portion of these forces with new material at the rate of 123,000 per annum so long as the war should last—a rate somewhat exceeding 10,000 recruits per month. Of those 123,000 annual recruits, 83,000 were to supply losses by death and discharges from service (exclusive of discharges for expiration of term of enlistment); 34,000 for desertions and missing in action; and 6,000 to supply other losses specified and unspecified.

The excess of the mortality due to disease and accident, over that due to wounds in action, became at this time a noticeable fact in the volunteer army of the United States, as in all other armies—two-thirds of the deaths of the officers and five-sixths of those of the men resulting from disease and accident; the remaining one-third and one-sixth, respectively, being caused by wounds received in battle.

It appeared from the returns that the general mortality of the army had been gradually increasing since the commencement of the war, and that the rate for the autumnal months was 1·7 times that indicated by the returns for the summer period, and the winter rate in turn double 1·7 times that of autumn.

To supply losses among the enlisted men in the Eastern armies required recruits at the rate of 18·8 per 1,000 per month, or 226 per 1,000 per annum; of which latter proportion 32 was the number required to supply the annual loss by death; 100 the annual loss by discharge from service, chiefly from disability; 79 the annual loss from missing in action and from desertions; and 15 to supply the loss from other causes.

To supply such losses in the Western armies required recruits at the rate of 19·5 per 1,000 per month, or 134 per 1,000 per annum; of which latter proportion 96 were required to supply the annual loss from deaths; 101 the loss from discharges from service, mainly from disability; 35 the loss from missing in action and from desertions, and 2 from other causes.

The desertions from the army in the autumn of 1862 became so great as to cause the appointment of officers to arrest and return such persons. An order of Gen. Buell, dated near Florence, Alabama, on June 24, stated that 14,000 officers and soldiers were absent from the various divisions of his army. Some had gone without any authority, and others with the permission of officers not authorized to grant it. Sickness was generally stated to be the cause of this absence, but in many cases it had notoriously ceased to exist. In September the War Department issued the following order:

Orders respecting Special Provost Marshals, and defining their duties.

WAR DEPARTMENT, ADJUTANT-GENERAL'S OFFICE,
WASHINGTON, *Sept.* 24, 1862.

First. There shall be a Provost Marshal General of the War Department, whose headquarters will be at Washington, and who will have the immediate supervision, control, and management of the corps.

Second. There will be appointed in each State one or more Special Provost Marshals, as necessity may require, who will report to, and receive instructions and orders from the Provost Marshal General of the War Department.

Third. It will be the duty of the Special Provost Marshals to arrest all deserters, whether regulars, volunteers, or militia, and send them to the nearest military commander, or military post, where they can be cared for and sent to their respective regiments; to arrest, upon the warrant of the Judge Advocate, all disloyal persons subject to arrest under the orders of the War Department; to inquire into and report treasonable practises, seize stolen or embezzled property of the Government, detect spies of the enemy, and perform such other duties as may be enjoined upon them by the War Department; and report all their procedings promptly to the Provost Marshal General.

Fourth. To enable Special Provost Marshals to discharge their duties efficiently, they are authorized to call on any available military force within their respective districts, or else to employ the assistance of citizens, constables, sheriffs, or police officers, so far as may be necessary under such regulations as may be prescribed by the Provost Marshal General of the War Department with the approval of the Secretary of War.

Fifth. Necessary expenses incurred in this service will be paid on duplicate bills certified by the Special Provost Marshals, stating the time and nature of the service, after examination and approval by the Provost Marshal General.

Sixth. The compensation of special Provost Marshals will be ——— dollars per month, and actual travelling expenses and postage will be refunded on bills certified to under oath and approved by the Provost Marshal General.

Seventh. All appointments in this service will be subject to be revoked, at the pleasure of the Secretary of War.

Eighth. All orders heretofore issued by the War Department, conferring authority upon other officers to act as Provost Marshals (except those who have received special commissions from the War Department, are hereby revoked.

By order of the Secretary of War.

L. THOMAS, Adjutant-General.

The operations of the surgical department have been aided by humane and benevolent associations. The horrors of battle were assuaged by ministers of mercy, and the services of the medical profession were voluntarily and gratuitously offered on every occasion. Relief associations in every State did much to comfort and assist the sick and wounded in camps and hospitals, and their vigilant superintendence perhaps operated to check the negligence, abuse, and fraud that too often prevail even in such institutions. Religious congregations and societies also tendered to the Government their church buildings for hospitals, while their pastors ministered to the patients.

The subsistence of the armies during the year was reported as good and wholesome. Fresh beef had generally been supplied to the armies in the field on the hoof, to lessen, as far as possible, the quantity of transportation required, and in larger proportion of the ration to marching columns. It was stated by the general-in-chief—Halleck—that no armies in the world were so well supplied as the armies of the United States.

CHAPTER XXVII.

The Campaign against Vicksburg—The Plan of Gen. Grant—The loss of Holly Springs: its consequences—Movement of Gen. Sherman toward Vicksburg—Haines' Bluffs—Attack of Gen. Sherman on Chickasaw Bluffs—Failure—Address to his Troops—Movement up the Arkansas River—Capture of Arkansas Post—Retires to Young's Point—Arrival of Gen Grant—Work on the Canal opposite Vicksburg—Floods—Queen of the West runs the Batteries at Vicksburg—Her Expedition down the Mississippi—Captures—Loss of the Queen of the West—Scenes up the Red River—Approach of the Enemy's Gunboats—The Indianola runs the Batteries—Her Destruction—Attempt of Gen. Grant to cut a Channel to Lake Providence: also one to Moon Lake—Expedition of Admiral Porter—Its Failure.

AFTER the battles of Fredricksburg and Murfreesboro, the armies engaged in those conflicts remained inactive for some time. Meanwhile the Federal Government pushed forward its plan of gaining the Mississippi River and cutting off the communication between the Southern States on its opposite sides by the capture of Vicksburg and Port Hudson. Its importance

H. W. Smith, N.Y.

U. S. Grant

LIEUT.-GEN. U.S. ARMY

New York, D. Appleton & Co.

was thus stated by Gen. Sherman at St. Louis after the close of the war: The possession of the Mississippi River is the possession of America; and I say that had the Southern Confederacy (call it by what name you may), had that power represented by the Southern Confederacy held with a grip sufficiently strong the lower part of the Mississippi River, we would have been a subjugated people, and they would have dictated to us if we had given up the possession of the lower Mississippi." The campaign against Vicksburg really commenced about the 28th of November. At that time, the forces of Gen. Grant were at Lagrange, three miles east of Grand Junction, on the Cairo and New Orleans Railroad, with garrisons at Columbus, Humboldt, Trenton, and Jackson, in Tennessee, and Bolivar and Corinth in Mississippi. These forces were designated as the Army of West Tennessee. The Confederate forces were at Coldwater and Holly Springs, about twenty miles distant.

The plan of Gen. Grant was, that Gen. Sherman should take command of the forces at Memphis in Tennessee, and Helena in Arkansas, and descend the river on transports with the gunboat fleet, and make an attack on Vicksburg by the 29th of December, and that Gen. McClernand should take the forces at Cairo and move down to Vicksburg, thus reënforcing Gen. Sherman soon after his attack on the town. Meanwhile Gen. Grant was to advance rapidly upon the Confederate troops in Mississippi north and east of Vicksburg, which formed the main body of their army, and keep them fully employed, and, if they retreated to Vicksburg, arrive there with them, ready to coöperate with Gen. Sherman.

Large reënforcements and supplies were received, and the advance of Gen. Hamilton's corps, on the 28th of November, began to move in the direction of Holly Springs, which was reached on the 29th. By the 1st of December, Gen. Grant's forces had arrived, and were chiefly encamped at Lumpkin's Mills, south of Holly Springs, and seven miles north of the Tallahatchie River. The Confederate force, now under the command of Gen. Pemberton, retired to that river, and finally fell back beyond Granada. Meanwhile Gen. Grant advanced on Oxford, and on the 20th of December an attack was suddenly made in his rear, by a Confederate force under Gen. Van Dorn, on the garrison under Col. Murphy at Holly Springs, which surrendered. The prisoners were paroled, and the supplies collected there for Gen. Grant's army were destroyed; also a large quantity of cotton which had been purchased of the people in the vicinity.

This surrender of Holly Springs is thus noted in the orders of Gen. Grant:

HEADQUARTERS THIRTEENTH ARMY CORPS, DEPARTMENT OF THE TENNESSEE, HOLLY SPRINGS, MISS., *December*, 23, 1862.

* * * * * * *

It is with pain and mortification that the General commanding reflects upon the disgraceful surrender of this place, with all the valuable stores it contained, on the 20th inst., and that without any resistance, except by a few men, who form an honorable exception; and this, too, after warning had been given of the advance of the enemy northward the evening previous. With all the cotton, public stores, and substantial buildings about the depot, it would have been perfectly practicable to have made in a few hours defences sufficient to resist, with a small garrison, all the cavalry brought against them, until the reënforcements, which the commanding officer was notified were marching to his relief, could have reached him.

The conduct of officers and men in accepting paroles, under the circumstances, is highly reprehensible, and, to say the least, thoughtless. By the terms of the Dix Hill cartel, each party is bound to take care of their prisoners, and to send them to Vicksburg, Miss., or a point on James River, Va., for exchange or parole, unless some other point is mutually agreed upon by the Generals commanding the opposing armies. By a refusal to be paroled, the enemy, from his inability to take care of the prisoners, would have been compelled either to have released them unconditionally, or to have abandoned all further aggressive movements for the time being, which would have made their recapture and the discomfiture of the enemy almost certain.

It is gratifying to notice, in contrast with this, the conduct of a portion of the command, conspicuous among whom was the Second Illinois cavalry, who gallantly and successfully resisted being taken prisoners. Their loss was heavy, but the enemy's was much greater. Such conduct as theirs will always insure success.

Had the commandant of the post exercised the usual and ordinary precautions for defence, the garrison was sufficiently strong to have repulsed the enemy, saved our stores from destruction, and themselves from capture.

The General commanding is satisfied that a majority of the troops who accepted a parole did so thoughtlessly, and from want of knowlege of the cartel referred to, and that in future they will not be caught in the same way.

By order of Major-General U. S. GRANT.
JNO. A. RAWLINS, Asst. Adjutant-General.

The post was under the command of Col. Murphy, who was surprised and captured with all his force except a small body of cavalry. The enemy estimated the stores destroyed as follows: "1,809,000 fixed cartridges and other ordnance stores, valued at $1,500,000, including 5,000 rifles and 2,000 revolvers; 100,000 suits of clothing and other quartermaster's stores, valued at $500,000; 5,000 barrels of flour and other commissary stores, valued at $500,000; $1,000,000 worth of medical stores; 1,000 bales of cotton, and $600,000 worth of sutlers' stores."

On the same day an attack was made at Davis's Mills, a little further north, which was bravely repulsed. Near Jackson, Tennessee, an attack was made by a body of cavalry under Col. Forrest on the 19th. The telegraph wire was cut and the railroad destroyed. On the next day Humboldt was captured and an attack made on Trenton. Other stations on the railroad, as Dyer's, Rutherford, and Keaton, were taken on the same day. The purpose appeared to be to destroy every railroad bridge from Columbus to Corinth, and thus cut off the communications and supplies of Gen. Grant. The consequence of these movements was to make Gen. Grant fall back upon Holly Springs,

This left the Confederate Gen. Pemberton at liberty to concentrate his forces at Vicksburg to resist Gen. Sherman. Thus that part of the plan of the campaign against Vicksburg, which related to the movements of Gen. Grant by land, was unsuccessful. The approach of the wet season of the year, the destruction of the railroads, and the difficulty and delay in making a further advance, caused the forces of Gen. Grant soon to be withdrawn for the purpose of joining Gen. Sherman before Vicksburg.

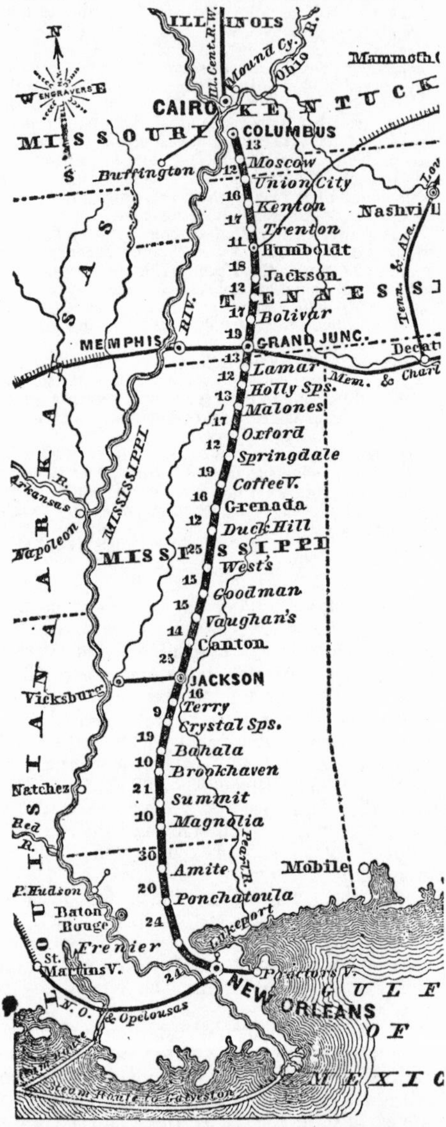

Meanwhile Gen. William T. Sherman, who had been stationed at Memphis, embarked with one division on the 20th of December, and dropped down to Friar's Point, the place of rendezvous. On the next day he was joined by Admiral Porter, in his flagship, with the gunboats Marmora, Capt. Getty, and Conestoga, Capt. Selfridge, to act as a convoy. The main body of the naval force was at the mouth of Yazoo river. On the same evening the troops at Helena, making another division, embarked in transports, and came to Friar's Point.

The arrangements were completed by the military and naval commanders during the next forenoon, the 22d, and the fleet got under way, and moved down just below the mouth of White river, where it came to, at sunset. On the next day it descended to Gaines's Landing, and at two P. M. came to anchor, to await the arrival of those transports in the rear, and also a division of troops from Memphis. Half of the town of Gaines's Landing was destroyed by fire while the army was there. Similar destruction had also been made at Friar's Point. These acts led to stringent measures on the part of Gen. Sherman.

On the night of the 24th and the morning of the 25th, the fleet arrived at the mouth of the Yazoo river. The fleet consisted of more than sixty transports, with a number of ironclad and other gunboats, and several mortar boats. The Yazoo is a deep, narrow, and sluggish stream, formed by the Tallahatchie and Yallobusha rivers, which unite in Carroll county, Mississippi. It runs through an alluvial plain of extreme fertility, about 290 miles, and empties into the Mississippi river twelve miles above Vicksburg.

By this time Gen. Grant's communications in his rear had been cut off, and he had been compelled to fall back. The confederate forces in his rear retired toward Vicksburg, where they had already begun to concentrate, both from the east and the west, although these facts were unknown to Gen. Sherman.

It was supposed by the Federal forces that they would now receive the coöperation of Gen. Banks and Admiral Farragut. The former had left New York, near the close of the year, with a considerable military force, for New Orleans, where the latter commanded the naval forces.

On the 26th, the expedition, under convoy of the gunboats, moved up the Yazoo, and the troops were landed at various points from the junction of Old River with the Yazoo to Johnson's Farm, a distance of about three miles, without opposition. The distance from Vicksburg was about eight miles. A strong position, known as Haines's Bluff, some distance above on the river, was held by the Confederate forces, and in the mean while attacked by the gunboats De Kalb, Cincinnati, Louisville, Benton, and Lexington. It was the plan of Gen. Sherman to attack Vicksburg in the rear. For this purpose he was engaged, on the 28th, in getting his forces into position.

The bluffs on which Vicksburg is built take their rise a little below the city, and extend in a direction north of northeast to the Yazoo river, terminating in Haines's Bluff, a distance of twelve or fifteen miles. They were fortified throughout their entire length. These bluffs front the Mississippi and Yazoo rivers. The ascent is abrupt and precipitous, and the only approach to the city by land from up the river is by climbing their face. In the rear the ground is high and broken, and somewhat rolling. It falls off gradually to the Big Black river.

The line of the Yazoo here is nearly northeast. It is six miles distant from the bluffs at Old river, and passes along their face until, at Haines's Bluff, the river and the bluffs come together. This junction is nine miles from Vicksburg by the road along the foot of the bluffs, and twenty-three miles from the Mississippi by the course of the Yazoo river. On the triangular-shaped bottom land between the bluffs and the Yazoo down to the Old river, the troops were disembarked for the purpose of getting in the rear of Vicksburg and capturing it.

About one third of the distance down the Yazoo from Haines's Bluff, a bayou puts off from the river at nearly right angles, until it approaches the bluffs, when it turns and follows their base until it empties into the Mississippi. It is called the Chickasaw bayou. Between this bayou and the bluffs is a plain, upon which the timber had been felled to form an abatis. The banks of the bayou are quite steep, and about two hundred feet apart. At the base of the bluffs, through their whole length, rifle pits had been dug, in the rear of which, upon the face of the bluffs, single-gun batteries had been planted at short intervals from Vicksburg almost to Haines's Bluff. At various commanding points along the range, both on its face and upon the summit, field works were thrown up for the reception and protection of light artillery whenever it might be needed.

Parallel with, and about half a mile north of the Chickasaw bayou, is a deep slough, having no connection with the river. As it approaches the base of the bluffs, it makes a sharp turn and enters Chickasaw bayou near the point where the latter makes its angle as it strikes the bluffs. In the latter part of its extent it contains but little water; its bottom, however, is a quicksand, which does not afford good footing. The bottom land of the Yazoo is covered with a dense growth of cypress trees: much of it is quite clear and free from undergrowth, while in other parts it is quite thick.

The first troops landed, on the 26th, were a brigade, under Gen. Blair, of Gen. Steele's division, and a brigade from each of the divisions under Gens. M. L. Smith and Morgan. They were ordered to advance two miles into the country, and make a thorough reconnoissance in the direction of the bluffs. The brigade from Gen. Morgan's division found the rebels in force about two miles inland. The other brigades met with no opposition. No conflict took place.

The force of Gen. Sherman was organized in four divisions as follows: First division, three brigades, under Brig.-Gen. George W. Morgan; second division, three brigades, under Brig.-Gen. Morgan L. Smith; third division, three brigades, under Brig.-Gen. A. J. Smith; fourth division, four brigades, under Brig.-Gen. Frederick Steele. The brigade commanders of this fourth division were Gens. Frank P. Blair, jr., John M. Thayer, C. E. Hovey, and Col. Hassendurbel.

Under the plan of attack, Gen. Steele was to hold the extreme left, Gen. Morgan the left centre, Gen. M. L. Smith the right centre, and Gen. A. J. Smith the extreme right. The division under Gen. Smith, however, not having arrived, Gen. Blair was placed on the right centre. All the divisions were to converge toward the point of attack on the bluffs. The remainder of the division of Gen. Steele was landed on the 27th above the Chickasaw bayou, to operate on that part of the line. The entire day was spent in getting the troops ashore. The bank of the river was overgrown with brush, and the ground was so soft that it was necessary to build roads for moving the wagons and artillery. At night the command had advanced only two miles from the shore.

On the same day, the 27th, the divisions on the centre, including Gen. Blair's brigade, advanced slowly toward the bluffs, in order to give time to Gen. Steele to come into position on the left. A battery of the enemy was found near the point designated for junction with Gen. Steele, not far from the angle of the bayou, and silenced. The night ensuing was cold and frosty, and the troops bivouacked without fires.

On the next day, the 28th, the enemy was driven across the Chickasaw, and night closed with the troops of Gen. Sherman in full possession south of the bayou, with one bridge thrown across, and with two bridges partly constructed. While reconnoitring the ground and directing the movement of some infantry, Gen. M. L. Smith was severely wounded in the hip, and the command of his division devolved upon Gen. David Stuart. Meanwhile, Gen. Steele had pushed forward his command. The slough on his right was deep and impassable, and on the left the ground had become swampy and full of small pools, so as to be also impassable. The only line of approach to the bluffs was along a narrow levee or causeway, which was exposed throughout to the enemy's artillery. Three attempts were made to approach the causeway, but the destruction of the troops was so manifest that they were withdrawn. Gen. Sherman, under this state of affairs, ordered Gen. Steele to return to the river, reëmbark and land on the lower side of the Chickasaw, thus holding still the extreme left, and advance upon its bank until he met Gen. Morgan. It was too late in the evening of the 28th when the troops were fairly on shore below the bayous to move farther. At this time the division of Gen. A. J. Smith came up and took its position on the right of the line. It had remained at Milliken's Bend as a support to a force sent out under Col. Wright to cut the Shreveport railroad on the west side of the Mississippi opposite Vicksburg.

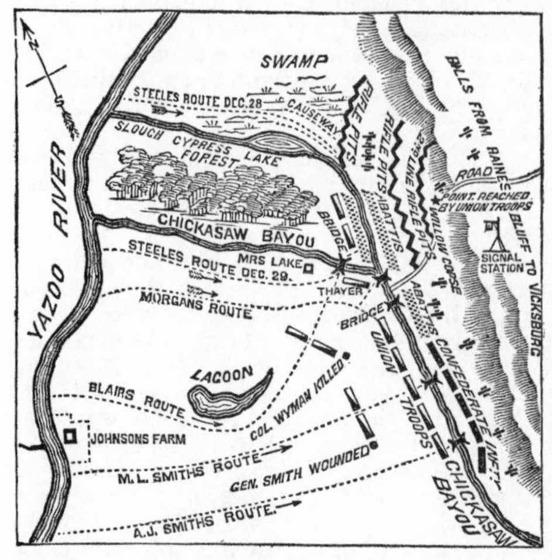

The situation of the forces at this time was as follows: Gen. Morgan was in position on the south side of the Chickasaw; near its angle, at the base of the bluffs, and on his immediate right, was Gen. Blair's brigade; Gen. M. L. Smith's division, under Gen. Stuart, was on the right centre, and Gen. A. J. Smith was moving up to the extreme right. Gen. Steele was coming up on the left to act as a reserve to Gen. Morgan.

At daylight on the 29th, the Confederate batteries began to fire upon Gen. Morgan's position, and continued it for an hour, although with little effect. With several cessations the cannonade was kept up during the forenoon. Occasionally engagements of infantry, as the opposing regiments came in reach of each other, took place. Several detachments were throwing bridges across the bayou, for the purpose of making an assault on the bluffs. The brigade of Gen. Blair had crossed the bayou before it turned along the bluffs, and was in position at the front of the hill, with a small abatis and a deep ditch between it and the point it designed to assail. On his right, at the point where the bayou makes its angle, was Gen. Morgan. Next to him was Gen. Stuart, and on the extreme right was Gen. A. J. Smith, preparing to throw a bridge across.

No order had been issued by Gen. Sherman appointing an hour for the assault. But by order of Gen. Morgan, Gen. Blair advanced, and Gen. Thayer, of Gen. Steele's brigade, came up for his support. The difficulties of crossing the ditch, and passing the abatis, were such, that the line of Gen. Blair was thrown into some disorder, which, however, it soon recovered, and moved forward upon the Confederate works. The first movement was over a sloping plateau, raked by a direct and enfilading fire from heavy artillery, and swept by a storm of bullets from the rifle pits. Undauntedly the brigade passed on, and in a few moments drove the enemy from their first range of rifle pits, and took full possession of them. Halting for a moment, the brigade pushed forward and took possession of the second line of rifle pits about two hundred yards distant. The batteries were above this line, and their fire still continued. A prompt and powerful support was necessary to make the attempt to capture them.

Simultaneously with the advance of Gen. Blair, an order was given to Gen. Thayer, of Gen. Steele's division, to go forward with his brigade. He crossed the bayou by the same bridge as Gen. Blair, and, entered the abatis at the same point, and deflecting to the right, came out upon the sloping plateau, about two hundred yards to the right of Gen. Blair, and at the same time. As he reached the rifle pits, with a heavy loss, he perceived that only one regiment, the Fourth Iowa, Col. Williamson, had followed him. After his movement commenced, the second regiment of his brigade had been sent to the right of Gen. Morgan as a support. The other regiments had followed this one. Notice of this change of the march of the second regiment, although sent, had failed to reach Gen. Thayer. With little hope of success, he bravely pushed forward into the second line of rifle pits of the enemy on the right of Gen. Blair. Here, leaving the regiment to hold the position, he hurried back for reënforcements. Meanwhile, Gen. Blair, vainly waiting for support, descended in person to persuade the advance of more troops. He, and Gen. Thayer, both failed in their efforts, and were obliged to order their commands to retire.

While Gen. Blair was urging the advance of more troops, his brigade fought with desperation to win the way to the top of the crest. Some fifty yards above the second line of rifle pits was a cluster of small willows. Thither many of the enemy, driven from the rifle pits, had fled. They were promptly pursued by the Thirteenth Illinois, and driven out by a hand-to-hand contest. They were supported at once by the other regiments of the brigade, but the position was exposed to a hot fire of the enemy's batteries. Meantime, a Confederate infantry force was concentrated to attack them, and after a sharp struggle the latter were forced back to the second line of rifle pits, when Gen. Blair's order to retire was received. The division of Gen. Morgan was not brought over the bayou in time to engage in the assault. The division of Gen. Stuart encountered so much difficulty in constructing their bridges over the bayou, under a hot fire of the enemy, that only one regiment finally crossed over. The bridge was then commanded by a flanking fire of the enemy, which prevented others from crossing. The regiment which had crossed returned after dark. A notice of the intended movement on the left had not been given to the division commanders on the right of Gen. Morgan. The division of Gen. Smith was so near to Vicksburg, and the strength of the enemy before him so great, that an assault would have been fruitless. Several sharp encounters, however, took place.

The real assault on the left was made by about three thousand men, and the loss was about eight hundred.

As soon as the assault on the left was concluded, Gen. Sherman determined to make another. A brigade, under the command of Gen. Hovey, was advanced to Gen. Blair's position at the mouth of the bayou, which was to assault the hill, supported by Gen. Morgan and the brigades of Gens. Blair and Thayer. The attack, however, was not made during the remainder of the day; and the next morning developed two new batteries of the enemy in position, and a portion of a new line of rifle pits. Firing was, however, kept up by both sides during that day; and on Wednesday, the 31st, a flag of truce was sent in by Gen. Sherman, and the dead were buried.

Afterward, on the 31st, arrangements were made to attack Haines's Bluff, which was supposed to be defended by a small force. The design, as formed between Admiral Porter and Gen. Sherman, was for a combined naval and land assault on the extreme Confederate right, with a view of getting a position on the bluffs, in the expectation that by so doing they would secure the key to the Confederate position, and compel the enemy to withdraw from the entire range of bluffs and form a new line at Vicksburg. It was planned to land the division of Gen. Steele out of range of the guns of the bluffs, and that they should immediately storm and carry the position. At the same time, the gunboats were to make an attack. The troops were made ready to embark at 2 o'clock A. M. of the next day, but a dense fog having settled on the river prevented their departure. The purpose evidently having become known to the enemy, it was finally given up.

The unexpected strength of the position of the enemy being manifest, and the failure of the forces under Gen. Grant to attack in the rear while Gen. Sherman made the attack in front, entirely disconcerted the original plan upon which the movement of Gen. Sherman was made. The loss of his communications by Gen. Grant, and the necessity for him to fall back, prevented this simultaneous attack on the front and rear of Vicksburg, and probably its capture at this time. It was supposed that the first assault under Gen. Sherman might have been successful if properly supported, so far as related to gaining the crest of the bluffs, although it was not thought that his force could have held it. Gen. Sherman, therefore, resolved to withdraw, and on Thursday night and Friday morning, January 2d, the troops were embarked and moved down to the mouth of the Yazoo river. The entire loss suffered in this expedition was 191 killed, 982 wounded, and 756 missing. Among the former was Lieut. Erwin, in command of a gunboat. Gen. McClernand, who had been ordered to proceed from Cairo, was at the mouth of the Yazoo on the arrival of Gen. Sherman. The former officer then took the command, and ordered the forces to Milliken's Bend, about twelve miles up the river.

On the 4th of January, Gen. Sherman issued the following order:

HEADQUARTERS RIGHT WING ARMY OF TENNESSEE,
STEAMER FOREST QUEEN, MILLIKEN'S BEND,
January 4th, 1863.

Pursuant to the terms of General Order No. 1, made this day by General McClernand, the title of our army ceases to exist, and constitutes in the future the Army of the Mississippi, composed of two "army corps;" one to be commanded by General G. W. Morgan, and the other by myself. In relinquishing the command of the Army of the Tennessee, and restricting my authority to my own corps, I desire to express to all commanders, to soldiers and officers recently operating before Vicksburg, my hearty thanks for the zeal, alacrity, and courage manifested by them on all occasions. We failed in accomplishing one great purpose of our movement—the capture of Vicksburg; but we were part of a whole. Ours was but part of a combined movement in which others were to assist. We were on time; unforeseen contingencies must have delayed the others. We have destroyed the Shreveport road, we have attacked the defences of Vicksburg, and pushed the attack as far as prudence would justify, and having found it too strong for our single column, we have drawn off in good order and good spirits, ready for any new move. A new commander is now here to lead you. He is chosen by the President of the United States, who is charged by the Constitution to maintain and defend it, and he has the undoubted right to select his own agents. I know that all good officers and soldiers will give him the same hearty support and cheerful obedience they have hitherto given me. There are honors enough in reserve for all, and work enough too. Let each do his appropriate part, and our nation must in the end emerge from the dire conflict purified and ennobled by the fires which now test its strength and purity. All officers of the general staff not attached to my person will hereafter report in person and by letter to Major-General McClernand, commanding the Army of the Mississippi, on board the steamer Tigress at our rendezvous at Haines's Landing and at Montgomery Point. By order of

Major-General W. T. SHERMAN.

J. H. HAMMOND, Assistant Adjutant-General.

Subsequently, on the 8th, Gen. Pemberton, who had fallen back from before Gen. Grant, and had taken command at Vicksburg, issued the following address to his troops:

HEADQUARTERS DEPARTMENT OF MISSISSIPPI AND
LOUISIANA, VICKSBURG, *January 8th.*

The Lieut.-General commanding this department of the army desires to express to its troops his high appreciation of their gallant demeanor in the defence of this important position. All praise is due them, not alone for so bravely repulsing the renewed assaults of an enemy vastly superior in numbers, but especially for the cheerful and patient endurance with which they have submitted to the hardships and exposures incident to ten successive days and nights of watchfulness in trenches, rendered imperatively necessary by the close proximity of the opposing armies, while all have performed their duties with benefit to their country and honor to themselves. Still, as must ever be the case in war, fortune has favored unequally those who by her favor held the posts of honor, and by their own resolute courage availed themselves of their opportunity; to them special thanks are due. It will be a proud and agreeable duty of the Lieutenant-General commanding to claim for them from their country the distinction and honor they so justly deserve.

(Signed) J. C. PEMBERTON,
Lieutenant-General Commanding.

At the time of the arrival of Gen. McClernand, a plan had been agreed upon between Gen. Sherman and Rear-Admiral Porter to attack Arkansas Post. The reasons for making this attack were that there was time to do it while Gen. Grant was moving his army to Memphis; the blow would be entirely unexpected by the enemy; the Federal forces were amply sufficient to make a victory certain, which would be valuable in restoring the spirit of the troops disheartened by their recent failure, which was not understood in its true light. On the other hand, the Confederate force up the Arkansas river had shown considerable activity by sallies in which they had captured two steamers bearing supplies to the army below.

Gen. McClernand approving of the enterprise, the forces moved up the Mississippi to Montgomery Point, opposite the mouth of White river.

White river, one of the principal streams in Arkansas, rises a few miles east of Fayetteville, and flows in a northeasterly direction into Missouri about one hundred miles. It then returns into Arkansas, and pursues a southeasterly course, and enters the Mississippi about fifteen miles above the mouth of the Arkansas. It is navigable by steamboats three hundred and fifty miles.

On Friday, Jan. 9th, the ironclads Louisville, De Kalb, and Cincinnati, with all the light-draft gunboats, moved up the White river, followed by the fleet of transports. After ascending the White river about fifteen miles, the fleet passed through a cut-off to the left, eight miles in length, into the Arkansas river. Thus the White river empties by one channel into the Mississippi, and by another into the Arkansas, when it has a higher stage of water than the Arkansas. When the Arkansas is higher than the White river, one of the Arkansas currents comes through the cut-off and out by the White river into the Mississippi.

It was about 11 o'clock A. M. when the fleet passed into the Arkansas. This is, next to the Missouri, the longest affluent of the Mississippi river. It rises near the Rocky mountains, and flows through nearly the centre of the State of Arkansas, exceeding two thousand miles in length, and navigable, during nine months of the year, about eight hundred miles from its mouth.

About half past four in the afternoon, the fleet moved to the shore, and preparations were made to land three miles below the fort. The artillery and wagons were brought on shore during the evening and night, and in the morning the troops were landed and marshalled in the fields bordering on the north bank. The attack, however, was begun by the gunboats.

The Arkansas river, in its descent toward the Mississippi, makes here a sharp elbow by flowing north, then turning abruptly to the east, and after a short distance turning again as abruptly to the south. On the left bank, at the point where the river turns to the east, the fort of Arkansas Post was located. Its guns commanded the river as it stretched to the east, and even after the turn to the south.

The advance of the troops was along the outside bank of this curve of the river, and it was expected the attack on the fort would be made during the day, but at sundown they were not in position. The division of Gen. Stuart, by order of Gen. Sherman, had moved along the bank, passing two rows of rifle pits which had been abandoned, and reached the point for an attack, but the corps of Gen. Morgan had not then deployed on the left. Orders were then issued by Gen. McClernand for the troops to get into position during the night, so as to make an attack in the morning. The force of Gen. Sherman worked its way through the forest and marsh round to the right, so as to invest the fort, while a brigade was thrown across the river to prevent the arrival down of reënforcements to the rebels.

The fort, which was called "Fort Hindman," was a regular square bastioned work, one hundred yards each exterior side, with a deep ditch about fifteen feet wide, and a parapet eighteen feet high. It was armed with twelve guns, two of which were eight inch and one nine inch. The number of troops which it contained was about five thousand, under the command of Brig.-Gen. Churchill.

During the evening of the 10th, the fort was bombarded by the ironclads Cincinnati, Lieut.-Commander Geo. L. Bache; De Kalb, Lieut.-Com. John H. Walker, Louisville, Lieut.-Com. R. L. Owen, all under the orders of Rear-Admiral Porter. The bombardment continued over a half hour, and the firing was active on both sides. The distance of the boats from the fort was about four hundred yards.

About noon on the 11th, the fleet was notified, by order of Gen. McClernand, that the army was ready, and a joint attack was made. The gunboats took a position within about three hundred yards of the fort and opened fire. The fort had opened upon them as soon as they came in sight. At the same time a battery of Gen. Sherman's began to fire, and the troops were advanced to attack. It was not long before the heavy guns of the fort were silenced by the gunboats, but the action on the part of the military grew more severe until four o'clock, when the enemy were so far overcome as to raise the white flag. A rush was immediately made, both by the land troops and naval force, to occupy the works, and the surrender was made complete. The loss of Gen. McClernand was about six hundred, of whom one hundred and twenty were killed. The Confederate loss was less, owing to the shelter of their troops. About sixty-five were

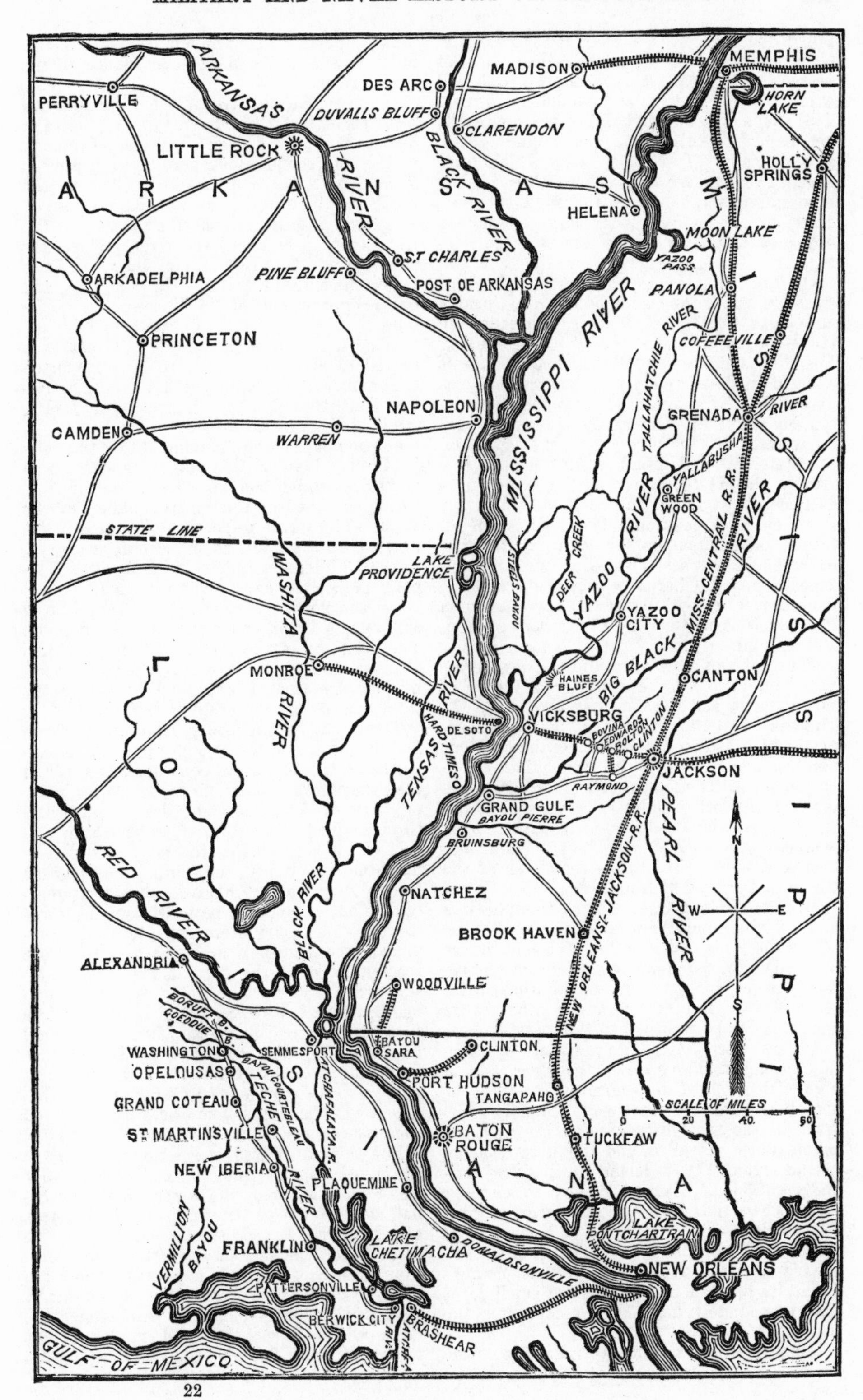
MEMPHIS
MADISON
DES ARC
PERRYVILLE
ARKANSAS
DUVALLS BLUFF
CLARENDON
HORN LAKE
LITTLE ROCK
BLACK RIVER
HOLLY SPRINGS
A R K A N S A S
HELENA
MOON LAKE
YAZOO PASS
ST. CHARLES
ARKADELPHIA
PINE BLUFF
POST OF ARKANSAS
PANOLA
MISSISSIPPI RIVER
PRINCETON
TALLAHATCHIE RIVER
COFFEEVILLE
NAPOLEON
GRENADA
RIVER
CAMDEN
WARREN
YALLABUSHA
GREEN WOOD
STATE LINE
DEER CREEK
YAZOO
RIVER
MISS. CENTRAL R.R.
LAKE PROVIDENCE
STEELS BAYOU
WASHITA
YAZOO CITY
RIVER
MONROE
HAINES BLUFF
BIG BLACK
CANTON
TENSAS RIVER
VICKSBURG
DE SOTO
HARD TIMES
BOVINA
EDWARDS
BOLTON
CLINTON
JACKSON
RAYMOND
GRAND GULF
BAYOU PIERRE
BRUINSBURG
PEARL RIVER
NEW ORLEANS-JACKSON-R.R.
RED RIVER
BLACK RIVER
NATCHEZ
BROOK HAVEN
N
W
E
S
ALEXANDRIA
WOODVILLE
L O U I S I A N A
M I S S I S S I P P I
BORUFF B.
COEODUE B.
WASHINGTON
SEMMESPORT
BAYOU SARA
CLINTON
OPELOUSAS
BAYOU COURTEBLEAU
TECHE
ATCHAFALAYA R.
PORT HUDSON
TANGAPAHO
SCALE OF MILES
0
20
40
60
GRAND COTEAU
ST. MARTINSVILLE
BATON ROUGE
TUCKEAW
NEW IBERIA
RIVER
PLAQUEMINE
LAKE PONTCHARTRAIN
VERMILLION BAYOU
FRANKLIN
LAKE CHETIMACHA
DONALDSONVILLE
NEW ORLEANS
PATTERSONVILLE
BERWICK CITY
BRASHEAR
GULF OF MEXICO

killed and eighty-three wounded. The ironclads were struck by many balls. A shot passed through a porthole of the De Kalb and exploded, killing two and wounding fifteen. Two shells entered portholes of the Louisville and exploded, killing one and wounding ten, two mortally. The other boats which were engaged escaped without serious injury. Seven thousand prisoners, eight thousand stand of arms, twenty cannon, and a large amount of ordnance and commissary stores were captured.

On the 15th, an expedition in light-draft steamers, under the command of Gen. Gorman and Lieut.-Com. J. G. Walker, proceeded up the White river and captured the towns of Des Arc and Duval's Bluff. The former is situated in Prairie county, Arkansas, and was once a thriving commercial town. It is situated on the White river, and is about fifty miles north east of Little Rock, the capital of the State. Duval's Bluff, a little below Des Arc on the White river, was the station of a Confederate camp, and an earthwork fort. It is an elevated position. The expedition returned to Napoleon on the 19th. Some prisoners and a few guns were captured by the expedition. St. Charles, a village on the Arkansas river, a short distance above Arkansas Post, was also captured by a force sent by Gen. McClernand.

The next two days after the engagement at Fort Hindman were devoted to the care of the wounded and the burial of the dead. On Thursday, the 15th, the corps of Gen. Sherman, which had embarked during the previous night, proceeded down the Arkansas river to Napoleon, at its mouth. The rifle pits were levelled, the fort completely blown up and destroyed, and a hundred wagons which had been captured were burned. On the 18th, Gen. McClernand embarked with the remainder of the troops and arrived at Napoleon.

Meanwhile Gen. Grant, leaving Memphis in a swift steamer, met Admiral Porter at the cut-off up the White river, on the 18th, and thence proceeded to Napoleon, where future movements were arranged in consultations with Gens. McClernand, Sherman, and others. On the same day he returned to Memphis.

Orders were immediately issued by Gen. McClernand to move down the river, and at eight o'clock on the next morning, the 19th, the signal for departure was given. Shortly afterward all the transports were on the way. A severe storm prevailed, and the fleet came to at the foot of Ozark Island until it had partially subsided. It then moved to Chicot's Bend, where the principal portion were moored for the night. On the next day, the fleet moved down to Milesia, and by two o'clock of the following day, the 21st, it arrived at Young's Point, its place of destination. A small force was immediately landed, to reconnoitre the country.

Young's Point is on the western side of the Mississippi river, about nine miles above Vicksburg, and nearly opposite the mouth of the Yazoo river.

On the 22d, the troops were landed and posted a little farther down the river, so as to defend the line of a canal which had been commenced a year previous, across the peninsula formed by a curve of the river, first to the north and then to the south. The purpose of this canal had been to afford a passage for the transports up or down the river, beyond the reach of the batteries at Vicksburg. A little below the extreme point of the peninsula, and on the opposite side of the Mississippi, is Vicksburg.

Meantime the army of Gen. Grant was moved to Memphis, thence to be transported to Young's Point. On the 20th, Gen. McArthur left Memphis, on fourteen transports, with his corps. He had been preceded by other bodies of troops, making at that time one hundred and twenty-five transports with troops and stores which had left. The forces of Gen. Grant consisted of the veteran soldiers of the West. The naval force was also greatly increased by the addition of several ironclads, as the Chillicothe, Indianola, Lafayette, Eastport, and a number of other gunboats.

On the 2d of February, Gen. Grant arrived at Young's Point and assumed the command. The divisions of the Army of Tennessee had also reached there, excepting the one commanded by Gen. Logan, and excepting the troops occupying the posts in Tennessee.

The attack on Vicksburg, from up the river, had demonstrated the strength of its defensive works on the north, and convinced Gen. Grant that they were too strong to be carried without a very heavy loss. The first step for him to accomplish, therefore, was the transportation of his army below the city, in order to make an attack from the south. The passage by the river was too hazardous to be attempted. The formidable batteries on the river front at Vicksburg were capable of destroying all the transports. Work was therefore recommenced on the canal across the peninsula, on the western side of the river, which had been located by Brig.-Gen. Williams at the first attempt to capture the city. This canal had been improperly located, its upper terminus being in an eddy, and the lower terminus being exposed to the enemy's guns; nevertheless it was thought that it would be completed sooner than a new one could be constructed. While this work was in progress, the river continued to rise rapidly, and great labor was required to keep the water out of the canal, and also out of the camps of the laborers and soldiers. In addition, the rain was incessant, and the magnitude of the work was, from these causes, grealy increased. The earth taken out of the excavation was placed on the west side, and thus formed an embankment or levee, which it was supposed would prevent the water from flooding the country on that side, and the ground on which nearly all of the army was encamped. As the canal cut the peninsula at right angles, the troops were encamped west of it and behind this embankment. On the 8th of March, when the enterprise promised success within a short time, the dam across the mouth of the canal gave way, owing to a rapid rise of the river and the great pressure of the water. When it broke there was a difference of eight feet between the bottom of the canal and the surface of the water in the river. The violence of the torrent as it rushed through swept away all the implements of labor, and the canal was full in a few minutes. The embankment had not been completed, and the water soon began to pour over. A spectator thus describes the scene: "Some regiments that were in exposed positions had to gather up tents and camp equipage in hot haste and confusion and run for the levee. Several companies on the lower side of the peninsula were cut off and had to be ferried to the main body of the army. The embankment of the Vicksburg and Shreveport railroad, which cut the peninsula longitudinally, prevented the water from flooding the northwest quarter. But that was considered insecure; the troops were all ordered to move their quarters to the levee."

Some delay was caused by the efforts to repair the damages, but it soon became manifest that, with the existing high stage of the water, some other plan would have to be adopted to get below Vicksburg with the transports.

At the commencement of the work on the canal, Gen. Grant, having more troops than could be employed at Young's Point to advantage, caused a channel to be cut from the Mississippi into Lake Providence on the west side of the Mississippi, and another into Coldwater river by the way of the Yazoo Pass, on the east side of the Mississippi. From the former of these routes no great expectations were entertained by Gen. Grant. He thought possible, however, that a route might be opened there through which transports might pass into the Mississippi, and enable him to coöperate with Gen. Banks below. By the Yazoo Pass he expected to get into the Yazoo by way of the Coldwater and Tallahatchie rivers, with some light gunboats and a few troops, and destroy some Confederate transports in that stream and some gunboats on the stocks. With such views the work on these channels was commenced.

While these operations were pushed forward, other measures for the annoyance of the enemy were also taken. A steamer called the "City of Vicksburg" was daily noticed lying under the batteries of the city, and it was known that farther down the river there was a number of transports rendering great service to the Confederate authorities by bringing supplies to their troops at Vicksburg and at Port Hudson, another strong position below. A movement was planned to destroy these means of transportation. Orders were therefore given to Col. Charles E. Ellet to prepare the ram steamer Queen of the West for running down below the batteries. This steamer was a wooden freight vessel, strengthened so as to carry a prow of iron. To protect her machinery from injury by the shot and shells of the batteries at Vicksburg, three hundred bales of cotton were placed about it, and her steering wheel was removed and placed behind the bulwarks of her bow. Her armament consisted of a large 30-pounder rifled Parrott gun on her main deck as a bow gun, one 20-pounder, and three 12-pounder brass howitzers on her gun deck. Besides these she had fifty or sixty rifles, carbines, cutlasses, pistols, &c. Her crew consisted of a first, second, and third master, two pilots, three engineers, blacksmiths, carpenters, and deck hands; also a squad of twenty-six soldiers. It was planned that she should start before daybreak on the morning of the 2d of February. At the appointed time the steamer was under way, but her steering apparatus in its new position controlled her movements so poorly that it was necessary to replace it in its original position. This was important, as the destruction of the City of Vicksburg would depend in part upon the accuracy of the blow of the Queen of the West. The detention which ensued prevented her from passing round the point of the peninsula into view from the Confederate batteries until sunrise, when she was instantly greeted by a shell that passed between her smoke chimneys and struck the water about three hundred yards behind her. After the sound of the first shot broke the stillness of the morning, the Confederate artillerists sprang to their pieces, and a hundred guns were fired with a wonderful celerity. Only three or four shots had struck her before she reached the front of the city. The first object now to be accomplished was the destruction of the steamer City of Vicksburg, which was made fast to the bank about the centre of the bend of the river, where the current ran very rapidly. To strike an unerring blow it was necessary for the Queen of the West to round to amid the storm of balls and shells, and move directly across the river against her victim. As she approached the steamboat and the city, the enemy, thinking that she had been disabled, and that her commander had concluded to surrender, raised enthusiastic cheers, which ceased as the ram struck the steamer. The wide guards of the Vicksburg, overlapping the deck of the Queen, even to the barricade of cotton bales, received the force of the blow and prevented the prow of the ram from reaching her hull. At the same time the current caught the stern of the Queen and swung her round side by side with the Vicksburg. This action of the current had been anticipated by Col. Ellet, and the starboard bow gun had been loaded with incendiary shells. It was now fired into the Vicksburg. At the same time the shells from the batteries had set on fire the cotton on the

Queen, and it was evident that to repeat the blow would involve the loss of the steamer. The effort was then made to turn her head out toward the stream, which, owing to the action of the wind and current, was, after some delay, accomplished. She then proceeded down the stream with all hands at work to extinguish the fire. Meantime the discharge from the batteries became quick and incessant, and she now received most of the dozen shots which hit her from the artillery and the sharpshooters on the shore. No material injury, however, was done, and she anchored below the outlet of the canal until one o'clock P. M., when she proceeded down the river.

On this expedition, down the river, her officers captured, below Natchez, and burned three small steamers, the Moro, Berwick Bay, and A. W. Baker; one of them was laden with pork, and another with molasses and sugar. She ran fifteen miles up the Red river, and returned on the fifth for a supply of coal. During the night a flatboat loaded with coal was cast loose in the stream, and passing the batteries safely, floated down to the steamer.

On the night of the 10th of February, this steamer started on another expedition down the Mississippi. The first object of the expedition was to capture Confederate steamers. It was also proposed to run up the Big Black river, which empties into the Mississippi at Grand Gulf, to visit the Atchafalaya, and perhaps the Red river, and, if practicable, to pass the batteries at Port Hudson, and effect a junction with the fleet below under Com. Farragut. A tender was provided for the Queen of the West in the steamer De Soto, a small ferry boat once running between De Soto, the termination of the Vicksburg, Shreveport and Texas railroad, across to Vicksburg. The batteries at Warrenton, eight miles below, were passed without molestation. At Taylor's Point, above Natchez, at the plantation once owned the late President Taylor, a short stop was made. It was found to be occupied by friendly owners. Natchez was next passed, and on Wednesday evening the steamer reached the mouth of Old river, into which Red river runs. This was the channel of the Mississippi before the cut-off was formed. The Red river extends from the northern side of Old river, first northwesterly, and then nearly west, across the State of Louisiana, into Texas. At high water it is navigable to Paris, nine hundred and sixty miles from New Orleans.

Passing the night at anchor at the mouth of Old river, on the next morning, the 12th, leaving the De Soto as a guard near the mouth of Old river, the Queen of the West entered the Atchafalaya, which flows north and empties into Red river just above its junction with Old river. A train of eleven army wagons was captured about five miles up the river, and at Semmes's port, ten miles farther up, seventy five barrels of beef and a mail with despatches was taken, but a Confederate steamer at that place had escaped. Returning down the river near dark, the steamer was fired on at the point where the wagons had been captured, and the first master mortally wounded. A landing was not made, but the steamer returned to the anchorage of the previous night. On the next morning Col. Ellet, having been informed of the parties who fired on the boat, returned and destroyed the dwellings, mills, and negro quarters on six sugar plantations above the mouth of the Atchafalaya. During the afternoon the steamers entered the Red river, and moved up as far as the mouth of Black river, at dark, where they anchored for the night. The Black river, formed by the junction of the Washita and Tensas rivers, flows south and empties into the Red river, a short distance above the mouth of the Atchafalaya. At daylight on the next morning they were under way up the river. About ten o'clock, the Era, No. 5, a steamer of one hundred tons, was discovered approaching. At the same time she discovered the Queen, and attempted to turn for the purpose of escaping, when a shot from the former demolished her wheelhouse, and her officers surrendered. Fourteen Texan soldiers and a number of citizens were found on board. The former were paroled and the latter dismissed, except a quartermaster, having $28,000 in Confederate funds, and two lieutenants. The boat was loaded with 4,500 bushels of corn in the ear, destined for the Confederate forces at Little Rock. Nothing further of importance was discovered during the passage of the next twenty miles up the river. In fact the stream is so crooked in some parts, that a distance of two miles across the land would strike a point to reach which a steamer would be obliged to go twenty miles. Thus information was easily sent of the approach of hostile vessels. Some twenty miles farther up was located Fort Taylor, a post which was supposed to be manned by about one hundred and fifty men, with two or three guns. It was situated on the south bank of the river, just above a bend which its guns commanded, that was made by an abrupt turn of the river to the north. From the point opposite this bend a long bar projected, on which the water is shallow, and it is necessary to "hug" the south shore to avoid being driven on the bar by a strong eddy.

The Era had been left with the three prisoners under a guard about twenty miles below. It was about nightfall as the Queen approached the bend of the river, with the De Soto a considerable distance astern. The pilot of the captured Era had been forced to assist at the wheel, owing to the intricacies of the channel. Upon turning the point, the Queen struck upon the bar and became fast aground in a position in which none of her guns were effective. The guns of the fort immediately opened upon her with fearful accuracy and rapidity. The shot and shell struck all about her. The lever of the engine was shot away, the escape pipe broken, and the immediate roar of steam that enveloped the vessel showed that her steam chest had been penetrated. Every thought of saving the steamer was given up, and the exertions of all were made to save themselves. Many threw bales of cotton overboard and floated on them down to the De Soto a mile below, among whom was Col. Ellet. The fort seeing there was no reply to their guns, and conceiving from the rush of steam that something had happened, slackened their fire and sent boats to reconnoitre. By this force the remainder of the crew were captured, and the boat made a prize.

Meanwhile the De Soto approached as near the point as was safe, and picked up those who were floating, and sent a boat for the crew, which was almost captured by the enemy, who had already reached the Queen. Finding that soldiers were collecting on the shore, the De Soto was turned and slowly floated down the stream. Three miles below she ran aground and unshipped her rudder, and for the next fifteen miles and during three hours she was unmanageable, and moved with the current. As she reached the Era at eleven o'clock, a second rudder was unshipped, and she became unmanageable again, when Col. Ellet ordered her to be blown up.

It was about twelve o'clock at night before the Era was under way. It was known to Col. Ellet that the swift gunboat Webb was at Alexandria, about sixty miles up the river, and he was confident that pursuit would be made after him by her. All hands were set to work to throw overboard the corn with which the Era was laden, and amid fog, thunder, lightning and rain, she worried her way out of the Red river into the Mississippi by morning. All that day, which was Sunday, with no fuel but some of the corn with which she had been laden, and cypress found on the banks too wet to make steam enough to give her headway, the fleeing steamer attempted to get up the river. She had made scarcely forty miles in twenty-four hours. At Union Point she was run aground and detained three hours in getting off. After passing Ellis's Cliffs, the black chimney of a passing steamer was discovered over the fog which enveloped her hull. The black smoke from her chimney showed that she burned coal, and that it was a Federal steamer. It was the Indianola, and all fear of the Webb was over. Scarcely was the Era well alongside of the Indianola and the fog had lifted a little, when the Webb hove in sight. A brief pursuit of her was made by the two boats, without success. The Era was then furnished with supplies, and sent up to Admiral Porter.

The Indianola, which came so fortunately to the rescue of Col. Ellet, was one of the finest of the ironclad gunboats of the squadron: she was new, and was 174 feet long, 50 feet beam, 10 feet from the top of her deck to the bottom of her keel, or 8 feet 4 inches in the clear. Her sides (of wood) for five feet down were thirty-two inches thick, having bevelled sticks laid outside the hull (proper), and all of oak. Outside of this was three-inch thick plate iron. Her clamps and keelsons were as heavy as the largest ships. Her deck was eight inches solid, with one-inch iron plate, all well bolted. Her casemate stood at an incline of 26½ degrees, and was covered with three-inch iron, as were also her ports. She had a heavy grating on top of the casemate that no shell could penetrate, and every scuttle and hatch was equally well covered. She was ironed all round, except some temporary rooms on deck, and, besides the amount of wood and iron already stated, had coal bunkers seven feet thick alongside of her boilers, the entire machinery being in the hold. She had seven engines—two for working her side wheels, two for her propellers, two for her capstans, and one for supplying water and working the bilge and fire pumps. She had five large five-flued boilers, and made abundance of steam. Her forward casemate had two 11-inch Dahlgren guns, and her after casemate two 9-inch. Her forward casemate was pierced for two guns in front, one on each side, and two aft, so that she could fire two guns forward, one on each side, and four at an angle sideways and astern. She had also hose for throwing scalding water from the boilers, that would reach from stem to stern, and there was communication from the casemates to all parts of the vessel without the least exposure. The pilot house was also thoroughly ironclad, and instant communication could be had with the gunners and engineers, enabling the pilot to place the vessel in just such position as might be required for effective action. She left her anchorage at the mouth of the Yazoo, about ten o'clock on the night of February 13th, to run below the batteries at Vicksburg. The night was hazy and cloudy, and thus exceedingly dark. After passing entirely through the fleet, and reaching the vicinity of the upper end of the canal, she shut off steam entirely, and suffered the current to bear her along. Its rate was about four miles an hour. In perfect obscurity she rounded the point, and drifted fairly beneath the formidable batteries. The tide bore her down directly toward the levee of the city. Lights were everywhere numerous, and the voices of citizens and soldiers sounded as if they were close alongside. Still the black and noiseless mass drifted along, almost rubbing the bank, yet undiscovered. The whole levee was patrolled by sentinels, and at one spot a camp fire was dimly burning. As the drifting vessel approached this point, a soldier stooping down gathered some faggots and threw them into the fire. A bright blaze flashed up for a moment, exposing everything within its sphere. The Indianola was seen by a soldier, who discharged his musket at her. At that discharge the soldiers everywhere along the bluff sprang to arms. A battery near the centre of the city fired a gun, rockets were sent off, soldiers on the bank discharged their muskets into the darkness, and indications of excitement were manifest everywhere. The boat had been discovered running the blockade, but no one knew where she was. Five minutes passed after the first gun was fired, and another had not followed. At last it became necessary to start the wheels in order to get steerage way on the steamer. The noise of the steam drew forth a second and third gun, and a discharge of musketry, and again all was still. The boat drifted on a few moments in silence, when the steam was again let on, and she dashed down the river, regardless of any noise that might be made. Battery after battery now opened upon her until twenty shots were fired, and she had passed uninjured beyond their reach. The steamer was under the command of Lieut.-Com. Brown, and continued on down the river, until she met the Era as above stated. After pursuing the Webb, in vain, as far as the mouth of Red river, the Indianola proceeded up that stream in search of Confederate transports, and kept up a watch off the mouth of the Atchafalaya river. Here her commander learned that the Queen of the West had been repaired and might soon be down. As the narrowness of the Red river made it difficult to manœuvre a long boat like the Indianola, while the Queen was much shorter, Commander Brown determined to return to the mouth of the Big Black river, and attempt to pass up that stream, and reach if possible the bridge of the Vicksburg and Jackson railroad. This had been one of the objects for which the steamers had run the blockade. The Big Black river empties into the Mississippi at Grand Gulf, forty miles below Vicksburg. It rises in the northern part of the State of Mississippi, and flows southwesterly, passing about fifteen miles east of Vicksburg.

On Tuesday morning, Feb. 24th, the Indianola reached the mouth of the Big Black, and in the afternoon made preparations to move up the river, when two steamers were descried approaching. These proved to be the Confederate gunboat Webb and the Queen of the West. The Webb was a powerful boat and one of the swiftest on the river. They immediately attacked the Indianola, and, chiefly by striking her with their rams, so shattered her as to endanger her sinking, when she was surrendered and immediately run ashore.

A few days afterward a flatboat was fitted up by Admiral Porter to appear like a gunboat, and set adrift in the river without a pilot or crew. As it passed the batteries at Vicksburg, it was supposed to be a formidable ram, and they fired fiercely. It escaped uninjured however, and floated on down the river. Information of its approach was sent to the Queen of the West, lying under the batteries at Warrenton, eight miles below Vicksburg, and she immediately fled down stream. The Indianola was undergoing repairs near where she was taken, and the authorities at Vicksburg, thinking that she would be recaptured by the ram, issued an order to burn her up. This order was sent down by a courier to the officer in charge of the boat. A few hours later, and another order was sent down countermanding the first, it having been ascertained that the monstrous craft was nothing else than a coal-boat. But before it reached the Indianola she had been blown to atoms: not even a gun was saved.

Meanwhile, the work of cutting channels from the Mississippi to Providence Lake, on the west side, and to Moon Lake, on the east side, was progressing rapidly.

Lake Providence is a few miles south of the boundary line between Arkansas and Louisiana. It is situated in Carroll parish, Louisiana, about one mile west of the Mississippi river, and about seventy-five miles above Vicksburg. It is about six miles in length. Two streams flow out of the lake to the south, Moon bayou and Tensas river. The former, after running about a hundred miles, unites with the latter. The two continue south, and unite with the Washita, and are called after the junction Black river, which empties into the Red river, as is stated on a preceding page. By cutting a channel from the Mississippi to Lake Providence, Gen. Grant thought a communication might be had through that lake down the Tensas and Black into the Red river, and thence through the Atchafalaya, with Gen. Banks at New Orleans. This route avoided the batteries at Vicksburg and Port Hudson. The canal to the lake was finished so as to let in the water on the 16th of March. The flood was so great as to inundate a large district of country, some of which was fine land for growing cotton. Some boats passed into Lake Providence, but the uncertainty of the channel of the Tensas river, and the interest which was now excited by the Yazoo Pass expedition, together with the unimportant results to be anticipated by removing a large force to the Red river or below, caused a diversion from this route to others presenting more certain prospects of success against Vicksburg.

Eight miles below Helena, in Arkansas, and on the opposite side of the river, is a little lake, known as Moon Lake. The passage from the Mississippi across the lake to the mouth of the Yazoo Pass is about eight miles; thence through the Pass proper to the Coldwater river, twelve miles. The Coldwater, a narrow stream, runs south, empties into the Tallahatchie, which continues to flow south, and unites with the Yalobusha, forming the Yazoo river, which empties into the Mississippi, a few miles above Vicksburg. By opening a wider channel from the Mississippi into Moon Lake, it was the opinion that the inner streams would be rendered more easily navigable, in consequence of an increase of water, so that some smaller gunboats and a few troops could destroy the enemy's transports in the Yazoo, and their gunboats which were building. In ordinary stages of water, steamboats could ascend the

Yazoo and Tallahatchie to the mouth of the Coldwater. The region of country through which these streams flow, especially the Yazoo, is very fertile, producing a large quantity of cotton, and furnishing considerable supplies to the rebel army at Vicksburg.

The expedition consisted of two of the largest and heaviest ironclad gunboats, one ram, six light-draft gunboats, three barges laden with coal, three steam tenders, and fifteen or eighteen transports. The passage from the Mississippi to the mouth of the Pass, after the improvement made upon it, was not attended with much difficulty. On the morning of the 25th of March it entered the mouth of the Pass. The tortuous stream was a hundred feet wide, and in some parts less. On its banks were cypress, sycamore, and gigantic cottonwood trees, whose branches formed a perfect arch over the stream. At the upper end the current rushed with great rapidity through the channel, and lower down were strips of bottom land, which were overflowed, and gave to it greater width, and, consequently, less rapidity. In the narrow and crooked passage it was necessary to resist the force of the current by the back revolution of the wheels of the boats, and by lines fastened from tree to tree as they moved along. Three days were thus passed in making a distance of about twelve miles, and reaching the Coldwater. Smokestacks were swept away, and much of the light upper works of several of the boats. The principal difficulty in the Pass arose from the activity of the enemy, who would close one end while the Federal force was opening the other. In this manner time was gained to prepare to resist the progress of the expedition by fortifying at the mouth of the Tallahatchie.

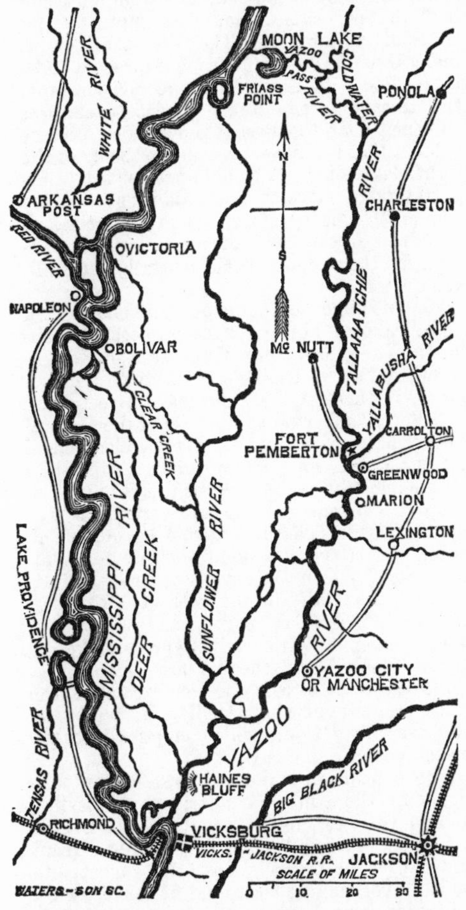

On the 2d of April the expedition proceeded down the Coldwater. This stream was a little wider than the Pass, so that the branches of the trees seldom met over head, but its current was more sluggish, and its channel equally tortuous. Two mortar boats now joined the expedition, adding their force to the heavy guns on the other boats. As it advanced it was further reënforced, until it consisted of eighteen transports, five small gunboats, and two of a large size, the Chillicothe and the De Kalb. The advance consisted of one division of Gen. McClernand's corps, which had been stationed at Helena, under command of Brig.-Gen. L. F. Ross, and the 12th and 17th Missouri regiments from Gen. Sherman's corps, as sharpshooters, on the gunboats. The mouth of the Coldwater was reached with only some damage to the light work, wheels, and rudders of the transports.

Proceeding down the Tallahatchie, the expedition arrived within ten miles of Greenwood on the 11th. Greenwood is a small village on the Yazoo river, just below the junction of the Tallahatchie with the Yallobusha, forming the Yazoo. Just below the position of the Federal transports, the Tallahatchie turns to the eastward, bending in the form of a horseshoe, and resumes its southerly course at a point nearly south of that where the transports were. The base of the peninsula formed by this bend, being the narrowest part, and nearly a mile across, was occupied by a Confederate fortification. It consisted of a single line of breastworks facing westerly, and composed of cotton bales and earth, and flanked on the right by a battery of three heavy guns fronting the river. Other field pieces were in position on the works. On the right flank of the line, a defence or raft of logs had been constructed, to serve as a blockade of the river. Directly in front of the breastworks was a deep slough, extending across the peninsula, and admirably serving the purpose of a ditch. The slough was close to the base of the works at the upper end, but gradually receded from them at the lower, where it was several hundred yards distant. Beyond the slough there was an almost impenetrable canebrake, backed by an extensive forest. Below this fortification on the river, and in the arc of the bend, the Yallobusha flows in from the northeast, and forms its junction with the Tallahatchie. The village of Greenwood is upon the Yazoo, four miles below. The object of the fortification at this location was not only to stop the fleet from passing below, but also to prevent its passing up the Yallobusha river, on which a number of the enemy's steamers had sought refuge, and on the bank of which also was the important town of Granada.

The Confederate force was estimated above five thousand men, under the command of Gen. Tilghman, who surrendered Fort Henry, in Kentucky. On the morning of the 11th a reconnoissance was made by the gunboat Chillicothe, Lieut.-Commander Foster. The boat approached within a short distance of the fortification, and fired several shots, and was hit four times in return by heavy shot from rifle pieces. At the same time detachments from the Forty-sixth and Forty-seventh Indiana regiments were sent out to feel the Confederate position on the land side. A considerable body of the enemy's skirmishers were encountered, who were driven across the slough and into the works, when the detachments were withdrawn. In the afternoon the Chillicothe was ordered to engage the fortification. After she had fired seven rounds, a 64-pound shell from the enemy passed through a half-open port, striking upon the muzzle of a gun, in which a shell had just been placed preparatory to cutting the fuse. Both shells exploded at once, by which three men were killed and eleven wounded. At this time orders were received to withdraw from the engagement. During the ensuing night a force was sent to throw up a battery facing the enemy's works, west of the slough, and in the edge of the timber. A single 30-pound Parrott gun was mounted, and the work concealed by brush from the view of the enemy. Subsequently another gun was mounted. No attack was made on the 12th, in consequence of the absence of the mortar boats. After some delay, on the 13th, the engagement was commenced about half past ten A. M. by the land batteries. The gunboats Chillicothe and De Kalb soon after approached and opened their fire. It now appeared that the fortification mounted a rifled 64-Parrott and three 24-Dahlgrens, and a small field battery. These guns were protected by a parapet composed of seven tiers of cotton bales, covered on the outside with eight feet of earth. The contest was bravely maintained for some time, when the fire of the enemy was suspended, but no disposition to surrender was shown. The gunboats and battery kept up the fire, but without any success in reducing the works. The Chillicothe was struck thirty-four times, but not severely injured. The DeKalb suffered more, in consequence of some shot penetrating her casemates, by which one man was killed and five wounded.

The impracticable nature of the approach to the fort by foot soldiers on the west, in consequence of the overflow or slough, rendered it necessary that the gunboats should silence the guns of the enemy, and enable the transports to run down and land troops immediately on the fort itself. But all attempts to silence the fort by the gunboats proved unsuccessful, and the guns of the battery were withdrawn, and the expedition put on the defensive. After a few days it began to retire.

Meantime, Gen. Grant had been led to believe, as the navigation proved better than was expected, that it was possible to make this the route for obtaining a foothold on high land above Haines's Bluff, and had sent forward a division of Gen. McPherson's corps, commanded by Brig.-Gen. J. F. Quimby, and had ordered some small-class steamers for transporting the army. The seventeenth corps, under Gen. McPherson, was also directed to be in readiness to move, and one division from the thirteenth and fifteenth corps each, was collected near the Pass. But it soon became evident that a sufficient number of boats of the right class, could not be obtained for the transportation of more than one division. On the 23d of March, therefore, orders were given to withdraw all the forces operating in that direction, for the purpose of concentrating at Milliken's Bend.

At this time another expedition had started under Admiral Porter, for the purpose of reaching the Yazoo below Fort Pemberton and Greenwood, and above Haines's Bluff. Such a movement, if successful, would leave Greenwood and Fort Pemberton to the rear of the Federal forces, and necessarily cause it to be abandoned. At the same time, about thirty Confederate steamers could be captured or destroyed. The route to be pursued by this expedition was up the Yazoo river to Cypress bayou, which enters that river at a point opposite the landing place of Gen. Sherman's troops when attacking the bluffs in the rear of Vicksburg, thence into Steele's bayou, and along that watercourse, and through Cypress Lake, to Little Black Fork, thence into Deer creek. Following this stream for some distance, the route branches off along Rolling Fork into the Big Sunflower river, which empties into the Yazoo above Haines's Bluff.

The expedition under Admiral Porter, consisted of the gunboats Pittsburg, Louisville, Mound City, Cincinnati, and Carondelet, with a number of small transports. Gen. Grant stated that the principal obstacles appeared to be the overhanging trees, and he sent forward a pioneer corps for their removal. Soon after, Admiral Porter sent back for a coöperating military force, and Gen. Sherman was promptly sent with one division of his corps. The number of steamers suitable for the navigation of these bayous being limited, most of the force was sent up the Mississippi to Eagle Bend, a point where the river runs within one mile of Steele's bayou, thus avoiding an important part of the difficult navigation. The cause of the failure of this expedition is thus explained by Gen. Grant:

"The expedition failed, probably, more from

want of knowledge as to what would be required to open this route, than from any impracticability in the navigation of the streams and bayous through which it was proposed to pass: the want of this knowledge led the expedition on until difficulties were encountered, and then it would become necessary to send back to Young's Point for the means of removing them. This gave the enemy time to move forces to effectually checkmate further progress, and the expedition was withdrawn when within a few hundred yards of free and open navigation to the Yazoo."

In addition to these several routes, another was prospected by Capt. F. E. Prime, as Chief Engineer, and Col. G. G. Pride, through the bayous, which run from near Milliken's Bend and New Carthage on the south, through Roundaway Bayou into the Tensas River. This route was found to be practicable, and work was commenced on it. With the aid of three dredge boats, it proceeded rapidly, and one small steamer and a number of barges were taken through the channel thus opened. About the middle of April, however, the river commenced falling so rapidly as to render it impracticable to open this water communication between Milliken's Bend and New Carthage. At the same time the roads between them became dry and passable, and thus made the water communication unnecessary.

On March 25th the ram Lancaster was lost in attempting to run the batteries at Vicksburg in order to gain the fleet of Admiral Farragut below. The Switzerland got through badly cut up.

CHAPTER XXVIII.

Object of Gen. Grant to reach the rear of Vicksburg—His Movements—Transports and Gunboats run the Batteries—Attack on Grand Gulf—Crossing the Mississippi by the Army—Change of base by Gen. Grant—Raid of Col. Grierson through Mississippi—Advance of Gen. Grant to the Big Black River—Battles—Occupation of Jackson—March on Vicksburg—Battles—March of Gen. Sherman to the Yazoo—Investment of Vicksburg—Siege—Surrender—Results.

THE object of Gen. Grant now was to find a route by which he could place his army with its supplies below Vicksburg, so as to approach it in the rear, where alone it was supposed to be weak and assailable, with the hope of success. As soon, therefore, as he had directed a water communication to be opened from a point on the Mississippi, near Milliken's Bend, to New Carthage, he determined to occupy the latter place. It was the first point below Vicksburg that could be reached by land at the stage of water existing at that time, and the occupancy of which, while it secured a point on the Mississippi River, would also protect the main line of communication by water. Major-Gen. McClernand, therefore, with the Thirteenth army corps, was, on the 29th of March, ordered to move to New Carthage. The Fifteenth and Sixteenth corps were to follow, moving no faster than supplies and ammunition could be transported to them. The movement was necessarily slow, in consequence of the bad state of the roads. As the advance reached Smith's Plantation, two miles from New Carthage, it was found that the levee of Bayou Vidal was broken in several places; and in consequence of the overflow of water, New Carthage was made an island. All the boats in the different bayous in the vicinity were collected, and others were built, but the transportation of the army was exceedingly tedious. Another route was therefore found, by making a further march of twelve miles around Bayou Vidal, to a point called Perkins's Plantation. The whole distance to be marched from Milliken's Bend to reach water communication below was thirty-five miles. Over this distance it was necessary to transport by wagons, with bad roads, the supplies of ordnance stores and provisions with which to commence the campaign on the opposite side of the river.

At the same time that the occupation of New Carthage was ordered, preparations were made for running transports and a gunboat fleet below the batteries of Vicksburg. The gunboats selected were the Benton, Capt. Greer; Lafayette, Capt. Henry Walke; Price, Capt. Woodworth; Louisville, Capt. Owens; Carondelet, Capt. McLeod Murphy; Pittsburg, Capt. Wm. Hoel; Tuscumbia, Capt. Shirk, and Mound City. All of these boats except the Price were ironclad. Each had taken, for additional protection, baled cotton, hay, railroad iron, timber, chains, or whatever else might be suitable. The transports which were selected were the Forest Queen, Capt. Dan. Conway; Henry Clay; and Silver Wave, Capt. McMillan. These boats took a quantity of supplies for the army, and bales of cotton and hay were placed around the most important parts of their machinery. The night of the 16th of April was fixed for the expedition to start. Everything was in readiness before dark. The plan decided upon was that the ironclads should pass down in single file, with intervals between the boats of a few hundred yards, and that when in front of the batteries they should engage them with their broadside guns, and, under cover of the smoke, the transports should endeavor to pass unseen. A spectator of the exciting scene has thus described it:

"Lights twinkled busily from the Vicksburg hillsides until about 10 o'clock, when they disappeared, and about the same moment song and laughter on our side were hushed, as a shapeless mass of what looked like a great fragment of darkness was discerned floating noiselessly down the river. It was the Benton. It passed and disappeared in the night, and was succeeded by another bank of darkness, the Lafayette, with the Price lashed to her starboard side. And thus they continued, as if huge shadows detached themselves from the darkness above, floated across the vision, and disappeared in the darkness below. Ten of these noiseless shapes revealed themselves and disappeared.

"Three quarters of an hour passed. People heard nothing save their own suppressed breathings; saw nothing save a long low bank of darkness, which, like a black fog, walled the view below, and joined the sky and river in the direction of Vicksburg. And all watched this gathering of darkness, for in it were thunders and lightnings and volcanoes, which at any instant might light up the night with fierce irruptions.

"So long a time passed without anything occurring that people began to believe the enemy had determined, for some malevolent purpose, to allow the fleet to pass below without obstruction. However, this supposition was hardly broached ere it was contradicted most emphatically. At just a quarter before eleven, two bright sharp lines of flame flashed through the darkness, at the extreme right of the Vicksburg batteries; and, in an instant, the whole length of the bluffs was ablaze with fire. The fleet, which had rounded the Point, and now lay squarely before the city, at once responded by opening their ports, and pouring their full broadside of twenty-five heavy guns, charged with grape and shrapnel, directly against the city.

"A great cloud of smoke rolled heavily over the gunboats, and in this the three transports entered and made their 'best time' down the river. The Forest Queen, which was in the advance, received a shot in the hull and another through the steam drum, which disabled her instantly. The Henry Clay, that came next, was stopped, to prevent her running into the other, and at the same moment was struck by a shell that set her cotton on fire. The crew, demoralized by the stoppage and terrified by the fire, ran aimlessly around for a few moments, then launched the yawl, sprang into it, and pulled for the shore. The pilot, finding that no engineers obeyed the bells, stayed a short time until the fire began to seethe around him, when he seized a plank, jumped overboard, and was picked up by a gunboat. The Clay, in the mean time, became a great blazing mass, that floated down the river until it disappeared below Warrenton. Had she been manned by men of nerve, the fire would have been extinguished and the boat carried through safely. The fact of her floating so far shows that her hull was uninjured.

"The Forest Queen was taken in tow by a gunboat, and towed below without further damage. The Silver Wave did not receive a scratch.

"The Vicksburg batteries were passed in about an hour and a quarter. Upon reaching Warrenton batteries, the gunboats took the initiative by pouring in their broadsides on the instant they reached position; and so continuous and terrific was their fire that the enemy scarcely attempted a response."

No one on board either of the transports was injured, and Gen. Grant immediately ordered six more to be prepared in like manner for running the batteries. Accordingly the Tigress, Anglo-Saxon, Cheeseman, Empire City, Horizona, and Moderator left Milliken's Bend on the night of the 22d of April, and five of them got by, but in a somewhat damaged condition. The Tigress received a shot in her hull below the water line, and sunk on the Louisiana shore, after passing the last of the batteries. In tow of these transports, twelve barges loaded with forage were sent, one half of which got through in a condition to be used. The transports injured in running the blockade were repaired by order of Admiral Porter, and in a very short time five of them were in running order, and the remainder in a condition to be used as barges in the movement of troops.

As the number of transports below Vicks-

GUNBOATS PASSING VICKSBURG

burg was limited, Gen. Grant found it necessary to extend his line of movement by land to Hard Times in Louisiana. By the circuitous route it was necessary to take, the distance was increased to seventy miles from Milliken's Bend.

On the 29th of April, the thirteenth corps of the army had reached the Mississippi, and the seventeenth was well on the way. Gen. Grant then embarked so much of the thirteenth as could be got on board the transports and barges, and moved to the front of Grand Gulf. This was a strong position on the east bank of the Mississippi, below the mouth of the Big Black river. The plan was that the gunboats under Admiral Porter's command should silence the fortifications, and under cover of the gunboats the troops should land and carry the place by storm.

At eight o'clock in the morning the attack was commenced by the gunboats, and continued fiercely for more than five hours. The following is the despatch of Admiral Porter respecting the attack:

FLAG SHIP BENTON, BELOW GRAND GULF, MISS., *April 29th*, 1862.

Hon. Gideon Welles, Secretary of the Navy :

I have the honor to inform you that, by an arrangement with General Grant, I attacked the batteries at Grand Gulf this morning, which were very formidable. After a fight of five hours and thirty minutes, we silenced the lower batteries, but failed to silence the upper one, which was high, strongly built, had guns of very heavy caliber, and the vessels were unmanageable in the heavy current. It fired but feebly toward the last, and the vessels all laid by and enfiladed it, while I went up a short distance to communicate with General Grant, who concluded to land the troops and march over to a point two miles below Grand Gulf. I sent the Lafayette back to engage the upper battery, which she did, and drove the persons out of it, as it did not respond after a few fires. At 6 P. M. we attacked the batteries again, and, under cover of the fire, all the transports passed by in good condition. The Benton, Tuscumbia, and Pittsburg were much cut up, having twenty-four killed and fifty-six wounded; but they are all ready for service.

We land the army in the morning on the other side, and march on Vicksburg. DAVID D. PORTER, Acting Rear-Admiral.

Gen. Grant, who was a spectator of the scene, says: "Many times it seemed to me that the gunboats were within pistol shot of the enemy's batteries. It soon became evident that the guns of the enemy were too elevated and their fortifications too strong to be taken from the water side. The whole range of hills on that side were known to be lined with rifle pits. Besides, the field artillery could be moved to any position where it might be useful in case of an attempt at landing." He therefore determined to run the enemy's batteries again, and to turn his position by effecting a landing at Rodney, or at Bruinsburg, between Grand Gulf and Rodney. Rodney is a small village on the east bank of the Mississippi, some miles below Grand Gulf. Bruinsburg is a small place between the two others. A reconnoissance was made to a point opposite Bruinsburg, and information was obtained from a negro that there was a good road from that place to Port Gibson. Gen. Grant determined to make the landing on the east side of the Mississippi, at Bruinsburg. Accordingly the troops were immediately ordered to land at Hard Times, and march across to the point below Grand Gulf, and at dark the gunboats again engaged the batteries, and all the transports were run by. They received but two or three shots during the passage, and these caused no injury.

At daylight on the morning of the 30th, the work of ferrying the troops across the Mississippi was commenced both by the gunboats and the transports. The thirteenth corps, as soon as landed and supplied with three days' rations, was started on the road to Port Gibson. The seventeenth corps followed as rapidly as it could be taken across the river. Port Gibson was a flourishing village on Bayou Pierre, 28 miles from its mouth, and about 65 miles southwest from Jackson, the capital of Mississippi. It was connected with Grand Gulf by a railroad.

About two o'clock on the next morning, May 1st, the advance of the enemy was met eight miles from Bruinsburgh, on the road to Port Gibson. They were forced to fall back, but as it was dark, were not pursued far until daylight. Then Gen. McClernand with his corps pressed forward within four miles of Port Gibson. Here the road divided in opposite directions. Both branches, however, led to Port Gibson. The enemy took a position on each branch, and thus divided the pursuing force. The nature of the ground was such that a very small force could easily retard the progress of a much larger one for several hours. The roads run on narrow, elevated ridges, with deep and impenetrable ravines on each side. The corps of Gen. McClernand was so divided that on the right were the divisions of Gens. Hovey, Carr, and Smith, and on the left the division of Gen. Osterhaus. The three former succeeded in driving the enemy from position to position steadily back toward Port Gibson. On the left, Gen. Osterhaus was unable to move the enemy until he was reënforced by a brigade of Gen. Logan's division, which was the advance of Gen. McPherson's corps. Another brigade of the same division was sent to Gen. McClernand on the right, and the enemy were so badly repulsed there as to be able to make no further stand south of Bayou Pierre. Late in the afternoon, Gen. Osterhaus was successful in repulsing the enemy, whom he pursued toward Port Gibson, but night closing in and the enemy making the appearance of another stand, the troops slept upon their arms until daylight. On the morning of the 2d, it was found that the enemy had retreated across Bayou Pierre, on the Grand Gulf road, and a brigade of Gen. Logan's division was sent to divert his attention whilst a floating bridge was thrown across the Bayou at Port Gibson. This bridge was completed, and Gen. McPherson's corps passed over and marched eight miles to the north bank of Bayou Pierre, built a bridge over that stream, and the advance commenced passing over it at five o'clock on the following morning. On the 3d, the enemy were pursued to Hawkinson's Ferry, with slight skirmishing all day, during which quite a number of prisoners, mostly stragglers, were taken. The following despatch from Gen. Grant was sent to Washington:

GRAND GULF, *May 7th.*

To Major-General Halleck, General-in-Chief:

We landed at Bruinsburg, April 30, moved immediately on Port Gibson, met the enemy, 11,000 strong, four miles south of Port Gibson, at 2 o'clock A. M., on the 1st instant, and engaged him all day, entirely routing him, with the loss of many killed and about 500 prisoners, besides the wounded. The enemy retreated toward Vicksburg, destroying the bridges over the two forks of the Bayou Pierre. These were rebuilt, and the pursuit was continued until the present time. Besides the heavy artillery at this place, four field pieces were captured, and some stores, and the enemy was driven to destroy many more. The country is the most broken and difficult to operate in I ever saw. Our victory has been most complete, and the enemy is thoroughly demoralized.

Very respectfully, U. S. GRANT,
Major-General Commanding.

These movements of Gen. Grant had caused the evacuation of Grand Gulf, and Admiral Porter, upon making a movement to attack that position on the 3d, found that it had been abandoned. He then sent the following despatch to the Navy Department:

FLAG SHIP BENTON, GRAND GULF, MISS.,
May 3d, 1863.

To the Hon. Gideon Welles, Sec'y of the Navy:

SIR: I have the honor to report that I got under way this morning with the Lafayette, Carondelet, Mound City, and Pittsburg, and proceeded up to the forts at Grand Gulf, for the purpose of attacking them again if they had not been abandoned.

The enemy had left before we got up, blowing up their ammunition, spiking their large guns and burying or taking away their lighter ones. The armament consisted of thirteen guns in all. The works are of the most extensive kind, and would seem to defy the efforts of a much heavier fleet than the one which silenced them.

The forts were literally torn to pieces by the accuracy of our fire. Col. Wade, the commandant of the batteries, was killed; also his chief of staff. Eleven men were killed that we know of, and our informant says many were wounded, and that no one was permitted to go inside the forts after the action, except those belonging there.

We had a hard fight for these forts, and it is with great pleasure that I report that the navy holds the door to Vicksburg. Grand Gulf is the strongest place on the Mississippi. Had the enemy succeeded in finishing the fortifications, no fleet could have taken them.

I have been all over the works, and find them as follows: One fort, on a point of rocks 75 feet high, calculated for six or seven guns, mounting two 7-inch rifled and one 8-inch, and one Parrott gun on wheels, which was carried off. On the left of this work is a triangular work, calculated to mount one heavy gun.

These works are connected with another fort by a covered way and double rifle pits extending a quarter of a mile, constructed with much labor, and showing great skill on the part of the constructor. The third fort commands the river in all directions. It mounted one splendid Blakely 100-pounder, one 8-inch and two 30-pounders. The latter were lying burst or broken on the ground.

The gunboats had so covered up everything that it was impossible at first to see what was there, with the exception of the guns that were dismounted or broken. Every gun that fell into our hands is in good condition, and we found a large quantity of ammunition. These are by far the most extensively built works, with the exception of those at Vicksburg, that I have seen yet, and I am happy to say that we hold them.

I am dismounting the guns, and getting on board the ammunition.

Since making the above examination, new forts have been passed nearly finished. They had no guns mounted, but were complete of the kind as regards position, and had heavy field pieces in them.

(Signed) DAVID D. PORTER,
Acting Rear-Admiral, Com'g Mississippi Squadron.

Gen. Grant now made the necessary arrangements for changing his base of supplies from Bruinsburg to Grand Gulf. From Milliken's Bend to New Carthage a water communication had been opened by the Roundaway bayou, and troops occupied positions along the route from Milliken's Bend to Dallas and thence to New Carthage. A strong body also occupied Richmond, situated in the angle formed by the junction of the Brashy with Roundaway bayou.

When the army moved from Milliken's Bend, the fifteenth corps, under Maj.-Gen. W. T. Sherman, remained to be the last to follow. Gen. Sherman had also been ordered to make a demonstration on Haines's Bluff, in order to prevent heavy reënforcements leaving Vicksburg to assist the Confederate forces at Grand Gulf. Gen. Sherman moved upon Haines's Bluff, landing his forces on the south bank of the Yazoo, and the attack was made chiefly by the gunboats, on the 6th of May. The ironclads De Kalb and Choctaw, with other gunboats, engaged the batteries for six hours, during which the Choctaw was struck fifty-four times. The enemy displayed a strong force, and anticipated a battle. On the 7th the expedition returned, and the military part prepared to join Gen. Grant. It was entirely successful in preventing reënforcements to the enemy at Port Gibson.

It had been the purpose of Gen. Grant, up to the time of crossing the Mississippi, to collect all his forces at Grand Gulf, and to get on hand a good supply of provisions and ordnance stores, before moving against Vicksburg from the south. He had also determined, in the mean while, to detach an army corps to coöperate with Gen. Banks on Port Hudson, and effect a junction of forces. But this plan was given up by him in consequence of learning that Gen. Banks could not return to Baton Rouge from his position west of the Mississippi before the 10th of May; and that by the reduction of Port Hudson he could not join Gen. Grant with more than 12,000 men. The delay also for the arrival of Gen. Banks at Baton Rouge, and then for the reduction of Port Hudson, would be so great that the addition of 12,000 men to his forces would not make him relatively so strong for the attack upon

Vicksburg, as if it was at that time promptly made. Another reason for a change of his first plan, and in favor of a prompt movement on Vicksburg, was the information that troops were expected at Jackson from the Southern cities under command of Gen. Beauregard.

Meanwhile the army was lying at Hawkinson's Ferry, waiting for wagons, supplies, and the arrival of Gen. Sherman's corps. Hawkinson's was the lowest of three ferries over the Big Black below the railroad. Hall's and Baldwin's were the names of the others. It was on a new military road from Grand Gulf to Vicksburg.

In order to facilitate Gen. Grant's operations by destroying the enemy's lines of communication and preventing the early concentration of reënforcements, a cavalry raid of unusual boldness was made in the rear of Vicksburg. Col. Benj. H. Grierson, commanding the first cavalry brigade, had proposed a descent into the State of Mississippi, without meeting the approval of the commanding general until the 1st of April, when he was instructed to prepare for an expedition. The force was stationed at Lagrange about fifty miles east of Memphis, and four miles west of the junction of the Mississippi and Charleston railroad. On the 17th, Col. Grierson was ordered to move his force, consisting of the 6th Illinois cavalry, Col. Loomis, 7th Illinois, Col. Edward Prince, and 2d Iowa, Col. Edward Hatch, out on the road to Ripley. Feints had previously been made from Lagrange, Memphis, and Corinth, in orto divert the attention of the enemy from the real movement. Early on the next day, the 18th, the force proceeded to Ripley : from that village, the 2d Iowa, advancing on the left flank of the column, took a southeasterly direction, and crossed the Tallahatchie about five miles northeast of New Albany. Meanwhile the main body proceeded directly south and crossed the river two miles east of New Albany. At the same time a battalion of the 7th Illinois marched on the right flank and crossed the river at New Albany. Skirmishing was kept up throughout the day by all the forces with detached bodies of the enemy, who were on both sides of the river, but unable to impede the progress of Col. Grierson. At night the 6th and 7th encamped about four miles south of New Albany, and the 2d Iowa about four miles east of that place. About midnight an attack was made upon this regiment, which was promptly repulsed. On the morning of the 19th a detachment was ordered by Col. Grierson to proceed eastward, another to move back to New Albany, and a third to march northwest toward King's Bridge, where a Confederate force under Maj. Chalmers was reported to be encamped. These movements were designed to lead the enemy to believe that the object of the expedition was to break up the different military organizations in that part of the country. This was successful. About nine o'clock the main body resumed its march in a southerly direction, with the 2d Iowa on its left flank. The various detachments which had been sent out soon joined the main column, and the whole force proceeded to Pontotoc. A small Confederate force was here encountered, and pursued through the town by the advance, and their entire camp equipage was captured, and also four hundred bushels of salt, which were destroyed at night. Col. Grierson encamped six miles south of Pontotoc, on the road leading to Houston.

Early the next morning, Major Lall, of the 2d Iowa, with about one hundred and seventy-five of the least effective portion of the command, one piece of artillery, and all the prisoners, moved northward, on the return to Lagrange. The object of Col. Grierson, in ordering this movement, was to relieve his command of incumbrances, and to lead the enemy to believe that the expedition had retraced its steps. The march southward was then resumed, and the force encamped that night about ten miles beyond the town of Houston.

On the next day, the 21st, Col. Hatch, of the 2d Iowa, was ordered to move his command toward Columbus, and destroy as much of the Mobile and Ohio railroad as possible, to attack Columbus if the opposing force was not too strong, and march thence to Lagrange, taking such route as he might consider to be the most suitable. In this movement, Col. Hatch was quite successful. It entirely misled Gen. Chalmers, who was in pursuit of Col. Grierson, and gave the latter a start of two or three days. The main body now continued its march to Starkville, and captured a mail, which was destroyed. At Dismal Swamp, four miles from Starkville, a halt was ordered, and a part of the command continued on five miles farther to one of the principal tanneries in the State, which was destroyed, with a large stock of boots, shoes, saddles, and leather.

On the 22d, the command again united and marched twenty-seven miles, nearly to Louisville, Mississippi. The deep streams and marshes made the route very difficult and perilous. On the next morning the command reached Philadelphia; here a mail was captured and destroyed. About daylight, on the next morning, Newton was reached, where two trains of cars, loaded with all kinds of quartermaster and commissary stores, ammunition, and shells, were captured, and their contents destroyed. One bridge was destroyed about half a mile east of the place, and three heavy trestlework bridges ten miles farther up the railroad. On the 25th, Col. Grierson reached Nichols's Plantation, seven miles west of Montrose. A more southerly route was now pursued. At Raleigh a halt was ordered for the night, and a scout sent to cut the telegraph wires on the railroad between Lake Station and Jackson. On arriving within seven miles of the railroad, a regiment of Confederate cavalry was met, which had left Brandon in search of Col. Grierson. They were on the direct road to his camp, and only fourteen miles distant. The scout succeeded in misleading the enemy, and returned safely to camp. Col. Grierson immediately moved his command over Leaf river, and destroyed the bridge, thereby preventing the possibility of a surprise in the rear. The command then moved on to Westville, and crossed the Pearl river at a point ten miles distant from the latter place. Two battalions, which had been sent out in advance, under Col. Prince, moved rapidly to the railroad station at Hazelhurst, and captured forty cars, loaded with shell ammunition, quartermaster's and commissary stores.

When south of Starkville, Capt. Forbes, of Co. B, 7th Illinois, was ordered to march to Macon. As he approached within a short distance of that place, he found it occupied by a considerable force of the enemy. He then moved to Newton, and thence to Enterprise, one hundred miles east of the main body of Col. Grierson's force. Here he sent a flag of truce to Col. Goodwin, commanding the Confederate force in the place, and demanded his surrender. Col. Goodwin requested one hour in which to determine his reply. But Capt. Forbes, finding the enemy to be stronger than he had supposed, and having accomplished his object in diverting their attention, before the expiration of the hour commenced a rapid movement to join Col. Grierson, then more than a day's march distant. Taking a westward course, he soon struck the route of the main body at Pearl river, and effected a junction. Near Gallatin a 32-pound Parrott gun, destined for Port Gibson, was captured and spiked. Five miles east of Gallatin, a detachment was sent to the railroad at Bahala, which destroyed the track, several cars, water tanks, and a considerable amount of other property, and cut the telegraph wires. On the morning of the 28th, Brookhaven was entered by the advance so suddenly that two hundred of the enemy were surprised and made prisoners. A large number of muskets and five hundred tents, at a camp of instruction, were destroyed. The main body, after leaving Gallatin, encountered a cavalry force under Col. Garland, when a skirmish ensued, in which several of the enemy were killed and others taken prisoners. A feint, for the purpose of deceiving the enemy, was made toward Port Gibson, and another toward Natchez, when the main body marched to Brookhaven.

On the 30th, Col. Grierson moved in a southerly direction, and destroyed all the bridges between Brookhaven and Bogue Chito Station. At the latter place fifteen cars, partly loaded with army stores, were destroyed, together with the depot and other railroad buildings. The force then marched to Summit, where twenty-five freight cars were destroyed. Thence Col. Grierson moved from the railroad to a point between Magnolia and Liberty, for the purpose of reaching the Clinton road. Finding a regiment of the enemy's cavalry at Wall's bridge, on the Tickfaw, a dash was made upon them, in which eight or ten were killed, several wounded, and the rest put to flight. The loss of Col. Grierson was one killed and five wounded. Moving then east of the Tickfaw a short distance, the march was continued directly southward. At Edwards's bridge another regiment of the enemy's cavalry was posted, purposely to dispute the passage. A battalion was sent to engage them, while the main body moved on in the direction of Greensburg. Only a few brief skirmishes took place with this regiment.

The march thus far had proved a constant surprise to the inhabitants, and as it was supposed that Col. Grierson would return to Lagrange,

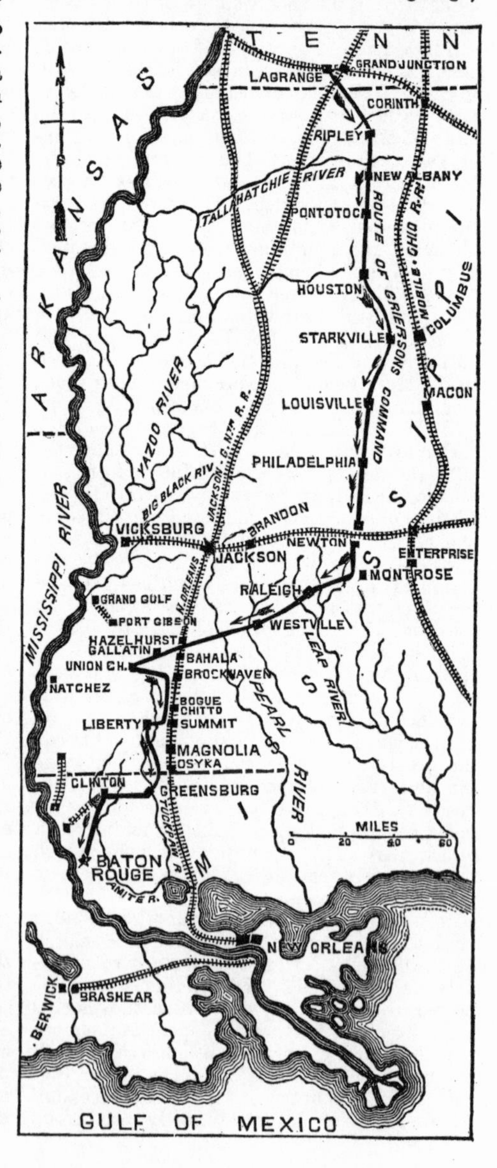

arrangements had been made to cut off his retreat. It was apparent now that his intention was not to return, but to march through the State. Preparations were therefore made at Osyka to stop his progress. It was well known that to advance any farther south it would be necessary for him to cross several bridges. Hence a regiment of Confederate cavalry was so posted as to flank his force, while a body of infantry was thrown in his front, to hold him in check until the cavalry could make an attack upon his flank and rear. Col. Grierson, understanding his danger, at once ordered a charge upon the infantry, and, with one dash, broke through their lines, and soon left them far in the rear. Fortunately he met with no loss, and continued his march south to Greensburg, thence direct to Clinton. About ten miles above that town he crossed the Amite river. On the Big Sandy creek a camp of partisan rangers was found, which he attacked, and destroyed one hundred and fifty tents, with the camp equipage and private baggage. Several horses were also captured. He then marched on the Greenville Spring road toward Baton Rouge. About ten miles from the latter place he suddenly came upon a force of cavalry, under Col. Stewart, and captured the entire body. About four o'clock in the afternoon of the 1st of May he entered the city of Baton Rouge, Louisiana. In seventeen days the troops had marched over eight hundred miles through the heart of the State of Mississippi. A large number of the enemy were killed and wounded, and it was estimated that over four millions of property were destroyed. On two important railroads communications were cut off with strong positions of the enemy. Over a thousand prisoners and more than twelve hundred horses were captured, and great excitement was created throughout the State.

Meantime, as the army of Gen. Grant lay at Hawkinson's Ferry, waiting for supplies and the arrival of Gen. Sherman's corps, demonstrations were made to induce the enemy to think that route and the one by Hall's Ferry, next above on the Big Black river, were objects of much solicitude to Gen. Grant. Reconnoissances were made on the west side of the Big Black river, extending within six miles of Warrenton.

On the 7th of May an advance was ordered. Gen. McPherson's corps were required to keep the road nearest Black river to Rocky Springs. Gen. McClernand's corps moved on the ridge road running from Willow Springs, and Gen. Sherman followed, with his corps divided on the two roads. All the ferries were closely guarded until the troops were well advanced. It was the intention of Gen. Grant here to hug the Big Black river as closely as possible with Gen. McClernand's and Gen. Sherman's corps, and thus get them to the Jackson and Vicksburg railroad, at some point between Edwards's Station and Bolton. Gen. McPherson was ordered to move by way of Utica to Raymond, and from thence into Jackson, destroying the railroads, telegraph, public stores, &c., and then push west to rejoin the main force. Gen. Sherman moved forward on the Edwards's Station road, crossing Fourteen Mile creek at Dillon's Plantation. Gen. McClernand moved across the same creek farther west, sending one division of his corps by the Baldwin's Ferry road as far as the river. At the crossing of Fourteen Mile creek, both Gens. McClernand and Sherman had considerable skirmishing with the enemy to get possession of the crossing. On the evening of that day, May 11th, Gen. Grant sent the following despatch to Maj.-Gen. Halleck, at Washington:

> My force will be this evening as far advanced along Fourteen Mile creek, the left near Black river, and extending in a line nearly east and west, as they can get without bringing on a general engagement. I shall communicate with Grand Gulf no more, except it becomes necessary to send a train with a heavy escort. You may not hear from me again for several weeks.

That night Gen. McClernand's corps was near Black river. Gen. Sherman, in the centre of the line, was at and beyond Auburn; and Gen. McPherson, about eight miles to the right, with his corps, had advanced a few miles north of Utica. Corn, salt meat, and live stock were found abundant.

On the next morning, Tuesday, May 12th, Gen. McClernand's advance drove in the enemy's pickets, and brisk skirmishing ensued for an hour or two, with little loss on either side. By noon the enemy had disappeared from his front. Gen. Sherman early set a division in motion, which came upon the enemy at the crossing of Fourteen Mile creek. The cavalry advance was fired upon from the thick woods that skirt the stream, and was unable, owing to the nature of the ground, to make a charge or clear the enemy from their position. A battery was brought forward, supported by two regiments, and skirmishers thrown out, who drove the enemy slowly until a brigade was thrown upon their right and left flanks, when they withdrew toward Raymond. The principal resistance to the line of march was, however, in front of Gen. McPherson. At ten o'clock his advance, under Gen. Logan, came upon a Confederate force, estimated at ten thousand, but which proved to be two brigades under Gens. Gregg and Walker, posted on Fondreu's creek, about two miles south of Raymond. Brisk skirmishing began at once, which soon brought on a general engagement. The enemy was almost wholly concealed at first by the woods bordering the stream, behind which their forces were posted. Their artillery was on an eminence, which commanded the Federal approach. The battle continued for three hours, when the enemy, after heavy loss in killed, wounded, and missing, withdrew in two columns, the principal one taking the road to Jackson. Gen. McPherson immediately occupied Raymond.

Gen. Grant was at this time with Gen. Sherman's corps, and had ordered that corps and also Gen. McClernand's to move toward the railroad from Vicksburg to Jackson by parallel roads, the latter in the direction of Edwards's Station, and the former to a point on the railroad between Edwards's Station and Bolton. But he afterward ordered these two corps to march to Raymond, in consequence of being informed that the enemy had retreated to Jackson after the defeat near Raymond, and also that reënforcements were daily arriving at Jackson, and that Gen. Joseph E. Johnston was hourly expected there to take the command in person. He says: "I therefore determined to make sure of that place, and leave no enemy in my rear."

On the next day, the 13th, Gen. McPherson moved to Clinton, and destroyed the railroads and telegraph, and captured some important despatches from Gen. Pemberton to Gen. Gregg, who had command on the previous day in the battle of Raymond. Gen. Sherman moved to a parallel position on the Mississippi Springs and Jackson road, and Gen. McClernand moved to a point near Raymond.

On the 14th, Gen. McPherson and Gen. Sherman each advanced from his respective position toward Jackson. The rain had fallen in torrents during the night before, and it continued to fall until about noon, thus making the roads at first slippery, and then miry. Nevertheless, the troops marched in excellent order and spirits about fourteen miles, when they came upon the enemy. The main body of their force in Jackson had marched out on the Clinton road, and encountered Gen. McPherson about two and a half miles from the city. A small force of artillery and infantry also took a strong position in front of Gen. Sherman, about the same distance out from Jackson.

On the march of Gen. McPherson from Clinton toward Jackson, Gen. Crocker's division held the advance. All was quiet until he reached a hill overlooking a broad open field, through the centre of which, and over the crest of the hill beyond, the road to Jackson passed. On the left of this latter hill the enemy had posted his artillery, and along the crest his line of battle. As the Federal force came within range, the artillery of the enemy opened fire. The battery of the First Missouri was moved to the left of a cotton gin in the open field, and returned the fire for nearly an hour, when the guns of the enemy were withdrawn. Meantime, Gen. Crocker had thrown out two brigades to the right and left of his battery, supported by another brigade at a proper distance, and had also pushed forward a strong line of skirmishers, and posted them in a ravine in front, which protected them from the fire of the enemy. After a little delay they were again advanced out of cover, and a desultory fire ensued between the opposite lines of skirmishers, in which the enemy, owing to the nature of the ground, had the advantage. At length Gen. Crocker, seeing the necessity of driving the rebels from the crest of the hill, ordered a charge along the line, the execution of which has been thus described: "With colors flying, and with a step as measured and unbroken as if on dress parade, the movement was executed. Slowly they advanced, crossed the narrow ravine, and, with fixed bayonets, reached the crest of the hill in easy range of the rebel line. Here they received a tremendous volley, which caused painful gaps in their ranks. They held their fire until they were within a distance of thirty paces, when they delivered the returning volley with fearful effect, and, without waiting to reload their muskets, with a terrific yell, they rushed upon the staggered foe. Over the fences, through the brushwood, into the inclosure, they worked their way, slaughtering on the right and left without mercy. The enemy, astonished at their impetuosity, wavered and fell back, rallied again, and finally broke in wild confusion." They finally retreated north, but without further damage.

When Gen. Sherman encountered the enemy, he soon discovered the weakness of the latter by sending a reconnoitering party to his right, which had the effect of causing them to retreat from that part of their line. A few of the artillerists, however, remained in their places, firing upon Gen. Sherman's troops until the last moment, evidently having been instructed to do so with the expectation of being captured in the end.

At this time Gen. McClernand occupied Clinton with one division, Mississippi Springs with another, Raymond with a third, and his fourth division and Gen. Blair's division of Gen. Sherman's corps were with a wagon train, still in the rear near Auburn. At the same time Gen. McArthur, with one brigade of his division of Gen. McPherson's corps, was moving toward Raymond on the Utica road. It was not the intention of Gen. Grant to move these forces any nearer Jackson, but to have them in a position where they could be in supporting distance if the resistance at Jackson should prove more obstinate than there seemed any reason to expect.

On the retreat of the enemy, Gen. McPherson followed directly into the city of Jackson. A fine battery of six pieces was found, and around the Deaf and Dumb Institute, which was used as a hospital, tents enough were seized to encamp an entire division. The commissary and quartermaster's stores were in flames. The Governor and State Treasurer had withdrawn, taking the State funds and papers. All citizens officially connected with State or Confederate Governments had also left. Many soldiers remained, besides a large number in the hospital.

At night, Gen. Grant, who with Gen. Sherman's corps had arrived at Jackson, was informed that Gen. Johnston, as soon as he had satisfied himself that Jackson was to be attacked, had ordered Gen. Pemberton peremptorily to march out from Vicksburg and attack the Federal rear. Availing himself of this information, he immediately issued orders to

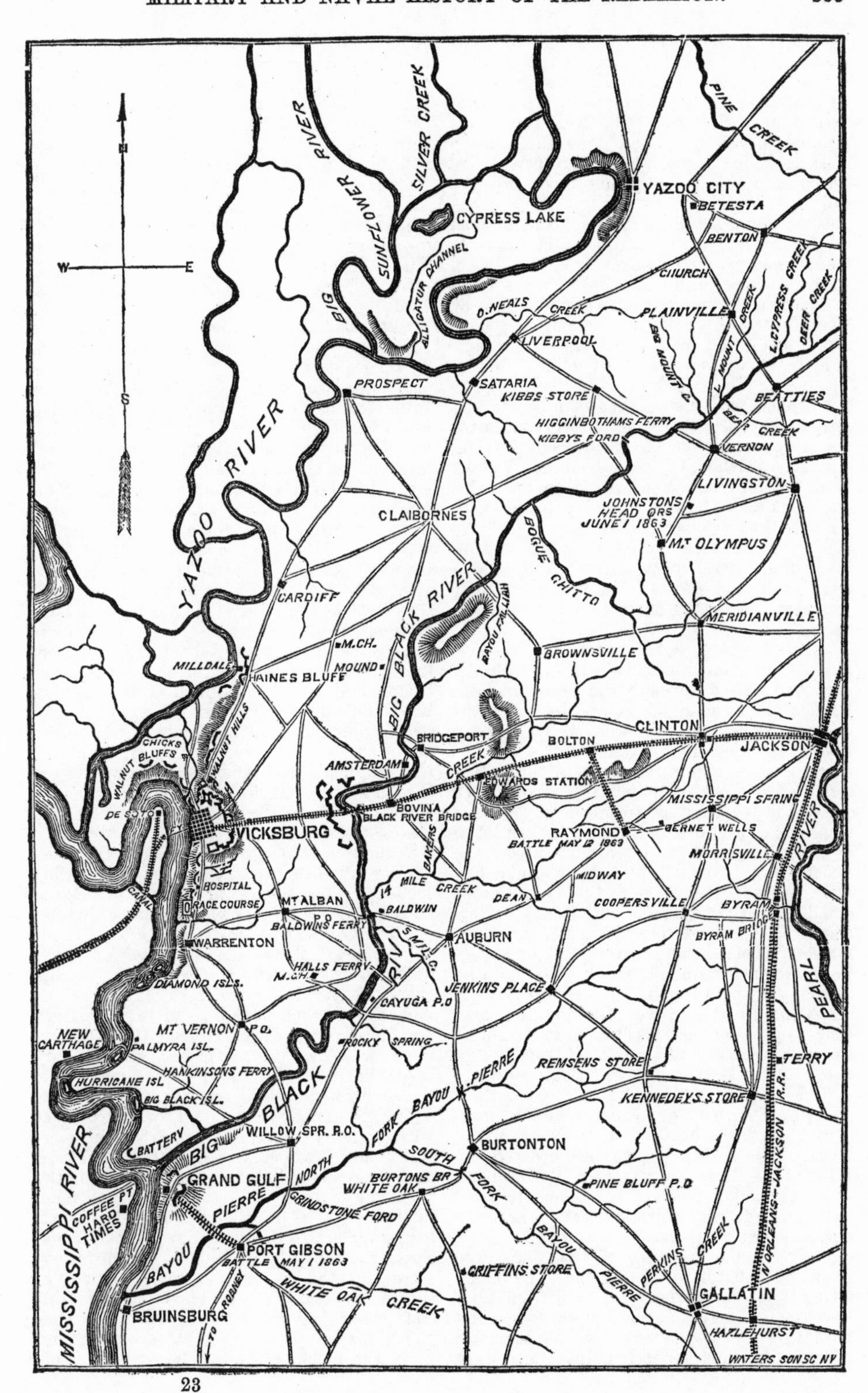
N
W
E
S
YAZOO CITY
BETESTA
BENTON
PINE CREEK
SILVER CREEK
BIG SUNFLOWER RIVER
CYPRESS LAKE
ALLIGATOR CHANNEL
CHURCH
O. NEALS CREEK
PLAINVILLE
LIVERPOOL
L. CYPRESS CREEK
DEER CREEK
PROSPECT
SATARIA
KIBBS STORE
BEATTIES
HIGGINBOTHAMS FERRY
KIBBYS FORD
BEAR CREEK
VERNON
LIVINGSTON
YAZOO RIVER
CLAIBORNES
JOHNSTONS HEAD QRS JUNE 1 1863
MT OLYMPUS
BOGUE CHITTO
CARDIFF
MERIDIANVILLE
BIG BLACK RIVER
BAYOU FALLIAH
M.CH.
MOUND
BROWNSVILLE
MILLDALE
HAINES BLUFF
WALNUT HILLS
CHICKS
WALNUT BLUFFS
BRIDGEPORT
BOLTON
CLINTON
JACKSON
AMSTERDAM
CREEK
EDWARDS STATION
BOVINA
BLACK RIVER BRIDGE
DE SOTO
VICKSBURG
MISSISSIPPI SPRING
RAYMOND
BERNET WELLS
BATTLE MAY 12 1863
MORRISVILLE
BAKERS
HOSPITAL
RACE COURSE
14 MILE CREEK
MIDWAY
CANAL
MT ALBAN
DEAN
COOPERSVILLE
BYRAM
P.O
BALDWIN
BALDWINS FERRY
BYRAM BRIDGE
WARRENTON
AUBURN
5 MIL. C.
HALLS FERRY
M.CH
DIAMOND ISLS.
JENKINS PLACE
PEARL RIVER
CAYUGA P.O
MT VERNON P.O.
NEW CARTHAGE
PALMYRA ISL.
ROCKY SPRING
REMSENS STORE
TERRY
HANKINSONS FERRY
HURRICANE ISL
BIG BLACK ISL.
FORK BAYOU PIERRE
KENNEDEYS STORE
BIG BLACK
BATTERY
WILLOW SPR. P.O.
BURTONTON
NEW ORLEANS—JACKSON R.R.
MISSISSIPPI RIVER
GRAND GULF
NORTH
SOUTH FORK
BURTONS BR
WHITE OAK
PINE BLUFF P.O
COFFEE PT
HARD TIMES
GRINDSTONE FORD
PIERRE
BAYOU
PORT GIBSON
BATTLE MAY 1 1863
PERKINS CREEK
GRIFFINS STORE
BAYOU PIERRE
WHITE OAK CREEK
GALLATIN
BRUINSBURG
TO RODNEY
HAZLEHURST
WATERS SON SC NY

Gen. McClernand, and to Gen. Blair of Sherman's corps, to face their troops toward Bolton, with a view to reaching Edwards's Station by marching on different roads, which converged near Bolton. Gen. McPherson was ordered to retrace his steps on the Clinton road, early on the morning of the 15th. Gen. Sherman was left in Jackson to destroy the railroads, bridges, factories, workshops, arsenals, and everything valuable for the support of the enemy. On the afternoon of the 15th, Gen. Grant proceeded as far west as Clinton, through which place Gen. McPherson's corps had passed to within supporting distance of Gen. Hovey's division of Gen. McClernand's corps, which had moved that day on the same road to within one and a half mile of Bolton. The country from Jackson to Bolton is rugged and broken, with a succession of hills and valleys, precipitous steeps and deep ravines, over and through which the road passes. Gen. Grant, on reaching Clinton, about five o'clock P. M., ordered Gen. McClernand to move his command early the next morning toward Edwards's Station, marching so as to feel the enemy, if he encountered him, but not to bring on a general engagement unless he was confident he was able to defeat him. Gen. Blair was also ordered to move with Gen. McClernand.

Early the next morning, two persons employed on the Jackson and Vicksburg railroad, who had passed through the army of Gen. Pemberton on the night before, were brought to the headquarters of Gen. Grant. They stated that the force of Gen. Pemberton consisted of about eighty regiments, with ten batteries of artillery, and that the whole force was estimated at near twenty-five thousand men. They also described the positions taken by the enemy, and his intention to attack the Federal rear. Gen. Grant had determined to leave one division of Gen. Sherman's corps one day longer in Jackson, but after this information he resolved to bring his entire command up at once, and accordingly sent orders to him to move with all possible speed until he came up with the main force at Bolton. A despatch was sent to Gen. Blair at the same time, to push forward his division in the direction of Edwards's Station with all possible despatch. Gen. McClernand was also ordered to establish communication between Gen. Blair and Gen. Osterhaus of his corps, and to keep it up, moving the former to the support of the latter. Gen. McPherson was also ordered forward at 5.45 A. M., to join Gen. McClernand. The information received was communicated to Gen. McClernand, with instructions as to the disposition of his forces.

Early on the morning of the 16th, Gen. Grant left Clinton for the advance, and on arriving at the point where the road from Raymond to Bolton crosses the Jackson and Vicksburg railroad, he found Gen. McPherson's advance and his pioneer corps engaged in rebuilding a bridge on the latter road, that had been destroyed by the cavalry of Gen. Osterhaus's division, which had gone into Bolton the night before. On reaching the front, Gen. Grant found Gen. Hovey's division of the thirteenth corps at a halt, with his skirmishers and the enemy's pickets near each other. Gen. Hovey was bringing his troops into line, ready for battle, and could have brought on an engagement at any moment. The enemy had taken up a very strong position on a narrow ridge. His left rested on a height where the road made a sharp turn to the left, as it approached Vicksburg. The top of the ridge and the precipitous hillside to the left of the road were covered by a dense forest and undergrowth. To the right of the road the woods extended a short distance down the hill, and then were cultivated fields on a gentle slope spreading into an extensive valley. Gen. Hovey's division was disposed for the attack on the road and into the wooded ravine and hillside, while Gen. McPherson's force, excepting Gen. Ransom's brigade, which arrived after the battle, were thrown to the right of the road, which was properly the enemy's rear. Still Gen. Grant would not allow an attack to be commenced by his troops until he could hear from Gen. McClernand, who was advancing with four, divisions, two of which were on a road intersecting the Jackson road about one mile from the position occupied by the above-mentioned troops, and about the centre of the enemy's line; the other two divisions were on a road still farther north, and nearly the same distance off. Learning that Gen. McClernand was distant two and a half miles, Gen. Grant sent orders to him to push forward with all rapidity. Meanwhile the continued firing between Gen. Hovey's skirmishers and the enemy grew into a battle by eleven o'clock. At first this division bore the brunt of the conflict, but finding the enemy too strong for them, one brigade and then another of Gen. Crocker's division of Gen. McPherson's corps was ordered to reenforce them. Meanwhile Gen. Logan's division of McPherson's corps was working upon the enemy's left and rear, which weakened exceedingly their attack in front. Here their force outnumbered the Federal force. Gen. McClernand was, however, expected momentarily upon the field. But he did not arrive until the enemy had been driven from the field after a terrible contest of hours, in which he met with a heavy loss in killed, wounded, prisoners, and artillery. It appeared afterward that the road to Vicksburg, after following the ridge in a southerly direction about one mile, intersecting one of the roads to Raymond, turned almost to the west, down the hill and across the valley in which Gen. Logan was operating on the rear of the enemy. One brigade of his division had, unconscious of this fact, penetrated nearly to this road, and compelled the enemy to retreat to avoid capture. As it was, much of his artillery and Gen. Loring's division of his army were cut off, besides the prisoners captured.

On the request of Gen. Hovey for more re-enforcements, just before the rout of the enemy commenced, Gen. Grant ordered Gen. McPherson to move what troops he could by a left flank to the enemy's front. Proceeding to the front, and expecting every moment to see the enemy, Gen. Grant found, on reaching what had been his line, that he was retreating. Upon arriving at the Raymond road, Gen. Grant perceived a column of troops on the left and on the next ridge, which proved to be Gen. Carr's division of Gen. McClernand's corps. To the left, Gen. Osterhaus's division of the same corps soon after appeared with his skirmishers well advanced. Gen. Carr was ordered to pursue the enemy with all speed to Black river, and to cross it if he could, and Gen. Osterhaus was ordered to follow. The pursuit continued until after dark, and a train of cars loaded with commissary and ordnance stores and other property was captured. Gen. Grant states that "the delay in the advance of the troops immediately with Gen. McClernand was caused, no doubt, by the enemy presenting a front of artillery and infantry, where it was impossible, from the nature of the ground and the density of the forest, to discover his numbers. As it was, the battle of Champion's Hill, or Baker's Creek, was fought mainly by Gen. Hovey's division of McClernand's corps, and Gens. Logan's and Quimby's divisions (the latter commanded by Brigadier-General M. M. Crocker) of McPherson's corps."

Orders were now sent back to Gen. Sherman to turn his corps toward Bridgeport, and Gen. Blair was expected to join him at that place. Bridgeport was on the Black river, and some miles north of the railroad. By crossing the river at that point, Gen. Sherman would be on the flank of the enemy, if they made a stand at the railroad crossing of the river.

At daylight on the next morning, the 17th, the pursuit was renewed, with the corps of Gen. McClernand in the advance. The enemy was found strongly posted on both sides of the Black river, at a point where the bluffs on the west side extended to the water's edge, but the east side was an open cultivated bottom of nearly one mile in width, and surrounded by a bayou of stagnant water from two to three feet in depth and from ten to twenty feet in width, extending from the river above the railroad to the river below. Along the inside line of this bayou the enemy had constructed rifle-pits, with the bayou serving as a ditch on the outside and immediately in front of them. The division of Gen. Carr occupied the right in investing this position, and the brigade of Gen. Lawler occupied the right of the division. After a few hours' skirmishing, Gen. Lawler discovered that by moving a portion of his brigade under cover of the river bank, he could get a position from which the enemy could be successfully assaulted. He accordingly ordered a charge. Notwithstanding the level ground over which a portion of his troops had to pass without cover, and the great obstacle of the ditch in front of the enemy's works, the charge was gallantly and successfully made, and in a few minutes the entire garrison with seventeen pieces of artillery were the trophies of this brilliant movement. The enemy on the west bank of the river immediately set fire to the railroad bridge and retreated, thereby cutting off all chance of escape for any portion of his forces remaining on the east bank.

By this time, Gen. Sherman had reached Bridgeport on the Black river above. The only pontoon train was with him. By the morning of the 18th, he had crossed the river and was ready to march on Vicksburg. Gens. McClernand and McPherson caused floating bridges to be constructed during the night, and were ready to cross their troops by eight o'clock on the next morning.

Early that morning, Gen. Sherman commenced his march by the Bridgeport and Vicksburg road, and, when within three and a half miles of Vicksburg, he turned to the right to get possession of Walnut Hills and the Yazoo river. This was successfully accomplished before night. Gen. McPherson crossed the Black river above the road to Jackson, and came into the same road with Gen. Sherman, but in his rear. His advance arrived after nightfall at the point where Gen. Sherman turned to the right. Gen. McClernand moved by the Jackson and Vicksburg road to Mount Albans, in the rear of Vicksburg, and there turned to the left to get into the Baldwin's Ferry road. By this disposition the three army corps covered all the ground their strength would admit of, and by the morning of the 19th the investment of Vicksburg was made as complete as could be by the forces under the command of Gen. Grant.

In the march from Bruinsburg to Vicksburg, only five days' rations were issued, and three of these were taken in haversacks at the start, and soon exhausted. It was a period of twenty days before supplies could be obtained from Government stores, during which all other subsistence was obtained from the country through which the army passed. It was abundantly supplied with corn, bacon, beef, and mutton. The march was commenced without wagons except such as could be picked up. Communications were at once opened with the fleet above Vicksburg, and Gen. Grant's base for supplies was changed from Grand Gulf to the Yazoo. The movements by which this was effected are thus described in a despatch from Rear-Admiral Porter to the Secretary of the Navy:

FLAG SHIP BLACK HAWK,
HAINES'S BLUFF, YAZOO RIVER, *May 20th.*

To Hon. Gideon Welles, Secretary of the Navy:

On the morning of the 16th I came over to the Yazoo to be ready to coöperate with Gen. Grant, leaving two of the ironclads at Red River, one at Grand Gulf, one at Carthage, three at Warrenton, and two in the Yazoo, which left me a small force. Still I disposed of them to the best advantage. On the 18th, at meridian, firing was heard in the rear of Vicksburg, which assured me that Gen. Grant was approaching the city. The cannonading was kept up furiously for some time, when, by the aid of glasses, I discovered a company of artillery advancing, taking position, and driving the rebels before them. I immediately saw that Gen. Sherman's division had come on to the left of Snyder's Bluff, and that the rebels at that place had been cut off from joining the forces in the city.

I despatched the DeKalb, Lieut.-Commander Walker, the Choctaw, Lieut.-Commander Ramsay, the Romeo, and Forest Rose, all under command of Lieut.-Commander Breese, up the Yazoo, to open communication in that way with Gens. Grant and Sherman. This I succeeded in doing, and in three hours received letters from Gens. Grant, Sherman, and Steele, informing me of this vast success, and asking me to send up provisions, which was at once done. In the mean time, Lieutenant-Commander Walker in the DeKalb pushed on to Haines's Bluff, which the enemy had commenced evacuating the day before, and a party remained behind in the hopes of destroying or taking away a large amount of ammunition on hand. When they saw the gunboats they ran out and left everything in good order, guns, forts, tents, and equipage of all kinds, which fell into our hands.

As soon as the capture of Haines's Bluff and the fourteen forts was reported to me, I shoved up the gunboats from below to fire on the hill batteries, which fire was kept up for two or three hours. At midnight they moved up to the town and opened on it for about an hour, and continued at intervals during the night to annoy the garrison. On the 19th I placed six mortars in position, with orders to fire night and day as rapidly as they could.

The works at Haines's Bluff are very formidable. There are fourteen of the heaviest kind of mounted eight and ten inch and seven and a half inch rifle guns, with ammunition enough to last a long siege. As the gun carriages might again fall into the hands of the enemy, I had them burned, blew up the magazine, and destroyed the works generally. I also burned up the encampments, which were permanently and remarkably well constructed, looking as though the rebels intended to stay some time. Their works and encampments covered many acres of ground, and the fortifications and rifle pits proper of Haines's Bluff extend about a mile and a quarter. Such a network of forts I never saw.

As soon as I got through with the destruction of the magazines and other works, I started Lieut.-Com. Walker up the Yazoo river with sufficient force to destroy all the enemy's property in that direction, with orders to return with all despatch, and only to proceed as far as Yazoo City, where the rebels have a navy yard and storehouses.

In the mean time Gen. Grant has closely invested Vicksburg, and has possession of the best commanding points. In a very short time a general assault will take place, when I hope to announce that Vicksburg has fallen after a series of the most brilliant successes that ever attended an army.

There has never been a case during the war where the rebels have been so successfully beaten at all points, and the patience and endurance shown by our army and navy for so many months is about being rewarded. It is a mere question of a few hours, and then, with the exception of Port Hudson, which will follow Vicksburg, the Mississippi will be open its entire length.

(Signed) D. D. PORTER,
Com'g Mississippi Squadron.

The result of the expedition to Yazoo City is thus described in the report of Lieut. Walker, addressed to Rear-Admiral Porter:

U. S. STEAMER BARON DE KALB,
MOUTH YAZOO RIVER, *May 23d.*

SIR: I have the honor to report that in obedience to your order I started from Snyder's Bluff on the 20th, with the DeKalb, Choctaw, Forest Rose, Linden, and Petrel, on an expedition to Yazoo City. Arriving at Haines's Bluff, I landed a force and spiked an 8-inch gun on the fort there, and burned the carriage. I also burned some forty tents left standing, and a steam sawmill.

Arriving at Yazoo City at 1 P. M., 20th, I was met by a committee of citizens, who informed me that the place had been evacuated by the military authorities, and asking protection. The navy yard and vessels had been fired by the enemy. I sent a working party to insure the destruction of everything valuable to the rebels. The vessels burned were the Mobile, a screw vessel, ready for plating; the Republic, which was being fitted out for a ram; and a vessel on the stocks—a monster, 310 feet long, 75 feet beam. The navy yard contained five saw and planing mills, an extensive machine shop, carpenter and blacksmith shops, and all necessary fixtures for a large building and repairing yard, which, with a very large quantity of lumber, were burned. I also burned a large sawmill above the town. Most of the public stores had been removed; such as I found in town were taken on board the vessels or destroyed. Enclosed I send a list of articles removed or destroyed by Acting Volunteer Lieut. Brown, the officer detailed for that purpose. In the hospital I found and paroled 1,500 prisoners, a list of whom I enclose.

Returning, I left Yazoo City this morning, arriving here at 4 P. M. At Liverpool Landing, in a sharp bend in the river, we were attacked by some field guns, and about 200 riflemen concealed in the bushes, and for a few minutes the firing was very sharp. The enemy retreated as soon as the vessels got into position to use their guns with effect. The Petrel, Linden, and Choctaw were struck with shot, but received no particular injury. Sergt. Stockinger, of this vessel, was killed by a rifle shot. The Linden had five wounded, the Petrel two, and the Choctaw one. Most of the wounds are slight.

After the storming of their position on the Big Black river, the Confederate force fell back to Vicksburg, which they reached about eight o'clock on Sunday night, the 17th. Their army was immediately reorganized, and placed as follows: Gen. Smith's division on the extreme left, Major-Gen. Forney in the centre, and Major-Gen. Stephenson on the right. Brig.-Gen. Bowen's division of Missourians held the reserve.

It has been stated that by the morning of Tuesday, the 19th, Vicksburg was invested by the Federal army. During that day there was a continued skirmishing, and Gen. Grant was not without hope of carrying the works. He found his forces insufficient to entirely invest the works. There was therefore danger that the two bodies of the enemy, under Gens. Johnston and Pemberton, might yet effect a junction, as it was known that the former was receiving large reënforcemsnts from Gen. Bragg's army in Middle and Eastern Tennessee. He therefore ordered a general assault to be made at two o'clock in the afternoon. This was made by the fifteenth army corps, which arrived in time before the works on the previous day to get a good position. The thirteenth and seventeenth corps succeeded in gaining an advanced position covered from the fire of the enemy. A Confederate report of the action of Tuesday is as follows: "On Tuesday morning, before daylight, they opened fire from their batteries, our guns responding immediately and with fine effect, compelling the enemy to shift their batteries several times. At the same time the enemy endeavored to throw forward a body of sharpshooters, but were prevented by the fire of our men from so doing. The artillery duel and sharpshooting continued for about three hours, when Gen. Pemberton rode up and ordered our men to cease firing, as he desired no artillery duels. In obedience to the order, our men ceased firing, and the result was that next morning, the enemy, emboldened by our silence, approached one hundred yards nearer than they were the day before, without any opposition. On Tuesday the enemy made their first assault on the line of works held by Brig.-Gen. Shoup's brigade of Louisianians. They marched up in one solid column, our men withholding their fire until the enemy had approached within thirty yards of the lines, when they opened a terrific volley of musketry. The enemy wavered a moment, and then marched forward. They were again met by another volley, when they broke and fled under cover of the hills. This was the only attempt made on that day to force our lines, and the attempt was evidently made more with the intention of 'feeling' our lines than with any serious idea of storming them."

By the 21st, the arrangements of Gen. Grant for drawing supplies of every description were completed, and he determined to make another effort to carry Vicksburg by assault. His reasons for this are thus stated: "I believed an assault from the position gained by this time could be made successfully. It was known that Johnston was at Canton with the force taken by him from Jackson, reënforced by other troops from the east, and that more were daily reaching him. With the force I had, a short time must have enabled him to attack me in the rear, and possibly to succeed in raising the siege. Possession of Vicksburg at that time would have enabled me to turn upon Johnston and drive him from the State, and possess myself of all the railroads and practical military highways, thus effectually securing to ourselves all territory west of the Tombigbee, and this before the season was too far advanced for campaigning in this latitude. It would have saved Government sending large reënforcements much needed elsewhere; and, finally, the troops themselves were impatient to possess Vicksburg, and would not have worked in the trenches with the same zeal, believing it unnecessary, that they did after their failure to carry the enemy's works."

Accordingly, orders were issued on the 21st for a general assault on the whole line, to commence at 10 A. M. on the next day. This assault is thus described by Gen. Grant: "All the corps commanders set their time by mine, that there should be no difference between them in the movement of assault. Promptly at the hour designated, the three army corps then

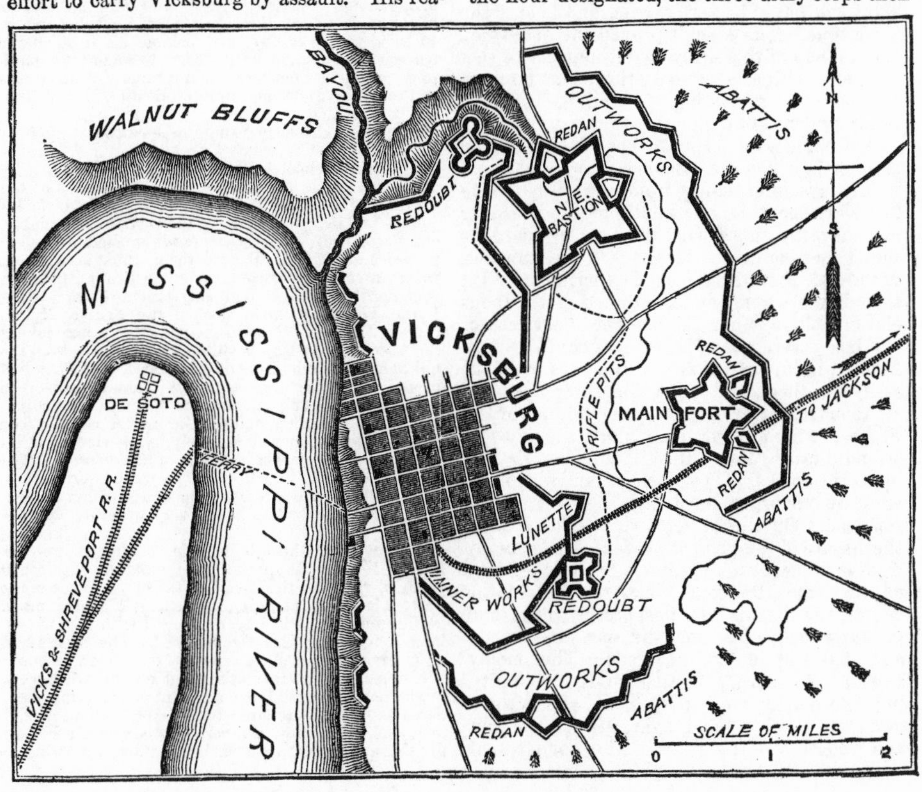

in front of the enemy's works commenced the assault. I had taken a commanding position near McPherson's front, and from which I could see all the advancing columns from his corps, and a part of each of Sherman's and McClernand's. A portion of the commands of each succeeded in planting their flags on the outer slopes of the enemy's bastions, and maintained them there until night. Each corps had many more men than could possibly be used in the assault, over such ground as intervened between them and the enemy. More men could only avail in case of breaking through the enemy's line or in repelling a sortie. The assault was gallant in the extreme on the part of all the troops, but the enemy's position was too strong, both naturally and artificially, to be taken in that way. At every point assaulted, and at all of them at the same time, the enemy was able to show all the force his works could cover. The assault failed, I regret to say, with much loss on our side in killed and wounded; but without weakening the confidence of the troops in their ability to ultimately succeed.

"No troops succeeded in entering any of the enemy's works, with the exception of Sergeant Griffith, of the Twenty-first regiment Iowa volunteers, and some eleven privates of the same regiment. Of these none returned except the sergeant and possibly one man. The work entered by him, from its position, could give us no practical advantage, unless others to the right and left of it were carried and held at the same time. The assault proved the quality of the soldiers of this army. Without entire success, and with a heavy loss, there was no murmuring or complaining, no falling back, or other evidence of demoralization."

A Confederate report thus describes the manner in which the assault was met by them: "The days intervening from the 19th to the 22d were spent in one continued bombarding and sharpshooting during the day; in the night they generally ceased firing. On the morning of the 22d, the enemy opened a terrific fire with their Parrott guns, and continued it till about eleven o clock, when the bombardment ceased, and heavy columns of the enemy could be seen forming in line of battle. Our forces were all ready for them, and eager for their advance. At about a quarter to twelve, the column of the Federal army advanced all along the lines in splendid order, and with a loud cheer dashed up to the works. They were gallantly responded to by our brave boys, and the first charge repulsed. On the extreme right of our lines, the nature of the ground prevented the enemy from making any heavy attack, but on the right of the centre, the centre, and the left of the centre, the assault was desperately made and gallantly met. But once did our lines break, and that was in Lee's brigade. The enemy gained a temporary footing on the rifle pits, but Lee quickly rallied his men, and, after a desperate hand-to-hand fight, drove them out and reoccupied the lines. The engagement at this point and at the right of the line, held by Brig.-Gen. L. Herbert, was of a terrible nature, the Federals having thrown their best troops on these works. Five times did they charge, and each time were repulsed. The last charge on the right of Brig.-Gen. Herbert's lines was made by an Irish regiment (the Seventeenth Wisconsin), carrying the green flag of Erin. They came at a double quick up the hill, each man in the front rank furnished with ladders to reach the works. Three times they essayed to plant their ladders, but were prevented by the obstinate resistance offered by the consolidated Twenty-first and Twenty-third Louisiana regiments. At the third charge they came within ten yards of the line, but two volleys of buckshot from the shotguns of our forces compelled them to make a precipitate retreat from the front of our works. At about 2 o'clock they made their last charge, and were again repulsed, when they retired, and did not attempt any further demonstration that day. The loss of the enemy on that day is estimated by competent parties at not less than from 8,000 to 10,000, while our loss was between 800 and 1,000 in killed and wounded."

The following despatch of Rear-Admiral Porter to the Secretary of the Navy, describes the part taken in this conflict by the naval force:

MISSISSIPPI SQUADRON, FLAG SHIP BLACK HAWK, May 23, 1863.

SIR: On the evening of the 21st I received a communication from Gen. Grant, informing me that he intended to attack the whole of the rebel works at 10 A. M. the next day, and asking me to shell the batteries from 9.30 until 10.30, to annoy the garrisons. I kept six mortars playing rapidly on the works and town all night, and sent the Benton, Mound City, and Carondelet up to shell the water batteries and other places where troops might be resting during the night.

At seven o'clock in the morning, the Mound City proceeded across the river, and made an attack on the hill batteries opposite the canal. At eight o'clock I joined her in company with the Benton, Tuscumbia, and Carondelet. All these vessels opened on the hill batteries and finally silenced them, though the main work on the battery containing the heavy rifled gun was done by the Mound City, Lieut.-Commanding Byron Wilson. I then pushed the Benton, Mound City, and Carondelet up to the water batteries, leaving the Tuscumbia, which is still out of repair, to keep the hill batteries from firing on our vessels after they had passed by. The three gunboats passed up slowly, owing to the strong current, the Mound City leading, the Benton following, and the Carondelet astern. The water batteries opened furiously, supported by a hill battery on the starboard beam of the vessels. The vessels advanced to within 440 yards (by our marks), and returned the fire for two hours without cessation, the enemy's fire being very accurate and incessant.

Finding that the hill batteries behind us were silenced, I ordered up the Tuscumbia to within 200 yards of the batteries, but her turret was soon made untenable. Not standing the enemy's shot, I made her drop down. I had been engaged with the forts an hour longer than Gen. Grant asked. The vessels had all received severe shots under water, which we could not stop up while in motion, and not knowing what might have delayed the movement of the army, I ordered the vessels to drop out of fire, which they did in a cool, handsome manner. This was the hottest fire the gunboats have ever been under, but owing to the water batteries being more on a level with them than usual, the gunboats threw in their shells so fast that the aim of the enemy was not very good. The enemy hit our vessels a number of times, but, fighting bow on, they did but little damage. Not a man was killed, and only a few wounded. I had only ammunition enough for a few minutes longer, and set all hands to work to fill up from our depot below.

After dropping back I found that the enemy had taken possession again of one of the lower hill batteries, and was endeavoring to remount his guns, and had mounted a 12-pounder field piece to fire at General McArthur's troops, which had landed a short time before at Warrenton. I sent the Mound City and the Carondelet to drive him off, which they did in a few moments.

I beg leave to enclose a letter from Gen. McArthur, explaining why he did not, to use his own expression, take advantage of the result gained by the gunboats.

I have since learned through General Grant, that the army did assault at the right time vigorously. In the noise and smoke we could not hear or see it. The gunboats were, therefore, still fighting when the assault had proved unsuccessful. The army had terrible work before them, and are fighting as well as soldiers ever fought before, but the works are stronger than any of us dreamed of. Gen. Grant and his soldiers are confident that the brave and energetic generals in the army will soon overcome all obstacles and carry the works.

(Signed) DAVID D. PORTER,
Acting Rear-Admiral, Com. Miss. Squadron.
Hon. G. Welles, Secretary of the Navy.

Gen. Grant now determined upon a regular siege of Vicksburg, and immediately began to mine the lines. The orders given to the enemy, by Gen. Pemberton, forbade the waste of ammunition, and thus Gen. Grant was able to commence throwing up works and erecting forts within a short distance of the opposing line of breastworks. The firing upon the town was made only during the day, until the 26th of May, after which it was continued day and night. The mortars on the peninsula opposite Vicksburg opened fire on the 25th, and continued it until the surrender. It was estimated at Vicksburg that as many as 6,000 mortar shells were thrown into the town every twenty-four hours, and on the line in the rear of the city, as many as 4,000 in the same time. Of the women and children remaining in the city, three were killed and twelve wounded during the siege. During about five days after the siege commenced, the troops in the city were allowed full rations. At the expiration of that time, they were gradually reduced to the following amount: four ounces of flour, four ounces of bacon, one and a half ounce of rice, two ounces of peas, not eatable, and three ounces of sugar, making a total of fourteen and a half ounces of food daily. The extent of the works, and the limited number of the Confederate troops, required every man to defend their lines, and no time was allowed to rest. Whole companies laid back of their breastworks for three weeks without leaving the line for a moment. The sharpshooters of Gen. Grant's army were regarded by the enemy as splendid shots, and after the first few days of the siege it was dangerous for any one of the enemy to look over their breastworks. In one instance, a hat placed on a stick, and held above a port for two minutes, was pierced by fifteen balls. The sharpshooters of the enemy were no less expert. The garrison was buoyed up with the hope of relief by an attack upon the rear of Gen. Grant's army by Gen. Johnston, who was gathering troops in Mississippi.

Meantime every effort was made to strengthen the force under the command of Gen. Grant. He had already ordered a division under Gen. Lanman and four regiments at Memphis to join him. He now brought forward the divisions of Gens. Smith and Kimball, of the sixteenth army corps, and placed them under the command of Maj.-Gen. C. C. Washburn. On the 11th of June, Maj.-Gen. F. J. Herron's division, from the department of Missouri, arrived, and on the 14th, two divisions of the ninth army corps, Maj.-Gen. J. G. Parke commanding, reached Vicksburg. These two divisions were a part of the forces of Gen. Burnside, commanding in the Department of Ohio. This increase of the forces of Gen. Grant enabled him to make the investment of Vicksburg more complete, and at the same time left him a large reserve with which to watch the movements of Gen. Johnston.

These reënforcements were arranged by placing Gen. Herron's division on the extreme left, south of the city. Gen. Lauman's division was placed between Gens. Herron and McClernand. Gen. Smith's and Gen. Kimball's divisions and the force under Gen. Parke were sent to Haines's Bluff. This place was now fortified on the land side, and every preparation made to resist a heavy force. About the 25th of June, Gen. Johnston crossed the Big Black river with a portion of his force, and everything indicated that he would make an attack. The position of Gen. Grant before Vicksburg having been made as strong against a sortie of the enemy as their works were against an assault, he placed Gen. Sherman in command of all the troops designated to look after Gen. Johnston. The force so designated, in addition to that at Haines's Bluff, was one division from the thirteenth, fifteenth, and seventeenth army corps each, and Gen. Lauman's division. As Gen. Johnston did not make the attack at the time it was expected, Gen. Grant determined to attack him as soon as Vicksburg was taken. He accordingly notified Gen. Sherman that another assault on Vicksburg would be made at daylight on the 6th of July, and ordered him to have up supplies of all descriptions, and to be ready to move upon the receipt of further orders, if the assault should prove successful. Gen. Sherman made his preparations immediately, and was ready to move earlier than the time appointed.

On the 6th of June an attack was made on Milliken's Bend, in which the enemy were repulsed. The Union loss was 101 killed, 285 wounded, and 266 missing. Gen. Halleck, in his report, says: "It is represented that the colored troops, in this desperate engagement, fought with great bravery, and that the rebels treated this class of prisoners of war, as well as their officers, with great barbarity. It has not been possible, however, to ascertain the correctness of the representations in regard to the treatment of these prisoners." A number of skirmishes also took place along the Tensas from Lake Providence to Richmond. The great object of the enemy in these movements was ultimately to approach Vicksburg from the west. All this time the works of the siege were pushed forward. But from the 22d of May to the 25th of June, no attempt upon the city of any serious nature was made, with the exception of the attack of the gunboat Cincinnati, for the purpose of silencing one of the land batteries. The report of this attack was thus made by the officer in charge:

MISSISSIPPI SQUADRON, FLAG SHIP BLACK HAWK, ABOVE VICKSBURG, *May 27th*, 1863.

To Rear-Admiral D. D. Porter:

SIR: In obedience to your order, the Cincinnati got under way this morning at seven o'clock, and steamed slowly down until a little abreast of where the mortars lie. When we rounded to, the enemy fired several shots from a gun called "Whistling Dick," but soon gave it up. At half past eight, with a full head of steam, we stood for the position assigned us. The enemy fired rapidly and from all their batteries. When abreast of our pontoon, and rounding to, a ball entered the magazine, and she commenced sinking rapidly. Shortly after the starboard tiller was carried away. Before and after this the enemy fired with great accuracy, hitting us nearly every time. We were especially annoyed by plunging shots from the hills, and 8-inch rifled and 10-inch smooth-bore shots did us much damage. The shots went entirely through our protection—hay and wood. And now, finding that the vessel would sink, I ran her up stream as near the right-hand shore as our damaged steering apparatus would permit. About ten minutes before she sank we ran close in, got out one plank, and put the wounded ashore. We also got a hawser out to make fast to a tree to hold her until she sank. Unfortunately, the men ashore left the hawser without making it fast. The enemy were still firing, and the boat commenced drifting out. I sang out to the men to swim ashore, thinking we were in deeper water (as was reported) than we really were. I suppose about fifteen were drowned and twenty-five killed and wounded, and one probably taken prisoner. This will sum up our whole loss. The boat sank in about three fathoms of water; she lies level and can easily be raised, but lies within range of the enemy's batteries. The vessel went down with her colors nailed to her mast, or rather to the stump of one, all three having been shot away. Our fire, until the magazine was drowned, was good, and I am satisfied did damage. We only fired at a two-gun water battery.

Very respectfully, &c.,
GEO. M. BACHE, Lieut. Commanding.

The progress of the mining operations was such, that on the 25th of June a fort, on the immediate right of the Jackson road, was blown up. It was occupied by the Third Louisiana regiment. Its destruction had been anticipated by the enemy, and most of the force was previously withdrawn to an inner line of intrenchments, so that only a few men were wounded by the explosion. As soon as it had been destroyed, a strong column advanced to storm the line, which was met by a force of the enemy, consisting of the Sixth Missouri, and a bloody contest ensued, in which the loss was severe on both sides. The Federal force then retired.

On the 29th of June, the same portion of the enemy's line was again blown up, but no attempt to charge was made. All attempts to countermine, on the part of the enemy, were signally unsuccessful, owing to the position of Gen. Grant's works. The state of affairs within the city at this time is thus described by a Confederate officer: "About the thirty-fifth day provisions began to get very scarce, and the advent of Gen. Johnston's relieving force was anxiously and momentarily looked for. Mule meat was the common fare of all alike, and even dogs became in request for the table. Bean meal was made into bread, and corn meal into coffee, and in these straits the garrison patiently dragged on the weary length of one day after another, under a scorching sun, the stench from the unburied corpses all around alone causing the strongest minded, firmest nerved to grow impatient for the day of deliverance. The enemy pushed their works: they blew up several forts, and with them the garrison, and attempted to charge; but the meagre and famished yet steadfast garrison still defiantly held the key of the Mississippi. But everything must have an end. Gen. Pemberton learned from Gen. Johnston that he could not afford him relief, and as the garrison was too famished and reduced to cut its way out, he determined to capitulate."

On the 3d of July, about half past seven in the morning, a flag of truce was seen on the crest of a hill above the camp of Gen. Burbridge. An officer was sent to escort the bearers of it, two Confederate officers, blindfold, to the tent of Gen. A. J. Smith, whose front they entered. These officers were Major-Gen. Bowen and Col. Montgomery, of Virginia. They were the bearers of the following despatch from Lieut.-Gen. Pemberton to Gen. Grant:

HEADQUARTERS, VICKSBURG, *July 3d*, 1863.

Maj.-Gen. U. S. Grant, commanding U. S. Forces:

GENERAL: I have the honor to propose to you an armistice for blank hours, with a view of arranging terms for the capitulation of Vicksburg. To this end, if agreeable to you, I will appoint three commissioners to meet a like number to be named by yourself, at such place and hour to-day as you may find convenient. I make this proposition to save the further effusion of blood, which must otherwise be shed to a frightful extent, feeling myself fully able to maintain my position a yet indefinite period. This communication will be handed you, under a flag of truce, by Major-Gen. James Bowen.

Very respectfully, your obedient servant,
JOHN C. PEMBERTON.

To this despatch Gen. Grant replied as follows:

HEADQUARTERS DEPARTMENT OF TENNESSEE, IN THE FIELD NEAR VICKSBURG, *July 3d*, 1863.

Lieut.-Gen. J. C. Pemberton, commanding Confederate Forces, &c.:

GENERAL: Your note of this date, just received, proposes an armistice for several hours, for the purpose of arranging terms of capitulation, through commissioners to be appointed, &c. The effusion of blood you propose stopping by this course can be ended at any time you may choose, by an unconditional surrender of the city and garrison. Men who have shown so much endurance and courage as those now in Vicksburg will always challenge the respect of an adversary, and I can assure you will be treated with all the respect due them as prisoners of war. I do not favor the proposition of appointing commissioners to arrange terms of capitulation, because I have no other terms than those indicated above.

I am, General, very respectfully, your obedient servant, U. S. GRANT, Major-General.

Gen. Bowen, the bearer of Gen. Pemberton's letter, expressed to Gen. Smith a strong desire to converse with Gen. Grant, and accordingly Gen. Grant, while declining this, requested Gen. Smith to say if Gen. Pemberton desired to see him, an interview would be granted between the lines, in McPherson's front, at any hour in the afternoon which Gen. Pemberton might appoint. A message was soon sent back to Gen. Smith, appointing three o'clock as the hour. At that time Gen. Grant, with his staff and Gens. McPherson, Ord, A. J. Smith, and Logan, was at the place, which was a fruit orchard midway between the front of the two contending forces. Gen. Pemberton soon came, attended by Gen. Bowen and Col. Montgomery. As the two commanders drew near each other, both, as though involuntarily, paused. The slight embarrassment was brought to a close by Col. Montgomery, who stepped forward and formally introduced them. They shook each other by the hand, and, after a few words, Gen. Grant proposed a private conversation, which was accepted, and the two generals stepped aside. The conference closed by Gen. Grant saying that he would send his proposition in writing. After an interview with his officers at his headquarters, Gen. Grant sent the following letter, by Gen. Logan and Col. Wilson, to Gen. Pemberton:

HEADQUARTERS DEPARTMENT OF THE TENNESSEE, NEAR VICKSBURG, *July 3d*, 1863.

Lieut.-Gen. J. C. Pemberton, commanding Confederate Forces, Vicksburg, Miss.:

GENERAL: In conformity with agreement of this afternoon, I will submit the following proposition for the surrender of the city of Vicksburg, public stores, &c. On your accepting the terms proposed, I will march in one division as a guard, and take possession at eight A. M. to-morrow. As soon as paroles can be made out, and signed by officers and men, you will be allowed to march out of our lines—the officers taking with them their regimental clothing, and staff, field, and cavalry officers one horse each. The rank and file will be allowed all their clothing, but no other property. If these conditions are accepted, any amount of rations you may deem necessary can be taken from the stores you now have, and also the necessary cooking utensils for preparing them. Thirty wagons also, counting two two-horse or mule teams as one, will be allowed you to transport such articles as cannot be carried along. The same conditions will be allowed to all sick and wounded officers and privates as fast as they become able to travel. The paroles for these latter must be signed, however, whilst officers are present authorized to sign the roll of prisoners.

I am, General, very respectfully,
Your obedient servant,
U. S. GRANT, Major-General.

About the dawn of day, on the morning of July 4th, the following reply was received from Gen. Pemberton:

HEADQUARTERS, VICKSBURG, *July 3d*, 1863.

Major-Gen. U. S. Grant, commanding United States Forces, etc.

GENERAL: I have the honor to acknowledge the receipt of your communication of this date, proposing terms for the surrender of this garrison and post. In the main, your terms are accepted; but in justice both to the honor and spirit of my troops, manifested in the defence of Vicksburg, I have the honor to submit the following amendments; which, if acceded to by you, will perfect the agreement between us: At ten o'clock to-morrow, I propose to evacuate the works in and around Vicksburg, and to surrender the city and garrison under my command by marching out with my colors and arms, and stacking them in front of my present lines, after which you will take possession. Officers to retain their side arms and personal property, and the rights and property of citizens to be respected. I am, General, yours, very respectfully,

J. C. PEMBERTON, Lieutenant-General.

To this letter Gen. Grant immediately replied as follows:

HEADQUARTERS DEPARTMENT OF THE TENNESSEE, BEFORE VICKSBURG, *July 4th*, 1863.

Lieut.-Gen. J. C. Pemberton, commanding Forces in Vicksburg:

GENERAL: I have the honor to acknowledge your communication of 3d July. The amendments proposed by you cannot be acceded to in full. It will be necessary to furnish every officer and man with a parole, signed by himself, which, with the completion of the rolls of prisoners, will necessarily take some time. Again, I can make no stipulation in regard to the treatment of citizens and their private property. While I do not propose to cause any of them any undue annoyance or loss, I cannot consent to leave myself under restraint by stipulations. The property which officers can be allowed to take with them will be as stated in proposition of last evening; that is, officers will be allowed their private baggage and side arms, and mounted officers one horse each. If you mean by your proposition for each brigade to march to the front of the lines now occupied by it, and stack their arms at ten o'clock A. M., and then return to the inside and remain as prisoners until properly paroled, I will make no objections to it. Should no modification be made of your acceptance of my terms by nine o'clock A. M., I shall regard them as having been rejected, and act accordingly. Should these terms be accepted, white flags will be displayed along your lines, to prevent such of my troops as may not have been notified from firing upon your men.

I am, General, very respectfully, your obedient servant.

U. S. GRANT,
Major-General U. S. Army.

To this letter the following answer was received:

HEADQUARTERS VICKSBURG, *July 4th*, 1863.

Major-Gen. U. S. Grant, commanding U. S. Forces, &c.:

GENERAL: I have the honor to acknowledge the receipt of your communication of this date, and in reply to say that the terms proposed by you are accepted.

Very respectfully, your obedient servant,
J. C. PEMBERTON, Lieutenant-General.

Of the terms of the surrender, Gen. Grant thus speaks in his report: "These terms I regarded more favorable to the Government than an unconditional surrender. It saved us the transportation of them North, which at that time would have been very difficult, owing to the limited amount of river transportation on hand, and the expense of subsisting them. It left our army free to operate against Johnston, who was threatening us from the direction of Jackson; and our river transportation to be used for the movement of troops to any point the exigency of the service might require."

At ten o'clock on the 4th, the Confederate forces marched out and stacked arms in front of their works, while Gen. Pemberton appeared for a moment with his staff upon the parapet of the central front. The city was immediately after occupied by the divisions of Gens. Logan, J. E. Smith, and Herron.

The part taken by the naval force in these operations is thus summarily described by Rear-Admiral Porter, in a despatch to the Secretary of the Navy, as follows:

U. S. MISSISSIPPI SQUADRON,
FLAG SHIP BLACK HAWK, *July 4th*, 1863.

SIR: I have the honor to inform you that Vicksburg has surrendered at last to the United States forces, after a desperate but vain resistance. That she has not done so sooner has not been for want of ability on the part of our military commanders, but from the magnitude of the defences, which were intended to repulse any force the Government could possibly send there. What bearing this will have on the rebellion remains yet to be seen, but the magnitude of the success must go far toward crushing out this revolution, and establishing once more the commerce of the States bordering on this river. History has seldom had an opportunity of recording so desperate a defence on one side, with so much courage, ability, perseverance and endurance on the other; and if ever an army was entitled to the gratitude of a nation, it is the Army of the Tennessee and its gallant leaders.

The navy has necessarily performed a less conspicuous part in the capture of Vicksburg than the army; still it has been employed in a manner highly creditable to all concerned. The gunboats have been constantly below Vicksburg in shelling the works, and with success coöperating heartily with the left wing of the army. The mortar boats have been at work for forty-two days without intermission, throwing shells into all parts of the city, even reaching the works in the rear of Vicksburg and in front of our troops, a distance of three miles. Three heavy guns placed on scows, a nine-inch, ten-inch, and a one-hundred-pounder rifle were placed in position a mile from the town, and commanded all the important water batteries. They have kept up an accurate and incessant fire for fourteen days, doing all the damage that could be done by guns under such circumstances. Five eight-inch, two nine-inch, two forty-two-pounder rifles, four thirty-two-pounder shell guns have been landed, at the request of the different generals commanding corps, from the gunboats, and mounted in the rear of Vicksburg; and whenever I could spare the officers and men from our small complement, they were sent to manage the guns, with what ability I leave the general commanding the forces to say.

In the mean time, I stationed the smaller class of gunboats to keep the banks of the Mississippi clear of guerillas, who were assembling in force, and with a large number of cannon, to block up the river and cut off the transports bringing down supplies, reënforcements, and ammunition for the army. Though the rebels on several occasions built batteries, and with a large force attempted to sink or capture the transports, they never succeeded, but were defeated by the gunboats with severe loss on all occasions. Without a watchful care over the Mississippi, the operations of the army would have been much interfered with; and I can say honestly that officers never did their duty better than those who have patrolled the river from Cairo to Vicksburg. One steamer only was badly disabled since our operations commenced, and six or seven men killed and wounded.

While the army have had a troublesome enemy in front and behind them, the gunboats, marine brigade, under Gen. Ellet, and a small force under Gens. Dennis and Mower, have kept at bay a large force of rebels, over twelve thousand strong, accompanied by a large quantity of artillery. Though offered battle several times and engaged, they invariably fled, and satisfied themselves by assailing half-disciplined and unarmed blacks. The capture of Vicksburg leaves a large army and naval force free to act all along the river, and I hope soon to add to my department the vessels which have been temporarily lost to the service, viz., the Indianola and Cincinnati. The effect of this blow will be felt far up the tributaries of the Mississippi. The timid and doubtful will take heart, and the wicked will, I hope, cease to trouble us, for fear of the punishment which will sooner or later overtake them.

There has been a large expenditure of ammunition during the siege. The mortars have fired seven thousand mortar shells, and the gunboats four thousand five hundred. Four thousand five hundred have been fired from the naval guns on shore, and we have supplied six thousand to the different army corps.

DAVID D. PORTER,
A. R.-Admiral, comm'ng Mississippi Squadron.

Hon. GIDEON WELLES, Sec'y of the Navy.

The result of his operations is thus summed up by Gen. Grant: "The result of this campaign has been the defeat of the enemy in five battles outside of Vicksburg; the occupation of Jackson, the capital of the State of Mississippi, and the capture of Vicksburg and its garrison and munitions of war; a loss to the enemy of thirty-seven thousand (37,000) prisoners, among whom were fifteen general officers; at least ten thousand killed and wounded, and among the killed, Generals Tracy, Tilghman, and Green; and hundreds, and perhaps thousands, of stragglers, who can never be collected and reorganized. Arms and munitions of war for an army of sixty thousand men have fallen into our hands, besides a large amount of other public property, consisting of railroads, locomotives, cars, steamboats, cotton, &c., and much was destroyed to prevent our capturing it.

"Our loss in the series of battles may be summed up as follows:

	Killed.	Wounded.	Missing.
Port Gibson	130	718	—
Fourteen Mile Creek (skirmish)	4	24	5
Raymond	69	341	32
Jackson	40	240	6
Champion's Hill	426	1,842	189
Big Black railroad bridge	29	242	2
Vicksburg	545	3,688	303

"Of the wounded, many were but slightly wounded, and continued on duty; many more required but a few days or weeks for their recovery. Not more than one-half of the wounded were permanently disabled."

On Saturday, the 11th of July, the force of Gen. Pemberton, having been paroled, marched from Vicksburg, and arrived at the Big Black river at night. Thence they were distributed to different parts of the South.

On the 13th of July, the President addressed the following letter to Gen. Grant:

EXECUTIVE MANSION, WASHINGTON, *July 13th*, 1863.

MY DEAR GENERAL: I do not remember that you and I ever met personally. I write this now as a grateful acknowledgment for the almost inestimable service you have done the country. I wish to say a word further. When you first reached the vicinity of Vicksburg, I thought you should do what you finally did—march the troops across the neck, run the batteries with the transports, and thus go below; and I never had any faith, except a general hope that you knew better than I, that the Yazoo Pass expedition and the like could succeed. When you got below and took Port Gibson, Grand Gulf, and vicinity, I thought you should go down the river and join Gen. Banks, and when you turned northward, east of the Big Black, I feared it was a mistake. I now wish to make the personal acknowledgment that you were right and I was wrong.

Yours, very truly, A. LINCOLN.

Major-General GRANT.

Major-Gen. Halleck, the General-in-Chief, in his annual report, thus speaks of Gen. Grant's operations: "When we consider the character of the country in which this army operated, the formidable obstacles to be overcome, the number of forces and the strength of the enemy's works, we cannot fail to admire the courage and endurance of the troops, and the skill and daring of their commander. No more brilliant exploit can be found in military history. It has been alleged, and the allegation has been widely circulated by the press, that Gen. Grant, in the conduct of his campaign, positively disobeyed the instructions of his superiors. It is hardly necessary to remark, that Gen. Grant never disobeyed an order or instruction, but always carried out to the best of his ability, every wish or suggestion made to him by the Government. Moreover, he has never complained that the Government did not furnish him all the means and assistance in its power, to facilitate the execution of any plan he saw fit to adopt."

After the capture of Vicksburg, Gen. Grant reported that his troops were so much fatigued and worn out with forced marches and the labors of the siege, as to absolutely require several weeks of repose, before undertaking another campaign. Nevertheless, as the exigencies of the service seemed to require it, he sent out those who were least fatigued on several important expeditions, while the others remained at Vicksburg, to put that place in a better defensive condition for a small garrison.

Immediately upon the surrender of the city, Gen. Sherman, with his force increased by the remainder of both the thirteenth and fifteenth corps, moved in pursuit of Gen. Johnston. When Gen. Grant moved his army from Jackson to Vicksburg, Gen. Johnston moved north to Canton. It now became the object of Gen. Johnston to collect a force to attack the rear of Gen. Grant. His energies were thus devoted during the whole siege of Vicksburg. Yet the country had been so exhausted of men to fill the army in Virginia, a force could not be obtained sufficient to rescue Vicksburg. With the troops which he had collected, he now approached the rear of the Federal army. The country for fifty miles around Vicksburg had —by orders of Gen. Grant on the 26th of May —been laid waste by Gen. Blair, who drove off the white inhabitants and burned the grist mills, cotton gins, and granaries, and destroyed the crops.

The result of the expedition of Gen. Sherman is thus stated in the despatches of Gen. Grant:

VICKSBURG, *July 15th.*

To Major-Gen. Halleck, General-in-Chief:

General Sherman has Jackson invested from Pearl river on the north to the river on the south. This has cut off many hundred cars from the Confederacy. Sherman says he has force enough, and feels no apprehension about the results.

Finding that Yazoo City was being fortified, I sent Gen. Herron there with his division. He captured several hundred prisoners, five pieces of heavy artillery, and all the public stores fell into our hands. The enemy burned three steamboats on the approach of the gunboats. The De Kalb was blown up and sunk in fifteen feet of water, by the explosion of a shell.

Finding that the enemy was crossing cattle for the rebel army at Natchez, and were said to have several thousand there, I have sent troops and steamboats to collect them, and destroy all their boats and means for making more.

(Signed) U. S. GRANT, Major-General.

VICKSBURG, *July 18th.*

To Major-Gen. H. W. Halleck, General-in-Chief:

Joe Johnston evacuated Jackson the night of the 16th instant. He is now in full retreat east. Sherman says most of his army must perish from heat, lack of water, and general discouragement.

The army paroled here have, to a great extent, deserted, and are scattered over the country in every direction.

General Ransom was sent to Natchez to stop the crossing of cattle for the eastern army. On arrival, he found large numbers had been driven out of the city to be pastured. Also, that munitions of war had recently been crossed over to wait for Kirby Smith. He mounted about 200 of his men and sent them in both directions. They captured a number of prisoners, 5,000 head of Texas cattle, 2,000 head of which were sent to Gen. Banks, the balance have been and will be brought here. In Louisiana they captured more prisoners, and a number of teams loaded with ammunition. Over 2,000,000 rounds of ammunition were brought back to Natchez with the teams captured; and 268,000 rounds, besides artillery ammunition, were destroyed. (Signed) U. S. GRANT, Major-Gen. Commanding.

The destruction of property at Jackson was most complete. On the south the railroad was injured as far as Brookhaven, a distance of fifty miles. On the north it was torn up at intervals for twenty miles. At Jackson extensive machine shops, five locomotives, and a large number of cars were destroyed by fire. The road east was torn up at intervals to Brandon, fifteen miles. The bridges at Jackson, some of which were costly, were also destroyed. This destruction secured Gen. Grant in the undisturbed possession of the western part of the State. The city was formerly one of the most prosperous in the Southern States. It was thus described at the time of its capture: "As the seat of government, it has the capitol buildings, the penitentiary, the governor's house, the asylum for the deaf and dumb and the insane; and in addition a fine court house, two excellent hotels, large blocks of stores, a cotton factory, a couple of founderies, grist mills, and a large number of splendid residences. The site of the city, upon the right bank of the Pearl river—a stream of rare beauty—is very fine. The business portion is divided into small lots, and the buildings, generally of brick, are placed in compact blocks. The portion for residences, however, is in marked contrast with the other. Here the lots contain from one acre to five, and in the suburbs over ten acres, according to the ability or taste of the owners. These grounds are laid off in excellent taste. Neatly trimmed hedges line the gravelled walks. The luxuriant shrubbery and gorgeous flowers of the genial South greet the eye in endless profusion and variety. Beautiful arbors, in some cool, shady spot, invite the stranger. And trees, loaded with ripened figs and peaches, and all that is delicious, bend to the hand that will pluck their treasures. In the midst, as far as possible removed from the dust and din of the street, and embowered in magnificent liveoaks and grand old cedars, stand the mansions. They are as different as the varied tastes and conditions of their respective owners, but they all bear an air of comfort and luxury, which proclaims the cultivated tastes and generous fortunes of their occupants. The buildings are not only models of architectural taste, but they are furnished with unusual richness, amounting in many cases to extravagance. This was the Jackson of the past. The Jackson of to-day is quite another place, for the fortunes of war have borne heavily upon it. The penitentiary, one of her fine hotels, her cotton factory, founderies, a whole block of stores, several warehouses, and the railroad bridge and depot buildings were destroyed while the Federal troops occupied the city in May. The reoccupation and evacuation by the Confederate armies cost her another large block of stores and the other hotel. The present occupation by the Federal army has well-nigh served to blot the place from existence. The first few hours were devoted by our soldiers to ransacking the town, and appropriating whatever of value or otherwise pleased their fancy, or to the destruction of such articles as they were unable to appreciate or remove. Pianos and articles of furniture were demolished, libraries were torn to pieces and trampled in the dust, pictures thrust through with bayonets, windows broken and doors torn from their hinges. Finally, after every other excess had been committed in the destruction of property, the torch was applied. From that hour to the present, there has scarcely been a moment when the citizens could not walk the streets by the light of blazing buildings. The entire business portion of the city is in ruins, with the exception of a few old frame buildings, which the citizens must have long regarded as an injury to the place. One residence after another has been burned, until none of the really fine ones remain, save those occupied as quarters by some of our general officers. The State house and court house and insane asylum are preserved and under guard. It is not improbable, however, that they, together with all the remaining residences worth anything, will be fired by our rear guard when we leave the city to-night. Of the Jackson of a few days ago, not above one fourth of the houses remain, and they are nearly all the residences of the poorer classes."

Another circumstance attended the return of the force of Gen. Sherman to Vicksburg, which is so peculiar to army movements into the Southern States, that a mention of it should not be omitted.

"The return of the army from Jackson was the occasion of a remarkable exodus of negroes. There were few able-bodied young men among them, for it is the policy of the masters to move that class farther south, and leave only the old and helpless behind them. But all the old men and women and the young children in the whole region of country around Jackson—those who have been a burden upon their masters, and will necessarily be dependent on our charity—accompanied the army on its return, in large numbers. Every species of vehicle, and an untold number of broken-down horses and mules, were pressed into the service by the contrabands *en route* for Vicksburg. Their effects consisted of a wonderful quantity of old clothing and bedding, and dilapitated furniture, which they seemed to regard as of inestimable value. The transportation, however, was not sufficient for all, and hundreds, carrying as many as possible of the movable articles, trudged along on foot. All seemed animated by a fear that our rear guard would overtake, pass, and leave them behind, and such a straining of energies, hurrying and bustling, were never before known among the whole black creation. The soldiers were particularly struck with the ludicrous appearance presented by the darkies, and the tedium and fatigue of the march were often relieved by good jokes cracked at their expense, which served to convulse the whole brigade with laughter.

"The minds of all of them are filled with the most extravagant ideas of the North. It is to them a country of ease and plenty and happiness, and say and do what you will, as soon as the military blockade is made less stringent, they will go North, if they accomplish the distance on foot. They don't feel safe here, not even those whose owners are dead."

A military and naval force was sent to Yazoo City, on the 13th.. It took three hundred prisoners, captured one steamer and burned five, took six cannon, two hundred and fifty small arms, and eight hundred horses and mules. No loss on our side was reported. Small expeditions were also sent against Canton, Pontotoc, Granada, and Natchez, Mississippi. At Granada, a large amount of railroad rolling stock was destroyed. The other expeditions were also successful, meeting with very little opposition. As soon as his army was supplied and rested, Gen. Grant sent a force under Gen. Steele to Helena, to coöperate with Gen. Schofield's troops against Little Rock, and another, under Gens. Ord and Herron, to New Orleans, to reënforce Gen. Banks for such ulterior operations as he might deem proper to undertake.

After Gen. Grant left Vicksburg to assume the general command east of the Mississippi, Gen. McPherson moved with a part of his force to Canton, Mississippi, scattering the enemy's cavalry, and destroying his materials and roads in the centre of that State.

CHAPTER XXIX.

Campaign of Gen. Banks—The Naval Force—Action with the Batteries at Port Hudson—March of Gen. Banks west of the Mississippi—Action at Brashear—Advance upon Alexandria—Its Capture—March to Semmesport—Crossing the Mississippi—Attack on Port Hudson—Its Investment—Siege—Surrender.

THE military operations before Vicksburg were only the prominent features of a great campaign extending from Washington to New Orleans. The movements of General Banks, particularly against Port Hudson, which fell with the fall of Vicksburg, and the advance of General Lee upon Washington, one object of which was to make a diversion in favor of Vicksburg, or rather to take advantage of the concentration of so large a force at such a distance, were incidents of the same campaign. Gen. Banks's arrival in New Orleans at the close of 1862 has been stated. The fleet, which arrived at the same time, consisted of twenty-six steam vessels and twenty-five sailing vessels, and the military force about ten thousand men. Immediately upon his arrival, General Banks took the position of General Butler as commander of the Department of the Gulf, and the latter reported at Washington. The leading objects of Gen. Banks's expedition were to strengthen the military force in Louisiana, and to coöperate in opening the Mississippi—two points on the banks of which were known to be strongly fortified, Port Hudson and Vicksburg. It was anticipated that these works might be reduced in a short time, and that the strength of General Banks might be sufficient for a movement on Texas. But it was soon perceived, after his arrival in New Orleans, that military affairs were in such an uncertain condition that the moment for immediate activity could not be determined. Meanwhile General Banks devoted his attention to the arrangement of affairs at New Orleans. Nothing of importance occurred, unless it was a small affair on the Teche River, in which Commander Buchanan, of the gunboat Calhoun, was killed, early in January. In March, Gen. Banks had concentrated his force at Baton Rouge, numbering nearly twenty-five thousand men. On the 13th a military movement on Port Hudson was ostensibly commenced, to divert the attention of the enemy, while the vessels ran above the batteries. The naval force was under the command of Admiral Farragut. Its result was to transfer a portion of the fleet above Port Hudson, where it could coöperate with the force above, and also cut off supplies to the enemy from Red River. Maj.-Gen. Halleck, in his annual report, says: "Had our land forces invested Port Hudson at this time, it would have been easily reduced, as its garrison was weak. This would have opened communication by the Mississippi River with Gen. Grant at Vicksburg. But the strength of the place was not then known."

The naval force consisted of the frigates Hartford, Mississippi, Richmond, and Monongahela, and the gunboats Albatross, Genesee, Kineo, Essex, and Sachem, and six mortar schooners. They reached Profit's Island, five miles below Port Hudson, early the next morning. At one P. M., the mortars and the gunboats Sachem and Essex, being in position, opened fire on the batteries at Port Hudson. The line of the batteries commenced below the town and extended on the face of the bluff, midway between the crest and the river bank, about three and a half miles. At nine and a half o'clock that night the signal to advance was made. The Hartford, Capt. Palmer, with Admiral Farragut on board, with the gunboat Albatross, Lieut.-Com. Hart, lashed to her side, took the lead. The Richmond, Capt. Alden, the gunboat Genesee, Commander McComb, the Monongahela, Capt. McKinstry, the Kineo, Lieut.-Com. Waters, and the Mississippi, Capt. Melancthon Smith, followed in the order named. The mortars meanwhile kept up their fire. Soon after, rockets were sent up by the enemy to give warning of the approach of the fleet. As the vessels approached the batteries opened fire, which was replied to. At the same time fires were kindled by the enemy on the opposite bank of the river, which revealed the position of the vessels. The Hartford and Albatross were successful in running above the batteries, but the smoke from their fire obscured the river before the other vessels. The Richmond received a shot through her steam drum, and was compelled to drop down out of fire and anchor. Three of her crew were killed and seven wounded. The Monongahela, after her captain was seriously injured, also dropped down the river and anchored.

The Kineo received a shot through her rudder post, and her propeller was made foul by a hawser, which rendered her unmanageable, and she floated down and anchored. After the guns of the batteries were got into range the fire was so accurate and constant as to threaten the destruction of every gunboat in the fleet. The Mississippi grounded under the guns of a battery astern, another on the bow, and others opposite to her. The enemy, upon discovering her position, concentrated their nearest guns upon her. She continued her fire for some time after getting aground. Capt. Smith, finding it to be impossible to get her off, determined to abandon her. He then ordered the engines to be destroyed, the guns to be spiked, and the vessel to be set on fire. The officers and crew were then hurried off to the shore opposite the batteries. Some of the crew are supposed to have jumped overboard, a few were taken prisoners, and the rest proceeded down the shore and were taken off by the other vessels. Of two hundred and thirty-three officers and men, twenty-nine were missing. The vessel, after becoming lighter by burning her top, drifted off, and, floating down the stream, finally blew up. Her armament consisted of nineteen eight-inch, one ten-inch, one twenty-pound Parrott, and two small howitzers in the tops.

Meanwhile, at three o'clock on Friday afternoon, Gen. Grover's division marched out of Baton Rouge, followed in the evening by Gen. Emory's division, and on the next morning by that of Gen. Augur. The army reached Springfield road crossing without a skirmish. The headquarters of Gen. Banks were established here, which was about seven miles from Port Hudson. During Saturday the entire body of cavalry and some infantry regiments were sent out on the Bayou Sara road toward Port Hudson, and down the Ross and Springfield Landing roads to reconnoitre. One or two sharp skirmishes took place with a force of Confederate cavalry and infantry sent out from Port Hudson and deployed as skirmishers in the woods. Toward evening the enemy retired within their intrenchments. Two Federal officers were wounded. On Sunday morning orders were issued to return to Baton Rouge, which was accomplished by evening. On the next day, an attempt to open communication with Admiral Farragut by sending a small force across the point of land opposite Port Hudson—the fourth effort to cross the point—was successful, but Admiral Farragut had moved up the river. The difficulties were caused by a flood. The rebels had cut the levee above.

The attention of Gen. Banks was now turned to that part of the State west of New Orleans and bordering on the Teche river. Opposite New Orleans, on the other side of the Mississippi river, commences the New Orleans and Opelousas railroad, which runs westwardly a distance of eighty miles to Brashear. This place is situated on the Atchafalaya river where it flows out of Lake Chetimacha into the Gulf of Mexico. Nearly opposite, on the western side of the river, is Berwick City, situated at the junction of the Teche river, or bayou, with the Atchafalaya. The Teche river commences in St. Landry parish, a few miles from Opelousas, and flows southeast in a very tortuous course for two hundred miles. During high water it is navigable nearly its whole length. On the banks of this river flourish the finest sugar-cane plantations in the State. The chief towns on the river are Franklin, Martinsville, and Opelousas.

A considerable force of the enemy was at this time stationed within supporting distance on the Teche. It had been kept there to repel a threatened invasion up that stream by the Federal force under Gen. Weitzel. The planters, supposing the Confederate force sufficient for their protection, had put in their crops as usual. When Gen. Weitzel made the first attempt to advance up the river, with the intention of establishing his headquarters at Franklin, the river was obstructed a few miles above its mouth. To prevent these obstructions from being removed, the enemy had thrown up earthworks, extending from the bank of the river back to an impassable swamp, and planted a battery. Here Gen. Moulton, with fifteen hundred men, aided by the gunboat Cotton, made such a stubborn resistance, that Gen. Weitzel was obliged to fall back. The enemy, supposing his object had been to capture the gunboat, removed her stores and ammunition immediately afterward, and burned her; thus showing that they apprehended a defeat on another attack. Subsequently the water washed a channel round the obstructions, and the passage up ceased to be disputed at that point. But much more formidable works were constructed a few miles above Pattersonville, and earthworks thrown up on the opposite side of the river, to prevent a flank movement by land or water. The distance at this point from the river back to the swamp was about three fourths of a mile. A small force could thus hold at bay here one greatly superior in numbers. Several thousand troops of the enemy were posted here, and those below were expected to fall back as the Federal force advanced.

It was to this region, comprising the parishes or counties of Terrebonne, Lafourche, Assumption, St. Mary, and St. Martin, that Gen. Banks now transferred his army from Baton Rouge. His object was the reclamation of this rich country, which had furnished inestimable supplies to the enemy, and which sustained a dense slave population. Having concentrated his forces at Brashear, Gen. Weitzel's brigade was crossed over to Berwick on the 10th of April. The landing was not disputed, but a reconnoissance discovered a force of the enemy, which retired. On the next day, Saturday, the infantry advanced a short distance. On Sunday, the division of Gen. Emory crossed, and the combined force made an advance, which the enemy opposed, but not obstinately. In this order the Federal column advanced, feeling its way, while the enemy, whose forces were commanded by Gen. Taylor, slowly retired upon their fortified position a few miles above Pattersonville. On the 13th there was considerable fighting, mostly with the artillery, in which the Diana, a Federal gunboat, captured about four weeks previous, bore a conspicuous part. On the morning of Saturday, the 12th, the division of Gen. Grover left Brashear on the gunboats Clifton, Estrella, Arizona, and Calhoun, and transports, and proceeded up the Atchafalaya, into Lake Chetimacha. The object was to get into the rear of the enemy, and if possible cut off his retreat if he evacuated his position, or to attack him in rear at the time of the attack in front. Some difficulties delayed the expedition, but it effected a landing early the next morning, about three miles west of Franklin, near a spot called Irish Bend. At this time the gunboat Queen of the West, which had been captured previously by the enemy, was blown up and destroyed on the lake. Skirmishing immediately ensued with a small force of the enemy, that fell back as Gen. Grover advanced. His position was about eleven miles distant from Gen. Banks. At Irish Bend the enemy seemed to be determined to make a stand, and a sharp struggle followed, in which they were forced to retire to the woods and canes. On this retreat they destroyed the gunboat Diana and the transports Gossamer, Newsboy, and Era No. 2, at Franklin. This success of Gen. Grover was followed by the evacuation of the works before Gen. Banks. Early on Tuesday morning, the cavalry and artillery, followed by Gen. Weitzel's brigade, with Col. Ingraham's force of Gen. Emory's division as a support, followed the enemy. So rapid was the pursuit that the enemy was unable to remove the transports at New Iberia, and five, with all the commissary stores and ammunition with which they were loaded, were destroyed at that place, together with an incomplete iron-clad gunboat. On Thursday, the army reached New Iberia. A foundery for the manufacture of cannon and other munitions of war was immediately taken possession of, as a similar one had been seized two days before at Franklin. Two regiments were also sent to destroy the tools and machinery at the celebrated salt mine of the town. Thus far about fifteen hundred prisoners had been captured, and more than five hundred horses, mules, and beef cattle taken from the plantations. The Federal loss was small. The entire force of the enemy was about ten thousand men.

On the next day, the 17th, the army moved forward, but Gen. Grover, who had marched from New Iberia by a shorter road, and thus gained the advance, met the enemy at Bayou Vermilion. Their force consisted of a considerable number of cavalry, one thousand infantry, and six pieces of artillery, massed in a strong position on the opposite bank. They were immediately attacked and driven from their position, but not until they had succeeded in destroying by fire the bridge across the river. The night of the 17th and the next day was passed in rebuilding the bridge. On the 19th, the march was resumed, and continued to the vicinity of Grand Coteau; and on the next day the main force of Gen. Banks occupied Opelousas. At the same time, the cavalry, supported by a regiment of infantry and a section of artillery, were thrown forward six miles to Washington, on the Courtableau. On the 21st, no movement was made, but on the next day, Brig.-Gen. Dwight, of Gen. Grover's division, with detachments of artillery and cavalry, was pushed forward through Washington toward Alexandria. He found the bridges over the Cocodrie and Bœuf destroyed, and during the evening and night replaced them by a single bridge at the junction of the bayous. A steamer had just been burned by the enemy, but the principal portion of her cargo, which had been transferred to a flat, was captured. Orders were also found there from Gen. Moore to Gen. Taylor, in command of the Confederate force, directing him to retreat slowly to Alexandria, and, if pressed, to retire to Texas.

Another expedition, under Lieut.-Col. Blanchard, was sent out by way of Barre's Landing, to examine the Bayou Courtableau in the direction of Bute-a-la-Rose, but he found the roads impassable four miles beyond Barre's Landing. The steamer Ellen was captured by him, which proved a timely assistance. Previously Bute-a-la-Rose had been taken by orders of Gen. Banks, with its garrison of sixty men, two heavy guns, and a large quantity of ammunition. The result of the expedition thus far is thus stated by Gen. Banks: "We have destroyed the enemy's army and navy, and made their reorganization impossible by destroying or removing the material. We hold the key of the position. Among the evidences of our victory are two thousand prisoners, two transports, and twenty guns taken, and three gunboats and eight transports destroyed."

On the 6th of May, Admiral Porter appeared before Alexandria with a fleet of gunboats, and took possession of the town without opposition. On that evening the cavalry of Gen. Dwight dashed into the place, and the next morning the advance of Gen. Banks arrived. Alexandria is the capital of Rapides parish in Louisiana. It is situated on the Red river, about one hundred and fifty miles from its mouth, and in the centre of a rich cotton-growing region.

The country thus occupied by Gen. Banks was the most fertile portion of the State of Louisiana. His movements had been so rapid that the enemy had been allowed no opportunity to make a stand against him after their defeat near Franklin. The capture of Alexandria and the attack on Fort de Russe below, was reported by Admiral Porter, with his movements, thus:

MISSISSIPPI SQUADRON, FLAG SHIP GENERAL PRICE, GRAND GULF, MISS., *May 13th.*

To Secretary Welles:

SIR: I had the honor to inform you from Alexandria of the capture of that place, and the forts defending the approaches to the city, by the naval force under my command. Twenty-four hours after we arrived the advance guard of United States troops came into the city. Gen. Banks arriving soon after, I turned the place over to his keeping. The water beginning to fall, I deemed it prudent to return with the largest vessels to the mouth of the Red river. I dropped down to Fort de Russe in the Benton, and undertook to destroy these works. I only succeeded, however, in destroying the three heavy casemates commanding the channel and a small water battery for two guns. About 600 yards below it I destroyed by bursting one heavy thirty-two pounder and some gun carriages left in their hurry by the enemy.

The main fort, on a hill some 900 yards from the water, I was unable to attend to. It is quite an extensive work, new and incomplete, but built with much labor and pains. It will take two or three vessels to pull it to pieces. I have not the powder to spare to blow it up. The vessels will be ordered to work on it occasionally, and it will be soon destroyed. In this last-mentioned fort was mounted the 11-inch gun, which I am led to believe lies in the middle of the river, near the fort, the rebels throwing it overboard in their panic at the approach of our gunboats. The raft which closed the entrance I have blown up, sawed in two, and presented to the poor of the neighborhood. I sent Commander Woodworth in the Price, with the Switzerland, Pittsburg, and Arizona, up Black river to make a reconnoissance, and he destroyed a large amount of stores, valued at $300,000, consisting of salt, sugar, rum, molasses, tobacco, and bacon.

(Signed) DAVID D. PORTER,
Acting Rear-Admiral,
Commanding Mississippi Squadron.

While at Opelousas, Gen. Banks issued the following order:

HEADQUARTERS DEPARTMENT OF THE GULF, 19TH ARMY CORPS, OPELOUSAS, *May 1st*, 1863.

The Major-General commanding the Department proposes the organization of a corps d'armée of colored troops, to be designated as the "Corps d'Afrique." It will consist ultimately of eighteen regiments, representing all arms—infantry, artillery, cavalry—making nine brigades, of two regiments each, and three divisions of three brigades each, with appropriate corps of engineers, and flying hospitals for each division. Appropriate uniforms, and the graduation of pay to correspond with the value of services, will be hereafter awarded.

In the field, the efficiency of each corps depends upon the influence of its officers upon the troops engaged, and the practical limits of one direct command is generally estimated at 1,000 men. The most eminent military historians and commanders, among others, Thiers and Chambray, express the opinion, upon a full review of the elements of military power, that the valor of the soldier is rather acquired than natural. Nations whose individual heroism is undisputed, have failed as soldiers in the field. The European and American continents exhibit instances of this character, and the military prowess of every nation may be estimated by the centuries it has devoted to military contest, or the traditional passion of its people for military glory. With a race unaccustomed to military service, much more depends on the immediate influence of officers upon individual members, than with those that have acquired more or less of warlike habits and spirit by centuries of contest. It is deemed best, therefore, in the organization of the Corps d'Afrique, to limit the regiment to the smallest number of men consistent with efficient service in the field, in order to secure the most thorough instruction and discipline, and the largest influence of the officers over the troops. At first they will be limited to five hundred men. The average of American regiments is less than that number.

The Commanding General desires to detail, for temporary or permanent duty, the best officers of the army, for the organization, instruction, and discipline of this corps. With their aid he is confident that the corps will render important service to the Government. It is not established upon any dogma of equality, or other theory, but as a practical and sensible matter of business. The Government makes use of mules, horses, uneducated and educated white men, in the defence of its institutions. Why should not the negro contribute whatever is in his power for the cause in which he is as deeply interested as other men? We may properly demand from him whatever service he can render. The chief defect in organizations of this character has arisen from incorrect ideas of the officers in command. Their discipline has been lax, and, in some cases, the conduct of their regiments unsatisfactory and discreditable. Controversies unnecessary and injurious to the service have arisen between them and other troops. The organization proposed will reconcile and avoid many of these troubles.

Officers and soldiers will consider the exigencies of the service in this department, and the absolute necessity of appropriating every element of power to the support of the Government. The prejudices or opinions of men are in no wise involved. The coöperation and active support of all officers and men, and the nomination of fit men from the ranks, and from the lists of non-commissioned and commissioned officers, are respectfully solicited from the Generals commanding the respective divisions.

By command of Major-Gen. BANKS.
RICHARD B. IRWIN, A. A. G.

The subsequent movements of Gen. Banks in this part of the State met with no serious opposition from the enemy. After the investment of Vicksburg, his forces were concentrated at Simmesport for an advance against Port Hudson. Meanwhile the division of Gen. Sherman, which had been quartered at New Orleans, was not inactive. A brigade was sent out under Gen. Nickerson, for the purpose of attacking any forces that the enemy might have in the neighborhood of Lake Pontchartrain. The first Texas cavalry, under Col. Davis, pushed as far as Tickfaw Station on the railroad, and captured a large amount of cotton, lumber, corn, and bacon. A lieutenant and eight men were made prisoners, among whom were fourteen Choctaw Indians. In this neighborhood a large tannery was also destroyed, and a large car shop, the Tangipaha bridge, and other valuable property. On the lake, four schooners, with cargoes of contraband goods, were burned.

The division of Gen. Augur had returned to Baton Rouge, from which a force was sent out that penetrated to a point on the railroad between Clinton and Port Hudson. A body of the enemy were encountered and routed. Of this body five were killed, several wounded, and twenty-five prisoners taken with their horses and accoutrements. About the same time Col. Grierson captured near Port Hudson three hundred head of cattle. The squadron, meanwhile, was anchored at the head of Profit's Island, not attempting any hostile demonstrations, except the mortar vessels, which at night threw a few shells into Port Hudson.

About the middle of May all the available force near the river was concentrated at Baton

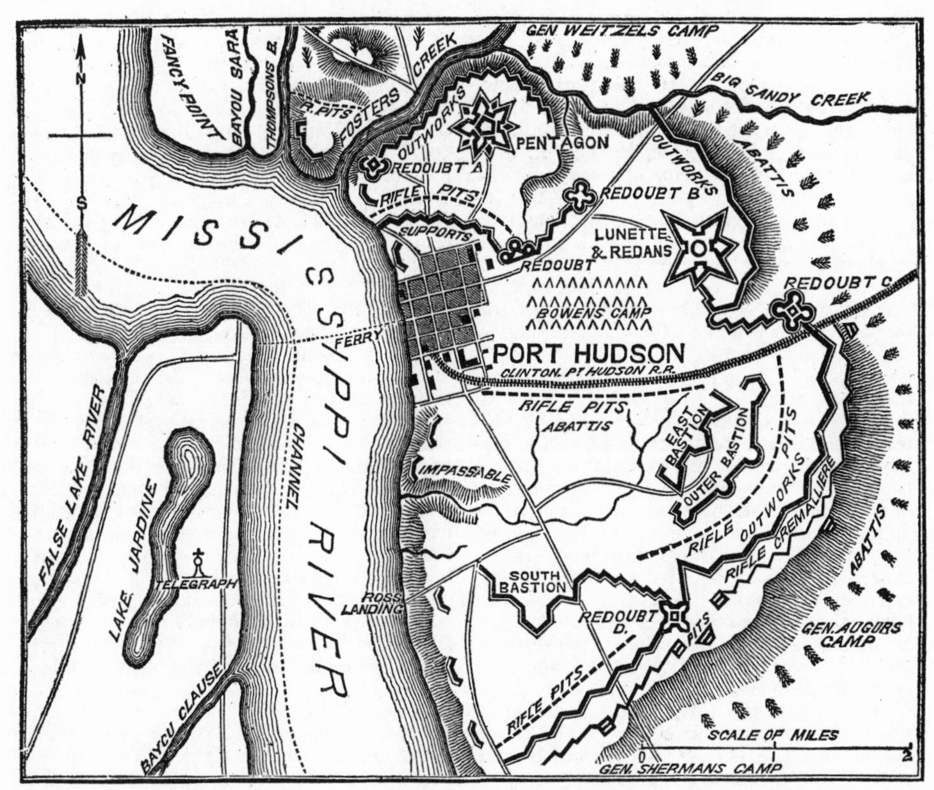

Rouge, to assist in the attack on Port Hudson. Thence Gens. Augur and Sherman moved to the south and east of that position, to coöperate with Gen. Banks. From Simmesport Gen. Banks moved his army to invest Port Hudson. A portion of his infantry was transported in steamers, and the residue with the artillery and cavalry and wagon train moved down on the west bank of the river, and thence across to Bayou Sara, which is five miles above Port Hudson, on the east bank of the Mississippi river. It was on the 21st of May that Gen. Banks landed, and on the next day a junction was effected with the advance of Maj.-Gen. Augur and Brig.-Gen. Sherman. His line occupied the Bayou Sara road. On this road Gen. Augur had an encounter with a force of the enemy, which resulted in their repulse with heavy loss. On the 25th, the enemy was compelled to abandon his first line of works. On the next day Gen. Weitzel's brigade, which had covered the rear in the march from Alexandria, arrived, and on the morning of the 27th a general assault was made on the fortifications.

Port Hudson, or Hickey's Landing, as it was called some years ago, is situated on a bend in the Mississippi river, about twenty-two miles above Baton Rouge, and one hundred and forty-seven above New Orleans. Approaching Port Hudson by water from below, the first batteries were situated on a bluff about forty feet above high water mark. Thence three series of batteries extended along the river above Port Hudson to a point on Thompson's creek, making a continuous line about three and a half miles in extent. Above Thompson's creek is an impassable marsh, forming a natural defence. From the lower battery began a line of land fortifications, of semi-circular form, about ten miles in extent, with Thompson's creek for its natural terminus above. The guns were of heavy caliber; in addition to which there were light batteries, that might be easily taken to any part of the line. The position was under the command of Col. Frank Gardner.

The fire of the artillery of Gen. Banks opened about six o'clock on the morning of the 27th, and continued with animation during the day. At ten o'clock, Gen. Weitzel's brigade, with the division of Gen. Grover—reduced to about two brigades—and the division of Gen. Emory, temporarily reduced by detachments to about a brigade, under command of Col. Paine, with two regiments of colored troops, made an assault upon the right of the enemy's works, crossing Sandy creek, and driving them through the woods into their fortifications. The fight lasted on this line until four o'clock, and was very severely contested. On the left, the infantry did not come up until later in the day; but at two o'clock an assault was commenced on the works on the centre and left of centre, by the divisions under Maj.-Gen. Augur and Brig.-Gen. Sherman. The enemy was driven into his works, and the Federal troops moved up to the fortifications, holding the opposite sides of the parapet with the enemy. On the right, the troops continued to hold their position; but on the left, after dark, the main body, being exposed to a flank fire, withdrew to a belt of woods. The skirmishers remained close upon the fortifications. On the extreme right, the first and third regiments of negro troops were posted. Of their behavior in action, Gen. Banks thus reports: "The position occupied by these troops was one of importance, and called for the utmost steadiness and bravery in those to whom it was confided. It gives me pleasure to report that they answered every expectation. In many respects their conduct was heroic. No troops could be more determined or more daring. They made during the day three charges upon the batteries of the enemy, suffering very heavy losses, and holding their position at nightfall with the other troops on the right of our line. The highest commendation is bestowed upon them by all the officers in command on the right. Whatever doubt may have existed heretofore as to the efficiency of organizations of this character, the history of this day proves conclusively to those who were in condition to observe the conduct of these regiments, that the Government will find in this class of troops effective supporters and defenders. The severe test to which they were subjected, and the determined manner in which they encountered the enemy, leaves upon my mind no doubt of their ultimate success. They require only good officers, commands of limited numbers, and careful discipline, to make them excellent soldiers." The entire loss in killed, wounded, and missing, since landing at Bayou Sara to this time, was nearly a thousand, including some of the ablest officers of the corps, among whom was Gen. Sherman.

A bombardment of the position had been made by the fleet under Admiral Farragut, for a week previous to this assault. Reconnoissances had discovered that the defences were very strong, consisting of several lines of intrenchments and rifle pits, with abatis of heavy trees felled in every direction. The upper batteries on the river were attacked by the Hartford and Albatross, which had run the blockade, and the lower by the Monongahela, Richmond, Genesee, and Essex.

On the 14th of June, after a bombardment of several days, another assault on Port Hudson was made. The position of Gen. Banks's forces at this time was somewhat changed, forming only a right and left without a centre, and, joined together, making a right angle. The division of Gen. Grover, on the upper side of Port Hudson, extended a distance of nearly four miles from the river toward the interior, within supporting distance of Gen. Augur's division. This was on the west side of the enemy's fortifications, and extended a distance of three miles to the river, and within hailing of the fleet. At this time, looking from the extreme northeasterly range of the enemy's rifle pits toward the river, on the upper side of Port Hudson, a long line of earthworks could be seen, glistening with bayonets, and protected by a deep ditch nearly twelve feet in width. Within short range, enfilading breastworks commanded every approach to the position of the enemy. The defences of the enemy formed nearly a right angle, both lines of which extended to the river, and enclosed a sharp bend. The point of attack was the extreme northeasterly angle of the enemy's position. For some days previous, several pieces of their artillery had been dismounted by the Federal fire and abandoned, while those in position were rendered useless by the fire of the sharpshooters. Two regiments were detailed as sharpshooters, who were to creep up and lie on the exterior slope of the enemy's breastworks, while another regiment—each soldier having a hand grenade besides his musket—followed. These grenades were to be thrown over into the enemy's position. Another regiment followed with bags filled with cotton, which were to be used to fill up the ditch in front of the breastworks. After these regiments came the others of Gen. Weitzel's brigade. Following these as a support were the brigades of Col. Kimball and Col. Morgan. These forces under Gen. Weitzel were designed for the attack on the right. In conjunction, on the left, moved the old division of Gen. Emory under Gen. Paine, forming a separate column. Both divisions were under the command of Gen. Grover, who planned the attack. It was expected that Gen. Weitzel's command would make a lodgment inside of the enemy's works, and thus prepare the way for Gen. Paine's division. The advance was made about daylight, through a covered way, to within three hundred yards of the enemy's position; then the field consisted of deep gullies covered by brush and creeping vines. The fire of the enemy was incessant, but a part of the skirmishers succeeded in reaching the ditch, where they were immediately repulsed by an enfilading fire. But little was therefore accomplished with the hand grenades, as they were at once caught up by the enemy, and hurled back. Meanwhile the assaulting column moved forward as rapidly as possible, and made a series of desperate assaults on the works, but the enemy were fully prepared, and lined every part of their fortifications with heavy bodies of infantry.

It was a part of the general plan of attack that a feint should be made on the extreme left by Gens. Augur and Dwight. This assault was made, and the fighting was extremely desperate on the part of the forces under Gen. Dwight. At length all the assaulting columns were compelled to fall back under the deadly fire of the enemy, and the fighting finally ceased about 11 o'clock in the morning. The loss of Gen.

Banks was nearly 700 in killed and wounded. Meantime the first parallel encircling the outer line of the enemy was pushed forward, and the skirmishers were posted in rifle pits so near that skirmishes were of constant occurrence at night. A small force of the enemy's cavalry hovered in the rear of Gen. Banks's army, without making any serious demonstrations.

The withdrawal of Gen. Banks's force from the west side of the Mississippi was followed by great activity on the part of the enemy, for the purpose of recovering the places held by a small body of Federal troops, and to cause a diversion from Port Hudson. Opelousas was reoccupied by a considerable Confederate force; the west bank of the Mississippi was lined with squads of the rebels, who fired upon every boat which passed. A raid was made upon Plaquemine by a body of Texans, who burned two steamers lying there. They were driven out by Lieut. Weaver, commanding the gunboat Winona. On the 17th of June, an attack was made on the Federal pickets at La Fourche, which was repulsed. On the next day it was repeated with the same result. On the 23d, Brashear City was captured by a confederate force under Gens. Green and Mouton. A camp of slaves, or contrabands, as they were called, was attacked by the enemy, and large numbers killed. Immense quantities of ammunition, several pieces of artillery, three hundred thousand dollars' worth of sutler's goods, sugar, flour, pork, beef, and medical stores, of vast amount, were also captured. On the 28th, an attack was made on Donaldsonville, and the storming party succeeded in getting into the fort. But the gunboats opened a flanking fire above and below the fort, and drove back the supporting party, so that the enemy broke and fled. Of those who had entered the fort, one hundred and twenty were captured and nearly one hundred killed.

Other movements on the part of the enemy were made at this time, which indicated great activity, and enabled them to destroy much Federal property. No embarrassment however was caused to the position of Gen. Banks. The enemy, in short, recovered the La Fourche, Teche, Attakapas, and Opelousas country, and captured Brashear, with fifteen hundred prisoners, a large number of slaves, and nearly all the confiscated cotton.

After these two attempts to reduce Port Hudson by a land assault, on the 27th of May and 14th of June, the purpose to make another was given up by Gen. Banks, until he had fully invested the place by a series of irresistible approaches. He was thus engaged in pushing forward his works when Vicksburg was surrendered. Information of this surrender was sent to Gen. Banks, and it was made the occasion for firing salutes and a general excitement in his camp, which attracted the attention of the enemy, to whom the surrender was communicated. Gen. Gardner, upon receiving the information, sent by flag of truce, about midnight of the 7th, the following note to Gen. Banks:

HEADQUARTERS, PORT HUDSON, LA., *July 7th*, 1863.

To Maj.-Gen. Banks, commanding United States Forces near Port Hudson:

GENERAL: Having received information from your troops that Vicksburg has been surrendered, I make this communication to request you to give me the official assurance whether this is true or not, and if true, I ask for a cessation of hostilities, with a view to the consideration of terms for surrendering this position.

I am, General, very respectfully,
Your obedient servant,
FRANK GARDNER, Major-General.

To which Gen. Banks thus replied:

HEADQUARTERS DEPARTMENT OF THE GULF, BEFORE PORT HUDSON, *July 8th*, 1863.

To Maj.-Gen. Frank Gardner, commanding C. S. Forces, Port Hudson:

GENERAL: In reply to your communication, dated the 7th instant, by flag of truce, received a few moments since, I have the honor to inform you that I received, yesterday morning, July 7th, at 10.45, by the gunboat General Price, an official despatch from Major-Gen. Ulysses S. Grant, United States Army, whereof the following is a true extract:

"HEADQUARTERS DEPARTMENT OF THE TENNESSEE, NEAR VICKSBURG, *July 4th*, 1863.

"*Maj.-Gen. N. P. Banks, commanding Department of the Gulf:*

"GENERAL: The garrison of Vicksburg surrendered this morning. The number of prisoners, as given by the officer, is 27,000, field artillery 128 pieces, and a large number of siege guns, probably not less than eighty. Your obedient servant,
"U. S. GRANT, Major-General."

I regret to say, that under present circumstances, I cannot, consistently with my duty, consent to a cessation of hostilities for the purpose you indicate.

Very respectfully, your obedient servant,
N. P. BANKS.

The following further correspondence then took place:

PORT HUDSON, *July 8th*, 1863.

GENERAL: I have the honor to acknowledge the receipt of your communication of this date, giving a copy of an official communication from Major-Gen. U. S. Grant, United States Army, announcing the surrender of Vicksburg.

Having defended this position as long as I deem my duty requires, I am willing to surrender to you, and will appoint a commission of three officers to meet a similar commission appointed by yourself, at nine o'clock this morning, for the purpose of agreeing upon and drawing up the terms of the surrender, and for that purpose I ask for a cessation of hostilities.

Will you please designate a point outside of my breastworks, where the meeting shall be held for this purpose?

I am, very respectfully, your obedient servant,
FRANK GARDNER, Commanding C. S. Forces.

HEADQUARTERS U. S. FORCES, BEFORE PORT HUDSON, *July 8th*, 1863.

To Maj.-Gen. Frank Gardner, commanding Confederate States Forces, Port Hudson:

GENERAL: I have the honor to acknowledge the receipt of your communication of this date, stating that you are willing to surrender the garrison under your command to the forces under my command, and that you will appoint a commission of three officers to meet a similar commission appointed by me, at nine o'clock this morning, for the purpose of agreeing upon and drawing up the terms of the surrender.

In reply, I have the honor to state that I have designated Brig.-Gen. Charles P. Stone, Col. Henry W. Birge, and Lieut.-Col. Richard B. Irwin, as the officers to meet the commission appointed by you.

They will meet your officers at the hour designated, at a point where the flag of truce was received this morning. I will direct that active hostilities shall entirely cease on my part until forther notice, for the purpose stated. Very respectfully yours, etc.,

N. P. BANKS, Maj.-Gen. Commanding.

The following are the articles of capitulation mutually agreed upon and adopted:

ART. 1. Maj.-Gen. Frank Gardner surrenders to the United States forces under Maj.-Gen. Banks, the place of Port Hudson and its dependencies, with its garrison, armaments, munitions, public funds, and materials of war, in the condition, as nearly as may be, in which they were at the hour of cessation of hostilities, namely, 6 o'clock A. M., July 8th, 1863.

ART. 2. The surrender stipulated in article one is qualified by no condition, save that the officers and enlisted men comprising the garrison shall receive the treatment due to prisoners of war, according to the usages of civilized warfare.

ART. 3. All private property of officers and enlisted men shall be respected, and left to their respective owners.

ART. 4. The position of Port Hudson shall be occupied to-morrow, at 7 o'clock A. M., by the forces of the United States, and its garrison received as prisoners of war by such general officers of the United States service as may be designated by Maj.-Gen. Banks, with the ordinary formalities of rendition. The Confederate troops will be drawn up in line, officers in their positions, the right of the line resting on the edge of the prairie south of the railroad depot; the left extending in the direction of the village of Port Hudson. The arms and colors will be piled conveniently, and will be received by the officers of the United States.

ART. 5. The sick and wounded of the garrison will be cared for by the authorities of the United States, assisted, if desired by either party, by the medical officers of the garrison.

The formal surrender was made on the 9th of July. Gen. Andrews, Chief of Staff of Gen. Banks, with Col. Birge leading his column, followed by two picked regiments from each division, with Holcombe's and Rowle's batteries of light artillery, and the gunners of the naval battery, entered the fortifications. The enemy were drawn up in line, with their officers in front of them, on one side of the road, with their backs to the river. The Federal troops were drawn up in two lines on the opposite side of the road, with their officers in front. Gen. Gardner then advanced, and offered to surrender his sword with Port Hudson. In appreciation of his bravery, he was desired to retain it. He then said: "General, I will now formally surrender my command to you, and for that purpose will give the order to ground arms." The order was given, and the arms grounded. The surrender comprised, besides the position, 6,233 prisoners, 51 pieces of artillery, two steamers, 4,400 lbs. of cannon powder, 5,000 small arms, and 150,000 rounds of ammunition. The loss of Gen. Banks from the 23d to the 30th of May was about one thousand. The village of Port Hudson consisted of a few houses and a small church, which had been nearly destroyed by the cannonade. The wounded and sick of the garrison suffered the most from want of medical stores. The provisions of the garrison were nearly exhausted.

The surrender of Port Hudson enabled Gen. Banks to turn his attention to other points which had been temporarily and necessarily neglected. His further movements are stated in subsequent pages.

CHAPTER XXX.

Movement of Gen. Burnside to cross the Rappahannock—Storm—The Army returns to Camp—Gen. Hooker takes command—Movement of Gen. Hooker across the Rappahannock—The Battle of Chancellorsville—Losses—The death of Gen. "Stonewall" Jackson.

AFTER the battle of Fredericksburg on the 13th of December, 1862, the army, under Maj.-Gen. Burnside, remained inactive for some weeks. Its position was opposite Fredericksburg. Indications of some movement, however, were manifest about the 16th of January. The roads were dry, and, on the night of the 16th, the pontoons were brought up from Belle Plain, and with the utmost secrecy taken near the river some distance above. An order to march had been twice issued and countermanded. On the 17th it was issued again, requiring each soldier to have three days' rations and sixty rounds of cartridges. The army at this time was as strong in numbers and material as it had ever been. It was supposed that the forces of Gen. Lee had been somewhat reduced by the withdrawal of small bodies to reënforce other points. His army was composed of eight divisions, commanded by Gens. A. P. and D. H. Hill, Early, Hood, Walker, Ransom, McLaws, and Anderson. Each division consisted of four to five brigades, and each brigade had from five to seven regiments. It was the intention of Gen. Burnside to move his army a few miles further up the Rappahannock, and cross at the fords and make an attack upon the flank of Gen. Lee. On the next day the order was postponed. The enemy in the mean time were on the alert, and expecting an attack at any time. On Tuesday, the 20th, Gens. Hooker and Franklin moved in heavy order, with tents, &c., toward Hartwood Church, which is directly north of the United States ford of the Rappahannock, which is twelve miles above Fredericksburg. Gen. Sigel moved in the afternoon in the same direction. The movement of Gen. Hooker was made by a road three miles north of the river, and concealed from the view of the enemy's pickets on the south bank. That night, at ten o'clock, a storm from the northeast commenced with high wind and torrents of rain. The march began the next morning at daylight, but the roads had become almost impassable. In every gully, batteries, caissons, supply wagons, ambulances, and pontoons were mired. All day there was a constant and exhausting struggle of men, horses, and mules with the mud. On Wednesday night the wearied troops lay down in their blankets. The storm still continued. During the next day an effort was made to concentrate on the high table land near Banks's Ford. It now became too manifest that it would be impossible to get the army through the freshly cut roads to the river, so that the fords could be reached. On Friday the storm abated, but further progress was necessarily suspended, and on the next day the movement was abandoned, and the army returned to its former quarters.

On Monday, the 26th, Gen. Burnside issued the following address, surrendering the command of the army to Gen. Hooker:

HEADQUARTERS ARMY OF THE POTOMAC,
CAMP NEAR FALMOUTH, *January 26th*, 1863.

By direction of the President of the United States, the Commanding General this day transfers the command of this army to Major-Gen. Joseph Hooker.

The short time that he has directed your movements has not been fruitful of victory or any considerable advancement of our lines, but it has again demonstrated an amount of courage, patience, and endurance that under more favorable circumstances would have accomplished great results.

Continue to exercise these virtues. Be true in your devotion to your country and the principles you have sworn to maintain. Give to the brave and skilful general who has long been identified with your organization, and who is now to command you, your full and cordial support and coöperation, and you will deserve success.

In taking an affectionate leave of the entire army, from which he separates with so much regret, he may be pardoned if he bids an especial farewell to his long-tried associates of the ninth corps. His prayers are that God may be with you, and grant you continued success until the rebellion is crushed.

By command of Major-Gen. BURNSIDE.
LEWIS RICHMOND, A. A. G.

At his own request, Gen. Burnside was relieved of his command, and the President immediately conferred it upon Gen. Hooker. The views under which this command had been accepted by Gen. Burnside were thus stated by him in his testimony before a committee appointed by Congress to investigate the conduct of the war:

On the 7th or 8th of November, I received an order from the President of the United States, directing me to take command of the Army of the Potomac, and also a copy of an order relieving Gen. McClellan from that command. This order was conveyed to me by Gen. Buckingham, who was attached to the War Department. After getting over my surprise, the shock, &c., I told Gen. Buckingham that it was a matter that required very serious thought; that I did not want the command; that it had been offered to me twice before, and I did not feel that I could take it; I counselled with two of my staff officers in regard to it, for, I should think, an hour and a half. They urged upon me that I had no right, as a soldier, to disobey the order, and that I had already expressed to the Government my unwillingness to take the command; I told them what my views were with reference to my ability to exercise such a command, which views were those I had unreservedly expressed, that I was not competent to command such a large army as this; I had said the same over and over again to the President and Secretary of War; and also that if matters could be satisfactorily arranged with Gen. McClellan, I thought he could command the Army of the Potomac better than any other general in it.

On the same day when Gen. Burnside retired, Gen. Hooker, on assuming the command, issued the following address to the army:

HEADQUARTERS, CAMP NEAR FALMOUTH,
January 26th, 1863.

By direction of the President of the United States the undersigned assumes command of the Army of the Potomac.

He enters upon the discharge of the duties imposed by the trust with a just appreciation of their responsibility. Since the formation of this army he has been identified with its history; he has shared with you its glories and reverses, with no other desire than that these relations might remain unchanged until its destiny should be accomplished.

In the record of your achievements there is much to be proud of, and, with the blessing of God, we will contribute something to the renown of our arms and the success of our cause. To secure these ends your commander will require the cheerful and zealous coöperation of every officer and soldier in the army. In equipment, intelligence, and valor the enemy is our inferior. Let us never hesitate to give him battle whenever we can find him.

The undersigned only gives expression to the feelings of this army when he conveys to our late commander, Maj.-Gen. Burnside, the most cordial good wishes for his future.

My staff will be announced as soon as organized.

JOSEPH HOOKER,
Maj.-Gen. Commanding Army of the Potomac.

Gens. Sumner and Franklin were at the same time relieved of the command of the right and left divisions of the army. The following is the official order of the President under which these changes were made:

HEADQUARTERS OF THE ARMY,
WAR DEPARTMENT, ADJUTANT-GENERAL'S OFFICE,
WASHINGTON, *January 28th*, 1863.

I. The President of the United States has directed:

First. That Maj.-Gen. A. E. Burnside, at his own request, be relieved from the command of the Army of the Potomac.

Second. That Maj.-Gen. E. V. Sumner, at his own request, be relieved from duty in the Army of the Potomac.

Third. That Maj.-Gen. W. B. Franklin be relieved from duty in the Army of the Potomac.

Fourth. That Maj.-Gen. J. Hooker be assigned to the command of the Army of the Potomac.

The officers relieved as above will report in person to the Adjutant-General of the Army.

By order of the Secretary of War,

E. D. TOWNSEND,
Assistant Adjutant-General.

On the 26th of January, the Senate of the U. S. Congress adopted the following resolution:

Resolved, That the Committee on the Conduct of the War be instructed to inquire whether Maj.-Gen. A. E. Burnside has, since the battle of Fredericksburg, formed any plans for the movement of the Army of the

Potomac, or any portion of the same; and if so, whether any subordinate generals of said army have written to or visited Washington to oppose or interfere with the execution of such movements, and whether such proposed movements have been arrested or interfered with, and, if so, by what authority.

The report of the committee, which was published in April, 1863, thus states the proceedings under the resolution:

Under that resolution, your committee proceeded to take the testimony of Maj.-Gens. A. E. Burnside and John G. Parke, and Brig.-Gens. John Newton, John Cochrane, and Wm. W. Averill. That testimony brings to light the following facts:

Shortly after the battle of Fredericksburg, Gen. Burnside devised a plan for attacking the enemy in his front. The main army was to cross at a place some six or seven miles below Fredericksburg. The positions for the artillery to protect the crossings were all selected; the roads were all surveyed, and the corduroy was cut for preparing the roads. At the same time a feint of crossing was to be made some distance above Falmouth, which feint could be turned into a positive attack should the enemy discover the movement below; otherwise the main attack was to be made below.

In connection with this movement of the main army, a cavalry expedition was organized, consisting of twenty-five hundred of the best cavalry in the Army of the Potomac, one thousand of whom were picked men. The plan of that expedition was as follows: Accompanied by a brigade of infantry detailed to protect the crossing of the Rappahannock, it was to proceed to Kelly's Ford; there the thousand picked men were to cross, and to proceed to the Rapidan, and cross that river at Racoon Ford; then to go onward and cross the Virginia Central railroad at Louisa Court House; the James river at Goochland or Carter's, blowing up the locks of the James River canal at the place of crossing; cross the Richmond and Lynchburg railroad at a point south of there, blowing up the iron bridge at the place of crossing; cross the Richmond, Petersburg, and Weldon railroad where it crosses the Nottoway river, destroying the railroad bridge there; and then proceed on by Gen. Pryor's command, and effect a junction with Gen. Peck at Suffolk, where steamers were to be in waiting to take them to Aquia creek. To distract the attention of the enemy, and to deceive them in regard to which body of cavalry was the attacking column, at the time the thousand picked men crossed the Rappahannock a portion of the remaining fifteen hundred was to proceed toward Warrenton; another portion toward Culpepper Court House; and the remainder were to accompany the thousand picked men as far as Racoon Ford, and then return. While this cavalry expedition was in progress, the general movement was to be made across the river.

On the 26th of December an order was issued for the entire command to prepare three days' cooked rations; to have their wagons filled with ten days' small rations, if possible; to have from ten to twelve days' supply of beef cattle with them; to take forage for their teams and their artillery and cavalry horses, and the requisite amount of ammunition—in fact, to be in a condition to move at twelve hours' notice.

Shortly after that order was issued, Gen. John Newton and Gen. John Cochrane—the one commanding a division and the other a brigade in the left grand division, under Gen. William B. Franklin—came up to Washington on leave of absence. Previous to obtaining leave of absence from Gen. Franklin, they informed him and Gen. William F. Smith that when they came to Washington they should take the opportunity to represent to some one in authority here the dispirited condition of the army, and the danger there was of attempting any movement against the enemy at that time.

When they reached Washington, Gen. Cochrane, as he states, endeavored to find certain members of Congress, to whom to make the desired communication. Failing to find them, he determined to seek an interview with the President for the purpose of making the communication directly to him. On proceeding to the President's House, he there met Secretary Seward, to whom he explained the object of his being there, and the general purport of his proposed communication to the President, and requested him to procure an interview for them, which Mr. Seward promised to do, and which he did do.

That day the interview took place, and Gen. Newton opened the subject to the President. At first the President, as Gen. Newton expresses it, "very naturally conceived that they had come there for the purpose of injuring Gen. Burnside, and suggesting some other person to fill his place." Gen. Newton states that, while he firmly believed that the principal cause of the dispirited condition of the army was the want of confidence in the military capacity of Gen. Burnside, he deemed it improper to say so to the President "right square out," and therefore endeavored to convey the same idea indirectly. When asked if he considered it any less improper to do such a thing indirectly than it was to do it directly, he qualified his previous assertion by saying that his object was to inform the President of what he considered to be the condition of the army, in the hope that the President would make inquiry and learn the true reason for himself. Upon perceiving this impression upon the mind of the President, Gens. Newton and Cochrane state that they hastened to assure the President that he was entirely mistaken, and so far succeeded that at the close of the interview the President said to them he was glad they had called upon him, and that he hoped that good would result from the interview.

To return to General Burnside. The cavalry expedition had started; the brigade of infantry detailed to accompany it had crossed the Rappahannock at Richard's Ford, and returned by way of Ellis's Ford, leaving the way clear for the cavalry to cross at Kelly's Ford. The day they had arranged to make the crossing, General Burnside received from the President the following telegram: "I have good reason for saying that you must not make a general movement without letting me know of it."

Gen. Burnside states that he could not imagine, at the time, what reason the President could have for sending him such a telegram. None of the officers of his command, except one or two of his staff, who had remained in camp, had been told anything of his plan beyond the simple fact that a movement was to be made. He could only suppose that the despatch related in some way to important military movements in other parts of the country, in which it was necessary to have coöperation.

Upon the receipt of that telegram steps were immediately taken to halt the cavalry expedition where it then was (at Kelly's Ford) until further orders. A portion of it was shortly afterward sent off to intercept Stuart, who had just made a raid to Dumfries and the neighborhood of Fairfax Court House, which it failed to do.

Gen. Burnside came to Washington to ascertain from the President the true state of the case. He was informed by the President that some general officers from the Army of the Potomac, whose names he declined to give, had called upon him and represented that Gen. Burnside contemplated soon making a movement, and that the army was so dispirited and demoralized that any attempt to make a movement at that time must result in disaster; that no prominent officers in the Army of the Potomac were in favor of any movement at that time.

Gen. Burnside informed the President that none of his officers had been informed what his plan was, and then proceeded to explain it in detail to the President. He urged upon the President to grant him permission to carry it out, but the President declined to do so at that time. Gen. Halleck and Secretary Stanton were sent for, and then learned, for the first time, of the President's action in stopping the movement, although

Gen. Halleck was previously aware that a movement was contemplated by Gen. Burnside. Gen. Halleck, with Gen. Burnside, held that the officers who had made those representations to the President should be at once dismissed the service.

Gen. Burnside remained here at that time for two days, but no conclusion was reached upon the subject. When he returned to his camp he learned that many of the details of the general movement, and the details of the cavalry expedition, had become known to the rebel sympathizers in Washington, thereby rendering that plan impracticable. When asked to whom he had communicated his plans, he stated that he had told no one in Washington except the President, Secretary Stanton, and Gen. Halleck; and in his camp none knew of it except one or two of his staff officers, who had remained in camp all the time. He professed himself unable to tell how his plans had become known to the enemy.

A correspondence then took place between the President, Gen. Halleck, and Gen. Burnside. Gen. Burnside desired distinct authority from Gen. Halleck, or some one authorized to give it, to make a movement across the river. While urging the importance and necessity of such a movement, he candidly admitted that there was hardly a general officer in his command who approved of it. While willing to take upon himself all the responsibility of the movement, and promising to keep in view the President's caution concerning running any risk of destroying the Army of the Potomac, he desired to have at least Gen. Halleck's sanction or permission to make the movement. Gen. Halleck replied that while he had always favored a forward movement, he could not take the responsibility of giving any directions as to how and when it should be made.

Gen. Burnside then determined to make a movement without any further correspondence on the subject. He was unable to devise any as promising as the one just thwarted by this interference of his subordinate officers, which interference gave the enemy the time, if not the means, to ascertain what he had proposed to do. He, however, devised a plan of movement, and proceeded to put it in execution. As is well known, it was rendered abortive in consequence of the severe storm which took place shortly after the movement began.

Gen. Burnside states that, besides the inclemency of the weather, there was another powerful reason for abandoning the movement, viz., the almost universal feeling among his general officers against him. Some of those officers freely gave vent to their feelings in the presence of their inferiors. In consequence of this, and also what had taken place during the battle of Fredericksburg, &c., Gen. Burnside directed an order to be issued, which he styled General Order No. 8. That order dismissed some officers from the service, subject to the approval of the President, relieved others from duty with the Army of the Potomac, and also pronounced sentence of death upon some deserters who had been tried and convicted.

Gen. Burnside states that he had become satisfied that it was absolutely necessary that some such examples should be made, in order to enable him to maintain the proper authority over the army under his command. The order was duly signed and issued, and only waited publication. Two or three of his most trusted staff officers represented to Gen. Burnside that should he then publish that order, he would force upon the President the necessity of at once sanctioning it, or, by refusing his approval, assume an attitude of hostility to Gen. Burnside. The publication of the order was accordingly delayed for the time.

Gen. Burnside came to Washington and laid the order before the President, with the distinct assurance that in no other way could he exercise a proper command over the Army of the Potomac; and he asked the President to sanction the order, or accept his resignation as major-general. The President acknowledged that Gen. Burnside was right, but declined to decide without consulting with some of his advisers. To this Gen. Burnside replied, that if the President took time for consultation he would not be allowed to publish that order, and therefore asked to have his resignation accepted at once. This the President declined to do.

Gen. Burnside returned to his camp, and came again to Washington that night at the request of the President, and the next morning called upon the President for his decision. He was informed that the President declined to approve his order No. 8, but had concluded to relieve him from his command of the Army of the Potomac, and to appoint Gen. Hooker in his place. Thereupon Gen. Burnside again insisted that his resignation be accepted. This the President declined to do; and, after some urging, Gen. Burnside consented to take a leave of absence for thirty days, with the understanding that, at the end of that time, he should be assigned to duty, as he deemed it improper to hold a commission as major-general and receive his pay without rendering service therefor. Gen. Burnside objected to the wording of the order which relieved him from his command, and which stated that it was at his own request, as being unjust to him and unfounded in fact; but upon the representation that any other order would do injury to the cause, he consented to let it remain as it then read.

The foregoing statements of the facts proved, together with the testimony herewith submitted, so fully and directly meet the requirements of the resolution, referred to them, that your committee deem any comment by them to be entirely unnecessary.

Subsequently a letter appeared from Gen. Cochrane, of which the following is an extract:

I have no copy of my evidence, nor have I seen Gen. Newton's. But I remember to have stated explicitly that I knew nothing of Gen. Burnside's plan; that I knew only of the dispirited condition of the troops, and the sense of apprehension which depressed them, and that I recognized it as a duty to communicate this knowledge to those whose duty it was to apply it. This much I testified that I had said to the President; and I then further said to the committee that had I been the depository of the commanding general's plans, and the possessor of facts which would necessarily have baffled those plans, and have involved the army in irretrievable ruin, I would have considered it no less than treason not to have disclosed the facts—that I was impressed that another defeat, then and there, would have been fatal to our cause; and that it was upon my deepest loyalty that I had spoken—that the geese had doubtless disturbed the sleeping Roman sentinel, when their alarm saved the capital from the Gauls; but that I had never heard that the geese had been punished for disturbing the sentinel, though I had heard that they had been honored for saving the state.

The following has appeared as so much of the order No. 8 as relates to the dismissal and relief of certain officers:

General Order No. 8.

HEADQUARTERS ARMY OF THE POTOMAC, *Jan. 23d*, 1863.

* * * * *

First. Gen. Joseph E. Hooker, Major-General of Volunteers and Brigadier-General of the United States Army, having been guilty of unjust and unnecessary criticisms of the actions of his superior officers, and of the authorities, and having, by the general tone of his conversation, endeavored to create distrust in the minds of officers who have associated with him, and having, by omissions and otherwise, made reports and statements which were calculated to create incorrect impressions, and of habitually speaking in disparaging terms of other officers, is hereby dismissed the service of the United States, as a man unfit to hold an important commission during a crisis like the present, when so much patience, charity, confidence, consideration, and patriotism are due from every soldier in the field. The order is issued subject to the approval of the President of the United States.

Second. Brig.-Gen. W. T. H. Brooks, commanding First Division, Sixth Army Corps, for complaining of the policy of the Government, and for using language tending to demoralize his command, is, subject to the approval of the President of the United States, dismissed from the military service of the United States.

Third. Brig.-Gen. John Newton, commanding Third Division, Sixth Army Corps, and Brig.-Gen. John Cochrane, commanding First Brigade, Third Division, Sixth Army Corps, for going to the President of the United States with criticisms upon the plans of their commanding officer, are, subject to the approval of the President, dismissed from the military service of the United States.

Fourth. It being evident that the following named officers can be of no further service to this army, they are hereby relieved from duty, and will report in person without delay to the Adjutant-General of the United States Army:

Maj.-Gen. W. B. Franklin, commanding Left Grand Division.

Maj.-Gen. W. F. Smith, commanding Sixth Army Corps.

Brig.-Gen. Sam. D. Sturgis, commanding Second Division, Ninth Army Corps.

Brig.-Gen. Edward Ferrero, commanding Second Brigade, Second Division, Ninth Army Corps.

Brig.-Gen. John Cochrane, commanding First Brigade, Third Division, Sixth Army Corps.

Lieut.-Col. J. H. Taylor, Acting Adjutant-General Right Grand Division.

By command of Maj.-Gen. A. E. BURNSIDE.

LEWIS RICHMOND, Assistant Adjutant-General.

The testimony of Gen. Burnside, in relation to this order, from which the committee condensed their abstract, was as follows:

I went to my adjutant-general's office, and issued an order, which I termed General Order No. 8. That order dismissed some officers from service, subject to the approval of the President, and relieved others from duty with the Army of the Potomac. I also had three sentences of death upon privates for desertion, which I had reviewed and approved, subject, of course, to the approval of the President, as I had no right to do any of these things without that approval. I had sent my own body guard over into Maryland, and had succeeded in capturing a large number of deserters. I had organized a court-martial, the one which is now in session down there trying some two hundred and fifty deserters.

I told my adjutant-general to issue that order (No. 8) at once. One of my advisers—only two persons knew of this—one of them, who is a very cool, sensible man, and a firm friend, told me that, in his opinion, the order was a just one, and ought to be issued; but he said that he knew my views with reference to endeavoring to make myself useful to the Government of the United States instead of placing myself in opposition to it; that all of these things had to be approved by the President of the United States, at any rate, before they could be put in force; that he did not think I intended to place the President in a position where he either had to assume the responsibility of becoming my enemy before the public, at any rate, thereby enabling a certain portion of my friends to make a martyr of me to some extent, or he had to take the responsibility of carrying out the order, which would be against the views of a great many of the most influential men in the country, particularly that portion of the order in reference to the officers I proposed to have dismissed the service. I told the staff officer that I had no desire to place myself in opposition to the President of the United States in any way; that I thought his (my staff officer's) view of the matter was the correct one; but that I had indicated in that order the only way in which I could command the Army of the Potomac. I accordingly took this order, already signed and issued in due form, with the exception of being made public, to the President of the United States, and handed him the order, together with my resignation of my commission as a major-general. I told him that he knew my views upon the subject; that I had never sought any command, more particularly that of the Army of the Potomac; that my wish was to go into civil life, after it was determined that I could no longer be of any use in the army; that I desired no public position of any kind whatever. At the same time I said that I desired not to place myself in opposition to him in any way, or to do anything to weaken the Government. I said he could now say to me, "You may take the responsibility of issuing this order, and I will approve it;" and I would take that responsibility, if he would say that it would be sustained after it was issued, because he would have to approve of it, for I had no right to dismiss a man or condemn a man to death without his approval. In case that order (No. 8) could not be approved by him, there was my resignation, which he could accept, and that would end the matter forever, so far as I was concerned; that nothing more would be said in reference to it. I told him he could be sure that my wish was to have that done which was best for the public service, and that was the only way in which I could command the Army of the Potomac. The President replied to me, "I think you are right. * * * [The suppressions here, in the body of Gen. Burnside's report of the President's answer, are made by the committee.] But I must consult with some of my advisers about this." I said to him, "If you consult with anybody you will not do it, in my opinion." He said, "I cannot help that; I must consult with them." I replied that he was the judge, and I would not question his right to do what he pleased.

The President asked me to remain all that day. I replied that I could not remain away from my command; that he knew my views, and I was fixed and determined in them. He then asked me to come up that night again. I returned to my command, and came up again that night, and got here at six o'clock in the morning. I went to the President's, but did not see him. I went again after breakfast, and the President told me that he had concluded to relieve me from the command of the Army of the Potomac, and place Gen. Hooker in command. I told him that I was willing to accept that, as the best solution of the problem; and that neither he nor Gen. Hooker would be a happier man than I would be if Gen. Hooker gained a victory there. The President also said that he intended to relieve Gen. Sumner and Gen. Franklin. I said that I thought it would be wise to do so, if he made the change he proposed to make. Gen. Sumner was a much older officer than Gen. Hooker, and ought not to be asked to serve under him.

On the 26th of April Gen. Burnside assumed the command of the Department of the Ohio. An invasion of Kentucky was at that time threatened by the Confederate forces.

The inclemency of the season was such that no movements could now be attempted by the Army of the Potomac or its adversary on the opposite side of the Rappahannock at Fredericksburg. Some raids by the enemy and some movements of cavalry were the only operations.

On the 12th of March a bold and successful raid was made by the enemy as far within the Federal lines as Fairfax Court House in Virginia. Brig.-Gen. Stoughton was taken from his bed and carried off, and a detachment from his brigade, with guards, horses, &c., captured.

On the 17th of March a sharp conflict took place between a body of cavalry, under Gen. Averill, and a similar force of the enemy near

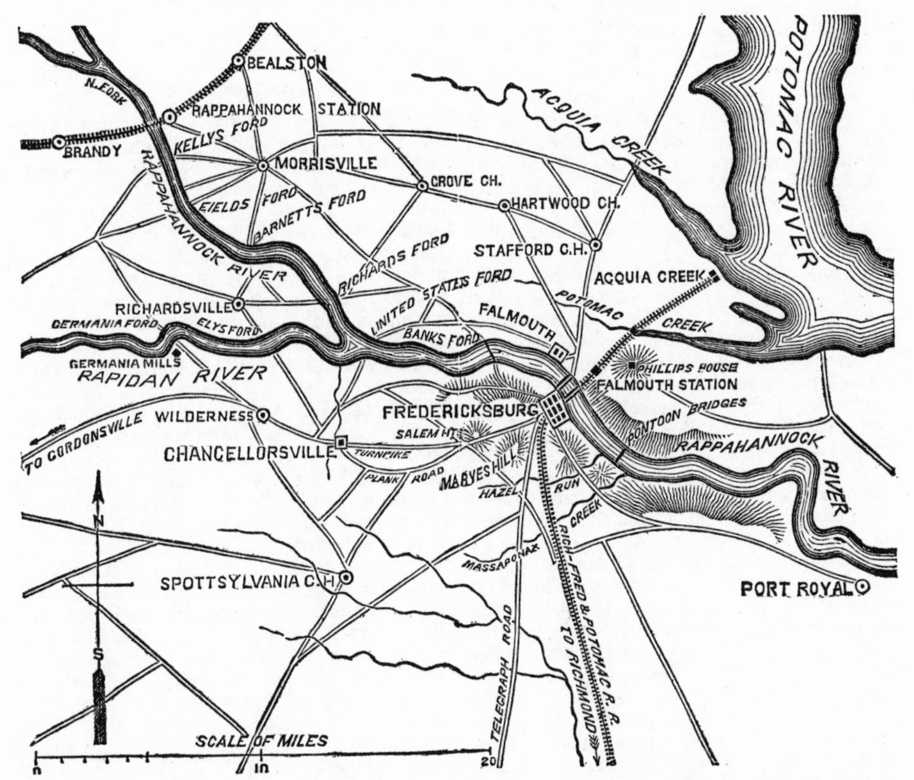

Kelly's Ford. About forty of Gen. Averill's force were disabled, and about eighty of the enemy made prisoners.

On the 13th of April, an expedition of cavalry, infantry, and artillery, under Major-Gen. Stoneman, proceeded in detachments to Warrenton, Bealton, Rappahannock bridge, and Liberty. Small bodies of Partisan Rangers were met with, but no opposition was encountered. Thence he moved to the fords of the Rapidan and took possession of them. These operations were made in advance of a general movement of the army across the Rappahannock to attack Gen. Lee. The stormy weather which ensued delayed this movement until the 27th of April.

The army of Gen. Lee, in its encampments near Fredericksburg, held a line running from northwest to southeast; its right wing was extended as far down as Port Royal on the Rappahannock, and its left wing rested above Fredericksburg on the same river. In this position it had only two main lines of retreat, one toward Richmond by railroad, and the other toward Gordonsville. The strength of this army was about seventy thousand men.

The army of Gen. Hooker consisted of seven corps, and numbered about one hundred and twenty thousand men. Under his plan of attack three corps were massed below Fredericksburg, to cross there and make a feint attack on the enemy, when two of the corps were to return immediately after crossing and join the other four corps, meanwhile crossing at several fords ten and twenty miles above Fredericksburg. The object of Gen. Hooker by moving down on the left of the enemy, was to force him to fight outside of his intrenchments, or to fall back on Richmond.

Falmouth, the position occupied by Gen. Hooker's army, is nearly opposite Fredericksburg, on the north bank of the Rappahannock. About twelve miles above, the Rapidan, a small river, unites with a stream heretofore called the North Fork, to form the Rappahannock. Lately, however, the North Fork has been called Rappahannock, and the Rapidan has been spoken of as a tributary. The United States Ford is abont one mile below the mouth of the Rapidan. Banks's Ford is about midway between the United States Ford and Falmouth. Kelly's Ford, where the four corps crossed the North Fork, or the Rappahannock as it is now called, is about twenty miles above Falmouth. Germania Ford, where the same force crossed the Rapidan, is about twelve miles south of Kelly's Ford, at a place called Germania Mills. The troops crossed here by wading. The water was up to the armpits, and with a rapid current. The bottom of the river was rocky.

On Monday morning, April 27th, the eleventh corps, under Maj.-Gen. Howard, the twelfth, under Maj.-Gen. Slocum, and the fifth, under Maj.-Gen. Meade, marched westward on the several roads leading to Kelly's Ford, which the advance under Gen. Howard reached on Tuesday forenoon. A brigade of this corps had been guarding the ford since the movement of cavalry under Gen. Stoneman. The pontoon boats had been moved into a creek behind the bluff at the Ford. About two hundred and fifty men of the 73d Pennsylvania and 154th New York immediately crossed in boats and occupied the bank of the river. Skirmishers were deployed to the right and left, but no enemy, excepting a few pickets who retired, was to be found. The remainder of the two regiments crossed in boats whilst the bridge was building. That evening the eleventh corps crossed, and the twelfth bivouacked on the shore.

Early on Wednesday morning, the twelfth corps crossed over, followed by Gen. Stoneman's cavalry force and the fifth corps. The wagon trains were sent back from Kelly's Ford and parked near Banks's Ford. The advance moved directly to Germania Ford on the Rapidan. The fifth corps, under Gen. Meade, crossed the Rapidan in the afternoon, a little lower down. On the next morning, Thursday, an advance was made to Chancellorsville, at the junction of the Orange Court House road with a road to Culpepper, between five and ten miles distant from the ford. The three corps were massed at this place at night, and Gen. Hooker arrived and made it his headquarters. On Wednesday, the second corps, under Gen. Couch, took a position at Banks's Ford, five miles above Fredericksburg. Some skirmishing had occurred with small bodies of the enemy, which retired. The cavalry force of Gen. Stoneman was sent to cut the communication of Gen. Lee's army by railroad with Richmond.

Meanwhile the remaining three corps of the army had been put in motion. The first corps, under Maj.-Gen. Reynolds, the third, under Maj.-Gen. Sickles, and the sixth, under Maj.-Gen. Sedgwick, moved from their camps on Monday night and took a position two miles below Fredericksburg. Early on the next morning, one division of the sixth corps crossed two miles below Fredericksburg, and one division of the first corps about one mile farther down. Some skirmishing took place, and the enemy held their position; at the same time bridges were thrown over and demonstrations made as if the intention was to cross a large force over. On the next day, Wednesday, the third corps, under Gen. Sickles, was detached and ordered to cross at United States Ford and join Gen. Hooker at Chancellorsville. On the next day Gen. Hooker issued the following order:

General Order No. 47.

HEADQUARTERS ARMY OF THE POTOMAC,
CAMP NEAR FALMOUTH, VA., *April 30th*, 1863.

It is with heartfelt satisfaction that the Commanding General announces to the army that the operations of the last three days have determined that our enemy must either ingloriously fly or come out from behind his defences and give us battle on our own ground, where certain destruction awaits him. The operations of the fifth, eleventh, and twelfth corps have been a succession of splendid achievements.

By command of Major-Gen. HOOKER.
S. WILLIAMS, Ass't Adj't-Gen.

Such was the position of Gen. Hooker's forces on Friday morning. About noon, the fifth and twelfth corps, under Gens. Meade and Slocum, were advanced by separate roads toward Fredericksburg. The former moved to the left and the latter to the right. The advance of Gen. Meade's corps was led by the second division under Gen. Sykes. In about an hour it encountered the enemy, and heavy firing ensued, which continued for three fourths of an hour, gradually extending toward the right wing. Orders were then sent by Gen. Hooker, whose headquarters were in the large house known as Chancellorsville, for the two columns to fall slowly back. This order was systematically obeyed, and everything became quiet until about four o'clock, when the enemy appeared in line of battle, in an open field fronting a dense wood, on the right of Gen. Hooker, and about a mile from Chancellorsville. A vigorous fire of artillery was opened on both sides, which continued until night, when the enemy retired. This movement was regarded as indicating a disposition on the part of Gen. Lee to feel the Federal lines and ascertain the strength of their position and force. Meanwhile Gen. Hooker had caused intrenchments to be thrown up by his army. On the next day, Saturday, the first corps, under Gen. Reynolds, was ordered to join Gen. Hooker at Chancellorsville. It arrived in the afternoon at United States Ford, and was ordered into position on the right.

During Friday night the enemy were observed cutting a road past the Federal picket line on the right, and wagons were seen passing up the road on Saturday. As no attack was made during the forenoon, it was determined to ascertain the nature of the movement on the right, by a reconnoissance in force under Gen. Sickles. The divisions of Gens. Birney and Whipple, with Gen. Barlow's brigade from Gen. Howard's corps, were pushed to the front. This force soon became more or less engaged, especially with the artillery and the sharpshooters as skirmishers. Prisoners who were taken reported that the wagon train which had been seen was composed mainly of ordnance wagons and ambulances, following a column of troops under the command of Gen. Jackson. It was perceived at once that the object of Gen. Jackson was to make a sudden and fierce attack upon the extreme right. To defeat this object Gen. Sickles was ordered to push forward, and Gen. Birney advanced with great vigor, cutting in twain a column of the enemy still moving up the road. Gen. Williams's division of Gen. Slocum's corps, which had been ordered to coöperate, then commenced a flank movement on the enemy's right, which promised great success. It was supposed that in consequence of this movement, Gen. Jackson would endeavor to retreat to escape a capture, or, if he made an attack on the right, that the eleventh corps would be sufficient to resist him. On the contrary, about five o'clock, a terrific volley of musketry on the extreme right announced that he had commenced his operations. The division of Gen. Schurz, which he first assailed, almost instantly gave way. Thousands threw down their arms and streamed down the road toward headquarters. The enemy pressed his advantage. The division of Gen. Devens, infected by the demoralization in front, soon followed the fugitives. Gen. Howard, the commander of the corps, with all his vigor and resolution could not stem the retreating torrent. The brigades of Cols. Bush, Beck, and McLean maintained themselves as long as possible, but finally gave way in good order before superior numbers.

Gen. Hooker now sent to the aid of Gen. Howard the second division of the third corps, under Maj.-Gen. Berry. Their batteries, under Capt. Best, were moved on a ridge running across the road, and after a short but sanguinary contest, the advance of the enemy was checked. This disaster compelled the recall of Gens. Sickles and Slocum. Gen. Williams's division found a portion of their works filled with the enemy, and Gen. Sickles could not communicate with the rest of the army by the way he had advanced, and only at great risk by any other route. This was the state of affairs at dark. A bright moon soon appeared, and a night attack was ordered to restore the communications. Gen. Wood's brigade of Gen. Birney's division made the attack at eleven o'clock, aided by the guns massed on the ridge in front of the enemy. This attack was successful and restored the communications. The enemy fell back nearly half a mile. The effect of the enemy's movement was to compel Gen. Hooker to contract his lines and assume the defensive, protected by breastworks and intrenchments.

During the night, the first corps, under Maj.-Gen. Reynolds, and the fifth corps, under Maj.-Gen. Meade, were transferred to Gen. Hooker's right, and set to work vigorously to intrench themselves. The position of the latter corps on the left was taken by the eleventh corps, which was reorganized during the night, and then assigned to a point where but little fighting was anticipated, and where they were protected by the work made on the previous day by the fifth corps. At the same time the force of Gen. Lee opposite the Federal right was strongly reënforced.

At 5 o'clock on Sunday morning, the enemy could be seen up the plank road about a mile and a half from the Chancellor House, which was still retained as the headquarters of Gen. Hooker. The Federal line was formed with the division of Gen. Berry on the right, that of Gen. Birney next on the left, and Gens. Whipple and Williams supporting. By half past five, Gen. Berry became engaged, and a terrible conflict ensued. The infantry of the enemy were advanced in overwhelming numbers for the purpose of crushing the Federal line, but the forces of Gens. Sickles and Slocum held them in check. The struggle became desperate, hand to hand, and the carnage great. It continued until 8.45 A. M., without the slightest intermission, when there was a temporary suspension on the Federal side, occasioned by getting out of ammunition. The position was, however, held by the bayonet for nearly an hour, until a supply was received, and an order was given to fall back to the vicinity of the Chancellor House. The contest now raged in this vicinity. Gen. Hooker's headquarters were withdrawn at ten o'clock. The house was burned by a shell of the enemy. The engagement continued until 11.30 A. M., when the musketry fire ceased. Gen. Hooker, acting on the defensive, had been compelled to contract his lines still further, and would perhaps have recrossed the Rappahannock that day except for the advantages expected to be gained by the movement of Gen. Sedgwick below Fredericksburg, and that of the cavalry force under Gen. Stoneman.

Several attempts were made by the enemy during the afternoon to force the lines of Gen. Hooker, but without success.

The following despatch, relative to the operations of Saturday and Sunday, was sent to Richmond by Gen. Lee:

MILFORD, *May 3d*, 1863.

To President Davis :

Yesterday Gen. Jackson penetrated to the rear of the enemy. We drove him from all his positions from the Wilderness to within one mile of Chancellorsville. He was engaged at the same time in front by two of Longstreet's divisions. Many prisoners were taken, and the enemy's loss in killed and wounded is large. This morning the battle was renewed. He was dislodged from all his positions around Chancellorsville, and driven back toward the Rappahannock, over which he is now retreating. We have again to thank Almighty God for a great victory. I regret to state that Gen. Paxton was killed, Gen. Jackson severely and Gens. Heth and A. P. Hill slightly wounded.

R. E. LEE, General Commanding.

On Saturday, May 2d, Gen. Sedgwick was ordered to cross the Rappahannock, move upon Fredericksburg, and march out on the plank road toward Chancellorsville, until he connected with the right under Gen. Hooker, and to destroy any force he might meet on the road. By twelve o'clock that night, the three divisions composing the sixth corps were all across, and waiting orders. The main force of the enemy had been concentrated on their own left to resist Gen. Hooker. The first division, under Gen. Brooks, was left to guard the crossing and occupy the enemy in front. At four o'clock A. M., on Sunday, the head of the corps was in motion toward Fredericksburg. At the edge of the town it was halted, the batteries brought into position, and the first line of the enemy's intrenchments in the rear carried with considerable loss. At noon the division of Gen. Howe was scattered over the heights, looking out for and pursuing the enemy, when orders were received to move on and join the other divisions, which had gone through the city. The height and the city were thus abandoned, to be occupied soon after by the enemy. About five o'clock, the advance was overtaken a few miles out of Fredericksburg, engaged in a brisk fight with the enemy. The division of Gen. Howe was deployed to the left of the road over a broken country, with the left wing to the rear, so as to confront the enemy reoccupying the heights and massing in the rear. In this position Gen. Sedgwick's force remained in line of battle during the night, distant about six or seven miles from Gen. Hooker. By morning of the 4th, the enemy appeared in strong force in front and on the hills to his left. About 4 P. M. they moved up to attack, and Gen. Sedgwick's artillery opened fire on every quarter, but could not check their slow and steady advance, before which he gradually fell back toward Banks's Ford. The engagement was hot, and lasted until 9 P. M., with a loss to Gen. Sedgwick of nearly four thousand. That Monday night he recrossed the Rappahannock. The crossing was effected in good order, with the camp equipage, mule trains, etc., except a few of the latter, which were taken when the enemy first appeared in rear at Fredericksburg. All the work on the left was performed by this corps of Gen. Sedgwick. It built three bridges, constantly skirmished with the enemy, stormed the heights of Fredericksburg, and advanced to support the right, when it was flanked by a heavy force of the enemy and forced to retreat across the river.

The movements of the enemy in this affair were thus reported by Gen. Lee:

To His Excellency President Davis:

At the close of the battle of Chancellorsville on Sunday, the enemy was reported advancing from Fredericksburg on our rear. Gen. McLaws was sent to arrest his progress, and repulsed him handsomely.

That afternoon, learning that his forces consisted of two corps, under Gen. Sedgwick, I determined to attack him, and marched back yesterday with Gen. Anderson, and united with McLaws early in the afternoon, and succeeded, by the blessing of Heaven, in driving Sedgwick over the river.

We have reoccupied Fredericksburg, and no enemy remains south of the Rappahannock or in the vicinity.

R. E. LEE, General Commanding.

While these operations were going on under Gen. Sedgwick, the enemy made no serious attack upon Gen. Hooker. On Monday, at daylight, they placed guns on the heights, which commanded the ground north of United States Ford, and began shelling the trains of Gen. Hooker. These guns were soon silenced by the twelfth corps, which relieved the eleventh, and now occupied the extreme left. During the day, the enemy continued to feel the lines of Gen. Hooker from the extreme left to right, making vigorous feints, driving in pickets, picking off artillery horses and officers on horseback. It was in one of these forays that Gen. Whipple was mortally wounded in the spine, while standing against a tree in his own camp, supposing himself to be in perfect security. Gen. Hooker continued during the day to strengthen his position with a second line of rifle pits. During Monday night slight skirmishing continued along the lines, with frequent volleys of musketry from some portion of the rifle pits. Batteries of flying artillery were used to shell the camps, which changed position as often as guns were brought to bear upon them. Thus the Federal troops were harassed and exhausted during the night.

Early on Tuesday all the pioneers and men, with extra tools, were employed on the roads leading from the army back to United States Ford. Old roads were repaired and new ones cut through the woods. The trains and artillery commenced moving toward the river early in the evening. The rain then was falling rapidly, and the night became quite dark. The crossing commenced at ten o'clock, and at three o'clock on Wednesday morning all the wagons and mule trains and artillery had passed the bridges, and the passage of the infantry commenced. The second corps, under Gen. Couch, led the advance. The fifth corps, under Gen. Meade, formed the rear guard, with Gen. Sykes's division of regulars to cover the retreat. The passage of the river was effected without any disturbance from the enemy. The dead on the battle field of Tuesday were left unburied, and many of the wounded remained behind. The rapid rise of the river prevented the immediate advance of Gen. Lee.

The movements of the cavalry force, under Gen. Stoneman, do not appear to have produced any advantage in favor of Gen. Hooker. As has been stated, the storms which ensued prevented active movements by Gen. Stoneman until the 29th of April. On that day he crossed at Kelly's Ford. The division of Gen. Averill moved to the Orange and Alexandria railroad, and encountered two regiments of the enemy, who retired toward Gordonsville. Thence he proceeded to Culpepper, and dispersed a force of the rebels there, capturing their rear guard, and seizing a large amount of flour, salt, and bacon. The enemy were pursued by way of Cedar mountain toward the Rapidan. Here he received a despatch from Gen. Stoneman, desiring him to push the enemy as vigorously as possible, and keep him occupied. On the 1st, scouting parties were sent up and down on both sides of the Rapidan. On the 2d, orders were received by him to join Gen. Hooker at United States Ford at once.

Gen. Stoneman, after crossing at Kelly's Ford, moved the main body of his command across Fleshman's creek, and encamped for the night in an open field. On the next day, the 3d, Gen. Buford crossed the Rapidan, two miles below Racoon Ford, and drove a body of infantry from the ford, where Gen. Gregg crossed later in the day. A lieutenant and thirteen privates of an artillery company were captured here. At night the whole force bivouacked one mile from the river. On the next day the march was commenced, and at Orange Spring a force of the enemy, approaching by railroad, barely escaped capture. That night the command encamped at Greenwood, one mile from Louisa Court House, through which the Virginia Central railroad passes, connecting Gordonsville with Richmond. On the next day, the 2d of May, a squadron of the 10th New York, under Col. Irwin, was sent five miles above the town, and another of the same regiment, under Major Avery, was sent the same distance below, to destroy the track of the road, while Col. Kilpatrick took possession of the town. The track was torn up for some distance, the telegraph cut, and some commissary stores seized. In the afternoon the command moved to Thompson's Four Corners. From this place, as headquarters, several expeditions were sent out. On the next morning Col. Wyndham proceeded to Columbia, on the James river, where the Lynchburg and Richmond canal crosses the river. An unsuccessful attempt was made to destroy the aqueduct. Five locks were injured, three canal boats, loaded with commissary stores, and five bridges, were burned, and the the canal lock cut in several places. A large quantity of commissary stores and medicines in the town were also destroyed. Another detachment, under Capt. Drummond, of the 5th cavalry, destroyed the bridge over the James river at Centreville. Other small parties were sent out in different directions, and some skirmishing took place with small parties of the enemy. At the same time a force, consisting of the 10th New York and 1st Maine, with two pieces of artillery, was sent out under Gen. Gregg, to destroy the railroad bridge at Ashland, while Col. Kilpatrick, with the Harris Light, and 12th Illinois, Lieut.-Col. Davis, were to go between Ashland and Richmond, destroying the railroad, bridges, &c. Gen. Gregg destroyed the bridge across the South Anna on the road from Columbia to Spottsylvania; thence he moved east, and destroyed the road to Beaver Dam Station. He then turned north to the Richmond and Gordonsville turnpike, sending out a detachment to burn the Ground Squirrel bridge. That night he bivouacked eight miles from Ashland. A detachment sent out to burn the bridge at Ashland found it too strongly defended. Some portions of the railroad track, however, were destroyed. Leaving Col. Kilpatrick and Lieut.-Col. Davis, Gen. Gregg returned on the next day to Gen. Stoneman. On the night of the 4th, Gen. Gregg moved near Yanceyville, and was followed the next day by Gen. Stoneman and Gen. Buford's command. On the 5th, the retrograde movement commenced, and crossing Racoon Ford, on the Rapidan, the command arrived at Kelly's Ford, on the North Fork. Meantime, the advance of Col. Kilpatrick was made, and thus subsequently reported by him:

By directions from Maj.-Gen. Stoneman, I left Louisa Court House on the morning of the 3d instant, with one regiment (the Harris Light Cavalry) of my brigade; reached Hungary, on the Fredericksburg railroad, at daylight on the 4th; destroyed the depot and telegraph wires and railroad for several miles; passed over to Brook turnpike, drove in the rebel pickets; down the pike, across the brook, charged a battery, and forced it to retire within two miles of the city of Richmond; captured Lieut. Brown, aide-de-camp to Gen. Winder, and eleven men within the fortifications; passed down to the left of the Meadow bridge on the Chickahominy, which I burned; ran a train of cars into the river; retired to Hanovertown on the peninsula; crossed and destroyed the ferry boat just in time to check the advance of a pursuing cavalry force; burned a train of thirty wagons loaded with bacon; captured thirteen prisoners, and encamped for the night five miles from the river.

I resumed my march at 1 A. M. of the 5th; surprised a force of three hundred cavalry at Aylett's; captured two officers and thirty-three men; burned fifty-six wagons, the depot, containing upward of twenty thousand bushels of corn and wheat, quantities of clothing and commissary stores, and safely crossed the Mattapony, and destroyed the ferry again just in time to escape the advance of the rebel cavalry pursuit. Late in the evening I destroyed a third wagon train and depot a few miles above and west of the Tappahannock on the Rappahannock, and from that point made a forced march of twenty miles, being closely pursued by a superior force of cavalry, supposed to be a portion of Stuart's, from the fact that we captured prisoners from the 8th, 1st, and 10th Virginia cavalry. At sundown discovered a force of cavalry drawn up in line of battle about King and Queen Court House. Their strength was unknown, but I at once advanced to the attack, only to discover, however, that they were friends—a portion of the 10th Illinois cavalry, who had become separated from the command of Lieut.-Col. Davis, of the same regiment.

At 10 A. M., on the 7th, I found safety and rest under our own brave old flag within our lines at Gloucester Point. This raid and march around the entire rebel army—a march of nearly two hundred miles—has been made in less than five days, with a loss of one officer and thirty-seven men, having captured and paroled upward of three hundred men.

At the same time, Lieut.-Col. Davis, of the 12th Illinois, was ordered to penetrate to the Fredericksburg railroad, and, if possible, to the Virginia Central, and destroy communications. If he crossed the Virginia Central he was to make for Williamsburg on the peninsula. Leaving the main body on the South Anna, on Sunday, May 3d, he passed down the bank of that river, burning a bridge, and, dispersing a mounted party of the enemy, struck the railroad at Ashland. Here he cut the telegraph, tore up some rails, and burned the trestlework bridge south of the town. At the same time a train of cars, filled with sick and wounded, arrived, and was captured. The prisoners were paroled, and the locomotives disabled. Twenty wagons, with horses, were destroyed, and several horses taken. Leaving at 6 P. M., a train of eighteen wagons was met and destroyed, and Hanover Station reached at 8 P. M. Here thirty prisoners were captured, and the railroad line broken. The depot, storehouses, and stables, filled with government property, were destroyed, also a culvert and trestlework south of the station. Among the property destroyed were more than one hundred wagons, a thousand sacks of flour and corn, and a large quantity of clothing and horse equipments. The command then moved down within seven miles of Richmond, and bivouacked until eight o'clock the next morning. It then marched for Williamsburg, but at Tunstall's Station, near White House, encountered a train of cars, filled with infantry and a battery of three guns. This force formed in rifle pits, so that Col. Davis, by a charge, could not penetrate their line: he therefore determined to cross the Pamunkey and Mattapony, and proceed to Gloucester Point. He thus reports the result of his movements:

Our total loss in the expedition has been two commissioned officers and thirty-three enlisted men; we brought with us one hundred mules and seventy-five horses, captured from the enemy. We captured, in the course of our march, a much larger number, which we could not bring in. The amount of property destroyed is estimated at over one million of dollars.

Respectfully submitted,

H. DAVIS, Lieut.-Colonel Commanding.

The army of Gen. Hooker, after recrossing, as before stated, moved immediately to its original camp opposite Fredericksburg.

On the 6th, Gen. Hooker issued the following address to his army:

General Orders No. 49.

HEADQUARTERS ARMY OF THE POTOMAC, *May 6th*, 1863.

The Major-General Commanding tenders to this army his congratulations on its achievements of the last seven days. If it has not accomplished all that was expected, the reasons are well known to the army. It is sufficient to say, they were of a character not to be foreseen or prevented by human sagacity or resource.

In withdrawing from the south bank of the Rappahannock before delivering a general battle to our adversaries, the army has given renewed evidence of its confidence in itself, and its fidelity to the principles it represents. On fighting at a disadvantage, we would have been recreant to our trust, to ourselves, our cause, and our country. Profoundly loyal and conscious of its strength, the Army of the Potomac will give or decline battle whenever its interest or honor may demand. It will also be the guardian of its own history and its own arm. By your celerity and secrecy of movement, our advance and passage of the rivers was undisputed, and on our withdrawal not a rebel ventured to follow.

The events of last week may swell with pride the heart of every officer and soldier of this army. We have added new lustre to its former renown. We have made long marches, crossed rivers, surprised the enemy in his intrenchments, and, wherever we have fought, have inflicted heavier blows than we have received. We have taken from the enemy five thousand prisoners; fifteen colors; captured and brought off seven pieces of artillery; placed *hors du combat* eighteen thousand of his chosen troops; destroyed his depots filled with vast amounts of stores; deranged his communications; captured prisoners within the fortifications of his capital, and filled his country with fear and consternation. We have no other regret than that caused by the loss of our brave companions, and in this we are consoled by the conviction that they have fallen in the holiest cause ever submitted to the arbitrament of battle.

By command of Major-General HOOKER.

S. WILLIAMS, Assistant Adjutant-General.

On the 7th, Gen. Lee issued the following address to his army:

General Orders No. 59.

HEADQUARTERS ARMY NORTHERN VIRGINIA, *May 7th*, 1863.

With heartfelt gratification, the General Commanding expresses to the army his sense of the heroic conduct displayed by officers and men, during the arduous operations in which they have just been engaged.

Under trying vicissitudes of heat and storm, you attacked the enemy, strongly intrenched in the depths of a tangled wilderness, and again on the hills of Fredericksburg, fifteen miles distant, and, by the valor that has triumphed on so many fields, forced him once more to seek safety beyond the Rappahannock. While this glorious victory entitles you to the praise and gratitude of the nation, we are especially called upon to return our grateful thanks to the only Giver of victory, for the signal deliverance He has wrought.

It is, therefore, earnestly recommended that the troops unite on Sunday next in ascribing to the Lord of Hosts the glory due His name.

Let us not forget, in our rejoicings, the brave soldiers who have fallen in defence of their country; and, while we mourn their loss, let us resolve to emulate their noble example. The army and the country alike lament the absence for a time of one to whose bravery, energy, and skill they are so much indebted for success.

The following letter from the President of the Confederate States, is communicated to the army as an expression of his appreciation of its success:

I have received your despatch, and reverently unite with you in giving praise to God for the success with which he has crowned our arms.

In the name of the people, I offer my cordial thanks to yourself and the troops under your command, for this addition to the unprecedented series of great victories which your army has achieved.

The universal rejoicing produced by this happy result will be mingled with a general regret for the good and the brave who are numbered among the killed and wounded.

R. E. LEE, General.

On the 8th, the following despatch was sent by the Secretary of War to the Governors of the Northern States:

WASHINGTON, *May 8th*, 1863.

The President and General-in-Chief have just returned from the Army of the Potomac. The principal operations of Gen. Hooker failed, but there has been no serious disaster to the organization and efficiency of the army. It is now occupying its former position on the Rappahannock, having recrossed the river without any loss in the movement. Not more than one third of Gen. Hooker's force was engaged. Gen. Stoneman's operations have been a brilliant success. Part of his force advanced to within two miles of Richmond, and the enemy's communications have been cut in every direction. The Army of the Potomac will speedily resume offensive operations.

(Signed) E. M. STANTON, Secretary of War.

On the same day, the President issued the following proclamation, preliminary to executing the law for obtaining soldiers by enrolment and draft. It would appear that the events on the Rappahannock had hastened the decision to put the law for this object in operation, and the proclamation notified all foreigners who had merely declared an intention to become citizens of the United States, that after sixty-five days they would be liable to draft, if found in the country.

By the President of the United States of America:

PROCLAMATION.

Whereas, the Congress of the United States, at its last session, enacted a law, entitled an act for the enrolling and calling out the national forces, and for other purposes, which was approved on the 3d day of March last; and whereas, it is recited in said act that there now exists in the West and South an insurrection against the authority thereof, and it is under the Constitution of the United States the duty of the Government to suppress insurrection and rebellion, to guarantee to each State a republican form of government, and to preserve public tranquillity; and whereas, for these high purposes, a military force is indispensable, to raise and support which all persons ought willingly to contribute; and whereas, no service can be more praiseworthy and honorable than that which is rendered for the maintenance of the Constitution and Union, and consequent preservation of free government; and whereas, for the reasons thus recited, it was enacted by said statute that all able-bodied male citizens of the United States, and persons of foreign birth who shall have declared on oath their intention to become citizens under and in pursuance of the laws therof, between the ages of 20 and 45 years, with certain exceptions not necessary to be here mentioned, are declared to constitute the national forces, and shall be liable to perform military duty in the service of the United States, when called on by the President for that purpose; and whereas, it is claimed by and in behalf of persons of foreign birth within the ages specified in said act, who have heretofore declared on oath their intention to become citizens under and in pursuance of the laws of the United States, and who have not exercised the right of suffrage or any other political franchise under the laws of the United States or of any of the States thereof, are not absolutely concluded by their aforesaid declaration of intention from renouncing their purpose to become citizens; and that on the contrary such persons under treaties or the law of nations retain a right to renounce that purpose and to forego privilege of citizenship and residence within the United States under obligations imposed by the aforesaid act of Congress:

Now, therefore, to avoid all misapprehensions concerning liability of persons concerned to perform the service required by such enactment, and to give it full effect, I do hereby order and proclaim that no plea of alienage will be received or allowed to exempt from obligations imposed by the aforesaid act of Congress any person of foreign birth who shall have declared, on oath, his intention to become a citizen of the United States, under the laws thereof, and who shall be found within the United States at any time during the continuance of the present insurrection and rebellion at or after the expiration of the period of sixty-five days from date of this proclamation; nor shall any such plea of alienage be allowed in favor of any such person who has so as aforesaid declared his intention to become a citizen of the United States, and shall have exercised at any time the right of suffrage or any other political franchise within the United States under laws of any of the several States. In witness whereof I have hereunto set my hand and caused the seal of the United States to be affixed. Done at the city of Washington, this 8th day of May, in the year of our Lord 1863, and of the independence of the United States the 87th.

(Signed) ABRAHAM LINCOLN, President.
W. H. SEWARD, Secretary of State.

Previously, while the movements of Gen. Hooker were in progress, the following military orders were issued. The object appears to have been to prevent the transmission of premature and unreliable reports to Halifax, Nova Scotia, and by steamer to Europe:

WASHINGTON, *May* 1, 1863.

To Major-Gen. Wool, Commanding at New York:

By virtue of the act of Congress authorizing the President to take possession of railroad and telegraph lines, &c., passed February 4th, 1862, the President directs that you take immediate military possession of the telegraph lines lately established between Philadelphia and Boston, called the Independent Telegraph Company, and *forbid* the transmission of any intelligence relating to the movements of the army of the Potomac or any military forces of the United States. In case this order is violated, arrest and imprison the perpetrators in Fort Delaware, reporting to this Department. If the management of the line will stipulate to transmit no military intelligence without the sanction of the War Department, they need not be interfered with so long as the engagement is fulfilled. This order will be executed so as not to interfere with the ordinary business of the Telegraph Company.

By order of the President:
EDWIN M. STANTON, Secretary of War.

The official statement of the killed and wounded of Gen. Hooker's army was as follows:

Officers killed,	154
Enlisted men killed,	1,358
Officers wounded,	624
Enlisted men wounded,	8,894
Total	11,030

Some of the wounded remained on the field of battle at least ten days, as appears by the following, which was made public:

HEADQUARTERS ARMY OF THE POTOMAC,
Tuesday, May 12, 1863.

Dr. Luckley, medical director in charge of our wounded on the field, reports that they are all comfortable, and are about twelve hundred in number. An ambulance train has been sent for them. They are expected to return to camp by to-night.

A flag of truce from Gen. Lee stated that he had exhausted his medicines and hospital stores, and fresh supplies were sent over for the wounded of Gen. Hooker's army. The number of prisoners taken was estimated by the enemy at eight thousand. It was an overestimate.

The loss of the enemy in numbers was less than that of Gen. Hooker, but far greater in the importance of the officers. Among their wounded was Gen. Jackson, who subsequently died. Upon hearing that he was wounded, Gen. Lee addressed to him the following letter:

CHANCELLORSVILLE, *May 4th.*

To Lieutenant-Gen. T. J. Jackson:

GENERAL: I have just received your note, informing me that you are wounded. I cannot express my regret at the occurrence.

Could I have directed events, I should have chosen for the good of the country to have been disabled in your stead. I congratulate you upon the victory which is due to your skill and energy.

Most truly yours,
R. E. LEE, General.

Gen. Jackson had gone some distance in front of his line of skirmishers, on Saturday evening, May 2d, and was returning about eight o'clock, attended by his staff and part of his couriers. The cavalcade, in the darkness of the night, was supposed to be a body of Federal cavalry, and fired upon by a regiment of his own corps. He was struck by three balls, one through the left arm, two inches below the shoulder-joint, shattering the bone and severing the chief artery; another ball passed through the same arm between the elbow and wrist, making its exit through the palm of the hand; a third ball entered the palm of the right hand, about the middle, passed through and broke two bones. He suffered for a week, during which his wounds improved, but sunk under an attack of pneumonia. The following order was issued by Gen. Lee:

General Order No. 61.

HEADQUARTERS ARMY OF NORTHERN VIRGINIA, *May 11th*, 1863.

With deep grief the Commanding General announces to the army the death of Lieut.-Gen. T. J. Jackson, who expired on the 10th instant, at 3.15 P. M. The daring, skill, and energy of this great and good soldier, by the decree of an all-wise Providence, are now lost to us; but while we mourn his death, we feel that his spirit still lives, and will inspire the whole army with his indomitable courage and unshaken confidence in God as our hope and strength. Let his name be a watchword to his corps, who have followed him to victory on so many fields. Let officers and soldiers emulate his invincible determination in defence of our beloved country.

R. E. LEE, General.

CHAPTER XXXI.

Position of the hostile Armies on the Rappahannock—The Military Departments—Advance of Gen. Lee toward the Shenandoah Valley—Capture of Winchester and Martinsburg—Invasion of Maryland and Pennsylvania—Calls for Troops from the Northern States—March of Gen. Hooker's Army—Plans of Gen. Lee—The Enemy in Pennsylvania.

THE armies confronting each other at Fredericksburg, now remained inactive for some time. A movement of a small force of Confederate cavalry near the Baltimore and Ohio Railroad, during the last week in April, was made, by which some injury was done to that road, and an alarm created on its borders. On the 1st of June, the Federal force at West Point, on the York River, under Brig.-Gen. Gordon, was withdrawn, and a cavalry dash from Gloucester was made by Col. Kilpatrick through the adjacent counties, for the purpose of joining his force with that of General Stoneman. At this time, also, some cavalry movements took place along the Rapidan, and such changes were observed in the appearance of the enemy's camp at Fredericksburg as created an impression that some of his force might have been withdrawn. This induced Gen. Hooker to make a reconnoissance in force on the 5th of June. The division of Gen. Howe, of the sixth corps, was sent across the river below Fredericksburg. Some skirmishing ensued, and the enemy developed so much strength as to create the impression that the mass of his forces had not been removed.

On Tuesday, the 9th of June, two brigades of Gen. Pleasanton's cavalry, under command of Gen. Buford, made a reconnoissance to Culpepper. The force was supported by two batteries of artillery, and two regiments of infantry, as a reserve. On Monday night, the force bivouacked near Beverly Ford, on the Rappahannock. Beyond the ford was a semi-circular belt of woods, with a range of rifle-pits near the edge; and a line of pickets guarded the fords on the southern bank of the river. The cavalry crossed at 4 A. M., the 10th New York in advance, and drove the pickets back to the rifle-pits, and then charged upon the pits. The combat was severe, but the enemy were driven from their pits and the woods. Falling back upon their artillery, they maintained their position until twelve o'clock, when Gen. Buford's artillery reached the ground, and the action was renewed. Gen. Pleasanton took command of the Union force before it was over. Gen. Stuart also arrived on the Confederate side. The Federal loss was about three hundred and sixty. Among the killed was Col. B. F. Davis, who led the cavalry force from Harper's Ferry at the time of its surrender in 1862. The enemy's loss was somewhat larger. The number of the enemy taken prisoners was about two hundred. In reply to a communication from Gen. Pleasanton, relating to the men left in the hands of General Stuart, the latter subsequently stated that the dead had been decently buried, the wounded humanely attended by his surgeons, and the prisoners sent to Richmond; but that no parties would be permitted to visit the field by flag of truce, for the purpose of procuring the remains of friends, and that all future communications must be sent by the flag-of-truce boat to City Point, Va.

Positive information was obtained by this reconnoissance that the Confederate forces were preparing for a movement, either against Washington or into the State of Maryland. An apprehension of an aggressive blow from the enemy, now existed. Where, or in what manner the attempt would be made to strike the blow, no one could foretell. A threat had been made to invade Maryland and Pennsylvania with a considerable force, in retaliation for the raids made by Col. Grierson in Mississippi and Cols. Kilpatrick and Davis in Virginia. The cavalry force of Gen. Pleasanton, on its return, brought information that the enemy had been moving in strong force westward, through the town of Sperryville, toward Luray, in the Shenandoah valley; that the column so moving was three hours and a half in passing the town, and was composed of infantry and artillery. The movement of Gen. Pleasanton also developed that the enemy were massing their cavalry on the Upper Rappahannock for some purpose. On the 11th of June, a force, consisting of two hundred and fifty of the enemy's cavalry, crossed the Potomac at Edward's Ferry, and attacked the company of the 6th Michigan on picket at Seneca. This company gradually fell back toward Poolesville. The enemy burnt their camp and recrossed the river, where they remained for some time, assuming a threatening appearance.

On the 8th of June, the Richmond (Va.) press spoke of a movement of Gen. Lee, in these words: "It is too generally known to raise any question of prudence in speaking of it, that Gen. Lee has put his army in motion. His designs are known only to himself, and those with whom it was his duty to confer. A few days will disclose them to the public, who are willing to wait patiently, in full confidence that the result will vindicate the wisdom of what he undertakes. A forward movement on his part has been for some time anticipated by the enemy, and is regarded with very perceptible uneasiness."

The facts were as follows: The position occupied by Gen. Hooker, opposite Fredericksburg, being one in which he could not be attacked to advantage, Gen. Lee determined to draw him from it. The execution of this purpose by him embraced the relief of the Shenandoah valley from the Federal troops that had occupied the lower part of it during the winter and spring, and, if practicable, the transfer of the scene of hostilities north of the Potomac. It was thought that the corresponding movements on the part of Gen. Hooker, to which those contemplated by Gen. Lee would probably give rise, might offer a fair opportunity to strike a blow at the army under Gen. Hooker, and that in any event that army would be compelled to leave Virginia, and possibly to draw to its support troops designed to operate against other parts of the Confederacy. In this way it was supposed that the Federal plan of campaign for the summer would be broken up, and a part of the season of active operations be consumed in the formation of new combinations and the preparations that they would require. Other valuable results, it was hoped by Gen. Lee, would be attained by military success.

The movement of Gen. Lee began on the 3d of June. Gen. McLaws's division of Gen. Longstreet's corps left Fredericksburg for Culpepper Court House; and Gen. Hood's division, which was encamped on the Rapidan, marched to the same place. They were followed, on the 4th and 5th, by Gen. Ewell's corps, leaving that of Gen. A. P. Hill to occupy the Confederate lines at Fredericksburg. The forces of Gens. Longstreet and Ewell reached Culpepper on the 8th, at which point the Confederate cavalry under Gen. Stuart was concentrated. Gen. Jenkins, with his cavalry brigade, had been ordered to advance toward Winchester, to coöperate with the infantry in the proposed expedition in the lower part of the Shenandoah valley, and at the same time Gen. Imboden was directed with his command to make a demonstration in the direction of Romney, in order to cover the movement against Winchester, and prevent the Federal troops at that place from being reënforced by the troops on the line of the Baltimore and Ohio railroad. Both of these officers were in position when Gen. Ewell left Culpepper Court House, on the 16th of June.

On the 9th of June, the War Department issued a general order (No. 172) establishing two new military departments, as follows:

1. The Department of the Monongahela, embracing that portion of the State of Pennsylvania west of Johnstown and the Laurel Hill range of mountains, and the counties of Hancock, Brooke, and Ohio, in the State of Virginia, and the counties of Columbia, Jefferson, and Belmont, in the State of Ohio. The command of this department is assigned to Major-Gen. William T. H. Brooks, with his headquarters at Pittsburg.

2. The Department of the Susquehanna, embracing that portion of the State of Pennsylvania east of Johnstown and the Laurel Hill range of mountains. The command of this department is assigned to Major-Gen. Couch, with his headquarters at Chambersburg.

The following is the list of the military geographical departments and their commanders at this time:

Department of the Tennessee—Maj.-Gen. U. S. Grant.
Department of the Cumberland—Maj.-Gen. W. S. Rosecrans.
Department of the Ohio—Maj.-Gen. A. E. Burnside.
Department of NewEngland—Maj.-Gen. John A. Dix.
Department of the Gulf—Maj.-Gen. N. P. Banks.
Department of North Carolina and Department of Virginia—Maj.-Gen. J. G. Foster.
Department of the Northwest—Maj.-Gen. John Pope.
Department of Washington—Maj.-Gen. S. P. Heintzelman.
Department of the Monongahela—Maj.-Gen. W. T. H. Brooks.
Department of the Susquehanna—Maj.-Gen. Darius N. Couch.
Department of Western Virginia—Brig.-Gen. B. F. Kelly.
Department of New Mexico—Brig.-Gen. James H. Carlton.
Department of the Pacific—Brig.-Gen. G. Wright.
Department of Key West—Brig.-Gen. J. M. Brannan.
Department of Kansas—Maj.-Gen. James G. Blunt.
Middle Department—Maj.-Gen. Robert C. Schenck.
Department of the South—Brig.-Gen. Q. A. Gillmore.
Department of Missouri—Maj.-Gen. John M. Schofield.

On the 12th of June, the Governor of Pennsylvania issued the following proclamation:

In the name and by the authority of the Commonwealth of Pennsylvania, by Andrew G. Curtin, Governor of the said Commonwealth:

A PROCLAMATION.

Information has been obtained by the War Department that a large rebel force, composed of cavalry, artillery, and mounted infantry, has been prepared for the purpose of making a raid into Pennsylvania. The President has therefore erected two new departments, one in Eastern Pennsylvania, to be commanded by Major-General Couch, and the other in Western Pennsylvania, to be commanded by Major-General Brooks. I earnestly invite the attention of the people of Pennsylvania to the general orders issued by these officers on assuming the command of their respective departments.

The importance of immediately raising a sufficient force for the defence of the State cannot be overrated. The corps now proposed to be established will give permanent security to our borders. I know too well the gallantry and patriotism of the freemen of this Commonwealth to think it necessary to do more than commend this measure to the people, and earnestly urge them to respond to the call of the General Government and promptly fill the ranks of this corps, the duties of which will be mainly the defence of our own homes, firesides, and property from devastation. ANDREW G. CURTIN.

On the same day, Gen. Couch assumed the command of the Department of the Susquehanna, with his headquarters at Harrisburg, Penn. In consultation with Governor Curtin, they were of the opinion that the danger of an invasion of the State of Pennsylvania was certain. The Federal Government was therefore requested by the Governor to suspend all recruiting for the regular or volunteer service within the State, so that the citizens could be available in its defence. The request was granted. At the same time Gen. Couch issued the following order, calling for volunteers:

DEPARTMENT OF THE SUSQUEHANNA, CHAMBERSBURG, *June 12th*, 1863.

The undersigned assumes command of this department. In view of the danger of the invasion now threatening the State of Pennsylvania by the enemies of the Government, a new military department has been made by direction of the War Department, embracing all the territory of Pennsylvania east of Johnstown and Laurel Hill range of mountains; headquarters at Chambersburg.

To prevent serious raids by the enemy, it is deemed necessary to call upon the citizens of Pennsylvania to furnish promptly all the men necessary to organize an army corps of volunteer infantry, artillery, and cavalry, to be designated the "Army Corps of the Susquehanna." They will all be enrolled and organized in accordance with the regulations of the United States service, for the protection and defence of the public and private property within the department, and will be mustered into the service of the United States to serve during the pleasure of the President or the continuance of the war. The company and field officers of the departmental corps will be provisionally commissioned by the President upon the recommendation of the General Commanding. They will be armed, uniformed, and equipped, and, while in active service, subsisted and supplied as active troops of the United States. When not required for active service to defend the department, they will be returned to their homes subject to the call of the Commanding General.

Cavalry volunteers may furnish their own horses, to be turned over to the United States at their appraised value, or allowance will be made for the time of actual service, at the rate authorized by law. All able-bodied volunteers between the ages of eighteen and sixty will be enrolled and received into this corps.

The volunteers for the State defence will receive no bounty, but will be paid the same as like service in the army of the United States, for the time they may be in actual service, as soon as Congress may make an appropriation for that purpose.

If volunteers belonging to this army corps desire, they can be transferred to the volunteer service for three years or during the war, when they will be entitled to all the bounties and privileges granted by the acts of Congress.

The General Commanding, in accordance with the foregoing general authority, calls upon all citizens within his department to come forward promptly to perfect the company organizations under United States regulations, to wit: one captain, one first lieutenant, one second lieutenant, sixty-four privates as the minimum and eighty-two as the maximum standard of each company.

The General Commanding specially desires that citizens of this district recently in the army should volunteer for duty in this army corps; thereby, from their experience, adding greatly to the efficiency of the force for immediate defensive operations; each company organization to be perfected as soon as possible, and report the name of the officers in command, the number of men, and the place of its headquarters, in order that they may be promptly furnished with transportation to the general rendezvous, which will be at Harrisburg. Any person who will furnish forty or more men who will be enrolled, if otherwise unobjectionable, will be entitled to a captaincy.

Any person who will bring twenty-five or more men, under the above conditions, will be entitled to a first lieutenancy, and every person who will bring fifteen or more men, under the same conditions, to a second lieutenancy. On their arrival at the place of rendezvous they will be formed into regiments. So far as practicable, and as may be found consistent with the interests of the public service, companies from the same locality will be put together in the regimental organizations.

For the present all communications will be addressed to Harrisburg. The chiefs of the respective organizations will report accordingly.

DARIUS N. COUCH, Major-Gen'l Commanding.

At the same time Gen. Brooks assumed command of the Department of Monongahela, with his headquarters at Pittsburg, and proceeded to prepare to resist any attempt at an invasion.

Meantime, the force which Gen. Hooker had sent across the Rappahannock on a reconnoissance had intrenched its position and remained on the plain below Fredericksburg, and two bridges were constructed over the river. The enemy fortified themselves strongly, and waited for any demonstration. There were evidently about ten thousand men in their first line of defences, and others were visible upon the ridges and in the woods, within supporting distance. New earthworks appeared every morning on the heights; picket firing was constant, and occasionally their artillery opened fire. It was known that troops had been hurrying up for some time from Southeastern Virginia and North Carolina, and that the army of Gen. Lee had been reorganized and made to consist of three large corps, under Gens. Longstreet, Ewell, and A. P. Hill. Although the force displayed in Fredericksburg was large, yet Gen. Lee was supposed to be at Culpepper on the 12th, with the corps of Gens. Longstreet and Ewell, for the purpose of attacking the right of Gen. Hooker, and preparations were made to resist him. On the 13th it was manifest that the movements of Gen. Lee in the direction of Culpepper, had been made on a larger and more extensive scale than was at first supposed, and embraced nearly the whole of his army, leaving near Fredericksburg not more than ten thousand men. Such a movement removed every doubt of his intention to assume the offensive.

There existed at this time many considerations to encourage Gen. Lee in this movement. The army of Gen. Hooker had been reduced, not only by the losses in the battle of Chancellorsville, but by the departure of nearly twenty thousand men, who had enlisted, some for two years, and some for nine months, and whose term of service had now expired. No aid to him could be expected from the West. The Confederate authorities had declared that Gen. Johnston should be strengthened sufficiently to attack Gen. Grant in the rear and raise the siege of Vicksburg. This declaration, on their part, had caused the Federal Government to make every exertion to defeat it. All the troops which could be spared in the West were sent to Gen. Grant. The force of Gen. Burnside, in the Department of Ohio, was included. This not only compelled the latter to remain inactive, but actually exposed Ohio and Western Virginia. The entire levy of nine-months' men would go home in June, and the Federal Government had made no call for others in their place, and had not in reality succeeded in obtaining by enlistment any number of troops except the free and slave blacks it had been successful in organizing. There were also reasons why the army of Gen. Lee should take the field. It was now well known to the Confederate Government that it would be unable to reënforce Gen. Johnston, so that the siege of Vicksburg could be raised; a counteracting effort was therefore necessary in some quarter. The supplies which might be obtained by an invasion of the North were also greatly needed.

It was the purpose of Gen. Lee, if possible, to strike a most decisive blow. For this object an army of nearly one hundred thousand men had been collected in the field. It was first contemplated by Gen. Lee to enter Pennsylvania, and keep the army of Gen. Hooker fully occupied. Meantime, a body of chosen troops were to be detached from the forces of Gen. Beauregard, at Charleston, and Gen. Bragg, in Tennessee, and concentrate at Culpepper, for the purpose of making an attack on Washington. It was thought that the Federal Government, thus divided between a fear of leaving Pennsylvania defenceless, and the necessity of protecting the seat of government, would be obliged to fail signally in one quarter or the other. Either Washington would fall, or the chief towns of Pennsylvania and all the rich regions surrounding them would come into the possession of Gen. Lee's army.

Gen. Hooker penetrated the object of Gen. Lee in concentrating upon the Upper Rappahannock before it was too late. As early as the 12th of June he began to send his sick and wounded to Washington, and to remove his stores. A most formidable invasion by Gen. Lee was soon developed.

On Friday, the 12th of June, it was ascertained at Winchester that a large body of the enemy were moving up the Shenandoah valley. On Saturday an attack was made by the advance of the enemy, under Gen. Rhodes, upon Berryville, which was held by Gen. McReynolds as an outpost of Winchester. The force of Gen. McReynolds was about three thousand men, and the position was midway between Winchester and Snicker's Gap, through which the enemy advanced. The attack was repelled with vigor and firmness for some time, when, in consequence of overwhelming numbers, a retreat upon Winchester was commenced. The 6th Maryland, Col. Horne, with Capt. Alexander's 1st Maryland battery covered the retreat, and maintained their ground until, the enemy closing around them, they were compelled to abandon their guns. A large part of the regiment were made prisoners, but were not disarmed, and, in the confusion which ensued during the darkness of the evening, withdrew unobserved, being familiar with the roads, and escaped.

On the same day, early in the morning, the pickets of Maj.-Gen. Milroy, at Winchester, were driven in by the advance of Gen. Ewell, with the divisions of Gens. Early and Johnson. A detachment was sent out to feel their strength, and an artillery fire was kept up for some time. Gen. Milroy, then in command at Winchester, had a force of seven thousand men, with three batteries of field artillery, and six siege pieces, in a fort. As the forces of the enemy increased during the day, the advanced regiments of Gen. Milroy were compelled to fall back to the cover of the town. Some guns, posted in the outskirts, prevented the enemy from crossing Mill creek that day; but all the country southward from the creek was free to them. During the morning of Sunday, and, in fact, all day, skirmishing took place between the 18th Connecticut and 87th Pennsylvania regiments and the skirmishers of the enemy's force, who were posted in the woods, a mile east of Winchester, on the Berryville road, and extending across to the Front Royal road on the southeast. The Federal troops kept close in upon the town, while the enemy came up to the eastern side of the public cemetery, across which the principal firing took place. About half past four P. M. the skirmishers of the enemy charged up the Berryville and Front Royal roads to the edge of the town, but by a well-directed fire were repulsed in confusion. A charge was now ordered by Gen. Milroy to be made by these two regiments, but the enemy were found to be so well supported in the distant woods that the regiments were compelled to get back as soon as they could.

About five o'clock P. M. the enemy appeared in strong force, with two eight-gun batteries, directly west of the main fort north of the Romney road, which runs directly west from the town, and about fifteen hundred yards from the outworks. These were held by the 110th Ohio, and company L, 5th regiment artillery. After getting his batteries into position and opening fire, Gen. Ewell massed his infantry, and charged across the fields to the very muzzles of the Federal guns, although the latter were fired vigorously. Without a pause, the enemy crossed the ditch, came over the breastworks, and planted their colors on the embankment. The Ohio regiment was driven from the works at the point of the bayonet. Some escaped back

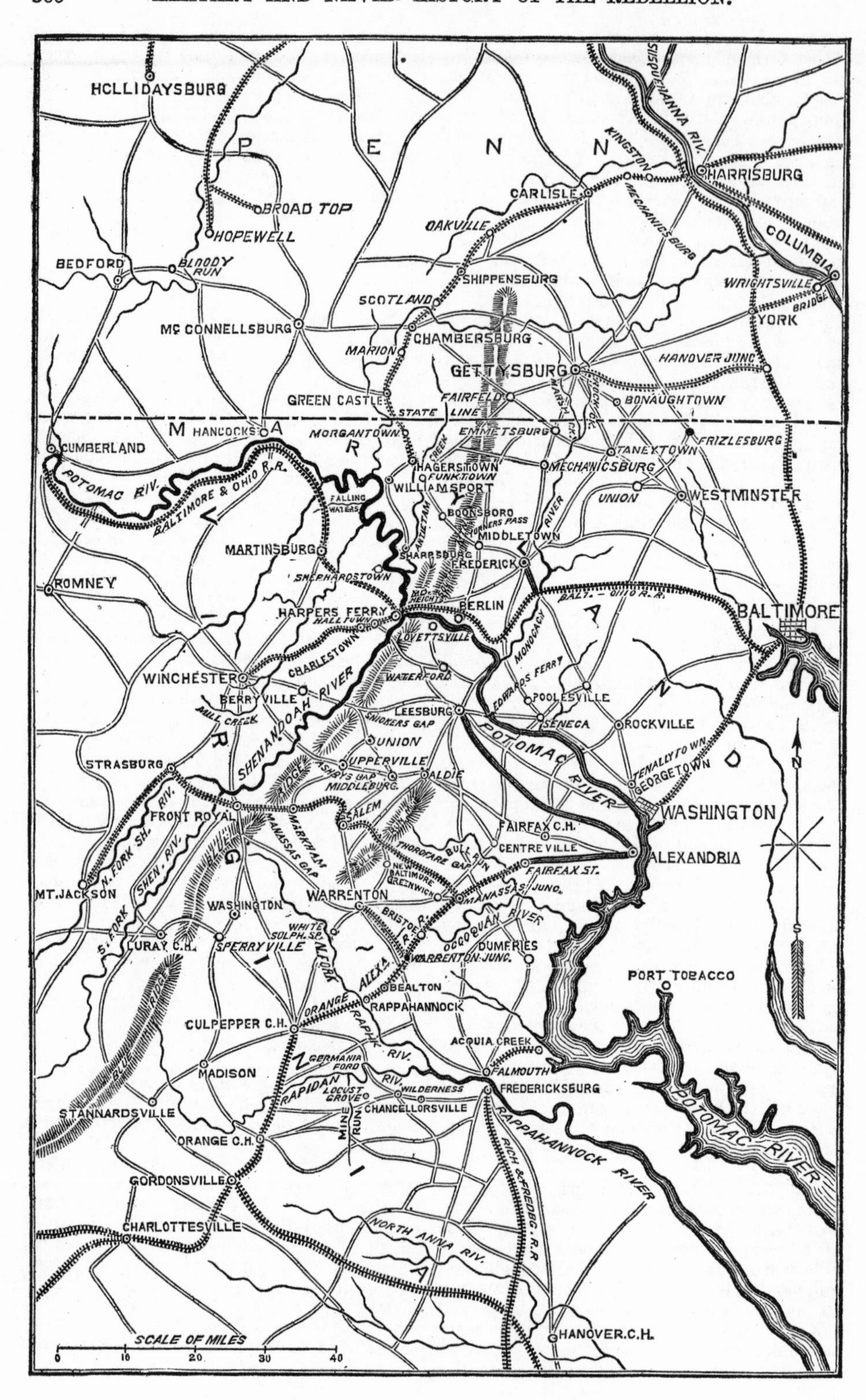
HOLLIDAYSBURG
BROAD TOP
HOPEWELL
BEDFORD
BLOODY RUN
MC CONNELLSBURG
CARLISLE
KINGSTON
MECHANICSBURG
HARRISBURG
SUSQUEHANNA RIV.
COLUMBIA
WRIGHTSVILLE
BRIDGE
YORK
HANOVER JUNC.
OAKVILLE
SHIPPENSBURG
SCOTLAND
CHAMBERSBURG
MARION
GETTYSBURG
FAIRFELD
BONAUGHTOWN
GREEN CASTLE
STATE LINE
P E N N
M A R Y L A N D
HANCOCKS
CUMBERLAND
MORGANTOWN
EMMETSBURG
FRIZLESBURG
TANEYTOWN
MECHANICSBURG
HAGERSTOWN
FUNKTOWN
WILLIAMSPORT
UNION
WESTMINSTER
POTOMAC RIV.
BALTIMORE & OHIO R.R.
FALLING WATERS
BOONSBORO
TURNERS PASS
MIDDLETOWN
MARTINSBURG
SHARPSBURG
FREDERICK
ROMNEY
SHEPHARDSTOWN
BALT. - OHIO R.R.
BALTIMORE
HARPERS FERRY
BERLIN
LOVETTSVILLE
CHARLESTOWN
WINCHESTER
WATERFORD
EDWARDS FERRY
POOLESVILLE
MONOCACY
BERRYVILLE
SHENANDOAH RIVER
MILL CREEK
LEESBURG
SNICKERS GAP
SENECA
ROCKVILLE
UNION
POTOMAC RIVER
STRASBURG
UPPERVILLE
ASHBY'S GAP
ALDIE
MIDDLEBURG
TENALLYTOWN
GEORGETOWN
WASHINGTON
FRONT ROYAL
SALEM
MARKHAM
MANASSAS GAP
FAIRFAX C.H.
CENTREVILLE
BULL RUN
ALEXANDRIA
THOROFARE GAP
FAIRFAX ST.
NEW BALTIMORE
GREENWICH
MANASSAS JUNC.
MT. JACKSON
N. FORK SH. RIV.
SHEN. RIV.
S. FORK
WASHINGTON
WARRENTON
BRISTOE
OCCOQUAN RIVER
WHITE SOLPH. SP.
LURAY C.H.
SPERRYVILLE
DUMFRIES
WARRENTON JUNC.
PORT TOBACCO
BEALTON
RAPPAHANNOCK
ORANGE ALEXA. R.R.
CULPEPPER C.H.
ACQUIA CREEK
GERMANIA FORD
FALMOUTH
MADISON
RAPIDAN
LOCUST GROVE
WILDERNESS
CHANCELLORSVILLE
FREDERICKSBURG
POTOMAC RIVER
STANNARDSVILLE
MINE RUN
ORANGE C.H.
RAPPAHANNOCK RIVER
RICH & FREDBG. R.R.
GORDONSVILLE
CHARLOTTESVILLE
NORTH ANNA RIV.
V I R G I N I A
BLUE RIDGE
HANOVER C.H.
SCALE OF MILES
0 10 20 30 40
N
S

to the main fort, and the remainder were captured or killed.

Gen. Milroy, finding that the enemy were on the east, south, and west of him, and were moving toward the Martinsburg road, which runs north from the town, ordered all the troops and artillery from the south and east into the line of earthworks encircling the main works, when the contest between the Federal artillery and that of the enemy continued until night. At that time the second brigade, under Col. Ely, occupied the town and the space to the main fort on the northwest; the first brigade, under Gen. Elliott, occupied the main fort, and the third, under Col. McReynolds, was posted in the Star fort, north of the main fort. Soon after dark the enemy charged across the ravine between their new position and the main fort, but met such a fire as quickly repulsed them. Quiet then prevailed.

At one o'clock, on Monday morning, Gen. Milroy called a council of brigade commanders, and it was decided to abandon the position, and retreat to Harper's Ferry. The troops were then quickly put in motion, taking nothing except what they had upon their persons. They marched on the road to Martinsburg about four miles, when they encountered a strong force of the enemy, upon whom an advance was made and repulsed. The 18th Connecticut and 5th Maryland regiments, being on the left of the line, were captured almost entire. Of the remainder, about 1,600 reached Maryland Heights; about 400 Hancock and Cumberland, and about 1,700 Bloody Run. Three full batteries of field artillery, and all the siege guns in the Star fort and the main fort, were taken by the enemy; also the quartermaster's and commissary's stores, the ammunition of all kinds, 6,000 muskets, 200 wagons with horses and mules, and all the private baggage of officers and men. The dead and wounded were left on the field and along the roadside as they fell. On Tuesday a large train of wagons, which had left Gen. Milroy early on Sunday, arrived at Harrisburg. It had not been molested.

Maj.-Gen. Milroy had previously rendered himself very obnoxious to the enemy, in consequence of rigorous measures adopted by him in Western Virginia. Their hatred to him was so bitter that a reward of ten thousand dollars was offered for his head.

Subsequently a court of inquiry was ordered, preliminary to a court martial, upon the conduct of Gen. Milroy at Winchester. The report of the Judge Advocate-General, with the evidence elicited, was laid before the President, who rendered the following decision:

In June last a division was substantially lost at and near Winchester, Va. At the time it was under Gen. Milroy, as immediate commander in the field, Gen. Schenck, as department commander at Baltimore, and Gen. Halleck, as commander-in-chief at Washington. Gen. Milroy, as immediate commander, was put under arrest, and subsequently a court of inquiry examined chiefly with reference to disobedience of orders, and reported the evidence.

The foregoing is a synoptical statement of the evidence, together with the Judge Advocate-General's conclusions. The disaster, when it came, was a surprise to all. It was well known to Gen. Schenck and Gen. Milroy for some time before that Gen. Halleck thought that the division was in general danger of a surprise at Winchester; that it was of no service there commensurate with the risk it incurred, and that it ought to be withdrawn. But, although he more than once advised its withdrawal, he never positively ordered it.

Gen. Schenck, on the contrary, believed the service of the force at Winchester was worth the hazard, and so did not positively order its withdrawal until it was so late that the enemy cut the wire and prevented the order reaching Gen. Milroy. Gen. Milroy seems to have concurred with Gen. Schenck in the opinion that the forces should be kept at Winchester, at least until the approach of danger; but he disobeyed no order upon the subject.

Some question can be made whether some of Gen. Halleck's despatches to Gen. Schenck should not have been construed to be orders to withdraw the force and obeyed accordingly; but no such question can be made against Gen. Milroy. In fact, the last order he received was to be prepared to withdraw, but not actually to withdraw till further order—which further order never reached him.

Serious blame is not necessarily due to every serious disaster, and I cannot say that in this case either of these officers is deserving of serious blame. No court martial is deemed necessary or proper in the case.

A. LINCOLN.

Maj.-Gen. Halleck, in his annual report, dated Nov. 15th, says:

Winchester and Martinsburg were at this time occupied by us simply as outposts. Neither place was susceptible of a good defence. Directions were therefore given on the 11th of June to withdraw those garrisons to Harper's Ferry; but these orders were not obeyed, and on the 13th Winchester was attacked and its armament and a part of the garrison captured.

On Sunday, the 14th, about 4 P. M., Gen. Rhodes, who had been instructed, after dislodging the force at Berryville, to cut off the communications between Winchester and the Potomac, appeared before Martinsburg, north of Winchester, and demanded its surrender of Gen. Tyler, who was in command. This was refused, and an attack was made, which Gen. Tyler resisted until dark. He then prepared to evacuate the position. This movement being discovered by the enemy, the attack was renewed, and a bloody contest followed, which was kept up until he reached the Potomac river. He then crossed at Shepherdstown, and subsequently moved to Harper's Ferry with his forces.

The following is Gen. Lee's report of the taking of Martinsburg:

CULPEPPER COURT HOUSE, *June 18th*, 1863.

Gen. S. Cooper, Adjutant and Inspector-General:

GENERAL: On the afternoon of the 14th, Gen. Rhodes took possession of Martinsburg, capturing several pieces of artillery, more than two hundred prisoners, and a supply of ammunition and grain.

Our loss was one killed and two wounded.

R. E. LEE, General.

Gen. Lee subsequently reported that more than four thousand prisoners, twenty-nine pieces of artillery, two hundred and seventy wagons and ambulances, with four hundred horses, were captured in these operations, besides a large amount of military stores.

On Monday morning a body of the enemy's cavalry, under Col. Jenkins, estimated at two thousand in number, crossed the Potomac at Williamsport, north of Martinsburg, without opposition, and immediately moved northward through Hagerstown to Greencastle, Pennsylvania, and thence to Chambersburg, where they arrived on Tuesday night. There was no Federal force at either of these places to oppose them. The only hostile acts of this force were the seizure of horses, cattle, and forage; goods were purchased at stores and paid for in Confederate scrip. On Tuesday afternoon a small force of Confederate infantry crossed the Potomac at Williamsport, for the purpose of guarding the passage until the return of the cavalry expedition.

The Baltimore and Ohio railroad managers, on seeing the approaching danger, had removed from their road all cars and engines for the space of one hundred miles, between Harper's Ferry and Cumberland.

The rest of the force which advanced up the Shenandoah valley was massed in the vicinity of Harper's Ferry, apparently threatening an attack upon that place, although it remained quiet. A band of guerrillas, under Col. Moseby, numbering about one hundred and fifty, on Saturday entered Loudon county, Va., and spread themselves about from Halltown to Waterford in small squads. On Sunday and Monday they were slightly reënforced. On Wednesday this force crossed the Potomac, and captured a small squad of home guards stationed there. They afterward intercepted a train of twenty-two freight cars, most of which were empty, that were returning to Baltimore from Harper's Ferry. The cars were burned, and the locomotives badly injured. The enemy then returned to the Virginia side of the river, but maintained their pickets along the banks. The force at Chambersburg, taking all the negroes with them, returned on Wednesday night to Hagerstown. The bridge at Scotland, five miles east of Chambersburg, was burned by them. From Hagerstown a detachment was sent to McConnellsburg, where it arrived on Friday morning, the 19th. The town was completely surprised, and large numbers of horses and cattle were captured. Many of the horses were returned upon the intercession of the owners. Goods were obtained from the stores in large quantities. The enemy then retired, but on the next day, a small body of them were captured in the neighborhood by a regiment of New York cavalry.

McConnellsburg is the capital of Fulton county, Pennsylvania. It is situated on the turnpike from Philadelphia to Pittsburg, and is seventy miles west of southwest from Harrisburg. The population is about eight hundred.

A small force appeared at Hancock, Md., on the 18th, and burned the canal boats there, but were driven off by a cavalry force from the command of Col. Gallagher, attached to the corps of Gen. Kelly. Cumberland, further west on the Potomac, was occupied by about nine hundred cavalry under Col. Imboden, on the 17th. No damage, however, was done. All the bridges on the Baltimore and Ohio railroad, from Harper's Ferry to Cumberland, a distance of one hundred miles, were destroyed. West of Cumberland the road was torn up at Brady's Station, which was east of New Creek, where the Federal forces were stationed. Meantime small bands of cavalry were sent out from Hagerstown and Frederick, to seize horses and cattle, large numbers of which were captured and driven across the Potomac to the Confederate army. These operations produced an unparalleled excitement in Washington and throughout the Northern States. They were regarded as indicating the approach of Gen. Lee with an immense army. It was known that he had commenced a movement, and that the Army of the Potomac was also in motion, but all information of the position of each army was carefully withheld from the knowledge of the public. Under this uncertainty, all measures taken by the Government for defence, which became known, tended to increase the excitement. Vast efforts were made with the utmost promptness and vigor, to prepare to resist successfully the invasion.

Upon the first complete news of the attack upon Winchester, the President issued the following proclamation:

Whereas, the armed insurrectionary combinations now existing in several of the States are threatening to make inroads into the States of Maryland, West Virginia, Pennsylvania, and Ohio, requiring immediately an additional military force for the service of the United States:

Now, therefore, I, Abraham Lincoln, President of the United States, and Commander-in-Chief of the Army and Navy thereof, and of the militia of the several States when called into actual service, do hereby call into the service of the United States one hundred thousand militia from the States following, namely:

From the State of Maryland ten thousand.
From the State of Pennsylvania fifty thousand.
From the State of Ohio thirty thousand.
From the State of West Virginia ten thousand.

To be mustered into the service of the United States forthwith, and to serve for the period of six months from the date of such muster into said service, unless sooner discharged; to be mustered in as infantry, artillery, and cavalry, in proportions which will be made known through the War Department, which department will also designate the several places of rendezvous.

These militia are to be organized according to the rules and regulations of the volunteer service, and such orders as may hereafter be issued.

The States aforesaid will be respectively credited under the enrolment act for the militia service rendered under this proclamation.

In testimony whereof I have hereunto set my hand and caused the seal of the United States to be affixed.

Done at the city of Washington, this 15th day of June, in the year of our Lord 1863, and of the independence of the United States the eighty-seventh.

By the President: ABRAHAM LINCOLN.
WM. H. SEWARD, Secretary of State.

On the same day, a telegraphic despatch was sent to Governor Seymour of New York, calling for twenty thousand militia immediately. On the same day the Governor replied, and ordered the troops out, as appears by the following sub-orders:

HEADQUARTERS FIRST BRIGADE N. Y. S. N. G., NEW YORK, *June 15th*, 1863.

By order of the Commander-in-Chief of the State of New York, the several regiments of this brigade will hold themselves in readiness to depart for Philadelphia at once, on short notice. By order of

Brigadier-General C. B. SPICER.

R. H. HOADLEY, Brigade Major and Inspector.

WILLIAM D. DIMOCK, Aide-de-Camp.

Order No. 3.

HEADQUARTERS, 543 BROADWAY, NEW YORK, *June 15th*, 1863.

Commandants of regiments of the Third Brigade N. Y. N. G., are hereby directed to report to General Wm. Hall, at his quarters, at six o'clock on Tuesday morning, by order of the Commander-in-Chief, Horatio Seymour, to be ready to go to Philadelphia at once, on short service.

The brigade drill for the 17th inst. is hereby countermanded. By order, General WM. HALL.

J. K. SMITH, Quartermaster.

The response of the Governor of New York was thus approved by the authorities at Washington:

WASHINGTON, *June 15th*, 1863.

GOVERNOR SEYMOUR: The President directs me to return his thanks, with those of the Department, for your prompt response. A strong movement of your city regiments to Philadelphia would be a very encouraging movement, and do great good in giving strength to that State.

EDWIN M. STANTON, Secretary of War.

The Governor of Pennsylvania, on the same day, issued the following proclamation:

The State of Pennsylvania is again threatened with invasion, and an army of rebels is approaching our borders. The President of the United States has issued his proclamation, calling upon the State for fifty thousand men. I now appeal to all the citizens of Pennsylvania, who love liberty and are mindful of the history and traditions of their Revolutionary fathers, and who feel that it is a sacred duty to guard and maintain the free institutions of our country, who hate treason and its abettors, and who are willing to defend their homes and firesides, and do invoke them to rise in their might and rush to the rescue in this hour of imminent peril. The issue is one of preservation or destruction. It involves considerations paramount to all matters of mere expediency, and all questions of local interest. All ties—social and political—all ties of a personal and partisan character, sink by comparison into insignificance. It is now to be determined by deeds, and not by words alone, who are for us and who are against us. That it is the purpose of the enemy to invade our borders with all the strength he can command, is now apparent. Our only defence rests upon the determined action of the citizens of our free commonwealth.

I therefore call upon the people of Pennsylvania, capable of bearing arms, to enroll themselves in military organizations, and to encourage all others to give aid and assistance to the efforts which will be put forth for the protection of the State and the salvation of our common country.

ANDREW J. CURTIN, Governor.

At the same time, he sent a message to the Governor of New Jersey, requesting the aid of troops from that State. The Secretary of War also sent a request to the Governor for troops. The Governor of New Jersey immediately issued the following call for men:

EXECUTIVE CHAMBER, TRENTON, N. J., *June* 16, 1863.

JERSEYMEN: The State of Pennsylvania is invaded. A hostile army is now occupying and despoiling the towns of our sister State. She appeals to New Jersey, through her Governor, to aid in driving back the invading army. Let us respond to this call upon our patriotic State with unprecedented zeal.

I therefore call upon the citizens of this State to meet and organize into companies, and report to the Adjutant-General of the State as soon as possible, to be organized into regiments as the militia of New Jersey, and press forward to the assistance of Pennsylvania in this emergency. The organization of these troops will be given in general orders as soon as practicable.

JOEL PARKER.

S. M. DICKINSON, Private Secretary.

On the 16th, the Governor of Maryland issued the following proclamation:

Whereas, the President of the United States, by his proclamation of the 15th instant, calling into the service of the Government the militia of several of the States now threatened with invasion by the insurgents in arms against the Union, has designated ten thousand men as the quota of Maryland, required for the special purpose of protecting her own soil, it becomes us to respond with the least possible delay earnestly and effectually to the call thus made upon us. The entire want of any efficient organization of the militia of the State makes it necessary to provide the required force either by volunteers or by draft. The term of their service will be six months, and the State will be credited under the recent enrolment act with the number thus furnished.

Whether we look to the purpose for which this force is required, to the success or efficiency of its operations, or to the probable movements of other States embraced in the same appeal, every consideration connected with the subject demands that the call should be met by an offer of volunteers. When our own territory is threatened by an invader, let it never be said that we lacked the spirit to meet the emergency or looked to others to provide for our defence.

Whilst, therefore, measures will immediately be taken to provide by draft from the recent enrolment whatever of the force now called for is not promptly furnished by volunteers, I would earnestly appeal to the patriotism and pride of every Marylander so to respond to the call now made upon them as to leave no necessity to raise a single company by any compulsory process.

The ten thousand men required of us will be organized into eight regiments of infantry, one regiment of cavalry, and two batteries of artillery, and though required to be of the maximum standard, they will be mustered into the service of the United States, armed and equipped, whenever they can muster the minimum number required in each.

The volunteer militia organizations now existing in the city of Baltimore and other parts of the State, are earnestly invited to call their members together and make their respective commands a nucleus for the formation of a complete regiment.

Whenever a battalion or company, or a majority of their respective members, shall make such offer of their services, they will report to Major Wharton, No. 65 Fayette street, who will designate a place of regimental rendezvous, and an effort will be made to obtain from the War Department permission to muster in the several companies, as soon as formed, without waiting for the complete regimental organization.

In witness whereof I have hereunto set my hand and affixed the great seal of the State, this 16th day of June, 1863. A. W. BRADFORD.

WM. B. HILL, Secretary of State.

The Governor of West Virginia issued the following order to commanding officers:

The commandants of regiments and companies of Virginia militia will immediately call their companies and regiments together, to be held in readiness to go to the field at an hour's warning, and will provide such means as shall be effectual in giving immediate notice to all. Arms and equipments will be furnished at the several places of rendezvous.

The enemies of our liberty and prosperity are again threatening our peaceful homes.

Citizen soldiers, stand by your firesides and defend them against the common foes of a free government.

Make every available spot a rifle pit from which to slay the enemy.

You know the roads and the passes. Show yourselves to be worthy of your sires, who gave you the inestimable blessings of freedom and independence.

F. H. PIERPOINT, Governor.

The Governor of Ohio made the following appeal to the citizens of the State:

STATE OF OHIO, EXECUTIVE DEPARTMENT,
COLUMBUS, O., *June 15th*, 1863.

TO THE PEOPLE OF OHIO.

Lee's rebel army is advancing in force upon Pennsylvania, Western Virginia, and the eastern portion of our own State. To meet this horde of rebels, the President of the United States has, by proclamation, called out one hundred thousand militia for the period of six months, unless sooner discharged. Of this force, thirty thousand are called from Ohio; and now, gallant men of Ohio, will you promptly respond to this necessary call, without hesitancy? I have assured the President that you would do so. Remember that our own sacred homes are threatened with pillage and destruction, and our wives and daughters with insult. To the rescue then at once, and thus save all that is dear to men. As we have but few, if any, regularly organized companies of volunteer militia, I can but invite and implore you to duty. The few companies which have been recently organized are requested to repair at once, with their entire force, to the camps hereinafter indicated. All others will go forward in squads and be organized into companies after their arrival in camp, for which purpose efficient officers will be designated. Railroad transportation has been duly provided, and every provision necessary for the comfort of the men after their arrival in camp. A reasonable allowance will be made to each volunteer for his subsistence when *en route* to the camp. The pay and allowance for clothing will be the same as that of the volunteer service. Should more respond than the Government requires, the surplus men will be returned to their homes free of all expense to themselves, with the regular pay for the period necessarily absent.

The military committees of the several counties are especially requested to exert themselves in securing a prompt response to this call. The troops will all be organized into regiments and well armed before being ordered into service.

And now, fellow citizens of the State, in the name and behalf of the best Government on earth, let me implore you to lay aside all other duties and obligations, and come forward promptly and cheerfully for the preservation of all that is dear to us. You will thus secure the gratitude of your children's children, and the smiles and blessings of Heaven.

DAVID TOD, Governor.

The utmost activity now prevailed to hasten forward troops to the centre of Pennsylvania. In New York, the Major-General of the First Division of State militia issued the following order:

HEADQUARTERS FIRST DIVISION N. Y. S. M.,
NEW YORK, *June 16th*, 1863.

The regiments of this division are directed to proceed forthwith to Harrisburg, in Pennsylvania, to assist in repelling the invasion of that State.

The United States Quartermaster and Commissary will furnish transportation and subsistence upon the requisition of regimental quartermasters, countersigned by the colonels.

The term of service will not exceed thirty days.

Commandants of brigades and regiments will report to the Major-General the numbers ready for transportation, and will receive directions as to the route and time of embarkation.

Each man will provide himself with two days' cooked provisions.

By order of Major-Gen. CHAS. W. SANFORD.
J. H. WILCOX, Division Inspector.

This division consisted of four brigades. The first brigade, under Gen. C. B. Spicer, was composed of the 1st, 2d, 3d, 71st, and 73d regiments. The second brigade, under Gen. Chas. Yates, was composed of the 4th, 5th, 6th, and 12th regiments. The third brigade, under Gen. Hall, was composed of the 7th, 8th, 37th, and 55th regiments. The fourth brigade, under Gen. Ewen, was composed of the 11th, 22d, and 69th regiments.

On that day there went forward the 7th regiment, 650 men. On the 18th, the 8th, 371 men; 11th, 762 men; 23d, 626 men, and 71st, 737 men. On the 19th, the 5th, 828 men; 12th, 684 men; 22d, 568 men; 37th, 693 men; 65th, 555 men, and 74th, 504 men. On the 20th, the 4th, 560 men; 13th, 496 men; 28th, 484 men; 56th, 476 men. On the 22d, the 6th, 656 men; 52d, 351 men; 69th, 600 men. On the 23d, the 67th, 400 men. On the 24th, the 55th, 350 men; 68th, 400 men. On the 26th, the 47th, 400 men. On the 27th, the 21st, 600 men. On July 3d, the 17th, 400 men; 18th, 400 men; 84th, 480 men. The total number sent between the 15th of June and the 3d of July was 13,971 men. During the same time scattered detachments of volunteers in the State to the number of 1,827 men were organized and equipped and ordered to Harrisburg.

On the 19th of June the following despatch was sent to the Adjutant-General of the State:

WAR DEPARTMENT, WASHINGTON CITY,
June 19th, 1863.

To Adjutant-General Sprague:

The President directs me to return his thanks to His Excellency Gov. Seymour, and his staff, for their energetic and prompt action. Whether any further force is likely to be required will be communicated to you to-morrow, by which time it is expected the movements of the enemy will be more fully developed.

(Signed) EDWIN M. STANTON,
Secretary of War.

Again, on the 27th, the following despatch was sent to the governor of the State by the Secretary of War:

WAR DEPARTMENT, WASHINGTON CITY, *June* 27, 1863.

DEAR SIR: I cannot forbear expressing to you the deep obligation I feel for the prompt and cordial support you have given the Government in the present emergency. The energy and patriotism you have exhibited I may be permitted personally and officially to acknowledge, without arrogating any personal claims on my part, to such service, or any service whatever.

I shall be happy always to be esteemed your friend,
EDWIN M. STANTON.

His Excellency HORATIO SEYMOUR.

The Governor of New Jersey, in answer to the request of the Governor of Pennsylvania, for the further services of the nine months' men, then returning from the war, immediately tendered the services of the 22d regiment, which had not been disbanded. It left for Harrisburg on the 17th. Other regiments of nine months' volunteers, then returned, tendered their services. By the 20th more than two thousand men had gone forward. Some single companies proceeded to Harrisburg. The entire State sent forward several thousand men. On the 22d the Governor ordered the troops to return home, as the emergency had apparently passed.

In Pennsylvania, the first efforts of the Governor were directed to obtain troops from Washington. These failed entirely. On the 16th he issued the following appeal to the people of Philadelphia:

To the People of Philadelphia:

For nearly a week past it has been publicly known that the rebels in force were about to enter Pennsylvania. On the 12th instant, an urgent call was made on the people to raise Department Army Corps for the defence of the State. Yesterday, under the proclamation of the President, the militia was called out. To-day a new and pressing exhortation has been given to furnish men, but Philadelphia has not responded.

Meanwhile the enemy is six miles this side of Chambersburg and advancing rapidly.

Our capital is threatened, and we may be disgraced by its fall, while the men who should be driving these outlaws from our soil are grumbling about the possible term of service for six months. It was never intended to keep them beyond the continuance of the emergency.

You all know this by what happened when the militia was called out last autumn. You then trusted your Government, and were not deceived. Trust to it again now. I will accept men without reference to the six months. If you do not wish to bear the ignominy of shirking from the defence of your State, come forward at once. Close your places of business and apply your hearts to the work. Come in such organizations as you can form. Gen. Couch has appointed Lieut.-Col. Ruff to superintend your organization. Report to him immediately. (Signed) A. G. CURTIN,
Governor.

At the same time the Governor gave notice that he would receive men without the requirement of six months' service, and arrangements were made with the railroads to furnish transportation to Harrisburg upon application of the officers of militia companies. On the 16th, Lancaster sent five hundred men to Harrisburg, and Reading a regiment. The militia at Harrisburg were reorganized and armed. On the 17th thousands of men reached Harrisburg from different parts of the State. The following list of some of the organizations shows that the interior of the State was aroused to action:

One hundred and twenty-seventh regiment (Col. Jennings), Harrisburg, 1,000 men.
First Pennsylvania Militia (Col. R. A. Lamberton), Harrisburg, 1,000.
Capt. William H. Connechan, Bradford, 105 men.
Capt. J. M. Gregory, Lehigh, 70 men.
Capt. J. H. Holion, Lehigh, 70 men.
Capt. J. M. Broomall, Delaware, 71 men.
Capt. G. T. Waters, Northampton, 53 men.
Capt. William R. Ash, Chester, 100 men.
Capt. J. G. Eicholtz, Chester, 53 men.
Capt. J. B. Davis, Northumberland, 50 men.
Capt. John McClay, Northumberland, 71 men.
Capt. William Stoel, Chester 50 men.
Capt. W. McVeigh, Chester, 60 men.
Capt. W. M. Hinkson, Chester, 45 men.
Capt. W. C. Dickey, Chester, 48 men.
Capt. E. F. James, Chester, 63 men.
Capt. George B. Thomas, Chester, 57 men.
Capt. Charles Roberts, Chester, 40 men.
Capt. R. D. Townsend, Chester, 16 men.
Capt. A. Ricketts, Luzerne, 56 men.
Capt. R. F. Clark, Columbia, 90 men.
Capt. J. B. Grantiers, Bradford, 71 men.
Capt. J. D. Jenkins, Chester, 82 men.
Capt. James Dickson, Luzerne, 40 men.
Capt. H. Bloss, Northampton, 35 men.
Capt. J. F. Ramsey, Montour, 70 men.
Capt. D. A. Smith, Schuylkill, 105 men.
Capt. T. J. Sleppy, Columbia, 31 men.
Capt. Wm. B. Mann, Philadelphia, 100 men.
Spencer Miller's battery.

By the 20th about twenty-five thousand citizens of Pennsylvania had taken the field. The imperfection of the militia law of the State was such that no regimental or brigade organizations were in existence. A few days later, as the army of Gen. Lee entered the State, and the serious character of the invasion became apparent, the Governor issued the following address:

Pennsylvanians! In the name and by the authority of the Commonwealth of Pennsylvania, Andrew G. Curtin, Governor of the said Commonwealth:

A PROCLAMATION.

The enemy is advancing in force into Pennsylvania. He has a strong column within twenty-three miles of Harrisburg, and other columns are moving by Fulton and Adams counties, and it can no longer be doubted that a formidable invasion of our State is in actual progress.

The calls already made for volunteer militia in the exigency, have not been met as fully as the crisis requires.

I therefore now issue this my proclamation, calling for sixty thousand men, to come promptly forward to defend the State. They will be mustered into the service of the State for a period of ninety days, but will be required to serve only so much of the period of muster as the safety of our people and the honor of our State may require. They will rendezvous at points to be designated in the general order to be issued this day by the Adjutant-General of Pennsylvania, which order will also set forth the details of the arrangements for organization, clothing, subsistence, equipments, and supplies.

I will not insult you by inflammatory appeals. A people who want the heart to defend their soil, their families, and their firesides, are not worthy to be counted men. Heed not the counsels of evil-disposed persons, if such there be in your midst. Show yourselves what you are—a free, loyal, spirited, brave, vigorous race. Do not undergo the disgrace of leaving your defence mainly to the citizens of other States. In defending the soil of Pennsylvania we are contributing to the support of our National Government and vindicating our fidelity to the national cause. Pennsylvania has always, heretofore, responded promptly to all the calls made by the Federal Government, and I appeal to you, now, not to be unmindful that the foe that strikes at our State, strikes through our desolation at the life of the republic.

Our people are plundered and driven from their homes solely because of their loyalty and fidelity to our free institutions.

People of Pennsylvania, I owe to you all my faculties, my labors, my life. You owe to your country your prompt and zealous services and efforts. The time has now come when we must all stand or fall together in the defence of our State, and in the support of our Government. Let us so discharge our duty that posterity shall not blush for us.

Come heartily and cheerfully to the rescue of our noble commonwealth. Maintain now your honor and freedom.

Given under my hand and the great seal of the State, at Harrisburg, this the 26th day of June, in the year of our Lord one thousand eight hundred and sixty-three, and of the Commonwealth the eighty-seventh.

By the Governor, A. G. CURTIN.

ELI SLIFER, Secretary of the Commonwealth.

In Maryland, on the 16th, various uniformed organizations of Baltimore tendered their services to the Governor for six months. Vigorous efforts were made to enlist recruits under the call of the President, with small success. The troops, however, which could be raised were retained for the defence of Baltimore.

From Delaware, two regiments, the 5th and 6th, numbering 1,919 men, raised for State defence, were sent into Maryland, and placed as guards of the railroads.

From West Virginia no troops came forward at this time.

Offers of troops for the emergency were made by the Governors of several States to the President. But their distance from the scene of operations, or the impression that the force at hand was sufficient, prevented the acceptance of them.

The call of the President for one hundred thousand men served to authorize the reception of troops for the emergency, which could be put into the field at once, but there was not sufficient time to create new organizations, or to fill up regiments partly organized.

Meantime the construction of defensive works was immediately commenced at Harrisburg, which was supposed to be the first point of attack. The records of the State and the specie in the banks were removed to places of security.

The scenes in that capital, on the 16th, were thus described by a spectator:

The morning broke upon a populace all astir, who had been called out of bed by the "beat of the alarming drum," the blast of the bugle, and the clanging of bells. The streets were lively with men, who were either returning from a night's work on the fortifications, or going over to relieve those who were toiling there. As the sun rose higher the excitement gathered head. All along the streets were omnibuses, wagons, and wheelbarrows, taking in trunks and valuables, and rushing them down to the depot, to be shipped out of rebel range. The stores, the female seminaries, and almost every private residence, were busy all of the forenoon in swelling the mountain of freight that lay at the depot. Every horse was impressed into service, and every porter groaned beneath his weight of responsibilities.

The scene at noon at the depots was indescribable, if not disgraceful. A sweltering mass of humanity thronged the platform, all furious to escape from the doomed city.

At the bridge and across the river the scene was equally exciting. All through the day a steady stream of people on foot and in wagons, young and old, black and white, was pouring across it from the Cumberland valley, bearing with them their household gods and all manner of goods and stock. Endless trains, laden with flour, grain, and merchandise, hourly emerged from the valley, and thundered across the bridge and through the city. Miles of retreating baggage wagons, filled with calves and sheep tied together, and great old-fashioned furnace wagons, loaded with tons of trunks and boxes, defiled in continuous procession down the pike and across the river, raising a dust that marked the outline of the road as far as the eye could see.

The proceedings at Pittsburg, for the defence of that city, were thus described on Friday, the 19th:

Work on the city defences is still progressing vigorously, and some of the more important works are now ready to receive the guns. The number of men employed on the fortifications yesterday was four thousand six hundred and five. The works are on Herron's Hill, on Harrison's Hill, on Mount Washington, on Squirrel Hill, and on Negley's Hill. There are upward of five thousand men in the trenches to-day, and with such a large working force it cannot take many days to finish the works now in hand. Gen. Bernard, with a competent staff of engineers, was engaged in laying out new works yesterday on the outer side of the Alleghany, so as to render the city secure against an advance from that direction. Works have also been laid out near Turtle creek and other important points.

The activity in Baltimore to prepare for defence is thus reported:

The work of erecting barricades progressed rapidly on Friday and Saturday, and on Sunday morning the entire circle of the city was completed and ready for military occupation at any moment that the scouts should announce the approach of the enemy. The erection of lines of intrenchments and fortifications on all the approaches to the city have also progressed rapidly. On Saturday about one thousand colored men were gathered by the police from different sections of the city, causing much excitement among that portion of our population as they were marched out to the different locations for the defensive works. At night another force was secured to relieve those who had been at work throughout the day, and another relief gang was provided on Sunday morning and evening, so that rapid progress has been made, and the works are now ready for immediate use.

Meanwhile the movements of Gen. Lee upon the headwaters of the Rappahannock had been made in such force as to lay Gen. Hooker under the necessity of hastily breaking up his camp at Falmouth, and taking new positions to meet this demonstration. On Saturday, the 13th, his army began to move from Falmouth, and during Sunday the stores were removed from Aquia Creek to Alexandria by twenty-six steamers, employed for that purpose. The storehouses and railroad buildings were not destroyed at that time, as the gunboats commanded the place. On the 21st, a small party of the enemy burned the quartermaster's buildings and the wharf. The buildings and wharf known as Urba Switch were not burned.

On Sunday morning the force on the Fredericksburg side recrossed, and on that day the last of Gen. Hooker's army left Falmouth. The corps of Gens. Longstreet and Ewell, of the Confederate army, passed through Culpepper just one week previous, and the latter marched into the Shenandoah valley against Winchester, &c.

The march of Gen. Hooker's army was rapid, and at times disorderly. Bridges broke down beneath the teams; droves of horses became frightened, and rushed through the column like a tornado; and the men, choked with dust, straggled into the fields in search of water and rest under the inviting shadows of the trees. On Sunday night the troops encamped at Dumfries, which is about midway between Falmouth and Fairfax. The design of Gen. Lee in massing his troops at Culpepper, to fall upon the right of Gen. Hooker, and intercept his communications by land with Washington, was thus defeated. A few guns were heard in the direction of Thoroughfare Gap; but with this exception everything seemed quiet along the lines. On Monday the army advanced to the neighborhood of the Bull Run battle field. The third corps reached Manassas Junction in the morning; the first and eleventh arrived at Centreville; and the second, fifth, sixth, and twelfth corps came up at night. Thus the whole country south of the Occoquan was left to the enemy. During the march, the cavalry acted on the flanks, and rendered great service in making reconnoissances. Gen. Gregg and his division operated in the neighborhood of Warrenton and White Sulphur Springs. Gen. Duffie's division, previously Gen. Averill's, moved to the base of the Blue Ridge, near Ashby's Gap. Gen. Buford, with the regulars, occupied Thoroughfare Gap, preventing an approach of the enemy through that passage. Col. Tyler, temporarily in command of Gen. Wyndham's brigade, guarded the Orange and Alexandria railroad. The defence of Washington had been the object of Gen. Hooker's movements thus far, and he occupied the position which he considered to be best to defeat any designs of the enemy upon that city. It remained therefore for Gen. Lee to attack Gen. Hooker in the old intrenchments before Washington or to move into Maryland.

On Wednesday, the 18th, a detachment of cavalry, consisting of the 2d and 4th New York, 6th Ohio, 1st Massachusetts, under command of Col. Kilpatrick, and the 1st Maine of Gen. Gregg's brigade, encountered a body of Confederate cavalry, under Col. Rosser. Col. Kilpatrick was leading the advance of the Federal cavalry, moving from Fairfax Court House to Aldie. The enemy's force, consisting of cavalry and mounted infantry, coming from the direction of Snicker's Gap, reached Aldie two hours in advance of the Federal force, and, learning of the approach of the latter, posted themselves in commanding positions. Col. Kilpatrick charged upon them and drove them through the town, beyond which a stand was made, at a point where a Confederate battery of four guns was posted in the road to Ashby's Gap. The enemy occupied the wooded hills and stone walls toward Snicker's Gap. Here a desperate contest ensued for three hours, during which repeated charges were made on each side. The arrival of the 1st Maine, Col. C. S. Douty, gave such strength to Col. Kilpatrick as caused the enemy to retire. During the retreat toward Ashby's Gap, they were attacked near Middleburg by the 1st Rhode Island, Col. Duffie, which had come up through Thoroughfare Gap. The loss was severe on both sides. Several prisoners were taken by Col. Kilpatrick. This force defeated was the advance of a larger force of Gen. Stuart, who was moving to the right and rear of Gen. Hooker.

On Saturday, the 21st, another cavalry contest took place, which was thus reported by Gen. Pleasanton, who commanded the Federal force:

HEADQUARTERS CAVALRY CORPS,
CAMP NEAR UPPERVILLE, 5.30 P. M., *June 21st.*

Brig.-Gen. S. Williams:

GENERAL: I moved with my command this morning to Middleburg, and attacked the cavalry force of the rebels under Stuart, and steadily drove him all day, inflicting a heavy loss at every step.

I drove him through Upperville into Ashby's Gap. We took two pieces of artillery, one being a Blakely gun, and three caissons, besides blowing up one; also, upward of sixty prisoners, and more are coming in; a lieutenant-colonel, major, and five other officers; besides a wounded colonel, and a large number of wounded rebels left in the town of Upperville. They left their dead and wounded upon the field; of the former I saw upward of twenty. We also took a large number of carbines, pistols, and sabres. In fact it was the most disastrous day to the rebel cavalry. Our loss has been very small both in men and horses. I never saw the troops behave better or under more difficult circumstances. Very heavy charges were made, and the sabre used freely, but always with great advantage to us. A. PLEASANTON, Brig.-Gen.

On Monday, June 15th, the day on which Gen. Hooker's army reached the neighborhood of Bull Run, Gen. Milroy retreated from Winchester and Gen. Tyler from Martinsburg, as above stated. It would have been dangerous for Gen. Lee to have attacked Gen. Hooker in the advantageous position which he now held. Gen. Lee reports as follows:

The whole army of Gen. Hooker withdrew from the line of the Rappahannock, pursuing the roads near the Potomac, and no favorable opportunity was offered for attack. It seemed to be the purpose of Gen. Hooker to take a position which would enable him to cover the approaches to Washington City. With a view to draw him farther from his base, and at the same time to cover the march of A. P. Hill, who, in accordance with instructions, left Fredericksburg for the valley as soon as the enemy withdrew from his front, Longstreet moved from Culpepper Court House on the 15th, and, advancing along the east side of the Blue Ridge, occupied Ashby's and Snicker's Gaps. His force had been augmented while at Culpepper by Gen. Pickett, with three brigades of his division.

The cavalry, under Gen. Stuart, was thrown out in front of Longstreet to watch the enemy, now reported to be moving into Loudon. On the 19th his cavalry encountered two brigades of ours, under Gen. Stuart, near Aldie, and was driven back with loss. The next day the engagement was renewed, the Federal cavalry being strongly supported by infantry, and Gen. Stuart was in turn compelled to retire.

The enemy advanced as far as Upperville, and then fell back.

The attention of Gen. Hooker was so occupied by the attempts to seize Thoroughfare Gap, Aldie, and portions of the Orange and Alexandria railroad, as to make it appear to be the intention of Gen. Lee to move upon the Federal army from these points. So skilfully was this done that the impression prevailed in the North that the blow would be struck at Gen. Hooker's army in its position, and that the emergency in Pennsylvania had passed away. Thus, on this ground, the Governor of New Jersey considered it safe to recall the troops from Pennsylvania. Meanwhile, Gen. Lee was gathering the fruits of the surrender of Winchester, and preparing to move his army across the Potomac. The demonstrations of Gen. Ewell in Pennsylvania having failed to cause the army of Gen. Hooker to leave Virginia, and as it did not seem disposed to advance on Gen. Longstreet, the latter was withdrawn to the west side of the Shenandoah. At the same time the progress of Gen. Ewell rendered it necessary that Gen. Lee should be within supporting distance. As soon therefore as the fords of the Potomac between Harper's Ferry and Williamsport were well seized by his advance, his main body began to move. This was as early as Sunday, the 21st—the day of Gen. Pleasanton's cavalry skirmish. On that day, Gen. Lee issued the following order to his army:

HEADQUARTERS ARMY NORTHERN VIRGINIA, *June 21st*, 1863.

While in the enemy's country, the following regulations for procuring supplies will be strictly observed, and any violation of them promptly and rigorously punished:

I. No private property shall be injured or destroyed by any person belonging to or connected with the army, or taken, except by the officers hereinafter designated.

II. The chiefs of the commissary, quartermaster, ordnance, and medical departments of the army will make requisitions upon the local authorities or inhabitants for the necessary supplies for their respective departments, designating the places and times of delivery. All persons complying with such requisitions will be paid the market price for the articles furnished, if they so desire, and the officer making such payment shall take duplicate receipts for the same, specifying the name of the person paid, and the quantity, kind, and price of the property, one of which receipts shall be at once forwarded to the chief of the department to which such officer is attached.

III. Should the authorities or inhabitants neglect or refuse to comply with such requisitions, the supplies required shall be taken from the nearest inhabitants so refusing, by the order and under the direction of the respective chiefs of the departments named.

IV. When any command is detached from the main body, the chiefs of the several departments of such command will procure supplies for the same, and such other stores as they may be ordered to provide, in the manner and subject to the provisions herein prescribed, reporting their action to the heads of their respective departments, to which they will forward duplicates of all vouchers given or received.

V. All persons who shall decline to receive payment for property furnished on requisitions, and all from whom it shall be necessary to take stores or supplies, shall be furnished by the officer receiving or taking the same with a receipt specifying the kind and quantity of the property received or taken, as the case may be, the name of the person from whom it was received or taken, the command for the use of which it was received or taken, and the market price. A duplicate of said receipt shall be at once forwarded to the chief of the department to which the officer by whom it is executed is attached.

VI. If any person shall remove or conceal property necessary for the use of the army, or attempt to do so, the officers hereinbefore mentioned will cause such property, and all other property belonging to such person, that may be required by the army, to be seized, and the officer seizing the same will forthwith report to the chief of his department the kind, quantity, and market price of the property so seized, and the name of the owner.

By command of Gen. R. E. LEE.
R. H. CHILTON, A. A. and I. G.,
Lieut.-Gen. R. S. EWELL, Com'g 2d Army Corps.

The following correspondence, which was intercepted by Gen. Hooker, shows the general plans of Lee at this time:

ADJUTANT-GENERAL'S OFFICE, RICHMOND, *June 28th*, 1863.

Gen. R. E. Lee, commanding Army Northern Virginia, Winchester, Va.:

GENERAL: While with the President last evening, I received your letter of the 23d instant. After reading it to the President, he was embarrassed to understand that part of it which refers to the plan of assembling an army at Culpepper Court House, under Gen. Beauregard. This is the first intimation that he has had that such a plan was ever in contemplation, and, taking all things into consideration, he cannot see how it can by any possibility be carried into effect.

You will doubtless learn, before this reaches you, that the enemy has again assembled in force on the peninsula, estimated between 20,000 and 30,000 men, from 6,000 to 10,000 of whom are reported to be in the vicinity of White House, and the remainder at Yorktown. It is impossible to say whether the estimated number is correct, as the several accounts vary and are not deemed altogether trustworthy; but the estimate, making due allowance for errors, is quite near enough to satisfy the most incredulous that he is in this vicinity in sufficient force, in cavalry, artillery, and infantry, to do much harm, whether his purpose be to make a demonstration on Richmond, or to confine himself to raids in breaking your communications and devastating the country. His efforts in the last case may prove more successful than in the first, if we may judge by what took place at Hanover only two days ago, when about 1,000 or 1,200 of his cavalry suddenly appeared there, and did some execution in breaking the railroad and burning a bridge, some buildings, public stores, &c. It is important that this raid took place only about two days after Gen. Corse's brigade had left there for Gordonsville. Had it remained at Hanover Junction, it is reasonable to suppose that most of the enemy's cavalry would have been either destroyed or captured, and the property saved from injury. Every effort is being made here to be prepared for the enemy at all points, but we must look chiefly to the protection of the capital. In doing this we may be obliged to hazard some other points. You can easily estimate our strength, and I suggest for your consideration whether, in this state of things, you might not be able to spare a portion of your force to protect your line of communication against attempted raids by the enemy.

Very respectfully, your obedient servant,
S. COOPER, Adjutant-General.

LETTER FROM JEFF. DAVIS.

RICHMOND, *June 28th*, 1863.

GENERAL: Yours of the 23d I received this evening, I hasten to reply to the point presented in relation to the forces on the coasts of South Carolina and Georgia. The hopes indulged as to our operations at the time which would intervene between the discharge of the enemy's trained troops and the substitution of them by others have been disappointed by the very error against which it was sought by warning to guard. Grant reached the river, got reënforcements, made intrenchments, and Gen. Johnston continues to call for reënforcements, though his first requisition was more than filled by withdrawing troops from Gens. Beauregard and Bragg. Gen. Bragg is threatened with attack, has fallen back to his intrenched position at Tullahoma, and called on Buckner for aid.

Gen. Beauregard says that no troops have been withdrawn by the enemy from his front since those returned to Newbern, and that his whole force is necessary to cover his line. This being in answer to a proposition to follow a movement of the enemy, said to be to the west, with all his disposable force, pointing him at the same time to the vital importance of holding the Mississippi, and communicating the fear that Vicksburg would fall unless Johnston was strongly and promptly reënforced. D. H. Hill has a small force, part of which has been brought here. Clingman's brigade is near Wilmington, Colquith's at Kingston, Martin's nominal, on the railroad at Weldon, and C. Cook's, Ransom's, and Jenkins's have been brought here; the two last temporarily from the defence of Petersburg and the country thereabout.

Wise's brigade is, as you left it, engaged in the defence of Richmond, and serving in the country to the east of the city. The enemy have been reported in large force at the White House, with indications of an advance on Richmond. We are organizing companies for home duties, and the spirit of resistance is increasing. Corse's brigade, in accordance with your orders, has been left at Hanover Junction. All the artillery, I am informed, was taken away, and the single regiment of infantry, which constituted the guard for the bridges, proved unequal to the duty, as you have no doubt learned. Reënforcements were ordered to go up, but some delay occurred, and they arrived too late to save the bridge or the brave guard which had unsuccessfully defended it. The Yankees, reported to be three regiments of cavalry, returned from the Central road in the direction of Hanover (old town), and nothing has been heard of them since.

It was stated that Gen. H. F. Lee was captured at the house of Mr. Wickham, but I trust it will prove to be one of the many startling rumors which the newsmongers invent. The advance of your army increases our want of cavalry on the north and east of the city; but except one regiment from North Carolina, I do not know of any which we can expect soon to be available to us. In yours of the 20th you say: "If any of the brigades I have left behind for the protection of Richmond can, in your opinion, be spared, I should like them to be sent to me." It has been an effort with me to answer the clamor to have troops stopped or recalled to protect the city and the railroad communications with your army. Corse's brigade has gone, and Wise's is the only other left by you. Cook's was in North Carolina, and Davis's brigade was sent to complete Heth's division in the place of Cook's; and Ransom's and Jenkins's constitute the defences of the south side as far as Weldon, and are relied on for service elsewhere from Wilmington to Richmond.

Gen. Ely is positive that the enemy intend to attack here, and his scouts bring intelligence, which, if I believed it, would render me more anxious for the city than at any former time. I do not believe that the Yankees have such force as is stated, but they have enough to render it necessary to keep some troops within reach, and some at Petersburg, at least until Suffolk is truly evacuated. Do not understand me as balancing accounts in the matter of brigades. I only repeat that I have not any to send you, and enough to form an army to threaten, if not capture Washington, as soon as it is uncovered by Hooker's army. My purpose was to show you that the force here and in North Carolina is very small, and I may add that the brigades are claimed as properly of their command. Our information as to the enemy's intentions may be more full and trustworthy hereafter. It is now materially greater than when you were here.

Very respectfully and truly yours,

JEFF. DAVIS.

The advance of the Confederate army, which crossed the Potomac, was the corps of Gen. Ewell. It passed from Williamsport to Hagerstown, which was still held by Col. Jenkins, and at noon, on the 22d, entered Greencastle, Penn., which is on the railroad from Hagerstown to Chambersburg. The distances on this line are as follows: from Hagerstown to Morganstown, 4 miles; to the State line, 5 miles; to Greencastle, 11 miles; to Marion, 16 miles; to Chambersburg, 22 miles. On the 23d, Chambersburg was reoccupied by the Confederate force under Gen. Ewell. Gen. Knipe, who was in command there, as the outpost of the Federal forces under Gen. Couch, collected in the valley, fell back in the direction of Carlisle to the main body.

In order to retain the Federal army on the east side of the mountains after it should enter Maryland, and thus leave open the Confederate communications with the Potomac through Hagerstown and Williamsport, Gen. Lee ordered Gen. Ewell to send a division eastward from Chambersburg to cross the South Mountains.

On the 24th, a detachment from Gen. Ewell's force advanced within twelve miles of Carlisle, on the railroad from Chambersburg to Harrisburg. The distances on that line were as follows: from Chambersburg to Scotland, 5 miles; to Shippensburg, 11 miles; to Oakville, 18 miles; to Carlisle, 34 miles; to Mechanicsburg, 44 miles; to Harrisburg, 52 miles. On the 24th, Gen. Lee crossed the Potomac into Maryland, in the vicinity of Shepherdstown. At the same time, the main body of his army crossed at the fords at Shepherdstown and Williamsport. The movement continued up the Cumberland valley, on the west side of the Catoctin Mountains. The advance was made in two divisions, one by way of the Harrisburg and Chambersburg Railroad toward Harrisburg, and the other from Gettysburg eastward to the Northern Central Railroad from Baltimore to Harrisburg, and thence to York and Lancaster, in Pennsylvania.

On Saturday the 27th, Carlisle, on one line of advance, was occupied at noon, and the advance continued to Kingston, 13 miles from Harrisburg. On the other line of advance, Gettysburg was occupied by a force from Hagerstown on the 26th; and at noon on the 27th, the same force had reached the Northern Central Railroad, at a point between York and Hanover Junction. This was about fifty miles north of Baltimore, and thirty miles south of Harrisburg. The same evening, York was occupied without resistance, and several bridges on the Northern Central Railroad were destroyed. On the 28th, this advance continued to the Susquehanna, opposite Columbia. The bridge across the river here consisted of twenty-eight spans, and was a mile and a quarter in length. It was burned by the order of the officer in command of the Federal force at Columbia—Col. Frick. The Confederate cavalry and artillery were close upon the structure when it was fired. On the same day, the advance from Carlisle approached within four miles of Harrisburg, where some skirmishing took place.

On the previous day, Gen. Lee, at Chambersburg, issued the following order to his army:

General Order No 27.

HEADQUARTERS ARMY OF NORTHERN VIRGINIA,
CHAMBERSBURG, PA., June 27th, 1863.

The Commanding General has observed, with marked satisfaction, the conduct of the troops on the march, and confidently anticipates results commensurate with the high spirit they have manifested. No troops could have displayed greater fortitude, or better performed the arduous marches of the past ten days. Their conduct in other respects has, with few exceptions, been in keeping with their character as soldiers, and entitles them to approbation and praise.

There have, however, been instances of forgetfulness, on the part of some, that they have in keeping the yet unsullied reputation of the army, and that the duties exacted of us by civilization and Christianity are not less obligatory in the country of the enemy than in our own.

The Commanding General considers that no greater disgrace could befall the army, and through it our whole people, than the perpetration of the barbarous outrages upon the innocent and defenceless, and the wanton destruction of private property, that have marked the course of the enemy in our own country. Such proceedings not only disgrace the perpetrators and all connected with them, but are subversive of the discipline and efficiency of the army, and destructive of the ends of our present movement. It must be remembered that we make war only upon armed men, and that we cannot take vengeance for the wrongs our people have suffered, without lowering ourselves in the eyes of all whose abhorrence has been excited by the atrocities of our enemy, and offending against Him to whom vengeance belongeth, without whose favor and support our efforts must all prove in vain.

The Commanding General therefore earnestly exhorts the troops to abstain with most scrupulous care from unnecessary or wanton injury to private property; and he enjoins upon all officers to arrest and bring to summary punishment all who shall in any way offend against the orders on this subject.

R. E. LEE, General.

On the 28th, the Confederate force at York made a demand on the authorities for $100,000 in United States Treasury notes, 200 barrels of flour, 40,000 pounds of fresh beef, 30,000 bushels of corn, 1,000 pairs of shoes, socks, &c. On that day, also, the enemy captured a train of one hundred and seventy-eight wagons and one thousand mules, between Rockville and Tenallytown, a few miles from Georgetown, D. C. Also a number of Federal officers were captured near Rockville, by a body of Confederate cavalry which had crossed the Potomac near Seneca, in the rear of Gen. Hooker's army; and at Edwards' Ferry, fifteen barges loaded with government stores were captured and burned by a body of Confederate cavalry. On the same day, this force of cavalry appeared at numerous points in Montgomery County, and seized horses. Some came as near to Washington as Silver Spring, on the Seventh-street road. These were portions of cavalry under Gen. Stuart. On the advance of Gen. Lee, Gen. Stuart was left to guard the passes of the mountains, and to observe the movements of the Federal army, with instructions to harass and impede as much as possible any attempt by it to cross the Potomac. With this view he followed its movements, and advanced as far east as Fairfax Court House. He then crossed the river at Seneca, and marched through Westminster to Carlisle. At this time the army of Gen. Lee was situated as follows: The main body, embracing the corps of Gens. Longstreet and Hill, were at and near Chambersburg, where Gen. Lee also was. The divisions of Gens. Rhodes and Johnson, of Gen. Ewell's corps, were in the vicinity of Carlisle and Harrisburg. The division of Gen. Early, of the same corps, was at York, where it was joined on the 27th by the brigade of Gen. Gordon. The cavalry, under Col. White, had advanced to the Susquehanna.

But the extreme point of the Confederate advance had been reached. On the 28th, orders were issued for both lines of advance of Gen. Ewell's corps to fall back on Gettysburg, to which point Gens. Longstreet and Hill were moving by the Chambersburg turnpike. The reason of this was the approach of the Army of the Potomac. Gen. Lee had made preparations to march upon Harrisburg, but on the night of the 27th information was received by him that the Federal army had crossed the Potomac and was advancing northward, and that the head of the column had reached South Mountain. As his communications with the Potomac were thus menaced, he resolved to prevent the further progress of the Federal army in that direction by concentrating his forces on the east side of the mountain.

CHAPTER XXXII.

Position of the Army of the Potomac—Gen. Hooker relieved by Gen. Meade—Concentration of the Enemy near Gettysburg—Opening of the Battle—The Battle—Retreat of Gen. Lee—Pursued by Gen. Meade—Coöperating Movements elsewhere—Advance of Gen. Rosecrans in Tennessee against Gen. Bragg—Raid of Gen. John Morgan in Ohio.

ON the 22d, the army of Gen. Hooker occupied the line of the Potomac on the Virginia side of the river, up to and beyond Leesburg. At the same time it held all the gaps of the Bull Run range. By Saturday, the 27th, they had advanced, and lay at and in the vicinity of Frederick, Maryland. On that day, an order was issued by the War Department to Gen. Hooker, to transfer the command of the army to Maj.-Gen. Meade, who commanded the Fifth corps, and to report himself at Baltimore. On the next day, Gen. Hooker issued the following order:

HEADQUARTERS ARMY OF THE POTOMAC,
FREDERICK, MD., *June 28th*, 1863.

In conformity with the orders of the War Department, dated June 27th, 1863, I relinquish the command of the Army of the Potomac. It is transferred to Maj.-Gen. George G. Meade, a brave and accomplished officer, who has nobly earned the confidence and esteem of the army on many a well-fought field. Impressed with the belief that my usefulness as the commander of the Army of the Potomac is impaired, I part from it, yet not without the deepest emotion. The sorrow of parting with the comrades of so many battles is relieved by the conviction that the courage and devotion of this army will never cease nor fail; that it will yield to my successor, as it has to me, a willing and hearty support. With the earnest prayer that the triumph of its arms may bring successes worthy of it and the nation, I bid it farewell.

JOSEPH HOOKER, Maj.-Gen.

This order was followed by the subjoined address from Gen. Meade:

HEADQUARTERS ARMY OF THE POTOMAC,
June 28th, 1863.

By direction of the President of the United States I hereby assume command of the Army of the Potomac. As a soldier, in obeying this order, an order totally unexpected and unsolicited, I have no promises or pledges to make. The country looks to this army to relieve it from the devastation and disgrace of a hostile invasion. Whatever fatigues and sacrifices we may be called upon to undergo, let us have in view constantly the magnitude of the interests involved, and let each man determine to do his duty, leaving to an all-controlling Providence the decision of the contest. It is with just diffidence that I relieve, in the command of this army, an eminent and accomplished soldier, whose name must ever appear conspicuous in the history of its achievements; but I rely upon the hearty support of my companions in arms to assist me in the discharge of the duties of the important trust which has been confided to me.

GEORGE G. MEADE, Maj.-Gen. Commanding.

This change was so entirely unexpected, both by the public generally and the army, that nothing could exceed the surprise which it occasioned. The reasons for the change have not yet been made known, except that Gen. Hooker was relieved at his own request. The impression upon the army was thus described:

The report of the change soon extended to the several corps, and their commanders hastened to bid farewell to the General. By three o'clock a large number of officers had assembled, and soon after Gen. Hooker appeared in the avenue before his tent. Some time was spent in social intercourse, and to the last all formalities were dispensed with. The parting was painful to every one, particularly to those who had become endeared to the General by old associations. Gen. Hooker was deeply grieved. He had been identified with the Army of the Potomac, he said, since its organization, and had hoped to continue with it to the end. It was the best army of the country, worthy of the confidence of the nation, and could not fail of success in the approaching struggle. He spoke of his successor as a glorious soldier, and urged all to give him their earnest support.

Gen. Meade was totally surprised by the order appointing him commander of the Army of the Potomac, and deeply felt the weight of responsibility resting upon him. His appointment gives universal satisfaction, and all express a determination to extend their heartiest coöperation.

An order for the movement of the army was issued on the same day by Gen. Meade. The sixth and eleventh corps, which were at Middletown, in the valley between the Catoctin and the Blue Ridge, were moved east to Frederick, and then directly up the Monocacy valley, on the west side of the stream, through Mechanicsburg and Emmitsburg, toward Gettysburg. The second and fifth corps crossed the Monocacy to the east, three miles above Frederick, and moved northeast through Union to Frizelburg, which is near the State line. The third and twelfth corps took the Middleburg road. The sixth corps crossed the Monocacy, east of Frederick, and moved to Westminster. These routes took the army into such a position that it could cover Baltimore, or cross the Susquehanna below Harrisburg, or prevent any movement of the Confederates toward Washington. On Tuesday forenoon, the first and eleventh corps were at Emmitsburg; the second and fifth at Frizelburg; the third and twelfth at Taneytown, and the sixth at Westminster. The Federal force at Harper's Ferry at this time was supposed to be about eleven thousand. It was incorrectly represented to Gen. Meade to be destitute of provisions, and that he must immediately supply it, or order the abandonment of the place. Accordingly, a few hours after he assumed the command, he assented to an order drawn up by an officer of Gen. Hooker's staff, directing Gen. French to send seven thousand men of the garrison to Frederick, and with the remainder, estimated at four thousand, to remove and escort the public property to Washington. This order was unknown in Washington till too late to be countermanded. It was not entirely executed when Gen. Meade ordered the reoccupation of that point.

At this time, Gen. Lee's forces had withdrawn from York and Carlisle, and from Chambersburg, and were concentrating on Gettysburg. The corps of Gens. Longstreet and Hill, forming the main army, were moving eastward, while Gen. Meade was moving northward. This movement would bring Gen. Lee on the flank of Gen. Meade's army. On Tuesday morning, Gen. Meade changed the line of march of all his corps, except the first and eleventh, toward Gettysburg. The first and eleventh were then moving in that direction. At the same time, Gen. Meade issued the following address to his army:

HEADQUARTERS ARMY OF THE POTOMAC,
June 30th, 1863.

The Commanding General requests that previous to the engagement soon expected with the enemy, corps and all other commanding officers address their troops, explaining to them the immense issues involved in the struggle. The enemy is now on our soil. The whole country looks anxiously to this army to deliver it from the presence of the foe. Our failure to do so will leave us no such welcome as the swelling of millions of hearts with pride and joy at our success would give to every soldier of the army. Homes, firesides, and domestic altars are involved. The army has fought well heretofore. It is believed that it will fight more desperately and bravely than ever, if it is addressed in fitting terms.

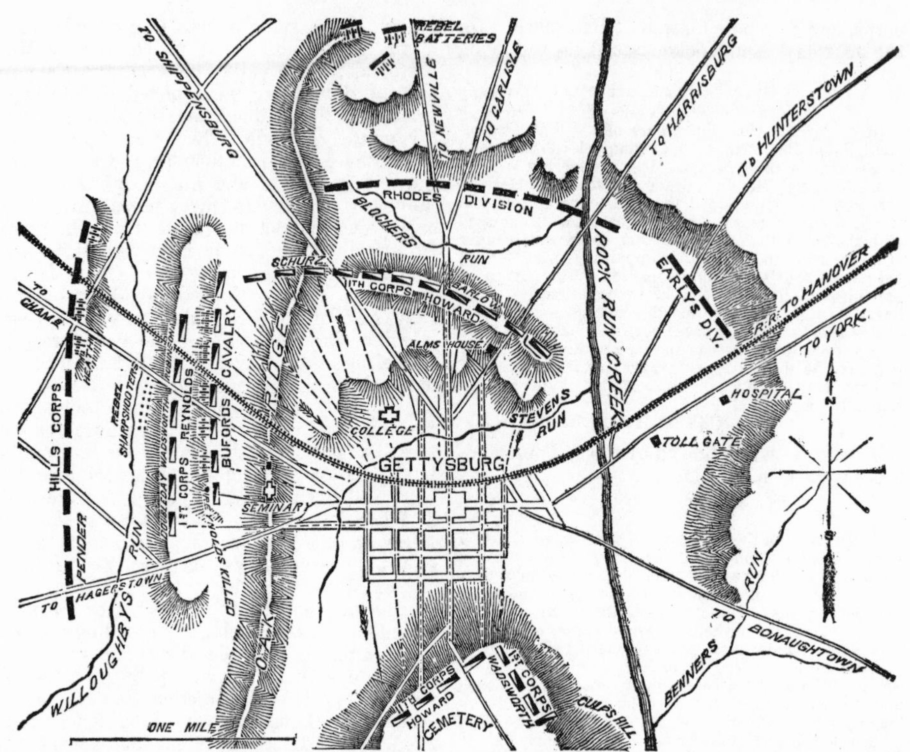

Corps and other commanders are authorized to order the instant death of any soldier who fails to do his duty at this hour.

By command of Major-Gen. MEADE.

S. WILLIAMS, Assistant Adjutant-Gen.

Gettysburg, whither both armies were moving, was not only the capital of the county in which it is located, but a central point to which many roads converged. The road from Westminster, by which the sixth corps was advancing, comes in on the southeast; that from Taneytown, by which the third and twelfth were advancing, comes in on the south, which was the route also of the second and fifth; that from Emmitsburg, by which the first and eleventh corps were advancing, comes in on the southwest; that from Chambersburg, by which the Confederate corps of Gens. Longstreet and Hill were advancing, comes in on the northwest; and those from Harrisburg and York, by which the corps of Gen. Ewell was advancing, come in on the northeast.

On Wednesday morning, Maj.-Gen. Reynolds, in command of the first corps, advanced on the Emmitsburg road from Marsh creek to Gettysburg, where he arrived about ten o'clock, and marched directly through the town. A body of the enemy, being the advance of Gen. Heth's division of Gen. Hill's corps, was discovered to be posted on the road that came in from Chambersburg on the northwest. They were driven back by Gen. Buford's cavalry. The division, coming up, drove back the cavalry. At this time the first corps appeared. The first division, under Gen. Wadsworth, was in the advance. The division of Gen. Doubleday followed and formed on the left, and that of Gen. Robinson on the right. The position occupied was a ridge northwest of the town, which sloped to the west, into a little open valley of ploughed fields and meadows. Beyond the valley is a ridge of higher land thickly wooded. The valley runs in a southwesterly direction. Across this valley the line of Gen. Reynolds advanced somewhat hastily, almost before it was well formed, and soon encountered a heavy force of the enemy's infantry, by which it was driven, but fell back in good order. The impetuosity of the enemy caused them to press the right centre too rashly, and, by a movement of the left centre upon the flank of the foe, a large number were taken prisoners. The advance of the enemy was broken soon after, and Gen. Reynolds prepared to go forward. His line advanced as before, and drove the enemy from the valley and over the ridge at the farther side, with a heavy loss by the severe fire of the foe. His line of skirmishers was now thrown out some distance from the hill, and Gen. Reynolds, upon going out to it to reconnoitre, was killed by a shot from the enemy.

The eleventh corps now arrived, and Gen. Howard assumed the command of the whole field, while Gen. Schurz took command of the eleventh corps. Gen. Doubleday now commanded the first corps.

It being reported that the enemy were now massing a force north of the town to attack the rear of the first corps, the first and third divisions of the eleventh corps were ordered across the rear of the first corps to take up a position on the right, and Gen. Steinwehr was stationed as a reserve on Cemetery Hill, immediately south of the town. This force of the enemy was the advance of Gens. Rhodes and Early's divisions falling back from the Susquehanna. At this time, about half past two P. M., the enemy advanced in force against the first corps, which slowly fell back to its original position, northwest of the town. Here it was somewhat reënforced and prepared to make a stand. The force of the enemy advanced across the open space in line of battle, while their batteries shelled the position of the first corps to cover the advance. At short range it met a fire so sharp and well served as to cause it to reel and fall back. The line was again formed and reënforced, and once more advanced, but with no better success. By this time the divisions of Rhodes and Early had come up from the east, and Pender's division of Gen. Hill's moved up on the right to the support of Gen. Heth. Another charge was now made by the whole force of the enemy. Their superior numbers enabled them to threaten both flanks of the Union force. The main effort was directed against the left, and, notwithstanding a brave resistance, such advantages were gained that the first corps was ordered back to the town. By this movement the left of the eleventh was uncovered, and a heavy advance completely on its right flank compelled it to retire. The enemy advanced and took possession of the town, while the two corps fell back and occupied the western slope of the hill south of the town, held by Gen. Steinwehr.

Gen. Lee says: "The attack was not pressed that afternoon, the enemy's force being unknown, and it being considered advisable to await the arrival of the rest of our troops. It had not been intended to fight a general battle at such a distance from our base, unless attacked by the enemy; but finding ourselves unexpectedly confronted by the Federal army, it became a matter of difficulty to withdraw through the mountains with our large trains. At the same time the country was unfavorable for collecting supplies while in the presence of the enemy's main body, as he was enabled to restrain our foraging parties by occupying the passes of the mountains with regular and local troops. A battle thus became, in a measure, unavoidable. Encouraged by the successful issue of the engagement of the first day, and in view of the valuable results that would ensue from the defeat of the army of Gen. Meade, it was thought advisable to renew the attack."

At dusk the third and twelfth corps arrived and took positions, the former on the ridge extending south and to the left of Cemetery Hill, and the latter on the same ridge as it curved to the right of the hill. At 11 P. M., Gen. Meade arrived and examined the position. He then posted the several corps in the following order: the twelfth, under Gen. Slocum, on the right; the eleventh, Gen. Howard, next; the first, Gen. Doubleday, the second, Gen. Hancock, the third, Gen. Sickles, in the centre; the fifth, Gen. Sykes, arrived the next morning, and was placed on the extreme left. The line stretched in a semicircle, having its convex centre toward Gettysburg, with the extreme toward the southwest and south. The heights on which the troops were posted sloped gently down from their front.

On the part of the enemy, Gen. Anderson's division of Gen. Hill's corps, and Gen. McLaws's division of Gen. Longstreet's corps arrived late in the evening within a mile or two of the town, and bivouacked for the night. Early on the next morning, Gen. Hood's division of Longstreet's corps arrived, and their line of battle was soon after formed.

The key of Gen. Meade's position was Cemetery Hill, a little distance south of the town, and on the northern slope of which the town itself is situated. It was so called because the burial place of the town was there. Its summit was east of the road which runs south to Taneytown. The ridge passed to the west of this road and ran south along its west side, and was occupied by the second, third, fifth, and sixth corps respectively, in line of battle. On the continuation of the ridge to the east and southeast was a part of the eleventh and the twelfth corps. On this part of the line the ridge was rocky and thickly wooded, and some defences were thrown up on Thursday morning by Gens. Geary and Williams. The ridge from Cemetery Hill directly south was open and clear, and the troops there faced to the west. The left flank of Gen. Meade rested upon a sharp, rugged, and almost perpendicular peak, covered with original forest growth. At the foot of the ridge on the west was a narrow valley between one and two miles in width, on the western side of which is another ridge, somewhat lower and running nearly parallel, and mostly covered with heavy timber. The line of battle of the enemy was formed on the slope of this ridge, with Gen. Ewell's corps on the left. Beginning at the town, Gen. Early's division was at the extreme right, then Gen. Rhodes's; on the right of his division was the left of Gen. Hill's corps, commencing with Gen. Heth's division, then Gens. Pender and Anderson's divisions. On the right of Gen. Anderson's division was the left of Gen. Longstreet's corps, Gen. McLaws's division being next to Gen. Anderson's, and Gen. Hood's on the extreme right of their line and opposite the extreme left of Gen. Meade. Neither the division of Gen. Ewell's corps nor that of Gen. Pickett of Longstreet's corps had at this time arrived. Gen. Pickett had been left at Chambersburg to protect the Confederate rear and escort their reserve train. Gen. Johnson had been operating near Harrisburg.

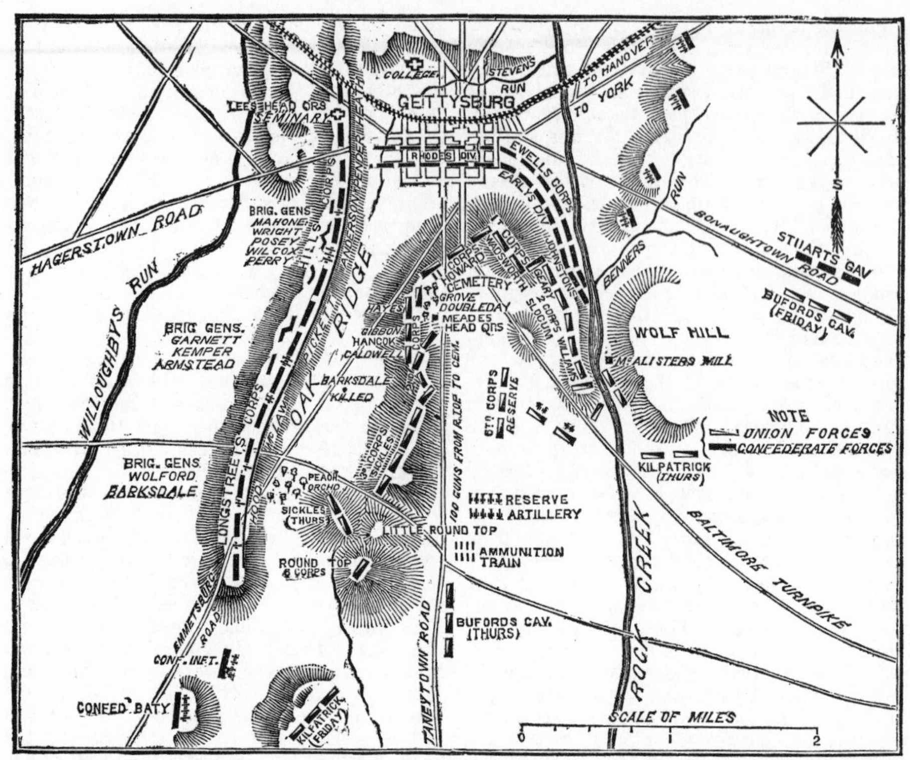

On the ridge occupied by Gen. Meade, a hundred guns were in position facing the enemy. The reserve artillery was in the rear, about equidistant from the extreme points of the line. The Union cavalry was east of the creek on the road to Baltimore. The artillery of the enemy in position was nearly one hundred and fifty guns.

During Thursday forenoon some skirmishing took place, but no movement of importance was made. On the Confederate side, about the middle of the afternoon, Gen. Lee issued orders for the commanders to prepare for a general attack upon the Federal centre and left. The movement was to be commenced by Gen. Longstreet and followed up on his left in quick succession by the respective divisions of Gen. Hill's corps. The movements in consequence of these orders were in progress when sharpshooters were sent out by Gen. Sickles, being one regiment, under command of Col. Berdan. They advanced in the woods about a mile beyond the Emmitsburg turnpike, reconnoitering, and reported that the enemy were moving large masses to turn the Union left. On this report Gen. Sickles moved up to a ridge in front, which he deemed a more commanding position to repel the attack. On this ridge, which he considered as commanding to a great extent the position he previously occupied, he formed his line. His right rested in the peach orchard, which is in the angle formed by the Emmitsburg road and a cross road running about southeast and connecting the Emmitsburg road with the road to Taneytown. The rest of the line extended in a southerly direction, with the left resting on the Round Top Hill. He had hardly got into position when the enemy made their anticipated attack. After resisting it about two hours, and the fifth corps failing to come to his support as promptly as was expected, he fell back to his original position upon the crest of the hill, where a most desperate assault was made by the troops of Gen. Longstreet. The line was strengthened by Gen. Meade, by ordering up the fifth corps to the position it afterward occupied on the left of the third. Two divisions were also sent from the twelfth corps, as no attack was threatened on the right. This formidable opposition and the precipitate and rugged character of the slope effectually repulsed all the efforts of Gen. Longstreet, with great loss, however, on both sides. According to the order of Gen. Lee, the advance was to commence from the right and be taken up along the whole line. With the advance of Gen. Longstreet a part of the division of Gen. Anderson moved upon the centre of Gen. Meade. As Gen. Sickles fell back, the second corps, under Gen. Hancock, came to his aid on his right, assisted by a portion of the first corps. These troops encountered a part of McLaws's and Anderson's divisions. The battle grew fearful. The enemy pressed forward unrestrained. Gen. Sickles was wounded in the leg, and the command of his corps devolved on Maj.-Gen. Birney. Gen. Hancock was wounded in the thigh, and Gen. Gibbons in the shoulder. The first and second wavered. The enemy pressed up to the very guns of the batteries, which were exposed to capture. The sixth corps, under Gen. Sedgwick, although weary with a march that day, hurried with shouts to the support, and the enemy staggered and drifted slowly back. A strong force was now pushed on their left flank, which pressed well to their rear along the Emmitsburg road, and the Confederates retired. At this time Gen. Ewell got his forces forward and made a desperate dash on the twelfth corps, under Gen. Slocum, on the extreme right, which had been weakened to support the centre and left. For fifteen minutes the attack was furious, but the sixth corps came to its support followed by the first corps, and the struggle continued with some advantages to the enemy until 9 o'clock, when he retired, having lost the day in every quarter. It was stated that the divisions of Gens. Pender and Heth, of Gen. Hill's corps, remained inactive.

Gen. Lee thus reports the operations of the day:

In front of Gen. Longstreet, the enemy held a position from which, if he could be driven, it was thought that our army could be used to advantage in assailing the more elevated ground beyond, and thus enable us to reach the crest of the ridge. That officer was directed to endeavor to carry this position, while Gen. Ewell attacked directly the high ground on the enemy's right, which had already been partially fortified. Gen. Hill was instructed to threaten the centre of the Federal line, in order to prevent reënforcements being sent to either wing, and to avail himself of any opportunity that might present itself to attack.

After a severe struggle, Longstreet succeeded in getting possession of and holding the desired ground. Ewell also carried some of the strong positions which he assailed, and the result was such as to lead to the belief that he would ultimately be able to dislodge the enemy. The battle ceased at dark.

During the night, Gen. Meade sent the following despatch to Washington:

The enemy attacked me about four P. M. this day, and, after one of the severest contests of the war, he was repulsed at all points. We have suffered considerably in killed and wounded. Among the former are Brig.-Gens. Paul and Zook, and among the wounded, Gens. Sickles, Barlow, Graham, and Warren slightly. We have taken a large number of prisoners.

On the next morning, the following further despatch was sent:

The action commenced again at early daylight upon various parts of the line. The enemy thus far have made no impression upon my position. All accounts agree in placing the whole (rebel) army here. Prisoners report Longstreet's and A. P. Hill's forces much injured yesterday, and many general officers killed. Gen. Barksdale's (of Mississippi) dead body is within our lines. We have thus far about sixteen hundred prisoners.

The action thus commenced was chiefly an artillery fire directed upon the line of Gen. Meade, which slackened after a few hours. On the right of Gen. Meade, the contest was close and more severe. It commenced at daylight, by an attempt on the part of the twelfth corps, under Gen. Slocum, to drive Gen. Ewell farther back. This attack met with a prompt response from Gen. Ewell. The fiercest assaults were made upon the positions of Gens. Geary and Berry, which fell back a short distance until supported by Gen. Sykes's division of the fifth corps and Gen. Humphrey's of the third. The struggle was now evenly contested for some time, when a further reënforcement arrived and took such a position as to enfilade the enemy, causing his force to retire, and at 11 o'clock A. M. a general quiet prevailed.

The movements of the enemy thus far had been made rather to cover up his designs than as serious efforts against Gen. Meade. The battle of the previous day had demonstrated that the issue of the struggle turned on the occupation of Cemetery Hill. To get possession of this spot was therefore the object of the enemy. Early in the morning, preparations had been made by Gen. Lee for a general attack upon Gen. Meade's whole line, while a large force was concentrated against his centre for the purpose of taking the ground it occupied. Gen. Longstreet massed fifty-five guns of long range upon the crest of a slight eminence, just in front of the extreme right of Gen. Hill's corps, and a little to the left of the heights upon which they were to open fire. At the same time, Gen. Hill massed some sixty guns along the hill, still farther to his left and in front of the same heights. The position of these guns was near the Bonaughton road, near the York road, near the Harrisburg road, and along the Seminary ridge to a point beyond Round Top. The artillery on Cemetery Hill was thus subject to more than a half circle of cross fires. At 1 o'clock the signal gun was fired, and the cannonading commenced. The fire of the enemy was thus concentrated on the position held by the eleventh and second corps. It drew a most terrific response from the Federal batteries. It is thus described by a spectator in the Union army:

"The storm broke upon us so suddenly that soldiers and officers—who leaped, as it began, from their tents, or from lazy siestas on the grass—were stricken in their rising with mortal wounds, and died, some with cigars between their teeth, some with pieces of food in their fingers, and one at least—a pale young German, from Pennsylvania—with a miniature of his sister in his hands. Horses fell, shrieking such awful cries as Cooper told of, and writhing themselves about in hopeless agony. The boards of fences, scattered by explosion, flew in splinters through the air. The earth, torn up in clouds, blinded the eyes of hurrying men; and through the branches of the trees and among the gravestones of the cemetery a shower of destruction crashed ceaselessly. As, with hundreds of others, I groped through this tempest of death for the shelter of the bluff, an old man, a private in a company belonging to the 24th Michigan, was struck, scarcely ten feet away, by a cannon ball, which tore through him, extorting such a low, intense cry of mortal pain as I pray God I may never again hear. The hill, which seemed alone devoted to this rain of death, was clear in nearly all its unsheltered places within five minutes after the fire began."

A spectator in the Confederate army has thus described this artillery contest: "I have never yet heard such tremendous artillery firing. The enemy must have had over one hundred guns, which, in addition to our one hundred and fifteen, made the air hideous with most discordant noise. The very earth shook beneath our feet, and the hills and rocks seemed to reel like a drunken man. For one hour and a half this most terrific fire was continued, during which time the shrieking of shell, the crash of fallen timbers, the fragments of rocks flying through the air, shattered from the cliffs by solid shot, the heavy mutterings from the valley between the opposing armies, the splash of bursting shrapnel, and the fierce neighing of wounded artillery horses, made a picture terribly grand and sublime, but which my pen utterly fails to describe. After the firing had continued for little more than an hour, the enemy's guns began to slacken, and finally all were silenced save some six or eight, which were in a clump of woods a little to the left of the stone fence." After the firing had continued about three hours, Gen. Howard, of the second corps, slackened his fire to allow his guns to cool: it was supposed by the enemy that they were silenced, and that the time had now come to make an irresistible attack. Their storming party was now moved up. The division of Gen. Pickett, which had arrived since the previous day, led the advance, supported on the right by Gen. Wilcox's brigade of Gen. Anderson's division, and on the left by Gen. Heth's division, commanded by Gen. Pettigrew. The troops of Gen. Pickett's division advanced in splendid order. On his left, the command of Gen. Pettigrew emerged from the woods, and swept down the slope of the hill to the valley beneath, and some two or three hundred yards in the rear of Gen. Pickett. As it entered the conflict, the line wavered, being raw soldiers, and wanting the firmness of nerve and steadiness of tread of the advance. As the advance came under the fire of the first and second corps, the enemy ceased firing from their batteries. Their ammunition was exhausted. The advance of Gen. Pickett, composed chiefly of Virginians, pressed forward. A terrible fire of grape, shell, and canister from forty guns is opened upon them. They waver not, but cross the Emmitsburg road, and approach the masses of infantry. Gen. Gibbon, in command now of the second corps, walks composedly along the ranks, saying: "Hold your fire, boys—they are not near enough yet." They come still nearer—then, with bayonets at the charge, sweep up to the rifle pits. A line of fire flashes from the second corps, and hundreds go down, but they do not falter. They charge over the pits. Gen. Gibbon orders his men to fall back to the rear of the batteries. It is done without confusion, to allow the artillery to use grape. Still on they press, up to the muzzles of the guns. Meanwhile, the hot fire has thrown the division of Gen. Pettigrew into the utmost confusion. Their line is broken; they are scattered over the plain, and flying panic stricken to the rear. Gen. Pettigrew was wounded, but still retained command, and vainly strove to rally his men. The moving mass rushes to the rear, and Gen. Pickett was left to contend alone. Strong flanking bodies were moved round to gain his rear. His officers were falling on every side, and he gave the order to fall back. In doing this they were pressed with great vigor, and a large number were made prisoners. Their retreat was finally covered by a brigade under Gen. Wright, which was moved forward by Gen. Lee for that purpose. While this assault was made, the extreme right and left were threatened by Gens. Ewell and Longstreet. Nothing further transpired during the evening and night.

The following despatch was, soon after the conflict, sent by Gen. Meade to Gen. Halleck:

HEADQUARTERS ARMY OF THE POTOMAC,
NEAR GETTYSBURG, *July 3d*—8.30 P. M.

To Major-General Halleck, General-in-Chief:

The enemy opened at one o'clock P. M., from about one hundred and fifty guns. They concentrated upon my left centre, continuing without intermission for about three hours, at the expiration of which time he assaulted my left centre twice, being, upon both occasions, handsomely repulsed with severe loss to them, leaving in our hands nearly three thousand prisoners. Among the prisoners are Maj.-Gen. Armistead, and many colonels and officers of lesser note. The enemy left many dead upon the field, and a large number of wounded in our hands. The loss upon our side has been considerable. Maj.-Gen. Hancock and Brig.-Gen. Gibbon were wounded.

After the repelling of the assault, indications leading to the belief that the enemy might be withdrawing, an armed reconnoissance was pushed forward from the left, and the enemy found to be in force. At the present hour all is quiet.

The New York cavalry have been engaged all day on both flanks of the enemy, harassing and vigorously attacking him with great success, notwithstanding they encountered superior numbers, both of cavalry and artillery. The army is in fine spirits.

(Signed) GEORGE G. MEADE,
Major-General Commanding.

On the next day, Gen. Meade issued the following address to his army:

General Order No. 68.

HEADQUARTERS ARMY OF THE POTOMAC,
NEAR GETTYSBURG, *July 4th.*

The Commanding General, in behalf of the country, thanks the Army of the Potomac for the glorious result of the recent operations. Our enemy, superior in numbers and flushed with the pride of a successful invasion, attempted to overcome or destroy this army. Utterly baffled and defeated, he has now withdrawn from the contest.

The privations and fatigues the army has endured, and the heroic courage and gallantry it has displayed, will be matters of history to be ever remembered.

Our task is not yet accomplished, and the Commanding General looks to the army for greater efforts, to drive from our soil every vestige of the presence of the invader.

It is right and proper that we should, on suitable occasions, return our grateful thanks to the Almighty Disposer of events that, in the goodness of His providence, He has thought fit to give victory to the cause of the just.

By command of Major-General MEADE.
S. WILLIAMS, A. A. General.

On the same day, President Lincoln issued the following announcement:

WASHINGTON, D. C., *July 4th*, 1863—10 A. M.

The President of the United States announces to the country, that the news from the Army of the Potomac, up to 10 o'clock P. M., of the 3d, is such as to cover the army with the highest honor—to promise great success to the cause of the Union—and to claim the condolence of all for the many gallant fallen; and that for this he especially desires that on this day, "He whose will, not ours, should ever be done," be everywhere remembered and reverenced with the profoundest gratitude.

(Signed) ABRAHAM LINCOLN.

On Saturday, the 4th, Gen. Ewell's division was withdrawn from its position in the town and the hills southeast of it, and placed behind the defences on the Seminary ridge, and both armies were engaged, with strong working parties, in burying their dead and taking care of the wounded. The morning was hazy, and from noon until night the rain fell in torrents. During the whole day the enemy sent forward such of their wounded as could bear removal, toward Hagerstown. Late in the afternoon their artillery and wagon trains also commenced moving in the same direction. At dark their whole army was put in motion, taking the road to Fairfield, and crossing South Mountain at Waterloo Gap. The position of Gen. Meade's army was now looked upon by the enemy as almost impregnable. The fighting for three days had nearly exhausted the ammunition of the Confederate army.

On Monday, the 6th, Gen. Lee reached Hagerstown, and took position with his army. On Tuesday the advance of Gen. Meade reached Funktown, six miles south of Hagerstown.

Meanwhile, Gen. Couch, who was in command of this department, had proceeded to organize the raw troops which had been called out, as they came in. His nucleus for this provisional army was the troops from New York. The first division organized was put under the command of Gen. W. F. Smith, and placed opposite Harrisburg, to resist an attack. Upon the retreat of the enemy from the neighborhood of that place, Gen. Smith immediately followed them with about six thousand men, a small number of cavalry, and two batteries of artillery. He advanced to Carlisle, where he was met by W. H. F. Lee, who expected to find Gen. Ewell there, and attacked with artillery. Gen. Smith was so strongly posted, that Lee soon retired and Gen. Smith followed. Meantime, Gen. Couch organized another division, and placed it under the command of Maj.-Gen. Dana. Before this was on its way, Gen. Couch moved his headquarters to Chambersburg, to superintend the entire movement. Gen. Smith, with his troops shoeless and living upon the country, joined the Army of the Potomac; and Gen. Dana pushed forward, and had reached Greencastle when Gen. Lee crossed the Potomac. Other reënforcements were sent to Gen. Meade. The entire Federal loss at Gettysburg was 2,834 killed, 13,790 wounded, and 6,643 missing. That of the enemy was larger: 4,500 of his dead were buried by the Union soldiers, 26,500 wounded fell into their hands, and 13,-621 prisoners were taken; also three guns, forty-one standards, and 24,978 small arms.

Meanwhile, Gen. Lee's forces fell back toward the river at Williamsport. On the 11th, Gen. Lee issued the following address to his troops:

General Order No. 16.

HEADQUARTERS ARMY OF NORTHERN VIRGINIA,
July 11th, 1863.

After the long and trying marches, endured with the fortitude that has ever characterized the soldiers of the Army of Northern Virginia, you have penetrated to the country of our enemies, and recalled to the defences of their own soil, those who are engaged in the invasion of ours. You have fought a fierce and sanguinary battle, which, if not attended with the success that has hitherto crowned your efforts, was marked by the same heroic spirit that has commanded the respect of your enemies, the gratitude of your country, and the admiration of mankind.

Once more you are called upon to meet the enemy, from whom you have torn so many field names that will never die. Once more the eyes of your countrymen are turned upon you, and again do wives and sisters, fathers and mothers, and helpless children lean for defence on your strong arms and brave hearts. Let every soldier remember, that on his courage and fidelity depends all that makes life worth having—the freedom of his country, the honor of his people, and the security of his home. Let each heart grow strong in the remembrance of our glorious past, and in the thought of the inestimable blessings for which we contend; and, invoking the assistance of that higher Power, which has so signally blessed our former efforts, let us go forth in confidence to secure the peace and safety of our country. Soldiers, your old enemy is before you. Win from him honor worthy of your right cause, worthy of your comrades dead on so many illustrious fields.

R. E. LEE, General Commanding.

The pursuit by Gen. Meade is thus stated in his report: "The 5th and 6th of July were employed in succoring the wounded and burying the dead. Major-Gen. Sedgwick, commanding the sixth corps, having pushed the pursuit of the enemy as far as the Fairfield pass and the mountains, and reporting that the pass was very strong—one in which a small force of the enemy could hold in check and delay for a considerable time any pursuing force—I determined to follow the enemy by a flank movement, and accordingly, leaving McIntosh's brigade of cavalry and Neil's brigade of infantry to continue harassing the enemy, I put the army in motion for Middletown, and orders were immediately sent to Major-Gen. French, at Frederick, to reoccupy Harper's Ferry, and send a force to occupy Turner's Pass, in South Mountain. I subsequently ascertained that Major-Gen. French had not only anticipated these orders in part, but had pushed a cavalry force to Williamsport and Falling Waters, where they destroyed the enemy's pontoon bridge, and captured its guard. Buford was at the same time sent to Williamsport and Hagerstown. The duty above assigned to the cavalry was most successfully accomplished, the enemy being greatly harassed, his trains destroyed, and many captures of guns and prisoners made.

"After halting a day at Middletown to procure necessary supplies and bring up trains, the army moved through South Mountain, and by the 12th of July was in front of the enemy, who occupied a strong position on the heights near the marsh which runs in advance of Williamsport. In taking this position, several skirmishes and affairs had been had with the enemy, principally by the cavalry and the eleventh and sixth corps. The 13th was occupied in reconnoissances of the enemy's position and preparations for an attack. But on advancing on the morning of the 14th, it was ascertained that he had retired the night previous by the bridge at Falling Waters and ford at Williamsport. The cavalry in pursuit overtook the rear guard at Falling Waters, capturing two guns and numerous prisoners. Previous to the retreat of the enemy, Gregg's division of cavalry was crossed at Harper's Ferry, and, coming up with the rear of the enemy at Charlestown and Shepardstown, had a spirited contest, in which the enemy was driven to Martinsburg and Winchester, and pursued and harassed in his retreat.

"The pursuit was resumed by a flank movement of the army, crossing the Potomac at Berlin and moving down the Loudon Valley. The cavalry were immediately pushed into several passes of the Blue Ridge, and having learned from servants of the withdrawal of the Confederate army from the lower valley of the Shenandoah, the army (the third corps, Maj.-Gen. French, being in advance) was moved into Manassas Gap, in the hope of being able to intercept a portion of the enemy in possession of the Gap, which was disputed so successfully as to enable the rear guard to withdraw by the way of Strasburg. The Confederate army retiring to the Rapidan, a position was taken with this army on the line of the Rappahannock, and the campaign terminated about the close of July."

On the 14th, Gen. Meade sent the following despatches to Washington:

HEADQUARTERS ARMY OF THE POTOMAC, July 14th—3 P. M.

H. W. Halleck, General-in-Chief:

My cavalry now occupy Falling Waters, having overtaken and captured a brigade of infantry, 1,500 strong, two guns, two caissons, two battle-flags, and a large number of small arms. The enemy are all across the Potomac. GEO. G. MEADE, Major-General.

HEADQUARTERS ARMY OF THE POTOMAC, July 14th—3.30 P. M.

Major-Gen. Halleck, General-in-Chief:

My cavalry have captured five hundred prisoners, in addition to those previously reported. Gen. Pettigrew, of the Confederate army, was killed this morning in the attack on the enemy's rear-guard. His body is in our hands. G. G. MEADE, Major-General.

The first of these despatches was subsequently denied by Gen. Lee, as follows:

HEADQUARTERS ARMY NORTHERN VIRGINIA, July 21st 1863.

Gen. S. Cooper, Adj't and Inspector-General C. S. A.:

GENERAL: I have seen in the Northern papers what purports to be an official despatch from Gen. Meade, stating that he had captured a brigade of infantry, two pieces of artillery, two caissons, and a large number of small arms, as this army retired to the south bank of the Potomac on the 13th and 14th instant. This despatch has been copied into the Richmond papers; and as its official character may cause it to be believed, I desire to state that it is incorrect. The enemy did not capture any organized body of men on that occasion, but only stragglers and such as were left asleep on the road, exhausted by the fatigue and exposure of one of the most inclement nights I have ever known at this season of the year. It rained without cessation, rendering the road by which our troops marched toward the bridge at Falling Waters very difficult to pass, and causing so much delay that the last of the troops did not cross the river at the bridge until 1 A. M. on the morning of the 14th.

While the column was thus detained on the road, a number of men, worn down with fatigue, laid down in barns and by the roadside, and though officers were sent back to arouse them as the troops moved on, the darkness and rain prevented them from finding all, and many were in this way left behind. Two guns were left on the road; the horses that drew them became exhausted, and the officers went back to procure others. When they returned, the rear of the column had passed the guns so far that it was deemed unsafe to send back for them, and they were thus lost. No arms, cannon, or prisoners were taken by the enemy in battle, but only such as were left behind, as I have described, under the circumstances. The number of stragglers thus lost I am unable to state with accuracy, but it is greatly exaggerated in the despatch referred to.

I am, with great respect, your obedient servant,
R. E. LEE, General.

This despatch of Gen. Lee was subsequently contradicted by Gen. Meade in the following statement, which is important, as containing the details of some of the operations to harass the retreat of the Confederate army across the river:

HEADQUARTERS ARMY OF THE POTOMAC, August 9th, 1863.

Major-Gen. Halleck, General-in-Chief:

My attention has been called to what purports to be an official despatch of Gen. R. E. Lee, commanding the rebel army, to Gen. S. Cooper, Adjutant and Inspector-General, denying the accuracy of my telegram to you, of July 14th, announcing the result of the cavalry affair at Falling Waters.

I have delayed taking any notice of Lee's report until the return of Brig.-Gen. Kilpatrick, absent on leave, who commanded the cavalry on the occasion referred to, and on whose report from the field my telegram was based. I now enclose the official report of Brig.-Gen. Kilpatrick, made after his attention had been called to Lee's report. You will see that he reiterates and confirms all that my despatch averred, and proves most conclusively that Gen. Lee has been deceived by his subordinates, or he would never in the face of the facts now alleged have made the assertion his report claims.

It appears that I was in error in stating that the body of Gen. Pettigrew was left in our hands, although I did not communicate that fact until an officer from the field reported to me he had seen the body. It is now ascertained from the Richmond papers that Gen. Pettigrew, though mortally wounded in the affair,

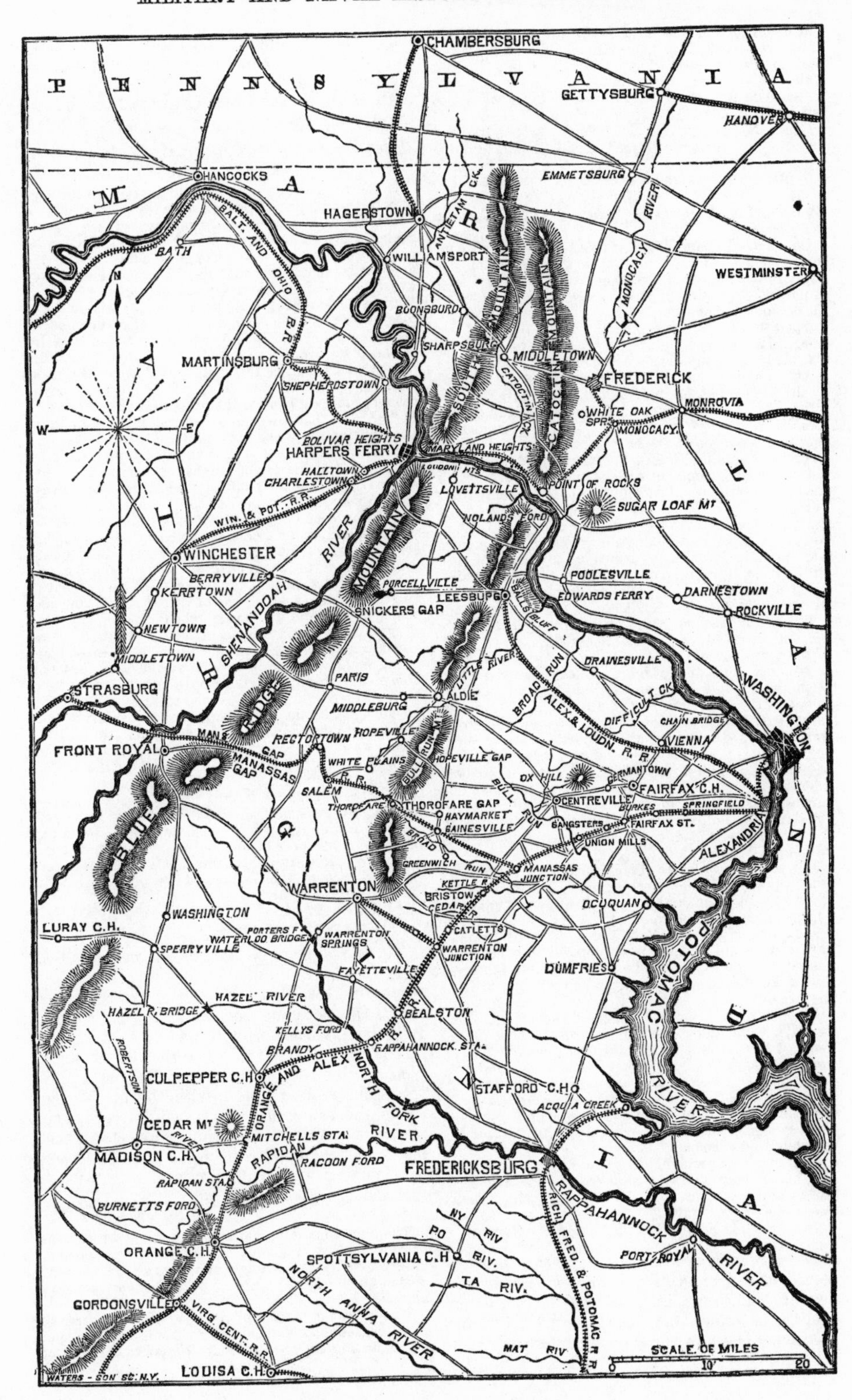
PENNSYLVANIA
MARYLAND
VIRGINIA
CHAMBERSBURG
GETTYSBURG
HANOVER
EMMETSBURG
HANCOCKS
HAGERSTOWN
WILLIAMSPORT
WESTMINSTER
BATH
BALT. AND OHIO R.R.
BOONSBURO
SHARPSBURG
MIDDLETOWN
FREDERICK
MARTINSBURG
SHEPHERDSTOWN
WHITE OAK SPRS
MONROVIA
MONOCACY
BOLIVAR HEIGHTS
HARPERS FERRY
MARYLAND HEIGHTS
HALLTOWN
CHARLESTOWN
LOUDON HTS
LOVETTSVILLE
POINT OF ROCKS
SUGAR LOAF MT
NOLANDS FORD
WIN. & POT. R.R.
WINCHESTER
BERRYVILLE
KERRTOWN
POOLESVILLE
PURCELLVILLE
LEESBURG
EDWARDS FERRY
DARNESTOWN
ROCKVILLE
SNICKERS GAP
NEWTOWN
MIDDLETOWN
STRASBURG
PARIS
DRAINESVILLE
WASHINGTON
ALDIE
MIDDLEBURG
CHAIN BRIDGE
VIENNA
FRONT ROYAL
MANASSAS GAP
RECTORTOWN
HOPEVILLE
WHITE PLAINS
HOPEVILLE GAP
OX HILL
GERMANTOWN
FAIRFAX C.H.
SALEM
THOROFARE GAP
HAYMARKET
GAINESVILLE
CENTREVILLE
SPRINGFIELD
FAIRFAX ST.
UNION MILLS
ALEXANDRIA
MANASSAS JUNCTION
WARRENTON
BRISTOW
CATLETTS
OCCOQUAN
LURAY C.H.
WASHINGTON
SPERRYVILLE
WATERLOO BRIDGE
WARRENTON SPRINGS
WARRENTON JUNCTION
FAYETTEVILLE
DUMFRIES
POTOMAC RIVER
HAZEL RIVER
HAZEL R. BRIDGE
BEALSTON
KELLYS FORD
BRANDY
RAPPAHANNOCK STA.
CULPEPPER C.H.
ORANGE AND ALEX R.R.
NORTH FORK RIVER
STAFFORD C.H.
ACQUIA CREEK
CEDAR MT
MITCHELLS STA.
MADISON C.H.
RAPIDAN
RACOON FORD
FREDERICKSBURG
RAPIDAN STA.
BURNETTS FORD
RAPPAHANNOCK RIVER
ORANGE C.H.
SPOTTSYLVANIA C.H.
PORT ROYAL
NORTH ANNA RIVER
RICH. FRED. & POTOMAC R.R.
GORDONSVILLE
VIRG. CENT. R.R.
SCALE OF MILES
10
20
LOUISA C.H.
WATERS - SON SC. N.Y.

was taken to Winchester, where he subsequently died. The three battle flags captured on this occasion and sent to Washington, belonged to the 40th, 47th, and 55th Virginia regiments of infantry.

Gen. Lee will surely acknowledge these were not left in the hands of stragglers asleep in barns.

(Signed) GEO. G. MEADE,
Major-General Commanding.

HEADQUARTERS THIRD DIVISION CAVALRY CORPS,
WARRENTON JUNCTION, VA., *August 7th.*

To Colonel A. J. Alexander, Chief of Staff of Cavalry Corps:

COLONEL: In compliance with a letter just received from the headquarters of the cavalry corps of the Army of the Potomac, directing me to give the facts connected with the fight at Falling Waters, I have the honor to state that, at 3 A. M. of the 14th ult., I learned that the enemy's pickets were retiring in my front. Having been previously ordered to attack at 7 A. M., I was ready to move at once.

At daylight I had reached the crest of hills occupied by the enemy an hour before, and, a few minutes before 6, Gen. Costar drove the rear guard of the enemy into the river at Williamsport. Learning from citizens that a portion of the enemy had retreated in the direction of Falling Waters, I at once moved rapidly for that point, and came up with this rear guard of the enemy at 7.30 A. M., at a point two miles distant from Falling Waters. We pressed on, driving them before us, capturing many prisoners and one gun. When within a mile and a half of Falling Waters, the enemy was found in large force, drawn up in line of battle on the crest of a hill, commanding the road on which I was advancing. His left was protected by earthworks, and his right extended to the woods on our left.

The enemy was, when first seen, in two lines of battle, with arms stacked, within less than 1,000 yards of the large force. A second piece of artillery, with its support, consisting of infantry, was captured while attempting to get into position. The gun was taken to the rear. A portion of the 6th Michigan cavalry, seeing only that portion of the enemy behind the earthworks, charged. This charge was led by Major Webber, and was the most gallant ever made. At a trot he passed up the hill, received the fire from the whole line, and the next moment rode through and over the earthworks, and passed to the right, sabring the rebels along the entire line, and returned with a loss of thirty killed, wounded, and missing, including the gallant Major Webber, killed.

I directed Gen. Costar to send forward one regiment as skirmishers. They were repulsed before support could be sent them, and driven back, closely followed by the rebels, until checked by the 1st Michigan and a squadron of the 8th New York. The 2d brigade having come up, it was quickly thrown into position, and, after a fight of two hours and thirty minutes, routed the enemy at all points and drove him toward the river.

When within a short distance of the bridge, Gen. Buford's command came up and took the advance. We lost twenty-nine killed, thirty-six wounded, and forty missing. We found upon the field 125 dead rebels, and brought away upward of fifty wounded. A large number of the enemy's wounded were left upon the field in charge of their own surgeons. We captured two guns, three battle flags, and upward of fifteen hundred prisoners.

To Gen. Costar and his brigade, Lieut. Pennington and his battery, and one squadron of the 8th New York cavalry of Gen. Buford's command, all praise is due. Very respectfully, your ob't servant,

J. KILPATRICK, Brigadier-General.

On the 7th of July, despatches were received at Washington announcing the surrender of Vicksburg, and, on the 14th, further despatches announcing the surrender of Port Hudson. The news of the surrender of Vicksburg was welcomed with salutes of artillery in a large number of the principal cities in the Northern States.

On the 15th, the President issued the following proclamation:

By the President of the United States of America:

A PROCLAMATION.

It has pleased Almighty God to hearken to the supplications and prayers of an afflicted people, and to vouchsafe to the army and the navy of the United States, victories on the land and on the sea so signal and so effective, as to furnish reasonable ground for augmented confidence that the Union of these States will be maintained, their Constitution preserved, and their peace and prosperity permanently restored. But these victories have been accorded not without sacrifices of life, limb, health, and liberty, incurred by brave, loyal, and patriotic citizens. Domestic affliction, in every part of the country, follows in the train of these fearful bereavements. It is meet and right to recognize and confess the presence of the Almighty Father, and the power of His Hand, equally in these triumphs and in these sorrows.

Now, therefore, be it known that I do set apart Thursday, the 6th day of August next, to be observed as a day for National Thanksgiving, Praise, and Prayer, and I invite the people of the United States to assemble on that occasion in their customary places of worship, and, in the forms approved by their own consciences, render the homage due to the Divine Majesty for the wonderful things He has done in the nation's behalf, and invoke the influence of His Holy Spirit to subdue the anger which has produced and so long sustained a needless and cruel rebellion, to change the hearts of the insurgents, to guide the counsels of the Government with wisdom adequate to so great a national emergency, and to visit with tender care and consolation throughout the length and breadth of our land all those who, through the vicissitudes of marches, voyages, battles, and sieges, have been brought to suffer in mind, body, or estate, and finally to lead the whole nation—through the paths of repentance and submission to the Divine Will—back to the perfect enjoyment of union and fraternal peace.

In witness whereof I have hereunto set my hand and caused the seal of the United States to be affixed.

Done at the City of Washington, this fifteenth day of July, in the year of our Lord one thousand eight hundred and sixty-three, and of the Independence of the United States of America the eighty-eighth.

[L. S.]

By the President: ABRAHAM LINCOLN.
WILLIAM H. SEWARD, Secretary of State.

The movements of Gen. Meade in pursuit of Gen. Lee were in detail as follows:

On the 18th, his headquarters were moved across the Potomac; on the 19th, they were at Lovettsville; on the 20th and 21st, at Union; on the 22d, at Upperville; on the 23d, at Markham Station; on the 24th, at Salem; and on the 25th, at Warrenton, with the army occupying the same line which it did two months previous. Active operations now closed, and on the 30th, Gen. Meade issued the following proclamation to the inhabitants:

HEADQUARTERS ARMY OF THE POTOMAC,
July 30th, 1863.

The numerous depredations committed by citizens, or rebel soldiers in disguise, harbored or concealed by citizens, along the Orange and Alexandria railroad, within our lines, call for prompt and exemplary punishment.

Under the instruction of the Government, therefore, every citizen against whom there is sufficient evidence of his having engaged in these practices, will be arrested and confined for punishment or sent beyond the lines. The people within ten miles of the railroad are notified that they will be held responsible in their persons and property for any injury done to the trains, road, depot, or stations, by citizens, guerillas, or persons in disguise; and in case of such injury they will be impressed as laborers to repair all damages. If these measures should not stop such depredations, it will become the unpleasant duty of the undersigned, in the execution of his instructions, to direct that the entire inhabitants of the district of country along the railroad be put across the lines, and their property taken for Government purposes.

GEORGE G. MEADE, Maj.-Gen. Commanding.

Some movements were made during the advance of Gen. Lee into Pennsylvania, which were important, being intended to serve as diversions. One made by a portion of the forces under Gen. Dix, from Fortress Monroe, up the peninsula toward Richmond, is mentioned in the correspondence between Mr. Davis and Gen. Lee, on a preceding page. The effect of this movement is there stated. Gen. Getty, of the seventh corps, was sent by Gen. Dix to the White House, at the junction of the Pamunkey with the York river. In this position he threatened both Richmond and the communications of Gen. Lee. From the White House a force was sent out to occupy Tunstall's Station, on the railroad to Richmond. Lanesville, on the other side of the Pamunkey, was also occupied, and an advance was made to Hanover, by which several prisoners were captured, among whom was Brig.-Gen. H. F. Lee, a son of Gen. R. E. Lee.

The advance of Gen. Rosecrans against the army of Gen. Bragg commenced at this time. It is hereafter stated. On the Confederate side a "raid" was made by the Partisan Ranger, John Morgan, into the States of Kentucky, Indiana, and Ohio, in which he designed to sweep everything before him, attracting the public attention entirely to himself, and breaking all the railroad communications by which reënforcements for the defence of Louisville, Kentucky, could be sent. Immediately upon this, Gen. Buckner, from Tennessee, was to dash into Kentucky with the force under his command, which was very considerable, capture Louisville, and then, in coöperation with Gen. Morgan, make an attack upon Cincinnati. By the advance of Gen. Rosecrans sooner than was expected, Gen. Buckner could not be spared for this movement.

Gen. Morgan, with about four thousand men, was in Tennessee at this time, south of the Cumberland river, and making a feint upon Tompkinsville, just over the line in Kentucky. Tompkinsville is the capital of Monroe county, 140 miles south of southwest of Frankfort, the capital of the State, and 10 miles from the Cumberland river. A small Union force was stationed at Columbia, the capital of Adair county, Kentucky, an important position to defend the State from a threatening enemy on the south bank of the Cumberland. On the 20th of June, Brig.-Gen. Hobson was ordered by Gen. Judah to move to Tompkinsville, then apparently threatened by Gen. Morgan. This opened the gate for Gen. Morgan, who immediately crossed the Cumberland at Burksville, the capital of Cumberland county. Thus having the start, Gen. Morgan moved rapidly on to Columbia, where a brave defence was made by Capt. Carter, with one hundred and fifty men of Col. Wolford's Kentucky regiment, who were, however, forced to retire with the loss of their leader. Thence Gen. Morgan attacked, on July 4th, Col. Moore, posted with a few hundred men at Green river bridge, who made a firm resistance. He next marched, on the 5th, to Lebanon, and demanded the surrender of the place by Col. Hanson, who, with his regiment, the 20th Kentucky, was stationed there. This was refused, and an attack was immediately made and bravely resisted for seven hours, when the enemy began to set fire to the town, and Col. Hanson surrendered to save its entire destruction. Lebanon is the capital of Marion county. It is 60 miles south by west of Frankfort. All the northern portion of the town, with the county clerk's office and the records, was burned. The soldiers who surrendered were marched in front to Springfield, and compelled to keep pace with the cavalry. The distance was ten miles, and passed in an hour and a half. The Union loss was five killed and several wounded; the Confederate loss was six killed and ten wounded. From Springfield, Gen. Morgan moved to Shepherdsville; thence to Bardstown, on the 6th.

On Tuesday, the 7th, the advance of his force reached Brandenburg on the Ohio river, forty miles below Louisville. During the day, the steamer McCombs, bound up the river, stopped, as usual, at Brandenburg, to take on passengers and freight. As soon as she touched the shore she was boarded by a number of the enemy and seized. Everything was taken that would serve the purpose of the captors, and the boat was run out into the river and anchored. Some time afterward, the steamer Alice Dean approached, when signals of distress were raised on the McCombs, and the Dean was induced to come alongside without a suspicion of the actual circumstances. She was then boarded and seized. On the next day, Wednesday, the force of Gen. Morgan, consisting of eleven regiments and over four thousand men, with ten pieces of artillery, including two howitzers, were taken across the river in these boats. The Dean was then burned, and also the wharf at Brandenburg, but the McCombs was given up.

In the mean time, Gen. Hobson, after some delay, commenced the pursuit. He started on the 4th, but being encumbered by a wagon train, and the roads being bad, he advanced only ten miles in five hours. On the next morning, the infantry, wagons, and artillery were left behind, and the pursuit made with cavalry. From 4 P. M. to 11 P. M. a halt was made. The march was then continued during the remainder of the night, and, on the next morning, Brig.-Gen. Shackelford was met with cavalry and artillery. Proceeding to Lebanon, Col. Wolford and his brigade there joined. Orders were also received by Gen. Hobson from Gen. Burnside, in command of the department, directing him to assume full command, and to pursue until the enemy was captured.. The command then marched toward Bardstown, until 1 A. M. After two hours' rest the pursuit was resumed. At night, a halt was made until rations could be obtained by the Louisville and Nashville railroad. The pursuit was renewed early on Tuesday, the 7th, and by night the force was within nine miles of Brandenburg. Gen. Hobson, wishing to coöperate with the gunboats and make a night attack, proceeded with a small escort to Rock Haven. Here he found that the gunboats had gone up the river. It was 1 A. M. before he returned. The men being so overcome with fatigue and want of sleep that it was almost impossible to arouse them, he reluctantly concluded to wait until daybreak. Pushing on at that time, he reached the river as the last boat with the enemy had crossed.

During the night the enemy marched toward Corydon, in Indiana, which they reached early the next forenoon. Some opposition was made to their progress by the inhabitants. Great excitement, however, prevailed in the State. A proclamation was issued by Gov. Morton, ordering all the able-bodied citizens in the southern counties of the State under arms. From Corydon, Gen. Morgan moved by the way of Greenville and Palmyra to Salem. At Palmyra a force of three hundred and fifty Home Guards had concentrated, having fallen back from near Corydon to that place. Considering their inability to retard the progress of the enemy, they also fell back to Salem. So sudden, however, was the entrance of the enemy into Salem, that these Guards were all made prisoners and subsequently paroled. At Salem, the depot of the Louisville and Chicago railroad was burned. Orders were also issued by Gen. Morgan to burn all the mills and factories in the town, but upon the payment of one thousand dollars for each mill and factory, they were spared. The railroad track was torn up, the water tank near the town burned, and one passenger and three freight cars. Three bridges between Salem and Farrabee's Station were also destroyed. Good horses were taken wherever found, and the whole command was remounted. From Salem the enemy moved to Canton, in Washington county, four and a half miles distant. Here over one hundred horses were taken, and, joining his left column with the right, which entered the town by way of Harristown, Gen. Morgan moved in the direction of Vienna, in Scott county, on the line of the Jeffersonville railroad. About 11

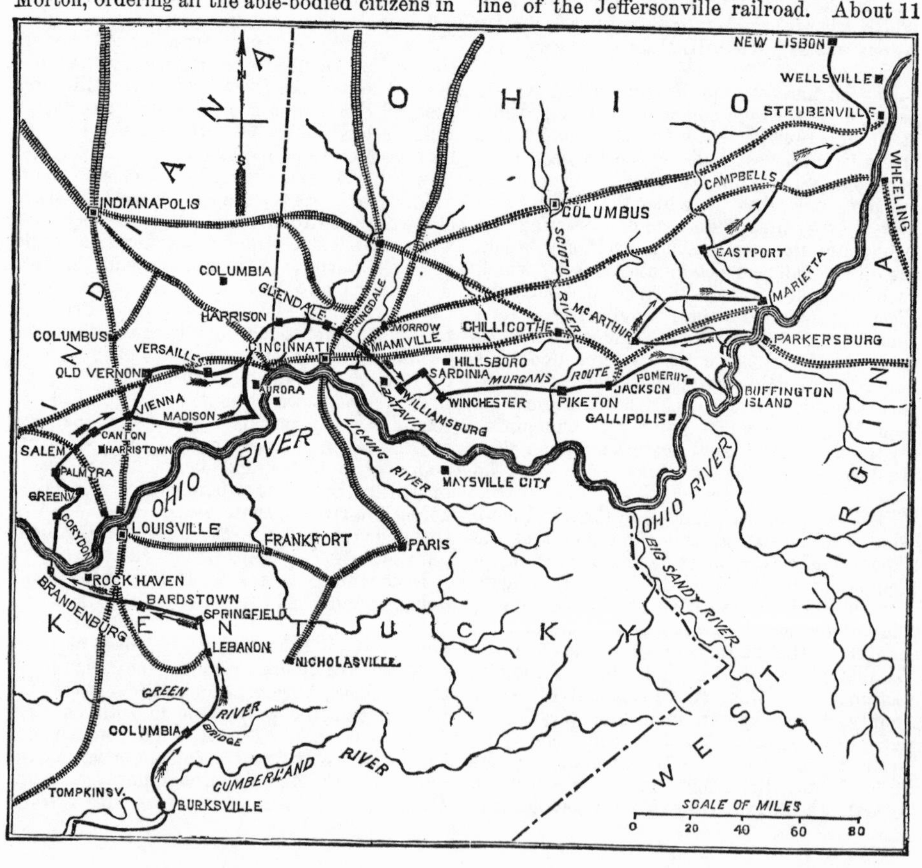

P. M. on Friday night the advance reached Vienna, and at 2 o'clock on the next morning the rear guard arrived. Here a railroad bridge was burned, and the depot and station house. Private property for the first time was here respected. At Vienna, the force of the enemy was divided into two columns, one of which marched north and the other started in the direction of Madison. The advance of the column marching north, appeared before Old Vernon, in Jennings county, on Saturday, at 6 P. M., the 11th of July. The place was held by a force under Gen. Love or Col. Barkham. A surrender was demanded by Gen. Morgan and refused. A half hour was then given for the removal of women and children. At the expiration of that time the Union force moved out to meet the enemy, and found that they had retired. Pursuit was made and a number captured. From Vernon they moved southward and tore up the track of the Madison and Indianapolis railroad, and cut the telegraph wires. They also destroyed a portion of the Ohio and Mississippi railroad west of Vernon. Thence the enemy moved eastward, and reached Versailles at 1 P. M. on Sunday. A party of sixty-three advanced to Osgood, and burned the bridge on the Ohio and Mississippi railroad. The enemy now moved in several parties. A large body encamped ten miles northwest of Aurora, on Sunday night, and proceeded thence to Harrison. Another portion crossed the Indianapolis and Cincinnati railroad, between Sunman and Van Wedden's stations, and passed on to Harrison on Monday. A large force crossed the same road at Harman's, and proceeded to the Ohio State line. At Van Wedden's the water tank and part of the track were destroyed. Horses were taken in all places, and those broken down left behind. During Monday, the 13th, the enemy continued moving eastward. In the evening, one division crossed the Coleraine turnpike just beyond the ten-mile post from Cincinnati, and thence advanced through Glendale and Springdale. A detachment went by the way of Camp Monroe, where the Government had been keeping large numbers of horses and mules for the use of the army. These had been removed only a few hours previous. A halt of a few hours was made near Glendale, and the march was then continued through Sharon and Reading to Montgomery. The inhabitants everywhere were required to furnish provisions. From Montgomery the enemy crossed to Miamiville.

A body also crossed the Little Miami railroad at Dangerous Crossing, between Miamiville and Branch Hill. At this spot they placed some ties and rails across the track near a declivity, and as the train from Morrow came down, about a quarter past 7 A. M., the locomotive was thrown from the track, the fireman killed, and the engineer badly bruised. In a few minutes the enemy came out of the woods and fields, and made prisoners of about two hundred recruits who were on the train. While the cars were burning they were paroled. Some skirmishing took place during the day. Arrangements were now made by means of gunboats to cut off the retreat of the enemy across the river, if they should attempt it. Forces were also gathering to stop the progress of Gen. Morgan, and his movements became more rapid. On Tuesday afternoon, the 14th, he reached Williamsburg, east of Batavia, in Clermont county, and near the line of Brown county. On Wednesday, he passed through Brown county, and, on Thursday morning at 9 A. M., through the town of Sardinia, sixteen miles southwest of Hillsboro, the capital of Highland county. At noon he was at Winchester, southeast of Hillsboro, and forced the citizens to prepare a dinner for his men. Afterward he moved to Piketown, which surrendered without opposition. Very little depredation was done except taking horses and provisions. Burning the bridge over the Scioto, he next moved toward Jackson, where he arrived in the evening, and remained until joined by his whole force. Thence he started for the Ohio river near Pomeroy.

In the mean time, Gen. Hobson, who arrived at the Ohio river in pursuit as the last of the enemy's force had crossed, sent the steamer McCombs to Louisville, to obtain other boats to aid in crossing. By night, quite a fleet had arrived, and the force was taken over before morning. Pursuit was immediately commenced on Wednesday. The command was fed by the inhabitants of the towns, but as Gen. Morgan had swept the horses from both sides of the road, and left only those which were broken down, the advantage was greatly in his favor. The men whose horses failed, pressed forward on foot until they could obtain others. Day after day passed, but still the enemy kept about the same distance ahead. For nearly twenty days and a distance of nearly seven hundred miles, this pursuit continued day and night, before the foe was reached. The local force of Indiana which was sent against Gen. Morgan, came no farther than the borders of the State. The first attempt to check his advance was made when he reached Piketon. A considerable force was at this time at Chillicothe, north of the latter place, and Col. Runkle, in command, planned to move over the Marietta railroad to Hampden, and then to Jackson, in advance of Gen. Morgan.

It was now manifest that the enemy aimed to reach the Ohio river at Gallipolis or Pomeroy. The inhabitants commenced cutting trees, which fell across the roads and delayed his progress. The militia in the adjoining counties rushed to arms. At the same time, the forces of Gen. Morgan had been constantly diminishing, by the exhaustion of some and the capture of others, until scarcely a fourth remained. These were harassed now at every step. Notwithstanding several skirmishes, they reached the river, and attempted to cross at Buffington island, near Pomeroy, but were driven back by the gunboats. Gen. Hobson had thus overtaken him, and a large portion of the force was captured, on the 21st, near Kyger's Creek. Gen. Morgan and about five hundred, however, escaped, and were not captured until the 26th, about three miles south of New Lisbon, near Wellsville, where he hoped to cross the river. Gen. Shackelford immediately sent to Gen. Burnside's headquarters the following despatch:

HEADQUARTERS IN THE FIELD,
Three miles south of New Lisbon, Ohio, *July 26th*, 1863.

To Col. Lewis Richmond, A. A. G.;

By the blessing of Almighty God I have succeeded in capturing Gen. John H. Morgan, Col. Chike, and the remainder of the command, amounting to about four hundred prisoners. I will start with Morgan and staff on the first train for Cincinnati, and await the General's order for transportation for the remainder.

J. M. SHACKELFORD,
Col. Commanding.

CHAPTER XXXIII.

Measures taken in the Insurrectionary States to recruit their Armies—The Army of the United States—Conscription—The Draft: how made—Riots in New York, Boston, and elsewhere—Employment of Colored Troops—Proceedings relative thereto—Organization of Hospitals—Expenditures—Materials—Ordnance and Small Arms.

It may not be out of place here to state the measures which were adopted to provide and maintain the vast military forces on each side. The acts of the Richmond Congress, passed in 1862, authorized Mr. Davis to call into the military service all white residents of the Confederate States between eighteen and forty-five, except exempts, or such part of them as in his judgment might not be necessary for the public defence. Under this authority all those between the ages of eighteen and thirty-five, forming the first class, were called into the field in 1862. The enrolment of the second class, between thirty-five and forty-five, was also completed, and a portion of the troops called out. At the close of 1862 the Confederate armies were larger than at any previous or subsequent period. This force was subsequently reduced by desertions during the winter, and by the withdrawal from service of many of the Maryland and Kentucky volunteers, whose terms had expired, and who were regarded as exempts. The force was considered to be sufficient to resist the advance of the Federal troops, until the march of Gen. Grant to the rear of Vicksburg demonstrated its weakness. At this time the relative physical abilities of the two antagonists were distinctly shown, for while the North reenforced Gen. Grant with ease to the extent he deemed necessary, the South were unable to reenforce Gen. Johnston sufficiently to enable him to threaten Gen. Grant. The resources of the States west of the Mississippi were cut off from the Confederacy, and besides the forces of Gens. Lee, Beauregard, and Bragg, and the detachments at important points, sufficient troops were not to be had to save Vicksburg. The defeat of Gen. Lee at Gettysburg, and the subsequent falling back of Gen. Bragg from Middle Tennessee, required the most active efforts to recruit the Confederate armies in order to maintain their positions. The first official act of the government to obtain more soldiers consisted in a proclamation issued July 15th, 1863, of which the following is an extract:

Now, therefore, I, Jefferson Davis, President of the Confederate States of America, do, by virtue of the power vested in me as aforesaid, call out and place in the military service of the Confederate States all white men residents of said States, between the ages of eighteen and forty-five years, not legally exempted from military service; and I do hereby order and direct that all persons subject to this call and not now in the military service, do, upon being enrolled, forthwith repair to the conscript camps established in the respective States of which they may be residents, under pain of being held and punished as deserters, in the event of their failure to obey this call, as provided in said laws.

It was estimated that the number which this conscription would bring out would be as follows:

Alabama,	10,393	Florida,	1,200
Georgia,	12,230	Mississippi,	9,000
North Carolina,	14,000	South Carolina,	6,500
Tennessee,	6,000	Virginia,	18,000
			77,323
Arkansas,	5,000	Louisiana,	8,000
Mississippi,	9,000	Texas,	5,000
			27,000

The total estimate was 104,323. That portion to be contributed by the States partly in possession of the Federal forces cannot be considered otherwise than as over-estimated. Some of the number liable had also gone voluntarily to the field, which would make the estimate about 75,000 men.

A report of the Conscript Bureau presented to Congress estimated the number of exempts in the four States under its charge as follows: Virginia, 20,370; North Carolina, 22,807; South Carolina, 5,814; Georgia, 15,837—total, 65,031. It was further estimated that the number of substitutes put into the army was from 20,000 to 25,000; and that, in addition, there were over 10,000 fraudulent substitute papers held by persons not in the service. According to some of the estimates of the press, only about 90,000 persons remained in the States entirely under Confederate control, who would be liable to conscription, under the above proclamation of July 15th.

The great source of weakness to the army was desertion, straggling, and absenteeism. So large was the number of those thus absent, that a half or three-fourths of them, added to the forces in the field, were estimated to be sufficient to give success at all points. As a measure toward effecting their return to the service, Jefferson Davis, on the 1st of August, issued an earnest appeal to them:

I call on you, then, my countrymen, to hasten to your camps, in obedience to the dictates of honor and of duty, and summon those who have absented themselves without leave, who have remained absent beyond the period allowed by their furloughs, to repair without delay to their respective commands, and I do hereby declare that I grant a general pardon and amnesty to all officers and men within the Confederacy, not absent without leave, who shall, with the least possible delay, return to their proper posts of duty; but no excuse will be received for any delay beyond twenty days after the first publication of this proclamation in the State in which the absentee may be at the date of the publication. This amnesty and pardon shall extend to all who have been accused, or who have been convicted and are undergoing sentence for absence without leave or desertion, excepting only those who have been twice convicted of desertion.

Finally, I conjure my countrywomen—the wives, mothers, sisters, and daughters, of the Confederacy—to use their all-powerful influence in aid of this call, to add one crowning sacrifice to that which their patriotism has so freely and constantly afforded on their country's altar, and to take care that none who owe service in the field shall be sheltered at home from the disgrace of having deserted their duty to their families, to their country, and to their God.

Given under my hand, and the seal of the Confederate States, at Richmond, this 1st day of August, in the year of our Lord, one thousand eight hundred and sixty-three.

[SEAL.]

JEFFERSON DAVIS.

No bounties appear to have been paid to volunteers after the passage of the conscription act, in 1862. Nor were any efforts made to fill up the quotas of States by contributions to volunteers, as was done in the Northern States.

Under the depreciation of the currency, the pay of the soldiers sunk to an insignificant sum; and, to prevent local disturbances, measures were taken in the several States to provide for their destitute families.

At the session of Congress at the close of 1863, an act was introduced which declared every man between the ages of eighteen and fifty-five to be in the military service for the war. Thus every one between these ages was made subject at once to the articles of war, to military discipline, and military penalties; and, upon failure to report for duty at a military station within a certain time, he was liable to the penalty of death as a deserter.

For the supply of the army a commissary agent was appointed for each county, or one for two or three counties, who was charged with the duty of purchasing and impressing supplies in his territory for the use of the army.

The report of the Secretary of War, made near the close of the year, alluded to desertion, straggling, and absenteeism, and said that the effective force of the army was but little over one-half or two-thirds of the men whose names were on the muster rolls. He recommended the repeal of the substitute and exemptive provisions, and that all having substitutes be put back into the field, and stated that the privileges which Congress granted, to put in substitutes, could be regularly and constitutionally abrogated by the same power.

On January 1st, 1863, the army of the United States, comprising the regular troops, and the volunteers obtained under the various calls made by the President since the commencement of the war, numbered probably between 600,000 and 700,000 men. Of the whole number of men voluntarily raised to that date no precise statement can be afforded, the information furnished by some of the reports being so obscure that it is difficult to decide to which class of service (that of the individual States or of the General Government), the troops furnished belonged.

The troops actually in service at the close of 1862, comprising three years', two years', twelve months', nine months' men and regulars, represented organizations amounting originally to an aggregate of 1,200,000; but among these the casualties of the field, diseases of the camp, discharges for physical disability, and desertions, had made fearful inroads, some regiments having within a year of their enlistment been reduced to less than the strength of a couple of full companies. As an illustration at once of the bravery of the troops and of the rate at which the army is depleted, Gen. Meade stated in reply to an address of welcome from the mayor of Philadelphia, that from March, 1862, when the Army of the Potomac left its lines in front of Washington, to the close of 1863, not less than a hundred thousand men in it had been killed and wounded.

In view of the serious loss of disciplined troops which would be caused by the return home of the two years', twelve months', and nine months' regiments, comprising an aggregate of about 65,000 men, whose terms of enlistment would expire during the summer and autumn of 1863, the Government early in the year took measures to obtain the passage of an Enrolment and Conscription Act, authorizing the President to recruit the army when necessary, by drafting from the able-bodied male citizens of the country between the ages of twenty and forty-five.

The conscription act became a law on March 3d; in the succeeding May and June the enrolment was effected in most of the States, and early in the former month a draft of 300,000 men was ordered, the conscription commencing in the several districts into which the country was divided by the provost marshal general and his assistants, as soon as the enrolment was completed and the quota in each assigned.

For making the draft, one-fifth of the number of men enrolled in the first class was adopted as the quota of a district. The main object was to apportion the number among the States, so that those previously furnished and those to be furnished would make a given part of their available men, and not a given part of their population; and a sufficient percentage was called for to make a given number. In consequence of thus basing the calls for men, those States which contained more females than males were really charged with a greater quota than those in which there was an excess of males. Some of the Western States with quotas nearly the same as some of the Eastern, not only furnished their quotas and a large excess besides, but had a larger proportion of males left than Eastern States which had not entirely filled their quotas and were therefore deficient. This deficiency was not probably from unwillingness to answer the call, but from a want of men, while the excess was attributable, in some degree, to the surplus of men. Thus the States to which the largest credits were to be given really had a larger proportion of men remaining than those to which a deficiency was charged.

Of those who were drawn, including the fifty per cent. additional, over eighty per cent. reported in accordance with the orders of the boards. Of all examined, about thirty per cent. were exempted on account of physical disability; another thirty per cent. were exempted under the provisions of the second section of the act above quoted, or found not liable on account of alienage, unsuitableness of age, non-residence, etc. About forty per cent. of the men examined have been held to service; about one-half of these paid the commutation of $300; about two-thirds of the remainder furnished substitutes, and the other third went in person to the field. Thus, if the number drafted is supposed to be 150, then deduct 20 per cent. for those not reported, it becomes 120; then deduct 60 per cent. or 72 for exempts, it becomes 48 who were held for service; then deduct one-half for those who paid commutation, and it becomes 24. Of this number two-thirds (16) furnished substitutes, and the other third (8) went to the field. In this proportion the enrolment of 3,113,305 would have sent into the field 66,043 as conscripts, 132,686 as substitutes—total, 198,129 men.

Indeed several of the Western States were not subjected to the draft on account of an excess of volunteers, and in other Western States the quota was quite small from the same cause. A bounty of $300 was so generally paid by cities, counties, and States, that drafted men could either retain it and go to the field, or purchase a substitute who was not liable to military service.

The draft was forcibly resisted in New York, Boston, and other places.

In New York, after several postponements, Col. Nugent, the provost-marshal, was directed to prepare the central office of the acting assistant provost-marshal-general, for the immediate execution of the provisions of the act for enrolling and calling out the national forces. The several deputies received official requisitions direct from the President, calling for specified numbers of men, and were instructed to commence operations on the 11th of July. In compliance with this order Provost Marshal Jenkins, of the ninth Congressional district of New York, publicly announced through the press, that on Saturday, the 11th, the ballots would be publicly counted at the corner of Forty-sixth street and Third avenue, and that immediately thereafter the wheel would be turned and the draft begin. Rumors of popular dissatisfaction were heard on every side, trouble was apprehended, and the police were notified to hold themselves in readiness for any emergency. On Saturday morning a large crowd assembled at the appointed place, but as every thing was conducted quietly, systematically, and fairly, no opportunity for disturbance occurred. The day passed pleasantly, the crowd were in good humor, well-known names were saluted with cheers, and at night as the superintendent of the police passed out from the office, he remarked that there was no danger to be apprehended; the Rubicon was passed, and all would go well. The names of the conscripts were published by the press of Sunday morning, with incidents, jocular and otherwise, connected with the proceedings. In the neighborhood in which the initial working of the law was attempted, an excitable element of the city's population resided. Very many poor men were, by the turn of the wheel, forced instantly, as it were, from home and comfort, wrested from the support of a needy family, to be sent they knew not whither, unless to the battle field, or, perhaps, to the grave. Such were the apprehensions of many imprudent persons who were liable to the draft, and such their anxieties for the fate of their wives and children, that associations were formed to resist it, at the last alternative, with bloodshed. Some of the inhabitants of the 9th district met in secret places on Sunday, and resolved to resist the further drafting by force, and, if necessary, to proceed to extremity. On the following morning, Monday the 13th, organized parties of men went from yard to yard, from shop to shop, to compel the workmen to leave their labor and join the several processions which were wending their way toward the corner of Third Avenue and Forty-sixth street. Unconscious of impending danger, Captain Jenkins, with his assistants, prepared for the morning's work, and in the presence of a great multitude, many of whom had crowded into the little room, the draft recommenced, a few names were called and registered, when a huge paving stone came crash through the window, and shivered into a thousand pieces the glass, knocked over two or three quiet observers, upset the inkstand on the reporters' table, and astonished somewhat the officials. Hardly had their surprise found expression in words before a second and a third stone was sent straight from the crowd among the officials and reporters behind the railing. As if emboldened by these acts, the crowd developed instantly into a mob, and with frantic yells passionately rushed upon the place, breaking down the doors, throwing helter-skelter the furniture, smashing into fragments the tables and desks, and venting their fury over the remains of the boxes connected with the office. The wheel was taken up stairs and eventually saved, but nothing else was spared from absolute wreck. The marshal escaped uninjured, as did the reporters; but one of the deputies, Lieutenant Vanderpoel, was badly beaten and taken home for dead. Having destroyed the material of the office, the enraged multitude thought of an additional outrage, and regardless of the women and children who occupied the upper portion of the house, sprinkled camphene upon the lower floor and set the place ablaze. In two hours from that time the entire block, of which this was the corner building, was a pile of smoking brick and mortar. At an early stage of the proceedings, Chief Engineer Decker, of the Fire Department, arrived, but the incendiaries had taken possession of the hydrants, and would not allow the engines to be worked. After much persuasion and an exhibition of absolute heroism, Chief Decker obtained permission to restrain the flames from further devastation, but it was too late to be of service. Police Superintendent Kennedy was attacked by the mob and nearly killed.

In the meantime, word had been sent to the lower part of the city, that the long threatened resistance had been made, and that success had crowned the efforts of the anti-conscriptionists. The most exaggerated rumors obtained ready currency, and while every one from the mayor to the ward-constable stood aghast, all business was suspended, and the voice of trade was hushed. There were no troops in the city, the militia regiments being nearly all on duty in Pennsylvania; the force in the several forts in the harbor was small, and the Navy Yard, at Brooklyn, could spare but a few marines. While therefore Maj.-Gen. Sandford, on the part of the State militia, Maj.-Gen. Wool, on behalf of the General Government, Mayor Opdyke, as the chief magistrate of the city, and their several staffs, were "consulting," the mob, whose proportions had attained the size of an army, had resolved itself into a peregrinating column of incendiaries, and was in the successful pursuit of an uninterrupted career of murder, pillage, and arson. No person was sacred from their touch, and before the day had passed, gangs of thieves joined the crowd, and availing themselves of the general disturbance, reaped vast harvests of money and other *desiderata*, which they unblushingly took from the pockets and persons of their proprietors. Several members of the press, in pursuit of their normal avocations, were maltreated and abused. A noticeable case was that a reporter, then of the "New York Times," who was surrounded by a set of ruffians on the corner of 46th street and Third avenue. Without a moment's parley, they robbed him of his watch, chain, diamond pin, and wallet, knocked him down, raised the cry of "Abolitionist!" and left him to the tender mercies of the crowd. Supposing him to be a spy, the rioters kicked and trampled upon him, pulled him by the hair up and down the streets, and only let him alone when some firemen interfered in his behalf. He was carried to a neighboring engine-house, and barely escaped being stoned to death by a second crowd, which had gathered about the door, and whose volleys of missiles broke every window in the house. A fortunate incident attracted their attention, and the wounded man was permitted later in the day to retire.

While the up-town mob was delighting itself in the destruction of a brown stone block in Lexington Avenue, a detachment of marines, some fifty in number, with muskets and blank cartridges, were sent to quell the riot. Taking a Third avenue car, at the Broadway junction, they started for 46th street. Information reached the mob that the soldiers were coming, and they prepared to receive them. Tearing up the rails, they rendered it impossible for the car to be drawn beyond 43d street, and at that point several thousand men, women, and children stood anxiously waiting for the storming party of fifty. Many of them, particularly the women, were armed with pieces of thick telegraph wire, which they had broken from the lines, and which, as will be seen, they used with great effect. Such a scene has rarely been witnessed; the men were sober and quiet, but malignant and fearful in their aspect; the women, on the contrary, were merry, singing and dancing; they cheered their husbands, chatted gaily with bystanders, and boasted of what should yet be done by their brawny arms. As the car, containing the marines, reached the centre of the block, the lieutenant in command ordered the men to leave and form in line. Small groups and gatherings of women and children greeted them with hisses and derisive cheers; to these they paid no attention, but marched toward the larger mob at the corner. The lieutenant called upon the crowd to disperse, but no further notice was taken of the command than a sullen refusal; he then ordered his men to fire, which they did, with blank cartridges, and of course, with blank effect. The smoke had not cleared away before the infuriated mob rushed with vengeance upon the little band, broke them into confusion, seized their muskets, trampled them under foot, beat them with sticks, punched them with the long wires, and laughed at their impotence. Several of the marines managed to escape into the side streets, but each fugitive had his gang of temporary pursuers, and quite a number were killed, while all were terribly beaten. From this moment the spirit of the mob seemed changed. Resistance was no longer thought of: attack was the watchword. A squad of police attempted to arrest some of the ringleaders at this point, but they were signally defeated, badly beaten, and one of them was killed. Elated with this triumph, excited by the spilled blood, and the instinct of passion, the mob seemed beside themselves, and proposed an immediate onslaught upon the principal streets, the hotels, and other public buildings.

Against the negroes there seemed to exist a peculiar animosity, and incidents of barbaric cruelty occurred. The restaurants and hotels whose servants were of this class, were taken possession of by the rioters, who broke windows, smashed furniture, maltreated guests, and sought to kill the fleeing and terrified servants. In the afternoon, by which time the whole city was in alarm, the crowd had increased to great numbers, when some one suggested that the Colored Half Orphan Asylum was not far from their immediate neighborhood. The asylum was a substantial edifice, erected a few years since, on Fifth avenue, between Forty-third and Forty-fourth streets, and afforded a home to between 700 and 800 children. Its destruction was at once resolved upon, and headed by a gang of half-grown men, the crowd rapidly moved on the asylum. Entering it by doors or windows, they ransacked every room, drove the women and nurses out, and flung the children hither and thither, kicked and cuffed the little ones without regard to humanity, and after throwing everything they could lay their hands upon into the street, deliberately set fire to the building. Here, too, Chief Decker interfered. With one hand he extinguished the flames, with his person barred the progress of the rioters, and strove by the force of words to deter them from their purpose. But his efforts were in vain. With fearful yells and screams, the boys set fire again to the doomed building, while the men looked sternly on, and the women walked off laden with the spoils.

About the same hour, an attack was made upon the armory in Second avenue, corner of Twenty-first street. The object was to secure rifles and muskets which it was known the Government had stored there. Early in the day, the police authorities had placed a squad of men in charge of the building, with instructions to guard it and to prevent the entrance of any one. Against an army of three or four thousand rough men it was no easy task to defend the building. Sledge hammers and stones soon broke open the doors, when a grand rush was made, and the men began to push in. The police knew their duty, and did it; their first volley killed two men, and a subsequent discharge three others; but then the crowd pushed on more vigorously. A severe hand-to-hand fight ensued among those at the door, while the crowd outside stoned the windows, breaking every pane of glass in the building. Finding resistance useless, the police retired and effected an escape through a rear door. The building was instantly fired, and soon fell a mass of blackened ruins.

In the lower part of the city, the evidences of riotous demonstrations were confined to attacks upon colored men, and a threatened demolition of the Tribune newspaper office. Toward five o'clock, the Forty-sixth street crowd made its way to the park, where they joined a smaller gathering of boys and men, who had been hooting and sneering at the establishment of the New York Tribune, and subjecting its inmates generally to an unpleasant inquisition. After some delay, the more venturesome approached the doors of the office. These were locked, but a few vigorous pushes broke them, and the crowd rushed in. The counters and desks were broken up, and preparations were made for a grand illumination, when a detachment of police suddenly made its appearance, and charged full upon them. So sudden was the attack that a panic seized them, and they fled like chaff before the wind.

The assaults upon negroes were among the most fiendish features of the proceedings. It was estimated that, during the twenty-four hours, at least a dozen unfortunate colored persons were brutally murdered, while some were beaten, forced to jump into the river, or driven from the city. A colored man residing in Carmine street, was caught by a mob of about four hundred men and boys, as he was leaving his stable in Clarkson street. Instantly an attack was made upon him, and he was beaten and kicked until life was seemingly extinct, and then his body was suspended to a tree, a fire kindled beneath it, the heat of which restored the sufferer to consciousness, while the smoke stifled him.

Several fierce battles were fought between the police and the mob, in which the former were invariably the victors. During the day and night, the city was protected solely and only by this arm of the civil service.

The office of Provost-Marshal Manierre was on Broadway near Twenty-eighth street. At nine o'clock drafting was begun there, but in consequence of the disturbances in the 9th district, at twelve o'clock it was suspended. Shortly afterward the mob arrived and entered and sacked the office, set fire to the building, and destroyed the entire block, of which the office was the centre building. The famous Bull's Head Hotel, on Forty-fourth street, between Lexington and Fifth avenues, shared the fate of other fine structures, and was burned to the ground, because its proprietor declined to furnish liquor. The residences of Provost-Marshal Jenkins and Postmaster Wakeman, the 23d precinct station house, and two brown stone private dwellings on Lexington Avenue, were totally destroyed by fire; several members of the police were killed and many badly wounded, some twenty negroes were murdered, and a number of marines stoned to death.

The Board of Aldermen of the city met at half past one o'clock, P. M., but a quorum not being present, that body adjourned.

It was the general belief, that a decided action on the part of the board in providing means whereby poor men, who should be drafted, would be furnished with substitutes, would at once check the riot; and to meet this view, Alderman Hall had proposed this resolution:

Whereas, It is apparent that the three hundred dollar clause in the National Enrolment act of the late Congress is calculated to inflict great privations upon the poorer classes of our citizens; therefore, be it

Resolved, That the Committee on National Affairs be, and they are hereby, instructed to report to this board a plan whereby an appropriation can be made, to pay the commutation of such of our poorest citizens as are likely to be most sorely affected by the enforcement of a conscription.

Maj.-Gen. Wool was in command of the Department of the East, with his headquarters in New York, and about noon issued the following call to "veteran volunteers":

The veterans who have recently returned from the field of battle, have again an opportunity of serving, not only their country, but the great emporium of New York, from the threatened dangers of a ruthless mob.

The Commanding General of the Eastern Department trusts that those who have exhibited so much bravery in the field of battle, will not hesitate to come forward at this time, to tender their services to the mayor, to stay the ravages of the city by men who have lost all sense of obligations to their country, as well as to the city of New York.

JOHN E. WOOL, Major-General.

P. S.—These men are requested to report to Major-General Sandford, corner of Elm and White streets, on Tuesday, July 14th, at 10 A. M.

The next morning at eight o'clock, several colonels of returned volunteer regiments called upon their former commands to rally, and in pursuance of orders from Gen. Wool, Gen. Harvey Brown assumed command of the Federal troops in the city.

The mob had full control of the city, and omitted no opportunity of breaking laws or violating ordinances, until midnight, when a heavy rain dispersed them.

On Tuesday the spirit of the riot was more malignant. Governor Seymour having arrived in the city, issued the following proclamation:

NEW YORK, July 14, 1863.

To the People of the City of New York:

A riotous demonstration in your city, originating in opposition to the conscription of soldiers for the military service of the United States, has swelled into vast proportions, directing its fury against the property and lives of peaceful citizens. I know that many who have participated in these proceedings would not have allowed themselves to be carried to such extremes of violence and of wrong, except under an apprehension of injustice, but such persons are reminded that the only opposition to the conscription which can be allowed, is an appeal to the courts.

The right of every citizen to make such an appeal will be maintained, and the decision of the courts must be respected and obeyed by rulers and people alike. No other course is consistent with the maintenance of the laws, the peace and order of the city, and the safety of its inhabitants.

Riotous proceedings must, and shall be put down. The laws of the State of New York must be enforced, its peace and order maintained, and the lives and property of all its citizens protected at any and every hazzard. The rights of every citizen will be properly guarded and defended by the Chief Magistrate of the State.

I do, therefore, call upon all persons engaged in these riotous proceedings, to retire to their homes and employments, declaring to them that unless they do so at once, I shall use all the power necessary to restore the peace and order of the city. I also call upon all well-disposed persons not enrolled for the preservation of order, to pursue their ordinary avocations.

Let all citizens stand firmly by the constituted authorities, sustaining law and order in the city, and ready to answer any such demand as circumstances may render necessary for me to make upon their services; and they may rely upon a rigid enforcement of the laws of this State against all who violate them.

HORATIO SEYMOUR, Governor.

It was soon urged upon the governor that measures more rigorous must be taken; and becoming convinced that such was the case, he was induced to declare the city in a state of insurrection.

This proclamation, however, produced but little effect, and the second day was in many of its features the worst of the four. The stores were closed in all parts of the city; no signs of trade were visible. Between the several military officers, into whose hands the defence of the city and the suppression of the riot were committed, there were difficulties of which no one could obtain a satisfactory explanation. General Wool as commanding general of the Department of the East, was in supreme control of the regular troops, and he delegated departments of his small command to General Brown and General Sandford, at different times, so that it was difficult for his more immediate subordinates to know the authority of each. The police were true to their great trust, and won for themselves an honorable record. The principal feature of these twenty-four hours was the onset upon the negroes, which was attended with fearful atrocities. Whenever a negro was found, death was his inexorable fate. Old men and infirm women were beaten without mercy; whole neighborhoods were burned out; the life of no person of color was safe for a moment in the presence of the infuriated mob. On several occasions during the day the military and the rioters were brought face to face. Twice an attempt was made to resist the progress of the soldiers, but ball cartridges were used and the rioters fled. Lieut. Wood, in command of 150 "regulars" from Fort Lafayette, was directed to disperse a crowd of perhaps 2,000 men, who had assembled in the vicinity of Grand and Pitt Streets. On the approach of the soldiers, the lieutenant called upon the crowd to disperse. A volley of stones was the reply. He then ordered his men to fire above the crowd, which being done without apparent effect, he directed them to fire and take aim. The result was 12 dead men, several wounded, and a general flight. Two children were among the killed. In this way the mob was frequently broken up, but as it would continually reorganize, it became necessary to adopt some plan of absolute and general dispersion. The citizens generally prepared to defend themselves and their property. The governor was induced to speak from the steps of the City Hall to an immense gathering of the people, among whom were undoubtedly many who had been engaged in the riots. The governor made a few remarks, intended to allay the popular excitement, and earnestly counselled obedience to the laws and the constituted authorities. He also read a note explanatory of what he had done about the draft. The governor was listened to with great respect, and the reading of the letter caused general satisfaction among his hearers.

The murder of Col. O'Brien was, perhaps, the most fearful of the many incidents which occurred. Commissioned to disperse a mob in the Third Avenue, he gallantly charged upon them with an efficient detachment of troops, and succeeded in breaking the front and turning the face of the rioters. Having sprained his ankle during the excitement, he stepped into a drug store in 32d street, while his command passed on. The store was soon surrounded, and the proprietor fearing it would be sacked begged the colonel to get away as soon as possible. With a brave heart O'Brien went out among the crowd alone; and while parleying with them a treacherous blow from behind laid him senseless upon the pavement. The crowd fell upon the prostrate form, beating and bruising it. For hours the bleeding body was drawn up and down the street, receiving a brutal treatment almost unparalleled, after which it was carried, with shouts and groans, to his residence, where the same conduct was repeated. A priest with kindly courtesy interfered, and read over the dead body the prayers of its church, after which he directed the remains to be taken into the house. Hardly was his back turned, however, when a brutal fellow stamped upon the corpse, and his example was followed by many others.

Events followed each other in rapid succession. The Secretary of War ordered home the militia regiments that were doing duty in Pennsylvania, and the rioters became, to a great extent, "demoralized," their leaders having been killed or taken prisoners. The stages and cars were withdrawn from the streets until Thursday, when, by order of the Police Commissioners, the regular running was resumed.

By this time it had become generally known that the draft was suspended. The municipal authorities had passed a relief bill to pay $300 commutation, or substitute money, to every drafted man of the poorer classes. These facts contributed greatly to appease the mob, though they had been practically subdued by the gallant conduct of the regular troops, the militia, and the police. The riot ceased as an organized operation, on the 16th instant. A large force of cavalry patrolled the disaffected districts on the evening of that day, and met with no armed opposition. On the morning of the 17th the cavalry found and took possession of seventy stands of revolvers and carbines, and several casks of paving stones, which had been secreted by the rioters, and also captured several prisoners. On the 18th instant, Maj.-Gen. Wool was relieved of the command of the Department of the East by Maj.-Gen. Dix, by orders of the President, dated the 15th. Gen. Harvey Brown who had been in command of the city and harbor of New York (under General Wool) during the riots, was relieved on the 17th instant by Brig.-Gen. Canby.

The twelve militia regiments had by this time returned from Pennsylvania. Detachments from their number, amounting to over 1,000 men, were constantly on duty for many days after the suppression of the riots, and the entire 1st division was ready to support them at short notice. But there was not the least symptom of a renewal of the disturbances, although rioters were arrested by civil processes, tried, and sent to prison, from day to day.

The number of persons killed during these terrible riots is not known. The mortality statistics for the week, at the city inspector's office, show an increase of 450 over the average weekly mortality of the year. About 90 deaths from gunshot wounds were reported at his office. It was said—but this is, doubtless, incorrect—that the remains of many of the rioters were secretly taken into the country and buried there. A large number of wounded persons probably died during the following week. Governor Seymour in his annual message states that the "number of killed and wounded is estimated by the police to be at least one thousand." The police and the regular and local military forces suffered but little in comparison with the mob. With regard to the militia of the 1st division, General Sandford gives the exact figures of their losses in a portion of the riots. He says that "one private soldier was killed, and twenty-two men dangerously, and fifty officers and soldiers slightly, wounded, at the defeat of the mob in 42d street, the storming of the barricade erected by the rioters in 29th street, and in the other conflicts which followed."

The losses by the destruction of buildings and other property were originally estimated at $400,000. A committee was appointed by the county supervisors to audit claims for damages, for all of which the county was responsible under the law, and for the payment of which a large appropriation was made. The aggregate of the claims far surpassed the highest expectations, amounting to over $2,500,000. The committee disallowed many, and cut down most of the remainder 50 per cent. At last accounts over $1,000,000 had been paid to claimants, and it was supposed that $500,000 more would be needed for the same purpose.

On the night of the 15th of July a riot broke out in Boston, under the following circumstances: Two of the provost marshal's assistants were engaged in distributing notifications to drafted men, when one of the officers was struck by a woman, at whose house a notification had been left. An attempt being made to arrest the woman, a number of her friends collected and attacked the officer, severely beating him. A police force was soon upon the ground, and succeeded in temporarily quelling the disturbance; but a crowd lingered in the vicinity of the scene, and increased as night approached, and the military authorities thought it best to order out the Lancers, the 11th battery (Captain Jones), the 44th regiment, three companies from Fort Warren, a company of regulars from Fort Independence, and a squad of the second cavalry from Readsville, to check the riot which was believed to be imminent. The entire police force was also placed on duty, and stationed at points where difficulties were most likely to occur. About 8½ P. M. a crowd of men and boys, estimated at from 500 to 1,000, gathered in front of the armory of the 11th battery, in Cooper Street, and although warned off by Captain Jones, the commanding officer, threw a shower of stones and bricks at the building, breaking the windows and the door, and wounding several of the soldiers. The mob then attempted to carry the building by storm, and had succeeded in forcing an entrance, when a gun loaded with canister shot was fired into them with terrible effect, but they did not break and run until a bayonet charge was made upon them. Six or eight persons were killed on the spot, and a large number wounded. Simultaneously with the attack on the armory a mob of several hundred persons broke into the gun store of Thomas P. Barnes, in Dock Square, and carried away about a hundred muskets and a large quantity of pistols and bowie knives. They next made a rush at the gun store of Wm. Read and Son, Faneuil Hall Square, but the police had received information of the intended attack, and were on hand in time to repel it. One of the rioters was shot by the police, and a few others were slightly injured. The formidable array of military and police, and the promptness with which they had quelled disturbances thus far, seemed to frighten the rioters at this stage of operations, and they gradually dispersed. The only other riotous incident of note during the night was an attempt to set fire to the armory in Cooper Street, in the absence of the guard. The fire was soon discovered and extinguished.

At Portsmouth, N. H., there was some trouble on the day of drafting. An excited throng of men, women, and children, gathered about the provost marshal's office, which was in charge of volunteers from Fort Constitution, and U. S. marines from the navy yard, under command of Col. Marston. A large police force was also in attendance, and instructed to disperse the crowd. Two men who resisted were taken to the station house. About 9½ P. M. an attack was made upon the station house by about 100 friends of the arrested parties, but was repelled by the small force of police then on the ground. A squad of soldiers from the provost marshal's office was sent to their assistance, and charged upon the mob with bayonets, dispersing it instantly. Two of the police and four of the rioters were wounded, but none reported killed; and there was no further obstruction to the draft in Portsmouth.

A disturbance which threatened at one time to assume formidable proportions occurred in Holmes County, Ohio, in June. It appears that on the 5th of that month, Elias Robinson, an enrolling officer, was stoned out of Richland township by a party of men, of whom the names of four were known. Captain Drake, the provost-marshal of that district, went with a posse of men to the village of Napoleon, in the above named township, to arrest those persons, and found them in the upper story of a house, armed and ready for resistance. They refused to surrender, saying that they would not consent to be tried by court-martial. On the promise, however, that they should be tried by the U. S. court at Cleveland, they gave themselves up, and the party started for Wooster. But before Capt. Drake had succeeded in getting his prisoners beyond the limits of Holmes County he was overtaken by an armed force of 150 men, who ordered the prisoners from the wagons, took revolvers from several of Capt. Drake's men, and surrounding Capt. Drake with a score of rifles pointed at his breast, demanded that he should take an oath never to enter Holmes County on such business again, on penalty of death. It is said that he refused to take the oath, and also to give up his pistols. The rescuers finally let him and his posse go, and carried the prisoners back to their homes. On the 12th and 13th the enrolling officers were also driven out of two of the townships of Holmes County.

The draft resulted, in twelve States in which it was enforced, in adding about 50,000 men to the army, and in the accumulation of a fund of $10,518,000, derived from commutations under what was known as the "Three Hundred Dollar clause" of the act, which was reserved for the procurement of recruits by bounties.

Previous to 1863 the employment of colored soldiers in the United States service was confined to two or three localities. At Hilton Head, South Carolina, Gen. Hunter had caused the able-bodied negroes from the neighboring plantations to be formed into regiments and drilled by competent officers; and Gen. Butler, finding in New Orleans a colored corps of the Louisiana State militia, raised under the certificate of a former governor of the State, placed it in the service of the Government, and encouraged the formation of similar organizations. These troops were originally intended chiefly for local service, or if sent beyond the localities in which they were raised, were to be employed to garrison posts which the unacclimated Northern soldiers could not safely occupy during the unhealthy season. Public opinion had not yet decided that they could become an integral portion of the army, and as such be available for every species of military service, notwithstanding that Congress, by two acts passed in July, 1862, had expressly authorized the employment of colored men as troops.

The first of these, known as the Confiscation Act, permitted the President to employ as many persons of African descent as he might deem necessary and proper for the suppression of the rebellion; and for that purpose to organize and use them in such manner as he might judge best for the public welfare. The second act authorized him to receive into the service of the United States for any species of labor or military or naval service for which they might be found competent, persons of African descent, who should be enrolled and organized under such regulations, not inconsistent with the Constitution and the laws, as he might prescribe; and should receive $10 per month and one ration per day, of which monthly pay $3 might be in clothing.

Both laws were made with reference to those persons who by force of arms or by provisions of statutes had been recently freed from bondage; and the important class of colored soldiers from the free States was probably not then in the contemplation of Congress. Many considerations were urged upon the President to induce him to exercise the power conferred upon him in a restricted sense only. The employment of negroes as laborers upon fortifications, teamsters, boatmen, and in similar capacities, was declared legitimate and sufficient for the present needs of the country; but, in the opinion of many, the arming of any considerable body of such persons was a measure fraught with ominous consequences. Whether or not these reasons were deemed conclusive, it is certain that, previous to 1863, the number of persons of African descent employed as soldiers was exceedingly limited. But with the commencement of the year a vigorous movement was initiated in various parts of the country to organize colored regiments, and especially to bring to the aid of the Government the latent strength of the large negro population in the seceded States.

On January 12th Mr. Stevens, of Pennsylvania, introduced into the House of Representatives a bill authorizing the President to raise, equip, and organize 150,000 colored troops, which, after being amended so as to provide for the enlistment of not over 300,000, was passed, February 2d, in the face of a determined opposition from members of the border States, and from some friends of the administration. A similar bill, introduced by Mr. Sumner in the Senate, having been reported back from the Committee on Military Affairs, with a recommendation that it should not pass, on the ground that sufficient authority to raise such troops was conferred by the act of 1862, no further action was taken on either bill. The subject had, however, been by this time very generally discussed, both in and out of Congress, and in deference to the wishes of a large portion of the community, and of many prominent public men, including officers of experience, the President determined to exercise, to their fullest extent, the powers conferred upon him by the act of 1862. Congress having in the Conscription Act avoided making any distinction between white and colored citizens, and required them equally to be enrolled and drafted in the armies of the United States, the policy of the administration thenceforth became clearly defined, and "persons of African descent," as well in the free as in the slave States, were declared to be available as soldiers.

The initiative in raising colored regiments in the free States was taken by Governor Andrew, of Massachusetts, acting in conformity with the following order from the Secretary of War:

WAR DEPARTMENT, WASHINGTON CITY,
January 20, 1863.

Ordered that GOVERNOR ANDREW, of Massachusetts, is authorized, until further orders, to raise such number of volunteer companies of artillery for duty in the forts of Massachusetts and elsewhere, and such corps of infantry for the volunteer military service, as he may find convenient. Such volunteers to be enlisted for three years, unless sooner discharged, and may include persons of African descent, organized into separate corps. He will make the usual requisitions on the appropriate Staff Bureaus and officers for the proper transportation, organization, supplies, subsistence, arms, and equipments of such volunteers.

(Signed) EDWIN M. STANTON,
Secretary of War.

Recruiting offices were immediately opened by the governor, and, as the colored population of Massachusetts was inconsiderable, agents were sent into neighboring States, where the scruples of the people or of the executive prevented the enlistment of troops of this class. In reply to inquiries, Governor Andrew announced that these regiments would be numbered, organized, considered, and treated in every respect precisely as other regiments previously sent into the field by Massachusetts; and, on the authority of the Secretary of War, he pledged the honor of the United States to them in the same degree and to the same rights with all other troops. Other free States subsequently sanctioned the enlistment of colored soldiers, including Rhode Island, Pennsylvania, New York, Ohio, and Kansas.

The Government having matured its plans with regard to the negro population whom the progress of the war had brought within the Union lines, Gen. Thomas, adjutant-general of the United States, was despatched in March to the Southwest, charged with the organization of colored troops, and the establishment of a labor system in the Mississippi valley. In the discharge of these duties he visited Memphis, Helena, and other points on both sides of the Mississippi as far south as Vicksburg.

Under the impulse given by this action of the Government, recruiting for colored regiments proceeded with considerable activity in Tennessee, Mississippi, Louisiana, and North and South Carolina, and before the close of the year was in progress in parts of Virginia and other districts in possession of the Federal arms, as also in Maryland and in the District of Columbia. Gen. Banks, commanding the Department of the Gulf, was so well satisfied with the black troops, which he found in the service on his arrival in New Orleans, and was so confident in the ability and disposition of the negroes to become good soldiers, that he ordered a whole army corps to be raised, consisting of eighteen regiments of five hundred men each, to be called the "Corps d'Afrique."

The enlistment of negroes in the rebel States, or of colored refugees from such States, was attended with little or no difficulty in respect to claims of service or labor from such persons. The owners were, for the most part, enemies, and after the Emancipation Proclamation of the President the question of property was considered definitively settled. When, however, the Government determined to make requisitions upon the colored population of the border slave States, or upon those portions of the seceded States expressly excepted from the operation of the Emancipation Proclamation, it became necessary to adopt some rule of compensation for slaveholders, whose rights might be affected. With this view an order was issued, on October 3d, from the War Department, directing the establishment of recruiting stations in Maryland, Missouri, and Tennessee, and prescribing the method of enlistment. "All able-bodied free negroes, slaves of disloyal persons, and slaves of loyal persons, with the consent of their owners," were declared eligible for military service, and the State and county in which the enlistments were made were to be credited with the recruits thus obtained. Loyal slaveowners offering slaves for enlistment were to receive $300 for each recruit accepted, upon filing a deed of manumission for him, and making satisfactory proof of title. But if within thirty days from the date of opening enlistments, a sufficient number of recruits should not be obtained to meet the exigencies of the service, then enlistments might be made by slaves, without requiring the consent of their owners; the latter were to receive the compensation, and upon the same terms provided for owners offering their slaves for enlistment. Special boards were also appointed for each State to determine all claims of owners, and to further the objects of the order.

The number of colored soldiers obtained from the sources above described has been variously stated; but it appears by the report of the bureau of enlistments, created in May, that by December, 1863, over 50,000 men had been organized and were in actual service.

The regular army of the United States, before the commencement of the present war, seldom numbering in its ranks more than 12,000 or 13,000 men, and with a medical and hospital service corresponding to its limited numbers, had little need of special rules of hygiene, or the elaboration of any extensive system of regulating the health and physical comfort of its forces.

The first step in the way of prevention of disease in the army must be taken in the *examination of recruits*. The ignorance or incompetence of the examining surgeons in the first two years of the war, and sometimes it is to be feared baser motives, led to great abuses in this respect. "Thousands of incapacitated men," says Surgeon-General Hammond, "were in the early stages of the war allowed to enter the army, to be discharged after a few weeks' service, most of which had been passed in the hospital. Many did not march five miles before breaking down, and not a few never shouldered a musket during the whole time of their service. * * * * Cases of chronic ulcers, varicose veins, epilepsy, and other conditions unfitting men for a military life, came frequently under my notice. The recruits were either not inspected at all by a medical officer, or else the examination was so loosely conducted as to amount to a farce. I know of several regiments in which the medical inspection was performed by the surgeon walking down the line and looking at the men as they stood in the ranks." There was great improvement in these examinations after the autumn of 1862.

At the commencement of the war, the War Department had no hospitals, save a few post and garrison establishments of antiquated design, and whose aggregate capacity was less than that of a single one of the magnificent structures since erected. In the battles of the spring of 1862, though new hospitals were erected with the utmost rapidity, consistent with their thorough adaptation to the wants of the patients, they were inadequate to accommodate the tens of thousands of the sick and wounded who needed care, and the Government was compelled to solicit the admission of its patient sufferers into the civil hospitals in the large cities. In this way many were provided for in Baltimore, Philadelphia, New York, Boston, Pittsburg, Cincinnati, St. Louis, and Louisville. The pushing forward of the new hospitals to completion, as well as the erection of others, meantime occupied the energies of the Quartermaster-General and the Surgeon-General, both men of extraordinary executive ability, and in the autumn of 1862, they were able to announce their readiness to accommodate in their own hospitals all their sick and wounded. In the construction and administration of those hospitals the Surgeon-General laid down these principles to be observed:

1st. That they should be capable of being well ventilated.

2d. That each should be sufficiently capacious for the number of inmates it was to contain.

3d. That they should admit of good drainage.

4th. That they should be provided with a sufficient number of windows.

5th. That the kitchen, laundry, and other offices of administration, should be separated from the wards, well arranged, and of ample size.

6th. That efficient water-closets, ablution, and bathing accommodations should be provided.

7th. That they should be amply supplied with water and gas, or other means of illumination.

8th. That the furniture of all kinds should be of suitable quality.

9th. That the officers and attendants should have their proper respective duties assigned to them, and that they should be in number sufficient for the wants of the sick.

10th. That proper rules should be established for the government of the hospital, for the diet of the inmates, and for preserving order and an efficient state of police.

The medical department has performed a herculean labor in the erection and fitting up of 233 general hospitals, in different parts of the country, beside a very considerable number of post and garrison hospitals. These hospitals are generally temporary structures, intended to last, without material repairs, for ten years.

The idea of a hospital, conceived by most non-professional readers, is that of a huge barrack-looking building or buildings, three or four stories in height, gloomy in appearance, and into whose cavernous walls many a poor unfortunate enters, but very few return to the life and bustle of the outer world. This typical hospital is as far as possible from the conception of Surgeon-General Hammond, or the able medical directors and surgeons who were his coadjutors in planning and superintending the construction of the General Hospitals of the army. They started with certain fundamental ideas of construction, which were carried through all their hospitals. The first of these was ridge ventilation, or the supplying a way of egress for the foul air of the ward by an opening of from ten inches to three feet at the ridge or apex of the roof, protected from the admission of rain, snow, or violent winds by a false roof, raised four inches above the true one, and projecting over it on each side about two feet. A perforated iron plate near the floor and behind each bed admitted the fresh air, which passed thus upwards, and forced the foul air through the roof opening. This formed the summer ventilation. In winter the fresh air was admitted around the stove from below, and passing between the stove and an outer casing of zinc, which surrounded it, was distributed through the room; while a large, square, wooden tube, open at the bottom, and extending to the roof, received and enclosed the pipe of the stove to its termination above the ridge, and thus became the ventilator of that portion of the ward.

Another new feature in the construction of these hospitals was the entire separation of the wards from the administrative portion of the hospital, and the making of each ward a single one-story pavilion, removed so far from every other ward or building, that it could have the benefit of the sun and the free circulation of pure air on both sides of it throughout the day, while at the same time one end of each ward opened from a corridor which would serve as a covered hall for exercise to the convalescing patients, and through which there was communication with the administrative buildings. The pavilions were to have their long diameter, where possible, a north and south line. Another point insisted upon was that no patient should have less than 1,000 (except under very peculiar circumstances not less than 1,200) cubic feet of space, and the air of this, by the system of ventilation, constantly changing.

The pavilions were to be raised at least one foot, generally two, above the ground; the floors to be coated with a mixture of beeswax and oil, to prevent any liquid from soaking into them; the baths and water-closets to be at the extreme end of the pavilions, and form an angle with them, and to be connected with such a system of sewerage as would convey all offensive matters and odors away instantly. A ward or pavilion was not to contain more than fifty-two beds, and these were to be placed in pairs with three feet space between the two, and each pair to be placed between the windows; the two beds, occupying an average space of fifteen feet in the length of the ward, and of seven and a half feet in width, and a passage way of ten feet to extend through the middle of the ward for its whole length, thus making the width of each ward twenty-five feet, and its length, if it contains fifty-two beds, about two hundred and twenty feet; the additional twenty-five feet being occupied with water closets, scullery, &c., at one end, and wardmasters', nurses' rooms, and mess room at the other. In the practical application of these principles, it has been found better not to have the wards quite so long, and they generally contain only thirty-six or forty-eight beds, some only twenty-four); or, if there were fifty-two, they occupied somewhat less than fifteen feet to the pair. The first large hospital built upon the principles presented by the surgeon-general, was the West Philadelphia Hospital, situated at the intersection of Forty-fourth and Spruce Streets, half a mile outside of the limits of the city of Philadelphia. We subjoin an engraving (fig. 1) of the general plan. The corridors are each 860 feet long, 14 feet wide, and 13 feet high, and serve as mess rooms for the pavilion. There are thirty-four pavilions, *b b b*, each 24 feet wide, and 13 feet high at the eaves; they are now of unequal length, ranging from 150 to 250 feet. Between the corridors is the administrative building, *a*. There are three kitchens, *c c c*; two laundries, *d d*; a chapel, *e*; store rooms, *f f*; a mess room for special occasions, *g*; two buildings for officers' quarters, *h h*; boiler room, *i*; residence of surgeon in charge, *k*; water tanks, *l*; barber shop and printing office, *m* and *n*; boiler and tank, *o*; smoking rooms, *p p*; reading and lecture room, *q*; knapsack room, *r*; guard room, *s*; stable, *t*; guard, *u*. The pavilions are 21 feet apart, which is too close by at least ten feet. The building is of wood, lathed and plastered on the outside. Its cost, aside from furniture, exceeded $200,000. It has 3,124 beds. The number of medical officers was fifty-two, beside eighteen medical cadets, and of cooks, nurses, and other attendants, four hundred and sixty-four. There were also three chaplains.

A still finer example of a great military hospital, the largest in the world, was the Mower General Hospital, at Chestnut Hill, Philadelphia. This vast establishment consisted of 50 pavilions, each 175 feet long, 20 wide, exclusive of the water closet and scullery which

(Fig. 1.)

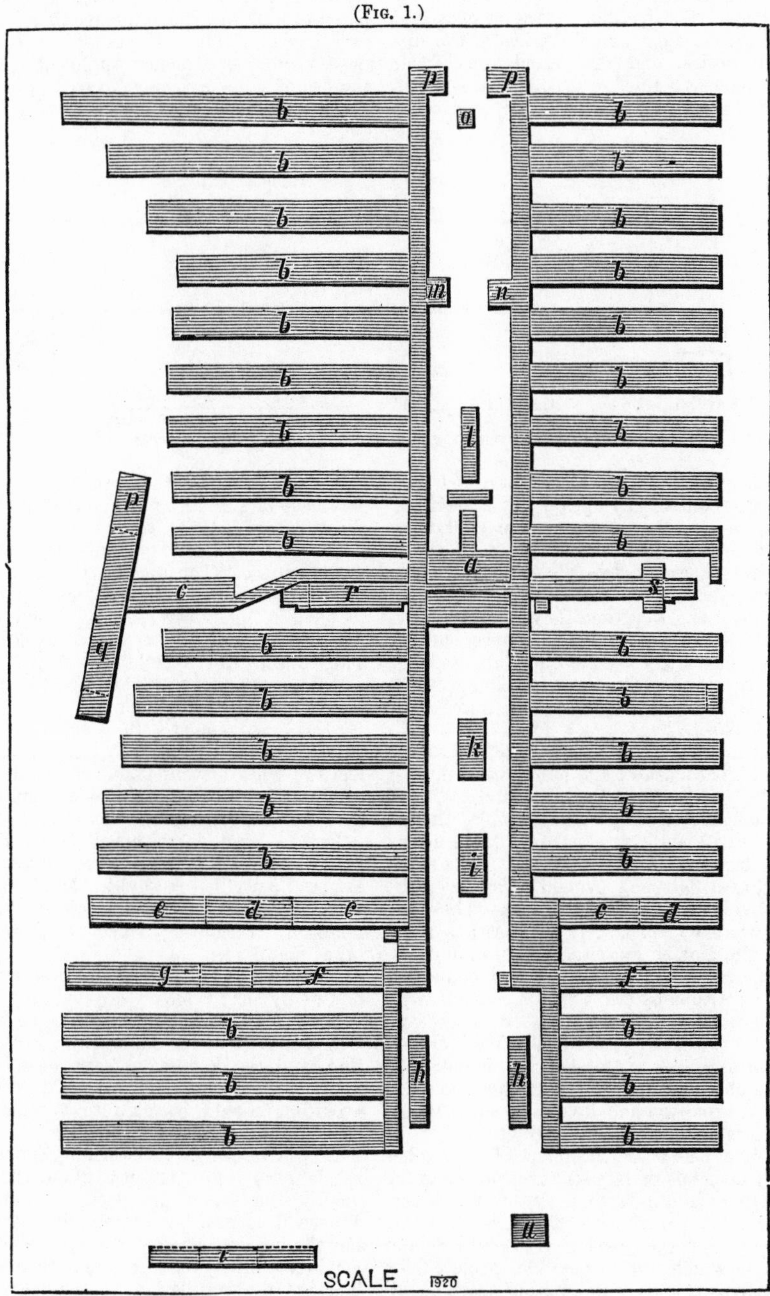

GROUND-PLAN OF WEST PHILADELPHIA HOSPITAL.

projected from the pavilion, 14 feet high to the eaves, and 19 feet to the ridge. These pavilions projected in radii from a corridor of flattened ellipsoidal form, 16 feet wide, and 2,400 feet long, enclosing an area of 541,466 square feet. Across the shorter diameter of the ellipsoid, as well as around its circumference was a railroad for moving food, fuel, furniture, carrying the patients to their wards, &c. The administrative portion of the building was in the central plot. The pavilions were twenty feet apart at the corridor, and forty feet at the distant extremities, and the circulation of air around them was thus secured. The sides of the corridor were almost entirely composed of glass sashes, which, in summer, were entirely removed. During inclement weather they were closed, and the corridor furnished with fifty large stoves, and used as an exercise hall, for those patients who were able to leave their ward. To each ward, at the end nearest the corridor, a mess room was attached, sufficiently large for the use of those patients who were able to leave their beds. The following plan (fig. 2) shows

(Fig. 2.)

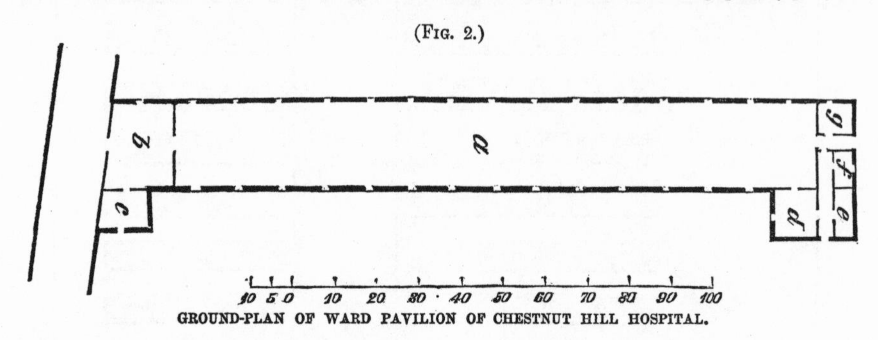

GROUND-PLAN OF WARD PAVILION OF CHESTNUT HILL HOSPITAL.

the arrangement of a ward pavilion in detail: *a* is the ward room occupying 150 feet in length of the pavilion, and twenty feet wide, containing fifty-two beds; *b*, the mess room; *c*, scullery; *d*, bath room; *e*, water closet; *f*, ablution room; *g*, wardmaster's room. The pavilions are four or five feet narrower than they should be, and when the beds are all full there are but 960 cubic feet of air to each patient; but as this is constantly changed by the admirable ventilation, it is nearly sufficient. The number of beds is 3,320. There was a force of 622 officers, attendants, guard, &c., attached to the hospital. The cost of the buildings was over $250,000. The McClellan Hospital, situated in the neighborhood of Philadelphia, though smaller (1,040 beds), was, perhaps, more nearly perfect than any other yet erected. The corridor was of a flattened ovoidal form, from the ends of which the pavilions project. These pavilions were wider, larger, and farther apart than at the Mower Hospital. The administrative building was in the centre and connected with the corridor by two straight passage ways. In the ground-plan (fig. 3), *a* is the main corridor; *b b b*, wards; *c*, administrative building, two stories high; *d*, kitchen; *e*, laundry; *f*, clothing and guard rooms; *g*, engine room; *h*, stable; *i*, provision and knapsack store room; *k*, quarters of medical officers in charge.

We give below ground-plans of two other military hospitals of large size, each arranging the pavilions in a different way, but all observing the same principles. The first was the Hammond General Hospital, at Point Lookout (fig. 4), in which sixteen pavilions project from a circular corridor. The administrative building was the wide structure at the upper side of the circle, and the kitchen, laundry, guard room, dead house, &c., were in the centre. The pavilions here are 40 feet apart at the corridor, and 75 feet at the farther end. They are 145 feet long, 25 feet wide, and 14 feet high to the eaves, and 18 to the ridge. The ventilation is perfect. Each patient has 1,116 cubic feet of space. The second, the Lincoln General Hospital, at Washington city (fig. 5), had its pavilions placed *en echelon*, along a corridor, forming two sides of an acute-angled triangle. The administrative building was at the apex, and the kitchen, &c., inclosed within the angle. This hospital accommodated 1,200 patients. By this arrangement a thorough ventilation of each ward was secured, while all the wards had the same direction and received the rays of the sun at the same time—a matter of considerable importance.

In the West, large hospitals on some one of these, or similar plans, were erected at St. Louis, Louisville, Nashville, Madison, Evansville, and New Albany, Indiana; and others at Madison, Wisconsin; Davenport, Iowa; and other points.

For field hospitals, the hospital tent is undoubtedly preferable to any building. Where a camp is somewhat permanent, the improved Crimean tent with double walls, ridge ventilation, and the admission of pure air near the floor, answers a good purpose. In both, special attention should be paid to ventilation, and over-crowding carefully avoided.

In the lighting and warming of hospitals, special care is now taken to avoid vitiating the air by the gases produced by combustion. Where it is possible, illuminating gas is used, but the vitiated air, and carbonic acid gas, are conducted off by chimneys in such a way as to increase the ventilation of the ward. If gas cannot be obtained, the vegetable oils or paraffine, spermaceti, or wax candles are preferable to any other modes of illumination. Coal or petroleum oils, camphene and burning fluid, ir-

(Fig. 3.)

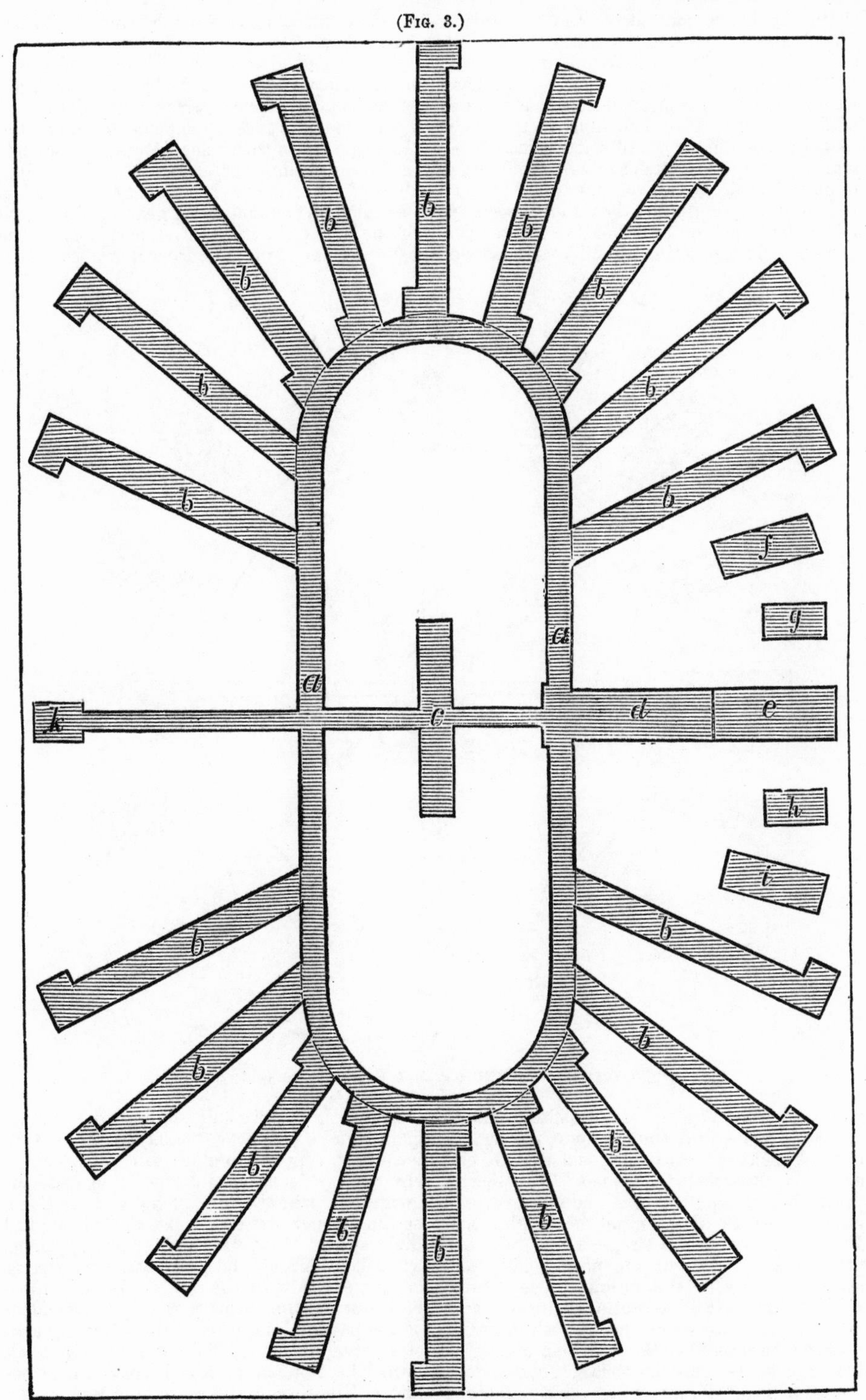

M'CLELLAN HOSPITAL, PHILADELPHIA.

ritate the lungs, and affect the respiration. The animal oils give off carbon, carbonic acid, and carburetted hydrogen in too large quantity to be desirable. The heating of the hospital wards should be connected as far as possible with the ventilation. The usual method is by stoves, though in some, hot water is introduced with advantage. Ruttan's system would seem to possess advantages over any other plan of warming and ventilation, but, so far as we are aware, has not been introduced. The temperature in cold weather is carefully watched, and is not allowed to vary much from 64° to 66° Fahrenheit.

The *alimentation* of the soldier is one of the most important items in the hygienic condition of an army. Great attention had been paid by the medical and commissary officers of the Government, to the arrangement and character of the ration, in order to furnish such combinations of food, and of such quality, as should be best adapted to maintain the health and strength of the soldier in its greatest perfection. The rations of most of the European armies are defective in these respects. The quantity of meat is generally too low, and in some, the supply of fresh meat and vegetables, and of coffee and sugar, is altogether inadequate. The fearful prevalence of typhus fevers, and of scurvy and other cachectic diseases, in the British and French armies in the Crimean war, was unquestionably owing to the poor quality and scanty quantity of the rations. The British soldier receives at home stations sixteen ounces of bread, and twelve ounces of flesh meat uncooked; on foreign stations, sixteen ounces of bread, or twelve ounces of biscuit, and sixteen ounces of meat, fresh or salt. This is charged to him at three and a half pence per day abroad, or four and a half pence per day at home. Coffee, sugar, pepper, potatoes, salt, or whatever else he may need, he must purchase from his own funds, where and how he can. In a few of the foreign stations, as at Hong Kong and the Cape of Good Hope, rice, sugar, coffee, and salt, in insufficient quantities, are issued as component parts of the ration. In the United States army, the ration is wholly independent of the pay, and consisted of the following articles: bread or flour, 1 lb. 6 oz.; fresh and salt beef, 1 lb. 4 oz., or pork or bacon, 12 oz.; potatoes, 1 lb. three times a week; rice, 1 $\frac{6}{10}$ oz.;

(FIG. 4.)

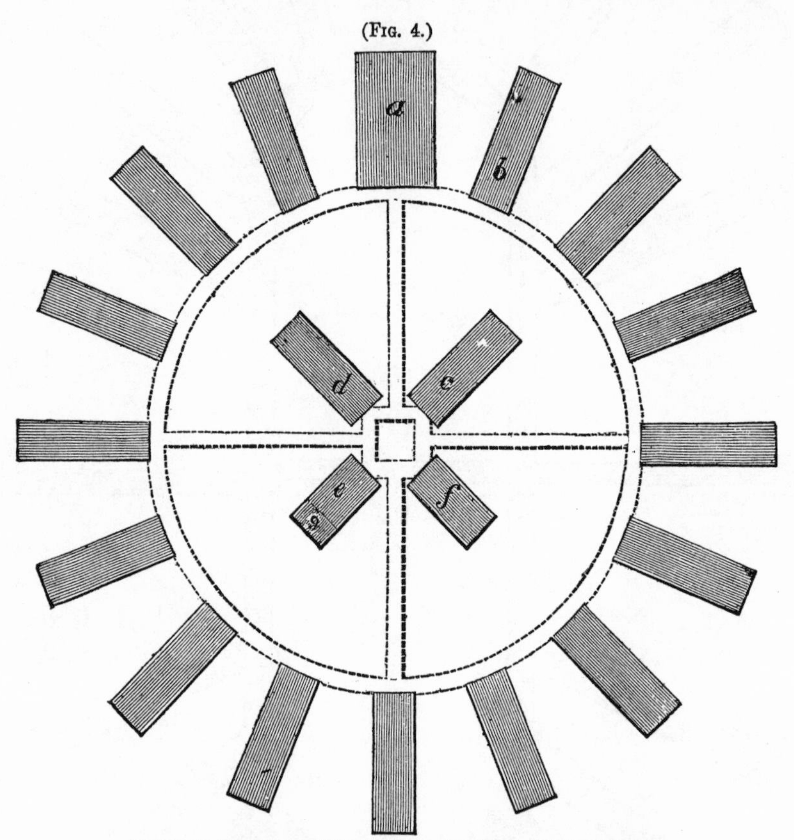

GROUND-PLAN OF HAMMOND GENERAL HOSPITAL, POINT LOOKOUT.

coffee, 1 $\frac{6}{10}$ oz.; or tea, $\frac{24}{100}$ of an oz.; sugar, 2 $\frac{4}{10}$ oz.; beans, $\frac{64}{100}$ of a gill; vinegar, $\frac{32}{100}$ of a gill; salt, $\frac{16}{100}$ of a gill; in addition to the above, 1 lb. of sperm candles, or 1¼ lbs. of ad-

(Fig. 5.)

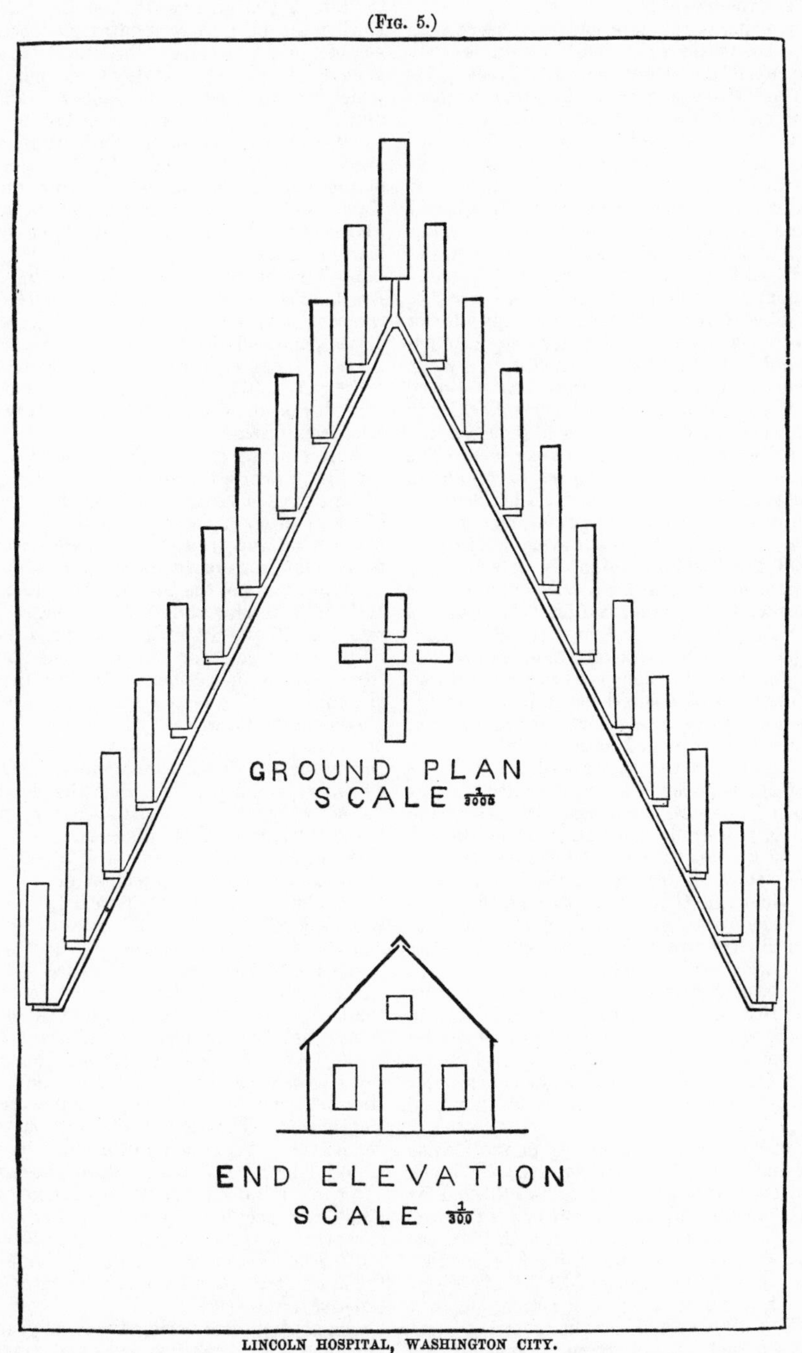

LINCOLN HOSPITAL, WASHINGTON CITY.

amantine candles, or 1½ lbs. of tallow candles, and 4 lbs. of soap, are issued to each hundred rations. Pepper has also been recently added to the ration, and extra issues of pickles, fruits, and other vegetables made, whenever the medical officers considered them necessary for the health of the troops.

It is owing to the care and persistence with which the various hygienic measures were urged upon the army, and the great pains taken to instruct and train the army surgeons and nurses in the hospitals for their duties, that the army of the United States, composed almost wholly of volunteers, whose whole mode of life had been changed by their new vocations, the greater part of them entirely ignorant of the laws of health, with surgeons who had, for the most part, no previous training in military medicine or surgery, and many of whom were utterly unfitted for their duties, maintained a lower sick rate as well as a lower rate of mortality than any other army in modern times. This result was reached, too, while the regions in which the army was stationed have in general been exceedingly unhealthy to the unacclimated, quite as insalubrious as any part of Spain, Portugal, or the Crimea. The attainment of so gratifying a result was due in a great degree to the United States Sanitary Commission, which, by its careful, regular and special medical inspections of every army corps, and all the hospitals, promptly detected any violations of hygienic laws, and took measures to correct them; published brief medical and surgical tracts from the pens of the ablest military physicians in the country and Europe, and placed copies in the hands of every army assistant surgeon and medical cadet in the army; trained many of the best nurses for camp, field, and hospital; provided anti-scorbutics in vast quantities where they were needed, and by its ministrations to the sick and wounded, and its stores of cordials, medicines, delicacies, and clothing, powerfully aided in restoring the disabled to service. The assistance thus rendered to the medical department of the Government, with which the Commission ever acted in perfect harmony, saved many thousands of lives, and made the army far more effective than it otherwise could have been.

A brief comparison of the medical statistics of the British army in the Peninsular war, in the war with Russia, and in times of peace, with those of the army of the United States during the recent war, will show conclusively the beneficial results of the strict attention paid to hygiene in the latter.

The average annual mortality in the British army during the Peninsular war was 165 men out of every thousand. Of these 113 died by disease or accident, and 52 by wounds received in action. From 1803 to 1812 the average annual death-rate of the entire British army abroad was 80 per 1,000;—71 by disease or accident, and 9 by wounds in action. This, it should be remembered, was in a veteran army composed, not of raw recruits, but of men hardened to exposure by years of service, a class of men far less liable to illness than raw recruits just from the farm, the store, or the workshop. In July, August, and September, 1854, the British army in the Crimea lost at the rate of 293 men per thousand, per annum. During the next three months, October, November, and December, the loss was at the annual rate of 511 to every thousand, 443 of which was by disease. In January, 1855, the mortality was at the rate of 1,174 to every 1,000—equal to the entire destruction of the army in ten months, and 1,143, or 97 per cent. of this loss was by disease. During the first three months of that year the death-rate was 912 out of every thousand, and 98 per cent. of it from disease.

During the entire campaign of 2½ years, April, 1854, to June, 1856, the annual death-rate was 232 per 1,000, of whom 202 were from disease, and only 30 from wounds received in action. In other words, during the campaign of 2½ years, 582 of every thousand men died from disease or wounds and 505 of every thousand from disease.

According to the Register General's report for the year 1861, the mortality among the home troops of Great Britain in that year was 91·24 in every thousand in a time of peace, and among the troops abroad the mortality from sickness averaged 100 in every thousand.

In the armies of the United States from April 15th, 1861, to May 18th, 1862, the entire death-rate was 53 per 1,000, per annum, of which only 44 per cent. or less than one-half was from disease or accident. During the year and three months next ensuing the loss from wounds in battle was very large, and during a portion of the time there was a large percentage of sickness from typhoid fever, diarrhœa, dysentery, small pox, etc., but the death-rate did not reach the ratio of the first year. On the 30th of June, 1863, there were in the general hospitals 91 men for each 1,000 of the army, and in field hospitals 44 out of every 1,000, making in all 135 of each 1,000 sick or wounded, of whom 110 were cases of sickness, and 25 of wounds or casualties. This far surpasses the British army even in time of peace. In 1861 the British troops in China had, in southern China, 283 out of every 1,000 constantly sick, and in northern China 205 out of 1,000. Among the home troops, the admissions into hospital were 1,025 of 1,000 mean strength, and 545 of every 1,000 were constantly sick. The careful weeding out of incompetent surgeons and inefficient nurses, the material improvement in the ambulance service, and the admirable construction of the new hospitals, in respect to temperature and ventilation, exerted a powerful influence, notwithstanding the terribly destructive battles, in diminishing the mortality, and promoting the recovery of the sick in the army.

The expenditures during the fiscal year ending June 30th, 1863, for arms and munitions of war, furnished by the Ordnance Department for sea coast and frontier fortifications, and for the forces in the field, amounted to $42,313,630.

The cannon, small arms, accoutrements, and equipments for men and horses, and ammunition obtained during the same period by purchase and manufacture, were as follows:

1,577 field, siege, and sea-coast cannon, with carriages, caissons, and other implements.
1,082,841 muskets and rifles for foot soldiers.
282,389 carbines and pistols for mounted troops.
1,251,995 cannon balls and shells.
48,719,862 pounds of lead and lead bullets.
1,435,046 cartridges for artillery.
259,022,216 cartridges for small arms.
847,273,400 percussion caps.
3,925,369 friction primers.
5,764,768 pounds of gunpowder.
919,676 sets of accoutrements for men.
94,639 sets of equipments for cavalry horses.
3,281 sets of artillery harness, each set for two horses.

The quantities of the principal articles of ordnance materials in the control of the department at the beginning of the war, the quantities of those articles that have since been procured, and the quantities of those articles on hand June 30th, 1863, are shown in the following table:

ARTICLES.	On hand at beginning of the war.	Procured since the war began.
Siege and sea-coast artillery....	1,052	1,064
Field artillery..................	231	2,734
Firearms for infantry..........	437,433	1,950,144
Firearms for cavalry...........	81,268	338,124
Sabres........................	16,933	837,555
Cannon balls and shells........	363,591	2,552,744
Lead and lead bullets, in lbs...	1,301,776	71,776,774
Cartridges for artillery.........	28,247	2,238,746
Cartridges for small arms......	8,292,300	522,204,816
Percussion caps...............	19,808,000	749,475,000
Friction primers...............	84,425	7,000,000
Gunpowder in lbs..............	1,110,584	13,424,363
Saltpetre, lbs..................	2,923,348	5,231,731
Accoutrements for infantry....	10,930	1,831,300
Accoutrements for cavalry.....	4,329	194,465
Equipments for cavalry horses.	574	266,581
Artillery harness (double).....	586	16,660

ARTICLES.	Issued since the war began.	On hand for issue, June 30, 1863.
Siege and sea-coast artillery....	2,088	927
Field artillery..................	2,481	484
Firearms for infantry.........	1,550,575	836,231
Firearms for cavalry..........	327,170	32,226
Sabres........................	271,817	32,571
Cannon balls and shells.......	1,745,586	1,180,749
Lead and lead bullets in lbs....	50,045,515	23,024,025
Cartridges for artillery	2,274,490	492,504
Cartridges for small arms.....	378,584,104	151,913,012
Percussion caps...............	715,036,470	74,246,530
Friction primers..............	6,082,505	1,005,629
Gunpowder in lbs..............	13,071,073	1,462,874
Saltpetre, lbs..................	none.	8,155,079
Accoutrements for infantry....	1,680,220	162,010
Accoutrements for cavalry.....	195,298	2,496
Equipments for cavalry horses.	211,670	5,552
Artillery harness (double).....	17,485	1,767

At the commencement of the civil war the amount of ordnance in the country was not large, though sufficient for all emergencies which had thus far occurred. The Secretary of War reported that there were in the possession of the United States, at the beginning of the war, 1,052 pieces of siege and sea-coast artillery of all calibers, and 231 pieces of field artillery. These were of a great variety of sizes, and some of them in unfit condition for service. The larger sea-coast artillery were mostly columbiads, or, as they are called in Europe, Paixhan guns—smooth-bore cast-iron guns, cast solid and bored. A few were Rodman guns, smooth bores, cast hollow, and with a water core which gave the inner surface of the cannon the character of chilled iron. The smaller guns were of a great variety of patterns and material—cast-iron, bronze, and brass—and their projectiles ranging from three to forty-eight pounds. The whole field artillery actively organized consisted of seven batteries, each of four guns, smooth bore, six and twelve-pounder howitzers. There was not at that time a single rifled cannon in the United States service. The Navy Department had on hand, on the 4th of March, 1861, 2,966 guns of all calibers. Of these, 1,872, or nearly two-thirds, were thirty-two pounders, of six different patterns; 107 were twelve-pounders, of two patterns; 29 were twenty-four pounders; 575 were eight-inch guns, of four different patterns; 27 were ten-inch guns; 305 were nine-inch Dahlgrens; 19 ten-inch Dahlgrens, and 32 eleven-inch Dahlgrens. Nearly or quite one-half of these guns were captured by the enemy or destroyed at the burning of the navy yard at Portsmouth, Va. Only 555 in all were on board ships, and of these nearly one-fourth were on the ships destroyed at that time. Of the army artillery, it is doubtful if there were five hundred pieces in serviceable condition at the command of the Government at the beginning of the war, and in the navy the amount of all calibers did not exceed one thousand. Some of the States, and some private individuals, possessed a few pieces, usually of small calibre. There had been for some years before the public, several inventions for the purpose of applying the principle of *rifling*, which had been so successful in small arms, to cannon, but none of these had been adopted by the Government, or were in use in the field batteries or forts under the control of the War Department, or in the vessels of the navy. The adaptation of the system of rifling invented by Charles T. James for small arms, was proposed, and repeated experiments were made with it, but it was found to require material modifications, and the death of the inventor by the explosion of his own cannon, in October, 1862, caused the abandonment of the efforts at improvement of that gun. Capt. R. P. Parrott, of the West Point foundry, had invented, just previous to the war, a rifle cannon, which, with some improvements in the projectiles and the method in rifling, proved the most successful of the numerous attempts at producing rifled cannon in this country. It was a muzzle loader (the breech-loading cannon having proved objectionable), and consisted of a cast-iron gun, much lighter than ordinary, but having a "reinforce" or cylindrical jacket of wrought-iron shrunk around the breach at the seat of the charge.

The charge for the 8-inch or 200-pounder gun, was 16 lbs. The projectiles weighed about 150 lbs., and the ranges as ascertained in the siege of Charleston, were somewhat greater than those of the 100-pounder. At the greatest elevation the range attained exceeded five miles. The 300-pounder weighed 26,000 lbs., used a charge of 25 lbs., and a projectile weighing 250 lbs. At an elevation of 35° it has thrown this formidable missile over five and one-fourth miles.

For siege purposes, for attacks on fortifications by vessels of the Monitor type, and for naval conflicts requiring great weight of metal, the Government adopted the Rodman guns of 8, 10, 13, 15, and 20-inch caliber, and the Dahlgren of 9, 10, and 11-inch caliber, the latter exclusively for the navy. Both these guns are smooth bores, though a very few of the Dahlgrens have been rifled. The Rodman gun, named after Major Rodman of the regular army, who is the inventor and superintendent of its manufacture, is of iron, cast hollow, and the core is kept cool during the casting by a constant stream of cold water passing through it.

The following table shows the weight of each size, the service charge, and the weight of the solid shot thrown by each:

Size of Gun.	Weight.	Service Charge.	Weight of solid shot.
Eight-inch....	9,240 lbs.	10 lbs.	65 lbs.
Ten-inch	15,400 "	18 "	128 "
Thirteen-inch.	38,000 "	30 "	294 "
Fifteen-inch ..	49,000 "	50 "	430 "
Twenty-inch..	116,000 "	100 "	1,000 "

Of the 9, 10 and 11-inch Dahlgren guns, about 804 had been made since the war commenced, and about 200 more were to be furnished by the close of the year 1863. Of the Rodman guns, the number has been over 2,000.

For field service the ten and twenty-pound Parrott, the brass twelve-pounders (Napoleons, as they are generally called), and for light artillery the steel cannon manufactured by Krupp, of Prussia, and the Wiard guns, were all in use, though the preference was given to the first three. The Wiard gun is a breech loader, with a long and slender barrel, except at the breech, which is very bulky, and composed of successive layers of hard and soft metals.

The Confederates introduced a new rifled gun into their service, invented by Capt. Brooke, one of their artillery officers. It seems to bear a strong resemblance to the Blakely (English) and Treadwell guns, and is hooped with iron or steel bands closely adherent to the cannon, not merely at the seat of the charge, but along its whole length. Dr. Girard, a French writer formerly resident in this country, and who has, since the war, visited Charleston, describes it as follows: "An attentive observer would not fail to remark the circular bands closely united to the piece, and which are destined to give a better resisting force. With regard to its rifling it is on the system of inclined planes instead of grooves. The projectiles are of forged (wrought) iron. Those I had an opportunity of examining were adapted to 7-inch guns. Their form is elongated, cylindrical nearly their entire length, with the exception of the front part, which is slightly conical and rounded at its periphery. The two extremities are vertical. The hinder part which presents itself to the breech of the piece bears on its circumference a bell-mouthed groove, and receives a copper ring whose ends nearly meet at the end of the projectile. The projectile has bands of copper running round it, one about four inches from the front, and the other close to the hinder part. These bands alone are destined to take the rifling of the piece. The mean length of these projectiles is 12 inches, their posterior diameter $6\frac{84}{100}$, their anterior diameter $6\frac{87}{100}$, and their weight from 116 to 120 lbs. At a distance of 260 yards, and with a charge of 12 lbs. of powder, they penetrated four iron plates of two inches each, backed with 18 inches of oak, the whole fixed against a clayey cliff."

The form and material of the projectiles for rifled ordance were a matter of profound study and research with numerous inventors. The Government, after a great number of careful and thorough trials, gave the preference to the inventions of four manufacturers, viz.: the Parrott, Shenkl, Hotchkiss, and Sawyer projectiles. The Parrott projectile, whether shell or shot, is long, pointed at the anterior extremity, and of smaller circumference in the centre than at either extremity. The base alone fits closely to the bore of the cannon, and has a ring of soft brass or a cup of the same metal, which by the expansive force of the gas of the projecting charge, is driven into the grooves to an extent sufficient to give it the rotary motion, and the extensive range of the rifle. The Hotchkiss and Sawyer projectiles use a metallic alloy of lead and antimony as a jacket to be forced into the grooves of the rifled ordnance, and the Shenkl missile applies papier maché to the same purpose. In all three, the softer material is driven upon the tapering spindle of the iron which forms the body of the projectile, from its posterior portion, by the force of the expansion produced by the ignition of the powder, and held there by shoulders projecting from the iron itself, and the rotary motion is thus imparted nearer the centre of gravity than in the Parrott projectile. The Roberts projectile has a core of iron tapering to a point at the posterior end, with a shoulder near the anterior extremity, and the soft metal (lead and antimony) which forms the jacket is in sufficient quantity to render the projectile cylindrical in form, and is forced forward by the action of the gas so as to check all windage and make the anterior portion of the projectile heaviest. The inventor claimed for it better range, less deflection, no danger of stripping, and economy of cost of the missile itself, and of wear or injury to the gun. His shell projectile, constructed externally in the same way, is a percussion shell, for which he claims safety from accidental explosion, and certainty of explosion at the moment of impact.

The improvements in the construction of small arms brought into notice by the war, have been even more remarkable than those which have been made in cannon. The old classification of breech and muzzle loaders is still maintained; but while, for the greatest possible accuracy in target-shooting, or that capacity for hitting with almost unerring certainty a small object at very long range, which has been displayed by some of our sharpshooters, the American target rifle, with its "telescopic sight," "false muzzle," and "starter," have no equal, the weapon is too heavy (weighing from 26 to 50 lbs.), and too delicately constructed, to answer for military service or for hunting, where it must be carried by the huntsman. The Springfield government rifle, a muzzle loading weapon without the adjuncts named, to insure perfect accuracy, is nevertheless as good a muzzle-loading rifle as can be made for military use, where weight, facility of carriage, and ease of handling are concerned.

It is worthy of note, however, that all the improvements in the rifle which have been made within ten years past have been confined to the breech-loading weapon. Breech-loading guns may be divided into two general classes, the first including those which may be loaded with loose powder and ball, or a paper, linen, or metal cartridge requiring a cap for its ignition, and the second those which use a metallic cartridge, having the fulminating composition in its base, which is fired by a blow of the hammer directly upon the cartridge itself. This last class may be further subdivided into those which use only a single metallic cartridge, and require reloading after each shot, and the magazine, or repeating rifle, in which a number of cartridges are inserted in a receptacle prepared for them, and which may then be fired in rapid succession till the magazine is emptied.

The metallic cartridge certainly possesses

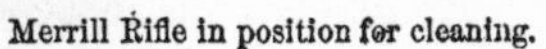

Merrill Rifle in position for cleaning.

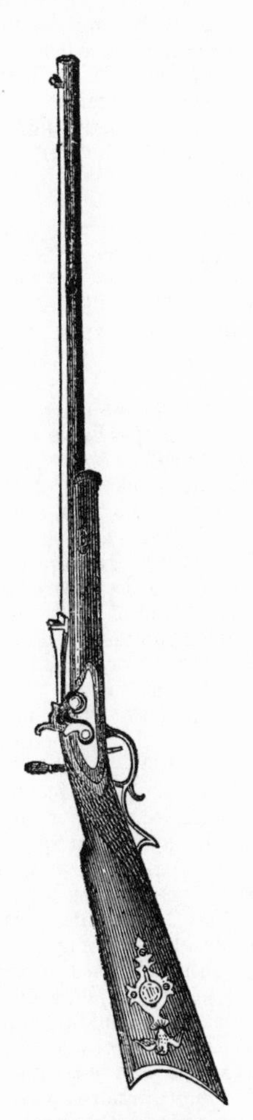

Merrill's Sporting Rifle.

some advantages over the ordinary paper or linen cartridge, or over the method of loading with loose powder and ball. It is water-proof, avoids the difficulty of loading in the ordinary way. Where, in the excitement of battle, the bullet is often put in before the powder, obviates the necessity of measuring the charge, does away with the ramrod, the priming wire, and the percussion cap, and enables the soldier to deliver his fire with great rapidity, without sacrificing precision or aim. The principal and most serious objections to them are their liability to premature explosion in the hands of the gunner (which seems to be obviated in some of the rifles using this cartridge), and the danger of their explosion from concussion, as by a serious blow on the cartridge-box of the soldier, or its being struck by a bullet or a fragment of shell.

The first of the breech-loading rifles which have come into very general use was SHARPS', a very simple but effective weapon, using ordinarily a patent cartridge with a conical ball, the cartridge enclosed in stout linen, but capable of being used effectually also with loose powder and ball. It may be fitted with Sharps' or Maynard's primer, or with a percussion cap. The rifle is small, light, and has a very long range, and is thus an excellent weapon for cavalry service, for which purpose it has been largely used.

The MERRILL rifle, the invention of a Baltimorean, belongs to the same class as Sharps', and like it uses the prepared paper cartridge and conical ball, or the ordinary round ball with loose powder. It is fired with the common percussion-cap. It is said not to be liable to fouling or to the escape of gas at the breach, and to possess a range fully equal to the Sharps'. It is so simple in its construction that muzzle-loading rifles of any pattern can be easily and without weakening transformed into breech-loaders, on its plan, and the Government have caused large numbers of rifles to be thus changed with great advantage. Two drawings are subjoined (see previous page), showing the construction of the military rifle and the sporting-rifle complete. The cavalry carbine of the Merrill patent weighs but 6¼ lbs. and the infantry rifle but 9 lbs.

ASHCROFT'S rifle, another new weapon belonging to the same class, is highly commended by Mr. H. W. S. Cleveland, author of "Hints to Riflemen," and decidedly one of the highest authorities in this country on the subject of rifles for military or sporting use. "The breech block of this rifle is constructed with a cylindrical gas-check, which enters the breech of the barrel and shuts against a shoulder; and this gas-check being slightly concave in its external form, the effect of the explosion is to strengthen and thereby to lengthen it, so as to press it against the shoulder, and effectually to prevent the slightest escape of gas. The proof that it does so is afforded by the fact that it has been fired eight hundred times in succession without cleaning, and the working of the parts was as easy at the last as at the first, and the gas-check itself remained as bright and unsullied as before it was used, which would not have been the case had there been any escape of gas." . . . . "The whole arrangement of the working parts is admirably simple and effective, and no breech-piece of solid metal could be more safe and unyielding than this when fixed in position; and by a very simple arrangement, it is impossible to fire the gun till this position is attained." Mr. Cleveland made a thorough experiment of the powers of this rifle, in comparison with several others, as to the penetration of the shot at thirty yards. The target was made of inch pine boards, free from knots and of even grain, and it exceeded all others except the Greene rifle, of which we shall speak presently, which was a much longer weapon, and used a heavier bullet and a much larger charge of powder. As compared with the Sharps' rifle of the same length and using the same cartridge, its average penetration was found to be one inch greater.

GREENE'S rifle, patented by Lieut. Col. J. Durell Greene, United States Army, in 1857, and now manufactured at Worcester, Mass., is a weapon of great merit. Though a breech-loader, its construction is entirely different from any other rifle in the market. It has been introduced into the French and Russian service, and is regarded with great favor in both. This is the only rifle manufactured in this country on the Lancaster system of rifling, that is, with an elliptic instead of a grooved bore, which imparts the rotary motion by giving the longest diameter of the ellipse a turn of three-fourths in the length of the barrel. The bullet is round, but assumes the elliptic shape on entering the barrel, though the variation from a sphere is but slight. The peculiarities in the construction of the gun are as follows: a cylinder of iron containing a breech-plug, which slides backward and forward within it, is inserted at the breech of the barrel, and moved forward by a projecting knob, which moves in a slot on the top of the barrel till it closes the breech, when it is turned to the right and secured in place by shoulders. The knob is held by a catch, which may be loosened by pressing a pin at the breech of the barrel. The hammer is on the under side, in front of the guard, and the nipple is so arranged that the fire is first communicated at the forward end of the cartridge, thus insuring the ignition of all of the powder. The cartridge has the bullet in its base, with a greased wad between it and the powder, which, with the bullet, packs the joint perfectly at every discharge, and prevents the slightest escape of gas. After each discharge this bullet is pushed forward by the breech plug to the end of the chamber, the cylinder is then drawn back, and the cartridge inserted in the slot which is thus opened. The cylinder is then pushed forward, pressing the cartridge before it, and the knob being turned to the side and the nipple capped, the gun is ready to fire. The movements are perfectly simple, and all the parts are strong and well adapted to stand the rough usage of military service. The Greene rifle is made with a 36-inch barrel, and this size carries a bullet weighing 575 grains or $1\frac{1}{5}$ ounces, and requires a charge of 88 grains of powder. With this charge its power of penetration is greater at thirty yards than any other of the modern rifles with the possible exception of the Whitworth, in which a leaden bolt, not a ball, is used. In Mr. Cleveland's experiments with ten different rifles, this penetrated his target of pine boards thirteen inches, while the Ashcroft penetrated eleven inches, and the others ranged from six to ten inches. It is fair to say, however, that the others had all shorter barrels, ranging from twenty to thirty-one inches, and carried smaller bullets, the charge of powder being also less.

The MAYNARD rifle, invented in 1851 by Dr. Edward Maynard, of Washington, D. C., but since that time considerably improved, is a most ingenious instrument, and for efficiency, strength, and simplicity has hardly been equalled. It is remarkably compact, and without any sacrifice of strength. The barrel can be disconnected from the stock by the removal of a single pin, and the whole gun can then be packed in a case 20×6×1 inch. Barrels of different calibre, either for shot or rifled, may be fitted to the same stock and changed in a few seconds. Springs, bolts, and catches are not used in this rifle, but the ends required are attained by the careful adjustment and excellent finish of the several parts, which work with mathematical precision, and give it the solidity of a mass of steel, which is not affected by any strain to which it can be exposed. The ammunition is contained in a metallic cartridge, having an aperture in the base through which the fire is communicated from the cap. These cartridges are so constructed that when charged, by means of a very simple implement which accompanies every gun, the ball is not only of necessity mathematically exact in its position, but is held, without compressing the cartridge (as is done in the self-exploding cartridges) simply by being fitted to it, so firmly that it cannot be moved after being placed in the chamber (which is enough larger than the calibre to admit of the presence of the cartridge), in any direction except with a perfectly true delivery through the calibre. The cartridges can be used over and over again for an indefinite period, being loaded by the gunner himself. There is also an arrangement for using loose ammunition, the ball being first inserted at the breech, and followed by a cartridge or charger, which is simply filled from the flask at each shot. By a recent improvement the empty cartridge after firing is started from its place by the act of raising the breech for reloading, so that it may easily be withdrawn.

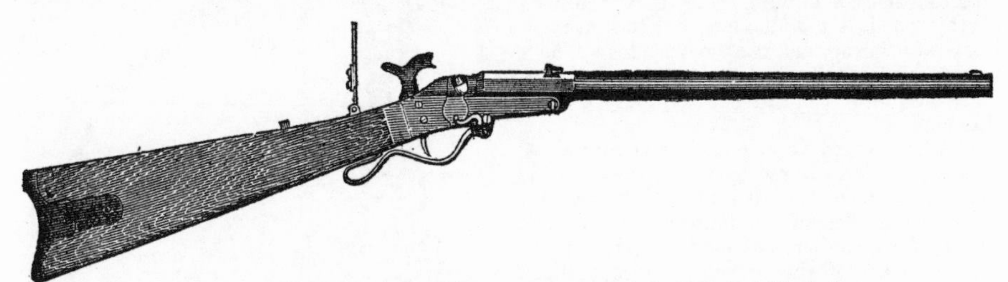

MAYNARD RIFLE.—Fig. 1. Showing Rifle loaded, cocked, and with back sight raised.

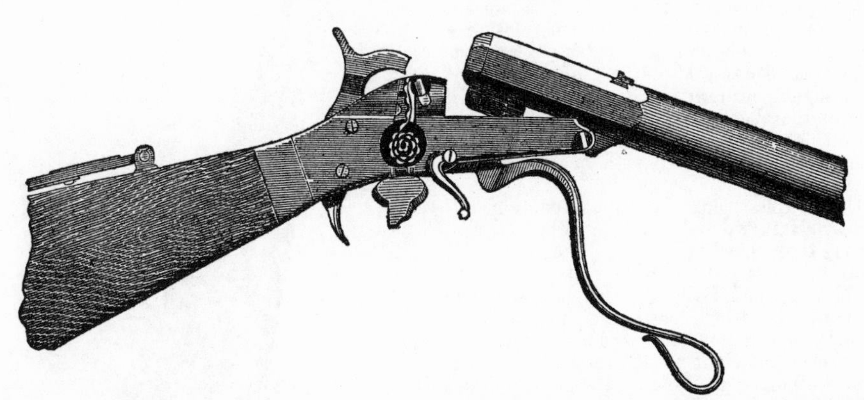

MAYNARD RIFLE.—Fig. 2. Showing Rifle in position to receive the cartridge, and with the magazine also opened, showing the primer.

The Maynard primer, used in connection with this rifle, and invented for it by Dr. Maynard, consists of a narrow strip of varnished paper of double thickness, having deposits of fulminating powder in cells between the two, at equal distances apart. Each strip contains three dozen of these cells, equivalent to the same number of caps. The strip is coiled in a magazine concealed beneath the lock-plate, and brought up by the motion of a wheel in the act of cocking, so as to bring a cell directly upon the top of the nipple. The fall of the hammer explodes it and at the same time cuts off the paper behind, so that it is not seen again till the gun is again cocked. Mr. Cleveland, after long experience, prefers the smaller sized barrel ($\frac{35}{100}$ inch calibre) to the larger, which is of half inch calibre, as being better adapted to its charge. He says of this smaller calibre, "In accuracy and force I have never seen it surpassed by any gun fit for field service." We subjoin two cuts of this rifle, one showing it loaded, cocked, and with back sight raised; the other in position to receive the cartridge, and with the magazine opened, showing the primer.

The SMITH's patent breech-loading rifle, manufactured by Poultney & Trimble of Baltimore, is another very simple, yet accurate and effective rifle. The cuts show its construction as completely as any description. There is nothing about it which can get out of order. Its range is 2,000 yards or more, and it can be fired ten times a minute. The cartridge used for this rifle is a metallic one, but the case collapses after firing, and can be withdrawn by a single motion of the finger. It has not the fulminating powder, but uses an ordinary percussion cap.

The BURNSIDE rifle belongs to the same class. It is now manufactured by the Burnside Rifle Co. in Providence, and is a breech-loader, having a breech-piece of wrought iron morticed to receive the chamber and movable breech-pin. The upper end of this breech-piece is screwed to the lower end of the barrel, which is of cast-steel and rifled with a gain-twist. The opening and closing the guard and its attachments are analogous to those of opening and closing a door by a thumb-latch and catch. The cartridge is similar to that of the Smith rifle; but by a slight peculiarity in its construction, and that of the chamber and perforated platinum case which fits to it, it is water and air-tight when loaded. It is fired with a common percussion cap.

Of the rifles using the self-exploding metallic cartridge, two only have much reputation, among those which are not repeating guns, and must be recharged for every shot. These are F. Wesson's and Ballard's. The WESSON rifle is light, the 24-inch barrel weighing only six pounds, and the 28 and 34-inch barrels not over seven and eight pounds respectively. Dr. I. J. Wetherbee, of Boston, an experienced and skilful shot, gives the result of extensive trials of this rifle with others, and gives it the preference over all others in accuracy, penetration, and range, and thinks it equal in rapidity of firing to most others. The 28 and 34-inch barrels he regards as preferable to the 24-inch. At the Massachusetts State trial of breech-loading arms at Readville, the Wesson rifle placed twenty successive shots in the target at 200 yards, and 50 shots were fired from it in less than five minutes. The annexed cuts repre-

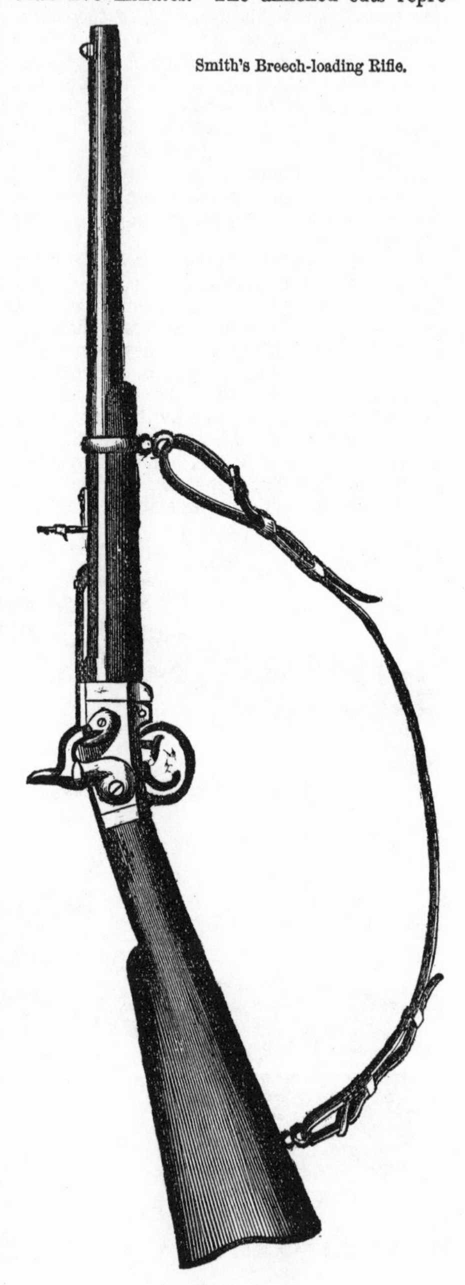

Smith's Breech-loading Rifle.

sent it in position for loading, and ready to fire. In loading, the breech is elevated by a movement somewhat like that of the Maynard. The empty cartridge is then withdrawn by hand, a new one inserted, and the barrel restored to its place, in which it is held by a

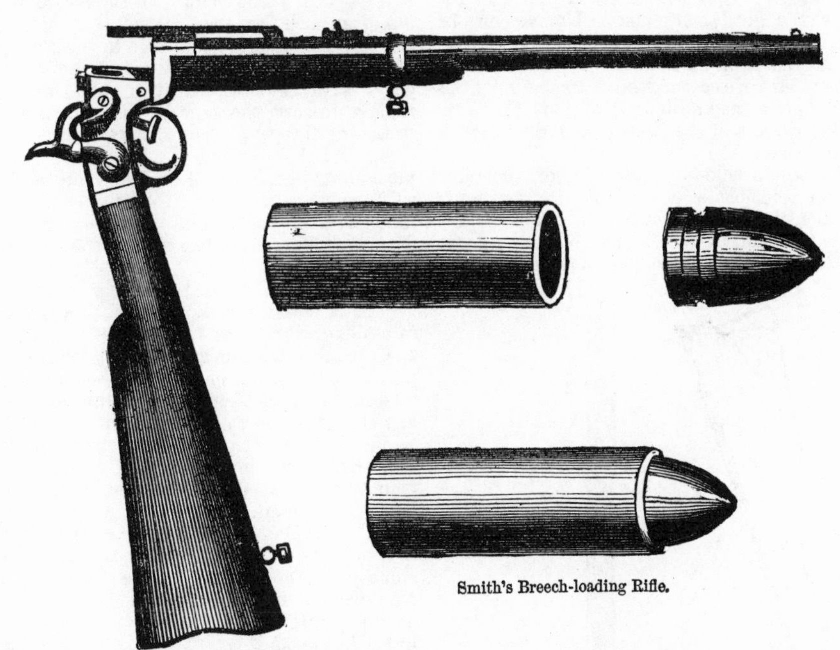

Smith's Breech-loading Rifle.

catch, which is loosened by a trigger in front of the one by which the piece is discharged. The hammer cannot be drawn back beyond half-cock till this catch has secured the barrel in its place. The piece is remarkable for elegance of form and perfection of mechanical finish.

The Ballard military rifle is so arranged

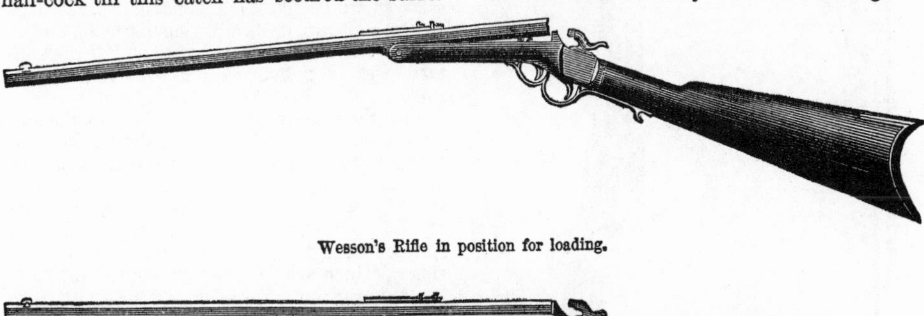

Wesson's Rifle in position for loading.

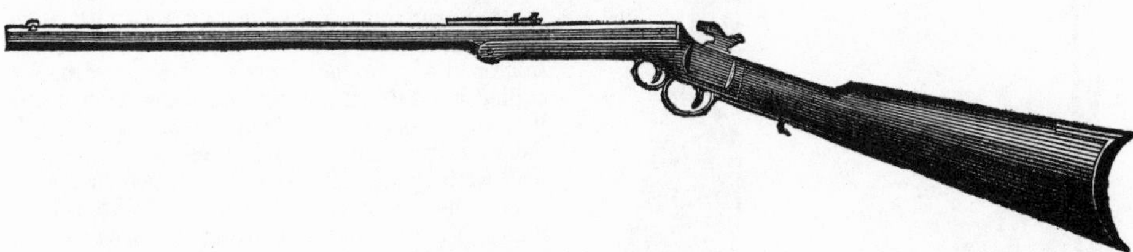

Wesson's Rifle ready to fire.

that it may be used with the metallic cartridge or with the ordinary soldiers' cartridge, to be fired with a cap. The breech of the rifle is opened for the insertion of the cartridge, by drawing down the guard, when the breech-block sinks perpendicularly, carrying the hammer with it, and throwing it back to half-cock. The empty cartridge is then removed by means of a finger-piece under the barrel, attached to a slide, which pushes out the cartridge by pressing against its flange, and is then restored to its place by a spring. The rifle shoots with great accuracy, putting every shot into a six-inch ring at four or five hundred yards, in the hands of a good marksman. The velocity of its shot is somewhat less than that of the Wesson, Maynard, or Colt rifles.

There are three models of repeating arms which have gained a high reputation: Colt's revolving rifles, and the Henry and Spencer repeating rifles.

The Colt's rifle is constructed on the same general principle as his pistols. A revolving chamber, fitted either for five or six shots, receives the charges, which may be either loose powder and ball or cartridges; a rammer, which is moved by a lever, insures their being sent home perfectly true, and the balls fit so exactly to the bore of the chambers as to close them hermetically. The calibre of the barrel being .02 of an inch less than that of the chambers, the ball is necessarily forced to fit itself exactly to the grooves, which are seven in number, and cut with a gain twist (that is, revolving more rapidly toward the muzzle than toward the breech of the gun.) The charge is fired with a cap, and the working of all the parts is simple and exact. Like all of the weapons from this famous manufactory, the excellence of the material and workmanship are not surpassed. The annexed cuts give an idea of the construction of this rifle:

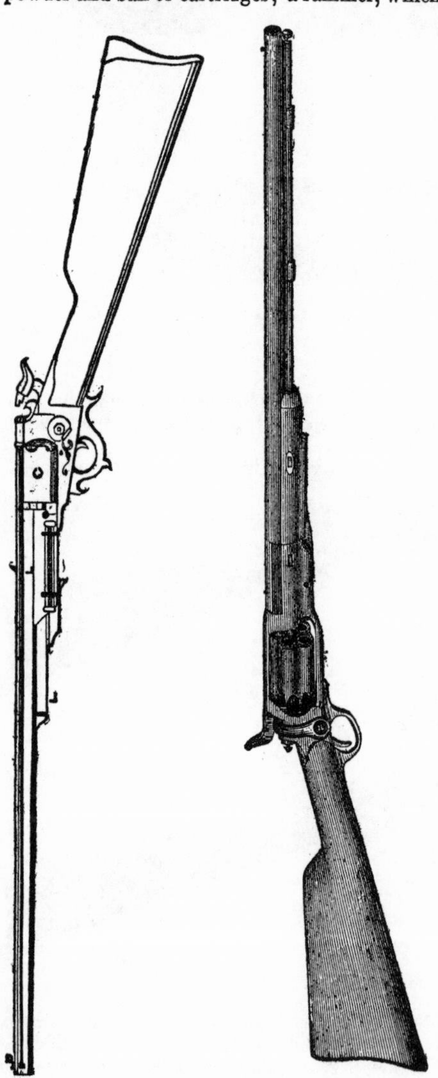

Colt's Rifle.

Mr. Cleveland states that he has with open sights placed ten successive shots from this rifle in a nine-inch ring at two hundred yards, and Lieutenant Hans Busk, of the Victoria Rifles, placed forty-six out of forty-eight shots inside a twenty-four-inch ring at four hundred yards, and the other two less than an inch outside, while eighteen of the forty-eight were inside a ring eight inches in diameter. He says: "For efficiency and strength of shooting nothing can beat it." General Marcy, U. S. A., pronounces it the most reliable and certain weapon to fire that he has ever used, and says, that if he were alone upon the prairies, and expected an attack from a body of Indians, he is not acquainted with any arm he would as soon have in his hands as this. The objections to it are, that it takes longer to load than any of the other breech-loaders; but when loaded, its five or six shots can be delivered with great rapidity); it is not so easy to clean as the metallic cartridge rifles, and is liable to be affected by dirt and rust in its working parts to an extent which would be objectionable to its military use. For hunting purposes it is admirable.

The Spencer repeating rifle is a comparatively new arm, having been patented in 1860. It uses the metallic self-exploding cartridge, and has a magazine in the breech of the gun securely protected from all danger of accidental explosion, containing, in the army and navy rifle seven, and in the sporting rifle nine, cartridges, which are fed successively to the chamber by means of a spiral spring, and with such precision as to avoid the possibility of their not taking the grooves properly. An ordinarily skilled marksman can discharge the seven loads in twelve seconds, and whole platoons of soldiers waiting for the word of command can fire with good aim once in three seconds. When the seven charges are fired, the rifle is held with the muzzle pointing downward, and a tube being withdrawn, which contains the spiral spring which pushes the cartridges forward, they are dropped into the magazine and the tube replaced. The operation requires but a very short time, and the soldier or sportsman is ready to fire his seven shots again. The gun is not liable to foul or to get out of order, and its range and force are good. It will throw a ball two thousand yards, and will seldom miss its mark at from seven hundred to a thousand. At a distance of from thirty to fifty yards, it will penetrate a pine target to a depth of from nine to thirteen inches. It was used with terrible effect by the Union troops at Gettysburg and Chickamauga, and in some other battles of the war. At Gettysburg, it was said by eye-witnesses that the head of the column (opposed to the troops armed with this weapon), as it was pushed on by those behind, appeared to melt away or sink into the earth, for though continually moving it got no nearer. Acting Brigadier-General John T. Wilder, of the Army of the Cumberland, in command of a brigade of mounted infantry armed with this rifle, wrote on the 28th of November, 1863, that at Hoover's Gap, June 24th, 1863, one of his regiments defeated a rebel brigade of five regiments, killing and wounding over five hundred, while their own loss was only forty-seven; and that from April to November his command had captured over 2,800 officers and men, losing as prisoners

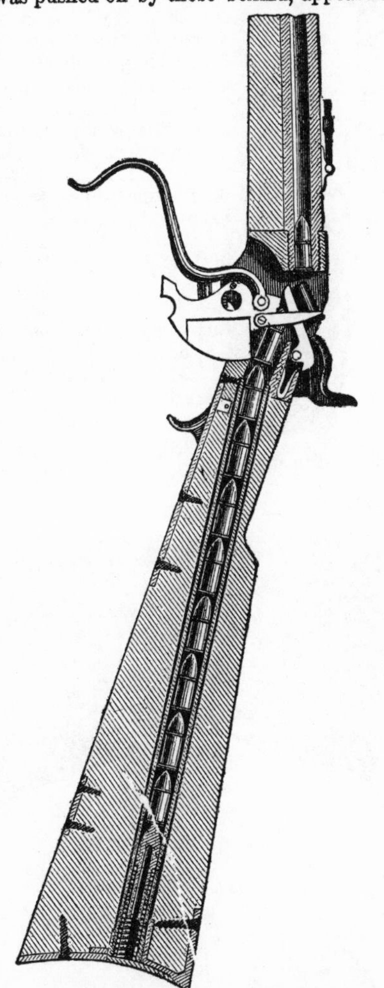

Section of carbine, showing cartridges in magazine, with lever down and breech open.

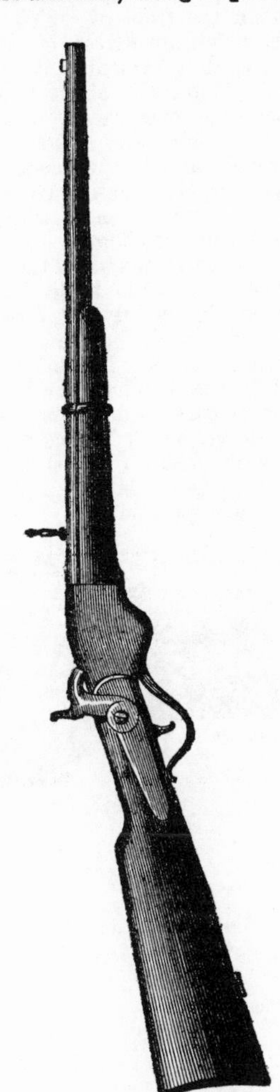

Spencer Rifle.

in the same period only six men. The subjoined cuts exhibit fully the mechanism of the magazine and lock.

Henry's repeating rifle is a still later invention, patented, we believe, in 1861. The principal novelty in this gun is the magazine and the manner of loading from it. It consists of a metal tube under the barrel, extending its entire length, of sufficient diameter to admit the cartridges freely. A section of this tube near the muzzle contains a spiral spring to throw the cartridges upon a carrier-block in the rear, and by means of a metallic sleeve five inches in length, embracing the barrel of the gun at this point, can be revolved upon the axis of the bore so as to open the magazine, and admit the introduction of the cartridges, of which it holds fifteen. Upon closing it, after filling, the spring throws a cartridge upon the carrier-block, which, by a forward movement of the trigger-guard, is raised to a level with the chamber, the hammer, by the same movement, being carried to a full cock. A reverse movement of the guard, bringing it to its place again, forces the cartridge into the chamber, and the gun is ready to fire. The ammunition is fixed, metal cased, with fulminate or cap in the rear. The hammer, upon falling, strikes a rod, or breech-pin, upon the front of which are two sharp points, which are driven into the rear of the cartridge, thus exploding it. The weight of the gun complete is about 10 pounds; it has six shallow grooves, each $\frac{1}{10}$ of an inch in width, with a gaining twist. The cartridge weighs 295 grains. In an experiment at the Ordnance Department, Washington, 120 shots were fired in five minutes fifteen seconds, including the time spent in reloading.

The following cuts show the construction of the rifle. The little projecting piece on the under side, in the first cut, directly in front of the shoulder, at the breech of the barrel, is the finger-piece connected with the follower on the end of the spiral spring. To load the magazine this finger-piece is drawn up to the lower end of the sleeve, which is then turned far enough to allow the follower to rest on the edge of the magazine, where it is held in place till the cartridges are dropped in.

Henry's Repeating Rifle.

This gun is not remarkable for accuracy at long distances, but at one hundred yards or thereabouts it is a very effective weapon. The sudden reduction of half the thickness of the barrel for five inches from the muzzle probably impairs its accuracy at long range. Its magazine, being in a thin metallic tube under the barrel, is liable to be indented by a shot or accidental blow, which would prevent the cartridges from sliding down, and as they cannot be easily introduced into the barrel in any other way, this would render the gun nearly useless. The necessity of leaving an open slit for the finger-piece to slide in exposes the contents of the magazine to the influence of dust and wet, which would tend to clog the passage and rust the spiral spring. Still this weapon has many excellent points, and in its method of loading, the capacity of its magazine, and its rapidity of firing, it surpasses any other repeating rifle. It is stated on good authority that Col. Nelter, while raising a

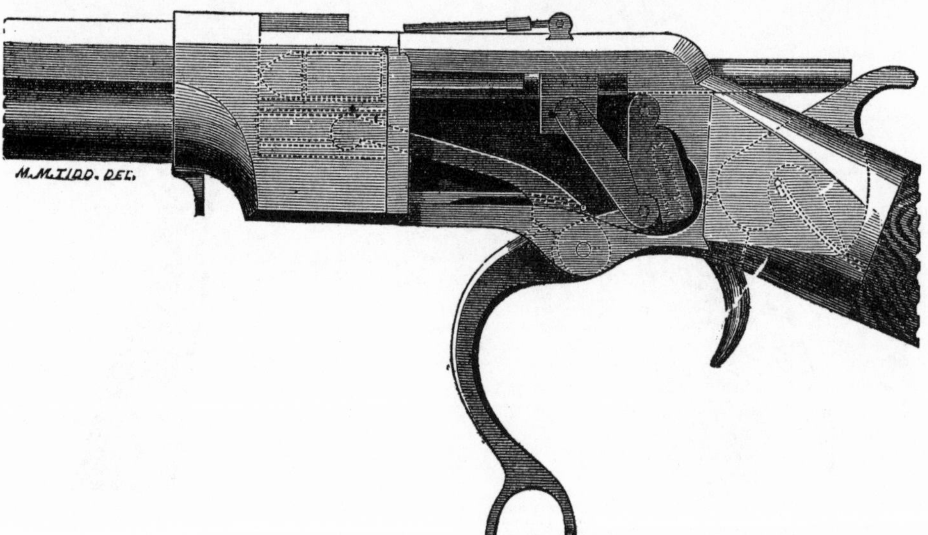

Sectional view of working parts, showing the operation of removing the empty cartridge and cocking the hammer.

regiment of Kentucky volunteers at Owensboro', Kentucky, sent out fifteen of his men armed with this rifle on a scout. They were attacked by a rebel force of two hundred and forty soldiers in an open lane where there was no shelter, and owing to their capacity to maintain a rapid and continuous fire, they successfully repulsed and drove from the field the entire rebel force. Capt. James M. Wilson, Co. M, 12th Kentucky cavalry, was attacked in his own house by seven mounted guerrillas armed with Colt's revolvers. He sprang for a log cabin across the street where he had his Henry rifle, Colt's revolver, etc., and though his clothing was riddled by their shot, gained it without a wound, and seizing his Henry's rifle, killed five of his assailants with five shots; the other two sprung for their horses, one of these he disabled with his sixth shot, and killed with the seventh; the other he killed with the eighth. The State of Kentucky, in consequence of this feat, armed his company with this rifle.

The WHITWORTH rifle, which is manufactured either as a breech or muzzle-loader, is the only English rifle which fairly competes with our American breech-loaders. As a breech-loading rifle it has been manufactured only by Westley Richards. It has a hexagonal bore and fires a hexagonal bolt an inch and a half in length, though only $\frac{44}{100}$ of an inch in diameter. This bolt weighs 517 grains. The bore is constructed with a complete turn in twenty inches, or one and a half turns in the length of the barrel, which is thirty inches. The charge of powder is seventy-six grains. It is a very efficient weapon of great range, though lacking somewhat in precision, is not liable to foul, but its cartridge, which is made of paper, is so long and narrow as to be liable to burst on the march.

CHAPTER XXXIV.

Operations of the Florida and Alabama—The bark Tacony—Capture of the Chesapeake—Damage to Federal Commerce—Increase of the Federal Navy—Operations of the North Atlantic Squadron—Operations of the South Atlantic Squadron—Attack on Fort McAllister—Attack on Charleston—Capture of the Atlanta—Other Naval Operations.

THE most important operations of the Confederate navy were those performed by the armed sea-going cruisers, whose depredations upon commerce cost the United States many millions in money, and almost paralyzed the shipping interest in the chief seaports. The commencement of 1863 found the Alabama, before mentioned, actively cruising among the West Indies. In the middle of January the Oreto, afterwards called the Florida, slipped out of Mobile, where she had taken refuge some months previous, and joined the Alabama in her work of destruction; and in the beginning of April the Japan, subsequently named the Georgia, escaped from the Clyde, and proceeding to the neighborhood of Ushant Island, on the French coast, was there armed and equipped as a privateer. "Sailing sometimes under the English and sometimes under the rebel flag," says Secretary Welles, "these rovers, without a port of their own which they can enter, or to which they can send a single prize for adjudication, have roamed the seas, capturing and destroying the commercial ships of a nation at peace with Great Britain and France; but yet when these corsairs have needed repairs or supplies, they have experienced no difficulty in procuring them, because it had been deemed expedient to recognize the rebels as belligerents. Not one of the many vessels captured by these rovers has ever been judicially condemned as a legal capture. Wanton destruction has been the object and purpose of the captors, who have burnt and destroyed the property of their merchant victims."

During the first three months of 1863 the Alabama and Florida cruised with impunity in the West India waters, finding no difficulty, when hard pressed, in taking refuge in neutral ports, or within a marine league of the shore of a neutral Government, and meeting with abundant sympathy from the local authorities and the population. Fulfilling few of the obligations of armed cruisers, they yet demanded and received all the favors accorded to nations having open ports. The Federal war vessels, on the other hand, were invariably subjected to the rules of national law in their strictest construction. The vigilance of the flying squadron under acting Rear Admiral Wilkes, which was organized to protect American interests in that quarter, and especially to guard the treasure ships in their transit to and from Aspinwall, finally made the neighborhood too hot for the Alabama and Florida, and in April they steered southward, and recommenced their work of destruction off the coast of South America, where many valuable prizes fell into their possession, which were almost invariably burned, or bonded, the crews being despatched to the nearest available port. In May the two privateers parted company, the Alabama proceeding to the Cape of Good Hope, while the Florida sailed northward, and on July 8th ventured within 60 miles of New York. After remaining several days in this dangerous neighborhood, she repaired to Bermuda, and about the middle of August turned up on the track of the Liverpool and New York packets. Then, after capturing a few prizes near the British Isles, she put into Brest for repairs.

In the early part of August the Alabama, accompanied by the Tuscaloosa, a captured merchantman, transformed into an armed tender, arrived at Capetown, where an enthusiastic ovation awaited them. One of the first acts of the privateersmen was to capture the American ship Sea Bride, within a marine league of the land. The American consul protested against this proceeding, and also against the admission of the Tuscaloosa, before legal condemnation, into Simon's Bay, as a violation of the Queen's proclamation of neutrality, but could obtain no redress. Soon afterward the Georgia, which ever since her equipment as a privateer had sailed southward along the African coast, burning and plundering on her way, also arrived at Capetown.

Early in February, 1863, the Vanderbilt, one of the largest and fastest steamers in the United States Navy, was put into commission for special service against privateers in the West India waters, and her commander was ordered, should he be satisfied that the Alabama and Florida had left that locality, to proceed down the South American coast to Rio Janeira, and thence to the Cape of Good Hope. In derogation of these orders, Admiral Wilkes, soon after the arrival of the Vanderbilt in the West Indies, transferred his flag to her and detained her in his possession until the middle of June, many weeks after the departure southward of the privateers. The latter, in consequence, were enabled to do immense damage to American commerce in the Southern Atlantic, and the plans of the Navy Department for their capture were frustrated. The Vanderbilt finally reached Rio Janeiro in the middle of July, and proceeding thence to Capetown via St. Helena, arrived at the former place in September. The rebels, however, were by this time on the alert, and kept out of the way of the Vanderbilt, which returned to the United States in the latter part of the year, having accomplished nothing important during her cruise. Subsequent to September the Alabama proceeded to the East Indies, and took many valuable prizes in that quarter, while the Georgia returned to France.

Early in May the Florida, while cruising in the West Indies, captured the brig Clarence, which was fitted out as a privateer and supplied with a crew, under command of Lieut. Charles W. Read, formerly a midshipman in the U. S. navy. The Clarence immediately steered northward, keeping near the Florida and Carolina coasts, and taking several valuable prizes on the way. On June 12th, when within 30 miles of the capes of Virginia, she captured the bark Tacony, to which vessel Lt. Read transferred his command. For the next twelve days he pursued a career of uninterrupted success among the unsuspecting merchantmen and fishing vessels which he encountered; but ascertaining that Union cruisers were on his track, he burned the Tacony, to avoid recognition, and on the 24th transferred his crew and guns to the captured schooner Archer. He then made for Portland harbor, with the intention of burning two gunboats building there and cutting out the revenue cutter Caleb Cushing. At sunset he came to anchor near the entrance of the harbor, and soon after midnight, the moon having then gone down, rowed direct to the Cushing in two boats with muffled oars, boarded the vessel, and having overpowered the crew, started for sea. No sooner was the Cushing missed from her anchorage than the Forest City and Chesapeake, two merchant steamers, were manned with troops and armed volunteers, and started in pursuit. A short distance from the harbor they overhauled her, and having no guns capable of coping with her heavy armament, made preparations to board, perceiving which the rebels took to their boats, after firing half a dozen shots at the steamers. Soon after the Cushing blew up. The boats, however, were captured, as also the Archer, and the whole crew securely confined.

On December 17th the steamer Chesapeake, plying between New York and Portland, was seized on her passage to the latter place, when about twenty miles northeast of Cape Cod, by sixteen of her passengers, who represented themselves as belonging to the Confederate States. The captain was put in irons, one of the engineers killed and thrown overboard, and the first mate wounded. The crew and passengers, with the exception of the first engineer, retained to manage the steamer, were subsequently put ashore in a boat, and the Chesapeake sailed to the eastward. Upon the reception of the news in the United States, a fleet of cruisers started in pursuit, and on the 17th the Chesapeake was captured by the Ella and Anna, in Sambro harbor, Nova Scotia, and with a portion of her crew, was carried to Halifax and delivered to the authorities. The prisoners were released by a mob, but the Chesapeake was subsequently restored to her American owners by an order of the chief colonial tribunal.

Of the amount of damage inflicted by rebel cruisers upon American commerce no complete estimate has been made. While at Capetown in September, Captain Semmes stated that the total number of captures made by the Alabama amounted to fifty-six vessels, which he supposed would involve a direct loss of four million dollars, beside the loss of freight, the high rates of insurance, and other embarrassments caused by the danger of carrying goods in American bottoms. The captures of the Florida were estimated by her commander in September at seventy-two, and their total value at $15,000,000, which is evidently exaggerated. Yet this is but a small part of the loss then sustained by American commerce, as will be seen by the following figures:

	Value under American flag.	Value under Foreign flags.
Foreign carrying trade in 1860.	$234,000,000	$150,000,000
Foreign carrying trade in 1862.	150,000,000	238,000,000
Foreign carrying trade first two quarters in 1863............	55,090,000	146,000,000

Of the extent to which the city of New York has suffered, the following table, showing how the carrying business, of which she once enjoyed a large share, has been transferred to foreign flags, is sufficiently indicative:

Foreign trade of the port of New York, for the quarter ending June 30th.

1860.	In American vessels.	In foreign vessels.
Value of goods imported......	$35,197,101	$13,242,622
" " exported.......	27,401,225	12,776,229
Total trade.	$62,598,326	$30,918,851
1863.		
Value of goods imported......	$12,731,819	$30,139,557
" " exported......	10,762,011	35,760,296
Total trade...............	$23,403,830	$65,889,853

A part of this change is doubtless in consequence of the active employment of so many American ships for purposes connected with the war; but, after making allowance for this fact, a sufficient number of vessels could be found for commercial purposes, were not shippers deterred by fear of capture from employing them as carriers. The success of their cruisers already afloat, and the ease with which they could be built and equipped in foreign countries, prompted the Richmond Government to contract for others, and during the year the Alexandra, a fast steamer of the Alabama class, and two iron-clad rams, the latter undertaken by Laird, of Liverpool, ostensibly for the "Emperor of China," or the "Viceroy of Egypt," were under construction in England. The vigilance of the American minister and the consuls prevented the completion of these, and at the close of the year they were temporarily in the possession of the British government, subject to the decision of the courts. The Alexandra case, after being carried to the House of Lords, on appeal from the Court of Exchequer, was decided against the Government, and the vessel was restored to her owners.

The growth of the Federal navy was very rapid. The classes of vessels, and aggregate armament and tonnage of the navy, including all the vessels building, at the close of 1863, were as follows:

	No. of vessels.	No. of guns.	Tonnage.
Iron-clad steamers, coast service.	46	150	62,518
Iron-clad steamers, inland service.	29	152	20,784
Sidewheel steamers............	203	1,240	126,517
Screw steamers................	198	1,578	187,892
Sailing vessels................	112	1,323	70,256
Total	588	4,443	467,967

During the year there were removed from the navy by various casualties, 34 vessels, having an aggregate of 166 guns and 15,985 tons. Of these twelve were captured by the enemy, three were destroyed to prevent their falling into the hands of the enemy, four were sunk in battle or by torpedoes, and fifteen were lost by shipwreck, fire, and collision. In the last-named category were the iron-clads Monitor and Weehawken, which foundered at sea in stormy weather.

The fleet in active service at the close of 1863 comprised 384 vessels of all classes, distributed as follows: Potomac Flotilla, 19; North Atlantic Squadron, 72; South Atlantic Squadron, 76; Eastern Gulf Squadron, 39; Western Gulf Squadron, 68; Mississippi Flotilla, 85; West India Squadron, 3; East India Squadron, 2; Mediterranean Squadron, 1; Pacific Squadron, 7; special service, 6; miscellaneous, &c., 6.

The grades of the officers had been changed by Congress, and new ones established. The number of officers of the higher grades was as follows:

	Active list.	Reserved list.	Retired list.
Rear-Admirals...............	6	..	8
Do. Acting..........	5	..	..
Commodores.................	18	..	33
Captains......................	*36	10	15
Commanders..................	†72	15	7
Lieutenant-Commanders........	144	..	..
Lieutenants.....................	55	..	8

The number of seamen in service on July 1st, 1863, including those on the Mississippi Flotilla, was about 34,000, and during the year enlistments averaged over 2,000 a month. In 1862 the average was 1,529 a month. The demand was altogether in excess of the supply of trained and experienced seamen, notwithstanding the marked decrease in the shipping business which the ravages of the Confederate privateers had caused; and the men enlisted were, for the most part, of the class known as landsmen, having little or no knowledge of a seafaring life.

One cause for this deficiency was the operation of the Enrolment and Conscription Act of 1863, which provided no exemption for sailors or mariners, a class of men whom most nations foster and cherish by special laws, and who were formerly expressly exempted by act of Congress from militia duty. But the chief cause was to be found in the high bounties offered for enlistment into the army, under the influence of which many sailors, whose services would be much more valuable afloat than on shore, were induced to become soldiers.

Congress therefore authorized bounties to be offered to sailors as well as soldiers, and measures also were taken to transfer sailors who had enlisted in the army into the naval service. The result was to rapidly fill up the deficiencies in the quota of seamen, and to fill the receiving ships to overflowing. In the latter part of 1863 the practice was also introduced of putting on shipboard rebel prisoners who had taken the oath of allegiance to the United States, and desired to enter the national service, but were unwilling to subject themselves to the risk of summary execution if recaptured while serving in the Federal army.

During 1863 six squadrons were maintained by the United States Government along the Atlantic seaboard, and in the Western waters, viz.: 1. The North Atlantic Squadron, Acting Rear-Admiral S. P. Lee. 2. The South Atlantic Squadron, Rear-Admiral S. F. Dupont, who was

* Beside one not recommended for promotion.
† Beside 18 not recommended for promotion.

relieved, July 6th, by Rear-Admiral J. A. Dahlgren. 3. The Eastern Gulf Squadron, Acting Rear-Admiral T. Bailey. 4. The Western Gulf Squadron, Rear-Admiral D. G. Farragut, who was temporarily relieved in July by his second in command, Commodore H. H. Bell. 5. The Mississippi Flotilla, Rear-Admiral D. D. Porter. 6. The Potomac Flotilla, Commodore A. A. Harwood. There were also small squadrons on the Pacific and East India stations, and a number of vessels were employed in searching for rebel privateers and on other special service.

The operations of the North Atlantic Squadron comprised chiefly blockade duties along the coasts of Virginia and North Carolina. So effective was the service that along the entire station all intercourse with the enemy was cut off, with the single exception of the port of Wilmington, the closing of which was difficult on account of its two inlets, thirty miles apart, flanked by extensive batteries. A few steamers from the Clyde and elsewhere, of light draught, succeeded, under cover of the darkness, in eluding capture, but most even of that description of vessels fell into the hands of the blockaders, or were run on shore and destroyed.

On January 14th the screw steam gunboat Columbia, Lieutenant Joseph O. Couthouoy, while cruising between Federal Point and Masonboro' inlet, was wrecked on the bar off the latter place, and before assistance could be procured from her consorts, was too much broken up by the sea to be got off. On the afternoon of the 15th, the Penobscot anchored near her, and by means of a surf-line succeeded in rescuing about thirty of the crew; but a heavy gale setting in at nightfall, she was obliged to run to sea again. Early the next morning several rebel shore-batteries opened upon the Columbia, and later in the day the Penobscot, Cambridge, and Genesee approached her. The surf was too high, however, to enable them to render any assistance to Lieut. Couthouoy, who, being helpless against the fire of the enemy, was compelled, in the afternoon, to surrender the remaining officers and crew, forty in number. He had previously spiked and thrown overboard his guns, drowned the powder in his magazines, and destroyed his signals.

On the morning of March 14th an attack was made by the troops under General D. H. Hill upon Fort Anderson, an unfinished earthwork on the left bank of the Neuse, opposite Newbern, which was garrisoned by a single regiment of volunteers. The fort had no guns mounted, and the troops in Newbern were unable to render assistance. The gunboats Hunchback and Heitzel, however, assisted by the Shawsheen and some smaller vessels, came promptly to the rescue, and by a well-directed fire silenced the enemy's artillery, consisting of fourteen pieces, and by compelling the retreat of Hill saved the fort. A nine-inch shell from the Heitzel dismounted and broke a Parrott gun, and killed and wounded a number of rebels. The enemy were followed and harassed in their retreat up the Neuse River by several light-draught vessels.

During the attack on Suffolk, Virginia, in the latter half of April, the small fleet of United States gunboats on the Nansemond took a distinguished part. On the 14th the Mount Washington, Stepping Stones, and Commodore Barney, the first named being at the time disabled, succeeded, with but slight loss, in silencing a formidable battery; and on the 19th Lieut. R. H. Lamson, with the Stepping Stones, aided the land forces under Gen. Getty in capturing a battery of five guns, manned by one hundred and sixty-one men.

In June and July a number of small gunboats coöperated in the expeditions up the York, Pamunkey, and Mattapony Rivers undertaken for the purpose of occupying West Point and threatening Richmond. There were also during the year joint army and navy expeditions, chiefly in the nature of reconnoissances, up the James, Piankatank, Ware, and other rivers of Virginia, and among the inlets between the York and the Rappahannock, most of which were attended by substantial successes. Similar operations were conducted at various times along the shallow sounds and inlets of North Carolina, and in the Roanoke and Chowan Rivers.

During the latter half of the year, and particularly after the harbor of Charleston had been rendered inaccessible to blockade runners, Wilmington became the chief port of resort on the Atlantic coast for vessels of this class. The addition to the blockading fleet of several swift steamers, newly built at the national yards, or captured, greatly increased the risk of entering Cape Fear River, by either inlet, and, in consequence, many valuable prizes were taken, and nearly as many vessels were driven ashore and destroyed.

On July 12th the Penobscot, Lieut.-Com. De Haven, succeeded, after a short chase, in driving the iron steamer Kate ashore on Smith's Island, where she was immediately deserted by her officers and crew. A boat was sent in to get her off, but, as the tide was falling, this was found impossible, and arrangements were made to burn her, should the attempt to float her off at high water prove ineffectual. At noon a battery was brought to the beach by the rebels, the fire from which drove out the party from the Penobscot. Under these circumstances, the Kate was ordered to be set on fire by shells, and was rendered, as was supposed, totally unserviceable, together with her cargo. Upon the departure of the Penobscot the enemy immediately stripped the Kate, and on the night of the 31st succeeded in floating her off, the damage to her hull proving to be slight. On the morning of August 1st she was discovered on her way to Fort Fisher, on Federal Point, the northern side of New Inlet, towed by a number of small boats, and the Mount Vernon, James Adger, and Iroquois at once bore toward the shore to cut her out. The enemy abandoned her at the approach of the blockading vessels, and, the Mount Vernon running alongside, in the midst of a severe fire from the rebel batteries at New Inlet and Zuk's Island, fastened a hawser to her port bow and by great exertions towed her out of the range of the fire. The Kate proved to be a new steamer, very fast, and built entirely of iron. Her machinery had been removed, but her hull was scarcely injured.

At daylight, on Aug. 18th, the steamer Hebe attempted to run into Wilmington by the New Inlet entrance; but being intercepted by the Niphon, she headed for the shore, a few miles above Fort Fisher, and her crew escaped in boats. As it was blowing too hard to get her off, a boarding party was sent from the Niphon to destroy her. Two Whitworth guns soon after opened fire from the beach upon the ship, which was found to be hard aground in 7 feet of water. The boat from the Niphon having been swamped almost as soon as she reached the Hebe, and the violence of the gale preventing the blockading vessels from sending effective assistance, nearly the whole boarding party was compelled to wade ashore and surrender to a force of Confederate cavalry and riflemen which had meanwhile arrived. The Hebe was then set on fire by shells from the Shokokon, and burned to the water's edge. The enemy, however, succeeded during the next few days in discharging a portion of the cargo in a damaged state; whereupon the Minnesota, running up to within 600 yards of the wreck, drove the rebels from their battery and completed the destruction of the hull and machinery. A party then landed and brought off the two Whitworth guns.

The most serious disaster of the year on this station was the loss of the ironclad, Monitor, Commander Bankhead, the celebrated pioneer vessel of her class, which foundered at sea in a gale, south of Cape Hatteras, on the night of Dec. 30th, 1862. The Monitor left Hampton Roads in tow of the side wheel steamer Rhode Island, on the 29th, the weather being then pleasant, and until 7 P. M. of the 30th, the voyage was unattended by any special incident. At that hour the wind, previously light, hauled round to the southward, gradually increasing in violence until midnight, with a heavy sea. As the swell increased the Monitor began to tow badly, and the bilge pumps, which during the day had kept her free from water, were no longer available. At 8 P. M. she labored heavily, the seas completely submerging the pilot house, and washing over and into the turret, and at times into the blower pipes. It was observed that when she rose to the swell, the flat under surface of the projecting armor would come down with great force, causing a considerable shock to the vessel and turret, and thereby loosening the packing around its base. The Rhode Island was several times signalized to stop, with a view of ascertaining whether the Monitor would ride easier, but she immediately fell off into the trough of the sea, and the water in her hold continued to gain steadily. The centrifugal pump was then started, and notwithstanding it worked well, the water had by 10½ P. M. risen several inches above the level of the engine room floor. Signals of distress were now made to the Rhode Island, which despatched two boats to the assistance of the Monitor, and at considerable risk the steamers came alongside of each other. While getting the men into the boats (a very hazardous operation, in consequence of the heavy seas breaking entirely over the deck of the Monitor), the sharp bow of the ironclad came into such dangerous proximity to the Rhode Island, that the latter was obliged to steam ahead, to avoid being stove near her water line. During the absence of the boats the rapidly rising water put out the fires in the Monitor, and her engines having stopped, she rolled into the trough. By letting go her anchor her head was again brought to the sea and the remaining crew and officers were taken off, except a few who, stupefied by fear, refused to leave the ship and went down with her. Several men had previously been washed overboard and drowned. At about 1 A. M. of the 31st, she disappeared. One of the boats from the Rhode Island employed in the last trip from that vessel did not return, and was supposed to have been swamped. It was however picked up on the morning of the 31st, by the schooner A. Colby, and the crew were safely landed at Beaufort. The total casualties of the Monitor were four officers and twelve men missing.

"I am firmly of the opinion," says Commander Bankhead, in his official report of the disaster, "that the Monitor must have sprung a leak somewhere in the forward part, where the hull joins on to the armor, and that it was caused by the heavy shocks received as she came down upon the sea. The bilge pumps alone until 7 P. M. had easily kept her free, and when we find that all her pumps a short time after, with a minimum capacity of 2,000 gallons per minute, not only failed to diminish the water, but, on the contrary, made no perceptible change in its gradual increase, we must come to the conclusion that there are, at least, good grounds for my opinion."

On the morning of June 24th, the blockader Sumter, while cruising off Smith's Island in a dense fog, came into collision with the transport General Meigs, from the effects of which she soon after sunk, being very rotten. The officers and crew got off in boats, and were taken on board the schooner Jamestown, but everything else in the ship went down with her.

The field of operations embraced by the South Atlantic squadron, although unchanged, com prised the coasts of South Carolina and Georgia and the northeast coast of Florida, and at the commencement of the year the greater part of the squadron was engaged in the blockade of Charleston, or stationed at Port Royal. Early in January the first instalment of ironclads destined to operate against Charleston arrived, and with a view of testing the efficiency of this class of vessels, Admiral Dupont ordered Commander Worden, with the Montauk, to enter Ossabaw Sound and attempt the capture of Fort McAllister, at Genesis Point, on the Great Ogeechee river, under cover of which was lying the steamer Nashville, recently fitted by the enemy for a privateer, and which was waiting to run the blockade. On the morning of January 27th, the Montauk, supported by several small gunboats, opened fire upon the fort, which proved to be a formidable casemated earthwork with bomb proofs, and mounting nine guns. The enemy's practice was excellent, but under the fire of the Montauk's 15 and 11-inch guns their fire slackened. Owing to obstructions in the river, the Montauk was unable to advance within effective range, and having expended her shells she retired. She was struck thirteen times but received no injury.

Early on the morning of January 29th the iron propeller Princess Royal, four days out from Bermuda, attempted to run past the blockading fleet into Charleston. The U. S. gunboat Unadilla, Lieut. Quackenbush, apprised of her approach by a blue light from the schooner Blunt, slipped her cable and stood in shore, firing a couple of shots at the Princess Royal. The latter was then run ashore and abandoned by her captain, supercargo, pilot, and some of the petty officers. A boat's crew from the Unadilla at once took possession of the prize, which several hours later, with assistance from other vessels of the blockading fleet, was got off without sustaining any injury. Her cargo proved to be one of the most valuable taken in the course of the war, consisting of two complete engines of great power, intended for iron-clads, beside rifled guns, arms, ammunition, medicines, and a variety of miscellaneous articles. The Princess Royal was two days later taken to Port Royal and subsequently sent to Philadelphia for adjudication.

The loss of the Princess Royal was a severe blow to the enemy, who, ascertaining on the next day that she was still lying at anchor off Charleston harbor, organized a daring scheme to recover possession of her, and at the same time to inflict as much damage as possible upon the blockading squadron. Accordingly at 4 A. M. of the 31st the iron-clad steam rams Palmetto State, Lieut. Rutledge, and Chicora, Commander Tucker, in the former of which was Flag officer D. N. Ingraham, commanding the station, ran out from Charleston by the main ship channel, and aided by a thick haze commenced an onslaught on the blockaders. The latter at that time consisted of the steamers Housatonic, Mercedita, Ottawa, Unadilla, Keystone State, Quaker City, Memphis, Augusta, Stettin, and Flag, beside the pilot boat Blunt, and some smaller vessels. Most of these were of the light class of purchased vessels, the ironclads and two of the heaviest men-of-war, the Powhatan and Canandaigua, being at Port Royal coaling or repairing. The Mercedita, Captain Stellwagen, was the first vessel attacked, and was almost immediately rendered helpless by a 7-inch shell from the Palmetto State, which, entering her starboard side, exploded in the port boiler, blowing a hole in its exit from four to five feet square, and killing and wounding several men. So suddenly had the ram come upon her in the haze, that it was impossible to bring any of her guns to bear, and further resistance being useless, Captain Stellwagen, in reply to a demand for surrender, announced that he was in a sinking state. An officer from the Mercedita was immediately sent on board the ram and tendered the surrender of the officers and crew, who were paroled.

The Palmetto State, leaving the Mercedita to her fate, then made for the Keystone State, Commander Le Roy, which was also at the same time assailed by the Chicora. The Keystone State returned their fire vigorously, but having been set on fire in her forehold by the explosion of a shell, was obliged to keep off for a few minutes until the flames could be got under. Commander Le Roy then turned his ship and with a full head of steam bore down upon the nearest ram at a speed of twelve knots, intending to sink her. He also trained his guns for a plunging fire at the moment of collision; but before this could occur a shot passed through both steam chests of the Keystone State, rendering her powerless. Ten rifle shells also struck her, mostly in the hull, near or below the water line, and about the same time the fire in her forehold burst out again, and the engineers reported the ship taking in water rapidly. Commander Le Roy accordingly hauled down his flag, but finding that the enemy were still firing upon him, he directed the colors to be rehoisted and the fire to be resumed from the after battery. At this moment the Augusta, Memphis, and Quaker City came up, and by diverting the attention of the rams, enabled the Keystone State to get out of the range of the fire. Subsequently she was taken in tow by the Memphis and reached Port Royal in a very crippled state, about one fourth of her crew being killed and wounded. The Mercedita also arrived there on the same evening without assistance, having succeeded in temporarily stopping the hole in her side and in getting up steam in her uninjured boiler.

Meanwhile the rams carried on a sort of running combat with several of the blockading fleet, which, having no guns capable of making an impression on ironclads, kept prudently aloof. Upon the approach of the Housatonic, the only heavy man-of-war then on the station,

Flag-officer Ingraham deemed it prudent to retire, and at about $7\frac{1}{2}$ A. M. both rams took refuge in the swash channel, and subsequently anchored in shoal water near the shore, to the eastward of Fort Moultrie. They remained here until 5 P. M., attended by several small steamers, and then disappeared behind Fort Moultrie. One of them, while returning into the harbor, had her pilot house carried away by a shot from the Housatonic. During this attack the Princess Royal, which was the principal object of contest on both sides, lay quietly at her anchorage. After the retreat of the rams she got to sea, and arrived safely at Port Royal.

The raid had failed of its object, and beyond the temporary disabling of two vessels of the blockading squadron, no practical advantage had been gained by the enemy. But as the latter maintained telegraphic communication with Richmond, and could send north their own statements of the occurrence several days in advance of despatches from the fleet, it was determined to forestall the Union accounts, and, if possible, induce foreign powers to believe that the fleet before Charleston had been dispersed and the blockade raised. Accordingly the Richmond papers of the 2d of February published despatches from Charleston announcing as the result of the naval engagement of Jan. 31st, two U. S. vessels sunk, four set on fire, and the remainder driven away. The following "official proclamation" was also given:

HEADQUARTERS LAND AND NAVAL FORCES,
CHARLESTON, S. C., *January 31st*, 1863.

At about five o'clock this morning the Confederate States naval force on this station attacked the United States blockading fleet off the harbor of the city of Charleston, and sank, dispersed, and then drove out of sight for a time the entire hostile fleet; therefore we, the undersigned commanders respectively of the Confederate States naval and land forces in this quarter, do hereby formally declare the blockade by the United States of the said port of Charleston, S. C., to be raised by a superior force of the Confederate States, from and after this 31st day of January, A. D. 1863.

[Signed] G. T. BEAUREGARD, Gen'l Com'g.
D. N. INGRAHAM, Flag-officer,
Commanding Naval Forces.
[Official] THOS. JORDAN, Chief of Staff.

"Yesterday evening (Jan. 31st)," said another despatch, "Beauregard placed a steamer at the disposal of the foreign consuls to see for themselves that no blockade existed. The French and Spanish consuls, accompanied by Gen. Ripley, accepted the invitation. The British consul with the commander of the British war steamer Petrel, had previously gone five miles beyond the usual anchorage of the blockaders, and could see nothing of them with glasses. Late in the evening four blockaders reappeared, but keeping far out. This evening a larger number of blockaders are in sight, but keep steam up, evidently ready to run." And it was subsequently announced that the consuls held a meeting on the night after the above proclamation was issued, and decided unanimously that the blockade had been legally raised.

The publication of these despatches caused considerable uneasiness at the North. It was not doubted indeed that despatches from Admiral Dupont would put an entirely different face upon the matter, but apprehensions were entertained in some quarters that statements of this kind going abroad, uncontradicted by other evidence, might be only too readily seized upon by unfriendly powers as a pretext for insisting that the blockade had been raised, and that having been once raised, it could not be declared renewed without formal notice from the United States authorities. These fears, however, proved groundless. Foreign journals or governments declined to be influenced by *ex-parte* statements, and despatches from the blockading fleet showed that nothing approaching a raising of the blockade had been effected.

For the purpose of fortifying his own statements, Admiral Dupont subsequently sent an official refutation of the Beauregard and Ingraham proclamation, and the rebel despatches, dated Feb. 10th, and signed by nearly all the commanding officers of vessels that were lying off Charleston harbor on the morning of Jan. 31st. "We deem it our duty," they observe, "to state that the so-called results are false in every particular—no vessels were sunk, none were set on fire seriously. * * * So hasty was the retreat of the rams that, although they might have perceived that the Keystone State had received serious damage, no attempt was ever made to approach her. The Stettin and Ottawa, at the extreme end of the line, did not get under way from their position till after the firing had ceased, and the Stettin merely saw the black smoke as the rams disappeared over the bar. The rams withdrew hastily toward the harbor, and on their way were fired at by the Housatonic and Augusta until both had got beyond reach of their guns. They anchored under the protection of their forts and remained there. No vessel, iron-clad or other, passed out over the bar after the return of the rams in shore. The Unadilla was not aware of the attack until the Housatonic commenced firing, when she moved out toward that vessel from her anchorage. The Housatonic was never beyond the usual line of the blockade." They also state that no vessel ran in or out of the port during the day, and that no attempt was made to run the blockade, and conclude as follows: "We do not hesitate to state that no vessel came out beyond the bar after the return of the rams, at between 7 and 8 A. M., to the cover of the forts. We believe the statement that any vessel came anywhere near the usual anchorage of any of the blockaders, or up to the bar, after the withdrawal of the rams, to be deliberately and knowingly false. If the statement from the papers, as now before us, has the sanction of the captain of the Petrel and the foreign consuls, we can only deplore that foreign officers can lend their official positions to the spreading before the world, for unworthy objects, untruths patent to every officer of this squadron." Previous to the preparation of this paper the blockading fleet before Charleston had been strengthened by the New Ironsides, Powhattan, and Canandaigua.

On January 30th, the gunboat Isaac Smith, Lieutenant Conover, while engaged in reconnoitring the Stono river, was obliged to surrender to a rebel land force. She had passed some miles beyond Legaréville, as she had been in the habit of doing for weeks previous, and was on her way back, when three shore batteries, previously concealed, opened a concentrated fire upon her from heavy rifled guns. Lieut. Conover replied with vigor, and endeavored to steam down past the batteries, but a shot in the Smith's steam chimney effectually stopped the engine, and with no wind, little tide, and boats riddled with shot, she was left at the mercy of the enemy. Resistance appearing useless, the ship was surrendered, after 24 men had been killed and wounded. It subsequently appeared that, from information communicated by a deserter, the enemy had planned the ambuscade by which the Smith was captured, and had aimed at her boiler and machinery, which were very much exposed.

On the morning of Feb. 1st, the Montauk again engaged Fort McAllister, at a distance of about 1,400 yards, the water being too shoal to permit her to approach nearer. Some injury was done to the parapets of the fort, and the Montauk was hit 46 times, but without receiving material damage. For eight months previous the privateer Nashville had been lying under the protection of the fort, watching an opportunity to run the blockade; and to prevent any attempt by the gunboats to cut her out, the river had been staked and a line of torpedoes laid across the channel. She had been frequently observed close under the fort, ready to make a dash if the opportunity offered, or quietly waiting for an ironclad to tow her to sea. On the morning of the 27th, a reconnoissance discovered the Nashville aground, and Commander Worden seized the opportunity to bring the Montauk close up to the obstructions in the river, and commence a bombardment upon her. In less than 20 minutes the Nashville was in flames from exploding shells, and half an hour later her magazine blew up with terrific violence, leaving not a vestige of the vessel in sight. The Montauk was struck five times by shots from Fort McAllister, and while she was dropping down beyond the range of the enemy's guns a torpedo exploded under her, inflicting a slight amount of injury.

By this time several additional ironclads had arrived at Port Royal, and for the purpose of subjecting their various mechanical appliances to the full test of active service, before entering upon more important operations, Admiral Dupont ordered them to make a concentrated attack on Fort McAllister. This took place on March 3d, the Passaic, Capt. Drayton, the Patapsco, Commander Ammen, and the Nahant, Commander Downes, participating, under the command of Capt. Drayton. The Passaic, by skilful pilotage, was brought up to within about 1,000 yards of the fort, and for eight hours withstood its chief fire, retiring only when her ammunition was expended. Few of her shots failed to strike above the parapet of the fort; but beyond disfiguring the face of the work they effected no injury which a night's work would not repair; and, in the opinion of Capt. Drayton, the fort could "not be made untenable by any number of ironclads which the shallow water and narrow space would permit to be brought in position against it." The Passaic was struck 34 times in all, 9 shots being against her side armor, 13 against her deck, 5 against her turret, and 2 against her pilot house. In all these parts of the vessel the bolts were more or less started by the violence of the concussion; and indentations, varying from half an inch to 2 inches, were made in the armor. A 10-inch mortar shell, loaded with sand, fell on the deck over the bread room, crushing in the planking, and would have gone through, had it not struck on a beam. "Had it been loaded with powder instead of sand," said Capt. Drayton, "it might have set the vessel on fire. This certainly does not say much for the strength of the deck, the injury to which has been so much more serious than to that of the Montauk, that I must attribute it to a worse class of iron, unless heavier guns have been mounted since the attack made by Commander Worden." Everything about the guns and carriages was reported to have worked well, except that the concussion of the 15-inch gun broke all the bolts holding the side of the box to the turret. The Patapsco and Nahant were unable to approach so near the fort as the Passaic, and received but a slight fire from the enemy, who directed their efforts chiefly against the latter. The Patapsco was struck but once, and the Nahant not at all. Satisfied with the experiment (for such the engagement had been on the part of the ironclads), Capt. Drayton immediately returned to Port Royal, where the Passaic, and also the Montauk, underwent repairs.

By the commencement of April, the preparations, which for many months previous had been making for a combined attack by the ironclads upon the fortifications of Charleston harbor, were completed, and on the morning of the 6th the whole fleet crossed the bar, with the intention of reducing Fort Sumter on the same day, and thence proceeding up to the city. But the weather becoming so hazy as to prevent the pilots from seeing the ranges, the attack was deferred until the next day, and the fleet anchored about five miles from Fort Sumter. At noon, on the 7th, this being the earliest hour at which, owing to the state of the tide, the pilots would consent to move, signal was given by Admiral Dupont from his flag-ship, the New Ironsides, for the vessels to weigh anchor. According to the plan of attack the vessels were to form in the following order ahead, at intervals of one cable's length: 1. Weehawken, Capt. John Rogers; 2. Passaic, Capt. Percival Drayton; 3. Montauk, Commander John L. Worden; 4. Patapsco, Commander Daniel Ammen; 5. New Ironsides, Commodore Thomas Turner; 6. Catskill, Commander George W. Rodgers; 7. Nantucket, Commander Donald McN. Fairfax; 8. Nahant, Commander John Downes; 9. Keokuk, Lieut. Commander Alexander C. Rhind. The squadron was then to pass up the main ship channel without returning the fire of the batteries on Morris Island, unless signalized to do so, and was to take up a position to the northward and westward of Fort Sumter, and engage its northwest face at a distance of from 1,000 to 800 yards. A squadron of reserve, consisting of the Canandaigua, Unadilla, Housatonic, Wissahickon, and Huron, under the command of Capt. Joseph H. Green, of the Canandaigua, was ordered to remain outside the bar, and be in readiness to support the ironclads, when they should attack the batteries on Morris Island, which would be subsequent to the reduction of Fort Sumter.

The chief works erected by the enemy for the defence of Charleston may be thus briefly described: On the upper or north end of Sullivan's Island a powerful sand battery guarding Maffit's Channel; another large sand battery, called Fort Beauregard, between this and the Moultrie House; Fort Moultrie, which had been greatly strengthened since the commencement of the war; Fort Sumter, built upon an artificial island in the middle of the channel, near the entrance of the inner harbor, and about 1½ miles west of Fort Moultrie; Battery Bee, adjoining Fort Moultrie, on the western extremity of Sullivan's Island; the Mount Pleasant battery on the mainland between Sullivan's Island and Cooper river; Castle Pinckney, built on an island about a mile distant from Charleston; all, with the exception of Sumter, being on the right or northerly side of the harbor. On the other side of the harbor, in the immediate vicinity of the city, was the Wappoo battery on James Island, commanding the embouchure of Ashley river; next to which was Fort Johnson, and between it and Castle Pinckney, Fort Ripley, a work erected on an artificial island in what is known as the "Middle Ground." On Cumming's Point, Morris Island, opposite Fort Moultrie, was Battery Gregg, and a mile south of this Fort Wagner, an extensive sand battery of the most powerful construction. Finally, at Light House Inlet, which divides Morris Island from Folly Island, was another fortification covering the landing at that place. Within a few days of the attack the enemy also erected a new sand work between the two last mentioned. The number of guns mounted on these works was estimated at several hundred, comprising the heaviest smooth-bore ordnance, and many rifled pieces of English manufacture; and as an additional means of protection, the channel between Fort Sumter and Sullivan's Island was obstructed by rows of floating casks supporting torpedoes and other submarine obstacles, and in that between Sumter and Cumming's Point were no less than four rows of piles extending nearly up to Charleston.

At half past twelve the fleet began to move, the Weehawken, the leading ship, having a pioneer raft attached to her bows for the purpose of exploding torpedoes and clearing away obstructions. Almost immediately her raft became deranged, and nearly an hour was consumed in putting it in position. At half past one the vessels were again under way and moved slowly up toward Fort Sumter, passing the works on Morris Island, which held an ominous silence. They then steered toward the entrance of the inner harbor, intending to pass between Fort Sumter and Sullivan's Island, and shortly before 3 o'clock came within effective range of these positions. At 2.50 P.M. the guns of Fort Moultrie opened upon the Weehawken, followed shortly after by all the batteries on Sullivan's Island and Morris Island, and by Fort Sumter. The remainder of the squadron followed steadily in the wake of the leading ship, which, however, upon reaching the entrance of the channel between Sumter and Sullivan's Island, encountered obstructions of so formidable a nature, that Capt. Rodgers considered it impossible to pass through them. He accordingly turned his ship to gain a better position for attack, and his movements being followed by the vessels immediately behind him, the line, in consequence of the narrowness of the channel, and the force of the tide, was thrown into some confusion. The New Ironsides, in attempting to turn, was caught in the tideway, refused to obey her rudder, and became in a degree unmanageable; while, to add to the complication, the Catskill and Nantucket, which kept in her wake, fell foul of her, and for fifteen minutes the three vessels were in a dead lock. On this occasion, and once subsequently, the Ironsides was obliged to come to anchor to avoid drifting ashore, in which case she would inevitably have been lost.

Nothing now remained but for the admiral to make signal to the fleet to disregard the movements of the flag-ship, and take up such positions as might seem most available. This was at once done, and shortly before 4 o'clock the remaining eight vessels were ranged opposite the northeast front of Sumter, at distances varying from 550 to 800 yards. The enemy during this time had not been idle, and from Forts Beauregard, Moultrie, and Sumter, Battery Bee and Fort Wagner, the concentrated fire of 300 guns was poured upon the devoted fleet, exceeding probably in rapidity and power any cannonade previously known in warfare. To this the eight ironclads could oppose but 16 guns. During the climax of the fire 160 shots

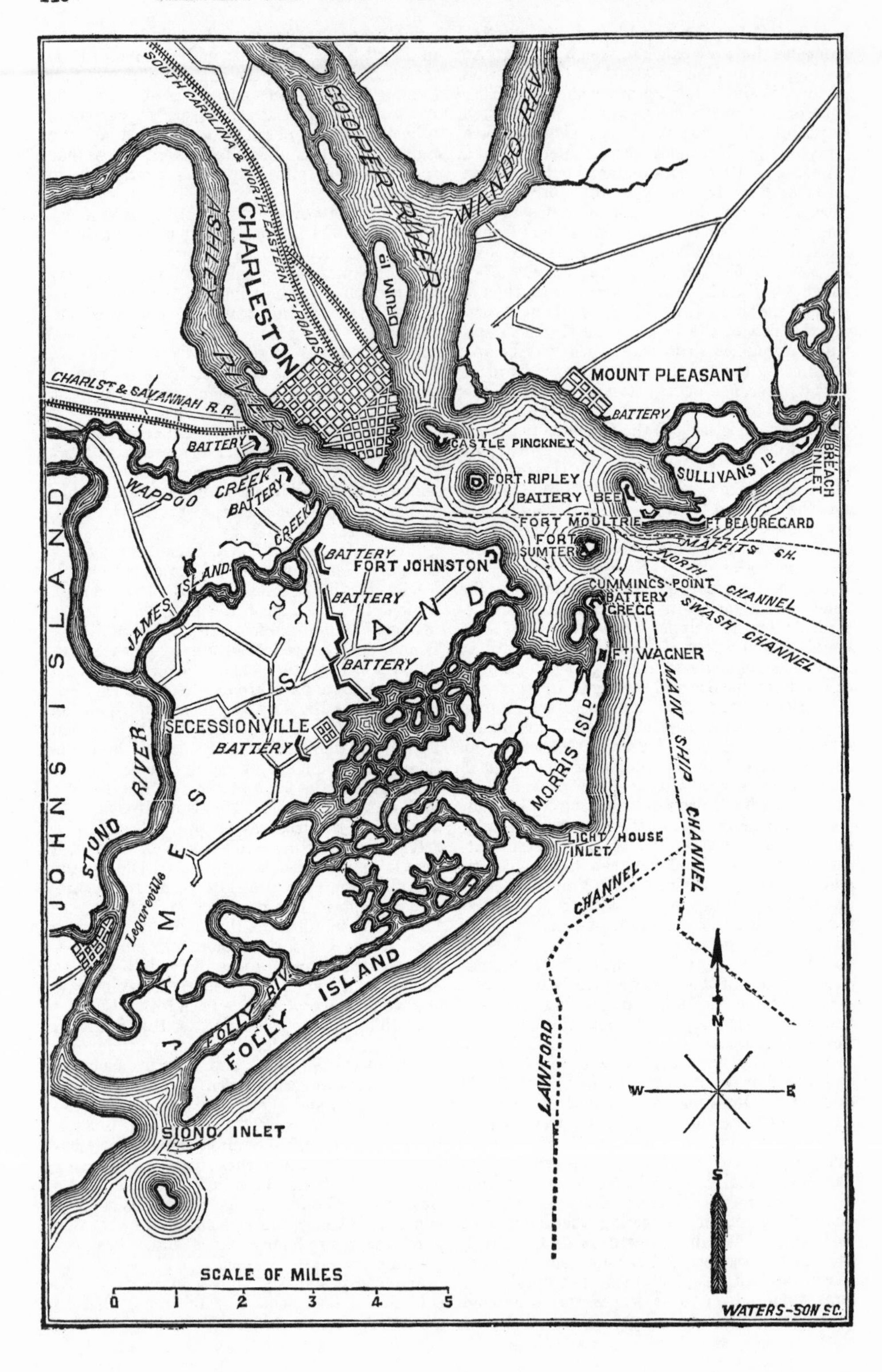
SOUTH CAROLINA & NORTH EASTERN R. ROADS
COOPER RIVER
WANDO RIV.
ASHLEY RIVER
CHARLESTON
DRUM ID.
MOUNT PLEASANT
CHARLST. & SAVANNAH R. R.
BATTERY
CASTLE PINCKNEY
SULLIVANS ID.
BREACH INLET
WAPPOO CREEK
FORT RIPLEY
BATTERY BEE
FORT MOULTRIE
FT. BEAUREGARD
FORT SUMTER
MAFFITS CH.
FORT JOHNSTON
NORTH CHANNEL
CUMMINGS POINT
BATTERY GREGG
SWASH CHANNEL
JAMES ISLAND CREEK
FT. WAGNER
JOHNS ISLAND
SECESSIONVILLE
MORRIS ISLD.
MAIN SHIP CHANNEL
STONO RIVER
JAMES ISLAND
LIGHT HOUSE INLET
Legareville
CHANNEL
FOLLY RIV.
FOLLY ISLAND
LAWFORD
N
W
E
S
SIONO INLET
SCALE OF MILES
0 1 2 3 4 5
WATERS-SON SC.

were counted in a single minute, and officers described the projectiles as striking their vessels sometimes as rapidly as the ticking of a watch. It is estimated that from first to last the enemy fired not less than 3,500 rounds of ammunition.

Placed in the focus of this tremendous fire, the ironclads fought at a disadvantage which rendered their offensive power of little effect. The confined space in which they were obliged to manœuvre called for unusual vigilance on the part of their commanders in avoiding collisions, as also in keeping clear of the floating obstructions and submerged batteries against which the tide was constantly bearing them. The dense clouds of smoke which hung over the water proved an additional source of embarrassment. They, nevertheless, entered resolutely upon the work before them, and directed their principal attack against Fort Sumter. Upon receiving the order to disregard the movements of the flag-ship, Lieut. Commander Rhind gallantly ran his vessel, the Keokuk, up through the others to within 550 feet of the fort, where she became a special target for the enemy. During the short period that she was able to retain this position, she was struck 90 times in the hull and turrets, 19 shots piercing her at and below the water line, and others entering her turret. The vessel was in fact so completely riddled, that her commander, fearing she could not much longer be kept afloat, withdrew from action at the end of half an hour, and succeeded in getting her to anchor out of range of fire. She was kept afloat during the night by means of her pumps, but sank the next morning. The Keokuk was only able to fire three times during the engagement, one of her guns having been almost immediately disabled, and the other rendered unavailable by casualties to the crew. She differed in construction and strength from the other ironclads of the squadron, and her side and turret armor of an average thickness of $5\frac{1}{2}$ inches, proved entirely insufficient to withstand the terrible fire to which she had been subjected.

The remaining vessels, though suffering no calamity comparable in extent with that of the Keokuk, were more or less damaged by the fire from the forts. The Nahant had her turret so jammed as effectually to prevent its turning, and the pilot house became nearly untenable in consequence of flying bolts and nuts. The Passaic was unable to use her 11-inch gun after the fourth fire, and had her turret temporarily jammed. The Patapsco lost the use of her rifle gun after the fifth fire, owing to the carrying away of her forward cap square bolts; and the Nantucket had her 15-inch gun permanently disabled after the third fire. The Weehawken, Montauk, and Catskill were obstructed in the use of their guns only by the obstacles to navigation above mentioned. The New Ironsides never got nearer than within 1,000 yards of the enemy's fire, and directed her chief attention to Fort Moultrie, against which, however, she was unable to discharge but a single broadside.

At 4.30 P. M. Admiral Dupont observing signs of distress on the part of several of his ships, made signal to withdraw from action, intending to resume the attack the next morning. The reports, however, which the different commanders made on that evening respecting the injuries to their vessels, the character of the obstructions in the inner harbor, and the number and weight of the enemy's guns, convinced him of the "utter impracticability of taking the city of Charleston with the force under his command." During the forty-five minutes that the fleet had been under the hottest concentrated fire of the enemy, one vessel had been wholly, and four partially disabled, and in the opinion of the admiral another half hour would have sufficed to put the remainder *hors de combat*. To compensate for these damages, nothing had been effected by the ironclads beyond some injuries to the east wall of Fort Sumter—a result which confirmed the admiral in his opinion that the opposing forces were too unequal to justify him in renewing the contest. The nine ships of the squadron had been able to fire but one hundred and thirty-nine shots against Fort Sumter in reply to the thousands of shells, solid shot, and steel pointed bolts hurled against them from six or seven different forts; and there was good reason to suppose that even had Sumter been silenced, the obstructions beyond would have been impassable, and the fire from the forts have sunk every vessel attempting to go up the harbor. This opinion, however, was not shared by all. Under these circumstances Admiral Dupont not only determined not to renew the fight, but to recross the bar and return with the ironclads to Port Royal; being prompted to the latter course partly by the necessity of making repairs, and partly by his belief that the anchorage inside or outside the bar was unsafe for vessels of the Monitor class. On the 12th the whole fleet, with the exception of the New Ironsides, which anchored outside Charleston bar, returned to Port Royal.

The casualties of the fleet were remarkably few, considering the fierceness of the enemy's fire, and resulted in almost every case from flying bolts and concussions within the turrets. But one man died of injuries received, and about twenty-five were wounded, principally on the Keokuk and Nahant. In some of the vessels no casualities whatever were reported. The Passaic was struck 35 times, the Nahant, 36 times, the Patapsco, 47 times, the Nantucket, 51 times, the Montauk, 14 times, and the Catskill, 20 times. Many of the shots made but slight indentations in the turrets and side armor, but in every ship repairs of greater or less extent were considered necessary. The Ironsides escaped with comparatively little injury, having during the whole engagement been out of range of the severest fire. The capabilities of the ironclads in contests of this nature were proved. In explanation of his failure to renew the attack, Admiral Dupont wrote as follows to the Navy Department, on the 15th:

> Any attempt to pass through the obstructions I have referred to, would have entangled the vessels and held them under the most severe fire of heavy ordnance that has ever been delivered; and while it is barely possible that some vessels might have forced their way through, it would only have been to be again impeded by fresh and more formidable obstructions, and to encounter other powerful batteries, with which the whole harbor of Charleston has been lined. I had hoped that the endurance of the iron-clads would have enabled them to have borne any weight of fire to which they might have been exposed; but when I found that so large a portion of them were wholly or one-half disabled, by less than an hour's engagement, before attempting to overcome the obstructions, or testing the power of the torpedoes, I was convinced that persistence in the attack would only result in the loss of the greater portion of the iron-clad fleet, and in leaving many of them inside the harbor, to fall into the hands of the enemy. The slowness of our fire, and our inability to occupy any battery that we might silence, or to prevent its being restored under cover of the night, were difficulties of the gravest character; and until the outer forts should have been taken, the army could not enter the harbor or afford me any assistance.

On the 13th the President despatched the following telegram to Admiral Dupont:

> Hold your position inside the bar near Charleston; or, if you shall have left it, return to it and hold it until further orders. Do not allow the enemy to erect new batteries or defences on Morris Island. If he has begun it, drive him out. I do not herein order you to renew the general attack. That is to depend on your own discretion or a further order.
>
> A. LINCOLN.

And by another order, dated on the succeeding day, he directed him, should he not succeed in taking the batteries on Morris Island or Sullivan's Island, to continue the demonstration for a time, and to make "the attempt a real one, though not a desperate one, if it affords any considerable chance of success." In reply, Admiral Dupont said that he should use every exertion to push forward the repairs of the iron-clads, and get them inside the bar. "I think it my duty, however," he observed, "to state to the department that this will be attended with great risk to these vessels from the gales which prevail at this season, and from the continuous fire of the enemy's batteries." He urged various objections to a further employment of them against the works on Morris Island, but expressed his willingness to obey all orders with the utmost fidelity, even should his judgment be opposed, and to renew, if necessary, the attack on Charleston, although he thought such a measure "would be attended with disastrous results, involving the loss of the coast."

In the early part of June, Admiral Dupont, having reason to believe that the Atlanta and other rebel iron-clads at Savannah were meditating an attack upon the blockading vessels in Warsaw Sound, despatched the Weehawken, Captain John Rodgers, and the Nahant, Commander J. Downes, thither to prevent any disaster to the fleet. The Atlanta, originally a swift and powerful British steamer called the Fingal, had early in the war run the blockade of Savannah, and been converted by the enemy into an iron-clad at a great expense. She was 191 feet in length and 40 feet beam, somewhat over 1,000 tons in measurement, and had a low deck, with a casemate or covered iron-plated house in the centre, with sloping sides and ends, in which was her battery, consisting of two 6-inch and two 7-inch rifled guns. Of these the former were broadside guns, and the latter worked on a pivot, either as broadside or bow and stern guns. She was further armed with a powerful ram, and had attached to her bow a submarine torpedo, charged with about fifty pounds of powder. No efforts had been spared to render her formidable, and it was believed by the enemy that her speed, her heavy armament, and her ram, would render her more than a match for any two vessels of the Monitor type. They therefore boldly steamed down the sound at dawn of June 17th, followed by several small steamers conveying pleasure parties who were to be the witnesses of her triumph. At a few minutes past four she was perceived by the Federal iron-clads, which were lying at anchor near the mouth of Wilmington River, and they at once prepared for action. The Weehawken being nearest the enemy got under way first and stood up the sound, followed by the Nahant, which, having no pilot, was ordered by Capt. Rodgers to keep in the wake of his vessel. A few minutes before five the Atlanta, which was then lying across the channel awaiting the attack of the Federal steamers, fired a single shot at the Nahant, which failed to take effect. The Weehawken steamed steadily toward the Atlanta, and when about three hundred yards distant opened upon her with her 15-inch gun. Drifting one hundred yards nearer, she discharged both her guns, upon which the Atlanta hauled down her colors, and ran up a white flag in token of surrender. The signal was not understood until after another discharge from the Weehawken, when all firing ceased, and the prize was taken possession of, after a contest of scarcely fifteen minutes, in which the Weehawken alone had participated.

On examination it was found that the enemy had been struck four times. The first shot knocked a hole in her casemate, without, however, going through, and scattered over the enclosed decks great quantities of wood and iron splinters, by which upward of forty men were stunned and wounded, one of whom subsequently died. This is believed to have been the first shot from a 15-inch gun fired in a naval combat, and according to the rebel officers its effect was to demoralize the whole crew of the Atlanta. The second shot struck the edge of the overhang; the third knocked off the top of the pilot house, wounding two pilots and stunning the men at the wheel, and the fourth struck a port stopper in the centre, breaking it in two and driving the iron fragments through the port. The first and third shots decided the battle, the former, as Captain Rodgers observed, having taken away the desire to fight, and the latter the ability to get away. The captured prisoners amounted to 145, officers and men, and the hull of the Atlanta was so little injured that in a short time she was enabled to take her place among vessels of her class in the United States navy.

The combat was characterized by the Secretary of the Navy as "the most marked and extraordinary in the service during the year, and in some respects one of the most significant and instructive naval battles of the war." Whatever opinions may have been entertained of the efficacy of iron-clads against forts of masonry or sand, few could doubt after this that when iron-clads were pitted against iron-clads their execution could be of the most decisive character. The Monitor class of vessels, which had fallen into temporary disfavor after the attack on Fort Sumter, became again popular, and were recognized as likely to be of the highest value in harbor or coast defence. The brevity of the conflict and the complete disabling of the Atlanta also reconciled many to the heavy ordnance carried by these vessels, the efficacy of which had been a subject of some dispute among professional men.

Notwithstanding the failure of the attack of April 7th, the Government was unwilling to relinquish further efforts against Charleston, and as the tone of Admiral Dupont's letters indicated that he was opposed to a renewed attack upon the forts, it was determined to relieve him by the appointment of Rear-Admiral Foote. That officer dying in New York before his departure, Rear-Admiral Dahlgren was appointed to the command of the squadron, and entered upon his duties on July 6th. Previous to this date the demonstrations against Charleston had been exclusively naval, but with the arrival of Gen. Gillmore as commander-in-chief of the military department of the South, arrangements were made for combined operations by the land forces and the iron-clads.

The chief maritime disaster on this station was the loss of the Weehawken, which sank at her moorings on the morning of Dec. 6th, during the prevalence of a northwesterly gale, carrying with her to the bottom four of her engineers and twenty-six of her crew. The remainder of the ship's company escaped in the boats, or by jumping overboard at the moment of going down. The most of those who perished were probably drowned in the turret and immediately below it, while seeking to force their way through the narrow openings which afford the only means of escape. The disaster was at the time attributed to her hatches being unclosed.

The proper station of the Western Gulf squadron was along the Gulf coast from Pensacola to the Rio Grande, but owing to military movements in Mississippi and Louisiana, Rear-Admiral Farragut (having been promoted to the new grade) was obliged to employ many of his vessels in the Mississippi and Red Rivers, in active coöperation with the land forces. For the same reason he gave his chief attention to this portion of his squadron, leaving the blockade of the coast to his subordinates.

The operations of the Mississippi fleet, like those of the preceding, were almost exclusively undertaken in conjunction with the land forces. Important services were rendered by the gunboats in patrolling the Tennessee and Cumberland Rivers, and dispersing the guerrillas who fired upon supply steamers and transports. To the gunboats on the Ohio, which in July coöperated with the land forces in the pursuit of Morgan, was in a considerable degree due the capture of that leader and his force.

The flotilla on the Mississippi numbered upward of a hundred vessels, carrying 462 guns, with crews amounting in the aggregate to 5,500 men. Thirteen of these were efficient iron-clads, 33 "tin-clads," so called from being less heavily plated than the others, and the remainder consisted of despatch and auxiliary vessels, rams, &c. There were also a number of iron and tin-clads in the course of construction.

The number of vessels captured by the several squadrons from the commencement of the war to Nov. 1st, 1863, was 1,045, classified as follows: steamers, 179; ships, 15; barques, 26; brigs, 30; schooners, 547; sloops, 131; yachts and small boats, 117. The value of all the prizes sent to admiralty courts for adjudication is estimated by Secretary Welles at upward of $13,000,000; and the value of those condemned, the costs and amounts distributed, are shown in the following table:

	No. of Cases.	Gross amount of sales.	Costs and expenses.	Net amount for distribution.
Boston........	13	$864,322 15	$25,188 44	$839,133 71
New York.....	89	2,218,263 29	281,162 07	1,937,735 21
Philadelphia...	57	*1,859,434 76	149.806 06	1,670,512 97
Key West.....	71	1,432,952 30	133,291 55	1,304,053 51
Washington....	44	72,091 62	11,966 12	60,909 08
Illinois........	11	91,619 28	5,993 40	85,625 88
Total....	285	$6,538,683 40	$607,407 64	$5,897,970 36

The number of prizes captured in 1863 by the four principal coast squadrons considerably exceeded 300, of which about one-third were steamers, in many cases built expressly for blockade running, and loaded with valuable cargoes.

* The sum of $89,115.73 allowed to claimants by decree of court.

CHAPTER XXXV.

Situation of Gen. Rosecrans—Attack on Fort Donelson—Expeditions of Colburn, Sheridan, Hall, and Col. Streight—Advance of Gen. Rosecrans—Retreat of Gen. Bragg—Movement of Gen. Burnside—Other Movements—Occupation of Chattanooga—Further advance of Gen. Rosecrans—Battle of Chickamauga—Firmness of Gen. Thomas—Army concentrates at Chattanooga.

BEFORE proceeding to state the important movements of the army under Gen. Rosecrans which took place at this time, it may be proper to notice its situation subsequent to the battle of Stone River in the beginning of the year. The operations of the Army of the Cumberland, under Maj.-Gen. Rosecrans, during 1862, closed with the battle of Stone River, near Murfreesboro. This battle took place on the last days of 1862 and the first of 1863. On the 5th of January the headquarters of the army were established at Murfreesboro. The army occupied a position in front of the town, and a series of extensive earthworks, completely encircling it, were constructed for the purpose of making it a depot of supplies and the base of future operations. The railroad track and the bridges in the rear toward Nashville were also repaired. On the 9th of January the army was divided into three corps, designated the Fourteenth, Twentieth, and Twenty-first, and commanded respectively by Gens. Thomas, McCook, and Crittenden. Active operations were, however, suspended, owing to the rains of the season. Large supplies were collected in consequence of the rise of the Cumberland River at Nashville and Murfreesboro. But the enemy was not idle. His cavalry overran the country, and men and wagons belonging to Gen. Rosecrans were often captured by him. The object was to cut off the communications of the Army of the Cumberland and its supplies. Thus also many of the steamers on the Cumberland River were captured and burned.

On the 31st, Brig.-Gen. Jeff. C. Davis, with a division of infantry and two brigades of cavalry, under Col. Minty, moved from camp on an expedition in the direction of Rover and Franklin. The force was absent thirteen days, and during that time some portion of it visited Middletown, Unionville, Versailles, Peytonville, Franklin, Hillsboro, Kinderhook, and Triune. The cavalry captured one hundred and forty-one prisoners, including two colonels, one major, four captains, and several lieutenants, with two men severely injured.

On the 3d of February an attack was made on Fort Donelson, in another part of this department. On the 2d, the Confederate Col. Forrest, with nine hundred men, had taken a position at Palmyra, for the purpose of interrupting the navigation of the Cumberland. On the next day he advanced upon the fort both from above and below. The garrison consisted of nine companies of the 83d Illinois, a battalion of the 5th Iowa cavalry, Flood's battery, and some wounded men, under command of Col. A. C. Harding. The battery consisted of four rifled guns, and in addition there was a pivot of thirty-two pounder rifled, mounted on the northwest corner of the fort. At half-past one in the afternoon a flag of truce was sent in by Col. Forrest, demanding a surrender of the fort and garrison. This was promptly refused, and preparations for defence were made. The attack was immediately commenced, and kept up with numerous charges, which were gallantly repulsed, until eight o'clock in the evening, when another demand for a surrender was made. It was again promptly refused, and the enemy retired in confusion. The Federal loss was thirteen killed, fifty-one wounded, and twenty taken prisoners, without including a captain and twenty-six men who were captured on the same day while on a scout; also one gun, twenty-five mules, and forty-two horses. The Confederate loss was estimated at two hundred and fifty killed, six hundred wounded, and one hundred and five prisoners.

A period of inactivity now ensued, which was suddenly broken by the defeat and capture of a Federal brigade at Spring Hill on the 5th of March. On the preceding day an expedition, under the command of Col. John Colburn, consisting of part of the 33d and 85th Indiana, 22d Wisconsin, and 19th Michigan, numbering fifteen hundred and eighty-nine men, together with the 124th Ohio, and six hundred cavalry and one battery of six small guns, was ordered to proceed from Franklin to Spring Hill, ten miles south, on the Columbia turnpike. Soon after commencing the march, the enemy were encountered, and after a sharp skirmish, repulsed. Moving forward about two miles, they were again encountered, but, owing to the late hour, the command encamped. Starting again on the next morning, the 124th Ohio being in the rear of the wagon train, the enemy was again met, after an advance of two miles, and sharp skirmishing was kept up for some distance. The enemy was then found in full force under Gen. Van Dorn and Col. Forrest. A severe struggle ensued, which was protracted until Col. Forrest had taken a position in the rear, when Col. Colborn, finding his ammunition failing, and his retreat cut off, surrendered. Thirteen hundred and six men were made prisoners. The cavalry were not engaged, and, with the artillery, escaped. The Confederate force consisted of cavalry and mounted infantry, composing six brigades, under the command of Maj.-Gen. Van Dorn. The whole force of Gen. Van Dorn had been at Spring Hill for three days, preparing to make an attack on Franklin.

Meanwhile a successful expedition was made by Gen. Sheridan, with his division, and Col. Minty, with a force of eight hundred cavalry. Several sharp skirmishes took place, and a portion of the force which captured Col. Colburn was overtaken at Thompson Station and driven from the field, and the force of Gen. Van Dorn was followed to Duck river, when the expedition returned to Franklin.

On the 18th of March, an expedition, consisting of the 105th Ohio, 80th and 123d Illinois, and an Indiana battery, and one company of 1st Middle Tennessee cavalry, numbering about fourteen hundred men, under the command of Col. A. S. Hall, left Murfreesboro and moved in the direction of Liberty. That night Gainesville was occupied, and on the next morning an advance was made, when a slight skirmish ensued. The enemy slowly retired on the turnpike down Smith's Fork, followed by Col. Hall, until they were found drawn up in line across the road. Finding, upon a reconnoissance, that he was greatly outnumbered, Col. Hall fell back toward Murfreesboro, with the object of drawing the enemy after him. That night he encamped at Auburn, seven miles from Liberty, and on the next morning, the 20th, took up a position at Milton, twelve miles northeast of Murfreesboro. Here he was attacked by the Confederate force under Gen. John Morgan, who, after a fight of three and a half hours, withdrew from the field. Four captains, two lieutenants, and fifty-seven men were left on the field as dead or mortally wounded. Their total loss was estimated at nearly four hundred. Ten prisoners, eight horses, and fifty-three stands of arms were captured. The loss of Col. Hall was six killed, forty-two wounded, and seven missing. The force of the enemy was about two thousand.

A large number of expeditions, similar to those above stated, were sent out at different times; often with much success. About the 10th of April another attack was made on Maj.-Gen. Gordon Granger, at Franklin, by the Confederate force, under Maj.-Gen. Van Dorn. The force of Gen. Granger consisted of the divisions of Brig.-Gens. Baird and Gilbert, sixteen hundred men and sixteen guns, and Brig.-Gen. Smith's cavalry brigade of eleven hundred and twenty-eight men; also a cavalry force of sixteen hundred men and two guns, under Col. Stanley. The only artificial defence was an uncompleted fort, which mounted two siege guns and two three-inch rifled guns. Its elevation was about forty feet above the surrounding country, and it commanded most of the approaches to Franklin, north of the Harpeth, and all from the south except a small portion of the surface covered by a few blocks of houses. Gen. Granger's camp was on the north side of the river, about two thirds of a mile distant from the town. Gen. Baird was ordered to hold in check any force attempting to cross the fords below the town, and Gen. Gilbert was placed in a position to meet any attack in front, or to reënforce either flank. Gen. Stanley was stationed out four miles on the road to Murfreesboro, and Gen. Smith's cavalry were held in reserve to reënforce Gen. Stanley. This force, however, was sent under a misapprehension to Brentwood. An attack was made by Gen. Van Dorn upon Gen. Granger's front, which was repelled and afterward turned upon Gen. Stanley, who was driven back by overpowering numbers before reënforcements could reach him. After this the enemy withdrew. The force of the enemy was estimated at nine thousand cavalry and two regiments of infantry, and his loss at about three hundred. The loss of Gen. Granger was thirty-seven killed, wounded, and missing.

On the 20th of April, a force, consisting of Maj.-Gen. Reynolds's division, Col. Wilder's mounted brigade, and seventeen hundred cavalry, under Col. Minty, left Murfreesboro to capture or disperse any Confederate force at McMinnsville. At night the cavalry encamped between Readyville and Woodbury. Early the next morning the force moved on, and, approaching the town, the pickets of the enemy were discovered. Forming a line, they opened fire, and were charged upon and driven through the town. The entire force thus dispersed consisted of seven hundred men. The wagon train had left the town for Chattanooga about an hour before the arrival of the Federal force, but, by hard pressing, three wagons were captured, and eight or nine men. Other movements were made by this force, which resulted in the capture of one hundred and thirty prisoners, the destruction of a trestlework below Morrison's, the burning of the railroad buildings, one locomotive, and two cars, at that place, the burning of the railroad bridge across Hickory creek, and the capture there of a large amount of bacon and other commissary stores. A large amount of property and stores, including a cotton factory and other Government buildings, was destroyed at McMinnsville, and a large number of horses and mules brought in. No casualties occurred to the Federal force.

On the 29th of April, a force of five hundred men, under Col. Watkins, captured a camp of the enemy, taking one hundred and thirty-eight prisoners.

About the same time an expedition was fitted out for Northern Georgia, consisting of the 51st Indiana, 80th Illinois, and portions of two Ohio regiments, under command of Col. A. D. Streight. The force numbered about eighteen hundred men, and the instructions given to Col. Streight were as follows:

HEADQUARTERS, DEPOT OF THE CUMBERLAND,
MURFREESBORO, *April 8th*, 1863.

Colonel A. D. Streight, 51st Indiana Volunteers:

By special field order, No. 94, paragraph 8, you have been assigned to the command of an Independent Provisional Brigade, for temporary purposes. After fitting out your command with equipments and supplies, as you have already been directed in the verbal instructions of the General commanding this department, you will then proceed by a route of which you will be advised by telegraph, to some good steamboat landing on the Tennessee river, not far above Fort Henry, where you will embark your command, and proceed up the river. At Hamburg you will communicate with Brig.-Gen. Dodge, who will probably have a messenger there, awaiting your arrival. If it should then appear unsafe to move farther up the river, you will debark at Hamburg, and, without delay, join the force of Gen. Dodge, which will then be *en route* for Iuka, Mississippi. If, however, it should be deemed safe, you will land at Eastport, and form a junction with Gen. Dodge. From that point you will then march in conjunction with him to menace Tuscumbia; but you will not wait to join in the attack, unless it should be necessary for the safety of Gen. Dodge's command or your own, or unless some considerable advantage can be gained over the enemy without interfering with the general object of your expedition. After having marched long enough with Gen. Dodge to create a general impression that you are a part of his expedition, you will push to the southward and reach Russellville or Moulton. From there your route will be governed by circumstances; but you will with all reasonable despatch push on to Western Georgia, and cut the railroads which supply the rebel army by way of Chattanooga. To accomplish this is the chief object of your expedition; and you must not allow collateral or incidental schemes, even though promising great results, to delay you so as to endanger your return. Your quartermaster has been furnished with funds sufficient for the necessary expenses of your command; you will draw your supplies and keep your command well mounted from the country through which you pass. For all property taken for the legitimate use of your command, you will make cash payments in full to men of undoubted loyalty, give the usual conditional receipts to men whose loyalty is doubtful; but to rebels, nothing. You are particularly commanded to restrain your command from pillage and marauding; you will destroy all depots of supplies for the rebel army, all manufactories of guns, ammunition, equipments, and clothing for their use, which you can without delaying you so as to endanger your return. That you may not be trammelled with minute instructions, nothing further will be ordered than this general outline of policy and operation. In intrusting this highly important and somewhat perilous expedition to your charge, the General commanding places great reliance on your prudence, energy, and valor, and the well-attested bravery and endurance of the officers and men in your command. Whenever it is possible and reasonably safe, send us word of your progress. You may return by way of Northern Alabama or Northern Georgia. Should you be surrounded by rebel forces, and your retreat cut off, defend yourself as long as possible, and make the surrender of your command cost the enemy as many times your number as possible. A copy of the general order from the War Department, in regard to paroling prisoners, together with the necessary blanks, are herewith furnished you; you are authorized to enlist all able-bodied men who desire to join the "Army of the Union." You must return as soon as the main objects of your expedition are accomplished.

Very respectfully, your obedient servant.

J. A. GARFIELD,
Brigadier-General and Chief of Staff.

The following additional instructions were sent by telegraph to Col. Streight:

April 9th, 1863.

The written instructions you have received, are designed to cover the cases you allude to. It is not necessary that a manufactory be directly in the employ of the rebels, to come under the rule there laid down. If it produces any considerable quantity of supplies, which are likely to reach the rebel army, it is to be destroyed. Of course, small mills, that can only supply the necessaries of life to the inhabitants, should not be injured. Any considerable amount of supplies likely to reach the rebel army, are to be destroyed. If you dress your soldiers in the costume of the enemy, they will be liable to be treated as spies: you should not do this without the consent of the men, after they have been fully advised of the consequences.

J. A. GARFIELD,
Brigadier-General and Chief of Staff.

Under these instructions, Col. Streight embarked on steamers at Nashville, with his command, and landed near Fort Donelson on the Cumberland river. He then proceeded across the country to the Tennessee river, while the steamers descended to the Ohio and came up the Tennessee to meet him. Thence he proceeded to Eastport, and formed a junction with Gen. Dodge's force then marching upon Tuscumbia, and defeated the Confederate troops stationed there, with considerable loss to them. Thence he moved to Northern Georgia, aiming to reach the important points of Rome and Atlanta. Meanwhile Gen. Dodge, with his force, turned southward, to make a sweeping raid in Northern Alabama, and return to his headquarters at Corinth.

No sooner had Col. Streight commenced his march than information of his movements was received by Gen. Forrest and Col. Roddy, who, with a cavalry force, happened to be within striking distance. By a rapid movement they came upon the rear of Col. Streight, and commenced a running fight, which continued for four days, during which there were two severe battles and several spirited skirmishes. The Federal troops thus marched over a hundred miles toward the heart of the State, destroying bridges, and large supplies of corn collected for the Confederate army, a large foundery for the manufacture of cannon and shot, and seizing all the animals needed. Strict discipline was also maintained, and the inhabitants were not needlessly harassed. The Confederate force finally increased to overwhelming numbers, and Col. Streight, having expended his ammunition, and his men becoming exhausted, was compelled to surrender at a point fifteen miles from Rome, in Georgia. His men, numbering thirteen hundred, were paroled and sent to Virginia, and exchanged about two months afterward. But his officers were retained and imprisoned, on the demand of the Governor of Georgia, by whom they were claimed as having incurred the penalty fixed by a statute of the State for inciting slaves to rebellion. It was charged, at the time of the surrender, that negroes were found in Col. Streight's command, who were uniformed and bearing arms. This was denied by the privates, who asserted that only five or six negroes were with the command, and they had started with it from Nashville. This imprisonment of Col. Streight caused the Federal Government to suspend the exchange of Confederate officers, and subsequently to imprison Gen. John Morgan and his officers in the penitentiary of Ohio. Col. Streight was then released from imprisonment as a felon, and, subsequently, Gen. Morgan escaped.

At this time, the authorities at Washington were led to believe that large detachments were going from Gen. Bragg's army to reënforce Gen. Johnston in Mississippi. Gen. Rosecrans was therefore urged to take advantage of this opportunity to drive Gen. Bragg back into Georgia, and thus secure East Tennessee from the possession of the enemy. Gen. Burnside was also ordered to coöperate with him. The following correspondence occurred between Gens. Halleck and Rosecrans:

MURFREESBORO, TENN., *June 11th*, 1863.

Your despatch of to-day is received. You remember that I gave you, as a necessary condition of success, an adequate cavalry force. Since that time I have not lost a moment in mounting our dismounted cavalry as fast as we could get horses. Not more than three hundred remain to be mounted. The 5th Iowa, ordered up from Donelson, arrived to-day. The 1st Wisconsin will be here by Saturday. My preliminary infantry movements have nearly all been completed, and I am preparing to strike a blow that will tell. But to show you how differently things are viewed here, I called on my corps and division commanders and generals of cavalry, for answers in writing to the questions:

First—From your best information, do you think the enemy materially weakened in our front? Second—Do you think this army can advance at this time with reasonable prospect of fighting a great and successful battle? Third—Do you think an advance advisable at this time? To the first, eleven answered no; six, yes, to the extent of ten thousand. To the second, four, yes, with doubts; thirteen, no. To the third, not one yes; seventeen, no.

Not one thinks an advance advisable until Vicksburg's fate is determined. Admitting these officers to have a reasonable share of military sagacity, courage, and patriotism, you perceive that there are graver and stronger reasons than probably appear at Washington, for the attitude of this army. I therefore counsel caution and patience at headquarters. Better wait a little to get all we can ready to insure the best result. If, by so doing, we, perforce of Providence, observe a great military maxim—not to risk two great and decisive battles at the same time—we might have cause to be thankful for it. At all events you see that, to expect success, I must have such thorough grounds that when I say "Forward," my word will inspire conviction and confidence where both are now wanting. I should like to have your suggestion.

W. S. ROSECRANS, Major-General.

To Maj.-Gen. H. W. HALLECK, General-in-Chief.

WASHINGTON, *June 12th*, 1863.

GENERAL: Your telegram of yesterday is just received. I do not understand your application of the military maxim not to fight two great battles at the same time. It will apply to a single army, but not to two armies acting independently of each other. Johnston and Bragg are acting on interior lines between you and Grant, and it is for their interest, not ours, that they should fight at different times, so as to use the same force against both of you. It is for our interest to fight them, if possible, while divided. If you are not strong enough to fight Bragg with a part of his force absent, you will not be able to fight him after the affair at Vicksburg is over, and his troops return to your front.

There is another military maxim, that "councils of war never fight." If you say that you are not prepared to fight Bragg, I shall not order you to do so, for the responsibility of fighting or refusing to fight at a particular time or place, must rest upon the general in immediate command. It cannot be shared by a council of war, nor will the authorities here make you fight against your will. You ask me to counsel them to caution and patience. I have done so very often, but after five or six months of inactivity, with your force all the time diminishing and no hope of any immediate increase, you must not be surprised that their patience is pretty well exhausted. If you do not deem it prudent to risk a general battle with Bragg, why can you not harass him, or make such demonstrations as to prevent his sending more reënforcements to Johnston? I do not write this in a spirit of fault finding, but to assure you that the prolonged inactivity of so large an army in the field is causing much complaint and dissatisfaction, not only in Washington, but throughout the country.

Very respectfully, your obedient servant,

H. W. HALLECK, General-in-Chief.

Maj.-Gen. ROSECRANS, Murfreesboro, Tenn.

HEADQUARTERS DEPARTMENT OF THE CUMBERLAND,
MURFREESBORO, *June 21st*, 1863.

GENERAL: In your favor of the 12th inst., you say you do not see how the maxim of not fighting two great battles at the same time, applies to the case of this army and to Grant's. Looking at the matter practically, we and our opposing forces are so widely separated, that for Bragg to materially aid Johnston, he must abandon our front substantially, and then we can move to our ultimate work with more rapidity, and less waste of material on natural obstacles. If Grant is defeated, both forces will come here, and then we ought to be near our base. The same maxim that forbids, as you take it, a single army fighting two great battles at the same time—by the way, a very awkward thing to do—would forbid this nation's engaging all its forces in the great West at the same time, so as to leave it without a single reserve to stem the current of possible disaster. This is, I think, sustained by high military and political considerations. We ought to fight here, if we have a strong prospect of winning a decisive battle over the opposing force, and upon this ground I shall act. I shall be careful not to risk our last reserve without strong grounds to expect success.

W. S. ROSECRANS, Major-General.

Maj.-Gen. H. W. HALLECK, General-in-Chief.

On the 24th of June, Gen. Rosecrans commenced a series of movements for the purpose of bringing on a conflict between his forces and those under the command of Gen. Bragg, or to cause the latter to retire. His plan was to create the impression of a main advance from Murfreesboro upon Gen. Bragg's centre and left, by feint movements and demonstrations with the smaller portion of the army in the direction of Shelbyville, while the decisive blow should be struck by marching rapidly with the main body upon Gen. Bragg's right, and, after turning or defeating it, to move upon Tullahoma, by way of Manchester. Thus he would seize the enemy's base and lines of communication from that point.

The twentieth corps, under Gen. McCook, was selected to make the advance on the right. About 7 o'clock on the morning of the 24th, the division of Gen. Sheridan advanced on the Shelbyville road, preceded by five companies of the 30th Indiana mounted infantry, under Lieut.-Col. Jones. As it came in sight of the enemy's outposts, it halted and bivouacked on each side of the road in the wood. The divisions of Gens. Johnson and Davis advanced six miles on the same road, and then turned to the left on the road to Liberty Gap.

The morning was stormy, but, before daybreak, the mounted infantry, under Col. Wilder, marched along the road leading to Manchester, followed by Gen. Reynolds with the remainder of his division. After some hours, Gens. Negley and Rousseau followed in the same direction. The instructions to Col. Wilder were to advance within a few miles of Hoover's Gap, and there halt until the infantry came up, and then to carry the works. Learning, however, that the works commanding the Gap were not occupied, he moved forward and took possession of them, before the enemy were sufficiently aware of his approach to make any serious resistance. At the same time he pushed forward to the other extremity of the Gap, and took up a position commanding the road and the enemy's camp. In this movement he captured a train of nine wagons and a drove of beef cattle. The enemy immediately prepared for an attack, and came on in such overwhelming numbers that they would have been successful, had not reënforcements arrived to the aid of Col. Wilder. The fighting continued for two hours, during which the loss of the command was sixty-three killed and wounded. The loss of the enemy was represented by prisoners as exceeding five hundred.

Meanwhile, the portion of the corps of Gen. McCook which took the road to Liberty Gap, encountered a force of the enemy near the entrance of the Gap. Gen. Willich, whose brigade led the column, was ordered by Gen. Johnson to drive the enemy. This was done so promptly that their tents, baggage, and supplies were captured. Col. Baldwin was then sent forward to clear the upper end of the Gap, where the enemy were soon found, in a force consisting of a brigade of infantry and a battery of artillery. After a sharp and short combat they were driven out, and their position occupied. On the next day, Gen. Johnson held the position which his command had won, in order to continue the delusion of the enemy as to the real designs of Gen. Rosecrans. Skirmishing was kept up by the enemy along the front, and, between three and four o'clock in the afternoon, a formal attack in line of battle was made. A sharp struggle ensued, but after two hours the enemy abandoned the contest. The occupation of these gaps gave to Gen. Rosecrans the command of the position, and as soon as he advanced through them to Manchester and Winchester, he flanked Gen. Bragg at Tullahoma, and obliged him to retreat. This was commenced at once; and on the first of July, Gen. Rosecrans, learning of the retreat of Gen. Bragg, rapidly advanced his forces. Gen. Thomas moved on the Manchester road, and Gen. McCook on the one from Tullahoma. Gen. Thomas moved rapidly, in order to strike the enemy, who were moving directly east to the military road, five miles east of the railroad, and parallel with it. The enemy however, reached the crossing of Elk river before he was overtaken by the advance of Gen. Thomas. The division of Gen. Negley encountered the rear of Gen. Hardee at a point four miles north of Elk river. The resistance made here by Gen. Wheeler was so stubborn, that Gen. Negley was delayed until the trains of the enemy had crossed the river. During the night, their reserve of artillery, consisting of twenty-six pieces, crossed the river at Estelle Springs, and reached Tin Mountain. After crossing, the rear of the enemy burned the bridges, and took up positions in works hastily thrown up on the opposite side, in order to delay the crossing of Gen. Thomas as long as possible, and to enable their infantry and trains to get into the mountains. At the same time heavy rains commenced, and the river rose very high. Gen. Crittenden took possession of the road from Dechard through Tracy City to Chattanooga, and thus forced Gen. Bragg to take the roads across the mountains. On the 2d, Gen. McCook moved so as to flank the road to Winchester and the mountains. At the same time, Gens. Rosecrans and Brannan moved to the upper crossing of Rock creek, to strike the rear of the enemy, who were to be detained by Gen. Negley. But Gen. Negley, mistaking the firing of a cavalry brigade on the right flank of the enemy for that of Gen. Rosecrans, opened with two batteries, and caused them to retreat precipitately to the mountains. On the morning of July 4th, the whole Federal force advanced to the foot of the mountains at Cowan, and found the enemy in full retreat upon Chattanooga. At the same time, Shelbyville was occupied by Gens. Stanley and Granger, and the former pushed on as far as Huntsville in Alabama.

This retreat of Gen. Bragg from Tennessee had a demoralizing effect upon his forces, and discouraged the friends of the Confederacy in Tennessee. The result of these operations of Gen. Rosecrans thus far was to recover Middle Tennessee, and to preserve Kentucky from an invasion. His losses in these operations were 85 killed, 462 wounded, and 13 missing. The loss of the enemy in killed and wounded is unknown, but 1,634 were made prisoners, and six pieces of artillery, many small arms, much camp equipage, and large quantities of commissary and quartermaster's stores were taken.

Gen. Bragg, having returned to Chattanooga on the south side of the Tennessee river, now fortified his position, and threw up defensive works at the crossing of the river and as far up as Blythe's Ferry.

The first object of Gen. Rosecrans was to repair the railroad from Nashville to Stevenson in Alabama. At Stevenson the Nashville railroad unites with the Memphis and Charleston road. Stevenson is thirty-seven miles west of Chattanooga, on the line of the latter road. Having completed his preparations, Gen. Rosecrans commenced his movement on Chattanooga and its covering mountain ridges on the southeast, on the 16th of August. On that day, Gen. Thomas moved from Decherd, with the division of Gen. Payne in advance. This division had been stationed at the University on the Cumberland mountains. The corps moved over the mountains on a line nearly parallel with the Nashville railroad to Stevenson: it crossed the Tennessee river at or near Bridgeport, Alabama, by a pontoon bridge. On the 16th, Gen. Johnson's division of Gen. McCook's corps left Tullahoma, and passed through Winchester on the forenoon of the 17th. Gen. Davis's division followed in the afternoon. Gen. Sheridan's division moved from Cowan on the same day, and joined the rest of the corps at Salem, ten miles from Winchester, on the Huntsville road. There the corps moved in column, accompanied by its artillery and baggage, crossing the mountains, and striking the Tennessee river at Bellefonte, Alabama, twelve miles east of Stevenson. Gen. Crittenden's corps moved eastward to feel the strength of the enemy, and to cross north of Chattanooga. The front of the entire movement extended from the head of Sequatchie valley in East Tennessee to Athens in Alabama, thus threatening the line of the Tennessee river from Whitesburg to Blythe's Ferry, a distance of one hundred and fifty miles.

On the 26th, a part of Gen. Davis's division crossed at Caperton's Ferry, about six miles below Bridgeport. The remainder of the division followed in a few days, and also Gen. Johnson's division of the same corps; on the 2d of September, Gen. Sheridan, of the same corps, crossed at Bridgeport, followed by the infantry and artillery of Gen. Brannan's division. Gen. Negley, of Gen. Thomas's corps, crossed at the same time at Caperton's Ferry. By the 8th of September, Gen. Thomas had moved on Trenton in Georgia, having seized Frick's and Stevens's Gaps on the Lookout mountain. Gen. McCook had advanced to Valley Head and taken Winston's Gap, while Gen. Crittenden had crossed to Wauhatchie, communicating on the right with Gen. Thomas, and threatening Chattanooga by the pass over the point of Lookout mountain. The first mountain barrier south of the Tennessee being thus successfully passed, Gen. Rosecrans decided to threaten the enemy's communication with his right, while the centre and left seized the gaps and the commanding points of the mountains in front. On the 9th, Gen. Crittenden made a reconnoissance which developed the fact that the enemy had evacuated Chattanooga on the day and night previous. The corps of Gen. Crittenden therefore took immediate possession of Chattanooga, which had been the object of the campaign, while Gen. Rosecrans, with the remainder of the army, pressed forward through the difficult passes of the Lookout mountain, apparently directing his march upon Lafayette and Rome.

At the same time when Gen. Rosecrans commenced his forward movement on the 16th of August, Gen. Burnside left Camp Nelson in Kentucky for East Tennessee. Gen. Burnside assumed command of the Department of Ohio in March. On the 30th of that month, Gen. Gillmore engaged and defeated a large force of the enemy under Gen. Pegram, near Somerset, Kentucky. The other operations which had taken place consisted of an attempted raid in Harrison county, Indiana, from which the enmy were driven back with a loss of fifty-three made prisoners; a movement under Col. Saunders, with two pieces of artillery, the first Tennessee cavalry and some detachments from Gen. Carter's command, by which the railroad near Knoxville and the bridges at State creek, Strawberry Plains, and Mossy creek were destroyed, and ten pieces of artillery, one thousand stand of arms, and five hundred prisoners were captured, with a loss of one killed, two wounded, and a few missing; also the raid of Gen. Morgan into Kentucky, Indiana, and Ohio, which is stated on a previous page. The departure of the ninth army corps to reënforce Gen. Grant, delayed somewhat Gen. Burnside's preparations for an active campaign in East Tennessee. The necessity, however, of his coöperating with the movements of Gen. Rosecrans, compelled him to take the field without awaiting the return of this corps.

At this time Gen. Buckner was in command of the Confederate forces in East Tennessee, with his headquarters at Knoxville. His force numbered about twenty thousand men, who were not supplied in the best manner with ordnance. This force was sufficient to have retarded the progress of Gen. Burnside through either the Cumberland, Big Creek, or Wheeler's Gap in the mountains; but he avoided that route. Concentrating his forces at Crab Orchard, on the southerly edge of Lincoln county, Kentucky, Gen. Burnside prepared for the movement over the mountains. The infantry were mounted, the cavalry and artillery were furnished with picked horses, and the division was attended with large droves of packed mules, loaded with commissary stores, in order that its movements might not be impeded by the slow progress of wagon trains. On the afternoon of August 21st the march commenced, with Gen. S. P. Carter in the advance. After an advance of thirteen miles, a halt was made at Mt. Vernon, the capital of Rockcastle county, Ky. On the 23d the march commenced at 4 A. M., and was continued over some of the wildest and most mountainous parts of Kentucky, twenty-six miles, to London. On the next morning the army was in motion toward Williamsburg, the capital of Whitley county, Ky., twenty-nine miles distant. On the 25th there were heavy rains, and no movement was made. On the 26th the movement continued to the place where the roads from Somerset and Williamsburg meet, about four miles beyond the State line, in Scott county, Tennessee. Here the army rested during the 27th and 28th, and was joined by Maj.-Gen. Hartsuff. On the 29th the movement was continued, with the mounted brigade of Gen. Shackelford in the advance. At midnight the banks of the New river were reached, and the next day the army encamped at Montgomery, in Morgan county, Tennessee, having made, during the two days, a march of forty miles. The movement continued on the 31st, and, on the 1st of September, Gen. Burnside, with an escort, proceeded to Kingston, while the army took a shorter road to Loudon bridge, leaving Kingston to its right. At Loudon, the East Tennessee and Georgia railroad crossed the Holston river over a fine bridge more than two thousand feet in length. To save or to destroy this bridge, as the situation should demand, was undoubtedly one of the objects of the forced march. The distance from Knoxville is thirty-nine miles. The artillery came into position, on the 2d, within easy range of this bridge, just in time to see the rear of the enemy pass over and apply the torch to the structure. It was entirely consumed. By the fire of the artillery several of the enemy were killed and wounded. The march then continued to Leoni Station, twenty-two miles from Knoxville. On the next day it was resumed to Knoxville, which had been occupied on the 1st by the advance. As Gen. Burnside approached Knoxville the inhabitants turned out to welcome him. His reception is thus described by a spectator: "As we neared Knoxville, the evidences of the intense devotion to the Union dwelling in the hearts of the people became more and more apparent. Along the entire route, especially the last ten or fifteen miles, the whole population seemed gathered on the roadside to give welcome to the Yankees. On the appearance of Gen. Burnside on the outskirts of the town, the news of his arrival spread, and everybody, rich and poor, the lame and the halt, rushed out to greet him. It was no vulgar curiosity to see a man famous in the world's history—it was the greeting of an oppressed people to their deliverer. Uncovered, and at a slow pace, the general rode through the streets to his headquarters. His progress was constantly impeded by the rushing of men to his horse's side to seize him by the hand and say, 'God bless you.' On arrival at headquarters, a large crowd assembled in the yard, and were clamorous for speeches. Brig.-Gen. S. P. Carter, a native of East Tennessee, came forward, and in a few words congratulated them on their deliverance. In response to repeated calls, Gen. Burnside then appeared and said, that although his profession was arms, and not speaking, yet he would take the occasion to say that, from the moment he took command of the Department of Ohio, it had been his fervent wish to lead an army into East Tennessee, to their deliverance; and he took great pleasure in saying that he had come with means sufficient, with their assistance, to hold the country permanently and securely.

"On the conclusion of the speaking the garrison flag of the United States was flung from the portico, and the crowd rushed up and seized it in their hands, many of them pressing it to their lips. While this was passing at headquarters, the troops had been waylaid all over the city, and carried off by violence to be feasted, without money and without price, on the best which the land afforded. Not officers merely; their bounteous hospitality knew no difference in rank among their deliverers."

At Knoxville, three locomotives and a large number of cars and railroad machine shops were taken possession of. A large train was also captured twelve miles northwest on the road to Virginia. On the 4th a movement was made upon Cumberland Gap. At Tazewell a slight skirmish took place with a small force of the enemy under Col. Carter. At daylight on the morning of the 7th, the Gap was invested, and its surrender demanded by Gen. Shackelford. Gen. Frazier, commanding the enemy's force, refused, and stated that he was prepared to hold out. It appeared that the enemy had a large quantity of grain in the gap, with a mill, which they used to grind it. During the ensuing night an expedition was sent out by Gen. Shackelford, which succeeded in destroying the mill. The enemy still refused to surrender, but on the arrival of Gen. Burnside, on the 9th, terms were agreed upon, and a surrender made unconditionally. The officers, however, were allowed to retain their side arms. About forty wagons, two hundred mules, four thousand pounds of bacon, two thousand bushels of wheat, a large quantity of other stores, and ten pieces of artillery, were surrendered. The number of prisoners was about two thousand. The march of Gen. Shackelford to the Gap, a distance of fifty-two miles, was made in sixty hours.

Meantime a column of cavalry ascended the valley to Bristol, driving the enemy across the Virginia line, and destroyed the railroad bridges over the Holston and Watauga rivers, so as to prevent their return into East Tennessee. The main body of Gen. Burnside's army was now ordered by the general-in-chief to concentrate on the Tennessee river, from Loudon west, so as to connect with Gen. Rosecrans's army, which reached Chattanooga on the 9th of September.

At this time the authorities at Washington were led to believe that Gen. Lee was receiving reënforcements from Gen. Bragg. The slight resistance made by the enemy in East Tennessee, and his abandonment without defence of such an important position as Chattanooga, rendered plausible the reports of spies and deserters from Gen. Lee's army, that reënforcements were arriving there. Fearing, therefore, that Gen. Rosecrans's army might be drawn too far into the mountains of Georgia, where it could not be supplied, and might be attacked before reënforcements could reach it from Gen. Burnside, Gen. Halleck sent the following despatch to Gen. Rosecrans:

HEADQUARTERS OF THE ARMY, WASHINGTON, D. C.,
September 11th, 1863.

Maj-Gen. Rosecrans, Chattanooga:

Gen. Burnside telegraphs from Cumberland Gap that he holds all East Tennessee above Loudon, and also the gaps of the North Carolina mountains. A cavalry force is moving toward Athens to connect with you. After holding the mountain passes, on the west of Dalton, or some other point on the railroad, to prevent the return of Bragg's army, it will be decided whether your army shall move farther south into Georgia and Alabama.

It is reported here by deserters that a part of Bragg's army is reënforcing Lee. It is important that the truth of this should be ascertained as early as possible.

H. W. HALLECK, General-in-Chief.

On the same day the following despatch was sent to Gen. Burnside:

HEADQUARTERS OF THE ARMY, WASHINGTON, D. C., September 11th, 1863.

Maj.-Gen. Burnside, Cumberland Gap:

I congratulate you on your success. Hold the gap of the North Carolina mountains, the line of the Holston river, or some point, if there be one, to prevent access from Virginia, and connect with Gen. Rosecrans, at least with your cavalry. Gen. Rosecrans will occupy Dalton, or some point on the railroad, to close all access from Atlanta, and also the mountain passes in the west. This being done, it will be determined whether the movable force shall advance into Georgia and Alabama or into the valley of Virginia and North Carolina. H. W. HALLECK, General-in-Chief.

On the next day, Gen. Rosecrans replied that he was sufficiently strong for the enemy then in his front, and that there were indications that the enemy intended to turn his flanks, and cut off his communications; he therefore decided that Gen. Burnside should move down his infantry toward Chattanooga, on his left, and that Gen. Grant should cover the Tennessee river toward Whitesburg to prevent any raid on Nashville. He was of the opinion that no troops had been sent from Gen. Bragg's army; but that Gen. Bragg was receiving reënforcements from Gen. Loring in Mississippi.

On the 13th, Gen. Foster, in command at Fortress Monroe, sent a despatch to Washington, stating that trains of cars had been heard running all the time, day and night, for the previous thirty-six hours, on the Petersburg and Richmond railroad, evidently indicating a movement of troops in some direction. On the morning of the 14th, he further stated that Gen. Longstreet's corps was reported to be going south, through North Carolina.

At this time Gen. Meade had been directed to ascertain—by giving battle, if necessary—whether any of Gen. Lee's troops had left. On the 14th he reported to Gen. Halleck as follows: "My judgment, formed on a variety of meagre and conflicting testimony, is, that Gen. Lee's army has been reduced by Gen. Longstreet's corps, and perhaps by some regiments from Gens. Ewell and Hill."

Upon receiving the despatches of the 13th, Gen. Halleck sent the following telegrams to Gens. Burnside, Rosecrans, Hurlbut, Grant, and Sherman:

HEADQUARTERS OF THE ARMY, WASHINGTON, D. C., September 13th, 1863.

Maj.-Gen. Burnside, Knoxville:

It is important that all the available forces of your command be pushed forward into East Tennessee. All your scattered forces should be concentrated there. So long as we hold Tennessee, Kentucky is perfectly safe. Move down your infantry as rapidly as possible toward Chattanooga, to connect with Rosecrans. Bragg may merely hold the passes of the mountains to cover Atlanta, and move his main army through Northern Alabama, to reach the Tennessee river and turn Rosecrans's right, and cut off his supplies. In this case he will turn Chattanooga over to you, and move to intercept Bragg.

H. W. HALLECK, General-in-Chief.

HEADQUARTERS OF THE ARMY, WASHINGTON, D. C., September 13th, 1863.

Maj.-Gen. Rosecrans, Chattanooga:

There is no intention of sending Gen. Burnside into North Carolina. He is ordered to move down and connect with you. Should the enemy attempt to turn your right flank through Alabama, Chattanooga should be turned over to Burnside, and your army, or such part of it as may not be required there, should move to prevent Bragg from reëntering Middle Tennessee. Hurlbut will aid you all he can, but most of Grant's available force is west of the Mississippi.

H. W. HALLECK, General-in-Chief.

HEADQUARTERS OF THE ARMY, WASHINGTON, D. C., September 13th, 1863.

Maj.-Gen. Hurlbut, Memphis:

I think, from all accounts, that Steele is sufficiently strong. All your available force should be sent to Corinth and Tuscumbia, to operate against Bragg. Should he attempt to turn Rosecrans's right and recross the river into Tennessee, send to Gen. Sherman, at Vicksburg, for reënforcements for this purpose. Gen. Grant, it is understood, is sick in New Orleans.

H. W. HALLECK, General-in-Chief.

HEADQUARTERS OF THE ARMY, WASHINGTON, D. C., September 13th, 1863.

Maj.-Gen. Grant or Maj.-Gen. Sherman, Vicksburg:

It is quite possible that Bragg and Johnston will move through Northern Alabama to the Tennessee river, to turn Gen. Rosecrans's right and cut off his communications. All of Gen. Grant's available forces should be sent to Memphis, thence to Corinth and Tuscumbia, to coöperate with Rosecrans, should the rebels attempt that movement.

H. W. HALLECK, General-in-Chief.

On the 14th, the following telegrams were sent to Gens. Foster, Burnside, and Hurlbut:

HEADQUARTERS OF THE ARMY, WASHINGTON, D. C., September 14th, 1863.

Maj.-Gen. Foster, Fortress Monroe:

Information received here indicates that part of Lee's forces have gone to Petersburg. There are various suppositions for this. Some think it is intended to put down Union feeling in North Carolina, others to make an attempt to capture Norfolk; others again to threaten Norfolk, so as to compel us to land reënforcements there from the Army of the Potomac, and then to move rapidly against Meade. Such was the plan last spring, when Longstreet invested Suffolk. It will be well to strengthen Norfolk as much as possible, and to closely watch the enemy's movements. I think he will soon strike a blow somewhere.

H. W. HALLECK, General-in-Chief.

HEADQUARTERS OF THE ARMY, WASHINGTON, D. C., September 14th, 1863.

Maj.-Gen. Hurlbut, Memphis:

There are good reasons why troops should be sent to assist Gen. Rosecrans's right with all possible despatch. Communicate with Sherman to assist you, and hurry forward reënforcements as previously directed.

H. W. HALLECK, General-in-Chief.

HEADQUARTERS OF THE ARMY, WASHINGTON, D. C., September 14th, 1863.

Maj.-Gen. Burnside, Knoxville:

There are several reasons why you should reënforce Rosecrans with all possible despatch. It is believed that the enemy will concentrate to give him battle. You must be there to help him.

H. W. HALLECK, General-in-Chief.

At the same time, Gen. Schofield, in command of the Department of Missouri, and Gen. Pope, in command of the Northwest Department, were ordered to send forward to the Tennessee line every available man in their departments; and the commanding officers in Indiana, Ohio, and Kentucky, were ordered to make every possible exertion to secure Gen. Rosecrans's line of communications. Gen. Meade was also urged to attack Gen. Lee's army while in its present reduced condition, or, at least, to prevent him from sending off any more detachments. More troops were not sent into East Tennessee or Georgia, on account of the impossibility of supplying them in a country which the enemy had nearly exhausted. Gen. Burnside's army was on short rations, and that of the Cumberland inadequately supplied.

On the 14th of September, the army of Gen. Rosecrans was occupying the passes of Lookout mountain, with the enemy concentrating his forces near Lafayette, to dispute his further advance. The threatened movements of Gen. Bragg to the right and left proved to be merely cavalry raids to cut Gen. Rosecrans's lines of supplies, and threaten his communication with Gen. Burnside. His main army was only awaiting the arrival of Gen. Longstreet's corps to give battle in the mountains of Georgia. It had already been reënforced by troops from Gen. Johnston in Mississippi, and by the prisoners captured at Vicksburg and Port Hudson, and released on parole, who had been declared by the Confederate authorities to be exchanged.

The line of Gen. Rosecrans's army extended at this time from Gordon's Mills to Alpines, a distance of some forty miles. By the 17th, they were brought within supporting distance, and on the morning of the 18th a concentration was begun toward Crawfish Springs.

The advance of Gen. Rosecrans's army can be traced in a few words. The Tennessee river, west of Chattanooga, in its general direction runs southwest. Skirting it is the Racoon range of mountains. Sand mountain, where the army passed over, is a part of this range. After marching over a plateau of twelve or fifteen miles in width, Sand mountain is descended, and the Lookout valley is gained. This valley is about two miles wide, and runs southwest. It is bounded on the east by the Lookout mountains, running parallel with the Racoon range. The right wing, under Gen. McCook, and the centre, under Gen. Thomas, had been in this valley two or three days when Chattanooga was evacuated. Early on Wednesday, the 9th, both corps were in motion to pass the Lookout range. They had only two passes by which to cross—one eight miles south of Trenton, and the other at Valley Head, more than twenty miles south of Trenton. At Valley Head the rugged mountain melts away into a wild scattering of hills, near which the road is abruptly turned through winding valleys, with a steep and stubborn spur before the summit is gained. After reaching the summit, a plateau gently rolling, about twelve miles in width, is found. There are groves and fields, and smooth-flowing streams, where the imagination pictured crags and cascades. At Valley Head, Gen. McCook's corps passed over Lookout mountain, and reached Alpines, in the valley, called Broomtown valley, on the 10th. Gen. Thomas took the middle gap, and passed through without opposition. At the same time Gen. Crittenden moved south of Chattanooga toward Gordon's Mills, a distance of twelve miles. Bounding Broomtown valley, on the east, is another parallel ridge, known as Taylor's ridge. It is not a formidable barrier, and is crossed by a number of good roads toward Lafayette, where Gen. Bragg was. The first opposition to the present advance of the army took place at Alpines, on Wednesday, the 9th, when a cavalry division had a brisk fight with the enemy, which continued two hours, with the loss of four killed and twelve wounded. The enemy retired, leaving a few dead. When Gen. Thomas passed through the central gap, he found himself in McLemore's Cove or valley, a strip of country enclosed between Lookout mountain and Pigeon mountain, a spur of Lookout, striking northeast from it, and gradually melting away as it approaches the Chickamauga river. To reach the same valley in which Gen. McCook's corps was, Gen. Thomas was compelled to pass through one of the gaps of Pigeon mountain. He therefore, on the 12th, ordered Gen. Negley to feel his way through the central pass. In obeying the order he was suddenly attacked by the divisions of Gens. Witters and Stuart, of Gen. Bragg's army, upon his front and flanks, with such energy as compelled his hasty retreat, with a loss of some forty killed and wounded. The advance of Gen. Rosecrans's army thus far in pursuit of the enemy, had been made under the impression that, as Chattanooga had fallen without resistance, Gen. Bragg was weak, and the Confederate Government unable to reënforce him; there would, therefore, be no fight north of the Coosa river. This sudden show of strength against Gen. Negley, therefore, created alarm. The question now was, whether this demonstration of the enemy indicated a purpose of giving battle, or whether it was a movement to secure a safe retreat. Gen. Rosecrans decided it to be the former. The next day, Gen. McCook was moving back over the Lookout mountain, with orders to close on the centre, and Gen. Crittenden, at Gordon's Mills, put in a good defensive position.

Lafayette, the capital of Walker county, thirty-two miles from Chattanooga, and eighteen from Dalton, was supposed to be the place where the enemy were concentrating. In their front was the Pigeon mountain. This range was the highest at the southern extremity, where it is separated from the Lookout mountain by Doherty Gap, a long and heavy pass. Two miles north is a less elevated gap, called Rape; seven miles farther north is Blue Bird, a rugged pass; three miles farther is Dug Gap, affording a good passage for an army. This was easily defended, and held by Gen. Bragg. Two and a half miles farther is Catlet's, through which runs a mountain stream and a good road; this was also held by Gen. Bragg. Two miles farther is Worthing, a rough road over the mountain, and impassable for artillery. Wicker is a good wagon road, where the mountain has diminished to a hill; a mile and a half beyond, an undulating country commences. The country lying between Pigeon and Lookout mountains is called McLemore's Cove, as above stated, about twenty miles long and eight broad. West of Pigeon mountain is Chickamauga valley, which separates it from Missionary ridge, a mere range of hills, and west of which is another valley separating the latter from Lookout mountain. This last range runs up within two miles of Chattanooga, and terminates abruptly at the Tennessee river, with a bluff two thousand feet high.

At the time of the repulse of Gen. Negley was the most favorable moment for Gen. Bragg to attack Gen. Rosecrans. The corps of Gen. McCook was separated from Gen. Thomas by a march of nearly three days. Gen. Crittenden could not reënforce Gen. Thomas without exposing Chattanooga, and Gen. Thomas could not move to Gen. Crittenden's position without exposing Gen. McCook. Slow as Gen. Bragg was in collecting his forces and advancing, the great battle which followed was begun before Gen. Rosecrans had recovered from the results of the position of his forces. Gen. McCook joined Gen. Thomas on the 17th, with his weary troops, and as heavy clouds of dust were discovered on Pigeon mountain by the signal officers, his corps and the right of the centre were formed into line of battle, which was maintained all the afternoon in McLemore's Cove. As the morning of the 18th broke, gray and chilly, the troops were ordered on the march. Gen. Thomas's corps pressed on toward Gordon's Mills, and Gen. McCook's moved up directly in his rear. At Gordon's Mills, Gen. Ward was stationed with two brigades. During the forenoon of this day, Gen. Granger, situated on the left of Gen. Ward, made a reconnoissance across the Chickamauga at Reid's bridge, with two brigades, and ascertained beyond a doubt that Gen. Longstreet's corps had joined Gen. Bragg. Cols. Minty and Wilder were sent with their commands, the former to watch Ringgold road crossing, and the latter to resist any advance from Napier Gap. Early in the afternoon the enemy made an attack from the two roads. Heavy cannonading ensued, but Cols. Minty and Wilder held their ground gallantly until a body of the enemy's infantry, having crossed at one of the several fords in the river, was fast gaining their rear, when they were compelled to retire. This proved to be the extreme left of the enemy.

Toward evening, Gen. McCook's corps pitched their tents at Lee's Mills, in McLemore's Cove; but hardly was this done before an order from Gen. Rosecrans directed them to move northward to Pond Spring, seventeen miles south of Chattanooga. Wearied as were the men, they marched silently and without straggling. All night there was a constant rumbling of wagons, and a ceaseless tread of troops. Gen. Crittenden being ahead of Gen. Thomas, had thrown Gen. Van Cleve's division on the left of Gen. Wood at Gordon's Mills, and Gen. Palmer's on his right, Gen. Thomas pushed still farther to the left. Gen. Johnson's two brigades were given to Gen. Thomas, and posted on Gen. Van Cleve's left, while Gen. Negley, who was already in position at Owen's Gap, a short distance south of Crawfish Spring, thirteen miles from Chattanooga, was ordered to remain there, and temporarily attached to Gen. McCook's corps.

The operations of the Confederate army up to this time had been as follows: In consequence of the flank movement of Gen. Rosecrans on the right of Gen. Bragg, in the month of June, the latter retreated from Shelbyville and Tullahoma toward Chattanooga, which was occupied in the first week of July. The brigade of Gen. Anderson, of Gen. Polk's corps, was ordered to Bridgeport for purposes of observation. The remainder of the corps of Gen. Polk was retained in and around Chattanooga; and Gen. Hardee's corps was distributed along the line of the railroad to Knoxville, with Tyner's Station, nine miles from Chattanooga, as the centre. The headquarters of Gen. Bragg were at Chattanooga. On the 21st of August the corps of Gen. Crittenden succeeded in reaching the town with artillery, from the heights overlooking the Tennessee river and the town. This bombardment was regarded by the enemy as announcing that Gen. Rosecrans's plans were completed and about to be executed. The effect was to cause the removal of Gen. Bragg's headquarters beyond the range of fire, and the removal of stores to points of convenience on the railroad in the rear, and the withdrawal of Gen. Anderson from Bridgeport. In consequence of the advance of Gen. Burnside into East Tennessee, the Confederate Gen. Buckner was now ordered to evacuate Knoxville and occupy Loudon; and in consequence of a demonstration reported to have been made by Gen. Rosecrans at Blythe's Ferry, on the Tennessee river, opposite the mouth of the Hiawassee, he was further ordered to fall back from Loudon to Charleston, and, soon after, to the vicinity of Chattanooga. On the 1st of September, Gen. Bragg was informed of the crossing of Gen. Rosecrans at Caperton's Ferry for three days, and that he was moving across Sand mountain, in the direction of Wills's valley and Trenton. This report was regarded by him as incredible, but soon after confirmed by the occupation of Trenton by Federal cavalry and by its advance up the Wills's valley railroad in the direction of Chattanooga as far as Wauhatchee, within seven miles, as a covering force to the advance of the infantry column at Trenton.

The following topographical view will assist in the comprehension of the subsequent movements: Chattanooga is situated on the Tennessee river, at the mouth of the Chattanooga valley—a valley following the course of the Chattanooga creek, and formed by Lookout mountain and Missionary ridge. East of Missionary ridge, and running parallel with it, is another valley—Chickamauga valley—following the course of Chickamauga creek, which, like the Chattanooga creek, discharges its waters into the Tennessee river—the first above, and the last below the town of Chattanooga, and has with it a common source in McLemore's Cove, the common head of both valleys, and formed by Lookout mountain on the west and Pigeon mountain to the east. Wills's valley is a narrow valley, lying to the west of Chattanooga, formed by Lookout mountain and Sand mountain, and traversed by a railroad, which takes its name from the valley, and which, branching from the Nashville and Chattanooga railroad, where the latter crosses the valley, has its present terminus at Trenton, and future at Tuscaloosa, Alabama. The distance of Bridgeport from Chattanooga is twenty-eight miles, of Caperton's Ferry about forty, and of Trenton something over twenty. Ringgold is eighteen miles from Chattanooga, on the Georgia State road, and Dalton some forty, at the point where the Georgia State road connects with the East Tennessee railroad. Rome is sixty-five miles southwest of Chattanooga, on the Coosa river, at the point of confluence of the Etowah and Oostenaula. The wagon road from Chattanooga to Rome, known as the Lafayette road, crosses Missionary ridge into Chickamauga valley at Rossville, and, proceeding in a southwesterly direction, crosses Chickamauga creek, eleven miles from Chattanooga, at Lee's and Gordon's Mills, and, passing to the east of Pigeon mountain, goes through Lafayette, distant some twenty-two miles from Chattanooga, and Summerville, within twenty-five miles of Rome. From Caperton's Ferry there is a road leading over Sand mountain into Wills's valley at Trenton, and from Trenton to Lafayette and Dalton, over Lookout mountain, through Cooper's and Stevens's Gap into McLemore's Cove, and over Pigeon mountain by Plug Gap. The road from Trenton, following Wills's valley, exposed, by easy communications, Rome, and, through it, Western Georgia and Eastern Alabama, with easy access to the important central positions, Atlanta and Selma.

Gen. Bragg, believing that a flanking movement was the object of Gen. Rosecrans by his advance on the left, ordered Lieut.-Gen. Hill, on Monday, September 7th, to move with his corps toward Lafayette, Gen. Polk to Lee's and Gordon's Mills, and Maj.-Gen. Buckner, with the Army of East Tennessee, and Maj.-Gen. Walker, with his division from the Army of Mississippi, to concentrate at Lafayette, and Brig.-Gen. Pegram to cover the railroad with his cavalry. These dispositions having been made of the Confederate forces, Maj.-Gen. Crittenden, commanding the left wing of the Federal army, which had not moved with the right and centre, but had been left in the Sequatchie valley, crossed the Tennessee river at the mouth of Battle creek, and moved upon Chattanooga. Maj.-Gen. McCook, commanding the right wing, was thrown forward to threaten Rome, and the corps of Maj.-Gen. Thomas was put in motion over Lookout mountain, in the direction of Lafayette.

A charge of incapacity was subsequently made against Gen. Bragg, because he did not at this time fall upon Gen. Thomas with such a force as would have crushed him; then turned down Chattanooga valley, throwing himself between the town and Gen. Crittenden, and crushed him; then passed back between Lookout mountain and the Tennessee river into Wills's valley, and cut off Gen. McCook's retreat to Bridgeport; thence moved along the Cumberland into the rear of Gen. Burnside, and defeated him. But Gen. Bragg now threw a force forward into McLemore's Cove, which resisted the advance of Gen. Thomas, as above stated. It was on such a limited scale as only to check this advance, and was thence withdrawn to Lafayette. Within thirty-six hours after this force retired, Gen. Rosecrans had recalled Gen. McCook, and concentrated him with Gen. Thomas in McLemore's Cove. Meantime, Gen. Crittenden, after occupying Chattanooga, did not stop to fortify it, but moved on toward Ringgold to cut off Gen. Buckner, who was understood to be moving to the support of Gen. Bragg. On reaching the point on the Georgia railroad at which Gen. Buckner crossed, and discovering that he was too late, he turned toward Lafayette to follow him. Moving up the Chickamauga, on the east side, he was confronted by a force of Confederate cavalry under Gens. Pegram and Armstrong, which retired before him until supported by a large body of infantry, when Gen. Crittenden, declining a battle, fell back on the Chickamauga, and crossed at Gordon's Mills. This brought the whole of Gen. Rosecrans's force on the west side of the Chickamauga within easy supporting distance.

Gen. Bragg now moved his army by divisions, and crossed the Chickamauga at several fords and bridges north of Gordon's Mills, up to which he ordered the Virginia troops, which had crossed many miles below, and near to which he attempted to concentrate. At this time the right of Gen. Rosecrans really rested on Gordon's Mills. Gen. Thomas had moved on until his left division, under Gen. Brannan, covered the Rossville road. Gen. Baird was on Gen. Brannan's right, then followed successively Gens. Johnson's, Reynolds's, Palmer's, and Van Cleve's divisions. Gen. Wood covered Gordon's Mills ford. Gen. Negley, four miles farther south, held Owen's Gap. Gens. Davis and Sheridan were on the march south of Gen. Negley. Gen. Wilder, with four regiments and a light battery, was posted at the right, near Gordon's Mills. Gen. Gordon Granger's forces were held in reserve some distance back on the Rossville road. Such was the position on Saturday, the 19th. The battle which now ensued opened about ten o'clock. The first attack of the enemy was upon the left wing of Gen. Rosecrans, which the enemy endeavored to turn, so as to occupy the road to Chattanooga. But all their efforts for this object failed. The centre was next assailed and temporarily driven back, but, being promptly reenforced, maintained its ground. As night approached, the battle ceased and the combatants rested on their arms. Gen. Bragg now issued an order dividing the forces of his army into two corps or wings. The right was placed under the command of Lieut.-Gen. Polk, and the left under Lieut.-Gen. Longstreet. The former was composed of Lieut.-Gen. Hill's corps of two divisions, under Maj.-Gen. Cleburn and Maj.-Gen. Breckinridge; with the division of Maj.-Gen. Cheatham, of Lieut.-Gen. Polk's corps, and the division of Maj.-Gen. W. H. T. Walker. The left was composed of the divisions of Maj.-Gen. Stewart, and Brig.-Gens. Preston Johnston, of Maj.-Gen. Buckner's corps; with Maj.-Gen. Hindman's, of Lieut.-Gen. Polk's corps, and Gens. Benning's and Lane's and Robertson's brigades of Maj.-Gen. Hood's division, and Gens. Kershaw's and Humphrey's, of Maj.-Gen. McLaws's division. The front line of the right wing consisted of three divisions, Breckinridge's, Cleburn's, and Cheatham's, which were posted from right to left in the order named. Maj.-Gen. Walker was in reserve. The line of the left wing was composed of Stewart's, Hood's, Hindman's, and Preston's divisions, from right to left, in the order named.

Toward morning of the next day the army of Gen. Rosecrans changed its position slightly to the rear, and contracted the extended lines of the previous day. Trains were moving northward on all the roads in the rear of Chattanooga, and the wounded were taken from the hospitals, which had become exposed by the concentration of the forces to the left. Gen. Thomas still held the left, with the divisions of Gens. Palmer and Johnson attached to his corps and thrown in the centre. Gen. Brannan was retired slightly, with his regiments arrayed in echelon. Gen. Van Cleve was held in reserve on the west side of the first road in the rear of the line. Gens. Wood, Davis, and Sheridan followed next, the latter being on the extreme left. Gen. Lytle occupied an isolated position at Gordon's Mills.

Orders were given by Gen. Bragg to Lieut.-Gen. Polk to commence the attack at daylight on the next morning. These orders were immediately issued by him; but prior to giving the order to move forward to the attack in the morning, Gen. Polk discovered that, owing to a want of precaution, a portion of the left wing, amounting to a whole division, had been formed in front of his line, and that if the order to make the attack at daylight was obeyed, this division must inevitably be slaughtered. The battle was finally opened about half past nine A. M., by a forward movement of Gen. Breckinridge, accompanied by Gen. Cleburn, against the left and centre of Gen. Rosecrans. Division after division was pushed forward to assist the attacking masses of the enemy, but without success. The ground was held by Gen. Thomas for more than two hours. Meantime, as Gen. Reynolds was sorely pressed, Gen. Wood was ordered, as he supposed, to march instantly by the left flank, pass Gen. Brannan, and go to the relief of Gen. Reynolds, and that Gens. Davis and Sheridan were to shift over to the left, and close up the line. Gen. Rosecrans reports that the order was to close up on Gen. Reynolds. Gen. Wood says that Gen. Brannan was in line between his and Gen. Reynolds's division.

A gap was thus formed in the line of battle, of which the enemy took advantage, and, striking Gen. Davis in his flank and rear, threw his whole division into confusion. Passing through this break in Gen. Rosecrans's line, the enemy cut off his right and centre, and attacked Gen. Sheridan's division, which was advancing to the support of the left. After a brave but fruitless effort against this torrent of the enemy, he was compelled to give way, but afterward rallied a considerable portion of his force, and by a circuitous route joined Gen. Thomas, who had now to breast the tide of battle against the whole army of the enemy. The right and part of the centre had been completely broken, and fled in confusion from the field, carrying with them to Chattanooga their commanders, Gens. McCook and Crittenden, and also Gen. Rosecrans, who was on that part of the line. Gen. Garfield, his chief of staff, however, made his way to the left and joined Gen. Thomas, who still retained his position. His ranks had now assumed a crescent form, with his flanks supported by the lower spurs of the mountain, and here, "like a lion at bay, he repulsed the terrible assaults of the enemy."

About half past three P. M., the enemy discovered a gap in the hills, in the rear of the right flank of Gen. Thomas, and Gen. Longstreet commenced pressing his columns through the passage. At this time, Maj.-Gen. Granger, who had been posted with his reserves to cover the left and rear, arrived on the field. He instantly attacked the forces of Gen. Longstreet, with Gen. Steadman's brigade of cavalry. The conflict at this point is thus described by Gen. Halleck: "In the words of Gen. Rosecrans's report, 'swift was the charge, and terrible the conflict; but the enemy was broken.' A thousand of our brave men killed and wounded paid for its possession; but we held the gap. Two divisions of Longstreet's corps confronted the position. Determined to take it, they suc-

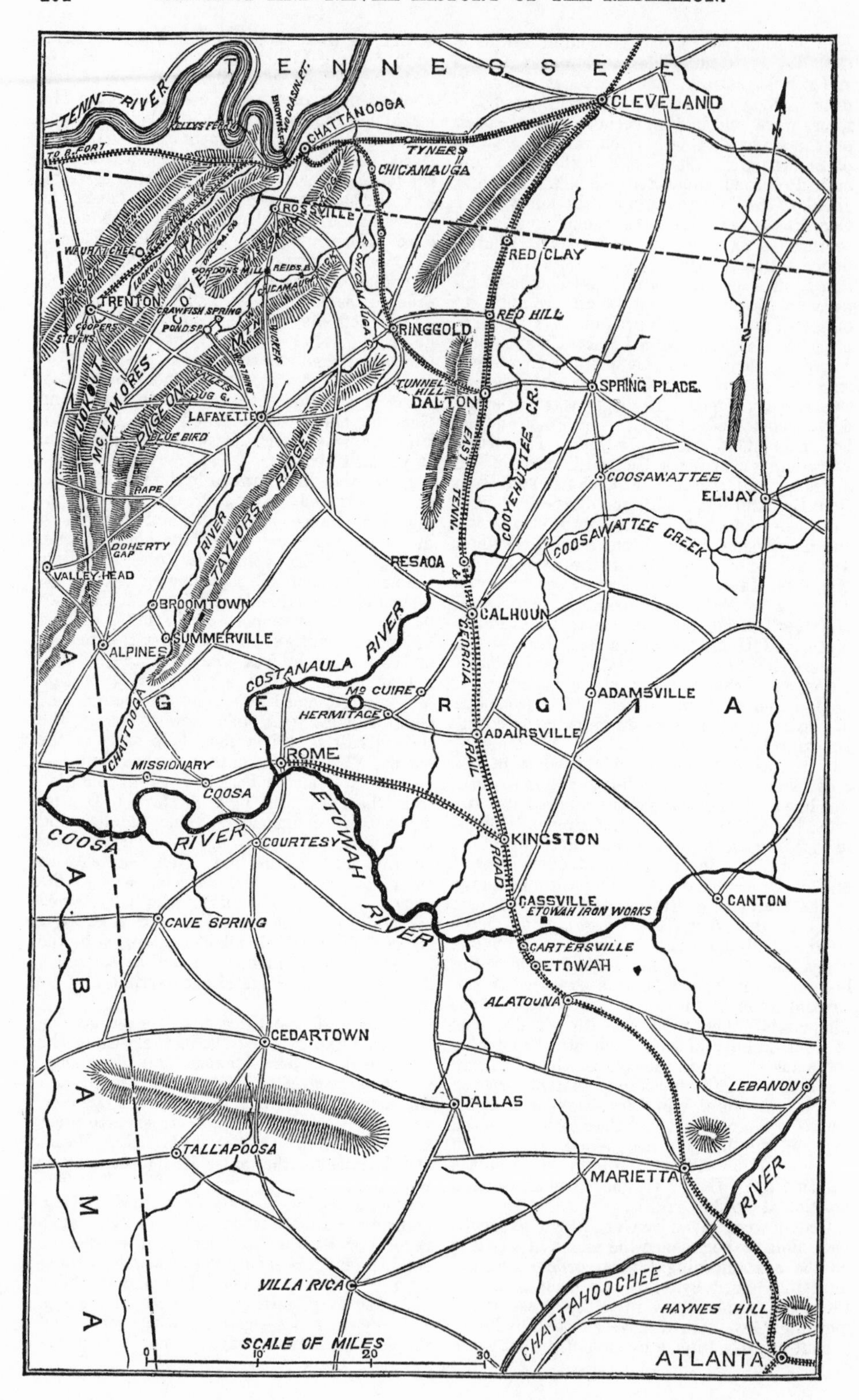
TENNESSEE
TENN RIVER
CHATTANOOGA
CLEVELAND
TYNERS
CHICAMAUGA
ROSSVILLE
RED CLAY
TRENTON
CRAWFISH SPRING
RED HILL
RINGGOLD
TUNNEL HILL
DALTON
SPRING PLACE
LAFAYETTE
BLUE BIRD
PIGEON
COVE
McLEMORES
LOOKOUT
TAYLORS RIDGE
COOSAWATTEE
ELIJAY
COOSAWATTEE CREEK
COOYEHUTTEE CR.
EAST TENN. & GEORGIA RAIL ROAD
RESACA
DOHERTY GAP
VALLEY HEAD
BROOMTOWN
CALHOUN
SUMMERVILLE
ALPINES
COSTANAULA RIVER
Mc CUIRE
HERMITAGE
ADAMSVILLE
G E O R G I A
ADAIRSVILLE
ROME
MISSIONARY
COOSA
CHATTOOGA
COOSA RIVER
ETOWAH RIVER
COURTESY
KINGSTON
CASSVILLE
ETOWAH IRON WORKS
CANTON
CAVE SPRING
CARTERSVILLE
ETOWAH
ALATOUNA
ALABAMA
CEDARTOWN
LEBANON
DALLAS
TALLAPOOSA
MARIETTA
CHATTAHOOCHEE RIVER
VILLA RICA
HAYNES HILL
SCALE OF MILES
0 10 20 30
ATLANTA

cessively came to the assault. A battery of six guns placed in the gorge poured death and slaughter into them. They charged within a few yards of the pieces, but our grape and canister, and the leaden hail of musketry, delivered in sparing but terrible volleys, from cartridges taken in many instances from the boxes of their fallen companions, was too much even for Longstreet's men. About sunset they made their last charge, when our men, being out of ammunition, moved on them with the bayonet, and they gave way, to return no more. In the mean time the enemy made repeated attempts to carry Gen. Thomas's position on the left and front, but were as often thrown back with great loss. At nightfall the enemy fell back beyond the range of our artillery, leaving Gen. Thomas victorious on his hard-fought field."

During the night Gen. Thomas fell back to Rossville, leaving the dead and most of the wounded in the hands of the enemy. Gen. Sheridan, who had been cut off by the advance of the enemy, as he was upon the extreme right, gathered his brigades and struck across Missionary Ridge directly to the west. The enemy were in possession of the country north of him. As he reached the top of the ridge, he caused the "assembly" to be blown, and picked up all the stragglers from the other divisions that he could find. He had lost three pieces of artillery, but in his progress met a whole battery which had been abandoned, and took it in charge. Passing the enemy's flank, and regaining the road on the ridge, he turned east through Rossville, and, without halting, reënforced Gen. Thomas at midnight. The position near Rossville was held during Monday without serious molestation, and in the night the force was withdrawn to Chattanooga.

The loss of Gen. Rosecrans in these battles was 1,644 killed, 9,262 wounded, and 4,945 missing, which, with a cavalry loss of 1,000, makes 16,851. In material, his loss was 36 guns, 20 caissons, 8,450 small arms, and 5,834 infantry accoutrements. He captured 2,003 prisoners. The loss of the enemy in killed, wounded, and missing, was reported at 18,000.

After Gen. Rosecrans's retreat to Chattanooga, he withdrew his forces from the passes of Lookout Mountain, which covered his line of supplies from Bridgeport. These were immediately occupied by the enemy, who also sent a cavalry force across the Tennessee above Chattanooga, which destroyed a large wagon train in the Sequatchie valley, captured McMinnsville and other points on the railroad, and thus almost completely cut off the supplies of Gen. Rosecrans's army. The line of the railroad at this time was well defended. The enemy's cavalry were attacked by Col. McCook, at Anderson's cross roads, on the 2d of October, by Gen. Mitchell, at Shelbyville, on the 6th, and by Gen. Crook, at Farmington, on the 8th.

On October 2d, Gen. Rosecrans issued an order, of which the following is an extract:

Army of the Cumberland: You have made a grand and successful campaign; you have driven the rebels from Middle Tennessee. You crossed a great mountain range, placed yourselves on the banks of a broad river, crossed it in the face of a powerful, opposing army, and crossed two other great mountain ranges at the only practicable passes, some forty miles between extremes. You concentrated in the face of superior numbers; fought the combined armies of Bragg, which you drove from Shelbyville to Tullahoma, of Johnston's army from Mississippi, and the tried veterans of Longstreet's corps, and for two days held them at bay, giving them blow for blow, with heavy interest. When the day closed you held the field, from which you withdrew, in the face of overpowering numbers, to occupy the point for which you set out—Chattanooga.

You have accomplished the great work of the campaign; you hold the key of East Tennessee, of Northern Georgia, and of the enemy's mines of coal and nitre. Let these achievements console you for the regret you experience that arrivals of fresh hostile troops forbade your remaining on the field to renew the battle, for the right of burying your gallant dead, and caring for your brave companions who lay wounded on the field.

When it was known at Washington that Gen. Longstreet's corps had probably gone to the aid of Gen. Bragg, the authorities ordered to Tennessee the forces of Gen. Grant at Vicksburg, and also appointed him to the command of the forces in the field in Tennessee. Before information was received in reply from Gen. Grant, who was at New Orleans, Gen. Hooker was, on the 23d of September, sent to Tennessee, in command of the Eleventh and Twelfth corps of the Army of the Potomac, which were detached for that object. They were assigned to protect General Rosecrans's line of communication from Bridgeport to Nashville.

CHAPTER XXXVI.

General Grant ordered to the command at Chattanooga—Defeats Gen. Bragg—Movements of Gen. Burnside in East Tennessee—Position of the Armies in Virginia—Advance of Gen. Meade to Mine Run—Gen. Gilmore's Operations before Charleston—Captures Morris Island—Opens fire on Fort Sumter and Charleston—Movements of Gen. Banks in Texas—Operations in Missouri and Arkansas—Operations against the Indians in Minnesota—Desolations by the Armies.

On the 18th of October, Gen. Grant having arrived at Louisville, Ky., assumed command of the consolidated Departments of Tennessee, Cumberland, and Ohio, by order of the President. The Department of Ohio had comprised the States of Ohio, Michigan, Indiana, Illinois, Western Virginia, and Kentucky, east of the Tennessee River, including Cumberland Gap, with the headquarters at Cincinnati, Ohio. That of the Cumberland had comprised the portion of the State of Tennessee east of the Tennessee River, and such parts of Northern Alabama and Georgia as may be taken possession of by the United States troops, with headquarters in the field. That of Tennessee had comprised Cairo, Illinois; Forts Henry and Donelson, Tennessee; Northern Mississippi, and the portions of Kentucky and Tennessee west of the Tennessee River, with headquarters in the field.

Major-Gen. G. H. Thomas was placed in the immediate command of the Department of the Cumberland, and Maj.-Gen. W. T. Sherman in that of the Department of Tennessee. Gen. Rosecrans was relieved. Gens. McCook and Crittenden were ordered to Cincinnati, and their corps consolidated into one.

At this time the army was at Chattanooga, which is situated in a bend of the Tennessee River. The flanks rested on its banks—the right at Chattanooga Creek, near the base of Lookout Mountain, and the left at Citico Creek. The picket lines followed these two creeks for a distance, and then passed across the low grounds between, which lie also between the foot of Missionary Ridge and the high grounds about the town upon which the defensive works were constructed. These works were connected by a strong line of rifle-pits. Behind this line and around the town the greater portion of the army was bivouacked, for very little camp equipage was to be had. This was the only point held by a Federal force south of the river, while the north side was occupied entire with troops stationed to guard the points above. The base of the army at Chattanooga was at Stevenson and Bridgeport, and was supplied from depots at Louisville and Nashville, by a single track of railroad. The south side of the river from Lookout Mountain to Bridgeport was in possession of the enemy, and the river road on the north side was rendered impassable by their sharpshooters stationed on the opposite bank. It was thus necessary to bring all supplies to the army over a distance of fifty or sixty miles, taking the road from Bridgeport up the Sequatchie valley, over the mountains into the Anderson road, thence to Chattanooga. The Tennessee was crossed by pontoon bridges, constructed from such materials as the forest and the town could afford. The storms rendered the roads nearly impassable, and the army was in danger of starvation.

Gen. Hooker had arrived at Bridgeport with the Eleventh and a portion of the Twelfth corps, and Gen. Sherman was on the route from Memphis. The first movement was to open the river, and secure a shorter land communication with the base. For this purpose the boats for a new pontoon bridge were filled with armed men at Chattanooga, and floated down in the night past Lookout Point, to a place known as Brown's Ferry, where they landed on the south side of the river, and took possession of two hills, after only a slight skirmish with the picket at the point of landing, and a feeble resistance from a brigade of infantry and regiment of cavalry stationed in the valley beyond the hills. The boats then crossed the river, and brought over more troops to hold possession, by whom a bridge was immediately constructed, about nine hundred feet in length, in five hours. The distance between this bridge and the one at Chattanooga was one and a half mile by land, and about eight miles by water. On the next day Gen. Hooker crossed the river at Bridgeport, and moved up, uniting with the force at Brown's Ferry. This opened the river, the road to Kelly's Ferry, and the direct road to Bridgeport, as well as the river road on the north side around the bend. This successful movement is thus explained by a spectator in the camp of the enemy:

The enemy were several miles distant, and the smoke of their bivouac fires resting above the tree tops indicated a halt. Subsequently the column resumed its motion, and during the afternoon the long, dark, thread-like line of troops became visible, slowly wending their way in the direction of Chattanooga. On Lookout Peak, gazing down upon the singular spectacle—a *coup d'œil* which embraced in curious contrast the beauties of nature and the achievements of art, the blessings of peace and the horrors of war—were Gens. Bragg, Longstreet, and others, to whom this bold venture of the enemy opened at once new vistas of thought and action. Infantry, artillery, and cavalry, all glided silently by, like a procession of *fantocini* in a panorama, until, among all the "sundown's sumptuous pictures" which glowed around us, there was not one like that of the great, fresh, bustling camp, suddenly grown into view, with its thousand twinkling lights, its groups of men and animals, and its lines of white-topped wagons, now strung like a necklace of pearls around the bosom of the hills. The Federals had succeeded in effecting a junction with the army of Chattanooga.

The question which naturally arises is, why did not Gen. Bragg throw his army in front of the advancing columns and check the movement? The answer is in the shape of one of those stolid facts which even strategy cannot always stir. On Monday night Gen. Thomas—or perhaps Grant, for he is now in Chattanooga—crossed a force of six thousand men, first over the Tennessee at the edge of the town, then over the neck of land known as the Moccasin, and finally over the river again at Brown's Ferry, in rear of Chattanooga, where, after a brief skirmish with one of our regiments, they took possession of the hills and commenced the work of fortification. Simultaneously with this movement, a column at Bridgeport, consisting of the Eleventh corps, Gen. Howard, and Twelfth corps, Gen. Slocum, the whole under command of Gen. Joe Hooker, started up the valley.

Under these circumstances, an interposition of our forces across the valley would in the first place have required the transfer of a considerable portion of our army from the east to the west side of Lookout Mountain, thereby weakening our line in front of Chattanooga, while the enemy reserved his strength; secondly, it would have necessitated a fight on both our front and rear, with the flanks of the Federals protected by the mountains; and finally, had we been successful, a victory would only have demoralized two corps of the Yankee army, without at all influencing the direct issue involved in the present investment of Chattanooga.

Gen. Longstreet, however, who from the peak had

carefully watched the march of the eleventh corps, determined to make an attack for another purpose—namely, to capture, if possible, a large park of wagons and its escort, numbering, as was supposed, from fifteen hundred to two thousand men, who still remained in the rear.

The attack thus proposed was made during the night, and the result was that, at five o'clock the next morning, the enemy had abandoned the entire country west of Lookout creek. These operations saved the army from starvation, for the situation of affairs was such that Chattanooga must be held at all hazards.

A steamboat had been built and another had been captured. The latter was now loaded with two hundred thousand rations. It ran the blockade of Lookout mountain, and arrived safely at Brown's Ferry. The point of Lookout mountain between Chattanooga and Lookout creek was still held by pickets and an infantry force of the enemy, while their batteries on the top commanded some distance each way. The steamboat passed to the pontoon bridge ground until the battle of Missionary ridge, thus covering the line of communication, and then in connection with the other boat ran regularly to Kelly's Ferry from Bridgeport, reducing the wagon transportation to ten miles over good roads. An interior line of defence, sufficient to hold Chattanooga with a small force, was now constructed, and the plans were matured for accomplishing the main object of the campaign, which was the clearing of East Tennessee of the enemy.

When Gen. Sherman reached the vicinity of Bridgeport with his corps, Gen. Longstreet had been detached with his command from the army of Gen. Bragg, and sent on an expedition against Knoxville. This weakened Gen. Bragg and exposed Gen. Burnside to danger. The plan therefore adopted by Gen. Grant was to attack Gen. Bragg, and to follow it by a movement in the rear of Gen. Longstreet. The forces of Gen. Bragg held Missionary ridge, the Chattanooga valley, and Lookout mountain, with their left resting on the latter, and their right on the ridge near the tunnel of the Knoxville and Chattanooga railroad. Their pickets occupied the south bank of the Tennessee river for miles above, and their supplies were brought by the railroad from Atlanta and Dalton. The mass of Gen. Bragg's force was in the Chattanooga valley, between Lookout mountain and Missionary ridge, and on that slope of Lookout, thus being very nearly on his centre. The ridge was heavily posted with artillery. The plan adopted by Gen. Grant for the attack, and the manner in which it was executed, were thus described by a spectator: "A division of Gen. Sherman's troops were to be sent to Trenton, threatening the enemy's left flank. Under cover of this movement, Gen. Sherman's main body was to march up by Gen. Hooker's lines, crossing the Brown's Ferry bridge mostly at night, thence into a concealed camp on the north side of the river, opposite South Chickamauga creek. One division was directed to encamp on the North Chickamauga; about 120 pontoons were to be taken under cover of hills and woods, and launched into the North Chickamauga; these were to be filled with men, to be floated out into the Tennessee and down it, until opposite the South Chickamauga (about three miles below), to effect a landing on that bank, and throw up works; the remainder of the command were to be taken across in the same boats, or a portion of them; the Tennessee and South Chickamauga were to be bridged, and then the artillery crossed and moved at once to seize a foothold on the ridge, taking up a line facing the enemy's right flank near the tunnel. Gen. Howard's corps of Gen. Hooker's command was to cross into the town by the two bridges, and fill the gap between Gen. Sherman's proposed position and the main body of Gen. Thomas's army. Gen. Hooker, with the remainder of his force and the division sent to Trenton, which should return, were to carry the point of Lookout, and then threaten the enemy's left, which would thus be thrown back, being forced to evacuate the mountain and take position on the ridge; and then the Federal troops, being on both flanks, and upon one flank threatening the enemy's communications, were to advance the whole line or turn the other flank, as the chances might dictate. Then a part of the force was to follow as far as possible, while Gen. Sherman destroyed the railroad from Cleveland to Dalton, and then pushed on to relieve Knoxville, and capture, disperse, or drive off Gen. Longstreet from before it.

"Gen. Smith, chief engineer, took personal charge of the preliminaries necessary for the move on the left flank. The pontoons were put in the Chickamauga; the men encamped; the bridge trains ready to debouch at the proper point; and so completely was every thing arranged that no confusion whatever occurred. Artillery was posted on the side of the river to cross fire in front of the point of landing, and force the same, if necessary.

"On Monday, November 24th, an armed reconnoissance was made by Gen. Thomas on his left, which developed the enemy's lines and gave to Gen. Thomas a line of battle in advance of his picket lines, at the same time allowing the eleventh corps (Howard's) to come into the position assigned it. At midnight the men entered the pontoons, floated down, and effected a landing. At daylight the pontoniers were at work, and at noon the Tennessee river was bridged by a pontoon bridge 1,400 feet long, and the rest of Gen. Sherman's troops crossed with his artillery. He then pushed out to the ridge and took up his position, and Gen. Howard communicated with him, his force having marched to its place. Gen. Hooker's forces formed a line of battle running up and down the side of the mountain and sweeping around the point, and, at night of the same day (the 24th), held what he had gained and communicated with Gen. Thomas's right. That night the enemy evacuated Lookout Mountain top, and fell back from his front to the ridge. Thus, on Tuesday night, Gen. Bragg was threatened on both flanks, and with a heavy line of battle in his front. It was difficult for him to determine what the Federal move would be. His railroad must be held at all hazards from Gen. Sherman. The amount of Gen. Hooker's force he could distinctly see. He reënforced his right very heavily, leaving enough to hold his left and front, as he supposed. On the 25th, Wednesday, Gen. Sherman commenced to move. Two hills were taken. From the third he was several times repulsed, and he moved around more force, as if to get in rear of Gen. Bragg's line, and the latter then commenced massing against him. The critical moment had now arrived. Gen. Hooker moved his columns along the Rossville road toward Gen. Bragg's left, and this drew still more force from the latter's centre.

"General Grant now ordered Gen. Thomas to advance and take the rifle-pits at the base of the mountain. The Army of the Cumberland, remembering Chickamauga and impatient by reason of remaining spectators of the operations of Gens. Sherman and Hooker for two days, went forward with a will; drove the enemy in disorder from his lower works; and went on, heedless of the heavy artillery and musketry hurled against them from the crest of the ridge. Half-way up they seemed to falter, but it was only for breath. Without returning a shot they kept on, crowned the ridge, captured thirty-five out of the forty-four pieces of artillery on the hill, turned some of them against the masses in Gen. Sherman's front, and the routed line fell back, while the rest of Gen. Bragg's army, including Bragg and Hardee, fled, routed and broken, toward Ringgold. Thousands of prisoners and small arms and quantities of munitions of war were taken. Gen. Hooker took up the pursuit, and that night Mission Ridge blazed resplendent with Union camp-fires. The next day Gen. Hooker pushed the enemy to Ringgold, where he made a show of stubborn resistance, but was forced to retire. Gens. Sherman and Howard pushed for the railroad, which they smashed completely. About sixty pieces of artillery and a thousand prisoners were captured." When the attack was planned, orders were sent to Gen. Burnside to lure Gen. Longstreet as far away as possible, and fall back to a position where he could stand a siege and subsist from the country. Some skirmishes with the enemy still in East Tennessee, had previously taken place. On the 21st of September, one occurred between Col. Foster and a body of the enemy near Bristol, and on the 10th and 11th of October a sharp engagement took place at Blue Springs. The enemy was defeated with a heavy loss in killed and wounded, and one hundred and fifty prisoners. The Federal loss was about one hundred. Subsequently Gen. S. Jones, who had held a threatening position with a small force of the enemy near the Virginia line, moved down on the north side of the Holston river to Rogersville, with some three thousand five hundred cavalry, and surprised the garrison at that place, and captured four pieces of artillery, thirty-six wagons, and six hundred and fifty men.

Previous to the advance of Gen. Longstreet into East Tennessee, Gen. Burnside had occupied Philadelphia, and other points on the south side of the Holston river with small garrisons. Some of these forces were surprised and six or seven guns captured, with forty wagons, and between six and seven hundred prisoners. The remainder retreated to Loudon. Upon receiving the orders from Gen. Grant, Gen. Burnside moved from Knoxville toward Loudon, to meet Gen. Longstreet. The latter placed his main force on the north side of the river Holston, but sent his cavalry up the south side, expecting that it would slip into Knoxville during Gen. Burnside's absence, and thus compel him to make a flank retreat. But the cavalry of Gen. Burnside was also on the south side of the Holston with a small force of infantry, and they fell back into the works, thus covering the town on that side. Gen. Burnside also fell back to Campbell's Station, and made a stand. A contest ensued for several hours in which Gen. Longstreet was repulsed. Gen. Burnside then withdrew to the neighborhood of Knoxville, and fortified his position. Gen. Longstreet then came up and commenced a siege. Knoxville was surrounded by Gen. Longstreet on the 17th and 18th of November. A constant fire was kept up on the line of Gen. Burnside until the evening of the 28th, when an attack was proposed on a small fort mounting six guns, on a hill near the town, and commanding the approaches to it on that side of the river. The fort was occupied by the 29th Massachusetts, the 79th New York and two companies of the 2d, and one of the 20th Michigan. On its front and flanks was once a thick field of pines, which had been cut down with the tops falling in all directions, making an almost impassable mass of brush and timber. A space around the fort was cleared. The ditch in front was about ten feet deep, and parapet nearly twenty feet high. The assault was made near daylight, on the 29th, by the Confederate brigades of Gens. Bryan and Humphrey, with a party from Wolford's. The enemy advanced in three lines and made the attack fiercely, but all attempts to scale the sides of the fort failed, and they were finally repulsed with a loss of two hundred killed and wounded, and several hundred made prisoners. Meantime the force of Gen. Burnside was closely pressed, and provisions became so scarce, that his troops were put on half rations of bread.

After the battle of Chattanooga, the pursuit of the enemy was discontinued through want of strong animals to draw the artillery

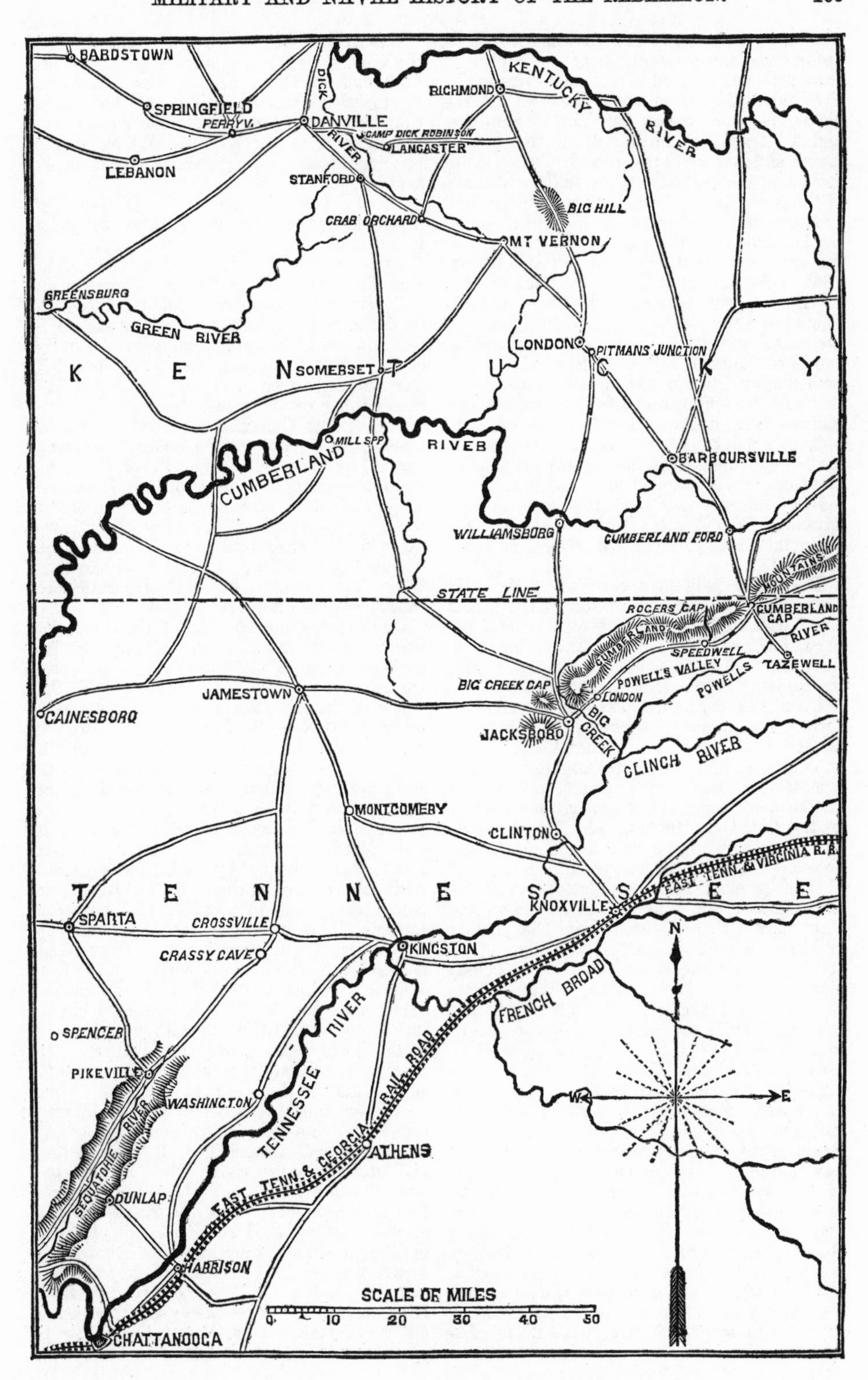
BARDSTOWN
SPRINGFIELD
PERRYV.
DANVILLE
DICK RIVER
CAMP DICK ROBINSON
LANCASTER
RICHMOND
KENTUCKY RIVER
LEBANON
STANFORD
CRAB ORCHARD
BIG HILL
MT VERNON
GREENSBURG
GREEN RIVER
LONDON
PITMANS JUNCTION
K E N T U C K Y
SOMERSET
MILL SPP
CUMBERLAND RIVER
BARBOURSVILLE
WILLIAMSBORG
CUMBERLAND FORD
MOUNTAINS
STATE LINE
ROGERS GAP
CUMBERLAND
CUMBERLAND GAP
RIVER
SPEEDWELL
TAZEWELL
POWELLS VALLEY
POWELLS
BIG CREEK GAP
LONDON
JAMESTOWN
CAINESBORO
JACKSBORO
BIG CREEK
CLINCH RIVER
MONTGOMERY
CLINTON
EAST TENN. & VIRGINIA R. R.
T E N N E S S E E
KNOXVILLE
SPARTA
CROSSVILLE
CRASSY CAVE
KINGSTON
N
FRENCH BROAD
SPENCER
TENNESSEE RIVER
RAIL ROAD
PIKEVILLE
WASHINGTON
W
E
SEQUATCHIE RIVER
ATHENS
EAST TENN. & GEORGIA
DUNLAP
HARRISON
SCALE OF MILES
0 10 20 30 40 50
CHATTANOOGA

and supply trains; but Gen. Sherman being reenforced by the eleventh corps, and a part of the fourth, commenced his march for Knoxville. Five miles above Loudon at Davis's Ford, the eleventh corps crossed the Little Tennessee, and at Morgantown seven miles further up, the fourth and his own corps crossed. The eleventh moved on the next day to Louisville, a distance of thirty-one miles. The other troops moved to Marysville. All were on the south side of the Holston. On the night of December 3d, the cavalry of Gen. Sherman reached Knoxville. This movement turned the flank of Gen. Longstreet, and he raised the siege and retreated toward Rutledge on that night. On the next day, the fourth arrived at Knoxville, and in conjunction with Gen. Burnside's forces immediately commenced a pursuit. Gen. Longstreet fell back into the border of Virginia, and took a strong position. Gen. Burnside was subsequently relieved from the command of the Department of the Ohio at his own urgent request, and Gen. Foster assigned to its command.

It was during this siege that Gen. Averill advanced from Western Virginia, and cut the communications of Gen. Longstreet, as hereatfer stated.

The other military operations of the year 1863, were, with the exception of the attack on Charleston, of a less conspicuous and important character. Some of them, however, were designed to be made in coöperation with the principal movements above stated.

Upon the departure of Gen. Longstreet's corps to reënforce Gen. Bragg, the remainder of Gen. Lee's army near Orange Court House, in Virginia, assumed a threatening attitude against Gen. Meade, and manœuvred to turn his left flank while at Culpepper Court House. At this time Gen. Hooker had left with nearly two corps to reënforce Gen. Rosecrans in Tennessee. The forward movement on the part of the Confederate army commenced on Thursday, October 8th, when Gens. Anderson and Heth moved their divisions from the vicinity of Peyton's Ford and Rapidan Bridge, up to and beyond Orange Court House. On Friday morning Gen. Wilcox's brigade moved from Barnett's Ford, and forming the rear of Lieut.-Gen. A. P. Hill's column, the troops proceeded to Madison Court House. At the same time, the corps of General Ewell followed, consisting of the divisions of Gens. Rhodes, Johnson, and Early. Meanwhile a show of force was still kept up in front of Gen. Meade on the Rapidan, by burning heavy camp fires, and maintaining the regular picket force in front. In the afternoon Gen. Stuart's cavalry began to advance, keeping on the right of the infantry, and rested at night near Madison Court House. On Saturday, the 10th, the infantry crossed the Robinson river near Criglersville, and soon after a skirmish took place between Gen. Stuart and a body of New York infantry, in which many of the latter were made prisoners.

Gen. Meade was now aware of the object of the enemy, and by Saturday night his whole force had left Culpepper and was falling back. His march was along the line of the railroad running from Alexandria. The enemy were encountered at times, and occasionally skirmishing ensued, but a general engagement was avoided.

On the 11th the main body of Gen. Lee's army reached Culpepper, and were compelled to halt during the day to furnish provision to the troops. On his advance Gen. Lee had left Gen. Fitz Lee with his division of cavalry and a detachment of infantry to hold his lines south of the Rapidan. This force was attacked by Gen. Buford on Saturday, and a sharp skirmish ensued; but the enemy being reënforced by Gen. Stuart's troops, Gen. Buford fell back across the Rappahannock.

On the 12th Gen. Lee advanced in two columns, with the design of reaching the Orange and Alexandria railroad north of the river, and intercepting the retreat of Gen. Meade. A cavalry skirmish occurred at Jeffersonton, but the Rappahannock at Warrenton Springs was reached that afternoon, when the passage was disputed by Federal cavalry and artillery. Upon the advance of a Confederate force these troops fell back.

On Tuesday morning, the 13th, the march was resumed, and the two columns reunited at Warrenton in the afternoon, and halted. On the next morning the advance of Gen. Lee was continued, a portion of his army moving by way of New Baltimore toward Bristoe's Station, and the rest, accompanied by the main body of the cavalry, proceeding to the same point by Auburn and Greenwich. Near the former place a skirmish took place between Gen. Ewell's advance and a body of Gen. Meade's troops. The retreat of Gen. Meade was conducted by direct parallel roads, while the enemy in their advance were compelled to march by difficult and circuitous routes. They were thus unable to intercept the retreat. The rear guard of Gen. Meade consisted of the second corps, under Gen. Warren. It had reached Bristoe's Station, and about noon on the 14th it was suddenly attacked by Gen. Hill, who, with two brigades of the enemy, had arrived in advance. Gen. Warren immediately arranged his corps for action, and a sharp struggle ensued, which lasted for some hours, when the enemy were repulsed with a loss of five guns and a large number killed, wounded, and four hundred and fifty made prisoners. The Federal loss was fifty-one killed, and three hundred and fifty-nine wounded. After remaining in possession of the field during the night, the second corps fell back across Broad Run. Gen. Meade then fortified his position beyond Bull Run, extending his line toward the Little River turnpike. The enemy now ceased to advance further. Gen. Meade held a strong position, and if it could have been turned by the enemy he could readily have retired to the intrenchments around Washington and Alexandria. After destroying the railroad from Cub Run southwardly to the Rappahannock, the enemy retreated on the 18th to the line of that river, leaving their cavalry in front of Gen. Meade.

During the next day the cavalry of Gen. Meade advanced, before whom Gen. Stuart retired, until an attack was made on their flank, near Buckland, by Gen. Fitz Lee, who had moved from Auburn. A severe action ensued, and the enemy advanced nearly to Haymarket and Gainesville, where the infantry were encountered, and the former retired.

When the advance of Gen. Lee from the Rapidan commenced, orders were sent to Gen. Imboden to advance down the Shenandoah valley and guard the gaps of the mountains on the Confederate left. Having performed this duty he marched on the 18th upon Charlestown, and, surrounding the place, captured nearly all of the force stationed there, with their stores and transportation. Upon an advance of the force at Harper's Ferry, Gen. Imboden retired with his booty.

Gen. Halleck states the loss in the cavalry corps during these operations to have been 74 by casualties and 885 missing. Gen. Lee states that in the course of these operations 2,436 prisoners were captured, of which 436 were taken by Gen. Imboden. The loss of the enemy is not stated.

On the 7th of November Gens. Sedgwick and French attacked the enemy at Rappahannock Station and Kelly's Ford, and captured several redoubts, four guns, eight battle flags, and about two thousand prisoners. The Federal loss in killed and wounded was three hundred and seventy.

About the 20th of November an advance was made by Gen. Meade from the position held at that time, under the impression that Gen. Lee was either retreating south from the Rapidan, or was preparing for a movement in some other quarter. The intention was to ascertain the position of Gen. Lee's forces, and to bring on a contest with them. Upon this advance the enemy fell back and took up a strong position behind Mine Run, southwest of Chancellorsville. The strength of the position, and the risks attending an assault, were such that the army of Gen. Meade withdrew from the front of the enemy, and resumed its previous camps around Brandy Station, on the Orange and Alexandria railroad.

In West Virginia the force was too small during the year to attempt any important campaign by itself; but it acted mainly on the defensive, in repelling raids of the enemy and breaking up bands of guerillas.

When Gen. Lee's army retreated across the Potomac in July last, Brig.-Gen. Kelly concentrated all his available force on the enemy's flank, near Clear Springs, ready to coöperate in the proposed attack by Gen. Meade. They also rendered valuable services in the pursuit after Gen. Lee had effected his passage of the river.

On the 24th of July Col. Toland attacked the enemy at Wytheville, on the East Tennessee and Virginia railroad, capturing two pieces of artillery, 700 muskets, and 125 prisoners. Our loss was 17 killed and 61 wounded. The enemy's killed and wounded were reported to be 75.

In August Gen. Averill attacked a force of the enemy under Gen. Sam. Jones, at Rocky Gap, in Greenbrier county, capturing one gun, 150 prisoners, and killing and wounding some 200. The Federal loss in killed, wounded, and missing, was 130.

On the 11th of September Gen. Imboden attacked a small force of Federal troops at Moorefield, wounding 15 and capturing about 150.

On the 5th of November Gen. Averill attacked and defeated the enemy near Lewisburg, capturing three pieces of artillery, 100 prisoners, and a large number of small arms, wagons, and camp equipage. The enemy's loss in killed and wounded was estimated at 300.

In December, Gen. Averill, with the 2d, 3d, and 8th Virginia mounted infantry, 14th Pennsylvania, Dobson's battalion of cavalry, and Ewing's battery, advanced into Southwestern Virginia, and, on the 16th, destroyed the Virginia and Tennessee railroad at Salem. At the same place three depots were destroyed, containing 2,000 barrels of flour, 10,000 bushels of wheat, 100,000 bushels of shelled corn, 50,000 bushels of oats, 2,000 barrels of meat, several cords of leather, 1,000 sacks of salt, 31 boxes of clothing, 20 bales of cotton, a large amount of harness, shoes, and saddles, equipments, tools, oil, tar, and various other stores, and 100 wagons. The telegraph wire was cut, coiled, and burned for a half mile. The water station, turn-table, and three cars were burned, the track torn up, and the rails heated and destroyed as much as possible, in six hours. Five bridges and several culverts were destroyed over an extent of fifteen miles. A large quantity of bridge timber and repairing materials were also destroyed. On returning, Gen. Averill found six separate commands under Gens. Early, Jones, Fitz Lee, Imboden, Jackson, and Echols, arranged in a line extending from Staunton to Newport, on all the available roads, to intercept him. Having captured a despatch of the enemy, by which their positions were made known, Gen. Averill marched from the front of Jones to that of Jackson during the night, crossed the river and pressed in the latter's outposts, and passed him. In the meantime, forces were concentrating upon Gen. Averill at a place called Calaghan's, over every available road but one, which was deemed impracticable. Over this one he crossed the top of the Alleghanies with his command, and arrived at Beverly on the 21st, with a loss of six drowned, four wounded, and ninety missing, and having captured about two hundred prisoners and one hundred and fifty horses.

In North Carolina, during the year 1863, no important operations were carried on against the enemy in consequence of the weakness of the Federal force. It acted chiefly on the defensive, and held the important positions which had been previously captured.

In March the Confederate general, Pettigru, with a large force of infantry and artillery, made an unsuccessful demonstration on Newbern. The loss of Gen. Foster, in command of the Federal forces, was two killed and four wounded. In April, Gen. Hill laid siege to Washington, on the Tar river. The town had only a small garrison and was slightly fortified. Gen. Foster, who was there at the time, caused the works to be so strengthened, that they were held until reënforcements arrived from Newbern to raise the siege.

In May an expedition was sent against a camp of the enemy at Gum Swamp, which captured one hundred and sixty-five prisoners and military stores. In July another expedition was sent against Rocky Mount on the Tar river, which destroyed the bridge at that place, and a large amount of property belonging to the enemy. No further operations of importance took place in North Carolina during the year. The Department of North Carolina was united with that of Virginia, under the command of Gen. Dix, until the latter was transferred to the command of the Department of the East, when Gen. Foster assumed the command. The latter was subsequently transferred to the Department of the Ohio, and Gen. B. F. Butler appointed to the command of the Department of Virginia and North Carolina.

After abandoning the siege of Washington in April, Gen. Hill marched toward Nansemond to reënforce Gen. Longstreet, who was investing Suffolk, in Southeastern Virginia. Upon failing in his direct assault upon the place, Gen. Longstreet began to establish batteries for its reduction. The defence of the place was conducted by Gen. Peck, under the command of Gen. Dix, who made every preparation of which it was capable, and retarded the construction of the enemy's works until the attempt was finally abandoned. The Federal loss during these operations was forty-four killed, two hundred and one wounded, and fourteen missing. They captured four hundred prisoners.

About the 20th of June, while Gen. Lee was advancing into Pennsylvania, all the available forces under the command of Gen. Dix, being about eighteen thousand men, were moved up the York river and landed at the Whitehouse, for the purpose of threatening Richmond, of destroying the railroad bridges over the South and North Anna rivers, which were on Gen. Lee's line of communication, and doing as much damage as possible to the enemy, besides occupying the attention of a large body of his force. One of the bridges over the South Anna was destroyed by an expedition under Col. Spear, and the quartermaster's depot at Hanover Station. On his return he brought back thirty-five army wagons, seven hundred horses and mules, and Gen. Fitzhugh Lee, the son of Gen. R. E. Lee, as a prisoner. The other bridge over the South Anna was not destroyed, but the railroad track between it and Richmond was torn up for a considerable distance, and the bridge at Ashland Station, on the same road, eleven miles out of Richmond, was completely demolished and burned, as also the depot. After remaining at the Whitehouse three days, Gen. Dix received orders to return with his forces for the purpose of reënforcing Gen. Meade. At that time he had completely cut off Gen. Lee's communications with Richmond by way of the two railroads crossing the South Anna river, and had control of the whole country from the Pamunkey to the Rappahannock.

The small force in the Department of the South caused a suspension of active operations until March, 1863. An attack upon Fort Sumter and Charleston had long been contemplated by the Navy Department, and it was represented that the operation of the ironclads would be greatly aided by a land force prepared to assist the attack, and to occupy any work reduced by the navy.

Gen. Foster was, therefore, sent with a considerable force and a large siege equipage to assist the naval attack. But not proving acceptable to Gen. Hunter, then in command, he returned to North Carolina, leaving his troops and siege equipage. The naval attack on the fort was made upon April 7th, and is described elsewhere, but was rather unsuccessful, and nothing apparently remained to be done by the land forces. It was now represented by the Navy Department that a second attack upon Fort Sumter and Charleston was preparing, and that its success required the military occupation of Morris Island, and the establishment of land batteries on that island to assist in the reduction of the fort. As this was a task requiring engineering skill, it was assigned to Gen. Q. A. Gillmore, who took the command of the department. On the night of the 3d of July he commenced his advance upon Charleston by the movement of troops to Folly Island. There they remained as secret as possible, and erected batteries to cover those of the enemy on the south ends of Morris Island. On the 10th the entire force which was required having arrived, the batteries opened upon the enemy, and when their guns were silenced a charge was made by the infantry, who had crossed to the island in boats, and the works captured. A despatch from Gen. Gillmore thus reports his movements:

HEADQUARTERS DEPARTMENT OF THE SOUTH,
IN THE FIELD, MORRIS ISLAND, S. C., *July 12th*, 1863.

Major-General H. W. Halleck, General-in-Chief:

SIR: I have the honor to report that at five o'clock on the morning of the 10th instant I made an attack upon the enemy's fortified position on the south end of Morris Island, and, after an engagement of three

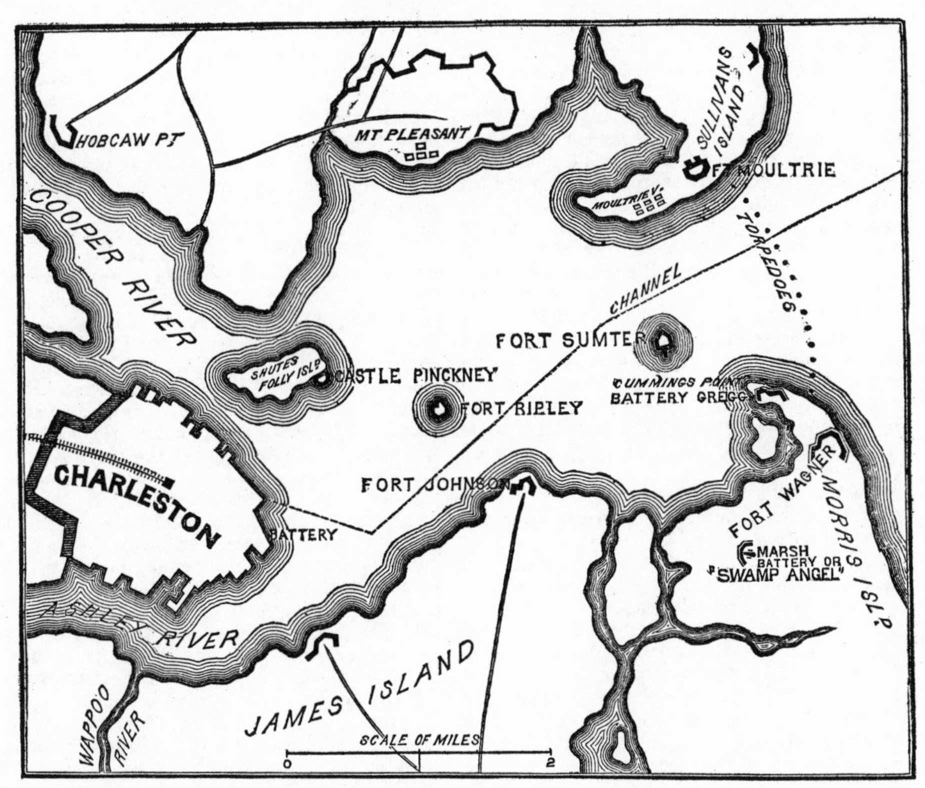

hours and a quarter, captured all his strongholds upon that part of the island, and pushed forward my infantry to within six hundred yards of Fort Wagner.

We now hold all the island except about one mile on the north end, which includes Fort Wagner and a battery on Cummings' Point, mounting at the present time fourteen or fifteen heavy guns in the aggregate.

The assaulting column was gallantly led by Brig.-Gen. Strong. It landed in small boats under cover of my batteries on Folly Island and four monitors led by Rear-Admiral Dahlgren, which entered the main channel abreast of Morris Island soon after our batteries opened. The monitors continued their fire during the day mostly on Fort Wagner.

On the morning of the 11th instant, at daybreak, an effort was made to carry Fort Wagner by assault. The parapet was gained, but the supports recoiled under the fire to which they were exposed and could not be got up. Our loss in both actions will not vary much from one hundred and fifty in killed, wounded, and prisoners. We have taken eleven pieces of heavy ordnance and a large quantity of camp equipage.

The enemy's loss in killed, wounded, and missing, will not fall short of two hundred.

Q. A. GILLMORE, Brig.-Gen. Commanding.

The portion of Morris Island not yet taken by Gen. Gillmore was well fortified. Fort Wagner was a strong work, constructed of immense timbers and rafters covered over with earth and sand some twenty feet thick. Its distance from Fort Sumter in an air line was about a mile and a half, and four and a half miles from Charleston. On the part of the island called Cummings' Point was Battery Gregg, about three-fourths of a mile from Fort Sumter. Morris Island is about five miles long and some three or four miles wide. Along the sea coast is an irregular ridge made of sand heaps, which is about half a mile wide, the rest of the island is low, level, marshy land, much of which is flooded at high tide. The Confederate forces on the island were under the command of Brig.-Gen. Harrison, of Georgia; Fort Sumter, which stands within the entrance, and nearly in the centre of the harbor, was under the command of Col. Rhett. The walls were protected by tiers of sand bags in the inside, some twenty feet thick, thus making an obstruction of brick and sand some twenty-six feet. Fort Moultrie is nearly opposite Sumter, on the north side of the harbor, and distant about one and one-fourth miles. Up the harbor on the southern side is Fort Johnson, one and one-fourth miles distant. About a mile beyond, in the middle of the harbor, on the "middle ground," is Fort Ripley. Castle Pinkney is in the same line, and on the north side of the harbor at the mouth of the Cooper river. There were, in addition, numerous batteries at various points on all the islands and the front of the city, and also works facing the land attack on James Island. The whole number of guns in position and afloat for the defence of Charleston, was estimated at three hundred and seventy-six.

The naval force under Admiral Dupont, composing the South Atlantic blockading squadron, consisted of sixty-one vessels of all classes, mounting three hundred and ninety-six guns. But iron clads, carrying in all about thirty-four guns, were expected to take the active part in the operations in the harbor.

After the failure of the assault upon Fort Wagner, Gen. Gillmore set to work to bring his heavy guns into position, not only for an attack upon Wagner, but upon all the works of the enemy, and also to throw shells into Charleston. The form of the contest now consisted in pushing forward the siege works and annoying the enemy as much as possible with sharpshooters and shells. The enemy acted in the same manner. Fort Johnson night and day threw shells, which burst above the workmen in the trenches. Wagner was kept quiet by the ship Ironsides and the monitors, while these in turn were attacked by the guns of Gregg and Sumter.

On the 18th of July, about twelve heavy guns were in position, besides eight or ten mortars, within eight hundred yards of Fort Wagner, and Gen. Gillmore determined on making another attack. It was commenced at noon by Gen. Gillmore's batteries and the frigate Ironsides; five monitors, two mortar schooners, and three wooden gunboats soon joined in. The enemy replied briskly from Fort Wagner, Battery Bee, beyond Cummings's Point, and the guns on the southwestern face of Fort Sumter. Their fire was chiefly directed against the vessels, occasionally a shell was thrown at the batteries. Soon after four o'clock the fire of Fort Wagner ceased. It was known that one gun had been dismounted and another was supposed to have exploded. Under the impression that the works were evacuated, another attempt to occupy them was determined upon. For this purpose two brigades consisting of the 7th Connecticut regiment, the 3d New Hampshire, the 9th Maine, the 76th Pennsylvania, and the 48th New York, under Brig.-Gen. Strong, and the 7th New Hampshire, 6th Connecticut, 62d Ohio, 100th New York, and 54th Massachusetts (colored), under Col. Putnam, were ordered forward from behind the sand hills. The brigades were formed in line on the beach, with the regiments disposed in columns, the colored regiment being in advance. This movement was observed at Fort Sumter, and a fire was opened on the troops but without effect. At dark the order was given for both brigades to advance, Gen. Strong's leading and Col. Putnam's within supporting distance. The troops went forward at quick time and in silence, until the 54th Massachusetts, led by Col. Shaw, was within two hundred yards of the work, when the men gave a fierce yell and rushed up the glacis, closely followed by the other regiments of the brigade.

The enemy, hitherto silent, opened upon them furiously with grape, canister, and a continuous fusilade of small arms. The negroes, however, plunged on, and many of them crossed the ditch, although it contained four feet of water, gaining the parapet. They were dislodged, however, in a few minutes with hand grenades, and retired, leaving more than one-half of their number, including their colonel, dead upon the field. The 6th Connecticut regiment, under Lieut.-Com. Rodman, was next in support of the 54th, and they also suffered terribly, being compelled to retire after a stubborn contest. The 9th Maine, which was next in line, was broken up by the passage of the remnant of the repulsed colored regiment through its lines, and retired in confusion, excepting three companies which stood their ground.

It now devolved upon the 3d New Hampshire regiment to push forward, and, led by Gen. Strong and Col. Jackson in person, they dashed up against the fort. Three companies gained the ditch, and wading through the water, found shelter against the embankment. Here was the critical point of the assault, and the second brigade, which should have been up and ready to support their comrades of the first, were unaccountably delayed. Gen. Strong then gave the order to fall back and lie down on the glacis, which was obeyed, without confusion.

While waiting here, exposed to the heavy fire, Gen. Strong was wounded. Finding that the supports did not come, Gen. Strong gave the order for his brigade to retire, and the men left the field in perfect order.

Soon afterward the other brigades came on, and made up for their tardiness by their valor. Rushing impetuously up the glacis, undeterred by the fury of the enemy, whose fire was not intermitted, several of the regiments succeeded in crossing the ditch, scaling the parapet, and descending into the fort. Here a hand-to-hand conflict ensued. The troops fought with desperation, and were able to drive the enemy from one side of the work to seek shelter between the traverses, while they held possession for something more than an hour. This piece of gallantry was unfortunately of no advantage. The enemy rallied, and, having received reënforcements, made a charge upon them and expelled them from their position by the force of numbers. One of the regiments engaged in this brilliant dash was the 48th New York, Col. Barton, and it came out almost decimated. The 48th was among the first to enter the fort, and was fired upon by a regiment that gained the parapet some minutes later, under the supposition that it was the enemy. About midnight the order was given to retire, and the troops fell back to the rifle pits outside of their own works. The loss in killed, wounded, and missing, was fifteen hundred and thirty.

Gen. Gillmore now made his preparations to bombard both Wagner and Sumter, and the city of Charleston.

Meantime a correspondence took place between the opposing commanding officers.

Under date of Headquarters Department of South Carolina, Georgia, and Florida, Charleston, S. C., July 4th, 1863, Gen. Beauregard says that it is his duty, in the interests of humanity, to address Gen. Gillmore, with a view of effecting some understanding as to the future conduct of the war in this quarter. And then, after alluding to the expedition set on foot by his predecessor, Maj.-Gen. Hunter, to the Combahee river, which seized and carried away negro slaves off plantations on its banks, ravaged the plantations, &c., he says he does not propose to enter upon a discussion touching that species of pillaging, but desires to acquaint Gen. Gillmore formally that more than one plantation was pillaged, buildings burned, and crops destroyed—acts which were not rendered necessary by any military exigency.

Then he takes up the question of the employment of negroes, and quotes Napoleon, to show the "atrocious consequences which ever resulted in the employment of a merciless, servile race as soldiers;" that Napoleon refused to employ the serfs in his campaign against Russia, because he dreaded the results of a civil or intestine war. He characterizes all who call to their aid such material, in the language of the publicists, as barbarians, &c. In conclusion, he asks whether the acts which resulted in the burning of the villages of Darien, Ga., and Bluffton, and the ravages on the Combahee, are regarded by Gen. Gillmore as legitimate measures of war, which he will feel authorized to resort to hereafter.

Gen. Gillmore addresses Gen. Beauregard from Morris Island, under date of July 18th. He states that, while he and his Government will scrupulously endeavor to conduct the war upon principles established by usage among civilized nations, he shall expect from the commanding general opposed to him full compliance with the same rules, in their unrestricted application to all the forces under his command.

Gen. Beauregard, under the date of July 22d, 1863, says he is at a loss to perceive the necessity for the remark that Gen. Gillmore will expect from him "full compliance with the same rules established by usages of civilized nations, &c., in their unrestricted application to all his forces," inasmuch as he is wholly unaware that any departure from the same has ever been alleged on his part, or by any of his troops, from the established laws and usages between civilized peoples; and then he calls for more specific charges.

In reply to Gen. Beauregard's despatch of the 22d ultimo, Gen. Gillmore, on the 5th of August, after noticing the remark of Gen. Beauregard that he was at a loss to perceive the necessity for his statement that he (Gen. G.) should expect a full compliance on his (Gen. B.'s) part with the same rules, &c., in their unrestricted application to all the forces under his command, states that he considered his remarks as pertinent and proper at the time. Events, he adds, since transpired, show them to have been eminently so. In proof he quotes the circumstances of agreement for mutual paroling and returning to their respective commands the wounded prisoners in our hands. "You declined," Gen. Gillmore goes on to say, "to return the wounded officers and men belonging to my colored regiments, and your subordinate in charge of the exchange asserted that the question had been left for after consideration." He could but regard this transaction as a palpable breach of faith on Gen. Beauregard's part, and a flagrant violation of Gen. B.'s pledges as an officer.

The first works erected by Gen. Gillmore after taking possession of Morris Island, were the construction of parallels. These extended from the beach on the right to the marsh on the left. The first was distant from Fort Wagner one thousand two hundred yards. The second, and principal one, was so constructed that its left was six hundred and seven yards from Wagner, and its right seven hundred and fifty yards. The third was four hundred and twenty-five yards from Wagner. The parallels were built in an oblong direction with the length of the island, having the highest points resting on the marsh. The rifle pits forming the foundation of the first parallel were thrown up shortly after the troops gained possession of the lower part of the island. These pits were thrown up in a single night, and used first in the attack on Fort Wagner, on July 18th. The interstices were subsequently filled, and the first parallel constructed. It was two hundred and twenty-five yards. The length of the second parallel was three hundred and twenty-five yards. The siege guns used for the offensive were mounted in the rear of this parallel. Its distance from Fort Sumter was three thousand three hundred and fifty yards. The third parallel was one hundred yards in length. On the left of the parallels earthworks were constructed, containing guns of heavy caliber. Their mean distance from Fort Sumter was four thousand one hundred yards. Still farther to the left, on the marsh, another earthwork was constructed facing Fort Sumter. On this was mounted a gun called "Swamp Angel." The "Marsh" is a vast growth of cane, bordering on Light House Inlet and Morris Island, directly facing James Island, which runs parallel with Morris Island. It is about a mile wide, and borders the island nearly its whole length. At low tide it is dry, but at high water there is about four feet of water over its whole extent. Scows were procured and loaded with bags of sand, and at every tide floated into the marsh, and piled on the selected spot. They sank down in their watery bed and rapidly disappeared, but the process was still continued with each renewing tide, until an immense bank, towering six feet above the tops of the canes, was visible. Strong traverses were erected, and after due time given for it to settle, the gun was placed on one of the scows, and floated through the canes at high tide to the site of the battery, where it was moored and soon mounted, the work having all been done at night, it being in full view of Fort Johnson and James Island batteries.

On the night of August 13th, the Federal works were advanced within four hundred and twenty yards of Wagner, without any suspicion of the enemy. Soon after daylight, a fire was opened from Wagner, Gregg, and Sumter, which continued for two hours, and answered with great vigor from the Federal batteries. On the 15th all the forts of the enemy from Johnson Island, on the left, to Fort Wagner, on the right, opened fire, and continued it at intervals of fifteen minutes. For the first time fire was opened upon Fort Sumter by the Federal batteries. A 200-pounder Parrott was brought to bear on the fort, for the purpose of testing the powder to be used in these guns. Seven shots were fired, a distance of two and five-eighth miles, the first three fell short, but of the remaining four, two went directly through the gorge wall, a short distance above the sally port, and two struck the parapet, and sent an immense amount of brick and mortar into the ditch and into the fort. The solid shot, which went through, made holes from four to five feet in diameter.

On the morning of August 17th, Gen. Gillmore, having completed his batteries, which numbered about sixty pieces, and obtained the range, his guns opened fire upon Fort Sumter. The fleet consisting of the frigate Ironsides and the Monitors, aided by some wooden gunboats, made an attack, at the same time, upon Forts Gregg and Wagner. The latter was completely silenced, and the former nearly so. The Monitors Passaic and Patapsco then moved nearer to Fort Sumter, and opened fire on it. In the afternoon the fleet retired, except so much as was required to prevent remounting the guns in Fort Wagner. The fire from the batteries upon Fort Sumter continued through the day and night.

The bombardment of Fort Sumter had now been regularly commenced by Gen. Gillmore. The following is the daily report by the enemy of its effect:

CHARLESTON, Thursday, *August 20th.*

The firing of the Parrott guns upon Fort Sumter to-day was exceedingly heavy, but not so accurate as heretofore. About noon the flag was shot away, but soon replaced. No casualties are reported. Col. Alfred Rhett is commanding, and the garrison is stout-hearted.

The battery of Parrott guns is distant from Sumter two five-eighth miles. The missiles used are 200-pound bolts, eight inches in diameter, two feet long, with flat heads of chilled iron. Shells of the same dimensions are also used.

Up to Wednesday night, the third day of the attack, 1,972 of these missiles struck Sumter, and including to-day 2,500 have struck. The damage is of course considerable, and for the last two days all the guns on the south face of the fort have been disabled.

Yesterday, about four o'clock, the iron-clads formed in line of battle to renew the attack on Sumter, but the fort opened at long range from the east face, and they retired without attacking. To-day the Ironsides and two Monitors kept up a fire on Wagner at intervals, and the Yankee sappers have begun to make approaches on that battery from the nearest work. A shot from Wagner disabled one of the Parrott guns, and the James Island batteries, under Lieut. Col. Yates, exploded two of the enemy's ammunition chests.

CHARLESTON, Friday, *August 21st.*

The fire of the enemy's land batteries has been heavier than ever to-day. A new battery of Parrott guns opened on Sumter this morning, and the fires have been concentrated upon the east battery and its guns. The south wall of the fort is now a pile of rubbish. On the north the wall is also crumbling into a heap of ruins. The flag has been shot away twice to-day, and six times during the attack. The flag-staff is shot off, and the flag flies from the ruins of the south wall.

Just before sunset Sumter fired several shots at the Ironsides, which was engaging Battery Wagner.

A Monitor this morning fired at Sumter while making a reconnoissance, but was not replied to. There is no report of casualties.

The sappers are making a regular approach on Battery Wagner.

CHARLESTON, Saturday, *August 22d.*

From 5 o'clock A. M. until 7 o'clock P. M. yesterday, the enemy's fire on Fort Sumter was very heavy. Nine hundred and twenty-three shots were fired, and seven hundred and four struck the fort, either outside or inside. The eastern face of the fort was badly battered. Some guns on the east end and the northeast face were disabled. The flag was shot down four times. Five privates and two negroes were wounded.

The enemy's fire on Wagner caused five casualties, including Capt. Robert Pringle, killed.

At 11 o'clock last night a communication from the enemy, unsigned, was sent to Gen. Beauregard, demanding the surrender of Sumter and the Morris Island batteries, with a notification that the city would be shelled in four hours if the demand was not complied with. Gen. Beauregard was on a reconnoissance, and Gen. Jordan returned it for the signature of the writer.

About two o'clock this morning the enemy began throwing shells into the city from a battery on the marsh between Morris and James Islands, and distant five miles from the city. Twelve 8-inch Parrott shells fell in the city, but caused no casualties. The transaction is regarded as an outrage on civilized warfare. The shelling had a good effect in hastening the exodus of non-combatants.

At daylight this morning the enemy opened fire vigorously on Sumter. The Ironsides has since opened. Sumter is replying. Wagner is firing briskly on the enemy's advanced works, 450 yards from our battery.

CHARLESTON, *August 22d.*

The fire of the enemy's land batteries has been kept up on Fort Sumter, and more guns disabled. There was only one casualty.

There was also a heavy fire on Battery Wagner from the fleet and land, also on Battery Gregg. The casualties at Wagner were one officer and four privates.

Gen. Gillmore's demand for the surrender of Fort Sumter and Morris Island, with a threat to shell Charleston in four hours from the delivery of the paper at Wagner, was signed and returned at seven o'clock this morning.

Gen. Beauregard, in his reply, charges inhumanity and violation of the laws of war, and affirms that if the offence be repeated he will employ stringent measures of retaliation.

Up to this time the threat to shell the city has not been executed.

CHARLESTON, Sunday, *August 23d.*

To-day the land batteries opened from south to north, and the Monitors from east to west, coming close up. The fire was very damaging. The east wall was cracked and breached, and the shot swept through the fort. A shell burst, wounding Lieut. Boylston, Col. Rhett, and three other officers.

The fort is now in ruins. Col. Rhett is ordered to hold this outpost even as a forlorn hope, until relieved or taken. Col. Gaillard was killed.

Gen. Gillmore sent a communication at 11 o'clock, giving notice that at 11 o'clock to-morrow he would open fire on Charleston.

CHARLESTON, Monday, *August 24th.*

The enemy's fire on Sumter slackened to-day. The fleet has not participated. At 12 o'clock last night the enemy's guns opened fire on the city, firing fifteen 8-inch Parrott shells. No casualties resulted. Non-combatants are leaving the city in continuous streams.

On the 24th of August, Gen. Gillmore sent the following despatches to Washington:

HEADQUARTERS DEPARTMENT OF THE SOUTH,
MORRIS ISLAND, S. C., *August 24th*, 1863.

To Maj.-Gen. H. W. Halleck, General-in-Chief:

SIR: I have the honor to report the practical demolition of Fort Sumter as the result of our seven days' bombardment of the work, including two days of which a powerful northeasterly storm most seriously diminished the accuracy of our fire.

Fort Sumter is to-day a shapeless and harmless mass of ruins. My chief of artillery, Col. J. W. Turner, reports its destruction so far complete, that it is no longer of any "avail in the defence of Charleston."

He also says that "by a longer fire it could be made more completely a ruin and a mass of broken masonry, but could scarcely be made more powerless for the defence of the harbor."

My breaching batteries were located at distances ranging between 3,320 and 4,240 yards from the works, and now remain as efficient as ever. I deem it unnecessary, at present, to continue the fire upon the ruins of Fort Sumter.

I have also, under a heavy fire from James Island, established batteries on my left, within effective range of the heart of Charleston city, and have opened with them, after giving Gen. Beauregard due notice of my intention to do so.

My notification to Gen. Beauregard, his reply thereto, with the threat of retaliation, and my rejoinder, have been transmitted to the army headquarters.

The projectiles from my batteries entered the city, and Gen. Beauregard himself designates them as the "most destructive missiles ever used in war."

The report of my chief of artillery, and an accurate sketch of the ruins of Fort Sumter, taken at 12 M. yesterday, six hours before we ceased firing, are herewith transmitted.

Very respectfully, your obedient servant,
Q. A. GILLMORE,
Brigadier-General Commanding.

OFFICE OF CHIEF OF ARTILLERY, DEPARTMENT OF THE SOUTH, MORRIS ISLAND, S. C., *August 23d*, 1863.

Brig.-Gen. Q. A. Gillmore, Commanding Department of the South, Morris Island, S. C.:

GENERAL: I have the honor to report the effect that our breaching batteries have had upon Fort Sumter, and the condition of that work to-night, at the close of the seven days' bombardment.

The gorge wall of the fort is almost a complete mass of ruins. For the distance of several casemates about midway of this face the ramparts are removed nearly, and in places quite to the arches, and but for the sand bags, with which the casemates were filled, and which have served to sustain the broken arches and masses of masonry, it would have long since been entirely cut away, and with it the arches to the floor of the second tier of casemates. The debris on this point now forms a ramp reaching as high as the floor of the casemates. The parapet wall of the two northeasterly faces is completely carried away, a small portion only being left in the angle made with the gorge wall, and the ramparts of these faces are also a total ruin. Quite one half of our projectiles seem to have struck the parade and parapet of these two faces, and judging from the effect they have had upon the gorge wall within our observation, the destruction of masonry on these two sides must be very great, and I am of opinion that nearly every arch in these fronts must be broken in. But one gun remains in position on these two fronts. This is in the angle of the gorge, and I think unserviceable.

The ruin extends around, taking in the northeasterly face as far as can be seen. A portion of this face adjoining the angle it makes with the southeasterly face is concealed, but from the great number of missiles which have struck in this angle during the last two days, it cannot be otherwise than greatly damaged, and I do not think any guns can be left on this face in a serviceable condition.

The ramparts on this angle, as well as in the southeasterly face, must be ploughed up and greatly shattered; the parapet on this latter face being torn off in many places, as we can see, and I hardly think the platforms of the three remaining guns on this face could have escaped.

With the assistance of a powerful glass, I cannot determine that more than one of these guns can be used. The carriages of the others are evidently more or less shattered, and such is the ruin of the parapet and parade in the immediate vicinity of this gun that it probably could not be served for any length of time.

In fine, the destruction of the fort is so far complete that it is to-day of no avail in the defence of the harbor of Charleston; by a longer fire it can be made more completely a ruin and a mass of broken masonry, but could scarcely be more powerless for the defence of the harbor.

I therefore respectfully submit my opinion that a continuance of our fire is no longer necessary, as giving us no ends adequate for the consumption of our resources.

Very respectfully, your obedient servant,
JOHN W. TURNER,
Colonel and Chief of Artillery.

WATERS-SON SC.

The correspondence mentioned in the preceding despatch commenced on the 21st. On that day Gen. Gillmore addressed the following note to Gen. Beauregard:

HEADQUARTERS DEPARTMENT OF THE SOUTH, MORRIS ISLAND, S. C., *August 21st*, 1863.

To Gen. G. T. Beauregard, Commanding Confederate Forces, Charleston, S. C.:

GENERAL: I have the honor to demand of you the immediate evacuation of Morris Island and Fort Sumter by the Confederate forces. The present condition of Fort Sumter, and the rapid and progressive destruction which it is undergoing from my batteries, seem to render its complete demolition within a few hours a matter of certainty. All my heaviest guns have not yet opened.

Should you refuse compliance with this demand, or should I receive no reply thereto within four hours after it is delivered into the hands of your subordinate at Fort Wagner for transmission, I shall open fire on the city of Charleston from batteries already established within easy and effective range of the heart of the city.

I am, General, very respectfully, your obedient servant, Q. A. GILLMORE, Brig.-Gen. Commanding.

To this note Gen. Beauregard replied as follows:

HEADQUARTERS DEPARTMENT OF SOUTH CAROLINA, GEORGIA, AND FLORIDA, CHARLESTON, S. C., *August 22d*, 1863.

SIR: Last night, at fifteen minutes before eleven o'clock, during my absence on a reconnoissance of my fortifications, a communication was received at these headquarters, dated "Headquarters Department of the South, Morris Island, S.C., August 21st, 1863," demanding "the immediate evacuation of Morris Island and Fort Sumter by the Confederate forces," on the alleged grounds "that the present condition of Fort Sumter, and the rapid and progressive destruction which it is undergoing from my batteries, seem to render its complete demolition within a few hours a matter of certainty;" and that if this demand were "not complied with or no reply thereto received within four hours after it is delivered into the hands of your (my) subordinate commander at Fort Wagner for transmission," a fire would be opened "on the city of Charleston from batteries already established within easy and effective range of the heart of the city." This communication to my address was without signature, and was of course returned.

About half past one o'clock one of your batteries did actually open fire, and threw a number of heavy shells into the city, the inhabitants of which, of course, were asleep and unwarned.

About nine o'clock this morning the communication alluded to above was returned to these headquarters, bearing your recognized official signature, and it can now be noticed as your deliberate official act.

Among nations, not barbarous, the usages of war prescribe that when a city is about to be attacked timely notice shall be given by the attacking commander, in order that non-combatants may have an opportunity for withdrawing beyond its limits. Generally the time allowed is from one to three days; that is, time for the withdrawal in good faith of at least the women and children. You, sir, give only four hours, knowing that your notice, under existing circumstances, could not reach me in less than two hours, and that not less than the same time would be required for an answer to be conveyed from this city to Battery Wagner. With this knowledge, you threaten to open fire on the city, not to oblige its surrender, but to force me to evacuate these works, which you, assisted by a great naval force, have been attacking in vain for more than forty days.

Batteries Wagner and Gregg and Fort Sumter are nearly due north from your batteries on Morris Island, and in distance therefrom varying from half a mile to two and a quarter miles. The city, on the other hand, is to the northwest, and quite five miles distant from the battery opened against it this morning.

It would appear, sir, that, despairing of reducing these works, you now resort to the novel measure of turning your guns against the old men, the women, and children, and the hospitals of a sleeping city, an act of inexcusable barbarity from your own confessed point of sight, inasmuch as you allege that the complete demolition of Fort Sumter within a few hours by your guns seems to you "a matter of certainty."

Your omission to attach your signature to such a grave paper must show the recklessness of the course upon which you have adventured; while the facts that you knowingly fixed a limit for receiving an answer to your demand, which made it almost beyond the possibility of receiving any reply within that time, and that you actually did open fire and throw a number of the most destructive missiles ever used in war into the midst of a city taken unawares, and filled with sleeping women and children, will give you a "bad eminence" in history, even in the history of this war.

I am only surprised, sir, at the limits you have set to your demands. If, in order to attain the abandonment of Morris Island and Fort Sumter, you feel authorized to fire on this city, why did you not also include the works on Sullivan's and James's Island—nay, even the city of Charleston in the same demand?

Since you have felt warranted in inaugurating this method of reducing batteries in your immediate front, which were found otherwise impregnable, and a mode of warfare which I confidently declare to be atrocious and unworthy of any soldier, I now solemnly warn you that if you fire again on the city from your Morris Island batteries without giving a somewhat more reasonable time to remove non-combatants, I shall feel impelled to employ such stringent means of retaliation as may be available during the continuance of this attack.

Finally, I reply, that neither the works on Morris Island nor Fort Sumter will be evacuated on the demand you have been pleased to make. Already, however, I am taking measures to remove all non-combatants, who are now fully aware of and alive to what they may expect at your hands.

Respectfully, your obedient servant,

G. T. BEAUREGARD, Gen. Com'g.

To this letter Gen. Gillmore made the following response:

DEPARTMENT OF THE SOUTH, HEADQUARTERS IN THE FIELD, MORRIS ISLAND, S. C., *August 22d*, 9 P. M.

G. T. Beauregard, Commanding Confederate State Forces, Charleston, S. C.:

SIR: I have the honor to acknowledge the receipt of your communication of this date, complaining that one of my batteries has opened upon the city of Charleston, and thrown a number of heavy rifle shells into that city, the inhabitants of which, of course, were asleep and unwarned.

My letter to you demanding the surrender of Fort Sumter and Morris Island, and threatening, in default thereof, to open fire upon Charleston, was delivered near Fort Wagner at 11.15 o'clock P. M. on the 21st instant, and should have arrived at your headquarters in time to have permitted your answer to reach me within the limit assigned, namely, four hours.

The fact that you were absent from your headquarters at the time of its arrival may be regarded as an unfortunate circumstance for the city of Charleston, but it is one for which I clearly am not responsible. This letter bore date at my headquarters, and was officially delivered by an officer of my staff. The inadvertent omission of my signature doubtless affords ground for special pleading, but it is not the argument of a commander solicitous only for the safety of sleeping women and children and unarmed men.

Your threats of retaliation for acts of mine, which you do not allege to be in violation of civilized warfare, except as regards the length of time allowed as notice of my intentions, are passed by without comment. I will, however, call your attention to the well established principle, that the commander of a place attacked, but not invested, having its avenues of escape open and practicable, has no right to expect any notice of an intended bombardment other than that which is given by the threatening attitude of his adversary. Even had this letter not been written, the city of Charleston has had, according to your own computation, forty days' notice of her danger. During that time my attack upon her defences has steadily progressed. The ultimate object of that attack has at no time been doubtful.

If, under the circumstances, the life of a single non-combatant is exposed to peril by the bombardment of the city, the responsibility rests with those who have first failed to apprize the non-combatants, or secure the safety of the city, after having held control of all its approaches for a period of nearly two years and a half, in the presence of a threatening force, and who afterward refused to accept the terms upon which the bombardment might have been postponed. From various sources, official and otherwise, I am led to believe that most of the women and children of Charleston were long since removed from the city. But, upon your assurance that the city is still full of them, I shall suspend the bombardment until 11 o'clock P. M. to-morrow,' thus giving you two days from the time you acknowledged to have received my communication of the 21st instant.

Very respectfully, your obedient servant,
Q. A. GILLMORE,
Brigadier-General Commanding.

The effect of the shells first fired at Charleston is thus described by a citizen: "Between one and two o'clock, Saturday morning, the enemy commenced firing on the city, arousing the people from their slumbers. Twelve 8-inch shells fell into the city, thirteen in all having been fired. Fortunately no person was injured. Several shells flew in the direction of St. Michael's steeple, and fell either in the vacant lots in the burnt district on King street, or more generally struck in Queen and Rutledge, where an 8-inch shell tore up the plank-road, and dug a large hole in the ground. Another shot entered the warehouse of G. W. Williams and Co., at the corner of Hayne and Church streets, entered the roof, and exploded in the upper story, making a large opening in the brick wall of the Medical Purveyor's storehouse next door, and scattering things in great confusion. Some loose straw or packing was set on fire by the explosion, which caused the alarm bell to ring, and brought out the firemen. It was extinguished with little effort before it had made any progress. Four shells fell in this locality. One large piece was picked up and exhibited at the guard-house, where it was the subject of much curiosity. There was a good deal of excitement and some surprise expressed at the enemy being able to reach the city from his present position. The battery is located in the marsh between Morris and Black Islands, distant fully five miles from Charleston."

On Wednesday, August 26th, Gen. Gillmore, having completed a fourth parallel and sap, which extended very close to Fort Wagner, determined to possess a ridge of sand which interposed, and was necessary to the success of his operations. It was constantly occupied by a strong body of the enemy's pickets, and at night by a force protected by rifle pits. A bombardment of the position was made just before dark, after which it was carried by the 24th Massachusetts. One company of North Carolina troops was captured. On the 7th of September, Morris Island was evacuated by the enemy, which is thus reported by Gen. Gillmore:

DEPARTMENT OF THE SOUTH, HEADQUARTERS IN THE FIELD, *September 7th*, 1863.

Maj.-Gen. H. W. Halleck, General-in-Chief:

GENERAL: I have the honor to report that Fort Wagner and Battery Gregg are ours. Last night our sappers mined the counter-scarp of Fort Wagner on its sea point, unmasking all its guns, and an order was issued to carry the place by assault at 9 o'clock this morning, that being the hour of low tide.

About 10 o'clock last night the enemy commenced evacuating the island, and all but seventy-five of them made their escape from Cummings's Point in small boats.

Captured despatches show that Fort Wagner was commanded by Col. Keitt, of South Carolina, and garrisoned by 1,400 effective men, and Battery Gregg by between 100 and 200 men.

Fort Wagner is a work of the most formidable kind. Its bomb-proof shelter, capable of containing 1,800 men, remains intact after the most terrific bombardment to which any work was ever subjected.

We have captured nineteen pieces of artillery and a large supply of excellent ammunition.

The city and harbor of Charleston are now completely covered by my guns.

I have the honor to be, General, very respectfully, your obedient servant, Q. A. GILLMORE,
Brigadier-General Commanding.

On the night of the 7th, an assault was made by an expedition on Fort Sumter. The flotilla consisted of between twenty-five and thirty boats, manned by over one hundred sailors, under Lieutenant Commandant Williams, and a hundred marines, under Capt. McCawley. The entire force was commanded by Commander Stephens, of the Patapsco. The boats were towed within a short distance of the fort, when they advanced. Three boats, under Commander Williams, Lieut. Remey, and Ensign Porter, landed, and the parties attempted to run up the ruins to the parapet, when they were fired upon by musketry, and hand grenades were thrown down upon them. The slope was so sharp that they were unable to reach the parapet. The signal was given from the fort, and in an instant all of the batteries of the enemy opened on the fort and shelled it terribly. Three boats were smashed, and all who landed were either killed or captured. Lieut. Bradford, of the marines, was mortally wounded and captured. Among others captured were Commander Williams, Lieut. Remey, Lieut. Preston, Lieut. Bower, Lieut. Bunce, Dr. Wheeler, and Ensign Porter. Forty or fifty sailors and marines were killed and wounded. The entire list of casualties was about eighty. The remainder of the command retired safe.

The captured forts on Morris Island were enlarged and new batteries erected by Gen. Gillmore, which effectually commanded Fort Sumter, and could aid any naval attack on Charleston. But little further progress, however, was made in the siege during the remainder of the year. The forts of the enemy were occasionally bombarded severely, and the shelling of Charleston at intervals, during day and night, was continued. The portion of the city within the reach of the shells was greatly injured, and entirely abandoned by its inhabitants. An attempt was made by the enemy to blow up the frigate Ironsides, with a torpedo, on the night of October 5th. It failed of success, and did no serious damage to the vessels.

Some further operations took place in the Department of the Gulf during the year. After the capture of Vicksburg, Gen. Banks was reënforced by Gen. Grant, and an expedition was fitted out under Gen. Franklin to occupy the mouth of the Sabine river, in Texas. It consisted of a force of four thousand men, and the naval steamers Clifton, Sachem, Arizona, and Granite City. The squadron was under the command of Lieut. Crocker. The defences at the pass were supposed to consist of two 32-pounders, *en barbette*, and a battery of field pieces, and two boats used on the bay, which had been converted into rams. The plan was that the squadron should make the attack alone, assisted by about one hundred and eighty sharpshooters divided among the four vessels, and, having driven the enemy from his defences and destroyed or driven off the rams, the transports were then to advance and land their troops.

Sabine Pass is the name of the outlet from Sabine Lake into the Gulf of Mexico. Sabine Lake is an expansion of the Sabine river about five miles from its entrance into the Gulf of Mexico, at the southwest extremity of Louisiana. Its length is 18 miles and its breadth 9 miles. Sabine river rises in Hunt county, Texas, and flows in a direction east of southeast until it strikes the eastern boundary of the State. From this point it pursues a southerly course, forming the boundary between Texas and Louisiana. It is very shallow at its mouth. The whole length of the river is estimated at 500 miles.

Early on the morning of Sept. 8th, the Clifton stood in the bay and opened on the fort, to which no reply was made. At 9 A. M. the Sachem, Arizona, and Granite City, followed by the transports, stood over the bar, and, with much difficulty, owing to the low water, reached an anchorage about two miles from the fort at 11 A. M. About the middle of the afternoon the Sachem, followed by the Arizona, advanced up the eastern channel to draw the fire of the forts while the Clifton advanced up the western channel. The Granite City remained to cover the landing of a division of troops under Gen. Weitzel. No reply was made to the fire of the gunboats until they were abreast of the forts, when eight guns opened fire upon them. Three of these were rifled. Almost at the same moment the Clifton and Sachem were struck in their boilers and both vessels enveloped in steam. The Arizona, not having room to pass the Sachem, then backed down the channel until she grounded by the stern, when the ebb-tide caught her bows and swung her across the channel. White flags were raised on the Clifton and Sachem, and within twenty minutes they were taken in tow by the enemy. The naval force of the expedition being thus disabled, the transports moved out of the bay. The Arizona was got afloat during the night and followed. The expedition then returned to Brashear City. The officers and crews of the Clifton and Sachem and about ninety sharpshooters who were on board were captured, and the loss in killed and wounded was about thirty. After remaining at Brashear City some time, the military force moved to Franklin and Vermillionville.

On the 27th of October an expedition under Gen. Banks put to sea from New Orleans. It consisted of about twenty vessels accompanied by the gunboats Owasco, Virginia, and Monongahela, and was destined to the mouth of the Rio Grande river, which is the boundary line between Texas and Mexico. During the first three days out the weather was pleasant. On the fourth a "norther" prevailed, and one light draft steamer and two schooners were lost, but no lives. On the 31st the expedition anchored off the mouth of the river and on the next day a force was landed on Brazos Island. By the 4th the troops were all landed, and on the next day, Gen. Banks, preceded by a small body of infantry and artillery, entered Brownsville on the Rio Grande river. A small body of the enemy under Gen. Bee attempted to destroy the public property, and retired on the approach of the Federal force. Subsequently Corpus Christi and the coast of Texas to within one hundred miles of Galveston were occupied. Gen. Banks successfully prosecuted the campaign thus begun in Texas, the extent and results of which more properly belong to the records of 1864.

In Missouri and the Department of the Frontier, those portions of the Confederate army of the Trans-Mississippi Department, which was under command of Gens. Hindman, Sterling Price, and Marmaduke, maintained a restless activity.

Early in January, 1863, a force of five or six thousand men, under Gen. Marmaduke's command, comprising a portion of the troops which had been so signally defeated at Crawford's Prairie (as described on a former page) a month before, proceeded down the Arkansas river to Spadry's Bluff, near Clarksville, Ark., and thence marched rapidly north toward Springfield, Mo., with the intention of seizing and destroying the large amount of Federal commissary and quartermaster stores accumulated there for the supply of the Army of the Frontier. The design of Gen. Marmaduke in proceeding so far eastward before making a movement northward into Missouri was to avoid all chance of collision or interference with his plans by Gens. Blunt and Herron. He hoped to reach Springfield and accomplish his purpose before they could obtain intelligence of his approach, and this once accomplished, those Federal generals and their army, deprived of all supplies, would, almost of necessity, be compelled either to surrender to Gen. Hindman or fly from North-western Arkansas. The scheme was well planned and circumstances indicated that it would be successful. Springfield had some defensive works, but they were not completed, and the Federal troops which were necessary to its adequate defence, were scattered widely over the entire region of South-western Missouri, two or three companies in a place. When, on the afternoon of the 7th of January, it was ascertained that the Confederate force had burned Lawrence Mills, and were then marching on Ozark, and would certainly appear before Springfield the next day, Brig.-Gens. Brown and Holland, who were in command there, the one of the Missouri State militia and the other of the enrolled Missouri militia, exerted themselves to the utmost to call together a force adequate to the defence of the town, but their most strenuous efforts only sufficed to bring together about 1,100 men, of whom 400 were either convalescents in the hospitals or those who had just been discharged from those institutions, and the remainder were in about equal numbers Missouri State militia and enrolled Missouri militia, almost wholly raw troops. The commissary and quartermaster's stores were sent north toward Bolivar, only enough being reserved to maintain the siege, which were placed in one of the forts. The Confederate force (or rather about one-half of it, not far from three thousand men) appeared before the city about one P. M. on the 8th, and commenced firing with solid shot at once, without giving any notice for the removal of non-combatants. The fighting which followed was irregular, and occasionally the Confederates gained some advantages; but the courage of the new Federal troops seemed to increase under fire, and late in the afternoon they commenced driving the enemy from one position after another, till at night the battle ended, having continued five hours, when the Confederates retreated, carrying with them a part of their wounded. The Federal loss was 14 killed, 145 wounded and 5 missing. The Confederates lost 41 killed, and over 160 wounded, of whom 80 were left in the town as prisoners. The next day the garrison of the town were ready to renew the battle, but found that the Confederates had escaped, and they were too feeble to make a vigorous pursuit.

Before proceeding from Ozark to Springfield, Gen. Marmaduke had detached Gen. Porter with nearly 3,000 men to follow the road south of the Ozark mountains to Hartsville, and having made what captures he could there, to rejoin the main force again at or near Marshfield, having in view, probably, the extension of his expedition either to Lebanon or Bolivar. On the 9th, Gen. Porter occupied Hartsville, but evacuated it that night, and moved toward Marshfield. Gen. Fitz Henry Warren, in command of that Federal military district, sent from Houston on the 9th of January Col. Merrill, with 850 men, to Springfield to reënforce the Federal garrison there. They reached Hartsville on Saturday, the 10th, and learned that Gen. Porter had been there the day previous. Leaving Hartsville at 3 P. M. they marched to Wood's Forks, on the road toward Springfield, by nightfall, and encamped in line of battle. The next morning (Jan. 11th), at daybreak, they encountered Gen. Marmaduke's forces marching from Springfield, and though the Federal position was an unfavorable one, Col. Merrill fought till 9 o'clock A. M., when the Confederates withdrew in a southerly direction. Sending out a pursuing force of cavalry, and himself returning toward Hartsville, Col. Merrill soon found that the Confederates were also marching toward Hartsville, and, as it afterward appeared, had formed a junction with Gen. Porter's command. Col. Merrill immediately ordered a forced march, and arrived in Hartsville in time to take a strong position, and awaited their attack. Firing commenced on both sides at a little after 11 A. M., and the battle raged till half-past 4 P. M., the Confederates charging repeatedly upon the Federal position, but being met at short musket range by so terrible a fire that they were compelled to fall back each time. At length, finding themselves unable to make any impression on the Federal garrison, the Confederates retreated, going at first toward Houston, but early the next morning they turned their faces southward, and moved rapidly toward the Arkansas line, near the north fork of White river. Their losses had been very heavy; Brig.-Gen. Emmet McDonald, and acting Brig.-Gen. Porter, two colonels, a major, a captain, and two lieutenants being among the killed, and several other officers severely wounded. Their entire loss was over 300 killed and wounded, and 29 prisoners. The Federal loss was 7 killed, 64 wounded, and 7 missing.

A portion of Gen. Marmaduke's force made their way to Van Buren Creek, and 300 of them were taken prisoners, on the Julia Roan, on the 28th of January. The greater part, however, descended the White river, and, with Marmaduke himself, camped at Batesville, Ark., from which town they were driven, after a sharp fight, by the Federal Col. Waring, on the 4th of February, a considerable number of the Confederates being killed and wounded, and a colonel and a number of privates being captured.

Gen. Marmaduke now repaired to the headquarters of the Confederate army corps in Arkansas, at Little Rock, and the next two months were spent by the generals of that corps mainly in enlarging and disciplining their force. The guerilla bands in Arkansas and Missouri made frequent dashes into the towns, and occasionally stopped steamers on the Missouri river, and plundered, captured, and murdered Federal citizens and soldiers, as in the case of the Sam Gaty, on the 28th of March, but these were only the acts of the irregular and bushwhacking troops in Missouri, and they generally met with swift retribution from the militia scouts and cavalry parties who patrolled all sections of that State. There was no considerable movement of Confederate troops till the latter part of April.

On the 17th of April, the Confederate general, Cabell, left Ozark, Arkansas, with two thousand men, two pieces of artillery, and three days' rations, to attack Fayetteville, Arkansas, which had been so many times a battle ground, and was then garrisoned by two regiments of Federal troops (the 1st Arkansas infantry and the 1st Arkansas cavalry), under the command of Col. M. La Rue Harrison. The attack was made on the 18th about sunrise, and after nearly six hours' severe fighting the Confederates were thoroughly defeated and in full retreat for Ozark. Gen. Marmaduke and his superior officer, Maj.-Gen. Sterling Price, having at last collected a sufficiency of troops, mostly Texans, and a large portion of them cavalry, to render an expedition into Missouri probably successful, sought and obtained permission to attempt the capture and destruction of Cape Girardeau, at that time the depot of supplies for a portion of Gen. Grant's army. The Confederate force, which consisted of Price's (1st) army corps of the trans-Mississippi Department, numbering somewhat more than ten thousand men, under the command of Gen. Marmaduke, left Little Rock, Arkansas, about the middle of April, and on the 20th had crossed the State line, and following the course of the St. Francis river, reached Fredericktown, Mo., about the 22d. From this point they marched upon Cape Girardeau, and came before the town on the 25th. The garrison there was under the command of Gen. John McNeil, and consisted of one thousand seven hundred men, mostly militia. Gen. McNeil had reached Cape Girardeau on the night of the 23d, and had taken immediate measures for the removal of the Government stores into Illinois, and had sent to St. Louis for reënforcements. Confident of success, the Confederates, though repulsed in their first attack, demanded on Saturday night (25th) the surrender of the town, the demand being made by acting Brig.-Gen. Carter, whose brigade was in the advance. Gen. McNeil replied at once, declining to surrender, as he believed himself capable of maintaining its possession. Fighting was not resumed till 10 A. M. of the 26th, when Gen. Marmaduke again demanded a surrender, threatening to storm the town in case of refusal. Gen. McNeil again refused, and after nearly five hours' fighting, in which the Federal artillery, which was admirably served, caused great havoc among the Confederate troops, Gen. Marmaduke retreated southward. He was pursued closely by Gen. Vandever and Gen. McNeil, and harassed severely, but succeeded in escaping into Arkansas, on the 2d of May. His loss in the battle of Cape Girardeau was sixty killed and about three hundred wounded. In his retreat he also lost a considerable number of killed and wounded, and many prisoners.

On the 6th of May a Federal force of about one thousand cavalry, and about the same number of infantry, under command of Col. (acting brigadier-general) Powell Clayton, left Helena, Arkansas, on an expedition to the region of Arkansas, lying between the White and St. Francis rivers, to break up a band of guerillas, and destroy Confederate stores accumulated there. The infantry went only as far as Snitzn's and then returned to Mariana. The cavalry proceeded to the vicinity of Taylor's Creek, a large detachment, however, going to Mount Vernon, and at these points, on the 11th of May, the two small bodies of cavalry, one numbering two hundred and thirty men, and the other seven hundred and twenty-five, had each a severe fight with separate brigades of Marmaduke's division, and both repulsed them with heavy loss to the Confederates.

On the 20th of May, the Federal forces, about one thousand two hundred in number, under the command of Col. William A. Phillips, near Fort Gibson, Indian Territory, were attacked by the Confederates, under Col. (acting brigadier-general) Coffey, commanding a force of five regiments. After a desultory fight, in which, through the cowardice of the Creek regiment, the Federal troops lost a part of their cattle, Col. Phillips succeeded in driving the Confederate troops over the mountain, and finally, in complete disorder, across the Arkansas river. The loss on the Federal side was about twenty-six in killed, wounded, and missing; that of the Confederates considerably larger. There were repeated skirmishes in this and other portions of the department, but no severe fighting in the Indian Territory, till July 15th, when Maj.-Gen. Blunt crossed the Arkansas river near Henry Springs, in that territory, and on the 16th attacked a superior force of Confederates under Gen. Cooper, which he completely routed, they leaving their dead and wounded on the field. The Federal loss was seventeen killed and sixty wounded, while that of the Confederates was one hundred and fifty killed (buried on the field by the Federal troops), four hundred wounded, seventy-seven prisoners, and one piece of artillery and one hundred stand of arms captured. After several subsequent skirmishes with the Confederates, Gen. Blunt descended the Arkansas river, and on the 1st of September occupied Fort Smith, Arkansas. The army of the frontier having been greatly depleted to furnish reënforcements to Gen. Grant, while he was engaged in the siege of Vicksburg, the Confederate generals in the Trans-Mississippi Department took advantage of the fact to make an attack on Helena, Arkansas, where the Federal general, Prentiss, was in command, with a force of about four thousand troops. Here again Gen. Sterling Price and Gen. Marmaduke found scope for action. The Confederate attack was made on the 4th of July, with a force of about fifteen thousand men. It was commenced about daylight, and, at first, they were successful in capturing a small fort forming a part of the outworks, but the gunboat Tyler, coming up opportunely, and opening upon them with its heavy guns, they were compelled to abandon it with severe loss. Determined not to relinquish their purpose, the Confederates fought desperately, charging repeatedly, and with large masses, upon the defences of the town, attacking now the north, and now the south side, but everywhere they met with the same terrible resistance from the Federal fire at short range, and from the large missiles from the gunboat; and at length, utterly foiled at every point, having lost over one thousand in killed and wounded, and more than one thousand one hundred prisoners, the Confederates fell back, and though remaining for a day or two in the vicinity, in hope of an opportunity to renew the attack, finding the Federal garrison reënforced, retreated to the interior of Arkansas.

After the surrender of Vicksburg, the Federal Gen. Steele was sent to Helena, with a considerable force, and instructed to form a junction with Gen. Davidson, who was moving south from Missouri, by way of Crowley's Ridge, west of the St. Francis, and with the combined force drive the Confederates south of the Arkansas River. Having effected this junction and established his depot and hospitals at Duvall's Bluff, on the White River, Gen. Steele, on the 1st of August, advanced against the Confederate army, which fell back toward Little Rock. After several successful skirmishes, he reached the Arkansas River, and threw part of his force upon the south side, to threaten the Confederate communications with Arkadelphia, their depot of supplies, and flank their position at Little Rock. Gen. Marmaduke was sent out with a cavalry force to beat the Federals back, but was completely routed. Seeing what must be the inevitable result of this movement of Gen. Steele, the Confederate Gen. Holmes destroyed what property he could, and after a slight resistance retreated with his army in great disorder, pursued by the Federal cavalry, and on the 10th of September Gen. Steele, with the Federal army, entered the capital of Arkansas. His entire losses in killed, wounded, and missing, in this whole movement, did not exceed one hundred. He captured one thousand prisoners, and such public property as the Confederates had not time to destroy. The Federal cavalry continued to press the retreating Confederates southward; but a small force, which had eluded pursuit, and moved eastward, attacked the Federal garrison at Pine Bluff, on the Arkansas, south of Little Rock, hoping to recapture it and thus cripple the Federals and break their communications. The attempt, which was made on the 28th of October, was repulsed with decided loss on the part of the Confederates, and the same day the Federal cavalry occupied Arkadelphia, and the Confederates retreated toward the Red River. This completely restored Arkansas to the Federal authority, except a small district in the extreme southwest, and the region of Northwest Arkansas, over which the guerrilla and other irregular troops of the Confederates continued to roam, in their plundering excursions into Missouri, Kansas, and the Indian Territory. Some of these were conducted on a large scale, and were accompanied by acts of most atrocious inhumanity. On the 20th of August one of the guerrilla leaders, who had assumed the name of Quantrell, or Quantrile, with a force of eight hundred, entered the city of Lawrence, Kansas; murdered in cold blood one hundred and twenty-five of its citizens, and burned the greater part of the city, destroying property to the value of over $2,000,000. He was pursued as soon as troops could be raised, and forty or fifty of his men killed. The Confederate Gen. Cabell, collecting together as many of the guerrillas and Indians as possible, and some of the routed troops, driven from Little Rock and its vicinity, started with a force variously estimated at from 4,000 to 10,000, in the latter part of September, from the Choctaw settlements of the Indian Territory, crossed the Arkansas River east of Fort Smith, and on the 1st of October, a detachment of his troops, under Gen. Shelby, joined Coffey at Crooked Prairie, Mo., intending to make a raid into Southwestern Missouri. This combined force, numbering 2,000 or 2,500 men, penetrated as far as the Missouri River at Booneville, but were pursued by the Missouri militia, and finally brought to a stand about eight miles southwest of Arrow Rock, on the evening of the 12th of October, Gen. E. B. Brown, who commanded the Federal troops, fought them till dark that evening, and, during the night, having detached a small force to attack them in the rear, renewed the battle the next morning at eight A. M. After a sharp contest they fled, completely routed and broken up, with a loss of several hundred in killed, wounded, and prisoners. They were pursued to the Arkansas line, and prisoners gleaned all the way. Gen. Marmaduke, who seems to have been with Gen. Cabell, attempted to advance from Fayettville, Ark., to reënforce them, but found them so thoroughly disorganized that the case was hopeless.

Early in October a desperate effort was made to capture and murder Gen. Blunt and his staff, who was at this time marching toward Fort Scott, Kansas. Three hundred Confederate soldiers in Union uniform approached him as he with his escort was in advance of his wagons. The escort, consisting of a hundred men, broke when the Confederates commenced firing on them, and seventy-eight of the hundred, including Major Curtis, a son of Gen. Curtis, were captured, and murdered after their capture. Gen. Blunt succeeded in rallying fifteen of the escort, and with these he advanced on his assailants, who retreated, till he found an opportunity of moving south, and joining the remainder of his command. These men, who thus murdered their prisoners, were under the command of Quantrell. The Confederates supposed that Gen. Blunt had been killed, and greatly rejoiced over his death. On the 20th of October Gen. Blunt was relieved from the command of the Army of the Frontier, and Gen. McNeil appointed his successor.

With these last convulsive throes, the active existence of the Confederate authority in Arkansas died out. On the 12th of November a meeting was held at Little Rock, to consult on measures for the restoration of the State to the Union, and was succeeded by others in different parts of the State.

The most atrocious outrage of the war was the attack of Col. Quantrell and his band of

Confederate guerrillas upon the thriving city of Lawrence, on the 21st of August, 1863. The attack was made in the early morning, and entirely without warning. The citizens, unarmed, were unable to make any defence, and were many of them shot down in the streets in cold blood. The Eldridge House, the largest hotel in the city, and all the stores on Massachusetts Street, the principal business street, were plundered and burned, as were many dwellings and stores in other parts of the city. Two hundred and five men were killed and many others wounded. No women or children were killed or wounded, though one assailant snapped his pistol at Miss Lydia Stone, a heroic woman, who had exposed her life for the preservation of others. Several of the churches were destroyed, and the property stolen and burned was estimated to exceed the value of $2,000,000. Quantrell, the leader of the gang, had been at one time a resident of Lawrence. Senator Lane (General James H. Lane) was in Lawrence at the time, but succeeded in avoiding the guerrillas, and as soon as they left the town raised such force as could be gathered and started in pursuit. Some thirty or forty of the guerrillas were overtaken and slain, but the remainder got away safely with their plunder. Much indignation was felt by the citizens of Kansas at the alleged remissness of General Ewing, who was in command of the district of Kansas and Western Missouri, and of General Schofield, who commanded the Department of Missouri. Two days after the attack, General Ewing issued the following order:

KANSAS CITY, MO., August 23, 1863.

All persons living in Jackson, Cass, and Bates Counties, Missouri, and that part of Vernon County included in this district, except those living within one mile of the limits of Independence, Hickman's Mill, Pleasant Hill, and Harrisonville, and except those in Kaw township, Jackson County, north of this creek and west of the Big Blue, embracing Kansas City and Westport, are hereby ordered to remove from their present places of residence within fifteen days from the date hereof.

Those who within that time prove their loyalty to the satisfaction of the commanding officer of the military station nearest their present places of residence, will receive from him certificates stating the fact of their loyalty and the names of the witnesses by whom it can be sworn. All who have received such certificates will be permitted to remove to any military station in this district, or to any part of Kansas except the counties on the eastern border of the State. All others shall remove out of this district. Officers commanding companies and detachments serving in companies, will see that this paragraph is promptly obeyed.

All hay or grain in the field or under shelter in the district from which the inhabitants are required to remove within reach of the military stations after the 9th of September next, will be taken to such stations and turned over to the proper officers there, and a report of the amount so turned over made to the district headquarters, specifying the names of all loyal owners and the amount of such produce taken from them. All grain and hay found in such districts after the 9th of September next, not convenient to such stations, will be destroyed.

Quantrell and his band of marauders for some time hovered around the Kansas border.

The Department of the Northwest was not without its disturbances, though the wholesale massacres of the previous year were, happily, not repeated. During the spring and early summer there were occasional outrages on the part of the Sioux of Minnesota and Dakota, who penetrated the lines, although a guard of 2,000 men were stationed along the frontier, and murdered about 30 persons. About a dozen of these assassins were captured or killed. Early in June General Sibley started with a force of between two and three thousand men for Devil's Lake, in Dakota Territory, 500 miles from St. Paul's, and sent General Sully, about the same time, with a large body of cavalry, up the Missouri, to coöperate with him in cutting off the retreat of the savages. On the 3d of July, Little Crow, the principal chief of the Sioux, who had been actively engaged during the winter and spring in endeavoring to raise the Sioux and Yanktonians to make another attack upon the settlers in Minnesota, and had endeavored to obtain guns and ammunition from British America, was killed by Mr. Sampson, about six miles north of Hutchinson, Minnesota. He was not fully identified till some time after. The cavalry force under General Sully failed to connect with General Sibley, and that General encountered the Indians, near Missouri Conteau, on the 25th of July, and engagements followed between that date and the 29th, at Big Mound, Dead Buffalo Lake, Stony Lake, and on the banks of the Missouri. In these engagements between 60 and 70 of the Indians were killed and as many more wounded. The loss of General Sibley's troops was five killed and four wounded. On the 3d of September General Sully encountered and defeated a body of Indians at Whitestone Hall, about 130 miles above the little Cheyenne. A part of these Indians had previously been engaged against Gen. Sibley. A large number of them were killed and wounded, and 156 taken prisoners. Gen. Sully's loss was 20 killed and 38 wounded. The Indians fled across the Missouri, and most of them, it is believed, took refuge in Idaho Territory, where they were, late in the year, guilty of some outrages.

In January, 1863, roving bands of Indians committed some thefts, robberies, and murders in the western part of what is now called Idaho Territory, in the vicinity of Bear River. Acting Brig.-General Connor, in command in that region, marched with a force of 275 men to Bear River, a distance of 140 miles, through deep snows, in which 76 of his men were disabled by frozen feet, and with 200 men attacked the Indian stronghold, in which 300 warriors were assembled, and after a hard-fought battle of four hours, destroyed the entire band, leaving 224 dead upon the field. His own loss was 14 killed and 49 wounded. Since that time the Indians in that quarter have been quiet.

At the close of 1863 the federal armies had made large progress. The State of Missouri was placed beyond the danger of an invasion.

The military power of the enemy in Arkansas was broken, and the greatest portion of the State made subject to the army of the Union. The occupation of the mouth of the Rio Grande, in Western Texas, had destroyed one outlet from the Confederacy to foreign countries, and the commerce which thereby existed. The capture of Vicksburg and Port Hudson removed from the banks of the Mississippi every military station of the enemy, by which the navigation of that river could be closed. It broke up the facilities for communication between the States east and west of that river, and, with the occupation of the eastern part of Tennessee, gave the Federal arms the entire control of that State. It brought under the same control a part of the States of Mississippi and Louisiana on the shores of the river. In the East there was no material change in the position of military affairs. No operations of any magnitude had taken place in the Departments of Virginia and North Carolina. And with the exception of the siege of Charleston, the same is true of the department of the South, embracing the States of South Carolina, Georgia, and Florida. The territory thus lost by the enemy embraced some of the most important districts for producing grain and cattle in the Southern States. It also contained some valuable deposits of nitre, used for the manufacture of gunpowder. The Secretary of War, in his annual report, in December, said: "The success of our arms during the last year has enabled the Department to make a reduction of over two hundred millions of dollars in the war estimate for the ensuing fiscal year."

The desolation caused by the war is almost indescribable. The condition of Mississippi will serve as an illustration. When Gen. Grant's army advanced as far south as Oxford and the Yallabusha at the close of 1862, the inhabitants had an opportunity to purchase a few of the most indispensable articles of clothing and household economy, but in the part of the State between Jackson and Granada there had not been even the most meagre stock of goods taken for three years. The destitution of the poor there reduced them almost to a state of barbarism. Of the fifty plantations on the road from Lagrange, Tennessee, to Holly Springs, Mississippi, only five were occupied. The rest were abandoned, and in a majority of instances the buildings were burned. On the 26th of May, an expedition, consisting of the 10th Missouri, 7th Kansas, and 15th Illinois cavalry and 9th Illinois mounted infantry, left Corinth for the purpose of a raid through a portion of country which had escaped the ravages of war. The expedition passed to Florence, Ala., and Savannah, Tenn., and returned to Corinth on the 31st, being absent five days and nights. What it accomplished in so short a space of time is thus described:

We burned seven cotton factories, costing an average of $200,000 each. The Southern Confederacy had offered for the largest $1,000,000 containing three hundred looms. They employed on an average one hundred men and the same number of women and children each. But their contents were more valuable than the buildings and machinery, having a large amount of stock and manufactured goods on hand. A large amount of steam flouring and saw mills was likewise burned. A number of blacksmiths' and wagonmakers' shops were destroyed, they being employed on Government work, and containing large numbers of wagons, arms of all kinds, &c., &c. A ton of powder, a large number of arms of English manufacture, 600,000 rounds of fixed ammunition, each cartridge having the crown of England stamped upon it, and several boxes containing shell, were destroyed. A number of dwelling houses were accidentally burned by our shells. The splendid bridge near Florence was burned. All along the route, both going and returning, our command marched in line through the waving wheat, just ripe, utterly destroying it. An immense ("immense" is not the word—language cannot describe the scene—the smoke arising from burning corn cribs in every direction, and for miles each side of our path) amount of forage was destroyed; some was passed by on account of the close proximity of dwelling houses. Large quantities of meat, &c., were used, but more wasted and destroyed. The people appear to think that starvation is staring them in the face; but let their Government protect them, and they will no doubt fare very well. We captured two majors, two captains, four or five lieutenants, and about one hundred men. A large Rebel flag was also captured. An immense amount of stock —horses, mules, oxen, cows, carriages, &c., &c.—was taken and turned over to the Government. About twenty men, who have escaped conscription by lying in the bush and other places of concealment, accompanied us into camp, and are joining some one of our regiments here. We brought about one thousand contrabands—men, women, and children—about two hundred and fifty of them joining the negro brigade. And all with a loss of less than thirty wounded and missing.

About the same time an expedition consisting of six brigades, and numbering about ten thousand men, moved up between the Big Black and Yazoo Rivers. The object was to destroy the resources of the country, to prevent the enemy from subsisting their armies, and to drive out any force that might be in that region. The results of the expedition are thus described:

We have marched over a hundred miles in a week during the hottest kind of weather. We destroyed all the forage and supplies and cotton, and drove off all the cattle, horses, and mules between the two lines for a distance of fifty miles. We met no considerable body of the enemy, and had only one or two slight skirmishes; but we ascertained where the enemy was concentrating, and gained much valuable information which may be of use hereafter. It was made our painful but imperative duty to destroy every thing—corn, cotton, meat, mills, and cotton gins—that we could find, sparing only dwellings and a small supply of provisions for each family. The command will rest here for a day or so, and then return to Vicksburg, which cannot hold out very long against our forces.

The number of locomotives and cars destroyed on the railroads of Mississippi during the year is stated to have been seventy-seven of the former, and about six hundred of the latter. Owing to the destruction of bridges it was impossible to remove a large portion of the former after they were captured.

On the 1st of August Gen. Grant issued the following order recommending that in the region subject to his arms the freedom of the negroes should be acknowledged, and instead of compulsory labor, contracts upon fair terms should be made between master and servants:

HEADQUATERS DEP'T. OF THE TENNESSEE,
VICKSBURG, MISS., *August* 1st, 1863.

1. All regular organized bodies of the enemy having been driven from those parts of Kentucky and Tennessee west of the Tennessee River, and from all Mississippi west of the Mississippi Central Railroad, and it being to the interest of those districts not to invite the presence of armed bodies of men among them, it is announced that the most rigorous penalties will hereafter be inflicted upon the following class of prisoners, to wit: All irregular bodies of cavalry not mustered and paid by the Confederate authorities; all persons engaged in conscription, or in apprehending deserters, whether regular or irregular; all citizens encouraging or aiding the same; and all persons detected firing upon unarmed transports. It is not contemplated that this order shall affect the treatment due to prisoners of war captured within the districts named, when they are members of legally organized companies, and when their acts are in accordance with the usages of civilized warfare.

2. The citizens of Mississippi within the limits above described are called upon to pursue their peaceful avocations, in obedience to the laws of the United States. Whilst doing so in good faith, all United States forces are prohibited from molesting them in any way. It is earnestly recommended that the freedom of negroes be acknowledged, and that instead of compulsory labor contracts upon fair terms be entered into between the former masters and servants, or between the latter and such other persons as may be willing to give them employment. Such a system as this, honestly followed, will result in substantial advantages to all parties.

All private property will be respected except when the use of it is necessary for the Government, in which case it must be taken under the direction of a corps commander, and by a proper detail under charge of a commissioned officer, with specific instructions to seize certain property and no other. A staff officer of the quartermaster or subsistence department will, in each instance, be designated to receipt for such property as may be seized, the property to be paid for at the end of the war on proof of loyalty, or on proper adjustment of the claim, under such regulations or laws as may hereafter be established. All property seized under this order must be taken up on returns by the officer giving receipts, and disposed of in accordance with existing regulations. * * * *

4. Within the county of Warren, laid waste by the long presence of contending armies, the following rules to prevent suffering will be observed: Maj-Gen. Sherman, commanding the Fifteenth army corps, and Maj.-Gen McPherson, commanding the Seventeenth army corps, will each designate a commissary of subsistence, who will issue articles of prime necesity to all destitute families calling for them, under such restrictions for the protection of the Government as they deem necessary. Families who are able to pay for the provisions drawn will, in all cases, be required to do so.

On the march of Gen. Sherman from Eastport, Miss., where his army abandoned the Memphis and Charleston Railroad, to reënforce Gen. Grant at Chattanooga, his force was subsisted on the route.

A very limited amount of supplies was brought by wagons, but the whole country for miles on either flank was stripped of every article of food and every pound of forage. The citizens were sorely pressed, but the safety and sustenance of armies were balanced against this fact, and decided in favor of the latter. All animals capable of carrying a soldier, his gun and blanket, were pressed into the service, and almost the whole command consequently arrived mounted.

CHAPTER XXXVII.

Progress of Civil Affairs—Finances of the Insurrectionary States—Decay of Railroads—Crops—Mission of Mr. A. H. Stephens—His Report—President Lincoln's Statement of the Condition of Affairs—His Amnesty Proclamation—Efforts to secure the advantages of the Emancipation Proclamation—Freedmen—Federal Finances—Confiscation—Exchange of Prisoners.

THE progress of civil affairs is too important to be overlooked. The year 1863 did not exhibit much advance in a commercial point of view. The expectations that had been entertained of an immediate renewal of trade as a necessary consequence of the opening of the Mississippi, and the continued occupation of the Atlantic coast of South and North Carolina, and the penetration of the troops into the Texan country, were not realized; and the foreign commerce of the country was greatly contracted in face of the improved harvests in Europe. These have enabled the people to dispense with much of the breadstuffs and provisions which were the main staples of the national export.

Extensive regulations were adopted by the Government of the United States relative to trade with the inhabitants within the lines of the army in the insurrectionary States. The results, however, were very limited.

In the insurrectionary States the currency exerted a most unfavorable influence on their internal affairs, and very seriously diminished the hopes of the people of ultimate success in the war.

At the commencement of hostilities, the impression was universal that the war would be short. The most distinguished politicians, the wisest commercial men and capitalists of all classes, indeed every household, acted upon this view. Hence, every one was soon embarrassed for the want of hundreds of small articles, which might have been procured at cheap rates if the parties had been able to look only a few months into the future. This same short-sightedness controlled the financial affairs of the

Confederacy. Its loans were to be in bonds, and its currency was to be paper. The capital invested in the bonds was drawn principally from banks, from merchants who had been driven out of business, and from trust estates and charitable institutions. Such sources were soon exhausted, and it became impossible to make further progress in bonding by appeals to the patriotism of the people, in consequence of their peculiar habits. There were no great money capitalists in the community. The capital of the people consisted mainly in lands and negroes, and the habits of the wealthy for generations had kept them in one channel—that of producing cotton, tobacco, and rice—the surplus products to be invested in lands and negroes. This thirst for land and negro investments absorbed the millions of income, and kept the people generally in debt as much as a year's income. There existed no millionnaire bankers, merchants, manufacturers, and other moneyed capitalists, that lived in splendor on incomes derived from money at interest. Such people as those were not in a situation to invest in bonds; nor was it reasonable to expect them to volunteer to invest in bonds at the expense of incurring new debts, or with the necessity of selling property. Many, very many planters who subscribed to the cotton loan sold the bonds immediately, and invested the proceeds in the payment of debts, or in land and negroes, and were unwilling afterward to sell, even to aid the Government, any of their agricultural products for less than the highest market value for currency. Many were not willing to sell for currency at any price. The consequence of this was an act of impressment on the part of the Government, and starvation to towns and villages, and all that class of persons who live on fixed incomes.

The following is a statement of the finances at the close of the third quarter of 1863:

Receipts from January 1st to September 30th, 1863.

For eight per cent. stock	$107,292,900
For seven per cent. stock	38,737,650
For six per cent. stock	6,810,050
For five per cent. call certificates	22,992,900
For four per cent. call certificates	482,200
Cotton certificates, act of April 21st, 1862	2,000,000
Interest on loans	140,210
War tax	4,128,988
Treasury notes	391,623,530
Sequestration	1,862,556
Customs	934,798
Export duty on cotton	8,101
Patent fund	10,794
Miscellaneous, including repayments by disbursing officers	24,498,217
Total	$601,522,893

Expenditures during same period.

War Department	$377,988,244
Navy Department	38,437,661
Civil, Miscellaneous, etc.	11,629,278
Customs	56,636
Public debt	32,212,290
Notes cancelled and redeemed	59,044,449
Total expenditures	$519,368,559
Total of receipts	601,522,893
Balance in treasury	$82,154,334

Brought forward	$82,154,334
From which is to be deducted the amount of Treasury notes which have been funded and brought in for cancellation, but have not yet been regularly audited, estimated	65,000,000
Total	$17,154,334

The public debt (exclusive of the foreign loan) at the same period, was as follows:

Funded.

Eight per cents	$207,128,750
Seven per cents	42,745,600
Six per cents	41,006,270
Six per cent. cotton interest bonds	2,035,000
Total	$292,915,620

Unfunded.

Treasury notes: general currency	$603,632,798
Two-year notes	8,477,975
Interest notes at 3.65	627,450
Interest notes at 7.30	122,582,200
Under $5	4,887,095
Five per cent. call certificates	26,240,000
Total	$766,447,519
Deduct amount of Treasury notes funded and cancelled	65,000,000
Total	$701,447,519

In order to estimate the amount of Treasury notes in circulation at the date of this report, there must be added the further sum of one hundred millions for the two months which have elapsed since the date of the above schedules. The balance of appropriations made by Congress, and not drawn on September 30th, stood as follows:

War Department	$395,502,698
Navy Department	24,413,645
Civil, Miscellaneous, etc.	56,240,996
Customs	294,460
Total	$476,451,799

The estimates submitted by the various departments for the support of the Government, were made to July 1st, 1864, the end of the fiscal year, and were as follows:

Legislative Department	$309,005
Executive "	52,850
Treasury "	22,583,359
War "	438,078,870
Navy "	13,624,945
Post Office "	8,908
State "	544,409
Justice "	222,587
Total	$475 498,493

If these estimates be extended to embrace the remaining six months of the same year, they must be doubled, and that sum added to the undrawn appropriations would make an aggregate of $1,427,448,778.

The Confederate currency was sold during the year at six cents, and less, on the dollar. This depreciation was followed by most disastrous effects. The staple property of the country became worth two or three, and in some cases four, times its old value. But most of the articles of consumption, such as food and clothing, were from five to one hundred times their former value.

The most serious consequence which resulted from the depreciation of the currency, was the refusal of the agriculturists to sell their produce for the Government notes, or to sell only at the highest price. This determination, if adhered to, would result in the destruction of the army from a lack of supplies, and the starvation of the people who were engaged in other industrial pursuits in towns and cities. In anticipation of this danger, an act was passed by Congress in the beginning of the year, which authorized the Government to seize or impress all the produce necessary for the army. It provided that a board of commissioners should be appointed in each State, who should determine, every sixty days, the prices which the Government should pay for each article of produce impressed within the State. A central board of commissioners was also appointed for all the States. The act authorized the agents of the Government to seize all the produce of the farmer, except so much as was necessary to maintain himself and family. For this produce the agent paid at the rate fixed by the State commissioners. The operation of the act created an unparalleled excitement among the people.

The embarrassment which arose from this state of affairs was greatly increased by the decay of the railroads. The means of transportation possessed in the Southern States became more and more limited during each year of the war. In Virginia the railroads were on the point of giving out at the beginning of 1863. Their rate of speed was reduced to ten miles an hour as a maximum, and their tonnage diminished from twenty-five to fifty per cent. This change in the rate of speed and quantity of freight was made through necessity. The wood work of the roads had rotted, and the machinery was worn out, and owing to the stringent enforcement of the conscription law among the men employed by the railroad companies, they had not been able, with all their efforts, to renew the one or repair the other. This failure extended to the roads in all the States. The scarcity of iron for rails was another serious injury, which could not be repaired. In this respect, the pressure of the blockade was more severely felt than in any other. So completely were these roads a part of the military system, that serious apprehensions existed that the armies might be obliged to fall back from some of their positions in consequence of the difficulty of getting to them food for men and horses. The country in the vicinity of the armies, had been stripped of its provisions and forage, and they depended for their existence and the maintenance of their positions upon the railroads. The better the roads were, the more certain were the supplies of the troops and their ability to resist all the efforts of the Federal army to occupy the country.

In two instances the Government made roads, to complete the internal system, where gaps existed. From Selma, in Alabama, to Meridien, in Mississippi, a link was built which completed this great highway from west to east, and superseded the necessity of a long detour by Mobile, and rendered useless any attempt by the forces at Pensacola to cut off communication by destroying the railroad which connects Montgomery with Mobile. The other instance was the line, of fifty miles in length, between Danville, in Virginia, and Greensborough, in North Carolina. By this work the Government was relieved from a dependence upon the line of railroad which runs from Richmond through Petersburg and Weldon, and which has for years been the great highway between the North and the South.

But while the armies were exposed to want, from the probable inability of the roads to transport sufficient provisions, the situation of the inhabitants in some parts of the Confederacy was equally critical, from the same cause. The northern part of Virginia, the fruitful valley of the Shenandoah, and the eastern section of North Carolina, produced in ordinary times most of the grain which supplied bread to the South, and which was exported to South America. Each of these districts was now in possession of the Federal forces. In Middle Tennessee agriculture was suspended, and the aged men, women, and children who adhered to the Confederacy, were forced to retire still farther south and increase the number of mouths to be fed there. Another source of supply, the North Carolina fisheries, which annually yielded millions of herring, besides shad to be salted, was also cut off. The wheat crop of 1862 was an unusually poor one; and although a sufficiency of grain for the year's supply of food was grown, the limited means of transportation possessed by the Confederacy were taxed to the utmost to bring this grain from the remote corners of States to the spots where it was demanded for consumption—to bring the food and the mouths together. Such was the aspect relative to provisions, in the beginning of the year. It was evident that a great change must be made in the production to enable the country to surmount these evils. The Government, foreseeing the danger, made vigorous appeals to the people.

These were followed by appeals from the governors of several States to their citizens, and by resolutions of legislative bodies. A very extensive effort was also made to secure the planting of more wheat and corn.

The crops during the summer were represented to be good, but as the latter part of the year approached, the apprehensions of a scarcity were manifest. It was said, "the coming winter will be one of unusual trials." In October the following facts occurred at Richmond. One firm sent one hundred barrels of flour to be sold at $27, while the price in the stores was from $65 to $75, and promised to the city all the flour on hand and all the tolls they might receive at Government prices. Another firm offered to sell all the flour sent for consumers without any charge for commissions. Another offered to grind all the wheat purchased by the city, at the cost of labor. The city of Richmond established a Board of Supply to purchase articles of necessity to be sold to the poor at cost.

Petersburg did the same, and the Secretary of War instructed the officers of the Government to facilitate the labors of these committees. All the churches and civic societies undertook to support their own poor. One firm, after strenuous efforts for several days, were unable to purchase a lot of flour for the accommodation of their customers, and concluded that the farmers were prevented from sending in their wheat because they were required to sell it at $5 per bushel. That there was an abundance in the country, and to spare, no one doubted. On the 29th of October, beef was quoted in Richmond at a dollar to a dollar and a half per pound. The butchers said they were unable to get cattle, and might be compelled to close their stalls. By an arrangement between the butchers and the Government, it ought to have sold at sixty-five to seventy cents per pound.

The condition of the supplies in Charleston was thus described:

Since the necessaries of life have reached the very exorbitant rates which they now command, our city fathers have been most zealously laboring for the benefit of the citizens at large, and with what success, the thousands who are now daily supplied with flour, rice, &c., at less than half the current market prices, can gratefully testify. The action of the council in this matter, as well as for the supply of fuel, has tended very materially to check the inflation of prices, which, but for this course, would be much higher. Yesterday afternoon one hundred and fifty cords of wood were distributed in quarter-cord lots to six hundred families, at the rate of twelve dollars per cord.

It was reported that in Southeastern Alabama and Southwestern Georgia, fifty per cent. more hogs had been raised than at any previous season of the year. The crops of wheat gathered in those sections were unusually large. In North Carolina the agents of the city of Petersburg were quite successful in procuring supplies. It was asserted that either North or South Carolina, Georgia, or Alabama, could furnish a sufficient supply for the population of Richmond.

Notwithstanding the general stringency of the blockade, many trips were made by vessels to Charleston and Wilmington during the early part of the year, with great profit to the owners. The officers of the Government owned many of these vessels. A large number, however, were captured.

The relations of the Confederate States with foreign nations underwent no favorable change during the year. England and France steadily declined to treat with them as independent States. Their views were approved by all the other States of Europe. It finally became evident that the simple recognition, not accompanied or followed by any thing in the shape of intervention, would be fruitless. The successes of the North also were such as to create the conviction in Europe that the time for declaring the seceded States to have established their independence had not arrived.

The Proclamation of Emancipation to all persons held as slaves in certain States and Districts, issued by President Lincoln on January 1st, 1863, caused great excitement in the Southern States. It is stated that the "Executive Government of the United States, including the military and naval authorities thereof, will recognize and maintain the freedom of such persons;" also, "such persons will be received into the armed service of the United States," &c. Its immediate effect was expected to arise under these clauses. The Confederate Congress took action at once on the subject. It was at first contemplated to make slaves of all free negroes found with arms in their hands; to kill all slaves found armed, and to hand over to the State authorities all their officers, to be dealt with according to the laws of the States relative to persons exciting insurrection. Severe measures were proposed in the Confederate Congress. These, however, were not adopted, and the subject was referred to the discretion of the President. Whether any extreme measures were inflicted upon these soldiers or their officers during the year, was not officially known. It was finally considered that, under the law of nations, a belligerent could employ against his antagonist any persons whom he could obtain, and, therefore, free negroes captured as Federal soldiers were entitled to be treated as prisoners of war. On the 23d of April an "Address to Christians throughout the World" was issued at Richmond, signed by ninety-six clergymen of all denominations. After asserting that "the Union cannot be restored," and that the Confederate Government is a fixed fact, the address proceeds to say:

The recent proclamation of the President of the United States, seeking the emancipation of the slaves of the South, is, in our judgment, a suitable occasion for solemn protest on the part of the people of God throughout the world.

The address charges President Lincoln with intending to produce a general insurrection of the slaves, and such an insurrection "would make it absolutely necessary for the public safety that the slaves be slaughtered; and he who would write the history of that event, would record the darkest chapter of human woe yet written." The proclamation, however, liberated no slaves except such as could come within the lines of the Federal armies. The political aspect of the proclamation was discussed at some length in the message of Mr. Davis to the Richmond Congress in January.

The difficulties which had arisen relative to the exchange of prisoners, and the threats of retaliation for some occurrences on each side, which were regarded by the other as unjustifiable acts of cruelty, was made the ostensible occasion for a mission by Vice-President Stephens to Washington, which he thus reported:

RICHMOND, *8th July*, 1863.

His Excellency, Jefferson Davis:

SIR: Under the authority and instructions of your letter to me of the 2d instant, I proceeded on the mission therein assigned, without delay. The steamer, Torpedo, commanded by Lieut. Hunter Davidson, of the navy, was put in readiness as soon as possible, by order of the Secretary of the Navy, and tendered for the service. At noon, on the 3d, she started down James River, hoisting and bearing a flag of truce after passing City Point. The next day (the 4th) at about one o'clock, P. M., when within a few miles of Newport News, we were met by a small boat of the enemy, carrying two guns, which also raised a white flag before approaching us. The officer in command informed Lieut. Davidson that he had orders from Admiral Lee, on board the United States flagship Minnesota, lying below, and then in view, not to allow any boat or vessel to pass the point near which he was stationed without his permission. By this officer I sent to Admiral Lee a note stating my objects and wishes, a copy of which is hereto annexed, marked A.

I also sent to the admiral, to be forwarded, another in the same language addressed to the officer in command of the United States forces at Fort Monroe. The gunboat proceeded immediately to the Minnesota with these despatches, while the Torpedo remained at anchor. Between 3 and 4 o'clock, P.M., another boat came up to us, bearing the admiral's answer, which is hereunto annexed, marked B.

We remained at or about this point in the river until the 6th inst., when, having heard nothing further from the admiral, at 12 o'clock M., on that day, I directed Lieut. Davidson again to speak the gunboat on guard, and to hand to the officer on board another note to his admiral. This was done. A copy of the note is appended, marked C. At half-past 2 o'clock P. M., two boats approached us from below, one bearing an answer from the admiral to my note to him of the 4th. This answer is annexed, marked D. The other boat bore the answer of Lieut. Col. W. H. Ludlow to my note of the 4th, addressed to the officer in command at Fort Monroe. A copy of this is annexed, marked E. Lieut.-Col. Ludlow also came up in person in the boat that brought his answer to me, and conferred with Col. Ould, on board the Torpedo, upon some matters he desired to see him about in connection with the exchange of prisoners. From the papers appended, embracing the correspondence referred to, it will be seen that the mission failed from the refusal of the enemy to receive or entertain it, holding the proposition for such a conference "inadmissible."

The influences and views that led to this determination after so long a consideration of the subject, must be left to conjecture. The reason assigned for the refusal of the United States Secretary of War, to wit: that "the customary agents and channels" are considered adequate for all needful military "communications and conferences," to one acquainted with the facts, seems not only unsatisfactory but very singular and unaccountable; for it is certainly known to him that these very agents, to whom he evidently alludes, heretofore agreed upon in a former conference in reference to the exchange of prisoners (one of the subjects embraced in your letter to me), are now, and have been for some time, distinctly at issue on several important points. The existing cartel, owing to these disagreements, is virtually suspended, so far as the exchange of officers on either side is concerned. Notices of retaliation have been given on both sides.

The effort, therefore, for the very many and cogent reasons set forth in your letter of instructions to me, to see if these differences could not be removed, and if a clear understanding between the parties as to the general conduct of the war could not be arrived at before this extreme measure should be resorted to by either party, was no less in accordance with the dictates of humanity than in strict conformity with the usages of belligerents in modern times. Deeply impressed as I was with these views and feelings, in undertaking the mission, and asking the conference, I can but express my profound regret at the result of the effort made to obtain it; and I can but entertain the belief that, if the conference sought had been granted, mutual good could have been effected by it; and if this war, so unnatural, so unjust, so unchristian, and so inconsistent with every fundamental principle of American constitutional liberty, "must needs" continue to be waged against us, that at least some of its severer horrors, which now so eminently threaten, might have been avoided.

Very respectfully,
ALEXANDER H. STEPHENS.

During the year no signs of yielding up were exhibited by the Confederate Government, or by the Governments of any of the seceded States. On the question of submission to the Federal Government, no organized body manifested any assent, but on the contrary the most determined opposition. The Federal Government, on the other hand, continued steadfast and onward in the policy it had adopted. The views of President Lincoln on the state of the country are thus given in his message to Congress, Dec. 8th, 1863:

When Congress assembled a year ago, the war had already lasted nearly twenty months, and there had been many conflicts on both land and sea, with varying results. The rebellion had been pressed back into reduced limits; yet the tone of public feeling and opinion, at home and abroad, was not satisfactory. With other signs, the popular elections, then just past, indicated uneasiness among ourselves, while, amid much that was cold and menacing, the kindest words coming from Europe were uttered in accents of pity that we were too blind to surrender a hopeless cause. Our commerce was suffering greatly by a few armed vessels built upon and furnished from foreign shores, and we were threatened with such additions from the same quarter as would sweep our trade from the sea and raise our blockade. We had failed to elicit from European Governments any thing hopeful upon this subject. The preliminary Emancipation Proclamation, issued in September, was running its assigned period to the beginning of the new year. A month later the final proclamation came, including the announcement that colored men of suitable condition would be received into the war service. The policy of emancipation and of employing black soldiers gave to the future a new aspect, about which hope, and fear, and doubt contended in uncertain conflict. According to our political system, as a matter of civil administration, the General Government had no lawful power to effect emancipation in any State, and for a long time it had been hoped that the rebellion could be suppressed without resorting to it as a military measure. It was all the while deemed possible that the necessity for it might come, and that, if it should, the crisis of the contest would then be presented. It came, and, as we anticipated, it was followed by dark and doubtful days.

Eleven months having now passed, we are permitted to take another review. The rebel hordes are pressed still farther back, and, by the complete opening of the Mississippi, the country dominated by the rebellion is divided into distinct parts, with no practical communication between them. Tennessee and Arkansas have been substantially cleared of insurgent control, and influential citizens in each, owners of slaves and advocates of slavery at the beginning of the rebellion, now declare openly for emancipation in their respective States. Of those States not included in the emancipation proclamation, Maryland and Missouri, neither of which, three years ago, would tolerate any restraint upon the extension of slavery into new Territories, only dispute now as to the best mode of removing it within their own limits. Of those who were slaves at the beginning of the rebellion, full one hundred thousand are now in the United States military service, about one-half of which number actually bear arms in the ranks; thus giving the double advantage of taking so much labor from the insurgent cause, and supplying the places which otherwise must be filled with so many white men. So far as tested, it is difficult to say they are not as good soldiers as any. No servile insurrection, or tendency to violence or cruelty, has marked the measures of emancipation or arming the blacks. These measures have been much discussed in foreign countries, and contemporary with such discussion the tone of public sentiment there is much improved At home the same measures have been fairly discussed, supported, criticized, and denounced, and the annual elections following are highly encouraging to those whose official duty it is to bear the country through this great trial. Thus we have the new reckoning. The crisis which threatened to divide the friends of the Union is past.

Looking now to the present and future, and with reference to a resumption of the national authority within the States wherein that authority has been suspended, I have thought fit to issue a proclamation, a copy of which is herewith transmitted.

On examination of this proclamation it will appear, as is believed, that nothing is attempted beyond what is amply justified by the Constitution. True, the form of an oath is given, but no man is coerced to take it. The man is only promised a pardon in case he voluntarily takes the oath. The Constitution authorizes the executive to grant or withhold the pardon at his own absolute discretion; and this includes the power to grant on terms, as is fully established by judicial and other authorities. It is also proffered that if, in any of the States named, a State Government shall be, in the mode prescribed, set up, such Government shall be recognized and guaranteed by the United States, and that under it the State shall, on the constitutional conditions, be protected against invasion and domestic violence. The constitutional obligation of the United States to guarantee to every State in the Union a republican form of government, and to protect the State in the case stated, is explicit and full.

But why tender the benefits of this provision only to State Governments set up in this particular way? This section of the Constitution contemplates a case wherein the element within a State, favorable to republican government, in the Union, may be too feeble for an opposite and hostile element external to or even within the State; and such are precisely the cases with which we are now dealing. An attempt to guarantee and protect a revived State Government, constructed in whole or in preponderating part from the very element against whose hostility and violence it is to be protected, is simply absurd. There must be a test by which to separate the opposing elements, so as to build only from the sound; and that test is a sufficiently liberal one which accepts as sound whoever will make a sworn recantation of his former unsoundness.

But if it be proper to require, as a test of admission to the political body, an oath of allegiance to the Constitution of the United States and to the Union under it, why also to the laws and proclamations in regard to slavery? Those laws and proclamations were enacted and put forth for the purpose of aiding in the suppression of the rebellion. To give them their fullest effect, there had to be a pledge for their maintenance. In my judgment they have aided, and will further aid, the cause for which they were intended. To now abandon them would be not only to relinquish a lever of power, but would also be a cruel and astounding breach of faith.

I may add at this point, that while I remain in my present position I shall not attempt to retract or modify the emancipation proclamation; nor shall I return to slavery any person who is free by the terms of that proclamation, or by any of the acts of Congress. For these and other reasons it is thought best that the support of these measures shall be included in the oath; and it is believed the executive may lawfully claim it in return for pardon and restoration of forfeited rights, which he has clear constitutional power to withhold altogether, or grant upon the terms which he shall deem wisest for the public interest. It should be observed also that this part of the oath is subject to the modifying and abrogating power of legislation and supreme judicial decision.

The proposed acquiescence of the national executive in any reasonable temporary State arrangement for the freed people is made with the view of possibly modifying the confusion and destitution which must, at best, attend all classes by a total revolution of labor throughout whole States. It is hoped that the already deeply afflicted people of those States may be somewhat more ready to give up the cause of their affliction, if, to this extent, this vital matter be left to themselves; while no power of the national executive to prevent an abuse is abridged by the proposition.

The suggestion in the proclamation as to maintaining the political framework of the States on what is called reconstruction, is made in the hope that it may do good without danger of harm. It will save labor and avoid great confusion.

But why any proclamation now upon this subject? This question is beset with the conflicting views that the step might be delayed too long or be taken too soon. In some States the elements for resumption seem ready for action, but remain inactive, apparently for want of a rallying point—a plan of action. Why shall A adopt the plan of B, rather than B that of A? And if A and B should agree, how can they know but that the General Government here will reject their plan? By the proclamation a plan is presented which may be accepted by them as a rallying point, and which they are assured in advance will not be rejected here. This may bring them to act sooner than they otherwise would.

The objections to a premature presentation of a plan by the national executive consists in the danger of committals on points which could be more safely left to further developments. Care has been taken to so shape the document as to avoid embarrassments from this source. Saying that, on certain terms, certain classes will be pardoned, with rights restored, it is not said that other classes, or other terms, will never be included. Saying that reconstruction will be accepted if presented in a specified way, it is not said it will never be accepted in any other way.

The movements, by State action, for emancipation in several of the States not included in the Emancipation Proclamation, are matters of profound gratulation. And while I do not repeat in detail what I have heretofore so earnestly urged upon this subject, my general views and feelings remain unchanged; and I trust that Congress will omit no fair opportunity of aiding these important steps to a great consummation.

In the midst of other cares, however important, we must not lose sight of the fact that the war power is still our main reliance. To that power alone can we look, yet for a time, to give confidence to the people in the contested regions, that the insurgent power will not again overrun them.

Until that confidence shall be established, little can be done anywhere for what is called reconstruction. Hence our chiefest care must still be directed to the army and navy, who have thus far borne their harder part so nobly and well. And it may be esteemed fortunate that, in giving the greatest efficiency to these indispensable arms, we do also honorably recognize the gallant men, from commander to sentinel, who compose them, and to whom, more than to others, the world must stand indebted for the home of freedom disenthralled, regenerated, enlarged, and perpetuated.

PROCLAMATION.

Whereas, in and by the Constitution of the United States, it is provided that the President "shall have power to grant reprieves and pardons for offences against the United States, except in cases of impeachment;"

And *whereas* a rebellion now exists whereby the loyal State Governments of several of the States have for a long time been subverted, and many persons have committed and are now guilty of treason against the United States;

And *whereas*, with reference to said rebellion and treason, laws have been enacted by Congress, declaring forfeitures and confiscation of property and liberation of slaves, all upon terms and conditions therein stated, and also declaring that the President was thereby authorized at any time thereafter, by proclamation, to extend to the persons who may have participated in the existing rebellion, in any State or part thereof, pardon and amnesty, with such exceptions and at such times and on such conditions as he may deem expedient for the public welfare;

And *whereas* the Congressional declaration for limited and conditional pardon accords with well-established judicial exposition of the pardoning power;

And *whereas*, with reference to said rebellion, the President of the United States has issued several proclamations, with provisions in regard to the liberation of slaves;

And *whereas* it is now desired by some persons heretofore engaged in said rebellion to resume their allegiance to the United States, and to reinaugurate loyal State Governments within and for their respective States;

Therefore, I, Abraham Lincoln, President of the United States, do proclaim, declare, and make known to all persons who have, directly or by implication, participated in the existing rebellion, except as hereinafter excepted, that a full pardon is hereby granted to them and each of them, with restoration of all rights of property, except as to slaves, and in property cases where rights of third parties shall have intervened, and upon the condition that every such person shall take and subscribe an oath, and thenceforward keep and maintain said oath inviolate; and which oath shall be registered for permanent preservation, and shall be of the tenor and effect following, to wit:

I, —— ——, do solemnly swear, in presence of Almighty God, that I will henceforth faithfully support, protect, and defend the Constitution of the United States and the Union of the States thereunder; and that I will, in like manner, abide by and faithfully support all acts of Congress passed during the existing rebellion with reference to slaves, so long and so far as not repealed, modified, or held void by Congress, or by decision of the Supreme Court; and that I will, in like manner, abide by, and faithfully support all proclamations of the Presicent, made during the existing rebellion, having reference to slaves, so long and so far as not modified or declared void by decision of the Supreme Court. So help me God.

The persons excepted from the benefits of the foregoing provisions are all who are or shall have been civil or diplomatic officers or agents of the so-called Confederate Government; all who have left judicial stations under the United States to aid the rebellion; all who are or shall have been military or naval officers of said so-called Confederate Government above the rank of colonel in the army or lieutenant in the navy; all who left seats in the United States Congress to aid the rebellion; all who resigned commissions in the army or navy of the United States and afterwards aided the rebellion; and all who have engaged in any way in treating colored persons, or white persons in charge of such, otherwise than lawfully as prisoners of war, and which persons may have been found in the United States service as soldiers, seamen, or in any other capacity.

And I do further proclaim, declare, and make known, that whenever, in any of the States of Arkansas, Texas, Louisiana, Mississippi, Tennessee, Alabama, Georgia, Florida, South Carolina, and North Carolina, a number of persons, not less than one-tenth in number of the votes cast in such State at the Presidential election of the year of our Lord one thousand eight hundred and sixty, each having taken the oath aforesaid, and not having since violated it, and being a qualified voter by the election laws of the State existing immediately before the so-called act of secession, and excluding all others, shall reëstablish a State Government which shall be republican, and in nowise contravening said oath, such shall be recognized as the true Government of the State, and the State shall receive thereunder the benefits of the constitutional provision which declares that "the United States shall guarantee to every State in this Union a republican form of government, and shall protect each of them against invasion; and, on application of the Legislature, or the executive (when the Legislature cannot be convened), against domestic violence."

And I do further proclaim, declare, and make known, that any provision which may be adopted by such State Government in relation to the freed people of such State, which shall recognize and declare their permanent freedom, provide for their education, and which may yet be consistent as a temporary arrangement with their present condition as a laboring, landless, homeless class, will not be objected to by the national executive.

And it is suggested as not improper that, in constructing a loyal State Government in any State, the name of the State, the boundary, the subdivisions, the constitution, and the general code of laws, as before the rebellion, be maintained, subject only to the modifications made necessary by the conditions hereinbefore stated, and such others, if any, not contravening said conditions, and which may be deemed expedient by those framing the new State Government.

To avoid misunderstanding, it may be proper to say that this proclamation, so far as it relates to State Governments, has no reference to States wherein loyal State Governments have all the while been maintained. And, for the same reason, it may be proper to further say, that whether members sent to Congress from any State shall be admitted to seats constitutionally, rests exclusively with the respective houses, and not to any extent with the executive. And still further, that this proclamation is intended to present the people of the States wherein the national authority has been suspended, and loyal State Governments have been subverted, a mode in and by which the national authority and loyal State Governments may be reëstablished within said States, or in any of them; and, while the mode presented is the best the executive can suggest, with his present impressions, it must not be understood that no other possible mode would be acceptable.

Given under my hand, at the city of Washington, the eighth day of December, A. D. one thousand eight hundred and sixty-three, and of the Independence of the United States of America the eighty-eighth.

[L. S.]

ABRAHAM LINCOLN.

By the President:

William H. Seward, Secretary of State.

The efficacy of the Emancipation Proclamation was probably very imperfectly manifested during 1863. On the one hand, it did not appear to make free any slave by its own operation during the year. All those became free who came in contact with the armies or within the military lines. This freedom would have been obtained equally as well without the existence of the proclamation, for all officers and soldiers had been forbidden to restore fugitives to rebel masters. On the other hand, it tended to awaken a great sympathy among the slaves for the Union cause, which held out to them the promise of certain freedom by its success; it presented a strong stimulus to free blacks to enter the army and fight for a cause which would give freedom to their race; it also stimulated the unconditional Union men in Maryland, Missouri, and Louisiana, to make every effort to change the constitutions of the former States so as to secure immediate emancipation. But the great efficacy of the proclamation was expected to become apparent at a future day, when the insurrectionary States should be recovered to the Union. In short, it made emancipation the policy of the Administration, and encouraged the friends of that great cause to make every exertion to secure its speedy accomplishment. But it must not be supposed that this policy was adopted without opposition. The President nowhere during the year stated that it was any thing more than a measure for the preservation of the Union, and limits himself to this position. The opposition to the Administration protested against it. The friends of the Administration, known as Union men, approved of it as a war measure, and a resolution to this effect passed the Republican State Convention of New York. The friends of the Administration, known as unconditional Union men, not only warmly approved of the proclamation, but demanded a most vigorous enforcement of it, by every method.

It now remains to notice the efforts which were made to secure the advantages of the proclamation, and the new questions which arose in connection with those efforts. The first movement was to bring the colored men into the field as soldiers, which has been previously related. On the 27th of January a bill was introduced into Congress to authorize the President to raise one hundred and fifty thousand colored volunteers. On the 31st of July the President issued an order declaring that the Government would give the same protection to all of its soldiers; and that if the enemy should sell or enslave any one because of his color, the offence should be punished by retaliation upon the enemy's prisoners. An opinion had already been given by the attorney-general, Mr. Bates, that the colored man was a citizen of the United States; and upon his appearance in the field under arms, it was insisted by many that he should possess all the rights and enjoy all the privileges peculiar to that citizenship. He should become a voter, they argued, and eligible to public office. A few went still further, and advocated an entire wiping out of all civil and social distinctions between the whites and blacks, and an establishment of all the intimate relations which exist between persons of one and the same race.

But while the able-bodied men among the freedmen were thus enlisted in the military and naval service of the United States, and many of the women found employment in the vicinity of the camps, garrisons, and hospitals, there was a much larger class who were not able-bodied, some of them capable of performing some labor, others feeble, decrepit, and helpless. In the regions which were occupied by Federal troops, the planters who sympathized with the Southern Confederacy had generally fled southward, taking with them or sending before them their able-bodied slaves, and leaving to the mercy of the invading army the old and decrepit, and the children who were too young to be of much value. Those who escaped, too, and came into the Union lines, often encountered great hardships in doing so, and in many instances arrived sick, half-starved, and with only a few rags for clothing. It was obviously the duty of the Government to provide in part at least for these poor creatures, and to furnish employment for such of them as were able to work, that they might sustain themselves and their more helpless kindred. There were, however, serious practical difficulties in the way. On the Mississippi, especially below Vicksburg, it was a matter of difficulty to obtain a sufficiency of rations for the soldiers, to say nothing of the 30,000 or 40,000 helpless colored people who looked to the Government for food; and the Government ration was not well adapted to the freedmen, who had been accustomed all their lives to corn bread and bacon. Clothing the Government had not, and could not procure, except for the uniforms of its soldiers. These sick, helpless, feeble, and infirm persons, and all who were not employed with the army, were therefore collected in camps at different points, and rations furnished them, such clothing as could be collected provided, and appeals made to the people of the North for new and second-hand clothing to supply their needs. Generous responses were made to these appeals, and vast quantities of clothing forwarded. Those who were capable of performing some labor, were presently employed on the abandoned plantations, which were leased under certain restrictions to tenants for one year.

This plan would have answered a tolerable purpose had the lessees of the plantations been honest, upright, humane men; but, with few exceptions, they were adventurers and camp followers, who were ready to turn their hands to any opportunity of getting gain by the oppression of the poor, the weak, or the defenceless. The wages prescribed were much smaller than were paid by the planters for the hire of slaves for the same work when cotton was but ten cents a pound, while at this time it was worth seventy cents; the clothing, which by the terms of the contract was to be furnished at cost, was actually supplied at a most exorbitant profit; and while a portion of their wages ($2 per head) was withheld for medical attendance, no physician was ever allowed to see them, and no medicines furnished on most of the plantations. The provisions concerning families were also shamefully evaded, and on many plantations every rainy day, or day when there was no opportunity for work, was deducted, and even the little pittance which remained was not paid, nor were they furnished with food according to agreement. In short, the plan inured, in its results, wholly to the benefit of the lessees, many of whom made large fortunes on the single year's labor. There were of course some exceptions, though but few, to this state of things. Fifteen small plantations were leased by negroes themselves, some of whom cultivated them by the aid of their own families, while others employed a number of other negroes. They all did well; and in a few instances in which men of a high and humane character leased plantations, and carried out their contracts in the spirit in which it had been conceived, they found the people whom they employed grateful and contented, and willing to labor faithfully, while their own receipts were such as amply compensated their exertions and expenditure.

Meantime the suffering, sickness, and mortality at many of the camps where the feeble and infirm freedmen were collected, were terrible. James E. Yeatman, president of the Western Sanitary Commission, visited these camps from Cairo to Natchez, in the autumn of 1863; and while in some of them the freedmen employed by the Government in chopping wood or other work, supported themselves and those dependent upon them in tolerable comfort, in others, and these the largest camps, there had been great distress and frightful mortality—the result of overcrowding, want of ventilation, malarious localities, the prevalence of small-pox, want of medical attendance, poor and insufficient food, and lack of clothing. Many of the people under these causes were seriously affected with *nostalgia*, or home-sickness; their condition being more wretched than it had been on the plantations. At the camp at Natchez, where there had been 4,000 freedmen, the number was reduced to 2,100 by deaths, from fifty to seventy-five having died per day during July and August; at Young's Point, near Vicksburg, the mortality had been equally great for three months; De Soto and President's Island were among the worst of these camps. Camp Holly Springs and Camp Shiloh near Memphis, Helena, and the Freedman's Hospital, were in better condition, and some of them had good schools for the instruction of those who desired to learn to read.

About 35,000 colored people were gathered in these camps between Cairo and Natchez, and about four-fifths of them under proper management could have earned their own support.

Near the close of the year, the management of these Infirmary farms and camps, as well as of the whole matter of leasing plantations and employing the freedmen, passed from the War Department to the Treasury Department, and the special agent appointed by the latter Department, in conjunction with Mr. Yeatman, perfected the regulations for the year 1864, guarding so far as was possible against all chances of fraud or ill treatment on the part of the lessees, placing them under strict supervision, increasing the wages of the freedmen about three fold, and making them a first lien on the crop. The tax payable to Government on the crop was also increased, and one-fourth applied to the support of schools for the colored children, and another fourth to the maintenance of the infirmary farms. Medical attendants were also to be provided for each district, and the money reserved paid to them by the district superintendent, and they were required to attend strictly to the health of the people of their districts.

Great attention was paid to the establishment of schools for the education of the freedmen, and to the imparting of religious instruction to them, especially at Port Royal, Roanoke Island, Norfolk, and at the Freedmen's village, Arlington, opposite Washington, D. C., under the direction of the Freedmen's Relief Societies, the American Missionary Association, the Free Mission Society, &c. In North Carolina, the land on Roanoke Island was assigned to the freedmen for cultivation, and they supported themselves comfortably.

But the questions relative to freedmen were generally regarded as of less importance compared with the greater one which arose relative to the relations of the insurrectionary States to the Federal Government, and which involved the *status* of the slave at the close of the civil war. Previous to the adoption of emancipation as a principle and a policy of the Government, it had been held by all except those who were looking to ultimate emancipation, that it was only necessary for the Southern States, in good faith, to send representatives to Congress where vacant chairs were in place for them, to restore their States to their original position in the Union. But now, under the operation of the principle of emancipation, they could not recover their position as slaveholding States, but must appear as non-slaveholding States. The problem thus to be solved was to accomplish the reappearance of the slaveholding insurrectionary States in the Union, with the shackles of their slaves knocked off, with their bondmen and women and children sent forth as free. A problem of this magnitude called into exercise for its solution the ablest intellects of the unconditional Union men, or emancipationists. In the first place, it assumed that the United States should prescribe the terms and conditions of the reappearance of the insurrectionary States in the Union, and be able to secure their reappearance upon those terms. To accomplish this measure involved the entire subjugation of those States, the extinction of their existing governments, and the creation of new ones.

The operations of the Federal Treasury during the year 1863, were successfully conducted. The enactment by Congress of a national banking law has proved a support of public credit; and the general legislation in relation to loans fully answered the expectations of its favorers.

The receipts during the year from all sources, including loans and the balance in the Treasury at its commencement, were $901,125,674.86, and the aggregate disbursements $895,796,630.65, leaving a balance on the 1st July, 1863, of

$5,329,044.21. Of the receipts there were derived from customs, $69,059,642.40; from internal revenue, $37,640,787.95; from direct tax, $1,485,103.61; from lands, $167,617.17; from miscellaneous sources, $3,046,615.35; and from loans, $776,682,361.57; making the aggregate, $901,125,674.86.

Of the disbursements there were for the civil service, $23,253,922.08; pensions and Indians, $4,216,520.79; for interest on public debt, $24,729,846.51; for the War Department, $599,298,600.83; for the Navy Department, $63,211,105.27; for payment of funded and temporary debt, $181,086,635.07; making the aggregate, $895,796,630.65; and leaving the balance of $5,329,044.21.

But the payment of funded and temporary debt having been made from moneys borrowed during the year, must be regarded as merely nominal payments, and the moneys borrowed to make them as merely nominal receipts; and their amount, $181,086,635,07, should therefore be deducted both from receipts and disbursements. This being done, there remains as actual receipts, $720,039,039.79; and the actual disbursements, $714,709,995.58, leaving the balance as already stated.

In January, 1863, Mr. John P. Usher was appointed Secretary of the Interior to succeed Mr. Smith, appointed judge of the U. S. District Court of Indiana. The Cabinet of Mr. Lincoln was thus composed as follows:

William H. Seward, New York, Secretary of State.
Salmon P. Chase, Ohio, Secretary of the Treasury.
Edwin M. Stanton, Pennsylvania, Sec'y of War.
Gideon Welles, Connecticut, Secretary of the Navy.
John P. Usher, Indiana, Secretary of the Interior.
Montgomery Blair, Maryland, Postmaster-General.
Edward Bates, Missouri, Attorney-General.

Intercourse of a private nature was allowed between the citizens of the Northern and Southern States, under certain simple regulations, as follows:

1. No letter must exceed one page of a letter sheet, or relate to any other than purely domestic matters.
2. Every letter must be signed with the writer's name in full.
3. All letters must be sent with five cents postage enclosed if to go to Richmond, and ten cents if beyond.
4. All letters must be enclosed to the commanding general of the Department of Virginia, at Fortress Monroe. No letter sent to any other address will be forwarded.

At intervals, females and children were granted passes to go South, under certain regulations.

The power of the Government to confiscate the property of the inhabitants of the insurgent States, early commanded the earnest attention of Congress, and led to a full discussion of the extent of this power, the manner of its exercise, and the restrictions imposed by the Constitution. The results of the examination were the enactment by Congress of the act of August 6th, 1861, and of the act of July 17th, 1862. The distinctive features of these laws were, that the first provided for the confiscation of property actually used in aiding, abetting, or promoting the measures of the rebels, while the second freed the slaves and confiscated all other property of persons assisting, engaged with or giving aid or comfort to the rebellion. By an order of the President under date of November 13th, 1862, and a subsequent one extending the directions of the first, the Attorney General was charged with the superintendence and direction of all proceedings under the two acts of Congress above referred to, in so far as concerned the seizure, prosecution, and condemnation of the estate, property, and effects coming under the operation of the same. Attorney General Bates, on the 8th of January, 1863, issued "General Instructions to District Attorneys and Marshals relative to proceedings under the acts of Congress for confiscation." These instructions provided generally that—

1st. All seizures were to be made by the Marshal under the written authority of the District Attorney.

2d. A true return thereof by the Marshal to the District Attorney.

3d. A record by the District Attorney of every order of seizure, and one by the Marshal of every return.

4th. That the District Attorney should exercise vigilance in executing the law and care to avoid hasty and improvident seizures.

5th. State laws directing seizures should be conformed to as nearly as may be, consistently with the objects of the acts of Congress.

6th. That property seized by the military officers might be received by the Marshal, who should make return thereof to the District Attorney.

7th. After seizure the District Attorney to proceed in the proper court for the condemnation of the property seized.

In pursuance of these instructions, proceedings were commenced in several districts to enforce the provisions of both laws.

With regard to the exchange of prisoners, the commencement of 1863 found the cartel agreed upon by Gens. Dix and Hill in the preceding July in full force and operation. The preponderance of prisoners on either side was not great, and notwithstanding certain acrimonious correspondence and retaliatory proclamations of the previous year, exchanges proceeded regularly at City Point on the James River, the chief place appointed for that purpose, to the mutual relief and advantage of the hostile parties.

The first indication of approaching complications was afforded by the message of Jefferson Davis to the Confederate Congress on Jan. 14th, in which he used the following language:

So far as regards the action of the Government on such criminals as may attempt its execution [referring to President Lincoln's emancipation proclamation of Jan. 1st, 1863], I confine myself to informing you that I shall, unless in your wisdom you deem some other course more expedient, deliver to the several State authorities all commissioned officers of the United States that may hereafter be captured by our forces in any of the States embraced in the proclamation, that they may be dealt with in accordance with the laws of those States providing for the punishment of criminals engaged in inciting servile insurrection.

On May 1st, the Congress, after mature deliberation, passed a series of resolutions in conformity with these views.

The effect of the resolutions was to withhold from exchange, if captured, a certain class of soldiers of the United States army, who were not regarded by the enemy as prisoners of war. As no colored soldiers had up to this time fallen into their hands, notwithstanding a large number of colored persons employed as ambulance and wagon drivers, laborers, servants, and in other capacities, had been captured by them and never accounted for, no direct issue seemed to be raised, and it remained for future events to develop one. The cartel was in reality interrupted when the resolutions became the law of the Confederacy, but its operation was not practically stopped until several months afterwards, and then for reasons only partially connected with the position taken by the rebel authorities on this point.

The cartel of July, 1862, had been so arranged that a correct return of prisoners could be kept by both sides, in order that a balance sheet might at any time be struck between them. For this purpose City Point and Vicksburg were selected as points of exchange. But under a liberal interpretation of the cartel it became the practice for the commanders of opposing armies to parole and exchange prisoners at will, without the formality of sending them to the rear for transportation to the points of exchange, or designating such points. In consequence of this course it became impossible to determine with accuracy the balances between the contending parties; and the United States Government, for the purpose, among other things, of making its generals conform strictly to the regulations of the cartel in the matter of paroles, issued, on May 22d, a code of instructions compiled by Dr. Francis Lieber, and known as general orders No. 100, in which it was provided that captures, to be valid, "must be reduced to possession," and that when the Government did not approve of a parole, the officer or man paroled must return to captivity. This was sent to Robert Ould, Confederate agent of exchange at City Point, on May 22d, accompanied by a note from Col. Ludlow, the Federal agent at Fortress Monroe, in which he stated that, together with the cartel, it would govern the U. S. army. He added:

I would invite your special attention to article seven of the cartel, which provides that all prisoners of war shall be sent to places of delivery therein specified. The execution of this article will obviate much discussion and difficulty growing out of the mode, time, and place of giving paroles. No paroles or exchanges will be considered binding except those under the stipulations of said article, permitting commanders of two opposing armies to exchange or release or parole at other points mutually agreed on by said commanders.

On July 3d, Gen. Lee received his final repulse at Gettysburg, and on the 4th he retreated toward the Potomac. A number of prisoners taken by him during the battles of the three previous days still remained upon his hands, and being unable to take these with him into Virginia he paroled and released them on the spot. Gen. Meade at once disavowed these paroles as having been made in violation of a liberal interpretation of the cartel, which required prisoners, when exchanged or paroled at a distance from either of the points of exchange, to be so exchanged or paroled at a point mutually agreed upon by the commanders of the opposing armies. In the present case nothing of the kind had been attempted, and the enemy, by showing his inability to remove his prisoners, failed to prove that he had reduced them to actual possession. Hence the Federal Government not only held these paroles to be invalidated, but ordered the officers and men to return to duty. The rebels complained bitterly of this proceeding, maintaining that the Federal Government had undertaken to supplement the cartel by its general orders, by which the basis of exchanges had been affected without previous agreement.

The battle of Gettysburg was followed by the unconditional surrender of Vicksburg and Port Hudson, by which the number of prisoners falling into the Federal hands was enormously increased. In both instances the commanders of the opposing armies, acting under the authority of the cartel, mutually agreed upon a place for the delivery of the prisoners on parole. The Port Hudson prisoners were accordingly sent to Mobile. Mr. Ould nevertheless undertook to release these men from their obligations, ostensibly because they were not exchanged at City Point or Vicksburg, the two places specially mentioned in the cartel (although that instrument provided for other arrangements, which in this instance were literally fulfilled), but really as a retaliatory measure to offset the disavowal of the Gettysburg paroles, and also, there is good reason to believe, for the purpose of filling up the depleted ranks of the rebel army. Other prisoners, to the number of several thousands, were for similar reasons subsequently absolved from their paroles. The proceedings above related involved no slight amount of acrimonious correspondence, extending over a considerable period, but cannot be said to have permanently interrupted the system of exchanges then in operation.

Previous to July no engagement had occurred in which colored troops had fallen into the hands of the enemy. But the capture of a number of the 54th Massachusetts (colored) regiment, at the assault on Fort Wagner in Charleston harbor, showed that the enemy were determined to carry out literally the provisions of the resolutions of May 1st. To protect this class of soldiers from these harsh measures, the following retaliatory order was issued by the President:

EXECUTIVE MANSION, WASHINGTON, July 30th.

It is the duty of every Government to give protection to its citizens of whatever class, color, or condition, and especially to those who are duly organized as soldiers in the public service. The law of nations and the usages and customs of war, as carried on by civilized powers, permit no distinction as to color in the treatment of prisoners of war as public enemies. To sell or enslave any captured person, on account of his color, and for no offence against the laws of war, is a relapse into barbarism and a crime against the civilization of the age. The Government of the United States will give the same protection to all its soldiers, and if the enemy shall sell or enslave any one because of his color, the offence shall be punished by retaliation upon the enemy's prisoners in our hands.

It is therefore ordered that for every soldier of the United States killed in violation of the laws of war, a rebel soldier shall be executed, and for every one enslaved by the enemy or sold into slavery, a rebel soldier shall be placed at hard labor on the public works, and continue at such labor until the other shall be released and receive the treatment due to a prisoner of war.

ABRAHAM LINCOLN.

By order of the Secretary of War.

E. D. TOWNSEND, Ass't Adj.-Gen.

Of the fate of the negroes captured at Fort Wagner no certain intelligence reached the Federal Government for several weeks, the rebels maintaining a strict silence on the subject; but Secretary Stanton, ascertaining soon after that three colored men captured on board the gunboat Isaac Smith in the Stono River, had been placed in close confinement, ordered three rebel prisoners of South Carolina to be held as hostages for them, and directed this fact to be communicated to the Confederate Government.

During the whole year not a single instance occurred of a negro soldier, or a commissioned officer of a negro regiment, being exchanged, or recognized as a prisoner of war. On the other hand, no instance came to light of the execution by the Confederate authorities of the death penalty upon prisoners of this class. A suspension of exchanges and a long correspondence now ensued.

The report of the Commissary-General of Prisoners, accompanying the Secretary of War's annual report of Dec., 1863, showed that the number of Confederate officers and men captured by the Federals since the beginning of the war, is: 1 lieutenant-general, 5 major-generals, 25 brigadier-generals, 186 colonels, 146 lieutenant-colonels, 244 majors, 2,497 captains, 5,811 lieutenants, 16,563 non-commissioned officers, 121,156 privates, and 5,800 citizens. Of these, the Federals had on hand at the date of the report, 29,229 officers and men, among whom were 1 major-general and 7 brigadiers. There had been 121,937 Confederates exchanged, against 110,866 Federal soldiers returned. The exchanges of officers on both sides were computed at their exchangeable value in privates.

Of the treatment of Federal prisoners by the rebel authorities, the accounts of exchanged surgeons, officers, and men, generally concurred in describing it as bad. Many had even denounced it as unnecessarily cruel. The enemy, in palliation of these complaints, alleged that the Union prisoners were placed on an equality, as respects rations and clothing, with their own soldiers, and that they did not receive the comforts which might be reasonably expected, simply because it was not in the power of the Confederate authorities to give them. This, in the opinion of several exchanged surgeons, who were in the habit of making daily visits to the prison hospitals in Richmond, would not account for the dreadful mortality in those buildings, averaging, at certain periods, upward of fifty persons a day. Toward the close of 1863, the Federal Government was permitted to send supplies of food and clothing to these prisoners; but charges of misappropriation of them having been made, the permission was, in December, revoked.

A somewhat remarkable episode of this period was the plot set on foot by the rebel authorities to liberate 2,500 of their officers confined on Johnson's Island, in Lake Erie, and in connection with this act to burn or destroy Buffalo and other lake cities. The expedition intended for this purpose was to rendezvous in Canada, surprise the Federal garrison on Johnson's Island, liberate the prisoners, convey them to Canada in vessels provided for that purpose, and forward them by Halifax to Nassau or Bermuda; the greater part of the funds being specially devoted to paying their passage to one of these points.

These facts coming to the knowledge of the American consul-general in Montreal, he at once laid them before the governor-general of Canada. The Canadian authorities gave the subject immediate attention, and by November 11th enough had been discovered of the plans of the rebels to authorize the governor-general to inform Lord Lyons, the British minister at Washington, by telegraph, of the existence of the plot. Lord Lyons at once communicated his despatch to the United States Government, and at midnight of the 11th a despatch was sent by Secretary Stanton to the mayors of Detroit, Buffalo, and other Western cities.

The prompt movement of troops to the scene of danger, and the precautions taken by the local authorities in the lake cities, had the effect of averting the threatened catastrophe, and in a few days tranquillity was restored.

CHAPTER XXXVIII.

Position of the Armies at the beginning of 1864—Gen. Sherman's march to Meridian—Opposing movements of the Enemy Gen. Gilmore's movements in Florida—Battle of Olustee—Campaign of Gen. Banks on the Red River—Battles—Co-operation of Gen. Steele—Its Results—Capture of Fort Pillow and slaughter of the Garrison—Unsuccessful Operations in North Carolina.

At the commencement of the year, 1864, the Army of the Potomac, under Gen. Meade, was near Culpepper Court House, in Virginia, with the army under Gen. Lee in front and south of him. The Confederate Gen. Early had been ordered to command the forces in the Shenandoah valley, with his headquarters at Staunton. The Federal forces held Winchester, Martinsburg, and Harper's Ferry, and occupied the line of the Baltimore and Ohio Railroad in Western Virginia. Gen. Burnside was still at Knoxville, in East Tennessee, with a line of communication into Kentucky. Eastward of him was Gen. Longstreet, with a division of the Confederate army. The army of Gen. Grant was in front of Chattanooga, in the southeast corner of Tennessee, and a force of the enemy before him at Dalton, under Gen. Bragg. The following address to his soldiers had been issued by Gen. Grant, near the close of 1863:

HEADQUARTERS MILITARY DIVISION OF THE MISSISSIPPI, IN THE FIELD, CHATTANOOGA, TENN., December 10, 1863.

The General commanding takes this opportunity of returning his sincere thanks and congratulations to the brave Armies of the Cumberland, the Ohio, the Tennessee, and their comrades from the Potomac, for the recent splendid and decisive successes achieved over the enemy. In a short time you have recovered from him the control of the Tennessee River, from Bridgeport to Knoxville. You dislodged him from his great stronghold upon Lookout Mountain, drove him from Chattanooga valley, wrested from his determined grasp the possession of Missionary Ridge, repelled with heavy loss to him his repeated assaults upon Knoxville, forcing him to raise the siege there, driving him at all points, utterly routed and discomfited, beyond the limits of the State. By your noble heroism and determined courage, you have effectually defeated the plans of the enemy for regaining possession of the States of Kentucky and Tennessee. You have secured positions from which no rebellious power can drive or dislodge you. For all this the General commanding thanks you collectively and individually. The loyal people of the United States thank and bless you. Their hopes and prayers for your success against this unholy rebellion are with you daily. Their faith in you will not be in vain. Their hopes will not be blasted. Their prayers to Almighty God will be answered. You will yet go to other fields of strife; and with the invincible bravery and unflinching loyalty to justice and right which have characterized you in the past, you will prove that no enemy can withstand you, and that no defences, however formidable, can check your onward march.

By order of Major-General U. S. GRANT.
T. S. BOWERS, Ass't Adj.-Gen.

The line of communication of Gen. Grant extended to Nashville by the railroad, through Stevenson and Murfreesboro'. Florence and Corinth were also held by a Federal force until the earlier portion of the year, when the former was occupied by the enemy. Military posts consisting of fortifications and heavy guns, with negro troops, were established on the Mississippi River at Cairo, Columbus, New Madrid, Fort Pillow, Memphis, Helena, Goodrich's Landing, Vicksburg, Natchez, Port Hudson, Baton Rouge, New Orleans, and Forts Jackson and St. Philip. There were also forces at other points adjacent to these. A large force was under the command of Gen. Banks, in New Orleans, with detachments at Brashear City, and at Brownsville, on the Rio Grande. Gen. Steele occupied Little Rock, Arkansas, with a considerable force, and Gen. Rosecrans, in command of the department, had a small body of troops in Missouri. The military positions on the coast of North Carolina and South Carolina remained unchanged.

The number of troops in the field at the commencement of the year can be only indefinitely estimated. Between October, 1863, and May, 1864, seven hundred thousand new troops took the field, as stated by Senator Wilson in Congress. A portion of these supplied the place of the three years' men whose term of service expired in 1864. A large majority of the latter, however, reënlisted.

The number of Confederate troops in the field known as veterans, in the beginning of the year, was as follows: That portion of the Southern army which constituted the force under Gen. Lee (counting in Gen. Longstreet, who commanded a portion of his army), numbered ninety thousand troops. This is also counting in the troops which were in the vicinity of Abingdon, Lynchburg, and other portions of Southwestern Virginia and East Tennessee, formerly under Gen. Samuel Jones, who was detached from Gen. Lee's army late in September, 1863, to operate against Gen. Burnside, and afterwards under the command of Gen. Breckinridge. At Richmond and at Petersburg there were, not counting in citizens and home guards, about three thousand men. Between Petersburg and Weldon there were one thousand men. Along the railroad, between Weldon and Wilmington, there were at least six thousand men. The forces under Gen. Pickett numbered eight thousand men. Imboden and Moseby together had four thousand men—all guerrillas. This swelled the army in Eastern Virginia and North Carolina to one hundred and twelve thousand strong.

The second great army in the Confederacy was that under Gen. Johnston, a large portion of which was cavalry. The army known as the Army of the Tennessee was composed of two corps, each having six divisions of infantry, amounting to thirty-six thousand men. There were also several divisions of cavalry, numbering at least eighteen thousand men, making an aggregate of fifty-four thousand. This included the four divisions sent to reënforce Gen. Polk, and the two divisions sent to Mobile, and the entire cavalry under Wheeler, Wharton, and John Morgan. Gen. Johnston also had command of all the Confederate forces in Georgia, Alabama, and Mississippi, except those at Savannah, Mobile, and under Forrest, who had an independent (roving) commission. Before the arrival of Gen. Sherman at Meridian, Gen. Polk had eighteen thousand troops, only two thousand of which were veterans.

The forces in South Carolina and at Savannah, under Gen. Beauregard, and in Florida, under Gen. McCown, numbered ten thousand. This only included the veterans, or old soldiers, as the armies in these three localities above mentioned a little later numbered twenty-five thousand men.

The next regular armies of the Confederacy were the Trans-Mississippi forces, scattered in different portions of Arkansas and Texas, and all under the command of Lieut.-Gen. Kirby Smith, the army in Arkansas under Gen. Holmes, and the army in Texas under Gen. Magruder; the old soldiers of which numbered twelve thousand men.

The forces at Mobile, under Gens. Maury and Claiborne, numbered about eight thousand. The forces under Gen. Forrest, and under Chalmers, Lee, and Richardson, amounted to six thousand, which included all the veterans in the rebel service.

To this may be added, however, in the same line, twelve thousand soldiers engaged in important prison guard, and in the hospitals and quartermasters' and commissary departments. There were also about two thousand men engaged in the guerrilla warfare on the banks of the Mississippi. No other guerrilla bands of importance existed in Gen. Grant's department. There was not a single squad in Kentucky, East and Middle Tennessee, Northern Alabama, or Northern Georgia. There were still several guerrilla organizations in West Tennessee and Northern Mississippi. The people themselves had rid the country.

The total of these veterans was two hundred and twenty-four thousand; to these were added, at the beginning of the year, one hundred and twenty thousand conscripts, making the number in the service three hundred and forty-four thousand.

The earliest operations of importance, in 1864, consisted of a movement under Gen. Sherman from Vicksburg, Mississippi, to Meridian, Alabama; another under Gen. Smith, from Memphis, Tennessee, to coöperate with Gen. Sherman; another under Gen. Grant's orders, from Chattanooga, Tennessee, upon Dalton, Georgia, and another under Gen. Schofield, who relieved Gen. Burnside, upon the forces under Gen. Longstreet, in East Tennessee.

Upon the return of Gen. Sherman from East Tennessee to Chattanooga, his command was stationed at Scottsboro', Alabama, and thence along the Memphis and Chattanooga Railroad, to Huntsville. Near the end of January, Gen. Sherman went to Memphis and Vicksburg, to command an expedition. Corinth was abandoned, and the Memphis Railroad eastward of Lagrange to Huntsville, and a large body of troops sent down the Mississippi to Vicksburg.

The following letter was addressed by Gen. Sherman, at this time, to his adjutant-general, relative to the course to be pursued by subordinate commanders of military districts to the inhabitants:

HEADQUARTERS DEP'T OF THE TENNESSEE,
VICKSBURG, January 31, 1864.

Major R. M. Sawyer, Ass't Adj.-Gen. Army of the Tennessee, Huntsville.

DEAR SAWYER: In my former letter I have answered all your questions, save one, and that relates to the treatment of inhabitants known or suspected to be hostile, or "secesh." This is in truth the most difficult business of our army as it advances and occupies the Southern country. It is almost impossible to lay down rules, and I invariably leave this whole subject to the local commanders, but am willing to give them the benefit of my acquired knowledge and experince.

In Europe, whence we derive our principles of war, as developed by their histories, wars are between kings or rulers, through hired armies, and not between peoples.

The war which prevails in our land is essentially a war of races. The Southern people entered into a clear compact of Government, but still maintained a species of separate interests, history, and prejudices. These latter became stronger and stronger, till they have led to a war which has developed the fruits of the bitterest kind.

We of the North are, beyond all question, right in our lawful cause, but we are not bound to ignore the fact that the people of the South have prejudices which form part of their nature, and which they cannot throw off without an effort of reason, or the slower process of natural change. Now, the question arises, should we treat as absolute enemies all in the South who differ from us in opinion or prejudice, kill or banish them; or should we give them time to think, and gradually change their conduct so as to conform to the new order of things, which is slowly and gradually creeping into their country?

When men take arms to resist our rightful authority, we are compelled to use force, because all reason and argument cease when arms are resorted to. When provisions, forage, horses, mules, wagons, etc., are used by our enemy, it is clearly our duty and right to take them, because otherwise they might be used against us.

In like manner, all houses left vacant by an inimical people are clearly our right, or such as are needed as storehouses, hospitals, and quarters. But a question arises as to dwellings used by women, children, and non-combatants. So long as non-combatants remain in their houses and keep to their accustomed business, their opinions and prejudices can in nowise influence the war, and therefore should not be noticed. But if any one comes out into the public streets and creates disorder, he or she should be punished, restrained, or banished, either to the rear or front, as the officer in command adjudges. If the people, or any of them, keep up a correspondence with parties in hostility, they are spies, and can be punished with death or minor punishment.

These are well-established principles of war, and the people of the South having appealed to war, are barred from appealing to our Constitution, which they have practically and publicly defied. They have appealed to war, and must abide its rules and laws. The United States, as a belligerent party claiming right in the soil as the ultimate sovereign, have a right to change the population, and it may be and is, both politic and just, we should do so in certain districts. When the inhabitants persist too long in hostility, it may be both politic and right we should banish them and appropriate their lands to a more loyal and useful population. No man will deny that the United States would be benefited by dispossessing a single prejudiced, hard-headed, and disloyal planter, and substituting in his place a dozen or more patient, industrious, good families, even if they be of foreign birth. I think it does good to present this view of the case to many Southern gentlemen, who grew rich and wealthy, not by virtue alone of their industry and skill, but by reason of the protection and impetus to prosperity given by our hitherto moderate and magnanimous Government. It is all idle nonsense for these Southern planters to say that they made the South, that they own it, and that they can do as they please—even to break up our Government, and to shut up the natural avenues of trade, intercourse, and commerce.

We know, and they know, if they are intelligent beings, that, as compared with the whole world, they are but as five millions are to one thousand millions—that they did not create the land—that their only title to its use and usufruct is the deed of the United States; and if they appeal to war, they hold their all by a very insecure tenure.

For my part I believe that this war is the result of false political doctrine, for which we are all as a people responsible, viz.: that any and every people have a right to self-government; and I would give all a chance to reflect, and when in error to recant. I know slave owners finding themselves in possession of a species of property in opposition to the growing sentiment of the whole civilized world, conceived their property in danger, and foolishly appealed to war; and by skilful political handling involved with themselves the whole South on the doctrines of error and prejudice. I believe that some of the rich and slaveholding are prejudiced to an extent that nothing but death and ruin will extinguish, but hope that as the poorer and industrial classes of the South realize their relative weakness, and their dependence upon the fruits of the earth and good will of their fellow-men, they will not only discover the error of their ways, and repent of their hasty action, but bless those who persistently maintained a Constitutional Government, strong enough to sustain itself, protect its citizens, and promise peaceful homes to millions yet unborn.

In this belief, whilst I assert for our Government the highest military prerogatives, I am willing to bear in patience that political nonsense of slave rights, State rights, freedom of conscience, freedom of press, and such other trash as have deluded the Southern people into war, anarchy, bloodshed, and the foulest crimes that have disgraced any time or any people.

I would advise the commanding officers at Huntsville, and such other towns as are occupied by our troops, to assemble the inhabitants and explain to them these plain, self-evident propositions, and tell them that it is for them *now* to say, whether they and their children shall inherit the beautiful land, which, by the accident of nature, has fallen to their share. The Government of the United States has in North Alabama any and all rights which they choose to enforce in war, to take their lives, their homes, their lands, their every thing, because they cannot deny that war does exist there, and war is simply power unrestrained by constitution or compact. If they want eternal war, well and good—we will accept the issue and dispossess them, and put our friends in possession. I know thousands and millions of good people who, at simple notice, would come to North Alabama and accept the elegant houses and plantations now there. If the people of Huntsville think different, let them persist in war three years longer, and then they will not be consulted. Three years ago, by a little reflection and patience they could have had a hundred years of peace and prosperity, but they preferred war; very well, last year they could have saved their slaves, but now it is too late—all the powers of earth cannot restore to them their slaves any more than their dead grandfathers. Next year their lands will be taken, for in war we can take them, and *rightfully*, too, and in another year they may beg in vain for their lives. A people who will persevere in war beyond a certain limit, ought to know the consequences. Many, many people, with less pertinacity than the South, have been wiped out of national existence.

My own belief is, that even now the non-slaveholding classes of the South are alienating from their associates in war. Already I hear crimination. Those who have property left, should take warning in time.

Since I have come down here, I have seen many Southern planters who now hire their negroes, and acknowledge that they knew not the earthquake they were to make by appealing to secession. They thought that the politicians had prepared the way, and that they could part in peace. They now see that we are bound together as one nation, by indissoluble ties, and that any interest or any people that set themselves up in antagonism to the nation, must perish.

While I would not remit one jot or tittle of our nation's rights, in peace or war, I do make allowances for past political errors and false prejudices. Our national Congress and Supreme Courts are the proper arenas in which to discuss conflicting opinions and not the battle-field.

You may not hear from me again, and if you think it will do any good, call some of the people together, and explain these my views. You may even read to them this letter, and let them use it, so as to prepare them for my coming.

To those who submit to the rightful law and authority, all gentleness and forbearance, but to the petulant and persistent secessionists, why, death is mercy, and the quicker he or she is disposed of, the better. Satan, and the rebellious saints of heaven, were allowed a continuance of existence in hell, merely to swell their just punishment. To such as would rebel against a Government so mild and just as ours was in peace, a punishment equal would not be unjust.

We are progressing well in this quarter. Though I have not changed my opinion that we may soon assume the existence of our National Government, yet years will pass before ruffianism, murder, and robbery will cease to afflict this region of our country.

Truly your friend,

(Signed) W. T. SHERMAN,
Major-General Commanding.

The advance of Gen. Sherman's movement, consisting of the 17th corps, under Gen. McPherson, left Vicksburg on February 3d, in light marching order, with rations for some days. The enemy were encountered after crossing the Big Black River, during the day, and some skirmishing ensued. The encampment was made that night on the west side of Baker's Creek, the enemy appearing in line of battle on the opposite side. The Confederate force consisted of about two thousand cavalry under Gen. Whitworth, who was in command from Jackson westward. At Canton there was

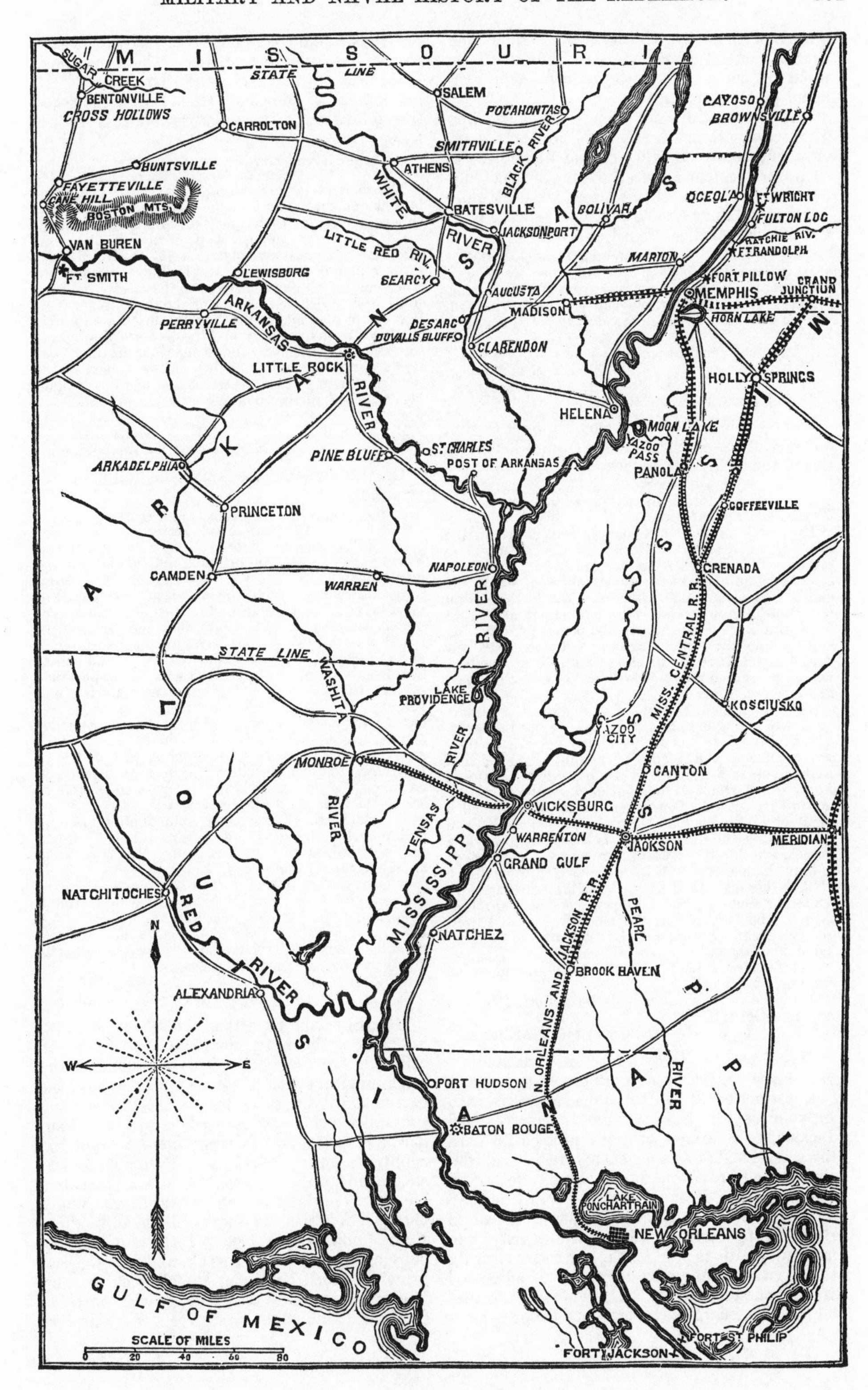
MISSOURI
STATE LINE
SUGAR CREEK
BENTONVILLE
CROSS HOLLOWS
CARROLTON
SALEM
POCAHONTAS
SMITHVILLE
HUNTSVILLE
ATHENS
FAYETTEVILLE
CANE HILL
BOSTON MTS.
BATESVILLE
WHITE RIVER
BLACK RIVER
JACKSONPORT
VAN BUREN
FT. SMITH
LITTLE RED RIV.
LEWISBURG
SEARCY
AUGUSTA
MADISON
PERRYVILLE
ARKANSAS
DESARC
DUVALLS BLUFF
CLARENDON
LITTLE ROCK
RIVER
HELENA
ARKADELPHIA
PINE BLUFF
ST. CHARLES
POST OF ARKANSAS
PRINCETON
CAMDEN
WARREN
NAPOLEON
ARKANSAS
STATE LINE
WASHITA
LAKE PROVIDENCE
MONROE
TENSAS RIVER
VICKSBURG
WARRENTON
GRAND GULF
NATCHITOCHES
RED RIVER
NATCHEZ
ALEXANDRIA
MISSISSIPPI
LOUISIANA
PORT HUDSON
BATON ROUGE
LAKE PONCHARTRAIN
NEW ORLEANS
GULF OF MEXICO
SCALE OF MILES
0 20 40 60 80
FORT JACKSON
FORT ST. PHILIP
CAYOSO
BROWNSVILLE
BOLIVAR
OCEOLA
FT. WRIGHT
FULTON LOG
HATCHIE RIV.
FT. RANDOLPH
MARION
FORT PILLOW
MEMPHIS
GRAND JUNCTION
HORN LAKE
HOLLY SPRINGS
MOON LAKE
YAZOO PASS
PANOLA
COFFEEVILLE
GRENADA
MISS. CENTRAL R.R.
KOSCIUSKO
YAZOO CITY
CANTON
JACKSON
MERIDIAN
PEARL RIVER
N. ORLEANS AND JACKSON R.R.
BROOK HAVEN
MISSISSIPPI
N
W
E

a force of about five thousand men under Gen. Loring, and at Meridian Gen. Polk with ten thousand more. The latter officer was in command of the department.

The preparations for Gen. Sherman's expedition had attracted the attention of the enemy, and many unaware of the difficulties of such a movement across the country, had supposed his object might be an attack on Mobile. The uncertainty which existed is shown by the following order, issued at a later date:

MOBILE, February 10, 1864.

DEAR SIR: I have just been informed by General Polk that the enemy is moving from Morton against Mobile. It is, therefore, my duty to ask all persons who cannot take part in the defence of the city to leave it.

I am, sir, very respectfully yours,
DABNEY MAURY,
Major-General Commanding.

To Col. JOHN FORSYTH, Mobile.

The Governor of Alabama, upon the first advance of the Federal troops from Vicksburg, issued the following address to the people:

EXECUTIVE DEPARTMENT OF ALABAMA,
MONTGOMERY, February 6, 1864.

To the People of Alabama:

The recent action of Congress has deprived the State of much of the materials of the second-class militia. It is important to the defence of the State, that Alabama shall have more troops subject to the call of her Commander-in-chief. We have, within the State, the materials for an efficient army. It needs nothing but the spirit, the prompt and willing spirit to fight, as men ought to fight, to guard our firesides and drive the hireling Yankee from our borders. We are threatened with raids into the heart of the State.

As your Executive Chief I call upon the middle aged, the young men and boys, to organize into companies at once, and report, without delay, that they are organized and ready. I cannot suppose that Alabamians will wait to be drafted into the service. The enthusiastic reënlistment of our veteran troops in the Virginia and Tennessee armies has caused a thrill of joyful hope to animate the hearts of even the croaking and despondent. If these battle-scarred heroes, who for three years have carried their lives in their hands, ready to be sacrificed in the defence of their homes and liberty, are willing to battle on while the feet of a hated foe press our soil, shall we at home be laggards in the race of glory? I trust no such damning stigma shall rest upon the honored name of Alabama.

I confidently expect a hearty, prompt, and noble response to this call.

The rolls of companies will be reported to the Adjutant-General.

T. H. WATTS, Governor of Alabama.

The force of Gen. Sherman consisted of two corps under Gen. McPherson and Hurlbut, estimated at thirty thousand men, with sixty pieces of light artillery. He reached Jackson on February 6th, and pressed forward toward Meridian. The enemy fell back, destroying all provision, and making a desert of the country. From Jackson Gen. Sherman crossed the Pearl River, and passed through Brandon to Morton. Here the enemy had made dispositions for a battle, but retired during the night. On the next day the army advanced and reached Meridian. The enemy state that all the Confederate Government property was previously removed, and nearly all the machinery of the railroad company. The force under Gen. Polk fell back across the Tombigbee. On his arrival at Meridian Gen. Sherman issued the following congratulatory address to his troops:

HEADQUARTERS, DEPARTMENT OF THE TENNESSEE,
MERIDIAN, MISS., February 15, 1864.

The General Commanding conveys his congratulations and thanks to the officers and men composing this command for their most successful accomplishment of one of the great problems of the war. Meridian, the great railway centre of the Southwest, is now in our possession, and by industry and hard work can be rendered useless to the enemy, and deprive him of the chief source of supply to his armies. Secrecy in plan and rapidity of execution accomplish the best results of war; and the General Commanding assures all that by following their leaders fearlessly and with confidence they will in time reap the reward so dear to us all—a peace that will never again be disturbed in our country by a discontented minority.

By order of W. T. SHERMAN,
Major-General Commanding.

On the same day he issued the following instructions:

HEADQUARTERS, DEPARTMENT OF THE TENNESSEE,
MERIDIAN, MISS., February 15, 1864.

1. The destruction of the railroads intersecting at Meridian is of great importance, and should be done most effectually. Every tie and rail for many miles in each direction should be absolutely destroyed or injured, and every bridge and culvert should be completely destroyed. To insure this end, to General Hurlbut is entrusted the destruction east and north, and to General McPherson the roads west and south. The troops should be impressed with the importance of this work, and also that time is material, and therefore it should be begun at once and be prosecuted with all the energy possible. Working parties should be composed of about one-half the command, and they should move by regiments, provided with their arms and haversacks, ready to repel attacks of cavalry. The other half in reserve will be able to watch the enemy retreating eastward.

2. Colonel E. F. Winslow, commanding cavalry, will keep his cavalry in advance of the party working eastward, and will act as though this army were slowly pursuing the enemy.

3. Special instructions will be given as to the general supply train; and the troops now in Meridian will, under proper brigade parties, collect meal, meat, and supplies. The destruction of buildings must be deferred till the last moment, when a special detail will be made for that purpose.

By order of W. T. SHERMAN,
Major-General Commanding.

Gen. Sherman reports that while at Meridian he made "the most complete destruction of railroads ever beheld." This was done on the road running south as far as Quitman; on the east as far as Cuba Station, twenty miles; and two miles north to Lauderdale Springs. Lauderdale County was already desolate, and the country between Meridian and Demopolis was sterile and unproductive. While at Meridian he heard nothing of the cavalry force under Gen. W. S. Smith, who was ordered to be there from Memphis by February 10th; and after occupying the town for a week, and his supplies growing short, he began to fall back toward Vicksburg, making a circuit by the north to Canton. This place was reached February

26th. His total loss was reported at one hundred and seventy men killed and wounded.

Meantime, Gen. W. S. Smith, who was ordered to report to Gen. Sherman at Meridian, moved from Memphis on February 11th, with a force of seven thousand men, consisting of cavalry and a brigade of infantry. After two days the expedition reached the Tallahatchie. A demonstration was made westward by the infantry toward Panola, thus attracting the attention of a force of the enemy, while the cavalry moved eastward to New Albany, where the river was crossed without opposition. Gen. Smith then pushed forward, and in the vicinity of Houston encountered some troops under Col. Gholson. They fell back to a swamp, where a considerable force was concentrated. Finding it impossible to turn either flank of this position, Gen. Smith moved rapidly eastward, while a demonstration was made in front of the enemy as if an attack was intended. On the same day he surprised and entered Okalona. The 9th Illinois cavalry, Lieut.-Col. Burgh, was then sent to Aberdeen to endeavor to secure a crossing of the Tombigbee. On the next morning Col. Grierson was sent forward with a brigade to support the 9th, with directions to threaten Columbus strongly. With the remaining force Gen. Smith advanced along the railroad toward West Point, tearing up the track and burning all the corn he found. The quantity which he destroyed is reported as nearly a million of bushels, with about two thousand bales of cotton. During this portion of the march negroes flocked to Gen. Smith by hundreds, mounted on their masters' horses and mules. They welcomed Gen. Smith as their deliverer whenever he met them: "God bless ye; has yer come at last? We've been lookin' for you for a long time, and had almost done gone give it up," was the cry of many. They bid farewell to their wives and children and marched in the van.

Hearing that the enemy was concentrated in heavy force at West Point, the brigade at Aberdeen was called over by a forced march to the railroad, at a station fifteen miles north of West Point. Two miles north of this station Gen. Smith encountered a force of the enemy, which fell back, after a sharp skirmish, through the town to a swamp on the right. Gen. Smith now found the enemy on his front in strong force, holding all the crossings of the swamp on the right; also on the line of the Octibbeha in front, and that of the Tombigbee River on his left. He could attack only with light carbines, as his horses were useless on the marshy ground. The enemy were armed with muskets and rifles. Gen. Smith was also now encumbered with pack-trains, and mules and horses captured, numbering about two thousand, beside as many negroes. To guard these his effective force was reduced, and he therefore determined to make a demonstration in front, and at the same time fall back with his trains and his main body to Okalona. This movement was successfully executed, although the enemy pressed closely, under the command of Gens. Forrest, Lee, and Chalmers. At Okalona, on the 22d, Gen. Smith was attacked, and suffered severely in the loss of men, besides five howitzers. His retreat that day was followed up. Under cover of the night he moved toward Pontotoc. This movement is thus described: "Picture to yourself, if you can, a living, moving mass of men, negroes, mules, and horses, of four thousand or five thousand, all *en masse*, literally jammed, huddled, and crowded into the smallest possible space; night setting in; artillery and small arms booming behind us; cavalry all around and ahead, moving on, on, on over fences, through fields and brush, over hills and across mud-holes, streams, and bridges, and still on, on into the night, until the moon rises on the scene and shows us some of the outlines of this living panorama. I forgot to say that in this crowd were a lot of prisoners, too, once or twice attempting to escape, followed by the swift report of the revolver, once with bitter consequences to the escaping prisoners."

During the day the enemy had moved on each flank, with the evident design of reaching the Tallahatchie River in advance, and forming a junction to prevent the crossing of Gen. Smith and capture his whole force; but, by marching all night, he safely crossed the river at New Albany. On the 23d the rear guard had skirmishing all day. On the 25th the advance reached Memphis, at 11 P. M., having marched nearly fifty miles that day. It was reported that a million bushels of corn were destroyed, many miles in length of the Memphis and Ohio Railroad, bridges, cotton-gins, and buildings. Says one: "We have probably devoured fifty thousand hams, some eggs, chickens, turkeys, milk, and butter by wholesale, and such *et ceteras* as can be found in so rich a country as we have passed through." The captured stock and trains were brought off safely. The loss was less than two hundred killed and captured. The expedition failed to make a junction with Gen. Sherman.

When the expedition of Gen. Sherman returned toward Vicksburg, a detachment was sent up the Yazoo River, accompanied with some gunboats. Yazoo City was attacked, but the enemy held it until reënforced. An amount of stores and cotton was destroyed. The Federal loss was about fifty killed and wounded. The general results of this movement, including those of Gens. Sherman and Smith, is stated to have been as follows: One hundred and fifty miles of railroad, sixty-seven bridges, seven hundred trestles, twenty locomotives, twenty-eight cars, several thousand bales of cotton, several steam mills, and over two million bushels of corn were destroyed. Some prisoners were captured, and upwards of eight thousand negroes and refugees came in with the various columns.

Many dwellings and all the outbuildings and farming utensils were destroyed.

The expedition of Gen. Sherman was generally supposed to be designed for the capture of Mobile. But, however that may have been, no official statement has been made. As it advanced toward Meridian, a force was detached from the army of Gen. Johnston, formerly commanded by Gen. Bragg, near Dalton, in Georgia, and sent to reënforce Gen. Polk. Two divisions of Gen. Hardee's Corps, under Gens. Stewart and Anderson, composed this force. To counteract this movement of the enemy, another was set on foot by Gen. Grant, then in command at Chattanooga. This consisted of an advance of the Fourteenth Corps, under Gen. Palmer, upon Dalton. It commenced on February 22d. The divisions of Gens. Jeff. C. Davis, Johnson, and Baird participated on the right, or direct road to Dalton, and the division of Gen. Stanley, under command of Gen. Crufts, on the left. This latter division had been encamped at Cleveland, and formed a junction with the main force between Ringgold and Tunnel Hill. The advance of the main force passed to the left of the Chickamauga battle-field, over Taylor's Ridge and through Ringgold Gap. A small force of the enemy was seen here, who retired. Ringgold, twenty-three miles from Chattanooga, was occupied that night. On the next day the column moved at daylight, and during the forenoon there was constant skirmishing with the cavalry of the enemy. At noon Gen. Crufts made a junction, and the whole corps moved forward in line of battle, with cavalry in advance and on the flanks, until it reached the vicinity of Tunnel Hill. On the ridge were four pieces of artillery, under Gen. Wheeler, which soon opened fire. These were dislodged in a short time by. the 2d Minnesota and 9th Indiana batteries, and the ridge occupied about 4 P. M. The advance continued and the cavalry force pressed forward in pursuit of the few scattered enemies, until it was checked by a cross-fire from six guns, at Rocky Fall, in a gorge through which the railroad and turnpike passes. The enemy succeeded in holding that position for the night. On the next morning, after considerable heavy fighting, the corps advanced into the town and captured about a hundred and fifty prisoners. The movement was immediately continued upon Dalton, distant seven miles from Tunnel Hill. The corps descended through the gaps into the Rocky Fall valley, the division of Gen. Crufts being on the left, Gen. Johnson on the right, Gen. Baird on the left centre, and Gen. Davis on the right centre. During the whole forenoon there was lively skirmishing, and the enemy's force evidently increased in numbers. Gen. Palmer advanced cautiously within two miles of Dalton, when it appeared that preparations had been made by the whole of Gen. Johnson's army to receive him. Considerable activity was perceptible in the interior of the enemy's works, and their cavalry began to hover about the flanks of Gen. Palmer's corps. Deserters reported that two divisions which had started toward Mobile had returned. Gen. Palmer now fell back to Tunnel Hill. His loss in the expedition was about three hundred and fifty killed and wounded. That of the enemy is unknown. Some prisoners were taken by Gen. Palmer. On March 10th he had fallen back to Ringgold.

The movement in East Tennessee consisted merely in an advance toward the position of Gen. Longstreet, who was then reported to be retreating into Virginia. He finally joined the army of Gen. Lee with his command.

In the Department of the South, authority was given to Gen. Q. A. Gillmore commanding, on December 22d, 1863, to undertake such operations as he might deem best on a conference with Admiral Dahlgren commanding the naval force. On the 13th of January the President wrote to Gen. Gillmore as follows:

EXECUTIVE MANSION, WASHINGTON, January 13, 1864.

Major-General GILLMORE: I understand an effort is being made by some worthy gentlemen to reconstruct a legal State Government in Florida. Florida is in your department, and it is not unlikely you may be there in person. I have given Mr. Hay a commission of major and sent him to you with some blank books and other blanks to aid in the construction. He will explain as to the manner of using the blanks, and also my general views on the subject. It is desirable for all to coöperate; but if irreconcilable differences of opinion shall arise you are master. I wish the thing done in the most speedy way possible, so that when done it be within the range of the late proclamation on the subject. The detail labor will of course have to be done by others, but I shall be greatly obliged if you will give it such general supervision as you can find consistent with your more strictly military duties. A. LINCOLN.

On January 14th Gen. Gillmore proposed to the War Department to occupy the west bank of the St. John's River in Florida, and establish small depots there preparatory to an advance west. On the 22d of January he was informed by the Secretary that the matter was left entirely to his judgment and discretion with the means at his command. On January 31st Gen. Gillmore again wrote to the Secretary that the objects to be obtained by the operations were:

1st. "To procure an outlet for cotton, lumber, timber, &c.

2d. "To cut off one of the enemy's sources of commissary supplies, &c.

3d. "To obtain recruits for my colored regiments.

4th. "To inaugurate measures for the speedy restoration of Florida to her allegiance in accordance with the instructions which he had received from the President, by the hands of Major John Hay, Assistant Adjutant-General."

On the same day Gen. Gillmore issued the following order:

HEADQUARTERS DEPARTMENT OF THE SOUTH.
HILTON HEAD, S. C., January 31, 1864.

GENERAL ORDERS No. 16.—In accordance with the provision of the Presidential Proclamation of Pardon and Amnesty, given at Washington on the 8th day of December, in the year of our

Lord one thousand eight hundred and sixty-three, and in pursuance of instructions received from the President of the United States, Major John Hay, Assistant Adjutant-General, will proceed to Fernandina, Florida, and other convenient points in that State, for the purpose of extending to the citizens of the State of Florida an opportunity to avail themselves of the benefits of that Proclamation, by offering for their signature the oath of allegiance therein prescribed, and by issuing to all those subscribing to said oath certificates entitling them to the benefits of the Proclamation. Fugitive citizens of the State of Florida, within the limits of this Department, will have an opportunity to subscribe to the same oath and secure certificates in the office of the Post Commander at Hilton Head, South Carolina.

By command of Maj.-Gen. Q. A. GILLMORE.
ED. W. SMITH, Ass't Adj.-Gen.

Orders were issued to Brig.-Gen. Truman Seymour on February 5th to proceed to Jacksonville, Fla., and effect a landing and push forward his mounted force to Baldwin, seventy miles from Jacksonville. It was the junction of the railroads from Jacksonville and Fernandina. On the 6th the expedition, consisting of twenty steamers and eight schooners, under convoy of the gunboat Norwich, left Hilton Head and arrived at Jacksonville on the next day, February 7th. When the landing of the troops commenced a small body of the enemy in a wood adjacent to the town fired three shots, thus wounding two or three persons. A company of colored troops went in pursuit, and the enemy after firing a few shots fled.

About twenty-five families remained in Jacksonville. They were chiefly women and children, and all professed to be in favor of the Union. The railroad was in running order to Tallahassee. Provisions and cattle were abundant. Gen. Joseph Finegan was in command of the forces of the enemy.

In the afternoon of the 8th the march to the interior of the State was commenced. The forces were divided into three columns, commanded respectively by Cols. Barton, Hawley, and Henry. Col. Barton took the main road, Col. Henry took the road to the right of that, and Col. Hawley one still further to the right. After an advance of three miles the three roads united on the line of the railroad. Here the infantry bivouacked for the night, and Col. Guy V. Henry, with the 40th Massachusetts infantry, the independent battalion of cavalry and Elder's horse battery B, 1st artillery, pushed forward on a reconnoissance. It was dark when the movement commenced at a brisk trot toward Lake City. For the distance of five miles none of the enemy were seen. The country through which the force passed was low, level, and marshy. On each side the road was flanked by pine forests. The soil was that of fair farming land to Lake City, but beyond it becomes a rich sandy loam. A mile and a half from Camp Finegan a picket station was discovered, but the pickets had fallen back to the reserve post. Pressing forward, after a short stop, Col. Henry soon came in sight of Camp Finegan on the right. About two hundred cavalrymen were seen drawn up in line of battle. Having no apprehension from this force, he continued his advance, and three miles beyond surprised and captured a camp of artillery containing four guns, camp and garrison equipage, including wagons, tents, commissory stores and officers' baggage. Three prisoners were taken. The remainder of the force escaped to the woods. This body was falling back, and had not anticipated so rapid an advance of the Federal force. Early on the next morning the advance reached Baldwin, a place of fifteen buildings. Here three cars, two of which were filled with corn, a three-inch rifled gun, a considerable quantity of cotton, rice, tobacco, and other stores were captured. At evening Gens. Gillmore and Seymour arrived.

On the 10th Col. Henry continued his advance. At Barber's Station a thousand barrels of turpentine and five hundred pounds of bacon were captured. An advance guard was then sent forward to see if the enemy were in position to defend the south fork of the St. Mary's river, while the remainder of the force cautiously followed. The enemy in small force were found defending the fork, when a skirmish ensued, in which four were killed on the Federal side and thirteen wounded. Two of the enemy were killed and three wounded, when they fled to the woods. Their force was about one hundred and fifty men. At 6 P. M. Col. Henry reached Sanderson, forty-miles from Jacksonville. The place had been abandoned by the enemy, and a large amount of stores committed to the flames. On the 11th the command encamped five miles from Lake City, which was held by the enemy but evacuated during the night. This was unknown to Col. Henry, and, as he was without infantry, he retraced his steps to Sanderson. The most important property captured was as follows: Two twelve-pounder rifled guns, two six-pounder guns, one three-inch gun, two other guns, five caissons, a large quantity of ammunition, an immense supply of camp and garrison equipage, four railroad cars, one hundred and thirteen bales of cotton, four army wagons, one hundred and five horses and mules, a large stock of saddlery, tanning machinery, three thousand and eighty-three barrels turpentine, six thousand bushels corn; three large warehouses were destroyed. On the 11th telegraphic communication was established between Jacksonville and Baldwin, and on that day Gen. Gillmore sent instructions to Gen. Seymour not to risk a repulse in advancing upon Lake City, but to hold Sanderson unless there were reasons for falling back, and also in case his advance met with serious opposition to concentrate at Sanderson and the south fork of the St. Mary's. On the 13th Gen. Seymour was further instructed to concentrate at Baldwin without delay. This was done at once. Meantime, Col. Henry was sent toward the left to capture some railroad trains at Gainsville on the Fernandina and Cedar Keys railroad. This resulted in a skirmish with a

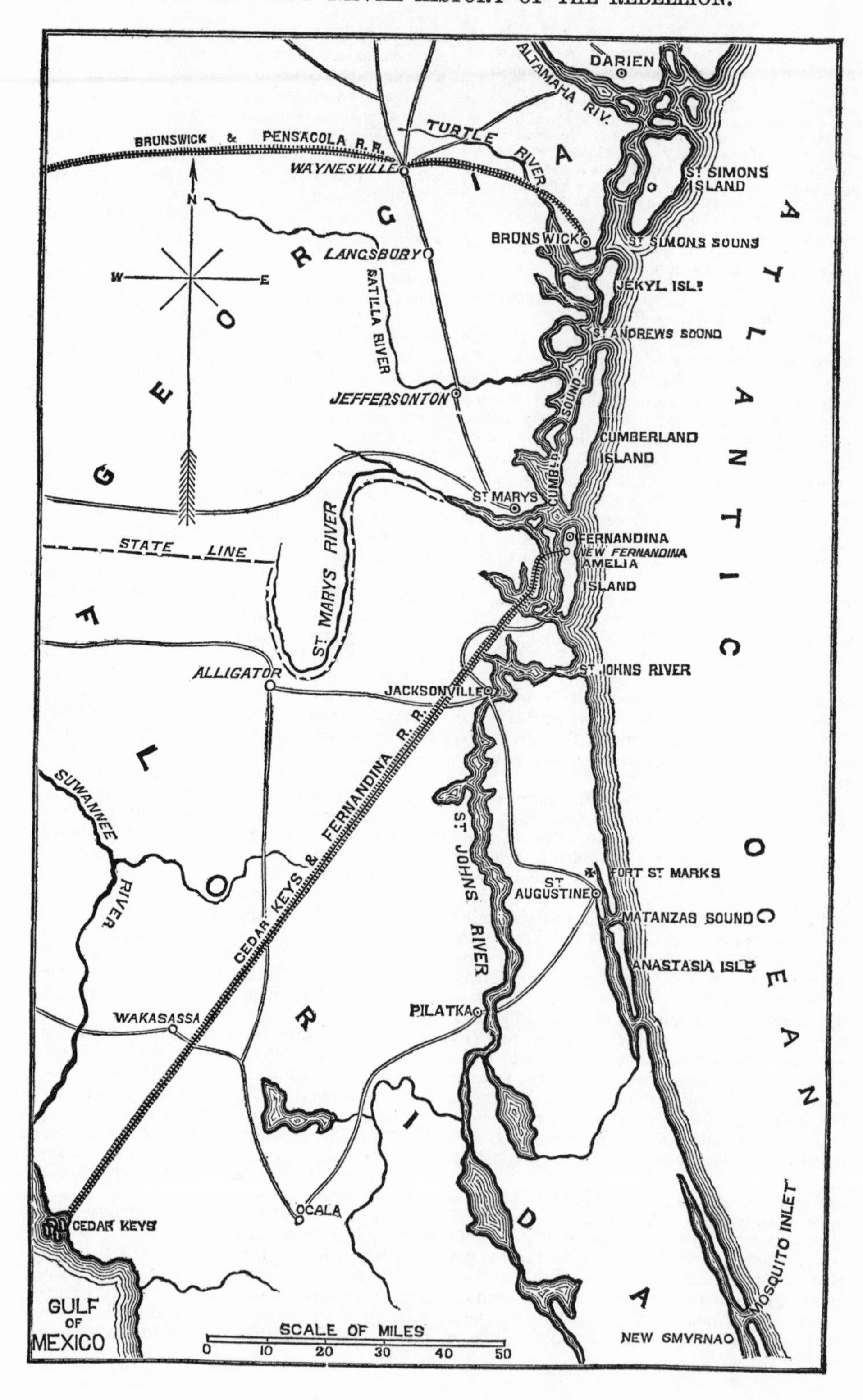
DARIEN
ALTAMAHA RIV.
TURTLE RIVER
BRUNSWICK & PENSACOLA R.R.
WAYNESVILLE
ST SIMONS ISLAND
BRUNSWICK
ST SIMONS SOUNS
LANGSBURY
SATILLA RIVER
JEKYL ISLD
ST ANDREWS SOUND
JEFFERSONTON
CUMBLD SOUND
CUMBERLAND ISLAND
GEORGIA
ST MARYS
FERNANDINA
NEW FERNANDINA
AMELIA ISLAND
STATE LINE
ST MARYS RIVER
ATLANTIC OCEAN
ALLIGATOR
ST JOHNS RIVER
JACKSONVILLE
CEDAR KEYS & FERNANDINA R.R.
SUWANNEE RIVER
ST JOHNS RIVER
FORT ST MARKS
ST AUGUSTINE
MATANZAS SOUND
ANASTASIA ISLD
FLORIDA
WAKASASSA
PILATKA
OCALA
CEDAR KEYS
MOSQUITO INLET
GULF OF MEXICO
SCALE OF MILES
0 10 20 30 40 50
NEW SMYRNAO
N
W
E

body of East Florida cavalry, which was repulsed. A reconnoissance was also made along the Georgia State line by Col. Scammon, destroying several small works of the enemy. After arranging with Gen. Seymour for the construction of certain defences at Jacksonville, Baldwin, and the south fork of the St. Mary's, Gen. Gillmore departed to Hilton Head. His understanding was that no advance would be made by Gen. Seymour without further instructions, and not until the defences were well advanced. It was the intention of Gen. Gillmore to construct several works capable of resisting a *coup de main* at Jacksonville, Baldwin, Pilatka, and perhaps one or two other important points, so strong that two or three hundred men would be sufficient at each. His desire was to see the lumber and turpentine trade on the St. John's River revived, and to give assurance that the occupation of the river was intended to be permanent.

On Thursday the 18th, the force of Gen. Seymour at Jacksonville left camp with ten days rations, and advanced on the line of the railroad sixteen miles. On the next day it moved seventeen miles to Barber's Station, the roads having been bad on the whole route. On the 20th the troops were in motion at an early hour, the light cavalry in advance. The line of march was across the south fork of the St. Mary's, and up the road to Sanderson, nine miles distant. The day was beautiful. The sky was clear overhead, and the savannahs which stretched out on each side of the sandy road winding through the pine woods, were warm with the sunshine. Sanderson was reached without a halt. There the infantry made a short halt, but the cavalry kept its position about two miles in advance. The march was resumed at midday toward Lake City. Gen. Seymour's force, consisting of five thousand men, moved in three columns, Col. Hawley's brigade on the left, Col. Barton's in the centre, and Col. Scammon's regiment on the extreme right. The cavalry in advance were led by Col. Henry with Elder's battery. In the rear was the colored brigade led by Col. Montgomery. About six miles from Sanderson the enemy's mounted pickets, thirty or forty in number, were met and driven in after exchanging shots. The main body hurried forward a distance of two miles, when three or four cannon shot of the enemy fell among the head of the column. Skirmishing commenced immediately. The artillery dashed into position on the gallop, the infantry on the double-quick step, and in a brief period of time a severe battle was progressing. Elder's battery unlimbered at the head of the road, Hamilton's to the left, and Langdon's on the extreme left, opening at short range with canister shot. The artillery of the enemy consisted of four or five guns, and was badly served at first, being fired too high to do injury. Gen. Seymour's line of infantry was well formed for the position. With the exception of a small field of a few acres, it was in the woods, amid a heavy growth of pine timber, and with swampy ground intervening between it and the enemy, of whose position nothing was known. The battle lasted for three hours. Two of the Federal batteries were disabled early in the action. The 7th New Hampshire broke, but was rallied again. The 8th U. S. colored fought well until the loss of their leader, when they fled. The contest closed at dusk, and Gen. Seymour finding his force repulsed with some loss, and the colored reserve unequal to the emergency, retired from the field leaving his dead and wounded. The retreat for a short distance was conducted in successive lines of battle, but finding the enemy were not disposed to follow the line was changed, and the force retired in column, Barton's brigade bringing up the rear covered by the cavalry and Elder's battery. A halt was made at Sanderson, six or seven miles, coffee cooked, and some attention given to the wounded. From Sanderson to Barber's Station, says a writer, "ten miles, we wended or crawled along, the wounded filling the night air with lamentations, the crippled horses neighing in pain, and a full moon kissing the cold, clammy lips of the dying." On the next morning the retreat was continued to Baldwin, where the cavalry of the enemy made their appearance. Many of the wounded were here sent on cars drawn by mules to Jacksonville, and Gen. Seymour, knowing that the enemy was following in force, ordered the commissary stores, worth about sixty thousand dollars, to be destroyed, and resumed his march to Jacksonville. His loss in killed, wounded, and missing was about twelve hundred.

The following despatch from the Governor of Florida presents the enemy's account of the battle:

TALLAHASSEE, FLA., February 21.

TO PRESIDENT DAVIS: I have just received the following despatch from Gen. Finegan, dated yesterday:

"I met the enemy in full force to-day, under Gen. Seymour, and defeated him with great loss. I captured five pieces of artillery, hold possession of the battle-field, and the killed and wounded of the enemy. My cavalry are in pursuit. I don't know precisely the number of prisoners, as they are being brought in constantly. My whole loss, I think, will not exceed two hundred and fifty killed and wounded. Among them I mourn the loss of many brave officers and men."

I understand that Gen. Finegan also captured many small arms.

(Signed) JOHN MILTON, Governor.

Gen. Seymour now occupied Jacksonville with his forces, and the enemy took up a position at Camp Finegan, eight miles distant, toward Baldwin. The following correspondence passed, at this time, between Gen. Seymour and Gen. Finegan commanding the enemy's force:

HEADQUARTERS DISTRICT OF FLORIDA, D. S.
JACKSONVILLE, FLA., Feb. 23, 1864.

SIR: In view of the inconveniences to which the wounded prisoners in your hands, since the action of the 20th, near Olustee, Florida, may be unavoidably subjected, I have the honor to propose that they may be paroled, and delivered within my lines as soon as possible, and Capt. G. S. Dana, of my staff, the bearer of this communication, is authorized to make such arrangements therefor as may be convenient, and a horse car or ambulance will be sent for the wounded, at such times as may be designated, should this proposal be acceded to.

The body of Col. C. W. Fribley was left on the field at Olustee. If there have been any means of identifying his person, I request that his grave may be so marked, that at some future day his family may be able to remove his remains.

I am, General, very respectfully,
Your obedient servant,
T. SEYMOUR,
Brigadier-General Commanding.

To the General commanding the Confederate forces in Florida.

HEADQUARTERS DISTRICT EAST FLORIDA,
BALDWIN, FLA., Feb. 24, 1864.

Brig.-Gen. T. Seymour, Commanding United States forces, Jacksonville:

GENERAL: I have the honor to acknowledge the receipt of your communication of the 23d inst., proposing "that the wounded prisoners left by you on the field of battle, at Ocean Pond, on the 20th inst., be paroled and sent within your lines, and requesting that, if the body of Col. C. W. Fribley, left on the ground, can be identified, that his grave be marked, so that at some future day his family may be able to remove his remains."

In reply, I have to state that the wounded prisoners have been sent forward and properly taken care of, and will be kept to await the future action of my Government in reference to a general exchange of prisoners.

I regret to state that the body of Col. Fribley has not been identified.

Very respectfully, your ob't serv't,
JOSEPH FINEGAN.
Brigadier-General Commanding.

HEADQUARTERS DISTRICT OF FLORIDA, D. S.,
JACKSONVILLE, FLA., Feb. 25, 1864.

GENERAL: Notwithstanding the information contained in your communication of the 24th inst., respecting the body of the late Col. Fribley, that it has not been identified, I have the honor to urge that measures be taken to ascertain the possession of some of the articles upon his person, with a view to the return of some of them to his widow, at this place. The accompanying memorandum may serve to assist in whatever investigation you may decide to institute.

And I feel assured that whatever can be done by you to mitigate the sorrow that is the lot of a most deserving and greatly suffering lady, will be cheerfully accorded.

And any remuneration that may be desired or necessary to procure any part of the personal memorials mentioned in this memorandum, will be duly forwarded to the parties having them in possession.

I have further to request, if the arrangement can be made, that Mrs. Fribley herself, accompanied by the adjutant of the late colonel, may be permitted to pass within your lines, in the hope of obtaining more information than can perhaps otherwise be anticipated.

The circumstances of this contest will certainly not be injuriously affected by such a concession to humanity.

Respectfully, your obedient servant,
T. SEYMOUR, Brig.-Gen. Commanding.

Brig.-Gen. Joseph Finegan, Commanding Confederate forces East Florida.

HEADQUARTERS DISTRICT EASTERN FLORIDA,
February 26, 1864.

GENERAL: I have the honor to acknowledge the receipt of your communication of the 25th inst., and to reply that I will cause the proper inquiries to be made to obtain the information sought for in your letter, and will, as soon as practicable, forward you a reply by flag of truce.

I regret to say that I consider it at present objectionable, for reasons which it is needless for me to state, but which will doubtless be appreciated by yourself, to grant a permit for Mrs. Fribley and the adjutant of her late husband's regiment to visit the battle-field of Ocean Pond. At a future day these obstacles may be removed.

I am, very respectfully, your obedient servant,
(Signed) JOSEPH FINEGAN,
Brigadier-General Commanding.

Brig.-Gen. T. Seymour, Commanding United States forces Jacksonville, Florida.

HEADQUARTERS DEPARTMENT SOUTH CAROLINA,
GEORGIA AND FLORIDA, March 4, 1864.

District of Florida headquarters, forces in the field.

GENERAL: In further reply to your communication of the 25th of February, 1864, I have the honor to forward through you to the widow of the late Col. Fribley, an ambrotype, supposed to be the one referred to in the memorandum accompanying your communication.

Traces have also been discovered of his watch, a letter from his wife to himself, and his diary, and steps have been taken to recover possession of them. If successful, the two former articles will be forwarded.

That I may not be misunderstood, it is due to myself to state that no sympathy with the fate of any officer commmnding negro troops, but compassion for a widow in grief, has induced these efforts to recover for her relics which she must naturally value.

Very respectfully, your obedient servant,
(Signed) W. M. GARDNER,
Brigadier-General Commanding.

To Brigadier-General T. SEYMOUR,
Comm'g United States forces, Jacksonville, Fla.

A small Federal force remained at Jacksonville for several months, and many raids in different directions were made by portions of it. No important military operations took place. The movement to reorganize the State ceased after the battle at Olustee.

Early in the year, a concentration of forces at New Orleans commenced. To these were added a portion of the forces of Gen. Sherman. After his return to Vicksburg from his expedition to Meridian, a considerable body of his troops moved to join Gen. Banks, while the division of Gen. A. J. Smith remained at Vicksburg, ready to coöperate. It was the purpose of Gen. Banks to open the region of Western Louisiana to trade, and scatter or destroy the forces of the enemy. During only the months of March and April the Red River has sufficient water to be navigable by the largest vessels.

In the beginning of the month of March, the division of Gen. Franklin, who formerly held a command in the army of the Potomac, moved from New Orleans by the railroad to Brashear City, thence along the Bayou Teche and Opelousas, to Alexandria. This was substantially the same route as was taken by the army in the previous year, under Gen. Banks. and described in previous pages of this volume. In the mean time the most formidable fleet ever seen in the western waters had been collected under Rear-Admiral Porter, at the mouth of the Red River. It consisted of twenty powerful armed steamers of all classes.

from the light to the heaviest draught. Among them were the monitors Ozark, Osage, Neosho; the ironclads Benton, Carondelet, Pittsburg, Mound City, Louisville, Essex, and Chillicothe; the rams Price, Choctaw, Lafayette, besides the lighter boats, Blackhawk, Ouachita, Champion, and Tyler.

On the 10th of March, about ten thousand troops under Gen. A. J. Smith embarked in twenty transports at Vicksburg, and proceeded to join the fleet. This force consisted of the first and third divisions of the sixteenth army corps, and the first and fourth divisions of the seventeenth. It was intended to unite with the force of Gen. Banks, to which was subsequently to be added the force under Gen. Steele from Arkansas. The principal force of the enemy was under Gen. Richard Taylor, at Shreveport. Bodies of troops under Gen. Price and Gen. Walker were also moving to unite with it.

On the next afternoon the transports arrived at the mouth of Red River, and joined the fleet. On the next day, Saturday, the 12th, the fleet moved up the old Red River, into the Atchafalaya, and in the afternoon anchored at Semmesport. The town had ceased to exist; a few chimneys marked the former site. It was burned by Col. C. R. Ellet, in retaliation for the firing upon his steamer, the Queen of the West; and afterward entirely destroyed by Col. John Ellet, during the siege of Port Hudson, to prevent the construction of batteries by the enemy, and a traffic across the river. Hearing nothing from Gen. Banks, Gen. Smith disembarked a portion of his troops on the next day, and sent a brigade under Gen. Mower to reconnoitre in the vicinity of Yellow Bayou. The enemy had broken up their camp and retired. Two extensive earthworks in an incomplete state were found. A distance further five teams loaded with tents were overtaken. The latter were burnt, and the teams loaded with sugar and molasses, and taken to the fleet. It was now decided that the column should march overland to Fort De Russy, a distance of thirty miles, whither it was supposed the enemy had retreated. At daybreak, on Monday morning, the force started in light marching order, with the brigade of Gen. Mower in advance. They had advanced scarcely five miles before they were beset by the enemy's cavalry, in front and rear. This continued until the position of the enemy, known as Fort De Russy, was approached in the afternoon. It consisted of two distinct and formidable earthworks, connected by a covered way; the upper part facing the road mounted four guns, two field and two siege; the lower work, commanding the river, was a casemated battery of three guns. Only two guns were in position in it, one a 11-inch Columbiad, and an 8-inch smooth bore. On each side were batteries of two guns each, making in all eight siege and two field-pieces. As the line moved up to the edge of the timber, the upper work opened with shell and shrapnel, against which two batteries were brought to bear. The cannonading continued for two hours. A charge was then ordered, and as the men reached the ditch, the garrison surrendered. The Federal loss was four killed and thirty wounded; that of the enemy, five killed and four wounded. The prisoners taken were twenty-four officers and two hundred men. Considerable ammunition and stores were found, besides a thousand muskets. A portion of the fleet arrived as the fort surrendered. Gen. Smith ordered the works to be destroyed. This portion of his troops were then embarked on the transports, and reached Alexandria, one hundred and forty miles from the Mississippi River, on the evening of the 16th. They were followed by the remainder of the forces and the fleet. The enemy retired before the advance, destroying two steamboats and considerable cotton. During the first week, the gunboats rescued upwards of four thousand bales of cotton, and large quantities were brought in by the negroes. The fleet was detained by the low water on the falls above Alexandria, its depth being only six feet, whereas nine feet were required to float the largest gunboats. Three formidable iron-clad rams of the enemy were reported to be at Shreveport, about four hundred and fifty miles above the Mississippi River. On the 19th, Gen. Stone, chief of Gen. Banks' staff, arrived and reported that the latter was at Opelousas. On the 20th, the cavalry force under Gen. Lee, attached to the command of Gen. Banks, reached Alexandria, after marching from Franklin across the Teche country. Meantime detachments from Gen. Smith's command had been sent forward, and captured several small bodies of the enemy.

On the 21st, Natchitoches was taken, with two hundred prisoners and four pieces of artillery. It is about eighty miles from Alexandria. On the 26th, the force of Gen. Smith as the advance, left Alexandria for Shreveport, to be followed by the troops of Gen. Banks then arriving. Shreveport was the destination of the expedition. It had been the capital of the Confederate State Government. Its situation is in almost the extreme northwestern corner of Louisiana, and at the head of navigation on the Red River. The enemy were reported to have a strong force there, and large quantities of cotton and military stores were expected to be captured. The coöperation of Gen. Steele in command at Little Rock, Arkansas, was also expected by Gen. Banks. Twelve of the gunboats and a fleet of thirty transports were able to pass over the shoals, and moved up the river in coöperation with the land forces. On the 4th of April, Gen. Banks' column reached Nachitoches. Here he remained two days.

On Wednesday, the 6th, the army moved from Nachitoches for Shreveport, with Gen. Lee's cavalry in advance. The infantry marched seventeen miles, and the cavalry reached

Crump's Hill four miles further, and half way between Natchitoches and Mansfield. On the 7th, Gen. Lee pushed forward, maintaining a constant skirmish with the enemy, until he arrived at a position two miles beyond Pleasant Hill. Here the main body of the enemy's cavalry, under Major-Gen. Thomas Green, was encountered by the advance of Gen. Lee's cavalry, consisting of a brigade under Col. H. Robinson. Heavy skirmishing ensued for two hours and a half, when Gen. Green fell back upon the Con-

federate infantry and artillery at Bayou du Paul. Col. Robinson finding the enemy in an increased force, halted for the night and to await reënforcements. Early the next morning, the infantry brigade of the 4th division of the 13th corps, under Col. Landrum, joined him, and the advance was resumed and continued until 2 o'clock P. M., driving the enemy before them for seven miles. The main force of the enemy now appeared, occupying a strong position in the vicinity of Sabine Cross roads east of Mansfield. They were partly concealed in a dense wood with an open field in front and the Shreveport road passing through their lines. Major-Gen. Taylor was in command. Major-Gen. Green commanded the left wing, Brig.-Gen. Mouton the right, with Gen. Walker's division still further to the right, and two cavalry regiments on the extreme right. Meantime Gen. Ransom arrived on the field with the remaining brigade of the 4th division of the 13th corps. The entire division numbered 2,600 men. The 19th corps, under Gen. Franklin, were in camp nine miles in the rear, and Gen. A. J. Smith, with about one-half of the 16th and 17th corps, was nearly twenty miles in the rear. The Federal artillery consisted of the Chicago Mercantile battery, the 1st Indiana battery, Nim's Massachusetts battery, and battery G, 5th regular artillery. Col. Landrum's brigade took a position on the right and centre with all the batteries except one, and Gen. Ransom's brigade on the left with Nim's battery supported by Col. Dudley's cavalry brigade, while Col. Robinson's cavalry protected the wagon train, and Col. Lucas acted on the right. Gen. Banks had, in the meanwhile, arrived on the field, and at once sent couriers for Gen. Franklin to hasten forward with all possible despatch. Heavy skirmishing commenced at 5 o'clock, and in a short time the skirmishers were driven in by the enemy advancing in force, when the engagement became general on the right and centre. To sustain this portion of the line, which was heavily pressed, the left was necessarily much weakened. This was observed by the enemy, who massed upon their right and dashed upon the left of Gen. Banks, which was soon driven back, and four guns of Nim's battery captured. Not horses enough were alive to drag it from the field. Meantime the right continued fiercely engaged and the centre was pressed back, when the right also gave way. The loss of the Chicago battery and the 1st Indiana soon followed. Gen. Cameron came up with a brigade of Indiana troops belonging to the third division of the 13th corps, and advanced to the front, but was unable to resist the force of the enemy. Gen. Franklin with staff, also arrived on the field in advance of his division. The line continued to fall back slowly until the baggage trains blocked up the roads in the rear so that the troops could not easily pass, when a panic ensued. The enemy now pursued for three and a half miles, when their advance was checked and driven back by Gen. Emory's division. Here the conflict ended for the day. Six guns of the Chicago battery, two of battery G, four of the 1st Indiana, and six of Nim's battery were left on the field, with two howitzers of the 6th Missouri. The loss of Gen. Banks was estimated at two thousand killed, wounded, and missing. His force on the field was about eight thousand. The force of the enemy was much larger. Gen. Mouton was among the badly wounded of the enemy.

As it was now known that Gen. Smith with his force had marched to Pleasant Hill and halted, Gen. Banks determined to withdraw to that place for the sake of concentrating his forces, and of the advantageous position which he could there occupy. The movement commenced at ten o'clock at night, and before daylight the rear of the army was well on the road. The enemy during the night had pressed his pickets down on Gen. Banks' front, but failed to discover the retreat of the troops as it was conducted with the greatest silence and expedition. Becoming aware of it in the morning, he followed after with his main force, his cavalry being in advance, but the cavalry failed to come up with the rear under Gen. Emory, before it had arrived at Pleasant Hill about seven o'clock in the morning. Col. Gooding, of the cavalry division, was then sent out on the Shreveport road to find the enemy. About a mile up the road the advance was seen approaching in strong force.

The battle-ground was an open field on the outside of the town of Pleasant Hill on the Shreveport road. It was open and rolling, and ascended both from the side of the town and from the side on which the enemy were approaching. A belt of timber extended almost entirely around it. The division of Gen.. Emory was drawn up in line of battle on the sloping side, with the right resting across the Shreveport road. Gen. McMillen's brigade formed the extreme right of the line, with his right resting near the woods, which extended along the whole base of the slope and through which the enemy would advance. Gen. Dwight's brigade was formed next with his left resting on the road, Col. Benedict's brigade formed next, with his right resting on the road and a little in the rear of Gen. Dwight's left. Two pieces of Taylor's battery were placed in the rear of Gen. Dwight's left on the road, and four pieces were in position on an eminence on the left of the road and in rear of Col. Benedict. Hibbard's Vermont battery was in the rear of the division. Gen. Smith's division, under command of Gen. Mower, was massed in two lines of battle fifty yards apart with artillery in rear of Gen. Emory's division. The right of the first line rested on the road, and was composed of two brigades: the first brigade on the right commanded by Colonel Linch; the second brigade on the left commanded by Colonel Shaw. The 3d Indiana battery (Crawford's) was posted in the first line of battle, and on the right of the 89th Indiana. The 9th Indiana battery (Brown's) was in position on the right of the first brigade. The Missouri battery occupied ground on the right of the 89th Indiana.

The second line was composed of two brigades. The 13th corps were in reserve. Skirmishing continued through the day, and at 4 P. M. the enemy's line of battle was formed. Gen. Green's division was posted on the extreme left; Gen. Mouton's division, under command of Brig.-Gen. Polignac, on Gen. Green's right; Gen. Walker on Polignac's right, and Gen. Churchill's division of Arkansians and Missourians on the extreme right. About 5 P. M. the enemy appeared on the field at the edge of the woods, and the battle began by the Federal batteries opening upon him with case shell as he advanced at double-quick. The left under Col. Benedict came into action first, and soon after the right and centre were engaged. The contest now became fierce on both sides, when Gen. Emory's division, pressed by overwhelming numbers, fell back up the hill to the 16th corps, which was just behind the crest. The enemy rushed forward and were met by Gen. Smith with a discharge from all his guns, which was followed by an immediate charge of the infantry, by which the enemy were driven rapidly back to the woods, where they broke in confusion. Night put an end to the pursuit. The Taylor battery lost on the advance of the enemy was recovered, and also two guns of Nim's battery. Five hundred prisoners were also taken. Early on the next morning, leaving the dead unburied and the muskets thrown on the field, the army commenced its march back to Grand Ecore, thirty-five miles from Pleasant Hill, to obtain rest and rations.

The entire losses of the campaign thus far were stated to be twenty pieces of artillery, three thousand men, one hundred and thirty wagons, twelve hundred horses and mules, including many that died of disease. The gains were the capture of Fort De Russy, Alexandria, Grand Ecore, and Natchitoches, the opening of Red River, the capture of three thousand bales of cotton, twenty-three hundred prisoners, twenty-five pieces of artillery, chiefly captured by the fleet, and small arms and considerable stores. A large number of citizens enlisted in the service in Alexandria, and the material for two colored regiments was gathered, and five thousand negroes, male and female, abandoned their homes and followed the army.

Meanwhile Rear-Admiral Porter ascended the falls with twelve gunboats and thirty transports, and reached Grand Ecore when the army was at Natchitoches preparing for an immediate march. As the river was rising slowly the advance was continued with six smaller gunboats and twenty transports, having army stores and a part of Gen. Smith's division on board. Starting on the 7th of April, Springfield Landing was reached on the third day. Here a large steamer sunk in the river obstructed further progress; and information was received that the army had met with a reverse. Orders also came to Gen. Smith's troops to return to Grand Ecore with the transports. The fleet, therefore, turned back, but was constantly annoyed by the enemy on the bank of the river. Two of the fleet at Grand Ecore were found above the bar, and not likely to get away until there was a rise of water in the river.

The continued low water in the Red River, and the difficulty of keeping up a line of supplies, caused the army to fall back to Alexandria. The march commenced in the afternoon of April 21st, by starting the baggage train with a suitable guard. At 2 o'clock the next morning the army began silently to evacuate its position, Gen. Smith's force forming the rear guard. Soon after daylight the enemy observing the movement began his pursuit, but with so small a force that only slight skirmishing

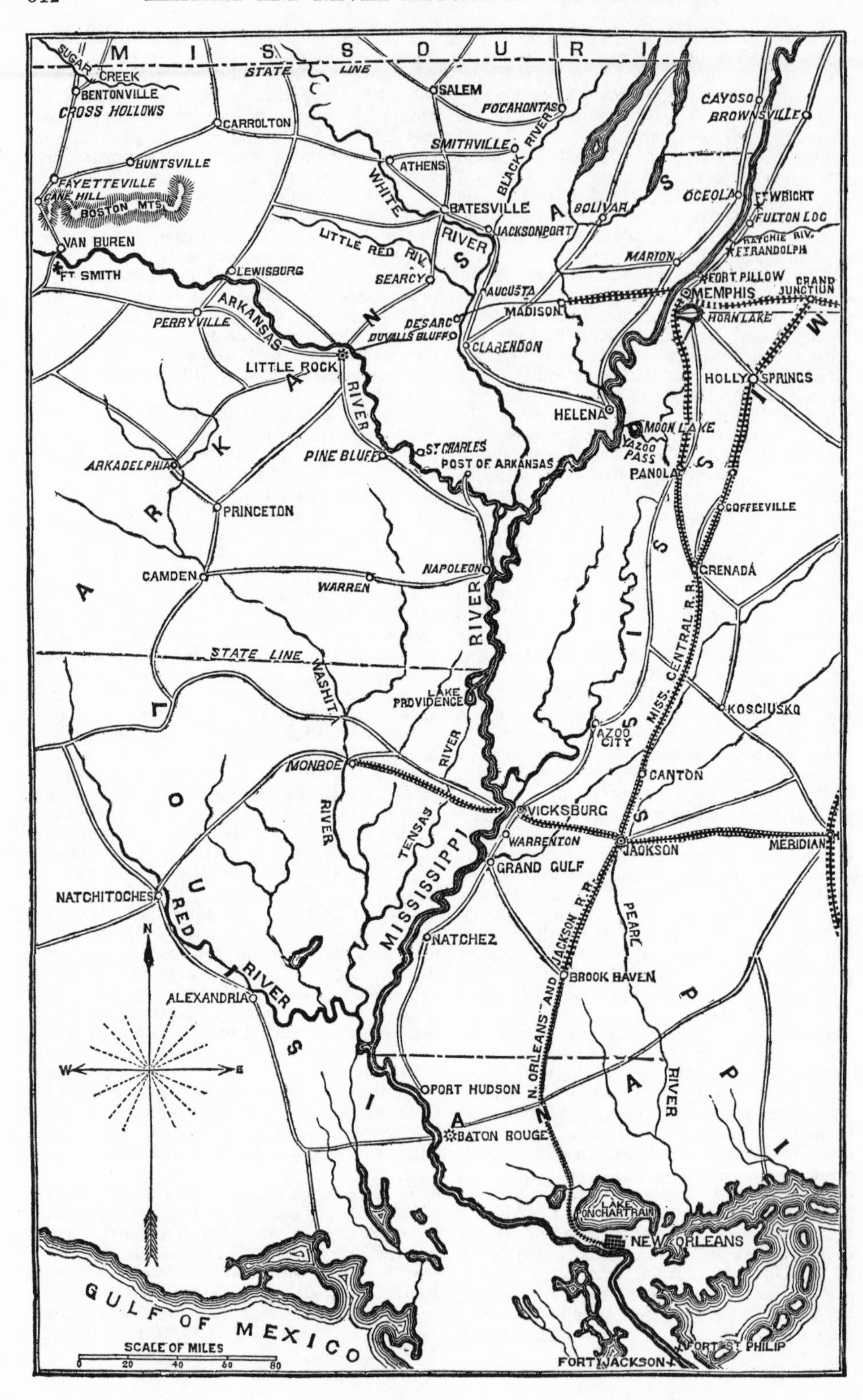
MISSOURI
STATE LINE
SUGAR CREEK
BENTONVILLE
CROSS HOLLOWS
CARROLTON
HUNTSVILLE
FAYETTEVILLE
CANE HILL
BOSTON MTS.
VAN BUREN
FT. SMITH
SALEM
POCAHONTAS
SMITHVILLE
ATHENS
BLACK RIVER
WHITE RIVER
BATESVILLE
JACKSONPORT
LITTLE RED RIV.
LEWISBURG
SEARCY
AUGUSTA
ARKANSAS
PERRYVILLE
MADISON
DESARC
DUVALLS BLUFF
CLARENDON
LITTLE ROCK
RIVER
HELENA
ST. CHARLES
PINE BLUFF
POST OF ARKANSAS
ARKADELPHIA
PRINCETON
CAMDEN
WARREN
NAPOLEON
STATE LINE
WASHITA
LAKE PROVIDENCE
MONROE
TENSAS RIVER
RIVER
VICKSBURG
WARRENTON
GRAND GULF
MISSISSIPPI
NATCHITOCHES
RED RIVER
NATCHEZ
ALEXANDRIA
PORT HUDSON
BATON ROUGE
LAKE PONCHARTRAIN
NEW ORLEANS
FORT JACKSON
FORT ST. PHILIP
GULF OF MEXICO
SCALE OF MILES
0 20 40 60 80
N
W
E
CAYOSO
BROWNSVILLE
OCEOLA
FT. WRIGHT
FULTON LDG
HATCHIE RIV.
FT. RANDOLPH
BOLIVAR
MARION
FORT PILLOW
MEMPHIS
GRAND JUNCTION
HORN LAKE
HOLLY SPRINGS
MOON LAKE
YAZOO PASS
PANOLA
COFFEEVILLE
GRENADA
MISS. CENTRAL R.R.
KOSCIUSKO
YAZOO CITY
CANTON
JACKSON
MERIDIAN
N. ORLEANS AND JACKSON R.R.
PEARL RIVER
BROOK HAVEN
ARKANSAS
LOUISIANA
MISSISSIPPI

took place. After moving thirty miles, the army bivouacked for the night. On the next morning the march was resumed, six miles to the crossing of Cane River. Here the enemy appeared in a strong position to dispute the crossing of the river. A flank movement through an almost impassable wood was made upon the enemy's position, from which he was driven, and the crossing secured. The pursuit was continued by the enemy until Alexandria was reached on the 27th.

Although Gen. Banks had declared in the commencement of the campaign that his occupation of the country would be permanent, such was now the state of affairs as to require his withdrawal, the season having passed for operating with any chance of success. Preparations for this object were soon commenced. The position of the fleet was most serious, and its extrication is thus related by Rear-Admiral Porter:

MISSISSIPPI SQUADRON, FLAGSHIP BLACK HAWK,
MOUTH RED RIVER, May 16th, 1864.

SIR: I have the honor to inform you that the vessels lately caught by low water above the falls at Alexandria, have been released from their unpleasant position. The water had fallen so low that I had no hope or expectation of getting the vessels out this season, and, as the army had made arrangements to evacuate the country, I saw nothing before me but the destruction of the best part of the Mississippi squadron.

There seems to have been an especial Providence looking out for us in providing a man equal to the emergency. Lieut.-Col. Bailey, Acting Engineer of the 19th Army Corps, proposed a plan of building a series of dams across the rocks at the falls, and raising the water high enough to let the vessels pass over. This proposition looked like madness, and the best engineers ridiculed it; but Col. Bailey was so sanguine of success that I requested to have it done, and he entered heartily into the work. Provisions were short and forage was almost out, and the dam was promised to be finished in ten days or the army would have to leave us. I was doubtful about the time, but I had no doubt about the ultimate success, if time would only permit. Gen. Banks placed at the disposal of Col. Bailey all the forces he required, consisting of some three thousand men and two or three hundred wagons. All the neighboring steam-mills were torn down for material; two or three regiments of Maine men were set at work felling trees, and on the second day after my arrival in Alexandria, from Grand Ecore, the work had fairly begun.

Trees were falling with great rapidity, teams were moving in all directions, bringing in brick and stone; quarries were opened; flat-boats were built to bring stone down from above, and every man seemed to be working with a vigor I have seldom seen equalled, while perhaps not one in fifty believed in the undertaking. These falls are about a mile in length, filled with rugged rocks, over which at the present stage of water it seemed to be impossible to make a channel.

The work was commenced by running out from the left bank of the river a tree dam, made of the bodies of very large trees, brush, brick, and stone, cross-tied with heavy timber, and strengthened in every way which ingenuity could devise. This was run out about three hundred feet into the river; four large coal barges were then filled with brick and sunk at the end of it. From the right bank of the river, cribs filled with stone were built out to meet the barges, all of which were successfully accomplished, notwithstanding there was a current running of nine miles an hour, which threatened to sweep every thing before it.

It will take too much time to enter into the details of this truly wonderful work; suffice it to say that the dam had nearly reached completion in eight days' working time, and the water had risen sufficiently on the upper falls to allow the Fort Hindman, Osage, and Neosho, to get down and be ready to pass the dam. In another day it would have been high enough to enable all the other vessels to pass the upper falls. Unfortunately, on the morning of the 9th inst., the pressure of water became so great that it swept away two of the stone-barges which swung in below the dam on one side. Seeing this unfortunate accident, I jumped on a horse and rode up to where the upper vessels were anchored, and ordered the Lexington to pass the upper falls if possible, and immediately attempt to go through the dam. I thought I might be able to save the four vessels below, not knowing whether the persons employed on the work would ever have the heart to renew the enterprise.

The Lexington succeeded in getting over the upper falls just in time, the water rapidly falling as she was passing over. She then steered directly for the opening in the dam, through which the water was rushing so furiously that it seemed as if nothing but destruction awaited her. Thousands of beating hearts looked on anxious for the result.

The silence was so great as the Lexington approached the dam that a pin might almost have been heard to fall. She entered the gap with a full head of steam on, pitched down the roaring torrent, made two or three spasmodic rolls, hung for a moment on the rocks below, was then swept into deep water by the currents, and rounded to safely into the bank.

Thirty thousand voices rose in one deafening cheer, and universal joy seemed to pervade the face of every man present. The Neosho followed next—all her hatches battened down, and every precaution taken against accident. She did not fare as well as the Lexington, her pilot having become frightened as he approached the abyss, and stopped her engine when I particularly ordered a full head of steam to be carried. The result was that for a moment her hull disappeared from sight, under the water. Every one thought she was lost. She rose, however, swept along over the rocks with the current, and fortunately escaped with only one hole in her bottom, which was stopped in the course of an hour. The Hindman and Osage both came through beautifully without touching a thing, and I thought if I was only fortunate enough to get my large vessels as well over the falls my fleet once more would do good service on the Mississippi.

The accident to the dam, instead of disheartening Col. Bailey, only induced him to renew his exertions, after he had seen the success of getting four vessels through. The noble-hearted soldiers, seeing their labor of the last eight days swept away in a moment, cheerfully went to work to repair damages, being confident now that all the gunboats would be finally brought over. The men had been working for eight days and nights, up to their necks in water, in the broiling sun, cutting trees and wheeling bricks, and nothing but good humor prevailed among them. On the whole, it was very fortunate the dam was carried away, as the two barges that were swept away from the centre swung around against some rocks on the left and made a fine cushion for the vessels, and prevented them, as it afterward appeared, from running on certain destruction.

The force of the water and the current being too great to construct a continuous dam of six hundred feet across the river in so short a time, Col. Bailey determined to leave a gap of fifty-five feet in the dam, and build a series of wing dams on the upper falls. This was accomplished in three days' time, and on the 11th instant the Mound City, the Carondelet, and Pittsburgh came over the upper falls, a good deal of labor having been expended in hauling them through, the channel being very crooked, scarcely wide enough for them. Next day the Ozark, Louisville, Chillicothe, and two tugs also succeeded in crossing the upper falls.

Immediately afterward the Mound City, Carondelet, and Pittsburgh started in succession to pass the dam, all their hatches battened down and every precaution taken to prevent accident.

The passage of these vessels was a most beautiful sight, only to be realized when seen. They passed over without an accident except the unshipping of one or two rudders. This was witnessed by all the troops, and the vessels were heartily cheered when they passed over. Next morning at ten o'clock, the Louisville, Chillicothe, Ozark, and two tugs passed over without any accident except the loss of a man, who was swept off the deck of one of the tugs. By three o'clock that afternoon, the vessels were all coaled, ammunition replaced, and all steamed down the river with the convoy of transports in company. A good deal of difficulty was anticipated in getting over the bars in lower Red River—depth of water reported only five feet; gunboats were drawing six. Providentially, we had a rise from the back-water of the Mississippi—that river being very high at that time—the back water extending to Alexandria, one hundred and fifty miles distant, enabling it to pass all the bars and obstructions with safety.

Words are inadequate to express the admiration I feel for the ability of Lieut.-Col. Bailey. This is without doubt the best engineering feat ever performed. Under the best circumstances, a private company would not have completed this work under one year, and to an ordinary mind the whole thing would have appeared an entire impossibility. Leaving out his ability as an engineer—the credit he has conferred upon the country—he has saved the Union a valuable fleet, worth nearly $2,000,000; more, he has deprived the enemy of a triumph which would have emboldened them to carry on this war a year or two longer, for the intended departure of the army was a fixed fact, and there was nothing left for me to do in case that event occurred but to destroy every part of the vessels, so that the rebels could make nothing of them. The highest honors the Government can bestow on Col. Bailey can never repay him for the service he has rendered the country.

To Gen. Banks, personally, I am much indebted for the happy manner in which he has forwarded this enterprise, giving it his whole attention night and day; scarcely sleeping while the work was going on; attending personally to see that all the requirements of Col. Bailey were complied with on the instant.

I do not believe there ever was a case where such difficulties were overcome in such a short space of time, and without any preparation.

Previous to passing the vessels over the falls, I had nearly all the guns, ammunitions, provisions, chain cables, anchors, and every thing that could effect their draft taken out of them.

* * * * * * * *

I have the honor to be, very respectfully, your obedient servant,

DAVID D. PORTER, Rear-Admiral.

Hon. GIDEON WELLES, Secretary of the Navy, Washington, D. C.

The last of the gunboats passed the falls on May 12th, and Alexandria was evacuated on the next day. As early as 10 A. M. the town was discovered to be on fire in several places. Various opinions existed as to its origin, but nothing positive was known. It is situated on a plain, in the centre of a rich cotton-growing region, with six hundred inhabitants. The fire spread with great rapidity. Gen. Banks made some ineffectual attempts to stay the progress of the flames, and tore down several buildings, but the soldiers, it is said, did not work with much interest. An engine was drawn to the river, but the hose was found to be cut. The scenes attending the burning of the town now became appalling. A spectator thus describes it:

Women gathering their helpless babes in their arms, rushing frantically through the streets with cries that would have melted the hardest hearts to tears. Little boys and girls were running hither and thither crying for their mothers and fathers; old men leaning on a staff for support to their trembling limbs, were hurrying away from the suffocating heat of their burning homes. The helpless wives and children of absent husbands and fathers were almost in the twinkling of an eye driven into the streets, leaving every thing behind but the clothes they then wore. Owing to the simultaneous burning in every part of the city, the people found no security in the streets, where the heat was so intense as almost to create suffocation. Everybody rushed to the river's edge, being protected there from the heat by the high bank of the river. The steamboats lying at the landing were subjected to great annoyance, the heat being so great that the decks had to be flooded with water to prevent the boats from taking fire. Among those who thus crowded the river bank were the wives, daughters, and children, helpless and now all homeless, of the Union men who had joined the Federal army since the occupation of Alexandria. Their husbands had already been marched off in the front toward Semmesport, leaving their families in their old homes, but to the tender mercies of the Confederates. The torch had now destroyed their dwellings, their household goods and apparel, the last morsel of provisions, and left them starving and destitute. As might be expected, they desired to go along with the Federal army, where their husbands had gone. They applied to be allowed to go aboard the transports. They were refused! They became frantic with excitement. The officers of the boats were desirous of doing so, but there was the peremptory order not to allow any white citizen to go aboard.

It had been expected when the army arrived that the occupation would be permanent, and that protection would be given to all who came forward and took the oath of allegiance; while those who would not were threatened with banishment and confiscation of property. Hundreds came forward and took the oath. An election was held, and delegates were sent to the constitutional convention then in session at New Orleans. A recruiting office was opened, and a large number of white men were mustered into the United States service. Quite a number of permanent citizens of Alexandria took the oath, and were promised protection. Their houses and other property were now all reduced to ashes, and they turned out in the world with nothing, absolutely nothing, save the amnesty oath. They could not now go to the Confederates and apply for charity. They too applied to be allowed to go aboard the transports and go to New Orleans. They were refused in every instance!

The guns taken from the boats above the falls were bursted; and when every thing was ready, the fleet, last of all, moved away, leaving the place wrapped in a dense volume of smoke. The fleet proceeded down the river about ten miles, and laid up for the night. On the next day the advance of the army was overtaken by the fleet, and on the 16th both began to arrive at Semmesport. The Atchafalaya was crossed the next day by the army, by means of twenty-

DAM ACROSS THE RED RIVER, CONSTRUCTED BY COL. BAILEY.

two steamboats placed side by side, with their bows lashed firmly together. "A plank bridge was then laid across the bows of each, connecting them together, and forming a solid bridge across the stream, which was no sooner finished than it was covered with teams, and there was a constant stream of wagons, cavalry, and men, until the night of the 20th, when the last of Gen. Smith's division crossed over, and the bridge in five minutes was endowed with life, and broke into fragments and proceeded up the river."

Thence the army proceeded toward the Mississippi, encountering on the way a considerable force of the enemy, with whom a sharp skirmish ensued. It finally returned to New Orleans, and the fleet resumed its station on the Mississippi. This withdrawal of Gen. Banks left the enemy at liberty to move into Arkansas and operate against Gen. Steele, who was moving toward Shreveport.

It was expected that Gen. Steele, in command of the 7th army corps, at Little Rock, in Arkansas, would coöperate with Gen. Banks on his approach to Shreveport. For this purpose he left Little Rock, March 23d, with twelve thousand infantry and three thousand cavalry, under Gen. Carr. On the previous day Gen. Thayer, in command of the Army of the Frontier, left Fort Smith, with nearly five thousand men, to join Gen. Steele. About the same time Col. Clayton, with a small force, left Pine Bluffs on an expedition. Camden was the point of junction for the three commands. It was 120 miles distant from Little Rock, about 180 miles from Fort Smith, and 80 miles from Pine Bluffs.

It was known that a force of the enemy, about twelve thousand men, under command of Gen. Price, was in southwestern Arkansas, and occupied a line from Camden, at the head of navigation on the Washita River, west to Washington, in Hampstead County. Camden is an important position for all movements looking to the occupation of the Red River and confluent streams. Forage and subsistence were abundant in the region, and the army of the enemy was well clothed and in good spirits.

Camden was known to be well fortified. Gen. Steele, therefore, directed his march toward Washington, evidently with the design of flanking Camden and drawing out of the fortifications what forces might be there. On the 14th of April, having advanced one hundred and ten miles in twenty-two days, he first encountered a strong cavalry division under Gen. Marmaduke. This was at the Little Missouri River, sixteen miles west of Camden. Heavy skirmishing ensued. On the 16th Gen. Thayer arrived with his force. Crossing the Little Missouri at a point menacing Shreveport, Washington, or Camden, Gen. Steele concealed the real destination of the expedition, which was Camden, and marched beyond the junction of the roads, thus deluding the enemy into the belief that he intended to attack Shreveport. Acting upon this opinion, they withdrew and took a fortified position. From this they were driven by a flank movement of Gen. Steele, who pursued, apparently with vigor, and captured some prisoners, and then moving in a direct line to Camden. The enemy, having discovered his error, concentrated his cavalry, and attacked in front, flank, and rear, hoping to embarrass Gen. Steele, so that his own infantry might have time to regain the works at Camden. Their efforts were in vain, and Gen. Steele took possession of the town.

Col. Clayton, in advancing from Pine Bluffs, captured a pontoon bridge over the Saline, and attacked and dispersed a cavalry force and took a number of prisoners. He thus reported his movement:

PINE BLUFF, ARK., March 31, 1864.

Major Greene, A. A. Gen.:

The expedition to Mount Elba and Longview has just returned. We destroyed the pontoon bridge at Longview; burned a train of thirty-five wagons, loaded with camp and garrison equipments, ammunition, quartermaster stores, &c.; captured three hundred and twenty prisoners; engaged in battle at Mount Elba, yesterday morning, Gen. Docking's division, of about twelve hundred men, from Monticello; routed him, and pursued him ten miles, with a loss on his side of over one hundred killed and wounded; captured a large quantity of small arms, two stands of colors, many wagons, and over three hundred horses and mules. Our loss will not exceed fifteen in killed, wounded, and missing. We brought in several hundred contrabands. The expedition was a complete success, the details of which will be furnished in my official report, which will be forwarded in a few days.

POWELL CLAYTON, Col. Commanding.

It was soon known that Gen. Banks had failed in his object on the Red River. This, to some extent, endangered the command of Gen. Steele. The force of the enemy, estimated to reach twenty-five thousand men, could now, in part, be moved against Gen. Steele. As it was not his plan to act alone, but in conjunction with Gen. Banks, he now prepared to fall back. In addition to these circumstances, his communications were interrupted and Little Rock threatened. On the day following the occupation of Camden, the enemy appeared in force about six miles to the south. A pontoon bridge was put across the Washita River thirty miles east of Camden, by which a force of the enemy's cavalry crossed and cut off the supplies. Trees were also felled into the stream, and other obstructions made to the navigation. On the 21st, a foraging party, with one hundred and fifty wagons and an escort of nearly a thousand men, were sent to a point sixteen miles west. On the return, at Poison Springs, twelve miles west of Camden, the command was attacked by a strong force of the enemy. After a severe struggle of some hours, the force reached Camden, with a loss of two hundred and fifty men, four guns, and the trains, with a number of arms.

On the 23d Gen. Steele started a train of two hundred and fifty wagons, six ambulances, and an escort of two hundred cavalry and twelve hundred infantry, with four pieces of artillery, to Pine Bluffs for supplies for the army. The expedition was under the command of Lieut.-Col. Drake, of the 36th Iowa. On the 25th, an attack was made on the train, within six miles of the Saline River, by a cavalry force under Maj.-Gen. Fagan, which resulted in the capture or wounding of all the officers, nearly all the men—of whom two hundred and fifty were killed and wounded—four brass guns, and the wagon trains.

On the 26th Gen. Steele determined to evacuate Camden, and before daylight of the 27th the army had crossed, the pontoon bridge was secured, and the Washita River put between him and the forces of the enemy. The army was pushed forward over bad roads, and on the 28th camped at Princeton crossing, and on the next evening at the Saline crossings, Jenkins Ferry. During the night the enemy showed themselves in the rear. Whether they were in force, or only sufficient to harass by cavalry attacks until Gen. Kirby Smith's main force could intercept the march to Little Rock, was uncertain. Dispositions were, however, made by Gen. Steele to resist a large force. The bad condition of the roads, and the heavy rain which commenced, and the darkness, prevented the crossing of the Saline during the night. The pontoon bridge, however, had been laid, and a small portion of the force passed over. The remainder of the army encamped in the bottom lands of the river, to which it descended from a considerable elevation about four miles west of the stream. Gen. Salomon's division camped about two miles from the hill, and the line which it was to hold in the morning was protected on the left by the Saline and swampy bottom lands, and on the right by a bayou skirting the base of the uplands. In the morning the rain poured in torrents. The artillery, the trains, and men were to cross over the river. Soon after daylight skirmishing commenced in the rear, and a general engagement soon succeeded. The enemy consisted of all their forces in southwestern Arkansas, with some from Louisiana, under Gens. Smith, Price, Walker, Churchill, and others. Under Gen. Steele, the commands of Gens. Salomon, Thayer, Rice, Ingleman, and Col. Benton were engaged. The battle continued about seven hours, and resulted in the repulse of the enemy, and a loss to Gen. Steele of seven hundred in killed and wounded, although several stands of colors were captured and three pieces of artillery. The loss of the enemy in killed and wounded was also severe. The effect of the battle was not only to secure a safe retreat to Little Rock for Gen. Steele, where he arrived on the 2d of May, but also to relieve, for some time, that portion of Arkansas, and also Missouri, from the presence of the enemy. The following is Gen. Steele's address to his troops:

HEADQUARTERS DEPARTMENT OF ARKANSAS,
LITTLE ROCK, May 9.

To you troops of the 7th army corps, who participated in the recent campaign designed to coöperate with Gen. Banks' movement against Shreveport, the Major-General Commanding tenders his earnest and grateful thanks. Although you were compelled to fall back without seeing the main object of the expedition accomplished, you will have the satisfaction of knowing that you have beaten the enemy wherever he has met you in force, and extricated yourselves from the perilous position in which you were placed by the reverses of the coöperating column. This let loose upon you a superior force of the enemy, under one of their best generals, causing the loss of your trains and the total interruption of your communications, rendering it impossible for you to obtain supplies. You have fallen back over rivers and swamps, while pressed by a superior force of the enemy. This you have done successfully, punishing the enemy severely at the same time.

The patience with which you have endured hardships and privations, and your heroic conduct on the battle-field, have been brought to the notice of the Government, and will furnish a page in the history of this war of which you may well be proud.

F. STEELE, Maj.-Gen. Commanding.

For further details of military affairs under Gen. Steele. *see* subsequent pages.

The withdrawal of the forces of Gens. Sherman and A. J. Smith from Vicksburg to engage in the Red River expedition, afforded an opportunity for the irregular command of Gen. Forrest, with other detached forces of the enemy in Northern Mississippi and Southwestern Tennessee, to concentrate for an attack on the Federal posts in West Tennessee and Kentucky. Accordingly, on March 23d, Gen. Forrest left Jackson, Tennessee, with about five thousand men, marching north to Union City. Jackson is a station on the railroad from Cairo and Columbus to New Orleans, and about one hundred and seven miles from Cairo, and sixty miles from Union City, another station on the same railroad, where the line to Paducah and the one to Hickman commence. On the next day he arrived before Union City and summoned Col. Hawkins, with four hundred and fifty men of the 11th Tennessee Union cavalry, to surrender. The surrender of the place was made after resisting an assault, and also two hundred horses and five hundred small arms. This surrender was opposed by the officers under Col. Hawkins' command, and only one man had been injured when it was made. A force under Gen. Brayman, from Cairo, advanced within six miles for its defence; but on learning that it had surrendered, Gen. Brayman retired. Gen. Forrest next occupied Hickman, and then moved immediately north with Buford's division of his forces, direct from Jackson to Paducah. This place was occupied by Col. S. G. Hicks, 40th Illinois regiment, with six hundred and fifty-five men. Col. Hicks retired into Fort Anderson and there made a stand, assisted by the gunboats Peosta and Paw-Paw, belonging to the command of Capt. Shirk of the navy. Gen. Forrest then sent the following demand for a surrender:

HEADQUARTERS FORREST'S CAVALRY CORPS,
PADUCAH, March 25, 1864.

To Col. Hicks, commanding Federal forces at Paducah:

Having a force amply sufficient to carry your works and reduce the place, in order to avoid the unnecessary effusion of blood, I demand a surrender of the fort and troops, with all the public stores. If you surrender you shall be treated as prisoners of war, but if I have to storm your works you may expect no quarter. N. B. FORREST, Maj.-Gen. Com'ing.

Col. Hicks replied as follows:

HEADQUARTERS POST PADUCAH,
PADUCAH, KY., March 25, 1864.

Maj.-Gen. N. B. Forrest, commanding Confederate forces:

I have this moment received yours of this instant, in which you demand an unconditional surrender of forces under my command. I can answer, that I have been placed here by my Government to defend the post. In this, as well as all other orders from my superior officers, I feel it my duty as an honorable officer to obey, and must therefore respectfully decline surrendering, as you require. Very respectfully, S. G. HICKS, Commanding Post.

Two successive attacks upon the fort were now made by the enemy and repulsed. They next occupied the houses, and fired from behind them and from the windows, but were steadily held back. At half-past eleven P.M. they retired. During the evening a steamboat on the marine ways was burned, and also some houses. On the next morning Gen. Forrest proposed an exchange for some prisoners in Col. Hicks' hands, but the latter had no power to make the exchange. In the afternoon the enemy retired. Gen. Forrest reported that he held the town ten hours, and captured many stores and horses, burned sixty bales of cotton, one steamboat, and took fifty prisoners. His loss at Union City and Paducah he stated at twenty-five killed and wounded, and the prisoners captured at five hundred. The loss of Col. Hicks was fourteen killed and forty-six wounded. A large portion of the town was destroyed, partly by the guns fired from the fort upon the enemy, and partly by the enemy.

On the 12th of April an attack was made on Fort Pillow by Gen. Forrest, with Gen. Chalmers' division of his forces, of which Gen. Forrest led Bell's brigade, and Chalmers led McCulloch's. Fort Pillow is situated about seventy miles above Memphis, on the Mississippi River. Its garrison at the time of the assault consisted of nineteen officers and five hundred and thirty-eight enlisted men, of whom two hundred and sixty-two were colored troops, comprising one battalion of the 6th United States heavy artillery, formerly the 1st Alabama artillery of colored troops, under the command of Major L. F. Booth; one section of the 2d United States light artillery (colored), and one battalion of the 13th Tennessee cavalry (white), commanded by Major W. F. Bradford. Major Booth was the ranking officer, and was in command of the fort.

The troops which had served to garrison the fort were withdrawn in January, to accompany Gen. Sherman's expedition to Meridian, and others had been sent from Memphis subsequently to hold it.

Just before sunrise in the morning, April 12th, the pickets of the garrison were driven in. This was the first intimation which the force then had of an intention of the enemy to attack the place. Fighting soon became general, and about nine o'clock Major Bradford succeeded to the command and withdrew all the forces within the fort. They had previously occupied some intrenchments at some distance from the fort and further from the river.

This fort was situated on a high bluff, which descended precipitately to the river's edge, the ridge of the bluff on the river side being covered with trees, bushes, and fallen timber. Extending back from the river on either side of the fort was a ravine or hollow, the one below the fort containing several private stores and some dwellings, constituting what is called the town. At the mouth of that ravine and on the river bank were some Government buildings containing commissary stores.

The ravine above the fort was known as Cold Bunk Ravine, the ridge being covered with trees and bushes; to the right or below, and a little to the front of the fort, was a level piece of ground, not quite so elevated as the fort itself, on which had been erected some log huts or shanties, which were occupied by the white troops, and also used for hospital and other purposes. Within the fort tents had been erected, with board floors, for the use of the colored troops. There were six pieces of artillery in the fort, consisting of two 6-pounders, two 12-pounder howitzers, and two 10-pounder Parrotts.

The rebels continued their attack, but up to two or three o'clock in the afternoon they had not gained any decisive success. The Federal troops, both white and black, fought bravely, and were in good spirits. The gunboat No. 7—New Era, Capt. Marshall—took part in the conflict, shelling the enemy as opportunity offered.

Signals had been agreed upon by which the officers in the fort could indicate where the guns of the boat could be aimed most effectively. There being but one gunboat no permanent impression appears to have been produced upon the enemy, for as they were shelled out of one ravine they would make their appearance in the other. They would thus appear and retire as the gunboat moved from one point to another.

About one o'clock the fire on both sides slackened somewhat, and the gunboat moved out in the river to cool and clean the guns, having fired 282 rounds of shell, sharpnel, and canister, which nearly exhausted the supply of ammunition. The rebels having thus far failed in their attack, resorted to their customary flags of truce. The first flag conveyed a demand from Gen. Forrest for the unconditional surrender of the fort. To this Major Bradford replied, asking to be allowed an hour to consult with his officers and the officers of the gunboat.

In a short time a second flag of truce appeared with a communication from Gen. Forrest. He would allow Major Bradford twenty minutes in which to move his troops out of the fort, and if it was not done in that time, an assault would be ordered. To this Major Bradford replied that he would not surrender. Immediately after the second flag of truce retired, the rebels made a rush from the positions they had treacherously gained, while the flags of truce were sent in, and obtained possession of the fort, raising the cry of no quarter. But little opportunity was allowed for resistance. The Federal troops, black and white, threw down their arms, and sought to escape by running down the steep bluff near the fort, and secreting themselves behind trees and logs, in the bushes, and under the brush, some even jumping into the river, leaving only their heads above the water as they crouched down under the bank.

The scenes which now followed became a subject of investigation by a Committee of Congress, who state in their report as follows:

The rebels commenced an indiscriminate slaughter, sparing neither age nor sex, white or black, soldier or civilian. The officers and men seemed to vie with each other in the devilish work. Men, women, and even children, wherever found, were deliberately shot down, beaten, and hacked with sabres. Some of the children not more than ten years old, were forced to stand up and face their mothers while being shot. The sick and wounded were butchered without mercy, the rebels even entering the hospital buildings, and dragging them out to be shot, or killing them as they lay there unable to offer the least resistance. All over the hillside the work of murder was going on. Numbers of our men were gathered together in lines or groups and deliberately shot. Some were shot while in the river, while others on the bank were shot and their bodies kicked into the water, many of them still living, but unable to make any exertion to save themselves from drowning. Some of the rebels stood upon the top of the hill, or a short distance down its side, and called to our soldiers to come up to them, and as they approached shot them down in cold blood; if their guns or pistols missed fire, forcing them to stand there until they were again prepared to fire. All around were heard cries of "No quarter, no quarter;" "Kill the d—n niggers;" "Shoot them down." All who asked for mercy were answered by the most cruel taunts and sneers. Some were spared for a time only to be murdered under circumstances of greater cruelty. No cruelty which the most fiendish malignity could devise was omitted by these murderers. One white soldier, who was wounded in the leg so as to be unable to walk, was made to stand up while his tormentors shot him. Others who were wounded and unable to stand up were held up and again shot. One negro who had been ordered by a rebel officer to hold his horse was killed by him when he remonstrated. Another, a mere child, whom an officer had taken up behind him on his horse, was seen by Chalmers, who at once ordered the officer to put him down, and shoot him, which was done. The huts and tents in which many of the wounded had sought shelter were set on fire both that night and the next morning, while the wounded were still in them, those only escaping who were able to get themselves out, or who could prevail on others less injured than themselves to help them out; and even some of them thus seeking to escape the flames were met by these ruffians and brutally shot down, or had their brains beaten out. One man was deliberately fastened down to the floor of a tent, face upwards, by means of nails driven through his clothing and into the boards under him so that he could not possibly escape, and then the tent set on fire. Another was nailed to the side of a building, outside of the fort, and then the building set on fire and burned. The charred remains of five or six bodies were afterwards found, all but one so much disfigured and consumed by the flames that they could not be identified, and the identification of that one is not absolutely certain, although there can hardly be a doubt that it was the body of Lieut. Akerstrom, quartermaster of the 13th Virginia cavalry, and a native Tennessean. Several witnesses who saw the remains, and who were personally acquainted with him while living here, testified that it is their firm belief that it was his body that was thus treated. These deeds of murder and cruelty closed when night came on, only to be renewed the next morning, when the demons carefully sought among the dead lying about in all directions for any other wounded yet alive, and those they killed. Scores of the dead and wounded were found there the day of the massacre by the men from some of our gunboats, who were permitted to go on shore and collect the wounded and bury the dead. The rebels themselves had made a pretence of burying a great many of their victims, but they had merely thrown them, without the least regard to care or decency, into the trenches and ditches about the fort, or the little hollows and ravines on the hillside, covering them but partially with earth. Portions of heads and faces, hands and feet, were found protruding through the earth in every direction even when your committee visited the spot two weeks afterward, although parties of men had been sent on shore from time to time to bury the bodies unburied, and re-bury the others, and were even then engaged in the same work. We found evidences of this murder and cruelty still most painful. We saw bodies still unburied, at some distance from the fort, of some sick men, who had been fleeing from the hospital, and beaten down and brutally murdered, and their bodies left where they had fallen. We could still see the faces, and hands, and feet of men, white and black, protruding out of the ground, whose graves had not been reached by those engaged in reinterring the victims of the massacre; and although a great deal of rain had fallen within the preceding two weeks, the ground, more especially on the side at the foot of the bluff where the most of the murders had been committed, was still discolored by the blood of our brave but unfortunate men, and the logs and trees showed but too plainly the evidences of the atrocities perpetrated there. Many other instances of equally atrocious cruelty might be enumerated, but your committee feel compelled to refrain from giving here more of the heart-sickening details, and refer to the statements contained in the voluminous testimony herewith submitted. Those statements were obtained by them from eye-witnesses and sufferers. Many of them, as they were examined by your committee, were lying upon beds of pain and suffering; some so feeble that their lips could with difficulty frame the words by which they endeavored to convey some idea of the cruelty which had been inflicted on them, and which they had seen inflicted on others. In reference to the fate of Major Bradford, who was in command of the fort when it was captured, and who had, up to that time, received no injury, there seems to be no doubt. The general understanding everywhere seemed to be that he had been brutally murdered the day after he was taken prisoner. How many of our troops thus fell victims to the malignity and barbarity of Forrest and his followers cannot yet be definitely ascertained. Two officers belonging to the garrison were absent at the time of the capture and massacre. Of the remaining officers but two are known to be living, and they are wounded, and now in the hospital at Mound City. One of them (Capt. Porter) may even now be dead, as the surgeons, when your committee were there, expressed no hope of his recovery. Of the men, from three hundred to four hundred are known to have been killed at Fort Pillow, of whom at least three hundred were murdered in cold blood, after the fort was in possession of the rebels, and our men had thrown down their arms and ceased to offer resistance. Of the survivors, except the wounded in the hospital at Mound City, and the few who succeeded in making their escape unhurt, nothing definite is known, and it is to be feared that many have been murdered after being taken away from the fort. When your committee arrived at Memphis, Tennessee, they found and examined a man (Mr. McLogan) who had been conscripted by some of Forrest's forces, but who, with other conscripts, had succeeded in making his escape. He testifies that while two companies of rebel troops, with Major Bradford and many other prisoners, were on their march from Brownsville and Jackson, Tennessee, Major Bradford was taken by five rebels, one an officer, led about fifty yards from the line of march, and deliberately murdered in view of all those assembled. He fell, killed instantly by three musket balls, and while asking that his life might be spared, as he had fought them manfully, and was deserving of a better fate. The motive for the murder of Major Bradford seems to have been the simple fact that, although a native of the South, he remained loyal to his Government.

On the other side is the following statement by Lieut.-Gen. S. D. Lee, who was in command of the Confederate department. It is part of a letter on the subject, dated June 28th:

As commanding officer of this department, I desire to make the following statement concerning the capture of Fort Pillow—a statement supported in a great measure by the evidence of one of your own officers captured at that place. The version given by you and your Government is untrue, and not sustained by the facts to the extent that you indicate. The garrison was summoned in the usual manner, and its commanding officer assumed the responsibility of refusing to surrender, after having been informed by Gen. Forrest of his ability to take the fort, and of his fears as to what the result would be in case the demand was not complied with. The assault was made under a heavy fire and with considerable loss to the attacking party. Your colors were never lowered and your garrison never surrendered, but retreated under cover of a gunboat, with arms in their hands and constantly using them. This was true particularly of your colored troops, who had been firmly convinced by your teachings of the certainty of slaughter in case of capture. Even under these circumstances many of your men—white and black—were taken prisoners. I respectfully refer you to history for numerous cases of indiscriminate slaughter after successful assault, even under less aggravated circumstances. It is generally conceded by all military precedent that where the issue had been fairly presented and the ability displayed, fearful results are expected to follow a refusal to surrender. The case under consideration is almost an extreme one. You had a servile race armed against their masters, and in a country which had been desolated by almost unprecedented outrages.

I assert that our officers, with all the circumstances against them, endeavored to prevent the effusion of blood; and as an evidence of this, I refer you to the fact that both white and colored prisoners were taken, and are now in our hands. As regards the battle of Tishimingo Creek, the statements of your negro witnesses are not to be relied on. In their panic they acted as might have been expected from their previous impressions. I do not think many of them were killed—they are yet wandering over the country, attempting to return to their masters. With reference to the *status* of those captured at Tishimingo Creek and Fort Pillow, I will state that, unless otherwise ordered by my government, they will not be regarded as prisoners of war, but will be retained and humanely treated, subject to such future instructions as may be indicated.

Your letter contains many implied threats; these, of course, you can make, and you are fully entitled to any satisfaction that you may feel from having made them.

It is my intention, and that also of my subordinate officers, to conduct this war upon civilized principles, provided you permit us to do so; and I take this occasion to state that we will not shirk from any responsibility that your actions may force upon us. We are engaged in a struggle for the protection of our homes and firesides, for the maintenance of our national existence and liberty; we have counted the cost, and are prepared to go to any extremes; and though it is far from our wish to fight under a black flag, still, if you drive us to it, we will accept the issue. Your troops virtually fought under it at the battle of Tishimingo Creek, and the prisoners taken there state that they went into battle under the impression that they would receive no quarter, and, I suppose, with the determination to give none.

I will further remark, that if it is raised, so far as your soldiers are concerned, there can be no distinction, for the unfortunate people whom you pretend to be aiding are not considered entirely responsible for their acts, influenced, as they are, by the superior intellect of their white brothers. I enclose for your consideration certain papers touching the Fort Pillow affair, which were procured from the writer after the exaggerated statements of your press were seen.

I am, general, yours, respectfully,

S. D. LEE, Lieutenant-General.

The report of the enemy stated that Gens. Forrest and Chalmers "both entered the fort from opposite sides, simultaneously, and an indiscriminate slaughter followed. One hundred prisoners were taken and the balance slain. The fort ran with blood. Many jumped into the river and were drowned, or shot in the water. Over $100,000 worth of stores were taken, and six guns captured. The Confederate loss was seventy-five. Lieut.-Col. Reed, of the 5th Mississippi, was mortally wounded."

A party of the enemy on the capture of Fort Pillow made an advance against Columbus, Gen. Buford being in command of their force.

On the 13th he sent the following summons to the commander of the fort:

HEADQUARTERS CONFEDERATE STATES ARMY,
BEFORE COLUMBUS, KY., April 13, 1864.

To the Commander of the United States forces, Columbus, Ky:

Fully capable of taking Columbus and its garrison by force, I desire to avoid shedding blood. I therefore demand the unconditional surrender of the forces under your command. Should you surrender, the negroes now in arms will be returned to their masters. Should I be compelled to take the place by force, no quarters will be shown negro troops whatever; white troops will be treated as prisoners of war. I am, sir, yours,

A. BUFORD, Brig.-Gen.

This demand was refused, and Gen. Buford retired without making an attack. At the same time an excitement arose at Paducah, under apprehension of another attack of the enemy. The entire forces, however, retired to Bolivar, Trenton, and Grand Junction. Some further military operations in this part of the country, chiefly of a partisan nature, took place.

Some active operations took place in North Carolina. The important ports on the sounds, as Newbern, Washington, Plymouth, &c., had been held since their capture by the forces under Gen. Burnside. On the 1st of February, a force of the enemy under Gen. Picket, consisting of Gen. Hoke's brigade, with a part of Gens. Corse's and Clingman's, made an assault on the Federal outpost at Bachelor's Creek, eight miles from Newbern, and captured it with seventy-five prisoners. They then advanced toward Newbern, where an attack was greatly feared. Before daylight on the next morning a party in barges captured the gunboat Underwriter, with her officers and a portion of her crew. The steamer was aground, but so lay as to cover a portion of the fortifications between Fort Anderson and Fort Stevens, at Newbern. Gen. Picket thus reported his expedition:

KINSTON, February 3, 1864.

To Gen. S. Cooper:

I made a reconnoissance within a mile and a half of Newbern, with Hoke's brigade, and a part of Corse's and Clingman's, and some artillery; met the enemy in force at Batchelor's Creek, killed and wounded about one hundred in all, captured thirteen officers and two hundred and eighty prisoners, fourteen negroes, two rifled pieces and caissons, three hundred stand of small arms, four ambulances, three wagons, fifty-five animals, a quantity of clothing, camp, and garrison equipage, and two flags. Commander Wood, Confederate States navy, captured and destroyed the United States gunboat Underwriter. Our loss thirty-five killed and wounded.

G. E. PICKET,
Major-General Commanding.

The next movement of importance made by the enemy was the capture of Plymouth. This town is on the south bank of the Roanoke River, about eight miles from its mouth. The river flows in an easterly direction into Albemarle Sound. The town originally contained about one thousand inhabitants, but was burned by the Union fleet two years previously. It had been held for some time as a key to the river, and had been strongly fortified. A breastwork with strong forts at different points along the line, had been constructed. Another strong work, called Fort Gray, had also been constructed about a mile further up the river, opposite which a triple row of piles had been driven, to which torpedoes were attached, to serve as a protection to the fleet below. The enemy had a powerful iron-clad ram in the river above. Still further up there was another row of piles with torpedoes, near which a picket boat was stationed to watch the iron-clad. The Federal gunboats Southfield and Miami were anchored in the river opposite the town. The garrison of the town was about twenty-four hundred men, under command of Gen. Wessels. They composed the 85th New York infantry regiment, 101st Pennsylvania infantry regiment, 103d Pennsylvania infantry regiment, 16th Connecticut infantry regiment, two companies of the Massachusetts heavy artillery, two companies of the 2d North Carolina volunteers, two companies of the 12th New York cavalry.

The approach of the enemy was unknown, until they began to appear about 3 P. M., April 17th, in the rear of the town, driving in the Union pickets. A brisk artillery fire was soon opened upon Fort Gray, which continued with some vigor until near midnight. About daylight on the next morning the contest was renewed, and two charges were made during the forenoon, which were repulsed. In the afternoon, two guns of the enemy were captured by a sortie from the fort. The gunboats then took a position, one above and the other below the town, and the contest continued fiercely until night, when it ceased without any advantage to the enemy. Early the next morning the picket boat up the river reported that the iron-clad had passed down. The gunboats were immediately lashed together, to make a joint resistance to the iron-clad. This had scarcely been done when she appeared within a hundred yards. As they approached each other, the gunboats fired without effect. The ram first struck the Miami, and gliding off struck the Southfield on her left side, crushing in six or eight feet square. The Miami now fired a shell at the iron-clad, which rebounded and killed her captain, Flusser, and wounded eight persons. Becoming separated from the Southfield, the Miami was swung round by the current, and unable for a time to render further assistance. The Southfield was now rapidly sinking, and her crew took to the boats and fled. The Miami, after her loss, withdrew. The iron-clad, called the Albemarle, under command of J. W. Coke, came down to the mouth of the river, outside of which were four gunboats. Her position in the river cut off all hopes of sending reënforcements to Gen. Wessels, and he surrendered to Brig.-Gen. Hoke on the next day. This surrender was thus announced by Gen. Peck, in command of the department:

HEADQUARTERS OF THE ARMY AND DISTRICT OF NORTH CAROLINA, NEWBERN, N. C., April 21, 1864.

General Orders No. 66:

With feelings of the deepest sorrow the commanding general announces the fall of Plymouth, N.C., and the capture of its gallant commander, Brig.-Gen. H. W. Wessels, and his command. This result, however, did not obtain until after the most gallant and determined resistance had been made. Five times the enemy stormed the lines of the general, and as many times were they repulsed with great slaughter; and but for the powerful assistance of the rebel iron-clad ram, and the floating sharpshooter battery, the Cotton Plant, Plymouth would still have been in our hands. For their noble defence the gallant Gen. Wessels and his brave band have, and deserve the warmest thinks of the whole country, while all will sympathize with them in their misfortune.

To the officers and men of the navy the commanding general tenders his thanks for their hearty coöperation with the army, and the bravery, determination, and courage that marked their part of the unequal contest. With sorrow he records the death of the noble sailor and gallant patriot, Lieut.-Com. C. W. Flusser, U. S. Navy, who in the heat of battle fell dead on the deck of his ship, with the lanyard of his gun in his hand.

The commanding general believes that these misfortunes will tend, not to discourage, but to nerve the army of North Carolina to equal deeds of bravery and gallantry hereafter.

Until further orders, the headquarters of the subdistrict of the Albemarle will be at Roanoke Island. The command devolves upon Col. D. W. Wardrop, of the 99th New York infantry.

By command of Maj.-Gen. JOHN G. PECK.
J. A. JUDSON, Ass't Adj't-Gen.

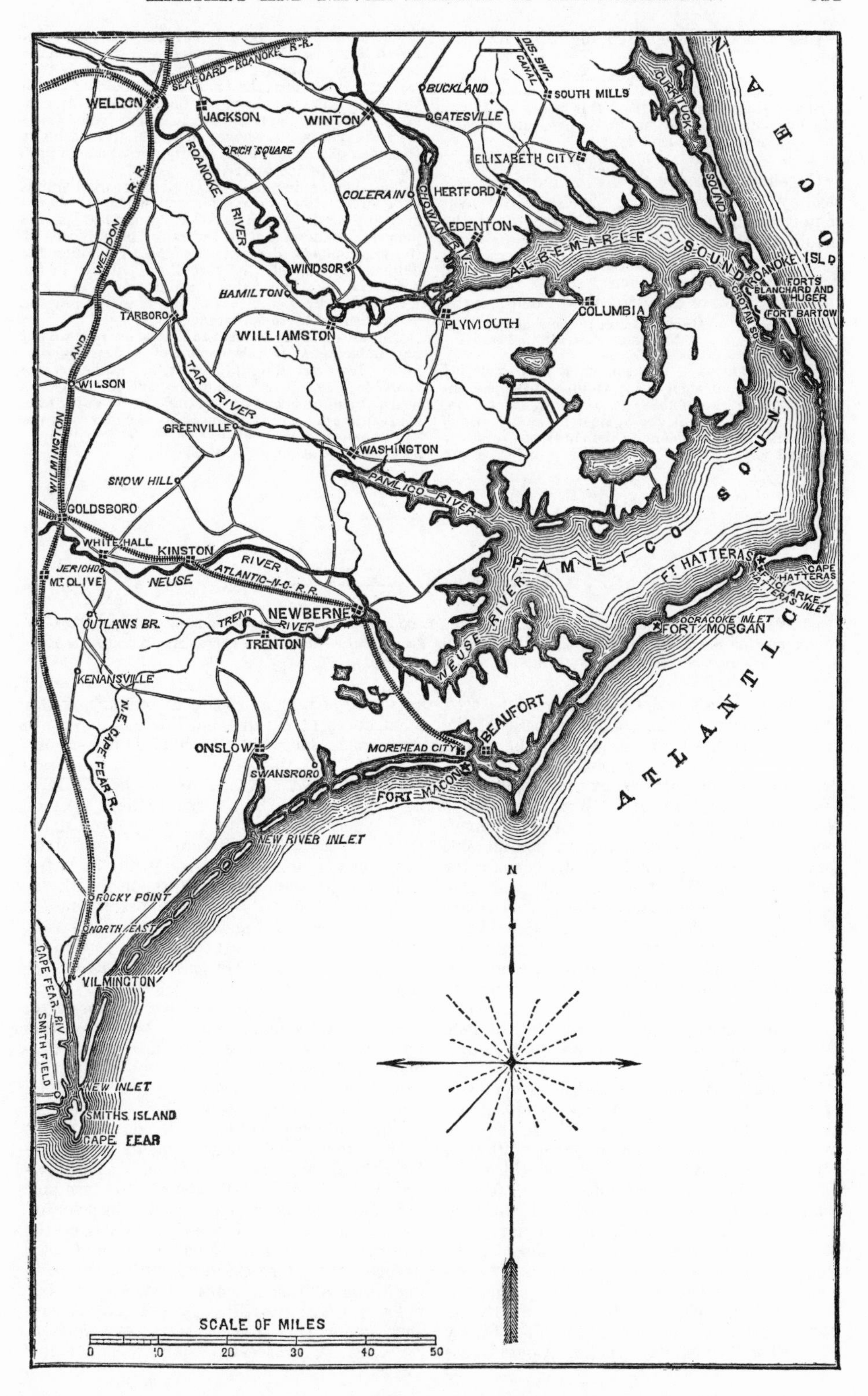
SEABOARD–ROANOKE R.R.
WELDON
JACKSON
RICH SQUARE
ROANOKE RIVER
WELDON AND WILMINGTON R.R.
BUCKLAND
DIS. SWP. CANAL
SOUTH MILLS
WINTON
GATESVILLE
ELIZABETH CITY
CURRITUCK SOUND
COLERAIN
HERTFORD
CHOWAN RIV.
EDENTON
ALBEMARLE SOUND
ROANOKE ISLD
FORTS BLANCHARD AND HUGER
FORT BARTOW
CROTAN SD.
WINDSOR
HAMILTON
TARBORO
WILLIAMSTON
PLYMOUTH
COLUMBIA
WILSON
TAR RIVER
GREENVILLE
WASHINGTON
SNOW HILL
PAMLICO RIVER
GOLDSBORO
WHITE HALL
KINSTON
NEUSE RIVER
ATLANTIC–N–C–R.R.
JERICHO
MT OLIVE
PAMLICO SOUND
FT HATTERAS
CAPE HATTERAS
FT CLARKE
HATTERAS INLET
OUTLAWS BR.
TRENT RIVER
NEWBERNE
TRENTON
OCRACOKE INLET
FORT MORGAN
KENANSVILLE
N.E. CAPE FEAR R.
BEAUFORT
ONSLOW
MOREHEAD CITY
SWANSBORO
FORT MACON
ATLANTIC OCEAN
NEW RIVER INLET
N
ROCKY POINT
NORTH EAST
WILMINGTON
CAPE FEAR RIV
SMITH FIELD
NEW INLET
SMITHS ISLAND
CAPE FEAR
SCALE OF MILES
0
10
20
30
40
50

Gen. Hoke thus reported his capture of the position:

PLYMOUTH, N. C., April 20, 1864.

To Gen. Braxton Bragg:

I have stormed and carried this place, capturing one brigadier, sixteen hundred men, stores, and twenty-five pieces of artillery.

R. F. HOKE, Brig.-Gen.

Only two places on the main land were now held by the Federal forces. These were Washington, on the Tar River, and Newbern, at the mouth of the Neuse. Washington was evacuated in the latter part of April, and burned. The following order of Gen. Palmer was issued for the purpose of detecting the incendiaries:

HEADQUARTERS DISTRICT OF N. C.,
NEWBERN, N. C., May 3, 1864.

General Orders No. 5.

While the troops of this command may exult and take just pride in their many victories over the enemy, yet a portion of them have, within a few days, been guilty of an outrage against humanity which brings the blush of shame to the cheek of every true man and soldier. * * * *

The commanding general had, until this time, believed it impossible that any troops in his command could have committed so disgraceful an act as this, which now blackens the fame of the Army of North Carolina. He finds, however, that he was sadly mistaken, and that the ranks are disgraced by men who are not soldiers, but thieves and scoundrels, dead to all sense of honor and humanity, for whom no punishment can be too severe.

The commanding general is well aware what troops were in the town of Washington when the flames first appeared. He knows what troops last left the place. He knows that in the ranks of only two of the regiments in the district of North Carolina the culprits now stand. To save the reputation of the command, it is hoped that the guilty parties may be ferreted out by the officers who were in Washington at the time of these occurrences.

This order will be read at the head of every regiment and detachment in this command, at dress parade, on the day succeeding its receipt, and at the head of the 17th Massachusetts volunteers and the 15th Connecticut volunteers, at dress parade, every day for ten consecutive days, or until the guilty parties are found.

By command of Brig.-Gen. I. N. PALMER.
J. A. JUDSON, Ass't Adj't.-Gen.

CHAPTER XXXIX.

Desultory Operations in Virginia—General Grant appointed Lieutenant-General—Reorganization of the Army of the Potomac—Gen. Sherman's Campaign against Atlanta—Its Plan—Battles—Manœuvres approaching Atlanta—Its Evacuation—Correspondence with the Authorities—Civilians sent away.

IN Virginia, a few desultory operations took place previous to the commencement of the great campaign of the year. On the 3d of January a supply train, consisting of two hundred animals, was captured by the enemy on its return from Petersburg, in West Virginia, to New Creek. A few of the men and animals escaped. The enemy, being in considerable force, now made several demonstrations for the purpose of reaching the Baltimore and Ohio Railroad, but were unsuccessful. On January 28th, a train from New Creek to Petersburg, laden with commissary stores for the garrison at the latter place, was attacked three miles south of Williamsport, and, after a sharp contest, captured by the enemy. The losses in this region in horses, wagons, stores &c., to Feb. 1st, was estimated at two hundred and fifty thousand dollars.

The headquarters of Gen. Meade, in command of the Army of the Potomac, was near Culpepper Court House. This position was occupied by that army from December, 1863, until May, 1864. The army of Gen. Lee, on the south side of the Rapidan, confronted it. A few reconnoissances were made, but without important results. A cavalry expedition into the neighborhood of Richmond was the most active movement at this period of the year. It commenced with the advance of the 8th corps, under Gen. Sedgwick, from Madison Court House, on Feb. 27th. A division under Gen. Birney followed on the next day. Madison Court House was occupied by a brigade of infantry, with a small force of cavalry, but the main force was encamped along the heights of Robertson's River. From this position pickets were sent out to the right and left. Gen. Birney's force occupied James City, a small village west of Culpepper. Meanwhile a cavalry force under Gen. Custer pushed forward by way of Madison Court House, in the direction of Charlottesville, the junction of the Alexandria with the Lynchburg Railroad. About the same time, in the afternoon of the 28th, Gen. Kilpatrick, with his division of cavalry and a portion of Gens. Merritt's and Gregg's divisions, with a light battery of six guns, being nearly eight thousand men, left Stevensburg for the lower fords of the Rapidan, intending to make a dash upon Richmond. This force crossed at Germania and Ely's fords, distant about sixty miles from Richmond. The command encamped on that night eight miles south of the Rapidan.

The headquarters of Gen. Lee were at Orange Court House, and the movements of the infantry with the command of Gen. Custer, toward Charlottesville, threatened to turn his left, and thus serve as a diversion in favor of the advance of Gen. Kilpatrick. Early on the morning of the 28th (Monday), Gen. Custer pushed forward across the Rapidan, and passing through Stannardsville arrived within four miles of Charlottesville. Here a body of cavalry under Col. Caskie were encountered. Six caissons, some camp equipage, and a few prisoners were captured, when the enemy rallied in force, and Gen. Custer fell back toward Ravenna River. Finding that the force of the enemy was considerable, the original intention of destroying the railway bridge and stores at Charlottesville was abandoned, and after burning three mills and a saddle factory the Ravenna was crossed, and the bridge burned. It now began to rain and freeze, and the night became exceedingly dark. Gen. Steadman's brigade being in advance, reached Madison Court House soon after daylight in the morning. Gen. Custer, however, was delayed by the difficulty of crossing streams with his artillery in the extreme darkness. Thus the enemy intercepted him near Stannardsville. By means of his artillery Gen. Custer held them in check until he could fall back upon a by-road, and thus avoid them. Madison Court House was reached at dusk on the 29th, with a number of horses and prisoners captured, and without the loss of a man.

In the meanwhile Gen. Kilpatrick resumed his advance on the next morning, to Frederick's Hall, on the Virginia Central Railroad. Here the track was torn up for some distance, and several officers of the enemy captured, and the carriages of several pieces of artillery destroyed. Col. Dahlgren was here detached with a portion of the force, and moved toward the James River Canal, and Gen. Kilpatrick advanced toward Ashland, on the railroad, twenty miles above Richmond. Here he rested on Monday night, and tore up a portion of the railroad track. Early the next morning he moved towards Richmond, on the Brooks' turnpike, and reached within six miles of that city. There he was met by a portion of the engineer troops and a few sections of light artillery, by which his advance was checked. A contest with artillery ensued for two hours, when Gen. Kilpatrick withdrew in the direction of Mechanicsville, burning the trestle work of the railroad accross the Chickahominy on his route.

The detachment under Col. Dahlgren penetrated as far as the farm of James A. Seddon, Confederate Secretary of War, and burned his barn and stables, and the flour and saw mills in the vicinity. On the canal a number of freight and other boats were destroyed, and a lock cut. A large number of horses were also seized. The ignorance or evil intention of their negro guide had misled the command, so that it was unable to join Gen. Kilpatrick at Ashland, and aid in the attack on Richmond, where it was supposed the enemy had few troops. It was afternoon, however, before he reached the vicinity of Richmond, advancing by the Westham or river road. As he approached nearer he was confronted on every road by superior numbers, and obliged to fall back.

He then attempted to reach the Peninsula through King's and Queen's county, where he encountered on the next day the 9th Virginia, Lieut.-Col. Pollard, and a sharp skirmish ensued. Col. Dahlgren was killed, and about sixty of his men captured. The remainder of the command, and the force of Gen. Kilpatrick, who had been obliged to move during the night by the pressure of the enemy, met a cavalry force sent out by Gen. Butler, from Williamsburg, near Tunstell's station on the York River railroad, and retired down the Peninsula. Their loss was about one hundred and fifty men killed and wounded, besides Col. Dahlgren. A number of prisoners were captured. The newspaper press at Richmond subsequently published the following address and orders, and asserted that they were found in the pocket of Col. Dahlgren. His connection with them has been denied, in the most positive manner, by the friends of Col. Dahlgren:

HEADQUARTERS, THIRD DIVISION,
CAVALRY CORPS, 1864.

Officers and Men—You have been selected from brigades and regiments as a picked command to attempt a desperate undertaking—an undertaking which, if successful, will write your names on the hearts of your countrymen in letters that can never be erased, and which will cause the prayers of our fellow soldiers now confined in loathsome prisons to follow you and yours wherever you may go. We hope to release the prisoners from Belle Isle first, and, having seen them fairly started, we will cross the James River into Richmond, destroy the bridges after us, and, exhorting the released prisoners to destroy and burn the hateful city, will not allow the rebel leader Davis and his traitorous crew to escape. The prisners must render great assistance, as you cannot leave your ranks too far, or become too much scattered, or you will be lost. Do not allow any personal gain to lead you off, which would only bring you to an ignominious death at the hands of citizens. Keep well together and obey orders strictly, and all will be well; but on no account scatter too far, for in union there is strength. With strict obedience to orders and fearlessness in their execution you will be sure to succeed. We will join the main force on the other side of the city, or perhaps meet them inside. Many of you may fall; but if there is any man here not willing to sacrifice his life in such a great and glorious undertaking, or who does not feel capable of meeting the enemy in such a desperate fight as will follow, let him step out, and he may go hence to the arms of his sweetheart, and read of the braves who swept through the city of Richmond. We want no man who cannot feel sure of success in such a holy cause. We will have a desperate fight; but stand up to it when it does come, and all will be well. Ask the blessing of the Almighty, and do not fear the enemy.

U. DAHLGREN, Colonel Commanding.

SPECIAL ORDERS AND INSTRUCTIONS.

Guides and pioneers, with oakum, turpentine, and torpedoes, signal officer, quartermasters, commissaries, scouts and pickets, and men in rebel uniforms —these will remain on the north bank and move down with the force on the south bank, not get ahead of them, and if the communication can be kept up without giving an alarm, it must be done; but every thing depends upon a surprise, and no one must be allowed to pass ahead of the column. Information must be gathered in regard to the crossings of the river, so that, should we be repulsed on the south side, we wlll know where to recross at the nearest point.

All mills must be burned and the canal destroyed, and also every thing which can be used by the rebels must be destroyed, including the boats on the river. Should a ferry boat be seized which can be worked, have it moved down. Keep the force on the south side posted of any important movement of the enemy, and in case of danger, some of the scouts must swim the river and bring us information. As we approach the city the party must take great care that they do not get ahead of the other party on the south side, and must conceal themselves and watch our movements. We will try and secure the bridge to the city, one mile below Belle Isle, and release the prisoners at the same time. If we don't succeed they must then dash down, and we will try to carry the bridge by storm. When necessary the men must be filed through the woods and along the river bank. The bridge once secured and the prisoners loose and over the river, the bridges will be burned and the city destroyed.

The men must be kept together and well in hand, and once in the city, it must be destroyed and Jeff. Davis and his Cabinet killed. Pioneers will go along with combustible material. The officer must use his discretion about the time of assisting us. Horses and cattle which we do not need immediately must be shot, rather than left.

Every thing on the canal and elsewhere, of service to the rebels, must be destroyed.

As Gen. Custer may follow me, be careful not to give a false alarm. The signal officer must be prepared to communicate at night by rockets, and in other things pertaining to his department. The Quartermasters and Commissaries must be on the lookout for their departments, and see that there are no delays on their account. The engineer officer will follow and survey the road as we pass over it, &c. The pioneers must be prepared to construct a bridge or destroy one. They must have plenty of oakum and turpentine for burning, which will be soaked and rolled into balls and be given to the men to burn when we get into the city. Torpedoes will only be used by the pioneers for burning the main bridges, &c. They must be prepared to destroy the railroads.

Men will branch off to the right with a few pioneers and destroy the bridges and railroads south of Richmond, and then join us at the city. They must be well prepared with torpedoes, &c.

The line of Falling Creek is probably the best to march along, or, as they approach the city, Good's Creek, so that no reënforcements can come up on any cars.

No one must be allowed to pass ahead, for fear of communicating news.

Rejoin the command with all haste, and if cut off, cross the river above Richmond and rejoin us. Men will stop at Bellona Arsenal and totally destroy it and every thing else but hospitals; then follow on and rejoin the command at Richmond with all haste, and, if cut off, cross the river and rejoin us. As Gen. Custer may follow me, be careful and not give a false alarm.

On the approach of Gen. Kilpatrick Richmond was in a defenceless condition. The Departments of the Government were closed and the clerks armed for defence. Men were collected from every quarter to oppose him. At the same time great consternation prevailed.

On the 29th of February an act of Congress to revive the grade of Lieutenant-General was approved by President Lincoln. He immediately sent the nomination of Maj.-Gen. Ulysses S. Grant to the Senate for confirmation. On March 3d this nomination was confirmed by the Senate. Gen. Grant was then in command of the army in Tennessee. He at once left his Department for Washington, and visited the President on March 9th. On presenting to him the commission as Lieutenant-General, in the presence of the Cabinet, Gen. Halleck, Gen. Rawlins, and Col. Comstock, of Gen. Grant's staff, the son of Gen. Grant, Mr. Lovejoy, of the House of Representatives, and others, the President rose and said:

GEN. GRANT: The nation's appreciation of what you have done, and its reliance upon you for what remains to do, in the existing great struggle, are now presented with this commission, constituting you Lieutenant-General in the Army of the United States. With this high honor devolves upon you, also, a corresponding responsibility. As the country herein trusts you, so, under God, it will sustain you. I scarcely need to add that with what I here speak for the nation, goes my own hearty personal concurrence.

To which Gen. Grant replied:

MR. PRESIDENT: I accept this commission with gratitude for the high honor conferred.

With the aid of the noble armies that have fought on so many fields for our common country, it will be my earnest endeavor not to disappoint your expectations.

I feel the full weight of the responsibilities now devolving on me, and I know that if they are met, it will be due to those armies, and, above, all to the favor of that Providence which leads both nations and men.

On the 11th of March Gen. Grant returned to Nashville, Tennessee. On the 12th, the following order was issued at Washington:

WAR DEPARTMENT, ADJUTANT GENERAL'S OFFICE,
WASHINGTON, March 12.

General Orders No. 98.

The President of the United States orders as follows: 1. Maj-Gen. Halleck is, at his own request, relieved from duty as General-in-Chief of the Army, and Lieut.-Gen. U. S. Grant assigned to the command of the Armies of the United States. The headquarters of the army will be in Washington and also with Lieut.-Gen. Grant in the field.

2. Maj.-Gen. Halleck is assigned to duty in Washington as Chief-of-Staff of the Army, under the direction of the Secretary of War and the Lieutenant-General commanding. His orders will be obeyed and respected accordingly.

3. Maj.-Gen. W. T. Sherman is assigned to the command of the military division of the Mississippi, composed of the Department of the Ohio, the Cumberland, the Tennessee, and the Arkansas.

4. Maj.-Gen. J. B. McPherson is assigned to the command of the Department and Army of the Tennessee.

5. In relieving Maj.-Gen. Halleck from duty as General-in-Chief, the President desires to express his approbation and thanks for the zealous manner in which the arduous and responsible duties of that position have been performed.

By order of the Secretary of War.

E. D. TOWNSEND, Ass't Adj't Gen.

On the 17th, Gen. Grant issued the following order:

HEADQUARTERS ARMIES OF UNITED STATES,
NASHVILLE, March 17, 1864.

General Orders No. 1.

In pursuance of the following order of the President—

EXECUTIVE MANSION,
WASHINGTON, D. C., March 10, 1864.

Under the authority of the act of Congress to revive the grade of Lieutenant-General of the United States Army, approved February 29th, 1864, Lieut-Gen. U. S. Grant, U. S. A., is appointed to the command of the Armies of the United States.

(Signed) A. LINCOLN.

I assume command of the Armies of the United States. My headquarters will be in the field, and until further orders will be with the Army of the Potomac. There will be an officers' headquarters in Washington, to which all official communications

H.W. Smith. N.Y.

W. T. Sherman

MAJ. GEN. U.S. ARMY

New York. D. Appleton & Co.

will be sent, except those from the army where headquarters are at the date of this address.

(Signed) U. S. GRANT, Lieut.-Gen. U. S. A.

On the 19th Gen. Grant left Nashville for Washington, and proceeded thence to the Army of the Potomac. On the 24th the following order was issued by Gen Meade, in command of the Army of the Potomac:

HEADQUARTERS ARMY OF THE POTOMAC, Thursday, March 24, 1864.

General Orders No. 10.

The following order has been received from the War Department:

WAR DEPARTMENT, ADJUTANT GENERAL'S OFFICE, WASHINGTON, March 23, 1864.

General Orders No. 15.

By direction of the President of the United States the number of army corps comprising the army of the Potomac will be reduced to three, viz., the 2d, 5th, and 6th corps; and the troops of the other two corps, viz., the 1st and 3d, will be temporarily reorganized and distributed among the 2d, 5th and 6th by the commanding general, who will determine what existing organizations will retain their corps badges and other distinctive marks. The staff and officers of the 2d corps, which are temporarily broken up, will be assigned to vacancies in the other corps, so far as such vacancies may exist. Those for whom there are no vacancies will cease to be considered as officers of the general staff of army corps.

2. Maj.-Gen. G. K. Warren is assigned by the President to the command of the 5th corps.

3. The following general officers are detached from the Army of the Potomac, and will report for orders to the Adjutant General of the army, viz.: Maj.-Gen. George Sykes, U. S. V.; Maj.-Gen. W. H. French, U. S. V.; Maj.-Gen. John Newton, U. S. V.; Brig.-Gen. J. R. Kenly, U. S. V.; Brig.-Gen. F. Spinola, U. S. V., and Brig.-Gen. Solomon Meredith, U. S. V.

By order of the Secretary of War.

E. D. TOWNSEND, Ass't Adj't Gen.

The following arrangements are made to carry out the provisions of the foregoing order:

The 2d, 5th, and 6th army corps will each be consolidated into two divisions. The 1st and 2d divisions of the 3d corps are transferred to the 2d corps, preserving their badges and distinctive marks. The 3d division of the 3d corps is transferred permanently to the 6th corps. The three divisions now forming the 1st corps are transferred to the 5th corps, preserving their badges and distinctive marks, and on forming the 5th corps they will be consolidated into two divisions.

The commanders of divisions transferred to the 2d, 5th, and 6th corps will at once report to the commanders of those corps for instructions. Brig.-Gen. J. B. Carr will report to Maj.-Gen. Hancock, commanding 2d corps, and Brig.-Gen. H. Prince to Maj.-Gen. Sedgwick, commanding 6th corps. The chief of artillery will assign eight batteries each to the 2d, 5th, and 6th corps; the batteries to be taken from those now with the corps and with the 1st and 3d corps. The batteries with the several corps in excess of the above allowance will join the artillery reserve.

The consolidation of divisions called for in this order will be made by the corps commanders concerned, who are authorized to rearrange the brigades of their respective commands in such manner as they may think best for the service. The reassignment of officers of the staff departments consequent upon the reorganization of the army, will be made upon the nomination of chiefs of the staff departments at these headquarters.

Special instructions will be given hereafter with respect to staff officers of the 2d corps, temporarily broken up.

The Major-General Commanding avails himself of the occasion to say that, in view of the reduced strength of nearly all the regiments serving in this army, the temporary reduction of the army corps to three is a measure imperatively demanded by the best interests of the service, and that the reasons for attaching the 1st and 3d corps for the time being to other corps, were in no respect founded on any supposed inferiority of those corps to the other corps of the army. All the corps have equally proved their valor in many fields, and all have equal claims to the confidence of the Government and the country. The 1st and 3d corps will retain their badges and distinctive marks, and the Major-General Commanding indulges the hope that the ranks of the army will be filled at an early day, so that those corps can again be reorganized.

By command of Maj.-Gen. MEADE.

S. WILLIAMS, Ass't Adj't Gen.

A concentration of troops was now commenced in preparation for a campaign against Richmond, in Virginia, by the Army of the Potomac, under Gen. Meade, and a campaign against Atlanta, in Georgia, by the Army of Tennessee, under Gen. Sherman. Gen. Grant continued to be present with the Army of the Potomac during the year. Gen. Meade was as truly the commander of that army as Gen. W. T. Sherman of the army operating in Georgia, and both these officers were equally under the command of Gen. Grant. His presence with the Army of the Potomac naturally led to his assuming a more direct and personal supervision of affairs in Virginia than he was able to do of the cooperative movement of Gen. Sherman in Georgia. The orders of Gen. Grant to Gen. Meade were of the most general character. The manner of executing them was left to the judgment and skill of the latter. It was now nine months since the Army of the Potomac had fought a general battle, and seven months since the Western army marched into Chattanooga—the last battle for the possession of which was fought in November.

The month of April passed in reorganizing both armies, and in making preparations for the campaign against Richmond and Atlanta.

It was the middle of March when Gen. Grant turned over the military division of the Mississippi, comprising the departments of the Cumberland, the Tennessee, and the Ohio, to Major-General W. T. Sherman, who had previously commanded the department of the Tennessee, to which Major-General McPherson was soon after assigned. In the succeeding month the general plan of the summer campaign, which contemplated a simultaneous advance upon Richmond by the army of the Potomac, and upon Atlanta from Chattanooga, by the several western armies, was matured, and Gen. Sherman at once bent every energy to the perfecting and enlargement of the communications between Nashville and Chattanooga, his primary and secondary bases, and to the accumulation in the latter place of a sufficient quantity of provisions and military stores. These went forward with great rapidity, and by the end of April the depots in Chattanooga were reported abundantly supplied for all immediate purposes.

At this time the headquarters of the armies of the Tennessee, the Cumberland, and the Ohio, were respectively at Huntsville, Chattanooga, and Knoxville; and on the 27th, Gen. Sherman having been notified by Gen. Grant that the Army of the Potomac would march from Culpepper on or about May 5th, and that he wished the movement from Chattanooga to commence at the same time, put his troops in motion toward the latter place. The total force under his command for offensive purposes, was as follows:

Army of the Cumberland, Major-Gen. Thomas Commanding.

Infantry	54,568
Artillery	2,377
Cavalry	3,828
Total	60,773
Guns	130

Army of the Tennessee, Major-Gen. McPherson Commanding.

Infantry	22,437
Artillery	1,404
Cavalry	624
Total	24,465
Guns	96

Army of the Ohio, Major-Gen. Schofield Commanding.

Infantry	11,183
Artillery	679
Cavalry	1,679
Total	13,559
Guns	28

making a grand aggregate of 88,188 infantry, 4,460 artillery, and 6,149 cavalry, or 98,797 men and 254 guns. The Army of the Cumberland comprised the 4th corps, Gen. Howard; the 14th corps, Gen. Palmer, and the 20th corps, Gen. Hooker; the Army of the Tennessee, the 15th corps, Gen. Logan; the 16th corps, Gen. Dodge; and later in the campaign, the 17th corps, Gen. Blair; and the Army of the Ohio, the 23d corps, Gen. Schofield. These armies were grouped on the morning of May 6th as follows: That of the Cumberland at Ringgold, on the Western and Atlantic Railroad, 23 miles southeast of Chattanooga; that of the Tennessee at Gordon's Mill, on the Chickamauga, eight miles west of Ringgold; and that of the Ohio, near Red Clay, on the Georgia line, about ten miles northeast of Ringgold. The enemy, comprising Gens. Hardee's, Hood's, and Polk's corps of infantry and artillery, and Wheeler's division of cavalry, the whole commanded by Lieut.-General Joseph E. Johnston, of the Confederate Army, lay in and about Dalton, fifteen miles south of Ringgold, on the railroad, the advance being at Tunnel Hill, a station about midway between the two places. Their cavalry were estimated by Gen. Sherman at 10,000 men, and the infantry and artillery at from 45,000 to 50,000, of whom much the greater part were veteran troops.

Topographically considered, the State of Georgia admits of three distinct divisions: 1. A mountainous region, embracing the northwest corner of the State, and which terminates at the Kenesaw Mountain, near Marietta, 120 miles from Chattanooga; 2. A gently undulating country extending from the mountainous region to a line passing in a northeasterly direction through Columbus, Macon, and Augusta; and 3. A level country extending to the seaboard, for the most part sandy and thickly covered with pine woods, and along the coast bordered by extensive swamps. The northwestern portion of the State, as far south as Atlanta, is almost exclusively a grain and grass-bearing region; the middle and eastern divisions being devoted chiefly to the cultivation of cotton. But its mineral wealth, particularly in iron ores, which abound among the mountains, has, since the commencement of the war, rendered the possession of this first-mentioned division a matter of prime importance to the Confederates. At Etowah, Rome, and Atlanta were large iron works in the employ of the rebel government, the capture and permanent occupation of which by a Union force would be likely to cause much embarrassment, not to speak of cotton and woollen mills at Roswell, Rome, and elsewhere, which turned out large quantities of fabrics for the use of the rebel troops.

Atlanta, lying near the boundary between the northwestern and middle divisions had, previous to the war, become an important centre of railroad communication and trade between the western and Atlantic and Gulf States, and one of the chief manufacturing towns of the South. It is laid out in a circle, two miles in diameter, in the centre of which was the passenger depot (since destroyed) of railroads radiating to Chattanooga, Augusta, Macon, and Montgomery; and the business portion of the town contained many fine blocks of warehouses for storing goods consigned from the north and northwest to the cotton regions of the South. Here also were established the machine shops of the principal railroads, the most extensive rolling mill in the South, foundries, pistol, and tent factories, and numerous works under the direction of the Confederate Government for casting shot and shell, and the manufacture of gun-carriages, cartridges, caps, shoes, clothing, and other military supplies. The population, numbering in 1860 about 15,000, had, subsequent to the commencement of the war, been increased by the arrival of refugees and government officials and employés to fully 20,000. In any event the capture of the place, with its vast stores and costly machinery, would so cripple the rebel resources, that the simple suggestion of such a contingency sent a thrill of alarm through the entire Confederacy. In the opinion of many its importance was not second even to that of Richmond. Strenuous efforts were accordingly put forth for its defence, and the line of approach along the Western and Atlantic Railroad, which is crossed by the Oostanaula and Etowah, branches of the Coosa River, which in turn is a branch of the Alabama, and by the Chattahoochee, and is girt as far as Marietta by ranges of rugged hills, was rendered as difficult for Sherman as the abundant

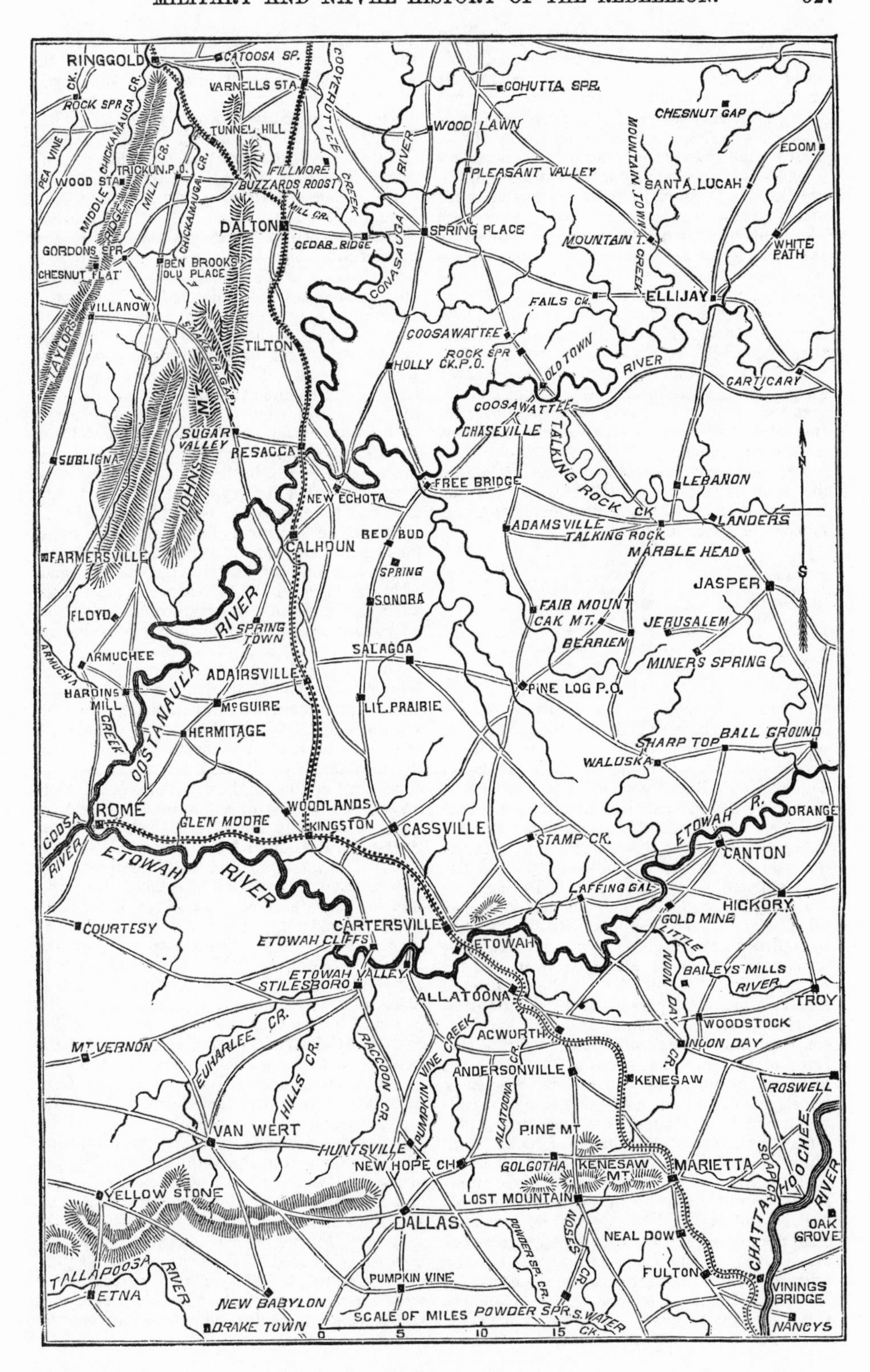
RINGGOLD
CATOOSA SP.
VARNELLS STA.
COOYEHUTTEE CREEK
COHUTTA SPR.
CHESNUT GAP
ROCK SPR
TUNNEL HILL
WOOD LAWN
MOUNTAIN TOWN CREEK
EDOM
PEA VINE CK.
CHICKAMAUGA CR.
FILLMORE
PLEASANT VALLEY
SANTA LUCAH
WOOD STA.
TRICKUN P.O.
BUZZARDS ROOST
MILL CR.
MIDDLE CHICKAMAUGA CR.
RIDGE
DALTON
SPRING PLACE
MOUNTAIN T.
WHITE PATH
CEDAR RIDGE
GORDONS SPR.
BEN BROOKS OLD PLACE
CONASAUGA RIVER
CHESNUT FLAT
ELLIJAY
FAILS CK.
VILLANOW
TAYLORS RIDGE
COOSAWATTEE
ROCK SPR
TILTON
SNAKE CR. GAP
HOLLY CK. P.O.
OLD TOWN
RIVER
CARTICARY
JOHNS MT.
COOSAWATTEE
CHASEVILLE
SUGAR VALLEY
TALKING ROCK CK.
RESACCA
SUBLIGNA
FREE BRIDGE
LEBANON
NEW ECHOTA
N
ADAMSVILLE
LANDERS
TALKING ROCK
RED BUD
CALHOUN
MARBLE HEAD
FARMERSVILLE
SPRING
JASPER
S
SONORA
FAIR MOUNT
OAK MT.
JERUSALEM
FLOYD
SPRING TOWN
BERRIEN
SALACOA
MINERS SPRING
ARMUCHEE
ARMUCHEE CREEK
ADAIRSVILLE
PINE LOG P.O.
HARDINS MILL
McGUIRE
LIT. PRAIRIE
OOSTANAULA RIVER
HERMITAGE
SHARP TOP
BALL GROUND
WALUSKA
ROME
WOODLANDS
ORANGE
COOSA RIVER
GLEN MOORE
KINGSTON
CASSVILLE
ETOWAH R.
STAMP CK.
CANTON
ETOWAH RIVER
LAFFING GAL
HICKORY
CARTERSVILLE
GOLD MINE
COURTESY
ETOWAH CLIFFS
ETOWAH
LITTLE RIVER
BAILEYS MILLS
ETOWAH VALLEY
STILESBORO
NOON DAY CR.
ALLATOONA
TROY
WOODSTOCK
ACWORTH
NOON DAY
MT. VERNON
EUHARLEE CR.
RACCOON CR.
PUMPKIN VINE CREEK
ALLATOONA CR.
ANDERSONVILLE
KENESAW
HILLS CR.
ROSWELL
PINE MT.
VAN WERT
HUNTSVILLE
CHATTAHOOCHEE RIVER
SOAP CR.
NEW HOPE CH.
GOLGOTHA
KENESAW MT.
MARIETTA
YELLOW STONE
LOST MOUNTAIN
DALLAS
OAK GROVE
POWDER SP. CR.
NOSES CR.
NEAL DOW
TALLAPOOSA RIVER
FULTON
PUMPKIN VINE
VININGS BRIDGE
ETNA
NEW BABYLON
POWDER SPR.
S. WATER CK.
SCALE OF MILES
0 5 10 15
DRAKE TOWN
NANCYS

resources at the disposal of Johnston would admit. Should the mountain region be traversed or turned, and the Chattahoochee be crossed by an invading army, the enormous strength of Atlanta itself still gave promise of a long and perhaps successful defence, while an active cavalry force operating on Sherman's flanks might so seriously interrupt his communications as to compel him to retrace his steps and abandon the campaign. His forces were also liable to daily depletion as he advanced by the necessity of garrisoning captured places as well as of guarding the line of railway, while Johnston, moving constantly nearer to his supplies and reënforcements, would probably be relatively stronger when he reached Atlanta than when he started. The consequences which defeat would entail upon either party seemed so disastrous that the campaign was watched with an interest hardly inferior to that attending the more extensive operations around Richmond.

For the convenience of reference the following table of stations on the Western and Atlantic Railroad, with their distances from Chattanooga, is appended:

	Miles.		Miles.
Boyce	5	Kingston	79
Chickamauga	10	Cass	86
Johnson	18	Cartersville	91
Ringgold	23	Etowah	95
Tunnel Hill	31	Altoona	98
Dalton	38	Ackworth	102
Tilton	47	Big Shanty	108
Resaca	56	Marietta	119
Calhoun	60	Vining's	130
Adairsville	69	Atlanta	138

A reconnoissance by Gen. Sherman of Gen. Johnston's position at Dalton satisfied him that an attack in front was impracticable, even should the enemy abandon their works at Tunnel Hill. Directly south of this eminence, through which passes the railroad by a tunnel eighteen hundred feet in length, opens a level valley about three miles long by half to three-quarters of a mile in width, bounded at its further extremity by "Rocky Faced Ridge," a steep, thickly-wooded and rugged eminence, which commands the approach to Dalton both by railroad and wagon road, and extends as an impassable barrier along its west side for many miles. The outlet to this valley is through a narrow mountain pass called Buzzard Roost, nearly midway between Tunnel Hill and Dalton, which by means of abatis, a formidable series of batteries, and a line of rifle-pits at its northern entrance, had been rendered absolutely impregnable to a force advancing along the railroad. On its northeast side Dalton was defended by strong works on Mill Creek. Gen. Sherman accordingly directed Gen. McPherson, with the Army of the Tennessee, to move rapidly southward from his position at Gordon's Mill, *via* Ship's Gap, Villanov, and Snake Creek Gap, upon Resaca, a station eighteen miles below Dalton, or upon any other point on the railroad which might prove more accessible. This movement, he supposed, would compel Gen. Johnston to evacuate Dalton, when Gen. McPherson would be in a position to harass the enemy's flank, while the main body of the Federal army pressed him from the north. While this flanking movement was in progress a strong feint of attack was to be made by Gen. Thomas in front of Buzzard Roost, and Gen. Schofield, with the Army of the Ohio, was directed to close up upon the latter's left.

On the 7th Gen. Thomas advanced from Ringgold toward Tunnel Hill, which was carried by the 14th corps under Gen. Palmer, after a brief skirmish, with the loss of a few men wounded. The slight resistance offered by the enemy indicated that they had no intention of defending the position, but only sought to hold Gen. Thomas in check until they could make good their retreat to the stronger position of Buzzard Roost. The Federal line was established on the same evening about a mile south of Tunnel Hill. On the 8th a demonstration in force was made against Rocky Faced Ridge and Buzzard Roost, which, on the 9th, was pushed almost to a battle. The 4th (Howard's) corps succeeded in carrying the ridge, but found the crest too narrow to enable it to attack the pass with any prospect of success. Gen. Schofield meanwhile came up on Gen. Thomas's left, which was held by Gen. Howard, and a brigade of his cavalry, while demonstrating against the enemy's right flank, met with some loss in an encounter with a superior force of rebel infantry.

On the 8th Gen. McPherson passed through Snake Creek Gap, surprising a rebel cavalry force sent to hold the position, and approached within a mile of Resaca, which he found too strong to be carried by assault. Apprehending, also, that if he should attempt to cross over to the railroad he might expose his left flank to an attack from the direction of Dalton, he fell back to a strong position at the west end of Snake Creek Gap, and reported to Gen. Sherman. The latter, finding that the demonstration on the enemy's flank had failed to compel him to evacuate his strong position, immediately determined to put the remainder of his army in motion for Snake Creek Gap; and on the 10th Gen. Hooker's (20th) corps, which held the right of Gen. Thomas's line, started for that place, followed on the succeeding day by the rest of Thomas's troops, with the exception of two divisions of Howard's corps and some cavalry, who were left to threaten the enemy in front of Buzzard Roost, and by Gen. Schofield's army; the three armies thus holding the same relative positions occupied by them at the commencement of the campaign. The Federal loss in the actions of the 8th and 9th was between 700 and 800 killed, wounded, and missing, the greater number being only slightly wounded.

Resaca, toward which Sherman was now moving, is situated on the Oostanaula, in a peninsula formed by the junction of that river with its northwest fork, the Conasauga, and across this peninsula the rebels had erected continuous lines of rifle-pits with strong field fortifications, particularly about the town, by means of which their flanks were protected on either river, and a line of retreat preserved across the Oostanaula. Friday, May 13th, was occupied by the troops in deploying through Snake Creek Gap and getting into position in Sugar Valley, a fertile tract beyond, much broken by hills, which are covered by a dense undergrowth, and on that account difficult of approach. The movement was covered by the cavalry under Gen. Kilpatrick, who, while pressing the enemy toward Resaca, fell into an ambuscade and received a severe flesh wound, which incapacitated him for several months for active duty. During the day the Federal lines were advanced toward Resaca, the right under McPherson resting on the Oostanaula, about two miles below the town, and extending thence northward so as to face it; the centre, under Gen. Thomas, closing up upon Gen. McPherson's left, and the left, under Schofield, striking the Conasauga near Tilton, a station on the railroad about midway between Dalton and Resaca. Beside the protection afforded by the two rivers, both flanks of the army were covered by heavy bodies of cavalry. The scene of these operations was a rugged, thickly-wooded country, abounding in steep hills and narrow ravines, through one of which, directly in front of the rebel lines, flows Camp Creek, a small stream emptying into the Oostanaula near Resaca.

Gen. Johnston was not long in detecting the object of Sherman's flanking march, and judging the position at Dalton to be no longer tenable, he moved rapidly southward on the 12th, and having the shorter line of march, reached Resaca with his entire force before the Union army had debouched from Snake Creek Gap. The divisions of Howard's corps left to watch Buzzard Roost, soon after occupied Dalton, which was found thoroughly stripped of supplies and almost deserted, and moving in the enemy's rear, effected a junction on the 14th with the Federal left, near Tilton. The successful turning of the rebel position at Dalton was justly considered a great step gained in the movement upon Atlanta; and even among the rebel troops there were many who thought that if their leader could not hold for more than four days a place so strongly fortified by nature, he would be unable to maintain himself for a long time at any of the remaining points north of Atlanta, no one of which was perhaps so capable of defence as Dalton.

The night of the 13th was employed by the rebels in strengthening their already formidable position by additional earthworks, and on the morning of the 14th they were in complete readiness for an attack, their right wing being held by Gen. Hardee, their centre by Gen. Hood, and their left by Gen. Polk. Skirmishishing commenced at an early hour, and the object of Gen. Sherman being to press Resaca at all points, while a force of infantry and cavalry crossed the Oostanaula and threatened Calhoun in the rear, the firing toward noon grew heavy along the whole rebel line. The Federal general had hoped to be able to turn the rebel left wing, and thus cut off their retreat, but the nature of the ground rendered this impossible. At 1 P. M. an attempt was made by Palmer's corps, holding the left centre, to break the enemy's line, and force him from an elevated position in the immediate front. To reach this point it was necessary to descend a hill in full range of rebel artillery, ford a stream thickly bordered with undergrowth and interlacing vines, and then, crossing a valley full of ditches and other obstructions, to mount the opposite eminence. In the teeth of a murderous fire of musketry and artillery, Palmer's troops charged down the hill and across the creek; but becoming speedily entangled in the obstructions, and unable to find shelter or to return with effect the plunging fire of the enemy, which caused havoc in their ranks, they were forced to retire, with a loss estimated at upwards of a thousand. About the same time, further to the left, Gen. Judah's division of the 23d corps and Newton's of the 4th corps, moving over comparatively level ground, succeeded, after a desperate struggle, in forcing the enemy to abandon an important position on their outer line. Although the Federal troops were unable to hold this, they succeeded in advancing their line and getting their artillery into a position to prevent the enemy from reoccupying the works. On the extreme left, that portion of the 4th corps which had arrived from Dalton, in concert with Gen. Schofield, maintained heavy skirmishing with the rebel right, the dense woods in that direction preventing the use of artillery, and effectually concealing the movements of troops on either side. The operations on Gen. McPherson's end of the line were, during the morning, of the same character.

At about 3 o'clock in the afternoon Gen. Johnston, perceiving that no serious impression had been made upon his lines, quietly massed a heavy force on the road to Tilton, with a view of turning the Federal left flank, held by Stanley's division of the 4th corps. The attack was delivered with impetuosity and in such overwhelming numbers, that Stanley's troops, after a stubborn resistance, were forced in confusion from a hill upon which they were posted. The rebels rushed on with loud yells across an open field west of the hill, and for a few moments matters wore a critical aspect. Fortunately, however, the movement of the rebel right had been early detected, and Hooker's corps sent from the centre to reënforce the Federal left. The timely arrival of a portion of his troops checked the rebel advance, and the scattered division of Stanley having been partially rallied, the rebels were at dusk driven back within their lines with severe loss. Meanwhile Gen. McPherson, taking advantage of the enemy's occupation with this movement, ordered Logan's (15th) corps, with a portion of the 16th, to cross Camp Creek and carry a hill and a line of rifle-pits on the enemy's extreme left, in front of Resaca, which was effected with slight loss. As the position was one which would enable the Federal General to pour a destructive enfilading fire upon the rebel works, and also to command the railroad and trestle bridges across the Oostanaula, a desperate effort was made soon after dark to retake it. Heavy columns of infantry with fixed bayonets moved up to the very crest of the hill, but recoiled under the steady fire of the Federal troops, and finally retired in confusion. At 10 P. M. the fighting terminated for the day. The result of the day's work was on the whole satisfactory to Gen. Sherman, as the Federal lines had nowhere been permanently forced back, while on their left and centre the rebels had lost positions of importance.

The night of the 14th was occupied by both armies in strengthening their positions, and the morning of the 15th opened with heavy skirmishing along the Federal centre, under cover of which troops were massed for an assault upon two fortified hills commanding each other, on the enemy's extreme right, which were considered the key to the whole position. For this purpose Gen. Hooker's corps had been shifted to the extreme left, and Gens. Howard's, Schofield's, and Palmer's troops moved to the right to fill up the gap occasioned by the withdrawal of Gen. Hooker. Shortly after 1 o'clock in the afternoon Gen. Hooker sent forward Butterfield's division as the assaulting column, supported by the divisions of Gens. Geary and Williams, and after several unsuccessful attacks the enemy were driven from a portion of their lines, and a lodgment was secured under the projecting works of a lunette, mounting four pieces of artillery. So severe, however, was the fire from rifle-pits beyond and on either side of this work, forming the inner rebel line, that further advance was impossible, and the Federal troops were fain to seek such shelter as was available, and content themselves with holding the position they had gained. Toward the close of the afternoon Gen. Hood's corps made a determined but unsuccessful effort to dislodge them, and subsequently, under cover of the darkness, a number of rebel prisoners were brought up, the ends dug out of the works, and the guns hauled out by means of ropes, under a destructive fire from the rebels. As soon as a breach was made our forces rushed in and captured the lunette after a desperate engagement. The guns seized were twelve-pounders. The flags of the 35th and 38th Alabama regiments were captured, with over two hundred prisoners. While these operations were in progress the enemy's attention was occupied by heavy skirmishing along the whole line.

During the night the enemy quietly abandoned Resaca, leaving behind a four-gun battery and a quantity of stores, and by dawn were well on their way to Kingston, thirty-two miles south on the railroad. Gen. Thomas's troops immediately occupied the town, and succeeded in saving the road bridge, but the railroad bridge, the most costly structure of the kind between Chattanooga and Atlanta, was destroyed by the enemy, with the exception of the stone piers. The total Federal loss in the two days' fighting was between 4,000 and 5,000 killed and wounded, upward of 2,000 of the latter being so slightly injured that they were returned to duty in two or three weeks. The rebel loss was stated by themselves at 2,500, which is probably not far from the mark. Fighting for the most part behind earthworks, and having the advantage of position, they necessarily suffered less than their opponents. Beside the eight guns and the stores already mentioned, they left about 1,000 prisoners in the hands of the Federals. According to Gen. Sherman nothing saved Gen. Johnston's army at Resaca but the impracticable nature of the surrounding country, which made the speedy passage of troops across the valley from Snake Creek Gap an impossibility. This fact enabled the rebel army to reach Resaca from Dalton along comparatively good roads, constructed beforehand by the foresight of their general. The latter was nevertheless severely criticized for this second abandonment of what was considered a defensible position, notwithstanding that the Richmond newspapers explained that his peculiar forte consisted in drawing an enemy after him, and then overwhelming him by a sudden attack. They also endeavored to derive consolation from a reputed caution of Gen. Scott to a Federal commander: "Beware of Lee advancing, and watch Johnston at a stand; for the devil himself would be defeated in the attempt to whip him retreating," which was extensively quoted in the Southern papers.

Soon after the discovery of Gen. Johnston's retreat, the cavalry divisions of Gens. Stoneman and McCook were thrown forward in pursuit, and during the 16th the army was occupied in crossing the Oostanaula. Gen. Thomas made the passage at Resaca, Gen. McPherson at Lay's Ferry, a few miles to the southwest, while Gen. Schofield, moving to the left of Thomas, crossed the Conasauga and Coosawattee, which unite near Resaca to form the Oostanaula. In this order the army marched southward on roads parallel to the railroad, finding no trace of the enemy until reaching the neighborhood of Adairsville, thirteen miles below Resaca, where Newton's division of the 4th corps had a smart skirmish with the rebel rear guard, who had posted their sharpshooters in an octagon cement building called "Graves House," for the purpose of delaying the advance. By the aid of artillery they were driven out, and on the 18th the 4th corps reached Kingston, four miles beyond which place the enemy were again discovered in considerable force on open ground. At Cassville, five miles east of Kingston, they were known to have constructed strong works; and on the 19th, in anticipation of a general engagement, Gen. Sherman directed Gen. Schofield to move down toward this place from the north, while Gen. Thomas closed up upon his right, and McPherson marched to Kingston to be in close support of Thomas. Gen. Johnston, however, declined the offer of battle, and during the night retreated across the Etowah, burning the road and railroad bridges behind him. A few days' halt for rest and refreshment was now allowed the army, and as the country north of the Etowah had been completely stripped by Gen. Johnston, it was necessary to await the arrival of supplies by railroad. The latter fortunately had received little injury at the hands of the enemy, and by the energetic labors of the repairing parties, who followed close behind the army, was put in running order to Kingston on the 20th, on which day trains arrived laden with supplies. By this means the army was soon restored to a condition of complete efficiency, and relieved of the necessity of looking after the wounded, who were sent back to Chattanooga. In like manner telegraphic communication with the latter place was kept open as the army advanced.

While these operations were in progress, Gen. Jeff. C. Davis, of Palmer's corps, on the 17th marched southwesterly from Resaca toward Rome, fifteen miles west of Kingston, which place he occupied on the 19th after a sharp fight, gaining possession of several forts, eight or ten guns of heavy caliber, large quantities of stores, and the valuable mills and foundries employed in the service of the Confederate Government.

Gen. Johnston had meanwhile taken a strong position at Allatoona Pass, in the Etowah Mountains, south of the Etowah River, which formed an almost impregnable barrier to a direct advance upon Atlanta by railroad. Gen. Sherman accordingly resorted to the same tactics which had proved so successful at Dalton; and having supplied his wagons with twenty days' provisions, and left garrisons at Rome and Kingston, he put his army in motion on May 23d for Dallas, a town lying about fifteen miles southwest of Allatoona Pass, and eighteen miles directly west of Marietta, a station on the railroad forty miles below Kingston, and twenty-four south of the Etowah River. He expected thus, by threatening Marietta, to compel the evacuation of Allatoona. The country between Dallas and the railroad is of the same impracticable character as that in which previous operations of the campaign had been conducted, being for the most part densely wooded, traversed by ranges of rugged hills, and cut up by frequent ravines. The roads were few and poor. Through this region, admirably adapted for defence, and of which the topography was scarcely known to the Federal general, the advance in the presence of a vigilant enemy had necessarily to be made with much caution, and it will be seen that several days were occupied with manœuvring for position and other movements, before any practical results were obtained.

In marching upon Dallas, Gen. McPherson, still holding the Federal right, made a somewhat wide detour to the southwest through Van Wert, while Gen. Thomas took a course nearly due south, having Gen. Schofield on his left flank. The movement had scarcely commenced before it was detected by Gen. Johnston, who having the shorter line to Dallas, marched in the direction of that place to cover the approaches to Marietta. On the 25th Hooker's corps, approaching Pumpkin Vine Creek on the main Dallas road, came into collision with parties of Hood's and Hardee's corps, and a severe engagement took place for the possession of a point known as the New Hope Church, where three roads meet from Ackworth [four miles south of Allatoona by rail], Marietta, and Dallas. By means of earthworks the enemy successfully resisted the advance of Gen. Hooker, and the night closing with a heavy rain storm, no further attempt was made to force the position. In this affair Hooker sustained a loss of about six hundred killed and wounded. Gen. Sherman then ordered McPherson to move up to Dallas, and Gen. Thomas to make a bold demonstration against New Hope Church, while Schofield overlapped the enemy's right wing. Owing to the difficult nature of the country, the 26th and 27th were occupied in perfecting these dispositions, and on the evening of the latter day his line extended in a semicircular direction northeast from Dallas, the enemy having his right resting on the road from Ackworth to Dallas, at a point three miles northeast of New Hope Church, and his left at a point nearly due east of Dallas. Heavy skirmishing attended these manœuvres, but as the density of the surrounding woods rendered the use of artillery impracticable, the casualties were not numerous. On the 28th, just as Gen. McPherson was on the point of closing up to Gen. Thomas in front of New Hope Church, in order to enable a further development of the Federal left wing, he was attacked by a heavy rebel force, whose repeated and desperate, though fruitless assaults had the effect of checking temporarily the contemplated movement. The Federal troops, protected by their breastworks, finally drove the enemy back with a loss of upward of two thousand killed and wounded.

After a brief pause, interrupted only by the customary skirmishing, renewed orders were given for the shifting of the Federal line to the left. The movement was now effected with comparative ease, and on June 1st, the roads to Allatoona and Ackworth being occupied, the cavalry divisions of Stoneman and Garrard were pushed forward to Allatoona Pass, which was carried with slight loss. Orders were immediately given to rebuild the railroad bridge over the Etowah, at Etowah Station, and on June 4th Gen. Sherman moved directly upon Ackworth. This manœuvre compelled Gen.

Johnston to abandon his intrenchments at New Hope Church, and move westward to the railroad to cover Marietta, and on the 6th the Federal army reached Ackworth, where it rested for several days. Allatoona Pass was at once fixed upon as a secondary base, and put in a defensible condition. A well-informed correspondent, summing up the results of the campaign to this date, observes: "We have in a month's time, with a force not very much superior to his, forced the enemy back nearly one hundred miles, obliging him to abandon four different positions of unusual strength and proportions; have fought him six times; have captured twelve guns, three colors, over two thousand prisoners, with considerable forage, provisions, and means of transportation; have placed at least fifteen thousand of his men *hors de combat*, and have destroyed several important foundries, rolling mills, iron works, &c., at Rome, and in the Allatoona Mountains."

On the 8th Gen. Blair reached Ackworth with two divisions of the 17th army corps, which were attached to Gen. McPherson's command, and a brigade of cavalry belonging to Gen. Garrard's division. These accessions compensated for the Federal losses in battle, and the garrisons left at Resaca, Rome, Kingston, and Allatoona, and on the 9th the army, refreshed by three days' much needed rest, and abundantly supplied with stores, moved forward to Big Shanty, the next railroad station south of Ackworth. Between this place and Marietta intervenes a mountainous district of vast natural strength, having three detached and well-defined summits, where Gen. Johnston had made his next stand. Kenesaw Mountain, the most easterly of these summits, is a double-peaked eminence, about 1,200 feet high, lying directly north and northwest of Marietta, and west of the railroad, and sending out a spur for several miles in a northeasterly direction. West of Marietta, on the road to Dallas, is Lost Mountain, and midway between the latter and Kenesaw, half a mile further to the north, is Pine Mountain, a rugged, cone-shaped peak, which may be said to form the apex of a triangle, of which Kenesaw and Lost Mountains constitute the base. The three eminences are connected by several ranges of lesser heights, seamed with ravines, and covered with a dense growth of oak and hickory, and upon their summits the rebels had erected signal stations which commanded an excellent view of all the general operations of the Federal forces. As the latter drew in sight, the most assailable points in this succession of mountain fortresses appeared bristling with cannon, and the spurs were alive with men constructing earthworks, felling timber for obstructions, and otherwise preparing for an obstinate resistance. The rebel front extended westward from the railroad, on which their right rested, about four miles, and comprised several successive lines of intrenchments. They had also some works on the ridge east of the railroad. "The rebel works," says the correspondent above quoted, "consisted of log barricades, protected by earth thrown against them, with a formidable abatis, and in many places a *chevaux-de-frise* of sharpened fence-rails besides. The thickness of this parapet (which really resembled a parallel) was generally six to eight feet at top, on the infantry line, and from twelve to fifteen feet thick at top where field guns were posted, or where fire from our artillery was anticipated."

The controlling point of the whole region is Kenesaw Mountain, which covers the railroad and the town of Marietta so effectually that a direct advance upon the latter place from the north would be well-nigh impossible. As the rebel lines were drawn, it constituted a stronghold or citadel in a deep reëntrant, Pine and Lost Mountains and the connecting ridges being in the nature of outworks, useful in retarding the approach of an enemy, but not absolutely essential as portions of a system of defences. The accounts of prisoners, deserters, and scouts, placed Gen. Johnston's force at nine divisions of seven thousand men each, which was probably somewhat above the mark; in addition to which an auxiliary force of fifteen thousand Georgia militia, called out by Governor Brown, was placed at his disposal. The latter, though comparatively undisciplined, did good service as laborers on fortifications, and were capable of offering considerable resistance behind earthworks. Hardee's corps occupied their right, Polk the centre, and Hood the left. Their cavalry, estimated at fifteen thousand, operated on the flanks, and in the Federal rear.

The order of the Federal advance was somewhat different from that previously observed during the campaign. Gen. McPherson's command was now transferred to the extreme left, and moved toward Marietta, having its right on the railroad, while Gen. Schofield, shifting to the right wing, marched for Lost Mountain. Gen. Thomas kept his old position in the centre, and moved on Kenesaw and Pine Mountains. Gens. Stoneman and Garrard covered the right and left wings with their cavalry, and McCook guarded the communications and rear. From the 9th to the 14th the Federal lines were gradually closed up toward the rebel position, Sherman's first object being to break the line between Kenesaw and Pine Mountains; and on the latter day, during a heavy cannonade by the 4th corps, the rebel Gen. Polk, commanding on Pine Mountain, was killed by the explosion of a shell. On the same night, the rebels, perceiving that Hooker's corps was moving around the base of the mountain to cut off their retreat, abandoned their works without loss of guns or material of war, and on the morning of the 15th the position was quietly occupied by Stanley's division of the 4th corps. A paper was found affixed to a stake, stating, "Here Gen. Polk was killed by a Yankee shell;" and from the reports of deserters it appeared that Gens. Johnston and

Hardee were standing near Gen. Polk when he was struck, and narrowly escaped death.

Gen. Johnston now drew back his centre about a mile, to a strong line of intrenchments in the rugged hills connecting Kenesaw and Lost Mountains, keeping his flanks on these two eminences. The 15th, 16th, and 17th, were occupied with incessant skirmishing, which told upon the spirits and endurance of the Federal army almost as much as a pitched battle. "The enemy," says a correspondent, "seems to have marked out this whole country, from the Allatoona Mountains to the Chattahooche, with line after line of rifle-pits and intrenchments and fortification. No sooner do we take possession of one formidable line of works than another confronts us, and each seems to be stronger than the preceding." On the extreme right during the afternoon of the 15th, Gen. Schofield carried the first line of the rebel works at the foot of Lost Mountain. During the 17th, the left and centre remained quiet, its line being so far advanced that a general engagement would otherwise have resulted. The right and right centre were pushed forward more than a mile, occupying a heavy line of intrenchments which the rebels had evacuated, and their main line at the foot of Lost Mountain, without serious loss. Toward evening, after much heavy skirmishing, the enemy's left was dislodged from the strong intrenchments at the Lost Mountain and in the rear of Kenesaw, and driven back upon his centre, the Federal army swinging around so as to threaten his flank. The movement occupied the whole day, and was rendered difficult by the thick growth of timber and underwood and the pertinacity of the skirmishers of the enemy. During the 18th, the right crowded the rebel left still further backward. The possession of the Dallas and Marietta road was secured, and the enemy pushed so hard at dusk that the 20th corps was in a line perpendicular to their own. The Federal troops met with considerable loss during the day, as in many places it was necessary to construct opposing works under the fiercest fire, especially from the enemy's sharpshooters; but from extreme right to extreme left the rebel skirmishers were steadily driven, and many of them killed and wounded. Several hundred prisoners were also taken. These made the number taken since the 11th about one thousand.

Apprehending that his position on Lost Mountain was in danger of being enveloped, Gen. Johnston, on the night of the 18th, under cover of the darkness and a violent storm of rain, drew in his left flank toward Kenesaw, which he made his salient, his right wing being thrown back to cover Marietta, and his left behind Nose's Creek, for the purpose of guarding his railroad communication with the Chattahooche. The abandoned works on Lost Mountain, and the line of breastworks connecting it with Kenesaw, were at once occupied by the Federal troops, and during the 19th the enemy was steadily pressed at all points. On the evening of that day our left held the base of Kenesaw on its north face, and the first ridge of hills running thence to the northeast, while our right lay to the west and rear of Kenesaw, and within three miles of Marietta. During these operations the rain fell almost incessantly, and the roads were rendered so heavy that a general movement would have been impossible. The most that could be attempted was to press the enemy without cessation, and harass him by constant skirmishing. The fact that under such discouraging circumstances so many strong positions were carried, testifies to the discipline and endurance of the troops.

The operations of the 20th and 21st were of a similar character to those above described, but on the 22d the enemy made a sudden attack upon portions of Gens. Hooker's and Schofield's troops on the Federal right, near what is known as the "Kulp House," and was handsomely repulsed, leaving his dead, wounded, and many prisoners behind him. The Federal centre was now established squarely in front of Kenesaw, but it required so many men to hold the railroad and the line running along the base of the mountain, that but a small force was left with which to attempt a flank movement to the right. So small was it that Gen. Sherman hesitated to push it vigorously toward the railroad, in the rear of Marietta, for fear that it might be altogether detached from the army and exposed to disaster. He therefore contented himself with extending his right along the enemy's flank, hoping that Gen. Johnston would thereby be induced to weaken his centre sufficiently to render an assault in that direction practicable. "Although inviting the enemy at all times," says Gen. Sherman in his official report, "to make such mistakes, I could not hope for him to repeat them after the examples of Dallas and the 'Kulp House;' and upon studying the ground, I had no alternative but to assault his lines or turn his position. Either course had its difficulties and dangers. And I perceived that the enemy and our own officers had settled down into a conviction that I would not assault fortified lines. All looked to me to 'outflank.' An army to be efficient must not settle down to one single mode of offence, but must be prepared to execute any plan which promises success. I waited, therefore, for the moral effect, to make a successful assault against the enemy behind his breastworks, and resolved to attempt it at that point where success would give the largest fruits of victory." The general point selected was the rebel left centre, in the belief that if this should be once forced, a road to the railroad below Marietta would be opened to the assaulting column, the enemy's retreat cut off, and their army overwhelmed in detail. Simultaneous with this an attack was directed to be made on Little Kenesaw by McPherson. The 27th was selected for the movement, and three days were allowed for preparation.

At 6 A. M., on the appointed day, Gen. Blair's (17th) corps, holding the extreme left of Gen. McPherson's line, moved toward the eastern point of the mountain to threaten the enemy's right, while Gen. Dodge's (16th) corps and Gen. Logan's (15th) corps assaulted the northern slope adjoining. The brunt of the attack was borne by three brigades of the 15th corps, which immediately scattered the enemy's skirmishers, and pushing on up the hill with impetuosity, carried part of the rebel rifle-pits. Some of the retreating enemy were captured while endeavoring to escape to a gorge which intervenes between the right and left halves of Kenesaw. Still pressing forward our troops arrived at the foot of a perpendicular cliff thirty feet high, from the crest of which the enemy formed in line of battle, poured a destructive plunging fire, and rolled down huge stones. Seeing it impossible to scale these cliffs our line halted, retired a short distance, and fortified on the extreme right. For the second and more important attack portions of Gen. Newton's division of the 4th corps, and of Gen. Davis's of the 14th corps, were selected. At a given signal the troops rushed forward with buoyant courage, charged up the face of the mountain amidst a murderous fire from a powerful battery on the summit and through two lines of abatis, carried a line of rifle-pits beyond, and reached the works. The colors of several regiments were planted before the latter, and some of the men succeeded in mounting the ramparts, but the deaths of Gens. Wagner and Harker, and the wounding of Gen. McCook, the destructive fire of both musketry and artillery, and the difficulty of deploying the long columns under such fire, rendered it necessary to recall the men. Gen. Newton's troops returned to their original line, while Gen. Davis's 2d brigade threw up works between those they had carried and the main line of the enemy, and there remained. The whole contest lasted little more than an hour, but cost Gen. Sherman nearly three thousand in killed and wounded, while the enemy, lying behind well-formed breastworks, suffered comparatively slight loss. During the day Gen. Schofield had sharp skirmishing with the enemy's left wing, and Gen. Cox's division of the 23d corps pushed forward to a point nine miles south of Marietta and three from the Chattahoochee; but the important fighting was in the centre. The failure of the attack is to be attributed to the fact that Gen. Johnston did not allow himself to be deceived by the lengthened line which Gen. Sherman opposed to him. From his elevated position on the summit of Kenesaw he could see plainly that the main posts still confronted him, and that the flanking movement to his left was not in earnest. Contenting himself, therefore, with sending a single corps to watch the right wing, he held his main body to repel the assault on his centre.

It was not, however, the intention of Gen. Sherman to rest long under the imputation of defeat, and he almost immediately commenced preparations to turn the enemy's left, amusing Gen. Johnston, meanwhile, by a show of approaching his centre by saps. On July 1st, Gens. Hooker and Schofield advanced to the right some two miles, and on the 2d Gen. McPherson received orders to rapidly shift his whole force from the extreme left to the extreme right of the Federal lines, and push on to Nickajack Creek, which flows into the Chattahoochee, four miles below the railroad bridge. His place on the left, in front of Kenesaw, was occupied by Gen. Garrard's cavalry, while Gen. Stoneman's cavalry moved on his flanks to strike the river near Turner's Ferry, two miles and a half below the railroad bridge. The object of the movement was speedily detected by Gen. Johnston, who at once prepared to evacuate Kenesaw and fall back to the Chattahoochee. On the night of the 2d his rear guard abandoned the works which for upward of three weeks had been so resolutely assailed and defended, and before dawn of the 3d the Federal pickets occupied the crest of the mountain. Orders were immediately given for Gen. Thomas to move forward along the railroad to Marietta, and thence southward to the Chattahoochee, the rest of the army pressing rapidly toward Nickajack Creek to harass the enemy in flank and rear, and if possible to assail him in the confusion of crossing the river. Gen. Sherman himself, accompanying the Army of the Cumberland, entered Marietta at 9 o'clock on the morning of the 3d. During the retreat about two thousand prisoners, principally stragglers, fell into the hands of the Federal troops.

Gen. Johnston was too good a general to leave his movement uncovered, and Gen. Thomas pushing forward in pursuit, found him intrenched behind a fortified line at Smyrna, half way between the river and Marietta, having his flanks protected by Nickajack and Rottenwood Creeks. This, however, was but an advance line, his intention being to make his real stand in a series of works on the left bank of the river, and at the railroad bridge, where he had constructed a strong *tête de pont*. Again a flanking movement to the right was attempted, and with such success that on the night of the 4th Gen. Johnston fell back to the river, across which the main body of his army passed, Gen. Hardee's corps remaining on the right bank. Gen. Sherman then moved up to the Chattahoochee, and on the evening of the 5th Gens. Thomas's and McPherson's troops occupied a line extending from a short distance above the railroad bridge to the mouth of Nickajack Creek, while Gen. Schofield was posted in the rear near Smyrna as a reserve. Cavalry demonstrations were extended as far south as Campbelltown, fifteen miles below the railroad bridge. By these several manœuvres, and particularly by the shifting of Gen. McPherson's troops to the right, Gen. Sherman aimed to convey to Gen. Johnston the impression that it was his *left* flank that was to be turned; and in pursuance of the same strategy the Federal general having determined that the enemy's position was unassailable except by a flank movement across the river, amused his enemy by demonstrations south of the railroad bridge, as if he intended crossing there. His real object was, by rapidly shifting masses of troops from extreme right to extreme left, to turn the enemy's *right* flank, and seize and hold the vital strategic points in that direction.

Gen. Schofield was, accordingly, directed to move due eastward from his position at Smyrna to the Chattahoochee, and to make a crossing near the mouth of Soap Creek, eight miles north of the railroad bridge. This was successfully accomplished on the 7th, with the capture of a gun and a number of prisoners, and a lodgment was effected on high ground on the left bank, and a substantial bridge constructed. At the same time Gen. Garrard occupied Rosswell, a town near the Chattahoochee, nearly due north of Atlanta, and about seven miles above Gen. Schofield's crossing, where he destroyed some woollen and cotton mills which had supplied the rebel armies. In accordance with Gen. Sherman's orders he secured the ford at this place until a corps could be sent thither from the Army of the Tennessee on the right wing. On the 9th, while the enemy were amused by feints extending from Power's Ferry, four miles above the railroad bridge, to Turner's Ferry, three miles below it, a crossing was effected at Rosswell, and the river firmly bridged; and under cover of the same demonstrations Gen. Howard was enabled to throw a bridge across at Power's Ferry. Gen. Johnston at length took the alarm, and during the night of the 9th gave orders for another retreat. His heavy guns were removed to Atlanta, seven miles distant, Gen. Hardee's corps was safely crossed to the left bank, and at daylight of the 10th the railroad bridge, the road bridge, and the pontoons, were in flames. The rebel army then fell back toward the fortifications of Atlanta, abandoning the whole line of the river, although its left wing kept in the neighborhood of Turner's Ferry, in the expectation of an attack from that quarter. Leaving Gen. Johnston to his delusion, Gen. Sherman rapidly and quietly moved the rest of the Army of the Tennessee behind the line of our forces, to its old position on the extreme left, and busied himself with strengthening his bridges and collecting supplies, which, as early as the 8th, were brought by railroad within a mile of the railroad bridge.

A week's rest was now allowed the army, a sufficient force being detailed to the left bank of the Chattahoochee to secure the several positions there and occupy the works of the enemy. These proved to be of the most formidable character, and had evidently cost many months of labor, the lines extending for upward of five and a half miles along the river, with almost impenetrable abatis in front. The sudden abandonment of them caused more consternation to the enemy than any previous disaster of the campaign, as it was anticipated that here, in the immediate neighborhood of his supplies, Gen. Johnston could make a long and probably successful stand; or at least keep Gen. Sherman at bay until reënforcements from other parts of the confederacy should arrive. The catastrophe completed the long catalogue of complaints against this general which his enemies had sedulously arrayed before the public, and his removal was clamored for as indispensable to the salvation of the cause. The inhabitants of Atlanta in particular urged that the retreating policy had been followed far enough. It can hardly admit of a doubt, however, that he had conducted the campaign with prudence and skill, and considering his inferiority in numbers to Gen. Sherman, who was always in a condition to outflank him, he had probably delayed the Federal advance as long as it was possible.

On the 17th the whole army was across the Chattahoochee, with the exception of Gen. Davis's division of the 14th corps, left to watch the railroad bridge and the rear, and prepared to move upon Atlanta. The Army of the Cumberland now occupied the right wing and right centre, resting on the river just above the railroad bridge, the Army of the Ohio the left centre, and the Army of the Tennessee the left. In this order a grand right wheel was commenced, the right wing of the Army of the Cumberland serving as the pivot, which, on the evening of the 17th, brought the Federal line into a position about northeast of the railroad bridge, along what is known as the old Peach Tree road. On the 18th the left wing, swinging rapidly around, struck the Georgia Railroad, which connects Atlanta with Augusta, at a point two miles west of Stone Mountain, a vast elevation of granite towering over the surrounding country, fifteen miles northeast of Atlanta. With the aid of Gen. Garrard's cavalry, which moved on his flank, Gen. McPherson broke up a section of about four miles of the road, while Gen. Schofield occupied Decatur, six miles east of Atlanta, and Gen. Thomas brought his troops close up to Peach Tree Creek, a small stream rising five or six miles northeast of Atlanta, and flowing southwesterly into the Chattahoochee, near the railroad bridge. In these manœuvres our extreme left encountered little else than cavalry, supported by a few guns and a very inadequate force of infantry, an evidence that the enemy was still laboring under the delusion that his left and not his right was the real point of attack, and that Atlanta was to be approached from the southwest instead of from the northeast. Under these circumstances Gens. McPherson and Schofield were enabled, on the 19th, to pass with little trouble westward of Decatur, within the naturally strong defensive lines of Nance's and Peach Tree Creeks. Gen. Thomas, moving more directly from the north of Atlanta, found the enemy in larger force, but succeeded on the same day in crossing Peach Tree Creek in front of their intrenched lines.

The Federal line then held the arc of a circle, extending from the railroad between Atlanta and the river to some distance south of the Georgia Railroad, and in a direction north and northeast of Atlanta.

Meanwhile, on the 17th, Gen. Johnston had, in accordance with orders from the confederate war department, turned over his command to Gen. Hood, accompanying the act with the following farewell address to his troops:

HEADQUARTERS, ARMY OF TENNESSEE,
July 17, 1864.

In obedience to the orders of the War Department, I turn over to Gen. Hood the command of the Army and Department of Tennessee. I cannot leave this noble army without expressing my admiration of the high military qualities it has displayed so conspicuously—every soldierly virtue, endurance of toil, obedience to orders, brilliant courage.

The enemy has never attacked but to be severely repulsed and punished. You, soldiers, have never argued but from your courage, and never counted your fears. No longer your leader, I will still watch your career, and will rejoice in your victories. To one and all I offer assurances of my friendship, and bid an affectionate farewell.

J. E. JOHNSTON, General.

General Hood, on assuming command, issued the following address:

HEADQUARTERS, ARMY OF TENNESSEE,
July 18, 1864.

SOLDIERS: In obedience to orders from the War Department, I assume command of this Army and Department. I feel the weight of the responsibility so suddenly and unexpectedly devolved upon me by this position, and shall bend all my energies and employ all my skill to meet its requirements. I look with confidence to your patriotism to stand by me, and rely upon your prowess to wrest your country from the grasp of the invader, entitling yourselves to the proud distinction of being called the deliverers of an oppressed people. J. B. HOOD, General.

With this change in commanders commenced a change in the method of conducting the campaign, by which it was expected that the *morale* of the rebel army, weakened by the persistent Fabian policy of Gen. Johnston, would be fully reëstablished. The time for retreating had passed when the chief city of western Georgia lay almost in the grasp of Gen. Sherman; and the rebel army, which, to give Gen. Johnston due credit, had been kept in a compact body, and had experienced but insignificant losses of guns or material of war, was to be launched, after their well-known tactics, in fierce assaults upon the invader. With this view the command was given to Gen. Hood, who had an unequalled reputation among their generals for energy and impetuous bravery.

On the 20th the Federal lines converged still more closely around the northern and eastern sides of Atlanta, and as a gap existed between Gens. Schofield and Thomas, Stanley's and Wood's division of Gen. Howard's corps were moved to the left to connect with Gen. Schofield, leaving Gen. Newton's division of Gen. Howard's corps, with inadequate force, to hold an important position on the road leading from Atlanta to Buckhead. This weak point was soon detected by Gen. Hood, who determined to signalize his appointment to the chief command by an assualt which, at one blow, should retrieve the disasters of the campaign. Gen. Sherman also was well aware that his line was vulnerable at this point; and as there were indications during the morning of a concentration of troops on the enemy's right, as if to attack the left, orders were sent to Gen. Newton and the rest of the Army of the Cumberland to close rapidly up in the latter direction. Gen. Newton accordingly pushed forward to a prominent ridge, where, about two o'clock in the afternoon his troops stacked arms and made a temporary halt. Some prisoners, gathered up by the skirmishers, having reported that there was no considerable force of the enemy within a mile and a half, no apprehension of an attack seems to have been felt, and no preparations had been made beyond the accustomed piles of logs and rails, which the Federal troops constructed as a matter of course, whenever halting for any considerable time on new ground in presence of the enemy. Gen. Hood had meanwhile been massing his main body in the woods immediately in front of Gen. Newton and of Gen. Hooker, who was approaching from the right, expecting, by a sudden and overwhelming attack upon the columns while in motion, to cut the Federal army in twain. At 4 o'clock he advanced from his covert without skirmishers, and pushed directly for Gen. Newton's position. Notwithstanding the unexpectedness of his appearance, the Federal troops sprang instantly to their arms, and from behind their breastworks poured deliberate and deadly volleys into the dense masses of the Confederates, who were further kept in check by well-served batteries which Gen. Newton had posted on each of his flanks.

Almost at the instant of the attack on Gen. Newton, Gen. Geary's division of Gen. Hooker's corps was struck by the advancing columns of the enemy and thrown back in some confusion. But quickly rallying, it recovered its ground and kept the enemy in check until Ward's division could arrive to its assistance. The latter met the enemy's charge by a counter charge, and the two columns mingling in the shock of battle, the enemy, after a brief and fierce struggle, were driven back. Further to the right, and next to Geary, Williams' division, though attacked with desperation, stood manfully up to the work, and repulsed with heavy loss every onset of the enemy. After four hours of incessant fighting, the latter retired precipitately to his intrenchments, leaving on the field upward of six hundred dead, one thousand severely wounded, seven regimental flags, and a number of prisoners. His total loss was estimated by Gen. Sherman at five thousand. That of the Federal troops was one thousand nine hundred, of which the greater part fell on Gen. Hooker's corps, which fought wholly on open ground, and bore the brunt of the battle.

During the 21st the enemy kept within his intrenched position, commanding the open valley of Peach Tree Creek, his right beyond the

Georgia railroad to the east, and his left extended toward Turner's Ferry, at a general distance of four miles from Atlanta. In the course of the day a steep and strongly-fortified hill, about five hundred yards in advance of the skirmish line of the extreme Federal left, was gallantly carried by Gen. Leggett's division of the 17th corps, though with a loss of seven hundred and fifty men. Four desperate attempts were made by the division of Gen. Cleburne to regain the position, which completely commanded Atlanta and the two principal roads leading north and south from the city; but the enemy finally retired, baffled and severely crippled, leaving his dead and most of his wounded on the slope of the hill. He also lost about a hundred prisoners. Gen. McPherson immediately threw out working parties to the hill, with the intention of occupying it with strong batteries.

On the 22d the whole advanced line of the enemy was found abandoned, a circumstance which at first led Gen. Sherman to believe that they intended to surrender Atlanta without further contest. Gen. Hood, however, was only preparing to repeat, on a larger scale, the experiment of the 20th. By a show of retreating upon the city he hoped to decoy Gen. Sherman into a rapid advance, and then suddenly, with heavy masses of troops, to strike the Federal army while in motion, at such weak points as should present themselves. "It is now quite evident," says an army correspondent, writing on the 24th, "that the enemy, when they fell back out of their works, did not retire to the inner line around the city at all, though by taking that direction, and showing themselves in large numbers upon their works, they intended to make us believe they had done so. Gen. Hardee's corps, instead, marched during the night away round to the eastward, sweeping entirely the circle of the Federal left wing, and then, as we closed in around the city, and before the left wing had got in position, struck us upon the front, and also upon the flanks." Unsuspicious of this deep laid plan for his discomfiture, Gen. Sherman pushed his troops beyond the abandoned works, and found the enemy occupying in force a line of finished redoubts completely covering the approaches to Atlanta, and busily occupied in connecting these redoubts with curtains strengthened by rifle trenches, abatis, and chevaux-de-frise. This satisfied him that Gen. Hood meant to fight, and he immediately resumed the dispositions previously commenced for pressing the city on its eastern and northern fronts. As the Federal line closed in, the circle which it formed became so contracted, that the 16th corps, Gen. Dodge, which formed the right of the Army of the Tennessee, was thrown out of position, and fell behind the 15th corps, the latter thus closing up with Gen. Schofield, who held the centre. Gen. McPherson accordingly ordered Gen. Dodge to shift his position to the extreme left of the line, and occupy the hill carried by the 17th corps on the previous day, and which was still held by Gen. Leggett's division. At about 11 A. M., soon after this movement had commenced, Gen. McPherson met the commander-in-chief near the centre of the lines. "He described to me," says Gen. Sherman in his official report, "the condition of things on his flank and the dispositions of his troops. I explained to him that if we met serious resistance in Atlanta, as present appearances indicated, instead of operating against it by the left, I would extend to the right, and that I did not want him to gain much distance to the left. He then described the hill occupied by Gen. Leggett's division of Gen. Blair's (17th) corps as essential to the occupation of any ground to the east and south of the Augusta railroad, on account of its commanding nature. I therefore ratified his disposition of troops, and modified a previous order I had sent him in writing to use Gen. Dodge's corps, thrown somewhat in reserve by the closing up of our line, to break up railroad, and I sanctioned its going, as already ordered by Gen. McPherson, to his left, to hold and fortify that position."

At noon Gen. McPherson rode off to the left, where the enemy appeared to be making a slight cavalry demonstration. He had not been gone half an hour when the desultory skirmishing which had been going on in that quarter all the morning suddenly deepened into a loud crash of musketry, followed by rapid artillery firing, indicating the presence of the enemy in large force. Gen. Hood had in fact secured the opportunity which he desired, and apprehending rightly that a demonstration was least expected on the left flank, had massed Gens. Hardee's and Stewart's corps under the cover of the thick woods which skirt the railroad, and was preparing to attack the 16th and 17th corps while they were getting into position, his forts meanwhile holding the Federal centre and right in check. Gen. Sherman instantly transmitted orders to Gens. Schofield and Thomas to keep the enemy employed on all parts of their front, and the former was directed to hold as large a force as possible in reserve to sustain the left, should aid be needed.

Gen. McPherson, upon reaching the left, found the 16th corps just about moving into position to prolong the flank, and temporarily facing to the left in a direction perpendicular to our main line. Between the right of the 16th and the left of the 17th corps was a wooded space of about half a mile which was not occupied by any troops. Shortly after twelve o'clock the enemy emerged from the dense woods in front of these corps in three solid columns, and marched directly upon the 16th corps for the purpose of turning our whole line. Three desperate assaults were repelled by Gen. Dodge, in the last of which the enemy suffered severe loss from the well-directed fire of the Federal batteries. Finding that the attempt to break the lines had failed at this point, Gen. McPherson took advantage of a temporary lull in the fighting to ride through the woods to Gen. Giles A. Smith's division, which held the left of the 17th corps. A report that the enemy in heavy force were moving around the left of the 17th corps, and were pushing in through the gap above mentioned, as existing between it and the 16th (the attack on the 16th corps having, in fact, been a feint to draw attention from the real point of attack), induced him to hasten in that direction. After reaching the gap he gave directions to the only member of his staff who accompanied him, the rest having been sent with orders to different portions of the field, to obtain a brigade from Gen. Logan's command and throw it across the gap, and then, with a single orderly, struck into a cross road leading directly to Gen. Smith's position. Already, however, unknown to him, the enemy's skirmish line had advanced close up to this road, and when it was too late to retrace his steps he found himself within fifty feet of it. The rebel officer in command called upon him to surrender, but he only dashed his horse to the right of the road, and was almost immediately brought to the ground, mortally wounded, by a volley from the skirmishers. His body was for a time in the possession of the enemy, but was subsequently recovered and brought within the Federal lines. Upon hearing of this disaster, Gen. Sherman ordered Gen. Logan to assume command of the Army of the Tennessee.

The brigade (Wangelin's) ordered up from Gen. Logan's corps, arrived in time to partially check the enemy, but could not prevent him from getting a portion of his force in the rear of the 17th corps, while heavy masses of troops, principally from Gen. Stewart's corps, were pushed against the works held by Gen. Leggett on the hill, wrested from Gen. Cleburne the day before, and which they were evidently determined to retake at any sacrifice. Sweeping up in their advance the working party engaged upon the fortifications, the enemy bore heavily against Gens. Smith's and Leggett's divisions, which, attacked in front and rear, were obliged to fire alternately from behind their own breastwork and the old abandoned parapet of the enemy. Gen. Leggett's troops clung firmly to their important position on the top of the hill, against the fortified angle of which the rebels dashed their columns with desperate but fruitless energy. Gen. Smith had meanwhile been compelled to abandon his more exposed lines, but by a skilful movement he gradually withdrew his men, regiment by regiment, to a new line connecting on the right with Gen. Leggett, his left, refused, facing to the southeast. In executing this movement he was obliged to abandon two guns to the enemy. Against this new formation of the 17th corps the enemy could make no impression, but recoiled again and again before the deadly fire of the Federal troops, which mowed down whole ranks at a time, and covered the ground and ditches with dead and wounded men. A part of the rebel force that pushed for the gap between the 16th and 17th corps renewed the attack upon the right flank of the former, and upon its first advance captured a six-gun battery of the regular army, which was moving along unsupported and unapprehensive of danger. Gens. Sweeney's and Fuller's divisions soon checked the enemy's advance, and finally drove him back in confusion with the loss of many prisoners. At a critical period of the battle several of Gen. Sweeney's regiments were found to be without ammunition; but as it was indispensable that they should hold their position, their commander ordered them to meet the enemy with the bayonet, whereupon the latter broke and fled to the rear. At about half-past three o'clock the enemy desisted from his attack on our left flank, having gained no ground and suffered enormous losses, for which his capture of eight guns ill compensated.

Meanwhile two divisions of Gen. Wheeler's cavalry, with a section of artillery, took a wide circuit to the east and fell upon Decatur, now three miles in our rear, where Col. Sprague, with three infantry regiments, and a battery, was guarding a number of wagon trains filled with commissary and ammunition supplies. By a skilful disposition of his small force, Col. Sprague held the enemy in complete check until every wagon except three was sent to the rear of Gens. Schofield and Thomas, when he also fell back nearer the main body, having inflicted considerable damage upon the enemy and secured a number of prisoners. Gen. Wheeler's unopposed approach to Decatur was owing to the absence of Gen. Garrard's cavalry on a raid southeast of Atlanta.

About 4 P. M. a pause occurred in the battle, occasioned by Gen. Hood's massing troops for an assault upon Gen. Logan's (15th) corps, temporarily commanded by Gen. Morgan L. Smith, which held the right of the Army of the Tennessee behind substantial breastworks, immediately adjoining the 17th corps. At half-past 4 P. M., while just enough of an attack was maintained against the extreme left to occupy the attention of the troops in that quarter, a heavy force two lines deep marched directly toward the left of the 15th corps, driving before it a couple of regiments of skirmishers and capturing two guns. Protected by their works, Gen. Lightburn's brigade, which held this part of the line, for half an hour kept the enemy at bay by well-directed discharges from a battery of 20-pounder Parrotts; but a second strong rebel column now approached, which scarcely faltered beneath the volleys which ploughed its ranks in long furrows, and presently, to add to the perplexity of the situation, a third column was seen pouring in at the rear through a deep cut in the Georgia railroad. Finding that to hold their position would insure capture, Gen. Lightburn's troops retired in considerable confusion to the second line of breastworks, five hundred yards from the main line, and the abandoned works, with two batteries, fell into the hands of the enemy. The position gained by the latter, if allowed to be held by them, threatened such serious disaster that Gen. Sherman sent orders to Gen. Logan, which had already been anticipated by that general, to make the 15th corps regain its lost ground at any cost. In aid of this movement he posted certain batteries from Gen. Schofield's corps where they could shell the enemy and the works beyond, so as to prevent reënforcements. Just as the enemy were preparing to turn the captured Parrotts upon the inner Federal line, the 15th corps, supported by portions of Gen. Schofield's troops, advanced with loud cheers upon them; and after a desperate struggle, in the course of which both Federals and rebels at times fought hand to hand across the narrow parapet, the latter were driven out of the works and the guns retaken. Their retreat was accelerated by repeated discharges of grape and canister among their crowded ranks which caused an awful carnage. With this repulse the battle terminated.

This was by far the bloodiest battle yet fought in Georgia; and notwithstanding the complete defeat of the enemy at all points, the Federal army sustained an irreparable loss in the death of Gen. McPherson, described by Gen. Sherman as "a noble youth, of striking personal appearance, of the highest professional capacity, and with a heart abounding in kindness that drew to him the affections of all men." The heroic conduct of the Army of the Tennessee during the whole battle was in no slight degree owing to the desire to avenge the fall of their commander. The total Federal loss on the 22d was 3,722, of whom much the greater portion were killed and wounded. The enemy's dead alone in front of our lines numbered 2,200 from actual count, and of these 800 were delivered to the enemy under flag of truce. Their total loss in killed was computed by Gen. Logan at 3,240. Upwards of 3,000 prisoners, including 1,000 wounded, and many commissioned officers of high rank, beside 18 colors and 5,000 small arms, fell into the hands of the Federals. The enemy of course removed many of their dead and most of their wounded. Owing to the closeness and desperation of the conflict, the proportion of wounded to killed was much less than usual--probably not more than two to one—which would make their loss in wounded about 6,500, and their total loss in killed, wounded, and prisoners, more than 12,000.

As an important feature in his campaign, Gen. Sherman had contemplated, in addition to offensive operations against the enemy in the field, a series of expeditions against the several railroads by which supplies or reënforcements were brought to Atlanta. The first line of rebel communications selected to be broken was the railroad system connecting Atlanta with the southwest, comprising the Atlanta and West Point and the West Point and Montgomery roads; and on July 10, in accordance with orders long previously issued by Gen. Sherman, a body of 2,000 Federal cavalry, under Gen. Rousseau, started from Decatur, Ala., for Opelika, a station on the latter of these roads, in eastern Alabama, whence a road diverges cast to the important manufacturing town of Columbus, Geo., and thence to Macon. On the 13th Gen. Rousseau crossed the Coosa near the Ten Islands, routing a body of Alabama cavalry; passed rapidly through Talladega; skirmished again with the enemy at the crossing of the Tallapoosa; and on the 16th struck the West Point and Montgomery road at Loachapoka, ten miles west of Opelika. From this point to Opelika the railroad was well broken up, and the bridges and culverts destroyed, beside three miles of the branch toward Columbus and two toward West Point. Gen. Rousseau then turned north, and brought his command in safety to Marietta on the 22d, with a loss of less than thirty men.

The next operation was to more thoroughly disable the Georgia railroad. This had been broken up between Decatur and Atlanta as the army closed around the city; but as Gen. Sherman already contemplated prolonging his right toward the west and south of the town, and possibly abandoning his hold on the railroad, it became necessary to render the latter unavailable to the rebels. Gen. Garrard was therefore detached on the 21st, and ordered to proceed with his cavalry to Covington, forty-one miles east of Atlanta, and destroy the railroad bridges over the Yellow and Ulcopauhatchee Rivers, branches of the Ocmulgee. He returned in safety on the 24th, having completely destroyed the two bridges, of which that over the Yellow River was 550 feet in length, and the other 250 feet, and broken up the railroad for seven miles between the two. He also burned three trains of cars, numerous depots, minor bridges and culverts, 2,000 bales of cotton, a new and extensive hospital building at Covington, and a considerable quantity of commissary and quartermaster's stores, and brought in with him several hundred prisoners and negroes and many horses. He lost but two men in the expedition.

Having rendered the Georgia road useless to the enemy Gen. Sherman next turned his attention to the Macon and Western Railroad, connecting Atlanta with Macon, and the only avenue left for the conveyance of stores and ammunition to the rebel army. For the purpose of effectually crippling this, he organized his cavalry in two large bodies, to move in concert from each wing of the army, while simultaneously with this movement the Army of the Tennessee was to be shifted by the right toward East Point, a station six miles south of Atlanta, where the Atlanta and West Point and Macon and Western Railroads diverge from a common track. Gen. Stoneman was transferred to the left flank, and assumed command of his own cavalry and Gen. Garrard's, comprising an effective force of 5,000 men, while Gen. McCook, on the right flank, received his own command and the cavalry brought by Gen. Rousseau, amounting in the aggregate to 4,000 men. This joint force Gen. Sherman supposed was fully adequate to look after Gen. Wheeler's rebel cavalry, and to accomplish the work allotted to it, which was to rendezvous at Lovejoy's station on the Macon road, thirty miles south of Atlanta, on the night of July 28th, and there make such a complete destruction of the road as would lead to the speedy abandoment of Atlanta. At the moment of starting, Gen. Stoneman asked permission, after fulfilling his orders, to proceed with his own command to Macon and Andersonville, and release the Federal prisoners of war confined at those places. After some hesitation Gen. Sherman consented, stipulating, however, as a condition precedent, that the railroad should be effectually broken up and Wheeler's cavalry put *hors de combat*.

On the 27th the two expeditions started forth, Gen. Stoneman making for McDonough, a town about ten miles east of Lovejoy's, and sending Gen. Garrard to Flat Rock to cover his movement; and Gen. McCook keeping down the right bank of the Chattahoochee. Gen. Stoneman, however, almost immediately turned off toward the Georgia Railroad, which he followed as far as Covington, whence he struck due south, and to the east of the Ocmulgee, for Macon, distant sixty miles, in the neighborhood of which he arrived on the 30th. A detachment was sent east to Gordon, a station on the Georgian Central Railroad, where eleven locomotives and several trains loaded with quartermasters' stores were destroyed, together with several bridges between that place and Macon. But as he learned that the prisoners in Macon had on the previous day been sent to Charleston, Gen. Stoneman decided to return at once by the way he had come, without attempting to reach Macon or Andersonville. On the even-

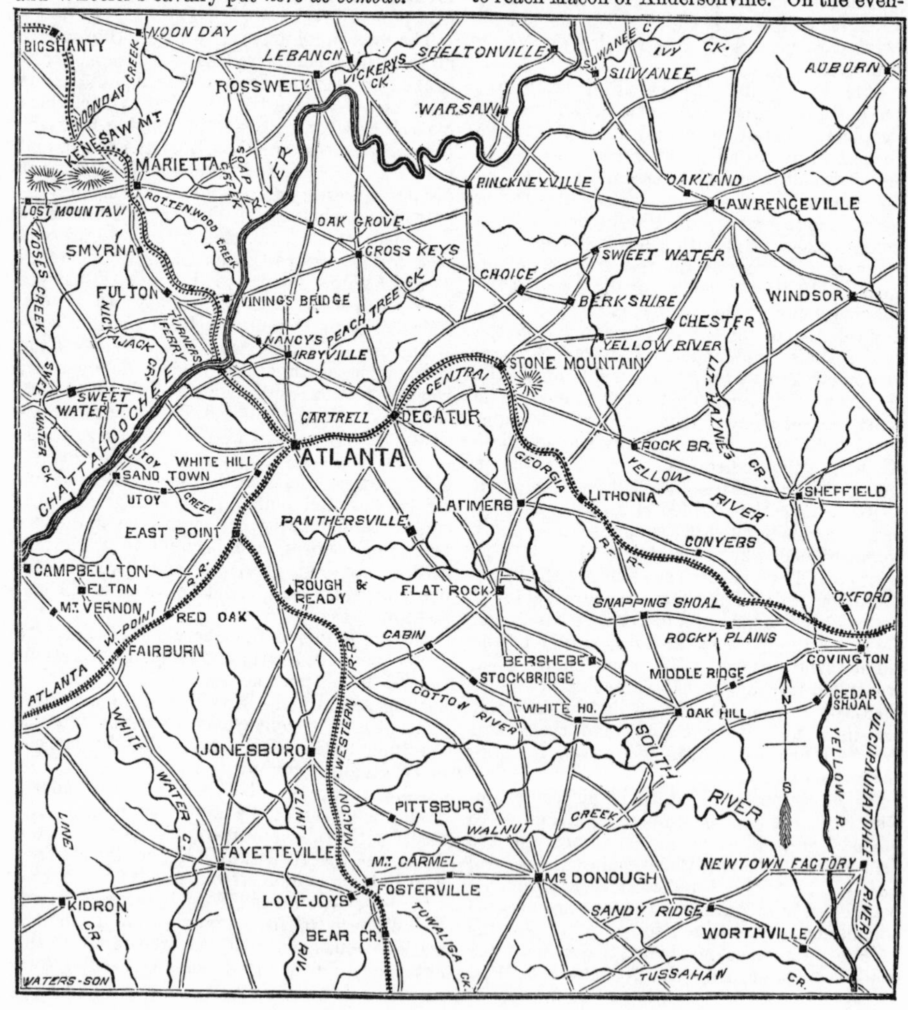

ing of the 30th he turned northward again, skirmishing on the way; and on the morning of the 31st, when about twenty miles from Macon, encountered a heavy force in his front. The country being unfavorable for cavalry operations, he dismounted a portion of his command, and threw them forward as skirmishers, but soon found himself surrounded. After various fruitless attempts to make head against the enemy, he gave directions to the greater part of his force to break through the opposing lines, and escape in the readiest manner possible, while he, with several hundred men and a section of artillery, occupied the attention of the enemy. He was finally overpowered and compelled to surrender. Of his three brigades one arrived safely within the Federal lines, one was attacked and somewhat scattered on the way back, and the third was captured with him. Gen. Garrard meanwhile, after waiting at Flat Rock for orders from Stoneman until the 29th, moved toward Covington, and learning that he had gone south from that point, returned to his position on the left flank of the army.

Gen. McCook, after reaching the neighborhood of Rivertown on the Chattahoochee, crossed on pontoons and made for Palmetto Station on the Atlanta and West Point Railroad, twenty-five miles south of Atlanta, where he destroyed a section of the road. He thence moved eastward upon Fayetteville and burned five hundred wagons belonging to the rebel army, besides killing eight hundred mules and capturing several hundred quartermasters' men, and reached Lovejoy's on the night of the 28th. Here he destroyed a section of the Macon and Western Railroad, but, hearing nothing from Stoneman, and finding his progress eastward barred by a constantly accumulating force of the enemy, he turned off to the southwest, and at Newman, a station on the Atlanta and West Point Railroad fifteen miles south of Palmetto, encountered a rebel infantry force coming up from Mississippi to Atlanta. After a severe fight with superior numbers he finally cut his way out, with the loss of five hundred men and all his prisoners, and reached the Chattahoochee, whence he arrived safely within the Federal lines. The damage done by the several expeditions scarcely compensated for the severe losses sustained by Gens. Stoneman and McCook, amounting to upward of fifteen hundred. Owing to the failure of Gen. Stoneman to concentrate with Gen. McCook at Lovejoy's, the communications with Atlanta were only temporarily interrupted, and the enemy gained at least a month's respite from their final catastrophe.

While the cavalry raid was in progress, the Army of the Tennessee was, pursuant to instructions, drawn out of its intrenchments on the left flank and moved *en echelon* to a position on the extreme right, the right flank being held by Gen. Logan's corps. This movement was directed by Gen. Howard, who on the 27th, by appointment of the President, assumed the command vacated by the death of Gen. McPherson. The line was thus prolonged due south, facing east, and south of Proctor's Creek. Apprehending that Gen. Hood might again improve the opportunity to attack the Federal army while in motion, Gen. Sherman on the 28th disposed of Gen. Davis's division of the 14th corps so that it might be within easy supporting distance of the flank of Gen. Howard's new line, in the event of a strong rebel demonstration in that quarter. The enemy was not slow to perceive that Gen. Sherman was gradually swinging around toward the Macon road, and to oppose the movement massed his troops in the same direction. About noon of the 28th Gen. Stewart's corps came out from Atlanta by the Bell's Ferry road, and, forming on open ground, advanced in long parallel lines upon Gen. Logan's troops, fortunately sheltered behind the customary breastworks of rails, expecting to find his flank "in air." For upward of four hours a series of desperate attacks were made upon Gen. Logan's position, which were uniformly repelled with loss. Again and again the rebel columns were brought up to the breastworks, only to recoil shattered and bleeding before the steady volleys of musketry and the incessant discharges of grape and canister by which they were assailed. The few officers and men who reached the rail piles were either killed or taken prisoners. Shortly after 4 o'clock the enemy retired, leaving his killed and wounded in our hands, and having experienced a total loss estimated by Gen. Sherman at five thousand. The Federal loss was under six hundred. By some inadvertency Gen. Davis's division failed to come up to the support of Gen. Logan, whereby an opportunity was lost to strike the assailing rebel columns in flank, and probably to put them to a disastrous rout.

About this time Gens. Hooker and Palmer resigned the command of their corps, and were succeeded, the former by Gen. Slocum, and the latter by Gen. Jeff. C. Davis. Gen. Slocum, however, being absent at Vicksburg, the command of the 20th corps was temporarily assumed by Gen. A. S. Williams. Gen. D. S. Stanley also succeeded Gen. Howard in command of the 4th corps.

Failing to dislodge Hood from Atlanta in this way, Gen. Sherman next resorted to a further extension of his right, in the hope of flanking him in that direction. The 23d corps, supported by the 14th, was accordingly, on the 5th and 6th of August, transferred from the left to a position somewhat below Utoy Creek, a small affluent of the Chattahoochee, where it joined on Gen. Logan's right and formed our right flank. Demonstrations of more or less importance were made against the enemy's works during the prolongation of the right, but everywhere he was found well protected behind an admirably constructed line of defences, within which was a second line, comprising a series of redoubts of great thickness of parapet and good command, connected throughout by a continuous infantry parapet, covered by abatis, cheveaux-de-frise, and other impediments of the most approved kind. This inner line of works completely enveloped Atlanta, and thence extended for six miles along the railroad track to East Point, previously described as jointly used by the Atlanta and West Point and Macon and Western Roads, thus covering the latter. The Federal army, instead of threatening the city on the north and east, was now so shifted from its first position that, while the extreme left covered the northern approaches to Atlanta, the extreme right was southwest of it, running parallel to the railroad. The Federal lines were drawn at an average distance of two and a half miles from the city, and between them and the rebel works intervened a narrow belt of rough and wooded country, the scene of constant skirmishing between the opposing forces. Thus Gen. Hood, though in inferior force to Gen. Sherman, having the advantage of interior lines, and acting strictly on the defensive behind almost impregnable works, seemed able to hold his position for an indefinite period. He had recently been reënforced by some veteran troops and by a body of several thousand Georgia militia, and had also added considerably to his fighting material by arming and organizing laborers, teamsters, and quartermasters' men, whose places were supplied by negroes.

A survey of the situation satisfied Gen. Sherman that Gen. Hood's lines could only be carried at a fearful sacrifice of life, and that in order to reach the Macon Road and control the supplies of Atlanta, a new movement by the right flank, in which nearly the whole army should participate, must be attempted. He accordingly determined to withdraw one corps to the intrenched position at the railroad bridge over the Chattahoochee, to protect communication with his base, and with his remaining troops to march rapidly to the southwest and south of the city, and crossing the two railroads, break them up in such a manner that immediate repairs would be impossible. The movement thus resolved itself into a raid, as the term is understood in modern military parlance, on a truly gigantic scale, and, if successful, would probably cut off Atlanta for months from its supplies and compel its evacuation. It involved, in brief, to use Gen. Sherman's own words, "the necessity of raising the siege of Atlanta, taking the field with our main force, and using it against the communications of Atlanta, instead of against its intrenchments." By the 16th of August his plans were completed; but, before commencing to put them in execution, he ascertained that Gen. Wheeler, with nearly the whole force of rebel cavalry, had moved round in a northeasterly direction to cut his communications between Marietta and Chattanooga. Thinking that in the absence of Gen. Wheeler the Federal cavalry might perhaps accomplish the task he had marked out for the whole army, he temporarily suspended his orders and directed Gen. Kilpatrick, recently returned to duty, to move across the railroads and tear them up thoroughly. Gen. Kilpatrick started on the 18th with a force of five thousand men, struck the Atlanta and West Point Road at Fairburn and the Macon road at Jonesboro, and Lovejoy's; but, being harassed by the enemy at each place, could effect no permanent damage. He finally returned on the 22d by way of Decatur, bringing one hundred prisoners, three flags, and one piece of artillery.

This satisfied Gen. Sherman that his original plan must be adhered to, and preparations for carrying it out were pressed with renewed activity. A battery of 4½-inch rifled guns was meanwhile put in position, and by its well-directed discharges impressed the enemy with the belief that regular siege operations were in progress, thus aiding to mask the new movement. It also materially interrupted the running of the rebel supply trains on the Macon road, and was the cause of several conflagrations in Atlanta. Notwithstanding the latter, the enemy held resolutely to their forts, with the evident intention of suffering the city to perish rather than abandon their position. On the night of the 25th, every thing being in readiness, and the wagons loaded with fifteen days' provisions, the 4th and 20th corps, occupying the extreme left, were moved quietly out of their intrenchments, and marched, the former to a position in the rear of the Army of the Tennessee, and the latter to the railroad bridge over the Chattahoochee and the adjacent ferries, which it was appointed to guard. On the succeeding night the 4th corps was moved southward toward Red Oak and Fairburn stations, on the Atlanta and West Point road, twelve or fifteen miles south of Atlanta, followed by the Army of the Tennessee, and on the morning of the 27th the whole front of the city was uncovered, except that portion occupied by the 23d corps, which alone remained within its intrenchments. In like manner the 23d corps was withdrawn from its intrenchments and formed the left of the new line, of which the Army of the Cumberland held the centre, and the Army of the Tennessee the right. These operations were viewed with undisguised wonder by the rebel troops from within their fortifications, and seemed to give color to the belief that Gen. Sherman had commenced a retreat. A skirmish line sent out toward the bridge, after the withdrawal of Gens. Thomas and Howard, encountered the 20th corps intrenched behind a strong *tête de pont*, and returned more bewildered if possible than before.

On the morning of the 28th, the Armies of the Cumberland and the Tennessee lay between Fairburn and Red Oak in a line facing east and north. The day was devoted to a thorough destruction of the West Point Railroad between these points, and some distance above. "It was done," says Gen. Sherman, "with a will. Twelve and a half miles were destroyed, the ties burned, and the iron rails heated and tortured by the utmost ingenuity of old hands at the work. Several cuts were filled up with trunks of trees, with logs, rock and earth, intermingled with loaded shells prepared as torpedoes, to explode in case of an attempt to clear them out." On the 30th the army was again in motion in a southeasterly direction, aiming to strike the Macon Railroad from Rough and Ready to Jonesboro. Gen. Hood now began to understand the object of Gen. Sherman's movement; but still ignorant, apparently, that nearly the whole Federal army was moving upon his communications, he contented himself with sending Gens. Hardee and S. D. Lee's corps to Jonesboro, where they intrenched, remaining in Atlanta with Gen. Stewart's corps and the militia. Gen. Howard, marching due east from Fairburn, arrived within half a mile of Jonesboro on the evening of the 30th; but encountering Gens. Hardee and Lee, he halted for the night in a strong position, and proceeded to throw up intrenchments. The remainder of the army, moving *en echelon* to the left, did not succeed in reaching the railroad.

Meanwhile the 15th corps, having seized a prominent hill which formed the key to the enemy's position, took post in the centre of the Army of the Tennessee, the 16th somewhat retired, holding the extreme right, and the 17th the left. The 15th corps spent the night in intrenching, and early next day, before the right and left flanks had taken up their advanced position, the enemy burst in masses on the 15th corps, but were steadily and repeatedly repulsed, losing several general officers, including Major-Gen. Anderson, mortally wounded, and five colonels and majors (wounded) taken prisoners, besides upward of three thousand rank and file killed, wounded, and captured. The Federal loss was slight, as the men fought behind breastworks. It was observed that the rebel attacks lacked the enthusiasm and dash which had characterized the severe assaults before Atlanta. During the 31st the 23d and 4th corps reached the railroad near Rough and Ready, and commenced destroying it north and south from that point, in the same thorough manner which had characterized their operations on the West Point road.

Upon the repulse of the enemy on the afternoon of the 31st, Gen. Sherman directed Gen. Howard to hold him in his fortifications until the remainder of the army could close in upon him. The 14th corps only, having a comparatively short distance to travel, succeeded in getting up to Jonesboro on September 1st, the other two being too far from the field, and too much embarrassed by the difficult character of the country and the want of good roads, to move with rapidity. At 4 P. M. the 14th corps, which had taken position on the left of the Army of the Tennessee, was ordered to assault the enemy's works, Gen. Sherman fearing that, if he waited for the arrival of Gens. Schofield and Stanley, darkness might intervene, and the enemy escape without a fight. The troops steadily advanced under a withering fire of musketry and artillery, and after a desperate conflict of two hours drove the enemy from their works, capturing two batteries—one of them Loomis' battery, captured at Chickamauga, some battle flags, and a large number of prisoners, including Gen. Govan and the greater part of his brigade, forming part of the celebrated "fighting division" of Gen. Cleburne. Darkness now setting in, Gen. Hardee was enabled to fall back seven miles to Lovejoy's, where he intrenched himself in a naturally strong position. Had Gens. Stanley and Schofield succeeded in coming up in season, he would in all probability have been overwhelmed and forced to capitulate.

Meanwhile, in Atlanta on the 1st, all was excitement and consternation, as it gradually transpired that the main body of the Federal army lay between the city and Gen. Hardee. Gen. Hood at once gave orders for the evacuation of his works, and the destruction of such stores and ammunition as could not be removed. The removal of all the supplies and ammunition that the transportation facilities of the army would permit commenced early in the morning, and was continued throughout the day. Large quantities of provisions were also distributed to the people, and the several bodies of troops, as they were withdrawn from the defences and went through the city, were allowed access to the public stores. The rolling stock of the railroads, consisting of about one hundred cars and six engines, was concentrated near the rolling mill before dark, by which time all the troops had passed through, with the exception of the rear guard, left to prevent straggling. The cars were then laden with the surplus ammunition, and together with the locomotives, depots, and store houses, and every thing, in fine, which would be of use to the Federal army, fired about midnight. The flames lit up the heavens for many miles, and the explosion of the ordnance trains was distinctly heard by the army in front of Jonesboro, and by Gen. Slocum at his position on the Chattahoochee. The latter sent out a heavy reconnoitring column at daybreak on the 2d, which, pushing forward without opposition, entered the city at 9 o'clock, where it was met by the mayor, who made a formal surrender, at the same time requesting protection for non-combatants and private property. This having been freely granted, Gen. Ward's division marched into the city with drums beating and colors displayed, and the national flag was raised over the Court House amidst hearty cheers. Eleven heavy guns were found in the fortifications, beside a number subsequently exhumed; and among the additional spoils were three uninjured locomotives, three thousand muskets in good order, a quantity of tobacco, and other stores. Of the valuable machinery in the workshops part had been removed to

Augusta and Macon, and part destroyed. "We have," says Gen. Sherman, in his despatch announcing the capture of Atlanta, "as the result of this quick, and, as I think, well-executed movement, twenty-seven guns, over three thousand prisoners, and have buried over four hundred rebel dead, and left as many wounded that could not be removed. The rebels have lost, besides the important city of Atlanta and their stores, at least five hundred dead, twenty-five hundred wounded, and three thousand prisoners; whereas our aggregate loss will not foot up fifteen hundred. If that is not success I don't know what is."

Of the losses in killed, wounded, and missing, sustained by the Federal army up to this period, the following table, based upon the most trustworthy information at present attainable, may be considered to give a fair estimate:

Skirmishing from Chattanooga to Resaca............	1,200
Battle of Resaca....................................	4,500
Skirmishing from Resaca to Allatoona...............	500
Battles around Dallas..............................	3,000
Battle of Kenesaw Mountain, July 27th.	3,000
Lesser contests around Kenesaw, June 9th to July 1st	4,500
Skirmishing between Kenesaw and the Chattahoochee	1,000
Battle of July 20th.................................	1,900
" of July 22d.....................................	3,700
" of July 28th....................................	600
Skirmishing from July 17th to August 28th..........	3,000
Fighting at Jonesboro, August 31st and Sept. 1st.....	1,500
Losses in cavalry raids..........................	2,000
	30,400

Of the total number, less than one-sixth come under the head of missing. The loss in cannon was fifteen pieces—ten in the battle of July 22d, three taken from Stoneman, and two abandoned by McCook. Notwithstanding these casualties, amounting to nearly a third of the force with which he set out from Chattanooga, Gen. Sherman was enabled to report, after the fall of Atlanta, that by the arrival of reenforcements, recruits, furloughed men and convalescents, he had maintained his original strength. Of the rebel losses it is more difficult to form an estimate, but the following is believed to be reasonably correct:

Loss in skirmishing from Chattanooga to Atlanta....	6,000
Battles at Resaca..................................	2,500
" around Dallas....................................	3,500
Battle of Kenesaw Mountain........................	1,000
" of July 20th..	5,000
" of July 22d......................................	12,000
" of July 28th.....................................	5,500
Lesser contests around Atlanta.....................	1,500
Battles at Jonesboro................................	5,000
	42,000

The enemy lost more than twenty general officers, killed and wounded, according to their own showing, besides from forty to fifty pieces of cannon, of which eight were 64-pounders, and over 25,000 stand of small arms. Their loss in colors was also much greater than that of the Federals.

Gen. Hood, upon abandoning Atlanta, directed his march toward McDonough, whence moving west he succeeded in forming a junction with Gens. Hardee and Lee. On the 2d Gen. Sherman followed in Gen. Hardee's traces, but finding him intrenched in a position of great strength, and learning the capitulation of the city, he desisted from further attack, and on the 4th gave orders for the army to proceed by easy marches in the direction of Atlanta. On the 8th the Army of the Cumberland encamped around the city, that of the Tennessee about East Point, and that of the Ohio at Decatur. Atlanta itself was held by Gen. Slocum's (20th) corps.

Previous to the departure of the cavalry under Gen. Wheeler, on their raid against the railroad communications of Gen. Sherman, as mentioned above, the latter had enjoyed a comparative immunity from such demonstrations. This was mainly the result of the skilful dispositions which he had made for guarding the road between Atlanta and Chattanooga. In the latter place he had also wisely accumulated a sufficient quantity of stores to render him in a measure independent of Nashville, in the event of any interruption of travel between the two places. He consequently felt little immediate uneasiness upon hearing of the departure of Gen. Wheeler, but rather congratulated himself that he was at a critical moment superior to the enemy in cavalry. Gen. Wheeler left Atlanta soon after the miscarriage of Gen. Stoneman's raid, with a mounted force of six thousand men, and moving around to the north-east, struck the Western and Atlanta road near Adairsville, just midway between Atlanta and Chattanooga. Here he succeeded in capturing nine hundred beef cattle. He next approached the road at Calhoun, nine miles north of Adairsville, where he committed some damage, and on August 14th made his appearance at Dalton, of which place, "to prevent the effusion of blood," he demanded the immediate and unconditional surrender. Col. Leibold, who held the town with five hundred or six hundred men, replied that he had "been placed there to defend the post, but not to surrender." Apprising Gen. Steedman, in command at Chattanooga, of his danger, he kept Gen. Wheeler at bay until the next day, when reënforcements arrived from that place, by whose aid the enemy were driven off in confusion. Gen. Wheeler then passed up into East Tennessee, leaving the Federals to repair at their leisure the damage he had done, and in a few days the railroad was again in good running order between Atlanta and Chattanooga. He subsequently destroyed a considerable portion of the road between Chattanooga and Knoxville, and moving west during the latter part of August and first week of September, made strenuous efforts to interrupt railroad and telegraph communication between Chattanooga and Nashville; but being pursued by Gens. Rousseau, Steedman, and Granger, he was speedily driven toward Florence, and thence into Northern Alabama. The damage committed by him between Chattanooga and Atlanta was so slight, that Gen. Sherman, writing from the latter place on September 15th, was enabled to say, "Our roads and telegraphs are all repaired, and the cars run with regularity and speed."

The news of the capture of Atlanta reached

Washington on Sept. 2d, and immediately elicited the following expression of thanks from President Lincoln:

EXECUTIVE MANSION, WASHINGTON, Sept. 2.

The national thanks are tendered by the President to Maj.-Gen. Sherman and the gallant officers and soldiers of his command, before Atlanta, for the distinguished ability, courage, and perseverance displayed in the campaign in Georgia, which, under Divine Power, resulted in the capture of the city of Atlanta.

The marches, battles, sieges, and other military operations that has signalled this campaign, must render it famous in the annals of war, and have entitled those who have participated there, to the applause and thanks of the Nation.

(Signed) ABRAHAM LINCOLN.

Orders were also given for the firing of national salutes at the principal arsenals, and the 11th of September was appointed a day of solemn national thanksgiving for the signal successes of Gen. Sherman in Georgia, and of Admiral Farragut at Mobile. The following is Gen. Sherman's congratulatory address to his troops:

HEADQUARTERS MILITARY DIVISION OF THE MISS.,
IN THE FIELD, ATLANTA, GA., Sept. 8.

Special Field Orders No. 68.

The officers and soldiers of the Armies of the Cumberland, Ohio, and Tennessee, have already received the thanks of the nation through its President and Commander-in-Chief; and it now remains only for him who has been with you from the beginning, and who intends to stay all the time, to thank the officers and men for their intelligence, fidelity, and courage displayed in the campaign of Atlanta.

On the first of May our armies were lying in garrison, seemingly quiet, from Knoxville to Huntsville, and our enemy lay behind his rocky-faced barrier at Dalton, proud, defiant, and exulting. He had had time since Christmas to recover from his discomfiture on the Mission Ridge, with his ranks filled, and a new commander-in-chief, second to none of the Confederacy in reputation for skill, sagacity, and extreme popularity.

All at once our armies assumed life and action, and appeared before Dalton; threatening Rocky Face we threw ourselves upon Resaca, and the rebel army only escaped by the rapidity of its retreat, aided by the numerous roads with which he was familiar, and which were strange to us.

Again he took post at Allatoona, but we gave him no rest, and by a circuit toward Dallas and subsequent movement to Ackworth, we gained the Allatoona Pass. Then followed the eventful battles about Kenesaw, and the escape of the enemy across Chattahoochee River.

The crossing of the Chattahoochee and breaking of the Augusta road was most handsomely executed by us, and will be studied as an example in the art of war. At this stage of our game our enemies became dissatisfied with their old and skilful commander, and selected one more bold and rash. New tactics were adopted. Gen. Hood first boldly and rapidly, on the 20th of July, fell on our right at Peach Tree Creek, and lost.

Again, on the 22d, he struck our extreme left, and was severely punished; and finally again, on the 28th, he repeated the attempt on our right, and that time he must have been satisfied, for since that date he has remained on the defensive. We slowly and gradually drew our lines about Atlanta, feeling for the railroads which supplied the rebel army and made Atlanta a place of importance.

We must concede to our enemy that he met these efforts patiently and skilfully, but at last he made the mistake we had waited for so long, and sent his cavalry to our rear, far beyond the reach of recall. Instantly our cavalry was on his only remaining road, and we followed quickly with our principal army, and Atlanta fell into our possession as the fruit of well-concerted measures, backed by a brave and confident army.

This completed the grand task which had been assigned us by our Government, and your General again repeats his personal and official thanks to all the officers and men composing this army, for the indomitable courage and perseverance which alone could give success.

We have beaten our enemy on every ground he has chosen, and have wrested from him his own Gate City, where were located his foundries, arsenals, and workshops, deemed secure on account of their distance from our base, and the seeming impregnable obstacles intervening. Nothing is impossible to an army like this, determined to vindicate a Government which has rights wherever our flag has once floated, and is resolved to maintain them at any and all costs.

In our campaign many, yea, very many of our noble and gallant comrades have preceded us to our common destination, the grave; but they have left the memory of deeds on which a nation can build a proud history. Gens. McPherson, Harker, McCook, and others dear to us all, are now the binding links in our minds that should attach more closely together the living, who have to complete the task which still lies before us in the dim future.

I ask all to continue as they have so well begun the cultivation of the soldierly virtues that have ennobled our own and other countries. Courage, patience, obedience to the laws and constituted authorities of our Government; fidelity to our trusts, and good feeling among each other; each trying to excel the other in the practice of those high qualities, and it will then require no prophet to foretell that our country will in time emerge from this war, purified by the fires of war, and worthy its great founder, Washington. W. T. SHERMAN, Maj.-Gen. Com'ng.

Upon arriving in Atlanta, Gen. Sherman determined that the exigencies of the service required that the place should for the present be appropriated exclusively for military purposes, and orders were immediately issued for the departure of all civilians, both male and female, excepting those in the employment of the Government. The following conveys the intentions of Gen. Sherman:

HEADQUARTERS POST OF ATLANTA,
ATLANTA, GA., Sept. 5, 1864.

General Order No. 3.

All families living in Atlanta, the male representatives of which are in the service of the Confederate States, or who have gone south, will leave the city within five days. They will be passed through the lines and go south.

All citizens from the North, not connected with the army, and who have not authority from Maj.-Gen. Sherman or Maj.-Gen. Thomas to remain in the city, will leave within the time above mentioned. If found within the city after that date, they will be imprisoned.

All male residents of this city, who do not register their names with the city Provost-Marshal within five days and receive authority to remain here, will be imprisoned. WM. COGSWELL,
Col. Commanding Post.

A truce of ten days was accordingly proposed, in a letter from the Federal general to Gen. Hood, then encamped near Lovejoy's, to which the latter made the following reply:

HEADQUARTERS ARMY OF THE TENNESSEE,
OFFICE CHIEF OF STAFF, Sept. 9, 1864.

Major-Gen. Sherman, Comm'g U. S. forces in Georgia:

GENERAL: Your letter of yesterday's date, borne by James W. Ball and James R. Crew, citizens of

Atlanta, is received. You say therein: "I deem it to be to the interest of the United States that the citizens residing in Atlanta should remove," etc. I do not consider that I have any alternative in the matter. I therefore accept your proposition to declare a truce of ten days, or such time as may be necessary to accomplish the purpose mentioned, and shall render all the assistance in my power to expedite the transportation of citizens in this direction. I suggest that a staff officer be appointed by you to superintend the removal from the city to Rough and Ready, while I appoint a similar officer to control their removal further south; that a guard of 100 men be sent by either party, as you propose, to maintain order at that place; and that the removal begin next Monday.

And now, sir, permit me to say that the unprecedented measure you propose, transcends in studied and ingenious cruelty all acts ever before brought to my attention in the dark history of war.

In the name of God and humanity I protest, believing that you will find you are expelling from their homes and firesides the wives and children of a brave people.

I am, General, very respectfully, your obedient servant, J. B. HOOD, General.

Official: McA. HUMMETT, Lieutenant, etc.

Accompanying the above letter was one addressed to Col. Calhoun, Mayor of Atlanta, as follows:

HEADQUARTERS ARMY OF THE TENNESSEE, September 9, 1864.

Hon. James M. Calhoun, Mayor:

SIR: I have the honor to acknowledge the receipt of your letter touching the removal of the citizens of Atlanta, as ordered by Gen. Sherman. Please find inclosed my reply to Gen. Sherman's letter. I shall do all in my power to mitigate the terrible hardships and misery that must be brought upon your people by this extraordinary order of the Federal commander. Transportation will be sent to Rough and Ready to carry the people and their effects further South.

You have my deepest sympathy in this unlooked for and unprecedented affliction.

I am, sir, very respectfully, your obedient servant, J. B. HOOD, General.

The following is Gen. Sherman's reply to Gen. Hood:

HEADQUARTERS MILITARY DIVISION OF THE MISSISSIPPI, IN THE FIELD, ATLANTA, GA., Sept. 10, 1864.

Gen. J. B. Hood, Commanding Army of the Tennessee, Confederate Army:

GENERAL: I have the honor to acknowledge the receipt of your letter of this date at the hands of Messrs. Ball and Crew, consenting to the arrangements I had proposed to facilitate the removal south of the people of Atlanta, who prefer to go in that direction. I inclose you a copy of my orders, which will, I am satisfied, accomplish my purpose perfectly. You style the measure proposed "unprecedented," and appeal to the dark history of war for a parallel as an act of "studied ungenerous cruelty." It is not unprecedented; for Gen. Johnston himself very wisely and properly removed the families all the way from Dalton down, and I see no reason why Atlanta should be excepted. Nor is it necessary to appeal to the dark history of war, when recent and modern examples are so handy. You, yourself, burned dwelling-houses along your parapet, and I have seen to-day fifty houses that you have rendered uninhabitable, because they stood in the way of your forts and men.

You defended Atlanta on a line so close to the town, that every cannon-shot, and many musket-shots from our line of intrenchments, that overshot their mark, went into the habitations of women and children. Gen. Hardee did the same at Jonesboro, and Gen. Johnston did the same, last summer, at Jackson, Miss. I have not accused you of heartless cruelty, but merely instance those cases of very recent occurrence, and could go on and enumerate hundreds of others, and challenge any fair man to judge which of us has the heart of pity for the families of "brave people." I say it is a kindness to those families of Atlanta to remove them now at once from scenes that women and children should not be exposed to; and the brave people should scorn to commit their wives and children to the rude barbarians, who thus, as you say, violate the laws of war, as illustrated in the pages of its dark history.

In the name of common sense, I ask you not to appeal to a just God in such a sacrilegious manner—you who, in the midst of peace and prosperity, have plunged a nation into civil war, "dark and cruel war," who dared and badgered us to battle, insulted our flag, seized our arsenals and forts that were left in the honorable custody of a peaceful Ordnance Sergeant, seized and made prisoners of war the very garrisons sent to protect your people against negroes and Indians, long before any overt act was committed by the "to you" hateful Lincoln government, tried to force Kentucky and Missouri into the rebellion in spite of themselves, falsified the vote of Louisiana, turned loose your privateers to plunder unarmed ships, expelled Union families by the thousand, burned their houses, and declared by act of Congress the confiscation of all debts due Northern men for goods had and received. Talk thus to the marines, but not to me who have seen these things, and will this day make as much sacrifice for the peace and honor of the South as the best-born Southerner among you. If we must be enemies, let us be men, and fight it out as we propose to-day, and not deal in such hypocritical appeals to God and humanity. God will judge me in good time, and He will pronounce whether it be more humane to fight with a town full of women, and the families of a "brave people" at our backs, or to remove them in time to places of safety among their own friends and people.

I am, very respectfully, your obedient servant, W. T. SHERMAN, Maj.-Gen. Com'g.

The following is the truce agreed upon between the two generals:

HEADQUARTERS MILITARY DIVISION, MISSISSIPPI, IN THE FIELD, ATLANTA, GA., Sept. 10, 1864.

Special Field Order No. 70.

1. Pursuant to an agreement between Gen. J. B. Hood, commanding the Confederate forces in Georgia, and Maj.-Gen. W. T. Sherman, commanding this Army, a truce is hereby declared to exist from daylight of Monday, September 12, until daylight of Thursday, September 22—ten (10) full days—at a point on the Macon Railroad known as Rough and Ready, and the country round about for a circle of two (2) miles radius, together with the roads leading to and from, in the direction of Atlanta and Lovejoy station, respectively, for the purpose of affording the people of Atlanta a safe means of removal to points south.

2. The Chief Quartermaster at Atlanta, Col. Easton, will afford all the citizens of Atlanta who elect to go south all the facilities he can spare to remove them, comfortably and safely, with their effects, to Rough and Ready station, using cars and ambulances for that purpose; and commanders of regiments and brigades may use their regimental and staff teams to carry out the object of this order; the whole to cease after Wednesday, 21st inst.

3. Maj.-Gen. Thomas will cause a guard to be established on the road out beyond the camp ground, with orders to allow all wagons and vehicles to pass that are used manifestly for this purpose; and Maj.-Gen. Howard will send a guard of one hundred men, with a field officer in command, to take post at Rough and Ready during the truce, with orders, in concert with a guard from the Confederate army of like size, to maintain the most perfect order in that vicinity

during the transfer of these families. A white flag will be displayed during the truce, and a guard will cause all wagons to leave at 4 P. M. of Wednesday, the 21st instant, and the guard to withdraw at dark, the truce to terminate the next morning.

By order of Maj.-Gen. W. T. SHERMAN.
L. M. DAYTON, Aide-de-Camp.

The civic authorities made a final appeal to Gen. Sherman to revoke or modify his order, which, with his reply, is here appended:

ATLANTA, GA., September 11, 1864.

Major-General W. T. Sherman:

SIR: The undersigned, Mayor, and two members of Council for the City of Atlanta, for the time being the only legal organ of the people of the said city to express their wants and wishes, ask leave most earnestly but respectfully to petition you to reconsider the order requiring them to leave Atlanta. At first view it struck us that the measure would involve extraordinary hardship and loss, but since we have seen the practical execution of it, so far as it has progressed, and the individual condition of many of the people, and heard the statements as to the inconvenience, loss, and suffering attending it, we are satisfied that the amount of it will involve in the aggregate consequences appalling and heart-rending.

Many poor women are in an advanced state of pregnancy; others having young children, whose husbands, for the greater part, are either in the army, prisoners, or dead. Some say: "I have such a one sick at my house; who will wait on them when I am gone?" Others say: "What are we to do; we have no houses to go to, and no means to buy, build, or rent any; no parents, relatives, or friends to go to." Another says: "I will try and take this or that article of property; but such and such things I must leave behind, though I need them much." We reply to them: "Gen. Sherman will carry your property to Rough and Ready, and then Gen. Hood will take it thence on;" and they will reply to that: "But I want to leave the railroad at such a place, and cannot get conveyance from thence on."

We only refer to a few facts to illustrate, in part, how this measure will operate in practice. As you advanced, the people north of us fell back, and before your arrival here a large portion of the people here had retired south; so that the country south of this is already crowded, and without sufficient houses to accommodate the people, and we are informed that many are now staying in churches and other outbuildings. This being so, how is it possible for the people still here (mostly women and children) to find shelter, and how can they live through the winter in the woods? no shelter or subsistence; in the midst of strangers who know them not, and without the power to assist them much if they were willing to do so.

This is but a feeble picture of the consequences of this measure. You know the woe, the horror, and the suffering cannot be described by words. Imagination can only conceive of it, and we ask you to take these things into consideration. We know your mind and time are continually occupied with the duties of your command, which almost defers us from asking your attention to the matter, but thought it might be that you had not considered the subject in all of its awful consequences, and that, on reflection, you, we hope, would not make this people an exception to mankind, for we know of no such instance ever having occurred—surely not in the United States. And what has this helpless people done, that they should be driven from their homes, to wander as strangers, outcasts, and exiles, and to subsist on charity?

We do not know as yet the number of people still here. Of those who are here, a respectable number, if allowed to remain at home, could subsist for several months without assistance; and a respectable number for a much longer time, and who might not need assistance at any time.

In conclusion, we most earnestly and solemnly petition you to reconsider this order, or modify it, and suffer this unfortunate people to remain at home and enjoy what little means they have.

Respectfully submitted,

JAMES M. CALHOUN, Mayor.

E. E. RAWSON, } Councilmen.
S. C. WELLS, }

GEN. SHERMAN'S REPLY.

HEADQUARTERS MILITARY DIVISION OF THE MISSISSIPPI, IN THE FIELD,
ATLANTA, GA., September 12, 1864.

James M. Calhoun, Mayor, E. E. Rawson, and S. C. Wells, representing City Council of Atlanta:

GENTLEMEN: I have your letter of the 11th, in the nature of a petition, to revoke my orders removing all the inhabitants from Atlanta. I have read it carefully, and give full credit to your statements of the distress that will be occasioned by it, and yet shall not revoke my order, simply because my orders are not designed to meet the humanities of the case, but to prepare for the future struggles in which millions, yea, hundreds of millions of good people outside of Atlanta have a deep interest. We must have Peace, not only at Atlanta, but in all America. To secure this we must stop the war that now desolates our once happy and favored country. To stop war we must defeat the rebel armies that are arrayed against the laws and Constitution, which all must respect and obey. To defeat these armies we must prepare the way to reach them in their recesses provided with the arms and instruments which enable us to accomplish our purpose.

Now, I know the vindictive nature of our enemy, and that we may have many years of military operations from this quarter, and therefore deem it wise and prudent to prepare in time. The use of Atlanta for warlike purposes is inconsistent with its character as a home for families. There will be no manufactures, commerce, or agriculture here for the maintenance of families, and sooner or later want will compel the inhabitants to go. Why not go now, when all the arrangements are completed for the transfer, instead of waiting till the plunging shot of contending armies will renew the scene of the past month? Of course I do not apprehend any such thing at this moment, but you do not suppose that this army will be here till the war is over. I cannot discuss this subject with you fairly, because I cannot impart to you what I propose to do, but I assert that my military plans make it necessary for the inhabitants to go away, and I can only renew my offer of services to make their exodus in any direction as easy and comfortable as possible. You cannot qualify war in harsher terms than I will.

War is cruelty, and you cannot refine it; and those who brought war on our country deserve all the curses and maledictions a people can pour out. I know I had no hand in making this war, and I know I will make more sacrifices to-day than any of you to secure peace. But you cannot have peace and a division of our country. If the United States submits to a division now, it will not stop, but will go on till we reap the fate of Mexico, which is eternal war. The United States does and must assert its authority wherever it has power; if it relaxes one bit to pressure it is gone, and I know that such is not the national feeling. This feeling assumes various shapes, but always comes back to that of Union. Once admit the Union, once more acknowledge the authority of the National Government, and instead of devoting your houses, and streets, and roads, to the dread uses of war, I, and this army, become at once your protectors and supporters, shielding you from danger, let it come from what quarter it may. I know that a few individuals cannot resist a torrent of error and passion such as has swept the South into rebellion; but you can point out, so that we may know those who desire a Government and those who insist on war and its desolation.

You might as well appeal against the thunder-storm as against these terrible hardships of war. They are inevitable, and the only way the people of Atlanta can hope once more to live in peace and quiet at home is to stop this war, which can alone be done by admitting that it began in error, and is perpetuated in pride. We don't want your negroes, or your horses, or your land, or any thing you have, but we do want and will have a just obedience to the laws of the United States. That we will have, and if it involves the destruction of your improvements we cannot help it. You have heretofore read public sentiment in your newspapers, that live by falsehood and excitement, and the quicker you seek for truth in other quarters, the better for you.

I repeat, then, that, by the original compact of government, the United States had certain rights in Georgia, which have never been relinquished and never will be; that the South began war by seizing forts, arsenals, mints, custom-houses, &c., &c., long before Mr. Lincoln was installed, and before the South had one jot or tittle of provocation. I myself have seen in Missouri, Kentucky, Tennessee, and Mississippi, hundreds and thousands of women and children fleeing from your armies and desperadoes, hungry and with bleeding feet. In Memphis, Vicksburg, and Mississippi, we fed thousands upon thousands of the families of rebel soldiers left on our hands, and whom we could not see starve. Now that war comes home to you, you feel very different; you deprecate its horrors, but did not feel them when you sentcar-loads of soldiers and ammunition, and moulded shell and shot, to carry war into Kentucky and Tennessee, and desolate the homes of hundreds and thousands of good people, who only asked to live in peace at their old homes, and under the Government of their inheritance.

But these comparisons are idle. I want peace, and believe it can only be reached through Union and war; and I will ever conduct war purely with a view to perfect and early success.

But, my dear sirs, when that peace does come, you may call on me for any thing. Then will I share with you the last cracker, and watch with you to shield your homes and families against danger from every quarter. Now you must go, and take with you the old and feeble, feed and nurse them, and build for them in more quiet places proper habitations to shield them against the weather until the mad passions of men cool down, and allow the Union and peace once more to settle on your old homes at Atlanta. Yours in haste,

W. T SHERMAN, Maj.-Gen.

In another communication to the Mayor Gen. Sherman ordered the latter to announce to the citizens:

The government will furnish transportation south as far as Rough and Ready; north, as far as Chattanooga. All citizens may take their movable property with them. Transportation will be furnished for all movables. Negroes who wish to do so may go with their masters; other male negroes will be put in Government employ, and the women and children sent outside the lines.

For the purpose of contributing to the comfort of those who were under orders to remove, an extension of the truce was subsequently obtained. The difficult and delicate task of superintending the departure of these persons was not effected without charges of cruelty and peculation against the Federal officers, with which for several weeks the Southern press teemed. Gen. Sherman, in a letter of Sept. 25, says: "The truth is, that during the truce 446 families were moved south, making 705 adults, 860 children, and 470 servants, with 1,651 pounds of furniture and household goods on the average to each family, of which we have a perfect recollection by name and articles."

CHAPTER XL.

Reorganization of the Army of the Potomac—Plans of Gen. Grant—Advance of the Army under Gen. Grant—Crosses the Rappahannock—First Day's Battle—Position of the Armies at Night—Burnside's Reserve brought on the Field—Subsequent Battles—March to the Left—Battles at Spottsylvania Court House—Thanksgivings at the North—Disposal of the Wounded.

THE Army of the Potomac, under Gen. Meade, in its reorganization was reduced to three corps, as stated on previous pages. Maj.-Gen. Warren was assigned to the command of the 5th army corps. The consolidation of divisions and arrangement of brigades was made as follows: The commanding officer of the 1st division of the old 5th corps was ordered to consolidate the three brigades into two brigades, to be designated as the 1st and 2d brigades, 1st division, 5th army corps. The old 2d division, 5th corps, was consolidated into one brigade, and designated as the 3d brigade, 1st division, 5th corps, commanded by Brig.-Gen. R. B. Ayres. The old 3d division, 5th corps, remained as the new 3d division, 5th army corps. The 2d brigade of the 3d division, 1st army corps, was transferred to the 2d division, 1st army corps, and this division afterwards designated as the 2d division, 5th army corps. The 1st brigade of the 3d division, 1st army corps, was transferred to the 1st division, 1st army corps, and this division afterwards designated as the 4th division, 5th army corps. The designating flags of the old 3d brigade, 1st division, 5th army corps; of the old 2d division, 5th army corps; of the old 2d brigade, 2d division, 5th army corps, and of the 3d division, 1st army corps, were ordered to be turned in to the corps quartermaster.

The following was the assignment of general officers to commands in the consolidated corps:

1—Brig.-Gen. J. S. Wadsworth, commanding 4th division.

2—Brig.Gen. S. W. Crawford, commanding 3d division.

3—Brig.-Gen. J. C. Robinson, commanding 2d division.
4—Brig.-Gen. Charles Griffin, commanding 1st division.
5—Brig.-Gen. R. B. Ayres, commanding 3d brigade, 1st division.
6—Brig.-Gen. L. Cutler, commanding 1st brigade, 4th division.
7—Brig.-Gen. Henry Baxter, commanding 2d brigade, 2d division.
8—Brig.-Gen. J. J. Bartlett, commanding 2d brigade, 1st division.
9—Brig.-Gen. James Barnes, commanding 1st brigade, 1st division.
10—Brig.-Gen. J. C. Rice, commanding 2d brigade, 4th division.

The 2d corps was commanded by Maj.-Gen. Hancock. The original regiments of the 2d corps were consolidated into two divisions, with a new assignment of division and brigade commanders.

The division formerly known as the 1st division of the 3d corps, commanded by Maj.-Gen. Birney, was designated as the 3d division of the 2d corps. The division formerly known as the 2d division of the 3d corps, to which Brig.-Gen. Carr had been assigned as commander, was afterwards known as the 4th division of the 2d corps. Each of these divisions had been reduced to two brigades. The following was the arrangement of divisions and assignment of commanders:

FIRST DIVISION.

Brig.-Gen. T. C. Barlow.
First Brigade—Col. N. A. Miles, 61st New York.
Second Brigade—Col. T. A. Smyth, 1st Delaware volunteers.
Third Brigade—Col. P. Frank, 52d New York.
Fourth Brigade—Col. J. R. Brooke, 55th Pennsylvania.

SECOND DIVISION.

Brig.-Gen. John Gibbon.
First Brigade—Brig.-Gen. A. S. Webb.
Second Brigade—Brig.-Gen. J. P. Owens.
Third Brigade—Col. S. S. Carroll, 8th Ohio.

THIRD DIVISION.

Maj.-Gen. D. B. Birney.
First Brigade—Brig.-Gen. J. H. Ward.
Second Brigade—Brig.-Gen. A. Hayes.

FOURTH DIVISION.

Brig.-Gen. J. B Carr.
First Brigade—Brig.-Gen. G. Mott.
Second Brigade—Col. W. R. Brewster, 73d New York.
Chief of Artillery, Col. Tibball.

Sixth corps was commanded by Gen. Sedgwick.

The old 3d division, 6th corps, was broken up, one brigade (Shaler's) going to the 1st division; the 2d (Wheaton's and Eustis') going to the 2d division. The 3d division, 3d corps, was transferred to the 6th corps, and Gen. Prince was assigned to the command of it. The three brigades of this division were consolidated into two, under Gen. Russell and Gen. Morris.

FIRST DIVISION.

Brig.-Gen. H. G. Wright.
First Brigade—Brig.-Gen. A. T. A. Torbett.
Second Brigade—Col. E. Upton, 121st New York.
Third Brigade—Col. H. Burnham, 5th Maine volunteers.
Fourth Brigade—Brig.-Gen. A. Shaler.

SECOND DIVISION.

Brig.-Gen. G. W. Getty.
First Brigade—Brig.-Gen. F. Wheaton.
Second Brigade—Col. L. A. Grant, "Fremont Brigade."
Third Brigade—Brig.-Gen. T. H. Neill.
Fourth Brigade—Brig.-Gen. A. L. Eustis.

THIRD DIVISION.

Brig.-Gen. H. Prince.
First Brigade—Brig.-Gen. W. H. Morris.
Second Brigade—Brig.-Gen. D. A. Russell.
Col. C. H. Tompkins, 1st Rhode Island artillery, commanding artillery.

The cavalry corps of this army was placed under the command of Gen. P. H. Sheridan, previously in service at the West. Brig.-Gen. Kilpatrick, in command of the 3d cavalry division, was transferred to the command of the cavalry in the Army of the Cumberland, under Major-Gen. Sherman; Gen. Pleasanton was relieved from the command of his cavalry corps, and ordered to report to Gen. Rosecrans; Gen. Sykes was ordered to report to Gen. Curtis; Gen. Newton was ordered to report to Gen. Sherman; Gen. French was ordered to report at Philadelphia; Gen. Meredith was ordered to report at Cairo; Gens. Ricketts, Gibbon, and Wadsworth, were ordered to report to Gen. Meade for assignments to command.

The following were the addresses of Gens. Pleasanton, Newton, and French, on parting with their commands:

HEADQUARTERS CAVALRY CORPS, ARMY OF THE POTOMAC, March 25, 1864.

General Orders No. 14.

Having been relieved from duty with the Army of the Potomac, the regret of separation from the many personal associations established in the cavalry corps becomes more impressive by the devotion, generosity, and noble daring that has been exhibited throughout one of the most eventful periods in the history of the war. The brave seek no higher tribute than the confidence of their commander. Your glorious deeds testify to the trust you have maintained so sacredly. Continue to be animated by the same spirit that now guides your colors to victory, and you will reap the reward of duty to yourselves, your country, and your God.

A. PLEASANTON, Major-General.

HEADQUARTERS FIRST CORPS, March 25, 1864.

In relinquishing command, I take occasion to express the pride and pleasure I have experienced with you, and my profound regret at our separation.

Identified by its services with the history of this war, the 1st corps gave at Gettysburg a crowning proof of valor and endurance, in saving from the enemy the strong position upon which the battle was fought. The terrible losses suffered by the corps on the 1st of July, attest its supreme devotion to the country. Though the the title of the corps may not survive the present changes, history will not be silent upon the magnitude of its services.

JOHN NEWTON, Major-General.

HEADQUARTERS THIRD ARMY CORPS, BRANDY STATION, March 24, 1864.

General Orders No. 26:

Having been detached from the Army of the Potomac, in consequence of its reorganization into three corps, I desire to express the personal feelings of regret with which the order is received. The consolidation of the corps gives this army greater strength. The generals to command them are conspicuous for their gallantry and ability. Only known in the department where bullets whistle, there is a strong probability that I may soon meet in the field those brave soldiers with whom I have been so long associated with pride and distinction.

WM. H. FRENCH, Major-Gen. Volunteers.

The following officers composed the staff of Gen. Grant in the field:

Brig.-Gen. John A. Rawlins, Chief of Staff; Lieut.-Col. T. S. Bowers, Ass't Adj't Gen.; Lieut.-Col. C. B. Comstock, Senior Aide-de-Camp; Lieut.-Col. O. E. Baca Babcock, Aide-de-Camp; Lieut.-Col. F. T. Dent, Aide-de-Camp; Lieut.-Col. Horace Porter, Aide-de-Camp; Lieut.-Col. W. L. Dupp, Ass't Insp.-Gen.; Lieut.-Col. W. R. Rowley, Sec.; Lieut.-Col. Adam Badeau, Sec.; Capt. E. S. Parker, Ass't Adj't-Gen.; Capt. George K. Leet, Ass't Adj't-Gen., in charge of office at Washington; Capt. P. T. Hudson, Aide-de-Camp; Capt. H. W. Jones, Ass't Quartermaster, on duty at headquarters; First-Lieut. Wm. Dunn, jr., 83d Indiana volunteers, Acting Aide-de-Camp.

At the same time the 9th corps of the army, at Annapolis, was filled up, partly with colored troops, and placed under the command of Major-Gen. Burnside, its former commander.

About the 23d of April, this corps moved to Washington, were reviewed by President Lincoln, and proceeded to Culpepper Court House, and were united to the Army of the Potomac.

Early in March Major-Gen. Sigel had been placed in command of the active forces in the Department of Western Virginia, for the purpose of coöperating with Gen. Grant by way of the Shenandoah valley. Those forces were largely increased.

The forces of Major-Gen. Butler, in command at Fortress Monroe, were also largely increased. Major-Gen. W. F. Smith, from the Western army, was assigned to the command of the 18th corps, and Major-Gen. Q. A. Gillmore, from the Department of the South, was assigned to the command of the 10th corps. Major-Gen. Foster was ordered to the command of the Department of the South. He had previously been in command in North Carolina.

On the 21st of April the Governors of Ohio, Indiana, Illinois, and Iowa, tendered to the President the services of one hundred thousand men for one hundred days. The object of this tender of men, the service in which they were to be engaged, and the reasons for the same, are fully stated in the following proclamation of the Governor of Illinois:

To the people of the State of Illinois:

On the 21st of April, the Governors of Ohio, Indiana, Illinois, Iowa, and Wisconsin, submitted to the President of the United States a proposition to furnish volunteers from their respective States for the coming campaigns:

WAR DEPARTMENT, WASHINGTON, April 21, 1864.

To the President of the United States:

First—The Governors of Ohio, Indiana, Illinois, Iowa, and Wisconsin, offer to the President infantry troops for the approaching campaign.

Second—The term of service to be a hundred days, reckoning from the date of muster into the service of the United States, unless sooner discharged.

Third—The troops to be mustered into the United States service by regiments, when the regiments are filled up according to regulations to the minimum strength. The regiments to be organized according to the regulations of the War Department. The whole number to be furnished within twenty days from date of notice of the acceptance of this proposition.

Fourth—The troops to be clothed, armed, equipped, subsisted, transported, and paid as other United States infantry volunteers, and to serve in fortifications or wherever their services may be required, within or without their respective States.

Fifth—No bounty to be paid the troops, nor the service charged or credited on any draft.

Sixth—The draft for three years service to go on in any State or district where the quota is not filled up; but, if any officer or soldier in the special service should be drafted, he shall be credited for the service rendered.

JOHN BROUGH, Governor of Ohio.
O. H. MORTON, Governor of Indiana.
RICH'D YATES, Governor of Illinois.
W. M. STONE, Governor of Iowa.

The foregoing proposition of the Governors is accepted, and the Secretary of War is directed to carry it into execution.

A. LINCOLN.

APRIL 23d, 1864.

I shall not set forth the various reasons which induced the Executive of these States to submit their proposition. It will be sufficient for you to know that it is evident from the circumstances which surround us, that the battles which are to decide the fate of the country are soon to be fought. The enemy has, during the past winter, been concentrating all his stength for the summer campaign which is before us. It is of the utmost importance to meet them with the greatest force, and with the most overwhelming numbers which it is possible to bring to bear.

You are also aware that the country which has already been wrested from the grasp of the enemy is of vast extent, embracing many States and Territories, many thousands of miles of seacoast, and the whole length of the Mississippi River, and of most of her tributaries, and that to hold this country and these long lines of sea and river coast requires large stationary forces.

The strongholds, forts, garrisons, cities, and towns, situated as they are in the midst of populations which are for the most part disloyal, and ready to rise upon the withdrawal of our troops, are almost innumerable, and require by far the greater part of our immense army in their protection and defence. In this view of the case, the Executives of the most Western States believed that the efficiency of the army might be immensely increased by a volunteer force, to be immediately raised, which should occupy the points already taken, and release our veteran troops, and send them forward to join the main body of the army, which is soon to engage the forces of the enemy. It will be apparent also that, while these forces are to be employed in fortifications, and at such points as the Government may require them now, in the future, also, they will place in the hands of the States the means to repel invasion from their borders, suppress insurrection, and maintain the peace.

The mode of enlistments, places of rendezvous, and all information pertaining to organization, &c., will be communicated to you by the adjutant-general of the State.

I make my appeal to the State of Illinois, to respond to the Government with her full quota of 20,000 men in the next twenty days. Although the State has thus far exceeded her quota under all calls by so many thousands, I doubt not she will stand ready to strengthen the arm of the Government in this trying hour, and that she will send this timely necessary relief to her gallant sons now in the field, and who have so distinguished her proud name upon every battle-field of the war. It is confidently hoped that by the timely aid which may thus be given our veteran army, the last blow may be given this wicked rebellion, and the Government reëstablished, the Union restored, and all the blessings of a stable and lasting peace secured.

Though in the North and in the South the notes of preparation for the conflict fill the land, yet for the first time have I fully seen the beginning of the end of this frightful war. All that is now required is, that the Government put forth its power at the right time, and in the right place.

The people of Illinois have confidence in her sons, and in the great commander, Gen. Grant, whom she has given to the country, as well as in the armies under his command. Let us do all in our power to uphold and strengthen their arms.

Glorious Illinois, in every period of this war you have done your duty. The shining achievements of your sons are the admiration of the world. In this most eventful hour you will not fail.

RICHARD YATES, Governor.

The address of the Governor of Indiana was as follows:

EXECUTIVE DEPARTMENT, INDIANAPOLIS, April 23, 1864.

To the people of Indiana:

The Governors of Ohio, Illinois, Iowa, Wisconsin, and Indiana, have offered to raise for the service of the General Government eighty-five thousand men for the period of one hundred days, to perform such military service as may be required of them in any State. They will be armed, subsisted, clothed, and paid by the United States, but receive no bounty. They will be mustered into the service of the United States for the period designated, the time to commence from the date of muster.

The importance of making the approaching campaign successful and decisive is not to be over-estimated, and I feel confident that this call will be promptly and fully responded to.

I need not enter into the reasons which have induced the making of this offer, and its acceptance by the Government, as they will be suggested to all by the condition and position of our military affairs.

I therefore call for twenty thousand volunteers, to rendezvous at such places as may be hereafter designated, and to be organized under instructions given by the Adjutant-General. Existing organizations of the Indiana Legion, offering their services, will be preserved when the regiment or company is filled to the minimum number, under the regulations governing the army of the United States.

O. P. MORTON, Governor of Indiana.

The following order was issued in Ohio:

COLUMBUS, April, 24th, 1864.

General Orders No. 12.

The regiments, battalions, and independent companies of infantry of the National Guard of Ohio are hereby called into active service for the term of one hundred days, unless sooner discharged. They will be clothed, armed, equipped, transported, and paid by the United States Government. These organizations will rendezvous at the nearest eligible places in their respective counties, the place to be fixed by the commanding officer, and to be on a line of railroad where practicable, on Monday, May 2, 1864, and report by telegraph to these headquarters at four o'clock P. M. of the same day the number of men present for duty. The alacrity with which all calls for the military forces of the State have been heretofore met, furnishes the surest guarantee that the National Guard will be prompt to assemble at the appointed time. Our armies in the field are marshalling for a decisive blow, and the citizen soldiery will share the glory of the crowning victories of the campaign, by relieving our veteran regiments from post and garrison duty, to allow them to engage in the more arduous labor of the field. By order of the Governor,

B. R. COWEN, Adjutant-General of Ohio.

The plan of Gen. Grant was more comprehensive than the mere capture of the city of Richmond. His purpose was to secure the machinery of the Confederate Government, and to destroy the army of Gen. Lee. Other movements were therefore necessary in connection with the one made under his own direction. The first of these was to be made by Gen. Sigel up the Shenandoah Valley toward Staunton with the view of taking possession of the Virginia Central Railroad, and ultimately holding Lynchburg on the Virginia and Tennessee Railroad. The next of these movements was to be made by Gen. Averill moving toward the same great railroad with the design of striking it near Salem or Wytheville. The next was to be made by Gen. Crook moving with a strong force and abundant supplies from Charleston, Va., toward Dublin Depot (Newbern), on the same railroad. The remaining movement on the west was to be made up the eastern side of the Big Sandy River, toward Abingdon, on the same railroad. It was intended that these different forces should strike the Virginia and Tennessee Railroad about the same time, at Abingdon, Wytheville, Dublin Depot, and Staunton, and should afterwards unite centrally west of Lynchburg, and march against that town. This combined movement comprehended a large aggregate of forces, to wit: 12,000 men by the Big Sandy route, under Gen. Burbridge; 4,000 under Gen. Crook, moving from the lower Kanawha; 2,500 cavalry under Gen. Averill, from northwest Virginia, and the army of Gen. Sigel, numbering nearly 12,000.

On the south side of Richmond it was intended by Gen. Grant to capture and hold Petersburg by a heavy force, under the command of Gen. B. F. Butler. Thus holding Petersburg and Lynchburg, all southern communication with Richmond would be cut off. The progress and results of these respective coöperating movements will be stated on a subsequent page.

On the 3d of May Gen. Meade issued the following address to the army:

HEADQUARTERS ARMY OF THE POTOMAC, May 3, 1864.

SOLDIERS: Again you are called upon to advance on the enemies of your country. The time and the occasion are deemed opportune by your Commanding-General to address you a few words of confidence and caution. You have been reorganized, strengthened, and fully equipped in every respect. You form a part of the several armies of your country—the whole under an able and distinguished general, who enjoys the confidence of the Government, the people, and the army. Your movement being in coöperation with others, it is of the utmost importance that no effort should be spared to make it successful.

Soldiers! The eyes of the whole country are looking with anxious hope to the blow you are about to strike in the most sacred cause that ever called men to arms. Remember your homes, your wives, and children; and bear in mind that the sooner your enemies are overcome the sooner you will be returned to enjoy the benefits and blessings of peace. Bear with patience the hardships and sacrifices you will be called upon to endure. Have confidence in your officers and in each other.

Keep your ranks on the march and on the battlefield, and let each man earnestly implore God's blessing, and endeavor by his thoughts and actions to render himself worthy of the favor he seeks. With clear conscience and strong arms, actuated by a high sense of duty, fighting to preserve the Government and the institutions handed down to us by our forefathers, if true to ourselves, victory, under God's blessing, must and will attend our efforts.

GEORGE G. MEADE, Maj.-Gen. Com'ding.

S. WILLIAMS, Ass't Adj. Gen.

On the same day camp was broken up, and with six days' rations the army was put in motion in light marching order. About 2 P. M. the division of cavalry commanded by Gen. Gregg, with a part of the canvas pontoon train, moved toward Richardsville and were engaged till late at night in repairing the roads to Ely's Ford. Soon after midnight a crossing was prepared by throwing two bridges over to the south shore. At the same time Gen. Wilson, in command of the 3d cavalry division, advanced to Germania Ford, eight miles above, and there prepared another bridge with canvas pontoons. About midnight the 2d corps, under Maj.-Gen. Hancock, began to move down the Stevensburg and Richardsville road to Ely's Ford. The entire corps were on the march before 3 A. M., and crossed soon after daylight. At the same time the 5th corps, under Maj.-Gen. Warren, began to move. The advance, consisting of two divisions of infantry and a portion of artillery, passed through Stevensburg soon after midnight, closely followed by the remainder of the corps, and destined to Germania Ford. This corps was closely followed by the 6th corps, under Maj.-Gen. Sedgwick, which left its camp at 4 A. M. It was the forces at Culpepper Court House which moved by the old plank road and crossed at Germania Ford. Those at Brandy Station, Catlett's, &c., on the Alexandria railroad, moved by the old turnpike, crossing the Rappahannock at Ely's Ford, four miles below the junction of the Rapidan and the Rappahannock rivers. Germania Ford is about twelve miles and Ely's Ford about four miles from Chancellorsville. Orange Court House is about twenty-seven miles and Wilderness Tavern about twenty-two miles from Chancellorsville. From points between Chancellorsville and Wilderness Tavern, roads lead to Gordonsville, Louisa Court House and Frederick's Hall, on the Virginia Central Railroad, in distances varying from twenty to thirty miles. From these places there are good roads leading direct to Richmond, which is distant between forty-two and fifty-four miles; and also good roads to Hanover Junction.

The crossing was effected during the day by these three corps without opposition. The pickets of the enemy withdrew quietly from the river, and the cavalry of Gen. Gregg advanced toward Chancellorsville without finding the enemy anywhere in force. Gen. Wilson's cavalry moved up the road to Parker's store, toward Orange Court House, the position of the enemy. The infantry and artillery followed in the direction of Chancellorsville and the Wilderness. The 2d corps camped on the old battle-field at Chancellorsville; the 5th at the old Wilderness Tavern, and the 6th at the Tavern and at Germania Ford.

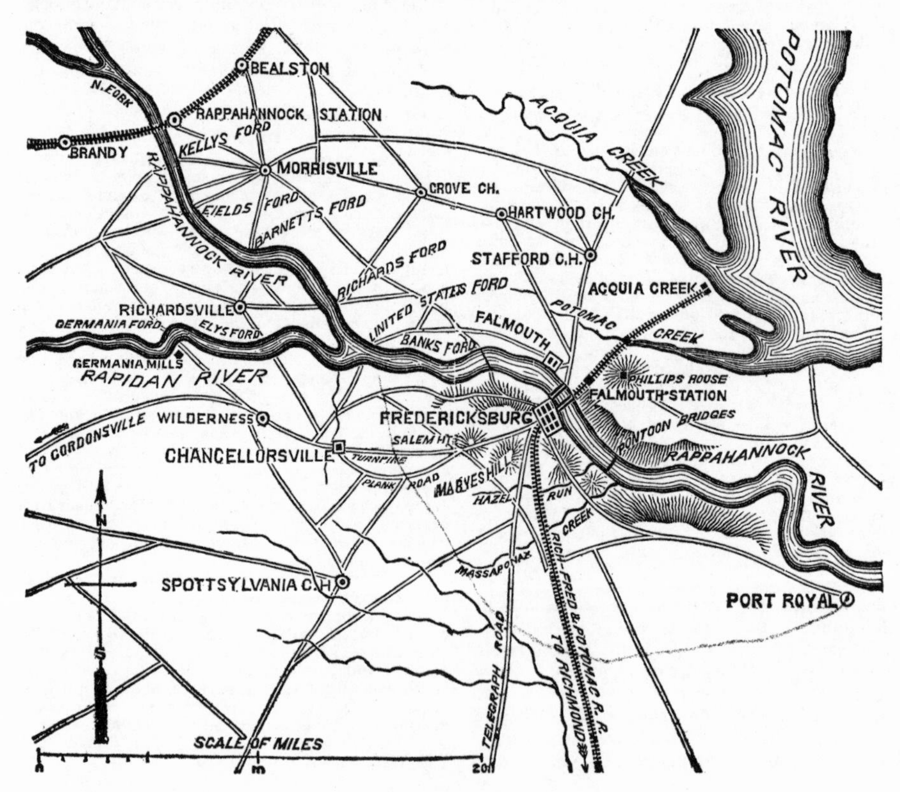

The 9th corps, under Gen. Burnside, was encamped at Warrenton. On May 1st he issued the following address to his troops:

HEADQUARTERS 9TH ARMY CORPS,
WARRENTON JUNCTION, VA., May 1, 1864.

The General commanding publishes the following instructions to the men just entering the service of the country. He expects that every old soldier who has learned their value by experience, will join in impressing their importance on those who are now to share with him the honor of a soldier's life.

On the march no soldier should quit the ranks, on any pretence whatever, without permission of his commanding officer. The army is about to move into the country of an active enemy, with no friendly force behind or near it, and every straggler runs the risk of Libby Prison or a bullet.

No soldier should leave camp without his musket; nor, on any consideration, whether on the march or in action, take off the haversack, canteen, or cartridge-box.

He should sleep with his arms within reach.

Washing the feet at night, soaping the stockings, and greasing the shoes will prevent foot-soreness.

Cavalry and artillery should husband their forage. Every soldier should endeavor to make his rations hold out longer than the time for which they were issued. A little saving may save a day's starving. It is well to make little bags, or some secure packages, for coffee, salt, and sugar. If mixed in the haversack they become worthless.

Blankets and overcoats should never be thrown away, no matter how tired or hot one may be. Cold nights follow hot days. The chief point in health and comfort is to sleep warm. At the same time the recruit should not overload his knapsack; by endeavoring to carry many comforts he may be compelled to throw away all.

He should never waste a cartridge nor a cap; the time may come when every one will tell.

When on picket duty he must remember that the safety of the whole army may depend upon his vigilance. He should observe and report every unusual sound. If attacked he must remember that a cool and determined party, acting on the defensive and properly protecting themselves, can keep at bay many times their number, and thus give time to their comrades to form and come to their support.

In action he should keep cool, not loading in haste, but tearing the cartridge and pouring in all the powder before putting in the ball. He should aim deliberately, aim low, and pull the trigger slowly. One shot in five minutes, well aimed, is better than five in a minute without aim.

He should never leave the ranks to carry off the wounded without permission of his officer; the ambulance attendants will take care of them, and he must feel that his first duty is to stand by his comrades in the fight.

Spies and persons in citizen's dress found lurking in our lines with hostile intent, should be immediately turned over to the Provost Guard.

Prisoners of war, wounded or not, should be treated with that soldierly kindness and consideration which the 9th corps has always honorably shown, and which is due to an open enemy.

The General Commanding desires to express to the 9th corps that he feels the same confidence in them now that he has ever felt in times past, and has ever found just cause for feeling. He believes that they will do their duty thoroughly and heartily on all occasions and under all circumstances.

By command of Maj.-Gen. BURNSIDE.
EDWARD M. NEILL, Ass't Adj.-Gen.

Acting as a reserve upon the advance of the army Gen. Burnside followed to the banks of the Rapidan, but did not cross over.

The army of Gen. Lee consisted of three corps under Lieut.-Gens. Longstreet, A. P. Hill, and Ewell, and occupied a position around Orange Court House, south of Culpepper Court House.

The plan of Lieut.-Gen. Grant in his advance upon Richmond was to follow a line nearly corresponding to the route of the Fredericksburg and Richmond railroad, making his base at Aquia Creek. For this purpose he moved down the right of the position of Gen. Lee, and was prepared either to accept a battle from him on the Rapidan or to continue his march to Spottsylvania Court House. But Gen. Lee would not consent to be outflanked, and ultimately endanger his railroad communication with Richmond. He, therefore, prepared to resist the progress of Lieut.-Gen. Grant, and commenced a rapid movement of his forces parallel with the course of the river. Lieut.-Gen. Longstreet's corps started from Gordonsville, Lieut.-Gen Hill took the plank road, and Lieut.-Gen Ewell the old turnpike which joins the plank. The two latter arrived in front of Lieut.-Gen. Grant's forces on Thursday morning. Early on that morning his forces began to move. The 5th corps, under Maj.-Gen. Warren, advanced from its position near Wilderness Tavern along the roads leading to Orange Court House, five miles to Parker's Store. It is here that the Germania Ford road debouches into the old turnpike. This point is in Spottsylvania county, about eight miles above Chancellorsville, and twenty below Orange Court House. The whole face of the country in that neighborhood is thickly covered with an undergrowth of field pines, cedars, and scrub oaks, and therefore utterly unfit for the use of cavalry or artillery. Maj.-Gen. Sedgwick with the 6th corps was to follow, and Maj.-Gen. Hancock with the 2d corps was to stretch southwesterly from Chancellorsville toward Shady Grove Church. Gen. Sheridan covered the extreme left beyond Maj.-Gen. Hancock, with the object of finding the enemy's cavalry under Gen. Stuart. The effect of these movements was to bring Maj.-Gen. Sedgwick on the right, Maj.-Gen. Hancock on the left, and Maj.-Gen. Warren in the centre of the line extending nearly five miles. The centre was thrown a little forward, the wings not having reached the best position, and then the action commenced.

At noon, Gen. Griffin, whose advance had been driven in, was ordered to push the 1st division of the 5th corps out to the right and left of the turnpike and feel the enemy. An advance of less than a mile, stretching across the turnpike, brought them in contact with the enemy under Lieut.-Gen. Ewell, posted on a wooded declivity. A sharp engagement ensued for an hour, when the pressure of the enemy could no longer be resisted. Gen. Griffin's division was driven back, leaving two pieces of artillery in the enemy's hands. The 4th division, under Gen. Wadsworth, and the 2d, under Gen. Robinson, now advanced, relieving Gen. Griffin, and holding the enemy in check. The Federal loss was about one thousand men.

The next movement of the enemy was to press between the corps of Gens. Warren and Hancock on the left centre. Here the contest commenced about 3 P. M. In anticipation of this movement Gen. Hancock's advance had been checked, and his corps was rapidly moving to close the gap between it and the centre. One division of the 6th corps, under Gen. Getty, had been detached and moved to the left, taking position on the right of the Orange Court House plank road. The advance, consisting of the 1st brigade of the 2d division of the 2d corps, had scarcely formed a junction with Gen. Getty, when the enemy, belonging to Lieut.-Gen. Hill's corps, made a powerful attack upon them. The position was held with the utmost obstinacy. Meanwhile the remainder of Gen. Hancock's corps arrived and attacked on the enemy's front and right. The divisions of Gens. Birney, Barlow, and Gibbons, took an active part, and the contest became exceedingly bloody. Such was the nature of the undergrowth that there was little opportunity to use artillery. The furious fire of the enemy's musketry was seldom surpassed. After the contest had stubbornly continued for two hours, a portion of Gens. Wadsworth's and Robinson's divisions of the 5th, moved out to turn the flanks of Gen. Hill's corps. The contest continued here until late in the night, and closed with a loss of a thousand killed and wounded, among whom was Gen. Alexander Hayes. The effort of the enemy to penetrate the left centre failed.

On the right the fighting commenced with an attack by Gen. Sedgwick, who advanced his line. In the afternoon the enemy advanced to drive him back, during which they made a desperate effort to turn his right. In this extremity he sent a request to Gen. Burnside, who had that day crossed over, to close up and assist him. At this time the attack of the enemy was repulsed, but near nightfall it was renewed again with great vigor. A most desperate engagement ensued, which continued until two hours after dark, when the indecisive conflict closed. Three hundred of the enemy had been taken prisoners, and they in turn claimed the capture of a thousand during the day.

The following is Gen. Lee's despatch:

HEADQUARTERS ARMY NORTHERN VIRGINIA, May 5, 1864.

Hon. Secretary of War:

The enemy crossed the Rapidan at Ely's and Germania Fords. Two corps of this army moved to oppose him, Ewell's by the old turnpike and Hill's by the plank road. They arrived this morning in close proximity to the enemy's line of march. A strong attack was made upon Ewell, who repulsed it, capturing many prisoners and four pieces of artillery.

The enemy subsequently concentrated upon Gen. Hill, who with his and Wilcox's divisions, successfully resisted the repeated and desperate assaults. A large force of cavalry and artillery on our right were driven back by Rossan's brigade. By the blessings of God, we maintained our position against every effort until night, when the combat closed. We have to mourn the loss of many brave officers and men.

Gallant Brig.-Gen. J. M. Jones was killed, and Gen. Stafford, I fear, mortally wounded, while leading his command with conspicuous valor. R. E. LEE.

No despatch was sent from Lieut.-Gen. Grant.

During the day the 9th corps, under Gen. Burnside, had come upon the field after a forced march. It was distributed as occasion required on the right, right centre and left centre. The Federal line continued substantially as during the day, stretching northwest and southeast, nearly parallel to a line from Germania Ford to Chancellorsville. Gen. Grant had thus been successful in covering the fords by which all his teams were yet to pass, and which it was absolutely necessary to keep open in order to preserve his line of communication, and which were threatened by the rapid and bold movement of Gen. Lee from west to east.

On the next day, Friday, May 6th, the battle consisted of a succession of fierce attacks made by each side. Both had more or less intrenched their positions by felling timber and covering it with earth, or with slight earthworks. An advance had been ordered on the right, at 5 A. M., by Gen. Grant, but before it took place the firing of the pickets had commenced and increased until six o'clock, when the engagement became general. The interval of ground between the opposing lines was fought over in some places as many as four or five times, the combatants driving each other in turn from the opposite lines of rifle-pits. Gen. Seymour with a provisional division on the extreme right, and Gen. Wright's 1st division of the 6th corps, next adjoining, were first engaged, and Gen. Ricketts' was next involved. An effort made on the part of the enemy to flank was repelled, and the line pushed a few hundred yards ahead, but without any decisive advantage. At 8 and half-past 10 o'clock the right was again pressed by the enemy. The firing at each period extended all along the line. The efforts of the enemy appeared to be intended to break through the separate corps. The gaps, however, were closed by the 9th corps. Earthworks were thrown up whenever and wherever practicable, and proved to be of invaluable service. On the left the engagement commenced at the same time as on the right. Gen. Hancock pressed the enemy some distance, until being reënforced they held their ground. Soon a severe assault was again made on the left, followed up along the line with such vigor as nearly to involve the whole in confusion. Reënforcements from Gen. Burnside checked the advance of the enemy, and relieved the left and centre. Before noon Gen. Wadsworth, commanding the 4th division of the 5th corps was shot in the forehead and instantly killed.

At noon the contest was comparatively suspended, and Gen. Grant concentrated his lines, interposing the greater part of Gen. Burnside's corps between Gens. Warren and Hancock. The left was also brought forward a little toward the centre from the Brock Road, to which it had been driven. These movements had hardly been completed when the forces of Gens. Longstreet and Hill renewed the attack on the left and centre with great fury, and drove them back. The fight was fiercest at the junction of these two corps and Gen. Crawford's 3d division of the 5th corps. Gen. Carr's 4th division of the 2d corps, and Gen. Stevenson's division of the 9th corps, suffered the most heavily. The latter division being on Gen. Hancock's right gave way, and the enemy rushed through the gap. Their advance was checked by an attack on the flank by Gen. Carrol's brigade of Gen. Hancock's corps, and they retired with much loss. The centre and left then recovered their former position.

Toward night the battle was renewed on the right. The assault of the enemy was sudden and furious, and the 2d brigade of the 3d division, under Gen. Seymour, on the extreme right, was panic-stricken, and, with Gen. Shaler's brigade, were overwhelmed and their commanders captured. Gen. Seymour had taken command of this brigade only on the previous night, and did every thing that skill and bravery could effect. The whole right wing, if not the whole army, was now in peril. Gen. Sedgwick, however, rallied and held his troops, thus saving the army from the threatened destruction. The enemy, not perceiving the havoc which they had made, or not knowing the condition of the right wing, and exhausted with the severe efforts of the day, retired in the darkness which now prevailed. No further effort was made to cut off the army from Germania Ford, even when it was nearly successful. The loss on the right wing was about 6,000, of which 4,000 occurred during this assault of the enemy. The total of the two days' battles was estimated at 15,000. Among the killed were Gens. Hayes, Wadsworth, and Webb of Gen. Grant's army. Of the enemy's, Gens. Jones, Jenkins, and Pickett were killed, and Gens. Longstreet, Pegram, and Hunter severely wounded. Gen. Longstreet was struck in the neck below the Adam's apple. The ball passed along the clavicle, fracturing it, and came out on the shoulder, cutting some important nerves of the arm. He was unable to take the field until near the close of the year.

At the close of the day both armies held substantially the same line as on the previous evening, and the intervening space was occupied by the dead and wounded. Gen. Grant had strengthened his left, and during the night preparations were made to strengthen the right, and to repair the disaster on that flank.

During these two days Gen. Grant's cavalry had occupied a position covering the rear and left, and prevented flanking movements by the cavalry of the enemy. On Friday, as Gen. Hancock's corps advanced to battle, the enemy charged and captured several hundred of the 18th Pennsylvania cavalry.

On Saturday, the 7th, brisk skirmishing ensued along the lines. Gen. Gordon's brigade of the enemy cut off the communication of Gen. Sedgwick with Germania Ford, and the latter was withdrawn toward Wilderness Tavern. Gen. Burnside's corps was moved out on the road to Spottsylvania Court House. It was evident in the afternoon that Gen. Lee was withdrawing his main force toward Spottsylvania Court House, and orders were issued to the surgeons in charge of the hospitals to remove their sick and wounded to Ely's Ford, and the supply trains were ordered to move in the night to the vicinity of Todd's tavern. Subsequently Fredericksburg was occupied by some of Gen. Grant's forces, and made a depot for the wounded and a basis for supplies.

The following despatches were sent by Gen. Lee to Richmond:

HEADQUARTERS ARMY NORTHERN VIRGINIA, May 7, 1864—8 P. M.

Honorable Secretary of War:

Gen. Gordon turned the enemy's extreme right yesterday evening and drove him from his rifle-pits. Among the prisoners captured are Gens. Seymour and Shaler. A number of arms were also taken. The enemy has abandoned the Germania Ford road and moved his pontoon bridge toward Ely's. There has been no attack to-day—only slight skirmishing along the line. (Signed) R. E. LEE.

HEADQUARTERS ARMY NORTHERN VIRGINIA, May 8.

Honorable Secretary of War:

The enemy have abandoned their position and are marching toward Fredericksburg. I am moving on the right flank. (Signed) R. E. LEE.

During the afternoon a battle took place between the cavalry. The loss was about two hundred and fifty on each side. At dark the 2d corps began to move by way of Brock's road, followed by the 5th corps on the same route. Gens. Burnside and Sedgwick moved on the old Chancellorsville road, and arrived on the field near Spottsylvania at noon on Sunday. Gen. Warren reached a point about three miles from Spottsylvania Court House, after marching all of Saturday night. About the same time Gen. Ewell's corps, with a portion of Gen. Longstreet's, had arrived. A sharply-contested action ensued in a field to the left of the Brock road, which stretched away to the east, toward the Spottsylvania and Fredericksburg road. The country was rolling, and dotted here and there with thick groves of pine and cedar for the distance of a mile from the point where the Wilderness terminates in the open country. A contest between cavalry had taken place in front of Gen. Warren, and some artillery was seen, but it was inaccurately reported that there was no infantry. As the advance of Gen. Warren passed down the road, shells were thrown at it with great activity, and the enemy fell back, making only a slight resistance. On reaching a triangular clearing known as Alsop's farm, of a hundred acres, the artillery of the enemy was found to be stationed there. Beyond the clearing was Ny Run, a small stream affording no obstacle to the advance of troops. The wooded ground rises beyond in ridges. The Union batteries were stationed to the right, commanding those of the enemy. The infantry advanced through the clearing and came upon three lines of the enemy, the last of which was behind earthworks. Here the struggle took place with the greatest violence, and continued some hours, during which Gen. Warren held his ground. In the afternoon a brigade of the 6th corps came to his assistance, and the enemy were driven from their position. The Federal loss was thirteen hundred. Many officers were wounded, among whom was Gen. Robinson, who was shot in the knee. Several brigades lost their commanders, and the 4th Michigan was finally commanded by a first lieutenant. The 1st Michigan, two hundred strong, came out of the fight with twenty-three men. The day was intensely hot, and many suffered from sun-stroke.

Monday was comparatively quiet in the morning, followed by cannonading and skirmishing, but no general battle. While superintending the mounting of artillery, Gen. Sedgwick was killed by a ball from a sharpshooter entering his head. The centre of the the line formed on Sunday was held by Gen. Warren, with the 2d corps, Gen. Hancock, on the right, and the 6th corps, Gen. Wright, lately Gen. Sedgwick, on the left. Toward night, on Monday, Gen. Grant ordered another advance on the enemy. The right, with Gens. Birney's and Gibbon's divisions in advance, followed by Gen. Carroll's brigade, crossed over to the south bank of a branch of the Po River. Here a severe battle with both infantry and artillery ensued. Each side alternately charged. At night the enemy held Spottsylvania Court House, and Gen. Hancock slowly retired his corps, after suffering heavy losses. During the day an attack, directed on Gen. Wilcox's division of the 9th corps, was met and repulsed.

The following despatches from Mr. Stanton, the Secretary of War, relative to the preceding operations, were sent to the public press:

WASHINGTON, May 8—9 A. M.

To Gen. John A. Dix, New York:

We have no official reports from the front; but the Medical Director has notified the Surgeon General that our wounded were being sent to Washington, and will number from six to eight thousand.

The Chief Quartermaster of the army of the Potomac has made requisition for seven days' grain, and for railroad construction trains, and states that the enemy is reported to be retiring. This indicates Gen. Grant's advance, and affords an inference of material success on our part.

The enemy's strength has always been most felt in his first blows, and his efforts having failed, and our forces, not only having maintained their ground, but preparing to advance, lead to the hope of full and complete success; for when either party falls back, disorganization by straggling and desertion commence, and the enemy's loss in killed and wounded must weaken him more than we are weakened. Nothing later than my last night's despatch has been received from Gen. Butler.

A despatch from Gen. Sherman, dated at 5 o'clock P. M. yesterday, states that Gen. Thomas had occupied Tunnel Hill, where he expected a battle, and that the enemy had taken position at Buzzard Roost Pass, north of Dalton. Skirmishing had taken place, but no real fighting.

Nothing later from Gen. Banks.

You may give such publicity to the information transmitted to you as you deem proper.

It is designed to give accurate official statements of what is known to the department in this great crisis, and to withhold nothing from the public.

EDWIN M. STANTON, Secretary of War.

WASHINGTON, May 8—5 P. M.

Maj.-Gen. John A. Dix, New York:

We are yet without any official despatches from the Army of the Potomac, except those referred to this morning from the Medical Director and Chief Quartermaster, and nothing additional has been received by the Department from any other source. It is believed that no fighting took place yesterday.

A part of the wounded arrived in ambulances this morning at Rappahannock Station, and are on the way in by railroad. The Department will probably receive despatches by that train, which will arrive to-night.

A despatch from Gen. Butler, just received, and which left him yesterday, states that a demonstration had been made by his forces on the railroad between Petersburg and Richmond, and had succeeded in destroying a portion of it, so as to break the connection; that there had been some severe fighting, but that he had succeeded. He heard from a rebel deserter that Hunter was dangerously wounded Pickett also, and Jones and Jenkins were killed.

Nothing further has been heard from Gen. Sherman.

EDWIN M. STANTON, Secretary of War.

WASHINGTON, May 9—10:45 A. M.

Maj.-Gen. John A. Dix:

We have intelligence this morning, by agents direct from the army, as late as Saturday evening, but no official reports. The general result may be estimated as a success to our arms.

The fighting on Friday was the most desperate known in modern times.

I deeply regret to say that the country will have to mourn the death of that accomplished soldier, Brig.-Gen. Wadsworth, who was struck in the forehead by a ball, at the head of his command, while leading them against one of the enemy's strongest positions. His remains are in our hands in charge of Col. Sharpe. Gen. Webb was wounded. Gen. Jones, of the rebel army, was killed.

The condition of our army is represented to be most admirable. Their cool, determined courage, has in every instance proved too much for the desperate fury of the rebels, who have been driven at all points. There has been no straggling.

At the latest accounts Hancock was pushing forward rapidly, by the left, to Spottsylvania Court House, and yesterday heavy cannonading was heard at Aquia Creek from that direction.

We have lost some prisoners. One regiment, the 7th Pennsylvania reserves, charged through an abatis of the enemy, but were unable to get back, and most of them were captured. We have also taken a large number of prisoners, supposed to be more than we lost. The wounded had not yet arrived at the point where the trains were to receive them. The Medical Director reports that a large proportion are slightly wounded. Artillery was not used on either side the last two days.

There is nothing later from Gen. Butler than the dates of my last despatch.

Gen. Sherman was heard from last night. He had been all day reconnoitring the enemy's position, and would attack to-day.

EDWIN M. STANTON, Secretary of War.

WASHINGTON, May 9—11:30 A. M.

Maj.-Gen. John A. Dix:

This Department has just received from Gen. Butler the official report of Gen. Lee of the operations of Friday. He says their loss in killed is not large, but they have many wounded. He grieves to announce that Gen. Longstreet was severely wounded, Gen. Jenkins killed, and Gen. Pegram badly wounded on Thursday, and that it is supposed that Gen. Stafford will recover. He thanks a merciful God that every advance on their (Gen. Grant's) part has been repulsed. He states that our forces attacked them and caused some confusion. Gen. Wadsworth's body fell into their hands; but our reports this morning state that it is now in our possession, under charge of Col. Sharpe, as stated in my first despatch this morning.

The belief here is that Lieut.-Gen. Grant is achieving a complete victory.

EDWIN M. STANTON, Secretary of War.

WASHINGTON, May 9—4 P. M.

Maj.-Gen. John A. Dix:

Despatches have just reached here direct from Gen. Grant. They are not fully deciphered yet, but he is "on to Richmond." We have taken two thousand prisoners.

EDWIN M. STANTON, Secretary of War.

The last official despatch.

WASHINGTON, May 9—4, P. M.

A bearer of despatches from Gen. Meade's headquarters has just reached here. He states that Lee's army commenced falling back on the night of Friday. Our army commenced the pursuit on Saturday.

The rebels were in full retreat for Richmond by the direct road.

Hancock passed through Spottsylvania Court House at daylight yesterday.

Our headquarters at noon yesterday were twenty miles south of the battle field.

We occupy Fredericksburg. The 22d New York cavalry occupied that place at eight o'clock last night.

The depot for our wounded is established at Fredericksburg.

EDWIN M. STANTON, Secretary of War.

The President, on the 9th, also issued the following proclamation:

EXECUTIVE MANSION, WASHINGTON, May 9, 1864.

To the Friends of Union and Liberty:

Enough is known of the army operations within the last five days to claim our especial gratitude to God. While what remains undone demands our most sincere prayers to and reliance upon Him (without whom all human effort is vain), I recommend that all patriots, at their homes, in their places of public worship, and wherever they may be, unite in common thanksgiving and prayer to Almighty God.

ABRAHAM LINCOLN.

The excitement produced throughout the North by these despatches was very great. Washington also was almost wild with enthusiasm over what was regarded as a great victory achieved by the Army of the Potomac over the army under Gen. Lee. In the evening the feelings of the people found vent in a congratulatory visit to the President, which is thus reported:

"A procession was formed in front of Willard's Hotel about half-past eight this evening, headed by the band of the 27th Michigan regiment, and proceeded to the White House. After several patriotic airs had been performed by the band, in response to the cheers and calls of the multitude assembled, the President came forward, and was introduced to the people by Senator Foster, of Connecticut.

"He returned his thanks for the compliment paid him, and said that we had won a great victory, for which we should return thanks to the Almighty, who had smiled upon and blessed our efforts, and also to Gen. Grant and his brave officers and soldiers, to whose heroism and sacrifices we were indebted, under Providence, for this triumph. We had won a great victory, but we must not be prematurely sanguine, for although much had been done, there was a great deal of work yet to do before the rebellion could be suppressed and the Union restored. There was one thing which he desired to say to them, and that was, that while Gen. Grant had met with stubborn resistance, he had not been forced back in the slightest degree from the line upon which he had started, and was now moving forward upon the line which he had marked out before the movement commenced. He had every confidence in Gen. Grant, and believed that he would accomplish the great work which he had yet to do.

"Enthusiastic cheers were given for the President, Gen. Grant, Gen. Meade, and our brave armies, after which the crowd retired in a quiet and orderly manner."

The thanksgiving recommended by the President was very generally observed by the churches on the following Sunday. As an instance, the rector of Trinity Church, New York, issued the following:

TRINITY RECTORY, May 13, 1864.

The reverend the clergy of this parish are requested, on the approaching feast of Whitsunday, to offer solemn thanksgivings to Almighty God for the answer to the prayers of his people, and for the great mercies extended to this nation by His Divine Providence during the past week. The form of thanksgiving set forth and authorized by the Bishop of this diocese will be used immediately after the general thanksgiving, at each service during the day.

MORGAN DIX, Rector of Trinity Church.

The following is a report of the manner of observance:

After the usual initial exercises had been gone through, the prayer for victories, to be found in the prayers at sea in the Episcopal book of common prayer, was read.

Dr. Vinton then ascended the pulpit and preached the sermon, taking his text from St. John, seventh chapter and thirty-ninth verse:—"The Holy Ghost is not yet." The preacher only briefly alluded to our victories in the course of his discourse. He said that the day of Pentecost had again dawned on the world; but the anniversary of the Christian year came that day, not ushered in like the fast days of the world formerly, but with the booming of cannon and hurrahs echoing in the air, and the rejoicing which all the people of this land were now expressing for their victories.

The rest of the preacher's discourse was strictly confined to remarks on the coming of the Holy Ghost, and in conclusion he said we should now especially give God thanks for all the favors we have received at His hands.

The despatches of the Secretary were continued as follows:

WASHINGTON, May 10, 1864.

To Major-Gen. Dix:

Despatches have been received this evening from Maj.-Gen. Grant, dated at one o'clock yesterday.

The enemy have made a stand at Spottsylvania Court House. There had been some hard fighting; but no general battle had taken place there.

I deeply regret to announce that Maj.-Gen. Sedgwick was killed in yesterday's engagement at Spottsylvania, being struck by a ball from a sharpshooter. His remains are at Fredericksburg, and are expected here to-night. [A ball entered his eye and passed through his head, killing him instantly.]

The army is represented to be in excellent condition, and with ample supplies.

Gen. Robinson and Gen. Morris are wounded. No other casualties to general officers are reported.

Gen. H. G. Wright has been placed in command of Sedgwick's corps.

Gen. Grant did not design to renew the attack to-day, being engaged in replenishing from the supply train, so as to advance without it.

EDWIN M. STANTON, Secretary of War.

On Tuesday morning, the 10th, Gen. Grant's forces occupied substantially the same position as on the previous day. His line stretched about six miles on the northerly bank of the Po, and took the general form of a crescent, the wings being thrown forward. The 2d corps, across the Po, now held a line on the right, nearly parallel to the road from Shady Grove Church to the Court House. The 5th corps held the centre, being on the east side of the Po, and the 6th corps held the left, facing toward the Court House. Further on the left was the 9th corps, under Gen. Burnside. Several batteries covered the right and others the left centre. In front was a dense forest. The enemy held Spottsylvania and the region north of the Court House. His left rested on Glady Run, sweeping northward and sheltered by strong works long before made in anticipation of this emergency. His right curved in a similar direction, and rested on the Ny River, and his centre, a little thrown forward from the right and left centres, was posted on commanding ground. His position was well supported by breastworks, and along the centre was the forest and underbrush, lining a marsh partially drained by the run. The conflict opened in the morning by a terrific fire of artillery, which was incessant during all the forenoon. A most vigorous and gallant attack was then made by the 5th corps, and by Gens. Gibbons' and Birney's divisions of the 2d corps, on the centre of Gen. Lee's army. The losses of Gen. Grant were most severe in the repeated charges by which the enemy was driven to his rifle-pits. Brig.-Gen. Rice, commanding the 2d brigade of the 4th division of the 5th corps, was killed at this time. In the mean time the enemy had attacked and turned Gen. Barlow's division of the 2d corps, on the right; but it was finally extricated without great loss. Toward the close of the day a most energetic assault was made along the whole line, in which the enemy's works were scaled, and more than a thousand prisoners taken, with several guns, by Gen. Upton's 1st brigade of Gen. Wright's 1st division of the 6th corps, which was in the advance of this onset. His position being too far in advance of the residue of the army to be held, he was compelled to fall back with the prisoners which he had taken. The Federal losses throughout the day were estimated to exceed ten thousand; and the total loss thus far, thirty-five thousand. The enemy's loss was supposed to be equally severe.

The following despatches from the Secretary of War, relative to this contest at Spottsylvania, were published:

WASHINGTON, May 11, 1864.

Maj.-Gen. John A. Dix:

Despatches from the Army of the Potomac have just reached here, bearing dates to 5 o'clock P. M. yesterday.

Both armies at that time held their positions at Spottsylvania Court House, without any material change. The enemy had been driven to their breastworks.

The 6th corps, under Gen. Wright, had carried the first line of the enemy's rifle pits.

There had been heavy skirmishing during the day.

Our wounded had reached Fredericksburg, and during the night some were brought up to Washington.

The Surgeon General reports that ample supplies of nurses, surgeons, and medical stores have gone forward.

There has been nothing heard from Gen. Sherman or Gen. Butler since my last despatch of yesterday.

EDWIN M. STANTON, Secretary of War.

WASHINGTON. May 11—11:30 P. M.

Maj. Gen. John A. Dix:

Despatches from Gen. Grant, dated at 8 o'clock this morning, have just reached this department. He says:

"We have now ended the sixth day of very hard fighting. The result to this time is much in our favor. Our losses have been heavy as well as those of the enemy. I think the loss of the enemy must be greater. We have taken over five thousand prisoners in battle, while he has taken from us but few except stragglers.

"I propose to fight it out on this line, if it takes all summer."

The Government is sparing no pains to support him.

EDWIN M. STANTON, Secretary of War.

The following despatch of Gen. Lee was sent to Richmond:

SPOTTSYLVANIA COURT HOUSE, VIA GURNEY'S, May 10, 1864.

The Honorable Secretary of War:

Gen. Grant's army is intrenched near this place, on both sides of the Brock road. Frequent skirmishing occurred yesterday and to-day, each army endeavoring to discover the position of the other. To-day the enemy shelled our lines and made several assaults with infantry against different points, particularly on our left, held by Gen. R. H. Anderson, The last, which occurred after sunset, was the most obstinate, some of the enemy leaping over the breastworks. They were easily repulsed, except in front of Gen. Doles' brigade, where they drove our men from their position, and from a four-gun battery there posted. The men were soon rallied, and by dark our line was reëstablished and the battery recovered.

A large body of the enemy moved around our left on the evening of the 9th, and took possession of the road about midway between Shady Grove Church and the Court House. Gen. Early, with a part of Hill's corps, drove them back this evening, taking one gun and a few prisoners.

Thanks to a merciful Providence, our casualties have been small.

Among the wounded are Brig.-Gens. Hayes and H. H. Walker.

R. E. LEE.

On the next day, Wednesday, the 11th, the position of the two armies was nearly the same as on the previous day. The enemy still held and covered the town with a crescent-shaped line. Their centre was very strong and posted securely, with rifle-pits in front and the strip of forest covering it, well guarded with lines of skirmishers. During the morning there was a brisk skirmishing, which died away at noon.

Some reconnoitring movements were made, and the enemy, apprehending an attack on their left, moved artillery from their right to left, toward the point threatened. During the afternoon rain fell for the first time since the army moved. It was determined during the day to make an assault early the next morning on the enemy's left, where their batteries were so strongly posted as to annoy Gen. Grant's lines. The 2d corps was selected to make this movement. Soon after midnight, in the darkness and storm, Gen. Hancock changed the position of his corps from the extreme right to the left, filling up the space between Gens. Wright and Burnside. It was then near ground well commanded by the enemy, and requiring a quick advance in the morning.

On Thursday the 12th, at the dawn of day, veiled by the twilight and by a dense fog, the 2d corps moved up to the enemy's lines. Gen. Barlow's 1st division and Gen. Birney's 3d division formed the first line; Gen. Gibbon's 2d division and Gen. Mott's 4th formed the second line. The advance of Gen. Barlow marched in column of battalions doubled on the centre. As the corps moved over the rugged and woody space intervening the excitement increased, until it broke out in a rush at the hostile intrenchments. These the corps leaped, with loud cheers, and dashed among the astonished enemy, compelling their surrender in mass. An entire division was surrounded, and officers and men captured. Three thousand prisoners and two generals—Maj.-Gen. Edward Johnson and Brig.-Gen. G. H. Stewart—were taken. So complete was the surprise that the hostile officers were taken at their breakfast, and within an hour after the start of the corps Gen. Hancock reported as follows: "I have captured from thirty to forty guns. I have finished up Johnson, and am now going into Early." The second line of rifle-pits was immediately stormed, and after a stubborn resistance wrested from the enemy. A heavy cannonade then commenced all along the line, to which the enemy replied with the utmost spirit. The whole line now pressed up to support the 2d corps. The 9th corps rushed in on the extreme left, converging toward the penetrated space, and joined its right to the left of the 2d corps. The 6th corps advanced against Gen. Ewell's left, and on the extreme right Gen. Warren's corps became hotly engaged. About 9 o'clock the enemy began to charge desperately upon the 2d and 9th corps, to recover the lost works. For three hours a bloody fight continued. At noon, however, they abandoned for a time the attempt to retake the position so obstinately held. But the further advance of Gen. Hancock had been successfully checked. Most of the captured cannon were covered by the guns of the sharpshooters, and neither party were able to bring them off. Meantime the right and centre had charged the enemy's position with great intrepidity, but without success, his position being found impregnable. Every avenue of approach was swept by a most destructive fire of artillery, and his force was strong enough to hold the position against twice the attacking numbers.

Gen. Meade now sought to turn the enemy's right; and after a temporary lull in the afternoon, began to crowd his troops down toward the left, still keeping up his artillery and infantry fire. The rain began to fall at noon, but the carnage went on until night. The enemy finding that the Federal right had been merely holding him in front from reënforcing his right, and had now abandoned his front, also concentrated on his right. Every inch of ground was fought over with desperation. The dead and wounded lay thickly strewn along the ground, and heaped up where the fight was hottest. After fourteen hours, night fell on one of the severest contests of the war. The movement of Gen. Hancock in the morning was the first decided success of the campaign, having secured an advance of a mile in the line at that point. About three thousand prisoners were reported to be captured. The loss in killed and wounded was estimated at ten thousand, and that of the enemy was supposed to be equally severe. The artillery which had been captured remained on disputed ground, and was subsequently withdrawn by the enemy.

On Friday the 13th it was soon apparent that the enemy had withdrawn his main force on the left, by falling back to a new defensive position. The storm increased, and rendered the roads very heavy. Skirmishing and artillery firing were kept up by small bodies of the troops during the day. At noon Gen. Meade issued the following address to his army:

HEADQUARTERS ARMY OF THE POTOMAC,
May 13, 1864.

SOLDIERS! The moment has arrived when your commanding officer feels authorized to address you in terms of congratulation.

For eight days and nights, without almost any intermission, through rain and sunshine you have been fighting a desperate foe in positions naturally strong, and rendered doubly so by intrenchments.

You have compelled him to abandon his fortifications on the Rapidan, to retire and to attempt to stop your progress, and now he has abandoned the last intrenched position, so tenaciously held, suffering in all a loss of eighteen guns, twenty-two colors, eight thousand prisoners, including two general officers.

Your heroic deeds, noble endurance of fatigue and privation, will ever be memorable. Let us return thanks to God for the mercy thus shown us, and ask earnestly for its continuance.

Soldiers! Your work is not over. The enemy must be pursued, and, if possible, overcome. The courage and fortitude you have displayed render your Commanding General confident that your future efforts will result in success.

While we mourn the loss of many gallant comrades, let us remember that the enemy must have suffered equal if not greater losses.

We shall soon receive reënforcements which he cannot expect. Let us determine, then, to continue vigorously the work so well begun, and, under God's blessing, in a short time the object of our labors will be accomplished.

(Signed) GEORGE G. MEADE,
Major-Gen. Commanding.

Official: S. WILLIAMS.

On Saturday the 14th, the enemy appeared to have fallen back a little, but to be still holding the Court House tenaciously. Gen. Meade's line finally stretched nearly at right angles across the Fredericksburg and Spottsylvania road, with Gen. Hancock's corps on the right, Gen. Burnside's 9th on the right centre, Gen. Wright's 6th on the left centre, and Gen. Warren's 5th on the left. The position of the enemy seemed to be a semicircular line of earthworks with rifle-pits here and there, well established on commanding heights, and the whole flanked right and left by dense woods. A part of the works appeared to be sodded, showing an old construction, and great activity was manifest in strengthening the position. Gen. Grant's forces soon commenced to throw up military works, and both armies were diligently at work with the spade. On the extreme left there was considerable fighting. In the afternoon Gen. Meade narrowly escaped capture or injury, being in a house near which the enemy made a sudden and unlooked-for charge.

On this day Gen. Lee issued the following address to his army:

General Order No. 41.

HEADQUARTERS ARMY OF NORTHERN VA., May 14, 1864.

1. The General Commanding takes great pleasure in announcing to the army the series of successes that, by the favor of God, have recently been achieved by our arms.

2. A part of the enemy's force threatening the Valley of Virginia, has been routed by Gen. Imboden and driven back to the Potomac, with the loss of their train and a number of prisoners.

3. Another body of the enemy under Gen. Averill, penetrated to the Virginia and Tennessee Railroad, at Dublin depot. A portion of his force has been dispersed by Gens. Morgan and W. E. Jones, who are in pursuit of the remainder.

4. The army of Gen. Banks sustained a severe defeat in Western Louisiana by the forces of Gen. Kirby Smith, and retreated to Alexandria, losing several thousand prisoners, thirty-five pieces of artillery, and a large number of wagons. Some of the most formidable gunboats that accompanied the expedition were destroyed to save them from capture.

5. The expedition of Gen. Steele into Western Arkansas has ended in a complete disaster. Northern journals of the 10th inst. announce his surrender, with an army of nine thousand men, to Gen. Price.

6. The cavalry force sent by Gen. Grant to attack Richmond has been repulsed, and retired toward the Peninsula. Every demonstration of the enemy south of James River has, up to this time, been successfully repelled.

7. The heroic valor of this army, with the blessing of Almighty God, has thus far checked the principal army of the enemy, and inflicted upon it heavy losses. The eyes and hearts of your countrymen are turned to you in confidence, and their prayers attend you in your gallant struggle. Encouraged by the success that has been vouchsafed to us, and stimulated by the great interests that depend upon the issue, let every man resolve to endure all and brave all, until, by the assistance of a just and merciful God, the enemy shall be driven back and peace secured to our country. Continue to emulate the valor of your comrades who have fallen, and remember that it depends upon you whether they shall have died in vain. It is in your power, under God, to defeat the last great effort of the enemy, establish the independence of your native land, and earn the lasting love and gratitude of your countrymen, and the admiration of mankind. R. E. LEE, General.

The following despatches were sent by the Secretary of War:

WASHINGTON, May 13—2:30 P. M.

To Major-General John A. Dix:

A despatch from Lieut.-Gen. Grant has just been received, dated near Spottsylvania Court House, May 12, 6:30 P. M. It is as follows:

"The eighth day of battle closes leaving between three and four thousand prisoners in our hands for the day's work, including two general officers and over thirty pieces of artillery. The enemy are obstinate, and seem to have found the last ditch. We have lost no organization, not even a company, while we have destroyed and captured one division (Johnson's), one brigade (Dobbs'), and one regiment entire of the enemy."

EDWIN M. STANTON, Secretary of War.

WASHINGTON, May 13—6:30 P. M.

Major-General Dix:

The following despatch from Mr. Dana has just reached this department.

EDWIN M. STANTON, Secretary of War.

SPOTTSYLVANIA COURT HOUSE, VA., May 13—8 A. M.

Hon E. M. Stanton, Secretary of War:

Lee abandoned his position during the night, whether to occupy a new position in the vicinity or to make a thorough retreat is not determined.

One division of Wright's and another of Hancock's are engaged in settling this question, and at half-past 7 A. M. had come up on his rear guard. Though our army is greatly fatigued from the enormous efforts of yesterday, the news of Lee's departure inspires the men with fresh energy.

The whole force will soon be in motion; but the heavy rains of the last thirty-six hours render the roads very difficult for wagons and artillery.

The proportion of severely wounded is greater than on either of the previous days' fighting. This was owing to the great use made of artillery.

WASHINGTON, May 13—6:55 P. M.

Major-General Dix, New York:

The Acting Surgeon General reports that of five hundred patients from the recent battle-field admitted into the Harwood Hospital, not one will require any surgical operation, and that, in his opinion, two-thirds of the whole number of wounded will be fit for service in thirty days.

Reënforcements are going forward to the Army of the Potomac.

EDWIN M. STANTON, Secretary of War.

WASHINGTON, May 15—9 A. M.

To Major-General Dix:

An official despatch from the battle field at Spottsylvania yesterday morning, at half-past 6, states that during the preceding night (Friday) a movement was made by the 5th and 6th corps to our left, and an attack was to have been made at daylight, but no sound of battle had been heard from that quarter. This manœuvre, it is said, if successful, would place our forces in Lee's rear, and compel him to retreat toward Lynchburg.

No cannon nor any sound of battle was heard yesterday at Belle Plain or Fredericksburg, which affords ground for inference that Lee had retreated during Friday night, and before the advance of the 5th and 6th corps.

Nothing later than half-past 6 A. M. of yesterday has been received from the army by the department. All the wounded that had reached Belle Plain yesterday evening have arrived here.

The surgical report from the headquarters of the army states that the condition of the supplies is satisfactory, and the wounded are doing well. The medical director at Belle Plain reports that every thing at that point is satisfactory. The surgical arrangements have never been so complete as now.

Gen. Sheridan's command had reached the left bank of Turkey Island at 3 o'clock yesterday afternoon, and have formed their junction with the forces of Gen. Butler.

EDWIN M. STANTON, Secretary of War.

On the 15th, 16th, and 17th, offensive operations were suspended. The roads had been made impassable by the rains.

It was at first supposed that the wounded in these terrible battles would be sent to Rappahannock Station, and thence by railroad to Washington. But the guerrillas of the enemy were so numerous in the rear of Gen. Grant's army as to prevent this arrangement. The trains were therefore withdrawn to Washington. At first hospitals were established on the field. But on Friday, the 6th, a number of slightly wounded men, who had been ordered to the rear, made their way to Fredericksburg under an escort of fourteen armed men. On entering the town, they were fired on by the citizens with such arms as could be obtained. They, however, succeeded in passing out and proceeded to Aquia Creek, where they were taken up by a gunboat and carried to Washington. Fredericksburg was occupied by a force of Gen. Grant, and hospitals established. Surgeons and nurses were immediately sent forward from Washington, Philadelphia, Harrisburg, Trenton, New York, and Albany, and other cities, to render assistance. The vessels in the employment of the Sanitary Commission were loaded with hospital supplies, and despatched with relief agents and nurses. The most severely wounded were retained at the hospitals in Fredericksburg, but others were transported to the Government hospitals in the northern cities. The Christian Commission had a large number of persons, with stores at hand, to afford relief. The Government also did every thing in its power to succor the wounded. The losses by the battles of the first eight days were variously estimated. The following is a statement which does not include the 9th corps:

	Killed.	Wounded.	Missing.	Total.
Second corps	1,100	7,000	1,400	9,500
Fifth corps	1,200	7,500	1,300	10,000
Sixth corps	1,000	6,000	1,200	8,200
Total	3,300	20,500	3,900	27,700

If the losses in the 9th corps are added to the above, and supposed to be in the same proportion, the entire loss will reach thirty-five thousand men.

On the 14th the first detachment of the hundred days' volunteers reached Washington. Many of them were sent into the army under Gen. Grant before their term of service expired.

CHAPTER XLI.

Strength of the Army of the Potomac—Coöperating Movements—Cavalry Raid to cut Gen. Lee's Communications—Advance of Gen. Averill in West Virginia—Advance of Gens. Crook and Sigel—Defeated by Gen. Breckinridge—Movement of Gen. Butler up the James—Attempts to cut the Railroads—Attack on Fort Darling—Expedition of Gen. Kautz.

The number of troops in the Army of the Potomac, when it crossed the Rapidan, has been variously stated at 120,000 and 150,000. The army consisted of four corps, each of which, with full ranks, would have numbered about forty thousand men. The ranks, however, were not full. No official statement of the numbers has been made. But there were various coöperating movements in which large forces were engaged. Gen. Butler moved up the Peninsula with a force between forty and fifty thousand strong, to cut the southern communications with Richmond. Another force, about fifteen thousand strong, moved up the Shenandoah valley, under Gen. Sigel, and from Western Virginia under other commanders, for the purpose of cutting the railroads running from the west and southwest to Richmond. It evidently must have been the opinion of Gen. Grant that the army of Gen. Meade would have been sufficient to cope with the forces of Gen. Lee. But, to secure ample provision for that object, the corps of Gen. Burnside was added as a reserve against all contingencies. After the first day's encounter, it was found necessary to order up this reserve in haste, and in the subsequent battles every brigade was fully employed as a part of the ordinary force. The subsequent and immense reënforcement required by Gen. Grant, after the battles at Spottsylvania Court House, served to show the unexpected great strength of the enemy in the field.

Several coöperating movements were in progress during the advance thus far of Gen. Grant. On Monday the 9th of May, the cavalry force connected with Gen. Grant's army commenced an advance to cut the communications between Gen. Lee's army and Richmond. At daylight the march began, with Gen. Merritt's 1st division in advance, Gen. Wilson's 3d division in the centre, and Gen. Gregg's 2d division in the rear. The movement was first toward Fredericksburg. At a distance of three miles from that city the column turned to the right and passed round the right flank of the enemy to the south of Spottsylvania Court House, on the road to Childsburgh, at which place a halt was made. Moving thence on the same road southerly and westerly, they forded the North Anna River at Anderson's bridge, two miles below Beaver Dam, about dusk. Gen. Custer's brigade took possession of the railroad station and captured a train of cars having on board three hundred and seventy-eight Union wounded and prisoners on their way to Richmond. These prisoners had been captured by the enemy during the late operations. The trains of cars, with the depot of supplies, were quickly set on fire, and two locomotives, three long trains, and a large quantity of bacon, meal, flour, and other supplies for Gen. Lee's army, were destroyed. The ties and bridges were burned, and the rails twisted so as to become useless. Meantime the enemy came up and attacked the flank and rear of the column, and captured many prisoners of the 6th Ohio. At night the column bivouacked on both sides of the North Anna.

Early on the next morning the enemy began to shell the camp, and the column moved south, the advance being annoyed by the enemy as it proceeded. The South Anna was crossed at Ground Squirrel bridge, and the bridge destroyed. The bivouac at night was near Goodall's, but the sharpshooters of the enemy caused some annoyance. Early on the next morning, the 11th, the 1st brigade of the 2d division under Gen. Davies was sent seven miles east to Ashland, on the Richmond and Fredericksburg Railroad. There the depot was burned and a considerable quantity of stores destroyed; also six miles of railroad, three culverts, two trestle bridges, several Government buildings, a locomotive, and three trains of cars. On the return the force was fired upon from the houses, and about thirty men were left in the enemy's hands. In the mean time the column had advanced and destroyed the track on the same road at Glen Allen station. The nearer it approached Richmond, the more opposition was made to its progress. At Yellow Tavern the cavalry of the enemy, concentrated under Gen. Stuart, made an attack on the advance under Gen. Devin. A sharp contest ensued, during which the brigades of Gens. Custer, and Gill, and Wilson came to his support, and the enemy were driven toward Ashland. Advancing still further toward Richmond, the picket defences were entered, and in a charge by Gen. Custer's brigade a hundred prisoners and a section of artillery were captured. In the conflict Gen. J. E. B. Stuart and Col. Pate, of the enemy, were fatally wounded. On the next morning the column turned toward Meadow Bridge, on the Chickahominy. It had been destroyed, but was rebuilt under a galling fire from the enemy, and crossed. The column next reached Mechanicsville and Coal Harbor, and encamped toward night at Gaines's Mill. On the next day the march was pursued by the way of Bottom bridge to Turkey Bend, where supplies were obtained from Gen. Butler.

Two movements were made by the forces in the Shenandoah valley and Western Virginia, which were designed to act against Lynchburg. The first, in May, miscarried, and the plan was afterwards altered. It was determined to carry it into effect in June. According to the original plan, at the time when Gen. Grant crossed the Rapidan, May 4th, Gen. Sigel was in motion upon Staunton, Gen. Crook upon Dublin depot, and Gen. Averill upon Wytheville, with the design, after destroying that town and the lead mines, to unite with Gen. Crook at Dublin depot, for a march toward Lynchburg in connection with Gen. Sigel. A movement by the Big Sandy, under Gen. Burbridge, upon Abingdon, and to prevent the advance of the enemy from the southwest, was not ready. The enemy, upon the advance of Gen. Sigel, ordered Gen. Breckinridge to move in haste further east, with all the troops he could collect, to oppose him, thus leaving Gens. Jenkins and McCausland, with a scattered force of fifteen hundred men, to resist Gen. Crook. Further to the southwest, on the line of the Lynchburg and Tennessee Railroad, the enemy happened to have a larger force than anywhere else on that route. Gen. W. E. Jones, in command, at once despatched Gen. Morgan further east. By making a forced march from Saltville, he arrived at Wytheville in advance of Gen. Averill. The latter, with a cavalry force of two thousand men, left camp at Charleston, Va., on May 1st, with three days' rations and two days' forage, and moved day and night over mountain paths until the evening of the 8th, when a cavalry force of the enemy was encountered near Jeffersonville, Va. This force was repelled, and a detour made by way of Princeton. On the 9th Gen. Averill left Tazewell Court House for Wytheville, in order to cut the railroad thirty miles lower down than it was to be cut by Gen. Crook. Cove Mountain Gap, near Wytheville, was reached on the 10th, and the enemy found to be in possession of the latter place. A conflict ensued, which, it is asserted by the enemy, resulted in the defeat of Gen. Averill, with a heavy loss in killed, wounded, prisoners, and horses, and prevented his reaching Dublin station and forming a junction with Gen. Crook before the latter had retired from that place. The following is Gen. Averill's address to his command, made some days later:

HEADQUARTERS CAVALRY DEPARTMENT, WEST VIRGINIA, Monday, May 23, 1864.

General Order No. 5:

The Brigadier-General commanding Cavalry Division, desires to express his sincere thanks to the officers and men of the division, for the uncomplaining fortitude with which they have endured the terrible vicissitudes incident to their recent march of three hundred and fifty miles, over mountains without roads, and the unwavering courage with which they attacked and held a superior force of the enemy near Wytheville, on the 10th, thereby enabling another command to accomplish its purposes without the opposition of overwhelming numbers. Your country will remember your heroism with gratitude; and the noble sacrifices and sufferings of our fallen comrades will be cherished forever in our memories. The 14th Pennsylvania and 1st Virginia cavalry first received the shock of battle, while the 2d and 3d Virginia cavalry and 34th Ohio infantry established a line which the enemy had reason to respect and remember. Great credit is due to the brigade commanders, Brig.-Gen. Duffie and Col. Schoonmaker, for the energy and skill they displayed. While the conduct of all was admirable and deserving the praise of the Brigadier-General commanding, he desires, without making invidious distinction, to express his high appreciation of the steady and skilful evolutions of the 2d Virginia cavalry, under Col. Powell, upon the field of battle. It was a dress parade, which continued without disorder, under a heavy fire, during four hours.

The purposes of the enemy were foiled by the engagement. The railroad was reached and destroyed, New River crossed, and the baffled columns of the enemy arrived in time to witness the destruction which all the energies of their superior force, even with artillery, failed to prevent.

(Signed) W. W. AVERILL,
Brigadier-General Commanding.

WILL RUMSEY, A. A. G.

Gen. Crook moved from Charleston, Va., at the same time with Gen. Averill. His object was to strike the Virginia and Tennessee Railroad at Dublin Station. His force consisted of the 23d, 34th, and 36th Ohio, forming the first brigade; the 12th, 91st Ohio, 9th and 14th Virginia, forming the second brigade; the 3d and 4th Pennsylvania Reserves, 11th and 15th Virginia, forming the 3d brigade. He proceeded without opposition nearly to Princeton, where two companies of the enemy, one of cavalry and one of infantry, were encountered and driven off. Near the southwestern base of Lloyd's Mountain, about four miles from Dublin depot, a more considerable force of the enemy was found. These were under the command of Gen. Jenkins. When he was killed, Gen. McCausland took the command.

After some skirmishing and manœuvring for a position, the enemy were attacked in front and flank and driven through Dublin to New River bridge. The Union loss was one hundred and twenty-six killed and five hundred and eighty-five wounded; and that of the enemy was severe, but unknown. On the next day an attack was made on the enemy's position near the bridge, and it was destroyed. The expedition proceeded as far as Newberne, on the Virginia and Tennessee Railroad, ninety-nine miles from Bristol, destroying the railroad for some distance. The resistance of the enemy, with the approach of a strong force under Gen. Morgan, caused Gen. Crook to abandon the design of the expedition against Lynchburg and withdraw to Meadow Bluff, in Greenbrier County.

The force in the Shenandoah valley, numbering about fifteen thousand men, was placed under the command of Gen. Sigel. He advanced to the vicinity of New Market, about fifty miles from Winchester, on the west side of the Masanuttan range of mountains, and nearly midway between Mount Jackson and Harrisonburg. His command was designed to coöperate with Gen. Grant, as before mentioned, up the Shenandoah valley, and occupy Gordonsville and Lynchburg, and thus destroy the western communication of Gen. Lee s army, and aid to isolate Richmond.

On the 13th of May Gen. Sigel's advance encountered the advance of Gen. Breckinridge. Some skirmishing ensued, which was renewed on the next day, and also on Sunday. Gen. Sigel, however, continued to advance, and brought a part of his forces into position, one division still being in the rear. About 3 P. M. the enemy moved to attack. A hot contest ensued, which resulted in the defeat of Gen. Sigel, with a loss of a thousand stand of small arms, six pieces of artillery, and seven hundred men. The loss of the enemy was also large. Gen. Sigel fell back in disorder, abandoning his hospitals, and destroying a portion of his train, and retreated to Cedar Creek, near Strasburg. The enemy failed to pursue in force. These results to Gens. Averill, Crook, and Sigel, caused a suspension of that part of the plan of Gen. Grant which consisted in destroying the Virginia and Tennessee Railroad, and the occupation of Lynchburg.

The next important movement in coöperation with Gen. Grant, was made on the southeast side of Richmond, from Fortress Monroe up the James River. The 18th corps, under Maj.-Gen. M. F. Smith, and the 10th corps, under Maj.-Gen. Q. A. Gilmore, composed the military force of the movement, under the command of Maj.-Gen. B. F. Butler. These forces were concentrated at Yorktown and Gloucester as if designed for a movement up the York River. At the same time a brigade under Col. S. F. Alford, 3d New York, landed at West Point, up the York River, and commenced building the wharves, &c. On the 4th of May orders to move were issued, and the troops embarked on board the transports. After dark on the 5th, the vessels began to move down the York River, and up the James River, preceded by three army gunboats under command of Brig.-Gen. Graham; by the double-enders Eutaw, Mackinaw, and Osceola; four monitors, the Tecumseh, Canonicus, Saugus, Onondaga, and the iron-clad Atlanta, and by the smaller gunboats Commodore Morris, Hunchback, Commodore Jones, Dawn, Delaware, Putnam, and Sheshonee.

As the fleet proceeded up the James River, a regiment of negro troops, under Gen. Wild, were landed at Wilson's Wharf, on the north bank, below Charles City Court House. This was done for the purpose of preventing the interruption of water communication. At Fort Powhatan Landing, a little above on the south bank of the river, two regiments of the same brigade were landed for the same object. At City Point, the division of Gen. Hinks, with some other troops, and a battery were landed. At this place the flag of truce boat was lying with four hundred and fifty prisoners brought up on the previous day for exchange. The remainder of the force proceeded up the river, and landed on the south bank at Bermuda Hundred, which is three or four miles above

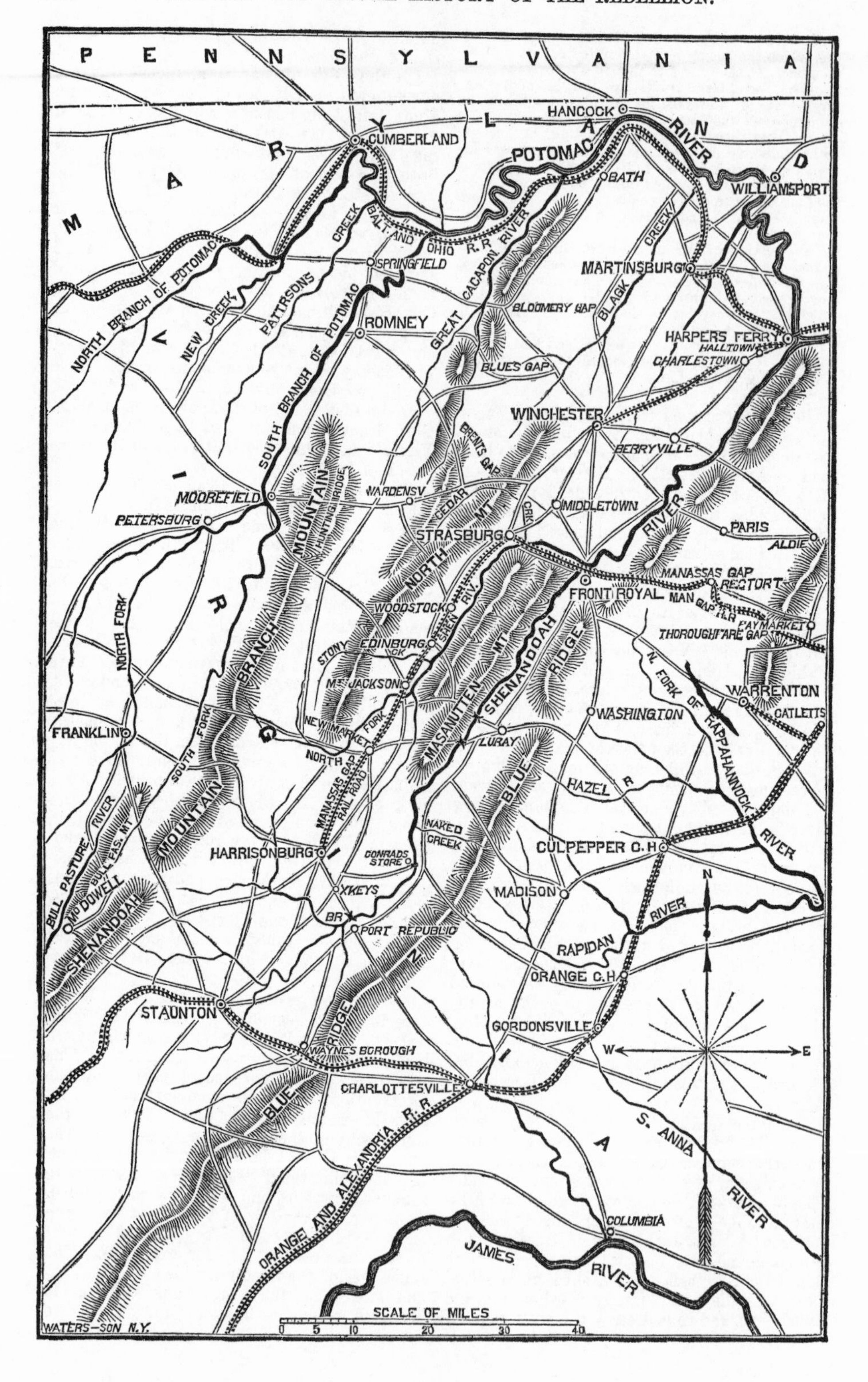
PENNSYLVANIA
MARYLAND
VIRGINIA
HANCOCK
CUMBERLAND
POTOMAC RIVER
BATH
WILLIAMSPORT
BALT. AND OHIO R.R.
CREEK
SPRINGFIELD
CACAPON RIVER
GREAT
MARTINSBURG
BLACK CREEK
NORTH BRANCH OF POTOMAC
NEW CREEK
PATTERSONS CREEK
SOUTH BRANCH OF POTOMAC
ROMNEY
BLOOMERY GAP
HARPERS FERRY
HALLTOWN
CHARLESTOWN
BLUES GAP
WINCHESTER
BRENTS GAP
BERRYVILLE
MOOREFIELD
PETERSBURG
MOUNTAIN
HUNTING RIDGE
WARDENSV
CEDAR CRK
MIDDLETOWN
STRASBURG
NORTH MT
PARIS
ALDIE
MANASSAS GAP
RECTORT
FRONT ROYAL
MAN GAP R.R.
HAYMARKET
THOROUGHFARE GAP
WOODSTOCK
N. SHEN. RIV.
SHENANDOAH
RIDGE
NORTH FORK
BRANCH
STONY CK
EDINBURG
MT JACKSON
MASANUTTEN MT
N. FORK OF RAPPAHANNOCK
WARRENTON
CATLETTS
WASHINGTON
FRANKLIN
SOUTH FORK
NEW MARKET
NORTH FORK
LURAY
BLUE
HAZEL R
MANASSAS GAP RAIL ROAD
RIVER
BULL PASTURE RIVER
BULL PAS. MT
MOUNTAIN
NAKED CREEK
HARRISONBURG
CONRADS STORE
CULPEPPER C.H
MADISON
XKEYS
MC DOWELL
SHENANDOAH
BR
PORT REPUBLIC
RAPIDAN RIVER
ORANGE C.H
STAUNTON
GORDONSVILLE
WAYNESBOROUGH
CHARLOTTESVILLE
BLUE RIDGE
ORANGE AND ALEXANDRIA R.R
S. ANNA RIVER
N
W
E
COLUMBIA
JAMES RIVER
SCALE OF MILES
0 5 10 20 30 40
WATERS—SON N.Y.

the mouth of the Appomattox River. Immediately upon landing, the troops intrenched themselves, with the gunboats covering their flank on the water. On the same day, Gen. Butler sent the following despatch relative to his proceedings to Gen. Grant:

OFF CITY POINT, VA., May 5, 1864.

Lieutenant-General Grant, Commanding Armies of the United States, Washington, D. C.:

We have seized Wilson's Wharf Landing. A brigade of Wild's colored troops are there. At Fort Powhatan Landing two regiments of the same brigade have landed. At City Point Hinks' division, with the remaining troops and battery, have landed. The remainder of both the 18th and 10th army corps are being landed at Bermuda Hundred, above the Appomattox.

No opposition experienced thus far. The movement was apparently a complete surprise. Both army corps left Yorktown during last night. The Monitors are all over the bar at Harrison's Landing and above City Point. The operations of the fleet have been conducted to-day with energy and success. Gens. Smith and Gilmore are pushing the landing of the men. Gen. Graham, with the army gunboats, led the advance during the night, capturing the signal station of the rebels.

Col. West, with eighteen hundred cavalry, made several demonstrations from Williamsburg yesterday morning. Gen. Kautz left Suffolk this morning, with his cavalry, for the service indicated during the conference with the Lieutenant-General.

The New York, flag of truce boat, was found lying at the wharf, with four hundred prisoners, whom she had not time to deliver. She went up yesterday morning.

We are landing troops during the night—a hazardous service in the face of the enemy.

BENJ. F. BUTLER, Maj.-Gen. Commanding.
A. F. PUFFER, Captain and A. D. C.

Gen. Kautz, above mentioned, left Suffolk on the 5th, and forcing a passage over the Black Water, advanced to Stony Creek, on the Weldon and Petersburg Railroad, and burned the bridge over that stream. A part of the force of Gen. Beauregard moving from Charleston to Richmond, had previously crossed over, and contested the further progress of Gen. Kautz, who then moved through Surry and Prince George counties to City Point, which he reached on the 8th.

On the 5th, also, Col. West, with two regiments of cavalry—the 1st and 2d colored—made a demonstration on Williamsburg, above Yorktown, on the Peninsula. He advanced to the Pamunkey River, stopping at the White House, and returned to Williamsburg on the next night. On the 7th he advanced over nearly the same ground again, but met with more opposition, than on his previous expedition. Subsequently his force was embarked on transports, and landed at Bermuda Hundred.

On the 6th, Gen. Butler caused reconnoissances to be made of the position of the enemy. On the 7th, an expedition consisting of five brigades under Brig.-Gen. Brooks was sent forward for the purpose of cutting the Petersburg and Richmond Railroad. When within two miles of the railroad, the cavalry advance came on the enemy in a strong position, from which they opened fire upon the mounted rifles. The cavalry fell back to the infantry line, which deployed as skirmishers, and slowly advanced with a strong support in line of battle. The enemy were now steadily driven, with some loss to both sides, back to their main line in front of the railroad. Here a sharp contest took place, during which some of the railroad was torn up, and a railroad bridge, crossing one of the tributaries of the Appomattox, was set on fire and totally consumed. The increase of the force of the enemy finally compelled Gen. Brooks to retire, leaving some of his dead and wounded on the field, and with an estimated loss of two hundred and fifty.

At the same time when Gen. Brooks' main column started, a brigade under Gen. Heckman, with Belger's Rhode Island battery, moved out on another road, and meeting a force of the enemy, drove them back on the railroad, but were unable to penetrate far.

The Petersburg and Weldon Railroad was supposed to be an important route by which supplies were brought to Richmond. For the purpose of disabling this line more effectually, another advance was made on the 9th.

Three divisions from the 10th corps, under Gens. Terry, Ames, and Turner, and two from the 18th, under Gens. Weitzel and Wistar, moved from camp at daylight, and reached the railroad at four points without opposition. Gen. Terry's division occupied Chester station, about fourteen miles from Richmond, and destroyed the track. Gen. Turner moved on his left toward Petersburg, until he came up with Gen. Ames' division, each destroying the road. Four miles was thus finished before noon, and the column began to move toward Petersburg, the division of Gen. Weitzel leading the advance. The enemy were met near Swift Creek. A desultory skirmish began, which was continued until the line of battle was formed and pushed forward. The fire on both sides then increased, and artillery was brought into action. Gen. Ames' division formed on the left, then Gens. Weitzel's, Turner, and Terry in the order named. The enemy were steadily driven back, with considerable loss on both sides. At night the enemy had fallen back to their batteries across the creek, and the skirmishers confronted each other on opposite sides. During the night the enemy formed in a column, and advanced about one o'clock, either to test the strength of the pickets, and to determine if the force had been withdrawn, or to capture a battery. The pickets on their approach fell back to the main line; and as they came well up, a destructive fire of musketry was opened upon them. Three charges were thus made in the dark, and repulsed, when the enemy withdrew, leaving sixty dead on the field. In the morning they made an attack upon the right flank, for the purpose of turning it, but without success. In the afternoon a similar attack was made on the left, which was repulsed with some loss on both sides. At night the forces had returned to their original

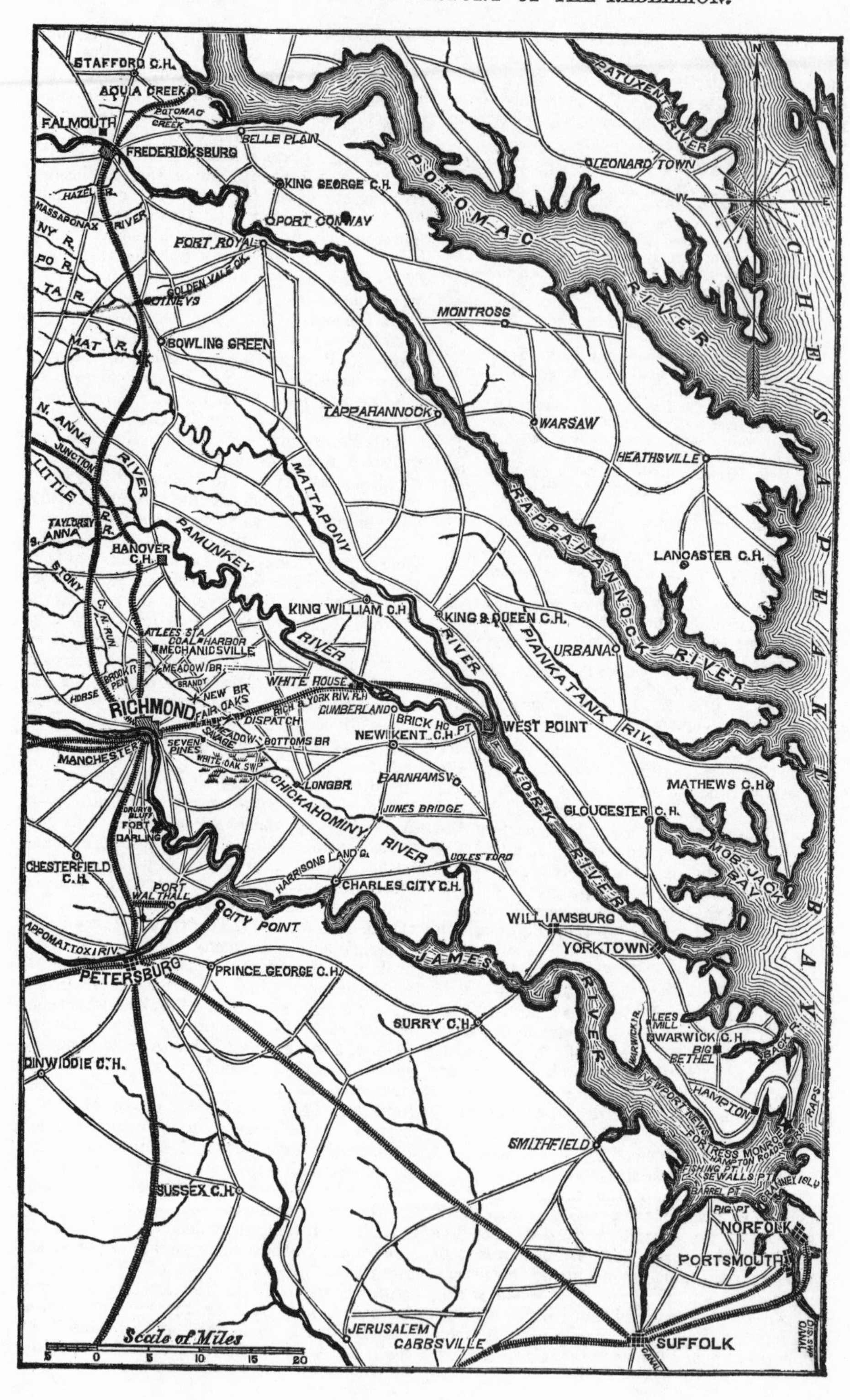
STAFFORD C.H.
AQUIA CREEK
POTOMAC CREEK
FALMOUTH
FREDERICKSBURG
BELLE PLAIN
LEONARD TOWN
PATUXENT RIVER
POTOMAC RIVER
KING GEORGE C.H.
PORT CONWAY
PORT ROYAL
HAZEL R.
MASSAPONAX RIVER
NY R.
PO R.
TA R.
GOLDEN VALE CK.
GUINEYS
MONTROSS
MAT R.
BOWLING GREEN
TAPPAHANNOCK
WARSAW
N. ANNA RIVER
JUNCTION
LITTLE R.
TAYLORSV
S. ANNA
HANOVER C.H.
STONY
PAMUNKEY
MATTAPONY
RAPPAHANNOCK RIVER
HEATHSVILLE
LANCASTER C.H.
CHESAPEAKE BAY
KING WILLIAM C.H.
KING & QUEEN C.H.
PIANKATANK RIV.
URBANA
ATLEES STA.
COAL HARBOR
MECHANICSVILLE
MEADOW BR.
BRANDY
NEW BR.
HORSE
RICHMOND
FAIR OAKS
DISPATCH
RICH & YORK RIV. R.R.
WHITE HOUSE
CUMBERLAND
BRICK HO. PT.
WEST POINT
RIVER
SEVEN PINES
SAVAGE
MEADOW
BOTTOMS BR.
NEW KENT C.H.
MANCHESTER
WHITE OAK SWP.
LONG BR.
BARNHAMSV.
CHICKAHOMINY RIVER
JONES BRIDGE
MATHEWS C.H.
GLOUCESTER C.H.
YORK RIVER
DRURYS BLUFF
FORT DARLING
CHESTERFIELD C.H.
HARRISONS LAND'G.
CHARLES CITY C.H.
MOB JACK BAY
PORT WALTHALL
CITY POINT
WILLIAMSBURG
YORKTOWN
APPOMATTOX RIV.
PETERSBURG
PRINCE GEORGE C.H.
JAMES RIVER
SURRY C.H.
LEES MILL
WARWICK R.
WARWICK C.H.
BIG BETHEL
BACK R.
DINWIDDIE C.H.
NEWPORT NEWS
HAMPTON
RIP RAPS
SMITHFIELD
FORTRESS MONROE
HAMPTON ROADS
FISHING PT.
SEWALLS PT.
CRANEY ISL'D.
BARREL PT.
PIG PT.
SUSSEX C.H.
NORFOLK
PORTSMOUTH
JERUSALEM
CARRSVILLE
SUFFOLK
CANAL
DIS. SWP. CANAL
Scale of Miles
5 0 5 10 15 20

position. The 11th was a day of quiet and rest to the army save that portion engaged in strengthening the intrenchments.

On Thursday, the 12th, a heavy force from both corps was sent out, under Gens. Gillmore and Smith, and at the same time an expedition of cavalry, under Gen. Kautz, for the purpose of cutting the railroad communication between Richmond and Danville. Leaving a sufficient force under Gen. Ames to watch the enemy at Petersburg, Gen. Gillmore advanced on the left up the railroad toward Chester station and Richmond. Gen. Smith, with the 18th corps and a division of the 10th, advanced in the same direction on the right, up the turnpike between the railroad and the James River. A little above Werbottom church the skirmishers in advance met the enemy and drove them back a mile or more. They then made a determined stand in a strong position, and a sharp engagement ensued. Finally the enemy retired slowly to a new position, where they again made a stand, and were again driven from it. The skirmishing continued until dark, when the command of Gen. Smith had advanced to Proctor's Creek, within about three miles of Fort Darling, and within sight of that work. The weather during the day was hot and sultry, and a number of cases of sunstroke occurred.

Meanwhile Gen. Gillmore moved from his position to Chester Junction, and thence up the railroad toward Richmond, reaching Chesterfield Court House, on the enemy's right, without any real opposition. Continuing his advance, and diverging still further to the right, he reached a formidable earthwork, stretching from west of the railroad across to the James River, which was strongly constructed, and well supplied with embrasures for artillery. This proved to be the outer line of defence about Fort Darling. The movement of Gen. Smith had caused the enemy to concentrate in his front, so that no heavy force appeared before Gen. Gillmore. Throwing forward the 24th Massachusetts and 10th Connecticut as skirmishers, with some sharpshooters and a battery or two in position to annoy the enemy and occupy his attention, Gen. Gillmore sent the brigade of Col. Hawley through the woods on the right, which surprised the enemy and entered the right flank of the work in the rear. The enemy made a sharp resistance, but were driven to the rear by the brigade of Col. White advancing and occupying the line. Finding their position turned by this movement, the enemy on the next morning—Saturday, the 14th—under cover of a vigorous demonstration, abandoned the whole line, and withdrew to the second, a stronger line of works, about three-fourths of a mile distant.

A despatch of Gen. Butler on the morning of the 14th says:

> We are still before the base of the enemy's works at Drury's Bluff, Fort Darling. The enemy are here in force. Gen. Gillmore, by a flank movement with a portion of his corps and a brigade of the 18th corps, assaulted and took the enemy's works on their right. It was gallantly done. The troops behaved finely. We held our lines during the night, and shall move this morning.

Two hours later he added:

> Gen. Smith carried the enemy's first line on the right this morning at 8 A. M. Loss small. The enemy have retired into three square redoubts, upon which we are now bringing our artillery to bear with effect.

The redoubts into which the enemy had retired commanded the outer line of their defences, and it was necessary that Gen. Butler should obtain possession of these to enable him to secure his position. His artillery was therefore brought to bear upon them, and with the aid of the sharpshooters the enemy's guns were silenced. About 9 P. M. the enemy attempted to advance on Gen. Butler's line near the Petersburg turnpike, but after a short engagement they withdrew within their work. On the next day, at noon, they again advanced, and attacked Gen. Heckman's brigade; a contest with musketry ensued, which continued for four hours, when they withdrew within their works. On the next morning, Monday, May 16th, under cover of a thick fog, the enemy made an attack on the line of Gen. Butler. The attack was made on the right, with cavalry, artillery, and infantry. The extreme right next the James River was held by Gen. Heckman's brigade. Next the river were two squadrons of colored cavalry, then came the 9th New Jersey infantry, then the 23d Massachusetts, then the 25th and 27th Massachusetts, all of Heckman's brigade, of Weitzel's division, of Gen. Smith's corps. Gen. Gillmore's corps held the left and left centre. The line of battle was the fortifications, except on the extreme right, where they did not extend down to the river. Prominent among the batteries on the right was battery E of the 3d New York artillery, of twenty-pounder Parrotts, and the 1st Rhode Island battery. On the right, in reserve, Col. Drake's brigade of the 10th corps was temporarily posted. A narrow belt of timber screened the reserves from the view of the enemy on the right. The advance of the enemy reached the rear of the 9th New Jersey before the attack was made. Gen. Heckman finding he could not hold his position, began to fall back. The enemy, however, charged upon him in overwhelming numbers, and his force was broken and driven from the field, and he was made a prisoner. At the same time a force of the enemy moved down the turnpike, and attempted to surprise Ashby's battery of twenty-pounder Parrott's. Most of the guns were saved, but the loss was heavy in men. The Rhode Island battery also lost one gun. Having forced back the right, a heavy attack was made on the entire line of the 18th corps, with feints along the line of the 10th corps; and the entire right was forced back some distance after several hours of severe and sanguinary conflict. The loss was severe on both sides in killed and wounded, and some prisoners were taken. After thus gaining a portion of their first line of intrenchments, the enemy massed their forces on the 10th corps to drive it back. Repeated charges were made, which were desperately resisted and driven back at all points. Finally, ceasing their efforts to force the position of the 10th corps, and leaving their dead and wounded on the field before its line, the enemy again massed on Gen. Smith's front and attacked his left. Gen. Gillmore immediately ordered Gen. Turner to attack the enemy on their flank, and also ordered Gen. Terry to support him. Gen. Turner's attack had hardly commenced, before Gen. Gillmore was ordered by Gen. Butler to retire and strengthen Gen. Smith's corps by forming in his rear. The troops fell back slowly and in order, repulsing every attempt of the enemy to quicken their movements, until they ceased to follow up and fell back to their first line of intrenchments. At half-past two o'clock the fighting, which had been going on with more or less violence along the whole line, ceased, and preparations were made by Gen. Butler to draw off his forces from the field and return to his intrenchments. The artillery was sent to the rear, except a section to cover the rear guard. The ambulances, loaded with wounded, and the supply trains, were despatched to the rear, and finally the entire army fell back. The enemy did not pursue. During the action of the morning, a brigade of the enemy attacked the force guarding the extreme left on the roads from Petersburg under Col. Dobbs, and after a sharp struggle drove him back toward Gen. Butler's intrenchments, but finally gave up the pursuit. The loss of Gen. Butler was estimated at twenty-five hundred. That of the enemy was severe, but the amount unknown.

The despatch relative to the above operations was as follows:

WAR DEPARTMENT, WASHINGTON, May 17, 9 P. M.

Major-General Dix:

Despatches from Gen. Butler, just received, report the success of his expedition under Gen. Kautz, to cut the Danville road and destroy the iron bridge across the Appomattox.

On Monday morning the enemy in force, under cover of a thick fog, made an attack upon Smith's line, and forced it back in some confusion and with considerable loss. But as soon as the fog lifted, Gen. Smith reëstablished his lines, and the enemy was driven back to his original lines.

EDWIN M. STANTON, Secretary of War.

The cavalry expedition under Gen. Kautz returned on the 17th. On the night of the day on which he started, Gen. Kautz reached Midlothian coal-pits, where he remained an hour. No injury was done to public property here, but a considerable amount of private property was destroyed. Thence he proceeded to Coalfield station, where he arrived between 10 and 11 o'clock. The depot building and water-tank here were destroyed, the telegraph wire torn down, and some hundred feet of the railroad track ripped up. Thence he advanced at daylight upon Powhatan station, which was reached at 8 A. M. The railroad was torn up, and the depot and water-tank destroyed. An advance was next made to destroy the iron bridge at Mattaox station. This was found to be too strongly guarded by the enemy, and the column turned to the right and reached Goode's bridge about 4 P. M. This bridge had been partly destroyed, but was repaired by Gen. Kautz, who pushed on and reached Chula station at 10 P. M. The enemy sent a locomotive from Mattaox to reconnoitre, which was captured and destroyed. On the morning of the 14th the column faced about and recrossed Goode's bridge, approaching Mattaox. Here a fight took place with the enemy, who were in a strong position, and after a loss of about thirty Gen. Kautz retired. The column now moved to the south, and crossed the Appomattox at Devil's bridge, which they were compelled to rebuild, reaching Finney Mill at 12 M. Here the 5th Pennsylvania, under command of Maj. Kleinz, was sent to the left near to Mansboro', on the road to Petersburg, to convey the impression that Gen. Kautz was about to move on that point. The march was then resumed, and, arriving within six miles of the Petersburg and Lynchburg road, Gen. Spear was sent with his brigade to destroy the road at Wilson's station, while the main column moved on to Welville, where they arrived at about 4 P. M. After waiting patiently until 5 P. M. for a train that was due at that hour from Petersburg, but which did not come, Gen. Spear destroyed the railroad property at Wilson's, and, moving up the road, rejoined Gen. Kautz at Wellville, just as the latter had finished tearing up the track and burning the depot.

The column arrived at Black's and White's at 10 P. M., and found large supplies of forage and rations. These were dealt out with a liberal hand to the exhausted men and horses: and the track and other railroad and government property having been destroyed, the force moved a few miles further on, and bivouacked at 2 A. M.

On the 15th, at 7 A. M., the column set out for Lawrenceville, and after a long march, passing through Jonesborough and Edmonds, arrived at that place at dusk. A large amount of property was destroyed here, and large quantities of corn and bacon distributed to the men. At daylight the march was resumed with the intention of striking the Petersburg road at Hickford. Finding a strong force of the enemy at Stony Point ready to receive him, Gen. Kautz turned directly north. After marching eight or ten miles, the advance came to a stand in the centre of an immense pine forest, at a loss how to proceed. The road to the right was followed, and Jarrett's station reached at 5 P. M. The track of the railroad was again torn up, and the troops marched to Freeman's bridge, arriving about midnight. Thence they moved to Belcher's Mills, Heart's station, and City Point.

The naval part of the forces had been chiefly employed in keeping the river open to navigation, and in removing the obstruction and torpedoes. In order to remove torpedoes, the shore near where they were placed was first shelled by the gunboats, to drive away any body of the enemy. A boat with a complement of men was then sent ashore to do the work. At the first place of landing, opposite Turkey Bend, they captured one large torpedo. The next landing was made under the bluff above which stands the mansion of Gen. Pickett, where they captured six more of the same size, making seven in all. There was great difficulty in cutting the strings of the torpedoes, as they led up the bluff, where the person exploding them is generally stationed. Great coolness and discretion had to be used in handling them. The officers waded up to their arm-pits in the water to get at them, which was very dangerous, as they knew not but that at any moment the string might be pulled from above and the torpedo exploded. All they had to depend upon to prevent this was the boat's crew, stationed on the bluff as sharpshooters, Each of the torpedoes contained about seventy-five pounds of powder. They were taken out of the stream, and, after considerable difficulty, successfully emptied of their contents.

On the 6th one of the smaller gunboats, Com. Jones, was destroyed by a torpedo. About fifty of the crew were killed and wounded. This was an instance of the most complete destruction by a submarine battery to which any vessel has been subjected, her annihilation being utter and instantaneous. The torpedo was fired amidships and directly under her, upraising the centre of the ship, which burst asunder as the explosion rent the air; and then, amid a cloud of smoke and steam, the body of her hull and upper works, rent into a thousand pieces, and, worst of all, numbers of her unfortunate crew, were propelled into the air, and fell like a shower of missiles from the crater of a volcano. When the smoke drifted from the scene the sunken framework and ribs of the destroyed vessel were all that remained, except innumerable splintered relics of the wreck, which covered the waters around the fatal spot. Two other boats, the Sheshonee and the Brewster, were destroyed by an explosion, not, however, of a torpedo.

The forces of Gen. Butler reached their intrenchments on Monday night, the 16th. On the next day scouts reported that two heavy columns of the enemy, with large trains, were passing down the turnpike to Petersburg. It was supposed that the trains were either carrying supplies for the moving column, or were sent to Petersburg to be loaded with supplies for Gen. Lee's army, or the forces at Richmond. The capture or destruction of any portion of them, therefore, appeared to be desirable. Accordingly, about 9, P. M., Gen. Foster, chief of Gen. Gillmore's staff, with a body of cavalry and nfantry, moved quietly out to the picket lines, and a few hundred yards beyond. There he stationed pickets on different roads to guard against an attempt to cut him off, and began to move up the road leading to the turnpike. In a moment or two he encountered the pickets of the enemy, and attempting to capture them received a heavy fire from the pickets and a force of the enemy behind them. Finding they were in too great force he made an attack on another portion of the line, but with the same result. He then returned to camp. This existence of the enemy in so large a force in his front caused Gen. Butler to make extraordinary exertions to complete other works on his defences. On the river he was covered by the gunboats under Rear-Admiral S. P. Lee.

At daylight on the 18th the enemy appeared and drove back the picket line within a few hundred yards of the breastworks. But their advance was checked after a heavy skirmish. They then commenced throwing up works directly in front of Gen. Butler's lines, either for the purpose of laying siege to his position, or to prevent him from reaching again the railroad to destroy it. On Thursday, the 19th, they put two or three light batteries in position and commenced vigorously shelling the lines. No assault was made, and their guns finally became silent during the remainder of the day. At midnight, however, they advanced in force on the pickets along nearly the entire line. The sharp fire of the pickets retarded their advance, but they crowded forward and the reserves were ordered up by Gen. Butler. A sharp fight ensued which lasted nearly an hour, when the enemy retired with considerable loss. At daylight on the 20th they began to shell the lines and camps, and to push the pickets strongly. The pickets of Gen. Ames were driven back from the rifle-pits thrown up on the picket line, and Gen. Terry's line was forced back under a heavy fire. The position thus obtained by the enemy was too important to be given up. A brigade, under Col. Howell, was therefore sent to retake the rifle-pits and establish a firm line there. This was accomplished after heavy fighting, with considerable loss on both sides. The attack was renewed again on the next day, but no advantage was gained by the enemy. Meantime the work on the fortifications of Gen. Butler was continued night and day, and all cover for the enemy's sharpshooters cleared away. Thus the failure of the expedition on the west to destroy the Virginia and Tennessee Railroad, and occupy Lynchburg, and the failure of Gen. Butler to capture and occupy Petersburg, enabled the enemy to concentrate against Gen. Grant. The forces of Gen. Breckinridge were immediately added to the army of Gen. Lee, and Richmond was held by the troops of Gen. Beauregard, which had opposed Gen. Butler. Gen. Grant, on the other hand, proceeded to organize new expeditions against Lynchburg, putting Gen. Hunter in the place of Gen. Sigel, and pressed forward himself to capture Petersburg.

CHAPTER XLII.

Concentration of Troops under Gen. Lee—Attempt to turn the Right of Gen Grant's Line—New Movement to the Left—Gen. Grant reaches the North Anna—Position of the Armies—Gen. Grant crosses the Pamunkey—Reënforcements from Gen. Butler—Battle at Coal Harbor—Failure of the attempt to push the Enemy across the Chickahominy—Crossing the James—Movement of Gen. Butler on Petersburg—Failure—Other Movements—Gen. Grant before Petersburg—Condition of the Army.

THE army of Gen. Grant had remained inactive during the 16th, 17th, and 18th, before Spottsylvania. On the afternoon of the 18th the enemy in force made an effort to turn the right of Gen. Grant's line. It was held by some regiments of heavy artillery, acting as infantry, comprising the 1st Massachusetts, 15th, 2d, 6th, and a battalion of the 4th New York, all under Col. Kitchings, who fell back across an open field under cover of some woods. Repeated attempts were made by the enemy to drive them further, but without success. Subsequently a charge was made, driving the enemy back across the open field, which was held. Night put an end to the conflict. The loss of Col. Kitchings was about eleven hundred men. About four hundred of the enemy were made prisoners.

The following is the despatch of the War Department:

WAR DEPARTMENT, WASHINGTON, May 20—6:30 P. M.

Major-General Dix:

This afternoon we have despatches dated at half-past eight this morning, from Gen. Grant.

Last evening an effort was made by Ewell's corps to turn our right. They were promptly repulsed by Birney's and Tyler's divisions, and some of Warren's troops that were on the extreme right. About three hundred prisoners fell into our hands, besides many killed and wounded. Our loss foots up a little over six hundred wounded and one hundred and fifty killed and missing.

General Grant says that probably our killed and missing are over-estimated.

Over twenty-five thousand veteran reënforcements have been forwarded to Gen. Grant. The condition of the army and his contemplated operations are entirely satisfactory. The army is abundantly supplied.

Major-General Hunter has been placed in command of the Department of West Virginia, including the Shenandoah valley.

On the night of the 20th the troops were moving all night to new positions; and on the next morning the general headquarters were broken up, and nearly the whole army was in motion. At 12 o'clock, P. M., of the 20th the cavalry left their camp in the woods near Massaponax Church, and advanced toward Guineas' station, on the Richmond and Fredericksburg Railroad. The pickets of the enemy, firing only a few shots, withdrew before the advance until they reached Guineas' bridge on the river Ny, a short distance from the station. Here an inclination to make a stand and oppose the advance was shown. They were, however, soon driven from the bridge. At Downer's bridge another stand was made, and the position held for some time. At Bowling Green the enemy made no stand, but assembled at Milford station in considerable force. On an eminence a little to the left of the station the enemy had mounted a battery, and thrown up some rifle-pits. A battery accompanying the cavalry was put into position, and occupied the enemy whilst a flank movement to the left was made. This was executed with success, and the enemy made a hasty retreat across the Mattapony. Six officers and sixty-six soldiers were surprised and captured. Milford station had been, until the previous day, the base for supplies to the army under Gen. Lee. But obtaining information of the contemplated movement, the enemy had removed their stores before the arrival of the cavalry.

Soon after midnight on the night of the 20th the 2d corps moved from its position on the Ny, near Spottsylvania Court House, and followed the road thus opened by the cavalry. Nothing unusual occurred during the march to Bowling Green. The corps then crossed the Mattapony at Milford bridge, and about a mile from the river Gen. Hancock halted his column and formed a line of battle in a commanding position on the crest of a range of hills. The enemy's cavalry followed close in the rear during the march and picked up the stragglers.

At six o'clock on the morning of the 21st the 5th corps, under Gen. Warren, left the position occupied by them and pushed on in the rear of Gen. Hancock. As the column approached the bridge across the Mattapony at 4 P. M., it was delayed by a detachment of the enemy's cavalry posted in the woods that skirt the river on both sides of the road. They were soon driven out with a slight loss. During the day the whole army was in motion. The weather had become fine and the roads well settled. On Sunday, the 22d, the following despatch was sent from the War Department:

WAR DEPARTMENT, WASHINGTON, May 23—10 P. M.

Major-General Dix:

On Friday evening General Grant commenced a movement for the purpose of compelling Lee to abandon his position at Spottsylvania. It has thus far progressed successfully.

Longstreet's corps started south at one o'clock Friday night, an hour and a half after Hancock moved. Ewell's corps followed Longstreet's last night.

The indications are that the rebel army has fallen back behind the North Anna. Hoke's brigade has joined Lee.

The movement of General Grant has thus far been

accomplished without any severe engagement or serious interruption.

We now occupy Guineas' station, Milford station, and south of the Mattapony on that line. No despatches have been received to-day from General Butler.

Despatches from Kingston, Ga., state that General Sherman's forces are resting and replenishing their supplies. EDWIN M. STANTON,
Secretary of War.

On the next morning the following additional despatch was sent from the Department:

WASHINGTON, May 23, 1864.

Major-General Dix:

We have no official reports since my last telegram from General Grant or General Butler.

Official reports of this Department show that within eight days after the great battle at Spottsylvania Court House many thousand veteran troops have been forwarded to General Grant.

The whole army has been amply supplied with full rations and subsistence.

Upwards of twenty thousand sick and wounded have been transported from the fields of battle to the Washington hospitals and placed under surgical care.

Over eight thousand prisoners have been transported from the field to prison depots, and large amounts of artillery and other implements of an active campaign brought away.

Several thousand fresh cavalry horses have been forwarded to the army, and the grand Army of the Potomac is now fully as strong in numbers, and better equipped, supplied, and furnished, than when the campaign opened.

Several thousand reënforcements have also been forwarded to other armies in the field, and ample supplies to all.

During the same time over thirty thousand volunteers for a hundred days have been mustered into the service, clothed, armed, equipped, and transported to their respective positions.

This statement is due to the chiefs of the army staff and bureaux, and their respective corps, to whom the credit belongs.

EDWIN M. STANTON, Secretary of War.

The 9th corps, under Gen. Burnside, began to move on the 21st. Early in the afternoon orders were given to leave the line of works thrown up in their front. The movement was covered by a sortie of Gen. Ledlie's brigade of Gen. Crittenden's division, who deployed in front in skirmish line with two regiments held in reserve. The enemy were driven some distance toward Spottsylvania Court House. Meanwhile the rest of the corps moved out of the works, and by night were far on the road. The march was kept up steadily until eleven o'clock, when a short halt was ordered.

Finding the enemy in force on the road proposed, the route was abandoned. The column retrograded a few miles on the Richmond and Fredericksburg telegraph road, and thence moved to the southeast. At 9 o'clock on the next morning a halt of an hour was made, and then the march was resumed, crossing the railroad near Guineas' station, and arriving at Bowling Green at 4 P. M. On the next morning the march was continued to Milford station.

The 6th corps moved after the 9th, and filed into the intrenchments as vacated by the 9th. The sortie of Gen. Ledlie had rallied the enemy on their main line, and they advanced in considerable force upon the 6th corps, but were met with such a fire as caused them to retreat with severe loss. Subsequently it followed the route of the 5th corps. On the 22d the entire army was in a new position, facing westerly from Milford to Guineas' station.

On Monday forenoon, May 22d, the advance of the army reached the North Anna River. The 5th corps arrived, by the telegraph road, in the neighborhood of Jericho Mills. The 2d corps arrived in the afternoon, and took position on the left of the 5th, extending to the railroad. In front of the army there were three fords of the North Anna, known as Island, Jericho, and Chesterfield, or Taylor's Bridge fords. The latter is about a mile above the railroad crossing of the river, and the next, or Jericho ford, about four miles further up. The 2d corps arrived at Taylor's bridge about the time when the 5th arrived at Jericho. About a hundred rods in front of Taylor's bridge is a small stream called Long Creek, parallel with the North Anna, and forming a junction with it below the railroad, thus giving a peninsular form to the land between. The bridge across the North Anna was commanded at its entrance by a redan whose extremities were covered by the river, and its flanks swept by artillery in field-works on the opposite bank, as well as by infantry in rifle-pits. The peninsula formed a broad open space between the redan and the 2d corps drawn up in front. Gen. Barlow's division occupied the right of the railroad, Gen. Birney's was in front of the peninsula, and Gen. Gibbon's on the right, while the 5th corps was on the right on the Milford road, and about four miles up from the railroad. Skirmishing commenced in front of Gen. Birney, and his batteries opened upon the enemy at 4 P. M. His division was ordered to charge and carry the works, and, if possible, get possession of the bridge across the river. A brilliant charge was made without a halt until the enemy was driven across the bridge, and guns so placed as to command it. The loss was about five hundred on each side. No effort was made to cross that night, but the bridge was then held by a small command. About 11 P. M. the enemy made a sortie from his works and endeavored to retake the bridge, but after a spirited skirmish of about twenty minutes he was driven off. About midnight another attack was made with a much larger force. The enemy got possession of the bridge and held it for some time, and made several attempts to burn it, but were finally forced to retire. Early the next morning the 2d corps crossed the river.

About the time when the bridge was taken by the 2d corps, the 5th corps effected a crossing and took a position on the south bank, and threw up some breastworks. Soon after they were attacked by a heavy force of the enemy, which was repulsed after causing a loss of about five hundred. Their own loss was unknown.

This attack was renewed during the night. About dark Gen. Burnside's corps came up and took position between Gens. Hancock and Warren, and made preparations to cross, while the 6th corps took the right of the 5th. On the next day, the 24th, the army crossed the river, and considerable skirmishing took place along the whole line with a loss of about five hundred. During the day a portion of the cavalry force under Gen. Sheridan reached the army, returning from James River. On the 25th, contrary to general expectation, the enemy were found strongly posted in force within two miles of Gen. Grant's lines. They lay in the form of a triangle, with the apex reaching nearly to the North Anna River, between the points where Gens. Warren and Hancock crossed with their corps. Their ground was found to be admirably chosen and extensively fortified. The formation of their line gave them every facility for a quick movement of troops from one flank to the other. A successful assault would have involved immense slaughter. As the apex of the enemy's position stretched toward the North Anna, his right wing resting on a formidable marsh and extending across the railroad, protected it and covered the junction. His left wing ran along Little River. New movements were therefore made by Gen. Grant. His plan was to recross the North Anna and march by the left flank. The swelling of the streams by the recent rains made it prudent to commence it as soon as possible. To cover the movement a strong demonstration was made during Thursday on the left of the enemy. Some divisions of cavalry attacked his left, whilst the 3d division of Gen. Sheridan's cavalry moved up the Virginia Central Railroad and began to burn the track. Under cover of this attack, on Thursday evening the 27th, the 6th corps quietly and swiftly withdrew to the north bank of the river, followed by the other corps in quick succession, and moved out easterly for the Pamunkey. The rear was protected by Gen. Hancock. At the same time a strong skirmish line was left in front to engage the enemy's attention and disarm suspicion.

At 9 o'clock on the next morning, Friday the 28th, Hanover Ferry and Hanovertown were occupied by a portion of Gen. Sheridan's cavalry, who captured seventy-five of the enemy. At 10 A. M. the 1st division of the 2d corps arrived, followed closely by the remainder of the corps. Hanovertown is on the Pamunkey River, fifteen miles from Richmond, and sixteen miles from the White House, on the same river. Thirteen miles east of the White House is West Point, where the Mattapony and the Pamunkey join and form the York River. Transports with supplies for the army were already on the way to the White House, to which the base of the army was now changed. On Saturday the 28th the troops continued to arrive all day, and the crossing of the Pamunkey was secured. The enemy had previously occupied Hanover Court House, and in the mean time extended his lines southerly. The despatch of the War Department relative to these movements was as follows:

WASHINGTON, May 28—9:50 P. M.

To Major-General Dix:

An official despatch from the headquarters of the Army of the Potomac, at Magahick Church, ten miles from Hanovertown, dated yesterday afternoon at five o'clock, has just been received.

It states that our army was withdrawn to the north side of the North Anna on Thursday night, and moved toward Hanovertown, the place designated for crossing the Pamunkey.

At 9 o'clock yesterday (Friday) morning Sheridan, with the 1st and 2d divisions of cavalry, took possession of Hanover Ferry and Hanovertown, finding there only a rebel vidette. The 1st division of the 6th corps arrived at 10 A. M., and now hold the place, with sufficient force of cavalry and infantry and artillery to resist any attack likely to be made upon them. The remainder of the corps is pressing forward with rapidity. Weather fine and perfect.

A later despatch dated at 7 o'clock this morning (28th), from Headquarters, Magahick Church, has also been received. It reports that every thing goes on finely; weather clear and cool; the troops came up rapidly and in great spirits, and that the army will be beyond the Pamunkey by noon.

Breckinridge is at Hanover Court House with a force variously reported from three thousand to ten thousand. Wickham's and Lomax's brigades of cavalry are also there.

The despatch further states that, after seizing Hanover Ferry yesterday, General Torbert captured seventy-five cavalry, including six officers; that the rebel cavalry is exceedingly demoralized, and flees before ours on every occasion.

No despatches from any other field of operations have been received to-day.

EDWIN M. STANTON, Secretary of War.

On Saturday two divisions of cavalry, under Gens. Torbert and Gregg, were pushed toward Mechanicsville as a reconnoissance of the enemy's line. Near the Tolopatomy Creek, a tributary of the Pamunkey, a sharp engagement took place with a cavalry force of the enemy, which resulted in forcing them back some distance, leaving a part of their dead and wounded. The loss of the Union force was about four hundred, and that of the enemy was supposed to be not less.

On Sunday, the 29th, the whole army was across the Pamunkey, and fronted southwest about three miles from the river. Reconnoissances were made from each corps, followed up by a gradual advance. The enemy appeared to be in force, distant about six miles, and beyond the Tolopatomy Creek, holding Shady Grove and Mechanicsville with his extreme right, and his centre in front of Atlee's station on the Virginia Central Railroad, and his left covering Hanover Court House.

On Monday, the 30th, the forces of Gen. Lee were reported to be on the Mechanicsville road south of the Tolopatomy Creek, with his right resting on Shady Grove. The right of Gen. Grant's army, consisting of the 6th corps under Gen. Wright, extended in the direction of Hanover Court House. The right centre was held by Gen. Hancock on the Shady Grove road, and the left centre by Gen. Warren on the Mechanicsville road. Gen. Burnside held the left, and a little in rear. The right and rear were covered by the 3d division of cavalry under Gen. Wilson. The divisions of Gens. Torbert and Gregg were advanced on the left flank. The division of Gen. Torbert held the Old Church Tavern Cross Road with a picket force extending on the road to Coal Harbor. A movement of the enemy was made about 2 P. M. upon these pickets, who were driven in, and a sharp engagement ensued, with a loss of eighty or ninety on each side, when the enemy were driven back. About 5 P. M. an attack was made on Gen. Warren's corps, which was gradually moving to the left along the Mechanicsville road, by a reconnoitring division of Gen. Ewell's corps with two brigades of cavalry. The turning of Gen. Warren's flank was endangered, which was prevented only by the timely arrival of reënforcements. A sharp engagement followed, and the enemy were forced to retire by a road parallel to the Coal Harbor road. Gen. Meade, upon being informed of the situation of Gen. Warren, ordered an attack along the whole line. Gen. Hancock alone received the order in time to attack before dark, and immediately advanced upon the enemy's skirmish line, captured their rifle-pits, and held them all night. Gen. Warren held his position near Mechanicsville, and the enemy moved down troops to prevent any further dangerous concentration on his right. An effort was made to dislodge Gen. Hancock at midnight, but without success.

On Tuesday, the 31st, the army of Gen. Grant was further reënforced by the arrival of the 18th corps under Gen. Smith. This corps, being a part of the command of Gen. Butler, embarked on transports at City Point, and moved with celerity down the James River and up the York River to the White House, which was the base of supplies for Gen. Grant's army.

After the retirement of Gen. Butler to his intrenchments on the 20th, little fighting occurred. An attack was made on his post at Wilson's Wharf, on the northerly bank of the James, held by two regiments of negro troops, on the 24th, by a body of cavalry under Gen. Fitz Lee. A demand for surrender was made, which Gen. Wild declined, when the skirmishing line was speedily driven in, and furious charges made on the works. After a contest of three or four hours the enemy withdrew, leaving twenty-five dead on the ground. On the 26th a reconnoissance discovered the enemy in considerable force. The position of Gen. Butler now was such that his communication and supplies were perfectly secure. Both flanks of his remaining force were covered by gunboats.

On Tuesday, May 31st, the headquarters of Gen. Grant were about five miles southeast of Hanover Court House, and less than that distance west of Hanovertown. In front of that position, facing westerly on its right and southwesterly on its left, the line of battle of the army extended a distance of six miles across Tolopatomy Creek. The right was held by Gen. Wright's 6th corps, next Gen. Hancock's 2d corps, next Gen. Burnside's 9th corps, and Gen. Warren's 5th corps on the left. The position of the enemy was on the westerly bank of a creek running southeast, and a tributary to the Tolopatomy before the latter turns to the northeast to the Pamunkey. Their line closely followed in general direction that of Gen. Grant's army. The right was held by Gen. A. P. Hill. the centre by Gen. Longstreet's corps, and the left by Gen. Ewell. In this position they covered the Chickahominy, which is the outer line of defence for Richmond and the Virginia Central Railroad, with cavalry supports thrown out on the left as far as Hanover Court House, and on the right to Bottom Bridge. This was the theatre of operations of the Army of the Potomac in 1862, when the approach to Richmond was made across the Chickahominy, before which the enemy were now strongly drawn up.

On Tuesday there was desultory firing through the day along the whole line. Gen. Grant already contemplated a movement by the left, and the 1st division of cavalry, under Gen. Torbert, were ordered forward to reconnoitre thoroughly the ground in the vicinity of Coal Harbor, and to hold it at all hazards for the occupation of infantry. While there a sharp fight ensued with a body of the enemy's cavalry, which resulted in Gen. Torbert's holding the desired ground.

On the next day, June 1st, an effort was made by a division of the enemy under Gen. Hoke, to get possession of Coal Harbor. This was repulsed by Gen. Sheridan. Subsequently Gen. Hoke was reënforced, and about noon checked the further advance of Gen. Sheridan on the left. On the previous night the 6th corps was detached from the right, and marched from Shady Grove to Coal Harbor, where they arrived soon after the close of the above affair. It formed in line on the right of the Gaines' Mill road, with Gen. Ricketts' division on the right, Gen. Russell's in the centre, and Gen. Neill's 2d on the left. About 3 o'clock the 18th corps, under Gen. Smith, from the White House, came into the field, and formed on the right of the 6th corps, with Gen. Martindale on the right, Gen. Brookes in the centre, and Gen. Devens on the left. Their march, like that of the 6th corps, had been severe, over a distance of twenty-five miles. A charge by the 18th corps was ordered at once, and, without stopping, they crossed an open field to a strip of wood, and took and held the first line of the enemy's rifle-pits, capturing six hundred prisoners. A lodgment was also effected in the enemy's line further to the right, but the position proved to be completely commanded by a redoubt in the second line of the enemy, and, amidst a heavy fire, it was abandoned. During the night the enemy made desperate efforts to

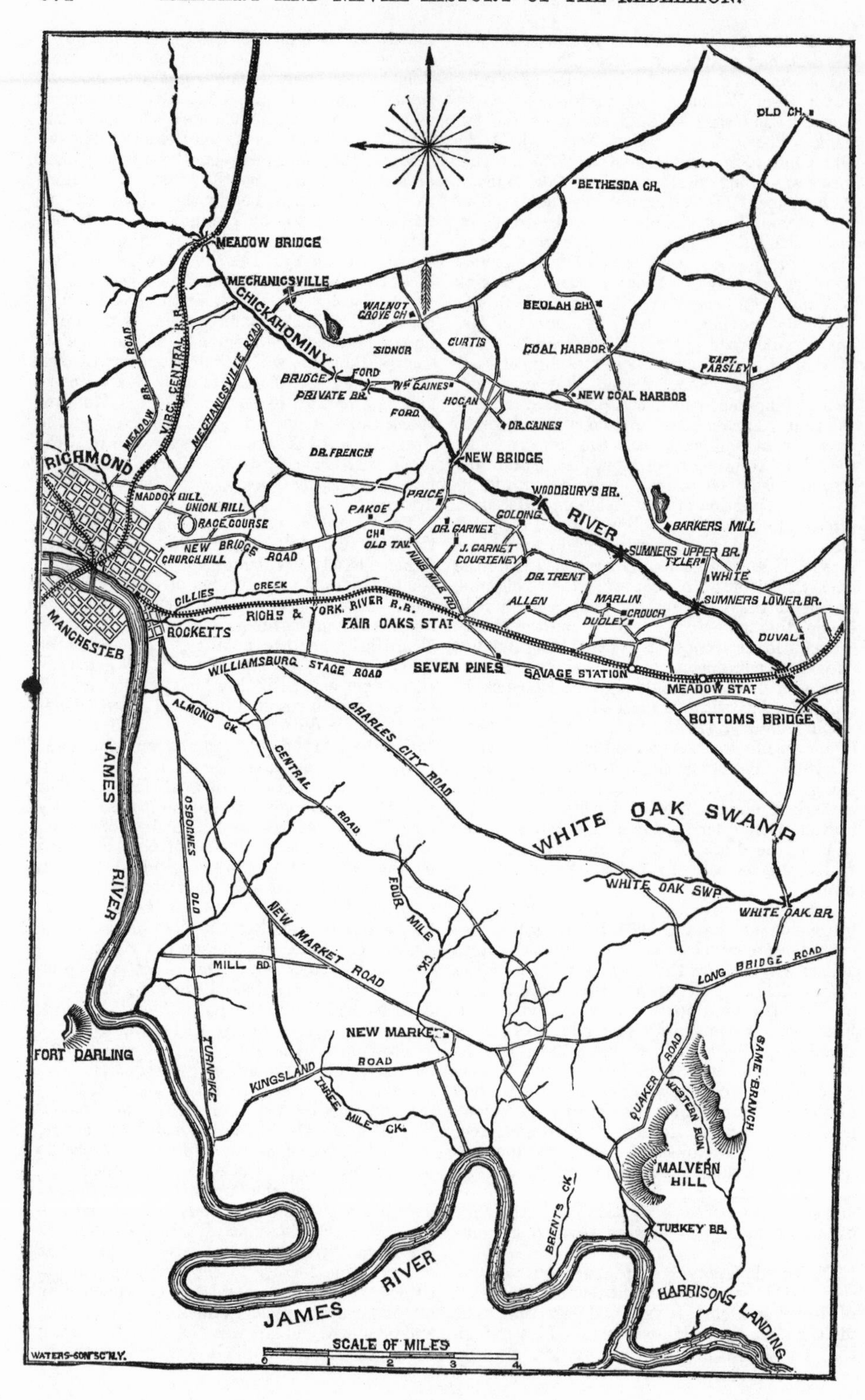
OLD CH.
BETHESDA CH.
MEADOW BRIDGE
MECHANICSVILLE
CHICKAHOMINY
WALNUT GROVE CH.
BEULAH CH.
SIDNOR
CURTIS
COAL HARBOR
CAPT. PARSLEY
BRIDGE
FORD
Wm. GAINES
PRIVATE BR.
HOGAN
NEW COAL HARBOR
FORD
DR. GAINES
MEADOW BR. ROAD
VIRG. CENTRAL R.R.
MECHANICSVILLE ROAD
DR. FRENCH
NEW BRIDGE
RICHMOND
MADDOX HILL
UNION HILL
RACE COURSE
PRICE
PAKOE
WOODBURYS BR.
GOLDING
RIVER
DR. GARNET
BARKERS MILL
CH.
OLD TAV.
NEW BRIDGE ROAD
CHURCH HILL
J. GARNET
COURTENEY
NINE MILE RD.
SUMNERS UPPER BR.
TYLER
WHITE
DR. TRENT
GILLIES CREEK
ALLEN
MARLIN
CROUCH
SUMNERS LOWER BR.
RICHd. & YORK RIVER R.R.
FAIR OAKS STAT
DUDLEY
MANCHESTER
ROCKETTS
DUVAL
WILLIAMSBURG STAGE ROAD
SEVEN PINES
SAVAGE STATION
MEADOW STAT
BOTTOMS BRIDGE
ALMOND CK
CHARLES CITY ROAD
CENTRAL ROAD
JAMES RIVER
OSBORNES OLD TURNPIKE
WHITE OAK SWAMP
FOUR MILE CK.
WHITE OAK SWP.
WHITE OAK BR.
NEW MARKET ROAD
MILL RD
LONG BRIDGE ROAD
FORT DARLING
NEW MARKET
ROAD
KINGSLAND
THREE MILE CK.
QUAKER ROAD
WESTERN RUN
SAME BRANCH
MALVERN HILL
BRENT'S CK
TURKEY BR.
JAMES RIVER
HARRISONS LANDING
SCALE OF MILES
0 1 2 3 4
WATERS-SON SC. N.Y.

regain the rifle-pits, and succeeded in annoying the troops with an enfilading fire. Their charges, however, were repelled. The loss of the Union troops was about two thousand; the enemy being behind breastworks, probably suffered much less. The change in the line now had brought Gen. Wright to the extreme left, between whom and the 5th corps was now the 18th under Gen. Smith. During the entire day there had been warm work along the whole line, in which the artillery took a part toward night. Several distinct charges were made by the enemy, which were repulsed. No careful estimate of the losses in this part of the field during the day was made, but it was supposed not to exceed a thousand. The loss of the enemy was severe. The result of the day was the complete occupation and holding of Coal Harbor, which was an important position both as commanding the road to the White House, whence supplies were brought, and also in reference to a subsequent crossing of the Chickahominy.

In the night it was determined by Gen. Grant to make the attempt to push the enemy across the Chickahominy, and to secure a place to ford that stream. The 2d corps was therefore advanced from the extreme right to the extreme left, in order to increase the force in that direction. It reached its position about noon the next day, Thursday, June 2d. The attack which was to have been made on that evening, owing to the heavy rain which ensued, was postponed until the next morning, Friday. Considerable skirmishing had taken place during the day, and a charge was made upon the 5th and 9th corps, without gaining any special advantage.

At half-past 4 o'clock on Friday morning the army was in motion. Its line extended from Tolopatomy Creek across the road from Coal Harbor to the Chickahominy. The ground consisted of woodlands, swamp, and open fields. The skirmishers were promptly advanced, and the whole line was soon engaged in a terrific battle. From Gen. Hancock's corps on the extreme left the brigades of Gens. Gibbon and Barlow moved boldly forward, exposed to shot and shell, up the ascent on which the enemy in their front had concentrated their men and artillery. They drove out the enemy, and for a moment were in possession of their position. Being in advance of the line, they were exposed to a most destructive enfilading fire of the enemy. At the same time the second line of the enemy was massed and hurled upon them. Thus overwhelmed in front, and swept by a fire on the flank, these divisions were now driven out of the intrenchments, but not until they had secured a color and three hundred prisoners. Falling back about fifty yards they were under a partial cover of the ridge. Here they intrenched themselves, and remained through the day. So far had they advanced that one of the enemy's batteries was captured and nearly turned against them when the retreat was ordered. The 18th and the 6th corps adjoining the second along the line charged forward with not less gallantry, and carried the first line of the enemy's intrenchments, but were received with a most destructive enfilading fire. After an obstinate conflict they were forced back, yielding the position which they had taken, and occupied another close to the enemy's works, which they intrenched. On the right the 5th and 9th corps were advanced; but the conflict here was not so severe, as the force of the enemy was massed on their right. Still further to the right the 3d division of cavalry, under Gen. Wilson, were engaged with a force of the enemy under Gen. Hampton, but without important results. The contest was continued with more or less vigor throughout the day. The enemy were found too strongly posted to carry their works, and all efforts to cross the Chickahominy at that point were repelled. The loss was nearly seven thousand in killed, wounded, and prisoners. The enemy lost many prisoners, but the advantages under which they fought prevented their loss from being so severe. The following despatches were issued by the War Department:

WASHINGTON, June 4, 1864.

To Major-Gen. Dix:

Despatches from Gen. Grant's headquarters, dated 3 o'clock yesterday, have just been received. No operations took place on Thursday. Yesterday, at half-past 4 o'clock A. M., Gen. Grant made an assault on the enemy's lines, of which he makes the following report:

"We assaulted at half-past 4 A. M., driving the enemy within his intrenchments at all points, but without gaining any decisive advantage. Our troops now occupy a position close to the enemy, some places within fifty yards, and are remaining. Our loss was not severe, nor do I suppose the enemy to have lost heavily. We captured over three hundred prisoners, mostly from Breckinridge."

Another later official report, not from Gen. Grant, estimates the number of our killed and wounded at about three thousand. The following officers are among the killed:

Col. Haskell, 36th Wisconsin; Col. Porter, 8th New York heavy artillery; Col. Morris, 66th New York.

Among the wounded are Gen. R. O. Tyler—seriously—will probably lose a foot; Col. McMahon, 164th New York; Col. Byrnes, 28th Massachusetts—probably mortally; and Col. Brooke, 53d Pennsylvania. EDWIN M. STANTON, Sec'y of War.

WASHINGTON, June 5—1 P. M.

Major-Gen. Dix:

A despatch from Gen. Grant's headquarters, dated half-past 8 o'clock last night, has been received. It states that "about 7 P. M. yesterday, Friday, 3d of June, the enemy suddenly attacked Smith's brigade, of Gibbon's division. The battle lasted with great fury for half an hour. The attack was unwaveringly repulsed. Smith's losses were inconsiderable."

At 6 P. M., Wilson, with his cavalry, fell upon the rear of a brigade of Heth's division, which Lee had thrown around to his left, apparently with the intention of enveloping Burnside. After a sharp but short conflict, Wilson drove them from their rifle-pits in confusion. He took a few prisoners. He had previously fought and routed Gordon's brigade of rebel cavalry. During these fights he lost several officers, among them Col. Preston, 1st Vermont cavalry, killed; Col. Benjamin, 8th New York cavalry, seriously wounded.

Our entire loss in killed, wounded, and missing

during the three days' operations around Coal Harbor will not exceed, according to the Adjutant-General's Report, seven thousand five hundred.

This morning, Saturday, June 4, the enemy's left wing, in front of Gen. Burnside, was found to have been drawn in during the night.

Col. Cesnola, in command of five thousand men, arrived there yesterday, having marched from Port Royal. EDWIN M. STANTON, Sec'y of War.

The position gained, however, was held, and during the next day, Saturday, June 4th, the erection of temporary breastworks was busily prosecuted. At 9 o'clock at night the enemy made a fierce attack on the corps of Gen. Hancock, Smith, and Wright, but after a severe loss they were repulsed.

On Sunday, the 5th, the lines continued close to each other. The sharpshooters of the enemy endangered any person exposed in the rifle-pits, and many officers and men were fatally wounded. Meanwhile the work on the intrenchments, when practicable, was kept up. Soon after dark the enemy made a sudden dash on Gen. Smyth's brigade of the 2d division of Gen. Hancock's corps. They met with a sharp resistance, and were soon repelled with a disproportionably large loss. On Monday the picket-firing was continued, with some change of position in bodies of the troops, and with the work on the intrenchments. At midnight an attack was made on Gen. Burnside's corps on the right, but soon repelled. The nearness of the lines of the two armies made the battle-fields of Friday disputed, and the dead still remained upon it unburied and the wounded were unrelieved. A correspondence ensued relative to these dead and wounded, between Gens. Grant and Lee. It resulted in an armistice of two hours, during which the dead and wounded were carefully removed. Meanwhile the 5th corps was detached from its position on the right centre and withdrawn to the rear. Its place in the line was filled by a transfer of the 9th corps from the extreme right. Commissary supplies had been constantly sent forward to the army from the White House, with some reënforcements of hundred days' men and convalescents. New earthworks were built, extending along the course of the Chickahominy, and everywhere the enemy built parallel works a few hundred yards distant. On Tuesday, June 7th, the enemy making a reconnoissance, attacked the 9th corps in the afternoon, but were vigorously repelled. Of the 5th corps detached during the night from their position in the line, the divisions of Gens. Griffin and Cutler, moved rapidly down toward Sumner's bridge, on the Chickahominy. The enemy at the bridge were in force, and opened with rather heavy guns on the approaching column. They were soon driven from the bridge, but continued to command it with their artillery. During Wednesday and Thursday there was no change of position. On the latter day, the cavalry under Gens. Torbert and Gregg were pushed further to the left. On Friday some skirmishing of cavalry took place on the right. The work of intrenchment was continued, and an advance was pushed as far as Bottom bridge, the next below the railroad crossing of Chickahominy. The enemy kept pace, confronting the advance, and fortifying at the bridge. On the same day the destruction of the railroad to the White House was begun from Despatch station easterly. The rails and ties were removed to the White House, and shipped on barges.

On Sunday night, June 12th, the movement for crossing the James River commenced. The line of the enemy extended from Bottom bridge along the Chickahominy, nearly parallel to which was the line of Gen. Grant, and both intrenched. Bottom bridge was commanded by the enemy, and could not be used for crossing. The next were Long bridge, six or seven miles, and Jones's bridge, ten or twelve miles below.

On Sunday night, June 12th, the army began to move. The 2d and 5th corps moved to Long bridge, over which they crossed, and took the road due south to Wilcox's wharf, twelve miles distant on the James' River, and a little west of Charles City. The 6th and the 9th corps at the same time marched to Jones's bridge, by which they crossed the Chickahominy and advanced rapidly to Charles City Court House, about nine miles nearly south of the bridge and a mile from the James' River. The 18th corps about the same time marched to the White House, embarked on transports and proceeded directly to Bermuda Hundred, on the south side of the James' River, being the headquarters of Gen. Butler. The points designated for the crossing of the other corps were Powhatan's and near Wilcox's Wharf, where pontoons had already been prepared by Gen. Butler. During all Sunday night and Monday the troops moved forward, and at evening the advance reached Wilcox's wharf. On Tuesday the crossing of the James commenced, and was completed on Wednesday. The movement had been attended with some slight skirmishing with the enemy, with a loss of not more than four hundred men.

Meanwhile deserters having reported that the force of the enemy at Petersburg had been greatly reduced, a demonstration against that city, was made by a portion of the forces under Gen. Butler at Bermuda Hundred. It was determined that Gen. Gillmore, with thirty-five hundred men, crossing the Appomattox, should move by the turnpike road and assault the city, while Gen. Kautz, with a cavalry force of fifteen hundred men, should make a circuit of the place and attack it on the southerly or southwesterly side, and thus, as the movement was simultaneous, both forces might enter the city together. At the same time another demonstration was to be made upon Fort Clifton, The movement commenced on Monday night. June 8th. Gen. Gillmore encountered no serious opposition until within two miles of the city, when he met the enemy's skirmish line and briskly drove it back. On arriving in front of the city where the fortifications could be closely examined, he found them too strong for the force at his command to attempt, and accordingly withdrew about noon and returned to camp in the evening. Meanwhile Gen. Kautz had forced the enemy's intrenchments and reached the streets of the city, sharply engaged in fighting. But the force of the enemy concentrating against him, he was forced to retire. Some prisoners were taken, and the loss was about twenty men. Two gunboats and a battery engaged Fort Clifton during the morning with a brisk fire.

Petersburg, a city of eighteen thousand inhabitants, is situated on the south bank of the Appomattox River, twenty-two miles south of Richmond, and ten miles from the James River at City Point. The Appomattox empties into the James at City Point. It is navigable to Petersburg for vessels of one hundred tons, and to Waltham, six miles below, by larger vessels. The city is connected with City Point by a railroad. The road from Richmond to North and South Carolina also passes through it. The river at this point runs nearly northeast to the James. The city was defended by several series of strong earthworks, consisting not only of square redoubts, but also of well-established and commanding rifle-trenches.

On Wednesday, June 15th, a reconnoissance was made by the cavalry, by which it was discovered that the corps of Gen. Hill occupied the region southeast of Richmond in strong force. At 1 o'clock on the morning of the same day the 18th corps, which had arrived on the previous evening from the White House, started for Petersburg. The Appomattox was crossed by a pontoon-bridge near Point of Rocks. The route was nearly the same as that taken by the advance of Gen. Gillmore on a previous day. Skirmishing of the advance with the enemy commenced at daylight. A row of rifle-trenches with two twelve-pounders was carried by a body of colored troops under Gen. Hinks' command later in the day. In the afternoon the movement resulted in forming a line of battle in front of the outer intrenchments of the enemy, about two miles from Petersburg. Just before sunset the order was given to carry the works by assault. The whole line rapidly advanced under a hot artillery fire from the enemy, and swept the entire range of rifle-pits with great gallantry. The enemy broke and deserted their intrenchments, losing sixteen guns, a battle flag, and three hundred prisoners. The Union loss was about five hundred. The position was held, but no further advance was made. It was supposed that, if a supporting force had been at hand, the second line of works might have been carried with comparative ease. The force of the enemy in the city was small, but reënforcements were received by them previous to the arrival of the other corps of Gen. Grant's army. The troops which held Petersburg composed the command of Gen. Beauregard. A portion of them had confronted Gen. Butler, and some had been in Richmond.

The cavalry under Gen. Kautz, which preceded the 18th corps, had moved out to the extreme left against the works near the Norfolk Railroad and on the Baxter road. The position of the enemy was, however, too strong to be carried, and Gen. Kautz retired.

Meanwhile the other corps of the army were approaching as rapidly as possible. Gen. Birney's division of the 2d corps arrived at evening and occupied the captured intrenchments. During the night the remainder of the corps came up.

On Thursday morning a part of the 10th corps, under Gen. Terry, was sent out to reconnoitre in front of Gen. Butler's position. The skirmishers soon drove the enemy, and his line was penetrated and carried, and the railroad subsequently reached near Port Walthall Junction. About two miles of the track were torn up, when the enemy came down in such force that Gen. Terry was obliged to retire.

Early in the morning Gen. Birney sent out a force under Gen. Egan and carried a redoubt on his left, with a loss of about a hundred. Meantime the troops of the enemy were crowded forward so rapidly that it became necessary to wait for Gen. Burnside's corps to come up. The intrenchments of the enemy ran semicircularly from the river on the north of the city to the river on the south. Their northern extremity was also strengthened by batteries on the opposite side of the Appomattox. In the afternoon the corps of Gen. Burnside arrived and a line of battle was formed, with the 18th corps under Gen. Smith on the right, the 2d corps under Gen. Birney during this assault, which was commanded by Gen. Hancock, and the 9th under Gen. Burnside on the left. At 6 o'clock an attack was made, and continued for three hours. Gen. Birney's division, on the right of the centre corps, carried the crest in his front and held it firmly. On the left of Gen. Birney's division the advance of Gen. Barlow found more difficulty, from the concentration of the enemy in front. A charge was made by the brigades of Gens. Miles and Griffin, which succeeded in gaining a foothold of the rifle-pits outside of the stronger works. But the troops were so annoyed by the enemy that Gen. Barlow determined to make an assault. But the enemy cut off his skirmish line in front, amounting to three hundred men, with their officers. Gen. Burnside also prepared to make an assault, but the enemy opened so severely as to frustrate it. The right took no important part in the contest. After three hours the assault was suspended. The loss was between fifteen hundred and two thousand. That of the enemy, as they held an advantageous position, was much less.

Early on Friday morning, June 17th, the assault was renewed by an order of Gen. Burnside to Gen. Patten's division to take the works in their front. The brigade of Gen. Griffin, supported by that of Gen. Curtin, dashed forward, carrying the position and capturing six guns, sixteen officers, and four hundred men, with a loss of about five hundred men. A pause now ensued, but skirmishing was kept up by the picket lines, and there was a moderate fire of artillery. In the afternoon Gen. Patten's division was relieved by that of Gen. Ledlie. An advance of this latter division was ordered, under cover of artillery, upon the enemy's breastworks, from which, after a desperate contest, they were driven, and the position carried, with the capture of some prisoners. Gen. Burnside was now about a mile and a half from the city and threw some shells into it. Several attempts were made by the enemy to recover the intrenchments during the day, but without success. About 9 o'clock at night, however, a desperate attempt to retake them was made and succeeded. In this affair about two hundred prisoners were made on each side. The loss of the division was estimated at a thousand. The rest of the line during the day was engaged in skirmishing, without any attempt at decisive assault. On the right the 18th corps had been withdrawn and returned to the intrenchments at Bermuda Hundred. The 5th corps, under Gen. Warren, had come and massed on the left in the rear of Gen. Burnside's 9th corps. The 2d corps was commanded by Gen. Birney, as Gen. Hancock was suffering from an old wound.

The proper dispositions were now made for a vigorous assault early on Saturday morning the 18th. The line was formed by the divisions of Gens. Martindale and Hinks, of the 18th corps, on the right, extended by the 6th, 2d, 9th, and 5th, in the order named, to the left. On sending out skirmishers preparatory to the assault, at 4 A. M., it was found that the enemy had withdrawn to an inner series of defences. New arrangements, therefore, became necessary. At noon a general advance of the 2d, 9th, and 5th corps was ordered. From the 2d corps an assaulting column of three brigades was sent forward, while the rest of the corps threw out double lines of skirmishers to divert the attention of the enemy. The men moved promptly up to the works to be assaulted, which were situated near the Petersburg and City Point Railroad. As they came out from cover, they were received by such a desperate enfilading fire from the left, that they retired without reaching the breastworks, leaving their dead and wounded on the field. In the afternoon a second storming party was organized to commence the attack from Gen. Mott's position. His division, with detachments from the other two of the corps, advanced in two columns about 5 P. M., but were received with such a destructive fire from concentrated batteries and musketry, as to force them back with terrible loss, in spite of the greatest bravery on their part.

The 9th corps, on the left of the 2d, was prompt to act during the day. There was brisk skirmishing, but no decisive advantage was gained. The line was established during the afternoon across the Petersburg and Norfolk Railroad.

On the left of the 9th, the 5th corps, at the time of the attack of the 2d, made a determined and vigorous advance against the south side of the Norfolk Railroad, and was partially successful. In the evening their efforts were again renewed, but were foiled by the enemy. The division of the 18th, on the extreme right, experienced the same results as the other troops. The operations of the day had been unsuccessful. The loss of the four days' operations was estimated above ten thousand men.

On Sunday, June 19th, there was skirmishing and considerable artillery fire, but no decisive movement. The loss was estimated at a hundred men. The 6th corps, heretofore on the north side of the Appomattox, now took a position on the right, and the colored division of Gen. Ferrero, of the 9th corps, arrived, and was posted in front. At night the enemy made an attack on the centre of the line, but were driven back. During the afternoon an attack with infantry and artillery was made on Gen. Butler's lines at Bermuda Hundred by a division of Gen. Longstreet's corps under Gen. Pickett. At the same time, three ironclads from Richmond made their appearance near Dutch Gap, but retired before the fleet of Admiral Lee. During the same night, squads of the enemy made their appearance along the James River and destroyed the wharfs at Wilcox's and Westover landings.

Monday, the 20th, was unusually quiet near Petersburg. Some demonstrations of the enemy's cavalry were near the White House, but without any serious result to the convalescents there.

On Tuesday, the 21st, a movement was made to occupy and destroy the railroad from Petersburg to Weldon. On the previous evening the 2d corps moved from its entrenchments on the right centre to the left, and its position was occupied by the 9th and a part of the 18th. In the morning, crossing the Petersburg and Norfolk Railroad, it marched as rapidly as possible in a southerly direction. A division of the 5th and one of the 6th corps moved out in support. Before noon, the 2d corps halted, and in the afternoon a division, under Gen. Barlow, with sharpshooters skirmishing in advance, was sent forward and found the enemy's lines in the neighborhood of the Jerusalem road, which bisects the region between the Norfolk and the Weldon Railroad. The position was known as Davis Farm, about three miles below Petersburg, and a mile from the railroad. The enemy proved to be in force, with artillery planted in earthworks. They advanced to attack, and a severe skirmish ensued, and the advance line of Gen. Barlow was withdrawn, and rejoined the column. The loss was about a hundred men. A reconnoissance toward Petersburg, at the same time, was attended with no results. So threatening was the aspect of the enemy on the left, that a squadron

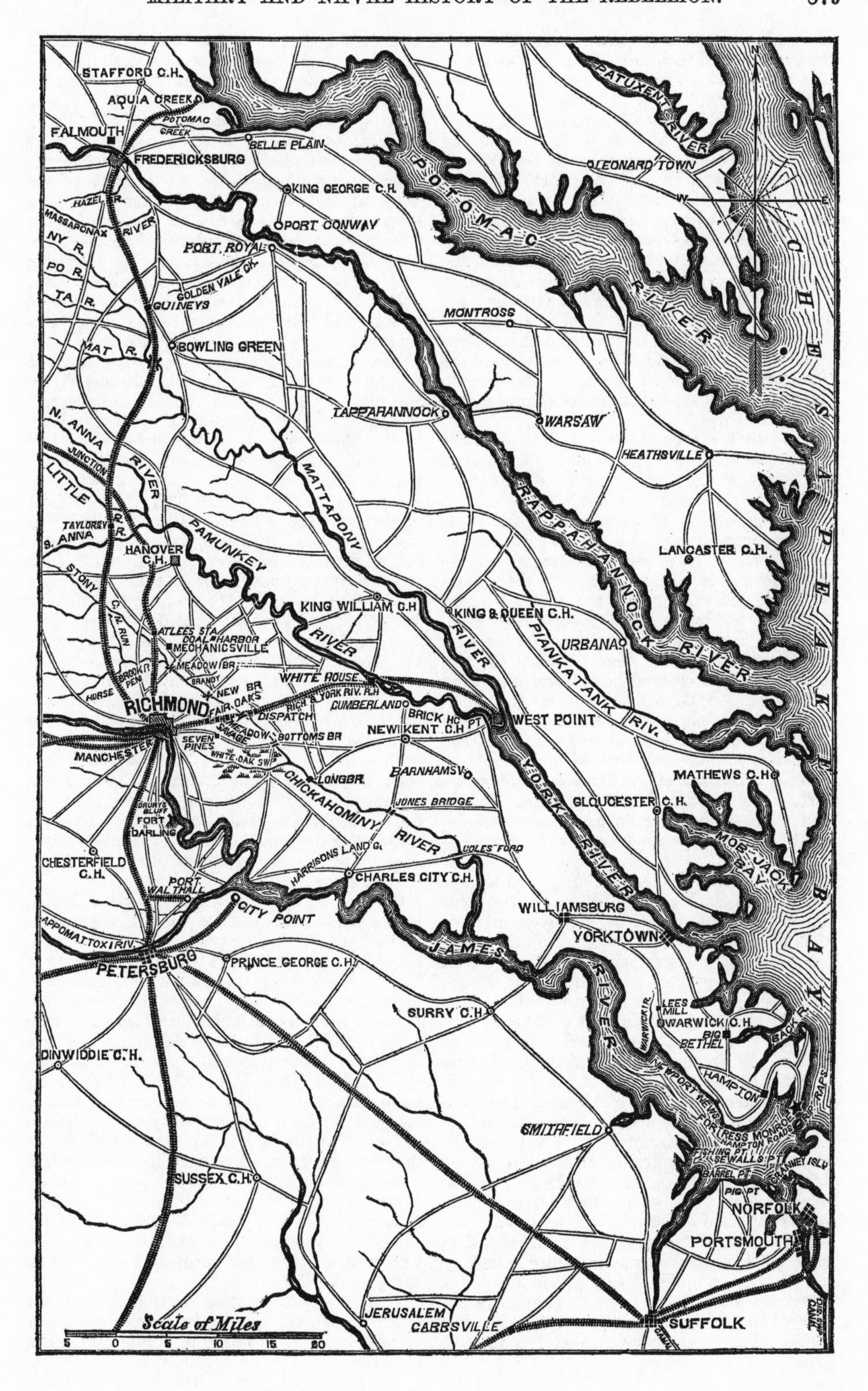
STAFFORD C.H.
AQUIA CREEK
POTOMAC CREEK
FALMOUTH
FREDERICKSBURG
BELLE PLAIN
KING GEORGE C.H.
PORT CONWAY
PORT ROYAL
HAZEL R.
MASSAPONAX RIVER
NY R.
PO R.
TA R.
GOLDEN VALE CK.
GUINEYS
MAT R.
BOWLING GREEN
MONTROSS
POTOMAC RIVER
PATUXENT RIVER
LEONARD TOWN
TAPPAHANNOCK
WARSAW
HEATHSVILLE
N. ANNA RIVER
JUNCTION
LITTLE R.
TAYLORSV.
S. ANNA
MATTAPONY
PAMUNKEY RIVER
RAPPAHANNOCK RIVER
LANCASTER C.H.
HANOVER C.H.
STONY
KING WILLIAM C.H.
KING & QUEEN C.H.
URBANA
PIANKATANK RIV.
ATLEES STA.
COAL HARBOR
MECHANICSVILLE
MEADOW BR.
BRANDY
NEW BR
WHITE HOUSE
RICHMOND
FAIR OAKS
RICH & YORK RIV. R.R.
DISPATCH
CUMBERLAND
BRICK HO. PT.
WEST POINT
MANCHESTER
SEVEN PINES
SAVAGE
MEADOW
BOTTOMS BR
NEW KENT C.H.
WHITE OAK SWP
CHICKAHOMINY RIVER
LONG BR.
BARNHAMSV.
JONES BRIDGE
MATHEWS C.H.
GLOUCESTER C.H.
YORK RIVER
MOB JACK BAY
DRURYS BLUFF
FORT DARLING
CHESTERFIELD C.H.
HARRISONS LAND G.
COLES FORD
CHARLES CITY C.H.
PORT WALTHALL
CITY POINT
WILLIAMSBURG
YORKTOWN
APPOMATTOX RIV.
PETERSBURG
PRINCE GEORGE C.H.
JAMES RIVER
SURRY C.H.
LEES MILL
WARWICK C.H.
BIG BETHEL
DINWIDDIE C.H.
NEWPORT NEWS
HAMPTON
FORTRESS MONROE
HAMPTON ROADS
SMITHFIELD
FISHING PT.
SEWALLS PT.
BARREL PT.
CRANEY ISL'D
PIG PT.
NORFOLK
PORTSMOUTH
SUSSEX C.H.
JERUSALEM
CARRSVILLE
SUFFOLK
CHESAPEAKE BAY
Scale of Miles
5 0 5 10 15 20

of cavalry was sent to protect that flank, and the corps retired to form position for the night.

In the lines east of Petersburg comparative quietness prevailed. The bridges across the Appomattox, between Petersburg and Pocahontas, the village on the Richmond side of the river, were shelled daily by the batteries of Gen. Grant. On the same day, the 21st, a division of the 10th corps, under Gen. Foster, crossed the James, at a point between Aikin's Landing and Four Mile Creek, and occupied Deep Bottom, about ten miles from Richmond. On the opposite side of the river, about six miles from Gen. Foster, the enemy had a battery at a position called Howlett's. In this position he threatened, to some extent, the southeast approaches to Richmond. At the same time the 18th corps moved from Bermuda Hundred to Petersburg, and occupied the position vacated by the 6th corps.

Early on Wednesday, the 22d, the movement against the railroad was resumed. The object was to cut off the communication with Petersburg from the south. At the same time a cavalry expedition was sent about ten miles further south, under Gen. Wilson, to destroy the railroad. The general movement was designed to consist of an advance of the 2d and 6th corps directly against the road. The 2d corps was on the left of the Jerusalem road, with Gen. Gibbon's division resting its right on the left of the road. Gen. Griffin's division of the 5th corps was on the further side. The position of Gen. Gibbon was so near the works of the enemy that any further advance by him would bring on a general engagement. The advance was, therefore, ordered for the left of the line, consisting of the divisions of Generals Barlow and Mott, and the 6th corps. It was to have been made at daybreak, but was delayed by each corps apparently waiting for the other to lead. At length each corps was ordered to advance independently, and to protect its own flank as connection between was not made. The line was deployed in open style, covering a large extent of ground, until it approached the presence of the enemy, in more intricate ground, when the left of the 2d, under Gen. Barlow, was pressed well in toward the right, thus opening a gap between it and the 6th corps. Gen. Barlow threw out flanking regiments to protect himself. But no sooner was the entire line of the 2d corps in position, and Gen. Barlow's division had commenced to intrench, when it was attacked on the flank by the enemy. In its advance, the 2d corps had separated from the 5th, on its right, and the 6th was now far distant, on the left and rear. The enemy took advantage of the error. One entire division, with Mahone's brigade, pushed through the interval. The flank of Gen. Barlow was instantly rolled up and a large number made prisoners. This movement of Gen. Barlow's force quickly uncovered the flank of Gen. Mott's division, and exposed him to the same danger. Gen. Mott at once fell back, with the loss of many made prisoners, and thus exposed the left flank of Gen. Gibbon's division. The line of intrenchments occupied by Gen. Mott was now captured by the enemy, who thus pressed Gen. Gibbon in front and rear. Several regiments were captured, with McKnight's battery, before the enemy were checked by the bravery of the 20th Massachusetts. The broken corps was soon rallied and a new line formed, and further attacks of the enemy repulsed. The 6th corps was also attacked on its left flank by a division of Gen. Hill's command, and its advance line driven back, thus widening the gap between it and the 2d. In the evening, Gen. Meade getting both corps well in order, directed an advance. The 6th recovered its former line and the 2d a part of its line, and intrenched for the night. At daylight the enemy appeared, strongly intrenched, before the Weldon Railroad. The loss of the day included about two thousand made prisoners, four guns, and some colors.

On the next day, the 23d, Gen. Wright moved out to the extreme left, and finding that the enemy had not advanced so far, sent out a reconnoitring force to the railroad. They reached it unopposed and cut the telegraph. The 3d, 4th, and 11th Vermont regiments were then sent forward to hold the road. But they had hardly reached it when they were attacked on their flank by a division of the enemy under Gen. Anderson, and their position was turned at once. Several hundred were taken prisoners, and some were killed and wounded. The enemy, elated with success, pushed the troops back to the main body, and then began a general attack. The line was withdrawn toward evening to the cover of the breastworks. The loss of the enemy in these two days was disproportionately small. Elsewhere, during the day, nothing of importance occurred.

On Friday, the 24th, the enemy opened with artillery upon the position of Gen. Stannard's division of the 10th corps. After an hour, a charge was made, which was repulsed with a loss to the enemy of one hundred and fifty prisoners, besides some killed and wounded. No important movements were made in other parts of the line. During the evening, the cavalry force under Gen. Sheridan, while marching from the White House to the James River, were attacked by the enemy and a bloody struggle ensued. The enemy were finally driven off, after a loss by Gen. Sheridan of four to five hundred men. His trains were saved from capture.

On the next day, the 25th, the principal demonstration was made in front of Gen. Burnside's position. It consisted of the advance of a strong skirmish line, which was easily repulsed.

The cavalry expedition of Gen. Wilson set out from the camps near Prince George Court House, on the morning of June 22d. His force was between six and eight thousand men, with three batteries of four guns each. The column moved to the Petersburg and Weldon Railroad at Reims' station. Here it took up and burned the track for several hundred yards, the water-tank, depot, and public buildings. It thence moved to Sutherland's station, on the Petersburg and Lynchburg Railroad, and advanced to Ford's station in the evening. Here two locomotives, sixteen cars, a depot, and a few stores were burned, and several miles of the road destroyed. On the next morning Gen. Kautz advanced toward Burkesville, which he reached in the afternoon, and destroyed the property of the road as at the other stations. Meanwhile the main body followed, and encountered in the afternoon a body of the enemy near Nottoway. A sharp conflict ensued until night, when the enemy retired. On the 24th the column reached Keysville, and bivouacked for the night. About eighteen miles of the road, besides other property, were destroyed during the day. On the next day the bridge over Staunton River was reached, but it was found to be well defended by the enemy. The return of the expedition now commenced. On the route they were so harassed by the enemy as barely to escape capture. On Thursday and Friday, July 1st and 2d, they arrived within the lines, in straggling parties, in a most pitiable and wretched condition, both men and horses being jaded and worn beyond description after their hard march, severe fighting, and the relentless harassing of the enemy. The entire wagon train, the ambulance train, all the guns (sixteen), nearly all their caissons, and many horses had been lost, and between ten and fifteen hundred men. More than a thousand negroes had been collected and followed the column, but most of them were recaptured by the enemy. It was asserted that about fifty miles of the Danville Railroad had been destroyed. A movement was made by the 6th corps to aid the expedition, on learning its situation, but without important results.

The weather at this period was exceedingly hot, and the army suffered greatly. At the same time a drouth prevailed, water became scarce, and the dust rose in clouds at every movement. The condition of the army at this time is thus described by the "Army and Navy Journal":

The medical and commissary department had been well conducted, but it is not too much to say that the troops were thoroughly worn out. While their spirit and enthusiasm were, and always have been, beyond all praise, the fatigues of so extraordinary a campaign had been overpowering. Officers experienced its effects as well as men. Their conspicuous bravery had stretched out, dead or wounded, commissioned officers of all grades, not by hundreds, but by thousands, before the James was crossed. The effect was apparent in some want of skill and experience in succeeding battles. Captains were sometimes commanding regiments, and majors brigades. The men missing the familiar forms and voices that had led them to the charge, would complain that they had not their old officers to follow. On the other hand, more than one leader of a storming party was forced to say, as he came back from an unsuccessful attempt against the outworks of Petersburg, "My men do not charge as they did thirty days ago." A few commanders, too, showed the fatiguing effects of the campaign by a lack of health, by a lack of unity and harmony, or of alertness and skill. The last attacks on Petersburg show clearly how the campaign was telling on men and officers, and the two achievements on the Jerusalem road of the 22d and 23d of June, put the matter beyond all doubt. On the former occasion, the gallant 2d corps, whose reputation is unexcelled, fell back, division after division, from the enemy's onset, and one of the very finest brigades in the whole army was captured, with hardly a shot fired. In our account at that time the probable cause of the disaster was intimated. But when, in addition to this, the Vermont brigade of the 6th corps was badly cut up on the following day, it became clear that the rapidity of the fighting must be checked awhile. The pace was now too great. There was need of rest, recruitment, and some reorganization.

CHAPTER XLIII.

The Second Movement against Lynchburg—Gens. Crook, Averill, and Hunter—Movement of Gen. Morgan—Advance of Gen. Hunter—Capture of Staunton, Lexington, &c.—He retreats to West Virginia—Invasion of Maryland—Defeat of Gen. Wallace—Approach of the enemy to Baltimore—Attack on Washington—The Enemy retire—Other Movements—Changes in the command of the Army of the James—Explosion of a Mine before Petersburg—Battle at Reams' Station—Hatcher's Run.

THE second movement against the Virginia and Tennessee Railroad, and for the occupation of Lynchburg, thereby to coöperate with Gen. Grant against Richmond, commenced about May 31st. Gen. Sigel was removed from the Department of Western Virginia, and Gen. Hunter placed in command.

The commands of Gens. Crook and Averill, which retired to Meadow Bluff, were reorganized and prepared for a simultaneous advance upon the Virginia and Tennessee Railroad and Lynchburg. Gen. Burbridge, in Kentucky, was ready to move upon extreme Southwest Virginia, so as to prevent any advance from that direction upon the rear of the combined forces about to move against Lynchburg. The position of the enemy at this time was most unfavorable for opposing these movements. Gen. Breckinridge, with the only Confederate force of importance west of the Blue Ridge, had been withdrawn to the army of Gen. Lee, leaving nothing but a few small brigades of inferior cavalry, about two regiments of infantry, and a small brigade of dismounted troops acting as infantry. To supply the place of Gen. Breckinridge, the little force of Gen. McCausland was sent from Dublin depot to the front of Staunton, and Gen. W. E. Jones was ordered to take all the troops to the same position which he could move from Southwest Wirginia. Gen. Jones, accordingly, got together all the Confederate troops west of New River, dismounting the brigades of cavalry, and moved to Staunton. He thus left in the extreme southwest only a few disjointed bodies of cavalry, and Gen. Morgan's command to oppose the advance of Gen. Burbridge. As this force was too small to effect that object by meeting Gen. Burbridge in front, with the slightest hope of success, it was resolved, as the only chance of saving the Southwest, that Gen. Morgan should dash boldly into the heart of Kentucky, and thus draw Gen. Burbridge away. This was expected to be successful, especially as Gen. Burbridge had much more to lose in Kentucky than the enemy had in Southwest Virginia.

On Sunday, June 29th, Gen. Morgan at the head of two thousand men passed through Pound Gap, on the border of Kentucky. At the same time a body of Gen. Burbridge's command was moving eastward and passed by Gen. Morgan. From Pound Gap he moved to Paintville, thence a scouting party was sent in advance to pick up horses. This body passed to Hazel Green, Owingsville, Flemingsburg, and Maysville, without resistance, thence to Mount Sterling, where a force from Gen. Burbridge overtook them. Other parties appeared in various places, but the main force moved to Cynthiana and Lexington, and approached Frankfort. Property was taken everywhere, the railroads destroyed, and bridges burned. Gen. Hobson, with a force of sixteen hundred men, was captured, and by the 12th of June Gen. Burbridge, with his whole command, was near Paris in full pursuit of Gen. Morgan. At Cynthiana a conflict took place, in which Gen. Burbridge reports that he killed three hundred and took as many more prisoners. He says: "Our loss in killed and wounded was about one hundred and fifty. Morgan's scattered forces are flying in all directions; have thrown away their arms, and are out of ammunition, and are wholly demoralized." Thus, by these movements, Gen. Burbridge was lured back to Kentucky and Southwest Virginia, for a time secured to the enemy. The rest and reorganization required by Gen. Burbridge's command, detained him until all the available reënforcements in Kentucky were required by Gen. Sherman in his progress to Atlanta.

Meanwhile the other parts of the general movement were in progress; Gen. Hunter, after assuming the command of the Department, issued the following order:

General Order No. 29.

HEADQUARTERS, DEPARTMENT WEST VIRGINIA,
IN THE FIELD, * * * *

It is of the utmost importance that this army be placed in a condition for immediate efficiency.

We are contending against an enemy who is in earnest, and if we expect success we too must be in earnest. We must be willing to make sacrifices—willing to suffer for a short time that a glorious result may crown our efforts. The country expects that every man will do his duty; and this well done, the protective care of a kind Providence will certainly ensure to us a complete success.

I. Every tent will be immediately turned in for transportation to Martinsburg, and all baggage not expressly allowed by this order will be at once sent to the rear. There will be but one wagon allowed to each regiment, and these will only be used to transport spare ammunition, camp kettles, tools, and mess-pans. Every wagon will have eight picked horses or mules, two drivers and two saddles. One wagon and one ambulance will be allowed to department headquarters, and the same to division and brigade headquarters. The other ambulances will be under the immediate orders of the Medical Director.

II. For the expedition on hand, the clothes that soldiers have on their backs, with one pair of extra shoes and socks, are amply sufficient. Every thing else in the shape of clothing will be packed to-day and sent to the rear. In each knapsack there must be one hundred rounds of ammunition, carefully packed; four pounds of hard bread, to last eight days; ten rations of coffee, sugar, and salt, and one pair of shoes and socks, but nothing else.

III. Brigade and all other commanders will be held strictly responsible that their commands are amply supplied on the march. Cattle, sheep, and hogs, and if necessary, horses and mules must be taken and slaughtered. These supplies will be seized under the direction of officers duly authorized, and upon a system which will hereafter be regulated. No straggling or pillaging will be allowed. Brigade and other commanders will be held responsible that there is a proper and orderly division of the supplies taken for our use.

IV. Commanders will attend personally to the prompt execution of this order, so that we may move to-morrow morning. They will see that in passing through the country in this way—depending upon it for forage and supplies—great attention is required of every commanding officer toward the enforcement of strict discipline.

V. The commanding general expects of every officer and soldier of the army in the field an earnest and unwavering support. He relies with confidence upon an ever kind Providence for a glorious result. The lieutenant-general commanding the armies of the United States, who is now vigorously pressing back the enemy upon their last stronghold, expects much from the Army of the Shenandoah, and he must not be disappointed.

VI. In conclusion, the major-general commanding makes it known that he will hold every officer to the strictest accountability for the proper enforcement of discipline in all respects; and that, on the other hand, he will never cease to urge the prompt promotion of all officers, non-commissioned officers, and enlisted men who attract recognition by their gallantry and good conduct.

By command of Maj.-Gen. HUNTER.
CHARLES G. HALPINE, Ass't Adj.-Gen.

His first movement was made from the neighborhood of Cedar Creek nearly to Woodstock. The guerrillas in the rear soon became troublesome, and were partially successful in destroying his communications. The advance continued through Woodstock, Mount Jackson, New Market, to Harrisonburg. On leaving this place the column was divided into two parts, one of which took the road by Port Republic, and the other the direct route to Staunton. The movement to Port Republic was a demonstration against the right of the enemy, and it encountered a movement on their part against the Federal left. At the same time the main body advanced in the direction of Mount Crawford, and met the enemy on North River, twelve miles from Staunton. A hot conflict ensued, as well here as at Port Republic, but the enemy were steadily driven on the North River, which exposed their right, and thus compelled it to fall back. At the same time Gen. Crook was approaching from the west, and the enemy in falling back retired toward Waynesboro' on the east. The loss of Gen. Hunter was two hundred and fifty. That of the enemy was severe, and included the commanding general, W. E. Jones. Staunton was immediately occupied by Gen. Hunter. Stores and railroad property of a large amount were captured.

The advance of Gens. Crook and Averill from Meadow Bluff was commenced on May 31st. They moved through Lewisburg, White Sulphur Springs, &c., to the Gaston depot on the Virginia Central Railroad by June 5th. This is about forty miles below the terminus of the road. Here the work of destruction commenced. The track was torn up, and bridges and culverts destroyed for a distance of ten miles. Thence the force moved over North Mountain, through Pond Gap to Staunton, and arrived on the 8th of June. The enemy attempted constantly to impede their progress.

On June 10th the consolidated command of Gen. Hunter marched from Staunton on the road through Middlebrook to Lexington, Gen. Crook's command being in advance. Three miles from Staunton the enemy, under Gen. McCausland, were posted behind rail breastworks, designed to delay the movement as much as possible. The steady advance, however, dislodged them, driving them ahead. Seventeen miles from Staunton they managed to kill two men and wound two others, when a strong force of cavalry dispersed them for that day. In the forenoon of the 11th Lexington was reached. The enemy had burned the bridge over the James, and were posted on the high bank opposite. They were driven off with artillery, after which the river was crossed at the fords and the town occupied. On Sunday, the 12th, the Military Institute and the house of Gov. Letcher were burned. Ten minutes were allowed to remove any property from the latter. A number of canal boats were destroyed, and considerable ammunition seized. A bronze statue of Gen. Geo. Washington, cast upon the orders of the legislature of Virginia, was taken down and subsequently transported to Wheeling, Va. On the 13th Gen. Averill was ordered to Buchanan, and the whole force followed on the next day. On Thursday, the 16th, Liberty was reached, and seven miles of railroad and the culverts and bridges destroyed. On the 17th the advance under Gen. Crook arrived within eight miles of Lynchburg at 10 A. M., and halted for the main force to come up. It arrived at 3 P. M., and moved on within an hour. After an advance of two miles the first position of the enemy was reached. They immediately opened with a brisk cannonade, but were soon driven back two miles to their line of breastworks with considerable loss to both sides. Night coming on Gen. Hunter was compelled to halt. All night the whistles of locomotives were heard in Lynchburg, bringing reënforcements from Richmond. On the next day the enemy appeared in force, and advanced to turn the right of Gen. Hunter's force. After a sharp struggle they were driven back to their breastworks, which were protected by others in the rear. The position of the enemy now appeared to Gen. Hunter to be so strong, and his numbers so great, as to destroy all hope of success with his army, now on limited rations. In the afternoon, therefore, the trains were started back, and at 9 P. M. the command commenced retreating, and marched until 1 A. M. the next morning, when they arrived within five miles of Liberty. At 9 A. M. the march was renewed until 2 P. M., when a halt was made three miles southwest of Liberty. The enemy followed close, and the skirmishing was continually heavy. The rear was brought up by Gen. Crook. At 6 P. M. the command was again on the march, and reached Bonsack's depot at 10 A. M. of the 20th, where a halt for rest was made. At 8 P. M. the march was resumed, via Buford's Gap, for Salem, which was reached at 5 o'clock on the next morning. The enemy continued a hot pursuit, and on the 21st captured ten pieces of artillery in a deep gap. Six were recaptured. That night the command rested all night for the first time since leaving Lynchburg. New Castle, in Craig County, was reached at 6 P. M. on the 22d. On the night of the 25th Meadow Bluff was reached by the force, being without supplies, except such as could be obtained from the sparse inhabitants of a mountainous country. On the 27th rations were obtained, and Gen. Hunter arrived at Loup Creek during the next day. On the same day the following despatch from Gen. Hunter was issued by the War Department:

WASHINGTON, June 28—4 P. M.

Maj.-Gen. Dix:

The following despatch has just been received from Gen. Hunter:

"I have the honor to report that our expedition has been extremely successful, inflicting great injury upon the enemy, and victorious in every engagement. Running short of ammunition, and finding it impossible to collect supplies while in the presence of an enemy believed to be superior to our force in numbers and constantly receiving reënforcements from Richmond and other points, I deemed it best to withdraw, and have succeeded in doing so without serious loss to this point, where we have met with abundant supplies of food. A detailed report of our operations will be forwarded immediately. The command is in excellent heart and health, and ready, after a few days' rest, for service in any direction."

Nothing later than my telegram of this morning has been received from Gen. Grant or Gen. Sherman.

EDWIN M. STANTON, Secretary of War.

The operations of the expedition were commented upon unfavorably by two newspapers in West Virginia. They were temporarily suppressed by Gen. Hunter. His reasons for this suppression, as well as his views of the condition of his men during the retreat, will be found in the annexed portion of a letter written by him:

HEADQUARTERS DEP'T OF WEST VIRGINIA.
CUMBERLAND, MD., July 13, 1864.

To his Exc. A. I. Boreman, Governor of West Virginia.

SIR: I have the honor to acknowledge the receipt of your communication dated July 10th, 1864, relative to the case of James E. Wharton, Esq., editor and proprietor of the "Parkersburg Gazette," and have first to state, in reply, that about two hours previous to the receipt of your letter orders had been given to the provost-marshal for Mr. Wharton's release, and he had been released before your letter reached my hand. And now a few words as to the causes which led to Mr. Wharton's arrest, and the temporary suppression of his journal.

As to the "criticism on your (my) conduct" in which Mr. Wharton indulged, and to which you refer, I agree with you that there was, of course, no offence whatever. It was merely a matter of taste on his part; nor was it noticed by me until you called my attention thereto as one of the possible causes for my action. But Mr. Wharton, in the editorial which led to the suppression of his paper, stated, first, that "Gen. Hunter, with his command, have principally passed through our city (Parkersburg) on their way east." This was contraband news, and was utterly untrue. Much less than one-tenth of my command had passed through Parkersburg, and I was detained there for some time after the appearance of the article, hurrying forward the balance.

In the second place Mr. Wharton went on to say, in the same article: "We were sorry to see so much suffering among them. They were completely worn out, and many in the division had died of starvation." . . . . . . "The sufferings of the soldiers in their movement from Lynchburg to Charleston were terrible, and they half require rest and surgical care."

That there was "some suffering" amongst the troops is true. The business of the soldier is one in which "suffering" forms an inevitable part. But on careful inquiry, personally and through many officers employed for the purpose, I have failed to discover even a report of any one case of death from hunger; while, on the other hand, my medical director, Surgeon Thomas B. Reed, an officer of large military experience and excellent judgment, assures me that, despite the certain limited privations and great fatigues of the march, the health of the command was, throughout, far better than the average health of soldiers quietly resting in their camps. . . . .

I have the honor to be, sir, with very sincere respect, your most obedient servant,

D. HUNTER, Maj.-Gen. Commanding.

The reason for his retreat through West Virginia was stated to be that "the return march down the Shenandoah to Staunton, was flanked by the railroad from Lynchburg to Waynesboro', and that Hunter with his whole command must, therefore, have been cut off and destroyed or captured, had any such movement been attempted."

Simultaneously with the beginning of the movement against Richmond, a cavalry raid was made by Gen. Sheridan from New Castle Ferry on the Pamunkey River to Gordonsville, the junction of the Virginia Central Railroad with the road to Alexandria. His report of the expedition was as follows:

I crossed the Pamunkey River on the 7th instant, marching via Aylett's, and encamped on Herring Creek.

On the morning of the 8th I resumed the march, via Polecat station, and encamped three miles west of the station.

On the 9th I marched through Childsburg and New Market, encamping on E. N. E. Creek, near Young's bridge.

On the 10th I marched via Andrews' Tavern and Leiman's store, crossing both branches of the North Anna, and encamped at Buch Childs, about three miles northeast of Trevilian station.

My intention was to break the railroad at this station, march through Mechanicsville, cut the Gordonsville and Charlottesville Railroad near Lindsay's house, and then to march on Charlottesville; but on our arrival at Buch Childs I found the enemy's cavalry in my immediate front.

On the morning of the 11th Gen. Torbert, with his division, and Col. Gregg, of Gen. Gregg's division, attacked the enemy. After an obstinate contest they drove him from successive lines of breastworks, through an almost impassable forest, back on Trevilian station.

In the mean time Gen. Custer was ordered with his brigade to proceed by a country road so as to reach the station in the rear of the enemy's cavalry. On his arrival at this point the enemy broke into a complete rout, leaving his dead and nearly all of his wounded in our hands; also twenty officers, five hundred men, and three hundred horses.

These operations occupied the whole of the day. At night I encamped at Trevilian station, and, on the morning of the 12th inst., commenced destroying the railroad from this point to Lorrain Court House. This was thoroughly done, the ties burned and the rails rendered unserviceable.

The destruction of the railroad occupied until 3 o'clock of this day, when I directed Gen. Torbert to advance with his division and Gen. Davis' brigade of Gen. Gregg's division in the direction of Gordonsville and attack the enemy, who had concentrated and been reënforced by infantry during the night, and had also constructed rifle-pits at a point about five miles from Gordonsville. The advance was made, but as the enemy's position was found too strong to assault, no general assault was made. On the extreme right of our lines a portion of the Reserve brigade carried the enemy's works twice, and was twice driven therefrom by infantry. Night closed the contest. I found, on examination of the command, that there was not a sufficiency of ammunition left to continue the engagement.

The next day trains of cars also came down to where we were engaged with the enemy. The reports of prisoners and citizens were that Pickett's old division was coming to prevent the taking of Gordonsville. I, therefore, during the night and next morning, withdrew my command over the North Anna, via Carpenter's ford, near Miner's bridge. In addition, the animals were for the two entire days in which we were engaged without forage. The surrounding country afforded nothing but grazing of a very inferior quality, and generally at such points as were inaccessible to us. The cavalry engagement of the 12th was by far the most brilliant one of the present campaign. The enemy's loss was very heavy. They lost the following named officers in killed and wounded:—Col. McAllister, commanding a regiment, killed; Brig.-Gen. Rosser, commanding a brigade, wounded, and Col. Custer, commanding a regiment, wounded. My loss in killed and wounded will be about five hundred and seventy-five. Of this number four hundred and ninety are wounded. I brought off in my ambulances three hundred and seventy seven—all that could be transported. The remainder were, with a number of rebel wounded that fell into my hands, left behind. Surgeons and attendants were detailed, and remained in charge of them. I captured and have now with me three hundred and seventy prisoners of war, including twenty commissioned officers. My loss in captured will not exceed one hundred and sixty. They were principally from the 5th Michigan cavalry. This regiment gallantly charged down the Gordonsville road, capturing fifteen hundred horses and about eight hundred men; but were finally surrounded and had to give them up. When the enemy broke they hurried between Gen. Custer's command and Col. Gregg's brigade, capturing five caissons of Pennington's battery, three of which were afterwards recaptured, leaving in their hands two caissons.

The contest at Trevilian was reported by Gen. Lee to be a rebel victory.

The retirement of Gen. Hunter to West Virginia, with his army in such condition as to need rest and reorganization, left the Shenandoah valley open to the unresisted occupation of the enemy. At the same time the state of affairs at Petersburg permitted Gen. Lee to detach a force for the invasion of Maryland, and perhaps cause troops to be recalled from Gen. Grant for the defence of Washington. Rumors of the advance of the enemy down the Shenandoah valley preceded their appearance by some days. On Saturday, July 2d, they first reached the region of Martinsburg. On the news of their approach, Gen. Sigel determined to evacuate Martinsburg and a part of the stores were removed, including nearly all the rolling stock of the railroad company, and heavy trains loaded with supplies for Gen. Hunter. A quantity of valuable stores, however, were lost. The enemy first appeared at North Mountain, eight miles north of Martinsburg, which compelled Gen. Sigel to fall back to Harper's Ferry. On Saturday, July 3d, he was attacked at Leetown, and quickly driven from his position, and moved to the strong position of Maryland Heights, which he held. The main line of the enemy's advance was by way of Martinsburg and North Mountain, across the Potomac to Hagerstown. A panic spread over the region, and the inhabitants fled with such property as they could hastily seize and remove. At Fredrick, Md., on the 5th, all the Government stores were loaded on railroad trains, and preparations made for an immediate evacuation of the city. On the same day Hagerstown was occupied and the stores plundered, and a requisition made on the inhabitants for $20,000. This money was paid and the raiding party left. The Baltimore and Ohio Railroad was held by the enemy as far down as Sandy Hook, and much of the track torn up. The following were the orders of the commanding officer of the enemy to his force:

HEADQUARTERS CAVALRY DIVISION,
VALLEY DISTRICT, June 28, 1864.

The following directions for the march of this command will hereafter be strictly observed:—

Before the march begins on each morning the rolls of each company will be called after mounting, and the adjutant of each regiment will keep a list of the names of all deserters.

Before dismounting at camp in the evening the rolls will again be called, and the brigade commanders will report to these headquarters the number of men absent at each roll call.

The habitual order of the march will be in column of "fours," but on narrow roads by "twos." The distance between the head of one brigade and the rear of the other will be two hundred yards. When artillery and ambulances accompany the brigades, those assigned to each brigade will follow immediately in rear of their brigades. During the march the brigades in rear will regulate their movements by those in front.

Regular halts will be made during the march, and neither officers nor men will leave the column, except at such halts, unless by the written consent of the brigade commander, and such permission will not be granted unless for important reasons.

Brigade, regimental, and company commanders will pass frequently from front to rear of their respective commands, to see that the column is at all times well closed up. Brigades will alternate in the march daily. A rear guard will be placed behind each brigade, and no person, except staff officers or couriers, will be permitted to fall behind such guard.

All the wagons of this division will march together under direction of the division quartermaster.

The quartermasters of the command will constantly accompany their respective trains. One man, dismounted when practicable, will go with each wagon to assist the driver. He will remain with the wagon. No other parties will be permitted with the train, except when a guard shall be necessary. The quartermasters will be held responsible that no others accompany the wagons. No other wagons or conveyances than those allowed from army headquarters will be allowed.

Upon reaching camp, officers and men must remain in their camps, and commanders will establish proper camp guards.

Immediately upon fixing the headquarters of the brigade the commanders will report their locality to division headquarters.

The utmost order and perfect quiet will be preserved upon the march and in camp. The silly practice of whooping and hallooing is strictly forbidden.

Destruction of the fences and crops of the farmers is positively prohibited, and such outrages will be paid for from the pay of the officers of the command nearest where such depredations may be committed.

Greatest care must be taken of ammunition. Not a cartridge must be fired unnecessarily. An important campaign is commenced, and upon its results depend more than we can estimate.

The Major-General commanding asks and expects from every man of his command a hearty and cheerful compliance with orders, assuring all that they shall reap and enjoy the full fruits of whatever their labors and privations may obtain.

By command of Maj.-Gen. RANSOM.
WALTER K. MARTIN, Asst.-Adjt.-Gen.
Brig.-Gen. NED MCCAUSLAND, com'dg brigade.
N. FITZHUGH, Asst.-Adjt.-Gen.

On the same day the President issued a call for twelve thousand militia from Pennsylvania, twelve thousand from New York, five thousand from Massachusetts, and the various Governors issued proclamations calling out the troops, and the militia began to assemble.

On Wednesday there was some skirmishing with a few of the enemy's cavalry, between Hagerstown and Frederick. The Federal force from Hagerstown fell back toward Chambersburg. At various points along the Potomac and north there was some skirmishing.

On Thursday, a reconnoitring force sent out by Gen. Wallace from Monocacy, was quickly repulsed by the enemy. Boonsboro' and Middletown were occupied by them, and they advanced within a few miles of Frederick, and threw some shots into the city. Before morn-

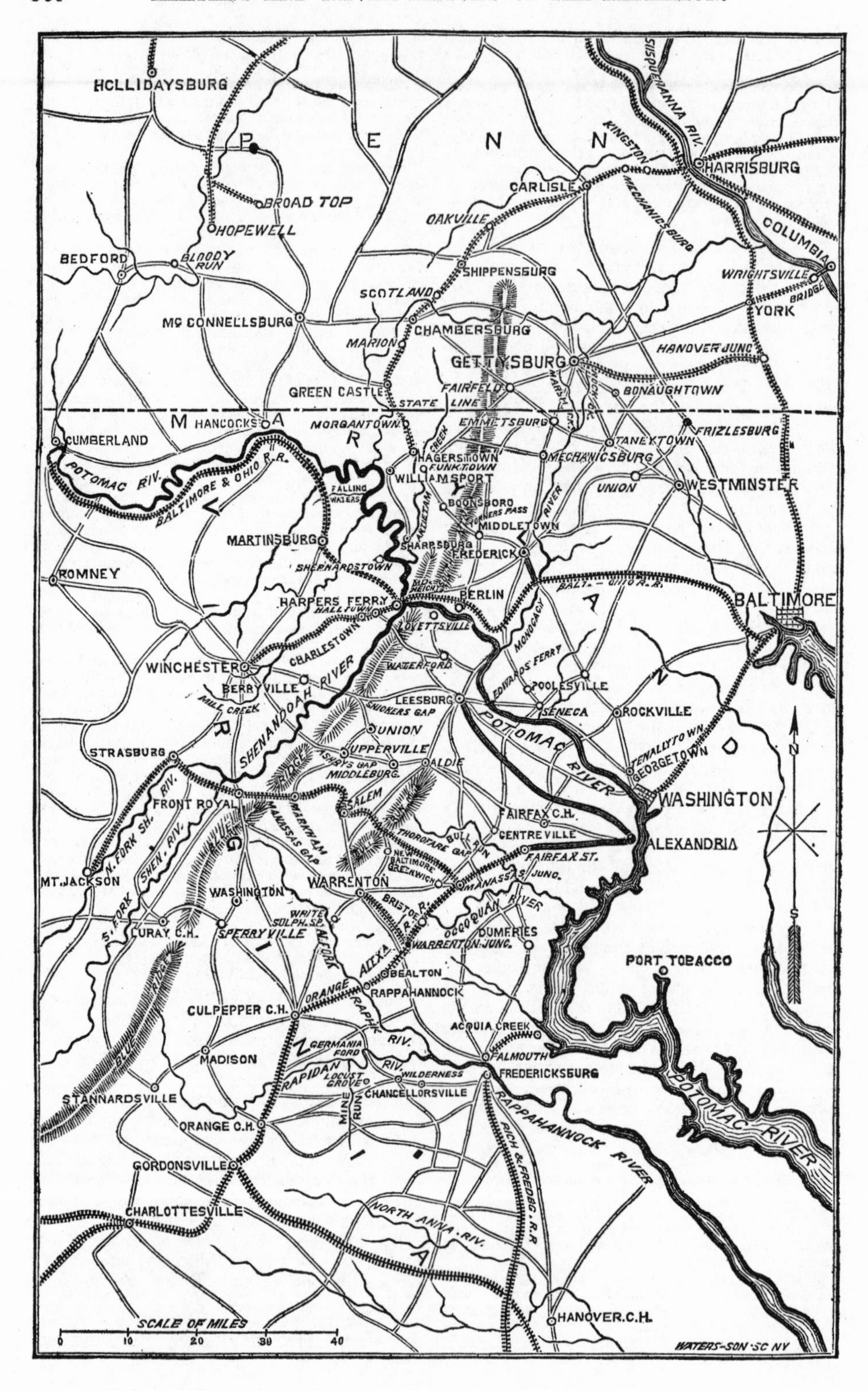
HOLLIDAYSBURG
P E N N
BROAD TOP
HOPEWELL
BEDFORD
BLOODY RUN
CARLISLE
KINGSTON
HARRISBURG
SUSQUEHANNA RIV.
MECHANICSBURG
COLUMBIA
OAKVILLE
SHIPPENSBURG
WRIGHTSVILLE
BRIDGE
YORK
SCOTLAND
MC CONNELLSBURG
CHAMBERSBURG
MARION
GETTYSBURG
HANOVER JUNC
GREEN CASTLE
FAIRFELD
BONAUGHTOWN
STATE LINE
M HANCOCKS A
MORGANTOWN
EMMETSBURG
FRIZLESBURG
CUMBERLAND
R
TANEYTOWN
HAGERSTOWN
FUNKTOWN
MECHANICSBURG
POTOMAC RIV.
BALTIMORE & OHIO R.R.
WILLIAMSPORT
UNION
WESTMINSTER
FALLING WATERS
BOONSBORO
TURNERS PASS
MIDDLETOWN
MARTINSBURG
SHARPSBURG
FREDERICK
SHEPHERDSTOWN
ROMNEY
BERLIN
HARPERS FERRY
HALLTOWN
LOVETTSVILLE
BALTIMORE
MONOCACY
CHARLESTOWN
WATERFORD
WINCHESTER
EDWARDS FERRY
BERRYVILLE
POOLESVILLE
MILL CREEK
LEESBURG
SENECA
ROCKVILLE
SNICKERS GAP
UNION
SHENANDOAH RIVER
STRASBURG
UPPERVILLE
ASHBYS GAP
MIDDLEBURG
ALDIE
POTOMAC RIVER
TENALLYTOWN
GEORGETOWN
WASHINGTON
FRONT ROYAL
SALEM
N. FORK SH. RIV.
SHEN. RIV.
MANASSAS GAP
FAIRFAX C.H.
CENTREVILLE
BULL RUN
THOROFARE GAP
ALEXANDRIA
FAIRFAX ST.
MT. JACKSON
NEW BALTIMORE
GREENWICH
MANASSAS JUNC.
WARRENTON
WASHINGTON
S. FORK
BRISTOE
OCCOQUAN RIVER
WHITE SULPH. SP.
LURAY C.H.
SPERRYVILLE
DUMFRIES
WARRENTON JUNC.
BEALTON
PORT TOBACCO
RAPPAHANNOCK
CULPEPPER C.H.
ORANGE
RAPP'K RIV.
ACQUIA CREEK
GERMANIA FORD
FALMOUTH
MADISON
FREDERICKSBURG
RAPIDAN
LOCUST GROVE
WILDERNESS
CHANCELLORSVILLE
STANNARDSVILLE
MINE RUN
POTOMAC RIVER
ORANGE C.H.
RAPPAHANNOCK RIVER
GORDONSVILLE
RICH & FREDBG. R.R.
CHARLOTTESVILLE
NORTH ANNA RIV.
HANOVER C.H.
SCALE OF MILES
0
10
20
30
40
WATERS-SON SC NY

ing of the 8th they withdrew to another quarter. The country on all sides was scoured for horses, forage, provisions, and money. On the 8th, another party from Harper's Ferry entered Hagerstown from Williamsport, and again plundered the inhabitants and burned some buildings. The enemy still occupied the road to Frederick with their main body behind Catoctin Mountain. In the evening of the same day, Gen. Wallace withdrew with his force from Frederick to Monocacy Junction. At sunrise on the next morning, the 9th, the enemy entered and levied a contribution on the inhabitants. About 9 A.M. they advanced against Gen. Wallace, who occupied a position on the east side of the Monocacy River, with his batteries protecting the railroad and the turnpike. The attack of the enemy was made on his left under Gen. Ricketts, with varying success for some hours, when it was forced to give way. At the same time the right of Gen. Wallace was outflanked by the enemy, who, appearing in the rear, poured in a reverse fire and swept off about six hundred men and officers, including Gen. Tyler. Gen. Wallace now fell back, and the enemy pursued him some miles toward Ellicott's Mills on the Baltimore turnpike. His loss was about twelve hundred men, with six cannon. The command under Gen. Ricketts had been sent forward from Petersburg by Gen. Grant. The force of the enemy consisted of a column which crossed the Potomac at Williamsport, and another which had besieged Gen. Sigel for four days in Harper's Ferry.

The disaster to Gen. Wallace created great excitement in Washington and through the Northern States. Washington appeared to be in imminent peril, and reënforcements were hurried forward. The 19th army corps, which had been sent from New Orleans to reënforce Gen. Grant, was at this time entering the Chesapeake Bay. It was at once sent to Washington. One corps of Gen. Grant's army—the 6th, under Gen. Wright—was detached from the lines before Petersburg, and also sent to Washington. Gen. Wallace, in command at Baltimore, was superseded by Gen. Ord. Meantime the enemy, after tearing up some of the railroad from Frederick to Baltimore, sent their main body south of it and detached a cavalry force toward the Northern Central Railroad from Harrisburg, Penn., to Baltimore. This cavalry expedition overran Eastern Maryland. Twenty-five miles of the Northern Central road were destroyed, and on Monday, the 11th, a force appeared on the Baltimore, Wilmington, and Philadelphia road, and captured and set on fire the trains at Magnolia station, seventeen miles south of Havre de Grace. In one train Maj.-Gen. Franklin was captured, but afterwards made his escape. Some damage was done to the track, and Gunpowder bridge was partially burned. The cavalry, heavily loaded with plunder, came within six miles of Baltimore, then turning southward they joined the force near Washington, which had been sent in that direction to guard against surprise. Part of it halted before Fort Stevens, on Seventeenth Street. Toward evening their sharpshooters had become so annoying, and their presence at the Capital so humiliating, that an attempt was made by Gen. Augur to dislodge them. A brigade of veteran infantry was detached along Seventeenth Street road, which encountered them, and a sharp skirmish ensued. The enemy were driven off, leaving about a hundred dead and wounded on the field. The Federal loss was between two and three hundred. While this demonstration was made before Washington, the rest of the enemy's force were moving across the Potomac, and on Wednesday morning the whole force was approaching the river and the invasion was ended.

On the retreat they were cautiously followed by a column from Washington, under Gen. Wright, consisting of the 6th corps and a division of the 19th. He crossed the Potomac below Edward's ferry and moved to Leesburg. At the same time a portion of one train was captured by the cavalry under Gen. Crook, with some of the teamsters and guard, and the rear driven through Snicker's gap after a sharp fight. The enemy, however, held the ferry across the Shenandoah with two guns, and checked the pursuit. On Monday, July 18th, the command of Gen. Wright and the cavalry under Gen. Crook, excepting a body sent to guard Ashby's gap, passed through Snicker's gap to the ferry. The infantry began to cross below the ferry. The cavalry also crossed, and forming a line with the brigade of Col. Wells on the left, and that of Col. Thorburn on the right, hotly engaged the enemy. As the latter were concentrating on the right, Gen. Wright began to cross the 6th corps to meet the enemy's concentration. But they charged the line with violence, and at length turned the right and drove it with some confusion across the ford. Finding the right giving way, Col. Wells withdrew the left, and the troops recrossed the river with a loss of three hundred. The force sent to Ashby's gap drove the enemy through the gap and across the river, but the latter finding their rear attacked, hurried back in force and compelled the command to retire with a loss of two hundred. The enemy now leisurely moved toward Winchester and Strasburg, and the force of Gen. Wright crossed the Shenandoah. They soon halted and recrossed, returning to Leesburg, whence Gen. Crook moved to Harper's Ferry, and Gen. Wright to Washington. On the 19th, the same day on which the enemy were overtaken at Snicker's ferry, Gen. Averill moved from Martinsburg toward Winchester, and encountered a cavalry force near Darksville. On the next morning he pressed toward Winchester, where he met the enemy, and a contest ensued for three hours, during which Gen. Averill captured four guns, several hundred small arms, and about two hundred prisoners. The total loss of the enemy was between three and four hundred. The force of the enemy at hand caused him to halt in his advance.

The entire force of the enemy in this invasion was not far from 20,000 men. It included two infantry corps under Gens. Breckinridge and Rhodes, a division of cavalry under Gen. Ransom, and three batteries of artillery. The whole was under the command of Maj.-Gen. Jubal Early. Leaving a considerable force to guard his rear, about fifteen thousand crossed the Potomac. His loss was about fifteen hundred. A large amount of property was destroyed, five thousand horses driven off, one of the greatest panics was excited, and several thousand men were withdrawn from Gen. Grant's army.

Gen. Crook, after returning toward Harper's Ferry joined Gen. Averill, and on July 23d there was considerable skirmishing at Kernstown, four miles beyond Winchester, and the Federal cavalry were driven back on the main body. On the next day the enemy pressed his advantage, and the cavalry were driven back in great rout through Winchester toward Bunker Hill. The breaking of his cavalry forced Gen. Crook to retreat. His command consisted of the cavalry under Gens. Averill and Duffie, and two divisions of infantry, about ten thousand men. The enemy being in greater strength outflanked him, and compelled a retreat from point to point. After the first struggle Gen. Early halted his main force about five miles north of Winchester, but his cavalry kept up a hot pursuit to Martinsburg. The loss of Gen. Crook from all sources was about twelve hundred, among whom was Col. Mulligan, killed. On the next day a sharp artillery engagement took place at Martinsburg, but Gen. Crook, having gained time to get off most of his trains, again fell back, and on the succeeding day crossed the Potomac into Maryland, without molestation by the enemy. Their loss in these affairs was considerable. None, however, were taken prisoners.

The enemy now held the west bank of the Potomac from Williamsport to Shepardstown. In Maryland and southern Pennsylvania the scenes in anticipation of the previous invasion were renewed—the panic—the frightful stories, fugitives, and the roads blocked with every species of property, which its owners were endeavoring to remove to a place of safety. The Federal troops rallied again, and on the 27th it was found that the enemy was not opposite Williamspoint. On the next day, Gen. Kelly crossed and reoccupied Martinsburg, which the enemy had already evacuated. On the next day, the 29th of July, a force of the enemy crossed the Potomac, and advanced on Chambersburg, in Pennsylvania. On the next day, Saturday, they dispersed some troops at Carlisle barracks, and a force of two or three hundred mounted men entered Chambersburg and set it on fire. A part of the inhabitants, with their valuable property, had gone off on the previous day. The enemy demanded a ransom of $500,000, which not being paid, about two-thirds of the town, or two hundred and fifty houses, were burned. The inhabitants who remained made no opposition.

During the forenoon the enemy withdrew. Immediately afterwards Gen. Averill entered the town, and without stopping to extinguish the flames set out in pursuit. On Thursday evening previous he had retreated from Hagerstown toward Carlisle. During Friday he was driven back to Greencastle by the force of the enemy which on that day crossed the Potomac, and a part of his train lost. At night the enemy turned toward Chambersburg, and Gen. Averill on the next morning began to follow after them through St. Thomas, Loudon, and McConnellsburg. The force from Chambersburg having reached their reserves, were overtaken by Gen. Averill toward evening, eight miles beyond McConnellsburg. Skirmishing took place until dark. On the next day Gen. Averill followed to Hancock, where the enemy checked the pursuit by felling trees and burning bridges behind him.

On Saturday, Col. Mosby, a partisan ranger, with about fifty men crossed the Potomac at Cheat ferry, pushed up the towpath to Adamstown, captured the picket there, consisting of thirty or forty cavalry, cut the telegraph wire, robbed a few stores, and quickly retired. This affair created great alarm at Frederick, Monocacy, and Poolesville. It stopped the railroad trains in the neighborhood, and gave rise to a report that Gen. Early was invading Pennsylvania with forty thousand men.

The band of Col. Mosby on its return encountered a superior force at Conrad's ferry, with which a slight skirmish occurred. The panic, however, increased. Gen. Couch telegraphed to the authorities at Pittsburg that "it is believed Breckinridge is marching west." All business was immediately suspended, and on Sunday a public meeting was held to prepare for defence. On Monday, August 1st, Gov. Curtin called the State Legislature to assemble on the 9th to take prompt measures in so great a crisis. At the same time Gen. Couch examined the defences on the Ohio and Monongahela Rivers. The 6th corps started for the scene of action on hearing of the defeat of Gen. Crook. Leaving Georgetown on July 26th, it bivouacked at Rockville at night. On the next day it marched to Hyattstown and reached the Monocacy on Thursday, and passing through Frederick encamped at Jefferson. On Friday evening it reached Halltown, three miles from Harper's Ferry. The force at that point, on Saturday, the day that Chambersburg was burned, consisted of the 6th corps, a part of the 19th, and the infantry of Gen. Hunter, under Gen. Crook. On that day orders came to move in pursuit of Gen. Early's army, which was reported to be ravaging Pennsylvania. The whole force, with an immense wagon-train, marched hard during that day and the next, losing some men by sunstroke, but finding no enemy. After a severe march they arrived at Frederick quite exhausted, and rested.

The small force of the enemy which had been in Maryland moved from Hancock on the Cumberland road, as above stated, the pursuit of Gen. Averill being checked by felling trees, &c. Gen. Kelly with his command in Western Virginia now started to intercept this advance. On Monday afternoon the enemy reached Folck's mill, three miles from Cumberland, and attacked Gen. Kelly, who was protecting the town. The skirmish continued until dark, and the enemy during the night fell back to Oldtown, leaving his killed and wounded, some wagons and ammunition. During the afternoon previous a force of five hundred men had been posted at Oldtown, under Col. Stough, to cut off the enemy's retreat. In the morning this force was attacked by the enemy, and, after a sharp skirmish, routed. The colonel and ninety men were made prisoners. The loss of the enemy in killed and wounded was about thirty; the Federal loss in this respect was much less. On Thursday, August 4th, the enemy made an attack on Gen. Crook, but were foiled, and during the night withdrew on the road to Moorefield. At that place he was overtaken by Gen. Averill and routed with the loss of his artillery, many wagons, and five hundred prisoners. The loss of Gen. Averill was about fifty. On Thursday, the 4th, a panic prevailed in Harrisburg, caused by a report that the enemy had crossed the Potomac, and was invading the North. Gov. Curtin issued a proclamation calling out thirty thousand militia, and the inhabitants in the Cumberland valley commenced another grand removal.

The result of these operations was to secure an organized defence under the command of Gen. Sheridan for the defence of the valley. This force, by orders of Gen. Grant, consisted of the 6th and 19th corps, the division of infantry under Gen. Crook, and the division of cavalry under Gen. Torbert, with four brigades of Gen. Hunter's cavalry.

The changes made before Petersburg during the operations of the enemy in Maryland, consisted chiefly in the transfer of troops to thwart them. The army of Gen. Grant continued more quiet than at any time since his campaign was commenced. The principal firing during this period was on the right and right centre, where Gen. Grant's lines were persistently pushed forward, and Petersburg and the batteries of the enemy monotonously shelled. Some skirmishes at different points also occurred by which a few men were lost on each side.

On July 1st a movement was made by a body of troops under Gen. Birney from Hilton Head, up the North Edisto River. They disembarked at White Point for the purpose of penetrating the country as far as practicable. The enemy were found in strong positions, and after some skirmishing the force withdrew. An attempt was also made to seize Fort Johnson on the northern end of James Island, by crossing Morris Island. The enemy were found to be strong and on the alert, and the force was withdrawn.

About the same time, July 3d, Gen. Dennis with a force of three thousand men moved out from Vicksburg to destroy the railroad from Jackson to Canton. Jackson was easily occupied, but on the return, an attack of the enemy was made upon the rear, and a sharp skirmish followed. The loss was about two hundred on each side. Some other movements were made at this time in Mississippi and Missouri partaking of a guerrilla character.

In the latter part of July some changes were made in the commanders of the corps of the army of the James River. An order from the War Department relieving Gen. Butler was rescinded by Gen. Grant, and the former was retained in command. Gen. Smith was relieved from the command of the 18th corps and succeeded temporarily by Gen. Martindale, and then permanently by Gen. Ord, of the 8th corps. Gen. Gillmore was relieved of the command of of the 10th corps, succeeded temporarily by Gens. W. H. H. Brooks and Terry, and permanently by Gen. Birney of the 2d corps.

The line of Gen. Grant extended at this time a distance of twenty miles. On the right, north of the James, at Deep Bottom, Gen. Foster's division of the 10th corps had been for some time in possession of an intrenched camp. This position served to prevent any sudden demonstration on the right flank by the enemy, who were in possession of Malvern Hill, and also checked any effort by them to blockade the river against gunboats and transports by field artillery. At the same time it furnished a good base for threatening an advance on Richmond from the southeast, or for making a feint in that direction. In the rear of Gen. Foster's position a pontoon bridge crossed the James which was thoroughly protected by gunboats, but in his front a large force of the enemy prevented an advance. On July 21st a second bridge was thrown across the James at Strawberry Plains a little further down, and on the next day a brigade of the 19th corps crossed over and held the head of the bridge. Constant skirmishing with the enemy followed for some days, and so threatening was the demonstration that a division was added to their force in front of Gen. Foster. On Tuesday, July 26th, rapid artillery firing, intermingled with musketry, was kept up during the forenoon. At evening it was renewed with the addition of the gunboats, and continued through the night. At 4 P. M. of the same day the 5th corps moved from the extreme left, followed by the cavalry under Gen. Sheridan to the James River at Jones's Neck. Before daylight they began to cross on a pontoon bridge, which had been muffled with hay and grass. A line of battle was then formed with Gen. Sheridan's cavalry on the extreme right, and the 2d corps next at Strawberry Plains, the brigade of the 19th corps on its left, and Gen.

Foster in his old position on the extreme left, at Deep Bottom.

The position of the enemy was in front of the 2d corps. They occupied rifle-pits, defended by one battery. An advance upon them was made by the 2d corps, during which Gen. Miles's brigade under cover flanked the whole position under a brisk charge. The enemy immediately retreated, losing their guns and some prisoners. A mile further in the rear they took a new position on a ridge. The Federal loss during the day was about a hundred. On the next day the demonstrations were continued, and a cavalry battle took place on the right with a loss of about two hundred and fifty. On Friday about four hundred empty wagons were taken across on the bridges as if an advance on Malvern Hill was to be made in great force. Nearly twenty thousand men and twenty cannon had thus been sent north of the James. Meanwhile the enemy hurried off a considerable force from Petersburg to meet these demonstrations, and during Thursday still more were sent. On Thursday evening, therefore, the 3d division of the 2d corps was secretly removed to Petersburg. After some skirmishing with the enemy on Friday afternoon, the rest of the 2d corps and the cavalry, after dark, retraced their steps and arrived before daybreak at Petersburg. At this place there had been the usual cannonade during the four preceding days.

All those movements were preliminaries to the explosion of a heavy mine which had been planted under one of the enemy's heaviest works. It had been suggested by Lieutenant-colonel Pleasants of the 48th Pennsylvania regiment, who with his regiment had been accustomed to mining before the war. By them the whole work was accomplished. It was begun on June 25th. It started in the side of a ravine in front of the 9th corps and pushed toward a formidable fort of the enemy situated about two thousand yards from Petersburg. The distance to be mined was about five hundred feet. The gallery was made in the usual shape, being about four feet wide at the bottom and sloping up to the top. Its height was about four and a half feet. A ventilating shaft was sunk near the entrance. The ground rose toward the enemy's position, and the tunnel was sloped upwards as it advanced. When the fort was reached, it was about twenty feet overhead. Wings were extended to the right and left, so that the main gallery might open into two diverging galleries, running along the outer line of the fort. Eight chambers were formed in these latter, separated by sand-bags and wood. Wooden pipes ran about a hundred feet from the magazines toward the mouth of the gallery, and were connected there by a hose or fuse which extended the rest of the distance. The chambers were charged with four tons of powder. After its completion a delay of some days ensued, during which the feint at Deep Bottom was made.

Every effort to conceal the work was made, but it was supposed that the enemy were aware of its existence.

The plan of assault was to explode the mine and immediately to open a cannonading from every gun on the line. Under cover of this concentrated fire, which might somewhat unnerve the enemy, a storming party was to rush through the gap made by the explosion and endeavor to carry the enemy's position beyond. In the rear of his first line was a strong crest, which commanded Petersburg. Tbe Federal lines were less than a hundred and fifty yards distant from the enemy at the nearest points. The approach to the part to be charged, which was about the same distance, had been made difficult by abatis and entanglements. Nearly a hundred heavy guns had been brought up by Gen. Grant, some of which were eight-inch and some even heavier.

The assaulting force was the 9th corps, supported by the 18th corps, with the 2d in reserve on the right, and the 5th on the left, the whole closely massed, and leaving only the necessary garrisons to hold the more distant intrenchments. This force was in position soon after midnight on Friday, July 29th. The 9th corps was arranged with Gen. Ledlie's division in advance, Gens. Wilcox and Potter's next in support, and the colored division, in command of Gen. Ferrero, in the rear. The fuse was to be lighted at 3½ o'clock A. M. But, owing to dampness, the fire went out in the gallery. It was renewed after much delay, but the explosion did not take place until twenty minutes of five o'clock, and after sunrise. A heaving and trembling of the earth was followed by huge clouds of earth and all the contents of the fort, as guns, caissons, limbers, and the soldiers which manned them being thrown into the air. To the spectators it resembled a great fountain in appearance; then, poising for a moment, it quickly descended. A crater, one hundred feet or more in length and half as wide, and a depth of twenty feet, with heaps of ruins, remained where once stood a six-gun fort, its camp equipage, and two hundred men. Immediately after the explosion, the cannonading from a hundred guns commenced. Gradually recovering from his surprise the enemy began to respond, and soon their entire line was engaged. Meantime, after a few minutes' delay, Gen. Marshall's brigade, of Gen. Ledlie's division, began to advance across the deadly plain. The supporting brigades spread out and enveloped the flanking rifle-pits, capturing about two hundred prisoners. The breach was gained, and the troops began to reform for assault. Instead of bursting at once upon the frowning crest, four hundred yards distant, the advance brigades were suffered to throw up intrenchments and spend time in getting two guns to bear on the enemy. Meanwhile the latter rallied and poured a terrific enfilading fire upon the captured fort. At length the 7th corps was re-formed, after a fatal delay, and with Gen. Potter's division on the right, Ledlie's in the centre, and Wilcox on the left, under cover of the fire of two guns, began the charge. At every step, the fire of the enemy in front and on each flank, concentrated with greater fury upon them and ploughed their ranks with slaughter. The charge was checked on the side of the crest, there was a halt, and finally the whole line, wavering under terrible odds, recoiled to the fort. The colored division of the corps remained. As a forlorn hope, it was despatched to do what the other three had failed in attempting. It rushed forward over the four hundred yards which separated it from the enemy only to meet the fate of its comrades. When once broken, it plunged headlong into the fort, upon which the enemy now concentrated their fire. It was evident the day was lost, and the question now was, how best to save the troops. Efforts were made by a division of the 18th and another of the 10th corps to distract the attention of the enemy, but they proved to be useless. His fire was directed straight upon the dismantled fort, now become a slaughter-pen, in which were huddled the fragments of the 9th corps, hoping for relief from their comrades who lay in their intrenchments, two hundred yards distant. Then squads of men began the work of retreating. But the enemy kept up a destructive cross-fire over every rod of the space between the fort and the Federal lines. The retreating movement, however, was kept up. Meanwhile, the enemy made several charges upon the ruins of the fort, which were bravely resisted by some of the officers and the remnants of the corps. About noon, however, a general retreat was ordered, a considerable part of the survivors of the assault having already crossed to the rear. Those who remained in the fort having exhausted their ammunition and being left unsupported by the rest of the army, were captured about 2 P. M. by a final charge of the enemy.

The Federal loss was estimated at five thousand; that of the enemy, one thousand, of whom two hundred were made prisoners. The dead lay on the field for thirty six hours, when they were removed under a flag of truce.

On Friday, Aug. 5th, a mine was exploded by the enemy. No assault followed. On the 7th there was a sharp skirmish and an artillery duel in front of the 9th corps. In the afternoon of the 9th another duel with heavy mortars occurred on the right and right centre. On the same day an ordnance boat was receiving fixed ammunition at City Point, when, by dropping one of the cases, the whole cargo was exploded. On several succeeding days, before Petersburg, only picket and artillery firing took place.

On August 10th, preparations were made for digging a canal at Dutch Gap. A great bend in the James River forms a peninsula called Farrar's Island, which a neck of land, less than half a mile wide, connects with the north shore. This isthmus it was proposed to cut by a canal. Such canal would save a circuit of six miles in a bend crowded with obstructions and torpedoes and guarded by gunboats of the enemy. If occupied, it would also flank the strong position of the enemy at Howlett's, where his heavy batteries swept the river. It would compel him to construct a new and more extended line of defence, requiring a larger force of men to defend it, and also bring Gen. Grant's forces dangerously near to Fort Darling. The prosecution of the work was continued through the remainder of the year, although often seriously and dangerously annoyed by the enemy. One of the last acts of Gen. Butler, while in command on the James, was an unsuccessful attempt to remove, by an explosion of powder, the earth at the entrance of the canal.

The state of operations at this time, as viewed by Gen. Grant, is expressed in the following letter:

HEADQUARTERS ARMIES OF THE UNITED STATES,
CITY POINT, VA., August 16th, 1864.

To Hon. E. B. Washburne:

DEAR SIR—I state to all citizens who visit me that all we want now to insure an early restoration of the Union is a determined unity of sentiment North. The rebels have now in their ranks their last man. The little boys and old men are guarding prisoners, guarding railroad bridges, and forming a good part of their garrisons for entrenched positions. A man lost by them cannot be replaced. They have robbed the cradle and the grave equally to get their present force. Besides what they lose in frequent skirmishes and battles, they are now losing from desertions and other causes at least one regiment per day.

With this drain upon them the end is not far distant, if we will only be true to ourselves. Their only hope now is in a divided North. This might give them reënforcements from Tennessee, Kentucky, Maryland, and Missouri, while it would weaken us. With the draft quickly enforced the enemy would become despondent, and would make but little resistance. I have no doubt but the enemy are exceedingly anxious to hold out until after the Presidential election. They have many hopes from its effects.

They hope a counter revolution; they hope the election of the Peace candidate. In fact, like "Micawber," they hope for something to "turn up." Our Peace friends, if they expect peace from separation, are much mistaken. It would but be the beginning of war with thousands of Northern men joining the South because of our disgrace in allowing separation. To have "peace on any terms" the South would demand the restoration of their slaves already freed; they would demand indemnity for losses sustained, and they would demand a treaty which would make the North slave-hunters for the South. They would demand pay for the restoration of every slave escaping to the North.

Yours, truly, U. S. GRANT.

On August 18th the 5th corps marched to Reams' station, on the Weldon Railroad, and surprised a body of the enemy guarding it, and took possession of the road. On the next day an impetuous attack was made upon their right by three brigades of the enemy under Gen. Mahone. The pickets and an advanced regiment were quickly driven back to the breastworks, and the enemy rushed through a gap in the line, separating the divisions of Crawford and Wilcox. A desperate engagement now ensued. At the same time the left of the line was attacked by the enemy under Gen. Heth, and the temporary intrenchments carried. On reaching the second line the enemy was brought to a stand, and then driven back with great slaughter. At this time reënforcements had arrived, consisting of the 1st and 2d divisions of the 9th corps. The lines were thus finally rallied and the enemy driven back, retrieving in a measure the disaster at the outset. The Federal loss was estimated between 3,500 and 4,000. The enemy claimed to have captured 2,700 prisoners. The Weldon Railroad was thus recovered by the enemy as far as Yellow Tavern, but the position first taken by Gen. Warren was held.

On August 28th, Gen. Grant issued the following order:

HEADQUARTERS ARMIES OF THE U. S., IN THE FIELD,
VIRGINIA, August 28th, 1864.

Special Orders No. 82.

Hereafter deserters from the Confederate army, who deliver themselves up to the United States forces, will, on taking the oath that they will not again take up arms during the present rebellion, be furnished subsistence and free transportation to their homes, if the same are within the lines of the Federal occupation.

If their homes are within such lines, they will be furnished subsistence and free transportation to any point in the Northern States.

All deserters who take the oath of allegiance will, if they desire it, be given employment in the Quartermaster's and other departments of the army, and the same remuneration paid them as is given to civilians employed for similar services.

Forced military duty, or services endangering them to capture by the Confederate forces, will not be exacted from such as give themselves up to the United States military authorities.

By command of Lieut.-Gen. GRANT.

T. S. BOWERS, A. A. G.

Affairs now remained quiet until September 10th, when the brigade of Gen. De Trobriand captured a portion of the enemy's pickets, inflicting a loss of one hundred to one hundred and fifty. On the 16th a body of the enemy's cavalry marched around in the rear of Gen. Meade's left at Reams' station, and captured the 13th Pennsylvania and a herd of 2,500 cattle. They were pursued by cavalry, but the pursuit was repulsed and they retired at leisure.

On September 14th the Secretary of War sent forward the following despatch:

WAR DEPARTMENT, September 14.

Major-General Dix, New York:

Lieutenant-General Grant telegraphs this department in respect to the draft as follows:

CITY POINT—10:30 A. M., September 13.

Hon. Edwin M. Stanton, Secretary of War:

We ought to have the whole number of men called for by the President in the shortest possible time. Prompt action in filling our armies will have more effect upon the enemy than a victory over them. They profess to believe, and make their men believe, there is such a party North in favor of recognizing Southern independence that the draft cannot be enforced. Let them be undeceived. Deserters come into our lines daily who tell us that the men are nearly universally tired of the war, and that desertions would be much more frequent, but they believe peace will be negotiated after the fall election. The enforcement of the draft and prompt filling up of our armies will save the shedding of blood to an immense degree. U. S. GRANT, Lieutenant-General.

The following telegram has been received from Major-General Sherman on the same subject:

ATLANTA, GA.—6:30 P. M., Sept. 13.

Hon. E. M. Stanton, Secretary of War:

I am very glad to hear that the draft will be enforced. First, we want the men; second, they come as privates to fill up our old and tried regiments, with their experienced officers already on hand; and third, because the enforcement of the law will manifest a power resident in our Government equal to the occasion. Our Government, though a Democracy, should in times of trouble and danger be able to wield the power of a great nation. All well.

W. T. SHERMAN, Major-General.

The draft is ordered to commence in all the States and districts where the quota is not filled by volunteers, on Monday, the 19th, and will go on until completed. Volunteers and substitutes will be received and credited to as late a period as possible. Volunteering is still progressing with vigor in most of the States. EDWIN M. STANTON,
Secretary of War.

A call for 500,000 men had been issued by the President on July 18th.

On Sept. 28th a movement was made by Gen. Grant on the north of the James. It was predicated on the belief that only a small force of the enemy occupied the works on the north side of the river, and a hope was entertained that by a sudden movement and a rapid advance the capture of Richmond might be the result. At the same time it was assumed that if the advance was successfully resisted it could only be accomplished by the withdrawal of a force from the south side of the river, which would materially aid the army of the Potomac in a contemplated movement on the enemy in the vicinity of Petersburg. Gen. Ord with the 18th corps was ordered to cross the James at Aikin's Landing, eight miles above Deep Bottom, and to mass his troops quietly on the north bank, and at daylight to advance against the enemy's works in his front with the utmost celerity, in order that no reënforcements might reach the enemy in time to oppose the movement. After capturing the works on Chapin's Farm, it was designed that he should without delay advance against the rear defences of Chapin's Bluff, and, after capturing these, destroy the bridges across the James and continue his advance toward Richmond, capturing the enemy or driving them before him, and effectually protecting his rear by the destruction of the bridges. At the same time Gen. Birney, on the afternoon of the 28th, with the 10th corps, moved to Bermuda Hundred and crossed the river during the night. A division of colored troops of the 18th corps was added to his force. Gen. Birney was ordered, by a rapid movement at daylight, to capture the enemy's work in front of Deep Bottom and gain possession of the New Market road leading to Richmond; thence to advance as rapidly as practicable toward Richmond, assaulting any works occupied by the enemy which he might meet, and establish communication or a connection with Gen. Ord at the Mill road, distant about seven miles from Richmond. Gen. Birney had captured the enemy's works at 8½ A. M., and by nine o'clock his second division was on the advance toward Richmond on the New Market road. Communication was established with Gen. Ord, as directed, by 10½ o'clock, and Gen. Grant, being on the field, expressed his gratification with the progress. The strong inner defences of Chapin's Bluff were soon encountered, and preparations were made to assault them. Gen. Ord had carried the first line of the enemy's works in his immediate front, capturing some fifteen pieces of artillery, and was then preparing to act in conjunction with Gen. Birney upon the enemy's line of fortifications. As the works were evidently very formidable, it became necessary to organize a regular assaulting column. This delayed the assault until 2 P. M. Meantime reënforcements were sent to the enemy, and as the assaulting column advanced they could be seen entering the works. From this cause and the strength of the works, the assault was unsuccessful, although the troops behaved with great gallantry. Two regiments only of the colored division reached one of the rebel forts, where they found a ditch ten feet wide and eight feet deep between them and the parapet. More than a hundred of these brave fellows jumped into the ditch and assisted some of their comrades to mount the parapet by allowing them to climb up on their shoulders. About a dozen succeeded in mounting the parapet by these means. But this force which had bravely pushed on was far too small to capture the fort, and was therefore compelled to retire, leaving their comrades in the ditch of the fort. But these were unable to make good their escape, as it would have been certain death to leave the the ditch and return to the troops, and were afterwards compelled to surrender. About eight hundred men were lost in this assault in killed, wounded, and prisoners. On the 30th the enemy attempted to recapture the works which had been taken, but without success. On the same day Gen. Warren attacked and carried the enemy's lines on their extreme right, and captured a number of prisoners. At the same time Gen. Meade attacked and carried the enemy's line near Poplar Grove Church.

On Oct. 7th the enemy made a vigorous and partially successful effort to turn the right flank of the Army of the James. Gen. Anderson, with one brigade of cavalry and two of infantry, surprised the Federal cavalry and routed the force on the right and captured many of them. Upon encountering the main body near New Market the enemy were repulsed and abandoned the Central road. The loss was about five hundred, that of the enemy was some larger, including one hundred and fifty prisoners.

On the 27th a movement was made by a portion of the 2d and 5th corps against the enemy's position at Hatcher's Run. A severe engagement ensued, in which the troops of both corps were driven back with severe loss. They, however, held their original position. The following is Gen. Grant's despatch respecting this movement:

CITY POINT, Oct. 27—9 P. M.

To Hon. Edwin M. Stanton, Sec'y of War:

I have just returned from the crossing of the Boylston plank road with Hatcher's Creek. Our line now extends from its former left to Armstrong's mill, thence by the south bank of Hatcher's Creek to the point above named. At every point the enemy was found intrenched and his works manned. No attack was made during the day further than to drive pickets and cavalry inside of the main work. Our casualties have been light, probably less than two hundred killed, wounded, and missing. The same is probably true with the enemy. We captured, however, seven loaded teams on their way to Stony Creek to the enemy, about a dozen beef cattle, a travelling forge, and from seventy-five to one hundred prisoners. Butler extended around well toward the Yorktown road without finding a point unguarded. I shall keep our troops out where they are until toward noon to-morrow, in hopes of inviting an attack.

(Signed) U. S. GRANT, Lieut. General.

The following is Gen. Lee's despatch:

HEADQUARTERS ARMY OF NORTHERN VIRGINIA, October 28th, 1864.

Hon. James A. Seddon, Secretary of War:

Gen. A. P. Hill reports that the attack of Gen. Heth upon the enemy upon the Boylston plank road, mentioned in my despatch last evening, was made by three brigades under Gen. Mahone in front and Gen. Hampton in the rear. Mahone captured four hundred prisoners, three stands of colors, and six pieces of artillery. The latter could not be brought off, the enemy having possession of the bridge.

In the attack subsequently made by the enemy Gen. Mahone broke three lines of battle, and during the night the enemy retired from the Boylston plank road, leaving his wounded and more than two hundred and fifty dead on the field.

About 9 o'clock P. M., a small force assaulted and took possession of our works on the Baxter road, in front of Petersburg, but was soon driven out.

On the Williamsburg road, yesterday, Gen. Field captured upward of four hundred prisoners and seven stands of colors. The enemy left a number of dead in front of our works and returned to his former position to-day. R. E. LEE.

The subsequent movements during the year were comparatively unimportant. Both armies prepared such quarters as to enable them to retain their positions during the winter.

CHAPTER XLIV.

The Sanitary Commission—Its Organization—Objects—Means of Transportation—Preventive Service—General Relief—Special Relief—Field Relief—Auxiliary Relief Corps—Receipts—Expenditures—Western Commission—Other Sanitary Commissions—Christian Commission—Organization—Objects—Services—American Union Commission—Objects.

Some notice should be given to those charitable organizations which were designed to relieve the sufferings of the wounded soldiers. Their agents were not only present on the field of these unparalleled battles, but they had accompanied the armies in every campaign.

The proclamation of the President of the United States on the 15th of April, 1861, announcing the beginning of a civil war, and calling for 75,000 volunteer soldiers, not only brought to light the patriotic feeling of the masses of American citizens, who hastened to enrol themselves among the volunteer defenders of the country, but evoked a deep feeling of sympathy, and a desire to aid in the good work on the part of those who from age, profession, or sex, were debarred the privilege of giving their personal service in the field. Soldiers' aid societies, to furnish lint, bandages, hospital clothing, and delicacies, as well as nurses for the sick and wounded, sprung up on every hand; their zeal was often mingled with inexperience and ignorance, and the Medical Bureau of the War Department, nearly as ignorant as they of the immense duties and responsibilities which would soon overwhelm it, turned a cold shoulder to their offers of aid; but the motives which prompted them in their benevolent offers were worthy of all praise. Among these aid societies, many of them organized within two or three weeks after the President's proclamation, was one, "The Woman's Central Association of Relief," in New York, which had among its officers some gentlemen of large experience in sanitary science, and of considerable knowledge of military hygiene. These sought to give to its labors a practical character from the beginning, and they urged upon the association the importance of ascertaining at once what the Government would and could do, and then making arrangements to coöperate with it and supplement its deficiencies. Prominent among these gentlemen was Rev. Henry W. Bellows, D.D., who had previously won a high reputation by his efforts for improving the sanitary condition of our large cities.

Other organizations of gentlemen were attempting by different, yet in the main similar measures, to render assistance to the Government. Among these were the "Advisory Committee of the Board of Physicians and Surgeons of the Hospitals of New York," and "The New York Medical Association for furnishing Hospital Supplies in aid of the Army," both new associations, called into existence by the exigencies of the war. Fraternizing with each other, as they well might, since they all looked to the accomplishment of the same end, these associations resolved to send a joint delegation to Washington to confer with the Government, and ascertain by what means they might best coöperate with it for the benefit of the soldiers of the nation.

The idea of organizing a Commission which should unite and energize all these as yet isolated societies, and apply their contributions to the best advantage in aid of the Medical Bureau and the sick and wounded soldiers, seems to have been suggested to the delegation at the very outset of their mission.

On the 18th of May, 1861, Messrs. Henry W. Bellows, D.D., W. H. Van Buren, M.D., Elisha Harris, M.D., and Jacob Harsen, M.D., representatives of these three associations, drew up and forwarded to the Secretary of War a communication setting forth the propriety of creating an organization which should unite the duties and labors of the three associations, and coöperate with the Medical Bureau of the War Department to such an extent that each might aid the other in securing the welfare of the army. For this purpose they asked that a mixed commission of civilians, military officers, and medical men, might be appointed by the Government, charged with the duty of methodizing and reducing to practical service the already active but undirected benevolence of the people toward the army.

On the 22d of May, R. C. Wood, M.D., then Acting Surgeon-General, and subsequently in charge of the Western Medical Department, followed this communication by a letter addressed to the Secretary of War, urging the establishment of the desired Commission as a needed adjunct to the new, extensive, and overflowing duties of the Medical Bureau.

On the 23d of May, the delegation addressed to the Secretary of War a "Draft of powers, asked from the Government, by the Sanitary delegates to the President and Secretary of War." In this paper the powers desired were stated as follows:

"1. The Commission being organized for the purposes only of inquiry and advice, asks for no legal powers, but only the official recognition and moral countenance of the Government, which will be secured by its public appointment. It asks for a recommendatory order, addressed in its favor to all officers of the movement, to further its inquiries; for permission to correspond and confer, on a confidential footing, with the Medical Bureau and the War Department, proffering such suggestions and counsel as its investigations and studies may from time to time prompt and enable it to offer.

"2. The Commission seeks no pecuniary remuneration from the Government. Its motives being humane and patriotic, its labors will be its own reward. The assignment to them of a room in one of the public buildings, with stationery and other necessary conveniences, would meet their expectations in this direction.

"3. The Commission asks leave to sit through the war, either in Washington, or when and where it may find it most convenient and useful; but it will disband should experience render its operations embarrassing to the Government, or less necessary and useful than it is now supposed they will prove."

Concerning the objects of the Commission, the delegation say:

"The general object of the Commission is through suggestions reported from time to time to the Medical Bureau and the War Department, to bring to bear upon the health, comfort, and morale of our troops, the fullest and ripest teachings of sanitary science, in its application to military life, whether deduced from theory or practical observations, from general hygienic principles, or from the experience of the Crimean, the East India, and the Italian wars. Its objects are purely advisory."

They indicate the following specific objects of inquiry:

"1. *Materiel of the Volunteers.* The Commission proposes a practical inquiry into the *materiel* of the volunteer forces, with reference to the laws and usages of the several States, in the matter of inspections, with the hope of assimilating the regulations with those of the army proper, alike in the appointment of medical and other officers, and in the vigorous application of just rules and principles to recruiting and inspection laws. This inquiry would exhaust every topic appertaining to the original *materiel* of the army, considered as a subject of sanitary and medical care.

"2. *Prevention.* The Commission would inquire with scientific thoroughness into the subject of diet, cooking, cooks, clothing, huts, camping grounds, transports, transitory depots, with their expenses, camp police, with reference to settling the question how far the regulations of the army proper are or can be practically carried out among the volunteer regiments, and what changes or modifications are desirable from their peculiar character and circumstances? Every thing appertaining to outfit, cleanliness, precautions against damp, cold, heat, malaria, infection, and unvaried or ill-cooked food, and an irregular or careless commissariat, would fall under this head.

"3. *Relief.* The Commission would inquire into the organization of Military Hospitals, general and regimental; the precise regulations and routine through which the services of the patriotic women of the country may be made available as nurses; the nature and sufficiency of hospital supplies; the method of obtaining and regulating all other extra and unbought supplies, contributing to the comfort of the sick; the question of ambulances and field services, and of extra medical aid; and whatever else relates to the care, relief, or cure of the sick and wounded, their investigations being guided by the highest and latest medical and military experience, and carefully adapted to the nature and wants of our immediate army, and its peculiar origin and circumstances."

The President and Secretary of War were not at first disposed to look with any great favor upon this plan, which they regarded rather as a sentimental scheme concocted by women, clergymen, and humane physicians, than as one whose practical workings would prove of incalculable benefit to the army which was rapidly coming into existence. The earnestness of its advocates, their high position, and the evidence which was adduced that they only represented the voice of the nation, produced some effect in modifying their views; and when the Acting Surgeon-General asked for it, as a needed adjuvant to the Medical Bureau, likely soon to be overwhelmed by its new duties, they finally decided, though reluctantly, to permit its organization. Accordingly the Secretary of War, on the 9th of June, decided on the creation of such a Commission, the President approving. The title first given to the new organization was "The Commission of Inquiry and Advice in respect of the Sanitary Interests of the United States Forces," but was subsequently changed to "The United States Sanitary Commission."

It was composed of the following gentlemen: Rev. Henry W. Bellows, D.D., President, New York; Professor A. D. Bache, Vice-President, Washington; Elisha Harris, M.D., Corresponding Secretary, New York; George W. Cullum, U. S. A., Washington; Alexander E. Shiras, U. S. A., Washington; Robert C. Wood, M.D., U. S. A., Washington; William H. Van Buren, M.D., New York; Wolcott Gibbs, M.D., New York; Cornelius R. Agnew, M.D., New York; George T. Strong, New York; Frederick Law Olmsted, New York; Samuel G. Howe, M.D., Boston; J. S. Newberry, M.D., Cleveland, Ohio. To these were subsequently added Horace Binney, Jr., Philadelphia; Rt. Rev. Thomas M. Clark, D.D., Providence, R. I.; Hon. Joseph Holt, Kentucky; R. W. Burnett, Cincinnati, Ohio; Hon. Mark Skinner, Chicago, Illinois; Rev. John H. Heywood, Louisville, Kentucky; Professor Fairman Rogers, Philadelphia; J. Huntington Wolcott, Boston; Charles J. Stillé, Philadelphia; Ezra B. McCagg, Chicago, Ill.; and nearly six hundred associate members, in all parts of the country.

It is a matter of wonder that in a field so wholly new the delegation should have so fully comprehended the duties which would be incumbent upon the Commission, and the range of its future operations. There were indeed certain features of its work which, of necessity, could only be developed by the bitter experiences through which it was called to pass; and in the end, the great lack in the Government medical service compelled it to assume more of the executive and less of the advisory functions. Still it has never failed to bear in mind that it was created to aid by its advice, counsel, and, where needed, its direct help, the medical department of the Government service.

Under its charter, it at once proceeded to organize its action and to appoint committees from its members to visit every camp, recruiting-post, transport, fort, hospital, and military station, to ascertain and report all abuses, and to perfect such organization as might insure a higher degree of health and comfort for the soldiers.

The medical members of the Commission undertook to consider the questions which might arise concerning the diseases of the camp, and their medical and surgical treatment, from the highest scientific point of view; and guided by the rich and abundant experience of European army surgeons, to prepare brief medical and surgical tracts adapted to the wants of the volunteer surgeons of the army. Among these tracts, of which many thousands have been circulated, were, "Advice as to Camping;" "Report on Military Hygiene and Therapeutics;" "Dr. Guthrie's Directions to Army Surgeons on the Battle-field;" "Rules for preserving the Health of the Soldier;" "Quinine as a Prophylactic against Malarious Diseases;" "Report on the value of Vaccination in Armies;" "Report on Amputation;" "Report on Amputation through the Foot and at the Ankle-joint;" "Report on Venereal Diseases;" "Report on Pneumonia;" "Report on Continued Fevers;" "Report on Excision of Joints for Traumatic Cause;" "Report on Dysentery;" "Report on Scurvy;" "Report on the Treatment of Fractures in Military Surgery;" "Report on the Nature and Treatment of Miasmatic Fevers;" "Report on the Treatment of Yellow Fever;" "Report on the Treatment of Infectious Diseases," etc.

Three committees were appointed, one to communicate the matured counsels of the Commission to the Government, and procure their ordering by the proper departments; a second to maintain a direct relation with the army officers and medical men, with the camps and hospitals, and by all proper methods to make sure of the carrying out of the sanitary orders of the Medical Bureau and the War Department; and a third to be in constant communication with the State Governments, and the public benevolent associations interested in the army.

This plan of organization was approved by the Secretary of War, on the 13th June, 1861, and on the 21st of that month the Commission issued its first address to the public. This was soon followed by an appeal to the Life Insurance Companies, and another to men of wealth throughout the country, for aid in the prosecution of its work. The members of the Commission, as such, received no compensation, but the purposes of the organization would require a very considerable number of paid employés, and would involve heavy expenses for publications and supplies, which could only be purchased with money. A considerable number of associate members were elected at this time, who gave their services in raising means for the operations of the Commission, and Ladies' Associations, in all parts of the country, prepared clothing and supplies of all sorts, and forwarded them to its depots.

The members of the Commission visited, during the summer of 1861, the different camps of the widely-extended armies of the republic, and carefully inspected and reported upon their sanitary condition and needs.

The necessity of the services of the agents of the Commission on the field immediately after, or, when practicable, during the progress of, important battles, was felt, as soon as such battles occurred. At first, owing to the difficulties of procuring transportation for its supplies to the field, in consequence of the dependence of the Medical Bureau upon the Quartermaster's Bureau for transportation, it could not reach the field so early as its officers desired, and in some of the earlier battles there was great suffering (partially ameliorated, it is true, by individual effort and enterprise) in consequence. But the Commission soon found it necessary to have its own independent transportation, and this both by land and water, its hospital transports, its wagons and ambulances, and its ambulance railroad cars. In July, 1863, it added to these the plan of attaching to each army corps a Superintendent of Relief, with his assistants, wagons, ambulances, and supplies, to remain constantly with his corps and minister to its needs.

The transportation of the wounded soldier from the battle ground to the field-hospital, as well as to the more remote camp, post, or general hospital, is a matter of importance. If roughly and unskilfully performed, the wounded man not only suffers severely, but his injuries may be rendered mortal. At first it was the practice in the army for the line officers to detach two men who were uninjured from the ranks to bear off each wounded man; but this weakened the force so much in a severe battle (the bearers seldom returning to their place), that it was finally prohibited, and only the ambulance men of the regiment, or the members of the band, aided sometimes by the chaplain, or by civilians, assisted in that duty. An ambulance corps was organized in connection with the Army of the Potomac in the autumn of 1862, but did not attain much efficiency till the spring of 1863. Congress, at its session of 1863-'64 extended its provisions to the other armies of the republic. By its provisions each regiment in going into battle is entitled to three ambulances, with their drivers, and six stretcher-bearers, who are commanded by a sergeant, the stretcher-bearers marching with the regiment into battle, and the ambulances being drawn up in rear between the army and the field hospital; the ambulance force of the regiments forming a brigade, being under the command of a second lieutenant, that of a division being commanded by a first lieutenant, and the force attached to a corps by a captain who is responsible to the medical director of the army. The ambulances to be provided with stretcher-hooks and seats, and with water, cordials, bandages, etc. The wounded are brought off by these arrangements promptly and with comparatively little suffering. As a matter of fact, however, there have been usually but two ambulances to a regiment, and sometimes but one.

The different means of transportation adopted deserve notice. In most of the armies the U. S. army hand-litter or stretcher is now in use for carrying men off from the field, but some of the smaller outlying bodies of troops, and occasionally detachments of cavalry, are not provided with them. For these, as well as for the larger bodies of troops early in the war, the hand-litter made with guns and blankets, has been extemporized; for this purpose the edges of the blanket are rolled over the guns, and tied firmly with twine, and two stout sticks are also tied transversely across at the head and foot serving as handles for the bearers. This being laid on the ground, the wounded man is placed gently upon it with his knapsack under his head, and the bearers, standing between the guns, carry him with comparative comfort. The Indian litter is made by taking two stout saplings, and attaching to them three cross-pieces about two and a half or three feet apart by cords and notches; the sick or wounded man being placed on his blanket, this frame-work is placed over him and the blanket knotted to it. By three bent twigs and an additional blanket a kind of wagon top can be made to this in case of storm. Dr. James R. Wood has invented an admirable hand-litter of canvas, with the sides bound with very strong rope with loops at suitable distances and the cross-pieces of steel. This can be rolled up in small compass for transportation, and needs only a couple of poles, easily obtainable for use at any time. Panniers to be fitted on the backs of mules or horses (the former are preferable) are of service in mountainous districts where wheel carriages are inadmissible. The French use them to some extent in their ambulance corps. One of the panniers receives a man sitting, the other, one in a recumbent or partially recumbent position. It is necessary that the animals, whether horses or mules, should have been trained specially for this service. A horse or mule litter for transporting a wounded man in a recumbent position, by means of two horses, one before, the other behind the litter, was ordered by the U. S. Army Medical Board in 1860, but has not been very generally introduced. It is convenient for a mountainous country, but requires too many horses and men for a single soldier. The two-wheeled ambulance, known as Cherry's Cart, which may be used either as an ambulance or transport, found at first considerable favor in the army, though Dr. (now Medical Inspector, U. S. A.) Coolidge's two-wheeled ambulance soon superseded it, and proved an admirable conveyance for wounded men on smooth and good roads, though too light for the rough and horrible routes over which most of our campaigning has been conducted. Surgeon General Hammond ordered, in 1863, four-wheeled ambulances to be drawn by two horses, which proved preferable to any others in the service. They were intended to convey ten or twelve persons sitting, or two sitting and two or three lying down. A still better four-wheeled ambulance, also drawn by two horses, has, within a few months past, been perfected by Dr. B. Howard, late a surgeon in the U. S. Army, and has been adopted in the service, and received the approval of the Sanitary Commission (*fig*. 3). It is beyond question the most admirably contrived conveyance for sick or wounded men over roads of any description which has ever been constructed, and seems to leave no room for further improvement. It admits of the transportation of six persons sitting, or two recumbent, or one recumbent and three sitting, and gives to the sitter all the advantages of a corner seat with cushion, for support, while the josting and shaking of an ordinary ambulance is entirely prevented by the use of semi-elliptic springs with counterpoise springs inside, and rubber buffers to receive any sudden shock (*figs*. 4, 5, 6). The badly wounded are brought on the litters of the ambulance, which are well cushioned and slid into place in the ambulance on steel rollers, and steadied in their position by loops and guys. A tank of fresh water is placed underneath the seats and beds, and the water can be drawn from the rear end of the ambulances (*figs*. 7, 8). There are also contrivances for the suspension of fractures of the lower extremities without motion, and for suspending, if necessary, additional stretchers in the ambulance. There are also hooks on the sides of the ambulance for carrying folded stretchers, and compartments for the necessary simple cordials, lint, bandages, &c. It is in short a complete flying hospital (*fig*. 9).

It has sometimes been necessary to transport the sick and wounded to hospitals remote from the battle-fields, either for the sake of a more healthful climate, or to afford them better hospital accommodation and greater facilities for recovery. In the earlier years of the war, this was done, when it was possible, on steamboats or steamships chartered as transports. They were often fearfully crowded and exposed to great suffering in their voyages, and where, as was the case after the battles of the Peninsula and Antietam in 1862, the voyage was made by sea, the rolling of the vessels in the gales they often encountered, increased the agony and caused the death of many of the helpless sufferers. Subsequently, where transportation by railroad was necessary, they were carried in passenger cars, or oftener in box or freight cars, with straw laid upon the floors. In this way many thousands were brought from Chattanooga to Nashville and Louisville, in the autumn of 1863, and a large number in the spring

Fig. 3.

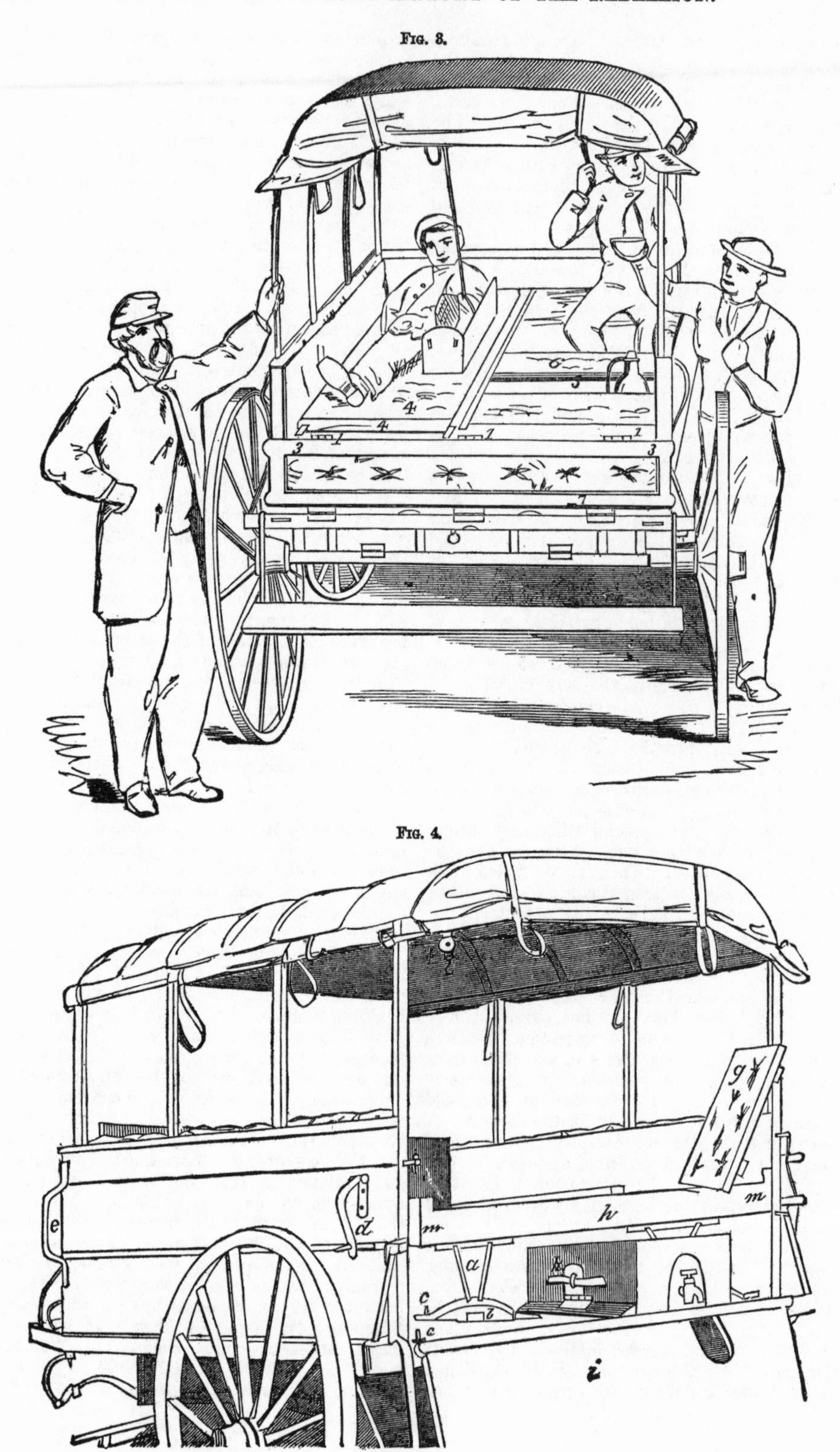

Fig. 4.

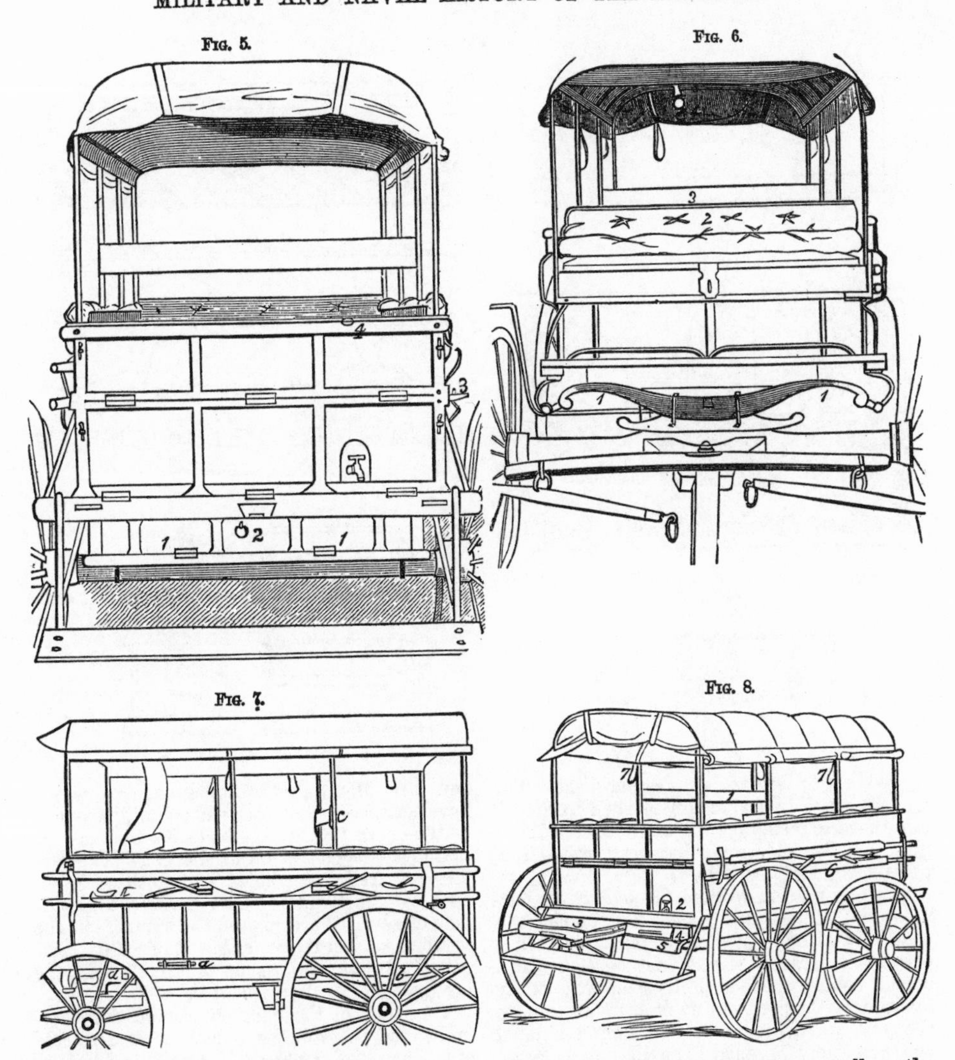

Fig. 5. Fig. 6. Fig. 7. Fig. 8.

and summer of 1864. The Sanitary Commission, desirous to relieve the suffering thus caused, ordered the construction of a number of hospital cars, from drawings made by Elisha Harris, M.D. In these cars the seats are removed, and the stretchers in which the patients are brought suspended upon gutta percha or rubber loops, and secured from swaying. There were five or six of them on the Atlanta, Chattanooga, Nashville, and Louisville route, with the surgeon's car in the centre of the train, with kitchen, dispensary, nurses, assistant-surgeons, and apothecaries in attendance, and the sick and wounded had the same care and attention they could have had in the best regulated hospitals. The same number have been constantly running between Washington, New York, and Boston.

The introduction of new and more deadly missiles into modern warfare considerably modified the methods of treatment as well as the diagnosis and prognosis of gunshot wounds. The old round bullet produced wounds far less formidable than those inflicted by the Minié ball or the shell, which played so prominent a part in the battles of this war. The round musket-ball had a much lower initial velocity, was readily deflected from its course by coming in contact with bone, tendon, or even firm muscular tissue, and if it penetrated the large cavities, usually made a clean perforation of a diameter but little larger than its own. The Minié, on the contrary, made a ragged, ugly wound, and passed straight on through muscle, tendon, cartilage, and bone, producing terrible comminuted fractures of the latter; and if it did not pass entirely through, usually came to the skin on the opposite side from that which it perforated, and lying there, presenting its long diameter to the surface, left a large and

FIG. 9.

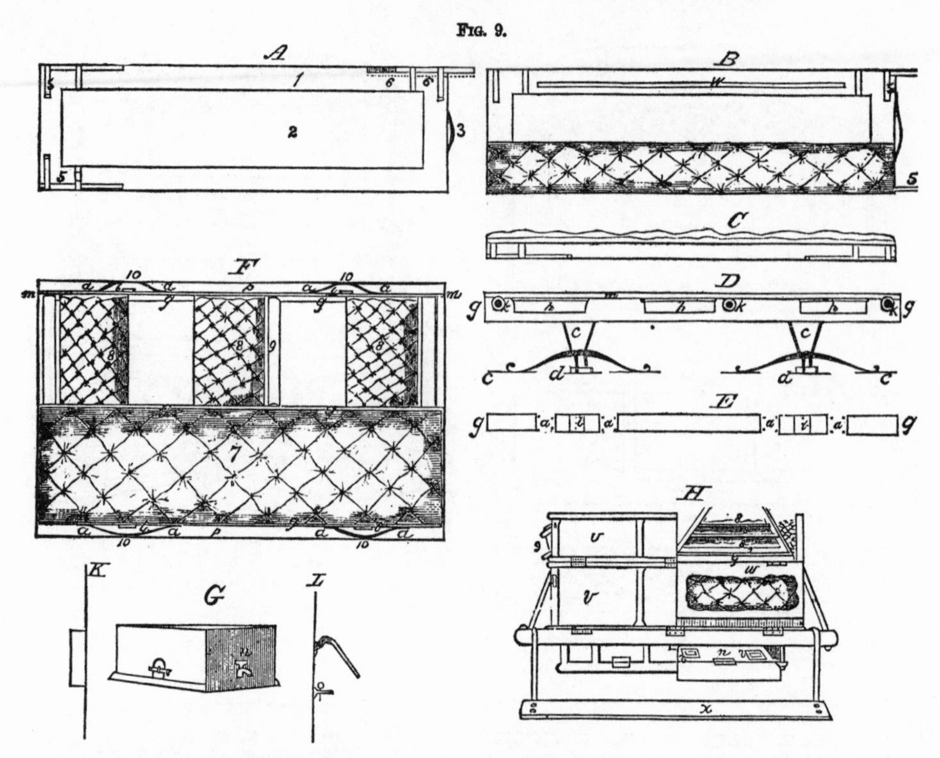

ragged cavity in its last resting-place. The wounds made by fragments of shell were still more severe, mangling the unfortunate subject most cruelly, and producing destructive fractures and sloughing wounds.

The Commission worked throughout in harmony with the United States Government, and especially with the Medical Bureau, to which it proved of great service. That bureau, which at the commencement of the war was utterly inadequate, though from no fault of its own, to the vast work before it, was soon regulated and admirably organized, having a corps of three thousand skilful and responsible surgeons, and fifteen thousand hired nurses experienced in their duties.

But even with this large force, trained as it had been by the arduous duties to which it had been called, there were numerous instances where the most perfect working of the Government machinery could not remedy suffering and misery which a more flexible system could relieve. The presence of incipient scurvy among the troops on Morris Island, and the forces engaged in the siege of Vicksburg and Port Hudson, was detected and remedied by the sending at once of large amounts of fresh vegetables and anti-scorbutics by the Commission to those points, which reached them promptly, and arrested the disease, while, by the necessarily slow movements of the Government, many weeks must have elapsed ere the needed remedies could have been furnished, and meantime half the forces engaged would have perished. "Potatoes and onions," says one of the energetic lady agents of the Commission in Chicago, "captured Vicksburg." "The supplies of fresh vegetables and anti-scorbutics sent by the Sanitary Commission to Morris Island, saved the army of the South," is the testimony of an impartial but thoroughly competent witness, who spent ten months in the hospitals of that department in 1863.

The work of the Sanitary Commission comprehended the following distinct departments of labor: 1st. *The preventive service, or Sanitary Inspection*, which required a corps of Medical Inspectors, whose time was passed with each army corps in the field, visiting camps, hospitals, and transports; skilful and experienced physicians, who watched the perils from climate, malarious exposure, from hard marching or active campaigning, from inadequate food or clothing, growing out of imperfect facilities of transportation, and reported to the Chief Inspector of that army, and through him to the Chief of Inspection at headquarters, for remedy, or to the Associate Secretary in charge, or to relief agents under their control, and thus saw to the supplying of the needs of that portion of the army, and the adoption of the necessary measures for the improvement of its sanitary condition. From the reports of these inspectors the materials were gathered which were digested into such forms as to be of permanent value in the Commission's Bureau of

Statistics. To this department belonged also the corps of Special Hospital Inspectors, selected from the most learned and skilful physicians of the country, who, from time to time, made the circuit of all the general hospitals of the army (numbering nearly three hundred), and reported upon their wants, condition, progress, *personnel*, and capacity for improvement. The substance of these reports was confidentially made over to the Surgeon-General. A third agency, in connection with this preventive service, was the preparation and circulation of the medical tracts already named, and information important and indispensable to the officers, soldiers, and especially the medical men in the field.

2. *The Department of General Relief.*—The supplies of food, clothing, bandages, hospital furniture, clothing, and bedding, delicacies for the sick, stimulants and cordials for the wounded on the field, the sick and wounded in camp, field, regimental, post, and general hospitals, came from the branches of the Commission, of which there were twelve, having depots in Boston, New Haven, New York, Philadelphia, Cincinnati, Cleveland, Chicago, Buffalo, Pittsburg, Detroit, Columbus, and Louisville. Each of these branches, which were variously denominated as Ladies' Aid Societies, Relief Associations, etc., had its distinctly defined field, from which it drew its supplies, and had from one hundred and fifty to twelve hundred auxiliary aid societies, in the towns, hamlets, and villages, and, in the cities, in the different churches of its field. The stores collected by the branch were received at its depot, opened, assorted, each kind by itself, repacked, and reports of the number and amount of the supplies thus accumulated were sent every week to the principal office of the Commission, or to the Associate Secretary of the Eastern or Western Department, as the case might be, and shipped, according to orders received, to the depots of distribution, Washington, D. C., Camp Distribution, Va., Baltimore, Md., Harper's Ferry, Va., Annapolis, Md., Camp Parole, Md., Norfold, Va., City Point, Va., Newbern, N. C., Beaufort, S. C., New Orleans, La., or to the army where they were needed, with the utmost promptness, One of these branches (the "Woman's Central Association of Relief") reported, among the stores forwarded from its depot, from May 1, 1861, to November 1, 1864, 599,780 pieces of clothing, 89,898 pieces of bedding, and over 90,000 packages of fruit, vegetables, jellies, wine, condensed milk, beef stock, groceries, pickles, lemonade, etc., of a total value of over a million of dollars. The "Northwestern Sanitary Commission," the branch of the U. S. Sanitary Commission at Chicago, had sent to the depots of distribution from its organization to December 31, 1864, supplies to the value of $230,645.02, and had expended besides for the purposes of the Commission, about $57,000 more. The supplies thus furnished were distributed with great care to avoid waste, and to supplement the food, clothing, and medicines which the Government was bound to furnish—the object being to do what the Government could not, and to avoid duplicating its supplies of what it could and should furnish. Care was exercised also to avoid imposition, while no sufferer in need was allowed to suffer when the Commission could supply his wants. The Commission was national in its character, and supplied the soldiers of one State as readily as those of another. Nay, more—the rebel wounded, when left on the field, or in temporary hospitals within the Union lines, or when sent to camps and hospitals as prisoners, uniformly received its bounty and its assiduous care. It had in this matter, at times, to contend, both among the people and on the field, with that exclusive feeling which would limit its beneficence to the soldiers of a single State or regiment; but oftenest the agents of these local organizations, from the feeling which such exclusiveness caused among the soldiers, turned their stores into the depots of the Commission, and themselves aided in their distribution to the soldiers, without distinction of locality. The Field Relief Superintendents, already mentioned, who accompanied each army corps, belonged to this department of general relief.

3. *The Department of Special Relief.*—This department was under the general superintendence of Rev. F. N. Knapp, Associate Secretary of the Commission for the East, at Washington, and of Dr. J. S. Newberry, Associate Secretary for the West, at Louisville. It furnished "Homes" to soldiers, where shelter, food, and medical care and general superintendence were furnished for those soldiers who were not yet under the care of the Government, or had just got out of their care, or had somehow lost their status, and could not immediately regain it—recruits, or men on leave, sick leave or furlough, going to and fro; men without skill to care for themselves, ignorant, underwitted, or vicious; men discharged prematurely from the hospitals, men found in the streets, or left behind by their regiments. Of these classes about seven thousand five hundred were accommodated daily or nightly in the homes of the Commission at Alexandria, Harrisburg, Baltimore, Washington, Buffalo, Cincinnati, Cairo, Paducah, Camp Nelson, Louisville, New Albany, Nashville, Columbus, Cleveland, Detroit, Memphis, and New Orleans.

There were also belonging to this department six lodges—homes on a smaller scale—where the wearied soldier, sick or feeble, might await his opportunity of obtaining his pay from the Paymaster-General; or landing sick from a steamer or cars, and unable to reach the hospital to which he might belong, could find rest, food, and medical care, till he could be transferred to the hospital, or was able to rejoin his regiment. There were also at Annapolis, Md., and at Washington, D. C., "Homes for the Wives, Mothers, and Children of Soldiers," fitted up and supplied by the Commission, where these friends of the sick and wounded soldier, coming with scanty means to minister to his necessities, could find comfortable food and shelter. Besides these, "feeding stations" for the supply of the sick, wounded, and famished soldier, passing to and from the field, were established, usually temporarily, but sometimes permanently, on the route from Louisville to Nashville, Chattanooga, Atlanta, &c., and in the Shenandoah valley, at City Point, and elsewhere. The hospital cars, of which there were several, between Washington, New York, and Boston, and between Louisville and Chattanooga, Tennessee, fitted up with hammocks, in rubber slings, and with a small kitchen for preparing the necessary food for the sick and wounded, and under the charge of a skilful surgeon, belonged to this department; as also the Sanitary steamers, the Clara Bell, on the Mississippi, the New Dunleith, on the Cumberland, and the Elizabeth, on the Potomac. These were used both for the transmission of necessary supplies, and the transportation of the wounded. In this department, also, the commission established agencies at Washington, Philadelphia, New York, Louisville, and New Orleans, for obtaining for the soldiers and their families pensions, bounties, back pay, transportation, aid in correcting the soldiers' papers, where there were errors in form, or recovering them their positions when they had wrongfully been set down as deserters, and saving them from sharpers. The Commission also established Hospital Directories at Washington, Philadelphia, New York, and Louisville. In these four directories were registered the names of all soldiers in the United States general hospitals, and as far as possible the regimental and post hospitals throughout the country, and these were constantly receiving additions from the reports sent regularly from such hospitals. By applying to these Directories, information was furnished to friends without cost, other than that of postage or telegram, of the location and condition of any soldier who was or had been within a year an inmate of any United States military hospital. At the Washington office of the Commission, the names of patients in the hospitals in Eastern Virginia, Maryland, District of Columbia, North Carolina, South Carolina, Florida, and Louisiana, were recorded; at Philadelphia, those in Pennsylvania hospitals; at New York, those in New York, New Jersey, and New England; at Louisville, those in Western Virginia, Ohio, Indiana, Illinois, Missouri, Iowa, Kentucky, Tennessee, Mississippi, and Arkansas. The officers in charge required the name, rank, company, and regiment of the person inquired for, and where he was when last heard from. About 900,000 names were thus recorded, and the information afforded by these directories to the friends of the sick and wounded was of incalculable value, often leading to the preservation of life, and to the relief of that most terrible mental anguish, the torture of a dread uncertainty.

Still another measure of special relief, on which the Commission expended more than $30,000, was the sending of supplies, so long as it was permitted, to our soldiers who were prisoners at Richmond, Salisbury, and Andersonville, and there undergoing the terrors of cold, nakedness, and starvation. It also sent on every flag-of-truce boat from Fortress Monroe ample stores of clothing, cordials, nourishing food, medicine, and restoratives, for the poor fellows who were exchanged, and who, but for this timely relief, would have many of them died on the voyage. It organized a system of furnishing fresh supplies to the hospitals around Washington at prime cost, which it brought from Philadelphia in arctic cars, thus preventing frauds, and the commissions formerly obtained by the hospital stewards, and furnishing more and better supplies to the inmates of the hospitals for less money. It caused reforms to be instituted in our own convalescent and parole camps, and in the prison camps of the rebels, which our Government held as prisoners, promoting the health and comfort of both in every possible way. Its agents and superintendents often brought off men under fire from the battle-field, and four of them were taken prisoners by the rebels after Gettysburg, and notwithstanding the kindnesses bestowed by the Commission on rebels, wounded and prisoners, were subjected to the meagre fare and filth of Libby prison and Castle Thunder, for months, when two of them were finally released on parole.

4. *The Department of Field Relief.*—The Commission maintained a chief inspector for the armies of the East, and another for the military division of the Mississippi, whose duty it was to superintend the work of field relief. He had under his command a superintendent and assistant-superintendent of such army, two field storekeepers and two messengers, and one or more relief agents to each army corps. These relief agents were furnished with one or more wagons of supplies and ambulances, and moved with their corps in the field, ministering to the wounded on the field, furnishing bandages, cordials, and nourishment, and aiding the surgeons and assistant-surgeons in the field hospitals. They also rendered assistance and supplied deficiencies in the care of the sick in camp. The expenditure of the Commission for the Field Relief Department exceeded $190,000.

5. Still another department of the Sanitary Commission's work was its *Auxiliary Relief Corps.* This was first organized in May, 1864. Its object was to supply the deficiency of systematic personal attendance and work in the hospitals, or among the wounded on the field. It employed in the Eastern armies (in Virginia and the Department of the South) forty men regularly, and the number was increased during the severe battles of May and June, by volunteers, to one hundred and fifty. In all, four hundred different agents were employed, and more than seventy-five thousand patients served with suitable food, delicacies, cordials, clothing, &c., &c., previous to Jan. 1, 1865. Personal

ministrations to the sick and wounded, in the way of conversation, writing letters, supplying them with stationery, postage stamps, newspapers, magazines, and books, also formed a part of the duties of this corps.

In these labors it constantly had the aid and coöperation of the Medical Department, and, where it could be bestowed, that of the Quartermaster's Department; and the generals and commanding officers in the field have, almost without exception, given it their hearty sanction and assistance. Without these, its work would have been fourfold more expensive than it was; but even with this assistance, it necessarily had to incur large expenditures, and distributed supplies to an immense value. At the commencement of its work, when it was expected that the war would be a brief one, it made its appeals to the public for fifty thousand dollars, a sum which it was thought would suffice to accomplish its purposes; but with the increasing proportions of the war, increasing means were found necessary. While, of most descriptions of supplies, their stock derived from the branches was ample, there were some, such as the best qualities of wines and brandies, quinine, &c., which could only be obtained by cash purchases. The transportation of their supplies, though much of it was given by railroad companies, was still very expensive, while the maintenance of their homes, lodges, offices, and directories, required a heavy outlay. The Commission, as such, received no compensation, and of its officers, the President, Vice-President, and Treasurer, received no pay; while the Associate Secretary for the West, having left his residence and practice at Cleveland for Louisville in the Commission's service, had a moderate salary. The Commission regarded it necessary for the proper performance of its extensive, varied, and onerous duties, to employ paid agents, and had in its employ about two hundred. To none of them were salaries paid so large as they could receive in other business, but they remained in the work because they loved it. The aggregate salaries, previous to May, 1864, was about $15,000 per month, and of other expenses from $30,000 to $35,000 per month, making a total sum of $45,000 to $50,000 per month; but with the progress of the gigantic campaigns, and the terrible battles, both East and West, in the months of May, June, July, and August, 1864, this expenditure was greatly increased. For the months of May and June alone the outlay was $525,000, and for the season more than $1,000,000; the expenditure of supplies varied with the occurrence of great battles. During, and immediately after, the battles at Gettysburg, supplies to the value of $75,000 were distributed there. To the Army of the Cumberland, within ten days after the disastrous battle of Chickamauga, six thousand packages were sent; and immediately after Chattanooga, five thousand packages and boxes went forward.

The receipts of the Commission, from its organization in June, 1861, to Oct. 1, 1864, were in money $3,083,124.58; of this amount about $1,000,000 was received from the States and territories on the Pacific slope, including about $700,000 from California alone. Aside from this, its branches received in money to December, 1864, about $2,000,000, which had been expended in the purchase of supplies, in local relief, and in the support of establishments of special relief under their direct charge. Its expenditures for the same period were $2,467,958.55, and in the months of October and Nov., $263,000, making its total expenditure from June, 1861, to Dec., 1864, $2,731,203.79. The value of articles received in kind as contributions by the Commission, from June, 1861, to Oct., 1864, was $8,406,272.78, of which $5,286,439.85 consisted of bedding, hospital furniture, and wearing apparel; $1,362,560.42, of hospital food and delicacies; $298,437.28, of miscellaneous supplies, and the remainder unspecified articles. The branches of the Commission, twelve in number, had furnished supplies to local institutions, soldiers' families, hospitals, etc., to the amount of between two and three millions more. Previous to July 1, 1864, the cost of distribution was only 3.76 per cent. of the amount distributed. The heavy expense of chartering steamers and employing auxiliary relief agents, etc., during the campaign of 1864, increased the cost of distribution to 4.88 per cent. of the value of the supplies distributed.

During the autumn and winter of 1863–'4, and the spring and summer of 1864, a series of fairs were held in several of the principal cities of the Union, in the interest of the Commission and its branches. These fairs were more gigantic in their conception and execution, and yielded larger returns than any enterprises of the kind ever attempted in this country. The Chicago fair, the first held, realized about $80,000 net; that at Boston, about $140,000; Cincinnati, $240,000; Albany, 80,000; Cleveland, about $80,000; Brooklyn, N. Y., $401,000; New York City, $1,200,000; Pittsburg, $100,000; Baltimore, $55,000; Philadelphia, $1,080,000. Several of the smaller cities collected at fairs for the same object, from $10,000 to $20,000. These sums were not, except in the case of the New York and Philadelphia fairs, paid wholly into the treasury of the parent Commission, a part, and in some cases the whole, being reserved for the purchase of supplies and material, and the support of local institutions for the soldiers or their families.

II. The Western Sanitary Commission. This organization was entirely distinct from the United States Sanitary Commission, but, like that, knew no State boundaries, but ministered alike to the needs of soldiers from all the States, though from its location it had only supplied the wants of western armies, and of the freedmen and white refugees of the Mississippi Valley. It derived its first authority to act from an order of Maj.-Gen. Fremont.

The authority conferred by the order was recognized and confirmed by Maj.-Gen. Halleck, who added Dr. S. Pollak to the Commission, and still later, viz., December 16, 1862, by an order from the Secretary of War (Hon. E. M. Stanton), extending the field of its labors, and reappointing the members of the Commission as at first constituted.

This Commission did not devote its attention to as wide a range of topics as the United States Sanitary Commission, but confined itself to the work of superintending hospitals, furnishing supplies, appointing nurses, visiting and caring for the sick and wounded of the army of the Southwest Frontier, the District of East Arkansas, the armies operating on both sides of the Mississippi, and the Mississippi Naval Flotilla; it acted at all times in concert with the Medical Directors and Inspectors of these armies, and on account of their efficient supervision of the condition and sanitary wants of the armies under their charge, did not find it necessary to appoint separate medical inspectors. It had the superintendence of twelve hospitals (one for officers and another for military prisoners), having accommodations for about eight thousand patients, besides ten large hospital steamers and floating hospitals; it established Soldiers' Homes and Soldiers' Lodges at St. Louis, Memphis, and Columbus, Ky., and agencies at Helena, Milliken's Bend, and Springfield, Mo., and prepared, published, and distributed a large edition of a "Treatise on the Preservation of the Health of the Soldier, the cooking of food, the preparation of diet for the sick, the duties of nurses and attendants, and the organization and general management of hospitals." During 1863 and 1864 it gave special attention to the necessities of the freedmen in the Mississippi Valley, and its officers interested themselves in the adjustment of wages and in securing just and considerate treatment of the emancipated slaves from those who have rented the plantations, which had been abandoned by rebel owners. The Commission expended about $40,000 in the relief of freedmen. It also kept a registry of the location and condition of invalid and wounded soldiers in the Western armies. It also provided to a considerable extent for the large number of white refugees from the States in insurrection, who drifted into St. Louis, and were in a condition of great suffering.

The Western Sanitary Commission received from its organization to January, 1865, a little more than $1,000,000 in cash, of which $500,000 was the net result of a fair held in St. Louis in May, 1864; and about $2,000,000 in supplies.

III. Other Sanitary Commissions. Two or three of the Western States established organizations dependent partly upon legislative grants, and partly upon contributions, for the care of the sick and wounded soldiers of their respective States, and their families, to which they gave the name of "State Sanitary Commissions."

They generally expended their moneys for those services which might be more appropriately rendered to a soldier by his own State, or its representatives, than by others, such as the furnishing means of reaching home during a furlough, or of reaching his regiment when he had been detained from it by sickness; the procuring of the allotment of his pay or bounty, or the rendering him contented by the care of his family. The Indiana State Sanitary Commission, fostered and prompted by the energetic and patriotic Governor of that State, accomplished much good in this way, and up to February, 1864, had expended $320,000 in its succor of Indiana soldiers. The Iowa State Sanitary Commission was also very efficient. It expended $175,500 to February 1, 1864. An organization of a similar character, though not with the same name, existed in Wisconsin, having originated with the late lamented Governor, Louis P. Harvey, who lost his life in a journey to the field of Shiloh, to distribute its bounties. It contributed largely to the aid of the soldiers, and its benefactions were not confined to those from Wisconsin. In Illinois there was an officer called a Commissioner-General, whose function it was to collect stores and supplies from the towns and counties of the State, and send them forward for distribution after each great battle. In New York, a State Soldiers' Depot was established in July, 1863, in Howard Street, New York City, and received an appropriation from the State Legislature of $200,000, which combined the character of a Soldiers' Home, hospital, and reading-room, and had its couriers on each train on which New York and other soldiers came from the Army of the Potomac, and met them coming from other points, by steamers or otherwise, cared for the comfort of the sick and wounded, administering, under the direction of its surgeon, cordials and nutriment while in transit, protected them from the sharpers who would plunder them, and in every way looked after their interests. It expended since its organization in June, 1863, to February, 1865, about $65,000 in money, and distributed clothing, etc., to the amount of over $10,000 more. It fed and lodged over 15,000 soldiers, and gave aid and counsel to thousands more.

One of the best of the institutions of this class was "The New England Soldiers' Relief Association," located at 194 Broadway, New York, and organized April 3, 1862. Its founders and supporters were New England men and women, but its doors were opened to, and its charities lavished upon, the soldiers of every State. That a soldier was on furlough, or sick or wounded, discharged or in trouble, was ever a sufficient passport to its halls and its sympathies. Since its organization, to January, 1865, it received, registered, lodged, fed, aided and clothed, sick and wounded or disabled soldiers from thirty-one States, the District of Columbia, the regular army, the navy, and the Invalid Corps, to the number of about 45,000, and fed or lodged, and rendered assistance to many thousands more, who were not sick, wounded, or disabled. It had a Hospital Record and Directory, very full and complete, of the inmates of all the military hospitals of New York and New England, which was kept up to date by daily reports from each hospital, and gave full particulars in regard to the location, condition, and final disposition of each patient. This register contained about 40,000 names, and was so complete that the Sanitary Commission, in February, 1864, relinquished theirs for that Department in its favor. It had a good hospital for the sick or wounded soldiers, with a skilful surgeon, careful attendants, and assiduous volunteer night watches; furnished an asylum to those unfortunate soldiers who, discharged from the service without means, found themselves homeless and shelterless, giving them a home till employment could be provided for them. It also interested itself in procuring transportation, bounties, and back pay for the soldiers, and furnishing information to the friends of those who were sick, or had died, relative to procuring their dues. Religious services were conducted every Sabbath at its rooms. Much of the service rendered, including that of the Superintendent, was voluntary, and without compensation. The Superintendent of this Association acted also in the capacity of State Military Agent for the States of Maine, New Hampshire, Vermont, Massachusetts, Wisconsin, Minnesota, and Indiana, and was authorized to render such assistance as might be needed to the soldiers of those States coming to New York.

From the commencement of the war the Young Men's Christian Associations, in most of the larger cities and towns of the loyal States, had contributed largely, not only in money and supplies, to the relief and comfort of the soldiers, but in personal service.

At a convention of these Christian Associations, held in New York, November 16, 1861, it was resolved to organize from the representatives of these bodies a United States Christian Commission, and the following persons were appointed: Rev. Rollin H. Neale, D.D., Boston; George H. Stuart, Esq., Philadelphia; Rev. Bishop E. S. Janes, D.D., New York; Rev. M. L. R. P. Thompson, D.D., Cincinnati; Hon. Benjamin F. Manierre, New York; Gen. Clinton B. Fisk, St. Louis; Rev. Benjamin C. Cutler, D.D., Brooklyn; Hon. John V. Farwell, Chicago; Mitchell H. Miller, Esq., Washington; John D. Hill, M.D., Buffalo. During the succeeding year Mr. Manierre and Rev. Dr. Cutler resigned, and their places were filled by the appointment of Jay Cooke, Esq., of Philadelphia, and Rev. James Eells, D.D., of Brooklyn. To these were subsequently added John P. Crozer, of Philadelphia; Charles Demond, of Boston; Rev. W. E. Boardman, Ex. Off., Philadelphia; Hon. George F. Patton, Bath, Maine; Rev. James Pike, Sanbornton Bridge, N. H.; Edward S. Tobey, Boston; Rev. Francis Wayland, D.D., Providence, R. I.; Rev. Heman Dyer, D.D., New York; Hon. William E. Dodge, New York; Nathan Bishop, LL.D., New York; Morris K. Jesup, New York; Joseph Patterson, Philadelphia; Rev. Bishop M. Simpson, D.D., Philadelphia; Hon. J. G. Smith, Gov. of Vt.; G. S. Griffith, Baltimore; Hon. W. T. Willey, Morgantown, W. V.; A. E. Chamberlain, Cincinati; Rev. R. J. Breckinridge, D.D., Lexington, Ky.; Rev. S. D. Storrs, Atchison, Kansas;. J. B. Roberts, San Francisco; Hon. James W. Nye, Carson City, Nevada; Hon. W. A. Buckingham, Norwich, Conn.; Walter S. Griffith, Brooklyn, N. Y.; Samuel B. Caldwell, Brooklyn, N. Y.; Rev. Charles Hodge, D.D., Princeton, N. J.; Stephen Colwell, Philadelphia; Horatio G. Jones, Philadelphia; William Frew, Pittsburg; Prof. M. L. Stoever, Gettysburg; Rt. Rev. Alfred Lee, D.D., Wilmington, Del.; Hon. Francis H. Pierpont, Alexandria, Va.; Rt. Rev. C. P. McIlvaine, D.D., Cincinnati, Ohio; Hon. Schuyler Colfax, South Bend, Ind.; Hon. John Owen, Detroit; Walter S. Carter, Milwaukee; Hon. Hiram Price, Davenport, Iowa; Rev. E. Lehman, Chaska, Minn.; Rev. S. Cornelius, Portland, Oregon; Hon. John Evans, Denver City. Col.

Mr. George H. Stuart, of Philadelphia, was elected President, and served in that capacity. Three or four months were consumed in arranging its plan of operations, in obtaining the approval of the President of the United States, the Secretary of War, the Secretary of the Navy, the General in command, and the Surgeon General. It was then deemed best to remove its headquarters to Philadelphia, and Rev. William E. Boardman was appointed General Secretary. There were added, in 1864, a Secretary of the Home organization, and a Secretary of the Field organization.

The general character of the duties of the Commission was defined at the meeting that brought it into existence; its grand object as avowed was to promote the physical comfort and the spiritual welfare of the brave men of the army and navy, in the field, in the hospital, the prison, or wherever they might be found. Like the Government, it embraced within the range of its influence the whole Union, and provided for the material and spiritual necessities of suffering humanity without regard to race, creed, or position. It aimed to save life in the hour of peril, to ameliorate the condition of our soldiers and seamen, to perform in the midst of the war the offices of a kind friend, to supply, as far as possible, the place of home, to furnish opportune and substantial relief when required, to bind up the wounds, to pour in the wine and the oil of love and peace, to speak a word of sympathy and encouragement to the suffering and depressed, to bring the influences of the Gospel to bear upon those who were far from home and its privileges, exposed to the dangers and temptations peculiar to the camp, to arrest the thoughtless in their course and reclaim the wayward, to send forth the living, practical teacher, to whisper Christian consolation to the dying, the wounded, and heavy-laden in heart.

In addition to the general executive committee and its central office in Philadelphia, the Commission had its agencies, its branch organizations, in the principal cities and towns of the land, engaged in collecting stores and procuring funds to carry on the work in the field. It had its extensive bases of supplies for the different armies, and its carefully organized corps of permanent agents, thoroughly acquainted with the wants of the soldiers and prepared to forward stores upon a requisition given by those in proximity to the scene of action. It maintained a constant supervision over the camp and field-hospitals, and when special emergencies arose demanding extraordinary activity and energy, during and after every battle, its representatives were present dispensing with a bountiful hand whatever might contribute to the comfort and immediate relief of the wounded. It sent forth ministers and laymen, voluntary agents, who labored without compensation to distribute with their own hands, under the direction of the surgeons, the stores gathered together, to circulate the Scriptures, religious newspapers and tracts, reading of a moral and instructive character, and lead men to repentance and a Christian life. It aided the surgeon, helped the chaplain, followed the army in its marches, went into the trenches, coursed along the picket-line, and ministered personally to the suffering and the distressed. Its influence was felt wherever the dying, the wounded, the sick, and the afflicted were to be found. It furnished clothing to the destitute, nutritious food to the sick, books for military hospitals, posts, and gunboats, a supply of paper, envelopes, ink, pens, pencils, and the thousand comforts which were gratefully appreciated by the soldier, and which the Government could not provide. It cheered with the consolations of religion those appointed to die; and as the soul passed from the body it received its dying words, and communicated the sad record to the bereaved at home. It administered Christian burial when practicable, and marked the place of interment for the satisfaction of distant friends. Besides the more private appeals and personal instructions given by the delegates in the tent and the hospital, public services were held from day to day, especially during the winter campaigns; chapels were erected, and meetings for prayer, conference, and preaching organized. The Secretary of the Commission compendiously but clearly set forth its system and work as follows:

I. DIVISION OF THE ARMY FIELD.

GENERAL.—1. Armies near Richmond. 2. Army in the Shenandoah Valley. 3. Army of the Cumberland, etc. 4. Armies along the Southern Mississippi. 5. Armies in Missouri, Arkansas, and Kansas. 6. The navy, southern coast, and gulf supplied from New York.

SPECIAL.—Stations and corps organizations.

A station in each great army centre when the army is at rest, and a moving organization in each corps when the army moves.

Out-stations to meet wants of various sections.

Permanent stations in all great permanent centres.

II. MEN AND WOMEN FOR THE FIELD.

1. *Agents.*—Permanent—paid.

One field agent for each general division, five in all, with assistants in the larger fields.

One station agent or corps captain for each station or corps organization, with teamsters.

2. *Delegates* for six weeks, or longer, unpaid; from two to ten at each station, as needed; and at City Point, forty to fifty. Three hundred the full corps. Over three thousand in all have served.

3. *Managers of Diet Kitchens.*—About sixty ladies employed.

III. APPLIANCES.

1. Barrack chapels, store, and subsistence rooms, at permanent camps.

2. Chapel, store, and subsistence tents, at all movable stations.

3. Churches, houses, etc., detailed by Government, at most permanent stations.

4. Wagons and teams, four-horse, for each moving organization; two-horse for such stations as require them.

5. Special diet kitchens in field hospitals, managed under direction of the surgeons, by Christian Commission lady managers.

IV. LABORS.

1. *Hospital.*—Preaching; prayer-meetings; personal intercourse with soldiers; and distribution.

2. *Field.*—The same—at all stations, and along the lines; at all out-stations, isolated posts, batteries, etc.

3. Battle-field work.

4. Individual relief, aid, and information, at special request.

5. Forwarding home money for soldiers in service, and effects of deceased soldiers.

6. Managing special diet kitchens, under medical authorities.

V. WHAT IS DISTRIBUTED.

Battle-field, hospital, and special diet kitchen stores; such as shirts, drawers, socks, handkerchiefs, towels, bandages, lint, farina, corn-starch, crackers, cordials, dried fruits, canned fruits, fresh apples, grapes, peaches, etc., onions, potatoes, ice, syrups, jellies, pickles, etc., Jamaica ginger, condensed milk, Bibles for hospitals and Bible-classes; Testaments to all soldiers. Scriptures in German, French, and other foreign languages. Gunboat libraries, hospital libraries, soldiers' books, weekly and monthly religious papers, over four hundred thousand a month; tracts, Silent Comforters, etc.

The General Government cheerfully furnished the free transportation of men and supplies over all military railways, and generously granted many privileges and accommodations, restricted only by absolute military necessity. Railroad and steamboat companies under proper regulations, very generally gave passes for the delegates of the Commission and for the transportation of their stores. The telegraph wires, without charge, were used for the transmission of despatches on business with the Institution, and every information and opportunity afforded to enable the Commission to carry forward its appropriate and benevolent work intelligently and successfully. The whole army was accessible to the labors of the Commission. Its delegates were welcomed at all points, its authority regarded, and its influence felt. Its voluntary, unpaid delegates were men of the highest position and character, bishops and pastors of the largest and most influential churches in city and country, lawyers and physicians of eminence, merchants and manufacturers, students of colleges and theological seminaries, etc. The American Bible Society granted largely of Bibles and Testaments in different languages; the Tract and Publication Societies, and publishers of religious and moral books, periodicals, and newspapers, of their several issues; and ladies of the highest respectability gave themselves to the work, under its auspices, of providing for the necessities of the suffering soldier.

The expenditures as well as the receipts of the Commission increased each year in a rapidly-expanding rate. In 1862, the first year of its existence, its entire receipts were $231,256.29, of which only $50,000 or $60,000 were in cash, the remainder being in supplies and facilities of transportation, etc., granted to it. In 1863 the total receipts of the central and branch offices of the Commission were estimated at $916,837.65: of which $358,239.29 was in money, and the remainder in stores, grants, and railroad and telegraph facilities, and the estimated value of the services of delegates. In 1864 the total estimated receipts were $2,882,347.86: of which $1,297,755.28 was in money; $1,160,508.37 in hospital stores; $33,084.38 in publications donated; $72,114.83 in Bibles and Testaments from the American Bible Society. The estimated value of volunteer delegates' services was $169,920; the value of railroad, steamboat, and other transportation facilities, $106,765; value of telegraphic facilities, $26,450; rents of warehouses and offices donated, $6,750.

The total aggregate of receipts for the three years ending Jan. 1, 1865, was $4,030,441.80. Since that period not far from $400,000 in money has been received, and very large amounts of hospital supplies.

The following general summary of the work and distribution of the Commission for the year 1864, will give some idea of its activity and usefulness:

Boxes of hospital stores and publications distributed during the year..	47,103	
Value of stores distributed..........		$1,714,261 85
Value of publications distributed....,		446,574 26
Value of stationery distributed.....		24,834 71
Value of 205 chapels and chapel tents erected during last winter and the present in the various armies.....		114,359 78
Copies of Bible and Testaments and portions of Scriptures distributed during the year..................	569,594	
Copies of Hymn and Psalm-books distributed during the year.......	4,815,923	
Copies of bound library books distributed during the year..........	33,872	
Copies of magazines and pamphlets distributed during the year.......	346,536	
Copies of religious, weekly, and monthly newspapers distributed during the year..................	7,990,758	
Copies of pages of tracts...........	13,681,342	
Copies of "Silent Comforter," etc....	3,691	
Delegates commissioned during the year...........................	2,217	
Aggregate number of days of delegate service......................	78,869	
Average number of delegates constantly in field during the year....	217	
Number of delegates now in the field........................	276	
Balance of cash on hand at the central office, January 1st, 1865......		$5,420 12

With these should be mentioned the Union Commission. This, like the Sanitary and Christian Commissions, was called into existence by the exigencies of the war. The contending armies surging to and fro over extensive regions of country had desolated them completely, seizing not only garnered but growing crops, cattle, horses, and mules, and destroying ruthlessly dwellings, barns, and fences, often applying the torch to those edifices which shot and shell had spared. From these desolated regions, often infested with guerrillas, whose murderous malignity spared neither age nor sex, fled their wretched inhabitants, mostly women and children, homeless and penniless, nearly naked and often starving, wearied, sick, and dying, seeking shelter and sustenance within the Union lines, at Nashville, Vicksburg, and Memphis. Military necessity forbade their remaining in these advanced posts of the Union armies; and rendering them what assistance could be spared in the way of food, the Government shipped them to Cairo, Louisville, St. Louis, Cincinnati, and other points. Here they were landed, sick, helpless, and friendless. Neither State nor municipal charity could legally be bestowed upon them; but that they might not perish, benevolent societies were organized which did what they could to shelter, clothe, and feed them, and provide places for them in the country. These organizations were local, called into existence by the emergency, and had not any central organization or means of mutual coöperation. Meanwhile the demand for help was increasing with fearful rapidity. In June, 1864, the present President of the American Union Commission, visiting the West with other gentlemen as a delegate of the United States Christian Commission, became deeply affected with the sufferings and necessities of these poor refugees, and after free conference with other patriotic and benevolent men, East and West, it was resolved to organize a Commission, having for its object the care and welfare of these refugees, and their eventual restoration, so far as was possible, to homes and home comforts. Most of these people were the wives and children of Unionists, who had either been killed or imprisoned for their loyalty, or were serving in the Union armies as soldiers of the nation. To leave their families to perish would have been unworthy of a great and noble people. A small portion, under the teachings of southern demagogues, were, in spite of their sufferings, still disloyal; but they, too, were starving, and Christianity forbade refusing succor to them. It was foreseen, too, that with the close of the war would arise other needs no less imperious, and demanding an enlarged and national charity. Industry must be revived in the regions wasted by war; desolated homes must be rebuilt, and farms stocked anew and supplied with the implements of husbandry and with seeds for crops. The confiscated lands must be made accessible to settlers, and emigration of the right character guided and stimulated. Free schools must be organized and sustained for a time in part by northern capital. Loyal presses, too, must be established, and the social structure renovated and placed upon its new basis of freedom, order, and law. While this change was going on, though superintended mainly, and supported in part by persons who had previously resided in the regions to be reclaimed, aid would be required for some time from those sections which had not been despoiled by the ravages of war. To the various local refugee societies letters were addressed, and their coöperation, counsel, and suggestions sought. These organizations welcomed with great cordiality the new movement, and united with it as branches, or entered into harmonious coöperation with it. The American Union Commission, as thus organized, had its headquarters in New York city, but included auxiliaries in Boston, Baltimore, Pittsburg, Cincinnati, Chicago, Cairo, Memphis, Nashville, Charleston, and other points. Its officers were Rev. Joseph P. Thompson, D. D., President; Rev. Lyman Abbott, Corresponding Secretary; H. G. Odiorne, Esq., of Cincinnati, Western Secretary; H. M. Pierce, LL.D., Recording Secretary; A. V. Stout, Esq. (President of Shoe and Leather Bank), Treasurer; and an Executive Committee of six members. Its fundamental article, approved, as was the whole work and purpose of the Commission, by the Government, stated that it "is constituted for the purpose of aiding and coöperating with the people of those portions of the United States which have been desolated and impoverished by the war, in the restoration of their civil and social condition upon the basis of industry, education, freedom, and Christian morality.

About the 1st of October, 1864, the Commission was fully organized for its work, and found at first abundant occupation in relieving the immediate necessities of homeless refugees, who were brought from the South in Government transports and landed upon the wharves in the most destitute condition. Nearly 100,000 were thus thrown upon the charity of the benevolent during seven or eight months of 1864–'65. The Commission gathered them into barracks or "homes" at St. Louis, Cairo, Louisville, Cincinnati, Indianapolis, New York, and other points in the North, fed, clothed, and provided them with medical care, and where it was possible procured for them places, where, by their own industry, they could obtain a livelihood. Experience in other organizations proved that the retention of large numbers in camps and barracks in a state of idleness, was injurious alike to their health, their morals, and their subsequent efficiency, and hence the Commission sought as speedily as possible to place all who were able to work in situations where they might obtain their bread by their labor. The extraordinary campaigns of General Sherman, and the sudden collapse of the rebellion, rendered a different system necessary in the Seaboard States. It was neither practicable nor desirable to bring the thousands who flocked into Savannah, Charleston, Wilmington, Newbern, Goldsborough, Petersburg, and Richmond, to the North. They must be aided in their dire necessity at home, and as soon as practicable assisted to sustain themselves. Provisions were accordingly shipped to Savannah, Charleston, Newbern, Richmond, and other points, and careful and trustworthy agents despatched with them to see to their honest and faithful distribution. Pauperism, or the dependence upon charity without effort at self-help, was sternly discouraged; the cities were districted, and the applicants visited at their homes.

The Commission disbursed in money and clothing from its New York office in six months, $70,000, and the various auxiliary boards probably fully as much more. (The Boston Branch expended $32,000.) Schools were opened in Richmond and other cities of the South. Seeds and agricultural implements were also furnished to the impoverished people of the Southern States, that they might be able to resume their long interrupted industry.

CHAPTER XLV.

Position of Gen. Sherman at Atlanta—Position of Gen. Hood: his Movements—Operations of Gen. Forrest—The failure to interrupt the Federal Communications—Plans of Gen. Sherman—His Orders—Distribution of his Army—Advance of the Left Wing—Excitement in Georgia—Advance of the Right Wing—Reaches the Ogeechee—Demonstration toward Augusta—Advance between the Ogeechee and Savannah Rivers—Scouts reach the Coast—Reduction of Fort McAllister—Investment of Savannah—Its Evacuation—Further Proceedings.

During the month of September, the Federal army in and about Atlanta were allowed to rest from the fatigues of active military duty, and many were sent home on furlough. The railroad was employed to its utmost capacity to bring forward supplies and recruits, and much was done in the construction of barracks, and in strengthening the defences of Atlanta. All this seemed to indicate Gen. Sherman's intention to make the city a base for further operations southward, and to hold it with a powerful garrison. From his recent experience of the facility with which a cavalry force could temporarily interrupt his long line of railroad communication,* he was disposed to hasten this work, and the end of the month found Atlanta transformed into a considerable depot of supplies, and so protected by works that a moderate force could hold it against an enemy numerically much superior. The departure of the great body of the inhabitants, by lessening the number of persons to be subsisted, added to the capacity of the garrison to withstand a protracted siege.

Gen. Hood, meanwhile, kept his forces in the neighborhood of Jonesboro, receiving his supplies by the Macon road. His army numbered about 40,000 men, exclusive of the Georgia militia; and, as if to show that no immediate offensive movement was contemplated, the latter were withdrawn from him by Gov. Brown soon after the evacuation of Atlanta, through the following communication:

EXECUTIVE DEPARTMENT,
MILLEDGEVILLE, Sept. 10th, 1864.

Gen. J. B. Hood, Commanding Army of Tennessee:

GENERAL: As the militia of the State were called out for the defence of Atlanta during the campaign against it, which has terminated by the fall of the city into the hands of the enemy, and as many of them left their homes without preparation, expecting to be gone but a few weeks, who have remained in service over three months (most of the time in the trenches), justice requires that they be permitted, while the enemy are preparing for the winter campaign, to return to their homes, and look, for a time, after important interests, and prepare themselves for such service as may be required when another campaign commences against other important points in the State. I, therefore, hereby withdraw said organization from your command, in the hope that I shall be able to return it with greater numbers and equal efficiency, when the interests of the public service require it. In this connection, I beg leave to tender to you, general, my sincere thanks for your impartiality to the State troops, and for your uniform courtesy and kindness to me individually. With assurances of my high consideration and esteem, I am, very respectfully, your obedient servant,

JOSEPH E. BROWN.

To allow their principal Southern army to rust in inactivity, was not, however, the intention of the rebel authorities, who, whatever public statements they might make as to the insignificance of Gen. Sherman's conquest, knew that it was a vital blow aimed at the heart of the Confederacy, and that this was the belief of the Southern people. Something must be done, and that speedily, to arrest the progress of the Federal army, or Georgia, and perhaps the Gulf States, would be irretrievably lost. In this emergency Jefferson Davis started on a tour of inspection through the South, and at Macon, on Sept. 23d, delivered a public address on the crisis, so marked by indiscreet admissions that many of the Confederate papers at first refused to believe that it was genuine. He alluded with undisguised vexation to the depletion in Gen. Hood's ranks caused by absenteeism, and promised, if the deserters would return to duty, that Gen. Sherman should meet "the fate that befell the army of the French Empire in its retreat from Moscow. Our cavalry," he said, "and our people, will harass and destroy his army as did the Cossacks that of Napoleon; and the Yankee general, like him, will escape with only a body-guard." These remarks foreshadowed a new policy, borrowed from that which Gen. Sherman himself had so successfully employed in the capture of Atlanta, and which, considering the long catalogue of rebel reverses in Georgia, had the merit of boldness, if not of farsightedness. The whole army of Gen. Hood, it was decided, should rapidly move in a compact body to the rear of Atlanta, and, after breaking up the railroad between the Chattahoochee and Chattanooga, push on to Bridgeport and destroy the great railroad bridge spanning the Tennessee River at that place. Should this be accomplished, Atlanta would be isolated from Chattanooga, and the latter in turn isolated from Nashville, and Gen. Sherman, cut off from his primary and secondary bases, would find Atlanta but a barren conquest, to be relinquished almost as soon as gained, and would be obliged to return to Tennessee. Atlanta would then fall from lack of provisions, or in consequence of the successful attacks of the Georgia militia.

In connection with this movement, Gen. Forrest, confessedly their ablest cavalry officer, was already operating in Southern Tennessee, where the Federal force was barely adequate to prevent him from interrupting communications between Nashville and Chattanooga. Not the least favorable result anticipated from this movement was the restoration of the *morale* of their army, which, dispirited by constant retreats and reverses, its leaders naturally supposed would be encouraged to greater efforts by an aggressive campaign. On the other hand, the effect of abandoning their conquests, to meet a defeated army operating in their rear, would be likely to perplex and disconcert the Federals. Such was the ingenious plan devised by the authorities, and, to a less able general than Sherman, its vigorous execution might have been productive of enormous disaster, including, of course, the abandonment of the conquests gained during a long and arduous campaign. The sequel will show that he was fully master of the situation, and that the boasts of the rebel papers, that "the great flanker was outflanked," were destined to prove illusive.

A week sufficed to complete Gen. Hood's arrangements, and by the 2d of October his army was across the Chattahoochee and on the march to Dallas, where the different corps were directed to concentrate. At this point he was enabled to threaten Rome and Kingston, as well as the fortified places on the railroad to Chattanooga; and there remained open, in case of defeat, a line of retreat southwest into Alabama. From Dallas he advanced east toward the railroad, and, on the 4th, captured the insignificant stations of Big Shanty and Ackworth, effecting a thorough destruction of the road between the two places. He also sent a division under Gen. French to capture the Federal post at Allatoona Pass, where he had ascertained that a million and a half of rations for the Federal army were stored, on which he probably depended to replenish his commissariat. The natural strength of the position was such that ten thousand men could easily hold it against ten times their number, as long as their supplies held out, besides cutting off railroad communications between Chattanooga and Atlanta. This of itself might have compelled the evacuation of the latter city, and was a sufficient inducement to make the attack.

Gen. Sherman, however, aware that his seat in Atlanta was insecure while this long line of communications lay so exposed to interruption, had anticipated and partially provided against such a movement as this; and immediately upon hearing that Gen. Hood had crossed the Chattahoochee, he despatched Gen. Corse with reënforcements to Rome, which he supposed the enemy were aiming at. During the previous week he had sent Gen. Thomas with troops to Nashville to look after Forrest. His bridges having meanwhile been carried away by a freshet which filled the Chattahoochee, he was unable to move his main body until the 4th, when three pontoons were laid down, over which the armies of the Cumberland, the Tennessee, and the Ohio crossed, and took up their march in the direction of Marietta, with fifteen days' rations. The 20th corps, Gen. Slocum, was left to garrison Atlanta. Learning that the enemy had captured Big Shanty and Ackworth, and were threatening Allatoona, and alive to the imperative necessity of holding the latter place, Gen. Sherman at once communicated by signals instruction to Gen. Corse at Rome to reënforce the small garrison and hold the defences until the main body of the Federal army could come to his assistance. Upon receiving the message Gen. Corse placed nine hundred men on the cars, and reached Allatoona before the attack of French. With this addition the garrison numbered 1,700 men, with six guns.

Early on the morning of the 5th, Gen. French, with 7,000 troops, approached Allatoona, and summoned the Federal commander, "in order to save the unnecessary effusion of blood," to make an immediate surrender; to which the latter replied: "I shall not surrender, and you can commence the unnecessary effusion of blood whenever you please." The battle opened at 8 A. M., and was waged hotly until 2 o'clock in the afternoon. Driven from fort to fort, until they reached their last defence, the garrison fought with an obstinacy and desperation worthy of the great stake for which they contended. Their general was wounded early in the action, but relaxed in no degree his efforts to repel the enemy. On one occasion the opposing forces mingled in a bayonet charge. During the heat of the contest Gen. Sherman reached the summit of Kenesaw Mountain, whence he repeatedly signalled, to Gen. Corse to hold out to the last. The announcement of approaching succor animated the garrison to renewed exertions, and they threw back the assaulting columns of the enemy again and again, finally compelling them to retire, beaten and disheartened, in the direction of Dallas. Their retreat was hastened by the rapid approach of Stanley's (4th) corps from the direction of Pine Mountain. The enemy left 700 to 800 killed, wounded, and prisoners in the hands of the Federals, and their total loss must have exceeded 1,000. The garrison lost 600 men. The town of Allatoona was reduced to a mere wreck by the severe fire of the enemy, and all the Federal artillery and cavalry horses were killed; but the valuable stores were saved, and the fort and pass held. The only important injury done by the rebels, was the destruction of six or seven miles of railroad between Big Shanty and Allatoona, which Gen. Sherman immediately commenced to repair.

For several days subsequent to the fight at Allatoona, Gen. Sherman remained in the latter place, watching the movements of Hood, who, he suspected, would march for Rome, and thence toward Bridgeport, or else to Kingston.

The 23d corps, commanded by Gen. Cox (Gen. Schofield, its commander, having previously been ordered to look after the defences of Chattanooga), was at once sent toward the former place, and, by the 10th, the whole army was on the march thither. Gen. Hood, however, crossing the Etowah and avoiding Rome, moved directly north, and on the 12th Stuart's corps of his army appeared in front of Resaca, the defences of which were held by Col. Weaver with 600 men and three pieces of artillery. The garrison immediately took to the rifle-pits surrounding the works, and kept the enemy's skirmishers at bay, and in the midst of a brisk contest a flag of truce approached, with the following message:

HEADQUARTERS ARMY TENNESSEE,
IN THE FIELD, Oct. 12th, 1864.

To the Officer Commanding the United States forces at Resaca, Ga.:

SIR: I demand the immediate and unconditional surrender of the post and garrison under your command; and should this be acceded to, all white officers and soldiers will be paroled in a few days. If the place is taken by assault, no prisoners will be taken.

Most respectfully, your obedient servant,
J. B. HOOD, General.

To which Col. Weaver replied:

HEADQUARTERS SECOND BRIGADE,
THIRD DIVISION, FIFTEENTH ARMY CORPS.

To Gen. J. B. Hood:

Your communication of this date just received. In reply, I have to state that I am somewhat surprised at the concluding paragraph, to the effect that "if the place is carried by assault, no prisoners will be taken." In my opinion, I can hold this post. If you want it, come and take it.

I am, General, very respectfully, your most obedient servant, CLARK R. WEAVER, Comd'g Officer.
W. W. MCCAMMON, A. A. A. G.

During the whole day continuous masses of rebel troops were passing the forts, but no serious attack was made upon the garrison, the enemy being more intent upon destroying the railroad toward Dalton than wasting their time or strength upon the reduction of a post, the possession of which they wisely considered would be of no particular advantage to them. During the night they captured, after a gallant resistance, a block house at Tilton, garrisoned by part of the 17th Iowa regiment. Throughout the 12th and the 13th the work of destruction continued, the enemy gradually passing to the north, out of sight of Resaca, and on the evening of the latter day the advance of Gen. Sherman's army arrived from Rome, followed on the 14th by the main body, which encamped around Resaca for the night.

Meanwhile the rebel army, pursuing its devastating march north, reached Dalton on the 14th, and, in consequence of the negligence of the Federal scouts, surrounded the fort, garrisoned by the 44th colored regiment, Col. Johnston, before adequate preparations for defence could be made. A demand for surrender similar to that sent to Col. Weaver was at once made, which was refused. But Col. Johnston, discovering that the beleaguering force comprised the whole of Hood's army, and that Buzzard Roost and other important points commanding his work had been occupied, subsequently surrendered his whole command. The 14th and 15th were employed by the enemy in continuing the destruction of the railroad as far as Tunnel Hill, which, whether through want of time or scarcity of gunpowder, they neglected to mine. They found no rolling stock of consequence on the road, and beyond the destruction of a few box-cars did little damage to this species of property. The approach of the Federal columns now warned Gen. Hood to move off to the west, and the 16th found him in full retreat for Lafayette, followed by Gen. Sherman, who, instead of marching along the railroad to Dalton, pushed for Snake Creek Gap, through which, in spite of obstructions accumulated there by Hood, he rapidly passed. At Ship's Gap he captured part of the 24th North Carolina regiment, stationed to delay his march. From Lafayette the enemy retreated in a southwesterly direction into Alabama through a broken and mountainous country, but scantily supplied with food for man or beast; and passing through Summerville, Gaylesville, and Blue Pond, halted at Gadsdens, on the Coosa River, 75 miles from Lafayette. Here he paused for several days, receiving a few reënforcements brought up by Gen. Beauregard, who had on the 17th assumed command of the Confederate military division of the West in the following address:

HEADQUARTERS MILITARY DIVISION OF THE WEST,
October 17th, 1864.

In assuming command at this critical juncture of the Military Division of the West, I appeal to my countrymen of all classes and sections for their generous support and confidence. In assigning me to this responsible position, the President of the Confederate States has extended to me the assurance of his earnest support. The Executives of your States meet me with similar expressions of their devotion to our cause. The noble army in the field, composed of brave men and gallant officers, are strangers to me, and I know that they will do all that patriots can achieve. The history of the past, written in the blood of their comrades, but foreshadows the glorious future which lies before them. Inspired by these bright promises of success, I make this appeal to the men and women of my country to lend me the aid of their earnest and cordial coöperation. Unable to join in the bloody conflicts of the field, they can do much to strengthen our cause, fill up our ranks, encourage our soldiers, inspire confidence, dispel gloom, and thus hasten on the day of our final success and deliverance.

The army of Sherman still defiantly holds Atlanta. He can and must be driven from it. It is only for the good people of Georgia and the surrounding States to speak the word, and the work is done. We have abundant provisions. There are men enough in the country liable to and able for service to accomplish this result. To all such I earnestly appeal to report promptly to their respective commands; and let those who cannot go see to it that none remain who are able to strike a blow in this critical and decisive hour. To those soldiers, if any, who are absent from their commands without leave, I appeal in the name of their brave comrades, with whom they have in the past so often shared the privations of the camp and the dangers of the battle-field, to return at once to their duty. To all such as shall report to their respective commands, in response to this appeal, within the next thirty days, an amnesty is hereby granted. My appeal is to every one, of all classes and conditions, to come forward freely, cheerfully, and with good heart to the work that lies before us.

My countrymen, respond to this call as you have done in days that have passed, and, with the blessing of a kind and overruling Providence, the enemy shall be driven from your soil. The security of your wives and daughters from the insults and outrages of a brutal foe shall be established soon, and be followed by a permanent and honorable peace. The claims of home and country, wife and children, uniting with the demands of honor and patriotism, summon us to the field. We cannot, dare not, will not fail to respond. Full of hope and confidence, I come to join in your struggles, sharing your privations, and with your brave and true men to strike the blow that shall bring success to our arms, triumph to our cause, and peace to our country. G. T. BEAUREGARD, General.

Gen. Hood still retained his special command, subject to the supervision or direction of Gen. Beauregard, and his army, after remaining a few days in Gadsden, moved, about the 1st of November, for Warrington, on the Tennessee River, 30 miles distant. Gen. Sherman meanwhile remained at Gaylesville, which place his main body reached about the 21st, watching the enemy's movements. During the retreat of Gen. Hood into Northern Alabama, he had frequent opportunities to join battle with his pursuers, which he uniformly declined.

The injuries to the railroad were confined to two sections, and covered about 28 miles of track: viz., 7 miles between Big Shanty and Allatoona, and 21 miles between Resaca and Tunnel Hill. So rapidly were the repairs effected, that, by the 20th, the road was in running order from Resaca to Atlanta; and on the 28th, while Gen. Hood was still lying at Gadsden, trains again left Chattanooga for Atlanta. Whatever, therefore, might be the final result of Hood's flanking movement, it had entirely failed to interrupt the Federal communications to a degree that would compel the evacuation of Atlanta. Without permanently disabling the railroad, he had been driven with loss across the mountains south of Chattanooga into Alabama; had cut himself entirely adrift from that admirable railroad system which had so long kept his army supplied, and had left Georgia and the whole Southeast open to the invaders. He perhaps felt himself compensated for these disasters by the opportunity, now temptingly presented to him, to carry the war into Middle Tennessee and Kentucky, and plunder the richly-stored cities and farms of those States, forgetting that a general who had shown such fertile resources during a long and trying campaign, was still opposed to him, with more than double his own force.

It was undoubtedly a part of Gen. Sherman's plan to remain at Atlanta no longer than would suffice to accumulate stores and thoroughly strengthen the defences; after which he would continue his march southward. This, with a determined and unbroken enemy in his front, was likely, to judge from previous experience, to prove a tedious and dangerous operation. To relieve himself of the presence of that enemy was the problem to be solved. When, therefore, Gen. Hood crossed the Chattahoochee on his flanking march upon the Federal communications, it was with mingled feelings of hope and apprehension that he was watched by his vigilant adversary; hope, that he would finally place himself in the position where he was actually found on the 1st of November; and apprehension, lest he should again retire to his camp near Jonesboro. It will be remembered how apparently slow was the pursuit of the rebel army by Gen. Sherman after the former had crossed the Chattahoochee, and how readily it seemed to escape into Alabama, and thence march toward the Tennessee. To those who had witnessed the brilliant campaign to Atlanta, the Federal general's lack of energy and tardiness of movement seemed unaccountable. In the light of subsequent events it would now appear that Gen. Sherman, making only a show of following his adversary, deliberately lured him into Northern Alabama, for the purpose of pursuing an uninterrupted march with his own army through the heart of Georgia. The ill-advised plan of Gen. Hood had given him the very opportunity which he desired, and he prepared at once to avail himself of it.

Anticipating that his army was unnecessarily large for his purpose, he detached from it the 4th and 23d corps, which were ordered to Tennessee, *via* Chattanooga and Bridgeport, to reenforce Gen. Thomas. This left him four corps—the 14th, 15th, 16th and 17th—which had accompanied him from Atlanta, and the 20th left to garrison that place. Two armies were thus formed, of which the former, in conjunction with such forces as Gen. Thomas had in Tennessee, was fully able to cope with Gen. Hood; while the latter, as events proved, was more than sufficient for the Georgia expedition. For several days Gen. Sherman retained his main force at Gaylesville, throwing out strong reconnoissances in the direction of the enemy, as if bent upon watching and thwarting his movement toward the Tennessee. But no sooner had he ascertained that Gen. Hood had started, than he moved his whole army eastward to Rome, with the exception of the two corps sent to Gen. Thomas, and commenced in earnest the preparations for his new campaign. Being no longer under the necessity of coping with an active enemy in his front, he had no further occasion to keep up a long line of railroad communication with a fortified base in his rear. The original plan, therefore, of provisioning Atlanta and using it as a secondary base, which would have required large details of troops, was willingly abandoned, and, in consequence, the place itself, and the greater part of the railroad connecting it with Chattanooga, became practically useless. To garrison and guard either, would be a simple waste of resources; and as it would be an act of needless generosity to leave them for the enemy to use, their destruction became a necessity. The army, once fairly started from Atlanta on its march through Georgia, was to cut loose from all bases and mainly subsist upon the country. This plan, so daring in its conception as to recall the achievements of the greatest generals of antiquity, appears to have been matured and carefully elaborated by Gen. Sherman long previous to its execution, and, upon being laid before the authorities at Washington, received their cordial approval.

During the first ten days of November every locomotive and car on the Chattanooga and Atlanta Railroad was employed in conveying North the inmates of the hospitals, and such supplies of all kinds as there was time to remove. The vast supplies of provisions, forage, stores, and machinery which had accumulated at Atlanta, Rome, and other points, the surplus artillery, baggage, and other useless wagons—every thing, in fact, likely to impede the movements of the army, was gathered up and sent safely to Chattanooga. In return, the trains brought down to Gen. Sherman recruits, convalescents, furloughed men, and ordnance supplies. On the night of November 11th, the last train left Atlanta for the North, and the army, supplied with every man and horse and gun which it needed, and having 30 days' rations in his wagons, was prepared to move toward the coast.

The five corps mentioned above as constituting the army which Gen. Sherman reserved for his expedition, were concentrated into four, by assigning one of the two divisions of the 16th corps (the remaining divisions were in Tennessee) to the 15th corps, and the other to the 17th. The expeditionary army then comprised the 14th corps, Gen. Jeff. C. Davis; the

15th, Gen. Osterhaus commanding in the absence of Gen. Logan; the 17th, Gen. Blair; and the 20th, Gen. Slocum; beside four brigades of artillery, one for each corps, two horse batteries, and two divisions of cavalry. Gen. Barry, chief of artillery, in fitting out this important arm, withdrew every doubtful or suspicious horse, and supplied enough serviceable animals to give each artillery carriage eight horses, and each battery a reserve of twelve horses. The cavalry were equipped with equal care. The total force numbered between 50,000 and 60,000 picked men, constituting one of the most effective armies ever organized. The following order of Gen. Sherman gives the plan of march and other details of the campaign:

HEADQUARTERS MIL DIV. OF THE MISSISSIPPI, IN THE FIELD, KINGSTON, GA., Wednesday, Nov. 9th.

Special Field Order No. 120.

1. For the purpose of military operations, this army is divided into two wings, viz.: The right wing, Maj.-Gen. O. O. Howard commanding, the 15th and 17th corps. The left wing, Maj.-Gen. H. W. Slocum commanding, the 14th and 20th corps.

2. The habitual order of march will be, whenever practicable, by four roads, as nearly parallel as possible, and converging at points hereafter to be indicated in orders. The cavalry, Brig.-Gen. Kilpatrick commanding, will receive special orders from the Commander-in-Chief.

3. There will be no general trains of supplies, but each corps will have its ammunition and provision train, distributed habitually as follows: Behind each regiment should follow one wagon and one ambulance; behind each brigade should follow a due proportion of ammunition wagons, provision wagons, and ambulances. In case of danger, each army corps should change this order of march by having his advance and rear brigade unincumbered by wheels. The separate columns will start habitually at 7 A. M., and make about fifteen miles per day, unless otherwise fixed in orders.

4. The army will forage liberally on the country during the march. To this end, each brigade commander will organize a good and sufficient foraging party, under the command of one or more discreet officers, who will gather, near the route travelled, corn or forage of any kind, meat of any kind, vegetables, corn meal, or whatever is needed by the command; aiming at all times to keep in the wagon trains at least ten days' provisions for the command and three days' forage. Soldiers must not enter the dwellings of the inhabitants or commit any trespass; during the halt, or a camp, they may be permitted to gather turnips, potatoes, and other vegetables, and drive in stock in front of their camps. To regular foraging parties must be entrusted the gathering of provisions and forage at any distance from the road travelled.

5. To army corps commanders is entrusted the power to destroy mills, houses, cotton gins, etc., and for them this general principle is laid down: In districts and neighborhoods where the army is unmolested, no destruction of such property should be permitted; but should guerrillas or bushwackers molest our march, or should the inhabitants burn bridges, obstruct roads, or otherwise manifest local hostility, then army corps commanders should order and enforce a devastation more or less relentless according to the measure of such hostility.

6. As for horses, mules, wagons, etc., belonging to the inhabitants, the cavalry and artillery may appropriate freely and without limit; discriminating, however, between the rich, who are usually hostile, and the poor or industrious, usually neutral or friendly. Foraging parties may also take mules or horses, to replace the jaded animals of their trains, or to serve as pack-mules for the regiments or brigades. In all foraging, of whatever kind, the parties engaged will refrain from abusive or threatening language, and may, when the officer in command thinks proper, give written certificates of the facts, but no receipts; and they will endeavor to leave with each family a reasonable portion for their maintenance.

7. Negroes who are able-bodied and can be of service to the several columns, may be taken along; but each army commander will bear in mind that the question of supplies is a very important one, and that his first duty is to see to those who bear arms.

8. The organization at once of a good pioneer battalion for each corps, composed, if possible, of negroes, should be attended to. This battalion should follow the advance guard, should repair roads and double them if possible, so that the columns will not be delayed after reaching bad places. Also, army commanders should study the habit of giving the artillery and wagons the road, and marching their troops on one side; and also instruct their troops to assist wagons at steep hills or bad crossings of streams.

9. Capt. O. M. Poe, Chief Engineer, will assign to each wing of the army a pontoon train, fully equipped and organized, and the commanders thereof will see to its being properly protected at all times.

By order of Maj.-Gen. W. T. SHERMAN.

L. M. DAYTON, Aide-de-Camp.

The following order issued by Gen. Slocum to the troops under his immediate command gives additional directions for the conduct of the march:

HEADQUARTERS TWENTIETH CORPS, ATLANTA, GA., Nov. 7th, 1864.

[*Circular.*] When the troops leave camp on the march about to commence, they will carry in haversack two days' rations salt meat, two days' hard bread, ten days' coffee and salt, and five days' sugar. Each infantry soldier will carry sixty rounds of ammunition on his person. Every effort should be made by officers and men to save rations and ammunition; not a round of ammunition should be lost or unnecessarily expended. It is expected that the command will be supplied with subsistence and forage mainly from the country. All foraging will be done by parties detailed for the purpose by brigade commanders, under such rules as may be prescribed by brigade and division commanders. Pillaging, marauding, and every act of cruelty or abuse of citizens will be severely punished. Each brigade commander will have a strong rear guard on every march, and will order the arrest of all stragglers. The danger of straggling on this march should be impressed upon the mind of every officer and man of the command. Not only the reputation of the corps, but the personal safety of every man, will be dependent, in a great measure, upon the rigid enforcement of discipline and the care taken of the rations and ammunition.

By command of Maj.-Gen. SLOCUM.

H. W. PERKINS, Asst. Adj.-Gen.

A glance at the map will show that two parallel lines of railway, having a general southeasterly direction, connect Atlanta with the Atlantic seaboard, one terminating at Charleston, 308 miles distant, and the other at Savannah, 293 miles distant. The former line is composed of the Georgia Railroad, 171 miles in length, connecting Atlanta with Augusta, and of the South Carolina Railroad, extending from Augusta to Charleston, 137 miles; and the latter, of the Western and Macon road,

103 miles in length, connecting Atlanta with Macon; and of the Central Georgia road, 190 miles long, connecting Macon with Savannah. From Augusta there also runs a cross-road, due south, to Millen, on the Georgia Central road, 53 miles in length, which affords a second route from Atlanta to Savannah, ten miles longer than that through Macon. The average width of the belt of country embraced between the two main lines as far eastward as Augusta and Millen is about 40 miles; eastward of those points the country gradually expands to a width of nearly 100 miles.

The Georgia road, from Augusta to Atlanta, since the capture of the latter place, had lost much of its importance; but all the others, including that between Augusta and Millen, were essential links in the great chain of communications between the northern and southern portions of the Confederacy; and their destruction, which was one of the objects of the expedition, would sever the Gulf States as completely from Virginia and the Carolinas, as the trans-Mississippi States were cut off from the rest of the Confederacy after the fall of Vicksburg and Port Hudson. The country included in this

railroad system was probably the richest and most populous of Georgia, containing the capital, Milledgeville, and many other important towns; and all accounts concurred in describing it as abundantly supplied with horses, cattle, and subsistence for an invading army. Here also had been conveyed for greater safety large numbers of slaves from the exposed parts of the rebel States. Not less important than these facts was the additional one, that, with the exception of a few brigades of cavalry under Gen. Wheeler, and such troops as could be gathered from Wilmington, Charleston, or Savannah, there was nothing but the Georgia militia to oppose the progress of Gen. Sherman. Under every circumstance, therefore, the two lines above described seemed likely to offer the most feasible route to the coast. The ultimate objective point of the expedition, whether Charleston or Savannah, it was left to circumstances to determine.

On the 11th of November the army was distributed as follows: the 14th corps, with which was Gen. Sherman, at Kingston; the 15th and 17th corps on the Powder Spring road, a little west of the Chattahoochee; and the 20th corps at Atlanta. The latter, after the appointment of Gen. Slocum as commander of the left wing of the army, was commanded by Gen. Williams. On the morning of the 12th the 14th corps moved out of Kingston, leaving a brigade to cover the last shipment north of supplies and rolling stock. This was completed in the afternoon; a parting message, "All is well," was sent to Chattanooga by the telegraph wires, which were then cut, and by nightfall not a soldier of the expeditionary army remained north of Kingston. Following the line of the railroad, the 14th corps thoroughly destroyed every mile of track between Kingston and the Chattahoochee, and every building that could be of any possible use to the enemy. Some instances of wanton destruction by negroes and stragglers occurred, including churches and unoccupied buildings in Kingston, Ackworth, Marietta, and elsewhere; but, in general, private property was respected wherever the main body of the corps marched. On the evening of the 10th, Gen. Corse's division of the 15th corps had burned the public buildings and machine shops of Rome. On the 14th the corps reached the Chattahoochee, and on the afternoon of the 15th marched into Atlanta. On the latter day, the 15th and 17th corps went into camp two miles south of the city, and the 20th corps marched out to a position somewhat further east. On the 7th, while the latter corps alone garrisoned Atlanta, a brigade of rebel cavalry which had been watching their opportunity, made a dash at the defences, but were easily driven off. They nevertheless continued their demonstration—which they called the "Siege of Atlanta"—for several days, until constrained by the approach of the main Federal army to retire. The several corps having been newly supplied with clothing and such equipments as were necessary from the depots in Atlanta, and every thing valuable to the Government removed, the torch was, on the evening of the 15th, applied to the store houses, machine shops and depot buildings, the most substantial of which had previously been mined. For many hours the heavens were lighted up by the flames of this vast conflagration, which was rendered more awful by the roar of exploding shells and magazines, and, by dawn of the 16th, all that was valuable of the city which, next to Richmond, had furnished more material for prosecuting the rebellion than any other in the South, lay in ashes. As far as was possible, private property was spared, and the city rendered of no immediate use to the enemy.

The army being now concentrated and ready to march, Gen. Sherman caused the following order to be promulgated:

HEADQUARTERS MILITARY DIVISION OF THE MISSISSIPPI, IN THE FIELD, KINGSTON, GA., Nov. 8th, 1864.

Special Field Orders No. 119.

The General Commanding deems it proper at this time to inform the officers and men of the 14th, 15th, 17th, and 20th corps, that he has organized them into an army for a special purpose, well known to the War Department and to Gen. Grant. It is sufficient for you to know that it involves a departure from our present base, and a long and difficult march to a new one. All the chances of war have been considered and provided for, as far as human sagacity can. All he asks of you is, to maintain that discipline, patience, and courage which have characterized you in the past, and hopes through you to strike a blow at our enemy that will have a material effect in producing what we all so much desire—his complete overthrow. Of all things, the most important is that the men, during marches and in camp, keep their places, and not scatter abroad as stragglers and foragers, to be picked up by a hostile people in detail. It is also of the utmost importance that our wagons should not be loaded with any thing but provisions and ammunition. All surplus servants, non-combatants, and refugees, should now go to the rear, and none should be encouraged to encumber us on the march. At some future time we will be enabled to provide for the poor whites and blacks who seek to escape the bondage they are now suffering under.

With these few simple cautions in your minds, he hopes to lead you to achievements equal in importance to those of the past.

By order of Gen. W. T. SHERMAN.

L. M. DAYTON, Aide-de-Camp.

On Nov. 16th the whole army marched eastward in four columns, the two under Slocum, with which was Gen. Sherman, following the railroad toward Augusta, while the right wing, under Howard, moved along the Macon and Augusta road. Each wing had cavalry moving on its flanks. Whether the immediate objective was to be Augusta or Macon, or both, it was no part of the Federal general's plan to divulge. To perplex the enemy and divide his forces by pretended demonstrations on places widely separated, he judged would be most likely to ensure him a speedy and uninterrupted march to the coast.

Gen. Howard's command, of which the 15th corps formed the right wing, followed the the railroad as far south as Jonesboro, where the mounted troops of Iverson essayed to make a stand, but were quickly dispersed by Kilpatrick. Thence the column moved east through McDonough and Jackson to the Ocmulgee, which it crossed at Planter's Factory, and passing south, through Monticello and Hillsboro, and between Milledgeville and Clinton, on the 22d struck the Georgia Central Railroad, with its left wing at Gordon, twenty miles east of Macon; the right wing being extended westward toward Griswoldville. In conjunction with the operations of this column the greater part of the Federal cavalry, under the immediate command of Gen. Kilpatrick, made a detour on the extreme right, through Griffin and Forsyth, toward Macon, within five miles of which place he was ordered to demonstrate. The rebels at first believed this to be another raid on a large scale; but learning of the approach of Gen. Howard's column they made haste to concentrate at Macon all their available troops, consisting of some cavalry under Wheeler, a small body of regulars, and several brigades of militia. They still remained in ignorance of Gen. Slocum's movement in the direction of Augusta, but believed Macon to be the main objective point of Gen. Sherman. On the 20th about eight hundred Federal cavalry, with four cannon, made a feigned attack on East Macon, two miles east of the city, which though resulting in little loss on either side, very effectually accomplished its purpose of deceiving the enemy. At one period of the fight a rebel battery was captured in a daring charge by the Federal troops, who, however, having no means of carrying off the guns, were obliged to relinquish them to the enemy. The Federal cavalry finally retired in the direction of Griswoldville after destroying several miles of railroad east of Walnut Creek.

Upon striking the Georgia Central Railroad, on the 22d, the 15th and 17th corps immediately began to destroy the track and the road bed between Gordon and Griswoldville in that thorough manner in which previous experience had rendered the troops adepts. It was while this work was going on that the most serious battle of the campaign up to this date took place. A brigade of infantry, with a section of artillery and some cavalry, under Gen. Walcot, forming the extreme right wing of the 15th corps, had been thrown forward to

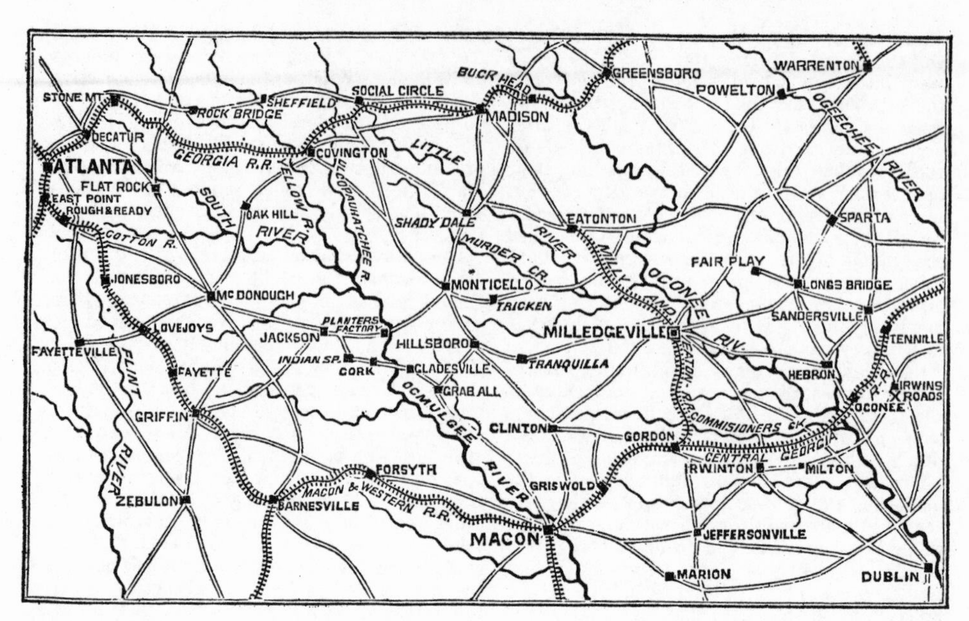

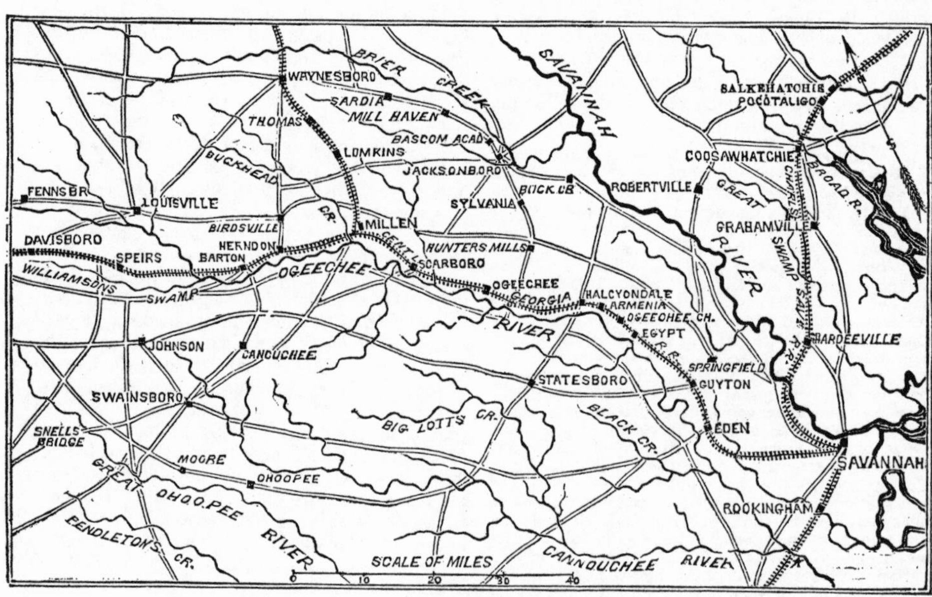

The above Maps represent a belt of country about 80 miles in width and 260 in length, which may be said to have been covered by the operations of the expeditionary army. The lines of march pursued by the four main columns did not, perhaps, extend to the extreme limits of this region; but there is little of it east of the Atlanta and Macon Railroad and west of the Savannah River which was not visited by the cavalry or foraging parties. By reference to the text the movements of the several columns, down to the invest ment of Savannah, can be readily traced.

Griswoldville, to continue the demonstration against Macon so successfully commenced by Gen. Kilpatrick two days previous. After burning the principal buildings in the town, the troops took position in a wood, protected in front by an open morass, and threw up a rail barricade. At 2 o'clock in the afternoon a rebel force about five thousand strong was perceived approaching from the direction of Macon. The Federal cavalry fell slowly back on either flank of the infantry, protecting them from attack in flank and rear, and leaving the enemy no alternative but to make a direct front attack. The latter, comprising several brigades of militia under Gen. Phillips, with a part of Hardee's old command brought up from Savannah, advanced with considerable confidence; and with that ignorance of danger common to raw troops, attempted to carry by storm the Federal position. Six desperate assaults were made, which Gen. Walcott's troops from behind their breastworks repelled with ease and with trifling loss, while the enemy, exposed to a withering fire and part of the time floundering in the morass, paid dearly for their temerity and inexperience. They finally retired toward Macon, leaving three hundred dead upon the field, and having met with a total loss estimated at two thousand five hundred, including Gen. Anderson severely wounded. Their own estimate placed their loss at six hundred and fourteen, which, from all the facts attainable, is manifestly an under estimate. Macon could easily have been taken by Gen. Howard after this encounter, but the Federal commander-in-chief, from prudential motives, did not deem it advisable to make the attempt. His base being, in technical language, "in the air," the capture of a place of so little intrinsic importance, now that its railroad connections were severed, was not essential to the plan of the campaign.

Meanwhile the left wing of the expeditionary army pursued its march along the Augusta and Macon Railroad in two parallel columns, of which the left or outer one was the 20th corps. The 14th corps was accompanied by Gen. Sherman in person. The latter, having destroyed the railroad effectually as far as Covington, turned thence, on the 19th, southeast toward Milledgeville, while the 20th corps, which had previously marched somewhat north of the railroad, continued the work of detruction as far as Madison, sixty-nine miles east of Atlanta and one hundred and two west of Augusta. This was intended to be a demonstration against the latter city, and the more completely to deceive the enemy the Federal cavalry moving on this wing was sent as far east as Union Point, seventy-five miles from Augusta. From Madison the 20th corps marched nearly due south through Eatonton to Milledgeville, where its advance arrived on the 21st, followed on the next day by the 14th corps, which passed through Shady Dale and Eatonton. Neither corps encountered any opposition worth mentioning during the march. At the time the expedition started from Atlanta the Georgia Legislature was in session at Milledgeville. The announcement of the approach of Kilpatrick's cavalry gave them at first no alarm, Macon being supposed to be the place aimed at, and the movement itself a raid. But when on the 18th it was ascertained that Gen. Howard's wing was moving through McDonough in a southeasterly direction, and that Gen. Slocum was evidently approaching from the north, an almost ludicrous panic and consternation seized upon the whole body of legislators, who, with Gov. Brown, fled in unseemly haste to Augusta with such valuables as could be packed within a few hours. On the morning of the 20th, two days after the departure of the legislature, a small party of Federal scouts dashed into the town, which was at once surrendered to them by the Mayor.

For several days previous to the evacuation of Atlanta, rumors of the probability of such an event were prevalent both in the loyal and disloyal States. By the latter the movement was supposed to have been forced upon Gen. Sherman by the aggressive campaign of Hood in Tennessee, and to promise substantial advantages to the rebel cause, no doubt being entertained that the Federal general, unable to maintain his communications with Chattanooga, had resolved to abandon his recent conquest and march back to Tennessee. The evacuation of Atlanta was in fact claimed as a rebel triumph. The cavalry advance toward Macon became in that light merely a demonstration to cover the retreat of the main body. When, however, the real purpose of Gen. Sherman became apparent, the unprepared condition of Georgia to oppose such a movement seems for the first time to have occurred to the State and Confederate authorities. Uttering almost in a single breath predictions of the speedy overthrow of Sherman and appeals to the people to rally against the invader, they exhibited in reality a degree of alarm which had any thing but an encouraging effect upon the public mind. On the 18th the following characteristic appeal was issued by Gen. Beauregard from his headquarters at Corinth, ~~Ala.~~:

To the People of Georgia:

Arise for the defence of your native soil! Rally around your patriotic Governor and gallant soldiers. Obstruct and destroy all the roads in Sherman's front, flank, and rear, and his army will soon starve in your midst. Be confident. Be resolute. Trust in an overruling Providence, and success will soon crown your efforts. I hasten to join you in the defence of your homes and firesides.

G. T. BEAUREGARD.

Simultaneous with this came the following appeal from one of the Georgia Senators in the Confederate Congress:

RICHMOND, Nov. 18.

To the People of Georgia:

You have now the best opportunity ever yet presented to destroy the enemy. Put every thing at the disposal of our Generals, remove all provisions from the path of the invader, and put all obstructions in his path.

Every citizen with his gun and every negro with his spade and axe can do the work of a soldier. You can destroy the enemy by retarding his march.

Georgians be firm, act promptly, and fear not.

(Signed) B. H. HILL.

I most cordially approve the above.

JAMES A. SEDDON, Sec'y of War.

And this also from the Georgia delegation in the lower house of Congress:

RICHMOND, Nov. 19, 1864.

To the People of Georgia:

We have had a special conference with President Davis and the Secretary of War, and are able to assure you that they have done, and are still doing, all that can be done to meet the emergency that presses upon you. Let every man fly to arms. Remove your negroes, horses, cattle, and provisions from Sherman's army, and burn what you cannot carry. Burn all bridges, and block up the roads in his route. Assail the invader in front, flank, and rear, by night and by day. Let him have no rest.

JULIAN HARTRIDGE, MARK BLAUFORD,
J. H. REYNOLDS, Gen. N. LESTER,
JNO. T. SHEWMAKER, JOS. M. SMITH.

One of the last acts of Gov. Brown, before his hurried flight from Milledgeville, was to issue a proclamation ordering a levy *en masse* of the whole free white population of the State between the ages of sixteen and forty-five years, except the legislature and judiciary, ordained ministers of the gospel, railroad employés and telegraph operators, and all persons physically unable to bear arms. They were required to undergo military service for forty days, and failure to report at the designated places was to be considered equivalent to desertion. Should the directors or superintendents of railroad companies refuse to afford proper coöperation with the military authorities they were to be sent immediately to the front. Pursuant to a resolution of the Legislature the Governor also offered pardon to the prisoners in the penitentiary at Milledgeville if they would volunteer and prove themselves good soldiers. About a hundred accepted the offer. These preparations came manifestly too late to offer any other than a feeble resistance to the advance of Gen. Sherman's well-appointed army; and whatever opposition the latter did encounter during the remainder of the campaign was due to the efforts of such fragmentary bodies of Confederate troops or organized State militia as could be hastily concentrated.

But few of the troops that reached the neighborhood of Milledgeville entered the town, two or three regiments only being detailed to do provost guard duty and destroy public property. The magazines, penitentiary, arsenals, depot buildings, factories, and storehouses, with seventeen hundred bales of cotton, were burned; but the Capitol and the private residences received no injury, and, as far as possible, pillage was prevented. The principal of the State Asylum, and other persons, expressed their gratitude to Gen. Sherman that order was so fully maintained. Some stores and about twenty-five hundred small arms fell into the possession of the Federal troops, and in the penitentiary were found some Federal prisoners of war. A number of sick rebels were also captured in the hospital.

While the left wing was enjoying a temporary rest at Milledgeville, the right advanced steadily along the Georgia Central Railroad to the Oconee, destroying every mile of track in its march. The rebels became aware at last that Macon was not to be seriously attacked, and by extraordinary exertions succeeded in getting Gen. Wheeler across the Oconee, in the neighborhood of the railroad bridge, where, aided by a body of militia under Gen. Wayne, he was prepared to dispute the passage. Upon reaching the bridge on the 23d, Gen. Howard found it too well guarded to effect a crossing except with considerable loss. A day or two was occupied with skirmishing across the river banks to occupy the enemy's attention, while the 15th corps was pushed down to a ford eight miles below the railroad, where a pontoon was laid without much difficulty. The rebel forces then made a precipitate retreat, and by the 26th the whole right wing was across the river and moving eastward along the railroad, which was destroyed as the column advanced. The left wing crossed the Oconee near Milledgeville without opposition on the 24th, and moved in a southeasterly direction toward Sandersville, a town lying a little north of the Georgia Central Railroad, and about 15 miles east of the river. This movement hastened the retreat of Gen. Wayne. The 14th corps now took post on the left flank of this column, which position it held during the remainder of the campaign. On the 26th, the 14th and 20th corps, marching on parallel roads, entered Sandersville simultaneously, driving out a body of rebel cavalry which essayed to impede their advance; and on the 27th and 28th both wings were temporarily encamped between Sandersville and Irwin's Cross Roads, a few miles south of the railroad. About this time Gen. Sherman transferred his quarters from the left wing to the 17th corps, then at Tennille, a railroad station near Sandersville.

After the demonstration toward Macon, ending with the action at Griswoldville, Gen. Kilpatrick shifted his cavalry force to the left wing. Remaining a day or two at Milledgeville to recruit, he started thence on the 25th in the direction of Waynesboro, a station on the Augusta and Millen Railroad, 75 miles due east, for the purpose partly of covering the passage of the main body of the army across the Ogeechee, the next great river on the route east of the Oconee, and partly of conducting a feint toward Augusta. On the 27th, a few hundred of his cavalry, under Captains Hays and Estes, dashed into Waynesboro, burned the railroad bridge over Briar Creek in the neighborhood, and after inflicting other damage, fell back on the succeeding day to the main cavalry body which lay east of the Ogeechee, in the neighborhood of Louisville. One of the prime objects of the advance was to surprise Millen and release the Federal prisoners confined there; but nothing more than a demonstration in that direction was attempted, information reaching Gen. Kilpatrick that the enemy had for weeks previous been gradually removing the prisoners to some less exposed point in Southern Georgia.

On the 28th the 14th corps struck the Ogeechee River at Fenn's Bridge, 15 miles northeast of Sandersville, crossed on pontoons after some hours' delay, and marching down the left bank of the river reached Louisville on the 29th. The 20th corps at the same time moved along the railroad, which from Davisboro station immediately south of Fenn's bridge, follows for about 20 miles a course parallel with the Ogeechee. The 17th and 15th corps moved south of the railroad, the 15th, with which was Gen. Howard, covering the right flank of the army. The cavalry under Gen. Wheeler fell back steadily in the path of the advancing columns, seeking to delay their movements, and during the 28th and 29th had much sharp skirmishing with the Federal cavalry in the neigborhood of Louisville. Up to this time the objective point of Gen. Sherman was as much an uncertainty to the rebel leaders as at the commencement of the campaign; but in the appearance of Gen. Kilpatrick on the left flank of the Federal army, and especially in the occupation of Louisville by the 14th corps, Gen. Wheeler fancied he detected an intention to move in force upon Waynesboro, and thence to Augusta, 30 miles further north. That he should be thus deceived was part of the plan of Gen. Sherman, who gladly witnessed the rebel cavalry moving to the north to obstruct the supposed advance upon Augusta, and thus leaving him at liberty to cross the Ogeechee with his main body. On the 30th, the 20th and 17th corps, which had been actively engaged for several days in destroying the railroad between Tennille station and the river, succeeded in crossing with little difficulty, the former at the railroad bridge, and the latter near Barton station, a few miles further east. The 15th corps pursued its march in a parallel line with the other columns on the right bank of the river. The Ogeechee was naturally a line of great strength to the enemy, who might have made its passage a costly effort to the Federal army. That three of its four corps should have, under these circumstances, crossed without loss was esteemed one of the most brilliant pieces of strategy witnessed during the campaign.

On the morning of Nov. 30th Gens. Baird's and Morgan's divisions of the 14th corps moved forward a short distance on the road toward Waynesboro, which was the signal for Gen. Kilpatrick to renew, in coöperation with these troops, his demonstration against Augusta. For the purpose also of expediting Gen. Wheeler's movement to the north, the remaining division of the 14th corps demonstrated on the same day against his left flank. This had the desired effect, and during Dec. 1st that general rapidly fell back before the Federal advance. During the 1st 2d and 3d constant skirmishing took place between the Federal and rebel cavalry, the latter being gradually pushed beyond Waynesboro. On the 3d they were found strongly posted on the railroad, two miles northeast of the town, with heavy rail barricades in front, and a swamp and railroad embankment on either flank. Two or three vigorous charges by the Federal cavalry sufficed to drive them from their defences with considerable loss. Up to this point Baird's division of the 14th corps formed the infantry support to the cavalry. The remaining divisions of this corps upon reaching Buckhead Creek had turned east to Lumpkin's station on the Augusta and Millen Railroad, 10 miles south of Waynesboro, where on the 3d and 4th they destroyed a considerable portion of the track. They then marched in a southeasterly direction for Jacksonboro, 20 miles east of Millen, where, on the 5th, they united with Gens. Kilpatrick and Baird, who having finished their demonstration against Augusta, moved rapidly south from Waynesboro on the 4th.

Meanwhile the 20th and 17th corps advanced steadily along the railroad, and on Dec. 2d the latter reached Millen. The 20th corps passed somewhat north of Millen, through Birdsville, and thence marched southeast, while the 15th corps moved in two columns to the west of the Ogeechee River, a day's march in advance of the main body. The whole army, pivoting, it may be said, upon Millen, now swung slowly around from its eastern course, and moved in parallel columns directly southward, all, with the exception of the 15th corps, marching down the peninsula formed by the Ogeechee and Savannah Rivers. The 17th corps followed the railroad, destroying it from Millen downward. The success of the feint toward Augusta was now demonstrated in the fact that Gen. Sherman was pursuing an uninterrupted march to the coast, with his army well in hand, while a large rebel force was concentrated in Augusta, too far in the rear of the Federal army to check its progress for a day, and utterly useless for offensive purposes. Even when it was ascertained that Gen. Sherman was moving south from Millen, the enemy appear to have been uncertain whether Savannah, Darien, Brunswick, or even Port Royal harbor was to be his objective point. After the deflection of the Federal march southward from Millen, however, they admitted that Gen. Sherman might possibly escape.

As the Federal army continued its advance down the peninsula between the Savannah and Ogeechee Rivers, it became apparent to Gen. Hardee, who held Savannah with fifteen thousand men, a great part of whom were militia, that that city was to be the objective of Gen. Sherman. A line of works, stretching from river to river, had been erected to delay the Federal advance; and for the purpose of preventing an attack upon the Savannah and

Gulf Railroad, which was being employed to its utmost capacity to bring supplies and re-enforcements to the city, a force was sent across the Ogeechee, which it was supposed would offer effectual resistance to the progress of the 15th corps. The greater part of the latter, however, had crossed to the east bank of the Ogeechee, on the 7th, near Eden, and on the succeeding day Gen. Corse's division was pushed forward between the Little and Great Ogeechee, thirteen miles in advance of the main column, to the canal connecting the Ogeechee with the Savannah. The canal was quickly bridged, and the division intrenched in a strong position on the south side, the enemy, after a brief resistance, abandoning their advanced lines, and taking refuge within the fortifications proper of Savannah. Other portions of the 15th corps were immediately brought up to support Gen. Corse, and on the 9th a detachment moved forward to the Savannah and Gulf Railroad, destroyed the track for several miles around Miller's station, and captured a train of eighteen cars, with many prisoners, thus cutting off communication between Savannah and the South.

While the extreme right was thus closing in upon the rear of Savannah, the main body moved south by rapid marches between the Ogeechee and Savannah Rivers. The weather, which had been for the most part favorable during the first half of the campaign, became rainy after the columns passed Millen, and the swampy regions of the coast, which the army had now entered upon, offered serious obstacles to rapid marching. But, inspired by continued successes and the prospect of soon opening communications with the fleet on the coast, the troops pushed forward with no more delays than were caused by bridging streams or corduroying swamps, and on the evening of the 10th the advance of the several columns had reached positions varying from three to eight miles distant from Savannah. On the march the left wing struck the Savannah and Charleston Railroad where it crosses the Savannah River, from which point southward the track was thoroughly destroyed. The enemy showed considerable resistance as the Federal army approached the city, and the 14th and 17th corps sustained some loss in skirmishing. A number of men having been wounded by the explosion of shells and torpedoes, buried and concealed in the road, the rebel prisoners were placed in front of the columns, and compelled to remove them. Kilpatrick covered the rear, and kept at bay such scattered bodies of cavalry as attempted to harass the march. The 11th and 12th were occupied in putting the troops in position, establishing batteries, erecting breastworks, and in other operations connected with a regular investment, and on the latter day the army was concentrated so as to form a semicircle, extending from the Savannah River to the Savannah and Gulf Railroad. The line was about ten miles long, the extreme left, held by the 20th corps, being about three miles from the city, while the extreme right of the 15th corps, resting on the railroad, was eleven miles distant. Next to the 20th corps came the 14th, and next to that on the right the 17th. Everywhere the troops encountered a strong line of earthworks, having heavy guns in position, and held apparently by a large force. These were the exterior fortifications of Savannah, and although of considerable extent, were so flanked by a series of impassable swamps stretching across the peninsula, as to be capable of easy defence. All the openings to these morasses, as well as the roads leading through them, had been fortified with extreme care, and could hardly be carried without severe loss.

Meanwhile, as early as the 9th, Capt. Duncan and two scouts had been sent from the 15th corps on the hazardous enterprise of penetrating the enemy's lines and reaching the coast, for the purpose of communicating with the fleet, which it was known was on the alert for intelligence from Gen. Sherman's army. Embarking in a small skiff on the Ogeechee, at nightfall, they paddled down the river until warned by the approach of day to conceal themselves in the rice swamps. On the night of the 10th they resumed their voyage, and creeping past Fort McAllister and the picket boats during a rain storm, emerged into Ossabaw Sound, where, on the morning of the 11th, they were picked up by the Federal gunboat *Flag*, which immediately conveyed them to Hilton Head. Gen. Foster, commanding the department, was at once summoned from Pocotaligo, where he was demonstrating against the Charleston and Savannah Railroad in aid of Gen. Sherman's movement, and received from the scouts Gen. Howard's despatch of the 9th: "We have had perfect success, and the army is in fine spirits." This was the first direct intelligence from the expeditionary army since its departure from Atlanta, and its reception in the North a few days later caused universal rejoicing. The greater part of the available naval force on the station being already in the Savannah River for the purpose of co-operating with the army, nothing remained to be done but to send a few vessels around to Ossabaw and Wassaw Sounds to endeavor to open communications. Wassaw Sound, into which empties the Wilmington River, being nearer the city, was carefully explored by Gen. Foster and Admiral Dahlgren, and both there and in Ossabaw Sound the gunboats were directed to make frequent signals with the shore.

Gen. Sherman having determined that Ossabaw Sound, which forms the mouth of the Ogeechee, afforded the most practicable means of communicating with the fleet, immediately took measures to reduce Fort McAllister, which commands the water approaches in that direction. This work, situated on the right bank of the Great Ogeechee, about six miles from the Sound, was one of the strongest of its class in the South, and had successfully resisted attacks by the Monitor fleet in January and March, 1863. It comprised three half bastions and two curtains, and mounted twenty-one guns, several of which were 8-inch and 10-inch pieces. Every line of approach, both by land and water, was swept by howitzers and field-pieces placed on the bastions, and along its front extended a ditch forty feet wide and of great depth, into whose bottom were driven heavy palisades. Outside of the ditch was a formidable line of abatis, and beyond this the land approaches were thickly planted with torpedoes. The fort had received additions in armament and garrison since the naval attacks, and was now held by two hundred and fifty men, commanded by Major Anderson and Captains Clinch and White.

On the evening of the 12th Gen. Hazen's division of the 15th corps, to which was assigned the duty of assaulting the fort, marched from its position on the Savannah and Gulf Railroad toward Kingsbridge over the Great Ogeechee, distant about six miles. This structure having been destroyed by the enemy, a new one, eighteen hundred feet in length, was erected during the night, and at daybreak of the 13th the column pushed on for Fort McAllister. At half-past four in the afternoon the work was completely invested, and the troops advanced to the assault in a single line, over an open space of six hundred yards, the greater part of which consisted of a rice swamp. The obstacles were formidable enough to have deterred veterans of more experience than those who formed the attacking column, and might have justified the erection of intrenchments and a system of gradual approaches, which would have involved a loss of valuable time and delayed the opening of communications with the fleet. "Carry the place by assault to-night if possible," was Gen. Sherman's order to Hazen, and the troops, fighting under the immediate eye of their commander, who was watching the action from a house-top some miles distant, and aroused to a high pitch of enthusiasm, pressed eagerly forward, regardless of bursting torpedoes or the fire from the fort. In an almost incredible short space of time the open ground was crossed, the abatis surmounted, and the ditch reached. A few minutes sufficed to remove the palisades, and the men, with loud cheers, swarmed over the parapet, shooting and bayoneting the gunners who refused to surrender, and planted the national colors upon the rampart. The assault occupied barely twenty minutes, and from first to last the storming column never wavered in its advance. The Federal loss was but twenty-three killed and eighty-two wounded, owing to the celerity of the movement, and that of the enemy amounted to fourteen killed and twenty-one wounded. Two hundred and eleven rebel officers and men were taken prisoners. On the succeeding day the latter were employed in removing the torpedoes buried around the fort.

Just previous to the assault Gen. Sherman detected a gunboat reconnoitring in the river below the fort, and at once opened communications with her by signals. No sooner was the fort taken than he embarked in a rowboat on the Ogeechee, and a few hours later was taken on board of the steamtug *Dandelion* in the cabin of which he wrote his first despatch to the Secretary of War as follows:

ON BOARD DANDELION, OSSABAW SOUND, 11:50 P. M., Dec. 13.

To-day, at 5 P. M., Gen. Hazen's division of the 15th corps carried Fort McAllister by assault, capturing its entire garrison and stores. This opened to us the Ossabaw Sound, and I pushed down to this gunboat to communicate with the fleet. Before opening communication we had completely destroyed all the railroads leading into Savannah and invested the city. The left is on the Savannah River, three miles above the city, and the right on the Ogeechee, at Kingsbridge. The army is in splendid order, and equal to any thing. The weather has been fine, and supplies were abundant. Our march was most agreeable, and we were not at all arrested by guerrillas.

We reached Savannah three days ago, but owing to Fort McAllister could not communicate; but now we have McAllister we can go ahead.

We have already captured two boats on the Savannah River, and prevented their gunboats from coming down.

I estimate the population of Savannah at twenty-five thousand and the garrison at fifteen thousand. Gen. Hardee commands.

We have not lost a wagon on the trip, but have gathered in a large supply of negroes, mules, horses, etc., and our teams are in far better condition than when we started.

My first duty will to clear the army of surplus negroes, mules, and horses. We have utterly destroyed over two hundred miles of rails, and consumed stores and provisions that were essential to Lee's and Hood's armies. The quick work made with McAllister and the opening of communication with our fleet, and the consequent independence for supplies, dissipates all their boasted threats to head me off and starve the army.

I regard Savannah as already gained.

Yours, truly,

W. T. SHERMAN, Major-General.

On the succeeding day he met Gen. Foster and Admiral Dahlgren in Wassaw Sound, where measures were concerted for opening permanent communication between the army and the fleet, and for efficient coöperation by the latter in the reduction of Savannah. The new base was established on the Ogeechee at Kingsbridge, and the obstructions in the river having been removed, a number of transports passed up on the 16th and 17th. On the 16th several tons of mail matter were distributed among the soldiers.

Meanwhile the lines of investment were steadily pressed around Savannah, prisoners being employed to remove the torpedoes buried by the enemy along the chief avenues of approach. On every side of the city but that fronting the river the investment was complete. By means of rows of piles, sunken vessels, and the guns of Forts Jackson, Lee, and Lawton, the enemy commanded the river to within a few miles of Fort Pulaski. Between the city and the South Carolina shore intervenes Hutchinson's Island, several miles in length, the upper end of which had been seized by Gen. Slocum as the Federal left wing approached the city. But the lower end, divided from the upper by a canal, was fortified and still held by the enemy; and somewhat below the island, on the South Carolina side, commences Union Causeway, traversing the extensive swamps intervening between Savannah and Charleston, and offering a practicable line of retreat to Gen. Hardee. To approach the city from the north, along the Carolina shore, through the wide stretch of swamps and rice-fields, artificially and skilfully flooded, seemed almost an impossibility, and the enemy relied confidently upon a protracted and perhaps successful resistance. On the 16th Gen. Sherman sent a formal demand for the surrender of Savannah, closing his despatch with Hood's words to the colored troops at Dalton. To this General Hardee replied that as his communications were still open and his men supplied with subsistence, he was able to withstand a long siege, and was determined to hold the city until his forces were overpowered.

Gen. Sherman now rapidly pushed forward his work, and by means of a substantial corduroy road traversing the swamps and rice-fields between Kingsbridge and the city, brought up heavy siege guns which by the 20th were put in position. Perceiving this, and also that preparations were making to close up the Federal lines on the left, Gen. Hardee seems to have become suddenly aware of the danger that menaced the city, and alive to the necessity of securing his own retreat while Union Causeway afforded an avenue of escape. On the afternoon of the 20th his troops were hurriedly set to work to destroy the navy yard and Government property, while the formidable iron-clads, Georgia and Savannah, moved up the river and commenced a furious fire on the Federal left, supported by several batteries. Under cover of this fire the garrison was transported during the night of the 20th, by steamboats, rowboats, and rafts to Union Causeway, and on the morning of the 21st the troops were well on their way to Charleston. Before leaving, they blew up the iron-clads and the fortifications below the city.

At dawn of the 21st the evacuation became known to the Federal pickets, and several regiments were sent forward to occupy the deserted intrenchments. A few hours later Gen. Sherman entered the city at the head of his body-guard, and received its formal surrender from the municipal authorities. The following despatch to the President announced this crowning success of the campaign:

SAVANNAH, GA., December 22.

His Excellency President Lincoln:

I beg to present you as a Christmas gift the city of Savannah, with one hundred and fifty heavy guns and plenty of ammunition, and also about twenty-five thousand bales of cotton.

W. T. SHERMAN, Major-General.

The following from Gen. Foster gives additional details of the capture:

STEAMER GOLDEN STATE, SAVANNAH RIVER, December 22—7 P. M.

To Lieut. Gen. Grant and Maj.-Gen. H. W. Halleck:

I have the honor to report that I have just returned from Gen. Sherman's headquarters in Savannah.

I send Major Gray, of my staff, as bearer of despatches from Gen. Sherman to you, and also a message to the President.

The city of Savannah was occupied on the morning of the 21st. Gen. Hardee, anticipating the contemplated assault, escaped with the main body of his infantry and light artillery on the morning of the 20th, by crossing the river to Union Causeway, opposite the city. The rebel iron-clads were blown up, and the navy yard was burned. All the rest of the city is intact, and contains twenty thousand citizens, quiet and well disposed.

The captures include eight hundred prisoners, one hundred and fifty guns, thirteen locomotives in good order, one hundred and ninety cars, a large supply of ammunition and materials of war, three steamers, and thirty-three thousand bales of cotton, safely stored in warehouses. All these valuable fruits of an almost bloodless victory have been, like Atlanta, fairly won.

I opened communication with the city with my steamers to-day, taking up what torpedoes we could see, and passing safely over others. Arrangements are made to clear the channel of all obstructions.

J. G. FOSTER, Major-General.

With the capture of Savannah ended the great winter campaign through Georgia, just five weeks after the Federal army left Atlanta. Within that period Gen. Sherman traversed at his leisure, and with a total loss of less than fifteen hundred men, a tract of country varying from sixty to twenty miles in width, and completely destroyed the great railroad quadrilateral of which Atlanta, Macon, Augusta, and Savannah formed the four corners. When it is recollected that from Atlanta to Madison on the Georgia road, and from the neighborhood of Macon to Savannah, the track was systematically torn up, beside considerable portions of the Milledgeville branch and the Augusta and Millen road, Gen. Sherman's estimate of 200 miles destroyed will seem under the mark. The work of destruction was carried on with a completeness and deliberation unknown to previous expeditions. Every rail was heated and twisted; every tie, bridge, tank, wood-shed, and depot building was burned, and every culvert blown up. For miles on the Georgia, Georgia Central, and Augusta and Millen roads, the track is carried over marshy territory by extensive trestle-work. This was all burned or otherwise injured beyond the possibility of immediate replacement. Almost from the moment of departure the army literally fed on the fat of the land, and fared probably better on the march than in camp. Live stock, poultry, Indian meal, sweet potatoes, sorghum syrup, and other luxuries were found in an abundance far exceeding the demands of the men, and many thousand head of cattle, horses, and mules were gathered up on the march and brought safely to the coast. The army is said to have encamped around Savannah with fifty days' rations of beef on the hoof. As a rule the regulations respecting pillaging were observed by the troops, but of necessity many instances occurred where private property, not necessary to sustain life or assist military operations, was appropriated by stragglers. Such occurrences are unavoidable in the unopposed progress of a large army through a well-stocked country. As was expected, large numbers of slaves, of both sexes and of all ages, seized the opportunity to gain their freedom, and followed in the wake of the several columns. The able-bodied men did good service as pioneers, teamsters, or laborers, and in many cases the places where horses, cattle, provisions, cotton, or valuables were concealed, were revealed by the colored fugitives. On several occasions this class of followers became so numerous as to impede the movements of the army and the trains. Many dropped off from time to time exhausted by the march; but from eight to ten thousand succeeded in reaching Savannah. Cotton was of course invariably burned where-ever discovered, and the loss is estimated at 15,000 bales. The most remarkable feature of the campaign was the trifling opposition which the enemy opposed to the expeditionary army, and the ease with which every attack was repelled. In every engagement, down to the smallest skirmish, the Federal troops, having an absolute faith in their leader which made them equal to any task he might impose, showed their superiority. The cavalry advance, supported occasionally by a division or two of infantry, and frequently engaging superior numbers, was found adequate for any thing which the enemy could oppose to them. Full half the loss sustained by Gen. Sherman was of stragglers and plunderers, surprised and captured by the enemy while out of the direct line of march.

Upon the surrender of Savannah, Gen. Geary was appointed military commander. The city was found uninjured, the Federal cannon having never opened upon it, and was crowded with refugees from the interior, many of whom were without the means of procuring food. Measures were adopted for supplying the wants of these persons, and stringent orders issued by Gen. Geary for the protection of peaceful citizens and their property against outrages by soldiers. The cotton was, however, appropriated by the United States Government, with the design of shipping it to the North for sale. The following order was issued by Gen. Sherman for the government of the city:

HEADQUARTERS MILITARY DIVISION OF THE MISSISSIPPI, IN THE FIELD, SAVANNAH, GA., Dec. 26th, 1864.

Special Field Orders No. 143.

The city of Savannah and surrounding country will be held as a military post and adapted to future military uses; but as it contains a population of some 20,000 people, who must be provided for, and as other citizens may come, it is proper to lay down certain general principles, that all within its military jurisdiction may understand their relative duties and obligations.

I. During war, the military is superior to civil authority, and where interests clash the civil must give way; yet where there is no conflict, every encouragement should be given to well-disposed and peaceable inhabitants to resume their usual pursuits. Families should be disturbed as little as possible in their residences, and tradesmen allowed the free use of their shops, tools, &c. Churches, schools, all places of amusement and recreation, should be encouraged, and streets and roads made perfectly safe to persons in their usual pursuits. Passes should not be exacted within the line of outer pickets, but if any person shall abuse these privileges by communicating with the enemy, or doing any act of hostility to the Government of the United States, he or she will be punished with the utmost rigor of the law. Commerce with the outer world will be resumed to an extent commensurate with the wants of the citizens, governed by the restrictions and rules of the Treasury Department.

II. The Chief Quartermaster and Commissary of the army may give suitable employment to the people, white and black, or transport them to such points as they choose, where employment may be had, and may extend temporary relief, in the way of provisions and vacant houses, to the worthy and needy, until such time as they can help themselves. They will select, first, the buildings for the necessary uses of the army; next, a sufficient number of stores to be turned over to the Treasury Agent for trade stores. All vacant storehouses or dwellings, and all buildings belonging to absent rebels, will be construed and used as belonging to the United States, until such times as their titles can be settled by the courts of the United States.

III. The Mayor and City Council of Savannah will continue and exercise their functions as such, and will, in concert with the commanding officer of the post and Chief Quartermaster, see that the fire companies are kept in organization, the streets cleaned and lighted, and keep up a good understanding between the citizens and soldiers. They will ascertain and report to the Chief C. S., as soon as possible, the names and number of worthy families that need assistance and support.

The Mayor will forthwith give public notice that the time has come when all must choose their course, viz.: to remain within our lines and conduct themselves as good citizens, or depart in peace. He will ascertain the names of all who choose to leave Savannah, and report their names and residence to the Chief Quartermaster, that measures may be taken to transport them beyond the lines.

IV. Not more than two newspapers will be published in Savannah, and their editors and proprietors will be held to the strictest accountability, and will be punished severely in person and property for any libelous publication, mischievous matter, premature news, exaggerated statements, or any comments whatever upon the acts of the constituted authorities; they will be held accountable even for such articles though copied from other papers.

By order of Maj.-Gen. W. T. SHERMAN.

L. M. DAYTON, Aide-de-Camp.

In marked contrast with the inhabitants of other Confederate cities captured during the war, the population of Savannah showed a desire to conform their conduct to circumstances, and refrained from open insults or efforts to vex or harass their captors. It does not appear that a bale of cotton, or indeed any thing of positive value, was destroyed by the citizens to prevent its falling into the hands of the Federal troops. A latent Union feeling was even developed, and at a meeting of influential citizens convened on the 28th, in pursuance of a call from Mayor Arnold, to take into consideration "matters relating to the present and future welfare of the city," the following resolutions were unanimously adopted:

Whereas, By the fortune of war and the surrender of the city by the civil authorities, Savannah passes once more under the authority of the United States; and whereas we believe that the interests of the city will be best subserved and promoted by a full and free expression of our views in relation to our present condition, we, therefore, the people of Savannah, in full meeting assembled, do hereby resolve,

1st. That we accept the position, and in the language of the President of the United States, seek to have "peace by laying down our arms and submitting to the national authority under the Constitution, leaving all questions which remain to be adjusted by the peaceful means of legislation, conference, and votes."

Resolved, 2d. That laying aside all differences and burying bygones in the graves of the past, we will use our best endeavors once more to bring back the prosperity and commerce we once enjoyed.

Resolved, 3d. That we do not put ourselves in the position of a conquered city asking terms of a conqueror, but we claim the immunities and privileges contained in the proclamation and message of the President of the United States, and in all the legislation of Congress in reference to a people situated as we are; and while we owe on our part a strict obedience to the laws of the United States, we ask the protection over our persons, lives, and property recognized by those laws.

Resolved, 4th. That we respectfully request his Excellency the Governor to call a convention of the people of Georgia, by any constitutional means in his power, to give them an opportunity of voting upon the question whether they wish the war between the two sections of the country to continue.

Resolved, 5th. That Major-General Sherman having placed as military commander of this post Brigadier-General Geary, who has, by his urbanity as a gentleman and his uniform kindness to our citizens, done all in his power to protect them and their property from insult and injury, it is the unanimous desire of all present that he be allowed to remain in his present position, and that for the reasons above stated the thanks of the citizens are hereby tendered to him and the officers under his command.

Finding the people so tractable and resigned to their condition, Gen. Geary exerted himself to protect them from oppression, and to maintain order; and several instances occurred of soldiers being severely punished for drunkenness, pillaging, or other improper acts. Measures were at once taken to prepare the Custom House and Post Office for the former uses, and by several of the insurance companies the propriety of establishing a National Bank, under the Act of Congress, was seriously considered.

CHAPTER XLVI.

General Sheridan takes command on the Upper Potomac—Attack on Fisher's Hill—March of Sheridan up the Shenandoah—Sudden Attack of the Enemy—Their Repulse and Pursuit—Guerrillas—Movements of Gen. Price in Missouri—Investment of Nashville by Gen. Hood—Battles—Retreat of Hood and pursuit by Gen. Thomas—Expedition against the Mississippi Central Railroad from Baton Rouge—Movements of Gen. Warren against the Weldon Road.

General Sheridan, after taking command of the army on the upper Potomac, held a strong position near the railroad from Harper's Ferry toward Winchester. On Sept. 14th a reconnoissance was made by Gen. Wilson within two miles of Winchester, which resulted in the capture of the 8th South Carolina infantry, numbering 136 men and 16 officers. On the 18th Gen. Gardner made an attack on Gen. Averill, at Martinsburg, but was repulsed. At this time the main body of Gen. Early's army was in the vicinity of Bunker Hill, northwest of the position held by Gen. Sheridan. By a rapid advance along the Winchester road Gen. Sheridan could gain the rear of the enemy, and he quickly embraced the opportunity. The 6th and 19th corps began to move at 3 A. M. on the morning of the 19th. Gen. Crook followed three hours later and joined the main column at the crossing of the Opequan. This advance was stubbornly resisted, and the first and second lines were temporarily thrown into confusion. But the artillery being brought into position, the ranks were reformed, and a severe contest ensued. At some points the opposing lines were not more than two hundred yards apart. By a successful cavalry charge the enemy were thrown into confusion and driven from the field. The enemy retreated toward Fisher's Hill, a short distance south of Strasburg, closely followed by Gen. Sheridan. That evening he sent the following despatch to Gen. Grant:

WINCHESTER, VA., Sept. 19, 7.30 P. M.

Lieut.-Gen. U. S. Grant:

I have the honor to report that I attacked the forces of Gen. Early over the Berryville pike, at the crossing of Opequan Creek, and after a most stubborn and sanguinary engagement, which lasted from early in the morning until 5 o'clock in the evening, completely defeated him, driving him through Winchester, capturing twenty-five hundred prisoners, five pieces of artillery, nine army flags, and most of their wounded. The rebel Generals Rhodes and Gordon were killed, and three other general officers wounded. Most of the enemy's wounded and all of their dead fell into our hands.

Our losses are severe; among them Gen. D. A. Russell, commanding a division in the Sixth Corps, who was killed by a cannon ball. Generals Upton, McIntosh, and Chapman were wounded.

I cannot yet tell our losses. The conduct of the officers and men was most superb. They charged and carried every position taken up by the rebels from Opequan Creek to Winchester. The rebels were strong in numbers and very obstinate in their fighting.

I desire to mention to the Lieut.-General commanding the army the gallant conduct of Generals Wright, Crook, Emory, Torbert, and the officers and men under their command. To them the country is indebted for this handsome victory.

P. H. SHERIDAN, Major-Gen. Commanding.

The force of Gen. Sheridan was composed as

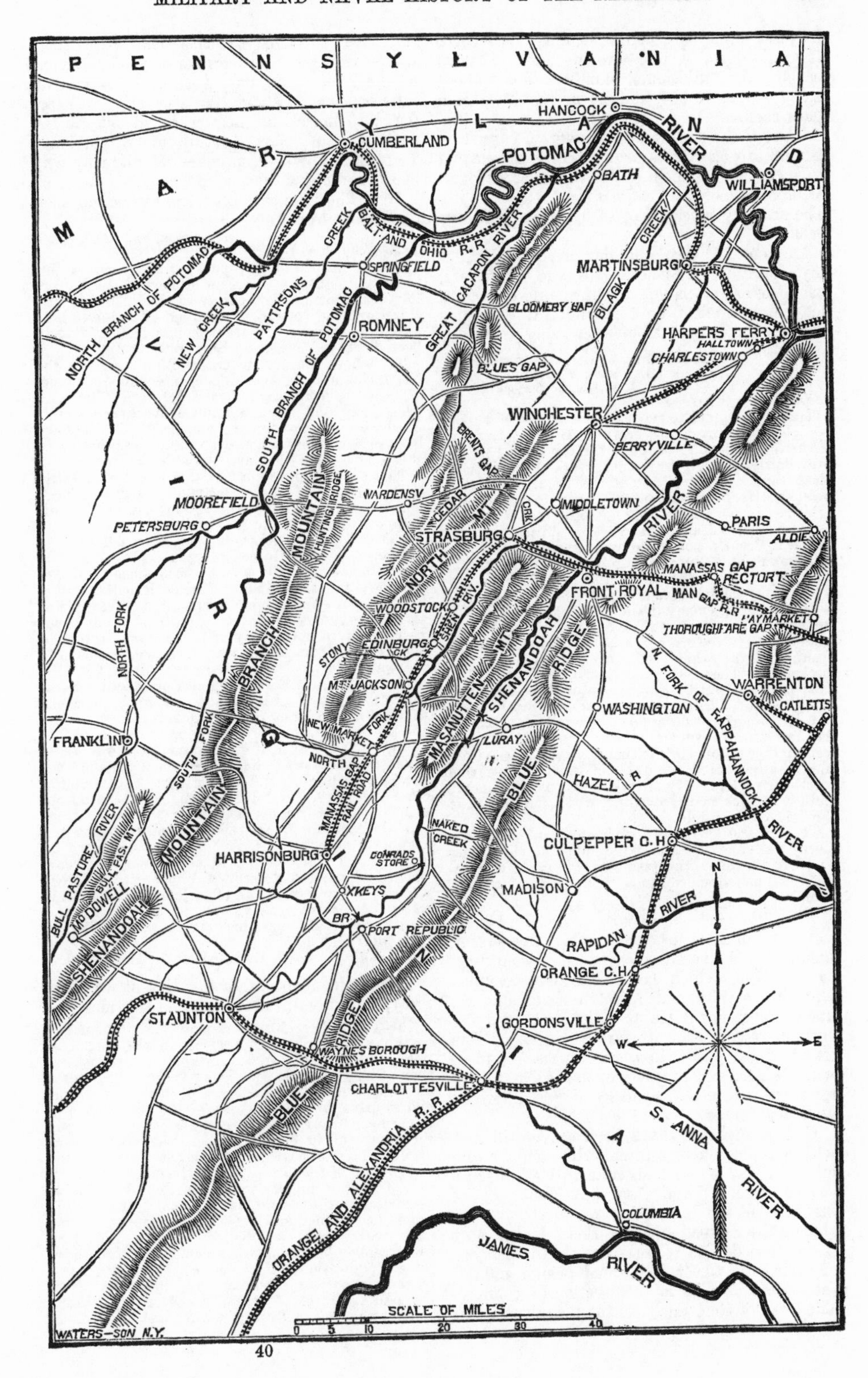
PENNSYLVANIA
MARYLAND
VIRGINIA
HANCOCK
CUMBERLAND
POTOMAC RIVER
BATH
WILLIAMSPORT
BALT. AND OHIO R.R.
CACAPON RIVER
GREAT
SPRINGFIELD
MARTINSBURG
BLACK CREEK
NORTH BRANCH OF POTOMAC
NEW CREEK
PATTRSONS CREEK
SOUTH BRANCH OF POTOMAC
ROMNEY
BLOOMERY GAP
HARPERS FERRY
HALLTOWN
CHARLESTOWN
BLUES GAP
WINCHESTER
BERRYVILLE
BRENTS GAP
MOOREFIELD
PETERSBURG
MOUNTAIN
HUNTING RIDGE
WARDENSV
CEDAR CRK
MIDDLETOWN
STRASBURG
PARIS
ALDIE
NORTH MT
MANASSAS GAP
RECTORT
FRONT ROYAL
MAN GAP R.R
HAYMARKET
THOROUGHFARE GAP
WOODSTOCK
EDINBURG
STONY CK
MT. JACKSON
MASANUTTEN MT
SHENANDOAH
RIDGE
N. FORK OF RAPPAHANNOCK
WARRENTON
CATLETTS
WASHINGTON
NORTH FORK
SOUTH FORK
BRANCH
FRANKLIN
NEW MARKET
NORTH FORK
LURAY
MANASSAS GAP RAIL ROAD
BLUE
HAZEL R
RIVER
BULL PASTURE RIVER
BULL PAS. MT
MOUNTAIN
HARRISONBURG
CONRADS STORE
NAKED CREEK
CULPEPPER C.H
MC DOWELL
SHENANDOAH
X KEYS
BR
PORT REPUBLIC
MADISON
RAPIDAN RIVER
ORANGE C.H
N
STAUNTON
RIDGE
GORDONSVILLE
W
E
WAYNESBOROUGH
CHARLOTTESVILLE
BLUE
ORANGE AND ALEXANDRIA R.R.
S. ANNA RIVER
COLUMBIA
JAMES RIVER
SCALE OF MILES
0 5 10 20 30 40
WATERS—SON N.Y.

follows: 6th corps, about 12,000; 19th corps (two divisions), 9,000; Crook's corps, 12,000; cavalry (three divisions), 10,000; artillery, about 2,000; total, 45,000, and 20 or 22 batteries, 6 guns each.

That of the enemy was known to consist of Gens. Early and Breckinridge's corps, amounting to about 20,000 men, exclusive of cavalry and artillery, which was estimated at 10,000 more. The artillery consisted of 14 batteries of 6 guns each.

On Sept. 22d Gen. Sheridan attacked the enemy's position at Fisher's Hill, and by forcing back the left of his line and throwing a force in his rear, compelled him to abandon it. He thus described and reported his success:

HEADQ'RS MIDDLE MILITARY DIVISION,
SIX MILES FROM WOODSTOCK,
11.30 P. M. September 22d.

Lieut.-General Grant:

I have the honor to report that I achieved a most signal victory over the army of General Early at Fisher's Hill to-day. I found the rebel army posted with its right resting on the north fork of the Shenandoah, and extending across the Strasburg valley westward to North Mountain, occupying a position which appeared almost impregnable.

After a great deal of manœuvring during the day, General Crook's command was transferred to the extreme right of the line on North Mountain, and he furiously attacked the left of the enemy's line, carrying every thing before him. While General Crook was driving the enemy in the greatest confusion, and sweeping down behind their breastworks, the Sixth and Nineteenth army corps attacked the works in front, and the whole rebel army appeared to be broken up. They fled in the utmost confusion. Sixteen pieces of artillery were captured, also a great many caissons, artillery horses, &c., &c.

I am to-night pushing down the valley. I cannot say how many prisoners I have captured, nor do I know either my own or the enemy's casualties. Only darkness has saved the whole of Early's army from total destruction. My attack could not be made until 4 o'clock in the evening, which left but little daylight to operate in.

The 1st and 3d cavalry divisions went down the Luray Valley to-day, and if they push on vigorously to the main valley, the result of this day's engagement will be still more signal. The victory was very complete.

(Signed,) P. H. SHERIDAN, Maj.-Gen. Com.

The number of prisoners taken was eleven hundred. The pursuit was made and continued to Staunton, which Gen. Sheridan occupied with his cavalry and inflicted much damage upon the enemy. He then leisurely and destructively fell back toward Strasburg. The losses of the enemy in these battles in killed, wounded, and missing was estimated at nearly ten thousand men. The losses of Gen. Sheridan were also severe.

On the night of the 27th Gen. Averill met with a repulse near Brown's Gap, and on the following day fell back six miles. He lost some twelve men. While Gen. Sheridan was at Staunton all public property was destroyed, including the railroad and factories. His cavalry then proceeded to Waynesboro for the purpose of destroying the iron railroad bridge and all the barns and mills in that section of country. The force of Gen. Early, in the mean time, had retreated through Brown's Gap with their wagon trains, but on learning of the operations of the Federal cavalry, Kershaw's division of infantry and Fitzhugh Lee's cavalry were ordered to march in their rear and cut off the command of Gen. Torbert at Waynesboro. The latter, however, marched all night by way of Staunton and escaped.

Gen. Sheridan thus reported his march back to Woodstock:

WOODSTOCK, VA., Oct. 7, P. M.

To Gen. U. S. Grant:

I have the honor to report my command at this point to night. I commenced moving back from Port Republic, Mount Crawford, Bridgewater, and Harrisonburg yesterday morning. The grain and forage in advance of these points had previously been destroyed in coming back to this point.

The whole country, from the Blue Ridge to the North Mountain, has been made untenable for a rebel army. I have destroyed over 2,000 barns filled with wheat, hay, and farming implements, over 70 mills filled with wheat and flour; four herds of cattle have been driven before the army, and not less than 3,000 sheep have been killed and issued to the troops.

This destruction embraces the Luray and Little Fork Valleys as well as the main valley. A large number of horses have been obtained, a proper estimate of which I cannot now make.

Lieut. John R. Meigs, my engineer officer, was murdered beyond Harrisonburg near Dayton. For this atrocious act all houses within an area of five miles were burned. Since I came into this valley from Harper's Ferry, up to Harrisonburg, every train, small party, and every straggler has been bushwhacked by people, many of whom have protection papers from commanders who have been hitherto in that valley.

The people here are getting sick of the war; heretofore they have had no reason to complain, because they have been living in great abundance.

I have not been followed by the enemy up to this point, with the exception of a small force of rebel cavalry that showed themselves some distance behind my rear guard. To-day a party of 100 of the 8th Va. cavalry, which I had stationed at the bridge over the North Shenandoah near Mount Jackson, was attacked by McNeil with seventeen men while they were asleep, and the whole party dispersed or captured. I think they will all turn up. I learn that 56 of them had reached Winchester. McNeil was mortally wounded and fell into our hands. This was most fortunate, as he was the most daring and dangerous of all bushwhackers in this section of the country.

(Signed) P. H. SHERIDAN, Major-Gen.

A correspondent, who was present with the army, thus describes the scenes of this march:

The atmosphere, from horizon to horizon, has been black with the smoke of a hundred conflagrations, and at night a gleam, brighter and more lurid than sunset, has shot from every verge. The orders have been to destroy all forage in stacks and barns, and to drive the stock before for the subsistence of the army. The execution of these orders has been thorough, and in some instances, where barns, near dwelling houses, have been fired, has resulted in the destruction of the latter. In no instance, except in that of the burning of dwellings within five miles, in retaliation for the murder of Lieut. Meigs, have orders been issued for the burning of houses, or have such orders been sanctioned by Gen. Sheridan. Such wholesale incendiarism could not have been pursued, however, without undue license being taken by the worst class of soldiers, and there have been frequent instances of rascality and pillage. Indiscriminating (for with such swift work discrimination is impracticable), relentless, merciless, the torch has done its terrible business in the centre and on either side of the valley. Few barns and stables have escaped. The gardens and cornfields have been desolated. The cattle, hogs, sheep, cows, oxen, nearly five thousand in all, have been driven from every farm. The poor, alike with the rich, have suffered. Some have lost their all.

"The wailing of women and children mingling with the crackling of flames, has sounded from scores of dwellings. I have seen mothers weeping over the loss of that which was necessary to their children's lives, setting aside their own, their last cow, their last bit of flour pilfered by stragglers, the last morsel that they had in the world to eat or drink. Young girls with flushed cheeks, and pale with tearful or tearless eye, have pleaded with and cursed the men whom the necessities of war have forced to burn the buildings reared by their fathers, and turn them into paupers in a day. The completeness of the desolation is awful. Hundreds of nearly starving people are going north. Our trains are crowded with them. They line the wayside. Hundreds more are coming —not half the inhabitants of the valley can subsist on it in its present condition. Absolute want is in mansions used in other days to extravagant luxury.

A committee, consisting of thirty-six citizens and the same number of magistrates, appointed by the county court of Rockingham for the purpose of making an estimate of the losses of that county by the execution of Gen. Sheridan's orders, made an investigation and reported as follows:

Dwelling houses burned, 30; barns burned, 450; mills burned, 31; fencing destroyed (miles), 100; bushels of wheat destroyed, 100,000; bushels of corn destroyed, 50,000; tons of hay destroyed, 6,233; cattle carried off, 1,750; horses carried off, 1,750; sheep carried off, 4,200; hogs carried off, 3,350; factories burned, 3; furnace burned, 1. In addition to which there was an immense amount of farming utensils of every description destroyed, many of them of great value, such as McCormick's reapers, and threshing machines; also household and kitchen furniture, money, bonds, plate, &c., &c., the whole loss being estimated at the enormous sum of $25,000,000.

As Gen. Sheridan moved down the valley toward the Potomac River, he was followed close by the enemy's cavalry in considerable force, under Gen. Rosser, the infantry being further in the rear. On Oct. 9th the head of the column of infantry having entered Strasburg by the eastern road, while the rear was some four miles further south, and the enemy following the cavalry on the western road had advanced so far as to bring the infantry upon their right rear, the cavalry under Gens. Custer and Merritt turned and made an attack. At the same time a report spread among the enemy's cavalry that the Federal infantry were flanking them. They immediately gave way, and a stampede ensued. The pursuit continued to Columbia Furnace, seven miles south of Fisher's Hill. The loss of the enemy was eleven pieces of artillery and about three hundred men. Gen. Sheridan then continued to fall back as far as Cedar Run. While at this position, on Oct. 19th, his force was suddenly attacked by the enemy before daylight, and his lines thrown into confusion with every prospect of a serious disaster. The left flank of the 8th corps was turned and the army driven back four miles with the loss of twenty-four pieces of artillery. At this moment Gen. Sheridan arrived on the field, and re-forming his lines, awaited the attack of the enemy. This was made at 1 P.M. and repulsed. At 3 P.M. Sheridan attacked the enemy and completely routed him, capturing fifty-four pieces of artillery, including his own pieces. His despatch from the battle-field to Gen. Grant was as follows:

CEDAR CREEK, VA., Oct. 19, 10 P.M.

Lieut.-Gen. Grant, City Point:

I have the honor to report that my army at Cedar Creek was attacked at Alacken this morning before daylight, and my left was turned and driven in in confusion. In fact, most of the line was driven in confusion, with the loss of 20 pieces of artillery. I hastened from Winchester, where I was on my return from Washington, and found my army between Middletown and Newton, having been driven back about four miles. I here took the affair in hand and quickly marched the corps forward, formed a compact line of battle to repulse an attack of the enemy, which was done handsomely at about 1 o'clock, P.M. At 3 P.M., after some changes of the cavalry from the left to the right flank, I attacked with great vigor, driving and routing the enemy, capturing, according to the last report, 43 pieces of artillery and very many prisoners. * * * *

I have to regret the loss of Gen. Bidwell, killed, and Gens. Wright, Grover, and Ricketts, wounded. Wright is slightly wounded. Affairs at times looked badly, but by the gallantry of our brave officers and men disaster has been converted into a splendid victory. Darkness again intervened to shut off greater results. I now occupy Strasburg. As soon as practicable I will send you further particulars.

(Signed) P. H. SHERIDAN, Maj.-General.

On the next day he further reported as follows:

CEDAR CREEK, VA., Oct. 20, 11.30 A.M.

To Lieut.-Gen. Grant, City Point:

We have again been favored by a great victory, won from disaster, by the gallantry of our officers and men. The attack on the enemy was made at 3 P.M., by a left half-wheel of the whole line, with a division of cavalry turning each flank of the enemy. The whole line advanced.

The enemy, after a stubborn resistance, broke and fled, and were pushed with vigor. The artillery captured will, probably, be over fifty pieces. This, of course, includes what were captured from our troops early in the morning. At least 1,600 prisoners have been brought in; also wagons and ambulances in large numbers. This morning the cavalry made a dash at Fisher's Hill and carried it; the enemy having fled during the night, leaving only a small rear guard.

I have to regret the loss of many valuable officers killed and wounded. Among them is Col. James Thorburn, commanding a division of Crook's command, killed; Col. Sherwood, commanding a brigade, but would not leave the field. I cannot yet give a full account, as many of our men who were captured in the morning have since made their escape and are coming in. Ramseur, commanding a division in Early's army, died this morning.

(Signed) P. H. SHERIDAN.

The enemy were pursued nearly to Mt. Jackson. The loss of Gen. Sheridan's army in the morning was between 800 and 1,000 taken prisoners. He took afterwards from 1,500 to 2,000 of the enemy prisoners, and 300 wagons and ambulances. The losses in killed and wounded on either side have not been reported.

They are known to have been severe. With the exception of a few affairs of small consequence, this closed the military operations in the Shenandoah valley for the remainder of the year; Gen. Early's force took a position further up the valley, while Gen. Sheridan's army was scattered in detachments widely separated. On Nov. 14th the President issued the following order:

War Department, Washington, Nov. 14th, 1864.

Ordered by the President:—1. That the resignation of George B. McClellan as major-general in the United States Army, dated November 8th, and received by the Adjutant-General on the 10th inst., be accepted as of the 8th of November.

2. That for personal gallantry, military skill, and just confidence in the courage and patriotism of his troops displayed by Philip H. Sheridan on the 19th of October, at Cedar Run, whereby, under the blessing of Providence, his routed army was reorganized, a great national disaster averted, and a brilliant victory achieved over the rebels for the third time in pitched battle within thirty days, Philip H. Sheridan is appointed Major-General in the United States Army, to rank as such from the 8th day of November, 1864.

By order of the President of the United States.

E. D. TOWNSEND,
Assistant Adjutant-General.

All that district of country west of Washington and immediately south of the Potomac River was infested with guerrillas throughout the year. Col. Mosby was their leader. Many of their expeditions were conducted with great boldness. Sometimes they came within a few miles of Washington. On one occasion during the year they captured a passenger train on the Baltimore and Ohio Railroad, between Harper's Ferry and Martinsburg. A rail was removed, and the train thus running off the track was brought to a stop. Their proceedings have been thus graphically described:

In an instant we heard the guerrillas entering the cars from both ends. Surmising their errand, I jerked my watch from my pocket, handed it to a lady companion, telling her to secrete it, which she did. Just then one of the fellows stood before me with a pistol close to my head and demanded my pocket book. I obeyed with commendable diligence. He passed on to relieve my neighbor of hat, coat, watch and pocket book. Another of the band approached, pistol in hand, "Here, you d—d Yank, hand over your watch." "You're too late," I answered promptly, "it is gone." The fellow seemed satisfied with this and went on.

A very demonstrative fat lady, seated near the end of our car, just then jumped up, caught one of the rebels in her arms. "Oh my love, my dear man, you will not kill me," she screamed, and at the same time clinging to him until in ungallant anger he roared, "Confound you, let me go; I will lose my part of the plunder with your stupidity." We were then ordered out, as the train was to be set on fire. On leaving the cars we had to climb a steep sand bank about twenty feet high, there to await further orders. The passengers in the sleeping-cars fared worse, as all, with one exception, lost their hats, coats, boots, watches, and money. When they were ejected from their quarters, and ascended the hill, they presented a sorry appearance—just conscious of their loss, trembling with cold, and fearing they might be invited to visit Richmond. In one car there were sixty German emigrants bound for Ohio, who, when the thieves demanded their money, showed fight. To intimidate the rest, two men were instantly shot by the butchers and a woman wounded. The remainder were then ordered to leave the cars, but did not understand the command. Mosby ordered his men to fire the cars and burn the "damn Dutch." The conductor begged of him to hold on until he could find a man who could speak German. The poor creatures were at last made to understand. They left the car; it was set on fire, and the two men and one wounded woman left in the flames.

There were about thirty Union soldiers on board, unarmed, returning to their commands. Those were taken prisoners, and also forty or fifty of the passengers were ordered to fall in line to be taken off. About this time I felt a little nervous, not having any strong desire to visit Libby; but fortunately as I had a screaming babe in my arms I was not one of the chosen. The whole party were soon ordered to march. Then followed hurried, agonizing farewells, and the victims moved forward. We all supposed they were on their way to Richmond, but only the soldiers met with this fate. The citizens were taken a short distance to a piece of woods and thoroughly searched and robbed of whatever money they had left and the best of their clothes. Then arose a cry that the Yanks were in the woods; the guerrillas mounted and started off in a hurry, but in five minutes they were back and exclaimed, "a false alarm!" and they fell to plundering still further. By this time the mail, express, and baggage had been robbed, and what they generally did not want was in flames, and the gentlemen were left no extra clothing, and certainly no surplus cash.

One of the ladies of our party lost all her baggage. In vain she begged a plethoric-looking guerilla to spare her clothing and that of her child. "There are no valuables in the trunk; you certainly can do nothing with its contents," she pleaded. "Pooh," sneered the "chivalry," as he swaggered past her, "they will do to help on the flame," and help the flames they accordingly did.

It was then announced by one of the officers that every rider had a place for a woman in front of him on his horse, but this beastly threat was not carried out. They then made a final search, and saw the work was complete; the train had been burned, a paymaster with $63,000 robbed, the passengers plundered of their hats, coats, boots, watches and money, and, locking and burning the mail, express, and baggage, they made us a boisterous farewell.

Missouri became the scene of a hostile invasion under Gen. Price, in the autumn. Various rumors and threats had been in circulation among the enemy for some months previous. About the 21st of September these rumors ripened into a certainty by a movement of Gen. Sterling Price across the Arkansas with two divisions of cavalry and three batteries of artillery. He joined Gen. Shelby near Batesville, sixty miles south of the boundary line of the Missouri, and was prepared to advance with 15,000 to 20,000 mounted veterans. The Federal force then in the Department under Gen. Rosecrans consisted of 6,500 mounted men for field duty scattered over a country four hundred miles long, and three hundred broad, with partially organized new infantry regiments and dismounted men. These latter were employed to cover the great depots at St. Louis, Jefferson City, St. Joseph, Macon, Springfield, Rolla, and Pilot Knob, to guard railroad bridges and protect as far as possible the lives and property of citizens from the guerillas who swarmed over the whole country bordering on the Missouri River. At this time Gen. A. J. Smith being at Cairo with 4,500 troops was ordered to Missouri. Preparations were made to concentrate the forces as soon as it should become manifest what course Gen. Price would pursue, and the enrolled militia of the State made ready to take the field.

When it became evident that Springfield was safe from the blow, Gen. Sanborn moved with all his available cavalry to reënforce Rolla, where Gen. McNeil was preparing to secure the depots and supply trains, while Gen. Ewing, with the 47th Missouri volunteer infantry, detachments of the 1st, 2d, and 3d State militia, and the 14th Iowa, defended Pilot Knob on Sept. 27th, and proved the presence of the enemy's entire force in southeast Missouri. The defence of Gen. Ewing was a severe blow to the enemy, and allowed time for the enrolled militia and citizens of St. Louis to prepare for its defence. At this time it was covered only by Gen. Smith's infantry and three regiments of cavalry thrown as far as practicable toward the enemy.

In the midst of the preparations at St. Louis, the 132d, 134th, 136th, 139th, 140th, and 142d regiments of Illinois hundred days' volunteers arrived, which secured the safety of that city. Meantime the 1st, 2d, 3d, 4th, 10th, 11th, 13th, and 80th regiments of enrolled militia, and the National Guard of St. Louis, organized under Gens. Pike, Wolff and Miller, to support Gen. Smith's infantry, and turn the tide of invasion westward.

The troops of the central district of the State were concentrated by Gen. Brown at Jefferson City, and being reënforced by Gen. Fisk with all the available troops north of the Missouri River, they were prepared for the defence of the State capital. In these efforts the citizens coöperated with enthusiasm.

Meanwhile, Gen. Price with his army, after awaiting a day or two at Richwood's, and threatening St. Louis, started for the State capital. At the same time Gens. McNeil and Sanborn, with all their available cavalry, moved by forced marches and reached the point of danger a few miles in advance of Price, and, uniting with Gens. Fisk and Brown, saved the State capital, and struck another blow to the hopes of the invaders.

On Oct. 8th, Gen. Pleasanton assumed command at Jefferson City, and sent Sanborn with all his mounted force, four thousand one hundred strong, to follow the enemy and harass them until the remaining cavalry and infantry supports could come up. The rear-guard of the enemy was thus driven upon their main force near Burnville, and Gen. Price was kept between the Federal force and the Missouri River until the latter were joined on the 19th by the command of Winslow, consisting of fifteen hundred men who had followed the enemy from Arkansas. This formed a provisional cavalry division of sixty-five hundred men under Gen. Pleasanton exclusive of escort guards. On the 22d, this force fell upon Gen. Fagan at Independence and routed him, capturing two guns. On the 23d, the Big Blue was passed, and a contest with the main force of the enemy took place, by which they were driven by dark beyond the Little Santa Fé. On the 24th, after a march of sixty miles, the enemy were overtaken at midnight at Marais des Cygnes. Skirmishing began at 4 A. M. on the 25th with artillery, when the enemy were driven from the field with loss of mules, horses, etc. They fell back skirmishing to the Little Osage Crossing, where a charge was made upon two divisions of them by two advanced brigades under Cols. Benteen and Phillips, and eight pieces of artillery and nearly one thousand prisoners, including Gens. Marmaduke and Cabell, were captured. The pursuit was kept up by Gen. Sanborn's brigade with repeated and successful charges to the Marmiton, whence the enemy fled under cover of night toward Arkansas. Kansas troops and Gen. Benteen's brigade followed rapidly, and on the 28th Sanborn reached Newtonia, where the enemy made his last stand, in time to turn the tide of battle, which was going against Gen. Blunt, and routing the enemy, thus giving the final blow to the invasion.

The loss of the enemy was ten pieces of artillery, a large number of small arms, nearly all his trains and plunder, and, besides his killed, wounded and deserters, 1,958 prisoners. Gen. Price claimed to have added to his force 6,000 Missourians. All his schemes were defeated, and the injury done was confined to the narrow belt of country over which his army marched. The Federal loss was 346 officers and men. After crossing into Arkansas the force of the enemy became greatly reduced.

Some military operations took place in East Tennessee near the close of the year, the most important of which was the defeat of Gen. A. C. Gillem by the enemy under Gen. Breckinridge. On Nov. 12th Gen. Breckinridge attacked the Federal forces and drove them from their intrenchments. On the 13th he again attacked them near Russellville. Gen. Gillem gradually fell back in the direction of Knoxville, and was pursued by the enemy as far as Strawberry Plains. Gen. Gillem lost heavily in killed and wounded, besides several hundred prisoners. Later in the year an expedition from East Tennessee was made by Gen. Stoneman, in conjunction with Gen. Burbridge, with better success. On Dec. 12th Gen. Stoneman, with a mounted force of four thousand men, and the brigade of Gen. Gillem, moved against the enemy, who were drawn up at Kingsport, on the Holsten River, to dispute its passage. This force was flanked by Gen. Gillem, with a loss of a hundred men and a wagon train, and pursued to Bristol, where Gillem captured two hundred and fifty more, two trains of cars, five engines, and a large amount of stores. On Dec. 14th Gen. Burbridge advanced to attack Gen. Vaughn at Zollicoffer, but the latter withdrew to Abingdon, which was captured by Burbridge, with much stores. A portion of the salt-works at this point was also destroyed. The pursuit of Vaughn was continued by Gen. Gillem, with the support of Brown's brigade, and some loss inflicted on him. A force was also sent to the Virginia railroad near Glade Springs, which destroyed a large number of bridges and depots, a large amount of rolling stock, and the extensive iron works near Marion. Upon the advance of the Confederate Gen. Breckinridge it withdrew to Kentucky.

The operations in Middle Tennessee became very important near the close of the year. On Nov. 4th, Johnsonville, a depot for supplies on the Tennessee River, was attacked and destroyed by Col. Forrest. The value of property burned was estimated at more than six million dollars. This result was achieved by planting batteries on the opposite bank of the river and destroying the small gunboats which lay near the place for its protection.

The movement of Gen. Sherman's force toward Savannah, with the necessary reduction of the Federal forces in Tennessee, tempted Gen. Hood to advance into that State with the hope that by the coöperation of Gen. Breckinridge in East Tennessee, the entire State might be recovered and restored to the Confederacy. On Nov. 21st Gen. Hood began to move north from the Tennessee River for the capture of Nashville, and on the 23d his army took possession of Pulaski, which had been just evacuated by the small Federal force under Gen. Hatch. Pushing forward with some skirmishing, Columbia was occupied on the 26th. Meanwhile the force left under Gen. Thomas by Gen. Sherman, continued to fall back toward Nashville. The enemy appeared before Franklin on the 30th, and Gen. Schofield prepared to make a stand. The force of Gen. Hood, however, was divided into two columns, one to attack Franklin in front, and the other to move down Harpeth River, cross over it some distance east of Franklin, and endeavor to get into the Federal rear. At 4 P. M. on Wednesday, the 30th, Gen. Hood's main column made a heavy and persistent attack on Franklin in front, but Gen. Schofield, who was in command with 15,000 men, managed to hold his own until dusk, and then ordered a retreat. This was accelerated by the news of the flanking column having crossed Harpeth River several miles east of Franklin. The retreat was continued all night, and on Thursday at daylight reached a point seven miles south of Nashville, where Gen. A. J. Smith's corps was posted. The Confederate flanking column, after crossing Harpeth River attacked a Federal cavalry brigade, and compelled it to retreat. The force reached Gen. Smith's position about the same time as Gen. Schofield. The enemy followed both, and Gen. Smith being hard pressed abandoned his position and fell back to the outer line of the Nashville intrenchments, three miles from the town.

Great consternation prevailed in Nashville. Business was suspended. The citizens and the vast army of Government laborers were put under arms. The army of Gen. Thomas was put in line of battle three miles south of Nashville, and the enemy advanced to a point five miles distant. The intervening space became a scene of constant skirmishing. Meantime Gen. Hood proposed to blockade the Cumberland River, cut the Louisville and Nashville road, and thus compel Gen. Thomas to evacuate the city. To execute this purpose more effectively, he fell back from his works before the city to intrench himself in the Overton range of hills, and thus cut off Thomas from Rousseau at Murfreesboro, and with his cavalry and Breckinridge's forces cut off Bridgeport and Chattanooga.

Reënforcements were now sent to Gen. Thomas with the greatest despatch, and he determined to dislodge Gen. Hood from his position, which he had already begun to strengthen. Accordingly, early on Dec. 15th, a feint was made on Hood's right and a real attack upon his left, which resulted in driving it from the river below the city as far as Franklin's pike, a distance of eight miles. The train and headquarters of Gen. Chalmers were captured; another train of twenty wagons, together with a thousand prisoners and sixteen pieces of artillery. During the ensuing night Gen. Hood contracted his lines back to the Brentwood range of hills, massing on the Franklin pike to keep it open, in case of retreat, and to cover his large wagon train, which was moving by by-roads into the pike. On the next morning the battle was renewed. The Federal position remained unchanged from the previous day. Steedman on the extreme left, Wood connecting with him on the left of the Franklin pike. Garrard's division of A. J. Smith's corps connecting with the right of Wood's; next came McArthur, then Col. Moore, connecting with Gen. Schofield's left. Gen. Cox formed Schofield's right and Gen. Couch his left. Wilson's cavalry came up on Schofield's right, along the Hillsboro pike, with orders to operate south of the hills, and, if possible, turn the enemy's flank and cut off his retreat. Movements commenced at 10 A. M., and in the afternoon the action became close and obstinate. Near dusk the enemy began to give way, and a rout soon followed. They were pursued until dark through the gap of the hills and along the Franklin pike. Some four thousand prisoners were captured.

The following is Gen. Thomas's report of this day's conflict:

HEADQUARTERS DEP'T OF THE CUMBERLAND, EIGHT MILES FROM NASHVILLE, Dec. 16—6 P. M.

To the President of the United States, Hon. E. M. Stanton, and Lieut.-General Grant:

This army thanks you for your approbation of its conduct yesterday, and assure you that it is not misplaced. I have the honor to report that the enemy has been pressed at all points to-day on his line of retreat to the Brentwood Hill. Brig.-Gen. Hatch, of Wilson's corps of cavalry, on the right, turned the enemy's left, and captured a large number of prisoners. The number is not reported.

Maj.-Gen. Schofield's corps, next on the left wing of the cavalry, carried several hills, capturing many prisoners and six pieces of artillery.

Maj.-Gen. Smith, next on the left of Maj.-Gen. Schofield, carried the salient point of the enemy's line, with McMillan's brigade of McArthur's division, capturing sixteen pieces of artillery, two brigadier generals, and about 2,000 prisoners.

Brig.-Gen. Garrard's division, of Smith's command, next on the left of McArthur's division, carried the enemy's intrenchments, capturing all the artillery and troops of the enemy on the line.

Brig.-Gen. Wood's troops on the Franklin Pike took up the assault, capturing the enemy's intrenchments, and in his retreat also capturing eight pieces of artillery, something over 600 prisoners, and drove the enemy within one mile of the Brentwood Hill Pass.

Maj.-Gen. Stedman, commanding detachments of the different armies of the Military Division of the Mississippi, most nobly supported Gen. Wood's left, and took a most honorable part in the operations of the day. I have ordered the pursuit to be continued in the morning at daylight. Although the troops are very much fatigued, the utmost enthusiasm prevails.

I must not forget to report the operations of Brig.-Gen. Johnson, in successfully driving the enemy, with the coöperation of the gunboats under Lieut. Commander Fitch, from their established batteries on the Cumberland, below the city of Nashville, and of the success of Brig.-Gen. Croxton's brigade, in covering and protecting our right and rear in the operations of to-day and yesterday. Although I have no report of the number of prisoners captured by Johnson's and Croxton's command, I know they have made a large number.

I am also glad to be able to state that the number of prisoners captured yesterday greatly exceeds the number reported by telegraph. The woods, fields, and intrenchments are filled with the enemy's small arms, abandoned in the retreat. In conclusion, I am happy to state that all this has been effected with very small loss to us. Our loss probably does not exceed 300, and very few killed.

(Signed) G. H. THOMAS, Major-General.

Early on the next morning the Federal pursuit was renewed. A large number of wounded were captured on the road to Franklin, and also stragglers. The cavalry harassed the flanks and rear of the enemy and scattered any force that offered resistance. The following is Gen. Thomas's report of the 17th:

HEADQ'S DEPARTMENT OF THE CUMBERLAND,
Near FRANKLIN, TENN., Dec. 17th, 8 P. M.

We have pressed the enemy to-day beyond Franklin, capturing his hospitals, containing over 1,500 wounded, and about 150 of our wounded, in addition to the above. Gen. Knipe, commanding a division of cavalry, drove the enemy's rear-guard through Franklin to-day, capturing about 250 prisoners and five battle-flags with very little loss on our side. Citizens of Franklin represent Hood's army as completely demoralized. In addition to the captures of yesterday, reported in my despatches of last night, I have the honor to report the capture of Gen. Rucker, and about 250 of the enemy's cavalry, in a fight that occurred about 8 o'clock last night between Gen. Rucker and Gen. Hatch of our cavalry.

The enemy has been pressed to-day both in front and on both flanks. Brig.-Gen. Johnson succeeded in striking him on the flank just beyond Franklin, capturing quite a number of prisoners—number not yet reported. My cavalry is pressing him closely through, and I am very much in hopes of getting many more prisoners to-morrow.

GEO. H. THOMAS, Major-General.

The entire loss of the enemy was 13,189 in prisoners, including several general and nearly one thousand other officers of lower grades, and seventy-two pieces of artillery. During the same period over two thousand deserters were received. The Federal loss was about 10,000 in killed, wounded, and missing. Gen. Hood retired with his remaining force into the northern part of Alabama.

Some military expeditions were made near the close of the year. A force left Vicksburg under Gen. Dana, in the latter part of November, for the purpose of coöperating with Gen. Sherman by occupying the enemy in Mississippi. It reached the Mississippi Central Railroad on Nov. 25th, and after an obstinate engagement succeeded in destroying the Big Black River bridge. Several miles of the track of the railroad, including culverts, stations, 2,600 bales of cotton, two locomotives, four cars, twenty barrels of salt, and $160,000 worth of stores at Vaughan station were also destroyed.

About the same time an expedition organized under the direction of Gen. Canby, consisting of a cavalry force under Gen. Davidson, left Baton Rouge. Thence it marched to Tanghipiho and destroyed the railroad to Jackson, burning bridges and railroad buildings. Thence it moved to Franklinville, capturing a mail and prisoners. Thence it moved to West Pascagoula. These movements caused a great panic in Mississippi, and created alarm for the safety of Mobile, thus effectively coöperating with Gen. Sherman.

In December a force, consisting of five divisions under the command of Maj.-Gen. Warren, made a raid upon the Weldon Railroad. The Nottoway was reached about midday Dec. 8th, and destroyed; thence the railroad track was destroyed nearly to Bellfield station, twenty miles south. On the 10th the expedition started on its return, followed by crowds of negroes, and arrived after an absence of four days. Its loss was about a half dozen men.

At the close of the year the area of territory held by the Federal armies was about the same as at the end of the previous year. The war during the year had been the cause of immense destruction to the South, both in men and property. In the latter probably there is no parallel in modern history. Its effect was apparent in the exhausted condition of the country.

The Indians on the frontier maintained a hostile attitude during a portion of the year. The plan of operations of Maj.-Gen. Pope, who was in command, embraced three objects: first, the chastisement and subjection of the bands of savages on both sides of the Missouri River, who continued refractory and hostile; secondly, the protection of the overland route to Idaho, by the establishment of strong military posts within the Indian country; thirdly, the security of the Minnesota and Iowa frontier against raids.

Some conflicts took place between the Indians and Gens. Sibley and Sully in the northwest, and Curtis in Kansas, by which their numbers were greatly reduced, and their provisions and property destroyed. The ferocious hostile attitude of these border tribes continued unchanged.

Several events tending to disturb the friendly relations of the United States with other countries occurred during 1864. Raiding parties were organized in Canada by persons claiming to be in the service of the Confederate States, for the purpose of liberating the prisoners of war confined on Johnson's Island, and depredating on the property of citizens of the United States. One of these parties, organized by one Bennet G. Burley, consisting of some twenty men, seized the steamer Philo Parsons, running between the city of Detroit and Sandusky, after she had left Kelly's Island in the State of Ohio. They then captured the Island Queen at Middle Bass Island, Ohio, where they put ashore all the passengers. While here they forced Walter O. Ashley, the clerk of the Philo Parsons, at the peril of his life, to deliver over his money. Burley was arrested, charged with robbery, and claimed under the Extradition Treaty; and surrendered after a hearing before the Recorder of the city of Toronto.

On the 19th of October a party of men from Canada, twenty to thirty in number, well armed, entered the village of St. Albans, in Vermont, robbed the bank in the place of fifty thousand dollars, stole horses enough to mount all the party, fired on a crowd of unarmed citizens, wounding three men, one mortally, and setting fire to one of the hotels. The whole transaction occupied only three-quarters of an hour, and the band immediately started for Canada, where thirteen of the marauders were arrested and confined at St. John's. As soon as the outrage was reported to the Canadian authorities they did every thing in their power to arrest the perpetrators; and Mr. Seward, on the 21st of October, expressed to Mr. Burnlew, of the British Legation at Washington, his "sincere satisfaction" with their proceedings. Mr. Seward regarded the outrage as a deliberate attempt to embroil the governments of England and the United States, and involve them in a border war. But he rejoiced that the officers and agents on both sides of the frontier had acted together in good faith, and with due respect on each side for the lawful rights and authority of the other. This, he adds, "is in entire conformity with the wishes of the United States." It should be added, that a great proportion of the stolen money was found on the persons of the raiders captured, and was taken possession of by the Canadian police. Lord Lyons, when the transaction occurred, was at New York, but immediately returned to Washington. The legal proceedings in the case of the prisoners were not very rapidly despatched, and early in November Mr. Seward speaks rather angrily of the requisitions for the offenders whose crimes were committed on Lake Erie, and for the burglars and murderers who invaded Vermont, remaining unanswered. In fact, the latter were discharged by Judge Coursol on a supposed technical defect in the instrument under which they were tried, released from custody, and the money restored to them. They were thus discharged on December 14th, and again apprehended, and finally released.

It is proper here briefly to mention the revolution extensively produced in the science of offensive and defensive warfare, and particularly in the department of fortifications. The newly-developed powers of modern artillery, both as respects the greatly-enlarged calibres of siege and naval guns, and the application of the principle of rifling to guns of the largest calibres, have proved destructive to masonry forts, even when so constructed as to be regarded as impregnable. Fort Sumter, one of the strongest forts of its class ever erected on this continent, and Fort Morgan in Mobile Bay, also a work of great strength, were both completely reduced by artillery fire, the one from land batteries at a distance of from two to three miles, and the other by the concentrated fire of the naval squadron of Admiral Farragut. In the case of Fort Sumter this result was the more remarkable as after its capture in 1861 it was strengthened by all the resources known to engineering art, and its gorge wall, which previously was more than ten feet in thickness, was protected by an inner brick wall of twelve feet, and for a considerable portion of its height by a covering of sandbags on its outside. All its casemates were also strengthened, the traverses on its terre-plain enlarged, and every precaution possible made use of to make it impregnable. Yet seven days' bombardment at the long distances named, were sufficient to reduce it to a ruin incapable of bearing any important part in the defence of the city or harbor. On the other hand, the sandwork Fort McAllister effectually resisted the assault of the three iron-clads in March, 1863, and the sandwork Fort Wagner, though badly located, and not judiciously defended, yet resisted two vigorous and well-conducted assaults, a severe and almost continuous bombardment from Admiral Dahlgren's squadron, and a constant cannonade from heavy batteries on Morris Island, and was only abandoned when approached and mined by a regular siege, and was found to be but little injured. Fort Fisher, a more recent example of an earthwork of great strength, though situated too near the channel so as to be exposed to the fire of the monster guns of the monitors at short range, yet withstood with but slight injury the first assault of the squadron, which concentrated upon it a fire of 539 guns; and though it might have been silenced by the fire of the fleet at the second bombardment, would hardly have been captured but for the feint of a seaward attack, which called off the attention of the garrison from the actual assault by Terry's force.

From these and other trials of the comparative powers of resistance of masonry and earthwork fortifications, the ablest engineers of the country have come to the conclusion that the best material for fortifications in general is a pure quartz sand with natural slopes; and that where the batteries of fortifications are much exposed or can be approached within short range, they should be protected by heavy iron plating.

Major-General Gillmore, who ranks as one of the highest authorities on this subject, regards the erection of revolving iron turrets in the centre of the channels of approach to large cities as a very desirable addition to their means of harbor defence, as combining the advantages of long range and wide field of fire.

While there has been so marked a revolution in the minds of military men in regard to the subject of permanent fortifications, a change almost as marked has taken place in regard to the method of giving or receiving battle. Heretofore, when two armies have been opposed to each other in the field, and neither of them disposed to take advantage of the defences of a fortified town, they have met each other on the open plain or slope of hillside or valley without fortification, and the fortunes of the day have often been decided by a dashing charge of cavalry or the sudden assault of infantry with the bayonet. Such was the case in the earlier battles of the present war; but the troops on both sides have learned that a barricade even of the rudest character will stop many of the balls, shot, and shell which are sent on an errand of destruction toward them, and at every halt for the night or for a few hours the men, before attending to any other duty, run up barricades of rails which they cover with earth, and thus protect themselves in part from a sweeping assault like those at Shiloh and at Stone River, which would destroy or capture thousands. The primary barricade is thrown up with wonderful rapidity, and is tolerably complete within five or ten minutes. If not immediately assaulted, the men proceed to perfect it by digging a trench inside and throwing the earth outside, thus making the protection greater; by felling the trees and undergrowth in front and arranging it as an abatis; by palisades and wire entanglements, and by placing heavy logs on the top of the barricades for protection to the sharpshooters. During General Sherman's campaigns from Chattanooga to Atlanta, and from that city to Savannah, as well as in General Grant's campaigns in Virginia, these temporary fortifications were constantly erected; and in General Sherman's report of the Atlanta campaign he says of this practice: "The skill and rapidity with which our men construct them is wonderful, and is something new in the art of war."

Though but remotely connected with the subject of fortifications, yet as pertaining to the matter of coast defences, the introduction of stationary torpedoes as a subaqueous protection merits attention. In no previous war have they been used to the same extent as in this. Various forms have been devised, and the contrivances for exploding them at the right moment for destroying the vessels which approached them, have displayed a rare ingenuity. Though considerable injury has been done by them, five or six vessels having been destroyed, yet they cannot, on the whole, be regarded as successful, as not one in five hundred, and perhaps hardly one in one thousand, have accomplished the purpose for which they were designed. Their use as a means of harbor defence seems to be conceded as justifiable by all military authorities; and if they can be made more certainly effective, they will form a very formidable addition to the means of protection to the approaches to large cities.

CHAPTER XLVII.

Naval Operations—The Stonewall—Other Cruisers—Capture of the Roanoke—Increase of the Federal Navy—Operations of the North Atlantic Squadron—Blockade—Action with the Albemarle—Her Destruction—Operations in James River—Attack on Fort Fisher—Repulse—Correspondence—Attack Renewed—Capture of the Fort—West Gulf Squadron—Capture of the Forts at Mobile Bay—Action between the Kearsarge and Alabama—Capture of the Florida.

THE naval operations in 1864 remain to be described. The rams built in England for sea service, and which excited much anxiety near the close of the previous year, under a conviction that they were intended for the Confederates, were detained and bought by the English Government. None of this class of vessels were therefore built in English ports and suffered to enter the service of the Richmond Government.

During the hostilities in which Denmark was involved, a ram was built in a port of France for that Government. On the return of peace this ram was transferred to agents of the Government at Richmond, and placed under the command of Capt. T. J. Page, formerly of the U. S. Navy, and called the Stonewall. She made for the port of Ferrol, in Spain, and was there blockaded by the U. S. frigates Niagara and Sacramento. She subsequently escaped and reached Havana, and was there delivered to the Spanish government. During the year 1865, she was given up by the latter to the United States.

The cruisers were more numerous and exceedingly destructive. Previous to January 30, 1864, the number of merchant vessels of the United States destroyed by them was 193; tonnage, 89,704; value of vessels at $50 per ton, $4,485,200; value of cargo at $100 per ton,

$8,970,400. Total, $13,455,600. The number captured by the different vessels and by the enemy up to the above date, was as follows:

By	steamer	Sumter....	27	By	privateer	Calhoun...	3
"	"	Alabama...	66	"	"	Savannah..	1
"	"	Florida....	16	"	"	Lapwing...	1
"	privateer	Tacony....	16	"	"	St. Nicholas	3
"	steamer	Georgia....	10	"	"	Echo......	2
"	privateer	Jeff. Davis.	7	"	"	Conrad....	1
"	"	Retribution.	2	"	"	Coquette..	1
"	"	Sallie	1				
"	steamer	Winslow...	5				164
"	"	Nashville..	2				

The other merchant vessels (twenty-nine) were captured in Southern harbors and rivers. Of the vessels captured by the cruisers, seventeen were bonded, and all the others burned.

During 1864 a few captures were made by the Alabama before she was sunk by the Kearsarge. The Florida, Captain Morris, appeared off the coast of Virginia in July and captured six vessels, and destroyed afterwards a number, and was finally captured in the harbor of Bahia by a U. S. steamer.

Three more cruisers also made their appearance during 1864, viz.: the Tallahassee, Olustee, and Chickamauga. The steamer Tallahassee in August visited the entire length of the coast of the Northern States, and destroyed thirty-three vessels in ten days, one of which was a New York pilot-boat. The steamer Olustee was an iron vessel of 1,100 tons burthen, schooner rigged, with two screws and very fast. Several vessels were captured by her off the coast and bound to New York in the month of November. The steamer Chickamauga also captured several vessels, which were valued at $500,000.

The most important rams for harbor service were the Tennessee and Albemarle. For the details respecting these and also the Confederate gunboats, see other pages.

On September 29th the steamer Roanoke, a passenger and freight vessel running between New York and Havana, was captured by Lieutenant Braine and some companions, who had come on board as passengers as the vessel was leaving Havana in the afternoon. The officers and crew were overpowered, made prisoners, and the vessel headed for Bermuda, where a pilot was called on board. Braine went ashore and brought on board a party, and the vessel put to sea, soon overhauling a brig with coal and provisions.

These were taken aboard, and on the next day a vessel was sent to take off the passengers. The transfer was made together with a quantity of cotton, and the steamer set on fire. The passengers and crew were taken into Five Fathom Hole, and the purser and first mate went ashore to have the Confederates as pirates arrested, which was done, but after a trial by the British authorities they were discharged. The Roanoke had on board $17,000 in greenbacks, and $4,000 in gold.

A correspondence relative to this affair ensued between the Governor of Bermuda and the Home Government, and with Mr. Adams, the American Minister at London. The reasons on which Lieutenant Braine was discharged are stated in the following letter of Earl Russell to Mr. Adams:

FOREIGN OFFICE, January 21.

SIR: I have had the honor to receive your letter of the 21st ult. protesting against the proceedings of her Majesty's colonial authorities at Bermuda in the case of the steamer Roanoke, and enclosing copies of various documents relating thereto.

These papers refer to two different complaints. The one complaint is, that persons were enlisted at Bermuda with a view to make war on a State in amity with her Majesty. The other complaint is, that certain passengers proceeding from Havana in the United States vessel Roanoke, when five hours from Havana on their voyage, rose on the captain, made themselves masters of the vessel, destroyed her, and were afterwards permitted to land on the island of Bermuda. The answer to the first complaint is, that sufficient evidence to convict the persons accused was not produced, and consequently they could not be convicted. The answer to the second complaint is, that the person arrested for a supposed piratical act produced a commission authorizing that act as an operation of war, from the Government of the so-called Confederate States, which are acknowledged by her Majesty's Government to possess all belligerent rights.

(Signed,) I am, &c., RUSSELL.

Of all the systems adopted by the Federal Navy Department to accomplish the various and arduous objects rendered necessary by the outbreak of the war, not the least interesting is the manner in which an effective blockade of the Southern coast was secured. The length of coast to be blockaded was three thousand five hundred and forty-nine (3,549) miles. This is a greater extent than the whole coast of Europe from Cape Trafalgar to Cape North. The most serious attempts heretofore made by the great maritime powers of Europe consisted in endeavors to interdict trade at a few of the principal ports of a belligerent. The first steps of the department consisted in making every naval vessel available, recalling the foreign squadrons, increasing the force by building new vessels, and procuring for naval purposes from the merchant service every steamer which could be made a fighting vessel, and in enlarging the capacity of the navy yards, putting in requisition the foundries and workshops of the country for supplies of ordnance and steam machinery, augmenting the number of seamen, and supplying the deficiency of officers by selecting experienced and able shipmasters and others from the commercial marine. The next efforts of the department were directed toward securing several harbors, at comparatively equidistant points, as bases of operations for the several squadrons, where our naval vessels could receive their supplies, and maintain themselves at their stations and on their cruising ground without returning to northern ports for repairs and to refit. For this purpose various naval expeditions were organized. The first sailed from Hampton Roads in August, 1861, and captured the forts at Hatteras Inlet. This was followed, a few weeks later, by the capture of Port Royal, which secured a commodious harbor for the ships of the South Atlantic squadron. Early in the spring of 1862 New Orleans was captured. Other harbors and places were from time to time seized and occupied. From the outset, the blockade has been so effective as to be respected by the nations of Europe, and to cause a constant complaint by the enemy of its exhausting severity. Wilmington was the last port captured, and here blockade-running was more successful than at any other.

At Wilmington alone, sixty-five steamers, the aggregate value of which, with their cargoes, scarcely falls short of thirteen millions of dollars, were captured or destroyed in endeavoring to enter or escape.

On the interior rivers of the country the department also early commenced to put afloat a large fleet. It comprised more than one hundred vessels. They were to a great extent boats that had been employed in the carrying trade, but which were purchased, strengthened, and fitted for war purposes. They were necessarily inferior to naval built vessels in strength, lightly armed, and more liable to disaster. To insure a systematic and vigorous execution of the duties devolving upon this squadron, the waters traversed by it were divided into ten naval districts, each under the command of an experienced naval officer. The vessels in each district had their appropriate field of duty, but at the same time they were held ready to support each other when occasion required, and could be readily concentrated upon any emergency. The principal rivers thus traversed were the Mississippi, lower Ohio, Cumberland, and Tennessee. The effect of their operations on the Mississippi was to break up the combinations of the enemy, and sever their organizations. On the other rivers, peaceful citizens were protected and partisan bands dispersed.

COMPARATIVE STATEMENT OF THE NAVY, DECEMBER, 1863 AND 1864.

No. of vessels.	DESCRIPTION.	No. of guns.	No. of tons.
671	Total navy, December, 1864	4,610	510,396
588	Total navy, December, 1863	4,443	467,967
83	Actual increase for the year	167	42,429
26	Total losses by shipwreck, in battle, capture, &c., during the year	146	13,084
109	Actual addition to the navy from December, 1863, to December, 1864	312	55,513

VESSELS CONSTRUCTED FOR THE NAVY SINCE MARCH 4TH, 1861.

No. of vessels.	DESCRIPTION.	Guns.	Tonnage.
7	Screw sloops, Ammonoosuc class, 17 to 19 guns, 3,213 to 3,713 tons each	121	23,637
1	Screw sloop Idaho, 8 guns, and 2,638 tons	8	2,638
8	Screw sloops, spar deck, Java class, 25 guns, and 3,177 tons each	200	25,416
2	Screw sloops, spar deck, Hassalo class, 55 guns, and 3,365 tons each	50	6,730
10	Screw sloops, clippers, single deck, Contoocook class, 13 guns, and 2,348 tons each	130	23,480
4	Screw sloops, Kearsarge class, 8 to 12 guns, and averaging 1,023 tons each	40	4,092
6	Screw sloops, Shenandoah class, 8 to 16 guns, and 1,367 to 1,533 tons each	74	8,584
2	Screw sloops, Ossipee class, 10 to 13 guns, and 1,240 guns each	23	2,480
8	Screw sloops, Serapis class, 12 guns, and 1,380 tons each	96	11,040
4	Screw sloops, Resaca class, 8 guns, and 831 to 900 tons each	32	3,462
8	Screw sloops, Nipsic class, 7 to 12 guns, and 593 tons each	71	4,744
23	Screw gunboats, Unadilla class, 4 to 7 guns, and 507 tons each	123	11,661
9	Screw tugs, Pinta class, 2 guns, and 350 tons each	18	3,150
2	Screw tugs, Pilgrim class, 2 guns, and 170 tons each	4	340
13	Paddle-wheel steamers, double-enders, Octorara class, 7 to 11 guns, and 730 to 955 tons each	98	11,024
26	Paddle-wheel steamers, double-enders, Sassacus class, 10 to 14 guns, and 974 tons each	272	25,324
7	Paddle-wheel steamers, of iron, double-enders, Mohongo class, 10 guns, and 1,030 tons each	70	7,210
1	Paddle-wheel steamer, of iron, double-ender, Wateree, 12 guns, and 974 tons	12	974
141		1,442	175,986
	IRON-CLAD VESSELS.		
2	Sea-going casemated vessels, Dunderberg and New Ironsides	28	8,576
3	Sea-going turret vessels, Puritan, Dictator, and Roanoke	12	9,733
4	Double turret vessels, Kalamazoo class, 4 guns, and 3,200 tons each	16	12,800
4	Double turret vessels, Monadnock class, 4 guns, and 1,564 tons each	16	6,256
1	Double turret vessel, Onondaga, 4 guns, and 1,250 tons	4	1,250
4	Double turret vessels, Winnebago class, 4 guns, and 970 tons each	16	3,880
8	Single turret vessels, Canonicus class, 2 guns, and 1,034 tons each	16	8,272
9	Single turret vessels, Passaic class, 2 to 4 guns, and 844 tons each	21	7,596
20	Single turret vessels, Yazoo class, 1 to 2 guns, and 614 tons each	35	12,280
2	Single turret vessels, Sandusky and Marietta, 2 guns each	4	953
3	Single turret vessels, Ozark, Neosho, and Osage, 2 to 7 guns each	13	1,624
2	Casemated vessels, Tuscumbia and Chillicothe, 5 and 3 guns respectively	8	768
62		189	73,988
203	Total	1,631	249,974

The foregoing tabular statement exhibits the number and description of vessels that were constructed, or put in the course of construction, for the navy to the close of 1864. Some of them were built by contract; others by the Government, in the several navy yards. If there is added to the number those constructed under similar circumstances, and within the same period, that have been lost by shipwreck, in battle, &c., viz.: the sloops Housatonic and Adirondack, and the iron-clads Monitor, Weehawken, Keokuk, Indianola, and Tecumseh, the aggregate would be 210 vessels, 1,675 guns, and 256,755 tons. Picket-boats, and small craft built for especial purposes, are not embraced in this statement.

Various classes of vessels were constructed to meet the peculiar exigencies of the service. A class of small heavily-armed propellers was needed at the outset, and twenty-three were constructed as gunboats, after the type of the Unadilla, Pinola, and Wissahickon. They maintained a good reputation to the close of the war. They were well adapted for guarding the coast. A larger description was needed for ocean service, and four vessels of the class of the Ossipee, mounting each two guns of eleven inch, were built. There were also four vessels of slightly less tonnage constructed, carrying the same armament of which the Kearsarge is a type. The Shenandoah is a type of six vessels mounting each three eleven-inch guns, all of which sustain a high reputation. The heavy guns mentioned constitute the principal armament of the several classes named, but they each have in addition from two to six guns of less calibre. All of these vessels were screw steamers, suitable for sea cruising; but the shallow sounds and bays, the rivers and bayous, often narrow and tortuous, required a different class, drawing less water. To turn in these frequently restricted channels is difficult, and sometimes impossible; the necessities of the case, therefore, suggested the principle of a fighting vessel with a double bow and a rudder at each end. Twelve paddle-wheel steamers of this class, of which the Port Royal and Sonoma are types, were constructed. Others of the same class were the Sassacus, distinguished in the attack on the ram in Albemarle Sound, and the Metacomet, conspicuous in Mobile Bay. One of this class was sent round Cape Horn to San Francisco where she is on duty.

Of the monitor class of vessels only two, the Dictator and Puritan, were proposed for sea-service. Four turreted vessels have been built of wood and cased with iron, thus differing from the original monitors, which are exclusively of iron. One of them, the Monadnock, performed her trips from Boston to Hampton Roads with entire satisfaction. Her draught of water was twelve feet, and with two independent screws she had a speed of ten knots. Four other similar vessels of a still more formidable and invulnerable character were commenced. The only other sea-going iron-clad ships besides the two turreted vessels above mentioned, were the New Ironsides and the Dunderberg, a casemate vessel.

In its iron-clads the department experimented by the construction of different classes and sizes, both in wood and iron, propelled by one screw and by two screws working independently of each other. In its most recent constructions of the Miantonomah class, a wooden vessel with Ericsson turrets, a high rate of speed, perfect ventilation, impregnability, and the enormous battery of four 15-inch guns, were combined in a vessel of 1,564 tons, and drawing only twelve feet of water. These vessels were free from the disadvantage of fouling, which so greatly reduced the speed of iron ones.

In the steam vessels nearly every variety and type of engine, of valve gear, of rate of expansion, of surface condenser, of screw propeller, and of boilers, have been thoroughly tested.

As in previous years of the war the seacoast and inland waters of the United States were, in 1864, in charge of six different squadrons, viz.: 1. The North Atlantic Squadron, Acting Rear Admiral S. P. Lee, relieved October 12th by Rear Admiral D. D. Porter; 2. The South Atlantic Squadron, Rear Admiral J. A. Dahlgren, temporarily relieved between February and May by Commodore S. C. Rowan; 3. The East Gulf Squadron, Acting Rear Admiral T. Bailey, relieved in October by Acting Rear Admiral C. K. Stribling; 4. The West Gulf Squadron, Rear Admiral Farragut, relieved toward the close of the year by Acting Rear Admiral H. K. Thatcher; 5. The Mississippi Flotilla, Rear Admiral D. D. Porter, relieved November 1st by Acting Rear Admiral S. P. Lee; and 6. The Potomac Flotilla, Commander Foxhall A. Parker. The usual squadron in the Pacific was also maintained during the year, under the command successively of Acting Rear Admirals C. H. Bell and G. F. Pearson; while that in the West India waters was, as an organization, discontinued. A number of vessels were actively employed from time to time in cruising after rebel privateers and in special service; and small squadrons were also maintained in the Mediterranean and the East Indies.

The operations of the North Atlantic Squadron, which in the previous year were almost wholly confined to blockade duties, were sufficiently various and important in 1864 to call forth all the resources at the command of the Naval Department. Besides the blockade of Wilmington, which alone required a fleet double in size and effectiveness to the entire naval force in commission previous to the war, the inland waters of Albemarle and Pamlico Sounds had to be guarded against the formidable iron-clads which the rebels had for a long time been constructing in the Neuse and Roanoke Rivers; operations on an extensive scale, in concert with the army, were conducted in the James River; and in the latter part of the year occurred the terrific bombardment of Fort

Fisher by the most powerful naval armament which ever attacked a fortification. In fact, so multiform were the duties required of this squadron, that in order to ensure their proper fulfilment, it was in the spring divided into four separate squadrons, one of which was stationed in the James River, one in the Sounds of North Carolina, and two off Cape Fear River and the adjacent inlets. Each of these squadrons was placed under an efficient officer, and the general headquarters were established at Beaufort, North Carolina. The almost total closing of Charleston harbor, and the vigilant watch kept over Mobile, caused Wilmington to be the only port east of the Mississippi River accessible to blockade-runners; and so daring, and in many cases so successful, were the latter in evading the Federal cruisers, that complaints were freely uttered against the naval department for permitting the rebels to enter and depart from this port at their pleasure. "Many who have failed to make themselves acquainted," observed Secretary Welles in his annual report, "with the facts connected with the Wilmington blockade, have been free and severe in their censures of the manner in which it has been conducted. The intelligent officers of the naval and merchant service who have labored with untiring zeal and assiduity, and watched with sleepless vigilance through weary months of winter and summer, and in all weathers, stimulated by the hope of benefiting their country and receiving its thanks, as well as by every inducement of fame and pecuniary reward, if successful, do not concur in the opinion that the port of Wilmington can be entirely closed by blockade."

To one familiar, however, with the configuration of the land at the mouth, or rather mouths of the Cape Fear River, through which a vessel must pass in order to reach Wilmington, the injustice of condemning the navy for not more effectually blockading the place will be sufficiently apparent. For about thirty-five miles before reaching the ocean the Cape Fear River flows in a direction nearly due south, and directly in front of its mouth lies Smith's Island, on either side of which are the two principal entrances to the river. The southwest, or main channel, is about two and a half miles in width, has a depth of from ten to fourteen feet over the bar, and is protected by Fort Caswell, a casemated stone work on Oak Island, adjoining the mainland, and by the Light House battery on Smith's Island. The northeast entrance, known as New Inlet, is less than two miles wide, and shallower than the other, and is protected by Fort Fisher, a first-class casemated earthwork near Federal Point on the mainland, and by a series of batteries extending thence about six miles in a northerly direction along the seacoast. Owing to an extensive shoal, called the Frying Pan, extending around the southern and western sides of Smith's Island, the distance by sea between the two entrances is forty miles, while inside the island it is not above eight. To the natural advantages of the locality, greatly enhanced by the artificial defences, on which the best engineering skill of the Confederacy had been expended since the commencement of the war, must be added the shallowness of the water, which decreases in depth gradually and regularly to the shore line, so that none of the blockade-runners of light draught were under the necessity of making directly for either entrance, but could, by the lead, run close under the land, and protected by the batteries, pass in at their leisure. In escaping from the river such vessels found still less difficulty in eluding the Federal cruisers, as they could pass for some distance up or down the coast before making an offing, or proceed straight out to sea, trusting to darkness, fog, or a full head of steam to make their escape. For running the blockade of this port a peculiar class of steamers, of great speed and light draught, was constructed in England, and the enormous profits arising from a successful voyage, a single trip often paying many times the cost of the vessel, tempted the merchants of that country to embark largely in this illicit commerce. Nassau, Bermuda, and Halifax became their chief places of rendezvous, and from one or the other of these ports there was almost a daily departure for Wilmington.

On the other hand, the Federal cruisers were for the most part of too deep a draught to run near the shore, or enter the several lesser channels through which the blockade-runners could pass; still less to approach the numerous shallow inlets extending up and down the coast, into which the latter could take refuge. Such, also, was the nature of the coast, and the liability at some seasons of constant stormy weather, that it was almost impossible to station light-draught blockaders there on permanent duty. These facts will explain why, with fifty cruisers stationed at the two main entrances of the Cape Fear River, some of them the fastest in the service, and officered by men who had not their superiors in any service in intrepidity, energy, and professional skill, blockade-runners were nevertheless enabled to pass in and out with seeming impunity. When it is considered, also, that the latter have always a full head of steam on at the critical moment, and that their adversaries cannot be equally prepared, the chances in favor of the blockade-runners are greatly increased. Thus it happened that the blockade of Wilmington was repeatedly broken, and that the port itself became the central depot of the Confederacy for the reception of supplies from abroad. This result, however, was not accomplished without considerable sacrifice, and the steamers captured or destroyed off the mouth of the Cape Fear River averaged one a week subsequent to the closing of Charleston harbor by the monitor fleet under Admiral Dahlgren.

From an official statement of the results of blockade-running at Wilmington from January, 1863, to December, 1864, published in the "Manchester Guardian," it appears that the total ventures made by English capitalists and speculators, counting the values of ships and cargoes, amounted to more than sixty-six millions of dollars (£13,241,000). The quantity of cotton exported in twenty-two months (January 1st, 1863, to October 31st, 1864) was 137,937 bales, or 62,860,463 pounds, of which the larger part was Sea Island. The value of the export and import trade in one year (July 1st, 1863, to June 30th, 1864) was $65,185,000; the rebel government rating exchange at five for one. The total number of vessels which ran the blockade in fifteen months (October 1st, 1863, to December 31st, 1864) was 397. The average amount of capital invested by Englishmen in trading ventures with Wilmington during a period of fifteen months (October 1st, 1863, to December 31st, 1864), is stated in detail as follows:

	Entrances. 203.	Clearances. 194.	Total ventures. 397.
Ships at £15,000 each	£3,045,000	£2,910,000	£5,955,000
Cargoes—Inw'd (£12,000) Outward (£25,000)	2,436,000	4,850,000	7,286,000
Total	£5,481,000	£7,760,000	£13,241,000

The operations in the Sounds of North Carolina, with the exception of some unimportant reconnoissances and boat expeditions, commenced in April with the engagement between the gunboats Miami and Southfield and the rebel ram Albemarle, at Plymouth, near the mouth of the Roanoke River, of which an account is given in connection with Army Operations. The advantages gained by the Albemarle on this occasion, taken in connection with the reverses sustained at Plymouth by the land forces in garrison there, called for vigorous measures to prevent further disaster, including possibly the overthrow of the Federal naval supremacy in Albemarle Sound. Captain Melancton Smith was accordingly sent to assume command in the Sounds with several vessels of the double-ender class, and was directed to attack the ram at all hazards, and use every means to disable or destroy her. On the afternoon of the 5th of May, the Federal fleet being collected near the mouth of the Roanoke River, the Albemarle came out, followed by the Bombshell, a small armed tender, and at 4:40 proceeded to engage the gunboats. In accordance with instructions, the larger gunboats manœuvred to get alongside of their antagonist, and fire upon her ports or roof, which were her most vulnerable parts; but, owing to the neglect of the smaller vessels to obey the signals from the flag-ship, and to their rapid and indiscriminate fire, it became impossible for the larger ones to take a desirable position without risk of being riddled by their own friends. The contest was, consequently, for the first half hour of a somewhat desultory character. The gunboats eluded the efforts of the Albemarle to ram them, but their guns seemed to make no perceptible impression upon her. Soon after 5 o'clock the Sassacus, watching her opportunity, struck the enemy fairly abaft her starboard beam, causing her to careen until the water washed over her deck and casemate. In this position the two vessels remained for about ten minutes, the crew of the Sassacus throwing hand-grenades down the deck-hatch of the Albemarle, and trying in vain to get powder into her smoke-stack. Could another of the gunboats at this juncture have got up on the other side of the ram, she might have been seriously disabled, and perhaps compelled to surrender; but before this could be effected she swung clear of the Sassacus, and in parting sent a 100-pounder rifle shot clean through the starboard boiler of her antagonist, who, enveloped in blinding clouds of steam, was compelled to withdraw for a short time from action. About this time the colors of the Albemarle came down, whether by accident or design is not known; but she nevertheless maintained a general engagement with the gunboats until 7:30 P. M., when she retired up the Roanoke River. With the exception of the Sassacus, the gunboats sustained comparatively little injury, although several of them were struck by the rifle shots of the Albemarle. The latter had her boats knocked to pieces, her smoke-stock riddled, and one of her guns partially disabled, but in other respects seemed in as good condition as upon going into action. Her motive power was entirely uninjured, and the rifled projectiles of the gunboats, even when discharged at short range, rebounded harmlessly from her armored sides. Her tender, the Bombshell, was captured early in the fight.

The action, though without any definite results, reflected no little credit on the bravery and skill of the small Federal squadron, and showed that, with a proper effort, even by the class of vessels engaged, the Albemarle might be compelled to remain within the waters of the Roanoke. She showed herself again on May 24th at the mouth of the river, but retired rapidly up the stream toward Plymouth upon being approached by the gunboats. From reports of refugees and deserters, it also appeared that she suffered considerably in the action of the 5th, both in her outer plating and from the concussion caused by the fire of the gunboats. On the 25th a daring but unsuccessful attempt was made by five volunteers from the gunboat Wyalusing to destroy her by a torpedo, while lying at the wharf at Plymouth.

But though manifesting no disposition to reassume the offensive, the Albemarle was of sufficient importance to induce the naval department to take measures during the summer for her destruction. Lieut. W. B. Cushing, who had on previous occasions shown equal coolness and daring in conducting hazardous reconnoissances, was selected for the undertaking, and a small steam launch was equipped as a torpedo vessel and put under his charge. On the night of Oct. 27th he started up the Roanoke with a crew of thirteen officers and men who chiefly volunteered for the service, and passing several miles of the enemy's pickets unobserved, arrived within twenty yards of the Albemarle before being hailed by her lookouts. The torpedo boat was then steered under a full head of steam direct for the ram, which lay at her wharf at Plymouth, protected by a raft of logs extending outwards about thirty feet. Upon the alarm being given by the lookout, a confused fire of musketry was opened by the rebels, which had little effect. "Passing her closely," says Lieut. Cushing, "we made a complete circle, so as to strike her fairly, and went into her bows on. By this time the enemy's fire was very severe, but a dose of canister at short range served to moderate their zeal and disturb their aim. In a moment we had struck the logs, just abreast of the quarter-port, breasting them in some feet, and our bows resting on them. The torpedo boom was then lowered, and by a vigorous pull I succeeded in driving the torpedo under the overhang, and exploded it at the same time the Albemarle's gun was fired. A shot seemed to go crashing through my boat, and a dense mass of water rushed in from the torpedo, filling the launch and completely disabling her. The enemy then continued to fire at fifteen feet range and demanded our surrender, which I twice refused, ordering the men to save themselves, and removing my own coat and shoes. Springing into the river, I swam with others into the middle of the stream, the rebels failing to hit us." Lieut. Cushing succeeded in reaching the opposite shore, and during the next day made his way by stealth through the surrounding swamps to a creek some distance below Plymouth, where he found a skiff belonging to a rebel picket, in which he effected his escape to the fleet. Only one other of his party succeeded in escaping, the rest being either captured, killed, or drowned. The Albemarle was completely submerged by the explosion of the torpedo, and so remained long subsequent to the evacuation of Plymouth by the rebels. This daring feat excited the admiration of the rebel no less than of the Federal authorities, and obtained for Lieut. Cushing the thanks of Congress, and promotion to the next highest grade in the service. The main rebel defence of Plymouth being thus removed, Commander Macomb, the senior naval officer in the Sounds, availed himself of Lieut. Cushing's success to reëstablish the Federal supremacy of the lower Roanoke. With the vessels under his command he immediately pushed up the river to Plymouth, drove the rebels from their rifle-pits and batteries, and on Oct. 31st retook the town, capturing a few prisoners, beside cannon, small arms, and ammunition. Thenceforth during the year the Federal forces held undisturbed possession of the Sounds.

For some time previous to May, 1864, the James River had been left almost exclusively to the enemy, who availed themselves of this circumstance to place torpedoes in the channel and otherwise obstruct its navigation. With the movement of Gen. Butler's forces up the river on May 5th, for the purpose of coöperating in the grand campaign of Gen. Grant against Richmond, commenced a long series of naval operations, which, though of considerable importance, are so intimately connected with the military campaign in that quarter, as to form a subordinate part of the operations of the army. Hence a very brief outline of what was accomplished by this division of the North Atlantic squadron is all that it is necessary to give here. The land forces were safely convoyed up the river to their landing places at City Point and Bermuda Hundred, with no disaster to the fleet beyond the destruction by torpedoes of two small paddle-wheel gunboats, the Commodore Jones and the Shawsheen. Military operations having commenced near Petersburg, five iron-clads, including the captured vessel Atlanta, were stationed some distance above City Point to watch the rebel iron-clads and rams in the upper James, and if possible engage them in action, while the smaller vessels of the fleet were busily occupied in dragging the river for torpedoes, in assailing moving batteries or bodies of the enemy along the shore, or in minor expeditions. During the attack upon the colored garrison at Wilson's wharf, a portion of the fleet rendered good service in repelling the enemy. In June, much to the disappointment of Admiral Lee, who earnestly desired a brush with the enemy, obstructions were sunk in the channel at Trent's Reach, for the purpose of protecting, from any sudden attack by the rebel fleet, the numerous transports collected at City Point, the security of which was deemed of too great importance to the army to permit their defence to be intrusted to the navy alone. During most of the summer and autumn, the iron-clads had frequent combats with the enemy's vessels and the powerful batteries at Howlett's, the advantages from which, owing to the difficult navigation of the river, could never be pushed to any definite result.

The complex yet comprehensive plan which the Government adopted in the spring of 1864, for the overthrow of the rebel power, provided for the capture of the remaining seaports, through which munitions of war and pecuniary aid were received by the Confederacy. Wilmington, from the facility which it afforded for blockade-running, and its easy communication with Richmond, became early in the summer a prominent object of attack; and to guard against any doubtful issue in such an undertaking, preparations commenced early in the summer to equip a squadron, which, while amply able to overcome all resistance, should also represent the commanding position assumed within three years by the United States among the great naval powers of the world. The naval department had on several previous occasions offered to close the port of Wilmington, with the aid of a coöperating land force; but, in view of the failure at Charleston in 1863, declined, without such coöperation, to assume the responsibility of reducing the strong forts at the mouth of the Cape Fear River. In previous years the exigencies of the service had prevented the employment of land forces for this specific purpose; now it was determined to furnish troops enough to crown the expedition with success. The stubborn fighting between the Rapidan and the James entailed, however, such serious losses upon Gen. Grant, that all the surplus troops at the disposal of the Government were needed during the summer, to replenish the wasted ranks of the Armies of the Potomac and the James, and for months the contemplated expedition remained unorganized. The naval part of it alone, in consequence of the constantly-increasing number of vessels at the disposal of the naval department, seemed to make progress. As early as August, iron-clads and wooden steamers began to rendezvous at Hampton Roads, until in October a formidable fleet, numbering over fifty war vessels, and including the iron-clad New Ironsides and four monitors, was collected, of which Admiral Porter assumed command.

Long before December the squadron was at its rendezvous in readiness to sail; but it was not until the winter had fairly commenced that the necessary quota of troops could be furnished. The signal successes of Thomas and Sherman having disarmed all apprehensions with respect to the result of military operations in the South and Southwest, and the Armies of the Potomac and the James having been recently largely recruited, the Government early in December issued orders for the troops designated for the service to repair to Hampton Roads. These consisted of Gen. Ames's division of the 24th corps, and of Gen. Paine's colored division of the 25th corps, numbering together 6,500 effective men, both of which belonged to the Army of the James. Gen. Weitzel was designated as commander-in-chief of the military part of the expedition, but Gen. Butler subsequently accompanied it in that capacity, and on the 9th notified Admiral Porter that he was in readiness to move. Owing to stormy weather none of the vessels sailed until the 12th, when the transports and smaller war vessels, about 75 in number, took their departure, followed on the succeeding day by the New Ironsides and the heavy steam frigates.

After careful consideration it was determined that of the two entrances to the Cape Fear River, New Inlet could be the more successfully attacked. The narrow strip of land forming part of the east bank of the Cape Fear River, and terminating in Federal Point, offered, on the whole, better facilities for landing troops than any other part of the coast; and the capture of the works which protected it would not only give to the fleet the command of the river, and thus virtually close the port of Wilmington, but by cutting off Fort Caswell, which commands the other mouth of the river, would render the possession of that

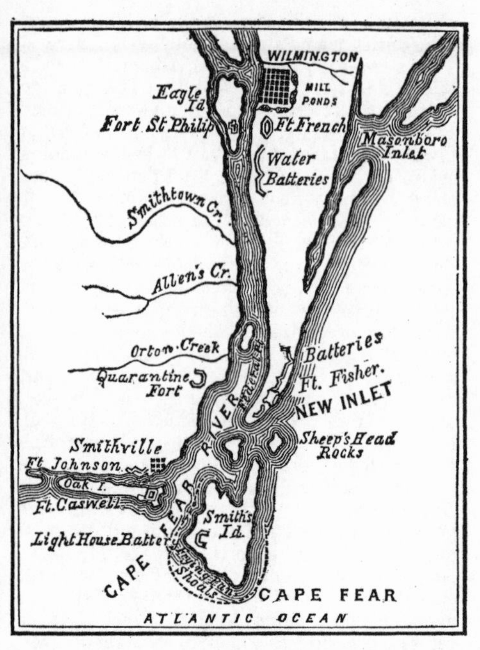

strong work of no further importance to the rebels. For the immediate defence of the inlet the rebels relied chiefly upon Fort Fisher, and a series of batteries, connected by rifle-pits, running thence in a southwest direction along the coast, at an average distance of two hundred yards from the beach, to what was called the "Mound Battery," situated near the extreme end of Federal Point. The fort and its connecting batteries, forming practically a single work, consisted of two fronts: the first, or land front, being four hundred and eighty yards in length and extending nearly across the narrow peninsula, while the sea front has a length of about thirteen hundred yards. The former was intended to resist any attack from troops approaching the fort from the north, and the sea front to prevent vessels from running through New Inlet or landing troops on Federal Point. The following more particular description of both fronts is given by Colonel Comstock, chief engineer of the military part of the expedition: "The land front consists of a half bastion on the left or Cape Fear River side, connected by a curtain with a bastion on the ocean side. The parapet is 25 feet thick, averages 20 feet in height, with traverses rising 10 feet above it and running back on their tops, which are from 8 to 12 feet in thickness, to a distance of from 30 to 40 feet from the interior crest. The traverses on the left half bastion are about 25 feet in length on top. The earth for this heavy parapet and the enormous traverses at their inner ends, more than 30 feet in height, was obtained partly from a shallow exterior ditch, but mainly from the interior of the work. Between each pair of traverses there was one or two guns. The traverses on the right of this front were only partially completed. A palisade, which is loopholed and has a banquette, runs in front of this face, at a distance of 50 feet in front of the exterior slope, from the Cape Fear River to the ocean, with a position for a gun between the left of the front and the river, and another between the right of the front and the ocean. Through the middle traverse on the curtain is a bomb-proof postern whose exterior opening is covered by a small redan for two field-pieces, to give flank fire along the curtain. The traverses are generally bomb-proofed for men or magazines. The slopes of the work appear to have been revetted with marsh sod or covered with grass, and have an inclination of 45 degrees or a little less. * * * There were originally on this front 21 guns and 3 mortars. * * * The sea front consists of a series of batteries, mounting in all 24 guns, the different batteries being connected by a strong infantry parapet so as to form a continuous line. The same system of heavy traverses for the protection of the guns is used as on the land front, and these traverses are also generally bomb-proofed." There was also a rebel battery, commanding the channel, on Zeeke's Island, two miles southeast of Fort Fisher, and several miles north of the latter were the Flag Pond Hill and Half Moon batteries, serving as outworks to it.

On December 15th the transports arrived off New Inlet, where, on the 18th and 19th, they were joined by the iron-clads, which, being obliged to put into Beaufort, N. C., for coal and ammunition, could not reach the rendezvous sooner. The heavy-armed frigates, on account of their slow sailing, arrived also a day or two after the transports. Scarcely was the whole fleet assembled than the weather, which had previously been fair, became threatening, and on the 19th the sea was too rough to admit of landing troops. On the 20th a gale set in from the northeast, and the transports, being now deficient in coal and water, and liable to disaster if they should attempt to remain at their anchorage, were directed to make for Beaufort. The war vessels rode out the gale, which lasted three days, in safety, the monitors acting unexpectedly well; and on the 23d, the wind having veered round to the west, Admiral Porter determined to improve what he considered a favorable opportunity, by commencing operations on his own account without waiting for the return of the transports. An important agent in the destruction or reduction of Fort Fisher was a vessel filled with powder, which it was designed to run ashore as near as possible to the fort and explode. The idea originated with General Butler, and was suggested by the accidental explosion at Erith, on the Thames, in England, on October 1st, of two barges and two adjoining magazines loaded with barrels of powder, by which eight or nine lives were lost, and much surrounding property was destroyed. It was supposed that a similar explosion of a vast mass of powder near the fort, the fleet meanwhile keeping at a respectful distance, would cause its walls to fall down, or some other serious disaster to occur, of which the attacking party might take advantage. The vessel selected for the purpose was the small gunboat Louisiana, purchased for operations on the North Carolina Sounds, and which, with a view of deceiving the rebels as to her true character, was disguised for the occasion as a blockade runner. She was then stored with two hundred and fifteen tons of powder, arranged as follows: Upon the berth deck was stowed a tier of barrels of powder with their heads taken out; over this sixty-pound bags of powder were piled in layers up to the top of the deck, and a house was constructed on the after deck, filled in the same manner. All were connected together by Gomez fuses, penetrating the mass, and uniting it at many points, every precaution being taken to insure, if possible, the instantaneous ignition of the whole mass. A simple method of firing these fuses by clock-work, timed as desired, was provided, three being provided in case one should fail. As a further precaution, in case the clock fuses should miscarry, the ends of the fuses were united at another point, and brought beneath a perforated framework of wood, in which were set lighted tapers, the lower end of the wicks penetrating the quick of the fuses. Five of these tapers were provided to insure success if other means failed; and, as a last precaution, it was arranged to fire the ship at a point remote from the powder at the moment of leaving it.

The vessel thus equipped was put in charge of Commander A. C. Rhind, who had associated with him Lieutenant G. W. Preston, Second Assistant Engineer Mullen, Acting Master's Mate Boyden, and seven men. The weather seeming auspicious for the enterprise on the 23d, Commander Rhind was directed, under cover of the darkness, to run his vessel aground directly opposite the fort, and proceed to explode her. Mr. Bradford, of the coast survey, had, the night previous, ascertained that a vessel of seven feet draught could be placed on the edge of the beach. The result of the undertaking is thus described by Admiral Porter:

At half-past ten P. M. the powder vessel started in toward the bar, and was towed by the Wilderness until the embrasures of Fort Fisher were plainly in sight. The Wilderness then cast off, and the Louisiana proceeded under steam until within two hundred yards of the beach, and about four hundred from the fort. Commander Rhind anchored her securely there, and coolly went to work to make all his arrangements to blow her up. This he was enabled to do, owing to a blockade-runner going in right ahead of him, the forts making the blockade-runner signals, which they also did to the Louisiana. The gallant party, after coolly making all their arrangements for the explosion, left the vessel, the last thing they did being to set her on fire under the cabin. Then taking to their boats, they made their escape off to the Wilderness, lying close by. The Wilderness then put off shore with good speed, to avoid any ill effects that might happen from the explosion. At forty-five minutes past one on the morning of the 24th the explosion took place, and the shock was nothing like so severe as was expected. It shook the vessel some, and broke one or two glasses, but nothing more.

To those watching the explosion from the fleet at several miles distance from the shore, it seemed scarcely louder than the discharge of a battery of light artillery; but at Newbern it was distinctly heard, and was supposed to be an earthquake. Not the slightest damage, so far as could be ascertained, was inflicted upon the fort, whose immensely thick walls of sand could probably have withstood the explosion of a dozen or more powder-ships.

Although the explosion had proved a failure and the transports were not yet in sight, Admiral Porter determined to proceed at once with the attack, hoping to damage the fort to such a degree that the troops, upon their arrival, would find comparatively little difficulty in carrying it by storm. Accordingly, at daylight of the 24th, the fleet stood in, in line of battle, toward the shore, and shortly before noon took up the positions previously assigned to them by the Admiral. The first line comprised the iron-clads, Ironsides, Monadnock, Canonicus, and Mahopac, which were anchored in line, about a length apart, at a distance of three-quarters of a mile from the fort, each having in its rear, within easy supporting distance, a gunboat to serve as a tender. A quarter of a mile behind the iron-clads was a line of heavy frigates, comprising the Minnesota, Colorado, Wabash, and vessels of similar calibre; and behind these another line, each vessel of which was anchored intermediate between those of the first line. Another division, consisting chiefly of gunboats, took position to the south and southeast of the forts, and to the left of the frigates, and still another was posted to the northward and eastward of the iron-clads, for the purpose of enfilading the works. The attacking squadron numbered thirty-three vessels of all kinds, mounting upward of four hundred guns, and was supported by a reserve of seventeen small gunboats with about one hundred guns.

Shortly before one o'clock the Ironsides opened upon the fort, followed by the monitors, and within half an hour afterwards the Minnesota, holding the left of the second line, succeeded in obtaining the range. The rebels kept up an active fire while the squadron was getting into position, but the terrific broadsides of the Ironsides almost immediately silenced all their guns on the northeast face of the fort; and by the time the last of the large vessels anchored and got its batteries into play, but one or two guns were discharged from any part of the fort, the incessant and tremendous fire of the fleet, surpassing any thing previously known in naval warfare, having driven the gunners within the shelter of their bomb-proofs. "In one hour and fifteen minutes after the first shot was fired," says Admiral Porter, "not a shot came from the fort. Two magazines had been blown up by our shells, and the fort set on fire in several places, and such a torrent of missiles were falling into and bursting over it, that it was impossible for any human being to stand it. Finding that the batteries were silenced completely, I directed the ships to keep up a moderate fire, in hopes of attracting the attention of the transports and bringing them in." In the latter part of the afternoon Gen. Butler arrived with a portion of his transports, and the fleet was signalled to retire for the night for safe anchorage. During the four or five hours that the engagement lasted, only one vessel, the gunboat Yantic, left the line to report damages, although several others were struck once or twice. The most serious disasters to the fleet were caused by the bursting of some of its own guns. Accidents of this kind occurred on the Ticonderoga, Yantic, Juniata, Mackinaw, Quaker City, and Susquehanna, resulting in the killing and wounding of between forty and fifty officers and men. The pieces which exploded were 100-pounder Parrott guns, and the effect was to cause a great distrust in this species of ordnance, as unfit for service, and, to use the language of Admiral Porter, "calculated to kill more of our own men than those of the enemy."

On the 25th the remaining transports arrived, and, in accordance with plans matured between the naval and military commanders on the previous evening, another attack upon the fort by the fleet was determined on, in coöperation with an assault by the troops upon the land face. Under cover of a detachment of gunboats, the disembarkation of the troops commenced, shortly after noon, on the beach about three miles above the fort. A portion of Curtis's brigade of Ames's division landed first, and pushed forward to reconnoitre the immediate approaches to the fort, the fleet meanwhile keeping up a slow and deliberate fire of just sufficient force to occupy the enemy's attention and prevent them from opening upon the troops. The reconnoitring column, accompanied by Gen. Weitzel in person, approached so near to Fort Fisher that several men in the skirmish line were wounded by fragments of shells from the fleet. From a point eight hundred yards distant Gen. Weitzel made a survey of the work, and the results of his personal observation, together with information previously received from trustworthy sources, induced him to report to Gen. Butler, upon his return to the transport fleet, that, under the circumstances, it would be "butchery to order an assault." This opinion coincided with that already formed by Gen. Butler, and orders were at once given to reëmbark the troops, all of whom, however, were not taken off until the next evening. During the advance of the reconnoitring column toward the fort, the garrisons of the Flag Pond and Half Moon batteries. numbering nearly three hundred officers and men, were captured.

The following correspondence subsequently passed between Gen. Butler and Admiral Porter:

HEADQ'RS DEP'T VIRGINIA AND NORTH CAROLINA, December 25, 1864.

ADMIRAL: Upon landing the troops and making a thorough reconnoissance of Fort Fisher, both Gen. Weitzel and myself are fully of the opinion that the place could not be carried by assault, as it was left substantially uninjured as a defensive work by the navy fire. We found seventeen guns protected by traverses, two only of which were dismounted, bearing up the beach and covering a strip of land, the only practicable route, not more than wide enough for a thousand men in line of battle.

Having captured Flag Pond Hill battery, the garrison of which, sixty-five men and two commissioned officers, were taken off by the navy, we also captured Half Moon battery and seven officers and two hundred and eighteen men of the 3d North Carolina Junior Reserves, including its commander, from whom I learned that a portion of Hoke's division, consisting of Kirkland's and Haywood's brigades, had been sent from the lines before Richmond on Tuesday last, arriving at Wilmington Friday night.

Gen. Weitzel advanced his skirmish line within fifty yards of the fort, while the garrison was kept in their bomb-proofs by the fire of the navy, and so closely that three or four men of the picket line ventured upon the parapet, and through the sally-port of the work, capturing a horse, which they brought off, killing the orderly, who was the bearer of a despatch from the chief of artillery of Gen. Whiting to bring a light battery within the fort, and also brought away from the parapet the flag of the fort. This was done while the shells of the navy were falling about the heads of the daring men who entered the work, and it was evident, as soon as the fire of the navy ceased because of the darkness, that the fort was fully manned again, and opened with grape and canister upon our picket line.

Finding that nothing but the operations of a regular siege, which did not come within my instructions, would reduce the fort, and in view of the threatening aspect of the weather, wind arising from the south-east, rendering it impossible to make further landing through the surf, I caused the troops, with their prisoners, to reëmbark, and see nothing further that can be done by the land forces. I shall therefore sail for Hampton Roads as soon as the transport fleet can be got in order.

The engineers and officers report Fort Fisher to me as substantially uninjured as a defensive work.

I have the honor to be, very respectfully, your obedient servant, BENJ. F. BUTLER.
Maj.-Gen. Comm'g.

To Rear Adm. PORTER, Commanding N. A. Blockading Squadron.

NORTH ATLANTIC SQUAD'N, U. S. FLAGSHIP MALVERN, OFF NEW INLET, December 26, 1864.

GENERAL: I beg leave to acknowledge the receipt of your letter of this date, the substance of which was communicated to me by Gen. Weitzel last night.

I have ordered the largest vessels to proceed off Beaufort, and fill up with ammunition, to be ready for another attack in case it is decided to proceed with this matter by making other arrangements. We have not commenced firing rapidly yet, and could keep any rebels inside from showing their heads until an assaulting column was within twenty yards of the works.

I wish some more of your gallant fellows had followed the officer who took the flag from the parapet and the brave fellow who brought the horse from the fort. I think they would have found it an easier conquest than is supposed. I do not desire, however, to place my opinion in opposition to Gen. Weitzel, whom I know to be an accomplished soldier and engineer, and whose opinion has great weight with me.

I will look out that the troops are all off in safety. We will have a west wind presently, and a smooth beach about three o'clock, when sufficient boats will be sent for them.

The prisoners now on board the Santiago de Cuba will be delivered to the Provost Marshal at Fortress Monroe, unless you wish to take them on board one of the transports, which would be inconvenient just now.

I remain, General, respectfully, your obedient servant, DAVID D PORTER, Rear Admiral.

To Maj.-Gen. B. F. BUTLER, Commanding, &c., &c,

For various reasons Admiral Porter was strongly opposed to abandoning the attack, and so expressed himself in his subsequent report to the Naval Department. "I don't pretend," he said, "to put my opinion in opposition to that of Gen. Weitzel, who is a thorough soldier and an able engineer, and whose business it is to know more of assaulting than I do, but I can't help thinking that it was worth while to make the attempt after coming so far." This was the view generally entertained by the public, who, accustomed of late to uninterrupted successes, chafed under this temporary check; and to the general dissatisfaction caused by the abandonment of the enterprise and the return of the troops to Fortress Monroe is doubtless partly to be attributed the order issued early in 1865, relieving Gen. Butler from the command of the Army of the James. The enemy, with some degree of reason, claimed that the result of the expedition was a triumph for their arms, notwithstanding that during two whole days Fort Fisher had been silenced by the guns of the fleet; and a congratulatory order was issued by Gen. Bragg, in which a high compliment was paid to Gen. Whiting, Col. Lamb, and the officers and men of the garrison. According to the rebel accounts the fort fired 662 shots on the first day of the attack and 600 on the second, and had 2 guns burst and 4 disabled. The garrison lost 3 killed and 55 wounded.

Admiral Porter remained off New Inlet a day or two after the departure of the transports, but finding it hopeless to attempt the reduction of the fort without the assistance of a land force, he withdrew his fleet to Beaufort, in the confident expectation that the troops would soon be ordered back again from Fortress Monroe. In this he was not deceived, for scarcely had the news of the abandonment of the expedition been received at headquarters, than orders were issued for a renewal of the attempt. On January 2d, Gen. Terry, commanding the 1st division of the 24th corps, Army of the James, was ordered to take command of the two divisions which had participated in the first expedition, to which was added a brigade under Col. Abbott from his own division, and two batteries, the whole numbering somewhat more than 8,000 men. With these he proceeded on the 5th to Fortress Monroe, and thence to Beaufort, where on the 8th he arranged with Admiral Porter a plan of operations against Fort Fisher. Owing to unfavorable weather the transports were unable to arrive off New Inlet until late on the night of the 12th. Next morning commenced the disembarkation of the troops at a point about five miles above the fort, the fleet, with the exception of the iron-clads, divided into three columns, covering the operation. One column moved a little to the northward of the landing place, to guard against any attack from the direction of Masonboro Inlet, and shelled the woods, which approach within about 300 yards of the shore, without, however, provoking any reply. With the aid of 200 boats from the fleet, besides steam tugs, nearly the whole of the troops were landed between 8 A. M. and 3 P. M., each man carrying three days' rations, and forty rounds of ammunition. A sufficient quantity of intrenching tools was also carried. The iron-clads, increased to five by the arrival of the monitor Saugus, meanwhile, from their old positions in front of Fort Fisher, had maintained a steady fire upon the work, in which, after the disembarkation of the troops was concluded, they received the coöperation of columns 1 and 2 of the fleet, comprising all the large vessels, which were posted very nearly as at the first attack. Column 3 remained to cover the landing and help get the field artillery, munitions, and commissary stores on shore.

The bombardment of the iron-clads was very effective, and that of the combined iron-clads and wooden ships, lasting from 4.30 P. M. to 6 P. M., the most tremendous, perhaps, in the annals of this or of any war, considering the weight of metal thrown, and the force with which it struck the fort. The iron-clads alone, with thirty guns, fired in the course of the day upward of 2,000 shells, or about four per minute; and during the grand bombardment it was reckoned that four shots were fired from the fleet each second, or about 20,000 in all. The rebels were pretty effectually kept within the shelter of their bomb-proofs while this *feu d'infer* continued, and could inflict but a trifling amount of damage upon the fleet. "Indeed," says Admiral Porter, "I do not see how they could fire at all after lines one and two got fairly anchored in position." At dark the wooden vessels drew off for the night, but the iron-clads remained at their anchorage, firing an occasional shell.

As soon as the troops were landed pickets were thrown out, who encountered the enemy's outposts; and from a few prisoners taken shortly afterward, it was ascertained that Hoke's division, stationed at Fort Fisher on the former attack, and which it was supposed had been sent south, was still in the neighborhood. Gen. Terry's first object after landing was to throw a defensive line across the peninsula from Cape Fear River to the sea, to protect his rear from an attack from the direction of Wilmington while he was operating against Fort Fisher. After two impracticable surveys, occupying many hours, a line was finally selected at 2 A. M. on the 14th, having an average distance of about two miles from the fort. Entrenchments were at once commenced, and by 8 o'clock on the morning of the 14th, a good breastwork, reaching from the river to the sea and partially covered by abatis, had been constructed. During the day this work was considerably strengthened, and the artillery, as fast as it was landed, was placed in position on the line. A careful reconnoissance satisfied Gen. Terry that, in view of the difficulty of conducting a regular siege on the narrow and exposed peninsula in such an inclement season of the year, the better policy would be to attempt an immediate assault. This decision coincided with Admiral Porter's views, and both commanders went heartily to work to arrange a plan of attack, the main feature of which, on the part of the navy, was to be a severe bombardment of the fort by the fleet, to cover the assaulting column, and to be continued against other parts of the work, after the assault had been commenced. It was also decided that the attack should be made at 3 P. M. of the 15th, and that the army should assault the western half of the land face, while a coöperating body of sailors and marines attacked the northeast bastion. A slow and deliberate fire was maintained against the fort during the day, with the object mainly of dismounting or disabling the guns on that part of the work where the assault was to be made, and also of demolishing the palisade sufficiently to admit the passage of troops.

At 11 A. M. of the 15th all the vessels of the fleet were in position and commenced a fire, "magnificent alike for its power and accuracy," which, as on previous occasions, silenced nearly every gun in the fort. Under its cover 1,600 sailors, armed with cutlasses, revolvers, and carbines, and 400 marines, and the whole commanded by Fleet Captain K. R. Breese, were landed on the beach, and by digging rifle-pits worked their way up within 200 yards of the fort. The troops selected for the assault were Ames's division, comprising the brigades of Curtis, Pennybacker, and Bell, while Paine's division of colored troops and Abbott's brigade held the intrenchments facing Wilmington, against which Hoke's troops, estimated at 5,000 strong, had begun to demonstrate. At 3.30 P. M. signal was made from the shore to the fleet to change the direction of the fire, in order that the troops might assault; and soon afterwards the sailors rushed with reckless energy toward the parapet of the fort, which at once swarmed with rebel soldiers, who poured in upon them a murderous fire of musketry. The marines, who were to have covered the assaulting party, for some unexplained reason failed to fire upon the rebels on the parapet, all of whom, in the opinion of Admiral Porter, an eye-witness of the fight, might have been killed. "I saw," he said, "how recklessly the rebels exposed themselves, and what an advantage they gave our sharpshooters, whose guns were scarcely fired, or fired with no precision. Notwithstanding the hot fire, officers and sailors in the lead rushed on, and some even reached the parapet, a large number having reached the ditch. The advance was swept from the parapet like chaff, and, notwithstanding all the efforts made by the commanders of companies to stay them, the men in the rear, seeing the slaughter in front, and that they were not covered by the marines, commenced to retreat; and, as there is no stopping a sailor if he fails on such an occasion on the first rush, I saw the whole thing had to be given up." The attack on this part of the fort, though a failure, diverted a part of the enemy's attention, and rendered the work laid out for the main storming column of troops much easier.

At the word of command, the division of Gen. Ames, which had been gradually drawn forward under the shelter of hastily-formed breastworks, rushed toward the fort, the brigade of Curtis taking the lead. The palisades had been so much injured by the fire of the fleet that a few vigorous strokes from the axemen sufficed to clear gaps for the passage of the troops, and in the face of a severe enfilading fire a lodgment was soon effected on the west end of the land front. Pennybacker's and Bell's brigades followed in rapid succession, the latter moving between the work and the river. "On this side," says Gen. Terry, "there was no regular parapet, but there was an abundance of cover afforded to the enemy by cavities from which sand had been taken for the parapet, the ruins of barracks and storehouses, the large magazine, and by traverses behind which they stubbornly resisted our advance. Hand to hand fighting of the most desperate character ensued, the traverses of the land face being used successively by the enemy as breastworks, over the tops of which the contending parties fired in each other's faces. Nine of these were carried, one after the other, by our men." At five o'clock, when about half of the land front of the fort had been thus captured, it became apparent that more troops were needed to support the assaulting column, and Abbott's brigade was ordered up, its place in the defensive line facing Wilmington being supplied by the sailors and marines. The attack then went on with redoubled fury, the fire of the navy meanwhile continuing upon that part of the work not occupied by the Federal troops, and upon the beach on Cape Fear River, under the apprehension that reënforcements might be thrown over there by the rebels from the right bank of the river. All this time signals between the land and naval forces were exchanged with great exactness, and the coöperation between the two services was in the highest degree harmonious and useful. By 9 P. M. two more traverses were carried, and an hour later Abbott's brigade drove the enemy from their remaining stronghold, and the occupation of the work was complete. The enemy fell gradually back to Federal Point, where, being cut off from further retreat, they surrendered unconditionally about midnight. About 4 P. M. Hoke had advanced against Paine's division, as if intending a general assault, but retired after a slight skirmish with the outposts. The garrison originally numbered over 2,300 men, of whom 1,971, with 112 officers, were captured. The rest were killed and wounded. Their commanders, Gen. Whiting and Col. Lamb, were captured, badly wounded. Of the three brigade commanders of Ames's division, Curtis and Pennybacker were severely, and Bell was mortally wounded, and the total Federal loss, according to official accounts, footed up as follows:

	Killed.		*Wounded.*		*Miss.*
	Officers.	Men.	Officers.	Men.	Men.
Curtis's brigade.......	2	35	18	166	9
Pennybacker's brigade.	7	24	15	183	72
Bell's brigade.........	2	15	4	105	—
Abbott's brigade......	—	3	2	18	11
Total...............	11	77	29	472	92
Aggregate........	....	..	....	......	691

The fleet suffered a loss of between two and three hundred in killed and wounded, principally in the assaulting column of sailors and marines, and two 15-inch guns were exploded on board the monitors. In other respects the ships experienced little damage.

The greater part of the guns of the fort were dismounted, or otherwise injured by the fire of the fleet, but the work itself received no damage which was not susceptible of immediate repair, its strength being about the same as before the bombardment. According to Admiral Porter, who had visited the Malakoff during the siege of Sebastopol, it was a much more formidable work than that celebrated stronghold, and its capture caused an almost unprecedented rejoicing throughout the United States. The capture of the fort having sealed the fate of the rebel supremacy in Cape Fear River, their remaining works covering the mouth of the river, including Fort Caswell and the forts at Smith's Island, Smithville, and Reeves's Point, together with the gunboats Chickamauga and Tallahassee, were destroyed or evacuated, whereby 169 guns and large amounts of ammunition and commissary stores fell into the hands of the Federals. Among the guns were some English ones of Sir William Armstrong's make. Admiral Porter immediately sent some of his light draught gunboats into the river, and by a skilful ruse decoyed several blockade-runners under the shelter of Fort Caswell, where they were of course speedily captured.

The operations of the South Atlantic Squadron were much curtailed by a variety of circumstances, the chief of which was the withdrawal of the greater part of the troops of the Department of the South, under Gen. Gillmore, to reënforce the Army of the James. Deprived of this necessary coöperative branch, Admiral Dahlgren found it impossible to make any serious demonstration against Charleston, and the fleet in that quarter was principally employed in blockade duties. A detachment of vessels coöperated in the St. John's River with the army movements in Florida in the spring, and subsequently in demonstrations against James's Island, Bull's Bay, and other places. On Feb. 17th the gunboat Housatonic was destroyed by a torpedo off Charleston, and two small armed steamers, the Columbine and Water Witch, fell into the enemy's hands in the course of the year.

The chief events in the history of the West Gulf squadron were those connected with the capture of the fortifications guarding the entrance to the bay of Mobile, and the consequent closing of that port against the blockade-runners. Although in many respects it was desirable to obtain possession of these works, the exigencies of the service in other quarters had not previously permitted the coöperation of so large a body of troops as was needed for the undertaking. The rebels availed themselves of this circumstance to construct several iron-clads and armed vessels, and threatened to raise the blockade of Mobile. Early in the year Admiral Farragut reconnoitred the approaches to the city, and offered, with the assistance of an iron-clad or two and a few thousand troops, to gain full possession of the bay; but as neither of these could at once be obtained, he was forced to confine himself to threatening demonstrations, although, as he privately informed the Naval Department, should the rebel iron-clads come out to attack his wooden fleet, the issue would necessarily be a doubtful one. He, however, expressed himself in readiness to measure his strength with Admiral Buchanan, whenever the latter should venture to offer battle, and kept his fleet in constant readiness for such a contingency.

At length, in the latter part of July, Admiral Farragut received an addition of four monitors to his squadron, the Tecumseh, Winnebago, Manhattan, and Chickasaw, and a coöperative land force under Gen. Granger was promised by Gen. Canby, commanding the military division of the southwest. The entrance to Mobile Bay is divided by Dauphin Island into two passages, the easterly of which is about four miles wide and twenty feet deep, and the other a shallow strait of not above five feet depth. On either side of the main channel stand Forts Gaines and Morgan, the former occupying the east end of Dauphin Island, and the latter the end of a long sandy point which makes out into the bay directly opposite. The channel runs close under the guns of Fort Morgan, and a large part of it had been obstructed with piles and torpedoes. Fort Morgan was a powerful stone, casemated work, mounting forty-eight guns, including some of very heavy calibre, and the armament of Fort Gaines consisted of twenty-one guns. About a mile distant from Fort Gaines, on Dauphin Island, was Fort Powell, a lesser work, adjoining which were a water battery and some earthworks. On the evening of Aug. 4th the monitors and wooden vessels were all assembled off the bar of Mobile Bay, and at 5.40 A. M. of the 5th the whole fleet moved up the bay in the following order, two abreast and lashed together: the Brooklyn with the Octorara on the port side, the Hartford and Metacomet, the Richmond and Port Royal, the Lackawanna and Seminole, the Monongahela and Kennebec, the Ossipee and Itasca, and the Oneida and Galena. Between the four first couples and Fort Morgan, at a distance of about two hundred yards from the latter, moved the monitors, headed by the Tecumseh, for the double purpose of keeping down the fire of the water-battery and parapet guns of the fort, and attacking the rebel iron-clads when the fort was passed. The object of coupling the wooden ships, an expedient as novel as it was ingenious, was to insure mutual protection by enabling each to tow along its consort, in case the latter should be crippled. The Admiral was on board his flag-ship the Hartford, and in order to get an unobstructed view of operations, and to give his orders with clearness, caused himself to be lashed to the main-top.

At about seven o'clock, as the head of the column came abreast of the fort, the latter opened fire, and the action soon became general. The enemy confidently expected, from the close quarters at which the fighting was to take place, to be able to sink or disable several of the attacking vessels. But here, as at the passage of the forts in Mississippi in 1862, Farragut converted what might well have seemed a disadvantage into a positive advantage to himself, by pouring such continuous broadsides into the fort as to drive the gunners from their guns, and enable the ships to pass with comparatively slight damage. At 7.40, while the firing was at its height, and the fleet making rapid progress in spite of the obstructions in its path, the monitor Tecumseh struck a torpedo, which blew a large hole through her bottom, just under the turret, and almost imediately she filled with water and sank. At this moment the Brooklyn, by backing her engines to avoid torpedoes, temporarily arrested the progress of the fleet, and the Admiral, regardless of torpedoes, at once dashed to the head of the column, first despatching a boat from the Metacomet to pick up the survivors of the Tecumseh. Of these only four officers and seventeen men were found; four swam ashore and were made prisoners, and the rest, with her commander, T. A. M. Craven, were drowned.

Soon after eight o'clock the whole column had passed the forts, with no serious disaster beyond the loss of the Tecumseh. The Oneida, which brought up the rear, and was consequently more exposed to the fire of the fort than the rest of the fleet, had her boiler penetrated by a 7-inch rifle-shell, and was deprived of motive power; but she was towed safely along by her consort, the Galena, and made good use of her guns until the fort was passed. Meanwhile the rebel fleet, consisting of the iron-clad ram Tennessee and the gunboats Selma, Gaines, and Morgan, had held a position inside the bay a little north of Fort Morgan, whence they poured a galling fire upon the fleet. The Tennessee, under the immediate command of Admiral Buchanan, made a dash at the Hartford and several other ships, during the passage of the fort, but subsequently sought shelter under its guns; and under the supposition that she had retired from the fight, Admiral Farragut ordered the fleet to cast off their couplings and come to anchor, with the exception of the light-draught gunboats, which were directed to pursue and destroy the Selma, Morgan, and Gaines. The Metacomet captured the Selma after a brisk engagement, but the Morgan and Gaines succeeded in getting under the protection of Fort Morgan. The former subsequently crept along the shore during the night into Mobile, but the latter was so seriously injured that she had to be destroyed. Several of the large ships were already at anchor, when, shortly before nine o'clock, the Tennessee was seen standing toward the Hartford, with the desperate intention apparently of fighting single-handed the whole fleet. Of the singular combat that followed, the following description is given by Admiral Farragut:

I was not long in comprehending his intentions to be the destruction of the flag-ship. The monitors, and such of the wooden vessels as I thought best adapted for the purpose, were immediately ordered to attack the ram, not only with their guns, but bows on at full speed, and then began one of the fiercest naval combats on record. The Monongahela, Commander Strong, was the first vessel that struck her, and in doing so carried away his own iron prow, together with the cutwater, without apparently doing her adversary much injury. The Lackawanna, Capt. Marchand, was the next vessel to strike her, which she did at full speed; but though her stem was cut and crushed to the plank ends for the distance of three feet above the water's edge to five feet below, the only perceptible effect on the ram was to give her a heavy list. The Hartford was the third vessel which struck her, but, as the Tennessee quickly shifted her helm, the blow was a glancing one, and as she rasped along our side, we poured our whole port broadside of 9-inch solid shot within ten feet of her casement. The monitors worked slowly, but delivered their fire as opportunity offered. The Chickasaw succeeded in getting under her stern, and a 15-inch shot from the Manhattan broke through her iron plating and heavy wooden backing, though the missile itself did not enter the vessel. Immediately after the collision with the flag-ship I directed Capt. Drayton to bear down for the ram again. He was doing so at full speed, when, unfortunately, the Lackawanna run into the Hartford just forward of the mizzen-mast, cutting her down to within two feet of the water's edge. We soon got clear again, however, and were fast approaching our adversary, when she struck her colors and run up the white flag.

She was at this time sore beset; the Chickasaw was pounding away at her stern, the Ossipee was approaching her at full speed, and the Monongahela, Lackawanna, and this ship were bearing down upon her, determined upon her destruction. Her smoke-stack had been shot away, her steering chains were gone, compelling a resort to her relieving tackles, and several of her port shutters were jammed. Indeed, from the time the Hartford struck her until her surrender, she never fired a gun. As the Ossipee, Commander Le Roy, was about to strike her, she hoisted the white flag, and that vessel immediately stopped her engine, though not in time to avoid a glancing blow. During this contest with the rebel gunboats and the ram Tennessee, and which terminated by her surrender at 10 o'clock, we lost many more men than from the fire of the batteries of Fort Morgan.

The Tennessee, as was effectually shown by the determined resistance which she made, was perhaps the strongest vessel ever constructed by the enemy. She was 209 feet in length, with a breadth of beam of 48 feet, had in the centre an external casement, with sloping sides, about 80 feet in length by 30 feet in breadth, and drew about 14 feet of water. Her deck was plated with 2 inches of wrought-iron, her sides with 4 inches, and her casemate with from 5 to 6 inches. Her armament consisted of 4 6-inch broadside rifles, and 2 7-inch pivot rifles, all of the Brooks pattern. But one shot, a 15-inch one from the Manhattan, penetrated her armor, and, in view of the hard pounding which she received, her injuries were on the whole inconsiderable. Admiral Buchanan lost a leg in the action, and ten or twelve of the crew were killed and wounded. The prisoners surrendered numbered 20 officers and about 170 men; and those on the Selma, 90 officers and men. The casualties in the fleet, exclusive of those on board the Tecumseh, were 52 killed and 170 wounded.

Meanwhile, on the 4th, a coöperative body of troops under Gen. Granger had landed on Dauphin Island, in accordance with an arrangement between Admiral Farragut and Gen. Canby, and commenced the siege of Fort Gaines. The rebel commander, Colonel Anderson, seeing that the Federal fleet held uninterrupted possession of Mobile Bay, concluded that further resistance was hopeless, and on the 7th surrendered his garrison of 818 men unconditionally. Fort Powell had been blown up by the rebels on the evening of the 5th. These obstructions being removed and Grant's Pass secured, the fleet was relieved from any apprehensions with regard to obtaining supplies; but it was nevertheless determined to complete the work originally undertaken by the capture of Fort Morgan, which still held out. The troops were accordingly transferred to the rear of the fort, and lines of investment drawn across the sandy spit on which it is situated. On the 22d, fire was opened from the shore batteries and the fleet, and on the next day Gen. Page, the rebel commander, surrendered unconditionally. When possession was taken of the work it was found that, with what Admiral Farragut called "childish spitefulness," he had destroyed many of the guns and other property which had been surrendered. Thenceforth during the year Mobile was effectually cut off from external commerce.

In the course of the year, says the Secretary of the Navy, "the three English-built piratical cruisers which, under the rebel flag, have, during the last two years, roamed the seas, robbing and destroying our merchantmen, shunning all armed antagonists, and have found refuge and protection, and too often supplies and other assistance, in neutral ports, have terminated their predatory career." These were the Alabama, the Florida, and the Georgia—the first sunk off Cherbourg by the Kearsarge, the second captured in Bahia harbor by the Wachusett, and the third captured at sea, off the coast of

Portugal, by the Niagara. Early in June the Alabama, after a prosperous career among the American merchantmen in the Southern Atlantic and Indian Oceans, returned to northern waters and put into Cherbourg. The Kearsarge, Captain John A. Winslow, then lying at Flushing, immediately sailed for Cherbourg to watch the movements of the Alabama; and on June 15th her commander received a note from Captain Semmes of the privateer, announcing his intention to fight the Kearsarge, and begging Captain Winslow not to depart until the two vessels could have an opportunity to measure their strength. As this was precisely what the Federal commander desired, he willingly awaited the movements of his adversary. The relative proportions and armaments of the two antagonists were as follows:

	Alabama.		Kearsarge.	
Length over all	220	feet	214¼	feet.
Length on water line	210	"	198½	"
Beam	32	"	33	"
Depth	17	"	16	"
Horse-power, two engines of.	300	each.	400	h. power.
Tonnage	1,150		1,030	

Armament of the Alabama.—One 7-inch Blakely rifle; one 8-inch smooth-bore 68-pounder; six 32-pounders.

Armament of the Kearsage.—Two 11-inch smooth-bore guns; one 30-pounder rifle; four 32-pounders.

The Kearsarge had twenty-two officers and one hundred and forty men, and the Alabama, so far as can be ascertained, about one hundred and forty officers and men, the greater part of the ship's company consisting of British subjects. Her gunners were trained artillerists from the British practice-ship Excellent. Availing himself of an ingenious expedient for the protection of his machinery, first adopted by Admiral Farragut in running past the rebel forts on the Mississippi in 1862, Capt. Winslow had hung all his spare anchor-cable over the midship section of the Kearsarge on either side; and in order to make the addition less unsightly, the chains were boxed over with inch deal boards, forming a sort of case, which stood out at right angles to the side of the vessel.

At twenty minutes past ten on Sunday morning, June 19th, the Alabama was seen standing out from Cherbourg harbor, accompanied by the French iron-clad Couronne, and followed by the steam yacht Deer-hound, whose owner, an Englishmen named Lancaster, was on board with his family, ostensibly to witness the engagement, but really, as it subsequently appeared, to act as a tender to the Alabama. Upon seeing the Alabama approach, Capt. Winslow kept out to sea a few miles, in order "that the positions of the ships should be so far off shore that no questions could be advanced about the line of jurisdiction." Upon reaching a point about seven miles from the land the Kearsarge put about, and steered directly for the Alabama, which first opened fire at a range of about a mile. The following account of the fight that ensued is given by Capt. Winslow:

Immediately I ordered more speed; but in two minutes the Alabama had again loaded, and fired another broadside, and following it with a third, without damaging us except in rigging. We had now arrived within nine hundred yards of her, and I was apprehensive that another broadside, nearly raking as it was, would prove disastrous. I accordingly ordered the Kearsarge sheered, and opened on the Alabama.

The positions of the vessels were now broadside to broadside, but it was soon apparent that Captain Semmes did not seek close action. I became then fearful lest, after some fighting, that he would again make for the shore. To defeat this I determined to keep full speed on, and with a port helm to run under the stern of the Alabama, and rake, if he did not prevent it by sheering and keeping his broadside to us. He adopted this mode as a preventive, and, as a consequence, the Alabama was forced, with a full head of steam, into a circular track during the engagement.

The effect of this manœuvre was such that, at the last of the action, when the Alabama would have made off, she was near five miles from the shore; and had the action continued from the first in parallel lines, with her head in shore, the line of jurisdiction would no doubt have been reached.

The firing of the Alabama from the first was rapid and wild; toward the close of the action her firing became better. Our men, who had been cautioned against rapid firing without direct aim, were much more deliberate; and the instructions given to point the heavy guns below rather than above the water line, and clear the deck with the lighter ones, were fully observed. I had endeavored with a port helm to close in with the Alabama, but it was not until just before the close of the action that we were in a position to use grape; this was avoided, however, by her surrender. The effect of the training of our men was evident; nearly every shot from our guns was telling fearfully on the Alabama, and on the seventh rotation on the circular track she winded, setting fore trysail and two jibs, with head in shore.

Her speed was now retarded, and by winding her port broadside was presented to us with only two guns bearing, not having been able, as I learned afterward, to shift over but one. I saw now that she was at our mercy, and a few more guns well directed brought down her flag. I was unable to ascertain whether they had been hauled down or shot away, but a white flag having been displayed over the stern, followed by two guns fired to leeward, our fire was reserved. Two minutes had not more than elapsed before she again opened on us with the two guns on the port side. This drew our fire again, and the Kearsarge was immediately steamed ahead and lay across her bows for raking.

The white flag was still flying, and our fire was again reserved. Shortly after this her boats were seen to be lowering, and an officer in one of them came alongside and informed us the ship had surrendered and was fast sinking. In twenty minutes from this time the Alabama went down, her mainmast, which had received a shot, breaking near the head as she sunk, and her bow rising high out of the water as her stern rapidly settled. The fire of the Alabama, although it is stated she discharged three hundred and seventy or more shell and shot, was not of serious damage to the Kearsarge. Some thirteen or fourteen of these had taken effect in and about the hull, and sixteen or seventeen about the waste and rigging.

The boats of the Kearsarge were at once sent to receive the officers and crew of the Alabama, but so rapidly did she go down that it was impossible to save them all without assistance. Capt. Winslow accordingly requested the Deer-hound, which had meanwhile come alongside, to assist in the rescue of his prisoners. The crew of the privateer were by this time struggling for their lives in the water, and many of the wounded men went down. In the confusion of the moment the Deerhound, after picking up forty-one persons, including Semmes, who was wounded, steamed off toward the English coast, and when observed had got too much the start to be overhauled. The total number brought on board the Kearsarge was sixty-nine, of whom seventeen were wounded; and twelve were picked up and carried into Cherbourg by two French pilot boats. Several of the wounded died soon after, and the total number of officers and men belonging to the Alabama who were landed in France or England, amounted to one hundred and fifteen. The casualties of the Kearsarge amounted to only three wounded. This most remarkable sea fight between single ships that has occurred within the century was witnessed by thousands of spectators on the French shore, and the result produced a profound impression in Europe and America. The conduct of Semmes in throwing his sword into the sea after surrendering, and also in allowing himself to be carried into a neutral port by the Deerhound, formed the subject of severe strictures in the United States.

The Florida, while lying in the neutral port of Bahia, Brazil, was captured by Capt. N. Collins of the Wachusett, as appears by the following brief report:

St. Thomas, W. I. Islands, Oct. 31.

Hon. Gideon Welles. *Sir:* I have the honor to report the arrival here of this ship, with the rebel steamer Florida in company. The Florida, with 58 men and 12 officers, was captured about 3 o'clock on the morning of the 7th of October, in the bay of San Salvador, Brazil, by the officers and crew of this vessel, without loss of life. We also captured five of the officers, including her commander. The remainder of her crew were on shore.

The Florida had her mizzen-mast and main-yard carried away and her bulwarks cut down. This vessel sustained no injury, A detailed report will be handed to you by Paymaster W. W. Williams.

Very respectfully your obd'nt serv't,
N. COLLINS, Com. U. S. Steam-sloop Wachusett.

In November the Florida was brought into Hampton Roads, and while lying there to await the decision of the delicate international questions which her capture evolved, was accidentally run into by a steam transport and sunk.

The Georgia was captured by the Niagara on August 15th. Although having no armament on board at the time, she was seized as a lawful prize, and sent to the United States for adjudication.

CHAPTER XLVIII.

Number of Southern Troops—Measures to arm the Slaves—Objections—Recruiting the Union Armies—Military Departments—Condition of the Southern States—Debt—Paper Currency—Peace Movements—Gilmore and Jacques—Unofficial Conference at Clifton—Proceedings at Fortress Monroe—Report of President Lincoln—Report of Messrs. Stephens, Hunter, and Campbell—Action of Congress relative to Slaves—Finances of the Federal Government—Exchange of Prisoners.

It is proper to notice the measures which had been adopted to maintain the large armies which fought the battles in 1864. The acts of the Congress at Richmond, by which their armies were formed, were revised at the beginning of 1864. On December 28, 1863, it was enacted that no person liable to military service should be permitted, or allowed to furnish a substitute for such service; on January 5, 1864, it was enacted that no person liable to military service should be exempted by reason of his having furnished a substitute. In February, a general military act was passed.

Under the provisions of this bill, almost the whole male population could be employed either in the army or in raising supplies. On the 5th of October, an order was issued revoking all details, furloughs, and temporary exemptions of men, between the ages of eighteen and forty-five. At the session in December, 1864, a new bill was introduced which omitted the exemption of fifteen field hands.

These acts were never executed strictly. In November the States of North Carolina and Georgia had respectively fourteen thousand and fifteen thousand exempts acting as State officers. More than thirty thousand were estimated to be exempted as State officers by the Conscription Bureau, and a hundred thousand from physical disability. The number of physicians exempted was estimated between three and four thousand; and farmers, one hundred and fourteen thousand.

No facts can at present be obtained by which to determine the strength of the armies in the field, or the real military power of the Confederacy. The following estimate was published at Richmond, Dec., 1864:

Number between 17 and 50 in 1860		1,299,700
Arrived at 17 since 1860		331,650
Total		1,631,350
Deduct for ordinary mortality	200,000	
For population within enemy's lines	340,515	
For losses in battle, and by unusual diseases	225,000	
		765,515
Remainder		865,835
Deduct 10 per cent. for exemptions for disability and other causes	86,584	
Prisoners in the enemy's hands	50,000	
		136,584
Subject to military duty		729,251
Left the country		36,462
Total		692,789

It was also stated at that time that if one-third of this number (230,932) were added to the army in the field, it would consist of

461,844 men. From this it might be inferred that the force then in the field was 230,912. This is about the number of veteran troops estimated to be in the service at the beginning of the year, to which 120,000 conscripts were added. The number of youths passing annually from sixteen to seventeen years of age, was estimated at 62,000.

The Secretary of War, in his report at the session of Congress in November, alludes to the enlistment of negroes as at that time unnecessary. He says:

While it is encouraging to know this resource for further and future efforts at our command, my own judgment does not yet either perceive the necessity or approve the policy of employing slaves in the higher duties of soldiers; they are confessedly inferior in all respects to our white citizens in the qualifications of the soldier, and I have thought we have within the military age as large a proportion of our whole population as will be required or can be advantageously employed in active military operations. If, then, the negro be employed in the war, the inferior is preferred to the superior agent for the work. In such a war as this, waged against foes bent with malignant persistence on our destruction, and for all that man holds priceless—the most vital work is that of the soldier, and for it wisdom and duty require the most fitting workmen. The superior instrumentalities should be preferred. It will not do, in my opinion, to risk our liberties and safety on the negro while the white man may be called to the sacred duty of defence. For the present it seems best to leave the subordinate labors of society to the negro, and to impose its highest, as now existing, on the superior class.

The use of the slaves as soldiers with the reward of freedom to those who survived, was strongly advocated during the year. From the beginning of hostilities they were the laborers on the fortifications in all parts of the Confederacy. At the same early period both the free and slave offered their services, and the former in considerable numbers enrolled themselves. In June, 1861, the Legislature of Tennessee passed an act to authorize the Governor to receive into the military service free persons of color between the ages of fifteen and fifty. Pay and rations were assigned to them. In September one regiment, numbering fourteen hundred, appeared on the field at the review of troops in New Orleans. In February, 1862, the subject of enrolling the free negroes was discussed in the Legislature of Virginia, and an act passed to provide for their enlistment. The next step was the threat to draft slaves to work on the fortifications when refused to hire them. This was made by Gov. Brown, of Georgia, in November, 1862. During the next year they were extensively employed as pioneers, sappers, cooks, nurses, and teamsters, and their employment as a military arm in defence of the country was advocated in Congress. In February, 1864, Congress passed an act making all "male free negroes (with certain exceptions) between the ages of eighteen and fifty," liable to perform such duties in the army, or in connection with the military defences of the country, in the way of work upon fortifications, or in Government works, etc., as the Secretary of War might from time to time prescribe, and providing them rations, clothing, and compensation. The Secretary of War was also authorized to employ for similar duty twenty thousand male negro slaves, and their owners were guaranteed against escape or death. He was authorized to impress the slaves when he could not hire them; and general orders No. 32, March 11, 1864, directed the enrolment of the free negroes, and their assignment to the performance of the duties mentioned in the act. Also the employment and impressment of slaves was ordered by the same general orders.

A bill to arm the slaves passed the House of Congress in the spring of 1865, but was lost in the Senate by one vote. The Legislature of Virginia instructed her Senators to vote for it. Whereupon it was reconsidered in the Senate in the following form:

A Bill to Increase the Military Forces of the Confederate States.

The Congress of the Confederate States of America do enact, That in order to provide additional forces to repel invasion, maintain the rightful possession of the Confederate States, secure their independence, and preserve their institutions, the President be, and he is hereby, authorized to ask for and accept from the owners of slaves the services of such number of able-bodied negro men as he may deem expedient, for and during the war, to perform military service in whatever capacity he may direct.

SECTION 2. That the General-in-Chief be authorized to organize the said slaves into companies, battalions, regiments, and brigades, under such rules and regulations as the Secretary of War may prescribe, and to be commanded by such officers as the President may appoint.

SEC. 3. That while employed in the service the said troops shall receive the same rations, clothing, and compensation as are allowed to other troops in the same branch of the service.

SEC. 4. That if, under the previous section of this act, the President shall not be able to raise a sufficient number of troops to prosecute the war successfully and maintain the sovereignty of the States and the independence of the Confederate States, then he is hereby authorized to call on each State, whenever he thinks it expedient, for her quota of three hundred thousand troops, in addition to those subject to military service under existing laws, or so many thereof as the President may deem necessary, to be raised from such classes of the population, irrespective of color, in each State, as the proper authorities thereof may determine.

SEC. 5. That nothing in this act shall be construed to authorize a change in the relation of the said slave.

The Senate amended it as follows:

Provided, That not more than twenty-five per cent. of the male slaves between the ages of eighteen and forty-five in any State shall be called for under the provisions of this act.

It was then passed and sent to the House, where the amendment was approved by the following vote:

YEAS.—Messrs. Anderson, Barksdale, Batson, Baylor, Blandford, Bradley, H. W. Bruce, Carroll, Clark, Clopton, Conrad, Darden, De Jarnette, Dickinson, Dupre, Elliott, Ewing, Funstein, Gaither, Goode, Gray, Hanley, Johnston, Keeble, Lyon, Machen, Marshall, McMullen, Menees, Miller, Moore, Murray,

Perkins, Read, Russell, Simpson, Snead, Staples, Triplett, and Villere—40.

NAYS.—Messrs. Atkins, Baldwin, Chambers, Colyar, Cruikshank, Fuller, Gholson, Gilmer, Hartridge, Hatcher, Herbert, Holliday, J. M. Leach, J. T. Leach, Logan, McCallum, Ramsay, Rogers, Sexton, J. M. Smith, Smith of North Carolina, Turner, Wickham, Wilkes, Witherspoon, Mr. Speaker—26.

When the bill was on its passage in the Senate, after the instructions of the Virginia Legislature, Mr. Hunter, of Virginia, said: When we left the old Government we had thought we had got rid forever of the slavery agitation; that we were entering into a new Confederacy of homogeneous States where the agitation of the slavery question, which had become intolerable under the old Union, was to have no place. But to his surprise he finds that this Government assumes the power to arm the slaves, which involves also the power of emancipation. To the agitation of this question, the assumption of this power, he dated the origin of the gloom which now overspreads our people. They knew that if our liberties were to be achieved it was to be done by the hearts and the hands of free men. It also injured us abroad. It was regarded as a confession of despair and an abandonment of the ground upon which we had seceded from the old Union. We had insisted that Congress had no right to interfere with slavery, and upon the coming into power of the party who, it was known, would assume and exercise that power, we seceded. We had also then contended that whenever the two races were thrown together, one must be master and the other slave, and we vindicated ourselves against the accusations of Abolitionists by asserting that slavery was the best and happiest condition of the negro. Now what does this proposition admit? The right of the central Government to put the slaves into the militia, and to emancipate at least so many as shall be placed in the military service. It is a clear claim of the central Government to emancipate the slaves.

If we are right in passing this measure we were wrong in denying to the old Government the right to interfere with the institution of slavery and to emancipate slaves. Besides, if we offer slaves their freedom as a boon, we confess that we were insincere, were hypocritical, in asserting that slavery was the best state for the negroes themselves. He had been sincere in declaring that the central Government had no power over the institution of slavery, and that freedom would be no boon to the negro.

He now believed, as he had formerly said in discussion on the same subject, that arming and emancipating the slaves was an abandonment of this contest—an abandonment of the grounds upon which it had been undertaken. If this is so, who is to answer for the hundreds of thousands of men who had been slain in the war? Who was to answer for them before the bar of Heaven? Not those who had entered into the contest upon principle and adhered to the principle, but those who had abandoned the principle. Not for all the gold in California would he have put his name to such a measure as this, unless obliged to do it by instructions. As long as he was free to vote from his own convictions nothing could have extorted it from him.

Mr. Hunter then argued the necessity of freeing the negroes if they were made soldiers. There was something in the human heart and head that tells us it must be so; when they come out scarred from this conflict they must be free. If we could make them soldiers, the condition of the soldier being socially equal to any other in society, we could make them officers, perhaps, to command white men. Some future ambitious President might use the slaves to seize the liberties of the country, and put the white men under his feet. The Government had no power under the Constitution to arm and emancipate the slaves, and the Constitution granted no such great powers by implication.

Mr. Hunter then showed from statistics that no considerable body of negro troops could be raised in the States over which the Government had control without stripping the country of the labor absolutely necessary to produce food. He thought there was a much better chance of getting the large number of deserters back to the army than of getting the slaves into it. The negro abhorred the profession of a soldier. The commandant of conscripts, with authority to impress twenty thousand slaves, had, between last September and the present time, been able to get but four thousand; and of these, thirty-five hundred had been obtained in Virginia and North Carolina, and five hundred from Alabama. If he, armed with all the powers of impressment, could not get them as laborers, how will we be able to get them as soldiers? Unless they volunteer they will go to the Yankees; if we depend upon their volunteering we can't get them, and those we do get will desert to the enemy, who can offer them a better price than we can. The enemy can offer them liberty, clothing, and even farms at our expense. Negroes now were deterred from going to the enemy only by the fear of being put into the army. If we put them in they would all go over.

In conclusion, he considered that the measure, when reviewed as to its expediency, was worse than as a question of principle.

A benevolent association, known as the Richmond Ambulance Corps, was early formed to look after the wounded in battle. Their agency was similar to the Sanitary Commission of the north. They have followed the Virginian army and been present in every battle. They have every appurtenance necessary in their humane vocation, such as hospital supplies, sugar, tea, coffee, etc., with utensils for preparing every thing on a large scale.

The stringency of the blockade compelled the inhabitants to manufacture the materials for war. The Ordnance Department organized twelve arsenals, eight armories, seven large harness shops, four powder mills, a laboratory for smelting lead, and many other small establishments. They supplied the army with two hundred field batteries, upwards of five hundred thousand small arms, several hundred thousand sets of infantry accoutrements, and millions of cartridges. A shoe establishment in Richmond, employed by the Government, made six hundred pairs daily. The material brought through the blockade in 1863, was estimated to be sufficient to put four hundred thousand men in the field.

So successful had been the manufacture of arms, that all the troops were provided with the best rifles, and the smooth bore nearly disappeared. The field artillery of the armies comprised more than a thousand pieces. The gun chiefly used was the 12-pounder Napoleon, to which had been added the 10-pounder Parrott. The number of cannon foundries built up since the commencement of the war was six; two of which had capacity to cast guns of the largest dimensions. Five powder mills were erected in different places, one of which alone was represented to be capable of producing all the powder required. Four hundred thousand percussion caps were manufactured in a day, and there was sufficient machinery to produce a million. The manufacture of the materials of war seemed to have reached such perfection, that it was asserted to be sufficient to supply all wants, without asking any thing from other countries.

During 1864 the number of men called for by the President of the United States to reenforce the army amounted in the aggregate to 1,500,000, although by an explanatory statement of the Provost Marshal General this number was in fact reduced to 1,200,000. Notwithstanding the impulse which the high bounties and premiums offered in 1863 gave to enlistments under the October call of that year for 300,000 men, the number of men realized seems to have been insufficient for the needs of the service, and on Feb. 1st, 1864, an order was issued by the President to draft 500,000 three years' men on March 10th, less the number enlisted or drafted into the service prior to March 1st, and not previously credited. This practically amounted to a call for 200,000, as appears by the following circular:

WAR DEPARTMENT, PROVOST MARSHAL GENERAL'S OFFICE, Feb. 1, 1864.

The President's order of this date, for a draft on tenth (10th) March for five hundred thousand (500,000) men, after deducting all who may be raised prior to March first (1) and not heretofore credited, is equivalent to a call for two hundred thousand (200,000) men in addition to the three hundred thousand (300,000) called for October seventeenth (17th). JAS. B. FRY, Prov. Mar. Gen.

By an order dated Jan. 14th, 1864, the Provost Marshal General also directed that the time for paying the bounty of $300 and $400, and the $15 and $25 premium, be extended to March 1st.

In anticipation of the momentous campaign which was impending, and the losses likely to be incurred by the troops in the field, the President on March 14th followed up his previous call by a supplementary one for 200,000 men, "to supply the force required to be drafted for the navy, and to provide an adequate reserve force for all contingencies."

The severe losses sustained by Gens. Grant and Sherman, the disasters connected with the Red River campaign, and other untoward circumstances, far more than neutralized the results obtained from the calls of February and March, and induced the President to make still another call on July 18th for 500,000 men, with the draft to take place on September 5th. Congress had meantime made important changes in the law of enrolment, as will be seen by the following extract from the proclamation:

Whereas, By the act approved July 4, 1864, entitled, "An act further to regulate and provide for the enrolling and calling out the national forces and for other purposes," it is provided that the President of the United States may, "at his discretion, at any time hereafter, call for any number of men, as volunteers, for the respective terms of one, two, and three years, for military service," and "that in case the quota, or any part thereof, of any town, township, or ward of a city, precinct, or election district, or of a county not so subdivided, shall not be filled within the space of fifty days after such call, then the President shall instantly order a draft for one year to fill such quota, or any part thereof, which may be unfilled;"

The allowance of credits having diminished the number of men to be obtained under this call to somewhat above 200,000 (although, according to the President's statement, 250,000 men were actually put into the army and navy under the call), a further call for 300,000 volunteers to serve for one, two, or three years, was issued on Dec. 20th. Quotas of States, districts, and sub-districts were directed to be assigned by the Provost Marshal General, and in case these should not be filled by Feb. 15th, 1865, a draft to supply the deficiency was ordered to commence forthwith.

The number of men called for during the year may be thus recapitulated:

Call of Feb. 1st	500,000
Call of March 14th	200,000
Call of July 18th	500,000
Call of Dec. 20th	300,000
	1,500,000

Deducting from this aggregate 300,000 men under the February call, who were really included in the October call of 1863, and 300,000 cancelled by credits on the July call, which made it equivalent to a call for 200,000, we have 900,000 as the number required to recruit the army and navy in 1864. If we also consider the December call as practically intended for 1865, the number is still further reduced to 600,000.

The fact that four calls for troops were made in the course of the year indicated either that the casualties of the service were greater than in any previous year of the war, or that the men called for were not in reality obtained, whatever the returns might show. The latter is in all probability the true cause of the frequency of the calls; and from their apparent inefficiency to recruit the army to an extent commensurate with the magnitude of its operations, it may be presumed that the military strength on January 1st, 1865, was not greater, if so great, as a year previous. The neglect of duty in the examining surgeons in passing men physically incapacitated for service, the frauds of bounty and substitute brokers, and the wholesale desertions of "bounty jumpers" (as those recruits or substitutes were called who systematically deserted after receiving their bounties, and often with the connivance of Government employés), reduced the number of enlistments to a comparatively small percentage; and hence the repeated calls of the President for additional men, instead of enormously increasing the strength of the army, barely enabled it to maintain its standard. On one point only an explicit official statement of the results of recruiting has been made public. The Provost Marshal General, in reference to the reënlistment of veteran volunteers during the fall of 1863, says: "Over one hundred and thirty-six thousand tried soldiers, who would otherwise, ere this, have been discharged, were secured for three years longer. Organizations which would have been lost to the service were preserved and recruited, and capable and experienced officers were retained in command. The force thus organized and retained has performed an essential part in the great campaign of 1864, and its importance to the country cannot be over-estimated."

A temporary addition was made to the army in the spring and summer of 1864 of a class of troops known as "Hundred-days men," numbering about 100,000, and voluntarily furnished by the governors of Ohio, Indiana, Illinois, Iowa, and Wisconsin. They were organized as regiments, and to serve one hundred days from the date of their muster into the service, unless sooner discharged. It was further stipulated that they should receive no bounty, nor be credited on any draft. Their services having been accepted, Congress appropriated $25,000,-000 for equipping them, and during May and June the hundred days' men went forward in large numbers to perform garrison duty and otherwise relieve old and disciplined troops, who were sent to the front.

Immediately after the call of July 18th for 400,000 men, the Provost Marshal General issued a series of instructions for the guidance of enlisting officers. The bounties provided by law were announced to be, for recruits—including representative recruits—(white or colored) for one year, $100; for two years, $200; for three years, $300. A first installment of bounty, amounting to one-third of the whole sum, was to be paid to the recruit when mustered in. The premiums previously paid for procuring recruits were discontinued, and neither drafted men nor substitutes, furnished either before or after the draft, were to be entitled to bounty from the United States. The "representative recruits," alluded to above, were those offered by persons not fit for military duty, and not liable to draft, from age or other causes, who desired to be personally represented in the army. The Provost Marshal General issued a circular to further this laudable project, and ordered the names of persons thus represented by recruits to be officially recorded. Many others, also, in anticipation of the draft, furnished substitutes for one, two, or three years, for whom they received no bounty from the General Government, although generally assisted by the town, county, or State in which they resided. The amount of these local bounties differed in different parts of the country. In the agricultural districts, where every able-bodied man could find abundant occupation during the harvesting season, it was no uncommon thing to offer from $1,200 to $1,500 for three years' recruits; and even among the large floating population of unnaturalized foreigners in the seaboard cities, from which substitutes were mainly drawn, the prices demanded were unprecedented in the history of the war.

The act of Congress of July 4th, 1864, having provided that the State Executive might "send recruiting agents into any of the States declared to be in rebellion, except the States of Arkansas, Tennessee, and Louisiana, to recruit volunteers, who should be duly credited to the States procuring them," a series of instructions on the subject were, on July 9th, promulgated by the War Department. The recruiting agents were to report through the commanding officers of certain designated rendezvous for the reception of this class of recruits, to the commander of the military district, department, or army in which such rendezvous might be situated, and were to be subject to all the rules and articles of war. Commanding officers were further directed to afford agents all reasonable facilities for the performance of their duties, to dismiss or arrest those guilty of improper conduct, and to prevent recruiting by unauthorized parties. Many of the States hastened to avail themselves of the opportunity thus offered to fill their quotas without drawing upon their population. Gov. Andrew, of Massachusetts, was one of the first to appoint recruiting agents, and the Executives of Ohio, Connecticut, Michigan, Maine, and other States, soon followed his example. Gov. Seymour, of New York, was among those who declined to act in the matter. In the opinion of many military men the new plan of recruitment within the lines of military operations, was objectionable; and commanding generals held it in particular disfavor on account of the opportunities it would afford for reckless and injurious competition among State agents, and for the infraction of sound military rules.

The result of the recruitment in the insurrectionary States was reported by the Provost

Marshal General as on the whole unfavorable, and the system was practically abolished.

The necessity of procuring substitutes from a class of the population not liable to draft, led to the enlistment of a large body of recruits of foreign birth, who had never been naturalized. Under these circumstances any considerable increase in the emigration from Europe to America was looked upon with suspicion by foreign governments or statesmen unfriendly to the United States, as having been caused by improper inducements, in violation of municiple law. It was even charged, by persons high in influence in England, that agents from the United States had visited Ireland and the British North American provinces, for the purpose of enlisting men in the army, and had despatched many recruits to America, ostensibly as mechanics or farm laborers. By a resolution adopted by the United States Senate, on May 24th, the President was requested to state if such was the fact.

The Secretary of State replied, that no authority to recruit abroad had been given by the United States Government, and that applications for such authority had been invariably rejected. The Government had no knowledge, he added, that any such recruits had been obtained in the provinces named, or in any foreign country.

Until 1864 the inferior standing of colored troops in the army with respect to bounty, pay, and pensions remained unchanged, notwithstanding the protest of the Secretary of War and other officials against the injustice thus done to men who shared all the dangers and privations of the war, and who were also liable to draft. The Army Appropriation Bill, passed in June, 1864, disposed of this vexed question by putting the colored soldiery on a footing with the white troops.

An order was soon after issued from the War Department to pay colored soldiers six months' full wages for the period embraced between January 1st and July 1st, 1864; and in August the Attorney-General, in accordance with the provisions of section 4, decided that colored men volunteering prior to 1864, were entitled to the same pay, bounty, and clothing, as other volunteers. By section 14 of the act of July 4, 1864, the widows and children of colored soldiers dying in battle, or of wounds or disease contracted in the military service, were declared entitled to pensions, provided such widows and children were free persons.

During the year colored troops continued to be enlisted into the army, principally in the Southern States, although several regiments, whose organization had commenced in the North in 1863, departed previous to July for the seat of war. If the statement of the Solicitor of the War Department be relied upon, upwards of 100,000 of this class of troops were enlisted in 1864. Opinions differed quite as much as in 1863, upon the propriety, politically considered, of employing negroes as soldiers, and upon their value in a military aspect; but toward the close of the year, in view of their soldierly conduct on various trying occasions, it seemed to become the settled conviction that they would form a useful branch of the service. The Corps d'Afrique organized by Gen. Banks in 1863, and intended to comprise about 15,000 men, was described in May, 1864, by an army correspondent in Louisiana, as greatly depleted in numbers by disease, by discharges for physical incapacity, and by desertions, and in consequence thoroughly demoralized. The rate of mortality among the men was said to have been unprecedented in the history of the war, and their idle, wasteful, and slovenly habits, it was alleged, made them unfitted for soldiers. On the other hand Adjutant-General Thomas, who had devoted several months of the previous year to organizing negro regiments in the South, and who had conceived a high opinion of their capacity, was amply confirmed in his views by his experience of 1864, and urged the necessity of enlisting more of this class of troops, as also of raising their pay.

The colored regiments continued to be officered by white men, who were subjected to an unusually strict examination by a board appointed for that purpose. Up to August, the total number of officers examined amounted to 2,471, of whom 1,486 were accepted.

Although desertions from the service during the year were not so numerous as in the early years of the war, when discipline was less strict, and the offence was considered in a less odious light, the number had still been sufficiently large to cause the Government considerable embarrassment. This resulted in a great measure from the inferior class of men enlisted into the army through the medium of bounty and substitute brokers, and from the unwise leniency shown by the Government to offenders. For a long time the death penalty seemed to have been practically abolished, and the activity of the Provost Marshals had in consequence little or no effect in lessening the number of absentees without leave. Unprincipled men, having no fear of execution before their eyes, risked the chance of recapture and the comparatively slight punishment which would follow, and escaped with their bounty money, a few weeks, or even days, after being mustered into the service. As an illustration of the extent to which the practice was carried, it is stated that out of a detachment of 625 recruits sent to reënforce a New Hampshire regiment in the Army of the Potomac, 137 deserted on the passage, 82 to the enemy's picket line, and 36 to the rear, leaving but 370 men, or less than 60 per cent., available for duty.

The desertions in the Army of the Potomac were greatly increased by a proclamation from Gen. Lee (intended as an offset to one issued by Gen. Grant), offering to send Federal deserters North. Thousands probably availed themselves of this opportunity, and found their way back to the loyal States, there perhaps to reënlist and again desert; and a small percentage entered the rebel service. The evil finally increased to such a degree that the death penalty was restored and unsparingly used. During the latter part of the year executions of deserters were almost of daily occurrence in the Army of the Potomac, and almost immediately a diminution in the number of cases was observable, which continued to the close of the war.

The total number of deserters of all kinds was estimated by Senator Wilson, in March, at 40,000. The Provost Marshal General reported 39,392 deserters and stragglers arrested by his officers between Oct. 1st, 1863, and Oct. 1st, 1864, and the total number arrested, from the establishment of the special bureau having charge of the matter to Oct. 1st, 1864, at 60,760.

On June 30th, 1864, 190 hospitals, with a capacity of 120,521 beds, were in active operation; and during the year the health of the entire army was reported better than is usual with troops engaged in arduous campaigns. At the close of the year the number of sick and wounded, both with their commands and in general hospitals, was less than 16 per cent. of the strength of the army. The number sick with their respective commands was 4 per cent., and in general hospitals 5 and $\frac{3}{10}$ per cent. of the strength. Of the 6 and $\frac{46}{100}$ per cent. wounded, nearly 1 per cent. were with their respective commands; the rest in general hospitals.

The supplies of ordnance produced during the year included 1,750 pieces of ordnance, 2,361 artillery carriages and caissons, 802,525 small arms, 794,055 sets of accoutrements and harness, 1,674,244 projectiles for cannon, 12,740,146 pounds of bullets and lead, 8,409,400 pounds of gunpowder, 169,490,029 cartridges for small-arms, in addition to large quantities partially made up at the arsenals. The supplies furnished to the military service during the same period included 1,141 pieces of ordnance, 1,896 artillery carriages and caissons, 455,910 small-arms, 502,044 sets of accoutrements and harness, 1,913,753 projectiles for cannon, 7,624,685 pounds of bullets and lead, 464,549 rounds of artillery ammunition, 152,067 sets of horse equipments, 112,087,553 cartridges for small-arms, and 7,544,044 pounds of gunpowder. The national armory at Springfield, Mass., was reported in a condition to turn out 300,000 of the best quality of rifle muskets annually. The stock on hand, at the close of the year, amounted to a million and a quarter, exclusive of the arms in the hands of the troops.

At the close of 1864 the military geographical departments were in charge of the following generals:

Department of the Tennessee—Maj.-Gen. O. O. Howard.
" of the Cumberland—Maj.-Gen. George H. Thomas.
" of the Ohio—Maj.-Gen. John M. Schofield.
" of the East—Maj.-Gen. John A. Dix.
" of the Gulf—Maj.-Gen. Stephen A. Hurlbut.
" of North Carolina and Virginia—Maj.-Gen. B. F. Butler.
Department of the Northwest—Maj.-Gen. John Pope.
" of Washington—Maj.-Gen. Christopher C. Augur.
" of Pennsylvania—Maj.-Gen. George Cadwallader.
" of Western Virginia—Maj.-Gen. George Crook.
" of New Mexico—Brig.-Gen. James H. Carlton.
" of the Pacific—Maj.-Gen. Irwin McDowell.
" of Kansas—Maj.-Gen. Samuel R. Curtis.
" of the Middle Department—Maj.-Gen. Lewis Wallace.
" of the South—Maj.-Gen. John G. Foster.
" of Missouri—Maj.-Gen. Grenville M. Dodge.
" of Arkansas—Maj-Gen. Joseph J. Reynolds.
" of the North—Maj.-Gen. Joseph Hooker.
" of the Mississippi—Maj.-Gen. Napoleon J. T. Dana.

The departments of the Tennessee, the Cumberland, and the Ohio, formed the military division of the Mississippi, of which Maj.-Gen. William T. Sherman assumed command in the early part of the year; and in May the departments lying west of the Mississippi were formed into the military division of West Mississippi, under the command of Maj.-Gen. E. R. S. Canby.

The several army corps, were, on Jan. 1st, 1865, commanded as follows:

*1st. Maj.-Gen. W. S. Hancock.
2d. Maj.-Gen. A. A. Humphreys.
3d. Discontinued.
4th Maj.-Gen. D. S. Stanley.
5th Maj.-Gen. G. K. Warren.
6th Maj.-Gen. H. G. Wright.
7th Maj.-Gen. J. J. Reynolds.
8th Maj.-Gen. Lewis Wallace.
9th Maj.-Gen. John G. Parke.
10th Discontinued.
11th do
12th do
13th Maj.-Gen. Gordon Granger.
14th Brig-Gen. Jefferson C. Davis.
15th Maj.-Gen. John A. Logan.
16th Maj.-Gen. Andrew J. Smith.
17th Maj. Gen. Frank P. Blair.
18th Discontinued.
19th Brig-Gen. W. H. Emory,
20th Brig-Gen. A. S. Williams.
21st Discontinued.
22d do
23d Maj.-Gen. John M. Schofield.
24th Maj.-Gen. E. O. C. Ord.
25th Maj.-Gen. Godfrey Weitzel.

The history of the insurrectionary States during 1864 presents them as absorbed in one great effort to maintain a successful war, the effects of which had reached every man and every family. The ardor of the early campaigns had passed away, and with it went the sanguine hopes of a speedy and certain triumph. Doubt, uncertainty of the result, and apprehension of the future, heretofore strangers, now found a place in every mind; yet, with the heroic resolution of once American citizens no words of fear or faintness were allowed to appear in their public or official proceedings. The tone of these documents was, however, more subdued, their extreme demands less often appeared, and the disappearance of passion softened all the intercourse with their opponents. These changes increased with the progress of the year, until at its close it might safely be said, that the Confederate States were no longer fighting for independence and a separate nationality, but for favorable terms of settlement.

Many of the elements which entered into such a struggle were abundant. The crops of 1864 were larger than those of 1863. At no time

* Reorganizing and not in active service.

during the year was there any lack of quantity. The difficulty was in the distribution. Manufacturers of necessary articles became prosperous. Paper-mills, in Georgia and other States, turned out large quantities. Cloth mills at Lynchburg, Mobile, Raleigh, Charleston, in Georgia, Alabama, and Mississippi, were in successful operation; their most important machinery having been imported from Europe. Establishments for the manufacture of cannon, small-arms, powder, shot, shell, percussion-caps, harnesses, wagons, ambulances, and all the materials of war, more than supplied the great demand.

The commerce of these States was carried on entirely by swift vessels running the blockade. Although limited, it was of great advantage to the Government and people. The latter, however, must have reached extreme destitution of some articles, but for the aid derived from the trade within the Federal lines.

The foreign relations of the States continued without change through the year. It appeared to be a stretch of presumption to expect France and England to recognize their independence. Recognition was of no practical value unless followed by armed assistance, and these countries were not in a condition to go to war with a friendly power to relieve one unknown, and of no strength on the ocean. The recognition of the Confederate States as a belligerent, while it deceived the people by exciting large expectations, was a great measure in favor of European powers, as it practically annihilated any opposition from the United States to their schemes and plans.

A change took place in the Treasury Department by the resignation of Mr. Memminger, and the appointment of Mr. G. A. Trenholm.

The operations of the Treasury for the six months, ending Oct. 1, 1864, present the following details; receipts, $415,191,550.

From four per cent. registered bonds, act 17th February, 1864	$18,363,500
From six per cent. bonds, $500,000,000 loan act, February 17, 1864	14,481,050
From four per cent. call certificates, act 17th February 1864	20,978,100
From tax on old issue of certificates, redeemed.	14,440,564
From repayments by disbursing officers	20,115,830
From treasury notes, under act 17th February, 1864	277,576,950
From war tax	42,294,314
From sequestration	1,338,732
From customs	50,004
From export duty	4,320
From coin seized by authority of the Secretary of War	1,653,200
From premium on loans	4,822,249
From soldiers' tax	908,622

Expenditures.

The expenditures during the same period are as follows:

War Department	$246,367,442
Navy Department	15,554,802
Customs	28,585
Civil, miscellaneous, and foreign intercourse	10,427,674
Total	$272,378,503
Public debt—for payment of interest	10,772,883
Public debt—for payment of principal	334,787,444
Total	$614,938,830

The balance in the treasury on 1st of April, 1864, was	308,282,722
The amount received since is	415,191,550
Total	$723,474,272
Deduct amount of expenditures	614,938,830
The balance in the treasury is	$108,535,442

The balance is made up as follows:

Treasury notes (new issue) and specie	$22,153,203
Treasury notes (old issue) to be cancelled	86,382,239
Total	$108,535,442

The Public Debt.

The public debt on the first of October, 1864, was as follows:

FUNDED DEBT.		
Total issue of bonds and stocks		$363,416,150
Total issue of call certificates		197,578,370
Total issue of certificates of indebtedness		19,010,000
Total issue of produce certificates, act April 21, 1862		$2,500,000
Amount of 7-30 interest notes, which have assumed the character of permanent bonds		99,954,900
Total		$682,459,420
Reduced by amount redeemed, to wit;		
Act May 16, 1861, principal	$2,976,000	
Act Aug. 19, 1861, principal	1,267,700	
Call certificates, act Dec. 24, 1861, six per cent	70,729,030	
Call certificates, act March 23,1863, five per cent	70,000,000	
Call certificates, act March 23, 1863, four per cent	1,825,000	
		$141,119,330
Total		$541,340,090
UNFUNDED DEBT.		
Amount 3-63 interest notes outstanding		$516,050
Total issue of treasury notes—old issue	$973,281,863	
Reduced by amount called in for cancellation	640,947,945	
		$324,209,818
Total issue treasury notes, new issue		283,830,150
Total funded and unfunded debt		$1,149,896,108

The Secretary says the foreign debt, consisting of a single item, is omitted; the whole amount, being £2,200,000, is adequately provided for by the cotton owned by the Government even at sixpence per pound, the quantity being about 250,000 bales.

In April, the note department of the Treasury was removed to Columbia, South Carolina. To increase the resources of the Government, heavy taxes were imposed.

The prices of articles in the markets did not decline during the year.

The position of the currency, on March 31st, was as follows:

Statement of the issue of non-interest-bearing Treasury Notes since the organization of the Confed. Government:

Fifty cents	$911,258 50
Ones	4,882,000 00
Twos	6,086,320 00
Fives	79,090,815 00
Tens	157,982,750 00
Twenties	217,425,120 00
Fifties	188,088,000 00
Total	$973,277,363 50

Statement showing the amount of non-interest-bearing Notes outstanding on March 31, 1864:

Act May 16, 1861—Ten-year notes	$7,201,375 00
Act Aug. 19, 1861—General currency	154,356,634 00
Act April 19, 1862—Ones and twos	4,516,509 00
Act Oct. 13, 1862—General currency	118,997,321 00
Act Mar. 23, 1863—General currency	511,182,586 50
Total	$796,254,425 50

The difference between the issues and the amount outstanding is the amount that had been redeemed.

Of all the difficulties encountered by the administrative bureau of the Government, the greatest was caused by the deficiency of transportation. With the coasting trade cut off and all the great rivers under command of the Federal fleet, the only reliance for internal trade and communication was necessarily on the railroads. These were never designed or provided with the means for the task now imposed upon them. They had, besides, suffered much from inability to command the supplies of iron, implements, and machinery, and from many sacrifices and losses in war. The deficiency in skilled labor was also a great embarrassment in requisite repairs. Some of the shorter and less important lines were thus sacrificed, and the iron and machinery taken for the maintenance of the leading roads, and for the construction of some essential and less exposed interior links of connection.

The military operations demanded all the energies of the people, and required the sacrifice of every private interest to secure their success. If these failed, their cause was lost. But armies could be raised and sustained only while hope invigorated the spirits of the people. In this respect the year 1864 brought the severest test which had yet been felt. The waning proportions of the military territory and of the armies to resist their foes, depressed the hopes of the rulers and people, and foreboded what the result would be. Hence unusual efforts were made to rouse their energies.

The question of Peace was present to every mind. But one view, however, controlled the Government and the majority of the people: when the North is prepared to acknowledge the independence of the Confederate States, the war will close and peace prevail. As there was not the slightest indication of such an act on the part of the North, all these parties urged forward the war. In North Carolina, during 1863, there were those who not only desired peace but demanded some immediate steps to be taken to open negotiations. In their minds the success of the Confederacy was considered impossible, as they sanguinely anticipated some favorable arrangements between the contestants.

The end of nearly four years of war presented the people of the Southern States under a Government in the exercise of every power of a national, central, military despotism. Conscription was carried to its last limit. Every man between seventeen and fifty was subject to military authority. None were exempt except on considerations of public interest. Direct taxes were laid in defiance of the theory of their constitution. Such vast amounts of paper money had been issued as to unsettle all values. The holders of this paper money were compelled to fund it or lose one-third. All the railroads were seized by the Government, and some were destroyed and others built. A universal system of impressment of property was established at Government prices in Government money. Of the exportations of the great staples the Government held the monopoly. Those citizens who were permitted to remain at home were required to execute a bond to furnish their products to the Government at its prices. The *habeas corpus* was suspended and a passport system was established. Notwithstanding all these sacrifices, the military operations had resulted in loss in every State, and the theatre of activity was reduced to three Atlantic States.

On the other hand, in the Union States a weariness of the war, or a laudable desire to put an end to the appalling horrors of the conflict, awakened in the mass of the people a strong wish for peace. So prevalent was this wish, that even unofficial individuals were tempted to undertake the preparation of the preliminaries. President Lincoln appears kindly to have indulged these inclinations, although they resulted in showing that neither side were willing to make any concession merely for the sake of peace.

The first of these movements, in point of time, consisted in a visit of Rev. Col. Jacques and Mr. J. R. Gilmore to Richmond, in which two interviews were had with Mr. Davis. The visit resulted in nothing, and the President appears to have taken no part in the matter further than to approve of their passage through the Federal lines, although the terms suggested in the conversations are the same as the President has advanced on every subsequent occasion. The following letter explains the manner in which a passage into the enemy's lines was obtained:

HEADQUARTERS ARMIES OF THE UNITED STATES,
CITY POINT, VA., July 8, 1864.

Gen. R. E. Lee, Commanding Confederate Forces near Petersburg, Va.

GENERAL: I would request that Col. James F. Jacques, 78th Illinois volunteer infantry, and J. R. Gilmore, Esq., be allowed to meet Col. Robert Ould, commissioner for the exchange of prisoners, at such place between the lines of the two armies as you may designate. The object of the meeting is legitimate with the duties of Col. Ould as commissioner. If not consistent for you to grant the request here asked, I would beg that this be referred to President Davis for his action.

Requesting as early an answer to this communication as you may find it convenient to make, I subscribe myself, very respectfully, your obedient servant, U. S. GRANT, Lieut.-Gen. U. S. A.

The following note opened the way for an interview with Mr. Davis:

SPOTTISWOOD HOTEL, RICHMOND, VA., July 17, 1864.

Hon. J. P. Benjamin, Secretary of State, C. S. A.

DEAR SIR: The undersigned, James F. Jacques, of Illinois, and James R. Gilmore, of Massachusetts, most respectfully solicit an interview with President Davis. They visit Richmond as private citizens, and have no official character or authority; but they are fully possessed of the views of the United States Government relative to an adjustment of the differences now existing between the North and the South, and have little doubt that a free interchange of views between President Davis and themselves would open the way to such official negotiations as would ultimate in restoring peace to the two sections of our distracted country.

They therefore ask an interview with the President, and awaiting your reply, are, most truly and respectfully, your obedient servants, JAS. F. JACQUES,
JAS. R. GILMORE.

Mr. Gilmore states the conversation between himself and Mr. Davis thus:

Gilmore.—Well, sir, be that as it may, if I understand you, the dispute between your Government and ours is narrowed down to this, Union or disunion?

Davis.—Yes, or to put it in other words, independence or subjugation.

Gilmore.—Then the two Governments are irreconcilably apart. They have no alternative but to fight it out. But it is not so with the people. They are tired of fighting, and want peace; and as they bear all the burden and suffering of the war, is it not right they should have peace, and have it on such terms as they like?

Davis.—I don't understand you; be a little more explicit.

Gilmore.—Well, suppose the two Governments should agree to something like this: To go to the people with two propositions: say, peace with disunion and Southern independence, as your proposition—and peace with union, emancipation, no confiscation, and universal amnesty, as ours. Let the citizens of all the United States (as they existed before the war) vote "yes" or "no" on these two propositions, at a special election within sixty days. If a majority votes disunion, our Government to be bound by it, and to let you go in peace. If a majority votes Union, yours to be bound by it and to stay in peace. The two Governments can contract in this way, and the people, though constitutionally unable to decide on peace or war, can elect which of the two propositions shall govern their rulers. Let Lee and Grant, meanwhile, agree to an armistice. This would sheathe the sword; and, if once sheathed, it would never again be drawn by this generation.

Davis.—The plan is altogether impracticable. If the South were only one State, it might work; but as it is, if one Southern State objected to emancipation it would nullify the whole thing; for you are aware the people of Virginia cannot vote slavery out of South Carolina, nor the people of South Carolina vote it out of Virginia.

Gilmore.—But three-fourths of the States can amend the Constitution. Let it be done in that way; in any way so that it be done by the people. I am not a statesman nor a politician, and I do not know just how such a plan could be carried out; but you get the idea—that the people shall decide the question.

Davis.—That the majority shall decide it, you mean. We seceded to rid ourselves of the rule of the majority, and this would subject us to it again.

Gilmore.—But the majority must rule finally, either with bullets or ballots.

Davis.—I am not so sure of that. Neither current events nor history shows that the majority rules, or ever did rule. The contrary, I think, is true. Why, sir, the man who should go before the Southern people with such a proposition, with any proposition which implied that the North was to have a voice in determining the domestic relations of the South, could not live here a day. He would be hanged to the first tree, without judge or jury.

Mr. Benjamin, Secretary of State, in an official letter to James M. Mason, commissioner in Europe, says:

Mr. Gilmore then addressed the President, and in a few minutes had conveyed the information that these two gentlemen had come to Richmond impressed with the idea that this Government would accept a peace on a basis of a reconstruction of the Union, the abolition of slavery, and the grant of an amnesty to the people of the States as repentant criminals. In order to accomplish the abolition of slavery, it was proposed that there should be a general vote of all the people of both federations, in mass, and the majority of the vote thus taken was to determine that as well as all other disputed questions. These were stated to be Mr. Lincoln's views.

The President answered, that as these proposals had been prefaced by the remark that the people of the North were a majority, and that a majority ought to govern, the offer was, in effect, a proposal that the Confederate States should surrender at discretion, admit that they had been wrong from the beginning of the contest, submit to the mercy of their enemies, and avow themselves to be in need of pardon for their crimes; that extermination was preferable to dishonor. He stated that if they were themselves so unacquainted with the form of their own Government as to make such propositions, Mr. Lincoln ought to have known, when giving them his views, that it was out of the power of the Confederate Government to act on the subject of the domestic institutions of the several States, each State having exclusive jurisdiction on that point, still less to commit the decision of such a question to the vote of a foreign people.

The next attempt to prepare the way for negotiations was of a semi-official character, and resulted in a clear statement by the President of his terms of settlement so indefinitely brought out in the preceding conversation. Mr. Horace Greeley, who was the active participant on the Union side, thus relates the origin of the correspondence which took place:

Some time since it was announced by telegraph from Halifax that Messrs. C. C. Clay, of Alabama, Jacob Thompson, of Mississippi (ex-United States Senators), Professor J. P. Holcombe, of the University of Virginia, and George N. Sanders, of Kentucky, had reached that city from Dixie *via* Bermuda, on important business, and all of these but Mr. Thompson (who was in Toronto) were soon quartered at the Clifton, on the Canada side of Niagara Falls. I heard soon after of confidential interviews between some or all of those gentlemen and leading Democrats from our own and neighboring States, and there were telegraphic whispers of overtures for reconstruction, and conditions were set forth as those on which the Confederates would consent to reunion. (I cannot say that any of these reports were authentic.) At length, after several less direct intimations, I received a private letter from Mr. Sanders, stating that Messrs. Clay, Holcombe, himself, and another, desired to visit Washington, upon complete and unqualified protection being given by the President or the Secretary of War.

As I saw no reason why the opposition should be the sole recipients of these gentlemen's overtures, if such there were (and it is stated that Mr. Clay aforesaid is preparing or to prepare an important letter to the Chicago Convention), I wrote the President, urging him to invite the rebel gentlemen aforesaid to Washington, there to open their budget. I stated expressly that I knew not what they would propose if so invited; but I could imagine no offer that might be made by them which would not conduce, in one way or another, to a restoration of the integrity and just authority of the Union.

The President ultimately acquiesced in this view so far as to consent that the rebel agents should visit Washington, but directed that I should proceed to Niagara, and accompany them thence to the capital. This service I most reluctantly undertook, feeling deeply and observing that almost any one else might better have been sent on this errand. But time seemed precious, and I immediately started.

The correspondence was as follows:

Mr. Jewett to Mr. Greeley.

NIAGARA FALLS, July 5, 1864.

MY DEAR MR. GREELEY: In reply to your note, I have to advise having just left Hon. George N. Sanders of Kentucky on the Canada side. I am authorized to state to you, for our use only, not the public, that two ambassadors of Davis & Co. are now in Canada, with full and complete powers for a peace, and Mr. Sanders requests that you come on immediately to me, at Cataract House, to have a private interview; or if you will send the President's protection for him and two friends, they will come on and meet you. He says the whole matter can be consummated by me, you, them, and President Lincoln. Telegraph me in such form that I may know if you come here, or they to come on with me.

Yours, W. C. JEWETT.

Mr. Greeley to President Lincoln.

NEW YORK, July 7, 1864.

MY DEAR SIR: I venture to enclose you a letter and telegraphic despatch that I received yesterday from our irrepressible friend Colorado Jewett, at Niagara Falls. I think they deserve attention. Of course I do not indorse Jewett's positive averment that his friends at the Falls have "full power" from J. D., though I do not doubt that he thinks they have. I let that statement stand as simply evidencing the anxiety of the Confederates everywhere for peace. So much is beyond doubt. I therefore venture to remind you that our bleeding, bankrupt, almost dying country, also longs for peace—shudders at the prospect of fresh conscriptions, of further wholesale devastations, and of new rivers of human blood; and a wide-spread conviction that the Government and its prominent supporters are not anxious for peace, and do not improve proffered opportunities to achieve it, is doing great harm now, and is morally certain, unless removed, to do far greater in the approaching elections. It is not enough that we anxiously desire a true and lasting peace; we ought to demonstrate and establish the truth beyond cavil. The fact that A. H. Stephens was not permitted a year ago to visit and confer with the authorities at Washington has done harm, which the tone of the late national convention at Baltimore is not calculated to counteract. I entreat you, in your own time and manner, to submit overtures for pacification to the Southern insurgents, which the impartial must pronounce frank and generous. If only with a view to the momentous election soon to occur in North Carolina, and of the draft to be enforced in the free States, this should be done at once. I would give the safe conduct required by the rebel envoys at Niagara, upon their parole to avoid observation and to refrain from all communication with their sympathizers in the loyal States; but you may see reasons for declining it. But whether through them or otherwise, do not, I entreat you, fail to make the Southern people comprehend that you, and all of us, are anxious for peace, and prepared to grant liberal terms. I venture to suggest the following plan of adjustment:

1. The Union is restored and declared perpetual.
2. Slavery is utterly and forever abolished throughout the same.
3. A complete amnesty of all political offences, with a restoration of all the inhabitants of each State to all the privileges of citizens of the United States.
4. The Union to pay four hundred million dollars ($400,000,000) in five per cent. United States stock to the late slave States, loyal and secession alike, to be apportioned pro rata, according to their slave population respectively, by the census of 1860, in compensation for the losses of their loyal citizens by the abolition of slavery. Each State to be entitled to its quota upon the ratification by its legislature of this adjustment. The bonds to be at the absolute disposal of the legislature aforesaid.
5. The said slave States to be entitled henceforth to representation in the House on the basis of their total, instead of their Federal population, the whole now being free.
6. A national convention, to be assembled as soon as may be, to ratify this adjustment, and make such changes in the Constitution as may be deemed advisable.

Mr. President, I fear you do not realize how intently the people desire any peace consistent with the national integrity and honor, and how joyously they would hail its achievement and bless its authors. With United States stocks worth but forty cents in gold per dollar, and drafting about to commence on the third million of Union soldiers, can this be wondered at? I do not say that a just peace is now attainable, though I believe it to be so; but I do say that a frank offer by you to the insurgents of terms which the impartial say ought to be accepted, will, at the worst, prove an immense and sorely needed advantage to the national cause. It may save us from a northern insurrection.

Yours, truly, HORACE GREELEY.

P. S.—Even though it should be deemed unadvisable to make an offer of terms to the rebels, I insist that, in any possible case, it is desirable that any offer they may be disposed to make should be received, and either accepted or rejected. I beg you to invite those now at Niagara to exhibit their credentials and submit their ultimatum. H. G.

President Lincoln to Mr. Greeley.

WASHINGTON, D. C., July 9, 1864.

HON. HORACE GREELEY: Dear Sir—Your letter of the 7th, with inclosures, received. If you can find any person anywhere professing to have any proposition of Jefferson Davis in writing, for peace, embracing the restoration of the Union and the abandonment of slavery, whatever else it embraces, say to him he may come to me with you; and that if he really brings such proposition, he shall, at the least, have safe conduct with the paper (and without publicity if he chooses) to the point where you shall have met him. The same if there be two or more persons.

Yours, truly, A. LINCOLN.

Mr. Greeley to the President.

OFFICE OF THE TRIBUNE, NEW YORK, July 10, 1864.

MY DEAR SIR: I have yours of yesterday. Whether there be persons at Niagara (or elsewhere) who are empowered to commit the rebels by negotiation, is a question; but if there be such, there is no question at all that they would decline to exhibit their credentials to me, much more to open their budget and give me their best terms. Green as I may be, I am not quite so verdant as to imagine any thing of the sort. I have neither purpose nor desire to be made a confidant, far less an agent, in such negotiations. But I do deeply realize that the rebel chiefs achieved a most decided advantage in proposing, or pretending to propose, to have A. H. Stephens visit Washington as a peacemaker, and being rudely repulsed; and I am anxious that the ground lost to the national cause by that mistake shall somehow be regained in season for effect on the approaching North Carolina election. I will see if I can get a look into the hand of whomsoever may be at Niagara: though that is a project so manifestly hopeless that I have little heart for it, still I shall try.

Meantime I wish you would consider the propriety of somehow apprising the people of the South, especially those of North Carolina, that no overture or advance looking to peace and reunion has ever been repelled by you, but that such a one would at any time have been cordially received and favorably regarded, and would still be.

Yours, HORACE GREELEY.

Hon. A. LINCOLN.

Mr. Sanders to Mr. Greeley.

[Private and confidential.]

CLIFTON HOUSE, NIAGARA FALLS, C.W., July 12, 1864.

SIR: I am authorized to say that Hon. Clement C.

Clay, of Alabama, Professor James P. Holcombe, of Virginia, and George N. Sanders, of Dixie, are ready and willing to go at once to Washington, upon complete and unqualified protection being given, either by the President or Secretary of War. Let the permission include the three names and one other.

Very respectfully, GEORGE N. SANDERS.

To Hon. HORACE GREELEY.

Mr. Greeley to the President.

OFFICE OF THE TRIBUNE, NEW YORK, July 12, 1864.

MY DEAR SIR: I have now information on which I can rely, that two persons duly commissioned and empowered to negotiate for peace are at this moment not far from Niagara Falls, in Canada, and are desirous of conferring with yourself, or with such persons as you may appoint and empower to treat with them. Their names (only given in confidence) are Hon. Clement C. Clay, of Alabama, and Hon. Jacob Thompson of Mississippi. If you should prefer to meet them in person, they require safe conduct for themselves and for George N. Sanders, who will accompany them. Should you choose to empower one or more persons to treat with them in Canada, they will of course need no safe-conduct; but they cannot be expected to exhibit credentials, save to commissioners empowered as they are. In negotiating directly with yourself, all grounds of cavil would be avoided, and you would be enabled at all times to act upon the freshest advices of the military situation. You will of course understand that I know nothing and have proposed nothing as to terms, and that nothing is conceded or taken for granted by the meeting of persons empowered to negotiate for peace. All that is assumed is a mutual desire to terminate this wholesale slaughter, if a basis of adjustment can be mutually agreed on; and it seems to me high time that an effort to this end should be made. I am, of course, quite other than sanguine that a peace can now be made, but I am quite sure that a frank, earnest, anxious effort to terminate the war on honorable terms would immensely strengthen the Government in case of its failure, and would help us in the eyes of the civilized world, which now accuses us of obstinacy, and indisposition even to seek a peaceful solution of our sanguinary, devastating conflict.

Hoping to hear that you have resolved to act in the premises, and to act so promptly that a good influence may even yet be exerted on the North Carolina election next month,

I remain yours, HORACE GREELEY.

Hon. A. LINCOLN, Washington.

President Lincoln to Mr. Greeley.

EXECUTIVE MANSION, WASHINGTON, July 15, 1864.

Hon. HORACE GREELEY, New York.

I suppose you received my letter of the 9th. I have just received yours of the 13th, and am disappointed by it. I was not expecting you to send me a letter, but to bring me a man or men. Mr. Hay goes to you with my answer to yours of the 13th,

A. LINCOLN.

President Lincoln to Mr. Greeley.

EXECUTIVE MANSION, WASHINGTON, July 15, 1864.

Hon. HORACE GREELEY: My Dear Sir—Yours of the 13th is just received, and I am not disappointed that you have not already reached here with those Commissioners. If they would consent to come on being shown my letter to you of the 9th inst., show that and this to them; and if they will come on the terms stated in the former, bring them. I not only intend a sincere effort for peace, but I intend that you shall be a personal witness that it is made. Yours, truly, A. LINCOLN.

Major Hay to the President.

UNITED STATES MILITARY TELEGRAPH, WAR DEP'T,
NEW YORK, 9 A. M., July 16, 1864.

His Excellency A. LINCOLN, President of the United States.

Arrived this morning at 6 A. M., and delivered your letter a few minutes after. Although he thinks some one less known would create less excitement and be less embarrassed by public curiosity, still he will start immediately, if he can have an absolute safe conduct for four persons to be named by him. Your letter he does not think will guard them from arrest, and with only those letters he would have to explain the whole matter to any officer who might choose to hinder them. If this meets with your approbation, I can write the order in your name as A. A. G., or you can send it by mail. Please answer me at Astor House. JOHN HAY, A. A. G.

President Lincoln to Major Hay.

EXECUTIVE MANSION, WASHINGTON, July 16, 1864.

JOHN HAY, Astor House, New York.

Yours received. Write the safe conduct as you propose, without waiting for one by mail from me. If there is or is not any thing in the affair, I wish to know it without unnecessary delay.

A. LINCOLN.

EXECUTIVE MANSION, WASHINGTON, D. C.

The President of the United States directs that the four persons whose names follow, to wit: Hon. Clement C. Clay, Hon. Jacob Thompson, Prof. James P. Holcombe, George N. Sanders, shall have safe conduct to the city of Washington, in company with the Hon. Horace Greeley, and shall be exempt from arrest or annoyance of any kind from any officer of the United States during their journey to the city of Washington. By order of the President,

JOHN HAY, Major and A. A. G.

Mr. Greeley's Reply.

NIAGARA FALLS, N. Y., July 17, 1864.

GENTLEMEN: I am informed that you are duly accredited from Richmond as the bearers of propositions looking to the establishment of peace; that you desire to visit Washington in the fulfilment of your mission, and that you further desire that Mr. George N. Sanders shall accompany you. If my information be thus far substantially correct, I am authorized by the President of the United States to tender you his safe conduct on the journey proposed, and to accompany you at the earliest time that will be agreeable to you.

I have the honor to be, gentlemen, yours,

HORACE GREELEY.

To Messrs. CLEMENT C. CLAY, JACOB THOMPSON, JAMES P. HOLCOMBE, Clifton House, C. W.

Messrs. Holcombe and Clay to Mr. Greeley.

CLIFTON HOUSE, NIAGARA FALLS, July 18, 1864.

SIR: We have the honor to acknowledge your favor of the 17th inst., which would have been answered on yesterday but for the absence of Mr. Clay. The safe conduct of the President of the United States has been tendered us, we regret to state, under some misapprehension of facts. We have not been accredited to him from Richmond as the bearers of propositions looking to the establishment of peace. We are, however, in the confidential employment of our Government, and are entirely familiar with its wishes and opinions on that subject; and we feel authorized to declare that, if the circumstances disclosed in this correspondence were communicated to Richmond, we would be at once invested with the authority to which your letter refers; or other gentlemen, clothed with full powers, would be immediately sent to Washington with the view of hastening a consummation so much to be desired, and terminating at the earliest possible moment the calamities of the war. We respectfully solicit, through your intervention, a safe conduct to Washington, and thence by any route which may be designated, through your lines to Richmond. We would be gratified if Mr. George N. Sanders was embraced in this privilege.

Permit us, in conclusion, to acknowledge our obligations to you for the interest you have manifested in the furtherance of our wishes, and to express the hope that in any event you will afford us the opportunity of tendering them in person before you leave the Falls. We remain, very respectfully, &c.,

C. C. CLAY, JR.
J. P. HOLCOMBE.

P. S.—It is proper to add, that Mr. Thompson is not here, and has not been staying with us since our sojourn in Canada.

Mr. Greeley's Reply.

INTERNATIONAL HOTEL, NIAGARA, N. Y., July 18, 1864.

GENTLEMEN: I have the honor to acknowledge the receipt of yours of this date by the hand of Mr. W. C. Jewett. The state of facts therein presented being materially different from that which was understood to exist by the President when he entrusted me with the safe conduct required, it seems to me on every account advisable that I should communicate with him by telegraph, and solicit fresh instructions, which I shall at once proceed to do. I hope to be able to transmit the result this afternoon; and at all events I shall do so at the earliest moment. Yours, truly,

HORACE GREELEY.

To Messrs. CLEMENT C. CLAY and JAMES P. HOLCOMBE, Clifton House, C. W.

Mr. Greeley to the President.

INDEPENDENT TELEGRAPH LINE,
NIAGARA FALLS, July 18, 1864.

Hon. ABRAHAM LINCOLN, President:

I have communicated with the gentlemen in question, and do not find them so empowered as I was previously assured. They say that "we are, however, in the confidential employment of our Government, and entirely familiar with its wishes and opinions on that subject; and we feel authorized to declare that, if the circumstances disclosed in this correspondence were communicated to Richmond, we would at once be invested with the authority to which your letter refers, or other gentlemen, clothed with full powers, would immediately be sent to Washington with the view of hastening a consummation so much to be desired, and terminating at the earliest possible moment the calamities of war. We respectfully solicit, through your intervention, a safe conduct to Washington, and thence by any route which may be designated to Richmond." Such is the more material portion of the gentlemen's letter. I will transmit the entire correspondence, if desired. Awaiting your further instructions, I remain yours,

HORACE GREELEY.

Messrs. Clay and Holcombe to Mr. Greeley.

CLIFTON HOUSE, NIAGARA FALLS, July 18, 1864.

To Hon. H. GREELEY, Niagara Falls, N. Y.:

SIR: We have the honor to acknowledge the receipt of your note of this date by the hands of Col. Jewett, and will await the further answer which you purpose to send to us. We are, very respectfully, &c.,

C. C. CLAY, JR.
JAMES P. HOLCOMBE.

Mr. Greeley to Messrs. Clay and Holcombe.

INTERNATIONAL HOTEL,
NIAGARA FALLS, N. Y., July 19, 1864.

GENTLEMEN: At a late hour last evening (too late for communication with you) I received a despatch informing me that further instructions left Washington last evening, which must reach me, if there be no interruption, at noon to-morrow. Should you decide to await their arrival, I feel confident that they will enable me to answer definitely your note of yesterday morning. Regretting a delay which I am sure you will regard as unavoidable on my part, I remain, yours truly, HORACE GREELEY.

To Hon. Messrs. C. C. CLAY, Jr., and H. P. HOLCOMBE, Clifton House, Niagara, C. W.

Messrs. Holcombe and Clay to Mr. Greeley.

CLIFTON HOUSE, NIAGARA FALLS, July 19, 1864.

SIR: Col. Jewett has just handed us your note of this date, in which you state that further instructions from Washington will reach you by noon to-morrow if there be no interruption. One or possibly both of us may be obliged to leave the Falls to-day, but will return in time to receive the communication which you promise to-morrow. We remain truly yours, &c.,

JAMES P. HOLCOMBE.
C. C. CLAY, JR.

To Hon. H. GREELEY, now at International Hotel.

The despatch which Mr. Greeley received from Washington, he thus explains: "Not feeling at liberty to concede this, I telegraphed to Washington for further instructions, and was duly informed that Major Hay, the President's private secretary, would soon be on his way to me. He reached the Falls on the 20th, and we crossed over to the Clifton, where Major Hay, after mutual introductions, handed Professor Holcombe the following paper in the handwriting of the President:

EXECUTIVE MANSION, WASHINGTON, July 18, 1864.

To whom it may concern:

Any proposition which embraces the restoration of peace, the integrity of the whole Union, and the abandonment of slavery, and which comes by and with an authority that can control the armies now at war against the United States, will be received and considered by the Executive Government of the United States, and will be met by liberal terms on other substantial and collateral points, and the bearer thereof shall have safe conduct both ways.

ABRAHAM LINCOLN.

"I left the Falls by the next train, leaving Major Hay to receive any response to the President's proffer, should any be made, but there was none."

Note from Major Hay to Mr. Holcombe.

INTERNATIONAL HOTEL, Wednesday July 20th.

Major Hay would respectfully inquire whether Professor Holcombe and the gentlemen associated with him desire to send to Washington by Major Hay any messages in reference to the communication delivered to him on yesterday, and in that case when he may expect to be favored with such messages.

Note from Mr. Holcombe to Major Hay.

CLIFTON HOUSE, NIAGARA FALLS, Thursday, July 21, 1864.

Mr. Holcombe presents his compliments to Major Hay, and greatly regrets if his return to Washington has been delayed by any expectation of an answer to the communication which Mr. Holcombe received from him on yesterday, to be delivered to the President of the United States. That communication was accepted as the response to a letter of Messrs. Clay and Holcombe to the Hon. H. Greeley, and to that gentleman an answer has been transmitted.

Messrs. Holcombe and Clay to Mr Greeley.

CLIFTON HOUSE, NIAGARA FALLS, July 21, 1864.

To HON. HORACE GREELEY:

SIR: The paper handed to Mr. Holcombe on yesterday in your presence by Major Hay, Assistant Adjutant-General, as an answer to the application in our note of the 18th inst., is couched in the following terms:

EXECUTIVE MANSION, WASHINGTON, D. C., July 18th, 1864.

To whom it may concern:

Any proposition which embraces the restoration of peace, the integrity of the whole Union, and the abandonment of slavery, and which comes by and with an authority that can control the armies now at war against the United States, will be received and considered by the Executive Government of the United States, and will be met by liberal terms on other substantial and collateral points, and the bearer or bearers thereof shall have safe conduct both ways.

ABRAHAM LINCOLN.

The application to which we refer was elicited by your letter of the 17th instant, in which you inform Mr. Jacob Thompson and ourselves that you were authorized by the President of the United States to tender us his safe conduct, on the hypothesis that we were "duly accredited from Richmond as bearers of propositions looking to the establishment of peace," and desired a visit to Washington in the fulfilment of this mission. This assertion, to which we then gave, and still do, entire credence, was accepted by us as the evidence of an unexpected but most gratifying change in the policy of the President—a change which we felt authorized to hope might terminate in the conclusion of a peace mutually just, honorable, and advantageous to the North and to the South, exacting no condition but that we should be "duly accredited from Richmond as bearers of propositions looking to the establishment of peace."

Thus proffering a basis for a conference as comprehensive as we could desire, it seemed to us that the President opened a door which had previously been closed against the Confederate States for a full interchange of sentiments, free discussion of conflicting opinions, and untrammelled effort to remove all causes of controversy by liberal negotiations. We, indeed, could not claim the benefit of a safe conduct which had been extended to us in a character we had no right to assume and had never affected to possess; but the uniform declarations of our Executive and Congress, and their thrice repeated and as often repulsed attempts to open negotiations, furnish a sufficient pledge that this conciliatory manifestation on the part of the President of the United States would be met by them in a temper of equal magnanimity. We had, therefore, no hesitation in declaring that if this correspondence was communicated to the President of the Confederate States he would promptly embrace the opportunity presented for seeking a peaceful solution of this unhappy strife.

We feel confident that you must share our profound regret that the spirit which dictated the first step toward peace had not continued to animate the counsels of your President. Had the representatives of the two Governments met to consider this question—the most momentous ever submitted to human statesmanship—in a temper of becoming moderation and equity, followed as their deliberations would have been by the prayers and benedictions of every patriot and Christian on the habitable globe, who is there so bold as to say that the frightful waste of individual happiness and public prosperity which is daily saddening the universal heart might not have been terminated, or if the desolation and carnage of war must still be endured through weary years of blood and suffering, that there might not at least have been infused into its conduct something more of the spirit which softens and partially redeems its brutalities?

Instead of the safe conduct which we solicited, and which your first letter gave us every reason to suppose would be extended for the purpose of initiating a negotiation in which neither Government would compromise its rights or its dignity, a document has been presented which provokes as much indignation as surprise. It bears no feature of resemblance to that which was originally offered, and is unlike any paper which ever before emanated from the constitutional executive of a free people. Addressed "To whom it may concern," it precludes negotiation, and prescribes in advance the terms and conditions of peace. It returns to the original policy of "no bargaining, no negotiations, no truces with rebels, except to bury their dead, until every man shall have laid down his arms, submitted to the Government, and sued for mercy."

What may be the explanation of this sudden and entire change in the views of the President, of this rude withdrawal of a courteous overture for negotiation at the moment it was likely to be accepted, of this emphatic recall of words of peace just uttered, and fresh blasts of war to the bitter end, we leave for the speculation of those who have the means or inclination to penetrate the mysteries of his Cabinet, or fathom the caprice of his imperial will. It is enough for us to say that we have no use whatever for the paper which has been placed in our hands. We could not transmit it to the President of the Confederate States without offering him an indignity, dishonoring ourselves, and incurring the well-merited scorn of our countrymen.

Whilst an ardent desire for peace pervades the people of the Confederate States, we rejoice to believe that there are few, if any, among them who would purchase it at the expense of liberty, honor, and self-respect. If it can be secured only by their submission to terms of conquest, the generation is yet unborn which will witness its restitution. If there be any military autocrat in the North who is entitled to proffer the conditions of this manifesto, there is none in the South authorized to entertain them. Those who control our armies are the servants of the people, not their masters; and they have no more inclination than they have right to subvert to social institutions of the sovereign States, to overthrow their established constitutions, and to barter away their priceless heritage of self-government.

This correspondence will not, however, we trust, prove wholly barren of good results.

If there is any citizen of the Confederate States who has clung to a hope that peace was possible with this administration of the Federal Government, it will strip from his eyes the last film of such delusion; or if there be any whose hearts have grown faint under the suffering and agony of this bloody struggle, it will inspire them with fresh energy to endure and brave whatever may yet be requisite to preserve to themselves and their children all that gives dignity and value to life or hope, and consolation to death. And if there be any patriots or Christians in your land who shrink appalled from the illimitable virtue of private misery and public calamity which stretches before them, we pray that in their bosoms a resolution may be quickened to recall the abused authority and vindicate the outraged civilization of their country.

For the solicitude you have manifested to inaugurate a movement which contemplates results the most noble and humane, we return our sincere thanks, and are, most respectfully and truly, your obedient servants,

C. C. CLAY, Jr.
JAMES P. HOLCOMBE.

Messrs. Clay and Holcombe to Wm. C. Jewett.

CLIFTON HOUSE, NIAGARA FALLS, July 20, 1864.

Col. W. C. JEWETT, Cataract House, Niagara Falls:

SIR: We are in receipt of your note admonishing us of the departure of Hon. Horace Greeley from the Falls, that he regrets the sad termination of the initiatory steps taken for peace in consequence of the change made by the President in his instructions to convey commissioners to Washington for negotiations unconditionally, and that Mr. Greeley will be pleased to receive any answer we may have to make through you. We avail ourselves of this offer to enclose a letter to Mr. Greeley, which you will oblige us by delivering. We cannot take leave of you without expressing our thanks for your courtesy and kind offices as the intermediary through whom our correspondence with Mr. Greeley has been conducted, and assuring you that we are, very respectfully, your obedient servants,

C. C. CLAY, Jr.
JAMES P. HOLCOMBE.

Mr. Greeley to Mr. Jewett.

INTERNATIONAL HOTEL, NIAGARA FALLS, July 20, 1864.

In leaving the Falls I feel bound to state that I have had no intercourse with the Confederate gentlemen at the Clifton House, but such as I was fully authorized to hold by the President of the United States, and that I have done nothing in the premises but in fulfilment of his injunctions. The notes, therefore, which you have interchanged between those gentlemen and myself, can in no case subject you to the imputation of unauthorized dealing with public enemies.

HORACE GREELEY.

To W. C. JEWETT, Esq.

No further attempts to open negotiations were made until December 28th, when the President and Secretary Seward met Commissioners from Richmond at Fortress Monroe. The particulars are thus stated by the President:

To the Hon. the House of Representatives:

In response to your resolution of the 8th inst., requesting information in relation to a conference held in Hampton Roads, I have the honor to state that on the date I gave Francis P. Blair, senior, a card written as follows, to wit:

"DECEMBER 28, 1864.

Allow the bearer, F. P. Blair, Sr., to pass our lines to go South and return.

(Signed) A. LINCOLN."

That at the time I was informed that Mr. Blair sought the card as a means of getting to Richmond, Va., but he was given no authority to speak or act for the Government. Nor was I informed of any thing he would say or do on his own account or otherwise.

Mr. Blair told me that he had been to Richmond and had seen Mr. Jefferson Davis, and he (Mr. Blair) at the same time left with me a manuscript letter, as follows, to wit:

"RICHMOND, VA., Jan. 12, 1865.

F. P. Blair, Esq.

SIR: I have deemed it proper and probably desirable to you to give you in this form the substance of the remarks made by me to be repeated by you to President Lincoln, &c. I have no disposition to find obstacles in forms, and am willing now, as heretofore, to enter into negotiations for the restoration of peace. I am ready to send a commission whenever I have reason to suppose it will be received, or to receive a commission if the United States Government shall choose to send one. Notwithstanding the rejection of our former offers, I would, if you could promise that a commission, minister, or other agent would be received, appoint one immediately, and renew the effort to enter into a conference with a view to secure peace to the two countries.

Yours, &c., JEFFERSON DAVIS."

Afterwards, with a view that it should be shown to Mr. Davis, I wrote and delivered to Mr. Blair a letter, as follows, to wit:

"WASHINGTON, Jan. 18, 1865.

F. P. Blair, Esq.

SIR: You having shown me Mr. Davis's letter to you of the 12th inst., you may say to him that I have constantly been, am now, and shall continue ready to receive any agent whom he, or any other influential person now resisting the national authority, may informally send me, with a view of securing peace to the people of our common country.

Yours, &c., A. LINCOLN.

Afterwards Mr. Blair dictated for and authorized me to make an entry on the back of my retained copy of the letter just above recited, which is as follows:

"JANUARY 28, 1865.

To-day Mr. Blair tells me that on the 21st inst. he delivered to Mr. Davis the original, of which the within is a copy, and left it with him; that at the time of delivering Mr. Davis read it over twice in Mr. Blair's presence, at the close of which he (Mr. B.) remarked that the part about our common country related to the part of Mr. Davis's letter about the two countries, to which Mr. D. replied that he understood it. A. LINCOLN."

Afterwards the Secretary of War placed in my hands the following telegram, indorsed by him, as appears:

"OFFICE U. S. MILITARY TELEGRAPH,
War Department.

[CIPHER.] The following telegram was received at Washington, Jan. 29, 1865:

'FROM HEADQUARTERS ARMY OF THE JAMES,
6.30 P. M., Jan. 29, 1865.

To Hon. E. M. Stanton, Secretary of War.

Ths following despatch is just received from Major-Gen. Parke, who refers it to me for my action. I refer it to you in Gen. Grant's absence.

(Signed) E. O. C. ORD, Maj.-Gen. Comdg.

'HEADQUARTERS ARMY OF THE JAMES.

The following despatch is forwarded to you for your action, since I have no knowledge of General Grant's having had any understanding of this kind. I refer this matter to you as the ranking officer present in the two armies. (Signed)

JOHN G. PARKE, Maj.-Gen. Comdg.'

"FROM HEADQUARTERS NINTH ARMY CORPS,
January 29, 1865.

Major-General John G. Parke, Headquarters Army of the Potomac.

Alexander H. Stephens, R. M. T. Hunter, and J. A. Campbell desire to cross my lines, in accordance with an understanding claimed to exist with Lieut.-Gen. Grant, on their way to Washington as Peace Commissioners. Shall they be admitted? They desire an early answer, so as to come through immediately. They would like to reach City Point to-night if they can. If they cannot do this they would like to come through to-morrow morning.

O. B. WILSON, Maj. Comdg. Ninth Corps.

Respectfully referred to the President for such instructions as he may be pleased to give.

EDWIN M. STANTON, Secretary of War."

JANUARY 29, 1865—8.30 P. M.

It appears that about the time of placing the foregoing telegram in my hands, the Secretary of War despatched to General Ord as follows, to wit:

"WAR DEPARTMENT, WASHINGTON CITY,
Jan. 29, 1865—10 P. M.

Major-General Ord.

This Department has no knowledge of any understanding by Gen. Grant to allow any person to come within his lines as commissioners of any sort. You will therefore allow no one to come into your lines under such character or profession until you receive the President's instructions, to whom your telegrams will be submitted for his directions.

EDWIN M. STANTON, Secretary of War."

[SENT IN CIPHER AT 2 A. M.]

Afterwards, by my directions, the Secretary of War telegraphed Gen. Ord as follows, to wit:

"WAR DEPARTMENT, WASHINGTON CITY, D. C.,
Jan. 30, 1865—10 A. M.

Major-General E. O. C. Ord, Headquarters Army of the James.

By the direction of the President you are instructed to inform the three gentlemen, Messrs. Stephens, Hunter, and Campbell, that a message will be despatched to them at or near where they now are without unnecessary delay.

EDWIN M. STANTON, Secretary of War."

Afterwards I prepared and put into the hands of Major Thomas T. Eckert the following instructions:

"EXECUTIVE MANSION, WASHINGTON, Jan. 30, 1865.

Major T. T. Eckert.

SIR: You will proceed with the documents placed in your hands, and on reaching Gen. Ord will deliver him the letter addressed him by the Secretary of War. Then, by Gen. Ord's assistance, procure an interview with Messrs. Stephens, Hunter, and Campbell, or any of them, and deliver to him or them the paper on which your own letter is written. Note on the copy which you retain the time of delivery and to whom delivered. Receive their answer in writing, waiting a reasonable time for it, and which, if it contain their decision to come through without further conditions, will be your warrant to ask Gen. Ord to pass them through as directed in the letter of the Secretary of War. If by their answer they decline to come, or propose other terms, do not have them passed through. And this being your whole duty return and report to me.

Yours truly, A. LINCOLN."

"CITY POINT, Feb. 1, 1865.

Messrs. Alexander H. Stephens, J. A. Campbell, and R. M. T. Hunter:

Gentlemen: I am instructed by the President of the United States to place this paper in your hands, with the information that if you pass through the United States military lines, it will be understood that you do so for the purpose of an informal conference on the basis of that letter, a copy of which is on the reverse side of this sheet; and that you choose to pass on such understanding, and so notify me in writing. I will procure the Commanding General to pass you through the lines and to Fortress Monroe under such military precautions as he may deem prudent, and at which place you will be met in due time by some person or persons for the purpose of such informal conference; and, further, that you shall have protection, safe conduct, and safe return in all events. THOMAS T. ECKERT,

Major and Aide-de-Camp."

Afterward, but before Major Eckert had departed, the following despatch was received from General Grant:

"OFFICE U. S. MILITARY TELEGRAPH,
[CIPHER.] War Department.

The following telegram was received at Washington, Jan. 31, 1865, from City Point, Va., 10:30 A. M., Jan. 31, 1865:

'*His Excellency Abraham Lincoln, President of the United States:*

The following communication was received here last evening:

"PETERSBURG, VA., Jan. 30, 1865.

Lieut.-Gen. U. S. Grant, Commanding Armies of the United States:

Sir: We desire to pass your lines under safe conduct, and to proceed to Washington to hold a conference with President Lincoln upon the subject of the existing war, and with a view of ascertaining upon what terms it may be terminated, in pursuance of the course indicated by him in his letter to Mr. Blair of Jan. 18, 1865, of which we presume you have a copy, and if not, we wish to see you in person, if convenient, and to confer with you on the subject.

Very respectfully, yours,
ALEXANDER H. STEPHENS,
J. A. CAMPBELL.
R. M. T. HUNTER."

I have sent directions to receive these gentlemen, and expect to have them at my quarters this evening awaiting your instructions.

U. S. GRANT, Lieut.-General,
Commanding Armies of the United States.'"

This, it will be perceived, transferred Gen. Ord's agency in the matter to Gen. Grant. I resolved, however, to send Major Eckert forward with his message, and accordingly telegraphed Gen. Grant as follows, to wit:

"EXECUTIVE MANSION, WASHINGTON,
Jan. 31, 1865.

Lieut.-Gen. Grant, City Point, Va.:

A messenger is coming to you on the business contained in your despatch. Detain the gentlemen in comfortable quarters until he arrives, and then act upon the message he brings as far as applicable, it having been made up to pass through Gen. Ord's hands, and when the gentlemen were supposed to be beyond our lines. A. LINCOLN."

[SENT IN CIPHER AT 1:30 P. M.]

When Major Eckert departed he bore with him a letter of the Secretary of War to Gen. Grant as follows, to wit:

"WAR DEPARTMENT, WASHINGTON, D. C., Jan. 30, 1865.

Lieut.-General Grant, Commanding, &c.

General: The President desires that you procure for the bearer, Major Thomas T. Eckert, an interview with Messrs. Stephens, Hunter, and Campbell, and if, on his return to you he requests it, pass them through our lines to Fortress Monroe by such route and under such military precautions as you may deem prudent, giving them protection and comfortable quarters while there, and that you let none of this have any effect upon any of your movements or plans. By order of the President,

EDWIN M. STANTON, Secretary of War."

Supposing the proper point to be then reached, I despatched the Secretary of State with the following instructions, Major Eckert, however, going ahead of him:

"EXECUTIVE MANSION, Jan. 31, 1865.

Hon. Wm H. Seward, Secretary of State:

You will proceed to Fortress Monroe, Va., there to meet and informally confer with Messrs. Stephens, Hunter, and Campbell on the basis of my letter to F. P. Blair, Esq., of Jan. 18, 1865, a copy of which you have. You will make known to them that three things are indispensable, to wit: 1st, the restoration of the national authority throughout all the States; 2d, no receding by the Executive of the United States on the slavery question from the position assumed thereon in the late annual message to Congress, and in the preceding documents; 3d, no cessation of hostilities short of an end of the war and the disbanding of all the forces hostile to the Government. You will inform them that all propositions of theirs not inconsistent with the above will be considered and passed upon in a spirit of sincere liberality. You will hear all they may choose to say and report it to me. You will not assume to definitely consummate anything. Yours, &c., ABRAHAM LINCOLN."

On the day of its date the following telegram was sent to Gen. Grant:

"WAR DEPARTMENT, WASHINGTON, Feb. 1, 1865.

Lieut.-General Grant, City Point, Va.:

Let nothing which is transpiring change, hinder, or delay your military movements or plans.

A. LINCOLN."

[SENT IN CIPHER AT 9:30 A. M.]

Afterward the following despatch was received from Gen. Grant:

"OFFICE U. S. TELEGRAPH, WAR DEPARTMENT.
[IN CIPHER.]

The following telegram was received at Washington at 2:30 P. M., Feb. 1, 1865, from City Point, Va., Feb. 1, 12:30 P. M., 1865:

'*His Excellency A. Lincoln, President of the United States:*

Your despatch is received. There will be no armistice in consequence of the presence of Mr. Stephens and others within our lines. The troops are kept in readiness to move at the shortest notice if occasion should justify it.

U. S. GRANT, Lieut.-Gen.'"

To notify Major Eckert that the Secretary of State would be at Fortress Monroe and to put them in communication, the following despatch was sent:

"WAR DEPARTMENT, WASHINGTON, Feb. 1, 1865.

T. T. Eckert, care Gen. Grant, City Point, Va.:

Call at Fortress Monroe and put yourself under the direction of Mr. S., whom you will find there.

A. LINCOLN."

On the morning of the 2d inst. the following telegrams were received by me from the Secretary of State and Major Eckert:

"FORTRESS MONROE, Va.—11:30 P. M., Feb. 1, 1865.

The President of the United States:

Arrived here this evening. Richmond party not here. I remain here. W. H. SEWARD."

"CITY POINT, Va., 10 P. M., Feb. 1, 1865.

His Excellency A. Lincoln, President of the United States:

I have the honor to report the delivery of your communication and my letter at 4:15 this afternoon, to which I received a reply at 6 P. M., but not satisfactory. At 8 P. M. the following note, addressed to Gen. Grant, was received:

'CITY POINT, VA., Feb. 1, 1865.

To Lieut.-Gen. Grant:

Sir: We desire to go to Washington City to confer informally with the President personally, in reference to the matters mentioned in his letter to Mr. Blair of the 18th of January, ult., without any personal compromise on any question in the letter. We have the permission to do so from the authorities in Richmond. Very respectfully yours,

ALEX. H. STEPHENS,
R. M. T. HUNTER,
J. A. CAMPBELL.'

At 9:30 P. M. I notified them that they could not proceed further unless they complied with the terms expressed in my letter. The point of meeting designated in the above would not in my opinion be insisted upon. I think Fortress Monroe would be acceptable. Having complied with my instructions, will return to Washington to-morrow unless otherwise ordered. THOMAS T. ECKERT, Major, &c."

On reading this despatch of Major Eckert's, I was about to recall him and the Secretary of State, when the following telegram of Gen. Grant to the Secretary of War was shown me:

"OFFICE U. S. MILITARY TELEGRAPH, WAR DEPARTM'T.

[IN CIPHER.]

The following telegram, received at Washington at 4:35 A. M., Feb. 2, 1865, from City Point, Va., Feb. 1, 1865:

'*Hon. Edwin M. Stanton, Secretary of War:*

Now that the interview between Major Eckert, under his written instructions, and Mr. Stephens and party has ended, I will state confidentially, but not officially, to become a matter of record, that I am convinced, upon conversation with Messrs. Stephens and Hunter, that their intentions are good and their desire sincere to restore peace and Union. I have not felt myself at liberty to express even views of my own, or to account for my reticence. This has placed me in an awkward position, which I could have avoided by not seeing them in the first instance. I fear now their going back without any expression to any one in authority will have a bad influence. At the same time I recognize the difficulties in the way of receiving their informal commissioners at this time, and I do not know what to recommend. I am sorry, however, that Mr. Lincoln cannot have an interview with the two named in this despatch, if not all three now within our lines. Their letter to me was all that the President's instructions contemplated to secure their safe conduct if they had used the same language to Capt. Eckert.

U. S. GRANT, Lieutenant-General.'"

This despatch of Gen. Grant changed my purpose, and accordingly I telegraphed him and the Secretary of War as follows:

"WAR DEPARTMENT, WASHINGTON, Feb. 2, 1865.

To Lieut.-Gen. Grant, City Point, Va.:

Say to the gentlemen that I will meet them personally at Fortress Monroe as soon as I can get there.

A. LINCOLN."

[SENT IN CIPHER AT 9 A. M.]

"WAR DEPARTMENT, WASHINGTON, D. C., Feb. 2, 1865.

To Hon. Wm. H. Seward, Fortress Monroe, Va.:

Induced by a despatch from Gen. Grant, I join you at Fortress Monroe as soon as I can come.

A. LINCOLN."

[SENT IN CIPHER AT 9 A. M.]

Before starting the following despatch was shown me. I proceeded nevertheless:

"OFFICE U. S. MILITARY TELEGRAPH, WAR DEPARTMENT.

[IN CIPHER.]

The following telegram was received at Washington, Feb. 2, 1865, from City Point, Va., 9 A. M., Feb. 2, 1865:

'*To Hon. W. H. Seward, Sec'y of State, Fortress Monroe:*

[Copy to Hon. E. M. Stanton, Secretary of War.]

The gentlemen here have accepted the proposed terms and will leave for Fortress Monroe at 9:30 A. M.

U. S. GRANT, Lieut.-Gen.'"

On the night of the 2d, I reached Hampton Roads, and found the Secretary of State and Major Eckert in a steamer anchored off the shore, and learned of them that the Richmond gentlemen were in another steamer, also anchored off shore in the Roads, and that the Secretary of State had not yet seen or communicated with them. I ascertained that Major Eckert had literally complied with his instructions, and I saw for the first time the answer of the Richmond gentlemen to him, which in his despatch to me of the 1st, he characterized as not satisfactory. That answer is as follows, to wit:

"CITY POINT, VA., Feb. 1, 1865.

To Thos T Eckert, Major and Aide-de-camp.

Major: Your note delivered by yourself this day has been considered. In reply, we have to say that we were furnished with a copy of the letter of President Lincoln to F. P. Blair, of the 18th of January ult. Another copy of which is appended to your note. Our intentions are contained in the letter, of which the following is a copy:

'RICHMOND, Jan. 28, 1865.

In conformity with the letter of Mr. Lincoln, of which the foregoing is a copy, you are to proceed to Washington City for an informal conference with him upon the issues involved in the existing war and for the purpose of securing peace to the two countries.

With great respect, your obedient servant,

JEFFERSON DAVIS.'

The substantial object to be attained by the informal conference is to ascertain upon what terms the existing war can be terminated honorably. Our instructions contemplate a personal interview between President Lincoln and ourselves at Washington; but with this explanation, we are ready to meet any person or persons that President Lincoln may appoint, at such place as he may designate. Our earnest desire is that a just and honorable peace may be agreed upon, and we are prepared to receive or to submit propositions which may possibly lead to the attainment of that end.

Very respectfully yours,

ALEXANDER H. STEPHENS,
R. M. T. HUNTER,
JOHN A. CAMPBELL."

A note of these gentlemen, subsequently addressed to Gen. Grant, has already been given in Major Eckert's despatch of the 1st inst. I also saw here for the first time the following note addressed by the Richmond gentlemen to Major Eckert:

"CITY POINT, VA., Feb. 2, 1865.

Thomas T. Eckert, Major and A. D. C.

Major: In reply to your verbal statement that your instructions did not allow you to alter the conditions upon which a passport would be given to us, we say that we are willing to proceed to Fortress Monroe, and there to have an informal conference with any person or persons that President Lincoln may appoint, on the basis of his letter to Francis P. Blair of the 18th of January ultimo, or upon any other terms or conditions that he may hereafter propose not inconsistent with the essential principles of self-government and popular rights, upon which our institutions are founded. It is our earnest wish to ascertain, after a free interchange of ideas and information, upon what principles and terms, if any, a just and honorable peace can be established without the further effusion of blood, and to contribute our utmost efforts to accomplish such a result. We think it better to add, that in accepting your passport we are not to be understood as committing ourselves to any thing, but to carry on this informal conference with the views and feelings above expressed.

Very respectfully yours, &c.,

ALEX. H. STEPHENS,
J. A. CAMPBELL,
R. M. T. HUNTER."

[NOTE. The above communication was delivered

to me at Fortress Monroe at 4.40 P. M., February 2, by Lieut.-Col. Babcock, of Gen. Grant's staff.

THOS. T. ECKERT, Major and A. D. C.]

"EXECUTIVE MANSION, Feb. 10, 1865.

On the morning of the 3d, the gentlemen, Messrs. Stephens, Hunter, and Campbell, came aboard of our steamer and had an interview with the Secretary of State and myself of several hours' duration. No question of preliminaries to the meeting was then and there made or mentioned. No other person was present. No papers were exchanged or produced, and it was in advance agreed that the conversation was to be informal and verbal merely. On my part the whole substance of the instructions to the Secretary of State, hereinbefore recited, was stated and insisted upon, and nothing was said inconsistent therewith, while by the other party it was not said that in any event or on any condition they ever would consent to reunion; and yet they equally omitted to declare that they would never so consent. They seemed to desire a postponement of that question and the adoption of some other course first, which, as some of them seemed to argue, might or might not lead to reunion, but which course we thought would amount to an indefinite postponement.

The conference ended without result.

The foregoing, containing, as is believed, all the information sought, is respectfully submitted.

ABRAHAM LINCOLN."

REPORT OF MESSRS. STEPHENS, HUNTER, AND CAMPBELL.

EXECUTIVE OFFICE, RICHMOND, February 6, 1865.

To the Senate and House of Representatives of the Confederate States of America:

Having recently received a written notification which satisfied me that the President of the United States was disposed to confer informally with unofficial agents which might be sent by me, with a view to the restoration of peace, I requested the Hon. Alexander H. Stephens, the Hon. R. M. T. Hunter, and the Hon John A. Campbell to proceed through our lines and to hold conference with Mr. Lincoln, or any one he might depute to represent him.

I herewith transmit, for the information of Congress, the report of the eminent citizens above named, showing that the enemy refused to enter into negotiations with the Confederate States, or any one of them separately, or to give to our people any other terms or guarantees than those which the conqueror may grant, or to permit us to have peace on any other basis than our unconditional submission to their rule, coupled with the acceptance of their recent legislation on the subject of the relations between the white and black population of each State. Such is, as I understand, the effect of the amendment to the Constitution which has been adopted by the Congress of the United States.

JEFFERSON DAVIS.

RICHMOND, VA., February 5, 1865.

To the President of the Confederate States:

SIR: Under your letter of appointment of the 28th ult., we proceeded to seek an "informal conference" with Abraham Lincoln, President of the United States, upon the subject mentioned in the letter. The conference was granted, and took place on the 30th inst., on board of a steamer in Hampton Roads, where we met President Lincoln and the Hon. Mr. Seward, Secretary of State of the United States. It continued for several hours, and was both full and explicit.

We learned from them that the message of President Lincoln to the Congress of the United States in December last explains clearly and distinctly his sentiments as to the terms, conditions, and method of proceeding by which peace can be secured to the people, and we were not informed that they would be modified or altered to obtain that end. We understand from him that no terms or proposals of any treaty or agreement looking to an ultimate settlement would be entertained or made by him with the Confederate States, because that would be a recognition of their existence as a separate power, which, under no circumstances, would be done; and for like reasons that no such terms would be entertained by him from the States separately; that no extended truce or armistice (as at present advised) would be granted, without a satisfactory assurance in advance of a complete restoration of the authority of the United States over all places within the States of the Confederacy.

That whatever consequence may follow from the reëstablishment of that authority must be accepted; but that individuals, subject to pains and penalties under the laws of the United States, might rely upon a very liberal use of the power confided to him to remit those pains and penalties if peace be restored.

During the conference the proposed amendment to the Constitution of the United States, adopted by Congress on the 31st ult., was brought to our notice. This amendment declares that neither slavery nor involuntary servitude, except for crimes, should exist within the United States, or any place within their jurisdiction, and that Congress should have power to enforce this amendment by appropriate legislation. Of all the correspondence that preceded the conference herein mentioned, and leading to the same, you have heretofore been informed.

Very respectfully, your obedient servants,

ALEX. H. STEPHENS,
R. M. T. HUNTER,
JOHN A. CAMPBELL.

The commerce of 1864 with Europe was limited in consequence of the increased duties on imports and the favorable harvests abroad, which diminished the demand for breadstuffs. The official statement of the Treasury Department gives the following results of the trade of the country for the fiscal years 1863 and 1864. The fiscal year ends on June 30th. The specie export for 1863 should be increased to $18,207,879, to embrace a large unusual shipment made from California to England for safety of transit.

Imports.	1863.	1864.
Goods	$252,731,939	$328,514,559
Specie	9,555,648	13,155,706
Total	$262,287,587	$341,670,265
Exports.		
Domestic produce	$249,856,649	$320,292,171
Foreign "	17,796,200	20,373,449
Specie	64,156,610	105,125,750
Total	$331,809,459	$445,791,370

The import valuations are in specie, being the invoice value. The export values are in legal tender prices. The advance in gold, as compared with legal tender notes and the increase of taxes, seriously affected the prices of articles sold for consumption.

Some modification allowing more freedom of trade was made in the conditions of commercial intercourse with places within the limits of the insurrectionary States during the year.

The financial affairs of the Government were successfully administered during the year.

The receipts from all sources, upon the basis of warrants signed by the Secretary of the Treasury, including loans and the balance in the Treasury, on the 1st day of July, 1863, were $1,394,796,007.62; and the aggregate disbursements, upon the same basis, were $1,298,056,101.89, leaving a balance in the Treasury, as shown by warrants, of $96,746,905.73.

Deduct from these amounts the amount of the principal of the public debt redeemed, and the amount of issues in substitution therefor, and the actual cash operations of the Treasury were: receipts, $884,076,646.57; disbursements, $865,234,087.86; which leaves a cash balance in the Treasury of $18,842,558.71.

Of the receipts, there were derived from customs $102,316,152.99; from lands, $588,333.29; from direct taxes, $475,648.96; from internal revenue, $109,741,134.10; from miscellaneous sources, $47,511,448.10; and from loans applied to actual expenditures, including former balance, $623,443,929.13.

There were disbursed, for the civil service, $27,505,599.46; for pensions and Indians, $7,517,930.97; for the War Department, $690,791,842.97; for the Navy Department, $85,733,292.77; for interest of the public debt, $53,685,421.69—making an aggregate of $865,234,087.86, and leaving a balance in the Treasury of $18,842,558.71, as before stated.

The public debt on the 1st day of July, 1864, as appears by the books of the Treasury, amounted to $1,740,690,489.49.

The action of Congress relative to slaves and free colored persons since the commencement of the war may be thus summarily stated. Slaves used for military purposes by the enemy were declared to be free; an additional article of war dismissed from service all officers who should surrender escaped fugitives coming within the lines of the armies; three thousand slaves in the District of Columbia were emancipated, and slaveholding forbidden: it was enacted that colored persons in the District should be tried for the same offences, in the same manner, and be subject to the same punishment as white persons, and that such persons should not be excluded as witnesses on account of color; and that colored schools should be provided, and the same rate of appropriation made to them as to schools for white children; and that there should be no exclusion from any railway car in the District on account of color; slavery was forever prohibited in all territory of the United States; a joint resolution was passed pledging the faith of the nation to aid non-seceding States to emancipate their slaves; all slaves of persons aiding the enemy, who should take refuge within the lines of the army, were declared free; it was enacted that no slave should be surrendered to any claimant until such person had made oath that he had not given aid and comfort to the rebellion; the President was authorized to receive into the military service persons of African descent, and such person, his mother, wife, and children, owing service to any person giving aid to the rebellion, were declared free; the mutual right of search was arranged within certain limits with Great Britain, in order to suppress the slave trade; the independence of Hayti and Liberia were recognized, and diplomatic relations with them authorized; colored persons, free or slave, to be enrolled and drafted the same as whites, the former to have the same pay as the latter, and the slave to be free; all fugitive slave acts were repealed; the coastwise slave trade was declared illegal; colored persons enabled to testify in all the courts of the United States; colored persons were authorized to carry the mails of the United States. Other measures were introduced but failed to pass.

The question of the proper disposition to be made of the vast number of persons of African descent who by the operation of the Emancipation proclamation, by the progress of the Union armies in various parts of the South, or the acts of Emancipation passed by the Constitutional Conventions of several of the States, became free, continued to excite the anxious attention of the Government and of the citizens of the United States. While some progress was made toward the solution of the difficulties, it cannot be said that any entirely satisfactory policy was adopted. Different sections required differences in detail in the management of freedmen. The number who had thus far obtained their freedom is not easily ascertained. In September, 1864, the Philadelphia "North American" published a carefully-prepared estimate for each State, making the aggregate amount 1,368,600. Mr. J. R. Gilmore (Edmund Kirke) had previously estimated the number at 1,555,225, while Jefferson Davis in the summer stated the number at 3,000,000, about three-fourths of the whole number in the country. Since that time, Sherman's march through Georgia, South and North Carolina, resulted in setting at liberty hardly less than 200,000, and victories in other quarters materially added to the number elsewhere. Whatever may have been the case in 1863, it hardly admits of a doubt that, including those set free by the Emancipation acts in Maryland, Western Virginia, and Missouri, the whole number of freedmen in 1864 did not fall much, if at all, short of 3,000,000. Of these nearly 250,000 were in the army, either as soldiers or teamsters, and probably more than twice as many more women, children, or old men were employed as servants, cooks, washerwomen, etc., etc., in the various camps, military posts, hospitals, etc., throughout the country. Of the remainder a large number picked up a living, more or less precarious, in the larger cities and towns of the West and South. Very few of them came North, the severe climate being disliked by the negro. Not far from a million and perhaps more than that number were employed upon plantations leased or permitted by the General Government, or worked for wages for farmers and planters in Missouri, Maryland, or Western Virginia, or did themselves become lessees of plantations, or were gathered in Freedmen's Home Colonies if feeble, aged, or infirm, and there supported from the proceeds of the labor of those who were able-bodied.

The Freedmen's Aid Societies, Commissions, and Associations, of which there were eighteen or twenty in the United States, were active and efficient in furnishing supplies, teachers, and religious instruction to the freedmen. They expended for these purposes during the three years ending January, 1865, nearly one million of dollars. Through their efforts a bill was introduced into Congress providing for the Establishment of a Freedman's Bureau in connection with the War Department which finally passed.

The statements of the number of prisoners exchanged to the close of 1864 by each party in the war are quite conflicting, and in the absence of the official documents of either, which were withheld from publication, and which, perhaps, would not agree in details, it is difficult to arrive at a satisfactory conclusion. The report of the Commissary General of prisoners, which accompanied Secretary Stanton's report at the close of 1863, stated that 121,337 of the enemy as prisoners had been exchanged against 110,866 Union prisoners; and that 29,229 still remained in Federal prisons. On the other hand the statistics kept by the clerk of Libby prison, at Richmond, showed that from the 1st of January, 1864, to December 19th, 31,630 Federal prisoners had passed the doors of that prison. This number is independent of twenty thousand captured at Spottsylvania and elsewhere in Virginia, and sent directly South. The statistics of the same prison made the number of those who passed its doors and departed as prisoners of war since the commencement of hostilities at 225,000.

Of the points in dispute between the authorities on each side and which caused temporary suspensions of the exchange, the most serious related to the negro prisoners.

This dispute was thus founded on principles which each party held to be fundamental, and yet were directly opposite. If the Federal Government yielded its assent to this doctrine, it would be an abandonment of the proclamation of emancipation, a breach of faith toward those men it had made free and accepted as soldiers in its service, and a direct recognition of the principle of property in man. On the other hand, if the Richmond authorities recognized the right of those fugitives from bondage to freedom, it would be an abandonment of the position for which they had been so long contending, and knock the corner-stone from under the whole fabric of slavery. The excess of prisoners finally became so large in the Federal hands, that the question upon which it was impossible to agree was temporarily waived. Another difficulty which existed early in the year, and at the close of the previous one, was a charge that the Federal Government departed from the original agreement.

From the date of the cartel until July, 1863, the enemy had an excess of prisoners. The Federal authorities after that date declared the cartel had been violated by the release from parole of the Vicksburg prisoners, and refused to proceed. They then proposed to exchange officer for officer and man for man. This was refused by the other side, on the ground that it was a departure from the cartel, and the exchange was suspended for some time on this ground. At length on August 10th, 1864, the Confederate Commissioner accepted these terms, "in view of the very large number of prisoners now held by each party and the suffering consequent upon their consequent confinement." The exchange, however, was not at the time resumed, as the question of slave soldiers was still under discussion.

This general suspension of an exchange and the rapid accumulation of prisoners became an additional cause of irritation to both parties. In the Federal hands there were between 60,000 and 70,000, and nearly as many in Confederate prisons. To the enemy there was an additional grievance arising from this detention. Their supply of men was limited; they needed every one for service in the field. In addition a large force was necessarily withdrawn from the field to guard the prisoners. Statements of great cruelty to Federal prisoners were now published and verified. Among them was the following appeal to the President, made by officers in confinement at Charleston:

CONFEDERATE STATES PRISON,
CHARLESTON, S. C., August —, 1864.

To the President of the United States:

The condition of the enlisted men belonging to the Union armies, now prisoners to the Confederate rebel forces, is such that it becomes our duty, and the duty of every commisioned officer, to make known the facts in the case to the Government of the United States, and to use every honorable effort to secure a general exchange of prisoners, thereby relieving thousands of our comrades from the horrors now surrounding them.

For some time past there has been a concentration of prisoners from all parts of the rebel territory to the State of Georgia—the commissioned officers being confined at Macon, and the enlisted men at Andersonville. Recent movements of the Union armies under General Sherman have compelled the removal of prisoners to other points, and it is now understood that they will be removed to Savannah, Georgia, Columbia and Charleston, South Carolina. But no change of this kind holds out any prospect of relief to our poor men. Indeed, as the localities selected are far more unhealthy, there must be an increase rather than a diminution of suffering. Colonel Hill, Provost Marshal General, Confederate States Army, at Atlanta, stated to one of the undersigned that there were thirty-five thousand prisoners at Andersonville, and by all accounts from the United States soldiers who have been confined there, the number is not overstated by him. These thirty-five thousand are confined in a field of some thirty acres, enclosed by a board fence, heavily guarded. About one-third have various kinds of indifferent shelter; but upward of thirty thousand are wholly without shelter, or even shade of any kind, and are exposed to the storms and rains, which are of almost daily occurrence; the cold dews of the night, and the more terrible effects of the sun striking with almost tropical fierceness upon their unprotected heads. This mass of men jostle and crowd each other up and down the limits of their enclosure, in storm or sun, and others lie down upon the pitiless earth at night, with no other covering than the clothing upon their backs, few of them having even a blanket.

Upon entering the prison every man is deliberately stripped of money and other property, and as no clothing or blankets are ever supplied to their prisoners by the rebel authorities the condition of the apparel of the soldiers, just from an active campaign, can be easily imagined. Thousands are without pants or coats, and hundreds without even a pair of drawers to cover their nakedness.

To these men, as indeed to all prisoners, there is issued three-quarters of a pound of bread or meal, and one-eighth of a pound of meat per day. This is the entire ration, and upon it the prisoner must live or die. The meal is often unsifted and sour, and the meat such as in the North is consigned to the soapmaker. Such are the rations upon which Union soldiers are fed by the rebel authorities, and by which they are barely holding on to life. But to starvation and exposure, to sun and storm, add the sickness which prevails to a most alarming and terrible extent. On an average one hundred die daily. It is impossible that any Union soldier should know all the facts pertaining to this terrible mortality, as they are not paraded by the rebel authorities. Such statements as the following, made by ——— ———, speaks eloquent testimony. Said he:—"Of twelve of us who were captured, six died; four are in the hospital, and I never expect to see them again. There are but two of us left." In 1862, at Montgomery, Alabama, under far more favorable circumstances, the prisoners being protected by sheds, from one hundred and fifty to two hundred were sick from diarrhœa and chills, out of seven hundred. The same percentage would give seven thousand sick at Andersonville. It needs no comment, no efforts at word painting, to make such a picture stand out boldly in most horrible colors.

Nor is this all. Among the ill-fated of the many who have suffered amputation in consequence of injuries received before capture, sent from rebel hospitals before their wounds were healed, there are eloquent witnesses of the barbarities of which they are victims. If to these facts are added this, that nothing more demoralizes soldiers and develops the evil passions of man than starvation, the terrible condition of Union prisoners at Andersonville can be readily imagined. They are fast losing hope, and becoming utterly reckless of life. Numbers, crazed by their sufferings, wander about in a state of idiocy; others deliberately cross the "dead line," and are remorselessly shot down.

In behalf of these men we most earnestly appeal to the President of the United States. Few of them have been captured except in the front of battle, in the deadly encounter, and only when overpowered by numbers. They constitute as gallant a portion of our armies as carry our banners anywhere. If released, they would soon return to again do vigorous battle for our cause. We are told that the only obstacle in the way of exchange is the status of enlisted negroes captured from our armies, the United States claiming that the cartel covers all who serve under its flag, and the Confederate States refusing to consider the colored soldiers heretofore slaves as prisoners of war.

We beg leave to suggest some facts bearing upon the question of exchange, which we would urge upon your consideration. Is it not consistent with the national honor, without waiving the claim that the negro soldiers shall be treated as prisoners of war, to effect an exchange of the white soldiers? The two classes are treated differently by the enemy. The whites are confined in such prisons as Libby and Andersonville, starved and treated with a barbarism unknown to civilized nations. The blacks, on the contrary, are seldom imprisoned. They are distributed among the citizens, or employed on government works. Under these circumstances they receive enough to eat, and are worked no harder than they have been accustomed to be. They are neither starved nor killed off by the pestilence in the dungeons of Richmond and Charleston. It is true they are again made slaves, but their slavery is freedom and happiness compared with the cruel existence imposed upon our gallant men. They are not bereft of hope, as are the white soldiers, dying by piecemeal. Their chances of escape are tenfold greater than those of the white soldiers, and their condition, in all its lights, is tolerable in comparison with that of the prisoners of war now languishing in the dens and pens of secession.

While, therefore, believing the claims of our Government, in matters of exchange, to be just, we are profoundly impressed with the conviction that the circumstances of the two classes of soldiers are so widely different that the Government can honorably consent to an exchange, waiving for a time the established principle justly claimed to be applicable in the case. Let thirty-five thousand suffering, starving, and dying enlisted men aid this appeal. By prompt and decided action in their behalf thirty-five thousand heroes will be made happy. For the eighteen hundred commissioned officers now prisoners we urge nothing. Although desirous of returning to our duty, we can bear imprisonment with more fortitude if the enlisted men, whose sufferings we know to be intolerable, were restored to liberty and life.

The exposure to artillery fire of officers who were prisoners was resorted to on two or three occasions as acts of retaliation, but it quickly led to explanations, and no injuries were the result. Arrangements were made by each party, on the approach of winter, to furnish their soldiers with blankets and other absolute necessities. Articles for Federal prisoners were sent to City Point from the North, and distributed as directed by agents of the rebels to prisoners in their hands. At the same time a thousand bales of cotton were shipped from Mobile to New York and sold. With the money thus obtained, blankets and other necessaries were provided for the rebel prisoners in Federal prisons. A contribution was also made up in England, and sent over for Confederate prisoners; but permission to deliver it was refused.

In November an exchange was resumed beginning first with the invalids and the sick, and carried forward very rapidly, on the basis of man for man, and officer for officer.

CHAPTER XLIX.

Progress of Military Operations—General Thomas' position in Tennessee—General Hood's position in Tennessee—Movement of the Enemy on the James River—Another Battle at Hatcher's Run—March of Gen. Sherman from Savannah—Capture of Columbia, S. C.—Evacuation of Charleston—Advance to Fayetteville—Transfer of Gen. Schofield to North Carolina—Capture of Wilmington—Advance of Gen. Sherman to Cheraw—Battle at Averysboro—Battle at Bentonville—Arrival at Goldsboro—Results of Sherman's March.

THE severe weather of the winter months caused no cessation in army operations. Maj.-Gen. Thomas, after pursuing the retreating forces of Gen. Hood from Tennessee, collected his troops at Eastport. Thence a considerable body of his men, consisting of the 23d corps under Gen. Schofield, were moved by railroad to the Atlantic coast and landed on the North Carolina shore. Another small portion was sent to Gen. Sherman at Savannah. To Gen. Thomas was now assigned the defence of that extended portion of the country from Atlanta north and westward, which belonged to the department under Gen. Sherman, when he commenced his march upon Savannah. The large garrisons which had been required at Memphis and other places on the Mississippi River, also in Tennessee and Kentucky, had been set free by his new position, and were able to join his forces. At the same time, the army of Gen. Hood had been fatally reduced. The situation of Eastport, on the Tennessee River, near the junction of the lines of Tennessee, Mississippi, and Alabama, placed the northern portion of the two latter States at the mercy of Gen. Thomas.

On Jan. 16th, 1865, Gen. Croxton, with a division of the 16th corps and the 1st division of cavalry, reconnoitred from Eastport toward Corinth, passing through Iuka and Brownsville. It appeared that a small force of Gen. Hood's army held Corinth, while the main body was at Tupelo. Thirty-five of the enemy were captured at the depot, and a hotel at Corinth burned. Deserters, averaging from thirty to fifty daily, were coming within Gen. Thomas's lines, from Hood's army. Subsequently a part of Gen. Hood's forces were marched by land eastward across the State of Georgia, to assist in opposing Gen. Sherman. This movement left Gen. Thomas free in the latter part of February to coöperate with Gen. Canby against Mobile, and Southern Alabama, and Mississippi.

Thus far the quiet of the Army of the Potomac, since its operations last described, had been undisturbed, except by those incidents usual to hostile armies when near each other. No important movement had been attempted. Under the call for troops in December, 1864, large numbers were going forward to fill its ranks. The withdrawal of a portion of the fleet and of the forces of the Army of the James for the second attack on Wilmington, tempted the enemy at Richmond to make a demonstration for the purpose of breaking the pontoon bridges over the James, and cutting the communication between the Federal forces on the two banks. If successful, it was undoubtedly the purpose to follow it up by an attack on the forces on the north bank. A fleet, consisting of the Virginia, Fredericksburg, and Richmond, ironclads carrying four guns each, and the wooden vessels Drewry, Nansemond, and Hampton, with two guns each, the Buford, one gun, the steamer Torpedo, and three torpedo boats, left Richmond on Jan. 23d. About midnight, the fleet passed Fort Brady, and began to pass the obstructions. A fire was now opened by the fort, to which the enemy replied, dismounting a hundred pounder in the fort, and escaping beyond its range. The chain in front of the obstructions beyond the lower end of the Dutch Gap Canal was cut, and the Fredericksburg passed through. But the Richmond, Virginia, and Drewry, in attempting to follow, grounded. The Drewry could not be got off, and was abandoned as daylight appeared, and was blown up subsequently by a shell from the battery on shore. The report of the affair by the enemy is as follows:

> The flagship of the expedition was the Virginia, commanded by Lieutenant Dunnington. The Richmond was commanded by Lieutenant Bell, who was First Lieutenant on the Alabama at the time of her fight with the Kearsarge. The Fredericksburg was commanded by Lieutenant Sheppard. The latter vessel, being of light draught, passed clean through the obstruction, but the others found a lower tier of obstructions deeply submerged, and which had not been moved by the freshet; the depth of water over them being impassable by vessels of their draught. The Virginia received a shot in the centre by a three hundred pounder Parrott shell, fired from a Yankee Monitor, being struck when trying to get off sunken obstructions in the river. The shot displaced a few of her bolts, and killed five of her crew. No other damage was done, but it was found that her engines were fouled, not in consequence of the shot, and that she was not in fighting order; in the mean time the fire of our vessels had completely silenced the Yankee shore batteries, and a number of shots were exchanged with the monitor, with what effect is not known. In consequence of the condition of the Virginia's engine, it was decided, on a consultation of the officers of the flotilla, to withdraw all vessels, which was done without further casualty. It had been impossible to survey the channel to any great extent on account of the enemy's picket fire, and the submerged obstructions of the river were found to be more effectual than they were supposed to be.

This was followed by shelling between the hostile batteries on the river throughout the day, and during the night the fleet returned to Richmond.

On the night of Jan. 31st, marching orders

were issued to the entire army at Petersburg, consisting of the 2d, 5th, 6th, and 9th corps. This was preparatory to another movement by the left, the plan of which was to throw a strong flanking column far beyond the right of the enemy's works, along Hatcher's Run, so that it might pass behind them and take them in reverse, and then, if possible, turn north and march upon the Southside Railroad. Meanwhile the rest of the army would form a connection between this corps on the left flank and press the enemy gradually back as far as possible toward the railroad. During the day and night following the issue of the orders, the usual preparations for a forward movement went on; troops and baggage were moved to the proper places, hospitals were cleared, the sick sent to City Point, and four days' rations distributed to the troops. Meanwhile a heavy fire was opened upon the enemy's lines at different points, to conceal the preparations on foot. This was kept up during portions of some nights in which the cars were kept incessantly running to mass troops and supplies on the right. The preparations for the movement were not completed until Sunday morning, the 5th. Gregg's division of cavalry had been ordered to move at 3 o'clock in the morning. The 5th corps, under General Warren, was to march at five, and the 2d corps under Gen. Humphreys, at six o'clock. The flanking column consisted of the 5th corps with Gregg's cavalry. The cavalry column moved down the Jerusalem plank road, and reached Reams' station soon after daybreak. The 5th corps moved along the Halifax road at 5 o'clock, with Gen. Ayres's division in advance, Gen. Griffin's next, and Gen. Crawford's in the rear. On the Vaughan road were the 2d and 3d divisions of the 2d corps, under Gen. Humphreys, who were expected to move directly upon the works at Hatcher's Run, while the 5th corps advanced around the right.

From Reams' station the cavalry advanced in the direction of Dinwiddie Court House, and encountered at Rowanty Creek, a tributary of the Nottoway, a portion of Hampton's cavalry, dismounted and sheltered by breastworks on the opposite bank, but commanding the bridge. After a short skirmish the bridge and the works were carried with a loss of about twenty men, and the capture of twenty-two prisoners. In a few hours two bridges were built for the troops and trains to cross. Meanwhile a portion of the cavalry advanced to Dinwiddie Court House, and captured some empty wagons, a mail, &c. Scouting parties also advanced up the Boydton road, and captured a few wagons. At night the force returned to Rowanty Creek, where Gen. Gregg bivouacked.

Meanwhile Gen. Humphreys, with the 2d and 3d divisions of the 2d corps continued his advance up the Vaughan road, encountering and driving in the enemy's pickets, and reaching the Run. The intrenchments of the enemy on the opposite bank were not very strongly manned, but the obstructions in the stream were such that the cavalry were driven back in an attempt to cross. The brigade of Gen. De Trobriand was then drawn up in line of battle, and the 99th Pennsylvania sent across in skirmish order, who carried the works at once with a small loss, and secured the fording of the stream. The enemy's small force were now driven back rapidly to the woods, and the brigade took a position on a hill beyond the ford, and throwing up intrenchments rendered itself secure. Previously, however, the 2d division, under Gen. Smyth, when within half a mile of the Run, turned off to the right on a path leading northeasterly toward Armstrong's mill and pond. After advancing three-fourths of a mile, the enemy were found in a strong position. Their pickets were driven in after a sharp encounter, and a line was formed connecting the left of the division with the right of the 3d, which Gen. Mott commanded. Temporary earthworks were thrown up and preparations made to resist an attack. Some skirmishing ensued between the pickets until 2 o'clock P. M., when a heavy artillery fire commenced, and an attack from the enemy was apparent. Under cover of the artillery fire the enemy pressed through the difficult swamp, and rushed upon the rifle-pits, which now partly covered the right of Gen. Smyth's division. He was received with such a sharp fire as forced him to fall back to the woods. A second and third attempt was made to carry the works, and turn the flank of Gen. Smyth, but each was repulsed. At dusk the fighting was over, and the lines remained secure. The loss of Gen. Smyth was about three hundred, and that of the enemy who made the attack somewhat larger.

During the night the 5th corps was brought into connection, on the left of the 2d corps, with the left of the 5th, covered by the cavalry of Gen. Gregg. The 6th and 9th corps were also so disposed as to render assistance to the 5th and 2d. In the morning the position of the troops was strengthened by constant work until noon. At this time Gen. Crawford's division of the 5th corps was sent toward Dabney's mills, in order to reach the Boydton plank road. The country through which the route lay was covered with woods, swamps, and ravines, cutting it up in all directions. At the same time the enemy, believing the Federal force had recrossed Hatcher's Run and abandoned the advance, had sent out Gen. Pegram with his division. About two miles above the Vaughan road his skirmishers met those of Gen. Crawford, and after a sharp contest were forced back toward his original position. The division of Gen. Evans came to the assistance of Pegram, and the advance of Gen. Crawford was checked. The division of Gen. Ayres was now sent to support Gen. Crawford, and a brigade of Griffin's to support Gen. Gregg, who was on the left, and had been engaged for some time with Lee's cavalry, which pressed his rear heavily. During a lull which happened, his force threw up breastworks. But toward evening they were attacked with great force by the enemy, and his pickets driven with his force into the works. The battle increased, and many of his officers were wounded. While this was taking place on the left of the Vaughan road, the infantry had again become furiously engaged on the right of the road by repeated attacks of the enemy along the line. Finally Gen. Gregg was driven out of his breastworks, and his line forced back to Hatcher's Run, where he soon found that a similar misfortune had happened to the infantry. It was not until the intrenched lines on the Vaughan road and Hatcher's Run, thrown up on the previous day, were reached, that the routed troops could be rallied. The enemy dashed forward with great elation, but were met by such a sharp fire from the intrenchments as caused them to fall back rapidly to the woods. Night put an end to the conflict. The following is a report by Gen. Lee of the operations of the day:

HEADQUARTERS ARMY NORTHERN VIRGINIA, Feb. 6, 1865.

General S. Cooper:

The enemy moved in strong force yesterday to Hatcher's Run. Part of his infantry, with Gregg's cavalry, crossed and proceeded on the Vaughan road, the infantry to Cattail Creek, the cavalry to Dinwiddie Court House, where the advance encountered a portion of our cavalry and retired.

In the afternoon parts of Hill's and Gordon's troops demonstrated against the enemy on the left of Hatcher's Run, near Armstrong's Mill. Finding him intrenched, they withdrew after dark. During the night the force that had advanced beyond the creek returned to it, and were reported to be recrossing.

This morning Pegram's division moved down to the right bank of the creek to reconnoitre, when it was vigorously attacked. The battle was obstinately contested several hours, but Gen. Pegram being killed while bravely encouraging his men, and Col. Hoffman wounded, some confusion occurred, and the division was pressed back to its original position. Evans's division, ordered by Gen. Gordon to support Pegram's, charged the enemy and forced him back, but was in turn compelled to retire. Malone's division arriving, the enemy was driven rapidly to his defences on Hatcher's Run.

The Union loss during the day was estimated at 1,500 to 2,000 men. The loss of the enemy was estimated as exceeding 1,000 men, including Gen. J. Pegram and Col. Hoffman, as killed.

During the night the works were strengthened, and early in the morning of the 7th the enemy made a demonstration on the skirmish lines of the cavalry and infantry on the right and left of the Vaughan road, but were repulsed. At noon the division of Gen. Crawford was sent out to make a reconnoissance, supported on the left by the division of Gen. Wheaton. The pickets of the enemy were encountered after an advance of about half a mile, and driven back to their works higher up the run between Armstrong's and Burgess's mills, and about two miles beyond the latter. A sharp fire of musketry ensued; but as Gen. Crawford was not prepared to force the lines, he drew his men back again to Hatcher's Run. The fighting by this column was kept up until night. During the day, the cannonading between the lines had been constant. The next day, the 8th, was devoted to throwing up intrenchments, and strong defensive works soon indicated the points at which the permanent lines were to be located. The enemy made no attempts to force the new positions, but appeared satisfied to give up the lower part of the run if no attempt was made by the Union forces on the Boydton plank road. The result of the entire movement had been to gain an advanced position on the enemy's right, which was held firmly, by completing the lines to Hatcher's Run, and extending the City Point railroad thither. Affairs now continued quiet for some time. Artillery duels were frequent along the lines before Petersburg, but no important movement was made. Large numbers of deserters from the enemy were constantly coming into the lines of Gen. Grant, often exceeding seventy a day for many days successively, and increasing to two hundred.

In the Shenandoah valley, small expeditions by one or the other party served to prevent a quiet state of affairs. Further west, the enemy captured Beverly on Jan. 11th. This was done by Gen. Rosser, who crossed the mountains, and early on the morning of Jan. 11th entered the place, making prisoners of four hundred of the garrison, consisting of seven hundred men, and dispersing the rest. They were asleep in their winter quarters, with no pickets out further than three hundred yards from their camp. A large amount of commissary and quartermasters' stores, with a great number of horses, were also taken. Again, on the 21st of February, a body of the enemy's cavalry, under Lieut. McNeil, dashed into Cumberland before daylight, surprised and captured the pickets, and carried off Maj.-Gens. Kelly and Crook. They were quietly seized in their beds with their staff officers, and taken to Richmond, and subsequently exchanged.

The success which attended the march of Gen. Sherman through Georgia, both in disheartening the Southern people and in destroying the communications between different parts of the Confederacy, determined the nature of the approaching campaign. The field of decisive operations was now reduced to three States, and if South and North Carolina were overrun it would not only cut off the resources of Gen. Lee's army at Richmond, but also result in concentrating an overwhelming force against him. Both combatants therefore prepared to put forth their final efforts. At Richmond, Gen. Lee was appointed as General-in-Chief; Gen. Johnston was ordered to the command in South Carolina; Gen. Hood was supplanted by Gen. Taylor in Alabama and Mississippi; Gen. Breckinridge was brought into the Cabinet as Secretary of War, which had already undergone a change by the displacement of Mr. Memminger as Secretary of the Treasury, and the appointment of Mr. Trenholm of South Carolina. On the Federal side Gen. Schofield, with a strong force, was placed in command in North Carolina, to prepare the way for the approach of Gen. Sherman, and Gen. Gillmore relieved Gen. Foster in the Department of South Carolina.

Immediately after taking possession of Savannah, Gen. Sherman began his preparations for a march through the Carolinas to Richmond; meanwhile Gen. Hardee with his command occupied Charleston. The first movement of Gen. Sherman was to send a part of Gen. Logan's 15th corps and Gen. Blair's 17th corps, both belonging to Gen. Howard's wing of his army, by transports to Beaufort, near Hilton Head. The important bridge where the railroad from Savannah to Charleston crossed the Pocotaligo, was the object of this movement. This bridge, 49 miles from Savannah and 55 miles from Charleston, being with the trestle work in the swamp a mile in length, was so necessary to the communication between the two cities, that frequent attempts had been made by the Union commanders of the department to destroy it. The force of the enemy had always proved strong enough to defeat these efforts. On Jan. 13th the advance from Beaufort began. The division of Gen. Hatch had taken a position near the bridge, with their guns turned on the railroad, when the 17th corps crossing the ferry at Port Royal on a pontoon bridge moved rapidly but cautiously to the railroad. The pickets of the enemy were driven away without difficulty. On the 15th an advance was made, the 17th corps being on the left, and Gen. Hatch on the right, and the railroad gained a little south of the bridge. The skirmishers pushed forward, encountering those of the enemy, who were supported by light artillery, and quickly drove them off, thus gaining the bridge. A brigade of the 17th followed, and carried it and the earth works at the further end. The enemy seeing they would lose possession of the bridge, attempted to burn it, but were defeated in their efforts by the rapid movements of the troops. The Federal loss was about fifty. The force of the enemy consisted of a detachment from Gen. Hardee's command, under Gen. McLaws. They were driven out, and the 17th corps occupied the railroad from Coosawatchie to the the Tallahatchie. A depot of supplies was established near the mouth of the creek, with easy water communication back to Hilton Head.

At the same time the left wing, under Maj.-Gen. Slocum, and the cavalry, under Maj.-Gen. Kilpatrick, were ordered to rendezvous near Robertsville and Coosawatchie, with a depot of supplies at Pureysburg on Sister's ferry on the Savannah River. Gen. Slocum caused a good pontoon bridge to be constructed opposite Savannah, and the "Union causeway" leading through the low rice fields opposite the city was repaired and "corduroyed." But before the time appointed for him to march, the heavy rains of January had swelled the river, broken the pontoon bridge, and overflowed the whole bottom, so that the causeway was four feet under water, and Gen. Slocum was compelled to look higher up for a passage over the river. He moved up to Sister's ferry, but even there the river with its overflowed bottoms was nearly three miles wide. He did not succeed in getting his whole wing across until during the first week in February.

Meanwhile the division of Gen. Grover of the 19th corps had been sent by Gen. Grant to garrison Savannah, and on Jan. 18th Gen. Sherman transferred the forts and city of Savannah to Gen. Foster, still commanding the Department of the South, and instructed him to follow on the coast the movements of the army under Sherman inland, by occupying Charleston and such other points as would be of any military value. The plan of Gen. Sherman was to strike direct for Goldsboro' in North Carolina, and open communication with the sea by the Newbern Railroad. For this purpose he ordered Col. W. W. Wright, Superintendent of Military Railroads, to proceed in advance to Newbern and to be prepared to extend the railroad out from that city to Goldsboro by March 15th. At the same time Gen. Sherman ordered his chief quartermaster and commissary, Gens. Easton and Beckwith, to complete the supplies at Sister's ferry and Pocotaligo, and follow the movement coastwise, and be prepared to open communication with him from Morehead City about the same time. Having completed his preparations, Gen. Sherman issued the order to march on January 19th. He left Savannah on the 22d

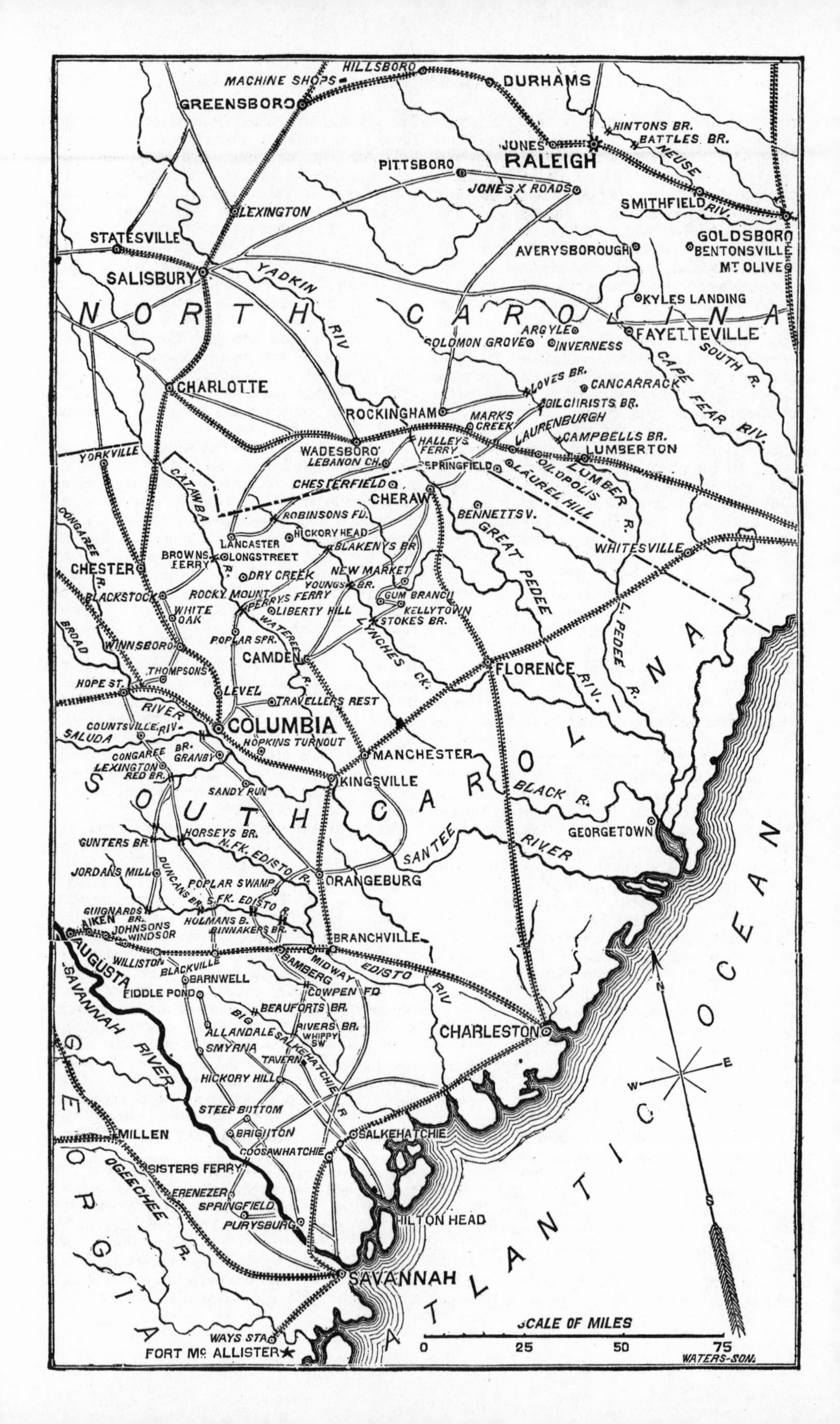

HILLSBORO
MACHINE SHOPS
DURHAMS
GREENSBORO
HINTONS BR.
BATTLES BR.
JONES
RALEIGH
NEUSE
PITTSBORO
JONES X ROADS
SMITHFIELD
RIV.
LEXINGTON
GOLDSBORO
STATESVILLE
AVERYSBOROUGH
BENTONSVILLE
MT OLIVE
SALISBURY
YADKIN
KYLES LANDING
N O R T H   C A R O L I N A
RIV
ARGYLE
FAYETTEVILLE
SOLOMON GROVE
INVERNESS
CAPE
SOUTH R.
LOVES BR.
CANCARRACK
FEAR RIV.
CHARLOTTE
GILCHRISTS BR.
ROCKINGHAM
MARKS CREEK
LAURENBURGH
CAMPBELLS BR.
HALLEYS FERRY
LUMBERTON
WADESBORO
YORKVILLE
LEBANON CH.
SPRINGFIELD
OILDPOLIS
LUMBER R.
LAUREL HILL
CATAWBA
CHESTERFIELD
CHERAW
BENNETTSV.
ROBINSONS FD.
CONGAREE R.
HICKORY HEAD
GREAT PEDEE
WHITESVILLE
LANCASTER
BLAKENYS BR.
BROWNS FERRY
LONGSTREET
CHESTER
NEW MARKET
DRY CREEK
YOUNGS BR.
GUM BRANCH
BLACKSTOCK
ROCKY MOUNT
PERRYS FERRY
KELLYTOWN
WHITE OAK
LIBERTY HILL
STOKES BR.
L. PEDEE R.
BROAD
WATEREE
LYNCHES
POPLAR SPR.
WINNSBORO
CAMDEN
FLORENCE
THOMPSONS
HOPE ST.
LEVEL
CK.
RIV.
RIVER
TRAVELLERS REST
COLUMBIA
COUNTSVILLE
SALUDA
HOPKINS TURNOUT
CONGAREE BR.
GRANBY
MANCHESTER
LEXINGTON
RED BR.
KINGSVILLE
BLACK R.
SANDY RUN
S O U T H   C A R O L I N A
HORSEYS BR.
GEORGETOWN
GUNTERS BR.
N. FK. EDISTO
SANTEE
RIVER
JORDANS MILL
DUNCANS BR.
POPLAR SWAMP
ORANGEBURG
GUIGNARDS BR.
S. FK. EDISTO R.
AIKEN
HOLMANS B.
JOHNSONS
BINNAKERS BR.
WINDSOR
BRANCHVILLE
AUGUSTA
WILLISTON
BLACKVILLE
BAMBERG
MIDWAY
EDISTO
RIV
SAVANNAH
BARNWELL
FIDDLE POND
COWPEN FD.
BEAUFORTS BR.
BIG
ALLANDALE
RIVERS BR.
WHIPPY SW.
SMYRNA
SALKEHATCHIE
TAVERN
CHARLESTON
HICKORY HILL
RIVER
N
E
W
S
STEEP BOTTOM
G E O R G I A
MILLEN
BRIGHTON
SALKEHATCHIE
COOSAWHATCHIE
SISTERS FERRY
OGEECHEE R.
EBENEZER
SPRINGFIELD
HILTON HEAD
PURYSBURG
SAVANNAH
ATLANTIC OCEAN
SCALE OF MILES
0
25
50
75
WAYS STA.
FORT MC ALLISTER
WATERS-SON.

and proceeded to Beaufort, and on the 24th reached Pocotaligo, where the 17th corps under Gen. Blair was encamped. The 15th corps at this time was somewhat scattered: the divisions of Gens. Wood and Hazen were at Beaufort; that of Gen. J. E. Smith was marching from Savannah by the coast-road, and that of Gen. Corse was still at Savannah, cut off by the storms and freshet in the river. The enemy supposed the object of Gen. Sherman was to reach Charleston, and had adopted the Salkehatchie River as his line of defence. On the 25th a demonstration was made against the Combahee ferry and railroad bridge across the Salkehatchie, for the purpose of occupying the enemy. The heavy rains had swollen the river so that water stood in the swamps for a breadth of more than a mile at a depth of from one to twenty feet. By making apparent preparations to cross the river, he was able, with a comparatively small force, to keep a considerably body of the enemy in front disposed to contest the advance on Charleston, although not having the remotest intention to move on that city. On the 27th Gen. Hatch's division evacuated its position on the Tullafuiney and Coosahatchie Rivers, and moved to Pocotaligo to keep up the feints already begun, and until the right wing should move higher up and cross the Salkehatchie about River's or Broxton's bridge.

By the 29th the roads back of Savannah had become sufficiently free of the flood to permit Gen. Slocum to put his wing in motion; and as he approached Sister's ferry the gunboat Pontiac was sent up by Admiral Dahlgren to cover the crossing. Meanwhile the division of the 15th corps had reached Pocotaligo, and the right wing had loaded its wagons and was ready to start. Gen. Howard was thereupon ordered to move the 17th corps along the the Salkehatchie as high up as River's bridge, and the 15th corps by Hickory Hill, Loper's cross-roads, Anglesey post office, and Beaufort bridge, leaving Gen. Hatch's division at Pacotaligo feigning to cross at the Salkhatchie bridge and ferry until the movement turned the enemy's position and forced him to fall back on the Edisto.

The march began on the 1st of February. All the roads northward had been held by the Confederate cavalry under General Wheeler, who had, with details of negro laborers, felled trees, burned bridges, and made obstructions to impede this march. The pioneer battalions, however, were so well organized that these obstructions were quickly removed. The felled trees were cleared away and bridges rebuilt by the heads of columns before the rear could close up. On February 2d the 15th corps reached Loper's cross-roads, and the 17th was at River's bridge. At this time Gen. Slocum was struggling with the floods of the Savannah at Sister's ferry. Two divisions of the 20th corps, under Gen. Williams, were on the east bank, and the cavalry of Gen. Kilpatrick had been able to cross over on the pontoon bridge. Gen. Sherman ordered Gen. Williams to march to Lawtonsville and Allandale, Gen. Kilpatrick to Blackville, by way of Barnwell, and Gen. Slocum to hurry the crossing at Sister's ferry as much as possible, and overtake the right wing on the South Carolina Railroad. At the same time Gen. Howard, with the right wing, was ordered to cross the Salkehatchie and push rapidly for the same railroad at or near Midway. The line of the Salkehatchie was held by the enemy in force, having intrenchments for infantry and artillery at River's and Beaufort bridges. The former position was carried on February 3d by Gens. Mower's and Smith's divisions of the 17th corps. The troops crossed the swamp, which was nearly three miles wide, and in which the water was from the knee to the shoulder in depth. The weather was severely cold, and the generals on foot led their commands and made a lodgment below the bridge, and turned on the brigade of the enemy which guarded it, and drove them in confusion toward Branchville. In this affair one officer and seventeen men were killed, and seventy wounded, who were sent to Pocotaligo. The 15th corps had been ordered to carry the Beaufort bridge, but this was evacuated by the enemy as soon as the crossing was effected at River's bridge. The position was strong both in its natural works and the line of works which defended the passage of the river. Gen. Sherman had now gained the peninsula formed by the Salkehatchie and Edisto Rivers, and threatened alike Augusta, Branchville, and Charleston. At Augusta Gen. D. H. Hill was in command with a considerable force, and Branchville was reënforced and works thrown up to render it more secure. The country in which the army was now moving was rich in forage and supplies. Turkeys, geese, ducks, chickens, nicely-cured hams, potatoes, honey, and an abundance of other luxuries, were obtained by the soldiers, and plenty of corn and fodder for the animals. The houses generally were deserted, although here and there women and children were found. Wide-spreading columns of smoke rose whereever the army went. The following correspondence relative to the destruction of dwellings took place on the dates therein named:

GRAHAMS, S. C., February 7, 1865.

GENERAL: I have the honor to propose that if the troops of your army be required to discontinue burning the houses of our citizens I will discontinue burning cotton.

As an earnest of the good faith in which my proposition is tendered, I leave at this place about three hundred bales of cotton unharmed, worth in New York over a quarter million, and in our currency one and a half millions. I trust my having commenced will cause you to use your influence to insure the acceptance of the proposition by your whole army.

I trust that you will not deem it improper for me to ask that you will require the troops under your command to discontinue the wanton destruction of property not necessary for their sustenance.

Respectfully, General, your obedient servant,
J. WHEELER, Maj.-Gen. C. S. A.

Maj.-Gen. O. O. HOWARD, U. S. Army, Com'ding, &c.

ANSWERED BY GENERAL SHERMAN.

HEADQU'RS MILITARY DIVISION OF THE MISSISSIPPI, }
IN THE FIELD, February 8, 1865. }

GENERAL: Yours, addressed to General Howard, is received by me. I hope you will burn all cotton, and save us the trouble. We don't want it; and it has proven a curse to our country. All you don't burn I will.

As to private houses occupied by peaceful families my orders are not to molest or disturb them, and I think my orders are obeyed. Vacant houses, being of no use to anybody, I care little about, as the owners have thought them of no use to themselves. I don't want them destroyed, but do not take much care to preserve them.

I am, with respect, yours truly,
W. T. SHERMAN, Maj.-Gen. Commanding.

Maj.-Gen. J. WHEELER, Commanding Cavalry Corps Confederate Army.

Upon the breaking of the line of the Salkehatchie the enemy retreated at once behind the Edisto at Branchville, and the whole army pushed at once to the South Carolina Railroad at Midway, Bamberg, and Graham's station. The troops immediately set to work to destroy the road, which had been of great importance to the enemy, both as a means of communication and for forwarding supplies from Augusta and northern Georgia to Richmond. From the 7th to the 10th of February the work was thoroughly done by the 17th corps, from the Edisto up to Bamberg, and from Bamberg up to Blackville by the 15th corps. As the 17th corps threatened Branchville, the enemy burned the railroad bridge and Walker's bridge below across the Edisto. Meanwhile Gen. Kilpatrick had brought his cavalry rapidly by Barnwell to Blackville, and turned toward Aiken, for the purpose of threatening Augusta without being drawn into any serious battle. Blackville is eighteen miles west of Midway, and forty-seven miles east of Augusta; Aiken is seventeen miles east of Augusta. In his progress he had serious skirmishes with Wheeler's cavalry, first at Blackville and afterwards at Williston and Aiken. On February 8th Gen. Williams, with two divisions of the 20th corps, reached the railroad at Graham's station, and Gen. Slocum reached Blackville on the 10th. This wing continued the destruction of the railroad from Blackville up to Windsor. By February 11th Gen. Sherman's force was along the railroad from Midway to Johnson's station. The effect was to divide the enemy's forces, which still remained at Branchville and Charleston on the one hand, and Aiken and Augusta on the other.

The movement on Orangeburg now commenced. The railroad from Augusta running nearly east to Branchville, there intersects with the railroad from Columbia to Branchville, running nearly south, and thence southeast to Charleston. Gen. Sherman at this time was operating west of Branchville on the railroad from that place to Augusta. He now strikes north to Orangeburg, the first important station on the road from Branchville to Columbia, and distant from Branchville seventeen miles. The next important station north is Kingville, where the road from Wilmington to Charleston intersects the Columbia and Charleston road, the latter portion of which is common to both. Orangeburg had a population of about three thousand, and was prettily situated on the north bank of the Edisto. From its position upon the ridge of high lands on which the railroad runs, it was really of more importance than Branchville, which the enemy had carefully fortified.

The 17th corps crossed the south fork of the Edisto at Binnaker's bridge, and moved directly for Orangeburg, while the 15th corps crossed at Holmon's bridge, and moved to Poplar Springs to act as a support. The left wing, which was still at work on the railroad, was ordered to cross the South Edisto at New and Guignard's bridges, and move to the Orangeburg and Edgefield road, and there await the result of the attack on Orangeburg. On the 12th the corps was before the north fork of the Edisto, and at an early hour engaged in skirmishing with the enemy at different points. A force was found intrenched in front of the Orangeburg bridge, but was swept away at a dash, and driven across the bridge, which was partially burned. Behind the bridge was a battery in position, covered by a cotton and earth parapet with extensive wings. While the division of Gen. Giles A. Smith was held close up to the Edisto, the other two were moved by Gen. Blair to a point about two miles below, where Gen. Force's division crossed by a pontoon bridge, and Gen. Mowers was held to act as a support. As soon as Force's division made their appearance coming up from the swamp, the enemy began to give ground, and Gen. Smith's division succeeded in gaining the bridge, and crossed over and occupied the enemy's position. The bridge was soon repaired, and by the middle of the afternoon the whole corps was in Orangeburg, and had begun to destroy the railroad. This work was done effectually by the corps to Lewisville, a distance of twelve miles. Gen. Blair was then ordered to push the enemy across the Congaree, and force him to burn the bridge. This was accomplished on the 14th. The Congaree River is formed by the Broad and Saluda Rivers, which unite at Columbia. After a southeast course of about fifty miles, it unites with the Wateree to form the Santee. Steamboats ascend to Columbia.

Gen. Sherman now directed his march straight for Columbia, distant fifty-one miles from Orangeburg. The advance of the 17th corps was along the State road, while the 15th corps crossed the north branch of the Edisto from Poplar Springs at Schilling's bridge, and took a country road which came into the State road at Zeigler's. The 20th corps moved north on a line west of the 15th, diverging toward Columbia; the 14th corps advanced in a line further west, and the cavalry on their left flank. On the 15th, the 15th corps discovered the enemy in a strong position at Little Congaree bridge, across Congaree Creek, with a work on the south side to cover their retreat across the bridge, and a well-constructed fort on the north side commanding the bridge with artillery. The ground in front was level and clear, but rendered very unfavorable by a fresh deposit of mud from a recent overflow. Gen. Woods, in command of the leading division, succeeded in turning the flank of the work south of the bridge by sending Stone's brigade through a cypress swamp on the left; and by following up the enemy, who immediately began to retreat, he was able to get possession of the bridge and the fort on the north side. The bridge had been somewhat injured by fire, and had to be repaired before the passage of the artillery. It was night, therefore, before the head of the column reached the bridge across Congaree River in front of Columbia. During the night the enemy shelled the camps from a battery on the east side of the Congaree above Granby. Early on the next morning, Feb. 16th, the head of the column reached the bank of the Congaree opposite Columbia, but too late to save the bridge over the river at that point, which had been set on fire by the enemy. Meanwhile the inhabitants of Columbia could be seen moving in great excitement about the streets, and occasionally small bodies of cavalry but no masses of troops. A single gun was fired a few times by the order of Gen. Sherman, at the railroad depot, to scatter the people who were seen carrying away sacks of corn and flour which his army needed. No manifestation of surrender was exhibited from the city.

Within an hour after the arrival of the head of Gen. Howard's column at the river opposite Columbia, the head of the column of the left wing under Gen. Slocum also appeared. Gen. Howard, instead of crossing in front of Columbia, moved three miles up to Saluda Factory, and crossed on the 16th, skirmishing with cavalry, and on the night of the same day made a bridge across Broad River, three miles above Columbia, by which he crossed over Stone's brigade of Wood's division of the 15th corps. Under cover of this brigade a pontoon bridge was laid on the morning of the 17th. Meanwhile Gen. Slocum moved up to cross the Saluda at Zion's Church, and thence to take the roads leading direct to Winnsboro. His object was also to break up the railroads and bridges about Alston.

Gen. Sherman thus describes the entrance to Columbia: "I was in person at the pontoon bridge (on the 17th), and at 11 A. M. learned that the Mayor of Columbia had come out in a carriage, and made a formal surrender of the city to Col. Stone, 25th Iowa infantry, commanding 3d brigade, 1st division, 15th corps. About the same time a small party of the 17th corps had crossed the Congaree in a skiff, and entered Columbia from a point immediately west. In anticipation of the occupation of the city, I had made written orders to Gen. Howard touching the conduct of the troops. These were to destroy absolutely all arsenals and public property not needed for our own use, as well as all railroads, depots, and machinery useful in war to an enemy, but to spare all dwellings, colleges, schools, asylums, and harmless private property. I was the first to cross the pontoon bridge, and in company with Gen. Howard rode into the city. The day was clear, but a perfect tempest of wind was raging. The brigade of Col. Stone was already in the city, and was properly posted. Citizens and soldiers were on the streets, and general good order prevailed. Gen. Wade Hampton, who commanded the Confederate rear guard of cavalry, had, in anticipation of our capture of Columbia, ordered that all cotton, public and private, should be moved into the streets and fired, to prevent our making use of it. Bales were piled everywhere, the rope and bagging cut, and tufts of cotton were blown about in the wind, lodged in the trees and against the houses, so as to resemble a snow-storm. Some of these piles of cotton were burning, especially one in the very heart of the city, near the Court House, but the fire was partially subdued by the labors of our soldiers. During the day the 15th corps passed through Columbia and out on the Camden road. The 17th did not enter the town at all; and, as I have before stated, the left wing and the cavalry did not come within two miles of the town.

"Before one single public building had been fired by order, the smouldering fires set by Hampton's order were rekindled by the wind, and communicated to the buildings around. About dark they began to spread, and got beyond the control of the brigade on duty within the city. The whole of Wood's division was brought in, but it was found impossible to check the flames, which, by midnight, had become unmanageable, and raged until about 4 A. M., when, the wind subsiding, they were got under control. I was up nearly all night, and saw Generals Howard, Logan, Woods, and others, laboring to save houses, and protect families thus suddenly deprived of shelter and of bedding and wearing apparel. I disclaim on the part of my army any agency in this fire, but, on the contrary, claim that we saved what of Columbia remains unconsumed. And, without hesitation, I charge Gen. Wade Hampton with having burned his own city of Columbia, not with a malicious intent, or as the manifestation of a silly 'Roman stoicism,' but from folly and want of sense in filling it with lint cotton and tinder. Our officers and men on duty worked well to extinguish the flames; but others not on duty, including the officers who had long been imprisoned there, rescued by us, may have assisted in spreading the fire after it had once begun, and may have indulged in concealed joy to see the ruin of the capital of South Carolina. During the 18th and 19th the arsenal, railroad depots, machine shops, foundries, and other buildings were properly destroyed by detailed working parties, and the railroad track torn up and destroyed to Kingsville and the Wateree bridge, and up in the direction of Winnsboro."

The following will show what troops first entered Columbia:

HEADQUARTERS FOURTH DIVISION,
SEVENTEENTH ARMY CORPS,
Near COLUMBIA, S. C., Feb. 17, 1865.

Brig.-Gen. Wm. W. Belknap, Commanding 3d Brigade:

SIR,—Allow me to congratulate you, and through you, Lieut.-Col. J. C. Kennedy, 13th Iowa Veteran volunteers, and the men under his command, for first entering the city of Columbia, on the morning of Friday, February 17th, and being the first to plant his colors on the capitol of South Carolina. While the army was laying pontoon bridges across the Saluda and Broad Rivers, three miles above the city, Lieut.-Col. Kennedy, under your direction, fitted up an old worn-out flat boat, capable of carrying about twenty men, and accompanied by Lieuts. H. C. McArthur and Wm. H. Goodell, of your staff, crossed the river in front of the city, and boldly advanced through its streets, sending back the boat with another procured on the opposite shore, for more troops, and on their arrival, with seventy-five men in all, drove a portion of Wheeler's cavalry from the town, and at eleven and a half o'clock A. M. planted his two stands of colors, one upon the old and the other upon the new capitol.

The swift current of the Congaree River and its rocky channel rendered his crossing both difficult and dangerous, and the presence of the enemy, but in what force unknown, rendered the undertaking still more hazardous. Lieut.-Col. Kennedy and his regiment are entitled to great credit for its successful accomplishment.

I have the honor to be, very respectfully,
Your obedient servant,
(Signed) GILES A. SMITH,
Brevet Major-General Commanding.

The consequences of the movements of Gen. Sherman thus far were a division of the forces of the enemy and the evacuation of Charleston. Gen. Hardee was in Charleston with about 14,000 men, expecting the approach of Gen. Sherman on his appearance in the neighborhood of Branchville. At Augusta, which was equally threatened, was Gens. D. H. Hill and G. W. Smith, who were so certain of the approach of Gen. Sherman that the public property was almost entirely removed from the city. A considerable cavalry force was at different points in South Carolina under Hampton, Wheeler, McLaws, and others. Gen. Beauregard, who had been in command at Charleston, was near the North Carolina line collecting forces and ready to take the command of troops from Hood's army with those under Hill. Gen. Lee, it is supposed, also sent some men into North Carolina. Gen. Sherman marched at once to Columbia, knowing that when once there Augusta could be easily taken. But if Augusta had been first captured, a concentration of the enemy might have been made at Columbia, which would have rendered its capture more difficult. Augusta was also of less importance after its railroad communication had been cut off. In the neighborhood of Charleston some skirmishing had taken place at intervals without any important results.

After Gen. Sherman destroyed the railroad in the neighborhood of Branchville, only one line remained open from Charleston. This was the road running north to Florence and Cheraw. It was the only line of retreat for Gen. Hardee, and as Gen. Sherman moved north it was necessary for the latter to secure it at once, as it was threatened. On Feb. 10th, Gen. Schemmelfennig, with a body of troops of Gen. Gillmore's command, laid a bridge across the creek separating Folly and Cole Islands from James Island, and effected a lodgment on the latter, about three miles southwest of Charleston. Skirmishers advanced and met the enemy about a mile distant on the Stono River. A gunboat and mortar schooner, and the iron-clads Augusta and Savannah, were now moved up the Stono, and, covering the flank of Gen. Schemmelfennig's troops, shelled the enemy. About 4½ P. M., Gen. Hartwell moved his whole brigade forward and carried the rifle-pits for the first time. The enemy retreated rapidly to his main works, leaving his dead and wounded, and losing about twenty prisoners. The Union loss was between seventy and eighty. Coöperating movements were made at the same time by the column under Gen. Hatch, which crossed the Combahee with slight loss and marched toward the South Edisto. No serious resistance was made to the advance in that region, which was accessible to the gunboats and defended only by small batteries on the river banks. The movement of Gen. Schemmelfennig being only a feint, his troops were withdrawn to Cole Island. A column under Gen. Potter, however, moved to Bull's Bay, as if designed to cut the northern railroad. On the night of the 17th the last of Gen. Hardee's troops left Charleston. The subsequent occupation of the city is thus described by official documents:

CHARLESTON, S. C., February 18,
via NEW YORK, Feb. 21, 1865.

Major-General Halleck, Chief of Staff:

GENERAL:—The city of Charleston and all its defences came into our possession this morning, with about two hundred pieces of good artillery and a supply of fine ammunition. The enemy commenced evacuating all the works last night, and Mayor Macbeth surrendered the city to the troops of Gen. Schemmelfennig at 9 o'clock this morning, at which time it was occupied by our forces. Our advance on the Edisto from Bull's Bay hastened the retreat.

The cotton warehouses, arsenals, quartermaster's stores, railroad bridges, and two iron-clads were burned by the enemy. Some vessels in the ship-yard were also burned. Nearly all the inhabitants remaining behind belong to the poorer class.

Very respectfully,
Q. A. GILLMORE, General Commanding.

HEADQUARTERS DEPARTMENT OF THE SOUTH,
CHARLESTON, S. C., Feb. 26, 1865.

Lieut.-Gen. U. S. Grant, and Maj.-Gen. W. H. Halleck, Chief of Staff, Washington:

An inspection of the Rebel defences of Charleston show that we have taken over four hundred and fifty pieces of ordnance, being more than double what I first reported. The lot includes 8 and 10-inch columbiads, a great many 32 and 42-pounder rifles, some 7-inch Brooks rifles, and many pieces of foreign make. We also captured eight locomotives and a great number of passenger and platform cars, all in good condition. Deserters report that the last of Hardee's army was to have crossed the Santee River yesterday, bound for Charlotte, N. C., and that it was feared that Sherman had already intercepted their march. It is reported, on similar authority, that the last of Hood's army, 12,000 strong, passed through Augusta last Sunday, the 19th, on the way to Beauregard. Georgetown has been evacuated by the enemy, and is now in our possession. Deserters are coming in constantly. We have over 400 already.

Q. A. GILLMORE,
Major-General Commanding.

The following is the report of Col. Bennett, who was the first to enter the city:

HEADQUARTERS UNITED STATES FORCES,
CHARLESTON, S. C., February 24, 1865.

Captain J. W. Dickinson, Acting Asst. Adjt.-General.

CAPTAIN: I have the honor to submit the following report of the evacuation and occupation of Charleston. On the morning of February the 18th I received information that led me to believe the defences and lines guarding the city of Charleston had been deserted by the enemy. I immediately proceeded to Cummings Point, from whence I sent a small boat in the direction of Fort Moultrie, which boat, when forty yards east from Fort Sumter, was met by a boat from Sullivan's Island, containing a full corps of band musicians abandoned by the enemy. These confirmed my belief of an evacuation. I had no troops that could be available under two hours, as, except in a few pontoon boats, there were no means whatever of landing troops near the enemy's works or into the city. I directed Major Hennessy to proceed to Fort Sumter and there replace our flag. The flag was replaced over the southeast angle of Fort Sumter at nine (9) o'clock A. M. I now pushed for the city, stopping at Fort Ripley and Castle Pinckney, from which works Rebel flags were hauled down and the American flag substituted. The guns in these works were in good order. There was mounted in Fort Ripley one Quaker gun bearing southeast. I landed at Mill's wharf, Charleston, at ten (10) o'clock A. M., where I learned that a part of the enemy's troops yet remained in the city, while mounted patrols were out in every direction applying the torch and driving the inhabitants before them.

I at once addressed to the Mayor of the city the following communication:

HEADQUARTERS UNITED STATES FORCES,
CHARLESTON, February 18, 1865.

Mayor Charles Macbeth, Charleston:

MAYOR: In the name of the United States Government I demand a surrender of the city of which you are the executive officer. Until further orders all citizens will remain within their houses.

I have the honor to be, Mayor, very respectfully, your obedient servant,

(Signed) A. G. BENNETT,
Lieut.-Col. commanding U. S. Forces, Charleston.

My whole force consisted of five (5) officers and the armed crews of two (2) small boats, comprising in all twenty-two (22) men. Both officers and men volunteered to advance from the wharf into the city; but no reënforcements being in sight, I did not deem it expedient to move on.

Public buildings, stores, warehouses, private dwellings, shipping, etc., were burning and being fired by armed Rebels, but with the force at my disposal it was impossible to save the cotton and other property. While awaiting the arrival of my troops at Mill's wharf, a number of explosions took place. The Rebel commissary depot was blown up, and with it is estimated that not less than two hundred (200) human beings—most of whom were women and children—were blown to atoms. These people were engaged in procuring food for themselves and their families by permission from the Rebel military authorities. The Rebel ram Charleston was blown up while lying at her anchorage opposite Mt. Pleasant Ferry wharf, in the Cooper River. Observing a small boat sailing toward the bay under a flag of truce, I put off to it, and received from a member of the common council a letter addressed to the General commanding United States forces at Morris Island or to the officer in command of the fleet. The following is a copy of the letter:

CHARLESTON, S. C., February 18, 1865.

To the General Commanding the Army of the United States at Morris Island:

SIR: The military authorities of the Confederate States have evacuated the city. I have remained to enforce law and preserve order until you take such steps as you may think best.

Very respectfully, your obedient servant,
CHARLES MACBETH, Mayor.

The deputation sent to convey the above letter represented to me that the city was in the hands of either the Rebel soldiery or the mob. They entreated of me in the name of humanity to interpose my military authority and save the city from utter destruction. To this letter I replied in the following terms:

HEADQUARTERS UNITED STATES FORCES, CHARLESTON
HARBOR, NEAR ATLANTIC WHARF, Feb. 18, 1865.

Mayor Charles Macbeth:

I have the honor to acknowledge the receipt of your communication of this date. I have in reply thereto to state that the troops under my command will render every possible assistance to your well-disposed citizens in extinguishing the fires now burning.

I have the honor to be, Mayor, very respectfully, your obedient servant, A. G. BENNETT,
Lieut.-Col. commanding U. S. Forces, Charleston.

Two (2) companies of the 52d Pennsylvania regiment and about thirty (30) men of the 3d Rhode Island volunteer heavy artillery having landed, I proceeded with them to the citadel. I here established my headquarters, and sent small parties in all directions with instructions to impress negroes wherever found, and to make them work the fire apparatus, until all fires were extinguished. I also sent a strong guard to the United States Arsenal, which was saved. As the troops arrived they were sent out to points in the city where were located railroad depots or any large buildings containing property, such as cotton, rice, tobacco, etc. It being apparent to me that I could not effectually save all that remained, I concentrated my guards wherever was stored the largest quantities.

I cannot at this time submit any account of, or estimate any value to, the property that has fallen into our possession. The most valuable items consist in cotton and rice. The cotton has not yet been secured. The rice is being given to the poor of the city to supply their immediate necessities.

Every officer and soldier exerted himself to a most willing performance of every allotted duty, yet I do not deem it invidious for me to make special mention of Lieutenant John Hackett, Co. M, 3d Rhode Island artillery, who volunteered to go alone to Fort Moultrie and there raise the flag. As also to speak of Major John A. Hennessy, Captain Samuel Cuskaden, and Lieutenant P. M. Burr, all of the 52d regiment Pennsylvania volunteers; and Lieutenant James F. Haviland, Acting Assistant Inspector-General of my staff, who accompanied me to the city; all of whose services were most highly valuable to me. Captain H. H. Jenks, 52d Pennsylvania volunteers, Acting Assistant Adjutant-General, also rendered important services. Although he remained at Morris Island, he was very efficient in facilitating the embarkation of my troops from there.

The flags from Fort Moultrie, Castle Pinckney, and Fort Ripley, and seventeen (17) signal pennants found in the city, were secured by the troops under my command.

I have the honor to be, Captain,
Very respectfully, your obedient servant,
(Signed) A. G. BENNETT,
Lieutenant-Colonel 21st regiment U. S. C. T.

A copy of the report of the evacuation and occupation of Charleston. JAMES F. HAVILAND,
First Lieutenant 127th Reg't N. Y. V., A. A. I. G.

Gen. Hardee, with about 12,000 men, moved

north, aiming to reach Charlotte in North Carolina. At the same time Georgetown, a seaport north of Charleston, was evacuated, and occupied by a naval force sent by Admiral Dahlgren. The force of Gen. Hood's army which had been sent eastward, having passed Augusta, was moving toward Charlotte, where Gen. Beauregard was in command. As the danger became more critical, the enemy sent Gen. Johnston to take the command, and he was again in a position to confront Gen. Sherman.

Meanwhile Gen. Sherman continued his march. The left wing and cavalry crossed the Saluda and Broad Rivers, and broke up the railroad about Alston and as high as the bridge across Broad River on the road to Spartansburg. Meanwhile the main body moved directly to Winnsboro, which Gen. Slocum reached on the 21st. Here the railroad was destroyed up to Blackstake's station, a distance of fifteen miles. The railroad runs from Columbia to Charlotte, N. C., one hundred and nine miles, thence to Greensboro, and branches to Lynchburg, Va., and Raleigh, N. C. The distance from Columbia to Winnsboro is thirty-nine miles. Gen. Slocum next turned to Rocky Mount, on the Catawba River, in a northeast direction. The 20th corps reached Rocky Mount on the 22d, and laid a pontoon bridge over the Catawba, and crossed on the 23d. The cavalry under Gen. Kilpatrick followed during the night ensuing, and moved up to Lancaster with instructions to keep up the feint of a general march on Charlotte, N. C., to which place Gen. Beauregard and the cavalry of the enemy had retreated from Columbia. The real aim of Gen. Sherman was to reach Cheraw and Goldsboro, N, C., where he could communicate with the naval forces. As has been already stated, a portion of Hood's army, consisting of Cheatham's corps, was aiming to make a junction with Gen. Beauregard at Charlotte, having been cut off by the rapid movement of Sherman on Columbia and Winnsboro. For three days, from the 23d to the 26th, the rains were heavy and the rivers became quite swollen, and the roads almost impassable. The 20th corps reached Hanging Rock on the 26th, and waited there for the 14th corps to get across the Catawba. The river had so swollen that the pontoon bridge broke, and was with difficulty restored by Gen. Davis.

Meanwhile the right wing had broken up the railroad to Winnsboro, and turned from thence to Peay's Ferry, where it crossed the Catawba before the heavy rain commenced. The 17th corps moved straight on Cheraw by the way of Young's bridge; and the 15th corps by Tiller's and Kelly's bridges. From the latter corps detachments were sent to Camden, to burn the bridge over the Wateree and the railroad depot, stores, &c. This was successfully done.

Several of the foragers, who, as a body, generally kept in advance of the troops, having been very cruelly treated by the enemy, Gen. Sherman wrote the following letter to Gen. W. Hampton:

HEADQUARTERS MILITARY DIV'N OF THE MISSISSIPPI, }
IN THE FIELD, Feb. 24, 1865. }

Lieut.-Gen Wade Hampton, Commanding Cavalry Forces, C. S. A.

GENERAL: It is officially reported to me that our foraging parties are murdered after capture, and labelled "Death to all foragers." One instance of a lieutenant and seven men, near Chesterfield, and another of twenty, "near a ravine eighty rods from the main road," about three miles from Feasterville. I have ordered a similar number of prisoners in our hands to be disposed of in like manner.

I hold about one thousand prisoners captured in various ways, and can stand it as long as you; but I hardly think these murders are committed with your knowledge, and would suggest that you give notice to the people at large, that every life taken by them simply results in the death of one of your confederates.

Of course you cannot question my right to forage on the country; it is a war right as old as history. The manner of exercising it varies with circumstances, and if the civil authorities will supply my requisitions, I will forbid all foraging. But I find no civil authorities who can respond to calls for forage or provisions, and therefore must collect directly of the people. I have no doubt this is the occasion of much misbehavior on the part of our men; but I cannot permit an enemy to judge or punish with wholesale murder.

Personally I regret the bitter feelings engendered by this war; but they were to be expected, and I simply allege that those who struck the first blow and made war inevitable, ought not, in fairness, to reproach us for the natural consequences. I merely assert our war right to forage, and my resolve to protect my foragers to the extent of life for life.

I am, with respect, your obedient servant,
W. T. SHERMAN, Maj.-Gen. U. S. A.

To which Gen. Hampton replied as follows:

HEADQUARTERS IN THE FIELD, Feb. 27, 1865.

Major-Gen. W. T. Sherman, U. S. Army.

GENERAL: Your communication of the 24th instant reached me to-day. In it you state that it has been officially reported that your foraging parties were "murdered" after capture, and you go on to say that you had "ordered a similar number of prisoners in your hands to be disposed of in like manner." That is to say, you have ordered a number of Confederate soldiers to be "murdered."

You characterize your order in proper terms, for the public voice, even in your own country, where it seldom dares to express itself in vindication of truth, honor, or justice, will surely agree with you in pronouncing you guilty of murder, if your order is carried out.

Before dismissing this portion of your letter, I beg to assure you for every soldier of mine "murdered" by you I shall have executed at once two of yours, giving, in all cases, preference to any officers who may be in my hands.

In reference to the statement you make regarding the death of your foragers, I have only to say that I know nothing of it; that no orders given by me authorized the killing of prisoners after capture, and that I do not believe that my men killed any of yours, except under circumstances in which it was perfectly legitimate and proper they should kill them.

It is a part of the system of the thieves whom you designate as your foragers, to fire the dwellings of those citizens whom they have robbed.

To check this inhuman system, which is justly execrated by every civilized nation, I have directed my men to shoot down all of your men who are caught burning houses. This order shall remain in force as long as you disgrace the profession of arms by allowing your men to destroy private dwellings.

You say that I cannot, of course, question your right to forage on the country. "It is a right as old as history." I do not, sir, question this right. But there is a right older even than this, and one more inalienable—the right that every man has to defend his home and to protect those who are dependent upon him; and from my heart I wish that every old man and boy in my country who can fire a gun, would shoot down, as he would a wild beast, the men who are desolating their land, burning their houses, and insulting their women.

You are particular in defining and claiming "war rights." May I ask if you enumerate among them the right to fire upon a defenceless city without notice; to burn that city to the ground after it had been surrendered by the authorities, who claimed, though in vain, that protection which is always accorded in civilized warfare to non-combatants; to fire the dwelling houses of citizens, after robbing them, and to perpetrate even darker crimes than these—crimes too black to be mentioned?

You have permitted, if you have not ordered, the commission of these offences against humanity and the rules of war. You fired into the city of Columbia without a word of warning. After its surrender by the Mayor, who demanded protection to private property, you laid the whole city in ashes, leaving amid its ruins thousands of old men and helpless women and children, who are likely to perish of starvation and exposure. Your line of march can be traced by the lurid light of burning houses, and in more than one household there is an agony far more bitter than that of death.

The Indian scalped his victim regardless of sex or age, but with all his barbarity he always respected the persons of his female captives. Your soldiers, more savage than the Indian, insult those whose natural protectors are absent.

In conclusion, I have only to request, that whenever you have any of my men "disposed of," or "murdered," for the terms appear to be synonymous with you, you will let me hear of it, in order that I may know what action to take in the matter. In the mean time I shall hold fifty-six of your men as hostages for those whom you have ordered to be executed. I am, yours, &c.,

WADE HAMPTON, Lieut.-Gen.

A small force of mounted men, under Capt. Duncan, was sent by Gen. Sherman to break up the railroad between Charleston and Florence, but were met by a division of cavalry under Gen. Butler, and after a sharp skirmish on Mount Elon, they were compelled to return without success.

Cheraw, to which Gen. Sherman was aiming, is a town on the right bank of the Great Pedee River, at the head of steam navigation. It had been a place of importance as a depot for cotton, and had about one thousand inhabitants. It is the termination of the northern railroad from Charleston through Florence, being distant from the latter forty miles, and from the former one hundred and forty-two miles.

On March 2d the advanced division of the 20th corps entered Chesterfield, a little northwest of Cheraw, encountering on the way the cavalry of the enemy under Gen. Butler, with whom skirmishing was kept up. On the next day, about noon, the 17th corps entered Cheraw. The force of the enemy in the place retreated across the Pedee, and burned the bridge. A considerable quantity of ammunition was captured in the town, and a number of guns which had been brought from Charleston on the evacuation of that city. These were destroyed, and also the trestles and bridges of the railroad as far down as Darlington, ten miles. An expedition of mounted infantry was sent to Florence, but it encountered both cavalry and infantry, and returned after doing no other damage than breaking up in part the road between the two places.

After a brief delay the march was resumed for Fayetteville, in North Carolina. The right wing crossed the Pedee at Cheraw, and the left wing at Sneedsboro. Fayetteville is the capital of Cumberland County, and was a flourishing town before the war, having a population exceeding seven thousand. It is on the left bank of Cape Fear River, at the head of navigation, and sixty miles south of Raleigh, the capital of the State, and one hundred miles northwest of Wilmington. It contained an arsenal, distilleries of turpentine, and cotton and flour mills. The 14th corps moved by Love's bridge, for the purpose of entering Fayetteville in advance, but the weather and road continuing bad it reached that place on March 11th, together with the 17th corps. They approached skirmishing with Gen. Wade Hampton's cavalry, which covered the rear of Gen. Hardee's army, as it retreated. It crossed the Cape Fear River and burned the bridge. The cavalry during the march had kept well on the left and exposed flank; but on the night of March 9th his three brigades were divided to picket the railroad. This was discovered by Gen. Hampton, who, early in the morning, dashed in and gained possession of the camp of Col. Spencer's brigade, and the house in which Gen. Kilpatrick and Col. Spencer had their quarters. The surprise was complete, but Gen. Kilpatrick quickly succeeded in rallying his men, on foot, in a swamp near at hand, and by a prompt attack, well followed up, he regained his artillery, horses, camp, and every thing except some prisoners. The enemy retired, leaving their dead behind.

The army remained at Fayetteville during three days, until March 15th. The United States arsenal, and a vast amount of machinery, which had formerly belonged to the arsenal at Harper's Ferry, were destroyed. Every building was knocked down and burned, and every piece of machinery broken up by the 1st Michigan engineers. The position of Gen. Sherman at this time is thus described by himself: "Up to this period I had perfectly succeeded in interposing my superior army between the scattered parts of my enemy. But I was then aware that the fragments that had left Columbia under Beauregard had been reënforced by Cheatham's corps from the West, and the garrison of Augusta, and that ample time had been given to move them to my front and flank about Raleigh. Hardee had also succeeded in getting across Cape Fear River ahead of me, and could therefore complete the junction with the other armies of Johnston and Hoke in North Carolina; and the whole, under the command of the skilful and experienced Joe

Johnston, made up an army superior to me in cavalry, and formidable enough in artillery and infantry to justify me in extreme caution in making the last step necessary to complete the march I had undertaken. Previous to reaching Fayetteville I had despatched to Wilmington from Laurel Hill Church two of our best scouts with intelligence of our position and my general plans. Both of these messengers reached Wilmington, and on the morning of the 12th of March, the army tug Davidson, Capt. Ainsworth, reached Fayetteville from Wilmington, bringing me full intelligence of events from the outer world. On the same day, this tug carried back to Gen. Terry, at Wilmington, and Gen. Schofield at Newbern, my despatches to the effect that on Wednesday, the 15th, we would move for Goldsboro, feigning on Raleigh, and ordering them to march straight for Goldsboro, which I expected to reach about the 20th. The same day, the gunboat Eolus, Capt. Young, United States navy, also reached Fayetteville, and through her I continued to have communication with Wilmington until the day of our actual departure. While the work of destruction was going on at Fayetteville, two pontoon bridges were laid across Cape Fear River, one opposite the town, the other three miles below."

While Gen. Sherman had been advancing to Fayetteville, some movements had taken place at Wilmington, N. C., intended to prepare the way for coöperation with him. It was on Jan. 15th that Gen. Schofield, with the 23d corps, left Gen. Thomas, as has been stated, for the Atlantic coast. The troops moved with their artillery and horses, but without wagons, by steam transports, to Cincinnati, Ohio, and thence by railroad to Washington, D. C., and Alexandria, Va. Although it was midwinter and the weather unusually severe, the movement was effected without delay, accident, or suffering on the part of the troops. In February an order was issued by the Secretary of War creating the department of North Carolina, and assigning Gen. Schofield to the command. The ultimate object of his operations was to occupy Goldsboro, N. C., and to open railroad communication between that point and the sea-coast, and further to accumulate supplies for Gen. Sherman's army and to join it, in its approach, at or near Goldsboro. Wilmington was made the first point to capture, as it would afford a valuable auxiliary base to Morehead City in the event of the junction being made at Goldsboro; and also as it would be of great value to Gen. Sherman in case the movement of the main army of the enemy or other circumstances should render advisable a concentration of Sherman's army at some point further south than Goldsboro.

With the 3d division of the 23d corps, under Major-Gen. J. D. Cox, Gen. Schofield reached the mouth of Cape Fear River on Feb. 9th, and landed near Fort Fisher. The other troops were to follow. Major-Gen. Terry, with about eight thousand men, then held a line across the peninsula, about two miles above the fort, and occupied Smithville and Fort Caswell on the south side of the river, while the naval squadron under Rear-Admiral Porter, occupied positions in Cape Fear River, and off the coast covering the flanks of Gen. Terry's line. On the west bank, Fort Anderson was occupied by the enemy with a collateral line running to a large swamp about three-fourths of a mile distant, and a line opposite Fort Anderson, running across the peninsula from Cape Fear River to Masonboro' Sound. This position was impregnable against a direct attack, and could be turned only by crossing the sound above his left, or passing around the swamp which covered his right. The first movement of Gen. Schofield consisted in pushing forward Gen. Terry's line on Feb. 11th, supported by Gen. Cox's division, which drove in the enemy's pickets, and intrenched in a new position close enough to the enemy's line to compel him to hold it in force. Efforts were then made to turn his left by the aid of a fleet of boats to cross the sound, but the weather prevented. Finally Gen. Schofield determined to attempt to turn the enemy's right. Gen. Cox's and Gen. Ames' divisions were crossed over to Smithville and joined by Col. Moore's brigade of Gen. Couch's division, which had just debarked. They advanced along the main Wilmington road until they encountered the enemy's position at Fort Anderson and the adjacent works. Here two brigades were intrenched to occupy the enemy, while Gen. Cox with the other two brigades and Gen. Ames' division moved around the swamp covering the enemy's right, in order to strike the Wilmington road in the rear of Fort Anderson. The distance to be travelled was about fifteen miles. The enemy, by means of their cavalry, discovering the movement of Gen. Cox, hastily abandoned their works on both sides of the river during the night of Feb. 19th, fell back behind Town Creek on the west, and to a similar position covered with swamps on the east. Thus the main defences of the Cape Fear River and of Wilmington were captured, with ten pieces of heavy ordnance and a large amount of ammunition.

On the next day Gen. Cox pursued the enemy to Town Creek, behind which he was found intrenched. The only bridge over had been destroyed. Gen. Terry, on the east bank, also encountered the enemy in superior force, and Gen. Ames' division was recrossed and joined him during the night. On the 20th Gen. Cox crossed Town Creek, and gaining the flank and rear of the enemy attacked and routed them, capturing two guns and three hundred and seventy-five prisoners, besides the killed and wounded. During the night he rebuilt the bridge, crossed his artillery, and advanced toward Wilmington without opposition. Meanwhile, Gen. Terry being unable to advance, so occupied the attention of the entire force of Gen. Hoke that he was unable to reënforce those defeated by Gen. Cox. On Feb. 21st Gen. Cox secured a portion of the enemy's bridge across Brunswick River, and passed a portion of his troops to Eagle Island, and threatened to cross the Cape Fear River above Wilmington. The enemy immediately set fire to his steamers, cotton, and military and naval stores, and abandoned the city. Early the next morning, Feb. 22d, Gen. Cox entered without opposition. The force in front of Gen. Terry fell back, and were pursued by him across Northeast River.

The Federal losses in these operations were about two hundred officers and men killed and wounded. That of the enemy was estimated at one thousand killed, wounded, and taken prisoners. Fifteen heavy and fifteen light guns were captured, with a large amount of ammunition.

As Gen. Schofield had no rolling stock at Wilmington, and was nearly destitute of wagons, he was compelled to operate from Newbern for the capture of Goldsboro. He had already sent to that place about 5,000 men, and ordered Gen. J. N. Palmer to move with as little delay as possible upon Kinston, in order to cover the workmen repairing the railroad. Gen. Ruger's division of the 23d corps was sent to reënforce Gen. Palmer, by way of Morehead City. As Gen. Palmer had not moved on the 25th, Gen. Cox was ordered to take the command and push forward at once. At the same time the division of Gen. Couch, which had just arrived at Wilmington, was prepared as rapidly as possible, together with the division of Gen. Cox, then under Brig.-Gen. Reilly, to join the column moving from Newbern by a land march from Wilmington. On March 6th the two divisions were ready to move for Kinston, and proceeded by way of Onslow and Richlands. On the 8th Gen. Cox had advanced to Wise's Forks, about one and a half miles below Southwest Creek, behind which the force of the enemy, consisting of Gen. Hoke's division and a small body of reserves, had retired. Meanwhile Gen. Cox sent two regiments, under Col. Upham of the 15th Connecticut, to secure the crossing of the creek on the Dover road. But the enemy having been reënforced by a portion of the old Army of Tennessee, recrossed the creek above the Dover road, and came down in the rear of Col. Upham's position, and surprised and captured nearly his entire command, about seven hundred men. They then advanced and endeavored to penetrate between Gen. Carter's and Gen. Palmer's divisions, occupying the Dover road and the railroad respectively, but were checked by Gen. Ruger's division, which was just arriving on the field. Only light skirmishing took place, from which the loss was small. As the enemy was equally as strong as Gen. Cox, and receiving reënforcements all the time, Gen. Cox intrenched his force to await the arrival of Gen. Couch. On the 9th the enemy pressed his lines strongly without making an assault; and on the 10th, having received further reënforcements, and perhaps heard of the approach of Gen. Couch's column, they made a heavy attack upon the left and centre of Gen. Cox, but were decisively repulsed with a heavy loss. They retired in confusion, leaving their dead and wounded and a large number of arms and intrenching tools. During the night they fell back across the Neuse and burned the bridge. The loss of Gen. Cox was about 300 in killed and wounded; that of the enemy was estimated at 1,500 in killed, wounded, and prisoners. During the night the column of Gen. Couch arrived. Gen. Schofield was delayed in crossing the Neuse until the 14th, for want of pontoons, when it was effected without opposition. Meanwhile the enemy had abandoned Kinston and moved rapidly toward Smithfield, to join the force under Gen. Johnston, to resist the advance of Gen. Sherman from Fayetteville. After occupying Kinston and repairing the bridge over the Neuse and the railroad track, Gen. Schofield moved on the 20th toward Goldsboro, which he entered on the evening of the 21st with slight opposition from the enemy.

Meanwhile Gen. Terry, with a portion of the command which had remained at Wilmington, moved from that point on March 15th, reaching Faison's depot on the 20th, and advanced to Cox's bridge, securing the crossing of the Neuse on the 22d.

The columns of Gen. Sherman commenced their march from Fayetteville on Wednesday, March 15th. His plan was, that Gen. Kilpatrick should move up the plank road to and beyond Averysboro, a village on the Cape Fear River, about forty miles south of Raleigh. Four divisions of the left wing, with as few wagons as possible, were to follow him; the rest of the train, under the escort of the two remaining divisions of the wing, were to take a shorter and more direct road to Goldsboro. In like manner Gen. Howard was to send his trains well to the right, under a good escort, toward Faison's depot and Goldsboro, and to hold four divisions light and ready to go to the aid of the left wing if it should be attacked while in motion. The weather continued bad, and the roads were almost impassable, requiring repairs at almost every foot to admit the passage of the wagons and artillery.

Gen. Kilpatrick advanced, followed by Gen. Slocum, who moved up the river or plank road on the 15th to Kyle's landing. About three miles beyond, at Taylor's Hole Creek, Gen. Kilpatrick encountered the rear-guard of the enemy, with which he skirmished heavily. At his request Gen. Slocum sent forward a brigade of infantry to hold a line of barricades. On the next morning the column advanced in the same order, and found the enemy in an intrenched position, with artillery, infantry, and cavalry. They were in front of the point where the road branched off toward Goldsboro through Bentonville. It appeared that Gen. Hardee, in retreating from Fayetteville, had halted in the narrow and swampy neck between the Cape Fear and South Rivers, in order to check the progress of Gen. Sherman, that time might be gained for the concentration of Gen. Johnston's forces in the rear at Raleigh, Smithfield, or Goldsboro. The force of Gen. Hardee was estimated at 20,000 men. Gen. Sherman found it to be necessary to dislodge him, both to gain possession of the road to Goldsboro and to keep up as long as possible the feint of an advance on Raleigh. The position of the enemy was a difficult one to carry, by reason of the nature of the ground, which was so soft that horses would sink everywhere, and even men could hardly make their way over the common pine barren.

Gen. Williams, with the 20th corps, was ahead, and Gen. Ward's division in the advance. This was deployed, and the skirmish line developed the position of a brigade of heavy artillery armed as infantry, posted across the road behind a light parapet, with a battery enfilading a clear field over which lay the way of approach. A brigade under Gen. Corse was sent by Gen. Williams to the left to turn this line. By a quick charge it broke the enemy's brigade, which retreated rapidly back to a second line better made and more strongly held. On the retreat the enemy were made to suffer by Winniger's battery of artillery, which had been put in position by Major Reynolds, chief of artillery. On the advance of Gen. Ward's division over the ground, three guns and 217 prisoners were captured. Of the latter 68 were wounded. Of the enemy's dead, 108 were buried by the troops. As the second line was developed, the division of Gen. Jackson was deployed forward on the right of Gen. Ward, and two divisions of Gen. Jefferson C. Davis' 14th corps on the left, well toward the Cape Fear River. At the same time Gen. Kilpatrick, who was acting in concert, was ordered to mass his cavalry on the extreme right, and in concert with the right of Gen. Jackson, to feel forward for the Goldsboro road. He succeeded in getting a brigade on the road, but it was attacked so furiously by a division of the enemy under Gen. McLaws, that it fell back to the flank of the infantry. Late in the afternoon the entire line advanced and drove the enemy within his intrenchments, and pressed him so hard that during the night, which was stormy, he retreated. In the morning he was followed by the division of Gen. Ward through and beyond Averysboro, when it became apparent that Gen. Hardee had retreated toward Smithfield instead of Raleigh. The Union loss was 12 officers and 65 men killed and 477 wounded. The loss of the enemy is unknown.

The division of Gen. Ward remained to keep up a show of pursuit, and the rest of Gen. Slocum's column turned to the right and built the bridge across the South River and took the road to Goldsboro. At the same time Gen. Kilpatrick crossed the river to the north in the direction of Elevation, and moved eastward, watching the left flank. The right wing of Gen. Howard was still working its way over the heavy roads toward Bentonville and Goldsboro. The cavalry of the enemy crossed in front of Gen. Sherman, to join their infantry at Smithfield, burning the bridges across Mill Creek. Smithfield is 22 miles northwest of Goldsboro, on the railroad leading from the latter place to Raleigh, and on the left bank of the Cape Fear River, 27 miles from Raleigh. Goldsboro is at the junction of the railroad from Raleigh to Newbern and that from Richmond to Wilmington.

On the night of the 18th Gen. Slocum's column encamped on the Goldsboro road, about five miles from Bentonville and twenty-seven miles from Goldsboro. The column of Gen. Howard was two miles south, and both columns had pickets three miles forward, at the junction of the roads leading to Goldsboro. The next movement is thus described by Gen. Sherman:—"All the signs induced me to believe that the enemy would make no further opposition to our progress, and would not attempt to strike us in flank while in motion. I therefore directed Gen. Howard to move his right wing by the new Goldsboro road, which goes by way of Falling Creek Church. I also left Slocum and joined Howard's column, with a view to open communication with Gen. Schofield, coming up from Newbern, and Gen. Terry from Wilmington. I found Gen. Howard's column well strung out, owing to the very bad roads, and did not overtake him in person until he had reached Falling Creek Church, with one regiment forward to the cross-roads near Cox's bridge across the Neuse. I had gone from Gen. Slocum about six miles when I heard artillery in his direction, but was soon made easy by one of his staff officers overtaking me, explaining that his leading division (Carlin's) had encountered a division of rebel cavalry (Dibbrell's), which he was driving easily. But soon other staff officers came up reporting that he had developed near Bentonville the whole of the rebel army under Gen. Johnston himself. I sent him orders to call up the two divisions guarding his wagon trains, and Hazen's division of the 15th corps, still back near Lee's store, to fight defensively until I could draw up Blair's corps, then near Mount Olive station, and with the three remaining divisions of the 15th corps come up on Gen. Johnston's left rear from the direction of Cox's bridge. In the mean time, while on the road, I received couriers from both Gens. Schofield and Terry. The former reported himself in possession of Kinston, delayed somewhat by want of provisions, but able to march so as to make Goldsboro on the 21st, and Gen. Terry was at or near Faison's depot. Orders were at once despatched to Gen. Schofield to push for Goldsboro, and to make dispositions to cross Little River in the direction of Smithfield as far as Millard; to Gen. Terry to move to Cox's bridge, lay a pontoon bridge, and establish a crossing; and to Gen. Blair to make a night march to Falling Creek

Church; and at daylight, the right wing, Gen. Howard, less the necessary wagon guards, was put in rapid motion on Bentonville."

It appears that on the advance of the head of Gen. Slocum's column from his camp on the night of the 18th, it first encountered Dibbrell's cavalry, but soon found its progress hindered by infantry and cavalry. The enemy attacked his advance and gained a temporary advantage, capturing three guns of Gen. Carlin's division, and driving the two advanced brigades back on the main body. Gen. Slocum at once deployed the two divisions of the 14th corps of Gen. Davis, and brought up on their left the two divisions of the 20th corps of Gen. Williams. These were placed on the defensive, and a line of barricades prepared. Gen. Kilpatrick also massed his cavalry on the left. In this position six assaults were made on the left wing by Gen. Johnston, with the combined forces of Gens. Hoke, Hardee, and Cheatham. During the night ensuing, Gen. Slocum got up his wagon train with its guard of two divisions, and Gen. Hazen's division of the 15th corps, which enabled him to make his position impregnable. Gen. Johnston had moved by night from Smithfield, with as little incumbrance as possible, for the purpose of overwhelming the left wing before it could be relieved. The right wing, in its advance to the aid of Gen. Slocum, found the cavalry of the enemy watching its approach without being able to offer any serious resistance until the head of the column encountered a considerable body behind a barricade, at the forks of the road near Bentonville, about three miles east of the battle field of the previous day. The cavalry were quickly dislodged, and the intersection of the roads secured. As the 15th corps advanced, Gen. Logan found that the enemy had thrown back their left flank, and constructed a line of parapet connecting with that toward Gen. Slocum, in the form of a bastion, with its salient on the main road to Goldsboro; thus interposing between Gen. Slocum with the left wing on the west, and Gen. Howard with the right wing on the east, while the flanks rested on Mill Creek and covered the road to Smithfield. Gen. Howard proceeding cautiously soon made strong connection with Gen. Slocum on the left, and at 4 P. M. of the 20th, a complete and strong line of battle confronted the enemy in his intrenched position, which put Gen. Johnston on the defensive, with Mill Creek and a single bridge in his rear. Gen. Sherman having nothing to gain by a battle, now pressed the enemy steadily with skirmishers alone, using artillery on the wooded space held by him, and feeling the flanks of his position, which were covered by swamps. On the next day, the 21st, a steady rain prevailed, during which Gen. Mower with his division, on the extreme right, had worked well to the right around the enemy's flank, and nearly reached the bridge across Mill Creek, which was the only line of retreat open to Gen. Johnston. Fearing the enemy might turn upon Gen. Mower with all his reserves, to overwhelm him, and perhaps yield his parapets for the purpose, Gen. Sherman ordered a general attack by his skirmish line, from left to right. Meanwhile Gen. Mower was able to regain his connection by moving to his left rear. During the night ensuing the enemy retreated toward Smithfield, leaving his pickets to fall into Gen. Sherman's hands, with many dead unburied and wounded in his field hospitals. At daybreak pursuit was made two miles beyond Mill Creek. The loss of the left wing about Bentonville was reported at 9 officers and 145 men killed, 51 officers and 816 men wounded, and 3 officers and 223 men missing; total, 1,247. Of the enemy, 167 dead were buried, and 338 made prisoners by the left wing. The loss of the right wing was 2 officers and 35 men killed, 12 officers and 289 men wounded, and 1 officer and 60 men missing; total, 399. Of the enemy, 100 dead were buried and 1,287 made prisoners by the right wing. The aggregate loss of Gen. Sherman, exclusive of the cavalry, was 1,646.

The result of this affair gave to Gen. Sherman full possession of Goldsboro, with the two railroads to Wilmington and Beaufort on the coast. The 22d was passed in burying the dead and removing the wounded at Bentonville, and on the next day all the troops moved to the camps about Goldsboro, already occupied by Gen. Schofield, there to rest and receive supplies of food and clothing.

During this march Gen. Sherman's army passed over an average breadth of forty miles of country, from Savannah to Goldsboro, and consumed all the forage, cattle, hogs, sheep, poultry, cured meats, corn meal, &c. It was stripped so bare as to make it necessary for the enemy to send provisions from other quarters to feed the inhabitants. It caused the abandonment by the enemy of the whole sea-coast from Savannah to Newbern, with the forts, dockyards, gunboats, &c. The real object of the march, says Gen. Sherman, "was to place this army in a position easy of supply, whence it could take an appropriate part in the spring and summer campaign of 1865." The troops remained in their camps during the remainder of the month of March. Meantime Gen. Sherman visited City Point and conferred with the President, Gen. Grant, and others.

CHAPTER L.

March of Gen. Sheridan from Winchester to the James River—Attack on the Army before Petersburg—Movement of Troops by the left of Gen. Grant—Battle near Five Forks—Cannonade of Petersburg—Assault on the City—Gen. Lee orders the evacuation of Richmond and Petersburg—Occupation of the latter by Union Troops—Occupation of Richmond by Gen. Weitzel—Retreat of Gen. Lee's Army—Pursuit by Gen. Sheridan—Surrender of Gen. Lee—Terms of Capitulation.

WHILE Gen. Sherman had been marching through the Carolinas, Gen. Grant was completing his preparations for the final conflict with Gen. Lee. Gen. Sheridan, in command in the Shenandoah valley, was ordered to join Gen. Grant, and for that purpose left his camp at Winchester on February 27th. His force consisted of the 1st division of cavalry under Gen. Merritt, the 3d under Gen. Custer, and one brigade of the 2d with four guns. The severe rains had swollen the rivers and made the roads bad. This stormy weather continued after the first few days during the march. The column passed through Kernstown, Middletown, Strasburg, and Woodstock, crossing the streams on the way without opposition. On the next day, the 28th, the march was made without opposition from Woodstock, through Edenburgh, to Hawkinsburgh. The north fork of the Shenandoah was crossed on a pontoon bridge, between Mount Jackson and New Market. In the crossing nine men of Gen. Custer's division were drowned. On the next day Gen. Sheridan passed through Harrisonburgh, Mount Crawford, Mount Sidney, and crossed Middle River, nine miles from Staunton, and camped four miles from that place, having advanced eighty-three miles in three days. The only skirmishing thus far took place at a point near the North River and Mount Crawford, between the brigade under Caphart and some cavalry of Gen. Rosser's division, who were trying to burn the bridge. The bridge was saved and several wagons of the enemy captured, with a loss of only six men.

Gen. Early, who had occupied Staunton, and was aware of the approach of Gen. Sheridan, instructed the inhabitants to remove their property, as he would be unable to retain possession of the town. Much property was therefore removed. During the night of March 1st, while the troops were encamped outside of Staunton, Gen. Devins' brigade of Merritt's division, moved to Staunton, drove the enemy's pickets through the town, and occupied it without opposition. Gen. Devin then turned to the left, marching easterly on the road toward Rockfish Gap, and destroyed the trestle bridge of the Virginia Central Railroad at Christina's Creek. On the 2d it rained heavily, but the column moved through Staunton toward Waynesboro, thirteen miles distant. At Fishersville, eight miles from Staunton, Gen. Custer's division being in advance, met the enemy's videttes and drove them back five miles to Waynesboro. Here he made a reconnoissance and discovered the enemy in position on some ridges along South River, with five guns. Placing the brigade of Gen. Pennington on the right, and Wells' on the left, with that of Caphart acting as a reserve, he advanced with the two forward regiments deployed as skirmishers and firing briskly. Immediately after firing a volley the entire line of the enemy broke, when the troops rushed upon them and captured 87 officers, 1,165 men, 13 flags, 5 cannon, over 100 horses and mules, and nearly 100 wagons and ambulances. Gen. Early lost his baggage but escaped to Charlottesville. Pursuit was made and Caphart's brigade crossing South River moved to Greenwood station, where it destroyed the depot, a train containing six pieces of artillery, and some commissary and ordnance supplies. Gen. Custer now waited for Gen. Merritt to come up, and both forces pushed on through Rockfish Gap to Charlottesville, eighteen miles. The prisoners were sent back to Winchester under a guard, which encountered some guerrillas on the way. At Charlottesville Gen. Sheridan remained two days. He says: "This time was consumed in bringing over from Waynesboro our ammunition and pontoon trains. The weather was horrible beyond description, and the rain incessant. The two divisions were during this time occupied in destroying the two large iron bridges, one over the Rivanna River, the other over Morse's Creek, near Charlottesville, and the railroad for a distance of eight miles in the direction of Lynchburg."

On March 6th Gen. Devin advanced with his division to Scottsville, whence light parties were sent through the country destroying all merchandise, mills, factories, bridges, &c. The division then proceeded along the James River Canal to Duguidsville, fifteen miles from Lynchburg, destroying every lock, and in many places the bank of the canal. The bridges at Duguidsville and Hardwicke had been burned by the enemy, and the pontoons were useless on account of the high water. At the same time the 3d division started from Charlottesville and proceeded down the Lynchburg Railroad to Amherst Court House, destroying every bridge, and in many places miles of the road. The bridges were numerous, and some of them five hundred feet in length. Abundant supplies were found in all places. The canal had been, says Gen. Sheridan, "the great feeder of Richmond." At Rockfish River the bank of the canal was cut, and at New Canton, where a dam is across the James, the guard lock was destroyed and the James River let into the canal, carrying away its banks and washing out its bottom. The dam was also partially destroyed. Among the captures were twelve canal boats laden with supplies, ammunition, rations, medical stores, &c. Gen. Custer was next sent to Ashland, and Gen. Devin to destroy the bridges over the South Anna. At noon on March 10th, the advance of Gen. Sheridan arrived on the banks of the Pamunkey, a few miles from Whitehouse, and soon crossed the river. On the 26th he reached City Point, and took a position in Gen. Gregg's old cavalry camp on the left and rear of the army.

The line occupied by Gen. Grant's army at this time extended a distance of about thirty miles. The extreme right was at Fort Harrison at Chafin's farm, north of the James River, where were also the outposts of the cavalry under Gen. Kautz. Thence it crossed the James in front of Bermuda Hundred and the Appomattox, and extended around Petersburg as far southwest as the bank of Hatcher's Run. This line was strongly intrenched everywhere, although the greater part of the army were on the left. The Army of the James, under Gen. Ord, was north of the James, forming the right wing, and the Army of the Potomac was south of the Appomattox, and formed really the left wing. From the Appomattox to Hatcher's Run there was a strong series of connected intrenchments. The first regular work on the line was Fort McGilvery; the next Fort Steadman; the next three-eighths of a mile further on, was Fort Haskell; the next Fort Morton, &c. Between the forts were mortar batteries, as follows: No. 8 near Fort McGilvery, No. 9 between that and Fort Steadman, No. 10 on the right of the latter fort and near it, and Nos. 11 and 12 on its left. Fort Steadman and the adjoining batteries were on an eminence known as Hare's Hill.

For some days previous to the arrival of Gen. Sheridan with his command, there had been indications of a change on the part of the enemy, such as might result in a dash on some part Gen. Grant's lines. About daylight, on March 25th, Gen. Gordon's old division and Bushrod Johnson's division of Lee's army were massed for a charge upon Fort Steadman, which covered about an acre of ground and had nine guns. At the same time the rest of Gen. Lee's army was arranged for an attack further down toward the left. At dawn Gordon's troops rushed forward to the attack. The space between the lines was about one hundred and fifty yards wide. They at once cleared their own abatis, charged across the interval, and up the ascent to Fort Steadman, and working through the abatis, carried the fort almost in an instant. The surprise was complete. In the fort was the 14th New York heavy artillery, and the line was guarded by Gen. McLaughlin's brigade of the 1st division of the 9th corps. The enemy immediately turned the guns of the fort against the rest of the line, and caused the abandonment of batteries 10 and 11 on the left, and battery 9 on the right. Upon these they dashed at once, and opened fire upon the troops as they escaped. Fort Haskell, however, soon gave them a check. The 3d division of the corps under Gen. Hartranft was quickly on the ground, and the batteries from all sides were speedily massed upon Fort Steadman. A terrible fire burst from the artillery, to which the enemy replied with the captured guns. Under this fire the division of Gen. Hartranft pressed up to retake the captured fort. The enemy at first resisted obstinately, and checked his progress with a loss of nearly two hundred killed and wounded. But the constant fire of the artillery and the pressure of Hartranft soon caused the enemy to fall back into the fort and then beyond it, down the hill, leaving all the captured guns in the endeavor to regain their own lines. A portion, however, were unable to escape, and about 1,758 were made prisoners, causing a total loss to the enemy of more than 2,000 men. The Union loss was nearly 1,000, in killed, wounded, and missing. No more firing took place at this point during the day. It was resumed at night when an attempt was made to repair the abatis. The affair was over before other Union troops arrived to give assistance. Later in the day a general forward demonstration was made along the line on the left, and a part of the enemy's skirmish lines captured with about 2,000 prisoners. Of this movement Gen. Grant reported thus:

"Our captures by the 2d corps were 365; by the 6th corps, 469, and by the 9th corps 1,049. The 2d and 6th corps pushed forward and captured the enemy's strong intrenchments, and turned them against him and still hold them. In trying to retake these the battle was continued until eight o'clock at night, the enemy losing very heavily. Humphreys estimates the loss of the enemy in his front at three times his own, and Gen. Wright, in his front, as double that of ours."

The following is Gen. Meade's congratulatory order to the army:

HEADQUARTERS ARMY OF THE POTOMAC, March 26, 1865.
General Orders No. 13.

The Major-General Commanding announces to the Army the success of the operations of yesterday.

The enemy, with a temerity for which he has paid dearly, massed his forces, and succeeded, through the reprehensible want of vigilance of the 3d brigade 1st division, 9th corps, in breaking through our lines, capturing Fort Steadman, and batteries 9, 10, and 11.

The prompt measures taken by Maj.-General Parke, the firm bearing of the troops of the 9th corps in adjacent portions of the line held by the enemy, and the conspicuous gallantry of the 3d division of this corps, for the first time under fire, together with the energy and skill displayed by Brigadier-General Hartranft, its leader, quickly repaired this disaster; and the enemy were driven from Fort Steadman and our lines, with heavy losses in killed and wounded, leaving in our hands eight battle-flags and over 1,900 prisoners.

The enemy being driven from the front of the 9th corps, the offensive was assumed by the 6th and 2d corps; the enemy by night was driven from his intrenched picket line, and all his efforts to recover the the same, which were particularly determined and persistent on the 2d corps front, were resisted and repulsed with heavy losses, leaving with the 6th corps over 400 prisoners, and with the 2d corps two battle-flags and over 300 prisoners.

The troops of the 6th corps, reported by Major-General Wright as engaged in these operations, were Getty's division, Keifer's brigade of Seymour's division, and Hamblin's and Edward's brigade of Wheaton's division.

Of the 2d corps, Major-General Humphreys mentions Miles' and Mott's divisions, and Smythe's brigade of Hays' division, supported by Griffin's division, 5th corps.

The result of the day was the thorough defeat of the enemy's plans, the capture of his strongly intrenched picket-line under the artillery fire of his main works, and the capture of ten battle-flags and about 2,800 prisoners—a result on which the Major-General Commanding heartily congratulates the army.

Two lessons can be learned from these operations: One, that no fortified line, however strong, will protect an army from an intrepid and audacious enemy, unless vigilantly guarded; the other, that no disaster or misfortune is irreparable, where energy and bravery are displayed in the determination to recover what is lost, and to promptly assume the offensive.

The Major-General Commanding trusts these lessons will not be lost on this army.

In conclusion, the Major-General Commanding desires to return his thanks to those commands of the army not specially mentioned in this order, for the promptness displayed by all, in their movements to different parts of the lines, under the exigencies of the hour. In connection with this subject, the promptitude of Major-General Warren and of Brevet Major-General Hunt, Chief of Artillery, in the early part of the operations, during the accidental absence of the Major-General Commanding, deserve commendation and thanks. GEORGE G. MEADE,
Major-General Commanding.

Indications were now more and more apparent of the weakness of Gen. Lee's forces, and the fall of Petersburg and Richmond. Gen. Grant immediately prepared for new movements of the highest importance, and considered that this attack of Lee was made to cover his designed retreat from Richmond.

On the 26th some sharp skirmishing broke out between the pickets of the 1st division of the 9th corps and their opponents, and the batteries joined in. It soon quieted down. On the 27th an attack was made by the enemy on Gen. Getty's division of the 6th corps by a small force of the enemy, which was repulsed after a sharp skirmish. On the same day orders were sent to the various field hospitals to remove the sick and wounded to City Point, and to keep the hospitals in readiness for any emergency that might arise. At 12 o'clock at night the whole army was put under marching orders, and the next day, the 28th, was passed in preparations for the movement. The plan was that the cavalry, under Sheridan, should advance to the left, as had been done so often before, followed by the 5th corps under Gen. Warren, and the 2d corps under Gen. Humphreys, while the other corps held the lines around Petersburg. For this purpose, on the 27th troops were selected from the 24th under Gen. Gibbon, and 25th under Gen. Birney, corps which belonged to the Army of the James, under Gen. Ord, and during the night marched across the river, leaving the remainder of the corps to garrison the position north of the James. At noon on the 28th, this force reached the headquarters of Gen. Meade, and early on the morning of the 29th marched into the lines as they were evacuated by the 2d corps.

About 6 A. M. of Wednesday the 29th, the cavalry began to move down the Jerusalem plank-road to Reams' station on the Weldon Railroad, in two columns, of which Gen. Crook commanded the right and Gen. Merritt the left. The bridge over Rowanty Creek was gone, and the creek not fordable. After a delay of four hours a bridge was built, and the advance under Crook crossed, and moved direct to Dinwiddie. The bad roads caused much delay. The town was occupied, and communication opened with Gen. Warren's corps on the right. It rained a little during the night, and very hard all of Thursday, the 30th. The roads became so bad as to block up the trains, and a part of the cavalry force was employed in guarding them. The rest moved up to the Boydton road.

Previous to the advance of the infantry, the left of the 6th corps extended to Hatcher's Run. The 2d corps extended down the run from the left of the 6th, at nearly a right angle, until reaching the crossing of the Vaughan road. The 5th corps was practically in reserve, and extended back at a right angle from the left of the 2d, in rear of the 6th. Early on the morning of the 29th the 2d corps moved along the Vaughan road, and was soon thrown into position along that road from Hatcher's Run to Gravelly Run, which unite at Monk's Neck to form Rowanty Creek. Works were thrown up to cover the corps from attack, but the enemy made no opposition. The 5th corps moved at the same time, and crossed Hatcher's Run. The route was along the road to Dinwiddie, until reaching the Quaker road, when the column turned abruptly to the right. About nine o'clock a connection was formed between the right of the 5th corps and the left of the 2d. The line of the former extended across the Quaker road, and within two or three miles of Dinwiddie. Some opposition had been made to the crossing of the 5th corps at Gravelly Run by a cavalry vidette, which was driven off after a short skirmish. Expecting an attack from the enemy, preparations were soon made by the troops, and about 3½ P. M. a division, under Gen. B. Johnson, attacked and drove in the skirmishers, and assailed with great force Gen. Griffin's division. Some batteries being in position opened upon the enemy, who had no artillery, and a sharp but short conflict ensued. Finding the force against him becoming too strong Johnson withdrew to his original position. The loss to the 5th corps was about five hundred, and that of the enemy was estimated at not far from the same number.

During the night, between 9 and 12 o'clock, a cannonade took place on the right of the

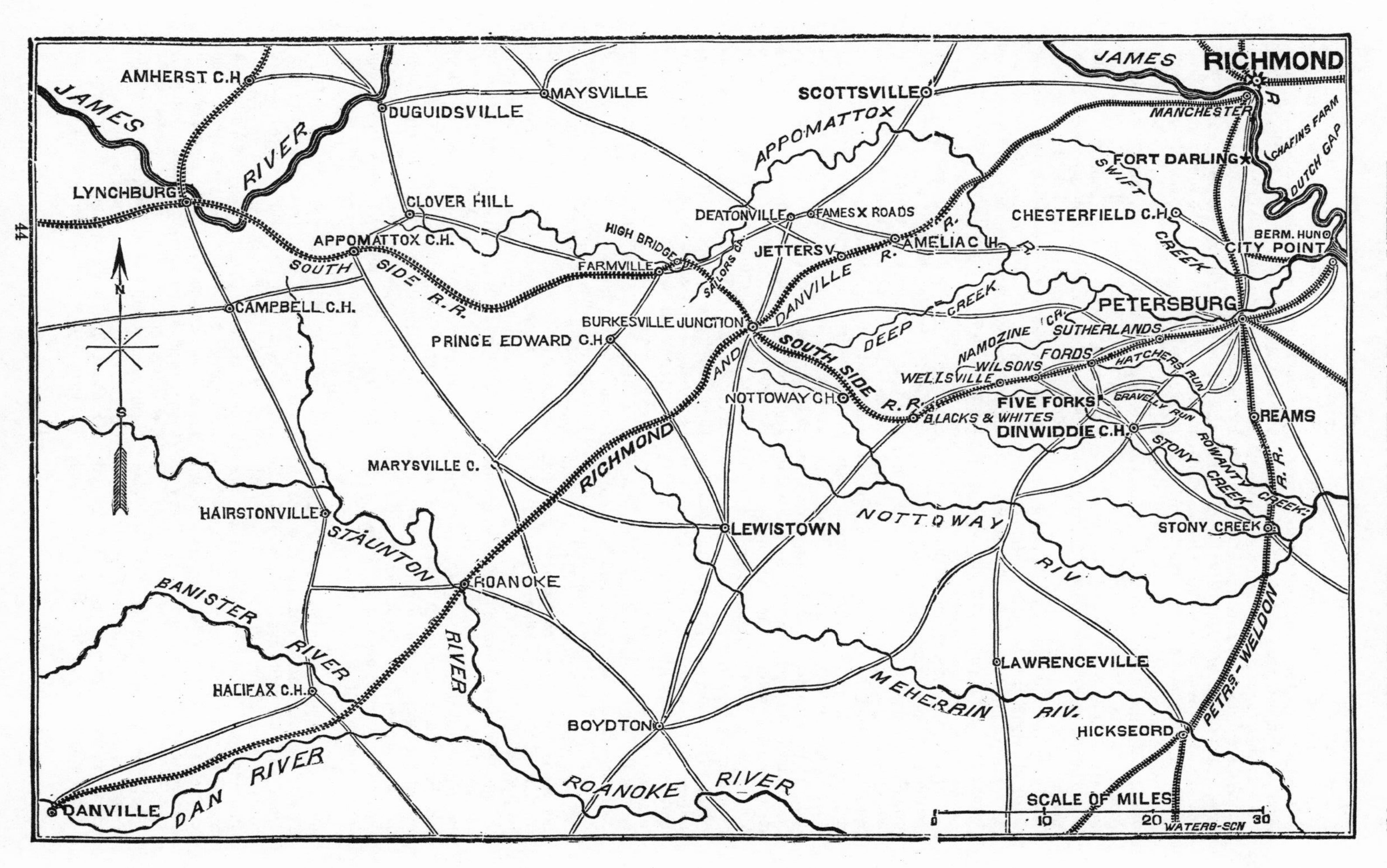
RICHMOND
JAMES
MANCHESTER
CHAFINS FARM
DUTCH GAP
FORT DARLING
SWIFT CREEK
CHESTERFIELD C.H.
BERM. HUN
CITY POINT
PETERSBURG
SUTHERLANDS
NAMOZINE CH.
WILSONS
FORDS
HATCHERS RUN
WELLSVILLE
FIVE FORKS
GRAVELLY RUN
BLACKS & WHITES
DINWIDDIE C.H.
REAMS
STONY CREEK
ROWANTY CREEK
R.R.
STONY CREEK
PETRS.-WELDON
HICKSEORD
LAWRENCEVILLE
MEHERRIN RIV.
NOTTOWAY RIV
LEWISTOWN
SCALE OF MILES
0
10
20
30
WATERB-SCN
AMHERST C.H.
JAMES RIVER
MAYSVILLE
DUGUIDSVILLE
SCOTTSVILLE
APPOMATTOX
LYNCHBURG
CLOVER HILL
DEATONVILLE
FAMES X ROADS
HIGH BRIDGE
SAILORS CR.
JETTERSV.
AMELIA C.H.
R.R.
APPOMATTOX C.H.
FARMVILLE
SOUTH SIDE R.R.
DANVILLE R.R.
DEEP CREEK
CAMPBELL C.H.
BURKESVILLE JUNCTION
PRINCE EDWARD C.H.
AND
SOUTH SIDE R.R.
NOTTOWAY C.H.
N
S
RICHMOND
MARYSVILLE C.
HAIRSTONVILLE
STAUNTON
ROANOKE
RIVER
BANISTER RIVER
HALIFAX C.H.
BOYDTON
DAN RIVER
ROANOKE RIVER
DANVILLE

line, in front of Petersburg. The loss was small on each side.

On the next day, Thursday, the 30th, Turner's division of the 24th corps was moved down the Vaughan road and across Hatcher's Run. It then turned to the right and advanced to make connection with the right of the 2d corps. A brigade of Gen. Foster's division then moved out and connected with the right of Turner, thus making the line complete. Field works were thrown up, and some skirmishing with the enemy took place. The two divisions of the 25th corps held a place between the right of the 24th and the left of the 6th. The 9th corps remained on the right of the 6th.

Early on the same day Gen. Sheridan connected his right with the left of Gen. Warren near the Boydton plank-road. The enemy had a strong line of intrenchments already erected to cover a position known as Five Forks. The force of Gen. Merritt was sent in that direction for the purpose of turning the right of the enemy, and the advance brigade, under Gen. Devin, soon encountered their cavalry, and drove them back to their works. Their infantry in turn drove back the advance. Their line of intrenchments covered the White Oak road, which runs from the Boydton road to the Southside Railroad. From the White Oak road toward Hatcher's Run the enemy were in strong force. All attempts to turn his right by cavalry were baffled.

Meanwhile some changes were made in the position of the different corps. The 5th at night occupied a position about a mile north of the junction of the Quaker and Boydton roads. During the day it had advanced westward about three-fourths of a mile, and lay fronting northward, with the pickets of Gens. Ayres's division within five hundred yards of the White Oak road, but at a spot between two and three miles west of its intersection with the Boydton road. The divisions of Gens. Crawford and Griffin were on the right successively. On the right of the 5th corps was the 2d, which now had its right near Hatcher's Run. Gen. Sheridan remained at Dinwiddie and covered the left. The movements of the day had been accomplished with skirmishing and some artillery firing, making the losses of the Union troops about two hundred.

The object now was to get possession of the enemy's position, known as Five Forks, by carrying which their right flank would be turned. At this point five roads meet in the woods, three of which run back to the Southside Railroad. The White Oak road was here strongly fortified with logs and earth, with its approaches blocked by fallen trees. Sharpshooters were also stationed to resist any advance.

Early on Friday morning, the 31st, Gen. Warren massed the division of Griffin in the rear of those of Gens. Ayres and Crawford, for an advance upon the White Oak road, which commences at the Boydton road and runs westward, crossing the Quaker road and the Claiborne, which latter extends northwestly to the Southside Railroad. About 8 o'clock the advance commenced toward the Dabney House, Ayres's division leading and supported by the other two. After moving about a half mile beyond the plank-road the enemy's skirmishers opened fire, at the same time falling back upon their main works, a mile and a half below the White Oak road. A severe fire was now opened upon the advance under Gen. Ayres, which broke and fell to the rear, followed by a vigorous charge upon them by the enemy. The attack of the enemy was so impetuous, and they were so well handled, that they swept the field, notwithstanding the obstinate resistance, Each division met the same fate until the whole 5th corps was driven back to the Boydton road, when Miles' division of the 2d corps came to their aid and checked the enemy. They now attempted to cut off Sheridan's cavalry, which were greatly exposed by the failure of the 5th corps to advance. The 2d division was on Stony Creek, southwest of Dinwiddie, consisting of three brigades—Smith's, Davies', and Gregg's—and holding the left of Sheridan's line. The brigade of Gen. Fitzhugh was next, and facing southeast, and next was Stagg's brigade, on Gravelly Run, six miles from Dinwiddie. About two miles from the latter place was Gibbs' brigade. Early in the afternoon the enemy attacked the left in force, but it held its ground. Davies' brigade, on the right of the extreme left, was next attacked, and, being flanked, was driven back with severe loss. The enemy next attacked the left centre, and forced it back, when the commands were faced into new positions, and reënforcements hurried up. At 5 P. M. the greater part of both divisions had been repulsed and driven back several miles to the Boydton road, and Gibbs' brigade had fallen back about a mile from Dinwiddie. The troops of Gen. Merritt were now reformed, and held a firm position on the right. The enemy, reënforced by the infantry which had driven the 5th corps, renewed the attack, but the artillery being in position, and a large force of cavalry having been rallied by Gen. Sheridan, the desperate charges of the enemy were successfully resisted, and they drew off to the woods. Meantime the 5th corps had been rallied, and advanced and regained the whole ground which had been lost. The division of Gen. Griffin captured the earthwork from which the enemy had issued, and advanced and took a position on the White Oak road, east of Five Forks. At the same time the 1st and 3d divisions of the 2d corps, next on the right, advanced, and a hot engagement with the enemy ensued. The latter resisted stubbornly, but at length withdrew, and the whole corps advanced three-fourths of a mile, capturing about one hundred and fifty prisoners. The two divisions of the 24th corps were on

BATTLE OF FIVE FORKS

the right of the 2d, and were thrown forward so as to coöperate with the general advance. The enemy had thus foiled the plans of the day; but owing to the strong force and the skilful handling of the numerous batteries in the field works he had been checked in turn, and forced to retire. At night the Federal right had advanced a few hundred yards from its position in the morning, and the left reached to the White Oak road, three-fourths of a mile from Five Forks, which was to the westward, and three miles from the intersection of the White Oak road with the Boydton road. The White Oak road from the extreme spot occupied, was held about one mile eastward. From that point the line ran in an irregular and semi-circular form to the 2d corps. The Union loss of the day was between 2,500 and 3,000; that of the enemy was less. Many prisoners were taken on both sides.

On the next day, Saturday, April 1st, the contest for the possession of Richmond was virtually decided. During the night Gen. Grant had placed the 5th corps, Gen. Warren, under the command of Gen. Sheridan. All night the troops had been busy throwing up works, corduroying roads, and bringing up trains. At 4 A. M. the enemy made an attack on Foster's division of the 24th corps. It had been expected, but they came so suddenly that the troops broke to the rear, and left them to raise their flag on the parapet. The troops were soon aroused and drove back the enemy. About fifty prisoners were captured on each side. This was followed by the roar of musketry and a cannonade all along the centre and right of the line. This soon quieted down. The command of Gen. Sheridan was now about 30,000 men, consisting of nearly four divisions of cavalry and three of infantry, and double the force which the enemy were able to concentrate against him. At the same time the army threatened the whole length of the extended line from Dinwiddie to Petersburg. The plan of operations by Gen. Sheridan appears to have been to break through the enemy's line in such a manner as to enclose Five Forks and its garrison, and to capture them. At daybreak the cavalry advanced under Gens. Custar and Devin, slowly driving the enemy toward the left of his works on the White Oak road. These divisions were dismounted, and fought with carbines, while the brigades of Gens. Gregg and Mackenzie remained in the saddle, so as to flank the enemy quickly. Thus the troops worked steadily up on all sides to the intrenchments of the enemy, who fell slowly back to their main position, delivering a most destructive fire. Thus Gen. Sheridan got a force well on the enemy's flank and rear, while the rest of the troops pressed slowly upon the front of his works. An attack was now to be made by the whole force, and about 3 P. M. the 5th corps was ordered forward to support the cavalry. It marched from its position, and was halted obliquely to the White Oak road. It was then swung round on its left wing as a pivot by advancing the centre and right. This brought it on one flank of the enemy, while the cavalry pressed the other. The enemy were pressed back slowly, and becoming aware of their dangerous position, a most deadly contest ensued for two hours. Being strongly intrenched, and having a battery in position, they raked the troops of Sheridan with a terrific fire. Several times his men, appalled by the slaughter, staggered back from the intrenchments; but by turns he urged, cheered, and drove them until the enemy were nearly surrounded on all sides and exhausted. With his ranks reduced and wearied, and seeing it to be useless to try longer to check the desperate onsets, the enemy rushed to the rear through the only outlet left for him. Sheridan, with overwhelming forces, pressed upon him, and a further bloody contest ensued. At 7½ P. M. the battle was over. The cavalry divisions of Gens. Custar and Mackenzie pursued and picked up many stragglers and fugitives. About four thousand prisoners were captured, several cannon, an ambulance and baggage train, several thousand muskets, and many flags. Sheridan's loss was estimated at not far from three thousand, while that of the enemy was as large, besides the prisoners. During the day the 2d corps had been making a general advance, engaged constantly with the enemy, and extending so as to connect with the 5th, and be ready to support them near the White Oak road. The 6th and 9th corps had not been engaged; but in order to coöperate in a manner with Sheridan, a general cannonade was opened along the front at 10 P. M. Enlivened by the news of Sheridan's success, the troops made it one of the hottest during the siege of Petersburg. During the day Gen. Warren was removed from the command of the 5th corps, and Gen. Griffin took his place.

At 4 A. M. on the next day, Sunday, April 2d, an assault all along the line by the 2d, 6th, 9th, 24th, and 25th corps commenced. The divisions of Gens. Turner and Foster, of the 24th corps, were brought up on both sides of Hatcher's Run in support of the 6th corps, and charged with it. The enemy opened a destructive fire while the troops were massing, and continued with such severity as often to check the advance. The 6th corps carried the two forts in its front, and the 3d division, under Gen. Seymour, after a severe fight, broke through to the Southside Railroad, and commenced to tear it up. The 24th corps, between the 6th and 2d, had been equally successful. The right division of the 2d corps and the two divisions of the 24th, captured one thousand prisoners and many guns, and carried the works up to the railroad. The 9th corps advanced simultaneously with the 6th, and after the severest fighting on the field, captured Fort Mahone, which covered the Jerusalem plank road. But the position was too important to be lost, and the enemy charged in turn to retake it, and were nearly successful, when, by the approach of the 6th corps on the left, he was once more driven back. The following telegraphic despatches relate the progress of the day:

CITY POINT, VA., April 2—2 P. M.
Hon. Edwin M. Stanton, Secretary of War:

At 10:45 A. M. Gen. Grant telegraphs as follows:

"Every thing has been carried from the left of the 9th corps. The 6th corps alone captured more than three thousand prisoners. The 2d and 24th corps captured forts, guns, and prisoners from the enemy, but I cannot tell the numbers.

"We are now closing around the works of the line immediately enveloping Petersburg. All looks remarkably well. I have not yet heard from Sheridan. His headquarters have been moved up to Banks' House, near the Boydton road, about three miles southwest of Petersburg." A. LINCOLN.

SECOND DESPATCH.

CITY POINT, VA., April 2—8:30 P. M.
Hon. Edwin M. Stanton, Secretary of War:

At 4:30 P. M. to-day Gen. Grant telegraphed as follows:

"We are now up, and have a continuous line of troops, and in a few hours will be intrenched from the Appomattox, below Petersburg, to the river above. The whole captures since the army started out will not amount to less than twelve thousand men, and probably fifty pieces of artillery. I do not know the number of men and guns accurately, however.

"A portion of Foster's division, 24th corps, made a most gallant charge this afternoon, and captured a very important fort from the enemy, with its entire garrison.

"All seems well with us, and every thing is quiet just now." A. LINCOLN.

During the afternoon of the same day Gen. Lee, finding his army no longer able to maintain its position, gave orders for the evacuation of Richmond and Petersburg. This was accomplished during the night. This evacuation was early discovered by the troops before those cities. As they advanced to take possession of Petersburg, the Mayor of the city appeared with the following communication:

To Lieut.-Gen. Grant, commanding the armies of the United States, or the Major-General commanding United States forces in front of Petersburg.

GENERAL: The city of Petersburg having been evacuated by the Confederate troops, we, a committee authorized by the Common Council, do hereby surrender the city to the United States forces, with a request for the protection of the persons and property of its inhabitants.

We are, respectfully, your obedient servants,
W. W. TOWNES, Mayor.
D'ARCY PAUL,
CHARLES F. COLLIERS.

Seldom was a city occupied by a besieging army with less disorder or damage to private property. A writer who was present says: "The citizens did not show themselves during the fore part of the day, but after discovering that our soldiers were orderly and well-behaved, with no disposition to disturb any one, they began to make their appearance at the doors and windows of their residences, and later in the day even entering familiarly into conversation, many of them expressing their joy quietly that the Confeds had gone, and hoping that the war would soon be over. For more than a month past rebel troops have been receiving less rations than ever before, only just enough being brought in to last from day to day. The citizens say they have suffered much, but it is well to take such stories with a good deal of allowance. The rebels managed to get away all their artillery, excepting one or two old Columbiads and a few heavy mortars, which they could not transport readily. The city presents a very cleanly and respectable appearance, and there are many residences here that would do no discredit to Fifth avenue, New York. Many of the houses in the lower part of the city have been badly injured by the shot and shell thrown from our batteries last summer, and since that time most of the houses located there have been vacant."

The occupation of Richmond is thus described:

WAR DEPARTMENT, WASHINGTON,
Wednesday, April 5—10:20 P. M.
To Major-General Dix:

The following details respecting the capture of Richmond and its occupation by the Union forces, have been telegraphed to this department from that city. EDWIN M. STANTON,
Secretary of War.

General Weitzel learned, at 3 o'clock on the morning of Monday, that Richmond was being evacuated, and at daylight moved forward, first taking care to give his men breakfast, in the expectation that they might have to fight. He met no opposition, and on entering the city was greeted with hearty welcome from the mass of the people. The Mayor went out to meet him and to surrender the city, but missed him on the road. Gen. Weitzel found much suffering and poverty among the population. The rich as well as the poor are destitute of food. He is about to issue supplies to all who take the oath. The inhabitants now number about twenty thousand, half of them of African descent.

It is not true that Jeff. Davis sold his furniture before leaving. It is all in his house, where I am now writing. He left at 7 P. M. by the Danville Railroad. All the members of Congress escaped. Hunter has gone home. Gov. Smith went with the army. Judge Campbell remains here.

Gen. Weitzel took here one thousand prisoners, besides the wounded. These number five thousand, in nine hospitals. He captured cannon to the number of at least five hundred pieces. Five thousand muskets have been found in one lot. Thirty locomotives and three hundred cars are found here. The Petersburg railroad bridge is totally destroyed; that of the Danville road partially, so that connection with Petersburg is not easily made. All the rebel vessels are destroyed except an unfinished ram, which has her machinery in her perfect. The Tredegar Works are unharmed, and the machinery was taken to-day under Gen. Weitzel's orders. Libby Prison and Castle Thunder have also escaped the fire, and are filled with rebel prisoners of war. Most of the editors have fled, especially John Mitchell. The *Whig* appeared yesterday as a Union paper, with the name of the former proprietor at the head. The theatre opens here to-night. Gen. Weitzel describes the reception of the President yesterday as enthusiastic in the extreme.

The fire in the city commenced in the Shockoe warehouse, filled with tobacco, as well as the large granary establishment on Carey Street near Twenty-third Street. It was very destructive, consuming quite one-third of the city; and in addition to destroying the War Department, the General Post-office, the Treasury building, several churches, and many stores, likewise destroyed the offices of the Richmond Enquirer, Dispatch, and Examiner; the Virginia Bank, the Farmers' Bank, and the Bank of Richmond.

On arriving in the city Gen. Weitzel, through his Adjutant-General, Major D. D. Wheeler, issued the following order:

HEADQUARTERS DEPARTMENT ARMY OF THE JAMES,
RICHMOND, VA., April 3, 1865.

Major-Gen. Godfrey Weitzel, commanding detachment of the Army of the James, announces the occupation of the city of Richmond by the armies of the United States, under command of Lieut.-Gen. Grant. The people of Richmond are assured that we come to restore to them the blessings of peace, prosperity, and freedom, under the flag of the Union.

The citizens of Richmond are requested to remain for the present quietly within their houses, and to avoid all public assemblages or meetings in the public streets. An efficient provost-guard will immediately reëstablish order and tranquillity within the city.

Martial law is, for the present, proclaimed.

Brig.-Gen. George F. Shipley, U. S. volunteers, is hereby appointed Military Governor of Richmond.

Lieut.-Col. Frederick L. Manning, Provost Marshal General, Army of the James, will act as Provost Marshal of Richmond. Commanders of detachments doing guard duty in the city will report to him for instructions. By command of Major-Gen. Weitzel,

D. D. WHEELER, Ass't Adj.-Gen.

Brig.-Gen. G. F. Shepley having been announced as Military Governor of Richmond, issued the following order:

HEADQUARTERS MILITARY GOVERNOR OF RICHMOND,
RICHMOND, VA., April 3, 1865.

1. The armies of the rebellion having abandoned their effort to enslave the people of Virginia, have endeavored to destroy by fire the capital, which they could not longer occupy by their arms. Lieut--Col. Manning, Provost Marshal General of the Army of the James and Provost Marshal of Richmond, will immediately send a sufficient detachment of the provost guard to arrest, if possible, the progress of the flames. The fire department of the city of Richmond, and all the citizens interested in the preservation of their beautiful city, will immediately report to him for duty, and render every possible assistance in staying the progress of the conflagration. The first duty of the armies of the Union will be to save the city doomed to destruction by the armies of the rebellion.

2. No person will leave the city of Richmond without a pass from the office of the Provost Marshal.

3. Any citizen, soldier, or any person whatever, who shall hereafter plunder, destroy, or remove any public or private property, of any description whatever, will be arrested and summarily punished.

4. The soldiers of the command will abstain from any offensive or insulting words or gestures toward the citizens.

5. No treasonable or offensive expressions insulting to the flag, the cause, or the armies of the Union, will hereafter be allowed.

6. For an exposition of their rights, duties, and privileges, the citizens of Richmond are respectfully referred to the proclamations of the President of the United States in relation to the existing rebellion.

7. All persons having in their possession or under their control any property whatever of the so-called Confederate States, or of any officer thereof, or the records or archives of any public officer whatever, will immediately report the same to Col. Manning, Provost Marshal.

In conclusion, the citizens of Richmond are assured that, with the restoration of the flag of the Union, they may expect the restoration of that peace, prosperity, and happiness which they enjoyed under the Union of which that flag is the glorious symbol.

G. F. SHEPLEY, Brig.-Gen. U. S. Volunteers,
and Military Governor of Richmond.

General Order No. 2.

HEADQUARTERS MILITARY GOVERNOR OF RICHMOND,
RICHMOND, VA., April 3, 1865.

No officer or soldier will enter or search any private dwelling, or remove any property therefrom, without a written order from the headquarters of the Commanding General, the Military Governor, or the Provost Marshal General.

Any officer or soldier, with or without such order, entering any private dwelling, will give his name, rank, and regiment.

Any officer or soldier entering a private dwelling without such authority, or failing to give his name, rank, or regiment, or reporting the same incorrectly, will be liable to immediate and summary punishment.

GEO. F. SHEPLEY,
Brig.-Gen. U. S. Volunteers, and Military
Governor of Richmond.

The following details were written by a correspondent at the time of the occupation: "The works in front of Richmond, which were wholly evacuated previous to our occupancy of the city to-day under Gen. Weitzel, consist of three strong lines, wholly enveloping it. The outer ones are continuous lines, the inner one consisting of a series of strong redoubts and bastion forts. All these works mount upwards of three hundred heavy guns, all of which we have taken, and would, when properly garrisoned, form an almost impregnable series of defences. As I rode along these lines they seemed, with the exception of the outer one, to have been most indifferently garrisoned; and but for the facility with which they could be reënforced at any time by bringing troops up the Petersburg road and crossing them on pontoons, the lines could have been carried by assault.

"The route which I pursued on entering the capital was that by the Osborn and Richmond pike, which leads in a nearly north and south direction, and quite parallel to the James River. After passing our picket line, the first work encountered was Fort Field, forming a part of the exterior line of defence. This work, which is a very strong one in itself, is surrounded by three lines of abatis and one of torpedoes. The torpedoes were carefully removed by the advanced guard of Weitzel. These lines of torpedoes were marked out by small flags for safety to the rebels, which flags they neglected to remove in their hasty flight. The camps were left entire —tents standing and furniture within. After passing this line we came upon the second line, which was equally as strong as the first, excepting as to abatis and torpedoes. The third line is just outside the edge of the town, is situated on high ground, and is well adapted to satisfy the conditions of defence. Each of the detached works forming this line sweep a portion of the line in front of it by its fire, and rendering that front line untenable when reached. These works, like the others, mount heavy guns, many of which were navy guns, probably captured at Norfolk in the early part of the war. Communication between these works and those on the other side of the river was maintained by four bridges, some of which were pontoon and some pile, in addition to the three railroad bridges at and in Richmond.

"The evacuation of the works and city was not generally understood by the troops and people till Sunday afternoon. The necessity of the movement was rendered imperative by Gen. Grant's successes on the left. At half-past three o'clock yesterday afternoon, Jeff. Davis, while in church, received a despatch from Gen. Lee, that immediate preparations must be made to evacuate Richmond and its defences at once, as he was wholly unable to make further headway against Grant's onset on the left. He added that his (Lee's) design was to endeavor to make Danville, and there fortify for a last grand stand.

"Davis left this city last night at eight o'clock by rail for Danville, his family having been sent out five days ago. On the train he had horses and carriages embarked, in case the road was interrupted, in order to easily make his way by these means. Governor Smith did not evacuate the Gubernatorial mansion until one o'clock this morning, when he fled, leaving Mrs. Smith behind, and all the furniture in his house, which he had heretofore threatened to burn. The residence of the Governor is now the headquarters of General Charles Devens, commanding a division in the 24th corps, now here. Mrs. General R. E. Lee, wife of the General-in-Chief, is also in the city."

The operations of Gen. Sheridan on the 2d, consisted in efforts to push the advantages thus far gained by him. On the 3d his object was to intercept the retreat of the enemy. The advance of the cavalry consisted of Custar's division. At Namozine Creek the rear guard of the enemy was found strongly intrenched behind earthworks covering the crossing. The bridge had been destroyed and trees felled across the road leading down to it. A section of artillery was opened in front, while the cavalry forded the stream and flanked the enemy's position. After a short skirmish the enemy retreated, leaving their path strewn with wagons, ambulances, dead and wounded horses and mules, caissons, boxes of ammunition, mess utensils, arms, accoutrements, blankets, &c. The enemy were overtaken beyond Namozine Church, and prisoners, horses, and arms were captured in abundance. A harassing pursuit was now kept up for twenty miles, during which about 350 prisoners, four cannon, two flags, and several ammunition wagons were captured. Night put a stop to its progress. Early on the next morning, Tuesday, April 4th, the pursuit was resumed, with Mackenzie's division in front and Custar's in the rear. The enemy were overtaken in the afternoon, and found posted with infantry and artillery in works about two miles from Bethany. Skirmishing began at once, and continued until dark, when the troops encamped, waiting for the rest of the column. Soon after 11 P. M. the cavalry were aroused and marched all night, reaching Jettersville about 6 o'clock in the morning, and there found the 5th corps, well intrenched across the railroad from Richmond to Danville. The 5th corps had started in pursuit, soon after the cavalry, on the 3d, under Sheridan's command. They arrived in sight of the Appomattox about 2 P. M. Thence it turned to the left without crossing the river, and moved along the Namozine road behind the cavalry, marching through Amelia County and crossing both Deep and Namozine Creeks. The distance made was sixteen miles, which ended in blocking the trains in the miry roads. Few people were to be seen, except those who had been slaves, many of whom followed the column. The march on the next day, Tuesday the 4th, was twenty miles, and brought the corps to Jettersville, where it was massed across the railroad in an open field. In the rear of the 5th corps followed the 2d, and in the rear of the 2d was the 6th. These two corps were under Gen. Meade on the river or Namozine road, but did not start until the 4th. After a long march the 2d reached Jettersville at 2 P. M. on the next day after the 5th.

When the cavalry reached Jettersville on the morning of the 6th, it was understood that Gen. Lee in his retreat from Richmond had got as far as Amelia Court House, while the Union troops were beginning to assemble at Jettersville. This place is on the railroad, about halfway between Burkesville and Amelia Court-House, and fifty-four miles southwest of Richmond. Amelia Court-House is on the same railroad, about forty-seven miles from Richmond. The cavalry division of Gen. Custar was immediately posted on the left of the 5th corps, and the 1st and Mackenzie's division still further to the left.

At the same time Gen. Davies' brigade of Gen. Crooks' division was sent toward Burkesville, to seize that station and ascertain the state of affairs in that direction. At Burkesville is the junction of the Richmond and Danville Railroad with the Southside Railroad from Petersburg, and fifty-two miles west of the latter place. Gen. Davies came upon the cavalry of the enemy at Fame's cross-roads, and attacking them, captured a large number of prisoners, 5 new Armstrong guns and caissons, and about 200 wagons, mostly empty, and 7 or 8 battle-flags. An infantry force then came to the support of the cavalry, and Gen. Davies was forced to retire with his prisoners, after burning the wagons. At 3 P. M. Gen. Sheridan learning this news, and finding the condition of the enemy, sent the following despatch to Gen. Grant:

JETTERSVILLE, April 5—3 P. M.

To Lieut.-Gen. U. S. Grant:

GENERAL:—I send you the enclosed letter, which will give you an idea of the condition of the enemy and their whereabouts. I sent Gen. Davies' brigade this morning around on my left flank. He captured at Fame's cross-roads five pieces of artillery, about two hundred wagons, and eight or nine battle flags, and a number of prisoners. The 2d army corps is now coming up. I wish you were here yourself. I feel confident of capturing the Army of Northern Virginia if we exert ourselves. I see no escape for Gen. Lee. I will send all my cavalry out on our left flank, except McKenzie, who is now on the right.

(Signed) P. H. SHERIDAN, Major-General.

LETTER.

AMELIA COURT HOUSE, April 5, 1865.

DEAR BRAMMIA:—Our army is ruined, I fear. We are all safe as yet. Theodore left us sick. John Taylor is well; saw him yesterday. We are in line of battle this evening. Gen. Robert Lee is in the field near us. My trust is still in the justice of our cause. Gen. Hill is killed. I saw Murray a few moments since. Bernary Perry, he said, was taken prisoner, but may get out. I send this by a negro I see passing up the railroad to Michlenburg. Love to all.

Your devoted son,

W. B. TAYLOR, Colonel.

Sheridan now proceeded to put his cavalry out on the left flank, and the slight skirmishing which took place indicated the contest of the next day.

Meanwhile the other corps of the army were approaching. On April 4th, Gen. Ord's column of the Army of the James, comprising two divisions of the 24th corps and one of the 25th corps, marched down the Cox's road from Sutherland's station, 10 miles west of Petersburg, on the Southside Railroad. Having separated from the main column, it moved on the direct road to Burkesville. Gen. Grant was with this force. After advancing along the railroad 15 miles, it encamped at night near Wilson's station. On the next day, the 5th, it advanced along the railroad to Black and White's, which it reached at 2 P. M. Thence it pressed forward, over good roads, to Nottaway Court House, 9 miles from Burkesville. Here the despatch of Gen. Sheridan was received by Gen. Grant, about 6½ P. M., and the two divisions of the 24th corps were immediately pushed forward to Burkesville, which they reached at 11 P. M. The division of the 25th corps remained at Black and White's. Gen. Grant himself went to Jettersville.

Of the 9th corps, two divisions on the 4th marched from Petersburg to Ford's station on the Southside Railroad, about 20 miles. On the 5th they advanced along the railroad to Wellsville, 41 miles from Petersburg, having in charge most of the army trains. On the next day, the 6th, they pressed forward, and arrived within 10 miles of Burkesville.

On the night of the 5th, after the skirmishing of the cavalry with the enemy, the army lay in line of battle, facing substantially to the north. The cavalry division of Gen. Mackenzie was on the left, next the 2d corps of infantry, with the 5th and 6th still further to the right, and the cavalry division of Gen. Custar on the right flank. At daylight in the morning Gen. Meade moved the three corps along the railroad in the direction of Amelia Court House, but learning that the enemy were retreating toward Farmville, the nearest station west on the railroad to Lynchburg, he changed the direction of the 2d and 5th corps from a northerly to a northwesterly one, with the 2d corps in advance, moving on Deatonsville, and the 5th on its right. At the same time the 6th corps faced about and moved by the left flank, taking position on the left of the 2d. The cavalry were on the extreme left. The 6th corps in its movement struck the road running from Deatonsville to Burke's station, a little south of the former place. It found the 2d corps engaged with the enemy at the front and right, and the cavalry on the left. Moving down the road toward Burke's station about a mile, it turned sharp to the right and proceeded across toward a nearly parallel road, on which the enemy was moving, and along which they had a line of intrenchments thrown up. Gen. Seymour's division of the corps carried the road held by the enemy about 4 P. M., and then turned to the right and advanced down the road against strong resistance. Gen. Wheaton's division was brought in on the left of Gen. Seymour's, and both swept down the road two miles. The enemy were there found reformed on the opposite bank of a deep and difficult creek, from which they were driven half a mile. At all points the enemy were driven during the day, and Lieut.-Gen. Ewell, Gen. Custis Lee, and three others, were captured, with a large number of men. The 5th army corps made a long march, but its position on the right prevented it from striking the enemy's column before it had passed. The Union loss was above 1,000. Five guns and many flags, caissons, and wagons were taken, besides prisoners. On the next day, the 7th, the 2d corps, with the 2d division of cavalry, found the enemy at Farmville, 16 miles west of Burkesville. A sharp contest ensued, causing a loss of several hundred men, among whom was Gen. Smyth. Other troops were brought up, but before the enemy could be reëngaged he was on the retreat again.

At High Bridge over the Appomattox, Gen. Lee crossed to the north side of the river, and two regiments sent by Gen. Grant to hold the bridge were captured by the cavalry of the enemy, and the bridge burned. The retreat of the enemy was now directly toward Lynchburg. The pursuit was made with great vigor, and stragglers were picked up at every step, and property dropped or partially destroyed by the enemy. During the day Gen. Grant addressed a letter to Gen. Lee, demanding a surrender of his army. On the 8th the enemy made most strenuous efforts, by hard marching, to extricate themselves; but at night they encountered Gen. Sheridan at Appomattox Court House, between themselves and Lynchburg. A sharp contest ensued, in which many of them were taken prisoners and their retreat checked. The 24th and 5th corps were in support of the cavalry, and during the night a strong position was taken across the main road, south of the enemy, the Appomattox River being on the north, and cutting him off from retreat in that direction. Early on the next morning Gen. Sheridan commenced a vigorous attack, and a warm engagement ensued until 9 A. M., when a flag of truce appeared in front of his line, with the information that hostilities had been suspended, in order to arrange terms of surrender. At this time Gen. Hancock was advancing, having left Winchester on April 4th, with a strong column, and moved up the Shenandoah valley for Lynchburg. Gen. Stoneman had already reached Boone, in North Carolina, in his march from East Tennessee, and would have aided in the capture of Gen. Lee's army if it had not surrendered. Gen. Sherman was also rapidly moving on Gen. Johnston in North Carolina, and cut off all possibility of his ultimately rendering any assistance to Gen. Lee.

The letter of Gen. Grant, addressed to Gen. Lee on the 7th, as above mentioned, was as follows:

April 7.

General R. E. Lee, Commander Confederate States Armies:

GENERAL:—The result of the last week must convince you of the hopelessness of further resistance on the part of the Army of Northern Virginia in this struggle. I feel that it is so, and regard it as my duty to shift from myself the responsibility of any further effusion of blood, by asking of you the surrender of that portion of the C. S. army known as the Army of Northern Virginia.

Very respectfully, your obedient servant,
U. S. GRANT,
Lieut.-Gen. Commanding Armies of the U. States.

To this note Gen. Lee replied as follows:

April 7.

To Lieut.-Gen. U. S. Grant, Commanding Armies of the United States:

GENERAL:—I have received your note of this date. Though not entirely of the opinion you express of the hopelessness of further resistance on the part of the Army of Northern Virginia, I reciprocate your desire to avoid useless effusion of blood, and therefore, before considering your proposition, ask the terms you will offer, on condition of its surrender.

R. E. LEE, General.

The following correspondence then ensued:

April 8.

To Gen. R. E. Lee, Commanding Confederate States Army:

GENERAL:—Your note of last evening, in reply to mine of same date, asking the conditions on which I will accept the surrender of the Army of Northern Virginia, is just received. In reply, I would say, that peace being my first desire, there is but one condition that I insist upon, viz.:

That the men surrendered shall be disqualified for taking up arms against the Government of the United States until properly exchanged.

I will meet you, or designate officers to meet any officers you may name for the same purpose, at any point agreeable to you, for the purpose of arranging definitely the terms upon which the surrender of the Army of Northern Virginia will be received.

Very respectfully, your obedient servant,
U. S. GRANT,
Lieut.-Gen. Commanding Armies of the U. States.

April 8.

To Lieut.-Gen. Grant, Commanding Armies of the United States:

GENERAL:—I received at a late hour your note of today, in answer to mine of yesterday. I did not intend to propose the surrender of the Army of Northern Virginia, but to ask the terms of your proposition. To be frank, I do not think the emergency has arisen to call for the surrender. But as the restoration of peace should be the sole object of all, I desire to know whether your proposals would tend to that end.

I cannot, therefore, meet you with a view to surrender the Army of Northern Virginia, but so far as your proposition may affect the Confederate States forces under my command, and lead to the restoration of peace, I should be pleased to meet you at 10 A. M. to-morrow, on the old stage-road to Richmond, between the picket lines of the two armies.

Very respetfully, your obedient servant,
R. E. LEE, General Confederate States Armies.

GEN. GRANT TO GEN. LEE.

April 9.

Gen. R. E. Lee, Commd'g Confederate States Armies:

GENERAL:—Your note of yesterday is received. As I have no authority to treat on the subject of peace, the meeting proposed for 10 A. M. to-day, could lead to no good. I will state, however, General, that I am equally anxious for peace with yourself; and the whole North entertain the same feeling. The terms upon which peace can be had are well understood. By the South laying down their arms they will hasten that most desirable event, save thousands of human lives, and hundreds of millions of property not yet destroyed.

Sincerely hoping that all our difficulties may be settled without the loss of another life, I subscribe myself, Very respectfully,
Your obedient servant,
U. S. GRANT, Lieut.-Gen. U. S. A.

GEN. LEE TO GEN. GRANT.

April 9, 1865.

GENERAL:—I received your note of this morning on the picket line, whither I had come to meet you and ascertain definitely what terms were embraced in your proposition of yesterday with reference to the surrender of this army.

I now request an interview in accordance with the offer contained in your letter of yesterday for that purpose. Very respectfully,
Your obedient servant,
R. E. LEE, General.
To Lieut.-Gen. Grant, Commanding U. S. Armies.

GEN. GRANT TO GEN. LEE.

April 9.

Gen. R. E. Lee, Commd'g Confederate States Armies:

Your note of this date is but this moment (11:50 A. M.) received. In consequence of my having passed from the Richmond and Lynchburg road to the Farmville and Lynchburg road, I am at this writing about four miles west of Walter's Church, and will push forward to the front for the purpose of meeting you.

Notice sent to me on this road where you wish the interview to take place will meet me.

Very respectfully, your obedient servant,
U. S. GRANT, Lieut.-Gen.

THE TERMS

APPOMATTOX COURT HOUSE, April 9.

Gen. R. E. Lee, Commd'g Confederate States Armies:

In accordance with the substance of my letter to you of the 8th instant, I propose to receive the surrender of the Army of Northern Virginia on the following terms, to wit:

Rolls of all the officers and men to be made in duplicate, one copy to be given to an officer designated by me, the other to be retained by such officers as you may designate.

The officers to give their individual paroles not to take arms against the United States until properly exchanged, and each company or regimental commander sign a like parole for the men of their commands.

The arms, artillery, and public property to be packed and stacked, and turned over to the officers appointed by me to receive them. This will not embrace the side-arms of the officers, nor their private horses or baggage.

THE MAJOR & KNAPP ENG. MFG. & LITH. CO. 449 BROADWAY, N.Y.

SURRENDER OF GENERAL LEE

This done, each officer and man will be allowed to return to their homes, not to be disturbed by United States authority so long as they observe their parole and the laws in force where they may reside.

Very respectfully,
U. S. GRANT, Lieut.-Gen.

THE SURRENDER.

HEADQUARTERS ARMY OF NORTHERN VIRGINIA, April 9, 1865.

Lieut.-Gen. U. S. Grant, Commd'g U. S. Armies:

GENERAL:—I have received your letter of this date, containing the terms of surrender of the Army of Northern Virginia, as proposed by you; as they are substantially the same as those expressed in your letter of the 8th instant, they are accepted. I will proceed to designate the proper officers to carry the stipulations into effect.

Very respectfully, your obedient servant,
R. E. LEE, General.

At 3½ P. M. the terms of capitulation were signed, and the utmost gratification prevailed through the army. The following is the form of the personal parole given by all the officers of Gen. Lee's army:

We, the undersigned, prisoners of war, belonging to the army of Northern Virginia, having been this day surrendered by Gen. R. E. Lee, commanding said army, to Lieut.-Gen. Grant, commanding the Armies of the United States, do hereby give our solemn parole of honor that we will not hereafter serve in the armies of the Confederate States, or in any military capacity whatever against the United States of America, or render aid to the enemies of the latter until properly exchanged in such manner as shall be mutually approved by the respective authorities.

Done at Appomattox Court House, Va., this ninth day of April, 1865.

This parole was countersigned as follows:

The above officers (or officer) will not be disturbed by the United States authorities as long as they observe their parole, and the laws in force where they may reside.
GEORGE H. SHARP,
General Assistant Provost Marshal.

The obligation of officers for the subdivisions under their command was as follows:

I, the undersigned, commanding officer of ——, do, for the within named prisoners of war, belonging to the Army of Northern Virginia, who have been this day surrendered by Gen. Robert E. Lee, Confederate States Army, commanding said army, to Lieut.-Gen. Grant, commanding Armies of the United States, hereby give my solemn parole of honor that the within named shall not hereafter serve in the armies of the Confederate States, or in military or any capacity whatever, against the United States of America, or render aid to the enemies of the latter, until properly exchanged in such manner as shall be mutually approved by the respective authorities.

Done at Appomattox Court House, Va., this ninth day of April, 1865.

The within named will not be disturbed by the United States authorities so long as they observe their parole and the laws in force where they may reside.

The surrender of Gen. Lee's army was followed by the voluntary surrender of all the troops in Northeastern Virginia, including those in the Shenandoah valley.

On the next day, the 10th, Gen. Lee issued the following farewell address to his army:

General Order No. 9.

HEADQUARTERS ARMY NORTHERN VIRGINIA, April 10, 1865.

After four years of arduous service, marked by unsurpassed courage and fortitude, the Army of Northern Virginia has been compelled to yield to overwhelming numbers and resources. I need not tell the survivors of so many hard-fought battles, who have remained steadfast to the last, that I have consented to this result from no distrust of them, but holding that valor and devotion could accomplish nothing that could compensate for the loss that would attend the continuation of the contest, I have determined to avoid the useless sacrifice of those whose past vigor has endeared them to their countrymen.

By the terms of agreement officers and men can return to their homes and remain there until exchanged. You will take with you the satisfaction that proceeds from the consciousness of duty faithfully performed, and I earnestly pray that a merciful God will extend you His blessing and protection. With an increasing admiration of your constancy and devotion to your country, and a grateful remembrance of your kind and generous consideration of myself, I bid you an affectionate farewell.

(Signed) R. E. LEE, General.

No official statement has been made of the number of officers and men surrendered. It is estimated that the army of Gen. Lee on evacuating Richmond consisted of not far from fifty thousand men. Large numbers abandoned the army and returned home, besides the killed, wounded, and prisoners taken during the pursuit. At the time of the surrender his total force was not far from twenty thousand men, this included all branches of the service, and leaving an effective force less than fifteen thousand men. The number of muskets surrendered scarcely exceeded ten thousand, and about thirty pieces of artillery. The total captures of artillery during the battles and pursuit amounted to one hundred and seventy guns. There were about three hundred and fifty wagons surrendered.

The War Department at Washington issued the following order on receiving the news of the surrender:

WAR DEPARTMENT, WASHINGTON, D. C., April 9—10 o'clock P. M.

Ordered: That a salute of two hundred guns be fired at the headquarters of every army and department, and at every post and arsenal in the United States, and at the Military Academy at West Point, on the day of the receipt of this order, in commemoration of the surrender of Gen. R. E. Lee and the Army of Northern Virginia to Lieut.-Gen. Grant and the army under his command; report of the receipt and execution of this order to be make to the Adjutant-General, Washington.

EDWIN M. STANTON, Secretary of War.

CHAPTER LI.

March of Gen. Stoneman from East Tennessee to Salisbury—Advance of Gen. Sherman upon Raleigh—Gen. Johnston proposes a Conference—The Conference and Terms agreed upon—Rejected at Washington—Surrender of Gen. Johnston's Army—March of Gen. Wilson in North Alabama—Capture of Mobile—Surrender of Gen. Taylor's Army—Surrender of Gen. E. Kirby Smith—Disbandment of the Armies—Farewell of Gen. Sherman—Farewell of Gen. Grant—Capture of Mr. Davis—Amnesty Proclamation—Measures to establish Civil Governments in the States—List of Army Officers.

THE cavalry column of Gen. Stoneman, already mentioned, as at Boone Court House, in North Carolina, at the time of the surrender of Gen. Lee, had left Knoxville, in East Tennessee, on March 10th. It struck the Central Railroad from Virginia to Tennessee at Wytheville and Christiansburg, in Virginia. Between these places thirty-three bridges were burned and twenty-five miles of the railroad destroyed. Thence it marched for Greensboro, in North Carolina, and on the 12th arrived at Grant's Creek, three miles from Salisbury. The enemy's line of defence for the town was on this creek, and defended by artillery and infantry. It was soon forced, with the capture of 14 guns and 1,104 prisoners. The town was occupied at 10 A. M., where the column remained for two days. During that time it destroyed four large cotton factories and 7,000 bales of cotton; four large magazines, containing 10,000 stand of small arms and accoutrements; 1,000,000 rounds of small arm ammunition, 1,600 rounds of fixed artillery ammunition, and 7,000 pounds of powder; 35,000 bushels of corn, 50,000 bushels of wheat, 160,000 pounds of cured bacon; 100,000 suits of gray uniforms and clothing, 250,000 army blankets, 20,000 pounds of harness-leather, 10,000 pounds of saltpetre, also a very large amount of sugar, salt, rice, and other stores, and medical supplies valued by the rebel medical directors at $100,000 in gold. In addition to the arsenals at Salisbury, establishments were fitted up, and filled with machinery sent from Raleigh and Richmond, all of which was destroyed.

Fifteen miles of railroad track and the bridges toward Charlotte were also destroyed. Thence Gen. Stoneman moved for the south side of the Catawba River and destroyed the railroad to the bridge, which was fatal to the armies of Lee and Johnston, who depended on that road for supplies and as their ultimate line of retreat.

Meanwhile the army of Gen. Sherman had been rested and recruited at Goldsboro, North Carolina. The men were all reclad, the wagons reloaded, and a fair amount of forage accumulated preparatory for a march to destroy or capture the army of Gen. Johnston. On April 6th Gen. Johnston's army was in and about Smithfield, and was estimated at 35,000, infantry and artillery, and from 6,000 to 10,000 cavalry. At daybreak on the 10th, Gen. Sherman's army was in motion. Gen. Slocum took the two direct roads for Smithfield; Gen. Howard made a circuit to the right, feigning to move up the Weldon road in order to disconcert the enemy's cavalry, while Gens. Terry and Kilpatrick moved on the west side of the Neuse River to reach the rear of the enemy between Smithfield and Raleigh. Gen. Schofield followed Gen. Slocum in support. The enemy's cavalry were met within six miles of Goldsboro by all the columns protected by the usual rail barricades. At 10 A. M. on the 11th, the 14th corps entered Smithfield, and the 20th was close at hand. Gen. Johnston had retreated rapidly across the Neuse River, and having the aid of the railroad to lighten his trains, could retreat faster than the pursuit could be made. The bridge over the Neuse had been burned and the roads had become heavy by rain. At this time the news of Gen. Lee's surrender was received, and Gen. Sherman immediately dropped his trains and marched rapidly in pursuit, reaching Raleigh at 7½ A. M. on the 13th, in a heavy rain. On the next day the cavalry pushed on to Durham station, the 15th corps followed as far as Morrisville station, and the 17th to John's station. By the 15th, although the rains were incessant and the roads almost impracticable, Gen. Slocum had the 14th corps near Martha's Vineyard, with a pontoon bridge laid across Cape Fear River at Avon's Ferry, the 20th corps, Gen. Mower commanding, being in support; Gen. Howard had the 15th and 17th corps stretched out on the roads toward Pittsboro, while Gen. Kilpatrick held Durham station and Capital Hill University. Gen. Johnston had retreated rapidly on the roads from Hillsboro to Greensboro, at which latter place he was. In this state of affairs Gen. Sherman received the following letter from Gen. Johnston:

HEADQUARTERS IN THE FIELD, April 14, 1865.

Major-General W. T. Sherman, Commanding United States Forces.

GENERAL: The results of the recent campaigns in Virginia have changed the relative military condition of the belligerents. I am therefore induced to address you in this form the inquiry whether, in order to stop the further effusion of blood and devastation of property, you are willing to make a temporary suspension of active operations, and to communicate to Lieut.-Gen. Grant, commanding the Armies of the United States, the request that he will take like action in regard to other armies, the object being to permit the civil authorities to enter into the needful arrangements to terminate the existing war.

I have the honor to be, very respectfully, your obedient servant,

J. E. JOHNSTON, General.

To this Gen. Sherman replied as follows:

HEADQ'RS MILITARY DIVISION OF THE MISSISSIPPI,
IN THE FIELD, RALEIGH, N. C., April 14, 1865.

Gen. J. E. Johnston, Commanding Confederate Army;

GENERAL: I have this moment received your communication of this date. I am fully empowered to arrange with you any terms for the suspension of further hostilities as between the armies commanded by you and those commanded by myself, and will be willing to confer with you to that end. I will limit the advance of my main column to-morrow to Morrisville, and the cavalry to the University, and expect that you will also maintain the present position of your forces until each has notice of a failure to agree.

That a basis of action may be had, I undertake to abide by the same terms and conditions as were made by Gens. Grant and Lee at Appomattox Court House, of the 9th instant, relative to our two armies, and, furthermore, to obtain from Gen. Grant an order to suspend the movements of any troops from the direction of Virginia. Gen. Stoneman is under my command, and my order will suspend any devastation or destruction contemplated by him. I will add that I really desire to save the people of North Carolina the damages they would sustain by the march of this army through the central or western parts of the State.

I am, with respect, your obedient servant,
W. T. SHERMAN, Major-General.

At the same time Gen. Sherman addressed to the Secretary of War and Gen. Grant the following letter:

HEADQ'RS MILITARY DIVISION OF THE MISSISSIPPI,
IN THE FIELD, RALEIGH, N. C., April 15, 1865.

Gen. U. S. Grant and Secretary of War;

I send copies of correspondence with Gen. Johnston to you, which I think will be followed by terms of capitulation. I will grant the same terms Gen. Grant gave Gen. Lee, and be careful not to complicate any points of civil policy. If any cavalry has retreated toward me, caution them to be prepared to find our work done. It is now raining in torrents, and I shall await Gen. Johnston's reply here, and will prepare to meet him in person at Chapel Hill.

I have invited Gov. Vance to return to Raleigh, with the civil officers of his State. I have met ex-Governor Graham, Messrs. Badger, Moore, Halden, and others, all of whom agree that the war is over, and that the States of the South must resume their allegiance, subject to the Constitution and Laws of Congress, and must submit to the National arms. The great fact was admitted and the details are of easy arrangement.

W. T. SHERMAN, Major-General.

On the 16th the following despatch was sent to Gen. Kilpatrick, at Durham station, and delivered by him to Gen. Sherman:

Major-General J. Kilpatrick, U. S. A.

GENERAL: The General Commanding directs me to arrange for a meeting between himself and Maj.-Gen. Sherman. In accordance with these instructions, I beg to inquire when and where this meeting can most conveniently be had. I suggest ten (10) o'clock, A. M., to-morrow as the hour, and a point on the Hillsboro road, equidistant from the picket of your command and my own, as the place for the proposed meeting.

I am, respectfully, yours,
NED WADE HAMPTON, Lieutenant-General.

The interview which followed with Gen. Johnston, five miles from Durham station, is thus reported by Gen. Sherman: "I agreed to meet Gen. Johnston in person at a point intermediate between our pickets on the 17th at noon, provided the position of the troops remained *statu quo*. I was both willing and anxious to consume a few days, as it would enable Col. Wright to finish our railroad to Raleigh. Two bridges had to be built and twelve miles of new roads made. We had no iron except by taking up the branch from Goldsboro to Weldon. Instead of losing by time I gained in every way, for every hour of delay possible was required to reconstruct the railroad to our rear and improve the condition of our wagon road to the front, so desirable in case the negotiations failed, and we be forced to make the race of near two hundred miles to head off or catch Johnston, then retreating toward Charlotte. At noon of the day appointed I met Gen. Johnston for the first time in my life, although we had been exchanging shots continually since May, 1863. Our interview was frank and soldier-like, and he gave me to understand that further war on the part of the Confederate troops was folly; that the 'cause' was lost, and that every life sacrificed after the surrender of Lee's army was the highest possible crime. He admitted the terms conceded to Gen. Lee were magnanimous and all he could ask; but he did want some general concessions that would enable him to allay the natural fears and anxieties of his followers, and enable him to maintain his control over them until they could be got back to the neighborhood of their homes, thereby saving the State of North Carolina the devastation inevitably to result from turning his men loose and unprovided on the spot, and our pursuit across the State. He also wanted to embrace in the same general proposition the fate of all the Confederate armies that remained in existence. I never made any concessions as to his own army or assumed to deal finally and authoritatively in regard to any other, but it did seem to me that there was presented a chance for peace that might be deemed valuable to the Government of the United States, and was at least worthy the few days that would be consumed in conference, and to push an enemy whose commander had so frankly and honestly confessed his inability to cope with me, were cowardly and unworthy the brave men I led. Inasmuch as Gen. Johnston did not feel authorized to exercise power over the armies in Texas, we adjourned to the next day at noon.

"I returned to Raleigh, and conferred freely with all my general officers, every one of whom urged me to conclude terms that might accomplish so complete and desirable an end. All dreaded the necessary laborious march after a fugitive and dissolving army back toward Georgia, over the very country where we had toiled so long. There was but one opinion expressed, and, if contrary ones were entertained, they were withheld, or indulged in only by that class who shun the fight and the march, but are loudest, bravest, and fiercest when danger is past.

"I again met Gen. Johnston on the 18th, and we resumed the conversation. He satisfied me then of his power to disband the rebel armies in Alabama, Mississippi, Louisiana, and Texas, as well as those in his immediate command, viz.: North Carolina, Georgia, and Florida. The points on which he expressed especial solicitude were lest their States were to be dismembered and denied representations in Congress, or any separate political existence whatever; and the absolute disarming his men would leave the South powerless and exposed to depredations by wicked bands of assassins and robbers. The President's (Lincoln) Message of 1864; his Amnesty Proclamation; General Grant's terms to General Lee, substantially extending the benefit of that Proclamation to all officers above the rank of colonel; the invitation to the Virginia Legislature to reassemble in Richmond, by Gen. Weitzel, with the supposed approval of Mr. Lincoln and Gen. Grant, then on the spot; a firm belief that I had been fighting to reëstablish the Constitution of the United States; and last, but not least, the general and universal desire to close a war any longer without organized resistance, were the leading facts that induced me to pen the 'memorandum' of April 18, signed by myself and Gen. Johnston. It was designed to be, and so expressed on its face, as a mere 'basis' for reference to the President of the United States and constitutional Commander-in-Chief, to enable him, if he chose, at one blow to dissipate the power of the Confederacy which had threatened the national safety for years. It admitted of modification, alteration, and change. It had no appearance of an ultimatum, and by no false reasoning can it be construed into an usurpation of power on my part."

Some complaint had appeared in the public press that the terms offered to Gen. Lee were too lenient. At the same time the assassination of President Lincoln took place, and public indignation was greatly aroused. In the midst of the excitement the memorandum of terms between Gen. Sherman and Gen. Johnston was received by the Government. It was as follows:

Memorandum or basis of agreement made this 18th day of April, A. D. 1865, near Durham's Station, and in the State of North Carolina, by and between Gen. Joseph E. Johnston, commanding the Confederate Army, and Maj.-Gen. W. T. Sherman, commanding the Army of the United States in North Carolina, both present:

1.—The contending armies now in the field to maintain their *status quo* until notice is given by the commanding-general of either one to its opponent, and reasonable time, say forty-eight hours, allowed.

2.—The Confederate Armies now in existence to be disbanded and conducted to the several State capitals, there to deposit their arms and public property in the State arsenal, and each officer and man to execute and file an agreement to cease from acts of war and abide the action of both State and Federal authorities. The number of arms and munitions of war to be reported to the Chief of Ordnance at Washington City, subject to future action of the Congress of the United States, and in the mean time to be used solely to maintain peace and order within the borders of the States respectively.

3.—The recognition by the executive of the United States of the several State Governments on their officers and Legislatures taking the oath prescribed by the Constitution of the United States, and where conflicting State Governments have resulted from the war, the legitimacy of all shall be submitted to the Supreme Court of the United States,

4.—The reëstablishment of all Federal Courts in the several States, with powers as defined by the Constitution and laws of Congress.

5.—The people and inhabitants of all States to be guaranteed, so far as the Executive can, their political rights and franchise, as well as their rights of person and property, as defined by the Constitution of the United States and of States respectively.

6.—The executive authority of the Government of the United States not to disturb any of the people by reason of the late war so long as they live in peace and quiet, abstain from acts of armed hostility, and obey laws in existence at any place of their residence.

7.—In general terms, war to cease, a general amnesty, so far the executive power of the United States can command, or on condition of disbandment of the Confederate Armies, and the distribution of arms and resumption of peaceful pursuits by officers and men, as hitherto composing the said armies, not being fully empowered by our respective principals to fulfil these terms, we individually and officially pledge ourselves to promptly obtain necessary authority and to carry out the above programme,

W. T. SHERMAN, Major-General,
Commanding the Army of the United States in North Carolina.

J. E. JOHNSTON, General,
Commanding Confederate States Army in North Carolina.

This was at once made public, accompanied with the following statement from the Secretary of War, Mr. Stanton:

This proceeding of General Sherman was unapproved for the following among other reasons:

1.—It was an exercise of authority not vested in General Sherman, and on its face shows that both he and Johnston knew that he (Sherman) had no authority to enter into such arrangement.

2.—It was a practical acknowledgment of the Rebel government.

3.—It undertook to reëstablish the Rebel State governments that had been overthrown at the sacrifice of many thousand loyal lives and an immense treasure, and placed arms and munitions of war in the hands of the Rebels at their respective capitals, which might be used as soon as the armies of the United States were disbanded, and used to conquer and subdue the loyal States.

4.—By the restoration of the Rebel authority in their respective States, they would be enabled to reëstablish slavery.

5.—It might furnish a ground of responsibility by the Federal Government to pay the Rebel debt, and certainly subjects loyal citizens of the Rebel States to the debt consummated by the Rebels in the name of the State.

6.—It puts in dispute the existence of loyal State governments, and the new State of Western Virginia, which had been recognized by every department of the United States Government.

7.—It practically abolished the confiscation laws, and relieved Rebels of every degree who had slaughtered our people, from all pains and penalties for their crimes.

8.—It gave terms that had been deliberately, repeatedly, and solemnly rejected by President Lincoln, and better terms than the Rebels had ever asked in their most prosperous condition.

9.—It formed no basis of true and lasting peace, but relieved Rebels from the pressure of our victories, and left them in condition to renew their effort to overthrow the United States Government, and subdue the loyal States, whenever their strength was recruited and an opportunity should offer.

At the same time the Secretary of War issued the following instructions to Gen. Grant:

WAR DEPARTMENT, WASHINGTON, April 21, 1865.

GENERAL: The memorandum or basis agreed upon between Gen. Sherman and Gen. Johnston, having been submitted to the President, they are disapproved. You will give notice of the disapproval to General Sherman, and direct him to resume hostilities at the earliest moment.

The instructions given to you by the late President, Abraham Lincoln, on the 3d of March, by my telegraph of that date addressed to you, express substantially the views of President Andrew Johnson, and will be observed by Gen. Sherman. A copy is herewith appended.

The President desires that you proceed immediately to the headquarters of Gen. Sherman and direct operations against the enemy.

Yours truly,
EDWIN M. STANTON, Secretary of War.
To Lieut.-Gen. GRANT.

COPY OF PRESIDENT LINCOLN'S INSTRUCTIONS.

WAR DEPARTMENT, WASHINGTON, March 3, 1865.

To Lieut.-Gen. GRANT:

The President directs me to say to you that he wishes you to have no conference with Gen. Lee, unless it be for the capitulation of Gen. Lee's army, or on some minor and purely military matter. He wishes me to say that you are not to decide, discuss, or confer upon any political question. Such questions the President holds in his own hands, and will submit them to no military conferences or conventions. Meantime you are to press to your utmost your military advantages.

EDWIN M. STANTON, Secretary of War.

Perhaps it may not be out of place to insert here the reasons briefly given by Gen. Sherman in his report, for his proceedings. They are as follows:

Immediately on my return to Raleigh I despatched one of my staff, Major Hitchcock, to Washington, enjoining him to be most prudent and careful to avoid the spies and informers that would be sure to infest him by the way, and to say nothing to anybody until the President could make known to me his feelings and wishes in the matter.

The news of President Lincoln's assassination, on the 14th of April (wrongly reported to me by telegraph as having occurred on the 11th), reached me on the 17th, and was announced to my command on the same day, in Field Orders No. 56. I was duly informed of its horrible atrocity and probable effects on the country. But when the property and interests of millions still living were involved, I saw no good reason why to change my course, but thought rather to manifest real respect for his memory by following after his death that policy, which, if living, I felt certain he would have approved, or at least not rejected with disdain.

Up to that hour I had never received one word of instruction, advice, or counsel as to the plan or policy of the Government, looking to a restoration of peace on the part of the Rebel States of the South. Whenever asked for an opinion on the points involved, I had always avoided the subject. My letter to the Mayor of Atlanta has been published to the world, and I was not rebuked by the War Department for it. My letter to Mr. ——— of Savannah, was shown by me to Mr. Stanton, before its publication, and all that my memory retains of his answer is that he said, like my letters generally, it was sufficiently emphatic, and would not be misunderstood. Both these letters asserted my belief that according to Mr. Lincoln's Proclamation and Message, when the people of the South had laid down their arms and submitted to the lawful powers of the United States, *ipso facto*, the war was over as to them; and furthermore, that if any State in rebellion would conform to the Constitution of the United States, cease war, elect Senators and Representatives to Congress, if admitted (of which each House of Congress alone is the judge), that State becomes instanter as much in the Union as New York or Ohio. Nor was I rebuked for these expressions, though it was universally known and commented on at the time. And again Mr. Stanton in person at Savannah, speaking of the terrific expense of the war and difficulty of realizing the money for the daily wants of Government, impressed me most forcibly with the necessity of bringing the war to a close as soon as possible for *financial reasons*.

On the morning of April 24th Gen. Grant arrived at Gen. Sherman's headquarters, and the latter was informed that the memorandum was disapproved, without reasons assigned, and he was ordered to give the forty-eight hours notice, and resume hostilities at the close of that time. Gen. Sherman immediately despatched the following note to Gen. Johnston:

HEADQ'RS MILITARY DIVISION OF THE MISSISSIPPI,
IN THE FIELD, RALEIGH, April 24, 1865.

Gen. Johnston, Commanding Confederate Armies:

I have replies from Washington to my communications of April 18. I am instructed to limit my operations to your immediate command, and not to attempt civil negotiations. I therefore demand the surrender of your army, on the same terms as were given to Gen. Lee, at Appomattox, of April 9, purely and simply. W. T. SHERMAN, Maj.-Gen.

Gen. Grant, although properly in command, left all the further measures to be executed by Gen. Sherman, and the presence of the former was even unknown to Gen. Johnston, who replied as follows:

[*Telegram.*]

HEADQUARTERS ARMY OF THE TENNESSEE,
IN THE FIELD, April 25, 1865.

Major-Gen. Sherman, U. S. A.

Your despatch of yesterday received. I propose a modification of the terms you offered; such terms for the army as you wrote on the 18th; they also modified according to change of circumstances, and a further armistice to arrange details and meeting for that purpose. JOS. E. JOHNSTON, General.

HEADQ'RS MILITARY DIVISION OF THE MISSISSIPPI,
IN THE FIELD, RALEIGH, April 25, 1865.

Gen Johnston: I will meet you at the same place as before, to-morrow, at 12 o'clock noon.

W. T. SHERMAN, Major-General.

[*Telegram.*]

Major-Gen. W. T. Sherman, Commd'g U. S. Forces:

GENERAL: I have had the honor to receive your despatch of yesterday, summoning this army to surrender on the terms accepted by Gen. Lee at Appamattox Court House. I propose, instead of such surrender, terms based on those drawn up by you on the 18th for disbanding this army, and a further armistice and a conference to arrange these terms.

The disbanding of Gen. Lee's army has afflicted this country with numerous bands having no means of subsistence but robbery—a knowledge of which would, I am sure, induce you to agree to other conditions. Most respectfully, your obedient servant,

J. E. JOHNSTON, General.

[*Telegram.*]

GREENSBORO' April 26, 1865—2 A. M.

Major-Gen. Sherman through Gen. Butler:

I will meet you at the time and place you designate. Is armistice with *status quo* renewed?

J. E. JOHNSTON, General.

Terms of a Military Convention entered into this twenty-sixth (26th) day of April, 1865, at Bennett's House, near Durham Station, North Carolina, between General Joseph E. Johnston, commanding the Confederate Army, and Major-General W. T. Sherman, commanding the United States Army in North Carolina.

All acts of war on the part of the troops under Gen.

Johnston's command to cease from this date. All arms and public property to be deposited at Greensboro, and delivered to an ordnance officer of the United States Army. Rolls of all the officers and men to be made in duplicate, one copy to be retained by the commander of the troops, and the other to be given to an officer to be designated by Gen. Sherman. Each officer and man to give his individual obligation in writing not to take up arms against the Government of the United States until properly released from this obligation. The side-arms of officers and their private horses and baggage to be retained by them.

This being done, all the officers and men will be permitted to return to their homes, not to be disturbed by the United States authorities so long as they observe their obligation and the laws in force where they may reside.

W. T. SHERMAN, Major-General,
Commanding U. S. Forces in North Carolina.
J. E. JOHNSTON, General,
Commanding C. S. Forces in North Carolina.
Approved:—U. S. GRANT, Lieut.-General.
RALEIGH, N. C., April 26, 1865.

On the next day Gen. Sherman issued the following order:

Special Field Orders No. 65.

HEADQ'RS MILITARY DIVISION OF THE MISSISSIPPI, IN THE FIELD, RALEIGH, N. C., April 27, 1865.

The General Commanding announces a further suspension of hostilities and a final agreement with Gen. Johnston, which terminates the war as to the armies under his command and the country east of the Chattahooche.

Copies of the terms of the convention will be furnished Major-Gens. Schofield, Gillmore, and Wilson, who are specially charged with its execution in the Department of North Carolina, Department of the South, and at Macon and Western Georgia.

Capt. Myers, Ordnance Department U. S. army, is hereby designated to receive the arms, etc., at Greensboro. Any commanding officer of a post may receive the arms of any detachment, and see that they are properly stored and accounted for.

Gen. Schofield will procure at once the necessary blanks, and supply the other Army Commanders, that uniformity may prevail, and great care must be taken that all the terms and stipulations on our part be fulfilled with the most scrupulous fidelity, while those imposed on our hitherto enemies be received in a spirit becoming a brave and generous army.

Army commanders may at once loan to the inhabitants such of the captured mules, horses, wagons, and vehicles as can be spared from immediate use, and the Commanding Generals of Armies may issue provisions, animals, or any public supplies that can be spared to relieve present wants, and to encourage the inhabitants to renew their peaceful pursuits, and to restore the relations of friendship among our fellow-citizens and countrymen.

Foraging will forthwith cease, and when necessity or long marches compel the taking of forage, provisions, or any kind of private property, compensation will be made on the spot; or, when the disbursing officers are not provided with funds, vouchers will be given in proper form, payable at the nearest military depot.

By order of Major-Gen. W. T. SHERMAN.
L. M. DAYTON, Ass't Adjutant-General.

Special Field Orders No. 66.

HEADQ'RS MILITARY DIVISION OF THE MISSISSIPPI, IN THE FIELD, RALEIGH, N. C., April 27, 1865.

Hostilities having ceased, the following changes and dispositions of troops in the field will be made with as little delay as practicable:

1. The 10th and 23d corps will remain in the Department of North Carolina, and Major-Gen. J. M. Schofield will transfer back to Major-Gen. Gillmore, commanding the Department of the South, the two brigades formerly belonging to the division of Brevet Major-Gen. Grover, at Savannah. The 3d division cavalry corps, Brevet Major-Gen. J. Kilpatrick commanding, is hereby transferred to the Department of North Carolina, and Gen. Kilpatrick will report in person to Major-Gen. Schofield for orders.

2. The cavalry command of Maj.-Gen. George Stoneman will return to East Tennessee, and that of Brevet Major-Gen. J. H. Wilson will be conducted back to the Tennessee River, in the neighborhood of Decatur, Alabama.

3. Major-Gen. Howard will conduct the Army of the Tennessee to Richmond, Virginia, following roads substantially by Lewisburg, Warrenton, Lawrenceville, and Petersburg, or to the right of that line. Major-Gen. Slocum will conduct the Army of Georgia to Richmond by roads to the left of the one indicated for Gen. Howard, viz., by Oxford, Boydtown, and Nottoway Court House. These armies will turn in at this point the contents of their ordnance trains and use the wagons for extra forage and provisions. These columns will be conducted slowly and in the best of order, and will aim to be at Richmond ready to resume the march by the middle of May.

4. The Chief Quartermaster and Commissary of the Military Division, Gens. Easton and Beckwith, after making the proper dispositions of their departments here, will proceed to Richmond and make suitable preparations to receive those columns and to provide them for the further journey.

By order of Major-Gen. W. T. SHERMAN.
L. M. DAYTON, Ass't Adjutant-General.

On the same day Gen. Johnston issued the following notice of surrender to his troops:

General Orders No. 18.

HEADQUARTERS ARMY OF THE TENNESSEE, April 27, 1865.

By the terms of a military convention made on the 26th instant, by Major-Gen. W. T. Sherman, United States Army, and Gen. J. E. Johnston, Confederate States Army, the officers and men of this army are to bind themselves not to take up arms against the United States until properly relieved from the obligation, and shall receive guarantees from the United States officers against molestation by the United States authorities, so long as they observe that obligation and the laws in force where they reside. For these objects duplicate muster-rolls will be made, and after the distribution of the necessary papers the troops will march under their officers to their respective States, and there be disbanded—all retaining personal property. The object of this convention is pacification to the extent of the authority of the commanders who made it. Events in Virginia, which broke every hope of success by war, imposed on its general the duty of sparing the blood of this gallant army, and saving our country from further devastation, and our people from ruin.

J. E. JOHNSTON, General.

On the 2d of May he issued the following farewell to his army:

General Orders No 22.

HEADQUARTERS ARMY OF THE TENNESSEE, NEAR GREENSBORO, May 2, 1865.

COMRADES: In terminating our official relations, I expect you to observe the terms of the pacification agreed upon, and to discharge the obligations of good and peaceful citizens to the powers as well as you have performed the duties of soldiers in the field. By such a course you will secure comfort and restore tranquillity to your country. You will return to your homes with the admiration of our people, won by the courage and noble devotion you have displayed in this long war. I shall always remember with pride the loyal support you have given me. I part from you with regret, and bid you farewell with feelings

of cordial friendship, and with earnest wishes that you may prosper. J. E. JOHNSTON, General.
J. E. KENNARD, Colonel, etc.

The number of men surrendered and paroled was not far from 25,000; 108 pieces of artillery were parked, with limbers, caissons, etc., complete. About 15,000 small arms were surrendered, and but little ammunition. A large number of men strayed away with guns, horses, mules, and wagons. A body of the cavalry, under Gen. Hampton, went south in the direction in which it was supposed Mr. Davis was moving. They subsequently disappeared, and their officers were classed among those paroled.

The column of Gen. Wilson, which has been already mentioned, was organized at Gen. Thomas's headquarters, in Nashville, for a cavalry expedition into Alabama. It was finely equipped in every respect, with plenty of good men, mostly veterans, horses, ammunition, supplies, pontoons, and wagons. The final rendezvous was Gravelly Springs, above Eastport, on the Tennessee River, and Selma, Montgomery, and Mobile. It numbered more than 15,000 men, consisting of the 1st division under Gen. McCook, the 2d under Gen. Long, the 4th under Gen. Upton, and the 5th under Gen. Hatch. The latter, however, was retained in reserve at Eastport. The movement commenced from Chickasaw on the 22d of March. Some of the enemy, consisting of Gen. Roddy's cavalry, were soon met, and driven back with constant skirmishing thirty miles to Plantersville. Here they made a stand on April 1st, until their flank was threatened, when they retired. The loss of each side in killed and wounded, thus far, was estimated at less than a hundred; three guns and two hundred prisoners were captured by Gen. Wilson. Pursuit was now made by the divisions of Gens. Upton and Long to Selma. There the enemy was found on April 2d, in line of battle outside of their works. Gen. Long having arrived first, formed and dismounted his men in the night, while the 4th division came up on the left. In the morning the skirmish line was advanced, and a brisk charge made. In a short time the enemy were driven from the field, and the intrenchments captured. Selma was immediately occupied. The killed and wounded of the Union forces was about two hundred, and that of the enemy supposed to be less. One hundred guns, one hundred and fifty officers, two thousand men, with many horses, mules, and supplies, were captured. The arsenal, with large stores of powder, percussion caps, shells, all the Confederate magazines, works, and buildings, four large furnaces, including the Red Mountain and Central iron works and machine shop, some dwellings, and vast stores of cotton were destroyed. On the 4th, Cahawba, a little southwest of Selma, was surrendered, and about seventy Federal prisoners were recovered. From Selma Gen. Wilson moved eastward, capturing Montgomery, West Point, Griffin, Lagrange, Columbus, and Macon. The following despatches from Macon relate his further proceedings:

HEADQUARTERS ARMY OF TENNESSEE,
April 21, 1865—9:30 A. M.

To Major-Gen. W. T. Sherman, through headquarters of Gen. Beauregard:

My advance received the surrender of this city with its garrison this evening. Gen. Cobb had previously sent me, under flag of truce, a copy of the telegram from Gen. Beauregard, declaring the existence of an armistice between all the troops under your command and those of Gen. Johnston. Without questioning the authority of this despatch, or its application to my command, I could not communicate orders in time to prevent the capture. I shall therefore hold the garrison, including Major-Gens. Cobb and G. W. Smith, and Brig.-Gen. McCall, prisoners of war.

Please send me orders. I shall remain here a reasonable length of time to hear from your.

J. H. WILSON, Brevet Maj.-Gen. U. S. A.

HEADQUARTERS CAVALRY CORPS, MILITARY DIVISION
MISSISSIPPI, MACON, GA., April 21, 1865.

Major-Gen. W. T. Sherman, through Gen. Johnston:

Your despatch of yesterday is just received. I shall at once proceed to carry out your instructions. If proper arrangements can be made to have sugar, coffee, and clothing sent from Savannah to Augusta, they can be brought hither by the way of Atlanta by railroad, or they can be sent by boat directly to this place from Darien. I shall be able to get forage, bread, and meat from Southeastern Georgia. The railroad from Atlanta to Dalton or Cleveland cannot be repaired in three months. I have arranged to send an officer at once, via Eufaula, to Gen. Canby, with a copy of your despatch. Gen. Cobb will also notify Gen. Taylor of the armistice. I have about three thousand prisoners of war, including Gens. Cobb, Smith, McCall, Mercer, and Robertson. Can you arrange with Gen. Johnston for their immediate release? Please answer at once. I shall start a staff officer to you to-morrow.

J. H. WILSON, Brevet Major-Gen. Comm'g.

Gen. Sherman, after the surrender of Gen. Johnston, went to Hilton Head, and caused supplies to be forwarded at once to Gen. Wilson. On May 1st Gen. Upton's division was sent to Augusta, and Gen. McCook's to Tallahassee, to receive the surrender of the garrisons and take charge of the public property, and execute the paroles required by the terms of surrender.

At the same time that Gen. Wilson was advancing against Selma and Montgomery, a movement was in progress for the capture of Mobile. This city was occupied by about fifteen thousand troops under Gen. Richard Taylor. The defences of the city had been most carefully constructed, and were under the command of Gen. Maury. In the harbor the enemy had several vessels, some of which were iron-clads; in addition to which its defences were regarded as almost impregnable. The Federal forces consisted of the 13th army corps under Gen. Granger, and the 16th under Gen. A. J. Smith, Gen. Canby being in chief command. Attached to these was a division of cavalry and a division of colored troops. With this force a strong fleet was in coöperation.

Mobile is situated on the west bank of the Mobile River, immediately above its entrance into the bay, and thirty miles north of the Gulf of Mexico. The site of the town is a level sandy plain, sufficiently elevated for drainage. The enemy had supposed that the attack would be made on the west, and on this side the city was most strongly fortified, but to no purpose in the final attack. The 16th corps, Gen. A. J. Smith, was landed on Dauphin Island, opposite Mobile Point, and reached Fort Gaines on March 12th. All the cavalry under Gen. Grierson, crossing Pontchartrain, reached Mobile Point, and on the 18th, every thing being in readiness, the march commenced. A brigade of the 3d division of the 16th corps, about two thousand strong, left Dauphin's Island to effect a landing on Cedar Point, above Fort Powell, and to clear the way for the rest of the corps. On the previous day a brigade of the 2d division of the 13th corps was landed on Mobile Point, to proceed as the advance of the corps on the mainland on the east side of the bay. At the same time Gen. Steele, in command of a division of colored troops at Pensacola and Barrancas, commenced a march across to Blakely on the Tensaw River, about twelve miles north of east of Mobile. On the 18th, the whole 13th corps under Gen. Granger followed the advance brigade, marching by land along the shore of Bon Secour Bay, which forms the southeasterly corner of Mobile Bay, near its mouth, and just north of Mobile Point, on which is Fort Morgan. Fish River, running south on the east side of Mobile Bay, empties into Bon Secour Bay, and the rendezvous of the army was fixed about eight miles from its mouth. On the 19th the 16th corps, under Gen. Smith, were taken in transports and moved across Mobile Bay, and disembarked at the rendezvous up the river by the night of the 21st. On the 22d and 23d the 13th corps, under Gen. Granger, which had been delayed in its march by the bad roads, began to arrive. Slight skirmishing occurred with the enemy along the route. The advance toward Spanish Fort at the head of Mobile Bay, on the east side, was made on the 25th. The 13th corps was on the left, direct for the fort, and the 16th corps on the right moving toward Blakeley. Constant skirmishing was kept up by the enemy, and the road was found to be thickly planted with torpedoes. On the 27th both corps marched into position, to invest Spanish Fort, and the enemy fell back toward Blakeley. At the same time the fleet got under way, and proceeded up the bay to Howard's Landing, below the fort. The Metacomet, Stockdale, Milwaukee, Cincinnati, Albatross, Winnebago, Genesee, and Osage, were ordered in toward the shore, and opened a cannonade, which the enemy did not return. The communication between the city and the fort was cut off by the fleet, with the loss of the Milwaukee and Osage blown up by torpedoes. The land forces brought up the artillery, and the appearance of a regular siege was presented. The fleet of the enemy at a distance also occasionally opened fire on the troops. On April 3d the investment was complete, and a fire was opened upon it both by land and water, which resulted in silencing the guns of the enemy by midnight. An hour afterwards the fort was surrendered with its dependencies. The number of men made prisoners was five hundred and thirty-eight and twenty-five officers. Gen. Canby reported that the major part of the garrison escaped by water. There was found in the fort five mortars and twenty-five guns.

Meanwhile Gen. Steele left Pensacola March 19th, and marched through Pollard toward Mobile. On the 25th he encountered the 6th Alabama cavalry at Mitchell's Creek, and a sharp contest ensued, in which the enemy were routed. Thence he continued his march toward Blakeley, and came in on the right of Gen. Canby.

After the surrender of Spanish Fort, the gunboat Octarora opened fire on Forts Tracy and Huger, near the mouth of the Tensaw River, but both works were abandoned by the enemy after spiking eight heavy guns. Blakeley was now invested by the gunboats in front, which had advanced up the river after the surrender of the forts and the removal of torpedoes, and by the troops on the land side. The works were carried by assault on April 9th, and two thousand four hundred prisoners and twenty guns taken. On the next day, the 10th, the enemy commenced evacuating Mobile, which was completed on the 11th by their retreat with their fleet up the Alabama River. On the next day it was surrendered to Gen. Canby and Rear-Admiral Thatcher, and occupied by the corps of Gen. Granger. Gen. Canby reported that he found in Mobile and its defences over one hundred and fifty guns, a very large amount of ammunition, and supplies of all kinds, and about one thousand prisoners. The Federal loss had been two thousand five hundred men, and that of the fleet fifty men.

On April 19th an officer of Gen. Taylor's staff arrived at Gen. Canby's headquarters with a flag of truce to make terms for the surrender of the troops east of the Mississippi. On May 4th surrender was executed. The delegation upon the Union side consisted of Gens. Canby, Osterhaus, Andrews; Col. Christenson; Capts. Barrett and Perkins; and, by invitation of Gen. Canby, Admiral Thatcher. At Citronelle, Alabama, where the conference was held, were found Gen. Taylor and staff, Commander Farrand, and Lieut. Commander Myers, of the Confederate navy, and a large concourse of other officers. After considerable discussion and consultation, ending at 7:30 P. M., the following conditions were agreed to and signed as the terms of surrender:

Memorandum of the conditions of the surrender of the forces, munitions of war, etc., in the department of Alabama, Mississippi, and East Louisiana, commanded by Lieut.-Gen. Richard Taylor, Confederate States army, to Major-Gen. Edward R. S. Canby, United States army, entered into on the 4th day of May, 1865, at Citronelle, Alabama:

1. The officers and men to be paroled until duly exchanged or otherwise released from the obligations of their parole by the authority of the Government of

the United States. Duplicate rolls of all officers and men surrendered to be made, one copy of which will be delivered to an officer appointed by Major-General Canby, and the other appointed by Lieut.-Gen. Taylor, officers giving their individual paroles, and commanders of regiments, battalions, companies, or detachments signing a like parole for the men of their respective commands.

2. Artillery, small arms, ammunition, and other property of the Confederate Government, to be turned over to the officers appointed far that purpose on the part of the Government of the United States. Duplicate inventories of the property surrendered to be prepared, one copy to be retained by the officer delivering, and the other by the officer receiving it, for the information of their respective commands.

3. The officers and men paroled under this agreement will be allowed to return to their homes, with the assurance that they will not be disturbed by the authorities of the United States as long as they continue to observe the conditions of their paroles and the laws in force where they reside, except that persons resident of Northern States will not be allowed to return without permission.

4. The surrender of property will not include the side-arms, or private horses, or baggage of officers.

5. All horses which are in good faith the private property of enlisted men will not be taken from them; the men will be permitted to take such with them to their homes to be used for private purposes only.

6. The time and place of surrender will be fixed by the respective commanders, and will be carried out by commissioners appointed by them.

7. The terms and conditions of the surrender to apply to the officers and men belonging to the armies lately commanded by Gens. Lee and Johnston, now in this department.

8. Transportation and subsistence to be furnished at public cost for the officers and men after surrender to the nearest practicable point of their homes.

R. TAYLOR, Lieut.-General.
E. R. S. CANBY, Maj.-General.

On the same day and at the same time and place, Commodore Farrand surrendered to Rear-Admiral Thatcher all the naval forces of the enemy then blockaded on the Tombigbee River, on the same terms as were granted by Gen. Canby to Gen. Taylor. The squadron was delivered up at Nanna Hubba Bluff on May 9th. The following vessels were surrendered: Jeff. Davis, Robert Watson, Magnolia, Marengo, St. Charles, Commodore Farrand, General Beauregard, Duke, Sumter, St. Nicholas, Reindeer, Admiral.

Among the officers surrendered were Commodore Ebenezer Farrand, of Florida; Commodore L. Rousseau, of Louisiana; Capt. Patrick W. Murphy, of North Carolina; Commander C. ap. R. Jones, of Virginia; Lieut. Julien Myers, of Georgia; Lieut. James D. Johnston, of Kentucky; Lieut. Chas. W. Hays, of Alabama; Lieut. Charles P. McGary, of North Carolina; Lieut. Robert T. Chapman, of Alabama; Lieut. F. B. Renshaw, of Florida; Lieut. E. Lloyd Winder, of Maryland; Lieut. John R. Eggleston, of Mississippi; Lieut. C. C. Simons, of Virginia; Lieut. John W. Bennett, of Maryland; Lieut. Thomas L. Harrison, of Virginia; Lieut. Joseph Fry, of Florida; Lieut. W. P. A. Campbell, of Tennessee; Lieut. Julian M Spencer, of Maryland; Lieut. James McBaker, Lieut. Edgar L. Lambert, and 110 others.

The detached forces of the enemy in various places east of the Mississippi were severally surrendered upon the same terms as embraced in those of the commanding officers, and by the middle of the month of May hostilities had ceased everywhere except west of the Mississippi River.

On learning the news of Gen. Lee's surrender, Gen. Kirby Smith, in command of the enemy's forces in Texas, issued the following order:

HEADQUARTERS TRANS-MISSISSIPPI DEPARTMENT,
SHREVEPORT, LA., April 21, 1865.

Soldiers of the Trans-Mississippi Army:

The crisis of our revolution is at hand. Great disasters have overtaken us. The Army of Northern Virginia and our Commander-in-Chief are prisoners of war. With you rests the hopes of our nation, and upon your action depends the fate of our people. I appeal to you in the name of the cause you have so heroically maintained—in the name of your firesides and families, so dear to you—in the name of your bleeding country, whose future is in your hands. Show that you are worthy of your position in history. Prove to the world that your hearts have not failed in the hour of disaster, and that at the last moment you will sustain the holy cause which has been so gloriously battled for by your brethren east of the Mississippi.

You possess the means of long resisting invasion. You have hopes of succor from abroad. Protract the struggle, and you will surely receive the aid of nations who already deeply sympathize with you.

Stand by your colors—maintain your discipline. The great resources of this department, its vast extent, the numbers, the discipline, and the efficiency of the army, will secure to our country terms that a proud people can with honor accept, and may, under the Providence of God, be the means of checking the triumph of our enemy and securing the final success of our cause. E. KIRBY SMITH, General.

At the same time public meetings were held in Texas, and resolutions to maintain the contest were adopted. The Federal Government immediately despatched a large force to New Orleans, under the command of Gen. Sheridan, preparatory to a campaign in Texas. Meanwhile, Col. Barret fought the last battle of the war. He had conducted a body of troops, on May 11th, from 300 to 500 strong, from Brazos to seize a camp of the enemy about fifteen miles above, on the Brownsville road, at Palmetto Ranch. His object was to secure horses and cattle. The camp of the enemy was captured and burned. But being delayed to secure horses, he was overtaken by a body of cavalry under Gen. Slaughter, with three pieces of artillery. A retreat was made with the enemy in pursuit, and a loss of about seventy-five men ensued, who were chiefly made prisoners, The following is Gen. Slaughter's report of the affair:

HEADQUARTERS WESTERN SUB-DISTRICT, TEXAS,
IN THE FIELD, May 13, 1865.

Captain L. G. Aldrich, Assistant Adjutant-General:

We attacked the enemy—about eight hundred strong—this evening at 3 o'clock, and drove him in confusion eight miles, killing and wounding about thirty and capturing eighty prisoners, with many arms and accoutrements. Owing to the scattered condition of the men, a halt was ordered. Captain Carrington's command coming up, he was again attacked and driven within one mile of Brazos, when darkness put an end to the pursuit. Had not our artillery horses broken down, we would, doubtless, have captured the whole command.

I cannot speak too highly of the sagacity of Colonel Ford and the gallantry of his command. Our loss was four or five severely wounded. We did not have three hundred in the fight, large numbers not having arrived.

J. E. SLAUGHTER, Brigadier-General Com.
Official: L. G. ALDRICH, Ass't Adjutant-General.

But the surrenders of Gens. Johnston and Taylor decided the course of events in the Trans-Mississippi Department. On the 23d of May, Brig.-Gen. Brent and several staff officers reached Baton Rouge, Louisiana, to consult with Gen. Canby on the terms of the surrender of Gen. Kirby Smith's army. The terms were arranged, and the surrender made on the 26th. They were as follows:

Terms of a military convention, entered into this 26th day of May, 1865, at New Orleans, La., between Gen. E. Kirby Smith, Confederate States army, commanding the Department of Trans-Mississippi, and Major-General E. R. S. Canby, United States army, commanding army and division of West Mississippi, for the surrender of the troops and public property of the military and naval authorities of the Trans-Mississippi Department:

1. All acts of war and resistance against the United States, on the part of the troops under Gen. Smith, shall cease from this date.

2. The officers and men to be paroled until duly exchanged, or otherwise released from the obligation of their parole by the authority of the Government of the United States. Duplicate rolls of all officers and men paroled to be retained by such officers as may be designated by the parties hereto—officers giving their individual paroles, and commanders of regiments, battalions, companies, and detachments signing a like parole for the men of their respective commands.

3. Artillery, small arms, ammunition, and other property of the Confederate States, including gunboats and transports, to be turned over to the officers appointed to receive the same on the part of the Government of the United States; duplicate inventories of the property to be surrendered to be prepared, one copy to be returned by the officer delivering, and the other by the officer receiving it, for the information of their respective commanders.

4. The officers and men paroled under this agreement will be allowed to return to their homes, with the assurance that they will not be disturbed by the authorities of the United States as long as they continue to observe the conditions of their parole and the laws in force where they reside; except that persons resident in the Northern States, and not excepted in the amnesty proclamation of the President, may return to their homes on taking the oath of allegiance to the United States.

5. The surrender of property will not include the side-arms, or private horses, or baggage of officers.

6. All horses which are, in good faith, the private property of enlisted men, will not be taken from them; the men will be permitted to take such with them to their homes, to be used for private purposes only.

7. The time, mode, and place of paroling and surrender of property will be fixed by the respective commanders, and it will be carried out by commissioners appointed by them.

8. The terms and conditions of this convention to extend to all officers and men of the army and navy of the Confederate States, or any of them, being in or belonging to the Trans-Mississippi Department.

9. Transportation and subsistence to be furnished at public cost for the officers and men (after being paroled) to the nearest practicable point to their homes.

S. B. BUCKNER,
Lieutenant-General and Chief of Staff,
for General E. KIRBY SMITH.
P. JOS. OSTERHAUS,
Major-General Volunteers and Chief-of-Staff,
for Major-General E. R. S. CANBY,
Commanding Military Division West. Mississippi.
J. N. GALLEHEW, Assistant Adjutant-General.

Additional terms were made later in the day for the rendezvous of the paroled troops in the trans-Mississippi Department near their homes, and also for the surrender of the Confederate navy under Capt. Carter.

The surrender of these armies left the military occupation of the rebellious States by the Federal forces unresisted and complete. The plan now adopted by the Government was, to retain in each State a sufficient military force to preserve peace, and to put down any opposition which might arise, and to disband the remainder of its armies, and to restore to civil rights all citizens who should take the oath prescribed in the amnesty proclamation of President Lincoln, which may be found on a preceding page. The effect of this was to oblige the person taking it to sustain the Federal Government and all its past acts relative to the emancipation of slaves.

The Army of the Potomac and the army under Gen. Sherman, with the exception of a comparatively small force retained in Virginia and North Carolina, were marched to the neighborhood of Washington, for a grand review and final dispersion. The review took place on the 22d and 23d of May. The mustering out of service was then commenced, and by July 1st nearly 800,000 men had been discharged. Gen. Sherman took leave of his troops by issuing the following order:

Special Orders No. 67.

HEADQ'RS MIDDLE DIVISION OF THE MISSISSIPPI,
IN THE FIELD, WASHINGTON, D. C., May 30, 1865.

The General Commanding announces to the Armies of the Tennessee and Georgia that the time has come for us to part. Our work is done, and armed enemies no longer defy us. Some of you will be retained in service until further orders. And now that we are about to separate, to mingle with the civil world, it becomes a pleasing duty to recall to mind the situation of national affairs when, but a little more than a year ago, we were gathered about the twining cliffs of Lookout Mountain, and all the future was wrapped in doubt and uncertainty. Three armies had come together from distant fields, with separate histories, yet bound by one common cause—the union of our country and the perpetuation of the Government of our inheritance. There is no need to recall to your memories Tunnel Hill, with its Rocky Face Mountain, and Buzzard Roost Gap, with the ugly forts of Dalton behind. We were in earnest, and paused not for danger and difficulty, but dashed through Snake Creek Gap, and fell on Resaca, then on to the Etowah, to Dallas, Kenesaw; and the heats of summer found us on the banks of the Chattahoochee, far from home and dependent on a single road for supplies. Again we were not to be held back by any obstacle, and crossed over and fought four heavy battles for the possession of the citadel of Atlanta. That was the crisis of our history. A doubt still clouded our future; but we solved the problem, and destroyed Atlanta, struck boldly across the State of Georgia, secured all the main arteries of life to our enemy, and Christmas found us at Savannah. Waiting there only long enough to fill our wagons, we again began a march, which for peril, labor, and results, will compare with any ever made by an organized army. The floods of the Savannah, the swamps of the Combahee and Edisto, the high hills and rocks of the Santee, the flat quagmires of the Pedee and Cape Fear Rivers, were all passed in midwinter, with its floods and rains, in the face of an accumulating enemy; and after the battles of Averysboro and Bentonville we once more came out of the wilderness to meet our friends at Goldsboro. Even then we paused only long enough to get new clothing, to reload our wagons, and again pushed on to Raleigh, and beyond, until we met our enemy, sueing for peace instead of war, and offering to submit to the injured laws of his and our country. As long as that enemy was defiant, nor mountains, nor rivers, nor swamps, nor hunger, nor cold, had checked us; but when he who had fought us hard and persistently offered submission, your General thought it wrong to pursue him further, and negotiations followed which resulted, as you all know, in his surrender. How far the operations of the army have contributed to the overthrow of the Confederacy, of the peace which now dawns on us, must be judged by others, not by us. But that you have done all that men could do has been admitted by those in authority; and we have a right to join in the universal joy that fills our land because the war is over, and our Government stands vindicated before the world by the joint action of the volunteer armies of the United States.

To such as remain in the military service your General need only remind you that successes in the past are due to hard work and discipline, and that the same work and discipline are equally important in the future. To such as go home, he will only say, that our favored country is so grand, so extensive, so diversified in climate, soil, and productions, that every man may surely find a home and occupation suited to his tastes; and none should yield to the natural impotence sure to result from our past life of excitement and adventure. You will be invited to seek new adventure abroad; but do not yield to the temptation, for it will lead only to death and disappointment.

Your General now bids you all farewell, with the full belief that, as in war you have been good soldiers, so in peace you will make good citizens; and if, unfortunately, new war should arise in our country, Sherman's Army will be the first to buckle on the old armor and come forth to defend and maintain the Government of our inheritance and choice.

By order of Major-General W. T. SHERMAN.
L. M. DAYTON, Assistant Adjutant-General.

At a later date Lieut.-Gen. Grant issued the following address to all the armies:

General Orders No. 108.

WAR DEPARTMENT, ADJUTANT-GENERAL'S OFFICE,
WASHINGTON, D. C., June 2, 1865.

Soldiers of the Armies of the United States;

By your patriotic devotion to your country in the hour of danger and alarm, your magnificent fighting, bravery, and endurance, you have maintained the supremacy of the Union and the Constitution, overthrown all armed opposition to the enforcement of the laws and of the proclamations forever abolishing slavery—the cause and pretext of the rebellion—and opened the way to the rightful authorities to restore order and inaugurate peace on a permanent and enduring basis on every foot of American soil. Your marches, sieges, and battles, in distance, duration, resolution, and brilliancy of results, dim the lustre of the world's past military achievements, and will be the patriot's precedent in defence of liberty and right in all time to come. In obedience to your country's call you left your homes and families and volunteered in its defence. Victory has crowned your valor, and secured the purpose of your patriotic hearts; and with the gratitude of your countrymen and the highest honors a great and free nation can accord, you will soon be permitted to return to your homes and families, conscious of having discharged the highest duty of American citizens. To achieve these glorious triumphs and secure to yourselves, your fellow-countrymen, and posterity the blessings of free institutions, tens of thousands of your gallant comrades have fallen and sealed the priceless legacy with their lives. The graves of these a grateful nation bedews with tears, honors their memories, and will ever cherish and support their stricken families.

U. S. GRANT, Lieutenant-General.

On May 5th an order was issued by Gen. Halleck, in command of the James River, declaring that all persons found in arms after May 26, against the authority of the United States in Virginia or North Carolina, would be treated as robbers and outlaws. A similar order was subsequently issued by the War Department, to be enforced in all States east of the Mississippi River. This caused the disbandment of all guerrilla organizations:

On April 29th the President issued the following proclamation:

EXECUTIVE CHAMBER, WASHINGTON, April 29, 1865.

Being desirous to relieve all loyal citizens and well-disposed persons residing in the insurrectionary States from unnecessary commercial restrictions, and to encourage them to return to peaceful pursuits, it is hereby ordered:

1. That all restrictions upon internal, domestic, and coastwise commercial intercourse be discontinued in such part of the States of Tennessee, Virginia, North Carolina, South Carolina, Georgia, Florida, Alabama, Mississippi, and so much of Louisiana as lies east of the Mississippi River, as shall be embraced within the lines of the national military occupation, excepting only such restrictions as are imposed by the acts of Congress, and regulations in pursuance thereof prescribed by the Secretary of the Treasury, and approved by the President, and excepting also from the effect of this order the following articles, contraband of war, to wit: Arms, ammunition, and all articles from which ammunition is manufactured; gray uniforms and cloth, locomotives, cars, railroad iron and machinery for operating railroads, telegraph wires, insulators, and instruments for operating telegraph lines.

2. All existing military and naval orders in any manner restricting internal, domestic, and coastwise commercial intercourse and trade with or in the localities above named, be and the same are hereby revoked, and that no military or naval officer in any manner interrupt or interfere with the same, or with any boats or other vessels engaged therein under proper authority pursuant to the regulations of the Secretary of the Treasury. ANDREW JOHNSON.

In relation to prisoners of war those who had been delivered on parole to Federal officers were declared exchanged, and those confined in the Southern States were released. The following orders were issued by the War Department respecting Confederate prisoners:

WAR DEPARTMENT, WASHINGTON, May 7, 1865.

Ordered—That all prisoners of war, except officers above the rank of colonel, who, before the capture of Richmond, signified their desire to take the oath of allegiance to the United States and their unwillingness to be exchanged, be forewith released on their taking said oath, and transportation furnished them to their respective homes.

In respect to all other prisoners of war, further orders will be issued.

The Commissary-General of Prisoners will issue the necessary regulations for preserving the requisite record of prisoners of war to be released under this order, the record to set forth the name of the prisoner, his place of residence, the organization to which he belonged, the time and place of capture, &c. The oaths of allegiance will be administered by commanding officers of the prisons, camps, and forts, who will send by telegraph daily reports of prisoners released to the Commissary-General of Prisoners. These reports will be consolidated for each day, and transmitted to the Secretary of War.

By order of the SECRETARY OF WAR.
James A. Hardie, Brevet Brig.-Gen., Inspector-Gen. U. S. Army.

WAR DEPARTMENT, ADJUTANT-GENERAL'S OFFICE,
WASHINGTON, June 6, 1865.

The prisoners of war at the several depots in the North will be discharged, under the following regulations and restrictions:

1. All enlisted men of the rebel army, and petty officers and seamen of the rebel navy, will be discharged upon taking the oath of allegiance.

2. Officers of the rebel army not above the grade of captain, and of the rebel navy not above the grade of lieutenant, except such as have graduated at the United States Military or Naval Academy, and such as held a commission in either the United States army or navy at the beginning of the rebellion, may be discharged upon taking the oath of allegiance.

3. When the discharges hereby ordered are completed, regulations will be issued in respect to the discharge of officers having higher rank than captains in the army or lieutenants in the navy.

4. The several commanders of prison stations will discharge each day as much of the prisoners hereby authorized to be discharged as proper rolls can be prepared for, beginning with those who have been longest in prison and from the most remote points of the country, and certified rolls will be forwarded daily to the Commissary-General of Prisoners of those discharged. The oath of allegiance only will be administered. But notice will be given that all who desire will be permitted to take the oath of amnesty after their release, in accordance with the regulations of the Department of State respecting the amnesty.

5. The Quartermaster's Department will furnish transportation to all released prisoners to the nearest accessible point to their homes, by rail or by steamboat.

By order of the President of the United States.
E. D. TOWNSEND, Ass't Adjutant-General.

Subsequently a commission was organized at Washington to investigate the treatment of Federal prisoners at Andersonville, which was charged to have been of a most cruel and barbarous nature.

The charitable organizations which had been called into existence by the war, now found the necessity for their services removed. In the brief but bloody campaigns of March and April, 1865, the Sanitary Commission continued its humane and noble work. The sick and wounded were cared for, their friends informed of their situation, their pensions, bounties, and back pay collected, and when the armies were disbanded the Soldiers' Homes were thrown open all along their various routes to welcome them, and agents of the Commission met them at railroad stations and steamboat landings to invite them to the homes and lodges, and protect them as far as possible from fraud. The Commission also greatly increased its claim agencies, which, without fee or reward, collected the arrearages and pay due to the soldiers, and established at its central office in Washington, with branches in all the principal cities, a bureau of information and employment, to secure to all soldiers desiring employment such situations as they were capable of filling. The receipts of the Commission were large during the spring months, but its disbursements were still larger. On the 1st of June, 1865, a second Sanitary Fair was opened at Chicago, Ill., for the purpose of raising funds for the maintenance of the claim agencies and other organizations of the Commission, which it was deemed desirable to continue in operation. About $325,000 above all expenses was received from this fair. On the 1st of July, 1865, the Aid Societies, auxiliary to the Commission, ceased their coöperative work, though many of them became auxiliary to the Commission as claim agencies. It was officially announced on the 26th of April, 1865, that the contributions to the Commission from California to that date amounted to $1,199,675.51; those of Nevada to $99,512.46; Oregon, $75,597.56; and Washington Territory, $20,753.92—making a total from the Pacific slope of $1,395,539.45. The Metropolitan Fair in New York yielded $1,184,146.72, and the Central Fair in Philadelphia, $1,035,398.96. The final campaign of the war demanded new efforts from the Christian Commission, and its agents labored with new zeal and energy. No official statement of its receipts during these months was made, but they are understood to have approached half a million of dollars, which was expended for the promotion of the physical, intellectual, and religious welfare of the soldiers and sailors. As the war closed the Commission disbanded and discontinued its work.

The Union Commission found, as it expected, a sphere of wider usefulness in the closing scenes of the war, and in the suffering which followed among the poorer classes of whites in the Southern States, and was actively engaged in endeavoring to improve their condition. It subsequently coöperated with the Freedmen's Bureau, the Western Sanitary Commission, and other similar institutions, in their useful labors.

A reduction of the naval force was made at the same time when the armies were disbanded. Volunteer officers resigned, men were discharged, and all vessels not needed for future service were sold. The steamer Webb, which had been used as a ram by the enemy on the Red River throughout the war, ran the blockade on that river, and passed down the Mississippi about April 24th, making an attempt to escape to the West Indies. Being pursued after passing New Orleans, and discovering the steamer Richmond coming up the river, her commander, Edward G. Reed, run her ashore, and setting her on fire, escaped, with nearly all the crew, to the swamps. The vessel was consumed. All the other vessels in the Confederate service were surrendered, as has been stated, except the Shenandoah, which was in Australia at the close of the war. She continued her operations, and caused great destruction among the whale-ships on the northwest coast of America.

Mr. Davis, who had acted as President of the insurrectionary States, on the evacuation of Richmond, hurried to Danville, Va., and immediately issued the following proclamation:

DANVILLE, VA., April 5, 1865.

The General-in-Chief found it necessary to make such movements of his troops as to uncover the capital. It would be unwise to conceal the moral and material injury to our cause resulting from the occupation of our capital by the enemy. It is equally unwise and unworthy of us to allow our energies to falter and our efforts to become relaxed under adverses, however calamitous they may be.

For many months the largest and finest army of the Confederacy, under command of a leader whose presence inspires equal confidence in the troops and the people, has been greatly trammelled by the necessity of keeping constant watch over the approaches to the capital, and has thus been forced to forego more than one opportunity for promising enterprise. It is for us, my countrymen, to show by our bearing under reverses, how wretched has been the self-deception of those who have believed us less able to endure misfortune with fortitude than to encounter dangers with courage.

We have now entered upon a new phase of the struggle. Relieved from the necessity of guarding particular points, our army will be free to move from point to point to strike the enemy in detail far from his base. Let us but will it and we are free.

Animated by that confidence in spirit and fortitude which never yet failed me, I announce to you, fellow-countrymen, that it is my purpose to maintain your cause with my whole heart and soul; that I will never consent to abandon to the enemy one foot of the soil of any one of the States of the Confederacy. That Virginia—noble State—whose ancient renown has been eclipsed by her still more glorious recent history; whose bosom has been bared to receive the main shock of this war; whose sons and daughters have exhibited heroism so sublime as to render her illustrious in all time to come—that Virginia, with the help of the people and by the blessing of Providence, shall be held and defended, and no peace ever be made with the infamous invaders of her territory.

If by the stress of numbers we should ever be compelled to a temporary withdrawal from her limits, or those of any other border State, again and again will we return, until the baffled and exhausted enemy shall abandon in despair his endless and impossible task of making slaves of a people resolved to be free.

Let us, then, not despond, my countrymen; but, relying on God, meet the foe with fresh defiance and with unconquered and unconquerable hearts.

JEFFERSON DAVIS.

Subsequently on understanding the true state of affairs, he proceeded further south with his family, designing to escape from the country by some port on the seacoast, but was captured at Irwinsville, Wilkinson County, Ga., on May 10th, with his family, his Postmaster, Gen. Reagan, his Private Secretary, Harrison, and others, with a train of five wagons and three ambulances. The captors were Lieut.-Col. Pritchard, of the 4th Michigan cavalry, and a body of his men. They belonged to the corps of Gen. Wilson. Davis was removed to Fortress Monroe, and retained as a prisoner in close confinement.

The plan adopted by the President for the restoration of the Southern people to their civil rights is explained in the following proclamation:

Whereas, The President of the United States, on the 8th day of December, A. D. eighteen hundred and sixty-three, and on the 26th day of March, A. D. eighteen hundred and sixty-four, did, with the object to suppress the existing rebellion, to induce all persons to return to their loyalty and to restore the authority of the United States, issue proclamations offering amnesty and pardon to certain persons who had directly or by implication participated in the said rebellion; and

Whereas, Many persons who had so engaged in said rebellion have, since the issuance of said proclamations, failed or neglected to take the benefits offered thereby; and

Whereas, Many persons who have been justly deprived of all claim to amnesty and pardon thereunder, by reason of their participation directly or by implication in said rebellion, and continued in hostility to the Government of the United States since the date of said proclamation, now desire to apply for and obtain amnesty and pardon.

To the end, therefore, that the authority of the Government of the United States may be restored, and that peace, order, and feeedom may be reëstablished, I, Andrew Johnson, President of the United States, do proclaim and declare that I hereby grant to all persons who have directly or indirectly participated in the existing rebellion, except as hereinafter excepted, amnesty and pardon, with restoration of all rights of property, except as to slaves, and except in cases where legal proceedings under the laws of the United States providing for the confiscation of property of persons engaged in rebellion have been instituted; but on the condition, nevertheless, that every such person shall take and subscribe the following oath or affirmation, and thenceforward keep and maintain said oath inviolate, and which oath shall be registered for permanent preservation, and shall be of the tenor and effect following, to wit:

"I, ——— ———, do solemnly swear, or affirm, in presence of Almighty God, that I will henceforth faithfully support and defend the Constitution of the United States and the Union of the States thereunder, and that I will, in like manner, abide by and faithfully support all laws and proclamations which have been made during the existing rebellion with reference to the emancipation of slaves, so help me God."

The following classes of persons are excepted from the benefits of this proclamation:

1. All who are or shall have been pretended civil or diplomatic officers, or otherwise domestic or foreign agents, of the pretended Confederate government.

2. All who left judicial stations under the United States to aid the Rebellion.

3. All who shall have been military or naval officers of said pretended Confederate government above the rank of colonel in the army or lieutenant in the navy.

4. All who left seats in the Congress of the United States to aid the Rebellion.

5. All who resigned or tendered resignations of their commissions in the army or navy of the United States to evade duty in resisting the Rebellion.

6. All who have engaged in any way in treating otherwise than lawfully as prisoners of war persons found in the United States service as officers, soldiers, seamen, or in other capacities.

7. All persons who have been or are absentees from the United States for the purpose of aiding the Rebellion.

8. All military and naval officers in the Rebel service who were educated by the Government in the Military Academy at West Point or the United States Naval Academy.

9. All persons who held the pretended offices of Governors of States in insurrection against the United States.

10. All persons who left their homes within the jurisdiction and protection of the United States, and passed beyond the Federal military lines into the so-called Confederate States, for the purpose of aiding the Rebellion.

11. All persons who have been engaged in the destruction of the commerce of the United States upon the high seas, and all persons who have made raids into the United States from Canada, or been engaged in destroying the commerce of the United States upon the lakes and rivers that separate the British Provinces from the United States.

12. All persons who, at the time when they seek to obtain the benefits hereof by taking the oath herein prescribed, are in military, naval, or civil confinement or custody, or under bonds of the civil, military, or naval authorities or agents of the United States as prisoners of war, or persons detained for offences of any kind either before or after conviction.

13. All persons who have voluntarily participated in said Rebellion, and the estimated value of whose taxable property is over twenty thousand dollars.

14. All persons who have taken the oath of amnesty as prescribed in the President's Proclamation of December 8, A. D. 1863, or an oath of allegiance to the Government of the United States since the date of said Proclamation, and who have not thenceforward kept and maintained the same inviolate—provided, that special application may be made to the President for pardon by any person belonging to the excepted classes, and such clemency will be liberally extended as may be consistent with the factsof the case and the peace and dignity of the United States.

The Secretary of State will establish rules and regulations for administering and recording the said amnesty oath, so as to insure its benefit to the people, and guard the Government against fraud.

In testimony whereof, I have hereunto set my hand and caused the seal of the United States to be affixed.

Done at the city of Washington, the twenty-ninth day of May, in the year of our Lord one thousand eight hundred and sixty-five, and of the independence of the United States the eighty-ninth.

ANDREW JOHNSON.

The proceedings of the President to restore a civil government to the Southern States, is explained in the following proclamation, issued in the case of North Carolina. A similar proclamation was issued, and a Provisional Governor appointed in each of the other States:

Whereas, The fourth section of the fourth article of the Constitution of the United States declares that the United States shall guarantee to every State in the Union a republican form of government, and shall protect each of them against invasion and domestic violence; and

Whereas, The President of the United States is, by the Constitution, made Commander-in-Chief of the Army and Navy, as well as Chief Executive Officer of the United States, and is bound by solemn oath faithfully to execute the office of President of the United States, and to take care that the laws be faithfully executed; and

Whereas, The Rebellion, which has been waged by a portion of the people of the United States against the properly constituted authorities of the Government thereof in the most violent and revolting form, but whose organized and armed forces have now been almost entirely overcome, has in its revolutionary progress deprived the people of the State of North Carolina of all civil government; and

Whereas, It becomes necessary and proper to carry out and enforce the obligations of the United States to the people of North Carolina, in securing them in the enjoyments of a republican form of government;

Now, therefore, in obedience to the high and solemn duties imposed upon me by the Constitution of the United States, and for the purpose of enabling the loyal people of said State to organize a State Government whereby justice may be established, domestic tranquillity insured, and loyal citizens protected in all their rights of life, liberty, and property;

I, Andrew Johnson, President of the United States, and Commander-in-Chief of the Army and Navy of the United States, do hereby appoint William W. Holden Provisional Governor of the State of North Carolina, whose duty it shall be, at the earliest practicable period, to prescribe such rules and regulations as may be necessary and proper for convening a convention composed of delegates to be chosen by that portion of the people of said State who are loyal to the United States, and no others, for the purpose of altering or amending the Constitution thereof, and with authority to exercise within the limits of said State all the powers necessary and proper to enable such loyal people of the State of North Carolina to restore said State to its constitutional relations to the Federal Government, and to present such a republican form of State Government as will entitle the State to the guarantee of the United States therefor, and its people to protection by the United States against invasion, insurrection, and domestic violence; provided that in any election that may be hereafter held for choosing delegates to any State convention as aforesaid, no person shall be qualified as an elector, or shall be eligible as a member of such convention, unless he shall previously have taken and subscribed the oath of amnesty as set forth in the President's proclamation, May 29th, 1864, and is a voter qualified as prescribed by the Constitution and laws of the State of North Carolina in force immediately before the 20th of May, A. D. 1861, the date of the so-called ordinance of secession; and the said convention when convened, or the Legislature that may be thereafter assembled, will prescribe the qualification of electors and the eligibility of persons to hold office under the Constitution and laws of the State—a power the people of the several States composing the Federal Union have rightfully exercised from the origin of the Government to the present time. And I do hereby direct:

1. That the military commander of the department, and all officers and persons in the military and naval service, aid and assist the said Provisional Governor in carrying into effect this proclamation; and they are enjoined to abstain from in any way hindering, impeding, or discouraging the loyal people from the organization of a State government as herein authorized.

2. That the Secretary of State proceed to put in force all laws of the United States, the administration whereof belongs to the State Department, applicable to the geographical limits aforesaid.

3d. That the Secretary of the Treasury proceed to nominate for appointment assessors of taxes and collectors of customs and internal revenue, and such other officers of the Treasury Department as are authorized by law, and put in execution the revenue laws of the United States within the geographical limits aforesaid. In making the appointments, the preference shall be given to qualified loyal persons residing within the districts where their respective duties are to be performed. But if suitable residents of the districts shall not be found, then persons residing in other States or districts shall be appointed.

4. That the Postmaster General proceed to establish post routes and put into execution the postal laws of the United States within the said State, giving to loyal residents the preference of appointment. But if suitable residents are not found, then appoint agents from other States.

5. That the district judge for the judicial district in which North Carolina is included, proceed to hold courts within said State, in accordance with the provisions of the act of Congress. The Attorney-General will instruct the proper officers to libel and bring to judgment, confiscation, and sale, and enforce the administration of justice within said State in all mat-

H. W. Smith, N. Y.

Andrew Johnson

PRESIDENT OF THE UNITED STATES

New York, D. Appleton & Co.

ters within the cognizance and jurisdiction of the Federal courts.

6. That the Secretary of the Navy take possession of all public property belonging to the Navy Department within said geographical limits, and put in operation all acts of Congress in relation to naval affairs having application to said State.

7. That the Secretary of the Interior put in force the laws relating to the Interior Department, applicable to the geographical limits aforesaid.

[L. S.] In testimony whereof I have hereunto set my hand, and caused the seal of the United States to be affixed.

Done at the City of Washington this twenty-ninth day of May, in the year of our Lord one thousand eight hundred and sixty-five, and of the Independence of the United States the eighty-ninth.

ANDREW JOHNSON.

WM. H. SEWARD, Secretary of State.

The Provisional Governors and date of appointment were as follows:

North Carolina, Wm. W. Holden, May 29.
Mississippi, Wm. L. Sharkey, June 13.
Georgia, James Johnson, June 17.
Texas, Andrew J. Hamilton, June 17.
Alabama, Lewis E. Parsons, June 21.
South Carolina, Benj. F. Perry, June 30.
Florida, William Marvin, July 13.

The following is a list of the officers of the War Department at the close of 1864; of the General Officers of the Regular Army in service subsequent to July, 1861; and of the Major and Brigadier-Generals of the volunteer army in service on Jan. 1, 1865, showing also where and how such general officers were employed at that date.

DEPARTMENT OFFICERS.

Officers not thus * designated are graduates of the Military Academy.

EDWIN M. STANTON, of Pennsylvania, *Secretary of War*.
PETER H. WATSON, *1st Assistant Secretary of War*. JOHN POTTS, *Chief Clerk*.
CHARLES A. DANA, *2d Assistant Secretary of War*.
HENRY W. HALLECK, *Chief of Staff*.

OFFICE.	NAME.	RANK.	Date of Commission.	Entry into service.	Born in.	Appointed from.
Adjutant General	Lorenzo Thomas	Brig.-Gen'l	3 Aug., 1861.	1 July, 1823.	Delaware	Delaware
Judge Advocate General.	Joseph Holt*	Colonel	3 Sept., 1862.	3 Sept., 1862.		Dist. Columbia
Inspector General	Randolph B. Marcy	do.	9 Aug., 1861.	1 July, 1832.	Massachus'ts	Massachus'ts
do.	Delos B. Sacket	do.	1 Oct., 1861.	1 July, 1845.	New York	New York
do.	Henry Van Rensselaer.	do.	12 Nov., 1861.	1 July, 1831.	New York	New York
do.	Edmund Schriver	do.	13 Mar., 1862.	1 July, 1833.	Pennsylvania	New York
Signal Officer Army	Albert J. Myer*	do.	3 Mar., 1863.	18 Sept., 1854.	New York	New York
Quartermaster General	Montgomery C. Meigs.	Maj.-Gen'l	15 May, 1861.	1 July, 1836.	Georgia	Pennsylvania
Comm. General of Sub	Amos B. Eaton	Brig.-Gen'l	29 June, 1864.	1 July, 1826.	New York	New York
Surgeon General	Joseph K. Barnes	do.		15 June, 1840.	Pennsylvania	Pennsylvania
Paymaster General	Timothy P. Andrews*.	Colonel	6 Sep., 1862.	22 May, 1822.	Ireland	Dist. Columbia
Chief Corps of Engineers.	Richard Delafield	Brig.-Gen'l		24 July, 1818.	New York	New York
Chief Ordnance Dep't	Alexander B. Dyer	do.		1 July, 1837.	Virginia	Missouri

GENERAL OFFICERS OF THE REGULAR ARMY IN SERVICE SINCE JULY, 1861.

NAME AND RANK.	Date of Commission.	Entry into service.	Born in.	Appointed from.	REMARKS.
Lieutenant-Generals.					
Winfield Scott	25 June, 1841	3 May, 1808	Virginia	Virginia	Retired Nov. 1, 1861.
Ulysses S. Grant	2 Mar., 1864		Ohio	Illinois	
Major-Generals.					
George B. McClellan	14 May, 1861	1 July, 1846	Pennsylvania	Ohio	Resigned Nov. 8, 1864.
John C. Fremont*	14 May, 1861	7 July, 1838	South Carolina	California	Resigned June 4, 1864.
Henry W. Halleck	19 Aug., 1861	1 July, 1839	New York	California	
John E. Wool*	16 May, 1862	14 April, 1812	New York	New York	Retired.
Ulysses S. Grant	4 July, 1863		Ohio	Illinois	Promoted.
Montgomery C. Meigs		1 July, 1836	Georgia	Pennsylvania	By brevet.
Joseph G. Totten	21 April, 1864	1 July, 1805	Connecticut	Connecticut	By brevet. Died in Washington April 22, 1864.
William T. Sherman	12 Aug., 1861		Ohio	Ohio	
Philip H. Sheridan	8 Nov., 1864		Massachusetts	Ohio	
George G. Meade	10 Aug., 1864				
George H. Thomas					
Brigadier-Generals.					
John E. Wool	25 June, 1841	14 April, 1812	New York	New York	Promoted.
William S. Harney*	14 June, 1858	13 Feb., 1818	Louisiana	Louisiana	Retired August 1, 1863.
Edwin V. Sumner*	16 Mar., 1861	3 Mar., 1819	Massachusetts	New York	Died March 21, 1863.
Joseph K. F. Mansfield.	14 May, 1861	1 July, 1827	Connecticut	Connecticut	Died September 18, 1862, of wounds received at Antietam.
Irwin McDowell	14 May, 1861	1 July, 1838	Ohio	Ohio	
Robert Anderson	15 May, 1861	1 July, 1825	Kentucky	Kentucky	Retired.
William S. Rosecrans	16 May, 1861	1 July, 1842	Ohio	Ohio	
Philip St. G. Cooke	12 Nov., 1861	1 July, 1827	Virginia	Virginia	
John Pope	14 July, 1862	1 July, 1842	Kentucky	Illinois	
Joseph Hooker	20 Sept., 1862	1 July, 1837	Massachusetts	California	
James B. McPherson	1 Aug., 1863		Ohio	Ohio	Killed near Atlanta, July 22, 1864.
George G. Meade	3 July, 1863		Spain	Dist. Columbia	
William T. Sherman	4 July, 1863		Ohio	Ohio.	Promoted.
George H. Thomas	27 Oct., 1863		Virginia	Virginia	
Winfield S. Hancock	12 Aug., 1864		Pennsylvania	Pennsylvania	
Andrew H. Reeder				Pennsylvania	Declined.
James W. Ripley	3 Aug., 1864	1 June, 1814	Connecticut	Connecticut	Retired.
Joseph G. Totten		1 July, 1805	Connecticut	Connecticut	Promoted.
John M. Schofield	20 Nov., 1864				
Oliver O. Howard	21 Dec., 1864				

LIST OF MAJOR AND BRIGADIER-GENERALS OF VOLUNTEERS, SHOWING WHERE AND HOW SAID GENERAL OFFICERS WERE EMPLOYED JANUARY 1, 1865.

NAME AND RANK.	STATION.	HOW EMPLOYED.
Major-Generals.		
John A. Dix	New York city	Commanding department of the East.
Nathaniel P. Banks	Washington, D. C.	Before Committee on Conduct of War.
Benjamin F. Butler	Bermuda Hundred, Va.	Commanding department of Virginia and North Carolina.
David Hunter	Washington, D. C.	Awaiting orders.
Ethan A. Hitchcock	Washington, D. C.	Commissioner of exchange of prisoners.
Irwin McDowell	San Francisco, Cal	Commanding department of the Pacific.
Ambrose E. Burnside	Providence, R. I.	Awaiting orders.
William S. Rosecrans	Cincinnati, Ohio	Awaiting orders.
John Pope	Milwaukee, Wis	Commanding department of the Northwest.
Samuel R. Curtis	Fort Leavenworth, Kansas.	Commanding department of Kansas.
Franz Sigel	Bethlehem, Penn	Awaiting orders.
Lewis Wallace	Baltimore, Md	Commanding middle department.
George Cadwalader	Philadelphia, Penn	Commanding department of Pennsylvania.
Edward O. C. Ord	In the field, Va	Commanding 24th army corps.
Samuel P. Heintzelman	Wheeling, W. Va	Member of general court-martial.
Joseph Hooker	Cincinnati, Ohio	Commanding Northern Department.
Silas Casey	Washington, D. C.	Commanding provisional brigades and member of board.
William B. Franklin	Wilmington, Del	President of retiring board.
Darius N. Couch	In the field, Tenn	Commanding 2d division, 23d army corps.
Henry W. Slocum	In the field, Tenn	Commanding left wing army of Georgia.
John J. Peck	New York city	Second in command department of the East.
Alexander McD. McCook	Baltimore, Md	Member of military commission.
John G. Foster	Hilton Head, S. C.	Commanding department of the South.
John G. Parke	Army of Potomac	Commanding 9th army corps.
Christopher C. Augur	Washington, D. C.	Commanding department of Washington.
Stephen A. Hurlbut	New Orleans, La	Commanding department of the Gulf.
Gordon Granger	Mobile Bay, Ala	Commanding district of West Florida and South Alabama.
Lovell H. Rousseau	In the field, Tenn	Commanding district of Tennessee.
George Stoneman	Louisville, Ky	Second in command department of the Ohio.
Oliver O. Howard	In the field, Ga	Commanding right wing army of Georgia.
Daniel E. Sickles	New York city	Off duty on account of wounds.
Robert H. Milroy	Tullahoma, Tenn	Commanding defences of Nashville and Chattanooga Railroad.
Daniel Butterfield	New York city	Member of general court-martial.
Winfield S. Hancock	Washington, D. C.	Organizing 1st army corps.
George Sykes	Fort Leavenworth, Kansas.	Awaiting orders.
David S. Stanley	In the field, Ga	Commanding 4th army corps. (On temporary leave of absence.)
James S. Negley	Pittsburg, Penn	Awaiting orders.
John M. Palmer	Carlinsville, Ill	Awaiting orders.
Frederick Steele	New Orleans, La	Under orders of Major-General Canby.
Abner Doubleday	Washington, D. C.	President of military commission.
Napoleon J. T. Dana	Memphis, Tenn	Commanding department of the Mississippi.
John A. Logan	In the field, Ga	Commanding 15th army corps. (On temporary leave of absence.)
James G. Blunt	Paola, Kansas	Commanding district of South Kansas.
George L. Hartsuff	New York city	President of general court-martial.
Cad. C. Washburne	Vicksburg, Miss	Commanding district of Vicksburg.
Francis J. Herron	Pittsburg, Penn	On temporary leave of absence.
Frank P. Blair	In the field, Ga	Commanding 17th army corps.
Joseph J. Reynolds	Little Rock, Ark	Commanding department of Arkansas.
John M. Schofield	In the field, Tenn	Commanding army of the Ohio.
Julius H. Stahel	Baltimore, Md	Member of general court-martial.
Carl Schurz	Bethlehem, Penn	Awaiting orders.
Gouverneur K. Warren	Army of Potomac	Commanding 5th army corps. (On temporary leave of absence.)
Alfred Pleasanton	St. Louis, Mo	Second in command department of the Missouri.
Andrew A. Humphreys	Army of Potomac	Commanding 2d army corps.
Quincy A. Gillmore		On tour of inspection of defensive works of the Mississippi.
William F. Smith		In mil. div. of W. Mississippi under special order of War Dep't.
James B. Steedman	In the field, Tenn	Serving in department of the Cumberland.
Edward R. S. Canby	New Orleans, La	Commanding military division of West Mississippi.
Horatio G. Wright	Army of Potomac	Commanding 6th army corps.
Andrew J. Smith	In the field, Tenn	Commanding detachment of the army of the Tennessee.
Grenville M. Dodge	St. Louis, Mo	Commanding department of the Missouri.
John Gibbon	Army of Potomac	Commanding 2d division, 2d army corps.
Peter J. Osterhaus	In the field, Ga	Commanding 1st division, 15th army corps.
Joseph A. Mower	In the field, Ga	Commanding 1st division, 17th army corps.
George Crook	Cumberland, Md	Commanding department of West Virginia.
Godfrey Weitzel	In the field, Va	Commanding 25th army corps.
Brigadier-Generals.		
Thomas W. Sherman	New Orleans, La	Commanding defences of New Orleans.
John D. Cox	In the field, Tenn	Commanding 3d division, 23d army corps.
Benjamin F. Kelley	In the field, W. Va	Commanding 2d infantry division department West Virginia.
A. S. Williams	Savannah, Ga	Commanding 20th army corps.
James B. Ricketts	Washington, D. C.	Severely wounded.
Orlando B. Wilcox	Army of Potomac	Commanding 1st division 9th army corps.
Henry H. Lockwood	Baltimore, Md	Commanding 3d sep. brigade 8th army corps.
Samuel D. Sturgis	Covington, Ky	Awaiting orders.
Henry W. Benham	City Point, Va	Commanding volunteer engineer brigade.
William F. Barry	Savannah, Ga	Chief of artillery, military division of Mississippi.
Lawrence P. Graham	Annapolis, Md	Member of board for examination of invalid officers.
Eleazer A. Paine	Monmouth, Ill	Awaiting orders.
W. T. Ward	In the field, Ga	Commanding 3d division 20th army corps.
John G. Barnard	City Point, Va	Chief engineer of armies operating against Richmond.
Innis A. Palmer	Newbern, N. C.	Commanding district of North Carolina.
Seth Williams	Army of Potomac	Assistant adjutant-general army of Potomac.
John Newton	Key West, Fla	Commanding district of Key West and Tortugas.

LIST OF MAJOR AND BRIGADIER-GENERALS OF VOLUNTEERS, &c.—(*Continued.*)

NAME AND RANK.	STATION.	HOW EMPLOYED.
George Wright	Sacramento, Cal	Commanding district of California.
John M. Brannan	Chattanooga, Tenn	Chief of artillery, department of Cumberland.
John P. Hatch	Morris Island, S. C	Commanding 1st sep. brigade, department of South.
Albin Schoepf	Fort Delaware, Del	Commanding post and military prison.
Thomas J. Wood	In the field, Tenn	Temporarily commanding 4th army corps.
Richard W. Johnson	Edgefield, Tenn	Commanding 6th division cavalry corps military division of Miss.
Adolph von Steinwehr	Wallingford, Conn	Awaiting orders.
George W. Cullum	West Point, N. Y	Superintendent of military academy.
Thomas J. McKean	Barrancas, Fla	Commanding district of West Florida.
Zealous B. Tower	In the field, Ga	Inspector general of fortifications military division of Mississippi.
Jefferson C. Davis	In the field, Ga	Commanding 14th army corps.
William S. Ketchum	War Department	On special duty.
John W. Davidson	New Orleans, La	Chief of cavalry military division of West Mississippi.
Thomas F. Meagher	In the field, Tenn	On duty in department of the Cumberland.
Andrew Johnson	Nashville, Tenn	Military Governor of Tennessee.
Eugene A. Carr	Little Rock, Arkansas	Commanding district of Little Rock.
Thomas A. Davis	Fort Leavenworth, Kansas	Commanding district of north Kansas.
William H. Emory	In the field, Va	Commanding 19th army corps.
Marsena R. Patrick	In the field, Va	Provost-marshal general armies operating against Richmond.
Orris S. Ferry	Philadelphia, Penn	Commanding district of Philadelphia.
Henry M. Judah	Louisville, Ky	Member of general court-martial and military commission.
John Cook	Springfield, Ill	Commanding district of Illinois.
John McArthur	In the field, Tenn	Commanding 1st division det. of the army of Tennessee.
Jacob G. Lauman	Burlington, Iowa	Awaiting orders.
Horatio P. Van Cleve	Murfreesboro, Tenn	Commanding post.
Speed S. Fry	Louisville, Ky	Awaiting orders.
Alexander Asboth	New Orleans, La	Sick in hospital.
Robert B. Mitchell	Omaha City, N. T	Commanding district of Nebraska.
Cuvier Grover	In the field, Va	Commanding 2d division 19th army corps.
Rufus Saxton	Beaufort, S. C	Commanding district of Beaufort.
Benjamin Alvord	Fort Vancouver, W. T	Commanding district of Oregon.
Napoleon B. Buford	Helena, Ark	Commanding district of eastern Arkansas.
Nathan Kimball	In the field, Tenn	Commanding 1st division 4th army corps.
Charles Devens	In the field, Va	Temporarily commanding 24th army corps.
Samuel W. Crawford	Army of Potomac	Commanding 3d division 5th army corps.
Henry W. Wessells	Washington, D. C	Commissary General of prisoners east of Mississippi.
John W. Geary	Savannah, Ga	Commanding 2d division 20th army corps.
Alfred H. Terry	In the field, Va	Commanding 1st division 24th army corps.
James H. Carleton	Santa Fé, N. M	Commanding department of New Mexico.
Absalom Baird	In the field, Ga	Commanding 3d division 14th army corps.
John C. Robinson	Albany, N. Y	Commanding district of northern New York.
Truman Seymour	Army of Potomac	Commanding 3d division 6th army corps.
Henry Prince	Louisville, Ky	En route to Savannah, Georgia.
Max Weber	Hagerstown, Md	Awaiting orders.
Jeremiah C. Sullivan	In the field, Va	Commanding 1st sep. brigade department West Virginia.
Albin P. Hovey	Indianapolis, Ind	Commanding district of Indiana.
James C. Veatch	Memphis, Tenn	Commanding district of West Tennessee.
William P. Benton	New Orleans, La	Awaiting assignment.
John C. Caldwell	Washington, D. C	President of military commission.
George S. Greene	New York city	Member of G. C. M. (wounded).
Samuel P. Carter	Knoxville, Tenn	Provost-marshal General of East Tennessee.
Erastus B. Tyler	Relay House, Md	Commanding 1st sep. brigade 8th army corps
Charles Griffin	Army of Potomac	Com'dg 1st div. 5th army corps. (On temporary leave of absence.)
George H. Gordon	Fort Monroe, Va	On duty in department of Virginia and North Carolina.
Stephen G. Burbridge	Lexington, Ky	Commanding district of Kentucky.
Washington L. Elliott	Mount Rozel, Ala	Commanding 2d division 4th army corps.
Albion P. Howe	Washington, D. C	Inspector of artillery.
Benjamin S. Roberts	New Orleans, La	Member of military commission.
Fitz Henry Warren	New York city	Member of military commission.
Morgan L. Smith	Vicksburg, Miss	Commanding post and defences.
Charles Cruft	In the field, Tenn	Commanding prov. division department of Cumberland.
Frederick Solomon	Little Rock, Ark	Commanding 1st division 7th army corps.
Henry S. Briggs	Washington, D. C	Member of general court-martial.
James D. Morgan	Savannah, Ga	Commanding 2d division 14th army corps.
August Willich	Cincinnati, Ohio	Commanding post.
Henry D. Terry	Washington, D. C	Member of general court-martial.
George F. Shepley	Norfolk, Va	Commanding district of Eastern Virginia.
John R. Kenly	Salisbury, Md	Commanding district of eastern shore of Maryland.
John P. Slough	Alexandria, Va	Military Governor and commanding district of Alexandria.
Gersham Mott	Army of Potomac	Commanding 3d division 2d army corps.
Henry J. Hunt	Army of Potomac	Chief of artillery.
Francis C. Barlow	On leave of absence	(Wounded).
Mason Brayman	Natchez, Miss	Commanding post and defences.
N. J. Jackson	Savannah, Ga	Commanding 1st division 20th army corps.
George W. Getty	Army of Potomac	Com'dg 2d div. 6th army corps. (On temporary leave of absence.)
Alfred Sully	Dubuque, Iowa	Commanding district of Iowa.
William W. Averell	Bath, N. Y	Awaiting orders.
Francis B. Spinola	Brooklyn, N. Y	Under trial by court-martial.
Solomon Meredith	Paducah, Ky	Commanding district of Western Kentucky.
Eliakim P. Scammon	Jacksonville, Fla	Commanding district of Florida.
Robert S. Granger	In the field, Ala	Commanding district of Northern Alabama.
Joseph R. West	Little Rock, Ark	Chief of cavalry, department of Arkansas.
George L. Andrews	Baton Rouge, La	Commanding district of Baton Rouge and Port Hudson.
Clinton B. Fisk	Macon, Mo	Commanding district of North Missouri.
Henry B. Carrington	Indianapolis, Ind	Commanding draft rendezvous.
William Hays	New York city	A. A. P. M. G., southern division of New York.
John H. King	In the field, Tenn	Commanding 1st brigade 1st sep. division, dep't of Cumberland.

LIST OF MAJOR AND BRIGADIER-GENERALS OF VOLUNTEERS, &c.—(*Continued.*)

NAME AND RANK.	STATION.	HOW EMPLOYED.
Israel Vogdes	Portsmouth, Va	Commanding defences of Norfolk and Portsmouth.
Adam J. Slemmer	Cincinnati, Ohio	President of board for examination of sick and wounded officers.
Lewis C. Hunt	New York city	Commanding defences of city and harbor.
Thomas H. Neill	In the field, Va	On duty in middle military division.
Thomas G. Pitcher	Indianapolis, Ind	A. A. P. M. G., State of Indiana.
Thomas W. Sweeney	Louisville, Ky	Under trial by court-martial.
Frank Wheaton	Army of Potomac	Commanding 1st division 6th army corps.
William P. Carlin	In the field, Ga	Commanding 1st division 14th army corps.
John S. Mason	San Francisco, Cal	A. A. P. M. G., for California and Nevada.
Romeyn B. Ayres	Army of Potomac	Commanding 2d division 5th army corps.
Richard Arnold	Wilmington, Del	Member of retiring board.
David McM. Gregg	Army of Potomac	Com'dg 2d cavalry division. (On temporary leave of absence.)
William B. Hazen	Savannah, Ga	Commanding 2d division 15th army corps.
Robert O. Tyler	Philadelphia, Pa	Wounded.
Alfred T. A. Torbert	In the field, Va	Chief of cavalry, middle military division.
Gilman Marston	Washington, D. C	On temporary leave of absence.
Michael K. Lawler	Memphis, Tenn	Commanding 1st brig. reserve corps, mil. div. of W. Mississippi.
George D. Wagner	Indianapolis, Ind	Awaiting orders.
William Dwight	In the field, Va	Commanding 1st division 19th army corps.
Lysander Cutler	Jackson, Mich	Commanding draft rendezvous.
James W. McMillan	In the field, Va	Commanding 2d brigade 1st division 19th army corps.
Sullivan A. Meredith	St. Louis, Mo	Member of general court-martial and military commission.
Joseph F. Knipe	In the field, Tenn	Serving with the army of the Tennessee.
E. W. Hincks	Hart's Island, N. Y. harbor	Commanding draft rendezvous.
John D. Stevenson	Harper's Ferry, W. Va	Commanding 3d division department of West Virginia.
James Barnes	Point Lookout, Md	Commanding St. Mary's district and prisoners' camp.
N. C. McLean	Lexington, Ky	Commanding 1st division district of Kentucky.
William Vandever	Louisville, Ky	On general court-martial.
Alex. Schemmelfennig	Bethlehem, Pa	Sick.
Edward Harland	Newbern, N. C	Commanding district of Newbern.
Charles K. Graham	In the field, Va	On special service in department of Virginia and North Carolina.
Samuel Beatty	Huntsville, Ala	Commanding 3d division 4th army corps.
John E. Smith	Savannah, Ga	Commanding 3d division 15th army corps.
Frank S. Nickerson	Searsport, Me	Awaiting orders.
Edward H. Hobson	Lexington, Ky	Commanding 1st brigade 1st division district of Kentucky,
Joseph D. Webster	In the field, Ga	Chief of Major-General Sherman's staff.
William Harrow	In the field, Ga	Commanding 4th division 15th army corps.
Joseph T. Copeland	Alton, Ill	Awaiting orders.
William H. Morris	New York city	Member of general court-martial. (Wounded.)
Thomas H. Ruger	In the field, Tenn	Commanding 1st division 23d army corps.
Elias S. Dennis	Memphis, Tenn	Commanding 2d brig. reserve corps, mil. div. of West Mississippi.
Thomas C. H. Smith	Milwaukee, Wis	Commanding district of Wisconsin.
Charles A. Heckman	In the field, Va	Commanding 3d division 25th army corps.
Mortimer D. Leggett	In the field, Ga	Commanding 3d division 17th army corps.
Davis Tillson	Knoxville, Tenn	Commanding 2d brigade 4th division 23d army corps.
Edward E. Potter	Hilton Head, S. C	Commanding district of Hilton Head.
Albert L. Lee	Washington, D. C	Before Committee on Conduct of War.
Egbert B. Brown	Rolla, Mo	Commanding district of Rolla.
John McNeil	St. Louis, Mo	Under trial by court-martial.
George F. McGinnis	New Orleans, La	On duty in department of Gulf.
Hugh Ewing	Louisville, Ky	Commanding 2d division district of Kentucky.
Daniel Ullman	Morganzia, La	Commanding United States forces.
George J. Stannard	St. Albans, Vt	Severely wounded.
Henry Baxter	Army of Potomac	Commanding 2d brigade 3d division 5th army corps.
John M. Thayer	Fort Smith, Ark	Commanding district of the frontier.
Charles T. Campbell	Milwaukee, Wis	Member of general court-martial. [rebels.
Halbert E. Paine	New York city	Commissioner for sending supplies to federal prisoners in hands of
Robert B. Potter	Army of Potomac	Com'dg 2d div. 9th army corps. (On temporary leave of absence.
Thomas Ewing, jr	St. Louis, Mo	Com'dg district of St. Louis. (On temporary leave of absence.)
J. A. J. Lightburn	Clarksburg, W. Va	Commanding post.
Henry H. Sibley	St. Paul, Minn	Commanding district of Minnesota.
Joseph B. Carr	Norfolk, Va	Commanding sep. brig. dep't of Virginia and North Carolina.
J. J. Bartlett	Army of Potomac	Commanding 3d brigade 1st division 5th army corps.
Patrick E. Connor	Camp Douglas, Utah Ter	Commanding district of Utah.
John P. Hawkins	Vicksburg, Miss	Commanding 1st division U. S. colored troops.
Gabriel R. Paul	Newport, Ky	Severely wounded.
Edward A. Wild	In the field, Va	On duty in 25th army corps.
Edward Ferrero	Bermuda Hundred, Va	Commanding defences of Bermuda Hundred.
Adelbert Ames	In the field, Va	Commanding 2d division 24th army corps.
William Birney	In the field, Va	Commanding 2d division 25th army corps.
Daniel H. Rucker	Washington, D. C	Chief depot quartermaster.
Robert Allen	Louisville, Ky	Chief Q. M. departments of the West.
Rufus Ingalls	City Point, Va	Chief Q. M. armies operating against Richmond.
Gustavus A. De Russey	Near Fort Corcoran, Va	Commanding division 22d army corps.
Alexander Shaler	Duvall's Bluff, Ark	Commanding 2d division 7th army corps.
Benjamin H. Grierson	Memphis, Tenn	Commanding cavalry division department of Mississippi.
Robert S. Foster	In the field, Va	Com'dg 1st div. 24th army corps. (On temporary leave of absence.)
Judson Kilpatrick	Savannah, Ga	Commanding 3d cavalry military division of Mississippi.
Alexander S. Webb	New York city	Member gen'l court-martial. (Under orders to army of Potomac.)
Alfred N. Duffie	Danville, Va	Prisoner of war.
Walter C. Whitaker	In the field, Tenn	Commanding 2d brigade 1st division 4th army corps.
Wesley Merritt	In the field, Va	Com'dg 1st cav. div. mid. mil. div. (On temporary leave of absence.)
George A. Custer	In the field, Va	Commanding 3d cavalry division middle military division.
William D. Whipple	Chattanooga, Tenn	Chief of Major-General Thomas's staff.
John C. Starkweather	Milwaukee, Wis	Awaiting orders.
Kenner Garrard	In the field, Ga	Commanding 2d cavalry division military division of Mississippi.
Charles R. Woods	Savannah, Ga	Commanding 1st brigade 1st division 15th army corps.
John B. Sanborn	Springfield, Mo	Commanding district of Southwest Missouri.

LIST OF MAJOR AND BRIGADIER-GENERALS OF VOLUNTEERS, &c.—(*Continued.*)

NAME AND RANK.	STATION.	HOW EMPLOYED.
Giles A. Smith	Savannah, Ga	Commanding 4th division 17th army corps.
Jasper A. Maltby	Vicksburg, Miss	Commanding brigade district of Vicksburg.
Thomas K. Smith	In the field, Tenn	Serving with det. of the army of Tennessee.
Walter Q. Gersham	New Albany, Ind	Wounded.
Manning F. Force	In the field, Ga	Commanding 1st brigade 3d division 17th army corps.
Robert A. Cameron	Thibodeaux, La	Commanding district of Lafourche.
John M. Corse	Savannah, Ga	Commanding 4th division 15th army corps.
John A. Rawlins	City Point, Va	Chief of General Grant's staff.
Alvan C. Gillem	In the field, Tenn	Commanding Governor's guard.
John W. Turner	Bermuda Hundred, Va	Chief of staff, department of Virginia and North Carolina.
Henry E. Davies	Army of Potomac	Commanding 1st brigade 2d cavalry division.
Andrew J. Hamilton	New Orleans, La	Under orders of Major-General Canby.
Henry W. Birge	In the field, Va	Commanding 1st brigade 2d division 19th army corps.
James H. Ledlie	Palatine Bridge, N. Y	Awaiting orders.
James H. Wilson	In the field, Tenn	Commanding cavalry corps, military division of Mississippi.
Adin B. Underwood	Newtonville, Mass	Wounded.
Augustus L. Chetlain	Memphis, Tenn	Commanding colored troops, State of Tennessee.
William A. Pile	Port Hudson, La	Commanding United States forces.
John W. Fuller	Savannah, Ga	Commanding 1st division 17th army corps.
John F. Miller	Nashville, Tenn	Commanding post.
Philip Regis de Trobriand	Army of Potomac	Commanding 1st brigade 3d division 2d army corps.
Cyrus Bussey	Little Rock, Ark	Commanding 2d brigade cavalry division, dep't of Arkansas.
Christopher C. Andrews	Steamer Niagara, Miss. river	En route to Morganzia, La. (On duty in department of Gulf.)
Edward M. McCook	In the field, Ga	Commanding 1st cavalry division, military division of Mississippi.
Lewis A. Grant	Army of Potomac	Commanding 2d brigade 2d division 6th army corps.
Edward Hatch	In the field, Tenn	Commanding 5th cavalry division, military division of Miss.
August V. Kautz	In the field, Va	Commanding cavalry division, dep't of Virginia and N. Carolina.
Francis Fessenden	Washington, D. C	Member of military commission. (Severely wounded.)
John F. Hartranft	Army of Potomac	Commanding 1st division 9th army corps.
Samuel S. Carroll	New York city	Member of general court-martial. (Severely wounded.)
Simon G. Griffin	Army of Potomac	Commanding 2d brigade 2d division 9th army corps.
Emory Upton	In the field, Tenn	Serving in dep't of the Cumberland. [army corps. (Wounded.)
John R. Brooke	Washington, D. C	Member board for examination of applicants for commissions in 1st
Nelson A. Miles	Army of Potomac	Commanding 1st division 2d army corps.
Joseph Hayes	Libby prison, Richmond, Va	Prisoner of war.
Byron R. Pierce	Army of Potomac	Commanding 2d brigade 3d division 2d army corps.
Selden Connor	Washington, D. C,	Severely wounded.
Joshua L. Chamberlain	Army of Potomac	Commanding 1st brigade 1st division 5th army corps.
Elliott W. Rice	Savannah, Ga	Commanding 1st brigade 4th division 15th army corps.
William F. Bartlett	Winthrop, Mass	Under medical treatment. [porary leave of absence.)
Edward S. Bragg	Army of Potomac	Commanding 1st brigade 4th division 5th army corps. (On tem-
Martin D. Hardin	Washington, D. C	Commanding division 22d army corps.
Charles J. Paine	In the field, Va	Commanding 1st division 25th army corps.
John B. McIntosh	Philadelphia, Pa	Severely wounded.
George H. Chapman	Winchester, Va	Member of military commission.
William Grose	In the field, Tenn	Commanding 3d brigade 1st division 4th army corps.
Joseph A. Cooper	In the field, Tenn	Commanding 1st brigade 2d division 23d army corps.
John T. Croxton	In the field, Tenn	Commanding 1st brigade 1st cavalry div. mil. div. of Mississippi.
John W. Sprague	Savannah, Ga	Commanding 2d brigade 1st division 17th army corps.
James W. Reilly	In the field, Tenn.	Commanding 1st brigade 3d division 23d army corps.
Luther P. Bradley	New Haven, Conn	Wounded. [leave of absence.)
Charles C. Walcutt	In the field, Ga	Commanding 2d brig. 4th div. 15th army corps. (On temporary
William W. Belknap	In the field, Ga	Commanding 3d brigade 4th division 17th army corps.
Powell Clayton	Pine Bluff, Ark	Commanding post.
Joseph A. Haskin	Washington, D. C	Chief of artillery, department of Washington.
James D. Fessenden	In the field, Va	Commanding 3d brigade 1st division 19th army corps.
Eli Long	Lexington, Ky	Wounded.
Thomas W. Eagan	Washington, D. C	Wounded.
Joseph R. Hawley	In the field, Va	Commanding 2d brigade 1st division 24th army corps.
William H. Seward, jr	Martinsburg, W. Va	Commanding post.
Isaac H. Duval	In the field, Va	Commanding 1st infantry division, department of W. Virginia.
John Edwards	Fort Smith, Ark	Commanding 1st brigade district of the frontier.
Thomas A. Smyth	Army of Potomac	Commanding 3d brigade 2d division 2d army corps.
Ferdinand Van Derveer	Hamilton, Ohio	Under orders to department of Cumberland.
Thomas C. Devin	In the field, Va	Com'dg 2d brigade 1st cavalry division middle military division.
Alfred Gibbs	In the field, Va	On duty in 1st cavalry division middle military division.
R. S. McKenzie	Army of Potomac	Commanding 2d brigade 1st division 6th army corps.
R. B. Hays	In the field, Va	Com'dg 1st brigade 1st inf. div., department of West Virginia.
James R. Slack	Memphis, Tenn	Com'dg 2d brig. 2d div. reserve corps, mil. div. of W. Mississippi.
Thomas J. Lucas	Indianapolis, Ind	On recruiting service.
E. J. Davis	Morganzia, La	Commanding cavalry brigade, department of Gulf.
Joseph Bailey	New Orleans, La	Commanding cavalry division, department of Gulf.
George L. Beal	In the field, Va	Commanding 1st brigade 1st division 19th army corps.
Henry G. Thomas	In the field, Va	Commanding 3d brigade 1st division 25th army corps.
Cyrus Hamlin	New Orleans, La	Commanding 3d div. U. S. colored troops, department of Gulf.

RECAPITULATION.

HOW EMPLOYED.	Maj. Generals.	Brig. Generals.	Aggregate.
On command	45	200	245
Before Committee on Conduct of the War	1	1	2
Awaiting orders	8	12	20
Commissioner for exchange and Commissary General of prisoners	1	1	2
Members of courts-martial, military commissions, &c	7	20	27
Off duty, on account of sickness or wounds	1	14	15
On special duty	2	12	14
On leave of absence	1	2	3
Under trial	....	3	3
Prisoners of War	....	2	2
Total	66	267	333

NAVY DEPARTMENT.

NAME.	DUTY.	Place of birth.	Where a citizen.	Date of original appointment.
Gideon Wells	Secretary	Connecticut	Connecticut	7 Mar., 1861
Gustavus V. Fox	Assistant Secretary	Massachusetts	Massachusetts	9 May, 1861
William Faxon	Chief Clerk	Connecticut	Connecticut	19 Mar., 1861
William Plume Moran	Clerk	Virginia	Virginia	8 Dec., 1852
do. do.	Disbursing Clerk			
Bureau of Yards and Docks.				
Joseph Smith	Chief of Bureau	Massachusetts	Massachusetts	25 May, 1846
William P. S. Sanger	Civil Engineer	Massachusetts	Dist. Columbia	15 Sept., 1842
John W. Bronaugh	Chief Clerk	Virginia	Dist. Columbia	4 June, 1849
Bureau of Navigation.				
Charles Henry Davis	Chief of Bureau	Massachusetts	Massachusetts	17 July, 1862
Benjamin F. Greene	Chief Clerk	New Hampshire	New York	19 Feb., 1863
Bureau of Ordnance.				
Henry A. Wise	Chief of Bureau	New York	New York	25 June, 1863
Richmond Aulick	Assistant	Connecticut	Virginia	28 June, 1863
C. E. Graves	Chief Clerk	Vermont	Vermont	9 Aug., 1861
Bureau of Equipment and Recruiting.				
Albert N. Smith	Chief of Bureau	Maine	Massachusetts	30 May, 1863
S. Henriques	Chief Clerk	Sweden	New York	2 Sept., 1862
Bureau of Medicine and Surgery.				
William Whelan	Chief of Bureau	Pennsylvania	Pennsylvania	1 Oct., 1853
Phineas J. Horwitz	Assistant to Bureau	Maryland	Pennsylvania	3 June, 1859
Bureau of Provisions and Clothing.				
Horatio Bridge	Chief of Bureau	Maine	Maine	1 Oct., 1854
Thomas Fillebrown	Chief Clerk	Maine	Maine	1 Sept., 1842
Bureau of Construction and Repair.				
John Lenthall	Chief of Bureau	Dist. Columbia	Pennsylvania	18 Nov., 1853
James W. Deeble	Chief Clerk	Dist. Columbia	Dist. Columbia	6 April, 1861
Bureau of Steam Engineering.				
Benjamin F. Isherwood	Chief of Bureau	New York	New York	25 July, 1862
William H. Allyn	Chief Clerk	Connecticut	Wisconsin	9 Jan., 1863

REAR ADMIRALS OF THE NAVY.

NAME.	State where born.	State of which a citizen.	Original entry into the service.	Date of present commission.
Active List.				
David G. Farragut,*	Tennessee	Tennessee	17 Dec., 1810	16 July, 1862
Louis M. Goldsborough	District Columbia	Maryland	18 June, 1812	16 July, 1862
Samuel F. Dupont	New Jersey	Delaware	19 Dec., 1815	16 July, 1862
Charles Henry Davis	Massachusetts	Massachusetts	12 Aug., 1823	7 Feb., 1863
John A. Dahlgren	Pennsylvania	Pennsylvania	1 Feb., 1826	7 Feb., 1863
David D. Porter	Pennsylvania	Pennsylvania	2 Feb., 1829	4 July, 1863
Retired List.				
Charles Stewart	Pennsylvania	New Jersey	†9 Mar., 1798	16 July, 1862
William B. Shubrick	South Carolina	South Carolina	20 June, 1806	16 July, 1862
Joseph Smith	Massachusetts	Massachusetts	16 Jan., 1809	16 July, 1862
Francis H. Gregory	Connecticut	Connecticut	16 Jan., 1809	16 July, 1862
Silas H. Stringham	New York	New York	15 Nov., 1809	16 July, 2862
Samuel L. Breese	New York	New York	17 Dec., 1810	16 July, 1862
Hiram Paulding	New York	New York	1 Sept., 1811	16 July, 1862

COMMODORES OF THE NAVY.

Active List.				
Thomas T. Craven	District Columbia	New York	1 May, 1822	16 July, 1862
Henry K. Hoff	Pennsylvania	South Carolina	28 Oct., 1823	16 July, 1862
Henry H. Bell	North Carolina	New York	4 Aug., 1823	16 July, 1862
William Smith	Kentucky	Missouri	4 Mar., 1823	16 July, 1862
John W. Livingston	New York	New York	4 Mar., 1823	16 July, 1862
Henry K. Thatcher	Maine	Maine	4 Mar., 1823	16 July, 1862
John S. Missroon	South Carolina	South Carolina	27 June, 1824	16 July, 1862
Robert B. Hitchcock	Connecticut	Connecticut	1 Jan., 1825	16 July, 1862
Stephen C. Rowan	Ohio	Ohio	1 Feb., 1826	16 July, 1862
Joseph Lanman	Connecticut	Connecticut	1 Jan., 1825	29 Aug., 1862
Thomas Turner	Virginia	Pennsylvania	21 April, 1825	13 Dec., 1863
Charles H. Poor	Massachusetts	District Columbia	1 Mar., 1825	2 Jan., 1863
Timothy A. Hunt	Connecticut	Connecticut	1 Feb., 1825	2 Jan., 1863
Sylvanus W. Godon	Pennsylvania	Pennsylvania	1 Mar., 1819	2 Jan., 1863
James S. Palmer	New Jersey	New Jersey	1 Jan., 1825	7 Feb., 1863
William Radford	Virginia	Missouri	1 Mar., 1825	24 April, 1863
John Rodgers	Maryland	Maryland	18 April, 1828	17 June, 1863

* Appointed Vice-Admiral December 21, 1864.

† As lieutenant.

COMMODORES OF THE NAVY.—(*Continued.*)

NAME.	State where born.	State of which a citizen.	Original entry into the service.	Date of present commission.
Retired List.				
John D. Sloat	New York	New York	12 Feb., 1800	16 July, 1862
William Mervine	Pennsylvania	New York	16 Jan., 1809	16 July, 1862
Thomas Crabbe	Maryland	Pennsylvania	15 Nov., 1809	16 July, 1862
John C. Long	New Hampshire	New Hampshire	18 June, 1812	16 July, 1862
John B. Montgomery	New Jersey	New Jersey	4 June, 1812	16 July, 1862
Cornelius K. Stribling	South Carolina	South Carolina	18 June, 1812	16 July, 1862
Joshua R. Sands	New York	New York	18 June, 1812	16 July, 1862
Charles H. Bell	New York	New York	18 June, 1812	16 July, 1892
Joseph R. Jarvis	Massachusetts	Maine	18 June, 1812	16 July, 1862
William C. Nicholson	Maryland	Maryland	18 June, 1812	16 July, 1862
Joseph B. Hull	New York	Connecticut	9 Nov., 1813	16 July, 1862
William H. Gardner	Maryland	Pennsylvania	6 Dec., 1814	16 July, 1862
T. Aloysius Dornin	Ireland	Maryland	2 May, 1815	16 July, 1862
Frederick Engle	Pennsylvania	Pennsylvania	6 Dec., 1814	16 July, 1862
John Rudd	Rhode Island	Virginia	30 Nov., 1814	16 July, 1862
William W. McKean	Pennsylvania	Pennsylvania	30 Nov., 1814	16 July, 1862
Charles Lowndes	Maryland	Maryland	28 Mar., 1815	16 July, 1862
John Marston	Massachusetts	Pennsylvania	15 April, 1813	16 July, 1862
Henry A. Adams	Pennsylvania	Pennsylvania	15 Mar., 1814	16 July, 1862
George F. Pearson*	New Hampshire	Massachusetts	11 Mar., 1815	16 July, 1862
John Pope	Massachusetts	Maine	30 May, 1816	16 July, 1862
Levin M. Powell	Virginia	Virginia	1 Mar., 1817	16 July, 1862
Charles Wilkes †	New York	New York	1 Jan., 1818	16 July, 1862
Henry Eagle	New York	New York	1 Jan., 1818	16 July, 1862
William M. Glendy	Virginia	Virginia	1 Jan., 1818	16 July, 1862
George S. Blake	Massachusetts	Massachusetts	23 April, 1818	16 July, 1862
Andrew A. Harwood	Pennsylvania	Pennsylvania	1 Jan., 1818	16 July, 1862
Theodorus Bailey	New York	New York	1 Jan., 1818	16 July, 1862
Hugh Y. Purviance	Maryland	Maryland	3 Nov., 1818	16 July, 1862
Cadwalader Ringgold	Maryland	Maryland	4 Mar., 1819	16 July, 1862
James L. Lardner	Pennsylvania	Pennsylvania	26 July, 1820	16 July, 1862

* Acting Rear Admiral.
† Reprimanded and suspended for three years from May 3, 1864. Two years of his suspension was remitted by the President, December 27, 1864.

BIOGRAPHICAL SKETCHES.

1861.

May 24.—EPHRAIM ELMER ELLSWORTH, a colonel of volunteers and the introducer of the Zouave drill and organization into the United States, born at Mechanicsville, Saratogo Co., New York, April 23, 1837, killed at Alexandria, Virginia, May 24, 1861. The financial misfortunes which overtook his father during Elmer's early childhood, prevented him from obtaining the object of his boyish ambition, a cadetship at West Point; but, passionately fond of study, he acquired a good English education. After brief engagements in mercantile employment in Troy and New York, he went to Chicago, and though not yet of age, commenced business for himself as a patent solicitor, and soon attained success and a handsome income; but through the fraud of one whom he had trusted was despoiled of his hard earnings. Instead of giving way to despondency, he turned his attention to the study of law, supporting himself meanwhile by copying law papers at night. But while thus rapidly familiarizing himself with the science of law, his predilection for the military profession was very strong; and having attained a thorough familiarity with the French *chasseur d'Afrique* or Zouave drill and organization, he resolved to form a Zouave corps in Chicago, with such modifications as he deemed desirable to better adapt it to this country and the genius of the people. The corps which he organized and of which he became the commander, was a remarkable one; the strictest abstinence from spirituous liquors and tobacco was enforced, and the drill was exceedingly severe in its gymnastic requirements. They had been organized less than a year when their extraordinary performances won them at the State Agricultural Fair a stand of colors, and in July, 1860, with their gallant commander at their head and bearing their prize colors, they visited the Eastern cities, and challenged competition in their military discipline and practice, and won golden opinions everywhere. On his return to Chicago he organized a Zouave regiment, which he offered to the governor for the defence of the State, as if in premonition of the coming struggle. During the autumn Ellsworth entered heartily into the political campaign, advocating the election of Mr. Lincoln. After the election he accompanied the President elect to Washington, where he received a lieutenant's commission preparatory to his entrance into the War Department, and had already matured in his own mind a reorganization of the militia of the country. The breaking out of the war changed his plans. At the proclamation of the President on the 15th of April, he hastened to New York, organized a Zouave regiment of 1,200 men from the Fire Department, and in three weeks marched at their head through Pennsylvania Avenue, Washington. He drilled his regiment assiduously, and, more than any other man could have done, tamed and controlled those restless and ungovernable spirits. On the 23d of May his regiment was ordered to Alexandria, which they reached early in the morning of the 24th. Seeing a secession flag flying over a hotel (the Marshall House), he entered and demanded of a man whom he met there, whose flag it was; the man, who was really the proprietor of the house, professed not to know, saying he was only a lodger; and Ellsworth, with two companions, ascended to the roof and took it down, wrapping it around his body. As he descended he said, "This is my trophy." "And you are mine," said Jackson, the proprietor, pouring the contents of his shot gun full into the breast of the colonel, and instantly falling himself from a musket ball through the head and a deadly bayonet thrust from one of Ellsworth's Zouaves, Francis E. Brownell. Jackson was captain of an artillery company in his own county. He was known by his neighbors as a man who united a dauntless courage with generous impulses. A week before his death a Union man from Washington had been seized in the streets of Alexandria, and a crowd threatened to shoot or hang him. He rescued him, and threatened to kill any man who should molest him. The body of Col. Ellsworth was borne sadly back to Washington, and the funeral services performed at the White House, with the President as chief mourner. From thence it was brought to his birthplace (Mechanicsville). A noble regiment, made up of one man from a town, in his native State, was raised as his fittest, though not his only monument.

June 10.—JOHN TROUT GREBLE, an officer of the United States army, born in Philadelphia, January 19, 1834, and killed in the battle of Great Bethel, Virginia, June 10, 1861. He acquired his early education at the Ringgold Grammar School and the Central High School of his native city, receiving his bachelor's degree at the latter in 1850, and immediately entered the United States Military Academy at West Point, where he graduated in 1854, with high rank in his class. On his graduation he was immediately commissioned as brevet second lieutenant in the 2d artillery, and stationed at Newport, R. I. In September of the same year he was made second lieutenant and sent to Tampa, Florida, where he served in the Indian troubles for two years, when he was compelled, in consequence of a severe fever, to return home on sick leave; but in the beginning of 1856 resumed his duties, acting a part of the time as quartermaster and commissary till December, 1856, when he was appointed acting assistant professor of Ethics in the Military Academy, the duties of which professorship he performed with credit and success till October, 1860, when, at his own request, he was detailed for active duty at Fortress Monroe. There he rendered efficient service in preventing the seizure of the fortress. On the 26th of May, 1861, he was sent to Newport News as master of ordnance, superintended the fortification of that point, and trained the volunteers to artillery practice. When the disastrous expedition to Great Bethel was planned, he was unexpectedly detailed to accompany it with two guns; and though in his own judgment it was ill-advised, and would probably prove fatal to him, he did not hesitate, but took an active part in its duties; and when the Federal troops were repulsed, by his admirable management of his guns protected them from pursuit and utter annihilation. Just at the close of the action, when he had given the order to withdraw from the field, he was struck by a cannon ball on the right temple and instantly killed.

June 10.—Major THEODORE WINTHROP, an officer of volunteers in the United States army, and an American author, born in New Haven, Conn., September 22, 1828, killed in the battle of Great Bethel, June 10, 1861. He graduated with high honors at Yale College in 1848, and soon after, partly to recruit his health, impaired by too close application, sailed for Europe, where he made an extensive tour mostly on foot. In Italy he formed the acquaintance of W. H. Aspinwall, of New York, and upon his return became tutor to his son, with whom he afterwards again visited Europe. Returning from this second tour, he entered the employ of the Pacific Mail Steamship Company and went to Panama, where he resided about two years. He then joined the unfortunate expedition of Lieutenant Strain, the exposures of which injured his health to such a degree that he was compelled to return to New York. He next engaged in the study of law, and was admitted to the bar in 1855. He first practised in St. Louis, but finding the climate unfavorable, he returned again to New York, where his fondness for literary pursuits drew him aside from his profession.

At the commencement of hostilities which resulted in the present war, he enrolled himself in the artillery corps of the 7th regiment, and subsequently was made acting military secretary and aid by Gen. Butler. His description of the forty-two days' campaign of the 7th regiment, in the June, July, and August numbers of the Atlantic Monthly, attracted much attention by its gracefulness and brilliancy, and the interest thus excited was afterwards heightened by his untimely death. In the autumn of 1861 Messrs. Ticknor and Fields, of Boston, published two works of fiction of considerable merit, "Cecil Dreeme" and "John Brent," which were found among his papers after his death.

June 17.—Col. HOLLOWAY, an officer of the Missouri State Guard, killed at the battle of the Big Blue, in Jackson County, Missouri. Had been a captain in the U. S. regular army, and was deeply deplored by Gen. Sterling Price's army. He had rendered great service in organizing Missouri troops, and there were few in that army and at that time who could fill his place.

June 27*th*.—JAMES HARMAN WARD, commander in the United States navy, son of Col. James Ward of Hartford, Conn.; born in that city in 1806, killed in the attack on Matthias Point, June 27, 1861. He was educated at the Vermont Military Academy at Norwich, and from thence entered Trinity College, Hartford. On the 4th of March, 1823, he received an appointment as midshipman on board of the Constitution, commanded by Commodore McDonough; rose to the rank of lieutenant on the 3d of March, 1831, and was attached to the Mediterranean squadron. For several years he was on the coast of Africa, and while there compiled his "Manual of Naval Tactics," published in 1858. In 1842–'43 he delivered in Philadelphia a popular course of lectures on Gunnery. He urged upon the Government the necessity of establishing a Naval School, and upon the opening of the school, was appointed one of the professors, and gave a series of lectures, subsequently published under the title of "Elementary Instructions on Naval Ordnance and Gunnery:" a work which has accomplished much in its effects upon naval science.

Soon after the introduction of steam into the navy, he gave the result of his observations in a work entitled "Steam for the Million," subsequently republished by Van Nostrand, New York. In 1853 he was made commander, and in 1857 was appointed to the command of the receiving ship North Carolina, lying at the Brooklyn Navy Yard. At the commencement of the war he was summoned to Washington to aid the Government by his counsels. Here he remained and organized the Potomac flotilla, to the command of which he was appointed on May 16, 1861. On the 31st, he, with the Freeborn, Anacosta, and Resolute, cannonaded the Confederate batteries at Aquia Creek, silencing three of them, and only retiring when his ammunition was exhausted. The next day, aided by the Pawnee, he resumed the attack, and succeeded in silencing the guns. On June 26th, on discovering that a battery was being erected at Matthias Point by the enemy, he sent to the Pawnee for aid to throw up breastworks; when completed, as the men were returning to the boats for the guns, a destructive fire was opened upon them by the enemy in ambush. The crew hastened to the steamer, the Freeborn covering their retreat. Capt. Ward gallantly stood at his post sighting one of the guns, when he was struck by a Minié ball and almost instantly killed. He was buried at Hartford, Conn.

July 5.—BENJ. J. BROWN, inspector-general, with the rank of colonel, on Gen. Slack's staff, who then commanded a division of the Missouri State Guard. He had held the position of president of the Senate of the State of Missouri, and was killed in the battle of Wilson Creek, in Missouri. He had participated in the battle of Carthage, and distinguished himself for dashing courage and cool judgment.

July 5.—RICHARD C. COXE, colonel in Missouri State Guard, killed at the battle of Carthage, in Missouri. At the opening of the war he lived in the town of Atchison, in Kansas, and took a prominent part in the Kansas troubles.

July 15.—ROBT. SELDEN GARNETT, an officer of the Confederate army, born in Virginia about 1821, and killed in the battle of Carrick's Ford, July 15, 1861. He entered West Point in 1837, and graduated 27th in his class in 1841, was appointed brevet second lieutenant of artillery on his graduation, and from July, 1843, to Oct., 1844, was assistant-instructor of infantry tactics at the military academy; was aide-de-camp to Gen. Wool in 1845, distinguished himself in the battles of Palo Alto and Resaca de la Palma, was promoted to a first lieutenancy in 1846, was aide-de-camp to Gen. Taylor through the Mexican war and until 1849, was breveted captain and major for gallant and meritorious conduct at Monterey and Buena Vista; transferred to the infantry in 1848, and promoted to a captaincy in 1851. From 1852 to 1854 he was commandant of the corps of cadets, and instructor in infantry tactics at West Point; appointed captain of the 1st regiment cavalry in 1805, and major of 9th infantry in the same month; was the commander in the operations against the Indians on Puget's Sound, Washington Territory, in 1856, and commanded the Yakima expedition in 1858. At the breaking out of the present war he took the side of the Confederates, was promoted to a brigadier-generalship, and assigned to the department of Western Virginia. Here, in July, Gen. McClellan attacked him, and after several days of alternate fighting and retreating, at the decisive action of Carrick's Ford, Gen. Garnett was killed and his forces routed. His body was carefully cared for by the Federal commander, and after being embalmed, was forwarded to his friends.

July 21.—Major SULLIVAN BALLOU, of the 2d Rhode Island regiment of volunteers, killed at the battle of Bull Run. He was born at Smithfield, R. I., March 28, 1829. In 1846 he entered Phillips' Academy at Andover, Mass., and subsequently Brown University. After remaining two years at the latter, he proceeded to the National Law School at Ballston, N. Y. In 1853 he was admitted to the Rhode Island bar, and practised his profession with little interruption in Smithfield and Providence until he left with his regiment for the seat of war. He was clerk of the House of Representatives of Rhode Island during the years 1854, 1855, and 1856, and the following year was Speaker of the House. In 1861 he held the office of Judge Advocate of the Rhode Island militia. He joined the army from a patriotic sense of duty, and his military career, though short, won him distinguished honor.

July 21.—FRANCIS S. BARTOW, a colonel of the 8th Georgia regiment, in the Confederate army, killed at the battle of Bull Run, in Virginia. At that battle he commanded a brigade, but at the head of the 8th Georgia regiment had charged a battery that was doing great havoc among Confederate troops, and had been repulsed. When Gen. Johnston, however, told him that the battery must be taken, he seized the standard of the 7th Georgia regiment and exclaimed, "I will do what mortal man can," and charged and took the battery, but was killed. "They have killed me," he cried, "but never give up the field." Col. Bartow was chairman of the military committee of the Richmond Congress, and upon his death that body paid a high tribute to his memory. His heroism in the battle of Bull Run, or Manassas Junction as it is called in the South, was so conspicuous as to attract the notice and eulogy of the entire Southern people. Some time before the battle, upon being told that Congress needed his services, he answered that his country needed his services on that field, and he would not leave until after the battle; and upon being told that he was too confident of success, and that the odds were very great in favor of the other side, he exclaimed with great fervor, "They can never whip us. We shall not count the odds. We may be exterminated, but never conquered. I shall go into this fight with the determination never to leave the field alive but in victory; and I know that the same spirit actuates my whole command. How, then, can they whip us?" On that sanguinary plateau near the Henry House, also fell Bartow, pierced through the heart by a Minié ball.

July 21.—BERNARD E. BEE, a brigadier-general in the Confederate army, killed at the battle of Bull Run. Gen. Bee was a native of South Carolina, and entered West Point from that State. He graduated fourth in his class, with high honors, in July, 1845, and entered the 3d infantry regiment. He served with marked distinction in the Mexican war, and was brevetted first lieutenant for gallant and meritorious conduct at the battle of Cerro Gordo, April 18, 1847 (March, 1849), in which he was wounded. He was brevetted captain for gallant and meritorious conduct at the storming of Chapultepec, Sept. 13, 1847 (March, 1847). He was afterwards adjutant. In subsequent wars with the Indians he achieved great success and distinction, winning the approbation of his native State, which presented him with a superb sword. Gen. Bee contributed in a large degree to the achievement of Confederate success at Bull Run. His stubborn resistance with his small force to the fierce charges and concentrated fire of artillery of the Federal troops, and his repeated and desperate charges subsequently upon being reenforced, rendered the plateau near the Henry House the bloodiest spot on the battle-field, and materially influenced the fortunes of the day. He died grasping the sword South Carolina had taken so much pride in presenting to him.

July 21.—Col. JAMES CAMERON, born at Maytown, Lancaster Co., Penn., March 1, 1801. In youth he engaged in various occupations, and at 19 years of age entered the printing office of his brother Simon, at Harrisburg. In 1827 he removed to Lancaster and assumed the editorship of the "Political Sentinel," studying law in the mean time in the office of the late President, James Buchanan. During the Mexican war he accompanied the volunteers of his State as sutler, in January, 1847. When the present war broke out he was living in retirement upon his estate on the banks of the Susquehanna, but upon urgent entreaty accepted the appointment of colonel of the 79th Highland regiment of the New York State militia, and from his election devoted himself assiduously to the duties of his position. In the battle of Bull Run, when his regiment was driven back before the terrible fire of the enemy, he would lead them up again and again with the shout, "Scots, follow me!" until he fell in the deadly charge.

July 21.— —— FISHER, colonel in the Confederate army, commanded the 6th North Carolina regiment; killed at Bull Run, in Virginia.

July 21.—Col. JOHN S. SLOCUM, born in the town of Richmond, R. I., Nov. 1, 1824. At the commencement of the Mexican war he obtained a commission in the army, and at Contreras received the brevet rank of captain for meritorious conduct. At the beginning of the present war Gov. Sprague appointed him colonel, and authorized him to raise a second regiment, which he speedily accomplished and again marched to the seat of war. At the battle of Bull Run his regiment led the advance of the division which crossed Cob Run and reached Bull Run at Sudley's ford, on the extreme left of the enemy's line. Here he bravely led on his regiment through the woods, and opened that terrible engagement, but fell almost in the beginning of the action.

July 21.—F. J. THOMAS, a colonel in the Confederate army. He was acting chief of ordnance on Gen. Joseph E. Johnston's staff, and was killed at the battle of Bull Run.

July 21.—Capt. OTIS H. TILLINGHAST, born at Homer, Cortlandt Co., N. Y., March 6, 1823. In 1847 he graduated with honor at the military academy at West Point, and was immediately appointed brevet second lieutenant in the 3d artillery, and joined Sherman's battery, under Gen. Taylor, at Saltillo, Mexico. In 1848 he was associated with the Mexican Boundary Commission, and in 1856 was appointed regimental quartermaster, and stationed in Florida. Soon after he was ordered to Fort Moultrie, where he remained until about the time of the insurrection. In July, 1861, Lieut. Tillinghast was appointed chief-quartermaster to Gen. McDowell's army, and attached himself to the division commanded by Col. Porter. Though his duties did not require him to take part in the battle, he entered with alacrity into the field, and fell early in the enagement, mortally wounded.

July 21.—Capt. LEVI TOWER, killed at the battle of Bull Run. Born in the village of Blackstone, Mass., August 18, 1835. He took a thorough classical course in the University Grammar School in Providence, and in due time entered Brown University, which he was subsequently compelled to leave in consequence of ill health. He was a member of the Pawtucket Light Guard, and with it joined the 1st regiment of Rhode Island volunteers.

July 22.—Col. WILLIAM D. KENNEDY, commander of the "Tammany" regiment of N. Y. volunteers. He was a prominent democrat of New York city, and a man of great energy and ability. He died at Washington of congestion of the brain.

Aug. 10.— —— CAWTHORN, colonel in the Missouri State Guard in the Confederate service. He had shown considerable ability and courage at the battle of Carthage, July 5, 1861. He commanded a brigade of cavalry in Gen. Rains' division, and was very badly wounded in the foot at Wilson's Creek, and refusing to permit amputation, he died after a few days of suffering.

August 10.—NATHANIEL LYON, a general of volunteers in the United States army, born at Ashford, Windham Co., Connecticut, July

14, 1819, killed at the battle of Wilson's Creek, Missouri, August 10, 1861. His mother was a daughter of Lieut. Daniel Knowlton, who served through the old French war and the Revolution. Gen. Lyon graduated at the Military Academy at West Point in 1841, and immediately received the appointment of second lieutenant in the 2d regiment of infantry. His first field of service was Florida, during the latter part of the Seminole war, where he distinguished himself as an able and energetic officer. He was subsequently stationed for several years at different posts on the western frontier. In 1847 he was promoted to a first lieutenancy, and upon the commencement of the war with Mexico was again ordered to active service. He joined Gen. Taylor at Monterey, and accompanied his regiment when it was detached from the command of Gen. Taylor and placed under that of Gen. Scott. He served at the bombardment of Vera Cruz and the battles of Cerro Gordo, Contreras, and Churubusco, and for "meritorious conduct" received the brevet rank of captain. At the close of the war with Mexico, Gen. Lyon was ordered to California, and detailed to service among the Indian tribes, who had become troublesome, and while engaged in this service was promoted to a full captaincy in 1851. From California Gen. Lyon was ordered to Kansas, during the height of the political troubles there, and used his influence to maintain order and calm the strife of partisans. Some of his articles written for the press at this period, bear evidence of great vigor of intellect, and earnest devotion to his country's good. Early in 1861 Capt. Lyon was placed in command of the United States arsenal at St. Louis; after the fall of Fort Sumter the possession of Missouri seemed to depend upon his energy and coolness. The police commissioners of St. Louis assumed to themselves the power of opposing the Government, and demanded that Capt. Lyon should confine his jurisdiction to the arsenal grounds; this he refused. Not long before the Governor of Missouri had authorized the formation of camps in various parts of the State. Taken in connection with the action of the commissioners, Capt. Lyon considered the concentration of these forces as an act of open hostility to the Government, and suddenly surrounded one of the camps, known as Camp Jackson, with a large force of the State "Home Guards" under Cols. Blair and Sigel, and, planting his guns on the heights, demanded of Gen. Frost, the commander of Camp Jackson, an immediate surrender; satisfied that he was unable to resist so large a force, Gen. Frost yielded up his whole command as prisoners of war. A few days later Gen. Harney arrived at St. Louis and assumed the command, and Capt. Lyon was appointed general of the 1st brigade of Missouri volunteers. He broke up a Confederate force at Potosi, and caused several important seizures of war material destined for Camp Jackson. Upon the removal of Gen. Harney, Gen. Lyon was placed in command of the department. Gov. Jackson and Gen. Price sought an interview with him, in which they insisted that no United States troops should march through or quarter in Missouri, although they had already allowed Confederate troops to do so. Lyon's reply was that the troops of the United States should march peaceably everywhere through the United States, offering insult to none, but would oppose every attack and crush every effort to molest them. Upon this Gov. Jackson withdrew from St. Louis and prepared for war. Gen. Lyon then took the field, but previously issued a proclamation to the citizens of Missouri, in which, after rehearsing the various acts of Gov. Jackson, he concludes: "If, in suppressing these treasonable projects, carrying out the policy of the Government, and maintaining its dignity, hostilities should unfortunately occur, and unhappy consequences should follow, I would hope that all aggravation of those events may be avoided, and that they may be diverted from the innocent and may fall on the heads of those by whom they have been provoked. In the discharge of these plain but onerous duties I shall look for the countenence and active coöperation of all good citizens, and I shall expect them to discountenance all illegal combinations or organizations, and support and uphold, by every lawful means, the Federal Government, upon the maintenance of which depends their liberties and the perfect enjoyment of all their rights."

Learning that Gov. Jackson and Gen. Price had commenced hostilities, Gen. Lyon moved toward Jefferson City with a small force, and upon his approach Gov. Jackson abandoned his position and retreated to Booneville, where a battle was fought on the 17th of June, which resulted in a complete victory, all the tents, ammunition, and supplies falling into Gen. Lyon's hands. Upon entering Booneville, he issued a proclamation, in which, after a statement of the facts in relation to the battle, he said: "I hereby give notice to the people of this State that I shall scrupulously avoid all interference with the business, rights, and property of every description recognized by the laws of the State, and belonging to law-abiding citizens. But it is equally my duty to maintain the paramount authority of the United States with such force as I have at my command, which will be retained only so long as opposition makes it necessary, and that it is my wish, and shall be my purpose, to visit any unavoidable rigor arising in this issue upon those only who provoke it."

He soon after moved forward to Springfield, an important town of Southwestern Missouri, driving the Confederates before him, and defeating them at Dug Spring, about fifteen miles from that town. Subsequent to the battle of Dug Spring, the Confederates received heavy reënforcements, and Gen. Lyon, after making several appeals to the Government for more troops, and receiving no response, called a council of war to determine upon the question of evacuating Springfield. Fearing any retrograde movement would be fatal to the cause, it was decided to attack Gens. McCulloch and Price in their camp at Wilson's Creek, though with scarcely any hope of success, as the Union force was but a little over five thousand, while the Confederate force was nearly twenty-five thousand. The battle was a desperate one, and Gen Lyon, after being twice wounded, was killed, while making a gallant charge at the head of the 1st Iowa regiment, which had lost its colonel. His body was subsequently conveyed to Connecticut, the home of his parents, and upon its way was received everywhere with marked respect. Military honors were paid to it at Cincinnati, Pittsburg, Philadelphia, Jersey City, and New York. The funeral oration was delivered by Galusha A. Grow, Speaker of the United States House of Representatives. In Congress, Senator Pomeroy delivered an eloquent tribute to his memory, and the following resolutions passed both houses:

Resolved, by the Senate and House of Representatives of the United States of America in Congress assembled—*First*, That Congress deems it just and proper to enter upon its records a recognition of the eminent and patriotic services of the late Brigadier-General Nathaniel Lyon. The country to whose services he devoted his life will guard and preserve his fame as a part of its own glory. *Second*, That the thanks of Congress are hereby given to the brave officers and soldiers who, under the command of the late General Lyon, sustained the honor of the flag, and achieved victory against overwhelming numbers at the battle of Springfield, in Missouri, and that, in order to commemorate an event so honorable to the country and to themselves, it is ordered that each regiment engaged shall be authorized to bear upon its colors the word "Springfield," embroidered in letters of gold. And the President of the United States is hereby requested to cause these resolutions to be read at the head of every regiment in the army of the United States.

Upon opening his will, it was ascertained that Gen. Lyon had bequeathed his entire property, $30,000, with the exception of some slight bequests, to the Government, to aid in the preservation of the Union.

Aug. 10.—CARY GRATZ, major in the Federal army, killed at the battle of Wilson's Creek, in Missouri, aged about 28 years. He was a native of Kentucky, and had large and influential connections in that State. For many years, however, he had been a highly esteemed commission merchant in St. Louis, where his untimely death was sincerely mourned.

Aug. 10.—CHARLES ROGGERS, major in the Missouri State Guard in the Confederate service, killed at Wilson's Creek, in Missouri, aged about thirty years. Major Roggers was an old resident of St. Louis, and a prominent politician. He early espoused the cause of the South, and was one of the association in St. Louis called minute men, before the war was actually commenced.

Aug. 10.—RICHARD HANSOM WEIGHTMAN, a colonel in the Missouri State Guard in the service of the Confederate States, killed at the battle of Wilson's Creek, or, as it is called in the South, "Oak Hills." He commanded a brigade of Missourians at that battle, and had organized and drilled them himself. They composed the best brigade then in that army. It was the excellent fighting of this brigade, and the military sagacity of its commander, that worsted Sigel's lines on the left of the line of battle. Col. Weightman was then sent to the right (Confederate left), when the long and sanguinary contest raged for the possession of Bloody Hill, where Gen. Lyon fell and where Col. Weightman was killed. He had manifested marked military abilities in the battle of Carthage, July 5, 1861, and distinguished himself by his reckless courage. He was a native of the District of Columbia, and the son of General Weightman. He entered West Point from the District of Columbia, and was a cadet from Aug., 1835, to April, 1837. He was expelled for cutting a brother cadet in the face with a knife, in a personal rencontre. With the same knife he killed the celebrated Santa Fé trader, F. X. Xaubrey, in a personal difficulty. He served in the Mexican war as captain in Major M. L. Clark's volunteer light artillery battalion from Missouri, and distinguished himself under Col. Doniphan at the battle of Sacramento; was additional paymaster until May, 1848, and mustered out of service August, 1849. Upon the organization of New Mexico, Col. Weightman was chosen provisionally United States senator from New Mexico, 1850. He afterwards represented New Mexico in the U. S. Congress, from the year 1851 to 1853. His loss to Gen. Price's army was very seriously felt. He had done much by his military acquirements and energy toward perfecting the organization and the discipline of Price's raw troops, and in that day of military ignorance none could be found able to fill his place.

Aug. 14.—Col. NOAH L. FARNHAM, born at Haddam, Conn., June 6, 1829. At 18 years of age he became a member of the New York "City Guard," and was on active duty at the time of the "Astor Place Riot." In 1857 he was elected second sergeant in the "Seventh Regiment," in which he was a recruit. When the "Seventh" left for Washington, Farnham was acting as first lieutenant, but upon Ellsworth's arrival at Washington with his regiment, he prevailed upon Farnham to accept the office of lieutenant-colonel of the Zouaves, and upon the death of Ellsworth he became colonel. When his regiment received orders to move on to Manassas he was confined to a sick bed, but rose, and, placing himself at the head of his men, hastened to the scene of action. Col. F. fought gallantly, but early in the engagement received a wound in his head, which, in his exhausted state, soon terminated fatally.

Sept. 10.—Col. JOHN WILLIAMSON LOWE, of the Ohio volunteers, killed at Carnifex ferry. He was born in New Brunswick, N. J., Nov. 15, 1809. When the Mexican war broke out, having some military knowledge, and feeling that his country needed his services, he accepted the command of the 4th Ohio regiment and went to the seat of war, serving until it was disbanded in 1848. When the rebellion began, he once more offered himself to his country. The 12th regiment was organized and he was unanimously chosen its colonel, and, united to the Cox brigade, they advanced up the Kanawha River. The only battle necessary to clear the Kanawha valley of the rebels was fought by the 12th, under Col. Lowe's command.

Sept. 15.—JOHN A. WASHINGTON, colonel in tho Confederate army, shot in a skirmish. He was a collateral descendant of the Washington family, and had been the proprietor of Mount Vernon, but sold it for $200,000 to the Mount Vernon Association.

Sept. 17.—Col. —— JOHNSTON, an officer of the Confederate army, killed in battle in Missouri.

Oct. 21.—EDWARD D. BAKER, an American senator and soldier, born in England about the beginning of the present century, and killed at the head of his column, at the battle of Ball's Bluff, Va., Oct. 21, 1861. He came to this country when five years of age, and found a home in Philadelphia, to which place his father, who was a member of the Society of Friends, was attracted by the large number of Friends in that vicinity. Before he reached the age of early manhood his father died and left Edward and a younger brother with no near relatives in this country, and portionless. Stout-hearted and self-reliant, the boy found work by which he could support his brother and himself, as a weaver, in a small establishment in South Street, Philadelphia. His leisure moments were earnestly occupied with reading, and most of his reading was of an instructive character. The West was then a region of romance, and its broad prairies and fertile soil presented attractions to those who looked forward to fortune in the future. Young Baker resolved to go thither, and taking his brother with him, the two youthful emigrants started westward with their packs upon their shoulders, with light hearts and purses as light. Crossing the then new States of Ohio and Indiana, they finally reached Springfield, Illinois, which Edward deemed the place for their future home. Here he soon commenced the study and the practice of law, and having a natural gift of oratory, to which his extensive reading had added a large vocabulary, he soon became one of the most popular advocates in the State. Uniting his fortunes with those of the Whig party, he soon won his way to political honors, and in 1846–'47 was elected to Congress from his district, and was fast becoming recognized as one of the leaders of his party, when the commencement of the Mexican war attracted his ardent spirit, and returning to Illinois he raised a regiment, and took it to the Rio Grande. Availing himself of a brief furlough, he resumed his place in Congress long enough to press his views and give his vote in behalf of the war, and hastened back to his regiment, which he overtook on the march from Vera Cruz. He distinguished himself in every action on the route to Mexico, and when Gen. Shields was wounded at Cerro Gordo, he succeeded to the command of the brigade, and led it through all the subsequent conflicts of the war. Returning to Illinois, he was again elected to Congress, and served his district there till 1850, when he visited Panama on business, and though attacked by the Chagres fever and compelled to return, he had learned too much of the new Eldorado of the West, California, to be contented to remain east of the Rocky Mountains, and in 1851 he removed to San Francisco, where he soon took rank as the leader of the California bar, and the most eloquent speaker in the golden State.

His impressive and touching oration over the body of his friend Broderick, will never be forgotten by those who heard it. He soon after removed to Oregon, where in 1860 he was elected to the U. S. Senate. He there distinguished himself as one of the firmest and loftiest patriots of the Senate, and in debate proved himself the most effective orator of that body. The taking of Fort Sumter fired his soul anew with military ardor, and on the 20th of April, at the mass meeting in Union Park, New York city, he delivered an address which thrilled the souls of all who heard it. He there pledged his personal services to the country as a soldier, and closed his speech with these impressive and eloquent words, which were greeted with a thunder of applause:

"And if, from the far Pacific, a voice feebler than the feeblest murmur upon its shore may be heard to give you courage and hope in the contest, that voice is yours to-day; and if a man whose hair is gray, who is well-nigh worn out in the battle and toil of life, may pledge himself on such an occasion and in such an audience, let me say, as my last word, that when, amid sheeted fire and flame, I saw and led the hosts of New York as they charged in contest upon a foreign soil for the honor of your flag; so again, if Providence shall will it, this feeble hand shall draw a sword, never yet dishonored—not to fight for distant honor in a foreign land, but to fight for country, for home, for law, for government, for constitution, for right, for freedom, for humanity, and in the hope that the banner of my country may advance, and wheresoever that banner waves, there glory may pursue and freedom be established."

The pledge thus made was speedily fulfilled. Though having a strong presentiment that he should fall in battle, he raised a fine regiment, called the California Regiment, which he led into the war, and had been nominated Brigadier-General, when the disastrous battle of Ball's Bluff occurred. He commanded a brigade in that battle, and after exhibiting the most heroic bravery and daring, exposing himself for some hours in the hottest of the fight, he fell pierced with six wounds. His colleague in the Senate, and Senators Latham and McDougal of California, and Sumner of Mass., pronounced touching and eloquent eulogiums on his memory.

Oct. 22.—William Lowell Putnam, a lieutenant of volunteers in the United States army, born in Boston, July 9, 1840, the grandson of Rev. Dr. Charles Lowell and Judge Samuel Putnam, educated partly in France, where he resided from 1851 to 1858, and subsequently trained in law and science in Harvard University; entered the 20th regiment of Massachusetts volunteers in 1861; was called to the field in September, and on the 21st of October, at the disastrous battle of Ball's Bluff, received a mortal wound while leading on his battalion to the rescue of a wounded officer. When borne to the hospital tent he declined the surgeon's assistance, bidding him go to those whom his services could benefit, as his life could not be saved. He died from his wound the next day. He was a young man of extraordinary genius, and of most lovely and blameless life, and the vast assembly who gathered in Boston to do honor to his last remains, responded most feelingly to the eloquent and touching portrayal of his character by his pastor, Rev. Dr. Bartol, and Rev. James Freeman Clarke.

Nov. 18.—Capt. George W. Snyder, died at Washington, D. C., aged 28 years. He was born in 1836 in New York. In 1852 he was appointed from the State of New York a cadet in the military academy at West Point, where he graduated with high honor, holding the rank of first captain. On leaving the academy he was appointed a second lieutenant of engineers, the highest promotion accessible to a recent graduate. He was attached in 1859 to the board of engineers under the presidency of Col. Thayer, of Boston. In the following year he was acting assistant professor of military and civil engineering at West Point. When trouble was anticipated at Charleston he was sent to that station as first engineer, assistant to Capt. Foster, and through the hardships consequent upon the siege of Fort Sumter, contracted the disease which ultimately proved fatal.

Dec. 26.—Gen. Philip St. George Cocke, an officer in the Confederate army, died in Richmond, Va., aged 53 years. Holding the State rights views of some of the leading men of Virginia, at the commencement of the present war he volunteered his services in the Confederate army of the Upper Potomac, and served as captain, colonel, and general. Upon the field of Bull Run he was commander of the 5th Confederate brigade. After a campaign of eight months he returned to his home, shattered both in mind and body, and in a paroxysm of insanity put an end to his life.

Dec. —.—George St. John Croghan, a colonel in the Confederate army, killed in a skirmish during Floyd's retreat from Cotton Hill, in Western Virginia. Col. Croghan was the son of the late Col. Croghan, of historical distinction in the North-Western campaign of the war of 1812. Col. George St. John Croghan was born in Kentucky. He invented a pack saddle for mules, which would convey three wounded men over the steep mountain passes of Western Virginia with almost the ease and comfort of an ambulance.

1862.

March 2.—Brig.-Gen. Frederick William Lander, an officer of volunteers in the United States service, born in Salem, Mass., December 17, 1822, died at Pawpaw, Va., March 2, 1862. He was educated at the Dummer Academy, Byfield, and completed his studies as engineer at Partridge's Military Academy in Norwich, Vt. After practising his profession a few years in Massachusetts, he was employed by the Government to conduct several important surveys, among which were two to determine the practicability of a railroad route to the Pacific, from the second of which, organized at his own expense, he was the only one who returned alive. In 1858 he had the command of an expedition to open a wagon road to California, across the plains. He made five explorations across the continent, as engineer, chief engineer, or superintendent, and for his celerity and efficiency was highly complimented by the Secretary of the Interior, in his official report. While engaged in this work his party were at one time attacked by the Indians, over whom they gained a complete victory, thereby ensuring safe conduct to the emigrant trains crossing the country. Of the appropriations made by Congress in two seasons alone for the construction of these roads, he brought back $100,000 of unexpended funds. At the commencement of the civil war, in 1861, he offered his services to Gen. Scott, "in any capacity, at any time, and for any duty," and was successfully employed on several important missions in the Southern States. After serving as a volunteer aid to Gen. McClellan in western Virginia, and participating in the capture of Philippi and the battle of Rich Mountain, he was, in July, 1861, commissioned brigadier-general, and assigned to an important command on the Upper Potomac. During the disaster at Ball's Bluff he was at Washington arranging for the opening of the Baltimore and Ohio Railroad. Receiving the intelligence of the action, he hastened to the spot, and in the skirmish which he had with the enemy opposite Edwards' Ferry, was wounded in the leg by a musket ball. Before the wound was healed he reported for duty, and was assigned the command of the forces at Romney, Va. A movement on the part of Gen. Jackson, threatening to outflank his troops, rendered it expedient for him to evacuate the position, which he did without loss, and soon after recovered it. Having discovered a Confederate camp at Bloomery Gap, he marched his four thousand men a distance of forty-three miles through deep snow, without rest and with little sustenance, and charging upon them completely routed the enemy, capturing seventeen commissioned officers and fifty privates. In this brilliant dash the Confederate commander and his staff surrendered to Gen. Lander, who, with a single aid, had outridden the rest of the force, and coming upon them at full gallop demanded their swords. In recognition of these services he received a special letter of thanks, written by the Secretary of War in behalf of the President. Soon after Gen. Lander was compelled, in consequence of his health, to apply for a temporary respite from military duties, but before his request could be complied with, he learned that the enemy were within his reach, and while preparing for a midnight attack, died suddenly with congestion of the brain. In personal presence Gen. Lander was commanding and attractive, and as a military leader combined a spirit of the most daring enterprise with clearness of judgment in the adaptation of means to results.

March 7.—Ben McCulloch, a general in the Confederate army, born in Rutherford Co., Tenn., in 1814, killed in the battle of Pea Ridge, March 7, 1862. He was a son of Alexander McCulloch, who fought under Gen. Jackson at the battles of Talladega, Tallahassee, and Horseshoe, during the Creek war. He attended school in Tennessee until he was 14 years of age, and from that time until 21 was mostly engaged in hunting, in which occupation he became highly skilled. This life gave him a taste for adventure, and, upon learning of an expedition of trappers to the Rocky Mountains, he made arrangements to join them; failing in this, however, he engaged to join the expedition of David Crockett to Texas, to take part in the revolution; but, arriving at Nacogdoches, the place of rendezvous, too late, he proceeded alone to the river Brazos, where he was taken sick, and did not recover until after the fall of the Alamo. In 1836 he joined the Texan army under Gen. Sam. Houston, and was assigned to the artillery. He served gallantly at the battle of San Jacinto, and afterwards settled in Gonzales Co., Texas, and was employed on the frontier, surveying and locating lands. Upon the breaking out of the Mexican war he raised a company of Texan rangers, and arrived at the seat of war four days after the battles of Palo Alto and the Resaca. His company were accepted by Gen. Taylor, and won great honor at the battles of Monterey and Buena Vista. He afterwards joined Gen. Scott's army, and for his gallant services at the taking of the city of Mexico, was appointed United States Marshal of Texas by President Pierce. In 1857 he was appointed, in conjunction with Ex-Governor Powell, commissioner to Utah. At the time of the inauguration of President Lincoln he was in Washington, it was believed, making arrangements, at the head of a body of secessionists, to take possession of the city; but, owing to the precautions of Gen. Scott, the idea was abandoned. He was subsequently made brigadier-general in the Confederate army, and assigned the command of the Arkansas forces. In June, 1861, he issued a proclamation to the people of Arkansas to assemble at Fayetteville to defend the State from invasion from Missouri. He commanded at the battle of Wilson's Creek, where Gen. Lyon was killed, and, it was said, having some misunderstanding with Gen. Price, surrendered the command to him. At the battle of Pea Ridge he led a corps of Arkansas, Louisiana, and Texas troops, and fell on the second day of the engagement.

March 7.—Gen. James McIntosh, an officer in the Confederate army, killed at the battle of Pea Ridge (or Elk Horn, as it is sometimes called), on the 7th of March, the first day of the battle. Gen. McIntosh succeeded to the command of that wing of the army commanded by Gen. Ben. McCullough, who had fallen early in the action. He had scarcely assumed command, when as he passed his old regiment, which was about to charge, he was enthusiastically cheered. His brave spirit could not withstand the temptation to place himself at their head, and lead the charge. He received the contents of a musket, loaded with buck-shot and ball, in the breast, and died instantly. It was said that the shot came from some of his own men; but the assertion has not been substantiated. At the time of his death he was regarded as the most dashing and accomplished cavalry officer in the Trans-Mississippi army of the South. Gen. McIntosh was born in Florida, and entered West Point military academy in 1845. Entered the army as brevet second lieutenant of the 1st infantry in 1849. In 1851 he was in the 8th infantry.

March 7.—Geo. W. Y. Slack, an officer in the Confederate army, was mortally wounded on the first day of the battle of Pea Ridge (or Elk Horn). He resided before the war in Linn County, Missouri, and was a member of the State Senate. He entered into the service of the State upon the first call of Governor Jackson, and was subsequently in all of Gen. Price's battles in Missouri, distinguished at all times for his coolness, courage, moderation, and good sense. He commanded a cavalry brigade at the battle of Wilson's Creek, and was severely wounded. Upon the transfer of the Missouri troops from the State to the Confederate service, in January, 1862, he resigned his position as general, and modestly entered the Confederate service as a private. He was chosen by the men formerly under his command, and temporarily assumed the command, as brigadier-general. Owing to the difficulty of communication with the government at Richmond, his appointment as general did not reach the army until after his death. In spite of all opposition, Gen. Slack had himself placed in an ambulance and attempted to follow the retreat of his troops, but was at length persuaded to allow himself to be secreted in a country house, declaring he would rather die than be captured. Parties of the Federal cavalry visited the house in search of him, but he feigned to be a private, and was not molested. His mortal wound was only half an inch above the one received at Wilson's Creek.

March 8.—Capt. CHURCHILL CLARK, an officer of artillery in the Confederate army, killed at Pea Ridge (Elk Horn). Capt. Clark was born in St. Louis, Mo., on the 12th of Sept., 1842. He entered the military academy at West Point, in 1859, appointed at large. He remained a cadet until June, 1861, when he resigned, and entered the Southern service as a cadet of the regular army. He was sent from Richmond as bearer of desptches to the Trans-Mississippi Department, and reported to Maj.-Gen. Sterling Price at Lexington, Mo. He was placed in command of two pieces of field artillery, and distinguished himself in the siege of Lexington. A guerdon was offered to him who should break the Federal flagstaff and bring down the flag, which was won by Capt. Clark, who sighted his own guns. His bravery and skill, and his youth, then only eighteen years old, won the respect and admiration of the army. He was highly complimented in general orders for his conduct in this engagement. When the army was reorganized at Springfield, Mo., Capt. Clark received a full battery of four guns from Gen. Price, and it was whilst in command of this battery, that on the second day of the battle of Elk Horn, his head was taken off by a cannon ball, just as he was limbering up his last gun, preparatory to a retreat. Capt. Clark had been ordered to retire, and had already withdrawn his other guns.

March 8.—Col. BENJAMIN A. RIVES, an officer in the Confederate army, killed at the battle of Pea Ridge (or Elk Horn). Col. Rives was born in Virginia, and married the daughter of Col. Towns, of Spottsylvania County in that State. Early in life he removed to Ray County, Missouri, where he settled, and practised the profession of medicine. He raised and tendered to Governor Claiborne F. Jackson the first military company that was raised in the State of Missouri to fight in behalf of the cause of the South. He subsequently commanded a regiment in Gen. Slack's brigade of cavalry, and at the battle of Wilson's Creek, as senior colonel, succeeded to the command of the brigade after the general was severely wounded. In January, 1862, upon the transfer of the troops from the State to the Confederate service, he was elected colonel of the third Missouri regiment, and was killed at the head of his regiment, gallantly maintaining his high reputation as a brave and skilful officer.

April 6.—Col. BLYTHE, an officer in the Confederate army, killed at the battle of Shiloh, in Tennessee. Col. Blythe was from Mississippi, and was formerly consul to Havana.

April 6.—Brig.-Gen. GLADDEN, an officer in the Southern army, killed at the battle of Shiloh. Gen. Gladden was born in South Carolina, but at the commencement of the war was a citizen of the State of Louisiana. He had distinguished himself in the war with Mexico, on the bloody fields of Contreras and Churubusco, and received honorable wounds in those engagements. He died in the belief that the Confederate arms had achieved a great victory, and exclaimed: "This is the best day of my life!"

April 6.—ALBERT SYDNEY JOHNSTON, a general in the Confederate service, born in Mason County, Kentucky, in 1803, was killed at the battle of Shiloh, April 6, 1862. He graduated at West Point in 1826, as lieutenant in the 6th infantry, served in the Black Hawk war, and in 1836 entered the Texan army as a private soldier. After several promotions, he succeeded Gen. Felix Houston in the chief command, and was involved in a duel with him in consequence. In 1838 he was appointed secretary of war, and the following year engaged in a successful expedition against the Cherokees. In 1840 he retired to private life for a time, in Brazoria County, Texas; but in 1846, at the solicitation of Gen. Taylor, he assumed the command of a volunteer Texan regiment against the Mexicans. At the siege of Monterey he served as inspector-general, and won himself much distinction. In October, 1849, he received from President Taylor the appointment of paymaster of the army, with the rank of major. In 1857 he conducted the expedition against the Mormons, and commanded the district of Utah, with the brevet rank of brigadier-general, until 1860, when he was removed to the command of the Pacific department, and stationed at San Francisco. His sympathies being upon the side of the Southern Confederacy, he was making arrangements to deliver the State of California to the Confederacy when he was unexpectedly superseded in his command by General E. V. Sumner, before his plans were completed. Upon his return to the East he was placed in an important command, and at the battle of Shiloh was commander-in-chief of the Confederate army of the West, and, in the first day of that sanguinary fight, when encouraging and urging forward his troops, was mortally wounded.

April 6.—Lieut. FITZ JAMES O'BRIEN died in Virginia, aged 33 years. He was born in Ireland, and came to this country about 1850. He was a brilliant writer, and also a poet of much merit. In April, 1861, upon the call for troops, he enlisted in the 7th regiment New York State militia, and in Jan., 1862, accepted an appointment upon the Staff of Gen. Lander, and in the short time of service prior to his death, distinguished himself as an officer of courage and daring. He was wounded in a skirmish on Feb. 16, and died from tetanus, following a severe surgical operation, which he bore with great fortitude.

April 6.—Col. EVERETT PEABODY, of the 25th Missouri regiment, was killed in the battle of Shiloh. He was born in Springfield, Mass., June 13, 1830, graduated at Harvard College in 1849, and adopted civil engineering as a profession, in which he rapidly distinguished himself. He was employed upon various railroads at the West, and in 1859 was chief engineer of the Platte County Railroad. When the war broke out he raised a battalion, was commissioned major, and employed in repairing and defending the railway communications of northern Missouri. He commanded 1,200 men at the siege of Lexington, and received a wound, which lamed him for life, notwithstanding which he reorganized his regiment, and upon joining Gen. Grant's army was assigned the command of a brigade under Gen. Prentiss on the exposed left wing, nearest the enemy, where in the unequal conflict he was killed.

April 6.—Col. KITT WILLIAMS, an officer in the Confederate army, killed at Shiloh.

April 7.—Col. WILLIAM PEGRAM was killed at the battle of Shiloh, Tenn. He was born in Virginia, but had resided for many years in Kentucky. Though a brother of Robert Pegram, commander of the Confederate steamer Nashville, he was a stanch loyalist, and raised a regiment of cavalry, which was in the engagement at Pittsburg Landing. At the time of his death he was acting brigadier-general.

April 7.—GEORGE M. JOHNSTON, Secession Provisional Governor of Kentucky, killed at Shiloh on the second day of the battle. He was the son of the hero of the battle of the Thames, and during a long public and private career had been regarded as one of the noblest sons of Kentucky. He served in the staff department the first day of the battle, but having had his horse killed under him, he entered a Kentucky infantry company that night, and was regularly "sworn in." On the second day he fell mortally wounded in the thickest of the fight. In making official mention of his death, Gen. Beauregard declared "that not Kentucky alone, but the whole Confederacy, had sustained a great loss in the death of this brave, upright, and able man."

April 8.—Prof. MILES J. FLETCHER, of the Indiana Asbury University, Greencastle, Ind., and State Superintendent of Public Instruction, was killed while on his way to aid the wounded, after the battle of Shiloh. He was a man of superior attainments, and of earnest loyalty and patriotism. During a part of the previous year he had added to his other duties that of assistant adjutant-general. In his message of Jan. 1863, Gov. Morton paid a tribute to his many virtues and excellencies.

April 10.—Gen. WM. HARVEY LAMB WALLACE died at Savannah, Tenn., from a wound received in the battle of Shiloh. He was born in Urbana, Ohio, July 8, 1821, was educated for the law, served in the Mexican war, and in 1853 was elected State attorney for the ninth judicial circuit of Illinois. He held command of the 11th regiment of Illinois volunteers, and joined the depot at Cairo during the early stages of the war. He held a command in the troops sent to attack Fort Henry, and distinguished himself in the siege of Fort Donelson, where he commanded a brigade in Gen. McClernand's division of Gen. Grant's army. For his gallantry upon that occasion he was made by Congress, on the 21st of March, a full brigadier-general, and with that rank went with the expedition up the Tennessee River.

April 25.—CHARLES FERGUSON SMITH, a major-general of volunteers in the United States service, born in Pennsylvania about 1806, died at Savannah, Tennessee, April 25, 1862. He was a son of the late Dr. Samuel B. Smith, U. S. A., graduated with honor at West Point in 1835, and was made second lieutenant of artillery on the 1st of July in the same year. In 1829 he was appointed assistant instructor in infantry tactics at West Point; in 1831 was promoted to the adjutancy, and in 1832 was made a first lieutenant. In 1838 he was appointed instructor in infantry tactics and commandant of cadets, and the same year was promoted to a captaincy. He took an important part in most of the battles during the Mexican war; in 1847 was brevetted major for gallant conduct in the battles of Pala Alto and Resaca de la Palma, in Texas, and at the battles of Monterey, Contreras, and Churubusco, won the successive brevets of lieutenant-colonel and colonel. In the same year he was appointed acting inspector-general in Mexico. On the 25th of November, 1854, he was made major of the 1st artillery, and the following year lieutenant-colonel of the 10th infantry. In Sept., 1851, he was promoted to the colonelcy of the 3d infantry, having the previous month been appointed brigadier-general of volunteers, and taken charge of the troops at Paducah, Ky. At the attack on Fort Donelson, the most brilliant charge was made by the troops under his command, and had much to do with the surrender. For his gallantry on that memorable occasion he was promoted to a major-generalship, and ordered to take possession of Savannah, Tenn., where he died of chronic dysentery contracted during the Mexican war, and fatally aggravated by his exposures in the campaign of the West.

May 18.—Gen. WM. H. KEIM died at Harrisburg, Pa., aged about 49 years. He was for several years a militia general, and in 1859 was elected surveyor-general of the State. At the commencement of the present war he accepted the position of major-general from Gov. Curtin, and was in Gen. Patterson's division on the Upper Potomac during the three months' service. In the fall of 1861 he was appointed a brigadier-general by the President, and joined McClellan's division, where a brigade, consisting chiefly of Pennsylvania regiments, was placed under his command. He died of a combined attack of typhoid fever and dysentery.

June 1.—Col. Oliver H. Ripley, of the 61st Pennsylvania regiment, killed in the battle before Richmond. He was born in Pittsburg in 1826, studied law under Bushrod Washington, Esq., served in the Mexican War, and upon his return resumed the practice of his profession, for which he possessed talents of the first order. As a soldier he possessed every necessary element—courage, endurance, and faith.

June 5.—Col. Albert Waldo Drake, died in South Windsor, Conn., aged 27 years. He entered the junior class in Yale after having been a member of Williams College, and graduated in 1857, studied law in Hartford and New Haven, and was admitted to the bar in 1859, in which year he was a member of the Connecticut House of Representatives. He afterwards commenced the practice of his profession in Hartford. At the beginning of the present war he was commissioned as first lieutenant of the 1st Connecticut volunteers, and distinguished himself with honor in the battle of Bull Run. He was subsequently appointed by the governor lieut.-colonel of the 10th Connecticut volunteers, and as such was engaged in the battle of Roanoke Island. He took part also in the capture of Newbern, and was then appointed colonel of his regiment.

June 6.—General Turner Ashby, an officer of cavalry in the Confederate army, killed in a skirmish near Harrisonburg, Virginia. He was the second son of the late Col. Turner Ashby, of "Rose Bank," Fauquier County, and Dorothia F. Green, daughter of the late James Green, Sr., of Rappahannock County, Virginia. The personal appearance of Gen. Ashby was not striking. He was of small stature, had a long black beard, and dark complexion. His eyes were dark and glittering. In battle his face was lighted up with the glow of excitement, and his eyes flashed like the blade of a cimeter. It was not generally known that the man who performed such deeds of desperate valor and enterprise, and who was generally pictured to the mind as a fierce, stalwart, and relentless adventurer, was as remarkable for his piety and devoutness as for his military achievements. His manners were a combination of gentleness with the most enthusiastic courage. It is said of him that when he gave his most daring commands he would gently draw his sabre, wave it round his head, and in a clear ringing voice command, "Follow me!" In his manner he was grave and silent, but courteous and gentle. He was singularly domestic in his tastes, and shunned the dissipations so common to young men. He had an enthusiastic love, however, for the chase and all field sports. He was an excellent and graceful horseman, and loved the horse. Gen. Ashby covered Gen. Jackson's (Stonewall) retreat from Kearnstown after the battle at that place. In his report Gen. Jackson says: "An official report is not an appropriate place to give a passing notice of the distinguished dead; but the close relations Gen. Ashby has borne to my command for the last twelve months justify me in saying that as a partisan officer I never knew his superior. His daring was proverbial; his powers of endurance almost incredible; his tone of character heroic, and his sagacity almost intuitive in divining the purposes and movements of the enemy." The death of his brother, Capt. Richard Ashby, saddened the life and changed the disposition of Gen. Ashby very materially. Capt. Richard Ashby had been engaged in a hand-to-hand contest in a skirmish, and had wounded his opponent, but in his retreat his horse proved false and fell. Capt. Ashby was caught, wounded, and beaten, and left for dead. He lived for several days, however, and died among his friends. But from that day Gen. Ashby always wore a sad smile; he was more silent and solemn and earnest than before. His behavior at his brother's grave was most touching. He stood over the open grave, took his brother's sword, broke it, and threw it in; clasped his hands and looked upwards, as if in resignation, and then pressing his lips, as if in the bitterness of his grief, while a tear rolled down his cheek, he turned without a word, mounted his horse and rode away. Thenceforth his name was a terror No dinner parties, no collations, no inducements could draw him away from his camp or his duties. He slept among his men, treated them as equals, and they idolized him. No matter at what time of night he was aroused he was wakeful and ready for battle. His passion for dangers was extraordinary. At one time, to encourage some militia whom he commanded, he advanced to the Potomac, and rode his white horse slowly up and down the bank. The Federal troops, with long ranged guns, were posted on the other side, and continually firing. When the balls were whistling by him thickest, Ashby would rein in his horse and stand perfectly still, the picture of daring and recklessness. At one time he was riding abreast of three hundred infantry, who were passing along the turnpike. All at once he wheeled his horse, and leaping the fence with drawn sword, cut his way right through them; then wheeling he did the same thing a second time. A week after this occurrence Ashby was dead.

June 18.—Col. James H. Perry, D.D., died of apoplexy at Fort Pulaski, Georgia, aged about 51 years. He was educated at West Point, served in the Texan War of Independence and through the Mexican campaign. At the commencement of the present war he was pastor of the Pacific Street M. E. Church at Brooklyn, N. Y., but from love of his country, and a sense of duty, resigned the pastorate of the church, and raised a regiment called the Continental Guards, which was accepted as the 48th N. Y. State volunteers. This regiment formed a part of Gen. Sherman's Port Royal expedition. At the time of his death he had command of Fort Pulaski.

June 21.—Charles Ellet, Jr., an American

engineer, born at Penn's Manor, Bucks Co., Pa., Jan. 1st, 1810, died at Cairo, Ill., June 21, 1862. He was a thorough master of his profession, and his name is identified with several of the most important works in the country. He designed and built the wire suspension bridge across the Schuylkill at Fairmount, Philadelphia, the first in the United States, and subsequently the suspension bridge across the Niagara River below the falls, and one at Wheeling, Va. He constructed the temporary track of the Virginia Central Railroad across the Blue Ridge, and contributed largely to the improvement of the navigation of the Kanawha River. He aided also in laying out the Baltimore and Ohio Railroad, and there are indeed hardly any of the Western or Middle States which do not furnish some lasting evidence of his professional skill. In 1846–'47 he was president of the Schuylkill Navigation Company. At the outbreak of the war, in 1861, he was residing at Washington, where he became deeply interested in the conduct of military matters, and devoted much attention to the use of rams in naval warfare. He projected a plan for cutting off the Confederate army at Manassas, which being rejected by Gen. McClellan, he wrote two pamphlets severely censuring his mode of conducting the campaign. The Navy Department having rejected his plan for the construction of rams for service on the Mississippi, he applied to the Secretary of War, and was successful. He was commissioned as colonel of engineers, and converted several powerful steamers into rams, which did effective service in the naval battle off Memphis, in which engagement he received the wound whereby he lost his life. He was the author of an "Essay on the Laws of Trade, in reference to the Works of Internal Improvement in the United States;" a paper "On the Physical Geography of the Mississippi Valley, with suggestions as to the Improvement of the Navigation of the Ohio and other rivers," published in "Transactions of the Smithsonian Institution;" a pamphlet on "Coast and Harbor Defenses, or the Substitution of Steam Battering Rams for Ships of War," and several other important and valuable scientific papers.

June 27.—Col. ISAAC M. TUCKER, of the 2d New Jersey regiment, was killed in the battle of Gaines' Mill. He was a resident of Newark, N. J., a member of the legal profession, and a man of much influence throughout the State. In 1856 he was a member of the State Republican Executive Committee. He was a true patriot, and his services to his regiment were most valuable. He was shot by the enemy while being borne wounded from the field.

June 30.—Col. GUILFORD D. BAILEY, was killed at the battle of the Seven Pines, aged 28 years. He was a native of New York, graduated at West Point in 1856, and was appointed to artillery service. Soon after his graduation he was ordered to Florida, and after a short service there was assigned to Forts Mackinaw, Snelling, and Leavenworth successively. When secession began he was in Texas, where he refused peremptorily to be included in Twiggs' surrender in 1861. Coming north, he was sent with Major Hunt's battery to reënforce Fort Pickens. Subsequently he raised a volunteer regiment in the northern part of New Jersey, and joined the Army of the Potomac, participating in all the battles until, as chief of artillery in Gen. Casey's division, he was mortally wounded.

July 24.—WILLIAM HENRY MILNOR, M.D., surgeon in the army, died at Savage's Station, near Richmond, Va., aged about 60 years. He was a son of the late Rev. Dr. Milnor, and at the time of his death Past Grand Master of the Masonic Order in the State of New York.

Aug. 5.—Brig.-Gen. ROBERT L. McCOOK, an officer in the Union service, shot by guerrillas near Salem, Alabama. He was a native of Jefferson County, Ohio, born in 1827. He was a man of fine attainments, and had early chosen the legal profession. He studied law in Columbus, and opened an office in that city when he was only 21 years of age. A few years later he removed to Cincinnati, where he acquired a large practice. At the first call for troops he raised a regiment of Germans for the war. During the two months that his regiment was in camp in Ohio, he had drilled them into a high state of perfection. In the campaign of Western Virginia in the summer and autumn of 1861 McCook and his "bully Dutchmen," as his regiment was called, were constantly on the alert, and at Rich Mountain, Cheat Mountain, in the various skirmishes on and near the line of the Baltimore and Ohio Railroad, and at Carnifex ferry, the skill, bravery, and daring of the commander, and the invincibility of the troops, were fully tested. Early in the winter Col. McCook was ordered with his command to Kentucky, and at Mill Springs the impetuosity of his regiment in their charge upon the enemy carried the day. Col. McCook was wounded in the engagement, but only remained away from his regiment long enough to recover sufficient strength to ride on horseback. For his gallant conduct at Mill Springs he was promoted to a brigadier-generalship, the Senate unanimously confirming the nomination, but he was so strongly attached to his "bully Dutchman," and they were so unwilling to have any other commander, that he never accepted the commission. He joined Gen. Buell's command after the evacuation of Bowling Green, but was not in any of the subsequent battles. At the time of the attack on him he was very sick, and was carried in an ambulance, one regiment and part of another of his brigade being in advance, and the remainder some distance in the rear. The guerrillas, who were partly residents of the vicinity, had been informed that he was to pass, and knowing his helpless condition, had lain in ambush for him while the regiments in advance passed. They came upon his escort in large force, overturned the ambulance, and shot him down in cold blood. His faithful driver and attendant bore him to the nearest house. He survived, though in terrible suffering, about 24 hours. His regiment, learning of the death of their commander, visited the scene, and seizing some of the guerrillas, hung them at once, and destroyed their houses. The McCook family have contributed more men to the war, probably, than any other in the United States. Maj.-Gen. Alexander McDowell McCook was a brother of the murdered general, and sixteen members of the family have been either in the army or navy.

Aug. 5.—Col. GEORGE T. ROBERTS, an officer in the Union service, and commander of the 7th regiment Vermont volunteers, killed at the battle of Baton Rouge, La. He was a native of Rutland, Vt., and the regiment which he commanded was one raised to form part of Gen. Butler's command on the Ship Island expedition. He was commissioned Feb. 12, 1862, and sailed for Ship Island on the 10th of the following month. Col. Roberts participated in the capture of New Orleans, and his regiment suffered severely in the battle of Baton Rouge, in which he lost his life.

Aug. 5.—Brig.-Gen. THOMAS WILLIAMS, an officer of the U. S. army, killed in the battle of Baton Rouge, La. He was a native of New York, born in 1818; was appointed a cadet at West Point from Michigan in 1833, and graduated in 1837; received the appointment of brevet second lieutenant in the 4th artillery during the same year; in 1840–'41 was acting assistant professor of mathematics at West Point; in 1844 was appointed an aide-de-camp on Gen. Scott's staff, and in the Mexican war won the brevets of captain and major for gallantry and meritorious conduct. He was promoted to a captaincy in 1850, and commissioned major in the 5th artillery in May, 1861, and in September of the same year appointed brigadier-general of volunteers. During the autumn of 1861 he commanded the forts at Hatteras Inlet, and when the Ship Island expedition was sent out was assigned to the command of one of the brigades. He commanded the forces in the first unsuccessful attack upon Vicksburg, projected and superintended the cutting of the canal intended to turn the course of the Mississippi away from Vicksburg; on the failure of this enterprise he was placed in command at Baton Rouge. He repelled with vigor and success the attack of the Confederate General Breckinridge on that place, but just at the close of the engagement, while bringing up a Michigan regiment to charge upon the enemy, he was slain. He was an able and skilful officer, and a very rigid disciplinarian.

Aug. 6.—Col. F. MCCULLOUGH, a guerrilla belonging to Porter's command, captured near Edina, Missouri. He was carried to Kirksville, where a court-martial was convened, before which he was tried and condemned to be shot to death with musketry the same afternoon. He received the announcement of his sentence with perfect composure, but protested against it. He leaned against the fence and wrote a few lines to his wife, which, with his watch, he delivered to the officer in command to give to her. On the way to the place of his execution he requested the privilege to give the command to fire, which was granted. All being ready, in a clear firm voice he said: "What I have done I have done as a principle of right. Aim at the heart. Fire!" The word taking the squad by surprise, one fired before the rest. He fell, and the remainder of the balls passed over him. He was despatched by another volley.

Aug. 9.—Lieut.-Col. L. H. D. CRANE, an officer in the Union service, at the time of his death acting colonel of the 3d regiment Wisconsin volunteers, killed at the battle of Cedar or Slaughter Mountain. He was a citizen of Ripon, Wisconsin, and had been for several years chief clerk of the Assembly of that State. He joined the regiment as major, but was soon promoted to the lieutenant-colonelcy, and at the time of the battle, owing to the illness of the colonel, was in actual command of the regiment. He was a genial, intelligent, and amiable man, beloved in his own neighborhood and State.

Aug. 22.—Gen. HEINRICH BOHLEN, an officer in the Union service, killed while opposing the attempts of the Confederate force to cross the Rappahannock. He was a native of Germany, but emigrated to this country a number of years since, and settled in Philadelphia as an importer of wines. At the commencement of the war he raised a regiment of his countrymen (the 75th Pennsylvania), which was subsequently attached to Gen. Blenker's division. He was promoted to a brigadier-generalship April 28, 1862, and attached to the Mountain Department, where he served under Fremont and Sigel, distinguishing himself for bravery and daring at the battle of Cross Keys. He was a man of devout and exemplary character. His son, Mr. J. B. Bohlen, who was on a visit to his native land, died in Baden-Baden on the same day with his father.

Aug. 27.—Col. FLETCHER WEBSTER, an officer of volunteers in the Union service, and at the time of his death colonel of the 12th regiment Massachusetts volunteers, died at Alexandria of wounds received in the second battle of Bull Run. He was the oldest son of Daniel Webster, and was born at Portsmouth, N. H., in 1812. He was educated at Dartmouth College, and served as Assistant Secretary of State under his father during the administrations of Presidents Harrison and Tyler. When Caleb Cushing went to China as American commissioner, Mr. Webster accompanied him as Secretary of Legation. Under the administrations of Presidents Pierce and Buchanan he held a position in the Boston custom house. When the call was made for troops in the spring of 1861, he was among the first to raise a regiment for the war, and was in active service till his death. He was shot through the lungs, and died of hemorrhage in a few hours. He was the last member of his family, a brother and sister having previously deceased.

Aug. 28.—Col. ISAAC H. MEANS, ex-governor of South Carolina, killed at the second battle of Bull Run. He was a colonel in the Confederate service.

Aug. 30.—Col. JAMES CANTWELL, an officer in the Union service, and at the time of his death colonel of the 82d Ohio regiment, killed at the battle near Gainesville, while rallying the left wing of his regiment, which had given way under the atack of an overwhelming force of the Confederates. He was a citizen of Kenton, Hardin County, Ohio, and volunteered in the service at the commencement of the war, having been lieutenant-colonel of the 4th Ohio regiment of three months' troops; when they were disbanded he raised the 82d regiment for the war, and received his commission as colonel Dec. 31, 1861.

Aug. 30.—Col. JOHN A. KOLTES, an officer in the Union service, and at the time of his death acting brigadier-general in Gen. Steinwehr's division, killed at the battle of Gainesville, Va. He was a native of Rhenish Prussia, born in 1823, and came to this country in 1846. In Prussia he had been a professor in one of the gymnasia or colleges. Shortly after his arrival here he joined a regiment from Pennsylvania which had volunteered for the Mexican war, and served throughout that war as orderly sergeant. After the close of the war he was for a time an officer of the Marine Corps, and was subsequently employed in the U. S. mint at Philadelphia. At the commencement of the present war he appealed to his countrymen to join him in defence of the Union, and succeeded in raising a regiment of Germans, whom he led to the field. He had been for four months acting brigadier-general in Steinwehr's division, and his friends had secured his promotion to that rank and were carrying his commission to him when they met his dead body as it was borne from the field.

Aug. 30.—Col. GEO. W. PRATT, an officer in the Union service, and at the time of his death colonel of the 20th regiment N. Y. State volunteers, was killed at the battle near Gainesville, Va. He was the son of Col. Zadock Pratt, formerly M. C. from Greene County, and had entered the volunteer service in the summer of 1861. He was an excellent officer, and highly esteemed in private life. He was killed while leading his men in a charge.

Aug. 31.—Col. THORNTON F. BRODHEAD, an officer of the Union army, and at the time of his death commander of the 1st Michigan cavalry regiment, died at Alexandria, Va., of wounds received the preceding day at the second battle of Bull Run. He was a native of New Hampshire, born in 1822, and was a son of Rev. John Brodhead, formerly a member of Congress from that State. He studied law at the Harvard Law School, and settled in his profession at Detroit, Mich. He served with distinction in the Mexican war as an officer in the 15th U. S. infantry, and was twice brevetted for gallant conduct in battle. At the close of the war he returned to the practice of his profession, and was soon after elected a member of the State Senate. In 1852 President Pierce appointed him postmaster of Detroit. At the commencement of the war he raised a cavalry regiment, at the head of which he served under Gens. Banks, Fremont, and Pope.

Sept. 1.—Maj.-Gen. PHILIP KEARNEY, an officer of volunteers in the United States army, born in the city of New York, June 2, 1815, was killed at the battle of Chantilly, Va., Sept. 1, 1862. He was of Irish descent, his great-grandfather having settled in Monmouth County, New Jersey, in 1716, and was a nephew of Gen. Stephen Watts Kearney. He studied law, but having a decided taste for military life, at the age of 22 accepted the commission of second lieutenant in the United States 1st dragoons, commanded by his uncle, and soon after was sent to Europe by the Government to study and report upon the French cavalry tactics. To accomplish this object he entered the military school at Saumur, in France, and from thence went to Africa, where he joined the 1st Chasseurs d'Afrique as a volunteer. By his daring exploits he attracted the attention of the French army, and was presented with the Cross of the Legion of Honor. In 1840 he returned home, and received the appointment of aide-de-camp to Gen. Macomb, and the following year was aide-de-camp to Gen. Scott, serving in that capacity until 1844. In 1846 he became captain of a company of dragoons, and from his private means provided for his men equipments and horses, and his corps formed the escort of Gen. Scott when he made his entrance into Vera Cruz. For gallant and meritorious conduct at the battles of Contreras and Churubusco he was brevetted major. While making a brilliant charge upon a battery at the St. Antonio gate of the capital, he lost his left arm. He had ordered the charge, but his men beginning to waver under a terrific fire, he dashed forward, and the troops, electrified by his example, followed, and slaughtered the Mexicans at their guns. After the Mexican war he was sent to California, and commanded an expedition against the Indians of the Columbia River, displaying during the campaign such tact and courage as won him the praise of the best military judges. In 1851 he resigned his commission, and, returning to Europe, devoted several years to military studies. During the Italian campaign of 1859, Major Kearney served as volunteer aid to Gen. Morris, a distinguished officer in the French army, and upon its conclusion he received from the Emperor Napoleon a second Cross of the Legion of Honor. He was residing in Paris when the present war broke out in 1861, and hastened home to offer his services to his country, and after some delay was appointed brigadier-general of volunteers, and placed in command of the New Jersey troops, and afterwards of United States volunteers. He distinguished himself at Yorktown, Williamsburg, Fair Oaks, White Oak Swamp, the Cross Roads, and Malvern Hills, and subsequently near Washington, under Gen. Pope. He was commissioned major-general July 4, 1862. As a disciplinarian, Gen. Kearney was second to none in the army, and his troops were enthusiastic in their admiration of his military ability.

Sept. 1.—ISAAC INGALLS STEVENS, a major-general of volunteers in the United States service, born in Andover, Mass., in 1817, killed in the battle near Chantilly, Fairfax Co., Va., Sept. 1, 1862. He graduated at West Point in 1839, ranking first in his class, and was commissioned second lieutenant of engineers. In 1840 he became first lieutenant, and was employed upon the fortifications of the New England coast until the Mexican war, at that time being adjutant of engineers. He was attached to Gen. Scott's staff, and for gallant and meritorious conduct at the battles of Contreras and Churubusco was brevetted captain, and major for his heroic conduct at the storming of Chapultepec, and the city of Mexico, where he received a severe wound from which he never fully recovered. His profound knowledge of the principles of war attracted the attention of his general, who spoke of him as "the most promising officer of his age." Upon his return to the United States he was selected by Prof. Bache to perform the duties of chief of the Coast Survey at Washington. In 1853 he resigned his commission and accepted the appointment of Governor of Washington Territory, where he became known as an able executive officer, displaying the most unremitting devotion to the interests of the Territory. During the administration of President Buchanan he represented Washington Territory as delegate in Congress for two terms. He was the chairman of the Breckinridge executive committee in the presidential campaign of 1860; but when the leaders of the party declared for secession, he openly denounced them, and stood by the Union, strongly urging President Buchanan to remove Secretaries Floyd and Thompson from the cabinet, and trust to the counsels of Gen. Scott. At the close of the session of Congress Gov. Stevens proceeded to Washington Territory, but upon hearing of the attack on Fort Sumter returned to Washington and offered his services to the Government. He was appointed colonel of the 79th New York Highlanders. He was commissioned brigadier-general of volunteers Sept. 28, 1861, and accompanied Gen. Sherman to South Carolina, where he bore a prominent part in all the battles near Port Royal. He was then transferred to North Carolina, whence he came to Virginia in the corps of Gen. Reno, and was promoted to the rank of major-general, his commission bearing date July 4, 1862. He was in all the skirmishes along the Rappahannock under Gen. Pope, and fought most gallantly in the battle near Bull Run. As he was bearing aloft the colors of one of his regiments, cheering on his men, he fell fatally wounded by a Minié ball passing through his head. In 1851 he published a work entitled "Campaigns of the Rio Grande and Mexico, with Remarks on the recent work of Major Ripley."

Sept. 1.—Gen. GEORGE B. TAYLOR, an officer of the Union army, died in Alexandria of wounds received at the second battle of Bull Run. He was a native of Clinton, Hunterdon County, New Jersey, and was born in 1808. At the age of 19 he entered the navy as a midshipman, but after a three years' cruise settled in New Jersey as a farmer. In the Mexican war he served first as lieutenant, and afterwards as captain in the 10th infantry. After the close of that war he resided for three years in California, and then returned to his native State, where he engaged in mining and manufacturing. At the commencement of the present war he was commissioned as colonel of the 3d New Jersey regiment, which, under Brig.-Gen. Runyon, formed a part of the reserve at Bull Run. When the three months' men were mustered out of the service, he reorganized his regiment and returned to the army, and was attached to the Army of the Potomac when it went to the peninsula. After the battle of West Point, Gen. Kearney was made a division commander, and Col. Taylor was placed in charge of the 1st brigade of N. J. volunteers. On the 9th of May, 1862, he received his commission as brigadier-general. In the hard fighting that followed before Richmond he performed his part manfully, and when the army returned to the Potomac he was prompt and ready with his brigade in the sharp battles southwest of Washington.

Sept. 6.—COL. BENJAMIN FRANKLIN LARNED, paymaster general of the U. S. army, died at Washington. He was born in Massachusetts in 1791, and on the 21st Oct., 1813, entered the army as ensign in the 21st regiment of infantry; he was promoted to a first lieutenancy in the summer of 1814, distinguished himself at the defence of Fort Erie, Aug. 13—15 of that year, and received the brevet rank of captain for his gallant conduct. In Jan., 1815, he was appointed regimental paymaster, and on the reduction of the army retained as paymaster of the 5th infantry, with the rank and pay of major. In 1847, when two deputy paymaster generalships were created, Major Larned was appointed to one of them with the rank of lieutenant-colonel, and on the death of Maj.-Gen. Towson, in 1854, he succeeded to the paymaster generalship by right of seniority, with the rank of colonel. Regarding it a matter of duty to aid in the work of reorganizing the department over which he presided, for the vast labors which were thrown upon it by the war, he toiled on, though with impaired health, till the office and its duties were completely systematized, when he sunk under the load and his overtasked powers gave way. He was greatly esteemed and beloved by all his acquaintance.

Sept. 14.—Brig.-Gen. —— GARLAND, an officer in the Confederate army, killed at the battle of Boonsboro, in Virginia, while endeavoring to rally his men. He fell pierced in the breast by a musket ball, and died upon the field.

Sept. 15.—DAVID EMANUEL TWIGGS, a major-general in the Confederate service, born in Georgia, in 1790, died in Augusta, Ga., Sept. 15, 1862. He entered the army as a captain in the 8th infantry in 1812, served throughout the war, and was afterwards retained in service as captain in the 7th infantry, with the brevet rank of major. In the Mexican war he held the rank of colonel of the 2d dragoons, but acted as brigadier, commanding the right wing in the battles of Palo Alto and Resaca de la Palma, and in the same month was made brigadier-general. He was subsequently brevetted major-general for gallant and meritorious conduct at Monterey, and presented with a sword by Congress. In 1847 he was in command of a division under Gen. Scott, and the following year was military governor of Vera Cruz. At the commencement of the present war he was in command of the Union troops in Texas, and through complicity with the Confederate leaders surrendered great quantities of military stores and material into the hands of the State authorities, and betrayed the troops under his charge to the Confederate authorities. For a short time he was in command at New Orleans, but very soon resigned, and after a retirement of a few months upon his estate in Mississippi, becoming alarmed at the approach of the Union troops, he removed to Augusta, Ga., where he died.

Sept. 16.—Col. DIXON H. MILES, an officer of the U. S. army, mortally wounded at Harper's Ferry, Va., by a shell thrown by the enemy after his surrender of the place. He was a native of Maryland, born about 1803, and was appointed a cadet at West Point from that State in 1819. He graduated in 1824, and received an appointment as brevet second lieutenant of the 4th infantry, and the same day was made second lieutenant of the 7th infantry. He was regimental adjutant from 1831 to 1836, and in 1836 was promoted to a captaincy. In Jan., 1839, he was appointed assistant quartermaster on the staff, with the rank of captain, but resigned his staff appointment in Sept., 1845. On the 9th of May he was brevetted major for gallant conduct at Fort Brown, Texas; and for his further meritorious conduct at several battles in Mexico, was brevetted lieutenant-colonel. In Feb., 1847, he was promoted as major of the 5th infantry, and in July, 1848, was civil and military governor of Jalapa, Mexico. In April, 1851, he was promoted to the lieutenant-colonelcy of the 3d infantry, and in 1857 and 1858 distinguished himself in several conflicts with the Apache and Navajoe Indians. In Jan., 1859, he was promoted to the colonelcy of the 2d infantry, and at the battle of Bull Run was in charge of the 5th division, and was ordered to cover the retreat. In Sept., 1862, he was intrusted with the command of the important post of Harper's Ferry, the retention and defence of which were essential to the complete success of the battles which followed. He asked for reënforcements, but they were not sent; one of his subordinates abandoned Maryland Heights, which commanded the main position, and finding the enemy approaching in large force, he surrendered the post with but slight resistance, and with it nearly 14,000 men as prisoners, and an immense amount of arms, ammunition, and stores.

Sept. 17.—Gen. LAWRENCE O'BRIEN BRANCH, an officer in the Confederate service, killed at the battle of Antietam. He was a son of Hon. John Branch, formerly governor of North Carolina, and was born in Halifax Co. in that State in 1820. He graduated at Nassau Hall College, Princeton, in 1838, studied law with his father, and practised his profession in Raleigh. In 1855 he was elected to Congress from the Raleigh district, and reëlected till 1861. After North Carolina passed the ordinance of secession, he entered the Confederate army first as colonel, but was soon promoted to a brigadier-generalship. At the battle of Newbern he had command of that important position, and subsequently took part in several of the battles in that State and on the peninsula.

Sept. 17.—JOSEPH KING FENNO MANSFIELD, a brigadier-general in the United States army, born in New Haven, Conn., December 22, 1803, was killed at the battle of Antietam, Sept. 17, 1862. At the age of fourteen he received a cadet's appointment, and entered the military academy at West Point, where he distinguished himself in military studies, passing through every grade of office in the cadet battalion, and during a portion of the fourth year acted as assistant professor in the department of natural philosophy. He graduated in 1822, standing No. 2 in a class of forty members, and was made a second lieutenant of the corps of engineers. For the next two years he was an assistant to the board of engineers, then assembled in New York, and engaged in planning fortifications for the defence of the harbors and cities on the coast. In 1832 he was promoted to be a first lieutenant, and for a few years following was engaged upon the construction of Fort Pulaski, though in the mean time occasionally being detached upon duty at other posts. On the 7th of July, 1838, he was appointed captain. He served in the Mexican war as chief engineer, under Gen. Taylor, was brevetted major for gallant and distinguished services in the defence of Fort Brown, Texas, in 1846, and the following September was brevetted lieutenant-colonel for gallant and meritorious conduct in the battles of Monterey, where he received no less than seven severe wounds. In 1847 he was brevetted colonel for his meritorious services at Buena Vista. On the 26th of May, 1853, he was appointed an inspector-general of the United States army, with the rank of colonel, which position he held at the breaking out of the war. In May, 1861, he was commissioned brigadier-general, and was placed in command of the department of Washington. He fortified the city on every side, crowned the heights of Arlington with earthworks, and took Alexandria. Upon the return of Gen. Wool to Fortress Monroe, he was sent to Hatteras, and afterwards to Camp Hamilton and Newport News. On the 10th of May he marched, with a division, to the attack on Norfolk, and, after the capture of that place, was assigned to the command of Suffolk, Va., where he acted as military governor. After the second battle of Bull Run, he was summoned to the court of inquiry at Washington, and, during the delay, becoming impatient for active duty, he was assigned to the command of the corps formerly under Gen. Banks, and, at the battle of Antietam, fell mortally wounded while cheering on his troops in a brilliant charge.

Sept. 17.—Col. J. H. Childs, an officer in the Union service, colonel of the 4th Pennsylvania cavalry, and at the time of his death acting brigadier-general, killed at the battle of Antietam. He was a citizen of Pittsburg, Pa., and entered the service in July, 1861. He had distinguished himself in several battles for courage, coolness, and skill, and at Antietam was in command of a brigade of cavalry.

Sept. 17.—Col. Augustus H. Coleman, an officer of the Union service, commanding the 11th Ohio regiment, killed at the battle of Antietam. He entered the service as major of the 11th regiment, at the beginning of the war, and after its reorganization, on the resignation of Lieut.-Col. Frizell, in Jan., 1862, was promoted to the rank of lieutenant-colonel, and soon afterwards of colonel. His regiment had done service in western Virginia as a part of Cox's brigade, and Col. Coleman had a high reputation for bravery and daring.

Sept. 17.—Col. Samuel Croasdale, an officer of the Union service, commanding the 128th Pennsylvania regiment, killed at the battle of Antietam. He was a citizen of Doylestown, Pa., and had a large practice in that town as a lawyer. Immediately after the President's proclamation of April 15, 1861, he volunteered as a private in Capt. Davis's company of three months' men. On their discharge he resumed the practice of his profession, but on the governor's call for nine months' men, in the summer of 1862, he opened a recruiting office and raised a full company of the citizens of Doylestown and vicinity in a few days. The 128th regiment, composed almost entirely of citizens of Berks, Lehigh, and Bucks Counties, was organized soon after, and he was appointed its colonel. After a few weeks' service in camps of instruction near Washington, the emergencies of the invasion of Maryland required the services of Col. Croasdale's regiment in the field, and it marched with the grand army from Washington. At Antietam, though a new regiment, it was assigned an important position, and Col. Croasdale was leading it forward through a tempest of shot and shell, when a musket ball passing through his brain killed him instantly.

Sept. 17.—Col. Roderick Matheson, an officer of the Union army, and commander of the 32d regiment N. Y. State volunteers (1st California regiment), killed at the battle of Antietam. He was a native of New York, but had resided for several years in California, and in May, 1861, left his home in that State and raised in New York city a regiment of Californians and those who had formerly resided on the Pacific coast. The regiment was completed about the 20th of June, 1861, and under Col. Matheson took part in the battle of Bull Run and in most of the subsequent battles in Virginia. His remains were sent to California, and buried with the honors of war at his former residence in that State.

Sept. 17.—Col. Hugh Watson McNeil, an officer in the Union service, and commander of the Pennsylvania "Bucktail" regiment, killed at the battle of Antietam while leading his regiment in a charge. He was a native of Seneca County, N. Y., and was of Scotch family, his father being a Cameronian clergyman; was born in 1830; was educated at Yale College, studied law at Auburn, and commenced practice in New York in 1857, but left his profession on account of ill-health; removed to Pennsylvania, and engaged in banking. At the commencement of the war he joined the Bucktail regiment as a private, but was soon chosen first lieutenant, and rose by successive promotions to the command.

Sept. 17.—Lieut.-Col. Philip J. Parisen, an officer in the Union service, at the time of his death in command of the 57th regiment New York State volunteers, killed at the battle of Antietam. He was a native of New York city, and entered the service Dec. 21, 1861, as major of the 57th, and early in 1862 was promoted to a lieutenant-colonelcy. He took part in most of the battles on the peninsula and in those of August in the vicinity of Washington. He was shot through the body and instantly killed while leading his regiment at Antietam.

Sept. 17.—Brig.-Gen. —— Stark, an officer in the Confederate army, killed at the battle of Sharpsburg, in Maryland.

Sept. 18.—Col. Henry W. Kingsbury, an officer of the U. S. army, commanding, at the time of his death, the 11th regiment Connecticut volunteers, died of wounds received the previous day at the battle of Antietam. He was a son of the late Major Julius J. B. Kingsbury, and was born in Connecticut in 1837. He entered West Point in 1856 and graduated in 1861, second in his class. Soon after his graduation he was assigned to the duty of drilling the volunteers at Washington, and after a short time put in command of a battery with the rank of captain. His thorough military knowledge and skill as an officer recommended him to the authorities of his native State, and he was offered the command of the 11th regiment. He acquitted himself nobly in his new position, and was regarded as an officer of great promise. In the battle of Antietam he was four times seriously wounded.

Sept. 19.—Lieut.-Col. WILDER DWIGHT, an officer of the Union service, lieutenant-colonel, at the time of his death, of the 2d Massachusetts volunteers, died in the hospital at Boonsboro', Md., of wounds received in the battle of Antietam. He was a son of William Dwight, of Boston, and was born about 1832, and graduated at Harvard University in 1853. He joined the 2d regiment at its formation, and had won the reputation of a brave and skilful officer. In the retreat of Gen. Banks down the Shenandoah valley in May, 1862, he was distinguished for his daring and the solicitude which he manifested for the safety of his men; and was taken prisoner during this retreat. At Antietam he was twice wounded. Three of his brothers are in the army.

Sept. 19.—Brig.-Gen. LEWIS HENRY LITTLE, an officer in the Confederate army, killed at the battle of Iuka, Miss. Gen. Little was the son of Col. P. Little, of Maryland, and was appointed from civil life in the regular army of the United States. Brevet second lieutenant of the 5th regiment of infantry, July 1st, 1839. In May, 1843, he was transferred to the seventh infantry; became first lieutenant April, 1845; brevetted captain for gallant and meritorious conduct at the battle of Monterey, Mexico, September 23d, 1846—brevet dated March, 1849. He was regimental quartermaster in March, 1847, and distinguished in the battle of Cerro Gordo. He was captain in the regular army in 1847. When the war broke out he was in command at Albuquerque, New Mexico. He resigned, and was appointed, by Gov. Jackson, of Missouri, adjutant-general in the State forces with the rank of colonel, and assigned to duty on the staff of Gen. Sterling Price. When the Missouri troops were transferred to the Confederate service Gen. Little was assigned temporarily to the command of them. At the battle of Elk Horn he handled his brigade with such courage and skill, and covered the retreat in so masterly a manner, that he soon after received the appointment from Richmond of brigadier-general. When Gen. Van Dorn was assigned to the command of the District of North Mississippi, Gen. Little succeeded to the command of Gen. Price's division, composed of the brigades of Hebert, Gates, Green, and Martin. While commanding this division he fell pierced by a Minié ball through the head.

Sept. 29.—WILLIAM C. PRENTICE, at Augusta, Ky., from wounds received in the conflict at that place on Sept. 27. He was the eldest son of Geo. D. Prentice, for many years editor of the "Louisville Journal," and a young man of remarkable powers. An intense Southern sympathy, in spite of the arguments, remonstrances, and entreaties of parents and friends, made him join the Confederate ranks, and after a brief service of five weeks he was fatally wounded. On his departure to join the Confederate force in Kentucky, his mother is said to have followed him four or five miles, with the hope of persuading him to return, but he declined her entreaties, saying, "Mother, I implore you not to ask me to stay. Honor calls me. I have talked long enough. I must now do something else, and show myself in my true colors."

Sept. 29.—WILLIAM NELSON, major-general of volunteers in the U. S. army, born in Maysville, Mason Co., Ky., in 1825, was killed at Louisville, Ky., Sept. 29, 1862. He entered the naval school at Annapolis at the age of fifteen, and, upon graduating, was appointed a midshipman in the U. S. navy. He was first attached to the sloop-of-war Yorktown, in commission for the Pacific, and soon after joined that squadron under Commodore T. Ap Catesby Jones. In 1846 he received his commission as passed midshipman, and was ordered to the frigate Raritan, attached to the home squadron, and flag-ship of Commodore Conner. In 1847 he was made acting master of the steamer Scourge, under the command of Com. Perry. At the siege of Vera Cruz, during the Mexican war, he won a high reputation in command of a navy battery. In 1854 he was promoted to the rank of master, and ordered to the frigate Independence, stationed in the Pacific. In 1858 he was ordered to the Niagara when she carried back to Africa the negroes taken from the steamer Echo. At the commencement of the present war he was on ordnance duty at the Washington navy yard, and was detailed to command the Ohio River fleet of gunboats, having received the rank of lieutenant commander, but was soon after transferred to the army for the purpose of influencing volunteers in Kentucky, his native State. He organized "Camp Dick Robinson," between Garrardsville and Danville, and another camp at Washington, in Mason Co. He fought several engagements with Humphrey Marshall, in some of which he was successful. In Sept., 1861, he was made brigadier-general, and appointed to the command of the second division of Gen. Buell's army. He won much distinction at the battle of Shiloh, was wounded at the battle of Richmond, Ky., and afterwards assumed command of all the forces in Louisville, having been made major-general of volunteers July 17, 1862. His overbearing nature made him unpopular with his associates, and he was shot in his hotel by Brig.-Gen. Jefferson C. Davis in a moment of resentment for his harsh and unjust treatment of that officer.

Sept. 29.—Gen. ISAAC PEACE RODMAN, a brigadier-general in the Union service, died near Hagerstown, Md., of wounds received in the battle of Antietam. He was a native of South Kingston, R. I., born Aug. 28, 1822. He received a good early education, and engaged while yet a youth in the woollen manufacture, and had attained a high reputation for the character of the goods manufactured by his firm, which were sold in all parts of the country. At the commencement of the war he was a member of the State Senate; but at once resigned his seat, recruited a company for the 2d Rhode Island regiment (Col. Slocum's), and went to the war as its captain. His company was the first to fire upon the enemy at the battle of Bull Run, and fought bravely throughout that battle. He was appointed lieutenant-colonel of the 4th Rhode Island regiment at its organization, and soon after promoted to the colonelcy of that regiment, which was detailed to the Burnside expedition. At Roanoke Island Col. Rodman took an active part, and at Newbern his regiment made the brilliant charge which won the day. His regiment also participated in the investment and reduction of Fort Macon; but before that was accomplished, Col. Rodman had received his commission as brigadier-general. An attack of typhoid fever, induced by over-exertion and exposure, rendered it necessary for him to come home on sick leave, and he only recovered in time to join Gen. Burnside at Fredericksburg. Here he found himself, though only a brigadier-general, in command of Gen. Parke's division. In the month of battles which followed, Gen. Rodman did his full share, quietly and unostentatiously. At South Mountain and Antietam he displayed military genius of a high order, and in the terrible conflict by which the stone bridge was carried and held, he was stricken down.

Oct. 4.—Col. —— Daly, an officer of the Southern army, killed at the battle of Corinth, while cheering and leading his men on to the attack. Col. Daly commanded the 13th Arkansas regiment.

Oct. 4.—Lieut. Samuel Farrington, an officer in the Southern service, killed at the battle of Corinth, Miss. Lieut. Farrington was a remarkably shrewd and able young officer. His devotion to the cause in which he had engaged was unsurpassed, if equalled At the breaking out of the war he resided in St. Louis, Mo., where he was in mercantile business, but was first lieutenant of an infantry company in the State service. When Gov. Jackson decided to carry the State out of the Union, and commenced war with the United States Government, Lieut. Farrington was ordered to guard the Gasconade bridge with a detachment of his men, and upon leaving the bridge burnt it. With the same detachment he was engaged in the battle of Boonville, the first fight made in the State of Missouri during the war. In the battle of Carthage he was on Gen. John B. Clark's staff, with the rank of colonel, and was distinguished for his courage, coolness, and ability. He commanded a regiment of infantry, as lieutenant-colonel, at the battle of Lexington, Mo. Upon the organization of Confederate troops in Missouri he resigned his commission in the State Guard, and accepted that of a lieutenant of artillery in the Confederate service, conscientiously believing that the cause in which he had taken up arms would be better served by all Missouri troops going into the army of the Confederate States. At the battle of Corinth a Parrott shot tore away his shoulder and half his breast. He turned his head half round, fell, and died instantly.

Oct. 4.—Gen. Pleasant Adam Hackleman, a brigadier-general in the Union army, killed at the battle of Corinth. He was a native of Franklin County, Indiana, born about 1817, was educated for the legal profession, and was prominent as a lawyer in the State. He became editor of the "Rushville Republican" about 1840, and continued as its editor till the commencement of the war. In 1841 he was a member of the Legislature of Indiana, and for several years afterwards clerk of Rush County. In 1847 and 1858 he was a candidate for Congress, but was defeated on both occasions. In 1860 he was a member of the Republican National Convention at Chicago, and in 1861 of the Peace Conference at Washington. In 1861 he was appointed colonel of the 10th Indiana regiment, and served in Gen. Banks' corps in Virginia; his gallant and meritorious conduct there occasioned his promotion to the rank of brigadier-general, April 28, 1862, and in June he was ordered to report to Gen. Grant, in the army of the Southwest. He took an active part in the battle of Iuka, and in the battle of Corinth was killed on the second day of the fight. He was a man of dignified and upright character, and of superior abilities.

Oct. 4.—Col. —— —— Rogers, a Confederate officer, killed at the battle of Corinth. He was from Texas, and was at that battle in command of a brigade. When, on the morning of the 4th, the Confederate troops, which had expected to capture Corinth with but a slight struggle, found themselves repulsed by the terrible fire of the Union battery Robinett, and were compelled to fall back into the timber for protection, Gen. Van Dorn called for volunteers to carry the battery by storm. Col. Rogers at once volunteered, and 2,000 men stepped from the ranks to accompany him. After addressing them a few words of encouragement, he gave the order to march, and they moved forward at a quick step, in solid column eight deep, directly in face of the battery. Before they reached it nearly one-half their number had fallen; but there was no faltering, the rear ranks stepped to the front and filled the gaps; they reached the outworks, and though twice driven back, succeeded the third time in planting their flag upon the parapet, when a volley from the guns of the inner works, at short range, killed a large number, among whom was the rashly brave Rogers. Gen. Rosecrans, in his general order after the battle, rendered the homage due from a chivalric foe to the brave man who led this attack, where death was so inevitable.

Oct. 4.—Col. JOSEPH L. KIRBY SMITH, of the 43d Ohio regiment, was killed at the battle of Corinth. He was born in 1836, was appointed a cadet of the Military Academy from New York, and graduated with the highest honors of his class in 1857; was at once appointed lieutenant of topographical engineers, accompanied the Utah expedition, was aide-de-camp to Gen. Patterson in 1860, and after his discharge appointed colonel of the 43d Ohio regiment, with which he served with distinction at Island No. Ten, his engineering abilities being brought almost constantly into requisition, and at the battle of Corinth, where he fell, had greatly distinguished himself for bravery and daring. He was a nephew of the Confederate general Edward Kirby Smith.

Oct. 6.—WILLIAM DEAN COLMAN, a captain and assistant adjutant-general in the U. S. volunteers, and one of the staff of Brig.-Gen. Stanley, 2d division, Army of the Mississippi, born in Salem, Mass., Sept. 15, 1827, the eldest son of Samuel Colman, publisher. On the breaking out of the war with Mexico he enlisted as a private in Walker's Mounted Rifles, and took an active part in the principal battles fought under Lieut.-Gen. Scott. When the first gun was fired by the confederates at Fort Sumter he was assistant postmaster at New Orleans, but, without stopping to count the cost, he abandoned all and hastened north to join the Union army. In the summer of 1861 he was appointed assistant quartermaster, and in December a major in the Missouri State Militia, where he was actively occupied in the most hazardous parts of that State till February, 1862, when he was ordered by Major-Gen. Halleck to the staff of Brig.-Gen. Stanley. On the 5th July he accepted from the president a commission as captain, and assistant adjutant-general of U. S. volunteers. He was in all the battles and skirmishes with Gen. Stanley, from New Madrid and Island No. Ten to the most memorable and sanguinary battle of Corinth on the 3d and 4th October, where he received a mortal wound, and died on the 6th after two days of severe suffering. He was buried with military honors, being much beloved and esteemed by Gens. Rosecrans, Stanley, and all on the staff, for his bravery, patriotism, and strict adherence to duty.

Oct. 8.—Gen. JAMES S. JACKSON, a brigadier-general in the Union service, killed at the battle of Perryville. He was a native of Kentucky, born about 1822, and educated for the bar. He had been some years in the practice of his profession, when at the commencement of the Mexican war he raised a regiment of volunteers, and served during the war. During his service in Mexico he had a difficulty with Col. Thomas F. Marshall, which resulted in a duel. On his return to Kentucky he resumed his practice first at Greenupsburg, and afterwards at Hopkinsville, Ky., and in 1860 was elected to Congress from the 2d congressional district of that State. In the autumn of 1861 he resigned his seat in Congress, and took command of the 3d regiment Kentucky cavalry, was an active participant in most of the battles of the winter and spring of 1861, and on the 16th of July was commissioned a brigadier-general. In the battle of Perryville he commanded a division of McCook's corps of the Army of the Ohio.

Oct. 8.—Gen. WILLIAM R. TERRILL, a brigadier-general of the Union army, killed at the battle of Perryville. He was a native of Virginia, born about 1832, and appointed from that State a cadet at the Military Academy, where he graduated in 1853, and was immediately appointed brevet second lieutenant of the 3d artillery, from which he was transferred to the 4th artillery in November following as second lieutenant. In 1855 he was appointed assistant professor of mathematics at West Point. In 1856 he was promoted to a first lieutenancy, and in May, 1861, was appointed captain in the 5th artillery, and assigned to duty on the coast survey. He soon after raised a regiment of volunteers, was sent to Kentucky, where he commanded a battery in Gen. McCook's division, was transferred to the command of a brigade, and for his gallant and meritorious conduct at the battle of Shiloh, was appointed brigadier-general of volunteers, his commission bearing date Sept. 9, 1862. At Perryville he was killed while urging forward his brigade against the enemy.

Oct. 9.—GEORGE WEBSTER, colonel of the 98th Ohio volunteer infantry, died of wounds received the preceding day in the battle of Perryville. He was born in Butler County, Ohio, in 1822. He volunteered in the Mexican war as a private soldier, but was promoted to be sergeant-major. After his return from Mexico he commenced the practice of law in Jefferson County, Ohio. In June, 1861, he volunteered as major of the 25th Ohio, and was promoted to a lieutenant-colonelcy in that regiment, and on the organization of the 98th regiment, in the summer of 1862, was appointed colonel. This regiment was ordered to join Gen. Buell's army, and at the battle of Perryville, Col. Webster was put in command of one of the brigades of Jackson's division of McCook's corps.

Oct. 11.—Capt. GREER TALLMADGE, quartermaster-general at Fortress Monroe, died of disease of the liver, at his quarters in that fortress. He was born in Dutchess County, New York, in 1826. He was the son of Hon. N. P. Tallmadge, late U. S. Senator from New York. He graduated at West Point in 1848, and was appointed brevet second lieutenant in the 1st artillery; early the following year he sailed with a detachment of United States troops for Fort Vancouver, Oregon Territory, where he was stationed for a year; returning in 1850 he was appointed aid to Gen. Wool, and after three years' service on his staff was ordered to Fort Niagara, and subsequently to Fort Ontario. In 1853 he was promoted to a first lieutenancy in the 4th artillery, and in 1857 accompanied the expedition to Utah, as an officer of Capt. (now General) Phelps' battery. In 1858 he was ordered to Fortress Monroe, and in May, 1861, promoted to the rank of captain in the quartermaster's department. The great labor of organizing the quartermaster's department for so large a force as was congregated in the military department of Fortress Monroe, and the added duties of assistant adjutant-general, which he discharged for a time, made his position one of great toil and responsibility, but they were admirably performed. The "contraband" idea put in practice by Gen. Butler, originated with him.

Oct. 16.—Gen. GEORGE B. ANDERSON, an officer in the Confederate army, died in Raleigh, N. C. He was born in Wilmington, N. C., in 1827, entered West Point from that State in 1848, graduated in 1852, and was appointed brevet 2d lieutenant in the 2d dragoons, promoted to be 1st lieutenant in 1855, and in 1858 appointed adjutant of his regiment with the rank of captain. He resigned in April, 1861, entered the Confederate army, where he was soon appointed brigadier-general, and at the battle of Antietam received a wound in the foot, which eventually proved fatal.

Oct. 20.—Major IRA L. HEWITT, a paymaster in the United States army, died in the city of New York. He resided for some years in Illinois, but emigrated to Texas in 1840, and had there become one of the associate justices of the supreme court of the State. At the commencement of the war, his attachment to the Union being known, his life was in danger, but he succeeded in escaping from the State by stratagem, and joining the army served at Ship Island and New Orleans under Gen. Butler, and when Col. A. J. Hamilton came north, accompanied him and was assigned to duty in New York.

Oct. 30.—ORMSBY MACKNIGHT MITCHEL, an American astronomer, and major-general of volunteers in the United States service, born in Union Co., Ky., Aug. 28, 1810, died of yellow fever, at Beaufort, S. C., Oct. 30, 1862. He received his early education at Lebanon, Warren Co., Ohio, and at 12 years of age began life for himself as clerk in a store in Miami, Ohio. In 1825 he received an appointment to a cadetship in West Point. In 1829 he graduated fifteenth in a class of 46, among which were Robert E. Lee and Joseph E. Johnston, late generals in the Confederate service. He was at once appointed assistant professor of mathematics, which position he occupied for two years. He subsequently studied law, was admitted to the bar, and practised in Cincinnati until 1834, when he was elected professor of mathematics, philosophy, and astronomy in the Cincinnati College. In 1845 he proposed the establishment of an observatory at Cincinnati, raising nearly the whole of the requisite amount by his own exertions, and was made director of the institution. To obtain the necessary apparatus he took a flying trip to Europe, visited London, Paris, and Munich, completed his contracts and returned to his college duties in the short space of fourteen weeks. In 1859 he was chosen director of the Dudley Observatory at Albany, retaining, at the same time, his connection with that at Cincinnati. As an astronomical lecturer, he was exceedingly popular, and among the monuments of his skill in perfecting the necessary apparatus for that department of science, is an instrument at Albany for recording right ascensions and declinations by electro-magnetic aid to within $\frac{1}{1000}$ of a second of time, and for the measurement, with great accuracy, of large differences of declination incapable of being reached by the micrometer.

Among his published works are: "Planetary and Stellar Worlds," "Popular Astronomy," and a treatise on Algebra. On the 1st of July, 1846, he commenced the publication of a periodical entitled the "Sidereal Messenger," which at the end of two years was discontinued for want of sufficient patronage. At the breaking out of the late rebellion, Professor Mitchel left his scientific pursuits and sought an opportunity of serving his country. In August, 1861, he was commissioned brigadier-general of volunteers, and ordered to the Department of the Ohio, under the command of Maj.-Gen. Buell. After the capture of Bowling Green and Nashville he made a forced march southward and seized the railway between Corinth and Chattanooga, thereby breaking the enemy's line of communication, and possessed himself of various points in northern Alabama, for which he was made a major-general. In July, 1862, he was relieved of his command, and, on the 17th of the September following, was appointed commander of the Department of the South, where he was making preparations for a vigorous campaign when he fell a victim to the yellow fever.

Nov. 3.—ISRAEL B. RICHARDSON, a major-general of volunteers in the United States service, born at Burlington, Vt., in 1819, died at Sharpsburg, Md., Nov. 3, 1862. He was a descendant of the Revolutionary hero, Gen. Israel Putnam, graduated at West Point in 1841, was appointed 2d lieutenant in the 3d infantry, and 1st lieutenant Sept. 21, 1846. He distinguished himself in nearly every important battle during the Mexican War; was brevetted captain for gallant and meritorious conduct at Contreras and Churubusco, and major for gallantry at Chapultepec; and so distinguished himself for bravery that he was known in the army by the sobriquet of "Fighting Dick." In March, 1851, he was promoted to a captaincy. In 1855 he left the army and retired to private life in Michigan. Upon the commencement of the late rebellion he promptly offered himself again to the Government, organized a regiment, the 2d Michigan volunteers, of which he was made colonel, and soon after was placed in command of a brigade, with which he covered the retreat of the army at Bull Run. His commission as brigadier-general dated back to May 12, 1861. At the battle of the Chickahominy he commanded a division of Gen. Sumner's corps, and won much honor upon that occasion. He received his commission of major-general July 4, 1862; distinguished himself at the battles of South Mountain and Antietam, in the latter of which he received the wound causing his death.

Nov. 5.—Col. CURREN POPE, commander of the 15th Kentucky regiment, died at Danville of wounds received at the battle of Perryville, on the 8th of October previous. He was a member of one of the most distinguished families of Kentucky, and was born in Louisville about 1813. He entered West Point as a cadet in 1829, and graduated in 1834, but soon after left the army to follow the profession of civil engineer. Early in the war a number of his relatives joined the Confederate army, but he adhered firmly to the cause of the Union, and abandoning his profession, raised the regiment which he commanded at the time of his death.

Nov. 6.—Gen. CHARLES DAVIS JAMESON died at Oldtown, Me., from camp fever, brought on by his exertions at the battle of Fair Oaks and the pestilential influence of the climate. He was born at Gorham, Me., Feb. 24, 1827; while yet very young, his parents removed to Oldtown, Me., where, after receiving a limited academic education, he at an early age embarked in the lumber business, and eventually became one of the largest manufacturers and shippers of lumber on the Penobscot. He had been an active adherent to the Douglas section of the democracy, and in 1860 was a Douglas delegate to the Charleston Convention, where he became convinced of the intentions of the Southern States to secede. At the commencement of the war he was one of the first, if not the first, of the prominent democrats of the State to offer his services to the Government, and was placed by Gen. Washburn in command of the first regiment which left that State for the beleaguered capital. In the battle of Bull Run he commanded this regiment (2d Maine) and distinguished himself by his bravery, and with his regiment protected the rear in its retreat to Centreville. For his conduct on that day he was appointed brigadier-general of volunteers, on the 3d of Sept., 1861. In the autumn of 1861 he was, without his knowledge or consent, nominated by the democrats of his own State for governor, and polled a heavy vote though defeated by the republican candidate. In the spring and early summer of 1862 he took an active part in the campaign on the peninsula, in Gen. Heintzelman's corps, and by his exertions there, both before and at the battle of Fair Oaks, contracted the fever which finally terminated his life. He ranked high as a disciplinarian and as a brave and competent commander.

Nov. 7.—Commodore GARRETT J. PENDERGRAST, commandant of the navy yard at Philadelphia, died in that city, aged 62 years. He was a native of Kentucky, and entered the navy when only 11 years of age, and had been in the service since that time, passing through all the grades. In 1860 he was flag officer of the home squadron, and did service at the commencement of the war in the protection of the important harbor of Hampton Roads. In the autumn of 1861 he was assigned to the command of the navy yard at Philadelphia. He died of paralysis.

Nov. 22.—Brig.-Gen. FRANCIS E. PATTERSON killed himself by the accidental discharge of his pistol in his tent at Fairfax Court House during the night. He was a native of Philadelphia, born in 1827, and had entered the army from civil life as second lieutenant of the 1st artillery in June, 1847. In March, 1855, he was promoted to a captaincy in the 9th infantry, then first organized. In May, 1857, he resigned, and devoted himself to civil pursuits. On the raising of the 115th Pennsylvania volunteers, Gov. Curtin offered him the command of the regiment, which he accepted, and acquitted himself so ably in the field, that on the 11th of April, 1862, he was appointed brigadier-general, and in the subsequent battles on the peninsula rendered efficient service.

Nov. —.—Gen. JOHN B. VILLIPIGUE, a brigadier-general of the Confederate army, died at Port Hudson, La., of pneumonia. He was born in South Carolina about 1834; it is said that his father was of French and his mother of Spanish extraction. He graduated at West Point in 1854; was appointed to a second lieutenancy in the 2d dragoons, and was promoted to a first lieutenancy in 1857, and assigned to service in the Southwest. In March, 1861, he resigned from the United States service, and at once accepted an appointment as colonel in the Confederate service. In Nov., 1861, he was wounded at the bombardment of Fort Pickens, and soon after was made a brigadier-general in the Confederate army. He was assigned to the command of Fort Wright, and retained it until the evacuation of that post; participated in the battle of Corinth in October, 1862, and was soon after assigned to the command of Mobile.

Nov. 27.—Gen. ALEXANDER EARLY STEEN (or STEIN), a Confederate officer, killed at the battle of Kane Hill, in Arkansas. A musket ball passed directly through his brain. He was appointed from civil life second lieutenant of the 12th infantry in the regular army of the United States, March 6th, 1847; was brevetted first lieutenant for "gallant and meritorious conduct" at the battle of Contreras and Churubusco, in Mexico, Aug. 2d, 1847—date of brevet August, 1848. His regiment was disbanded in July, 1848, and he was appointed second lieutenant of the 3d infantry, June 30th, 1852.

Dec. 6.—CLAIBORNE F. JACKSON, late Governor of Missouri, died at Little Rock, Ark., of cancer in the stomach. He was born in Fleming County, Ky., April 4, 1807, and emigrated to Missouri in 1822. In the "Black Hawk" war he raised a volunteer company, and served as captain. He was for ten or twelve terms a member of one or the other House of the Missouri Legislature, and for one term Speaker of the House. In the session of 1848 he drew up and carried through the Legislature the famous Jackson resolutions. He was one of the prime movers in the organization of the present banking system of Missouri, and for a number of years Bank Commissioner. In 1860 he was elected Governor. His own sympathy with secession, and his determination to draw the State into it, soon became evident; and having fled from the State capitol on the approach of Gen. Lyon in July, he was deposed by the State Convention, and Gov. Gamble appointed provisional governor in his place. He acted for a short time as a general in the Confederate army, but his disease, from which he had long suffered, becoming aggravated, he retired to Little Rock, where he died after some months of suffering.

Dec. 12.—Rev. ARTHUR B. FULLER, a Unitarian clergyman, and chaplain of the 16th regiment Massachusetts volunteers, killed while crossing the Rappahannock with a portion of his regiment, who had volunteered to cross the river, and drive off the sharpshooters who were preventing the laying of the pontoon bridges. He was born in 1824 at Cambridgeport, Mass., and was the son of Hon. Timothy Fuller, an eminent lawyer and member of Congress from 1817 to 1825, and a brother of the celebrated Margaret Fuller, Countess D'Ossoli. In his childhood the family removed to Groton, Mass., and by an accident in his boyhood Arthur lost an eye. He was fitted for college by his sister, and entered Harvard university in 1839, graduating in 1843. After studying theology at the Cambridge Divinity School, Mr. Fuller went to Illinois as a teacher and missionary, and after some years' labor there returned—first to Boston, and afterward to Watertown, Mass., where he was settled as pastor. He volunteered as a chaplain early in the war, and not only fulfilled his duties in that capacity unexceptionally, but by his earnest sympathy for the members of his regiment, and his careful solicitude for their health, their mental improvement, and their moral welfare, became the idol of his regiment, and exerted a powerful and salutary influence on other bodies of men in their vicinity. His patriotism and courage led him to risk all perils with his men, and when several companies of them volunteered as a forlorn hope in the mission of crossing the Rappahannock under a deadly fire, his prompt determination to go with them greatly stimulated their enthusiasm. He edited his sister's works, and had published several original volumes.

Dec. 13.—Brig.-Gen. GEORGE D. BAYARD, an officer of the United States army, was killed in the battle of Fredericksburg. He was a native of New York, born about 1836; he entered West Point as a cadet in 1852, and graduated in June, 1856, receiving immediately an appointment as 2d lieutenant of the 4th cavalry. On the 20th of Aug., 1861, he was promoted to a captaincy in his regiment, and was allowed leave of absence to take command of the 1st Pennsylvania volunteer cavalry attached to Gen. McCall's reserve corps, and participated in the various battles of that fighting corps. On the 20th of Nov., 1861, he made a most brilliant and successful dash at the head of his regiment upon Dranesville. On the 10th of June, 1862, he was nominated as brigadier-general of volunteers commanding cavalry, his commission dating from the 28th of April. During the autumn he had done excellent service with his brigade, making frequent dashes into the enemy's lines, and driving them from the gaps of the Blue Ridge. At Fredericksburg he was attached to Gen. Franklin's corps. He was buried with military honors at Princeton, N. J.

Dec. 13.—Gen. THOMAS R. R. COBB, of Georgia, an officer of the Confederate army, killed at the battle of Fredericksburg. Gen. Cobb was a brother of Major-Gen. Howell Cobb, and was an able and eloquent member of the provisional congress of the seceded States, in which body he served as chairman of the committee on military affairs.

Dec. 13.—Lieut.-Col. JOSEPH BRIDGHAM CURTIS was killed at Fredericksburg while leading his regiment in a charge. He was born in New York in 1836, and was a son of the late George Curtis president of the Continental Bank, and brother of the author, George Wm. Curtis. He had received an education as an engineer, and at the commencement of the war was a member of the engineer corps of the Central Park, and volunteered in the 7th regiment N. Y. S. M. as an engineer. Soon after that regiment was mustered out of the service he reëntered the volunteer army as adjutant of the 4th Rhode Island regiment, one of the regiments attached to the Burnside expedition. He distinguished himself at the capture of Roanoke Island for coolness and daring, and was soon after appointed by Gen. Rodman assistant adjutant-general on his staff. The ability he displayed in this position led to his promotion soon after, at Gen. Burnside's request, to the lieutenant-colonelcy of the 4th Rhode Island, and with his regiment he joined the Army of the Potomac on the peninsula, and was with it in that succession of terrible battles between the Rappahannock and Washington, and at South Mountain and Antietam. In the last-named battle his regiment was so cut up that it was by command of the general withdrawn from the field, but the lieutenant-colonel did not go with it; seizing the musket and cartridge box of a dead soldier, he joined the ranks of a Pennsylvania regiment and did duty as a private to the close of the battle. At Fredericksburg he was in command of the regiment, the colonel being disabled by a wound.

Dec. 13.—Brig.-Gen. MAXEY GREGG, of South Carolina, a Confederate officer, killed at the battle of Fredericksburg. He entered into the war at its commencement, and commanded the 1st South Carolina regiment, which was the first force from that State which arrived in

Virginia, and was hailed by the people upon its advent into Richmond with extraordinary demonstrations of honor and welcome. When the term of service of this regiment expired, it returned to South Carolina, but Col. Gregg remained in Virginia, and subsequently reorganized the regiment, which was afterwards constantly and conspicuously in service. Col. Gregg was shortly afterwards made a brigadier-general. Previous to the war Gen. Gregg, though devoted to the profession of law, had a wide and brilliant political reputation. In politics he was an extreme States' rights man, and stood with others in South Carolina at the head of that party. He took a prominent part in favor of the policy of reopening the slave trade; and with ex-Governor Adams, of South Carolina, being associated as leading representatives of that idea in the cotton States. He was a prominent member of the bar, and practised his profession with distinction and success in Columbia for over twenty years. As a military man he had a wide reputation for coolness and self-possession in danger. In battle he had the faculty of inspiring his troops with confidence and enthusiasm—not by words but by deeds.

Dec. 13.—Brig.-Gen. CONRAD FEGER JACKSON, was killed at the battle of Fredericksburg, where he commanded the brigade formerly known as Gen. Ord's. He was a citizen of Pennsylvania, and previous to the war had been connected with the Pennsylvania Central and Reading Railroads, where he was well and favourably known. Soon after the commencement of the war he was appointed colonel of the 9th regiment of the corps of Pennsylvania reserves, under the command of Gen. George A. McCall. The corps was ordered to Washington, July 22, 1861, and Col. Jackson's regiment entered that city on the 26th of that month with full numbers and completely equipped, and encamped near Seventh Street. They were subsequently ordered to Tenallytown, and formed part of the 3d brigade, then under command of Gen. E. O. C. Ord. The regiment was subsequently stationed on the heights south of the Potomac, and formed a part of the brigade which gained a victory at Dranesville. On the peninsula Col. Jackson distinguished himself at Mechanicsville and Gaines' Mills, and participated in the remaining contests of those memorable seven days. He also took an active part in the battles between the Rappahannock and Alexandria in the latter part of August; and having, on the departure of Gen. Ord to the West, been promoted to the command of the brigade, he led his troops into the action of South Mountain and Antietam. At Fredericksburg he was at the head of his troops, leading them on to a charge, when a rifle ball passed through his head, killing him instantly.

Dec. 31.—Col. JULIUS P. GARESCHÉ, chief of Maj.-Gen. Rosecrans's staff, was born in Cuba, of American parents, in 1821. At the age of 16 he entered West Point, and graduated in 1841. He served in the Mexican war, and during eight years previous to the secession was on duty at Washington as assistant adjutant-general. When the war broke out, his patriotic nature sought active service, and he accepted the appointment of chief of staff to Gen. Rosecrans, having previously declined a commission of brigadier-general, preferring to win the honor upon the field of service. From his long experience and thorough acquaintance with military science, he was eminently qualified for his duties, and rendered himself at once an invaluable aid to his commander. He was an earnest and devoted Christian, gentle and amiable in character and disposition, and was widely known for his benevolence to the poor and sympathy for those in affliction and sorrow. He was one of the founders of the Society of St. Vincent of Paul in Washington. His many virtues, added to his gentlemanly deportment and earnest devotion to his country, won the love of both officers and men, and his untimely death by a cannon ball, which took off his head, while on duty at the side of his commander, was alike a shock to the army and country. A few days after the battle his body was disinterred and taken to Cincinnati, from whence, after appropriate honors, it was forwarded to his family in Washington City.

Dec. 31.—Gen. ROGER W. HANSON, an officer in the Confederate army, killed at the battle of Murfreesboro (or Stone River as it is sometimes called). Gen. Hanson was born in Winchester, Ky., and was a son of Samuel Hanson, of the same State. Gen. Hanson, at the breaking out of the war, was a practising lawyer in Lexington, Ky., a prominent politician, and a staunch Union man of high reputation. His age was about thirty-four when he was killed.

Dec. 31.—Brig.-Gen. JAMES E. RAINS, an officer in the Confederate service, killed at the battle of Stone River. He was a native of North Carolina, graduated at West Point in 1827, and was appointed to the 7th infantry. He took part in the Seminole war in Florida, and was brevetted major for gallant and meritorious conduct in an action with the Indians near Fort King, April 28th, 1840, on which occasion he commanded the troops, and was wounded. In 1855 he was with his regiment in Washington Territory, and was appointed brigadier-general of the Washington Territory volunteers. When the war broke out he was a lieutenant-colonel of the 5th infantry, but his sympathies being with the Confederate cause, he resigned his commission, July 31st, 1861, and, according to Gen. Sterling Price's official report of the battle of Wilson's Creek, was acting as brigadier-general of the advance guard of the army which fought the battle, August 10th. He distinguished himself at the battle of Shiloh and Perryville, and at the battle of Stone River, where he lost his life, won much credit by his skill and daring.

Dec. 31.—Col. GEORGE W. ROBERTS, killed at the battle of Stone River, was born in Westchester county, Penn., Oct. 2d, 1833; graduated at Yale College in 1857, studied law, and practised his profession in his native county until the spring of 1859, when he removed to Chicago, Ill. The commencement of the war found him enjoying a prosperous business, but his patriotism led him to enter the army, and he began recruiting for the 42d regiment Illinois volunteers. On the 22d of July he received his commission as major of the regiment. The following September he was elected lieutenant-colonel, and upon the death of Col. Webb, was chosen colonel. With his regiment he took part in the memorable march of Gen. Fremont to Springfield. He distinguished himself in the faithful discharge of his duty at different points, but more especially by his valuable service during a midnight expedition in spiking a number of guns at the siege of Island No. 10. An upper battery of the enemy commanded the river so effectually that no boats could pass. Col. Roberts conceived the idea of spiking the guns, and selecting a dark and stormy night for the occasion, with only forty men in five small boats, he bravely accomplished his purpose. He afterwards distinguished himself at the battle of Farmington, Tenn. At the siege of Corinth he was in the advance, and was one of the foremost in entering the fortification of the enemy. He was in command of the first brigade, first division of the Army of the Mississippi, and won much honor during the campaign of 1862. At the battle of Stone River he had the advance of the 20th army corps, and drove the enemy to their breastworks. On the 31st his brigade engaged two divisions of the enemy at once, maintaining their ground until attacked by a third division. At one period of the engagement, observing a Confederate division driving some of our regiments before them, he asked permission of Gen. Sheridan to charge upon the enemy, and galloping before the 42d Illinois, he waved his cap and ordered them to fix bayonets. The men, fired by his bravery, rushed upon the foe with such force that they broke and fled in the wildest confusion. This discomfiture at such a juncture no doubt had its effect on the final triumph of the day. While gallantly inspiring his men to action he received the fatal bullet which ended his brave career

Dec. 31.—J. W. SCHAEFFER, acting brigadier-general of the U. S. volunteer service, killed at the battle of Stone River. He was a native of Pennsylvania, but was appointed to the service from Illinois. In the official report of the battle of Stone River, Gen. Rosecrans mentions his name with honor.

Dec. 31.—Brig.-Gen. JOSHUA WOODROW SILL, an officer of the United States army, killed in the battle of Stone River. He was born in Chillicothe, Ohio, Dec. 6, 1831; received a thorough English and classical education, and was appointed a cadet at West Point in 1849, where he graduated third in his class. In 1854 he received an ordnance appointment, and was stationed at Watervliet Arsenal, West Troy. The following year he was recalled as one of the instructors at West Point, and after serving two years in that capacity was ordered to Pittsburg Arsenal, and from thence, in 1858, to Vancouver, Washington Territory, to superintend the building of an arsenal there. Finding this impracticable, in consequence of the difficulty existing about Vancouver's Island with the British Government, he returned, and soon after was ordered to Fort Leavenworth. In 1860 he resigned his position in the army, and accepted the professorship of mathematics and civil engineering in the Brooklyn Collegiate and Polytechnic Institute. Upon the outbreak of the present war he resigned his position, and upon offering his services to the Governor of Ohio was appointed assistant adjutant-general of the State. In August, 1861, he was commissioned colonel of the 23d Ohio volunteers. He joined Gen. Nelson in his Kentucky expedition, and after his return was placed in command of a brigade, receiving the commission of brigadier-general July 29, 1862. Subsequently he commanded a division for a time, evincing great courage and skill, and upon the reorganization of the army under Gen. Rosecrans he was assigned a brigade in Gen. Sheridan's division, at the head of which he gallantly fought, and fell during the memorable Wednesday of the battle of Stone River.

1863.

Jan. 1.—WILLIAM B. RENSHAW, acting commodore of the naval squadron engaged in blockading Galveston, Texas, was killed upon his flag-ship, the Westfield. He was a native of New York, from which State he was appointed to the navy as a midshipman, Dec. 22d, 1831. In 1837 he passed the Examining Board, and received his warrant as a passed midshipman, and was attached to the North Carolina, at the New York navy yard. In 1841 he was promoted to a lieutenancy, and in 1861 became commander, and was ordered to the Ordnance Bureau at Washington, on special service. He was next transferred to the command of the United States steamer Westfield, under Admiral Farragut, and was by him assigned to the command of that portion of the squadron which blockaded Galveston. During the recapture of Galveston, the Westfield got hopelessly aground, and having a large supply of ammunition and two magazines of powder on board, Commodore Renshaw determined to destroy her rather than let her fall into the hands of the enemy. Having made due arrangements, and secured the safety of his men, he stayed behind to light the train before leaving; but a drunken man had, it is said, prematurely lighted the match, and the commodore, together with those in the small boats awaiting him, were involved in the general destruction. He was a faithful officer, and had spent thirty-one years in the service of his country.

Jan. 1.—Commander JONATHAN M. WAINWRIGHT, an officer in the U. S. navy, was killed upon the Harriet Lane during the attack upon Galveston, Texas. He was a native of New York, but a citizen of Massachusetts, from which State he was appointed to the United States navy as a midshipman, June 13th, 1837. He passed the Examining Board June, 1843, and received his warrant as a passed midshipman on that date. He was then engaged at the naval rendezvous in New York. On the 17th of September, 1850, he was promoted to a lieutenancy, and upon the commencement of the war was advanced to be a commander, and ordered to the Harriet Lane. He was a son of the late Bishop Wainwright, and had been twenty-five years in the United States service.

Jan. 2.—Lieut. EDWARD LEA, of the U. S. navy, was killed upon the Harriet Lane in the engagement before Galveston, Texas. He was a native of Maryland, but a resident of Tennessee, from which State he was appointed to the Naval Academy in 1851. After graduating he received an appointment to the Home squadron, and subsequently to the East India squadron. At the commencement of the war, being himself truly Union, notwithstanding his ties of relationship in the South, he was assigned to the Harriet Lane, then fitting out to join Admiral Porter's mortar flotilla in the bombardment of Forts Jackson and St. Philip.

Jan. 3.—Commander WILLIAM GWIN, of the United States navy, died in the hospital of his vessel, from wounds received in the action against the batteries on Haines's Bluff. He was born in Columbus, Indiana, in 1831, and entered the U. S. naval service as a midshipman in 1847, in which capacity he made one cruise off the coast of Brazil in the frigate Brandywine, flag-ship of the squadron, and off the coast of Africa. In June, 1853, he passed a satisfactory examination at the Naval Academy, and, with the rank of passed midshipman, was ordered to the Bainbridge, in which vessel he cruised off the coast of Brazil until 1856. On the 15th of September he was promoted to a lieutenancy. He was next ordered to the Pacific squadron, and, after a brief visit home in 1859, was assigned to the Mediterranean squadron. On the breaking out of the war he was ordered home, and assigned to the Cambridge, on blockading duty on the Atlantic coast. From this he was detached, January, 1862, and assigned to the command of the gunboat Tyler, of the Western flotilla, in which vessel he participated in the battles of Fort Henry and Fort Donelson. He also took part in the battle of Shiloh, at the time when the gunboats fired at night among the enemy, his vessel discharging one hundred and eighty-eight shells. On the 16th of July, 1862, he was made a lieutenant-commander under the late act of Congress in relation to officers in the navy. He distinguished himself in the expedition up the Yazoo River in company with the Carondelet, to meet the famous Confederate ram Arkansas; and his vessel, though sadly disabled, did not cease firing until she had passed through the entire squadron. After the explosion on the Mound City at St. Charles, by which her commander, Capt. Kelly, was so badly scalded, Lieutenant-Commander Gwin took command of that vessel, which he held until assigned to the Benton, the largest and most powerful vessel of the river fleet. While in charge of this gunboat he participated in the attack upon Haines's Bluff, during which he was mortally wounded.

Jan. —.—Brig.-Gen. EDWARD N. KIRK, an officer of volunteers in the U. S. service, died from wounds received at the battle of Stone River. He was born in Ohio, but subsequently removed to Sterling, Whiteside County, Illinois. In the autumn of 1861 he was instrumental in raising and organizing the 34th Illinois volunteers, of which he was chosen colonel. At the battle of Shiloh he acted as brigadier-general, and was also engaged in this capacity at the siege of Corinth. At the battle of Stone River he commanded one of the brigades in Johnson's division of McCook's corps, and was mortally wounded while bravely withstanding the enemy during that fierce encounter.

Jan. 11.—Col. EMMETT MACDONALD, an officer of the Confederate army, killed at the battle of Hartsville, in Missouri. He was born in Steubenville, Ohio, on the 25th of November, 1834. His father, Isaac MacDonald, was born in that beautiful and romantic spot known as Grey Abbey, on Strangford Loch, in the County of Down, Ireland. His mother, whose maiden name was Annie Wilson, was likewise born in Ireland, in the town of Lisburn, noted for its linen manufactures. Col. MacDonald was the descendent of a long line of warlike ancestors. The father of his grandfather was a Scottish chief of the MacDonalds of Glencoe. His great-uncle sympathized with the American colonies in their struggle for freedom with Great Britain, and he fought in their cause in South Carolina. His father was a "United Man," and was engaged in the Irish Rebellion in 1798. After receiving a liberal English education, Col. MacDonald, at the age of sixteen, located in St. Louis, and commenced business as collector and general agent. His leisure hours were devoted to the study of history, poetry, politics, and law. In 1859 he was admitted to the bar, and received the nomination for the position of assistant circuit attorney for St. Louis County, but was defeated in the election by the German vote. In the heat of the canvas he was challenged by Sylvan Carlin to fight a duel, which took place on Bloody Island, opposite the city of St. Louis. Two shots were exchanged with Kentucky rifles, at fifty paces, but neither party was injured. Friends interposed, and the difficulty was amicably arranged. He had another "affair of honor" not long after this occurrence, which was near not ending so happily. Being called on for satisfaction, he proposed to settle the matter on the spot, with Derringer pistols, across the table. The gentlemen took their places, and with the fatal weapons at the breast of each other, awaited the signal, but none of their numerous acquaintances in the room would give the word in so deadly an encounter. The cause of the difficulty proved to be a few words spoken in jest, and was soon explained. During the Kansas troubles MacDonald was captain of a company of mounted infantry in Bowen's battalion of Missouri volunteer militia, sent to the border to put a stop to the outrages committed by lawless bands of "Jayhawkers." He remained on the border six months, at the end of which time he was ordered to report with his command at Camp Jackson, near St. Louis, and was captured on the 10th of May, 1861, with the whole force in that encampment. MacDonald denied the legality of the capture, and refused to give his parole. All the rest of the prisoners gave their parole, under protest, and were released. Capt. Lyon, who had made the capture, sent MacDonald out of the State, to avoid the writ of habeas corpus, which was, however, issued and served upon him. But the prisoner was not then in his possession. Another writ was issued and served upon Col. McArthur, who then held MacDonald. Col. McArthur refused to obey the writ, and the return was so made to the court. In the mean time MacDonald was removed to Cairo, Ill. Upon the case being laid before Gen. McClellan, he ordered MacDonald to be handed over to the civil authorities, which was done, and he was discharged. He then joined Gen. Price's army, and led a portion of the Missouri cavalry at the battle of Carthage. It was by his interposition that a whole company of Gen. Sigel's noted regiment of Turners was saved from massacre. The company was captured in Sigel's retreat. It becoming known that this company had taken part in the massacre at Camp Jackson, the Missourians were almost uncontrollable. MacDonald sought and obtained permission from Gen. McCullough to protect all prisoners. He regaled them with two barrels of lager beer, paroled and sent them under escort through the Confederate lines. His treatment a few weeks later, by the Illinois troops, at Rolla, whither he had been sent with a flag of truce, was an ill return for his magnanimous behavior toward the captive Germans. Nothing but the protecting arm of the commander, Gen. Samuel Sturgis, saved his life. At the battle of Wilson's Creek he fought in the ranks of a Louisiana regiment. At the battle of Dry Wood he commanded a piece of field artillery. At the battle of Lexington, Mo., he commanded Bledroe's battery, that officer having been wounded at Dry Wood. Gen. Price, in his official report of the capture of Lexington, makes mention of the "gallant services" of Capt. MacDonald. At the battle of Pea Ridge, Capt. MacDonald commanded a battery of four field-pieces, and was complimented by Gen. Van Dorn on the field. His battery was in the battle of Farmington, in front of Corinth, Miss., where he was, as usual, distinguished for his contempt of danger. Whilst on a visit to Richmond, he took part as a volunteer in the ranks in the seven days fighting around that place. Subsequently he obtained permission to go to the Trans-Mississippi Department and raise a regiment of cavalry. On the 8th of January, 1863, he commanded a brigade under Gen. Marmaduke, in the attack on Springfield, Mo. At the battle of Hartsville he had come upon the field to remonstrate with the general commanding against keeping his regiment too far from the scene of action to take part in it, when seeing two pieces of Confederate artillery in danger of capture, he gathered a few stragglers together and made a charge, with the intention of bringing them off. He succeeded, but received two balls in the leg, and expired in four hours after. As he laid bleeding upon the field, he said: "Never mind me, take off the guns, boys." As he was being carried from the field, feeling that his life was ebbing with the crimson stream from his wound, he asked his assistants to draw the curtains of the ambulance aside, that he might hear the music of the battle and see the retreating enemy. His last words were: "Tell the general to remember the charge of the stragglers. It was a gallant charge." He was buried on the battle-field, but his remains were subsequently removed to St. Louis. The provost marshal of that city, Gen. Franklin A. Dick, issued an order for the seizure of the body and its burial in the soldier's graveyard. Kindred and friends begged the privilege of a decent burial for the deceased, but the provost marshal being inexorable, the brothers and sisters of Col. MacDonald gathered round the corpse, and gave the messengers, who had been sent to seize it, to understand that it must be done over their dead bodies. Appeal was made to Major-Gen. Curtis, commanding the department, and he generously revoked the order. The remains of Col. Emmett MacDonald were buried in the lawn of his sister's residence near St. Louis, but were recently removed to a lot in the Bellefontain Cemetery. Col. MacDonald possessed a remarkable personal appearance. His figure was good, and his face handsome, noble, and expressive. His height was about five feet ten inches, and his hair, which he wore very long, was as black as the raven's wing. He took an oath that he would not cut it until the independence of the Southern Confederacy was recognized. Col. MacDonald's death occurred on the same day that, years before, the edict was issued by William of Orange for the massacre of his ancesters, the MacDonalds of Glencoe.

Jan. 14.—Rev. JAMES HORTON DILL, a Congregational clergyman, died on board of a vessel on his way from Louisville to Nashville, whither he was going to join his regiment, of which he was chaplain. He was born in Plymouth, Mass., Jan. 1st, 1821, studied theology in New Haven, Conn., and was ordained pastor of the First Congregational Church in Winchester, Conn., Aug. 26th, 1846. In Feb., 1852, he was installed pastor of the First Congregational Church in Spencerport, New York. In 1859 he removed to Chicago, and became the pastor of the South Congregational Church. His devotion to his country led him to accept the chaplaincy of the 38th regiment of Illinois volunteers in the autumn of 1862. His death was hastened by his unsparing activity and devotion to the cause he had espoused.

Jan. 14.—Lieut.-Com. THOMAS BUCHANAN MCKEAN, of the U. S. navy, was killed at Bayou Teche, La. He was a native and citizen of Pennsylvania, from which State he was appointed to the Naval Academy as a cadet in October, 1851. He graduated in 1855, and was attached to the sloop Constellation, then stationed in the Mediterranean, in the squadron commanded by Commodore Breese. In 1858 he was promoted to be master, and ordered to the sloop St. Mary's in the Pacific squadron. In 1860 he was made a lieutenant, and attached to the steam sloop Mississippi, and, under the new act of Congress, became lieutenant-commander in 1861. He was next in command of the New London, the "black devil" of the Mississippi Sound, and subsequently of the gunboat Calhoun, on which he lost his life.

Jan. 24.—Lieut.-Col. WARREN STEWART, a cavalry officer in the U. S. service, was killed opposite Vicksburg. He first entered the United States service during the present war as captain of an independent cavalry company from Illinois, and was attached to Gen. McClernand's brigade. On the 2d of February, 1862, he was appointed acting adjutant-aid on Gen. McClernand's staff, with the rank of captain. He took an active part in the memorable battle of Fort Donelson. The several companies of cavalry connected with McClernand's brigade were next consolidated, under the title of Stewart's Independent Battalion of Cavalry, the command of which devolved upon him, with the rank of major, dating from February 1st, 1862. He was wounded at the battle of Shiloh, and was especially mentioned in his general's official report for his gallantry on that occasion. He also participated in the siege of Corinth, and subsequently was attached to the division stationed along the Memphis and Charleston Railroad. On the promotion of Gen. McClernand he was made lieutenant-colonel. He was engaged in destroying the ferry boats opposite Vicksburg, when he was killed by a shot from the enemy.

Feb. 19.—Commander MAXWELL WOODHULL, of the United States navy, was killed at Fort Marshall, Baltimore, aged about fifty years. He was visiting the forts around the city, in company with Gen. Butler and Gen. Schenck and staff, in whose honor a salute was fired; the gunner, supposing the whole party had passed out of range of the gun, fired a 32-pounder just as a fragment of the party came up; unfortunately Commander Woodhull received the whole charge, which caused his death in a few moments.

Feb. 22.—EDWARD SMITH GILBERT, a lieutenant-colonel in the U. S. volunteer service, died of consumption at Rochester, N. Y., aged 31 years. He was born in Livingston County, N. Y., graduated at Amherst College in 1855, and became professor of mathematics in the Collegiate Institute of Rochester, N. Y. Soon after the breaking out of the war he entered the military service as second lieutenant in the 13th regiment N. Y. volunteers. After the first battle of Bull Run he was promoted to a first lieutenancy, and a few months later to a captaincy, and transferred to the 25th regiment. During the peninsular campaign he rose to the rank of major. In one of the "seven days' battles" he was taken prisoner, and remained in Richmond until August. On rejoining his regiment he was promoted to the rank of lieutenant-colonel. His death occurred while at home on a furlough.

March 12.—HENRY N. FISHER, M.D., died in Washington, aged 29 years. After the disasters of the peninsular campaign he volunteered as physician and surgeon, to minister to the necessities of the sick and wounded soldiers, and made several trips between Harrison's Landing and New York on one of the transports. His faithfulness and efficiency recommending him to those in authority, he received an appointment as surgeon in the army, and for several months previous to his death had charge of Eckington Hospital, in the suburbs of Washington. His devotion and untiring energy in behalf of the suffering under his care, contributed to bring on the fever which cut him off in the dawn of manhood.

March —.—Acting Master ROBERT L. KELLY, of the U. S. navy, was killed during the attack upon Port Hudson. He was a native of the State of Rhode Island. During the early part of the war he performed important services in the North Atlantic squadron, after which he was transferred to the Western Gulf blockading squadron, where he was in active service on board the United States sloop Mississippi for more than a year. He held an important post as an officer of that ship, and in her last engagement fought his division nobly and courageously amid the shower of shot and shell until he fell lifeless upon the deck.

March 21.—Major-Gen. EDWIN VOSE SUMNER, an officer of U. S. volunteers, and brevet major-general in the U. S. army, born in Boston, Mass., in 1796, died at Syracuse, N. Y., March 21st, 1863. He was educated at the Milton Academy, Boston, and in March, 1819, was appointed second lieutenant in the 2d infantry, and served in the Black Hawk war. When the 2d regiment of dragoons was raised by Gen. Jackson, he was commissioned as its captain, and was for many years employed in service on the Indian frontier, and subsequently commanded the school of cavalry practice at Carlisle, Penn. He was promoted to be major in 1846, and in April, 1847, led the famous cavalry charge at Cerro Gordo; was wounded, and obtained the brevet of lieutenant-colonel. At Contreras and Churubusco he won much honor, and at the battle of Molino del Rey commanded the entire cavalry, holding in check 5,000 Mexican laucers. For his gallant conduct he received the brevet of colonel, and in July, 1848, was commissioned lieutenant-colonel of the 1st dragoons. At the close of the war he was placed in command of the department of New Mexico, In 1855 he was promoted to the colonelcy of the 1st cavalry, and the following year was in command at Fort Leavenworth, Kansas. In July of 1857 he led a successful expedition against the Cheyenne Indians, and in 1858 was appointed commander of the department of the West. In March, 1861, he was appointed brigadier-general in the regular army, in place of General Twiggs, and in March, 1862, appointed commander of the first army corps in the Army of the Potomac. At the siege of Yorktown he commanded the left wing, and was engaged in all the battles of the Chickahominy, during which he was twice wounded. For his services before Richmond he was made major-general of volunteers, and brevet major-general in the regular army. Upon the reorganization of the army Gen. Sumner was assigned to the 2d corps, and in the battle of Antietam was wounded. Subsequently he was placed in command of the right grand division of the Army of the Potomac, but, upon the appointment of Gen. Hooker as chief of that army, he asked to be relieved, and after a few weeks was ordered to the command of the army of the frontier. Upon the way thither he was taken sick, and died after a short illness, at Syracuse.

March 28.—Brig-Gen. JAMES COOPER, an officer of the U. S. volunteers, died at Columbus, Ohio, aged about 60 years. He was a native of Frederick County, Maryland, but removed many years ago to Pennsylvania, where he became a prominent whig politician, and was known as one of the leading advocates of the tariff of 1842. He was elected to the United States Senate, and served two terms with much ability, taking a prominent part in all the important questions that at that time agitated the country. A few years ago he took up his residence in Frederick City, Maryland, and after the breaking out of the war he was appointed the first brigadier-general; took command of all the volunteers in Maryland, and organized them into regiments. Subsequently he was appointed to the command of Camp Chase, near Columbus, Ohio, where he remained in the discharge of his duties until attacked with fatal illness.

April 10.—Dr. ROBERT WARE died in Washington N. C., aged 29 years. He was a native of Boston, Mass., studied at the Latin school in that city, graduated at Harvard College in 1852, and studied medicine with his father, Dr. John Ware, until May, 1854, when he went to Europe and remained until September, 1855, spending about six months of the time in Paris, studying in the French hospitals. On his return to this country he resumed his studies with his father, and graduated at the Medical School in 1856, when he began the practice of his profession in Boston. In July, 1857, he was appointed one of the district physicians of the Boston Dispensary. He was remarkably successful in his practice, which increased rapidly, as his father was intending to relinquish the profession to his son. On the breaking out of the war he was one of the first physicians to enter into the service of the Sanitary Commission, in which he continued until the close of the peninsular campaign in Virginia. Throwing his whole soul into the work of ministering to the wounded and dying, he spared himself neither night nor day. He was subsequently appointed surgeon of the 44th Massachusetts regiment, with which he left for the seat of war. On his arrival in North Carolina his arduous labors and exposures to the unhealthy climate brought on a fever, which speedily terminated his valuable life. In the eloquent language of one of the officers of the Sanitary Commission, he was "one who, through months of death and darkness, lived and worked in self-abnegation; lived in and for the sufferings of others, and finally gave himself a sacrifice for them."

April 12.—Lieut.-Col. EDGAR A. KIMBALL, killed at Suffolk, Va. He was born in Concord, N. H., in 1821, was educated as a printer, removed to Vermont, and became editor and proprietor of the Woodstock (Vt.) "Age," a liberal democratic newspaper. He distinguished himself in the Mexican campaign, and for his gallantry at Contreras, Churubusco, and Chapultepec, received the brevet of major. He was subsequently for a time in the office of the New York "Herald." Upon the breaking out of the war he again took the field, and received the commission of major of the 9th New York volunteers (Zouaves), May 13th, 1861, and the following August participated in a reconnoissance up the peninsula. At the battle of Roanoke Island, N. C., Feb. 7th, 1862, Major Kimball led his Zouaves along a narrow causeway commanded by the enemy's cannon, and at great peril carried the work and planted the Federal flag over it. On the 14th of February, 1862, he was promoted to the position of lieutenant-colonel, and soon after was placed in command of the regiment, which formed a portion of the 9th army corps. He participated in the reduction of Fort Macon, and was also engaged in the battles of South Mountain, Antietam, and Fredericksburg. The regiment was next transferred to Newport News, thence to Suffolk, Va. Here he unfortunately met his death, on the 12th of April, by a shot from General Michael Corcoran. Gen. Corcoran had occasion to pass Col. Kimball's camp on important duties connected with his command, before dawn of that day, and his right to pass being challenged by Col. Kimball, he announced his rank and position, and the urgency of his journey. By some strange perversity, Col. Kimball refused to accept his statement, and persisting in his determination not to allow him to pass, Gen. Corcoran, after giving him notice, fired upon him with fatal effect.

April 14.—BENJAMIN WELCH, late commissary general of the State of New York, died at Clifton Springs, aged 45 years. He studied law with the late Judge Mann, of Utica, N. Y., and was subsequently editor of the Utica "Democrat" and of the Buffalo "Republican." He was at one time State treasurer, and for four years commissary general of the State. In the spring of 1862 he accepted a position on General Pope's staff, and during the campaign of the following summer contracted the disease which subsequently proved fatal.

April 18.—Lieut.-Com. MCDERMOTT, of the U. S. gunboat Cayuga, was killed at Sabine Pass, while making a reconnoissance in company with Capt. Reed, of the gunboat New London. He was a brave man, a gallant officer, and a true patriot.

April 26.—Col. EDWARD COBB CHARLES died in New York from wounds received in the battle of Glendale. At the commencement of the war he went out with the 42d New York volunteers as lieutenant-colonel. At the battle of Ball's Bluff, Col. Cogswell, the commander of the regiment, was taken prisoner, and Lieut.-Col. Charles was promoted to the position thereby left vacant. He was in all the engagements from Ball's Bluff down to the last of the seven days' battles before Richmond. In the battle of Glendale he was severely wounded by a Minié rifle ball, and left for dead on the field. He was, however, taken prisoner, and lay for many weeks in a prison hospital. He afterwards came north on parole and was confined for some time. After undergoing some severe surgical operations mortification probably supervened, causing his death. His funeral took place from the City Hall, New York, and was attended by a large concourse of citizens, the old Light Guard joining in the procession.

May 1.—Brig.-Gen. R. D. TRACY, an officer in the Confederate service, a native of North Carolina, who entered the Confederate army from civil life. After serving for some time as colonel of a North Carolina regiment, he was promoted to the rank of brigadier-general in 1862, and was killed at the battle of Port Gibson, Miss.

May 1.—Lieut.-Col. WILLIAM WADE, an officer of artillery in the Confederate army, killed near Grand Gulf, on the Mississippi River. Lieut.-Col. Wade, at the breaking out of the war, was a prominent and highly respected merchant in St. Louis, Mo. At Camp Jackson, where Gen. Lyon captured the militia of St. Louis County, while in their camp, Lieut.-Col. Wade was on the staff of Brig.-Gen. Frost. By some mistake he was omitted in the parole. He soon after went South, and received from the Secretary of War of the Confederate Government a battery of six guns, with which he joined Gen. Price, at Rock River, in Missouri. The battery was divided into two batteries, and he was promoted to the rank of major. When the State troops were transferred from the State to the Confederate service, his battalion was reduced to a six-gun battery, to conform to Confederate regulations. At Elk Horn he distinguished himself for courage, and coolness, and ability. He was in the battles of Farmington, Iuka, and Corinth, Mississippi, in all of which his battery was conspicuous for its efficiency. His courteous and amiable manners endeared him to all who knew him. He was promoted to a lieut.-colonelcy only a short time before his death.

May 2.—Brig.-Gen. EDWARD F. PAXTON, an officer in the Confederate service, killed at the battle of Chancellorsville, Va. He was a native of Rockbridge County, Va., and received his military education at the Virginia Military Academy at Lexington. When "Stonewall" Jackson was made a brigadier-general he appointed young Paxton, to whom he was strongly attached, adjutant-general of his brigade, and on his own advancement promoted him adjutant-general of the division. When Jackson became commander of an army corps, he asked and obtained the appointment of Paxton as brigadier-general, and in this capacity he served at Antietam, Fredericksburg, and the beginning of the battle of Chancellorsville. He was killed on the same evening on which Jackson was mortally wounded.

May 3.—HIRAM GEORGE BERRY, a major-general of volunteers in the United States service, born in Thomaston (now Rockland), Maine, August 27th, 1824, killed at the battle of Chancellorsville, May 3d, 1863. In early life he had acquired the carpenter's trade, and followed the business for a few years, but was subsequently engaged, successfully, in navigation. He represented his native town in the State Legislature several times, and was mayor of the city of Rockland. Having a taste for military affairs he originated and commanded for several years the Rockland Guard, a volunteer company which had attained a very high reputation for its perfection of drill and discipline. At the commencement of the war he entered the volunteer service as colonel of the 4th regiment of Maine volunteer infantry. The regiment left Rockland on the 17th of June, 1861, arrived in Washington on the 20th, and went into camp on Meridian Hill on the 21st. On the 8th of July it crossed into Virginia, and on the 16th marched toward Centreville, where it arrived on the 18th. It participated in the battle of Bull Run, in acting Gen. Howard's brigade. After the battle it returned to Alexandria, and on the 24th to Meridian Hill. It was afterwards brigaded in Gen. Sedgwick's brigade of the Army of the Potomac, and when the army moved to the peninsula formed part of Gen. Birney's brigade, in Gen. C. S. Hamilton's division, and in that division participated in the siege of Yorktown. On the 4th of April, 1862, Col. Berry was made a brigadier-general of volunteers, his commission dating from March 17th, 1862, and was placed in charge of the third brigade of the third division of Heintzelman's third army corps. By this change he was separated from his regiment. In command of this brigade he participated in the battle of Williamsburg, where the coming of his brigade brought the first relief to the wearied and blood-stained heroes of Gen. Hooker's division; fought under Gen. Kearney at Fair Oaks, and won the special commendation of that daring and gallant officer for his indomitable bravery; bore a conspicuous part in the seven days' battles, and on the 4th of July, 1862, was, with Heintzelman's corps, highly complimented for his valor and endurance by the commanding general. On the 15th of August he moved with his brigade to Yorktown, and thence to Alexandria; thence to Warrenton Junction and Rappahannock, and on the 29th and 30th of Aug. took part with Kearney's division in the battles of Centreville and Manassas, or the second Bull Run. On the 1st of September he participated in the battle of Chantilly, where the gallant Kearney lost his life. During the campaign in Maryland he held with his brigade important fords on the Potomac, and thus cut off the retreat of the enemy. At the battle of Fredericksburg, Dec. 13th, 1862, Gen. Berry led his brigade in a charge upon a force considerably exceeding his own in numbers, and drove them back, thus relieving his division, then commanded by Gen. Birney, from imminent peril. For this brave act he was complimented by Gen. Birney in his report. In January, 1863, he was nominated by the President as major-general of volunteers, with rank dating from Nov. 29th, 1862, and was confirmed by the Senate on the 9th of March, 1863. He was then placed in command of the second division of the third army corps, which was at that time under the command of Major-Gen. Sickles. At the battle of Chancellorsville, after the fight of the eleventh army corps, who were pursued with great fury by Gen. Jackson's corps, Gen. Hooker selected Berry's division, which had been formerly his own division, and was one of the finest in the army. to charge upon the advancing foe, and stem the overwhelming wave which was sweeping his army to destruction. His order was characteristic, and showed his thorough appreciation of the courage and military skill of Gen. Berry. It was as follows: "Go in, General; throw your men into the breach; don't fire a shot—they can't see you—but charge *home* with the bayonet." They did charge *home*, and in the shock of battle which followed, the foe went down like grass before the mower's scythe. For three hours that division, almost alone, withstood the repeated assaults of a large body of Confederate troops flushed with their previous victory, and at last drove them back, and regained a portion of their lost ground. The battle was renewed early the next morning, and again Berry and his division were in front and received the first assault of the enemy. Intent upon driving them back, Gen. Berry headed one of his brigades in several successful bayonet charges, and in one of these was instantly killed by a shot from the enemy. Gen. Berry was not only a brave and skilful commander, but a most estimable man in private and social life, and his death caused deep sorrow among a wide circle of warmly attached friends.

May 3.—Lieut.-Col. DUNCAN MCVICAR was killed near Spottsylvania, Va. He was born in Scotland. At the commencement of the war he was a resident of Kingston, Canada, but his sympathies being upon the side of the Union, he came to the United States to aid in its maintenance. He first joined a company of light artillery in New York city, and proceeded to Rochester for recruits. He afterwards joined the Harris Guards, and rose to the office of lieutenant-colonel. During the peninsular campaign he commanded a battalion of his regiment then in the service on the Chickahominy. He was a brave and chivalrous officer, and lost his life while making a reconnoissance with a part of his men, and bravely assailing a force of the enemy which he encountered.

May 3.—Col. BENJAMIN RINGOLD was killed in the fight before Suffolk, Va. He entered the army as a captain, was promoted to be major, and subsequently became colonel of the 103d New York volunteers. He commanded his regiment at South Mountain, Antietam, and Fredericksburg. At Antietam he particularly distinguished himself by his bravery and daring in driving a Georgia regiment from a strong position at the point of the bayonet, and taking the colors of the regiment. He was for a long time attached to Col. Hawkins's brigade.

May 4.—Rev. FRANCIS EUGENE BUTLER died from wounds received in battle of Suffolk, Va., aged 38 years. He was a native at Suffolk, Conn., and for a number of years was engaged in mercantile pursuits in New York city, where he was well known as secretary of the New York Bible Society, as one of the founders of the Young Men's Christian Association, and as an active friend of other religious institutions. When twenty-nine years old he entered Yale College with the determination of fitting himself for the ministry. He graduated in 1857, after which he spent three years in the study of theology at Princeton, and subsequently one year at Andover. Having been licensed to preach, he supplied for a time the pulpit of a church in Bedford Springs, Penn., and afterwards that of the Second Presbyterian Church in Cleveland, Ohio. He was next engaged as minister of the Congregational Church in Paterson, N. J. When the 25th regiment of New Jersey volunteers was organized, he accepted the post of chaplain, and accompanied the regiment to Suffolk, Va. In an engagement near that place, May 3d, learning that some men of a Connecticut regiment on the right were suffering for want of surgical assistance, he went to their relief, and in so doing, being greatly exposed, he was shot by a sharpshooter and died the next day.

May 4.—JOSEPH B. PLUMMER, a brigadier-general in the United States volunteer service, died at Corinth, aged about 44 years. He graduated at West Point in 1841, in the same class with the late Gens. Lyon, Richardson, Reynolds, and Whipple, the late Col. Garesché, and Gens. Buell and Wright of the army of the United States. After serving with distinction in Florida and Mexico, he was stationed for several years at the West. At the commencement of the present war he was a captain of the First United States infantry, and accepted the command of a regiment of Missouri volunteers. In this capacity he participated in the battle of Springfield, and subsequently distinguished himself at the battle of Fredericktown, Mo., for which he was promoted to the rank of brigadier-general of volunteers. He participated in the campaign of the Mississippi River, and distinguished himself at Island No. 10, and other engagements in that vicinity. Becoming prostrated by his severe labors in the service, he obtained leave of absence to recruit his health. After a short visit to his family, he returned to his command while yet unfit for duty, and died the day after his arrival in the camp of Gen. Rosecrans, at Corinth.

May 5.—Col. WILLIAM OLIVER STEVENS died from injuries received in the battle near Chancellorsville, Va., aged 36 years. He was born in Belfast, Maine, was fitted for college at Phillips Academy, Andover, and graduated at Harvard College in 1848. After leaving college he studied law with his father in Lawrence, and subsequently with Hon. Thomas Wright of the same place, and went to Florida, where he practiced his profession for a few months, but was obliged to leave on account of the debilitating effects of the climate. In 1852 he went into the practice of his profession in Dunkirk, New York. In 1859 he was elected district attorney of Chautauque County, filled the office for two years to the entire satisfaction of the people, and resigned his position for the military service of his country, in 1861. He joined the Excelsior Brigade at Staten Island, as captain of a company raised in Dunkirk, was elected major before leaving the island, and took a conspicuous part in the battles of Williamsburg, Fair Oaks, White Oak Swamp, and Malvern Hill. In October, 1862, he was commissioned colonel, dating back to September, and his regiment was attached to the third army corps under Gen. Sickles. At the battle of Chancellorsville, May 3d, his horse being shot under him early in the engagement, he led his regiment on foot, and soon after received a mortal wound and was carried to the hospital, where, after enduring the most terrible suffering with heroic fortitude, he died the following Tuesday.

May 5.—Brig.-Gen. AMIEL W. WHIPPLE, an officer of United States volunteers, born in Greenwich, Mass., died at Washington, May 5, 1863, from wounds received at the battles near Chancellorsville. He graduated at West Point in 1841, was commissioned brevet second lieutenant in the 1st artillery, and then transferred to the topographical engineers. In 1841 he was engaged in the hydrographical survey of the Patapsco River, and in 1842 in surveying the approaches to New Orleans and the harbor of Portsmouth, N. H. In 1844 he was detailed as assistant astronomer upon the Northeast boundary survey, and in 1845 was employed in determining the northern boundaries of New York, Vermont, and New Hampshire. In 1849 he was appointed assistant astronomer on the Mexican boundary, and his journal while in Mexico was published by order of Congress. In the spring of 1853 he was ordered to direct the survey of the Southern Pacific Railroad. In July, 1855, he was promoted to be captain of topographical engineers, and the following year was appointed light-house engineer, and afterwards superintendent of the improvement of St. Clair Flats and St. Mary's River. In the spring of 1861 he was made chief engineer on the staff of Gen. McDowell; was present at the battle of Bull Run, and was afterwards employed on surveys for fortifications, and promoted major of engineers. Subsequently he was attached to the staff of Gen. McClellan, made brigadier-general of volunteers in May, 1862, and placed in charge of all the fortifications and garrisons on the south side of the Potomac. Shortly afterwards he was promoted to the command of a division in the ninth army corps, and at the time of his death was in command of the third division of the third corps.

May 7.—JOHN E. HOLMES died at Annapolis from the effects of confinement in a Richmond prison. He was born in Hartford County, Connecticut, in 1809, was educated in the Universalist Academy at Hamilton, N. Y., and commenced the study of law, but subsequently entered the ministry. After preaching three years he returned to the study of law, and was admitted to the bar in Illinois. In 1843 he removed to Jefferson, Wisconsin, and soon after became a member of the Territorial Council. In 1848 he was lieutenant-governor, and in 1852 was elected to the State Legislature, all of which positions he filled with honor and usefulness. When the war broke out he felt it his duty to devote his energies to the service of his country. In August, 1862, he received a commission, and at once entered upon his duties. He was taken prisoner at Brentwood, Tennessee, March 25th, 1863, was rapidly marched to Richmond, where he was imprisoned four weeks, and died immediately after being exchanged.

May 8.—Maj.-Gen. Earl Van Dorn, an officer in the Confederate service, was killed by Dr. Peters, of Maury County, Tennessee. He was born in Mississippi about 1823, graduated at West Point in 1842, and was appointed brevet second lieutenant United States 9th infantry; became second lieutenant in 1844, and first lieutenant in 1847; was brevetted captain for gallantry at Cerro Gordo, and major for gallantry at Contreras and Churubusco; distinguished himself at Chapultepec, and was wounded when entering the city of Mexico. From January, 1852, to June, 1855, he was treasurer of the Military Asylum at Pascagoula, Miss. He distinguished himself in three different expeditions against the Comanches in Texas, in one of which he was dangerously wounded. On the breaking out of the war he resigned his commission in the United States army, and accepting the position of colonel in the Confederate army, took command of a body of Texan volunteers, and entered into an engagement to get possession of the vast amount of military stores and equipments which the United States Government had collected in Texas. In the spring of 1861 he captured the steamship Star of the West at Indianola, and a few days after, at the head of eight hundred men, at Saluria he received the surrender of Major C. C. Sibley and seven companies of United States infantry, and the following month that of Lieut.-Col. Reeve and six companies of the 8th infantry. He was made brigadier-general and subsequently major-general, and took command of the trans-Mississippi district, January 19th, 1862; commanded at the battle of Pea Ridge, and was superseded by Gen. Holmes. Since the battle of Corinth, where he was unsuccessful, he had remained in comparative obscurity, but had been engaged in several attacks upon the outlying divisions of the Army of the Cumberland. He had made his headquarters for some months in Maury County, Tennessee, and while there injured the family of Dr. Peters, who, after attempting in vain to secure from him such reparation as it was in his power to make, at last took his life.

May 10.—Thomas Jonathan Jackson, a general in the Confederate army, born in Clarksburg, Harrison County, Va., January 21st, 1824, died at Guinea's station, on the Richmond and Fredericksburg Railroad, May 10th, 1863. The death of his father, in 1827, left him dependent upon an uncle, by whom he was brought up to a farmer's life. As a boy he was noted for gravity and sobriety of manners, and at 16 years of age is said to have been elected constable of Lewis County. Though indicating no special aptitude or taste for a military career, he obtained in 1842 the appointment of cadet at West Point, where he was graduated in 1846, 17th in a class of 59, which numbered among its members Generals McClellan, Stoneman, Foster, Couch, Réno, and others distinguished on both sides in the present war. At the academy he was far from being a brilliant pupil, mastering his studies with extreme difficulty, but learning thoroughly whatever he attempted. His disposition was retiring and taciturn, and at this, as well as at other periods of his life, he was afflicted with various forms of hypochondria, imagining that he had consumption, incipient paralysis, and other maladies.

He was immediately brevetted 2d lieutenant in the 1st artillery, and accompanied Magruder's battery to Mexico serving first under Gen. Taylor and subsequently under Gen. Scott. During the victorious campaign of the latter in the valley of Mexico he was promoted to a first lieutenancy, and for gallant conduct at Contréras, Churubusco, and Chapultepec, was successively brevetted captain and major. Returning home in impaired health, he resigned his commission in 1852, and was soon after appointed professor of mathematics in the Military Institute of Virginia, where he remained until the outbreak of the civil war. He performed his professional duties with conscientious fidelity, but in matters of discipline was too much of a martinet to become popular with the pupils of the school, who were accustomed to ridicule his peculiarities of manner and appearance, and his strict observance of a religious life. Thus the spring of 1861 found him scarcely known beyond the walls of the Institute, and not esteemed there as a soldier of more than ordinary promise. He embraced the cause of secession with enthusiasm, was commissioned a colonel by Gov. Letcher, of Virginia, and on the 3d of May appointed commander of the "Army of Observation" at Harper's Ferry, which a few weeks later he resigned to Gen. Joseph E. Johnston, retaining command of the infantry.

For several weeks he was employed in frequent manœuvres between Winchester and Harper's Ferry, encountering the Federal Gen. Patterson's advance at Falling Waters on July 2d; and on the 18th his brigade, consisting of five Virginia regiments, carefully disciplined by himself, was hurried off to Manassas, almost under the eye of Patterson, to reënforce Beauregard. He bore a distinguished part in the battle of Bull Run, where, in the language of the Confederate Gen. Bee, "Jackson stood like a stone wall;" and ever after that eventful day he was popularly known as "Stonewall" Jackson, and the troops commanded by him on the occasion as the "Stonewall Brigade." He remained with his brigade in the neighborhood of Centreville until October, having previously been commissioned a brigadier-general, and was then promoted to be a major-general and assigned to the command of the troops at Winchester, where he remained until early in the succeeding March, retiring only on the approach of the Union forces under Gen. Banks.

A reconnoissance made on the 18th and 19th of this month by Gen. Shields, commanding a division of Gen. Banks' corps, discovered Jackson posted in a strong position south of Winchester, and in immediate communication with powerful supports, for which reason the Union forces were concentrated near Winchester. On the 22d, Banks, with half of his corps, marched for Centreville to join the army of McClellan, and this fact having been communicated to Jackson by his scouts, the Confederate cavalry was ordered to drive the Union pickets back toward Kernstown, a small village, three miles south of Winchester, while the main body of the Confederates was pushed forward with secrecy and rapidity. Here on the morning of the 23d, Jackson, deceived evidently as to the strength of the Union army, made a vigorous attack upon Shields' left wing. Failing to make an impression there, he massed his troops for an assault upon the right, where Shields, in anticipation of such a movement, had concentrated a large force. One of the fiercest contests of the war ensued, but by unflinching energy the Unionists succeeded in driving the Confederates from a strong position behind a stone wall, and the latter at once yielded the field to their opponents, leaving behind two guns and other trophies. The swelling of the Shenandoah by rains having prevented the arrival of his supports, Jackson was compelled to retreat up the valley, disputing step by step the pursuit of Banks and Shields, until he reached the neighborhood of Harrisonburg, about sixty miles south of Winchester. From this point he was summoned with his command to Richmond, where the Confederates were collecting all their available strength, in anticipation of the advance of McClellan up the peninsula. But having suggested that he could better defend Richmond on the Shenandoah than on the Chickahominy he was allowed to remain where he was.

With a view of dislodging Jackson from this position two columns of Union troops were directed to operate in concert, one under Banks in the Shenandoah valley, and another under Fremont in the Mountain Department, to the west. Both were weak in numbers, and by the beginning of May the corps of Banks had been reduced, by the withdrawal of Shields' division, to less than 7,000 men. Jackson, however, by concentrating with Gens. Edward Johnson and Ewell, had increased his force to upward of 20,000. In conformity with the Union plans, Gen. Milroy, of Fremont's column, early in May marched with a small force eastward toward Buffalo Gap, for the purpose of threatening Staunton. Jackson at once moved to meet him, encountered the Union forces at McDowell on the 8th, and drove them back to Franklin, on the west side of the mountains, thus effectually preventing a junction between Fremont and Banks. Then rapidly retracing his steps, he collected all his available troops and turned upon Banks, who had been constrained by the depletion of his corps to fall back some distance from Harrisonburg.

On the 23d of May a portion of Jackson's army which had made a detour toward Front Royal on the Manassas Gap Railroad, surprised the small Union force under Col. Kenly, stationed there, and captured nearly the whole command. Banks, who was then at Strasburg, was not slow to perceive his critical position, with an enemy on his front and flank, and on the night of the 23d commenced a rapid retreat toward Winchester, sending his train in advance. The force which had moved upon Front Royal also pushed on to intercept him at Middletown, while Jackson with his main body followed vigorously in his rear, expecting by this movement to capture Banks's train, if not to put his whole army *hors de combat*. At Middletown the Union train was driven back upon the main body, whereupon Banks, ordering his troops to the head of the column, repulsed the enemy in his front, and succeeded, after hard fighting, which was continued at intervals along the line of march, in reaching Winchester. But Jackson was too close upon his rear to admit of his making a stand there, and almost immediately the retreat was renewed and not again ended until the Union troops reached the Potomac on the 26th, the Confederates pressing them continually on either flank and on their rear. A brigade under Gen. Gordon, left behind at Winchester to enable the main body and the train to get well forward, maintained for some time an unequal fight with Jackson, but was finally compelled to fall back.

Thus in less than three weeks Jackson had not only baffled the efforts of Fremont and Banks to capture him, but had driven the latter completely out of Virginia. A more important advantage gained by him for the Confederate cause was the diversion of McDowell's corps, then preparing to march upon Richmond, from its contemplated junction with McClellan, which, in the opinion of the latter general, would have sealed the fate of the Confederate capital. Jackson remained in the vicinity of the Potomac, between Williamsport and Harper's Ferry, until the 30th of May, when prudential motives counselled him to move southward. The excitement which his dashing raid created throughout the Northern States had caused a considerable accumulation of troops at Harper's Ferry, while Fremont on one flank and McDowell on the other were in motion to cut off his retreat. Accordingly, on the night of the 30th, after a fruitless attempt to carry the Federal position at Harper's Ferry, he hurried off toward Winchester, whence on the succeeding day his retreat was continued up the valley. On the afternoon of the 31st, Fremont's advance, which had hastened by forced marches over difficult mountain roads from Franklin, encountered the rear guard of Jackson near Strasburg, and a smart skirmish ensued, which was terminated by darkness without material advantage on either side.

Jackson's retreat now equalled in rapidity that of Banks' a week previous. He had however the advantage of having got his main body and train well forward, and his rear guard, covered by Ashby's cavalry, by delaying the march of Fremont, enabled the Confederates to pass safely through Strasburg. Part of the division of Shields, sent westward by McDowell to intercept Jackson, reached Front Royal, twelve miles from Strasburg, about the same time, so that the escape of the latter between both parties of his pursuers seemed almost miraculous. On the afternoon of June 1st, Fremont entered Strasburg only to find Jackson far in advance of him. Shields' advance guard now joined Fremont's force, while his main army passed up the valley along the south fork of the Shenandoah, Jackson and Fremont being on the north fork. It was thus the object of Jackson, though in superior force to Fremont, to avoid fighting a pitched battle, as the delay which would thereby be caused in his movements might enable Shields to flank him on the east. For seven days the pursuit was pressed with vigor by Fremont, Jackson having in some instances barely time to burn the bridges behind him, and being obliged to leave by the way much of his plunder and material; and on the 8th the two armies came into collision at Cross Keys, seven miles beyond Harrisonburg. A severe but indecisive engagement followed, terminating at nightfall, and under cover of the darkness Jackson pressed forward to secure the passage of the Shenandoah at Port Republic.

Shields had meanwhile made a parallel march with the retreating and pursuing armies, and his advance under Col. Carroll reached Port Republic on the 8th, while Jackson was fighting the battle of Cross Keys. Had the bridge over the Shenandoah been destroyed at this juncture, and had Carroll then pressed on to Waynesboro and rendered the Virginia Central Railroad impassable at that point, the position of Jackson would have been critical. But the latter, well aware of this plan to intercept him, again baffled his enemies by the celerity of his movements, and before Carroll had made preparations to destroy the bridge, drove him back toward his supports. The Confederate army then pushed silently and swiftly across the river, upon the banks of which Fremont arrived on the morning of the 9th, only to find the bridge in flames and his prey again snatched from his grasp. Gen. Tyler meanwhile came up to the assistance of Carroll, but being in insignificant force, was soon put to rout by Jackson, who proceeded by easy marches to Richmond. Pursuit was impossible by the Federal troops, and Jackson was needed for more important duties in the army of Lee. Thenceforth he held no independent command, but his management of the brief but exciting campaign of the Shenandoah had sufficed to make his name famous both in Europe and America; and his admirers claim that in no subsequent campaigns, when acting under the directions of a superior, did he exhibit such energy, decisiveness, and command of resources. His raid was of great benefit to the Confederate cause, and in no remote degree produced a series of disasters to the Federal arms, which for a time turned the scale against them.

On June 25th Jackson arrived at Ashland, about sixteen miles north of Richmond, whence, in accordance with Lee's plan of a flank movement on McClellan's right wing, he was directed to move to Cold Harbor and attack the rear of Fitz John Porter's corps, which alone occupied the left bank of the Chickahominy. During the 26th and 27th he was occupied with getting into position, and late on the afternoon of the latter day, his troops falling with irresistible fury on the exhausted forces of Porter, who had been contending for hours against superior numbers at Gaines' Mill, drove them toward the Chickahominy and gave the victory to the Confederates. On the 29th he moved across the Chickahominy, engaged McClellan's rear guard on the succeeding day at Frazier's farm, and on July 1st shared in the signal defeat of the Confederates at Malvern Hills, where his corps lost several thousand in killed and wounded. A pause then ensued in the military operations before Richmond, both sides being too shattered to desire to renew the contest immediately. But about the middle of July the movements of the army of Virginia under Gen. Pope induced Lee to send a force to cover Gordonsville, and Jackson with his old corps, and Ewell's division, were selected for this duty.

For several weeks he remained at Gordonsville. But learning on August 7th that Pope's advance was at Culpepper Court House, he marched rapidly in that direction with his whole force, hoping to cut it off before the arrival of reënforcements. On the 9th was fought the severely contested battle of Cedar Mountain, between Jackson and Banks, in which the latter was forced back about a mile toward his supports. But Jackson almost immediately retired across the Rapidan toward Orange Court House, to await the arrival of the main body of the Confederates, which was pressing forward under Lee to the invasion of Maryland. McClellan was also by this time in motion down the peninsula, and it became an object of paramount importance with Lee to overwhelm the small force under Pope before any portion of the Army of the Potomac could join it. About the 18th Lee effected a junction with Jackson, and on the next day the united Confederate army moved toward the Rapidan, Jackson keeping to the left with a view of flanking Pope. On the 20th the Rapidan was crossed, and for several days the Confederates harassed Pope by frequent attempts to cross the Rappahannock, which, it subsequently appeared, were intended to mask a flanking movement under Jackson toward Thoroughfare Gap in the Bull Run Mountains, and thence to Manassas in the Federal rear.

On the 24th and 25th Jackson made rapid

progress northward, moving by unfrequented roads, taking no unnecessary baggage or rations, and subsisting his men on roasted corn and whatever else the country might produce. On the 26th he passed safely through Thoroughfare Gap, and fell suddenly upon the small Union force at Manassas, capturing prisoners, cannon, and a large amount of stores. Learning this, Pope moved with his whole force to the rear, and stationed McDowell at Thoroughfare Gap to prevent the arrival of reënforcements for Jackson. The situation of the latter becoming somewhat critical, he evacuated Manassas on the 28th, and moved through Centreville toward Gainesville, to be in the neighborhood of his supports. Here, on the succeeding day, he was brought to bay by the united Federal forces, and had there been a proper concert of action between Pope and his generals, it seems impossible but that he should have been crushed before the arrival of Lee. As it was, he was pushed back toward the Bull Run Mountains, with fearful loss, but unbroken and defiant, and the golden opportunity was lost to the Federals. Longstreet had meanwhile forced his way through Thoroughfare Gap, followed, on the night of the 29th, by Lee, and on the 30th the Confederates confronted their foe with a united army and in greatly superior numbers. Jackson had a full share in the bloody battle of that day, and after the retreat of Pope across Bull Run, led his corps to the north of Centreville, with a view of turning the Federal right and severing their connections with Washington. Pope anticipated this movement by falling back a few miles to Germantown, where, on the evening of September 1st, a sharp action was fought, resulting in the repulse of the Confederates.

Lee was now ready for the invasion of Maryland, and Jackson was again pushed forward, as he had been during the whole campaign, to be the pioneer of the movement. On the 4th of September he occupied Leesburg, on the 5th he crossed the Potomac near the Point of Rocks, and on the morning of the 6th his advance entered Frederick, where, with a view of winning over the inhabitants to the Confederate cause, a proclamation was issued, promising them relief from the tyranny by which they were oppressed, and similar benefits. As a further means of conciliation, strict measures were taken to protect private property, and on Sunday, the 7th, Jackson, true to his devotional habits, publicly attended Divine service at the Presbyterian and German Reformed churches. The expected sympathy of the Marylanders, however, proved a delusion; recruiting for the Confederate army made little or no progress, and the approach of the Federal army under McClellan rendered it necessary for Lee, whose whole force was now concentrated at Frederick, to move in the direction of the upper fords of the Potomac, by which, in case of defeat, he might retire into Virginia.

One of the prime objects of the campaign was the capture of Harper's Ferry, then garrisoned by a considerable force of Federals, and containing large amounts of artillery and munitions of war. Accordingly detachments were sent to occupy Maryland Heights, in Maryland, and Loudon Heights, on the right bank of the Shenandoah, both of which command the place, while Jackson marched up the Potomac to Williamsport, and, crossing thence into Virginia, moved down to the rear of Bolivar Heights, the only point of Harper's Ferry which the Federals had fortified. The latter, though thus invested on three sides, might easily have maintained the post but for the unaccountable abandonment, by Col. Ford, of Maryland Heights, the occupation of which by the Confederates on the 13th and 14th decided the fate of the garrison. A furious cannonade from Maryland and Loudon Heights was opened on the 14th, while Jackson pressed the garrison in the rear. The attack was renewed on the morning of the 15th, and resulted, in a few hours, in the unconditional surrender of the place, with 11,000 troops and all the material of war.

Meanwhile the battle of South Mountain had been fought, and Lee, retreating before McClellan, was taking position behind Antietam Creek. Foiled by the vigor and celerity of Jackson in his effort to relieve Harper's Ferry, the Federal general concentrated his forces to give battle to Lee and drive him out of Maryland. No time, therefore, was to be lost by Jackson in forming a junction with his commander; and leaving Gen. A. P. Hill with his division to hold Harper's Ferry and finish paroling the prisoners, he crossed the Potomac at the Shepherdstown ferry on the 16th, and the same evening took post on the Confederate left wing on the historic field of Antietam. The hardest fighting of the succeeding day devolved upon him, and though the obstinate valor of the Federal troops availed to push him back some distance, the ground was gained at a cost of life never exceeded during the war. On the night of the 18th the Confederates quietly retreated into Virginia, and for several days Jackson was employed in destroying the Baltimore and Ohio Railroad track from near Harper's Ferry to the North Mountain, a distance of 30 miles. Scarcely had he accomplished this work when he was called upon to repel a reconnoitring party of Federals, who crossed the Potomac near Shepherdstown and were driven back with serious loss.

During October and November Jackson remained in the valley of Virginia, Lee having meanwhile occupied and fortified Marye's Heights, in the rear of Fredericksburg, in front of which Burnside lay, on the left bank of the Rappahannock. In the first week of December he was summoned thither by Lee, and upon his arrival took command of the right wing of the Confederate army, which he held during the eventful battle of the 13th. Though here, as at Antietam, the weakest point in the line was given him to defend, and though at one time he was in imminent danger of being flanked by Franklin, he held his ground till darkness ended the battle, at which time no important advantage had been gained in that quarter by the Federals. He even designed a night attack by massing his artillery in front and supporting the pieces with infantry, but was obliged, in consequence of a severe fire from the Federal batteries on the opposite side of the river, to abandon the project.

For several months Jackson remained at his headquarters, ten miles below Fredericksburg, employed chiefly in preparing the official reports of his battles. He still held command of the right wing, and for services in the battle of December 13th had been promoted to be a lieutenant-general. With the exception of cavalry expeditions and occasional reconnoissances, no operations were undertaken by Gen. Hooker from the time of assuming command of the Federal army, January 26th, until the latter part of April. On the 26th of that month, however, he commenced the execution of a plan which he had been long maturing, and which contemplated a flank movement by one portion of his army some distance above Fredericksburg, while another portion crossed the Rappahannock below the town, and menaced it from that quarter. By a skilful ruse Jackson's corps was detained in its old position below Fredericksburg, while the bulk of the Federal army crossed the Rappahannock and the Rapidan at various fords above, and on the evening of April 30th was concentrated to the number of four corps at Chancellorsville, about twelve miles west of Fredericksburg. The position of Hooker enabling him to threaten both Fredericksburg and Gordonsville, was strengthened during the ensuing day by the erection of breastworks and abatis. Lee was not slow to fathom the design of the Federal general, and leaving a single division to guard the heights he had so long occupied, he moved westward on the 29th of April, and threw up earthworks midway between Chancellorsville and Fredericksburg to arrest the progress of Hooker toward the latter place. During May 1st he reconnoitred the Federal lines, and finding them impregnable in the neighborhood of Chancellorsville by reason of the earthworks and abatis, he determined upon a flank movement upon Hooker's right, and selected Jackson to execute it.

The latter accepted the task with alacrity, and early on the morning of the 2d his corps commenced its march, moving toward the road leading to Germanna ford on the Rapidan, so as to strike the rear of the Federal right wing, occupied by the 11th corps under Gen. Howard. No suspicion seems to have entered the mind of any of the Federal generals that such a movement was in progress, the Confederate attack, if made at all, being expected in front of Chancellorsville, and no precautions had been taken to fortify this part of the line. Suddenly, at about six o'clock in the evening, Jackson fell like a thunderbolt upon the unprepared Federals, who were cooking supper, or engaged in various camp duties. Formation or order was impossible in the face of the impetuous charge of the Confederates, and in an almost incredibly short time the greater part of the 11th corps was routed and fleeing in a confused mass toward the Federal centre, which was, by this unforeseen disaster, pressed back upon Chancellorsville. By great exertion the fugitives were rallied behind other troops, and the advance of Jackson stayed. The latter, however, had no thought of pausing in his career, and having given orders to Gen. A. P. Hill to press forward in pursuit, reserving his fire unless cavalry approached from the direction of the enemy, he rode with his staff and escort to the front. It was now nearly nine o'clock, and quite dark, and in deference to the wishes of his staff, who thought he was exposing himself needlessly to the Federal skirmishers, Jackson turned his horse to ride back toward his own lines. In the growing obscurity the cavalcade was mistaken for Federal cavalry, and a South Carolina regiment, in literal conformity with the orders recently issued, fired a sudden volley into it, by which Jackson was wounded in both arms, and several of his staff killed outright. He fell from his horse, exclaiming, "All my wounds are by my own men," and almost immediately a Federal column, attracted by the firing, charged over the very spot where he lay, his staff scattering in all directions at their approach. The Federals were in turn repulsed, and in the midst of a terrific artillery fire, which swept down the Confederates by hundreds, he was placed on a litter and carried to the rear, receiving in the confusion of the moment severe contusions in his arms and sides.

His left arm was amputated on that same evening, and two days later he was removed to Guinea's station, on the Richmond and Fredericksburg Railroad. For several days he continued to improve, but on the 7th, while preparations were making to remove him to Richmond, symptoms of pneumonia appeared. On the evening of that day all pain left him, and with its cessation he began rapidly to sink. He died quietly on Sunday afternoon, the 10th, exclaiming, when told by his wife of his approaching end, "Very good, very good; it is all right!" and was honored with a public funeral in Richmond on the 12th, amidst unmistakable manifestations of sorrow. Throughout the seceded States he was not less profoundly mourned, the public regret being intensified by the reflection that their great general, like the eagle killed by arrows tipped with its own plumage, had fallen under the volleys of his chosen and devoted soldiery.

The character of Jackson was developed only during the two brief but momentous years which succeeded the outbreak of the war. Had secession never taken place he might have lived and died the obscure and eccentric professor which the spring of 1861 found him. In private life, in fact, he was, like others distinguished in his profession, a comparatively dull and uninteresting man, noticeable chiefly for the depth and earnestness of his religious convictions; and few could have predicted that under so quiet an exterior he concealed an impetuous bravery rivalling that of Ney and Lannes, and an energy, ripened judgment, and command of resources to which those generals could lay no claim. Of his capacity to undertake a large independent command no test was ever made, his celebrated campaign in the Shenandoah valley having been conducted with an army not exceeding 25,000 men. But as the lieutenant of another, executing important movements of an army wing, and anticipating almost intuitively the plans of his superior, he proved himself a genius of the first order; and one can readily appreciate the significance of Lee's remark, when learning the misfortune which had befallen his favorite general: "He is better off than I am. He lost his left arm, but I have lost my right." During his residence at Lexington he became a member of the Presbyterian Church, and at his death was a deacon in that denomination. Embracing, to its fullest extent, the doctrine of predestination, he was regarded by many as a fatalist, and his religious fervor seemed to rise with the progress of the war, approaching sometimes the verge of fanaticism. He attended service regularly on Sundays, never omitted his daily devotions, encouraged prayer meetings and revivals among his troops, and in reports and despatches announcing successes in the field, invariably ascribed the victory to divine interposition. To extreme simplicity of manners and dress, he united a transparent honesty of character, and a genuine humanity, which, in the midst of a civil war of unexampled fury, caused him to be respected alike by friends and foes. In person Jackson was of middle height and soldierly bearing, and his features, when not lightened up by eyes of singular brilliancy and expression, were in no respect remarkable.

May 11.—Col. John M. Wimer, a Confederate officer, killed at the battle of Hartsville, Mo. Col. Wimer had long been a citizen of high reputation and extensive influence in St. Louis, Mo. He had held many and various positions of public resonsibility in the city and State; among the most important, that of mayor of the city.

May 17.—Brig.-Gen. Lloyd Tilghman, an officer in the Confederate service, was killed at Champion Hill, Miss. He was a native of Maryland, graduated at West Point in July, 1836, and was appointed second lieutenant of the 1st dragoons; resigned September, 1836. He then became a division engineer of the Baltimore and Susquehanna Railroad, and subsequently surveyor of the Norfolk and Wilmington Canal, and the Eastern Shore Railroad. During the Mexican war he was a volunteer aid to Col. Twiggs in the battle of Palo Alto and Resaca de la Palma, and commanded a volunteer partisan party in Mexico, October, 1846. He was superintendent of defences at Matamoras, January, 1847; captain of volunteer artillery in Hughes's regiment for the Mexican war from August, 1847, to July, 1848, and the principal assistant engineer of the Panama division of the Isthmus Railroad in 1847. At the commencement of the war he went into the Confederate service.

May 16.—Lieut.-Col. —— Horney, an officer of the Federal army, killed at the battle of Champion Hills. Lieut.-Col. Horney was an officer of the 10th Missouri regiment, in Gen. Boomer's brigade at that battle.

May 22.—Gen. George Boardman Boomer, an officer in the Federal volunteer army, killed at Vicksburg, Miss. Gen. Boomer was born in Sutton, Worcester County, Mass., July 26th, 1832. He was the son of the Rev. Job Bordon Boomer. He went west at a very early age, and settled in St. Louis, where he pursued the business of bridge building throughout the State of Missouri, and succeeded remarkably well. He laid out and partially built the town of "Castle Rock," on the Osage River. When the guns of Sumter told that civil war had actually commenced, Gen. Boomer entered the army of the Union as colonel of the 26th regiment of Missouri volunteers, and as such was present at the surrender of Island No. 10 and at the battle of Iuka, Miss., where he greatly distinguished himself, but was severely wounded. He received two balls in his body, but would not leave the field until he received a third, which placed him *hors de combat.* At the battle of Champion Hills, near Vicksburg, Miss., he commanded the 2d brigade of Quimby's division, McPherson's corps, and behaved with such conspicuous gallantry and rendered such signal service that he was highly recommended for promotion. He was killed in a charge on the fortifications at Vicksburg. His remains were carried to St. Louis, Mo., and thence to Worcester, Mass., his native county, where his obsequies were performed with military honors.

May 23.—Col. J. Richter Jones, an officer of the U. S. volunteers, was killed near Newbern, N. C. He was born in 1804; received his academical education at the Germantown Academy, and graduated with high honors at the University of Pennsylvania in 1821. Having studied law, he was admitted to the Philadelphia bar in 1827, and continued to practise until 1836, when he was appointed a judge of the Court of Common Pleas for the county of Philadelphia, and held the office until his term expired by limitation under the new Constitution in 1847. When the war broke out he was residing near Laporte, Sullivan County, Pa. He promptly offered his services to the War Department, was commissioned colonel of a regiment he had raised, and located his camp in Roxborough. On the 8th of March, 1862, he left with his regiment, the 58th Pennsylvania volunteers, for Fortress Monroe, and was in the advance when the attack was made on Norfolk. He also performed some bold movements on the Blackwater. Subsequently he was transferred to the Department of North Carolina, and in January, 1863, his regiment was stationed near Newbern. A short time previous to his death he was in command of a brigade, in which position he evinced much ability as a military chieftain.

May 27.—Col. DANIEL S. COWLES, an officer of the U. S. volunteers, was killed in the assault at Port Hudson. At the commencement of the war he was engaged in the practice of law in Columbia County. He accepted the command of the 128th regiment of New York volunteers, made up, for the most part, of men of wealth and high social position. He was cool in council, brave in battle, and fell by a bayonet thrust while leading his men to the enemy's works.

May 27.—Lieut.-Col. WM. LOGAN RODMAN was killed in the attack on Port Hudson, Miss. He was born in New Bedford, Mass., March 7th, 1823; graduated at Harvard College in 1842, and soon after entered into mercantile business. He visited California during the gold excitement, and was absent two years, returning by way of Calcutta and the overland route through Europe. He was a member of the Common Council of New Bedford in 1852, and in 1860 and 1862 was in the Legislature. He enlisted in the service of the country, raised a company of volunteers, with whom, as their captain, he proceeded to the seat of war. His skill and bravery rapidly promoted him to the position, first, of major, and then of lieutenant-colonel, and in the assault, during which he lost his life, he bore a gallant part.

June —.—Brig.-Gen. MARTIN E. GREENE, an officer of volunteers in the Confederate army, killed at Vicksburg, Miss. Brig.-Gen. Greene was one of the most remarkable characters developed by the war. He entered into the contest with the serious, grim determination of a zealot. His private character was pure and chaste, unsullied by a single vice. The immorality and licenses of army life could never corrupt his strict principles, or divert him from his path of devout religious practices. He was never known to touch ardent spirits, and at home was a "class-leader" in the Methodist Church. After the capture of Camp Jackson, near St. Louis, Mo., May 10th, 1861, the country was so unsettled and dangerous that Gen. Greene organized and commanded a company of home guards for the protection of the families of the neighborhood of Paris from lawless bands of desperadoes. This body of men afterwards swelled to twelve hundred, and Greene organized it into a regiment, and became its colonel. Upon the advance of Gen. Price on Lexington, Gen. Curtis, with 2,800 men, advanced into Monroe County to capture Greene and his party, but the latter marched his men seventy miles, and arrived at Glasgow on the Missouri River the next day, where he captured a steamboat loaded with supplies for the garrison at Lexington, and safely crossed his troops to the south side. He reported to Gen. Price, and contributed by his determination, good sense, and sagacity to the capture of the garrison under Col. Mulligan, at Lexington. His men rolled hemp bales up the precipitous bluff on the bank of the river, and converted them into movable breastworks. The garrison fired hot shot at them, and ignited the combustible material; but nothing daunted, Gen. Greene had the bales saturated with water, and steadily the line advanced. The first line of Federal works was reached, and the hemp-bales, by means of skids, placed against the works, actually rolled over and advanced on the second line. Col. Mulligan seeing that this new mode of approach would be successful, surrendered the place. Gen. Greene was afterwards conspicuous for coolness and courage in all of Gen. Price's battles in Missouri. He was in the battles of Farmington, Iuka, Corinth, Big Black, and Baker's Creek. At Vicksburg he had a presentiment he would be killed. He wrote an affectionate letter to his wife, taking leave of her. In a few hours after a ball from the rifle of a sharpshooter passed through his head, killing him instantly.

June —.—Col. EUGENE IRWIN, an officer of the Confederate army, killed at Vicksburg, Miss. Col. Irwin was a son of James Irwin. His mother was a daughter of Henry Clay, of Kentucky, and he was a great favorite of his illustrious grandfather. In the neighborhood of Ashland, it was no unusual sight to see the great orator of the United States affectionately leading his little grandson, Eugene, by the hand, and listening with delight to his boyish prattle. Col. Irwin was born in Lexington, Ky., but at the commencement of the war was a merchant in New Orleans, Louisiana. He was distinguished for his reckless daring, and when killed was on the top of the breastworks at Vicksburg, in the hottest of the fight, gallantly waving his sword and animating his men by his rash example.

June 1.—Brig.-Gen. EDMUND KIRBY, an officer of U. S. volunteers, died in Washington, from wounds received at the battle of Chancellorsville. He was born in Brownsville, Jefferson County, New York, graduated at West Point, and joined the army in May, 1861. He was assigned to Ricketts' battery as second lieutenant, and upon the imprisonment of Gen. Ricketts by the enemy, assumed command of the battery, which position he retained until his death. He took a prominent and active part in all the battles in which the Army of the Potomac was engaged, and was promoted to a brigadier-generalship for his bravery at Chancellorsville.

June 1.—Major MASSETT, an officer in the U. S. volunteers, died at Memphis, Tenn. He was an Englishman by birth, but had been for the last twenty years a citizen of the United States. After the loss of a son, Col. Massett, killed at the battle of Fair Oaks, he abandoned a life of ease and comfort, and entered the army, with the rank of major of cavalry. As an officer he was brave and active, and spared neither body nor mind in the faithful performance of his duties.

June 9.—Col. BENJAMIN F. DAVIS, of the 8th N. Y. cavalry, was killed while leading a brigade to the charge. He was a native of Mississippi; but was appointed a cadet at West Point from the State of Alabama, in the year 1850; graduated in 1854, and was appointed brevet second lieutenant of the 5th infantry, and, in 1855, was transferred to the 1st dragoons, with the full rank. He distinguished himself in the conflict in New Mexico, June, 1857. In 1860 he was promoted to a first lieutenancy, and, continuing in the service when his State seceded, was, on the 30th of July, 1861, further promoted to a captaincy in the 1st dragoons, now 1st cavalry. At the battle of Williamsburg he so distinguished himself that he was nominated for a brevet of lieutenant-colonel. In June, 1862, he was placed in command of the 8th regiment of New York cavalry, and soon after was brevetted and confirmed major for his gallant withdrawal of the cavalry from Harper's Ferry.

June 11.—Rev. JAMES AVERILL died at Lafourche, La., aged 48 years. He was born in Griswold, Conn. He was fitted for college in the Plainfield Academy; graduated at Amherst College in 1837; pursued his theological studies at New Haven, where he graduated in 1840, and was ordained pastor of the church in Shrewsbury, Mass., June 22d, 1841. In 1848, his health being very poor, he was obliged to remit his labors, and subsequently was settled in Plymouth Hollow, Conn., Oct. 13th, 1852. After a ministry here of ten years, he asked for a dismission, and accepted the chaplaincy of the 23d regiment of Connecticut volunteers, which he accompanied to Louisiana. After a short but faithful service in this new field, he fell a victim to the climate, and died of intermittent fever, after an illness of two weeks. He was an ardent friend of the philanthropic and moral enterprises of the day, a staunch advocate of temperance, and a strong anti-slavery man.

June 23.—Lieut.-Col. ABEL SMITH died at the Hotel Dieu in New Orleans. He was in command of the 2d Duryea Zouaves (165th New York volunteers) at the battle before Port Hudson, and, while fighting at the head of his regiment, received the wound of which he afterwards died.

June 26.—ANDREW HULL FOOTE, an American rear-admiral, born in New Haven, Ct., Sept. 12th, 1806, died in New York, June 26th, 1863. At sixteen years of age he entered the navy as acting midshipman, and made his first cruise in the schooner Grampus, which formed part of the squadron operating, in 1823, under Commodore Porter, against the pirates of the West Indies. In the succeeding year he obtained a midshipman's warrant; in 1830 he was commissioned a lieutenant, and in 1838 he accompanied Commodore Read in his voyage of circumnavigation, as first lieutenant of the sloop John Adams, participating in the attack of the squadron upon the pirates of Sumatra. In 1841–'43, while stationed at the Naval Asylum in Philadelphia, he prevailed upon many of the inmates to take the temperance pledge, and was thus one of the first to introduce into the navy the principle of total abstinence from spirituous liquors. In his next cruise, as first lieutenant of the frigate Cumberland, he induced the crew to give up their spirit rations, to the manifest improvement of health and discipline; and he also personally superintended their religious instruction, often preaching on the berth deck to officers and men. In 1849–'52 he commanded the brig Perry, of the African squadron, and showed great vigilance in suppressing the slave-trade; and it is worthy of note that during the cruise not a drop of grog was served out to the crew, and not an officer or man was lost or disabled, or for any considerable period on the sick list, although the station is notoriously unhealthy.

In 1852 he was promoted to be a commander, and after serving on the "Naval Retiring Board," and in other capacities, he sailed in 1856, in command of the sloop Portsmouth, for the China station. At the time of his arrival, hostilities were imminent between the British and Chinese, and the latter, with a recklessness which subsequently cost them dear, fired from the Canton barrier forts upon a boat from the Portsmouth, at the stern of which the American flag was displayed. Receiving permission, after urgent solicitation, from his commanding officer, Commodore Armstrong, to resent this indignity, he anchored his ship opposite the largest of the forts, and on November 21st, with partial assistance from the sloop Levant, effected a practicable breach in its walls. Immediately a force of marines and sailors were landed, and the work carried by assault, Commander Foote being one of the first to enter with the stormers. The remaining forts, three in number, yielded successively to his attacks, and on the 24th the American flag waved over all of them. In view of the disparity of strength between the contending forces, the forts being massive granite structures, mounting 176 guns, and manned by 5,000 Chinese, the engagement was justly esteemed one of the most brilliant in the annals of the American navy, and Commander Foote received abundant congratulations and compliments from foreign officers on the station, who had been witnesses of his gallantry.

At the outbreak of the rebellion, Commander Foote was executive officer at the Brooklyn navy yard. In July, 1861, he was commissioned a captain, and in the September following was appointed flag officer of the flotilla fitting out in the Western waters. He entered upon his duties with great energy, and by the commencement of 1862 his vessels were completed and awaiting their crews and armaments, the work having been, in his own words, "the most difficult and arduous" of his life. Early in February the combined advance of the gunboats and land forces against the enemy in Kentucky and Tennessee was commenced, and on the 6th, Foote, without waiting for the arrival of the coöperating land forces under Gen. Grant, attacked, with seven gunboats, the strong works at Fort Henry, on the Tennessee River, and in two hours compelled an unconditional surrender. With the least possible delay, he transferred his fleet to the Cumberland River, and on the 14th opened fire upon Fort Donelson. The contest was maintained with great vigor on both sides for an hour and a quarter, and resulted in silencing the heavy water batteries of the enemy. The flag-ship St. Louis, and the Louisville, having at this juncture become unmanageable by injuries to their steering apparatus, drifted out of the fire, and the fleet was obliged to haul off, leaving the capture of the fort to the land forces.

Foote, though injured in the ankle by the fragment of a shot, and compelled to move upon crutches, proceeded up the river immediately after the surrender of the fort, and destroyed the Tennessee iron works at Clarksville. Then, after a brief respite at Cairo, he sailed with his fleet, considerably increased in efficiency, down the Mississippi, the Confederates evacuating their strong positions at Columbus and Hickman at his approach. He remained at his post during the tedious siege of Island No. Ten, but after the reduction of that place, was reluctantly compelled by intense suffering from his unhealed wound to apply for leave of absence, and early in May turned over his command to Commodore Davis. Upon being restored to health, he was placed in charge of the bureau of equipment and recruiting under the new organization of the navy, and in July the President appointed him one of the nine rear-admirals on the active list. In June, 1863, he was ordered to relieve Admiral Dupont in command of the South Atlantic blockading squadron, and died while making preparations for his departure for Charleston.

Apart from his professional career, Admiral Foote was noted as an active friend of religious and philanthropic enterprises, and when not absent on sea duties, frequently participated at the religious anniversary meetings in New York and elsewhere. While in command of the Western flotilla, he framed and enforced strict rules for the proper observance of Sunday, and for the prevention of profane swearing and intemperance. He had also some reputation as a writer, and in connection with his African cruise published "Africa and the American Flag," containing a general survey of the African continent, with remarks on the slave trade; beside a series of letters on Japan, which country he visited in 1857.

July 1.—John Fulton Reynolds, a major-general of United States volunteers, born in Lancaster, Pa., in 1820, killed at the battle of Gettysburg, July 1, 1863. He graduated at West Point on the 30th of June, 1841, and on the 23d of October following received his commission as second lieutenant in the 3d artillery. On the 13th of June, 1846, he was promoted to the rank of first lieutenant, and served throughout the Mexican war, winning the brevets of captain and major for his "gallant and meritorious conduct" at Monterey and Buena Vista. After his return from Mexico he was engaged in military service in California, and against the Indians on the Pacific coast. In 1852 he was appointed aid to Gen. Wool, and on the 3d of March, 1855, was promoted to a captaincy in the 3d artillery. On the 14th of May, 1861, he was appointed lieutenant-colonel of the 14th United States infantry. On the 20th of August, 1861, he was commissioned brigadier-general of volunteers, and appointed to the command of the 1st brigade of the Pennsylvania reserve corps, then under Gen. McCall. In June, 1862, the Reserves joined the Army of the Potomac on the peninsula, and Gen. Reynolds, on the 26th of June, 1862, participated in the battle of Mechanicsville, and the next day took part in the severe battle of Gaines' Mill. He was also engaged at Savage Station, and at Charles City Cross-Roads, where he took command of the division after Gen. McCall was taken prisoner, and at a late hour the same day was himself captured by the enemy and sent to Richmond. For his gallantry in these battles he received the brevets of colonel and brigadier-general in the regular army. After his release from Richmond, and on the 26th of September, he returned to the command of his division, and soon after assumed command of the 1st army corps, by virtue of seniority of rank. He commanded this corps in the first battle of Fredericksburg. In January, 1863, he was nominated major-general of volunteers. In the battles of Chancellorsville his corps took no active part, being in the reserve. On the 12th of June he was appointed to the command of the right wing of Hooker's army, having charge of three corps. He hastened forward to Gettysburg at the direction of the commanding general, and arrived there in the vanguard of the Union army, and bringing his little corps of eight thousand men into action against a Confederate force of three times their number, he rode forward to reconnoitre a grove in which the enemy had placed a large body of sharpshooters; and dismounting from his horse, approached a fence and looked over toward the wood, when he was struck in the neck by a rifle ball, and, falling upon his face, died in a few minutes.

July 2.—Brig.-Gen. William Barksdale, an officer in the Confederate service, was killed at the battle of Gettysburg. He was born in Rutherford Co., Tenn., August 21st, 1821. His early education was obtained in the Nashville University, after which he removed to Columbus, Miss., where he studied law and was admitted to the bar before he had attained his majority, becoming a successful practitioner. He was for a time one of the editors of the Columbus "Democrat," in which he sustained the principle of States' rights and the delegated powers of the General Government. During the year 1847 he participated in the Mexican war as a non-commissioned officer in the staff of the 2d Mississippi volunteers. In 1851 he was chosen a member of the State Convention to discuss the compromise measures proposed during the previous year. In 1853 he was elected to Congress on the general ticket, and became a leading member of the States' rights portion of the democratic party. During one of those memorable disturbances in the House of Congress, Mr. Barksdale assisted Mr. Brooks of South Carolina in his assault upon Hon. Charles Sumner. When the war broke out, he left his seat in Congress and joined the Confederate army. At the head of the 13th regiment of Mississippi volunteers he participated in the various campaigns in Virginia, and was promoted to the rank of brigadier-general, and placed in command of the 3d brigade of Major-Gen. Early's division of Lieut.-Gen. Ewell's corps in Gen. Lee's army. On the second day of the battle of Gettysburg, July, 1863, he was killed while in the act of leading on his men.

July 2.—Col. EDWARD EVERETT CROSS was killed at Gettysburg. He was born in Lancaster, N. H., and commenced life as a journeyman printer. He was for some time connected with the press in Cincinnati, and in 1854 he canvassed the State of Ohio for the American party. He was afterwards employed as agent of the St. Louis and Arizona Mining Company, in which he subsequently became a large stockholder. He made several trips across the plains, taking the first steam-engine that ever crossed the Rocky Mountains. When the war commenced he organized the 5th New Hampshire regiment, and was commissioned as its colonel. Under his command the regiment distinguished itself in many important engagements, and won an enviable reputation for bravery. He had been in command of a brigade several months, and was strongly recommended for a brigadier-general. He fell while gallantly fighting at the head of his regiment in the memorable battle of Gettysburg.

July 2.—Col. PATRICK H. O'ROURKE was killed at the battle of Gettysburg. He was a native of Ireland; was appointed a cadet to West Point from New York, and graduated in 1861, standing first in his class. He was assigned to a lieutenancy in the regular army, and placed in the engineers corps in service at Hilton Head and the works on Savannah River, where he greatly distinguished himself. When the 140th regiment was ready for the field, he was assigned to the command, and soon brought it up to a high degree of discipline. He possessed military talent of a high order, and was eminently prepossessing and courteous in all his ways. At the reduction of Fort Pulaski he behaved with great gallantry, and at Chancellorsville commanded a brigade with great honor to himself. At the battle of Gettysburg he mounted a rock, cheering on his men, when he was struck by the fatal bullet.

July 2.—Col. C. F. TAYLOR, an officer of U. S. volunteers, was killed at the battle of Gettysburg. He was born in 1840, and was a brother of Bayard Taylor, with whom a few years ago he travelled extensively in Europe. After his return he graduated at the Michigan University. His patriotic devotion to his country led him to organize a company in Pennsylvania under the first call of the President. He received a captain's commission from the governor, and his company was attached to the Bucktail regiment under Col. Kane. At the battle of Harrisonburg, Va., when Col. Kane was wounded, Capt. Taylor remained with that officer on the field, and they were both taken prisoners by the enemy. A few months later he was appointed colonel of the regiment, Col. Kane having been promoted as brigadier-general. When Gen. Burnside attempted to storm the heights of Fredericksburg, he led one of the charges with great gallantry and was twice wounded. While bravely leading a charge over Roundtop Summit, at the battle of Gettysburg, a ball entered his heart as he raised his sword above his head. His last words were, "Come on, boys: we'll take them all prisoners!"

July 2.—Brig.-Gen. STEPHEN H. WEED, an officer of U. S. volunteers, was killed at the battle of Gettysburg. He was a native of New York, graduated at West Point in July, 1854, and subsequently was made first lieutenant in the 4th United States artillery. When the 5th United States artillery was organized, he was appointed captain. His ability and genius as a commanding officer, and especially as an artillerist, had long been appreciated in the corps, and his brigadier-general's commission was the reward of his gallant services at the battles near Chancellorsville. At the time of his death he was commanding the 3d brigade of regulars, and was fighting manfully, when a bullet from the enemy struck his arm, and, passing into his lung, inflicted a terrible wound from which he died in a few hours. In trying to catch the dying commands of Gen. Weed, Lieut. Charles E. Hazlett, a young officer of the 5th artillery, was kneeling with his head bent close to that of Gen. Weed, when a bullet struck his forehead, felling him dead upon the bosom of his friend.

July 2.—SAMUEL KOSCIUSZKO ZOOK, a brigadier-general in the U. S. volunteer service, was killed in the battle of Gettysburg. He was born in Pennsylvania about the year 1823. When quite young he entered into the telegraph business, and made several important discoveries in electrical science, which gave him a wide reputation. When about twenty-five years of age he removed to New York, and became connected with the local military organizations of the city. In 1857 he was commissioned lieutenant-colonel of the 6th New York State militia, and at the outbreak of the war, though much out of health, went with his regiment to the seat of hostilities, and was appointed military governor of Annapolis. After his return, he recruited the 57th regiment of New York State volunteers, and, having been commissioned colonel, led it to the peninsula. During that long and bloody campaign he generally held command of a brigade, though without the rank or commission properly belonging to his position. On the 29th of November, 1862, he was commissioned brigadier-general, the appointment being confirmed in March, 1863. He was placed in command of his old brigade, and nobly distinguished himself at the battles of Chancellorsville and Gettysburg, on the latter field giving up his life.

July 3.—Brig.-Gen. LEWIS A. ARMISTEAD, an officer in the Confederate service, was killed at Gettysburg. He was a native of Virginia, and was appointed from that State a cadet at West Point in March, 1834. He remained in the Military Academy till October, 1836. On the 10th of July, 1839, he was appointed second lieutenant in the 6th infantry; he was advanced to a first lieutenancy in March, 1844; received the brevets of captain and major for gallant and meritorious conduct in the battles of Contreras, Churubusco, Molino del Rey, and Chapultepec, in 1847. In the last of these engagements he had led a storming party against the citadel. He attained a captaincy in March, 1854, and in 1859 commanded a detachment sent against the Indians from Fort Mohave, California, and attacked and routed them with great slaughter. He joined the Confederates early in the war and was appointed a brigadier-general in 1862. He was a brave officer.

July 3.—Brig.-Gen. ELON J. FARNSWORTH, an officer in the U. S. volunteer service, was killed at the battle of Gettysburg. He was born in Livingstone County, Michigan, in 1835, and was educated at the university of that State. In 1857 he went to New Mexico, and became attached to the United States commissary department, and subsequently was engaged in Utah in the same capacity. When the news of the war reached him in the summer of 1861, he hastened home to join the 8th Illinois cavalry, which his uncle, Gen. John F. Farnsworth, was then organizing. He was made battalion quartermaster, but was soon promoted to the captaincy of Company K of that regiment. During all the battles of the peninsula and in Gen. Pope's campaign he never missed a fight or skirmish in which his company was engaged. In May, 1863, he was placed upon Gen. Pleasanton's staff as aide. He was made brigadier-general only a few days before his death.

July 3.—Brig.-Gen. RICHARD B. GARNETT, an officer in the Confederate service, was killed at the battle of Gettysburg. He was a native of Virginia, entered the service of the United States army as second lieutenant of infantry, July, 1841, and was captain of the 6th infantry, May 9, 1855. When the war broke out he resigned to enter the Confederate service, and was engaged in most of the battles in Virginia. He was at first a colonel under Pegram and Floyd in Western Virginia, but soon after joining Lee's army was promoted to the command of a brigade. He had the reputation of being a capable officer.

July 3.—Maj.-Gen. WILLIAM D. PENDER, an officer in the Confederate service, was killed at the battle of Gettysburg. He was a native of North Carolina and appointed from that State to West Point, where he entered as a cadet in 1850 and graduated in 1854. He was appointed brevet second lieutenant in the 4th artillery in July, 1854, and second lieutenant of the 1st dragoons in March, 1855. He distinguished himself in several conflicts with the Indians in Washington Territory in September, 1858. He joined the Confederate army early in the war, and rose by successive promotions from the rank of colonel to that of major-general. He commanded a division of Gen. Hill's corps at the battle of Gettysburg.

July 3.—Col. J. K. MARSHALL, an officer in the Confederate service, was killed at Gettysburg. He was born in 1840, graduated at Lexington (Virginia) Military Institute in 1860, when he went to Edenton, North Carolina, and took charge of a private school. Upon the commencement of the war he accepted the captaincy of a volunteer company, and was subsequently elected colonel of the 52d regiment of North Carolina troops, taking the place of Col. Vance, who resigned because elected governor.

July 3.—Brig.-Gen. SEMMES, an officer of the Confederate army, killed at the battle of Gettysburg.

July 4.—Col. PAUL JOSEPH REVERE, an officer of U. S. volunteers, died of wounds received in the battle of Gettysburg. He was born in Boston, September 18, 1832, and was a grandson of Paul Revere of Revolutionary history. His early educational advantages were good, and in 1852 he graduated at Harvard College. When the war broke out, though occupying a high social position and surrounded by every thing calculated to make life pleasant, he at once volunteered his services in behalf of his country, and accepting the commission of major in the 20th regiment of volunteers, went to the seat of war. At the disastrous battle of Ball's Bluff his regiment behaved nobly, but lost heavily; he was taken prisoner, and, with his colonel, was confined in a felon's cell as a hostage for the privateersmen whom the United States Court had convicted as pirates. After his exchange he participated in the campaign on the James River, and at Antietam was on Gen. Sumner's staff, when he was complimented for his gallantry, having received a severe wound, which gave him a long winter of pain and seclusion. Upon his recovery he was promoted as colonel of the 20th regiment, and received his death wound in the first successful battle of the campaign.

July 12.—Commander ABNER READ, an officer of the United States navy, died from a wound received upon the Monongahela, at the batteries above Donaldsonville. He was a native of Ohio and about forty-two years of age at the time of his death; was educated at the Ohio University at Athens, which institution he left in his senior year in 1839, having received a midshipman's warrant. His first voyage was on the schooner Enterprise to the South American coast, having been detached from a ship-of-war destined to the Mediterranean, on account of some little difficulty with the captain previous to the sailing of the vessel. Prior to his examination, he spent a year in reviewing his studies at the Naval School in Philadelphia, and stood fifth in a class of forty-eight. He was at once detailed to the duty of acting sailing master, in which capacity he made several voyages and soon acquired the reputation of being one of the most skilful navigators in the service. At the breaking out of the Mexican war he was on the coast of Africa, but returned in time to make a cruise in the Gulf and participate in some naval operations near the close of the war. The progress of naval promotion being slow, he did not reach the rank of lieutenant until 1853, and in 1855 the Navy Retiring Board consigned him to the list of retired officers, but he was not long after reinstated by the Examining Board. Soon after the commencement of the war he was ordered for service to the Wyandotte, the command of which soon devolved upon him, and it was this vessel which performed such important service in saving Fort Pickens from falling into the hands of the enemy. In May, 1862, the health of Lieutenant Read was so much impaired that he was relieved of his command for a time in order to place himself under medical treatment. A severe fit of sickness prostrated him for some weeks, and before fully recovering his strength, he asked sailing orders and was assigned to the command of the gunboat New London. Proceeding at once to Ship Island he commenced cruising in the Mississippi Sound, and in eight days captured four valuable prizes. The exploits of this vessel won for it from the enemy the appellation of the "Black Devil," and it soon succeeded in breaking up the trade between New Orleans and Mobile. The New London captured nearly thirty prizes, took a battery at Biloxi, and had several engagements with Confederate steamers on the sound. A short time previous to his death he lost his left eye in an engagement at Sabine Pass. In June of 1863 he was placed in command of the steam sloop-of-war Monongahela. He was a skilful officer and a universal favorite throughout the navy.

July 14.—Col. HENRY T. O'BRIEN was killed by the rioters in New York city. He was a native of Ireland, but had resided for many years in New York city. Previous to the riot he had been for some time engaged in raising a three years' regiment (the 11th New York volunteers, or James T. Brady Light Infantry). Early on Monday, July 13th, he volunteered his service and those of his regiment to aid in suppressing the riot.

July 18.—Acting Brig.-Gen. HALDIMAND SUMNER PUTNAM, an officer of United States volunteers, was killed at the attack on Fort Wagner. He was born in Cornish, N. H., Oct. 15th, 1835, graduated at West Point in 1857, and from that time until a few months previous to the war, was stationed at different localities on the western frontier. When the war broke out, he was summoned to Washington and intrusted with special messages of the highest importance to carry to Fort Pickens. He accomplished his mission, and was returning to the North when he was seized by the military authorities at Mongomery, Alabama, and held in prison several days, but was finally released and came back to Washington. Soon after he was placed upon Gen. McDowell's staff, in which position he performed many arduous and important duties. He participated in the first battle of Bull Run, and won himself much honor by his bravery and devotion. When requested to take command of a regiment from his native State, he at first declined, upon the ground that he was too young for so responsible a position, but upon being further urged, he finally accepted, and on the 14th of January, 1862, departed with his regiment for the seat of war. During the first year of its service this regiment was stationed at Fort Jefferson, on Tortugas Island. Since then the command has been located at St. Augustine, Florida, Port Royal, S. C., and in the vicinity of Charleston, and though not engaged in any important action previous to the attack upon Fort Wagner, it has participated in many skirmishes and expeditions. For four or five months previous to his death he was acting brigadier-general, and was serving in that capacity when he fell on Morris Island. His forces consisted of the 7th New Hampshire volunteers, and several other regiments from the Middle States. At the attack on Fort Wagner he led his brigade gallantly into action, and fell while rallying his men, holding his position within the enemy's works.

July 18.—Col. ROBERT GOULD SHAW, an officer of colored volunteers, was killed during the assault upon Fort Wagner. He was the only son of Francis G. Shaw, of Staten Island, and was born about 1836. When the war broke out he enlisted as a private in the 7th regiment New York militia, and went to Washington. Before the three months' term of service expired, he sought and obtained a commission in the Massachusetts 2d, which subsequently won so much honor on many a battle-field. At the battle of Cedar Mountain his life was saved by his watch. He commanded the first regiment of colored soldiers from a free State ever mustered into the United States service, and although aware that, by the order of Mr. Davis, he ran the risk of dying upon the gallows if taken prisoner, he went forth ready to die in any way that might prove for the benefit of his country. He fell at the head of his regiment, when standing upon the parapet of Fort Wagner, which had been carried by assault.

July 19.—Major DANIEL McCOOK, an officer of United States volunteers, died of wounds received at the fight with Morgan's men near Buffington Island, Ohio. He was born in 1796. He was clerk in the Pension Office at Washington for two or three years previous to the commencement of the war, and for ten months previous to his death was a paymaster in the United States army. He had eight sons, who have all been in the service except one, Col. George W. McCook, attorney-general of Ohio.

July 30.—Brig.-Gen. GEORGE C. STRONG, an officer of United States volunteers, died from wounds received in the assault upon Fort Wagner, Charleston harbor, aged 30 years. He was born in Stockbridge, Vt. His father died when he was but eight years of age, and he was adopted in the family of his uncle, A. S. Strong, of Easthampton, Mass., under whose care he imbibed his first desire for military life. He entered West Point Academy in the class of 1857, and held the post of first captain of cadets for three years. After graduating he had charge of the Bridesburg arsenal, was thence transferred to Fortress Monroe, and thence to Mount Vernon, Alabama. He subsequently had charge of the Watervliet arsenel a short time, but on the breaking out of the war he applied for active service, and was placed on the staff of Gen. McDowell, at the battle of Bull Run, and was highly complimented for his efficiency in that battle. He was next appointed on the staff of Gen. McClellan, but shortly after was detailed as ordnance officer, by Gen. Butler, to the Department of the Gulf. He distinguished himself at Biloxi, and in the perilous adventure up the Tangipahoa River. He was a brave and skilful officer, and was honored and trusted by the men under his command. At the assault on Fort Wagner he commanded the assaulting column, and led it with the judgment and courage of a veteran.

July —.—Lieut.-Col. —— NAZER, of the New York Mounted Rifles, died at Washington of typhoid fever. He had acquired some distinction in the British army, having been an officer of the 90th Light Infantry. After leaving the British army, he was for some time treasurer of the Winter Garden, in New York. On the breaking out of the war he accepted the position of lieutenant-colonel of the New York Mounted Rifles, with which regiment he continued to serve up to the period of his death, and was on the eve of receiving the full colonelcy. He was an able officer, and his soldierly acquirements and high sense of honor won for him the respect and esteem of his whole division.

Aug. 6.—Capt. ROCK CHAMPION, an officer of the Confederate army, killed in a skirmish at Middleburg, Tenn. At the battle of Elk Horn or Pea Ridge, Capt. Champion commanded the escort of Brig.-Gen. D. M. Frost, and in the hottest of the fight charged a whole infantry regiment with his little band of eighteen. He took part in all the battles in Missouri. At the battles of Carthage, Wilson's Creek, &c., he commanded a regiment of infantry in the Missouri State Guard, and was distinguished for his intrepid courage. Whilst in command of a company of cavalry in North Mississippi, a romantic incident occurred in which Capt. Champion was the hero. A young lady, described as very beautiful, and the daughter of one of the wealthiest men of Northern Alabama, declared she would bestow her hand on the man who would kill the Federal colonel who commanded the town in which she resided, he having by his conduct while in command greatly incensed the inhabitants. Not long afterwards Gen. Roddy made a sudden attack upon the town, and in a hand to hand encounter Capt. Champion killed the Federal colonel. Learning then, for the first time, that a young lady had made such a declaration, he called upon her. She was as good as her word, and they were engaged to be married when Capt. Champion's command was ordered to Tennessee. In an engagement at Middleburg, Tennessee, he was killed. It is said he was so close to the soldier who shot him, that he ran his sword through his opponent, after receiving the wound, and that both fell and died together.

Aug. —.—Maj.-Gen. JOHN S. BOWEN, an officer in the Confederate army, died at Raymond, Miss. He was a native of Georgia, graduated at West Point in July, 1863, and was appointed brevet second lieutenant of mounted rifles. He resigned in May, 1856. He married in St. Louis, Mo., and was for a time an architect in that city. He commanded the 2d regiment of Missouri volunteer militia of the district of St. Louis, at the time Camp Jackson was captured, May 10, 1861; but having protested against the legality of the capture and the exaction of his parole at the time it was given, he escaped to the South, and disregarding his parole entered the Confederate army. He was afterwards exchanged for an officer captured by Gen. Price at Lexington, Mo., but published a card stating that he had never been legally a prisoner, and refused the benefit of the exchange. At Memphis he raised the 1st Missouri Confederate regiment of infantry, which, through the whole war, was hardly surpassed in gallantry, discipline, or drill. At the battle of Shiloh, Gen. Bowen, then acting brigadier general, was severely wounded. From this wound and a fever from which he was suffering when he went into the battle, he never entirely recovered. Gen. Bowen commanded the Confederate troops in the battle near Port Gibson in May, 1863, and made a very stubborn resistance to Gen. Grant's advance. He reported Grant's force at 20,000, his own at 5,500. He was in all the subsequent battles around Vicksburg, and bore a prominent part in the negotiations for the surrender of the city. Gen. Bowen was an excellent officer, and a soldier of spirit and courage. He is said to have died of mortification and sorrow for the fall of Vicksburg.

Aug. 6.—Brig.-Gen. LUCIUS MARSH WALKER, an officer of the Confederate army, killed in a duel by Gen. Marmaduke, also of the Confederate service, near Little Rock, Ark. Gen. Walker was born in Tennessee, and was a cadet at West Point in 1846. July 1, 1850, he was brevet second lieutenant of the 2d dragoons. He resigned on the 31st of March, 1852. At the breaking out of the war he lived in Arkansas. During the siege of Corinth he commanded a brigade in Hardee's corps, and in the campaign in Kentucky in the fall of 1862, he commanded a brigade in the same corps, and in Anderson's division. In November of the same year he was transferred to the Trans-Mississippi Department. The cause of the duel was something Gen. Marmaduke had said derogatory to the courage of Gen. Walker. The duel was of a deadly character, the terms being: weapons, revolvers—distance twelve paces; firing to commence at the word, and continue until one or the other should fall.

Aug. 11.—Lieut.-Col. GEORGE NAUMAN, an officer of United States volunteers, died at Philadelphia in the 61st year of his age. In 1819 he entered the Military Academy at West Point, and in 1821 was acting assistant professor of French in that institution; in 1823 he graduated, and was commissioned brevet second lieutenant in the 2d regiment of artillery, and the same year received his full second lieutenancy in the 1st regiment of artillery; was appointed assistant commissary of subsistence in March, 1828, and was assistant instructor of French at the Military Academy, from September, 1828, to August, 1829. In May, 1832, he was promoted to a first lieutenant. He served in the Florida war, where he distinguished himself, particularly in the battle of "Wahoo Swamp." He served throughout the war with Mexico under Gens. Taylor and Scott, and was twice promoted for "gallant and meritorious conduct." He commanded the 1st regiment of artillery; was "Commissioner of Prizes" at Vera Cruz, at the close of the war, and conducted the evacuation of that city by the United States army. He commanded Fort Washington, on the Potomac, from 1848 to 1852; served on the Pacific coast, from May, 1854, to January, 1861, having been promoted major of the 3d artillery; was inspector of artillery for the Department of Oregon and California, from May, 1858, to January, 1861, and for some months conducted the Artillery School at Fort Vancouver. He was promoted to the lieutenant-colonelcy of the 1st artillery, July, 1861, and was chief of artillery at Newport News, Va., in March, 1862, during the engagement with the "Merrimac," "Yorktown," "Jamestown," and other Confederate steamers. For the last year he was stationed at Fort Warren, in the harbor of Boston, engaged in preparing that work for a state of suitable defence. He was on the eve of promotion to a full colonelcy of artillery, and was on the way to Lancaster to visit his children, when he was attacked by sunstroke, and died in a few hours.

Aug. 14.—Commodore HENRY W. MORRIS, an officer of the United States navy, died in New York city in the 58th year of his age. He was a son of the late Thomas Morris, a conspicuous member of the New York bar, and subsequently United States marshal for the southern district of that State, and grandson of the celebrated Gouverneur Morris of Revolutionary memory. The subject of this notice entered the navy as midshipman, Aug. 21st, 1819. He was first stationed at the Brooklyn navy yard, but in 1820 he was ordered to the corvette Cyane, from thence to the sloop-of-war Ontario, and next to the frigate Constitution, at that time cruising in the Mediterranean. From 1828 to 1838, under the commission of lieutenant, he distinguished himself in various positions. From 1839 to 1845 he was on special duty in New York city, passing through six degrees of official promotion during the term of six years. He was then appointed to the command of the storeship Southampton, at that time belonging to the African squadron. In 1846 he was again ordered to the Brooklyn navy yard, where for the next five years he was awaiting orders. In the mean time he was promoted to the rank of commander, and in 1851 was appointed to the command of the rendezvous in New York until 1853, when he was ordered to the sloop-of-war Germantown, belonging to the Brazilian squadron. In 1855 he was transferred to the Mediterranean station, where he served as fleet captain under Commodore Stringham. Upon his return to America, he received in 1856 his commission as captain. Toward the close of 1861 he superintended the construction of the steam sloop-of-war Pensacola, at the Washington navy yard. In January, 1862, the Pensacola, under his command, successfully passed the line of Confederate batteries on the Potomac, and after anchoring a short time in Hampton Roads, set sail to join the blockading squadron in the Gulf of Mexico. The Pensacola took a brilliant part in all the attacks upon Forts Jackson and St. Philip, and upon the Chalmette batteries. After the capture of New Orleans, Commodore Morris was intrusted with the duty of holding the city and guarding the adjacent coasts. Under his many arduous duties his health became seriously affected, and after resisting for a time the entreaties of his friends, he was persuaded to come North to recruit his strength, but died soon after his arrival.

Aug. 14.—Brig.-Gen. BENJAMIN WELCH, Jr., an officer of United States volunteers, died at Cincinnati of congestive fever, acquired during the campaign in Mississippi. He was formerly a citizen of Ohio, but more recently of Columbia, Penn. He served during the war with Mexico, and for gallant conduct in the battle of Buena Vista was promoted to a lieutenancy. At the commencement of the war he entered the service as lieutenant-colonel of the 45th Pennsylvania, was subsequently promoted to the colonelcy of the regiment, and during 1863 was made a brigadier-general.

Aug. 26.—JOHN BUCHANAN FLOYD, a general in the Confederate army, born in Montgomery (now Pulaski) County, Va., in 1805, died at Abingdon, Va., Aug. 26th, 1863. He was graduated at the South Carolina College in 1826, subsequently practised law for several years in Virginia, and in 1836 emigrated to Helena, Arkansas, whence he returned in 1839 to Virginia. In 1847–'49 he represented Washington County in the House of Representatives, and from 1850 to 1853 he was governor of the State. As a delegate to the democratic presidental convention at Cincinnati in 1856, he exerted his influence in favor of the nomination of Mr. Buchanan, in whose interest he made speeches in many parts of the country during the ensuing canvass, and for whom he cast his vote in the electoral college of Virginia. President Buchanan rewarded his services by appointing him in March, 1857, Secretary of War. In that capacity he labored to the best of his ability to promote the rebellion of the Southern States, and to place them on a footing of strength commensurate with the importance of the conflict upon which they were about to enter; and there seems now to be little doubt that for several years previous to the election of Mr. Lincoln he was privy to the plot for overthrowing the Government. During 1860, in accordance with his orders, the army had been dispersed in the remotest part of the country, considerable portions being on the western frontier, in California, and Southern Texas, whence they could not readily be conveyed to the Atlantic seaboard; and in the same year an extensive transfer of arms from northern to southern arsenals was made, 115,000 muskets having been transferred by one order, and great quantities of cannon and ammunition by other orders.

No sooner had the secession of South Carolina paved the way for concentrated action on the part of the conspirators, than he began to avow openly his sympathy with the movement; and during the stormy discussions in the cabinet on the subject of reënforcing the forts in Charleston harbor, he was the most strenuous opponent of that measure, threatening to resign if it were consummated. On December 26th Major Anderson unexpectedly removed his garrison from Fort Moultrie to Fort Sumter, and upon the refusal of the President to order the entire withdrawal of the United States troops from Charleston harbor, Mr. Floyd tendered his resignation, and was succeeded by Mr. Holt. Soon afterwards he was indicted by the grand jury of the District of Columbia as being privy to the abstraction of bonds to the amount of $870,000 from the Department of the Interior in the latter part of 1860. He had, however, been permitted to retire from Washington, and was never subsequently brought to trial.

As a reward for his eminent services to the cause of secession, he was appointed, soon after the commencement of hostilities, a brigadier-general in the Confederate army, and in the summer and autumn of 1861 commanded, with Gens. Wise and Henningsen, in Western Virginia. The campaign was conducted by him with little skill or energy, and his retreat from Gauley Bridge, September 10th, after his defeat by Gen. Cox, with loss of baggage, camp equipage, and ammunition, was characterized by the Virginia papers of that period as the most disgraceful rout of the war. He was subsequently ordered to Kentucky, and commanded a brigade at Fort Donelson when that place was besieged by Gen. Grant, in February, 1862. From apprehensions that, if captured, he might be subjected to harsh treatment, while public opinion in the loyal States was embittered against him, he retired, on the night previous to the surrender of the fort, with Gen. Pillow and 5,000 men of the garrison, and made good his escape into Southern Tennessee and Alabama. Thenceforth he held no important command. A temporary reappearance in the field in the succeeding summer, under State authority, resulted in no practical success, and he died in retirement.

Aug. —.—Brig.-Gen. ROSWELL SABINE RIPLEY, died in Charleston, S. C. He was a native of Ohio, and appointed cadet from that State in 1839; he graduated seventh in his class, and was appointed brevet second lieutenant 3d artillery July, 1843; became second lieutenant in the 2d artillery in 1846, and first lieutenant March 3d, 1847. He was aide-de-camp to Gen. Pillow in 1847 and 1848; was brevetted captain for gallantry at Cerro Gordo, and major for gallantry at Chapultepec. In 1853 he resigned his commission and retired to private life. At the outbreak of the war he entered into the service of the Southern Confederacy, took a prominent part in the siege of Fort Sumter, and was wounded at the battle of Antietam. He was the author of "The War in Mexico" (2 vols., New York, 1849).

Sept 19.—Col. HANS C. HEG, acting brig.-gen. of United States volunteers, was killed at Chickamauga, aged 34 years. He was a Norwegian by birth, and came with his father to the United States when but 11 years of age, and settled in Wisconsin. In 1849, during the gold excitement, he went to California by the overland route, and after a stay of two years returned, and, purchasing a piece of land near Milwaukee, engaged in farming and mercantile pursuits until 1859, when he was elected by the Republican State Convention of Wisconsin to the office of commissioner of State Prisons. In 1861 he entered into the military service of his country as major of the 4th Wisconsin militia, and, on the

30th of September of the same year was commissioned colonel of the 15th regiment of Wisconsin volunteer infantry, composed mostly of Scandinavians. This regiment formed part of the forces under Gen. Pope in the reduction of Island No. 10, and was afterwards attached to Col. Buford's brigade, with which it participated in the surprise and capture of Union City, Tenn.; it also took a prominent part in the battle of Chaplin Hills near Perryville, Oct. 8th, 1862. With Gen. Buell's army, Col. Heg joined in the pursuit of Gen. Bragg's forces out of the State of Kentucky, and when the former was superseded by Gen. Rosecrans, he continued his command, and participated in the contests at Stone River and Murfreesboro. On the 29th of April he was placed in command of the third brigade of Davis's division, McCook's (20th) army corps, of the Army of the Cumberland. With this brigade he took part in all the movements of the 20th corps, resulting in the evacuation of Shelbyville, Tullahoma, and Chattanooga, and at Chickamauga, where he fell at the head of his forces on the second day of the fight.

Sept. 19.—Brig.-Gen. PRESTON SMITH, an officer of the Confederate army, killed during the last of the first day's battle at Chicamauga. He had entered the Confederate service as an officer of a Tennessee regiment, and rose by gradual promotion to the rank of brigadier-general. After dark, accompanied by his staff, he was reconnoitring the ground in his front, when he suddenly came upon a regiment of the opposing army, who fired a volley upon his party, killing him and nearly all of his staff.

Sept. 20.—Brig.-Gen. JAMES DESHLER, an officer of the Confederate army, killed on the second day of the battle of Chicamauga. Gen. Deshler was a graduate of West Point, and one of the most unassuming, gentle, and courteous gentlemen in the army. At the time of his death he commanded a splendid brigade of Texans, who idolized their commander.

Sept. 20.—Brig.-Gen. BEN. HARDIN HELM, an officer in the Confederate service, killed on the second day of the battle at Chickamauga (the river of death). Gen. Helm was born in Hardin County, Ky., in 1831, and entered West Point from that State in 1849. In 1851 he was brevetted second lieutenant of 2d dragoons, and resigned October, 1852, to take up the profession of law. He was a son of ex-Governor John L. Helm, a prominent politician of Kentucky. His mother was the daughter of that distinguished statesman known as "old Ben. Hardin of Kentucky." Gen. Helm's wife was a half sister of Mrs. Lincoln, wife of our late President. Immediately after the fall of Fort Sumter, President Lincoln sent Gen. Helm a commission as major in the regular army of the United States, but his sympathies being with the South, and holding a commission in the State Guards of Kentucky, under Gen. Buckner, he refused the commission tendered him by the authorities at Washington, and entered the Confederate service as a private. He immediately rose to the rank of colonel, and commanded the 1st Kentucky cavalry. In 1862 he was promoted to the rank of brigadier-general. He was in the battles of Perryville and Stone River, in which last he commanded a division. The Kentucky brigade which he commanded at Chickamauga went into action with one thousand seven hundred and sixty-three men, and came out with only four hundred and thirty-two.

Sept. 20.—Lieut.-Col. WILLIAM G. JONES, an officer of the U. S. volunteers, died at Chattanooga from wounds received at the battle of Chickamauga, aged 28 years. He graduated at West Point in 1860, and, after the usual respite, was ordered to join his company of the 8th infantry —to which he was attached as brevet second lieutenant—then serving in Texas. He participated in several Indian skirmishes; and at San Antonio was taken prisoner. In the fall of 1860 he became second lieutenant in the 10th infantry, and in the following spring was promoted to first lieutenant. In March, 1862, he was selected as aide-de-camp to Gen. Andrew Porter, then provost marshal general of the Army of the Potomac, which post he filled, with ability, until he was appointed lieutenant-colonel of the 71st Pennsylvania volunteer infantry, and the colonel being absent, took command of the regiment. In the battles of Peach Orchard, Glendale, White Oak Swamp, and Allen's Field, the regiment under his command won itself much honor; and for his conduct on these occasions he was rewarded with the brevets of captain and major. He was subsequently aid upon the staff of Major-General Sumner, in which capacity he distinguished himself at South Mountain and at Antietam. After the death of General Sumner he was appointed to the colonelcy of the 89th Ohio infantry; and it was while ably commanding this regiment of Crook's brigade, that he fell fighting nobly at the head of his men.

Sept. 20.—Brig.-Gen. WM. HAINES LYTLE, an officer of U. S. volunteers, was killed at Chickamauga, Ga. He was born in Cincinnati, Ohio, Nov. 2d, 1826, and his ancestors, for several generations, were noted as military men. He graduated with distinction at Cincinnati College; studied law, and, during the Mexican war, entered the military service of his country as a lieutenant of an independent company of foot soldiers. On the 21st of December, 1847, he was promoted to the captaincy, retaining his command until the regiment was disbanded, July, 1848. At the conclusion of the Mexican war he resumed the practice of his profession, and was soon after elected to the Ohio Legislature. Subsequently he was chosen major-general of the first division of Ohio militia, a position previously held by both his father and his grandfather. At the outbreak of the present war he accepted the colonelcy of the 10th Ohio volunteers, which, by its desperation in the fight, won the title of the "Bloody Tenth." He participated in the battle of Rich Mountain, where he won much honor. At Carnifex Ferry he commanded a brigade, and largely contributed to drive Gens. Floyd and Wise from that part of Virginia; and here he was severely wounded. When scarcely recovered he returned to the field and first took the command of the Bardstown Camp of Instruction, and then of the 17th brigade under General O. M. Mitchel, participating in the brilliant operations along the Memphis and Chattanooga Railroad. At the battle of Perryville he was again wounded, and fell into the hands of the enemy, but after a week's captivity was exchanged. For his gallant conduct he was made brigadier-general of volunteers in the spring of 1863, and from that time to his death served under Gen. Rosecrans. In addition to his talents as a soldier, he was a poet of much merit, though from his extreme modesty few of his productions have found their way into print. He fell at the battle of Chickamauga, by a bullet which pierced his brain, as he was gallantly leading a charge.

Sept. 22.—Major —— GRAVES, an officer of artillery in the Confederate army, mortally wounded at the battle of Chickamauga. Major Graves was a very recent graduate of West Point, and was a rashly brave but exceedingly efficient officer. At Fort Donaldson he commanded a battery, and was there captured with the remainder of the army. After his exchange, he was placed upon Gen. Breckenridge's staff as chief of artillery, with the rank of major, and was acting in that capacity when he was mortally wounded by a musket-ball through the bowels, and taken to Ringold, where he died.

Oct. —.—Brig.-Gen. CHARLES DIMMOCK, an officer of the Confederate army, died at Richmond, Va. He was born in Massachusetts, and was a cadet at West Point from Sept., 1817, until July, 1821. He graduated second in his class, and entered the army as brevet second lieutenant of 1st artillery, July, 1821, and from that time until July, 1822, he was acting assistant professor of engineering in the military academy at West Point. In 1826 he was assistant commissary of subsistence, and from Aug., 1831, to Aug., 1836, was quartermaster, when he was promoted to a captaincy. He was civil engineer on the railroad from Weldon, North Carolina, to Wytheville, Va., in 1836, and on the route of the Wilmington and Raleigh Railroad in 1837. He was engaged in the same capacity from 1837 to 1839 on the military road from the Upper Mississippi to Red River, and general agent of the Portsmouth and Roanoke Railroad in 1839 and 1841. He served in the army of the United States fifteen years. Since 1843 he had been superintendent of the Virginia State armory, and captain commanding State Guard. During the war he was chief of ordnance of the department of Virginia.

Oct. 2.—Major EDWARD B. HUNT, an officer of U. S. volunteers, born in Livingston County, N. Y., in 1822, died at the Brooklyn Marine Hospital, Oct. 2d, 1863. He was appointed to the Military Academy from his native State in 1841, graduated second in the class of 1845, was appointed second lieutenant in the corps of engineers, and was assigned to duty as assistant to the Board of Engineers for Atlantic Coast Defence. After serving in this capacity a year, he was called to fill the important position of principal assistant professor of civil and military engineering at the military academy, West Point, where he remained until 1849, when he was employed as assistant-engineer upon Fort Warren, Boston harbor, Mass. From 1851 to 1855 he was the assistant of Prof. Bache in the Coast Survey Bureau. From 1855 to 1857 he was engaged in engineer operations in Newport, R. I., and constructed and repaired many important lighthouse structures on the coast. In 1857 he was ordered to Key West, where for five years he assisted in the construction of fortifications and other defensive works on the island, receiving his captaincy while serving there, July 1st, 1859. It was chiefly through his instrumentality that the forts of Southern Florida were withheld from the Confederates after the war actually commenced. In 1862 he was appointed chief engineer of the 5th army corps, commanded by Maj.-Gen. Banks, and from this duty was relieved and placed on special service under the Navy Department, in order to superintend the construction of his submarine battery. While engaged in making some experiments with this battery, a shell prematurely discharged, immediately after which he descended into the caisson, and in attempting to ascend, being probably overcome by the gas, fell backward, striking his head, and causing concussion of the brain, from which he died the next day.

Oct. 14.—Brig.-Gen. HENRY F. COOK, an officer in the Confederate service, was killed at Bristoe Station. He was a native of Mississippi; served in the Mexican war as first lieutenant in Jefferson Davis's regiment of Mississippi volunteers; distinguished himself in the battle of Monterey, where he was wounded, and commanded Co. C in the battle of Buena Vista. He had joined the Confederate army early in the war, and had risen by successive promotions to the rank of brigadier-general in 1863.

Oct. 18.—Col. THOMAS RUFFIN, an officer in the Confederate service, died at Grace Church Hospital, Washington, from wounds received at the battle of Bristow Station. He was a native of North Carolina, but for a number of years was a citizen of Missouri, residing at Bolivar, Polk County, and was at one time State Attorney for that judicial circuit. Subsequently he returned to his native State, from which he was elected to Congress.

Oct. 29.—Col. CHARLES RIVERS ELLET, commander of the Mississippi marine brigade, died at Bunker Hill, Illinois, aged about 22 years. He was a son of the late Col. Charles Ellet, an accomplished engineer and the originator of the ram fleet, and was born in Philadelphia. To a thorough education he had added the advantages of foreign travel and a brief residence in Paris. He had made choice of the medical profession, and at the outbreak of the war was engaged in pursuing the requisite studies, in which he had already made such progress as to fill competently the place of assistant surgeon in one of the military hospitals. Preferring to follow the fortunes of his father he accompanied him westward in the spring of 1862, and commanded one of the rams at the action of Memphis, in which the elder Ellet received the wound which soon after proved fatal. After his father's death, on the organization of the Mississippi marine brigade by his uncle, now Gen. Alfred W. Ellet, he was promoted to a colonelcy, and when his uncle was commissioned brigadier-general of land troops, he was placed in command of the marine brigade. Choosing the ram Queen of the West as his headquarters, he made many daring expeditions on the Mississippi. He succeeded in running the Confederate batteries at Vicksburg, and was for some time engaged in cruising between that stronghold and Port Hudson. On the 10th of February, 1863, he started upon an expedition up the Red River, during which he captured the Confederate steamer Era No. 5 and some other vessels, and after ascending the river for some distance with success, his vessel was run aground by the pilot, in such position that she was disabled by the fire from a Confederate fort, and fell into the hands of the enemy; Col. Ellet, however, made his escape upon a bale of cotton and was picked up by the De Soto. During and after the siege of Vicksburg, Col. Ellet and his command rendered much valuable assistance to Gen. Grant, in keeping open his communications, and while engaged in these operations his health became so seriously affected by the noxious vapors of the river as to make it necessary to retire for a season to Illinois to rest. His death, which was the result of the disease he contracted, was very sudden.

Oct. 31.—Brig.-Gen. Louis Blenker, of U. S. volunteers, died in New Jersey, aged 51 years. He was born in the city of Worms, in the Grand Duchy of Hesse Darmstadt, and in his youth was apprenticed to a jeweller, but upon his majority enlisted in the Bavarian legion which was raised to accompany the newly-elected King Otho to Greece. From a private he rose to a sergeant, and when the legion was disbanded in 1837, received with his discharge the rank of lieutenant. With this rank he returned to Worms, whence he went to Munich to attend medical lectures with the view of becoming professor of medicine. Subsequently he changed his mind and entered into commercial pursuits. In 1849 he became a leading member of the revolutionary government in his native city, and having been appointed commander of the national guards, took an active part in the popular struggle of that period. After the revolutionary movement had been crushed he retired to Switzerland, and, being ordered to leave the country, he embarked at Havre for the United States, and settled on a farm in Rockland County, N. Y. Subsequently he removed to New York city, where he engaged in commerce until 1861. Upon the commencement of the war he raised the 8th regiment of New York volunteers, with which he marched to Washington, having been commissioned its colonel May 13th, 1861. After being encamped for some time on Meridian Hill, the regiment was incorporated with others into a brigade, of which Col. B. was appointed commander. The brigade was then attached to Gen. McDowell's army as a portion of Col. Miles's 5th division. During the battle of Bull Run this division acted as a reserve, and for his services at that time he was commissioned a brigadier-general, August 9th, 1861. He remained with the Army of the Potomac, commanding a division, until the commencement of the Yorktown campaign, when he was ordered to Western Virginia. Gen. Blenker participated in the battle of Cross Keys, June 8th, 1862, but was shortly after relieved of the command and was succeeded by Gen. Sigel. He was then ordered to Washington, where he remained for some time, and on March 31st, 1863, was mustered out of service.

Nov. —.—Brig.-Gen. Johnson K. Duncan, an officer who died in the Confederate service. He was a native of Pennsylvania; entered West Point in 1845, and upon his graduation was appointed brevet second lieutenant 2d artillery; was transferred to the 3d artillery Oct., 1849, as second lieutenant, and in Dec., 1853, was made first lieutenant. He resigned Jan. 31st, 1855, and upon the commencement of the war entered into the Confederate service as colonel. He was appointed brigadier-general from Louisiana, and commanded Forts Jackson and St. Philip at the time of the bombardment by Flag-officer Farragut.

Nov. 15.—Brig.-Gen. Conrad Posey, an officer in the Confederate service, died at Charlottesville from a wound received at Gettysburg. He was a native of Mississippi, and was made a brigadier-general early in 1863. He was an officer of much military talent.

Nov. 24.—Major Gilbert Malleson Elliott, of the 102d regiment N. Y. volunteers, was killed at Lookout Mountain. He was born in Connecticut in 1840, and removed to New York in early childhood. In 1857 he became a member of the Free Academy, and at once took the highest stand in scholarship and deportment, receiving the gold medal at four successive commencements, and the valedictory oration at his graduation. On the completion of his studies, he was impressed with a strong desire to enter into the service of his country, and in October of that year was commissioned first lieutenant. At Antietam he won himself much honor, and soon after was appointed ordnance officer in the second division of the 12th army corps, where he rendered most effective service during the battles of Chancellorsville and Gettysburg. Having previously received the rank of captain, he was subsequently appointed major, and was soon after placed in actual command of his regiment, both of his superior officers having been wounded, In September, 1863, the 12th army corps was transferred from the Army of the Potomac to the Army of the Cumberland, and in the storming of Lookout Mountain his regiment held the right of Geary's division in Gen. Hooker's first line of battle. During the hottest part of the engagement Major Elliott leaped upon a rock, either to cheer his men or for purposes of observation, and immediately received a ball from a sharpshooter, causing speedy death.

Nov. 25.—Brig.-Gen. WILLIAM P. SANDERS, an officer of U. S. volunteers, died at Knoxville, Tenn., of wounds received in the battle at Campbell's Station. He was a native of Kentucky, graduated at West Point in 1856, and entered the service as brevet second lieutenant 1st dragoons, and was transferred to the 2d dragoons in May, 1857. Soon after the commencement of the war, he was made captain of a company in the 6th regular cavalry, and took an active part in the peninsula campaign. He subsequently accepted the office of colonel of a volunteer regiment in Kentucky, and performed many valuable services in the West. A few months previous to his death he was appointed brigadier-general of volunteers, and was assigned to the command of the first division of cavalry in East Tennessee. He was a brilliant officer, a true patriot, and a thorough gentleman.

Nov. 29.—Col. MCELROY, an officer of the Confederate army, killed in Lieut.-Gen. Longstreet's attempt to take Knoxville, East Tenn. He fell mortally wounded in the ditch where, in an instant of time, the Confederates lost seven hundred men, and where the dead and wounded laid seven and eight deep. He commanded the 13th Mississippi regiment.

Nov. 29.—Col. THOMAS, an officer of the Confederate army, killed at the storming of Knoxville, Tenn. Col. Thomas fell mortally wounded in the ditch where so many Confederates fell, and into which hand-granades and ignited shell were thrown from the forts. He commanded the 16th Georgia regiment.

Dec. 13.—Gen. THOMAS J. GREEN, an officer in the Confederate service, died at his residence in Warren County, N. C., aged 62 years. He was a general in the Texas war of independence, a member of the Texan Congress, the leader of the Mier expedition, one of the band of "Mier prisoners," and subsequently historian of that transaction. He was afterwards a State senator in California, and major-general of the militia in that State.

Dec. 16.—JOHN BUFORD, a major-general of volunteers in the United States service, born in Kentucky in 1825, died at Washington, Dec. 16, 1863, of typhoid fever, contracted in service with the Army of the Potomac. His early training and education were carefully conducted, and his mental and moral development gave bright promise of future usefulness. He was appointed from Illinois, to the military academy at West Point, and graduated in 1848, standing well in his class, and in the estimation of all who knew him; was appointed brevet second lieutenant of 1st dragoons, and served on the Plains until the war broke out, when he promptly and heartily offered himself to the service of his country. His rare abilities as an officer attracted the attention of the Government, and he was early made a major in the Inspector-General's corps. His peculiar duties did not give him an opportunity to engage in the leading campaigns until 1862, when he was made a brigadier-general, simply as an acknowledgment of his military merits. In the early part of 1862 he fought under Gen. Pope in his Virginia campaign, succeeding Gen. Stoneman (who afterwards became his commander) on Gen. McClellan's staff, during the battle of Antietam. When the present cavalry organization of the Army of the Potomac was perfected, of which Gen. Stoneman was at that time the chief, Gen. Buford was assigned to command the reserve cavalry brigade. He was subsequently conspicuous in almost every cavalry engagement, and at Gettysburg commenced the attack on the enemy at Seminary Ridge, before the arrival of Reynolds on the 1st of July, and on the 2d of July rendered important services both at Wolff's Hill and Round Top. A short time previous to his death he was assigned to the command of the cavalry in the Army of the Cumberland, and had left the Army of the Potomac for that purpose. He was a splendid cavalry officer, and one of the most successful in the service; was modest, yet brave; unostentatious, but prompt and persevering; ever ready to go where duty called him, and never shrinking from action however fraught with peril. His last sickness was but brief, the effect, probably, of protracted toil and exposure. On the day of his death, and but a little while before his departure, his commission of major-general was placed in his hands. He received it with a smile of gratification that the Government he had defended appreciated his services, and gently laying it aside, soon ceased to breathe.

Dec. 17.—Commodore GERSHOM J. VAN BRUNT, of the U. S. navy, died at Dedham, Mass., aged 63 years. He was a native and a citizen of New Jersey, and entered the service November 3d, 1818. He received his commission of commodore July 16th, 1862, was in command of the Minnesota, which sailed from Boston soon after the commencement of the war, and took an active part in the reduction of the Hatteras forts, and in the blockading service at Hampton Roads. Subsequently he was entrusted by the Government with the supervision and equipment of Gen. Banks' New Orleans expedition, and at the time of his death was acting under the orders of the War Department as inspector of transports for the New England district. He was highly esteemed in the navy for his talents as an officer as well as for his intrinsic worth.

Dec. 22.—MICHAEL CORCORAN, a brigadier-general of U. S. volunteers, born in Carrowkeel, county Sligo, Ireland, Sept. 21st, 1827, died Dec. 22d, 1863, near Fairfax Court House, of injuries received by a fall from his horse. His father, Thomas Corcoran, was an officer in the British army, and saw service in the West Indies. On the mother's side he was a descendant of the Earl of Lucan, the title and estates of whose family were confiscated after the noble defence of Limerick, during the seventeenth century, and were conferred on the Bingham family for services rendered the British crown. Young Corcoran received the benefits of a good English education until his nineteenth year, when, through some influential friends, he received an appointment in the Irish Constabulary force; but the love of his country burned so strongly within him that he could not brook the oppression of British rule, and, fearing that some occasion might tempt him to break through all restraint, he resigned his commission in 1849, emigrated to this country, and settled in New York city. There he made many friends, and through their influence was appointed to an official situation in the post-office, and subsequently was clerk in the register's office. He commenced his military career as a private in Company I, 69th New York State militia. Displaying some amount of military talent, he rose successively from one grade to another, and in August, 1859, was elected colonel of the 69th. While holding this position, he attracted much public notice by his refusal to parade his regiment at the reception accorded to the Prince of Wales, upon his visit to New York city during the fall of 1860. He had not forgotten how England had persecuted and oppressed his countrymen, and declined to do homage to the son of a sovereign under whose rule some of the most worthy sons of Ireland had been banished. In this he was consistent with the spirit and principles of those heroes of Limerick from whom he had descended, and was fully sustained by the corps he commanded. By command of Major-Gen. Sandford he was subjected to a trial by court-martial, which was long, and contested upon his part with true Irish spirit and independence, and which was still pending when the war broke out. The President's call to arms fired all the patriotism of his soul; he called upon his men to stand by the flag of the Union and the sacred principles it involved. The court-martial was quashed. The Irish flocked to the ranks with all the enthusiasm of native-born citizens, and the 69th left New York for the seat of war, attended by a vast concourse of admiring people. The regiment was speedily sent to Virginia, where the men comprising it built, upon Arlington Heights, the famous "Fort Corcoran." At the disastrous battle of Bull Run, July 21st, 1861, the 69th won itself much honor. Their gallant colonel was taken prisoner, first sent to Richmond and afterwards to Charleston, S. C., where he was closely confined for nearly a whole year, being held most of the time as a hostage for some privateersmen who had been condemned as pirates. An exchange being finally effected, he was released, and was commissioned brigadier-general, dating from July 21, 1861. He next organized the Corcoran Legion, which took part in the battles of the Nansemond River and Suffolk, during April, 1863, and held the advance of the enemy upon Norfolk in check. In August, 1863, the Legion was added to the Army of the Potomac. On the 22d of December, Gen. Meagher, who had been paying a visit to Gen. Corcoran, was returning to Washington, when the latter, with some members of his staff, concluded to accompany him. Gen. Corcoran mounted upon Gen. Meagher's horse, and was somewhat in advance of the party. When near his headquarters, his companions found him lying senseless, his horse having fallen upon him. He was placed at once under medical treatment, but died without waking to consciousness.

Dec. 31.—Capt. GEORGE W. VANDERBILT, son of Commodore C. Vanderbilt, died at Nice, in the 25th year of his age. He graduated at West Point in the spring of 1860, and immediately entered the regular army with the rank of second lieutenant. He was first stationed at Fort Walla-Walla, in Washington Territory, where he remained until the war broke out, when he was ordered to Boston to take charge of the recruiting service at that place. In the spring of 1862 he received an appointment on the staff of Brig.-Gen. Tyler as assistant-adjutant general, with the rank of captain. He was regarded by his superiors as an officer of great promise. While in the discharge of his duties he contracted a disease incident to exposure in an unhealthy region, and resisting the importunities of his superior to accept a furlough for the recovery of his health, he was soon beyond the reach of medical skill. In the spring of 1863, finding himself seriously ill, he obtained a furlough, and left for Europe, where he secured the best medical advice, but too late; he continued to sink, and died the last day of the year, lamented by a large circle of relations and friends.

Dec. —.—Lieut.-Col. LACHLAN ALLAN MACLEAN, an officer of the Confederate army, killed in a personal encounter at Richmond, Ark., by Colonel Robert C. Wood, who had been at one time a member of Gen. Sterling Price's staff. Lieut.-Col. Maclean was born in Scotland, and was the son of Hector Maclean. He once lived in the State of Missouri, and taught school in Lexington. He had been chief clerk for John Calhoun, surveyor-general for the State of Arkansas and the territory of Nebraska, and proved himself so efficient that the entire business was entrusted to him. During the Kansas troubles he espoused the pro-slavery party and became a brigadier-general of volunteer forces in Kansas. At the time of his death he was the adjutant-general of Major-Gen. Sterling Price, and about forty-four years of age. He had the wild roving disposition of a border man, or of the Scottish Highlander, but the gentle and refined manners of the polished gentleman. His personal appearance was remarkably striking, his voice rich and mellow, and his taste for poetry and elocution chaste and cultivated. His friends, who have so often assembled around the camp-fire in the far West to hear his rehearsals, will long remember his "Dundee" and his "Antony and Cleopatra."

1864.

Jan. 8.—Rear-Admiral GEO. W. STORER, an officer of the U. S. navy, died at Portsmouth, N. H. Admiral Storer had served his country in its navy over half a century. He was born in New Hampshire, and was appointed a midshipman in the navy Jan. 16th, 1809. On July 24th, 1813, he was appointed a lieutenant, and ordered to the Independence, seventy-four guns. He was ordered to the old frigate Congress in 1818, and in 1819 to the Jura frigate. In 1820 he was ordered to the Constitution, then flag-ship of Commodore J. Rodgers, on the Mediterranean station, where he remained on a long cruise. In 1825 he was stationed at the Portsmouth navy yard. In 1828 he was promoted master commandant, which is ranked next to that of captain. He was placed in command of the sloop-of-war Boston (eighteen guns), and attached to the Mediterranean squadron in 1831. He remained in command of that ship until the end of the cruise, when he was again ordered to the Portsmouth navy yard, 1833. He was promoted captain, and put on waiting orders Feb. 9th, 1837. The following year he was put in command of the Potomac frigate, and ordered to the coast of Brazil. He returned in 1843, and awaited orders at Portsmouth, and was again attached to the navy yard at that place. In 1848 he commanded a squadron off the coast of Brazil. In 1851 he obtained a leave rendered necessary by the state of his health. After a short leave he reported for duty, and was put on waiting orders. He was then ordered to the Philadelphia Naval Asylum as Governor, in 1855. He was relieved in 1858 and placed on waiting orders. On the 16th of July, 1862, he was promoted rear-admiral, and placed on the retired list. His time was largely occupied after, as in fact before his promotion, as president of courts-martial and inquiry. He was fifty-five years in the naval service. Of that time he was at sea twenty-one years and nine months; twenty years on shore and other duties; unemployed twelve years and eight months. At the time of his death he was announced to preside over a court-martial to be held in New York city. He had lived to see the once small navy of a few ships grow to be scarcely inferior to any on the ocean. It was the dream of his youth and the pride of his manhood realized and gratified.

Jan. 12.—Col. EDWIN ROSE died at Jamaica, L. I. He was born in Bridgehampton, L. I. Feb. 14th, 1817, graduated at West Point, but resigned his position in the army in 1837, to enter the service of the State of Michigan as civil engineer. He reëntered the service in 1861, as colonel of the 81st New York volunteers, and served with honor through the peninsular campaign, when, his health becoming impaired, he accepted the appointment of provost-marshal of the First Congressional district of New York. He twice represented Suffolk County in the Legislature.

Jan. 20.—T. M. SAUNDERS, captain in the United States army, died at St. Paul, Minn. He was a native of Virginia. During the Crimean war he obtained a furlough and joined a British regiment. He was twice wounded at the battle of Inkermann. At the breaking out of the rebellion he continued firm in the support of the Government; and, upon receiving an autograph letter from Jefferson Davis, enclosing a commission as a brigadier-general in the Confederate Army, he returned it with the utmost indignation.

Jan. 29.—STEPHEN G. CHAPLIN, brigadier-general of United States volunteers, died at Grand Rapids, Mich. He entered the service as major of the 3d Michigan, was severely wounded at Fair Oaks, participated in the battles of Bull Run, Antietam, and Fredericksburg, and received his commission of brigadier in 1862. He was in command of the Grand Rapids camp of conscripts at the time of his death.

Jan. 31.—SOLON BORLAND, formerly a United States Senator from Arkansas, and brigadier-general in the rebel army, died in Texas. He was born in Virginia, educated in North Carolina, studied medicine, and settled in Little Rock, Ark., where he practised his profession. He served in the Mexican War as major of volunteers and aide-de-camp, and was taken prisoner; was elected United States Senator in 1849, and in 1853 appointed minister to Central America, where, in consequence of an altercation, he returned in 1854, and Greytown was bombarded by Com. Hollins in consequence of the insult offered him. He was afterwards appointed Governor of New Mexico, but declined. He was ardently in favor of secession, and on the 24th of April, 1861, long before the secession of the State, raised a body of troops and captured Fort Smith, Ark., in the name of the Southern Confederacy.

Feb. 5.—Rev. N. A. STAPLES, a Unitarian

clergyman, died in Brooklyn, in the 34th year of his age. He was a native of Mendon, Mass.; studied theology at the Meadville Seminary, under Dr. Stebbins; was for a time pastor of a church in Lexington, Mass., and subsequently of a church in Milwaukee. At the beginning of the war he was appointed chaplain to one of the Wisconsin regiments, resigning his pastorate to accept the post. Here, as ever, he was earnest and faithful in the discharge of his duties, and contracted the disease which finally terminated in death. He succeeded the Rev. Mr. Longfellow in the Second Unitarian Church of Brooklyn, where he discharged his duties as a pastor as long as his failing strength allowed.

Feb. 15.—Capt. ALLAN RAMSAY, of the United States Marine Corps, died at the headquarters of the Marine Corps, of small-pox. He was a son of Commodore William Ramsay, United States navy, and was on the Richmond during all her service on the Mississippi, before and after running past the batteries. He had been in fifteen engagements during the war.

Feb. 20.—Commander DAWSON PHENIX, U. S. navy, died in Philadelphia, aged 36 years. He entered the naval service in 1841, having been appointed from Maryland, his native State. His first orders were to join the Independence, then attached to the home squadron. Subsequently he served on board the frigate Savannah, of the Pacific squadron, and during a cruise of the Brandywine, also upon the steamer Princeton. In July, 1847, he was ordered to the naval school for promotion; was a passed midshipman in 1848, and the following year was ordered upon the coast survey, where he remained until July, 1850, when he was ordered to the Raritan, but was transferred to the sloop St. Mary's. In 1852 he was detached from that vessel and ordered to the Observatory at Washington, where he remained until October, 1853, when he was sent to the receiving-ship Philadelphia, and again to coast survey duty. In September, 1855, he was promoted to a lieutenancy, and afterwards served upon the Fredonia and the Lancaster. In 1861 he was promoted to be lieutenant-commander, and ordered to ordnance duty at Old Point Comfort, Va. A few months previous to his death he was assigned to the command of the gunboat Pocahontas.

Feb. 22.—Col. —— FRIBLEY, of the 8th United States volunteers (colored), was killed at Olustee, Florida, aged 28 years. He enlisted at the commencement of the war as a private in the 84th Pennsylvania, and rose to his position through good conduct and courage alone.

March 4.—Col. ULRIC DAHLGREN, an officer in the United States volunteer service, born in 1842, killed in a skirmish at King and Queen's Court House, Virginia, March 4, 1864. He was the son of Rear-Admiral John Dahlgren, and had received a very thorough education, and especially a careful training in the science of gunnery, which was his father's speciality. He had entered the navy as midshipman before the breaking out of the war, and at the time of the attack on Fort Sumter was travelling in the Southwestern States. Great efforts were made to induce him to join the rebels, but he refused indignantly; and hastening home, he assisted his father in the Ordnance Department; and when Gen. Saxton was in command at Harper's Ferry, and the place was first threatened, Commodore Dahlgren, having received orders to place a naval battery on Maryland Heights, sent his son Ulric to place the guns in position, and take charge of the battery. He executed this duty with great skill, and when Gen. Sigel relieved Gen. Saxton of his command, he found young Dahlgren at his post as captain of artillery, and took him at once upon his staff. Subsequently Gen. Sigel solicited and obtained his appointment as additional aide-de-camp with the rank of captain. He served in this capacity in Fremont's mountain campaign, distinguishing himself particularly at Cross Keys, and served through Pope's campaign, acting as chief of artillery under Sigel at the second battle of Bull Run, where he was specially commended by his general. During the movements in the autumn of 1862 he was actively engaged under Gen. Stahel in all his reconnoissances and raids, and when the Army of the Potomac moved down into Virginia, in November, 1862, he made that attack upon Fredericksburg at the head of Gen. Sigel's bodyguard, which has become famous in the history of the war. For this gallant act Gen. Burnside detailed him as special aid upon his staff. At the crossing of the Rappahannock, at the unfortunate battle of Fredericksburg, he was one of the first to land in that city. When the army went into winter quarters he rejoined Gen. Sigel, and when that general was relieved of command, Gen. Hooker applied to have Capt. Dahlgren transferred to his staff, which was done. He again distinguished himself at the battle of Chancellorsville, was with General Pleasanton in all the cavalry fights in the Bull Run Mountains and Aldie, joined Gen. Stahel's expedition to Warrenton as a volunteer, and led the most important reconnoissances then made. When Gen. Meade succeeded Gen. Hooker, he requested Capt. Dahlgren to remain on his staff. Before the battles at Gettysburg he obtained from Gen. Pleasanton a hundred picked men, with a roving commission, and among other distinguished services rendered the Union cause, scoured the country in search of a bearer of despatches, whom he knew to be on his way from Jefferson Davis to Gen. Lee, captured him and his escort, secured the despatches, and, by the most skilful manœuvring, succeeded in reaching Gen. Meade's tent after the first day's battle, and laid these important papers before him. Not waiting for thanks, he returned to his men, and harassed the enemy at every point, destroying their wagon trains, and attacking their rear-guard. On their retreat he led the famous charge into Hagerstown, when of five officers in the charge two were killed, he was wounded, and one of the remaining two was saved by the ball striking his scabbard. He was brought to Washington, and his leg amputated, and, owing to the severe inflammation which had set in, five operations were required before the wound would heal, and his life was despaired of. For his gallantry in this campaign he was made colonel, and as soon as he was able to move he was anxious to return to active service. In concert with Gen. Kilpatrick he planned the raid toward Richmond, fired with the hope of being able to release the Union prisoners then suffering so terribly at Libby Prison and Belle Island. Accepting with delight the most dangerous part of the duty, he was led into the midst of the enemy by his treacherous guide, and brutally murdered when endeavoring to fight his way out. His body was stripped and treated with indignity, and the rebels published, with abundant comments, papers which they asserted were found upon his person, giving instructions to his men to burn Richmond, and even photographed these papers, and sent copies to England. His friends asserted that they were base forgeries.

March 11.—Col. GEZA MIHOLOTZI died at Chattanooga from the effects of a wound received at Buzzard Roost. He was born in Pesth, Hungary, received a military education, and took part in the Hungarian revolution of 1848–'9; came to this country in 1850, settled in Chicago, and commenced the study of medicine under Dr. Valenta of that city. At the outbreak of the rebellion he raised a company for the three months' service, and was elected captain. In November, 1861, he was elected lieutenant-colonel of the 24th Illinois volunteer (infantry), and on the resignation of Col. Hecker, became colonel of the regiment. He served in several important battles, and as a regimental commander stood very high in the estimation of his military superiors.

March 15.—KENNEDY STEWART, M. D., surgeon in the United States navy, died in Philadelphia, aged 31 years. He was born at Easton, Pa.; graduated at Jefferson College in 1854, and the following spring was appointed to the navy. Not being assigned immediately to duty, he joined a merchant vessel, but hearing of the ravages of yellow fever at Norfolk and Portsmouth, he volunteered for service there, and was soon prostrated by the disease. On his recovery he joined the Preble, and participated in the battle between the rebel navy and the blockading squadron at the mouth of the Mississippi. At the capture of New Orleans he was on the Hartford, and was especially commended in the official report of that battle. In the summer of 1863 he was again ordered to the Gulf on board the Ticonderoga, and was with her until she returned to the Philadelphia navy yard for repairs.

March 23.—Col. HENRY VAN RENSELLAER, Inspector-General of the United States army, died in Cincinnati, aged about 53 years. He was a son of the late Stephen Van Rensellaer, graduated from the academy at West Point in 1831, but soon after resigned his connection with the army, married a daughter of the Hon. John A. King, of Jamaica, L. I., and went to take possession of a patrimonial landed estate in St. Lawrence County. In 1841 he was elected a member of the House of Representatives from his district, and served through the three sessions of the 27th Congress. For some years past he had resided in Cincinnati, but upon the breaking out of the rebellion offered his services to his country, and was made by Gen. Scott chief of staff, with the rank of brigadier-general. Upon the retirement of Gen. Scott, the subject of this notice was made inspector-general in the regular army, with the rank of colonel, and continued in the faithful discharge of the duties of his post until a few days prior to his death.

April 4.—Lieut.-Col. GEORGE H. RINGGOLD, an officer of the United States army, died at San Francisco, California, aged 50 years. He was a native of Hagerstown, Maryland, graduated at West Point military academy, July, 1833, as brevet second lieutenant in the 6th infantry, but resigned in 1837. During the Mexican war he was reappointed to the army as major and paymaster, and in 1862 was promoted to deputy paymaster-general, with the rank of lieutenant-colonel. He was truly loyal to his country, and although of Southern birth, firmly withstood all influences exerted to draw him from her allegiance. As a scholar he was endowed with rare attainments, was possessed of a decided poetic talent, an accomplished draughtsman, and amateur painter. He was the author of a book of poems, entitled "Fountain Rock, Amy Weir, and other Metrical Pastimes," published in 1863, and dedicated "To my Children."

April 8.—Maj.-Gen. ALFRED MOUTON, an officer of the Confederate army, killed at Mansfield, Arkansas. He was the son of the former Governor of Louisiana, who was also once Senator in the Congress of the United States. He was wounded in the battle of Shiloh, and was in all of Gen. Thomas Green's conflicts. He was regarded as one of the ablest and bravest officers in the Trans-Mississippi Department. At the time of his death he was commanding a division in Gen. Dick Taylor's army.

April 14.—Maj.-Gen. THOMAS GREEN, an officer of cavalry in the Confederate army, killed at Blains' Landing, on Red River, in an attack on the Federal gunboats and transports. Gen. Green was born in Virginia, and was the son of Chief-Justice Green, of Tennessee, who was also president of the Lebanon (Tenn.) law school. He went to Texas when he was only eighteen years of age. Gov. Sam. Houston, an excellent judge of human nature, discovered, at first sight, that Green and Ben. McCulloch, who were both about eighteen years of age, possessed extraordinary minds and abilities, and at the battle of San Jacinto placed them in command of all the artillery of the army. Gen. Green, Ben. McCulloch, and Jack Hays organized, commanded, and raised to the highest perfection, the Texas Rangers. Thomas Green commanded a company of Texas Rangers in Col. Jack Hays's regiment during the war with Mexico. After peace was declared he became clerk of the Supreme Court. At the breaking out of the war he entered the Confederate army, and commanded the 5th, the choicest regiment of cavalry from Texas. He was commander-in-chief at the battle of Valverde during the latter part of the fight, Gen. Sibley being too ill to remain in command. He also commanded the forlorn hope of five hundred Texans in the attack on Galveston and the capture of the Harriet Lane. After this feat he was ordered to report to Gen. Dick Taylor, and was put in command of the old Sibley brigade. He was in the battle of Bisland, where Gen. Taylor, in his report, called him the "Ney" and the "Shield and Buckler of his army." At Vermilion Bayou, where he had a fight with the Federal gunboats, he was seen to go to the river edge to get a drink of water. As he held the bucket to his lips two bullets passed through it, but Gen. Green neither took it from his mouth nor spilled a drop. A staff officer being sent to him to know how long he could hold his position, as there were hundreds of baggage wagons to get away, he answered: "Tell Gen. Taylor not to ask me how long I can hold the position, but to send me word how long he desires it held." About this time he was put in command of all the cavalry in Taylor's army and in the district in which that army operated. He was repulsed at Donaldsonville. At the battle of Bayou La Fourche he defeated Gens. Grover and Weitzel, and captured over five million dollars' worth of supplies. He defeated Gen. Washburne at Bayou Fordache in November, 1863. At Bayou Borbeaux he fought successfully two entire corps, and was made major-general for his achievements. He was then ordered to Texas and put in command of all the cavalry of the Trans-Mississippi Department. Gen. Green was a remarkable man, and was regarded in his department, and by all who knew him, as one of the few men who, during the whole war, had manifested real military genius.

April 17.—Rev. WM. H. GILDER, chaplain of the 40th New York regiment, died of smallpox at Culpepper, Va., aged 52 years. He was educated in the Wesleyan University, at Middletown, Conn., joined the Philadelphia Conference in 1833, and after preaching for several years in New Jersey, returned on account of failing health to Philadelphia, where he edited the "Christian Repository." He was for seventeen years engaged in the work of education: first as Principal of the Female Institute at Bordentown, N. J., and afterwards as President of Flushing Female College, L. I. In 1859 he resumed preaching, and in 1862 accepted a chaplaincy in the army, following his charge to every battle, until prostrated by disease terminating in his death.

April 18.—Lieut.-Com. CHARLES W. FLUSSER, of the United States navy, born in Maryland about 1832, killed near Plymouth, North Carolina, in a naval engagement, April 18th, 1864. Commander Flusser belonged to one of the oldest and best families in Maryland, but during his childhood his parents removed to Kentucky, from which State he was appointed a midshipman in the navy, July 19, 1847. His first cruise was made in the Cumberland. In 1849 he was sent to the Raritan, 40 guns, where he remained until the latter part of 1850. In 1851 he was ordered to the Saratoga, sloop-of-war, and in her made a cruise which lasted two years. In 1853 he was at the Naval Academy at Annapolis, preparatory to passing as passed midshipman. His warrant to that grade bore date of June 10, 1853.

At the close of the examination, after a brief recreation, he was ordered to the frigate Savannah, where he remained during the entire cruise, which ended on the 26th of November, 1856. During the cruise he was promoted to a lieutenancy, his commission bearing date September 16, 1855. In 1857 he was granted a leave of absence. Toward the close of the year, however, he was ordered to the Naval Academy as an assistant professor. He remained in that position until ordered to the brig Dolphin, in 1859. He made a cruise in her, returning late in 1860. He then was granted a leave of absence, in which position he was when the war broke out. He applied for active duty at once, when it was seen that war must ensue, and the Navy Department assigned him to the command of the purchased gunboat Commodore Perry, and with this vessel he took part in the naval attack by Commodore Goldsborough which preceded the capture of Roanoke Island on the 7th of February, 1862, by Gen. Burnside.

On the 3d of October, 1862, he took part in the shelling of Franklin, Virginia. More recently he has been in command of the gunboat Commodore Perry, in the North Atlantic Blockading Squadron, being stationed in North Carolina waters. At the time of his death he was in command of the Miami, in Albemarle Sound.

He was a skilful and intelligent sailor, a thorough and gallant officer, and a genial, accomplished, and high-toned gentleman. In habits he furnished an example of temperance and moderation.

He had been urgently besought by his Maryland friends, many of whom were secessionists, as well as by Commander Collins, and other Southern officers, to join the South, and was offered a high command; but he refused firmly and indignantly, and threw his whole soul into the cause of the Union.

April 24.—FRANKLIN HULSE CLACK died from wounds received during the battles of Mayfield and Pleasant Hill, Louisiana. He was a son of Commander Clack, U. S. N., was born in Florida, 1828, graduated at Mount St. Mary's College in 1845, and took the degree of Bachelor of Laws at Yale College, 1847. In 1851 he was appointed Secretary of Legation to Brazil, and after his return and settlement in New Orleans, was appointed U. S. District Attorney for Louisiana. On retiring from this position he continued the practice of law with great success.

April 25.—Rev. JAMES H. SCHNEIDER died at Key West, of yellow fever, aged 25 years. He was a son of Rev. Dr. Benjamin Schneider, missionary of the A. B. C. F. M. at Aintab, Syria, and was born at Broosa, Turkey, graduated at Yale College in 1860, and spent the three years following in teaching in the State Normal School, Bridgewater, Mass. It was his desire to enter into the service of his country, and being drafted, he at once reported in person for duty, was appointed lieutenant in the 2d regiment of U. S. colored troops, and subsequently chosen chaplain of the regiment, being ordained at Bridgewater, Oct. 27th, 1863. In entering the military service he declined an appointment as tutor in Yale College, and postponed his preparations for the work of a foreign missionary, upon which he had determined.

May 1.—Commodore WILLIAM DAVID PORTER, an officer of the United States navy, born in New Orleans, La., 1810, died of disease of the heart in New York city, May 1st, 1864. He was a son of Commodore David Porter, and elder brother of Adm. David D. Porter. He entered the service from Massachusetts, Jan. 1st, 1823, and was connected successively with the Franklin, Brandywine, Natchez, Experiment, United States, and Mississippi; and in 1843 was ordered to the home squadron. In 1849 he commanded the storeship Erie, and in 1851 was made commander of the Waterwitch. He projected and was the founder of the present light-house system, served through the Mexican war with distinction, and in 1855 was placed on a retired list by a secret Navy Board; four years later he was restored to his rank as commander by President Buchanan; was ordered to the United States sloop St. Mary's, and did important service on the Pacific coast. On the outbreak of the war he was ordered home, and though he had property in Virginia, and several of his family were in the rebel service, he proved faithful to the Government, and, laying aside all personal considerations, tendered to it his aid, and was assigned to the superintendence of the building of the iron-clad Essex, at St. Louis, which he named after his father's ship. In the attack on Fort Henry he commanded the Essex, and during the engagement was severely scalded by the steam issuing from the boiler, the thick plates of which had been penetrated by a ball. He also commanded the Essex at the attack on Fort Donelson, and fought his way in the same boat past all the batteries from Cairo to New Orleans. He caused the destruction of the ram Arkansas, above Baton Rouge, in Aug., 1862, and during the following month bombarded Natchez, attacked the Vicksburg batteries and Port Hudson. On the 16th of July, 1862, he was promoted from captain to commodore, after which he did but little active service, owing to an enfeebled state of health, which, as already stated, eventually resulted in heart disease. Commodore Porter had two sons in the Confederate service.

May 5.—Col. ALFORD B. CHAPMAN was killed at the battle of the Wilderness, aged about 27 years. He was a native of New York city, and had been for eight years previous to the war connected with the 7th militia regiment, N. G. At the commencement of the rebellion he raised a company, which was attached to the 57th regiment of New York volunteers, and, after several promotions, rose to the command of the regiment.

May 5.—Brig.-Gen. ALEXANDER HAYS, an officer of U. S. volunteers, was killed in the battle of the Wilderness, aged 40 years. He was a native of Pittsburg, Pa., graduated at West Point in 1844, was appointed brevet second lieutenant of the 4th United States infantry, and in June, 1846, was fully commissioned a second lieutenant of the 8th infantry. He was engaged in the Mexican war, and distinguished himself in several important battles. In 1848 he resigned his connection with the army and became engaged as an iron manufacturer in Venango Co., Pa., from which occupation he was called at the outbreak of the rebellion. Entering the volunteer service as colonel of the 63d Pennsylvania volunteers, he was appointed captain of the 16th regular infantry, dating from May 14, 1861, which regiment was attached to the Army of the Potomac, and during the peninsular campaign formed a portion of the 1st brigade 3d army corps. He participated with gallantry in the battles of Seven Pines and Fair Oaks, and was nominated for a brevet of major of the United States army, distinguished himself during the seven days' battles, and was nominated brevet lieutenant-colonel, took part in the Maryland campaign, and was made brigadier-general of volunteers Sept. 29, 1862. He was wounded at the battle of Chancellorsville, and at the battle of Gettysburg was in command of the 3d division of his corps, and of the whole corps for a time, after the wounding of Gen. Hancock. He led the 3d division through the battles of Auburn, Bristoe Station, and Mine Run. Upon the reorganization of the Army of the Potomac for the next campaign, Gen. Hays was placed in command of the 2d brigade, Birney's 3d division 2d corps, under Gen. Hancock.

May 5.—Brig.-Gen. A. G. JENKINS, a Confederate officer, killed in the battle of the Wilderness. He was a native of Virginia, had received his military education at the Virginia Military Institute at Lexington, and had distinguished himself in several actions in Western Virginia. He was in the advance of Lee's army before the battle of Gettysburg, and took part in that battle.

May 5.—Major-Gen. SAMUEL JONES, a Confederate officer, killed in the battle of the Wilderness. He was a graduate of West Point, appointed from Virginia, of which State he was a native, and at the opening of the war was captain in the 1st regiment of artillery, U. S. A. He resigned his commission in the army April 27, 1861, and was immediately appointed colonel, and soon after brigadier-general by the Confederate War Department, and early in 1860 was promoted to the command of a division, with the rank of major-general. He had been in command of the rebel forces in West Virginia until the spring of 1864, when he brought his contingent to reënforce Lee's army on the Rapidan.

May 5.—Gen. JOHN LLOYD died in New York city, aged 67 years. He was a native of Dutchess County, N, Y., was for many years a prominent dry goods merchant in New York, and latterly the head of the firm John Lloyd & Sons, real estate brokers. In his younger years he held the rank of major-general in the State militia.

May 6.—THOMAS COLDEN COOPER, a captain in the 67th regiment N. Y. State volunteers, was killed while leading a charge in the battle of the Wilderness. He was a native of Ohio, a man of fine education and culture, and previous to 1862 had been the principal of the New York Institution for the Blind for several years. Resigning his position there, he accepted an appointment as captain in the 67th New York volunteers.

May 6.—Brig.-Gen. JAMES SAMUEL WADSWORTH, of U. S. volunteers, born in Geneseo, Livingston County, N. Y., October 30th, 1807, killed in the battle of the Wilderness, May 6th, 1864. He was the son of James Wadsworth, an extensive landowner and philanthropist of Geneseo, under whose care he received a thorough rudimentary education, after which he was sent to Harvard College, and thence to Yale College, where he completed his studies. Soon after graduating he entered upon the study of law in Albany, finishing his course in the office of the great statesman and lawyer, Daniel Webster, and was admitted to the bar in 1833, but did not practise his profession, as the charge of his immense estate required his whole attention. A few years later Mr. Wadsworth turned his attention somewhat to local politics. A Federalist by education and a Democrat by conviction, he early took part in the "Free Soil" movement that divided the Democracy of the State, and gave a zealous support to the Presidential candidate of that party in 1848, and to the Republican candidates of 1856 and 1860. Like his father, he manifested a deep and active interest in the cause of education. He founded a public library at Geneseo; was a liberal subscriber to the endowment of Geneseo College; aided in the establishment of the school district library system, and in every way did what lay in his power to relieve suffering and diffuse the benefits of our free institutions. Acting as a commissioner to the Peace Convention held in Washington, in 1861, under an appointment from the Legislature of New York, when it became evident that war was inevitable, he was prompt to offer his services to the Government. When communication with the capital was cut off, he chartered two ships upon his own responsibility, loaded them with provisions, and proceeded with them to Annapolis, where they arrived most opportunely to supply the pressing necessities of the Government. Commencing his military career as a volunteer aide to Gen. McDowell at the first battle of Bull Run, upon the recommendation of that general, Wadsworth was appointed brigadier-general of volunteers August, 1861, and in March, 1862, became Military Governor of the District of Columbia. In the election of Governor of New York, in November, 1862, Gen. Wadsworth was the Republican candidate, but was defeated by Mr. Seymour. In the following December he was assigned to the command of a division in the Army of the Potomac. At Fredericksburg and Chancellorsville he displayed great military skill, and at Gettysburg his division saved the first day. Upon the reorganization of the Army of the Potomac for the campaign of 1864, Gen. Wadsworth was assigned to the command of the fourth division of the fifth corps, at the head of which he bravely met his death.

May 9.—JOHN SEDGWICK, a major-general of volunteers in the United States Army, born in Connecticut about 1815, killed near Spottsylvania Court House, Va., May 9th, 1864. He was graduated at West Point in 1837, 24th in a class of fifty members, among whom were Gens. Benham, Hooker, Arnold, French, and others of the Federal service, and the rebel Generals Bragg, Early, and Pemberton. He entered the Mexican war as first lieutenant of artillery, and was successively brevetted captain and major for gallant conduct at Contreras, Churubusco, and Chapultepec. He also distinguished himself at the head of his command in the attack on the San Cosmo gate of the city of Mexico. At the outbreak of the rebellion he held the position of lieutenant-colonel of the 2d United States cavalry. On April 25th, 1861, he was promoted to the colonelcy of the 4th cavalry, and on August 31st was commissioned a brigadier-general of volunteers, and placed in command of a brigade of the Army of the Potomac, which in the subsequent organization of the army was assigned to the 2d corps under Gen. Sumner, Gen. Sedgwick assuming command of the 3d division of the corps. In this capacity he took part in the siege of Yorktown, and the subsequent pursuit of the enemy up the peninsula, and greatly distinguished himself at the battle of Fair Oaks, where the timely arrival of Sumner's troops saved the day. In all the seven days' fighting, and particularly at Savage Station and Glendale, he bore an honorable part, and at the battle of Antietam he exhibited the most conspicuous gallantry, exposing his person with a recklessness which greatly imperilled his life. On this occasion he was twice wounded, but refused for two hours to be taken from the field. On December 23d he was nominated by the President a major-general of volunteers, having previously been made a brevet brigadier general of the regular army, and in the succeeding February he assumed command of the 6th army corps. At the head of these troops he carried Marye's Heights in the rear of Fredericksburg during the Chancellorsville campaign in May, 1863, and after the retreat of Gen. Hooker across the Rappahannock, succeeded only by very hard fighting in withdrawing his command in the face of a superior force, against which he had contended for a whole day, to the left bank of the river. He commanded the left wing of the Army of the Potomac during the advance from the Rappahannock into Maryland in June, and also at the succeeding battle of Gettysburg, where he arrived on the second day of the fighting, after one of the most extraordinary forced marches on record, and where his steady courage inspired confidence among his tried troops. During the passage of the Rapidan on November 7th, 1863, he succeeded, by a well-executed manœuvre, in capturing a whole rebel division with a number of guns and colors, for which he was thanked by Gen. Meade in a general order. In command of his corps he took part in the spring campaign of the Wilderness, under Gen. Grant, and on the 5th and 6th of May had position on the Federal right wing, where the hardest fighting of those sanguinary engagements took place. Three days later, while directing the placing of some pieces of artillery in position in the intrenchments in front of Spottsylvania Court House, he was struck in the head by a bullet from a sharpshooter, and instantly killed. Gen. Sedgwick was one of the oldest, ablest, and bravest soldiers of the Army of the Potomac, inspiring both officers and men with the fullest confidence in his military capacity. His simplicity and honest manliness of character endeared him, notwithstanding he was a strict disciplinarian, to all with whom he came in contact, and his corps was in consequence one of the best in discipline and *morale* in the army. He several times held temporary command of the Army of the Potomac during the absence of Gen. Meade, but on more than one occasion declined the supreme command.

May 10.—Count HERMANN HACKE was killed in the battle of Spottsylvania. He was a native of Prussia, and connected with the Prussian army, but obtained a furlough, and coming to this country procured a commission as first lieutenant in the 7th New York volunteers. Upon the expiration of his term of service he procured a commission as first lieutenant in the 52d New York volunteers, Hancock's corps, and fell while leading a charge at the head of his company. He was a brave and gallant soldier.

May 10.—JOHN M. JONES, a brigadier-general in the Confederate service, killed near Spottsylvania, Va., aged about 43 years. He was a native of Virginia, and graduated at West Point in the class of 1841. After serving as second lieutenant in the 5th and 7th regiments of infantry, he was appointed in 1845 assistant instructor in infantry tactics at West Point, which position he filled for several years. In 1847 he was promoted to a first lieutenancy and in 1853 to a captaincy in the 7th infantry, and accompanied his command in the Utah expedition. He resigned his commission in May, 1861, was appointed colonel of a regiment of Virginia volunteers, and in 1863 was promoted to the command of a brigade in Ransom's division of Longstreet's corps. In the latter capacity he took part in the rebel attack on Knoxville in the fall of 1863, and in the operations in the Wilderness and in the neighborhood of Spottsylvania immediately preceding his death.

May 10.—Col. CLAY PATE, an officer of the Confederate army, killed in a cavalry fight with Sheridan, near Yellow Tavern, on the road to Richmond. Col. Pate gained some distinction as a partisan leader during the troubles in Kansas. When the war commenced he raised a battalion of cavalry in Richmond, Va., which was soon after its organization merged into the 5th Virginia regiment, and he became lieutenant-colonel of the regiment. Col. Rosser being promoted, he became colonel, and was killed a few days after he received his promotion. He was a native of Virginia, and was 33 years of age at his death.

May 10.—Lieut.-Col. —— RANDOLPH, an officer of cavalry in Stuart's corps, killed at Yellow Tavern in a fight with Sheridan.

May 10.—THOMAS G. STEVENSON, a brigadier-general of U. S. volunteers, killed near Spottsylvania, Va., aged 28 years. He was the son of Hon. J. Thomas Stevenson, of Boston, and early manifested a predilection for military life, having risen from the ranks to be major of the 4th battalion of Massachusetts infantry, which position he held at the commencement of the war. He had an unsurpassed reputation as a drill-master, and his command, which was brought to a high degree of discipline, was the school of many young officers since distinguished in the national service. In the fall of 1864 he recruited the 24th regiment of Massachusetts volunteers, which originally formed part of Foster's brigade in Burnside's expedition to North Carolina, and as its colonel participated in the capture of Roanoke Island and Newbern, February and March, 1862, and in various minor operations immediately succeeding those events. After holding for some months the outpost defences of Newbern, he conducted several expeditions within the rebel lines, and on Sept. 6th successfully defended Washington, N. C., against an attack by a superior force. He had charge of a brigade in the movements on Goldsboro and Kingston, and in December, 1862, was appointed a brigadier-general; and when Gen. Foster, in Feb., 1863, organized the expedition for operations against Charleston, received command of a brigade in Gen. Naglee's division. Shortly after his arrival at Port Royal he was temporarily put under arrest by order of Gen. Hunter, for a casual expression of his disbelief in the policy of arming slaves, but was subsequently honorably acquitted of blame. His appointment as brigadier-general was confirmed in March, 1863, and during the succeeding summer he saw much active service in the neighborhood of Charleston, assisting in the reduction of Morris Island and the assault on Fort Wagner, where he commanded the reserves. He returned to the north in the fall to recruit his health, and subsequently was appointed by his old commander, Gen. Burnside, who had a high appreciation of his capacity, to command the 1st division of the 9th corps. He was killed at the head of his troops. As a disciplinarian he was greatly esteemed, and he showed also an energy and maturity of judgment which gave promise of a brilliant career as a soldier.

May 11.—JULIUS DANIELS, a brigadier-general in the rebel army from Virginia, killed in the battle of Spottsylvania.

May 11.—Brig.-Gen. J. B. GORDON, an officer of the rebel army, wounded in the skirmish between Sheridan's cavalry and the rebels near Richmond, died at Richmond, Va. He was a native of North Carolina, and entered the rebel service as major of the 1st regiment of North Carolina cavalry, and was advanced first to the command of his regiment and then to that of a brigade in Gen. Fitz Hugh Lee's division of rebel cavalry.

May 11.—Brig.-Gen —— Perrin, an officer of the rebel army from South Carolina, killed in the battle of Spottsylvania.

May 11.—JAMES CLAY RICE, a brigadier-general of United States volunteers, born at Worthington, Mass., Dec. 27, 1829, died from wounds received at the battle near Spottsylvania Court House, May 11th, 1864. His early life was spent in a struggle to obtain an education, and in 1854 he graduated at Yale College, with high honors. Shortly afterwards he went to Natchez, Miss., where he engaged in teaching, and edited the literary department of one of the local newspapers. He also pursued the study of law, and was admitted to the bar in that State. Returning to the North he continued his legal studies in New York, and in 1856 entered upon the practise of his profession, in which he was rapidly rising to distinction. At the outbreak of the war he entered the ranks as a private soldier in the New York Garibaldi Guard, and subsequently, by distinguished merit, attained the colonelcy of the 44th New York volunteers, or Ellsworth's regiment. He led this regiment through the battles of Yorktown, Hanover Court House, Gaines's Mill, Malvern Hill, and Manassas, and was only absent from Antietam because on a sick bed with typhoid fever. He was also at Fredericksburg under Gen. Burnside, at Chancellorsville under Gen. Hooker, where he was temporarily in command of a brigade, and at Gettysburg, where he greatly distinguished himself by his skill and gallantry. It was his brigade which, on the second day of the battle, held the extreme left of the line successfully under the repeated and desperate onsets of the enemy. For three hours Col. Rice fought incessantly, receiving no orders from any superior officer, arranging and disposing of his men with such skill and judgment that at the close of the day's fight he had extended his line so as to cover Round-Top Mountain, thus securing it against any flanking movement. For this and other gallant deeds he was warmly commended by Gen. Meade and earnestly recommended by him and Gens. Hooker and Butterfield, for the appointment of brigadier-general of volunteers. The President acquiesced in the wishes of these officers, the Senate confirming the appointment, and dating his commission from Aug. 17, 1863. In this position he took part in the operations of Mine Run, passed through the terrible battles of the Wilderness, and met his death at the head of his command, on the banks of the Po. He died shortly after amputation had been performed, his last words being, "Turn me over that I may die with my face to the enemy." Gen. Rice was a man of deep religious principle, a brave and skilful officer, and thoroughly devoted to his country.

May 11.—L. A. STAFFORD, a brigadier-general in the rebel army, died at Richmond of wounds received at the battle of the Wilderness. He was a native of Virginia.

May 12.—Baron VON STEUBEN was killed at Spottsylvania. He was a Prussian officer, came to this country and joined the 52d New York volunteers, and proved himself a gallant and faithful officer.

May 12.—Maj.-Gen. JAMES E. B. STUART, an officer in the Confederate service, born in Patrick County, Va., about 1832, died in Richmond, June 11th, 1864. He was graduated at West Point in 1854, commissioned a cavalry officer, and after reaching the rank of first lieutenant, resigned May 14, 1861. He had previously seen considerable active service in the Indian country, and was known as a fearless rider and brave soldier. He immediately entered the Confederate army, commanded the cavalry at the battle of Bull Run, was promoted a brigadier-general in September, 1861, and in the ensuing winter organized the cavalry forces of the enemy in Virginia. He first brought himself conspicuously into notice by his celebrated raid in the rear of Gen. McClellan's communications near Richmond, on June 13th and 14th, 1862, which was the immediate precursor and cause of the change of base soon after commenced by the Federal army, and also of the seven days' fighting. During the advance of Gen. Lee toward Maryland in the succeeding August he made a night attack, in the midst of a terrific thunder-storm, on Gen. Pope's headquarters, capturing many private papers and plans of campaign; and in October, a few weeks after the battle of Antietam, at the head of two thousand cavalry and four pieces of flying artillery, he crossed the Potomac between Williamsport and Hancock, and passing through Mercersburg and Chambersburg, rode completely round the Union lines, and recrossed the river into Virginia with the loss of but one man. This raid, though of little advantage beyond the capture of several hundred horses and the destruction of a few thousand dollars' worth of stores, was the most daring movement of the kind hitherto attempted during the war, and greatly enhanced Gen. Stuart's reputation as a cavalry officer. It was his last great success. At Beverly ford, in Virginia, and in Maryland and Pennsylvania, during the Gettysburg campaign, he was invariably worsted in his encounters with the Federal cavalry. He, however, rendered efficient service in protecting the retreat of Lee's army after the battle of Gettysburg. He was mortally wounded in an encounter with Gen. Sheridan's cavalry at Yellow Tavern, near Richmond, while endeavoring to cover that city against Federal raids, and died a day or afterwards.

May. 13.—CHARLES BROOKS BROWN died in a field hospital from wounds received the previous day in the battle at Spottsylvania Court House, Va., aged 29 years. He was a native of Cambridge, Mass., graduated at Harvard College in 1856, studied law, and was admitted to the Suffolk bar in 1858. He soon after removed to Springfield, Illinois, and entered upon the duties of his profession. In 1860 he returned to his native State and opened an office in Charlestown, and subsequently in Boston. Upon the outbreak of the war he enlisted as a private in a Cambridge company attached to the 3d regiment of Massachusetts volunteers, and afterwards in the 19th regiment Massachusetts volunteers, serving in the peninsular and other campaigns of the Army of the Potomac. Was wounded at the battle of Fair Oaks and again at Fredericksburg, and upon the expiration of his term of three years, reënlisted for another three years' service.

May 14.—Lieut.-Col. —— LLOYD was killed at Resaca. He was an officer of the 119th regiment of New York volunteers, and fell while leading a desperate charge upon the enemy.

May 16.—Brig.-Gen. WATT RANSOM, an officer of the Confederate army, killed at Burmuda Hundred.

May 22.—Col. —— FELLOWS, an officer of the Federal army, died at Key West. He was colonel of the 2d U. S. (colored) regiment. He was a native of New Hampshire, and graduated at the West Point military academy. Shortly after graduating, having been instrumental in raising the second colored regiment in the District of Columbia, he was appointed to the command of it as colonel, and soon manifested an ability which made his regiment one of the best colored regiments in the service. At the time of his death he was very little over 23 years of age. His personal appearance was very prepossessing, and his "suaviter in modo" won the esteem of both officers and men.

May 22.—Rev. SAMUEL FISKE, a captain of U. S. volunteers, died at Fredericksburg of wounds received at the battle of the Wilderness. He graduated at Amherst College in the class of 1848. He was the author of a series of Letters from Europe written some years since for the Springfield "Republican," signed by "Dunn Browne," and also a well-known college text-book, a translation of Eschenberg's "Manual of Greek and Roman Antiquities." When the war broke out he was pastor of a church in Madison, Conn., but from a patriotic love of his country entered the army, and after fighting bravely in several battles, was taken prisoner by the enemy, and detained for some time in Richmond. He was promoted to a captaincy previous to the battle of the Wilderness, in which he lost his life.

May 24.—Col. GEORGE B. HALL, an officer of U. S. volunteers, died at his residence in Brooklyn, from disease contracted in the service, aged 38 years. He was a son of ex-Mayor Hall of Brooklyn, entered upon his military career at the early age of 19 years as a private in the 165th regiment N. Y. S. M., rapidly rising through the several grades of promotion, until the commencement of the Mexican war, when he was offered and accepted the position of first lieutenant in the 1st regiment of New York volunteers. He distinguished himself at Vera Cruz, Cerro Gordo, Contreras, and particularly at Churubusco, and for his gallantry on several occasions was remembered by Gen. Scott, who, in 1853, recommended him to the Secretary of War as worthy of promotion to the rank of brigadier-general. In April, 1850, he was commissioned as major of the 13th regiment N. Y. S. M., and the following September was made lieutenant-colonel in the same regiment. While occupying a position in the City Inspector's Department, New York, the rebellion broke out, when he at once resigned and entered into the work of raising troops for the defence of the Union, was made colonel of the "Jackson Light Infantry," or 71st regiment N. Y. S. V., and was with it in every battle and skirmish in which it was engaged, from the Stafford Court House raid of 1862, to the battle of Fredericksburg.

May 26.—Commander EDWARD A. BARNET, an officer of the U. S. navy, died in New York city after a long and painful illness. On the 24th of June, 1837, he entered the United States naval service as midshipman from Pennsylvania, his native State. The first ship to which he was ordered was the sloop-of-war Ontario, on the West India station, carrying eighteen guns. He was, in 1840, transferred to the schooner Grampus, and in the following year to the sloop-of-war Levant. In 1842 he was attached to the schooner Wave, and during the following year he was attached to the naval school at Philadelphia. On the 29th of June, 1843, he was warranted a passed midshipman, and ordered to the steamer Princeton, where he remained until he was ordered to the East Indies as the naval storekeeper at Macao. In 1847 he was ordered to the sloop-of-war Dale, on which vessel he remained until January, 1848, when he was ordered to the receiving-ship Boston. He received his commission on the 4th of August, 1850, as lieutenant, and was ordered to duty on the Coast Survey, where he remained until October, 1851. His next orders placed him in the steam frigate San Jacinto, on the Mediterranean station. In 1853 he was ordered to the receiving-ship at Philadelphia. He was next in the sloop-of-war Jamestown, and in 1856 was ordered to the steam frigate Wabash, flag-ship of the Home Squadron, under Commodore Paulding. The flag-ship returned in 1858, and he was put upon waiting orders. In 1860 he joined the sloop-of-war John Adams, on which he remained until the commencement of civil war in the United States. The resignation of officers from the South in the United States naval service afforded him rapid promotion, and on the 16th of July, 1862, he was made commander, and ordered to the New York navy yard on ordnance duty. He was detached from the post in October of sixty-two, and was shortly after seized with the illness that resulted in his death. He was in the naval service about twenty-seven years—fourteen of which he was at sea; five years and nine months on shore and other duties; and seven years unoccupied. He was a valuable officer, and highly esteemed.

June 2.—Brig.-Gen. Geo. E. Doles, an officer of the Confederate army, killed near Cold Harbor. Gen. Doles was from Georgia, and commanded a division in Ewell's corps. He entered the service as captain of Co. A in the 4th Georgia regiment of infantry, and was soon after promoted to a colonelcy, and on Nov. 1st, 1862, was made brigadier-general. At the time the fatal shot struck him he was dismounted. His horse had been restive and troublesome, and he had sent him to the rear. The ball passed through his heart and out under his right arm, shattering the arm frightfully. His body was sent to Richmond, and thence to his native State. His merit and high qualifications procured him the recommendation upon which he was created brigadier-general. At the time of his death he was 34 years of age.

June 2.—Col. Jeremiah C. Drake, an officer of U. S. volunteers, was killed in the action at Cold Harbor, Va., aged about 38 years. He was a native of Herkimer County, N. Y., but removed to Wisconsin, and was for some time engaged in mercantile pursuits. Subsequently he removed to Rochester, N. Y., and commenced the preparatory studies for a collegiate course. He then entered the Madison University, passed through the academic course, studied theology, and upon the outbreak of the rebellion was occupying the pulpit of the Baptist Church at Westfield. Having a strong desire to enter into the service of his country, he volunteered in the 49th regiment New York, was elected captain, and shared in the disasters of the peninsular campaign. Upon the organization of the 112th New York he accepted the colonelcy of the regiment, and served with it during the siege of Suffolk, and afterwards in the siege of Charleston, under Gen. Gillmore. Col. Drake was appointed to command the 2d brigade, 3d division, 10th army corps, in the attack upon Richmond *via* James River, under Gen. Butler.

June 2.—Col. Lawrence M. Keitt, an officer in the Confederate army, died at Richmond of wounds received in the battle of the preceding day. Col. Keitt was a native of South Carolina; born Oct. 4, 1824; graduated at the College of South Carolina in 1843; studied law, and was admitted to the bar in 1845. In 1848 he was elected to the State Legislature, and in 1853 to Congress, to which he was thrice reëlected — his last term expiring in March, 1861. At the time of Preston Brooks' assault on Senator Sumner, in 1856, he was with Brooks, and exerted himself to prevent any of those present from interfering to rescue Sumner, and by word and act justified the ruffianly attack. In the winter of 1861 he left his seat in Congress, before the close of the session, to aid in carrying out the secession measures of South Carolina. He raised a regiment, and was in several of the earlier battles of the war as colonel. In 1863 he was an acting brigadier-general, but was at the time of his death in command of the 20th South Carolina regiment, esteemed one of the finest regiments in the rebel service till the campaign of 1864.

June 2.—Col. John McConihe, an officer of U. S. volunteers, was killed in the battle of Cold Harbor, Va., aged 29 years. He was a native of Troy, N. Y.; studied law with his father, Hon. Isaac McConihe, of that city, and at the law school at Albany; graduated at Union College in 1853, and was subsequently chosen one of the Board of Education. In 1856 he went to Omaha, and was appointed Private Secretary to the Governor, and was afterwards Adjutant-General of the Territory. On the breaking out of the rebellion he raised a company, was made its captain, participated in the Missouri campaign of 1861 and part of 1862, and was severely wounded in the battle of Shiloh. Returning to Troy, he was appointed lieutenant-colonel of the 169th New York, and did provost duty at Washington, participating also in the siege of Morris Island. Subsequently he served in Florida, in the peninsula under Gen. Butler, and finally under Gen. Grant.

June 3.—Col. Franklin A. Haskell, an officer of U. S. volunteers, was killed in the battle of Cold Harbor, Va., aged 35 years. He was a graduate of Dartmouth College in the class of 1854.

June 3.—Col. LEWIS O. MORRIS, an acting brigadier-general of volunteers, and captain in the 1st artillery in the regular army, was killed in the battle of Cold Harbor. He was a native of New York. His father was an officer in the regular army, killed at the siege of Monterey, and young Morris, though not educated at West Point, received a commission as second lieutenant on the 8th of March, 1847, and took part in the siege of Vera Cruz and the subsequent advance upon Mexico. From that time to the commencement of the present war he has been almost constantly in the field, and in April, 1861, had attained the rank of captain in the 1st artillery. In the winter of 1860–'61 he was stationed in Texas, and his company was the only one not surrendered to the rebels. He was immediately called to active service, and in the winter of 1862 was designated to direct the operations against Fort Macon, N. C., which he captured and afterwards commanded. In the summer of 1862, his health being impaired, he obtained a short leave of absence and returned to his home in Albany, N. Y., when he was soon after appointed colonel of the 113th N. Y. volunteer infantry, with whom he started for Washington, and reached that city when it was menaced by Lee's troops. He converted the regiment into one of heavy artillery in a very short time, and contributed materially to the defence of the city. The regiment was stationed at Fort Reno, but this inactive life did not suit the fiery spirit of Col. Morris, and he plead earnestly and repeatedly to be sent into the field. At the beginning of the campaign of 1864 his wish was gratified, and during all the battles from Spottsylvania till his death he commanded a brigade. He was greatly beloved and admired as an officer, and while a strict disciplinarian his urbanity and kindness of heart made him the idol of his men.

June 3.—Col. ORLANDO H. MORRIS, an officer of U. S. volunteers, was killed in the action at Cold Harbor, Va., aged 29 years. He was a son of Gen. Wm. L. Morris, and, when the war broke out, was a promising young lawyer in New York city. He assisted in the organization of the 66th regiment of New York volunteers, was commissioned its major in November, 1861, and served in that capacity through the peninsular campaign; was subsequently promoted to the colonelcy, and led his regiment at Chancellorsville, acting during part of the engagement as brigadier-general. During the recent severe battles under Lieut.-Gen. Grant, the 66th was very conspicuous, being in the advance of the attack which resulted in the capture of Gen. Johnson and his division.

June 3.—Col. PETER A. PORTER, an officer of U. S. volunteers, was killed at the head of his division at the battle on the Chickahominy, aged 36 years. He was a son of P. B. Porter, a major-general in the U. S. army, and now an extensive landholder in Niagara County, N. Y.; was a member of the Assembly in 1862, and, by his talents and integrity won a position of influence in the Legislature. When the President called for troops to repair the losses of the peninsular campaign, he raised a regiment, and taking command of it went to the war. He was stationed for some time on garrison duty at Baltimore, and while there was offered the nomination for Secretary of State on the Union ticket, but, true to his patriotism, declined the honor. He subsequently joined the Army of the Potomac, and was killed at the close of the first month of active service, while leading on a division which he was temporarily commanding.

June 3.—COL. EDWIN SCHALL, an officer of U. S. volunteers, was killed in battle at Cold Harbor, Va., aged 29 years. He was a son of Gen. Wm. Schall, and a native of Montgomery County, Pa.; was favorably known in civil life, and was twice elected Burgess of Norristown, Pa. He was educated for the law, and was also a graduate of Captain Partridge's Military Academy. At the commencement of the war he was editor of the "National Defender," published in Norristown, but abandoned his occupation, and in company of four brothers, joined the 4th regiment of Pennsylvania volunteers and was commissioned its major. He served with his regiment throughout its whole career, and participated in all its engagements, passing rapidly through the usual promotions. Subsequently he was transferred to the command of the 51st, and during several months of service in East Tennessee was in command of a brigade.

June 3.—Col. FREDERICK F. WEAD, an officer of U. S. volunteers, was killed in the battle of Cold Harbor, Va., aged 29 years. He was born in Malone, Franklin County, N. Y., graduated at Union College in 1856, studied law at Poughkeepsie, was admitted to the bar, and practised his profession in his native town until the breaking out of the rebellion in the spring of 1861, when he entered the U. S. service as First Lieutenant, in the 16th regiment of New York volunteers. In October, 1861, he was appointed one of Gen. Slocum's staff, with which he served through the peninsular campaign, and in 1862 was appointed lieutenant-colonel of the 98th regiment New York volunteers, and afterwards colonel. Subsequently his regiment was assigned to Gen. Heckman's brigade, forming a portion of the 18th army corps, under Gen. Smith. During the battle of South Richmond Gen. Heckman was taken prisoner, and the command of the brigade temporarily devolved upon Col. Wead. At the time of his death the 18th army corps was serving under Gen. Grant.

June 5.—Col. ARTHUR H. DUTTON, an officer of U. S. volunteers, was killed in the engagement near Bermuda Hundred. He was a native of Wallingford, Conn., graduated at West Point in the Engineer Corps in 1861, and at the time of his death held the rank of captain of engineers in the regular army. While on duty in North Carolina with his regiment, the 21st Connecticut volunteers, he served as chief of staff for Maj.-Gen. Peck, and subsequently held a similar position upon the staff of Maj.-Gen. W. F. Smith. After the battle of Drury's Bluff, in which he greatly distinguished himself, he was placed in command of the 3d brigade, which position he had held but a few days when he lost his life.

June 5.—Brig.-Gen. W. E. Jones, an officer in the Confederate army, killed at Piedmont, in West Virginia. Gen. Jones was an officer of cavalry, and reputed to be one of the best in the Confederate service.

June 7.—Gordon Winslow, M. D., D. D., a clergyman of the Episcopal Church, fell overboard from a transport and was drowned in the Potomac, aged 60 years. He was a native of Williston, Vt., graduated at Yale College, studied for the ministry, and became rector of a church in Troy, N. Y., and subsequently in Annapolis, Md. Afterwards he was for many years rector of St. Paul's, Staten Island, and chaplain of the Quarantine. At the commencement of the war he was appointed chaplain of the Duryee Zouaves, and accompanied the regiment in all its hard-fought battles. He also served with the Sanitary Commission, and upon the return of his regiment in 1863, was appointed Inspector of the Army of the Potomac for that Commission, and was returning from his labors in its behalf at Belle Plain, having in charge his wounded son, Col. Cleveland Winslow, when he met his untimely death. He had been a frequent contributor to the press, and was a man of high and liberal intellectual culture, and of a most genial and amiable disposition. His wife had been for many months engaged in ministering to the sick and wounded soldiers in Washington, and his two sons were officers of the Union Army. Rev. Hubbard Winslow, D. D., of New York, and Rev. Myron Winslow, D. D., missionary in Ceylon, were both brothers of the deceased.

June 11.—Col. Edward Pye, an officer of U. S. volunteers, died from wounds received at the battle of Cold Harbor, Va., aged 40 years. He was educated for the law, and soon after entering upon the practise of his profession rose to a high rank at the bar. When quite young he was appointed District Attorney for Rockland County, N. Y., and soon after County Judge and Surrogate. At the breaking out of the rebellion he at once made preparations for winding up his practice, accepted the command of a company in the 95th regiment New York State volunteers, then organizing under the name of the "Warren Rifles," and in the fall of 1861 entered into active service with the Army of the Potomac. Being promoted to a lieutenant-colonelcy, he led his regiment through the carnage of Antietam, followed the enemy across the Potomac to the Rappahannock, and shared in the battles of Fredersicksburg, Chancellorsville, and Gettysburg, receiving after the latter his commission as colonel. In the battles of the Wilderness and Spottsylvania he was often in the front ranks of the army, and in the battle of Cold Harbor, while leading an assault upon the breastworks of the enemy, received a rifle ball in the shoulder, and at the same moment was wounded by a shell, surviving these injuries but a few days.

June 14.—Leonidas Polk, a bishop of the Protestant Episcopal Church, and General in the Confederate service, born in Raleigh, N. C., in 1806, died near Marietta, Ga., June 14, 1864. He was graduated at West Point in 1827, and appointed a brevet second lieutenant of artillery; but having, through the influence of Bishop McIlvaine, then chaplain at West Point, been induced to study for the ministry, he resigned his commission in December, 1827, and three years later was ordained a deacon in the Protestant Episcopal Church. From 1831 to 1838 he officiated at various places in the South, and in the latter year he was consecrated Missionary Bishop of Arkansas and the Indian territory south of 36° 30′, with provisional charge of the dioceses of Alabama, Mississippi, and Louisiana, and the missions in the republic of Texas. In 1841 he resigned these charges, with the exception of the diocese of Louisiana, of which he remained bishop until the close of his life. The outbreak of the rebellion found him a strong sympathizer with the doctrine of secession. His education and associations were strongly Southern, and his property, which was very considerable in lands and slaves, helped to identify him with the project for establishing a Southern Confederacy. His familiarity with the Valley of the Mississippi prompted him to urge upon Jefferson Davis and the rebel authorities the importance of fortifying and holding its strategical points, and amidst the excitement of the time the influence of his old military training became uppermost in his mind. Under these circumstances the offer of a major-generalship by Davis was regarded not unfavorably, in spite of the sacred calling which he had followed during thirty years. He applied to Bishop Meade, of Virginia, for advice, who declined to give it, but referred him to Gen. Robert E. Lee, as one to whose judgment he might safely defer. Lee unhesitatingly advised him to accept the commision, and he at once did so. His first command extended from the mouth of the Arkansas River, on both sides of the Mississippi, to Paducah, on the Ohio, his headquarters being at Memphis; and his first general order, issued July 13th, declared that the invasion of the South by the Federal armies "comes bringing with it a contempt for constitutional liberty, and the withering influence of the infidelity of New England and Germany combined." It was under his general direction that the extensive works at Forts Donelson and Henry, Columbus, Ky., Island No. Ten, Memphis, and other points were constructed, and the skill with which they were selected for defence testifies to his thorough military training. He held this command until the spring of 1862, when, in consequence of the signal Federal successes in that part of the country, he was relieved and ordered to join Johnston's and Beauregard's army at Corinth. As commander of a corps he participated in the battle of Shiloh, and in the subsequent operations ending with the evacuation of Corinth. He afterwards held a command in the army of Gen. Bragg, took part in the battle of Perryville during the invasion of Kentucky in the autumn of 1862, and saw much hard fighting at the stubbornly contested battle of Murfreesboro. Still serving under Bragg, he fell back with him beyond Chattanooga before the steady advance of Gen. Rosecrans in the campaign of 1863, and had a share in the victory of Chickamauga. For disobedience of orders in this battle, whereby, as was asserted by Gen. Bragg in his official report, the Federal army was alone saved from annihilation, he was relieved from his command, and ordered to Atlanta. He was soon after appointed to command the camp of rebel prisoners paroled at Vicksburg and Port Hudson, and in the winter and spring of 1864 had temporary charge of the Department of the Mississippi. By skilful dispositions of his troops he prevented the junction of the Federal cavalry column under Gen. Smith with Gen. Sherman's army in southern Mississippi, and caused the campaign undertaken by the latter in February to result in no permanent advantage. His prestige being thus restored, he received orders to unite his force with that of Johnston at Resaca, and took command of one of the three corps of Gen. Johnston's army, which in the spring of 1864 attempted to withstand the advance of Gen. Sherman toward Atlanta. After participating in the chief engagements previous to the middle of June, he was killed by a cannon shot while reconnoitring on Pine Mountain, a few miles north of Marietta. About a year and a half before this he had been commissioned a lieutenant-general in the Rebel army. Gen. Polk never resigned his diocese, and, it was said, intended at the close of the war to resume his Episcopal functions. He had labored zealously in behalf of religious interests previous to the rebellion, and was described by his friends as of manly bearing, frank and cordial manners, and impressible and easily kindled temperament. He was buried in the yard of the Episcopal church in Augusta.

June 15.—Col. SIMON H. MIX, an officer of U. S. volunteers, was killed in a charge upon the rebel intrenchments at Petersburg. He was a native of Fulton County, N. Y., and learned the printing trade of his father, Peter Mix, for many years editor of the "Schoharie Patriot." Both father and son were among the earliest and firmest Republicans, and the latter was, in 1860, Republican candidate for Congress, but was beaten by a few votes by Hon. Chauncey Vibbard, Superintendent of the Central Railroad. At the commencement of the war the subject of our sketch dedicated himself to the service of his country. He was appointed major and finally colonel of the 3d cavalry regiment New York, which he was instrumental in raising, and died at its head.

June 15.—Col. —— RIELY, an officer of the Confederate army, killed at New Hope Church, in Georgia. Col. Riely was colonel of the 1st Missouri regiment of infantry (Gen. John S. Bowen's old regiment), and was sleeping in the trenches when a spherical-case shot from the Federal guns burst near the parapet, and an accidental ball mortally wounded him.

June 16.—Hon. ANDREW EWING, an officer in the Confederate service, died in Atlanta, Ga. He was a lawyer of eminence, and a politician of considerable importance, having for many years participated in the political controversies which mark the history of Tennessee. He represented the Nashville district, Tenn., in Congress during one term, and in February, 1861, was elected to represent Davidson County in the proposed State Convention, which was voted down by the people, being at that time a sincere Union man. Unfortunately he was subsequently drawn away from his allegiance to the Union, and took an active part against the Government. After the fall of Fort Donelson he left his home and became an exile, holding until he died some position in the rebel army.

June 20.—JOHN K. HARDENBROOK, Acting Assistant Surgeon U. S. A., died at Rush Barracks, Washington, D. C., in the 62d year of his age, of typhoid fever, contracted while in the discharge of his duties at L'Ouverture Hospital, Alexandria, Va. Dr. Hardenbrook was one of the oldest physicians of New York city, and for several years Secretary of the New York County Medical Society; also one of the first trustees of the Rutgers Female Institute, and was a member of one of the oldest Masonic Lodges in New York. He promptly offered his services in response to a call for more surgeons for the army, and was assigned to duty at Alexandria, where he labored faithfully in the discharge of his duties until attacked with the disease which terminated in death.

June 22.—WILLIAM WHEELER, an officer of United States volunteers, was killed near Marietta, Ga., aged 28 years. He was a native of New York city, graduated at Yale College in the class of 1855, and studied law until 1857, when he sailed for Europe. After passing the summer in travel, he continued the study of law at the University of Berlin, and subsequently visited Italy and Greece. In July, 1858, he returned to New Haven, and the following spring entered the Law School at Cambridge, Mass., where he received the degree of LL.D. in 1860. Soon after he opened an office in New York, and entered upon the practice of his profession, but upon the outbreak of the rebellion his patriotic impulses led him to accompany the 7th regiment of N. Y. S. N. G. to the defence of the Capital. After this temporary service he raised a company and was made lieutenant, and subsequently captain of the 13th Independent battery of N. Y. In the Shenandoah valley, and at Gettysburg, with the Army of the Potomac, and subsequently in the battle of Lookout Mountain, he bore an honorable part. He was afterwards appointed chief of artillery on the staff of Gen. Geary, 2d division, 20th army corps, and met his death while bravely holding an exposed position with his battery in the face of the enemy.

June 27.—Brig.-Gen. CHARLES G. HARKER, an officer of United States volunteers, was killed in the battle at Kenesaw, Ga. He graduated at West Point about 1857, and was appointed second lieutenant of the 9th United States infantry, and afterwards captain in the 15th regulars. At the breaking out of the war he was appointed to the colonelcy of the 65th Ohio, known as Sherman's brigade; participated in the battles of Stone River, Chickamauga, and Mission Ridge, in the latter being the first to pass the enemy's works, and took an active part in the East Tennessee campaign with the 4th army corps. He was commissioned brigadier-general for his gallantry at Chickamauga. He fell while bravely leading on his brigade, and within a few yards of the enemy's works.

June 27.—Col. OSCAR F. HARMON, an officer of United States volunteers, was killed at the battle of Kenesaw Mountain, Ga. He was a native of Wheatland, Monroe County, N. Y., studied law in the school of Prof. John W. Fowler, at Ballston Spa, N. Y., and in the office of Smith and Griffin, at Rochester, N. Y. In 1853 he removed to Danville, Ill., where he practised his profession with distinguished success until the summer of 1862, when, from a strong desire to serve his country in the army, he accepted the proffered command of the 125th regiment of Illinois volunteers, which position he held with increasing popularity until his death. In the terrible assault upon the rebel position at Kenesaw Mountain, his regiment was assigned a difficult point. The brigade commander, Gen. McCook, being dangerously wounded, the command devolved upon Col. Harmon, and while nobly cheering on his men he was struck by a ball in his breast, which immediately proved fatal.

June 30.—Col. WILLIAM WILSON, an officer of United States volunteers, killed by a fall from his horse at his farm in Westchester County, N. Y. He was the leader of the famous Wilson Zouaves, and served with his regiment in many positions of great danger and exposure, being stationed for several months at Santa Rosa Island, previous to the capture of Fort Pickens. His camp was once surprised while there, and made a gallant fight.

July 4.—Brig.-Gen. JAMES E. BLYTHE, an officer of the Indiana militia, died at Evansville, Ind., aged 45 years. He was a native of Lexington, Ky., graduated at Hanover College, Ind., in 1838, studied law in New Jersey, and was admitted to the bar in that State in 1840, and the following year removed to Evansville, where he entered upon the practise of his profession. His talents and learning enabled him in a short time to take his position among the leading members of the profession in the Supreme and inferior Courts of the State, and in the Courts of the United States. He was a prominent and influential member of the Constitutional Convention of Indiana in 1850–'51, and also of the House of Representatives of that State in 1859. During the years 1862 and 1863 he was brigadier-general of the active militia or Legion of Indiana, and through his exertions and influence the Legion of the border counties in the southwestern part of the State was organized and rendered sufficiently formidable for the prevention of raids.

July 6.—Brig.-Gen. SAMUEL A. RICE, an officer of United States volunteers from Iowa, died at Oskaloosa, Iowa, of wounds received in the battle of Jenkins' Ferry, in Arkansas. He was a native of New York, but had removed to Iowa, and engaged in civil pursuits, and soon after the opening of the war entered the service as colonel of the 33d Iowa volunteers. He soon distinguished himself for military skill and courage, and was put in command of a brigade, and on the 4th of July, 1863, at the battle of Helena, Ark., his command was conspicuous for its bravery and good conduct. For his meritorious conduct in this and subsequent battles, he was appointed brigadier-general, his commission dating August 4, 1863. He took an honorable part in every battle of the arduous campaigns of that and the succeeding year in Arkansas, up to the time of receiving his fatal wound.

July 7.—Col. CLEVELAND WINSLOW, an officer of U. S. volunteers, died in the hospital at Alexandria, Va., from wounds received at the battles near Mechanicsville, Va., aged 28 years. He was a native of Medford, Mass., and the eldest son of the Rev. Gordon Winslow, D. D. When the war commenced he was engaged in mercantile pursuits in New York city, but having some military knowledge from his connection with the militia, he raised a company of men and departed with the famous Duryea Zouaves for the seat of war, continuing with them for two years in all their engagements. Immediately upon the return of his regiment he raised another, and with it was engaged in all the important battles of the Army of the Potomac since that period.

July 11.—Col. P. STEARNS DAVIS, 39th regiment Massachusetts volunteers, an officer in the volunteer service, killed near Petersburg, Va.

July 17.—Col. DAN. McCOOK, an officer of United States volunteers, died in Steubenville, Ohio, of wounds received in the battle of Kenesaw Mountain, making the fourth member of the family who have fallen in the service of their country, and leaving two brothers only, who were at that time commanding Ohio regiments in the field.

July 20.—Brig.-Gen. ARMISTEAD L. LONG,

an officer of the Confederate army from Georgia, killed at the battle of Peach Tree Creek, Ga.

July 20.—Brig.-Gen. JOHN J. PETTUS, an officer of the Confederate army from Mississippi, formerly Governor of that State, killed at the battle of Peach Tree Creek, Ga.

July 20.—Brig.-Gen. GEORGE M. STEVENS, an officer of the Confederate army from Maryland, killed at the battle of Peach Tree Creek, Ga.

July 21.—Brig.-Gen. LUCIEN GREATHOUSE, of U. S. volunteers, killed in a skirmish near Atlanta, Ga., aged 21 years. He was a native of Carlinsville, Ill., graduated at Bloomington, studied law, and was admitted to the bar. At the commencement of the war he volunteered as a private, and after passing through every intermediate grade was commissioned colonel of the 48th Illinois, his regiment bearing a conspicuous part in the achievements of the Army of the Tennessee. He was made a brigadier-general only a day or two previous to his death.

July 22.—JAMES BIRDSEYE MCPHERSON, a major-general of United States volunteers, born in Sandusky County, Ohio, November 14th, 1828, killed near Atlanta, Ga., July 22d, 1864. He entered West Point from Ohio in 1849, and at the end of that year ranked second in his class. The two years following he stood first, graduating at the head of his class June 30th, 1853, and was at once appointed brevet second lieutenant of engineers and assistant instructor of practical engineering at the Academy, a compliment never before awarded to so young an officer. He was next appointed assistant engineer on the defences of New York harbor, and on the improvement of the navigation of the Hudson River, having previously been made full second lieutenant of engineers. In January, 1857, he was placed in charge of the construction of Fort Delaware, and subsequently of the erection of fortifications on Alcatras Island, San Francisco Bay, California, and was also connected with the survey of the Pacific coast. In December, 1858, he was promoted to first lieutenant, and in 1861 was ordered from the Pacific coast to take charge of the fortifications of Boston harbor. The same year he was made captain, and upon the appointment of Maj.-Gen. Halleck to the command of the Department of the West in November, he was chosen aide-de-camp to that general, and at the same time was promoted as lieutenant-colonel. In the expeditions against Forts Henry and Donelson he was chief engineer of the Army of the Tennessee, and subsequently was at Shiloh, and as colonel on Gen. Halleck's staff, held the chief engineering charge of the approaches to Corinth, which ended in its evacuation. On the 15th of May, 1862, he was made brigadier-general of volunteers, and appointed general superintendent of military railroads in the district of West Tennessee the following June. In September, 1862, Gen. McPherson held a position on the staff of Gen. Grant; and for his gallantry at Corinth was promoted to be major-general, dating from October 8th, rising to that position in the short space of nine years, and by merit alone. From that time till the close of the siege of Vicksburg, during which he commanded the centre of our army, his career was one course of triumph. Gen. Grant wrote of him: "He is one of the ablest engineers and most skilful generals. I would respectfully, but urgently, recommend his promotion to the position of brigadier-general in the regular army."

Upon this recommendation Gen. McPherson was immediately confirmed a brigadier-general in the regular army, dating from August 1st, 1863, and soon after conducted a column into Mississippi and repulsed the enemy at Canton. Subsequently Gen. McPherson's department was extended so as to embrace all the region bordering the Mississippi River, from Helena, Arkansas, to the mouth of the Red River, with headquarters at Vicksburg. In the memorable expedition to Meridian he was second in command to Gen. Sherman, and during the first Atlanta campaign his command was the Department of the Tennessee, including the entire 15th, 16th, and 17th corps. He distinguished himself at Resaca, Dallas, Allatoona, Kulp House, and Kenesaw. In the battles before Atlanta Gen. McPherson's grand division held the left of the line. In superintending the advance of his skirmish line he had ridden from left to right, and was returning when he was suddenly confronted by a party of the enemy in ambush, and received a shot in the breast causing almost instant death. Gen. McPherson was a man of indefatigable energy, tireless industry, and a bravery which almost amounted to recklessness. He always reconnoitred in person.

July 22.—Maj.-Gen. WILLIAM WALKER, an officer of the Confederate army, killed in the battle of the twenty-second of July, in front of Atlanta, Ga. Gen. Walker was from Georgia, and commanded principally Georgia troops. He was a graduate of West Point, and greatly distinguished himself in the war with Mexico, where he was severely and dangerously wounded a number of times. He was notorious particularly for three things: his reckless courage, the number of wounds he had received, and the habitual expression of "By G—, sir."

July 26.—Col. JAMES A. MULLIGAN, an officer of U. S. volunteers, born at Utica, N. Y., June 25, 1830; died July 26, 1864, from wounds received at the battle of Winchester, Va. He was of Irish descent, his parents having emigrated to this country a few years previous to his birth. In the autumn of 1836 his parents removed to Chicago, and after a few years' residence placed him in the University of St. Mary's of the Lake. He graduated in 1850, being the first graduate from the University, and in the same year commenced the study of the law. In 1851 he accompanied John Lloyd Stephens, the American author, on his expedition to the Isthmus of Panama. After remaining at Panama about a year, the deceased returned to Chicago, and in 1855 he was admitted to the bar, and immediately commenced practise in that city. During the winter of 1857 he was appointed to a clerkship in the office of the Interior at Washington. When the war broke out he obtained the requisite authority, and in a few weeks raised a fine regiment of Irishmen, the 23d Illinois infantry, afterwards known as "Mulligan's Brigade," was made colonel, and in July, 1861, left for the front. During the first month or two of service the regiment was actively engaged in Virginia and Missouri until September, when it was ordered to the defence of Lexington. For nine days Col. Mulligan held the town against heavy odds, praying for reënforcements; but reënforcements came not. Lexington fell into the hands of the rebels, and Col. Mulligan and his command were also captured. He was exchanged on the 25th of Nov., and returned to Chicago as the hero of Lexington. On his return he reorganized his regiment. In January, 1862, he was ordered with his regiment to proceed to New Creek, Va., and hold that post. From that date till the time of his reënlistment (in June, 1864), Col. Mulligan participated in several hard-fought battles.

In the battle of Winchester during a charge on the rebel lines he was mortally wounded; a squad of his men seeing him fall, attempted to carry him off the field, but seeing that the colors of his brigade were endangered, he turned to his bearers and exclaimed, "Lay me down and save the flag," repeating the order upon their hesitation. They obeyed him, and ere their return, he was borne off by the enemy, and soon after died in their hands. Col. Mulligan was at one time offered a commission of brigadier-general, but declined, preferring to remain with his old regiment. He was a peculiarly gifted writer, strictly temperate in all his habits, and an earnest, devoted Catholic.

July 27.—SILAS MILLER, colonel of the 36th regiment Illinois volunteers, died at Nashville, Tenn., from wounds received at the battle of Kenesaw Mountain, Ga., aged 25 years. He was born in Tompkins County, N. Y., but when very young removed to Aurora, Illinois, learned the printer's trade, pursuing his education in the mean time, and when the war broke out was diligently engaged in the study of law. In April, 1861, he enlisted in the volunteer service as a private, passing rapidly through the different grades of promotion, and doing important service in the early campaign of Missouri and Arkansas, and in Mississippi and East Tennessee; was taken prisoner by the enemy at the battle of Murfreesboro, and after his exchange was commissioned colonel of his regiment, participating with it in the fearful battles of Chickamauga and Mission Ridge, where he commanded a brigade. From thence he went with his command into East Tennessee, enduring with them one of the severest campaigns of the war. In January, 1864, he reënlisted, accompanied Gen. Sherman on his eventful campaign, and participated in all the engagements between Chattanooga and Kenesaw Mountain, where he received the fatal wound.

July 29.—ABRAHAM SIDDON COX, M. D., Surgeon-in-Chief of the 1st division, 20th corps, Army of the Cumberland, died in the officers' hospital, Lookout Mountain, Tenn., aged 64 years. Dr. Cox was a native of New York, and had been for many years one of the most eminent medical practitioners of New York city. At the opening of the war, with a rare patriotism, he relinquished his large practice and took an appointment as a surgeon in the army. His abilities were recognized, and he was promoted to be surgeon-in-chief of division; but the hardships and exposures of the Chattanooga and Atlanta campaigns had broke down his health and terminated his useful life.

Aug. 5.—Capt. TUNIS AUGUSTUS CRAVEN, U. S. navy, killed by the explosion of the Tecumseh by a torpedo, in Mobile Bay. He was a native of New Hampshire, and entered the navy as a midshipman, June 2, 1829, serving on different vessels until 1837, when, upon his own request, he was placed on the Coast Survey. In 1841 he was promoted to a lieutenancy, and was attached to the sloop-of-war Falmouth till 1843, when he was transferred to the receiving-ship North Carolina. Subsequently he was connected with the Pacific squadron, and again from 1850 to 1859 upon the Coast Survey, from which he was appointed to the command of the steamer Mohawk, of the home squadron, stationed off the coast of Cuba to intercept slavers. When the war broke out Capt. Craven was placed in command of the Crusader, and had an important share in preserving for the Union the fortress of Key West. In April, 1861, he was appointed commander of the new sloop Tuscarora, and was sent after rebel cruisers. At his own request he was placed in charge of the monitor Tecumseh, early in the present year, and joined the James River flotilla. Recently he was ordered to reënforce Admiral Farragut, and bravely met his fate during the assault on the defences of Mobile.

Aug. 5.—JOHN FARON, Chief Engineer U. S. navy, was lost by the sinking of the monitor Tecumseh, in Mobile Bay. He entered the service in 1840, being appointed from the State of New Jersey, of which he was a native. Upon the completion of the U. S. steam frigate Powhatan, he was attached to her as one of her officers, and served three years and a half in her, making a cruise in the Gulf, thence to China and Japan. He served as senior assistant on the Niagara during the laying of the Atlantic cable, and was in charge of the engine department of the San Jacinto when the rebel commissioners, Slidell and Mason, were captured, since which time he has been superintendent of the monitors built at the iron ship-building yard at Jersey City. Previous to the Tecumseh being commissioned, he was ordered to the Onondaga; but preferring to go to sea in a vessel of his own construction, he succeeded in getting detached and ordered to the Tecumseh, and had left a sick bed to be present at the engagement during which he lost his life.

Aug. 6.—Brig.-Gen. GRIFFIN A. STEDMAN, an officer of U. S. volunteers, killed near Petersburg. He was a native of Hartford, Ct., a graduate of Trinity College, and entered the service in 1861 as major of the 11th regiment Connecticut volunteers. On the resignation of the lieutenant-colonel he was advanced to that position, and in the battle of Antietam, where Col. Kingsbury, the commander of the regiment, was killed, he was wounded, but not fatally. Recovering, he commanded the regiment at Fredericksburg, and Chancellorsville, and Gettysburg. At the commencement of the campaign of 1864 he was put in command of a brigade, and fought through all the terrible battles of the campaign in such a way as to win the frequent commendation of his superior officers. After the explosion of the mine at Petersburg his brigade was much exposed to the assaults of the enemy, and in one of the frequent skirmishes which occurred he lost his life. His commission as brigadier-general did not arrive till after his death, though he had been acting in that capacity for several months.

Aug. 16.—Brig.-Gen. VICTOR J. B. GIRARDEY, an officer in the Confederate army, killed in the action near Richmond, Va. He was quite young, and had previously to the campaign of 1864 been provost marshal of Richmond.

Aug. 16.—Col. ABEL D. STREIGHT, U. S. volunteers, killed during an engagement at Dalton, Ga. He was a resident of Indianapolis when the war broke out, and when the call was made for three years' men, raised a regiment, of which he was made colonel, and took part in the campaign which placed Kentucky and Tennessee in the possession of the Union armies. In 1863 he led a cavalry force on a raid through Alabama, which, though well conducted, was but partially successful, and resulted in his being taken prisoner and confined in Libby prison. After a long period of privation and suffering, he made his escape and returned to his home in Indiana, but soon after rejoined his regiment in the field.

Aug. 16.—Brig.-Gen. DANIEL PHINEAS WOODBURY, U. S. volunteers, died at Key West, Fla., of yellow fever. He graduated at West Point in 1836, and was first commissioned in the 3d artillery, but in 1838 was made second lieutenant in the corps of engineers. In 1847 he was engaged in the survey of the Oregon route. In 1853 he was promoted to a captaincy, and previous to 1860 was engaged in the work of constructing Fort Jefferson, in the Tortugas. In May, 1861, he was appointed to superintend the construction of a part of the defences of Washington under Gen. Barnard, and the following year was made lieutenant-colonel of volunteers, and subsequently brigadier-general of volunteers, to date from March 19, 1862, and assigned to the command of the Engineer Brigade of the Army of the Potomac. During the whole of the peninsular campaign Gen. Woodbury's command was engaged in constructing bridges, railroads, earthworks, &c., and greatly assisted the army in its movements. After the appointment of Gen. Hooker to the army, Gen. Woodbury accepted an assignment to the Department of the Gulf, as commander of the district of Key West and Tortugas, arriving at his new post April, 1863. In June, 1863, he was promoted to be lieutenant-colonel of engineers in the United States army. He was the author of a work entitled "Sustaining Walls," 1854; also, "Theory of the Arch," 1858.

Aug. 21.—Commander JAMES M. DUNCAN, an officer of the U. S. navy, died in Brooklyn, N. Y., of disease of the heart, aged 44 years. He was a native of Madisonville, Ohio, entered the navy in 1837, and subsequently passed through a course of study at the naval school, Philadelphia. He took an active part in the Mexican war, and especially distinguished himself in the contest which preceded the annexation of California. The commencement of the present war found him serving as a lieutenant on the U. S. steamer Crusader, then just completing a two years' cruise after slavers on the coast of Cuba. In 1862 he was appointed commander, and assigned to the storeship Release, and subsequently to the monitor Weehawken, of which he had command when she went down in Charleston harbor, but was providentially on board the flag-ship at the time of the disaster. He was in command of the Norwich, and assisted in the bombardment of Fort Pulaski, and of Jacksonville, Fla. During his service on the Gulf blockade, Commander Duncan contracted the disease which terminated his life.

Aug. 21.—Col. A. F. DUSHANE, an officer of U. S. volunteers, killed before Petersburg, Va. He was at the time of his death acting as brigadier-general of the Maryland brigade.

Aug. 23.—Col. CARTER VAN VLECK, an officer of U. S. volunteers, died in a field hospital, near Atlanta, Ga., from a wound received in action. He was an eminent lawyer of Illinois, joined the 78th Illinois volunteers at the commencement of the war, and had recently been made colonel.

Aug. 29.—Dr. W. H. RULISON, Medical Director of the cavalry corps of the Army of the Shenandoah, killed near Winchester by a rebel sharpshooter. He was from Ohio, and had attained a high reputation for ability in his profession.

Sept. 1.—Brig.-Gen. ROBERT H. ANDERSON, an officer in the Confederate army from Georgia, a graduate of West Point, killed in the battle of Jonesboro, Ga.

Sept. 1.—Brig.-Gen. ALFRED CUMMING, an officer in the Confederate army from Georgia, a graduate of West Point, killed at the battle of Jonesboro, Ga.

Sept. 1.—Col. WILLIAM T. C. GROWER, an

officer of U. S. volunteers, killed at Jonesboro, Ga., while leading his troops against the rebel intrenchments, aged 25 years. He was a resident of New York previous to the war, and for several years was connected with the Metropolitan Bank. He entered the volunteer service in May, 1861, as captain in the 17th regiment N. Y. S. M., was promoted to the position of major, and passed through the various campaigns of the Army of the Potomac until the second battle of Bull Run, when he was wounded and disabled for nearly a year. He afterwards reorganized the regiment, serving with it in the Army of the Tennessee, and subsequently in the Army of the Cumberland.

Sept. 1.—Brig.-Gen. —— PATTEN, an officer in the Confederate army, killed at the battle of Jonesboro, Ga.

Sept. 2.—Col. DAVID IRELAND, an officer of U. S. volunteers, died at Atlanta, Ga., from a wound received at Resaca some months previous. He was a native of Scotland, entered the service in the 137th New York, and distinguished himself at the battles of Lookout Mountain, Mission Ridge, and Resaca, where he was severely wounded. At the time of his death he commanded the 3d brigade, 2d division, 20th corps.

Sept. 3.—Col. FREEMAN MCGILVERY, an officer of U. S. volunteers from Maine, died while under the influence of chloroform, undergoing an operation made necessary by a wound received at the battle of Chaffin's Farm. He was a skilful artillerist, and at the battle of Gettysburg, on the 2d of July, as chief of artillery in Sedgwick's corps, turned the fortunes of the day by the skill and promptness with which he planted his batteries, and the tenacity with which he held them to their work. At the time of his death he was chief of artillery in the 10th corps, Army of the James.

Sept. 3.—Major REID SANDERS, an officer in the Confederate service, a son of the Confederate Agent, George N. Sanders, died at Fort Warren, Boston, aged 27 years. He was sent as bearer of despatches from the Confederate Government to Europe, on a blockade-runner, but was captured and confined in Fort Warren as a prisoner of state.

Sept. 4.—Brig.-Gen. MILO S. HASCALL, an officer of U. S. volunteers from Indiana, who entered the service as colonel of one of the Indiana regiments, but was promoted to a brigadier-generalship in 1862. He handled his brigade with great skill and bravery in the battle of Stone River, where he was wounded, but returned to his command and participated in the battles of Chickamauga and Mission Ridge, and was active as division commander in the early battles of the Atlantic campaign. He was killed in an engagement near Franklin, Tenn.

Sept. 4.—Brig.-Gen. JOHN H. MORGAN, an officer of the Confederate army, killed at Greenville, Tenn. Gen. Morgan was born on the 1st of June, 1826, in the beautiful city of Huntsville, Ala. In 1830 he removed to Kentucky, and settled on the Tates Creek road, two miles from Lexington. At the breaking out of the war with Mexico his martial spirit took fire immediately, and he rushed to arms with the first who volunteered. He served in Humphrey Marshall's regiment of cavalry as first lieutenant, and was in the battle of Buena Vista. At the termination of twelve months from the time of enlistment his term of service expired, and he returned to Lexington, Ky., and organized a company for the war. The State of Kentucky having offered more troops than her quota amounted to, the captains of companies drew lots for acceptance or non-acceptance. Capt. Morgan lost, and his company returned to Lexington, where it was dismissed. In 1848 he married, but his wife died in 1861. He did a large business in bagging, lindsey, and jeans. He had in Lexington manufactories, where all of those articles were made. In September, 1861, he left Lexington with a part of his old State guard company, "The Lexington Rifles," numbering one hundred guns, and though Lexington was then occupied by the United States forces, he arrived safely at Bowling Green, then in possession of the Confederate troops, and there joined the standard of Gen. Buckner. At the battle of Shiloh Gen. Morgan commanded a squadron of cavalry. He soon after commenced his series of raids into Kentucky, in which he destroyed military stores and transportation amounting to many millions of dollars. He captured railroad trains loaded with supplies and soldiers, and burnt the trains and stores, and paroled the soldiers. He tore up railroad tracks, and burnt bridges, and destroyed culverts in the rear of the Federal army, and prevented timely reënforcements and regular and necessary military supplies from reaching the Federal armies. In this way he gave a constant and excessive annoyance. Nothing was safe except where guarded by large bodies of troops. He moved with such celerity that Union men and small bodies of troops in Kentucky knew not when they laid down at night in perfect security, but they would wake up next morning in the hands of the ubiquitous Morgan. On one day he was heard of hundred of miles away; on the next he was confronting them. He carried a telegraph operator with him, who tapped the wires sometimes, and at others took possession of offices at posts captured by Morgan, and so managed the telegraphing as that much of the purport of what was done in the State to intercept him became known to the daring raider. So renowned and dreaded did he make himself, that at length it became necessary to make a garrison of the State of Kentucky. Troops were stationed at all of the towns of any importance, and arrangements made for concentrating them at the shortest notice, upon any given point. As a partisan fighter, Gen. Morgan's talent was of a high order. But for the full development of such talent one must be untrammelled. Gen. Morgan, when placed under the orders of Gen. Bragg, at Tullahoma, Tenn., and by him placed on his right flank, did not gain reputation. Why? Because he was fettered by orders, and besides, that service was suited neither to him nor his men. Gen. Morgan originated the present mode of fighting cavalry, or mounted infantry, as all mounted men might now more properly be called. He also originated the idea of extensive cavalry raids to impair the strength and destroy the resources of an enemy. The mode of fighting alluded to consists in moving by circuitous routes with great rapidity to the distance of hundreds of miles, and thus avoiding the enemy's troops; then falling unexpectedly upon detached posts or bodies of men or army trains. When any fighting is to be done, dismount the men and let them fight with long ranged accurate guns, as infantry. For it is well known that only the best cavalry can cope with a line of infantry armed with the modern improved firearm; and that where such vast armies are in the field as the late war called out, it is impossible to keep them supplied with trained cavalry. It was for these reasons that John Morgan's mode of organizing mounted men, and fighting them on foot, has been so generally adopted in this country. It would have been better for the South if the idea of Morgan's raiding had never been originated, because the vast resources of men and horses at the command of the Federals general enabled them to organize and send through all the unprotected and productive parts of that country immense raiding expeditions, which spread devastation and suffering among countless thousands of women and children, whose natural protectors were in the southern armies, or had fled from the country to avoid military service. In 1863 he undertook a bold and extensive raid through Kentucky, Indiana, and Ohio. But he, and nearly his entire command, were captured, and himself and officers confined in the Ohio Penitentiary. Some time afterwards he escaped, and reached Richmond, Va., where he received an enthusiastic ovation. He subsequently undertook a raid into Tennessee, but being betrayed while stopping at a house, was surrounded during the night by a company of Union cavalry, and killed in his attempt to escape.

Sept. 5.—Col. James C. Clark, an officer of U. S. volunteers; died in Troy, from illness contracted during service in Louisiana, aged 49 years. He served in the peninsular campaign, and distinguished himself by his gallantry at Port Hudson. He was colonel of the 79th colored regiment, and at the time of his death was acting as brigadier-general.

Sept. 14.—Brig.-Gen. Joshua B. Howell, an officer of U. S. volunteers, was accidentally killed near Petersburg, Va., by being thrown from his horse, aged about 65 years. He was a brave officer, and had been wounded in several battles during the war. He was colonel of the 85th regiment of Pennsylvania volunteers, and had recently been made brigadier-general.

Sept. 14.—Major (Acting Colonel) Henry L. Patten, an officer of U. S. volunteers, died of wounds received in battle near James River, aged 28 years. He was a native of Kingston, N. H., graduated at Harvard College in 1858, spent a few years in teaching, and when the war broke out was studying law. He entered the army with the 20th Massachusetts regiment, served in the peninsular campaign, and especially distinguished himself at Fredericksburg, Gettysburg, and the battles of the Wilderness.

Sept. 19.—Brig.-Gen. A. C. Godwin, an officer in the Confederate service, killed at the battle Winchester, Va. He was a native of Portsmouth, Va., was formerly Provost-Marshal of Richmond, and was subsequently promoted colonel of a North Carolina regiment. A short time previous to his death he was made brigadier-general.

Sept. 19.—Maj.-Gen. Robert E. Rhodes, an officer in the Confederate service, killed in the battle at Winchester, Va. He was a native of Lynchburg, Va., graduated at the Virginia Military Institute, in the Class of 1848, and after a few years of professorship at that institution, removed to Alabama. In 1861 he entered the Confederate service as captain of the Mobile Cadets, and upon the organization of the 5th Alabama regiment, was appointed its colonel. Soon after the first battle of Manassas he was promoted to the rank of brigadier-general; was wounded at the battle of Seven Pines, and also at Sharpsburg; was present at Fredericksburg and at Chancellorsville, when he was made major-general; served through the Pennsylvania campaign with Early, in the defence of Lynchburg, and with the army of the valley of Virginia in 1864, throughout its marches and battles, commanding one of the two army corps of which it was composed, until he fell at Winchester.

Sept. 19.—Brig.-Gen. David A. Russell, an officer of U. S. volunteers, killed in battle near Winchester, Va. He graduated at West Point in 1845, served in the Mexican war, and was brevetted "for gallant and meritorious conduct at National Bridge and Cerro Gordo." In 1854 he was promoted to a captaincy in the 4th regiment of infantry in the regular army, and in August, 1862, was made major in the 8th infantry. He entered the volunteer service at the commencement of the present war as lieutenant-colonel of the 7th Massachusetts volunteers, attached to the 6th army corps, served with distinction through the important battles of 1862–'63, having been commissioned a brigadier-general November, 1862, and subsequently was in command of Gen. Howe's division, 6th army corps, and in that command served with distinction at Gettysburg, and in the campaign of Gen. Grant from the Rapidan to the James. In the summer of 1864 he was transferred to the command of a division in the army of the Shenandoah, where he met his death, gallantly fighting at the head of his troops.

Sept. 24.—Commodore THOMAS A. CONOVER, U. S. navy, died at South Amboy, N. J., aged 73 years. He entered the navy in January, 1812, his first cruise being on the Essex, commanded by Captain David Porter, during the war with England. His next service was under Commodore McDonough, on Lake Champlain. Promoted to a lieutenancy shortly after, he served on board the Guerriere in the Mediterranean, and subsequently in other vessels in various portions of the world until his promotion to the position of commander about 1835, in which capacity he commanded the John Adams sloop-of-war some years. In 1848 he was promoted to the rank of captain, and in the years 1857-'58 commanded the squadron on the coast of Africa, the old Constitution being his flag-ship. In July, 1862, on the creation by law of the grade of commodores in the navy, he received a commission as such. He had been in the service fifty-three years.

Sept. 29.—Brig.-Gen. HIRAM BURNHAM, an officer of U. S. volunteers, killed in battle at Chaffin's Farm. He entered the service as colonel of the 6th Maine volunteers, leading them with skill and gallantry through the peninsular campaign, at Antietam, and subsequently. At the second battle of Fredericksburg he distinguished himself for bravery and courage, and again at Gettysburg. In April, 1864, he was made brigadier-general, and during the campaign from the Wilderness to Petersburg, he bore a conspicuous part. A few weeks previous to his death he was assigned to a brigade in Stannard's division 18th corps.

Sept. 29.—Col. N. E. WELCH, an officer of U. S. volunteers, killed in battle near Chaffin's Farm. He was commissioned colonel in 1863, and was placed in command of the 16th Michigan regiment, at the head of which he was gallantly fighting when he met his death. He was regarded as one of the bravest and most skilful officers of the volunteer service.

Oct. 3.—Lieut. JOHN R. MEIGS, an officer of U. S. volunteers, killed by guerrillas near Harrisonburg. He was the only son of Maj.-Gen. Meigs, Quartermaster-General; graduated at West Point in 1863, at the head of his class, and with the highest honors, and was immediately sent to the field, where he highly distinguished himself during the campaigns in Maryland, Harper's Ferry, and the Shenandoah valley. At the time of his death he was engaged in making a military survey, in his capacity of Chief Engineer of the Army of the Shenandoah.

Oct. 5.—Col. JAMES REDFIELD, an officer of U. S. volunteers, was killed at the head of his regiment in the battle of Allatoona Pass, Ga., aged 40 years. He was a native of Clyde, Wayne County, N. Y., graduated at Yale College in 1845, studied law, and was for some time in the office of the Secretary of State (New York). He subsequently removed to Iowa, and was elected State Senator. At the outbreak of the rebellion he assisted in raising the 39th Iowa regiment, which he led through nearly all the hard campaigns of the Western army.

Oct. 6.—Col. J. C. THOMAS AMORY, an officer of U. S. volunteers, died of yellow fever at Newbern, N. C. He graduted at the military academy, West Point, in 1851, and was assigned to the 7th infantry, in which he obtained a first lieutenancy in 1855, and in 1861 a captaincy. In the latter year he was appointed colonel of the 17th Mass. volunteers, with which regiment he took part in Gen. Burnside's North Carolina expedition, participating in the capture of Newbern, where he remained stationed up to the time of his death. During nearly the whole of his service in North Carolina he was in command of a brigade.

Oct. 7.—Brig.-Gen. GREGG, an officer in the Confederate service, killed in battle near Petersburg, Va. He was commanding a Texas brigade at the time of his death.

Oct. 13.—Dr. EMIL OHLENSCHLAGER, late medical inspector on Gen. Sheridan's staff, was murdered by guerrillas near Winchester, aged 29 years.

Oct. 13.—Col. GEORGE D. WELLES, an officer of U. S. volunteers, died of wounds received in the battle near Strasburg. He was made colonel of the 34th regiment Massachusetts volunteers, August, 1862.

Oct. 14.—Col. JOHN P. SANDERSON, an officer of U. S. volunteers, and Provost Marshal General of the Department of Missouri, died at St. Louis. He had filled many important offices of trust during the war, among which was that of chief clerk of the War Department, during Mr. Cameron's term as Secretary. Before resigning that, he was appointed lieutenant-colonel of the 15th U. S. infantry, and soon after was commissioned colonel of the 13th U. S. infantry, with which he passed through the fearful contest of Chickamauga. Some months previous to his death he was appointed to the responsible office of Provost Marshal General at St. Louis.

Oct. 14.—Brig.-Gen. WADKINS, an officer in the Confederate service, killed in the battle of Resaca, Ga.

Oct. 18.—DANIEL BELL BIRNEY, a major-general of volunteers in the service of the United States, and at the time of his death commander of the 10th army corps, born in Huntsville, Ala., in 1825, died in Philadelphia, Oct. 18th, 1864. Gen. Birney was a son of the late Hon. J. G. Birney, an Alabama planter and statesman, who emancipated all of his slaves, and coming first to Cincinnati, and afterwards to Michigan, to advocate the cause of emancipation, was, in 1844, the candidate of the liberty party for the presidency. His son received his academical education in Cincinnati, and also studied law there, but after his admission to the bar was for two or three years engaged in mercantile pursuits. In 1848 he removed to Philadelphia and opened a law office, and soon acquired a large practice. He early connected himself with one of the volunteer militia companies of that city, and at the commencement of the war was active in raising a Philadelphia regiment under the three months' call, of which he was appointed lieutenant-colonel. At the expiration of their time of service, the men reënlisted under him as colonel, and the regiment joined the Army of the Potomac. In February, 1862, he was appointed brigadier-general, and served in all the battles of the peninsula, as well as those before Washington. In the battle of Fredericksburg he distinguished himself, and in the battle of Chancellorsville his brigade, in Berry's division, rendered efficient service in checking the advance of Jackson's troops after the panic in the 11th corps. After the death of Gen. Berry he took command of the division, being promoted to a major-generalship May 23d, 1863, and led it in the battle of Gettysburg, commanding the corps after Gen. Sickles was wounded. After the 2d corps had been recruited to about 40,000 men, he was assigned to the command of one of its divisions, and in the campaign of 1864 his bravery and skill had called forth the warm commendations of his superior officers. In pushing Lee back from the wilderness, in the movements toward the North Anna, the crossing of that river and the Pamunkey, in the actions of Hanover Court House and Bethesda Church, in the battle of Cold Harbor, and indeed in every battle of the campaign, his division was foremost in the very heart of danger. On the 23d of July Gen. Grant promoted him to the command of the 10th army corps, in the Army of the James. Early in October he was taken sick with malarious fever, and his constitution was so seriously impaired by the great exertions he had made at the time of the rebel attack on Kautz's cavalry corps, being then ill in bed, that it could not withstand the onset of the disease. He was brought home to Philadelphia, and though almost in a dying state, insisted on being borne to the polls (the State election being in progress) to vote before he was carried home. He was greatly esteemed and beloved both in the army and in Philadelphia.

Oct. 19.—Brig.-Gen. DANIEL D. BIDWELL, an officer of U. S. volunteers, killed in the battle of Cedar Creek, Va., aged about 48 years. He was born in the township of Buffalo, N. Y., where he became a prominent and influential citizen, and for more than twenty years was identified with the military organizations of the city. When the war broke out he was holding the office of police justice, but resigned his position and entered the 65th regiment of volunteers as a private, and was subsequently appointed brigade inspector. Upon the death of the captain of his company he resigned that position, accepted the command vacated, and withdrawing it from the regiment, reorganized it as an independent citizens' corps, thus forming the nucleus of what has since been known as the 74th regiment. In September, 1861, he was commissioned colonel of the 49th regiment, served with it through the peninsular campaign, and during the "seven days' battles" was in command of a brigade, continuing in charge from Harrison's Landing to Washington, and up to the time of the battles of South Mountain and Antietam, when he resumed command of his regiment. Col. Bidwell took a prominent part in the battles of Fredericksburg and Chancellorsville, commanded a brigade at Gettysburg, and when Gen. Grant took command of the armies in Virginia, was again placed in charge of a brigade, participating in all the battles near Petersburg. He was commissioned brigadier-general in July, 1864, and had served with honor in all the late battles in the Shenandoah valley, under Gen. Sheridan.

Oct. 19.—Col. JOSEPH THOBURN, an officer of U. S. volunteers, who entered the service in 1861 as colonel of the 1st regiment West Virginia volunteers, killed in the battle of Cedar Creek. He was a brave and able officer, and at the time of his death was commanding the 1st division of the Army of the Shenandoah. While rallying his men he was treacherously surprised and shot by a rebel officer in the Union uniform.

Oct. 20.—CHARLES RUSSELL LOWELL, an American soldier, born in Boston in 1835, died near Cedar Creek, Va., October 20th, 1864. He was educated at the Public Latin School of Boston, and in 1854, when scarcely nineteen years of age, graduated at Harvard College with the first honors. After several years of travel in Europe he entered into commercial pursuits, and at the outbreak of the present rebellion was superintendent of some iron-works in Maryland. He immediately sought service in the army, and was commissioned a captain in the Sixth regiment of regular cavalry. During the next two years he saw much service as a cavalry officer and as a member of Gen. McClellan's staff, and after participating in the peninsular campaign and in the military operations in Virginia and Maryland of the succeeding autumn, was appointed early in 1863 to command the 2d Massachusetts cavalry, then organizing in the neighborhood of Boston. In this capacity he on one occasion, by his coolness and personal courage, repressed a dangerous mutiny among a portion of his command. The regiment, upon being recruited to its full number, was sent to Washington, where for more than a year Col. Lowell held command of all the cavalry about the city, a post requiring no little vigilance and activity, in view of the daring depredations by Mosby's guerrillas, whom his troopers frequently encountered and dispersed. Becoming weary of this guard duty, and longing for the opportunity to serve in a regular campaign, he gladly transferred his command to Sheridan's army in the valley of the Shenandoah, and in every subsequent engagement and reconnoissance showed such ability and courage, that a brigadier-general's commission would undoubtedly have been soon conferred upon him, had he lived. He was mortally wounded at the battle of Cedar Creek, Oct. 19th, and died on the succeeding day. He had hitherto seemed to bear a charmed life, having had twelve horses killed under him within three years, and escaped without a wound. In social position, in culture, and in intellectual gifts, Col. Lowell was one of the most promising young men that New England has sent to the war. Almost every great quality belonging to the soldier seemed to be his, and his whole soul was absorbed in the cause for which he fought and died.

Oct. 20.—Maj.-Gen. STEPHEN D. RAMSEUR, an officer in the Confederate service, died of wounds received in the battle of Cedar Creek. He was commanding a division in Early's army.

Oct. 26.—Brig.-Gen. J. FAGAN, an officer in the Confederate service from Texas, killed in Kansas. He had been a prominent actor in most of the important Western battles, and distinguished himself for his bravery as commander of a regiment in the battle of Shiloh, and as a brigadier in the battle of Corinth.

Oct. 27.—Brig.-Gen. —— DEARING, an officer in the Confederate service, killed near Petersburg, Va.

Oct. 27.—Col. —— KIDDOO, an officer of U. S. volunteers, died from wounds received in battle near Richmond. He was in command of the 22d regiment U. S. colored troops.

Oct. 29.—Brig.-Gen. THOMAS E. GREENFIELD RANSOM, an officer of U. S. volunteers, born in Norwich, Vt., Nov. 29, 1834, died of dysentery at Rome, Ga., Oct. 29, 1864. In 1846 he entered Norwich University, continuing there, with the exception of a short interval, until the age of seventeen. In 1851 he entered upon the practise of his profession as an engineer, in Lasalle County, Ill. Three years later he embarked in the real estate business at Peru, in that State, and in 1855 removed to Chicago to become a member of a firm largely engaged in land operations. At a later period he removed to Fayette County, and while engaged in trade acted as an agent for the Illinois Central Railroad Company. At the commencement of the war he raised a company and proceeded to Camp Yates, at Springfield, April 24, 1861, where it was organized into the 11th Illinois volunteers, and upon the election of officers he was made major. After the expiration of the three months' service the regiment was reorganized and mustered in for three years, Ransom being elected lieutenant-colonel. On the night of the 19th of August, in a brilliant dash upon Charleston, Mo., he was severely wounded, and in consequence was granted a furlough of thirty days, but reported for duty upon the seventh day. He participated in the capture of Fort Henry, and led his regiment in the assault upon Fort Donelson, where he was again severely wounded, his clothing being pierced by six bullets, but he would not leave the field until the battle was ended. For his gallantry upon that occasion he was promoted to the colonelcy. At Shiloh, Col. Ransom led his regiment through the hottest part of the battle, and was mentioned by Maj. Gen. McClernand in his official report as "performing prodigies of valor, though reeling in his saddle and streaming with blood from a serious wound." He subsequently served upon the staff of Gen. McClernand, and also upon that of Gen. Grant, who has on several occasions borne testimony to his bravery as an officer. In January, 1863, Ransom was appointed brigadier-general, his commission dating from November, 1862. He won honor to himself at Vicksburg and during the Red River campaign, commanded a division until Gen. McClernand fell ill, when the command of the corps devolved upon him. In the disastrous battle of Sabine Cross-Roads, April, 1864, while fighting with a courage and bravery unsurpassed, he was severely wounded in the knee. The limb was examined by four surgeons, two advising amputation, and the others deeming it unnecessary. Subsequently Gen. Ransom was assigned to the command of the 4th division, 16th army corps, operating in the vicinity of Atlanta, from thence he was promoted to the command of the left wing of the corps, and finally to the command of the 17th corps. From the date of the capitulation of Atlanta, Gen. Ransom had suffered from a severe attack of dysentery, but no consideration would induce him to leave the post of duty. While his corps was in pursuit of Hood's army he directed its movements, though obliged to ride in an ambulance, being too weak to sit upon his horse, and soon after sank under the power of his disease. His career, though short, was brilliant. He was a man of fine genius, great military capacity, and of unblemished personal character.

Oct. 29.—Col. HENRY CLAY PATE, an officer in the Confederate service, killed during the engagement between Gens. Sheridan and Stuart's cavalry near Richmond, aged about 33 years. He was a native of Western Virginia, and was a speaker and writer of some distinction. He attained an unenviable notoriety as a "border ruffian" leader in the Kansas troubles of 1855–'58. On the breaking out of the war he raised a battalion of cavalry in Richmond, which was soon merged in the 5th Virginia cavalry, and being promoted to the rank of lieutenant-colonel, served through the principal battles in Virginia. He had but recently been made colonel.

Nov. 7.—Col. CORNELIUS W. TOLLES, Chief Quartermaster of Gen. Sheridan's army, died at Winchester, Va., of wounds received from guerrillas Oct. 11th, in the 37th year of his age. He entered the service of the United States in May, 1861, as first lieutenant of the 13th regiment of infantry, and received his appointment of quartermaster August, 1862. He served constantly in the field, discharging the duties of his position with zeal and fidelity, winning the confidence and esteem of commanders and subordinates. His health having given way under his severe labors, he was temporarily placed on duty as inspector; but, upon his recovery, he was appointed Acting Chief Quartermaster of the Middle Military Division. While actively engaged in the duties of this position, he published some valuable contributions to military literature in the "United States Service Magazine," the "Army and Navy Journal," and elsewhere.

Nov. 19.—Lieut.-Col. JAMES A. P. HOPKINS, an officer of U. S. volunteers, died in New York city. He entered the volunteer service with the 133d regiment N. Y. (2d Metropolitan), sharing with it in the siege of Port Hudson. He also fought with great bravery and skill in other engagements in the department of Gen. Banks. During the latter part of his career at the South he was appointed Chief of Police in the city of New Orleans, and subsequently received a commission as Chief of the United States Detective force of that city.

Nov. 25.—Maj. JOSEPH W. PAINE, an officer of U. S. volunteers, died suddenly in New Orleans, La. He was a native of Boston, Mass., and for several years was an associate editor and publisher, with William Mathews, of the "Yankee Blade." More recently he was connected with several of the leading life insurance companies of New York city, but continued to contribute to some of the principal Boston and New York journals. In the summer of 1863 he entered into the volunteer service as first lieutenant of the 13th New York cavalry, and in 1864 was commissioned major of the 4th U. S. colored cavalry, and at once proceeded to the Department of the Gulf. During the Red River campaign he did able and effective service, but in August was obliged to come North for the benefit of his health. While there he entered into the political campaign, supporting the Administration both with pen and voice. The second week in November he returned to New Orleans, before his health was sufficiently recruited, and died within a week of his arrival.

Nov. 26.—Col. FREDERICK BECKHAM, an officer of artillery in the Confederate army, killed at Columbia, Tenn., by a fragment of stone, which, being thrown into the air by the explosion of a shell from the Federal guns, struck him in the head and penetrated the brain. At the battle of Manassas, and indeed in many other severe battles fought by the Virginia army, he commanded a battery of field guns, and distinguished himself by his courage and ability. He was a graduate of West Point, and served some time on Gen. Hood's staff, when that officer was in the army of Virginia. When Gen. Hood was promoted to a lieutenant-generalcy, Col. Beckham was promoted to a colonelcy of artillery, January, 1864, and assigned to Hood's staff as chief of artillery of his corps in the Army of Tennessee.

Nov. 30.– Major-Gen. PATRICK CLEBURN, an officer of the Confederate army, killed at the battle of Franklin, Tenn. Gen. Cleburn was born in Ireland, but received his military education in the English army. When the war broke out it found Gen. Cleburn practising law in Arkansas, where his talents had raised him to the head of his profession. He entered the army as a private, and by his merit and successful engagements rose to the rank he bore when he fell. His division was thought invincible. His name was a tower of strength, and the tide of battle often changed on whatever part of the battle-field he and his division appeared. His command was composed of veterans from Texas and Arkansas. Gen. Cleburn's horse fell dead across the Federal breastworks, and he was mortally wounded himself, and died in a few moments.

Nov. 30.—Col. HUGH GARLAND, an officer of the Confederate army, killed at the battle of Franklin, Tenn. Col. Garland was from St. Louis, Mo., and had, by the death of Col. Riely, succeeded to the command of the 1st Missouri regiment of infantry only a short time before his death. At the time of his becoming colonel of his regiment, he was in Richmond on special duty, recruiting from exchanged prisoners, and rejoined his command at Kenesaw Mountain some time in June, 1864. He fell at the head of his regiment in the charge on the breastworks of Gen. Schofield's army. Col. Garland's personal appearance was very striking. He was nearly six feet two inches in height, and well proportioned, fair complexion, high smooth forehead, and light blue eyes; his manners were bland and courteous; his disposition noble and kind, and his gallantry and courage undoubted.

Dec. 9.—Lieut.-Col. LUCIUS M. SARGENT, an officer of U. S. volunteers, killed near Meherrin River, Va. He was a son of Lucius M. Sargent, the well-known author. He was in command of the 1st Massachusetts cavalry.

Dec. 11.—Col. J. HOWARD KITCHING, an officer of U. S. volunteers, formerly colonel of the 6th New York artillery, but of late in command of a provisional division in the Army of the Shenandoah, died from the effects of a wound received in the battle of Cedar Creek, at his father's residence, Dobbs' Ferry, N. Y. He was a native of New York, was well educated, and at the opening of the war enlisted as a private in the Lincoln cavalry. He was transferred soon after to the 2d New York artillery, in which he soon rose to the rank of captain, and by diligent study and observation made himself an accomplished artillerist and thorough military scholar. He served in every battle in which the 6th corps was engaged during the peninsular campaign, and in the autumn of 1862 became lieutenant-colonel of the 135th New York volunteers, afterwards the 6th New York artillery, of which regiment he became the commander on the promotion of Col. Morris to the brigadier-generalship. From the time of his receiving a commission as colonel he was almost constantly in command of a brigade, and repeatedly received the special commendation of his superior officers, especially that of

Gen. Meade, for his extraordinary gallantry in the action of the 19th of May. In the battle of Cedar Creek, Oct. 19th, his division bore the brunt of Gen. Early's attack, and fought with desperate valor. He was wounded in the ankle early in the action, but would not leave the field till the close of the battle; but erysipelas set in after the first operation, rendering a second necessary, under which he died.

Dec. 16.—Col. O. De Forrest, an officer of U. S. volunteers, died in New York. He was among the first to enter the army at the beginning of the rebellion, commanding the 5th New York cavalry until a short time after the battle of Gettysburg. During the Maryland and Pennsylvania campaign he commanded the 5th brigade of Gen. Kilpatrick's cavalry division, and distinguished himself as an excellent officer.

Dec. 24.—John Lawrence Fox, M.D., Fleet-Surgeon U. S. navy, died at his residence in Roxbury, Mass., aged 54 years. He was a native of Salem, Mass., graduated at Amherst College in 1831, and in 1837 entered the navy as assistant surgeon. In 1847 he received a full commission. A few months previous to his death he was appointed fleet-surgeon upon the staff of Admiral Porter, and his death was doubtless the result of overtaxing his system by the severe duties of his department.

Dec. 25.—Major John S. Fillmore, paymaster U. S. Army, died at his residence in Denver City, Colorado Territory. He was a native of the State of New York; was appointed paymaster by the Governor of Colorado in August, 1861, and was commissioned paymaster in the U. S. army by the President, in November, 1862.

1865.

Jan. 1.—Angus W. McDonald, a colonel of in the Confederate service, and for many years brigadier-general of Virginia militia, died in Richmond, Va. He was a native of New York, and was born in 1802. His father was a major in the United States army, and died during the war of 1812, at Buffalo, N. Y. The son was appointed a cadet at West Point, and graduated in 1817, and on his graduation was appointed third lieutenant in the artillery corps. He was promoted to a second lieutenantcy in February, 1818, and in April of the same year to a first lieutenancy. He resigned in January, 1819, and commenced the practice of law at Romney, Va. He had been for many years a brigadier-general of the militia in Virginia, and on the breaking out of the war received a commission as colonel of volunteers in the Confederate army. In June, 1864, he was captured by Gen. Hunter, near Lexington, Va., and was exchanged on the 14th of November.

Jan. 16.—Col. Louis Bell, of the 4th New Hampshire volunteers, acting brigadier-general, died of wounds received at Fort Fisher the preceding day. He was born in Chester, N. H., in 1836, and was the youngest son of the late Governor Samuel Bell. He graduated at Brown University in 1853, and commenced the practice of law at Farmington, N. H. In 1860 he was appointed Solicitor for Stafford County. In April, 1861, he was offered the captaincy of a company of the 1st New Hampshire regiment of three months' men, and served during the campaign. Returning home he was appointed lieutenant-colonel of the 4th New Hampshire volunteers, and upon the resignation of Col. Whipple, in March, 1862, was made commander of the regiment. Col. Bell was for some time a member of Gen. T. W. Sherman's staff, and was inspector general of the Department of the South from November, 1861, to March, 1862. Previously to the Wilmington expedition he had been several times temporarily a brigade commander, and had served bravely at Pocotaligo and at the siege of Fort Wagner. At the attack on Fort Fisher he commanded a brigade of Gen. Ames' division, and was mortally wounded while leading his men in an assault upon one of the traverses of that work. He was a brother of Chief Justice Bell, of Manchester, N. H., of the late Dr. Luther V. Bell, of the McLean Lunatic Asylum, and of Dr. John Bell, U. S. A.

Jan. 21.—Brevet Brig.-Gen. Charles Wheelock, colonel of 97th New York volunteers, died at Washington, D. C., from disease contracted in the service. He was a native and resident of Oneida County, N. Y., where he was engaged at the beginning of the war in a large and prosperous business, which he abandoned immediately after the fall of Fort Sumter, and devoted his whole time to raising men for the army, pledging himself to provide for their families. In the summer of 1861 he said to a friend: "I am worth, I think, in the neighborhood of $10,000. Half of this I have already given or pledged to aid the war, and if my country wants the other half it can have it, and myself into the bargain." Becoming impatient with the slow progress of the war, he soon after commenced raising a regiment on his own hook, fed and housed several hundred men at his personal expense for many months, and after a series of embarrassments and disappointments that would have disheartened almost any other man, completed its organization and marched it to the field. Entirely without military experience, and with but a very limited general education, he became one of the best volunteer officers in the service, and so signally distinguished himself that he was brevetted brigadier-general for bravery and good soldiership. He had seen much service, was engaged in many of the bloodiest battles in

Virginia, was taken prisoner, if we mistake not, at the second battle of Bull Run, and tasted for many months the sweets of prison life at Richmond, but was subsequently exchanged, when he rejoined his old regiment and did more gallant service in behalf of the old flag.

Jan. 29.—Dr. ROBERT MONTGOMERY SMITH JACKSON, Medical Inspector of the 23d army corps, and acting medical director of the Department of the Ohio, died at Chattanooga, Tenn. He was a native of Pennsylvania, and a resident of Cresson, Pa., at the commencement of the war. He was widely known throughout Pennsylvania, being distinguished for great force of character, decided opinion, and some eccentricity withal. He was a man of strong and generous feelings, and intense in his patriotism. As a scientific man he had few superiors in Pennsylvania. He was thoroughly versed in all departments of natural science, and as a geologist and botanist was specially distinguished. He was a member of the Pennsylvania Geological Commission, of which Professor Rogers was chief, and very much of the results of that survey are due to the skill and industry of Dr. Jackson. He was an enthusiastic mountaineer, and believed that in the pure air of the Alleghanies the enervated and listless inhabitants of cities and the lowlands would find health, strength, and energy. He published, some years ago a work called "The Mountain," which is distinguished by a love of nature, and by a scientific handling of the topics, which, without being too technical, is of a character to elevate the human mind and teach the reader to look "from nature up to nature's God." Some of Dr. Jackson's views are bold and startling, but his fine command of language, his chaste and vigorous style, places the book among the most remarkable of its kind ever written. Dr. Jackson was a member of the American Philosophical Society, Academy of Natural Sciences, and other learned institutions.

Jan. —.—Lieut.-Col. LEWIS LEDYARD WELD, U. S. C. T., formerly Secretary of the Territory of Colorado, died before Petersburg. He was a native of Hartford, Conn., born about 1834, and son of the late Lewis Weld, president of the American Asylum for the Deaf and Dumb. He graduated at Yale College in 1856, and studied law. In 1858 he removed to Leavenworth, Kansas, where he practised law for two years, writing frequently for the newspaper press. In 1862 he was made Secretary of Colorado, and was the first editor of the Denver Commonwealth. In 1863 he was made lieutenant-colonel of a colored regiment, and served with distinction through Grant's campaign till his death.

Feb. 6.—JOHN PEGRAM, a major-general in the Confederate service, mortally wounded in the battle of Hatcher's Run, and died in Petersburg the following day. He was a son of the late Hon. John Pegram, M. C. from Virginia in 1818 and 1819, but was born in South Carolina, to which State his father had removed. He graduated at West Point in 1855, and at the opening of the war was first lieutenant of 2d dragoons, but resigned on the secession of his State, and was soon after appointed to the command of a Confederate volunteer regiment, and in 1862 promoted to be brigadier-general. He was in most of the severe battles of the Army of Virginia, and in 1864 was made major-general. His division had distinguished itself throught the campaign of 1864–'65 for its persistent and desperate fighting, and its commander, Gen. John Pegram, was regarded by his superiors in command as one of the ablest division commanders in the army.

Feb. 6.—JOHN H. WINDER, a brigadier-general in the Confederate service, died at Florence, S. C., of apoplexy. He was a native of Maryland, the son of Gen. William H. Winder, of Baltimore, an officer in the war of 1812, and graduated at West Point about 1825. He served in the army with considerable distinction, took part in the Mexican war, and at the commencement of the rebellion was major and brevet lieutenant-colonel of the 3d artillery. He resigned, and entered the Confederate service, where he was soon made a brigadier-general, but was not employed in active service to any great extent. He commanded the post of Richmond, and had charge of the Union prisoners in Libby Prison and Belle Isle for some time, and was finally sent to Andersonville, Ga., in a similar capacity. When Sherman's expedition passed through Georgia, he left Andersonville and repaired first to Charleston, and afterwards to Florence, where he died.

Feb. 8.—Lieut.-Col. —— TREMAINE, of the 10th New York cavalry, died near Petersburg of wounds received at the battle of Hatcher's Run, Feb. 6th. He was the son of the Hon. Lyman Tremaine of Albany, and was born in Greene County, N. Y., in June, 1843; entered Hobart College in the fall of 1860, and remained till the summer of 1862, when unable longer to resist the calls of patriotism, he entered the army as adjutant of the 7th New York heavy artillery. He served with distinction in the defences of Washington, and subsequently as assistant adjutant-general, with the rank of captain, on the staff of Gen. Davies of the cavalry in Kilpatrick's division of the Potomac army. In this position he distinguished himself by his bravery and the prompt and intelligent discharge of his duties. In December, 1864, he was commissioned lieutenant-colonel of the 10th New York cavalry, in the command of which regiment he was wounded at Hatcher's Run in the battle of February 6th, and died on the following Wednesday. Col. Tremaine was distinguished for an unusual degree of generosity, firmness, and courage, great ability and entire devotion to the cause of his country.

Feb. 9.—Capt. JAMES MELVIN GILLISS, an officer of the U. S. naval service, and at the time of his death Superintendent of the National Observatory, was born in the District of Columbia in 1810, died in Washington, D. C., of apolexy, Feb. 9, 1865. He entered the navy as midshipman March 1, 1827, having enjoyed good previous advantages of education. He spent but little time afloat, his entire sea service amounting to only four years and seven months, his fondness and adaptation for astronomical studies having led to his being employed very early in that department of naval service. In 1838 he organized the first working observatory in the United States, and during the five following years collected and published his astronomical observations, the first American work of the kind published. In September, 1842, Lieut. Gilliss was appointed to plan and superintend the construction of a naval observatory, which was completed and furnished in 1845. On the 16th of November, 1848, he was ordered to proceed to Chili to make observations for the determination of the Solar Parallax, and remained there three years. Through his influence a naval observatory was established in that country, and he completed a series of observations of great value, not only in regard to the Solar Parallax, but to the constellations of the Southern Hemisphere, and to earthquakes, and other subjects relating to the physical geography of Chili. His observations have been published by the Government in a series of quarto volumes. In 1858 he visited Peru to observe the total eclipse of the sun, which was most complete and and protracted in that country, and in 1860 made the journey to Washington Territory for the same purpose. His observations in regard to both were of great importance, and went far toward settling several questions of interest in relation to the form and properties of the sun. On the flight of Lieut. Maury at the commencement of the war, Commander Gilliss was at once placed in charge of the Observatory (his appointment bearing date April 22, 1861), which he had constructed and equipped sixteen years before; a most beneficial change to the institution, which, under his charge, soon became one of the few first-class observatories in the world. He found a vast amount of work left in arrears by his predecessor, no reduction of the observations of the previous six years having been made. He applied himself to the work of bringing them up, and of adding new and valuable observations, with great industry, and perhaps with an assiduity which may have caused his untimely death. On the 16th of July, 1862, he was promoted to the rank of captain in the navy. He had won for himself a high reputation among the most eminent astronomers of the world by his profound astronomical knowledge and his eagerness in the pursuit of his favorite science. Shortly before his death he had made an official report to the Secretary of the Navy, detailing the scientific observations made in various observatories of the world, under his auspices or at his request, to ascertain the parallax of the planet Mars, and the result as approximating the exact distance from the earth to the sun. He possessed a rare degree of mechanical ingenuity, and had contributed many valuable improvements in the instruments of astronomical science. Thoroughly Union, he had given one son to his country's service, who, after a long imprisonment in one of the Southern prisons, had reached home the evening before his father's decease.

Feb. 12.—Col. —— Dean, of the 58th U. S. colored troops, was killed in Arkansas. He was on an expedition from Helena across the country to St. Francis River.

Feb. 22.—Lieut.-Commander Marshall C. Campbell, an officer of the U. S. naval service, and until a short time before his death instructor in seamanship and naval tactics in the Naval Academy, died in Baltimore, Md. He was born in Tennessee, in 1834, but was admitted to the Naval Academy from Mississippi, where his parents then resided, in February, 1850. He was a young officer, of fine attainments, and had spent nine years and seven months of the fifteen years he had been in the navy, afloat, his last cruise having closed in September, 1864. His assiduity in the performance of his duties had so far overtasked a somewhat feeble frame that he returned to Baltimore, now the residence of his widowed mother, only to die. Although from a State in rebellion, he was distinguished for his thorough attachment to the national cause.

March 10.—Maj.-Gen. William H. C. Whiting, an officer in the Confederate service, wounded at Fort Fisher, and taken prisoner, died at Governor's Island, N. Y., whither he had been removed. He was a native of New York, was born about 1825, and graduated at West Point in 1845, ranking very high in his class. He took part in the Mexican war, and was promoted rapidly for an officer of engineers, having attained the rank of captain of engineers in 1861, when he went over to the rebels, having resided for some years in Virginia. He was made a brigadier-general in 1862 and a major-general in 1863. In the autumn of 1864 he was put in command of Fort Fisher, and was in charge during both attacks.

March 25.—Brig.-Gen. William R. Terry, an officer in the Confederate service, killed in the assault on Fort Stedman, near Petersburg. He was a native of Virginia, and had been educated in the Lexington (Va.) Military Academy.

April 1.—Brevet Brig.-Gen. Frederick Winthrop (Colonel of the 5th New York volunteers and captain 12th infantry U. S. army), killed at the battle of Five Forks, Va., while leading the 1st brigade, 2d division, 5th corps. He was born in New York in 1840, joined the 71st regiment New York State militia in its three months' service at the beginning of the war as a private, and fought at Bull Run. In October, 1861, he was appointed captain in the 12th U. S. infantry (regular army), and continued in service until the battles of the Wilderness in 1864, when he was appointed colonel of the 5th New York regiment, and shortly afterwards brevetted brigadier-general for gallantry in the field. He was a cousin of the late Major Theodore Winthrop and of Robert C. Winthrop of Boston.

April 2.—Lieut.-Gen. AMBROSE POWELL HILL, an officer in the Confederate army, born in Culpepper County, Va., in 1824, killed in the assault on Petersburg, Va., April 2, 1865. His father was for many years a leading politician and merchant in Culpepper County. The future lieutenant-general entered the military academy in 1843, and graduated with fair standing in his class in 1847, in the same class with Gen. Burnside. There being no vacancy he received the brevet rank of second lieutenant in the 1st artillery, and on the 22d of August of the same year attained a full second lieutenancy. He was promoted to be 1st lieutenant in September, 1851, and in 1855 to be captain. In November of that year he was appointed an assistant on the United States Coast Survey, in which he continued till March 1st, 1861, when he resigned his connection with the regular army; and when Virginia seceded from the Union, he sought and received an appointment from Gov. Letcher as colonel of the 13th regiment of Virginia volunteers. He was attached to Johnston's army, and stationed at first at Harper's Ferry, and in the battle of Manassas, or Bull Run, came in with Johnston's troops in season to turn the issue of the battle. At Williamsburg, in May, 1862, he held the rank of brigadier-general, and distinguished himself as a gallant fighter in that battle. For his bravery in this battle he was made major-general, and on the 25th of June, 1862, formed one of the council of war held in Richmond. He took part in the battle of Mechanicsville on the 26th of June, and in the succeeding battles of what is known as "The Seven Days," he was a prominent actor, and gained a brilliant reputation for bravery and skill in the handling of his troops. He was actively engaged in the battles of Cedar Run, or Cedar Mountain, in the Groveton or second Bull Run battle, in the attack near Centreville on the 30th of August, at Chantilly, and in the campaign before Washington, in which Gen. Pope was the Federal commander. On the 14th of September, 1862, he captured Harper's Ferry, and made a forced march to Antietam Creek, where he ar-arrived in season to take part in that severe but indecisive battle, and on the 19th repulsed the Federal troops, who crossed the river in pursuit of the rebels, with heavy loss. In the battle of Fredericksburg, Dec. 13, 1862, his division formed the right of Jackson's force, and fought desperately, finally repulsing the Federal troops. At Chancellorsville, in May, 1863, his division formed the centre of Jackson's command, and participated in that flank movement, by which Hooker's right was so effectually crushed. When "Stonewall" Jackson received his death wound, the command devolved on Gen. Hill, who was himself severely wounded soon after. For his gallantry in this battle he was made a lieutenant-general, and placed permanently in command of one of the three great corps into which the Army of Virginia was divided. On the 1st, 2d, and 3d of July, 1863, he led his corps in the severe battle of Gettysburg, and though successful the first day, was unsuccessful on the second and third. In the autumn of 1863 he was concerned in the affair at Bristoe Station with a part of his corps, but was repulsed with serious loss. In the great battles of the spring of 1864, Gen. Hill was, next to Gen. Lee, the most prominent actor in the Army of Virginia. On the 5th of May, from 2 P. M. till long after nightfall, he was engaged in a most desperate but indecisive conflict, and the early dawn would have found him in a position of extreme peril had not Longstreet's corps been brought up to reënforce him at 2 A. M. The fighting of the 6th of May was very severe, and in this Hill took a full share, but it was no more decisive than that of the previous day. In the movement toward Spottsylvania Hill aided by his counsel, but his corps were not engaged. In the battle of Mechanicsville Hill's corps sustained the brunt of the attack, and under his eye fought with great heroism. In the battle of the 3d of June, at Cold Harbor, the corps were at first in reserve, but supported the other corps before the battle was over. On the 22d of June his corps and Longstreet's repulsed the attempt of the Federal troops to gain possession of the Weldon Railroad, and drove them back with severe loss. At the explosion of the mine on the lines of Petersburg, on the 30th of July, in the engagement at Reams' Station, on the 25th of August, in the battle of Hatcher's Run, Oct. 28–30, and the subsequent movements in that vicinity, in December, 1864, and February, 1865, Gen. Hill led his corps with great ability, and in almost every instance repulsed the Federal troops. When the final attack upon the South Side Railroad and the defences of Petersburg came (March 29–April 2), Gen. Hill was active and indefatigable in his exertions to repel the Federal attack, and on the 2d of April, for the possession of the works in front of Petersburg, his corps were opposed to the 6th, 9th, and part of the 25th Federal corps, almost single-handed, and then, as always, exposing himself to fire without hesitation, he was instantly killed by a rifle shot, and as time was pressing, the evacuation of the city being determined upon, was buried the same day.

April 5.—Col. HUGH H. JANEWAY, 1st New Jersey volunteer cavalry, killed at Fame's Cross-Roads, near Jetersville, Va. He was born in Jersey City, N. J., in 1842, entered the 1st New Jersey cavalry at the commencement of the war as second lieutenant, and rose steadily through every grade to the highest, being appointed colonel when but twenty-two years of age, at the written request of every officer in the regiment. He had been in every important battle of the Army of the Potomac, and had been twelve times wounded. He was a young man of extraordinary promise, and in his last as in every previous battle, he led his men into the fight, asking them only to follow his example. He had just seized the colors of his regiment and was in the act of carrying them forward, when a bullet entered his brain, and he died instantly.

April 6.—Brevet Brig.-Gen. S. T. READ, Chief of Staff to Gen. Ord, shot by the rebel Gen. Dearing, in a hand to hand conflict, at the High Bridge over the Appomattox, near Farmville, Va. Gen. Read was a native of Massachusetts, and had entered the service as captain of a company of unattached cavalry from that State in January, 1862. After considerable service in this capacity the several companies of cavalry having been organized into a battalion, he accepted a staff appointment, and distinguished himself at Gettysburg, where he was severely wounded, and subsequently in the battles of Grant's campaign. When Gen. Ord took a command in connection with the Army of the James, he gave him a position as chief of staff, which he retained when Gen. Ord was assigned to the command of the Army of the James. He had recently received a brevet promotion for gallantry in the field.

April 9.—Brig.-Gen. THOMAS A. SMYTH, commanding the 2d division 2d army corps, was mortally wounded near Farmville, Va., by a shot from a sharpshooter on the 6th of April, and died at Petersburg. He was born in Ireland, but emigrated to this country when a boy and settled at Wilmington, Del., where he engaged in the coachmaking business. At the opening of the war he recruited a company in Wilmington, and proceeded to Philadelphia and joined a three months' regiment then leaving for the Shenandoah valley. Returning home he was made major of the Delaware regiment then leaving for the seat of war, and rose gradually from that position to lieutenant-colonel and colonel, and soon was put in charge of a brigade, where he won a high reputation for his daring and skill. He was promoted to the rank of brigadier general in the summer of 1864, for his gallant conduct at Cold Harbor.

April 11.—Col. WILLIAM SERGEANT, 210th Pennsylvania volunteers, and captain of the 12th infantry, U. S. A., was wounded on the 31st of March near Petersburg, and died on board the boat coming from City Point to Fortress Monroe. He was born in Philadelphia in 1830, and was the son of the late Hon. John Sergeant, and brother of Mrs. Gen. Meade. He was educated for the bar, and had attained a high position, and represented his native city in the Legislature before the opening of the war. He volunteered early in the war, and soon after received an appointment as captain in the 12th U. S. infantry, in which position his gallantry in the peninsular and other campaigns attracted the attention of his superiors. He was subsequently called to the command of the 210th Pennsylvania volunteers, and in the duties of his new post was as remarkable for his personal bravery as for the military talent which he had developed. He was gentle, open hearted, and generous to a fault.

April 15.—ABRAHAM LINCOLN, sixteenth President of the United States, and Commander-in-Chief of the Army and Navy of the same. He was born in Hardin County, Kentucky, February 12, 1809, and died in Washington from a pistol-shot wound inflicted by an assassin, April 15, 1865. His father was very poor, and the region of Kentucky in which he lived afforded at that time but scant opportunities for education. At seven years of age he was sent to school for a short time, and his only text-book was an old copy of Dilworth's Spelling-Book. When he was in his eighth year, his father, tired of the hopeless struggle which even then crushed all the energies of the poorer white settlers in the slave States, sold his little homestead, and putting his family and his few household goods upon a raft, sought a new home in the then wilderness of Spencer County, Indiana, cutting his road with his axe through the dense forest during the last eighteen miles of his route. Rearing a log-cabin two or three miles distant from the nearest neighbor the family entered upon a pioneer's life. The mother of the future President, herself a woman of intelligence and piety, taught her boy to read and write, and encouraged the taste for books which even their circumstances could not wholly repress. When he was ten years of age she died. His father married again a year or two later, and the step-mother proved a kind and tender friend to the orphaned boy. When he was about twelve years old a Mr. Crawford, one of the settlers, opened a school in his own cabin, and young Lincoln attended and studied arithmetic and some of the other branches of a common school education. But few books had found their way into the wilderness of the "Pocket," as this portion of Indiana was called, but whenever one could be obtained his father always endeavored to procure the reading of it for him. In this way he became familiar with Bunyan's Pilgrim's Progress, Esop's Fables, Weems's and Ramsey's Life of Washington, a Life of Henry Clay, and perhaps a few other volumes. At the age of nineteen he made a trip to New Orleans in company with the son of the owner of a flatboat, who intrusted to the care of the two youths a valuable cargo. Attacked on their way down by a gang of thievish negroes, the two young men defended the property and drove off the plunderers, and pushing out into the stream succeeded in saving it from depredation.

In 1830 Mr. Lincoln's father determined upon another removal to Decatur, Illinois, and his son assisted him in settling in his new home, breaking the ground for a crop of corn, and building a rail fence around his farm. The winter which followed was very severe, and it required the utmost exertion of Abraham Lincoln, now a stalwart youth of twenty-one years, and his father, to keep the family in food, which was mostly obtained by hunting. Two years more were passed in working on a farm, or as clerk in a store. In 1832 the Black Hawk war occurred. Volunteers were called for, and young Lincoln enlisted and was at once made captain. He experienced considerable marching during the campaign, but had no opportunity of exhibiting his prowess as a fighter. After his return from the war he ran for the Legislature, but was defeated, though receiving a heavy vote. He next purchased a store and stock of goods, and was appointed postmaster. The store proved unprofitable and he sold out, but through the whole pursued his studies at every opportunity. Having acquired a knowledge of surveying, he spent the greater part of the next two or three years as government surveyor, and won a high reputation for the accuracy of his surveys. In 1834 he was a member of the Illinois Legislature, and after the session closed, devoted all his leisure time to the study of law. In 1836 he was admitted to the bar, and in April, 1837, removed to Springfield, Illinois, and commenced practice in partnership with Hon. John T. Stuart. He soon won a good reputation as an able pleader, both in civil and criminal practice. He was reëlected twice to the Legislature, where he formed the acquaintance of his subsequent political antagonist, Hon. Stephen A. Douglas. In 1840 he declined being a candidate for the Legislature, and though taking a deep interest in political matters, ranking as a Whig of the Henry Clay School, he sought no political preferment, but devoted himself assiduously to his profession, in which his ability had already gained him a commanding position. In 1844 he canvassed the State for Mr. Clay. In 1846 he was elected to Congress, and took his seat in 1847, the only Whig representative from Illinois, and probably the only one who could have been elected. During the single term in which he was a member of the House of Representatives there were several important questions before Congress, among others the Mexican War, the Right of Petition, the Abolition of Slavery in the District of Columbia, the Wilmot Proviso, the Pacheco Case, the River and Harbor Bill, the Modification of the Tariff, and the Abolishment of the Franking Privilege. In regard to all these questions Mr. Lincoln took a manly and decided action, voting generally with his party, but independently whenever he regarded their course as inconsistent with the highest rule of right.

In 1848 Mr. Lincoln was a member of the national convention which nominated Gen. Taylor for the Presidency, and subsequently canvassed Illinois in his favor. In 1849 he was the Whig candidate for United States senator from Illinois, but was defeated, the Democratic party having a majority in both branches of the Legislature. He now devoted himself most assiduously to his professional pursuits, though still watching with great eagerness the political measures before the country. In May, 1854, the Nebraska bill was passed, and the Missouri Compromise act repealed. This roused the majority of the people of the Northern States to a vigorous opposition, and Illinois, which had long been regarded as one of the most reliable of the Western States for the Democratic party, was revolutionized. Mr. Lincoln took a prominent part in the political campaign of the autumn of 1854. A United States senator was to be chosen in the place of Gen. Shields, who had supported the Nebraska bill, which Judge Douglas had originated. The State was carried by the Whigs, who had two candidates for the senatorship, Mr. Lincoln and Judge Trumbull, one of Whig and the other of Democratic antecedents. Regarding a division as disastrous at that time, and satisfied of Judge Trumbull's ability and integrity, Mr. Lincoln, with rare generosity, not only withdrew his name from the canvass, but persuaded his friends to support Trumbull, who was then elected.

In 1856 Mr. Lincoln's name was prominent before the first Republican national convention for the Vice-Presidency, receiving one hundred and ten votes on the informal ballot. His name headed the Republican electoral ticket in Illinois, and he took an active part in the canvass.

In 1858 the senatorial term of Judge Douglas being about to expire, the Republicans of Illinois at their State Convention on the 17th of June, 1858, at Springfield, nominated Abraham Lincoln as their candidate for United States senator. Judge Douglas was the candidate of the Democratic party; and, in accordance with Western custom, the two candidates canvassed the State in defence of their principles. The canvass was one of deep interest; great principles were at stake. Both the candidates were men of decided ability, and possessed the power of swaying their audiences—Judge Douglas by a rare talent for reaching the popular vein, and chiming in with the prejudices, the sympathies, and the passions of the people, and Mr. Lincoln by an irresistible logic, and a happy faculty of "putting things," which, by a few well-placed words, overturned and annihilated his adversary's positions. It would have been difficult to find two men better matched for a controversy. At first their meetings before the people were accidental; Judge Douglas spoke at Chicago on the 9th of July, and Mr. Lincoln on the 10th, and a week later both spoke on the same day at Springfield. On the 24th of July Mr. Lincoln challenged Judge Douglas to a series of debates on the principles involved in the campaign. The Judge accepted, and though the terms he proposed gave him four speeches to Mr. Lincoln's three, the latter made no objection. Seven of these debates were held in different parts of the State between the 21st of August and the 15th of October, and they were afterwards published in full from phonographic notes. The principles of the two parties were very thoroughly discussed, and the weak points of each fully exposed. The discussion was fair, open, and manly, and it was very generally conceded that Mr. Lincoln was unsurpassed in the mental tournament. The Republicans had a majority of about five thousand in the popular vote, but owing to the inequality with which the State was districted, and the pressure from other States, Mr. Douglas was reëlected to the Senate by a small majority of legislative votes.

During the next year and a half Mr. Lincoln visited Ohio, Kansas, and New York, and made several speeches of great ability on political questions. That delivered in New York and subsequently published, was one of the most effective and eloquent expositions of the policy of the Republican party, and served as a text-book for the orators of that party in the succeeding canvass. A speech delivered in Cincinnati to an audience largely made up of Kentuckians in the spring of 1860, in which he enunciated, in his own telling way, his abhorrence of slavery, is still remembered in that city for its extraordinary power. The Republican national convention, which assembled at Chicago on the 16th of May, 1860, was at first nearly equally divided between Mr. Seward and Mr. Lincoln as its candidate for the Presidency, but the preponderance for Mr. Lincoln soon became evident, and on the third ballot he was nominated, receiving three hundred and fifty-four out of four hundred and sixty-five votes, and by motion of Mr. Evarts, of New York, the nomination was made unanimous. The nomination with the platform was formally accepted by him, in a graceful letter, on the 23d of May, and was enthusiastically received by the Republican party throughout the country.

His opponents were divided (purposely, there was reason to believe, it being the design of the leaders at the South to make his election certain, that it might be used to effect a disruption of the nation) to a greater extent than ever before, there being three other tickets in the field, viz., Messrs Breckinridge and Lane, the candidates of the Pro-slavery Democrats; Messrs. Douglas and H. V. Johnson, the candidates of the Progressive Democrats; and Messrs. Bell and Everett, the representatives of a conservative party, mostly composed of those who had belonged to the old Whig party. On the 6th of Nov., 1860, the election took place, and Mr. Lincoln received 180 electoral votes out of 303, Breckinridge having 72, Bell 39, and Douglas 12. The popular vote was somewhat different in its proportions, Mr. Lincoln having a plurality of nearly 600,000, but not an absolute majority, while Douglas came next, Breckinridge next, and Bell last. The exact popular vote was: for Lincoln, 1,857,610; for Douglas, 1,291,574; for Breckinridge, 850,082; for Bell, 646,124.

No sooner was his election ascertained than the conspiracy which had long been smouldering in the Southern States burst out in full flame. During the four months which intervened between his election and his inauguration, six States—South Carolina, Mississippi, Alabama, Florida, Louisiana, and Texas—passed ordinances of secession, and appointed delegates to meet in convention at Montgomery, Alabama, on the 4th of February, a month before the inauguration. This convention adopted a provisional constitution for what they denominated the Confederate States, and chose Jefferson Davis President and Alexander H. Stephens Vice-President of their new government. Thus, before he had even left his home in Illinois to come to the capital and assume office, and nearly a month before his taking his official oath, the insurrectionists had organized a rebellion involving six States, and with a certainty that others would join them. It was not in consequence of any thing he had done, for he could not as yet perform any official act; nor was it in consequence of any thing which the leaders saw he had power to do, for they knew his views of the sanctity of an oath, and he would swear to maintain the constitution inviolate. Secession had been a foregone conclusion to be carried out at this time, if it could be made practicable.

On the 11th of February, 1861, Mr. Lincoln left his house in Springfieid, Illinois, to go to Washington, and enter upon his presidential duties. In the course of his journey he passed through Indianapolis, Cincinnati, Columbus, Pittsburg, Cleveland, Buffalo, Albany, New York, Trenton, Philadelphia, and Harrisburg. He met the Legislatures of Indiana, Ohio, New York, New Jersey, and Pennsylvania, which were then in session, at the capitals of those States, and everywhere along his way made brief addresses, the main scope of which was, that if the people only stood firm in maintaining the constitution and the Government, no power on earth could overthrow them. At Philadelphia information was communicated to him that a plot existed to assassinate him at Baltimore. The only precaution he took was to leave Harrisburg one train earlier than had been expected, the telegraph wires being mean time disconnected. He arrived in Washington on the morning of Saturday, Feb. 23d.

On the 4th of March, 1861, he took the oath of office, and delivered his inaugural address, a plain, straightforward talk with the nation. He began by showing, in the clearest way, that there was no ground for the apprehension which seemed to exist at the South that "their property, their peace, and their personal security were to be endangered." He declared that he took the oath to support the Constitution "with no mental reservations." He argued briefly and clearly the question of secession, averring that, in spite of all that had been done at the South, the Union was unbroken, and he should, to the extent of his ability, take care "that the laws of the Union be faithfully executed in all the States;" that in doing this there would be no bloodshed, "unless it be forced upon the national authority," but that the power of the Government would be used "to hold, occupy, and possess the property and places belonging to the Government, and to collect the duties and imposts;" and he closed his address with an earnest appeal to all who really loved the Union, to pause and consider "before entering upon so grave a matter as the destruction of our national fabric, with all its benefits, its memories, and its hopes." "In your hands, my dissatisfied fellow countrymen," said he, "and not in mine, is the momentous issue of civil war. The Government will not assail you. You can have no conflict without being yourselves the aggressors. You have no oath registered in heaven to destroy the Government, while I shall have the most solemn one to 'preserve, protect, and defend' it. I am loath to close. We are not enemies, but friends. We must not be enemies. Though passion may have strained, it must not break our bonds of affection. The mystic cord of memory, stretching from every battle-field and patriot grave to every living heart and hearthstone all over this broad land, will yet swell the chorus of the Union, when again touched, as surely they will be, by the better angels of our nature."

Mr. Lincoln found, upon entering upon the duties of his office, the credit of the Government greatly impaired by the uncertainty of the future, its navy scattered, and less than a dozen ships in serviceable condition to guard our coasts; the larger part of the small arms and cannon belonging to the Government in the hands of the States which had already seceded; forts, arsenals, mints, and vessels seized by the insurrectionists; the troops of our regular army deprived of their arms and sent home, by slow and devious routes, as paroled prisoners. The garrison of Fort Sumter was drawing nigh the point of starvation, and no supplies could be sent them except by running the fire of batteries. The attempt was made by a merchant vessel, but she was fired upon, and without waiting the surrender, which could not have been long delayed, the rebel leaders chose to bombard the fort, and take possession of it after a thirty-three hours' siege, on the 14th of April.

Then came the necessity of at once calling the nation to arms, and on the 15th of April the call for 75,000 men roused the people to the struggle which for four years to come was to task their energies and try their patience. The response from every northern State was cordial, prompt, and earnest. Men and means were pressed upon the Government in abundance. Kentucky, Missouri, Maryland, Delaware, and Virginia hung back, and some of them answered the call with insolent threats and defiance. Virginia soon after went over to the Rebels; the Governor of Missouri, foiled in his efforts to take the State in the same direction, fled from the State, and loyal officers took his place; Maryland, held in military possession, took up the national cause, and finally emancipated her slaves; Delaware, halting long between two opinions, at length raised troops for the Union; and Kentucky, attempting neutrality, found herself neutral only as the battle-field and plunder ground of the contending armies. An extra session of Congress had been called for July 4th. On the 19th of April the ports of the seceded States were declared under blockade. Washington, at first in extreme peril, was, not without bloodshed, soon strongly garrisoned. The President long cherished the hope that the war would be but brief, and that soon peace and union as of old would be restored. The battle of Bull Run dispelled in part this illusion; the nation began to harness itself for the work before it, and during the autumn and winter of 1861–'62 the President was heavily burdened with the cares and responsibilities so suddenly thrown upon him; finance, the raising and maintaining great armies throughout the country; settling the difficult Trent case, and adjusting temporarily the serious and delicate questions connected with slavery which were constantly arising, under the movements of Butler, Fremont, and other of the army commanders.

The year 1862, though cheered by some victories like those of Thomas, at Mill Spring, the grand forward movements of Halleck, Grant, and Buell through Kentucky and Tennessee, the capture of Island No. 10 and Memphis, of New Orleans and its guarding forts, of Beaufort and Port Royal, of Roanoke Island and Newbern, was on the whole one of gloom and anxiety for the President. But the dawn of the new year brought altered prospects. He had, after long and anxious deliberation, come to believe in the necessity of the proclamation of emancipation as a war measure, and the first day of the new year saw liberty proclaimed to all the slaves of the rebellious States. The victory of Stone River, the capture of Vicksburg and Port Hudson, and the opening of the Mississippi, the substantial exclusion of the Rebels from Missouri and Arkansas, the redemption of Tennessee, were all so many positive gains; while the disaster of Chancellorsville was more than redeemed by the glorious though bloody victory of Gettysburg, and the misfortunes of Chickamauga alleviated by the triumphant successes of Chattanooga. "Peace" said the President, reviewing these achievements of our armies, "does not look so distant as it did." He had anxiously sought for two years to bring the border States into the adoption of a system of emancipation, more or less gradual; and he was rewarded by the adoption of an emancipation constitution in the new State of West Virginia, and the emancipation of their slaves by Missouri and Maryland, while Congress abolished slavery in the District of Columbia, forbade it in all the territories, and struck from the statute books the fugitive slave laws.

The arrest of persons guilty of alleged treasonable acts or words, which, though not made in all cases by his order, he could not but sanction, occasioned some animadversions, and was explained by him in two lucid and able letters to the New York and Ohio committees who had addressed him on the subject. In 1864, the first few months of the year were rendered anxious by financial difficulties, the rapid depreciation of the national currency, the resignation of Secretary Chase, and the appointment of Mr. Fessenden. Then began in May those movements—unequalled in the history of modern times, by which, in less than a twelvemonth, the rebellion was crushed—Grant's great campaign, where each day's slaughter was almost that of an army, but in which, with a wonderful endurance and persistency, he held his adversary, till at last he yielded; that unparalleled march of a thousand miles, by which Sherman, making pauses only at Atlanta, at Savannah, and at Goldsboro, swept as with a besom of destruction through the hostile territory, and at last brought his foe to surrender; and that wisely-planned retreat of Thomas on Nashville, and his subsequent hurling of his troops upon the foe, pursuing them till they were scattered and broken. Meantime Mr. Lincoln had been, by a respectable majority in the popular vote, and a great majority in the electoral college, called for a second term to the Presidential chair, inaugurated amid the acclamations of thousands, though still not without some threats of assassination, he seemed about entering upon more halcyon days. Richmond and Petersburg had been evacuated, and his own feet had trodden the pavements of the late Rebel capital; Lee had surrendered, and Johnston was about to do so. Davis was a fugitive, and his abdication had been made without leaving a successor. War had substantially ceased, and the national banner was to float from the walls of Fort Sumter on the 14th of April, 1865, the anniversary of the day, four years before, which witnessed its humiliation. Pacification was to be the future work of the President.

Amid these joyous anticipations of the future, when the sad and wearied look which had so long hovered over his face seemed about to give place to one of serene satisfaction, the assassin, creeping stealthily from behind, as he sat with his family and friends in his box at the theatre, on the night of the 14th of April, 1865, fired, with fatal precision, the pistol shot, which, penetrating his brain, in a few hours terminated his life. The immediate assassin was an actor, by the name of John Wilkes Booth, but the assassination was a part of a conspiracy intended to cripple the Government by the simultaneous destruction of its principal executive officers, and it involved either as principals or accessaries, a number of persons. Nine of the more immediate actors suffered condign punishment, Booth being shot in the act of arresting him; Harold, Payne, Atzerot, and Mrs. Surratt hung; Arnold, Mudd, and McLaughlin imprisoned for life, and Spangler for six years. The excitement which the intelligence of his death caused throughout the nation, has never been paralleled in human history. The whole people were in tears; cities and villages were draped in mourning; all ranks and conditions lamented him as a father, and everywhere were seen the insignia of sorrow. When his body was borne through the cities through which he had passed as he came to enter upon his Presidency, it was greeted with unusual demonstrations of grief; the throngs in the streets were clad in the habiliments of wo, and with saddened countenances and streaming eyes watched the funeral train as it bore all that was mortal of the loved and honored President, a martyr for his country's sake, to the quiet grave in his prairie home. England poured forth her encomiums upon the dead, her widowed queen writing a most touching letter of sympathy to the bereaved consort of the President, while her poets vied with ours in chaunting his requiem. France, too, expressed in words and tones of sympathy her grief at our nation's bereavement, and the wave of grief sweeping over Europe found answering billows in the far-off Orient. China, Japan, and Siam sent their condolence.

Mr. Lincoln's character as a man and a chief magistrate may be summed up in a few words. He was honest in the best sense of the term; patient, forbearing, and forgiving; slow in arriving at conclusions, but when once settled in them, firm to obstinacy; endowed with a wisdom and tact not acquired in the schools, but which guided him in administration, sustained him in despondency, and rendered him calm and self-possessed in the hour of success; in short, a self-taught, large-hearted, clear-headed man.

April 17.—Charles H. Tyler, a brigadier-general in the rebel army, killed at West Point, Ga., in the battle at that point with Major-General Wilson's cavalry. He was a native of the South, and at the breaking out of the war a captain of dragoons in the U. S. army. His promotion was not rapid, and he had not apparently distinguished himself in the war.

April 21.—Col. Matthew Murphy, 69th regiment N. Y. volunteers, died in New York, from wounds received at the battle of Hatcher's Run, Feb. 4, 1865. He was a native of Ireland, born Dec. 26, 1840, but had come to the United States in childhood. At the commencement of the war he was a teacher in Public School No. 24, and from patriotic impulses entered as a private in the 69th, but soon rose from the ranks by his merit, and on the return of the regiment to this city was elected its colonel, reorganized and filled up the regiment, and led it again to the field. He had taken part in most of the prominent battles, and had won the reputation of a brave and gallant officer.

April 22.—William W. McKean, U. S. N., a commodore in the naval service of the United States, died near Binghamton, N. Y., after a brief illness. He was born in Pennsylvania in 1801, being the son of Judge McKean and a nephew of Governor McKean. He entered the navy from Pennsylvania in Nov. 1814, and had consequently been over fifty years in the service, twenty-five of them afloat. His last cruise was completed in June, 1862. In 1823–'24 he commanded a schooner in Porter's squadron, and was very active in suppressing piracy along the coast of Cuba, and among the islands of the West Indies. In 1860 he was sent on the special service of conveying the Japanese embassy home, and on his return was the first commander of the West Gulf blockading squadron. He received his commission as commodore July 16, 1862.

May 1.—Lieut. EDWIN J. DE HAVEN, U. S. N., died at Philadelphia. He was born in Philadelphia in 1819, and entered the navy in Oct., 1829, at the age of ten years. He had been nearly thirty-six years in the service, about one-half of it in the sea service, but owing to impaired vision had been placed upon the retired list. His last cruise was completed in Feb., 1857. He was a man of fine scientific abilities, and was often detailed for special service. He commanded the first Arctic exploring expedition, of which Dr. Kane wrote so graphic an account. He was for several years employed in the National Observatory under Maury, who was indebted to him for much of the reputation he had attained.

June 11.—Dr. WILLIAM WHELAN, U. S. N., surgeon and chief of bureau of medicine and surgery in the Navy Department, died at Washington, D. C. He was born in Philadelphia, Sept. 4, 1808. He graduated at Mount St. Mary's College, Emmittsburg, with the highest honors of his class, though quite young, and studied medicine under Dr. Samuel Jackson, of of Philadelphia, graduating M. D. at the University of Pennsylvania in 1828. He at once entered the navy as an assistant surgeon, and continued in it till his death. His first sea service was a cruise of over five years in the West Indies. On his return he was ordered to Boston, where he assiduously prepared himself for his second examination, and was assigned the first place in his class. He was promoted to be surgeon in 1837. He then made a cruise to the Pacific in the Falmouth, and was twice fleet surgeon to the Mediterranean squadron each time at the request of the commander of the fleet. In October, 1853, Dr. Whelan was appointed to the Medical Bureau by President Pierce, as successor to Dr. Thomas Harris. In 1862, under the four years rule, he was again nominated to the Senate by the President, and confirmed. In 1855, when on a tour of duty, he received a severe injury from a railroad accident, from which he never entirely recovered. As an executive officer, as well as a surgeon, he had won a high reputation for clearness of comprehension, decision, skill, and gentleness.

June 13.—Col. J. CLEVELAND CAMPBELL, 23d U. S. C. T., died at Castleton, N. Y., from injuries received at the explosion of the mine at Petersburg, July 30, 1864. He was born in New York in July, 1836, and graduated successively at the Free Academy, Union College, and the University of Göttingen. Early in the war he entered as a private in the 44th N. Y. volunteers, was soon promoted to be a lieutenant on Gen. Palmer's staff, was next adjutant of the 152d N. Y. volunteers, then captain in Upton's 121st N. Y. volunteers, and after passing a most brilliant examination was commissioned lieutenant-colonel, and finally colonel of the 23d U. S. C. T. He led his regiment into the hottest of the fight at Petersburg, when the mine exploded, and left in and around that awful crater nearly 400 of his men, killed or wounded. His lung was contused and ruptured by a bursting shell, which eventually caused his death.

June 23.—SAMUEL FRANCIS DU PONT, U. S. N., a rear-admiral in the navy of the United States, born at Bergen Point, New Jersey, September 27, 1803, died in Philadelphia, Penn., June 23, 1865. He was of French origin on his father's side, his grandfather being P. S. Du Pont de Nemours, the intimate personal friend of Madison and Jefferson. He was appointed a midshipman in the navy by President Madison, December 19, 1815. His appointment was made from Delaware, of which State he became a resident in his boyhood. His first cruise was in the Franklin, 74, under Commodore Stewart; from this he was transferred to sloop-of-war Erie, Captain Ballard. His second cruise was on the Mediterranean station in the Constitution, and twice subsequently he returned to the Mediterranean for three years in the North Carolina, 74, and in the sloop-of-war Ontario. He also served on the West India station and on the coast of Brazil in the frigate Congress, under Commodore Biddle. On the North Carolina he had been promoted to be sailing master, and in 1826 he was commissioned lieutenant and ordered to the schooner Porpoise. From 1835 to 1838 he served as executive officer on the Warren and Constellation, and from 1838 to 1842 on the Ohio, the flag-ship of Commodore Hull. In 1845, having been promoted to the rank of commander, he was ordered to the Pacific in command of the frigate Congress, bearing the flag of Commodore Stockton, and in 1846 was transferred to the corvette Cyane. The outbreak of the Mexican war brought his services into request. In the Cyane he captured San Diego, and landed John C. Fremont. He cleared the Gulf of California of Mexican vessels, capturing and destroying thirty. He took possession of La Paz, the capital of Lower California, spiked the guns of San Blaz, and established the blockade of Mazatlan, which latter port he subsequently assisted in capturing, leading the line of boats which entered the main harbor under the orders of Commodore Shubrick, in November, 1847. He was next despatched in the Cyane to defend Lower California against the Indians and Mexicans. He covered La Paz until it could be fortified, landed at San José with a force of one hundred marines and sailors, defeated and scattered a largely superior force of Mexicans, and rescued a small party under Lieut. Heywood, who were beleaguered in the Mission House. He led or took part in a number of expeditions into the interior, capturing many prisoners and coöperating with Col. Benton and Lieutenant (now Maj.-Gen.) Halleck, approaching from the north, scattered the Mexicans and Indians, and gained complete possession of the peninsula of California. In 1848 he returned to Norfolk in the Cyane after an absence of three years. After a service of forty years, sixteen as lieutenant and thirteen as commander, he was made a captain in 1855. In 1857 he was ordered to the command of the Minnesota, and sent on a special service to China, with W. B. Reed minister to that empire. After a cruise of two years, during which he visited Japan, Western India, and Arabia, he returned in June, 1859, to Boston, in the Minnesota. On the 1st of Jan., 1861, he was appointed to the command of the Philadelphia navy-yard, relieving Commodore Stewart. Here he was stationed at the commencement of the war, and by his promptitude and experience rendered great service in securing Washington. In June, 1861, he was made president of a Board called at Washington to establish a plan of naval operations from the examination of the records of the coast survey and other data.

On the division of the Atlantic squadron into two distinct commands, in September, 1861, Capt. Du Pont was appointed to the command of the South Atlantic squadron, where he remained until his recall on the 3d of June, 1863. His first enterprise afloat with his squadron was the brilliant bombardment and capture of Forts Beauregard and Walker, at the entrance of Port Royal Harbor, S. C., and the occupation by a joint land and naval force of the islands adjacent. This was justly regarded as one of the finest and most admirably conducted naval conflicts of the war. He also rendered essential service in the establishment of a very close blockade of the coast of Carolina and Georgia; in the occupation of Tybee Roads and Tybee Island, which gave the army their base for the reduction of Fort Pulaski; in the expedition for the destruction of the batteries on the mainland at Port Royal ferry; in the capture in March, 1862, of Cumberland Island and Sound, Amelia Island, the river and town of St. Mary's, Ga., Fernandina, Florida, and Fort Clinch. The inlets along the coast were also occupied or carefully examined, the rivers ascended, Jacksonville and St. Augustine, Florida, taken, and the yacht America, which had been sunk, was raised. At Charleston alone the blockade was ineffective, the force at command not being sufficient to cover completely the circuit from the bay to Stono, and the demands upon the navy rendering the reënforcement of the squadron impossible. The capture of Charleston, it was hoped, would complete the blockade, and in April, 1863, a resolute attempt was made, the rear-admiral himself leading the attack to bombard, and if possible pass Fort Sumter. It failed, one of the iron-clads being sunk and others disabled, and the brave admiral did not feel warranted in renewing the attack. The Secretary of the Navy deeming him distrustful of the iron-clads of the Monitor type, removed him from the command of the squadron, but his successor, with a larger fleet and an efficient coöperative land force, was no more successful.

On the 16th of July, 1862, while in command of the squadron, Captain Du Pont was made a Rear-Admiral, ranking second in the list. After his withdrawal from the South Atlantic squadron he held no active command, but served, as occasion required, on naval commissions and courts-martial. He had been active in the general improvement of the navy during all his period of service; had assisted in the organization of the Naval Academy, and was a member of the Light House Board; had twice aided in revising the Rules and Regulations of the Navy; was a member of the Naval Retiring Board; and had at various times contributed important papers on subjects relating to the interests of the naval service. Among these one on coast defences has been republished and widely circulated. He was a brave and accomplished sailor, a fearless and greatly beloved commander, an earnest, sincere, and consistent Christian. His death was occasioned by a sudden attack of quincy, a disease to which he had been for some years subject.

INDEX OF CONTENTS.

B

C

D

E

G

H

I

J

K

L

N

Q

R

S

T

THE END.